OBITUARIES FROM THE TIMES 1971-1975

including an Index to all Obituaries and Tributes
appearing in The Times during the years 1971-1975

Compiler: **Frank C. Roberts** (Home News Editor, *The Times* 1965-1968)

NEWSPAPER ARCHIVE DEVELOPMENTS LIMITED
MECKLER BOOKS

Newspaper Archive Developments Limited,
16 Westcote Road,
Reading RG3 2DF, England.

© Newspaper Archive Developments Limited, 1978
Distributed in north and south America by
Meckler Books
P.O. Box 405 Saugatuck Station,
Westport, Conn. 06880, U.S.A.

ISBN 0 903713 97 7
ISBN 0 930466 05 5

In preparing this volume valued advice and assistance were
received from Colin Watson Obituaries Editor
of *The Times*

Print and typography Consultant Graham Saunders

Manufactured in Great Britain by
Tonbridge Printers Ltd,
Shipbourne Road,
Tonbridge, Kent
and G. & J. Kitcat Ltd,
Shand Street,
London SE1

PREFACE

The Obituary columns of *The Times* are one of the most important parts of the record which the newspaper maintains. They are the earliest substantial account of many lives to be published and they are often the foundation on which subsequent references or brief lives are built.

Obituaries are prepared with great care. In many cases and in the majority of larger entries they are prepared some time before the deaths of their subjects, often by those who have known the subject well and often by scholars in their particular field. The names of *The Times* obituary writers are not divulged and the confidence in which they are written is carefully preserved.

In 1975 a volume of the obituaries from *The Times* between 1961 and 1970 was published. At the time it was promised that further volumes would be published in due course and this is the first of the subsequent volumes covering the years from 1971 to 1975. It is expected that subsequent volumes will also cover five-year periods. As in the first volume, what is published here is not a revision of what was published at the time. The length of each entry and the judgment it contains stand as they stood when first published, however inclined one might be to modify some of these judgments in the light of subsequent history. These books are records of contemporary judgments and stand as such.

This volume contains just over a thousand obituaries for the five-year period it covers. That represents approximately four obituaries for every week of publication, which means that the leading obituaries of the period are included.

The percentage of British entries is just below 60 per cent with the rest being overseas and this book does therefore contain almost all the major international figures who died in the first half of the 1970's. This is an international work of reference.

Thirteen of the obituaries are over 2,500 words in length and, of these, ten are international and only three are British, The British obituaries include the Duke of Windsor, Lord Reith (who created the BBC), and Lord Astor of Hever (who was for many years proprietor of *The Times*.)

The longest obituary published in this volume is that of Lyndon Johnson. It is perhaps the fact that he died within a few years of the end of his presidency that accounts for his having nearly twice as long an obituary as that of his fellow President of the U.S., Harry Truman.

Three artists were among the list of long obituaries: Shostakovich, Stravinsky and Picasso.

In a small number of cases, we have not republished obituaries of people who might have been expected to appear because the original obituary notice, written with the knowledge available at the time, now appears to be inadequate or possibly misleading. We have not published any of the appreciations that we received, in-interesting though many of them are.

The Times attaches great importance to maintaining as high a quality as possible for our obituaries. The first volume was generally welcomed as an important book of reference and at the same time as an extremely readable brief library of short lives. We hope that this volume which comes out nearer to the deaths it commemorates will serve the same purpose.

WILLIAM REES-MOGG
Editor of *The Times*

January 1978

COMPILER'S NOTE

In the obituaries of this half-decade, the Early Seventies from 1971 to 1975, the emphasis passes with the death of President Truman from those who directed policy and operations in the Second World War to two groups. One dominant group may be said to have reshaped the destinies of their own nations, like Khrushchev or de Valera, Nkrumah or Papa-Doc, Ayub Khan or Faisal of Saudi Arabia. The second group consists of men and women who were unique in their spheres for what they were and what they did —Picasso, Stravinsky, the Duke of Windsor, Coward, Chevalier, Moura Budberg, Josephine Baker, Madeleine Vionnet, "Coco", Chanel, Chichester, Reith, Goldwyn, Lindbergh or Wodehouse.

These are barely twenty of the thousand people included in this book. A longer list could pall, but their collected life-stories rival the selection in the earlier volume, which covered the Sixties. Now, with only half the period of ten years to be compressed between two covers, it has been possible to reprint a higher proportion of the obituaries appearing in *The Times* during the years 1971–1975.

The first volume was greeted as a work of contemporary history, and as a book in which to dip or browse. It led to public discussion of the role of the obituary in literature and journalism. And the book was accepted as being about life rather than death. On page 406 of this volume an obituarist quotes the late St.-John Perse, the French poet. Perse pointed out that "the birth of a book is the death of a tree" and that "few books are worth the tree they kill". However, the subjects of obituaries live again in these pages, and 1,000 lives re-told may well justify the death of their tree.

Obituaries From The Times is now established as a series. It has been possible, in this volume, to refer the reader, by asterisks inserted in the text, to related lives which appeared in the earlier volume. A consolidated list of these earlier subjects appears on pages 589–590.

Included in this volume, on pages 593–597, there is a guide to the obituaries, grouped according to the following spheres of activity: royalty and statecraft; public service and politics; armed forces; education; economics, trade and transport; law; philosophy and psychology; religion; science; medicine; industry and engineering; commerce and property; literature; history, geography, travel and exploration; journalism; art and architecture; music; theatre, broadcasting and cinema; and sport.

The obituaries are reprinted as they appeared in *The Times*, subject to minor changes of style—for instance to clarify the date of death— or to correct errors. In the earlier volume cross-headings used in the newspaper were reprinted to preserve the journalistic look of the obituary and to allow latitude in the make-up of pages. As cross-headings disappeared from *The Times* towards the end of the Sixties they do not appear in this volume.

F.C.R.

NOTE ON THE USE OF ASTERISKS IN THESE PAGES

In these obituaries of persons who died in 1971-75 there are many references to men and women who had died in the decade of the 'Sixties. An asterisk beside one of these names indicates that a biography of that person appears in *Obituaries from The Times 1961-70*, which is available also from Newspaper Archive Developments Limited. A list of these earlier biographies, with the year of death and page reference, is in pages 589-590 of this volume.

A

Paul Abbatt, who died on June 15, 1971 at West Byfleet, Surrey, was the husband of Marjorie Abbatt, and co-founder with her of a famous toyshop. It is difficult for those who know their celebrated toys to think of them as anything but inseparable partners.

This century has seen a revolution in private and official understanding of the role of play in the lives of children, and Paul Abbatt was one of the practical revolutionaries who helped to bring it about. Today a clear sign of his influence is the fact that all over Britain are shops that take toys seriously. To do so is no longer something peculiar to Paul and Marjorie Abbatt.

The contents of their London shop was never quite like the contents of other toyshops: as someone once remarked, at Christmas there is more evidence of solid beechwood than of tinsel. You can find the constituent parts of harbours, towns, bridges, sturdy wheelbarrows which not even the most perverse child can break up, chutes, climbing frames and above all bricks —"whole bricks, half bricks and quarters", which are beautifully squared and rounded, and in using which many a future civil engineer first learnt about construction.

Paul's personal history was indeed a series of rebellions against ready-made ideas, whether educational, social, religious or political. Born into a Lancashire family, Quakers since the 17th century, he was educated at Ackworth, Bootham and Trinity Hall, Cambridge, with the prospect of becoming a schoolmaster, and for some years taught mathematics and physics first at Sidcot School, later at more experimental schools and at Toynbee Hall. Asked long afterwards why he gave up teaching, he replied "to break through the barriers which separated me from life"—not the kind of remark he would make casually, nor yet the kind he would avoid.

Marjorie had always hoped to teach. They met at a children's camp in the New Forest, were married in 1930, and then spent a year in Europe studying theories about children's play.

Two years later they opened their toyshop in London. The idea was gaining acceptance that children could externalize their psychological troubles by playing with toys, and that the toy leaving most to the child's imagination was best for the purpose. Even so the opening of their shop was a brave venture. Originally they specialized in large bricks made by their own carpenters, later branching out as ideas for soundly-designed and attractive toys crystallized.

The influence of their ideas has been wide, and many toy designers, unsure of the viability of their plans, found support and encouragement from the Abbatts.

Paul Abbatt was a quiet, friendly, shy, playful, irreverent, kind, courageous, basically serious man whose need to discover himself was solved by him in a universal way, so that many more than he benefited. Children delighted in him, and he leaves behind him overlapping circles of affection among his relations, his business associates, the world of design, members of his staff, educationists in Europe and America, and his fellow members of the Arts Club.

June 16, 1971.

Colonel Rudolf Abel, who died in Russia on November 15, 1971, remained an almost total enigma, in spite of his great notoriety as the Soviet "master spy" who was exchanged in Berlin for Francis Gary Powers, the American U.2 pilot shot down over Russia.

Abel's real name is not known, although at least five aliases were recorded during his nine illegal years in North America before his arrest in 1957.

He was convicted for conspiracy to obtain and transmit defence information to the Soviet Union. But, as the fascinating book *Abel* by Louise Bernikow pointed out in 1970, the nature of the information he passed was never disclosed by either Americans or Russians.

No other member of his reputed espionage network is ever known to have been picked up—except Reino Hayhanen, his assistant, whose defection to the Americans produced Colonel Abel's arrest.

For want of an answer, Miss Bernikow suggests that Colonel Abel was the archetype of the modern "white espionage" agent, the covert expert who is prodigious at scanning and at distilling useful overt information from the flood of technical and general publications. Allen Dulles,* who was director of the Central Intelligence Agency at the time, later disputed her "master spy" attribution.

Reviewing the book *Strangers at the Bridge* by James Donovan, who was Colonel Abel's defence counsel, Dulles wrote that Abel "did not direct the entire Soviet espionage network in North America, but he was an important cog in their 'illegal network' ". That network was claimed to have been destroyed.

Donovan petitioned successfully against the death penalty (on the far-sighted ground that an exchange might be useful some day) and Colonel Abel began serving a 30-year term in the federal penitentiary in Atlanta.

The exchange of Abel for Powers, who had been shot down in 1960 and sentenced to 10 years' imprisonment in Russia, was urged upon President Kennedy* by Donovan, who then conducted "unofficial" negotiations with the Russians, leading to the extraordinary scene on Glienicker bridge on February 10, 1962.

The Russians made no acknowledgement that Colonel Abel was a spy until May 1965, and subsequently his role became blurred in the propaganda game of "our spies are better than yours", in which both sides indulged.

The Russians asserted that Colonel Abel had been a member of Soviet intelligence since 1927. His service inside Germany against Hitler was acclaimed in *Pravda* in May 1965 by Semichastny, then head of the K.G.B.

November 18, 1971.

General Creighton Abrams, the United States Army Chief of Staff, died on September 4, 1974 at the age of 59. He was Military Commander in Vietnam during the years in which the American military commitment in the war was gradually being reduced.

A modest man, with a fine sense of humour and an appreciation of classical music, Abrams abandoned the expensive and destructive policy of "search and destroy" missions which the United States forces had followed under his predecessor, General William Westmoreland. He substituted extensive small-unit patrolling and the widespread use of helicopters to re-establish control over the war in the field. At the same time the United States sought to win popular support by technical and agricultural assistance programmes.

The largest military action he directed was the American intervention in Cambodia in May 1970, which had to be prepared at very short notice and which, President Nixon claimed later, set back enemy objectives in the war for at least six months and allowed the programme of Vietnamization to go forward.

Creighton Abrams was born in Springfield, Massachusetts, in September 1914. Upon graduation from the U.S. Military Academy he received a commission as a Second-Lieutenant of Cavalry and served during the Second World War in the Fourth Armoured Division under General George Patton. He participated in all campaigns of the division as a Battalion or Combat Command Commander.

After the end of the war he was assigned to the War Department General Staff with the task of determining the United States base requirements in the Philippines following independence. In 1949 he returned to Europe as a tank commander in the First Infantry Division. Later he served as Corps Chief of Staff in Korea and Chief of Staff of the Armoured Centre at Fort Knox.

In 1956 he was promoted to Brigadier General and in 1959 returned to Europe as Assistant Division Commander of the Third Armoured Division. Later, after promotion to Major General, he was assigned as Deputy Chief of Staff at Headquarters U.S. Army, Europe.

In 1962 he returned to Washington as Deputy Chief of Staff for Military Operations, in which post he was responsible for the control of Federal troops in racial disturbances in Alabama and Mississippi.

In 1963 Abrams became Commanding General of Five Corps and was promoted to Lieutenant General. He was appointed to the rank of full General in September 1964 and was sworn in as Vice Chief of Staff, U.S. Army.

Abrams was made Deputy Commander, U.S. Military Assistance Command in Vietnam by President Johnson in April 1967. He became Commanding General in Vietnam in July 1968. His confirmation by the Senate as Army Chief of Staff in 1972 was delayed while an armed services committee investigated whether he knew about unauthorized air raids on North Vietnam in 1971. Eventually the Senate confirmed his appointment in October 1972.

September 5, 1974.

General Abye Ababa, former President of the Ethiopian Senate, was among those members of the Emperor's regime who were executed in Ethiopia on November 24, 1974.

He was born in 1918 in Addis Ababa. His father had two years previously rendered signal service to the Emperor during the battle at Sagalle, when the latter finally established his position by defeating a rebel army brought against him by his predecessor's father; and true to his nature the Emperor took special care of the son, who was sent to be educated at the Officer's Training School at Holetta and adopted the Army as a career.

He saw service with the partisans who fought alongside the British forces against the Italians in 1941. In 1942, after the Emperor had regained his throne, Abye

married his second daughter, the Princess Tsahai, who however died in childbirth the same year. Soon afterwards he was appointed Governor-General of Wollega Province, his first experience of administration, for which he soon gave evidence of exceptional aptitude. In 1946 he reverted to the Army as a Divisional Commander, and in 1949 became Acting War Minister, an appointment which was made substantive in 1951. In 1955 his career took a new direction, as he was appointed Ambassador in Paris, a post which he held for the next three years.

In 1958 the Emperor recalled him to Addis Ababa and appointed him Minister of Justice. He also attached him as his Special Representative to the Duke of Gloucester when the latter, with his Duchess, paid an official visit to Addis Ababa that year; for his services in this capacity he was created an honorary K.B.E.

In 1959 General Abye, as he had by then become, received still further advancement, being appointed Minister of the Interior and also Viceroy of Eritrea, the former Italian colony which had been controlled by virtue of a United Nations decision in 1952.

This last was a difficult post, for Eritrea was economically depressed and had never taken kindly to Ethiopian rule, and it was a measure of General Abye's firmness and competence that he was able not only to keep it quiet but also to prevent its being affected by the serious revolt which broke out in Addis Ababa in 1960.

November 28, 1974.

Emperor Haile Selassie of Abyssinia—See Ethiopia.

Dean Acheson, Secretary of State under President Truman, died on October 12, 1971 at his home in Maryland. He was 78.

Perhaps no American Secretary of State left a deeper mark on the world scene than he. His four years of office in President Truman's second Administration (1949 to 1953) saw the final emergence of the United States in a world role on the testing grounds of communist imperialism, years of imminent peril abroad and revolutionary change at home. In both situations Acheson's conduct of foreign policy, formulated to an unusual degree on his own initiative, had all the marks of a rare strategical ability exercised with the more poise and assurance from the six years he had served at the State Department as Assistant and Under Secretary. Few incumbents were better prepared for the top post or assumed office at a more challenging juncture, of which the Berlin blockade and Korea were immediate manifestations.

His fervent belief in collective security, already apparent in exploratory work on the United Nations and the Marshall Plan,

triumphed in April 1949 with the historic signature of the North Atlantic Treaty, the first military alliance concluded by the constituted Republic in peace time, with all it implied for American leadership of the free world. Acheson, having left the service in 1947 for lack of means, had no part in Washington's first circumscribed moves in response to alarmed measures in western Europe to resist Russian encroachment. His task, backed by Truman at every turn, was to ensure that the treaty did not suffer the fate of the old League of Nations commitment at the hands of a politically hostile Senate. His assiduous collaboration with Senator Arthur Vandenburg, the Republican leader, remains a model in the art of governing. In the upshot only a handful of Republican votes opposed ratification of an instrument that blew America's traditional isolation sky high.

Acheson's diplomatic talents were then turned at a long series of allied conferences to putting teeth into the Atlantic Pact, notably by convincing Europe of the sincerity of United States intentions in face of the inhibiting fact that under the Constitution there could be no guarantee of American armed assistance. Without his powerful arguments it might not have been enough to provide American troops and an American Supreme Commander, or to extend military credits to the war-torn Europeans. To surmount British and especially French aversions from German rearmament was a measure of his consummate skill in reducing so many different positions to a unified defence posture, an achievement that had Truman testifying that there would have been no Nato without Dean Acheson. Or, it might be added, without the warm, fertile relationship he established with Ernest Bevin, the British Foreign Secretary, for whom he had an unbounded admiration. In their lighter moments they could be as happy together as a couple of schoolboys. Some of their strategems could go awry, such as the formula they devised in the United Nations, enabling allied forces in Korea to cross the 38th parallel to the north in violation of proclaimed war aims.

This friendship of opposites certainly went deeper than the more formal but none the less constructive relations between Acheson and Sir Anthony Eden (later Lord Avon), men so similar in style and background that they were sometimes mistaken for each other. Phases of the Korean war, the Abadan oil crisis and the unavailing long-drawn efforts to create a European Defence Community especially engaged their endeavours to align common Anglo-American positions. In spite of divergences and occasional squalls, Acheson was usually found to be a loyal and discerning friend of British interests. Even beyond the claims of collective security his guiding principle was to negotiate from strength; and this, combined with his intellectual brilliance—some would say arrogance—and a cutting, sardonic humour, edged him towards intolerance. A strong streak of expediency in some of his policies was notably evident in the so-called "uniting for peace" measures he sponsored in the United Nations by which, as a means of side-tracking the Soviet veto in the Security Council, the General Assembly was empowered to act in international disputes. A revision of such questionable wisdom and legality might not have been devised had he paused to contemplate an Assembly nearly twice the size that it was then.

In face of a Republican Congress, Acheson's efforts to maintain a bi-partisan approach to international affairs were largely defeated by the vindictive mood of politicians bent on smearing Democratic rule and finding scapegoats for the alleged "sell-out" in China. His commendable action in appointing John Foster Dulles to handle the Japanese peace treaty was lost in the mounting hysteria of McCarthyism, with its drumming accusations that the State Department harboured a nest of espionage and subversion. Acheson, a proud man who did not suffer fools gladly, was in some respects his worst enemy. His personal loyalty to his subordinate, Alger Hiss, deeply implicated in the "pumpkin papers" spy case, was admirably foolhardy in a man holding public office; and the ordinary American was apt to bridle at the cultured, cosmopolitan air and mannerisms of speech and grooming widely resented as being too British. Hence, perhaps, the whispers that American policy was made in Whitehall.

Acheson's mother was Canadian. Of commanding presence, he came as near being a dandy as most Americans would allow in themselves; but beneath a supercilious bearing and trenchant expression he had great charm, warm sympathies, and a huge sense of fun. On most mornings he and his diminutive friend, Mr. Justice Felix Frankfurter* of the Supreme Court, would be seen walking to their offices from their Georgetown homes, a warming sight. As Acheson used to say, no man needing an atmosphere of approbation would serve as Secretary of State. If he was injured politically by a combination of smear tactics and personal foibles, few would gainsay that his eminent talents succoured and inspired the western cause at a dire turn of postwar history.

On the advent of President Eisenhower in 1953, returning to his Washington law practice, he assumed the mantle of elder statesman in the affairs of his party, aloof from the fray but sufficiently influential until the Kennedy era to frame the foreign policy plank of the Democratic platform. One of his many comments on the world scene, as waspish as ever, memorably portrayed Britain as a nation that had lost an empire and was still seeking a role.

Dean Gooderham Acheson was born at Middletown, Connecticut, on April 11, 1893, the son of Edward Campion Acheson by his marriage with Eleanor Gooderham. He was educated at Groton and at Yale, a privileged beginning. Having intended from his youth to be a lawyer, he went on to the law school at Harvard, where in 1918 he obtained his LL.B. During the war he served for a time in the Navy. At the time of Acheson's qualification as a lawyer, Mr. Justice Holmes and Mr. Justice Brandeis, the distinguished judges of the Supreme Court, used to pick the two most brilliant men of each Harvard class to assist them. Acheson, through the good offices of Felix Frankfurter, who was to remain a lifelong friend, was fortunate enough to be chosen by Justice Brandeis. Later he entered the law firm of Covington, Burling and Peebles.

In 1933, when the Democrats were launching the New Deal, Acheson had his first experience of office. Roosevelt appointed him Under-Secretary of the Treasury. This did not last long. With that stubborn integrity which was to cause him trouble nearly 20 years later, Acheson found himself unable to justify Roosevelt's unorthodox fiscal policies and soon was out of a job. But he did not waver in his loyalty to his party, to the President, or to Roosevelt's broad liberal approach to human problems; in this he differed from many members of his privileged class.

In 1939 Acheson became associated with the Government again as the head of a committee appointed by the Attorney General to study the problem of administrative tribunals. Two years later this body issued a report which was described as "a landmark in the history of administrative reform".

With the outbreak of war Acheson became a vigorous advocate of aid to Britain and is believed to have been the first to suggest the "bases for destroyers" deal. In 1941 he returned to the State Department, first as Assistant Secretary in charge of trade and commerce and later in charge of congressional relations and international conferences. In the six years that followed he served four Secretaries of State—Hull, Byrnes, Stettinus and General Marshall—and gained an experience unrivalled by any other non-career officer. Among his tasks were lend-lease (of which he said the United States wanted in return not gold or goods but a new world), the creation of U.N.R.R.A. and the drafting of the statute for the Food and Agriculture Organization, the preparations for the San Francisco Conference which created the United Nations, and the Acheson-Lilienthal report on control of atomic energy.

In 1945, the year the war ended, Roosevelt died and Truman succeeded to the presidency. There then was laid the foundation of a long, fruitful collaboration and staunch friendship between two apparently ill-assorted men, the cocky little small-town Missourian and the urbane, intellectual aristocrat who was now Under-Secretary of State.

It was Acheson who helped to obtain the approval of Congress for the decision to go to the aid of Greece and Turkey, which was an historic turning-point in the development of American policy. And it was Acheson who, in a little-noticed speech a month before General Marshall made his famous one at Harvard, outlined the substance of the generous and far-sighted offer to restore the European economy after the devastation and dislocation of the war.

Many of Acheson's admirers felt that as Secretary he was less receptive to new ideas than he had been when he occupied less exalted posts. In a kindlier climate these misgivings might have been disproved, but by 1950 American politics were poisoned by long-pent-up frustrations. The Republicans had been out of power for nearly 20 years and had been embittered by having success—at least apparently within their grasp—snatched from them by Truman's unexpected victory in 1948. It fell to Acheson to attempt to disentangle American foreign policy in the Far East from the failing fortunes of the Chinese Nationalists. The effort only succeeded in worsening Acheson's relations with Congress. He was notably independent of mind and did not always succeed in disguising his feelings. "Letting the dust settle in China" was an unlucky phrase; and it is clear enough from Acheson's book, *A Citizen Looks at Congress,* that however much he tried to control himself, he often became irritated and impatient with the waste of time involved in answering congressional questions and discouraged by the adjustment of policies to fit congressional prejudices.

Persecuted, vilified and perpetually embattled as the Secretary of State was in Washington, his ability to explain and justify American foreign policy to America's allies remained unequalled and abroad his reputation stood high. At home he did not shrink from telling American audiences that the development of positions of strength from which it should be possible to negotiate successfully with the Soviet Union required real sacrifices. When the challenge came in Korea in June 1950, the decision to intervene had to be taken by the President, but there is no doubt that he and Acheson saw eye to eye. Acheson has often been most unfairly blamed, particularly by Republicans, for "inviting" the Korean attack in a speech setting out the American defence line in the Pacific; this left Korea out in the cold. But in this Acheson was following the line laid down by the Department of Defence; moreover, he made it quite clear that while the United States could not, single-handed, undertake the defence of any country on the Asian mainland, an attack would be a matter for the United Nations.

The Korean War temporarily stilled controversy, but it sprang up again as the casualty lists lengthened.

In December 1950 the Republicans in the Senate and the House passed a resolution calling for Acheson's resignation. The President stoutly refused to consider it, but only a handful of courageous Democrats spoke up for the Secretary of State, and Acheson's influence abroad was weakened when it should have been most unassailable. By 1951 the country was more bitterly divided than ever by the open rift between General

7

MacArthur, commanding in Korea, and the Administration. MacArthur's eventual recall and the congressional investigation which followed presented themselves to Acheson's enemies as an opportunity to destroy the Secretary of State. Instead the old soldier faded away; it was Acheson, strongly supported by the Chiefs of Staff, who managed to convince his hearers that the MacArthur policy of extending the war would have been disastrous.

But at home he had become a political liability conspicuous even in an Administration doomed by the popular feeling that it was "time for a change". To win congressional agreement for the Administration's basic foreign policies, concessions had to be made elsewhere and an attitude of rigid anti-communism adopted; Acheson, it should be remembered, had no personal political following of his own, such as Cordell Hull had enjoyed. Damage was done to the very "coalition diplomacy" by which Acheson had always set such store. The emphasis fell more and more on military assistance and less on economic aid and the new world which Acheson had once envisaged. The last few months of office, after Eisenhower's landslide victory in November 1952 could be no more than a holding operation.

For nearly a year and a half Acheson refrained from commenting upon the policies of his successor. But foreign affairs remained his absorbing interest and by 1954 he felt free to criticize publicly the idea of "massive retaliation" and what he felt was a failure to pay sufficient regard to the views of America's allies. After the Democratic defeat in 1956, Acheson became the head of a new Democratic advisory subcommittee on foreign policy and was heard more frequently. Somewhat to the consternation of his fellow Democrats, he did not invariably take issue with Dulles; on the subject of a second summit conference in 1958, for example, his opposition was more adamant than that of either the President or Dulles. And his crushing rebuke to George Kennan for preaching disengagement in central Europe might have been drawn up by Dulles himself. Acheson did, however, urge review and revision of American policy towards Communist China, and in the crisis over the offshore islands of Quemoy and Matsu he expressed the deepest misgivings over the Administration's policy. His reward was to be attacked as an apostle of appeasement by Nixon in the congressional election campaign of 1958.

Although he was barred by the turn of the political tide from public office, Acheson's views and his experience were not wholly wasted, as those of public servants so often are in the United States. He was a witty and effective speaker, much in demand, and an accomplished writer. In his first book, *A Democrat looks at his Party,* he justified in intellectual terms his life-long attachment to the Democrats. In *A Citizen Looks at Congress* he was less hopeful; the division of authority built into the Ameri-

can system was, he felt, ill-suited to the conduct of foreign affairs in the twentieth century and he saw no cure for this save the rather remote one of an improvement in the quality of Congressmen and their adoption of a policy of no-interference. In view of Acheson's own experiences, such pessimism is not surprising.

Yet, in spite of all the harassment to which he had been subjected, he had helped to bring about a revolution in America's attitude to the world—and that of the world towards America.

Acheson married in 1917 Miss Alice Stanley, of Detroit. They had a son and two daughters, one of whom, Mary, married Mr. William Bundy.

October 13, 1971.

Achille van Acker, who died in Bruges on July 10, 1975 at the age of 77, was Prime Minister in four of Belgium's postwar coalition governments.

One of six children of a Bruges basketmaker, he left school at the age of 10 to help his father weave baskets for carrying shrimps and shellfish. Then, in a succession of jobs, among them boatman, docker, bookbinder and journalist, he began to take an active interest in the trade union movement.

His political career began in 1926 when he was elected to the Bruges City Council, and a year later he entered Parliament as a Socialist member for the city, a post he held almost continuously until 1974, when he retired from active politics.

From the start his main concern was to improve the social welfare of his fellow-countrymen. During the war, when the Socialist Party was banned by the Nazi occupiers, he played a major role in reorganizing the party and laying the foundations for the Belgian social security system.

As Prime Minister in three governments between 1945 and 1946 he was faced with the awesome task of beginning to rebuild the country's economy. His main achievements were to help revive coal production and to dampen the inflation which struck the country in the immediate post-war years.

The austerity campaign he waged during this period eroded some of his personal popularity, and although the Socialist Party led a series of coalition governments until 1949 he stepped down from the leadership in August 1946.

He was to become Prime Minister again for the last time in 1954 in the only Socialist coalition of the 1950s and 1960s. Subsequently, as an elder statesman, he was elected Speaker of the Lower House, an office he held until his retirement in 1974. Throughout his life, his lack of formal education never proved a handicap. Brought up in the Dutch language, he taught himself French and was an avid reader until his death.

His slightly authoritarian manner and his bluntness were sometimes not appreciated by some of his political colleagues, but his complete candour and the courage he displayed in taking unpopular decisions earned him universal respect.

Unlike his socialist contemporary, Paul-Henri Spaak, he was not well known outside Belgium, but inside the country his reputation was as high.

July 12, 1975.

Sir Grantley Adams, C.M.G., Q.C., former Prime Minister of the now defunct West Indies Federation, died in Bridgetown, Barbados, on November 28, 1971. He was 73.

He was one of the most convinced advocates of a federated West Indies, and as a politician attended every conference on federation from Montego Bay in 1947, through the London conferences in 1953 and 1956, to the London conference of 1961, which finally chose the date for independence. Indeed, his enthusiasm led him as long ago as 1938 to prepare a draft constitution for a federated West Indies, which he presented at the West Indies Labour Conference in British Guiana in that year. Thus his anger and dismay when the Federation was dissolved in 1962 were considerable, and he led a deputation to London to protest against the decision.

Throughout a long political life in his native island of Barbados, Grantley Adams proved himself to be an able, wily and, when the need arose, a fiery politician. He had a high reputation as an advocate and used his forensic skill in parliamentary debate. First elected to the Barbados House of Assembly in 1934, he became a member of the executive committee in 1941. In 1954 Mr. Adams, as he then was, became the first Premier of Barbados.

Outside the West Indies he gained an international reputation for his work as a leader of organized labour, and in 1948 as a member of the United Kingdom delegation to the inaugural United Nations meeting in Paris, where, though in his time he had been a severe critic of British colonialism, he defended it brilliantly against Russian attacks. In 1949 he was vice-president of the inaugural meeting of the Free Trade Unions of the World, which later became the International Confederation of Free Trade Unions. In 1953 he was an official representative at the Coronation of Queen Elizabeth II. He received his knighthood in 1957. When the federation came into being in 1958, Adams was elected Prime Minister after Norman Manley,* the Premier of Jamaica, had refused to stand for that office. His task was hard. He had to guide through its first difficult years a federation of islands of widely different character and the constitution under which he worked gave to the central government the serious weakness of inadequate financial control. Furthermore, with two of the most able politicians—Manley and Dr. Eric Williams of Trinidad—outside federal politics, Adams inevitably found himself as a small-island man running an administration largely staffed by small-island men. It was perhaps not surprising in the circumstances that he sometimes appeared to be still the Barbadan rather than the West Indian.

Opposition to Adams, and the feeling that he had not sufficient stature as an international politician, reached a high point at the time of the 1961 Constitutional Conference. At the preliminary talks in Port of Spain, and at Lancaster House, the personal antagonisms, the mutual suspicions and the battle royal between Jamaica on the one hand, wanting a weak central federation, and Trinidad and the small islands on the other wanting more power in the centre, drew the conference at times to the borderline of failure. When it was over, Grantley Adams was a disappointed man, but still sufficient of a believer in federation to decide to make the best of the baby which he had nurtured and which now appeared far sicklier than he would have hoped. Adams remained Prime Minister until 1962 when the Federation was dissolved after Jamaica and Trinidad had opted out.

He was born on April 12, 1898, and educated at Harrison College, Barbados, where he won the Barbados Classics Scholarship to Oxford. He was an undergraduate at St. Catherine's Society and took his B.A. in jurisprudence in 1924, in which year also he was called to the Bar by Gray's Inn. He returned to Barbados where he practised as a barrister and also spent many years as a journalist on local newspapers. He was at various times president of the Barbados Progressive League, the Barbados Workers' Union, the Labour Party, and the Caribbean Labour Congress. During his time in office in Barbados he initiated and implemented many reforms, including the introduction of adult suffrage, workmen's compensation, and a peasant loan system. He was married, and Lady Adams was at one time a school teacher in Barbados. He had one son, Tom.

Tall, lean, and slightly stooping, Grantley Adams was a man of caustic wit but considerable personal charm. His quiet courtesy belied the firebrand qualities that lay not far below the surface. He deserves to be remembered as the father of the West Indies Federation even if the role which he was able to play in it was strictly limited by a weak constitutional framework.

November 29, 1971.

Sir Walter Adams, C.M.G., O.B.E., who had a distinguished and varied career, died on May 21, 1975 in Salisbury, Rhodesia. He had gone to that country on May 17 to receive an honorary doctorate. He was 68.

He was Principal of the University College of Rhodesia and Nyasaland from 1955 to 1967, and from 1967 until 1974 Director of the London School of Economics and Political Science.

His reign there did not begin happily. Even before he had taken up his appointment a pamphlet criticizing some of his actions while in Rhodesia was put out by a group of students, and in the years 1968 and 1969 Houghton Street was constantly in the news for one reason or another; there were sit-ins by students (not all of whom were members of the school) sometimes accompanied by violence. Subsequently Adams closed the school for a period and two lecturers were dismissed. However in time dissent dwindled away to nothing and Adams's later years were relatively untroubled.

He was born on December 16, 1906, the son of Walter Adams, of Brighton, and was educated at Brighton, Hove and Sussex Grammar School and University College London, of which he was later elected a Fellow. From 1926 to 1934 he lectured in history at the college and during this period spent a year in the United States as a Rockefeller Fellow.

In 1933 he was so concerned over the plight of Jewish academics in Germany that he resigned his post at University College in order to become secretary of the Academic Assistance Council where he did notable work. In 1938 he joined the staff at L.S.E.

From 1942 to 1944 he was Deputy Head of the British Political Warfare Mission to the United States and in 1945 was appointed assistant Deputy Director-General of the Political Intelligence Department of the Foreign Office.

In 1946 Adams became the first secretary of the Inter-University Council for Higher Education Overseas, and took with both hands an opportunity to set his mark upon the creation of British universities in "developing" countries on a grand scale. Every home university provided a member of the council, in very many cases its vice-chancellor, and Walter Adams left the L.S.E. to become its secretary and for the first eight years of its life its man of destiny.

At the end of those eight years there were universities in Malta, Hong Kong and Malaya; and university colleges, offering "special relationship" London degrees, in the Sudan, Uganda, Nigeria, Ghana, and the West Indies; shortly to be followed, under the same momentum, by universities or university colleges in Rhodesia, Sierra Leone, Kenya, Tanzania, Zambia, Malawi, Mauritius, and the South Pacific. In the latter years, almost all the university colleges became independent universities, and further new universities were founded in Nigeria and Ghana.

This palpable success in university building in developing countries was owed largely to the imagination and good sense which Adams showed in devising the tactics of the operation. He was most successful in leading his council, with strong support from the chairmanships first of Sir James Irvine of St. Andrews, and later of Sir Alexander Carr-Saunders of the London School of Economics. In 1955 he went to Central Africa as Principal of the young University College of Rhodesia and Nyasaland in Salisbury, Southern Rhodesia.

He went as a dedicated missionary of inter-racial higher education, and under him the college must have seemed in the first years to be making a most promising start. It was situated in an area which was reserved for whites and whose residents undoubtedly welcomed the preservation of the system of residential segregation. Yet quite soon there was the beginning of a good social way of life on the campus, with white and black students of both sexes living together in the halls. This was a great triumph for Adams; and further, in spite of his preoccupation with the preservation at all costs of "university standards", the time would soon have come, under the Federation, when there would have been more black students than white. The college would have become an African style college but significantly inter-racial in a sense of its own.

But the coming of U.D.I. changed the situation. Black students were no longer forthcoming to the college from outside Rhodesia, and the niggardly expenditure inside Rhodesia on black secondary education made the African student body very small and of very slow growth. Also the Government, while it was willing to permit university education for a very restricted number of Africans who might be needed for the economy, was clearly hostile to any promotion by the college of any expansion of African higher education in a big way. Finally, and not unnaturally, the Government watched the college very closely and tightly on security grounds. In this situation Adams did two things, which may well have been consistent with his lifetime principles as he saw them, but which soon lost him his previous image as a vanguard fighter for university education for Africans; he insisted on his doctrine of "standards" for university admission, thereby keeping the proportion of black students in the college quite low, and he showed more patience than his old colleagues might have expected with a Government which was in principle unfriendly to the inter-racial aims of the college and from time to time took significant hostile action against it.

Through a bitterly difficult period for the college he stuck to his guns against a quite large body of critical opinion which was activistically inter-racialist and unwilling to flirt with appeasement of the Rhodesian Front, and in doing so played his cards from day to day a good deal closer to his chest than up-to-date university opinion can readily accept in a university principal.

Few men could have been less open to the accusation of racial prejudice, and the scurrilous and cruel attack on Adams at the time when his appointment was announced did not survive his arrival at the London School of Economics as its Director in the autumn of 1967 in succession to Sir Sydney Caine. It was, however, his misfortune to arrive soon before the peak of world-wide student unrest and violence that reached L.S.E. before the rest of the country. During this trying period in late 1968 and 1969 Adams showed himself morally and physically courageous, strong principled, firm in adherence to academic standards, utterly unwilling to condone breach of the fundamental decencies and integrity of academic life, yet patient, fair and understanding of the aspirations and generous feelings of youth.

Then and later he gave every encouragement to the move to bring students into greater participation in all areas where they could usefully and properly contribute. It was an obvious pleasure for him to be with and to talk to young people. A certain innate shyness limited his relations with older people, but those who worked closely with him soon became aware of his passionate concern with fairness to individuals whether students, staff or others.

He made a major contribution to improving and strengthening the school's arrangements for self-government. He had returned to it at a time when it had begun to outgrow administrative arrangements that had long served it well, so that there was an increasing danger of drifting from one ad hoc decision to another. His period of office saw the committee structure under his guidance tightened and systematized in a way that spread the decision-making more widely and reduced substantially the degree of personal intervention by the Director in the decision process.

He was made C.M.G. in 1952 and received a knighthood in 1970.

He married, in 1933, Tatiana Makaroff. They had three sons and one daughter.

May 22, 1975.

Max Adrian, the actor, died on January 19, 1973 at his home in Shamley Green, Surrey, at the age of 69.

His first appearance in London was at the Globe Theatre in 1927, in a walking-on part, and his subsequent work developed a versatility which was obviously part of his nature, for he was just as likely to appear in revue as in a classical play, in an obviously ephemeral modern comedy as in an ambitious and challenging intellectual role. Throughout the 1930s he played important roles in London, but he interspersed these with provincial repertory.

His entry to the classical theatre came with a modern dress version of *Troilus and Cressida,* in which he took the part of Pandarus, at the Westminster Theatre in 1938. In a short time he had added several important Shavian roles—the Dauphin in *Saint Joan* and Sir Ralph Bloomfield-

Bonnington in *The Doctor's Dilemma* among them—to his experience, and reached Restoration comedy at the Little Theatre in 1940, playing Sparkish in *The Country Wife.*

As a member of Sir John Gielgud's company at the Haymarket Theatre in 1944 and 1945 and on tour he was a remarkably fantastic Osric in *Hamlet,* Jeremy and Tattle in Congreve's *Love for Love,* Puck in *A Midsummer Night's Dream,* Delio in *The Duchess of Malfi* and Arnold in Maugham's* *The Circle.* His stylistic accuracy, an ability to find the exact idiom of each of these roles and a natural imaginativeness in inflection, gesture and timing made all this work admirable, while a natural sense of dramatic propriety kept his idiosyncratic gifts under control; he made as much of the parts as they were worth, and never tried to make more.

His subsequent work ranged as widely as his choice of parts in the 1930s, from revues to new plays, but rarely in the classics where he could have claimed a particular type of role as his own. In 1967 his one-man show drawn from the non-dramatic writings of Bernard Shaw, the playwright's personalia and opinions, presented a deeply understanding portrait of a complex character—Shaw impish, malicious, playful, outrageous, affectionate, angry and almost always eloquent.

Adrian's sense of style included a wit which could add to the roles that needed it. He could make the fantastic seem no more than everyday, and the ease with which he assumed Osric-like elaborations of manner was accompanied by a remarkably neat exactitude, even when making big effects. His voice was like no other heard on the English stage of his day, vestigially Irish and harshly attractive.

January 20, 1973.

Gregory Peter XV Cardinal Agagianian, former Prefect of the Sacred Congregation for the Propagation of the Faith, and Patriarch of Cilicia in Armenia, died in Rome on May 16, 1971. He was 75.

Agagianian, who was regarded as *papabile* before the Conclave that elected Pope John XXIII,* was among the most learned and certainly the finest linguist in the Sacred College. His position was unique as that of the first Russian to become a cardinal and as a Catholic of the Armenian rite. He was closely concerned with relations between the Holy See and the Eastern Churches; and, although the number subject to him as Patriarch was relatively small in comparison with the total number of Armenian Christians, he enjoyed widespread popularity throughout the Middle East. Of medium height and cordial manner, he was particularly easy of approach, and his gift of tongues made him an admirable emissary of the Holy See during his official visits to many countries.

Lazarus Agagianian was born on September 18, 1895 at Akhaltzikhe in Georgia, some 70 miles from the coast of the Black Sea. His father died when he was five years old, and his pastor, Mgr. Serge Der-Abrahamian, later Rector of the Pontifical Armenian College, Rome, was so impressed by his promise as a student that he sent him to Rome at the age of 11 to study for the priesthood at the Urban College. There he was considered too young for seminary life, but, through the personal intervention of Pope St. Pius X, who is said to have remarked: "This boy will yet give great service to the Church," he was allowed to stay.

He remained until 1919 in Rome, where he took a triple doctorate in philosophy and theology and Canon Law, and was ordained to the priesthood. His first appointment was to pastoral work among Roman Catholics of the Armenian rite at Tiflis during the crucial period after the Communist Revolution. He was there in 1921 when the Red Army occupied Tiflis and carried out the purge of nationalism ordered by Stalin in his native Georgia. The young priest escaped arrest and a few months later he was recalled to Rome on appointment as Vice-Rector of the Armenian College, under his former pastor. It was during his work at the college, of which he was rector for three years, that he added proficiency in most European languages to his knowledge of Latin, Greek, Hebrew and his native languages.

In 1935 Pope Pius XI appointed him as titular Bishop of Comana in Armenia and Apostolic Visitor of the Patriarchal Institute of Bzommar in Syria. Two years later the Synod of the Armenian Latin Hierarchy, meeting in Beirut, elected him as Patriarch. He took as Patriarch the name of Gregory, adding that of Peter, in accordance with the custom that obtained after the reconciliation with the Holy See of 1742.

For the following eight years the Patriarch was in Beirut, engaged in the care of his widely scattered flock, many of whom he was prevented from visiting by the 1939–45 war, but to many of whom he carried out a series of visitations, particularly in America after the end of hostilities.

In 1946 he was elevated to the Sacred College as Cardinal Priest with the title of St. Bartholomew on the Island. Thereafter he resided mainly in Rome with many curial duties as member of several congregations and commissions, among them the Congregations for Extraordinary Ecclesiastical Affairs and for the Eastern Church, and the Commission for the Codification of Oriental Canon Law, of which he became president. He was a member also of the Pontifical Commissions for Biblical Studies and for the authentic interpretation of Canon Law, and in 1958 he became a member of the Holy Office and of the Consistorial Congregation.

Apart from his visitations in America in 1951, he made a series of visits in following years to Persia, Palestine, Egypt and Iraq, and in 1954 he presided at the Marian Congress of Eastern Rites.

Appointed by Pope John XXIII as Pro-Prefect of the Sacred Congregation for the Propagation of the Faith, which has jurisdiction over all missionary regions as well as some in which hierarchies are established, he succeeded Cardinal Fumasoni-Biondi in 1960 as Prefect and Grand Chancellor of the Urban College. In the same year, in preparation for the Second Vatican Oecumenical Council, he became president of the Commission for the Missions and a member of the Central Commission, of which the Pope is president.

In March 1966, as head of the Church's missionary work, he preached in Westminster Cathedral at a mass offered in thanksgiving for the centenary of the founding by Cardinal Vaughan of England's own missionary society, the Mill Hill Missionaries. His last journey abroad was in July 1969, when he accompanied Pope Paul on his visit to Uganda.

He resigned as Patriarch and Catholicos of the Armenians in 1962 because of pressure of work in Rome; and in October 1970, shortly after celebrating his 75th birthday, he retired as Prefect of the Congregation for the Evangelisation of Peoples —the new name for Propaganda Fide.

May 18, 1971.

Fulque Agnew died on August 28, 1975 in Malawi at the age of 74. Though he inherited a baronetcy he discontinued the style of Sir and the use of the title.

Fulque Melville Gerard Noel Agnew was born in October 1900, son of Major Charles Hamlyn Agnew, third son of the eighth baronet, and Lilian, daughter of Lieutenant-General Sir J. Wolfe Murray, K.C.B. In 1928 he succeeded to the baronetcy, which was founded in 1629, on the death of his uncle, Sir Andrew Agnew, ninth baronet.

Agnew was a radical aristocrat, whose conventional career took a leftward turn about the time he succeeded to the baronetcy. While still a schoolboy of 16 he joined the Army during the holidays from Harrow, serving in the Machine Gun Corps and in the Royal Flying Corps in France, and was wounded and twice mentioned in dispatches.

After the war he was given a permanent commission and spent the next 12 years in the regular Army, both in India and as an intelligence officer in China. At one point in his Army career he was granted leave to take part in an Arctic expedition.

He resigned from the service in 1931 and spent the next eight years, until the outbreak of war, in travelling on the Continent and studying the rural economy of central, eastern and south-eastern Europe. He spent some time as a student at the Universities of Graz and Vienna.

When war broke out in 1939, Agnew was officially informed that he would not be allowed to join the armed forces because of the implications of some secret work in which he had been engaged in Central Europe in previous years. He thereupon enrolled as an undergraduate at Edinburgh University and graduated B.Sc. in 1943.

From 1943-47 he served in the Friends' Ambulance Unit and was engaged in relief work among refugees and displaced persons in the Middle East and in the Aegean Islands and thereafter in Italy and Austria. When communal strife broke out on a large scale in India, he was invited to assist the Indian Government to withdraw their refugees from Pakistan and to organize relief and rehabilitation measures among them. He remained as an adviser to the Indian Ministry of Refugees until the end of 1944, when he felt that foreign advice and assistance were no longer required.

From India he went to South Africa and farmed until 1953, when he was appointed Registrar of the University of Fort Hare, where he and Lady Agnew were a great source of strength to the African undergraduates. They made no bones about their opposition to apartheid, and when the control of the University College passed in 1959 to the Bantu Education Department, Agnew and his wife, a distinguished geographer, and seven other senior members of the staff were expelled because of their liberal principles.

In 1960 Agnew was appointed secretary of Cambridge University Department of Education, a post he held until he resigned at the end of 1965 to go to Malawi, where Lady Agnew had been elected Professor of Geography.

Agnew's work at Cambridge was very much appreciated both by his colleagues, who found him an able and humane administrator, and by the postgraduate students, who found his advice helpful in all manner of matters. But Africa called him and he responded, feeling that he could give more useful service for the rest of his working life in the University of Malawi than in an old-established university in England. He also felt that in Malawi he could carry on the work which had given him so much satisfaction at Fort Hare until he was arbitrarily dismissed for identifying himself with what he felt were the paramount African causes.

In 1937 he married Swanzie, daughter of the late Major Esmé Erskine, C.M.G., M.C., by whom he had one son, Crispin, born in 1944, who succeeds to the baronetcy.

September 10, 1975.

Conrad Aiken, the distinguished poet, short story writer, novelist, critic and autobiographer, died on August 17, 1973 at Savannah, Georgia, United States, aged 84. In whichever medium he wrote, Aiken was always first a poet. Yet he never quite

achieved, either in the United States or in Britain, the degree of recognition that his talent and originality warranted, and this although he did not lack the customary honours accorded to major American writers.

These included a Pulitzer Prize in 1930, the Chair of Poetry at the Library of Congress in 1950-52, a National Book Award in 1954, the Bollingen Prize in 1956, and the Gold Medal for Poetry of the National Institute of Arts and Letters in 1958. Significantly, though he had been publishing since 1914, most of these honours came to him in the last decades of his life.

Conrad Potter Aiken was of an Old New England family but was born in Savannah, Georgia, on August 5, 1889. At the age of 11 he was taken to New Bedford, Massachusetts, to be brought up there by a great-great-aunt, his father having killed himself and his wife. After schooling at Concord, he went to Harvard as a member of the famous Class of 1911, which included T. S. Eliot*, Van Wyck Brooks, Walter Lippmann, Robert Benchley and John Reed.

After Harvard, he worked for a time as a sports reporter but, having a small private income, soon devoted himself wholly to his own writing. In the early 1930s he went to England and settled at Rye. For some years he was London correspondent to *The New Yorker*. He returned to the United States on the outbreak of war and for the rest of his life lived mainly in Brewster, Massachusetts.

Despite the variety of forms he practised, Aiken's work from beginning to end was of a piece, bearing his own highly idiosyncratic signature. His description of his volume of poems *Preludes* (1931) seems to cover all his work: "an exploration of the fragmented ego, and a celebration of it and of the extraordinary world in which it *finds* itself, as well".

The most striking early expression of this exploration is probably *Senlin, and Other Poems* (1918), poems whose rhythms—though only their rhythms, for Aiken was essentially a romantic poet—often uncannily parallel those of Eliot's "Prufrock." The Senlin poems, like *Preludes*, are "a probing of the self-in-relation-to-the-world," and for Aiken the solid fabric of the world had been all but dissolved in the findings of Freud on the one hand and of Einstein on the other; with the result that in this middle period of his work, in his prose only less than in his verse, Aiken's writing was fluid, fluent, limpid, aspiring to the condition of music.

Aldous Huxley* dismissed him as an "agreeable maker of coloured mists." In fact, reality was always there, but it was reality shaped by dream, as though dream— or nightmare—was itself the fundamental reality.

This came out strongly not only in his poetry but also in the short stories, of which he was one of the twentieth-century American masters—the short stories were collected in 1966—and in the novels: *Blue Voyage* (1927), which among other things is an early example of the influence of Joyce's *Ulysses; The Great Circle* (1933); *King Coffin* (1935); and *The Conversation* (1940). It came out too in *Ushant* (1952), which Aiken significantly subtitled "an autobiographical narrative."

Viewed as straight autobiography, *Ushant* would be a maddening book. As it is, it is a remarkable experiment in self-revelation and an invaluable picture of London literary life between the wars, containing very frank renderings of friends such as Eliot (referred to throughout as "Tsetse") and the novelist Malcolm Lowry. It also recreates with much vividness the almost archetypal New England background in which Aiken had his roots.

It was to that sombre background, as well as to the contrasted and very different subtropical background of the Georgia of his early boyhood, that he returned in his later poetry, particularly in *Time in the Rock* (1936), *The Kid* (1947), *Skylight One* (1949), *Sheepfold Hill* (1958). In these poems of the New England experience his verse became tighter and more concentrated, as though approximating to the austerity of his ancestral acres.

Aiken was three times married: in 1912 to Jessie McDonald, by whom he had a son and two daughters, in 1930 to Clarice Mary Lorenz, and to Mary Augusta Hoover.

August 20, 1973.

Lord Ailesbury, the seventh Marquess, died on July 14, 1974, at the age of 70.

The only son of the sixth Marquess, he was educated at Eton and Christ Church, Oxford. In the Second World War while serving in the R.A.S.C. he was taken prisoner by the Germans before the evacuation of Dunkirk. In a book *I Walked Alone* (1950) he described how he jumped from the back of a moving lorry in Belgium and after many difficult weeks reached Gibraltar. He made his way by foot and bicycle and on one occasion had a ride in the car of a Nazi officer. On reaching Spain he was arrested, placed in a camp for political prisoners and eventually repatriated.

The tale of an extremely hazardous journey was told with an admirable modesty and, on occasions, splendid understatement. The author published it as the Earl of Cardigan, the name by which he was known during his father's lifetime. He was also the author of *Youth Goes East*, an account of a journey taken in the 1920s with his first wife and a friend in a Morris Oxford from the Hook of Holland to Athens; *Amateur Pilot*, which was about learning to fly; *The Wardens of Savernake Forest* (he was the 29th Hereditary Warden of the forest); and *The Life and Loyalties of Thomas Bruce*, one of his ancestors who was Gentleman of the Bedchamber to King Charles II and King James II.

Lord Ailesbury was a Justice of the Peace for Wiltshire, a former county councillor, and from 1950 to 1969 a Deputy Lieutenant.

He was three times married and is succeeded by his eldest son, Viscount Savernake.

July 17, 1974.

Henry Mann Ainsworth, one of the pioneers of the motor industry, died in Paris on January 24, 1971. He was 86.

Ainsworth joined the Hotchkiss company of Paris as a young engineer in 1904, and retired in 1949 but remained on the board as technical adviser.

He volunteered for service in the British Army in 1914, rising to the rank of captain and also being decorated with the British Military Medal, Inter-Allied Medal and the Star of Mons.

In 1916 he was released from active service to start a factory in Coventry, making Hotchkiss machine-guns, and he produced more than 50,000. In 1919 the factory was re-tooled and was the first one to mass-produce motor engines, these being sold to W. R. Morris, later Lord Nuffield*. The factory was eventually bought by Lord Nuffield.

Ainsworth returned to Paris in 1923 and built a factory producing not only Hotchkiss cars but also a light tank: more than 2,000 tanks were built for the French Government. In 1928 he was made a Chevalier de la Légion d'Honneur.

Ainsworth was a friend of Louis Renault, Gabriel Voisin, André Citroën and Paul Panhard. He created the St. Denis works of Hotchkiss, where he became technical director, then chairman and general manager. Between the wars Hotchkiss cars won the Monte Carlo Rally three years in succession.

In 1941 Ainsworth escaped from Paris just before it was overrun by the Germans and made his way via Portugal with his tank designs to the United States, where he was appointed tank production expert to the British Purchasing Commission in Washington. Lord Beaverbrook* appointed him Director-General of Tank Design and he was flown from America in a bomber.

In 1949 he was elevated by the French Government to the rank of Commandeur de la Légion d'Honneur for services to France. He was an early member of the management committee of the Automobile Club de France.

January 27, 1971.

Sir Bronson Albery, who was for many years either a managing director or chairman of the company controlling the Criterion, Wyndham's and New Theatres, and who also put his experience and enthusiasm at the service of the theatre in a wider sense through his connexions with the Old Vic and the Arts Council, died on July 21, 1971 in London after a long illness. He was 90.

His professional standing could hardly be better illustrated than by the fact that Bernard Shaw, to whom he was then known merely by reputation, entered into no written contract with Albery when *Saint Joan* was produced at the New in 1924.

His father James Albery was a playwright who had fallen out of the running, and his mother Mary Moore became the breadwinner by resuming her career on the stage a few years after the birth of the second of their three sons, Bronson, on March 6, 1881. He owed his first name to his parents' friendship with Bronson Howard, another playwright and brother-in-law of the actor-manager Charles Wyndham, whose leading lady Mary Moore became.

Bronson ("Bronnie") James Albery, whose father died in 1889, was educated at Uppingham, like his elder brother Irving Albery, and at Balliol College, Oxford, and was called to the Bar. He did not turn to theatrical management until 1914, soon after Charles Wyndham's retirement from the stage, and then in partnership not with his mother but with Allan Aynesworth the actor. Beginning with Cyril Harcourt's *A Pair of Silk Stockings*, they made three productions before the 1914-18 War broke out.

He served as a lieutenant in the R.N.V.R. from 1917 until 1919. At the beginning of 1919 Wyndham, who had become Bronson Albery's stepfather in 1916, died. Wyndham's son by his first marriage, Howard Wyndham, had returned from America some years before to help Mary Moore in the running of the family's three theatres. After the war he was joined by Bronson Albery, and on Mary Moore's death in 1931 they succeeded to the properties.

By that time Albery had shown how he proposed to make use of his managerial opportunities by espousing the cause of Sybil Thorndike and Lewis Casson*. The latter had their first experience of West End management, on a sharing basis, at the New in 1922, and in 1923 Albery entered into a partnership with them which lasted a little less than five years. It has been said, by Dame Sybil's biographer, Russell Thorndike, that the reason she first liked Albery was that he reminded her of Gerald du Maurier, and that he brought to the work of planning a flair for just how much of a good thing the public would take and would demand, in which the Cassons themselves were lacking. Certainly he was in favour of starting with *Advertising April*, a farce, as a contrast to the dramatic plays of Dame Sybil's recent season at the New, and certainly he had not been in favour of doing, as a successor to *Saint Joan*, a play by Lennox Robinson in which her role was too short to satisfy the expectations of her increased following. The first of their Shakespearian productions, *Cymbeline*, at the New, was described by Albery as "a failure, deservedly a failure"; of the other two, both designed, as *Saint Joan* had been, by Charles Ricketts, *Henry VIII* at the Empire fared better than *Macbeth* at the Princes.

His association with Michel Saint-Denis of the Compagnie des Quinze and with John Gielgud, who before he came into prominence at the Old Vic had been commended to Albery's attention by Mary Moore, began in 1931. In that year he transferred from the Arts Theatre Club, of which he was one of the three founder-directors, Saint-Denis's productions of two plays by André Obey, and at the same club-theatre he presented John Gielgud in a play submitted to him by the latter, Ronald Mackenzie's *Musical Chairs*. The one thing led to return visits to the New and Wyndham's by Saint-Denis's company which, through the break with naturalism in the productions and the collective rhythm of the acting, were to influence the work of English directors, designers and actors; the other thing led to John Gielgud's appearance in six more plays under the Howard Wyndham-Bronson Albery management.

Those plays included Gordon Daviot's *Richard of Bordeaux* (Gielgud's biggest personal success up to that time), *Hamlet* and Obey's *Noah*, under the direction of Saint-Denis, who had now settled in England with a view to setting up a drama school and a company. After Gielgud's contract with Albery had run out with *Romeo and Juliet* and *The Seagull*, and Saint-Denis had made the biggest success of his English career with a production of *The Three Sisters* for Gielgud, Albery lent himself to a scheme for the establishment of a theatre-centre with a repertory company and a programme of modern and classical plays, the whole to be linked with Saint-Denis's London school, by joining forces with the latter at the Phoenix during the latter half of 1938.

The times, with the Czech crisis culminating in Munich, and Munich pointing none knew whither, made detailed planning of the necessary kind impossible and demanded of the theatre something to which neither of the first two plays selected, a Russian play about the Ukraine in 1918 and a *Twelfth Night* under-cast notwithstanding the presence of Peggy Ashcroft and Michael Redgrave, was the answer. At the end of three months the season closed.

Albery, a governor of the Old Vic since 1936, had presented three Old Vic productions—*As You Like It* with Edith Evans, *Ghosts* with Marie Ney and *Macbeth* with Laurence Olivier—in the West End during 1937, and it was to him that Tyrone Guthrie, the Administrator of the Vic and of Sadler's Wells, turned for help in keeping their work alive during the Second World War, after the Wells was commandeered and the Vic damaged by bombing. Albery became administrator of the Ballet in 1941, and later was joint administrator with Guthrie of the drama and opera companies, which played alternately at the New Theatre during their London seasons, the plays including *Othello* and *The Merchant of Venice* with Frederick Valk and *Hamlet* with Robert Helpmann. Albery resigned as joint administrator in 1944, and a new triumvirate of which Olivier and Ralph Richardson were members took over the direction of the drama company; but the New remained the London home of both companies until the re-opening of the Wells in 1945 and of the Vic in 1950.

In 1945 Albery, who had been chairman simultaneously of the Society of West End Theatre Managers and of the Theatres' War Service Council, joined the Drama Panel of the Council for the Encouragement of Music and the Arts. Three years later, the Arts Council having been incorporated meanwhile, he was appointed to its executive committee and to the chairmanship of its drama panel. Knighted in 1949, he was sole drama representative on the executive when the Council severed the connexion with certain important play-producing companies, and when the affairs of the Old Vic, with which the Council continued to be associated, went through a period of crisis, ending with the return of Guthrie as administrator in 1951 and the winding up of schemes for training actors and rebuilding the stage, of which Michel Saint-Denis had been one of the three sponsors.

Albery was chairman of the Drama Advisory Committee of the British Council from 1952 until 1961, and was chairman of the Old Vic Trust while all plays in the First Shakespearian Folio were produced within five seasons, beginning with *Hamlet* with Richard Burton in 1953 and ending with *Henry VIII* with Gielgud and Edith Evans in 1958, and while funds were raised by tours overseas for the building of the Old Vic Annexe. He was still a director of the trust and a governor when the Old Vic Company played for the last time in the theatre before it became the temporary home of the National Theatre Company in 1963.

He had been president of the Repertory Players, a society for the production of new plays on Sunday night; and the early works of young playwrights presented by Howard Wyndham and himself included the first plays of Ronald Mackenzie, Gordon Daviot and Arthur Macrae, and the second play (*French Without Tears*) of Terence Rattigan. If he said that his proudest memory was of his association with Gielgud, Olivier, Ashcroft and Evans in *Romeo and Juliet* in 1935, those of *Saint Joan*, the Compagnie des Quinze—*Musical Chairs, Richard of Bordeaux* and *A Month in the Country*, staged jointly with Tennent Plays in 1943 with Valerie Taylor and Redgrave in the cast—assuredly came close behind.

Always ready to talk about the theatre, to laugh over it and to hear other people's opinions of it, he won friends for it wherever he went. As if he had not enough to do already, he made work for himself out of sheer kindness and for fun, as on an occasion in 1923, recalled by Tyrone Guthrie, when the young Guthrie, faced for the first time with the duties of assistant stage manager to a company that had hired the bar at the New Theatre for a rehearsal, was shown how to arrange the tables and chairs by an anonymous man who got down on his hands and knees with a tape measure, disguising his voice so that the visiting novice might not identify him. Nor did he, until his next meeting, which was almost 20 years later.

Albery married in 1912 Miss Una Gwynn Rolleston, by whom he had two sons and two daughters. His son Donald was joint managing director with him of Wyndham Theatres Ltd., and became sole managing director on his father's retirement.

Bronson Albery was a Chevalier of the Legion of Honour and until 1967 he was a Vice-president of the Actors' Benevolent Fund and Chairman of the Vic-Wells Association. From 1952 to 1953 he held office for the second time as President of the Society of West End Theatre Managers, an office of which the first holder was his stepfather, Charles Wyndham, in 1908.

July 22, 1971.

Winthrop Aldrich, formerly chairman of the Chase National Bank, and United States Ambassador in London from 1953 to 1957, died on February 25, 1974, at his home in New York. He was 88.

Lawyer, banker and financial statesman, he was the son of Senator Nelson W. Aldrich, who in his career had been chairman of the National Monetary Commission which played an influential part in the setting up of the Federal Reserve System. He was actively associated with the work of some leading philanthropic organizations.

Winthrop Aldrich entered banking after a successful career in the legal firm of Murray, Aldrich and Webb. He became president of the Equitable Trust Company in 1929 and, a year later, when Equitable Trust merged with the Chase bank, was made president of the combined organization.

He made his mark in the financial field in the years of the Depression. It was in no small part due to his recommendations that the Banking Act of 1934 dictated the separation of commercial banks from their securities affiliates.

Aldrich, a liberal Republican, spoke up strongly for unconditional aid to Britain in the early days of the Second World War and was the first president of the British War Relief Society. Later, he was to be equally staunch in his support for the Marshall Aid Plan.

For his "furtherance of the interests of the British Commonwealth in the Allied cause during the War" the King's Medal for Service in the Cause of Freedom was conferred upon him by King George VI in

1945. He was also made an honorary G.B.E.

In 1946 President Truman appointed Aldrich chairman of the President's Committee for Financing Foreign Trade. In the same year he was vigorous in his advocacy of the U.S. loan to Britain, testifying before a Congressional committee and speaking on other occasions in favour of the credit being granted.

His period as American Ambassador in London was coming to an end when the Suez crisis blew up. An idea of the part he played during this difficult time for Anglo-American relations can be deduced from the speech which the Prime Minister, Harold Macmillan, made at the dinner given in Aldrich's honour by the Pilgrims early in 1957. "From my personal knowledge I can tell you that he has played a remarkable and indeed historic role during these anxious weeks", Macmillan said. "We owe him a debt which we cannot easily repay."

Some of Aldrich's conclusions on the Suez affair were contained in a "footnote to history" which he contributed to *Foreign Affairs* in 1967. The use of force by Britain and France against Egypt had a catastrophic effect on Anglo-American affairs, he wrote; but he added that another event which had greatly damaged relations between the two countries was the failure of the United States to support a Belgian amendment at the United Nations aimed to enable the British and French to withdraw from Suez "without undue humiliation".

Winthrop Williams Aldrich was born in Providence, Rhode Island, on November 2, 1885 and was educated at Harvard, as many of his family had been before him. He graduated in 1907 and went on to take a degree in law.

When America entered the First World War he joined the U.S. Naval Reserve and served with it for two years.

He married in 1916 Harriet, daughter of Charles B. Alexander. They had two sons, of whom one survives, and four daughters. His wife died in 1972.

February 27, 1974.

C. H. O'D. Alexander, C.M.G., C.B.E., one of the most gifted of British chess masters, died on February 7, 1974 at the age of 64. He was twice British chess champion.

Conel Hugh O'Donel Alexander was born in Cork on April 19, 1909, the son of Professor C. W. L. Alexander. He was educated at King Edward's High School and King's College, Cambridge, where he took first class honours in mathematics. From 1932 to 1938 he taught at Winchester, and from 1938 to 1939 he worked for the John Lewis Partnership.

During the Second World War he was attached to the Foreign Office. After the war, until 1971, he worked for the Government Communications Headquarters at Cheltenham.

He married in 1934 Enid Constance Crichton Neate, and they had two sons.

Alexander was one of the most gifted, possibly the most gifted, of all British chess masters. Although he managed to play a considerable amount of chess, especially in the earlier part of his career, the demands of his profession left him with comparatively little time for its practice and study; otherwise he would certainly have been of true grandmaster class, and possibly even of world stature.

He first came on the chess scene when he won the British Boys' Championship at Hastings in 1926. Rapidly improving after his admission to Cambridge University, he won the university championship four times and distinguished himself by winning a beautiful game in the annual match with Oxford University against R. H. Newman.

By 1932, when he came second in the British championship, he was recognized as Britain's leading young player. In 1938 he won the British championship at Brighton; he repeated that success at Blackpool in 1956.

But it was in the international field that he really found his forte. It seemed that the more formidable the opposition, the greater his spirits mounted to overcome it. He played with great distinction for his country in the Olympiads at Folkestone 1933, Warsaw 1935, Stockholm 1937 and Buenos Aires 1939, and also after the war in 1954 and 1958. In individual international tournaments his greatest successes were equal second at Hastings 1938 with Keres, ahead of Fine and Flohr; first at Hastings 1947, and equal fifth at the Hilversum Zonal tournament of that year; equal fifth at the Staunton Memorial Tournament of 1951; and equal first with Bronstein at Hastings 1953.

Possessor of an attractive and incisive style, he won many brilliant games, notably against Botvinnik, Gligoric, Pachman and Szabo. He was chess correspondent for *The Sunday Times* and always wrote felicitously and lucidly about the game.

Among his writings were *Chess* (1937), *Alekhine's Best Games of Chess, Vol. III* (1946), *Learn Chess* (1963 with T. J. Beach), and *Spassky and Fischer: (World Chess Championship 1972)*.

With his passing the world of chess is bereft of a most valiant spirit and a firm and lifelong friend. He was a symbol of all that is best in British chess and will be remembered as such by those who knew him.

February 16, 1974.

Dr. Salvador Allende Gossens, who died when overthrown as President of Chile in an armed coup on September 11, 1973, was one of the most important leftwing leaders of Latin America; his only peer was Dr. Fidel Castro, Prime Minister of Cuba. The two men were personal friends but although their proclaimed goal was identical, the building of a socialist society in the Marxist mould, the essential importance of the two figures lay in the alternative methods each proposed to achieve it.

Allende was Chilean to the core and it is difficult to think of the "Chilean road to Socialism" without his political skills, which gradually came to dominate the entire left-wing movement in Chile and to make him four times candidate for the presidency, or without his deeply Chilean personality, the ability to combine a genuine popular touch with a stubborn determination to do things in a Chilean way and work out methods fitted to that country. Above all he was practical, even cautious in the established way of Chilean politics, as opposed to the passionate, wilful violence typical of the Latin American guerrilla which Dr. Castro basically portrayed.

The Chilean "socialist experiment" was rightly felt by Chileans to have significance not only for other Latin American countries. For Dr. Allende's government signified, from the day he took office in November 1970, after the outgoing majority Christian Democrats had given him the necessary vote in Congress, an attempt to begin building a socialist society in an undeveloped country while maintaining the framework of liberal parliamentary government Chile had received from leading European nations last century. France, Italy and Spain watched instinctively, despite the conflict with their domestic contemporary politics, the immensely complex process Allende was trying to achieve.

Many doubted the sincerity of his repeated pledges not to discard one or other of his fixed points. His steeliness of character, the complexity of his political makeup, which anyone coming into closer contact with the man sensed beneath the bonhomie, explained how he personally seemed confident he could reconcile them—if a sufficient number of his countrymen would stay with him and evolve as Chile evolved "her" socialism.

Allende helped found the Chilean Socialist Party in 1933 and through many years he helped powerfully amid party controversies on ideological goals and transitory methods to form the distinctive force it became among the world's Marxist socialist parties.

It broke away from the Chilean Communist Party founded after the Russian Revolution because its revolutionary Marxism shunned Moscow's tutelage as failing totally to analyse the Chilean reality and absurdly limited recruitment to a proletariat which was only beginning to exist.

Chile's socialism, recruited from all social classes, was unpuritanical, Latin in its acceptance of the force of individual personality, and "anti-imperialist", which meant Chile had not only to remake its own society but radically change the "colonial" economic relations existing with the world's rich countries, particularly the

United States.

Allende, the son of a Valparaiso lawyer, was born on July 26, 1908. His grandfather had been a founder of the Chilean Radical Party, one of the non-Marxist parties which was to make up Allende's "Popular Unity" government coalition in 1970.

The family background, and especially his mother, favoured modern ideas and at his lycée and at medical school Allende was actively advocating such ideas.

When in 1931 a popular uprising brought the end of the semi-Fascist Ibañez regime, Allende with a group of sympathizers led the takeover of Santiago University and was jailed by a military tribunal for "revolutionary activities". He later had difficulty in finding a post as a doctor in private practice and became a coroner's assistant. It was not until 1937 that he first got elected to Congress. From 1939 to 1942 he held office as Minister of Health.

Those early professional years undoubtedly moulded Allende as a Marxist politician; as a doctor he saw the malnutrition, the high infant mortality, the alcoholism, the bad housing, illiteracy and exploitation of the Chilean poor in the 1930s.

His emotional attachment to the masses and socialism—for all his tactical skills as a political leader—was accompanied by a virtual disinterest in economics or the mechanics of creating a socialist economy.

Allende was only declared the left's candidate for the fourth time in February 1970 after five months of haggling, and his campaign lacked the support of a left-wing experts' team which gave distinction to the 1964 campaign when he was defeated by Eduardo Frei. Previous failures had strained his following and brought rejection of his "electoralismo" by even a section of his own party which had come to believe in the Castroite guerrillas' road to power.

Allende himself was surprised by his September 4 victory and told impatient foreign journalists that night seeking an interview before he addressed the Santiago masses: "Gentlemen, I have waited 18 years for this moment, can't you now show a little patience?"

Two of his campaign promises were soon made good. He nationalized Chile's big copper mines previously partly owned by the United States, taking over the sales operation as well as production, and ended the diplomatic and economic boycott of communist Cuba by Chile. At first he moved cautiously in order not to provoke the United States further, but relations worsened to a point that, when addressing the United Nations in 1972, he accused United States corporations, banks and government agencies of "serious aggression". In particular he singled out the International Telephone and Telegraph Corporation and the Kennecott Copper Corporation who had "dug their claws into my country". He attacked the former for trying to stop him acceding to the presidency and the latter for bringing legal action against the state copper company in foreign courts.

His reputation for caution and compromise was shown during his dramatic and troubled years in office. A strike of truck-owners and shopkeepers in 1972 was solved temporarily by bringing into his cabinet senior members of the armed forces. This calmed the atmosphere enough to allow him to travel to Mexico, the United Nations, the Soviet Union (where soon after he was awarded the Lenin Peace Prize), and Cuba.

Mid-term elections, in which all seats in the Chamber of Deputies and half the Senate were at stake, showed growing support for his own Socialist Party within the Government's coalition and he cut the opposition's majority in congress slightly.

But this was only temporary relief for him as, in the Chilean winter of 1972, his Administration was plunged into its most serious crisis. After an abortive coup by a small section of the armed forces in June, the truck-owners again went on strike against the threat of nationalization. This time it spread to include professional workers, and street violence by the left and the right became a feature in the Latin American republic, which had a reputation for parliamentarianism and respect for the law.

The armed forces were again brought back into the cabinet but this time they were restless, only too aware that they were beginning to sacrifice their political neutrality.

With inflation running at what was believed to be the highest rate in the world, with his country dangerously polarized between the left and the right, with food and other goods in short supply, Allende, blaming all his ills on "the fascists", struggled to stop Chile from tipping over into civil war.

On September 11, 1973, the armed forces sided with the anti-Marxist opposition and deposed him in a violent coup. His last public statement, made while his palace and his suburban home were being bombed, was: "I will not resign. I will not do it. I am ready to resist with whatever means, even at the cost of my life, in that this serves as a lesson in the ignominious history of those who have strength but not reason."

Chile's attempt to create a socialist revolution through democratic means was over.

Allende could be a raspingly bitter speaker, a subtle Marxist debater, but also an eloquent spokesman for the Third World's poverty. The speech he gave when Queen Elizabeth made a state visit to Chile in November 1968, as president of the Chilean Senate, was a finely measured appeal to the rich nations.

Allende lived in a comfortable Santiago home completely within the personal style of the Chilean upper middle class to which he was born. He leaves a widow and three daughters.

September 13, 1973.

Norman Allin, the distinguished British oratorio and opera bass, died on October 27, 1973 at the age of 88.

Allin was born at Ashton-under-Lyne on November 19, 1884. He studied at the Royal Manchester College of Music from 1906 until 1910 with a view to becoming a teacher. But after marrying the mezzo-soprano Edith Clegg he decided to take up singing himself. His first appearance was at a concert in Manchester.

His stage debut was with the Beecham* Company at the Aldwych in 1916 as the Aged Hebrew in *Samson et Dalila.* He soon graduated to more substantial roles with that company, including Dosifei in *Khovanshchina* when the opera was first given in English, at Drury Lane.

His Covent Garden debut came in 1919, as Khan Khonchak, under Albert Coates. The same season he sang his first Gurnemanz, for which the beauty of his singing and the dignity of his acting were praised; and his first Boris.

In 1922 he became one of the directors, as well as the leading bass, of the newly formed British National Opera Company, and sang a variety of roles in the company's Covent Garden seasons, including a notable Mephistopheles and Sarastro.

In the international seasons later in the 1920s he sang, among other roles, Dr. Bartolo in *Le Nozze di Figaro,* a part he also took in the opening performances at Glyndebourne in 1934. Among his other roles were Hunding, Hagen and Ochs, all in English for the B.N.O.C., and Fafner in German at Covent Garden.

He also appeared in a variety of parts with the Carl Rosa Company from 1942 to 1949.

On the concert platform he sang everything from Purcell to Mussorgsky with the same facility. In his heyday, he was undoubtedly Britain's outstanding bass and in present circumstances would undoubtedly have had an international career of note. His voice was that rarity, a true, voluminous bass. It was once described as "a wonderful organ, and for all its majestic proportions as flexible as many a coloratura soprano's".

He was still singing with the same breadth and power well into his sixties, a sure test of the validity of his vocal method. His many records bear witness to the vitality and smoothness of his singing.

October 29, 1973.

Professor P. R. Allison, F.R.C.S., M.D., Nuffield Professor of Surgery in the University of Oxford, died in Oxford on March 6, 1974 at the age of 66.

Philip Rowland Allison, the son of J. R. Allison, was born at Selby, Yorkshire, on June 2, 1907 and was educated at Hymers College, Hull. He was one of a family of five, two others of whom became doctors. He entered the Leeds Medical School in

1924 and had a brilliant career, taking the B.Sc. with 1st Class Honours in Physiology in 1927, and the M.B., Ch.B. with 1st Class Honours in 1931. He became F.R.C.S. in 1932, when he was only 25, and Ch.M. in 1936.

Allison's ambition from the beginning was to become a leader in surgery and he lost no time on the way. After a series of junior appointments he was elevated to the staff of the General Infirmary at Leeds in 1936 and worked for five years as a general surgeon. By 1941 he had decided that his surgical field of choice was the chest and he became the first thoracic surgeon to be appointed to the General Infirmary at Leeds, eventually becoming surgeon to the Leeds Regional Hospital Board, and senior lecturer in thoracic surgery in 1949.

During the war he was thoracic surgical adviser to the Emergency Medical Service for his part of England, and he had a mobile thoracic surgical team ready to deal with air-raid casualties. By the end of the war he had established an international reputation in his field and it was generally held that he was the leading oesophageal surgeon in the world.

In 1953 the Chair of Surgery in Leeds became vacant and the surgeons there of one accord recommended Allison. His purpose now was clear. It was to be head of the best department of thoracic surgery in the Commonwealth, if not in the world. When, therefore, the university refused to promise all that he had asked for, he left Leeds and accepted the Nuffield* Professorship of Surgery at Oxford, which had become vacant.

Allison had learnt that it was not possible to maintain a lead in thoracic and cardiac surgery without ultra-modern equipment which is necessarily expensive. In spite of considerable initial resistance he built a first-class department which in retrospect was in no way extravagant. His main contribution to surgery in Oxford was to set an example of practice. He always insisted that he was not just a thoracic surgeon and his work extended over a wide field.

In the operating theatre he combined boldness and originality in conception with meticulous care in execution. He did his own post-operative dressings and spent much time in the instruction of his nurses so as to ensure the best team-work. His unit was, in fact, a small, closely-knit family.

Allison was a little below middle height with hair already white by the time he was 50. He always wore a bow tie, sometimes of unusual length and brightness, and this, with the handkerchief appearing from the breast pocket and the flower in the button-hole, gave the panache which physicians are prone to detect in successful surgeons and medical students love to caricature.

He married Kathleen Greaves in 1937 and they had two sons and one daughter.

March 7, 1974.

Ambrose, (Baruch Ambrose), one of the most popular band leaders of the big band era, died in Leeds on June 11, 1971. He was 70.

Earlier he had collapsed in a television studio where he was watching the singer Kathy Kirby, whose career he had done so much to forward, rehearse.

His golden years were those in the decade between the two world wars, but when the big bands began to lose their popularity Ambrose was faced with difficult times. In 1955 he remarked, ironically, "Once I played for the King of England; now I play for Teddy boys at five bob hops".

He was not overstating the case, for in the heyday of success his signature tune "When Day is Done" had been heard in more than one palace and he was as popular in the plushier restaurants and clubs of metropolitan America as in the West End.

In an interview in 1970 he remarked that there was a time when travelling did not mean dashing for a plane. "We used to get the Blue Train to Cannes", he said.

He was born Baruch Ambrose, the son of a Jewish wool merchant at Amherst Park, London. At 16 he was playing sixth fiddle at the Palais Royal in New York. He had been taken to America at the age of 11 by an aunt. At 17 he formed his own band.

It was at Ilford Palais, Essex, that Kathy Kirby, then 16, first became associated with the Ambrose band. She asked Ambrose if she could sing and when he heard her he recognized her talent. Later he became her manager and guided her to success.

Early in 1971 a record company, staging a revival of dance band music of the '30s, released an L.P. record of Ambrose's numbers.

June 14, 1971.

Florence Amery, C.I., widow of the Rt. Hon. L. S. Amery, C.H., for many years an outstanding figure in British political life, and mother of Julian Amery, M.P., died on February 18, 1975 at the age of 94. Her husband died in 1955.

She had the gifts—beauty, capacity, charm, understanding and a natural friend-liness—which made and kept friends wherever she went. Mrs. Amery would have been outstanding in any sphere, and if it had not been for her devotion to her husband and his career, as well as to her family, she could, and no doubt would, have created and followed a career of her own.

She had decided convictions, and some-times a forthright way of expressing them, but she had also the saving grace of toler-ance for the opinions of others, and it was part of her charm that she was a good and sympathetic listener.

For the greater part of their married life she invariably travelled with her husband on all the multitudinous foreign journeys which he had to make in the course of his political career, and she was also his con-stant companion and support in his polit-ical campaigns at home and throughout his long representation of the South (after-wards the Sparkbrook) division of Birming-ham. She helped him materially, as he so handsomely testifies in his three volumes of *My Political Life*, to serve his constituents and to retain their confidence.

She could speak persuasively but she ex-celled as an organizer and administrator who, by the very force of her personality and her capacity for visualizing the larger issues, could galvanize others into doing things, and often into achieving results which they may themselves have doubted.

This was particularly evidenced in her great work as chairman of the Indian Com-forts Fund, which throughout the 1939-45 War looked after the needs of Indian prisoners of war on the Continent and of Indian seamen in British ports.

In this way, her name became known throughout India. There, indeed, the com-forts fund, and the goodwill which it estab-lished, could well be her most abiding memorial. For this work she was created, in 1945, a Lady of the Imperial Order of the Crown of India.

Adeliza Florence Louise was born in the 1880s at Whitby, Ontario, the fourth daughter of John Hamar Greenwood, a barrister of substance, and a member of an old English family of West Riding origin which had afterwards settled in Radnor-shire. "Bryddie" Greenwood, as she was known in the family circle, was educated first at home and then at St. Hilda's Col-lege. She was a popular figure in her home town when Leo Amery met her on his visit to the Dominion in 1910.

There was a certain piquancy about their marriage, and Florence Greenwood's coming to settle in England as the wife of the man who was then by some regarded as an arch-Imperialist although in fact in his earliest days as a journalist on the *Man-chester Guardian* he had been dubbed a "pro-Boer". Her elder brother, Hamar Greenwood, was already in England and a rising star in the ranks of the Liberal Party.

Mrs. Amery had all the opportunities of employing her graces as hostess when her husband was Secretary of State for the Colonies in the early 1920s. Those were the days before the Dominions and the Com-monwealth were talked about much, but Florence Amery, Canadian born, and with an intense feeling for the links which bind Britain and the sister nations together, threw open her home for regular tea parties at which the London officials, and visitors from all parts of Britain overseas, could meet upon a common basis of friendship and association.

February 20, 1975.

Haj Amin el Husseini—See Jerusalem.

Lord Ampthill, C.B.E., the third baron, died on June 3, 1973. He was 76. The eldest son of the second Baron Ampthill, he was born on October 4, 1896, and succeeded his father in 1935.

In 1912, at the age of 16, Ampthill joined the Royal Navy as a midshipman after going through the Royal Naval Colleges at Osborne and Dartmouth. He served throughout the First World War, initially in H.M.S. Defence, which was sunk at Jutland with no survivors only a week after he had left her to join a sloop in the Mediterranean on promotion to sub-lieutenant.

Towards the end of the war he qualified as a submarine officer and took part in a number of underwater patrols in the North Sea.

From earliest childhood the Navy had been his predominant interest but, unhappily, he retired from the Service soon after the war for domestic reasons, thus putting an end to what might have been a distinguished naval career. However, after spending the inter-war years with an engineering company and in other business appointments he was recalled to the Navy with the rank of commander at the beginning of the 1939-45 war. After serving in the Torpedo and Mining Department of the Admiralty he joined the staff of Admiral Sir B. Ramsay and as Senior Administrative Naval Officer with the rank of captain he played an important part behind the scenes in the planning and execution of the naval aspects of the allied landings in North Africa and Europe. For his distinguished services in these campaigns he received the C.B.E., Chevalier Légion d'Honneur and Croix de Guerre with Palms (France) and the Order of the Legion of Merit (U.S.A.). His liaison duties with the United States Navy won him many American friends.

After the war Ampthill was appointed a director of a large public company with responsibility for manufacturing and production and in this capacity too he was able to use his outstanding administrative abilities to great effect. In this and throughout his career he was always intensely loyal to his subordinates, who responded with affection and respect.

Until 1971, when his health began to fail, he took a keen part in defence debates in the House of Lords as a staunch supporter of the Royal Navy.

He married in 1918 Christabel Hulme, daughter of Lieutenant-Colonel John Hart, by whom he had one son. The marriage was dissolved by divorce in 1937 and he married secondly that same year Sibell Faithfull, daughter of T. W. Lumley. She died in 1947 and he married thirdly in 1948 Adeline, daughter of Canon H. E. Hone, They had one son and one daughter.

The death of Lord Ampthill inevitably recalls the prolonged litigation of some 50 years ago in which he was intimately involved and which produced what *The Times*, in a leader of 1924, called a memorable judgment. Mr. John Hugo Russell, as Lord Ampthill then was, petitioned in 1922 for a divorce from his wife, whom he had married in 1918 and who gave birth to a son in October 1921. At the conclusion of a second hearing in March 1923 Mr. Russell was granted a decree nisi. Mrs. Russell's appeal to the Court of Appeal was dismissed. She then appealed to the House of Lords who, on May 30, 1924, by a majority of three to two, allowed her appeal.

The result was that she remained the lawful wife of Mr. Russell and the child remained the child of the marriage. In 1926, Mr. Justice Swift made a declaration that Geoffrey Denis Erskine Russell was the lawful child of his parents, John Russell and Christabel Russell.

The case of Russell v Russell established an important rule of law—namely, that no evidence can be given by a husband or a wife in any proceedings whatever to the effect that they have not had intercourse, if the effect of such evidence would be to bastardize a child born in wedlock. The leader in *The Times* commented on the social importance of the case, and explained that "For this reason it has been necessary to report at considerable length the painful and even repulsive evidence of a kind which would otherwise have found no place in these columns".

Two years later an Act of Parliament was passed restricting the reporting of evidence in divorce cases: as a result reporting was limited to the summing up of the judge, points of law submitted, a concise statement of the charges and counter-charges, and the identity of the parties.

June 4, 1973.

Lale Andersen, the German singer whose "Lili Marlene" became a hit with troops during the Second World War, died in Vienna in August 1972 at the age of 59.

She first recorded the sad, haunting song in 1939. It became a theme song for the Eighth Army men as well as for Rommel's desert troops.

The first version of the song, set in slow waltz time, was a flop; but Norbert Schultze, the German opera composer, gave the song a more sprightly tempo and soon it became the most memorable song of the war. It was broadcast over German radio to Afrika Korps troops fighting in North Africa, was heard by soldiers of the British Eighth Army, and became popular with both forces.

Towards the end of the war the song was banned by the Nazis.

After the war Lale Andersen enjoyed an international reputation, appearing with great success in Britain, the United States and Canada. She had recently published her autobiography, *The Sky has Many Colours.*

August 30, 1972.

Sir Donald Anderson, chairman of P. & O. Steam Navigation Company from 1960 to 1971 and probably the outstanding shipping man of his generation, died on March 20, 1973 at the age of 66.

He was one of the national directors chosen for the board of Times Newspapers Ltd. by Gavin Astor, now Lord Astor of Hever, when the company was formed. He was a diligent attender of board meetings and though he was always willing to place at the board's disposal his shrewd business sense he was never obtrusive.

Anderson emerged from retirement in spectacular style at the end of 1972 to play a decisive role in the movement to reject P. & O.'s proposed merger with the Bovis building group. By swinging his weight solidly against the merger he exercised a significant influence over many wavering shareholders.

He was also responsible for persuading Lord Inchcape to offer himself as a candidate for the chairmanship of P. & O. in the event of the bid's failure. The bid was subsequently defeated, Lord Inchcape was elected chairman, and thus for the second time Anderson was instrumental in the choice of a successor to the post.

Donald Forsyth Anderson was born on September 3, 1906 into one of the leading shipping families in the United Kingdom. He became a dedicated shipowner. He rose from a minor position in the firm of Anderson, Green and Company, ship managers and shipbrokers, to be head of the P. & O. Group, the largest independent shipping concern in the world. There was hardly an activity connected with the ship-owning side of the industry with which he was not at one time or another associated. When president of the Chamber of Shipping of the United Kingdom in 1953 he also held the chairmanship of the Shipping Federation—an office in which he served from 1950 to 1962—thus combining under one leadership the two national organizations which cover the commercial and personnel interests of the British merchant fleet.

The Anderson family, which is of Aberdeen origin, have been in the shipping business for over a hundred years. In the middle of the nineteenth century they built up their interest in shipping in the Aberdeen White Star Line. This developed into the Aberdeen and Commonwealth Line. The family business of Anderson, Green and Company, now well past its centenary, at one time managed the Orient Line, later merged with the P. & O. group.

It appeared an unfortunate accident of timing when Anderson, a man of positive and forceful disposition, took over the helm at P. & O. at a time when world shipping conditions were such that retrenchment was the order of the day. He nevertheless proceeded in the ensuing years to lead P. & O. and by example the rest of the industry into a vigorous programme of rationalization, reorganization, and above all diversification that became so marked a feature of British shipping in the late sixties. Under him P. & O., which in the 1950s was still firmly wedded to its century-old business of passenger and cargo liners, branched out into tankers, bulk-carriers and other specialized fields, sometimes alone, sometimes with partners who had an expertise to offer.

Undoubtedly the most important of these was the formation in the mid-sixties of the Overseas Containers consortium in which he was the prime mover. Through O.C.L., and the later A.C.T. consortium which it brought into being by a process of reaction, British liner shipping underwent (and is still undergoing) the most far-reaching transformation since the coming of steam, involving huge investment, new relationships between old rivals, and a radical upheaval in the life and work of thousands engaged in the movement of general cargo afloat and ashore. That the impetus for this vast process should have sprung from the largest, oldest, and until a short time before most conservative pillar of the old regime, was eloquent testimony to Anderson's far-sightedness, courage, and force of per-personality.

His one great fear about shipping was complacency—"a dangerous habit and as British as chilblains or beer"—and in his last speech as president of the Chamber of Shipping he gave expression to that fear. There was, he said, no divine law which laid it down that the British shipping industry must flourish. It was built at a time when it had great advantages—the first "run" at the steam engine, vast tonnages of coal to carry out and of grain to bring back, when Britain was the workshop of the world and the world's banker, broker and merchant. "Behind us", he emphasized, "we have a great position which our forefathers won; a wealth of commercial goodwill; a deep well of shipping experience and tradition in management, in operation, in sea-going personnel—factors of enormous value, but by themselves they do not guarantee shipowners a living from the world for five minutes."

Anderson had about him an air of distinction. Tall, sparely built, good-looking, with a strong characterful face denoting both sternness and humour, his tufted eyebrows concealed keen, penetrating eyes which gave a hint of the acute mind, combined with consummate skill, that made him so able an administrator. He would pucker his broad forehead in moments of concentration and often he gave the impression of speaking his thoughts aloud—but they were thoughts that rarely needed second thoughts.

"Lean and aggressive" was a description applied to him by one commentator, and he could certainly be aggressive in speech. His devotion to shipping and to his own group of companies in particular led him on one occasion to speak of "business parasites" who were trying to "suck the lifeblood" of the shipping industry by demanding bigger dividends. The speech was made at a relatively minor dinner of shipping staffs, but it attracted wide publicity and aroused angry reactions. Anderson made a handsome apology at the annual meeting of the P. & O., which followed quite soon.

His humour was dry and sometimes mordant, but his sharpest shafts were usually tempered by kindliness. He could make a brilliant speech without preparation or notes. With an expressionless face—it would have been called a "pan face" in theatrical circles—he would criticize with wit and wisdom men and matters of the moment in a seemingly effortless way which never failed to entertain. In his position as one of the leading shipowners in Britain he was much sought after as a speaker. He was never known to be dull.

In his relaxed moments he was a charming individual and a perfect host. On an informal trip from Tilbury to Southampton in the Iberia he did not disdain to appear in his shirt sleeves.

A strong individualist, Anderson recognized that there were spheres in which action even by the most powerful groups of shipowners would be of no avail and must be left to government. As chief spokesman of the industry he expressed appreciation of the praise given to shipowners officially and unofficially for maintaining Britain's position as a leading maritime nation and for shipping's contribution to the balance of payments and for the constant endeavours to keep the merchantile marine in a state of competitive efficiency. But, as he drily observed, tributes, like kind words, butter no parsnips and lay no keels.

Anderson was a keen rider to hounds. He had the reputation of being a fine horseman. His wife was the sister of Colonel Llewellyn, the owner of the well-known show-ring horse Foxhunter.

Donald Anderson was the second son of Sir Alan Garrett Anderson. His grandmother was Dr. Elizabeth Garrett Anderson, the first woman to qualify as a doctor in Britain. He went to Eton and on coming down from Trinity College, Oxford, where he took an M.A. degree, he entered the family business of Anderson, Green and Company. He joined the P. & O. Steam Navigation Company in 1934. He was appointed a director in 1943, a managing director in 1946 and deputy chairman in 1950. He succeeded Sir William Currie as chairman in 1960.

In 1939 he went to the Ministry of Shipping (subsequently the Ministry of War Transport). Two years later he was appointed to the British Merchant Shipping Mission to the U.S.A. in Washington, D.C., a post he retained until he rejoined the P. & O. in 1943. His presidency of the Chamber of Shipping in 1953-4 carried with it the chairmanship of the General Council of British Shipping, a body set up during the Second World War to coordinate the views of the Chamber and the Liverpool Steam Ship Owners' Association. The council was dissolved in 1963 when the Liverpool association joined the Chamber.

Anderson was the fourth member of his immediate family to become president of the Chamber. Both his grandfather and father occupied the position, as did his brother, Sir Colin Anderson. A distant cousin, Sir Kenneth Anderson, was president as far back as 1915 and two others—I. C. Geddes, a first cousin of Sir Alan Anderson, and Sir Austin Anderson, who belonged to another branch of the family, were also, in their turn, presidents—a remarkable record which has rarely, if ever, been beaten.

As chairman of the Shipping Federation, Anderson was also president of the International Shipping Federation, joint chairman of the National Maritime Board and chairman of the Merchant Navy Training Board. He was president of the Institute of Shipping and Forwarding Agents in 1955, president of the Institute of Marine Engineers in 1956 and chairman of the British Liner Committee from 1956-1958. He was honorary treasurer of the Royal Free Hospital. He was awarded the honorary rank of Captain R.N.R., in recognition of his outstanding support given through his shipping companies to the Royal Naval Reserve in the post-war years.

He was created a Knight Bachelor in 1954. In 1946 he was made an Officer of the Order of Orange Nassau for services to the Netherlands and in 1959 received the decoration of Commendatore of the Order Al Merito della Republica Italiana.

He married in 1935 Margaret Elaine, eldest daughter of Sir David R. Llewellyn, Bt. They had four daughters.

March 22, 1973.

Leroy Anderson, the American light music composer, died in May 1975 at the age of 66.

Anderson was famous for his popular concert style, and many of his compositions are firmly established in the light orchestra repertoire. His composition "Blue Tango" earned him celebrity in 1952 when it became the first strictly instrumental number to reach the top of the Hit Parade. It eventually sold over two million copies to become a major commercial success.

Anderson was born of Swedish ancestry in Cambridge, Massachusetts, in June 1908. At the age of 11 he studied music at the New England Conservatory and in the following year wrote his first composition, a minuet for string quartet.

He studied music at Harvard, and on graduation in 1929 became choirmaster and organist of the East Congregational Church in Milton, Massachusetts.

He remained there for six years and, though he conducted and arranged music for the Harvard University Band during this period, worked at a doctoral thesis on foreign languages with a view to becoming a teacher of languages. This knowledge of languages was to be put to use later in his life as a liaison officer and translator in the Second World War.

But in 1935 Anderson gave up his thesis and appeared in Boston and New York as a freelance conductor, composer and arranger. He made a strong impression on the conductor of the Boston Pops Orchestra, Arthur Fiedler, and was engaged as its permanent orchestrator.

His gift for garbing popular music with varied colours and an ability to combine popular and symphonic elements without creating any clash in style greatly enhanced his reputation. His first composition for the Pops Orchestra, "Jazz Pizzicato", was in 1937.

During the Second World War, Anderson was called up by the army and served first as a press and liaison officer in Iceland, before transferring to Military Intelligence in Washington.

Returning to the Boston Pops Orchestra after the war, he composed several more pieces, of which "Fiddle-Faddle" and "The Syncopated Clock" virtually launched him on his successful career. From that point Decca engaged him to record his work and he became one of America's best known semi-classical composers.

To a grasp of technique he brought a sense of humour and a flair for burlesque, and was particularly successful in injecting borrowed sounds from the extra-musical world—the ticking of clocks, the clicking of typewriters and the ringing of sleigh bells—into his music.

A spate of compositions followed his first recording contract, many of which are now titles firmly entrenched in the repertoire. Among these well known pieces are "Fiddle-Faddle", "Belle of the Ball", "Plink, Plank, Plunk", "Sleigh Ride", "A Trumpeter's Lullaby" and "Blue Tango".

"The Typewriter" was effectively used in 1959 in the film *But Not For Me*, starring Clark Gable.

Recalled to army service during the Korean War, Anderson again served with Intelligence. Back in civilian life he composed his first Broadway Musical score *Goldilocks* in 1958. Thereafter he conducted a number of major American light orchestras and made numerous recordings.

May 20, 1975.

The Rt. Rev. W. L. Anderson, who was Bishop of Salisbury from 1949 to 1962, died on March 5, 1972 at the age of 80.

Anderson had held three bishoprics and was the first bishop ever to have served in all three fighting services. His first love was the country, and his second the sea. He was always thankful to shake the dust of London from his feet and he made no pretence at ecclesiastical statesmanship, eschewing the kind of episcopal pronouncement which seems to be written to match its headlines. But he was a much beloved Father in God to his clergy and people, and was never happier than when he was moving among them from village to village on one of his many pilgrimages through his country diocese.

William Louis Anderson was born in Assam on February 11, 1892, the son of James Drummond Anderson, of the Indian Civil Service. He was educated at St. Paul's School, of which he was a scholar, and at Gonville and Caius College, Cambridge, where he was an Exhibitioner. He graduated in 1914 and became an Honorary Fellow of his College in 1950.

When he went up to Cambridge he joined the 1st King Edward's Horse and it was with that regiment that he went to France in 1914 as a Squadron Sergeant Major. He was always proud to have been an Old Contemptible and his regiment held him in high esteem and was represented at both his enthronements. In 1916 he was commissioned in the Royal Naval Air Service and two years later became a Captain in the newly-formed R.A.F. While serving in the Scilly Islands he sank an enemy submarine in a flying-boat attack and for this exploit was awarded the D.S.C.

After the war he returned to Cambridge and received his theological training at Ridley Hall; he was later chairman of its governing body. He was ordained in 1920 and became chaplain of his college and curate of Holy Trinity, Cambridge, where the vicar was then the Rev. Edward Woods, whom Anderson was to succeed as Bishop of Croydon. In 1922 he was commissioned in the Royal Navy as a chaplain, and served in H.M.S. Royal Oak before becoming Chaplain of the Royal Naval College, Dartmouth.

In 1928 he became vicar of the busy Birmingham parish of St. John, Sparkhill, moving four years later to St. John's, Meads, Eastbourne, at a time when that parish contained more than a score of private schools. As at Dartmouth, he was at his best with young people and quickly won their affection and their loyalty. He was thoroughly happy in a parish which also included the lighthousemen at Beachy Head, and from which he could walk straight on to the Sussex Downs.

In 1937 Archbishop Lang appointed him to the Suffragan Bishopric of Croydon. Like his predecessor, but unlike any of his successors, he also held the posts of Archdeacon, Rural Dean and Vicar of Croydon, together with an Honorary Canonry of Canterbury. This was a gruelling job in a setting which was not very congenial to him. Soon after his arrival his wife caught typhoid in an epidemic and, when war came, he was confronted with conditions which made each sphere of his "Pooh-Bah" appointment increasingly difficult to fulfil. The first bombs to be dropped inland fell on Croydon aerodrome in 1940 and Anderson was soon on the scene.

In 1942 Sir Winston Churchill* nominated him for the See of Portsmouth. At any time he would have been happy to go to a diocese which included such a historical naval port, but in wartime it was the one diocese for which his experience most fitted him and he was undoubtedly the man for the job. He was in his element from the start. Bishopswood at Fareham became a home from home for all ranks, and he was indefatigable in visiting service establishments as well as his parishes on the mainland and in the Isle of Wight.

He never took kindly to diocesan administration or finance, and the problems of a small new diocese with slender resources and an incomplete cathedral bore increasingly upon him in the years following the war. His translation in 1949 to the diocese of Salisbury gave him full scope for his pastoral gifts, while he was able to leave to others many of the tasks which he found most irksome. In 1964 he became chairman of the Churches' Council of Healing.

Gifted with a resonant and pleasing voice and with great charm of manner, he was always welcome as a preacher and speaker, and his wide parochial and pastoral experience made him a wise counsellor whom his clergy always delighted to see. He was an artist of no mean distinction and exhibited regularly in the Naval Artists' Exhibition.

He married in 1921 Gwendoline Victoria Mary Jones, who was his constant companion in all his episcopal visits, and who helped him to be "given to hospitality" on a scale now seldom found in bishops' houses. She died in 1957. There were two sons of the marriage. He married, secondly, in 1963, Jessie Vida Hearn.

March 7, 1972.

Lieutenant-General Aman Andom, who in 1974 had briefly assumed the functions of Head of State of Ethiopia, and who was executed in that country on November 24, 1974, was born in 1924 of a Lutheran family of Eritrea, at that time an Italian province, and was educated at an American school in Khartum.

By 1941 he had already seen service with Ethiopian partisans against Italian occupying forces in Western Ethiopia, and after the liberation of the country he became a regular soldier. He soon acquired a reputation for energy and ability, was sent on courses at the Cadet College in Khartum, at Camberley, and at Sandhurst, and rose to the rank of Major-General.

In 1962, when the Emperor's Imperial Guard revolted, Andom was serving on the Somali frontier and took no part. Later he appears to have been suspected by the ruling hierarchy of holding unorthodox or even subversive views, because in 1964 he was sent to Washington as Military Attaché.

The following year he was taken out of the Army and appointed a member of the then ineffectual Senate. There, however, his outspoken criticisms of the Administration further offended the Emperor, although they commended him to the liberal elements already active within the country.

Early in 1974 the serious provincial famine, badly mishandled by the Government, led to a popular uprising which forced the Emperor to dismiss his long-trusted ministers and to appoint a new Cabinet with a mandate to reform the Administration and root out corruption.

It proved ineffectual and in July it was replaced by a new team. Andom, whose Eritrean origin and religion were deemed assets in view of the conflict between Copts and Muslims, which had long plagued that province, was made Minister of Defence. He was at the same time promoted to Lieutenant-General and appointed Chief of Staff.

The reformist efforts of even the new ministers proved equally inadequate to satisfy the malcontents, who by now included an increasing number of military personnel, and effective power gradually became vested in the so-called Armed Forces Coordinating Committee, of which Andom, by virtue of his reputation and sympathies, became spokesman and titular head.

In September 1974 this body took over power, the Emperor was deposed and Andom became de facto Head of State until he was forced from office and arrested.

November 25, 1974.

Professor E. N. da C. Andrade, F.R.S., **the** eminent physicist, died on June 6, 1971. He was 83.

Andrade was a man of many talents and interests—individual in all that he did and touched. As a physicist, he pursued his own lines, convinced that not all physicists should be nuclear, and ranged widely in his work. More than competent as a theorist, ingenious in devising experiments, his researches had the elegance that comes from a matching of aim, method and execution. As a collector of Newton's works he was an enthusiast; and as a student of Newton, Hooke and, in general, of the early days of the Royal Society, he showed scholarship and imagination.

As expositor and editor he did much in many ways to promote interest in science. As a conversationalist he could be brilliant —often with a bite in the brilliance—and was then the life of any party. As a writer he could be as good as he chose to be, which was good by any standards. He liked to live well, and did. He was generous but suffered neither injury nor fools gladly; and was often his own worst enemy. An intellectual aristocrat, he would have fitted more comfortably into the eighteenth than into the twentieth century; but in any age he would have carried a flail, and with it driven himself, as well as sometimes lashing about him.

Andrade's best-known research was on the physics of metals. But he did work in at least two other fields and made discoveries in each. He was one of the first to bring some real science into the study of creep in metals. He introduced rational methods of

experiment, and showed how conditions for obtaining more informative measurements than before could be realized. He distinguished between temporary creep caused by the slipping of one plane on another in metal crystals, and permanent flow which becomes progressively more important at higher temperatures, and in many engineering applications is critical.

In the same field of research he developed methods of making pure, single crystals of metals in the form of wires or rods, found their properties to differ startlingly from those formed of many small crystals, and studied the nature of glide planes. Later industrial research on the development of single crystals—not, in fact, of metals—for possible use as materials grew directly from Andrade's work.

He worked also on the physics of liquids —an obstinately difficult subject in which he arrived at simplicity in special conditions —and on the movements of solid particles in various experiments used in teaching to illustrate the properties of sound-waves. His ingenuity in experiment showed here to advantage.

As a student of seventeenth-century science, and also as a speaker and writer, Andrade touched possibly his highest point in his Wilkins lecture to the Royal Society, given in 1949. His subject was Robert Hooke—Newton's versatile, proud, injured and much maligned contemporary—and the concluding section of his lecture developed into a speech for the defence such as cannot often have been heard in the Royal Society's meeting room, and which is deserving of study as an example of that rather specialized form of literature, the written speech.

The understanding of Hooke which he then showed suggested a recognized parallel with himself. Newton, the master, was however his main and abiding interest, and from 1948 onwards he was chairman of the committee of the Royal Society responsible for preparing the tercentenary edition of Newton's letters. He was also chairman of the society's library committee, of which he was a member for 23 years.

As an expositor of science at different levels Andrade was editor for physics of the fourteenth edition of *Encyclopaedia Britannica,* acted for many years as adviser to a firm of publishers, was science correspondent of *The Times* from 1945 to 1952, introduced speakers in the B.B.C.'s programme "Science Survey" in its original form, was a member of the Brains Trust, on three occasions gave the Royal Institution's Christmas lectures "adapted to a juvenile auditory", and was a prolific writer of books, several of which had long histories. For example, *The Atom,* first published as a yellow-back "Benn sixpenny" in 1927, wore well enough to provide a basis for *The Atom and its Energy,* published 20 years later. A more advanced book, *The Structure of the Atom,* was already in its third edition by 1927, and his *An Approach to Modern Physics* is a lineal descendant of

The Mechanism of Nature, first published in 1930 and translated into six languages.

As well as other books of his own— including verse—he was joint author with Julian Huxley of *Simple Science.* Since he was always a stickler for accuracy, and wrote to inform rather than to mystify, his contribution to the understanding of science must have been great indeed. He was also a crusader, under his own name and through the Royal Society, for clear and simple writing by scientists.

He was a Savage of long standing, and it was at this club that his varied interests and moods seemed, during many years, to find their most natural expression. Among his qualities was a dislike of seeing a wrong done behind his back to one he approved of; then, in any mood, he could take quick and direct action to end it, not looking for thanks.

Born in London on Decmber 27, 1887, Edward Neville da Costa Andrade was educated at St. Dunstan's College and at University College London, where his record was outstanding. First class honours in physics were followed by a succession of college scholarships, and then an 1851 Exhibition scholarship that took him in turn to Heidelberg (where he earned a Ph.D. *cum summa laude*), the Cavendish Laboratory, Cambridge, and back to University College London. Manchester University gave him a fellowship.

At this point war intervened, and while on active service in France as an officer of the Royal Garrison Artillery he was both mentioned in dispatches and elected to a fellowship by his own college—an honour which he appreciated the more from its timing. As a physicist with artillery experience he was, in 1920, appointed Professor of Physics at the Artillery College, Woolwich, a position which he held until 1928, when he was elected to the Quain Chair of Physics (at University College) of the University of London. The Fellowship of the Royal Society followed in 1935.

During the Second World War he was for four years Scientific Adviser to the Director of Scientific Research, Ministry of Supply; was a member of the Advisory Council of Scientific Research and Technical Development in the Ministry of Supply from its inception until 1942; and contended with the destruction of his department at the college by enemy action. He was a member of the Council of the Royal Society from 1942-44 and President of the Physical Society from 1943-45.

In 1949, when 61, he was appointed Director of the Royal Institution, Resident Professor, and Director of the Davy Faraday Laboratory. The appointment carried with it continued opportunities for research, and appealed also to his historical sense and liking for pleasant surroundings to live in. But there had long been two sides to the work of the institution; the limits of authority of the Director were subject to uncertainty; and possibilities of personal conflict existed. Trouble might have been foreseen, and in fact developed. He resigned in May 1952, but it was not until March of the next year that the last of an unhappy story was heard. For Andrade it was a tragedy, although he had much still to occupy him. His concern with Newton's letters continued, he had his writing, and for some years a room at the Royal School of Mines where he could still engage in research. In 1958 he was awarded the Hughes Medal of the Royal Society, to his evident pleasure.

At different times he had received a number of honours from France. He was a Chevalier de Légion d'Honneur, was a corresponding member of the Académie des Sciences, and was awarded the Grand Médaille Osmond of the Société Française de Métallurgie. The engineering significance of his work was recognized in 1941, when he gave the James Forest lecture of the Institution of Civil Engineers.

In 1965 he put his remarkable collection of books up for sale at Sotheby's, London, and they realized nearly £70,000.

He was twice married.

June 7, 1971.

Admiral Sir William Andrewes, K.B.E., C.B., D.S.O., who died on November 21, 1974, aged 75, was in command of the naval forces of the British Commonwealth at the disposal of the United Nations when war broke out in Korea in 1950.

His disposition and handling of these forces earned high commendation from the American chiefs with whom he served, and during the latter part of his time he was given command of the United Nations blockade and escort force.

William Gerrard Andrewes, second son of Canon G. T. Andrewes, of Winchester, was born in 1899. He entered Osborne as a naval cadet from Twyford School, Winchester, in September 1912, and went to sea as a midshipman of the battleship Canada in the Grand Fleet in July 1915. He was present at the Battle of Jutland.

After promotion to acting sub-lieutenant in September 1917 he joined the destroyer Walrus, in which he served until after the war. He attended a course at Cambridge University in 1919-20 and was afterwards promoted to Lieutenant from October 15, 1919.

Further destroyer service followed in the Versatile, and in 1921-23 he specialized in torpedoes, being retained on the staff of Vernon for 18 months after qualifying. He was torpedo officer of the 4th Submarine Flotilla on the China Station in 1925-27, then had further staff service in the Vernon, became torpedo officer of the battleship Warspite in 1930, and fleet torpedo officer on the China Station, in H.M.S. Kent, in 1931.

He was promoted to commander in December 1932, attended the course at the Staff College during 1934, and joined the Nelson as fleet torpedo officer in the Home Fleet. In July 1937 he went to the Rodney as executive officer, and a year later was promoted to captain and selected for the 1939 course at the Imperial Defence College.

At the mobilization for the Second World War he was appointed to command the seaplane carrier Albatross, but from February 1940 was for a short time chief staff officer to the Vice-Admiral, Dover.

For more than two years from April 1940, or during the most critical periods of the war, he was Assistant Director of Plans. Then in September 1942 he took command of the cruiser Uganda, in which he served in the Atlantic and the Mediterranean. He was mentioned in dispatches for his work during the invasion of Sicily, and received the D.S.O. for courage, leadership and devotion to duty during the landings on the mainland of Italy and in the operations at Salerno.

During the invasion of Normandy in 1944 he was chief staff officer for administration and the turn-round of shipping to the Commander-in-Chief, Portsmouth, and for this service was made a C.B.E. in the 1945 New Year Honours. In the autumn of 1944 he went to the Pacific as chief of staff to the Vice-Admiral (Q), in the rank of commodore, second class, and was serving there when the war ended.

From December 1945 he commanded the aircraft carrier Indomitable, engaged in trooping duties between the Far East and the United Kingdom until early in 1947, when he became chief of staff to the Commander-in-Chief at Portsmouth.

In January 1948 he was promoted to rear-admiral, and for the next two years was senior naval member on the directing staff of the Imperial Defence College. In the 1949 Birthday Honours he was made a C.B. In January 1950 he went to the Far East station as Second-in-Command and Flag Officer Commanding the 5th Cruiser Squadron. When war broke out in Korea five months later he was cruising in Japanese waters, and was placed in command of all vessels of the British Commonwealth which joined the forces at the disposal of the United Nations.

Early in the war, after the cruiser flying his flag had successfully shelled North Korean forces, the American naval commander sent a signal in praise of "Admiral Andrewes and his fast-firing crew", and he afterwards earned warm commendation from General MacArthur and other American commanders, and was awarded the American Silver Star.

He was promoted to vice-admiral in December 1950, and two months later was created a K.B.E. for distinguished service in Korean waters. He was Commander-in-Chief, America and West Indies station from 1951-53, and Deputy Supreme Allied Commander, Atlantic, 1952-53. He retired in 1956 after two years as President of the Royal Naval College, Greenwich.

In 1927 he married Frances Audrey, eldest daughter of Mr. H. G. Welchman, of Grove House, Winchester, and they had one son and one daughter.

November 22, 1974.

Sir Linton Andrews, former Editor of the *Yorkshire Post* and former chairman of the Press Council, died in Leeds on September 27, 1972. He was 86.

He edited the *Yorkshire Post* with ability and vigour from 1939 until 1960, when he retired and was made an executive director of the newspaper company (he had been a director since 1950). He was chairman of the Press Council from 1955 to 1959, and pursued a large number of other activities linked with his journalistic interests.

William Linton Andrews was born at Hull in 1886, son of William Andrews, author, publisher and antiquary, and was educated at Hull Grammar School and Christ's Hospital. He began work fresh from school as a reporter on the *Eastern Morning News* in his native city when he was 16 years of age. Then he went as a reporter to the *Huddersfield Daily Chronicle*.

After joining the *Sheffield Telegraph* Andrews signed, as a matter of form, an agreement containing a clause prohibiting him on leaving the company from working on any other newspaper in Sheffield or within a radius of 20 miles. He left in 1907 for freelancing in Paris, but later was offered a post on the *Sheffield Independent* with the prospect of another to write leading articles on the *Sheffield Evening Mail*. Andrews was sued by the *Telegraph* in what became known as "the Radius Case," and won on appeal, with union backing.

Andrews went on writing leading articles for the *Evening Mail* until it was forced to close down. He was next similarly employed on the short-lived *Southern Daily Post*, Portsmouth, and then wrote leading articles for the *Dundee Advertiser*, of which he later became news editor. He stayed in Dundee until the outbreak of war in 1914, when he immediately joined the Black Watch and served in France for three years. Later, in the *Leeds Mercury*, he described with discernment his experiences on the Western Front, and the serial was published as a book, *Haunting Years*. While at the front he wrote a personal narrative of the Battle of Neuve Chapelle and it came to the notice of Lord Northcliffe. As a result Andrews was invited to contribute to the *Daily Mail*, and after the war he worked on the paper for four years as a sub-editor.

In 1923 Andrews was appointed editor of the *Leeds Mercury*, when it was acquired by the *Yorkshire Post*, and for 16 years he gave to it a distinctive personality. Much of the space was devoted to sport and pictures, and the news columns—particularly those of Yorkshire news—were marked by a lively touch. Andrews wrote a daily column commentary over his initials, as well as many of the leading articles. He loved to master a crisis, and was ever a forthright champion of the rights of the journalist and the press.

After the outbreak of war in 1939 it was decided for economic reasons to merge the *Mercury* with the *Yorkshire Post.* Arthur Mann, editor-in-chief of the *Yorkshire Post,* resigned and retired, and the choice fell on Andrews to be his successor. To take over the outstanding position that Mann held was in itself not easy and Andrews had the additional difficulty of trying to combine the character of the *Mercury* with that of the *Post.* Although the circulation rose, he was not wholly successful in the latter task, not because of any lack of ability or ideas, but rather because the two characters were so distinct as to be almost incompatible. The two editors themselves were also very different: Mann the statesman-diplomatist type of editor, who wrote little himself but directed others what line to take, and who sought always a certain austerity; Andrews· the versatile, who wrote extensively and enjoyed doing so, and had a flair for the easier-to-read style of journalism.

Andrews continued to write his commentary, though not so frequently, and many leading articles. He never lost, but indeed developed, the habit of observation of details and quick decision that he gained in his earlier training. Thus he did his writing direct on to his typewriter, surprisingly quickly, and he could never comprehend why all others could not do so too. His future programme usually seemed to colleagues impossibly large. Yet he found time frequently to broadcast and to speak in public, to write letters and articles in other papers and magazines, to edit the *Transactions* of the Brontë Society, and to write several books on north country topography and people. He edited the history of the *Yorkshire Post,* which was published in 1954 to mark its second centenary. In February 1968, when he finally retired as a director, the board made him editor emeritus of the *Yorkshire Post* and a consultant.

Andrews was a foundation member of the Press Council and its first vice-chairman before becoming chairman; president of the Guild of British Newspaper Editors, 1952 to 1953; and president of the Institute of Journalists, 1946. He served at various times on the Court and Council of Leeds University, of which he was an honorary LL.D., the Scottish Regimental Association of Yorkshire, the Society of Yorkshiremen in London, the Association of Yorkshire Bookmen, the Leeds Philosophical and Literary Society, the Bradford English Society, Leeds Musical Festival Society, the Newspaper Press Fund, the joint editorial committee of the Newspaper Society and the Editors' Guild, the British committee of the International Press Institute, the council of the Commonwealth Press Union, and the committee of the sixth Imperial Press Conference—he was a delegate to the con-

ference in Canada in 1950 and to the Commonwealth Press Conference in India and Pakistan in 1961. In 1967 he was visiting Professor at Southern Illinois University, United States. He took a leading part on the National Council for the Training of Journalists, which administers the training scheme for juniors. In 1970, together with H. A. Taylor, he published *Lords and Labourers of the Press.* He was knighted in 1954.

He married in 1915 Gertrude, eldest daughter of Alexander Douglas, of Dundee. She died in 1958. There were no children.

September 29, 1972.

Ivo Andrić, the Yugoslav author, who was awarded the Nobel Prize for Literature in 1961, died on March 13, 1975 in Belgrade. He was 82.

He was born in Travnik, Bosnia, on October 10, 1892. His mother, widowed at the early age of 21, went to live with her parents at Vichegrad and here Andrić attended his first school. Later, he was sent to Sarajevo, and he studied philosophy at Zagreb, Vienna and Cracow. There was no question whether the boy was to work with his hands as his father had done in the fabrication of traditional-style coffee grinders.

He had always desired to write and even as a student he translated Walt Whitman and created his own poems. When, in 1917, as a member of the Young Bosnian Movement, he was imprisoned by the Austrians, he devoted his time to the reading of Kierkegaard and to the writing of a lyrical journal, in the manner of Ovid, *Ex Ponto.* There followed a volume of poems written in prose form with the title *Inquietudes.* Thus, by way of romantic narrative he turned to tales, short stories and novels.

On his release from prison, a career in the diplomatic service found him successively at Bucharest, Madrid, Brussels and Geneva. At the outbreak of the Second World War he was Minister in Berlin, and although he was not actually imprisoned he never wished to talk about those war years: "I have drawn a line through them", was the expression he used.

His biographer, Petar Dzadzic, tells us that Andrić's life flowed alongside his diplomatic career without jolts from outside events or change, rather as if all his energy flowed in the reality of his visions. Andrić himself affirmed that three centuries of Ottoman oppression followed by three-quarters of a century of Austrian rule had made of his "little country" a witch's cauldron of hate and passion.

In view of this, he published between 1924 and 1941 three volumes of tales, some of a cruel realism and some full of poetry, drawn from a rather mythical Bosnia, rich in legend and tradition. They were shaped in the silence and solitude imposed by the Serbo-Croatian language.

He compared the life he lived in Belgrade from 1941 onwards to that of the French writers under the occupation. The existence of the Maquis gave him the feeling of a greater liberty and transcended the material of his novels so as to give them a more universal meaning.

Of these, the first to be published was *Bosnian Story.* It is the chronicle of eight years of his native town Travnik, taken at the outset of the nineteenth century. *The Woman from Sarajevo* is a work in Balzac form, and *The Bridge on the Drina* (1945) is again a chronicle of an oriental town, but in this instance a survey spanning three and a half centuries. A number of his works were translated into English.

When the war put an end to his diplomatic career, Andrić continued to live quietly with his wife in the little Belgrade flat overlooking the Park of the Pioneers. His time was spent in writing, presiding over the Union of Yugoslav writers, reading his favourite authors, the French moralists of the eighteenth century, and translating Kafka, for whom he had a profound admiration.

March 14, 1975.

Archbishop of Apamea—See Mathew.

Stephen Arlen, C.B.E., managing director of Sadler's Wells Opera since 1966, died on January 19, 1972 after a short illness.

He was the moving spirit in the transfer of the company from Sadler's Wells Theatre to the London Coliseum. At the time of the change in 1968 he stated his main objective as being to give the company a new home "where the members can stretch themselves, where it will be possible to develop on all fronts—singing, production and design." On the whole, he had achieved that objective in a very short time, particularly in respect of the Wagnerian repertory and in such exciting, if controversial, productions as *The Damnation of Faust, Carmen* and *Tales of Hoffman.*

He believed strongly that opera must be made relevant for today, especially for young audiences who had probably never entered an opera house before. On that account, and because he was essentially a man of the theatre himself, he was anxious to bring into the house people with experience of the latest trends in the "straight" theatre. The epitome of a dynamic theatrical personality, he was always trying to achieve ideal standards for his company and its work.

He was born in Birmingham in 1913 and began his theatrical career as an actor at the age of 16. He then became a stage manager, in which capacity he worked on George Robey's last production, *The Bing Boys Are Here.* After more experience as a stage manager, in many musicals and plays, he joined the Bronson Albery Organization for Michel Saint-Denis's season at the Phoenix Theatre, and was also stage director for a production of Ibsen's *Ghosts* at the Vaudeville Theatre, starring Clifford Evans and Marie Ney.

He worked with E.N.S.A. in France during the "phoney" war in 1939. He joined the army as a private in The Buffs and then took up a commission in The North Staffordshire Regiment. At the end of the war he was production manager for *The Stars in Battledress*. Then in 1945 he became general manager for the famous Old Vic seasons at the New Theatre, working with George Devine, Michel Saint-Denis and Glen Byam Shaw, who was later to collaborate with him successfully at Sadler's Wells and the Coliseum as co-director.

In 1951 he went to Sadler's Wells as general manager, later becoming administrative director. In 1959 he was invited by the Belgian Minister of International Affairs to advise Maurice Huisman, director of the Monnaie Theatre in Brussels, on the reorganization of the principal Belgian national opera.

He was released by the Sadler's Wells Trust in 1962 to become administrative director of the National Theatre during its formative period. After its establishment he returned to Sadler's Wells and succeeded Norman Tucker as managing director in 1966. He was chairman of the British Centre of the International Theatre Institute and helped organize the institute's London conference in 1971, and was also with Walter Felsenstein, co-chairman of the Lyric Theatre Centre.

He was awarded the C.B.E. in 1968. He married first Narice, daughter of James Ingram; and second Iris Kells, the soprano.

January 20, 1972.

Louis Armand, the eminent French engineer, chairman of the European Atomic Agency (Euratom) in 1958-59, died on August 30, 1971. He was 66.

He will be especially remembered for the way in which he brilliantly reformed and reconstructed the French railway system after the Second World War.

His original impact on national events was as a mechanical engineer with the P.L.M. railway; in a study of corrosion in locomotive boilers his "Traitement Intégral Armand" of water became adopted generally.

When the Second World War came and the Germans overran France, Armand disappeared into the Resistance to organize sabotage of the enemy's movements by rail. He came to light involuntarily as a hostage of the Gestapo at Fresnes in 1944 and was held until immediately before the liberation of France.

He put his time in prison to good use, planning the revival of the wrecked railway network and pondering on technical advances, of which the system of 50-cycle 25 kV. electrification sponsored by him has spread from France to Britain and to other countries.

He emerged from the war a man far deeper and broader than the engineer, burly, confident, sparkling with energy. As Director-General of the S.N.C.F. he was in a position, and ready, to reconstruct his railways from the plans laid at Fresnes and from Marshall Aid so opportunely to hand. He made the S.N.C.F. the fastest, the most punctual, and technically the most advanced railway in the world, a lead which was not seriously challenged for over a decade by Japan, and for nearly two decades by Britain.

That done, his faith in himself and his dynamism demanded wider fields. He combined supreme direction of the S.N.C.F. with the Presidencies of first the French, then the European Atomic Energy Commission, of the French African Industries Development Bureau, and of the Channel Tunnel project.

In 1961 he became Secretary-General of the International Union of Railways, whose work under him became ever more international. Regardless of boundaries and curtains, the great Frenchman became the great European. At this time a friend said of him: "He has no superior in intellect. There is no problem, technical, political or economic, which he does not illuminate."

Armand was born on January 17, 1905 at Cruseilles in Haute-Savoie, of parents who were school teachers. He graduated from the École Polytechnique in 1926 and from the École des Mines, in which he was respectively second and first in his class. After a time as a mining engineer in Clermont-Ferrand he joined the P.L.M. railway in 1934 as a mechanical engineer. This career was interrupted by the war. In 1944 he was appointed Director of Works of the S.N.C.F., and in 1946 to the chief executive post, as Director-General.

Armand was an honorary K.B.E., a Grand Officier de la Légion d'Honneur; a Compagnon de la Libération (1944); and in 1963 he was elected a member of the Académie Française.

He was married in 1925 and had two sons and two daughters.

August 31, 1971.

Louis Armstrong, the jazz musician, died in New York on July 6, 1971, at the age of 71. He was the greatest trumpeter and one of the best singers in jazz.

He was born in New Orleans in 1900 and is said to have received his first musical training, on cornet, in the Waifs' Home where he was placed after being caught firing a revolver during the 1913 New Year festivities. Released two years later, he made a living working at odd jobs, selling papers and driving a coal cart, until in 1918 his increasing musical skill secured him a job in Kid Ory's band, replacing Joe "King" Oliver who had just left for Chicago.

The next two years he spent playing on the Mississippi river boats, then two more years in New Orleans until in 1922 he was summoned by King Oliver to join his legendary Creole Jazz Band in Chicago. It was Armstrong's growing reputation which had made Oliver, hitherto the most renowned New Orleans cornettist, send for him to play alongside him, and there was something neatly symbolic about the way in which it was soon realized that Oliver's second cornettist was now the greater player.

In 1924 Armstrong went his own way, meanwhile changing to trumpet from cornet, and the pattern of his life now reflected the spreading popularity of jazz, because after five years in Chicago, playing in bands which he seldom led but always starred in, he followed his fame to New York, where he starred at a Harlem ballroom and in a top revue at the same time. He went to California, worked his way back across the United States and then followed his fame again across the Atlantic, visiting London in 1932 and virtually remaining in Europe until 1935. From then until the end of his life he was an international figure, travelling everywhere and welcome everywhere.

He led a big band from 1936 to 1947; then in response to the renewed interest in small groups formed a band which, whatever the future personnel, was always called his All Stars, although this was most accurate a title in the early days when Earl Hines and Jack Teagarden were with him. With his All Stars he toured widely, to Latin America for example in 1956, to London for the first time in two decades the same year, and in 1957 to Africa. But he also appeared in films (notably *Satchmo The Great, New Orleans,* and *High Society*), played with symphony orchestras, produced a book and even surprised everyone in the early sixties by making a best-selling record of "Hello, Dolly".

His achievement as a jazz trumpeter was that he came at a time when jazz musicians' short variations on a theme were starting to turn into sustained melodic lines, seized instinctively on this development and carried it farther than anyone else. The recordings he made in the twenties display playing remarkable by any standards, but doubly so considering how recently jazz had begun to forge its own language. The way Armstrong soars up to a high note, peels off into a dive at exactly the right moment, alters the shading of a long note, separates notes crisply or slurs them together, steers a slow phrase into a sharp rhythmic figure, explores upper and lower register with equal mastery—this superb manipulation of a new language is staggering now, but in the twenties it created an effect on his fellow players which wholly identified him with jazz.

It would be unfair to contemporaries such as Jabbo Smith and Red Allen to present him entirely as a lone pioneer; what was significant about his playing was that the intuitive sense of logic and balance with which he welded phrase to phrase, and the sheer breadth, power and nobility of his style suddenly opened up vistas of what future jazz soloists might achieve, and it is this liberating influence rather than any specific technique that was his greatest legacy. His singing presented the same warmth and grandeur on a different plane —his slightly surrealistic abandonment of the lyrics, often halfway through a song, and his abrasive but appealing voice were a good deal more human and appealing than most popular singing but would hardly have brought him into a recording studio if he had not also been a great trumpeter.

It is of course by his achievements inside the recording studio that he will now have to be remembered and the greatest of these undoubtedly took place before 1930, but although he was never quite so good again and became a star of entertainment as much as a great jazz musician there is still very fine music to be found on his post-1930 records. And we should remember, as Humphrey Lyttelton once pointed out in some of the wisest words ever written about Armstrong, that to him jazz was his native form of entertainment, not a music apart, and that the show business routines to which some people objected were as much an essential part of him as the great music.

He was at once a jovial yet dignified father figure of entertainment, a considerable comedian in his own right, the man who led the way in transforming jazz from a folk music into an art and the thorough professional who would never interpret his own life in such terms.

July 7, 1971.

Cecily Arnold, soprano, instrumentalist, lecturer and teacher, died on October 5, 1974. She was 78.

A pupil of Charles Phillips, she went to the Royal College of Music after the First World War, studying singing under Frederick Sewell and composition under S. P. Waddington, and afterwards completed her training with Louise Trenton.

Her purity of tone, smoothness of phrasing and clarity of diction, combined with an obvious sense of sympathy and commitment, soon proved her a recitalist of note. Equally arresting was her sense of professional dedication; her work, whether she was called upon to learn the title role in Gluck's *Alceste* in three weeks or to give the premiere of Beryl Price's settings of poems by Cavalcanti, was to her a constant privilege.

Her good-humoured enthusiasm and unassuming artistry as a lecturer commended her to audiences of all types and ages. She was at home both on the campus at Berkeley and working with C.E.M.A. in a bomb-shelter in war-time London. But if any

spot had a particular place in her affections it was the Geffrye Museum in London; she was a devoted supporter of its work and her last songs there were of an outstanding intensity.

In 1927 she married Eric Marshall Johnson, and with him during and after the Second World War she formed the nucleus of the Old Music with Old Instruments Consort, whose personnel also included at various times Edgar H. Hunt, Desmond Dupré and Thurston Dart. She edited music for the consort and joined in writing a short series of booklets to accompany the consort's work. The first of these contained a commendatory foreword by Canon F. W. Galpin.

To arouse interest in older music—especially in that of the English lutenist song composers (for which her voice was admirably suited) and in the practically unknown repertory for viols (into which she was an indefatigable researcher, and for the sake of which she made herself as competent on the treble viol as she was on the harpsichord and clavichord)—was perhaps her main achievement. But it would be a mistake to judge, as one might from her publications, that this was her only concern. Certainly she herself would prefer to be remembered for her renderings of Delius's songs; the composer gave them his delighted approval over five remarkable evenings at Grez-sur-Loing in 1932 and in consequence allowed her to give in London in the same year the first performance of his last song, a setting of Verlaine's "Avant que tu ne t'en ailles".

October 22, 1974.

Bishop of Arundel and Brighton—See **Cashman.**

Sir Noel Ashbridge, who died aged 85 on June 4, 1975, was as much responsible as any man for the excellence of the B.B.C.'s technical services, which enabled the Corporation to meet successfully the challenging demands of wartime broadcasting, and in peacetime also to lead the world.

Small, unassuming, without jargon, he could with a word bring far greater engineers and scientists than himself back to commonsense. He had visions, but they were always practical.

Noel Ashbridge was born on **December 10, 1889,** the fourth son of John Ashbridge of Wanstead. Educated at Forest School, he graduated in engineering at King's College, London. He spent some time at Yarrows and British Thomson-Houston; his future was decided by the First World War in which he served throughout.

From the Royal Fusiliers he was transferred to the Royal Engineers, and in 1915 was one of the first to operate wireless equipment in the front line.

Although he returned to heavy electrical

engineering on demobilization, his interest led him in 1920 to join Marconi's. He took part in the design of some of the earliest wireless receivers. More important, he became assistant to Captain P. P. Eckersley at Writtle 2MT, the first station to send out regular weekly broadcast programmes.

When the British Broadcasting Company was formed in 1922, Eckersley was appointed its first Chief Engineer. Ashbridge joined him from Writtle four years later. When Eckersley left the B.B.C. in 1929, Ashbridge succeeded him as Chief Engineer.

For the next twenty-three years Ashbridge led an evergrowing and increasingly expert team of B.B.C. engineers. He had to make innumerable recommendations with no precedents to guide him. Eckersley had proposed the regional broadcasting scheme, which involved the first use of high powered transmitters. It was Ashbridge who largely carried it out.

Thereafter developments multiplied. In 1932 the B.B.C. Empire shortwave service was started. Out of it grew the great development of the B.B.C.'s wartime services and the world-wide coverage of the Overseas Division of the B.B.C. In 1936 there was the start at Alexandra Palace of the world's first public television service.

In 1936, also, Ashbridge began the preparation of plans for broadcasting in the event of war. For these, too, there were no precedents. The task was a severe one. There was the double requirement that the nation should be assured of a continuing broadcasting service and that this should not give directional help to enemy bombers. Both requirements were met.

After the war Ashbridge led the B.B.C. engineers in setting up the Home, Light, and Third programmes, in spreading television through the country as fast as the Government would allow, and in developing v.h.f., of which he was an early advocate.

From 1943 to 1948 Ashbridge was Deputy Director-General of the B.B.C. first under Robert Foot, then under William Haley. He brought his common-sense to this role also, but he was not well equipped for it. He had no programme experience or knowledge of wider affairs.

In the Corporation's major reorganization of 1948 the post was abolished. Ashbridge joined the new Board of Management as Director of Technical Services. In 1952 he retired under the age limit. He then served on the Board of the Marconi Company for seven years.

Ashbridge, who was knighted in 1935, was also a Knight of the Danish Order of Dannebrog. He gave valuable service to many organizations in his profession and served on a number of committees.

He was President of the Institution of Electrical Engineers in 1941-42, and Chairman of the Radio Research Board 1952-57. A man of few words, he combined neatness of thinking with thoroughness in execution. Few men have given such important service with such few airs.

Lady Ashbridge, who was the daughter

of Rowland Strickland of Erith, and whom he married in 1926, died in 1948. They had two daughters.

June 6, 1975.

Amy (Mrs. Peter) Asher—See Shuard.

Daisy Ashford (Mrs. Margaret Devlin), author of that small comic masterpiece *The Young Visiters* which she wrote when she was nine, died at Hellesdon, Norwich, on January 15, 1972 at the age of 90.

As a child she lived at Lewes, writing furiously after tea while her sisters were playing at shops; in this kind of atmosphere *The Young Visiters* was born. There were other books, including *The Hangman's Daughter, Where Love Lies Deepest,* all written before the author's career as a writer of fiction came to an end with her despatch to a convent school at Haywards Heath.

In 1919 the red notebook containing *The Young Visiters* turned up in a drawer and was lent to a friend who was recovering from influenza. The friend sent it to Frank Swinnerton, then reading for Chatto and Windus; Chatto published the book, which had an immediate success. In the spring of 1919 the *Daily Mail* described *The Young Visiters* as "the book over which half London is laughing, the other half having to wait while more copies are being printed."

When the question of an advance by the publishers was being discussed the author thought she would "go a dash" and named a sum of £10; Chatto offered £500. An introduction to the book was written by J. M. Barrie, though not before he had had the author to see him at the Adelphi, where he lived, to see if she were genuine. He was satisfied.

The book scores because the young author's sharp unblinking eye is matched by a disconcertingly frank style, a style that caused the first readers of the book to refuse to believe that *The Young Visiters* had been written by a child, and to suspect that the real author was Barrie.

The effect on the reader of the mis-spelt, unpunctuated view of High Life is immediate and unforgettable. The plot concerns the adventures of Ethel Monticue, rather a hoity-toity madam ("Ethel patted her hair and looked sneery"), who is admired by Mr. Salteena, ("an elderly man of 42 . . . I am parshial to ladies if they are nice I suppose it is in my nature. I am not quite a gentleman but you would hardly notice it but can't be helped anyhow"), and who eventually marries the handsome Bernard ("Bernard always had a few prayers in the hall and some whiskey afterwards as he was rather pious").

The plot is well worked out and the pace never slackens, but to many readers the joy of the book is in the incidental touches, for example the "privite compartments" at the "Crystal Pallace", occupied by Earls "and even Dukes" which the author conjured up after a visit to Hampton Court. Perhaps the most delightful portrait of all is that of the Prince of Wales, later Edward VII, to one of whose "levies" Mr. Salteena manages to gain admittance, to his supreme gratification. The Prince, wearing a "small but costly crown", confesses to a certain weariness of court life. "It upsets me said the prince lapping up his strawberry ice all I want is peace and quiut and a little fun and here I am tied down to this life he said taking off his crown being royal has many painfull drawbacks."

A dramatization of *The Young Visiters* was put on at the Court Theatre in 1920 and ran for over 100 performances. The book became a musical in 1968. By 1936 the book had gone through 19 impressions and it is estimated that over half a million copies have been sold. In the autumn of 1965 appeared *Love and Marriage,* which contained two early stories by Daisy Ashford and one by her sister Angela.

January 17, 1972.

Professor Arthur Aspinall, c.v.o., Professor of Modern History in the University of Reading from 1947 to 1965, and subsequently Professor Emeritus, died on May 2, 1972 at his home in the Isle of Man. He was 70.

He was born in the West Riding of Yorkshire in 1901. At first he intended to study chemistry, but entering Manchester University in the great days of H. W. C. Davis, Tout and Powicke, he turned to history. His doctoral thesis, characteristically completed in less than two years, formed the basis for his first publication, *Lord Brougham and the Whig Party* (1927). It at once demonstrated the solid foundation of scholarship which underlay his academic career.

His first appointment was as Lecturer in History at the University of Rangoon from 1925 to 1931, where he produced a monograph on *Cornwallis in Bengal.* He moved to a Lectureship at Reading University in 1931 and, despite later offers from elsewhere, remained there until his retirement. He was particularly proud to succeed to Sir Frank Stenton's Chair in 1947. Like Stenton, Aspinall was an exact scholar, with an unrivalled knowledge of the primary source materials for his period, the late eighteenth and early nineteenth centuries of British political history. He devoted his academic life to the publication of impeccable edited texts of the major correspondence of the period, so that every historian working in that field, now and in the future, will be heavily in his debt.

Aspinall made his reputation in 1938 with his monumental *Letters of George IV (1812-1830),* a work still unsurpassed for its editorial skill. This work also began a connexion with the Royal Archives at Windsor which continued to the end of his active life and which made him the foremost authority on the numerous family of George III. His greatest work was undoubtedly his *Later Correspondence of George III (1783-1810)* published in five volumes in 1962-70, and the companion *Correspondence of George, Prince of Wales (1770-1810)* in eight volumes between 1963 and 1971, completed after retirement and despite failing eyesight. These volumes stand as a permanent memorial to his astonishing industry and meticulous scholarship.

He also published the correspondence, among others, of Princess Charlotte; of Mrs. Jordan, mistress of William IV as Duke of Clarence; and of Charles Arbuthnot, Treasury politician and friend of Wellington. Other standard works included *Politics and the Press, c. 1780-1850,* the *Diary of Henry Hobhouse, 1820-47,* and his greatly expanded and definitive Raleigh lecture of 1952, *The Cabinet Council, 1783-1835.* For several years he served as editor of the forthcoming volumes in the *History of Parliament* dealing with the period 1790-1820, and though he relinquished this task on retirement his unrivalled knowledge of the archives enabled him to lay a secure foundation for others to build on.

He shared with a colleague the editorship of Volume XI in the *English Historical Documents* series. His research students and colleagues benefited greatly from his example of rigorous and exact scholarship, while his services to the history of the Royal Family were fittingly commemorated on his retirement by the award of the C.V.O.

His first wife, Gladys Shaw, whom he married in 1931, died suddenly on the eve of his retirement in 1965. He married Beryl Johnson in 1968. She survives him, with one son and one daughter of his first marriage.

May 6, 1972.

Colonel Lord Astor of Hever, a former chief proprietor of *The Times* and chairman of The Times Publishing Company from 1922 to 1959, died in the south of France on July 19, 1971. He was 85.

Although, owing to his enforced exile, the ending of this variously active and immensely fruitful life does not cut as many direct links with British affairs as it would have done at the time, he will none the less be mourned and missed in a great number of circles, and above all in Printing House Square.

He was a man who, once he had decided to interest himself in anything, was prepared to give it unlimited attention. *The Times,* the Middlesex Hospital, the Commonwealth Press Union, St. Bride's Church, the Phoenix Assurance Company, the Royal College of Music—many in those organizations can recount innumerable incidents of quiet care for their interests and devotion to the causes they served. No man could be more thorough; no man can have done good with a greater absence of fuss.

If we put *The Times* first it is because for over 40 years he regarded it as his paramount responsibility. Its independence, its vigour, its health, its traditions, were his constant care. His love for it—the word is not too strong—was part and parcel of that passion for the cardinal things in English life which was at the heart of his happiness and guided all he did.

He was a rich man; he regarded his wealth as a trust. He lived sparely. Owing to his wounds in the First World War, whereby he lost a leg, he was always in discomfort and often in pain. He overcame his disability so thoroughly that many who came into contact with him did not know he had it. A keen player of many sports before the First World War—cricket, squash rackets, polo, golf—he never lost his interest in them afterwards, and in spite of his handicap played games well into his seventh decade. The shyest of men (to the point of inaudibility), he could also be one of the firmest. Kind, considerate, imaginatively thoughtful, dedicated to the public good, he was above all a man whom everyone instinctively and rightly trusted.

The Rt. Hon. John Jacob Astor, first Baron Astor of Hever, of Hever Castle in the county of Kent, was born in New York on May 20, 1886. He was the second son of the first Viscount Astor and of Mary Dahlgren, daughter of James W. Paul, of Philadelphia. His mother died in 1894. In 1890 his father moved to England and nine years later became a naturalized British subject.

From the age of four John Astor was brought up entirely in Britain. He first went to a preparatory school in Farnborough, then to Eton, where he remained from 1899 to 1905. He preserved a deep affection for Eton and retained a lively interest in its affairs to the last day of his life. He had been chairman and president of the Old Etonian Association. In 1905 he went to New College, Oxford. In 1906 he left it to join the 1st Life Guards. He had many natural qualifications to be a soldier, among them physical courage. In 1911 he was appointed A.D.C. to Lord Hardinge of Penshurst, then Viceroy of India.

When war broke out in 1914 he was one of the Old Contemptibles. He went to France with the Household Cavalry as a signalling officer. In October he was wounded at Messines. Returning to his regiment, and twice refusing staff appointments, he remained with it until September 1917. Early in 1918, after a gunnery course, he was posted to command the 520th Household Siege Battery. When commanding his battery in September 1918 he was dangerously wounded in 14 places. His arm was broken and his right leg had to be amputated. He was awarded the Legion of Honour.

After the war he retired with the rank of major. In 1927 he was appointed Honorary Colonel of the Kent Heavy Brigade, R.A., and in 1928 Honorary Colonel of the 23rd London Regiment. During the 1939-45 War he commanded the City Press Battalion of the Home Guard with the rank of lieutenant-colonel.

Before he was wounded Lord Astor of Hever excelled at games. He was in the Eton XI for two years, played rackets for the school and won for it the public schools' championship. Later he won the Army championship in singles and doubles, and won prizes in the 1908 Olympic Games. He was a good rider in steeplechases, and while in India won a reputation as a polo player. His war injuries did not kill these activities. He continued to play cricket and tennis and, lame though he was, he won the Parliamentary squash rackets in 1926 and 1927. He also continued to be a keen golfer. In 1924-25 he was captain of the Royal Cinque Ports Golf Club and he later became president of the Kent Golf Union and captained the London Press Golfing Society. He was president of the M.C.C. in 1937-38 and president of the Hurlingham Club, of which he had also been chairman. He was a keen shot and few things made him happier than his shooting parties at Hever. Painting and playing the organ were his non-athletic relaxations. He enjoyed his life at Hever to the full; the companionship of his dogs, tree-felling, good talk; and in the summer entertaining his friends on his yacht Deianeira.

In 1916 John Astor married Lady Violet Mary, the youngest daughter of the fourth Earl of Minto, formerly Governor-General of Canada and Viceroy of India. She was the widow of Lord Charles George Francis Mercer Nairne, younger son of the fifth Marquess of Lansdowne. It was the happiest of marriages. His wife became his companion and helper in all his activities. Many forms of recognition marked his career, but none pleased him more than that of the Freedom of Dover, which was conferred on him and on Lady Violet together. Lady Astor of Hever's death in January 1965 deprived him of the main solace of his exile.

There were three sons of the marriage, Gavin, Hugh and John. Gavin Astor now succeeds to the barony. He succeeded his father as chairman of The Times Publishing Company in 1959 and so remained until 1966, when Lord Thomson acquired control of *The Times*. Since 1967 he has been president of Times Newspapers Ltd.

The first Viscount Astor died in 1919. John Astor inherited the use of a great fortune. Hever Castle, which his father had given him shortly before, became his favourite home. Through the years he gave it constant thought and care.

After a short period of recuperation at the war's end John Astor found himself full of energy and anxious to have a serious purpose in life. He served for a period on the London County Council. In 1922 he entered the House of Commons as the Unionist member for Dover. In 1924 he had the unusual experience of needing to be elected twice. Returning from abroad, he made his first appearance in the new Parliament just at the moment when a division was about to be taken. He voted in it, overlooking the fact that he had not yet taken the oath. Through this inadvertence he had to be elected again. At the by-election he was unopposed.

Lord Astor of Hever became the predominant owner of *The Times* in 1922. Lord Northcliffe died in that year and Lord Astor of Hever acquired the majority of the shares in The Times Publishing Company, and also purchased the holding of the late Sir John Ellerman. Thereafter John Astor and John Walter* were the two chief proprietors of *The Times*.

Thus there began an association which was unreservedly for the good of the paper. At once the new owner regarded his acquisition as a high and serious responsibility; in what may be regarded as a statement of faith he wrote in the *Empire Review* in September 1923:

The Times supports no party, person or interest for any other reason than that it believes that party, person or interest to be in the right. No one is exempt from its criticism, but no one who deserves it need fear that its support will be withheld. Personal vendettas, mere sensationalism, or calculated demonstrations of how much the press can accomplish, are alike foreign to the basic principles of the paper. Again, it is a governing consideration of its direction that *The Times* ought, above all else, to deserve the confidence of the public. It may from time to time make unsound decisions upon questions of the day. No newspaper can hope to be exempt from ordinary human limitations, but its readers will know that, if it has erred, it has erred only after the gravest consideration within its power, and an earnest endeavour to discover the right".

Throughout the years of their joint responsibility for the editorial control of *The Times* John Astor and John Walter chose their staff carefully and then gave them their full confidence in discharging the terms of that trust set out above. They regarded their rights much as those which Bagehot described as the sovereign's—"to be informed, to encourage, and to warn". They never sought to impose their views. Their only concern was that whatever judgments were come to should have been made for the right reasons.

With this there went a constant care for the harmony and well-being of the staff. In addition to ensuring that the company provided for their health and comfort in working hours and for their pensions on retirement, John Astor did all in his power to encourage their games and pastimes. For many summers before the last war he and his wife entertained the staff, their wives and their friends at immense gatherings at Hever Castle, running sometimes to over 3,000 guests. John and Violet Astor were happy and friendly hosts. As each year was added to the last there grew a link of affection between John Astor and his staff that was intensely personal. It showed itself from time to time in gifts that were made to him by the staff on significant occasions. These he cherished.

The ownership of *The Times* at once brought John Astor into touch with other newspaper work. In what may be described as these outside activities, the Commonwealth Press Union had pride of place. He attended the third Imperial Press Conference at Melbourne in 1925 as treasurer. Later as president he was chairman of the succeeding conferences. He came to possess the confidence of the press of the whole Commonwealth in a way it has been given to few other men. Here too there was the same simple tenacity to principles and individual attention to people. A legion of newspapermen throughout the Commonwealth became his friends. In London he was chairman of the Press Club for over 28 years. When the Press Council was set up after the Second World War he was the automatic choice as its first chairman.

Medical work interested Lord Astor of Hever from the First World War onwards. His benefactions were many. The principal focal point of his interest was the Middlesex Hospital. In 1938 he became chairman of the governors. In 1948 it was disclosed that he had given the whole sum, £300,000, which the nurses' home had cost when it was built in 1931. In 1955 he gave £400,000 towards the rebuilding of the Middlesex Hospital Medical School, and in 1957 a further £50,000. He gave more than money, however. For him the hospital was a living thing. No one of its problems ever bored him: he took a lively interest in them all. Many medical students felt their hearts warm to the man who sat silent, smilingly smoking his pipe through their meetings.

To enumerate all his other activities would be to make too long a catalogue. He had been honorary secretary of the King's Roll National Committee, president of the British Legion in Kent, a vice-president of the British and Foreign Bible Society, and chairman of the advisory committee of St. Dunstan's. He was a Master of the Guild of St. Bride, and gave £25,000 towards the cost of restoration. Typically he set his heart on the church having a good organ. The way in which he interviewed organ makers and organists for months on end so that he could thoroughly understand the practical problems was part of his nature. Perhaps his most moving gesture was the production of a book commemorating the 28,000 Americans of all services who lost their lives while based in Britain during the Second World War. *Britain's Homage to 28,000 American Dead* was sent free of cost to all the next of kin who could be traced.

He was appointed a director of the Phoenix Assurance Company in 1931. He became chairman in 1952, relinquishing this post in 1958. He had also been a director of the Great Western Railway, Barclays Bank and Hambros Bank. He was interested in broadcasting from its birth and was a member of the Broadcasting Committees of 1923 and 1935. From 1937 to 1939 he was a member of the B.B.C. General Advisory Council. He was president of Dover Club, a Deputy Lieutenant for Kent, Justice of the Peace, and a Lieutenant for the City of London. He received honorary degrees from Perth, Australia (1925), London (1939), and McGill (1950).

In the 1956 New Year Honours John Astor was made a baron. It was characteristic of him that he pondered the offer of this for some time to make sure in his own mind that its acceptance would not appear to compromise the independence of *The Times*. His friends pointed out to him that he had done enough in other walks of public life to justify any honour. He was at that time recovering from a severe attack of rheumatoid arthritis. This had caused him to begin to cut down some of his public activities.

In May of 1955 he resigned from the chairmanship of the Press Council and withdrew from the leadership of the United Kingdom delegation to the Commonwealth Press Conference to be held in Australia in October. But, thanks to his habitual self-discipline having led him to follow absolutely the regimen his medical advisers had ordered, he made a complete recovery. He had retained enough interests to keep him fully occupied. It seemed as if he could look forward to a happy autumn to his days.

In 1962 a most severe blow fell upon him. The Finance Act of that year contained a clause which enforced that all people who died domiciled in Britain had to pay estate duty on property which they owned abroad. The purpose of the clause was the proper one of defeating those who had escaped this duty by exporting their money or other forms of estate shortly before they died. In Lord Astor of Hever's case he had imported his money into Britain throughout his life. Nevertheless, although the Trust which is the basis of the Astor fortune is a completely American one, and although none of the money had ever been in Britain, the clause was so badly drafted that his death in Britain would have caused the estate to be liable to its full effect. As he explained in a frank and dignified statement on September 1, 1962, his father had left the trust fund specifically for the grandchildren, and Lord Astor of Hever had no power to touch the trust capital, receiving only the income for his lifetime. In order to preserve the trust fund it was decided that he must as soon as possible take up foreign domicile. He had to give up almost all his English interests—one of the very few he retained was the chief proprietorship of *The Times*—to dispose of many of his belongings and to live abroad for the remainder of his days.

He settled at Pegomas near Grasse in the South of France so that his friends could visit him easily. In time he managed to surround himself once again with accustomed furniture and the routine belongings of daily life. They relieved his hurt a little. But the blow never ceased to be severe. He had been a lover of all things English. He had drawn happiness from his association with the Guards, with the Commonwealth, with the newspaper life of London, with the Middlesex Hospital and other medical ventures, with the City. To be forced to go abroad to die was the most cruel irony.

If there could be mitigation it came from the messages of sympathy which poured in upon him from every walk of life, and from the tributes which were paid to all he had done for them by one organization after another. They each knew they had lost a friend the like of whom they would never see again.

One of his later acts was typical of all his others. With the money he saved by living abroad and from the things he had been forced to sell he set up a charitable trust fund to help medicine and education in Britain.

July 20, 1971.

Miguel Angel Asturias, the Guatemalan novelist who was awarded the Nobel Prize for Literature in 1967, died on June 7, 1974 at the age of 74.

At the time of the award he acknowledged that the Swedish Academy had granted the prize symbolically for Latin American literature as a whole, as much as for him as an individual—a fair enough assessment since there are several other writers upon whom the prize might justly have been conferred. Yet in a flourishing generation of Latin American writing, Asturias's achievement was indeed considerable.

The earliest discernible characteristic of Asturias's work was his interest in the traditions of the Mayas, which he discovered not in Guatemala but through contact with French Maya scholars in the Musée de l'Homme in Paris. The fruit of this contact was his *Leyendas de Guatemala* (*Legends of Guatemala*, 1930), immediately acclaimed by Paul Valéry who wrote an introduction to it.

More notable was the novel *Hombres de Maiz* (*Men of Maize*, 1949). Writing in a tradition of Indianist novels several decades old in Latin America, Asturias was however the first Latin American writer to present the Indian fully and convincingly from within. The world was depicted in this novel as seen entirely through the eyes of a Guatemalan Indian; through spectacles made of magic, myth and metaphor. In a later novel, *Mulata de Tal* (*The Mulatta and Mr. Fly*, 1963), the fantasies of Indian legend had somewhat degenerated into an excuse to deploy fantasy, for its own sake, into a gratuitous surrealist romp. In the 1950s a very socially conscious Asturias began a trilogy of novels—*Viento Fuerte* (*Strong Wind*, 1951), *El Papa Verde* (*The Green Pope*, 1953) and *Los Ojos de los*

Enterrados (*The Eyes of the Buried*, 1961) —which sought to expose the abuses of American capital, and particularly of the United Fruit Company, in Central America. These novels have been criticized for an excessive tendentiousness, but there is often an impressive, angry passion pervading them which carries considerable conviction.

Asturias's fame rightly rests, however, in particular on one *tour de force, El Señor Presidente* (*Mr. President*, 1946), a novel which depicts with savage effect the claustrophobic terror deployed by a Latin American dictator. The novel deliberately avoids naming the exact place and time in which it is set; as a result its message becomes symbolic of a condition that has affected most Latin American—and not only Latin American—countries. Indeed its story of a doomed struggle between innocence and cynically corrupt powers foreshadows another great description of dictatorship—Lydia Chukovskaya's *The Deserted House*.

El Señor Presidente—and all Asturias's work—is written in a vastly rich Spanish. Some people think that Asturias has fallen into the trap of what Borges once called that mistaken belief that good writing involves the use of every single word in the dictionary. Asturias may have been occasionally verbose; he nevertheless wrote passages of great descriptive, sometimes compulsive power.

Born on October 19, 1899, Asturias was educated at the Instituto Nacional de Guatemala and the Universities of Guatemala and Paris. He entered the diplomatic service after the Second World War, and was appointed ambassador to El Salvador in 1953. After the overthrow of President Arbenz in 1954, Asturias went to live in Argentina and then moved to Europe. In 1966 he was awarded the Lenin Peace Prize and agreed to represent the new Guatemalan president, Mendez Montenegro, as ambassador in Paris. He resigned in 1970 to devote all his time to writing.

June 11, 1974.

The Ecumenical Patriarch Athenagoras, Archbishop of Constantinople and New Rome, who died in Istanbul on July 6, 1972 at the age of 86, was the spiritual leader of the 250 million members of the Orthodox Church, and an outstanding figure in the Christian Church.

In his inaugural address at the enthronement ceremony in 1949 he expressed the theme of church unity, which was the dominant interest of his life.

His historic meeting with Pope Paul VI at Jerusalem in 1964, which bridged a gulf of more than 900 years between the Churches of Rome and Constantinople, will always be regarded as one of the great landmarks of Christian history.

In a message to the Patriarch, delivered the following April by a delegation to Istanbul from the Vatican secretariat for Christian unity, the Pope wrote "With this visit we wish to renew the kiss of peace which we exchanged on the Mount of Olives".

Athenagoras, as much as Pope Paul and his predecessor Pope John,* had worked for years to create the conditions which made such a meeting possible, and it was his good fortune to see that dream fulfilled. Athenagoras always had a very close and warm feeling for Pope John and for his ideals, which he often expressed.

In 1965 Athenagoras formally annulled the excommunication pronounced by the Orthodox Church on the Church of Rome in 1054. This act was reciprocated by the Pope in Rome. Two years later Pope Paul VI visited Athenagoras in Istanbul.

When Athenagoras returned the visit later the same year, his journey was the first visit to Rome by a Patriarch of Constantinople since 1451. After a joint service in St. Peter's, Patriarch and Pope pledged themselves to work for full unity between Roman and Orthodox Catholics. The Patriarch spoke of their meeting as being that of "brother to a brother".

The opposition to his meetings with the Pope which faced Athenagoras from within his own Church, and particularly the diehards of the Church of Greece, underlines the complete difference of his position, in terms of ecclesiastical dominance, from that of the Pope.

The Pope is acknowledged as supreme in the Catholic world; but Orthodox Christianity is divided into autocephalous (self-governing) patriarchates and national churches, each independent in all its decisions from the Ecumenical Patriarch, who is regarded merely as *primus inter pares* among the patriarchs. In every major decision he has to persuade; he cannot command.

Further, the position of the Patriarch has been made infinitely more difficult than that of the Pope in that, since the establishment of the Turkish secular state by Kemal Ataturk in the 1920s, he has been a Turkish subject, with all the obvious limitations which such a condition implies.

At times when relations between Turkey and Greece have been extremely bitter, as for example during the troubles in Cyprus, the position of the Ecumenical Patriarch has exceeded that of all other Christian leaders in delicacy. It was a measure of the skill and temper of Patriarch Athenagoras that even at the peak periods of Turco-Greek tension, as in 1955, 1958, and 1964, he managed, while remaining true to his own Church and the Orthodox community, to keep good relations with Turkish leaders.

Since 1917 the chief problem of the Orthodox Church has been the division of the church between the Communist and non-Communist worlds. The larger part of the Eastern Church lay behind the iron curtain, in the Orthodox patriarchates of Russia, Romania, Bulgaria, Georgia, and other Communist countries.

When he was elected Ecumenical Patriarch in 1948 Athenagoras found the churches beyond the iron curtain slipping increasingly away from even the nominal suzerainty of Constantinople. There was the constant danger of a schism within the Orthodox church as serious as that which had rent the Christian church as a whole in the eleventh century.

Athenagoras boldly faced this problem, and by his constant striving for Orthodox unity achieved greater success than any of his predecessors in office. He saw Orthodox unity as the first step, and for him the most practical step, leading towards complete Christian unity. "We Orthodox must speak with one voice", he constantly said.

The increased contacts between East and West after the death of Stalin slightly eased this task. In 1959 Athenagoras went on a goodwill mission to all the Orthodox patriarchates and archbishoprics of the Middle East, and later he was the driving force behind the organization which culminated in the Pan-Orthodox conference in the island of Rhodes in 1961. All the Orthodox Churches from behind the iron curtain attended this conference (except Georgia, which was represented), and the conference was regarded as the first step towards a Pan-Orthodox synod to be convened at some future date. The Rhodes conference was an important event for the unity of the Orthodox Church.

At the end of 1960 the Russian Patriarch Alexeii* visited Athenagoras at the Phanar, the seat of the patriarchate, and there were also visits from the Bulgarian and other patriarchs. These visits were regarded by Orthodox circles as an acknowledgement of the spiritual supremacy of Constantinople within the Orthodox Church, and Athenagoras could be said to have done much to strengthen Constantinople in the position of primacy *inter pares* to which it is traditionally entitled.

Athenagoras went some distance to improve relations with Rome, unbridged since the days of the Great Schism of the eleventh century. In 1961 he received a pontifical mission at the Phanar headed by Monsignor Testa, Rector of the Pontifical Academy.

Though the Orthodox Church did not send observers to the Ecumenical Council in 1962 (it simply expressed good will for the council's work), Athenagoras, a strong supporter of union, was believed to have been personally in favour of such a move. The sending of two observers by the Russian Church, without previous consultation with Constantinople, was believed to have been a political decision in Moscow.

Athenagoras was born in 1886, the son of a village doctor in Epirus in northern Greece (at that time part of the Ottoman Empire). At the age of 17 he entered the Orthodox Theological Seminary on the island of Halki, near Istanbul, from which he graduated in 1910 and was ordained deacon. After various posts in Greece, he was elected in 1922 Metropolitan of Corfu and Paxos with the rank of Archpriest and

Bishop.

In 1930 he was elected Archbishop of America, where he remained for 18 years. He became the friend of several American Presidents, including Roosevelt, Truman and Eisenhower,* and learnt to speak fluent English. In 1948 he was elected Ecumenical Patriarch, the summit of a brilliant ecclesiastical career.

Both mentally and physically he was a man of stature. More than 6ft tall, with the magnificent beard worn by the Greek patriarchs, he reminded one of Michelangelo's "Jehovah". It was a memorable sight to see him celebrating the office in all the splendour of his Byzantine robes. He had a mind both flexible and subtle, attuned to the West, yet quite familiar with the East. He had the determination in the pursuit of chosen goals possessed by the Epirot Greek, allied to lucidity and wisdom, and the charity of a Christian.

Those who saw one quite unusual view of Athenagoras will never forget it. During the mammoth trial of the deposed leaders of the Menderes* regime on the island of Yassiada in 1960 and 1961, the Patriarch was called by the court to give evidence in the case in which the Menderes government was accused of having deliberately inspired the anti-Greek riots in Istanbul on September 6, 1955. It was a dramatic scene when the great bearded figure of the Patriarch entered the witness box. Rarely, if ever, has so eminent a dignitary given evidence in a court of law.

Everybody expected him to accuse Menderes; but he did not. He told the court he had personally no direct evidence that the Menderes government had provoked the riots. It was not the evidence that the judges wanted; but it was the word of a Christian, in which charity to the fallen won the battle against more understandable motives.

During his Patriarchate further progress was made in the traditional good relations between the Orthodox and Anglican churches. He was visited by two Archbishops of Canterbury, by Dr. Fisher in 1960 and by Dr. Ramsey in 1962. As a result of the second meeting it was decided to revive an earlier ecclesiastical commission of the thirties to examine differences of doctrine between the Anglican and Orthodox churches with a view to their harmonization, and this was a further step towards good relations. Dr. Ramsey even went so far on this occasion as to speak of "complete unity" between the two churches, at least on the basis of full intercommunication between them.

The Patriarch's zeal in the cause of unity took him to eastern Europe, and in 1967 he travelled to Britain, the first visit made by an Ecumenical Patriarch. The hope he expressed was that his visit might become a new starting point for greater progress.

It was always a pleasant and interesting experience to go to one of the Sunday lunches at the Patriarchate, where Athenagoras kept hospitable board not only for the whole Orthodox community of Istanbul but for friends or even passers-by. The bearded Patriarch would kiss intimate friends or honoured ecclesiastics on the top of the head, something which his great height made it easy for him to do. He was always approachable, and full of interest, as well as well-informed, about the outside world.

July 8, 1972.

Robert Atkins, C.B.E., the actor and director, who died on February 10, 1972 in a London hospital at the age of 85, had come fairly early to see the presenting of Shakespeare as his mission, and had done his utmost to carry it out wherever he found or was able to set up a theatre that he considered suitable.

He was probably at his best when working for Lilian Baylis, a manager as dedicated and determined as himself but not always congenial to him or in sympathy with him, at the Old Vic in the early 1920's. When he left, he had nearly 40 years of work before him, including many seasons in Regent's Park, with which his name became chiefly associated.

Born at Dulwich on August 10, 1886, Robert Atkins enrolled at R.A.D.A., Tree's Academy of Dramatic Art as it then was, in 1905, and in 1906 he was engaged at Tree's theatre, His Majesty's, where he appeared in some ten strongly cast, magnificently staged but textually abridged productions of Shakespeare. After leaving "my old Master", as he sometimes called Tree, Atkins served two other actor-managers, Martin Harvey and Forbes-Robertson, accompanying the latter to the United States, and he had also some service with F. R. Benson's companies behind him when he presented himself at the Old Vic in 1915.

Greet engaged him for the Old Vic—the company, including Sybil Thorndike and her brother Russell, visited Stratford-on-Avon in 1916—and reengaged him for a provincial tour on Atkins's demobilization after the war, but a letter he had written to Lilian Baylis while on service in Palestine, setting out ideas (which owed less to Tree's influence than to William Poëls's of the Elizabethan Stage Society) how Shakespeare should be produced, led to his appointment, in succession to Russell Thorndike and Charles Warburton, as play-director at the Old Vic for the 1920-21 season. He was allowed to build out an "apron" and to mask the footlights but not to remove them, since they were still wanted by the opera company which shared the stage and the weekly programme.

In each of his first four seasons just under 20 plays were produced, mostly at fortnightly intervals. During his fifth and last season, the normal run was increased to three weeks. The sum available for spending on new costumes and scenery for any production, which sometimes had to meet the needs of the opera company as well, was less than £15; for the rest, a permanent wardrobe was founded, old "flats" and cloths were painted and repainted, and a few rostrums and sets of steps were used again and again in different combinations. Under such conditions Atkins produced all the plays commonly assigned to Shakespeare except *Cymbeline*, whose turn came later. With *Troilus and Cressida* in 1923 he completed the Shakespearian cycle at Lilian Baylis's theatre, which thus became the holder of a world record.

A guest-appearance in Brussels at the invitation of the Belgian government in 1921, Atkins's staging of hitherto unproduced plays by Laurence Binyon, Gordon Bottomley and Halcott Glover, above all his giving *Peer Gynt* its first professional production in London, with Russell Thorndike as Peer, in 1922, had increased the prestige of the theatre, and furnished material for a campaign as a result of which funds were raised.

During the last months of his last season (1925) he played Autolycus, Macbeth, Sir Toby Belch—during each season he was accustomed to appear at intervals, and on occasions he had also directed the opera— and the old stock-company actor in Pinero's *Trelawny of the "Wells"*.

Thanks to Sydney Carroll, who established the Open Air Theatre in the gardens of the Royal Botanical Society in Regent's Park, opening with a revival of the black-and-white *Twelfth Night*, Atkins had the opportunity of conducting a new, predominantly Shakespearian adventure on a stage of raised turf against a background of bushes and trees. Between the first season in 1933 and the last season before the outbreak of the Second World War, through bad weather and through good—the takings varying from £16 on a wet night to £400 on a fine one—sometimes enlisting stars from the films and from the West End such as Anna Neagle, Fay Compton and Gladys Cooper, but more often relying on Shakespearians from his own and subsequent seasons at the Vic, Atkins made "Shakespeare in the Park", in spite of obtrusive microphones and of unevenness in the acting, a popular institution.

In the war-year 1941 he staged *The Taming of the Shrew* on a platform in Southwark Park before regaining access to the Royal Botanical Society's gardens, where even during the chaotic summer of Dunkirk he had produced one Shakespeare play, adding two others to it for matinées at the Vaudeville during the Blitz.

Before the war he had been a guest-producer on two occasions at Stratford-on-Avon, and he returned there in 1944 to conduct the last two wartime festivals, directing eight plays in each and reducing the distance between stage and stalls by raising the level of the apron stage. In London in 1946 he directed Claire Luce, who had played leads for him at Stratford-on-Avon, in a play by Clifford Bax* about Mary Stuart, and again took control at the Open Air Theatre, finding other backers after the withdrawal of the Arts Council grant, and continuing in management there until the end of the 1960 season.

February 11, 1972.

W. H. Auden, for long the *enfant terrible* of English poetry, who died on September 28, 1973 at the age of 66, emerges finally as its undisputed master. His earliest mature style in the 1930s was particularly influential, since it developed out of his efforts to break free from the fastidiousness, formlessness and *ennui* of twenties modernism.

It was Auden above all who showed how the full range of traditional forms could be revived in the service of the kind of moral and social realism that a world in crisis demanded. In this way he was in the vanguard of a versatile and publicly accessible art. He wrote cabaret songs, ballads, commentaries for films, words for cantatas and song-cycles, travel books, light verse and plays. Such a deliberate broadening of the appeal of his poetry led him to a simplicity of image and statement which was worth saying.

The lyrical concision and fertile scorn of *Poems* (1930) provided merely the groundbass upon which his later styles formed their eloquent variations. He could talk in poetry as no one since Byron, and was never happier than when following Pope, Horace or Marianne Moore. His best poems ("Spain 1937", for instance, or "In Praise of Limestone") have arguments, and these arguments, however brilliantly clothed in diction or metaphor, are of supreme importance. He was above all an intellectual poet.

To anyone who was young in the 1930s and troubled by the state of the world, Auden's death will mean that something of their past has died too; for thousands of those who would now be called "the involved" felt that Auden spoke up for them. Yet in later life Auden had second thoughts above some of the battle cries and hot attitudes of 40 years ago, and doubts about the influence of poets and poetry on great affairs.

In spite of long residence abroad Auden remained unalterably, unmistakably English; perhaps perversely W. S. Gilbert's line "For he is an Englishman" comes to the mind, yet it is not altogether inapposite, for Auden shared Gilbert's passion for and, in a different field, mastery of the English language; he delighted in its felicities, its quirks and subtleties (he was ever a dab hand at an unusual rhyme); he wonderfully enriched it in his work; and in later years spoke out loudly against the forces which he thought were debasing it. He remained always a craftsman working in English.

Wystan Hugh Auden was born on February 21, 1907 at York. His father, G. A. Auden, became Professor of Public Health at Birmingham University and as a children's psychologist no doubt contributed to his son's wide-ranging and scientific education. At Gresham's School, Holt, Auden read papers on "Enzyme Action" and "Folklore", played Caliban in *The Tempest*, organized and played in a recital of modern British music, and won prizes in English, Science and Latin prose. When he began to write poetry at the age of 15 his principal interests were mining and mineralogy. His early models were de la Mare and Hardy, though at Christ Church, Oxford, he discovered the work of T. S. Eliot*. He had gone up as an Exhibitioner in Natural Sciences, and switched to English after a term of P.P.E. His undergraduate poetry reflects the influence not only of Eliot, but of Old English verse, which was for him the principal attraction of the Oxford English School. His writing was intelligent, dense, allusive and precise, and his reputation at Oxford was enormous.

Auden spent some time in Germany after taking his degree, and for some years after that earned his living by teaching in prep schools. His keen interest in anthropology and psychoanalysis, and his belief that poetry should be clinical and observant, made his first volume, *Poems* (1930), intriguingly oracular and authoritative. It was an instant success. Much of his early poetry is in parts as difficult and personal as any of his predecessors'. *The Orators* (1932), for instance, one of the few modern poems that can stand comparison with *The Waste Land,* is at once a fantasizing analysis of a sick society and an examination of the predicament of the homosexual, though Auden was rarely explicit on this theme.

In the face of unemployment, the rise of Fascism and the approach of war, Auden found it impossible to maintain a detachment from politics. These subjects began to find their way into his poetry with a growing intensity which made him for a whole young generation the poetic and satiric exponent of the anti-Fascism of the Left, almost an English Brecht. The bulk of this work is found in the collections *Look, Stranger!* (1936) and *Another Time* (1940), though equally striking are the plays he wrote in collaboration with Christopher Isherwood for the Group Theatre. *The Dog Beneath the Skin* (1935), *The Ascent of F6* (1936) and *On the Frontier* (1938) in all their bold colours and natural sense of drama show, however, an increasing pessimism about the individual's hope of redeeming an unjust society.

Auden travelled widely in the later 1930s in Spain (he drove an ambulance for a time in the Civil War), in Iceland and China. From this perspective the world's problems seemed less and less soluble in political terms, and as a writer he felt limited by the English scene. In 1937 he was awarded the King's Gold Medal for Poetry. He went to the United States in the spring of 1939 and later became an American citizen, working out in his poetry historical and existential reasons for Christian belief.

His return to Episcopalianism had a variety of causes, but the final gesture seems to have coincided with the death of his mother (herself a High Anglican) in 1941. Auden adopted the new ideology with his customary gusto, and the long poems written in America at this time, *New Year Letter* (1941), *For the Time Being* and *The Sea and the Mirror* (1944) and *The Age of Anxiety* (1947), are his most ambitious works, the last being awarded a Pulitzer Prize.

They show immense technical virtuosity and also influences as various as Jung* and Henry James, besides making his current theological preoccupations dramatic and palatable, and dealing with the evil of Nazism from his usual bird's-eye perspective.

In 1945 he visited Europe as a major in the United States Strategic Bombing Survey, and wrote a report on the July 20 Plot against Hitler.

In 1948 he began to spend his summers on Ischia, and completed the libretto of *The Rake's Progress* (with his collaborator and friend Chester Kallmann) for Stravinsky. Another developing interest was literary criticism. *The Enchafèd Flood* (1950) was only one small fruit of a vast amount of stimulating teaching and lecturing in America during this decade.

In 1956 he was appointed Professor of Poetry at Oxford. The shorter poems that he wrote in this period are among his most relaxed and impressive, deriving much from a study of classical and medieval history.

In 1957 he won the valuable Feltrinelli Prize and bought his house at Kirschstetten, some miles outside Vienna. He published his most creative and suggestive collection of criticism, *The Dyer's Hand*, in 1962 and wrote a libretto for Hans Werner Henze (*Elegy for Young Lovers*).

Some critics regretted Auden's later manner which, with its frequent use of syllabic metres and a fondness for neologisms, did sometimes give his poems a deceptively playful and informal air. His collection *About the House* (1966) seemed in particular to be rather too domestic an approach to his perennial quest for the Good Life; and his ideal role of "minor Atlantic Goethe" only too true of a poet who had relinquished the roots that made his poetry great in the thirties. Such criticism was belied by the deep humanity and continuing technical excellence of his work, such as that contained in *City Without Walls* (1969).

Auden was given an honorary D.Lit. of Oxford in 1971; London made him an honorary D. Lit. in 1972. In that year he returned to live in the precincts of his old college.

The pale, seemingly bloodless face of his youth had long yielded to the celebrated crevices and cross-hatching of his maturer years.

Auden appeared to weather almost geologically, settling comfortably into his habitat with the modest assurance of one who could wear carpet slippers in the High, and who had taken his moral bearings accurately enough to be a flamboyant and naturally aphoristic conversationalist. He was one of those few in whose mouths even gossip attains a mythopoetic importance.

Auden's poetry was created in the turbulent wake of his intellectual exploration. He was restless and loved systems. He made his discoveries (whether of Homer Lane, Marx or Kierkegaard) well in advance of literary fashion, and was forever discarding outworn ideas and tinkering with his earlier poems.

W. H. Auden rescued poetry from its coterie image, made prosody and rhetoric respectable, and upheld a profitable belief that "even a limerick ought to be something a man of honour, awaiting death from cancer or a firing squad, could read without contempt".

But whatever we find to praise most in this abundant writer—his lyrical gift, his vivid ratiocination, his light verse, his metaphysical insight or his brilliant figurative powers—we owe to him above all our sense that the greatest poetry must observe, absorb and criticize the public events and social conditions of its own time.

October 1, 1973.

Lady Aylmer (Lady Aylmer-Jones)—See Byrne.

Michael Ayrton, the painter, sculptor and author, died on November 17, 1975 at the age of 54. A man of diverse interests, he essayed many art forms, ranging from graphic and plastic art to the novel.

He was born in London on February 21, 1921, the son of the poet and essayist Gerald Gould and the suffragette and later Labour Party Chairman Barbara Ayrton. Born Michael Ayrton-Gould, a reflection of his mother's feminist impetus, he eventually discarded his father's name. He was educated at Abinger Preparatory School, one of the most progressive of the day, but at 14 discontinued his formal education in favour of the study of art in Paris and Vienna. From his early 20s he exhibited prolifically, following an initial show at the Leicester Galleries with numerous shows at the Redfern and in Europe and the United States.

He soon showed that multiplicity of interests which was to be the hallmark of his artistic persona. He worked as a designer on John Gielgud's 1942 production of *Macbeth,* the 1944 Sadler's Wells *Le Festin de l'Araignée,* and the 1946 Covent Garden production of Purcell's *The Fairy Queen.*

He showed versatility as an illustrator of books and in the 1940s became known to a wider public as the youngest member of B.B.C. Radio's *Brains Trust.*

He had already produced his illustrations

for Webster's *The Duchess of Malfi* and for an anthology, *Poems of Death.* His own paintings at this period were for the most part in conventional and academic modes of representation, portraits, including a well-known drawing of Dylan Thomas, classical landscapes and still life.

He was also art critic of the *Spectator* from 1944 to 1946.

In 1952 he turned to sculpture, and though his work in plastic media seemed to veer in many cases sharply away from the conventions acknowledged by his pictures, his increasing regard for myth manifested itself.

In particular the myth of Daedalus and Icarus was to possess Ayrton, and from 1956 his work cast and recast his preoccupation with the classical story. It led him from an exhibition of 14 bronzes representing Icarus in 1961, through an illustrated prose and verse recreation of the myth entitled *The Testament of Daedalus* (1962), to one of his most curious commissions, the construction of a maze in the United States. This was the result of a novel by Ayrton entitled *The Maze Maker* (1967), this time a fictional treatment of the Minoan labyrinth and its Greek creator. The novel, which won him a Royal Society of Literature Award, brought a commission from an American banker, Armand Erpf, for a full-sized maze at his home in the Catskill mountains at Arkville, N.Y. Until immobilized by an arthritic condition, Ayrton continued to reflect in his work his fascination with the Daedalus legend and what it represented to him.

In other spheres into which he ventured, Ayrton performed with equal facility. He was a provocative essayist on art; wrote, directed and narrated a B.B.C. documentary on Berlioz; and won a prize at the Bergamo film festival for a film he made (with Basil Wright), *Greek Art.* He wrote a book on the Italian Gothic sculptor Giovanni Pisano, illustrated Aeschylus and Euripides, and explored his mythological preoccupations in a further book, *Fabrications* (1972).

Perhaps it was this very diversification, perhaps the sense he always felt of being a man out of his times, which seemed to prevent him from achieving an organic, integrated body of work in any medium. As a sculptor and painter he was erudite and versatile, but always a classicizer in an expressionist era. This conflict always fascinated him, but he never seemed to be able, as an artist, to express the paradox creatively.

November 19, 1975.

Field Marshal Ayub Khan, former president of Pakistan, died on April 20, 1974, of a heart attack in his house in Islamabad. He was 66.

He is likely to be one of those whose record will look better in historical perspective than it did in his lifetime. His

attempt was to establish for Pakistan a halfway house to democracy, but it failed; his experiment ended in chaos, with himself angrily repudiated by almost every political element in the country, and with the army stepping in again to impose order. The system which he had evolved was swept away root and branch.

Ayub defined his system as being an attempt to create a democracy that his people could understand and operate, and if there was a note of patronization in that, it reflected what was perhaps his own prime weakness as a political leader. His system never became the object of loyalty, or even of enthusiasm, just as—and partly because —the President himself never became the object of affection or symbol of national progress among his countrymen,

There was something about Ayub which prevented him from becoming a popular leader. Partly this may have reflected his self-identification with the landed, and indeed semi-feudal, power of what was then West Pakistan—this was no Nasser*, who could appeal to the nationalist middle class by giving them concessions, coupled with gestures towards the peasantry. But it was also a matter of personality. Ayub was stiff, almost unbending in manner, resentful of differences and opposition, susceptible to flattery. He could instil respect but not affection. Perhaps it was because, as a regular soldier, he regarded people as "other ranks" to be cared for and to be led.

On the surface at least, Ayub's decade of power, 1958 to 1969, was one of considerable achievement, and he brought Pakistan many of the things he had promised when, as commander-in-chief, he seized power— political stability, economic progress and a more respected standing in the world's affairs. Where he failed was at the political level. The prosperity which his supporters claimed he had produced was never more than a middle class boom, whose benefits did not percolate into the massed lower levels of society; social divisions and tensions were much sharpened in consequence. And the under-lying political problem for Pakistan, a country without natural coherence, that of unity, Ayub did worse than ignore—he denied that it existed. The result was that when after the collapse of his system the long-suppressed political forces were given their head, they began to pull the country to pieces. But still, the decade of Ayub promises to stand out as an oasis of order combined with progress, between two periods of political chaos and national stagnation.

Born on May 14, 1907, in a Pathan family of military tradition and some means, Ayub went to Aligarh Muslim University and then to Sandhurst. When the end of the Second World War came he was commanding an infantry battalion in Burma. After the departure of the British, promotion was rapid and by 1950 Ayub was commander-in-chief. From the beginning in Pakistan—unlike in India—

the army was drawn towards an active role in politics. In 1954 Ayub became the symbol of the developing political involvement of the soldiers when he became defence minister as well as commander-in-chief. His time in the cabinet was short, not much more than a year, but it was sufficient to confirm his contempt for politicians and conviction that the democratic political process had nothing to offer his country.

The ambitions of men such as Ayub himself and Pakistan's last constitutional president, Iskander Mirza, did much to warp the early growth of democracy in their country. Mirza stepped into a scene of mounting chaos and abrogated the constitution on October 7, 1958; three weeks later he was sent into exile in London when Ayub and his fellow generals took power themselves. Ayub declared himself President and before long he promoted himself to the rank of Field-Marshal. This self-indulgence, indicative perhaps of Ayub's basic humourlessness as well as vanity, led to the estrangement between himself and the army which was to be a factor in his downfall.

The new President moved vigorously into action. Martial law courts imposed draconic penalties, including flogging, on traders convicted of black-marketeering. A rigorous screening of corrupt civil servants was begun, leading to the dismissal of about 1,600. As is usual with new brooms, the authorities swept clean but not deep. The intervention of the army was welcomed, all confidence in the previous polity having been lost, and Ayub made sure that the army's popularity was not diminished by over-exposure. A few weeks after the coup, the troops were back in their barracks and the running of the country was in the hands of a purged and temporarily chastened civil service.

All civil liberties were now abolished, a rigorous press censorship was instituted, and a daunting array of penalties were promulgated, including death—which, in fact, was never imposed. The regime's bark was worse than its bite—but its bark, backed up with threats, was enough for the flimsy opposition.

The heart of the system that Ayub evolved—democracy of a kind "the people could understand and work"—was the structure of "basic democracy", a pyramid of local government designed to associate the people with administration. The "basic democrats", totalling about 80,000, were elected under universal direct franchise; but they then acted as an electoral college for the presidency and the national assembly. The Ayub system created an executive of almost untrammelled power, leaving the legislature impotent and irrevelant and the judiciary without any civil liberties to guard.

It was Ayub's first hope that his system could function without political parties, but it soon became apparent that this was not so, and Ayub finally had to lend his name to a revived splinter of the old Muslim League. When, in 1965, Ayub was re-elected president, it was a triumph of the self-stabilising element of the system, not of his own personal or partisan popularity. The system acted like a sea-wall, translating the surges of popular disaffection into ripples of discontent. The trouble with such a system is that it leaves no way to change except to smash the system itself.

It crumbled with astonishing suddenness. At the end of 1969, the regime apparently had nothing more to worry about than the celebration of a decade of progress under Ayub—the cult of personality being by then well-developed, indeed over-blown. Pakistan was the blue-eyed boy of the community of western aid specialists, a model of sagacious and steady use of assistance from abroad. By then student riots broke out, at first expressing disaffection with matters as petty as bus fares. The politicians saw an opportunity, jumped in as the students themselves felt their growing power, and the rioting spread and intensified. The target became not the transport services nor the university authorities, but the regime itself.

Now the fundamental weakness of the Ayub system was exposed. Its only sanction now lay where it had in the beginning—in the army.

But would the army really lend itself to the suppression of student-led mobs? Would Ayub in 1958 have let his troops be thus used to prop up the former regime, after it had lost all popularity? Corruption had emerged again—indeed it was never really eradicated—and the multiplying wealth of the wealthiest was regarded as a national scandal, not least in army circles. Ayub's own family, notably his sons, were judged to have profited more in the 10 years of his rule than could be explained by simple business acumen—especially as they had at the beginning been rather junior army officers.

Feeling that the army would not agree to be used as the big stick, Ayub parleyed and was lost. He promised not to stand again for the presidency. He undertook to oversee the demolition of his whole system, and to support a return to the parliamentary order he had kicked aside. But with disorder spreading, there was no way for him but to resign quickly. His own commander-in-chief, General Yahya Khan, stepped in, martial law was again declared, and the army was once more welcomed especially by those classes who saw in the spreading disorder a threat to their own positions. Ayub retired into silence and inconspicuousness.

There were calls for vengeance against him and his family but the ruling generals—perhaps from loyalty, or from intimations of their own future self-interest—gave these no encouragement. Ayub lived in the house he had built for himself in Islamabad, the new capital, and commuted often to the little state of Swat to fish.

He married Zubeida Khatoon and had four sons and three daughters.

April 22, 1974.

B

Josephine Baker, who died in Paris on April 12, 1975 at the age of 68, was, besides a singer and dancer, a resistance heroine of the Second World War and mother to a group of international orphans. The daughter of an American Negro mother and a Jewish travelling salesman father, she was born in St. Louis, Missouri.

She had her early schooling in Philadelphia and then went to New York, where she trained as a dancer and sang at nightclubs in the Harlem district. But it was in Paris that her international career really began when at the age of 19 she appeared with the Revue Nègre at the Champs-Elysées. Thereafter she was based in the city appearing in variety, revue, operetta, and films such as *Zou Zou* and *Princess Tam Tam*. From feats such as dancing on a mirror at the Folies Bergère wearing nothing but a string of rubber bananas round her waist, she built up a reputation as the Black Goddess of cabaret.

Yet her role in life was far from being confined to show-business. During the Second World War she joined the French Resistance and her activities gained recognition with the Croix de Guerre with Palm, the Legion of Honour and the Rosette of the Resistance.

But her deepest impulses were humanitarian. She was a campaigner for Civil Rights in the United States and in 1948 bought a chateau in Bergerac in south west France which, besides being a home, she ran as a multiracial orphanage for 12 orphans. These children who were known as her "rainbow tribe" came from 10 different countries and became her adopted family. It was more their welfare than the lure of the footlights which occasioned her stage appearances from her return to the Olympia, Paris, in October 1959 to her London Palladium show in 1974.

Here at 68, sporting a skin-tight cat-suit and a crest of enormous feathers, she vividly evoked the presence that, singing on a trapeze and throwing roses to her male admirers, had tantalized audiences at the Folies Bergère 30 years earlier. Yet, kindly but cool, she did not project sexuality so much as good comradeship and, in her delighted response to applause, she was very much a little girl.

Her way with a song, too, was very much that of a child, spontaneously delighted with, and almost as soon wearying of, a kitten. Attacking the first few bars with zest and refined intelligence, she would quickly relinquish it for another as though tired of it herself or fearing that we would tire of it.

This perfunctoriness perhaps explained why she had been content to remain so long away from a sphere which—as witness her changing a new microphone for one which had broken down, casually and perfectly in the rhythm of her song—was still emphatically her element.

She died with her career still at its peak, only five days after receiving a standing ovation from an audience including such stars as Sophia Loren, Alain Delon, Jeanne Moreau and Princess Grace of Monaco, at a gala performance of a revue celebrating her 50 years in show-business.

Three times married, to Pepito Abitano, Jean Lion and Joseph Bouillon, she is survived by her adopted family.

April 14, 1975.

Dr. Robert Baldick, F.R.S.L., Fellow of Pembroke College, Oxford, died on April 24, 1972. He was 44 and one of the most gifted and versatile scholars in the field of French literature and culture.

Born in Huddersfield on November 9, 1927 of an English father and a French mother, he was educated at Royds Hall Grammar School and then at the Queen's College, Oxford, where he was a pupil of Iain Macdonald, for whom he retained a lasting affection. In 1948 he obtained first class honours in schools, and stayed on to do research under the aegis of the great Oxford figure Enid Starkie*, whose vivacity, humour, enthusiasm and, at the same time, rigid and exact scholarship were so much in tune with his own approach to his subject and to life. It was she who suggested that he should turn his attention to the French author Huysmans, on whom he produced a remarkable thesis which obtained him his doctorate in 1952.

The book which he produced from this thesis in 1955 was widely acclaimed. Using a wealth of unpublished material, he transformed Huysmans studies by his full portrayal of the man and the author, hitherto a matter more of legend than of fact.

It was while in Paris, working on this subject, that Baldick met one of the greatest influences on his life, the scholar and bookseller Pierre Lambert. Lambert had devoted his life to Huysmans studies and to the collection of manuscript material relating to the period. He welcomed the young scholar with open arms; and, with a generosity unrivalled in academic circles, he recognized the capability of the young man, and opened up his archives to him. Robert Baldick became a kind of adopted son to Lambert and his wife, with whom he remained on the closest terms for the rest of his life. Lambert's wide circle of intellectual and literary friends soon became Baldick's, and this Paris stay was the basis for that even wider acquaintance with French literary circles which became his.

In 1953 he took up a post as assistant lecturer at Glasgow University, but almost immediately he was back in Oxford as a joint lecturer of Pembroke and University Colleges. In 1958 he was made a Fellow of Pembroke College and Tutor in French. This post he held until his death. He was a most stimulating teacher, whether it was in the tutorial or in the lecture theatre. He had the capacity for arousing great enthusiasm, and for making his pupils feel themselves part of the period with which he was dealing.

The work on Huysmans, published at so young an age, heralded a vast output of publications, all of which gave evidence of the same sympathy with French literary society of the nineteenth century. It was fitting that his last book, *Dinner at Magny's,* should have had on its cover a picture of various French literary figures (Flaubert, George Sand, etc.) at dinner, and that amidst them there should have been the unmistakable figure of Robert Baldick himself.

The most important of these other works were: *The Life and Times of Frédéric Lemaitre* (1962), *The Goncourts* (1960), *The Life of Henry Murger* (1961), and *The Siege of Paris* (1965). At the time of his death he was engaged on a major work on Zola.

A stream of excellent translations came from his pen, including translations from Huysmans, Flaubert, Sartre, Verne, Radiguet, Camus and many modern authors. In many of these he was helped by his wife Jacqueline. Baldick helped to raise the standard of translations into English; he also helped to raise the status of the translator. As editor of the Oxford Library of French Classics from 1962 to 1967, and as joint editor of Penguin Classics from 1964 onwards, he made sure that translators were paid a proper fee for what is a specialist job, and that the British public was introduced to the best of foreign literatures in translations that respected and did not betray the intentions of the author. He himself was chosen as translator for various French theatrical productions, notably Jean-Louis Barrault's *Rabelais* in London in 1971.

Amid all this he retained a zest for life which was outstanding in its vigour, humanity and capacity for humour. He was the best possible dining companion, and was with justification curator of Common Room of his college, acting as host to guests after dinner. He was a brilliant raconteur and at the same time a good listener to others. His membership of the Savile Club was another of his great enjoyments. He loved the good things of life and was wine steward of his college as well as a member of the Winegrowers of Châteauneuf du Pape.

Above all, he had a great capacity for friendship. The loss of three of his greatest friends—Pierre Lambert, Enid Starkie and Iain Macdonald—in the last three years had deeply saddened him.

By his first marriage, to Grace Adlam, he leaves three children, Julian, Christopher and Hilary; and by his second marriage, to Jacqueline Harrison, he leaves two children, Nicholas and Oriel.

April 25, 1972.

Cristobal Balenciaga, the most distinguished couturier of his time, died in Valencia, Spain, on March 23, 1972. He was 77.

Balenciaga, the Spanish-born Paris couturier whose influence on world fashion was decisive during the two decades that followed the Second World War, was born on January 21, 1895 at the fishing village of Guetaria, near San Sebastian. He came of humble parentage; and, though the information about his early years is scant, such stories as there are—the collar he is said to have sewn with bright beads when he was only five years old for the family cat, the preference he showed for sewing with his mother rather than helping his father with his boat, the suit he copied from a Drecoll model for the aging Marquesa de Casas Torres—all point to one thing: a precocious and, as it turned out, an abiding passion for dressmaking.

At the age of 20 he had opened his own dressmaking establishment at San Sebastian. Twenty-two years later, in 1937, he opened in Paris at No. 10 avenue George V, an address that was to become that of the greatest and most distinguished couturier of our times.

His reputation was already made before the war but it was the postwar period that established him as a creator in a class apart; indeed it can be said that he revolutionized world fashion at that time.

The main means of the change he brought about were the relaxing of the fitted line and, in a sense, the stylization of the female body. He began the process by letting out all seams, turning the dress in this way into an easy, casual garment, and the classic tailored suit into a two-piece with a short, straight jacket—an influence that governs suit structure to this day. At the same time he opened up the day neckline and cut sleeves to three-quarter length, both tendencies that were to have far-reaching effects on everyday styling for a decade or more. He also did away with the fitted coat, and by forcing the sloping shoulder line gave a new husky look to jacket and coat tops. The provocatively covered forms that resulted from these slow but powerfully directed movements led, first, to the loose tunic line of 1955, followed two years later by the sack.

His was a logical process of evolution yet paradoxically he was always ahead of other designers in styling and in daring; and it was the repeated return of all designers to the main Balenciaga direction that earned for him the term of "the designer's designer".

Balenciaga clothes were too uncompromising and indeed often too unflattering to be easy to wear, though André Courrèges, who worked for him for 10 years, held a different view. They have always demanded of the private clients that made up the bulk of his business unerring elegance and distinction as well as wealth—for the House of Balenciaga has the reputation of being the most expensive dressmaking house in the world.

Balenciaga was one of the few great couturiers who could carry out the whole operation himself, from cutting to finishing. His work rested on a solid technical basis; on that he built his aesthetic success.

He is reported to have said that the secret of harmony is balance, and that balance in clothes depends on the right disposition of the three essential ingredients that go to make up a model—cut, colour, ornamentation. It is this intractable pre-occupation with balance that gave to even the most startling Balenciaga model a look of satisfying solidity—almost at times of rugged sturdiness that seemed to stem from some deep peasant instinct in their creator. His love of rough textures, roomy styles, earthy colours, and styles that do not date, bears out this something fundamental in the genius of Cristobal Balenciaga. Cecil Beaton once said of him: "Proud, Spanish, classical, he is a strange rock to be found in the middle of the changing sea of fashion."

In 1968 he shut up shop. In one of his very rare interviews, and probably his last, given in 1971 to Prudence Glynn of *The Times*, he said: "The life which supported couture is finished. Real couture is a luxury, and a luxury which is just impossible to do any more."

He came out of retirement to design the wedding dress of Maria Del Carmen Franco, granddaughter of General Franco, who was married to Prince Alfonso de Borbon y Dampierre in 1972.

March 25, 1972.

Joseph Bamford—See **McAvoy.**

Evelyn Baring, 1st Baron Howick of Glendale—See **Howick.**

Captain C. D. Barnard, who made a number of historic long-distance pioneering flights in the years 1928 to 1930, died at his home in Brighton on August 7, 1971. He was the personal pilot of "the flying duchess," the Duchess of Bedford, who sponsored many of these flights.

Charles Douglas Barnard, who was born in 1895, obtained his flying certificate in 1915 while serving with the Royal Flying Corps. After the war he became a test pilot with the Sopwith Aviation Company, and from 1920 to 1927 was a pilot with the de Havilland* Aircraft Company, making the first London-Malta flight in 1923.

The first long-distance flight with the Duchess of Bedford was a tour of Europe and North Africa, covering more than 5,000 miles, in 1927. Two years later Captain Barnard piloted her Fokker monoplane, named the "Spider," to India and back in seven and a half days, covering the distance of approximately 10,000 miles in 88½ hours. The monoplane had a Bristol Jupiter engine of 500 hp. For this achievement he was awarded the gold medal of the Royal Aero Club. The following year they accomplished another record flight from London to Capetown and back, 19,000 miles in 20 days.

Among Captain Barnard's exploits was a record solo flight from London to Malta and back, non-stop each way, which he completed in 26 hours. For a few years afterwards he operated Barnard's Air Circus in England and India.

August 10, 1971.

Alfred Barnes, P.C., who died on November 26, 1974, aged 87, was Minister of Transport in the postwar Labour Government, and piloted through the Commons the Transport Act of 1947. He was for many years a leading figure in the Co-operative movement and was chairman of the Co-operative Party from 1924 to 1945. He sat as Co-operative Labour Member for East Ham, South, from 1922 to 1931 and from 1935 to 1955.

As the minister primarily responsible for getting on to the statute book one of the most complex and comprehensive measures of nationalization ever enacted, Barnes will always have a secure place in the history of the Labour Party. But there must also rank high in his services to the socialist cause his important contribution to the development of the Co-operative movement as a political force.

The cohesion it attained owed much to his endeavours. He was one of the most constructive thinkers in the movement and he brought to it uncommonly shrewd business ability and much administrative skill.

His approach to the formidable task of bringing inland transport under comprehensive control was practical and pragmatic. He saw no point in needless rigidity. He was criticized by some Labour backbenchers for the measure of freedom of choice he left in the carriage of goods by road, but that did not bother him. He always had an acute sense of the politically possible.

One of the secrets of his success was that he never worried. He believed that if a man worried over his job he was not really up to it. One of his habits was to sit down every morning and think over the events of the previous day so that he could base future action on the experience he had gained.

It was said of him that he rarely read a book. This was not strictly true, but he was certainly not addicted to what he called theoretical reading. He liked to get his facts at first hand.

He was no dialectician, and certainly no orator. His speeches, delivered in a flat, unhurried style, seemed loosely constructed and they were not always particularly grammatical. But invariably there was sound substance in them, and he could be surprisingly fruitful of ideas. He was a quiet man, unassuming, unpretentious, good humoured and tolerant, and with a courage in face of severe physical disability which earned him deep respect.

Alfred John Barnes was born at North Woolwich in 1887, the youngest of seven children of William Barnes, a docker. When he was eight, this "urchin in the slums", as he called himself later, lost a leg after a fairground accident. He went from elementary school to the Northampton Institute and the L.C.C. School of Arts and Crafts and became a skilled designer and worker in precious metals.

His revolt against the squalor he saw in the East End drove him into the I.L.P. and the Co-operative movement, and by the time he was 22 he was hard at work getting the unions of his trade to combine in a national organization. He got on to the management committee of the Stratford Co-operative Society in 1914, and in 15 months he was its president.

The formation in 1920 of the London Co-operative Society was largely a result of his endeavours to get neighbouring societies to unite. He became its first president and held the office for nine years.

He had always urged that the Co-operatives should seek direct parliamentary representation, and when the Co-operative Party was formed he became a member of the first executive committee. When he was returned to Parliament for East Ham, South, in 1922 he presented Co-operation to the House as an integral part of socialism and as a practical alternative to capitalist enterprise.

His views did not commend themselves to some Labour intellectuals. He believed in the closest collaboration between the Co-operative and Labour parties and played an important part in establishing their relations on a satisfactory basis. But he was always careful to ensure that there should be no risk of the complete absorption of the Co-operative Party.

November 27, 1974.

Dr. J. M. Barnes, Director of the Toxicology Unit at the Medical Research Council Laboratories, Carshalton, since 1947, died on September 24, 1975 at the age of 62.

The son of a Sheffield doctor, John Morrison Barnes was born on January 11, 1913, and educated at Repton, Trinity Hall, Cambridge, and the Sheffield Medical School where he took his clinical training. He qualified in 1936 and spent the Second World War in the R.A.M.C.

In 1947 the chemical industry asked the Medical Research Council to establish a unit to study the toxic properties of potentially useful materials. What was asked for was not a mere testing station but an independent expert unit to which materials could be referred for examination.

The Medical Research Council acceded to the request and appointed Dr. Barnes as director. His briefing fortunately was deliberately wide and somewhat vague. Dr. Barnes took full advantage of this pioneering effort and its wide-ranging scope and in a short time he had established the unit as a centre to which research workers came from all over the world.

He started off with beryllium, then coming to the fore as a potentially dangerous industrial hazard. Pesticides rapidly came to his notice as a toxic hazard, largely because of their indiscriminate use, and Dr. Barnes became the World Health Organization expert on this subject, chairing special expert groups on the subject and writing reports which are now standard references on the subject. In due course his unit became the W.H.O. international reference centre for the evaluation of the toxicity of pesticides.

For a period carcinogenicity took up much of his time and he and his colleagues were responsible for discovering the carcinogenicity of the nitroso compounds. He was early on to the toxicity of mercury, now a worrying international pollution problem, and was currently investigating the toxic effects of carbondisulphide, widely used in industry, on the heart.

A review of the subjects he covered in his unit reveals a width of scope that knew no national limits. Thus at one time his research programme included "Identification of Toxic Substances in the Smoke from Incense Sticks and Other Woods".

He was appointed C.B.E. in 1962, a token, and scarcely adequate, official recognition of one to whom industry, both employers and employees, as well as the inhabitants of the developing world with their dependence on safe pesticides for the full exploitation of their country's resources owe a heavy debt of gratitude.

September 30, 1975.

Sidney Barnes, the Australian cricketer, died on December 16, 1973, at the age of 57. He was a gifted and pugnacious player who, however, did not always serve either himself or the game to best effect by his brushes with authority.

The same brash confidence, efficiency and talents that ensured his success as a self-made man on and off the cricket field were hardly the ones to endear him to officialdom. The Australian cricketing hierarchy, until recent years, were not known for their tolerance of those who did not conform. In many ways Barnes, both in his own character and as a player, was perhaps born a decade too soon.

Sidney George Barnes was born in humble circumstances to the wife of a sheep farmer in a remote country district of Queensland. His father died before he was born; the family eventually moved to a Sydney suburb.

At the end of his first full Sheffield Shield season, Barnes was included in the 1938 Australian side to tour England. He broke a bone in his wrist during shipboard games on the journey to Europe and had his arm in plaster until halfway through the tour.

Barnes reached the peak of his individual skills and his notoriety as a nonconformer and exhibitionist when cricket resumed after the war. Now more heavily built, he crouched over his bat with the hands well down the handle, transformed from a free-driving strokemaker to a watchful back-footed accumulator. His square cut remained one of the most memorable strokes in post-war cricket, but the rest were often restrained in the interests of efficiency.

The change came about perhaps for two reasons. One was the understandable ambition to succeed in order to reap the consequent side benefits, and the other was his unselfish conversion at the age of nearly thirty to the role of opening batsman. With W. A. Brown not available for the 1946-47 series against England, it was Barnes who joined Arthur Morris in forming a superb first-wicket partnership, to which Sir Donald Bradman's powerful sides owed so much.

Outstanding feats by Barnes were often accompanied by controversy. When he made 234 against England at Sydney in the second Test of the 1946-47 series, he batted more than 10 hours and made the slowest double hundred in history. At one stage he appealed after almost every other ball against the light, hoping for a postponement until batting conditions improved. "We could have played on but it was a Test match and we just had to win", he confessed later.

At Lord's, in 1948, he said he would make a Test hundred and did so despite a duck in the first innings. On that tour his close and fearless fielding at short leg became widely discussed, with intimidation of the batsman always a possibility. Eventually, in the third Test at Manchester, a stroke from Dick Pollard caused Barnes to be carried off injured.

Already Barnes had crossed the Australian authorities by playing Lancashire League cricket, against their wishes, with Burnley in 1947; and the following year by having his wife in Britain during the Australian visit, contrary to the regulations of the time. Back in Australia he once crossed authority by vaulting the turnstile at a Test match, having given his player's ticket away. He declined the terms offered for the Australian tour of South Africa in 1949-50 because he felt they were not high enough.

Soon afterwards he took up journalism. His cricket writing was often acrimonious and wounding, though usually sound technically. A libel action concerned with his absence from the South African tour did nothing to calm the troubled waters, and a later attempt to return to cricket was marked by arguments with officials.

In his early days Barnes bowled occasional leg breaks and was also a capable wicketkeeper. Nine Test matches against England brought him 846 runs at an average of 70.50, which emphasizes his ability on the most important occasions. In all first class cricket he made a little over 8,000 runs, at an average of 53 plus, and hit 26 hundreds.

Those who knew him least were always the most critical of him. There were plenty who knew him well who admired him and only regretted that he did not always do justice to himself.

December 17, 1973.

Marian (Mrs. Donald) Barnie—See Veitch.

Sir Michael Barrington-Ward, K.C.V.O., C.B.E., D.S.O., chairman of the Operating Committee of the four U.K. railway companies from 1938-1947, and thereafter, until his retirement in 1953, a member of the Railway Executive, died on July 28, 1972 at the age of 85. He was a brother of R.M. Barrington-Ward, a former editor of *The Times.*

By birth into a clerical family, by education at Westminster and by training at Edinburgh University in engineering he inherited principles and developed standards. For one who was to become the Chief of Operations of the railways of Britain an uncompromising integrity and undeviating tenacity of purpose were a solid foundation for his pursuit of safety and punctuality.

In these matters his standards were absolute. Many of his junior officers remember, when they attempted the slightest compromise of his standards, the spare high-coloured figure levelly and bleakly handing down instant decisions to their shame. By getting these priorities right he brought his charge, the Southern Area of the L.N.E.R., to a high pitch of service.

In this he had not many assets but his principles and his standards. The L.N.E.R. was poor; "B.W." had to make do with few new locomotives or carriages, little new signalling and no new stations. When the war came in 1939 no one was therefore better qualified to lead the railways in times in which making-do was all—apart from an unconcealed impatience with those who would not make do; and, of course, except for the high courage with which he led railwaymen to work unsheltered through the blitz and the V1s and the V2s.

In 1944 close at hand outside his room at Marylebone there was the unheralded crash of an explosion. The eyes did not waver. The voice went levelly on with its sentence. It was easy to recall that he had won a D.S.O. in France in 1916 for towing loaded wagons out of an exploding ammunition dump. It was easy too to serve such a taskmaster with appreciation and affection.

Victor Michael Barrington-Ward was born on July 17, 1887, the third son of Canon M. J. Barrington-Ward, D. D., Rector of Duloe, Cornwall. He was educated at Westminster and at Edinburgh University, where he took a degree in engineering. He joined the Midland Railway as an assistant engineer but soon went into the army, first in the South Lancashire Regiment, then in 1915 in the Royal Engineers. In the Railway Operating Division of the Corps he rose to lieutenant-colonel, was mentioned in dispatches four times, received a French Army Citation and the Croix de Guerre with palm and the United States Medal of Freedom.

After the war he was briefly with the Midland Railway and with the Ministry of Transport. In 1922 he joined the North Eastern Railway and soon found his vocation in Operations. In 1923 he became District Superintendent at Middlesbrough; in 1927 Superintendent of the Western Section, Southern Area; in 1938 Superintendent of the Southern Area and Chairman of the National Operating Committee. In the early part of the war he was promoted Divisional General Manager; in 1947 a member of the Railway Executive. From 1948 to 1953 he was chairman of the Railway Clearing House.

He had been Miller Prizeman of the Institution of Civil Engineers and won the Operations Gold Medal of the Institute of Transport.

He married in 1920 Barbara, daughter of J. T. Pilling. They had three daughters. The marriage was dissolved in 1938. He married in 1938 Isobel, daughter of Dr. S. J. Kerfoot, by whom he had a daughter.

July 31, 1972.

Sir Ronald Baskett, O.B.E., Secretary of the Agricultural Research Council, who died on November 24, 1972, at the age of 71, would undoubtedly have gained greater worldly honours had he not consistently put the interests of his work and his co-workers before his own. Something of the "sacred hunger of ambitious minds" he certainly had, but nothing of selfish ambition.

He was quietly optimistic by nature, wholly without self-consciousness and, being always prepared to think the best of people, generally got the best out of them. But there was complete integrity, and much shrewdness also, in his open and generous character, and anyone who might try to take advantage of this apparently easygoing man would be liable to regret his error.

These characteristics stood Baskett in good stead when in October 1971 he was called out of his retirement to become Secretary of the Agricultural Research Council. The appointment was a temporary one, but it was not in his nature to act as a mere caretaker. For two years there had been rumours of major changes, inevitably causing anxiety and misunderstanding; the hostile reception accorded by scientists to the Rothschild proposals, published about the time of Baskett's appointment, did not provide the best atmosphere for the ensuing negotiations between the research councils and government departments. Through his previous experience as a re-

search director and civil servant Baskett was uniquely equipped to face this situation. He threw himself energetically into the complicated discussions with an honesty and dedication that could not fail to dispel misunderstanding. He knew how important it was to maintain the morale of the directors and staffs of the research institutes, and in negotiation he was concerned to secure recognition of their role in policy formation within any future organization. Though he did not live to see the final outcome of his endeavours he had, in his short time as secretary, served the A.R.C. with more than ordinary distinction.

When Baskett was appointed, in 1924, to a post in the Ministry of Agriculture for Northern Ireland, he became a founder member of the joint organization comprising the Agricultural Faculty of the Queen's University and the research divisions of the Ministry, which afterwards developed so successfully. He was appointed Professor of Agricultural Chemistry in 1935, and Chief Scientific Officer of the Ministry in 1947. Baskett specialized in animal nutrition, a subject to which he made notable original contributions and which he taught with enthusiasm and lucidity. He was one of the first to recognize the importance of quality in animal products, especially in relation to Northern Ireland's need to establish a firm basis for its export trade to the rest of the United Kingdom.

During the war, Baskett had to administer the rationing of feeding stuffs and fertilizers in Northern Ireland, onerous work that gave him valuable experience of the commercial world. He served from 1950 to 1952 as United Kingdom Agricultural Attaché in Washington, and on his return became Permanent Secretary to the Ministry of Agriculture, Northern Ireland; but the pull of research and teaching proved too strong, and in 1953 he reverted to Professor and Chief Scientific Officer.

When the directorship of the National Institute for Research in Dairying fell vacant in 1959, Baskett was persuaded to undertake it. Under Professor H. D. Kay the Institute had established a great international reputation which Baskett worthily maintained. He knew his staff well and had a great capacity for unobtrusive encouragement—he was renowned for the slowness of his passage through the Institute's premises because he stopped for a chat with nearly everyone he met. He improved relations between the Institute and the University of Reading, and established better channels of communication with the dairy industry. He succeeded in these, as in other things, because, as he might well have said, "it's astonishing what you can achieve if you don't try to get the credit for it."

Baskett served on many committees—on milk composition, on the veterinary profession, on higher education in the colonies, and others; in retirement he chaired a major inquiry into beef cattle improvement. He was appointed O.B.E. in 1947 and knighted in 1966; of the other honours that came his

way he was especially proud of the honorary D.Sc. from Queen's in 1963—a fitting tribute to an Englishman who really understood (and loved) Northern Ireland.

Baskett married Shirley Firth in 1927 and they had three sons; his family life was a rich and happy one.

December 4, 1972.

H. E. Bates, C.B.E., the short-story writer and novelist, died on January 29, 1974, in hospital at Canterbury. He was 68.

He published his first novel, *The Two Sisters,* at the age of 20. It had been accepted for Jonathan Cape by Edward Garnett, who became his mentor, in much the same way as he had been D. H. Lawrence's more than a decade earlier. Bates repaid the debt in 1950, with an attractive memoir of Garnett, which, from the very nature of the relation between them, was as much a piece of autobiography as of biography. Bates proved a more amenable pupil than Lawrence, perhaps because of the enthusiasms for Chekhov and Maupassant, Turgenev, Flaubert, and Bierce, he shared with Garnett. More than any English writers, these were his masters: Turgenev above all, whose influence, assimilated and made part of the author himself, was evident in his work from the beginning, in short stories and novels alike. During the first half of his career he was thought of primarily as a short-story writer. Later, his novels brought him a much wider readership, but it is on the short stories, and those written while still a young man, stories collected in the volumes *The Woman Who Had Imagination* (1934), *Cut and Come Again* (1935), *Something Short and Sweet* (1937), *The Flying Goat* (1939), and *The Beauty of the Dead* (1940), that his reputation will largely rest. Even when he seemed to be obsessed with the Larkin saga he continued to write short stories which showed glimpses of his old mastery.

Herbert Ernest Bates was born on May 16, 1905, at Rushden, Northamptonshire, of "simple country folk", to use his own phrase. He attended Kettering Grammar School but, as the list of writers who influenced him shows, was essentially self-educated. For a time he worked as a reporter on a country newspaper and then as a clerk in a leather warehouse. After the publication of *The Two Sisters,* apart from a brief interlude as an assistant in the children's department of a famous London bookshop, a job Garnett characteristically found for him, he devoted himself entirely to writing.

His stay in London was relatively short: by 1931 he was settled in Kent, in the village where he lived for the rest of his life except for the war years, during which he served in the R.A.F. there. His duties were in public relations, but public relations most imaginatively conceived, as is shown by the two collections of short stories about fighter pilots and bomber crews at war, *The Greatest People in the World* and *How Sleep the Brave,* written over the pseudonym of "Flying Officer X". Bates rose brilliantly to the occasion and the stories, wry, often poignant, still move the reader today.

Other fruits of his experience of wartime life with the R.A.F. were his novels *Fair Stood the Wind for France* and *The Purple Plain,* which dealt with the retreat from Burma.

Bates was always a countryman, and his best work was inspired by the English countryside. When, as occasionally, he dealt with life in London or in industrial slums, he was never quite convincing; it was as though he was writing out of memories of literature rather than from direct observation. In his stories of the country, however, and of life in small country towns, his observation never failed him, and he rendered English country life without sentimentality and in its most enduring aspects. At his best, scene and character exist in perfect balance, though the impression remains that he was secretly less interested in character than in scene. This is especially true of his later novels. The earlier ones, *The Two Sisters, Catherine Foster, Charlotte's Row, The Fallow Land* and *The Poacher,* had been largely carried by their author's strong lyrical impulse; when this faded, as it tended to do in the later fiction, what remained in the memory was a series of vignettes, of visual impressions, rather than any intense or revealing relationship between human beings.

Bates was a highly professional writer, but not even the careful craftsmanship of his postwar work could hide the fact that, in the novels at least, he relied too much on his strong visual sense, so that his characters were too plainly adjuncts of the scenes described, taking from them what life they had. At the same time, even when the creative pressure seemed low, he wrote with a precise felicity, a sure observation expressed in an unerring sense of words. He was, in no pejorative sense, a prose poet, and his best effects were obtained when his delight in the natural scene, his vivid apprehension of the moods of nature, of the changing seasons and the weather, crystallized into symbols of the states of mind of his characters. When this happened—and it did so time and again during the first 15 years of his career—he was without an equal in England in the kind of story he had made his own, and stood in the direct line of succession of fiction-writers of the English countryside that includes George Eliot, Hardy, and D. H. Lawrence.

His character, Uncle Silas, a shrewd, hard-living, lusty, nonagenarian peasant based on memories of a great-uncle, when projected on television, brought Bates an audience wider by far than his usual circle of readers. Bates developed and enlarged upon this Rabelaisian side of country life in his bucolic comedy of the welfare state, *The Darling Buds of May.* It was fearfully suc-cessful, was filmed and staged, and proved to be the forerunner of other Larkin episodes; to those who had admired the early Bates with his true feeling for the English countryside, life with the Larkins seemed crude stuff.

In his last years he published three admirably evocative volumes of autobiography, *The Vanished World, The Blossoming World* and *The World in Ripeness.* In 1970 he published his novella *The Triple Echo,* which was made into a successful film with Glenda Jackson and Oliver Reed in the leading parts. He reached an even wider audience through the stylishly directed Granada series *Country Matters* in which stories by himself and A. E. Coppard were adapted for the television screen. They proved immensely popular. Bates was created C.B.E. in June 1973.

Bates attempted the drama in *The Days of Glory,* wrote a critical study *The Modern English Short Story,* and was the author of several volumes of essays on country scenes and life.

He married in 1931 Marjorie Helen Cox and had two sons and two daughters.

January 30, 1974.

Fulgencio Batista, the dictator who dominated Cuban politics for 26 years until overthrown by Fidel Castro, died of a heart attack while driving from Madrid to Marbella on August 5, 1973. He was 72.

He was in the mould of the typical Latin American dictator. Ill-educated and pugnacious, he rose through the ranks of the army to become a tough sergeant and, with ambition and cunning, he was able to place himself at the forefront of the 1933 revolution against the Machado dictatorship. As head of the army he controlled or influenced Cuban political life until 1959, whether as President or whether behind the scenes.

Many intellectuals, students and businessmen never forgave him for sweeping aside the processes of democracy in 1952 when he led a bloodless coup. It was during the following years that Cuba became prosperous as the United States invested heavily in the island. He can be credited with building roads, schools and hospitals and passing social security and minimum wage laws. But charges of corruption became commonplace and he never narrowed the gulf between the rich and the poor. Fidel Castro, organizing guerrilla warfare in the Sierra Maestra, soon won support with promises of civil liberties and an end to poverty. Batista took more and more repressive and brutal measures to keep himself in power.

During his period of exile he tried to justify his long rule. He kept in contact with his former Cabinet but saw little of the thousands of Cuban fellow-exiles living in Europe and the United States. Batista wrote a number of books which combined a hatred of Castro and communism with bitter attacks on the United States who, he considered, had betrayed him in his hour of need.

Fulgencio Batista y Zaldivar was born at Banes, Cuba, in January 1901, of mixed blood. It was said that he had been orphaned at the age of 13 and was then taken into a school run by American Quakers. Before he joined the Cuban National Army in 1921 he had, by all accounts, tried a variety of occupations, among them those of agricultural worker, mechanic, carpenter, clerk and railwayman. He served a two-year enlistment in the army but later rejoined after taking a secretarial course, thereby qualifying himself for clerical work at army headquarters where he made the most of his opportunity to gain knowledge of the workings of the military system.

By the early 1930s the dictatorial regime of General Machado was running into serious difficulties; an attempt to stabilize the price of sugar, always the mainstay of Cuba's economy, failed and no great relief came from a programme of public works. As discontent grew widespread Machado took increasingly illiberal measures against it. After a particularly violent outbreak the United States Government offer of mediation was accepted. An amnesty was declared and constitutional and political reforms promised. The equivocations of Machado, who was apparently bent on resignation one minute and then decided to hang on to the reins of power the next, did nothing to allay national discontent and disillusion. A general strike broke out in 1933 and Machado fled the country.

Batista, a man of handsome presence and powerful personality, now came to the fore as a leader of the enlisted men's initiative which restored order. By September he had been appointed a colonel and Chief-of-Staff of the Constitutional Army appointed by the Government of Five. For many years to come he was to be a dominating force in Cuban affairs.

After the fall of President Ramon Grau San Martin, whose attempts at reform were short-lived, a military junta headed by Batista conferred office on Colonel Carlos Mendieta, who was promptly granted recognition by the United States and other governments. The collaboration of Batista and Mendieta proved effective if oppressive, for their measures were dictatorial and elections were postponed.

Between 1935 and 1940 Batista continued to rule Cuba through a succession of presidents but in the latter year stood himself, defeating Grau San Martin. During his full term which lasted until 1944, Cuba entered the Second World War on the side of the Allies and established diplomatic relations with the U.S.S.R. In 1944 Batista's candidate was defeated by Grau San Martin and Batista left the country to live in the United States.

He returned in 1949, was elected a senator, and in 1952 led a coup "to save the republic from chaos". He remained president for the next seven years.

His regime was sustained by an alliance

of the Army and the powerful trade unions, but his third term was anything but peaceful and by 1957 Cuba was in a state of great unrest, with the well-armed force of revolutionaries led by Fidel Castro carrying on widespread guerrilla warfare from the mountain fastness of Oriente province. In January 1959 Batista left Cuba for the Dominican Republic. Later he lived in Europe on the monies, said to be considerable, which he had invested in various European countries.

August 7, 1973.

Dr. Abdul Rahman al Bazzaz, a former Prime Minister of Iraq and one of the leading personalities to emerge in that country after its 1958 revolution, died on June 28, 1973 in Baghdad.

A Sunni Muslim, born in 1913, he graduated in law from Baghdad University and later took a Doctorate of Law at the University of London. In 1955 he became Dean of the Baghdad Law School, but a difference of view with the Royalist regime led to his dismissal the following year.

In 1959, after the *coup d'état* in which this regime was destroyed, the Republican Government which had replaced it appointed him President of the Court of Cassation, but in 1960 he fell out with General Kassim,* the then President, and after a short term of imprisonment was released and retired to Cairo. Early in 1963, after General Kassim's overthrow and murder in another *coup d'état*, he returned to Iraq and was soon appointed Ambassador to Cairo. He took a leading part in the negotiations which, in April 1963, led to an agreement between the Egyptians, Iraqis and Syrians to federate their countries within two years; the agreement, however, proved abortive and later in the same year Bazzaz was appointed Ambassador to the Court of St. James. In 1964 he also became Secretary-General to O.P.E.C. (the Organization of Petroleum-Exporting Countries), in which capacity the astuteness and powers of patient diplomacy for which he had already become known stood him in good stead.

In early September 1965 he became Deputy Prime Minister, Foreign Minister, and acting Minister for Oil in a new Government formed by the Head of the Iraqi Air Force, Brigadier Abdul Razzak. A main issue in Iraq at that time was how close the country's relations should be with Nasser's* Egypt, and Brigadier Abdul Razzak's predecessor had been forced out of office by a mass defection of ministers, who considered his policy to have been too anti-Egyptian. Within a fortnight, however, Abdul Razzak was himself forced into exile by a group of officers for being allegedly too pro-Nasser, and at this juncture the President, Field-Marshal Arif,* called upon Dr. Bazzaz to form a Government, evidently hoping that his experience

and qualities would succeed, where a succession of military officers had failed, in restoring political stability and democratic processes. Bazzaz accepted and formed a Government which, for the first time since the 1958 revolution, contained no serving officers.

With his new team Bazzaz displayed commendable energy in promoting administrative efficiency, which had declined as a result of the political instability of the previous years, and in tackling the numerous problems besetting the country, notably the perpetual friction, often amounting to open revolt, between the Kurdish minority and the central government. His main interest, however, clearly continued to reside in oil matters, in which his knowledge and experience were outstanding: he not only continued his efforts to resolve remaining differences between his Government and the Iraq Petroleum Company, but more than once went to New York on a self-imposed mission when important matters concerning relations between Arab governments and concessionary companies were being discussed in the O.P.E.C.

In the following year he fell victim to political intrigues and was forced out of office. He went to London, where during the next two years he spent an increasing proportion of his time; but in the summer of 1968 he decided, allegedly against the advice of his friends, to return to Baghdad.

He was arrested on arrival and throughout 1969 there were conflicting rumours about him. It was said that he was dead; that he had been sentenced to 15 years' imprisonment; that he had been brutally tortured; and that he would appear in a television "confession." In July of that year the Baathist regime in Iraq announced that it would try him, with 19 others, on charges of conspiring to overthrow the regime. Late in 1970 it was reported that he and certain other political prisoners had been released, and that he was back in his own home. In recent years it was reported that he had been paralyzed.

A man of considerable presence, possessed of a lively intelligence and great energy, Bazzaz represented his country in London with distinction at a time of great difficulty.

July 4, 1973.

Captain Stephen H. Beattie, v.c., who played a major role in the celebrated raid on St. Nazaire in 1942, died on April 24, 1975 at the age of 67.

Stephen Halden Beattie was born in 1908, the son of the Rev. Prebendary E. H. Beattie. Educated at Abberley Hall, and Rugby, he joined the Royal Navy and was Lieutenant-Commander at the time the decision was made to attack St. Nazaire.

The objectives of the Combined Operations force that sailed from England on March 26 were twofold—to ram the giant Forme Ecluse drydock, thus denying it as a

repair facility to the German battleship, Tirpitz, and secondarily, to cause as much damage to the U Boat pens as possible.

Beattie's role was the decisive one, as the commanding officer of the destroyer H.M.S. Campbeltown. Exhibiting the coolest seamanship under heavy fire from ships and shore batteries, he rammed the drydock caisson at high speed.

The subsequent detonation of the five tons of high explosive H.M.S. Campbeltown carried put the dock out of action for the remainder of the war.

Apart from its strategic value the raid was an important symbolic blow struck at the enemy-occupied Continent at a point in the war when the Allies had yet to take any significant initiative in the European theatre.

Beattie, who was captured along with 215 others of the raiding force, was awarded the V.C. for this feat, and spent the remainder of the war as a prisoner.

Beattie was promoted Captain in 1951 and was Senior Officer, Australian Frigate Squadron, from 1952 to 1954. He was Senior Naval Officer, Persian Gulf, from 1956 to 1958 and later commanded the cruiser H.M.S. Birmingham. He retired from the Royal Navy in 1960 but was Naval Adviser to the Ethiopian Government in 1965.

He was also a Chevalier, Legion of Honour and a Croix de Guerre with Palms. He is survived by a wife and four sons.

April 26, 1975.

General André Beaufre, who died suddenly on a visit to Belgrade on February 12, 1975, at the age of 73, was one of the foremost French military thinkers and the originator of a theory of nuclear deterrence which had far-reaching influence. His *Introduction to Strategy*, published in 1963, was described by Sir Basil Liddell Hart* as the most complete, the most carefully formulated treatise on strategy published in the present generation.

André Beaufre was born on January 25, 1902 at Neuilly sur Seine, near Paris. He was attached to Weygand's headquarters in Algeria in 1940, after the collapse of France, and thanks to his perfect knowledge of English took part in the Weygand*-Murphy discussions on the shipping of food supplies to North Africa. He was active in the resistance, and after a spell in prison became head of General Giraud's personal staff.

He fought in Tunisia and Italy, before joining the headquarters of Marshal de Lattre de Tassigny. But he was not merely an armchair soldier. As a colonel he commanded the last French column to cross northern Tonking during the Indo-China war, and his spells of active service alternated with service on the staff.

He helped to prepare the Suez expedition, and under General Sir Charles Keightley commanded the intervention force in

Port Said. He was then appointed Deputy Commander-in-Chief of the French forces in Germany, and Deputy Chief of Staff in charge of logistics at Shape.

In 1960 he was French representative on the Nato Military Standing Group in Washington, and retired the following year at his own request. This was the beginning of a second intensely active career as a military commentator and author of world repute.

He had no excessive sympathy for General de Gaulle's* policy towards Algeria, Nato and the army. His intellectual independence made him rather a lone wolf among military men, but his ideas were widely respected. He was one of the first with General Ailleret,* the former Chief of Staff of the French forces, to recognize the importance of the French nuclear deterrent.

In his *Introduction to Strategy,* he covered all aspects of modern warfare and the possibilities of stabilizing it at the level of conventional armaments without resorting to strategic nuclear weapons. He regarded French tactical nuclear weapons rather as a detonator for the American nuclear deterrent than as a direct deterrent.

He worked out a bipolar organization of the Atlantic Organization, in which Europe would be one of the poles of decision, and the use of nuclear arms would be coordinated, although their control would remain purely national. He was a frequent contributor to *Le Figaro* and other publications on strategic questions.

One of his last contributions was on President Sadat's visit to Paris. He had gone to Belgrade on a lecture tour at the request of the Council for Scientific Activities of the Yugoslav Army when he died of heart failure in his hotel.

February 14, 1975.

Hugh Beaumont, the theatrical manager, of whom it was said by Sir Tyrone Guthrie that more than any other single individual he could make or break the career of almost any worker in the British professional theatre, died on March 22, 1973 at his home in London. He was 64.

Even at the last, when there were those who considered him a spent force, he had in active preparation seven productions of "straight" and musical plays, for which by no means all the contracts had been signed, but the details of which, known in full to no one else, were like pieces of a jig-saw puzzle, waiting to be assembled, as circumstances permitted, in a picture pleasing and, if possible, profitable to himself.

He was born in 1908, by all accounts in South Wales—his real surname is a matter of doubt, his nickname "Binkie" was in general circulation—and it was certainly in Cardiff that he began his career as assistant manager of a theatre controlled by Howard and Wyndham. Some years later, after gaining further business experience at Philip

Ridgeway's Barnes Theatre, he came to know H. M. Tennent, a fellow worker for Howard and Wyndham, and, dissatisfied with the quality of the attractions which they were booking, they decided to go into production-management on their own account. They began operations at the Queen's, in 1936, with a failure. On Tennent's death in 1941, Beaumont became managing director. He continued to hold that position, the organization having proliferated to a point at which it was described in 1960 as by far the biggest and most important production firm in London, until his death.

What chiefly impressed people was, from his earliest days in management, this young man whose training had been on the business side, whose talk about his projects, conducted with the aid of a glib line in fashionable expressions, was amusing, unpretentious and commercial, and yet deadly accurate and shrewd in his assessment of artistic merit. He was, to quote Guthrie again, courteously, gently relentless in keeping his collaborators on their toes. He would compel an author of the eminence of Thornton Wilder to rewrite, and a company including Ruth Gordon and Eileen Herlie and directed by Guthrie himself, to re-rehearse. He believed that he knew what was needed, whether the production in question was a classic, a modern comedy, a musical, or a television play. He had, it may be, no theories, no philosophy, but he had standards. He may have aimed only at success, but what he achieved, more often than not, was excellence.

Among his productions, which require four columns of *Who's Who in the Theatre* for their listing, perhaps he deserves to be remembered above all for those in which he was the backer and counsellor of his friend John Gielgud: the classical seasons at the Phoenix and the Haymarket during the late war and at the Phoenix and the Lyric, Hammersmith, in the early 1950s. In striving to further the theatrical causes he believed in, he was, according to his colleagues, indefatigable: according to his critics, ruthless. When back-payment of entertainment tax, from which his non-profit-making subsidiary companies had hitherto been exempted, was claimed from him, he took the case right up to the House of Lords, and when he lost he devised other means of gaining a hearing, within the commercial, unsubsidized theatre, for the work he wished to promote.

One might call him a back-seat driver, but he issued his directions to the man or woman at the wheel in a manner that not even the most sensitive could consider rude. He did not want publicity for himself. He did not want money for its own sake. He wanted power. He wanted to do things. He wanted to continue playing the theatre-game which was his passion, his amusement and his life.

March 23, 1973.

S. N. Behrman, playwright, journalist and author, died on September 9, 1973 at the age of 80.

Though primarily remembered as a writer of successful plays, Behrman's journalism and general writing were anything but negligible. He was for long a star of the *New Yorker,* and his enjoyable and frequently sardonic portrait of the great art dealer Duveen had its origins in articles published in that magazine.

He had charm, wit and humour and a willingness to listen, and these attributes helped to bring him another success in *Conversations with Max,* which was based on interviews with Sir Max Beerbohm, conducted in Beerbohm's old age. Behrman wrote two admirable books of reminiscence, *The Worcester Account* and *Tribulations and Laughter,* published in Britain in 1972.

For something like 40 years he was a figure to be reckoned with on Broadway. A shrewd observer of manners, particularly of the well-to-do, his comedies with their polished dialogue and sometimes rather insubstantial plots might have been dismissed as drawing-room comedy if it were not noticed that the author, a man of sharp conscience and at bottom a moralist, also offered in them statements of contemporary truth. Behrman was an accomplished craftsman and his craft was never seen to better advantage than in *Jane,* which Behrman wrote from a story by Somerset Maugham* and in which Maugham, himself a master of the theatre, took a close interest. It was staged in London in 1947 with Yvonne Arnaud and Ronald Squire in the main roles and was given over 270 performances.

Berhman was in his early thirties when his play *The Second Man,* a 1927 vehicle for the Lunts, brought him international fame in the Broadway-West End theatre, and from then on he never had difficulty in getting a work on the stage, though not all he wrote achieved equal success.

When *The Second Man* was presented in London in 1928 with Noel Coward, Zena Dare, Raymond Massey and Ursula Jeans in the main parts it was thought by some people to be a Coward work written under another name.

Behrman's best-known plays include *Serena Blandish,* a dramatization of a novel by Enid Bagnold; *Meteor; Brief Moment; Biography; Rain from Heaven,* an early anti-Nazi play; *Amphitryon 38,* an adaption of Jean Giraudoux's work; *Wine of Choice; No Time for Comedy; I Know my Love;* and *But for Whom Charlie.*

No Time for Comedy was first put on in New York in 1939 with Laurence Olivier as the star. It went to London in 1941 and, with Rex Harrison, Lilli Palmer, Diana Wynyard* and Walter Fitzgerald in the leading parts, ran for over 300 performances.

Samuel Nathaniel Behrman was born in Worcester, Massachusetts, on June 9, 1893, the son of Joseph Feingold Behrman. He recalled in *The Worcester Account* that his father, a grocer, was a better student of the Talmud than he was a provider. Nevertheless he knew the value of learning and kept his son "immersed in assorted literature: Horatio Alger and Shakespeare in equal parts." The young Behrman studied at Clark University and Harvard and then tried to get a job.

He was not successful but he was fortunate to have the sympathy of his brothers, who supported him while he took an M.A. at Columbia. After this he worked for a time on *The New York Times Book Review* but was dismissed after it was discovered that while running a queries and answers column he had sent inquisitive letters to himself to relieve his boredom.

For several years thereafter he lived from hand to typewriter in the byways of Times Square reviewing books, writing articles and short stories, and collaborating in two plays which failed. After the success of *The Second Man* there were invitations from Hollywood, where he found lucrative employment on and off for many years. He wrote film scripts for the Greta Garbo films *Queen Christina, Anna Karenina* and *Two-Faced Woman.*

Behrman was a man of many friends.

In 1936 he married Elza Heifetz Stone, sister of the violinist Jascha Heifetz. He is survived by his widow, their son David, a stepson and a stepdaughter.

September 11, 1973

Hana Benesova, widow of Eduard Benes, former President of Czechoslovakia, died in Prague on December 2, 1974 and was cremated there on December 7.

Mrs. Benesova's death was not reported in the Czechoslovakian media, and only a brief announcement of her cremation was published in daily newspapers of December 9. Eye-witnesses said that about 3,000 people attended the cremation. Her husband died in September, 1948. After his death his widow lived in seclusion.

As a child, she lost her mother and her father, a minor railway official, and was brought up by an aunt who watched over her education and allowed her to go to Paris as a University student. In Paris, Hana Vlckova met Eduard Benes, a student about two years her senior, who had transferred from Prague University with the warm approval of his professor, Thomas Masaryk. The period of engagement was brief, and back in Prague the young couple worked as political partners; both longed for the overthrow of the Habsburg system and the full autonomy, if not the independence, of the Czech lands.

Two small events shortly before Sarajevo may have helped to change the course of history. Benes broke his leg while playing football, and the aunt left her niece a modest fortune. The broken leg saved Benes from an immediate call-up in July, 1914; his wife's legacy enabled him to give his own savings of about £300 to Thomas Masaryk, and

with that slender sum the campaign for Czech freedom was launched. A year later Benes had set up his headquarters in a fifth floor room in Paris, and his wife was in a Habsburg prison. They did not meet again until November 1918.

Mrs. Benesova stayed with her husband in Paris throughout the Peace Conference of 1919. She went with him on many visits to Geneva and during his 17 years as Foreign Minister she entertained with simple dignity in the Czernin Palace in Prague. With the aged Masaryk's retirement at the end of 1935, she became the first lady of the land, but she wished her predecessor, Dr. Alice Masaryk, to retain her leadership of the Czechoslovak Red Cross as well as many other duties.

When Munich brought Benes a second exile his wife was at his side in Putney, Chicago, Paris and again in London. He was still her first care, but she understood the frustrations and bewilderment of exile, and she gave strong support to Czech and Slovak women who found their way to London. Though she curtailed social duties in Britain, she always attended the Czechoslovak Independence Day service in St. Paul's.

The return to the Hradcany Castle was beset with difficulties, and in the summer of 1947, anxiety and overwork gave Benes a slight stroke. Mrs. Benesova insisted that he must remain at his country house in Sezimovo Usti. She paid almost her last visit to Prague as the President's wife when she broke to Dr. Alice Masaryk the news that her brother, Jan, had been found dead beneath the window of his flat in the Czernin Palace. Six months later, in September 1948, Benes died and his widow was given a substantial pension. The Gottwald Government took care that she did not leave the country, and a request to go to Switzerland for an eye operation was refused.

December 10 & 13, 1974.

David Ben-Gurion, for nearly 60 years one of the leaders of the Zionist Movement, and the first Prime Minister of Israel, died on December 1, 1973 at the age of 87.

Born at Plonsk in Russian Poland on October 16, 1886, he became an ardent Zionist at an early age, and at 20 settled in Palestine as a Labour pioneer, taking the name of a Hebrew warrior who was a hero in the struggle with Rome. He worked as a farm labourer and early began to organize Jewish Socialist groups. Later he went to Istanbul as a student in the Ottoman School of Political Science. Throughout his life he was devoted to study of the Hebrew bible and philosophy and history, Jewish and general. He taught himself ancient Greek, was master of the literature of half a dozen countries, and had a wide knowledge of Buddhism. He was possessed with a sense of the Messianic destiny of the Jewish people in his generation; and recognized that the

fostering of the Jewish consciousness involved respect for Jewish traditional observance.

After the entry of Turkey into the 1914-18 War on Germany's side, Ben-Gurion, like other subjects of enemy states in Palestine, was called on to accept Ottoman citizenship or leave the Ottoman Dominions. He went to the United States, where he married, and founded a party of Labour Zionists (Poale Zion), and the Pioneer (Hechalutz) movement for training young men and women for settlement in Palestine.

He took a leading part also in recruiting for the Judean battalions of the Royal Fusiliers, enlisted himself, and returned to Palestine in 1918 as a soldier of the British Forces. Thereafter he remained in Palestine, except for frequent missions abroad. He was the leader of Labour politics, and for long chairman of the Palestine branch of the Executive of the Jewish Agency, which was in effect the Zionist Organization. He had a big part in the formation in 1919 of the Histadruth, the General Federation of Jewish Workers. This was the only Jewish trade union organization of real consequence and the nucleus of the Socialist State in Mandatory Palestine. Three out of every four Jewish workers belonged to it. He formed within the Federation the Central Labour Party (M.A.P.A.I., meaning the Workers of Israel), and was its leader till his resignation in 1964.

Ben-Gurion was a political Zionist, whose life purpose was the creation of a state in which the Jews should have sovereignty.

In face of chronic Arab unrest and frequent Arab attacks on Jewish settlements, he organized Jewish Self-Defence (Haganah), which was an underground movement until the establishment of the state, and transformed it to an effective army. When the Royal Commission recommended in 1937 the partition of Palestine into Jewish and Arab states he was prepared to accept it; but in 1942 his influence led to the adoption by the Zionists in America of the programme of establishing Palestine as a Jewish state. His activist views brought him into conflict with Weizmann, who was then the President of the Zionist Organization.

Ben-Gurion was given his chance when the United Nations approved a plan for the partition of Mandated Palestine into two states. He accepted the plan, secured the support of a majority in the Jewish community, and on May 14, 1948 proclaimed the independent State of Israel in Tel Aviv. It secured quick recognition in the outside world; the first major powers to recognize it were the United States and the Soviet Union.

As the first Prime Minister of Israel he formed a Government on the basis of a broad coalition, with the object of uniting the country to face the immediate invasion of the Arab armies. He was Minister of Defence as well as Prime Minister, and master of the strategy of the campaign. During the struggle for independence he held a position comparable with that of Sir

Winston Churchill* during the Second World War. After the first election in January 1949 for a Constituent Assembly, there were rifts in the broad coalition; but he held together the Socialist Party and the religious groups then, and again after the second election in 1951. And he carried through fearlessly a policy of ingathering the dispersed tribes. In the autumn of 1953, being "spiritually weary", he retired to a collective settlement in the Negev, Sde Boker, and was out of office, but not out of politics, for 14 months. His retirement was part of an active campaign to inspire the young Israelis to pioneer in the Negev and on the frontiers.

In February 1955 he was called back as Minister of Defence, and in the summer of that year, after the third general election, became again Prime Minister, and formed a Coalition of four Left-Wing Parties, dropping the bourgeois General Zionists whom he had previously included. The security of the State against the mounting threats from Egypt was his principal concern. These took the form of persistent and bloody raids into Israel of terrorists armed by Egypt and based on Gaza and other places in Egyptian hands.

Having dropped the Foreign Secretary, Moshe Sharett*, who was against activism, he mobilized Israel's forces and launched the invasion of the Sinai Peninsula, acting in concert with the British and French Governments, who were anxious to bring down Abdel Nasser*. On November 7, after a lightning campaign of five days in which Israel forces occupied most of the peninsula, he declared that Israel would hold on to her conquest until Egypt made a settlement. Later, having received representations from President Eisenhower and warnings from the Soviet Union, he stated that the forces would withdraw when arrangement was made with the United Nations for posting an international emergency force on the Egyptian frontier. The assurance of free navigation in the Gulf of Aqaba, and the presence of a United Nations Force on the Sinai and Gaza frontier, gave Israel a sense of security, and strengthened the hold of Ben-Gurion on the nation. His party in the fourth general election gained a greater number of seats than ever before; and Ben-Gurion, when called on again to form a coalition Government, was in a stronger position with the other Labour parties to whom he turned.

He was apt to antagonize his colleagues by impetuous action or speech, as when in 1959 he approved the sale of munitions made in Israel to the German Federal Republic, and in 1960 made remarks at an archaeological meeting about the biblical story of the Exodus from Egypt, which angered respectively the left and the religious parties. In 1961 internal difficulties in the Coalition and his own party led him to demand a general election; and this time Mapai lost five seats. The vote reflected reduced confidence in him. Some of his actions had provoked a protest of the intellectuals against what seemed a dicta-

torial outlook.

He came out at this stage for electoral reform. Ben-Gurion believed that the existing system of strict proportional representation, which treated the whole country as one constituency and allocated seats to names on party lists, was impersonal and out of keeping with Jewish individualism. He wanted constituency elections, by direct vote, on the British model.

But no other party would support the change. He became involved also in a bitter and protracted dispute over Pinhas Lavon, who was Minister of Defence while Ben-Gurion was in retirement, and who was compelled to resign because of a deplorable security mishap. A Ministerial Committee cleared Lavon, but Ben-Gurion refused to accept its report and demanded a judicial reconsideration. Mapai was split on the issue, and in June 1963 he retired again in order to devote himself to writing the history of his times. He chose as successor Levi Eshkol,* then Minister of Finance, but soon quarrelled with him and Mapai over the "Lavon Affair" and electoral reform. By mid-1965 he was actively opposing the Mapai-led Government, had left Mapai and had formed a "progressive" Socialist party, Rafi, in which his chief supporter was General Moshe Dayan. That autumn Rafi contested the General Election but won only 10 out of 120 seats in the Knesset. His challenge to the Socialist "Establishment" had failed, although Rafi did not formally dissolve itself until December 1968, returning then to the Mapai fold. In the 1969 elections Ben-Gurion campaigned as virtually a one-man party and was returned to the Knesset.

His active political career was over and he retired to his "Kibbutz" or collective settlement of Sde Boker in the Southern desert of the Negev. There he devoted his time to the writing of books and newspaper articles, and to the creation of a "College of the Negev" in which intellectual achievement should be married with pioneering zeal. He never ceased to urge the quicker colonization of the southern desert.

To close the cultural and educational gap between the immigrants from Europe and those from oriental countries was another of his causes; and he insisted that every Jew describing himself as Zionist should live in Israel, or prepare his children to live there.

In international relations he held a unique position as a dynamic and realistic elder statesman with the heads of the big Western Powers and with the new states of eastern Asia and Africa.

He made Churchillian declarations on the need for understanding with the Soviet Union and Arab neighbours. There was no response, partly because he remained in the political wilderness and did not rejoin the reunified and expanded Socialist party. Ben-Gurion will be remembered for his fifteen years' leadership of the State of Israel, for his brilliant grasp of political realities when that state was in process of being created, and for his earlier, thirty years of patient work in welding a self-aware and deter-

mined Jewish community in Palestine. For most of his active political life he was both prophet and statesman, the leader and father of his people.

December 3, 1973.

Jack Benny, who died at his home in California on December 26, 1974 at the age of 80, was the leader of a generation of American comedians who grew to fame with the spread of radio in the early 1930s.

Born Benjamin Kubelsky in 1894, in Waukegan, Illinois, where his father ran a saloon, he went into vaudeville at the age of 15, but not on the stage. Instead, he was in the orchestra pit, already playing the violin that was, with his reputed frugality, to become a trademark of a lifetime in entertainment.

Returning to vaudeville after the 1914-18 War, in which he served in the United States Navy, Benny progressed from the pit to the stage, where he found work first as a stand-up comic, then as a dancer and eventually as a small-part actor in Broadway musicals.

In 1926 he went to Los Angeles, where he met and married Mary Livingstone who was to stay with him on stage and off throughout his long life. Billed by now as Benny K. Benny, he continued to work in musicals and occasionally as part of a piano and violin double act.

His real break did not come until 1932, in which year he went on radio for the first time as a guest of Ed Sullivan. "Hello folks," were his first broadcast words. "My name is Jack Benny. There will now be a short pause for everyone to say, 'Who cares?'"

Radio audiences did, however, care about him, to such an extent that he bought himself out of an already scheduled stage musical and started to work instead with the gravel-voiced Negro, Rochester, on the shows that were to make both his name and his fortune.

In spite of his repeated assurances to the contrary, Jack Benny was neither a mean man nor a mean violinist, although when he played his first serious concert one critic did note that the New York Philharmonic seemed to be out of tune with him. Another added simply: "Last night Jack Benny played Mendelssohn, and Mendelssohn lost". Yet beneath the wisecracks Jack Benny was serious enough about the violin to invest in a Stradivarius, and his work for innumerable charities was every bit as painstaking and as frequent as the jokes about his meanness. He once set up a trust fund to give every child in Waukegan 39 dollars, with the proviso that they could not cash the money until their thirty-ninth birthdays, by which time the value had multiplied many times over.

After the Second World War Benny moved his show, complete with Rochester, to television and carried it on there until changing public taste made it impossible to continue with the "Uncle Tom" character of Rochester. Alone, Benny continued to do television specials and concert and cabaret appearances until the very last months of his life.

His jokes remained, like the man himself, as polished, as urbane and often as acid as a page of the *New Yorker*. He leaves a widow and their adopted daughter.

December 28, 1974.

Nadia Benois, the author and painter (widow of Jona Ustinov and mother of Peter Ustinov, the actor and dramatist) died, aged 79, on February 8, 1975.

In artistic circles in London Nadia Benois was greatly loved as a woman, as she was admired as an artist. She was an irresistibly attractive personality; handsome, impulsive, generous, witty and gay, with a deep voice and a great laugh that warmed the heart.

In her youth—she was in her early twenties when first in London—she was startlingly beautiful. Few artists can have had a more fortunate ancestry. Born near St. Petersburg, she was the daughter of Louis Benois, architect to the Tsar and designer of the now demolished cathedral at Warsaw.

Her grandfather and great-grandfather were architects; and Alexandre Benois, the first painter to collaborate with Diaghilev in the Russian Ballet, and Albert Benois, a leading Russian water colourist, were her uncles.

The Benois family was originally French. On her mother's side Nadia Benois was descended from the Venetian Cavos family, who first introduced opera into Russia, founded the Russian National School of Music, and built opera houses in St. Petersburg and Moscow.

Nadia Benois studied painting under her uncle Alexandre and at the St. Petersburg Academy. In 1920 she married Jona Ustinov, an international journalist of Russian descent whose grandfather had migrated to Germany, and went to London, where Ustinov was then London correspondent of the Wolff Bureau, the German equivalent of Reuter's. When, inevitably, Ustinov came into conflict with the Nazis, he severed his connexion with the Wolff Bureau, and he and his wife and son became British subjects.

The first one-man show of works by Nadia Benois was held at Tooth's Galleries in 1929, and it delighted everybody by its general effect of happiness.

After executing small commissions for the theatre, Nadia Benois had her great opportunity in 1939, with designs for the costumes and setting of the ballet *The Sleeping Princess*, as produced at Sadler's Wells and in a gala performance at Covent Garden in aid of the Housing Centre.

Basing her treatment on reminiscences of the original production in 1890, Miss Benois avoided the exotic atmosphere of Bakst in favour of the cool and mannered elegance of illustrations to the original fairy tale. The passage of time during the "sleep" was indicated by a transition in the costumes from the sixteenth to the seventeenth century. Her brilliant success was not unworthy of her famous uncle.

February 10, 1975.

Michael Benthall, C.B.E., the theatrical director, died on September 6, 1974 at the age of 55. He succeeded Sir Tyrone Guthrie as Director of the Old Vic in 1953, a position he held until 1961. More recently he worked chiefly in the United States, where he directed the musical *Coco* in 1969.

The son of Sir Edward Charles Benthall, he was educated at Eton and Christ Church, Oxford, where he played Claudio in the O.U.D.S. production of *Much Ado About Nothing* in 1938, making his professional debut the same year in *Traitor's Gate* first in Newcastle and later in the West End. After playing small parts at the Old Vic and the Open Air Theatre, Regent's Park, he joined the Royal Artillery in 1939 and when he was demobilized in 1946 it was with the rank of major.

His career as a director had already been launched in 1944, when he co-directed *Hamlet* with Tyrone Guthrie at the Old Vic, and *Don Pasquale* at the Cambridge Theatre was the first of several opera productions, which included the 1947 *Turandot* at Covent Garden and the 1948 production of *Aida*.

After a production of *The White Devil* at the Duchess with Margaret Rawlings and Robert Helpmann, his first production at Stratford-on-Avon was *The Merchant of Venice* in 1947. This was revived in 1948, together with three new productions of his *Hamlet*, with Paul Scofield alternating the part with Helpmann, *King John* and *The Taming of the Shrew*. The productions were attacked for making picture and movement predominate over the text and the acting, but there were great advantages in the choice of the Victorian Gothic settings (designed by James Bailey) for *Hamlet* and the young Kenneth Tynan called Scofield's performance in the part the best he had seen.

Benthall's other major productions in 1948 were a very successful *Wild Duck* at St. Martin's with Anton Walbrook* as a comic Hjalmar, Mai Zetterling as a pathetic Hedvic, and Fay Compton as a cockney Gina. In 1949 he set his Old Vic production of *She Stoops to Conquer* in Rowlandson's cartoons, opening each scene with a tableau. Moving back into the nineteenth century, he set his Stratford *A Midsummer Night's Dream* in Victorian decor, again designed by James Bailey. His other Stratford production, *Cymbeline*, was less successful.

In 1950 he directed *As You Like It* in New York, and in 1951 he was the man Laurence Olivier chose to direct him and Vivien Leigh* in *Antony and Cleopatra* and *Caesar and Cleopatra* at the St. James's Theatre. It was inevitable that the Shaw play should come badly out of the comparison, and Benthall tried misguidedly to compensate by trying to disguise the difference of level between the two scripts. His Stratford production of that year was *The Tempest* with Michael Redgrave as Prospero, and was designed by Loudon Sainthill.*

When he took up his position at the Old Vic he launched into an ambitious five-year plan to stage all 36 plays in the Shakespeare First Folio. His 1956 *Othello* alternated Richard Burton and John Neville as Othello and Iago; and the final play, *Henry VIII* (1958), had John Gielgud and Edith Evans in it. His subsequent productions at the Old Vic included *The Cenci* and *Dr. Faustus*. He directed Terence Rattigan's *Man and Boy* in London and New York, and the 1966 *Macbeth* at Chichester with John Clements. He will also be remembered for two scenarios he wrote for the Sadler's Wells ballet, *Miracle in the Gorbals* and *Adam Zero*.

September 9, 1974.

W. O. Bentley, M.B.E., the inspiration behind the Bentley car and the man responsible for its design and racing triumphs, died in a nursing home at Woking, Surrey, on August 13, 1971.

Few marques of motor car could equal the Bentley for the "mystique" associated with its name and the numerous legends which grew from its racing record and the "Bentley Boys" who drove the big green cars to victory.

It is 40 years since the last of those meticulously-prepared machines received its finishing touches from the dedicated hands of the craftsmen at Cricklewood and went off on its extended road test. It is a lasting tribute to "W.O.," the quiet and precise engineer, that they are more highly esteemed than ever as the most sought-after of all the vintage motor cars.

Bentley's cars were skilfully designed and massively constructed, handsome to look at and exciting to hear. "W.O." disliked noisy engines and the "boom" or "burble" of the Bentley exhaust, suggesting controlled potency, was as much a trademark as the letter "B" on the radiator. Not for nothing had "W.O." been trained at the Doncaster locomotive works where there was a strong tradition of high engineering skill and majestic good looks.

Walter Owen Bentley was born in London on September 16, 1888, of Yorkshire background, the youngest of a family of nine children. From an early age he was fascinated by mechanical things and after leaving Clifton College he became an apprentice with the Great Northern Railway Loco Works at Doncaster. In 1909 he achieved his childhood ambition when he was made a second fireman, originally on local goods and passenger trains and finally on main-line expresses. At the end of his apprenticeship, however, he decided that the railways offered little scope as a career and turned to the internal combustion engine, mainly because of his interest in motor cycles, which had already won him a gold medal in the Welsh six-day trial.

The transition from two-wheels to four-wheels was the next stage in Bentley's competition career and, after driving a Quadrant in a number of trials, he bought a faster Rex. With this car he crashed without injury on the first lap of the 1909 Tourist Trophy and went off the road again the following year with a burst tyre. That year he joined the National Motor Cab Company, London, helping to run and maintain several hundred Unic taxis and waging unceasing war on any driver who attempted to tamper with the meters.

In 1912 Bentley, or "The Bun," as he was called by his family, joined forces with his brother H. M. Bentley and took over the London agency of three French cars: Buchet, La Licorne, and Doriot, Flandrin et Parant (the D.F.P.). It was at these premises in New Street Mews off Upper Baker Street that the first Bentley 3-litre Engine Ex-1 roared into life seven years later.

It was at this time that W.O. formed the philosophy which was to guide his future. His favourite of the three marques he was selling was the D.F.P., and with capital being limited he decided that the quickest and most effective publicity would come through racing. After winning the Aston hill climb in its first major outing, he went on to score a respectable number of successes at Brooklands and other speed venues, finishing well up in the two-day 1914 Tourist Trophy. But just as the firm was benefiting from his successes, war was declared and Bentley joined the Royal Naval Volunteer Reserve.

At first he worked on Clerget rotary engines at Chiswick and was then sent to Humbers' at Coventry, where he designed his own Bentley Rotary BR1 aero-engine. This was a great success and the BR2 engine was accepted for group manufacture at the Daimler headquarters.

In January 1919 the first car to carry his name was conceived in a top floor building in Mayfair and nine months later the first 3-litre engine burst into raucous song in New Street Mews. The first model, quite a lot of which was mocked up, appeared at the Motor Show at Olympia in November and the first complete car Ex-1 was road tested in January 1920.

With little financial backing, Bentley Motors struggled to get into production in small premises at Cricklewood and in September 1821 the first car was delivered.

Bentley fully realized the value of racing to attract sales and Bentley cars appeared at Brooklands, in several hill climbs and a single-car entry in the 1922 Indianapolis 500-mile race, where W. D. Hawkes and his riding mechanic, Browning, finished at an average of over 80 m.p.h.

In 1923 a rather sceptical Bentley was persuaded to attend the first Le Mans 24-hour race, where to his delight the privately-entered Bentley of Duff/Clement took fourth place. The following year, this talented pair put the Bentley marque truly on the map by winning the race and giving the small concern a new spirit of self-confidence. But as the result of a complete failure in the 1925 Le Mans race Bentley was severely criticized by his board and the company got into deep financial trouble. This was partially solved by the arrival of the late Captain Woolf "Babe" Barnato, son of the diamond king Barney Barnato, who bought the entire assets and became chairman of the company. Barnato competed with distinction at the wheel of Bentley cars in many races and helped guide the firm to its finest hour, but the writing was already on the wall.

The 1920s were the era of the "Bentley Boys"—the rip-roaring, scarf-flying men who drove his cars, such as Dr. "Benjy" Benjafield, Sir Henry Birkin, Glen Kidston, Jack and Clive Dunfee, S. C. H. "Sammy" Davis, George Duller, J. F. Duff, Woolf Barnato, Dick Watney, Frank Clement, Baron d'Erlanger, Jean Chassange, L. G. Callingham and R. C. Gallop. From 1927 onwards, fortune favoured the team and with the 3-litre, the 4½-litre and the 6½-litre models Bentley cars swept to victory at Le Mans for four years in succession, with Barnato sharing the winning car in 1928, 1929 and 1930. But in spite of these triumphs on the race-tracks, it was not enough to save the tottering firm. When the Wall Street crash came in 1929, followed by the slump in Britain, it went into a decline from which it could not recover.

In 1931 the company was acquired by Rolls-Royce, who out-bid Napiers, and W. O. Bentley went with it, helping develop the 3½-litre Rolls-Bentley at Derby. In 1935, when his contract was due to be renewed, he joined the Lagonda company and designed their big V12-engined car, one of which was third in the 1939 Le Mans race. During the 1940s war he worked on armaments at Lagonda and immediately after started to design a 2½-litre six-cylinder car to be sold as the Lagonda-Bentley. But Rolls-Royce intervened, claiming his name as a trade mark, and after long litigation Bentley retired from the automobile scene as a disappointed man.

Bentley was married three times. His first wife died after the 1914-18 War, and the second marriage was dissolved. In 1934 he married Margaret Roberts Hutton.

August 16, 1971.

Dr. Norman Bentwich, O.B.E., M.C., who died on April 8, 1971 at the age of 88, had been Attorney General, Government of Palestine, and for nearly 20 years was Professor of International Relations in the Hebrew University of Jerusalem. He was an exponent of Zionism in a moderate and scholarly form and a keen supporter of humanitarian causes.

Norman de Mattos Bentwich was born in London on February 28, 1883. His father, Herbert Bentwich (of the Inner Temple) was proprietor and editor of *The Law Journal* for many years; his mother was a sister of Solomon J. Solomon, R.A., the well-known portrait painter, and herself a woman of considerable artistic sensibility. From St. Paul's he went to Trinity College, Cambridge, as major scholar. He won the Yorke Essay Prize on two occasions and the Whewell Scholarship in International Law. He was called to the Bar by Lincoln's Inn in 1908. In 1912 he became Inspector of Courts under the Egyptian Ministry of Justice.

There he remained until the winter of 1915 when, on the entry of Turkey into the war, he joined the Camel Transport Corps. Operations on the Suez Canal and in Palestine revealed in him an unsuspected capacity for dealing with camels and other unfamiliar military things, and this bespectacled and scholarly lawyer won the M.C., and emerged from the war with the rank of lieutenant-colonel. He was appointed O.B.E. in 1918. During the Second World War he served for some time in the Ministry of Information and later in the Air Ministry.

His father was an early adherent of the Zionist movement and he himself was a convinced and active Zionist from his university days onwards. Never a leading figure in the Zionist Organization itself, with which indeed he was sometimes at loggerheads on questions of policy, he made his contribution to the Jewish national revival as an exponent in writing and speech of Zionist and Jewish ideals, and by personal participation in the Jewish life in Palestine and later of Israel.

In 1910 he helped to found and edit the *Jewish Review* (which appeared until 1914); his book *Philo Judaeus* appeared in 1910 and was followed by *Josephus* four years later and by *Hellenism* in 1919, the combination of a Hebraic and a classical education bearing good fruit.

In 1918 he became legal secretary to the British Military Administration in Palestine, and in 1921 the title of the office was changed to that of Attorney General. In that capacity he played a notable part in reshaping the legal system of the country, drafting laws for a developing society which have since been taken over by the State of Israel. He remained in office until 1931, refusing several offers of promotion outside his beloved Palestine. The Arabs were suspicious of a Jew holding such a key position, and there was an Arab attempt on his life after the disturbances of 1929. Characteristically, he pleaded that his assailants should go unpunished.

While he was convalescent in the South of France the Colonial Office decided that he should not return to Palestine, and, refusing positions elsewhere, he resigned from the service. The irony of the situation lay in the fact that his impartiality and moderation made him as suspect to the Jews as to the

Arabs. He shared the viewpoint of a small group of liberally minded idealists, headed by Dr. Magnes, president of the Hebrew University of Jerusalem, who strove for a bi-national state; and when in 1932 he delivered his inaugural lecture as Professor of International Relations at the Hebrew University (it was entitled "Jerusalem— City of Peace") the police had to be called to quell a riot started by the extreme Zionist element among the students. This first course of lectures was later published in English (*The Religious Foundations of Internationalism*, 1933) as well as in the Hebrew in which it had been delivered.

Though, except for part of the 1939-45 period, Bentwich visited Palestine every year, his Chair, which he retained until 1951, absorbed only a small portion of his energies. Together with Harry Sacher he re-established the *Jewish Review* in 1932; he became active in many organizations, some Jewish and some non-denominational, for the succour of refugees from Germany, serving as Director of the League of Nations High Commission for Refugees from 1933 to 1936; he became an adviser to the Emperor Haile Selassie when he was exiled from Abyssinia, and followed the Emperor to Addis Ababa shortly after British forces wrested his country from the Italians; after the war he was prominent in discussions concerning reparations and restitution to victims of the Nazis, working with the Anglo-Jewish Association and the Consultative Council of Jewish Organizations, for which he acted as representative at the United Nations. His energy was inexhaustible, and was shown particularly in the arduous journeys that he was making frequently to all parts of the world.

Among all the many causes which he served during his long career of public work, none was the object of such sustained devotion as the Hebrew University of Jerusalem, on whose behalf he laboured unremittingly both as chairman of the Friends of the Hebrew University in Great Britain, and, from 1951, as a vice-chairman of its international board of governors. The university made him an honorary Ph.D. in 1956. He had become an honorary LL.D. of Melbourne in 1938 and of Aberdeen in 1942.

He was a prolific writer. Besides the books already named there may be noted *Palestine of the Jews* (1919), *England in Palestine* (1932), *The Jews* (1934), *The Jews in Our Time* (1960), *Solomon Schechter* (1938), *Judah L. Magnes* (1955), *Judea Lives Again* (1944), *Israel* (1952). In the legal field may be mentioned the seventh edition of Westlake's *Private International Law* (1925), *The Declaration of London* (1911), the third edition of his father's *Privy Council Practice* (1937), and *The Mandates System* (1930). He published an autobiography, entitled *A Wanderer Between Two Worlds* in 1941 and carried on the story of his life to 1958 in *My Seventy-Seven Years*, printed in 1961. The foregoing does not complete the list of his books, and besides there were innumerable articles in both learned and popular periodicals on a wide variety of subjects.

He married in 1915 Helen Franklin, a niece of Viscountess Samuel. Mrs. Bentwich is a former chairman of the L.C.C.

April 10, 1971.

Professor J. D. Bernal, F.R.S., the distinguished physicist, died in London at the age of 70 on September 15, 1971. He was Professor of Physics at Birkbeck College, London, from 1937 and its first Professor of Crystallography from 1963 to 1968.

He occupied a remarkable position in our time, a symbol of underlying unities between diverse and at times almost irreconcilable seeming opposites; by profession a physicist, whose discoveries were of most importance in chemistry and biology; an exponent of peaceful cooperation who made outstanding contributions to the successful prosecution of the war; a link through many vicissitudes between east and west.

John Desmond Bernal was born in Ireland at Nenagh, co. Tipperary, on May 10, 1901, the son of Samuel George Bernal and Elizabeth Miller Bernal. His father's family had been settled in Ireland as small farmers for some generations, having come originally from Spain in 1644—one ancestor was ship's doctor to Columbus on his voyage across the Atlantic. His mother was an American journalist, a graduate of Stanford University. From the age of 14 he was educated in England at Stonyhurst College and Bedford School, and then at Emmanuel College, Cambridge, where he took Part I of the Tripos in Mathematics and in Chemistry, Geology, and Mineralogy; and Part II in Physics.

In this period he wrote his first serious scientific paper, a derivation of the 230 space groups using Hamiltonian quaternions (a very considerable achievement for an undergraduate) for which he was awarded a college prize. This paper was never published, on account of the expense involved, though accepted by the Cambridge Philosophical Society. But it was seen by Sir William Bragg, who offered Bernal his first research post at the Royal Institution on the strength of it. And very much later, in all of one night, it was read by Carl Herman at Stuttgart, and played some part in the developments which led to the construction of the International Tables for Crystallography.

At the Royal Institution, to which he went in 1922, Bernal was allotted space to construct his own X-ray tube and other apparatus. He set out to apply space group theory rigidly to the deduction of the crystal structure of graphite, and in the process developed the method of interpreting rotation photographs by the use of the reciprocal lattice charts which bear his name. (There is a crystallographic tradition that the first charts were drawn with the help of bootlaces in an inn on holiday in Wales). From graphite he became deeply interested in the problem of the metallic state, and then in the wider subject of crystal chemistry under the influence of V. M. Goldschmidt. With his appointment as lecturer in structural crystallography at Cambridge in 1927 (later, 1935, as Assistant Director of Research) he began a variety of new, highly important, researches. First among these were his measurements on Vitamin D, and a group of related sterols, which led to his realization that the then accepted Windaus-Wieland formula for the sterols could not possibly be correct and so to the adoption of the now accepted sterol skeleton. Other subjects he explored included Vitamin B1, the sex hormones, liquid crystals, Rochelle salt and various problems of coordination chemistry, the theory of muscular contraction, and the distribution of minerals in the earth's crust in relation to earthquake shocks.

In 1933 he took the first X-ray photographs of single crystals of a protein, pepsin, and followed this a year or two later, in collaboration with I. Fankuchen, with a remarkable series of experiments on tobacco mosaic virus. These defined both the size and the shape of the virus particle, and showed it to have a regular internal structure explored much later in his laboratory by R. Franklin and A. Klug. Also in 1933 he published with R. H. Fowler a paper on the structure and properties of water—which grew out of a conversation when fogbound at Moscow airport at 4 o'clock in the morning. This paper is a mine of ideas on the hydrogen bond and the liquid state, many of which he developed further in later papers, and particularly, the detailed geometrical theory of close packed liquids which he published in 1958-59. These different researches together led him to consider the conditions under which life could develop, some of which he discussed in his Guthrie lecture published with the title *The Physical Basis of Life* (1951).

In 1937 Bernal was appointed Professor of Physics of Birkbeck College, London. Organization of research there was interrupted almost immediately by the outbreak of war, when Bernal became scientific adviser to the Research and Experimental Department of the Ministry of Home Security. The story of his appointment is typical of the contradictions involved in his history. In 1935 a group of scientists in Cambridge, including Bernal, formed an anti-war group, which was gradually led to carry out a number of critical experiments on protection against air raids. Bernal discussed some of these at a luncheon party in Oxford, at All Souls, given by Sir Arthur Salter, at which Sir John Anderson was also present; after which Anderson is reported to have said that he would have Bernal as adviser "even if he were red as the flames in hell". At first, during the war, Bernal was primarily concerned with the physics of explosions and the consequent action necessary in air-raid precautions. As the blitz developed he himself helped to operate the method of bomb disposal he had advocated—the rapid removal of the contents of the bomb like blowing an egg. He examined in detail the statistics of bomb damage; at one point he calculated the probable effects of a raid of 500 bombers on Coventry, and saw his predictions altogether too accurately verified in the actual raid of 450 German bombers which took place a few weeks later.

After the last major blitz on London in 1941 he was transferred first to Bomber Command, and then to Combined Operations under Lord Mountbatten. Then began a series of journeys which took him all over the world, and more deeply still into the organization of the war—to Tripoli with Zuckerman, to study the effects of enemy and allied bombing, to Accra, to Brazil, to Quebec with Churchill* in 1943, to advise on artificial harbours, and then to Washington, and to Ottawa, where he was concerned with the construction of the fantastic ice ship, Habbakuk, conceived by Geoffrey Pike.

He returned before D-day to explore the landing beaches in Normandy—first in theory, and then in practice. Theory included geological texts, talks with Professor Goldschmidt, the study of early manuscripts, the *Roman de rue*, which described William the Conqueror's route along the coast, and archaeological discoveries of the Abbé de Huc. Practice involved a secret expedition to the Norman coast before D-day, and final verification on D-day plus two. After D-day came further journeys with Mountbatten to the Far East, Ceylon and Burma.

After the war, for a short time it seemed that Bernal would play as prominent a part in national reconstruction as in the war effort (he once said it was for him a period of intense respectability). At home he was appointed chairman of the Scientific Advisory Committee of the Ministry of Works; abroad he was concerned with the organization of Unesco, and of the European Economics Advisory Council, and paid visits to the United States, Sweden, Denmark, and India, to give advice on reconstruction. Research began again at Birkbeck College under his direction, not only in the fields of his early interest—proteins and viruses—but also on new topics—cements and building materials, semi-conductors, micro-focus X-ray tubes, and electronic computers. Gradually, however, as the cold war developed, Bernal found himself less and less in sympathy with government organization and intellectually isolated from many who had been his close friends during the war.

His interest in politics had begun early and violently during the Easter rebellion in Ireland in 1916, when he saw the burning of a big country house near his home and the finest streets of Dublin in smoking ashes. At Cambridge he abandoned the religion of his childhood—he had been brought up a Catholic—and moved towards Communism. From that time and throughout his life he belonged to a number of political organizations of varying degrees of left wing affiliation—just before the outbreak of the war he estimated he was a member of 60 different

committees (not quite all political) from which he resigned to take part in war research. Among the organizations which he helped to initiate or develop, were For Intellectual Liberty (1936), the Association of Scientific Workers (of which he was president 1947-49), the World Federation of Scientific Workers (vice-president 1946 to date), the Rassemblement Universelle pour la Paix in Brussels (1936), and the World Peace Council, founded in Wroclaw (1948), of which he was chairman (1959-60). Probably the most important aspect of this side of his life were the intimate friendships he formed, first with Langevin and Curie-Joliot in France; then, after the war, with Ilya Ehrenburg* in Moscow, and Kuomeijo in Peking. These, and other close friendships, grown during many visits in Eastern Europe and China, and the long conversations he had with Khrushchev and Mao Tse-tung, played a part in the steps by which scientific contacts between east and west were slowly re-established in the early 1950s. From 1958 to 1965 he was chairman of the World Council of Peace.

At the same time Bernal was a *philosophe* in the eighteenth-century sense of the term, one who reflected on society in order to promote its improvement. Indeed, it was an essential part of Bernal's creed that scientists should also be philosophers, in this sense. Here his natural bent for systematizing was reinforced by a Marxist view— he had no inhibitions about the label—of man's relations with nature and society. But the intellectual tradition to which Bernal belonged, while it certainly included Marx, was above all the tradition of Renaissance Rationalism and Humanism stemming from Leonardo da Vinci, Bacon and Comenius. The dominant idea running through all his writings was the belief in the possibility of human perfection through the use of human reason. His first book, *The World, the Flesh, and the Devil* (the three enemies of man's rational soul), published in 1932, a somewhat fantastic forecast of the future, contained the germ of much of his later, more serious thought. In *The Social Function of Science* (1939) he explored the possibility of the rational organization of scientific knowledge and techniques. *The Freedom of Necessity* (1949) is a collection of essays and lectures, linked together by the Spinozist theme—that man's freedom consists in understanding, and controlling, the human environment. In *Science in History* (1954) he sketched on a vast canvas the interrelations between science and society, from the earliest times until the predictable future, a subject which he had dealt with in more detail for one period and country in *Science and Industry in the Nineteenth Century*. *World Without War* (1958), was concerned with the problem of the rational organization of the world's resources—developing, in a systematic and quantitative form, his original thesis, that "permanent prosperity, no longer a Utopian dream, awaits the arrival of permanent peace". In 1967 he published *The Origin of Life*.

It is difficult to evaluate accurately his very varied contribution in so many different fields. He has solid achievements to his credit. But those who knew him will remember best, first his great learning, through which he carried the nickname, Sage, at Cambridge—and, secondly, his power of rapid synthesis. He would take hold of any new field of knowledge presented to him, and produce some fresh and illuminating thought, by so doing perhaps starting a whole new train of scientific research. As Sir Lawrence Bragg wrote of his contribution to crystallography in 1948: "No one has done more than he has as an explorer and pioneer. Time and again, when reviewing some branch of X-ray analysis which is now very active, we have to acknowledge that the first critical experiment was due to his inspiration."

Bernal received many and varied honours. He was elected a Fellow of the Royal Society in 1937, and received a Royal Medal in 1940. In 1945 he was awarded the Medal of Freedom with Palms of the United States, in 1953 the Lenin Prize for Peace, a Grotius Medal in 1959, and an Honorary Doctorate at Humboldt University. He was a foreign member of the Polish, Hungarian, Romanian, Bulgarian, and U.S.S.R. Academy of Sciences, and honorary professor of Moscow University.

He married in 1922, and had two sons.

September 16, 1971.

Peter Lorraine Ashton Berthon, co-designer of the B.R.M. racing car, who died in January 1971 while swimming near Durban, was closely connected with the international motor racing scene for nearly 40 years. He will be remembered as a brilliant engine designer, often hampered in the fruition of his far-seeing ambitions by insufficient capital. He was in his early sixties.

Throughout his engineering career, Berthon was connected with Raymond Mays, a former wool broker and racing driver of repute. It was in 1934 that Berthon joined a three-man syndicate with Raymond Mays and Humphrey Cook to launch the English Racing Automobiles—E.R.A.—racing car in a century-old mill house at Bourne, Lincolnshire, birthplace of Hereward the Wake.

The 1500c.c. car was successful, with many international victories, but in 1938 E.R.A. went out of business and Berthon left the team to help run an ageing E.R.A. as an independent team with Mays, which was well-known at the end of the Brooklands pre-war era.

Following distinguished service as a wartime R.A.F. pilot, Berthon rejoined Mays at the end of the war as the designer of the new British Racing Motors—B.R.M.—car which will go down in history as the most maligned of all Formula 1 racing cars. The Mays-Berthon team had visions of their new dreamchild conquering the motor racing world and indeed, at the start, it appeared that there was sufficient sponsorship from British industrial concerns to make the B.R.M. a race-winning reality.

Government support was pledged in 1947 and the B.R.M. was first displayed at Folkingham Airport, Lincolnshire, two years later. The V16 1½ litre-engined car was brilliantly conceived—perhaps too brilliantly, for the supercharged engine running up to 12,000 r.p.m. caused severe stress and strain. After some abortive race appearances the B.R.M. began to win races, but interest among the British Racing Motors Research Trust supporters waned and in 1952 the organization was bought out by Alfred (later Sir Alfred) Owen, of the vast Rubery Owen empire, and both Mays and Berthon joined the new partnership. Where the V16 had proved a costly failure, the new B.R.M. V8 designed by Berthon won for B.R.M. and Graham Hill the 1962 world championship.

January 20, 1971.

Edna Best, for many years a popular actress on the London stage, died on September 18, 1974 in a Geneva clinic. She was 74.

A player who had proved there was much more in her than audiences suspected in the days of her first success was lost to London when, after a number of appearances in America, Edna Best decided to settle there in 1939. Her rise had been so sudden that a quick fall might have been predicted, but she held her position long enough to show that it had been earned. She was there on the spot when the part of her lifetime came along—that of Tessa in the dramatized version of Margaret Kennedy's *The Constant Nymph*, produced by Basil Dean at the New Theatre in 1926 with, first, Noel Coward and later Sir John Gielgud as the musician Lewis Dodd.

Born at Hove on March 3, 1900, the daughter of Leonard William Best, she was trained by Kate Rorke at the Guildhall School of Music, appeared in *Charley's Aunt* at the St. James's Theatre, London, at Christmas 1917, and then toured in an American farce, *Fair and Warmer*, taking the part played in London by Fay Compton. In 1919 she followed Miss Compton in this part at the Prince of Wales, and later in the year deputized for her as the heroine of Somerset Maugham's* *Caesar's Wife*. In 1920 she had her first success in her own right, appearing in two short-lived plays at the Little, and in what was known as a "flapper" part at the St. James's during Henry Ainley's brief actor-management. One more popular comedy—*Brown Sugar*—and Edna Best, aged 21, had arrived.

She lost no ground with her Peter Pan; but *Polly with a Past* tested her too highly in 1921, and on this occasion the applause of her supporters proved embarrassing. "We hope injudicious admirers are not going to spoil Miss Edna Best" wrote the critic of *The Times* at the beginning of his notice.

With *The Lilies of the Field* she seemed to get started again, and she certainly made the most of her opportunities in Lonsdale's *Spring Cleaning*, wearing a monocle and an "Eton crop", and in Noel Coward's *Fallen Angels*, with Tallulah Bankhead* as her fellow-angel.

But the quality of her as Tessa in *The Constant Nymph* must have surprised all but the initiated, such as Coward himself, who had already had occasion to notice her "orderly course of accurate timing and almost contemptuous restraint."

There was something contemptuous about her restraint as Margaret Kennedy's heroine, too. She gave the impression that Tessa could have said, if she had wanted to, much more than she did; and Edna Best's achievement was to convince an audience that the girl had the heart and mind of an adult though her speech and bearing were those of an adolescent.

In her next play, *Come With Me*, also by Margaret Kennedy, she was partnered by Herbert Marshall* who became her husband after her marriage to Seymour Beard, the actor, had been dissolved. She and Marshall appeared in New York in Lonsdale's *The High Road,* and in London in Milne's *Michael and Mary* and Molnar's *The Swan* (1930). Their association in the theatre continued for two more years, but the marriage was then dissolved and during the remainder of the 1930s she had no regular stage partner in her work in England, which included appearances in Ivor Novello's *Murder in Mayfair* (1934), the Drury Lane pantomime (herself as Cinderella) of 1936, and J. B. Priestley's *Johnson over Jordan* (1939). Her performance as Sir Ralph Richardson's stage-struck wife was the last she gave in England before crossing the Atlantic.

In America during the 1940s and 1950s several of the parts she took were in New York productions of plays well known in London: Terence Rattigan's *The Browning Version* and *Harlequinade;* Captain Brassbound's *Conversion;* Anouilh's *Colombe;* Noel Coward's *Quadrille*. One of her appearances there on television was with Coward, as the wife in his less spectacular *Cavalcade—This Happy Breed*.

Edna Best was first seen on the screen in 1923 in *A Couple of Down and Outs,* and among the other films in which she appeared were *Tilly of Bloomsbury; Michael and Mary* with her husband Herbert Marshall; Alfred Hitchcock's *The Man who Knew Too Much; South Riding,* with Ralph Richardson and Glynis Johns, the film based on Winifred Holtby's novel.

By her marriage to Seymour Beard, Edna Best had twin sons, and by her marriage to Herbert Marshall a daughter, the actress Sarah Marshall. Edna Best's third husband, Nat Wolff, was associated with films and television in the United States and Mr. Wolff predeceased her.

September 19, 1974.

The King of Bhutan died on July 21, 1972 while on a visit to Nairobi. He was 44. King Jigme Dorji Wangchuk ruled his little Himalayan kingdom through a period of hastening change and occasional turbulence.

When he ascended the throne of the Druk Gyalpo (Dragon King) on the death of his father in 1952 Bhutan was still sealed off from the modern world, the mule tracks (which were the only ways of access) used only by traders bringing in salt and a few other commodities from Tibet, grain from India. The King's father had established the primacy of the throne over the monasteries and the monks who made up a sizable proportion of the Bhutia population, but otherwise the society was much as it had always been: the power of the King was absolute, serfs worked the estates of the monasteries and the royal family, and those who came in audience to the King prostrated themselves.

Beginning by freeing the remaining serfs—his father had started that process—and ending the practice of prostration, Jigme Dorji Wangchuk then moved cautiously to open his kingdom to outside influences. The reassertion of Chinese rule over Tibet, and the violent, often brutal social reforms that were instituted there persuaded him and his advisers of the need to close Bhutan's northern borders, and that made it necessary to improve communications with India. An agreement was made in 1959 by which India would lay roads into the kingdom, simultaneously increasing the subvention which Delhi had been paying to Bhutan since the British days.

The roads were long in building, the mountains made their construction difficult and slow, but their impact on the economy and society was quicker. Cash began to replace barter, the introduction of the wheel (hitherto unknown in Bhutan) and of trade goods from the south stimulated what had been an entirely static economy. The process of modernization, particularly as applied to the little army, made enemies, and in 1964 the King's right hand man and chief of his ministers, Jigme Dorji, was assassinated. The King, who was abroad at the time, flew back to Bhutan, landing by helicopter in one of his fortresses rather than at the place where troops were drawn up to receive him. But the army remained loyal.

The King gradually brought the Tsongdu, the national assembly, into a more positive role (it was at first little more than an advisory chamber) and progressively increased the powers of his ministers. His own position in Bhutan seemed politically unassailable; he was popular and travelled widely over the kingdom.

Bhutan is a sovereign state, and the King was determined that it would so remain, and made sure that India was given no encouragement to think that its treaty right to "advise on the conduct of Bhutan's foreign relations" entailed anything more than that. He declined repeated Indian offers to station troops in Bhutan, saying that if any troops moved in without his invitation they would be resisted as invaders. He went to Delhi in 1966 to get the promise of Mrs. Gandhi, the Indian Prime Minister, that India would let Bhutan be the judge of the timing of her entry into the United Nations, and that India would not attempt to obstruct it. That undertaking was given in writing—India belied Bhutanese misgivings by the generosity and friendliness of her treatment of this little neighbour. In 1971 Bhutan became a member of the U.N.

Jigme Dorji Wangchuk was educated in Bhutan, first by a tutor, later at a small school. He first visited Europe in 1949, spending six months in Scotland and England, and after 1960 became a regular visitor to Switzerland, where he first went for treatment after a heart attack. After that his health was never strong (he suffered too from the royal disease of fistula) but he never spared himself, lived much as his forebears had done—though taking advantage of such modern luxuries as glazing for the palace windows—and limited his trips abroad.

The King married Kesang Dorji, sister of his then chief minister, in 1951. They had one son and four daughters. The heir is Crown Prince Jigme Singhi Wangchuk.

August 4, 1972.

Princess Marthe Bibesco, the writer, died on November 29, 1973 in Paris, at the age of 85.

Although born into a distinguished Romanian family—her father was Jean Lahovary, Foreign Secretary, and her mother was a Princess Mavrocordato—she had long been known as one of the most outstanding women writers in the French language. She was elected a member of the Royal Belgian Academy in succession to the novelist Colette, and her book *Les Huits Paradis* was crowned by the French Academy.

Her novel *Catherine-Paris* was the first modern French novel to be selected by the Literary Guild in the United States; and it was published by Jonathan Cape at the same time. Among her early successes was also *Isvor, Country of Willows,* and her account of her meetings and impressions of Proust, *Au Bal Avec Marcel Proust.*

Like many cultured Romanians she was educated mostly in Paris. She wrote her first book, *Les Huits Paradis,* when she was 18. It was about her travels in Persia. She had married the important Prince George Bibesco; when they took a house in Paris Marthe Bibesco was recognized as one of the most beautiful women in Parisian society, and Frenchmen fell madly in love with her. She was only 16 when she married, gifted and rich: no wonder the unknown Proust was attracted by her.

Her books about Proust were especially subtle and understanding. In the first book, *Au Bal Avec Marcel Proust,* she describes graphically how she was not interested in the strange new writer at first and fled from him at the ball, but came to appreciate him in the end. But then her cousins, Princess Antoine and Emmanuel Bibesco, had become his closest friends. Her second volume, *The Veiled Wanderer,* is based on Proust's little-known letters to the Duc de Guiche, her cousin, and later the Duc de Gramont.

One of the fascinations of Marthe Bibesco was her intense gift to please men. Friendship was important to her, and she made any man she liked feel that he was the only man in the world for the moment. She was a marvellous conversationalist and extremely well read. Her Palace of Mogosea, a restoration of an old Venetian Brancovan palace, was the most splendid in Romania.

Even after the communists had confiscated the Bibesco estates she lived in an apartment on the Ile St. Louis in Paris, furnished with great elegance, with panels by Boucher and relics connected with Napoleon coming from Prince George Bibesco's mother, who had been a Princess Craraman-Chimay and was related to the Murat, Montesquiou and de Gramont families.

Princess Bibesco had a great success in England. She was a close friend of Sir Philip Sassoon, Ramsay MacDonald and the Churchill family. Indeed she wrote a study of Sir Winston Churchill.* After the Second World War she started her volumes of *Nymphe d'Europe*; in 1971 she published her *Confesseur et Les Poètes,* unpublished letters to her friend, Abbé Benois, from Marcel Proust, Paul Valéry, and Jean Cocteau;* and in 1972 her letters from Paul Claudel.

Princess Marthe Bibesco will be much missed; she was a unique personality, and her portraits by Boldini reveal what rare beauty she had.

November 30, 1973.

Professor Alexander Bickel, of Yale University, a leading authority on American constitutional law who became prominent in the Watergate legal controversies, died in New Haven, Connecticut, at the age of 49, in November 1974.

Bickel, a Romanian Jewish refugee, was taken by his parents to New York in 1939 when he was 15. A brilliant student, he graduated from the Harvard Law School, was admitted to the Bar and had a meteoric rise through the corridors of American legal power.

Soon after graduation he was made law clerk to Justice Felix Frankfurter* of the Supreme Court. He was also a prolific writer of books and articles.

In the autumn of 1973 he reached national prominence in helping precipitate the great "firestorm" that wrecked the Nixon presidency in October 1974. A strict constructionist, Bickel wrote in *New Republic* magazine an article suggesting that Nixon's only way out of his tapes battle with the courts lay, constitutionally, in dismissing the man who was suing him, namely Professor Archibald Cox, then special prosecutor.

He argued only that the President had the constitutional power, not that it was politic. Nixon's men, as General Alexander Haig later admitted, took intense interest, and about four weeks later the President proceeded to his first great folly, the dismissal of Professor Cox.

His successor, Jaworski, had greater powers, and when Nixon's second battle went to the Supreme Court, Bickel agreed the President had no choice but to submit.

November 11, 1974

Abebe Bikila, the Ethiopian athlete, who won gold medals for the marathon in successive Olympic Games, died on October 25, 1973 at the age of 46.

Abebe Bikila was the first of the great athletes of Africa to make their mark on the Olympic Games. His victory in the 1960 marathon in Rome was completely unexpected. Even those who had noted, from the entry list, that this unknown Ethiopian had a best time of 2hr. 21min., did not believe he could be a serious threat.

Bikila, then a member of the household guard to Emperor Haile Selassie, gained his victory in Rome by pulling away in the last 1,000 metres after advice from his coach to leave his effort late. What struck the press, waiting by the floodlit Arch of Constantine, was that his final barefoot steps were taken along the Appian Way, up which his Ethiopian ancestors had been brought as prisoners of the Roman Empire. In fact Bikila's father had fought as a guerrilla against the troops of Mussolini in the 1930s.

Four years later, in Tokyo, Bikila again became Olympic marathon champion, this time wearing warm-up shoes; and so determined to prove his freshness at the end of the traditional 26 miles 385 yards that he went through a series of physical jerks, to delight the crowd.

Bikila won that second gold medal on October 21, 1964. On September 16 he had had his appendix removed. Yet his winning time of 2hr. 12min. 11.2sec. in Tokyo was the fastest achieved for the classic event.

Bikila competed in his third Olympics in Mexico in 1968 without winning any medal. He was forced to drop out and instead had to concentrate on the first place of his countryman, Mamo Wolde.

The next year came tragedy. Bikila was injured so seriously in a car accident that he became paralysed. Even after treatment at Stoke Mandeville, he was confined to a wheelchair. His true fighting spirit was underlined when he took up archery and competed in the paraplegic Olympics. Now, at only 46, this quiet, lean man has finished the good fight.

October 26, 1973.

Sir George Binney, D.S.O., F.R.G.S., the explorer, died on September 27, 1972. He was 72.

During the twenties he took part in three Oxford expeditions to the Arctic—two of which he led. In 1924 on the third expedition the party explored the little-known North-East Land of Spitzbergen by making aerial surveys, surveys from the coast, and sleigh journeys. He later described the exploration, which occurred in conditions of round-the-clock daylight, in *With Seaplane and Sledge in the Arctic* (1925); the sledging parties accomplished their arranged journeys, but the seaplane was less successful.

Binney received the Back Award of the Royal Geographical Society and the Gold Medal de la Roquette of the Geographical Society of Paris for his journey across North-East Land. Binney served with the Hudson's Bay Company from 1926 to 1931 and as a result of his journeys through Eskimo country published *The Eskimo Book of Knowledge* in 1931.

During the Second World War Binney served with the Royal Naval Volunteer Reserve. While he was assistant commercial attaché at Stockholm from 1940 to 1942 Binney was knighted for "special services in the supply of valuable war material". He was said to have been the brains behind the blockade-running attempt by 10 Norwegian ships from Gothenburg in 1942. He was awarded the D.S.O. in 1944 for outstanding leadership and skill.

From 1931 to 1939 he worked for the United Steel Co. Ltd. Binney was educated at Eton College and at Merton College, Oxford, and was editor of *Isis* in 1920.

He was twice married.

September 30, 1972.

Lord Birkenhead, the second Earl, who died on June 10, 1975 at the age of 67, achieved considerable distinction as a biographer of the major figures of his own era.

He was born in 1907, the son of F. E. Smith, the celebrated "F.E.," who became the first Earl of Birkenhead, and Margaret Eleanor, the second daughter of the Rev. H. Furneaux, a Fellow of Corpus Christi College, Oxford.

From his earliest days he was never able to forget the tremendous figure of his father who had himself been intensely aware of the iron character and narrow religious views of his West Riding mining ancestry against which his own father had rebelled.

Frederick Winston Furneaux Smith was educated at Eton, and Christ Church College, Oxford. Though he did not attain the academic distinction his father had at Oxford, he nevertheless was universally popular, hunting and being a member of the Bullingdon Club.

From 1938 to 1939 he was Parliamentary Private Secretary to the Secretary of State for Foreign Affairs. He became a Lord-in-Waiting to King George VI in 1938, continuing until 1940. He was again King George's Lord-in-Waiting from 1951 to 1952, and from 1952 to 1955 Lord-in-Waiting to the Queen.

He had also joined the 53rd (Oxfordshire Yeomanry) Anti-Tank Regiment in 1938, and became a Captain in 1940. He served at the Staff College in 1941 and became a Major the following year. He then attended the Political Intelligence Department of the Foreign Office and took part in the British Military Mission to the Yugoslav partisans in 1944 and 1945.

But it was before the war that his attention was turned to literature and journalism and in particular the field of biography where he was later to make his mark. His first essay in this field was the daunting task of writing the official biography of his father, *Frederick Edwin, 1st Earl of Birkenhead,* the two volumes of which were published in 1933 and 1935.

The task was a formidable one, not only because of his (at that stage) relative lack of political experience but by virtue of the author's proximity to the powerful character of his subject. Nevertheless the result was by no means a partisan study and was pursued for the most part with the meticulous conscientiousness which made him an always competent, if perhaps seldom inspired, biographer.

His second work, *Strafford* (1938), was undertaken in the light of extant studies on the subject by historians of standing, but was well received and, like much of what he wrote, does not fail to make a contribution to historical analysis of the struggle between King and Parliament.

Lord Birkenhead's career as a biographer continued with *Lady Eleanor Smith—a Memoir* (1953), and a return to a revision and condensation of his biography of his father, with *F.E.* in 1959.

This involved some drastic rewriting and recasting, in particular the dispelling of the almost legendary story of the gypsy blood which had been dear to the mythology of the Smith family. But the result was greater objectivity than he had achieved in the performance of the 1930s—a portrait still filial, but by no means uncritical.

The Prof. in Two Worlds, a biography of Professor Lindemann, Baron and later Viscount Cherwell (1961), and *Halifax* (1965) are both open to the objection that they lean towards over-partiality to their subjects, but *Walter Monckton* (1969) is an able and objective portrait.

Altogether his works, if they do not reach the pinnacle of the art of biography on which stand the classics of the genre, are always authoritative and to be respected.

He married, in 1935, the Hon, Sheila Berry, an author in her own right. They had one son and one daughter.

Lord Birkenhead is succeeded by his son, Viscount Furneaux.

June 11, 1975.

Justice Hugo Black, doyen of the U.S. Supreme Court to which he was appointed by President Roosevelt in 1937, a judge famed for his defence of individual liberties, died on September 25, 1971 at the age of 85. He retired on September 17.

His dissenting opinions as leader of the court's liberal wing found him often in a minority of one—far more often than any in the long succession of fellow judges, at least 20 of them, whom he outlived during his long tenure.

For him the Bill of Rights was sacrosanct, a position once taken to the length, off the bench, of arguing that the libel and slander laws infringed constitutional freedoms of press and speech. He held that it was time enough for government to step in to regulate people "when they do something, not when they say something".

It was sufficiently remarkable that a Jeffersonian liberal of such forthright conviction should come from the Deep South; far more so that he could survive exposure as a past member of the Ku-Klux-Klan and win the respect of most Americans for the courage and tenacity of his views. There was nothing of the crank or extremist about Black, a "joiner" with all the Southerner's relaxed charm and a cordial man in private life. During his 10 years in the United States Senate he was never taken for a "Red", not even for a radical in that most conservative of chambers. During a visit to England in 1967 he said to *The Times* diarist: "I don't know the origin of my beliefs; I just formed them as I went along."

He played a vigorous game of tennis into his 80s, nearly 40 years after his doctor had advised him to desist. In his resolve to stay young and active he was not the man to act on the dispensation by which the nine members of the Supreme Court may retire on full pay at the age of 70, for all his criticism before his own appointment of the "old men" who refused to resign. Black, with little more than a year's experience of the judiciary as a police court judge at Birmingham, Alabama, emerged from the political storm over Roosevelt's ill-advised attempt to "pack" the court by appointing alternates to judges who chose to stay on after the discretionary retiring age. Although many shared the President's anger at the court's rejection of much of his New Deal legislation, the proposed remedy—for most historians his greatest blunder—was deeply resented by most senators, who buried the Bill, as a move to override the traditional separation of power for blatant political purposes. Not, however, by Black, one of the staunchest supporters of the New Deal and of the President's efforts to bring the court to heel.

All this had been power politics, and a seat on the bench was soon to fall vacant, the first since Roosevelt came to office. In nominating Black, a doughty liberal of 51, as an associate justice he undoubtedly acted out of revenge. Only five judges in a century had come from the Senate, and members would need to go back on the club rules to reject one of their fellows. As it was, they sent the nomination to committee, the first time since 1888 that a member appointed to public service by the White House had not been endorsed without debate. In face of bitter attacks from Republican opponents, Black was duly confirmed by 63 votes to 16 and lost no time in being sworn in.

He was in Europe when, less than a month later, the Ku-Klux-Klan bombshell fell. A Pittsburgh journalist, who won a Pulitzer prize for his disclosures, produced records showing that Black had joined an Alabama lodge in 1923, a form of insurance practised by many coming men in the South. The President, in no doubt that the bullet was intended to ricochet, was highly embarrassed. If he or the Senate had been aware that his man had taken a secret oath against large groups of Americans, Black would not have gone to the Supreme Court. On returning, he went on the radio to explain that he had left the Ku-Klux-Klan before his election to the Senate and he invited friendly consideration for his liberal record in Congress. Such candour can disarm American public opinion; whether it mollified Roosevelt never became clear.

Attempts to bar Black on legal grounds were equally rejected by the court of Chief Justice Hughes when the new young judge took his seat. The Ku-Klux-Klan incident may have served to sharpen his view of individual freedoms, an *idée fixe* that admitted no compromise. He was in a minority of one 12 times in his first term; throughout, he was invariably on the side of free speech, trial by jury, safeguards of the Fifth Amendment, and the long struggle for racial equality, however fiercely his native South denounced him as a traitor. In such issues Black was always on the barricades with terse, pungent opinions more notable for their clarity than for legal intricacies.

One of his earlier judgments, written for the majority, set aside the conviction of a Florida negro because a confession had been extorted by third degree methods. Undaunted by interests of state, he opposed the Smith Act which outlawed the Communist Party; in his view, to advocate the violent overthrow of government was no good reason to be sent to prison. In 1951 he strongly dissented from Chief Justice Vinson's ruling against 11 communist leaders, arguing that "the benefits derived from free expression are worth the risk." A few years later the court ordered the release of five communists convicted in California and the retrial of nine others. Black again dissented because all 14 were not acquitted.

He was against attempts to ban literature from the mails on grounds of their alleged obscenity, and in 1962 wrote a majority opinion against school prayers. "It is no part of the business of government," he ruled, "to compose official prayers for any group of the American people."

He had previously concurred in a case brought by Jehovah's Witnesses that school children could not be compelled to salute the American flag, a ceremony that meant "nothing but fear of spiritual condemnation."

General sympathy with the trade unions was reflected in a dissent in 1941 from a ruling that upheld the right of state courts to prohibit picketing. It was he 11 years later who wrote the majority opinion denouncing President Truman's move to prevent a steel strike by taking over the industry. "The founders of this nation," he said, "entrusted the law-making power to the Congress alone in both good and bad times."

In his last opinion, delivered on June 30, 1971 on a ruling that newspapers could publish secret Pentagon (defence department) papers on the Vietnam war, he wrote: "The founding fathers gave the free press the protection it must have to fulfil its essential role in our democracy. The press was to serve the governed, not the governors."

Hugo La Fayette Black was born on February 27, 1886, in Harlan, Alabama, in moderate circumstances and, orphaned at an early age, was brought up by a brother. As a schoolboy, he was a keen "court fan;" while others played their games he sat in the local court room, drinking in its wisdom, and soon decided to be a lawyer. He worked his way through the University of Alabama where a fleeting attraction to medicine was surrendered to his first love, and he took his law degree in 1906.

In 1927 he became a Senator for Alabama, after winning the Democratic nomination. He soon made his presence felt in Washington, and after election to a second term in 1932 became one of the most vigorous New Dealers in Congress. He was in the vanguard leading to the creation of the Tennessee Valley Authority, and his Bill for a 30-hour week was widely conceded to have laid the basis for Roosevelt's National Reconstruction Act. Black became a force in the Senate as chairman of special committees investigating air-mail contracts and lobbying activities.

Black, simple in tastes and habits, was a Freemason and a Baptist. In 1921 he married Josephine Patterson Foster, who died in 1952, leaving two sons and a daughter. Several years later, at the age of 71, he married his secretary, Mrs. Elizabeth De-Meritte.

September 27, 1971.

Professor Lord Blackett, O.M., C.H., F.R.S., one of the most eminent experimental physicists of his generation, died on July 13, 1974 aged 76.

A former President of the Royal Society, a Nobel prize winner, honoured by universities all over the world, he had received all the rewards of a great professional scientist; and he stood out among scientists through the power and elegance of his researches, through his contributions to military thinking, through the independence of his political attitudes, and through the distinction of his personality.

He had occupied physics chairs at Birk-beck College, London University, at Manchester University and at Imperial College, where he was Professor Emeritus and a Fellow.

He was awarded something like a score of honorary degrees by universities at home and overseas and had sat on many of the most influential and significant committees in his own country. He was President of the British Association in 1957-58.

Patrick Maynard Stuart Blackett was born on November 18, 1897. His grandfather had been vicar of Croydon, his father was a stockbroker; he was born into an upper middle-class environment in the age—as he himself said—when Kipling was the poet of an Empire just passing into decline. This orthodox background affected him in two ways: he rebelled, with the strength and decision of a powerful nature, against its political assumptions, and that rebellion lasted all his life; but what also lasted all his life was the natural authority, the sense of responsibility and command, of the people among whom he was born. It was according to the family pattern that he went into the Navy, and was trained at Osborne and Dartmouth; it was like him that he took it for granted, enjoyed being a naval officer, and came out top of his class.

He was present at the Battle of the Falkland Islands before he was seventeen, and at Jutland before he was nineteen. In the closing months of the 1914-18 War, as a sub-lieutenant in a destroyer, his thoughts went to the design of a gun-sight. He knew he had a scientific talent but it was boredom, not dislike for the service, that led him to speculate vaguely about changing his career. When the war ended, the Admiral sent a number of bright young officers to Magdalene on a six months' rehabilitation course; he went according to orders, not of his own volition. He had not been a month in Cambridge, however, before he realized that this was the life for him. Within another fortnight he had resigned his commission; he never lacked confidence, and he did not doubt that he could make a success of academic science.

Right from the beginning, he was marked out as a brilliant member of Rutherford's Cavendish Laboratory. In addition to his intellectual strength, he had a first-class nose for which problem would go, and which would not go. He had, in addition, great skill and love of experimentation for its own sake. This love he never lost. To a greater extent than in most scientific intellectuals, he thought with his hands, and this gift kept him at direct individual research throughout his career. In many ways, his scientific talents were more like Rutherford's than those of any other of Rutherford's pupils. This did not assist their personal relations, which were never easy: they were both born to be patriarchs, and there was room for only one patriarch in the Cavendish. Nevertheless, Blackett had already made his reputation by the end of the twenties. By his classical development of the cloud-chamber, he was able to study the collision of nuclear particles with a new refinement. As well as being in the heart of nuclear physics he showed the interest in some of the long-standing "old-fashioned" problems which he retained all his life: he found time to develop an ingenious method for measuring specific heats.

He was a picturesque figure in the Cambridge of the period. One of the most handsome of men, he drew attention whenever he stalked in his dignified stride through the streets. After holding a by-fellowship at Magdalene, he became a Fellow of King's. Happily married, recognized as a rising star of physics, he had most of the luck a young man could want; but his social conscience, which had not been in action while he was in the Navy, did not let him rest. As an undergraduate he had become friendly with Kingsley Martin,* later editor of the *New Statesman*, and Blackett soon became committed to the left. During the twenties, he began to take on the position that he never abandoned or budged from. Of the left-wing scientific figures between the two wars, he was, along with Bernal, much the most distinguished as a scientist. He was also probably the toughest-minded, the most pragmatically useful, as a political thinker. Deep in his heart, he might be compensating for the privileges among which he was brought up; but in expression, thought and action, he was as practical and authoritative about politics as he was about physics.

In 1933 he brought off his most spectacular piece of scientific work. He discovered the positive electron, while almost simultaneously, and quite independently, C. D. Anderson was making the same discovery in the United States. Anderson was a few weeks ahead with his publication, but the credit was shared, and it was for this research among others that 15 years later Blackett was awarded the Nobel Prize for Physics. In the same year, 1933, he left Cambridge for the Physics Chair at Birkbeck College. About this time he was starting his investigations into cosmic rays, the second of his three main groups of researches. As an unexpected side result, he was drawn into military science, in which he thus happened to acquire a good deal of training before 1939.

Brought into the Air Defence Committee in 1936 by Tizard, always a good judge of intelligence, Blackett was better prepared for his war jobs than any of his scientific contemporaries; and in the war made perhaps the most striking and original contribution of any of them. While scientific adviser to A.A. Command, he initiated the main principles of what became known as "Operational Research." With Coastal Command, aided by a scientist of genius, E. J. Williams, and a set of able men attracted by his leadership, he showed what a kind of variational analysis could do, even in the untidiest and most cluttered problems of war. At the Admiralty, from 1942-45, he was Director of Operational Research and brought the method to a higher point of usefulness than in any other department and

any other country in the war. His aim, as he said himself, was to find numbers on which to base strategy, not gusts of emotion. He later applied the same method, with devastating effect, to economic problems, as in his famous address to the British Association in 1957.

In the war he was one of the most effective scientific figures on either side, using great powers with his customary authority. Immediately after the war, he went through the only obscure period of his adult life. He was thought to be committed too far to the left for a Labour Government to employ with ease; he had also attracted the envy of lesser men. So he retired to Manchester, where in 1937 he had been elected to the Langworthy Professorship, and went back to his research on cosmic rays. His love for doing things with his own hands supported him, at a time when he was right out of public life: he was also supported by the academic honours, including the Nobel prize, rolling in. But there is no doubt that he felt ill-treated; he was too much in the habit of command to like being left out of affairs. He felt more isolated still when in 1948 he published an essay on the military and political consequences of atomic energy. Most of what he said in this book, and his later one, *Atomic Weapons and East-West Relations* (1956), is now accepted as platitudinous: at the time it seemed to many to be inhumanly cold, perverse, and probably pro-communist.

When he moved to Imperial College in 1953, however, he entered a period of Augustine serenity. He was busy with his third major personal research, this time on rock magnetism; his scientific eminence, which had never been in doubt, was now more than ever acclaimed, nationally and internationally; of all his brilliant contemporaries, he was proving himself the best stayer and the most continuously creative. He loved living in London: there remained about him a vestigial air of the intelligentsia of the twenties. Even more handsome as an aging man than as a young one, he was as much a figure in the King's Road as he had once been in King's Parade. In affairs he had become at last a kind of scientific elder statesman, trusted in quarters where he used to be thought a dangerous radical.

The crown of his career was still to come. During the 13 years when the Labour Party was out of office, he was one of a group of scientists which met regularly to suggest plans for scientific and technological policy: this group, of which he was the senior member, became influential when Harold Wilson succeeded to the leadership of the party. It was Blackett's thinking that led directly to the creation of the Ministry of Technology as soon as the Wilson government was formed. In no other way, Blackett had argued, could enough technological innovation be brought into industry within five or 10 years. It was at his insistence that the revival of the computer industry was made a first priority; he personally presided over the official committee on computers within

the Ministry. Typically, he did not enter open politics, but was content to work for a year as a civil servant, paying courteous deference to his official superiors. He remained deputy chairman of the Minister's Advisory Council throughout the administration's life, and also personal scientific adviser to the Minister. He had refused many honours: in the style of a radical of the twenties he would not take any title, though he liked being called Professor; in 1965 he accepted a C.H.

The greatest honour of all, and the one which gave him nothing but pleasure, was on the way. In November 1965 he was elected President of the Royal Society. This was the one piece of recognition that he had wanted for himself: in his periods of isolation he had thought it would never happen, and had accepted that as the price for standing firm by unpopular attitudes. But, under Florey's* leadership, the Royal Society itself was changing, and with general approval gave Blackett the highest honour in its power. When it happened, his reserve and austerity broke down altogether; his first Presidential speech took him more emotional effort than anything in his public life. He was appointed to the Order of Merit in 1967 and became a life peer in 1969.

He married in 1924 Constanza Bayon. They had one son and one daughter.

July 15, 1974.

Beatrice Mary Blackwood, F.S.A., who won international fame as an anthropologist and ethnologist at the Pitt Rivers Museum, Oxford, died on November 29, 1975 aged 86. She had pursued her remarkable career right up to the time of her death.

The eldest child of James Blackwood of St. John's Wood, she read English at Somerville College from 1908 to 1912, and returned in 1918 to read for the Diploma in Anthropology, which she passed with distinction.

She took her B.A. and M.A. together in 1920, when membership of Oxford University and the conferment of degrees were open to women for the first time. In 1923 she added the B.Sc., while holding a demonstratorship in the Department of Human Anatomy.

Then she was awarded a research fellowship to spend three years at field work in the United States and Canada. She turned her attention to the Pacific when appointed Lecturer in Ethnology, and carried out field research in the Northern Solomons for Yale University, and in New Guinea and New Britain for the Pitt Rivers Museum, for which she made outstandingly fine collections.

This exemplary field work was rewarded with the Rivers Memorial Medal of the Royal Anthropological Institute in 1943, and she was elected a Fellow of the Society of Antiquaries in 1948. Her single-minded devotion to anthropological field research and studies of museum collections put her in permanent demand on the councils of learned societies, like the Royal Anthropological Institute, of which she was to become vice-president, the Folklore Society, and international research bodies.

This brought her close friends and associates in all corners of the world, with whom by tireless energy she maintained contacts of inestimable value to her museum, the Pitt Rivers, which she served with characteristic sustained energy until the very end.

In collaboration with the late curator, T. K. Penniman, she edited the Pitt Rivers Museum's Occasional Papers on technology. Her major published work was *Both Sides of Buka Passage* (1935), on her work in the Solomons, and frequent contributions to learned journals also followed from her field work.

But she herself was proud of the fact that, owing to her small stature and fearlessness, she used to be the first to be sent into caves with small entrances "to make sure" (as she said) "that it would be all right for the men to follow."

December 2, 1975.

Joan Blakeman—See Woodward.
Admiral Carrero Blanco—See Carrero.

James Blish, the well-known science fiction writer, died on July 30, 1975 in Henley-on-Thames, after a long illness. He began his professional life writing for the pulp magazines, turning his hand to anything, even to stories of sports he had never seen ("I still don't know what they actually *do* in basketball," he said recently).

His first science fiction story was published in 1940, since when he produced a growing number of novels and stories of a highly personal excellence. Among them are *Fallen Star, Titan's Daughter, A Torrent of Faces* (one of the most imaginative and enchanting of over-population novels, written over a 20-year period with Norman Knight), his celebrated *A Case of Conscience,* the two linked eschatological novels, *Black Easter* and *The Day After Judgment,* and the novels comprising the *Cities in Flight* sequence, currently enjoying fresh popularity in new paperback editions. Blish would also wish his lovingly researched and prolix *Doctor Mirabilis,* a fictionalized life of Roger Bacon, to be remembered.

Born in New Jersey in 1921 Jim Blish was a graduate of Rutgers and Columbia Universities, with a solid scientific background. His dedication to the SF field—and dedication was very much a feature of his life, whether to friends or work—manifested itself in the time-consuming jobs he undertook, including editing an ill-fated magazine, *Vanguard,* and reviewing under the name of William Atheling Jr.; two volumes of his criticism have been published.

He published poetry, and essays on James Branch Cabell, and he also wrote many of the widely successful Star Trek paperbacks, claiming against the derision of friends that they helped to introduce younger readers to SF. Blish was his own man. Like C. S. Lewis,* whom Blish greatly admired, he had a rare belief that the republic of letters was all one.

Long an anglophile—and responding in particular to the success of his novels published in Britain by Faber and Faber since 1957—Blish and his wife moved to England, with their cats, in 1968. Since then they lived near Henley-on-Thames, both bravely fighting the illness which slowly beat him.

Blish was, in Hardy's phrase, a crusted character; yet talking to him, with the immense reservoir of science, literature, music, and various esoteric subjects on which he could draw, often with dry humour, was never less than a pleasure. He leaves behind him unfinished works on James Joyce (on whose writings he was a respected expert), witchcraft, and the operas of Richard Strauss.

He was twice married, first to Virginia Kidd, the American literary agent, by whom he had a son and a daughter, and secondly, to Judy Ann Lawrence, the artist and writer.

July 31, 1975.

Sir Arthur Bliss, C.H., K.C.V.O., Master of the Queen's Music since 1953, who died on March 27, 1975 at the age of 83, at his London home, was an internationally respected musician.

He was a distinguished and fairly prolific composer of music (some 130 works are credited to him), much of it durably outstanding, in most available genres. In his youth he had been an able pianist, though modest about his talent, and he remained a convincing and accomplished conductor, not only of his own compositions. For a period he served as a musical administrator, reluctant but industrious, to the B.B.C.; he was a conscientious, efficient committee chairman.

As a composer Bliss first made his name with lively, invigorating experiments in unusual combinations of timbre, somewhat indebted to Stravinsky and the French "Armistice" school of composers. During the mid-1920s, at about the time when he contracted his long and happy marriage, his music became more consciously British in manner and eventually more traditional in language—perhaps to the advantage of his personal communicative eloquence, for his music remained quite distinctive. Music for dramatic purposes—theatre, film, ballet opera, radio—can be seen as a guideline throughout Bliss's composing life. Even in non-dramatic works there was often a literary or pictorial or delineatory element more or less apparent behind the notes; Bliss recognized this—"There is only a little of the spider about

me...I am more of a magpie type."

We may sense that his concertos are, to some degree, musical portraits of their original exponents. Solomon, Campoli, Rostropovich, in the viola sonata Lionel Tertis, in the *Introduction and Allegro* Stokowski and the Philadelphia Orchestra, seem to be enshrined in sound next to, or even above the musical personality of the composer. Certainly Bliss derived creative stimulus from executant musical virtuosity, as he makes plain in his autobiography *As I Remember* (1970), where we discover also his vivid response to travels abroad and to the literature of other countries.

He and his music won many a success abroad. To foreign listeners it may have sounded as typically English as its composer with his handsome military bearing (legacy of First World War service in France where, as an officer in the Grenadier Guards, he was wounded twice and mentioned in dispatches) and courteous, jovial disposition. The music and the man were, in truth, more internationalist than Little Englander.

It was indeed from New England that Bliss sprang on his father's side. Arthur Edward Drummond Bliss was born in Barnes, London, on August 2, 1891, and was educated at Rugby and Pembroke College, Cambridge, where he took the degrees of B.A. and Mus.B. in 1913, his mentors there including Charles Wood and E. J. Dent. His mother, who died when he was four, was English and a keen amateur pianist; her three sons were all musically gifted.

Young Arthur Bliss's early musical enthusiasms were Schubert and Beethoven; then, thanks to a young music master at Rugby, Debussy and Ravel. Before leaving school he had succumbed to the spell of Elgar who was subsequently to befriend and encourage him. At Cambridge and then during a short studentship at the Royal College of Music in London, before wartime enlistment took him from there, he experienced his first taste of Schoenberg and the repertory of Diaghilev's Russian Ballet. Composition studies with Stanford proved uncongenial but Bliss was much helped and stimulated by Vaughan Williams and Holst, as by his fellow-students Howells, Goossens* and Arthur Benjamin.

Bliss had been composing since 1910, and a piano quartet in A minor won a wartime prize. Eventually he suppressed all his music written before *Madam Noy* in 1918: this is the first of several pieces in which voices are integrated, as if instrumentally, into unconventional chamber musical textures—*Rhapsody* (1919) and *Rout* (1920) explored this idea further with, respectively, vocalises and nonsense syllables. *Rout* was the most successful of these, twice encored at its first performance, and still sometimes to be heard nowadays. A solo tenor voice, singing meaningless but euphonious words, was also incorporated in the piano concerto (1920); Bliss soon thought better and omitted the voice, but revised the concerto more thoroughly as a two-piano concerto in 1924, and subsequently in 1968 for the two-piano three-hands Sellick-Smith duo. Controversy attended these early works, likewise the entertaining *Conversations* for a mixed instrumental quintet (the first sets a committee meeting to music) and the incidental music for Shakespeare's *The Tempest* which brought drums into the auditorium to accompany the opening scene.

Bliss was acquiring a reputation as a tearaway, but when Elgar procured for him a commission from the Three Choirs Festival Bliss responded with the substantial and highly inventive as well as exhilarating *Colour Symphony* (1922), a work that may now be recognized as the start of the mature Bliss. He directed the first performance at Gloucester, having been active as a conductor since returning from the war: his appointment in 1921 to Portsmouth Philharmonic Society allowed him to strengthen his classical repertory, while in London he chiefly conducted new or recent music including the premiere of Vaughan Williams's *Shepherds of the Delectable Mountains*.

In 1923 Bliss accompanied his father and family on a visit to the United States. He settled in Santa Barbara, California, to work as conductor, lecturer, pianist, and occasional music critic, as well as composer. Here in 1925 he married Trudy Hoffmann, daughter of an American naturalist. The wedded couple decided to make their home in London but the American experience left its mark in works written expressly for Monteux* and the Boston Symphony Orchestra and for Stokowski and the Philadelphia Orchestra, as well as the oboe quintet commissioned by Mrs. Sprague Coolidge.

A new type of vocal composition, with anthologized texts drawn from several periods and united only by subject matter, occupied Bliss in the *Pastoral* for mezzo-soprano, flute, chorus and strings plus timpani, a work of special charm conceived on a holiday in Sicily. The same method of assembling texts was followed in the *Serenade* (1929) and, most important, the choral symphony *Morning Heroes*, written for the 1930 Norwich Festival and designed to exorcise the composer's nightmares of wartime in the trenches. Bliss reverted to the anthology in two later sacred choral works, *The Beatitudes* for the 1962 Coventry Festival, and *Mary of Magdala* for the 1963 Worcester Festival. *Morning Heroes* is arguably the finest of all Bliss's compositions, though an alternative choice might be the splendid *Music for Strings* which Adrian Boult and the Vienna Philharmonic introduced at the 1935 Salzburg Festival, or the *Checkmate* ballet written for what is now the Royal Ballet on its first visit to Paris, or the new piano concerto, Bliss's bold tribute to the people of the United States at the New York World's Fair in 1939.

Bliss had approached music for ballet via film music, first and most notably with his orchestral score for *Things to Come* (1934-

35), not only greatly successful but a landmark in the history of music for the cinema. A later film, *Men of Two Worlds* (1945) involved the composition by Bliss of another piano concerto movement entitled *Baraza*, with obbligato male chorus—it had a certain vogue at that time when films about piano concertos were popular, and a year later Bliss wrote *Theme and Cadenza*, a fragment of a violin concerto, for a radio play by his wife, though this is chiefly significant because the collaboration then with Alfredo Campoli was to be furthered in 1955 with Bliss's violin concerto for him.

The outbreak of war in 1939 found Bliss, his wife and their two daughters, on holiday in New England after the premiere of the piano concerto. He was persuaded to remain in America where he worked as visiting professor at Berkeley in the University of California, but in 1941 he returned to London and gave his services to the B.B.C., first as Assistant Overseas Music Director, and then as Director of Music, a task he found "restricting," not least because he was not composing music, and had left his family in America. In 1944 he left the B.B.C. and composed his second ballet, *Miracle in the Gorbals*, an impressive piece of music-theatre though the music has proved more durable than the ballet. A third ballet, *Adam Zero* (1946), was even more quickly dropped though Bliss preferred it of his various ballet scores.

This involvement with music for the theatre (extending back to music for *As You Like It* at Stratford on Avon in 1919) was leading Bliss to opera. During the war he had planned with Stephen Spender an opera on Homer's *Odyssey*, but this came to nothing. Bliss's first and major operatic achievement was *The Olympians*, with libretto by J. B. Priestley, first produced at Covent Garden in 1949. It was a qualified success, handicapped partly by the young opera company's collective inexperience and by the exigencies of postwar controls. Bliss's second opera, *Tobias and the Angel* (1960), was designed for television, written in collaboration with Christopher Hassall*; it was more convincingly judged and would bear revival, especially in the revised form as a two-act stage opera. There may have remained some doubt whether Bliss had the born opera composer's individual attitude to characterization of the singing voice. Two late works acquitted him of this charge, a concert scena, *The Enchantress* written for Kathleen Ferrier in 1951, the year in which Bliss was knighted, and the song-cycle, *A Knot of Riddles* for baritone and 11 instruments, commissioned for the 1963 Cheltenham Festival (of which Bliss was the loyal and energetic president for many years), a work of real subtlety and charm.

Bliss was appointed Master of the Queen's Music in 1953. He took his responsibilities seriously, composing many short occasional pieces for royal or otherwise festive events. He remained alert and industrious well into his ninth decade of life. Among his later works special mention must be made of the

second string quartet composed for the Griller Quartet in 1950, the piano sonata written for Noël Mewton-Wood in 1952, and the cello concerto for Rostropovich (1970), all works of outstanding brilliance and fire. Bliss's creative ingenuity is further attested by the orchestral *Meditations on a Theme of John Blow* (1955) where, as in *The Beatitudes,* the composer contrives more diversity of expressive content than the *donnée* would suggest, particularly in the sphere of menace or aggression which always drew on an imposing vein in Bliss's inventive circulation.

In 1956 he led a musical deputation to Soviet Russia, the first from Britain since the war. Its members were acclaimed and Bliss returned next year as a judge of the Tchaikovsky Piano Competition. In 1963 he was awarded the Gold Medal of the Royal Philharmonic Society, and in 1964 an honorary doctorate of music by Cambridge University for whose musical quincentenary celebrations he composed his *Golden Cantata* to poems by Kathleen Raine. He received doctorates from Edinburgh, Glasgow, London and Bristol, and held many influential honorary appointments, honouring them in deeds as well as in the name.

March 29, 1975.

Edmund Blunden, C.B.E., M.C., the distinguished poet and writer, and Professor of Poetry at Oxford from 1966 to 1968, died on January 20, 1974.

Edmund Blunden chose to end his biography of Shelley with a quotation from the poet in which he affirmed that individual poems were properly to be recognized "as episodes to that great poem, which all poets, like the cooperating thoughts of one great mind, have built up since the beginning of the world." This Platonic doctrine appealed to Blunden's remarkable feeling for poetic continuity, and may be fitly applied to his own work. His death at the age of 77 concludes one such long and rich episode.

Edmund Charles Blunden was born in London on November 1, 1896. Two years later the family moved from London to Yalding in Kent, where the father was a schoolmaster—and organist and choirmaster. Blunden attended first the local grammar school, but soon won a scholarship to Christ's Hospital, Horsham, becoming senior "Grecian" in due course. He was deeply devoted to the school, and his consciousness of those early "Old Blues," Coleridge and Leigh Hunt and Charles Lamb, influenced him all his life. They were his gateway into letters, and he was soon to emulate their literary achievements. In 1914, the year he gained the senior classics scholarship at Queen's College, Oxford, he printed privately at Horsham two pamphlets of verse: *Poems* and *Poems Translated from the French.*

But the outbreak of the First World War changed everything and within a few months he was serving as a volunteer with The Royal Sussex Regiment. He gave an account of his service in Flanders in *Undertones of War*, but that classic alone hardly describes the full impact made on him by the war. He felt an intense loyalty not only to his immediate comrades in the regiment but to all of his generation, without respect to nationality, who had shared the hell of the trenches, and was haunted throughout life by its memories. In 1916 he was commissioned and in 1917 was awarded the Military Cross.

He took up his scholarship after demobilization in 1919, but, finding himself unable to settle down to academic life, he left Oxford for London in 1920 to become assistant to Middleton Murry on *The Athenaeum*. When *The Athenaeum* merged with *The Nation* in 1921, under the editorship of H. W. Massingham, he continued as a regular contributor until his appointment as Professor of English in the University of Tokyo in 1924. He married Mary Daines in June 1918. There were a son and a daughter by this first marriage. In 1933 he married Sylva Norman, a writer who later came to share his enthusiasm for Shelley and other Romantics.

The war had been unable to interrupt entirely his studies or his writing. He had always a book with him in the trenches, and in 1916 he printed three pamphlets of verse. But he did not make a name for himself as a poet until the publication of *The Waggoner* in 1920 and *The Shepherd* in 1922, which won him the Hawthornden Prize. At one time it was usual to refer to Blunden as a "Georgian" on the strength of his appearance in the final volume of Sir Edward Marsh's *Georgian Poetry*, but the genius he showed in those two books of his own could not be so easily classified. He did not owe his poetic character to any temporary fashion. He sprang from the central tradition of English verse, continuing it in terms of his own peculiar vision. He knew the Elizabethans well but began to feel also at home with the seventeenth-century metaphysicals.

Time and again he caught, either deliberately or with unconscious sympathy, the genuine accent of such poets as Herbert and Traherne and Vaughan; and his English renderings of the Latin verse of the period, especially Milton's, are among his most felicitous translations. Dryden, Collins, the Wartons, and Christopher Smart were among his favourites of the following period, but his deepest affection was reserved for the Romantics—Coleridge, Shelley, Keats, and the lesser lights. He wrote at length or commented on or edited works by all the poets mentioned; and coming down in time, he gave his whole-hearted admiration to Thomas Hardy, publishing a study of him in 1941. His allegiance was to poetry itself, rather than to any of its schools, and though he was prompt to help and encourage the many young poets who appealed to him, he was scrupulous never to try to divert them from their individual tacks.

The Waggoner and *The Shepherd* are misleading titles if they are interpreted to mean that Blunden was essentially a pastoral poet. The pastoral vein in English verse was especially dear to him, but in his own poetry, though he could brilliantly visualize the country scene and country folk, he interpreted nature in the light of the tensions and complexities of his age. Nature was an idyll of his childhood—a bright unattainable vision seen retrospectively through the screen of war and its congregated ghosts—and was for him an ironic or pathetic commentary on the bewildering present, never an escape from its demands. He was, in his own words, "too old a realist" to be tricked by appearance or sentiment. He rediscovered John Clare, and edited his poems from manuscript, in collaboration with Alan Porter, in 1921, which marks one of his allegiances, but he was also the editor of Wilfred Owen, which points to another.

Undertones of War was written while he was in Japan and on publication in 1928 was immediately recognized as a masterpiece. Here he never obtrudes himself upon the reader and is the interpreter of, rather than a commentator on, events, catching exactly not only the horrors and devastation of the conflict but the humanity, humour, and courage of his comrades. The prose is as admirable in its way as his verse of the time, unaffected and yet ready to draw on all the resources of rhythm and image. In spite of the Second World War intervening to distract attention from the First, the book's lustre is undimmed.

He returned from Tokyo in 1928 and renewed his connexion with *The Nation*, but in 1930 he was elected a Fellow and Tutor of English at Merton College, Oxford. He made an excellent tutor, and many of his pupils became lifelong friends. His first collected volume of verse appeared in 1930, and in the same year his admirable biography of Leigh Hunt was published. His knowledge of the Romantic period was extraordinary, in sympathy and detail, and, with the modesty and generosity that were his most characteristic traits, he was always ready to share it with other scholars. His gift of books to Keats House, Hampstead, should be mentioned in this connexion. But his range was not confined to the Romantics. There was hardly an aspect of English literature—or, for that matter, of English painting—in which he was not equally well versed.

He published several volumes of poetry during the 1930s. He wrote fluently and easily, with a remarkable talent for occasional verse, but he might have done better to have been more selective in his choice for publication, for some of the poems written at this time fall short of his best. He was, however, always being asked for contributions, and it went against his generous temperament to disoblige. His fatigue, rather than decline, was due not to any failure of power but to the extreme perturbation roused in him by the threat of approaching war. All the old spiritual wounds were set aching and his grasp on poetry seemed occasionally to grow relaxed. His answer to the charge that he published too that time was the poet's best editor. A much was, however, Walter de la Mare's—second collected volume of his poetry came out in 1940.

At the outbreak of war he served for a time with the University O.T.C., giving instruction in map reading, a subject in which he delighted, but in 1943 he resigned his Fellowship and returned to London, as a staff writer on *The Times Literary Supplement*. He was from early years a practised reviewer, and a collection of articles contributed to the *Literary Supplement* had appeared under the title of *Votive Tablets* in 1931.

His marriage to Miss Norman was dissolved in 1943. He married Claire Poynting in 1944; there are four daughters by the marriage.

Once the shock of war had been accepted he quickly recovered his poise and began to write poetry with his earlier intensity. *Shells by a Stream* (1944) and *After the Bombing* (1949) contain some of his most mature poems. They show the lyrical grace, the felicitous phrasing, the keen observation, and the deliberative intelligence of his earlier work, but their rhythm is tauter and their imagery sharper, in response to the moral and emotional stresses of the time. He was active, too, in prose. *Cricket Country* (1944), his delightful, digestive account of cricket—a game which had engaged his entire devotion from childhood, as both a keen player and spectator—was highly successful; and in scholarship his *Shelley, a Life Story* (1946) was equally popular.

He returned to Japan in 1947 as Cultural Liaison Officer to the British Mission. The appointment was a wise choice. He was regarded with the greatest esteem and affection in that country—sentiments which he fully reciprocated—and in 1950 was elected to the Japan Academy, the highest honour that could be paid. He was created C.B.E. in 1951. He held the honorary degree of D.Litt. from the universities of Leeds and Leicester.

He resumed his work on *The Times Literary Supplement* in 1949, but returned to the Far East as Professor of English in the University of Hongkong in 1955. A year later he received the Queen's Gold Medal for Poetry. Once again he gained the immediate respect and admiration of his students. Wherever he chanced to live or whomever he lived among, his sincerity, modesty and gentleness, his wisdom and knowledge, his humour and generosity, and his rare poetic temperament won him devoted friends.

In February 1966, he was elected Oxford Professor of Poetry in succession to Robert Graves. He polled 477 votes. Robert Lowell, the American poet, received 241 votes.

Blunden wrote much and variously—only a few of his many writings have been referred to here—and the problem he set in classification may have helped to divert attention in recent years from his achievement. Nor did he call attention to himself by sharing in any of the literary controversies of his time: being an ally of no party, he was adopted by none. The diversity of his prose and the range of his scholarship alone would have been sufficient for an ordinary reputation, but in the long run Blunden's will rest on his poetry—one of the most admirable illustrations of the English tradition in our time, and an episode "to that great poem."

January 22, 1974.

Dr. Thomas Sherrer Ross Boase, M.C., President of Magdalen College, Oxford, from 1947 to 1968, died on April 14, 1974. He was 75.

He was born on August 31, 1898, the son of C. M. Boase, and educated at Rugby. He served in the 1914-18 War with the Oxford and Bucks Light Infantry and was awarded the Military Cross. In 1919 he went up to Magdalen College, Oxford, as Exhibitioner in History, and from then, in spite of a 10-year period of absence, he was continuously concerned with Oxford. He was from the beginning a university rather than a college man. As an undergraduate, by his own choice, he never resided in college, but preferred to live in lodgings, and many of his closest friends were members of other foundations, especially Balliol and New College. He was also prominent in the Urquhart *salon* and was a regular visitor to the Chalet.

Although his interest in history, especially medieval history, was always strong, his overriding preoccupation was always with pictures and to only a slightly less extent with architecture and sculpture. Hence it was no surprise when, after a distinguished career at Hertford College from 1922-37 as Tutor in History and Dean, he became Professor in the History of Art at London and Director of the Courtauld Institute. This post he held until 1947, but was taken away from it from 1939-45 on government service in the Middle East in the Second World War. He had, however, already established himself as an authority on Art History and became a Trustee of the National Gallery, 1947-53, and a member of the advisory council of the Victoria and Albert Museum, 1947-70. In 1950 he became a governor of the British Museum, and in 1952 of the Shakespeare Memorial Theatre.

As an art historian his knowledge was as wide-ranging as his tastes were catholic. In the *Oxford History of English Art,* of which he was himself the general editor, he wrote with equal competence the volumes dealing with the twelfth and the nineteenth centuries. Vasari and the art of the crusading states were the subjects of his Slade Lectures at Oxford, and his contributions to the *Journal of the Warburg and Courtauld Institutes* included both a valuable study of the architectural history of his own college and a monograph on the sculptor J. G. Lough.

When, in 1947, the Presidency of Magdalen was vacated by President Tizard, the Fellows with remarkable speed and unanimity elected Boase as his successor. He had indeed every qualification for the post. In addition to being a Magdalen man who had constantly maintained his interest in and contact with the college, he was thoroughly well versed in the intricacies of university politics and had also achieved great distinction both in his chosen field of study and in complicated and controversial administration elsewhere. He was already a well-known figure in the university and was almost at once elected to the Hebdomadal Council. In due course he became Vice-Chancellor and held that difficult and onerous post from 1958 to 1960 with great dignity and distinction, and in 1960 received the honorary degree of D.C.L. at Harold Macmillan's first Encaenia as Chancellor. Soon afterwards he withdrew from university politics to devote more time to the college and to his own work.

The choice of Boase as President of Magdalen College was a very happy one. He tried to guide the college rather than to govern it and although his views, which he often held strongly, did not always agree with those of the majority of the Fellows, his sense of what was politically possible always saved him from pressing them to a point at which he might have caused a serious split in college. With undergraduates he was particularly good. He handled them with the sympathy and tact which comes from long experience; he knew them well and many became his friends. Indeed his circle of friends from Oxford, from his British Council days or from artistic connexions, was so large that he found a ready welcome in almost any part of the world.

He never liked or understood accounts, and, as a good Scot, he had a natural bent towards frugality which his colleagues did not always share. He felt strongly that economy was a good thing which deserved more attention than it usually received. But in this as in other matters he accepted with good grace decisions of which he did not personally approve.

April 15, 1974.

Dr. Jaime Torres Bodet, the Mexican diplomat and writer, died in Mexico City on May 13, 1974 at the age of 72.

He was elected Director-General of Unesco at the Beirut General Conference in 1948, an obvious choice to succeed Julian Huxley, as he had shown interest in Unesco from the start.

At that point in its history, Unesco needed a man who could represent the less developed countries of the world in their genuine aspirations towards world peace, a higher standard of literacy, and intellectual and moral betterment.

Torres Bodet was already known as an educational reformer. He spoke fluent French, was a poet and novelist of distinction, and had diplomatic experience which his predecessor lacked. During his four years at Unesco he was able to mobilize the support of Latin American and Arab states, although often at the risk of antagonizing the larger countries who were contributing most to Unesco's budget.

Torres Bodet was particularly interested in Unesco's work on fundamental education, agriculture and health, and cooperated actively with F.A.O. and W.H.O.

From the time of his election in Beirut, Torres Bodet had warned that it would be a shortsighted policy to embark on too many projects. In his efforts not to spread Unesco's budget too thin, he met mounting opposition from his own secretariat and executive.

This opposition came to a head at the General Conference in Florence in 1950, and Torres Bodet felt it necessary to present an ultimatum: either he must have a vote of confidence that Unesco was contributing to the cause of world peace, or he must resign. The Conference gave him a unanimous vote of confidence and he continued as Director-General until 1952, when the total budget he had asked for was drastically cut.

He felt he could no longer do useful work, and presented his final resignation. His critics said that he had been too touchy but for him the issues were fundamental.

His poetry was distinguished, and he wrote essays on subjects ranging from Proust and Beethoven to the dances of Madras and the need for communication between eastern and western cultures.

May 15, 1974.

U. V. Bogaerde, who was appointed first art editor of *The Times* in 1922 and held that position until he retired in 1957, died on November 5, 1972. He was 80.

He was on *The Times* for 45 years—apart from service with the Army in the 1914-18 War—starting in 1912 as a black and white artist. Throughout that long period he was continually engaged in experiments that heralded successive advances in photography and the reproduction of news photographs as well as other illustrations.

Ulric Van den Bogaerde, when he joined *The Times* in 1912 at the age of 20, was an accomplished young artist. The only illustrations then appearing in *The Times* were in the advertisements, and Bogaerde extended their range to the editorial columns with his own drawings of such subjects as the livery company halls of the City, and London's chop houses.

He also illustrated some of the Russian supplements that *The Times* published in the early days of the 1914-18 War, and later in 1914 took over the make-up and illustrations for *The Times History of the War.* The paper had not then any photographers and Bogaerde had himself to dash off, for example, to Scarborough and other places on the north-east coast to take pictures of damage done by German cruisers.

At the same time an important part of his work lay in improving the reproduction of drawings and photographs. Lord Northcliffe, who had been chief proprietor of *The Times* since 1908, took an active personal interest in the development of half-tone and photogravure processes—and working for "the Chief" was often a stimulating experience.

This experimental work was interrupted by the First World War, during which Bogaerde served with the Army in France and Italy. It was restarted—again under the direct inspiration of Northcliffe—with fresh enthusiasm in 1919.

Then suddenly, in March 1922, Northcliffe, in an early morning telephone call, demanded that a page of half-tone news photographs, complete with captions, be brought to him at Carlton Gardens by midday. Bogaerde achieved the seemingly impossible by collecting staff from their scattered homes in taxis. When he duly handed the page of pictures to Northcliffe at his house the Chief approved it, saying: "It will do, and it is to go into the paper tonight for tomorrow—and from then on a page of pictures every day!"

It was, as Bogaerde used to recall, a staggering order, even by Northcliffe's impetuous standards. Indeed, the Chief himself rang up on the third morning to ask: "Can you keep it up six days a week? It wants some doing, you know." Bogaerde, now installed as art editor, started his department with one photographer and one photographic printer; processing was done in one of the smallest rooms in Printing House Square; and the dark room was in what had been the first John Walter's stables.

The art department rapidly expanded; one of Bogaerde's earliest successes was the development, in cooperation with technicians whose aid he enlisted, of a plate and lens that would take a clear, well defined photograph inside a theatre by ordinary stage lighting. This, in 1923, was an exciting achievement.

Again, in 1939, the outbreak of war halted the range of experiments in which Bogaerde had taken so keen and fruitful an initiative. But in the postwar years such was the pace of technical development that when Bogaerde retired in 1957 newspaper illustration was being carried out through the transmission of original photographs by wire or radio to the art department, where they were fed straight into an electronic engraving machine.

Bogaerde had lived for some years near the village of Fletching in Sussex where, in his retirement, he found abundant interest in gardening and rural pursuits as well as his lifelong hobby of painting.

He married in 1919 Margaret, daughter of Mr. Forest Niven, and their elder son is the distinguished actor Dirk Bogarde.

November 6, 1972.

Charles E. Bohlen, the distinguished American diplomat, died in Washington on January 1, 1974. He was 69.

No diplomat had a more steadying influence on United States relations with the Soviet Union than he. His memoirs, *Witness to History*, had recently been published.

Patronage and political whim bear so strongly on Washington's top diplomatic appointments that it takes a special ability applied in some special situation to give the career officer much chance of preferment. "Chip" Bohlen's special ability was in Russian affairs, which made him the indispensable man to most of the five Presidents and eight Secretaries of State under whom he served. He was Roosevelt's interpreter at Teheran and Yalta, sometimes the only other American present at the President's secret talks with Stalin, and the notes he made on these crucial Allied war conferences provide much of the diplomatic history of the period.

Bohlen, every inch a professional, was much the "European" American. Holding a Harvard degree in European history, urbane and worldly-wise, he had a zestful quality, an ironic humour, to spice a natural reserve. There was a vigorous athletic poise about him, and he made friends easily. No one did more within the limits of diplomacy to give an underlying continuity to Washington's Russian policies, if the thread was often lost amid wilder flights of political and public reactions. In this, he had the advantage of having gone to Moscow as a young vice-consul in 1934 as soon as the United States extended diplomatic recognition to the Soviet Government. From then on the Russian thread ran almost unbroken through his 40 years in the foreign service. Increasingly, he became the Russian expert to whom the White House and State Department listened: no mere Kremlinologist, he.

Unlike some American diplomats of fact and fiction, he had the language. After Harvard, perhaps it was a trip round the world in a tramp steamer that lured him to the foreign service in 1929. From Prague, his first overseas post, he was transferred to Paris—one of six young officers selected to study Russian pending official recognition of the Soviet regime. On full-time active duty, he took a three-year course at L'École Orientale des Langues Vivantes, spent his summers studying the local background at such places as Riga, and put in a lot of time at Paris cafés trying his accent on White Russian emigrés. He became so fluent that he was to astonish Stalin by explaining in Russian the intricacies of American baseball; after his last tour in Moscow he reckoned that he must have spent 4,000 hours in diplomatic talks with Russian officials.

To be at the elbow of Allied leaders in most of the secret diplomacy of the war and after had a ring of high adventure. Bohlen might not have gone so far, however, without marked attributes of perception and judgment, not to say discretion. He could speak bluntly and was soon known as a good man at a conference. For nearly 25

years he was in and out of Moscow, a milestone as it were of his promotions. After a spell in Washington, he went back in 1937 as second secretary, promoted to Consul, and saw the gathering war clouds of the Ribbentrop-Molotov Pact. In 1940, the Tokyo Embassy called for a Russian expert and he was interned in Japan for six months after Pearl Harbour—an experience shared by Kennan in Berlin. Repatriated, he served at the State Department as acting head of East European affairs and in 1943 was in Moscow again with Cordell Hull for the Three-Power conference of Foreign Ministers. He stayed on at the Embassy as first secretary and in 1944 was recalled to Washington for special assignments.

Herein lay the twist of chance that put Bohlen's star in the ascendant. Accompanying Averell Harriman, then Ambassador in Moscow, to the Cairo conference in 1943, he had formed a friendship with Harry Hopkins, *éminence grise* of the White House, who asked him all sorts of questions and liked his informed, unbiased answers. He so impressed Hopkins that he subsequently persuaded Roosevelt to fill a long-felt want by appointing him White House liaison officer with the State Department.

In this capacity, extended for a time by President Truman, with whom he attended the Potsdam conference, Bohlen was on the inside of history. He was privy to Roosevelt's private talks with Stalin at Teheran, and before Yalta went to London with Hopkins in the hope, it was said, of putting Sir Winston Churchill* in a more amiable mood for concessions that the President was to make there.

Going on to Paris, they found de Gaulle* "neither very responsive nor very conciliatory".

With the onset of the cold war, his experience and judgment were even more valuable. He had certainly seen too much of the Russians to have any easy conviction that they would succumb to trumpet blasts of psychological warfare from Washington.

He was at Dumbarton Oaks and San Francisco for the birth of the United Nations. When hopes of success looked bleakest it was he who gave Harriman the idea of urging the President to send Hopkins to talk directly with Stalin. Although Hopkins by then had retired from government service, all three flew to Moscow and the deadlock was broken.

Bohlen at this period was in all the White House discussions on Russia and interpreted at Truman's meeting with Molotov on the Polish question. He worked closely with Secretary James Byrnes in the Council of Foreign Ministers, notably in preparing the Paris peace conference. It had now become the custom for each delegation to brief the press on the broad course of the sessions— highly selective and misleading though such accounts could be. As the American briefing officer, Bohlen won the esteem and friendship of many correspondents. General Marshall, as Secretary of State, made him his personal adviser on Soviet affairs at about the time he reached the rank of counsellor. He had a hand in exchanges about occupation difficulties in Germany leading to the Berlin blockade; went with Marshall to Moscow in 1947 for the abortive meeting of Foreign Ministers; and was in London next year with General Bedell Smith,* then Moscow Ambassador, for further western discussions on the Berlin situation. A two-year term from 1949 as Minister at the Paris Embassy gave him a change of scene, though not in the France of his youth.

For half his career Bohlen worked in virtual secrecy, known to his friends as a man of boundless energy, and amusing conversationalist keen on golf and cards. He became a *cause célèbre* in March 1953, when Senator Joseph McCarthy and other right-wing Republicans tried to block Senate approval of his nomination by President Eisenhower* as Ambassador in Moscow. They pounced on the chance of making a scapegoat of Roosevelt's right-hand man for the "appeasement" of Yalta. Bohlen was confirmed unanimously in committee after saying that he would not rewrite the history of Yalta to suit anyone's prejudices. The McCarthyites, returning to the charge in full session, called him "part and parcel of the Acheson-Hiss-Truman group in the State Department—the group we promised to repudiate when in power". There were insinuations of damaging information in secret files of the F.B.I. that made him a bad security risk. Delay was inevitable and, with Kennan already recalled, Dulles was not to get a successor to Moscow before Stalin died.

Of greater import at home, Eisenhower was facing his first challenge from McCarthyism within two months of taking office. Some feared that he might withdraw the nomination. But the President, smarting under the affront to his executive authority, fully backed Bohlen.

Within the limits of an Ambassador's influence, Bohlen's cool powers of appraisal were invaluable during his four years in Moscow. In various ways, however fitfully, they marked the beginning of a new era of détente. The need to contain Russian policies from a position of strength was not inconsistent, in his view, with coexistence; he was always one of those who foresaw that the real enemies were Russia and China. He was hardly helped by the Dulles doctrine of "massive retaliation" or by gratuitous ideas about liberating Russia's "captive" satellites that were to have hollow echoes in the Hungarian rising of 1956. No one was better qualified to interpret the process of de-Stalinization. No adviser had a more constructive hand in attempts to mend East-West relations at the Geneva Four-Power summit conference of 1955. He saw the "spirit of Geneva" flicker out at the subsequent meeting of foreign ministers, and within a year was back in the diplomatic storms of Hungary and the Suez crisis. His instructions were to restrain Russian intervention in the Suez affair. Among the exchanges he handled was a proposal by

Marshal Bulganin that the United States join Russia in ending the fighting by force; Eisenhower replied that such action was unthinkable.

Bohlen could only deny in 1957 that he was leaving Moscow against his will, but his transfer as Ambassador in Manila had all the look of exile to those aware of his difficulties with some of Dulles's positions. Delicate negotiations affecting military bases in the Philippines were pending, and the post ranked for a full pension, which he could have taken at the age of 54. Instead, after the death of Dulles in 1959, he was persuaded by Christian Herter,* the new Secretary, to return to the State Department as special assistant for Soviet affairs. He went back in the afterglow of Khrushchev's visit to President Eisenhower, whom he would have accompanied on the return visit to Russia if an American U2 aircraft had not first been caught spying there.

It was not to the France of fond recollection that Bohlen returned as Ambassador in 1962, but to an almost obsessive anti-Americanism in Gaullist policies, suggesting something more implacable than differences of national interest. In the acutely sensitive state of Franco-American relations, President Kennedy preferred to rely on Bohlen's cool professional skills rather than on the more personal diplomacy of General James Gavin, his predecessor. Bohlen's considerable achievement, recognizing the inherent weakness of de Gaulle's Russian hand, was to maintain a pained moderation at the diplomatic level, in face of American anger at French interference in Vietnam and at what looked to many people like a systematic attempt to wreck the Atlantic alliance. After the withdrawal from Nato he had the sorry task of negotiating the liquidation of American bases in France, but insisted that this was not a bilateral issue. Too many Americans were buried on French soil, he said, to talk of a quarrel between France and the United States.

He could only wait and watch as relations progressively deteriorated, and in 1967 was chosen by President Johnson to become Deputy Under-Secretary of State for Political Affairs. There were those who thought that President Nixon might appoint him Secretary of State, a not too fanciful assessment of an eminently professional career.

Charles Eustis Bohlen was born in August 1904, at Clayton, New York, of a banking family related to the German von Bohlens who married into the Krupp empire. Much of his early childhood was spent in South Carolina, and the family moved in 1916 to Massachusetts. He attended St. Paul's Academy before going on to Harvard. He met his wife, Avis Thayer, in the early Moscow days while she was visiting her brother, Charles Thayer, a young service colleague of Bohlen's whose later novels have a Moscow background.

January 3, 1974.

Dr. Pierre Boissier, who was killed in an accident on April 26, 1974 while on a civil defence exercise near Geneva, was one of the outstanding intellectual figures in the international committee of the Red Cross with which he had been associated for more than a quarter of a century. He was 53.

A nephew of Leopold Boissier, a former president of the I.C.R.C., he took a law degree at Geneva University. From 1948 onwards he carried out many missions as a committee delegate. He was involved in critical situations in Cyprus, the Middle East, India and Vietnam. In September 1970 he was one of the I.C.R.C. team that negotiated the release of passengers after the multiple hijacking to Zerka air strip in Jordan. He had been a member of the committee itself since July 1973.

It was, however, as an exponent of the concept of the Red Cross movement and as its historian that he had become best known. He was one of the founders of the Henry Dunant Institute which he had directed since 1966. In this capacity he was responsible for training those young Swiss, usually lawyers, doctors, businessmen and engineers, who volunteer for I.C.R.C. emergency assignments.

He also was particularly concerned with establishing the points of reference that can make the Geneva Convention seem relevant in countries whose circumstances have put humanitarianism at a premium.

April 29, 1974.

Hector Bolitho, who died on September 12, 1974, although in no sense one of the leading literary figures of the day, was a prolific writer who had the gift of choosing interesting subjects for his biographies and the power of writing about them in such a way as to arouse interest. He was one of those writers who win for themselves a limited but faithful public.

Henry Hector Bolitho was born at Auckland, New Zealand, in 1898, the son of Henry and Ethelred Frances Bolitho. As a young man he travelled in the South Sea Islands, and when in 1920 the Prince of Wales visited New Zealand Bolitho went through that country with him and told the story of the tour in his first book, *With the Prince in New Zealand.* Two years later he went to England, and he spent a year wandering in Africa, Australia, Canada, America and Germany. His book, *The Letters of Lady Augusta Stanley,* and *Solemn Boy,* a novel, appeared in 1927 and thereafter he published one or more works in almost every year.

In his *The New Zealanders* (1928), a contribution to the Outward Bound Library, he fulfilled the purpose of its promoters and gave an excellent account of his fellow countrymen. *The Glorious Oyster* (1929) was a pleasant, easily written little book of no great pretensions, and in the same year he published *The Later Letters of Lady*

Augusta Stanley. He collaborated with the then Dean of Windsor (Dr. A. V. Baillie) in *A Victorian Dean* (1930), a memoir of Arthur Stanley, the mid-Victorian Dean of Westminster.

Ever since his travels with the Prince of Wales Bolitho had had a romantic attachment to royalty, and his work at Windsor brought him once more into that aura which he was readily content to breathe for the rest of his life. In 1932 he published his *Albert the Good*, printing in it a number of letters which the Prince Consort had written during his married life to his elder brother, Ernest, and which had not been previously published. In *Alfred Mond: First Lord Melchett* (1933) he had an interesting subject whom he regarded as a great man "by the quality of his mind and inspiration". The next year he published *Beside Galilee: a Diary in Palestine* and followed it up by *The Prince Consort and His Brother* (1934). *Victoria, the Widow and Her Son* (1934) carried the story begun in *Albert the Good* to the end of the great Queen's reign. His exuberant loyalty caused him to depict the relations of his two subjects as more harmonious than most researchers would suggest.

James Lyle MacKay, First Earl of Inchcape (1936) was another careful and interesting biography and a few months after it *Marie Tempest* appeared. Then he reverted to the royal family and in 1937 published the lives of *Edward VIII* and *George VI*, and edited *Further Letters of Queen Victoria* (1938). Just before the war he wrote *Romania Under King Carol* (1939) and, having made a lecture tour of the United States, published *America Expects* in 1940. Two years later Bolitho's *War in the Strand* appeared.

During the war he served with the rank of squadron leader in the R.A.F.V.R. and edited the *R.A.F. Journal*, and he also collaborated with Sir Terence Rattigan in a play *Greyfarm*, which was produced in New York. After it he took advantage of his experience in the R.A.F. to write the history of Coastal Command in *Task for Coastal Command*. He then devoted himself exclusively to the affairs of the royal family and produced in quick succession *The Romance of Windsor Castle, The Reign of Queen Victoria, A Century of British Monarchy* and *Their Majesties.*

He published *Jinnah, Creator of Pakistan*, in 1954, and in 1962 a volume of reminiscences, *My Restless Years.*

September 21, 1974.

Dr. Edith Bone, who at the age of 68 wrote *Seven Years Solitary*, an account of her imprisonment by the A.V.O., the Hungarian Secret Police, died on February 14, 1975 aged 86. It was one of the most heroic, and witty, records of human endurance in modern times.

Born in Budapest in 1889, the daughter of a well-to-do Hungarian family, she learnt English from an English governess, and qualified as a doctor, studying in Germany and in France. A visit to Russia with a Red Cross delegation in 1918 to help in the repatriation of Hungarian soldiers added Russian to the four languages she already spoke.

In Russia she joined the Communist Party, and in 1932 she went to England and became a British subject. She remained a maverick of the Communist Party, speaking her mind, constitutionally unable to toe the party line, or indeed any line, and making her living by translating and interpreting.

In 1949 she visited Hungary and was taken, on her way to the airport, by the secret police and imprisoned in the worst possible conditions, sometimes in total darkness, without paper, pencil, books or as much as a comb for her hair, in a vain attempt to make her confess to being "an English spy." A staged trial condemned Dr. Bone, then aged 60, to 15 years' imprisonment.

While her British friends kept up a constant flow of inquiries, which were turned aside by the Hungarian authorities, Dr. Bone, imprisoned by those she thought her friends, disciplined herself to ignore thoughts of self-pity or hopes for the future, and with the help of an iron will, a strong constitution, an unusual sense of humour, and a well stocked mind, fought back at the authorities in every way she could.

Kept in solitary confinement for seven years, she was released by the Hungarian Revolution in 1956, and, still wearing prison clothes, reached the British Legation and left for Austria on the last available transport before the frontier was closed. Her book was a remarkable witness to the power of the human spirit in adversity, and is part of the literature which deals with man's unconquerable mind.

February 17, 1975

Vice-Admiral Sir Stuart S. Bonham-Carter, K.C.B., C.V.O., D.S.O., who died on September 5, 1972 at the age of 83, served with distinction in the two world wars. He commanded a blockship at Zeebrugge in 1918 and, from 1940 to 1945, had varied service in commands from Halifax to Malta, particularly in the protection of convoys to North Russia.

He was the youngest rear-admiral in the Service in 1939, and might have risen to the highest commands but for a spell of ill-health in 1943. Of jovial appearance and mien, he was always good company and, in spite of a slight stammer, an excellent raconteur. He was universally popular with officers and men, and had all the qualities for a well-loved leader.

Stuart Sumner Bonham-Carter was born on July 9, 1889, the younger son of Lothian George Bonham-Carter, of Buriton House, Petersfield. He entered the Britannia as a naval cadet in 1904. Early in 1918 he was among the volunteers selected to prepare for the raid on Zeebrugge on St. George's Day. In this operation he commanded the blockship Intrepid, which he sank in the canal, making good his escape with another officer and four petty officers in a Carley raft until picked up later by a motor launch. The award to him of the D.S.O. stated that he "handled his ship with great skill and coolness in a position of considerable danger under heavy fire. Great credit is due to him for his success in sinking the Intrepid in the Bruges Canal."

When the Second World War began in 1939, he was Naval Secretary to the First Lord, a post he had taken up in May. But an office desk was distasteful to him, and he was not sorry when a brief illness compelled him to relinquish it. He was soon afloat, however, hoisting his flag in January 1940 in the Third Battle Squadron. This force was based at Halifax, where he assumed charge of the British ships in Canadian waters, and quickly established most cordial relations with the American Navy near his station.

Among his ships in the autumn of 1940 were the 50 old American destroyers transferred for service in the Royal Navy, which were commissioned in Canada and sent to their various war stations. After relinquishing command at Halifax, Rear-Admiral Bonham-Carter was appointed to command the 18th Cruiser Squadron in the Home Fleet. With this force he saw much arduous service in 1942 in the protection of Russian convoys, during which his flagship was twice torpedoed. By December 1942 he had become a vice-admiral, and was appointed Flag Officer-in-Charge at Malta. This command he had to relinquish owing to ill health at the end of May 1943 and on December 31 of that year he was placed on the retired list, but in 1944 and 1945 he was back in service as a commodore of convoys.

He married in 1933 Eve, widow of Brigadier C. R. Lloyd, Indian Army, and daughter of Donald Shaw, and had one daughter.

September 7, 1972.

Georges Bonnet, the former French Foreign Minister, who was one of the main architects of the 1938 Munich agreements, died in Paris on June 18, 1973. He was 83.

As foreign minister in the years immediately preceding the Second World War, he worked for an understanding with Nazi Germany and became a leading advocate of the appeasement policy, which won him popularity at the time but subsequent sharp criticism. The Munich agreements, which gave parts of Czechoslovakia to Germany, were also signed by Britain and Italy.

Bonnet reached the most important point of his career when he became Foreign Minister in the Radical-Socialist government headed by Edouard Daladier* in April 1938. In that same year, he had been Président du Conseil himself but for a brief moment. He was to remain Foreign Minister until the outbreak of war in September 1939, when Daladier dropped him because of his record as an appeaser.

The thirties showed British and French statesmanship at a very low ebb, the two democracies standing by hesitant while Hitler scored victories which undermined their security. If it was the British under Neville Chamberlain who took the lead in the appeasement policy, which culminated in the Munich agreements of September 1938, it must be said that strong political forces in Britain always opposed appeasement and public opinion frequently reacted against it. Also, Chamberlain's appeasement policy ended after German entry into Prague.

In France, open dislike of appeasement was shown by the communists—until the Russo-German Pact in 1939—by about half of the Socialist Party and by a few isolated figures such as Mandel, and, on the right, de Kerilliis and Marin. The general mood of the country was dread of war, accompanied by a gloomy determination to defend French soil if need be. There was a determination among most politicians, except those plotting to link France with the dictators, to stick to the British alliance at all costs. Bonnet was not one of the totally identifiable pro-Germans, but one of his close friends, Elie du Bois, a strong anti-fascist, records that long before Bonnet became Foreign Minister, he was known for his advocacy of an understanding with Germany. "How could you think this possible with a maniac such as Hitler when Briand, under far more favourable circumstances, failed with Streseman?" du Bois asked. The reply was that the inadequacy of the French army and the weakness of the economy made reconciliation essential.

Naturally, Bonnet approved of Munich and of Chamberlain's efforts to win over Mussolini. When he invited Ribbentrop to Paris in December 1938 to sign the Franco-German declaration of good will, Bonnet was, in the eyes of many Frenchmen, only doing the counterpart of Chamberlain in the private agreements after Munich which Daladier had not been asked to sign. When, in September 1939, Mussolini proposed a second Munich, Bonnet's formal note stating that France could not negotiate while German troops were in Poland was as stiff as that of Lord Halifax. In the official French documents of the period Bonnet is "covered" —but he had the opportunity of editing these documents.

Without going too deeply into this murky period, it is evident from German and Polish sources that Bonnet had given Ribbentrop the idea that, after Munich, issues between Germany and Czecholovakia would not be raised by France. The Polish ambassador had told his Government that, after the Ribbentrop visit to Paris, he was convinced that the French Government would work towards getting rid of her obligations to Poland. Bonnet's real attitude to the Mussolini proposals for saving peace in September 1939 has also been questioned. During Sumner Welles's visit to Paris in the spring of 1940, Bonnet, no longer a minister, informed him that a strong peace party existed in France. The most convincing evidence of Bonnet's views and behind-the-scenes actions when Foreign Minister, was the approval of him by Right-wing pro-Fascist or pacifist groups, of which the notorious *Je Suis Partout* was one.

Born at Bassillac in the Dordogne in 1889, of a family connected with important Radical-Socialists such as Jules Ferry and Waldeck Rochet, it was not surprising that Georges Étienne Bonnet abandoned a promising career in the civil service and in 1924 entered politics and, a year later, was selected by Painlevé as Minister for the Budget. His administrative ability and tireless energy subsequently ensured him a place in no less than 12 governments. The Popular Front government of Leon Blum mistrusted him but sent him to Washington as ambassador. He was recalled to become Minister of Finance for the fourth time.

He was a man of outstanding gifts, although even his friends admitted that his capacity for hard work was accompanied by deviousness of character. He had misty blue eyes and a mumbling, hesitant speech, though he always knew his subject well. A friend wrote of him: "When he walks, he does not go straight but moves sideways in such a manner that all one sees of him is a long powerful nose that seems to scent every danger and every prey."

Having been a member of the Grand Council during the Vichy regime, he suffered a period of eclipse after the war. He wrote two volumes of political memoirs in which he tried, with considerable ability, to exculpate himself. As the Radicals and the moderate Right recovered some of their former influence during the IVth Republic, Bonnet returned to the Palais Bourbon, being elected Deputy for the Dordogne in 1956-58, and re-elected in 1958. During the 1914 war he won the Croix de Guerre and among other decorations he held was the Grand Cross of St. Michael and St. George.

June 19, 1973.

Joachim Bonnier, the bearded Swedish racing driver, was killed at Le Mans on June 11, 1972. He was 42.

Bonnier was far more than a talented and experienced racing driver. He was also a multi-lingual ambassador and spokesman for the sport throughout the world.

As a Grand Prix driver between the years 1957 and 1969, Bonnier was a regular campaigner in such famous marques as Maserati, B.R.M., Porsche, Cooper, Lotus, Honda and McLaren cars, and took part in more than one hundred events qualifying for the drivers' world championship. He scored numerous places but his only world championship victory was in the 1959 Dutch Grand Prix, when he gave B.R.M. its first major victory.

Although Bonnier dropped out of formula one racing during the 1969 season, he remained active in motor sport as both a driver and team entrant in international sports car events for the manufacturers' championship, first as Scuderia Filipinetti and then as Écurie Bonnier. One of his last victories was in the Jarama Spain two hours race in November 1971.

Bonnier was born in Stockholm on January 31, 1930, the second son of an eminent professor of genetics. After completing his studies in Sweden, Paris and Oxford Bonnier served his apprenticeship in his uncle's powerful newspaper and magazine publishing group, the Bonniers Aktiebolag. He made his competition début in 1948 in a Scandinavian dirt road rally and after serving for three years in the Swedish navy as a lieutenant (destroyers) he turned to ice racing in 1953, a favourite form of Scandinavian motor sport.

From 1955 onwards Bonnier moved through the ranks of saloon and sports car racing to formula one Grand Prix racing and there are few circuits round the world where the tall elegant Swede, who looked like a Viking chieftain, did not race with considerable success. In relating his crowded career as a racing driver it is only possible to highlight his victories in such diversified events as the Stockholm Grand Prix 1955, the Avus ring and the Rome Grand Prix 1956, the Finnish Grand Prix 1957, the Naples Grand Prix and the Freiberg Hill climb 1958, the Targa Florio 1960 and 1963, the formula two German Grand Prix and the Modena Grand Prix 1960 and the Nürburgring 1,000 kilometres in 1966.

In 1961 Bonnier became the first vice-president of the newly-founded Grand Prix Drivers' Association (G.P.D.A.) and since then had campaigned unceasingly to make motor racing circuits, cars and emergency equipment more efficient to help save drivers' and spectators' lives.

Bonnier, who lived in a Swiss mansion, was married in 1960.

June 12, 1972.

Aleck Bourne, M.A., M.B., F.R.C.S., F.R.C.O.G., the eminent gynaecologist, who died on December 27, 1974 at the age of 88, was before he retired consulting gynaecologist at St. Mary's Hospital and to the Samaritan Hospital for Women and consulting obstetric surgeon to Queen Charlotte's Hospital.

Aleck William Bourne was born on June 4, 1886, the only son of the Rev. W. C. Bourne, of Barnet. He was educated at Rydal School and at Downing College, Cambridge, where he obtained a first class Natural Science Tripos in 1908.

Entering St. Mary's Hospital with a senior University scholarship he qualified as M.R.C.S., L.R.C.P. (1910), and from this time until the outbreak of the 1914-18 War held residential and other appointments at St. Mary's, Queen Charlotte's and the Samaritan. In 1911 he obtained the M.B., B.Ch., Cambridge, and the F.R.C.S. England.

He served as a surgical specialist in Egypt and France during 1914-17, being attached successively to the 17th and 2nd General Hospitals, and after the war he rapidly acquired a large consulting practice in obstetrics and gynaecology.

During his time at Queen Charlotte's, in association with Professor J. H. Burn, he published important original work on uterine action in labour and in response to various drugs. He examined in his specialty for the universities of Cambridge and Birmingham and for the conjoint diplomas of the Royal College of Physicians and the Royal College of Surgeons.

In 1925 he was elected a foundation Fellow of the Royal College of Obstetricians and Gynaecologists and was curator of its museum, which he founded in 1938 and built up during the following years. He was president of the Obstetrical and Gynaecological Section of the Royal Society of Medicine in 1938-39.

Bourne was the author of many valuable contributions to the literature of his specialty, his best known writings being *A Synopsis of Midwifery and Gynaecology* and *Recent Advances in Obstetrics and Gynaecology*, jointly with Leslie Williams, and, jointly with Sir Eardley Holland, was editor of *British Obstetric and Gynaecological Practice*.

In 1938 Bourne came into the public eye when he operated to terminate the pregnancy of a girl aged 14 years and nine months, who had been criminally assaulted and raped by some soldiers in a London barracks. The operation was done in St. Mary's Hospital and Bourne himself drew the attention of the police to his intervention.

He was tried at the Central Criminal Court in July 1938 on a charge of procuring abortion and was acquitted. His action was described by the *Lancet* as "an example of disinterested conduct in consonance with the highest traditions of the profession."

Since the Act of 1861 the only recognized justification for the operation was probable danger to the life of the pregnant woman should the pregnancy be allowed to continue.

But in his summing-up of Rex v Bourne (1939, 1 K.B., 687) *Macnaghten, J.* said: "If the doctor is of opinion, on reasonable grounds and with adequate knowledge, that the probable consequences of the pregnancy will be to make the woman a physical or mental wreck, the jury are quite entitled to take the view that the doctor, who, under these circumstances and in that honest belief, operates, is operating for the purpose of preserving the life of the mother."

Bourne was a whole-hearted advocate of state medicine and expounded his views in a Penguin special, *Health of the Future*

(1942), which attracted much attention. He was a man of wide interests which included literature and his garden. His chief sport was racing in small yachts.

He was a member of several yacht clubs and in 1933 won the Royal Corinthian Yacht Club's cup for the best cruiser of the year without a paid hand. He married in 1912 Bessie, eldest daughter of Mr. G. W. Hayward, of Barnet. There were three daughters of the marriage.

December 30, 1974.

Elizabeth Bowen, C.B.E., who died on February 22, 1973, at the age of 73, was a novelist and short story writer of subtlety and distinction.

Elizabeth Dorothea Cole Bowen, novelist. was born in Dublin on June 7, 1899 of an Anglo-Irish family that had lived at Bowen's Court, County Cork, since the time of Cromwell. Taken to England when she was seven, she went to school at Downe House, Kent. During the First World War she worked in a hospital for shell-shock cases in Dublin and after the war lived for some years in Italy. Her first book, *Encounters*, a collection of short stories, appeared in 1923, her first novel, *The Hotel*, in 1927. A highly conscious artist, as a novelist Elizabeth Bowen worked in that tradition of English social comedy which takes in both Jane Austen and Henry James. This to say she wrote at once as moralist and psychologist, though the social comedy, in the Austen sense, was stronger in the earlier novels, such as *The Hotel*, which was set in Ireland among the Anglo-Irish gentry, than in the later. Her special talent first clearly emerged in *To the North* (1932), which was followed by *The House in Paris* (1935) and *The Death of the Heart* (1938), which all in their different ways explore the Jamesean theme of the confrontation of innocence and experience.

By general consent *The Death of the Heart* is her finest novel; in it, all her gifts came together. Prominent among them was her uncanny ability to match scene and weather with her characters' moods, as is instanced in the opening episode in which Anna Quayne and St. Quentin are shown on a bridge over the frozen lake in Regent's Park. A description of great vividness of a winter scene in London, by indirection it renders the frozen heart of Anna as she is faced with the unwelcome though accepted intrusion into her narrow family circle of her sister-in-law Portia, a girl on the threshold of adolescence. The novel brings out, too, the largeness of Elizabeth Bowen's charity; nobody in the tragi-comedy is wicked, and the tragi-comedy is shown as from good intentions divorced from natural affections.

Her acute sensibility to place and to the atmosphere of place at a particular of time stood Elizabeth Bowen in good stead when she wrote her next novel *The Heat of the*

Day (1949). During the Second World War she worked in the Ministry of Information and at night was an air-raid warden, one of what she calls in the novel "the intimate and loose little society of the garrison." *The Heat of the Day* is not entirely successful but, all the same, is perhaps the most detailed evocation we have of what it was like to live in London during the war years. The atmosphere of the place and the time, of the beleaguered city, is rendered in almost mediumistic rapport. Wartime London is the element in which the characters have their being. This sense of the unique quality of those years is caught even more intensely in her short stories of the period collected in *The Demon Lover* (1945).

Her later novels, *A World of Love* (1955), in which she returned to Ireland for the scene of her action, *The Little Girls* (1964), and *Eva Trout* (1969) were less enthusiastically received by reviewers and public; but they continued to demonstrate a powerful and subtle imagination striving, sometimes indeed straining, to pin down the novelist's vision in the exact words necessary to render it.

In 1942 she published *Bowen's Court*, a history of the family house that she inherited in 1931 and is now demolished. *The Shelbourne* (1951) was a history of the famous Dublin hotel. *A Time in Rome* (1960) was a notable travel book. She gathered together the best of her literary journalism in *Collected Impressions* (1950), which contains her "Notes on Writing a Novel," a work which seems certain to survive as a classic statement of the novelist's art.

Very tall, and gauntly handsome, she was a woman of great personal distinction; and she did not allow the stammer with which she was inflicted to prevent her from becoming a highly successful broadcaster in the B.B.C. Third Programme and a lecturer in great demand in American universities.

February 23, 1973.

Sir Maurice Bowra, C.H., Warden of Wadham College, Oxford, from 1938 to 1970 died on July 4, 1971. He was 73.

By his death Oxford has lost the most remarkable figure of his time in the university. A passionate interest in human beings, for themselves, for what they did and particularly for what they wrote, carried him from ancient China through classical antiquity, the Renaissance, Mont Parnasse and Russia to modernist poetry; and such was his literary sensitivity, his enthusiasm and above all his genius for communication, that generations of undergraduates and young dons have felt that they owed to him their first real grasp of the infinite variety of civilization; so deep too was the impression he made that even the most critical have usually absorbed more than they realize of his outlook and of his style.

These were intensely original and catching,

and, remarkably, they made their mark not on the second-rate but men of independent genius. His influence can be detected on writers of such diverse gifts as Cyril Connolly, Rex Warner, C. Day-Lewis, John Betjeman, Osbert Lancaster, Isaiah Berlin and A. J. Ayer, and there are others, such as Evelyn Waugh* and Henry Green, who have owed something to his inspiration. But while this width of learning and sagacity are evident in his voluminous writings, his style on paper, though eminently orderly and lucid, tends to lack vitality and is quite unlike the scintillating, shimmering and sometimes thunderous wit of his conversation. Posterity will have no measure of his true greatness.

Nor will those who met him only in his later years, when his short round figure had lost some of the bounce and energy that made it such an exciting part of the Oxford scene and when increasing deafness began to cut him off from those immediate contacts with strangers, especially the young, at which he had excelled.

He was born on April 8, 1898 at Kinkiang on the Yangtse. His father, Cecil Arthur Vernon Bowra, was a Commissioner in the Chinese Customs Service, as his father had been before him. Vivid experience in the Far East in infancy and boyhood may have served to kindle his imagination. In 1903 he went to England but made further visits to the East in 1909 and again in 1916: on the way home that year he was held up in a Petrograd starving and on the edge of revolution; there he began his study of Russian.

He was at school at Cheltenham and was elected to a classical scholarship at New College in 1915. From August 1917 to the end of the First World War he served in France with the Royal Field Artillery; an experience which left him with no great love of the military and a profound and lasting loathing for war and the cruelty and stupidity that goes with it.

On going up to New College he at once became the acknowledged leader of a circle of exceptionally brilliant undergraduates among whom only one, J. B. S. Haldane,* could rival his range and none his wit and fluency. He was already enormously well read: Anatole France, whose wide range may have served as a model, was a favourite with him just then. And already in his freshman days he was as fully armed as he ever became with his gifts of swift epigram and verbal ingenuity. Of his tutors Alec Smith (later Warden Smith) won him by his humanity and was in many ways his model as tutor, Dean and Warden; while Gilbert Murray's sense of style and attitude to scholarship, so Bowra himself claimed, shaped his whole academic life.

After obtaining firsts in Classical Moderations and Greats, he became in 1922 classical tutor and Fellow of Wadham. At various times he was Dean and Senior Tutor, and in 1930-31 was appointed Proctor. His boundless hospitality made Wadham in those days the most familiar of all Oxford colleges to many Londoners: a hospitality memorable above all for his special brand of conversation. In developing a theme, whether about men or books, he would push on to extremes of exaggeration and, sometimes, fantasy, which might appear hilariously funny at the time only for the verbal and imaginative dexterity, but which depended for their real effect on an originality and an element of truth that gave an edge to all he said and which only a very few great "wits" command.

But the social side of his life, while important to him and to the many who shared it, absorbed only a tiny part of his energies. He was intensely proud of his college and devoted himself to its affairs, not only in the business of administration but by entering into easy friendly relations with undergraduates, and by working hard to raise its intellectual standards.

At the early age of 40 he was elected Warden (in 1938). During the war little could be done for the college but he faced the problem of returning ex-servicemen in 1945 with characteristic foresight and radicalism. He filled what had been a small college to bursting-point, some said beyond it, and then moved on at once to deal with the consequences; to build up the teaching strength, to increase accommodation for undergraduates, to answer the new demands of the sciences, above all to turn quantity into quality. An additional fellow, an extra room, another first, nothing pleased him more, and the improvement he achieved in the intellectual standing of the college and in its buildings, which during his time as warden were renovated and much extended, is the memorial he would most have valued.

In all this he was supported by devoted colleagues, but it was Bowra who gave the impetus and the optimism that made it possible to succeed. More than that, his own experience during and after the First World War, together with his natural humanity, helped him to understand the problems of his generation and to solve them as humanely as Alec Smith had solved those of Bowra's own undergraduate days. Clever and less-clever alike had their faith in civilized life restored by his sympathy, generosity, excitement, wit and, when needed, anger. His response to the special problems of later generations of undergraduates was less spontaneous but on any matter of principle unerringly right.

When, for example, in 1968 some undergraduates wanted to have their objections to the proctorial system heard by the Privy Council, Bowra was the first to give them public support, and in answer to the objection "Why should they?" answered simply "Because they are entitled to and because they want to." More and more demands were made on his time, by the university, by other universities and institutions in the United Kingdom and abroad (he played a conspicuous part in the foundation of the British Institute in Teheran in 1962), by friends and admirers, academic and literary, throughout the world, and to all these he gave lavishly; but none of them ever took precedence over the claims of Wadham's humblest undergraduate or youngest don.

In 1951-54 Bowra was vice-chancellor. For many years both before and after this he did full service on the various important bodies of the university—the Hebdomadal Council, Chest, General Board and Clarendon Press.

He was an efficient administrator; his power of swift thought enabled him to polish off business quickly. In the chair he was staccato and relevant; he brought in his fun and jokes in moderation and he made everyone feel lively. As vice-chancellor he prided himself in taking special trouble with new appointments, and, whatever the extra demands on him, he greatly raised the standard of hospitality and consideration shown to honorands and other distinguished visitors to Oxford, to many of whom he became, if he was not already, the university's most distinguished name. More important, in the university, as already in his college, he was trying to face, not always successfully, those problems of growth, finance, administration and admissions which were not generally recognized for a decade or more.

Bowra's extraordinary powers of concentration were such that he never let this other work interfere with his studies or the copious flow of his writings. Most of these are concerned with literary criticism. Though not a great critic he had two important assets: an unerring eye for the best in literature, and an ability to communicate his enthusiasm for it. He reached a wide circle of readers, and there can be few of them whose horizons have not been in some way enlarged by his books.

In his classical writings, as in his lecturing, his aim, like that of his master, Murray, was to keep the Greeks alive; and though his style was not such a delicate instrument as Murray's, his grasp of the Greek mind was more direct and realistic, and found a ready response in the audience for which he wrote, namely the generations which came after the First World War. His *Ancient Greek Literature* (1933), an excellent short survey, *The Oxford Book of Greek Verse in Translation* (1937), of which he was the editor, and which contained many of his own verse translations, *The Greek Experience* (1957), perhaps the best book of its kind yet written, *Landmarks in Greek Literature* (1966), aimed at diffusing knowledge and understanding of the Greek world to a wide public; much earlier he collaborated with H. T. Wade-Gery, a friend and colleague whose stimulating influence can be seen in some of his best work, in a translation of *Pindar's Pythian Odes* (1928), which deserves to be more widely known.

His more specialized works of scholarship are somewhat unequal. *Early Greek Elegists* (1938) is a slight though useful introduction; *Sophoclean Tragedy* (1944) lacks his customary insight; and his edition of the text of *Pindar* (1935) has now been superseded. But *Tradition and Design in the Iliad* (1930) and *Greek Lyric Poetry*, in its revised form

(1961: first edition 1936), are lasting contributions to classical studies; and above all his book on *Pindar* (1964) is a masterly performance, rivalling the standard work of Wilamowitz. Besides these, Bowra wrote many valuable articles, the most important up to 1953 being collected in *Problems in Greek Poetry;* and it is in this smaller compass that he did some of his best work.

He was always at pains to see literature in the context of the society in which it was written; his main concern was with ideas rather than words. He despised perfectionism and pedantry alike as forms of laziness, wasting on minutiae time better spent on grappling with larger tasks; and he never paraded his knowledge of secondary literature. This sometimes led to errors and omissions in his work; but it also led critics to underestimate his scholarship, learning and originality.

His specifically classical interests, however, accounted for only a part of his output. In *The Heritage of Symbolism* (1943) he showed his skill in the interpretation of modern poets. In a similar field was the *Creative Experiment* (1949), on which Pasternak commented that it was the best interpretation of him that he had seen. (In 1943 he had already published his *Book of Russian Verse* including more of his own verse translations.) On the earlier masters he wrote *From Virgil to Milton* (1945), *The Romantic Imagination* (1949) and *Heroic Poetry* (1952); the last was heroic in another sense—its range was probably beyond the capacity of any other living scholar. In 1955 he published *Inspiration and Poetry* and in 1962 a remarkable work, *Primitive Song,* a study of oral poetry surviving in Africa and elsewhere.

But here too some of his best work was on a smaller scale: In *General and Particular* (1964) is a selection of these shorter essays which includes some of the outstanding lectures which he gave in Oxford and elsewhere, *The Meaning of a Heroic Age* (Earl Grey Lecture, Newcastle 1957) and *Poetry and the First World War* (Taylorian Lecture, Oxford 1963). In 1966 he published his *Memories,* a deliberately selective account of his own life up to 1938 and of the people he knew. In this book he appropriately shed the stiffness of his more formal writing and conveyed something of the tones which made his conversation memorable: and though it is not uniformly successful—least, perhaps, in its set-piece character-sketches—it reveals its author's observation and humanity as well as his wit. *On Greek Margins* was published in 1970.

Bowra became an Honorary Fellow of Wadham College and an Honorary D.C.L. of Oxford University in 1970. *Periclean Athens,* his last book, was published in 1971.

His services to scholarship were widely recognized. He was awarded the Conington prize at Oxford in 1930, was made a Doctor of Letters in 1937 and from 1946 to 1951 was Professor of Poetry. He became a member of the British Academy in 1938 and from 1958 to 1962 was its President. He was awarded honorary doctorates by Trinity College, Dublin, and by the Universities of Wales, Hull, St. Andrews, Paris, Aix-en-Provence, Columbia and Harvard where he also gave the Charles Eliot Norton lectures on poetry in 1948-49. He was knighted in 1951, was a Commandeur de la Légion d'Honneur and a Knight-Commander of the Greek Royal Order of the Phoenix.

To the outsider he could appear a formidable and sometimes unsympathetic figure, disturbingly frank and non-conformist to the old (he was a free-thinker, an epicure and an uninhibited advocate of pleasure), determinedly old-fashioned to the young. He was also extremely sensitive to criticism, especially when it came from someone on whose loyalty he relied, and in his younger days there were periods of estrangement even from his best friends.

But at his most wrathful—and no one then could rival his verve and wit in denigration—he was careful to say nothing that would really damage a friend, and those who knew him well were absolutely confident of his generosity and rock-like loyalty. They also knew that the old were usually shocked because they themselves were not flexible enough to keep up with him and that the young were puzzled because they could not see through the manners of a past generation to the real Bowra.

He was a young radical who stayed both young and radical to the end; that he always tended to the Left in politics, the non-professional Left, was only one accidental result of this extraordinary ability to keep abreast of the modern world. He saw through new pomposities, pretensions and hypocrisies as he had seen through the old, and was devastating in his invective against them, but his mind was always open to new ideas of value and they could find no more energetic or eloquent advocate. Above all he was a passionate apostle of toleration, and hated cruelty and injustice in any form; nor did he stop at words in helping their victims at home and abroad.

Older friends of Bowra could see in him an emblem of the survival of civilized values; younger friends (and difference of age was never any bar to real friendship) learnt from him to distinguish what was really valuable from what was merely prejudice. It was not his erudition, it was not even his wit, that was the secret of his influence. It was his deep-rooted and passionate belief in certain attributes of civilization, in the comfortable life, in the value of art and of the pursuit of truth, and, most of all, in human freedom. On these central issues he was adamantine.

Some have seen in Bowra a man of action *manqué,* whose energies and talents called for a wider sphere than the academic world to which he confined them. But for all his strength and shrewdness, he lacked the qualities of ruthlessness and calculation which go with the pursuit and exercise of power; and this lack made him greater as a human being than many men of his time who possessed them.

July 5, 1971.

Lord Boyd Orr, C.H., F.R.S., internationally known for his work on nutrition, and first Director-General of the United Nations Food and Agriculture Organization, died at his home near Brechin, Angus, on June 25, 1971 in his 91st year.

The man who was a doctor for a month became a pioneer in the movement to relate health and agriculture, and to raise the food standards of the world. He was made a Companion of Honour in 1968 for services to human and animal nutrition.

John Boyd Orr was born at Kilmaurs, Ayrshire, on September 23, 1880. He was the son of R. C. Orr and Annie Boyd. His father was a "bonnet laird," a small property owner and quarrymaster. His mother was a woman of strong intellect and determination, qualities which were as pronounced in her son as the "Boyd" which he put in his title. His native countryside was that of the Covenanters, and the tradition of the conventicle was part of his upbringing by parents stern in the ways of the minority sect of the Free Church.

John was bred for the church (two of his brothers were ordained as ministers) but while studying for his M.A. degree at Glasgow University, on his way to a divinity course, he strayed into the zoology classes where the teaching of Darwinism diverted him from the fundamentalism of his parents' sect. He gave up the idea of becoming a minister and, with his M.A. degree, became a schoolteacher for four years. (The relic of his theological phase was his *History of the Scotch Church Crisis of 1904.*) He returned to Glasgow University to study for his medical degree. Following his graduation in medicine, he gained the Barbour Scholarship and, for his M.D. thesis, the coveted Bellahouston Gold Medal and the invitation of the great surgeon, Sir William McEwen, to become his assistant.

His career as a doctor lasted a month, as a *locum tenens.* He had, as in the case of the ministry, a conscience-crisis. As a medical student "walking the wards" of the Glasgow hospitals, he had been distressed by the diseases of poverty, the malnutrition and rickets of the slum-children, for which the doctors had no physic; and his brief experience of practice confirmed a resolve. He returned to the university to do postgraduate research on metabolic disease and became a D.Sc.

He was offered the post of Director of Animal Nutrition Research at Edinburgh University. His laboratory was a cellar. He had scarcely taken up his new appointment when the First World War broke out and he joined the R.A.M.C. On the battlefields he won the M.C. (with Bar) and the D.S.O.

as regimental medical officer with the Sherwood Foresters, in a comradeship with miners which influenced his subsequent research. He transferred to the Navy in an inter-service inquiry into the physical requirements of servicemen and was at sea in the "Q-ships."

At the end of the war he returned to his £380-a-year post and his cellar-laboratory. From this grew the Rowett Research Institute for Animal Nutrition, the Reid Library, the Duthie Experimental Stock Farm, the Imperial Bureau of Animal Nutrition, and Strathcona House, a "club" for the world's nutritionists. His persuasiveness and his capacity for fund-raising were responsible for all of those.

His later career as a scientist-statesman overshadowed the substantial research record which made him a Fellow of the Royal Society. One of his earliest contributions (with Professor E. P. Cathcart) was *Energy Expenditure of the Infantry Recruit in Training*. Even more significant, in terms of modern agriculture, were the studies of the mineral requirements of animals. One of his colleagues in these inquiries was Walter Elliot (later Minister of Agriculture, Health, etc.,) who gained his D.Sc. at the Rowett Institute. In the 1920s his most impressive field work was the investigation of the pastures of East Africa. It was primarily concerned with mineral deficiencies and soil-exhaustion but, typically, he added a clinical unit to investigate the effects on the human population, the Masai and Kikuyu. This report, apart from pioneering the regeneration of pastures, is a classic in social-medicine.

By reference, his professional concern was with farm animals. He protested that he had no difficulty in persuading farmers of the virtues of nutrition—because they could prove in terms of their stocks that it paid dividends—but that he could not convince anyone that the same was true of children. Stretching his research mandate during the economic crisis, he carried out a feeding experiment among 1,500 children of unemployed Lanarkshire miners. He fed them, at school, with the skimmed milk which was being thrown away by the farmers who could not sell it. The results were convincing, and school milk and school meals have consistently reaffirmed them since, but no one listened then.

As a critic of the marketing boards (because they were "organizing shortage") he was allowed to undertake, with Government financial help, the survey which became *Food, Health and Income*. Short memories have forgotten the political impact of that scientific measurement of poverty and hunger. It was embarrassing to the Government. Economists were engaged to reexamine his figures, with results which were even more embarrassing because he had shrewdly modified them so that when they were "corrected" they came out worse. He was made a Knight Bachelor, and appointed to the food commissions.

Food, Health and Income had world-wide repercussions. Similar inquiries were carried out in 19 countries, including the United States, and the analysis of *Hunger in the midst of Plenty* led to the setting up of the Mixed Commission of the League of Nations, under Lord Astor.* This "marriage of health and agriculture," as Stanley (later Viscount) Bruce* called it, was the forerunner of the U.N. Food and Agriculture Organization. The news reached Sir John Boyd Orr in Aberdeen as a telegram from Frank MacDougall, economic adviser to the Australian delegation. It read: "Be of good cheer, Brother Orr, for we have this day lighted in Geneva such a candle as, by God's grace, shall never be put out."

The report, and the popular discussions and "committees against malnutrition" which were set up, created a public awareness which simplified the introduction of rationing at the outbreak of war. Sir John Boyd Orr, combining Directorship of the Rowett with the Professorship of Agriculture at Aberdeen, served on the Ministry of Food commissions and made an eventful journey to the United States. He was nominally delivering lectures, but his self-appointed mission was to see President Roosevelt and Vice-President Henry Wallace.* He was successful and was, in part, responsible for what became the Hot Springs Conference which, however, he did not attend because officialdom still regarded him as unorthodox. Nevertheless he made a dramatic intervention as a "ghost" in the film *World of Plenty*, which was shown to a full meeting of delegates.

When the Quebec Conference was called in 1945 to give effect to the Hot Springs intentions and bring the Food and Agriculture Organization into being, Sir John Boyd Orr was in the House of Commons as Independent M.P. for Scottish Universities. He was not included as a delegate but was invited by the Labour Government to go as a technical adviser. He made only one speech. When the conference began with discussions on the appointment of a director-general he had already packed his bags and had climbed to the Heights of Abraham for a farewell view. Like the Elders of the Congregation, a deputation followed him and led him back to the Chateau Frontenac. By unanimous vote, he was acclaimed the first Director-General of F.A.O. In almost his first speech, he reproached the statesmen for the organization they had created: "The hungry are crying out for bread and we are going to give them pamphlets."

Before he had properly established his headquarters in Washington, he appalled the official world by summoning in May 1946 a conference of producer and consumer nations to deal with the famine which threatened 75m. people. Contrary to all expectations, that conference agreed on self-denying ordinances to share supplies with the more desperate countries. Britain accepted the bread-rationing which it had not had even in the worst days of the war. Other countries did similar things. The famine of 1946 did not happen. The conference called for a scheme which would ensure that food would be available at prices fair to the farmers and consumers. It might have been the ventriloquial voice of Boyd Orr giving himself instructions. He produced a scheme for a World Food Board and fought for it with untypical heat. After one impassioned intervention at Geneva, an awe-struck delegate declared "He had the fire of God in his belly and he belched."

The subsequent attrition of his scheme discouraged him. Governments were nervous of this Old Testament prophet in modern idiom and hedged him round with officialdom; he resigned. Attlee made him a peer as Baron Boyd Orr of Brechin Mearns (1949). His own university honoured him. He found himself simultaneously elected Lord Rector by vote of the students and Chancellor by vote of the graduates. He became Chancellor. He was awarded the Nobel Peace Prize in 1949, and disbursed the prize among the organizations working for peace. When reminded that he would want the money to travel, he said he could always sell a cow. Metaphorically, he sold a lot of cows. He visited the U.S.S.R., China, India, the Middle East and Latin America.

In 1915 he married Elizabeth Pearson Callum, of West Kilbride, whose warm and winsome personality charmed people wherever the couple went in six continents. She was engrossed in all his work and devoted to all his enterprises. In his years of retirement, without a secretary at his farm in the foothills in the Grampians, she typed his world-wide correspondence, with two fingers. It was an ideally happy marriage, tragically marred by the death of "Billy," their only son, on a Coastal Command mission during the war. She was his inseparable companion abroad and whenever he was from home in Britain he telephoned her ("The Boss") every evening. His elder daughter, Judy, while serving as a doctor in India, married Lt. Col. Kenneth Barton, who returned to farm the land adjoining Boyd Orr's property, near Edzell, Angus. His younger daughter, Minty, whose sculptures have been shown in the Paris salons, married David Lubbock, who had assisted him in his nutrition surveys and had joined him in F.A.O., and who took a farm in the same neighbourhood. The three farms "in the family" combined to provide the diversified agriculture in which Boyd Orr maintained his professional interest. In this happy family, his seven grandchildren knew as "Popeye" the man who was revered by millions.

This lean, long-jawed Scot, with eyebrows like eaves above deceptively mild blue eyes, was a spellbinder. He had no tricks of oratory and an uncompromising Scots accent, yet he could bring conferences of government officials to their feet cheering his forthrightness and obvious sincerity. His latter-day *persona* was a combination of all his careers. He was by instinct a doctor who wanted to do something for his patient without waiting for the laboratory reports. In research, he was a cautious scientist, but in nutrition he insisted that scientific facts should "work for their living". He was a practical farmer but his acres extended round the whole world.

The preacher who rejected the pulpit became the evangelist of peace through plenty.

June 26, 1971.

Air Commodore John David Boyle, C.B.E., D.S.O., who died, on September 25, 1974, at the age of 90, was one of the earliest officers of the Royal Flying Corps.

Although he never rose to the highest rank, he was a pioneer of military flying, and did much to endow what was then an infant service with the *esprit de corps* which grew so quickly in the Royal Air Force.

"Jack" Boyle was born in 1884, the fourth son and the seventh child of the 7th Earl of Glasgow. He was eight years old when his father, a retired naval captain, was appointed Governor of New Zealand, and he received his early schooling at Wanganui in that country before proceeding to Winchester. In 1906 he was gazetted into The Rifle Brigade; but he soon became infected with the new excitement of flying, and was seconded in 1912 to the Royal Flying Corps. His younger brother Alan, who died in 1958, had some years before built the first British monoplane, and set up several cross-country records which remained unsurpassed for some months.

Alan's Royal Aero Club Certificate was numbered 13, No. 1 being held by Moore-Brabazon;* Jack Boyle's was No. 51. His lifelong grief was that he was retained for too long during the First World War on training duties because of his gifts as a pilot. But between those years and his retirement in 1932, he did much spadework, commanding stations in England and Iraq, and acting as Senior Air Staff Officer to the Air Defence of Great Britain. Recalled to the service in 1939, he spent three years in the siting of new operational airfields all over Britain.

On July 8, 1974, he celebrated his ninetieth birthday at his home near Portpatrick in Wigtownshire. The occasion was marked by a large gathering of family and friends, an interview with him on the B.B.C., the honour of a fly-past over his house by four Buccaneers of the Royal Air Force, and a telegram of congratulations from the Queen.

Boyle married first, in 1913, Ethel, daughter of Sir Henry Hodges, Judge of the High Court in Victoria; she died in 1932. The elder son of this marriage, Major Richard Boyle, M.C., of The Black Watch, was killed in the Rhine crossing in 1945; the younger, Squadron Leader Peter Boyle, R.A.F., was killed in a flying accident in 1959, after having been shot down and

taken prisoner in 1944. He married secondly in 1935 Marie, daughter of John Gibb, of Orford, Suffolk, who survives him.

September 26, 1974.

Mary Boyle, collaborator with the Abbé Breuil,* died in France on December 22, 1974, at the age of 93. She was the second daughter and fourth child of Rear-Admiral R. H. Boyle. She was born on August 11, 1881, at Highlandman, Perthshire. Educated at home, she and her two sisters were the despair of 14 governesses. Both parents and her stepmother had died by the time she was 18.

Six months of the following two years were spent in Switzerland and Italy, studying languages and art and forming life-long friendships. There followed a prolonged period of ill health during which she lived for some time in the house of Dr. Walter Smith, celebrated preacher and poet, who encouraged her to use his extensive library.

During the 1914-18 War she was a "Belgian matron" in a house for 60 refugees in Glasgow, and a market gardener. When peace came, she went to Grenoble University and gained in three months a "Certificat de Littérature française". Later she lectured in the United States in universities, schools and clubs on the painted caves of France and Spain, borrowing plates of the Abbé Breuil's copies of Altamira cave.

In Italy, Mary Boyle had met Professor F. C. Burkitt and his family. She met the Abbé Breuil while with the Burkitts in Cambridge, where he received an honorary degree in 1920. Four years later the abbé offered to teach Mary Boyle all he knew of prehistory; it was Professor F. C. Burkitt who urged her to accept. Their association lasted 37 years.

To write a brochure on the cave of Barma Grande near Mentone was the first task set by the abbé. Later he told her to write a popular book going backwards in time from the Iron Age; the result, *In Search of our Ancestors*, sold on both sides of the Atlantic. A previous book *Man before History* was used by the Parents' National Educational Union (P.N.E.U.).

For eight years, whenever lecturing did not keep the abbé in Paris, Mary Boyle worked with him in the cave of La Mouthe near Les Eyzies in the Dordogne. For another eight years they studied together the dolmens and *allées couvertes* of Brittany.

In Paris, Mary Boyle worked beside the abbé in his flat, writing translations and letters, reading the newspapers and books for which he had no time. Separate knowledge was shared: he spoke of rock paintings in the Spanish Levant, she of Italian Primitives. They travelled together to Florence, later to Rome, London, Scotland, Spain and Portugal, and more than once a year to the Dordogne. When the abbé went to Peking, the Red Sea, and Abyssinia, he

sent Mary Boyle to study with his greatest friend, the Abbé Obermaier, who held the chair of Prehistoric Archaeology in Madrid University. She learned to read and translate Spanish and wrote the English translation of *The Cave of Altamira* (Duke of Alba's edition).

The Second World War separated the abbé and his Scottish collaborator—but only temporarily. In the middle of the war Mary Boyle was closely involved in a plan, put up by Field Marshal Smuts, to find the abbé—then in Portugal—and get him first to Lourenço Marques and then to South Africa. Despite the intense difficulties of war-time travel Mary Boyle accomplished her mission. For several years she and the abbé, who was attached to Witwatersrand University, worked together in South Africa until the end of the war enabled them to return to France.

Beyond the Bounds of History, with a text in English by Mary Boyle, was prefaced by Field Marshal Smuts who, on visits to Paris after the war, twice sent her and the abbé out again to Africa. There, peacetime conditions enabled them to undertake expeditions in the field, studying and copying the rock paintings in which the abbé had for long been deeply interested.

They finally returned to France in 1951, planning a series of books on the rock paintings of Southern Africa. *Four Hundred Centuries of Cave Art* was published in both French and English.

While the fifth volume in the Southern Africa series, dealing with paintings in Southern Rhodesia, was in press, the Abbé Breuil died at his home in the country at Isle-Adam in August 1961. Mary Boyle was beside the abbé as he crossed his last frontier. Thus ended this very remarkable Catholic and Protestant, French and British companionship.

Mary Boyle was a Fellow of the Society of Antiquaries of Scotland and a Chevalier of the Legion of Honour.

January 3, 1975.

Sir Daniel (Mr. Justice) Brabin, a Judge of the High Court since 1962, died on September 22, 1975 at the age of 62.

In 1965 he was asked by the Home Secretary, Sir Frank Soskice, to conduct an independent inquiry into the case of Timothy Evans, who was hanged in 1950 for the murder of his infant daughter. The inquiry took 32 days and Brabin's report, published in October 1966, ran to 158 pages.

In his report Brabin gave it as his opinion that Evans probably did not murder his daughter. He suggested that John Reginald Halliday Christie, who in 1953 confessed to strangling six women, probably killed the child and that Evans probably murdered his wife, Beryl.

Evans and his wife and their child lived

at 10 Rillington Place, Notting Hill, London, the home of Christie. Christie was also hanged.

The judge believed that it was impossible now to come to a conclusion on the guilt or innocence of Evans "beyond reasonable doubt" in either case. Shortly after the report was published Evans was granted a posthumous free pardon.

Daniel James Brabin, the son of William Henry Brabin, was born on August 14, 1913 and educated at Douai School and Trinity Hall, Cambridge. He was a pupil of Lord Shawcross and was called to the Bar by the Inner Temple in 1936. He became a Master of the Bench in 1960. In the Second World War he saw service in the Royal Artillery and won a Military Cross in 1945. He took silk in 1951 and was Recorder of Bolton from 1953 to 1962.

He married in 1949 Mary, daughter of John McParland.

September 24, 1975.

James J. Braddock—Jim Braddock, the former world heavyweight boxing champion—died in North Bergen, New Jersey, on November 29, 1974. He was the hero of one of those rare "rags to riches" stories which have always encouraged deprived young men to make their living in the ring. He was 68.

Braddock, who was born on December 6, 1905, won the world title by outpointing Max Baer in June 1935. Yet, a year before, he was making such a failure of his career, which included an unsuccessful challenge in 1929 for Tommy Loughran's light-heavyweight title, that he was forced to apply for public relief as unemployed.

In June 1934 Braddock was brought in as a late substitute against a rated opponent named Corn Griffin, and he upset the odds with a second-round knockout. After two more victories he was matched with Baer and, although the odds were 10 to 1 against his winning the title, he succeeded and earned himself the nickname of "Cinderella Man."

Unluckily for Braddock, his first title defence fight in June 1937 was against the talented Joe Louis. Braddock gave one of the most courageous exhibitions ever seen by a heavyweight champion, putting Louis down in the first round before he was himself knocked out in the eighth. The Cinderella Man, whose 12-year professional career embraced 84 bouts, of which he lost 19, fought only once more, a points victory over Britain's Tommy Farr.

But the days of poverty were happily over now for, by a secret contract arranged just before his only title defence, Braddock and his manager, Joe Gould, gained a sizable cut of all Louis's purses for the next 10 years.

December 2, 1974.

Sir Lawrence Bragg, C.H., O.B.E., M.C., F.R.S., joint Nobel prizewinner for Physics in 1915 at the age of 25, and formerly Fullerian Professor of Chemistry at the Royal Institution, London, Superintendent of the House and Director of the Davy Faraday Research Laboratory, died on July 1, 1971 at the age of 81.

William Lawrence Bragg was born in Adelaide, South Australia, on March 31, 1890, the elder son of William Henry Bragg (afterwards Sir William Bragg, O.M.), who was then Professor of Physics and Mathematics at Adelaide University. He was educated at St. Peter's College, Adelaide, and at Adelaide University. After his father's appointment to the Cavendish Professorship of Physics in Leeds University in 1909, young W. L. Bragg went to Trinity College, Cambridge, where he was Allen Scholar and where he later, in 1914, became a fellow and lecturer in natural sciences, and was awarded the Barnard Medal. Later, when he had become the Cavendish Professor of Experimental Physics at Cambridge, he admitted that he had done no physics at school and expressed his view that "it does not matter very much what boys are taught so long as they are taught to work well and work hard and efficiently."

In 1912, before his college course was completed, he and his father spent much of the summer vacation discussing some experiments just carried out in Germany, in which a crystal placed in a narrow pencil of X-rays had given a pattern of black spots (a diffraction pattern) on a photographic plate. When he got back to Cambridge University he thought much more about these experiments and produced a simple geometrical explanation of the phenomenon in terms of the selective reflection of the X-ray beam by regularly-spaced planes of atoms within the crystal. It followed from this that these diffraction patterns might be used to determine the various geometrical arrangements of atoms in crystals of different types.

Since very fine crystals were available in the collection in the Mineralogy Department of the university, W. L. Bragg borrowed some of these and took X-ray photographs of them. It was against the rules to remove them from the collection; but a sympathetic young lecturer, Professor Hutchinson, organized a black market (as Bragg later described it) for this enterprising student and taught him a great deal of crystallography into the bargain. At the suggestion of the Professor of Chemistry, Professor Pope, Bragg began by studying crystals of rocksalt, sylvine and other similar substances, and published the first "X-ray analysis of crystal structure" in the *Proceedings of the Royal Society, June 1913.*

These experiments preceded a short period of most fruitful collaboration between father and son in the old Physics Laboratory of the University of Leeds for which, in 1915, they were jointly awarded

the Nobel Prize for Physics. "It was a glorious time", he afterwards wrote, "when we worked far into every night with new worlds unfolding before us in the silent laboratory."

From 1915 to 1919 W. L. Bragg was technical adviser on sound-ranging in the map section, G.H.Q. France, and in 1918 he was awarded the M.C. and O.B.E. Then he succeeded Sir Ernest (later Lord) Rutherford as Langworthy Professor of Physics in the Victoria University of Manchester, a position he occupied for 18 years. He energetically tackled the problems of restaffing a department severely depleted by the war, and of dealing with a great influx of ex-service and other students, but at the same time he built up a splendid research team, consisting of men many of whom have since become famous not only in Britain but all over the world.

In 1921 he married Alice Grace Jenny, the elder daughter of Albert Hopkinson, by whom he had two sons and two daughters, and whose charm and character (she was Mayor of Cambridge during part of his tenure of the Cavendish professorship) greatly helped him throughout his professional career. In the same year he became a Fellow of the Royal Society, on whose council he served in 1931–33.

Following his early work on the atomic structures of some simple salts and oxides, W. L. Bragg undertook the investigation of those complex minerals, the silicates, of which the earth's crust is largely composed. He later described this as "one of the most exciting and aesthetically satisfying researches with which I have been associated"; and of this work it was said that through it "a chemical riddle has been transformed into a system of simple and elegant architecture".

The work on silicates was preceded and followed by researches on the structures of metals and alloys and their phase changes. In his presidential address to Section A of the British Association in 1948 he recalled that "a young John's student called Edward Appleton* was the first whom I ever had to work with me. We investigated the structure of metal crystals together in 1914". When, in 1938, after a short period as Director of the National Physical Laboratory, W. L. Bragg was appointed the successor of Lord Rutherford as Cavendish Professor of Experimental Physics at Cambridge, he had Edward Appleton as his fellow professor in the Cavendish Laboratory.

To have succeeded in both these diverse fields of structural research—minerals and metals—would have been enough for many men, but not for W. L. Bragg. He had always, since the days when his imagination had been fired by C. T. R. Wilson's lectures at Cambridge, been interested in X-ray diffraction as a branch of optics; and he initiated methods which have since gone far towards replacing earlier laborious trigonometrical calculations by rapid optical devices based on the analogy of the diffraction or visible light ("lightning calculations with light", he called them). He was also keenly interested in the relationships between the atomic structure and the physical and mechanical properties of solids (for one of the results of the X-ray diffraction technique was to establish the fact that *all* solids are essentially crystalline, in that the atoms of which they are built up form a periodically repeating, symmetrical pattern, different for every solid).

He designed a model of a metal which consisted of a raft of little bubbles, which became widely used for teaching, and which illustrated, among other things, the plastic flow of metals when distorted and the reason for their practical weakness as compared with their theoretical strength. But this was only one of the many attractive lecture and research experiments that he devised. In fact, like his illustrious father, he had a real genius for communicating his scientific knowledge to either an expert or to a lay audience. He was not the type of scientist who is only happy when he can write down equations and solve them.

It was for this reason that his final outstanding success was as Fullerian Professor of Chemistry and Resident Professor at the Royal Institution, a position that had been occupied by a succession of world-famous scientists, including Humphrey Davy, Michael Faraday, John Tyndall, James Dewar and William Henry Bragg. He was simultaneously the Director of the Institution's Laboratories and here, from 1954, he built up a new research team whose main interest was one that had grown to fascinate him in his later years at the Cavendish Laboratory—the problem of the structure of proteins, or, as it might indeed be called, the problem of life. He retired in 1966.

The Christmas lectures for children at the Royal Institution, initiated by Faraday in 1826, and continued in an unbroken succession ever since, had been justly famous from their beginning. Many people, both scientists and non-scientists, admitted in later years that their interest was first aroused by attending these lectures or by reading the books that were based on these courses "adapted to a juvenile auditory", given at the Royal Institution. W. L. Bragg gave the set of six Christmas lectures on "Electricity" in 1934–35 and the success of this tradition gave him the idea that young people from the schools in and around London might benefit tremendously from having such courses arranged throughout the whole academic year.

Honours were of course showered upon him. He received the Hughes Medal of the Royal Society in 1931, a Royal Medal in 1946 and the Roebling Medal of the Mineralogical Society of America in 1948. During the Second World War he acted as Co-ordinator of British, Canadian and American Military Research; and he was knighted in 1941. He held many honorary doctorates, from Dublin, Leeds, Manchester, Lisbon, Paris, Brussels, Liège, Durham, Cologne and St. Andrews; and he was an honorary member or a foreign member of many academies and societies. He was a member of the B.B.C. General Advisory Council, 1952; and of the Scientific Advisory Council, 1954. Besides numerous scientific papers he also wrote *X-rays and Crystal Structure* (with W. H. Bragg) 1915; *The Crystalline State*, 1934; *Electricity*, 1936; and *Atomic Structure of Minerals,* 1937. The last-named book was based on a course of lectures that he gave in 1934 at Cornell University, U.S.A.

July 2, 1971.

Sir John Braithwaite, chairman of the London Stock Exchange Council from 1949 to 1959, died on April 5, 1973 at the age of 88.

During his 10 years of office he was responsible for many reforms within the Stock Exchange itself and for the improvement in the relations between the London market, the public and other stock exchanges. When he retired he could look back on many changes, some of which, like the opening of the Visitors' Gallery and the making of a film, would have been considered revolutionary when he was first elected to the governing body in the 1930s. It was during his tenure of the chairmanship that the Stock Exchange compensation fund was established to protect the public against loss through the default of members of the exchange.

Braithwaite was the driving force behind the campaign to impress upon the general public that the Stock Exchange is a national institution by showing how it works and how it helps to provide the funds needed by the Government, insurance companies, pension funds, commercial undertakings and a variety of other enterprises.

Born in 1884, John Bevan Braithwaite came of a stockbroking family. His father, Joseph Bevan Braithwaite, was a partner in a family firm founded in 1825 and built up mainly by a great-uncle who joined the firm in 1833 after migrating from Kendal, Westmorland.

He was educated at Leighton Park School, Reading, from which he went to Owen's College which is now Manchester University. He then entered the family firm where, as he later said, "I did every job bar licking the stamps". After 4½ years' training in every department, and becoming a member of the London Stock Exchange at 23, he entered the partnership. Working steadily up the ladder he later became a senior member of the firm. In 1937 he was elected to the then governing body of the Stock Exchange, the Committee for General Purposes. He became a deputy chairman in 1946 and chairman in 1949.

Soon after his first election in 1937 Braithwaite took a keen interest in improving the relations between the London and provincial exchanges, which at that time left a good deal to be desired, and in 1939 he was chairman of the joint conference, the first of its kind ever held, which laid the foundations for the close and happy relations which now exist throughout the stockbroking profession.

He lectured and spoke on Stock Exchange matters in many parts of the country; he was for 11 years a governor of the London School of Economics; and prior to nationalization he was a director of several electric companies and chairman of the City of London Electric Lighting Company.

He was a discerning collector of Oriental porcelain and English water-colours, and also possessed a small but eclectic library, leaning rather to Elizabethan and 17th century writers.

In 1957, on the 254th anniversary of the death of Samuel Pepys, he gave the address at the annual Memorial Service at St. Olave's, Hart Street, entitled "Samuel Pepys, Amateur Musician".

He was a great lover of music and, if pressed, admitted to amateur arranging, composition and conducting. He took an active interest in the rebuilding of the City's own theatre—the Mermaid.

He married in 1908 Martha Janette, daughter of J. A. Baker. They had two sons and a daughter. His wife died in 1972.

April 6, 1973.

Warwick Braithwaite, F.R.A.M., the conductor, died at the age of 75 on January 18, 1971. He was active in the opera house and the concert hall for more than 50 years.

Born on January 9, 1896, in Dunedin, New Zealand, he went to England in 1916 to study at the Royal Academy of Music, as Goring Thomas Compositions Scholar; during his years at the Royal Academy he won the Challen Gold Medal and the Battison Hayes Prize.

In 1919 he became conductor to the O'Mara Opera Company and joined the British National Opera Company as répétiteur in 1921. Braithwaite moved to broadcasting almost at the birth of the new medium: in 1922 he became assistant musical director, and musical director of the Western Region, based in Cardiff, to the then British Broadcasting Company, forging links with Wales which led him to the conductorship of the Cardiff Music Society and the Welsh National Orchestra.

From 1932 to 1940 he was conductor of Sadler's Wells Opera, finding time to conduct Sir Robert Mayer's Children's Concerts during the long illness of Sir Malcolm Sargent* in 1934, and to take charge of opera at the Royal Academy of Music in 1937 and 1938. From 1940 to 1946 he was conductor of the Scottish Orchestra, and of Sadler's Wells Ballet in 1948. This took him to the staff of Covent Garden, first as conductor of ballet and then of opera in 1953. He spent the next year as conductor of the National Orchestra of New Zealand, and was artistic director of the National Opera of Australia in 1954 and 1955.

Braithwaite went to England primarily as a would-be composer, but he counted composition only as one of his hobbies. He was a first-rate craftsman, and his book *The Conductor's Art* concerns itself with the technique, and not the mystique, of conducting; it is direct, thorough and helpful. His reputation went beyond the organizations with which he was officially connected, and he was heard from time to time with every major British orchestra.

Warwick Braithwaite was married in 1931; he leaves two sons, one of them Nicholas Braithwaite, the conductor, and a daughter.

January 20, 1971.

The Rev. Prof. Samuel George Frederick Brandon, Professor of Comparative Religion in the University of Manchester since 1951, died on October 29, 1971 as a result of an infection contracted in Egypt. He was 64.

He was born in Devon, and educated at the College of the Resurrection, Mirfield, and the University of Leeds, where he graduated in 1930. After his ordination in 1932 he served curacies at St. Mark's Church, Ford, Devonport and Westward Ho!

Enlisting as a chaplain in 1939, he was at the Dunkirk evacuation in 1940, and subsequently served throughout the North African and Italian campaigns. During these years he organized a study scheme for officers and men of all denominations who were contemplating ordination. He also acquired a close knowledge of and an interest in military affairs which was never to leave him, even though overlaid by other concerns. He continued after the war to serve in a chaplains' department, and it was while serving in Austria in 1951 that he was invited to occupy the vacant Manchester chair of Comparative Religion.

He was perhaps not an obvious candidate for the post, having had no previous teaching experience at any university level, but he had been a student of comparative religion ever since his Mirfield days (this at a time when comparative religion was held to be a somewhat suspicious activity in an Anglican priest); interest had been succeeded by intense application; and by 1951 he had written his first comparative book, *Time and Mankind*, in which he had launched what was to become his distinctive thesis, that religion originates in man's consciousness of, and reactions to, the passing of time. Also in 1951 had appeared *The Fall of Jerusalem and the Christian Church*, in which he had examined the significance of the fall of Jerusalem in A.D. 70 for the growth of the early Christian communities.

It was on the strength of these two books, which had come to the notice of Professor E. O. James, that Professor Brandon was

appointed, and the areas of study they represent continued to form the twin foci of his interest throughout the remainder of his academic career. His other comparative works, *Man and His Destiny in the Great Religions; Creation Legends of the Ancient Near East; History, Time and Deity;* and *The Judgment of the Dead*, elaborate the time theme and its implications.

They exhibit a breadth of reading and a passion for exact scholarship second to none. But it was in his other area, that of Christian origins, that Professor Brandon was to achieve a renown bordering on notoriety. That this was so was due to his two books *Jesus and the Zealots* and *The Trial of Jesus of Nazareth*, in which he presented the thesis that Jesus had been executed by the Romans for sedition, and that various indications in the Gospels pointed to Jesus's movement having had something in common with other revolutionary movements of the first century, notably that of the Zealots.

It was unfortunate that these books should have appeared at a time when various protest movements in the West were entering a more violent phase than hitherto; and rather to his consternation, Professor Brandon found himself reported at length in *The Times* and found his "violent Jesus", the revolutionary from Nazareth, being adopted energetically by the Christian wings of the protest movement, particularly in America.

Professor Brandon cared for none of these things. The ideal which motivated him was genuine historical curiosity— the desire to find out the *Wie es eigentlich gewesen* —and if this led him on an occasion to place undue reliance on hypothetical constructions he was doing no more than practically all historians have always done.

He had a great love of scholarship for its own sake. He loved teaching, as successive generations of Manchester students will testify; and he was always ready to offer his help, whether to potential research students in search of a project, or to the latest literary enterprise which seemed to need support and weight. His productivity was legendary (achieved by the most disciplined use of time). Apart from the books already mentioned, he edited and wrote well over half of a dictionary of comparative religion, published in 1970; and on the more popular level he wrote extensively for *History Today*, and *Man, Myth and Magic*, believing that if scholars were not prepared to write for the people, others would—and the people would suffer.

But those who saw in Professor Brandon only the scholar totally obsessed by his subject, though they saw a great deal, did not see all. As a man he was gentle, generous and wise—naturally reserved, but possessed of great warmth and a rare sense of humour. He was the best of colleagues; not the best of chairmen, being far too courteous ever to hurry a meeting along; an expansive talker and a good listener, he was always ready to assume responsibility; as a

senior professor he was a Pro-Vice-Chancellor of Manchester University from 1967 to 1970; and in 1970 in Stockholm he was appointed secretary-general of the International Association for the History of Religion, an onerous duty which he would much rather not have accepted, but which he took on for the sake of his subject.

Students at Manchester in a Faculty of Theology were sometimes at a loss to know quite how to reconcile Professor Brandon's Anglo-Catholic past with his often expressed belief that religion is essentially an expression of man's heart and soul. On this point, he was always reticent, but he continued to the end to exercise his priestly functions when called upon to do so, and although intellectually convinced of the dispensability of much institutional religion, retained an emotional attachment to the church. He used, for instance, to say that to have been an Anglo-Catholic is the best possible training for a comparative religionist, since the Catholic knows by experience what to the Protestant must remain only inference—the vast importance of the visual and kinetic dimensions of the religious experience. He regretted, too, that the world of music was closed to him.

If the subject of comparative religion today enjoys a fair esteem in Britain, and if it is looked on as something more than a dubious fringe activity, then that is due in very large measure to the precept and example of Professor Brandon over the past 20 years. It is difficult to imagine what the subject will be like without him, his enthusiasm and his integrity.

He married in 1934 Ann Miles, and leaves one surviving son.

November 2, 1971.

Owen Brannigan, the distinguished bass singer, died in hospital at Newcastle upon Tyne on May 10, 1973. He was 65. He was born in Northumberland on March 10, 1908 and retained throughout his career a firm connexion with his North Country roots. After studying at the Guildhall School of Music, which he did part-time while working as a joiner in Slough, he made his stage debut with Sadler's Wells Opera in 1943 as Sarastro. He had, in fact, been heard by Joan Cross in a B.B.C. broadcast and she invited him to join the company. He remained with the company, singing most of the principal bass roles, until 1948 and returned to it for a further spell, 1952 to 1958.

In 1945 he created the part of Swallow in *Peter Grimes* and later sang the same role at Covent Garden. The following year he created the part of Collatinus in Britten's *The Rape of Lucretia* and in 1947 Superintendent Budd in *Albert Herring*, both at Glyndebourne. Britten then wrote the parts of Noye in *Noyes Fludde* and Bottom in *A Midsummer Night's Dream* specially for him; both were memorable and often repeated interpretations.

Brannigan was perhaps even better known as an oratorio than as an opera singer, and he was also a regular broadcaster. He was a characterful Handelian bass (a Somnus in a stage performance of *Semele* for the Handel Opera Society remains keenly in the mind) and a rousing recitalist, always including a selection of his beloved North Country Songs in his programme. He sang regularly from 1944 onwards at the Proms where he often appeared in the Gilbert and Sullivan evenings. He recorded many of the bass roles in the Savoy operas under Sir Malcolm Sargent.*

He also created roles in Malcolm Williamson's operas, *Our Man in Havana, The Violins of Saint Jacques* and *English Eccentrics*, and in John Gardner's *The Moon and Sixpence*.

Brannigan's voice was a full, resonant bass, capable of considerable flexibility, which was helpful in the many buffo roles he was called on to play. However, he liked to consider himself as much a dramatic bass as a comic one, and he was a particularly effective Osmin, a role that comes somewhere between the two. He had a natural gift for characterization, never so aptly displayed as in the part of Bottom, in which he projected the role's endearing as well as its ridiculous side. On the radio, he was an amusing raconteur, and here, as much as on the stage and in real life, his cheerful, colourful personality was much to the fore. He will be sorely missed by opera and concert-goers in Britain.

May 11, 1973.

Pierre Brasseur, who died suddenly in Brunico, Italy, on August 14, 1972 while acting in a film, was one of the leading French actors of his generation, both on stage and on screen. He was known primarily as an expansive, romantic performer, first as a tempestuous jeune premier, and latterly as something approaching a Gallic Donald Wolfit.

He was born in Paris in 1905, of a theatrical family, his real name being Espinasse (Brasseur was his mother's maiden name.) He began on the stage very young, playing a great variety of small roles, graduating to leading roles about 1929, when he appeared with great success in *Le Sexe faible.* With the advent of the talkies he was a natural recruit; he made some silent films from 1925, but in the 1930s he came into his own, being associated particularly with roles in the romantic, melancholy, larger-than-life screenplays of Jacques Prévert, notably *Quai des Brumes* (1938), *Lumière d'été* (1942), *Les Enfants du Paradis* (1944), *Les Portes de la nuit* (1946), and *Les Amants de Vérone* (1948).

In 1949 he made a spectacular comeback to the stage in *Le Bossu,* and thereafter divided his time between stage and screen. Among the important plays he appeared in

were the first production of Claudel's *Partage de Midi*, Sartre's *Le Diable et le bon Dieu* and *Kean* (in which, in the showy role of the English actor as imagined by Dumas and re-created by Sartre, he scored one of his greatest triumphs), Anouilh's *Ornifle*, de Montherlant's *Don Juan* and those two international standbys of mature actors, the talk-pieces *Dear Liar* and Shaw's *Don Juan in Hell* from *Man and Superman*. He also ventured, surprisingly but very effectively, into more modern drama by playing the role of the father in the French production of Pinter's *The Homecoming*.

Meanwhile his film career was crowded, if seldom rising to the heights of his earlier films. Mostly he was cast in very conservative films by very conservative, commercial directors, but occasionally his peculiar qualities were recognised by the younger generation of French film-makers, as in Franju's *Les Yeux sans visage* (in which he played a variation of the traditional mad scientist) and Borowszick's *Goto, L'île d'amour*, where his flamboyant style made him perfectly at home among the film-makers' gothick imaginings.

In less extravagant parts he was not so easy to cast; he really belonged spiritually to the era of the spectacular actor-manager, and seemed somewhat confined in the understated modern theatre and cinema. He was also something of a writer, publishing poems and several stage plays, as well as a book of memoirs, *Ma Vie en vrac* (1968). He was married twice, first to Odette Joyeux and second to Lina Magrini; he had one son by his first wife.

August 16, 1972.

Helene Brecht—See Weigel.

Walter Brennan, the American character actor who appeared in nearly 120 films and won three Oscars as best supporting player, died in California on September 21, 1974. He was 80.

He entered films in the early 1920s and served a long apprenticeship as a stuntman and a bit-part actor. Then a small but telling appearance in *Barbary Coast* (1935) brought him a contract with the producer, Sam Goldwyn. Brennan played a one-eyed boatman called Old Atrocity, ferrying travellers from ship to shore in San Francisco. A piece of dialogue from the film became famous. Challenged on his "cargo" (who was in fact Miriam Hopkins), he replied: "A white woman." Told that he was lying, Brennan retorted: "No I ain't. She's whiter than a hen's egg."

Brennan was born in Swampscott, Massachusetts, on July 25, 1894. After graduating from technical college he was a hobo in New England before serving with the American forces in France during the First World War. After 1918 he travelled in Britain and Europe, returned to the

United States and became a bank clerk, and was on his way to Guatemala in search of fresh adventures when he happened to stop off in Hollywood. His first film appearance was in 1923.

During his long wait for recognition, Brennan developed a strong comedy technique—notably in Hoot Gibson Westerns—and learnt to play characters much older than himself; both attributes were to prove invaluable in his later career. He was chosen for *Barbary Coast* after being spotted by Goldwyn in King Vidor's *The Wedding Night*, and he went on to win his three Oscars in the next five years—for *Come and Get It; Kentucky;* and a brilliant portrayal of Judge Roy Bean in *The Westerner,* directed by William Wyler in 1940. He was in steady demand thereafter and still active in films in his mid-seventies.

Brennan will be remembered chiefly as a comedy player, particularly in the Western, where he effected a notable gallery of garrulous old-timers: the characterization probably reached its peak in the old jailkeeper, Stumpy, who helped John Wayne against the bad men in a celebrated Western of the late 1950s, *Rio Bravo*. The director, Howard Hawks, had made *Barbary Coast* and *Come and Get It,* and he seemed to have a special rapport with Brennan, who also worked with him on *Sergeant York; To Have and Have Not* (providing fine support to the Bogart/Lauren Bacall team); and another distinguished Western, *Red River*.

Brennan was equally adept, when given the opportunity, at portraying evil on the screen, and gave a memorable performance as the father of the Clanton gang in John Ford's version of the Wyatt Earp story, *My Darling Clementine*. His other films ranged from Fritz Lang's famous *Fury* in 1936 to the more recent *Bad Day at Black Rock, The Far Country, How the West was Won*, and the 1969 comedy Western, *Support Your Local Sheriff*. He was a regular television performer from the mid-1950s, spending five years in the series, *The Real McCoys*.

He married in 1920 and had two sons and a daughter.

September 23, 1974.

Zena Brett—See Dare

Havergal Brian, the composer, died at Shoreham, Sussex, on November 28, 1972. He was 96.

Until a few years ago his work was hardly known, if known at all, by modern music lovers. He was immensely prolific but his music was little played; nevertheless, he continued to compose, and by the time he was 93 had 32 symphonies to his name. No. 32 was first performed in 1971 by the Kensington Orchestral and Choral Society in St. John's, Smith Square, London, to mark the composer's 95th birthday.

In the early years of the century he won considerable reputation as a progressive and promising composer. The change of taste precipitated by the 1914 War set English music developing in directions which Brian was not prepared to follow, and he dropped out of the running, though he never gave up composition.

William Havergal Brian was born on January 29, 1876 at Dresden, Staffordshire. Both his parents worked in a pottery factory. He received his only general education in the choir of St. James's Church. He left school at the age of 12, but in the same year became deputy organist of St. James's, and three years later obtained his first salaried post as an organist. The money he thus earned he used to pay for lessons in harmony and counterpoint from a local musician named Theophilus Hemming. J. G. Halford, a Birmingham conductor, gave him advice on the orchestra and lent him scores, but apart from this Brian was self-educated in the higher principles of musical composition.

From the age of 18 Brian was profoundly influenced by the music of Elgar, who was then just coming to the fore as a writer of choral works, and it was on Elgar's recommendation that a partsong setting of Shakespeare's Shall I Compare Thee to a Summer's Day? by Havergal Brian was chosen as a test piece for the Morecambe Musical Festival of 1905. From that time onwards Brian's partsongs were much used at competitive musical festivals on the Lancashire coast and at the Midland Festival.

Among Brian's larger compositions may be mentioned the orchestral works A First English Suite and the overture For Valour, introduced to London at Promenade Concerts in 1908 by Sir Henry Wood; a symphonic poem Hero and Leander performed in Hanley by Sir Thomas Beecham* in the same year; Variations on an Old Rhyme, Festal Dance, and the comedy overture Doctor Merryheart, all of which attracted attention by their rich sense of humour.

The choral works of this period were a grandscale setting of By the Waters of Babylon, performed in Hanley in 1908 and again at the Musical League Festival in Liverpool in 1909, and a cantata entitled A Vision of Cleopatra, performed at the Southport Musical Festival of 1909 under Sir Landon Ronald. All his vocal music shows a refined, educated taste—his literary taste stretching from Herrick to Donne and Yeats.

The war of 1914 profoundly affected Brian. The hearty humour of his early works turned to satire in his opera The Tigers, composed during the war years, and his style grew more complex and elaborate. His works for the next 25 years were all, with the exception of a violin concerto composed in 1935, written on the vastest scale for orchestras so large that they stood outside the practical policy of the concert hall. Five symphonies and a setting of

Shelley's Prometheus Unbound were his chief preoccupations during these years. The Gothic Symphony (No. 2), completed in 1919, is written on a scale that can be compared only to that of Mahler's Eighth Symphony in its demand for solo voices, multiple choirs, children's choir, and four brass bands à la Berlioz's Requiem, as well as a huge orchestra with a number of unusual instruments. The Third and Fourth Symphonies are for orchestra alone, the Fifth has a choral finale, and the Sixth, Wine in Summer, is a song symphony with a baritone soloist, to words by Lord Alfred Douglas.

The Gothic Symphony was published and described by Tovey as a masterpiece; Beecham, Harty, Wood and Goossens* all wished to perform it, but its vast expense put it beyond their reach and it was not until 1966, the year of Brian's ninetieth birthday, that Sir Adrian Boult conducted a performance in a crowded Albert Hall. The army of performers included 500 singers; the vast orchestra had about 50 brass and 30 woodwind players.

The growing terseness and economy of Brian's later symphonies—his Twenty-sixth was composed in 1966—seems to be the result of the progress of his musical imagination rather than a series of attempts to confine his imagination within the boundaries of the practical.

The Twelfth Symphony, composed in 1957, another short, single-movement work, made an immediate impression at a Promenade Concert in 1966.

One or two broadcasts from his wealth of unheard music kept Brian's name from complete oblivion, and was the result of the championship of Dr. Robert Simpson and a few other musicians of importance and influence.

Brian seems to have endured almost complete neglect with remarkable courage and high spirits, as though to have written the works which lay unplayed on his shelves was reward enough, but it is clear that neglect had its inevitable effect on his music. All his explorations after 1914 were carried on, so to speak, in the dark; he had no facilities for readjustment and revision in the light of actual performance, so that there are moments of technical uncertainty in all the later music we have heard.

Though the size of some of his works transcends Elgar, Strauss or even Mahler at their vastest, he never, either in harmony, melodic quality or the use of his materials, suggests discipleship to them or to others. The music is always entirely his own, sturdy, vigorous and rich in feeling. The courage of his persistency was heroic, and few English musicians can escape a sense of shame when they contemplate his vast output of unplayed, unpublished works.

November 29, 1972.

___

Ann Bridge—See Lady O'Malley.

___

Tony Brise, who was an outstanding Grand Prix motor racing prospect as a driver, died in the Elstree plane crash with the champion driver, Graham Hill, on November 29, 1975. He was 23.

Though his own Formula 1 career began only at the tragic Spanish Grand Prix in April 1975—a race which was stopped when a car driven by Rolf Stommelen crashed, killing several people at the trackside—he had shown consistent promise and astuteness as a racing prospect.

Graham Hill signed him up as a member of his own team, and, though his first outing in the Belgian Grand Prix saw him drop out with engine failure, he claimed his first world championship point when he finished sixth in his next race, the Swedish Grand Prix.

He had also registered resounding wins in the single seater world, and recorded a runaway victory in the John Player Formula Atlantic Championship in 1975. He was twice awarded the Grovewood Award for the best young prospect in motor racing.

The son of the former motor racing driver, John Brise, he is survived by a wife, Janet.

December 1, 1975.

___

Sir Harry Brittain, K.B.E., C.M.G., died on July 9, 1974 at the age of 100.

His death removed from public life a most colourful personality. Newspapermen will long remember him for his far-sighted vision which led to the foundation of the Commonwealth Press Union. He was a co-founder of the Pilgrims Club and it was always one of his great aims to bring the English speaking peoples on both sides of the Atlantic into closer contact. During the 1914-18 war he was largely responsible for the welfare and entertainment of members of the American Forces during their stay in Britain. For 11 years he was Conservative Member of Parliament for Acton; with Sir Arthur Pearson he founded the Tariff Reform League; and he was a vice-president of the English Speaking Union. He was an indefatigable worker and propagandist for any cause he espoused; few men can have sat on more committees than he.

Harry Brittain's cheerful personality brought him a host of friends in every part of the world. He was rarely seen at a public function, even in distant parts of the Commonwealth, without a carnation in his buttonhole; and a carnation, apricot in colour and shot with scarlet and orange, was named after him and received a high award at the Chelsea Flower Show.

He was born at Ranmoor, near Sheffield, on December 24, 1873, the son of W. H. Brittain, and educated at Repton and Worcester College, Oxford, where he gained honours in law. He went through a business training in Sheffield and was called to the Bar by the Inner Temple in 1897 but never practised. His thoughts were already turning to big business in general and to the newspaper industry in particular. He acted as private secretary to Sir William Ingram and then joined Sir Arthur Pearson, with whom he worked in the creation of the Tariff Reform League and the Tariff Commission and in 1902 was working on the staff of the *Standard,* and the *Evening Standard.*

It was doubtless his association with Pearson that turned his thoughts to the House of Commons. He was elected Conservative member for Acton at the coupon election of 1918 and he held the seat until 1929. He made witty speeches and was always heard with attention and it was something of a surprise to his friends that he never obtained junior Ministerial rank.

He had been director of the Anglo-Russian Trust which had been a successful concern before the Russian revolution. One of its issues was for £5m. for the purpose of conveying fresh water to Baku. This had been guaranteed by both the Imperial Government and the municipality of Baku. When the old Russia ceased to exist the shares turned into waste paper and the millions of pounds' worth of bonds suffered a somewhat similar fate.

Brittain's chief memorial is the Commonwealth Press Union, for the creation of which he must be given sole credit. The story of its origin is told in *Pilgrims and Pioneers,* the first of his volumes of reminiscences. He was staying in Canada in 1907 when the thought came to him that a determined effort should be made for the encouragement of inter-Empire knowledge and understanding. He felt that this could best be done by organizing in London a gathering of editors or proprietors of the Empire's newspapers to show them something of the "old country" and to thrash out many mutual problems and interests. His idea was that this should be followed by the formation of a permanent organization with headquarters in London and with branches throughout the Empire and by meetings in each of the great Dominions at regular intervals. He discussed the plan with John Dafoe, the great editor of the *Winnipeg Free Press,* and encouraged by his enthusiastic support he got to work as soon as he returned to England. He tackled Lord Burnham, Frank Newnes, C. P. Scott, St. Loe Strachey, Bruce Ingram and Lord Northcliffe, and they all urged him to go ahead. Northcliffe volunteered to act as treasurer if Brittain would serve as secretary. A guarantee fund was formed and the Imperial Press Conference met for the first time in London in June 1909. The dinner of welcome was marked by a memorable speech by Lord Rosebery which Brittain afterwards described as the greatest speech that he had ever heard. The conference was a triumphant success and had at least two important results—the reduction of cable rates to every part of the Empire and the formation of a permanent body to carry on the work which the conference had begun.

The Empire Press Union was founded a few months later and when at its conference in Canada in 1950 it was decided to change its name to the Commonwealth Press Union it was Harry Brittain who moved the necessary resolution. He saw the change with nostalgic regret, but without misgivings. Until the end of his long life he took the greatest interest in the Union's fortunes.

His second greatest interest was the Pilgrims Club, of which he was one of the founders in July, 1902 as a result of an informal meeting at which General Joseph Wheeler ("Hellfire Joe" of the American Civil War), Colonel Bryan Mahon, C. S. Rolls, and Harry Brittain were elected as a provisional committee. Lord Roberts was appointed president and the club's first function was a dinner in his honour in the following month. The dinner was arranged at two days' notice and General Wheeler and Brittain rushed round London in a cab to secure the attendance of the important guests whose support they wanted for the new undertaking. Since then few American men of mark have come to Britain without being received by the Pilgrims, and it has become the accepted custom for the newly-arrived American Ambassador to Britain and the newly-appointed British Ambassador in Washington to be entertained by them. The Pilgrims of America were founded in the United States in 1903. Later the two organizations formed the Pilgrims Club and a member elected on either side of the Atlantic becomes a member of the sister society. Brittain was the effective head of the Pilgrims until he resigned the chairmanship in 1918 and was elected vice-president.

Brittain received great support in all his work from his wife, whom he married in 1905. She was Alida Luisa, only daughter of Sir Robert Harvey and an amateur harpist of considerable ability. There were a son and a daughter of the marriage. Lady Brittain died in 1943. He married, secondly, in 1961, Muriel Leslie, daughter of H. Leslie Dixon.

July 10, 1974.

Professor C. D. Broad, Fellow of Trinity College, Cambridge, and Emeritus Knightbridge Professor of Moral Philosophy in the University of Cambridge, died on March 11, 1971.

Charlie Dunbar Broad was born in London on December 30, 1887, the only child of Charles Stephen Broad and his wife Emily Gomme. He was educated at Dulwich College, and in 1906 entered Trinity College, Cambridge, as a major scholar in natural science. He took a first in part I of the natural sciences tripos in 1908, and a first with distinction in part II of the moral sciences tripos in 1910. In 1911 he was elected to a prize fellowship at Trinity for a dissertation which formed the basis of his first book, *Perception, Physics and Reality.* This was published in 1914.

Broad left Cambridge in 1911, and was successively assistant to the Professor of Logic at St. Andrews, lecturer in logic at Dundee, and Professor of Philosophy at Bristol.

He returned to Trinity in 1923 to succeed McTaggart, his former director of studies and supervisor, as fellow and lecturer in moral sciences. Broad was appointed university lecturer in moral science in 1926, and Sidgwick lecturer in 1931. He was elected to the Knightbridge Professorship in 1933.

He was a Litt.D. and as an exceptional case also an honorary Sc.D. of Cambridge, an honorary LL.D. of Aberdeen, Bristol, and Dublin, and an honorary Doctor of Philosophy of Uppsala. He was elected a fellow of the British Academy in 1926 and later of Academies in Sweden, Finland and the United States.

Broad's chief published works were his *Scientific Thought* (1923), *The Mind and its Place in Nature* (1925), *Five Types of Ethical Theory* (1930), and the monumental *Examination of McTaggart's Philosophy* (1933-38). He also published a large number of articles in various philosophical periodicals some of which were subsequently collected in his *Ethics and the History of Philosophy* (1952) and *Religion, Philosophy and Psychical Research* (1953).

Broad's philosophical writings were distinguished by an exceptional combination of analytic and constructive gifts as well as by immense versatility, thoroughness and clarity. In his youth he was influenced by Russell, Whitehead and Moore, by W. E. Johnson and by G. F. Stout; but his own ideas and approach were importantly different from those of any of his contemporaries.

His characteristic procedure was as follows. He would state the problem with which he was concerned in a clear and precise form, distinguishing carefully between the different meanings of the various terms employed; he would then explain all the alternative solutions that were theoretically possible and discuss the reasons for and against each of them; and finally he would work out in great detail and with the utmost care that particular solution which seemed to him to be the most plausible.

The range of his philosophical interests included the theory of knowledge, the logic of induction and of probability, the philosophy of physics and of biology, philosophical psychology, and ethics. In each of these fields he illuminated every problem which he discussed. In particular, in the theory of knowledge his "sensum" theory, which has led some historians of philosophy to regard him as one of the leading contemporary "realists", forms perhaps the fullest, clearest and most coherent philosophical theory of perception worked out in recent times.

Like his predecessor in the Knightbridge Chair, Henry Sidgwick, Broad was keenly interested in psychical research. He joined the Society for Psychical Research in 1920, was president of the society in 1935 and in 1958, and took a prominent part in its work. Some of his views on the various topics falling within this field are contained in *The Mind and its Place in Nature*, and in *Religion, Philosophy and Psychical Research*.

March 15, 1971.

Sir John Brocklebank, fifth baronet and tenth chairman of Cunard, who died in Malta on September 13, 1974, came of a family associated with shipping for nearly two centuries. He was 59.

John Montague Brocklebank was the son of Sir Aubrey Brocklebank, and was born on September 3, 1915. He was educated at Eton and Cambridge, but at both he tended to be distinguished more in athletic than academic spheres. He took a pass degree in history—for which, he confessed, his only excuse was a cricket blue. His father sent him to be apprenticed in a shipyard and the man who was to become chairman of the Cunard company thus spent the first 15 months of his business career gaining knowledge of ships in a practical manner.

From his shipyard apprenticeship he went to the Cunard company. In 1939 he joined the Army, his abandonment of the sea being solely due, as he ruefully admitted, to sea-sickness. He spent much of his military life in a German prison camp. He joined the board of Cunard in 1951 and was elected deputy chairman two years later. On the death of Colonel D. H. Bates he was, in 1959, elected chairman of the boards of the Cunard Steam-Ship Company, Ltd, and Cunard White Star, Ltd. He came reluctantly to the position when he was only 43 years of age, at a difficult time in the Cunard company's affairs.

Declining transatlantic sea travel was affecting Cunard's profits considerably and during his six years of office Brocklebank had to face one crisis after another. One of the first fruits of his chairmanship was a vigorous reorganization scheme. Staff in a number of shore establishments—not excluding the head office in Liverpool, known to many British seamen as the Kremlin—was top-heavy and substantial pruning was necessary. This the new chairman carried out, for behind his friendly, quiet, nervous manner, was, where commercial matters were concerned, an almost ruthless strain. Valuable land property was sold, outstandingly that of the company's New York skyscraper.

Only a year after his appointment, Cunard went "into the air", purchasing Eagle Airways. This was followed by an application to operate a North Atlantic passenger service. The licence was granted, but later revoked after an appeal by the British Overseas Air Corporation. In 1962, however, there was a link-up of the two organizations. B.O.A.C.-Cunard was born,

with the shipping company holding 30 per cent of the shares. He never lacked courage and this was shown in his vetoing of the obsolete Q3 concept of a replacement for the aging Queen Mary, and his discussions with the Government which led to the loan of some £17m. towards the building of a Q4—today's QE2—which would be more "flexible" than the original models.

When he resigned the chairmanship of Cunard in 1965, owing to ill-health, the board of directors paid tribute to his "whole-hearted devotion to the company's interests over six very difficult years" and expressed their gratification at his acceptance of the honorary presidency of both the Cunard and Brocklebank companies and of the position of a consultant to the group.

Until his resignation Brocklebank was chairman of the family firm of Thos. & Jno. Brocklebank Ltd (the company retains the archaic abbreviations of an earlier age). He was a member of the council of the Chamber of Shipping of the United Kingdom and he was elected chairman, in 1965, of the Liverpool Steam Ship Owners' Association. He was a past president of the Institute of Shipping and Forwarding Agents.

He married in 1950 Pamela Sue, daughter of Mr. W. H. Pierce, O.B.E. They had one son, Mr. Aubrey Thomas Brocklebank, who succeeds to the baronetcy.

For a year or two in the thirties Sir John was a leg-break bowler good enough to get anyone out on his day. He took 10 wickets for Cambridge in the University match of 1936 and in spite of playing very little first-class cricket at the time was chosen for the Gentlemen against the Players in 1939. He spun the ball like a top, though like most wrist spinners who do that he found control elusive. An ebullient person, he was probably every bit as happy dropping a leg break on the spot as being at the helm of one of the world's great shipping companies.

September 17, 1974.

Sir Denis Brogan, Professor of Political Science in the University of Cambridge from 1939 to 1968, and subsequently Professor Emeritus, died at Cambridge on January 5, 1974 at the age of 73.

During a period when understanding America became essential to an appreciation of world affairs, he did more than anyone else to explain American life and institutions to a European audience. He was also the leading British expert on modern French history. Through journalism and the radio he became one of the best-known academics in the country at large.

Brogan was born in Glasgow on August 11, 1900, the eldest son of Denis Brogan and Elizabeth Toner. He was educated at local schools, but was ill more or less continuously between the ages of 12 and 18 and so had time to read a great deal on his

own. He went on to Glasgow University, then to Balliol and Harvard. He had lived in Paris, Rome and New York before spending more than a night in London, and this helped to give him a remarkable detachment of view about his adopted country. He became in due course a lecturer at University College London, at the London School of Economics, and then a fellow and tutor at Corpus Christi College, Oxford. In 1939 he succeeded Sir Ernest Barker as Professor at Cambridge and became a fellow of Peterhouse.

In 1933 Brogan published his first book, *The American Political System*. Breaking away from any conventional approach, this became the standard exposition of its subject and had a big impact on university teaching. Written in a vivid style, it was none the less based on the closest and most careful study. Not content with mere detailed analysis, he suggested some reforms, including a revolution in the whole attitude of the American people to the practice of self-government.

Brogan's initial interest in France came from Dumas père, and these two countries then occupied him in turn for the rest of his life. After his *Proudhon* (1934) and *Abraham Lincoln* (1935) *The Development of Modern France 1870-1939* appeared in June, 1940. Coming at the moment of France's collapse, it possessed a poignant interest. This substantial and highly concentrated volume was essentially narrative history, but narrative directed to illustrate the changes in modern French society. France in this period became an urban, industrial state, but at the same time she lost her European predominance to Germany, and this put dangerous psychological stresses on her people. Weaknesses in the Executive had exposed the French state to corrupt justice and irresponsible parliamentarianism. Perhaps there was undue concentration in this book on the play of parties and parliamentary fencing, as there was certainly too little on culture. But probably it was the most solid and satisfying achievement in a lifetime of scholarship.

U.S.A., an Outline of the Country, its People and Institutions (1941) was another admirable piece of work and brought entirely up to date. *Politics and Law in the United States* was published in the same year, a book which showed what a large place was given to written law in American government, and incidentally how the Supreme Court functioned best when it acted as a political rather than a judicial body. *Is Innocence Enough?* appeared about the same time. Once again good style went with good polemical sense, and though he may have committed some errors in tact in the distribution of his castigations, he scored some convincing points against the naïve illusions of the Left between the wars. He especially attacked the ignorance of Europe shown for example by Bernard Shaw. He also hit a sensitive target when he explained that what irked the rulers of Germany long before the rise of Hitler was "not the injustice of Versailles, but the loss of the war".

Brogan himself, in the Second World War, worked chiefly for the Information Services, especially directing his attention to the two-way communication between Britain on the one hand and France and the United States on the other. He began to suffer again from ill health at this period but this did not interfere much with his output. As an editor of the *Dictionary of National Biography*, as a leader-writer for *The Times*, as a writer of innumerable book reviews and letters to the newspapers, he was able to employ to excellent effect his fantastic memory and range. As a regular broadcaster on "Transatlantic Quiz", and later on "Round Britain Quiz", he was to become one of the first of a new race of dons who combined academic distinction with wide popular celebrity. He turned more and more to a popular audience, for example in *The English People* (1943) and *The American Problem* (1944). In this last book he was at pains to stress what marked Americans off from Englishmen rather than to show what united these kindred stocks. *The Free State*, in 1945, was a propaganda tract aimed at the Germans, explaining the difficulties and imperfections of democracy, but suggesting that "life is on its side, and so is the whole western tradition of which Germany is a part". Some people objected that the author was here confusing the theory of the free state with the practice of English parliamentarianism. He then wrote *French Personalities and Problems* (1946) and *American Themes* (1948), here collecting together some of his casual writings.

A novel, *Stop on the Green Light*, was a light-hearted fantasy that came out under a pseudonym in 1950. It was followed the next year by another forthright tract, *The Price of Revolution*. This perhaps laboured a truism, but it did so with learning and intelligence. We were perforce living in an age of revolution, but one could have too much of a good thing. The experience of Russia, Turkey, Mexico, Japan was called on to show how every political remedy had its price, and violent remedies a necessarily high price. "The impatience of the young is not an excuse for the abandonment of responsibility by their elders who have noticed how quickly the rosy dawn turns into a hangover." Liberty and order had been won with great difficulty, but they could be easily lost.

After another gap there were other books, *An Introduction to American Politics* (1955). *Roosevelt* and *The French Nation from Napoleon to Petain (1814-1940)* in the same year. *America in the Modern World*, in 1960, was more critical of the United States than his earlier books had tended to be. McCarthyism, the economic imperialism of the United States in Cuba and South America, the concentration on private enterprise to the occasional exclusion of public service, these were blemishes which he acknowledged and examined. But

already before the Kennedy era he saw that the period of American complacent self-satisfaction was over, and that the most penetrating criticism there was self-criticism. In the preface to *American Aspects* (1964) he spoke of "the fascination all aspects of American life have had for me since I first read *The Last of the Mohicans, Buffalo Bill* (in paperback) and Mark Twain in the days of President Taft".

Brogan was not an original thinker, and his books were not so much profound or methodical as entertaining and suggestive. His real skill was in presenting information rather than in analysing it or drawing conclusions. He possessed a tremendously tidy and well-stocked mind, and he could be informative and amusing on almost any subject at all. These qualities gave a particular value to the numerous reviews he wrote for *The Times Literary Supplement* for something like 40 years. The allusiveness which made his earlier reviews—and books —difficult going later came more under control. He learnt how not to overload a point with marginal irrelevances and how not to scintillate so much that a reader was dazzled. As a person, despite his shyness, he was an easy and much-liked colleague, a witty companion, who unashamedly enjoyed good food and drink, and a teacher who was generous of his time with undergraduates. He was, too, always ready to put himself at the service of the Liberal Party, and of international movements like the United Nations Association; and he dashed about the world giving lectures. In spite of a photographic memory which gave him a wonderful command of everything he encountered in his vast and rapid reading, he was the perfect model of the absent-minded professor, capable of undertaking lecturing engagements in different countries on the same night, repeatedly getting into the wrong train, and going to meetings on the wrong day.

He possessed a number of honorary doctorates in France, was a Chevalier de la légion d'honneur and a Commander of the Order of Orange-Nassau. He was also a director of Hamish Hamilton, an honorary fellow of Corpus Christi College, Oxford, an honorary fellow of Peterhouse, Cambridge, in 1967 and a Fellow of the British Academy. He was knighted in 1963.

He married the well-known archaeologist, Miss Olwen Kendall, by whom he had three sons and a daughter.

January 7, 1974.

Dr. Jacob Bronowski, the mathematician and scientist, died on August 22, 1974, in the United States at the age of 66.

Bronowski was born in 1908 in Poland, but lived in Germany during the First World War. He went to England in 1920 and read mathematics at the University of Cambridge from 1927 to 1930. He was a Wrangler in that year, and continued

mathematical research at Cambridge from 1930 to 1933. In the following years, he published numerous papers in algebraic geometry and topology, and more recently in mathematical statistics and in mathematics applied to biology. He was Senior Lecturer at the University of Hull from 1934 to 1942.

He left university teaching in 1942 to become head of a number of statistical units dealing with the economic effects of bombing. In his wartime research he was a pioneer in the development of operational research methods. He was Scientific Deputy to the British Chiefs of Staff Mission to Japan in 1945 and wrote the classical British report, *The Effects of the Atomic Bombs at Hiroshima and Nagasaki*. From 1945 to 1950 he was engaged in research for the Government in applying mathematical methods of analysis and forecasting to the economics of industry. In 1950, he became Director of the Coal Research Establishment of the National Coal Board. There he was responsible for the research which culminated in the discovery of the new process for making smokeless fuel. He was in charge of the full development of this process as Director-General of Process Development in the National Coal Board from 1959 to 1963.

Bronowski was on loan to Unesco as head of the Projects Division in 1947, and on leave of absence as Carnegie Visiting Professor to the Massachusetts Institute of Technology in 1953. During his stay at the Institute he delivered lectures on *Science and Human Values* which initiated discussion of the two cultures, and which have since become famous in book form.

He was the author of two widely known books on literature: *The Poet's Defence* (1939) and *William Blake, A Man Without a Mask* (1944). He was well known for his radio and television talks and dramas. These included *The Face of Violence*, which won the Italia prize for the best dramatic work broadcast throughout Europe during 1950 and 1951, and *The Abacus and The Rose: A New Dialogue on Two World Systems* which was broadcast by the B.B.C. Third Programme in 1962 as one of the programmes to celebrate the fortieth anniversary of the Corporation.

The combination of scientific and literary interests made Bronowski a leader in the modern movement of scientific humanism. His book *The Common Sense of Science* reinterprets the development of scientific ideas in a way which makes them meaningful to scientists and non-scientists at the same time. His later works included a book of intellectual history, *The Western Intellectual Tradition* (with Professor Bruce Mazlish), and a book of his television programmes on the concepts of modern science, entitled *Insight*.

In January 1964 Bronowski joined the Salk Institute for Biological Studies in San Diego, California, as senior fellow, becoming director of the Council for Biology in Human Affairs in 1970.

After being away from British television and radio for a decade (he had been a popular member of the *Brains Trust*), Bronowski returned in 1973 to present a 13-part series for the B.B.C. called *The Ascent of Man*, which won him the Royal Television Society's silver medal for outstanding creative achievement. He spent more than two years making the programme, travelling in more than 30 countries, to trace the history of science and mankind from prehistoric times.

He married in 1941 Rita Coblentz and they had four daughters.

August 23, 1974.

Clive Brook, an actor well-known both on stage and in films, died on November 17, 1974 at the age of 87.

He was one of the several English players whose diction and stage experience gave them a great advantage in the early days of talking pictures, but his reputation had already been made by then in silent films.

Clive Brook was born in London on June 1, 1887. He joined The Artists Rifles as a private in 1914, and was commissioned six months later. Later he served in the Machine Gun Corps. It was not until after his demobilization that he adopted acting as his chosen profession. His first appearance on the stage was in *Fair and Warmer* in the provinces; and his first appearance in London was made at the St. Martin's Theatre in February 1920, in *Just Like Judy*. Thereafter he was regularly employed on the stage, and also began to appear in English silent films, playing the lead opposite Betty Compson in *Woman to Woman*.

In 1924 Brook was put under contract by one of the founder producers of the American film industry, Thomas Ince, and went to Hollywood. His good looks, poise and elegance made him a leading man who was much in demand, especially in films with a sophisticated society background, and after a few years he was given a long-term contract by Paramount, and co-starred with their leading lady, Florence Vidor.

The coming of sound increased his popularity still further. One of his first sound films was *The Laughing Lady*, which he made with Ruth Chatterton,* whose waning fortunes it instantly revived. Two outstanding pictures followed shortly afterwards—*Shanghai Express* and *Cavalcade*. In the former, a highly melodramatic adventure story directed by Josef von Sternberg, he had Marlene Dietrich as his leading lady, while in *Cavalcade*, Hollywood's adaptation of Noel Coward's play, he took the part of Robert Marryot in a distinguished English cast which included Diana Wynyard* and Ursula Jeans.

In 1934 he returned to England to make *Loves of the Dictator, Love in Exile, Lonely Road, Action for Slander* and *Return to Yesterday*. During the war years he appeared in *Convoy, Freedom Radio, Breach of Promise, The Shipbuilders* and *Flemish Farm*. He also produced, adapted, directed and played in *On Approval*, with Beatrice Lillie in 1944.

After the war, he returned to the stage, and enjoyed a notable success at Wyndham's as Michael Wentworth in *The Years Between*. Thereafter he concentrated on the theatre, and appeared in a number of plays in London, on tour and in America, where he made his first stage appearance at Newhaven, Connecticut, in 1950 as Josiah Bolton in *Second Threshold*. Later he turned to television, being seen in *Second Threshold, The Giaconda Smile* (in which he had appeared on the London stage some 10 years previously), *The Play's the Thing*, and *The Judge's Story*.

As an actor he was handicapped, in his younger days, by being typed as the reserved and sophisticated English gentleman (many of the still pictures from his earlier films show him in immaculate evening dress), but his range was far wider than that. He was never a demonstrative or emotional player, but his performances had power, authority and polish. The record books of the cinema credit him with having starred in more than 90 films, in itself a remarkable achievement.

He married in 1920 Miss Mildred Evelyn, and the children of the marriage, Faith and Lyndon Brook, have both had successful theatrical careers.

November 19, 1974.

Basil Brooke, 1st Viscount Brookeborough —See Brookeborough.

Sylvia Lady Brooke, Ranee of Sarawak, died on November 11, 1971 at the Queen Elizabeth Hospital in Barbados at the age of 86.

Lady Brooke was the widow of Sir Charles Vyner Brooke*, the Rajah of Sarawak, who died eight years earlier. He succeeded his father in 1917 and in 1946 ceded the country to the Crown and retired to London where he spent his remaining years, retaining his title Rajah of Sarawak.

The Hon. Sylvia Leonora Brett was the second daughter of the second Viscount Esher, and she married Sir Charles Vyner Brooke in 1911. In 1912 the old Rajah, suspicious of what he called the "Esher influence", decreed Vyner's younger brother heir presumptive to Vyner if the latter had no male issue, though he became reconciled to his daughter-in-law before his death. There were three daughters of the marriage, Leonora, Elizabeth and Valerie.

Lady Brooke published several books, among them *Queen of the Head-hunters* (1970). In this book she tells of her courtship. Vyner Brooke, the third son of Sir Charles Brooke, second Rajah of Sarawak, and Margaret de Windt, Ranee of Sarawak, chose Sylvia as his wife when she was 17. Despite parental disapproval, an abortive elopement and some years of separation, they did at last get married. Vyner was a shy man; he was terrified not only of Sylvia's intellectual friends but also of the socially great. In Sarawak, Sylvia, as Ranee, always had to walk 4ft behind her husband because he walked with God under his umbrella. Later, their daughters, given the title of princesses by the press, made the headlines with marriages to an earl, an all-in wrestler, a dance-band leader and various others; while Sylvia, when the cash grew short, lectured in the United States as "The Queen of the Head-hunters".

Her conventional childhood involved playing with the royal children from Windsor. She was presented without success at Court. Meanwhile she won a £20 prize from *The Woman at Home* for a short story. Her literary mentors were J. M. Barrie, who sponsored her first volume of short stories, and Bernard Shaw, who wrote her charmingly coquettish letters.

November 13, 1971.

Lord Brookeborough, K.G., P.C., C.B.E., M.C., who was Prime Minister of Northern Ireland from 1943 to 1963, died on August 18, 1973 at the age of 85.

A staunch representative of the Anglo-Irish aristocracy and an unyielding believer in the Protestant ascendancy, he had a far-reaching effect on the province's political life. The sectarian strife now tearing at the fabric of Northern Ireland's society is in part attributable to the immobility imposed in his long period of political leadership.

Brookeborough was a man of courage, conviction and great charm. But his political sense was seriously found wanting by the intransigence with which he excluded the Roman Catholic minority from responsibility and participation. He believed that, being basically republicans, they were not in a constitutional sense to be trusted.

He laid the foundation of his reputation in his early days as Prime Minister. With Dublin neutral, Belfast was a base for the Allies: a back door firmly shut on the enemy.

The union with England was his abiding concern and he would allow nothing to compromise it. While Northern Ireland M.P.s at Westminster took the Conservative whip, his Government at Stormont re-enacted most of the Attlee Government's social measures.

When he resigned the Premiership of Northern Ireland in March 1963, he was Ulster's longest-serving Prime Minister, having held office for two months short of 20 years. He had also established a United Kingdom record by holding government office continuously for 33 years.

The Right Hon. Sir Basil Stanlake Brooke, first Viscount Brookeborough, of Colebrooke, co. Fermanagh, and a baronet, both in the Peerage of the United Kingdom, was born on June 9, 1888 of a family which was one of the oldest settled in Northern Ireland from England. He was the eldest son of Arthur Douglas Brooke, and he traced his ancestry back to Sir Basil Brooke, knighted by Queen Elizabeth I. For many generations since they have been known as "The Fighting Brookes". Some of his later ancestors did battle for William of Orange on the Boyne, and they supplied a long and distinguished line of sailors, soldiers, statesmen and administrators through the centuries.

Basil Brooke went to Winchester, and afterwards passed through the Royal Military College, Sandhurst, before he was commissioned to the Royal Fusiliers. Later he transferred to the 10th Hussars, fought with them throughout the First World War, taking part in the Dardanelles campaign, was awarded the M.C., the Croix de Guerre with Palm, and was mentioned in dispatches.

He had in 1907 succeeded to the family baronetcy and the Colebrooke Park Estates, before returning to Ulster after the war ended. In 1921 he became a Senator in the first Northern Ireland Parliament, but retired a year later to assume full-time duties as a Commandant of the Special Constabulary in his own county. He was then 33. He had been out of Ireland for most of his young manhood, and he was now brought for the first time into close touch with the welter of problems with which both South and North were bemused following upon the state of virtual civil war in the South, and the creation of Ulster as a separate province. Brooke's post in co. Fermanagh was near enough to the Free State border to be a dangerous one, and both he and the men whom he commanded were often in peril.

For seven years after resigning from the Senate he remained out of the active political scene at Stormont, but in many other ways served the Province, and his party's relentless campaign to preserve the Union. But in 1929, under strong pressure from his friends, he agreed to stand for the Northern Ireland Parliament and was elected for Lisnaskea.

His impact upon practical politics was immediate. In 1933 the Premier, Sir James Craig, as he then was, made him Minister of Agriculture, a post which he retained until 1941. Under his direction as a practical agriculturist himself, the farming and allied industries in Ulster were transformed. Large and far-reaching schemes for the marketing of milk, eggs and meat were introduced, the farmers were encouraged and aided to increase proficiency in cultivation, and within these seven or eight years the Ulster countryside assumed a prosperity which it had never known before.

With the outbreak of war in 1939, the Irish Free State remained stubbornly neutral. Lord Craigavon had died while still Premier, a post in which he was succeeded by that other veteran Ulsterman, John M.

Andrews, who counted Brooke among the ablest members of his Cabinet, and as the strain of the war developed he transferred him from agriculture to the Ministry of Commerce and Production. It was the ideal choice, and under his guidance the Ulster contribution to the war effort developed enormously.

He made frequent journeys to London for consultation. He countered the suggestion to the British Premier and his ministers that those workers in Ulster still unemployed should be moved to English factories, by demanding that the raw materials and the instruments of output should be supplied to Northern Ireland, so that Ulster's men and women could work at home. In particular, he arranged for the lifting of the Limitation of Supplies Order so that the Province might receive additional quantities of many materials—as, for example, textiles and metals—so that Ulster was able still more enormously to increase its war output.

In May 1943 John Andrews, then 72, and feeling the burden of his years and office, resigned as Premier. Sir Basil Brooke was the inevitable successor, and with the support and goodwill of everybody he retained the portfolio of Commerce, and for the remaining two years of the war held both offices.

It was a period of intense strain, because from time to time his concentration upon the war effort was deflected by events in Eire, and he suffered deep personal losses in the fighting. But he maintained all his many-sided activities, and in particular made and maintained wide contacts with officers of all ranks in the American and other Allied Forces in Northern Ireland.

With the end of the war he was able to turn his attention to those other issues which his country, like others, had to face in the process of transformation. It was here again that his experience, energy and force of character were so manifest. He was particularly active in his efforts to consolidate and extend the industrial developments in Ulster.

Otherwise he constantly countered the attempts from Dublin to end partition, declaring that he was a Unionist first and a Conservative second, always making it clear that both his Government and himself sought no interference in the affairs of Eire, and proclaiming Ulster's desire to live in friendly neighbourliness with the south.

In the spring of 1955 he returned with his wife from a protracted tour of Australia and New Zealand, during which he had explained his policy and had negotiated concerning the import restrictions on Ulster's exports, especially linen.

He led the Unionist Party at the polls at five Ulster general elections, 1945, 1949, 1953, 1958 and 1962. Only once was he opposed in his constituency, Lisnaskea, and he then defeated a Nationalist opponent.

His leadership came under criticism early in 1963 from a group of Unionist backbenchers who were mainly concerned about

directorships held by other members of the Government. The split was healed and Lord Brookeborough was given a unanimous vote of confidence. But a serious operation which coincided with this affair forced him to retire from office. He declined an earldom.

Although it attracted little criticism in Great Britain at the time, his refusal to bring the Roman Catholic minority into active participation in public affairs stands out in retrospect as a serious blemish on his political record. In that respect his mind was prejudiced to an extent that damaged the political development of the province.

He was also, by modern standards, casual in his approach to his political duties. Lord O'Neill of the Maine, who succeeded him as Prime Minister, wrote of him that he was good company and a good raconteur, and those who met him imagined that he was relaxing away from his desk. But, O'Neill said, they did not realize that there was no desk.

In the last three years of his life, years in which the Stormont institution came under its greatest strain and eventually crumbled, Brookeborough made only occasional forays into political life. In 1972 he appeared next to William Craig on the balcony of the Stormont Parliament building, a diminutive figure beside the leader of the Vanguard movement who was rallying Right-Wing Unionists against the Government.

He opposed the Westminster White Paper on the future of Northern Ireland and caused some embarrassment to his son, Captain John Brooke—the Unionist chief whip and a Faulkner man—by speaking against the Government's proposals on the night before the Assembly elections.

In his private life he was a man of the simplest and most modest tastes and habits. His greatest recreation was farming, and he won many awards. But he also liked shooting, fishing and golf.

He was created C.B.E. in 1921, and made a Privy Councillor of Northern Ireland in 1933. He was created a Viscount in 1952.

He married, in 1919, a kinswoman, Cynthia, daughter of Captain and the Hon. Mrs. Sergison, of Cuckfield Park, Sussex, and they had three sons, two of whom were killed in action during the Second World War. The surviving son, John Warden Brooke, succeeds to the viscountcy.

Lord Brookeborough's wife died in 1970, and in 1971 he married Sarah Eileen Bell Calvert, widow of Cecil Armstrong Calvert, F.R.C.S.

August 20, 1973.

Roy Brooks, the London estate agent, well-known for his frank and piquantly humorous property advertisements, died on August 30, 1971 at the age of 55.

His direct approach to the selling of property began after the Second World War. At first glance the advertisements, under the name of E. H. Brooks & Son, in the Sunday papers, appeared orthodox. Then came the straight talk: "bedroom suitable for child or large dwarf"; "a nice house in a nasty part of Westminster"; "decor repulsive"; "so-called garden"; and other fairly brutal comments. The forthright approach was highly successful and brought Brooks a lot of business.

A man of spirit and enthusiasm with a strongly developed social conscience, he stood unsuccessfully as Labour candidate at Aldershot in the general election of 1959.

He also did journalistic and radio work, and appeared on television in programmes concerned with property.

After the Hungarian revolution he was associated with a house for refugee children. Another of his schemes was the modernization of a house for Recidivists Anonymous—a society for old lags determined to go straight.

September 1, 1971.

Sir (George) Lindor Brown—See Sir Lindor Brown.

Ivor Brown, C.B.E., F.R.S.L., who died on April 22, 1974 at the age of 82, was among the most prolific writers of his generation. The trenchant, witty articles that he contributed during the 1914-18 War to Orage's *New Age* were followed by a flow of journalism and books that never stopped. Even when he was editing *The Observer,* from 1942 to 1948, he continued to do dramatic criticism and much other writing.

He wrote for many years for the *Manchester Guardian* and later for *The Times.* The *Saturday Review* and *Punch* were among the weeklies for which he worked. The exercise of composing seemed to be as effortless for him as it had been for Chesterton. He did not chuckle to himself as the words came, as Chesterton did, but his hand moved smoothly and steadily, almost as though it were automatic, and his countenance as he wrote was as relaxed as that of a man in a club armchair. Only occasionally would he sit back, stumped for a thought or a word, biting his handkerchief in deepest gloom. Heavily built, given to sometimes disconcerting silences, he could, when the mood was on him, be as entertaining in talk as he invariably was on paper.

Ivor John Carnegie Brown was born in Penang on April 25, 1891. He came of an Aberdeenshire family; his grandfather, a minister of the Church of Scotland, followed Dr. Chalmers at the Disruption. His father, a graduate of Aberdeen, took up practice in the Malay States. The boy was sent home to school at Cheltenham and went on to Balliol. On graduating he was for a short time in the Civil Service, but in 1913 abandoned that career to take up literary work.

During the 1914-18 War he was a conscientious objector. He was keenly interested in the progressive politics of the time. He lectured for the Oxford Tutorial Classes Committee and wrote in forward-looking journals. In two books on *English Political Theory* and *The Meaning of Democracy* he showed the early bent of his mind.

In 1919 there began with his appointment to the London staff his long association with the *Manchester Guardian.* From the first his interests included the theatre; and as part of his duties was to write dramatic criticism it fell to him to interpret the great outburst of new and experimental modes of play-writing that followed, especially on the Continental stage, the 1914-18 War. His reactions to the "expressionists" like the Capek brothers, to Pirandello and to their counterparts in the United States like Elmer Rice* and Eugene O'Neill are collected in a volume, *Masques and Phrases,* compiled from his contributions to the *Manchester Guardian, Saturday Review* and *New Statesman* among other journals. It remains a valuable commentary on a remarkable chapter in the history of the theatre.

Brown was too active and had too well stored a mind to be content with concentration on the stage. Throughout a number of years he contributed to the *Manchester Guardian* a series of Saturday articles on the social and literary trends of the day that gave him a high place among stylists. They are collected in such volumes as *Brown Studies* and *I Commit to the Flames.* His outlook was that of a rationalist and a reformer, but a fastidious choice of words and a pervasive vein of ironical humour made him, even at his most polemical, an engaging writer. His delight in exposing contemporary follies ran sometimes to fiction, notably in a modern variant on *Candide* entitled *Master Sanguine,* and in a picture of the disaster that may befall a simple seaside resort through over-development, *Marine Parade.*

In 1926 Brown was appointed Shute lecturer on the Art of the Theatre at Liverpool University, and in 1939 Professor of Drama to the Royal Society of Literature. When C.E.M.A.—the Council for the Encouragement of Music and the Arts, later to become the Arts Council—was set up in the war years, he was made its Director of Drama. He had by then been for some years the dramatic critic of *The Observer* and a frequent contributor to its literary columns. When, in 1942, J. L. Garvin retired from the editorship, Brown was appointed to the post. He continued to be its chief dramatic critic, but at the same time found scope for his gift for social and political commentary in witty "middle articles" and, on occasion, in well turned satiric verse.

By many readers he will be remembered affectionately for his "word books". They began with *A Word in your Ear,* published in 1942; and 30 years later, in *A Charm of Names,* he was still sharing his connoisseurship with an appreciative public. His interest was not merely etymological—he had a delight in words, and with this delight went a sharp concern for their correct usage. In *No Idle Words* (1949), for example, he was astringent about the use of "evocative", "integrated" and "overall", and this examination of current use and misuse was to be found in most of his subsequent excursions into the world of words. It would, none the less, be quite wrong to look on him as a pedant; there might be the little lecture on what was seemly and what was not, but there was also the pleasant Brownian ramble, in which philology, literary allusion and personal reminiscence came tumbling out along the way, making Ivor Brown such excellent company to a multitude of readers.

His interest in William Shakespeare and his curiosity about "the man behind the plays" was lifelong. Typically, he refused to defer automatically to the professors and the scholars, and his *Shakespeare* (1949) had a breezy, common sense, no-nonsense air about it. It was a popular success and went into a fourth edition in 1963. It was followed by other Shakespearian studies: *Shakespeare in his Time, How Shakespeare spent the Day, Shakespeare and his World,* and *The Women in Shakespeare's Life.*

Brown was a keen lover of the open air and was never happier than when walking the moors and hills of Scotland, Wales or Derbyshire. He had too a fondness for the Scandinavian nations, and in the difficult years after the war did much by lecturing in Denmark to reestablish cultural links with that country, a service recognized by the conferment upon him by the King of Denmark of a Knighthood of the Order of Dannebrog.

He published a number of novels, books on Shaw, Dickens, Somerset Maugham*, and Conan Doyle, on London and Balmoral; a true professional man of letters, he was never happier than when engaged on a piece of writing. He was chairman of the British Drama League from 1954 to 1965 and a Fellow of the Royal Society of Literature. In 1957 he was created C.B.E.

He married Irene Hentschel, who shared his interest in the theatre and who, under her maiden name, had directed many successful plays. There were no children of the marriage.

April 23, 1974.

Sir Lindor Brown, C.B.E., F.R.S., Principal of Hertford College, Oxford, died on February 22, 1971 at the age of 68.

Lindor Brown was educated at Boteler Grammar School, Warrington, and at the University of Manchester, where he took physiology honours, going on to qualify medicine in 1928. He began his career in physiology as a lecturer in B. A. MacSwiney's department in Leeds.

A decisive step came when in 1934 he joined Sir Henry Dale's* laboratory at the

National Institute for Medical Research, then at Hampstead. This laboratory has been one of the chief nurseries of British medical science. Brown joined at the beginning of its *anni mirabiles*, when Dale and his colleagues laid the foundation of the theory of chemical transmission (the theory, now widely accepted, that nerves excite activity in the structures they control, not by the electrical eddy currents of the nervous impulse but by the release of a specific chemical substance).

Brown brought to the collaboration a beautiful technique, great resourcefulness, and an eye for simple decisive experiment. With Dale's retirement Brown became head of the physiology and pharmacology division, and led its wartime activities in research into the physiology of diving and submarine life. Here his ability to secure friendly collaboration, not only among scientists, but (much more remarkable) between executive officers and backroom boffins, produced a co-operation between the Royal Navy and the Medical Research Council that is still fruitful.

With the return of peace the laboratory returned to its normal activities but it was not long before University College London claimed him, in 1949, as its Jodrell Professor of Physiology. There he began his work on the release of the sympathetic transmitter. He had been elected to the Royal Society in 1946; in 1955 he became its Biological Secretary, a post he held, over the time of the tercentenary celebrations, until 1963.

During this period he went to the Waynflete Chair in Oxford, and became a Fellow of Magdalen. He enjoyed only a brief respite from Royal Society duties before being appointed to the Franks Commission of Inquiry into the working of the university. Apart from these appointments, he had throughout his career done much for physiology and medical science; notably as secretary of the Physiological Society and then as its foreign secretary, and on the *Journal of Physiology*'s editorial board; as President of the International Union of Physiological Sciences; and as a member of the Medical Research Council, and later of the (now transmogrified) Council for Scientific and Industrial Research.

In 1967 he was appointed Principal of Hertford College, an election happily coinciding with the transformation and lightening of Radcliffe Square and Catte Street by the newly cleaned face of the college. In his period of office, so tragically cut short, he became much beloved by his colleagues and members of the college, present and past. He inaugurated the college's major appeal for funds for the building of a third quadrangle of the college. He continued to be active in scientific research and negotiated the endowment of two Senior Research Fellowships in the college, in conjunction with the University engineering and computing laboratories.

Lindor Brown brought to all he did a highly individual personality, long familiar at meetings of the Physiological Society; a light-hearted perspicacity quick to deflate the pompous; an array of anecdotes suitable for any company (and a puckish pleasure in occasionally mismatching them); and a strong prejudice in favour of the young. He never lost his pleasure in working (in any material) with his own hands, his delight in craftsmanship, whether traditional or modern, and his enjoyment in scientific collaboration (his list of co-workers is long and distinguished).

He married a fellow medical student, Jane Rosamond, daughter of Professor C. H. Lees, F.R.S., and had four children. All those who enjoyed the family's hospitality (often, as a physiologist's wife learns, impromptu and at irregular hours), his numerous colleagues, and friends all over the world will miss greatly his invigorating presence.

February 23, 1971.

Pamela Brown, the actress, who had contributed something distinctive to the theatre ever since the intelligence of her work and her remarkable, incandescent personality and striking good looks were first recognized during the early days of the Second World War, died on September 18, 1975 at the age of 58.

She was born on July 8, 1917. Ill health, whereby her stage career was often to be interrupted, originally promoted it, for after her recovery from a long illness, contracted in her fifteenth year, it was decided that she should not go back to school at Ascot but should train to be an actress instead.

Accordingly she studied at R.A.D.A., and in 1936 played a season at the Shakespeare Memorial Theatre, Stratford-on-Avon. This was followed by engagements in South Africa, at the Oxford Playhouse, at Perranporth and at the Old Vic. She returned in 1940 to the Oxford Playhouse where, at the suggestion of a critic who had been much impressed by her, James Agate, she was cast as Hedda Gabler and in other leading parts.

Her success was confirmed in 1942 by her performance as Claudia in Rose Franken's play of that name in London. She appeared with the Old Vic company in the West End as Ophelia to Robert Helpmann's *Hamlet* and as Goneril to Olivier's *Lear*, and with Gielgud's company in Wilde and Congreve in America. She again played with Sir John in Christopher Fry's *The Lady's not for Burning*—the author had been with her at the Oxford Playhouse and wrote the part of the suspected witch specially for her—and during his classical season at the Lyric, Hammersmith, where, however, she was less successful as his Millamant in *The Way of the World* than as Aquilina the courtesan in *Venice Preserv'd*.

Apart from Franken and Fry, the contemporary dramatists in whose plays she appeared in London included Aldous Huxley* (*The Gioconda Smile*), Charles Morgan (*The River Line*), Wynyard Browne (*A Question of Fact*) and Enid Bagnold (*The Chalk Garden*). Later she was seen in New York in *The Country Wife* and in Maurice Evans's revival of *Heartbreak House*, and in England on television with Sir Laurence Olivier in *John Gabriel Borkman* and with Dame Edith Evans in *Hay Fever*.

Pamela Brown played a number of parts in British films from 1941 onwards, including that of Jane Shore—a non-speaking part, but in her hands an eloquent symbol of clandestine love and of conspiracy—in Sir Laurence Olivier's *Richard III*. This was in 1955. Later films in which she had parts were *Cleopatra; Becket; Secret Ceremony;* and *Lady Caroline Lamb*. On television she was seen recently in *Mary and Louisa* with Faith Brook and Anton Rodgers. This was one of the London Weekend series "Affairs of the Heart", plays inspired by the stories of Henry James.

She was formerly married to Peter Copley, the actor.

September 20, 1975.

Sir John Bruce, C.B.E., T.D., F.R.S.E., F.R.C.S.E., Emeritus Professor of Clinical Surgery in the University of Edinburgh, and Honorary Surgeon to the Queen in Scotland, died on December 30, 1975 at the age of 70.

He was one of the last of the general surgeons who lent such lustre to British surgery during the present century, which in practice meant that his main domain was the gastro-intestinal tract. A sound and safe, if not original, surgeon, his main claim to fame was as a catalyst in an era when, largely as a result of developments in biochemistry, anaesthesia and antibiosis, surgery was blossoming out with almost explosive force into realms and activities that had hitherto been more or less forbidden territory. Bruce was wise enough to realize that this was not his forte, but he gave every encouragement to his staff and others to take the plunge into these enticing new spheres.

In this he was aided by an outgoing nature. He was a *bon viveur* who loved company, and was never happier than when arguing—whether with his colleagues or his juniors. He had the traditional Scottish gift of the gab which could ignore the remorseless moving hands of time and talk until the sun arose over the horizon announcing the approach of yet another day. Not the least of his claims to fame was that he was no narrow nationalist. The world was his parish, so far as surgery was concerned. Hence the number of lectures he delivered and the number of external examinerships he held in all five continents.

Success, however, never turned his head, and right to the end there was still recognizable in him the "lad o' pairts" who had graduated with honours in 1928. Over the years he developed many of the mannerisms of his old chief, Sir John Fraser, for whom he had an almost idolatrous admiration. He may never have acquired the polish of his old chief, but a somewhat comparable physical build, combined with the mannerisms, would on occasions produce a most striking similarity.

John Bruce was born on March 6, 1905, and graduated with honours from Edinburgh University in 1928, proceeding to his Fellowship of the Royal College of Surgeons of Edinburgh in 1932. He was appointed assistant surgeon to the Royal Infirmary, Edinburgh, in 1935, and surgeon to the Western General Hospital, Edinburgh, in 1946. Ten years later he was appointed to the Regius Chair of Clinical Surgery in Edinburgh, a post he held until his retirement in 1970.

He spent the entire period of the Second World War in the R.A.M.C., first in Norway, where he was mentioned in dispatches, and then as Brigadier-Consulting Surgeon to the 14th Army, S.E.A.C., and in Burma, where he was again mentioned in dispatches. He never lost his interest in the Services, and after the war he was a member of the advisory boards of both the Army and the R.A.F.

In his time he was President of the Royal College of Surgeons of Edinburgh, the Association of Surgeons of Great Britain and Ireland, and the International Federation of Surgical Colleges. He was an honorary fellow of the College of Surgeons of England, Ireland, America, Canada, Australasia, South Africa, and Denmark, and an honorary member of the Academy of Medicine of Malaya. His visiting professorships were almost equally prolific—the universities of California, Copenhagen, Ohio, Wisconsin, and Cincinnati, as well as the Sir Arthur Sims Commonwealth Professorship. He was an honorary LL.D. of the University of Alberta, and an honorary D.Sc. of the University of Pennsylvania. To these must be added an impressive list of eponymous lectureships.

Apart from his presidential and eponymous lectures, and the 2nd Edition of the *Manual of Surgical Anatomy* for which he was responsible, he was not a prolific writer. It was as a bedside teacher in the old style of clinical teaching that he excelled. In the ward and in the operating theatre he was in his element—stimulating and provocative, but always understanding and always ready and willing to help the dresser or junior colleague who sought his professional help and guidance. In his passing Edinburgh has lost one of its surgical characters and a staunch upholder of the great surgical tradition of a medical school that includes Lister, Stiles, Wilkie and Fraser in its surgical roll of honour.

He was appointed C.B.E. in 1945 and knighted in 1963. He married, in 1935, Mary Whyte Craig.

December 31, 1975.

Avery Brundage, Honorary Life President of the International Olympic Committee (I.O.C.), died on May 8, 1975 aged 87.

Brundage was the colossus of the modern Games, which he dominated during the most turbulent period in their history. He was elected President in 1952 for a period of eight years (according to the constitution) and reelected for three successive periods of four years before yielding office in 1972 to Lord Killanin, of Ireland.

Lord Killanin's first duty in his new office was to announce that Avery Brundage had been elected Honorary Life President.

It was Brundage's misfortune to hold office during a period when the movement was rarely free of political tension, as it grappled with the problems of two Germanies, two Koreas, two Chinas, a divided South Africa and a division of opinion over Rhodesia.

Finally, it became embroiled in the Middle East conflict in 1972, when, in all, 17 lives were lost during the Games of the XXth Olympiad at Munich. When the news was received at 6.30 am on September 5 that two Israelis had been killed and the others held hostage in the Olympic Village, Brundage, a month short of his eighty-fifth birthday, immediately drove to the Olympic Village to take a personal hand in the deliberations.

It was typical of a man whose physical durability had been a source of admiration to those who came in contact with him in later life. He was still clear of mind and unflagging in the face of wearisome debate, sometimes protracted to the small hours. His voice remained strong and his tread firm, though a growing deafness, added to congenitally poor eyesight, had become a handicap.

From the moment of taking office Brundage was confronted with the German problem, which, for a time, represented an Olympic triumph. Unlike the United Nations, the I.O.C. refused to recognize two nations and it was not until 1968 that two German teams took part in the Olympic Games, and even then, at Grenoble for the Winter Games and Mexico in the summer, they used one flag and one (Olympic) anthem. Not until 1972, indeed, did the Germans compete as two nations, with separate anthems and flags.

The two Koreas were successfully accommodated as two nations, though not without occasional friction over extraneous issues. There was, however, no solution to the Chinese puzzle and it was a matter of deep personal regret to Brundage, strongly attracted to the Orient, that mainland China could not be lured back to the fold during his term of office.

He was unwilling, however, to pay the price acceptable to the United Nations—the inclusion of the mainland to the exclusion of Taiwan, an example later followed by a number of international sports federations as China kept up its preparations for applying for readmission to the Olympic Movement in April 1975.

When South Africa were excluded from the 1964 Games in Tokyo, it was decided to send a commission to examine conditions in that country to help to decide whether or not they should be allowed to compete at Mexico City in 1968. The commission, under the chairmanship of Lord Killanin, gave guarded approval to the South African proposal for a mixed team and the I.O.C. accordingly invited the South Africans to Mexico City.

There followed such an outcry, with the threat of a massive boycott by African nations and certain sympathizers, that the invitation, to Brundage's lasting regret, was later withdrawn, officially because the safety of the South African team could not be guaranteed in Mexico City. This was cynically regarded as an unworthy compromise, though in the light of events many were later inclined to change their minds.

A number of people, variously estimated between 200 and 500, were shot down during a demonstration before the Games opened, and four years later there was to be the dramatic, and bloody, confrontation with Arab terrorists. In 1970 South Africa, which had until then been a member of the Olympic committee of nations, though unable to compete, was expelled from the movement altogether.

In 1972 Rhodesia provided something of an echo of the South Africa experience. When African nations gave notice of withdrawing from the Munich Games, Brundage threatened them with expulsion, on the ground that they were allowing politics to interfere with sport. He charged them with "naked blackmail". In the event Brundage had to make a humiliating withdrawal, when a majority of his I.O.C. colleagues (there were 70 of them at the meeting) decided that the "invitation should not be sustained". He was, he said, "shocked" by the vote.

But if there was one issue above all others that Brundage became associated with it was the vexed question of amateurism. He had no time for professionalism, which he once said belonged to the circus. "Trained seal" was his pet term of scorn for the professional sportsman. Thus he insisted on the strict interpretation of amateurism established when the modern Games were founded at the end of the last century. Through constant iteration, he unwittingly coined a multiple adjective to crystallize his philosophy—"cleanpureandhonest".

As the evidence mounted that transgressions were the rule rather than the exception, he yet maintained his position and there were murmurs among his own members of "dictator" and "megalomaniac".

The I.O.C., under Brundage's direction, took action against doubtful competitors, whether of sexual abnormality or under the influence of drugs, and strove, with some success, to protect the Games from commercial exploiters. It had less success in controlling its own affairs and seemed powerless, quick though it was to diagnose the illness, to find a cure for what the

French members called "gigantisme".

Though Brundage frequently inveighed against the growth of the Games, each surpassed its predecessor in sheer size. The Moscow games of 1980 may exceed even the enormous Munich and Montreal (1976) commitments unless Lord Killanin can clothe idle words with flesh and blood. Excessive nationalism, similarly, has gone on unchecked, for all the passionate pleas, at I.O.C. meeting after meeting, for urgent action.

Brundage first became associated with the Olympics in 1912 when he competed for the United States in the pentathlon and decathlon at Stockholm. The war ended and he began to scale the heights of administration. He was elected President of the United States Olympic Committee in 1929. He became a member of the I.O.C. in 1933 and took over the reins of office from Sigfrid Edström, of Sweden, in 1952.

There are two views of Brundage's position during the Berlin Olympics in 1936. Some argued a withdrawal, but Brundage took the view that the Games could contribute to peace and international friendship. A few years later he became Chairman of the "Keep America out of the War" committee. He resigned the day after Pearl Harbour.

Brundage suffered the Winter Games with little grace. He refused to attend skiing events at Grenoble in 1968, as a protest against commercial intrusion, and he was largely instrumental in having Karl Schranz, an Austrian skier, disqualified at Sapporo in 1972 for no publicly disclosed reason.

At the following I.O.C. plenary session he explained that Alpine skiers, as a breed, were not true amateurs and an example had had to be made of the principal transgressor. His final words on the Winter Games were contained in his last address to an I.O.C. session, at Munich in 1972, when he wished them "a decent burial" at Denver in 1976. After that Denver withdrew, in the face of environmental protest, and the Games, switched to Innsbruck, show little sign of moribundity.

Brundage was born at Detroit on September 28, 1887, and moved with his family to Chicago six years later. Orphaned at 11, he was cared for by a variety of aunts and uncles, but the domestic upheaval had little effect on his maturing process. After a successful school career, at the Chicago English High and Manual Training School, he went on to gain an engineering degree at the University of Illinois.

Because of defective eyesight (his only physical shortcoming until later years), the First World War found him not in uniform and in Europe but in Washington, where he laid the foundations of a construction business that flourished to such purpose that at one point in his career he claimed to have built nearly a half of Chicago, including the biggest factory in the city for Henry Ford. He managed to remain solvent during the depression and emerged to amass a fortune of such magnitude that he was able

to give the city of San Francisco his collection of Oriental art worth more than £20m. in 1967 and still remain a millionaire to much the same amount.

Brundage married a talented musician, Elizabeth Dunlap, in 1927 and established a home at Santa Barbara, California. But during his busy years of presidency he was able to spend only a few weeks a year there. He used to say that he had a house at Santa Barbara, an office in Chicago and lived in an aircraft. Elizabeth Brundage died, childless, in 1971.

In 1972 he was married again, to Princess Mariann Reuss, then 36. Princess Mariann said at the time that their first two children would be given names beginning with A and B, to match her husband's initials. But there were no children of the marriage.

May 10, 1975.

Sir Frederick Brundrett, K.C.B., K.B.E., who died on August 1, 1974 at the age of 79, was Scientific Adviser to the Minister of Defence, and Chairman of the Defence Research Policy Committee from 1954 to 1959.

During the Second World War he was closely involved in the recruitment of scientists and scientific workers to the government service. His principal scientific work was concerned with the development of short-wave radio, in which he played a leading part in the period between the two world wars.

The thing most remembered of Brundrett's time as Scientific Adviser to the Minister of Defence, and earlier as deputy to Tizard and Cockcroft*, was the extent to which he gained and held the confidence of successive Chiefs of Staffs of the Services—and this in the days before the united Ministry of Defence. They not only trusted his handling of the Defence Research and Development programmes but they soon came to welcome his down-to-earth advice and help in resolving many more directly military problems and arguments of priority between competing Service developments. A weekend in seclusion at Greenwich or Camberley, with Brundrett in attendance to tackle an impasse among the Chiefs, would as likely as not result in a Brundrett working party with agreed terms of reference that put all on notice that a solution could and would be reached.

He was born on November 25, 1894, the son of Walter Brundrett, and educated at Rossall School and Sidney Sussex College, Cambridge, where he was a wrangler. He joined the wireless branch of the R.N.V.R. in 1916 and was later engaged in research work on underwater communications with submarines. On demobilization in 1919 he went to the scientific side of the Admiralty and was allocated to the signal school, where he remained until 1937, when he was promoted Principal Scientific Officer and transferred to the headquarters of the Chief of the Royal Naval Scientific Service.

He was promoted superintending scientist in 1939, Assistant Director of Scientific Research in 1940, Deputy Director in 1942, and in 1946 Chief of the Royal Scientific Service in succession to Sir Charles Wright.

Brundrett was appointed Deputy Scientific Adviser to the Minister of Defence in 1950, and four years later succeeded Sir John Cockcroft as Scientific Adviser and Chairman of the Defence Research Policy Committee.

On retirement from these posts he was appointed Chairman of the Air Traffic Control Board. He was a Civil Service Commissioner from 1960 to 1967, and for six years from 1960 Chairman of the Naval Aircraft Research Committee, Aeronautical Research Council.

Brundrett was widely known as a successful farmer, and he brought his common sense and scientific approach to bear on many aspects of agriculture, including the management of contagious abortion in cattle. He was Chairman of the Council of the Red and White Friesian Cattle Society. He was a dedicated follower of most sports and a notable hockey player, who captained the Hampshire county XI and the Civil Service XI before the Second World War.

He married in 1920 Enid, daughter of G. R. James, of Cambridge. Their only son was killed in Italy in 1944.

August 6, 1974.

The Duke of Buccleuch, a leading Scottish landowner, died in hospital in Edinburgh, aged 78, on October 4, 1973.

He had been Chancellor of the Order of the Thistle since 1966 and Lord Lieutenant of Roxburgh since 1932. He was Unionist M.P. for Roxburgh and Selkirk from 1923 to 1935; and was Captain-General of the Royal Company of Archers. He was Lord Steward of the Household of King George VI from 1937 to 1940; and was a former Governor of the Royal Bank of Scotland.

He was a brother of the Duchess of Gloucester.

He inherited vast estates and priceless treasures which he looked after with superb efficiency and pride, and was always delighted to share the beauty of his possessions with anyone who showed interest. Apart from his political and military interests, forestry in all its aspects was his main preoccupation and all his estates are a model of timber husbandry. He was a first class shot, a gifted athlete, and would have been a cricketer of importance had not the First World War intervened.

He was Master of the family pack of hounds which roamed over a great area of wonderful hunting country. His long partnership with Summers, huntsman of the Duke for 50 years, was almost symbiotic in its instinctive partnership. In everything he did his physical energy seemed to be astonishing. He moved from one house and estate to another, and even after two hip operations at the age of 70, thought nothing of dancing into the small hours. To some he seemed to retain many of the indelible characteristics of his ancestor Charles II—a caustic sense of humour, combined with a kindly interest in everything and everyone, and above all a tremendous joy of living.

Walter John Montagu-Douglas-Scott, K.T., P.C., G.C.V.O., eighth Duke of Buccleuch, tenth Duke of Queensberry, was born on December 30, 1894, the eldest son of the seventh duke. As Earl of Dalkeith he was at Eton from 1908 to 1913, and went up to Christ Church, Oxford.

He received his commission as second lieutenant in the Grenadier Guards in September, 1914, and served in the First World War with the 1st Battalion and also with the 3rd Battalion of the Royal Scots and on the staff, being promoted captain in 1918.

In 1920 he went to Canada as A.D.C. to the Duke of Devonshire, the Governor-General.

He commanded the 4th Border Battalion the King's Own Scottish Borderers from January 1923 to January 1929, when he was gazetted colonel in the T.A.

He was elected Unionist member for Roxburgh and Selkirk in 1923, and held the seat until he succeeded to the dukedom in October 1935 on the death of his father. A few weeks later he gave away his sister on her marriage to the Duke of Gloucester.

The Duke married in 1921 Vreda Esther Mary, daughter of the late Major W. F. Lascelles, and had a son and two daughters.

The Duke was created G.C.V.O. in 1935. He became a Privy Councillor in 1937 and a Knight of the Thistle in 1949. He bore the Third Sword at the Coronation of Queen Elizabeth II.

The Earl of Dalkeith, Conservative M.P. for Edinburgh, North, who succeeds him in the dukedom, was born on September 28, 1923. He was injured in a hunting accident in 1971 and has been confined to a wheelchair.

October 5, 1973.

Patrick Buchan-Hepburn, 1st Baron Hailes —See Hailes.

Pearl S. Buck, the American novelist, author of the best-seller *The Good Earth* and winner of the Nobel Prize for Literature in 1938, died at her home at Danby, Vermont, on March 6, 1973. She was 80.

Her literary achievement, though notable, was not quite so high as it seemed in the first flush of her evocation of the Chinese scene and its pieties of hearth and home. Her knowledge of China, more especially of the north, was born of long residence there, and the sincerity with which she pursued the single inspiration of her work was never in question. Nor could it be denied that her semi-biblical cast of narrative style,

while tending towards monotony, matched her descriptions of immemorial peasant custom in China. The fidelity to life of her projection of Chinese thought and character, however, is another matter. Other Western interpreters of China, not to speak of Chinese themselves, have hesitated to endorse her view of the habit of mind of the Chinese peasant, and their attitude gains point from the somewhat glossy romanticism that became increasingly evident in Mrs. Buck's later work. Nevertheless, the intimacy with which she wrote of everyday Chinese life and conditions was never without effect, and in the circumstances of 1938 the honour conferred upon her by the award of the Nobel Prize for Literature in that year carried widespread approval.

The child of American parents who were both missionaries in China, Pearl Sydenstricker was born in West Virginia on June 26, 1892. At the age of four months she accompanied them on their return to the remote interior, in the Yang-tse valley, and stayed there until she was seventeen, having apparently learned to speak Chinese before she could fully speak English. In the United States she completed her education at Cornell University, then went back to China as a missionary and teacher and married Dr. J. L. Buck, head of the department of rural economics at Nanking University. During the next twenty years or so her love and admiration of the enduring virtues of life lived close to the soil of China were nourished by all that she experienced and observed there. In 1933 her strictures on certain aspects of missionary work, following as they did a certain amount of unimaginative criticism of her novel, *The Good Earth*, led to her resignation of the position she had held under the American Presbyterian Board of Foreign Missions.

Mrs. Buck's first novel, published in the United States in 1930, was *East Wind, West Wind*, a study of the conflict of the old and the new in China illustrated in the marriage of a European-trained doctor and a girl whose mind is enclosed within the traditional sanctions of Chinese family life. A perceptive and intelligent piece of work, it made no great stir. In the following year, however, came *The Good Earth*, and Mrs. Buck stepped into immediate and generous recognition, which was probably much assisted in the United States a few months later by the Japanese occupation of Manchuria. Other novelists both in America and Britain had written vividly and sympathetically of China, but none had seemed to be able to create a picture of the commonplaces of Chinese life "from the inside". This was, or appeared to be, Mrs. Buck's achievement. *The Good Earth*, designed as the first volume in a trilogy covering the history of the three generations of the house of Wang and spanning the transition from an established order of things to the modern period of Western contagion and unrest, made instructive and absorbing reading. Its somewhat too obviously poeticized simplicity of utterance helped rather than

hindered popular favour. The book was awarded the Pulitzer Prize for fiction in 1932 and was subsequently made into a film in which Luise Rainer, who won an Academy award for her performance, starred with Paul Muni.

Other volumes appeared in fairly rapid succession. A short novel, *The Young Revolutionist*, gave warning of Mrs. Buck's weaknesses of sentiment and style, but she recovered with the middle volume of the trilogy, entitled *Sons*, published in the same year. Then came *The Mother* (1934), another illuminating and tenderly written story of peasant life in the north, and after that *A House Divided* (1935), the third and concluding part of the story of the house of Wang. From this point the level of Mrs. Buck's fiction tends to decline, though she still produced good work. There were biographies, in the not too successful form of novels, of the father and mother; there were novels in which she abandoned China, again not too successfully, for the contemporary American scene; in *The Patriot* she wrote once more, and very nearly at her best, of Chinese nationalism in the making; in *Dragon Seed* (1942) she attempted to describe life in the Japanese-occupied regions of China, but marred her effect both by a lack of detachment and the conspicuous incongruity of her biblical accent. She produced several volumes of short stories of the popular magazine variety and also turned her hand to a translation of an enormous Chinese novel of the early part of the fifteenth century, *All Men are Brothers*. The emotionalism that gained on her in her later fiction is specially marked in *The Promise*, a story of the courage of the Chinese troops, the incompetence and cowardice of the British, and the general inspiration of the American idea during the retreat in Burma in 1942.

With the entry of the United States into the war in 1941 Pearl Buck lectured and wrote on the subject of democracy, America and the awakening of the East. Hers was an overriding sympathy with China and the Chinese, and the airy and inexperienced character of much of her political criticism may be attributed to genuine missionary zeal.

After the end of the Second World War she continued to produce a steady stream of novels and in 1955 *My Several Worlds*, an autobiography.

She was twice married—first to J. L. Buck, by whom she had a daughter who was mentally retarded and about whom she wrote a book. Her second marriage was to Richard Walsh, her publisher.

She adopted a number of children and, on making her home in the United States, worked for handicapped children; started an adoption society for children of mixed race; and set up a foundation for educating the American children of American servicemen. Her second husband died in 1960.

March 7, 1973.

Baroness Marie Budberg ("Moura" to an exceptionally large circle of friends and acquaintances all over the world) died in Italy on October 31, 1974.

For nearly four decades she was in the centre of London's intellectual, artistic and social life. She shared homes with H. G. Wells, Maxim Gorky and Sir Robert Bruce Lockhart.* But these three liaisons, openly admitted and fully accepted, each constituting a very different phase in her long life, were the least of her claims to fame. In early autumn 1974, she left London to live in Italy.

Author, translator, production adviser on plays, films and television programmes, an occasional actress herself (mostly in striking silent parts), sometimes a stage or costume designer, historical researcher and artistic codirector, publishers' reader of manuscripts in five languages and during the Second World War managing editor of *La France Libre*, a devoted matriarch to her own large family, a solid friend and ever ready mother confessor to people of the utmost variety, a *grande dame* but equally at her ease with the poor and humble, a generous hostess, an invaluable guest, this fantastic woman was unique.

Baroness Marie Budberg was the third and youngest daughter of Count Ignaty Platonovitch Zakrevski, the scion of a large noble family who won distinction in many fields, especially in the administration, the army and at court. Moura's direct ancestor was one of Empress Elizabeth I's children, born in 1742 of her secret marriage to Alexis Rasumovski.

Moura's father inherited a family estate near Kiev, in the Ukraine, and two town houses, one in Kharkov, also in the Ukraine, and one in St. Petersburg. He was a prosperous landowner and he belonged to the upper crust of the ruling classes.

He studied law at the Imperial Law School in St. Petersburg, later became a member of the Senate, a combination of a high administrative department and Supreme Court, and a member of the Imperial Council, Russia's Upper House. He held strong liberal views and was a passionate "Dreyfussard".

He even wrote a letter to Emile Zola and also appealed to the Senate to intervene in favour of Dreyfus. Instead, his fellow Senators expelled him. He died in 1905. His wife, née Boreisha, from Moscow, survived him for 14 years.

Moura was born in the Kharkov house in 1892. The family usually spent its summer in the Ukraine and its winters in St. Petersburg. Passionate linguists, both of them, her parents insisted that she and her two sisters be brought up in five languages. Foreign governesses and teachers made them equally proficient in Russian, French, English, German and Italian.

At the age of 12 she was sent to one of St. Petersburg's best known high schools for girls, Princess Obolensky's, and at 16 she was dispatched to Cambridge where she spent six months at Newnham polishing her English. In Russia at the time women were not admitted to the universities but there were special so-called "superior women's courses" for them which enjoyed university status. She joined one of these and specialized in literature.

In 1911 she married John Benckendorff who was then a second secretary at the Russian Embassy in Berlin, and they stayed there until the outbreak of the First World War. On their return to Russia she joined the army and she established herself in St. Petersburg as a young society matron.

She was a wartime nurse in a hospital, took part in various charitable and public organizations and, in fact, did all the things that were then fashionable for people of her class. By then she also had two small children to look after, a son, Paul, and a daughter, Tanya.

It so happened that in January 1914 H. G. Wells paid a brief visit to St. Petersburg and that they met socially. When he returned in 1920, at the invitation of the Bolsheviks, she of all people was assigned to be his guide and interpreter, a curious coincidence considering their subsequent great romance which lasted until he died in 1946.

She first met Bruce Lockhart in 1918. In his *Memoirs of a British Agent,* he has described in full with quite unusual frankness or indiscretion the love affair that followed; also his own and her troubles with the Soviet Secret Police.

Meanwhile she had got in touch with her husband who was still in the army and told him of her affair with Bruce Lockhart. They agreed to meet at his estate in Estonia and both set out on foot for the reunion. She was caught, arrested and brought back to the capital while he was killed by his own peasants soon after reaching the house.

She badly needed a job, and obtained an introduction to Maxim Gorky who at the time was heading a huge publishing project called World Literature. With her knowledge of languages (he knew none, despite many years of residence in Capri), she was just the person he wanted. She became his private secretary, personal translator, literary adviser and eventually enamorata.

After the death of her mother in 1919 she moved into Gorky's large flat which was shared by a curious motley of writers, artists and theatrical people. They all pooled their miserable rations which added up to enough for everyone, and Moura also brought along her French chef who contrived to make quite good meals out of the poorest material. Gorky's wife, later a lifelong friend of Moura's, was in charge of this small community.

In the autumn of 1921 Gorky left Soviet Russia, partially because he was genuinely ill (he had suffered from lung trouble for years) and partially because of the growing tension in his relations with the Soviet Government. He arranged for Moura to join him in Germany and at first they lived near Berlin, but later in the Black Forest.

He did not feel at ease in Germany and for a time they moved to Czechoslovakia but did not like it either, and finally they settled in Sorrento where they stayed for several years. But in the twenties Moura visited London several times as well as Estonia, where her children were in their father's house. In 1933 Gorky decided to return to the Soviet Union, but she refused to go with him. That year she went back to London for good, took her children over, and began a totally new life.

She had no difficulty in finding plenty of translation work: H. G. Wells and many other literary celebrities saw to that. She also met plenty of publishers and theatrical people who needed her advice and offered her a great variety of jobs. For several years Sir Alexander Korda retained her as a permanent personal assistant with regular office hours and a regular salary, but with most variegated assignments.

Her romance with H. G. Wells began quite soon after she had settled down in London. Harold Nicolson* tells in his diary for November 7, 1933, about an unsuccessful dinner party Wells gave at which everybody expected him "to announce his engagement to Moura, but for some reason no announcement could be made".

Little did Nicolson know that only a few hours before the dinner, while riding with Moura in a taxi, Wells had told her of his intention and she replied that if that was really what he wanted to do, she would prefer to throw herself out of the cab there and then. She loved Wells deeply and enjoyed his company enormously, but she did not wish to be married again. Besides, during the years of turmoil in Russia she already had acquired a second husband, a handsome young Baltic baron by the name of Budberg.

In later years she used to say that had he not been a hopeless gambler she might perhaps have stayed with him for the rest of her life. But since his gambling was incurable, poor Budberg was rapidly divorced and given a transatlantic ticket—one way.

For many years she was at home four or five times a week from 6.00 to 7.30, when a considerable amount of alcohol was absorbed and many cigarettes were smoked. But she could drink any sailor under the table without batting an eyelid. These were not formal cocktail parties and people just dropped in.

Guests varied from ambassadors and peers of the realm to stage and literary celebrities, but there were also some men and women who were boring nonentities. She was equally kind to all of them.

How she found time for work, which she took most seriously, it is hard to understand. But she produced more than 30 books and hundreds of notes, memoranda, drawings and summaries of texts and ideas. Her resilience was astounding. Tall, corpulent, with a large handsome face, she commanded attention wherever she went.

To those whose life she touched she will always remain an unforgettable person. But for those who knew her well, and especially the small circle of really close friends, her going leaves a vacuum that nothing can fill. There is an old American saying that fits her well: "After they made that one, they broke the mould."

November 2, 1974.

Marshal Semyon Mikhailovich Budënny, who died on October 27, 1973, would have ranked in history as one of the great heroes of the Russian Civil War of 1918-20 if only he had died soon afterwards; but, having lived to the ripe old age of 90, he is more likely to be remembered as one of the great incompetents of the Second World War.

Even after his lamentable record of 1941, he remained, with his legendary, almost "Wilhelmian" moustache, one of the most picturesque public figures in the Soviet Union, though his role since the end of the last war was little more than decorative. He was a genuine museum piece; both in the highly mechanized Second World War and, later, in the age of nuclear arms. He still looked and behaved like a dashing cavalry sergeant of a bygone age.

The Soviet regime inherited him from the Tsarist army. He was born in 1883, the son of a small Cossack farmer. As a private in a Cossack cavalry regiment he fought in Manchuria during the Russo-Japanese War of 1904-05. He was then scarcely literate; but in 1908 he graduated with distinction, according to his official biography, from the St. Petersburg Riders' School.

As a non-commissioned officer he fought bravely in the First World War, but after the October Revolution, unlike so many other Cossacks, he supported unequivocally the new Soviet regime. It was indeed during the Civil War of 1918-20 and the Soviet-Polish War of 1920 that the Budënny legend was born.

As early as February 1918 he formed a Cossack cavalry unit which fought the Whites on the Don; by August 1918 he headed a cavalry regiment of 1,500 sabres; in March 1919 a cavalry division; and soon afterwards the famous "horse army", the *Konarmiya Budiennavo*, a powerful striking force in that war, in which tanks were still few and far between.

Under Budënny the Red Cavalry played an important part in the battles of Tsaritsyn (the future Stalingrad) in the winter of 1918-19. But Budënny's greatest victory was in the autumn of 1919, when his troops smashed the White cavalry corps under Generals Mamontov and Shkuro during General Denikin's abortive "advance on Moscow".

Budënny's cavalry fought in the Soviet-Polish war of 1920 and took part in the final liquidation of the Whites that autumn. The dashing cavalryman became a hero of Soviet folklore. A more realistic, tragic, and at times sordid, picture of life among Budënny's rank-and-file soldiers during the Polish campaign was provided by one of the Russian literary masterpieces of the 1920s, Isaac Babel's *Konarmiya.*

Later his personal popularity as a *miles gloriosus* was illustrated when numerous localities in Russia and as many as 3,215 *kolkhozes* were named after him.

He joined the Communist Party in 1919, and after the Civil War became very much a member of the Soviet establishment. He was still far from being a highly educated officer. In the 1920s he was placed in charge of the Red Army's stud farms. It was not until 1932, when he was nearly 50, that he graduated from the Frunze Military Academy. Then his progress was rapid.

A great favourite of Stalin, with whom he had been closely associated during the Tsaritsyn fighting in the Civil War, he was appointed commander of the Moscow military district in 1937, the year of the great army purges; and in 1939 deputy commissar of defence.

At the outbreak of war in June 1941, Budënny was also appointed commander-in-chief of the "South-West Direction". (At that time the front was divided into three "directions", Voroshilov* commanding in the north, Timoshenko* in the centre, and Budënny in the south, i.e., in the Ukraine.)

Voroshilov and Budënny were both Civil War heroes, both "political" generals enjoying Stalin's special favour, and both totally incapable of dealing with the Nazi *Blitzkrieg.*

Budënny, having lost his head completely during the battle of Kiev, was replaced by Timoshenko; but it was too late, and what followed was one of the most disastrous encirclements of the Second World War.

The Kiev disaster was later the subject of much controversy, Khrushchev, who was Budënny's top political commissar, attributing it to a grave error on Stalin's part, and not to Budënny's incompetence. But the fact remains that the more "modern" generals of the Red Army, men like Zhukov, Konev, Rokossovsky* or Vasilevsky, had no respect for Budënny's military talents.

Except for his one short reappearance at the front as commander of an army group during the disastrous Caucasus retreat in the summer of 1942, Stalin refrained from giving him any highly responsible army posts during the rest of the war. Although a marshal of the Soviet Union since the 1930s, Budënny's role became little more than decorative. Nevertheless he continued as a loyal Stalinite, to be personally favoured by the commander-in-chief, though other generals, guilty of lesser disasters than he, had been demoted and even shot.

After the war, covered like a Christmas tree with medals and decorations, Budënny was invariably present at all great ceremonies, Red Square parades and receptions. Outwardly he was the jovial, back-slapping type, a heavy eater and drinker. A profiteer of the army purges of 1937-39, he never showed any regret for what had been done to his fellow generals.

After Stalin's death, he became a favourite with Khrushchev, and welcomed the latter's attempt to put the blame for the Kiev disaster on Stalin.

October 29, 1973.

Nikolai Bulganin, chairman of the Council of Ministers of the Soviet Union, i.e., Prime Minister, from 1955 to 1958, died on February 24, 1975. He was 79.

After Stalin's death in 1953 Bulganin became a deputy Prime Minister and Minister of Defence in the government of Malenkov, but during the power struggle between Malenkov and Khrushchev Bulganin lent his support to the latter. After Khrushchev's victory Bulganin replaced Malenkov as Prime Minister.

Bulganin became a familiar world figure as Soviet Prime Minister and travelling companion of Khrushchev on international visits in the mid-1950s. With his silver hair and trim goatee beard he appeared as a smooth contrast to the blunt Khrushchev.

The era of "B and K"—as western newspapers dubbed them—lasted from February 1955 until March 1958, when he was summarily replaced by Khrushchev as Prime Minister.

After his fall he was appointed head of the economic council of Stavropol and in December 1974 he was reported to have confessed to having been prominent in the councils of the "anti-party" group which included Molotov, Malenkov, Kaganovitch, clashed over policy with Khrushchev, and attempted to oust him.

In March 1960, reliable Moscow sources said that Bulganin had been relieved of the Stavropol post at his own request and was living in retirement near Moscow on a state pension of some 350 roubles (£163) a month. However, he did not entirely vanish from human ken and in January 1964 was seen "chatting gaily" with Khrushchev at a Kremlin party.

In 1970 he attended the funeral of Molotov's wife* in Moscow.

In later years he was seen frequently on the central Moscow boulevards leaning on a stick and watching groups of old-age pensioners playing chess and dominoes in the open air.

Nikolai Alexandrovitch Bulganin was born on June 11, 1895 at Nizhny Novgorod (later Gorky). His father was a clerk in a local factory. He received his early education in the modern language school in his native town. Shortly after the February revolution in 1917 Bulganin, then 22, joined the Bolshevik party. After the October Revolution he was appointed to a leading post in the Cheka (All-Russian Extraordinary Commission for the Suppression of Counter Revolution, Sabotage and Speculation) which he held until 1922.

After the withdrawal of the forces sent to aid the White Russian commanders, and the consolidation of the revolution, Bulganin was redirected to a leading post in connexion with the attempt to establish a stable Soviet economy, and for the next five years, from 1922-27, his energies were utilized by the Supreme Economic Council.

In 1931 he was elected president of the Moscow Council of Workers' Deputies. In the same year he was elected Mayor of Moscow, a post which he continued to hold until 1937.

By 1934, Bulganin had risen considerably inside the Communist Party organization, and in that year he was elected to membership of the central committee, and in 1937 was appointed to the post of president of the Council of People's Commissars of the R.S.F.S.R. (Russian Socialist Federal Soviet Republic). By the following year, he had risen a further stage, and was appointed a vice-president of the Council of People's Commissars of the U.S.S.R. In addition to this post during the years immediately preceding the Nazi attack on Russia, from 1938-41, he headed the directorate of the State Bank of the U.S.S.R.

In the initial period of the German invasion, a number of old soldiers were directed to leading military commands in the army. Among these was Bulganin. In 1941 he was a member of the military council for the defence of Moscow, and from 1941 to 1943 was a member of the military council on the West Front. In 1942 he was appointed a lieutenant-general in the Red Army. Until 1944 he held other military posts—among these being membership of the military council of the second Baltic Front and the first White Russian front.

With the successful conclusion of the war, Bulganin was appointed in 1946 Vice-Minister of the Armed Forces of the U.S.S.R. and in the following year Minister of the Armed Forces of the U.S.S.R. in succession to Stalin. He was promoted to the additional post of vice-president of the Council of Ministers of the U.S.S.R. in 1947 and held both these posts until 1949. In the same year he was promoted to the rank of Marshal of the Armed Forces of the Soviet Union.

Bulganin's ability and experience had earned considerable prestige for him in the Communist Party and in 1948 he was elected to full membership of the Politburo. He was relieved of his duties as Minister of the Armed Forces in 1949, being succeeded by Marshal Vassilevsky, and he then concentrated on his work in the councils of the Politburo, and as vice-president of the Council of Ministers.

Although during Stalin's lifetime he played like the others a subservient role and was never a very distinct figure, he quickly managed to exploit the opportunities that arose after Stalin's death. In the rivalry between Malenkov, Molotov and Khrushchev versus Beria, he was able to exercise much influence on the situation through his control of the armed forces. Having been trained as a member of the Cheka under its notorious Commissar, Felix Dzierzynski, a Pole, he better than anybody

else understood how to draw the net round Beria. After Beria's liquidation, he was honoured with the decoration of the Order of the Red Star.

Whether he had any real enthusiasm for the various Khrushchev policy innovations, notably that for coexistence, is difficult to know. Although he gave lip service in speeches and put his signature to a number of "letters" to western statesmen, in all probability he regarded it, as Lenin did, as a temporary expedient. But under Khrushchev's directing hand, he became the first Soviet Prime Minister to step outside the borders of his country in the attempt to give expression to the coexistence policy. China was visited, after that India, Burma and even Great Britain, where he is remembered as presenting a somewhat lugubrious contrast to the ebullient Khrushchev.

It was while Bulganin and Khrushchev were visiting Britain that Commander Crabb, the Naval frogman, disappeared. There were tales that he had vanished in Portsmouth Harbour while paying an underwater call on the new Russian cruiser which had brought the Russians to Britain.

A headless body wearing a frogman's suit was found near Chichester 14 months later and it was accepted at the inquest that it was Commander Crabb.

February 26, 1975.

Sir Christopher Bullock, K.C.B., C.B.E., the country rector's son who became the civil head of the Air Ministry at the age of 39, and was later dismissed from the Civil Service, died at his home in London on May 16, 1972, aged 80.

His dismissal from the post of Permanent Secretary to the Air Ministry followed the findings of a board of inquiry appointed to investigate certain conversations between Sir Christopher and representatives of Imperial Airways concerning the possibility of his future association with that company.

The inquiry found that his conduct was "completely at variance with the tenor and spirit of the code which clearly precludes a civil servant from interlacing public negotiations entrusted to him with the advancement of his personal and private interests". A minute by the Prime Minister commented that he was glad to observe no question of corruption was involved.

This brought to an unhappy conclusion a career in the Civil Service described at the time as of exceptional and varied brilliance. From Rugby, where he was captain of the Running Eight, he went to Trinity College, Cambridge, where he took many scholastic prizes, and then won first place in the open competitive examination for the Home and Indian Civil Service in 1914.

He chose India, but after the outbreak of war joined the Rifle Brigade (Special Service). Seconded to the Royal Flying Corps he served first as an observer and then as a pilot in Egypt, and was wounded. This

brought him home in 1917, and to the Air Ministry, where his promotion was rapid. He acted as principal private secretary to successive Secretaries of State, and his ability in these posts and for two years as assistant secretary in the Ministry led to his appointment as Permanent Secretary in June 1930, although because of illness this did not become effective until the following January.

Here he played a leading part in the evolution of the Empire air mail scheme, against what he described as a good deal of opposition before the Cabinet finally endorsed the report he drafted; and he was deputed to negotiate with South Africa, Australia and India before the plan was carried through.

After leaving the service he joined the boards of several public companies, and later retired.

Christopher Llewellyn Bullock, born in November, 1891, was the second son of the Rev. Ll. C. W. Bullock, rector of Great and Little Wigborough, Essex. He married in 1917 Barbara May, daughter of Henry Lupton, of Torquay, and they had two sons. He was appointed C.B.E. in 1926 and knighted in 1932.

May 19, 1972.

Dr. Ralph Bunche, former United Nations Under Secretary-General for political affairs, died on December 9, 1971 in New York. He was 67.

Although Ralph Bunche was perhaps best known to the world as the Nobel Peace Prize-winning negotiator of the Armistice Agreements between Israel and her Arab neighbours after the Middle East war of 1948, his whole career, both in the United States and in world affairs, was spent in the attempt to reconcile extremes and to build up the basis of understanding upon which alone peaceful settlements of longstanding conflicts can be worked out.

Starting out as a political and social scientist at a time when being black was anything but an advantage, he was in turn professor, field investigator in colonial Africa and Asia and later in the United States, government servant and, for many years, the doyen of international civil servants, an international mediator of the highest skill and reputation, and one of the principal architects of United Nations peace-keeping operations.

Ralph Johnson Bunche was born in Detroit, Michigan, on August 7, 1904. His father was a barber and his mother a housewife and enthusiastic amateur pianist. His early years were spent in Detroit and in Albuquerque, New Mexico, to which his parents had migrated in an attempt to cure the tuberculosis which left Bunche an orphan at 13. Thereafter he and his sister were reared by their maternal grandmother, Mrs. Lucy Johnson, a tiny but formidable lady to whom, throughout his life, Bunche gave credit for whatever success he might have had. It was she who imbued him with a rugged self-respect, self-dependence and pride in his race. She insisted on his going to the University of California in Los Angeles, at a time when Ralph himself was perfectly content with a job as a carpet-layer and with the raffish life of the young men of the Los Angeles ghetto which is now Watts.

U.C.L.A. awakened Bunche to the possibilities of the world outside the ghetto. A number of teachers, recognizing his unusual character and ability, encouraged him, and he was especially inspired by a series of lectures by the famous Harvard professor and Negro intellectual, W. E. B. Du Bois.* He graduated with honours from U.C.L.A., and went on to Harvard for a doctorate in government and international relations. He did post-doctoral work on colonial conditions at Chicago Northwestern, the London School of Economics and—extraordinary for a coloured man—the University of Cape Town. He resisted all attempts by the South African authorities to dissuade him from working at the latter institution after it was discovered that the distinguished academic was also black.

Bunche had become a member of the faculty of Howard University, Washington, in 1928 and soon became head of the Department of Political Science. In 1930 he married one of his students, Ruth Ethel Harris. During 1938-40 he collaborated with Gunnar Myrdal in the classic survey of the Negro in America which was published in 1944 as Myrdal's *An American Dilemma.* During field trips in the South for this project Myrdal and Bunche, a highly suspect combination both intellectually and racially, had some narrow escapes and were run out of a number of Southern towns.

During the war Bunche worked in Washington on African affairs in the organization that became the Office of Strategic Services, and in 1944 he was invited to join the State Department, again specializing in African and Colonial Affairs. He was a member of the United States delegation to Dumbarton Oaks (1944), to the 1945 San Francisco Conference which drew up the United Nations Charter, to the preparatory meetings of the United Nations in London and to the First General Assembly of the United Nations in 1946.

Trygve Lie,* the first Secretary-General of the United Nations, requested Bunche's services in 1946, and he subsequently became a permanent member of the United Nations Secretariat in 1947. He served as Secretary of the first United Nations mission to Palestine in 1947, and in 1948 he was assigned to accompany the United Nations mediator, Count Folke Bernadotte, to the Middle East.

He escaped being assassinated with Bernadotte in Jerusalem in September 1948 only because he was held up at an Israeli checkpoint on his way to meet Bernadotte for an inspection trip. The French colonel who took Bunche's place in the car was killed. The United Nations Security Council at once appointed Bunche as acting United Nations mediator in Bernadotte's place, and in this capacity from January to July 1949 he directed the negotiations on the island of Rhodes and elsewhere which finally resulted in the four Armistice Agreements between Israel and the Arab States. Bunche's assignment to this task was fortuitous, since the three-man Conciliation Commission which was to try to negotiate the agreements failed to arrive in Rhodes, apparently in the belief that the task was hopeless. The entire responsibility therefore fell on Bunche, whose negotiating skill, tact, imaginativeness and sheer physical stamina dominated the proceedings and led to an unexpectedly successful outcome. For this feat Bunche received the Nobel Peace Prize in 1950.

Bunche's permanent post in the United Nations Secretariat from 1947 to 1954 was as Principal Director of the Department of Trusteeship and Information from Non-Self-Governing Territories, a position in which he was a firm, if discreet, promoter of decolonization. His enormous knowledge and experience of the colonial world played a vital part in the establishment of the United Nations Trusteeship system and in the United Nations' role in preparing for the wave of decolonization which broke in the later 1950s and 1960s.

In January 1955 Dag Hammarskjöld,* recognizing Bunche's exceptional character, ability and international prestige, appointed him Under-Secretary in his own office so that he could undertake special political and other assignments for the Secretary-General.

Under Hammarskjöld Bunche was the main organizer and director of United Nations operations in the Middle East during and after the Suez crisis of 1956, and especially of the United Nations Emergency Force in the Middle East, a pioneering and novel effort in international organization.

A new challenge for United Nations peace-keeping emerged suddenly in the Congo in July 1960. Hammarskjöld, apprehensive of possible trouble after the declaration of Congolese independence on June 30, 1960, sent Bunche to Leopoldville to represent him at the independence celebrations and told him to stay on for a while to see what assistance the United Nations might usefully give to the new Congo Government. Hammarskjöld's apprehensions were soon justified when, less than a fortnight after independence, following the mutiny of the Army and the Belgian military intervention, President Kasavubu* and Prime Minister Lumumba* appealed to the United Nations for military and civilian assistance to get rid of the Belgian troops, to reestablish law and order and to keep the public administration of the country running. Bunche found himself overnight at the head of a completely improvised United Nations military and civilian operation of as yet unknown size and strength in a vast country where chaos and anarchy reigned and where a rising tide of violence was fed and complicated by powerful external interests, both political and commercial.

Bunche responded to this extraordinary situation with his usual quiet and indefatigable good humour. He worked day and night, oblivious of riots, mutinies, panics and often very difficult physical conditions. He took in his stride arrest by the mutinous Congolese army, the importunities of innumerable ambassadors, ministers, operators and private citizens, and the caprices and occasional tirades of the Prime Minister. In two weeks the United Nations operation was functioning in all parts of the Congo except Katanga and was virtually the sole instrument of public security and public administration. It was a remarkable achievement. At the end of August, however, Bunche found that his increasingly strained relations with Lumumba were beginning to make him dangerously ineffective in critical times and he asked Hammarskjöld to relieve him.

In 1964 Bunche was the guiding spirit in setting up of the United Nations Peace-keeping Force in Cyprus and in 1965 he directed the large and complicated operation which observed the cease-fire after the India-Pakistan war and which ended with withdrawal of the Indian and Pakistani forces to their previous positions. He also made a hazardous preliminary reconnaissance of the situation in Yemen and set up the United Nations Observation Mission which operated in that country from 1963 to 1964.

Intensely loyal to those he worked for and to those who worked for him, Bunche was, above all, devoted to the principles of the United Nations and believed that his most important achievement was the building up of the United Nation's peace-keeping capacity. He had no illusions about the shortcomings of the United Nations, but he was utterly convinced that it must, and could, be made to work and was therefore undismayed by the interminable frustrations of the political work of the Organization. To work at the United Nations, he used to say, one *had* to be an optimist.

December 10, 1971.

Roger Burke, editor of the *New Law Journal,* who died suddenly in London on December 19, 1974, was aged 37.

A man of great energy and many talents, he was born in co. Cork and educated in London.

He joined the Army at an early age and was attached to the Parachute Regiment in Cyprus. During his five year Army service he became middleweight boxing champion, winning 57 out of his 60 fights.

A spell in the Inland Revenue followed and soon revealed a quick understanding of tax law and practice which enabled him to set up as a tax consultant, particularly to solicitors. He branched out into free-lance journalism, with contributions, mainly on tax matters, appearing regularly in about

30 newspapers and periodicals.

He married in 1957, and with his wife founded a fortnightly research and information service on parliamentary and local government and economic affairs. Indeed his involvement in local government led him to become a member of the Bexley Council and Bexley Arts Council, chairman of the Bexley housing committee and a governor of several schools. He was the first general secretary of Amnesty International.

In 1969 he joined Butterworths, the law publishers, working on *Simon's Taxes*. He continued to write in his spare time, and published several books on local government matters. When Tom Harper gave up the editorship of the *New Law Journal*, Butterworths turned to Burke as his natural successor.

From July 1971, when he became editor, Burke's lively style and particularly his outspoken comments on the law and the legal establishment, contributed much to the *New Law Journal*'s success.

It is significant that reforms or amendments of the law often followed criticism in the *New Law Journal*. Burke leaves a widow and two teenage daughters.

December 23, 1974.

John Percy Burrell, the director of plays, who died on September 28, 1972 at Champaign, Illinois, was jointly responsible with Sir Ralph Richardson and Sir Laurence Olivier for forming the Old Vic Company that made history at the New Theatre during the last theatrical season of the Second World War, the first season of the postwar period and part of the two following seasons.

Burrell, born in India on May 6, 1910 and educated at Shrewsbury School, had for three years been producer and director at the Barn Theatre, Shere, before in 1937 he joined the staff of the London Theatre Studio which Michel Saint-Denis, the former director of the Compagnie des Quinze, had set up with the encouragement of Tyrone Guthrie and John Gielgud. Burrell there found himself the colleague of George Devine and Marius Goring.

From the studio he moved to Toynbee Hall as director of drama and thence, after serving in the War Office, to the B.B.C., where he remained as drama director, also directing in the "live" theatre a very strongly cast revival of *Heartbreak House*, until invited to join Richardson and Olivier, specially released from their war service, in raising and directing perhaps the most brilliant and adventurous of all the Old Vic companies in the long history of Lilian Baylis's old theatre.

Burrell was himself responsible for directing *Arms and the Man*, *Richard III* (with Olivier) and *Uncle Vanya* during the first season, both parts of *Henry IV* (with Richardson as Falstaff and Olivier as Hot-

spur and Shallow) in the second season, and later *The Alchemist* (with George Relph as Subtle), *Saint Joan* (with Celia Johnson), *The Government Inspector* (with Alec Guinness) and *The Way of the World* (with Edith Evans, the Millamant of the 1920s, now appearing as Lady Wishfort).

It is noteworthy that Harcourt Williams, a director of the plays in Miss Baylis's time and a member of the Burrell-Richardson-Olivier company for two seasons, did not take the view that the first named and least well known of the triumvirate was no match for the other two in the matter of supplying leadership and guidance. In Williams's opinion, the gathering up of the threads of the old organization, blown apart by the war, and the weaving of them into a reserved and slightly different pattern, was the work of three men of cultural integrity and unquestioned ability.

The directing at the Haymarket of *The Heiress*, with Richardson and Peggy Ashcroft, in 1949, for which Burrell was originally nominated, was not completed by him.

His last work as a director in London appears to have been done at the Westminster in 1952. Subsequently he was associated with the American Shakespeare Festival Theatre and Academy at Stratford, Connecticut.

October 4, 1972.

Sir Frederick Burrows, G.C.S.I., G.C.I.E., the last Governor of Bengal, died on April 20, 1973.

He had one of the most remarkable careers of any man springing from the ranks of the workers in this century. The son of a railwayman, he was for many years employed as a porter on the old Great Western Railway and he served first as a private in the Grenadier Guards during the 1914-18 War. In November 1945 Clement Attlee, then Prime Minister, recommended him as Governor of Bengal, and his appointment by the King made him the first trade union leader to become head of an Indian Province.

His tenure of that office was brief, but his name is still held in the highest regard throughout what used to be the Indian Empire, but especially in the province he ruled, and in Ceylon, where he had previously spent many useful months as a member of the Commission of Inquiry into Constitutional Reform.

Frederick John Burrows was born in 1887 in Herefordshire, and was educated at local board schools, from which he went straight into railway work. With only three breaks—those involving his war service from 1914 to 1918, his three years' duties as president of the National Union of Railwaymen, and his work on the Ceylon commission—Burrows was always a working railwayman until he went out to Ceylon, and only two or three days before the announcement of

his appointment as Governor of Bengal he was at the branch meeting of the N.U.R. at Ross-on-Wye, near his home, as an ordinary member.

In contrast with others of his colleagues who have in the past been selected for such posts, he was never a great national figure in the Labour movement or, indeed, beyond his association with his own organization, an outstanding personality in the trade union world. He had, however, been for a number of years a member of the executive committee of the National Union of Railwaymen, and also of its Great Western sectional council, in the days before nationalization. It was not until 1943, when he was elected president of the N.U.R., that he became familiar to men and women in the wider sphere, but he at once attracted attention for the skill with which for three years he led it, for his firmness of principle, combined with his moderate way of stating his position, and his statesmanlike conception of the proper relations between the greater unions and the nation.

Indeed, it was largely in consequence of his display of these attributes, and of his patience and tact as a negotiator, that Churchill* selected him as one of the Labour members of the commission to go to Ceylon early in 1945, to inquire into constitutional reforms there. When Burrows returned, having completed also his term of office as president of the N.U.R., he was perfectly prepared to go back to his family cottage at Ross-on-Wye and resume his work as a railway checker, such was his modesty, without fuss, or without any effort to seek a post more consonant with the responsibilities with which he had, for some years then, been entrusted. He was, however, soon afterwards appointed to the Colonial Advisory Board.

Burrows went out to India in the following February with the misgivings of many people, although with the good will of everybody. His equipment consisted only of the brief period he had served on the National Executive of the Labour Party, during which he had devoted himself considerably to foreign and Dominion affairs, the months he spent in Ceylon, and his work on the Colonial Advisory Board.

Indeed, it was said at the time that before joining the Ceylon Constitutional Reform Commission he had never been known to make a public reference to Indian affairs. And yet, in Bengal, he was a success from the start. It was the charm of his personality, aided by his intelligent, well informed and understanding wife, his qualities of diplomacy, and the pains which he took at once to get at the heart of the Bengalis, that won him first their respect, and then their trust and admiration.

He was treading in the footsteps of men like Lord Brabourne, Sir John Herbert, and Sir John Anderson, and was immediately succeeding R. G. Casey, in a post of almost overbearing responsibility and anxiety, with India from end to end in a state of seething unrest. There was probably less tension or disturbance in Bengal during his administration there than in any other part of what was then still the Indian Empire; and when the province was, after the Indian Independence Act became law, divided into West Bengal attached to India, and East Bengal with a portion of Sylhet added to Pakistan, the separation of the two parts was carried through practically without serious incident, while the Punjab witnessed at the same time the greatest migration, with the most tragic suffering in human history.

The end of British rule in August 1947, and the creation of independence, ended automatically, of course, the days of the British governors. Eighteen months is a very brief period for a man to be able to make his mark in such high office, but it can truly be said that Burrows returned to Britain in the knowledge that it had sufficed for him to secure a sure place in the history of India under Britain.

It was typical of him that, on returning to England, although made chairman of the Agricultural Land Commission, he took up the threads of his own personal life once more in the seven-roomed cottage, Thrushes Nest, at Ross, where he had lived as a railwayman for so many years before going to India.

Burrows was created a G.C.I.E. in 1945 and a G.C.S.I. in 1947. He was a magistrate and a deputy lieutenant for Herefordshire, and had served on the Lord Chancellor's Committee on Legal Aid for Poor Persons.

He married, in 1912, Dora Beatrice, daughter of Mr. J. Hutchings, of Hereford. While in India she was awarded the Kaisar-i-Hind Gold Medal. They had one son and one daughter. His wife died in 1968.

April 24, 1973.

Larry Burrows, probably the greatest trouble-shooting photographer of the post-war period, died during the fighting in Vietnam on February 10, 1971. For twenty years he roamed the trouble-spots of the world, but it was particularly the war in Vietnam which he made his field of operations. He had been continuously in and out over the last eight years, building up an international reputation, and winning more photographic awards than he could remember—as many as ten in a single year.

Burrows covered the Suez crisis, the American landing in the Lebanon, the Mosul uprising in Iraq, the Congo and many more. He was roughed up, beaten up, arrested, and had his camera smashed in several continents.

Burrows won the Robert Capa Award in 1964 and 1966, on both occasions for "superlative photography requiring exceptional courage and enterprise." His first real success was in 1947—he covered the blowing up of the Heligoland U-boat pens. He and an A.P. man chartered an old D.H. Dragon Rapide. They were supposed not to go nearer than nine miles from Heligoland, but talked the pilot into coming in 500ft above the island. When they found it impossible to photograph through the Plexiglass window, they knocked it out with an axe and tossed for the first shot. Burrows managed to shoot 11 pictures in all and got two pages in *Life* for the story.

Burrows was a Londoner in his middle forties, who got his job carrying photographs round a Fleet Street office. At the age of sixteen he moved to *Life* magazine, with which he remained for his whole working life. Bad eyesight kept him out of the war, and he served thirteen months in the coalmines before rejoining *Life*.

His home for the last decade had been in Hongkong, from which he covered a photographic parish extending from India to New Zealand. Burrows was an "equipment man". "When I take the lot with me there are twenty-six cases." He would spend hours bolting a camera into a helicopter, and was prepared to work eight months to complete a picture story of the air war in Vietnam to his satisfaction. Colleagues, editors and military men alike paid tribute to his outstanding courage.

Though his task in life was a grim one, he was a man of intense feeling, and hated the war which so much fascinated him. "My deepest wish" he said "is to be around to photograph North and South Vietnam at peace when all the trouble is over."

A devoted family man, Larry Burrows leaves a wife and two children.

February 12, 1971.

Sir Cyril Burt, Professor of Psychology, University College London, from 1931 to 1950 and since then Professor Emeritus, died on October 10, 1971 at the age of 88.

For over 40 years he had been the leading figure in Britain in the applications of psychology to education and the development of children, and to the assessment of mental qualities.

Born in March 1883, the son of Dr. C. Barrow Burt, a house-physician at the Westminster Hospital, he developed an early interest in medicine. Later his father took a practice in Warwickshire, near to the family seat of the Galtons. Burt learnt much physiology from accompanying him on his rounds, and was inspired by hearing of Sir Francis Galton's studies of heredity and mental measurement. However he obtained classical scholarships at Christ's Hospital, and then at Jesus College, Oxford, and attributed his lifelong interest in educational selection and examinations partly to his own success.

Though reading classics he attended Gotch's and J. S. Haldane's lectures, and was allowed to take psychology as a special subject under William McDougall. Influenced also by Karl Pearson, he began his work on tests of mental traits and their statistical inter-relations; and with Keatinge (Reader in Education) he started the first child guidance clinic in England, where backward and delinquent children came for mental examination.

After a period at Würzburg, where another early interest was encouraged, namely the psychology of artistic and musical appreciation, he became an assistant to Sherrington at Liverpool, lecturing to medical students on physiology, psychology and psycho-analysis. Here he published his study of sex differences in mental traits and his finding, from tests of preparatory and other schoolboys at Oxford, that the more highly intelligent individuals were characterized chiefly by superiority in reasoning powers. The conception of an hierarchy of mental functions, ranging from the most general and abstract down to the simpler memory, sensory and muscular capacities, which subdivide into the various more specialized talents, was fundamental to his later work on the structure of mind. It has by now won very general acceptance, as against the contrasting theories of Charles Spearman, who stressed the single common factor in all kinds of abilities, and of American workers in this field who emphasize, rather, the diversity and independence of mental faculties.

After a short period as Assistant Lecturer to C. S. Myers at Cambridge, Burt was invited in 1913 by the farsighted educational administrators of the London County Council to become the first psychologist appointed to an education authority anywhere in the world. The ensuing seven years were among the most fruitful of his whole career. His duties were concerned chiefly with the classification of pupils, with the mental defective at one end of the scale and the scholarship winner at the other; also with the diagnosis and amelioration of backwardness, maladjustment and delinquency in the school population. His studies of the incidence, causes and treatment of subnormality were models of the scientific yet genuinely psychological approach.

By contrasting large groups of subnormal and normal children in respect of background and environmental characteristics, physical traits and health, abilities and temperamental traits, school histories and leisure occupations, he was able to show objectively the complexity of factors underlying abnormality and to disprove many over-simplified and biased explanations. Often, also, he lived in the slums to study delinquents at first-hand. *The Young Delinquent*, published in 1925, is still the outstanding source of information on this topic, and *The Backward Child* (1937) has been hardly less influential. However Burt's views, propounded in *The Subnormal Mind* (1935), on the origins of neurotic behaviour, which derived largely from McDougall's theories of human instincts, have become outmoded.

To assist in accurate assessment, Burt translated and adapted the intelligence scale of Binet and Simon, and likewise revised the later American versions. While with the

L.C.C. he prepared a comprehensive series of tests of educational attainments, including accurate standards of performance for children of different ages; and he carried further his studies of statistical techniques for analysing test scores. His survey of *The Distribution and Relations of Educational Abilities* was published in 1917, *Mental and Scholastic Tests* in 1921, and a *Handbook of Tests for Use in Schools* in 1923. Many of these tests are still the standby of educational psychologists in schools or child guidance clinics. He was a pioneer, also, in the construction of intelligence and attainment tests which could be given to large groups of pupils at one time, and which became so important in the selection of 11-year children for grammar school education.

Shortly after the war he rejoined Myers to become head of the vocational guidance section of the National Institute of Industrial Psychology, and evolved the basic methods of all-round assessment and interviewing from which have sprung guidance movements in most European and Commonwealth countries, including the British Youth Employment Service, and personnel selection in the armed forces. In 1924 he became Professor of Education (part-time) at the London Day Training College, now the Institute of Education, and played an equally important role in the promotion of the child-guidance and schools psychological services. From 1931 to 1950 he was Professor of Psychology at University College London, and was largely absorbed in the training of British and Commonwealth psychologists, though continuing to contribute prolifically to psychological journals.

He also produced his most far-reaching volume on *The Factors of the Mind* in 1940.

He received the honour of knighthood in 1946. In 1947 with Sir Godfrey Thomson, he became the first editor of the *British Journal of Statistical Psychology,* in whose pages may be found a continuous stream of his studies of mental measurement. But in addition he was an excellent popular lecturer, and provided attractive series of talks on B.B.C. programmes. It was characteristic of him to show boundless generosity in helping younger psychologists who followed his lead, though he was sometimes more difficult with colleagues who took an independent line. Those who submitted queries, or technical reports, were habitually greeted almost by return of post with many closely-typed foolscap pages of the most valuable, and erudite, advice.

He married Joyce, daughter of P. F. Woods, herself a doctor and gynaecologist.

October 12, 1971.

Richard Burton, one of the dwindling band of British Open golf champions, died on January 30, 1974 in hospital, aged 66.

His victory came at St. Andrews in 1939; and as seven years elapsed before the next Open was played, Burton's career as a golfer was to a certain extent frustrated by lack of opportunity in the years when his game had reached its peak. Yet he played in the Ryder Cup matches of 1935, 1937 and 1949, winning both his foursomes, but losing three singles.

He was strong and stood well over 6ft., which explains a suggestion of looseness in his swing. He had a reputation for wildness in a wind, but it was blowing at St. Andrews when he came to the last two holes needing a five and a four to beat the American challenger, Johnny Bulla. He made his five at the Road Hole and then sent one of his huge drives up the eighteenth, stopping only just short of the Valley of Sin. To the alarm of spectators he took a deep-faced blaster for his short run-up to the green, but played it well and holed the putt for a three, winning by two strokes.

Apart from his long driving, putting was the strong point of his game. He demonstrated this after the war, when in one of the last events he won, in 1949 at Hollingbury Park, Brighton, he had rounds of 68, 66, 64, 68 for a total of 266, the lowest four-round tournament total ever recorded at that time in Britain. He finished 12 strokes ahead of the field.

Burton, who was born at Darwen, Lancashire, was attached to the Hooton club at Sale before moving to Coombe Hill.

February 2, 1974.

Dr. Vannevar Bush, the American scientist and engineer who was a central figure in the development of nuclear fission and the atomic bomb, died in Belmont, Massachusetts, on June 28, 1974 at the age of 84.

Graduating as an electrical engineer in 1913, he served in the United States Navy and then became an assistant professor at the Massachusetts Institute of Technology. He later was made Vice-President of the Institute and Dean of the Engineering Faculty. In 1938 he was elected President of the Carnegie Institution, where he began to coordinate research in various scientific fields. This was to lead to his appointment at the outbreak of the Second World War as Chairman of the United States National Defence Research Committee, and in 1941 Director of the Office of Scientific Research and Development.

President Roosevelt had been impressed by Bush's work and style. When a group of scientists were invited to the White House to discuss the plans needed if the nation were to become involved in global war, Bush—so the story goes—handed the President his recommendations set forth in four paragraphs on a single sheet of paper.

In Washington he directed the work of some 30,000 physicists, chemists, engineers and doctors, and became best known to the public as the man who commanded the "Manhattan Project"—the undertaking that produced the atomic bomb.

When the first experimental atomic explosion was to take place at the New Mexico testing grounds, and with zero hour approaching, someone remarked to Bush that they were all rather close. "Dr. Bush," he said, "if this thing goes off, the President will have to look for a new director for the O.S.R.D." "If it does not, he will, too", Bush replied.

After the war he was active in governmental and educational committees and became a director of Merck, Sharp and Dohme International, the pharmaceutical company. He was Chairman of the corporation at the Massachusetts Institute of Technology from 1957 to 1959, becoming honorary chairman after that.

An amiable, pipe-smoking New Englander (he once remarked that the reason why he could work with the British was because "they smoke pipes and can get together far better than those deluded chaps who smoke cigarettes"), Bush was always outspoken. He discomfited the United States space researchers in 1960 by declaring that placing a man in space was little more than a stunt. "The man can do no more than an instrument—in fact he can do less," he said. He believed that other fields of research should come first, particularly medical research.

His publications included *Modern Arms and Free Men*, a discussion of the role of science in preserving democratic institutions, and *Pieces of the Action*, a rambling and fascinating account of his varied life. Besides numerous American awards, he was made an honorary K.B.E. in 1948.

In 1916 he married Phoebe Davis and they had two sons.

July 1, 1974.

Colonel Frank Bustard, one of the great shipping pioneers of recent years, died at his home in Haslemere on January 22, 1974 at the age of 87 after a short illness.

He was the father of the "ro-ro" revolution. Using converted tank landing craft, he started services between Britain, Ireland, and the Continent after the war, which led to the huge drive-on ferry fleet of today, rivalling the container-ship in its fundamental impact on sea transport.

Bustard was a man of zest, enthusiasm, and ideas. The youngest of four sons of John and Alice Bustard, an old Liverpool Unitarian family, he joined the White Star Line as an apprentice under J. Bruce Ismay and quickly rose to be passenger traffic manager.

Transatlantic liners were still in their heyday, with fierce rivalries, particularly between Cunard and White Star, and it was typical of Bustard that he refused to join the forced merger between the two lines in 1934, preferring to start a rival concern with which he hoped to introduce new standards of tourist travel, with £10 fares to New

York.

For one reason or another it came to nothing and he joined up again in 1939. He had served in the Artists Rifles, King's Own (R.L.R.) in the First World War, being four times mentioned in dispatches and awarded the O.B.E. (Military). From 1939-45 he served in various aspects of Movement Control including the D-Day landings, again being twice mentioned in dispatches.

Joined by his sons John and Michael, he started the Transport Ferry Service in 1945 and over the next four years acquired seven tank-landing craft as the business expanded. When the time came to replace them with new vessels he sold out to the British Transport Commission in 1954, and retired from business in 1956. He remained active; the twinkle never left his eye.

He married in 1912 Nora Hamilton, of Liverpool, by whom he had four sons and a daughter. After her death in 1950 he married in 1952 Margaret Wilkinson Sands, by whom he had a son.

January 23, 1974.

Professor Sir James Butler, M.V.O., O.B.E., the educationist and historian, died on March 2, 1975 aged 85.

James Ramsay Montagu Butler was born in 1889, the son of H. Montagu Butler, once Headmaster of Harrow, but by that time Master of Trinity College, Cambridge, and of Agnata, the daughter of Sir James Ramsay the historian, herself a classical scholar of distinction.

In 1902 Butler went to Harrow, the headmaster's house, and in due course became head of the school. In 1907 he entered Trinity as a major scholar. His academic achievements both in classics and history were outstanding and he also became president of the Union.

In 1913 he won a fellowship at his college with a thesis, which he substantially published in 1914 as a book, *The Passing of the Great Reform Bill*, a remarkable piece of work for a young man, and possibly his best book. In the 1914-18 War he served first with the Scottish Horse in the Dardanelles and Egypt and then at the War Office as a staff officer under Sir William Robertson.

At the end of the war he joined the League of Nations section of the Peace Conference at Paris. In 1919 he returned to Trinity but in 1922 he was elected as an independent to serve in Parliament as a member for Cambridge University. He was not by temperament well suited for politics, and at the general election of 1923 was displaced by his cousin, Sir Geoffrey Butler. He returned to academic work. In 1928 he became a Tutor of Trinity and from 1931 to 1938 was Senior Tutor.

There were those to whom this seemed a humdrum sequel to such brilliant beginnings, but they had probably mistaken the nature of the qualities in which Butler excelled, and also underestimated the value of the work he was doing.

Butler, with his tact, his clarity of mind and his unusual integrity, was peculiarly well fitted for the task, and seldom has the work been better done. In 1939 he rejoined the Army and did intelligence work first at headquarters in France, and then, after sharing in the retreat through Dunkirk, in England. Towards the end of the war he helped to organize and run an establishment at Wimbledon to train men to take up posts in occupied territory.

After the war he became chief historian for the official military history which was being planned, and in 1947 he became Regius Professor of Modern History at Cambridge. Again his gifts for unobtrusive but effective academic administration were called upon. For instance he piloted a rather bitterly contested reform of the historical Tripos to a successful conclusion, and played an important part in securing the application of the large sum collected as a memorial to Field Marshal Smuts to the promotion of the study of the affairs of the British Commonwealth at Cambridge.

His professorship ceased in 1954, but he continued his work for the history of the war. Besides organizing the work of other scholars he was wholly responsible for writing Vol. II of the series on the *Grand Strategy* which covered September 1939 to June 1941, and together with J. M. A. Gwyer for Vol. III in the same series covering June 1941 to September 1942. From 1955 to 1960 he was Vice-Master of Trinity College and he was knighted in 1958. In 1960 he published a life of his friend Lord Lothian.

Butler's life was fortunate because destiny provided him with a series of important tasks in the organization of scholarship and education. The best of such work must be intelligent but self-effacing, and the instinct to keep himself out of the picture came naturally to Butler.

He was an affectionate man of great charm with a natural gaiety and an instinct for hospitality, which contrasted attractively with his own tastes in life which were austere; but there was in him a gentle remoteness of character which sometimes made intimacy difficult.

Perhaps his greatest pleasure was in rock climbing, and he felt, also very strongly, the attraction of hills and wild places, particularly of the Highlands of Scotland. He was unmarried, and lived most of his life in rooms in college. His was not however in any way a cloistered existence, for his interests were wide and friends numerous.

March 3, 1975.

Frederick Victor Butterfield, the oldest man in Britain, died in a Harrogate nursing home on March 8, 1974 aged 110. Born in Thirsk in 1864, Butterfield was a year old at the time of President Lincoln's assassination.

He qualified as a dispensing chemist in 1885 after five years' training without wages, and when prescriptions were written in Latin. He went to London to work in the pharmacy of Savory and Moore in Bond Street which enjoyed the privilege of dispensing medicines for Queen Victoria's household, only to return north in 1893 to open his own dispensary on Station Bridge, Harrogate.

His extraordinary longevity bestowed upon him every accolade of age. He was not only Harrogate's oldest resident but the Pharmaceutical Society's oldest member; he was not only believed to be the Stock Exchange's oldest active investor but the country's oldest and most consistent voter, for he was proud of the fact that he had voted for the Conservative Party at every general election since 1890, including the February 1974 election, which fittingly coincided with his birthday celebrations.

Butterfield was a businessman until 1970 when his pharmacy closed on the death of his son at the age of 75. He had never failed to watch its progress closely from the day he had bought it, and rumour had it that his was the hand that guided it for almost 80 years.

An avid reader and an early riser, it was his custom to be called each morning at six o'clock, so that after washing and dressing he could devote himself without interruption to his three morning newspapers and absorb himself in their City pages.

March 11, 1974.

Rear-Admiral Sir Anthony Buzzard, the second baronet, C.B., D.S.O., O.B.E., who was Director of Naval Intelligence from 1951 to 1954, died on March 10, 1972 in Guildford. He was 69.

The years when he was Director of Naval Intelligence were to see the defection to Russia of Burgess and Maclean, and in a wider context the death of Stalin and the dismissal of General MacArthur from command of the United States forces in Korea for threatening to extend the war into China.

All these called for examination and comment from the intelligence point of view. He was a forceful protagonist of his beliefs, prepared to argue with his colleagues of the other services on practically every aspect of a case, and when his opinions were rejected he showed little personal animosity; indeed defeat seemed rather to fortify him for the next battle.

Buzzard was one of the founder members of the Institute of Strategic Studies which brought together theologians, military experts and politicians to discuss problems of mutual concern. When it appeared, some years later, that the Institute was not spending enough time discussing the moral criteria which should inform decisions on war and peace, Buzzard and a number of other Christians were instrumental in setting up the Conscience of Christian Approaches to Defence and Disarmament.

In C.C.A.D.D., on the working party of the British Council of Churches on defence and disarmament, and in the international Red Cross, Buzzard was concerned to see that Christian standards were upheld and, above all, to find what was possible in the impossible situations which so often arise in international affairs.

He was constantly persuading his colleagues to learn from past failures and so to learn the art of peacekeeping. Priority, in the last years of his life, was given to the situation in the Middle East. Just before the outbreak of war in June 1967, Buzzard wrote a pamphlet which was published by the Church of England Board for Social Responsibility's committee on international affairs with the title *The Middle East*.

He became chairman of the Middle East Advisory Committee of the British Council of Churches and wrote another pamphlet *Israel and the Arabs—the Way Forward* (1967). He suggested ways in which reconciliation might be effected. He believed that a system of guarantees could be made by the "middle" powers which would provide an opportunity for Arab and Israeli to talk together and to find a lasting peace.

Buzzard was made a D.S.O. for his conduct in command of the destroyer Gurkha when she was sunk by aircraft, in 1940, fighting to the last moment. In 1941 he was awarded the O.B.E. for distinguished services in the action in which the Bismarck was destroyed. His later career during the war included service in the War Cabinet Offices and the command of an aircraft-carrier in the Pacific.

Anthony Wass Buzzard was born on April 28, 1902, the eldest son of Sir E. Farquhar Buzzard, Physician-in-Ordinary to King George V. He entered the Royal Navy as a cadet at Osborne College and, from Dartmouth, as a midshipman, he went to sea in 1919 in the battleship Iron Duke.

In 1939, Buzzard was given command of the large destroyer Gurkha. Her short but extremely busy and varied fighting career came to a gallant end in the North Sea when she was bombed and sunk by German aircraft, with her gun-crews continuing to fire until the water drove them from their guns. It was an episode which showed the determination that lay behind Buzzard's pleasant and unassuming manner.

In 1941 he became commander of the battleship Rodney, and received his promotion to captain's rank the same year. He was appointed Assistant Director at the Admiralty Plans Division, for duty as a member of the inter-service Joint Planning Committee on the staff of the War Cabinet.

Buzzard returned to active service in 1944 in command of the aircraft-carrier Glory and he took part in the operations of the British Pacific Fleet against the Japanese. After the war he was given the command of a Royal Naval air station in England,

and later the command of the cruiser Superb.

At tennis, Buzzard only just failed to become the champion player of the Navy. He competed in a number of service championship matches at Wimbledon and, as a sub-lieutenant, he won the doubles on three occasions, each time with a different partner.

He married in 1932 Margaret Elfreda, the daughter of Sir Arthur Knapp. They had two sons and one daughter. Buzzard succeeded his father in 1945; the heir to the baronetcy is his son, Anthony Farquhar Buzzard.

March 11, 1972.

Cecily Byrne, the actress, who was Lady Aylmer, wife of Sir Felix Aylmer (-Jones), died on June 30, 1975. She was a most sensitive and accomplished actress much occupied in the London theatre between the wars.

Born in Birmingham, she was Sir Barry Jackson's* niece (the daughter of his sister Minnie); she appeared in several of his early enterprises, in the improvized theatre at his home—where John Drinkwater remembered "a small girl with very long pigtails"—and later with the Pilgrim Players, the amateur company from which the Birmingham Repertory would rise. On the famous evening of February 15, 1913, she acted Viola in *Twelfth Night*, the first production at Jackson's theatre in Station Street; Felix Aylmer was Orsino, and Drinkwater, under the name of John Darnley, Malvolio.

During ensuing years Cecily Byrne had many parts at the Repertory. She is recalled for her Rosalind in *As You Like It*; Ethel (with song) in Hankin's *The Cassilis Engagement*; Kate in *She Stoops to Conquer*; Miranda in *The Tempest*; Alice in Drinkwater's *The Storm*—which the dramatist said she played with a fine spring of nervous energy—Petronell in the first performances of *The Farmer's Wife* (1916), and very much else. In 1915 she had been in London for a while, understudying Madge Titheradge* in *Gamblers All*; when at length she established herself on the London stage she was seldom in need of an engagement.

She returned to Birmingham in December 1919 with her husband, Mr. Felix Aylmer, to play Lady Teazle in *The School for Scandal*.

Intellectually and physically Cecily Byrne could grace any stage. Her repertory experience had made her richly adaptable and her long London record included such parts, notable in their day, as Drinkwater's Mary Stuart (Everyman revival, 1923); Margaret, the hostess in Lonsdale's *Spring Cleaning* (St. Martin's, 1925), Elsie in the same author's *The High Road*, (Shaftesbury, 1927), the Countess in *By Candle Light* (Prince of Wales, 1928), Mrs. Lennox in

Galsworthy's last play, *The Roof* (Vaudeville, 1929), Mrs. Darling in *Peter Pan* on several occasions, and Anne in Lonsdale's *The Way Things Go* (Phoenix, 1950).

During the early summer of 1944 she had been a nobly-spoken Hermione in *The Winter's Tale* at Regent's Park; and she repeated this in the autumn at the Birmingham Repertory—a production in which the young Paul Scofield was the Clown.

July 4, 1975.

James Francis Byrnes, who died on February 9, 1972 at the age of 92, was President Truman's Secretary of State from 1945 to the beginning of 1947.

That the cold war should have begun while Byrnes was in charge of American foreign policy was ironic, for in domestic affairs his reputation was that of a conciliator. He had a remarkable record of public service in all three branches of the federal Government, first as a member of the House of Representatives and the Senate, then as a Justice of the Supreme Court, and during the war as Roosevelt's unofficial "Assistant President" in charge of the home front.

Although Byrnes had been the intimate adviser of two Democratic Presidents, he broke with his party in 1952 and voted for General Eisenhower.*

Byrnes was born on May 2, 1879, in Charleston, South Carolina, of poor parents, learned shorthand to support his family, and was admitted to the Bar in 1903. After four years as a journalist, he became an official court reporter and later practised law. From 1911 to 1925 he was a member of the House of Representatives and in 1931 was elected to the Senate for the first of two six-year terms. In Congress he spoke little, but he was a hard worker and made friends easily. He became invaluable to Roosevelt, partly as an astute party manager but chiefly as a link between the President and the conservative southern Democrats. He cared little for the theory of government, but he was a practical politician of great skill and warmth.

Byrnes was regarded as a moderate liberal and in June 1941 Roosevelt appointed him to the Supreme Court. But with America's entry into the war he was persuaded to resign and to become, first, Director of Economic Stabilization and in 1943 the head of the Office of War Mobilization. His task was to oversee and coordinate the great complex of agencies created to direct resources into the war effort, speed production and regulate civilian consumption. Tightening America's belt did not make him popular; in particular the trade unions resented his freeze of wage rates.

Largely for this reason, he was denied the vice-presidential nomination in 1944; it went to Senator Truman. When the President died less than a year later and the inexperienced Truman succeeded him,

Byrnes would have been less than human if he had not felt a pang of resentment. Before then, however, he had accompanied Roosevelt to Yalta and this proved a stepping-stone to the State Department. The exchanges between Roosevelt, Stalin and Churchill* were taken down in Byrnes's shorthand, and his report on them to Congress struck many as more lucid and incisive than that of the President.

Truman began by leaning on the experienced Byrnes, took him to Potsdam, and soon after made him Secretary of State. He was confirmed unanimously by his old friends in the Senate and always enjoyed good relations with Congress.

Byrnes was a fast learner, but he knew little of foreign affairs. Although his memoirs show that his suspicions about Soviet intentions had been aroused early in 1945, he began with high hopes of achieving a settlement of the war and was prepared to meet the Russians halfway—to London it seemed, at first, at the expense of the British. At the Moscow conference Byrnes was so accommodating over Bulgaria and other satellites that he was hauled over the coals by President Truman, though this may have been due to the President's resentment because Byrnes announced policies without first consulting the White House.

After the London conference early in 1946, a policy of "firmness and patience" was substituted for that of conciliation and by September, at Stuttgart, Byrnes was taking a hard line against Russian violation of the Potsdam agreement on reparations and promising that the United States would not withdraw its troops from Germany as long as those of other occupying powers remained there. Byrnes has been criticized for not insisting on a showdown on Germany and Austria in 1946 and for moving on to other issues, but it is important to remember that America had demobilized much of its Army and that public opinion was not ready to abandon its hopes of cooperation with the Russians.

The most vocal attack on Byrnes came from the opposite quarter, from those who felt that he was being unnecessarily provocative and that more generous policies and a more friendly approach would dissolve Russian intransigence. This was the theme of Henry Wallace's* famous attack on Byrnes in September 1946, which led to Wallace's disappearance from the Cabinet. Byrnes rightly threatened to resign unless the President dismissed his Secretary of Commerce.

It cannot be claimed that Byrnes was a creative or far-sighted Secretary of State, but he held the fort.

His memoirs, *Speaking Frankly*, give a candid if anecdotal account of his problems at this time.

In 1906 Byrnes married Miss Maud Busch.

February 10, 1972.

C

Amilcar Cabral, who was assassinated in Conakry, capital of Portuguese Guinea, on January 20, 1973, had become recognized through his work and writings as one of the outstanding political leaders and thinkers of modern Africa.

Born of African origin in 1926, at Bafata in what was then the Portuguese West African colony of Guiné, he spent part of his youth in the colonial capital of Bissau, but was able, thanks to his family's relatively comfortable position, to go to secondary school and then to the University of Lisbon, where he qualified as an agricultural engineer in 1951.

Already determined to find ways of working for his country's independence, he served for two years in the Colonial Administration of Guiné. His opinions became offensive to the governor of the colony, and Cabral transferred to Angola. There, late in 1956, he helped to form the earliest important nationalist grouping of that colony, the M.P.L.A. (Popular Movement for the Liberation of Angola).

A few months earlier, during a visit to his mother in Bissau, he also formed with five others a nationalist movement in Guiné, P.A.I.G.C. (African Independence Party of Guiné and Cape Verde). This small clandestine grouping pressed for political concessions by organizing strikes and demonstrations, but decided in September 1959, after the particularly violent repression of a strike in the Bissau docks, to prepare for armed action. It was from this period that Cabral began to demonstrate the personal qualities of patience, courage and political farsightedness which were soon to make him, as well as the movement that he led, into a most formidable opponent of continued Portuguese colonial rule. Though urged by foreign advisers to launch a revolt in 1960 and then in 1961, Cabral refused. They would begin, he said, only when the political work had been completed.

Launched eventually in January 1963, the armed uprising of the P.A.I.G.C. survived all Portuguese efforts at repression, and went from strength to strength. Cabral continued to see the war strictly as a political instrument; and his main effort went into creating a new political and social structure of self-rule in the wide regions which the guerrillas of the P.A.I.G.C. successively cleared of the Portuguese army.

January 22, 1973.

Sir Stanford Cade, K.B.E., C.B., F.R.C.S., F.R.C.P., F.R.C.O.G., the eminent surgeon and authority on the treatment of cancer by radium and other forms of radiation, died on September 19, 1973. He was 78.

The son of Samuel Kadinsky, of St.

Petersburg, he was born on March 22, 1895 and educated in Brussels and at King's College London, from which he gained an entrance scholarship to Westminster Hospital Medical School. He had a successful academic course, gained the Bird Prize and Gold Medal, and qualified M.R.C.S., L.R.C.P. in 1917. Thereafter he held several resident posts in Westminster Hospital and decided to specialize in surgery.

He carried out some research work at King's College, took the coveted F.R.C.S. England in 1923 and later in the following year was elected to the surgical staff of Westminster Hospital. Later he was appointed surgeon to the Radium Institute and Mount Vernon Hospital. At this time he changed his name by deed poll.

He was fortunate in having as his senior colleagues several distinguished surgeons—Walter Spencer, Arthur Evans, Ernest Rock Carling—who appreciated his merit and encouraged his activities. The very next year (1925) he gave a Hunterian Lecture at the Royal College of Surgeons on the subject of regional anaesthesia, to which he had devoted attention; and two years later (1927), in collaboration with Arthur Evans, published a paper on the treatment of cancer of the tongue by radium.

Great developments were then taking place in radiation treatment and Ernest Rock Carling (later Sir Ernest) was taking a leading part in that development, in which Cade eagerly joined.

In 1931 Cade assisted Walter Spencer in the production of the third edition of Butlin's book on diseases of the tongue, and two years later he gave another Hunterian Lecture at the College of Surgeons in which he dealt with the treatment of cancer of the tongue and pharynx.

His reputation and experience grew rapidly and he was collecting his views into book form when the Second World War broke out. Cade was appointed Consulting Surgeon to the Royal Air Force with the rank of Air Vice-Marshal.

In 1940 he published the first edition of his remarkable work on *Malignant Disease and its Treatment by Radium,* which at once became a standard reference book on the subject. A second and larger edition in four volumes was published in 1948-1952.

At the end of the war began Cade's most brilliant period. He was acknowledged leader in the surgery of malignant disease, was extremely busy in private and hospital practice, was constantly in demand to deliver special lectures, and in 1949 was elected to the Council of the Royal College of Surgeons.

His association with the College of Surgeons was close and fruitful. He took the work seriously and played his part in the great surge of development which was at that time reviving the college.

The peak of his professional career was attained when in 1958 he was elected president of the International Cancer Congress held in London. About the same time (1959) he was awarded the Fothergillian Gold

Medal of the Medical Society of London. Many other distinctions came to him.

Stanford Cade was rather below medium height, and possessed a friendly manner and kindly disposition. He was a very hard worker and undoubtedly advanced considerably the knowledge and practice of surgery and radio-therapy in the treatment of cancer. He was a good speaker and had a rich fund of anecdotes.

In 1920 he married the eldest daughter of William Agate of Paisley. It was a happy union and they had three daughters. Lady Cade died in 1951. In her memory Sir Stanford instituted at the Royal College of Surgeons a Lady Cade Medal which was to be awarded to a Royal Air Force Medical Officer for notable work affecting that Service.

September 21, 1973.

Major Robert Cain, v.c., who won his award for sustained valour at the Battle of Arnhem in 1944, died on May 2, 1974. He was 65.

At the time of the battle he was attached to The South Staffordshire Regiment, 1st Airborne Division. The citation to his V.C. described how, throughout the whole course of the Battle of Arnhem, Major Cain showed superb gallantry. Early in the battle, a rifle company of The South Staffordshire Regiment he was commanding was cut off and for six days was closely engaged by the enemy. In one instance, armed with a Piat, Major Cain went out alone to deal with an approaching Tiger tank, and although wounded he continued firing until he immobilized it. Later, leaving cover and taking up position in open ground, he drove off three more tanks.

During the days of the battle he was everywhere where danger threatened, encouraging his men by his fearless example, refusing rest and medical attention. When the enemy made a concerted attack on his position, Major Cain, armed with only a light 2-inch mortar, by daring leadership of his few remaining men completely disorganized the enemy, who withdrew in disorder. His power of endurance and leadership were the admiration of all and his coolness and courage under incessant fire could not be surpassed.

Born on January 2, 1909, he was educated at King William's College, Isle of Man.

May 4, 1974.

Joseph Maria Laurens Theo Cals, the Netherlands Prime Minister from April 1965 to November 1966, Minister of Education from 1952 to 1963, and one of the two chairmen of the Commission appointed to draw up a reformed constitution, died in hospital in The Hague on December 30, 1971 after a long illness. He was 57.

He was born in Roermond, in the south of the Netherlands in July 1914. At the age of 26 he had completed his law studies at Nijmegen University. After the German occupation of the Netherlands ended in 1945 he began a political career which led within three years to the offer of a post of State Secretary at the Ministry of Education. Initially he turned the offer down because he felt he needed more parliamentary experience. Two years later he accepted the appointment. After two years as State Secretary he became, at the age of 38, Minister of Education. He held this post for 11 years.

He was a member of the largest Dutch political party, the Roman Catholic K.V.P. Both within and outside the party he was seen as a radical left wing politician but did not leave the party in 1966 when the left wing split. During his period as Minister of Education he laid the foundations for the present Dutch education system. The Mammoetwet in 1963 changed the rigid structure of secondary education in Holland into a more subtle scheme which enabled scholars to change course in midstream, and late developers to switch into a higher stream; and laid emphasis on a broad fundamental education programme with specialization deferred as long as possible.

In 1963 he returned to the Second Chamber as a Member of Parliament. His appointment as Prime Minister in 1965 came as a surprise. He led a Cabinet composed of members of the K.V.P., the Socialists and the Protestant Anti-Revolutionary parties. This "Roman Red" Cabinet, as it was known in Holland, had to deal with serious economic problems, riots in Amsterdam and fierce opposition to the marriage of Crown Princess Beatrix to the former West German diplomat Claus von Amsberg. Cals was, however, too radical for some of the members of his own party. The Cabinet fell after a vote of no confidence was introduced by the present Dutch Minister of Foreign Affairs, Norbert Schmelzer, also a member of the K.V.P. In 1967 Cals and Professor A. M. Donner were appointed chairmen of the Royal Commission for the reform of the constitution and voting system.

He leaves a widow and five children.

January 1, 1972.

Arthur Calwell, leader of the Opposition in the Australian Parliament from 1960 to 1967, died in Melbourne on July 8, 1973 at the age of 76.

No man ever came nearer to being Prime Minister of Australia, in 1961, and no man in Australia ever suffered such an electoral defeat, only five years later. It was a personal tragedy, and it is possible that a Labour government in 1961 may have been good for Australia. That year, leading Labour for the first time into a general election against the omnipotent Menzies,

Calwell reduced his record majority of 32 to the narrowest possible working majority of one. The result surprised Calwell much less than everyone else because he had fought his campaign with a devastating surge of released emotion after almost nine years as deputy to the erratic, very trying Dr. Evatt.*

Thereafter Calwell's political fortunes, and his judgment, declined with the fortunes of his party. He was much to blame. So was the archaic party which allowed itself to be led for too long by a lovable old man with most of its worst prejudices. In November 1966 Calwell suffered a record electoral defeat, at the hands of Harold Holt* whom (as a politician) he rather despised. Calwell resigned as leader of the Opposition on February 8, 1967. He retired, like Scullin, to the back benches but he went on speaking and fighting for Australia's interests, as he saw them.

Within 24 hours of his resignation he was warning the Labour party against turning itself into another Conservative party. The point needed making. Calwell's career ended with a disappointment as big as his ambition, but his early achievement was very great. In 1945 he became Australia's first Minister for Immigration, a post which admirably suited his tremendous energy and patriotism. He made immigration a matter of faith, converting even the most distrustful. He toured Europe in 1947 but it was typical of Calwell's insularity that he did not go back again in any one of the 14 years before he very nearly became Prime Minister.

Under Calwell's leadership the Labour party represented, very necessarily, the spirit of Australian nationalism, "one-eyed" sometimes but always angrily independent. Calwell's courage kept him voicing really liberal views which Australians tended to forget under their empirical, self-styled Liberal government.

Again, it was Calwell's campaign in 1961 which reminded people of their duty to keep up the value of social services in a society inclined to be selfish, with so much affluence and opportunity for the young and strong. But he had of course his weaknesses. Twice in his lifetime Calwell saw the Australian Labour movement split asunder. When he became leader he was determined not to court a third disaster. He became a reluctant dragon, devoting himself to compromise and seeming to condone the "popular front" behaviour of Labour's extreme left wing. As a Roman Catholic and a Melbourne man, living in the stronghold of the Democratic Labour Party, he suffered because of sectarianism and his anger against the D.L.P. was so great that he would defend whatever it attacked, including "unity tickets" with communist candidates in trade union elections. This practice was virulent in Victoria. Significantly this was the only state in which Labour did not win a seat from the government in 1961. So Calwell's understandable weakness probably cost him the office he wanted more than anything else.

But even this weakness had its obverse side, where courage showed. A devout Catholic, Calwell was also a fiercely loyal Labour man. This determination lost him the friendship of Dr. Mannix,* the Roman Catholic Archbishop of Melbourne and buttress of the D.L.P. It was grievous for a man whom Pope Paul VI made Knight Commander of the Order of St. Gregory the Great in 1963.

Calwell was sentimental, tough, and friendly, with a gnarled sort of face (large hooked nose and massive jaw) and a voice which was always harsh and husky, as if he were permanently at the end of some long speech on the Yarra Bank, Melbourne's equivalent of Hyde Park Corner, where he sharpened his considerable eloquence as a young man. He loved words (and disputation) and he would use words with a fine relish for their endless possibilities. He once advocated summit talks because "propinquity is everything, in international as in love affairs".

Arthur Augustus Calwell was born in Melbourne, Victoria, on August 28, 1896, the eldest of seven children of a policeman. His paternal grandfather was an American who went out to Victoria in the gold rush of 1853 and married a girl from Wales. His mother was a Roman Catholic, the daughter of Irish immigrants to the United States. His great-grandfather was a member of the state legislature of Pennsylvania. "I was born in west Melbourne and grew up in the crowded inner area, with its cottages built on 14ft frontages and even less, and with evidence of human misery visible to all", wrote Calwell. After leaving school he became a clerk in the state public service.

By 1931 he was president of the state branch of the Labour Party. In 1940 he entered the House of Representatives in Canberra. When Curtin became Prime Minister in 1941, Calwell was not invited to join the government, although a big man in Victoria. He had to wait until 1943, partly because he had opposed conscription for service overseas.

July 10, 1973.

Basil Cameron, C.B.E., who died on June 26, 1975 at the age of 90, began his musical career as a violinist but spent most of it in conducting.

George Basil Cameron was born at Reading on August 18, 1884. He went to school at Tiverton and studied his music in York under Editha Knocker for violin and Tertius Noble of the Minster for other instruction. Thence he went in 1902 to the Berlin Hochschule for four years. Between 1906 and 1912 he earned his living as a violinist, but then obtained the post of conductor of the Torquay Municipal Orchestra.

The experience he had at Torquay, and subsequently at Hastings (1923-1930) and Harrogate (1924-1930) in popularizing classical music stood him in good stead when in the Second World War he found himself assisting Sir Henry Wood at the Promenade Concerts during the blitz. On at least one occasion there was an all-night session at Queen's Hall in which the audience was drawn into the extemporary provision of a non-stop programme. These war seasons associated him so firmly with the Proms that he remained thenceforth as one of the associate conductors.

Between the end of his Hastings appointment, in which he was succeeded by Julius Harrison, and his return to London, he had spent eight years in America as conductor of the orchestra at San Francisco and Seattle.

Since his repertory was wide and his tastes catholic, he at one time or another conducted all the London orchestras and undertook engagements with the principal orchestras of Amsterdam, Berlin, Prague and Budapest. He normally gave the impression of being a sound if slightly stolid conductor, but he was a man of finer sensibilities than that, and every now and again he could fire an orchestra into deeply felt or blazingly effective interpretations.

The steady aspect of his musicianship made him an infallible stand-by in emergencies, and if he never became a virtuoso of the modern type he rendered long and varied service to English orchestral music. He was created C.B.E. in 1957. He was unmarried.

June 28, 1975.

Dr. Maurice Campbell, O.B.E., F.R.C.P., who died on August 7, 1973 at the age of 81, was one of the leading British authorities on diseases of the heart. He was physician to Guy's Hospital and to the National Hospital for Diseases of the Heart, and had been joint editor (and was later consulting editor) of the *British Heart Journal* since its inception in 1938.

John Maurice Hardman Campbell was born on September 3, 1891, the son of John Edward Campbell, F.R.S., and Sarah Hardman. He was educated at Winchester, of which he was a Scholar, and at New College, Oxford, where he took a first class in physiology in 1914 and was elected to a Senior Demyship at Magdalen College. He continued his medical training at Guy's Hospital, where he was elected to a Hilda and Ronald Poulton Fellowship, and held in succession the posts of demonstrator of physiology, chief assistant to the Neurological Department, and medical registrar. He graduated B.M., B.Ch. in 1916 and proceeded to the D.M. in 1921.

During 1916-19 he served as a captain, R.A.M.C., in Mesopotamia and North Persia. He was appointed assistant physician to Guy's Hospital in 1927 and became full physician in 1934. He was a Beit Memorial Research Fellow in 1923-27, and he was also Medical Officer to the Commercial Union Assurance Company and to the Scottish Widows' Life Assurance Society. He was elected F.R.C.P. London in 1929 and filled the offices of examiner (1944-45), councillor (1948-50) and Lumleian lecturer (1946).

It was as a pioneer collaborator in the field of heart surgery, however, that Campbell came into his own after the 1939-45 War. He himself once recalled how the first time he and Russell (later Lord) Brock lunched together after the war the latter talked about the surgical relief of mitral stenosis. As Campbell commented: "Probably he and I did not realize how this talk would change our lives." Change their lives it did. Lord Brock leapt to the fore as a pioneer heart surgeon, with Maurice Campbell acting as his cardiological adviser. It was a partnership which was to become famous, and it put Guy's Hospital in the forefront of heart surgery. Writing many years later, Campbell recalled: "They were exciting times. Before the war my patients had been mostly in their sixties; now they were mostly in their teens or younger, and so much could be done for them."

He was a past-president of the British Cardiac Society and a past-chairman of the British Heart Foundation. He was an enthusiastic member of the Sherlock Holmes Society and an equally keen ornithologist.

He married in 1924 Ethel Mary, daughter of Captain Chrimes, C.B.E. They had two sons and three daughters.

August 9, 1973.

Professor Francis Camps, who died on July 8, 1974 at the age of 67, was one of the best-known and respected experts in forensic medicine Britain has ever produced.

Francis Edward Camps was born on June 28, 1905, the eldest son of a doctor. Educated at Marlborough College, Guy's Hospital, the School of Tropical Medicine at Liverpool, and at Neuchâtel University, Switzerland, Camps qualified in 1928.

After periods as house physician at Guy's Hospital and in general practice he became pathologist at Chelmsford & Essex Hospital, where he specialized in bacteriology and epidemiology, proceeding to the London M.D. in 1933. During the thirties he became drawn to forensic medicine and carried out autopsies for the Essex Coroner, but it was not until after the Second World War that he turned to forensic medicine as a full-time career. He started lecturing at the London Hospital Medical College in 1945, being appointed Lecturer in 1953, Reader in 1954, and Professor in 1963, retiring in 1970. After his retirement he was made Professor Emeritus.

He built up a department of forensic medicine at the London second to none in the world. Under his leadership it constantly expanded, and the scope of the work undertaken embraced all aspects of legal medicine, clinical, pathological, serological and toxicological. People from all over the world visited his department; many stayed to work in it. Perhaps the greatest legacy Camps left to forensic medicine is the number of young men he trained who continue the subject as specialists in their own right. He was lecturer in forensic medicine at the Royal Free Hospital Medical School and the Middlesex Hospital Medical School.

From 1960 to 1962 he was Director of Laboratories of the Royal Institute of Public Health and Hygiene. He was tireless in his enthusiasm and advocacy of his subject, and he served on many committees, the most notable perhaps being the B.M.A. Special Committee on the Recognition of Intoxication in the Relation of Alcohol to Road Accidents in 1951, the Coroners' Rules Committee of the Home Office in 1953, the Mortuaries Committee of the Ministry of Housing and Local Government in 1955, and the Home Office Scientific Advisory Council.

He was one of the original founders of the British Association in Forensic Medicine in 1950 and served as its president from 1958 to 1960. He was the mainspring behind the formation of the British Academy of Forensic Sciences in 1959, serving as its president in 1963 and as its secretary-general from 1960.

Camps was blessed with exceptional stamina and he accomplished in hours what would have taken lesser men days. He got through a prodigious amount of work, not only in mortuaries and in the courts, but in lecturing, writing and latterly broadcasting. Throughout his life he put his heart and soul into his chosen career, never sparing himself.

He was particularly interested in promoting and improving forensic medicine and he missed no opportunity of doing so. His output of published work was formidable and at least four of his books are landmarks in forensic medicine. His particular interests within the speciality were in poisons and drugs, especially alcohol and drug addiction. He travelled all over the world visiting medico-legal centres and attending congresses and meetings, to which he almost always contributed.

His was a household name to the general public through the enormous number of famous cases in which he was involved as a pathologist. As a person he was an impressive figure, radiating vitality, urging himself and others on, never tiring, always enthusiastic. He had great personal charm and was an excellent host. No snob he, for he was equally at home with medical students as with the leaders of his profession, and no organization or person who asked his help was rebuffed.

July 10, 1974.

Former Archbishop of Canterbury—See Fisher of Lambeth.

Professor Norman Capon, M.D., F.R.C.P., F.R.C.O.G., died on January 7, 1975, at the age of 82.

Capon was one of the founder fathers of the modern British school of paediatrics which has played such a prominent part in raising the standards of child health in Britain during half a century.

He may not have achieved as much public acclaim as some of his fellow paediatricians but from his beloved Liverpool, in which he spent his entire professional career, he exerted an influence that was respected by all concerned with the health and welfare of the rising generation.

Norman Brandon Capon was born on June 14, 1892 and was educated at Liverpool College and Liverpool University, where he graduated with first class honours in medicine and gynaecology in 1916. After three years in the R.A.M.C. he returned to civilian practice and proceeded to his M.D. with special merit in 1921. The following year he took his Membership of the Royal College of Physicians of London and nine years later was elected F.R.C.P.

Having chosen paediatrics as his special interest he rapidly established the high reputation that he was to retain throughout his whole career, culminating with his appointment to the chair of child health in Liverpool University which he held from 1954 to 1957.

He was an original member of the British Paediatric Association, later becoming president, and his fellow members showed their appreciation of his services to paediatrics by electing him an honorary member. He had also served as president of the section of paediatrics of the Royal Society of Medicine.

His services were much in demand as a lecturer. In 1947 he was convocation lecturer, National Children's Home, and two years later he was the Charles West lecturer in the Royal College of Physicians in London.

In 1954 he delivered the Lloyd Roberts lecture in Manchester and the following year he delivered the Blackham Memorial lecture.

He was not a prolific writer but everything he wrote was characterized by that careful precision and thought which he brought to all his work and which were the basis of the high respect in which he was held not only by his students and colleagues in Liverpool but also by his fellow paediatricians throughout Britain.

Particularly was this so in the case of the newborn child, an aspect of paediatrics in which he was particularly interested and which accounted for the high opinion held of him in obstetrics circles, culminating in their electing him a Fellow of their college in 1957.

January 10, 1975.

Lord Cardigan—See Ailesbury.

Sir Neville Cardus, C.B.E., who died on February 28, 1975, aged 85, began as a sickly child in a Manchester slum, and ended as an octogenarian who had richly fulfilled his two-fold ambition, to make a name as a music critic and a writer on cricket.

He had no formal training in either field. The start of cricket for him was bowling for hours at a bucket, shielded by a broad piece of wood. Music came to him naturally and gave him his first chance of getting into print. As a sporting writer, he ranks with the old masters of the art from Hazlitt to Bernard Darwin*; his cricket books became classics in his lifetime.

A versatile all-round journalist, Cardus delighted in commenting on the contrasts he had known in the social scene over the years. He could talk as well as he wrote and was as welcome in exalted music circles as among cricketers in a pub. No compliment pleased him more than that he had made many people wish they had actually been at a cricket match or actually attended a concert. He wrote on cricket as a cricketer; on music as a listener.

Born on April 2, 1889, Cardus was brought up in the home of his grandfather, a retired policeman. He never knew his father and the most he ever heard of him was that he had been one of the first violins in an orchestra.

In his *Autobiography* (1947) he wrote that his Aunt Beatrice, "a great and original girl", frankly, and his mother, more discreetly, joined "the oldest of professions".

A brief Board school education was interrupted by an illness which kept him in bed for nearly a year. Earning his first money as a pavement artist, he went on to scrape a living from a miscellany of odd jobs, selling papers in the street, delivering the washing for his mother and aunts, pushing a handcart for a builder, and serving as a junior clerk.

Learning to spin an off-break that whipped up viciously, he played as an occasional pro in club cricket, and answered an advertisement for an assistant to William Attewell, the old Nottinghamshire player and head coach at Shrewsbury School. He was taken on, and stayed for five seasons from 1912 to 1916. One day the headmaster, Alington (later headmaster of Eton and Dean of Durham), found him on the field reading Gilbert Murray's translation of the *Medea* of Euripides. This happy chance led to Alington making him his private secretary. Cardus always acknowledged his debt to Alington, who gave him the run of the library. But the clerical headmaster never shook his young assistant's faith in free thinking.

Having volunteered in August 1914 for military service and been rejected—"not to my surprise or dismay"—owing to extreme short sight, he was placed in an awkward dilemma when Alington went to Eton. He became a casual labourer and sold policies covering funeral expenses among the poor for a burial society. Escape from this dreary task came when he wrote to C. P. Scott asking for employment in the counting house of the *Manchester Guardian* and enclosing cuttings of what little he had written. Scott was impressed and took him on briefly as secretary, and, later, invited him to join his staff as a reporter at 30s a week, with 10s for expenses. This was in 1917, and for the next two years he did all sorts of work for the paper.

He became its cricket correspondent by chance. In March 1919 he suffered a breakdown and, after he returned to the paper, the news editor, later editor, W. P. Crozier, suggested that he might convalesce by spending a few days at Old Trafford. His first cricket report appeared in June 1919. Next year he began writing on cricket every day, covering the most important matches up and down the country and his salary was raised to £5 a week. Between 1920 and 1939 he wrote roughly 8,000 words a week on cricket every summer from mid-May to August, nearly 2,000,000 words in 20 years.

He brought to this an unusual combination of qualities. First, he was a player in his own right who knew from first-hand experience how professionals reacted, and, secondly, he had absorbed the passion for writing good prose which was the tradition of Scott's young men. He put everything that was in him into his reports, catching the atmosphere of a ground, the personalities of the men in the field, the excitement and the tedium of the day's play—all distilled through his literary and musical enthusiasms. For him, Macartney was the Figaro of cricket, Maclaren the Don Quixote with his stonewalling partner, Makepeace, as Sancho Panza, and J. W. Hearne* the Dickensian Turveydrop of the crease. This often bewildered the players he was writing about, but they respected him for his technical knowledge of the game. He put his experiences as "Cricketer" into a number of books, including *A Cricketer's Book; Days in the Sun; The Summer Game; Cricket; Good Days; Cricket all the Year Round* and *Close of Play.*

Delighting in cricket, he never wavered in his regard for music as his first string. He had first got into print in 1910 with an article in *Musical Opinion* on "Bantock and style in music", which tempted him to throw up his job as a clerk and devote himself to freelance journalism. But a postal order for only 7s 6d in payment for this article made him prudent, and he stuck to his job. He wrote musical articles in his early days in the *Manchester Guardian,* acting as assistant to its great critic, Samuel Langford, who taught him much, and with whom he always maintained a disciple-to-master relationship. He succeeded Langford in 1927, and held the post up to 1940 when he went to Australia. After his return to England, he had a spell on the staff of *The Sunday Times* in 1948-49, and rejoined the *M.G.* as its London music critic in 1951. From 1941-47 he was with the *Sydney Morning Herald,* and, later, he again visited Australia to broadcast on music for one hour weekly.

Reflecting on the two themes which engaged him, he once confessed, "I could say that the Hammerclavier Sonata was the last thing that Beethoven wrote, and I'd get a couple of dozen letters, perhaps, 75 per cent from foreigners. But, if I said that Hutton made 363 at the Oval in 1938 I'd get thousands from Yorkshire alone." He admitted, though, that "cricket opened my door of escape; cricket brought me enough economic independence whereby to educate myself". His books on music, some of which were translated into German and Swedish, included *Ten Composers; Musical Criticisms of Samuel Langford; Kathleen Ferrier Memorial Book; Talking of Music; A Composer's Eleven; Sir Thomas Beecham*: A Portrait; Gustav Mahler: His Mind and His Music, Vol I;* and *The Delights of Music.*

He married in 1921 Edith Honorine King, who died in 1968. There were no children. He was made C.B.E. in 1964 and knighted in 1967.

March 1, 1975.

Ottilie, Lady Carnarvon—See **Losch.**

Edward John Carnell, Britain's great pioneer of science fiction, died unexpectedly on March 23, 1972. He was 59.

Ted Carnell's life was dedicated to science fiction from the days when the term was unknown, through its period as a term of opprobrium, to its present state as a viable form of expression. The changed role of the genre owes much to Ted Carnell's work.

He attended Britain's first S.F. convention in 1937, together with "fans" who were later to become writers, Arthur C. Clarke and Eric Frank Russell. From then on his administrative abilities came to the fore. He was made treasurer of the newly-founded Science Fiction Association, and was instrumental in transferring another newly-founded organization, the British Interplanetary Society, from Liverpool to London. Later, Carnell edited the B.I.S.'s journals and publications for a while.

During the Second World War, he served as a gunner in Combined Ops., and was strenuously involved in commando raids, and more than one beach-head invasion.

After the war, he seized on the opportunity to publish *New Worlds*— a magazine later in its history to receive sizable Art Council grants and be banned by W. H. Smith—which he had prepared for publication in 1939. The magazine, backed by dedicated fans of S.F., soon found its way to a regular publisher and a regular public. It became a monthly early in 1954.

Carnell added a sister magazine, *Science Fantasy* and later *Science Fiction Adventures.* All prospered. All appeared regularly and paid their authors regularly. British science fiction writers were thus provided with a reliable native market for their work, instead of having to sell to the United States. All the great and small names appeared in Carnell's magazine.

Carnell moved into agenting, becoming the first British literary agent to specialize in S.F. He was extraordinarily diligent and built up world wide connexions. Among the authors he represented, in whole or in part, were John Christopher, Damon Knight, Frederik Pohl, Michael Moorcock, J. G. Ballard, Samuel Delaney, and Brian Aldiss.

Science fiction made only one or two odd hard-cover appearances in England before the early 50s. When the boom began, Carnell was the adviser to whom bewildered publishers turned. He was thus instrumental in introducing many of the leading American writers to Britain.

He was a founder member of the Science Fiction Book Club, remaining on its selection panel with Kingsley Amis and Dr. George Porter for many years. He was one of the four founders of the International Fantasy Award in 1951, before the current Hugos and Nebulas were thought of. Carnell saw his tiny kingdom grow to a small empire, but no empire builder he—writers were his friends whose success he encouraged but never exploited.

When *New Worlds* was sold to another publisher in 1964, Carnell quietly handed over his battered editorial chair to Michael Moorcock and launched a regular series of anthologies, *New Writings in S.F.,* which provided a market for less well known names. He never lost heart or interest, even during painful illness. He was a modest man, with many more friends than he realized, all over the world.

He is survived by his widow, son and daughter.

March 25, 1972.

Georges Carpentier, the former world light-heavyweight boxing champion and one of the most celebrated European sportsmen, died on October 28, 1975 at the age of 81.

François Mauriac* wrote of Carpentier "this kind of man of honesty so dear to Pascal". Arnold Bennett said of him "He might have been a barrister, poet, musician, Foreign Office attaché, or Fellow of All Souls, but not a boxer."

Yet this lean, debonair, unarguably handsome man was a boxer, and of such ability that the American expert Nat Fleischer ranked him as the seventh best light-heavyweight of all time. Carpentier, who was born on January 12, 1894, fought in every one of the eight major professional divisions from flyweight up to heavyweight—apparently a unique record. Just after the First World War his victories over British opponents made him a legend there.

As a heavyweight Carpentier brushed aside the challenge of Joe Beckett,* Bombardier Billy Wells* and, with an advantage of nearly 2 stone in weight, beat Ted (Kid) Lewis* in the first round, though this victory was much disputed at the time. England regarded the charming Frenchman as unbeatable and so it seemed until July 2, 1921. On that day in Jersey City a crowd of 80,000, paying a million dollars, saw Carpentier, who had won the world light-heavyweight title from Battling Levinsky the previous year, smashed down by the world heavyweight champion, Jack Dempsey, in the fourth round. In Paris flares in the sky told the news and the city wept. From London Lloyd George sent Carpentier a cable saying "I admire you all the more." Outside the Jersey City arena kindly Americans said to a weeping patriot, "Don't cry, Frenchie."

Carpentier, then, was a god of sport to Europe. But one year later his own countrymen spat in his face when, undertrained, he was knocked out by the wild but immensely strong Battling Siki and lost his world light-heavyweight championship. It looked as though "Gorgeous Georges", as the Americans called him, would finish his blazing career in ignominy. But Carpentier came back to score his second first round knockout over Britain's Beckett and to show remarkable courage against the great Gene Tunney before being stopped in the 15th round. The French forgot the Siki defeat and Carpentier, equally popular on both sides of the Atlantic, proceeded into the kind of golden retirement which is the reward of so few champions of sport.

In the years that followed no one thought much about Carpentier's hard, early years in a coal mining town, his close relationship with his manager François Descamps or his French lightweight title won at 15 years of age. They forgot that Georges won a European championship at 17, and at 18 suffered dreadful beatings from the vicious Americans Frank Klaus and Billy Papke. It was all so long ago.

But still Georges Carpentier was treasured as the best image of a sport sometimes more noted for its tragedies than success stories. He made frequent visits to England, reported the Ali versus Cooper world championship for the *Sunday Telegraph*, and was virtually adopted by the British public as one of their own. To the end he was "le gentleman-boxeur".

October 29, 1975.

Admiral Luis Carrero Blanco, the Spanish Prime Minister (Presidente de Gobierno), was assassinated in Madrid on December 20, 1973. He was 70.

His death deprived the Spanish political scene of the man actively associated longer than anyone else with General Franco's regime, and the most faithful interpreter of the General's decisions.

Luis Carrero was born in Santoña, on the north coast of Spain, on March 4, 1903. At 15 he entered the Spanish Naval Academy, from which he passed out top of his year. His ship in 1925 formed part of the Hispano-French Squadron which covered Colonel Franco's landing at Al-Hoceima in Morocco, the operation which turned the tide of the Riff War.

A year later Carrero transferred to submarines, and in 1931 received his own command. As a loyal monarchist he obeyed Alfonso XIII's orders to accept the Republic. In the continuing climate of good relations between the French and Spanish navies, Carrero attended the French Naval Staff College as well as the Spanish, and in 1935 he was appointed an instructor at the Spanish Naval War College in Madrid.

He was still in Madrid when the Civil War began on July 18, 1936. He took refuge first in the Mexican and then in the French Embassy, and thus avoided the fate of the majority of his fellow naval officers, death at the hands of their crews at sea or firing squads ashore. From the French Embassy he made his way through Republican-held territory into France and out again into Nationalist-held territory, reporting for duty at Franco's headquarters in June 1937, just in time to play a useful role as liaison officer between the naval and land forces advancing beyond his native Santoña into Santander. He then commanded in turn a destroyer and a submarine before getting a staff appointment.

In 1941 General Franco brought Commander Carrero Blanco into his inner circle with the title of Under-Secretary to the Cabinet, but in effect as his private secretary in government. Several facets of Carrero's ability and thought commended him to the Spanish Head of State: his monarchism; his certainty that the rising of July 18 1936 against the Popular Front had been necessary to keep Spain from becoming a Soviet satellite; his conviction that without Franco's leadership the Nationalists would have lost; his doubts whether German air and naval power could triumph against the British; his private pro-French, or at least anti-German sympathies, yet preparedness, for tactical reasons, to voice or write sentiments pleasing to the Germans.

Carrero at the time believed that Spain could recover her ancient place as a Mediterranean naval power, but more easily after an Allied than a German victory in World War Two.

Like Franco he held discipline and adherence to the written law or regulation essential to good government, of ship or country alike; but the Nazi and Fascist elevation of the State above the individual was anathema to his monarchist and religious convictions. He could assent to the vague generalities of the "Principles" of Franco's politically all-embracing Movimiento, but not their strict Falangist interpretation. It was a time when anti-monarchist, pro-German Falangists plotted to overthrow Franco. In Carrero he had a man whom he could fully trust: indeed a man who thought and wrote so much like himself that which of the many newspaper articles of the period written under various pseudonyms were Carrero's and which were Franco's cannot be said with certainty. Carrero was kept on the active list of the navy and promoted accordingly to reach the rank of full Admiral in 1966.

In 1951 Carrero's post was raised to ministerial rank to give him a voice and a vote in government. The fact that his opinion was so often favoured by Franco, in the final decision, gave rise to talk of Carrero as the "eminence grise" of the regime; but it was Franco who spoke through a willing Carrero. Carrero was a device to obtain reaction to and uninhibited discussion of ideas and proposals in the Cabinet which few ministers would have dared to challenge if spoken from the Chair. It was from conviction nevertheless rather than as a most obedient servant that Carrero urged over the next 15 years the reinstitution of the monarchy and the naming of Prince Juan Carlos as the future King of Spain. It was he who brought to the notice of Franco the "technocrats" responsible for Spain's economic development on European lines and towards integration with Europe from the mid 1950s onwards.

Carrero Blanco's power increased as that of the Falange diminished, a gradual process culminating in his appointment in October 1967 to the post of Vice-Premier over an existing Cabinet and reappointment in that post in the next Cabinet, that of October 1969, in which there were no doctrinaire Falangists. It was a government whose composition warranted expectations that it would relax the regime's curbs on freedom of political expression and activity, and even give way to the ever more insistent demand by Churchmen that free trade unions should be permitted. The Falangists, angry over their exclusion from government and fearful that the official trade unions, their last stronghold, might be dismembered, immediately embarked on a campaign of violent demonstrations to supplement those inspired by socialists and others among workers and students. These manifestations were adduced by those who, with memories of the Civil War, had looked with disfavour at the small liberties granted over the previous 15 years as proof that any further relaxation of the curbs could lead only to another civil war.

The Church argued the exact opposite, that it was the continued lack of freedom which was fomenting the unrest which could end in civil war. In the event, in the years of Admiral Carrero's Vice-Premiership, 1967-73, years in which he chaired Cabinet meetings with increasing frequency in the absence of Franco, censorship of the printed word became stricter, associations previously held legal were ruled political and therefore illegal, sentences for political offences were stiffened, and the subservience of trade unions to government control was reaffirmed. Admiral Carrero's known religious convictions had led the anti-clericals to believe that he might bring Spain into line with modern Catholic thinking on social and political affairs. Far from it. In a speech in December 1972 he praised Franco in terms which gave grave offence to orthodox Catholics, and endorsed General Franco's earlier hints that he might have to act against Churchmen who criticized his regime.

At the beginning of June Admiral Carrero Blanco was appointed Head of Government under the terms laid down by the Ley Orgánica, or Constitution, prepared under Carrero's supervision and approved in 1966. He proceeded to form his own cabinet. He conceded the post of Vice-Premier to Torcuato Fernandez-Miranda, a man long associated with the Falange, but no out-and-out Falangist, and only one ministry to a member of the religious institute Opus Dei where there had been at least three previously, but this one man was the architect of Spain's economic development, Professor López Rodó. It was a cabinet, like all Franco's except the last, in which every shade of political opinion not directly opposed to the regime was represented.

Admiral Carrero wrote several books on naval history as well as innumerable political articles for newspapers. He leaves a widow, three sons (all in the Navy), two daughters, and 14 grandchildren.

December 21, 1973.

John Carter, C.B.E., who held a unique position in the world of bibliography and antiquarian bookselling, died on March 18, 1975 at the age of 69.

John Waynflete Carter was born at Eton on May 10, 1905. His father was the Rev. Thomas Buchanan Carter and his mother a member of the Stone family; and on each side there were long connexions with Eton College and King's College, Cambridge, at both of which Carter received his education, taking first classes in both parts of the Cambridge Classical Tripos.

In his last year he attended Housman's lectures on textual criticism and in due course became Housman's bibliographer and the editor of his *Collected Poems* and *Selected Prose*. Even as a schoolboy he had begun to collect the works of Catullus, and Housman's introduction to the Renaissance editors of the poet fired Carter with an ambition to edit his works, a plan not wholly abandoned until 40 years later, when his notable Catullus collection passed to the University of Texas.

From 1927 to 1939 and from 1946 to 1953 Carter was associated with the American publishing house of Scribner, and in the earlier period created an antiquarian bookselling department of that firm, which gained great prestige. His inquiring and scholarly mind was alert to changes of taste and new paths in book collecting and he had a large share in the expansion of interest in such subjects as early detective fiction and the evolution of binding styles. These activities were greatly stimulated by

his friendship with Michael Sadleir.

Carter's name will always be linked with that of Graham Pollard in the unmasking of the forger, Thomas James Wise, who had fraudulently manufactured, and with the utmost subtlety marketed, scores of "first editions" of small works by eminent Victorian authors. Carter and Pollard's celebrated exposure, *An Enquiry into the Nature of Certain Nineteenth Century Pamphlets*, 1934, is now a minor classic.

Its pioneering methods, especially in the chemical analysis of paper and the microscopic study of type, have passed into the text books of bibliography and librarianship. Its devastating final indictment of the then most eminent living bibliographer created a sensation which older bibliophiles will all recollect.

During Wise's lifetime parts of the story could not be told; further details, such as the complicity of Harry Buxton Forman and the shocking mutilation by Wise of early plays in the British Museum have been discovered since, and some additional forgeries have been identified. The *Enquiry*, however, remains perhaps the most dramatic, and certainly the most dramatically presented, piece of literary detection ever published. Plans for a new edition were in hand when Carter died.

Carter's post with an American firm and his marriage to an American, Ernestine Marie Fantl (later the well known fashion writer and associate editor of *The Sunday Times*), gave him a familiarity with book collectors and librarians on both sides of the Atlantic which has seldom been equalled. During the war he worked for the Ministry of Information and later for the British Information Services in New York and was responsible for the pamphlet, *Victory in Burma*, designed to tell the American public of the British share of the burden of war in the Pacific theatre.

Carter's success in New York led to him being seconded from Scribner's to be personal assistant to Sir Roger Makins, U.K. Ambassador in Washington, from 1953 to 1955: and for his services at this period he was created C.B.E.

His stature as a bibliographer had grown in the meantime. For his tenure of the Sandars Readership at Cambridge, 1947, he produced a series of lectures which made an elegant and lucid book on the evolution of bibliophily, *Taste and Technique in Book-Collecting*, 1948; and his *ABC for Book-Collectors*, first published in 1952, acquired best-selling status, combining the presentation of the maximum of information with much tart and lively comment.

Carter's career as a bookseller culminated in the tracking down and purchase of the Shuckburgh copy of the Gutenberg Bible, lost sight of for over a century. In 1953 the London branch of Scribner's, of which Carter was managing director, closed its doors and his unique experience of the American market was acquired by Sotheby & Co. His share in the sensational expansion of that firm, especially in bringing

American properties into the London auction room, was considerable.

Carter was a skilful propagandist for the promotion of book collecting, a persuasive lecturer and writer on the subject. He was for many years active on the council of the Bibliographical Society, of which he was president in 1968-69, a member of the editorial board of *The Book Collector*, and organizer of the bibliographical page of *The Times Literary Supplement*. He also was involved in the mounting of several notable exhibitions, especially "Printing and the Mind of Man", 1963.

The high standard of his scholarship he carried into other fields. Sartorially immaculate, he had a patrician air, accentuated by an eyeglass before which head waiters quailed. He had pronounced views on the correct composition of dry Martinis, on which he wrote a pamphlet: he was a lifelong devotee of the ballet. Eton and King's (and the Garrick Club) retained his affection to the end, and his election as a Fellow of Eton in 1967 gave him particular pleasure, as did news of the award of the Gold Medal of the Bibliographical Society (sadly, he died before any formal presentation could take place). To his intimates he was the gayest and most generous of companions.

March 19, 1975.

Pablo Casals, the world-famous cellist, died on October 22, 1973 at the age of 96.

It has become a cliché to say of any man that he became a legend in his own lifetime. In the case of Casals the cliché is exact truth. He influenced the musical life of the twentieth century at many points— as a master cellist whose innovations in technique and method have become common practice; as a conductor, a piano accompanist and a composer. He was, too, a man of strong principles which he held with a determination strong enough to withdraw him from the career of a virtuoso player in countries where he was admired, so that he might not seem to acquiesce in a political system which he bitterly rejected.

Pau Casals (he preferred the Catalan form of his Christian name) was born at Vendrell near Tarragona, on December 29, 1876. His first music teacher was his father, an organist, and by the time he was 12 Casals had obtained some degree of familiarity with, and some ability to play, all the orchestral instruments. His great love, however, was the cello, which he studied at the Royal Conservatoire in Madrid and later taught at the Conservatoire in Barcelona.

In 1895 he became cello soloist in the orchestra of the Paris Opera, and made his first appearance as a concert soloist, with the Lamoureux Orchestra in Paris and at the Crystal Palace concerts in London in 1898. In 1891 he had toured the United States, and if the absence of anything spectacular or meretricious about either his interpretations or his platform manner made recognition of his supreme musical gifts less rapid than has been the discovery of many instrumentalists less supremely musical, by 1910 he was generally accepted as the greatest cellist of the age.

It was through Casals that the unaccompanied Cello Suites of Bach, long regarded as little more than technical exercises, returned to the recital programme; he played them with a range of colour and a subtlety of phrasing which showed them to be works of imagination and eloquence worthy to stand beside their composer's music for solo violin. He was, too, a devoted player of chamber music, whose collaboration with the violinist Jacques Thibaud and the pianist Alfred Cortot* produced superb performances, and recordings as good as the technical standards of the time would permit, of the great classical trios.

After his second marriage, to the American Lieder singer Susan Metcalfe in 1914 (his first marriage, in 1906, to the Portuguese cellist Guilhermina Suggia, had ended in divorce), Casals appeared frequently as her accompanist.

In 1919 he formed the Barcelona Orchestra, for which he worked tirelessly and at some cost to himself until the outbreak of the Spanish Civil War in 1936. With his orchestra, many of the members of which were working men from Barcelona and its immediate neighbourhood, Casals brought orchestral music to an area where it had previously remained almost unknown, and it was his musicianship rather than his international prestige as a soloist which made him an inspiring conductor for whose ears no detail of a score was insignificant. When an English musician asked one of Casals's players to describe the great cellist as a conductor, he received the reply, "Casals is always satisfied with perfection." Casals conducted the Barcelona Orchestra in Paris, but his conducting debut in London was with the London Symphony Orchestra in 1925, and two years later he conducted some of the Beethoven Centenary Festival concerts in Vienna.

He was a convinced liberal driven into exile by the Spanish Civil War and the victory of General Franco. During the fighting he gave many concerts to bring relief to his fellow-countrymen, including one in London at which he played concertos by Haydn, Dvorak and Elgar. He continued his career after the Second World War, but in the late 1940s refused to play in Britain and America because of the tolerance shown by these two countries for the regime in Spain, just as he had refused to play in Fascist Italy, Nazi Germany, and Communist Russia. He continued to give master classes in the United States and for several years, after settling at Prades in the French Pyrenees, organized a festival there where chamber music and the works of Bach were given splendid performances by the pick of the world's instrumentalists, who were drawn there by the magic of Casals's playing, personality and reputation.

In 1963, however, he withdrew his embargo upon appearances in England and conducted his oratorio *El Passebre* (*The Manger*) in the Festival Hall, London. The concert was part of a world tour in which he conducted performances of the oratorio dedicated to world peace, a lengthy and exhausting effort which seemed to leave him undisturbed.

No other musician of our time has received such universal recognition; Casals's interpretations were never too romantic for the classically-minded, or too restrained for the romantics, and his old gramophone records still seem to set a standard for the performance of the entire cello repertory. Those more recent, belonging to the days of the long-player and high fidelity, reproduce not only his tone and phrasing and his infallibly just tempi—they capture something of the delight he felt at his cello by catching the sound of his voice as he sang his way with his instrument through the works in which he was engaged. His obvious integrity, too, the quality of direct single-mindedness which he displayed both in music and in the politics which demanded his self-denying ordinance, or his care for the Barcelona Orchestra at a time when his career as a virtuoso might have made him a very rich man, added to the attraction he exerted over audiences.

In other respects, too, Casals was a man of unusual generosity, quick to recognize the quality of accompanists and collaborators, and with a long memory for friends to whom, as often as possible, he would pay eloquent tribute. His devotion to Donald Tovey, who had dedicated his Cello Concerto to Casals, was typical of a loyalty that was not weakened in any way by the passing of time after Tovey's death, so that Casals would publicly wonder why every town in Britain did not put up a statue to the friend he believed to be "the greatest musical thinker since J. S. Bach."

If perfectionism and hatred of anything either facile or meretricious made him less than the easiest of men to work with—he was quite capable of using his bow to conduct an orchestra and set a tempo different from that given by the official conductor—his devotion to music and the simplicity and geniality of his personality made it natural not only to forgive but to admire him. As a conductor he was inspiring through the thoroughness and devotion of his work rather than through any technical brilliance or parade of personality; his compositions were the overflow of a full mind dedicated to his art, for music to him was a sacred rite. "Even his apparently inextinguishable pipe," a pianist said after rehearsing with him, "seemed to burn incense."

In 1957, after the death of his second wife, Casals married Miss Marta Montanez, a Puerto Rican who had previously been one of his students.

October 23, 1973.

The Rt. Rev. David Cashman, first Bishop of the Roman Catholic Arundel and Brighton diocese, died on March 14, 1971. He was 58.

Born in Bristol on December 27, 1912, David John Cashman studied for the priesthood at Cotton College, North Staffordshire, and the English College, Rome. He was the first priest to be ordained by Archbishop Godfrey, first Apostolic Delegate to Great Britain, who had been his rector at the English college. It was the beginning of a life-long friendship between the two men.

Father Cashman served only a year in the Birmingham archdiocese—as a curate at Stoke-on-Trent—before Archbishop Godfrey moved him to London to be his secretary at the Apostolic Delegation. The genial, gregarious Cashman proved an admirable foil for the rather shy, diffident Archbishop Godfrey.

The task of the Apostolic Delegate was a difficult one. He was a diplomat without official status but was a frequent negotiator with government officials. Cashman's aid proved to be invaluable.

On Archbishop Godfrey's appointment as Archbishop of Liverpool in 1953 Cashman continued his work at the delegation as secretary to Archbishop O'Hara* before being appointed in 1956 parish priest of Arundel, Sussex, and chaplain to the Duke of Norfolk, whose friend he had been for many years. He was created a domestic prelate by Pope Pius XII in the same year.

Two years later he returned to London to be consecrated titular bishop of Cantano and Auxiliary to Archbishop Godfrey, at that time Archbishop of Westminster.

Then in June 1965 Cashman was named first Bishop of the newly-created diocese of Arundel and Brighton, which covers the county of Sussex and the county of Surrey outside the Greater London boroughs.

Soon after the publication in July 1968 of Pope Paul's encyclical letter condemning artificial birth control Cashman issued a pastoral letter in which he said he shared the Pope's compassion for those to whom the encyclical had come as a disappointment and the source of great difficulties. He maintained that condemnation of birth control was not a condemnation of those who in temptation or through worry and other difficulties failed the moral law in this regard. He urged married couples to use the sacraments as much as possible provided they had "the goodwill in the course of time to keep perfect God's law in their marriage".

Cashman was one of the first bishops in England and Wales to call meetings of priests of his diocese to hold discussions on the Pope's encyclical on birth control.

Cashman was a keen sportsman. Some years ago he aroused the ire of animal lovers when he remarked in an interview that his favourite pastime was shooting birds and rabbits.

March 15, 1971.

Francis Milton Cashmore, F.R.I.B.A., died on July 13, 1971. By his death architecture loses an exponent whose influence on design spanned from the Heal building in Tottenham Court Road, London, of the early 1920s to the 32-storey Britannic House in Moorfields, headquarters of the British Petroleum Company. Senior partner in the firm of Joseph and F. Milton Cashmore & Partners, whose offices he had attended the day before he died, Cashmore, though 79, had maintained a remarkably open mind in the matter of architectural design, which enabled him to stay well abreast of the times.

Born in Hampstead in 1892, he was educated at University College School before being trained at the Regent Street Polytechnic school of architecture and at the Royal Academy Schools, where his mentor was Lutyens.

Qualifying A.R.I.B.A. in 1919, Francis Cashmore was in practice on his own for a short period, designing private houses at Alderley Edge, Cheshire, and the "Oxford & Cambridge" public house in the Hammersmith Bridge Road, where many a thirst occasioned by cheering the Boat Race crews has been slaked. In 1924 he joined the offices of Ashley and Winton Newman, and subsequently of Dunbar Smith and Cecil Brewer, for whom he worked on Heal's building, outstanding in its time and in the years since.

In the late 1920s, Cashmore joined the firm of Messrs. Joseph, of which he became a partner and, in 1960, senior partner. There he was associated with a range of buildings which included flats at Hurlingham and in the West End for the Prudential Assurance Company, and a whole series of offices for important companies, among them River Plate House, E.C.2; offices in Bishopsgate for Samuel Montagu; head offices for Alliance Assurance in Bartholomew Lane; and Shellmex House, built on the site of the Cecil Hotel in the Strand, for the Shell Company, for whom they also designed offices in Rio de Janeiro and Buenos Aires.

Other buildings designed in this period were the Denham Film Studios for Korda; the Bearstead memorial hospital, Stoke Newington; the Bath Club reconstruction in St. James's; and the new Gamage's store near Marble Arch.

After 1945 the firm became engaged in developments in the Moorfields area in the City, designing Longbow House and B.P. House before being commissioned by British Petroleum to design Britannic House, their headquarters in Chiswell Street. Cashmore and his partner, Niall Nelson, produced a monumental but sensitively designed 32-storey building for the site, completed in 1967, but Cashmore always regretted that there had been no comprehensive development plan for the area, and that the siting of other and smaller buildings in the neighbourhood was inopportune.

Cashmore was an excellent painter in water-colour and held an exhibition of his work in London in the 1960s. With his wife Josephine (who, with their two sons, survives him) he had played a not inconsiderable part in maintaining the character of Hampstead Garden Suburb where, for many years, he had lived.

July 23, 1971.

Sir James Cassels, who was a judge of the High Court from 1939 to 1961, died at the age of 94 on February 7, 1972.

He had had a varied and interesting career, first as a journalist, then at the Bar, and finally on the Bench, all of which he enjoyed with enthusiasm and to the full.

Born on March 22, 1877, he was the only son of Robert Cassels, who was one of the founders of the Metropolitan Police Courts Officials' Benevolent Society, and became assistant clerk at Bow Street and later at the South-Western Police Court.

James Dale Cassels was educated at what is now known as the Westminster City School, though in his days the name was prefaced by the word "United". While there he learned shorthand.

He began life as a reporter on the *Sussex Coast Mercury*. From there he went, at 10s. a week, to the *Chelsea News*, which also published the *Fulham Chronicle*. He carried out the many and varied tasks of a reporter and sometimes, when attending inquests, sat on the jury when the coroner found himself short of a juryman. In 1898 he joined the Parliamentary staff of the *Morning Post* as a sessional, which meant that he received a salary only when Parliament was sitting. During that time Gordon Hewart (later Lord Chief Justice of England) was in the Gallery as a sketch writer. Cassels later became a member of the permanent staff of the *Morning Post* and stayed for 14 years, first as a reporter and then as a sub-editor.

In 1908 Cassels was called to the Bar by the Middle Temple—of which he was Treasurer in 1947—joined the South-Eastern Circuit (of which he afterwards became leader) and read in the chambers of Walter Frampton, a well-known and greatly respected criminal law practitioner. He retained his association with the *Morning Post* until 1911, by which time he realized that working on a newspaper at night and conducting a case in county court or a criminal court next morning was a too vigorous burning of the candle at both ends. Thereafter he confined himself to practice at the Bar.

In the First World War he reached the rank of captain, went through the Battle of Arras and was twice mentioned in dispatches. He later served as a courts-martial officer. In 1919 he returned to practice and soon became busy. After a case in which he was led by F. E. Smith, later Lord Birkenhead, the latter gave Cassels his red bag. He acquired a reputation not only in criminal but also in civil cases, and he took silk in 1923. In London, too, he constantly appeared in its various criminal courts and in the King's Bench Division, and was sought after in libel and breach of promise cases.

His pleasant and genial personality made him effective with juries, and if there was a touch of humour in a case Cassels could be counted on to extract it. He was a man of generous instincts and though the foibles of his fellow men did not escape him, he had a wide and sympathetic appreciation of human nature.

In 1927 he succeeded Sir Edward Marshall-Hall as Recorder of Guildford and, two years later, he was made Recorder of Brighton. He was also Chairman of East Sussex Quarter Sessions. At the general election of November 1922 he won West Leyton for the Conservatives in a three-cornered fight and held the seat until his defeat by Labour in 1929. In 1931 he was returned for North-West Camberwell and held the seat until 1935. He was twice in 1938 appointed a Commissioner of Assize and in 1939 a judge.

In January 1950 two men, George Kelly and Charles Connolly, were charged at Liverpool Assizes with the murder, in March 1949, of Leonard Thomas, the manager of the Cameo Cinema, Wavertree. Both pleaded not guilty and the jury disagreed. At his subsequent trial on February 8, 1950, Kelly was found guilty. The second trial of Connolly came before Cassels on February 13 of the same year and, the prosecution offering no evidence on the charge of murder, the jury returned a verdict of not guilty.

The public were greatly concerned at the news that John Thomas Straffen had escaped from Broadmoor, a concern which turned to distress and anger when a child aged five years, Linda Bowyer, was later found dead. Straffen in July 1952 was tried before Cassels for the murder of the child and convicted, but was reprieved. In October 1955 Cassels tried three members of the Irish Republican Army concerning raids on the R.E.M.E. depot at Arborfield on August 13 of that year. On the counts in the indictment on which they were found guilty they were sentenced to imprisonment for life. Cassels also decided a number of important civil actions which found their way into the Law Reports.

His record of trials which went to the Court of Appeal was very good. It was said that soon after his appointment to the Bench a friend remarked: "I see that the Court of Appeal upset you yesterday", to which he replied: "No; they may have reversed me, but they didn't upset me."

That he fully justified his appointment, increased his stature and gained the admiration and respect of all who appeared before him was universally acknowledged. After his retirement he sat as Commissioner of Assize at Norwich in October and November 1961 and at the Central Criminal Court in June 1962 to assist in clearing up arrears, experiences which have rarely, if ever, fallen to the lot of a retired judge of the High Court.

He was three times married and is survived by his widow, Deodora, widow of Colonel Croft, and by a son and a daughter of his second marriage. The son is His Honour Judge F. H. Cassels.

February 8, 1972.

Professor Marchese Sir Aldo Castellani, the distinguished physician and specialist in tropical medicine, died on October 3, 1971. He was 94.

Aldo Castellani hailed from a distinguished Florentine family and was born there on September 8, 1877. After graduating with honours at the University of Florence, and subsequently studying under Professor W. Kruse in Bonn, he went to London in 1901, lured by the fame of Patrick Manson, to sit at his feet at the London School of Tropical Medicine which had just been founded. He was encouraged to do so by his compatriot, Dr. Louis Westenra Sambon, who, as Manson's counsellor, was firmly established there.

It was soon realized that the newcomer was someone exceptional, being possessed of great intelligence and having the advantage also of being a brilliant linguist. After passing the necessary examinations he was given his first great chance in June 1902 as a member of the Royal Society's Commission to Uganda on Sleeping Sickness, the terrible scourge which was then rampant on the shores of Lake Victoria. The other members were Dr. G. C. Low, Dr. N. Nabarro and Dr. Cuthbert Christy. At Entebbe he soon succeeded in proving that the trypanosome (June 12, 1902) *T gambiense* (discovered by Forde in 1901) was the cause of the dreaded sleeping sickness and that it occurred in the blood, the brain and in the cerebrospinal fluid. Though for some time he got confused with a streptococcus, this, his greatest discovery, was subsequently confirmed by Major-General Sir David Bruce.

His next appointment, on Manson's recommendation, was as bacteriologist to the Ceylon Government at the Laboratory in Colombo (1903-15). There he worked for twelve years and during that time he earned fame by fundamental discoveries in tropical medicine. These were the demonstration of the cause of yaws, a spirochaete (*spirochaeta pertenuis*) in 1906. Later he elaborated a reaction in the blood which was of considerable value in the diagnosis of typhoid fever and finally he isolated the fungus of that curious skin disease known as *Tinea imbricata*. He then became interested in dermatology and classified a number of tropical skin diseases with imposing Graeco-Latin names. Soon, however, he became involved in medical practice, gaining a high reputation, and was one of the first to inject salvarsan, which had just been elaborated by Ehrlich, as a cure for yaws and realized that it might produce severe reactions.

Early in 1915 he was called to Naples as a successor to Negri who discovered the bodies of rabies in the brain which bear his name, but soon he was involved in the First World War, at first with the Red Cross in Serbia, and was busy treating the dreaded typhus and typhoid fevers. It was there that he produced his tetravaccine which was widely used in later years, but unfortunately did not bear out its pristine promise.

In 1917 he was called to Paris as a member of the Interallied Sanitary Commission and came into contact with many celebrated personalities and collected many honours. He had the exceptional distinction of being Lieutenant Colonel in the Royal Italian Medical Service and an Admiral of the corresponding branch in the Italian navy at the same time.

With the advent of peace in November 1918, finding no opening in his native land, he turned up in London to plead with his master, Sir Patrick Manson, and shortly found himself appointed consultant to the Ministry of Pensions with headquarters at Roehampton. It was not long before he set up his plate in Harley Street and acquired a practice of unprecedented proportions, so that his patients had to be parked on the stairs, and it is claimed that on one auspicious occasion he could count three European queens in his consulting room at one and the same time.

In 1926 he joined the staff of the newly constituted Ross Institute at Putney and served there until it became incorporated with the London School of Hygiene and Tropical Medicine. Several years later, in 1934, he lectured on mycology also at the latter school, though his critics complained that he was perhaps too eager to find and name new species on insufficient grounds.

To add to his burdens he undertook the arduous duties of professor of Tropical Medicine in Tulane University, New Orleans, to which he paid short visits for several years.

During the unquiet years before the Second World War, and with the advent of the Fascist regime, he was, on several occasions, called to his native land to attend the Duce. As recounted in Ciano's diary, he diagnosed a duodenal ulcer and Mussolini was soon cured, demonstrating this happy event by jumping his Irish hunter round the course.

In 1928 he was created honorary K.C.M.G., which he lost in 1940; it was recently restored to him.

At the outbreak of the Italo-Ethiopian War he was appointed as Surgeon-General to the Italian Forces in the field.

In his final report on the health of this great army he was certainly over-optimistic. Never in the whole of history had such a feat been accomplished. Malaria had been abolished with quinine and a glass of Chianti, in contradistinction to our own disastrous experiences in two world wars, and typhus did not exist. At a lecture on this campaign at the Royal Society of Arts, he was acclaimed by Sir Humphrey Rolleston, President of the Royal College of Physicians, as the "greatest hygienist since Moses". This was a propaganda pep-talk, for it soon became apparent that the disease-rate had been much more serious than at first appeared.

At the outbreak of the Second World War and the entry of Italy into the fray Castellani was whisked away to Rome along with Count Grandi, the Italian Ambassador, and soon after reappeared in Tripoli and Cyrenaica as Director of Medical Services. After the Italian retreat he was in Rome acting as referee to the Italian Government for the prisoners of war, especially the British. After the armistice he left Italy for political reasons for Portugal, where he settled at Estoril as medical adviser to the exiled Italian Royal family and other European royalties. He was some time Professor of Pathology and Tropical Medicine in the Lisbon Institute, which has issued a panegyric on his achievements.

Castellani was a prolific writer and his publications were legion. He poured out papers, mostly on dermatology, but he was apt to let his imagination run riot and many will not agree with his description of the newer tropical diseases. At any rate his later works did not attain the standard of his earlier researches.

In 1912 he published with his friend, Dr. A. J. Chalmers, the dean of the medical school in Colombo, a *Manual of Tropical Medicine*, which became deservedly popular, but several years later a second edition appeared so immense and weighty as to become impracticable. He also produced in 1938 a book on tropical climatology and others on fungi and fungal diseases which led to some criticism. In addition he edited the *Journal of Tropical Medicine* for many years.

During his sensational and dramatic career Castellani was honoured by many governments and received a spate of honours, including the American Distinguished Service Cross and the French Knight Officer of the Legion of Honour.

Finally he wrote his memoirs, which appeared in 1960, one for British and the other, even more royal, for American consumption. They describe flamboyantly but vividly, and with a touch of humour, his extraordinary experiences with royalties and hobnobbing with other most important personages.

Castellani married Josephine, daughter of George Ambler Stead in 1907. He leaves a daughter, Jacqueline Lady Killearn, and three grandchildren.

October 5, 1971.

Egerton St. John (Jack) Catchpool, C.B.E., who died on March 13, 1971 at the age of 80, was secretary of the Youth Hostels Association from its inception in 1930 until 1950 when he became vice-president.

The idea, as Catchpool explained at a

meeting in London in January 1931, was to establish chains of hostels throughout the country at which young men and women could be accommodated at about 1s. a night while wandering through the countryside. Twenty-one years later there were some 300 hostels in England and Wales able to accommodate 14,000 young people overnight. He also played an important part in the development of the youth hostel movement throughout the world.

Catchpool transplanted the German idea of youth hostels on British soil; his personal influence, a peculiar blend of innocence and playful enthusiasm, wit, entire absence of swank, and extraordinarily practical mind, was one of the main factors in making the movement into one of the finest youth developments of modern times. In his autobiography, *Candles in the Darkness*, published in 1966, Catchpool told of his adventures in Russia while working for the Friends' War Victims Relief, and of the rehabilitation of Toynbee Hall after the Second World War.

Catchpool was born on August 22, 1890 and educated at Sidcot School, Woodbrooke Quaker College and Birmingham University. He was secretary of the Friends' Social Service Union in 1913-14 and between 1915 and 1919 served with the Friends' War Victims Relief Committee. From 1920 until he became secretary of the Y.H.A. he was sub-Warden of Toynbee Hall. He was president of the International Federation of Youth Hostels from 1938 to 1950. Between 1925 and 1931 he was a co-opted member of the L.C.C. Education Committee. In 1963-64 he was Warden of Toynbee Hall. Since 1957 he had been chairman of the Firbank Housing Society.

He married in 1920 Ruth Allason, daughter of Henry Lloyd Wilson. They had one son and four daughters.

March 16, 1971.

Peter Cazalet, who died at his home near Tonbridge, Kent, on May 29, 1973, aged 66, will be remembered for his many successes as National Hunt trainer to Queen Elizabeth the Queen Mother and his close friendship with the late Lord Mildmay, another patron of his Fairlawne stable in Kent.

He first took out a licence to train in 1939 and from a humble start with a few cheaply-bought horses soon built up a powerful stable, saddling his 1,000th winner before he reached the age of 60. Yet there was one particular ambition he never achieved and that was to win the Grand National. The ill-fated defeats of Davy Jones (1936), Cromwell (1948) and Devon Loch (1956) were calamities not easily forgotten.

It was mainly through the influence of Anthony Mildmay that the then Queen and Princess Elizabeth became racehorse owners. In 1949 Cazalet bought Monaveen to run in their joint names, and a huge crowd gave the royal steeplechaser a tremendous ovation when that same October he won at Fontwell Park. He was indeed the first horse to run for a Queen of England since the days of Queen Anne. It was also on this same little Sussex course that in 1972 he saddled the Queen Mother's 250th winner.

At Eton Cazalet was much more interested in cricket and rackets than in the Turf and it was not until his Christ Church years at Oxford that the fever gripped him. Besides representing the University at cricket, tennis and rackets—showing a talent which was shared by his brother Victor, three times amateur squash champion, and his sister Thelma—he found time to ride and win a number of point-to-points. From 1932 to 1938 he rode as an amateur, having spent two valuable years learning the secrets of race riding and stable management with "Sonny" Hall, an outstanding trainer of that era.

In the early thirties he collected a few jumpers at Fairlawne, his family's majestic estate near Tonbridge, with Harry Whiteman holding the trainer's licence. There he was joined by young Mildmay and Edward Paget, a London stockbroker with much riding experience. The three owners soon began to win races and attract attention, so when the last named finished second on Egremont in the 1932 Grand National there were high hopes for the future. Four years later came Davy Jones's tragic Aintree debacle, with Mildmay's mount running off the course between the last two fences. This bitter disappointment was soon to be effaced by the darker side of the war. Cazalet became a major in the 2nd (Armoured) Battalion of the Welsh Guards. Mildmay was one of his troop leaders.

Hostilities over, Fairlawne began to expand and prosper. There was now royal patronage and the Cazalet-Mildmay partnership was going from strength to strength. Yet tragedy and setbacks lurked around the corner. In 1948 Cromwell finished third at Aintree with his rider doubled up from cramp. Thus for the second time in a dozen years "m'Lord", as Anthony Mildmay had become affectionately known to many on the race-course, was thwarted from winning a Grand National which appeared to be within his grasp. His death two years later by drowning was a shock which deeply affected the whole Cazalet family. Then in 1956 the Aintree jinx once again struck Fairlawne when the Queen Mother's Devon Loch collapsed within a stone's throw of the winning post with the race at his mercy.

Cazalet finished the 1964-65 season with a then record of 87 winners. His stable by now had a great public following and many of his horses became firm favourites with racegoers, for there was no nonsense about their form. Such royal performers as Double Star II, The Rip, Laffy, Makaldar and Manicou spring readily to mind. Two idols which also drew the crowds were Guy Lawrence's elegant and dashing Rose Park and Bill Whitbread's brilliant but erratic Dunkirk. Not only did Fairlawne attract the best owners, but it employed many of the best jockeys. Among those who rode regularly for the stable were Tony Grantham, Bryan Marshall, Dick Francis, Bill Rees, "Gene" Kelly and David Mould.

Peter was a perfectionist. He did everything in style, whether it was scoring centuries for Eton at Lords, for Kent in the county championship, or when entertaining royalty at Fairlawne. Reserved and averse to publicity, he was admired and respected rather than loved by the racing public. The high standards he set made him at times appear to strangers as somewhat impatient and intolerant. Yet he never failed to keep the affection of those who knew him well, as he did the loyalty of those who worked for him.

He was a great family man and one of the proudest moments of his life was when his eldest son Edward, later a barrister, won his first race under rules in 1953. Another memorable occasion was when Cromwell, "m'Lord's" favourite horse, left by him to his sister Helen, won the Mildmay Memorial 'Chase at Sandown Park 20 months after Lord Mildmay's death. Peter's first wife Leonora, by whom he had a son and daughter, died tragically in 1944 after a minor operation. In 1949 he married Zara, the former wife of Lord Belper, and they had two sons.

May 30, 1973.

Robert Gascoyne-Cecil, 5th Marquess of Salisbury—See Salisbury.

Former Archbishop of Central Africa—See Paget.

François Cevert, the French racing driver, was killed on October 5, 1973 during practice for the United States Grand Prix at Watkins Glen, New York. He was 29.

A driver for the British Tyrrell Ford team, Cevert was said to have hit a barrier at an S-turn on the circuit, and he went over the guard rail.

He entered the grand prix ranks only in June 1970 in the Dutch Grand Prix, but he was already considered a future world champion. At the end of the 1971 season the dark-haired, good-looking Frenchman (brother-in-law of the French driver Jean-Pierre Beltoise, currently a member of the Marlboro-B.R.M. team) was placed third in the drivers' championship when his team mate Jackie Stewart won the title for the second time. With Stewart already champion for the third time, Cevert was again lying third in the championship struggle behind Emerson Fittipaldi. Driving with immense flair and natural ability, Cevert was placed second in six out of the 14 races of the 1973 series—the Argentine, Spanish, Belgian, French, Dutch and German grands prix—and third in the Swedish race.

His ability to follow team orders implicitly while playing the supporting role to Stewart was a vital ingredient in the Tyrrell team's success, and their several 1-2 wins in the dark blue cars were reminiscent of Fangio and Moss for Mercedes in years gone by.

It is ironical that Cevert should have been killed at Watkins Glen where he won his first and only Grand Prix victory in 1971; he was second in 1972.

Though inevitably he had to play second fiddle to Jackie Stewart in the Tyrrell team, his real talent and potential were never more clearly demonstrated than they were earlier in 1973 at the formidable Nürburgring circuit, when he was never more than three seconds behind the master—and both were far ahead of the rest of the field.

October 8, 1973.

Sir James Chadwick, C.H., F.R.S., who won the Nobel Prize for Physics in 1935 for his discovery of the neutron, died at the age of 82 on July 24, 1974.

Born in 1891, Chadwick began his career as a physicist under Rutherford at Manchester. There he investigated the gamma rays emitted by radio-active materials, most of the work being in cooperation with A. S. Russell. Shortly before the First World War he went to the Reichanstalt at Berlin to work with Geiger and was interned in the Ruhleben camp when war began. In camp Chadwick threw his whole energies into starting experimental research under the difficult conditions of working in a stable.

It was there that he met his future colleague, Charles Ellis, who learnt his physics from Chadwick, starting with quantum theory and radioactivity, since Chadwick's interest was in the work of Planck, Nernst and Rutherford. In Ruhleben, Chadwick, with Ellis's help, worked on the ionization which occurs in the oxidation of phosphorus, and also on the photo-chemical reaction of carbon monoxide and chlorine. Some equipment for this was obtained through the kindness of Professors Planck, Nernst and Lise Meitner*; the rest was constructed in the way that all prisoners of war learn.

When Rutherford went to the Cavendish Laboratory at Cambridge after the war he took Chadwick with him. His first piece of research there was the direct determination of the atomic number of an element through the scattering of alpha particles. In this classical experiment he used an annular scattering foil of metal at a fixed angle to increase the yield of the scattered particles. He cooperated with Rutherford in a truly epoch-making series of experiments on artificial distintegration of light elements by alpha particle bombardment, and for a period of about 10 years he was responsible for the detailed organization of research in an important section of the laboratory.

Chadwick at this time showed a complete allegiance to the modern ideas that were developing on atomic structure, and he had a great admiration for Niels Bohr*; but at the same time he was cautious in accepting the result of any experiment unless it met his own highly critical standard. He took a great pleasure in detailed experimental technique which was then largely a matter of personal skill with his own hands. In many respects his approach to an experiment was similar to his approach to a good wine— a subject which in those days had already attracted his interest. He was extremely kind to young scientists and would take infinite trouble over any experiment designed to test a theory put forward by a young researcher on the basis of the newly-discovered quantum mechanics.

His most famous work, however, owed little or nothing to theory; this was the discovery of the neutron in 1932, for which in 1935 he received the Nobel Prize for Physics. The apparatus which he used is preserved in the museum of the Cavendish Laboratory. Chadwick himself, in his Rutherford Memorial Lecture, delivered in 1953, described this discovery as follows: "Just before this event (the work of Cockcroft* and Walton), I had discovered a new particle of nuclear structure, the neutron, a discovery which resolved some grave difficulties in the nuclear structure, and which in the course of a few years was to lead to the development of atomic energy. In his Bakerian Lecture in 1920 Rutherford had predicted the existence of this particle and described some of its properties. The experimental results on which he seemed to base his prediction were in fact unreliable, but, as I learned from many discussions with him, his belief in the neutron did not grow out of these experiments, but from long and deep consideration of the problem of building up nuclei. I soon came to share his belief. In later years he was too occupied with outside duties for such adventures, and I pursued them myself. I mention this matter here to acknowledge my debt—in truth a small part of my debt—to Rutherford." This characteristically modest description of his work does not detract from the fact that Chadwick made one of the great scientific discoveries of all time.

In 1935, in common with many of Rutherford's co-workers at that time, he left the Cavendish to found a school in the provinces, being appointed to the Lyon-Jones Chair of Physics at the University of Liverpool. When he went there the physics department hardly existed as a research school and was not even wired for alternating current. None the less, one of the first things that Chadwick did was to order a cyclotron. The machine was completed in 1939 and with some modifications is still working. Most of the work with this piece of equipment was concerned with the nuclear disintegration of the light elements, in fact much of the experimental evidence for the so-called "stripping reactions" came from his school at Liverpool.

During the war Chadwick was deeply involved with the development of the uranium bomb, being probably the first Englishman to appreciate fully the danger that the enemy might produce one first. It was at Liverpool that the measurements were made of the cross section for fission of the light isotope of uranium, which proved its possibility. In 1943 he went to the United States as head of the British team and took with him all the senior members of his department at Liverpool.

While in the United States he undertook the very heavy responsibility of the coordination of the work of the American, British and Canadian teams.

He was knighted in 1945 and on his return from America he set himself to develop at Liverpool a nuclear physics school on a much larger scale. He obtained a new building for nuclear physics and the design of a very successful synchro-cyclotron was started at that time, though the machine did not come into operation until after he left Liverpool.

In 1948 he returned to Cambridge as Master of Gonville and Caius College and threw himself at once into the detailed administration of the college. His Mastership there has been marked by an insistence on high standards in scholarship and research of those elected to Fellowships, and by his great interest in and love for the college. He resigned the Mastership in 1958 and was made a Companion of Honour in 1970.

He married, in 1925, Aileen, daughter of H. Stewart-Brown, and they had twin daughters.

July 25, 1974.

Lord Chandos, K.G., P.C., D.S.O., M.C., died on January 21, 1972 at the age of 78.

Better known as Captain Oliver Lyttelton, Member of Parliament for Aldershot from 1940 to 1954, he had an exceptionally full life, having taken up three separate careers —in the City, in politics, and in industry. Before being appointed President of the Board of Trade in October 1940, Lyttelton had taken no part in politics, yet within a year he was a member of the War Cabinet, as Minister of State resident in the Middle East. For the last three years of the Coalition Government he was Minister of Production, and in the brief "Caretaker" Government he combined this with his former office at the Board of Trade. In the Conservative administration of 1951 he accepted the post of Colonial Secretary, though he would have preferred the Treasury. After three turbulent years dealing with troubles in Malaya and Africa, he returned to industry as chairman of Associated Electrical Industries, retiring at the end of 1963.

Lyttelton was quite unlike the popular image of either a city man or a captain of industry. His interests were more those of an eighteenth century patron of the arts, and his manner retained the social graces of the days of his youth. Moreover his approach to all matters remained completely open-minded, and to the end of his life he continued to look ahead, and to think—optimistically—about the future.

For these reasons he had the rare gift of attracting people, from all walks of life and all ages. He was, in fact, the friend of three Prime Ministers, Churchill,* Eden, and Macmillan. But in contrast to many of his political business colleagues he preferred to make himself accessible to any who wished to see him. His affable and genial manner immediately put visitors, particularly young people, at their ease; his immense store of anecdotes, told with skill and enjoyment, soon provoked laughter, and invariably disarmed even determined critics. These qualities, invaluable in politics for smoothing out difficulties and carrying awkward negotiations to success, may have led, in industry, to some lack of ruthlessness. For even when he felt that advantage was being taken of his good nature, he was incapable of dealing harshly with anyone. But all aspects of industry's role in modern society interested him, especially industry's responsibility for exploiting the advances of science and its duty to its workpeople. His advice was frequently sought by the Government on a wide range of matters, and he was often able to give decisive and effective leadership to the industrial community.

Part of the secret of his success lay in his zest for life. In his memoirs he reflected that he had seldom woken up in the morning, except when about to make an important speech, without feeling how good life was. The sentiment, and the reservation, were characteristic.

Oliver Lyttelton was born on March 15, 1893, the only son of Alfred and Dame Edith Lyttelton. His father had been Colonial Secretary under Balfour, and an outstanding sportsman, particularly as a cricketer. Oliver was sent to Eton and then to Trinity College, Cambridge, but without making his mark at either place.

The First World War was to be for him, as for all those of his generation who survived it, the great formative experience. Lyttelton volunteered for service as soon as war was declared, and in December 1914 he became a subaltern in the Grenadier Guards. From the early part of 1915 he was continuously on active service in France, winning both the D.S.O. and the M.C. and being mentioned three times in dispatches. Miraculously he was not wounded until April 1918 when he was Brigade Major in the 4th Guards Brigade.

Back in London at the age of 26, without a university degree, Lyttelton was advised not to follow his father into law, and instead he obtained a position in Brown, Shipley & Co., merchant bankers, as a clerk in the correspondence department. After less than a year, however, he was offered a job in the British Metal Corporation, shortly becoming manager and later managing director. For the next 20 years

there was no indication that he might one day become a public figure. But all the time he was acquiring experience and expert knowledge of the metal business.

Before the outbreak of war, Lyttelton had tried in vain to persuade the British Government to stockpile metals, but it was only when he became Controller of Non-Ferrous Metals in September 1939 that he was able to push through a plan for the long-term purchase of supplies which not only ensured that enough metal would be forthcoming for the war effort, but also incidentally saved the Government millions of pounds.

In July 1940 Mr. Churchill invited him to join the Government, and in October he became President of the Board of Trade and a member of the Privy Council. But it was not until November 26 that he became a member of Parliament, being returned unopposed for Aldershot, where Lord Wolmer had succeeded to the peerage. As president his main task was to see that the needs of the civil population made as little demand as possible on British industry. This required schemes to "concentrate" each industry into a few companies only, to allocate materials, and to introduce rationing and price controls widely. His introduction of clothes rationing, an intricate problem in any case, was made still more difficult by Churchill's obvious dislike of the idea.

Lyttelton was sent out to Cairo with the status of a member of the War Cabinet to establish the new post of Minister of State in the Middle East at the end of June 1941. For some time the war had been going badly in that area, and Churchill relates in his War Memoirs that he had been "extremely distressed by the apparent inadequacy of the Cairo staff". In a letter to General Wavell, Churchill explained that Lyttelton's prime duty would be "to relieve the High Command of all extraneous burdens, and to settle promptly on the spot . . . many questions affecting several departments or authorities which hitherto had required reference home". During the eight months he held this office Lyttelton formed the Middle East War Council, forced King Farouk* to accept a government with wider popular support, dealt with a currency crisis in Persia, and, with difficulty, came to an agreement about Syria with General de Gaulle*, who had been incensed by the terms of the Armistice granted to the Vichy French there.

In March 1942, Lyttelton returned to London as Minister of Production, a post he held until the end of the Coalition Government.

When the Labour government came to power in 1945 Oliver Lyttelton, as he says in his memoirs, "had to look around me for an income". The job he chose was the chairmanship of Associated Electrical Industries, a company then controlled by General Electric of America.

He left the company to rejoin the Conservative Government in 1951. After the

war he had emerged as the leading Conservative spokesman on financial and economic matters. It was, therefore, a surprise to many and, initially, to him, that he was made not Chancellor of the Exchequer but Colonial Secretary.

In his new post, however, he belied both appearances and expectations. As a member of the City wing of the Tory party par excellence, the Opposition expected to find him a reactionary. But Lyttelton had most of the outlook of the great Whigs. He was far too intelligent a man to believe that it was within the bounds of the politically possible to impede progress towards self-government. There was also a cynical streak in him which prevented him from agonizing too much at the imperfections of newly independent governments. He early made it plain that his arrival at the Colonial Office might betoken changes in tactics, personnel and pace, but not in the direction of policy.

Again, the Colonial lobby in Parliament rather expected him to remain aloof from coloured nationalist politicians. But Lyttelton, although he was a man of numerous prejudices, did not number colour prejudice among them. He got on famously with Orientals and Africans, provided they amused him and were congenial company. And it was surprising how many of them did—and how much they reciprocated his feelings. In Nigeria, he must have been about the most popular British Colonial Secretary who ever visited the country, and he was astute in exploiting his charm for political purposes. Flattery, he used to say, is the infantry of negotiation.

He could bully as well as flatter, and at times he rushed his fences. In Malaya he did so with outstanding success but in Central Africa his achievements were not enduring. In Kenya, during the Mau Mau rebellion, his great contribution was his ability to persuade the reluctant settlers to move forward politically, thereby helping weaken African support for the terrorists. This was accompanied by willingness to back strong measures in the suppression of violence. The combined formula worked.

It was after he returned to the A.E.I. chairmanship in 1954 until his retirement in 1963 that he made his greatest impact on the company and on the business world. He followed an enthusiastic expansion programme, raising in four years at the end of the 1950s no less than £59m from the public and more than doubling the size of the company. He strove to take the company into every area of the electrical industry, spending heavily on research and development and taking over such companies as Siemens Brothers. He centralized the management and made the name of Associated Electrical Industries much better known than that of the subsidiaries. He fostered the expansion of the Hotpoint domestic appliance subsidiary. He moved with the company into a palatial new headquarters at Grosvenor Place (now the home of the British Steel Corporation).

He was not, however, successful in making the company efficient and profitable enough to succeed in the more competitive conditions of the 1960s. The reorganizations and management plans looked good on paper and the company's annual report and accounts set a new high in standards of disclosure of information to shareholders and in glossy descriptions of the company's activities. The figures, however, were depressing. During Chandos's second period as head of A.E.I. the capital employed by the company rose from £58m to £150m, sales rose from £128m to £213m, but profits fell from £15.3m to £6.6m. Four years after Chandos's retirement A.E.I. was still relatively unsuccessful and it fell, after a controversial battle, to a takeover bid from the smaller G.E.C.

His activities ranged far wider than business. He became a Trustee of Churchill College, Cambridge, and of the National Gallery in 1958, and chairman of the National Theatre Board in 1962. This last appointment gave him special pleasure, because his mother had devoted much of her public life after the 1914-18 war to trying to establish a National Theatre.

In 1971 he became life president; his chairmanship was marked by rows with the executive of the National Theatre, in particular that concerning the staging of Rolf Hochhuth's play *The Soldiers* to which the Board objected in 1967. Chandos stated that while "all matters of artistic importance naturally are matters for the director" what he called "wide national policy" was the Board's responsibility. He also dealt with the building of a new theatre on the South Bank under mounting costs.

He was delighted by the success, both with critical and with popular opinion, of his memoirs, published at the end of 1962. They well reflect the range, wit and style of the author, and, characteristically, it was praise for the excellence of the prose which pleased him most. In 1968 he published *From Peace to War; A Study in Contrast (1857-1918)*.

In 1970 he became a knight of the Order of the Garter.

He married, in 1920, Lady Moira Godolphin Osborne, fourth daughter of the 10th Duke of Leeds. They had three sons (one of whom was killed on active service in Italy in 1944), and a daughter. His heir is the Hon. Antony Alfred Lyttelton.

January 22, 1972.

Gabrielle Chanel—"Coco" Chanel, la grande couturière—died on January 10, 1971 at the age of 87.

She reached a peak of fame and popularity in the 1920s when she succeeded in replacing the extravagant pre-war fashions with simple, comfortable clothes. The same cardigan jackets and easy skirts that she popularized then were revived in her successful come-back in the late 'fifties, and her famous Chanel No. 5 scent kept her name in the public eye throughout her long career.

She became something of a legend in the world of fashion; and a Broadway musical, based on her career and starring Katharine Hepburn, was put on in 1968.

Most sources suggest that "Coco" Chanel was born in 1883, although this fact, like so many others about her life, was a jealously guarded secret. Traditionally her nickname "Coco" was earned by her habit of riding in the Bois when the cocks were still crowing "Cocorico" but she later claimed that it was merely a respectable version of "cocotte".

Orphaned at an early age, she worked with her sister in a milliner's in Deauville, where she finally opened a shop in 1912. After a brief spell of nursing in the war, she founded a couture house in the Rue Cambon in Paris. There she worked, lived and entertained for much of the rest of her life, although she actually slept in the Ritz Hotel on the other side of the road.

Chanel sensed the profound need for change, renewal and emancipation that was sweeping the world in 1914 and set out to revolutionize women's clothing. It was her talent, drive and inspiration that brought about a complete metamorphosis of fashion in post-war years. She began by liberating women from the bondage of the corset. In 1920 she made the first chemise dress, and the "poor girl look", in contrast to the rich woman of pre-war years, was born. She succeeded in making women look casual but at the same time elegant by using the then revolutionary combinations of jersey, tweed and pearls. Dior was to say of her later: "with a black sweater and 10 rows of pearls Chanel revolutionized fashion".

In 1925 she made fashion history again with the collarless cardigan jacket. Her bias-cut dress was labelled by one critic "a Ford, because everybody has one". It was Chanel who introduced the shoe-string shoulder strap, the strapped sandal, the flower on the shoulder, the floating evening scarf, the wearing together of "junk" and real jewels. Chanel launched the vogue for costume jewelry, particularly rows of fake pearls, bead and gold chains and gee-gaw-hung bracelets.

At the height of her career, Chanel was said to be the wealthiest couturière in Paris. She was at that time controlling four businesses: the couture house, textile and costume jewelry factories, and perfume laboratories for her famous scent. At this time also her private life, particularly her friendship with the second Duke of Westminster, became a subject of constant public interest and speculation. But although Mademoiselle Chanel's engagement to Paul Iribe, a well-known artist and fashion sketcher, was reported in 1933, she never married.

In 1938, after a losing battle with the rising influence of Schiaparelli, Chanel retired from the couture scene. Sixteen years later she staged a spectacular comeback, roused into action it is said by irritation of seeing Paris fashion taken over by men designers. Her first post-war collection in 1954 was ill received by fashion critics, for instead of launching a new fashion revolution she went on from where she had left off—cardigan suits, short pleated skirts, crisp little blouses, short chiffon and lace dresses, masses of "junk" jewelry. But her timing proved to have been perfect. Rich and famous women once again adopted the Chanel look and when the French magazine *Elle* ran a Chanel pattern they received a quarter of a million requests for it.

In 1957 Chanel won the American Nieman Marcus award for fashion, but even without this official recognition her continuing influence was indisputable. Many different factors contributed to her success as a dress designer, but chiefly it was the result of immense flair coupled with ruthless good taste. In her own language she described all that she most disliked as *vulgaire*. Her clothes were the antithesis of that.

January 12, 1971.

Charles Henry Chapman, who died on July 15, 1972 at the age of 93, will for ever be associated with the characters of Charles Hamilton's fictional school Greyfriars whom he drew so graphically in the pages of the boys' paper *The Magnet* for nearly 30 years, as well as in various other magazines and books.

He especially portrayed the "Fat Owl" of the Remove Form at Greyfriars, Billy Bunter, with flair and humour and was certainly this famous schoolboy character's most definitive illustrator.

Charles Henry Chapman was born on April 1, 1879 at Thetford, Norfolk, and educated at Kendrick school, Reading, Berkshire. He showed an aptitude for art at school and on leaving studied drawing under Allen W. Seaby, professor of fine art at Reading university.

He was later apprenticed to an architect at Basingstoke but found he enjoyed turning out humorous drawings and cartoons more than applying himself to draughtsmanship and design. He began sending his work to London editors and in 1900 celebrated his 21st birthday by having a drawing accepted by a boys' magazine, *The Captain*.

Over the next few years his drawings appeared in numerous boys' magazines and comic papers until in 1911 Chapman joined the staff of *The Magnet*, which ran Frank Richards's (a pseudonym of Charles Hamilton) popular stories about Greyfriars School, Billy Bunter, Harry Wharton and Co., and the rest. He took over the illustrating work from an artist named Arthur Clarke who had died suddenly. Chapman did so well that his association with *The Magnet* continued until the paper's demise in 1940.

For nearly 30 years he drew Billy Bunter and the other ever popular Greyfriars characters, so helping to immortalize some of juvenile literature's most famous schoolboys. He also illustrated the long series of Bunter books from 1955 until they ended in 1965. Chapman was still drawing Billy Bunter for the entertainment of friends and collectors until recently and had lived for many years at Tokers Green, near Reading, Berkshire. He was active until a few weeks before his death, and often said that he owed his health and longevity to his regular habits of cycling, walking and taking a daily cold bath.

July 18, 1972.

Lt.-Col. F. Spencer Chapman—See Spencer Chapman.

Guy Chapman, O.B.E., M.C., an author of scrupulous and sensitive quality whose chief interest was in history, and who after the Second World War occupied the chair of modern history at Leeds University, died on June 30, 1972. He was 82.

Born on September 11, 1889, the son of G. W. Chapman, for many years official receiver in bankruptcy, Guy Patterson Chapman was educated at Westminster School and at Christ Church, Oxford, and was called to the bar on the eve of war in 1914. He was commissioned in The Royal Fusiliers, went out to France in the summer of 1915, and as a junior officer experienced a great deal of trench fighting during the next three years. He was awarded the M.C. and was twice mentioned in dispatches. After the armistice he served for some time with the army of occupation on the Rhine. He was made O.B.E. in 1919.

He returned to civilian life in 1920 and for most of the next twenty years was engaged in publishing in London. At one time he conducted a small publishing firm under his own name; but, though the firm never lacked enterprise and brought out works of scholarly and distinguished character, among them a translation of *Tallement des Réaux,* who at the time was known to only a handful of students of French historical memoirs in Britain, the business did not prosper. Though he came to writing relatively late, however, Chapman had always combined publishing with a strong leaning towards literary and historical scholarship. For some years he was engaged with John Hodgkin in compiling a bibliography of Beckford. This was published in 1930, when interest in the personal history of the "abbot" of Fonthill and the literary significance of the author of *Vathek* had still to be fully awakened. The bibliography marked a notable stage in the awakening. In the same year Chapman published a short novel, *A Painted Cloth.* Three years later came *A Passionate Prodigality,* an uncommonly vivid, truthful, and memorable description of trench warfare in France. The book has a high place in the literature of the First World War. It was republished in 1965.

Chapman's subsequent biography of Beckford, representing the labour of years among the manuscript sources and written with conspicuous skill and vigour, appeared in 1937. Although his interpretation at several points was disputed, the patient and searching analysis and the literary distinction of the work were generally recognized. A similar care and thoughtfulness were apparent in a stimulating study in a different field, *Culture and Survival,* published in 1940. In this compact little essay in sociology Chapman attempted to trace the relation between rising standards of life and a decline in fertility, between the collapse of a rural culture and the commercialization of leisure activities in the cities.

Soon after the book appeared he was appointed to the Army Educational Corps and took an energetic and prominent part in directing the work of the Army Bureau of Current Affairs. From 1945 to 1953 he held the chair of modern history at Leeds University. During this period he was engaged in close and often concentrated study of the politics and social history of the French Third Republic. Not until 1955, however, did he complete his labours on *The Dreyfus Case,* in which he produced what is almost certainly the fairest and clearest account in English of the historic *affaire.* The book is, indeed, a singularly just, temperate and impressive piece of work. *The Third Republic of France: The First Phase, 1871-1894* appeared in 1962 and *Why France Collapsed* in 1969.

Thoughtful and plain-spoken, though less tough-minded than he sometimes appeared to be, Chapman was a man of strong character and unaffected sensibility.

He married, in 1926, the writer Miss Storm Jameson.

July 1, 1972.

Ezzard Charles, world heavyweight boxing champion from June 1949 to July 1951, died on May 28, 1975 at the age of 53. He had been crippled by lateral sclerosis for a number of years.

Charles became champion after beating Jersey Joe Walcott on points in a colourless fight for the title which had been vacated by Joe Louis. He lost it to Walcott just over two years later in a seventh round knockout.

Charles was born in Lawrenceville, Georgia on July 7, 1921, and had a successful amateur career in which he won all 42 of his bouts.

His first professional fight was a three-round knockout victory over Medley Johnson and he thereafter established himself solidly with a string of 15 consecutive victories, 13 by knockouts.

Called up by the United States Army in 1943, he continued boxing and took part in many inter-allied tournaments in North Africa and Italy, all of which he won.

After discharge from the army he continued boxing professionally again and won the National Boxing Association version of the heavyweight championship by his victory over Walcott. But though he defended his title successfully eight times it was not until he had defeated Joe Louis, who came out of retirement to face him in 1950, that he was generally recognized as world champion.

Thereafter he successfully defended against Nick Barone, Lee Oma, and twice against Jersey Joe Walcott, who eventually knocked him out at his third attempt.

Charles was not a celebrated and never a popular champion but he was a boxer of considerable skill as well as being a sharp puncher. Arguably his courage and skill were most appreciated after he had lost the championship, during the first of his two comeback attempts against Rocky Marciano*. He withstood The Rock's fierce assault for 15 skilfully evasive and daring rounds though he lost on a points decision.

A second attempt against Marciano also failed, this time in the eighth round by a knockout, and set the seal on his ring decline.

He announced his retirement in 1956 and though he did return briefly to the ring two years later he did not box after 1959.

After his retirement, Charles helped with community projects in Chicago. He was elected to the Boxing Hall of Fame in 1970.

Ezzard Charles must have been one of the most underrated of all heavyweight champions, for he is best remembered for his two courageous losing battles with Rocky Marciano—the first of which went the full 15 rounds—and for having had the temerity to outpoint the fading, once great, Joe Louis.

Charles was perhaps at his best around 13st 3lb. But for the extra weight, which would have made it agony for him, in his prime, to sweat down to 12st 7lb, he could have been a great light-heavyweight. Indeed he was good enough, when still boxing in that somewhat unfashionable division, to knock out the legendary Archie Moore. Charles was inhibited in the ring, a psychiatrist hired by a news agency once decided, "because he loses the spontaneity he has in his dreams."

The factual explanation may have been that Charles never quite recovered from the trauma he suffered in 1948 when an opponent named Sam Baroudi died after being knocked out in the tenth round. Charles, once hailed as the Cincinnati Cobra, from then on became, according to close friends, a tamed tiger. He boxed once in Britain, in 1956, when he was disqualified for persistent holding in two rounds against Dick Richardson.

May 29, 1975.

Sir John Charles, K.C.B., M.D., a former Chief Medical Officer of the Ministry of Health, Ministry of Education, and the Home Office, died on March 31, 1971 at the age of 77.

John Alexander Charles was born on July 26, 1893, the son of John Charles, M.D., who practised for many years in Stanley, co. Durham. J. A. Charles was at school first at St. Bees and afterwards at the Royal Grammar School, Newcastle upon Tyne. In 1910 he entered the University of Durham College of Medicine, Newcastle upon Tyne, and qualified M.B., B.S., with 1st class Honours in 1916. In 1925 he took the D.P.H., Cambridge, with distinction; in 1927 the M.R.C.P. Lond.; in 1930 the M.D. (Durham) with commendation; and in 1935 he was elected F.R.C.P. Lond.

After holding house appointments at the Royal Victoria Hospital, Newcastle upon Tyne, Charles spent seven years as Captain R.A.M.C. (Special Reserve), with war service in France and Italy and postwar service in Germany.

He was appointed Medical Officer of Health, Newcastle upon Tyne at the end of 1932. In this capacity he achieved a high reputation. In addition to competent administration, he made important epidemiological, nutritional and public health inquiries. This work led to his appointment as a deputy chief medical officer of the Ministry of Health in 1944, and in 1950 he succeeded Sir Wilson Jameson* as chief medical officer of the three departments of State—Health, Education and Home Office, retiring in 1960.

In Charles's ten years of office as chief medical officer he gave much attention to the development and consolidation of the National Health Service. He witnessed a further decline in tuberculosis and diphtheria, and encouraged effective vaccination against poliomyelitis. Among many other subjects which engaged his attention and which are recorded in his annual reports were the mental health services under the new Act, the dental services, care of the aged, and the progress of maternity and child welfare work.

He visited various parts of the world in the interests of international health, being also president of the Executive Board of the World Health Organization (1957-58) and president of the twelfth World Health Assembly in 1959.

He took a considerable interest in medical history, being a founder member of the Faculty of History of the Society of Apothecaries. He was the author of papers on John Hunter, Mark Akenside, the physician-poet, and "Roger Bacon on the Errors of Physicians" (*Gideon de Laune Lecture,* 1960).

Charles was of medium height and clean-shaven. His manner was quiet and at times might even appear distant. Those who knew him well appreciated his kindly disposition, industry and whole-hearted devotion to duty.

In 1947 he married Madeleine Frances, daughter of Sir William Hume, C.M.G., M.D., F.R.C.P. They had a son and a daughter.

April 8, 1971.

Henri Charrière, the French ex-convict author of the best-selling book *Papillon,* died on July 29, 1973, in a Madrid clinic.

Charrière, who made of his life on Devil's Island, and while on the run before recapture, one of the best sellers of all times, was 66. He had cancer of the throat.

Papillon, the name Charrière took from the Paris underworld of the 1930s, sold more than 10 million copies, and was translated into some 20 languages. In France Charrière became a literary and social star overnight as his memoirs of life in French penal colonies in Guyana and refuge among jungle Indians appeared in the summer of 1969. It caught ideally the mass reading public of the holiday season, but the ex-convict's story proved no less successful later in all the countries of Europe, the United States and in Latin America itself.

Charrière always maintained that his life sentence, awarded when he was only 25 for the shooting of a Pigalle pimp, was based on a judicial blunder, with the real killer "Roger le Corse" (also known as "Papillon") never having been found. But "Papillon Rose", also known as "Le Juste", was found by the police and subsequently condemned for the killing.

The immense success of the book, including praise from François Mauriac* and President Georges Pompidou, led in 1970 to France's then Minister of Justice, M. René Pleven, according Charrière an official pardon, although French law forbids a condemned murderer from returning to the area where the crime was committed.

The public success produced, perhaps inevitably, a second reaction of a different kind—from various sides doubt was shed both on the veracity of Charrière's many adventures, and whether he was indeed the author or had been guilty of plagiarism.

Charrière took action in the French courts to protect his reputation from these allegations, particularly after the widow of another ex-convict asserted that he had made free use of her husband's unpublished memoirs of prison life. At a press conference "Papillon" himself once declared that the book was 75 per cent truth and 25 per cent invention.

Charrière was the son of a respectable small town schoolmaster in the Ardèche region of Central France. His mother died when he was 11 and after troubled schooldays he was put into the merchant navy. It was a bad conduct record while serving which prevented him from pursuing a professional career. He drifted into the Paris underworld of prostitution, robbery and crime.

After 13 years of jail life, Charrière obtained his freedom again when the Venezuelan authorities showed leniency and humanity, impressed by the Frenchman's ten bids to escape and resistance while on the run. He lived subsequently in Caracas until emerging with *Papillon* to become famous.

Charrière attempted a second success with *Banco* published in France in 1972, which completed his life story. Neither this, nor the film he made with a scenario written by himself, evoked anything like the same public response.

Charrière leaves a widow, a Venezuelan he married in 1971, having divorced his first wife, whom he had married when awaiting his original trial in 1931.

July 31, 1973.

The Rt. Rev. George Armitage Chase, M.C., Master of Selwyn College, Cambridge, from 1934 to 1946 and Bishop of Ripon from 1946 to 1959, died on November 30, 1971 at the age of 85.

Born on September 3, 1886, the third son of the Rt. Rev. F. H. Chase, sometime President of Queens' College, Cambridge, later Bishop of Ely, Chase came from Rugby with a scholarship to Queens', graduated in Classics and went on to first-class honours in Theology in 1910, winning the Carus Prize in 1909, the Crosse Scholarship in 1910, and the Hulsean Prize in 1912.

Ordained in 1911 he joined the staff of Portsea parish church under C. F. Garbett, whom he was to serve later as examining chaplain when Garbett became successively Bishop of Southwark, Bishop of Winchester, and Archbishop of York. In 1913 he was elected Fellow and Dean of Trinity Hall, and after more than four years as Chaplain to the Forces, during which time he won the M.C., he returned to Trinity Hall in 1919 as Senior Tutor, soon to become Vice-Master as well. Chase took a leading part, along with the Master, Dr. Bond, in knitting together a mixed bag of ex-service freshmen, and then in gradually achieving a healthy balance between academic and other interests.

He accepted the offer of the mastership of Selwyn College in 1934. Under his predecessor the college could point to a creditable record of achievement; what was most needed was a complete overhaul of internal administration, a sense of purpose and policy to be shown in such matters as the election of Fellows and the management of the meagre resources of the college, and closer contact with the rest of the university. In all this, as in the chairmanship of the College Meeting, Chase's wisdom and influence were at once felt.

Chase, however, was not only an administrator. Although he would not have claimed to be a profound scholar he kept abreast of current theological thought and writing and was an admirably lucid lecturer. As a preacher he adopted a straightforward form of approach, without adornment of style or emotional appeal, which was always expressive of the piety, single-mindedness, and common sense which marked his character.

At Trinity Hall he was largely responsible for, and contributed to, getting an organ built in the previously music-less chapel, and an organ scholarship founded for its proper use; the gift of a new organ was one of a number of benefactions, many of them anonymous, to Selwyn College. From 1936 to 1945 he represented the university as proctor in Convocation, in which office his colleague was his close friend, then Regius Professor of Divinity, Dr. C. E. Raven.*

It was a surprise to many who knew Chase's personal and administrative gifts that he was not called to the episcopate till he had passed his 60th birthday. But his strong physique and unremitting activity enabled him during his years as Bishop of Ripon to make a definite mark both in the diocese and in the wider fields of Church work. The diocese of Ripon includes the city of Leeds, with its strong Church tradition: the see city is distant 30 miles—an unfortunate addition to the burden of travelling—and the large number of purely country parishes extend up the Dales to the borders of Westmorland.

It was a surprise to those who knew that Chase's only parochial work had been a generation earlier in the spacious days of pre-1914 England, to discover how understanding he proved in the problems of pastoral and parochial life in the North of the 1950s. He knew his clergy and they trusted his judgments. He encouraged new evangelistic methods, as at Halton, to meet new conditions. He wisely but definitely supported reform in the administration of Baptism and Confirmation, matters to which his interest was particularly drawn through his secretaryship of the committee dealing with those matters at the Lambeth Conference of 1948, and of the subsequent Joint Committees of the Convocations on the subject. He was an excellent chairman of numerous diocesan committees.

He took also an increasing part in central Church work, particularly in the reform of Canon Law. Personally, though reserved, and in some ways never ceasing to be a bachelor don, he was readily approachable and entirely without pomposity. He worked immensely hard, and his principal recreation came from his love of classical music.

December 1, 1971.

Marshal Chen Yi, the former Chinese Foreign Minister, died in Peking on January 6, 1972. Chairman Mao Tse-tung and the Chinese Premier, Chou En-lai, attended his funeral in the Chinese capital on January 11.

Chen Yi, the brilliant guerrilla general who became Communist China's Minister of Foreign Affairs in 1958, was one of the most colourful figures in the Peking leadership. He had a reputation for being indiscreet and impulsive in his conversation, and was consequently a favourite of foreign journalists. But his mandarin family background made him suspect to the Chinese Communist Party ideologues, and he never wielded any important political power in Peking. He was widely regarded as one of the small but able band of more pragmatic party leaders loyal to the Prime Minister, Chou En-lai.

Chen Yi was born in 1901 in Loshan in the province of Szechuan, the son of a retired magistrate. At the end of the First World War he was one of those eager left-wing students who went to France to work and study.

Soon after returning to China he enrolled in the Communist Party, joined the Northern Expeditionary Army in Kiangsi and took part in the Nanchang Uprising in 1927. He became attached to Chu Teh's forces in South-West China, and was elected to the Central Executive Committee of the Provisional Government of the Chinese Soviet Republic based in Juichin in 1931. He did not accompany Mao Tse-tung in the Long March, but remained behind to direct the rear-guard action while the main forces of the Red Army set out.

He rose rapidly in the Red Army and was Commander of the Third Field Army which overran East China in 1948 and 1949. He was Mayor of Shanghai from 1949 to 1958. In 1954 he was appointed vice-premier of the State Council and vice-chairman of the National Defence Council. He was in the Chinese delegation to the Bandung Conference in 1955 and was made a Marshal of the People's Liberation Army in the same year.

His interests extended to language reform and scientific planning, and he was president of the All-China Association for Eliminating Illiteracy. He also played a leading role in the Tibetan question, heading the mission to Lhasa for the inauguration of the Preparatory Committee for the Tibet Autonomous Region for 1956. He became a member of the Party's Central Committee and Politburo and in February 1958 he succeeded Chou En-lai as Foreign Minister. He acted as Premier in Chou's absence early in 1959.

In recent years he was a frequent traveller abroad, particularly to Indonesia, Burma and Africa. He attended the Geneva Conference on Laos in 1961-62. He led the Chinese delegation to Indonesia for the preparatory conference of the 2nd Afro-Asian Conference in 1964, and played a leading role in the events surrounding the abortive Afro-Asian Summit Meeting at Algiers in the following year.

He gave a famous press conference in Peking in September 1965, when he condemned the United Nations' attitude to China's membership and implied that a number of conditions would have to be met before China would respond to any invitation to join.

Chen and his wife soon ran into criticism from Red Guard posters when the cultural revolution grew fierce in 1966 and in 1967. When his own ministry was infiltrated by radical factions he attacked the "rebels" who had so roughly set about the Foreign Ministry staff and returned ambassadors. The battle went on and in February 1968 no fewer than 91 members of the ministry, including many ambassadors, signed a wall poster defending Chen Yi.

The rigours of the struggle nevertheless wore him down. He was required to write a confession. Mao Tse-tung was quoted as complaining that his old friend Chen had lost 40lb. But whatever sympathy Mao felt for him did not stop the harrying of Chen by extremists or stop him fading from the scene. Before the cultural revolution ended he had ended his active life. A year before he died he was formally replaced.

January 12, 1972.

Dr. Eustace Chesser, L.R.C.P., L.R.C.S. (EDIN.), L.R.F.P.S. (Glas.) died on December 5, 1973 at the age of 71.

A psychiatrist of repute, it was to the sexual aspect of human relationships that he particularly devoted his attention, becoming an authority second to none in this field.

He championed abortion and homosexual law reforms when these subjects were taboo but lived to see his zealous work reach fruition. The wide sweep of his activities can be observed in the long list of organizations of which he was, at one time or another, an energetic member—the Society for the Study of Addiction, the Abortion Law Reform Association, the Medico-Legal Council, the Married Women's Association, the British Social Biology Council, the Homosexual Law Reform Society, the International Committee for Sexual Equality and many others.

Not only was he an outstanding therapist; he was, too, a prolific and controversial writer with a simplicity and clarity of style which made things easy for the man-in-the-street to understand. He wrote more than 30 books of which the first, *Love Without Fear* (published in 1941), is still a best-seller. It has sold in millions in many languages and must have enabled countless people on the threshold of life to experience with proper pleasure the act of sex in the context of a meaningful relationship. His provocative book *Is Chastity Outmoded?* caused a sensation when it appeared in 1962. In *Living With Suicide* (1967), the book by which, he once said, he would most like to be remembered, he wrote, "The right to choose one's time and manner of death seems to me unassailable". In addition to his books he wrote extensively for the press. He was also a frequent broadcaster on television and radio.

Eustace Chesser was born on March 2, 1902 and educated at George Watson's

School and qualified at Edinburgh in 1926. Before his interest in psychiatry took formal shape he was in general practice in Cinderford, Manchester and, through the years preceding the last war, very successfully in the West End of London. At that time he was clinical assistant at the Tavistock Clinic where he underwent a psychoanalysis, and thereafter entered upon his memorable psychiatric career.

As the years went by he became increasingly liberal in his interpretation of Freudian psychoanalytical concepts. His personality was such that he evolved his own dynamic methods. Jewish by birth, he discarded orthodox beliefs in favour of humanism, while never decrying the importance of a religious faith in others.

In 1969 he suffered a serious illness which he faced with calm, reflective courage but which left him physically incapacitated for the rest of his life. His recreations were listed in *Who's Who* as "ideas, places, people and things"; even after his illness his absorption in all four, particularly the first and third, never diminished. Eustace Chesser's special quality was that as an author, as a doctor and as a man he was equally impressive. As an author he was known to millions, as a doctor to thousands but as a man only to a privileged few. His candour, his hatred of hypocrisy and his indifference to convention were formidable and could embarrass those with superficial sensitivities but to his friends these things were refreshing. From him there emanated a power, a warmth and a radiance which were as enriching as they were unforgettable.

In 1926 he married Rose Morris, by whom he had a son and a daughter. She died in 1960. Secondly he married Sheila Blayney-Jones, who survives him.

December 6, 1973.

Former Bishop of Chester—See Crick.

Maurice Chevalier, the French comedian and actor, died on January 1, 1972. He was 83.

When Mistinguett died in 1956 a part of Paris died with her. She was the incomparable "Miss"—a symbol of a gaiety and warmth that had its origin in a little flowerseller from Les Halles.

Now Maurice Chevalier is dead, and Paris has lost another part of its history and its legend. He too represented the warmth and the gaiety of shabby little back streets, and the heart and soul of a great city. Age meant nothing to him. He was the same personality in youth as he was as a veteran actor. His popularity did not depend on his voice, or his style, or his charm. It had nothing to do with sex appeal. Mistinguett used to say of him, "Il a le fluide," and when challenged to define this could only shrug her shoulders in perplexity. Yet, to her, it was his supreme quality. By it she meant that he had the power to abolish the footlights and the orchestra pit, and to become one with his audience. They were united with him in a strange bond of intimacy. It is an indefinable quality, possessed only by a few great artists.

Chevalier was born at Menilmontant, a poor district outside Paris, on September 12, 1888, the son of Victor Charles Chevalier, a house painter, and Sophie Josephine, a lace-maker. The family were poor, and when Maurice was eight his father deserted them. Two years were then spent in a children's home (Chaplin was placed in an orphanage when he was five), and he went to work when still very young, earning a pittance in a number of trades. But the stage called him, as it called Chaplin, and his gaiety and friendliness soon won him a small niche as an entertainer. The music-hall was his obvious destination, and by the time he had reached his 'teens he was appearing at the Eldorado in Paris in a show aptly named *Le Beau Gosse*.

The turning point in his career occurred when he became Mistinguett's dancing partner at the *Folies Bergère* in 1910. It was sometimes said of him later that Mistinguett made him, but she herself always denied this. After all, for her he had *le fluide* and it was only necessary to teach him the technique of their trade, and to help him to become a true artist and professional. They worked together, on and off, for 10 years; and together they captured Paris. They became as much a part of it as the Eiffel Tower.

Chevalier joined the French Army in 1914, but was wounded and taken prisoner in his first engagement with the enemy, and spent more than two years in a prisoner-of-war camp. But in 1918 he was able to return to the Paris music-halls, and took up once again the threads of his career. He was soon back at the *Folies Bergère*, and he made his first appearance on the London stage at the Palace Theatre in February 1919 in *Hullo, America*.

The coming of sound in the cinema found him at the peak of his career; and his was exactly the type of personality of which the new talking pictures of Hollywood were so urgently in need. He could sing, dance and act reasonably well, but above all he had the power to project his personality from the screen. His casual, intimate style and seemingly effortless technique were in sharp contrast to the overacting and over-talking approach of so many of the existing film players.

It was now that his luck, which had changed so notably once he had left the misfortunes of his childhood behind, was again to give him exactly the opportunity he needed. It was Jesse Lasky who was generally considered to have started Chevalier on his American film career, but in fact it was M.G.M.'s most talented producer, Irving Thalberg, who first realized his potentialities and gave him a film test in Paris in 1928. Lasky saw the test, and later saw Chevalier at the Casino de Paris, where he was the darling of an audience composed largely of American and British tourists. Lasky quickly put him under contract and took him to New York, where he allowed Florenz Ziegfeld to use him for a few weeks in his *Midnight Frolic* on the New Amsterdam Roof before whisking him away to Hollywood.

His first picture was *Innocents of Paris,* which was made in haste and did not amount to very much, but which was an instant success, partly on account of Chevalier's personality, and partly because of his singing of its theme song, "Louise," which was to become part of his repertoire for the remainder of his life.

Hollywood was now about to enter its golden era of musicals. It had the best song writers in the world, and most of the best directors. Not all took kindly to the new and specialized technique of filming musicals, but there was one man who revealed an exceptional flair for them. This was the German, Ernst Lubitsch, and it was Chevalier's supreme good fortune to be directed in his second picture, *The Love Parade*, by this master craftsman. Lubitsch had style, elegance, wit—and a Continental sophistication which was rare in Hollywood.

Lasky chose a new young singer from Broadway called Jeanette MacDonald* to play opposite Chevalier in *The Love Parade*, and as a team they fitted perfectly into the Lubitsch pattern. The film was a triumphant success. From then on Chevalier had only to stay on in Hollywood to make himself a fortune and to become a film star known throughout the world. His pre-war American films included *Paramount on Parade, The Big Pond, The Playboy of Paris, The Smiling Lieutenant, One Hour With You, Love Me Tonight, A Bedtime Story, The Way to Love, The Merry Widow* and *The Man from the Folies Bergère*. He also made two British pictures, *The Beloved Vagabond* and *Break the News*.

During this time he did not forsake the stage, and continued to appear in Paris, New York and London.

During the Second World War he remained in France, performed in Paris from time to time, and paid at least one professional visit to prisoner-of-war camps in Germany. Certainly the Germans made many attempts to exploit him, and after the war he was obliged to answer charges of collaboration. Of these he was acquitted and in 1946 resumed his career, making a film under René Clair's direction called *Le Silence est d'Or*. This, though successful enough, was a long way from the opulent musicals of his hey-day in America; it seemed in the 1950s that his career as an international film star might be ended, although he continued to appear on the stage throughout the world.

Then in 1958 he made *Gigi* with Leslie Caron, and suddenly it seemed as though all the old magic was back again. Here was an elderly man looking back over his shoulder nostalgically to a romantic past, and serenading the beauty of woman as he had serenaded it all his life. The twinkle was there in his eye, the charm and the roguishness; but above all there remained the power to achieve that complete personal intimacy with his audience. Chevalier was home again, against his native background. The *gamin* had grown up into a *boulevardier*, but he was still a carefree youth at heart.

He will be remembered in many ways and in many parts, but always and above all with his straw hat tilted down over his nose, and his lower lip pouting a little like a naughty schoolboy, as he confided in his audience with that easy intimacy which made them feel that they were sitting opposite him on the other side of his fireplace, and sharing with him his confidences about life, about love and about women.

Chevalier was a holder of the Croix de Guerre and an officer of the Legion of Honour.

He was married in 1927 to Yvonne Vallée, the singer and dancer, but this marriage was dissolved in 1935.

January 3, 1975.

The death of **General Chiang Kai-shek,** President of the Chinese Nationalist Government in Taiwan, on April 5, 1975, at the age of 87, ended a long life of dedicated service to his country marred by a narrow view of its needs in an age of revolution.

Throughout his career a determination to cling to his own power always overrode any criticism of his rule.

For a time, when the new Government of a supposedly united China was set up at Nanking in 1928, he was looked to as the symbol of the country's new-found nationalism and this reputation was later revived during the war against Japan. At the war's end, however, the failings of the party he had led, added to the chaotic conditions in the country, were to bring down his regime in the civil war that had begun 22 years before when Chiang had savagely turned on his communist allies in the Kuomintang Party. He was defeated by a regime much more resoundingly nationalist than his own and far more ably led after Mao Tse-Tung's wartime reforms of the Chinese Communist Party.

Chiang had failed to be the successor of Sun Yat-sen either as a political magnet internally, or as one able to uphold his country's status externally. In particular his reliance on favourites and particular factions prevented any men of merit from rising to the top in his own party.

In a longer view his abilities were not so different from some of the warlords against whom he fought and with whom he bargained to gain power in the China

of the 1930s. At no time did he rule all of China. In 1928 the Government effectively controlled no more than four or five provinces. The manoeuvres to which he was reduced to maintain the appearance of a national government were to undermine any hopes he had of restoring it after the war.

His patriotism was unquestionable and his integrity was that of the old-style official. His desire to restore Chinese greatness was undoubted. Even his xenophobia, so obviously revealed in his book *China's Destiny*, was in keeping with Chinese tradition and the main stream of Chinese nationalism. But his grasp of China's economic needs was weak; his choice of advisers was prejudiced and often mistaken; his conservatism, though worthy in a sense, had little appeal to the younger generation.

One contrast between the unsuccessful Chiang and the successful Mao was in the ideological mixture by which they aimed to inspire a new China. There was always an unresolved conflict for Chiang Kai-shek between the old China and a new one. In great part he clung to the old Confucianism as a source of authority. He saw himself as a disciple of Sun Yat-sen yet he had never read Sun's writings until after Sun died. It is doubtful if Sun's three peoples principles could have contributed much to divert Chiang from his conservatism.

His second marriage to Soong Mei-ling (whose elder sister Soong Ching-ling had married Sun Yat-sen in 1915) was to bring with it an attachment to Christianity. The Soong family were Christian and Chiang owed his introduction to the western religion to his mother-in-law. He took it seriously, believing that some of its precepts would serve in the reform of China; in campaigns against recalcitrant warlords he was reported to have devoted time on the battlefield to Bible study. He was received into the Methodist Church in 1930.

The action was no less part of the modernizing polish for which he looked to his Americanized wife, along with some knowledge of English and of western etiquette. In 1934 the New Life movement exposed the hybrid character of the mixture of ideas by which he attempted to earn China's loyalty.

Like his successor Mao Tse Tung, Chiang showed no disposition to learn at first hand about the outside world. A visit to the Soviet Union in 1923 and the Cairo wartime conference in 1943 were his only journeys westward. His outlook and manners remained China-centred, the western imports serving only as a necessary reinforcement for China's regeneration. This pride in China was untouched by any real response to change in his own country. He remained a conservative all his life, blind to young minds, dominating China by military power, obdurate in face of appeals for change. He saw himself as the only possible saviour for China and this justified his own personal ascendancy. Authoritarian to the last in Taiwan, he routed out dissent there as much as he had done on the mainland.

Chiang Kai-shek (Chiang Chieh-shih in the Mandarin romanization) was born on October 31, 1887 at Fenghua in the province of Chekiang, growing up among the frugal, hardworking, obstinate people of the district where his forebears had farmed the land for centuries. Although the family was far from well off, Chiang received a good education, and at the age of 18 was sent to the Paoting Military Academy in north China as one of 40 students supplied by the province. After graduating at Paoting, Chiang was sent by the Government to Japan in 1907 for further military training. During his four years in Tokyo he spent much of his time with Chinese revolutionaries working for the overthrow of the Manchu regime, becoming a member of the secret society which was later reorganized into the Kuomintang. It was thus that he first met Sun Yat-sen, who recognized in him one of the rising hopes of the revolution.

In 1911 Chiang was thinking of leaving for Germany to complete his studies there when the revolution broke out in China. During the turbulent period which followed Yuan Shih-Kai's seizure of power Chiang took an increasing share in the perils of intrigue, faction, and revolt which eventually established Sun Yat-sen in office in Canton in 1917. Chiang also shared the dangers of Sun Yat-sen's insecure term of Canton and in the summer of 1922 sailed with him in the British gunboat in which he escaped to Hongkong. After a further period of intrigue in Shanghai, Chiang returned with Sun Yat-sen to Canton in 1923 when the latter's Government was reestablished in the south. Disappointed by the non-recognition of western powers, Sun Yat-sen turned his eyes towards Russia, and in response to Soviet overtures sent Chiang on a mission to Moscow, where four months were spent in studying the Soviet system.

Among the direct results of Chiang's visit to Moscow was the setting up in 1924, with the active backing of the powerful Russian adviser Borodin, of the Whampoa Military Academy, near Canton, to train young officers for the Kuomintang armies. Chiang was appointed president of the school, with General Blücher (Galen) as the chief of his Russian instructors. For two years Chou En-lai took charge of the political department. The death of Sun Yat-sen in the north the next year thus found Chiang in a position to assert his political claims as one of the four lieutenants named in the leader's will. The path was further cleared by his appointment as leader of the expedition against the warlords of the north, which gave him command of the best troops in the country. Chiang emerged from this welter of events the strongest man in China.

As early as 1926 Chiang fell out with the Communists but under Russian pressure they remained loyal to the Kuomintang until Chiang's treacherous massacre of communist workers who facilitated the entry into Shanghai in April 1927. Chou En-lai was one of those who narrowly escaped death on this occasion.

After the new government was set up in 1928 Chiang redoubled his efforts to unify his still far from united country. The biggest thorn in his side apart from the many warlords who survived to wield authority in their own provinces, was the Communist regime, which had established a stronghold first in Kiangsi, where five successive campaigns were necessary to dislodge them, after which their long march took them to a new base at Yenan in the north-west. In December of 1936 he went to Sian, capital of Shensi, to press the lagging campaign against the Communists, which had been entrusted to Chang Hsueh-liang, the displaced warlord of Manchuria. The Young Marshal, as Chiang was known, took advantage of the visit to seize Chiang and hold him for political ransom. After 13 days of refusing to compromise, Chiang was finally freed through the intervention of Chou En-lai who flew to Sian.

Faced by growing Japanese aggression Chiang sought by an adroit mixture of firmness and concession, at home as well as abroad, to postpone the evil hour as long as possible. Gradually public feeling against any further concessions to Japan, coupled with the drama of his arrest in Sian, left Chiang no choice but to resist. The hour struck with a clash between Japanese and Chinese troops at the Marco Polo bridge near Peking on July 7, 1937.

With a full sense of the realities, he resolutely embarked on a long war of attrition, the scorched-earth policy, and the building up of a fortress in the great provinces of the interior. In this way, in spite of appalling losses, the Chinese managed to contrive and survive until the Japanese attack on Pearl Harbour in December of 1941 brought about the grand alliance. The climax of his career was his visit to Cairo late in 1943 for the historic conferences with Churchill* and Roosevelt. The visit not only confirmed his position among the leaders of the allies but also attested China's full equality in the family of nations. The logical sequel to this, which came in the summer of 1945, was the surrender of the Japanese forces in China, followed by Chiang's triumphal return to Nanking in December of the same year.

The postwar chaos found Chiang and the government unequal to the task. The threat of civil war remained and General Marshall's mission of mediation had no success owing to intransigence on both Communist and Nationalist sides. Discussions in 1946 on the Communist behalf by Chou En-lai brought no change in Chiang's refusal to form a coalition of any kind. Elections for a national assembly in 1947 were a mere formality. Steadily the corruption and inefficiency of the Kuomintang increased and no measure was initiated to stop it. By then the civil war that had never really ceased was resumed. Communist forces concentrated in Manchuria and soon reduced the Nationalists to the larger towns.

By 1948 they had been driven out entirely with great loss of troops. In September of that year Tsinan was the first provincial capital to fall and thereafter the collapse was rapid. China was seized by inflation, support for the Kuomintang dwindled and with the fall of Peking and Tientsin at the turn of the year the fate of the Nationalist Government was no longer in doubt. At this point, in a peculiarly Chinese gesture, Chiang resigned the presidency and handed over to the Vice-President, Li-Tsung-jen, withdrawing to his home province of Chekiang. In fact he kept all the reins of power and prepared his eventual retreat to Formosa where emissaries were sent early in 1949. In April of that year Nanking fell to the Communists and the National Government moved first to Canton and then back to Chungking. Chiang meanwhile moved to Formosa with two divisions of his best troops and there resumed office as president.

By the end of 1949 the last Kuomintang forces had left the mainland and the plight of Taiwan looked no better than the mainland had. But the Communist assault in Korea brought American forces back into play and with it President Truman's decision to resist any attack from the mainland on Formosa. American aid to the Nationalist Government slowly began to build up again as the war continued in Korea. After its end the government in Taiwan, though never popular with the indigenous population whose memories of the massacre of 1947 were still fresh, began to feel more settled and with the departure to exile of some of the worst and most corrupt officials the regime pulled itself together in this confined area.

An economic success was linked to Japan's rise as a dominant force in trade and investment in the area together with better use of American aid. Saved from extinction by the Korean War the Nationalist Government was contrite over its failings and more ready to introduce such things as land reform when it was Taiwanese landlords and not the Kuomintang's own following that faced them.

For Chiang the role of the elder statesman was agreeable. Chiang could preside over a going concern while the Republic of China—as it called itself—enjoyed full American backing, diplomatic recognition, and the status of the China seat in the United Nations. Economic progress obliterated political unease; dissent went largely unpublicized. Every year Chiang promised a return to the mainland from which the "Communist bandits" would be driven out.

His claim that the Communists were puppets of the Russians looked foolish when the Sino-Soviet dispute erupted, but his self-assurance hardened with age. Even the final blow of President Nixon's rapprochement with Peking and a changeover of governments in the China seat at the United Nations left him unperturbed. True, he resorted to the often-used trick of retirement in face of apparent failure but his willingness to stand down from presidential office in February 1972 was rejected by the expected response of loyal supporters and he was reelected for his fifth six-year term in command.

April 7, 1975.

Sir Francis Chichester, K.B.E., who died on August 26, 1972, was in the great tradition of pioneer adventurers.

A small, quiet, unassuming man, he seemed impervious to hardship, danger and loneliness. His courage and willpower twice rescued him from what had seemed almost certain death, once after an air crash in Japan in 1931 and the second time when stricken with lung cancer shortly before he won the first single-handed transatlantic sailing race in 1960.

The son of a Devon rector, he was born on September 17, 1901 and educated at Marlborough. He had a bleak and lonely childhood. In his autobiography he describes his father as rather a tormented man who eventually "became a puritan of the severest kind . . . he seemed to be disapproving of everything I did and waiting to squash any enthusiasm". When Francis was bitten by a viper at the age of 11 his father sent him off to bicycle all alone to an infirmary four and a half miles away. It may be that in his later adventures he was still trying to win the approval and self-respect he was denied as a child. In any case, he developed early the habit of making his own life and accustoming himself to hardship.

His schooling was also grim—a long story of beatings and deprivations and petty restrictions. Marlborough seemed to him like a prison, with its appallingly deficient food and constant brutality. It was also very cold, and since only the senior boys were allowed near the fire Chichester typically decided to train himself to conquer the problem by wearing only a cotton shirt under his coat and sleeping under a sheet at night.

Here he did make some friends, and also did well in sport. He specialized in mathematics, which helped his navigation later. But he eventually decided that "real life is flowing past" and simply informed his housemaster that he was leaving at the end of term.

For a while he worked on a farm, but was soon sacked. After that, at the age of 18, he emigrated to New Zealand, where he worked on a sheep farm, as a miner, a salesman, and later a highly successful land agent. By the time he was 26 he was earning £10,000 a year. A friend, Geoffrey Goodwin, persuaded him to go into partnership in the aviation business and he was soon smitten by the urge to fly himself.

In 1929 he returned to England and after a short, intensive course of instruction set off for Sydney in a Gipsy Moth. In spite of crash landing in Libya he arrived safely and was given a hero's welcome as only the second man to fly solo from England to Australia. This was followed by an even more remarkable feat, the first east to west solo flight across the Tasman Sea. It required superb navigation in order to find two tiny islands en route, since his aircraft could not carry enough fuel for a non-stop crossing.

Later that year, however, he met with real disaster. Having reached Japan in an attempt to complete a round-the-world flight, he flew into some telephone wires when taking off from Katsuura, and crashed into the harbour.

Somehow he survived his severe injuries and, after a visit to England, returned to New Zealand. But the urge to fly had not left him and in 1936 he piloted a Puss Moth with one passenger from Sydney to England via Peking. In England he met and married Miss Sheila Craven (his first wife, Muriel Blakiston, died in 1929; they had one son, who died). She was to become a considerable influence in his life.

She had unshakable and unbounded confidence in him; it was remarkable how later, in his last great venture, when some were crying "woe" and asking "Should he . . .? Can he . . .? What if . . . ?" she never expressed the slightest doubt in her husband's ability to come through all his trials. She had sailed with him and had seen what manner of man he was and the range of his skills at sea.

After a further brief stay in New Zealand, which his new wife found uncongenial, he went back to Britain shortly before the war. His knowledge of navigation made him a considerable asset to the Royal Air Force, and he became senior navigation officer at the Empire Central Flying School.

When the war ended he became a map publisher—"by accident", as he put it in his autobiography—and after a difficult start the business prospered. But a routine existence did not suit him and, in response to a continuing urge for adventure, he took up ocean racing and cruising. He bought a second-hand boat which he renamed Gipsy Moth II, and also navigated the American Bill Snaith's Figaro in the 1957 Admiral's Cup races.

But a dark and terrible shadow was looming imminent in the shape of cancer of the lung. Within a few months he was desperately ill and given only a short time to live. Largely at his wife's insistence he refused an operation, and after months of despair, followed by slowly growing hope, he recovered in time to sail again during Cowes Week in 1959 and in the subsequent Fastnet race.

The next year he was fit enough to take part in the first single-handed transatlantic race, a recovery which he described as "miraculous". In his new Gipsy Moth III he won the race in a time of 40½ days. He was elected Yachtsman of the Year in the following November, and not long afterwards was awarded the Gold Medal of the Institute of Navigation.

Two years later he lowered his transatlantic record by nearly a week, arriving in New York on Independence Day and receiving a telegram of congratulation from President Kennedy*. But his declared aim of making the crossing in less than 30 days was not fulfilled until the 1964 race, when this success was dimmed by the knowledge that he had been beaten into second place by the Frenchman Eric Tabarly.

Still the restless urge for new achievements drove him on, and in August 1966 the spare, grey-haired bespectacled figure was waving goodbye once again. This time the aim was not, as had been originally supposed, to win the round-Britain race, but a voyage round the world in his new Gipsy Moth IV. He hoped to reach Sydney in under 100 days, which was the average time taken by the old Clipper ships.

Gipsy Moth IV—designed by Illingworth and Primrose—cost about £30,000. The hull was cold-moulded laminated wood to make as light a boat as possible.

At first he made good time, and for the first 5,000 miles kept up with the record-breaking run of the famous Cutty Sark. But a succession of calms, followed by fierce gales, set him back, and the last straw was when his self-steering gear broke. Briefly he gave up the attempt and headed for Fremantle, but typically he could not face the thought of failure and altered course for Sydney once again. He managed to rig a temporary substitute for the self-steering gear by using a small sail to operate the rudder.

He eventually arrived in Sydney seven days later than he had had hoped, to a fantastic welcome. Such fame as he had known before was as nothing to this. Suddenly he was an international hero, accorded front-page headlines in the world's newspapers.

Chichester was flooded with advice not to attempt the second half of the passage but, heedless of the fears expressed for his safety, he set sail again on January 29.

The day before he left Sydney he was appointed a Knight Commander of the Order of the British Empire "in recognition of his individual achievements and sustained endeavour in the navigation and seamanship of small craft."

Within three days he ran into the edge of a cyclone and the boat was knocked down by a huge wave. The astonishing old man merely cleared up the debris and carried on his course.

As he approached the Horn in mid-March 1967, a spell of fine weather which he had made the most of began to deteriorate, and it was in huge green seas towering between 15ft. and 20ft. over him that he was seen rounding the Horn by Murray Sayle, of Times Newspapers, flying precariously in a piloted small aircraft. Gipsy Moth was running under bare poles except for a spitfire jib, the smallest sail Chichester had. He was doing a good eight knots with a howling gale of 40 knots blowing him onward. As Sayle flew overhead taking the first pictures (which were published exclusively in The Times) of the epic passage, H.M.S. Protector kept a watchful eye on the intrepid old sailor—at a respectful distance.

Chichester actually rounded the Horn on Monday, March 20 at 11.10 a.m. local time (2.10 p.m. G.M.T.). In an exclusive message to The Times on March 22 he described how his cockpit was filled five times and how on one occasion it took him more than 15 minutes to drain it. He sailed out of the Forties on March 31 and on April 24 crossed the Line.

He completed his single-handed circuit of the world on May 28, 1967, passing Plymouth breakwater at 8.56 p.m., flanked by a protective naval escort to keep the huge armada of welcoming boats at a safe distance. Vast crowds assembled on the Hoe to watch the dramatic dusk home-coming. The Sound was littered with lights from the gathering of craft of every size. Overhead there was a constant buzzing of aircraft.

Champagne was drunk on board Gipsy Moth IV and then Chichester stepped ashore to be welcomed briefly by the Lord Mayor of Plymouth.

Early in June he was taken ill with a haemorrhage from a duodenal ulcer, and his return to London in Gipsy Moth, planned for the middle of the month, did not take place until early in July. He anchored at Woolwich on July 6 and on the following day was given perhaps the most remarkable of all his welcomes. He was dubbed knight with Drake's sword by the Queen at a ceremony in the Grand Square of the Royal Naval College, Greenwich, and then Gipsy Moth passed beneath Tower Bridge. At Tower Pier Chichester and his wife were greeted by the Lord Mayor of London, Sir Robert Bellinger. Ships' horns and sirens blared out a welcome, a fireboat shot jets of water into the air, and hundreds of people clustered on wharves, on the tops of buildings and on London Bridge to wave and cheer. After landing, Chichester drove in an open white car, watched and greeted by thousands of City workers, to the Mansion House, where the City Corporation lunched him, Lady Chichester and their son Giles on coq au vin and presented him with a silver and silver-gilt table decoration.

Gipsy Moth IV is now permanently dry-docked at Greenwich next to the Cutty Sark.

In 1971 Chichester crossed the Atlantic from Bissau in Portuguese Guinea to San Juan del Norte in Nicaragua in Gipsy Moth V—the 57ft. boat built for him at Crosshaven. Though he failed in his attempt to set a record of sailing more than 200 miles a day single-handed, he sailed the 4,000 miles in just over 22 days.

His last appearance in a long-distance event—The Observer Singlehanded Transatlantic Race in June 1972—was a sad anticlimax. Far from fit, he struck wretched weather; lost radio contact; was obliged to drop out of the race; and, with the aid of a Royal Navy crew, was finally brought home to Plymouth, where he entered hospital in a low state.

August 28, 1972.

Erskine Childers, who died on November 17, 1974, was the fourth President of the Republic of Ireland and the second Protestant to hold that office. He rose to high office in the republic from a background strikingly different from that of his ministerial colleagues.

He was the descendant of a staunch Unionist family of big landowners in co. Wicklow, the Bartons. He was of the second generation to join the nationalist cause.

His father, the Erskine Childers best known in Britain as the author of *The Riddle of the Sands* and as a distinguished naval flying officer in the First World War, had thrown in his lot with the Sinn Fein and supported de Valera in opposing the treaty and sticking out for a republic.

He was arrested by the Free State Government in 1922, and executed by a firing squad on a dubious charge of bearing arms. His son, then at an English public school, saw his father in the condemned cell just before the execution. The father asked him if he meant to go into Irish politics and he said he did.

The memory of this harrowing encounter always remained with him. His youthful promise made there was richly fulfilled. Deep filial piety combined in him with a capacity for mastering the essentials of a political or economic issue and with wide culture.

Erskine Hamilton Childers was born in London on December 11, 1905. His own family links in Ireland can be traced back about 400 years to Elizabethan planters in co. Fermanagh. His mother, Mary Alden Osgood of Boston, who completely identified herself with her husband's Irish loyalties, was a woman of forceful personality and she influenced her son in his ambition. He went to Gresham's School, Holt, and then to his father's old college, Trinity, Cambridge, where he took honours in the History Tripos.

He early joined the Fianna Fail party led by de Valera, serving first as advertisement manager of the Irish Press Ltd. and then, after a long spell as secretary of the Federation of Irish Manufacturers, in various ministerial posts. Beginning in 1944 as Parliamentary Secretary to the Minister for Local Government and Public Health, he rose steadily in position and influence.

As Minister for Posts and Telegraphs, 1951-54, he threw himself with enthusiasm into the building up of Radio Eireann. After heading the ministries of Lands, Transport and Power and, again, Posts and Telegraphs, he was promoted in 1969 to be Tánaiste (Deputy Prime Minister), an office

he combined with being Minister for Health.

By such activities as his support of a new role for the republic in Europe, he was one of those who sought to shape debate in the republic into a more constructive pattern at a time when the Northern Ireland crisis invited the reawakening of civil war politics in the south.

His endorsement of Jack Lynch in condemning violence on either side of the border was more emphatic than many of the other politicians, in a party which, although constitutional, has never forgotten that it owes its existence to the gun.

Before resigning to contest the presidency, Erskine Childers had sat for Monaghan, a border constituency historically part of Northern Ireland, and with both a significant Protestant population and areas sympathetic to, or liable to intimidation by, the Provisional I.R.A.

He consistently opposed violence at a time when the Unionists just across the border claimed the southern Government was doing nothing to curb the gunmen. But it certainly took courage for a Dail deputy from such a sensitive constituency to make the speeches he did.

Childers's usual air of modest gravity did not suggest a man temperamentally suited to the hustings. There could have been no greater contrast of style than that between him and his opponent in the contest for the presidency in 1973, Thomas O'Higgins, who threw himself into the battle with an almost American panache.

Childers, riding round the countryside with a group of Fianna Fail party aides in a motor-coach, was so restrained that he scarcely seemed to be electioneering at all.

Nevertheless he won, and gave a much needed boost to Jack Lynch and his party three months after the Fianna Fail defeat at the polls. It had been a traumatic time for a party which had been in power for 35 out of the previous 41 years. It is no disservice to Childers to say that he won office in a state where party label and personal lineage are of such importance.

Perhaps the greatest gap between promise and achievement concerned Childers' exercise of the presidency. During the election campaign, he had laid special emphasis on making the office a focus for the discussion of leading issues outside the area of party politics. He expressed particular interest in youth and the environment, and emphasized the need to look 20 years ahead, and to involve the best available talent in an exploration of the options facing a society which had rapidly moved from generations of austerity to near affluence.

He also suggested that, if elected, he would like to represent the republic by lecturing abroad on non-contentious subjects. But after winning the highest office in the state, he quickly found that the non-controversial area was a very limited one.

Within weeks of the election he caused a flurry when reports of an interview broadcast in the United States filtered back to

Dublin. During the questions and answers he was said to have emphasized several times that he was not giving his own opinion but was acting as a rapporteur of the Irish situation, and only on questions about which the political parties were completely at one.

Nevertheless, southern Irish governments are not used to the idea of the president, who is traditionally above politics, making comments on Irish unity. One of the paradoxes of the Irish scene is that most citizens of the republic feel unity to be a long way off, but for the highest citizen of all apparently to suggest that this is so was, and is, too near the bone.

Although he distinguished himself from his predecessor, de Valera, by regularly making public statements while in office, Childers soon learnt to confine himself to pronouncements on social issues such as the drink problem. While this is certainly acute in Ireland, the scope of his speeches became less ambitious than foreshadowed, and the elegant former vice-regal lodge in Phoenix Park did not become the intellectual and practical hub for which he had appealed.

Childers often seemed an unlikely participant in Irish politics, not only because of his accent which to Irish ears sounded acutely English. As holder of high office in a party pledged to the restoration of the Irish language as one of its chief objectives, he explained that failure to speak it was caused by his inability to master the required sounds. His declaration on taking office as president in June 1973, delivered in the first official language, Irish, did, however, earn him praise for his delivery.

He was twice married, first in 1925 to Ruth Dow by whom he had two sons and three daughters.

After her death Erskine Childers married in 1952 Margaret Dudley, a popular member of the British Embassy staff in Dublin who made a delightful hostess in their home on the outskirts of the city. They had one daughter. This was an ecumenical marriage. While his second wife was a Roman Catholic, he remained an active member of the Church of Ireland.

November 18, 1974.

Henry Blasius Masauko Chipembere, one of the decisive early nationalists in Central Africa, died in a Los Angeles hospital on September 24, 1975. He was 45.

In the 1950s, after receiving a B.A. degree from Fort Hare University College in South Africa, he became the first African district officer in Nyasaland (now Malawi). In 1956 he was among the first Africans elected to that colony's Legislative Council.

As a leader of the African National Congress of Nyasaland, he was an architect of its drive to independence and nationhood. As he told the Devlin Commission after the disturbances that engulfed Nyasaland in 1959, he and his younger colleagues had brought Dr. H. Kamuzu Banda back to Nyasaland after a long absence in order that their movement might have an older and experienced leader. With Dunduzu Chisiza and W. Kanyama Chiume, Chipembere organized the militant protests of that year. He was violent in speech, but gentle in feeling and moved mostly by patriotism and the energy of nationalism.

The son of one of Nyasaland's leading African clergymen, he remained ascetic in personal habit and dedicated, to the end of his life, to the future of his country. Detained with Banda and the others, Chipembere was thought to be the most resourceful and dangerous of the nationalists. He was therefore jailed for longer than others and, after being released, he was tried and convicted for uttering sedition. He was again imprisoned until late in 1961.

By 1962 Banda had established himself and the Malawi Congress Party in power. Chipembere became Minister of Local Government and then, with independence in 1964, Minister of Education. Yet he was never comfortable with Banda's autocratic methods as Prime Minister of Malawi.

Chipembere and the others had supposed that, when independence was achieved, Dr. Banda would become a figurehead, and they, as practical men who had lived with the people all their lives, would make and execute policy. Dr. Banda resisted this attitude and, using his constitutional powers, since the Governor was still head of state, threw them out of the Government. The ex-ministers became rebels and Chipembere organized an armed insurrection which, however, failed badly against Banda's superior organization.

Chipembere became an exile, first in Tanzania and then in the United States. Until his death he taught African history at California State University, Los Angeles, while completing a Ph.D. thesis on Malawi at the University of California, Los Angeles.

October 7, 1975.

Herbert Chitepo, who met a violent death on March 18, 1975 in Lusaka, Zambia, was a barrister by profession, but he lived with violence for several years as a Rhodesian nationalist leader in exile.

He had been chairman of the Zimbabwe African National Union (Z.A.N.U.) and, as an opponent of compromise either with rival Rhodesian African movements or with the Government in Salisbury, he organized guerrilla attacks against that Government in Rhodesia.

Chitepo was born in June 1923, and was educated first in Rhodesia and then in South Africa, where he graduated with a B.A. degree from Fort Hare University College in 1949. He then became a research assistant at the School of Oriental and African Studies in London, and read for the Bar, becoming Rhodesia's first African barrister.

He returned to Rhodesia in 1954 and built up an ample practice, partly in defending African nationalists in court. In turning gradually to politics and nationalism he took the familiar path of many from Africa and elsewhere who had studied in London. He went into voluntary exile in 1962 and was made the first African Director of Public Prosecutions in Tanganyika.

In Rhodesia the Rev. Ndabaningi Sithole and Joshua Nkomo attempted to form the Zimbabwe African People's Union (Z.A.P.U.), but the more radical Sithole broke away in 1963 to form Z.A.N.U., and Chitepo sided with Sithole, although outside Rhodesia he became chairman of Z.A.N.U. while Sithole was its president.

Chitepo moved to Zambia in 1966, and, as other Z.A.N.U. leaders were detained by the Rhodesian Government, he became the day-to-day leader of that group. He also hardened in his resolution against compromise, and was prominent in organizing opposition to the British proposals on a settlement there in 1971.

With the new move in late 1974 towards détente in southern Africa, fostered by President Kaunda of Zambia, among others, Chitepo's position became difficult; but when the rival nationalist groups nominally united under the umbrella of the African National Council (A.N.C.) he was made a senior official of A.N.C. in Zambia.

The sought-after unity has remained fragile, and will probably be further undermined, at least for a time, by a vacuum in Z.A.N.U. leadership after Chitepo's death.

March 19, 1975.

Esmé Church, who died on May 31, 1972 at Quenington, Gloucestershire, at the age of 79, was probably more highly esteemed by her fellow actors and actresses and by her associates in theatrical administration than by playgoers who judged of her importance solely by her performances on stage.

As a performer she was accomplished, but it is for the influence she had over younger players, both professional and amateur, and for the selfless spirit in which her work was done, that she will be remembered with most gratitude.

Born in February 1893, Esmé Church studied for the stage at the Guildhall School and at what is now R.A.D.A. A red-haired girl of 20, she was engaged by George Alexander for a part in a Pinero play, and in 1916 she joined Lena Ashwell's Concert Party for the entertainment of the troops, acting in England and France during the war and in Germany after the Armistice. Between 1920 and 1928 she remained a member of Lena Ashwell's company. Among the many parts she took at their own theatre, the Century in Bayswater, and elsewhere was Isolt to John Laurie's Tristan in John Masefield's* Tristan and Isolt.

After leaving Lena Ashwell she went to work for another great woman of the theatre, Lilian Baylis, as leading lady of the Old Vic Company, again playing opposite John Laurie.

Two years later she herself directed a summer season at the Greyhound, Croydon. An engagement to play the middle-aged novelist in Priestley's *Dangerous Corner* gave her the opportunity of working under Tyrone Guthrie in the same company with Marie Ney, an association that was renewed when the three joined forces in Miss Ney's first venture in actress-management. Esmé Church appeared in 1936 in two of the Ibsen plays presented in London by Leon M. Lion in conjunction with the newly formed Arts Theatre of Cambridge; of her Aunt Julia in *Hedda Gabler* Charles Morgan wrote in *The Times*: "the old lady is quietly alive; the rest are acting".

In the same year she returned at Miss Baylis's invitation to the Old Vic as head of the School of Acting. In addition to taking charge of students' training she directed a number of productions by the company itself: *As You Like It* in an eighteenth-century setting with Edith Evans as Rosalind; *Ghosts* with Marie Ney as Mrs. Alving; and, after Miss Baylis's death and a Mediterranean tour of which Esmé Church and Lewis Casson* were the joint-directors, two plays by Shaw, *The Devil's Disciple* with Robert Donat and *Saint Joan* with Constance Cummings, which opened at the Buxton Festival, but were prevented from reaching the Waterloo Road by the outbreak of the Second World War.

During the war years she worked in many parts of Great Britain; as director for H. M. Tennent in Scotland; as a member of the Old Vic Company on tour and in the West End; as director of the Young Vic 9 (a children's theatre) on tour and of *The Merchant of Venice* (with Frederick Valk as Shylock) and of an adaptation of Lewis Carroll's *Alice* stories (with Sybil Thorndike as two Queens), in the West End.

In 1944 Esmé Church accepted the invitation of the Bradford Civic group to become director of their playhouse in Chapel Street.

London did not again see Esmé's work until the early 1950s, and then as an actress in a play by Tyrone Guthrie, as director of a play by George Scott-Moncrieff about Mary Stuart (Marie Ney), and as a character described by Thornton Wilder as "fifty, florid, stout and sentimental" in his comedy *The Matchmaker*, directed by Guthrie. New York audiences had their first view of her in that same role in 1955.

At the beginning of the 1960s Esmé Church made two guest appearances with the Royal Shakespeare Company: at Stratford-on-Avon as the stage mother of Christopher Plummer's Richard III, and in London as one of the "costumed" letter-writers in John Barton's adaptation of the epistolary classic *Les Liaisons Dangéreuses*.

June 1, 1972.

Richard Church, C.B.E., poet, critic and novelist, died on March 4, 1972 at his home in Kent. He was 78.

It was as a poet in a tradition of authentic minor poetry that Church laid most valid claim to serious recognition. At his most felicitous he achieved a note of lyrical contemplation of telling quietness and candour, crystallizing a world of familiar discovery in the brief and direct statement of personal experience. If his verse seldom possessed a quality of strangeness or carried any perturbing force of suggestion, it was, on the other hand, in contrast with so much of the verse of his contemporaries, unfailingly lucid.

Sometimes, indeed, it was written with all too patent ease: like other and better poets, Church wrote a good deal more, no doubt, than was worth writing. But over a long poetic career he retained his own quiet and unmistakably personal colour. Always a busy literary journalist, he was a graceful if somewhat popular type of critic, while he also wrote sympathetically and well of country life, more particularly in the Home Counties. As a novelist he was less assured. His novels were gravely and deliberately undertoned, marked by passages of careful description and sober reflection, but for the most part conspicuously wanting in life.

But by far his most remarkable prose achievement consisted of the volumes of autobiography *Over the Bridge* (1955), vivid, inwardly searching and beautifully illuminated in detail (this won *The Sunday Times* Prize for Literature); *The Golden Sovereign* (1957), only a degree less fine and rounded in execution; and *The Voyage Home* (1964), in which he described the clash between the urge to write and the need to earn a living he experienced as a young civil servant, how the problem was solved, and his final progress to professionalism and the full literary life.

Born in London on March 26, 1893, the son of Thomas John Church, a Post Office worker, and Lavinia Annie Orton, he was educated at Dulwich Hamlet School and entered the Customs and Excise as a junior civil servant. He continued as a civil servant for many years, devoting his leisure to poetry and music, and then took the plunge from tedious security as a customs clerical officer into the shoals and currents of the profession of literary journalism. Book reviewing and the ordeal by drudgery of a publisher's reader were his chief financial standby over a fairly long period. He had published several slim volumes of verse before he won attention in 1926 with the dramatic monologue *Portrait of the Abbot,* in which, although the form did not quite suit him, his spare unrhetorical blank verse caught the lights and shades of the sceptical mind with revealing irony. Then followed *The Dream, Theme and Variations, Mood without Measure,* and in 1930 *The Glance Backward.*

Of the later books of poetry perhaps the most notable was the *Twentieth-Century Psalter* (1943), a sequence in which Church attempted to draw meaning for the contemporary mind from the horror and heroism of the years of war. A large volume of his *Collected Poems* was issued in 1948. Two years later Church brought out an anthology of *Poems for Speaking,* which he prefaced with a pointed critical argument, very much in keeping with the character of his own verse, that sound is the most potent element in poetry. Among the poems included in a new small collection published in 1957, *The Inheritors* (which won the Foyle's Poetry Prize) were several that had originally appeared in *The Times Literary Supplement.*

The earliest of his novels, *Oliver's Daughter,* appeared in 1930. Its merits of quiet observation and defects of rather listless and unimpassioned imagination are those of all his works of fiction, which are restricted in range and repetitive in theme. The author's talent did not, in fact, run at all spontaneously towards the novel. The book of his that made most impression was *The Porch,* published in 1937, a somewhat Gissing-like reconstruction of youth, into (which won the Foyle's Poetry Prize). were biography. It won the Femina-Vie Heureuse prize. Later novels included a sequel, *The Stronghold* (1939), *The Nightingale* (1952), a tale of classical antiquity rather simply translated in modern dress, and *The Dangerous Years* (1956), set in Paris between the wars.

Possibly the most attractive of his volumes of collected essays on country themes was *A Window on a Hill* (1951). Among other diverse undertakings of his that deserve to be mentioned are *A Portrait of Canterbury,* the verse play about Marlowe, *The Prodigal,* that he wrote for the Canterbury Festival in the Coronation Year 1953, and a small guide to the Royal Parks of London. He also published *London, Flower of Cities All* (1967) and *London in Colour* (1971). *The Little Kingdom,* on Kent, appeared in 1964.

Tall, spare, somewhat studious in appearance and a shade fastidious in habit, Church was always a welcome figure in literary society. He married first Caroline Parfett, and, after this marriage was dissolved, secondly Catherina Anna Schimmer, who died in 1965. They had one son and three daughters. He married thirdly Dorothy Beale.

March 6, 1972.

Captain Peter Churchill, D.S.O., well known for his work for the French Section of Special Operations Executive (S.O.E.) during the Second World War, died in Cannes on May 1, 1972. He was 63.

The son of W. A. Churchill, he was educated at Malvern and Caius College, Cambridge, where he read modern languages, for which he had a marked gift. His courier during his secret work in France was Odette Sansom, better known as Odette, who was later captured by the Germans on the same day as he.

In 1947 she and Captain Churchill were married. They were divorced in 1956 and both were again married, he to Jane Hoyle and she to Geoffrey Hallowes.

During his last illness she visited Captain Churchill in hospital in Cannes.

[A long tribute, describing Peter Churchill's gallant work, was attached to this obituary.]

May 2, 1972.

Dr. G. S. R. Kitson Clark—See **Kitson Clark.**

Lesley (Mrs. J. D.) Clark—See **Storm.**

Professor Sir Wilfrid Le Gros Clark, F.R.S., former Professor of Anatomy in the University of Oxford, and a Fellow of Hertford College, died on June 28, 1971. He was 76.

He was born in Hemel Hempstead in 1895, the second of three sons of the Rev. Travers Clark. From Blundell's School he went to St. Thomas's Hospital, where he qualified in 1916 and to which he returned as a Demonstrator of Anatomy, after spending the last two years of the 1914-18 War as an R.A.M.C. officer in France.

Teaching anatomy must have had little appeal for him in this period of his career for, two years later, he obtained the appointment of Principal Medical Officer of Sarawak, Borneo. In the three years during which he occupied this office he not only gained a considerable reputation as a medical practitioner, both in administrative circles and among the native population, but also laid the foundation for much of his later research. He returned to England as Reader in Anatomy at St. Bartholomew's Hospital, a post which was raised to a professorship in 1927. In 1929 he accepted the Chair of Anatomy in his old hospital, St. Thomas's, and five years later he moved to Oxford as Dr. Lee's Professor of Anatomy—a post which he occupied until 1962.

Considerable attention was being paid in the early 1920s to the question of the evolutionary relationships of the more primitive primates, the mammalian order to which man belongs, and stimulated by Sir Grafton Elliot-Smith, F.R.S. (then Professor of Anatomy at University College London). Professor Le Gros Clark undertook while in Borneo to make observations both on the rare spectral tarsier and, more particularly, on the tree-shrews which are indigenous to that country. He continued this work for a number of years in England, and its results were the subject of a series of papers first published in the proceedings of the Zoological Society, and later embodied in a book, *Early Forerunners of Man,* which appeared in 1934. In this book he also reviewed much of the comparative data which form the basis of opinions about the general evolution of the primates. An expanded revision of this book was published in 1959 under the title of *The Antecedents of Man*.

His interest in the problem of primate evolution received a new stimulus at the end of the Second World War as more and more fossil primate material was discovered in South and East Africa. Although at first sceptical of the claims that the South African fossils, *Australopithecinae*, had any greater relevance to the story of human evolution than other simian fossils, Le Gros Clark suddenly swung in favour of this view and into support of the position that had been taken up by Professor Dart and Dr. Broom. Le Gros Clark's conversion did not, however, resolve the issue, and he himself became somewhat impatient in the controversy. His own views were set out in 1955 in a short book entitled *The Fossil Evidence for Human Evolution*, and later in a British Museum booklet *The History of the Primates*, which has now gone through many editions. Neither of these works contains any reference to published data which conflict with the particular view about the evolutionary significance of the Australopithecines to which Le Gros Clark had added the weight of his name.

Le Gros Clark's early work on the tree-shrews had led him to the view that they should be classified among the primates rather than the insectivores, and through a survey of the anatomy of the brain, he was led into a very fruitful field of study— the investigation of the relation of the cerebral cortex to the big sensory nucleus of the brain, the thalamus, and the detailed tracing of the pathways followed by visual stimulations on their way from the eyes to the cerebral cortex. This work proved a stimulus to a great deal of research, both in Britain and abroad. Le Gros Clark was also responsible for the anatomical mapping of the hypothalamus, the part of the brain which controls visceral function, and he also devoted some of his attention to the anatomy of sensation, and in particular, to the anatomy of colour vision.

His influence was no less marked in teaching than it was in research. Owing to its preoccupation with the rote-learning of topographical details, anatomy in Great Britain had for years been sinking into the position of a Cinderella of the medical sciences. Le Gros Clark fought hard to revive the subject, by associating himself with the less hide-bound of his anatomical colleagues, by campaigning for a functional and experimental approach to the subject, and by cutting away at the dead-weight of anatomical detail which the student was expected to learn. His *Tissues of the Body* is now known to several generations of medical student, and he also contributed an important section to a reformed *Textbook of Human Anatomy*, edited by W. J. Hamilton, which has also had a useful influence on anatomical teaching in England. Le Gros Clark published his autobiography *Chant of Pleasant Exploration* in 1968. He

was one of the experts who exposed the Piltdown Man hoax in the fifties.

Le Gros Clark was elected to the Royal Society in 1935, and was awarded a Royal Medal in 1961. He was president of the Anatomical Society of Great Britain in 1952 and 1953, and president of the International Anatomical Congress which took place in Oxford in 1950. He was elected president of the British Association for 1961. He served on the Medical Research Council, and was an honorary member of several foreign scientific societies. He was also a member of the Salters' Company, of which he was Master in 1954.

In 1923 he married first Freda Constance Giddey (who died in 1963) by whom he had two daughters; in 1964, he married secondly Violet, widow of Dr. Leonard Browne.

June 29, 1971.

Sir Richard Clarke, K.C.B., O.B.E., died on June 21, 1975 at the age of 64. His death deprives British public life of a most remarkable personality.

Although Sir Richard "Otto" Clarke was widely known in governmental, academic and business circles, he was not very much in the public eye; but he had a major influence on national affairs and, for anyone who knew him, he was one of that very small group of people who make an immediate, powerful and lasting impression.

Richard William Barnes Clarke was born in 1910. He was educated at Christ's Hospital and was a Wrangler at Cambridge.

His career began with a short spell in the British Electrical and Allied Manufacturers' Association. This was followed by six years on the *Financial News*, up to the outbreak of war; during that period he was also a Visiting Lecturer at Cambridge University. Forty years ago, as a young newspaper man, he devised an Index of Ordinary Share prices which was to become the celebrated *F.T. Index*.

His journalistic training stood him in good stead in his subsequent career. It provided him with an ability to concentrate on essentials and gave him an extraordinary speed and lucidity in drafting. It was just before switching from journalism to public administration that he wrote a classic little study on the British economic blockade.

He then became one of that large but highly select band of temporary civil servants who, as certainly the more enlightened "regulars" will acknowledge, transformed the character of the British administrative machine, and made it capable of coping with the tasks of war in a way it would otherwise not have been able to.

He was successively in the Ministries of Information, Economic Warfare, Supply and Production, and spent one year—an extremely important one both for his own education and his future career—in the Combined Production and Resources Board

in Washington.

Like a few others, though in retrospect undoubtedly not a sufficient number, he decided to stay on in the Civil Service once the war was over. He became an Assistant Secretary in the Treasury, advancing rapidly to Under-Secretary and Third Secretary.

He and William (now Lord) Armstrong were the two principal authors of the reorganization of the Treasury which was carried out under Selwyn Lloyd's Chancellorship and which came into effect in 1962.

Its most important features were the combination of the Home and Overseas Finance Divisions (reverting to an earlier pattern) and the setting up of a National Economy Group (the predecessor and, later, the inheritor of the concept underlying the Department of Economic Affairs), reporting directly to the Permanent Secretary, though headed by a Third Secretary—unlike the two main Operating Divisions which were headed by Second Secretaries. Otto Clarke became one of these, being in charge of the supply side of the Treasury. He then moved on to become Permanent Secretary at the Ministry of Aviation and, during the last four years of his Civil Service career, he was Permanent Secretary of the Ministry of Technology.

When he retired in 1970, he continued to do a certain amount of work for the Civil Service, both at home and abroad, which resulted in a series of reports of great value in the highly important if somewhat esoteric fields of Government structure and administration. He also took a number of directorships in major companies.

This recital of the successive stages in his career shows a progress which, though not very common, is at the same time not altogether unusual. What was different about Otto Clarke was that he consistently brought to all his activities both exceptional qualities of intellect and high executive ability. Despite the fact that he, a wartime recruit, had reached the heart of the very citadel of orthodox Treasury control, he always retained a fresh and unorthodox approach to all problems with which he had to deal. He was exceptional in this respect: there were not many of those who stayed on after the War and became established Civil Servants who were able either to avoid continuing to be relative outsiders or, alternatively, to be wholly absorbed into the orthodoxies of the machine.

He did not suffer fools gladly, and even Ministers were not spared, where necessary, his polite yet incisive critical comments. But his keenest shafts were reserved for those of high but unmerited position; for the more humble, if they were truly anxious to understand and to do right, he had ample patience and much help to offer.

He could also be a most delightful companion. He had an enormous range of interests and knowledge, to which the wide variety of books in his library bore witness.

In the Civil Service he was treated with that respect which great ability always commands; but he was also regarded with a certain awe.

He played a decisive part in the management of the balance of payments in the immediate postwar period; and his role as the "rear link" in Whitehall for many of Britain's postwar international activities, the Marshall Plan, the whole range of activities connected with the European Recovery Programme, the economic and financial aspects of N.A.T.O., the Free Trade Area negotiations, and many others, was of crucial importance.

It is not generally known that after many false starts, with the aid of specially summoned outside "writers", it was Otto who wrote the triumphant short, succinct, yet comprehensive introductory report which was the European response to the Marshall speech.

Equally, it is not perhaps generally known that among the many official documents he wrote was that landmark in economic planning, the White Paper *Economic Survey 1947*, one of the important stages in the infusion of Keynesian doctrines into macro-economic management.

He played an outstanding part in guiding Whitehall thinking, at the same time being a splendid comrade-in-arms to those "in the field" whenever he could be tempted away from the fastnesses of Great George Street. Otto Clarke at work, for example, in an official car bringing him back from the airport after a Marshall Plan meeting in Paris, with the stub of a Stationery Office pencil writing on a wartime quality Stationery Office scribbling pad at a fantastic speed a detailed account of the meeting, with considered conclusions, virtually ready without correction to be printed as a Cabinet document, was an unforgettable experience.

Otto Clarke married in 1950 Brenda Pile (née Skinner). This, for both of them a second marriage, was an exceptionally happy one, and a great joy to behold to their close friends. Lady Clarke and three sons survive him.

Sir Richard was a keen and excellent chess player in his youth and played on a high board for Cambridge University in the early 1930s. He was a contemporary of the late C. H. O'D. Alexander and played on the second board to Alexander's first in the 1931 and 1932 matches against Oxford University, losing in 1931 and winning in 1932.

On leaving the university and entering the Civil Service he gave up active play but maintained a strong interest in the game and was particularly concerned with questions of advancing the quality of British chess so that it could do well in the international field.

Some 20 years ago he took on the organization of a rating system for players of the British Chess Federation. He became chairman of the B.C.F. Grading Committee and by dint of much skilful work succeeded in making the grading scheme as foolproof as possible. When, in 1970, the Friends of Chess organization was founded with the express object of improving the standing of British chess in the international field, he became chairman of its committee and threw all his energies into the work with utmost enthusiasm. His passing is a sad loss for British chess.

June 23, 1975.

The Rev. Philip Thomas Byard Clayton, C.H., M.C., D.D., perhaps better known as "Tubby" Clayton, founder padre of Toc H, died on December 15, 1972 at the age of 87.

He was born on December 12, 1885, at Maryborough, Queensland, the fifth and youngest child of the Rev. R. B. B. Clayton.

He was educated at St. Paul's School and was elected to a classical scholarship at Exeter College, Oxford, gaining the Milton prize for verse. At Oxford he made some mark as a speaker and had a great many friends; he graduated in 1909 with a first class in Theology, for he was a Rebecca Squire scholar in the university and destined for holy orders. Instead of going to a theological college he read with the Dean of Westminster, then Dr. Armitage Robinson, afterwards of Wells, living in the Deanery and incidentally acquiring much knowledge of the antiquities of the Abbey.

In response to an appeal by Dr. John Stansfeld, he helped in the work of the Oxford and Bermondsey Mission—"Bermondsey was the true cradle of Toc H"—where he met Alec Paterson, Donald Hankey, Basil Henriques*, Neville Talbot, Barclay Baron and Hubert Secretan.

In 1910 he was ordained and for four years served a curacy in the large parish of Portsea, where the vicars generally became bishops under that formidable man Cyril Forster Garbett, later Archbishop of York.

On the outbreak of war in 1914, he volunteered as an Army chaplain and served first in hospitals in France. The Senior Chaplain of the 6th Division, Neville Talbot (later Bishop of Pretoria), was looking for a rest-house to serve the troops in the bottle-neck of traffic surging to and from the Ypres Salient in Flanders. He knew that Clayton was the man to take charge of it and together they found the house. On December 11, 1915 Clayton started his unique rallying-point and continued to be, while officially the Garrison Chaplain of Poperinge, the genial host and inn-keeper at Talbot House until after the Armistice.

This "home from home", a "heaven in the hell of men's lives", was named after Neville's youngest brother, Gilbert Talbot, the most brilliant of the sons of the Bishop of Winchester, killed in action in the Ypres Salient five months previously. The spirit of the place generated by its host was denoted by the sign facing men as they entered and pointing back to the door, "Pessimists, Way Out". Clayton soon had his guests busy on jobs of service. Refreshment for body, mind, and soul was provided in the garden—a canteen, recreation and writing room, a library in the chaplain's room labelled "All rank abandon, ye who enter here" and above all in the loft, "the Upper Room". There Tubby installed a carpenter's bench, found in a garden shed, to serve as altar in a chapel used in turn by thousands of men, many for the last time, for the Ypres Salient alone took toll of a quarter of a million lives.

Talbot House was Tubby's base for frequent visits to troops in and near the front line. For a time a daughter-house was possible in the ruins of Ypres. The name, T.H. for short, became Toc H in the Morse signallers' language of the time. This nickname stuck to the postwar movement of which it was the birthplace and Tubby the founder.

In 1919 Clayton selected Knutsford Prison in Cheshire to be transformed into an Ordination Test School, of which he became chaplain and tutor. (The Service Candidates Ordination Fund and a first roll of candidates had been started during the war in Talbot House.) During the same period, in collaboration with his cousin, Dick Sheppard, then vicar of St. Martin-in-the Fields, and with Alec Paterson, shortly to become a Commissioner of Prisons, Tubby was planning to open a Talbot House in London. Between them they formulated a way of living, "Four Points of the Compass", to guide men keen to preserve and pass on the best of what experience in war had taught them. In 1920 the first residential house of many, "Toc H Mark I", was opened and Tubby had launched a movement "to teach the younger generation class-reconciliation and unselfish service". As a way of practical Christianity, one of its aims and methods was "to spread the Gospel without preaching it".

By 1922 Toc H had 40 branches and became an association incorporated by Royal Charter, the Prince of Wales being the active patron and Tubby the founder padre "for so long as he desires to hold the office". By dint of constant travelling and letter-writing Clayton built a movement which eventually numbered a thousand branches in Britain, several hundred overseas and the Toc H Women's Association of almost equal strength.

To provide a spiritual centre for the work of Toc H, the Archbishop of Canterbury, Randall Davidson, as patron of the living, appointed Clayton in 1922 to the benefice of All Hallows by the Tower. This most ancient of parish churches in the City of London became the guild church of Toc H, serving Free Churchmen as well as Anglican. He remained vicar until 1963.

In 1926 he planned and launched the Tower Hill Improvement Trust. Largely through the generosity of Lord Wakefield of Hythe, properties were acquired and clearances effected. The provision of Tower Beach as a playground for children was secured in 1934. The gardens and the public terrace on the site of a huge warehouse overlooking the Tower are permanent memorials to his unflagging work for the amenities of Tower Hill.

In the blitz of 1940 All Hallows Church was bombed and burnt, only the tower, some walls and the undercroft surviving. After the war Clayton toured the Dominions and the United States to secure gifts of money and material and raised sufficient to supplement the war damage grants for rebuilding. In fulfilment of Clayton's hopes, the headquarters of Toc H was moved in 1960 from Westminster to a freehold property at the corner of Trinity Square, opposite the guild church.

In the early part of the Second World War Clayton was with the Royal Navy in the Orkneys, establishing Toc H Services Clubs round Scapa Flow. Later he was at sea as chaplain to the Anglo-Saxon tanker fleet and to the Merchant Navy in the Indian Ocean and Mediterranean.

He was awarded the Military Cross in 1917 and was made a Companion of Honour in 1933. In 1954 he received the degree of Doctor of Divinity (Lambeth) "in recognition of his services to the Church through Toc H".

He was unmarried.

December 19, 1972.

Sir Alan Cobham, K.B.E., A.F.C., who died on October 21, 1973, aged 79, will be remembered as one of the earliest pilots to use aircraft for long-distance journeys.

To some extent his flights between 1921 and 1935 were exhibition efforts. They won him fame and publicity but they sought also to show how the aeroplane could be used for practical purposes, and so served as prophetic demonstrations. In the course of those exploits he used both landplanes and seaplanes, and although some of his air journeys were prolonged by mechanical and other handicaps, he succeeded more fully than any other early pilot in seizing the attention of ordinary people in many parts of the British Commonwealth and in awakening them to the possibilities of air transport.

He had a lively imagination, a shrewd judgment, endless perseverence and a store of tireless energy that kept himself and his helpers continuously aiming at their objective. Those qualities were to serve him as well in later life, when his piloting days were over, as they did in taking aircraft over unfamiliar terrain, for he had to drive his project for refuelling in the air through jungles of prejudice and distrust before he got it accepted first by the United States and at last by the Royal Air Force.

All his days he ran true to form. Just as ideas bubbled out of his enthusiasm for flying, and drove him to joy-riding, to air photography, to long taxi journeys, and then to immense undertakings like trips to the Far East, Australia and round Africa, so, when he came to running his air circuses, he never let difficulties deter him from adding new thrills or from keeping his appointments with his public; and similarly in launching his new business of flight refuelling, he experimented, demonstrated, modified and improved, and generally advanced the technique until the process of refilling tanks in the air became almost as simple as driving up to a petrol pump.

There was never any acceptance of defeat in Alan Cobham. He could be driven frantic by misfortunes; he could present a convincing picture of despair and disgust; he could grumble and complain like the best of soldiers; and he could drive and harass his helpers incessantly, but as he drove himself with equal vigour they stayed with him and were given a generous share in his successes. His temperament, methods and accent were those of the best type of Cockney, and he had a host of friends who smiled indulgently at his tantrums and his showmanship, and loved him for his essential kindliness and lack of pretensions.

Born on May 6, 1894, the son of Frederick Cobham, Alan John Cobham began with no obvious advantages. He was a grammar school boy who started work on a farm, had a job in a city warehouse, and, when the First World War broke out, promptly enlisted. He found himself in the artillery and was serving on the Aisne by September 1914. He had already developed an interest in aircraft and he was soon longing to get into the Flying Corps. It took three years of persistent applications to get him his transfer. When he came out of the R.A.F. in 1919, he joined two brothers in a joy-riding business.

After a year of relative prosperity—5,000 people were given their first "flip"—times became difficult and Cobham, down to his last £3, accepted employment as a photographic pilot with Airco Ltd. A year later he had a chance to join Geoffrey de Havilland* in his new company at Stag Lane, Hendon, and the succession of his long flights, largely in de Havilland aircraft, began. They grew out of his work as a demonstration and taxi pilot. First there was a trip in 1921 of 5,000 miles round Europe, then one of 8,000 miles embracing Europe and North Africa in 1922, together with a spectacular one-day journey from London to Belgrade and back.

In 1923 he had a passenger—Lucien Sharpe—on a 12,000 mile charter trip through Europe to Palestine, Egypt, up the Nile, along the North African coast, and home through Spain. By 1924 he had a new four-seater at his service and with it won a competition at Gothenburg. He was also the winner of the King's Cup that year, and towards the end of the year he set out to fly Sir Sefton Brancker to Rangoon and back. Each year now saw Cobham engaged on some new flying enterprise. In 1925-26 he went to the Cape and back; in 1926 to Australia and back; in 1927, in a Singapore flying boat, 23,000 miles round Africa; in 1931 on a survey flight up the Nile and on to the Belgian Congo.

Having demonstrated what aircraft could do to open up Africa and tighten the lines of communication with the Dominions, he constituted himself for the next four years the missionary of air transport in Britain, and also found a means of earning a living for himself as his own master. He organized a flying circus and barnstormed with it round the country, celebrating at each stand "national aviation day". He gave the crowds an exciting display, having engaged pilots who could do all the tricks right down to picking up a handkerchief from the grass with a spike at the wing-tip, and he gave many thousands their first brief taste of travel in an airliner, for in his later years on the road he had in his circus fleet an 18-seater!

Commercial air transport had overtaken and justified his missionary work by 1935, and the day of the air circus was over. Cobham now turned his attention to increasing the range of commercial aircraft without diminishing the payload. With his usual industry he worked out a system whereby a tanker aircraft could dangle a fuel hose to be grappled by a line and hook from a liner flying below, hauled in, connected to a hydrant in its tail so that fuel might flow by gravity from the tanker.

The system worked. It was employed off Ireland in 1939 to top up the tanks of the Imperial Airways flying-boats that made the first experimental commercial crossings of the Atlantic. It went on being improved in ways of making contact, and in means of making sure that the tanker and receiver would meet in the wide and cloudy spaces of the air. And yet air transport showed no sign of accepting the boon he offered. Nor did the R.A.F. Even through the early years of the war he could evoke no military interest in his system. Finally, the need to give escorting fighters longer range for their work with the day bombers over Germany brought the United States Army Air Force to his demonstrations.

From that point he could count his campaign as won, and he settled down to consolidate his victory. The somewhat clumsy grappling process of making a connexion was replaced by a system in which the receiving aircraft flew a probe into a funnel at the end of the tanker's hose and locked it home with the pressure of its own speed. A company was set up in the United States to exploit his patents. For a number of years fighters and bombers alike in the U.S.A.A.F. have been equipped for flight refuelling on the Cobham plan. Much less wholeheartedly, the R.A.F. followed suit.

In this activity Cobham won none of the glory that had belonged to his flying days, but he applied the same industry and tenacity and refused to let his visions be smothered by the apathy of others.

Thirty years after his long flight to Cape Town and back, he and Lady Cobham (whom he met in his joy-riding days, and who died in 1961) allowed themselves a party to celebrate the achievements that had gained him his knighthood. In the autumn of 1956 his friends in the flying world were invited to London. Nearly 500 joined him in his nostalgic backward glance, to find the same bustling organizer devoting his talents to hospitality, to give the same amused approval to the showmanship, and the same affection to the least self-conscious of egoists.

October 22, 1973.

Coco the Clown—See **Poliakov.**

Lord Cohen, P.C., who was a Lord of Appeal in Ordinary from 1951 to 1960, died on May 9, 1973. He had not only a distinguished career in the practice and administration of the law, but was also well known for his varied public and charitable activities.

Lionel Leonard Cohen, Baron Cohen, of Walmer, in the county of Kent, was born on March 1, 1888, his father being Sir Leonard Lionel Cohen, K.C.V.O. He was educated at Eton and New College, Oxford, obtaining a first class in history, and was called to the Bar by the Inner Temple in 1913 (of which he was made a Bencher in 1934 and elected Treasurer in 1954). During the 1914-18 War he served with the 13th Princess Louise's Kensington Battalion of The London Regiment, and later, after recovering from wounds received in action, he held a staff appointment.

On his demobilization he entered the chambers of Alfred Topham, afterwards Judge Topham, in New Square, Lincoln's Inn, and, as he had decided to practise at the Chancery Bar, he was admitted *ad eundem* as a member of Lincoln's Inn. He very soon acquired a substantial practice, which lay mostly in the field of company law (being given his red bag by Lord Simon—then Sir John Simon—at a very early stage) and by 1929 his practice had become so large that he was virtually compelled to take silk.

Lionel Cohen had a brilliant intellect and a very quick-thinking mind. He also had the capacity for taking infinite pains, and his drafting was a model of care, thoroughness and accuracy. On taking silk he shed the burden of drafting, and soon had a very considerable advisory practice, particularly in company matters, his opinions commanding the greatest respect in the City of London and in industry generally.

As a silk he was seen more in court than as a junior, but as an advocate he was less successful. His speed of thinking was the real cause for he left judge, opponent and witness too far behind, and he was inclined to omit to finish a sentence in his eagerness to pass on to the next. Nevertheless, his brilliance and the wide knowledge of the law which he had acquired within the Bar were universally recognized, and on the death of Mr. Justice Farwell in 1943 it was a foregone conclusion that he would be appointed to fill the vacancy, thus leaving the Ministry of Economic Warfare where he had been serving since 1939.

As a judge he really came into his own. He was relaxed, patient and courteous, so that every counsel who appeared before him enjoyed doing so, and every litigant, successful or otherwise, recognized that he had had a fair and impartial hearing, a tribute which it has, unfortunately, not in every case been possible to pay. He was elevated to the Court of Appeal in February 1946, when its membership was expanded. Here he confirmed and extended his already established reputation as a lawyer, being by this time versed in most branches of the law; so that in 1951 on the appointment of Lord Simonds to the Woolsack, it was again a foregone conclusion that Cohen should succeed him as a Lord of Appeal in Ordinary. In the House of Lords and in the Judicial Committee of the Privy Council his opinions and his judgments respectively bear the stamp of authority. He left his mark on the interpretation, administration and judicial making of the law.

He was a man of great charm, of which characteristic he was entirely unaware, and of essential kindliness. He also had that virtue so essential in those in whose hands responsibility is placed, namely, an innate sense of humility, which was plain to those who knew him well throughout his career. His absorbing hobby was golf, at which he was in his day very proficient; and whereas in the Army, at any rate during the 1914-18 War, the teaching was to identify a place by the nearest church, this, in the case of Cohen, was accomplished by reference to the nearest golf course. He was also a brilliant player of bridge.

Cohen's public services, apart from his devotion to the law, were many. Cohen was chairman of the Company Law Amendments Committee which sat from 1943 to 1945, and which made far-reaching recommendations for the reform of this branch of the law. The Government accepted in full the proposals made, and the Companies' Act of 1948 was the result. In 1946 Cohen was appointed a member of the tribunal (of which the then Master of the Rolls, Lord Greene, was chairman) established to assess the difficult and complicated questions of the amount of compensation for assets which were to be transferred to the National Coal Board. It was said that each of the leading counsel who argued on behalf of the various interests concerned received 13,000 guineas—which is some indication of the length and complexity of the inquiry.

In the same year Cohen was appointed chairman of the Royal Commission—which sat from 1946 to 1956—to determine what awards should be paid to inventors for the use of their inventions, designs, drawings, or processes by Government Departments and allied Governments during the Second World War. Among the many recipients of awards were Air Commodore Sir Frank Whittle for his invention of the jet engine, and Sir Robert Watson-Watt, who developed radar. In 1950 a Royal Commission was set up to inquire into the system of taxation of profits and income, of which Cohen was appointed chairman, but from which he retired in November 1951 on his being made a Lord of Appeal in Ordinary. Two air disasters—a Comet lost near Elba in January 1954 and another Comet lost south of Naples in the same year—were the subject of an inquiry over which Cohen presided. He and his assessors found that the cause was due to metal fatigue.

In August 1957 Cohen undertook a most onerous task, which raised many controversial matters, when he became chairman of the new independent Council of Prices, Productivity and Incomes. The terms of reference were: "Having regard to the desirability of full employment and increasing standards of life based on expanding production and reasonable stability of prices to keep under review changes in prices, productivity and the level of incomes (including wages, salaries and profits) and to report thereon from time to time". Three highly important reports were presented before Cohen resigned from the Council in September 1959 to give more time to his legal duties.

Cohen was a member of the Board of Governors of St. Mary's. He became an Honorary Fellow of New College, Oxford, in 1946, a Fellow of Eton from 1950 to 1960, and chairman of the College Committee of University College London from 1953 to 1963.

From 1934 to 1939 he served as vice-president of the Jewish Board of Deputies, and also held office in the Anglo-Jewish Association. He was never a Zionist, but for many years he was active for Jewish cultural institutions, the Hebrew University of Jerusalem, the Weitzman Institute of Science and the Anglo-Israel Archaeology Fund. In 1957 he visited Israel and lectured at the University on English company law, and on the Lionel Cohen Foundation, which had been established in his honour.

He married in 1918 Adelaide (who died in 1961), youngest daughter of Sir Isidore Spielmann. They had two sons and a daughter.

May 10, 1973.

Elizabeth Coles—See **Elizabeth Taylor.**

Marie Collier, the Australian soprano opera singer, died on December 8, 1971 when she fell from the window of a flat in Leicester Square, London. She was 44.

She was born and brought up near Melbourne and began her career in musicals. Then she took the role of Magda in an Australian production of *The Consul*, which toured all over the continent.

After being coached in Milan, Marie Collier went to England to be auditioned by Covent Garden, with whom she signed a contract in 1956. One of her first and best roles with the company was Musetta in *La Bohème*.

In the 1959-60 season she was lent to Sadler's Wells where she made her mark in the title role of Janacek's *Katya Kabanova* and in an interesting new production of *Tosca* by Dennis Arundell.

Back at Covent Garden she extended her repertory in the early 1960s with Santuzza (in Zeffirelli's production of *Cavalleria Rusticana*), Cio-Cio-San, Marie (in *Wozzeck*), Elisabeth in *Don Carlos,* and created the role of Hecuba in Tippett's *King Priam* (1962). Her break into wider than national circles came in the 1963-64 season when she tackled the title role in the first British performance of *Katerina Ismailova* at Covent Garden and Emilia Marty in Janacek's *The Makropulos Case* at Sadler's Wells. From then on she was in demand abroad not only for this kind of role but also for the regular lyric-dramatic parts, appearing in Vienna, New York (at the Metropolitan) and San Francisco with considerable success.

Perhaps she gained her greatest fame in 1965 by taking over at short notice from Callas in the Zeffirelli production of *Tosca* at Covent Garden. Her most recent appearances in Britain took place in 1970, when she played Santuzza at Covent Garden and again (very successfully) Emilia Marty with Sadler's Wells at the Coliseum where she was due to repeat the part in the New Year, 1972.

Her vibrant, lustrous voice and flamboyant, committed personality were particularly well suited to the Puccini heroines—Manon Lescaut and Minnie (in *The Girl of the Golden West*) were also her roles—and to the portrayal of more modern heroines. Anybody who has seen or heard her in one of her Janacek parts will cherish the memory.

She is survived by a husband and four children.

December 9, 1971.

Victor John Collins—See Stonham.

Padraic Colum, the Irish poet and man of letters, died at Enfield, Connecticut, on January 11, 1972 at the age of 90. He had been in a nursing home since suffering a stroke in the summer of 1970. He had long made his home in the United States.

Colum was one of the younger personalities of the Irish literary renaissance in the early years of this century and a promising figure in the Irish theatre movement inaugurated by Yeats and Lady Gregory. In the first two plays of his produced in Dublin he gave evidence of very real qualities as a playwright. If nevertheless he did not entirely succeed in the theatre, it was apparently because he lacked the gift, which

has been more highly prized in Ireland than the grim and forbidding Irish comedies of the past half-century would perhaps suggest, of making an audience laugh.

As a poet, however, his unselfconscious felicity in the world of Irish traditional song brought him immediate recognition. His was a consistency of imaginative mood and impulse, nourished on the custom and diction of the Irish countryside, that harked back to an authentic tradition of Elizabethan lyricism. In the texture of Colum's verse are deposited turns of Irish country speech that would have been familiar to Sidney and Spenser. To this echoing sympathy he added as a poet a finely individual delicacy of sense and a limpid intimacy of fancy—qualities that helped to make him, incidentally, an incomparable story-teller for children. He was one of the co-founders and regular contributors to the *Irish Review.*

Born at Longford on December 8, 1881, in a workhouse of which his father, Padraic Colum, was master, he was an undergraduate at Trinity College, Dublin. A young man of striking personal beauty, he acted in *Deirdre*, by "A.E." [G. W. Russell], which in 1902 was the real beginning of the Abbey Theatre. In the next year his own play, *Broken Soil*, with a tragic theme deriving, as an Irish critic of the period observed, from the temperament, religion and tradition peculiar to the Irish people, made a powerful impression. A year later he was included among the eight poets represented in the volume of *New Songs* edited by A.E.; while a year later still his second play, *The Land*, which draws from the Irish scene of those years the bitter moral that the strong go to America and the fools remain in possession, confirmed the impression made by the earlier play.

He was a railway clerk for some years, during which he published two books of poetry, *Wild Earth* and *Dramatic Legends*. In 1914 he went to the United States on what was intended to be a short visit only; in the event he made his permanent home there. Besides verse, he produced in *Castle Conquer* (1923) a novel of the Irish countryside of forty years earlier of a rare and telling poetic simplicity; the idiom of the dialogue is of a naturalness far removed from the studied convention of Anglo-Irish dialect. In that same year also Colum was officially invited to Hawaii in order to study native myth and folklore and to preserve them in written form. *At the Gateways of the Day: Tales and Legends of Hawaii* appeared in 1924, and a second volume of similar character, *The Bright Islands*, in 1926.

In a book of Irish impressions, *The Road Round Ireland* (1927), Colum brought a characteristically illuminated sensibility to his commentary on Ireland's past and present, and revealed a mastery of English prose. A similar mastery, directed to different ends, is apparent in his numerous volumes of retold tales, among the most notable of which are *The Adventures of*

Odysseus and the Tale of Troy, The Boy who knew what the Bird Said and *The Girl Who Sat by the Ashes.* A volume of Colum's *Collected Poems* appeared in 1932, and later books of verse included *The Story of Lowry Maen* (1937), a narrative poem, and *Flower Pieces* (1939).

He continued to write and publish into old age. *Collected Poems* appeared in 1953, *The Flying Swan,* a novel, in 1956 and *Images of Departure,* further poems, in 1968. In 1960 he published a biography of the Irish leader, Arthur Griffith, and a year earlier, with his wife, Mary, *Our Friend James Joyce.*

Mary Colum, the daughter of Charles Maguire, died in 1957 at the age of 70. She was a writer and critic who won a reputation in the United States and, until her death, was guest professor of Comparative Literature at Columbia University.

January 13, 1972.

Commander Sir Richard Colville, K.C.V.O., C.B., D.S.C., who served as Press Secretary to King George VI from 1947 to 1952, and as Press Secretary to the Queen from her accession in 1952 until 1968, died on June 14, 1975 aged 67.

He came from a family with a tradition of service to the sovereign as courtiers and as officers of the armed forces, and he began life as a sailor and served throughout the war in the Royal Navy until his retirement in 1947. His naval service included a term in the old Royal Yacht, the Victoria and Albert.

His appointment as Press Secretary in 1947 met with a mixed reception in the newspaper world of the day where it was felt that some more direct knowledge of the working of the press would have been an advantage. His forthrightness and uncompromising personality meant that his tenure of office was never entirely free from friction.

The appointment came immediately before the wedding of the then Princess Elizabeth, and during his period of office Colville coped with the press arrangements for many major royal occasions, including the Coronation in 1953, and the birth of all four of the Queen's children.

The royal wedding in 1947, into which he was plunged with so little time for preparation, was a severe test of his mettle and a testimony to his quality. He not only survived the experience, but won tributes for his handling of it. His knowledge of the way in which the press works grew, of course, with his experience. At the end of his long term of office, there were few people who were so intimately acquainted with all aspects of the media.

His character was set firmly in the period of his birth and education. He retained throughout his life an uncomplicated loyalty and an unqualified devotion to his sovereign, which were always his first principles in dealing with the press. He clung tenaciously to his own point of view, based on his view of the world and his principles, which were old fashioned in the best sense. He was always prepared with good humour to hear out an argument to the end. Friends soon came to know and appreciate a keen sense of humour and unfailing kindness.

His relations with the press organizations were close and intimate, and developed in an atmosphere of mutual respect. His absolute honesty and fair-handed administration were always recognized and admired.

In his dealings with the press, Colville was determined to win for the Royal Family a recognition of their right to a private life. That he won this in the end was a tribute to his tenacity. Thanks to his success the Royal Family felt able to encourage his successors to develop a more positive approach in their dealings with the press world.

He was made M.V.O. in 1950, C.V.O. in 1953, K.C.V.O. in 1965, C.B. in 1960, and D.S.C. in 1943.

He was a devoted family man and his retirement in 1968 was shadowed by the unexpected death of his wife, a daughter of General Birdwood, in 1972. She had provided throughout his years as Press Secretary a domestic environment into which the cares of office were not permitted to obtrude. His own courage after this blow, and the loss of a leg consequent upon illness which followed his retirement, will not be forgotten. He will be remembered with warmest affection by his colleagues, and by a multitude of people who dealt with him during his naval and official careers.

He leaves a son and two daughters, and grandchildren who had immensely cheered his last years.

June 17, 1975.

Dr. Edward Condon, a leading American physicist who assisted in development of the atomic bomb, died on March 25, 1974, in Boulder, Colorado, at the age of 72.

At the beginning of the Second World War, Condon was working for Westinghouse Electric Company, and contributed to the development of radar. Shortly afterwards he was persuaded to join Dr. Robert Oppenheimer* as a member of the team at Las Alamos, New Mexico, that produced the atomic bomb.

While he was director of the United States National Bureau of Standards he was harassed by the House of Representatives Un-American Activities Committee who were suspicious of his political views and those of his friends. One of the committee's reports in 1948 referred to him as "one of the weakest links in our atomic security". The chairman of that committee, J. Parnell Thomas, a New Jersey congressman, was later sent to prison for "padding his office payroll".

For the next seven years Condon was a controversial figure as he was continually investigated and cleared by every government department he had ever worked for, as well as the military.

President Truman leapt to Condon's defence, commenting on a public platform that scientific work indispensable for national security "may be made impossible by the creation of an atmosphere in which no man feels safe against the public airing of unfounded rumours, gossip and vilification". He then went across and shook Condon's hand.

In 1954 Condon gave up the attempt to be granted clearance which would give him access to classified information, after the Secretary of the Navy, prompted by the then vice-president Richard Nixon, suspended the clearance granted by the Defence Department and ordered yet another review.

Condon, who had been president of the American Association for the Advancement of Science and of the American Physical Society, became professor of physics at Washington University in St. Louis and at the University of Colorado. In 1966 he was asked by the Air Force to study Unidentified Flying Objects.

Two years and $500,000 later, the Condon report decided that nothing had come from the study of such objects in the past 21 years that had added anything to scientific knowledge.

He married Emilie Honzik in 1922 and they had three children.

March 27, 1974.

Cyril Connolly, C.B.E., the distinguished critic and author, died on November 26, 1974, at the age of 71. Cyril Connolly was born at Coventry on September 10, 1903. King's Scholar at Eton, with George Orwell, Anthony Powell, Henry Green, John Lehmann and Harold Acton among his contemporaries, Brackenbury Scholar at Balliol, his brilliance made an immediate mark. Sir Maurice Bowra, when Vice-Chancellor of Oxford many years later, remembered him as the cleverest boy of his generation.

And yet, as he himself well knew, he never fully lived up to his gifts. A man of acute self-knowledge, he had learnt, too early, perhaps, to take their exact measure. "The more books we read", runs the opening sentence of *The Unquiet Grave*, "the sooner we perceive that the only function of a writer is to produce a masterpiece". His two most enduring books, *Enemies of Promise* and *The Unquiet Grave,* close as they come to being precisely that, may also be regarded as apologies for his failure to assemble his forces for a full-scale attack on the respect of posterity.

Connolly was a hard man to know. His Irish fantasy made him a delightful companion when he chose; but he could also be challengingly uncouth. Sir Harold Nicolson* noted with astonishment his early habit of marking his place in a book at the breakfast table with a strip of bacon; and his friends, however devoted, retained a store of anecdotes which turned on similar quirks of manners and sense.

Partly he was revenging himself at such moments on a physical envelope which he found unsatisfactory. His aesthetic perfectionism extended to the appearance of the human race, and he resented for himself a tubby, loose-hung frame rather than that of the Apollo he felt he deserved to be. Women he cherished—he was three times married and a notable victim in the lists of love—and here again he suffered for not, in his own view, living up to the difficult role of a great lover. So that, as time passed, a sombre introspection, not lightened by a mixture of extravagant natural tastes, heavy necessary expenses and small financial resources, crushed his inborn wit and made him on the whole a melancholy companion, yet always capable of enchanting the company by a sudden shaft.

To his tried friends he was kindness itself, generous, inexhaustibly hospitable. He loved good food and drink (in studied moderation)—few things in life gave him greater pleasure than to inherit Richard Wyndham's excellent cellar; he enjoyed the best company and sang melodiously for his supper; and with the years his remembered jokes, if rarer, were no less treasured.

His journalistic career began under Desmond MacCarthy and Raymond Mortimer on *The New Statesman and Nation.* He acknowledged of these editors that they did much "to soften a coarse and violent streak in me which was always rebelling against literature, and which took refuge in a mutinous and iconoclastic sloth". He made an immediate reputation as a reviewer of new fiction. He may not have been a favourite with the novelists themselves, for he often used their work as a chopping block for the exercise of his wit, but how extraordinarily funny he could be may be seen in such pieces as "Ninety Years of Novel-Reviewing" and "Mr. Mossbros takes the Class", reprinted in *The Condemned Playground.* As the same volume shows he was a master parodist who used parody as a tool of criticism.

His most signal achievement in journalism, however, was as editor of *Horizon,* the monthly magazine he founded with Stephen Spender and Peter Watson on the eve of war in 1939. No magazine could have been less "official" or predictable than *Horizon;* but it held its own as a typically British institution throughout the war. It was in great demand outside Britain, and its value as an element in the outside world's idea of Britain when at war can hardly be exaggerated. It was especially appreciated in the United States. Orwell's most characteristic essays appeared in the magazine, as did Evelyn Waugh's* *The Loved One,* Mary MacCarthy's *Oasis,* and Augustus John's* autobiography; writers met in its pages for the first time included Angus Wilson, Denton Welch and J. Maclaren

Ross; it contained some of the best reporting of the war and its aftermath and was tireless in the interpretation of French art and thought during the first years of liberation.

Connolly conducted *Horizon* until 1950, when he brought it to a close largely because he had become bored with editorship. From then on he was a regular reviewer in *The Sunday Times*.

His secondary books included *The Rock Pool*, a disappointing novel rather in the manner of Norman Douglas's *South Wind*, *The Modern Movement*, a critical sketch of contemporary writing which displayed a foible for categorical list-making rather than original insight, *The Missing Diplomats*, reminiscences of Guy Burgess and Donald McLean, and collections such as *Ideas and Places* and *Previous Convictions*. A further collection of pieces, *The Evening Colonnade*, appeared in 1973.

Throughout, his taste was for what he called "the high peaks of the secondary range"—Horace, the Virgil of the *Georgics* and *Eclogues*, Villon, Montaigne, La Rochefoucauld, Leopardi. The choice helps to define the man. It was in *The Unquiet Grave*, an intimate journal made up of reflections and maxims, that he most completely revealed himself, in the guise of Palinurus, the helmsman of the Aeneid, who fell overboard while asleep at the tiller. The man who emerges was very much of his time: a liberal with little faith in the durability of liberal values, a hedonist with a nervous tendency to shy away from the reality of pleasure, a lover of the Mediterranean in all its aspects, yet at the same time a victim of *Angst*, self-doubting, sure of one thing only: that man justifies himself in the masterpieces of art.

Connolly was made C.B.E. in 1972.

November 27, 1974.

Lord Constantine, M.B.E., the spectacular and popular West Indian all-round cricketer, the greatest of all fieldsmen and an effective campaigner against colour prejudice, died in London on July 1, 1971. He was 69.

To a wide public in the nineteen-twenties and thirties he was the personification of emergent West Indian cricket and he used his standing as a games-player with judicious dignity to further the causes of political independence and social equality for his people.

He was born in Diego Martin, near Port of Spain, Trinidad, on September 21, 1901, the son of Lebrun Constantine—"Old Cons"—a sugar plantation foreman who was a member of the West Indian teams which toured England in 1900 and 1906, and the first West Indian to score a century in England.

Family practice with his father, his uncle, Victor Pascall, a slow left arm bowler for Trinidad, and his mother keeping wicket,

early instilled cricket into the younger Constantine. But obvious natural aptitude and keen fielding, rather than any outstanding figures, won him a place in the Trinidad team in 1921. He had played in only three first-class matches when he was told to be ready to join the 1923 West Indian side for England. On that tour, apart from a brave innings of 60 not out in a total of 97 against Derbyshire, he made an impression only by brilliant fielding at cover point. During the next five years in the West Indies, however, unremitting practice made him a genuinely fast bowler and a sure slip fieldsman while, through his fine eye, natural timing and speed of reaction, he became an explosive, if inconsistent, attacking batsman. Those years of application bore fruit in England in 1928.

In the three Tests of that summer—the first ever played by West Indies— he achieved no more than five wickets and 89 runs; but on the tour he became the first West Indian to perform the "double" of 1,000 runs and 100 wickets in a season.

Above all, a single match established him and his country's cricket in English public imagination. At Lord's in June, Middlesex, batting first, declared at 352 for six wickets and put out the West Indians for 230 in which only Constantine, with 86, scored more than 30. In the Middlesex second innings Constantine took seven wickets for 57. West Indies, needing 259 to win, were 121 for five, and apparently losing, when Constantine went in. He hit with such force that one straight drive broke the finger of the bowler, Hearne,* and went on to strike the pavilion rails and fly up into the seating. Constantine scored 103 out of 133 in an hour, and won the match for the West Indians by three wickets.

From that day until he retired from all play some 30 years later, Constantine attracted crowds as few other cricketers have ever done. In 1929 he was engaged by the Nelson club and except in 1939, when he joined the West Indies team in England, he continued as a League professional with considerable success for Nelson, Rochdale, Bootle, Crompton and Windhill until 1948.

For some years he bowled at such pace that he was menacing to the best batsmen even on good wickets. Of little more than average height, wide-shouldered and long-armed, he took a short, lively run and bowled off a fine leap with a high action and a full follow-through. He developed many variations, including a well disguised and controlled slower ball, which was often a leg break or googly and, as he grew older, took many wickets by guile and accuracy. In the deep field he made catches that seemed far beyond his reach, swooped to pick up at full speed with an apparently boneless ease, and his throwing, on or off balance, was strong and accurate; while close to the wicket his catching was bewilderingly quick and certain. As a batsman he was prepared to attack any bowler; he cut, pulled, hooked and drove exuberantly, produced some remarkable, spontaneous

strokes to counter the unexpected, and struck some blows of phenomenal length. The essence of his cricket was that by batting, bowling or fielding he might win any match from almost any situation.

Before he left the West Indies Constantine had, in the words of his fellow Trinidadian, C. L. James, "revolted against the revolting contrast between his first-class status as a cricketer and his third-class status as a man". Professionalism enabled him to settle in England to study law and to argue the causes of West Indian self-government and racial tolerance. In many Lancashire towns where he played cricket, there were children who had never before seen a coloured man; and, by speeches and lectures, and the publication of pamphlets, he did much to foster understanding of his people's problems. He and his wife fitted happily into Lancashire life and in 1963 the freedom of the Borough of Nelson was bestowed on him.

In 18 Test matches for West Indies between 1928 and 1939 he scored 641 runs at an average of 19.42 and took 58 wickets at 30.10. These are unimpressive figures but at Georgetown in 1930, his nine wickets for 122 linked with Headley's two centuries to give West Indies their first win in a Test match; and in his last Test, at The Oval in 1939, he took five English first innings wickets for 75 and then scored 78 out of 103 in less than an hour. Because he spent so much of his career in the leagues, he played only 194 innings in first-class cricket; scored 4,451 runs and took 424 wickets. Figures, however, cannot reflect his aggressive approach, tactical acumen or his quality as an athlete, entertainer and match-winner, nor prove the fact, which his contemporaries never doubted, that he was the finest all-round fieldsman the game of cricket has ever known.

He remained in England during the Second World War. From 1942 to 1947 he was a welfare officer, with particular responsibility for West Indian workers, in the Ministry of Labour and National Service, and received the M.B.E. for his services. In 1944 he took action against The Imperial Hotel, London for "failing to receive and lodge him" and won the nominal damages he sought.

In 1954, after a long struggle, he passed his Bar Finals and was called by the Middle Temple in 1954; he became an honorary Master of the Bench in 1963. He published his book *Colour Bar* in 1954. When he returned to Trinidad, he was called to the Bar there and elected as a People's Nationalist Movement member for Tunapuna to the first Trinidad Legislature, in which he became Minister of Works and Transport.

Disillusioned by politics, he did not stand for re-election in 1961 and in the following year was appointed High Commissioner for Trinidad and Tobago in London, a post he held until his resignation in 1964, after trying to help to solve difficulties in Bristol when busmen were said to be operating a colour bar. He subsequently practised in the English courts, wrote and broadcast on cricket, and, in 1966 became a member of the Race Relations Board. He was knighted in 1962. In 1967 he became Rector of St. Andrews University; in 1969 he became a life peer. He was also a governor of the B.B.C.

A man of quiet manner, religious conviction and high principles, Constantine was popular on all the many levels at which he lived and worked. He married, in 1927, Norma Agatha Cox; they had one daughter.

July 2, 1971.

Archbishop of Constantinople—See Archbishop Athenagoras.

Fernand Contandin—See Fernandel.

Sir James Cook, F.R.S., F.R.I.C., eminent both as a scientist and as a university administrator, sometime Regius Professor of Chemistry in the University of Glasgow and Vice-Chancellor of the Universities of Exeter and East Africa, died on October 21, 1975 at the age of 74.

Born in London on December 10, 1900, James Wilfred Cook graduated in chemistry at University College and became lecturer in chemistry at the Sir John Cass Technical Institute in 1920. There he worked with E. du Barry Barnett on the chemistry of anthracene derivatives and obtained his Ph.D. degree. During this time he supplied some anthracene derivatives to Sir Ernest Kennaway for his work on carcinogenesis and, as a result, Kennaway invited Cook to join the staff of the Royal Cancer Hospital in 1929. Cook remained at the Cancer Hospital for ten years, becoming Reader in Pathological Chemistry in 1932 and Professor of Chemistry in 1939.

It was there that he made his outstanding contribution to cancer research, first demonstrating the carcinogenicity of polycyclic benzenoid hydrocarbons and then isolating from coal tar its main carcinogenic component, which he showed to be the pentacyclic hydrocarbon, 3:4 benzpyrene. This work was of great importance since it showed, for the first time, that cancer could be induced by minute quantities of a pure chemical compound. Further work showed that this property was shared by other polycyclic hydrocarbons and that there was a revealing correlation between structure and carcinogenicity. The importance of the work was recognized by the award, jointly to Cook and Kennaway, in 1936 of the Prize of International Union Against Cancer and by Cook's election in 1938 to the Royal Society.

In 1939 Cook was appointed to the Regius Chair of Chemistry in Glasgow, which he occupied for sixteen years. The move from what was essentially a research post to the leadership of a large and vigorous university department with heavy teaching commitments Cook took in his stride, finding time also to serve, *inter alia*, as President of the Royal Institute of Chemistry from 1949 to 1951 and as a Member of the University Grants Committee from 1950 to 1954. In Glasgow his work on polycyclic hydrocarbons continued unabated while he added to it outstanding contributions to the chemistry of colchicine and the tropolones.

In 1954 he became Principal of the University College of the South West and negotiated the final metamorphosis of the College into the University of Exeter, of which he became, in 1955, the first Vice-Chancellor. During his eleven years in Exeter he guided and supervised the growth of the university from a small university college of fewer than a thousand students, preparing for London External Degrees, to a fully-fledged independent university of over two thousand students. This growth in numbers was accompanied by the erection of many fine new buildings, a task into which Cook threw himself with great energy; when the university made him an Honorary LL.D. in 1967 the Public Orator was able to say of him, with no exaggeration, "Si monumentum requiris, circumspice".

In Cook, the university found an able and energetic administrator, a wise leader, a devoted and successful advocate and, in truth, a second founder. During his time in Exeter, Cook served on many Government committees and showed a great interest in higher education in developing countries, especially in Africa. The honorary Directorship of the M.R.C. Carcenogenic Substances Research Unit, in Exeter, enabled him to keep in touch with organic chemistry.

When Cook retired from Exeter in 1965, it was obvious that he had much more valuable work to do and that his career had by no means ended. In 1966 he became Vice-Chancellor of the federal University of East Africa; in this post he most successfully welded the constituent colleges at Nairobi, Kampala and Dar-es-Salaam into a coherent whole, now unfortunately dismembered, and greatly raised their standing.

He retired from East Africa in 1970 only to become, in 1971, Chairman of the Academic Advisory Committee of the New University of Ulster, at Coleraine; he had already, since 1965, been Chairman of the Academic Planning Board and he devoted much thought to this new venture, travelling regularly to Northern Ireland to take part in the counsels of the new university.

His eminence was recognized by the knighthood conferred on him in 1963 and by honorary doctorates from five universities. He was Pedler Lecturer of the Chemical Society in 1950 and Davy Medallist of the Royal Society in 1954.

In 1930 he married Elsie Griffiths, by whom he had three sons; her death, in 1966, left him a very lonely man. He found happiness again when, in 1967, he married Vera Ford, who survives him.

Cook was not only exceptionally able, but also exceptionally hard-working and busy. Perhaps for this latter reason he presented to many a rather cold and aloof exterior; all those with whom he came into contact knew him to be just and fair in all his dealings.

October 24, 1975.

Dame Gladys Cooper, D.B.E., whose death at the age of 82 occurred on November 17, 1971 at her home at Henley on Thames, was an actress to whom the English theatre gave much in the way of opportunities in her youth, and who repaid it by giving much to the English theatre, through the matured vigour of her character and of her work whenever she returned from Hollywood and Broadway in later years.

She was known to the British public as in turn a picture-postcard beauty and golden-haired supporting player in Edwardian musical comedy, a straight actress who quickly developed into an actress manageress, and a freelance actress of international reputation in films and television as well as in the theatre. In 1967 she was created D.B.E.

Gladys Cooper was the eldest daughter by his second marriage of Charles Frederick Cooper, editor of *The Epicure*, a journal founded by himself. She was born on December 18, 1888 at Lewisham, and auditioned at a voice-trial at the Vaudeville Theatre in 1905, landing her first job with a touring company in Seymour Hicks's *Bluebell in Fairyland*. She made her London debut in a musical comedy in 1905, and in the following year was engaged by George Edwardes, impresario of the Gaiety and Daly's, for whom she worked in the chorus and understudied, and later played small parts in *The Girls of Gottenberg, Havana,* and *Our Miss Gibbs*.

She was already a picture-postcard beauty, and married to Herbert John Buckmaster, but, doubting whether she would become a star of musical comedy, she allowed herself to be considered for a part in a straight play adapted by Somerset Maugham,* which Charles Hawtrey was about to produce. The part was hers, but George Edwardes would not release her, and it was two years later that she made her first impression in the "legitimate" theatre as Cecily in a revival of *The Importance of Being Earnest*. Having held her own modestly in Shaw, Galsworthy, Arnold Bennett and Edward Knoblock, she was promoted by Gerald Du Maurier in 1913 to the leading part in a revival of Sardou's *Diplomacy*.

Soon after the outbreak of war in 1914, she accompanied Seymour Hicks's concert party to the British Front in France. Two comedies at the Playhouse, in one of which she played opposite Hawtrey, were followed by an invitation from Frank Curzon to join him in management at that theatre. During her first tenure she appeared in a melodrama and four comedies, two of them with Hawtrey. Although her return to it, after playing in Maeterlinck and Ellen Terry's old part in Wills's *Olivia*, was made in a dramatic role, her ambition to repeat the success of her Dora in *Diplomacy* was not gratified until the revival in 1922, with Du Maurier directing and with the cast wearing modern dress, of *The Second Mrs. Tanqueray*. It was a great night for the ex-Gaiety Girl. She proved that it was possible to be the most beautiful actress in the theatre and also to carry guns enough for the most famous of Pinero's dramatic heroines.

She fired as many guns, or more, as Sudermann's Magda, another role associated with Mrs. Patrick Campbell, and, having given herself a change in a French farce and as Peter Pan, she reverted to Pinero in a revival of *Iris*, which would not, however, have prospered if the cast had not been reinforced after a while by her partner in two films which she had made in the early 1920s, Ivor Novello. The date was out of Pinero, even of Pinero in a Molyneux model. It was necessary to find contemporary plays of the right weight.

There could have been no better vehicle for her and Gerald Du Maurier than Frederick Lonsdale's *The Last of Mrs. Cheyney* (comedy with a background of drama), and for her alone than Maugham's *The Letter* (all drama), which was her first venture as lessee of the Playhouse in 1927, and out of which she made £40,000 by the end of her first provincial tour. Thereafter the search for a suitable play, while it brought her Maugham's *The Sacred Flame, Cynara* (with Du Maurier) and a drama by a new writer, Keith Winter, was so arduous and so seldom wholly successful that she gave up the lease of the Playhouse after six years.

In 1934 Gladys Cooper made her American debut in Winter's *The Shining Hour*, and although it was followed by a successful season in London, in 1935 she returned to New York to play Desdemona and Lady Macbeth opposite the English-born actor Philip Merivale, whom—her marriage to her second husband, Sir Neville Pearson, Bt., being dissolved—she married in Chicago in May, 1937, while they were on tour together.

The Merivales appeared jointly in London under Basil Dean's direction in that same year, and in Shakespeare and Aristophanes in Regent's Park some months later; but before the end of 1938 they were both in New York in different plays, and it was there that Gladys Cooper received soon afterwards her first offer from Hollywood. Having finished the film *Rebecca*, she decided to stay on and, provided other film engagements were forthcoming, to make a home in California for her husband and herself which might also be used by the children of their previous marriages and by her sisters. She found herself engaged for a succession of parts such as Bette Davis's

screen mother in *Now, Voyager*, a nun in *The Song of Bernadette* (with Jennifer Jones) and a duchess in *Mrs. Parkington* (with Greer Garson), for some of which she received Academy Awards for the best supporting role of the year. From being totally unknown to American film-goers she came to receive more fan letters than she had had in London in her heyday; and so, what with work and the dislocation caused by the Second World War, she did not return to England until April 1945—and then to make a film, *Beware of Pity*—and did not reappear on a London stage until 1948—and then only on three months' leave from M.G.M.—when, a widow now in private life, she played opposite Francis Lister in Peter Ustinov's *The Indifferent Shepherd*.

After two years she was in England again, but in a comedy that was not thought worthy of her. It was her third post-war play, Noël Coward's *Relative Values*, that gave her, since she was perfect casting for the part of a shrewd, witty and beautiful white-haired dowager countess, the opportunity and, since it settled down to a long run, the time to reestablish herself in the post-war English theatre as a personality and a mistress of her craft.

After two more plays in London and Enid Bagnold's *The Chalk Garden* in New York, she answered an appeal to take over her old part in the London production of the last-named play, from which Edith Evans was forced to withdraw temporarily because of sickness. Gladys Cooper, now nearing her seventieth year, left Long Island within a matter of hours, arrived in London on the following morning, and played at the Haymarket that same night. Perhaps it was not surprising that her next play in London should have been an anticlimax, indeed a disaster, and that its two successors were quickly forgotten. But *A Passage To India* in New York in 1962 was at any rate a distinguished enterprise, and George Cukor's colour film *My Fair Lady* gave audiences all over the world the chance of seeing her, as Mrs. Higgins, wear Cecil Beaton's re-creations of the fashions of 1912, a year in which Gladys Cooper had once played six new parts successively on the West End stage.

She was seen as Mrs. Tabret in a revival of Maugham's *The Sacred Flame* in 1967, and later that year in *Let's All Go Down The Strand* by the late Hugh Williams and his wife, Margaret. In 1969 she appeared in another of Mr. and Mrs. Williams's plays, *His, Hers and Theirs*.

She celebrated her eightieth birthday while playing in Ira Wallach's *Out of the Question* at the St. Martin's on the night of December 18, 1968. The management had bought back all the tickets for the evening's performance and filled the stalls with her family and friends. At a point at which her stage grandson should have appeared, Robert Morley, her son-in-law in real life, who was not in the cast, came into view carrying a tray clinking with champagne and glasses.

She was back on the stage again in 1971 in a revival of *The Chalk Garden* at the Haymarket, playing the role she created in 1955 in New York. Illness compelled her to give up the idea of repeating her performance of it at the O'Keefe Centre in Toronto.

By her marriage to H. J. Buckmaster, which was dissolved, Gladys Cooper had a daughter Joan who married Robert Morley, the actor, and a son John who began his stage career in 1934. By her second husband, Sir Neville Pearson, she had a daughter who went on the stage under the name of Sally Cooper, and who married in 1961 the actor Robert Hardy.

November 18, 1971.

John Cooper, an outstanding British athlete who won two silver medals in the 1964 Olympics, was among those killed in a Turkish airline crash on March 3, 1974. He was 33.

Britain won four gold medals in the 1964 Olympic athletics but Cooper's silver medals in the 400 metres hurdles, and then the 4 x 400 metres relay, were arguably the best all-round performance by any member of that British team.

What made these successes all the more remarkable was that Cooper lacked suppleness for hurdling and basic speed for running on the flat. But his extraordinary competitive spirit pulled him from fourth to second behind the American Rex Cawley in the last few strides of the 400 metres hurdles. On the third stage of the 1,600 metres relay Cooper ran the greatest race of his career, with a 45.4sec. leg, though he had never before beaten 47sec.

Several months later Cooper, who was not one given to dramatic exaggeration, said that on the last bend of that relay leg his effort was so great that he blacked out. But he still maintained his poise to give the baton for the last lap to his friend and fellow Loughborough student, Robbie Brightwell, who ensured the silver medals went to Britain.

Cooper, who was married only in October 1973 after leaving teaching to work with Brightwell for a sports goods firm, was mentally as well as physically hard when it came to top class competition. For all his tenacity he had a no-nonsense brand of humour which brought him many friends in the sport.

March 5, 1974.

Sir (Vincent) Zachary Cope, M.D., M.S., F.R.C.S., consulting surgeon to St. Mary's Hospital, Paddington, died on December 28, 1974 at the age of 93.

His lasting claim to surgical fame rests upon his world-wide influence in improving the standard of early diagnosis of acute emergency conditions in the abdomen by his classic little book entitled *The Early Diagnosis of the Acute Abdomen*. Published in 1921, it has been translated into the French, Spanish, Portuguese, Italian, German and Greek languages and is still selling freely. During the Second World War he played a prominent part in the direction and best use of medical manpower and afterwards in the nation-wide survey of hospital accommodation. In his retirement he turned his attention to writing medical history.

Vincent Zachary Cope was born in Hull on February 14, 1881, being the youngest child of a Non-conformist minister. In 1890 the family moved to London where the rest of his life was spent. He was educated at the Westminster City School where in 1899 he was awarded the gold medal as head boy. Gaining a scholarship to St. Mary's Hospital Medical School he came under the influence of Augustus Waller, the inventor of the electrocardiograph, and Almroth Wright. After holding several junior appointments at St. Mary's and the London Temperance Hospitals he became surgical registrar to the former and in 1911 he was elected a member of the honorary staff, while in 1912 he became surgeon to the Bolingbroke Hospital, both of which institutions he continued to serve until the end of his active career.

His association with the Royal College of Surgeons of England was close and long continued. Taking his F.R.C.S. in 1901, he was elected to the council in 1940 and upon several occasions had delivered Hunterian and Arris and Gale Lectures. As vice-president he was appointed Bradshaw Lecturer in 1949 and Tomes and Vicary Lecturer in 1952. He took an active part in the affairs of the Royal Society of Medicine and the Medical Society of London of which he was Lettsomian Lecturer, Orator and President.

In 1941 Cope was appointed Sector Officer of No. 6 Sector of the Emergency Health Service of London, and thus began a long period of service with the Ministry of Health, which led to his becoming chairman of many committees dealing with manpower and hospital facilities.

He headed the team which surveyed the hospitals of the South-West region of England, their findings being published in a Blue Book. In 1949 the Minister of Health and the Secretary of State for Scotland set up a series of eight committees to consider the supply and demand, training and qualifications of eight groups of medical auxiliaries, and Cope was made chairman of each of these committees. This entailed heavy work but it was completed in 18 months and the report was issued in 1951. For all this devoted service Cope was knighted in 1953.

During his active life in practice Cope published monographs upon *The Surgical Aspects of Dysentery, Actinomycosis* and *The Treatment of the Acute Abdomen* in addition to his much more famous *Diagno-*

sis of the Acute Abdomen. After his retirement however he became interested in medical history. Under the general guidance of Sir Arthur McNalty he edited the volumes on Surgery and Pathology in the Medical History of the Second World War. He published biographies of Cheselden and Sir Harry Thompson, wrote the history of the Royal College of Surgeons of England and of St. Mary's Hospital Medical School. From his pen came also *Florence Nightingale and the Doctors, Six Disciples of Florence Nightingale, Famous General Practitioners*, a life of Sir John Tomes, and a short account of the career of Almroth Wright.

Zachary Cope was the soul of kindness and he could never bring himself to say an unkind word of any man; further, he was a delightful and most considerate chief with whom to work. In his later years he amused himself and others by writing verse and upon one occasion lectured to students for 30 minutes on the surgery of duodenal ulcer in this medium. When he was vice-president of the Royal College of Surgeons it fell to him to propose the toast of the guests at the annual Hunterian Dinner. The speeches had not been inspiring but Cope gave his whole speech in verse, much to the evident enjoyment and amusement of the royal guests who had graced the occasion with their presence. Many younger consultants and a host of general practitioners will remember him with affection as a wise and gentle surgeon, kind and considerate to his patients.

He was twice married; there is one daughter of the second marriage and she alone survives him.

December 31, 1974.

Bainbridge Copnall, M.B.E., F.R.B.S., President of the Royal Society of British Sculptors from 1961 to 1966, died on October 18, 1973 at the age of 70.

He was distinguished for his versatility, for his experiments with a wide range of methods and materials, and for the high standard of much of the resulting sculpture. His work ranged from the traditional portraiture and architectural carving of his early years to large-scale works in new media, like fibre glass, and to experiments with form in which representational elements mingled with abstract conceptions.

Edward Bainbridge Copnall was born in Cape Town, South Africa, in 1903 and went to England when he was small. He was educated at the Liverpool Institute and Skinners School, and received his art training at Goldsmiths College and the Royal Academy Schools. He left the latter in 1924 to earn a living as a portrait painter, and, as he himself put it, he painted all comers at nominal fees for several years, meeting with a modest success. In 1927 he met Eric Kennington, whose work made a deep impression on him. As a result he decided to

turn to sculpture as a medium of expression.

An important early commission was for decorative sculpture and painting for the new building of the Royal Institute of British Architects in Portland Place which was erected in 1931-34.

His range of work increased during the thirties and included wood carvings for the liners Queen Mary and Queen Elizabeth, illustrating the history of shipping; and engraved glass screens for the latter ship and for the Odeon Cinema in Leicester Square. Among his important sculptures during this period was one of the stone figures that occupy the corners of the river facade of the Adelphi building.

During the Second World War Copnall served as a camouflage officer in Northern Africa, the Near East and Italy, and lectured on deception and camouflage to a large number of troops. He was awarded the M.B.E. for his services. At the end of the war he was given a studio at the British School at Rome where he painted portraits of senior officers. On his return to England he was headmaster of the Sir John Cass College of Art from 1945 to 1953.

Always an experimenter with materials and new effects, in the 1950s he began making figures of fibre glass. Fibre glass and resin being light in weight and permitting a speedy technique Copnall realized its potentialities. His first figure in this medium was the "Swan Man" made for the I.C.T. building on Putney Bridge. This was followed by other large figures in fibre glass. While experimenting with various media, and making immense figures for buildings, Copnall continued to carve in stone and among his later works of this kind were the balcony fronts in Carrara marble of the office building that occupies the St. James's Theatre site, the subjects of the carvings being actors and playwrights associated with the theatre, among them Oscar Wilde, Sir George Alexander, Lord Olivier and Vivien Leigh*.

He married in 1927 Edith Muriel Dancy, by whom he had two sons and a daughter.

October 19, 1973.

Dr. Andrew Cordier, who died on July 11, 1975 at the age of 74, was one of the original members of the United Nations Secretariat and, as Executive Assistant to the Secretary-General, occupied for nearly sixteen years a central position in the development and activity of the organization under the Secretary-Generalships of Trygve Lie* and Dag Hammarskjöld.*

On leaving the United Nations he became Dean of the School of International Relations at Columbia University, a post which he combined with many other activities in the international world in which he was such a familiar figure.

Andrew Wellington Cordier was born near Canton, Ohio, on March 3, 1901. He graduated from Hartville High School in

1918 and taught at Greentown High School from 1919 to 1921. In addition to numerous honorary degrees he held a B.A. degree from Manchester College, Indiana, and a Ph.D. degree from the University of Chicago.

Cordier was Chairman of the Department of History and Political Science at Manchester College from 1927 to 1944, and lecturer on social sciences for the Indiana University Extension Division from 1929 to 1944. Between 1928 and 1961 he travelled extensively, studying crises in the Sudetenland, Danzig and, following the Chaco War, in Paraguay.

From 1944 to 1946 Cordier served in the State Department as expert on International Security and later as an expert in the United States delegation to the San Francisco Conference which founded the United Nations, and as adviser to United States Senator Arthur H. Vandenberg. In 1945 he was sent to London to assist in setting up the United Nations. He was appointed Executive Assistant to Trygve Lie, first Secretary-General of the United Nations early in 1946.

As Executive Assistant to the Secretary-General, Cordier was responsible for co-ordinating United Nations activities and programmes, much as a Chief of Staff does in a large military headquarters. He was also responsible for the organization of the sessions of the General Assembly and was the principal adviser on procedure and organization to the successive presidents of the General Assembly from 1946 to 1962.

Cordier's main motivation was a passionate interest in international organization and a deep loyalty to and love of the United Nations. He was one of those original members of the Secretariat who learnt early to subordinate national feelings to loyalty to the international organization and who devotedly served it to the exclusion of narrower or more factional interests.

A genial, burly, apparently rather bumbling man with a strong dislike of bureaucratic procedures, Cordier had a fantastic memory and a flair for informal negotiation and organization. Thus, without seeming to impose on or dictate to his secretariat colleagues and to national representatives, he kept the often tangled strings of United Nations operation firmly in his hands (and in his head) and was a most effective chief assistant to the Secretary-General.

This was not always easy. His first Chief, Trygve Lie, was, for all his physical bulk, a mercurial man, inclined to touchiness and unpredictable reactions, and Cordier very often found himself smoothing over or ironing out the results of some unexpected outburst or initiative of his Chief.

The characters and whims of the successive presidents of the Assembly, an office which tends to bring out latent megalomania, also presented a constant challenge to Cordier's good nature, powers of diplomacy and efficiency. That the machine ran as well as it did in the early years of the United Nations was due in considerable

measure to his steadiness and devotion.

The coordination of the Secretariat, especially in its initial years, required tact and elasticity. The McCarthy period, which chose targets freely and unscrupulously among American Secretariat officials, also put the United Nations staff under the most disagreeable strain in the years from 1951 to 1954. Cordier, as a senior and centrally-placed United States official, was in a very exposed position at this period.

Hammarskjöld's appointment as Secretary-General in April 1953 heralded a period of welcome change and constructive development in the affairs of the Secretariat. Starting diffidently and quietly, Hammarskjöld set about restoring the morale of the Secretariat and building up the confidence of governments in its objectivity and effectiveness. In this great and successful effort Cordier and Ralph Bunche were the closest collaborators of the Secretary-General.

Cordier, with his bluff good humour and warm personality, was an ideal complement to Hammarskjöld, the austere, intellectual Swede. It was a relationship of mutual respect and affection which lasted until Hammarskjöld's death in September 1961, and it says much for the strength of the mutual regard of the two men that both their professional and their personal relationships were undisturbed by the successive crises and challenges that confronted Hammarskjöld as Secretary-General.

Cordier would have been the first to say that these were the most rewarding and fascinating years of his life and that, after them, any other occupation would be something of an anti-climax.

The development of the potentialities of the Secretary-General's office were the central theme of a period which saw, among other events, the release of the United States prisoners in China, the first international conferences on the Peaceful Uses of Atomic Energy, the Suez crisis and the first United Nations force, and the Lebanese and Congo crises.

Despite his undoubted objectivity and loyalty to the United Nations, Cordier's American nationality was inevitably a potential target for attack from the Communist countries, and it is remarkable that this attack in fact only developed as late as 1960 in relation to the United Nations operation in the Congo. Cordier was sent to Leopoldville in September 1960, to take charge for the short period between Dr. Bunche's departure and the arrival of his successor as Officer-in-Charge in the Congo, Rajeshwar Dayal. His arrival in the Congo coincided with the crisis caused by the overt split between Prime Minister Lumumba* and President Kasavubu*, and the threat of serious disorders. To avert or circumscribe possible disorders, Cordier made the highly controversial decision to close temporarily the Leopoldville radio station and all airports. Whatever the merits of this decision, it was bound, affecting, as it did, Lumumba and a number of Soviet transport aircraft, to bring down a storm of criticism from the

Russians upon Hammarskjöld and upon Cordier.

He was supported loyally by Hammarskjöld in this episode, but it had already become necessary for Hammarskjöld to take cognizance of the pressure to reallot the national make-up of his immediate office, which at this time contained three senior Americans, Bunche, Cordier, and Heinrich Wieschhoff (who was killed with Hammarskjöld). Plans were therefore made to move Cordier to a post exclusively concerned with General Assembly affairs, a decision which, though it was inevitably a personal blow, he accepted loyally in the interests of the organization.

Cordier relinquished his post as Executive Assistant to C. V. Narasimhan of India in August 1961. One month later Hammarskjöld was killed. In early 1962 Cordier left the United Nations to become Dean of the new School of International Affairs at Columbia University.

At Columbia, Cordier built up the School of International Affairs, bringing into its work many figures who were, or had been, active in the international world. He also organized and raised funds for the great new building which was to house it. He remained active outside the University in a number of capacities, especially in ones concerning his late chief. He was a member of the American Committee for the Dag Hammarskjöld Foundation and organized the Hammarskjöld memorial lectures, later editing them for publication under the title *The Quest for Peace*. Other publications included (with K. L. Maxwell) *Paths to World Order* (1967), and (ed.) *The Public Papers of the Secretaries-General of the United Nations. Vols. 1-2 (1968-72)*.

Cordier is survived by his wife, a son and daughter and two grandchildren.

July 14, 1975.

Katharine Cornell, who died on June 9, 1974 aged 76, was among the most consistently admired and steadfastly modest American actresses of her time. Dark, tall, grave-voiced, not classically beautiful but compelling, she always suggested emotional reserves and never lost an audience's allegiance.

She was born in 1898, daughter of a Buffalo doctor who turned theatre manager. New York critics, when she acted there from 1916 to 1918 in a famous amateur company, the Washington Square Players, were already noticing her ability in long speeches. She went on to learn the professional business in "stock" at Buffalo and Detroit, made a sole London appearance in November 1919 as Jo in *Little Women,* and triumphed in New York as the loyal daughter in *A Bill of Divorcement* in 1921. She was now married to Guthrie McClintic who, after 1925, directed nearly all her plays.

During the 1920s, as a Broadway personage, entirely unaggressive, she was able to transform various tawdry pieces—*The Green Hat* for one. Although she was an ideal Candida, her talent far exceeded her parts until she entered management in 1931, choosing to play Elizabeth Moulton-Barrett, to which she brought all her tenderness and dignity, in Besier's *The Barretts of Wimpole Street,* after 28 other New York managements had refused it.

After this she seldom had a poor play. She played Juliet in 1934 with a touching truth. In 1936 her St. Joan expressed both the "village-girl-into-warrior" and the "dear child of God." Never letting her work lose its freshness (an article of faith with her), she had become the "first lady" of Broadway.

New York acclaimed her Oparre in *The Wingless Victory* (1936), her wise, loving Candida (1937), Linda in *No Time for Comedy* (1939 with Laurence Olivier), Masha in *The Three Sisters* (1942), and Shakespeare's Cleopatra (1947).

June 11, 1974.

Professor Charles A. Coulson, F.R.S., who died on January 7, 1974, was Professor of Theoretical Chemistry in the University of Oxford.

He was born at Dudley in 1910. He came of farming stock, though his father had already broken with tradition and was principal of the local technical college, a circumstance which no doubt influenced the son in his choice of a career.

He was educated at Clifton College and Trinity College, Cambridge, where he had a distinguished career, obtaining first class honours and a B in Part II of the Mathematical Tripos, followed by a first class in the Natural Science Tripos Part II (Physics). After a short period of research for his Ph.D., he was elected to a Fellowship at Trinity which he retained till 1938 when he left to take up a lectureship at St. Andrews. He returned south in 1945 to Oxford as one of the first Imperial Chemical Industries Fellows and Lecturers in Mathematics at University College, and in 1947 accepted a Professorship in Physics at King's College, London, returning finally to Oxford in 1952 to succeed E. A. Milne as the second Rouse Ball Professor of Applied Mathematics. He continued to hold this chair for twenty years, until in 1972 he became the first holder of a newly created chair of Theoretical Chemistry and head of a new department.

Coulson's first published paper, on the behaviour of monsoons, appeared in the *Quarterly Journal of the Meteorological Society* in 1931, while he was still an undergraduate, intending then to take up meteorological research. His interests subsequently centred in molecular physics and for a time he worked in the Low Temperature Research Station in Cambridge on the bacteriological effects of radio-active radiations. (He used occasionally to boast that he had been in turn meteorologist, mathematician, biologist, physicist and chemist). His many published papers dealt mainly with atomic and molecular structure and its chemical implications. He was the author of two much used textbooks on *Waves* and *Electricity and Magnetism* and a treatise on *Valence.*

Coulson, a Fellow of the Royal Society of Edinburgh since 1943, was elected to the Royal Society in 1950 and was the recipient of many academic honours, including the Sykes Gold Medal, the Pierre Lecompte de Nouy Prize, the Royal Society's Davy Medal and the Fellowship of the Royal Society of Liège. His university lectures were very carefully prepared and effectively delivered, attracting large undergraduate audiences, the largest theatre in the science area being regularly filled to capacity. He accepted invitations to lecture in most British universities, many European countries and America.

He spent much energy and effort in the organization of the new Mathematical Institute completed in 1963, and was happily involved in its activities for a long time. In this period, while he continued his more elementary lectures, he spent increasing effort and time on the organization of advanced study and research in theoretical chemistry, where his own reputation was increasingly recognized. His Tuesday colloquia on atomic and molecular structure were an important forum for the meeting of theorists and experimentalists. They were, indeed, one of the brightest features in the chemistry school at Oxford.

He founded a summer school for theoretical chemistry which was outstandingly successful. People went to it from all over Europe. When he became the first head of the new department of Theoretical Chemistry, it was a recognition of a development that had been created in Oxford through his own work.

Coulson was too young to have been one of the founders of modern theoretical chemistry, but he played a major part in developing and applying the basic principles. He was a disciple of the late Sir John Lennard-Jones and together they largely determined the course of the British school with its emphasis on the so-called molecular orbital method of treatment. He was a considerable originator of ideas but probably his more important role was as an expositor. In this, because of his grasp of the subject and his lucidity, he was superb both as a writer and as a lecturer. Because he combined high intellectual gifts with integrity and genuine friendliness, he had a profound influence on his research pupils and associates who venerated him. He thought of them as a family and the feeling was warmly reciprocated.

Brought up as a Methodist, he was deeply interested in religion and active in the life of the Christian Church, and was ever ready to accept invitations to preach and lecture. He was a former vice-president of the Methodist Conference. In 1965 he became chairman of Oxfam till 1971.

His family life (he was married in 1938 and had two sons and two daughters) was very happy, though his academic and religious commitments took him from home more than he would have liked.

January 8, 1974.

Professor W. H. B. Court, emeritus professor of Birmingham University, who died on September 30, 1971, was a scholar revered and respected by economic historians in Britain and abroad. He was 66.

Born in Cirencester in 1904, the son of a bookseller, he was set on an academic career by the inspiring influence of the headmaster of Newbury Grammar School, Edward Sharewood Smith, after his family moved to that town.

In 1923 he went to Cambridge to read history, having obtained a scholarship to Downing College. An admiration for R. H. Tawney's* work led to a research interest in the economic policy of the Calvinist colonizers of New England, and he went to Harvard as a Choate and Rockefeller fellow in 1927 to study this theme.

On his return however he was appointed to a post in the department of commerce at Birmingham University, and he was diverted to research in industrial history, the result being a classic study of regional industrial development, *The Rise of the Midland Industries* (1938). The powerful intellectual influence and close friendship of Sir Keith Hancock began to move Harry Court in the direction of imperial economic history, but the war intervened and he soon found himself in wartime administration in the Ministry of Shipping.

In 1948 Hancock offered him a place in the War Cabinet office to help with the official history of the war, and Court became responsible for the history of the coal industry in wartime, which made its appearance in 1951.

After the war Cambridge University Press wished to publish a short economic history of Britain, left unfinished at his death by Sir John Clapham. Court was invited to finish it, but his continuation grew into a separate volume, covering the period since 1750. This, published in 1954, has held the field as a textbook remarkably well considering the rapid changes and reinterpretations in modern British economic history, and it is still one of the most widely used in schools and universities. In 1965 he published an important collection of, and commentary upon, documents in British economic history between 1780 and 1914.

A volume of collected papers which he published in 1970, *Scarcity and Choice,* reflected his very wide interest in economic history, and was remarkable for the autobiographical essay "Growing up in an Age of Anxiety" which sensitively describes the formative years of a young academic in the shadow of the First World War.

Professor Court had in 1947 been invited to fill the newly created chair of economic history at Birmingham and to take the headship of a new department of economic and social history. He retired from the chair in 1970 but had continued to teach in the department until a few months before he died.

His distinction and the respect he commanded among his colleagues were recognized by his becoming Fellow of Downing College, Fellow of the British Academy and President of the Economic History Society. He had already made great progress with two projects which he had hoped would have been the fruit of a busy retirement: a study of the inter-relationship of war and economic history in the early twentieth century, and an addition of R.H. Tawney's unpublished papers which the Economic History Society had asked him to undertake.

Harry Court was a devoted academic whose scholarship was universally respected and whose quiet humility only served to emphasize his great and unconscious personal dignity. His consideration and kindness to his colleagues and his welcome to newcomers will be long remembered.

His width of reading and breadth of cultural interests were remarkable in an age of increasingly narrow specialization. But recent invasion of university life by political turbulence was not congenial to his gentle and rational temperament. He married in 1940 Audrey Kathleen, daughter of the Rev. A. E. Brown, C.I.E., and leaves a widow and three daughters.

October 6, 1971.

Dame Kathleen Courtney, D.B.E., well known in the United States and in Britain for her work, first for the League of Nations Union and afterwards for the United Nations Association, died on December 7, 1974, at the age of 96.

She was born on March 11, 1878, the daughter of Major D. C. Courtney, R.E., and was educated in private schools and at Lady Margaret Hall, Oxford. She took the Honours School of Modern Languages. Kathleen Courtney used that education, together with a clear vision and an exceptionally keen intelligence, in furthering the progress, first of women and later of mankind. She was hon. secretary of the National Union of Women's Suffrage Societies until 1914 when the First World War broke out. She was one of the founders of the Women's International League and afterwards did relief work with the Society of Friends in Austria, Poland and Greece. After studying the work of the League of Nations during many visits to Geneva she became a member of the executive committee of the League of Nations Union and did much speaking on its behalf. During the Second World War she continued this work and went on a highly successful speaking tour in the United States.

When the United Nations Association was formed in 1945, she became deputy chairman. In 1949 she was elected chairman of the executive and in the same year she was appointed joint president. She held both offices at the same time until she retired from the chairmanship in 1951.

Dame Kathleen was an admirable chairman. She was never confused nor misled by the multitude of resolutions, amendments and riders that came before her and was quite equal to a severe reprimand when she saw that it was needed. Yet her sternness was accompanied by a courtesy and grace which deprived it of sting. After much confused and blurred talk at a rather confused conference, Miss Courtney's speech would seem like a knife cutting through butter. She was a lively speaker with a sense of humour. Because of her wide knowledge of international affairs she was a great help in directing the policy of the United Nations Association. Her singleness of purpose and integrity shone through all her work. Her moral courage never failed and she had no thought of self in effort or achievement. She was created C.B.E. in 1946 and advanced to D.B.E. in 1952.

December 10, 1974.

Sir Noël Coward, died in Jamaica on March 26, 1973 at the age of 73.

Playwright, composer, director, actor, singer and dancer, he was also on occasion novelist, short-story writer and autobiographer, and he wrote fluent, entertaining light verse. None of the great figures of the English theatre has been more versatile than he. Whatever he had found to do was done with elegantly professional certainty of effect.

During his lifetime, his place in the theatre depended on no single vein of achievement but on his complete mastery of all the stage required for whatever work he had undertaken. One or two of his sentimental songs keep their place among the popular classics of light music; others, wittily mocking, are destined for a longer life. He had little voice, but no singer more naturally gifted could project the wit of these songs with half the effect of his own dry, *staccato* style. As an actor he carried naturalism to its farthest extremes, but in a number of roles like that of Lewis Dodd, the bohemian composer of Margaret Kennedy's *The Constant Nymph* in the 1920s and Shaw's King Magnus, in *The Apple Cart,* which he played in the Coronation season of 1953, he made every necessary effect with a delightful simplicity and punctuality, adding often to their weight by under-statement; he was too disciplined and conscientious an artist to essay what was beyond his capacity for effectiveness.

Posterity may reject his musicals as limited by the tastes and techniques of the 1920s and 1930s. His serious pieces—like *Cavalcade* among his musicals, *The Vortex* and *This Happy Breed* among his plays— may seem too easily sentimental to appeal to later ages, but they reflect the mood of their times with startling clarity. Of all his multifarious achievements, it is as a master of the comedy of manners that he is irreplaceable; his work in this special field is precisely written, and elegantly economical; it belongs to the classical tradition of Congreve, Sheridan, Wilde and Shaw.

Noël Coward was born at Teddington on December 16, 1899, the son of Arthur Coward, who worked for a firm of music publishers. His formal education was limited, for he made his first public appearance when he was 10, in a children's play *The Goldfish* at the Little Theatre. This brought an offer of a page boy's part, in *The Great Name,* from Charles Hawtrey, by whose skill, professionalism and disciplined craftsmanship Coward was permanently and beneficially influenced. Until 1915, when a mild attack of tuberculosis sent him for treatment to a sanatorium, he played a large number of juvenile parts. Because of his illness, when he reached military age in 1918 he was put into a labour battalion, but transferred from that to the Artists Rifles O.T.C.

After the war he joined Arthur Bourchier's company, but in 1920 he appeared in his own first play, a light and flimsy comedy, *I Leave it to You,* at the New Theatre; this was later followed by *The Young Idea,* and in 1923 he acted, sang and danced in *London Calling,* a revue of which he was part-author and part-composer. Changing his tone in 1925, he made his first great success with *The Vortex,* a somewhat melodramatic confrontation between a foolish, amorous middle-aged woman and the drug-taking Hamlet who was her son. In it, Coward found an authentic desperation in the self-conscious gaiety of the period after the First World War.

Hay Fever, written in a weekend in 1925, is a more dazzling achievement; like *The Importance of being Earnest,* it is pure comedy with no mission but to delight, and it depends purely on the interplay of characters, not upon elaborate comic machinery. This was followed by a series of musicals produced by C. B. Cochran which culminated in *Bitter Sweet,* probably the best of Coward's work for the musical stage, in 1929, and *Cavalcade,* a magnificently spectacular pageant of English history, from the death of Queen Victoria to the great slump, as it was seen through the eyes of an upper-middle-class family. *Cavalcade's* sincere, sentimental patriotism converted to Coward's cause many theatregoers who had distrusted the flippancy, the facility and the witty light-heartedness of his earlier work. Between the two musicals came *Private Lives,* a comedy as beautifully and smoothly made as *Hay Fever,* and no less witty but with a closer relevance to the moral concerns of its day. It exploits with inventive delight its author's gift for the retort discourteous, the comic inflation of the obvious, the urgent pursuit of the wild irrelevancy and his mastery of cleverly economical effect.

In the 1930s he was active in management in England and New York, in partnership with Alfred Lunt and Lynn Fontanne, and he continued to create plays and musicals with no less ease and effect, though for a time with less wit. In 1941, however, *Blithe Spirit* broke new ground, admitting the fantastic into his mocking picture of the age; it ran for nearly 2,000 performances. *Present Laughter*, written in the following year, displays moral perplexities like those of *Private Lives* against a theatrical background; the background is beautifully sketched and the problems are worked out with undiminished wit and hilarity. Between these two uncloudedly sunny plays came *In Which We Serve*, Coward's film in tribute to the Royal Navy, which he wrote and directed himself and in which he played the leading role. *This Happy Breed* achieved a working class *Cavalcade* of life between the two World Wars.

His later work, with occasional novels and short stories, a War Diary to link his pre-war autobiography *Present Indicative* to its post-war sequel, *Future Indefinite*, could not always recapture the wit and the tingling contemporaneity of his earlier plays. His musicals remained gracefully made and precise in effect, but they belong to the days before the war, and of his plays, only *Nude With Violin* and *Relative Values* seemed to awaken his sharp revelatory wit. Never idle, he made Feydeau's *Occupe-toi d'Amélie* into *Look after Lulu*, a typically Coward work even though it seemed unblushingly to allude to earlier effects and to earlier dialogue for effects he knew to be infallible. He appeared in small parts, beautifully observed, magnificently understated and extremely wittily played, in a variety of films in the later 1950s and the 1960s.

In 1964, a year in which Granada presented four of his plays on television under the omnibus title *A Choice of Coward*, he had the satisfaction of directing the National Theatre production of *Hay Fever* —the second modern play to be included in the National repertoire and the first play ever to be directed there by its author. This was followed by a musical version of *Blithe Spirit*, supervised but not written or composed by Coward, and by a revival of *Present Laughter*, with Nigel Patrick playing Coward's old part and directing. It ran for close on 400 performances at the Queen's. In 1972 Coward attended the first night of *Cowardy Custard* in London—a revue of his revue material. A revival of *Private Lives* with Maggie Smith and Robert Stephens opened in London. He also received an honorary degree from Sussex University.

"If and when", Coward had written in 1958, "she (success) chooses to leave me I shall not repine, nor shall I mourn her any more than I mourn other loved ones who have gone away. I do not approve of mourning, I only approve of remembering, and her I shall always remember gratefully and with pride."

By the time he reached his seventieth birthday in 1969, the year in which he was awarded a knighthood, it was possible to see how firmly the best of Coward's work was rooted in the English comic tradition. It is an attack in suitably comic terms on the insincere inflation of emotion, on the dishonesty of meaningless fine manners and unexamined conventions, and on the hypocrisy which masquerades as moral censoriousness; it rejects the easygoing, the undisciplined and the unprofessional. Claiming no more than, in the words of one of his songs, "a talent to amuse", Coward, his public had come to learn, amused them for their own good as well as their delight.

Coward was widely admired and loved in his own profession for his generosity and kindness to those who fell on hard times. Stories are told of the unobtrusive way in which he relieved the needs or paid the debts of old theatrical connexions who had no claim on him.

March 27, 1973.

John Cranko, the South African-born choreographer, died suddenly on June 26, 1973 after collapsing on an airliner that was taking him and the Stuttgart Ballet, of which he was director, back from the United States. The aircraft made an unscheduled stop in Dublin but Cranko was dead on arrival in hospital. He was 45.

Born in Rustenburg on August 15, 1927, John Cranko was educated in Johannesburg and started his career in Cape Town with the University of Cape Town Ballet and the Cape Town Ballet Club. His first ballet—a version of Stravinsky's *The Soldier's Tale*—was made when he was only 16 and three years later, when he went to England to join the Sadler's Wells Theatre Ballet, he had already composed several short works. Although engaged as a dancer, he showed Ninette de Valois a couple of his early creations. He was soon producing ballets for the company and by the 1950-51 season he was named as resident choreographer. In that season he composed his first great success, the witty *Pineapple Poll*, which has happily remained in the repertory ever since.

Within two years he was creating ballets both for the Sadler's Wells and Covent Garden stages, producing a remarkable sequence of handsomely crafted ballets, including *Bonne Bouche* (1952), *The Shadow* (1953), *The Lady and The Fool* (1954), culminating in his first full-length piece *The Prince of the Pagodas* (1957) which was additionally distinguished by being the first long British ballet with a specially commissioned score by Benjamin Britten.

His extraordinary fertility of invention also led him to work in the theatre—he wrote a review *Cranks* and he also staged works for the Paris Opera, for La Scala, Milan, and organized a season of ballets in collaboration with the painter John Piper at Henley-on-Thames. All this must seem but a prelude to his great achievement in Germany. Invited to produce *The Prince of the Pagodas* in Stuttgart in 1960, he was then asked to take responsibility for the Opera Ballet there, and in the following year he took up the post of Ballet Director. He swiftly succeeded in shaping a company that was ready to appear at the Edinburgh Festival of 1963 and which developed thereafter into one of the major companies of the world. His inspiring gifts as leader of the company, his creative fluency, and his deep-seated classicism—fruit of his training in the Petipa/Ashton repertory of the Royal Ballet—meant that the Stuttgart Ballet matured and grew safely as well as speedily.

His ballets covered an enormous range, from full-length works like *Onegin*, *The Taming of The Shrew*, *Romeo and Juliet* and *Carmen* (in which he showed Marcia Haydée to the world as a great ballerina) to short works that could be searchingly beautiful, like *Brouillards*, or outrageously funny like *Jeu de Cartes*. He had a uniquely theatrical approach to dancing; his narrative works were outstandingly effective and in everything he composed—serious ballets, experimental pieces like *Présence*, effortless comedies like *Taming of the Shrew*— Cranko showed a marvellous awareness of the possibilities of dance in the theatre. His monument is the fine company he created; which has been hailed in America and the U.S.S.R. as well as in Europe.

In a comment just after the news of his death had been announced, Kenneth MacMillan, director of the Royal Ballet and a friend and contemporary of Cranko, said: "Our careers went hand in hand. We worked together many times both in Stuttgart and London. His death is a great blow to the world of ballet and a great personal blow to me."

June 27, 1973.

Lord Crawford and Balcarres, the Premier Earl of Scotland, who gave service to the arts, died on December 13, 1975 at the age of 75.

David Robert Alexander Lindsay, 28th Earl of Crawford and 11th Earl of Balcarres, was born on November 25, 1900 and educated at Eton and Magdalen College, Oxford. His academic career was not particularly distinguished either at Eton or at Oxford; but he was brought up amidst the almost unbelievable treasures of his homes at Balcarres, at Haigh Hall, Wigan, and in Audley Square; inherited the scholarly tastes which had distinguished his ancestors for several generations; and at Eton formed a lifelong friendship with the master who shared his interests and lent him books on the fine arts.

In the First World War he was too

young to do more than get into uniform. On leaving Oxford, after serving for a time as Hon. Attaché in Rome, he was elected in 1924 as Conservative M.P. for the Lonsdale Division of Lancashire and so served until the death of his father in 1940 transferred him to the House of Lords, in which he sat as Baron Wigan. He had enjoyed the House of Commons, but the House of Lords, where from time to time he made effective speeches on subjects of which he had special knowledge, gave him more leisure for what was to be his life's work, the service of the arts in Britain.

In 1940 he was already a Trustee of the National Gallery; he was frequently reappointed to that board thereafter, and was presently associated, in several cases as Chairman, with the British Museum, the Tate Gallery, the National Galleries and the National Library of Scotland, the Fine Arts Commission, the Standing Commission on Museums and Galleries, the National and the Pilgrim Trusts, the National Art-Collections Fund, and less permanent bodies such as the Waverley Committee on the Export of Works of Art. He was a most valuable committee-man and an excellent chairman, businesslike without being aggressively so, and even-tempered, betraying his rare impatiences by signs seldom perceptible except to close friends.

Probably very few who sat with or under him failed to regard him not only with affection but also with admiration and respect for the care he took to master agenda and for the endless pains he was willing to devote to causes which he had at heart. When, for instance, in 1962, the Royal Academy announced unexpectedly that it was going to sell Leonardo da Vinci's cartoon of the Virgin and St. Anne, and the National Art-Collections Fund, almost at a moment's notice, undertook to try to raise the £800,000 required to save it for the nation, Crawford, its chairman, postponed an operation for which he was due and for the next four months spent almost every day at the appeal headquarters in the National Gallery organizing money-raising schemes, broadcasting, giving personal interviews, and writing personal appeals to possible donors and letters of thanks to generous subscribers. Many others helped, but the final success of the appeal, in face of difficulties, was due to him.

By the time that Crawford succeeded to the peerage the vast collections of the house of Lindsay had already been depleted by many sales, but enough remained to fill the three houses mentioned above, and when Balcarres became his sole residence, further sales were necessitated not only to meet estate duty but to make it possible to house the residue in the great house in Fife which overlooks the Firth of Forth.

Some collections were deposited on loan in libraries, but enough was retained to make Balcarres a veritable Aladdin's cave. To see their owner among these treasures was a delightful experience. That he should know the pictures and works of art was to be expected, but he was equally at home among the books and documents and at a visitor's request would lay hand at once on, say, the *editio princeps* of a minor Greek author or a letter of Mrs. Fitzherbert, and would discourse on the printer or the writer as informedly as on the pictures and the other artistic treasures.

Crawford had always intended that parts of his library should pass to the nation at his death as payment, in kind, of estate duty. It included The Borghese Collection of Pamphlets and Broadsheets, printed in the Vatican between the sixteenth and eighteenth centuries, a collection unrivalled anywhere in the world; a French Revolutionary and Napoleonic collection of pamphlets and newspapers, second only to the British Library collection; the most complete collection in existence of English Civil War newspapers; the Miscellaneous Broadsides, one of the largest existing collections of seventeenth century popular literature relating to a whole range of public and private affairs of the period; and the Luther Tracts, one of the finest private collections outside Germany.

It was a fear of his that the introduction of a wealth tax would compel him to sell these collections on the open market during his lifetime, simply to pay it, and he represented strongly the loss to the national heritage this would involve, in evidence he presented to the Select Committee on a Wealth Tax, earlier in 1975.

In the event, with the future of the wealth tax still an open question, the libraries for which he intended them will now benefit from these incomparable collections.

His committee duties took him often to London; as chairman he had to visit properties belonging or offered to the National Trust, and since he was a practised and agreeable speaker he was in demand to open new or refurbished museums and galleries; he also lectured in America on behalf of the National Art-Collections Fund.

No doubt he enjoyed much or most of this, but he was happiest at home, and if he occasionally complained it was less of labours elsewhere than of the too frequent absences from Balcarres which they entailed.

Crawford was created G.B.E. in 1951 and K.T. four years later, and was Deputy Lieutenant for Fifeshire. He held honorary doctorates of the Universities of Oxford, Cambridge, St. Andrews, London, Manchester, Exeter, York, Warwick and Amherst College, Massachusetts, and was Rector of the last from 1952 to 1955. He was also an honorary Royal Academician and fellow of several other professional bodies.

He married, in 1925, Mary, daughter of Lord Richard Cavendish and niece of the 9th Duke of Devonshire. They had three sons of whom the eldest, Lord Balniel, P.C., succeeds him.

December 16, 1975.

John Creasey, M.B.E., who died on June 9, 1973 at his home in Wiltshire, was almost certainly the world's most prolific writer of crime fiction. For fear of saturating the market, he used, at various times, more than 28 pseudonyms; J. J. Marric, Gordon Ashe, Anthony Morton, Jeremy York and Michael Halliday were the best known.

His output was astonishing. He could, and for many years did, write a book in a week, while maintaining a good standard of craftsmanship and literacy. At the last count there were 560 titles. The characters he created, especially The Toff, Commander Gideon, Inspector West and The Baron, became familiar all over the world.

Creasey was born at Southfields, Surrey, in 1908. His father was a cabinet maker and coachbuilder. He was educated at Fulham Elementary School and Sloane School, Chelsea. Leaving school at the age of 14 he became an office boy. By the time he was 19 he was probably the only office boy in London to possess 743 rejection slips from publishers. Then he sold an article, a few weeks later a short story, and the floodgates were opened. When he was 27, he gave up his job as a clerk in the Firestone Tyre Company and devoted himself, full-time, to writing.

The first book he ever possessed was *Bulldog Drummond* and he was determined to write the sort of story he enjoyed reading. *Seven Times Seven* (1932) launched him in this *genre*, and he soon followed it with a succession of books about a gentleman-adventurer, The Toff, and another series about a secret service organization, Department Z. In the next 25 years, the period of his maximum productivity, he wrote 333 full-length books. They included westerns (under the pseudonyms Tex Riley and Ken Ranger) and love stories, but most of them were thrillers of one kind or another.

As Gordon Ashe he indulged in his most direct imitations of Bulldog Drummond; as Michael Halliday he produced mild mystery novels for library readers; as Norman Deane he wrote spy stories during the war. With a straight Scotland Yard story, *Inspector West Takes Charge* (1942), he began, under his own name, what was to become perhaps his most popular series; it was certainly his own favourite for a long while, and heralded a new, more realistic, mood in his writing. His one attempt at a "straight" novel, *Adrian and Jonathan* (1954), which he wrote under the name of Richard Martin, passed unremarked.

He enjoyed the business side of his work. He liked to visit his publishers and agents all round the world. For publicity purposes, he designed a Toff tie and owned a Rolls-Royce marked with the Toff's symbol.

He experimented with publishing his own books in a paper-back edition, edited the *John Creasey Mystery Magazine*, and assiduously brought his early novels up to date for new editions. When he found that his books were not selling in America, he went to New York, studied the market and very successfully adapted his style to the prevailing fashion.

He was too facile to please the critics. When, in 1955, he published a documentary police novel, *Gideon's Day,* under the new pseudonym of J. J. Marric, he received far better reviews than he was accustomed to get under his own name. It was, in fact, one of the best books he ever wrote; it was turned into a good film and not such a good television series, and was followed by a long succession of almost identical Gideon stories, which became very popular on both sides of the Atlantic.

Creasey was impatient of intellectual criticism. His business, he believed, was to sell books and to entertain; but he took his work very seriously. He founded, and was first chairman of, the Crime Writers' Association. Typically, he was also a keen Rotarian. He was a tolerant teetotaller and gave up smoking when he was quite young.

At the 1950 general election he stood unsuccessfully as a Liberal candidate, but left the Liberal Party after the Suez crisis, in which he supported the Government. He then fought several by-elections under the label All Party Alliance, a name he created to promote the idea of a coalition Government, which would be drawn from all parties in proportion to the total votes cast for them at the election. Its policies, he hoped, would be those of national unity and common sense rather than those of sectarian dogma. At the Oldham by-election in 1968, he saved his deposit, collecting twice as many votes as the Liberal.

Lately, indefatigable as ever, he undertook another enterprise dear to his heart—a saga of novels, which was to tell the history of the Metropolitan Police embodied in several generations of the same families. He meant this series to be, at once, the vindication of his claim to be a serious writer, a tribute to the London police and a statement of his belief in law and order, decently and humanely administered. The first volumes—and quite a number of other Creasey novels—remain to be published.

He was married four times—on the last occasion, only a few weeks before he died —and had three children. In 1946 he was awarded an M.B.E. All his books were strengthened by a quality of rather unsophisticated goodness; they gave much pleasure and can have harmed no one.

June 11, 1973.

Admiral of the Fleet Sir George E. Creasy, G.C.B., C.B.E., D.S.O., M.V.O., who died on October 31, 1972 at the age of 77, had a distinguished career, alike in staff and command service, which was remarkable for its variety.

Though he had never before commanded a destroyer, he was a successful flotilla captain. Not long after being Director of Anti-Submarine Warfare during critical stages of the Battle of the Atlantic, con-

cerned with the destruction of enemy U-boats, he became Head of the British Submarine Service, responsible for the extension and development of under-water craft. Though he had never been directly associated with naval aviation, he was Flag Officer (Air) in the Far East. He was Chief Staff Officer to the Allied Naval Commander in the invasion of Europe, and after the war held more than one appointment on the Board of Admiralty.

George Elvey Creasy, the son of Leonard Creasy, was born on October 13, 1895. He entered the Navy as a cadet at Osborne in 1908, was at Dartmouth from 1910 to 1912, and passed out from the training cruiser Cornwall the following year. He served in the Grand Fleet and took part in the operations in the Heligoland Bight in 1917.

After serving as Assistant Director of Plans at the Admiralty in 1936-38, he took command of the Grenville and the 1st Destroyer Flotilla, Mediterranean. This was his command during the early months of the Second World War. The Grenville returned to join the Home Fleet, and after she was sunk by a U-boat in January 1940, he transferred to the Codrington.

In this ship he took to England Princess Juliana and her family after the invasion of Holland in May 1940, and afterwards took part in the evacuation from Dunkirk. For two years from September 1940, he was Director of the Anti-Submarine Warfare Division of the Naval Staff, and in 1942-43 commanded the battleship Duke of York. He was promoted to rear-admiral in July 1943. His next appointment was as chief staff officer to Admiral Sir Alexander Ramsay for the planning and execution of the naval operations for the Allied landing in Normandy in June 1944.

Three months later he was appointed Rear-Admiral (Submarines) and held the post for a period which saw the end of the war and the surrender of the German U-boats. It was a tribute to his all-round capacity that from submarines he turned to aircraft, taking up, in 1947, the post of Flag Officer, Aircraft Carriers and Air-Stations, British Pacific Fleet and East Indies. In 1948, he was promoted vice-admiral. Eight months later he succeeded Admiral Sir Philip Vian* as Fifth Sea Lord and Deputy Chief of Naval Staff (Air), and, in 1949, was transferred to another post on the Admiralty Board, that of Vice-Chief of the Naval Staff.

He was C.-in-C. Home Fleet from 1952 to 1954 and also C.-in-C. Eastern Atlantic under Nato. From 1954 to 1957 he was C.-in-C. Portsmouth and also C.-in-C. Home Station-designate and Allied C.-in-C. Channel Command under Nato. He was a Deputy Lieutenant for Essex.

He married in 1924 Monica, eldest daughter of Wilfred Ullathorne, and had one son.

November 2, 1972.

Sir Herbert Creedy, G.C.B., K.C.V.O., who died on April 3, 1973, ranked as one of the most notable Permanent Secretaries in the Civil Service in its prime, and his career was a remarkable one by any standard. For nearly 20 years he was Secretary and member of the Army Council, a position named, during his last 15 years' service, Permanent Under-Secretary of State for War. When he joined the War Office, the Boer War had not closed; three years later, the Army Council came into being, and 60 years still farther on, as senior of all living Army Councillors, he attended its obsequies.

Herbert James Creedy was born on May 3, 1878. He went to Merchant Taylors School, where his ability as a classical scholar was such that Sir James Jeans switched from classics to science to avoid his competition. At Oxford, he was a scholar of St. John's College and took a double first in Classical Moderations (1898) and Lit. Hum. (1900). He was Senior Scholar of St. John's from 1901 to 1905, and in 1931 his College elected him to an honorary fellowship. He joined the War Office in 1901, and two years later became private secretary to Sir Edward Ward, then Secretary of the War Office. Five years later he was promoted to take charge of the War Office central management branch. In 1913 he became private secretary to the Secretary of State, and thus began his long service to seven Secretaries of State: Colonel Seely, Asquith—for two periods when he was Prime Minister—Kitchener, Lloyd George, Derby, Milner, and Churchill*. In 1916 he became Assistant to the Secretary of the War Office in charge of the central management branch, while remaining private secretary.

In 1920 Sir Reginald Brade, Secretary of the War Office, retired through ill-health, and Creedy, still nominally in what is now the fifth administrative grade, succeeded him. Sir Charles Harris was later associated with him as Joint Secretary (Finance), and in July 1920 both became members of the Army Council. In 1924 Creedy became sole Permanent Under-Secretary of State for War and Accounting Officer, and held this post until he retired in 1939.

His rise to the permanent headship showed that his eminent qualifications included a positive answer to the historic question: "Is he fortunate?" The ill-health of others opened his way to becoming private secretary and then Secretary, and the tradition is that Sir Reginald Brade's illness was endured to the limits of tolerance, until a dangerous rival had disappeared.

After 1903 Creedy was never far removed from the central controls of the War Office; this may have seemed a narrow basis of experience, but after his accession his capacity for the position received universal recognition. He excelled in the frictionless management of an office governed by a council whose other members were politicians and soldiers. It was never an easy office, especially at the outset. In a rare moment of confidence he recalled how in his early tenure a military Army Councillor thought it natural to send for the Secretary. Creedy went and was infinitely helpful, but no similar episode occurred again. Once established, with the unequalled prestige of his associations, he steered his office and the Army through the reflux from the 1914 War, staved off mutilation in the slump, and only two years later encountered the increasingly frenetic rearmament period.

The story goes that on the morning of Kitchener's arrival at the War Office his first remark was: "There is no Army", and, on Creedy handing him a pen to give his signature, which failed to function, he murmured: "Dear me, what a War Office! Not a scrap of Army and not a pen that will write!"

Urbanity, an Army Councillor said, was a word invented to describe Sir Herbert Creedy. Yet few inspired more awe in their contemporaries. His bright glance missed nothing, particularly if it were out of place. When he read an official file several processes went on simultaneously; he was rapidly mastering its contents, reducing it to order, and reaching a decision. His happiness of phrase was the despair of imitators. But with all his talent for orderly procedure he never lost sight of main issues, and rarely failed to lead discussions to painless agreement on essentials.

So long a life provided an ample epilogue. During the Second World War he was member, and later chairman, of the Security Executive. Among other activities, he was secretary, and registrar, of the Distinguished Service Order, governor of Wellington College (1939-1953) and commissioner of the Royal Hospital Chelsea (1945-1957). He was feted and consulted as doyen by successors whose arrangements he treated with an etherealized benevolence. Many will remember him on his daily round of the St. James's quadrilateral; he later retired to Oxford from which he had set out at the turn of the century.

Creedy was made K.C.B. while still a private secretary. He was appointed K.C.V.O. in 1923 and G.C.B. in 1933. He was an Officer of the Order of St. John of Jerusalem, and received a number of foreign orders.

He married in 1904 Mabel Constance, daughter of S. J. Lowry. She died in 1958, and they had one daughter.

April 5, 1973.

Sir Archibald Creswell, C.B.E., who died on April 8, 1974, at the age of 94, was an outstanding authority on Islamic architecture and craftsmanship.

Keppel Archibald Cameron Creswell was born in London in 1879 and was educated at Westminster School and the City and Guilds Technical College. In 1916 he joined the Royal Flying Corps and later, as a staff-captain in the R.A.F. Middle East, was seconded to the government of occupied enemy territory as Inspector of Monuments, 1919-20. He then settled down in Cairo, where he lived for the rest of his life. He had found his métier in the single-minded study of Muslim building, first in Egypt and then throughout North Africa and the Near East. For pharaohs and pyramids and Greek or Roman colonialism he had no thought, but no Muslim monument was too remote and secluded to command his scholarly interest and his measuring tape.

In 1932 the Clarendon Press published the first of several massive volumes from his hand: two on *Early Muslim Architecture,* two on *The Muslim Architecture of Egypt,* and, quite recently, an elaborately revised edition of his first volume. These substantive publications, which are unlikely to be replaced for a long time to come, were supplemented by many papers in learned journals and by a *Bibliography of the Architecture, Arts and Crafts of Islam,* 1961. As a background to this untiring research work, he was Professor of Muslim Art and Archaeology at the Egyptian University, 1931-1951, and Professor of Muslim Architecture at the University of Cairo from 1956.

But no note on Creswell's life and work would be complete without reference to his personality. His small, neat figure, always impeccably dressed, with a high starched collar in the hottest weather, was familiar in the streets of Cairo and commanded respect and indeed fear in every situation—even during the height of the Suez crisis when he strode through the Cairene crowds carving a swath with his sword-like walking-stick.

For any sort of cruelty, even so venial a one as that of beating an overladen donkey, he had no tolerance. The sequence was inevitable: (i) Arab carter savagely belabours donkey; (ii) Creswell leans over the side of his open car and thrashes Arab carter; (iii) crowd assembles and blocks street; (iv) Creswell spots distant and reluctant policeman, leaps from car, thrashes his way through the crowd and collars policeman when on the point of escaping; (v) Creswell compels reluctant policeman to march offending carter in front of him to the nearest police station; (vi) crowd makes away with cart and donkey. To his last day, Creswell was unaware of the demise of the British Empire.

The C.B.E. accorded to him in 1955, his fellowship of the British Academy, his gold medal from the Royal Asiatic Society, and many other recognitions of his achievement as a scholar, were received with a proper appreciation, but his friends felt that the knightly spurs which came to him in 1970 were his just and most felicitous reward.

April 13, 1974.

The Rt. Rev. Douglas Henry Crick, Bishop of Chester, 1939-55, and honorary Assistant Bishop, Diocese of Gloucester, 1957-67, died on August 5, 1973. He was 88.

The second son of the Rev. Philip Crick, he was born on January 10, 1885 and attended as a scholar Winchester and New College, Oxford. Ordained deacon in 1908 after training at Bishop's Hostel, Liverpool, he served the first four years of his ministry as Assistant Chaplain in the Mersey Mission, afterwards going to be curate in charge of Maltby Colliery Village. In 1916 he returned for a short time to Winchester as a "college tutor" and had a further short spell of similar work at Bradfield, but school-mastering was not to be his vocation. In 1918 he became vicar of Wednesbury and for more than 20 years made his home in the diocese of Lichfield, being successively rector of Stoke on Trent (becoming a Prebendary of Lichfield in 1929), Archdeacon of Stoke on Trent in 1932 and Suffragan Bishop of Stafford in 1934 in succession to Dr. Crawfurd. Both in his Black Country parish and in the Potteries he proved himself a very capable incumbent with a pastoral heart; he was popular with both clergy and people.

He went to the see of Chester in abnormal times; opportunities were severely limited by war conditions and he had to carry on with a depleted band of clergy, for Cheshire had contributed more than its normal proportion of priests to the service of the Forces. He inherited a diocese whose administrative organizations, fresh from the master hand of Dr. Fisher, were in splendid order, and in war-time there was neither the need nor the opportunity to initiate new enterprises; the difficulty was to keep things going with so reduced a clergy. He was unsparing in going personally to the relief of his overdriven parish priests and all that his kindness and sympathy could do to lighten their burdens he undertook.

In 1955 the Bishop resigned the see of Chester and retired to the West country where he served as honorary Assistant Bishop in the diocese of Gloucester, and assisted in the parish of Chipping Campden.

He married in 1914 Evelyn, daughter of the Rev. J. C. Vernon. They had one son and three daughters. His wife died in 1960 and he married secondly in 1961 Mary, daughter of the Rev. B. Wright.

August 8, 1973.

Richard Crooks, the former Metropolitan Opera tenor, died on October 1, 1972 at his home near San Francisco. He was 72.

Crooks began his singing career in the church choir and at the age of eleven made his first public appearance in Mendelssohn's *Elijah.* After serving as a flying officer in the First World War he made his New York debut with the New York Symphony Society under Walter Damrosch; other engagements with this orchestra were followed by an extensive concert tour. During the next few years orchestral and festival engagements and recitals made him well known in America as a concert singer.

He made his opera debut in Germany in 1927, singing Cavaradossi in *Tosca* at Hamburg and Berlin, and made four European tours during the next five years, singing in Germany, Austria and the Scandinavian countries. Crooks appeared at the Metropolitan opera in 1933. For the next ten years he was one of the Metropolitan's leading tenors in Italian and French lyric parts. He toured Australia and Africa in 1936 and 1939 and, until his retirement in 1946, continued his concert activities in the United States.

Crook's singing was marked by musicianship and a consistently high standard of tone and vocal production, and he was an expressively sympathetic interpreter in both opera and concert.

October 2, 1972.

Richard Crossman, P.C., O.B.E., the Labour politician, who held high office during the Labour Government of 1964 to 1970 and who was M.P. for Coventry East from 1945 to 1974, died on April 5, 1974. He was 66.

His career is a classic illustration of the strength and limitations of the intellectual in politics, and more especially in Labour politics. Throughout his life, Crossman was an unrepentant believer in the potentialities of reason when applied to political problems. A brilliant intellect gave him an easy ascendancy over most of his adversaries in argument. They found themselves deluged by a stream of dazzling paradoxes, though they were also often disarmed by sallies of humour and unexpected gestures of intellectual chivalry.

In several ways, however, Crossman aroused deep suspicion. Like many other intellectuals in the radical tradition, he undoubtedly had an itch for power, and he wholly lacked the hypocrisy to conceal it. He often appeared to change his mind on issues of fundamental importance, a tendency for which politicians of more muddled mind and with a more empirical approach are easily forgiven; as a rationalist, however, Crossman always found himself under the necessity of justifying these charges in terms of absolute immutable principle. This involved him in complicated mental gymnastics which won the hearts of connoisseurs but aroused distrust in the majority of his parliamentary colleagues. In fact, he never indulged in fraudulent intellectual tricks.

Added to all this as a further handicap in Labour politics was his prosperous middle class background. Before he went into politics his life was spent on the lecturer's rostrum and at the administrator's desk; he could claim none of those redeeming features, such as a period of slumming

or experience as a field officer, which other socialists will sometimes accept as expiations of a happy childhood.

It is a tribute to the force of his personality and the unmistakeable brilliance of his talents that these disadvantages did not prevent him from achieving and keeping high office in two Labour governments. As Minister for Housing and Local Government, though not conspicuously successful in building houses, he showed a degree of freedom from the constricting influence of dogma which surprised many who did not understand the complexity of his make-up.

As Leader of the House of Commons, he was able to apply himself to what he had for long regarded as one of the chief dilemmas of political life in Britain—the difficulty of reconciling efficient, energetic and planned government with democratic control. He was replete with fertile ideas on this subject, but his attempts to put them into effect (by such devices as morning sessions and specialist committees) aroused considerable bewilderment at Westminster, and were apparently not destined to produce any lasting effect on the functioning of Parliament.

As Secretary of State for Social Services and head of the Department of Health (after Harold Wilson had amalgamated these bodies), he was able to take the first steps towards putting into effect his characteristically ambitious (but some would say excessively doctrinaire) plans for earnings-related pensions.

Nevertheless, it seemed appropriate that Crossman should end his career, as he had begun it, as a thinker and writer in the combative radical tradition. His brief but distinguished spell as editor of the *New Statesman* (a review on which he had served for many years before taking public office) confirmed the view that, for all the zest with which he had played the political game, one half of him had always looked on political activity mainly as a source of copy for journalism and material for scholarship.

His very last period in journalism was as a columnist on *The Times*, a role which gave some pleasure to him and much to the staff of *The Times* who worked with him.

Richard Howard Stafford Crossman was born in December 1907. His father, Mr. Justice Crossman, was a man of strong Conservative convictions and a close friend of Clement Attlee*; in later life, Crossman was fond of attributing Attlee's deep suspicions of him as a politician to the Labour leader's inability to forgive him for having broken the judge's heart by becoming a Socialist. After a brilliant career at Winchester, Crossman took firsts in Mods. and Greats at New College and stayed on there as a Fellow, Philosophy Tutor and, for a while, as Lay Dean.

But, as his early writings (notably *Plato Today*) proved, he was by nature a preacher rather than a scholar. While still a don, he became leader of the Labour group on Oxford City Council and, in 1937, he left

Oxford to lecture for the Workers' Educational Association, to become a member of the staff of the *New Statesman,* and to fight an unsuccessful by-election.

Crossman's fluent command of German and deep understanding of Germany (he was of German ancestry) took him, at the outbreak of war, to the German section of the B.B.C. His brilliant talents as a propagandist were soon appreciated, and he became in succession head of the German section of the Political Warfare Executive, deputy director of Psychological Warfare in North Africa and, in the last year of the war, second-in-command of the Psychological Warfare Division of S.H.A.E.F. His outstanding service during this period laid the foundation of his public career.

In 1945 Crossman was elected as Labour member for Coventry East, a constituency which he continued to represent until 1974. He soon made his mark as a rebellious backbencher, infuriating Ernest Bevin by his passionate advocacy of the Israeli cause and his bitter criticisms of a foreign policy founded, he maintained, on dependence on the U.S.A. He was also a prominent member of the Keep Left group, which sought to keep the Government faithful in its domestic policy to the pure word of Socialism.

Attlee's profound distrust of him, however, was for long an effective barrier to Crossman's progress in the Parliamentary Labour Party. His first serious exercise in official policy-making was as chairman of the group which devised Labour's pensions proposals, embodying the principle of "half-pay on retirement." These undoubtedly brought about a revolution in the party's thinking on a central issue of home policy but the calculations on which the proposals rested were competently pronounced to be wildly inaccurate, and helped, in some quarters, to confirm Crossman's reputation as an intellectual gadfly. As front bench spokesman on pensions under Gaitskell*, however, he acquitted himself admirably.

Unfortunately Crossman found Gaitskell's leadership of the party scarcely less restricting to his genius than Attlee's had been. Though never a committed Bevanite he was always critical of the decision to allow defence to depend almost entirely on the nuclear deterrent, and he also suspected Gaitskell's "revisionism" as a concession to capitalism, no doubt believing that any modernized version of the Socialist creed which might have become necessary could more suitably have sprung from his own fertile mind. His efforts to act as a mediator between Gaitskell and the Bevanites (diplomacy was never his strong point) tended to increase party disunity, and in 1960 he resigned from the Front Bench.

Harold Wilson's election to the leadership of the Labour Party on Gaitskell's death in 1963 owed much to Crossman's zealous campaigning, and gave Crossman his first chance of real authority in the leadership of the parliamentary party. As Minister of Housing and Local Government between

1964 and 1966, he proved a more efficient administrator than many had expected, in spite of often exasperating his civil servants. He also showed a commendable freedom from rigid Socialist dogma. At least two of his important legislative measures—a scheme for giving financial aid to those who did not qualify for tax relief in respect of their house mortages, and a new Rate Rebate Act to remedy some of the inequalities of local taxation—commanded widespread support.

So he came to the climax of his career, the Leadership of the House of Commons. The grand theme of his tenure of that office was that efficient and dynamic government could be reconciled with a high degree of freedom and influence for individual M.P.s. The most important of his innovations, morning sessions, has been widely recognized as a failure, and has been abandoned. Another innovation, specialist committees, though it still has some advocates, has not aroused much enthusiasm or produced much tangible result other than an aggravation of the burdens of backbenchers.

Crossman's attempt to maintain a liberal interpretation of the loyalty due from backbenchers to the Party Whip brought him into bitter conflict with Emmanuel Shinwell, the veteran of working-class politics, and this incident again emphasized his perennial handicap as a bourgeois intellectual in the Labour movement. In terms of sheer productivity, however, Crossman's leadership of the House was a success; in the course of his first session in that office, he broke the record for the number of Bills reaching the Statute Book.

Crossman's last office, that of Secretary of State for Social Services, and head of the Department of Social Security, which he occupied from the autumn of 1969 to Labour's defeat in 1970, did not greatly add to or subtract from his reputation. Much of his time was perforce spent in defending the controversial provisions of his Wages-Related Pensions Scheme, formulated in a White Paper in January 1969; but he also showed some outstanding humanity in his handling of some of his duties as head of the health department.

Few were surprised at his decision in 1970 to renounce the prospect of further Front Bench parliamentary work by becoming Editor of his beloved New Statesman, a perfect forum for the enfant terrible who could now also speak with the authority of the elder statesman. He soon showed that he had lost none of his vitality as a journalist; but the form of journalism in which few of his contemporaries surpassed him—pungent, intellectually sophisticated, critical analysis of public affairs—is today less fashionable among the radical vanguard than it was in Crossman's youth. It was ironic, therefore, but not unexpected, that Crossman's forced retirement from the New Statesman in 1972 should come about as part of a plan to make that review more up-to-date and less hidebound by old-fashioned standards and categories of thought.

Everyone who came in contact with Dick Crossman reacted to him; some were infuriated, and, indeed, everybody was infuriated at one time or another; others thought him too rude. But he was a very, very clever man and an interesting man and a congenial man. He belonged to a brilliant Oxford generation, a generation of intellectual conversationalists; he was younger than Sir Maurice Bowra but from the same college. They were not close friends but at worst they were very devoted old enemies. He will be missed in many places, not least by his friends in Printing House Square.

Crossman began to keep a political diary in 1952 when he was an Opposition backbencher without much hope of office. He felt that, if no one kept a chronicle, future historians would be unable to piece together any coherent picture of what went on inside the Bevan group. When, 12 years later, he became a Cabinet Minister, he continued keeping the diary, which he dictated on tapes each weekend at his home in North Oxfordshire.

He realized that a diary of his whole ministerial life, dictated while the memory was still hot, uncorrupted by "improvements", and giving a detailed account of what a minister did with his time, in his department, in Cabinet Committee and in the Cabinet itself, would have special historical value. During the next six years he recorded over 1,500,000 words, a detailed record of the Wilson administration of 1964-70. The first of the three volumes in which the greater part of the material will be published is to appear this autumn (1974) under the joint imprint of Hamish Hamilton and Jonathan Cape. Entitled The Diaries of a Cabinet Minister, Volume I, it covers his time as Minister of Housing from 1964 to 1966.

He was married three times.

April 6, 1974.

Lord Crowther, chairman of the Economist Newspaper, Limited, and editor of The Economist from 1938 to 1956, died on February 5, 1972 at London Airport, Heathrow. He was 64.

Crowther had been Chancellor of the Open University since 1969. He was chairman of the committee set up by the Government in 1968 to make a wide-ranging review of consumer credit. He was also chairman of the Commission on the Constitution, to examine the functions of the Government in relation to the various countries and regions of the United Kingdom.

By the death of Geoffrey Crowther the country lost perhaps the ablest of the "men of the thirties" who never sought, and indeed refused, the obvious places of public prominence. As an editor and as a commentator on the principles and practice of economics and politics he stood beside his famous predecessor, Walter Bagehot.

Crowther did not win the same unqualified national acclaim as a businessman as he had as a journalist. He had his share of successes, but his public image was strongly affected by the major controversies in which he became involved. He first became known as a powerful City figure when he played the major part in the early 1960s in the successful resistance by printers Hazell Sun to a take-over bid from the News of the World. To fight off the News of the World, Hazell Sun merged with another printing firm, Purnell, run by Wilfred Harvey, to form the British Printing Corporation.

It was not a happy merger and Crowther was again the leader in a boardroom battle which led to the removal of Wilfred Harvey from the board and a public scandal over deals done by the Purnell side which seemed to be more in the interest of the controlling family than for the benefit of the public shareholders.

British Printing was reorganized and the board was strengthened by bringing in accountants, civil servants, and businessmen from other industries, but although they were successful in stemming the flood of post-merger troubles they launched into some major disasters in the field of encyclopaedias and part-works. Crowther himself left the board soon after the biggest of the disastrous ventures—the joint company with Robert Maxwell's Pergamon Press, International Learning Systems Corporation—was started.

Crowther was more successful in the property field. In the early 1960s he gave his support to a small company headed by an unknown property man, then in his 20s, Nigel Broackes. Thanks to Crowther's wide range of City contacts, and particularly his directorship of the Commercial Union, Broackes was able to borrow the money to build one of the most successful property companies in the country, Trafalgar House Investments, which now owns, among others, such famous concerns as Trollope & Colls and the Cunard shipping company. Crowther himself left the board of Trafalgar House two years before he died after an unpublicized row over Broackes's wish to go into hotels, an area in which Crowther was already interested.

It was as chairman of Trust Houses, the hotel group which included such London luxury hotels as Grosvenor House and The Hyde Park, as well as the provincial chain of Trust Houses, that Crowther made his biggest mark on business. Under him the quality of the hotels was radically improved, the management system modernized and a well planned and ambitious expansion programme launched, including the £25m Post Houses programme. In 1970 Trust Houses was merged with the Forte catering and entertainments concern.

Trust Houses Forte is the largest hotel and catering group in Britain. In 1971, Crowther seemed in command of it. He was chairman himself and the reins of executive control were held by Michael Pickard, his protégé and the T.H.F. managing director. In January 1972 Crowther and his supporters were forced to resign from the board after a long and bitter public battle with Sir Charles Forte.

Ironically, Crowther was defeated at the game he had in the past proved successful in—boardroom power struggles fought in the back rooms by lobbying City figures, and in public by propaganda wars in the press. Sir Charles Forte proved the better tactician. He first secured a majority on the T.H.F. board by securing the removal of Pickard after the Pergamon Board of Trade inspectors had criticized him, and then winning the support of new directors. After Crowther had lost in the boardroom he gave his support to the Allied Breweries giant in their attempts to take over T.H.F. It was not enough. Sir Charles Forte borrowed £8m. to add to his own holding of T.H.F. shares and retained sufficient loyalty among the public shareholders to frustrate the Allied bid. For Crowther there was no alternative to resignation. It was a sad end to his most significant business venture.

Geoffrey Crowther was born on May 13, 1907, the son of the scientist Charles Crowther. From Leeds Grammar School and Oundle he went to Clare College, Cambridge, where he easily got first-class honours in modern languages and in economics. As a Commonwealth Fund Fellow he went on to study at Yale and Columbia University: it was during his stay in the United States that he met his future wife, Margaret Worth, whom he married in 1932.

Two years' work with a London merchant banking firm was followed by a special study of the Irish banking system, resulting in Crowther's appointment as economic adviser on banking to the Irish Government. The report on the Irish banking system which he drafted in this capacity is still a classic. He gave up this appointment in 1932 to join the editorial staff of *The Economist* under Walter Layton. He became assistant editor in 1935, and in 1938 succeeded Layton as editor, a position which he held until 1956. In that year he retired in order to become chairman of the Central Advisory Council for Education, continuing, however, to take an active part in the paper's concerns as managing director, then deputy chairman and finally chairman. As chairman of The Economist Newspaper Ltd., he developed its profitability and prestige, adding to its interest in 1964 the notable building development in St. James's Street.

Though he had no taste for the formal corridors of power, and was entirely lacking in political ambition for himself, Crowther held a special place, both when he was in journalism and afterwards, in the shaping of rational (and often radical) thought about national and international affairs. Publicly, this showed itself in his wartime work; in the Crowther Report on the development of educational policy; in his

shrewd and trenchant advice on matters of transport and urban development; in his down-to-earth advocacy of a European policy for Britain (which he saw as reinforcing and not rebuffing its essential American connexion); and in his only too rare published comments on the nation's ills and opportunities. Privately, he was always one of the few whose opinions mattered to those who had charge of the country and its business.

Under Crowther's editorship *The Economist* was revolutionized in format and in content. While retaining its specialist authority as a City periodical, it widened its appeal to the intelligent general public, lightened its style, and became one of the most influential weeklies in the world. Much of this achievement was undoubtedly due to Crowther's own writing; to his gift of getting to the heart of the matter, and to his blend of pungent common sense, steady principle, lucidity and pervasive wit. But his indirect influence was hardly, if at all, less important. He was in a special sense an inspired leader. *The Economist* was the model of a successful democracy.

Although he was always perfectly ready to be shot at in the editorial chair and even on occasion to be shot down, Crowther had an extraordinary gift both for eliciting and for formulating consensus; in spite of the wide variety of political attitudes, of temperaments and of expertise, represented at the weekly editorial conferences—which frequently had all the entertainment value of a combined Brains Trust and three-ring circus—*The Economist* spoke with a single voice, and its staff wrote with conviction because they were convinced.

During the war, Crowther held a succession of official positions, first with the Ministry of Supply, later with the Ministry of Information, then, from 1942 to 1945, with the Ministry of Production, where he was Deputy Head of the Joint War Production Staff.

It is matter for general regret that he wrote so little in permanent form. His one substantial work was the *Outline of Money* published in 1941; its combination of theoretical authority, practical expertise and stylistic liveliness gave it forthwith an unchallengeable position both with students embarking on serious studies and with the general public. His three previous books—*Ways and Means*, 1936, *Economics for Democrats*, 1939 (which is especially worth re-reading), and *Ways and Means of War*, 1940—were pithy, untechnical statements of the economic facts of life, based on a series of broadcast talks. He was an extremely successful broadcaster, but after the war he could rarely be tempted in front of the microphone.

He was knighted in 1957 for his services to journalism and in 1968 became a life peer.

February 7, 1972.

Professor Robert Cruickshank, who died on August 16, 1974 at the age of 74, was Sir Alexander Fleming's successor as professor of bacteriology at St. Mary's Hospital, London.

Although he had a brilliant academic career as a student, as a bacteriologist he tended more to the administrative side and it was in this capacity, both in the academic and the public health field, that he established himself as one of the leading members of his specialty. In thus forging a strong link between academic and public health bacteriology he played a most valuable part in an era when such collaboration was beginning to provide a cross-fertilization that has proved of inestimable benefit both to bacteriology (or micro-biology as it is now known) and public health.

Robert Cruickshank was born in September 1899. He graduated from Aberdeen University with honours in 1922 and proceeded to his M.D. with "highest honours" three years later. He held the Anderson Travelling Fellowship in Glasgow University from 1922 to 1924. There followed spells as resident medical officer in the Royal Hospital for Sick Children in Glasgow and in the Belvedere Hospital for Infectious Diseases. These two appointments, and particularly the latter, gave him a sound clinical training in bacteriological diseases which was to prove most useful to him when he finally settled in his specialty.

This he did in 1928 after a year as lecturer in malignant diseases in Aberdeen University when he was appointed lecturer in bacteriology in Glasgow University and bacteriologist to Glasgow Royal Infirmary. Eight years later when the London County Council reorganized its pathological services, he accepted an invitation to become one of its first group pathologists. He organized a most efficient wartime service.

In view of his success in this sphere it was not surprising that in 1945 he was appointed director of the Central Public Health Laboratory of the newly established Public Health Laboratory Service. Three years later he returned to the academic sphere as professor of bacteriology in St. Mary's Hospital and director of the Wright Fleming Institute of Microbiology. As successor to two outstanding and dominating personalities—in their own very different ways—Alexander Fleming and Almroth Wright, it was a difficult post to hold down but this Cruickshank did with consummate skill. In 1958 he returned north as professor of bacteriology in Edinburgh University, an appointment he held until his official retirement in 1966. Still active in mind and body, however, retirement was not for him and he immediately accepted an invitation to the University of the West Indies in Jamaica as professor of preventive medicine.

His writings were mainly articles in medical journals and he himself aptly described their scope as "embodying researches in the diagnosis and control of infectious

131

disease". He was also editor of the eleventh and twelfth editions of the leading British textbook on the subject, *Medical Microbiology*, a best-seller which he transferred from a small book, first published in 1925, to a two volume textbook largely written by past and present members of the staff of the microbiology department in Edinburgh. He was appointed C.B.E. in 1966 and in 1968 his own university awarded him an honorary LL.D.

August 19, 1974.

Group Captain S. D. Culley, D.S.O., who as a naval pilot achieved one of the most spectacular combat victories of the First World War, died at the age of 79 on June 10, 1975.

Born in the United States and educated there and in Canada, Stuart Douglas Culley entered the R.N.A.S. in 1917. In August of the following year the Harwich Striking Force under Admiral Tyrwhitt was being annoyed by Zeppelins off the Frisian Coast which were able to observe British troop movements without coming within range of the Force's guns.

Since attack by Britain-based aircraft was out of the question at that range, a lighter, capable of being towed at 32 knots by a destroyer, was built to serve as a rudimentary take-off deck for a Sopwith Camel fighter.

Culley volunteered to fly the aircraft without any previous practice at this type of take-off. On August 10, 1918, the Zeppelin, L53, one of the later generation of long-range Zeppelins, appeared at 18,000 feet. Culley's primitive flight deck was steamed to windward and he took off.

In full view of the watching Harwich Force, he climbed to 18,000 feet, destroyed the airship, and returned to land safely on the lighter, a feat which earned him the D.S.O. Alluding to the incident in later years, Tyrwhitt said of his then only 18-year-old pilot: "It was the grandest and bravest thing I have ever seen in my life."

Culley later joined the Royal Air Force and served in the Middle East and India. He was mentioned in dispatches in the Mohmand Operations in 1935 and again in the Syrian Campaign of 1941. He retired from the R.A.F. as a Group Captain in December 1945 and settled in Italy. The Camel aircraft is still preserved in the Imperial War Museum.

June 18, 1975.

Charles Cundall, R.A., R.W.S., who died on November 4, 1971 at the age of 81, was one of those painters whose work is proof that, however welcome creative experiments may be in the arts, there will always be room for the man who depends on training, discipline, experience, control, and crafts-manship.

Today, the standard of skill needs to be high if it is to be the chief source of success. In Cundall's case, this was so.

Charles Cundall was born on September 6, 1890 and was educated at Ackworth School, Yorkshire, the Royal College of Art, the Slade, and abroad. As a young man he was a designer of lustre ware at Pilkington's pottery and also designed stained glass. The outbreak of the 1914-18 War occurred before he had become fully established as an artist, and for some three years he served as an infantryman with The Royal Fusiliers. The war once over, his progress was steady.

Landscape was perhaps what he enjoyed most, but he was a practised portrait painter, and had notable skill in conveying crowd scenes. There is a celebrated example in the gallery adjoining Lord's cricket ground, showing a Test match in progress. There was also a time when Cundall worked a good deal in water-colour, and indeed some of his best oils, notably a view of Arklow in co. Wicklow, now in a private collection, have the simplicity and clarity of the water-colour at its most characteristic.

Cundall was a great traveller, and brought back memorable things from Spain (he was in Toledo, painting the Alcazar, a week before the siege began); Paris, where he painted the pre-war royal visit; the United States; and Canada, where, among other subjects, he painted the arrival of the King and Queen at Quebec, in May 1939.

A picture of his, "Coronation Day, 1937," was bought by Queen Mary and later given as a birthday gift to King George VI.

Cundall was elected A.R.A. in 1937 and a full Academician in 1944. During the war he served as a naval war artist. Later he took passage in a ship of the escort when King George VI and his Queen embarked in H.M.S. Vanguard, the last of the battleships, for a visit to South Africa in 1947. He was fond of telling how, when painting the royal party partly concealed by a flimsy screen, the present Queen Mother peeped over. Confronted with the shock of red hair to which time was so kind, she exclaimed: "Surely you must be Mr. Cundall!"

Cundall's work, often large-scale, may be seen at the Tate, Liverpool, Manchester, Bristol and elsewhere. He was an assiduous worker all his life, and remarkably consistent in his output. In later years he undertook a number of industrial commissions.

He married Jacqueline Pietersen in 1923, and they had one daughter.

November 6, 1971.

Philip Cunliffe-Lister, 1st Earl of Swinton
—See **Swinton.**

Dame Myra Curtis, D.B.E., who after a distinguished career as a civil servant was Principal of Newnham College, Cambridge, from 1942 to 1954, and was chairman of the committee which supervized the founding of New Hall, died in a nursing home at Bognor Regis on June 26, 1971.

Born in 1886 and educated at Winchester High School, now St. Swithun's, she read classics at Newnham, and entered the Civil Service in 1915, serving first in the War Trade Intelligence Department, and then from 1917-22 in the Ministry of Food. Her central work for the Civil Service was at the Post Office from 1924-37. War returned, and she became Assistant Secretary to the War Damage Commissioners, being made a Commissioner herself in 1943 after her move to Cambridge. And she was still to do valuable public service as chairman of an interdepartmental committee on the care of deprived children. On the strength of the Curtis Report a new social service was founded. A tireless worker and a good chairman who spared no pains to master the subject in hand, as well as an effective speaker and broadcaster, she amply earned her promotion to D.B.E. in 1949.

Meanwhile, at Cambridge. she soon found her way through the intricacies of wartime and peacetime regulations, and she played an important part in the negotiations which led to women becoming full members of the university in 1948. In 1052 she became the first woman member of the Council of the Senate.

Dame Myra loved planning and delighted in college building projects, so it was most fortunate that she was available to lend her energy to coordinating the movement initiated in several quarters for the foundation of a third college for women at Cambridge. As chairman of the committee appointed by the university to investigate the possibilities, she applied her administrative experience to great effect; and a year later, in 1954, when she retired from her distinguished reign at Newnham, New Hall opened with 16 undergraduates.

With admirable self-effacement she withdrew from Cambridge, now an honorary fellow of her college, and rarely went back. Her reward was always in the consciousness of work well done. Her impelling stimulus was ethical, not religious; and she disliked what she considered to be sentimentality. Though she could be sympathetic and farseeing in her advice to individuals, and was deeply attached to her friends, her outlook was primarily that of an administrator. Apart from reading, her greatest pleasures were gardening and cooking. She transformed a somewhat barren piece of college land singlehanded into a blooming garden; and in vacation she enjoyed running a small cottage and providing excellent meals from scanty materials. But Newnham and New Hall will not forget what they owe her.

June 29, 1971.

D

Dame May Curwen, D.B.E., President of the British Council for Aid to Refugees from 1962 to 1973, died on September 13, 1973 aged 84.

She did not start her notable career in the public service until she was approaching 30, but then she entered upon a course which was to provide her with two careers, one after another, and both of them of outstanding value to the community. For 30 years afterwards her life and efforts were devoted almost entirely to the Young Women's Christian Association; and then, upon her retirement from it, she accepted the post of chairman of The British Council for Aid to Refugees, in whose service she was indefatigable. She was a woman of great character and resource, of tremendous drive and organizing capacity, and every movement and cause to which she applied herself felt the impact of her strong personality.

Anne May Curwen was born on May 7, 1889 at Birkenhead, the daughter of William Curwen. She was educated at Birkenhead High School and Harrogate College; and after a few years at home she went up to Newnham College, Cambridge, taking first class honours in history.

Her first intention was to teach, and after graduating she became in 1914 history mistress at Orme Girls' School at Newcastle under Lyme, Staffordshire. Finding teaching not to her taste, she offered herself for work with the Scottish Women's Hospitals and soon afterwards was appointed organizing secretary. In the latter part of 1918 she went on behalf of the organization to Serbia, to help in organizing rehabilitation.

A year or so later she began her long association with the Y.W.C.A. by joining the finance department of the national staff. She was education secretary from 1920-30, and national general secretary from 1930-49.

The years of the Second World War severely taxed the resources of the association. As the enemy was cleared out of the occupied countries she travelled almost continuously through France, Belgium and Holland, arranging rest centres for nurses and servicewomen, a task which, with the coming of peace, she carried into Germany.

In retirement she could not be idle, and her acceptance of the urgent invitation to help the Council for Aid to Refugees was prompt and effective. In becoming chairman she was in some respects continuing both a service and a tradition.

She was not content to do her work from the London offices, but again set out on travels which took her over many parts of Europe, and she frequently spent weeks at a time in the camps which the council established, watching and attending to every detail of the work. She was particularly concerned about education, rehabilitation and training, and never lost that sense of compassion and humanity which was first aroused by her many months in South-Eastern Europe in 1918-19. She became president in 1962.

She added to her responsibilities by becoming United Kingdom delegate to the United Nations Refugee Fund from 1954-58; she was chairman in 1958. She was vice-chairman of the National Council for Social Service from 1956-70; chairman of the Women's Group on Public Welfare, 1948-60; and honorary secretary of the Consultative Committee of Women's Church Organizations, the last-named being an outward expression of her deeply religious personal life. She was vice-chairman of the United Kingdom committee of World Refugee Year, 1959-60. She was an omnivorous reader, and was renowned for her fine cooking at her hospitable Hampstead home.

She was made C.B.E. in 1943, and promoted to be a Dame of the Order in 1949. In 1922 she was awarded the Yugoslav Order of St. Sava (3rd class) for her work in Serbia. She was awarded the United Nations Nansen Medal in 1964.

September 15, 1973.

Bernard van Cutsem, the Newmarket trainer, who won the 1972 2,000 Guineas with the Duke of Devonshire's High Top, died in a London hospital in December 1975 at the age of 59.

He had been ill for a long time and since midsummer his 40-horse stables at Exning near Newmarket had been managed by his assistant, Mick Ryan.

Apart from High Top, probably the best horse he trained, van Cutsem also won the Irish 2,000 Guineas in 1970 with Decies. Other well known horses trained at his Newmarket stables were Park Top, Crowned Prince, Karabas and Noble Decree.

The son of Henry van Cutsem, he was born in 1916 and educated at Downside and Jesus College, Cambridge. He saw service in the Life Guards in the Second World War.

There are not many courses north of the Trent river at which Bernard van Cutsem did not have runners in the last 20 years or so, and his horses invariably had the shine and gloss on their coats, and an air of wellbeing, which might be expected from a former officer in the Life Guards. They were always immaculately turned out, and they won a great number of races of all types that ranged from the Observer Gold Cup with High Top and Noble Decree; the Champagne Stakes, also at Doncaster, with Crowned Prince and Otha; the Northumberland Plate with Amateur; the Portland Handicap with Mountain Call; and Redcar's William Hill Gold Cup with Mandamus.

In less important races he captured many prizes and always looked forward to his "Yorkshire Raids."

December 11, 1975.

Luigi Dallapiccola, doyen of Italian composers, died on February 18, 1975 at Florence. He was 71.

The leading exponent in Italy of 12-note music, he did not allow his adherence to it to overlay his native lyricism, as his lengthy list of choral and other vocal works would indicate.

He was born on February 3, 1904, at Pisino in Istria, then part of the Austro-Hungarian empire. Having decided at an early age to become a composer, he studied piano and harmony, finishing his theoretical studies at the Cherubini Conservatory in Florence, graduating in piano and composition.

He formed a duo with the violinist Materassi to perform modern scores, and became the Italian delegate to the International Society for Contemporary Music, for which he wrote one of his first important works, an orchestral Partita, with a soprano part in the final movement. First performed in 1933, it was also given at the I.S.C.M. Festival at Florence the following year. It made its composer's name.

His friendship with Berg brought him under the influence of the second Viennese school, which led him to write several significant works in a dodecaphonic style, although he used 12-note technique more as a means to an end than as an end in itself.

His works usually had a strong feeling of key, and in that sense tended to be nearer Berg than Schoenberg. That kind of modernism was frowned on in fascist Italy, and his kind of writing, together with his marriage to a Jewess, made him *persona non grata* under Mussolini's regime.

After the war he emerged as the leading Italian composer of his generation and his experiences led him to one of his most profound works, the opera *Il prigioniero* (1950), still performed regularly in Italy. In it, his sympathy with prisoners of all kinds found moving expression. It followed on his earlier operatic success, *Volo di notte,* based on a book by Saint-Exupéry.

Il prigioniero had a worthy companion and predecessor in the cantata, *Canti di prigionia,* dealing with the imprisonment of such figures as Mary Stuart and Savanarola. That and several of his other attractive vocal works were featured at the Three Choirs Festival at Worcester in 1969. It was attended by the composer, who gave several lectures notable for their lucidity, charm and self-deprecating humour.

The most important of his recent works was the opera *Ulysses,* given its premiere at the Berlin Festival in 1968. In this large-scale piece, Dallapiccola carried on what he then termed his continuing operatic theme of depicting "the struggle of man against some force much stronger than he", epitomized in the final scene in which Ulysses, alone in his boat, comes to place his trust in some superior being, whom he addresses as "Signore". The opera was produced in an English translation by Brian Trowell for Radio 3 in 1969, when it was acknowledged as a thought-provoking, if flawed work.

February 21, 1975.

Toti dal Monte—See Monte.

Admiral Sir Frederick Dalrymple-Hamilton, K.C.B., who was in command of H.M.S. Rodney at the sinking of the Bismarck in 1941, and was subsequently Admiral of the British Joint Services Mission in Washington, died on Boxing Day, 1974. He was 84.

Frederick Hew George Dalrymple-Hamilton was born in 1890, the younger son of Colonel the Hon. North Dalrymple-Hamilton of Bargany, Ayrshire, and grandson of the tenth Earl of Stair. He entered the Britannia as a cadet in 1905 and went to sea the following year. The first 30 years of his service were spent mostly in destroyers, which were always his delight—he commanded no fewer than three of them during the First World War. He also served three spells in the Royal yachts: as sub-lieutenant in the Victoria and Albert before the First War; as lieutenant-commander in the Renown during the Prince of Wales's cruise to India and the Far East in 1921; and again in Victoria and Albert from 1922 to 1924.

In 1936, as a captain, he was appointed to command the Royal Naval College at Dartmouth. It was an inspired choice, as many a naval officer who began his career during Dalrymple-Hamilton's three-year tenure will testify. His standards were high, but his touch was light; and he was splendidly supported in this and his subsequent shore appointments by his wife, despite her increasing and eventually total blindness. In some way his years at Dartmouth, with the opportunity they gave him of moulding so many young officers on the eve of the Second World War, could be considered as his greatest contribution to the Royal Navy.

But the real climax of his career came in 1941, when he was commanding the battleship Rodney. She was in North American waters when the hunt for the Bismarck began. The exigencies of "wireless silence" made it impossible to brief him in detail; but by a series of brilliant deductions concerning the possible intentions of the German captain, he contrived to bring the Rodney into the battle at precisely the right place and moment, knowing that his only son was already engaged in the fight as a junior officer in another ship.

Later promotions were as Flag Officer, Iceland, where he established close relations with the United States Navy, to whose officers he greatly endeared himself with his salty and unconventional sense of humour; as Naval Secretary to the First Sea Lord, Sir Andrew Cunningham*; and

to the command of the Tenth Cruiser Squadron in the Home Fleet. In this capacity he supported the invasion of Normandy, and had the satisfaction of witnessing the expulsion of the Germans from the ancestral home in the Cotentin Peninsula of his French great-grandmother the Duchesse de Coigny.

In 1945 he became Vice-Admiral, Malta; in 1946, Flag Officer, Scotland; and in 1948, Admiral, British Joint Services Mission in Washington. In this his last naval appointment, the friendships he had made in the United States Navy in Iceland and elsewhere stood him in good stead, and his eventual retirement in 1950 after 45 years of varied and distinguished service was regretted in Washington almost as much as in the Royal Navy.

He and his wife had long made their home at Cladyhouse, on the shore of Lochryan near Lochinch; but on the death of his elder brother he succeeded to the old and beautiful house of Bargany in Ayrshire, with its legendary acres of azaleas and rhododendrons.

He married in 1918 Gwendolen, daughter of Sir Cuthbert Peek, Bt., and leaves one son and two daughters. His wife died in November. The son, who succeeds to Bargany, is Captain North Dalrymple-Hamilton, C.V.O., D.S.C., M.B.E., R.N.

December 30, 1974.

Cardinal Jean Danielou, of the Society of Jesus, a distinguished theologian, writer and humanist, died on May 20, 1974. He was 69 years of age.

Throughout the period of transformation and upheaval undergone by the Roman Catholic Church since the Second Vatican Council, Cardinal Danielou played a prominent part as an ardent polemicist and defender of traditional values and beliefs. He was especially firm in his defence of the Papacy and of its supremacy, and inspired the "Letter of Loyalty and Obedience" sent to Pope Paul VI and signed by more than 100,000 believers. But he was not hostile to evolution and "Aggiornamento" in the Church, and played a prominent part in the ecumenical movement, especially in relations with non-Christians. His standpoint marked him out as a conservative in doctrinal matters, at a time when the French hierarchy was dominated by much more "progressive" bishops, but his conservatism was always enlightened, generous, and deeply spiritual.

Jean Danielou, the son of Charles Danielou, journalist, politician and minister, and of Madeleine Clamorgan, the founder of a famous institution for the education of young ladies, was born on May 14, 1905 at Neuilly sur Seine, just outside Paris. After studying at the Sorbonne, he entered the Society of Jesus in 1929 and was ordained in 1938, having in the meantime obtained doctorates of theology and of

letters. His doctorate thesis, "Platonisme and mystical theology after Saint Gregory of Nyssa", was to determine his career. He specialized in the history of the primitive Christian church, and Judeo-Christian theology, and became a professor, later dean, of the Paris Faculty of Theology. But he was also and always a pastor of youth, chaplain of the teachers' school at Sèvres, and of others. He vigorously encouraged young people in their hostility to rising fascism and naziism.

His literary activity was also considerable. He played a leading part in the jesuit periodical *Études*, and was the author of a number of works on the liturgy, theology, and the place of the Church in the modern world, including *Bible and Liturgy* (1950), *Theology of Judeo-Christianity* (1958), *Prayer, a political problem* (1965), and *Why the Church?* (1972). He made of the Cercle Saint Jean Baptiste, a meeting in Paris, a place of permanent exchange and contact between people of many religions. In the words of Father Michel Riquet, a distinguished fellow Jesuit and distinguished preacher, Cardinal Danielou's luminous and lively works were designed to give Christians the answer to the burning problems of their time, and were marked by the firm resolution to uphold a Christianity open to progress, but in the true tradition of the Apostles.

He participated in the work of Vatican II, and in the post-conciliar commissions as an expert. In 1969, he was made a Cardinal by Pope Paul, who had a great personal esteem for him. Three years later, he was elected a member of the French Academy, to the chair of Bossuet, in succession to Cardinal Tisserant, an election contested by progressive elements of the church as redolent of past "triumphalism". He was a Chevalier of the Legion of Honour.

May 22, 1974.

Bebe Daniels, who died on March 16, 1971 in London at the age of 70, enjoyed two notable careers in show-business, the second of which, begun in British radio during the war, made her and her husband, Ben Lyon, firm favourites of the British public and something of an institution even among those for whom their earlier careers in Hollywood were known only as a subject for their own jokes.

Bebe Daniels was born in Dallas, Texas, on January 14, 1901, and as her parents were actors she began an acting career early —at the age of four, to be precise, when she toured as the Duke of York in *Richard III*. The next year she was playing productions by Morosooa and Belasco, entered films with *The Squaw Man* (first version) in 1906, and by the time she was seven had played her first starring role on the screen, as the young heroine of *A Common Enemy*.

At the age of 13 she was starring opposite Harold Lloyd in a series of *Lonesome Luke* two-reel comedies, and shortly afterwards was put under contract by Cecil B. de Mille, for whom she played secondary roles in such films as *Male and Female, Why Change Your Wife,* and *The Affairs of Anatol.* From there she went on to a long-term contract with Paramount, officially achieved adult stardom in 1922, and by 1924 was playing opposite Rudolf Valentino in *Monsieur Beaucaire.* After this she played a number of light popular films with titles like *Miss Bluebeard, The Manicure Girl,* and *Wild, Wild Susan,* and coasted along very happily until the coming of sound.

For the talkies her pleasant singing voice and early stage training stood her in good stead, and she achieved one of her biggest film successes in *Rio Rita* (1929). Other musicals followed, *42nd Street* among them, as well as a few dramatic roles in films such as *Counsellor-at-Law.*

In 1935 she went to Britain and appeared in several British films, then on the stage—at the Holborn Empire in the George Black musical *Haw Haw,* at the Palladium in *Gangway,* and for more than two years at the Piccadilly and elsewhere in *Panama Hattie.*

It was in the early days of the war, though, that she found her warm and lasting place in the hearts of the British public, by choosing to stay on in Britain, with Ben Lyon, and continue through the worst days of the blitz to appear in their radio show *Hi Gang,* which she also largely wrote. She and her husband toured widely entertaining the troops, and after the war she received the Medal of Freedom from the American Government for war service. In 1945 she returned briefly to Hollywood as a film producer for Hal Roach and Eagle-Lion, but returned to Britain in 1948 and had lived there with her family ever since.

From 1950 they appeared in a succession of series of family comedies, *Life With the Lyons,* first on radio, then latterly on television and in the cinema. During this time nearly all the notable talents in British comedy script writing today passed through her "script factory" writing episodes for the series, and many have since paid tribute to her unfailing eye for a telling situation and her immaculate sense of comic timing, which provided invaluable training in the sheer craft of comedy.

She is survived by Ben Lyon and their two children, Barbara and Richard.

March 17, 1971.

Egmond D'Arcis, who died on December 7, 1971 at the age of 84, was for over 40 years the correspondent of *The Times* in Switzerland. For almost 60 years he was closely associated with alpine climbing and its organization. He was president of the International Union of Alpine Associations for many years.

D'Arcis's association with *The Times* began in the spring of 1921, when he was introduced to the paper by Hubert Walter, who after having been Special Correspondent in Paris immediately after the war had been sent to Geneva to watch the emergence of the League of Nations. Between 1914 and 1918 D'Arcis had done propaganda work for the British Embassy in Switzerland, and this, and family associations with England and his strong pro-British sympathies influenced Walter in his recommendation.

To begin with, D'Arcis concerned himself with the League of Nations as well as with Swiss news, but as the league took shape in Geneva it became the practice of *The Times* to send staff correspondents to cover its sessions—W. F. Casey (later Editor) and Harold Williams, the Foreign Editor, in the early days—and from then on D'Arcis confined himself to purely Swiss news. This restriction he happily accepted, perhaps the more so because he was writing regularly about his beloved mountains and mountaineering.

During the Second World War he again did propaganda work for Britain, this time in direct cooperation with H. G. G. Daniels, a former staff correspondent of *The Times* in Berlin and Paris. After the fall of France, Daniels produced a bulletin of British news (from the B.B.C.) in German in the Embassy in Berne and D'Arcis did the same in French in Geneva. For a time this was a clandestine operation; the typewritten bulletin was duplicated in D'Arcis's home until the Swiss authorities told him he could drop the subterfuge, by which they at least had never been deceived.

Meanwhile, he continued to act as correspondent of *The Times,* exploiting the possibilities of Switzerland as a source of news of Germany and France, an operation of some delicacy, as many of his best sources were necessarily secret. He found some help in the reasonableness of the Swiss censorship, which would on occasion point out that while a news item could not go out datelined "Geneva" there would be no obstacle if it appeared to originate from the "French frontier". He liked to recall that one of the censors, emerging from almost six years of anonymity, turned out to be a fellow mountaineer.

D'Arcis, short and sturdily built, started mountaineering in his youth, but those who knew him only in later life, quiet, unassuming and undogmatic, would not have suspected that he was one of the first to climb in the Swiss Alps without guides and thereby incur a great deal of criticism. In his early days he climbed many peaks and was one of the pioneers of the climbing and training schools of the Swiss Alpine Club.

He started skiing about 1903, at a time when few people went to the mountains in winter. About this time his all-the-year-round enthusiasm for the mountains spilled over into writing. His climbing, his work in the organization of mountaineering—he also shared in the formation of the first voluntary mountain rescue squad in Geneva—and his personal popularity led to his election in 1932 as president of the International Union of Alpine Associations, then newly formed. From then on, he was regularly reelected every three years, and the organization of the union, with its seat in Geneva, owed much to his enthusiasm and energy.

The alpine museum at Zermatt, the basis of which was the Seiler collection of accident relics, was primarily D'Arcis's idea; he was always a zealous guardian of alpine amenities. Some years ago he was the originator of the campaign that stopped the building of a cable railway to the summit of the Matterhorn. The petition against the scheme was signed by 1,800,000 people all over the world.

Besides his journalism, D'Arcis wrote two books: *En Montagne* (1935) and *Neiges Eternelles* (1945). He is survived by his wife, his constant companion, who shared his enthusiasms and delighted his friends with her vivacity.

December 8, 1971.

Phyllis Dare, the actress, who died on April 27, 1975 at the age of 84, was for years a leading lady of musical comedy, as was her elder sister Zena Dare; but, unlike her sister, she did not make a second, successful career for herself in straight comedy in later life. It seemed as if she remained in the world of musical romance, and when such work no longer came to her, she in effect retired. Her sister died in March.

Born on August 15, 1890, the daughter of Arthur Dones, a clerk in the Divorce Court, Phyllis was three and a half years younger than Zena, but they first appeared together, under the stage name Dare, in a pantomime in 1899, after which their next professional association was in 1940.

Seymour Hicks engaged Phyllis for a child's role in his *Bluebell in Fairyland* and entrusted her in 1905 with the heroine's role in *The Catch of the Season* in succession to Zena and to his wife Ellaline Terriss, for whom he had originally written it.

Phyllis Dare also succeeded the American star Edna May in *The Belle of Mayfair,* and soon afterwards had her first experience of singing a number by Paul A. Rubens, an Old Wykehamist, a former member of the Oxford University Dramatic Society and a prolific composer, for whom she was to work in three more of his musical plays.

It was not, however, in a Rubens show but in *The Arcadians* that she had her first long run. Her next pieces, *The Girl in the Train, Peggy* and Rubens's *The Sunshine Girl,* were all staged by George Edwardes, the father of musical comedy, the last two at the Gaiety Theatre; but according to its chronicler Macqueen-Pope,

Phyllis Dare was not the perfect leading lady for that theatre. She with her grace and repose was like a pearl, whereas what the Gaiety needed, and had previously had in Gertie Millar, was a glittering diamond.

Certainly it was not there but at the Adelphi that she played her next two leading roles, which proved to be the last of the series, for George Edwardes. After the outbreak of war in 1914, while Edwardes was still interned in Germany, she took service under Frank Curzon in a revival of Rubens's *Miss Hook of Holland. Tina,* produced shortly after Edwardes's death in 1915, in which Godfrey Tearle played opposite to her when not on duty as a cadet at Wellington Barracks, also had music by Rubens. The latter had become engaged to her, but his health deteriorated, and in November 1916 the engagement was broken off by common consent.

Rubens died some months later at the age of 40, and she was not seen again on the stage, apart from a brief appearance in revue, until the summer of 1919 at the opening of the Winter Garden, in company with what *The Times* called a bevy of demobilized comedians. According to the same critic, her acting and dancing in *Kissing Time* had improved to the point where they were now equal to her singing.

She brought all three aspects of her talent into play in Frederick Lonsdale's *The Lady of the Rose* and *The Street Singer*—the former was an adaptation by him—in the early 1920s. Her leading man in both was Harry Welchman, and Lonsdale intimated to Daly's audience that something more serious and dramatic than usual was contemplated in the first, by dispensing with an opening chorus and raising the curtain on a stage on which Phyllis Dare was pensively alone.

She was less well served in the musical plays that followed, for the fat parts in *Lido Lady* were those of the comedians Jack Hulbert and Cicely Courtneidge, while Edgar Wallace hardly supplied a fat part for anyone in *The Yellow Mask*; so that it was obvious by the end of the 1920s that if at nearly 40 she was to remain at the top of her profession she must look to the straight stage for her main opportunities.

Marie Tempest and Gladys Cooper had successfully made the change-over; Lily Elsie* looked like doing so, though she did not persevere; Zena Dare, having left the stage on her marriage and returned fifteen years later, was in the midst of attempting it.

The wife's role in the first London revival of Lonsdale's straight play *Aren't We All?* seemed to promise a good fresh start for Phyllis Dare, but there was an interval of seven years during which she was seen again on the musical stage in London and on tour, before her next straight role in a comedy thriller by Walter Hackett, to which her contribution was less important than that of the comedienne, Marion Lorne, the author's wife.

Authors and managers had difficulty in

"seeing" her in comedy roles. She hadn't the gaiety, the quietly mocking spirit of Zena, which Ivor Novello had now exploited to the advantage of them both. Phyllis still lived up to Macqueen-Pope's word for her in her musical-comedy days. She was still a pearl, and now that she was older, there was a certain gravity and aloofness about her.

She spent a lot of time on tour in the years preceding the Second World War and during it, in Dodie Smith's *Call it a Day,* with her sister again in a revival of Novello's *Full House*—Zena in Lilian Braithwaite's old part, Phyllis in Isabel Jeans's —and in Rose Franklin's *Claudia.*

The postwar years brought her supporting roles in three more comedies, the only worthy one that of the heroine's bitter adversary in a revival of Maugham's* *Lady Frederick,* dressed in the fashions of the 1880s. But in 1949 Ivor Novello had ready *King's Rhapsody,* in which there was a role not only for Zena Dare but, for the first time in a musical of his, for Phyllis too.

One was to be the mother, the other the faithful mistress, of a Ruritanian royalty to be played by Novello himself, and to the mistress he gave a song that had been no more than a half-success in a previous Novello musical, staged during the late war. Described in *The Times* as a mock-revolutionary ditty, as now sung at the Palace it was voted the best number in the new, sumptuous Novellian romance. Phyllis Dare, wrote Macqueen-Pope, could have taken as many encores as she liked.

Nearly eighteen months later Novello died while the play was still running, and at the end of seven more months, in October 1951, it closed. Thereafter Zena Dare continued her career, but Phyllis did not. She spent the years of her retirement mostly in Brighton. She was unmarried.

April 29, 1975.

Zena Dare (the Hon. Mrs. Brett), the actress, who died on March 11, 1975 at the age of 88, had a remarkable career in the theatre in the sense that it consisted of two careers, both successful, separated by 15 years during which she was in retirement.

When she left the stage after her marriage in 1911, she was a big name in musical comedy. She returned in 1926 to the legitimate theatre, where her name meant little; but when she left for good it had gained lustre from the success of numerous light plays, straight and musical, to which the urbanity and wit of her acting had contributed much.

Her death recalls the era of the picture postcard and millions of copies must have been sold of the four reigning beauties of the period, Marie Studholme, Gabrielle Ray and the Dare sisters, Zena and Phyllis. Zena Dare's sparkling personality decorated many a play for many a year.

Florence Hariette Zena Dones, the daughter of Arthur Dones, a clerk in the Divorce Court, was born (according to *Who's Who in the Theatre*) on February 4, 1887. She and her younger sister, Phyllis Dare, began their careers in the same London pantomime in 1899, but Zena's education continued, on her mother's insistence, for several more years in the intervals of further appearances in pantomime.

After touring in one of Seymour Hicks's many musical comedies, she was engaged for a West End role under Frank Curzon's management, but was released when Hicks needed someone to play the leading part which he had designed for his wife, Ellaline Terriss—and, incidentally, to dance an Irish jig with a shillelagh in her hand—in *The Catch of the Season.*

Having finished a spell of work for George Edwardes, most active of all Edwardian impresarios of musical comedy, she returned to play with Hicks at the recently opened Aldwych in *The Beauty of Bath* and in *The Gay Gordons,* a piece set in the Scottish Highlands on a Twelfth of August with herself as a gipsy who changed places with Ellaline Terriss as a millionaire's daughter.

She and Hicks later appeared together at the Coliseum, and it was at the newly reconstructed Hippodrome that she was last seen on the stage before becoming the wife in January 1911 of the Hon. Maurice Brett, second son of the second Viscount Esher. A daughter, a son and a second daughter were born of the marriage during the first six years of her 15 years' absence from the theatre.

At the age of 39 she came back not to the West End but to lead a touring company, without any big names in support of her, in Lonsdale's *The Last of Mrs. Cheyney.* She survived the exacting task for a late beginner in high comedy, to whom the learning of straight dialogue did not come easily, of playing opposite Noël Coward under Basil Dean's direction the part originally played by Lynn Fontanne in S. N. Behrman's *The Second Man;* and after a tour of South Africa with her own company, she stood in for a couple of weeks for Marie Tempest, the doyenne of London's comedy actresses, in the name part of St. John Ervine's *The First Mrs. Fraser.*

But her real opportunity of making a new niche for herself in the theatre was given to Zena Dare by Ivor Novello in the years immediately preceding and following the death of her husband, which occurred in 1934. The roles of Novello's stage mother in his *Proscenium,* of the murderer's mother in his *Murder in Mayfair,* and of the manageress of a beauty parlour in his Drury Lane musical *Careless Rapture* were exactly suited to her years and to her bent for mild caricature, which allowed her to mix frivolity with the romantic sentiment of Novello's work and so made the latter more palatable to his increasingly large public.

She had an intrinsically better part in

M. J. Farrell and John Perry's Irish comedy *Spring Meeting* in 1938, but soon after the beginning of the Second World War she and her sister Phyllis, reunited professionally for the first time since childhood, went on tour in a revival of one of Novello's lesser plays. The war years brought her roles in Sir John Gielgud's revival of a Barrie; as the Red Queen in *Alice Through the Looking Glass*; and in a new Lonsdale; but later in 1945 she rejoined Novello in his *Perchance to Dream*, a musical romance with a Regency and Victorian setting.

King's Rhapsody, its Ruritanian successor, with Zena as his royal mother and Phyllis as his faithful mistress, was the last Novello in which he himself was to appear. It had been running for almost 18 months at the Palace when he died in 1951, and it continued running for seven months after his death.

She spent some time in the cast of Noël Coward's *Nude with Violin,* having succeeded Joyce Carey as the bogus painter's widow; but her longest run of all was that of the Shaw-inspired musical *My Fair Lady* with which, after more than five years as Mrs. Higgins at Drury Lane and a season on tour, Zena Dare closed her career.

It was fitting that she should do so while wearing Cecil Beaton's witty versions of the fashions of the pre-1914 period, of which she had been one of the picture-postcard beauties in her own right. Her vivacity, grace and charm were indeed proof against age.

March 12, 1975.

Sir Robin Darwin, C.B.E., R.A., who died suddenly on January 30, 1974, was Principal of the Royal College of Art from 1948 to 1967; and from that year, when the college was given university status, until his retirement in 1971, he was its first rector and vice-provost.

He had been art master at Watford Grammar School and then at Eton College from 1933 to 1938. From 1939 to 1944 he worked at the camouflage directorate of the Ministry of Home Security, becoming its secretary.

After service with the Ministry of Town and Country Planning and the Council of Industrial Design, he was Director of the King Edward VII School of Art at Newcastle upon Tyne, and Professor of Fine Art at Durham University from 1946 to 1947. Then he succeeded P. H. Jowett at the Royal College of Art.

Robert Vere Darwin was born in 1910, the son of the late Bernard* and Elinor Darwin, and was thus great grandson of the author of *Origin of Species* and a descendant of Erasmus Darwin. He was educated at Eton and studied painting at the Slade School of Art in 1929.

His appointment to Eton at the age of only 23 was unexpected and followed the accidental death of his predecessor. Within a year the drawing schools, from being little more than a scene of discreet and genteel activity in drawing from the cast and painting from nature in water colours, had become a vital centre of the college's daily life. His enthusiasm set the place on fire, and he proved himself an inspiring teacher and a liberator.

He joined the Council of Industrial Design as training officer soon after its creation in 1944. His important contribution was a report on the training of industrial designers which was constructive as well as analytical and which paid particular attention to the proper place of the Royal College of Art within the national system of art education and training. He proposed a widening of the college's field of activity to include disciplines as various as light engineering, plastics technology and fashion design, and emphasized the importance of cultivating the relationship that existed between all branches of art and design.

His choice as principal of the Royal College of Art was one of brilliant imagination. He threw himself into his new role with the energy and gusto that he brought to every activity, setting up advisory committees of industrialists to analyse the needs of each industry that the college was to serve; developing academic and administrative systems that would win respect for the place and its products among those most sceptical of the art student's value in an industrial society; identifying designers practising in the various fields, cultivating their friendship and choosing from among them, and then infecting the chosen with his own enthusiasm.

He set store by the independence of the constituent schools. Their heads were expected to run them each in his own way so that each school developed its own special character and its own pride in its contribution to the central achievement. But still he emphasized the close relationship of the separate activities and the interest that each held for all. His staff were truly a team.

Within 15 years his vision and methods had earned success. The college, which had lost some of its identity through its wartime exile to Cumberland, was now generally regarded as the leading institution of its kind in the world. Its influence spread through the whole edifice of art education in Britain, thanks in part to the external activities of its principal, who was serving concurrently on the National Advisory Council on Art Education and the National Council for Diplomas in Art and Design.

Since his retirement Darwin had given his wisdom and experience to the Royal Academy of Arts, of which he was elected an associate in 1966 and a full academician in 1972.

Behind all his public activities he knew himself as a painter. At the Slade under Tonks and Steer he found himself a part of that rebel generation which included William Coldstream, Rodrigo Moyniham and Geoffrey Tibble. His painting always expressed the exuberance of his own nature.

He was a warm and constant friend and a marvellous travelling companion. He could be ruthless when too much concern for the feelings of others would have interfered with his duty, and so he made enemies. But surprisingly often they ended as his friends.

He married first Yvonne, daughter of the late H. J. Darby. He married secondly Ginette, daughter of the late F. W. Hewitt and Adriana Hugh-Smith and she survives him. He was knighted in 1964.

February 1, 1974.

Sir Peter Daubeny, C.B.E., the founder and, for a decade, the Artistic Director of the World Theatre Season at the Aldwych, died on August 6, 1975 at the age of 54.

It would be difficult to exaggerate either Peter Daubeny's fortitude or the extent of his influence on the English theatre. After being wounded at Salerno in 1943 and losing his left arm, he did not enjoy good health and was often in considerable pain, but bravely continued an abnormally active life. During the last 12 years of his life he spent the bulk of his time working in his World Theatre Season, travelling tirelessly all over the globe, like a theatrical Marco Polo, exploring the international scene as no impresario ever had before.

But it was long before 1964 that he began to change the face of Britain's insular theatre by importing foreign companies. There are few turning points in our postwar theatrical history as important as the 1956 visit of Brecht's Berliner Ensemble, which shifted playwrights, directors, designers and even casting directors to thinking more in socio-economic terms. Kenneth Tynan had already written copiously about Brecht, and Joan Littlewood had absorbed some of his ideas, but it was Daubeny who actually brought over three of his productions.

Born in Wiesbaden on April 16, 1921, into a military family with no theatrical connexions, Peter Daubeny spent a year training as an actor at Michel St. Denis's London Theatre Studio, and in the summer of 1939 he was taken on as a student at the Liverpool Repertory Theatre, but his acting career was cut short by the war. As a lieutenant in the Coldstream Guards he fought with the Eighth Army in North Africa until he lost his arm.

He had already decided on a career in theatrical management before being invalided back to Britain. With some help from Ivor Novello he succeeded in mounting the first play to be produced in London after V.E. Day—*The Gay Pavilion* by William Lipscombe. It came off after barely a month's run, but, having met S. N. Behrman socially, Daubeny was able to bounce back into the same theatre, the Piccadilly, two months later with *Jacobowsky and the Colonel*, Brecht's adaptation of a play by Werfel, directed by Michael Redgrave, who also played the Colonel.

Within the next four years, though still in his twenties, Daubeny was able to put on plays by Lonsdale (*But for the Grace of God*, with A. E. Matthews), Somerset Maugham (*Our Betters*), Ivor Novello (*We Proudly Present*), Noël Coward (a revival of *Fallen Angels* with Hermione Gingold and Hermione Baddeley) and a successful thriller, *The late Edwina Black*.

His international involvements began mainly with ballet companies. Between June 1951 and March 1952 he presented six foreign companies at The Cambridge, including the Ballets des Champs-Elysées with Jean Babilée, Zizi Jeanmaire and Roland Petit, Katherine Dunham's company and a company from India. In 1953 he brought over Sacha Guitry and the American National Ballet Company. Then in 1954 he organized Martha Graham's first visit to London.

Before his first World Theatre Season was launched with the sponsorship of the Royal Shakespeare Company in 1964 as a contribution to the celebrations for the 400th anniversary of Shakespeare's birth, he had been responsible for bringing a great many important companies to England. They included the Mozart Opera Company from Salzburg, Les Ballets Africains, Jean Vilar's Théâtre National Populaire, the Red Army Choir, the Compagnie Madeleine Renaud-Jean, Louis Barrault (in a programme of four plays, one of which was Claudel's *Christophe Colombe*, which gave London audiences one of their earliest experiences of "total theatre"), Edwige Feuillère's company, the Chinese Classical Theatre from Formosa, the New York Negro Ballet, the Moscow Art Theatre, the Comédie Française, the Swedish company from Malmo in Ingmar Bergman's production of Goethe's *Urfaust*, Jerome Robbins's Ballets U.S.A., Marie Bell's company in a Racine season and the Off-Broadway company in Jack Gelber's *The Connection*.

It has been said that the World Theatre Season became one of the strongest justifications for London's claim to be the world's theatrical capital: this is true, but we must not forget how much Daubeny had already done towards establishing the claim.

There is no need to list the companies or the productions which have been seen in the 11 seasons he organized, but what is not always realized is how often they provided cues for English productions. Jacques Charon's direction of the Comédie Française in Feydeau's *Un Fil à la patte* must have inspired the idea of inviting him to direct Feydeau's *A Flea in Her Ear* at the National, and Zuckmayer's *The Captain from Köpenick* might never have been done there if the Schiller Theatre from Berlin had not brought it to the previous year's World Theatre Season.

Nor can it be fortuitous that the Royal Shakespeare Company's decision to revive Dion Boucicault's *London Assurance* was taken just after the Abbey Theatre from Dublin had brought his play *The Shaughraun* to the 1968 World Theatre Season. And it was after Japanese Noh Theatre had featured in the 1967 season that Peter Brook introduced Noh techniques into his work on *The Tempest*.

When ill health prevented Peter Daubeny from organizing a World Theatre Season in 1974, it became obvious that no one could step forward to replace him. Who else would have the flair, the energy, the devotion and the time to travel round the world shopping for productions? It was good news that the doctors allowed him to produce another season in 1975, and, though it turned out to be below the standard he had set for himself, it should not be allowed to obscure the importance of his earlier achievements.

Made C.B.E. in 1967 and knighted in 1973, he was also showered with international honours, the Gold Cross of the Royal Order of King George I of Greece (1965), Cavaliere of the Order of Merit of the Italian Republic (1966), Gold Medal of Czechoslovakia (1967), Order of Merit of the German Federal Republic (1971), Legion of Honour (1971), and Polonia Restituta (1974). Italy conferred on him the rank of Commendatore of its Order of Merit only a few days before he died.

Sir Peter Daubeny published two books, *Stage by Stage* (1952) and *My World of Theatre* (1971). He married in 1948 and is survived by Lady Daubeny, a son, Nicholas, and a daughter, Caroline.

August 7, 1975.

Herman David, C.B.E., chairman of the All-England Lawn Tennis Club and a world authority on industrial diamonds, died at the age of 67 on February 25, 1974.

In his youth, he was a fine tennis player who could have achieved distinction had he been able to devote more time to the game. But it was as a tennis administrator, notably as chairman of the All-England Club and the Wimbledon championships committee, that he may be best remembered.

It would be invidious to suggest that any one man was responsible for ripping away the hypocrisy of "shamateurism" ("a living lie" as he put it in a memorable and oft-quoted phrase) and ushering in the era of open competition that led to the game's astonishing advance as a big-money spectator sport. But Herman David had as much to do with it as anyone. He raised the banner of rebellion; and he held it aloft until, after many battles had been lost, the cause was eventually won.

As a player he won many tournaments before the war and, at Wimbledon, took sets from such famous contemporaries as Fred Perry and Frank Shields and partnered another, Dorothy Round, in doubles. With Perry, he played singles for Britain in their 5-0 Davis Cup win over Romania at Torquay in 1932. As late as 1947, he reached the last 16 of the Wimbledon doubles with his brother Edmund. From 1953 to 1958 he was non-playing captain of the British Davis Cup team.

By this time he was also serving on the committee of the All-England Club. He had succeeded Dr. Colin Gregory as Davis Cup captain and in 1959, when Gregory died, David also succeeded him as chairman of the All-England Club. One of his first tasks was to call a special general meeting to consider amateurism and the possibility of an Open Wimbledon.

In 1964 the All-England Club put to the Lawn Tennis Association a motion that, in effect, suggested Britain should "go it alone" with an Open Wimbledon. For years, said David, the International Lawn Tennis Federation had been "wilfully blind" to the problems of the players. At that time the L.T.A. were not ready to defy the I.L.T.F. But David and like-minded progressives kept on fighting, and three years later they swung the L.T.A. behind them.

Fed up with "shamateurism", Britain sought to abolish all distinctions between amateurs and professionals. They announced that in April 1968 they would hold an Open tournament at Bournemouth. The I.L.T.F. threatened to suspend them. But Britain would not budge. In March 1968 the I.L.T.F. agreed to a limited number of Open tournaments, a compromise that led David to observe: "We got nearly all we wanted."

The barriers between amateurs and professionals were crumbling at last. In that winter of 1967-68 Britain launched a revolution that changed the history of the game; and David as ever, was in the front line.

He remained forthright and firm amid the difficulties that inevitably beset the game's sudden expansion as an honest and respectable profession in which players could earn their money openly. The wider war had been won. David concentrated now on the health of the tournament that had always been close to his heart—Wimbledon. His leadership had much to do with its astonishing capacity to survive weakened men's entries (forced upon it by disputes in which others sought to use Wimbledon's prestige and influence) that would have seriously damaged any other tournament.

David was always positive and bold in his integrity. In the controversies of recent years his attitude towards the I.L.T.F. seemed to soften a little. But his judgment was usually sound and it was always guided by patriotism and loyalty, plus the wisdom gained from the experience of many years in the service of the game. He left Wimbledon and the game as a whole in a healthier condition than he found them—and he would wish no better epitaph than that.

In 1934 he married Mavis Evans and they had one son and two daughters.

February 26, 1974.

Sir Martin Davies, C.B.E., F.B.A., formerly Director of the National Gallery, died on March 7, 1975 in a London hospital. He was 66.

He was born on March 22, 1908 and educated at Rugby School and King's College, Cambridge, where he studied modern languages. He joined the staff of the National Gallery in 1932 and rose steadily from Assistant Keeper until in 1968 he succeeded Sir Philip Hendy as Director. He retired as Director in 1973.

Although before 1945 he had published some scholarly articles, it was his catalogues of the National Gallery pictures appearing in the immediate postwar years which internationally revealed Davies's stature as a scholar. They were the fruit of intensive, scrupulous study of each picture catalogued, facilitated by the wartime storage of the pictures in Wales, of which he was effectively in sole charge.

The first catalogue to appear was that of the *Early Netherlandish School* in 1945, a school for which he had a special affection and to which he returned in his volumes of *Les Primitifs Flamands.* It was followed by catalogues of the French and British schools. In 1951 appeared the first edition of Davies's major work, the *Earlier Italian Schools* catalogue, of which he later published a revised edition.

The discreetly employed yet vast erudition, and the author's characteristic blend of scepticism with tenacity in research, established these volumes as unrivalled catalogues of any public collection of pictures. Their influence has probably been greater than is always recognized.

During his comparatively short tenure as Director, Davies sought to combine scholarly standards with cautious fostering of more popular approaches. Several distinguished acquisitions were made, including Titian's "Death of Actaeon", purchased after a successful public appeal, and the then recently discovered "S. Ivo" by Rogier van der Weyden, on whom he published his only monograph (1973).

A complete illustrated general catalogue of the collection was published during his directorship, as well as a new series of booklets, *Themes and Painters,* to which he himself contributed Crivelli and Rembrandt. Much of his time and thought were given to the building of the northern extension of the gallery, its largest addition since 1911, now nearing completion.
[This obituary was followed by a tribute from a reader.]

March 8, 1975.

S. O. Davies, MP. for Merthyr Tydfil since 1934, died at Merthyr General Hospital on February 25, 1972. He was 85.

Stephen Owen Davies was not nominated by Merthyr Labour Party for the 1970 general election. He fought the official Labour candidate and won with a majority of nearly 7,500. He sat as Independent Labour and was expelled from the official Labour Party.

He was one of the left wing "rebels", and time and again was a source of trouble to the official Labour Party leadership in the House of Commons. No disciplinary action seemed to moderate his extreme views, and he maintained a stubborn aggressive attitude.

He was particularly outspoken in his dislike of the United States and its policy, and on one occasion was openly rebuked at question-time by Clement Attlee. He gave the impression of having few political sympathizers among his Parliamentary colleagues; indeed, he tended deliberately to isolate and estrange himself from them. In 1961 he was one of five Labour rebels who had the whip withdrawn by the Parliamentary group after voting against Service estimates. It was restored in 1963.

In 1966 the Aberfan Disaster killed 144 people, 116 of them children. Davies told the inquiry into the disaster that he had repeatedly voiced fears about the stability of the Aberfan Tip. After the disaster, Davies spoke of new perils to Aberfan and demanded the removal of what was left of the tips. Richard Marsh, then Minister of Power, ordered an immediate inquiry. Davies resigned from the management committee of the Aberfan Disaster Fund in 1968. He said it was a "betrayal of principle" to use on the tips money given by people to the fund.

Three months later Davies was himself offered the freedom of the borough. He refused. "It would be superfluous", he wrote to the council, thanking them for their kindly gesture. "The confidence which the people have shown me over many years has given me the fullest satisfaction."

Davies's final blow at the party he had served for more than 30 years came when the election expenses of his 1970 campaign were published. They showed he had defeated the official Labour candidate for £212—the smallest expenses of any M.P. in the House.

Born in 1886, he entered the pits at the age of 12; matriculated from the coalface; graduated in arts at the University of Wales; and returned to work as a collier. In 1913 he became a check-weigher, and five years later was appointed miners' agent under the South Wales Miners' Federation at Dowlais, a post he held until 1933. From 1924 to 1934 he represented the Welsh miners on the Miners' Federation of Great Britain, and later became Chief Organizer to the South Wales Miners' Federation.

In 1934 the opportunity came for him to enter the House of Commons. R. C. Wallhead, who had sat for Merthyr Tydfil for many years, died, and Davies was chosen as his successor. But he had to fight a surprisingly difficult by-election. In addition to a Liberal opponent, Campbell Stephen stood as an Independent Labour candidate, and there was also a Communist candidate. His majority was 8,269, and at subsequent elections he was never seriously worried. In 1950, for instance, his majority was nearly 23,000.

Although he had an intense dislike of militarism in all forms, Davies denied he was a pacifist, declaring that a man who had fought the coal owners could never be a pacifist. He strongly opposed the United Nations' intervention in Korea, and in 1953 greatly angered the whole House by asking the Prime Minister "in view of the widespread revulsion of feeling against the United States in this country, if he would take steps to have the United States Embassy and consulates here closed within four weeks, and all United States armed forces withdrawn forthwith from British soil". Some Labour members attempted to get the question ruled out of order, but the Speaker said that the House must be careful to preserve the doctrine of free speech. To this the argument was raised that Davies's was obviously an abuse of free speech, but the Speaker adhered to his ruling. In the absence of the Prime Minister, the Leader of the House (then Mr. Crookshank*) replied that "the Prime Minister does not for one moment accept the mischievous and irresponsible assertions made, which are utterly without foundation". This was the occasion when Davies was publicly rebuked by his party leader.

Perhaps the most serious breach of discipline occurred in 1948, over the notorious Nenni telegram, when Davies was one of 22 left-wing Labour M.P.s, one of whom was subsequently expelled from the party, who signed the telegram of good wishes to the Nenni-Communist combination in the Italian parliamentary election. In November 1954 Davies was one of the seven Labour M.P.s who defied the instructions of their leaders by voting in the division on the London and Paris agreements. The party whip was withdrawn from all of them, after an acrimonious discussion at the party meeting, but they were readmitted early in 1955.

Davies was a strong advocate of Welsh Home Rule, and in 1955 introduced the Government for Wales Bill, but little came of it. In appearance Davies was anything but a revolutionary. Tall, with a not unpleasing personality, he had an outwardly quiet demeanour. But underneath fires were forever smouldering, and could be fanned into flame at the least provocation. He was for many years a member of Merthyr Corporation, and also served as mayor.

He married in 1934, and had two sons and three daughters.

February 26, 1972.

Sir Herbert Davis, a vice-chairman of Unilever Limited from 1943 to 1956, died on February 20, 1972. He was 80.

Born in 1891 he spent much of his boyhood in Hackney and was educated locally at the Grocers' School and at St. John's

College, Cambridge. There he read natural sciences and gained a First in two years, continuing to read for a History Tripos in which he took a Second.

Before leaving Cambridge two important events changed the course of his life. First, through undergraduate friends, he met his wife, Eva Fitzgerald Radford, whom he married in 1912. (Lady Davis died only some weeks ago). Secondly, the newly formed University Appointments Board persuaded him not to follow his choice of a career in the Indian Civil Service but rather to go into commerce. He was directed to Brunner Mond, who had very recently started an early form of management training scheme with selected graduates. On acceptance in 1912 Davis was appointed to the raw materials buying department of Joseph Crosfield Limited, the Warrington soap and chemicals firm, then controlled by Brunner Mond.

In the First World War he was seconded to the Government Department dealing with edible oil supplies. Here he did outstanding work and the work brought him into contact with all sides of the edible oils industry, including Jurgens Limited, the Dutch-owned margarine house. At the end of the war Jurgens offered him an appointment as assistant buyer, which he accepted. He spent some time buying on the Baltic Exchange but eventually Anton Jurgens appointed Davis one of his personal assistants.

With excess capacity throughout Europe, the 1920s were years of intense competition in the margarine industry and the fierce rivalry between Jurgens and their main competitors Van den Berghs led more than once to litigation. Eventually in 1927 the two companies merged to form the Margarine Union; Davis was at the centre of the litigation and subsequent merger, and became a secretary of the new group.

When the Margarine Union and Lever Brothers merged in 1929 to form Unilever, once again Davis was at the centre of the negotiations; indeed it was very probably one of his suggestions that led to the choice of Unilever as the final name of the new group.

From 1930 to 1939 Davis was chief architect of the rationalization and consolidation of Unilever's oil milling activities in the United Kingdom. In 1937 he was appointed to the board.

With the Second World War he was again seconded to Government service as Director of Oils and Fats. He was created C.B.E. in 1941 and was knighted in 1943. Under his direction his division was outstandingly successful not only in organizing the supply and distribution of oils and fats, but also in procuring supplies of the necessary vitamins A and D for the allied countries as well as for Britain. In January 1942 he was appointed a vice-chairman of Unilever.

Herbert Davis brought a quick and incisive brain, combined with complete intellectual integrity and detachment, to any discussion in which he took part. In spite of his own ability to think quickly, he never lost patience with others whose mental processes were slower and he earned not only the respect but affection of his subordinates.

February 22, 1972.

Dr. C. J. Massey Dawkins died on August 8, 1975 at the age of 70. He was a well known London anaesthetist who spread his anaesthetic wings widely, covering dentistry, paediatrics, obstetrics and geriatrics as well as the general field of anaesthesia.

He was one of the pioneers in the field of epidural anaesthesia and it was only in July 1975 that his presidential address on the use of epidural anaesthesia to the section of anaesthetics of the Royal Society of Medicine was published in the Society's *Proceedings*, Epidural anaesthesia, or block, is the modern successor to the older spinal anaesthesia, whereby the pain of an operation is relieved by interrupting the flow of the pain impulses to consciousness, by an injection round the spine. Full anaesthesia is therefore not needed, even though many surgeons and anaesthetists prefer to give in addition a light degree of general anaesthesia.

It was typical of Dr. Dawkins's human approach to his speciality that he concluded his presidential address with the comment "I would like to end on a more humane note . . . it is pleasant to see a patient regain consciousness on the operating table and shake hands with the surgeon, one lady going so far as to insist on kissing him."

Charles John Massey Dawkins was born on July 13, 1905, and was educated at Mill Hill School. Emmanuel College, Cambridge, and the Middlesex Hospital. He qualified in 1929, proceeding to his M.D. in 1936. He took to anaesthetics early in his professional career and in due course he became anaesthetist at University College Hospital, London, being senior anaesthetist from 1946 until his retirement in 1970. He was also dental anaesthetist to his old hospital as well as consulting anaesthetist to the Paddington Green children's hospital and several surburban and home county hospitals.

He was elected a Fellow of the Faculty of Anaesthetists of the Royal College of Surgeons of England in 1948, and he was serving as President of the Section of Anaesthetics of the Royal Society of Medicine at the time of his death. He was also an honorary member of the Finnish Society of Anaesthetists. He was an enthusiastic yachtsman and maintained a lifelong interest in the United Hospitals Sailing Club from home at Bradwell-Juxta-Mare, Essex.

He married, in 1930, Dr. Sylvia Mabel Ransford. They had one son and two daughters.

August 12, 1975.

Edith Day, who died in a London hospital in May 1971, was an American musical comedy actress who established a reputation in London in a single night.

It was in 1920 that she made her first London appearance at the old Empire Theatre in the musical comedy *Irene*, as the girl who lived in a New York tenement house and dreamed, on the fire escape staircase, of the hero who would one day come into her life.

At first a demure shrinking figure with her hair tied with a ribbon which seemed to have come straight off a chocolate box, her stature grew as her dreams materialised. By the end of the evening she had danced and sung her way into the hearts of her audiences who attended over 300 performances and who left the Empire humming one of the two songs which captured London, "Alice-blue Gown" and Irene O'Dare."

Born at Minneapolis on April 10, 1896, she made her first appearance in New York in *Pom Pom* during the First World War, but her first considerable success was in the American production of the musical comedy *Going Up* at the end of 1917, which ran for 350 performances. This was followed by *Irene,* which ran for 670 performances, but she left the American cast in the early days of the run to appear in London in the part which she had created.

She reigned supreme at Drury Lane from 1925 to the beginning of 1930, playing the leading part in *Rose Marie* (851 performances). *The Desert Song* (432 performances), *Showboat* (350 performances), and a revival of *Rose Marie* which scored another hundred performances. There is no doubt that she did much to ensure the success of the new Drury Lane policy of producing spectacular musical plays which Sir Alfred Butt* had inaugurated. Her third great success at Drury Lane was in *Showboat* in the part of Magnolia Hawks in which she easily held her own, despite the competition of two other great artists, Paul Robeson and Marie Burke, in addition to a mass of elaborate spectacle. Thereafter Miss Day appeared in London in *Rio Rita,* in a revival of *The Desert Song*, and in *Sunny River.*

In 1960 she appeared in Noël Coward's *Waiting in the Wings.* She was three times married. Her third husband, Henry Horne, died some years ago. Her son was killed in the Second World War.

May 3, 1971.

Cecil Day-Lewis, C.B.E., who in 1968 succeeded John Masefield as Poet Laureate, died on May 22, 1972 at the age of 68. He had been in poor health for some time.

From an early age he was a dedicated and copious poet, and naturally (though criticism was not really his forte) from time to time published books on his art or craft which were extremely successful (as, indeed, was his verse itself) in making available to a wider audience the preoccupations of a minority art. Though for a short time he worked at the conventional novel, his reputation in prose fiction was gained under the nom-de-plume of "Nicholas Blake" as a writer of deservedly popular detective stories. No assessment of his literary place could fail to take into account also his verse translations, particularly of Virgil, where it might well be argued that his strong sense of tradition yet readiness for sensible experiment found their most successful combinations.

He was born on April 27, 1904, the only child of the Rev. F. C. Day-Lewis, a clergyman in the Church of England. His mother died when he was very young and his relationship with his father was close. Mrs. Day-Lewis was Irish, and Ireland, where the poet spent much of his childhood (and, in later life, many holidays), provided him with that touch of exoticism English writers, even the most English of them, seem to search for. He never, for instance, lost an attractive slight lisp on his final rs, and enjoyed assuming a highly-convincing brogue for anecdotal purposes.

His childhood, schooldays at Sherborne, life at Wadham College, Oxford, his adoption and later rejection of communism are described in his excellent autobiographical book, *The Buried Day*. He was in the school second Rugby XV and played cricket for his house. He was also C.S.M. in the O.T.C. and while commanding a company of the Home Guard in the war showed himself an ingenious deviser of tactical exercises. Like Ireland, the Dorsetshire countryside became a permanent attachment and no doubt led him to his enthusiasm for Hardy. He very soon omitted his earliest poetry from the canon and it was with the volume *Transitional Poems* of 1929 that his reputation started to be made.

The date of his birth was crucially important. He was the oldest of "the Three"—Auden, Spender, Day-Lewis—with whom the "new poetry" of the early 'thirties was associated, but whether without the influence of Auden his own poetry would ever have become "new" may be doubted. Both Spender and MacNeice* added individual notes to the verse revival of those days, but Day-Lewis's most successful contribution was almost wholly in the voice of the Master:

Suppose that we, to-morrow or the next day,

Came to an end—in storm the shafting broken,

Or a mistaken signal, the flange lifting—

Would that be premature, a text for sorrow?

Such poetry was by no means mere plagiarism or pastiche (indeed, it is often memorable and powerful) but its manner did not completely overlay a much more conventional diction and way of feeling—a poetry, in fact, with Georgian roots. So that when, later in the 1930s, the influence of the style embodied in Auden's 1930

Poems receded, and his belief in socialism and the working-class began to be very directly (and touchingly) expressed in his verse, Day-Lewis ran foul of such sophisticated organs of the "new poetry" as *New Verse* and really only in the journalistic concept did he remain part of the avant garde.

After going down from Oxford he taught in schools for eight years, during which time he married his first wife, Mary King, by whom he had two children. It was not until the mid-thirties that he was able, at first through a contract for three conventional novels (by his own account failures) and later through his detective stories, to devote his whole time to writing. He wrote his first detective novel when in desperate need of £100 to mend the stone-tiled roof of his cottage; having read a vast number of detective novels he thought he ought to be able to write one himself. It was accepted by Collins and published in 1935.

The departure from the English literary scene of Auden and the public events that led to disillusionment with communism at the end of the 1930s may in retrospect be seen to have operated to the benefit of Day-Lewis as a writer. His later poetry no longer aspires to the radical in either form or content; however, that does not mean that it lacks technical interest or humanity —on the contrary. The "poeticisms", when they occur, seem much less venal, and the personal elements, because they no longer have to be related to public issues, are at once more moving and expressed with sharper detail.

Day-Lewis spent most of the war years in London, where he worked for the Ministry of Information. After the war he attracted large audiences as Clark lecturer at Cambridge in 1946, later as Professor of Poetry at Oxford, and in 1964-65 as Charles Edward Norton lecturer in Harvard. He served his fellow writers in many arduous ways, not least as Chairman of the Arts Council Literature Panel. He was made C.B.E. in 1950. From 1958 he was vice-president of the Royal Society of Literature, of which he was a Companion.

His second marriage to the actress Jill Balcon in 1951 increased his interest in the speaking of his own and other poets' verse and he became one of the outstanding poetry readers of his time. Though his working days were divided equally between his writing and his duties as director of the publishers, Chatto and Windus (whose poetry list he did much to enlarge, particularly in the direction of young or unfashionable poets), he continued to be a prolific producer of verse and prose. Not least he went on writing mystery stories but they were more often "crime novels" than mere puzzles, of greater depth than their counterparts of the 'thirties and 'forties, amusing and civilized though the latter always were (indeed, one or two are classics of the genre). Nor must his fiction for children be forgotten.

Day-Lewis was a handsome man, in

dress something of a dandy (in the best sense) and with a similar taste in such things as motor cars. In first coming into a room he might give the impression of austerity, but quite soon the mask would relax into its attractive lines of humour. He was, in fact, no mean anecdotalist, often against himself; at one time he had an hilarious story of catching his own dental plate before it could fly into the stalls after an impassioned end to a poetry reading.

No poet can be said to be a simple character, but there is little doubt that in his later years (for instance over the Poet Laureateship) Day-Lewis thoroughly enjoyed the fame that had come to him—as he soberly rejoiced in the affection and respect of his attractive and warm-hearted second wife, in their two children and in their Georgian house and its ambience in Greenwich. The successive blows to his health of later life he endured with stoicism, characteristically extracting a fund of stories from his medical and surgical experiences.

It may be asserted that for a writer who lived through some of the most atrocious years of human history his work as a whole is insufficiently disturbing; however, neither his years of success and happiness nor his capability of pleasing in many traditional modes ever led him to stop striving to depict nature and human nature as penetratingly as he was able. *The Whispering Roots*, a collection of poems published in 1970, was not only technically resourceful (like Hardy, he never ceased to explore the possibilities of metre and stanza-form), but also contained among the perennial response to physical experience, a new insight into personal destiny.

His sympathy with the oppressed had only a comparatively brief period of political expression, but it was an indication of his essential concern for others which endured in his wide circle of friends and his work for his professional brethren.

May 23, 1972.

Basil Dearden, who died in a car crash on the M4 near Brentford in March, 1971 was one of a generation of highly professional film makers who began their careers at Ealing Studios; unlike many of them, though, he continued to do good work when removed from the protective familiar atmosphere of Ealing under Sir Michael Balcon. He was 60.

Basil Dearden was born at Westcliff-on-Sea in 1911, and started out in show business as an actor. He worked in various repertory companies, doubling actor and stage manager, and toured the United States with the Ben Greet company in Shakespeare. For five years he was general stage manager with Basil Dean, and went with him to Ealing in 1937 as his assistant. In the next few years he turned his hand to all sorts of jobs round the studios—

writer, dialogue director, associate producer and finally director. The first few films he worked on were comedies by the most popular stars of the day, George Formby* and Will Hay; he wrote *Let George Do It* and co-directed three of Will Hay's last films, *The Black Sheep of Whitehall, The Goose Steps Out*, and *My Learned Friend*.

In 1943 he was given his first solo job in direction with *The Bells Go Down*, an effective picture of the firefighting service in wartime. More distinctive, though, was his atmospheric ghost story *Halfway House*, followed by collaboration on *Dead of Night*, a classic clutch of ghost stories on which several new talents at Ealing worked. In 1947 he made *Frieda*, which introduced Mai Zetterling to English films and Dearden to the topical problem picture (in this case the problem of a war bride in England)—a genre he was to be associated with throughout his career. Less characteristic, but still one of his most memorable films, was *Saraband for Dead Lovers* the following year; an outstandingly stylish costume melodrama made with unexpected flair and relish.

Dearden's later films at Ealing included one of the studio's biggest box office successes, *The Blue Lamp*, and many quiet, humane, rather anonymous films on such questions of the moment as probation (*I Believe in You*) and ethics in boxing (*The Square Ring*) and racing (*The Rainbow Jacket*). After the dissolution of Ealing and the sale of Ealing Studios, Dearden made a very charming Ealing-style comedy in *The Smallest Show on Earth* (1957), about the humours of running a small and antiquated cinema. This was one of the earliest films made by Dearden and Michael Relph formerly a designer at Ealing, as a producer-director team functioning as an independent unit. Under this arrangement nearly all Dearden's subsequent films were made, usually with him directing and Relph producing.

Dearden continued to direct prolifically throughout the 1960s, alternating problem pictures with lighter works. He himself was deeply serious about the problem pictures such as *Sapphire,* about colour discrimination; *Victim*, about homosexuality; and *Life for Ruth*, about religious objections to medical treatment. And certainly some of them, especially *Victim*, had a considerable effect as propaganda, though on the whole they have suffered the fate of most artistic propaganda in that their effectiveness has diminished considerably along with the urgency of the problems they deal with. It seems likely that his more lasting achievement in the cinema will turn out to be films like *The League of Gentlemen* (1960), a crisply effective perfect-crime thriller; *Khartoum* (1966), a resplendent return to period recreation on the last days of General Gordon; and *The Assassination Bureau* (1968), a lighthearted period fantasy. His last film, *The Man who Haunted Himself*, was released in 1970.

Basil Dearden was not—nor did he ever claim to be—in the big league of directors whose every work is marked with a distinctive personality. But he was an impeccable craftsman, serious and enterprising in his choice of subject, gifted with a real visual flair, in period subjects especially. Many more pretentious film makers have got further in critical estimation with a lot less.

He was married to Melissa Stribling and had two sons.

March 25, 1971.

Mgr. Josemaria Escriva de Balaguer y Albas–See Escriva.

Sir Gavin de Beer, F.R.S., F.S.A., who died suddenly on June 21, 1972, at the age of 72, was Professor of Embryology, University College London from 1945 to 1950 and Director of the British Museum (Natural History) from 1950 to 1960. From 1946 to 1949 he was president of the Linnean Society. He was awarded the Linnean Gold Medal in 1958 and the Darwin Medal of the Royal Society in the same year. He had been elected F.R.S. in 1940.

He was a prolific writer on a wide range of scientific and non-scientific subjects. De Beer did, in fact, bridge the so-called two cultures; he was entirely at home in both science and the humanities. In such books as *Embryology and Evolution* and *Embryos and Ancestors* he made important contributions to the study and understanding of his speciality but he wrote also with charm and assurance on Hannibal's route over the Alps and on Edward Gibbon.

Gavin Rylands de Beer, the son of H. C. de Beer, was born on November 1, 1899 and spent his childhood in Paris. At an early age he showed two of the characteristics which were to distinguish him—a most exceptional capacity as a linguist and extreme orderliness of mind; indeed these qualities were interrelated for few could acquire four languages simultaneously without disastrous results to the command of each. But de Beer's French and German were to become as perfect as his English, which was of a high literary quality, and his Italian lagged but little behind. It was at this early stage, too, that he first started foreign travel. After attending the École Pascal he returned to England to go to Harrow. Two years in the Grenadier Guards followed before he went to Magdalen as a Demy, taking a First in Zoology. Elected a Fellow of Merton in 1924, he became successively Senior Demonstrator in Zoology, Lecturer in Embryology and Reader in Zoology. He was a successful Sub-Warden at a time when the Warden had ceased to play an active part.

But neither the physical nor the intellectual climate of Oxford suited him and in 1938 he moved to London as Reader in Embryology at University College. Within a year he was back in uniform, ending as Lieutenant-Colonel with a record of some highly successful psychological warfare. He returned to University College as Professor, remaining there for five years. In 1950 he became Director of the British Museum (Natural History) and was knighted in 1954. He remained at the museum until his retirement from the public service.

Though a specialist in a rather narrow field his interests were enormously wide and his knowledge immense. He could have made a successful career in several other branches of science, to say nothing of becoming an historian, an author or a philologist. His curiosity was insatiable, his energy great and his memory prodigious. For him relaxation was reading, but reading of an intensity amounting to research. The information acquired was stored in a mind like the finest card index, to be produced without notice to solve some totally unrelated problem. Where did Hannibal cross the Alps? Whence came the inhabitants of Switzerland? What happened on the first ascent of Mont Blanc? The first of these questions was answered as definitely as it is ever likely to be by the application of scientific evidence as diverse as the seasonal flow of rivers and astronomy; the second by evidence ranging from glaciology to blood groups. The answer to the third was in collaboration with T. Graham. Rarely can more nails have been driven into the coffin of a myth.

His greatest hobby was Switzerland, particularly the history of Alpine travel. Here his knowledge, like his library, was unique. Walking tours and visits were often planned because of associations ranked almost higher than natural beauty. He wrote prolifically, in French as well as English, but he wrote because he wanted to and for no other reason.

Travellers in Switzerland, his exhaustive record of Alpine travel down the centuries, was the result of re-reading his entire Alpine library during the long periods of tedious inactivity imposed by firewatching and the like. But even if a book was slender and hastily composed, his rigorous standard of scholarship was maintained. His intolerance of lesser standards sometimes led to difficulty, since Alpine scholarship is often less scrupulous. A walker and a skier, he did not climb. He was however elected to the Alpine Club under the literary qualification and his work was recognized by the honorary degree conferred by the University of Lausanne.

Wearying of hotels and the attendant difficulty of working conditions, he spent most of his time when in Switzerland during the immediate pre-war years in a 17th-century chalet near Davos. Not content with knowing several languages, he set out to invent a new one. His addiction to nicknames and to calling objects by special names now found full scope, and friends staying at the chalet needed a word list; their halting attempts to master the idiom were apt to lead to extensions of the vocabulary. Life in the chalet also afforded opportunities for his taste for the milder forms of practical joking (had he not as a junior subaltern stacked the cards so that four senior officers playing bridge found themselves each with a complete suit?). Unfortunately he had to sell the chalet after the outbreak of war and the days of walking tours and skiing went with it.

After the war he helped in the founding of the Anglo-Swiss Society and was on its committee for a time. He also served on the council of the Ski Club of Great Britain. There followed a period of estrangement and friends were startled by the violence of his comments on things Swiss. He continued, however, to visit French-speaking Switzerland, temporarily rating the Jura above the Alps. The phase passed, but his visits to Switzerland never regained their earlier frequency or length; later a heart attack was to put the mountains out of bounds.

But Switzerland by no means absorbed all his energy and in no way lessened his affection for France. He did much for Anglo-French relations, particularly in the scientific and cultural fields. This work brought him the Legion of Honour and an honorary degree of the University of Bordeaux.

He married in 1925 Cicely Glyn, the younger daughter of the Rev. Sir Hubert Medlycott, Bt.

June 23, 1972.

Maurice Dekobra, the French novelist, and author of the best-seller *La Madone des Sleepings* (*The Sleeping Car Madonna*) died at the age of 88 on June 2, 1973.

Maurice Ernest Tessier was born in Paris on May 26, 1885, a few days after the state funeral of Victor Hugo. He was to change his name to Dekobra (a pun, he claimed, on the French "deux cobras") in 1906. His literary career spanned over 60 years, during which time he enjoyed the reputation of the most-read French author in the world: his novels were translated into 30 different languages, and sold over 10 million copies.

Early in the century Dekobra began working in journalism, a profession which allowed him to satisfy his two major passions: writing and travel. His first book, *Les Mémoires de Rat-de-Cave* (1912), was a humorous work and set the pattern for most of his early writings. It was not, however, until the 1920s that he made his real mark. Then, his inborn dromomania and peculiar literary talents combined to provide the ideal panacea for the "disillusioned post-war generation", and Dekobra embarked upon a series of so-called "cosmopolitan novels". His sensational best-seller *La Madone des Sleepings* (1925) added yet another touch of magic to the legendary Orient Express, and placed Dekobra top among the popular novelists of his day.

During the inter-war years he earned the reputation of an indefatigable globetrotter, travelling widely in Europe, America, and the Near and Far East. Part of Dekobra's success at this time was undoubtedly his genius for choosing titles: *Serenade to the Hangman, Confucius in a Tail-coat*, or even *Perfumed Tigers!*

During the Second World War Dekobra lived in New York and Hollywood, where he continued writing popular novels. From his return to Paris the rhythm of his life slowed, but almost imperceptibly. If his age and health prevented him from further travel, they certainly had little effect on his literary output. In 1951, at the age of 66, he wrote his first detective novel, *Opération Magali*, which won him the Prix du Quai des Orfèvres. Through the 60s he worked in collaboration with the authoress Anne-Mariel on a series of historical novels, and witnessed the revival of a number of his former best-sellers, among them *La Madone des Sleepings*—re-edited by Livre de Poche in 1967. He even attempted to write an up-dated sequel in 1972, with the title *La Madone des Boeings*. It would be unfair to judge the author on his last efforts. The fact that the new Madonna failed to recapture the magic of the old hardly detracts from Maurice Dekobra's standing as an amazing literary phenomenon, an author who became a legend in his own life-time.

June 5, 1973.

Lord Delacourt-Smith, P.C., for nearly 20 years general secretary of the Post Office Engineering Union, died on August 2, 1972. He was 55.

Delacourt-Smith had unusual qualities for a trade union leader. A university scholar and a research worker in earlier days, he was a thoughtful man and a Fabian, with the ability to work an argument through, who played little part in the power struggles in the movement. He was quiet in manner but impressive because he seldom spoke without a detailed knowledge of his subject.

Born in 1917, Charles George Percy Smith was educated at the County Boys' School, Windsor, and Wadham College, Oxford, where he was a scholar. He was Librarian of the Oxford Union and on leaving the university became at the age of 21 research assistant to the New Fabian Research Bureau and then an assistant secretary of the Civil Service Clerical Association.

After wartime service in the Royal Engineers and the Royal Army Service Corps, during which he was mentioned in dispatches, he became Labour M.P. for Colchester in the 1945 election and held the seat until 1950. From 1947 to 1949 he was Parliamentary Private Secretary to the Secretary of State for Commonwealth Relations.

In 1953 he left the assistant secretaryship of the Civil Service Clerical Association to become general secretary of the Post Office Engineering Union. One of his achievements as secretary was to work out a completely revised scheme for theoretical and practical training for Post Office engineers, and within the T.U.C. he actively supported the development of educational facilities for workers.

Charles Smith, as he was then, was a leading member of a Fabian Society group which gave evidence to the Donovan Royal Commission on Trade Unions and Employers' Associations, urging that all possible steps should be taken to end class divisions in British industry by giving staff status to manual workers, that industrial democracy should be widely extended by broadening the scope of bargaining, and that local labour courts should adjudicate over disputes concerning the interpretation of collective agreements. He and his colleagues favoured an incomes policy and thought trade unions should expand their social role, their educational programmes and their research facilities.

Smith was made a life peer in 1967 and two years later entered the Labour government as Minister of State in the Ministry of Technology. He was given leave of absence by his union and returned to it when Labour went out of office in 1970.

Delacourt-Smith acted as adviser to the Prison Officers' Association from 1956 to 1969. He was chairman of the staff side of the Civil Service National Whitley Council from 1962 to 1964, president of the Postal Telegraph and Telephone Workers' International in 1969. From 1960 to 1969 he was a J.P. He was a part-time member of the British Airports Authority from 1965 to 1969 and a member of the Shipbuilding Inquiry Committee in 1965 to 1966. In 1937 he married Margaret Hando and they had one son and two daughters.

August 3, 1972.

R. F. Delderfield, the dramatist and author, died at his home in Devon on June 24, 1972. He was 60.

Delderfield never attempted the ambitious, the revelatory or the grand. Always entirely a professional writer, he precisely understood his powers and their limits, working effectively within them to dramatize slices of identifiable life; places, situations and the people appropriate to them were clearly defined and accurately drawn.

He scored a resounding success and a run of more than 2,000 performances with *Worm's Eye View*, the funny side of life in the R.A.F. Careful craftsmanship, clearly defined characters, always types rather than personalities in a situation which avoided deliberate exaggeration, together with precision of aim and a basic honesty, were the virtues he brought to all his plays and not only to this spectacular aid to postwar cheerfulness. *Worm's Eye View* became a powerful influence, nudging later English farce towards the study of a comic proletariat instead of the comic bourgeoisie which had been its earlier business.

Although nothing else of his achieved comparable success, he wrote more than a dozen popular comedies, several historical romances for the stage, novels both numerous and long, and four studies of aspects of the life of Napoleon. He was a prolific and professional author who had the satisfaction of being widely read.

Ronald Frederick Delderfield was born in London in February 1912. He went to school at West Buckland and became a newspaper reporter. He was editor of the *Exmouth Chronicle* after the war, resigning the post in 1947. He served throughout the war in the R.A.F., and was a public relations officer at the Air Ministry.

Delderfield's first play, which was put on by a society bearing the name "New Plays", was a full-length character study of Pontius Pilate called *Spark in Judaea*. Two years later, in 1939, he had a play at the "Q" Theatre, *Printer's Devil*, for which he drew on his press experiences.

Reviewing the first night of *Worm's Eye View* in December 1945, *The Times* concluded that "this farcical comedy should thrive passing well on its incidental humour". It did rather more than that, answering for five years and 2,000 performances to an English appetite for the comedies of war. *Peace Comes to Peckham* (1947), about returning evacuees, exploited the same vein.

Several farces later Delderfield wrote *The Meyerling Affair*, first done on television in 1956 and then at the Pitlochry Festival the next year. This was a well-constructed play from the copious and conflicting material concerning the death of the Crown Prince Rudolph of Austria and his mistress in his hunting lodge at Meyerling in 1889. His talent for historical romance was exercised in some of his novels also.

Several of his plays were turned into films. But in his later years Delderfield turned from the stage to novel writing and to works of popular history, notably about Napoleon. *There was a Fair Maid Dwelling* (1960) is an example of his lighter style—a leisurely love story, a challenge, he himself described it, to "the sink, braces and bacteria school of postwar realism in drama and fiction".

There were other cultural trends of which he disapproved, and he once tried to enlist his fellow-writers in an association to agitate against horror films. Other of his novels presented, at unusual length, slices of life in a West Country valley; and he continued until the end of his life to make books out of his extensive reading in the life and times of Napoleon.

He married in 1936 May Evans. They had a son and a daughter.

June 26, 1972.

Terence de Marney, the actor and director, died in an accident on May 25, 1971 at the age of 62.

Born in London on March 1, 1909, his career in the theatre began in 1923 and continued almost without interruption, taking in occasional films, radio and television parts, ever since. De Marney's first stage appearance in 1923 was as a page boy in a sketch at the Coliseum.

A year later he was the office boy in *Brewster's Millions* and Jim Hawkins in an adaptation of *Treasure Island* at the Strand. He toured with Mrs. Patrick Campbell in *The Last of Mrs. Cheyne* and in 1930 played Gustave in *The Lady of the Camellias*. He toured South Africa as Raleigh in *Journey's End*, spent 1931 as director of the Connaught Theatre, Worthing, and in 1932, with his brother, the actor Derrick de Marney, he founded the Independent Theatre Club at the Kingsway Theatre, where he directed Emil Ludwig's *Versailles* and an adaptation of Schnitzler's novel *Fräulein Else*. In 1934 he played Tybalt in *Romeo and Juliet* at the Open Air Theatre and Giovanni in *'Tis Pity She's a Whore* at the Arts.

In the 1930s he played in sketches with which he toured the country's variety theatres in a revival of Sutton Vane's *Outward Bound* and in a variety of thrillers. This was, in a sense, the pattern of his later career which included Agatha Christie's *Ten Little Niggers* and *Dear Murderer,* a revival of Du Maurier's *Trilby;* he directed Louis Golding's *Magnolia Street Story* and *Master Crook,* originally called *Cosh Boy.* With his brother he alternated as Slim Callaghan in *Meet Slim Callaghan* at the Garrick and carried on the same role in the play's sequel *Slim Curves,* which he produced and directed. He also appeared in the radio serial role as the Count of Monte Cristo.

With Percy Robinson he wrote the stage thrillers *Whispering Gallery, Wanted for Murder* and *The Crime of Margaret Foley,* and he collaborated with Ralph Stock to write *Search.* In 1962 two very diverse roles in William Saroyan's double bill *Talking to You* provided him with an opportunity to demonstrate the extremes of his style.

Terence de Marney obviously relished the sinister, the indefinably frightening and the strange, but his range was not limited to them and he could provide romantic charm and sheer physical excitement. He acted decisively, and whenever it was necessary with real authority.

May 26, 1971.

Henry de Montherlant, who ended his life by shooting on September 21, 1972, was 76.

His death marks the disappearance from the French literary scene of one of its most distinguished, most independent and most controversial figures. Despite a devoted circle of admirers, Montherlant aroused the enmity of many of his fellow-countrymen, particularly of the younger generation. They considered him to be a haughty traditionalist in social and political matters who admired power and force too readily; they also saw him as a partisan of shifting and sometimes contradictory causes. It is to the credit of his detractors, however, that many of them—with, however, great reluctance—admitted that he had become, towards the end of his career, the greatest living French man-of-letters.

Henry-Marie-Joseph-Frédéric de Montherlant was born in Paris on April 21, 1896. His family could trace a clear, unbroken line of descent from the sixteenth century, and his own outstanding physical and intellectual gifts, together with his determination to embrace the most conflicting elements of experience, led to his being described as a Renaissance man born out of his time. After the early years which he devoted to a study of the Roman moralists, and during which he "discovered" Pascal, Chateaubriand, Nietzsche, Barrès and d'Annunzio, Montherlant fought in the First World War. He was wounded in 1918 and then served as an interpreter with the American Army until his demobilization in September 1919.

For the next five or six years Montherlant continued to read widely and to meditate on the significance of his wartime experiences. He also had careers as amateur footballer, sprinter and bullfighter in Spain. His enthusiasm for bullfighting was matched by his knowledge of technique and it was only in 1925, having been wounded by a bull, that he gave up his practice of the art, though not his love for it. This period of intense activity, intellectual as well as physical, saw the publication of Montherlant's first books.

In 1920 came *La Relève du matin,* a collection of essays praising school life, the uncompromising integrity of early adolescence and certain features of Catholicism. This was followed in 1922 by his first novel, *Le Songe,* which was less a story than a highly individual orchestration of certain themes, including his mixed feelings about the excitement and the horror of war and his praise of the virile comradeship of men at the expense of what he then held to be the compromises and weaknesses inseparable from love. Two years later came a striking collection of philosophically minded essays and poems on sport, *Les Olympiques.*

This was followed in 1926 by a second novel, *Les Bestiaires,* which skilfully wove the moods of irony, enthusiasm, harsh realism and poetic meditation round the theme of a young Frenchman's early contacts with Spain in general and bullfighting in particular.

By this time Montherlant had withdrawn from Europe. He was to spend the next 10 years outside France, mostly in North Africa. This is the period when his doctrine of *totalisme,* his attempt to embrace as many contrasting experiences as possible, became most obvious. It can be seen in the alternating sensualism and asceticism of works written, though not all published, at this time.

Perhaps it is set out most strikingly in the *récit* of 1929, *La petite Infante de Castille*. It also occurs in his collections of essays and novels. The former include: *Aux Fontaines du désir* (1927), *Mors et Vita* (1932), *Service inutile* (1935) and *Un Voyageur solitaire est un diable* (1961); the novels are: *L'Histoire d'amour de "La Rose de sable"* (1954), *Les Célibataires* (1934) and the first two volumes, published in 1936, of his *Jeunes Filles* tetralogy.

During the Second World War (which he had begun to foresee clearly by 1936) Montherlant appeared to some to have compromised himself, morally and politically, by certain essays in *Le Solstice de juin* (1941). It can hardly be disputed that here, as in *L'Equinoxe de septembre*, of 1938, he showed little political wisdom, and confused international realities with his own private mythologies. Nevertheless, it is typical of the ambiguity surrounding this period that *Solstice* and a general selection from his works were banned in several countries by the occupying German authorities. Later, in 1944, there is the significant fact that his flat in Paris was closely searched by the Gestapo.

During and after the war Montherlant began a new literary career as a dramatist. He scored particular successes with such plays as *La Reine morte*, *Le Maître de Santiago* and *Port-Royal*. This aspect of his work is that which people in Britain and in the United States know best, and several of his plays have been established for some time in the Comédie Française repertory.

Malatesta and *The Master of Santiago* were performed at the Lyric, Hammersmith, by Sir Donald Wolfit's* company in the 1950s, and *The Cardinal of Spain* was seen at the Yvonne Arnaud Theatre, Guildford, in 1969. Perhaps the most celebrated and controversial of his plays was *La Ville dont le prince est un enfant*, which was a study of homosexual passion set in a Roman Catholic boys' school and which he did not for some years allow to be performed.

After the resounding success of Jean Meyer's Paris production, Peter Daubeny took it to London for his World Theatre season in 1971.

In 1960, having repeatedly refused to put forward his candidature for the Académie Française and to make the expected preparatory visits to individual academicians, Montherlant was elected to membership by an overwhelming majority on the initiative of the *secrétaire perpétuel*.

Advancing years did not appear to weaken Montherlant's creative gifts, and in 1963 he made a splendid return to fiction with *Le Chaos et la nuit*. This was followed in 1965 by a new play, *La Guerre civile*, with a Roman setting which confirmed Montherlant's continuing ability to write astringent dialogue. His "Carnets" for the years 1958-64 were published in 1966 under

the title, *Va jouer avec cette poussière*, and a major literary event of 1967 was the appearance of the full original version of *La Rose de sable*—a novel of close on 600 pages devoted to the problems of French colonialism in North Africa. An outstanding new novel, *Les Garçons*, was published in 1969.

He was very much in the best French *moraliste* tradition and his distinctive gift to the world of letters lay most clearly, perhaps, in his ability to disturb the intellectual presuppositions of readers or audience—and to do so in a prose style of quite outstanding richness, vividness and beauty.

September 23, 1972.

Armand Denis, who brought wildlife safaris to millions of viewers throughout the world in films that he and his wife Michaela made, died in Nairobi on April 15, 1971. He was 74.

The husband-and-wife team of television explorers travelled throughout Africa, South America and the Far East in search of animal subjects. They first met in New York, and then again in Ecuador, before they were married in Bolivia and Michaela became her husband's assistant. In their search for material they found animals ranging from red ibis and the sea-cow to gorillas and armadillos.

In 1954 Armand and Michaela Denis received the award for the best television documentary of that year for their "Filming in Africa" series. Armand also made full-length films, including *Savage Splendour*.

This was described as the first full-length colour film to be produced in Africa.

Denis, the son of a Belgian judge, was born in Brussels and went to England as a First World War refugee, and took a degree at Oxford University in chemistry. He emigrated to America and became an American citizen. He began a career in chemical research as a Research Fellow at the Californian Institute of Technology, where his interests included radio, and helped to invent a device for automatic volume control. Then, through his interest in photography, he turned to filming animals.

Denis published his autobiography, *On Safari*, in 1963. In it he told how he once was a novice monk; helped Dr. Marie Stopes to translate a paper on the microstructure of coal; and told how his interest in wildlife was first quickened while working as a chemist at Farnborough. *Cats of the World*—a survey of 36 living species of cats—was published in 1964.

Denis settled in Kenya and was devoted to the conservation of game, which he did much to popularize.

April 16, 1971.

King Frederik IX, King of Denmark since 1947, died on January 14, 1972.

He was born in the last year but one of the nineteenth century, towards the end of the long reign of King Christian IX (1818-1906)—called "The Grandfather of Europe" because so many of his descendants mounted thrones. He was the father of Queen Alexandra, wife of King Edward VII.

The late king, his great-grandson, spent his early youth at the Danish court of pre-1914 days, but he was essentially a man of his time. Through his wisdom, tact and love of simplicity he proved a successful and popular king of a country where "few have too much, a fewer still too little". Though the Danes have little use for the outward show of monarchy and adopt a cynical attitude towards what remains of their aristocracy, they took the good-humoured King Frederik to their hearts, and always flocked in large crowds to cheer the royal family when they appeared in public.

The King established an easy relationship with his fellow-Danes and always appeared relaxed and happy. In Denmark it is quite usual for the newspapers to print cartoons of the royal family. These amused the King and he made a collection of them, just as he was always on the lookout for new jokes about himself, sometimes adding one or two of his own making.

He was a giant of a man, as befitting a king of a race descended from the Vikings. He stood 6ft. 3in., being immensely proud of his physique. On visits to London in his younger days he would often pay a call on his trainer, an ex-Olympic coach. His 45in. chest was tattooed with an elaborate Chinese dragon, and he was far from being offended when a picture showing his manly tattooed chest appeared in a popular English Sunday paper on the eve of his state visit to King George VI and Queen Elizabeth in 1951.

He was a hard-working constitutional monarch, keeping regular hours in his "office" in the Amalienborg Palace. In 1955 he supervised the making of a film *A Day in the King's Life,* showing him in his daily routine, receiving ministers, answering letters, presiding over meetings of the Council of State, and giving his fortnightly audiences at Christiansborg Palace when, in accordance with an old Danish custom, any Dane may ask to speak to his sovereign.

During the German occupation he and Queen Ingrid used bicycles and could occasionally be seen wheeling Princess Margrethe in her perambulator.

He had two great interests—music and the sea. When he was only 16 he conducted the Royal Life Guards Band, and until rheumatism made it too painful for him to raise his arm above his shoulder he often conducted the Danish Royal Symphony and the Royal Theatre Orchestras, but never in public, apart from a single performance at the Royal Theatre when, then Crown Prince, he conducted Mascagni's *Cavalleria*

Rusticana. He liked to conduct at private concerts to which he invited members of the diplomatic corps and friends from many walks of life. He also made records, which were sold for charity. His favourite composers were Beethoven and Wagner. The Royal Danish Ballet was not only royal in name: the King followed its activities closely and whenever the ballet returned from a foreign tour the Ballet Master would be invited to the palace to report, just like a foreign minister coming back from a mission abroad.

His love of the sea came naturally to him as a Dane. He joined the Royal Danish Navy as a cadet and worked his way up through every rank to Rear-Admiral in 1945. On his retirement from the active list he still had his "command" of the royal yacht Dannebrog, on which he spent perhaps the happiest time of his life, cruising in and out of Denmark's many islands, sailing her to Greenland and across the North Sea on his frequent sea visits to Britain, when Dannebrog would anchor in the Thames above Tower Bridge. The royal yacht ranked as a second home for the King and his family, and he and the Queen would spend the night on board when they paid official visits to Denmark's coastal towns, to avoid giving his hosts the trouble of accommodating them.

Born on March 11, 1899, the elder son of King Christian X and Queen Alexandrine, his family—the House of Schleswig-Holstein-Sonderborg-Glucksborg—has given princes and princesses to Great Britain, Imperial Russia, Sweden, Greece and Norway.

An important event in his early life came in 1920, when with his father King Christian and his brother Prince Knud he rode into liberated North Slesvig, part of the territory lost to Prussia in 1864 and restored to Denmark after the First World War. Twenty years later Denmark was overwhelmed by the German invasion, the second in less than a century. During these critical days the courageous attitude of King Christian, who refused to be cowed by the invaders, set a high example to the country and his son, the Crown Prince, who remained in Denmark throughout the war years.

In 1922 he was briefly betrothed to Princess Olga of Greece, sister of the late Duchess of Kent. Princess Olga later married Prince Paul of Yugoslavia.

In 1935 he married Princess Ingrid, the daughter of King Gustav Adolf of Sweden and his first wife, Princess Margaret of Connaught. They had three children. The eldest, who now succeeds her father, was Princess Margrethe, born during the German invasion in April 1940. She married, in 1967, Count Henri de Monpezat, a French diplomat, later created Prince Henrik of Denmark.

She was followed by two other children, both girls: Princess Benedikte, born in 1944, who married in 1968 the Prince of Sayn-Wittgenstein-Berleburg, a German; and Princess Anne-Marie, born in 1946—she is married to King Constantine of Greece.

On April 20, 1947, when the country had hardly recovered from the aftermath of the occupation, King Christian X died, and the next day the new ruler was proclaimed from the balcony of the Christiansborg Palace as King Frederik IX—Frederiks having alternated with Christians for 500 years. At the end of his speech to the assembled people, Queen Ingrid appeared on the balcony and the King grasped her hand and kissed her saying, "Now we two will march forward together following the example set us by the old King and Queen."

As King Frederik and Queen Ingrid had no son, the heir-presumptive was the King's brother, Prince Knud, but in 1953 the Danish constitution (which excluded women from the throne) was altered and a new law of succession was introduced, following a nation-wide plebiscite, preparing the way for accession of the present sovereign, Queen Margrethe.

The late king was an Honorary Admiral in the British Navy, Honorary Air Chief Marshal of the R.A.F., and Colonel-in-Chief of the Queen's Regiment, which includes The Buffs. Before the regimental amalgamation of the 1960s he was Colonel-in-Chief of The Buffs, carrying on an association going back to Prince George of Denmark, the consort of Queen Anne, who was Honorary Colonel of The Buffs. King Frederik was created a G.C.V.O. in 1948 when he visited London to open the exhibition of Danish art treasures at the Victoria and Albert Museum, and three years later, during his state visit to King George VI and Queen Elizabeth, he was made a Knight of the Garter. In 1957 King Frederik and Queen Ingrid entertained Queen Elizabeth and the Duke of Edinburgh when they paid their state visit to Denmark.

January 15, 1972.

Admiral Sir Michael Denny, G.C.B., C.B.E., D.S.O., who was Commander-in-Chief, Home Fleet, and Commander-in-Chief, Eastern Atlantic (N.A.T.O.) in 1954-55, died on April 7, 1972. He was 75.

Denny was chairman of the British Joint Services Mission, Washington, and United Kingdom Representative on the Standing Committee of N.A.T.O. Military Committee from 1956 to 1959. From 1959 to 1966 he was chairman of Cammell Laird, and later consultant.

Denny was a distinguished gunnery specialist. He served throughout two world wars, in the second of which his work ranged from that of senior naval officer at Aandalsnes during the Norwegian campaign to the command of an aircraft carrier in the Pacific.

He was chief staff officer during the Dunkirk evacuation. After the war his appointments included that of Third Sea Lord during an important period of technical development.

Michael Maynard Denny, born on October 3, 1896, was the son of Canon Edward Denny, M.A. He entered Osborne as a naval cadet from Queen Elizabeth's Grammar School, Wimborne, in 1909, and four years later passed out from Dartmouth second of the 65 cadets in his term.

Throughout the 1914-18 war he served in the Grand Fleet as midshipman in the Neptune and sub-lieutenant and lieutenant in the Royal Sovereign. After specializing in gunnery in 1919-20 he was selected for the advanced course, and in 1921 was appointed for experimental duties. This was the first of a series of such appointments; when not at sea he spent all his service until after he became a captain in gunnery experimental work. He was also awarded the Egerton memorial prize for gunnery.

Between 1922 and 1930, when he became a commander, he was gunnery officer in the Emperor of India, the Montrose, and 1st Destroyer Flotilla and the Nelson. He was fleet gunnery officer in the Mediterranean in 1932-34, and then executive officer of the cruiser Shropshire until promoted to captain in 1936. In 1937 he joined the Naval Ordnance Department as Assistant Director, and a year later was made Deputy Director, the post he held when war broke out again in 1939.

When the Germans invaded Norway in April 1940, he was appointed senior naval officer at Aandalsnes, where he served during the landing and withdrawal of the Allied troops. During the Dunkirk evacuation he had charge of what was known as the "Dynamo room" at Dover, which controlled all the movements of shipping engaged in this vast but hastily improvised undertaking. For services in Norway and at Dover he was created C.B.—a rare honour for a junior captain.

His next appointment was to the cruiser Kenya, which he commanded as flag captain to Rear-Admiral H. M. Burroughs in the raid on Vaagso in 1941. He saw much other active service in her, including convoys to North Russia and Malta. In 1942-43 he was chief of staff to the Commander-in-Chief, Home Fleet, Admiral Tovey, with rank of commodore 1st class, his work there and in the Kenya being recognized by the award of the C.B.E. In 1943, he took command of the aircraft carrier Victorious, and was in her in the Pacific until the war ended in August 1945. It was from this carrier that successful air strikes were directed against Okinawa, and Captain Denny was awarded the D.S.O. He was promoted to rear-admiral in 1945.

Denny became Assistant Chief of Naval Personnel and Director of Personal Services. From 1947 to 1949 he was Flag Officer (Destroyers) in the Mediterranean, and was promoted to vice-admiral in 1948. In 1949, he joined the Board of Admiralty as Third Sea Lord and Controller of the Navy and held this post for nearly four years, during which he became an admiral in 1952. He was promoted to K.C.B. in 1950.

He married in 1923 Sara Annie Esmé, daughter of Colonel Loftus Welman. She died in 1971.

April 11, 1972.

André Dunoyer de Segonzac—See Dunoyer.

Major Alexander P. de Seversky, the aircraft designer and aerospace consultant, died on August 24, 1974 in New York at the age of 80.

Born in Tiflis, Russia, in 1894, de Seversky was educated at the Imperial Naval Academy in Russia and the Military School of Aviation. On his first war mission he was shot down over the Gulf of Riga and lost his right leg. Returning to combat duties, he was accredited with shooting down 13 enemy planes. Assigned to Washington as an assistant naval attaché for air, he chose to stay permanently in the United States after the Russian Revolution.

Devoting all his energies to the development of aviation, he won acclaim for his work on the first automatic synchronous bombsight and, with Dr. Elmer Sperry, on gyroscopically stabilized flight instruments which lead to the introduction of the automatic pilot. He designed landing-gear for seaplanes and the first in-flight refuelling system. He designed and built all-metal amphibious aircraft as well as the P35, the first all-metal aircraft with fuel tanks in the wings, and the prototype of the P47 Thunderbolt fighter.

During the war he wrote *Victory Through Air Power,* in which he prophesied that the entire globe would eventually be dominated by air power, rather than land or sea power, and that nations would be able to hurl their long-range air forces at enemy countries in another hemisphere.

Both President Roosevelt and President Truman applauded his work. Roosevelt said that de Seversky "foresaw the technical necessity for the long-range escort fighter and devoted himself single-mindedly to its development". The United States was therefore able to win control of the air during the war.

He had founded two companies before the war, and later started the Seversky Aviation and Electronatum Corporation, which manufactured his wet-type electrostatic precipitator for air pollution control.

He married Evelyn Olliphant in 1925.

August 27, 1974.

Vittorio de Sica, for many years Italy's most popular film actor and one of her most talented and influential directors, died in Paris on November 13, 1974 at the age of 73.

He was born on July 7, 1901, at Sora, in the province of Frosinone, but moved with his family to Naples when he was only six days old. His childhood and early manhood were spent in Naples, a background which was later to be useful to him both as actor and as director.

At first he was intended for the law, a calling which might have exploited his eloquence and histrionic ability had he not been drawn to the stage as a more suitable outlet. After completing his military service he took up acting, and within a few years had established himself as one of the most talented and versatile stage actors in Italy, with a particular gift for light comedy.

His film debut came with the talkies, his first appearance being in *La segretaria di tutti* (1931). The next year he made the film that fixed his popular image for ever in the minds of the Italian public, *Gli unomini, che mascalzoni!* It was directed by Mario Camerini, master of the so-called "white telephone" school of prewar Italian films, a series of glossy and elegant light comedies or emotional dramas taking place among members of the fashionable aristocracy or upper middle classes.

Another famous comedy, *Daro un milione,* followed. From 1935 onwards he devoted his time almost entirely to films, becoming the most important and consistently successful of Italy's box office stars.

After a few years' appearing in a succession of successful, if not particularly distinguished, comedies and dramas, de Sica started to become interested in the production side of film making. In 1940 he wrote the script for one of his films, *L'avventuriera del piano di sopra,* and collaborated with Giuseppe Amato on the direction of another, *Rose scarlette.* Emboldened by the experience, he went on to direct by himself *Maddalena zero in condotta,* a comedy starring himself which achieved enormous popularity and confirmed his directorial skill.

This and the next film he directed, *Teresa Venerdi,* in which he appeared with Anna Magnani, were still comedies in the white telephone tradition, though handled with unusual finesse. But in 1943 he first showed his real distinction as a director with *I bambini ci guardano,* which he wrote and directed, but did not appear in.

After the Second World War his first film was the earliest of his mature masterpieces, *Sciuscia* (1946). It showed the full flowering of the neo-realist movement in its first phase; made entirely on location with non-professional actors, it told of the lives of two Neapolitan shoeshine boys, pathetic but self-possessed waifs leading a hand-to-mouth existence among the debris of the war. It also demonstrated de Sica's remarkable talent for directing children.

Ladri di biciclette (*Bicycle Thieves*), which de Sica directed in 1948, established him once and for all as one of the world's leading directors, and created a sensation wherever it was shown. With *Sciuscia* it must be one of the most lauded films in the history of the cinema, gaining innumerable awards and prizes, including an American Academy Award. In it de Sica worked again with Cesare Zavattini, the scriptwriter of *Sciuscia* and of most of his subsequent films.

It was a story of extreme poverty, made with deep humanity and understanding.

For his next film de Sica attempted something rather different: *Miracolo a Milano* was a poetic fantasy based on an original novel by Zavattini. To many it remains the most successful of all de Sica's films.

It was followed, after another two-year interval, by *Umberto D,* a pathetic study of old age and its problems; and then by de Sica's first English-speaking film, *Indiscretion,* starring Montgomery Clift and Jennifer Jones. That remains perhaps the most controversial of all his films: some critics regarded it as a betrayal of the neo-realist ideal, while others felt, with some show of reason, that even if the story was basically something out of a women's magazine, de Sica's direction and the acting of the principals gave it unusual depth and poignancy.

During those years de Sica had also kept up his acting, appearing in innumerable Italian films, some of them good, many far from good. His main reason for this activity, as he explained, was to raise enough money to finance the films which he himself wanted to direct, and which, with the exception of *Indiscretion,* were financed almost entirely with his own money.

In the middle and late 1950s a number of projects were shelved, and he devoted much time to setting up the most ambitious, an original Zavattini fantasy, *Il Giudizio Universale,* rather in the style of *Miracolo a Milano,* setting the Last Judgment in Naples. When finally made, this had little success. But the film he directed immediately before it, *La Ciocara* (*Two Women*), set him off on a new and far more prosperous stage of his career, achieving international box office success and bringing its star, Sophia Loren, a Hollywood Oscar.

From this followed in rapid succession a series of Sophia Loren vehicles, including an episode in *Boccaccio 70, Yesterday, Today and Tomorrow* and *Marriage, Italian Style,* as well as, more improbably and not very successfully, a version of Sartre's *The Condemned of Altona.* The other four Sophia Loren films, however, established de Sica as a big box-office director the world over, even if for admirers of his earlier work they carried him sadly far from the simple ideals of neo-realism.

A tentative attempt at renewal within the neo-realist style in the French-made *Un Monde nouveau* was given a very mixed reception, and de Sica returned again to big international production with the Peter Sellers comedy *After the Fox.*

Though his later films, whatever their commercial success, have been artistically disappointing, a handful of his earlier films —*Sciuscia, Ladri di Biciclette, Umberto D* —guarantee him a place in film history. At the moment their virtues are unfashionable and their defects at times painfully obvious; but undoubtedly the pendulum will swing again in their favour, and at the same time we may come to see more clearly that his finest work is to be found in those films—especially *Miracolo a Milano* and *Il Giudizio Universale*—where the realism is unashamedly leavened with eccentric fantasy. Those films at least are quite unlike anything else in the modern cinema.

De Sica's career, nevertheless, concluded with a film which was to prove his outstanding commercial triumph as well as one of the major critical successes of the later period of his activity. *Il Giardino dei Finzi Contini,* an elegant, understated recollection of the rise of Nazism as reflected in the individual experience of an aristocratic family and the circle of their acquaintances, won the 1972 United States Academy Award for the best foreign film of the preceding year.

November 14, 1974.

Astra Desmond, C.B.E. **(Lady Neame),** the distinguished English contralto, died on August 16, 1973. She was 80.

She had a voice both rich and flexible which brought her success on the concert platform and in oratorio. She was an admired Angel in *Dream of Gerontius* and had sung on many occasions under Elgar's direction. Nowhere was her intelligent musicianship more clearly displayed than in her recitals of *Lieder.*

Her outlook was anything but insular and her musical sympathies were broad. She took the trouble to acquaint herself with foreign languages in order to achieve a truer insight into European music. She was particularly successful with the songs of Grieg and Sibelius, about whose work she had written.

Though not primarily known as an opera singer she had appeared with the Carl Rosa Company (she was a former member of the Carl Rosa Trust); had sung Carmen and Delilah at Sadler's Wells, and Ortrud and Fricka at Covent Garden. In 1928 she sang in the first broadcast of Stravinsky's *Oedipus Rex.* She was Professor of Singing at the Royal Academy of Music from 1947 to 1963; a former president of the Incorporated Society of Musicians and of the Society of Woman Musicians; and a former member of the Arts Council Music Panel. She was made C.B.E. in 1949.

She was born Gwendolyn Mary Thomson in Torquay on April 10, 1893 and educated at Notting Hill High School and Westfield College, where she was a classical scholar. She studied singing with Blanche Marchesi and Louise Trenton, and in Berlin with Grenzenbach and von Bos.

She married in 1920 Sir Thomas Neame. They had three sons.

August 17, 1973.

Prince Alexander Desta, who had been deposed as Deputy Commander of the Imperial Ethiopian Navy, and was grandson of Emperor Haile Selassie I, was among those executed in Ethiopia on November 24, 1974.

He was born on July 7, 1934, the son of Ras Desta Ramtew, who was killed during the Abyssinian-Italian war, and of Princess Tenagne Work, Haile Selassie's only surviving daughter. He was educated at Dollar Academy in Scotland, and Wellington College in England.

After being trained at the Royal Naval College, Dartmouth, H.M.S. Britannia, where he graduated in 1951, Desta served in the aircraft carrier Triumph, the cruiser Gambia, and in 1955-56 with destroyers in the Mediterranean in Barossa.

Shortly after his return to Ethiopia his grandfather appointed him Deputy Commander of the newly-formed Ethiopian Navy. He was promoted Commodore in 1967 and to the rank of Rear-Admiral at the time of Princess Anne's visit in February 1973, when she was the Emperor's guest at the annual naval review.

Apart from his naval activities, Desta accompanied the Emperor on many of his state visits abroad and represented him at the independence celebrations of Nigeria, the Congo and Northern Rhodesia.

November 30, 1974.

Sir Humphrey de Trafford, BT., M.C., died on October 6, 1971 at the age of 79.

For nearly half a century he had a very close and active connexion with the British turf, first as an amateur rider and later as an owner, breeder and member of the Jockey Club and National Hunt Committee. His slight but dapper figure and his scarlet and white quartered racing colours were a familiar sight to racegoers on many racecourses where he often acted as a local steward.

As a young Coldstream Guards officer he proved to be a competent and fearless rider, characteristics which were to earn him a Military Cross in the First World War. In 1926 he founded a stud at Newsells Park, Barkaway, near Royston in Hertfordshire, and it was here that he bred most of his horses, including the classic winners Alcide and Parthia. The former, one of the outstanding horses of the century, won eight races worth £56,042 during his three seasons in training. His victories included the St. Leger in 1958 and the King George VI and Queen Elizabeth Stakes the following year. Alcide was unluckily beaten in the Ascot Gold Cup, and strained stomach muscles prevented him from running in and winning the Derby. Sir Humphrey, alas, was not always the luckiest of owners.

Parthia, however, won him the 1959 Derby and five other good races as well, before becoming a successful sire at Newmarket's Upend Stud. After eight years Sir Humphrey and his fellow shareholders sold their horse to Japan for a then quite princely sum. They perhaps did not foresee that within 12 months a filly by their sire, named Sleeping Partner, would win the Epsom Oaks for Lord Rosebery! Other winners that come to mind—and they all gave their enthusiastic owner equal pleasure—are Papillio, successful in the 1953 Goodwood Stakes, and Approval, who won the Observer Gold Cup at Doncaster in 1969 and the Dante Stakes at York in 1970.

Unlike some older members of the Jockey Club, Sir Humphrey always kept a keen interest in National Hunt racing. He had most of his horses with Captain Cecil Boyd Rochfort, who was succeeded on his retirement at Freemason Lodge, Newmarket, in 1969 by his stepson, Henry Cecil. But he also had a few horses with Willie Stephenson, whose stable was only a few miles from Newsells Park—the only trainer then holding a licence who could claim the distinction of having saddled a Grand National as well as a Derby winner.

A lifetime spent in racing gave Sir Humphrey the experience which many sought and which he was always willing to share. He became a steward of the Jockey Club from 1934-37 and served further terms in 1944 and 1951. His active participation in turf affairs leaves a gap that will not be easily filled.

The eldest son of Sir Humphrey Francis de Trafford, third baronet, he was born on November 30, 1891 and educated at the Oratory School and R.M.C., Sandhurst.

He was a Deputy Lieutenant for Hertfordshire, a Justice of the Peace and, in 1945, High Sheriff of the county.

He married in 1917 the Hon. Cynthia Cadogan, third daughter of Viscount Chelsea, second son of the fifth Earl of Cadogan, by whom he had four daughters. His wife died in 1966. The heir to the baronetcy is his brother, Mr. Rudolph de Trafford, O.B.E.

October 8, 1971.

Eamon de Valera, the Irish nationalist leader and President of the Republic of Ireland from 1959 to 1973, died on August 29, 1975 at the age of 92.

About a man who has been in turn a guerrilla commander, a political prisoner, a successful revolutionary, a partisan in civil war, a founder and leader of a political party, an elder statesman, and a head of state there will be found no consensus in the estimation of his contemporaries. By outsiders de Valera was thought of as a protoliberator from the bonds of empire, as an austere statesman of grave utterance with an honoured memory at the League of Nations, as the embodiment of whatever is consistent in the aspirations of the Irish nation. To part of his own people he was a hero of 1916, the last of the commandants to surrender, the one leader to survive the national struggle who never flinched in his purpose, the one man of his time with a preeminent claim to govern the Irish people. To another part he was a danger to the state, a politician of tricks and turns who was capable of disastrously wrong decisions, to whose actions most of the misfortunes of the country since 1921 were attributed, and that most dangerous of power-seekers, a man with an invincible sense of his own righteousness.

The complexity of his character adds to the difficulty of judgment. Gentle and courteous in private, he was often withering and autocratic in his public dealings. To know what the Irish people wanted, he once said, "I have only to examine my own heart". It was a way of short-circuiting democratic consultation to which he frequently resorted. There was a bleak integrity and refusal to count the cost about many of his actions that was in apparent contradiction to the transparent opportunism of others. The dialectical refinement and argumentative stamina with which he vindicated the settled principles of his policies were used with equal effect to justify his occasional tergiversation. Yet this much even his detractors must concede: he possessed unshakable courage and resolution, his patriotism was unalloyed and passionate, and in the flat years of post-revolutionary politics he was the only figure in Irish public life with magic to his name.

The most fateful moment of his career, and that by which all that followed must be judged, was when Griffith and Collins returned from London with the treaty of December 1921. It afforded neither political integrity for the island nor republican status for the 26 counties. It was, said de Valera, "neither this nor that". Certainly it compromised the full demands of Sinn Fein. Yet it gave the Free State effective and evolving independence, it was approved by a majority of the Dail, and it was assuredly acceptable to most of the Irish people. Was de Valera justified in these circumstances in repudiating the treaty and allying his unrivalled prestige and command of loyalty with the fanatics of armed resistance? There is no need to impugn his motives in order to conclude that he was wrong; for from that grave decision flowed an atrocious period of civil war, animosities that bevilled Irish politics for four decades and retarded the development of the country, and the continuance of the Irish Republican Army as a threat to civil order.

His subsequent conduct of the affairs of the state, creditable as it was in many ways, could not efface that disservice. He was Prime Minister for 16 years and then off and on for another five. He accomplished much: yet the two objectives of his later political career which seemed to be nearest to his heart, and on which he certainly expended most rhetoric—the end of partition and the restoration of Irish language—were as far as ever from accomplishment when at last in 1959 he sailed into the placid waters of the presidency.

There was a grandeur about his public career and a simple dignity in his bearing that eminently suited him for presidential office; for he held a place of honour in the history as well as in the contemporary affairs of his country. Tall; austere in his habits and his dress; grave and firm of countenance; soft, dry, and labyrinthine in speech; he dominated his countrymen, uniting and then dividing their loyalties as no man other than Parnell had done before him.

Eamon (it is the Irish form of Edward) de Valera was born in New York on October 14, 1882. His father, Vivion de Valera, a music teacher of poor health, was a native of Spain; his mother, Catherine Coll, had gone to America from co. Limerick in 1879. Vivion de Valera died when his son was two years old, and the child was sent to his mother's people in Limerick. He attended successively a national school, the Christian Brothers' Schools at Charleville and Blackrock College in co. Dublin. Later he took good degrees in arts and science at the Royal University of Ireland, taught mathematics in Rockwell College, Carysfort Training College and Holy Cross College, and became a mathematical lecturer in St. Patrick's College, Maynooth.

De Valera was imbued with nationalist ideas from an early age. During his period of schoolmastering he adopted and studied the doctrines of Sinn Fein, and attended constantly at the meetings of the Gaelic League, where he obtained a sound acquaintance with the Irish language. He joined the Irish Volunteers at their inauguration in 1913, and rose to officer's rank in the separatist section of that movement after the schism occurred with the Redmondite section. In 1914 he played an active part in the Howth gun-running, and he became adjutant of the Dublin Brigade of the Volunteers in 1915.

For all practical purposes de Valera's public career began with the Rising of 1916, when he commanded the force of insurgents stationed in Boland's Mill, Dublin. Militarily he was the most successful of the Irish leaders; Boland's Mill was the last post to be surrendered, and it was surrendered only on the orders of the insurgent Commandant-General. De Valera was tried and sentenced to death. The sentence was commuted to one of penal servitude for life, and he was imprisoned in Lewes gaol. There is no evidence that he was reprieved because of his American birth. It is more likely that he and another commandant, Thomas Ashe, were reprieved because by that time the unfavourable public effect of the executions was beginning to appear.

Early in 1917 the seat for East Clare fell vacant, and Sinn Fein nominated de Valera, whose part in the rising had made him a national hero. During the election the general amnesty of Irish political prisoners was proclaimed, and de Valera returned to Ireland. Immediately he found himself not only the parliamentary representative of East Clare, having polled more than twice

as any votes as his opponent, but, as one of the few insurrectionists to escape execution, the acknowledged leader of the republican element in the country. In accordance with Sinn Fein's political strategy, he abstained from taking his seat at Westminster and devoted himself, instead, to the reorganization of the Volunteers. His personal influence helped greatly to rally the dissipated elements of the movement, and his election to the presidency of Sinn Fein in the autumn of 1917 marked a significant step—the assimilation of Sinn Fein to the Volunteers.

Under the presidency of Arthur Griffith Sinn Fein had not been a republican organization; its objects had been cultural and in politics more or less constitutional. At the same time its branches permeated the country, providing an effective means for the dissemination of nationalist views. The Castle authorities sought to ridicule the insurrection by identifying it with Sinn Fein, an outlandish-sounding organization which in fact had had nothing to do with the rising. The trick had the opposite effect; for once the British, by executing the leaders of the rising, had invested a forlorn and mismanaged enterprise with the glory of martyrdom, Sinn Fein became the beneficiary of the new national sentiment. When under de Valera's presidency the republican and previously constitutional elements of nationalism were fused, an instrument was created more powerful even than that which Parnell had brought into being.

During the winter of 1917-18 de Valera toured, preaching the duty and organizing the means of armed rebellion against England. In April 1918 his campaign reached its height on the rumour that conscription would be applied to Ireland. He was arrested on a charge of treason and confined in Lincoln prison. In December, while he was still a prisoner, a general election, in which Sinn Fein swept the country, was held. In January the 73 Sinn Fein members constituted the first Dail Eireann in Dublin, reaffirmed their allegiance to the Republic proclaimed in 1916, and selected de Valera as their first President.

In February, through the agency of Michael Collins, he escaped from Lincoln and made his return to Ireland. For the next four months he was occupied in vain attempts to induce the Peace Conference to include Ireland in the scope of its deliberations. Meanwhile, the Volunteers and British troops were in daily conflict, and Ireland knew all the horrors of internal war. De Valera, constantly on the run, was at the heart of the Irish resistance. In June, however, leaving Griffith as Acting-President of the Republic, he went to the United States in search of money. The 17 months which he spent there were a medley of success and disappointment; but although he could not induce Washington to recognize the Irish Republic, he succeeded in his main object. When he returned to Ireland in December 1920 he had raised a loan of $6m for the Republican Government.

Guerrilla warfare raged all through 1920 and the first half of 1921, and the Dail functioned amid extreme difficulties and dangers. In May 1921 the second Dail Eireann was constituted, and in July the Truce was signed. De Valera went to London to meet Lloyd George, but the two reached no agreement on the matters at issue. De Valera invented and advanced the idea of "external association", an Irish republic in association with the British Commonwealth. But British constitutional thinking had not at that time advanced so far.

In October, on the invitation of Lloyd George, de Valera sent plenipotentiaries to London to conclude an acceptable treaty. A treaty was signed in December establishing the Irish Free State with Dominion status, and incorporating an oath of allegiance to the King. It was instantly denounced by de Valera, and approved by a majority of the Dail after prolonged and bitter debate. About the honours of that debate controversy continues to this day.

De Valera resigned his office as President of Dail Eireann, and he and his followers left the Dail, and did not appear in it again until 1927. Although he had ceased to be President of the Dail, de Valera was still President both of Sinn Fein and of the nominal Republic. All the enmity which he had borne against the British Government in Ireland was transferred after the Treaty to his fellows who had fallen so far from their faith as to accept Dominion status in a partitioned Ireland. For nearly a year he conducted, though at first equivocally, a campaign against the new Government which for horror matched anything in the previous three years. The Treaty party, in spite of the deaths of Griffith and Collins, showed unexpected competence and resolution, and early in 1923 the Republicans had been driven out of all save a few strongholds, and the leader instructed his followers to dump their arms and abandon the fight for the time being. In August he came out of hiding to contest an election in Clare. He was arrested on his political platform in Ennis, and did not regain his liberty until the following July.

De Valera's life during the next three years was quiet. His party, refusing to take the Oath of Allegiance, continued to abstain from the Dail. In 1926, however, the Government made nomination for the Dail conditional on an affidavit to take the oath. De Valera changed his tactics, and proposed at the annual Ard Fheis, or general convention, of Sinn Fein that the Republicans should take their seats. The proposal split Sinn Fein. The irreconcilables, who still refused to acknowledge the existing Dail, retained the title of Sinn Fein: de Valera's partisans, pledged now to legislative action, formed a new organization under the name of Fianna Fail.

While in opposition, Fianna Fail was organizing its programme for the next general election. Its principal points were the abolition of the oath, the retention of the land annuities which had been pledged to Britain by Cosgrave's financial agreements of 1923 and 1926, and the development of the Free State's resources towards a condition of self-sufficiency. The Government had improved the country's commerce with England, and there was virtually free trade between the two nations. In 1930-31 the world depression began to affect Ireland; cattle prices on the English market declined and the farmers began to experience vague doubts concerning the wisdom of free trade with England. Furthermore, those two years witnessed a revival of terrorist tactics by the Irish Republican Army, which had cast itself loose from de Valera's control as soon as he consented to take the oath (as an empty formality).

In 1931 the Government approved an Amendment to the Constitution which outlawed the I.R.A. and kindred Republican bodies, and established a military tribunal for the trial of political offences. This action helped to alienate the people from the Government. Furthermore, de Valera was now in control of a daily newspaper, *The Irish Press*: the funds for it he had collected by a visit to the United States in 1930, and for the first time the Cosgrave Government was opposed by a serious daily paper. In February 1932 Cosgrave appealed to the country, and the general election gave the Fianna Fail-Labour coalition a majority of five over all other parties.

De Valera formed a Government—a Government which, for all intents and purposes, consisted of himself. Virtually an autocrat within his Cabinet and party, he put his policies into immediate practice. He released the Republicans who had been gaoled by the military tribunal and, without officially notifying the British Government of his intention, introduced a Bill to abolish the oath. The Bill was carried in the Dail, but eventually was held up by the Senate which in turn de Valera abolished. When he defaulted on the current instalment of land annuities and demanded that the British claim to them should be tested by law, the British Government stipulated that the case in accordance with a decision of the 1930 Imperial Conference should be tried by an Empire tribunal. De Valera refused to negotiate on these terms. Thereupon Britain, in an attempt to recoup herself for the loss of the land annuities, imposed heavy import duties on Free State agricultural produce. De Valera retaliated with severe tariffs on British goods, and an economic war developed which was to cause almost untold trouble to the Free State and bring its agriculture to the verge of ruin.

He continued his campaign against the imperial connexion by studied disregard of the Governor-General. He then recommended his recall, and the nomination of a country shopkeeper as the next incumbent revealed his intention of degrading the dignity of the office and eventually abolishing it.

In spite of the dire results of his experiment in economic nationalism de Valera was returned to power, though not always with an absolute majority for his party in the Dail, at successive elections in 1933, 1937, and 1938. In this he was helped by his unrivalled political acumen, by the disorganized state of the opposition parties, and by the disastrous irruption into politics of General O'Duffy and his Blue Shirts. All the same, his redistributive social policies and his steady progress towards the next best thing to a republic were sufficiently in tune with the sentiments of a large enough part of the electorate.

He seized the occasion of the Abdication of King Edward VIII to slip through two Bills eliminating all the functions of the Governor-General from the Constitution and introducing a form of "external association" with the Crown and Commonwealth; and in 1937 he brought in a new Constitution in which the Irish Free State became Eire (which is the Irish for Ireland), with a president and a reformed senate. The Constitution laid juridical claim to the whole of the province of Ulster and accorded a "special position" to the Roman Catholic Church.

These unilateral moves, which in earlier days would have been highly provocative of the British, were accepted with equanimity on the English side of the Irish Sea, where the Irish question had fallen out of politics, where the conception of the Commonwealth had lost much of its formality, and where de Valera's moves were recognized as making little practical difference.

De Valera's stature was quickly recognized on the international stage at Geneva, where he was chairman of the Council of the League of Nations in 1932 and President of the Assembly in 1938. His speeches on behalf of collective security were straight and firm, and he was an advocate of action by the League against Japan in Manchuria and Italy in Abyssinia.

In the spring of 1938 the ruinous economic war between Britain and Ireland was at last called off. In London de Valera negotiated an agreement in three parts which secured generous terms for his country. First the British Government gave up the naval bases at Queenstown, Berehaven, and Lough Swilly and renounced its right to further naval facilities in Irish ports in time of war ("a more feckless act can hardly be imagined", was Sir Winston Churchill's* comment); next Ireland paid £10m. to compound for the land annuities and other suspended payments, and as a corollary the penal duties imposed by both sides were abolished; next a trade agreement was reached of great benefit to Irish agricultural production.

Two matters which de Valera kept in the forefront of domestic policies were the Irish language and partition. Irish as an official language in state affairs, its compulsory introduction into the school curriculum, some knowledge of it as a qualification for public office, these were ideas common to all the founders of the new state. De Valera alone among politicians never seemed to lose his enthusiasm in the face of overwhelming evidence of the policy's failure as a means of resuscitating the language. For him language was a badge of nationhood: "I believe that as long as the language remains you have a distinguishing characteristic of nationality which will enable the nation to persist. If you lose the language the danger is that there would be absorption".

Nor did the hopes of a United Ireland prosper any better. In fact every step in de Valera's progress to abolish links with the Crown drove that distant prospect farther into the distance. Partition was the ostensible reason for his policy of neutrality in the war—a policy which received the general endorsement of his countrymen, whose opportunities to become individual belligerents were unlimited.

In October 1939, at the instance of Churchill who was then First Lord of the Admiralty and apprehensive about defence of the Western Approaches, strong representations were made to de Valera to grant naval facilities at Berehaven. He was inflexibly opposed. The British Cabinet briefly considered coercion before dismissing it. The following summer a different approach was tried. Malcolm MacDonald was sent to Dublin with proposals under which a declaration by the British Government accepting the principle of a united Ireland together with a joint North-South working party for that purpose would be exchanged for Eire's entering the war on the side of the United Kingdom. De Valera, spotting that Belfast would still retain a practical veto and knowing that belligerency would disunite his people, did not warm to the proposal.

In the wake of Pearl Harbour Churchill had one more try. "Following from Mr. Churchill to Mr. de Valera. Personal. Private and Secret. Begins. Now is your chance. Now or never. 'A Nation once again'. Am ready to meet you at any time. Ends." De Valera's characteristically dry reply was, "Perhaps a visit from Lord Cranborne would be the best way towards a fuller understanding of our position here."

In some ways de Valera interpreted the obligations of neutrality in a sense convenient for Britain and its allies, in other ways he was unbendingly pedantic: he protested against the arrival of American troops in Northern Ireland, he declined the request of the United States, backed by Britain, to remove Axis consular and diplomatic representatives who were believed to be endangering allied security, and he made himself somewhat ridiculous by the nicety of calling on the German Minister in Dublin on May 2, 1945, to express his condolence on the death of Adolf Hitler.

De Valera was returned to power at two elections during the course of the war, but his unbroken period of office of 16 years came to an end in 1948, when an uneasy coalition of opposition parties secured a majority against him. He formed two more governments, in 1951-54 and 1957-59, but he had nothing new to offer his countrymen.

His presence at the centre of the stage prolonged the political division of Ireland along lines drawn in the 1920s, and kept a younger generation of politicians from their full inheritance.

In the summer of 1959, at the age of 78, and with his sight badly impaired, he allowed his name to go forward as a candidate for the presidency. His manner of going was characteristic of the turbulence of his long career. He was never one to scruple at altering the Constitution if he thought he could improve it. His last attempt was to substitute for proportional representation the British system of simple majorities in single-member constituencies, more favourable, it was felt, to his own party; and he so arranged things that the plebiscite on this issue should fall on the same day as the presidential election, hoping, his critics alleged, to confuse the constitutional issue with a test of his own undoubted prestige. The stratagem, if it was one, failed. He was duly elected President, but proportional representation remained.

When his term of office expired in 1966, he stood for re-election. He was opposed by T. F. O'Higgins, a much younger man belonging to the Fine Gael Party. De Valera was returned by a bare 10,000 majority in contrast to his majority of 120,000 in 1959. The cities turned against him, where the modernity of his opponent rang more true than de Valera's appeal to the visionary values of a united Gaelic Ireland.

As President he scrupulously refrained from political partisanship. His public visits abroad were few. He was in Italy on St. Patrick's Day 1962, and received from the hands of the Pope the insignia of the Supreme Order of Christ, the Vatican's highest decoration. In the summer of 1964 he visited the United States, whither he had been invited by President Kennedy* when the latter made his triumphal tour of Ireland shortly before his assassination. De Valera addressed a joint session of Congress to whom he expressed the hope that one day another representative of Ireland would be able to stand before them and announce that "our severed country has been reunited and the last source of enmity between the British people and the Irish people has been removed and at last we can be truly friends".

His second term of office expired in 1973, and the de Valeras retired to the modest seclusion of a convalescent home at Blackrock, co. Dublin, there to continue the regular observance of the religious duties which they had long practised.

Eamon de Valera had married in 1910 Miss Sinead ni Fhlannagain. She died at the beginning of 1975. There were five sons (one of whom is dead) and two daughters of the marriage.

August 30, 1975.

Margaret Devlin—See Daisy Ashford.

Thomas E. Dewey, who died on March 16, 1971 in Florida at the age of 68, will be remembered primarily as the most surprising loser of a Presidential election in the history of the United States. Other men have lost the Presidency by narrower margins, but no other has seemed so certain to triumph until the nation actually went to the polls.

If his defeat by Harry Truman in 1948 was the most spectacular event of his career, it was by no means the whole story. He belonged to what, despite popular misconceptions, is really a select band in American politics—those who have twice failed as their party's nominee for the Presidency and yet remained a force in the nation's counsels.

He was among General Eisenhower's earliest and most powerful backers; he remained an elder statesman of the Republicans and normally used his influence in a moderate and sensible way.

In his journey from isolationism to internationalism, and in the practical idealism with which he adjusted his thinking to the changing world, he mirrored the mental development of the American people during his years of maturity.

Yet, with all these gifts and his fine record, he was not of the highest political stature. There was not the sense of a great President being lost through the quirks of the electoral process. He had neither the personal magnetism of the outstanding political leader nor the vision of the statesman. What he did have was efficiency and a sharp intellect.

Thomas Edmund Dewey was born on March 24, 1902 at Owosso, a small town in Michigan where his father kept a store, acted as postmaster and ran a weekly newspaper. Tom was educated at the local municipal school, and as a boy helped his father with the paper and on his own account became agent for a national weekly, organizing a team of youngsters to sell subscriptions for him. He thus made enough money to take him to the University of Michigan where he assisted in producing the university paper and made his name as a debater.

Dewey held positions in several law firms, but the break-through came with his appointment at the age of 28 as Chief Assistant United States Attorney for the southern district of New York. In this post he was prosecutor in a number of sensational cases, and was able to begin building the position on which his early reputation depended as the representative of the law fighting the organized crime which was then at its height in New York.

For a short time he was District Attorney but, with the defeat of the Republican administration, returned to a lucrative private practice in 1933. Two years later, he was appointed by the Governor as a special prosecutor and investigator of crime and vice in New York. So successful was he in this task that in 1937 he was elected District Attorney.

He was a popular public figure and a natural choice as the Republican candidate for Governor in 1938. Although he was defeated, he waged such an impressive campaign that he became a leading contender for the Republican Presidential nomination in 1940, and were it not for the successful last-minute *coup* by Wendell Wilkie, Dewey might well have been chosen. As it was, he stood again for Governor in 1942 and was elected.

His administration was capable, his appointments shrewd, and his relations with the state legislature fruitful, and in 1944 he had little difficulty in becoming the Republican nominee for President. But his task was difficult. Not only was his opponent one of the most adroit politicians in the history of the United States—Franklin D. Roosevelt—but it was difficult to attack the conduct of affairs without seeming to criticize the nation's war effort.

There were also divisions within the party, and Dewey was easily defeated. He continued as Governor of New York and in 1948 stood again as the Republican candidate for the Presidency. This time his chances appeared really bright; in fact, the public-opinion polls did not bother to take any soundings for more than a week before the actual voting. The vigour and persistence of Truman's hard campaigning at local level—the last five"whistle-stop" campaigns—made up the leeway; Dewey was disappointed once again.

Tom Dewey returned then to private law practice after retiring as Governor in 1954. His wife, the former Frances E. Hull, whom he married in 1928, died in 1970. They had two sons.

March 17, 1971.

Jack R. Dick, the American businessman, the first portion of whose superb collection of sporting pictures was sold at Sotheby's in October 1973 for some £1.2m., died in New York on January 6, 1974.

He died in his mid-forties having, among other things, built up from nothing, and sold, a multi-million dollar cattle business, Black Watch Farms, and formed the largest and most important collection of English sporting pictures in the world. The paintings sold at Sotheby's represented only one quarter of the collection. He had also formed an important collection of French paperweights, paying some of the highest prices ever recorded at auction. He was a man of exceptional charm.

His fortune was based on Black Watch Farms, a type of cattle breeding unit trust. About 600 investors were attracted by the possibility of tax write-offs and breeding profits; at one point Black Watch Farms managed more than 30,000 head of cattle in 20 states. In 1963 he paid £63,000 for a prize Aberdeen-Angus bull at Perth.

Dick sold the operation in 1968 to a company called Bermec, receiving $5½ mil-

lion in cash and $30 million worth of stock in the new company, as he explained when in London in October 1973. "I was a very rich man on paper," he said. He furnished a palatial residence in Greenwich, Connecticut, called Hampton Court, and his life-style was nothing if not lavish. Even in that same month he was seen to tip a London airport porter with a £10 note.

His financial troubles started in 1971 when Black Watch Farms was declared bankrupt, shortly followed by Bermec. His $30 million worth of stock were suddenly worthless. To solve his financial difficulties it became imperative to sell his collection of sporting paintings.

The collection had taken him 15 years or so to build. He explained, in October 1973, how his interest in sporting pictures had arisen. He had started collecting cattle pictures and had soon managed to make "a pretty good corner".

But at the same time he was, in his own words, "the leading breaker of Arabian horses in the United States." So he started buying paintings of Arabian horses and this quickly led him to the great English school of sporting art. His fierce competition in the sale room with Paul Mellon for the best examples of the genre in the 1960s brought a sensational price spiral. He purchased works from many old English collections, with the constant help and advice of Ackermann's, the Bond Street dealers. In a short time he developed knowledge and an "eye" that rivalled the dealing fraternity themselves.

The first sale aroused exceptional interest at Sotheby's, for it was preceded by weeks of controversy and much transatlantic legal activity.

The pictures were sold, in effect, by Sotheby's on behalf of the United States Government, which was acting on its own behalf to secure payments of a tax debt incurred by Dick, and as trustee for other creditors with a claim on the pictures. Prices "went through the roof": George Stubbs's "Goldfinder", the centre piece of the sale, fetched £225,000, an auction record for the greatest of English sporting artists. Arthur Devis's "The Swaine Family" made £136,000, almost twice the pre-sale estimate; and Ben Marshall's "Mr. Wastall with his Jockey" climbed to £47,000, multiplying the estimate more than three times.

Dick leaves a widow, a son and a daughter.

January 9, 1974.

Professor Arthur Herbert Dodd, Professor of History at the University College of North Wales, Bangor, from 1930 to 1958, died at his home in Bangor, Gwynedd, in May 1975. He was 82.

A. H. Dodd was a member of a notable Wrexham family which included his brother, C. H. Dodd, the eminent New Testament scholar. He was educated at

Wrexham Grammar School and at New College, Oxford, where he had a distinguished academic record.

He had at first contemplated a career in the Civil Service but soon resolved that he was best fitted for academic work. He was appointed Lecturer in the Department of History at Bangor in 1919 under Sir John Lloyd, whom he succeeded as Professor in 1930. His first major work, *The Industrial Revolution in North Wales* (1933), was at once acknowledged to be an admirable pioneer study.

Thereafter he became increasingly attracted to the Tudor and Stuart periods. His attachment to the sixteenth century was further stimulated by the companionship of Sir John Neale and his colleagues when University College London was evacuated to Bangor during the Second World War—a link which he always greatly valued.

One of his later books was the popular *Elizabethan England*, first published in 1961. Welsh scholars, however, associate him primarily with seventeenth-century Wales and his *Studies in Stuart Wales* (1952), together with a number of erudite articles, were based upon extensive forays into the abundant and largely unexplored collections of family papers at Aberystwyth and Bangor. His work upon the political and social life of Stuart Wales will not soon be superseded.

A. H. Dodd's devotion to the adult education movement began in R. H. Tawney's* tutorial class at Wrexham in 1911 and it continued throughout his life. He was for many years Chairman of the North Wales District of the Workers' Education Association and he lectured regularly to an extra-mural class until a few months before his death. The degree of D.Litt., *honoris causa*, of the University of Wales was conferred upon him; and both he and his brother, C. H. Dodd, were made freemen of Wrexham.

His mind was tough and agile, but when engrossed in a problem he was apt to be oblivious of trifles. Indeed, his several minor tribulations by road and rail speedily passed from mere anecdote into legend, which did not at all displease him for he had a wonderful sense of fun.

His personality was warm and generous and his experiences as a soldier during the First World War gave him an added insight into problems confronting ex-service students after the Second. He will be remembered with abiding affection, especially by those who had the great good fortune to have been taught by him. He is survived by his widow and four daughters.

May 21, 1975.

Dr. Charles H. Dodd, C.H., who died on September 21, 1973 at the age of 89, was the most influential British New Testament scholar of the twentieth century.

After a full career of university teaching

and writing for both learned and popular readerships, he devoted another two decades of his long life to his part in the translation and literary work of the New English Bible, not only as Convener of the New Testament Panel, whose work was published in 1961, but as general director of the whole work, including the Old Testament and Apocrypha, leading to the publication of the complete Bible in 1970. Since 1966, when the Old Testament work became increasingly important, he shared the directorship with Sir Godfrey Driver, but from the inception of the whole operation Dodd's wise guidance and sensitivity to the claims of scholar and simple reader alike were indispensable.

His book on *The Authority of the Bible* (1928) displayed a discriminating concern for the place of the Scriptures in a liberal climate of religious opinion, and some 25 years later he wrote *According to the Scriptures* to show how the early Christians had appealed to the Old Testament in their own apologetics. His first popular book was on *The Meaning of Paul Today* (1920) and he published a splendid Romans, together with a technical study of *The Bible and the Greeks* and a widely ranging discussion of *History and the Gospel*.

Of even greater significance were two small books of 1935-36. *The Parables of the Kingdom* expounded the view that in the work of Jesus, defended in his parables, the kingdom of God had been inaugurated. (Dodd later modified this "realized eschatology" to take more account of the futurist elements.) *The Apostolic Preaching and its Developments* recovered the common message (or *kerygma*) of the early Church that in Jesus the prophecies had been fulfilled.

However, Dodd was greatest as a Johannine scholar. Prepared by a commentary on *The Johannine Epistles,* the two great works of his retirement, *The Interpretation of the Fourth Gospel* (1953) and *Historical Tradition in the Fourth Gospel* (1963), opened a new era in the discussion of the mystical and historical, Jewish and Hellenistic, elements in St. John.

Charles Harold Dodd was born in Wrexham on April 7, 1884. He was the eldest son of Charles Dodd, headmaster of an elementary school in Wrexham. He learnt Welsh as a schoolboy and this was to stand him in good stead later, when he became one of the very few New Testament scholars who could be called on to examine Welsh theses for higher theological degrees (in the University of Oxford). He also anticipated future developments at this period by becoming a local preacher when he was still a schoolboy. He went up to University College, Oxford as a classical scholar, where he both coxed one of the boats and got his First in Greats. The eight years after he took his degree were extremely diverse. For a short period he lectured in Classics at the University of Leeds and there (despite his lack of acquaintance with the stage) produced *The Clouds*. He was

elected Senior Demy at Magdalen College in 1907 and took the opportunity of spending a short time in the University of Berlin to study numismatics. It was on this subject that he published his first paper, *Samians at Zancle-Messana*, and there followed other papers on the same subject.

It was also in this early period that he developed his interest in archaeology and wrote a work which he never published on early Christian inscriptions in Italy. He helped Haverfield and Craister excavate the Roman settlement at Corbridge. In 1910, he joined Mansfield College to study theology and was ordained in 1912. He then left Oxford and went to Warwick for three years as minister of the Independent or Congregational Church. When he returned to Mansfield College in 1915, it was his intention to pursue the study of Church History and it was only after he had almost completed a book upon the period between Constantine and Theodosius that the teaching needs of Mansfield turned his interest to New Testament scholarship.

He was Yates Lecturer in New Testament Greek and Exegesis at Mansfield from 1915 to 1930. He still retained, however, his interest in affairs outside the academic sphere and he not only helped to arrange boys' camps in Merionethshire but also sang for the troops in Oxford during the 1914-18 War. He soon became recognized in the university and became a lecturer in New Testament Studies in 1927 and held both the Speaker's Lectureship and the Grinfield Lectureship on the Septuagint. In 1930 he succeeded A. S. Peake as Rylands Professor of Biblical Criticism and Exegesis in Manchester, where he remained for five years.

He was then elected at Cambridge to the Norris Hulse Chair of Divinity and so became the first non-Anglican Professor of Divinity at either university. He occupied this chair until his retirement in 1949. He was elected a Fellow of Jesus College in 1936 and became an honorary Fellow on his retirement from his chair in 1949. Two years later he was elected as honorary Fellow of his old College (University College) in Oxford. His work as a scholar by no means ended when he ceased to be an active university teacher. He was then able to bring to completion the Johannine studies which had occupied him for over 25 years and to produce several other works, smaller but of considerable importance. He was also able to accept the major responsibility for the new translation of the Bible and became general director of the whole scheme—an exacting and time-consuming task, to which he brought vision as well as unsparing toil.

In addition to being elected a Fellow of the British Academy, he was the recipient of numerous honorary degrees. He was an honorary doctor of Oxford, Cambridge, Manchester, Glasgow, Aberdeen, Wales and London Universities and held the honorary S.T.D. of Harvard and an honorary doctorate of Strasbourg. The honorary doctor-

ate of Theology was conferred on him at Oslo soon after the war, when Oslo University awarded honorary degrees for the first time in its history.

In 1961 he was created a Companion of Honour, in recognition of his work for the New English Bible.

Dodd combined to a very remarkable degree a range of knowledge unusual in these days of specialization with the accuracy and research of a trained scholar and with brilliant gifts of popular exposition. As preacher, lecturer and broadcaster he maintained a consistently high standard, and his many books showed a similar excellence in insight and clarity. At a period of acute and even extravagant theological tension his generosity of temper, soundness of judgment and breadth of knowledge gave him a unique position among contemporary scholars.

In his committee work on the preparation of the New English Bible Dodd stood out as an admirable expositor, clear, concise and persuasive. Very ready to listen, when necessary he could be decisive. He was impressive in his strong desire to remember the ordinary reader and by his courage in deserting tradition when it conflicted with a deeper truth.

He was a man of singular charm, very happily married to the widow of John Elliott Terry. With her genial efficiency and quiet humour, Mrs. Dodd made a perfect partner. Their children and grandchildren brought them much happiness.

September 25, 1973.

Thomas Dodd, the former Democratic senator for Connecticut censured in 1967 by his peers for diverting political funds for his personal use over a five year period, died in Old Lyme, Connecticut on May 24, 1971. He was 64.

Dodd, tipped as Johnson's vice-president at one time, was one of the few senators to receive the full wrath of the Senate through a censure motion—and the first since Senator Joseph McCarthy. The Senate's reprimand of Dodd, which spelt political ignominy for him, seemed lenient compared with the exclusion of Adam Clayton Powell, Representative for Harlem, by the House in the same year. Both had been accused of similar misdeeds. Dodd used extremely skilful defence tactics: after newspaper columnists had accused him of misconduct he himself asked for an investigation by the Ethics Committee. He fought the charges on the ground that he had broken rules which did not exist.

One certain asset of Dodd was his instinct for political survival. The image he projected during the eighteen-month inquiry was that of an aggrieved party rather than an offender. The four former staff members who passed his records on to the columnists were branded by him as victims of a "pathological desire for vengeance".

The columnists were, he said, "the most unscrupulous character assassins ever spawned by the American press".

Before the Committee he successfully gained a separate vote on the two main charges against him—one of double-billing airline tickets, the other of using campaign funds for his own use. The former was voted out. But on the latter he was found guilty. The Committee found that Dodd, a member of the foreign relations and judiciary committees, and chairman of two subcommittees, had collected more than £160,000 from testimonial dinners and campaign contributions—of which amount it claimed he had diverted about a quarter for his own personal use.

Thomas Joseph Dodd was born at Norwich, Connecticut, on May 15, 1907. He took a law degree at Yale in 1933 and two years later established the National Youth Administration programme in Connecticut. From 1938 to 1945 he was assistant chief of the civil rights section in the Department of Justice. He was chief trial counsel at the Nuremberg Trials after the Second World War, and went into private practice at Hartford in 1947. From 1953 to 1957 he was a member for Connecticut in Congress. In 1959 he became a Senator, being defeated in 1970. In the Senate he took part in the anti-Communist crusades, and also, as chairman of the Senate juvenile delinquency committee, warned against the danger of drugs.

May 25, 1971.

Sir Charles Dodds, M.V.O., F.R.S., the first baronet, Emeritus Professor of Biochemistry at London University, died on December 16, 1973 at the age of 74. He was Courtauld Professor of Biochemistry and Director of the Courtauld Institute of Biochemistry at Middlesex Hospital Medical School from 1927 to 1965.

Edward Charles Dodds was born on October 13, 1899, the only son of Ralph Edward Dodds. He was educated at Harrow County School and at the Middlesex Hospital Medical School, where he stayed throughout his career.

For upwards of forty years he played an outstanding part in many aspects of medical research, and particularly in the development of medical biochemistry, in matters relating to food and diet, in discoveries in endocrinology and in many aspects of the fight against cancer.

Dodds was a brilliant student and from his earliest days in medicine was clearly destined for a career of great distinction. He soon made his name as a teacher in the Bland Sutton Institute of Pathology and then was appointed Courtauld Professor of Biochemistry at London University at the age of 25, with the exciting task of building up the newly constructed Courtauld Institute of Biochemistry. He was its first director when it started in 1927 and he held the post until his retirement from the active staff in 1965, when he became Emeritus Professor.

He was one of the team of young men called in by Lord Dawson during the illness of King George V and his work was recognized when he was made M.V.O. in 1929.

With Dodds as its head, the new institute soon made a name for itself and became a leader in the development of medical biochemistry. A constant succession of papers came from his pen, describing his research work in a wide variety of subjects; the bibliography of his papers and books amounts to some 270 contributions.

He attracted other young workers, to whom he gave advice and encouragement but allowed the greatest freedom, so that the interests of his department and its contributions covered a very broad spectrum. The institute's reputation was also increased by its teaching and, in particular, the successful experiment of concentrating, within the institute, the teaching of all forms of chemistry, from inorganic of the premedical period up to chemical pathology of the clinical period.

Dodds was in great demand as a lecturer and adviser at home and abroad, and he received honours from many sources. He had obtained the degrees of M.D., D.Sc., and Ph.D. from London University; to them were added honorary doctorates from the Universities of Cambridge, Birmingham, Melbourne, Bologna, and Chicago. He was a Fellow of the Royal Institute of Chemistry and of the Royal Society of Edinburgh, and the honorary fellowships of the Royal College of Obstetricians and Gynaecologists, of the Royal College of Physicians and Surgeons of Glasgow, of the Royal Australasian College of Physicians, and of the American College of Physicians, were conferred on him.

He had honorary membership of many foreign medical and chemical societies and received numerous gold medals and prizes, including the Garton Prize and Medal of the British Empire Cancer Campaign, the Walker Prize of the Royal College of Surgeons, the Gold Medal in Therapeutics of the Society of Apothecaries, the Gold Medal of the Society of Chemical Industry, the Berzelius Medal of the Swedish Medical Society, the Medals of the universities of Ghent and Brussels, and the Pasteur Medal of the Société de Chimie Biologique Française.

Among the many statutory lectures that he gave were the Goulstonian lectures of the Royal College of Physicians, the Harvey lecture of New York University, and the three most important lectures of his own medical school, the Astor lecture, the Comfort Crookshank lecture, and the Sanderson Webb lecture. He was the Sims Travelling Professor of the Royal College of Surgeons in 1952.

He was elected a Fellow of the Royal Society in 1942 and later served as a member of council and as vice-president. He was knighted in 1954 and was created baronet in 1964. He was President of the Royal College of Physicians from 1962 to 1966.

Dodds was continually called to serve on official and charitable scientific bodies. For the Ministry of Agriculture, Fisheries and Food, he was chairman of the food additives and contaminants subcommittee of the Food Standards Committee, and also of the Advisory Committee on Poisonous Substances used in Agriculture and Food Storage. He was chairman of the Advisory Council on Scientific Research and Technical Development at the War Office.

He served as a member of the National Research Development Corporation of the Overseas Research Council, of the Council for Scientific Policy, and he was one of the first members of the Clinical Research Board of the Medical Research Council. He was for many years chairman of the scientific advisory committee of the British Empire Cancer Campaign, and chairman of the scientific advisory committee of the Fleming Memorial Fund for Medical Research, and he was also chairman of the committee of management of the Cancer Research Institute, Royal Cancer Hospital, and of the governing body of the Lister Institute; and vice-president of the Arthritis and Rheumatism Council.

Scientifically, perhaps the greatest original contribution made by Dodds was the work, in association with Wilfred Lawson, which led to the discovery of Stilboestrol. But there was much other work of great significance in other fields, such as insulin, the secretions of the pituitary, and the problems of hormones in cancer. In later years his particular strength was his ability to recognize promising new lines of research and to advise and encourage junior colleagues to perfect them.

He was brought up in the Bland Sutton Institute, where there was a tradition of cancer research, and that remained his most consuming interest throughout his life. He was associated with the British Empire Cancer Campaign from its foundation, and succeeded Lord Horder, by whom he was greatly influenced, as chairman of its scientific advisory committee. The work he did has had a great influence in determining the progress of cancer research in Britain.

Dodds's election as president of the Royal College of Physicians was a landmark; it was the first time the office had been held by one not practising clinical medicine. He succeeded when the new college building was nearing completion and had the task of stabilizing the college finances to meet greatly increased demands for maintenance and for increasing the college's scope of activities. For that he was admirably suited, as he had great ability and long experience in attracting generous financial support for the research work of his own institute.

For some years Dodds had been Harveian librarian at the college and he had a great interest in, and made contributions to, the study of English medical history. He was a staunch supporter of the Society of Apothecaries, of which he was master from 1947 to 1949. The historical interests of the society and its long tradition made particular appeal to him, and his unique knowledge and appreciation of good wine were responsible for the continued excellence of its cellar.

Despite his vast experience, Dodds was no great orator; he was shy, and public speaking was always something of an ordeal. For those who did not know him, his shyness sometimes made him seem rather unapproachable; but he had an exceptionally wide circle of devoted friends. To those who knew him well, his outstanding characteristic was his loyalty. He always remembered the help given to him when he was making his way, particularly by Lord Webb Johnson and later Harold Boldero, and he gave much time and thought to helping the careers of others.

There were demands for his services from many quarters, at home and abroad, but first and foremost throughout his life came his loyalty to his institute and to the Middlesex. Indeed, after his retirement he continued to serve as honorary director of its newly established Department of Rheumatology Research.

He married in 1923 Constance Elizabeth, only daughter of J. T. Jordan, and they had a son, Ralph Jordan Dodds, who was born on March 25, 1928, and who succeeds to the baronetcy. Lady Dodds died in 1969.

December 18, 1973.

Desmond Donnelly, former M.P. for Pembroke, who in 1968 resigned from the Labour Party, founded his own Democratic Party and then joined the Conservatives, was found dead on April 4, 1974. He was found to have taken his life while suffering severe depression. He was 53.

Donnelly's career was remarkable both for its independence—at no time could he have been described as a "party man"—and for the progressive change in his views. On his election to Parliament he was a "Bevanite"; later he broke with Bevan, and attached himself to Hugh Gaitskell*; later still he was to leave the Labour Party after 18 years, begin his own Democratic Party and eventually join the Conservatives.

Donnelly had heeded Churchill's* advice to the ambitious, "Make sure of your base", and his popularity in his constituency was very great. He was one of the few present-day politicians who could claim to have built up a genuinely personal following. He described his role in Pembroke as "a moulder of public opinion and dispenser of rough justice", and by a combination of words and deeds (he had a flair for public controversy which he put to good use, and he was in part responsible for the supertanker oil terminal harbour at Milford Haven), he made himself secure.

Desmond Louis Donnelly was born in 1920 in India. His father was a tea planter. He was of Irish ancestry and the first of

his family to return to Britain for a century. He was educated at the Bembridge School, Isle of Wight, and served from 1940 to 1946 in the Royal Air Force, reaching the rank of flight lieutenant. He first came to prominence when, at the outbreak of the last war, as a young player, he founded the "British Empire Cricket Eleven" which included players of the calibre of Keith Miller, Denis Compton and C. B. Clarke, and which played a good deal of war time cricket.

In 1945 he stood as Commonwealth candidate for Evesham and lost, and in 1946 as Labour candidate in co. Down. In 1946 he became editor of *Town and Country Planning*, and in 1948 the director of the Town and Country Planning Association. In the 1950 general election he stood as Labour candidate in Pembroke where he defeated the Liberal-Conservative candidate Gwilym Lloyd George (Lord Tenby*) by 129 votes, a Labour gain in what was elsewhere unrelieved disaster for the party. Donnelly, "an Englishman with an Irish name sitting for a Welsh seat", became a close associate of Aneurin Bevan.

However, he grew gradually disenchanted with "the great man" and his coterie, and when he became convinced that German rearmament was desirable, he broke with the Left. "I had gone very wrong," he said later. Since that time he took up positions that were to the right of the Labour Party. He was a strong opponent of the Campaign for Nuclear Disarmament, an early supporter of the Common Market, and a close associate of Hugh Gaitskell. He took a robust anti-Soviet line, in part due to his extensive travels in Russia, China and Eastern Europe. He never troubled to hide his disagreements with Harold Wilson, and it came as no surprise when, after Labour won the 1964 election, he was not even offered a junior post in the Government. Unabashed, he called publicly for a Liberal-Labour alliance, and gave notice, together with Woodrow Wyatt, that he would not vote for the renationalization of steel. This effectively postponed the measure until after the 1966 general election.

Fortified by the result in Pembroke where he retained his seat with a majority of 5,931, Donnelly took up an increasingly radical position. He advocated looser ties with the trades unions, "in which the unions do not look on the Labour Party as their pet poodle", was highly critical of the Government's handling of the economy, and then, after the devaluation of the pound had obliged the Government to reverse its policies "east of Suez", he resigned the party whip. At that time he wrote: "either the Government must change out of recognition, or it must go, and go this year. The alternative is Britain's ruin".

At a meeting of the Conservative Monday Club, where he received a two-minute ovation, he said that "Wilson should resign and leave public life". Donnelly, however, was not always consistent. Less than a year before he had said of the Prime Minister

that he was "the only leader capable of leading our country towards that future that all radicals and progressives demand". Clearly Donnelly's view of the future had changed. He felt strongly about Britain's world role, and believed that the Labour Government had abandoned it together with Britain's responsibilities to people in the Middle and Far East to whom it had given promises.

In 1967, now expelled from the Labour Party, he launched his own Democratic Party. He advocated, among other things, the abolition of the welfare state, a form of national service for all young people, and radical tax changes. The party contested unsuccessfully five seats in the 1970 election. Donnelly stood again for Pembroke but was defeated by the Conservative candidate. Ever the maverick, he abandoned the new party a year later and joined the Conservatives, explaining to Edward Heath that it was because of his views on issues such as Britain's entry into the Common Market and industrial relations reform.

He married Rosemary Taggart in 1947 and they had two daughters and a son.

April 5, 1974.

Lord Donovan, who died on December 12, 1971 at the age of 73, was a Judge of the High Court from 1950 to 1960, a Lord Justice of Appeal from 1960 to 1963, and a Lord of Appeal in Ordinary from 1963. In a comparatively short time after his appointment to the High Court Bench he gained in stature, displayed a judicial temperament and made an excellent judge in all the variety of work which came before him, qualities which he developed with great ability throughout the remainder of his judicial career.

At the Bar he had specialized in revenue work, but not long before he was appointed to the Bench revenue cases were transferred from the Queen's Bench to the Chancery Division. Accordingly, apart from a few occasions, the valuable service which he could have rendered in this increasingly difficult and complicated branch of the law was not used. However, he soon settled down to the work of the Queen's Bench Division, both civil and criminal, and quickly established a high reputation. With his clear and vigorous mind, harnessed to direct thought and speech, he listened to cases with the "unstrained attention of a Judge", allowed counsel to present their arguments without unnecessary interruption, but kept the hearings within bounds so that no time was wasted. He took the greatest care—indeed, he enjoyed fitting together the facts and evidence in a complicated case, and he showed a sound knowledge of the law. Though his was not an expansive nature, partly due to shyness, he took a balanced view of affairs, had a depth of common sense and understood his fellow creatures. His friendships were marked by generous and thoughtful actions. He was ever a champion of the underdog.

Terence Norbert Donovan was born on June 13, 1898. During the 1914-18 War he served in France with The Bedfordshire Regiment and later with the Royal Air Force. In 1920 he entered the Civil Service where he was engaged in the revenue department. The experience thus gained formed a sound basis when, like others who began their careers in the same way, he was later called to the Bar. In Donovan's case he was called by the Middle Temple in 1924, and he acquired a substantial practice in Revenue cases. He was also called to the Bar of Southern Rhodesia in 1937, when briefed in a case in that country. His practice grew, and future events justified his taking silk in 1945.

In politics Donovan represented the Labour interest, and was elected for the East Leicester Division in 1945. In the General Election in February 1950 he was returned for North-East Leicester. He did much good work on a number of committees. In 1945 he was appointed chairman of the British Government Legal Commission to Greece.

In the following year the important Denning Committee on Divorce procedure was set up and Donovan was one of its members, as he also was on the long-awaited Committee on Court-Martial Procedure, presided over by Mr. Justice Lewis, which sat from 1946-48.

It may fairly be said that few people had expected Donovan's appointment as a Judge. But in July 1950, while the Labour Party were still in power, he was offered a Judgeship, and, though he hesitated for some time before accepting it, his decision to do so was a wise one and proved to be fully justified.

As with all judges, it fell to his lot to try a number of cases which attracted public attention. Among them was what became known as the Brighton Trial, a long and arduous case, heard at the Central Criminal Court, when two police officers and another man were found guilty of conspiracy.

His name became nationally known as a result of the report of the Royal Commission on Trade Unions and Employers' Associations over which he presided from 1965 to 1968. The commission, the first to inquire into the general problems of industrial relations for more than 60 years, was appointed because of growing evidence of disorder in industry as shown by the growth in the number of unofficial strikes and inflationary wage movements.

When the composition of the commission was announced, including George Woodcock, the T.U.C. general secretary, Sir George Pollock, former director of the British Employers' Confederation, and others known to hold conflicting views, few expected a unanimous report. However, largely as a result of Lord Donovan's tactful and persuasive handling of the inquiry, the main body of the report was in the end signed by every member, though several added notes of reservation.

The Donovan Report, as it came to be known, was a disappointment to those who were advocating strong legislative regulation of industrial relations. The Labour Government initially, and the Conservative Government afterwards, both put forward legislative proposals which the commission had rejected and the new Industrial Relations Act bears little relation to the Donovan recommendations.

Nevertheless, the commission's analysis of what is wrong with the country's industrial relations and its suggested remedies have had an important influence on industrial behaviour. The main theme was that a division had developed between the formal system embodied in official institutions and the informal systems actually operated by managers, shop stewards, and workers. The central defect, the commission said, was the disorder in factory and workshop relations and the pay structures which resulted; and the solution was to be found in factory-wide or company agreements, the creation of which would depend primarily on the initiatives of boards of companies. Since the report, this analysis has become widely accepted, though the nature of the remedies has remained in dispute.

In 1925 Donovan married Marjorie Florence, daughter of Charles Murray, of Winchester, who survives him with their two sons and one daughter.

December 13, 1971.

Lewis Douglas, United States Ambassador to Britain from 1947 to 1950, died on March 7, 1974, at his home at Tucson, Arizona. He was 79.

Among the many posts he held was that of president of the United States Churchill Foundation, which provides scholarships and Fellowships, to enable American students to go to Churchill College, Cambridge for advanced studies.

He will be remembered in Britain as a wise counsellor and a very good friend, who never wavered in his faith in Britain's powers of recovery or in the imperative need of Anglo-American unity amidst the dislocation and menace of a world torn by war and revolution. No leading American figure, perhaps, with the exception of General Marshall himself, played a more notable or less obtrusive part in the counsels of Washington in furthering the early stages of the European Recovery Programme, and no envoy in London could have been more helpful or more sincerely persuasive in the task of reconciling the American and British points of view on disputed issues, among them the difficult issue of Palestine. Douglas held a conspicuously high place in the line of American Ambassadors in Britain since Walter Page.

Lewis William Douglas, the son of James Stuart Douglas, was born on July 2, 1894, at Bisbee, Arizona. He graduated from Amherst College in 1916 and then spent a year at the Massachusetts Institute of Technology, where he studied mining engineering; the family had extensive copper interests, his grandfather having become possibly the most successful mining engineer of his time. He enlisted in the United States Army in 1917, went out to France with the 91st Division, and as a first lieutenant fought in the Argonne and in Flanders.

After his return to civilian life he went back for a short time in 1920 to Amherst as instructor in history. But teaching did not seriously tempt him and he withdrew to Arizona, engaged in the family mining business and in insurance, farmed, wrote on economics, and in 1923 was elected to the Arizona House of Representatives, where he served for two years. Arizona sent him to Congress as representative at large in 1927, and during the following six years he became an able exponent in the House of financial orthodoxy, chairman of a special House economy committee, and a friend of Franklin Roosevelt.

He resigned his seat in Congress in 1933 in order to accept President Roosevelt's offer of the post of Director of the Budget. But Douglas, a firm advocate of economy in Government expenditure, soon found himself at odds with the monetary experiments of the New Deal and resigned some 18 months later. The experience, however, was not without influence upon his subsequent financial views.

He accepted a business appointment, which he abandoned in 1936, when he was appointed, largely on the strength of his administrative abilities, Principal and Vice-Chancellor of McGill University. He held the post for two years and returned to the States in order to become president of the Mutual Life Insurance Company of New York in 1940. But there was soon more urgent work for him to do. Early in 1942 he went to London to assist Averell Harriman with lend-lease, of which he had from the start been a stalwart supporter, and when he returned to Britain later in the year it was as deputy head of the United States war shipping administration. Hostilities over, he was for a short time assistant to General Clay in Germany.

In the discussions in America regarding financial aid to Britain Douglas came out unequivocally in favour of a gift of $4,000m. rather than a loan; he had a deeper insight than most experts in the United States into the financial realities of the after-war period in general and of Britain's position in particular. Then, in February 1947, President Truman nominated him as Ambassador in London. It was, for many, a surprise choice, but events were to prove how admirably sound it was. The new Ambassador rose commandingly to his opportunities in London and in Washington, where he made a particularly deep impression, for instance, on the Senate foreign relations committee in giving evidence before the passage of the European

Recovery Act. In the same way, the importance of his share in the diplomatic preparations for the North Atlantic Pact cannot be easily exaggerated.

The respect and affection he had inspired were still more strikingly apparent when in April 1949 he incurred serious injury to an eye while fishing.

A former national chairman of the English-Speaking Union of the United States, he was made an honorary G.B.E. in 1957.

He married, in 1921 Peggy Zinsser, daughter of Fred G. Zinsser. There were two sons and a daughter of the marriage. The daughter, Sharman, was a close friend of Princess Margaret.

March 9, 1974.

Douglas Douglas-Hamilton, 14th Duke of Hamilton—See Hamilton.

Sir George Dowty, industrialist, engineer and inventor, founder, chairman and chief executive of the Dowty Group, died at his home in the Isle of Man on December 7, 1975. He was 74.

George Herbert Dowty came to prominence in the aircraft industry and proceeded to apply the principles of his specialist products to other industries with such shrewdness that they were spread over a large part of the world. Within 30 years of an extremely modest start, he was the head of 10 companies in Britain, the Commonwealth and the United States and, although his labour force at home numbered only about 6,000, his turnover stood usually at some £20m. a year. Part of the secret of his prosperity lay in his readiness to give manufacturing licences to companies abroad, whereby he was relieved of purely industrial anxieties and yet was provided with a steady income which he devoted in large measure to research and development.

From the start, his interest in new ideas and in finding channels for their exploitation constituted his strength. He began as a draughtsman with no advantages but a lively mind and a stubborn determination not to shirk the consequences of his inventiveness. At that beginning he owed a good deal to the advice and encouragement of H. P. Folland, then chief designer of the Gloster Aircraft Company, where young Dowty was a draughtsman, but thereafter for 10 years, he had a thin and arduous time.

He had launched himself, in 1924, with an internally-sprung wheel for aircraft undercarriages. To his embarrassment, he received an order around £1,500 from Japan. Chiefly to satisfy that order, he founded a little company, rented a loft in Cheltenham at 2s. 6d. a week, employed himself at £3 a week and engaged the part-time services of two craftsmen who went to work for him in the evenings. When the work

for Japan ended, orders were hard to get. The infant company kept itself alive by making small articles for various markets—metal labels for gardeners, developing dishes for photographers and the like—but at the same time Dowty was at work on wheels and undercarriage legs for aircraft.

In 1934 he got an order for undercarriages for Gloster Gauntlet fighters and found himself launched on the development of those telescopic legs in which the landing shock was absorbed by the travel of one tube inside another, with a cushion of oil to lessen the ultimate jolt. Factory premises just outside Cheltenham were obtained and equipped. Production got under way and orders flowed in as re-armament gained impetus. In 1935 the company bought Arle Court, a mansion on the outskirts of the town, and turned it into a headquarters office with a dwelling for the chairman in part of it. There the chairman continued to live while research, development and testing departments grew up round it and turned it into the humming centre of the enterprise.

Dowty saw that as aircraft became bigger and heavier the shock-absorbing in undercarriage legs would make increasing demands on hydraulic systems. He set his team the task of foreseeing these demands. This meant providing for extremely high pressures in the fluids, and the question of seals which would remain effective under such pressures had to be tackled. Adjusting the length of travel at given loads to fluid pressures and seal capacities soon made this business an essentially specialist one and Dowty's became the designers of undercarriages for specific aircraft as well as the makers of components.

As a result of this work, Dowty made contact with the coal-mining industry, suggesting the use of hydraulic extending legs, instead of the old-fashioned wooden pit props, which could be used over and over again. When trials proved their efficiency, he went farther and designed a complete system of roof supports for use in mining, based on his hydraulic props. To claim that he undertook these advances himself would be an exaggeration but he remained the inspirer and director of a team of engineers and scientists who led a much harder life than any of the artisans in his workshops. Towards his workpeople he was a benevolent employer; towards his senior officials he was a generous, friendly but intensely demanding chief.

His hydraulics moved on to railway buffers and thence to a great variety of new applications. His imagination was always at work and it had behind it a sound training in modern engineering.

The seventh and twin son of William Dowty, of Pershore, he was educated at the Royal Grammar School, Worcester, and then in technical skills at the Victoria Institute. He had served an apprenticeship with Heenan and Froude and afterwards worked as a draughtsman with British Aerial Transport, Dunlop, A. V. Roe and

Gloster. He was just 23 when he set out on his own in that Cheltenham loft.

Thirty years later he served as president of the Royal Aeronautical Society, and was awarded the society's gold medal for the advancement of aeronautical science. He was president of the Society of British Aircraft Constructors in 1960-61 and treasurer of the Society of British Aerospace Companies in 1961-68.

He was a deputy lieutenant for Gloucestershire and an honorary freeman of Tewkesbury and Cheltenham.

December 9, 1975.

Thomas William Dreaper, the famous Irish National Hunt trainer, died on April 28, 1975 at his home in Kilsallaghan, co. Dublin. He was 76.

After a successful career as an amateur rider from 1922 to 1940 he turned to training, and saddled no fewer than ten winners of the Irish Grand National and five winners of the Cheltenham Gold Cup. During this golden era he handled a long succession of brilliant and talented steeplechasers, but it was his association with the Duchess of Westminster's Arkle, perhaps the greatest jumper of all time and certainly the foremost since the days of Dorothy Paget's Golden Miller, for which he will be best remembered.

In January 1972 he handed over his Greenogue stable to his 20-year-old son James, who has continued the run of family success.

Although somewhat elusive with strangers, he was a man of great charm and wisdom, completely dedicated to his profession. It was on his advice that the Duchess at Goff's Sale in 1960 bought an unnamed, unraced three-year-old for 1,150 guineas—later to be named Arkle after a mountain near her Scottish estate.

He was to win 27 of his 35 races, worth £74,623, before he shattered a pedal bone in 1966. He was put down in 1970.

Among Dreaper's distinguished owners at various times were: Lord Bicester, the Earl of Donoughmore, Lady Fingall, Colonel John Thompson and James Rank. It was for the last-named that he trained Prince Regent, 1942, and Shagreen, 1949, to win the Irish Grand National.

It was a great disappointment to him that while so many of the big steeplechase prizes in England and Ireland went his way, the Aintree Grand National always eluded him. It was a sad coincidence that he had Early Mist in his stable until James Rank's death in 1952, when most of his bloodstock was put up for sale. The following year this horse, carrying the colours of Joe Griffin and then trained by Vincent O'Brien, beat 30 rivals in this much-coveted race.

Nevertheless the strength of his steeplechasing team ensured him many other outstanding successes. Fortria won him two

Mackeson Gold Cups at Cheltenham in 1960 and 1962, Flying Bolt the Massey-Ferguson Gold Cup on the same course in 1965, and Fort Leney (1968) completed a fifth win for his stable in the Cheltenham Gold Cup.

Dreaper was a successful farmer as well as racehorse trainer. He always had an eye for talent and those who worked for him were chosen because of their special ability. Tim Hyde and the brothers Pat and Toss Taaffe, as riders, shared in most of his triumphs, and his staff at Greenogue were always loyal to a considerate and experienced master.

It was appropriate in his last season that he finished once again top of the National Hunt trainers in Ireland. In 1945 he married Eva Elizabeth Russell, by whom, apart from James, now running the stable, he had two daughters.

April 30, 1975.

Lieutenant-Colonel George Drew, former national leader of the Progressive Conservative Party, and Canadian High Commissioner in London from 1957 to 1964, died in Toronto on January 4, 1973. He was 78.

He led the Progressive Conservative Party between 1948 and 1956. As Prime Minister of Ontario before that, his victory in the provincial general election of 1943 began an unbroken 29 years of Conservative government in the province.

He had a long and honourable career in Canadian politics, both national and provincial, before his successful tenure of the Canadian High Commissionership in London. In the latter post, in which he succeeded a career diplomatist, his social gifts, for which Ottawa had offered more limited opportunities but which were always there, were a valuable asset.

Born in Guelph, Ontario, on May 7, 1894, he was the son of John J. Drew, K.C., and was educated in Guelph and then at the Upper Canada College in Toronto before he entered the University of Toronto to do the law course at Osgood Hall.

He was called to the Ontario Bar in 1920, but by then he had a useful military career behind him. In the First World War he served in the Artillery in France. He was wounded early in 1917, and after recuperating in Canada commanded the 64 Battery C.F.A.

Drew entered active politics through municipal affairs. He was also immersed in the law and it was 1936 before he took a prominent place in provincial politics.

He was chosen leader of the Conservative Party in Ontario in 1938, and a by-election in the following year at Simcoe East enabled him to assume control of the Opposition in the Legislature.

Harry Nixon, who succeeded Mitchell Hepburn in 1943, closed the gap between the Conservatives of Ontario and Ottawa, and Drew found it expedient to force an election. The Conservatives became the largest single party in the Legislature, though without a majority over the C.C.F. (Socialists) and Liberals together. The provincial election of June 1945 saw loyalty to Conservatism restored in Ontario.

In the provincial election of 1948 the Conservatives' majority was cut by 13 seats, and Drew lost his own seat but later that year he was chosen to succeed John Bracken, the federal leader of the Progressive Conservative Party who was retiring because of illness. Drew had many things in his favour—his vigorous campaign against Mackenzie King during the war, his sponsorship of the British connexion which the Liberals played down, his record of good government in Ontario, his vigour and confidence and the good looks that had won him the nickname "Handsome George".

No one could then foresee that Louis St. Laurent, the quiet Quebec lawyer, would develop into an esteemed national figure accepted as the representative Canadian of English-speaking Canada as well as of Quebec. Drew worked hard for national popularity on the same scale, but, though general esteem was his, he never at all rivalled St. Laurent.

No one ever doubted Drew's courage and pertinacity, but in the House of Commons it was often evident that he had not the quickness of mind and tongue to counter St. Laurent's suavity or break down Clarence Howe's blunt assertions that he knew best. Too often tactical advantages were not pressed home and telling arguments were weakened by repetition.

He was confirmed in the leadership in 1954. From then until the summer of 1956 Drew took, with John Diefenbaker, Donald Fleming and Davy Fulton, his full share of the Conservative assault against the Liberal citadel. The strenuous session from January to mid-August of that year left the Conservatives in a more hopeful position than for two decades. But Drew, who had not fully recovered from a severe attack of meningitis two years earlier, was a tired man. He resigned the party leadership in 1956—to be succeeded by Diefenbaker, who led the party to victory as the largest group in a no-majority House of Commons in June 1957.

His work in London was widely appreciated in Ottawa, especially his activity in development of greater trade and the exchange of visits between Canadian and United Kingdom businessmen. His knowledge of international affairs and Commonwealth relations made him a valued adviser during his years in London.

Drew married Fiorenza d'Arneiro, daughter of Edward Johnson, the tenor singer, who was manager of the Metropolitan Opera House, New York. They had one son and one daughter. She died in 1965. He married in 1966 Mrs. Phyllis McCullagh.

January 5, 1973.

Sir Godfrey Driver, C.B.E., M.C., Professor of Semitic Philology at Oxford from 1938 to 1962, died on April 22, 1975 at the age of 82.

Driver's immense learning made an important contribution to the New English Bible. Just as his father had been a moving spirit in the work of the Revised Version, so from 1947, when the new project began, Driver devoted himself heart and soul to the Old Testament part of the work and and in 1965 became Joint Director, with C. H. Dodd, of the whole enterprise.

His great knowledge of Semitic languages enabled him to make many quite new suggestions as to the meaning of rare words, and the finished Old Testament of the New English Bible bears his strong impress both in scholarship and in language. It was wholly appropriate that in 1968 he was knighted.

Godfrey Rolles Driver, son of the late Rev. Samuel Rolles Driver, D.D., Regius Professor of Hebrew and Canon of Christ Church, Oxford, was educated at Winchester and New College, entering both as a scholar. He became a Fellow of Magdalen in 1919, and served his college as Classical Tutor, Librarian and Vice-President.

In 1928 he was appointed Reader in Comparative Semitic Philology, and 10 years later the title of Professor was conferred upon him. He retired from his Chair in 1962. He was a most loyal son of both his college and his university in whose affairs he maintained a keen and active interest.

While he was still at school Driver assisted the late Sir Arthur Cowley with the proofs of the second edition of Gesenius's *Hebrew Grammar* (1910). After a distinguished record at Oxford in classics—he gained Gaisford Prizes for Greek Prose and Verse—Hebrew and Semitic studies increasingly claimed his attention. As an undergraduate he had already won the Junior Hall-Houghton Prize for Septuagint and the Pusey and Ellerton Hebrew Scholarship, and after graduation he was awarded the Senior Kennicott Hebrew Scholarship.

He remained throughout his life a fine classical scholar, but it was in the field of Hebrew and Semitic studies that he came to be recognized by scholars the world over as a foremost authority. Both in range and depth his knowledge of ancient Semitic languages was remarkable, and for over 40 years he made an outstanding contribution in books, articles, and reviews, to the elucidation of the Hebrew text of the Old Testament and of other ancient Semitic documents.

Three early books, all published in 1925, already revealed his mastery in the field of Semitic languages. They were *Letters of the First Babylonian Dynasty, A Grammar of the Colloquial Arabic of Syria and Palestine* and *Nestorius, The Bazaar of Heracleides* (edited from the Syriac text jointly with Dr. L. Hodgson). Collaboration with Sir John Miles resulted in the publication

10 years later of *The Assyrian Laws*, to which were added in due course two volumes, *The Babylonian Laws* (1952, 1955), all works of the highest scholarship and indispensable for the study of ancient Near Eastern law codes.

With *Problems of the Hebrew Verbal System* (1936), a subject in which Driver was wont to confess a traditional interest—his father's book on the Hebrew tenses was published in a third edition in 1892—he brought prominently to the notice of English readers the view, advocated especially by some German scholars, that Hebrew is a mixed language, and he showed how the Hebrew verbal system, as well as other elements in the language, derive from eastern and western strands of Semitic. His book is, as was his father's before him, a landmark in the history of the study of the subject.

In *Semitic Writing*, the Schweich Lectures for 1944 (second edition 1958), he brought a fresh approach to the study of the alphabet. He argued strongly for a close connexion between the Egyptian hieroglyphic system of writing and the Phoenician script. The Sinaitic script was not, he believed, the missing link between them, but one link in a complex chain of development.

Scarcely any discovery of ancient documents, whether seals, sherds, tablets, or scrolls, escaped Driver's attention. The tablets from Ras Shamra occupied him for many years.

When the Dead Sea scrolls were found, Driver at once entered the fray. With the passing of time his views about them changed radically. When it was decided to publish an edition of the collection of Aramaic documents acquired by the Curators of the Bodleian Library in 1943-44, which had already been worked on to some extent by other scholars, the final editing of them was entrusted to Driver. His edition appeared in 1954 (*Aramaic Documents of the Fifth Century B.C.*).

Driver was much in demand as an examiner in Old Testament and Semitic subjects. He was Visiting Professor at Chicago in 1925 and at Louvain in 1950. From 1933-40 he was Joint-Editor of the *Journal of Theological Studies*. He was President of the Bibliographical Society (1937-38) and of the Society of Historical Theology (1950-51) in Oxford, of the Society for Old Testament Study (1927), and of the International Organization for the Study of the Old Testament (1953). From 1935-39 he was Grinfield Lecturer on the Septuagint in Oxford.

He was made a Fellow of the British Academy in 1939, an honorary D.D. of Aberdeen (1946) and Manchester (1956), an honorary D.Litt. of Durham (1948), and an honorary Litt.D. of Cambridge (1964). He was appointed C.B.E. in 1958. A volume of essays, to which scholars in many countries contributed, was presented to him on the occasion of his seventieth birthday, and the autumn issue of the *Journal of Semitic Studies*, 1962, which contained articles by his former pupils, was dedicated to him.

He had a high sense of duty in all things, and he was always conscious of the debt which he owed to his father, whose memory he held in reverence.

Not all his time was spent in his study. He saw military and national service in two world wars—he won the M.C. in the first. He found time to inspect schools on behalf of the Ministry of Education, and many of his last years were devoted to the creation of the Institute of Oriental Studies in Oxford. He was a loyal churchman and served on the Council of Wycliffe Hall, Oxford. Like his father before him, he was a good and valued friend and contributor to *The Times*.

He married in 1924 Madeleine Mary, daughter of John Goulding, of Bridlington, and had three daughters.

April 24, 1975.

Stanley Lithgow Drummond-Jackson, a pioneer of intravenous anaesthesia in dentistry, died on December 7, 1975 at the age of 66.

Born in Gosforth, Northumberland, and educated at Barnard Castle School, and Edinburgh University Dental School, he qualified in 1931.

In 1932 he entered general practice in Huddersfield, intending at the same time to complete work for a higher dental degree. It was at this point he became interested in the possibilities of the drug hexobarbitone as a potential anaesthetic in dentistry. He thereafter abandoned his work for a higher degree and devoted his energies to the problems of pain control in dentistry, publishing his first paper on the subject in 1934.

During the Second World War he served with a field ambulance post in the 51st Highland Division, breaking his neck in an exercise shortly before D-Day.

After the war he returned to practice in Harley Street in 1946, and in 1948 published his book *Dental Practice Management*. His major work, *Intravenous Anaesthesia in Dentistry* appeared in 1952 and in the same year he made a film on the subject which had the same title.

In 1957 he and a group of colleagues founded the Society for the Advancement of Anaesthesia in Dentistry. Their intentions were for a small study group of about 40 members. Interest in this facet of dentistry was to grow until the society has, to-day, approaching 3,000 members and branches all over the world, notably in Australia and the United States.

The society started its own postgraduate courses in dental anaesthesia in 1958, initially at Drummond-Jackson's Wimpole Street home, but later transferred to University College London, where they continue to be given. He was also extensively in demand as a lecturer abroad, in Australia, New Zealand and the United States.

Clinical anaesthesia owes its very existence to dental surgeons, for it was their discovery. The pioneers were dentists who saw its possibilities and pursued them with fanatical enthusiasm. D.-J., as he was affectionately known to a worldwide circle of friends and associates, was in direct line with those pioneers. His contribution was to realize what a boon it was to the patient to be asleep for the unpleasant procedures of dentistry under a barbiturate injected into a vein; and sleep it was, with none of the unpleasant after effects of the other anaesthetics. This might not seem much—indeed he was not the first to use a barbiturate for this purpose, but it was forty-one years ago and at a time when two of the most eminent physicians of the day had, on the basis of their experience of cases of suicidal overdose, roundly condemned the use of barbiturates for any purpose whatsoever.

The timorous sheered off; it took a man of D.-J.'s courage to persevere, and he was right. But by flying in the face of what then became orthodox belief he incurred the disapproval of those who could speak with authority—the Establishment. Friction became inevitable when he brought out *Intravenous Anaesthesia in Dentistry* to popularize his method. But the society—S.A.A.D., as it came to be known—grew rapidly and by the 1960's as many as 250 dentists from far and wide, each time a fresh group, assembled twice a year to attend his three-day tutorials and demonstrations. Any anaesthetist who showed originality in the field of dental anaesthetics was at once offered the freedom of this platform; but essentially S.A.A.D.'s purpose was to propagate his method, and this endeared him still less in academic circles.

In his zeal to show how safe the method was and what scope it had, he overplayed his hand. He used it on occasion for excessively long cases and in excessive dosage —perfectly safe for him but not for others. The excess was picked up by a team of investigators and on the basis of this excess the whole method condemned in an article in the *British Medical Journal* in 1969. History had repeated itself.

D.-J., incensed by what he considered an unfair attack, brought in 1972, at his personal expense, a libel action against the British Medical Association and the authors of the paper. The action, hopelessly enmeshed in the intricacies of medical science, had though still in its early stages to be abandoned in its thirty-eighth day after what had already become the longest and probably the most costly hearing of such an action in the entire history of the London courts.

Those who knew D.-J. will remember him, not only for his extraordinary courage but also for his unfathomable kindness and generosity.

He is survived by his widow, Ruth.

December 10, 1975.

The death of **Jacques Duclos** on April 25, 1975 removed from the French political scene a man who was for many years a major figure in the French Communist Party.

One of its longest serving members—he joined the party at its formation in 1920—he gained considerable celebrity towards the end of his career when he polled a fifth of the votes in the first round of the 1969 Presidential elections following the departure of General de Gaulle.*

Some of this success was personal. Duclos was witty and had the ability to hold and amuse any audience, a gift which earned him some popularity in the Assembly so often bored by earnest but incompetent speakers. In 1969 he had lost none of the verve which had helped him win his first seat in the Assembly in 1926.

Yet Duclos was one of the party's toughest leaders and as a member, from an early age, of the Communist Executive, had performed all the mental back-somersaults required of leading Communists.

Born in 1896, the son of a carpenter and inn-keeper at Louey, a small village in the Pyrénées, Jacques Duclos started work at 11 as apprentice to a pastry cook at Tarbes. At 16 he went to Paris. Although with nothing but an elementary education his intelligence developed quickly; he read the French classics, particularly Balzac and Zola, and went much to the theatre. In 1914 he was torn between hatred of the Kaiser, the desire to see Alsace-Lorraine return to France and admiration for the great Socialist tribune Jean Jaurès.

He fought at Verdun and nearly lost both his legs as a result of prolonged immersion in filthy water. Later, he fought at the Chemin des Dames in the ill-fated Nivelle offensive of 1917 and was taken prisoner. After the war he took up political activity with the Anciens Combattants, met Henri Barbusse, whose novel *Le Feu* was making a great sensation, and Vaillant Couturier. After the Tours conference of the Socialist party, he joined the faction led by Marcel Cachin which became the French Communist Party.

At the age of 30, he was elected Communist Deputy for the 14th arrondissement of Paris, against Paul Reynaud*. He was a member of the Central Committee of the Politbureau in 1931 and in that year secretary of the party. In 1936, after the victory of the Popular Front, he became a Vice-President of the Assembly. By this time he already appeared to be the second man in the party leadership after Maurice Thorez.*

Although the Party approved the Hitler-Stalin Pact, its Deputies voted the war credits in September and Thorez rejoined his military unit after doing so. All the same, hundreds of militant Communists, outraged by the party's approval of the German-Russian pact, left the party. When the party was dissolved Thorez deserted, and most of the Communist leaders were arrested. Duclos went into hiding and throughout the war led a clandestine existence mainly in the suburbs of Paris. He became, with Frachon, the leader of the party and it was with him that Thorez, in Moscow, kept contact.

After the fall of France the Communists continued to oppose what they called the imperialist war. The main enemy was the Vichy regime and after that de Gaulle, the agent of British capitalism; about the German occupier, the clandestine *L'Humanité* was discreet. But Duclos, with the signature of Thorez, published the since much discussed "Appeal of July 10th" which enabled the Communists after the war to claim to have been the first party to resist the Germans and thereby to annul the hesitations and errors of the immediate past.

By the end of 1940 the propaganda line for which Duclos was responsible had become more anti-Nazi and groups began to stock arms. But it was not until Hitler invaded Russia that the Party line could become simple and effective, and French Communists patriots. In January 1943 the Party accepted, for official purposes, to come under the authority of the French National Committee in London.

In spite of his wartime role, Duclos was not one of the Communists who became Ministers in de Gaulle's provisional government after liberation.

Only once did he appear very much in the public eye. Although a Deputy, he was arrested in 1952 for being on the scene an hour after it had happened of a riot against Nato and General Ridgway. He was in his car with his wife, another Communist and two pigeons. The accusation of inciting the rioters obviously did not hold water and the more stupid one, that the pigeons were carriers (whereas they were destined for the casserole) brought ridicule on the authorities.

Throughout the postwar period, however, Duclos remained very much in the inner circle under Thorez and then Waldeck Rochet. He was therefore one of the people directly responsible for the cautious, not to say conservative, policy of the Party towards de-Stalinization and Hungary, and its "respectable attitude" in 1968.

That these policies, which were attacked by some Communists as dishonourable, were realistic from the point of view of maintaining Communism as a political force, is shown by Duclos' success in 1969.

His wife Gilberte, whom he married in 1937, was 16 years younger than himself, a State nurse and also a militant Communist. Duclos published, with Fayard, five volumes of his memoirs.

April 28, 1975.

Sir Val Duncan, O.B.E., chairman and chief executive of Rio Tinto-Zinc, who died on December 19, 1975 suddenly at the age of 62, was one of the leading industrial figures of his generation.

When he joined the Rio Tinto Company in 1948 as commercial manager it was an unremarkable copper mining company, based in south-west Spain. The merger with the Consolidated Zinc Corporation of Australia, the major Australian mining concern with roots going back to the earliest development of Broken Hill, formed the basis for the development of a major, British-based mining finance house. This process was further consolidated by the merger in 1968 with the American Borax group, whose development had been based on the borax deposits in Death Valley, California, and in Nevada.

John Norman Valette Duncan was born on July 18, 1913, the son of Norman Duncan, and educated at Harrow (of which school he became a Governor in 1971) and Brasenose College, Oxford. He was called to the bar in 1938. His war service was in the Royal Engineers, much of it on the staffs of Montgomery, Eisenhower* and Alexander.* After the war he was briefly Assistant Secretary at the German and Austrian Control Office and then assistant director of marketing at the National Coal Board, before joining Rio Tinto. He became managing director of Rio Tinto-Zinc in 1962 and chairman in 1964.

Under Duncan's very personal leadership, R.T.Z. diversified throughout the world. Its interests now cover every continent and its products range from emeralds to aluminium. Because of its operations in Canada, Australia and South Africa, R.T.Z. controls a substantial share of the world's proven uranium deposits. He saw early that the business of mineral extraction required close cooperation and understanding with the Governments of the countries where R.T.Z. was operating. It was also clear to him that R.T.Z.'s chosen field of expertise was highly sensitive, and local equity participation was an essential element of the strategy, if reasonable profits were to be made. Despite the diversification of the 1960s, however, R.T.Z. remained predominantly a copper producing group.

More recently, R.T.Z. has been experiencing a political reaction in its overseas operations. The potentially profitable copper and gold mining venture at Bougainville has become centrally involved in the independence movement of Papua New Guinea. The uranium deposits at Rössing, in South West Africa, are also now a greater cause for concern. At home R.T.Z. has come under criticism from environmentalists for its proposals to mine in Snowdonia and for the lead pollution from its Avonmouth smelter.

He was increasingly a public figure and spokesman for international industry. He defended vigorously the interests of responsible international business investment. In 1968 he was chairman, at the invitation of Michael Stewart, then Foreign Secretary, of a committee to report on the future of the foreign service. He was knighted in 1968 and was a director of the Bank of England and of B.P.

Val Duncan was a man of many friends, and they included people both inside and outside the world of business in which he worked. His quickness of understanding and his innate sympathy for other people made it delightful to work with him, or to find oneself in his company. As a business negotiator he was unsurpassed, and he used his skill to achieve negotiations which were fair to all sides, and fair to the public interest as well. He wanted to avoid deals which would turn sour later on. He used the same qualities of understanding and generosity to win for himself, and to retain, a wide circle of private friendships.

He was one of the three or four major creative figures in post-war British business. The present situation of Rio Tinto-Zinc, that great national asset, is a measure of his creative accomplishment. Yet he will be remembered by all who knew him for his care, his sympathy and his concern. He was a very gentle empire builder; he was a man who did a great deal to earn his country's precarious living in an exceptionally difficult period.

He married in 1950 Lorna, daughter of Robert Archer-Houblon. She died in 1963.

December 20, 1975.

André Dunoyer de Segonzac, the French painter, died on September 17, 1974 in Paris at the age of 90.

He had a place of distinguished independence in modern art as a painter in oils, a water-colourist, and an etcher and illustrator—water-colour and etching being the media in which he found freest and most brilliant expression. His achievement in the *art anglais* of water-colour was especially admired and sought after by collectors in England, and indeed he was an artist of a kind more often to be found in England than in France.

He was once described as "a country squire who put his acres on canvas" and the jesting remark is true enough to the impression conveyed of a countryman born and bred with an understanding of rural life in his bones. In the presence of his earlier winter landscapes one would imagine their author as a burly man in rough tweeds and thick boots with pipe in mouth, gun under arm and dogs at heel, tramping contentedly over the rough soil with an impartial eye for anything that suggested a picture or anything suitable for the pot that rose or scuttled away from him. It is necessary however to remember that he was also accustomed to the Parisian social round (his duality of interests and character often surprised his friends); so impressions of the ballet, the dance, the boxing-ring and of Paris itself add their sophisticated vividness to the graphic art in which he excelled.

Dunoyer de Segonzac was born on July 6, 1884 at Boussy-Saint-Antoine. From the Lycée Henri IV, where he studied mathematics and engineering, he went to the School of Oriental Languages to specialize in the dialects of the Sudan, and after graduation travelled in Africa to complete his studies. He also visited Sicily, Italy and southern Spain. At the age of 18, his artistic instincts awakened by these experiences, he returned to Paris and at first attended the studio of Luc-Olivier Merson, afterwards studying at the Académie Julian, at the École des Beaux Arts under Jean-Paul Laurens and the Académie de la Palette under Jacques-Émile Blanche.

Before 1914 he had already gained a considerable reputation though while he mingled with Fauvist and Cubist painters and was a friend of Apollinaire he was as immune from their theories and "isms" as he was from purely academic influence. He admired Cézanne, but the geometrical suggestions in Cézanne's work did not incline him, as they did others, towards Cubism.

During the First World War he served in the trenches as a corporal and sergeant and was later employed as a camouflage officer. As chief of camouflage at the front with the Third Army he won the Croix de Guerre. His war drawings, some of which appeared in *L'Élan* and *Le Crapouillot*, led to his taking up etching and in 1919 he was invited by René Blum to etch a series of plates from them. He found the new medium entirely congenial and in the course of his later career produced more than 1,500 etchings and etched illustrations.

Among the books he illustrated were: the *Tableau de la Boxe* by Tristan Bernard; Flaubert's *L'Éducation Sentimentale*, 1923; *Huit Illustrations de Guerre*, 1926; *La Treille Muscate* of his friend and neighbour at Saint Tropez, Colette, 1932; Virgil's *Georgics*, 1926 and onwards, eventually published by the artist himself in 1947; and *Quelques Sonnets de Ronsard*, 1956. The exquisite plates for the *Georgics* comprise the artist's masterpiece and one of the century's most beautifully illustrated books.

Between the oil paintings and the graphic art of Dunoyer de Segonzac there is a striking difference due to his sense of what was appropriate to a given medium. His oils, particularly the earlier landscapes, are blunt in drawing and executed with a heavy impasto applied with a palette knife. His water-colours fluently combine pen-drawing and colour. His etchings are distinguished by an exquisite delicacy and economy of line. From 1926, when his etchings were introduced at the Independent Gallery, his work was frequently exhibited in London. He had been an honorary member of the Royal Academy since 1947.

September 18, 1974.

Bishop of Durham—See Ramsey.

Marshal Enrico Gaspar Dutra, who was President of Brazil from 1945 to 1951, died in Rio de Janeiro on June 11, 1974, at the age of 89.

A slightly-built man, Dutra had a reputation as a hard worker who regulated his life with military efficiency. His period in the presidency divided the Vargas era in two, and was notable for the attempts made to strengthen the new constitution of 1946, with its emphasis on representative democracy.

Born on May 18, 1885 in Cuiabá, his military career was helped when he put down a communist revolt in 1935 in Rio de Janeiro. Vargas, the authoritarian central figure in Brazilian politics from 1930 to 1954, made him his Minister of War—a position he held from 1936 until 1945. He was responsible for modernizing the Brazilian army and, although an open admirer of German military efficiency, he supported cooperation with the Americans after Pearl Harbour and organized the Brazilian expeditionary force which fought in Italy.

Although known as a loyal Vargas man, Dutra led a coup against Vargas in 1945 when he tried to forestall elections and remain in power. In the elections Dutra won more than half the votes and became the first president to be installed by populist vote since 1926. He governed conservatively, banning the communist party in 1947 and breaking off diplomatic relations with the Soviet Union. In the general elections of 1950 the voters, discontented with economic policy, turned back to the more flamboyant politics of Vargas.

June 12, 1974.

Palme Dutt, a foundation member of the British Communist Party and a member of its executive from 1922 to 1965, died on December 20, 1974, aged 79.

Rajani Palme Dutt was born at Cambridge. His father, a surgeon, was a member of a prominent Bengali family; his mother was Swedish. Dutt was educated at the Perse School, Cambridge, and won a scholarship to Balliol College, Oxford, where he took a first class in Classical Moderations in 1916.

He was sent down from Oxford for engaging in antiwar activities, and served a prison sentence for refusing to serve in the forces. He was later allowed to return to take the Final School of Literae Humaniores in which he again took a first in 1918.

After a short spell of schoolteaching he became fully employed in the Labour Research Department, formerly the Fabian Research Department, where he specialized in international affairs. His first book, *The Two Internationals,* was published in 1920. He was a foundation member of the Communist Party and in 1921 he began publication of the *Labour Monthly,* a journal which he edited thereafter and which has provided guidance on the "party line".

In 1922 Dutt was appointed chairman of a commission to reorganize the party on "Bolshevik" lines, and later in the year he was elected to the central committee, on which he served continuously for 43 years. For several months in 1923-24 he also edited the *Workers' Weekly*, but a breakdown in health forced him to give this up. He lived in Brussels for several years afterwards.

In 1929, when under the tightening grip of Stalin's dictatorship the Comintern sought to eliminate signs of independence in the leadership of national communist parties, Dutt and Harry Pollitt were called upon to take control of the British party from J. R. Campbell and others.

Pollitt became general secretary and Dutt, as a member of the Politbureau, undertook various special duties which included the editorship of the *Daily Worker* in the years 1936 to 1938. The Pollitt-Dutt partnership worked well: Dutt provided the intellectual justification for the emotional rhetoric at which Pollitt was so effective.

The collaboration of the two men, which lasted for over 25 years, was broken for some months at the outbreak of war in 1939. Pollitt could not accept the sudden change of policy in Moscow, and temporarily gave up his post in the party; but Dutt adapted himself swiftly and took over the secretaryship for a time.

The invasion of Russia in 1941 was followed by an equally swift change of attitude by Dutt, which is reflected in his book, *Britain in the World Front* (1942).

In 1945 he stood as communist candidate for Parliament for the Sparkbrook division of Birmingham and in 1950 he stood for Woolwich, East. For more than 20 years before his retirement from the central committee in 1965, Dutt acted as vice-chairman of the party; and after retirement he carried on in charge of the International Department. He attended the twentieth Congress of the Russian Communist Party in 1956 and thereafter played an important part in resisting the criticism of the leadership at the time of the anti-Stalin campaign and the Hungarian revolution.

It may be that his greatest contribution to communism was in the development of the Indian party, the seeds of which he diligently sowed among Indian students in Britain between the wars. Yet, whatever damage he did to the British Empire in that period, he probably more than made up by his strong discouragement of rebellious tendencies in India in the critical years 1941-45.

December 21, 1974.

Dr. François Duvalier, President of Haiti since 1957, whose brutish tyranny one critic condemned as showing "a total disregard of the most elementary principles of life in an organized society", died on April 21, 1971. He was 64.

Duvalier, known affectionately as "Papa Doc" to his followers, was not averse to primitive chauvinistic demonstrations when it came to enforcing his writ. When 19 Army officers plotted against his regime in 1967, Duvalier personally commanded the firing squad which executed them. When he was excommunicated from the Roman Catholic church in 1960, he attended Mass in the cathedral at Port-au-Prince accompanied by an armed guard and carrying an automatic weapon himself.

He did not balk at using democratic trappings to give his regime a legal veneer. When he wanted to become President for life in 1964, he held a referendum in which all the voting papers were marked "Oui". There was speculation in 1965 that he would become an emperor like his predecessors, Dessalines and Henri-Christophe, but the distribution of portraits with the legend "François Premier" in public places did not herald the expected empire. The excesses of his dictatorship ran to arbitrary arrests, persecutions and summary executions in which whole families were exterminated. He used his personal gangster militia—nicknamed the "Tonton macoute" or bogymen —to prevent any popular rising. Instead thousands—among them the much-needed educated—fled. And Duvalier remained supreme to fend off some eight armed invasions by dissident exiles in 11 years.

In time, Duvalier mellowed. He was forced to reconsider his image abroad as tourism slumped and foreign aid was withdrawn. The show-trial of the British "spy" David Knox in 1968 marked a slight turning-point; it demonstrated to the outside world that death-sentences could be commuted in Haiti. His railings against the film *The Comedians*, made from Graham Greene's book, as "an attack on him", however, displayed a childish pique. He sued in the French courts asking for 10m. francs and was awarded one.

Duvalier's paternalistic oratory had initially captivated the impoverished Negro country people; he also exploited for his own ends the racial tension between the Negro majority and the mulatto élite minority. He played on their superstitions and their simple pride; he knew the voodoo rites they indulged in; and as a doctor who had come to cure "the nation's ills" after the fall of the Magloire regime he showed an ironic skill—conducting terrorism with all the gusto of a primitive possessed by a barbaric megalomania and racialist obsession. The patient, as a result, worsened.

François Duvalier was born in Port-au-Prince on April 14, 1907. He claimed to be a full-blooded Negro, like 19 out of 20 Haitians, and in his later years was certainly a Negro nationalist, but he probably had some European blood. He was a quiet and studious boy and young man. By mercurial Haitian standards he was gravity itself, reserved, dutiful and withdrawn. He shared the absorption common among his countrymen with the little nation's strange and exotic traditions, the legacy of the Creole-French, the West African jungle, and the careers of Toussaint, Dessalines and Henri-Christophe, but he was more systematic than most in studying them. Toussaint's phrase "My people are born to suffer" was

a favourite of Duvalier's in his early days as a young doctor, although it took on an altogether more depressing significance when he became a dictator presiding over the disintegration of any institutional order.

Duvalier had none of the taste for each day's pleasures which made life tolerable and even cheerful for a poor peasant, but although he was brought up in a devout Roman Catholic household, he was fascinated, psychologically as an outsider, by the pagan rites brought over from Africa and surviving—rustic, deprecated and mildly disreputable—in country places as "voodoo".

After school, where he took classics, Duvalier went in for medicine and had his doctorate from the national faculty in 1934. He served successively with two hospitals, and did useful and respected work as a country doctor. He wrote extensively on social and antiquarian matters, and brought out a book on the "evolution" of voodoo in 1944. After two years' graduate work on public health at Ann Arbor, he returned to a series of medical posts in the public service, and was supervisor of the campaign which brought the endemic contact infection of yaws under control in 1947-48 by a combination of penicillin and international cooperation. The Estime Government appointed Duvalier Secretary of Labour, a post he held when General Magloire took over by a coup in 1950.

At this point Duvalier's prestige was high, both as a public servant and a scholar. He was happily married to Simone Ovidenaud and had a young family of three daughters and a son. For four years he publicly opposed the regime and continued his practice. In 1954 he went underground, abandoned medicine except as a political recommendation—"a nation's ills demand a doctor"—and apparently allowed the darker side of his personality full play.

The Magloire regime, protesting good intentions, was in constant political and economic trouble, intensified by a disastrous hurricane in 1954. United States aid and food programmes kept the country from famine and economic collapse. In September 1956 Magloire proclaimed an amnesty and Duvalier came out of hiding to declare himself a candidate for President. The highly coloured stories about his underground days are legion—that he passed in disguise for a widow, that he trained as a marksman with the lugubrious epigram that "a doctor must sometimes take life to save it", and that he became an active celebrant of voodoo rite. He also seems to have come to an understanding with Generalissimo Trujillo*, dictator of the Dominican Republic in the eastern two-thirds of the island, although Trujillo was primarily responsible for a mass murder of Haitian squatters in 1937.

Magloire resigned in December, 1956, and a few months later Duvalier was overwhelmingly elected President in an election prepared and supervised by the army under General Kebreau, an officer trained like most of his colleagues by the U.S. Marine mission. Duvalier promised to "save the peasantry from superstition and dirt". Washington had high hopes of him, but they did not last long.

He first turned against the army, deposed Kebreau and almost certainly had him murdered, and increased the civilian militia. The rationale for this was that the army had exploited Haiti for years and must yield place to ordinary citizens. Later, without apology, Duvalier created a gangster militia later nicknamed "Tonton macoute" or "bogymen", whose qualifications were full Negro blood, loyalty to the President and a summary efficiency in their hatchet work. As things disintegrated, Duvalier decreed that only a member of this organization could attend the university, although most of its members were illiterate.

Then he turned on the church, largely manned by Frenchmen and Canadians because native clerics were few in a country 85 per cent illiterate. In December 1960 he put a censorship on the confessional newspaper *La Phalange* and expelled Archbishop Poirier. As a result he was excommunicated. Although Mme. Duvalier was of mixed blood, her husband indulged his prejudices against the mulatto élite and encouraged his thugs to arrest their women on charges of immorality. Many thousands of educated Haitians went into exile, many of them to French Africa. The poor fled to the Dominican Republic and Cuba, 50 miles across the straits. The administration became increasingly ludicrous, until the Tonton macoute insisted at gun-point on taking over American aid cargoes on the quays.

In 1959 Duvalier had easily fought off an invasion mounted from Cuba, and intensified repression. In 1961 there was an election for a unified legislature—one candidate for each seat, with "François Duvalier, President" on each paper. On this basis he declared himself reelected for another six years. Overseas the regime conducted itself with remarkable impertinence, playing on American fears of communism to keep the flow of aid going, which accounted for a third of the budget. Most of the rest went for military and paramilitary expenses. The Duvalier family and friends flourished, and his pretty daughters were celebrated for their high fashions. He himself became more of a recluse.

In 1962 the British and American Ambassadors were successively expelled after diplomatic protests about gangsterism. In May 1963, when his legal term was due to expire, Duvalier survived a major crisis which brought two forays by exiles and almost brought a war with the Dominican Republic. The United Nations and the Organization of American States were anxiously seized of the problem. By September President Bosch had been overthrown in Santo Domingo; and Duvalier, by congressional acclaim now entitled "Renovator of the Nation", was over the worst.

April 23, 1971.

E

Maurice Edelman, Labour M.P. for Coventry North West since 1974, died on December 14, 1975 at the age of 64. He had previously been the member for Coventry West from 1945 to 1950 and for Coventry North from 1950 to 1974.

He was deservedly considered one of the most glamorous figures on the Labour backbenches, one who rose to considerable eminence purely on the basis of hard work and literary talent. He had been a war correspondent in the Second World War, and, in his prolific writings since, he retained much of the dash associated with that profession.

Of debonair appearance, with a ready smile and an equally ready wit, he was an asset to any social occasion. Yet he was no mere dilettante, and in his closing years he became increasingly concerned with what he saw as the dangers to freedom posed by both the socialist state and the infiltration of the Labour Party by extremists.

Maurice Edelman was born in Cardiff in 1911 of humble Jewish stock. He was educated at Cardiff High School, whence he gained an exhibition in modern languages to Trinity College, Cambridge. After this he worked for some years in a City trading firm in which he became director of the continental department.

He visited most of the countries of Europe and, especially, made a study of Russia aided by fluent Russian, This served him in good stead later when he wrote for *The New Statesman* and *The Guardian* on Russian affairs. It also gave him the data for his Penguin Special, *How Russia Prepared*, a rather starry-eyed and (by his later standards) dreadfully uncritical eulogy of Russia's achievements, which appeared in 1942; but it was full of interesting material and briskly written.

He had already written another book about Soviet law with the sinister title, *G.P.U. Justice*, in 1938, and followed that up at the beginning of the war with a socialist attack on the capitalist style of running the war, *Production for Victory not Profit*. During the war, however, he had a more active role as a writer, because he became war correspondent for *Picture Post* in North Africa and France. He recorded these experiences in another Penguin, *France: the Birth of the French Republic*.

With this background it was not surprising that he was elected Labour Member of Parliament for West Coventry. It was not obvious then, perhaps, that he would remain, throughout a long career in the House, a backbencher. He was an active one, especially in foreign affairs.

He was a delegate to the Consultative Assembly of the Council of Europe from 1949 to 1951 and from 1965 to 1970, and Chairman of the Socialist Group in the Western European Union from 1968 to 1970. A fluent French speaker, he did much to improve Anglo-French relations. He was Vice-President of the Anglo-French Parliamentary Relations Committee, and President of the Alliance Française. He was made an Officer of the Legion of Honour in 1960 and received the Médaille de Paris in 1972. Unusually for a Labour member, he was an admirer of General de Gaulle*—but then, he was an admirer of Disraeli too.

The flow of books continued unceasingly throughout a busy public life. He wrote a number of novels, mostly about politics and usually characterized by thrills and suspense. Among them one should mention *Who Goes Home?* (1953), *Call on Kuprin* (1959) (set in Russia), and *The Prime Minister's Daughter* (1964). His most recent success was a novel about the life of Disraeli. He also wrote plays for television, one of them about Admiral Byng.

In recent years Edelman had become very concerned about the growth of government, and had persistently asked ministers about the jobs in their giving. Not long before he died he had written two articles for *The Times* suggesting that a Public Services Commission should take over the appointment of those who are at present given places because of the "old boy network". He had long since ceased to be enamoured of the Left or Russia, and was particularly incensed about the Soviet treatment of the Jews. He regarded the Prentice case as a dangerous portent and wanted to change the rules of the Labour Party to make it more difficult for small groups of activists to take over.

Among the gems of his wit we may remember his summing up of the newspapers: "I read the *Daily Express* for entertainment, *The Times* for serious instruction, the *News Chronicle* for moral uplift, *The Daily Telegraph* to find out what the Government's foreign policy is, and the *Daily Herald* out of loyalty."

He had a happy family life. He was married in 1933 to Matilda, daughter of K. Yates. He had two daughters.

December 15, 1975.

Group Captain H. R. A. Edwards, D.F.C., A.F.C., the distinguished oarsman, an Oxford Blue, a double Olympic gold medallist and formerly coach of the Oxford crew, collapsed at Hamble on December 21, 1972 and was taken to Southampton hospital but was dead on arrival. He was 66.

Hugh Robert Arthur Edwards, the son of the Rev. Robert Edwards and brother of E. C. T. Edwards who was also an Oxford rowing Blue, was born on November 17, 1906 and educated at Westminster and Christ Church, Oxford.

He was commissioned in the R.A.F. in 1931. A well-known racing pilot owning his own aircraft, he was placed second in the King's Cup air race in 1935. His brother had won the race four years earlier.

He served with distinction in the Second World War, winning the D.F.C. in 1944. He had won the A.F.C. a year earlier. While in command of a Coastal Command squadron equipped with Liberators he was returning from convoy escort when three engines of his aircraft failed. He brought the Liberator down in the sea some miles from the Seven Stones off the Cornish coast, and escaped by sculling himself into shipping lanes in a small escape craft. He retired from the R.A.F. in 1956.

With the death of "Jumbo" Edwards, rowing lost one of its most colourful and famous personalities. He will be remembered as not only one of the greatest oarsmen of all time but also as a famous coach, innovater and raconteur. The loss of Jumbo Edwards to the sport will be felt in almost every rowing nation of the world. His race record could only be described as phenomenal, reaching its peak at Long Beach, California, in the 1932 Olympic regatta, when Jumbo Edwards won two gold medals.

Edwards, rowing with Lewis Clive and representing Christ Church, Oxford, won his first gold medal in the Olympic regatta in coxless pairs. Then two days before the final of the coxless fours, Jumbo Edwards moved into the Thames Rowing Club coxless four to replace "Tig" Tyler who had been taken ill. After a hasty reshuffle in the crew's rowing order Jumbo Edwards steered the boat from the three seat and went on to gain his second gold medal. Edwards's feat of winning two gold medals in an Olympic regatta equals the record of John B. Kelly, father of Princess Grace of Monaco, who won the single and double sculls in Brussels in 1920.

Jumbo Edwards also gained a gold medal in eights in the 1930 Empire Games in Hamilton, Canada. He first appeared in the Henley Royal Regatta, rowing for Westminster School in the Ladies' in 1923, and also competed in the Diamond Sculls between 1928 and 1930. Altogether he won the Grand, Stewards and Goblets twice, and in 1931 set up another outstanding feat, winning the Grand, Stewards and Goblets in the same year.

The one victory which eluded him during his rowing career was a win in the Boat Race, in which he twice represented Oxford. In the 1926 race he rowed at five, behind his brother, and collapsed during the race half way along Chiswick Eyot. Yet Jumbo Edwards will be remembered as a successful boat race coach, particularly in the 1960s, and was chief coach of Oxford as recently as 1970.

As a coach he was distinguished for his courage in experimenting and introducing innovations to the sport. The use of long oars, "spade" blades, methods of calculating wind and water speeds and the power output of oarsmen, specially designed boats and the use of interval training for conditioning oarsmen were all methods introduced by Jumbo Edwards in Britain in the pursuit of greater speed. He was not always successful with his experiments but displayed a rare courage in following his convictions rather than slavishly copying other coaches and their methods. Jumbo Edwards was a trend setter in the sport.

Edwards was above all as a coach a supreme technician. Some felt that at times he was blinded with scientific aspects at the expense of other factors contributing to boat moving. Yet rowing experts such as Dr. Karl Adam of West Germany often paid tribute to many of Edwards's theories. British rowing owes more to Jumbo Edwards than any other person in the sport for attention to the science of boat moving.

In 1960 Jumbo Edwards was the Olympic coach to Britain's eight and in 1964 was appointed chief national coach to the ill-fated Nautilus club. Despite not being selected as a coach to the 1964 Olympic rowing team, Jumbo Edwards paid his own way and travelled by steamer to Tokyo. Oxford had no stauncher supporter.

December 23, 1972.

Lord Egremont, M.B.E., who died on June 6, 1972, was best known, as John Wyndham, for his long and happy association with Harold Macmillan. Their friendship and collaboration, that of statesman and private secretary, had no counterpart in modern political history. It extended over a period of more than 20 years; and, just as it was the most cordial, it was also one of the most productive of partnerships. He was 52.

When illness compelled Macmillan to relinquish the premiership in October 1963 Wyndham also retired from the centre of affairs, though he was still only 43 years of age. Thereafter, as Lord Egremont, he devoted much of his time to his huge estates in Sussex and Cumberland, to the numerous local duties attaching to a great landowner, to the galleries (especially the Wallace Collection) in which he was interested, and to writing. In recent years he had emerged as a light essayist of more than passing note and had published an engaging book of memoirs, which he called *Wyndham and Children First.*

John Edward Reginald Wyndham, born on June 5, 1920, became a baron (resurrecting an extinct family title as Lord Egremont) in the special list of honours which marked Macmillan's retirement. This accelerated his accession to the peerage by four years, for he was already destined to become the sixth Baron Leconfield, which he did on the death of his father in 1967. He continued to use the Egremont title, however ("You can't keep changing your name," he used to say).

Educated at Eton and Cambridge, he was turned down for the armed forces at the beginning of the war because of defective eyesight. He first met and joined Macmillan in 1940, when the latter was Parliamentary Secretary to the Ministry of Supply. When Macmillan was moved to the Colonial Office in 1942, Wyndham, by now nicely established as private secretary and confidant, went with him. Then, on New Year's Day 1943, they set off together for North Africa, where—with Cabinet rank—Macmillan was to become Churchill's* Minister Resident at Allied Force Headquarters in Algiers. Macmillan was then 48, Wyndham was 22. For the former, this was the first taste of real influence and power—in which the latter was to share for many years to come.

After the end of the war in Europe and the break-up of the coalition Government, Macmillan returned to London to become Secretary of State for Air in Churchill's caretaker administration. Wyndham accompanied him to the Air Ministry. With the fall of the caretaker Government in 1945 and Macmillan's departure from office he was transferred to Washington as private secretary to R. H. (later Lord) Brand*, head of the British Treasury Delegation, and was soon involved in the negotiations for the American loan.

He retired from the public service not long afterwards, but quickly "became bored", as he put it in his memoirs, "and went and joined the Conservative Research Department". There, under the chairmanship of R. A. Butler, he found himself working with Iain Macleod,* Reginald Maudling and Enoch Powell, who were not yet in Parliament, and was able to resume his association with Macmillan.

He stayed five years, following Maudling as head of the economic section, until, in 1952, he inherited the family estates on the death of his uncle Charles, the third Lord Leconfield. They amounted to some 70,000 acres, with Petworth House—which Egremont liked to call "the finest house in Europe"—as the most glittering jewel of all. The house, which then became his home, had already—and at his instigation—been made over to the National Trust, along with the park and an endowment of £300,000. Otherwise the estates remained in the family.

When Macmillan was appointed Foreign Secretary in the Eden Government in 1955, Egremont rejoined him. He was unable to continue serving when Macmillan became Chancellor, however, because he was still negotiating with the Treasury over death duties on his uncle's estate. The partnership, thus interrupted, was not resumed until Macmillan had succeeded Sir Anthony Eden as Prime Minister in January 1957. Thereafter, Egremont was never far from his side.

In his private secretary Macmillan had discovered years earlier a man who was, like himself, widely and deeply read, with a life-long love of literature and a strong, and ever-present, sense of history. Egremont also had an uncommonly good knowledge of painting, as befitted the custodian of the magnificent collection at Petworth. Socially and politically, he was rather in the mould of a Whig grandee. Beneath the flippant, casual manner that he affected more often than not, and his gifts as a raconteur, was a serious and sensitive nature. He could be very blunt, too, and he was always frank. He was shrewd and down to earth in his judgment of men and their motives. The independence, detachment and candour that he brought to his work at 10 Downing Street and elsewhere commanded general respect.

He had been in poor or indifferent health for a number of years and seriously ill since autumn, 1971. His death at the distressingly early age of 52 will be mourned in many quarters, and not least by his estate workers, for he was a good-natured and considerate employer.

Egremont was appointed M.B.E. in 1945; he became a Justice of the Peace for West Sussex in 1953 and was High Sheriff of the county in 1960.

He married a cousin, Pamela Wyndham-Quin, in 1947, and they had three children. The heir to the two baronies is their elder son, Max, who was born on April 21, 1948.

June 7, 1972.

Professor W. Ehrenberg, who died at his home in Wembley on November 19, 1975 at the age of 74, was one of the fast-dwindling band of brilliant physicists whom Germany lost when the Nazis came to power.

Werner Ehrenberg, the son of Albert and Hedwig Ehrenberg, was born on July 20, 1901 in Berlin and educated there and at Heidelberg, his first main interest being philosophy. Although crippled from boyhood by poliomyelitis, within two years of graduating he established himself as an experimentalist of the highest order by a series of publications on X-ray physics. From Berlin he moved to Stuttgart, extending his interests to electron diffraction and electrical conduction.

In 1933 he joined other distinguished refugees under the auspices of Professor P.M.S. (later Lord) Blackett at Birkbeck College, University of London. There he published work on cosmic radiation and neutron physics. From 1936 to 1945 work in an industrial laboratory gave less opportunity for publication, but he studied fresh fields of physics, including thermodynamics, on which he lectured at Birkbeck, where he returned in 1945 as one of Professor Bernal's research team. The years of study and the techniques developed in industry now bore rich fruit; pioneering work was done in several directions, including electron behaviour in insulators and the design of a novel X-ray tube, the latter with his student (now Professor) W. E. Spear, whose sister he married in 1952. As supervisor of a flourishing group of research students he inspired affection and admiration for his inexhaustible patience, generous resourcefulness, simplicity of manner, and total integrity.

In 1949 he and R. E. Siday predicted an important electron interference phenomenon which was re-discovered ten years later and verified experimentally.

His major work, *Electric Conduction in Semiconductors and Metals*, was published in 1958. In 1951 he was appointed Reader, and in 1962 Professor of Experimental Physics; headship of the Department followed in 1964.

The words "the motive of intellectual honesty is the supreme refinement of the motive of curiosity", from his inaugural lecture, reveal something of his standards. These, and the flexibility of mind that enabled him to move from philosophy to an extraordinary range of specialisms in physics, characterized his approach to the administrative tasks that came late in his career.

At that time he was one of the few senior scientists who believed that part-time study should remain Birkbeck's primary concern. As a Governor of the College in 1965-67 he had an important influence in the moves preparatory to the appointment by the University and the University Grants Committee of Lord Ashby's Academic Advisory Committee, whose report vindicated his views. He was also responsible for coordinating and approving the physics courses of the various colleges of the University of London, when the course-unit B.Sc. was introduced.

He became Professor Emeritus and after retirement in 1968 continued to examine, to supervise research and to participate actively in colloquia. In his final years he brought to bear on the preparation of a book on *Cause, Necessity and Chance* his remarkable combination of powers: a knowledge of classical philosophy and languages, united with a profound understanding of a great width of physics.

He leaves a widow and a daughter, Margaret.

December 2, 1975.

Elijah Muhammad—See Muhammad.

Allen Ellender, senior United States Senator, and chairman of the Appropriations Committee, died on July 27, 1972 at the age of 81. He was one of the last of the colourful old line Southern Democrats—with a maverick streak to his courtly conservatism.

He died while in the midst of a vigorous campaign for reelection from Louisiana to his seventh successive term—which would have made him the longest serving senator in American history. As it was he served 37 years.

Although he was virtually a founding member of the Senate's southern block, voting regularly with his Dixie colleagues against civil rights legislation, and the expansion of federal programmes, Ellender was also known for going his own way,

and being outspoken about it.

Unlike his predecessor, Senator Richard Russell, Ellender could not be counted upon for automatic approval of establishment defence and foreign policies. Most recently he opposed the A.B.M., and earlier he was a distinct nuisance in the Dulles era in promoting better relations with the Soviet Union.

Some of his trips provide lively footnotes to postwar history. As he lectured Presidents, from Eisenhower* to Kennedy*, so he delighted in admonishing foreign governments, particularly in the Third World.

The Congressional Record is replete with his folksy remarks. Once he noted "the canals of Venice are filled with water"; but more usually he caused a diplomatic stir, such as in his remark in 1962 that "the average African is incapable of leadership except through the assistance of Europeans".

A bouncy man of only five feet four, Ellender left his most solid legislative achievements in farm policy, having served for many years as chairman of the Agriculture Committee. He was author of the original school free lunch programme.

He was born into a struggling farming family in Montegut, Louisiana, but got a quick start in local politics after graduating in law from Tulane University. He became floor leader of the state house when Governor Huey Long was elected, and subsequently, as Speaker, was closely identified with the Long faction in state politics until the governor's assassination in 1935.

In the following year he was elected to the Senate, and thereafter was mostly unopposed for reelection in a state that comes closest to any in the union to being a "one party show".

A widower since 1949, Senator Ellender was renowned in Washington for his cooking of spicy "Cajun" Louisiana dishes, with which he regularly regaled national leaders, including presidents.

July 29, 1972.

Sir John Ellerman, the shipping millionaire, died on July 17, 1973, at the age of 63. Ellerman, the second baronet, was director of Ellerman Lines Ltd. He was also a noted zoologist.

Ellerman was reputed to be one of the richest men in Britain. He was extraordinarily shy and permitted few photographs to be taken of him.

He was born on December 21, 1909, the only son of Sir John Ellerman, the first baronet. He married in 1933 Esther, daughter of Clarence de Sola, of Montreal.

As a boy Ellerman was fascinated by small animals. His interest developed into serious study. In 1951, in collaboration with Sir Terence Morrison-Scott, who was then in charge of the British Museum's mammal room and later became Director of the British Museum (Natural History), he published the monumental *Checklist of Palae-arctic and Indian Mammals, 1758 to 1946*.

The book was a critical revision, based on the museum's unrivalled collections, of the systematic position of the mammals inhabiting an immense area of the earth's surface. It was followed in 1953 by *Southern African Mammals, 1758 to 1951*, by Ellerman and Morrison-Scott together with R. W. Hayman.

Ellerman was 23 when his father died leaving more than £17m. The first baronet was himself held to be Britain's richest man. The Ellerman fortune rested on shipping, land, breweries, newspapers and investment trusts.

The family business went on. Ellerman took a close personal interest but left the running of the business to others. The Ellerman fortune grew, eventually reaching and passing the level it had attained before death duties reduced it.

Ellerman was tall, lean, sensitive, and a keen music lover. He was a Gilbert and Sullivan expert and played the piano.

He had homes in Mayfair, France and South Africa. His liking for seclusion was well known and he became something of a mystery figure.

There is no heir to the baronetcy.

July 18, 1973.

Duke Ellington, the great jazz musician, died in New York on May 24, 1974 at the age of 75.

Edward Kennedy Ellington was born on April 29, 1899, in Washington D.C., where his father worked as a butler and later as a blueprint maker for the Navy. He had already started studying the piano in 1906 and at school showed signs of being gifted both musically and artistically. It was while he was at school that he gained the nickname "Duke", supposedly on account of his sartorial elegance. By 1916 he was earning a living painting commercial signs by day and playing the piano at night in the so-called stride style then beginning to be popularized by James P. Johnson.

In 1917 he refused the offer of a scholarship from the Pratt Institute of Fine Arts in Brooklyn so that he could continue his music, and in 1918 married Edna Thompson. The next few years he spent playing and organizing bands in Washington until 1922 when he made an abortive attempt to earn his living in New York. The next year he was back again, this time with more success, for he was soon leading a band at the Kentucky Club and beginning to make a name for himself. It was also at this time that he turned his attention to writing and composing, in which field his greatest achievements were to lie.

In 1927 he was invited take his band to the Cotton Club, a famous night-spot of the time, where he stayed for five years. There he made numerous records and broadcasts which for the first time brought his name to a wider public. As his grasp of writing grew surer, he gradually enlarged his orchestra, always enrolling musicians whose styles and techniques would blend with and broaden his orchestral palette, until he had laid the foundation for a personnel which would change surprisingly little over the years.

He finally left the Cotton Club in 1932 and in the next year made a highly successful tour of Europe. From then until 1942, when there was a recording ban in America, he made a profusion of fine records, the best of which are perhaps those dating from the early forties. The most popular of these, starting with "Mood Indigo" in 1930, were slow, occasionally sentimental performances, but they do not represent those most admired by other musicians.

In 1943 he inaugurated a series of annual concerts at the Carnegie Hall, at the first of which he presented a long work entitled "Black, Brown and Beige", the first in a series of larger scale works such as "Deep South Suite", "Blutopia", "Liberian Suite", &c. During this decade the personnel of his orchestra changed more rapidly than before and there was a general ebb in the popularity of big bands. In fact, when the fifties arrived, Ellington was virtually the only jazz musician still leading a large band and this was reflected in the somewhat lower quality of his output.

In the later fifties this trend was reversed. Some musicians who had been with him since the early thirties and left him in the early fifties came back to his orchestra—Lawrence Brown and Johnny Hodges for instance—and he made some fine records, notably a suite entitled "Such Sweet Thunder".

Duke Ellington was undoubtedly the greatest composer in jazz, but the use of the word "composer" may confuse anyone accustomed to classical usage. Improvization has always been more important in jazz than writing; the chief value of a jazz composition usually lies in the opportunities its harmonic framework gives to jazz soloists, which means that the composer is almost invariably subordinate to the musicians who interpret and elaborate on his work.

This never applied to Ellington for the simple reason that he always interpreted his own material through the medium of his orchestra. Many of its members possessed timbres and, in the case of the brass, muted techniques which are unique in jazz. Ellington wrote with these distinctive resources in mind—indeed, his pieces were often written in collaboration with one of his players or even changed during rehearsal at their suggestion. The result was a composition as much suited to the peculiar qualities of his orchestra as a building is planned to fit into an individual site.

Because they depended so heavily on the orchestral context for which they were written, his compositions were not compositions in the classical sense; it is impossible to separate Ellington's contribution from that of his men. On "East St. Louis Toodle-Oo", for example, a piece recorded in the late twenties, the brooding minor theme relies as much on its flexible interpretation by the muted trumpet of Bubber Miley as on its own inherent quality. "Clarinet Lament" and "Echoes of Harlem", recorded on the same day in 1936, are built around the clarinet and trumpet of Barney Bigard and Cootie Williams respectively and are unimaginable without them.

In the late thirties a new development became apparent in Ellington's music. Both jazz improvization and jazz composition were gradually becoming more ambitious, making it more difficult to satisfy the demands of both within a single piece. As a result, he tended to make his ordinary orchestral output more simple from the formal point of view and more and more to feature individual soloists; at the same time, he began to write more ambitious large scale works in which individual improvization did not play such a large part; and this division was present in his work ever since.

However, he never satisfactorily showed that he could work on a massive scale, perhaps because jazz itself never can. Significantly, his large works always took the form of suites, which were no more than separate pieces linked by a non-musical programme.

As a pianist Ellington was never a serious rival in the twenties to such colleagues as Fats Waller, James P. Johnson and Willie the Lion Smith. But alone among them he adapted his style as jazz evolved until by the forties he had developed a wry, casual yet percussive approach which makes him one of the most distinctive pianists in jazz. And yet even as a pianist he cannot be judged apart from his other capacities, for the flavour of his piano playing contributed as much to his orchestral sound as that of any of his sidemen.

No account of Ellington is complete without mentioning that he was one of America's better songwriters, having written such songs as "Mood Indigo", "Caravan", "Sophisticated Lady", "Don't Get Around Much Any More" and "I'm Beginning to See The Light". Even if not in the top flight, they brought him enough royalties in later years to enable him, it is said, to keep his beloved band on the road at a loss. He toured widely almost to the end—his last appearance in England was at a concert at Westminster Abbey—even though he had lost some of his most valued men, notably his co-writer Billy Strayhorn*, alto saxophonist Johnny Hodges, and tenor saxophonist Paul Gonsalves, who died only a few days before Ellington. All his life he had been honoured outside the jazz profession, from an early essay of praise by Constant Lambert to a special evening dedicated to him at the White House by President Nixon, though perhaps it was a greater tribute to have been awarded the French Legion of Honour. He received these, as he moved through life, with wit and dignity; when told not long before he died that a prize many people had thought he would get had been awarded elsewhere, he merely commented that fate did not want him to be too famous too soon.

What Ellington will be remembered by is the hundreds of fine records he made from the mid-twenties onwards which show how the rather verbose art of jazz can be successfully controlled in succinct statement. With his talent and technique he might easily have been tempted to overstrain the jazz medium, as Paul Whiteman* and Stan Kenton were, but by and large he accepted the limitations of the music and consequently his achievements were vastly greater. That posterity should only be able to judge him by his records may seem strange to a classical musician, but the essence of his art was that Ellington's music ceased to be his music when played by any other orchestra. Duke Ellington was the greatest figure in jazz history, perhaps because his achievements incorporated and enhanced the best of so many others. In the history of American music Duke Ellington towers far above such a figure as George Gershwin; posterity may decide that he is only surpassed by a very small handful of his fellow countrymen in any sphere of music.

May 25, 1974.

Sir Claude Elliott, O.B.E., headmaster of Eton from 1933 to 1949 and Provost from 1949 to 1964, died at the age of 85 on November 21, 1973.

Claude Aurelius Elliott, son of Sir Charles Elliott, K.C.S.I., Governor of Bengal, was born on July 27, 1888 and was educated at Eton, in College, and at Trinity, Cambridge. Apart from winning a first-class in each part of the History Tripos, he made no special mark at school or university. He pulled a valiant and competent oar in the Third Trinity boat, and was the centre of a small but very faithful circle of intimate friends. In 1910 he was elected a fellow of Jesus College and in 1913 was joint tutor with Edwin Abbot. During the 1914-1918 war he at first drove an ambulance near Ypres, and later was appointed to a post at the Admiralty under Sir Vincent Baddeley. For his work at the Admiralty he was made O.B.E.

He returned to Cambridge in 1919 to the busy life of a college don. He sat on several university commissions and syndicates, and was elected to the Council of the Senate. His ability in finance and his thoroughness made him a valuable member of various sub-committees of the council, and the bursarial committee of Jesus. And he was also in charge of historical studies in his college. As a lecturer, Elliott was clear and concise and had a good delivery, but eschewed with an almost too vigorous conscientiousness anything that was not strictly relevant to his special subject, medieval English history.

He was appointed headmaster of Eton in 1933. At first sight, perhaps, he seemed to lack some of the essential gifts which the headmastership of a great school demands. Though he handled educational problems as they arose with patience and thoroughness, they were not congenial to him, and perhaps he regarded them much as Dr. Johnson did, as schemes of political reform. Then again, a headmaster is expected to show interest in all his school's activities, and Elliott was far too honest a man to simulate with any conviction an enthusiasm for art and music. His personal appearance was modest and unassuming, and elderly visitors to Chapel would look in vain for the awe-inspiring majesty of Warre, the saintly austerity of Edward Lyttelton, or the winning and felicitous style of Alington's sermons and addresses. But anyone who thought that Elliott's shy manner and rather hesitating speech were the marks of a weak or timorous character would be quickly undeceived. He surveyed a problem carefully and long, and though ready to defer to the opinions of others in matters about which he did not feel strongly, in those which he considered questions of principle, he could be adamant.

To the staff—he was an admirable picker of masters—and to the boys he was always the same—courteous, patient, humorous, kind and above all absolutely natural. No one ever could have been more free from the little mannerisms and poses which supreme authority often acquires.

As the Second World War approached, the shadow of A.R.P. began to lie heavy on Eton life. Almost daily the headmaster was exposed to a spate of government regulations and private suggestions, the latter often couched in alarmist and hot-headed terms, advocating anything from disbanding the school, or removing it to Aberystwyth, to the total militarization of the curriculum; and no one could have stood up to these stresses with a cooler steadfastness than did Elliott. He was determined that Eton should carry on, that the boys should be as safe as possible short of flight, and that all should play their part in the country's ordeal.

He was a first-class mountain climber, of the classic school to which Provost Hornby before him had belonged. His mountain judgment was impeccable, his technique accomplished and safe; and he could, when he thought fit, climb with phenomenal power and pace. He was an authority on the Pyrenees and contributed the chapter on that range to *Mountain Craft*. With his brother Frank he was one of the first to ski regularly in the Alps, and to combine it with winter mountain ascents. He was President of the Alpine Club from 1950 to 1952.

In 1949 he was appointed by the King to be Provost of Eton in succession to Sir Henry Marten. It would be difficult to imagine a man more suited to the circumstances of the time at Eton. As soon as postwar regulations made it possible, the school was launched on a programme of building reconstruction far beyond anything it had ever attempted before. The stone and brickwork of the old buildings were repaired; almost every window in College Chapel had new stained glass to replace that destroyed by bombing—the great East window by Evie Hone, and others by John Piper. The wooden roof of the chapel was found to be irreparably damaged by the deathwatch beetle and was replaced by a splendid new stone vaulted roof; new science schools were built and three new boarding houses; others were brought up to the standard of modern requirements. No Provost since William Waynflete has left such a mark on the buildings of Eton.

He married in 1913 Gillian, daughter of Registrar F. T. Bloxham. His wife died in 1966. He is survived by their son.

November 24, 1973.

Leonard K. Elmhirst, chairman of the Dartington Hall Trust, died suddenly in California on April 16, 1974. He was 79.

Born on June 6, 1893 at Laxton in the East Riding, Elmhirst was the second eldest in a family of nine. About 1900 his father took over the ancient family estate of Elmhirst in Worsborough Dale, near Barnsley, and managed it himself. Young Elmhirst, therefore, had a strict grounding in farming and land management, enjoyed country pursuits and developed a keen sense of responsibility towards those around him. He had an orthodox education and went up to Trinity, Cambridge, in 1912 to read history and theology. Unfit for military service in 1914, he volunteered for the Y.M.C.A. overseas, and sailed for India in October 1915.

Elmhirst enjoyed working with Indians and took a keen interest in the problems of the country, especially rural poverty. In the following autumn he transferred to Mesopotamia where, after 12 months' strenuous work, he succumbed to fever. Returning to India, he acted as secretary to Lionel Curtis, then working on the preliminaries to the Montagu-Chelmsford reforms.

Demobilized in 1919, following a year's service in the army, he got himself to Cornell University, three weeks after the beginning of the autumn term, practically penniless. Generously helped, he earned his way along, and secured an agricultural degree within two years. During that time he worked actively for the Cosmopolitan Club (mostly for foreign students) and managed to save it from bankruptcy, with the help of Dorothy Whitney Straight, whose husband had studied in Cornell and died in France in 1917. In 1925, Dorothy Whitney Straight and Leonard Elmhirst were married.

Meanwhile Elmhirst had returned to India in the service of the poet, Rabindranath Tagore, to found the Institute of Rural Reconstruction at Sriniketan, now part of the All-India University of Visva-Bharati. Tagore wished Elmhirst to train young men in the practice of rural life and work, and help country people contend with modern civilization. Elmhirst took his first group of students into the Moslem, Hindu and Santali villages of the district early in 1922. The villagers were divided by all kinds of prejudices, but yielded gradually to patient and imaginative handling. After a year Elmhirst was able to hand over to his staff, and conduct Tagore on tours to China, Japan, South America and Italy, where the poet had an encounter with Mussolini.

In September 1925 Elmhirst and his wife completed the purchase of Dartington Hall, near Totnes, in Devon, a medieval manor house of great beauty, surrounded by 820 acres of farm and woodland. Like many other estates, it had been run down during decades of depression, and the outlook for agriculture was daunting. The Elmhirsts aimed at complete rehabilitation—to create an up-to-date rural enterprise offering not only good wages and physical amenities, but opportunities for a full life.

At first everything was run personally. Then, with quickening expansion a company was formed in 1929, and a Trust in 1931-32. The former looked after all the commercial enterprises; the latter maintained the estate (soon greatly enlarged), subsidized all the educational activities, and financed a big building programme. Most of the commerce was rural or local in character—farming, forestry, horticulture, cidermaking, sawmilling, textiles, etc.

Of the co-educational ventures, the co-educational boarding school was the best known, breaking much new ground and gaining a lot of publicity, some of it unwelcome. Today it is expanding to meet a growing demand for "free" education. The Arts Centre began by training local talent in music, dance and drama, as well as providing professional entertainments. Recently a residential music college has been founded. The theatre was thrown open to visiting and local companies; exhibitions, concerts and conferences regularly arranged; while, in August, the whole place was given over to the Summer School of Music, a separate organization which drew large numbers of music lovers to Dartington for a month. The Adult Education Centre was another venture, offering vocational classes and opportunities for social activity by local people. Research has been yet another fruitful field with, inter alia, departments of agricultural and forest economics, and a soil laboratory.

Finally the Trust constructed magnificent gardens, initiated far-seeing schemes of welfare and restored all the medieval buildings with fine scholarship and good taste.

Elmhirst led several lives at once. He did a vast amount of work for Exeter University, Devon County Council and many local organizations. His interest in the land was deep. He encouraged progressive husbandry on the estate and, after a visit to Russia in 1932, pioneered an experiment in artificial insemination, founding the Dartington Cattle Breeding Centre, which served south Devon and east Cornwall. He launched the International Conference of Agricultural Economists in 1929, a world

organization with which it linked the Institute of Agrarian Affairs, a department of the University of Oxford. He was no less effective in forestry. Dartington Woodlands Ltd. was notably successful, and, as president of the Royal Forestry Society of England and Wales, Elmhirst was able to safeguard the place of private forestry when new and radical legislation was enacted after the war.

Politically, though a member of the Labour Party, he treated every problem without dogmatic prejudice. It was this attitude that drew him towards P.E.P. (Political and Economic Planning) the non-party fact-finding organization, which he helped to found and actively sustained.

Elmhirst spent much of the last war in public service. He visited the United States three times on Government missions. In 1942 he led an Anglo-American mission to the Middle East to help raise agricultural production. In 1944 he was summoned to India by Lord Casey to act as his agricultural adviser after the famine in Bengal. Nehru* was a close friend, and it was due partly to their mutual respect that the great Damodar Valley scheme for irrigation and hydro-electricity was pushed through. In 1954 he was appointed a member of the Indian Rural Higher Education Committee.

A world citizen, yet English to the core, Elmhirst was deeply affected by social history and tradition. In short he was a great liberal-minded Englishman, in the direct descent of all those who have used their wealth and their talents for the benefit of fellow men. His first wife died in 1968. They had one son and one daughter. In 1972 he married Dr. Susanna Issacs.

April 18, 1974.

Lord Elton, who was General Secretary of the Rhodes Trust from 1939 to 1959, died on April 18, 1973. He was 80.

Poet and novelist in the earlier phase of his career, then most notably historical writer and essayist, Elton was an author of unusually varied parts. He produced nothing of the highest literary character, though his cultivation of mind is apparent in everything he wrote. Through most of his books runs a pronounced thread of anti-intellectualism—a deep distrust of superior mental capacity wherever it is not balanced by action and experience.

Although in this Elton was animated not only by good sense but by a sentiment of thoughtful sympathy for ordinary men and women and for homely things, it is possible that his somewhat defiant prepossession where intellectuals were concerned stood in his way as a writer. In its absence he might well have absorbed more of what specifically contemporary thought had to give.

As a politician he was an Imperialist of enlightened stamp, who truly believed in the civilizing record of the Empire and

Commonwealth. During the years between the wars, or at any rate in the earlier part of the period, he held mild Labour views, and in the declining phase of MacDonald's nominal ascendancy in the "National" Government was raised to the peerage. But his party convictions were never very strong—they declined easily, in point of fact, into a sort of benevolent, amorphous conservatism—and he was apparently glad to withdraw from polemical politics to the life of letters. By way of relief he served as Secretary of the Rhodes Trust, to which appointment he brought personal charm and sound judgment. Elton, who in private life was a sincere Christian, could indeed be relied upon to display these qualities.

The Right Honourable Godfrey Elton, first Baron Elton, of Headington, Oxfordshire, in the peerage of the United Kingdom, was born on March 29, 1892, the son of Edward Fiennes Elton, of Ovington Park, Hampshire, and Burleigh Court, Gloucestershire. He was brought up in easy circumstances at Crowthorne, Berkshire, where he acquired his enduring love of the Berkshire and Hampshire countryside. From Lockers Park preparatory school he went to Rugby, where he became Head of the School in 1910-11. Going from Rugby to Balliol, he received an honourable mention for the Ireland Scholarship in 1913 and in the same year was placed in the first class in Honour Moderations.

In the war of 1914-18 Elton passed his medical examination by "wangling" the eyesight test and was gazetted to a T.A. battalion, The Hampshire Regiment. Sent to India to complete his training, he went in October 1915 with a relief draft to the Persian Gulf and from there to Kut. He went all through the siege, suffered great hardship as a prisoner of war on a two-months' journey to Kastamuni, in Asiatic Turkey, and was in captivity for two and a half years, during which time he was apparently able to read a good deal of modern history.

In 1919 Elton was offered a Fellowship of Queen's College, Oxford, and a lectureship in Modern History. He remained a Fellow until 1939 (when he was made supernumerary Fellow), was dean from 1921 to 1923 and tutor from 1927 to 1934. He contested the Labour Thornbury Division of Gloucestershire in 1924 and 1929 and resigned prospective candidature and was expelled from the Labour Party as a supporter of MacDonald in September 1931.

Together with these political activities and his collegiate work went an active literary career. A book of verse, *Schoolboys and Exiles*, appeared in 1920; three years later Elton published *The Revolutionary Idea in France, 1789-1878*, in which he pursued an unexceptional argument as to the nature of gains made by the French Revolution; another volume of verse, *Years of Peace* (1925) brought into view once more his anti-intellectual bias of mind. In the following year appeared the earliest and most promising of his novels, *The Testament of*

Dominic Burleigh, a short book oddly charged with spiritual tension. Later novels —*Against the Sun* (1928) and *The Stranger* (1930)—more obviously dissipated their imaginative substance.

In devotion to Ramsay MacDonald, whose lead he followed in 1931, Elton acted as honorary political secretary of the National Labour Committee and for some six years edited its organ, the *News-Letter*. He did not play an outstanding part in debates in the Lords, but was nevertheless welcomed there by the handful of his party colleagues.

His books from 1931 onwards include *England Arise*, a sketch of the early history of the Labour Party, and a biography of MacDonald. There was interesting and at times lively matter in a discursive autobiographical volume, *Among Others* (1938), after which his two most notable volumes were, perhaps, *St. George or the Dragon* (1942), an onslaught on the intellectuals in even more dashing and possibly less discriminating terms than usual, and *Imperial Commonwealth* (1945), a reasoned declaration of political faith. He published *Simon Peter*, a study of discipleship in 1965 and *The Unarmed Invasion* in the same year.

Elton did useful service as a member of the Ullswater committee on the future of broadcasting appointed in 1935 (no account, incidentally, of his talents and capacities would be complete which omitted to mention his deserved success as a broadcaster), and from 1936 was chairman of the Road Accidents Emergency Council. He succeeded Lord Lothian as Secretary of the Rhodes Trust in May 1939. He was also, among other things, a Nuffield medical trustee.

He married, in 1921, Dedi, daughter of Gustav Hartmann, of Oslo, and had one son and two daughters. The heir is their son, the Hon. Rodney Elton.

April 19, 1973.

Sir Arthur Elton, a pioneer of the documentary film, who lived at Clevedon Court, Somerset, died in a Bristol nursing home on January 1, 1973. He was 66.

Arthur Elton, one of the most distinguished and influential members of the English documentary movement, was almost unique among his contemporaries in having experience of work on feature films before entering the field of documentary. When he came down from Cambridge in 1927 he immediately joined the scenario department of Gainsborough Films, where he worked until he became a member of the newly founded film unit of the Empire Marketing Board in 1931. Here he formed part of a group of enthusiastic young filmmakers under the leadership of John Grierson, among them Basil Wright and Edgar Anstey, and directed several short films, among them *Shadow on the Mountain, Upstream, Voice of the World* and *Aero Engine*.

After the Empire Marketing Board film unit had been taken over by the G.P.O. Elton became a producer for the Ministry of Labour for two years, making films like *Workers and Jobs* and *Men Behind the Meters*, as well as joining Edgar Anstey in the direction of his best-known film, *Housing Problems*, a series of filmed interviews with slum dwellers illustrated with scenes of their living conditions.

As proved the case with most of his contemporaries, with the passage of time Arthur Elton found himself more and more involved in the organization of film production to the virtual exclusion of actual direction, but perhaps in his case this process discovered for him his true vocation as encourager of talent in younger directors and technicians, many of whom would pay tribute to his constructive criticism and acute film sense, whether applied to minute technical exposition, to the poetic description of atmosphere or to any of the hundred and one functions of documentary between these two extremes. In 1937 he was associated with John Grierson and Basil Wright in the foundation of Film Centre as an organization which could provide a production set-up for documentaries of all kinds, and produced through it such films as *Dawn of Iran, Transfer of Power* and many more.

From 1941 to 1944 he played an important part in the wartime production of documentary as Supervising Producer to the Ministry of Information, as well as being president of the Scientific Film Association, a body in which he always took an enthusiastic interest, from 1943 to 1946.

At the end of the Second World War, he returned to Film Centre as producer, although he kept up his own official work, as film adviser to the Danish Government in 1946 and to the Control Commission in Germany the next year. He was elected a governor of the British Film Institute 1948-49, and became adviser to the Shell organization for a number of years before being appointed production head of Shell Films in 1957.

The Shell unit soon became, while under his supervision, one of the most enterprising and accomplished producers of documentaries during the fifties, when, thanks to Elton's work at Shell and Edgar Anstey's with British Transport Films, there was something of a revival in British documentary after a postwar eclipse.

Elton's documentation of Clevedon Court, his family home since 1709, and now a National Trust property, was superbly accomplished as a kind of by-product of his other activities. He also collected all the guide books and topographical pictures of the town and augmented the mass of local history already in the shelves of his family library.

The collapse of Clevedon pier in 1970 brought all his concern into focus. Believing passionately that this lovely and graceful construction was a great artefact of the great age of cast and wrought iron and the English genius for engineering, he became chairman of the Clevedon Pier Restoration Trust.

After restoring Clevedon Court and handing it over to the National Trust in 1960 he found his greatest local pleasure as chairman of the Clevedon Printing Co., Ltd. which publishes the weekly *North Somerset Mercury*, and his concern for community life in a community newspaper was therein expressed.

Elton, the tenth baronet, succeeded his father in 1951.

January 2, 1973.

Simon Elwes, R.A., a notable portrait painter, died on August 6, 1975 at the age of 73. Born in 1902, the son of the famous singer, Gervase Elwes, and Lady Winefride Elwes, daughter of the 8th Earl of Denbigh and Desmond, he was educated as Lady Cross School, Seaford, and The Oratory, Edgbaston.

From 1918 he was a student for a time at the Slade School where he showed that he had a natural gift and inclination towards portraiture. He did not however take too kindly to the rigours of general studies demanded by his professor (Henry Tonks) and he soon moved to Paris where he found an atmosphere more congenial to his development as a painter. He remained there until 1926.

When eventually he came into his own, his gifts fell naturally into place and proved him to be one of the most successful portrait painters of his time. He first exhibited, a portrait of Lady Lettice Lygon, at the Royal Academy in 1927 and thereafter his works were hung in its annual Summer Exhibition almost without a break until and including 1975. Among his sitters were the Duke and Duchess of York (later King George VI and Queen Elizabeth the Queen Mother), the Princess Royal,* Prince George and Princess Marina,* and, more than once, H.M. Queen Mary and Her Majesty the Queen, as well as famous personalities such as Sir Thomas Beecham* and the artist's brother, Mr. Justice Elwes.* In addition there were frequently flower pieces and landscapes in his contributions.

He was elected an Associate of the Royal Academy in 1956 and a full Academician in 1967. He was also president of the Guild of Catholic Artists and a distinguished member of the Royal Society of Portrait Painters. He had been created a Knight of Malta in 1929. During the Second World War he served in the 10th Royal Hussars, dealing with public relations and painting the portraits of many high-ranking Army officers in the Middle East.

After the war, a severe thrombosis deprived him of the use of the whole of his right side and thereafter, such was his spirit, he learnt to paint equally successfully with his left hand. Whatever the circumstances, he always displayed remarkable courage and gaiety, reflected perhaps in the buttonhole he invariably wore. He was a marvellous companion.

His painting was impressionistic, certainly in regard to his sympathetic response to the character and vitality of his sitter, qualities which he rendered in an enthusiastic and painterly manner. He knew how to construct a picture to enhance the individuality of the subject.

He married in 1926 the Hon. Gloria Rodd, daughter of the 1st Lord Rennell. They had four sons, one of whom died in infancy.

August 9, 1975.

Professor Walter Bryan Emery, C.B.E., formerly Edwards Professor of Egyptology in the University of London, died after a sudden illness in Cairo on March 11, 1971. He was 67.

Bryan Emery was the last survivor of a small group of British archaeologists who entered the Service of Antiquities of the Egyptian Government in the days when it depended largely on European assistance for the recovery and preservation of the ancient monuments of the lower Nile valley. Although in recent years he occupied the position of Field Director of the Egypt Exploration Society's excavations, his work at Saqqara was conducted under the aegis of both the Society and the Antiquities Service and thus he retained a connexion which, with enforced interruptions, spanned more than forty years.

Born in 1903, he received his early education in his native city of Liverpool. On leaving school he began a course of training to become a marine engineer, but he soon discovered that his real ambition lay in another direction, not, however, before he had taken an active part in the construction and proving trials of one of the few British battleships to be built between the two wars.

What had previously been no more than a keen interest now became a consuming passion, and in 1921 he went to Liverpool University to read Egyptology under Professor T. E. Peet. Two years later he decided to cut short his university studies and to accept an invitation from Sir Robert Mond to direct his privately-financed operations at Luxor, under the auspices of Liverpool University.

By 1926 he had excavated, protected and partly restored a dozen private tombs, including that of the Vizier Ramose, one of the finest tombs of the Eighteenth Dynasty. In the following year, again with the support of Sir Robert Mond, he conducted an exploratory mission to Armant, the site of the ancient city of Hermonthis. Classical historians had recorded that the burial-place of the sacred Buchis bulls lay in its vicinity, and Emery's aim was to find it.

The city and its environs covered a wide area, but Emery, by clever deduction and minute observation of the terrain and other physical features, selected immediately the right spot for his trial shaft and within three days he had found sufficient evidence of the correctness of his judgment to justify a full-scale excavation in the following season by the Egypt Exploration Society and Sir Robert Mond. It resulted in the discovery of not only the tombs of the bulls but also those of their mothers.

Having successfully launched these excavations Emery transferred his activities in 1929 to Nubia, where exploratory work had become urgently necessary owing to the Government's decision to increase the height of the Aswan dam and the consequent flooding of the low-lying archaeological sites south of it.

Assisted by L. P. Kirwan, he surveyed the two banks of the Nile from Wadi es-Sebua to Adindan, a distance of nearly 100 miles. It was exhausting work conducted under pressure, and much of it carried out in the heat of summer when the river was at its lowest level. At the very end of his survey he was rewarded by the discovery, at Ballana and Qustol near Abu Simbel, of the tombs of the kings of the pagan inhabitants of Lower Nubia from the fourth to the sixth centuries A.D., known to archaeologists as the X-group people.

The rich treasure recovered from these tombs now fills two rooms in the Cairo Museum, and even so only part of it can be shown. Quite suddenly, an important new branch of art had become known. The survey and the publication of its results occupied six years until 1935 when he was appointed Director of the Antiquities Service's excavations at North Saqqara. His task was to explore a cemetery of brick mastabas dating from the First Dynasty which was known to lie beneath the sand near the eastern edge of the high desert.

Within a few months of his appointment he had brought to light, from the superstructure of a mastaba which one of his predecessors had incompletely excavated, a magnificent collection of objects, including some astonishing works of art, all dating from the very beginning of Egypt's ancient history. But it was only the first of a succession of remarkable discoveries in these mastabas which extended, owing to enforced periods of inactivity, over the next 20 years.

With the outbreak of the Second World War in 1939 Emery dropped his spade for a weapon and took part in much of the early desert warfare until he was appointed Chief of Intelligence of the British Army in Egypt, attaining the rank of Lieutenant Colonel. Retiring from the army in 1946 he went back to Saqqara, but after one season lack of funds for excavation in the Antiquities Service compelled him to resign and he accepted an appointment at the British Embassy in Cairo, where he remained until he was elected to the Chair of Egyptology at University College London in 1951.

It was a post for which he was admirably suited and which he held with distinction for 19 years, retiring in 1970. By the terms of the endowment, the holder of the chair was required to teach for two terms only in each academic year, the intention being that he should spend the third term in Egypt instructing his more advanced students in practical field-work. Emery was thus able to combine his professorship at the university with the honorary post of Field Director of the Egypt Exploration Society and to resume his interrupted excavations at Saqqara. Political difficulties in 1956 again halted the work and Emery turned once more to Nubia, choosing the fortress and temple of Buhen on the Second Cataract as the object of his attention.

From this work he was able to discover much about the technique of warfare in the second millennium B.C. It also led to an unexpected gain when, in 1959, the Egyptian Government decided to build the new high dam at Aswan; Buhen lay within the territory to be submerged by the waters of the new reservoir, and, in the time available between the announcement of the plan and its execution, it would have been difficult to attend to the excavation of the fortress and the removal of the temple to Khartoum, both of which he was able to carry out. Moreover, he was also able to do some valuable work at Qasr Ibrim, another site in the doomed territory. But Emery's contribution to the Nubian emergency was not limited to excavation. He was also chairman of the committee appointed by Unesco to assist the Egyptian government authorities in the organization of the work and in the allocation of sites to the many expeditions sent by other countries to help in the rescue operations.

The Nubian crisis past, he was able to return to Saqqara in 1964 for what proved to be the last phase of his remarkable career. Having finished in 1955 the excavation of the large mastabas of the First Dynasty, he turned to a part of the site where he had already located a tomb of the Third Dynasty but had put off clearing it until time permitted. At the bottom of the burial shaft he found one of a series of interconnected tunnels which contained some hundreds of thousands of mummies of ibises; subsequently he found a similar tunnel with mummified baboons. Both of these creatures were sacred to the god of wisdom, Thoth.

Perhaps the most outstanding discovery of all was made at the end of his last season, when he located the tomb of the sacred cows, the mothers of the Apis-bulls buried in the Seapeum which Mariette had found in 1851. It was chiefly the clearance and conservation of this rock-hewn hypogeum which occupied Emery until a few days before his death.

March 13, 1971.

Emperor Haile Selassie of Abyssinia—See Ethiopia.

Charles Engelhard, the American industrialist and racehorse owner, died in Boca Grande, Florida, on March 2, 1971. He was 54.

He owned the racehorse Nijinsky, which in 1970 became the first "triple crown" classic winner in England for 35 years. The horse —regarded as one of the outstanding horses of all time—won the Derby, the St. Leger and the 2,000 Guineas. It also won a fourth classic—the Irish Derby. He was chairman of the Engelhard Minerals and Chemicals Corporation, whose three divisions refine and fabricate precious metals, deal on metal exchanges, and produce rare earth for scientific and industrial purposes.

Engelhard's other interests were diversified and included a sizable holding in a mutual fund operating in Europe. As well as being a highly successful man of business, Engelhard cut a substantial figure in social circles and was a vigorous sportsman. In fact the same shrewdness and determination which characterized his business dealings were evident in his pursuit of horse racing.

Engelhard was recognized as one of the leading owners of thorough-bred racehorses, and had stables in Ireland, England, France, South Africa and the United States.

Nijinsky, undoubtedly the greatest racehorse he ever owned, was syndicated as a stallion for a world record 5,400,000 dollars (£2,250,000 sterling).

Nijinsky, winner of 11 of his 13 races, won nearly £265,000 in prize money in his two years' racing. Engelhard paid £35,000 for the Canadian-bred colt at the Toronto yearling sales in 1968. Nijinsky's successes in 1970 made Engelhard a leading owner in Britain for the first time.

He had more than 50 horses in training in England and Ireland with five different trainers—Jeremy Tree, Fulke Johnson Houghton, J. F. Watts and J. W. Watts in England and Vincent O'Brien in Ireland. O'Brien had charge of Nijinsky, who won his first 11 races and looked like retiring with an unbeaten series of glittering successes; but he was inched out of victory in France's richest race, the Prix de L'Arc de Triomphe at Longchamp, and failed again three weeks later in England's Champion Stakes, his final race before being retired to stud. Nijinsky was ridden in most of his races by Lester Piggott.

The Engelhard business was started by Charles Engelhard's father, a German who emigrated to the United States in the 1890s. It was estimated he made over £10m.

Charles Engelhard, who was educated at Princeton University and saw service in the Second World War in the United States Air Corps, took over the family business soon after the end of hostilities and began to diversify its activities. He was a close friend of Harry Oppenheimer, head of the Anglo-American goldmining and De Beers diamond groups, and had a substantial stake in the Anglo-American empire.

March 3, 1971.

Erik Eriksen, Danish Prime Minister from 1950 to 1953, died of a heart attack at Esbjerg Hospital on October 7, 1972. He was 69.

Eriksen was first elected to the Folketing in 1935 and was Minister for Agriculture in two periods, before heading the coalition of his own Liberal Party and the Conservatives from 1950 to 1953.

Eriksen, who was born on the land, led a party which has always been a farmers' party but under his leadership began for the first time to seek support in towns. His greatest achievement was the Danish constitutional reform of 1953 in which the upper chamber (Landsting) was abolished, the voting age reduced to 21 years, and female throne succession introduced, paving the way for the present Queen Margrethe II to succeed to the throne.

The reform was very much the personal achievement of Eriksen; an attempt 14 years earlier to introduce similar reforms had failed. For many years his thinking dominated the Liberal Party, but his political career ended in 1965, when the party rejected his long-held dream of uniting with the Conservatives to form a strong liberal alternative to the Social Democrats.

The bride was willing at the time, but his own party was not, and he resigned as party leader in disappointment. Like many other Scandinavian politicians, he favoured Nordic cooperation and from 1964 until 1971 was chairman of the Nordic Association in Denmark.

He was a Liberal of the old school, deeply respected by his opponents and supporters. As a parliamentary speaker he was known for his wit, in spite of a very smooth form of delivery; and as a politician he had a vision and flexibility that made him the natural spokesman for all the Liberal opposition parties during many years under Social Democratic government.

Erik Eriksen studied to be a farmer in his youth, and in 1928 took over management of his father's farm, which he inherited 11 years later. But he also had an early interest in politics and got his political schooling in the Young Liberal organization, where he was national chairman from 1929 to 1932. Whenever public life permitted he returned to his farm, and it was there that he received Nikita Khrushchev during a state visit to Denmark. The meeting led to an argument between the two after Eriksen expressed doubts whether Russian collective farming was as effective as Khrushchev had claimed when the two men were strolling through some of the best-tended fields in Denmark.

Since resigning from the Liberal Party chairmanship in 1965, Eriksen managed his farm and followed a rather quiet life. But he reemerged on the public scene to support the campaign for E.E.C. membership.

He is survived by his wife and three sons.

October 9, 1972.

St. John Ervine, playwright and author, died on January 24, 1971 aged 87.

As a playwright Ervine held a high place among his contemporaries for the greater part of his professional career. Ervine's popularity was steadily maintained over a fairly long period—to some extent, no doubt, because his plays were diverse in kind.

Ervine established an individual reputation as dramatic critic for many years of *The Observer.* Though he tended, perhaps, to idealize the role of the actor-manager in the years before the 1914-18 War, nobody made out a better case against the more flagrant commercialization of the West End theatre in London in the years immediately after.

In criticism generally Ervine was acute and perceptive, though inclined to immoderation.

He was less well known as a novelist than as a playwright or controversialist, but perhaps his deepest powers of imagination and sympathy are revealed in the novels he wrote about his native Ulster.

St. John Greer Ervine, who was born in Belfast on December 28, 1883, came of a deep-rooted Ulster stock. His interest in the theatre was roused when as a small boy he sat in the gallery of the Theatre Royal in Belfast and saw Benson playing Shakespeare.

In 1907 he wrote a one-act play, *The Magnanimous Lover,* an unsparing little piece about Protestant self-righteousness in Northern Ireland, which was produced at the Abbey Theatre in Dublin in 1913. By that time he had written *Mixed Marriage* and *Jane Clegg,* both sincerely felt and moving in their unaffected dramatic realism. His next play, *John Ferguson,* attained a remarkable tragic power and dignity.

In 1914 Ervine produced his first novel, *Mrs. Martin's Man,* a strong, truthful and telling study of a lower-middle-class Ulster household. The theatre was still his chief concern, however, and in 1915 he became manager of the Abbey Theatre. Next year he joined the Army as a trooper in the Household Battalion and it was as a lieutenant in The Royal Dublin Fusiliers that he was wounded in France in May 1918 and lost a leg.

In 1920 appeared another novel, *The Foolish Lovers,* in which he took an Ulster hero to London. At about this time he also wrote a book on Sir Edward Carson and the Ulster movement, and in 1923 he brought out his study of Parnell, in which he kept a striking balance of judgment for all the emphasis of his Northern Irish point of view.

In the next few years came four plays: *The Ship; Mary, Mary, Quite Contrary; The Lady of Belmont* (a "sequel" to *The Merchant of Venice*); and *Anthony and Anna;* and another novel, intelligent and veracious, *The Wayward Man.* Then, in 1929, *The First Mrs. Fraser* was produced at the Haymarket Theatre, and Ervine frankly enjoyed his thumping success.

Most of Ervine's later work can only be

171

listed. Among the plays were: *People of Our Class; Boyd's Shop* (perhaps the best of them); *Robert's Wife; The Christies;* and *Friends and Relations;* none of the three plays produced after the Second World War —*Private Enterprise* (1947), *My Brother Tom* (1953), and *Esperanza* (1957)—was entirely happy in theatrical terms or was successful with the public.

For the rest there were books like *A Journey to Jerusalem*, which contained as much of opinion as of travel; *Sophia*, a novel of a too discursive stamp; and three books on the theatre.

Ervine's energies in this later period were chiefly devoted to biography. In 1934 came his careful, industrious study of General Booth, *God's Soldier*, a work which, though intellectually faulty, is at once an impressive tribute to the memory of a remarkable man and a valuable source book for the social historian. A less formal work of biography, *Craigavon: Ulsterman,* in 1949, similarly, has much to recommend it. Ervine published in 1952 a new "appraisal" of Oscar Wilde—an unjust piece of work and perhaps not conspicuously sensible. Four years later came a massive volume on *Bernard Shaw, His Life, Work and Friends.* Ervine had known and admired Shaw for many years.

During his later years he was a pillar of the "Individualist" movement. In the 1939-45 war he was an outspoken critic of Eire's neutrality. In 1932 he was appointed to the professorship of dramatic literature of the Royal Society of Literature in succession to Harley Granville Barker. He was a member of the Irish Academy.

January 25, 1971.

Mgr. Josemaria Escriva de Balaguer, who died in Rome on June 27, 1975 at the age of 73, was the founder and President-General of Opus Dei, the Roman Catholic organization whose members strive to achieve Christian perfection and bring Christian principles into professional and social life.

Opus Dei operates in all countries of western Europe, North and South America and in several nations in Africa, Asia and Australasia. In 1973 there were over 56,000 members belonging to 80 nationalities.

The organization, which has not been without its critics, has been particularly influential in Spain, for many of the technocrats to whom General Franco turned when he instituted a programme of economic reform and expansion in the 1950s were Opus Dei men and several are or have been Cabinet ministers.

Josemaria Escriva de Balaguer y Albas was born in Barbastro, Spain, in 1902. He obtained a Doctorate in Law at Madrid University, and one in Sacred Theology at the Lateran Pontifical University (Rome). He was ordained priest in 1925 and started his pastoral work in country parishes. Later he worked in poor districts of Madrid and among university students. He was Superior of the Seminary of Saragossa, Professor of Philosophy and Professional Ethics at the Madrid School of Journalism, and professor of Roman Law in Saragossa and Madrid. Mgr. Escriva de Balaguer was a domestic prelate to the Pope, Consultor to the Pontifical Commission for the Interpretation of the Code of Canon Law, Chancellor of the Universities of Navarre (Spain) and Piura (Peru), and member of the Roman Pontifical Academy of Theology.

On October 2, 1928, three years after his ordination and while he was living in Madrid, Mgr. Escriva founded Opus Dei. From then on his life coincided with the history and development of the association. He had lived in Rome since 1946 as the President-General of Opus Dei.

June 28, 1975.

Former Archbishop of Esztergom—See Mindszenty.

The former Emperor Haile Selassie of Ethiopia died in Addis Ababa on August 27, 1975 at the age of 83.

He was deposed in 1974 after a total reign of 46 years, preceded by 14 years of Regency. Despite his ignominious fall from power, he was the greatest ruler in Ethiopia's long history and the creator of the modern State, and his overthrow deprived his country of a unique stabilizing influence, the Organization of African Unity of a respected elder statesman, and the world of a picturesque and still respected personality.

He was a man of tenacious and dedicated purpose, which survived intact the ordeal of defeat and exile between 1936 and 1941. For 30 years after his restoration his authority, his talents, and his immense energy were devoted to the task of consolidating his country and modernizing its ancient institutions, and the great progress which it realized during his reign owed almost everything to his planning and execution. The power which he wielded until early 1974 was all but absolute, but was tempered by moderation based on profound religious conviction, which manifested itself particularly in clemency towards even those who had tried unsuccessfully to dethrone him.

Latterly, however, the very completeness of his authority seems to have become an obstacle to his comprehension of the ills afflicting Ethiopian society, and of the resentment which they were increasingly arousing, especially amongst the educated class of which he himself had been the creator; and it was this lack of comprehension which was primarily responsible for the outbreak in early 1974 of the popular revolt which led to his deposition.

Tafari Makonnen was born at Harar on July 23, 1892, the youngest son of Ras Makonnen, who was a cousin of the reigning Emperor Menelik and Governor of the province. His abilities were early recognized by his father, who arranged for him to be instructed by a priest from the French Mission; French consequently became the language which he spoke with greatest ease, and French thought and literature were to exercise a lasting influence on him.

Having survived, alone of a family of 11, the rigours of childhood, he was summoned to Addis Ababa by the Emperor Menelik, on whom his lively and inquiring mind made an immediate impression. His advancement was therefore swift. By the age of 13 he was a *dejazmatch*. That year his father died after naming him his heir. At 14 Tafari was Governor of Salali, and at 16 Governor of Sidamo, one of the richest provinces of the Empire. He was no more than 18 when he was entrusted with his father's old province of Harar, where he promptly launched a vigorous programme of reform. Its success and popularity were such that in 1916, on the deposition of Lij Yasu, Menelik's grandson and uncrowned successor, he was chosen by a council of notables as Regent and Heir to the Throne.

Almost immediately afterwards Tafari had to fight for his life against forces brought against him by Negus Mikhail, Lij Yasu's father, but he triumphed and from then onwards his authority was established.

From the first year of his Regency Tafari gave evidence of bold and progressive ideas. He founded new schools, endowing them from his private fortune, and encouraged the growth of foreign mission schools. Young men were sent abroad to receive a liberal or technical education and he followed with personal interest their progress in their studies. Social reforms were put in hand and their development was reflected in the changing face of the capital, in which hospitals, offices, and public buildings rose. Slavery was abolished. New contacts were established with the outside world. In 1922 the regent visited Aden, and two years later made a tour of Europe. He manifested eager interest in every sort of modern development: to the horror of his subjects, he insisted on making a flight in an aeroplane. The reputation of his country gradually grew, and in 1924 he won for her admittance to the League of Nations, on whose stage she was soon to play so sombre a part.

He had still to consolidate his own position. The capture of Lij Yasu (who had found sanctuary among the Muslims of the eastern deserts) was an important step forward; but he had also to reckon with the Empress Zauditu. On the death of Hapta Giorgis, the War Minister who held the balance of power between Regent and Empress, the two stood face to face. The trial of strength between them came in 1928 when Tafari's position was threatened by a rising of the Imperial Guard. He replied by surrounding the palace with his troops and compelled the Empress to recognize his new title of King.

Two years later she became seriously ill with diabetes and the Rases of the north seized the opportunity to rebel. Acting with his usual promptness, Tafari sent his troops northwards and bombarded the insurgents with propaganda leaflets from an aircraft, the first apparently ever to be used in that country. After a fierce struggle in which the rebellious Ras Gugsa, a former husband of the Empress, was killed, Tafari's troops emerged victorious. The news precipitated the death of the Empress. The seal was formally set on Tafari's power when in November of that year he was crowned King of Kings and founded a new dynasty under his baptismal name of Haile Selassie.

Under the gathering cloud of Italy's growing belligerence, the next five years brought forth more and quicker reforms. A Parliament was inaugurated, measures to put down the slave-trade were made effective, and the administration was centralized. Above all the new Emperor showed intense interest in education and plans for school development were pushed rapidly forward.

Militarily, however, the Italian invasion of Ethiopia, in October 1935, found the country virtually helpless. Once diplomatic action had failed to halt Mussolini, Ethiopian resistance against the well-equipped Italian forces was foredoomed. If the Hoare-Laval pact would have been a crushing blow to Ethiopia, the collapse of sanctions, and the arms-embargo imposed by the great powers were mortal ones. Yet for some months Haile Selassie gallantly sustained an unequal contest. On the battlefield he personally led his troops; he is said to have manned a machine-gun for two days without rest or food. When further resistance became impossible he went into exile with his family, first on board a British cruiser to Palestine and later to England, where he was sympathetically received. After a last personal appeal to the League of Nations, where his dignity and bearing made a deep impression even if they could produce no tangible result, he returned to England and settled down in Bath, where he became a familiar as well as a picturesque figure. In after years he frequently referred with gratitude to the kindness extended to him during this unhappy period.

The outbreak of war between Great Britain and Italy in June 1940 brought him new hope. He insisted on proceeding at the earliest possible moment to Khartum, whence partisan activities in Ethiopia were organized. In January 1941 he reentered his country from the Sudan at the head of a partisan force, which soon captured the province of Gojjam from the Italians. Three months later the converging strength of Allied columns under Generals Platt and Cunningham forced a surrender of the main Italian forces, and on May 5 the Emperor was able to return in triumph to his capital, five years to the day since his expulsion. In a speech on arrival he referred to it as "a day which men and angels could not have foreseen".

The Emperor at once threw himself into the task of reconstruction and rehabilitation. He was at first irked by the limitations placed on his sovereignty by the powers exercised by the British occupation forces, but by an Anglo-Ethiopian Agreement concluded in January 1942 most of these were relinquished to him and he thereafter exercised virtually absolute authority.

His first preoccupation was with internal security, which had always been difficult to establish in a country divided by formidable barriers of mountain and ravine and with poor communications; by the introduction of modern methods, notably the telegraph, the telephone, and internal air services, he eventually succeeded better than any predecessor had ever done in imposing his rule in the remotest areas. In other spheres of administration he sought assistance wherever it was offered, notably from the United States, but mindful of past experiences was careful not to lean too heavily on any one nation for advice or help. British influence, at first paramount, inevitably waned; though it remained strong in education, where the Emperor, having in 1942 declared English an official language on level terms with Amharic, employed large numbers of British or Commonwealth teachers in the State schools and in the University College of Addis Ababa, and Great Britain also helped to modernise the medical services. A British Military Mission to reorganize his army was however replaced in 1950 by an American one; while Swedish and American missions were brought in to create the nucleus of an Air Force, and later Norwegians to found a Navy.

Loans from the World Bank and the establishment of an American Highways Authority enabled the road-system left by the Italians to be maintained and extended, with benefit to both public security and the economy, though it remained inadequate for such a country.

Throughout these formative years the Emperor presided over every development affecting his people's welfare, inspiring, guiding, if necessary rebuking, personally visiting every new school, every military unit, every new enterprise. Deeply religious, he untiringly performed the duties assigned by tradition to his office in all the lengthy ceremonies of the Church; a devoted family man, he seldom appeared in public without a bevy of grandchildren, over whose lives and education he exercised an affectionate but close supervision; and his intelligence, his wit, and his quiet dignity never failed to impress the visitors who came in ever-increasing numbers from the outside world. They observed that his far from impressionable subjects still cast themselves before his car to call attention to a grievance, and gave spontaneous expression of their sympathy when he suffered personal affliction —notably when in 1957 his beloved second son was accidentally killed.

Externally the Emperor aimed at securing not only peace and independence for Ethiopia, but also international respect. His success was demonstrated when the United Nations Assembly in 1950 approved the federation to it of the former Italian colony of Eritrea. In 1954 he paid a state visit to Great Britain, the first of a series which he undertook with the object of calling world attention to the evolution of his state. In 1958 relations with Italy, whose nationals— Fascists excepted—he had protected ever since his restoration, were normalized by an agreement under which the Italian Government agreed, by way of war reparations, to construct gratis a hydro-electric project in the south. The Emperor also saw to it that Ethiopia played a full part in United Nations activities, supplying a contingent of troops for Korea and a larger one for the Congo besides being prominent in proceedings at New York; and he was particularly satisfied when in 1959 Addis Ababa was chosen as the centre for the newly-established Economic Commission for Africa.

He was equally insistent that his country's voice should be heard in the counsels of the emergent African states, and his foreign policy was gradually modified from pro-Western to "neutral" and pan-African, in harmony with the evolution of African opinion.

Only with the leaders of Somalia, whom he suspected of designs on his largely Somali-populated Ogaden Province, and of Egypt, whom he accused of intriguing among his Muslim subjects in Eritrea, was he unable to come to terms.

In 1955 the Emperor, determined to encourage the political evolution of his people, had promulgated a new Constitution which endowed the country with its first elected Chamber of Deputies. Elections for it, first held in 1957, succeeded beyond expectations, but the Emperor judged it wise to withhold real responsibility from the emergent Parliament.

As it turned out, this deprivation was too prolonged: for in 1960 came a first serious challenge to his authority. During his absence on a visit to Brazil his trusted personal bodyguard revolted and seized several members of his family and close adherents as hostages. The regular armed forces remained loyal and quickly suppressed the rising, but not before several of the hostages had been killed and sufficient sympathy with the insurgents had been expressed, especially by young educated Ethiopians, to suggest the existence of a serious political malaise. The Emperor, returning post-haste, dealt leniently with all but the two ringleaders, and exonerated his Crown Prince for having broadcast in their favour by publicly recognizing that he had acted under duress. He also attempted to meet the underlying discontent by bringing a few of the younger men into positions of responsibility.

Once stability had been restored the Emperor's predilection for foreign affairs seemed if anything to increase. In a Cabinet reshuffle he retained the portfolio of Foreign Affairs and kept it until 1966. He led Ethiopian delegations to Conferences of Non-aligned States at Belgrade in 1961 and of African States in Lagos in 1962, and in 1963 was host to the first Conference of Independent African States in Addis Ababa. He then went on a tour of North and West Africa, during which he participated in a successful mediation in a serious dispute between Algeria and Morocco.

In 1964 he attended a second conference of what had come to be called the Organization of African Unity (O.A.U.), and the consistently high quality of his addresses at these assemblies was a main cause of the organization's decision to set up its permanent headquarters in Addis Ababa, and of his being on occasion referred to as "The Father-Figure of African Unity".

In 1963 and 1964 he exchanged visits with President Tito of Yugoslavia, with whom he had struck up a friendship, and in 1964 toured the Iron Curtain countries, ending up with attendance at another Conference of Non-Aligned States, this time in Cairo. In 1965 he received a return state visit from the Queen and the Duke of Edinburgh, during which her Majesty bestowed on him, to his obvious pleasure, the baton of a Field-Marshal of the British Army to add to the Garter, G.C.B., G.C.M.G., and Chain of the Royal Victorian Order which he already held.

In 1966 the Emperor's personal disengagement from internal affairs, begun earlier, was continued by his relinquishment of the portfolios of Foreign Affairs and Education (the latter of which he had held since his restoration) and by his devolution to his trusted Prime Minister Aklilou Habte-Wold of the responsibility for selecting Cabinet Ministers and for day-to-day administration. His authority, however, remained supreme in all matters of importance, for Parliament remained comparatively ineffective and his ministers, individually or in council, would never have ventured to adopt a line of action of which he was known to disapprove.

But as the years went by the aging Emperor, despite his unremitting industry and constant travels, increasingly gave the impression of loneliness and of isolation from the common people. He had lost his staunch helpmate the Empress* in 1962, and his third son soon afterwards; and in 1972 the Crown Prince, with whom his relations had always been correct rather than close, became so ill as to require prolonged stay in hospital abroad.

In 1973 matters were brought to a head by a failure of the annual rains, which caused a disastrous famine in many districts where the population was already on the subsistence-level. Foreign relief, belatedly solicited by a Government apparently loath to recognize the emergency, was generously given, but both the communications and the administration were too defective to enable it to be effectively distributed; and to the discontent thus generated was added a steep rise of local prices, due to world causes but nevertheless crippling, which eventually

brought about a wave of strikes in the towns and a serious mutiny of the armed forces.

The malcontents were mostly professing loyalty to the Emperor's person, but made a series of demands which included the resignation of the Government, constitutional changes designed to secure greater popular participation in its successor, a searching enquiry into the accusations of official corruption, and sweeping reforms in land-tenure and labour relations. The Emperor found himself forced not only to grant substantial rises in army and labour pay but to promise constitutional changes, and it became clear that his long period of virtual autocracy had come to an end.

Throughout 1974 his authority declined. The stopgap Government under Lij Endelkatchew Makonnen which he had been forced to appoint in February gave way in July to another headed by Mikhail Imru, but it was already clear that the real power had passed into the hands of the Co-ordinating Committee of the Armed Forces, a body of comparatively junior officers animated by liberal ideas and zealous for a complete reform and reorganization of the administration.

Against the Emperor this body proceeded cautiously in view of his unique prestige; but step by step he was stripped of his powers and privileges and the process was accelerated by the popular indignation aroused by the assiduous circulation of reports accusing him and his family of self-enrichment at the expense of the common people.

One by one all his close adherents were removed or abandoned him; even the Church leaders with whom he had worked in close collaboration all his life found it politic to dissociate themselves from him. He became virtually isolated in the Jubilee (now renamed National) Palace, from which he could hardly stir for fear of encountering one of the increasingly frequent popular demonstrations calling for his removal. The inevitable end came in September, when the Committee seized power and proclaimed his deposition in favour of the ailing Crown Prince, himself deposed in the abolition of the Crown by the new government in March 1975.

He was subsequently accused by the armed forces coordinating committee of having exploited public funds for his own benefit, besides which it was alleged that he had a personal fortune of several hundred million pounds salted away in Swiss bank accounts.

After his deposition Haile Selassie was at first confined to a three roomed mud hut in the local army barracks, but later allowed to return to the Grand Palace at Addis Ababa, now the headquarters of the government.

It was at the palace that he underwent a prostate operation in June.

August 28, 1975.

Dr. Maurice Leon Ettinghausen, who died in Oxford on November 14, 1974 after a brief illness, aged 91, was probably the oldest active antiquarian bookseller on the international scene.

Born in Paris in 1883, he went to England in 1887. He was educated at St. Paul's, went up to Queen's College, Oxford, in 1902, and obtained a doctorate in Sanskrit from the Sorbonne in 1905.

After a brief association with the firm of Luzac and Company (Oriental Publishers and Booksellers) in London, he joined the Munich firm of Ludwig Rosenthal, "the founder of the modern school of antiquarian bookselling", as Ettinghausen called him in his memoirs.

Interned in Ruhleben Camp during the First World War, he joined the firm of Maggs Brothers after his return to England, and was manager of their Paris branch in the thirties. He settled in Oxford in 1940 where he was associate of A. Rosenthal Ltd. until the end of his life.

A passionate bookman of great erudition and versatility, Dr. Ettinghausen's career not only reflected, but also shaped a great epoch of collecting and bookselling. His dominant role in dealings with the great European and American collectors and institutions during his 20 years with Maggs Brothers has become bookselling history.

He produced a series of catalogues of incunabula, French, Spanish and Portuguese books and Americana of unprecedented lavishness and typographical excellence, and he was the principal negotiator in the purchase for the nation of the famous *Codex Sinaiticus* in 1933.

He wrote a volume of memoirs *Rare Books and Royal Collectors* (Simon and Schuster, New York, 1966) and a volume of correspondence between that erudite bibliophile King Manuel of Portugal, then living in exile at Twickenham, and himself was published by the Casa de Bragança in Lisbon in 1957.

November 20, 1974.

Air Chief Marshal Sir Donald Randell Evans, who was an innovator in night fighter tactics in the Second World War, died on April 9, 1975 aged 63. He was Commandant of the Imperial Defence College from 1968 until his retirement from the Royal Air Force in 1970.

He was born at Richmond, Surrey, and educated at the R.A.F. College, Cranwell, which he entered in 1930. His career after leaving Cranwell in 1932 included service with No. 45 Squadron in the Middle East and he joined Fighter Command, where he was an H.Q. signals officer at the outbreak of war. It was in 1941 that he was given command of a special unit engaged on the development of night fighter interception. While flying with this unit he personally shot down two enemy aircraft and was awarded the D.F.C. in 1942.

He afterwards went to H.Q. No. 11 Group, Fighter Command, as Group Captain in charge of night operations until he joined the Signals Special Planning Section at Mediterranean Air Command in 1943. There he was involved with the air signals planning for the Allied invasion of Sicily, duties he repeated when he returned to Britain to join the Allied Expeditionary Air Force for the Normandy landings.

After the war he graduated at the R.A.F. Staff College, commanded the Telecommunications Flying Unit at Defford from 1946 to 1948, and was Group Captain in charge of plans at Fighter Command H.Q. He took the 1956 course at the Imperial Defence College and was Senior Staff Officer at Fighter Command from 1957 to 1958. He was Commandant of the School of Land/Air Warfare from 1959 to 1961 when, as an Air Vice-Marshal, he became Assistant Chief of Defence Staff at the Ministry of Defence.

An important step was his appointment as Chairman of the Chiefs of Staff working party in the reorganization of the Ministry of Defence in 1963. With an already established reputation as a progressive mind on joint planning he worked closely with the then Chief of Defence Staff, Lord Mountbatten, to try to ensure that unification became a real integration of the policy-making functions of the three services, a step resisted at that time by some, less flexible, senior officers.

From 1964 to 1966 he was Air Officer Commanding, Technical Training Command, and from 1966 to 1967 was Air Secretary at the Ministry of Defence. After his retirement he was a consultant on military aviation matters to Ferranti, Edinburgh. He was made a C.B.E., 1944; C.B., 1955; and a K.B.E., 1964.

April 11, 1975.

Sir Edward Evans Pritchard—See Evans-Pritchard.

Merlyn Evans, the painter, died on October 31, 1973 at the age of 63.

Born in Cardiff in 1910, he studied first at the Glasgow School of Art and later at the Royal College of Art. In 1931 a travelling scholarship gave him a year abroad; he studied mainly in Paris and Berlin, becoming deeply impressed with the work of Klee and Kandinsky.

His mind was already developing towards abstract art; two years later he met and talked with such artists as Ozenfant,* Mondrian, Kandinsky and Giacommetti,* which strengthened his convictions on abstract work. By 1935 he was exhibiting in Paris, in 1936 at the International Exhibition of Surrealist Art, London, and in 1937 at the Salon de Mai.

During the war he served in the Eighth Army in North Africa and Italy, an ex-perience reflected in paintings later. His first one-man show was in 1949, followed by others in 1952, 1955 and 1958 at the Leicester Galleries. In 1956 came his first retrospective at the Whitechapel Art Gallery.

As well as painting he worked prolifically at etching and engraving, becoming a consummate master in that field. In 1958 he showed a powerful series of prints, "Vertical Suite in Black", fierce in intensity, influenced by his interest in African sculpture.

His work now figured in many international exhibitions—Sao Paulo, Tokyo, Kassel, Ljubljana, Carrara, Pittsburgh, and in 1960 at the Venice Biennale. In 1966 he was awarded a gold medal at the National Eisteddfod, of which he was particularly proud, himself a Welshman.

In 1967, at the invitation of the Chicago Art Institute, he staged a large exhibition of paintings, and later of prints at Philadelphia. While in the United States, where he stayed for several months, he visited and talked with some of the leading New York painters, in particular Rothko* and Newman. Later he exhibited in New York at the Marlborough-Gerson.

In 1972-73 came his Retrospective of Graphic Art at the Victoria and Albert Museum which revealed him as one of the most important British artists of the twentieth century in that field. His latest paintings were also exhibited in London. For the spring of 1974 a large exhibition of his work in Cardiff had already been planned. A film of his activities was completed.

Evans was a man of great compassion and tenderness. Although an abstract artist, his work reflects strong feelings and forebodings, being deeply concerned with the violence and sufferings of our times. His culture was deep: he was interested in philosophy, wrote poetry, and his powers of analysis were most trenchant.

In recent years he had also carried out architectural commissions. For years he was a teacher and many students at the Central School and Royal College were attracted by his great knowledge and breadth of sympathy.

He will be deeply missed by a wide circle of artists and friends.

His works are in many collections: the Tate Gallery, the British Museum, the V. & A. Museum, and the Museum of Modern Art, New York, to name but a few.

He is survived by his wife, Margerie Few, the concert pianist.

November 3, 1973.

Professor Trefor E. Evans, C.M.G., diplomat and academic, who died at Aberystwyth on April 16, 1974, aged 61, had previously been one of the most accomplished Arabists in the Foreign Service, and, by virtue of his understanding of and sympathy with Arabs, had been able to fill with distinction a number of difficult posts in Arab countries.

Born in Wales in 1913, he was educated at Cowbridge and Balliol, where he graduated in 1934, later taking a doctorate of philosophy at Hamburg. In 1937 he entered the Levant consular service, and after two years learning Arabic at Beirut, and a spell at Alexandria, he spent from 1941 to 1945 in the Embassy at Cairo. For much of this time he was private secretary to Lord Killearn*, the ambassador, for whose forcefulness he conceived a strong admiration, and whose wartime diaries he was, 30 years later, to edit for publication. In 1945 he became British consul at Damascus, at a time of acute Franco-Syrian strife, and later served successively in Aleppo, Beirut and the Foreign Office.

In 1952 he returned as Oriental counsellor to Cairo, where the Nasserite* revolution had just ousted King Farouk*; four years of service there ended with the Suez adventure of 1956. After two years at Berne he became in 1959 consul-general at Algiers, already in the throes of a revolution against the French; and, in 1962, when this ended in Algerian independence, he was appointed the first British ambassador to the new state. In 1964 he was transferred as ambassador to Damascus, and in 1967 to Baghdad. In all three of these posts he had to deal with highly nationalistic and left-wing governments, on whom his optimistic and sympathetic judgments were not always appreciated at home.

In 1969, after some soul-searching, he resigned from the Foreign Office to fill the chair of international politics at the University of Wales. He leaves a widow and two daughters.

April 19, 1974.

Sir Edward Evans-Pritchard, F.B.A., Professor of Social Anthropology in the University of Oxford from 1946 to 1970, died on September 11, 1973.

Edward Evan Evans-Pritchard, second son of the Rev. T. J. Evans-Pritchard, was born in Sussex in 1902. He was educated at Winchester and Oxford, where he read modern history. Under the influence of the late Professor C. G. Seligman he then did postgraduate work in anthropology at the London School of Economics.

From 1926 onwards he made many field expeditions to the Anglo-Egyptian Sudan and adjoining parts of East and North Africa. His first major academic appointment (1931) was to a chair of sociology at the Egyptian University, Cairo, which he held until 1934.

For the next few years he was research lecturer in African sociology at Oxford, a post that enabled him to spend much time in the field. During the Second World War he served as political officer in Syria and Cyrenaica, and was mentioned in dispatches. In 1946 he succeeded A. R. Radcliffe-Brown as Professor of Social

Anthropology at Oxford. He was a Fellow of All Souls from 1946 to 1970 and Sub-Warden from 1963 to 1965.

Evans-Pritchard's fieldwork was done mainly among the Azande and Nuer of southern Sudan. Through his writings about them those peoples have come to be among the best known of all primitive societies. Two of his early books, *Witchcraft among the Azande* (1937) and *The Nuer* (1940), were immediately and universally recognized as brilliant contributions to anthropological theory and methods of research, and did much to establish his reputation as the foremost British social anthropologist of his generation.

In 1940 he also edited, with Meyer Fortes, who 10 years later became Professor of Social Anthropology at Cambridge, a volume of essays on *African Political Systems*, which revolutionized the study of primitive government.

He was a prolific writer, especially on kinship, religion, and the history of anthropology; but none of his later works was as significant as those mentioned. His purely theoretical essays and lectures, notably on the relationship between anthropology and other social sciences, revealed a depth of scholarship unmatched by any of his contemporaries, but were sometimes too controversial and too neglectful of modern trends to meet with general approval.

He was a stimulating and provocative teacher, with a sardonic though occasionally malicious sense of humour. Under his guidance the Oxford school of social anthropology attracted students from many parts of the world and produced some of the leading modern teachers of the subject.

For several years, as a member of the now defunct Colonial Social Science Research Council, he was also instrumental in sponsoring a good deal of fieldwork in Africa and elsewhere, contributing thereby to the generally admitted preeminence of British scholars in that branch of anthropological investigation.

He was president of the Royal Anthropological Institute from 1949-51 and first chairman of the Association of Social Anthropologists of the British Commonwealth, a professional body of selective membership that he was largely instrumental in forming. He was also made an honorary member of both the Institut Française de Sociologie and the American Academy of Arts and Sciences.

In 1939 he married Ioma Heaton Nicholls, a daughter of a prominent South African politician and at the time one of his own students. Her sudden death in 1959 was a great shock to the many friends who had been charmed by her sunny disposition and gracious hospitality. He is survived by three sons and two daughters.

Evans-Pritchard became a Fellow of the British Academy in 1956. He was knighted in 1971.

September 14, 1973.

F

Sir Arthur Fadden, P.C., G.C.M.G., who died on April 22, 1973, at the age of 78, was Prime Minister of Australia for 40 days in 1941. But he will be remembered best as Treasurer of the Commonwealth.

Altogether he introduced a record number of eleven budgets, the last nine of which were consecutive and charted Australia through a period of unprecedented growth, when he managed to combat with fair success the dangers first of world-wide inflation and then of the American recession. He was leader of the Country Party from 1941 until he left the Federal Parliament in 1958.

He was a considerable person in his own right, but he had no illusions about the preeminence in Australian politics of Sir Robert Menzies, Leader of the Liberal Party, which was also the predominant partner from 1949 in the Liberal-Country Party coalition government. Fadden was content and, in fact, determined to serve with the utmost loyalty a Prime Minister whom others once sought to displace. This political devotion to a man whose personal qualities were very different to his own was one of Fadden's greatest services to Australia, for it enabled Sir Robert Menzies to leave the country often and for long periods on important government business and know that all would be well in Canberra on his return. Fadden was a sound and decisive administrator, who was acting Prime Minister on ten separate occasions covering a total period of 19 months.

Fadden was very much an Australian. He liked to be called "Artie", and he liked to leave his coat undone. He had the manner of an agreeable extrovert and was kindly, cheerful and open with everyone.

Arthur William Fadden was born on April 13, 1895 at Ingham, North Queensland. His father, Richard, was a policeman. Soon after he was born his family moved to the Mackay district where Arthur spent his boyhood. At the age of 15 he left Walkerston State School and became "rouseabout" for a gang of sugar cane cutters; he boiled their billy for tea, swept out their quarters and did other odd jobs. A cane inspector was impressed by the boy's quick wit and got him a job in the office of the Pleystowe sugar mill. In his spare time he studied accountancy by correspondence and was appointed assistant town clerk of Mackay at the age of 18. At 21 he was town clerk and a fellow of the Institute of Chartered Accountants of Australia. He played football and cricket for Mackay and was district boxing champion.

In 1916 he married Ilmer Thornber and they had two sons and two daughters. He moved to Townsville, building up a substantial accountancy practice there and then set up a branch office in Brisbane. In 1932 he agreed to stand as Country Party candidate for Kennedy at the elections to the State Legislative Assembly. He was elected

and became a severe critic of the Labour government.

In April 1939, after the death of the Prime Minister, Lyons, the Country Party, led by Sir Earle Page*, decided to withdraw from any coalition led by Sir Robert Menzies. Fadden strongly disagreed with Page's repudiation of Menzies' leadership and with several others resigned from the Country Party. Page became Prime Minister for three weeks and was succeeded before the end of April by Menzies.

Fadden soon rejoined the Country Party and in 1940, to resolve a deadlock between Page, McEwen and Cameron (who became Speaker), he was elected acting Leader of the Country Party. In 1941 he was confirmed as Leader, having proved his ability to lead and humour men of considerable ability and ambition.

In 1940 Fadden entered the Government as Minister assisting the Treasurer. Five months later he was made Minister for Air, and in October 1940 became Treasurer for the first time. Early in 1941, Sir Robert Menzies went to England, having appointed Fadden Acting Prime Minister during his absence. It was Fadden who defended in Australia the controversial decision to send Australian troops to Greece.

Sir Robert Menzies resigned in August 1941, believing that his resignation would reunite the government's ranks. A joint meeting of the Country Party and the United Australia Party, of which Menzies was still leader, elected Fadden to succeed him; and the Governor-General, Lord Gowrie, asked Fadden to form a government. He became Prime Minister at the age of 46.

The Government still depended on the votes of two Independents, who chose in September to support an Opposition vote of censure on the heavy budget which Fadden had introduced that month. The Government was defeated and Fadden resigned on October 7. Labour, under Curtin, took office. Sir Robert Menzies withdrew his claim to be Leader of the Opposition, and a joint meeting of the Country Party and the U.A.P. elected Fadden, who remained the Leader of the Opposition until July 1943. After the Federal elections in August that year he was succeeded by Menzies. Under both men the Opposition supported the Labour Government in its prosecution of the war.

When Labour was removed from office at the elections in December 1949, Sir Robert Menzies, as Leader of the Liberal Party (which he had fashioned from the old U.A.P.), became Prime Minister, and at once appointed Fadden Treasurer and Deputy Prime Minister. Early in July 1950 Menzies summoned a special meeting of Parliament to discuss Australia's reaction to the beginning of the Korean war. It approved the despatch of air and naval units to join the United Nations forces, and three days later Menzies was on his way to London and Washington by air. Fadden became Acting Prime Minister, with the world in yet another crisis and Australia deeply involved. On July 26 it was Fadden who announced that Australian ground forces would also be sent to Korea.

April 23, 1973.

Mary (Mrs. J. B.) Fagan—See Grey.

Professor G. Hamilton Fairley, a leading authority on the treatment of cancer by drugs, was killed on October 23, 1975 in a bomb explosion near his home in London. He was 45.

His main research interests were in tumour immunology—the study of resistance to cancer by the body's natural defence mechanisms.

Gordon Hamilton Fairley was born on April 20, 1930 and educated at Geelong Grammar School, Australia, Marlborough College, and Magdalen College, Oxford, before going to St. Bartholomew's Hospital, London, for his clinical studies. He qualified in 1954 and held house appointments at his own hospital, the Brompton Hospital, and the postgraduate medical school.

From 1958 to 1961 he held the Leverhulme Research Scholarship of the Royal College of Physicians, and during that time he began his research into the immune mechanisms in blood diseases, under the guidance of Sir Ronald Bodley Scott and Professor J. V. Dacie. In 1965 he was appointed to the consultant staff at St. Bartholomew's Hospital, where in 1970 he became director of the Imperial Cancer Research Fund's Medical Oncology Research Unit. Two years later, when the first chair of medical oncology was established at the unit, he was appointed professor.

Professor Hamilton Fairley's interests covered both clinical and basic research. Much of his time was spent in improving the combinations of drugs used in the treatment of the leukemias and related disorders such as Hodgkin's disease, but he was also concerned with ways in which the immunological response of the body to a cancer could be stimulated and strengthened.

He had published widely on both topics and was highly regarded in international circles of cancer research. He is survived by his wife, three daughters and a son.

October 24, 1975.

King Faisal—See Saudi Arabia.

Professor Lloyd A. Fallers, the distinguished American social anthropologist, died on July 4, 1974 at the age of 48.

"Tom", as he was universally called, was as much a member of the small community of British anthropologists as he was a respected figure in the much larger community of those working in the United States.

Born in Nebraska City on August 29, 1925, he was both undergraduate and graduate student at the University of Chicago and, apart from three years at Berkeley and a year at Princeton, he also did most of his teaching at Chicago. It was there that in 1973 he was named the Albert A. Michelson Distinguished Service Professor of Anthropology and Sociology in recognition of "his research and teaching and the leadership he has provided other scholars in the study of new nations".

It was his research work as a young man that first brought him into the British orbit. He was one of four American students chosen to receive British Government grants for work in a British colony with funds allocated by the then Colonial Social Science Research Council set up in 1945—grants made as a gesture of gratitude for the very generous help given to British anthropologists by different American research councils over the previous years. As a result of this award, Fallers spent the year 1949-50 at the London School of Economics as a Fulbright scholar and then took up a fellowship at the new East African Institute of Social Research attached to Makerere College—now Makerere University—in Uganda.

From 1950-52 he did a fine study of the Basoga, a Bantu people living on the northern shore of Lake Victoria, on whom he wrote his first book, *Bantu Bureaucracy* (1956). This was followed by studies on Soga land tenure (1956) and marriage (1957), together with a book which has attracted the interest of lawyers as well as anthropologists, *Law without Precedent* (1969).

Fallers identified himself very closely with the work of this new East African Institute, of which he was later to become director, and though much in the colonial situation was alien to him, both as an American and as a person, yet he showed unusual objectivity in studying current political and social situations, and sympathy, which is also rare, for the difficulties of government officials, European and African, struggling with the problems of their new world.

His interest in East Africa continued for many years and widened into studies of all developing countries. It was a concern which led him to make a second field trip, this time to Edremit, a coastal town in Turkey, in 1968-69. He was an active member of a famous seminar entitled the Committee for the Comparative Study of New Nations, started at the University of Chicago in 1960 by Professor E. Shils with the cooperation of C. Geertz, D. Apter and others. Later, in 1969, Fallers became its chairman.

Fallers was a product of the sociology and anthropology departments of Chicago University. He was a student of Robert Redfield, Fred Eggan and Edward Shils. He was also much influenced by the work of Max Weber, whose message was not at the time very prominent in the teaching of anthropology in British universities. It was basically Weber's theories as to the evolution of western type bureaucracies from traditional methods of inheriting or acquiring office which led Fallers to play such a prominent part in a comparative study of chieftainship at district and village levels carried out in Uganda and Tanzania by scholars associated with the E.A.I.S.R. He contributed to the resultant publication, *East African Chiefs*, edited by A. I. Richards (1960). It was also his interest in leadership which made him an enthusiastic and stimulating director of a study of leadership in Buganda, an important project of which the results were published under his editorship as *The King's Men: Leadership and Status in Buganda on the Eve of Independence* (1964).

In all these empirical studies, Fallers combined in a most unusual way a sense of theoretical issues with a fertile supply of ideas as to how each hypothesis could be tested. His was the practical suggestion that the changes in the type of official could best be tested by the collection of career histories on an ingenious sample basis. It was he who organized the gathering of the élite sample of politicians, editors, civil servants of Uganda and Buganda governments, clergymen, teachers, doctors, lawyers and large landowners which he used to form the basis of the Carnegie leadership study. Later he made similar inquiries in the Turkish town of Edremit.

The practical abilities he showed in organizing field projects showed themselves in more mundane ways at the institute. He was the carpenter or electrician called in a crisis. He often serviced the cars of his junior and even his senior colleagues. He had had to work his way through university and seemed to have acquired training in every art needed for life in the East Africa of that time. He was an accomplished pastry cook and even knew how to "joint" a sucking pig brought as a gift by a visiting chief, since it appeared that in one vacation he had been a butcher's assistant.

Fallers was a beloved Director of the Uganda Institute. His power of work was enormous and he was generous to a fault with the time and ideas he gave to the Fellows.

A senior Colonial Office official, consulted whether it was suitable to have an American, and a rather young American, as Director of a British Institute, replied that there was such a "shining decency" about Fallers that it was impossible not to trust him completely and this is a quality which will remain in the minds of his friends and students. At the University of Chicago his devotion to teaching and learning brought him great respect from the young as well as the old. He was most steadfast through a long illness and, although his physical strength was much reduced, he continued his research and did his teaching on crutches and from a wheelchair.

He leaves a widow, Margaret Chave

Fallers, also an anthropologist, who wrote with him a paper entitled *Social Roles in Edremit (Turkey)*. She was for some years principal of the demonstration school attached to the University of Chicago. He is also survived by two daughters.

July 8, 1974.

Captain Cyril Falls, C.B.E., died on April 23, 1971, aged 83.

Scholar, author and soldier, he was Military Correspondent to *The Times* from 1939 until 1953, and was Chichele Professor of the History of War at Oxford from 1946 until 1953. As a military historian he had a high reputation; as a journalist he will be specially remembered not only for his contributions to *The Times* but for his popular weekly articles which appeared in the *Illustrated London News* for over 20 years.

Falls was a delightful man of modest and unassuming character, and a charming and loyal friend. He was slightly built and always immaculately turned out. All his life he cultivated a somewhat military air which was enhanced by a brushed-up moustache. He prided himself upon having had an excellent tailor for over 40 years, and he used to say he was not conceited about anything except his clothes. A stranger was often surprised to find, behind this façade of rather dry formality, his warm, friendly personality and charm, his cultivated and intelligent mind and his keen sense of humour.

His interests were as varied as his tastes were catholic. He read widely and voraciously, and had a vast knowledge of French as well as of English literature. He loved music, riding, sailing, shooting and racing, and he knew a good deal about them all.

Falls was the best of companions and a stimulating and amusing conversationalist, and he made devoted friends wherever he went.

Cyril Bentham Falls was born in 1888, the elder son of Sir Charles Fausset Falls who was for some years M.P. for Fermanagh and Tyrone.

He was educated at Bradfield College, Portora Royal School, Enniskillen, at London University and abroad.

When the Ulster Division was formed in the First World War Falls, then a clerk in the Foreign Office, joined the 11th Battalion of the Royal Inniskilling Fusiliers. He served in France with his regiment, and on the staff of the 36th and 62nd Divisions as liaison officer with the French. He was a happy choice for liaison duties; the French liked him, and he liked the French generals and staff officers and got on well with them. He was mentioned in dispatches twice and was awarded the French Croix de Guerre with two citations.

He has put it on record that all through the war he felt that, if he survived, he would like to take a hand in writing the official history of the operations. This field was opened to him when he was asked to write the history of the 36th Ulster Division. He did this work in the Historical Section of the Committee of Imperial Defence where the war diaries were kept. Sir James Edmonds, the head of the historical section, liked his book and in 1923 offered him a place on his staff, first as assistant and then as senior historian. Falls continued in this employment until December 1939 when he became Military Correspondent to *The Times* in succession to Captain Basil Liddell Hart.* Although he had never done inside press work before, he had been an occasional contributor for some 15 years to *The Times* and *The Times Literary Supplement*, and his writing was already familiar to readers of *The Times* in the articles from "A Military Correspondent" which had been appearing since the outbreak of the war.

During the war Falls wrote for *The Times* a long series of well informed commentaries on the strategic and tactical aspects of the operations. In collecting information for this task he was helped by friends who held senior appointments in the General Staff and who had learned that his discretion was complete and that he was absolutely trustworthy so far as secrecy was concerned.

In addition to his articles for *The Times*, Falls undertook a great deal of other work of a journalistic nature, and delivered many lectures and broadcast talks. His articles in the *Illustrated London News* dealt with a wide range of subjects to do with world affairs, and were more often than not of a non-military character.

In 1946 he was appointed Chichele Professor of the History of War at Oxford, and he held this post for seven years. During his first years at Oxford he found special pleasure in his association with undergraduates of the war generation, some of them ex-majors, who were up at that time.

His Fellowship of All Souls College and the friendships he made there were always a joy to him.

In 1941 he delivered the Lees Knowles lectures at Cambridge University, taking as his subject the methods of modern war; and, in 1942, he delivered the Ludwig Mond lectures at the University of Manchester on "War—Science, Art or Business?" He was appointed a Trustee of the Imperial War Museum in 1947, in succession to Lord Mottistone.*

Thereafter until the end of his life he always had at least one book on the stocks. Although his output was large everything he wrote was historically reliable and bore the stamp of his native shrewdness, fairness and impartiality.

He was created C.B.E. in 1967.

He married in 1915 Elizabeth Heath and they had two daughters.

April 24, 1971.

Emily Faulder, who died on December 30, 1974, aged 91, was one of the original Universal Aunts. The idea of providing "anything for anyone at any time" came to Miss Gertrude Maclean, and in February 1921 she founded Universal Aunts in a small office in Sloane Street, London.

She was soon joined by Miss Faulder and to the astonishment of their friends the venture throve and became a successful business. Miss Maclean died in 1953 but Miss Faulder remained an active member of the board until she was over 80.

At the outset the aunts were mostly asked to meet children, to pack, to shop, to chaperone and to walk dogs. Later they acquired a bigger office, a telephone and a typist and in 1922 were turned into a company. A domestic agency was started and during the Second World War Universal Aunts were constantly being called upon to pack up houses and help with the evacuation of children.

Today, the staff is much larger; there are "outside" aunts recruited on a part-time basis and contacts in the principal European countries; "operations" generally may be more diverse and sophisticated but the demand for children to be met, luggage to be traced, presents packed for "foreign parts" and journeys to be mapped out never slackens.

January 4, 1975.

Sir Roy Fedden, M.B.E., a pioneer of the aircraft industry, died on November 21, 1973 at the age of 88.

He will be particularly remembered for his work with the old Bristol Aeroplane Company, of which he was chief engineer from 1920 to 1942, a period which saw the appearance of a famous range of Bristol aircraft engines, ranging from the Jupiter to the Centaurus.

Alfred Hubert Roy Fedden was born on June 6, 1885, the son of Henry Fedden. He was educated at Clifton College and Merchant Venturers College, Bristol, and served a three-year engineering apprenticeship. He joined the Brazil Straker Company, the works of Straker-Squire, in 1907 as a draughtsman, and became technical director responsible for all motor vehicle design and production. From 1914 to 1918 the factory, under his direction, produced large numbers of Rolls-Royce, Renault and Curtiss aero engines.

In 1920 he joined the Bristol Aeroplane Company as chief engineer, with a staff of 32, to found the engine division, taking with him the Jupiter aero engine design. He was responsible for the initiation and development of all Bristol aero engines, including the Jupiter, Mercury, Pegasus, Perseus, Taurus, Hercules and Centaurus. These engines were made all over the world under licence and were used extensively by the R.A.F.

He was special technical adviser to the

Minister of Aircraft Construction 1942-45, having left Bristol after a disagreement. From 1945 to 1947 he did research for the Ministry of Supply. He was aeronautical adviser to Nato, 1952-53; and from 1953 to 1960 was aircraft consultant to the Dowty group.

Fedden was knighted in 1942 for his services to aviation. He received many awards and distinctions, among them the honorary D.Sc. of Bristol University, the Royal Aeronautical Society's silver medal, the Manly Gold medal and the Guggenheim Trophy.

President of the Royal Aeronautical Society 1938, 1939 and 1945, he was made an honorary fellow of the society in 1954. He was on the board of governors of the College of Aeronautics, Cranfield, 1964-69. He published *Britain's Air Survival* in 1957.

He married in 1948 Norah Lilian, third daughter of Edgar Crew, of Clifton.

November 22, 1973.

Ethel Sophia Fegan, sometime librarian at Cheltenham Ladies' College and Girton College, Cambridge, and in her day a notable figure in the library world, died on August 4, 1975.

She was born in 1877 and educated at Blackheath High School and Girton College, where she took the Classical Tripos in 1900. While librarian at Cheltenham Ladies' College, from 1908 to 1917, she inaugurated courses of professional training in librarianship for a succession of senior girls, establishing one of the earliest schools of librarianship in Britain. She also evolved a sensible library classification for schools, further developed by her successor Miss Monica Cant and published by them jointly as *The Cheltenham Classification.* This work proved a godsend to school librarians, as did her excellent practical *School Libraries.*

Subsequently Miss Fegan was for twelve years librarian at Girton College. She reorganized the Girton library on scientific lines, and did much work on incunabula in other Cambridge libraries for Dr. A. W. Pollard's *Short-title Catalogue.* She also devilled indefatigably for Dr. A. C. Haddon, both privately and in the University Museum of Archaeology and Ethnology, where together they built up what is now the valuable Haddon Library. Under Dr. Haddon's influence, she qualified in 1929 for the Cambridge Diploma in Anthropology and her work took a new direction.

After a sabbatical year in Northern Nigeria she became a pioneer in the first official attempt to give an education to Mohammedan girls brought up in the medieval atmosphere of the Northern Nigerian Emirates. The liveliness of the first school at Katsina and the friendship established with Emir Al Hajji Muhammad Diko, C.M.G., and his principal wife—a first pupil—and courtiers were something

entirely new and inspiring. Expansion quickly followed, with a training college at Sokoto, inaugurated first for teachers and next for housewives.

Her work in West Africa did not end with retirement from the official education service. She toured the Gold Coast training librarians, and did two spells of service in one of the largest leper settlements of the Northern Emirates, where her humanity and linguistic vivacity found full scope.

On her return to Britain she did voluntary work in the Cambridgeshire County Archives until she was over 90.

August 19, 1975.

Walter Felsenstein, the post-war creator and director of East Berlin's Komische Oper, died on October 8, 1975 at the age of 74.

Over the past 28 years, the name of Walter Felsenstein became synonymous with the phrase *realistisches Musiktheater,* his term for the kind of operatic staging which brought him world-wide fame. Many—perhaps most—operatic connoisseurs with international experience came to regard Felsenstein as a unique genius of the theatre, the greatest since Stanislavsky.

In the postwar operatic world, only Wieland Wagner* wielded an influence even comparable to his. Born on May 30, 1901 in Vienna, Felsenstein died in East Berlin leaving a yawning vacancy with no one even on the horizon who could fill it completely.

In staging opera, Felsenstein demanded equal legitimacy for both music and drama to produce a *Gesamtkunstwerk,* a work of art in which all elements have equal weight. Relatively few singing artists passed his fearsome duplex muster, but those who did affectionately addressed him as Chef and accorded him an almost fierce loyalty and devotion.

In 1947 the military government in Berlin's Soviet Sector invited Felsenstein to establish a new company, the Komische Oper, in the rebuilt Metropol Theater in the Behrenstrasse, just south of the Unter den Linden. In founding the company, which proved to be his greatest accomplishment and his monument, Felsenstein became one of numerous Berlin residents who lived in one sector and worked in another. He remained the Komische Oper's director until he died.

Political developments, particularly the cold war and in 1961 the Berlin Wall, exposed Felsenstein to much political sniping from the Western side, for no one else except Bertolt Brecht lent the fledgling German Democratic Republic such international cultural allure. When East Germany erected the wall, all West Berliners employed in East Berlin had to choose between moving East or losing their jobs. In direct confrontation, Felsenstein presented to Walter Ulbricht what amounted to an ultimatum. As a result, the Komische Oper

alone retained all its West Berlin personnel, including charwomen, with their status and salaries in no way altered. Such exceptions earned the Komische Oper an only half-jocular nickname: "the third German state".

Felsenstein received East Germany's highest decorations and prizes, and also honorary doctorates from the universities in East Berlin and Prague. Whereas other major German opera directors present about 60 different works during a season, Felsenstein restricted his repertory to 12 at any one time. Before unveiling a new production he rehearsed it, quite literally, just as long as he felt necessary—sometimes for months. A sharp-eyed assistant scrutinized every single performance, and acted upon his copious notes during the subsequent rehearsals, which continued just as long as a work remained in the repertory. Thanks to such perfectionism, a production's fiftieth —or 100th, or 200th—performance might prove even fresher and more vibrant than an opening night.

Admiring colleagues and critics have written several entire books and almost countless articles about Felsenstein's art. Operatic pilgrims from all over the world regarded as inimitable many Felsenstein productions, among them *The Magic Flute,* two *Carmens* (the first one with Otto Klemperer), *Othello, La Traviata,* and *Tales of Hoffman,* all of them done in the language Felsenstein's audience spoke and understood. He also had the ability to take relatively unfamiliar works, such as Janacek's *The Cunning Little Vixen,* Prokofiev's *The Love for Three Oranges* or Offenbach's *Barbe-Bleu,* and stage them unforgettably. In recent years Felsenstein also resumed work in the dramatic theatre, in Munich and Vienna. Two former Felsenstein assistants, Götz Friedrich and Joachim Herz, remain in the forefront of operatic staging today.

Felsenstein is survived by his wife, Maria, and a son, Johannes.

October 10, 1975.

Fernandel, who must stand alongside Raimu and Jacques Tati as one of the best and most successful film comedians that France has ever produced, died in Paris on February 26, 1971 at the age of 67.

Before his last illness he was making the fifth in the series of Don Camillo films by which he will best be remembered. In them he played the part of a French priest, devious and full of native cunning, who was at loggerheads with the local communist leader. First in the series was *The Little World of Don Camillo* which he made in 1951.

His real name was Fernand Joseph Contandin and he was born in Marseilles on May 8, 1903. He was interested in acting from childhood, and organized theatricals when he was a schoolboy. After he had completed his military service, he toured the provinces as a singer and finally reached Paris in 1928 where he was given the chance to appear in a revue at the Concert Maytol. This led to a part in Sacha Guitry's film *Le Blanc et le Noir* which was produced by Marc Allegret in 1930. His was essentially a film comedian's face—long, expressive, comic and at times mournful, with a protruding jaw and tombstone teeth. His ability as a comedian was at once apparent, and it was his good fortune that it was recognized by some of the leading French film directors of the day. And notably by Marcel Pagnol.

For the first few years of his film career he was seen only as a comedian, but his considerable potential as a character actor was revealed when he played Saturnin in Pagnol's *Angèle* in 1933. It was chiefly as a comedian, however, that he was seen thereafter in a long succession of films stretching over a period of more than 40 years (he is said to have appeared in nearly 150). He became to France a comedian as native to his southern background as George Formby* was to the north of England. During the 1930s he was often seen in films that burlesqued the military way of life, and he also appeared as an honest, knockabout funny man in broad stories of lower class life.

Such parts came easily to him. Perhaps too easily, for he was capable of a far more exacting challenge.

His international fame was not long delayed. His name was to be found in the leading American film magazines by the end of the 1930s, after America had seen such films as Pagnol's *Harvest,* made in 1939, and *The Well Digger's Daughter,* in 1940, another Pagnol comedy in which he appeared with Raimu. In 1958 he was seen opposite Bob Hope in *Paris Holiday,* by which time his horselike countenance was known to filmgoers throughout the world.

But to the French he remained their own especial comedian, and this was confirmed when he was awarded a Legion of Honour for his work as a *marchand de bonheur* ("a trader in happiness"). He certainly brought enjoyment to millions during his long career on the screen.

March 2, 1971.

Jose Maria Ferreira de Castro, one of Portugal's leading writers and an outstanding democrat, died on June 30, 1974, aged 77.

Ferreira de Castro, born of a humble family, emigrated to Brazil when he was 12 years old. He first made a living in the Amazonian jungle as best he might, and continued his hazardous career in Belem at the age of 15. Among other things he turned his hand to bill-sticking, working on tramp steamers and writing for local newspapers about his experiences. He returned to Portugal in 1919 and continued his journalistic career.

A serial novel published in Belem in 1916 was followed by other stories and novels, and in 1930 his first major work *A Selva* was published. The novel, describing life in the Brazilian jungle, was translated into English under the title *Green Hell* and, with French, German and other European editions, sold hundreds of thousands of copies enabling him to travel freely.

He was a steady opponent of the Salazar* regime, but turned down a proposal that he stand for the presidency of the republic in 1958, the year when the late General Humberto Delgado* took up the challenge. He was elected president of the Portuguese Writers Society in 1962.

Other of his works include the novels *Emigrants, Eternity* and *Cold Land.* His last appearance was on May 1, 1974, when liberated Portugal celebrated its first free May Day for half a century. Ferreira de Castro was prominent among the crowd milling down Lisbon's central Avenida da Leberdade wearing a red carnation, symbol of the armed forces movement which brought in the new government.

July 4, 1974.

Sir Paul Fildes, O.B.E., F.R.S., former Director of Chemical Bacteriology at the Medical Research Council, died on February 5, 1971 at the age of 88.

During the Second World War he was a vigorous leader in the work on bacteriological warfare.

Paul Fildes, born in London in 1882, was the second son of Sir Luke Fildes, K.C.V.O., R.A., the painter. He went to Winchester, Trinity College, Cambridge and the London Hospital. As a medical student there he was attracted to research and indeed dabbled in it in William Bulloch's laboratory. After qualification in 1909 he joined Bulloch as an assistant bacteriologist and embarked upon what was to be over half a century of microbiological research.

The science of medical bacteriology was then in the first flush of its maturity, and Fildes soon established himself as one furthering its consolidation. Like other great bacteriologists of his generation, Fildes began by tackling the problems immediately to hand; his intellectual attitudes were formed and his interests focused during their solution. With James McIntosh, he spent the prewar years in extensive work on syphilitic infections, particularly syphilis of the nervous system; and on the treatment of the disease with Ehrlich's newly discovered arsenical compounds.

During the 1914-18 war he worked as a pathologist at the Royal Naval Hospital, Haslar, first as a civilian and then as a Surgeon Lieutenant-Commander in the R.N.V.R. Here the work to hand was the laboratory investigation of the large numbers of sufferers from dysentery invalided home from the Gallipoli campaign.

He returned in 1919, with a military O.B.E., to his post at the London Hospital; and his interests began to shift from clinical to those of microbial biochemistry, the field of his best contributions to science. Microbial biochemistry and genetics, later to be of outstanding importance in medical as well as general microbiology, were then embryonic. The flourishing state of British microbial chemistry today owes much to two pioneers: the biochemist Marjorie Stephenson, who at Cambridge concentrated largely on microbial enzymes, and Fildes, who concentrated on bacterial nutrition. Fildes's interest in nutrition was generated by his immediate postwar study of factors needed for the artificial culture of the influenza bacilli. These growth factors are obviously essential nutrients of the bacteria, which have to be supplied because the microbes themselves cannot synthesize them.

Next came his classical proof that tetanus bacilli grow in the animal body only when the tissues lose the oxidizing power which in normal tissue can suppress the essential metabolism of the bacilli. The value of a biochemical approach to microbiological problems was evident to Fildes; and in 1934 the Medical Research Council established for him a unit for bacterial chemistry at the Bland Sutton Institute of the Middlesex Hospital. With a staff that included B. C. J. G. Knight and Donald Woods, he investigated a number of bacterial growth factors, among them gases, vitamins and amino-acids; discovered a number of essential nutrients of known composition; and determined the sequence of enzyme reactions whereby a microbe synthesizes a complex substance from simpler chemicals. These were outstanding contributions to bacterial chemistry.

The 1939-45 war dispersed the unit, but not before Fildes had formulated a strategy for chemotherapy on the basis of the unit's work. Arguing from the dependence of the sequence of vital enzymic reactions on the supply of essential metabolites, he postulated that an essential metabolite of known structure might after chemical modification be no longer usable for growth, but would still combine with the appropriate enzyme and thus, by blocking an essential metabolic process, kill the microbe.

The strategy was based on Donald Woods's proof that the sulphonamide drugs act in this way. The strategy, which is still valid in principle, was successfully applied in that a number of inhibitors of bacterial growth were devised; but it has not been very successful in revealing new chemotherapeutic agents for treating infections, because most inhibitors devised in this way have proved to be toxic for the animal as well.

At the outbreak of the 1939-45 War, Fildes was one of the few senior bacteriologists in Britain who foresaw the need to counter the potential threat of bacteriological warfare. He wanted active study of the potentialities and limitations of possible agents as weapons, so that defences against the most likely forms of attack could be devised. He found it difficult to get support for research of this kind from his employer, the Medical Research Council. The Council was understandably but, in view of the reality of the threat, exaggeratedly reluctant to associate itself with even defensive work on what was regarded as a morally indefensible perversion of medical knowledge. By an informal compromise Fildes was in effect seconded to the Ministry of Supply and went with some of his immediate colleagues to the research establishment at Porton Down. Though he habitually denied any directorial role, Fildes was in fact a vigorous leader in the work on bacteriological warfare; and at the end of the war, when these activities were transferred to the new, separate Microbiological Research Establishment at Porton, he remained for many years its active adviser, and was for even longer the father figure of the establishment.

After three more years as director of the Bacterial Chemistry Unit, reconstituted in 1946 at the Lister Institute, he retired at the age of 67 to Howard (Lord) Florey's* Department of Pathology at Oxford, where for 13 years he worked fruitfully on virology. With characteristic caution, for in research Fildes always took the most immediate step from the known to the unknown, he chose to work on bacterial viruses, applying the techniques for exploring essential nutrients of bacteria to finding substances essential for their infection by viruses.

Fildes liked to be an independent worker with his own small group of colleagues. This liking is evident too in his founding, with three close colleagues, of the *British Journal of Experimental Pathology* in 1920, a journal independent of both supporting societies and publishers. He was a superb editor of that journal, as indeed he was of the great nine-volume *System of Bacteriology* published by the Medical Research Council in 1931.

Fildes was elected to the Royal Society in 1934, received its Royal Medal in 1953, and, at the age of 81, the Society's highest honour, the Copley Medal. He had the honorary degrees and fellowships of scientific societies usual to a person of his distinction.

Paul Fildes was by nature and upbringing conservative in outlook. In science he was conservative only in his almost doctrinaire scepticism; in all else he was a genuine progressive, his prejudices always yielding to logic. He was intellectually modest— once in private he questioned the propriety of his being a Copley Medallist in the same class as Pasteur—but justifiably proud of his achievements and a little vain about them. Some found him difficult; to most he was reserved and rather uncompromising in manner, with a quiet ruminative way of speaking that never varied, even in anger or when, as sometimes happened, he was being devastatingly rude. Those who got to know him had for him a lasting, if occa-

sionally rueful, affection, for he was a good friend, and a good companion with a charm and a sardonic humour of his own; and he revealed himself to them as a rigorously honest, kindly and generous man, He was unmarried.

February 6, 1971.

Professor H. P. R. Finberg, general editor of the *Agrarian History of England and Wales,* died on November 1, 1974 at the age of 74.

He was Emeritus Professor of English Local History at Leicester University.

Herbert Patrick Reginald Finberg was born at Rickmansworth on March 21, 1900, the son of Turner's biographer. His artistic inheritance found expression in his first career in the design and production of books. After only a third class in Lit. Hum. at Oxford he had to abandon hopes of working in academic philosophy, and went to work with Basil Blackwell and Bernard Newdigate at the Shakespeare Head Press before setting up his own press, the Alcuin, in a barn at Chipping Campden.

He strove there to print at the highest standards without having all the type handset, and cheerfully undertook jobbing printing alongside such well-received editions as Housman's *Poems* of 1929. In 1936 his press moved to Welwyn but foundered in the slump. He then became a director of the Broadwater Press, their Twickenham edition of Pope being a product of this period. In 1944 he became editorial director of Burnes Oates and Washbourne, where his life-long devotion to Roman Catholicism found expression in a series of liturgical works. At the same time his advisory work to H.M. Printers and the Ministry of Works is revealed in the elegant pages of such diverse publications as the *Coronation Service* (1953) and the Ministry of Works *Post-war Building Studies: the Housing Manual.*

His spare-time interests were at the same time unconsciously laying the foundation for his second career, as an academic historian, which began at the age of 52. One university librarian, introduced to Finberg "the master topographer", was amazed to find later that he had been talking to a Finberg whom he knew as the master typographer. The interest in local history had been first aroused by the genealogy of his wife's family, an inquiry which took him from Bedfordshire to Devon, and to the records of the Duke of Bedford's estates kept in London and Tavistock. Wartime holidays in Devon provided opportunity for fieldwork, and firewatching in Welwyn the occasion for writing, and by 1949 *Tavistock Abbey* was completed. At meetings of the Devon Association he began his own, and most fruitful, Devon association with W. G. Hoskins, then lecturer in economic history at Leicester. Their collection of essays, *Devonshire Studies,* proved to be a

formative volume in making English local history a respectable academic subject, demonstrating a union of conventional scholarly skills with a keen sense of local topography and the open air. When Hoskins went to Oxford in 1952 Finberg was strongly supported by Tawney* and Stenton as successor to him as Reader and Head of the Department of English Local History, although some academic eyebrows were raised at the appointment of someone without teaching experience.

By the time of his retirement in 1965 Finberg had served the University of Leicester and the cause of local history well. Six books of his own were not sufficient: he drew on his earlier publishing experience to launch and edit a brilliant series of *Occasional Papers in Local History;* to launch the *Agricultural History Review,* which he edited for 11 years; and the massive project for an *Agrarian History of England* of which he became general editor. From 1966-68 he was president of the British Agricultural History Society. In 1963 he was elevated to a chair, a recognition which did something to assuage his deep-rooted belief that academics were prejudiced against him by his late arrival in their midst.

Finberg also had the rare pleasure of delivering two inaugural lectures, one as Head in 1952 and one as Professor in 1964.

He had a very full retirement, not being one to rest on Emeritus laurels. Having seen the Tudor volume of the *Agrarian History* off the press in 1967 he took on editing and contributing to the volume dealing with the difficult earliest period. He also became a part-time research assistant at Leeds, working with Maurice Beresford on their handlist of medieval boroughs, and in 1968-69 was a Fellow of Clare Hall, Cambridge.

Finberg was a member of a committee of specialist advisers to the Vatican Council on vernacular liturgies. His *Manual of Catholic Prayer* (1962) was awarded the Belgian *Prix Graphica* in 1965: the translation was Finberg's own, a complement to the text of *The Missal in Latin and English* which he had published in 1949.

Himself so precise, imprecision in others offended his scholarly sense and he always took readily to controversy, theological as well as academic. An amiable man, he criticized others from the highest motives and was sometimes surprised that when one attacked the naughty academic animal it defended itself, and he sometimes corrected another's error as if he were correcting an errant galley proof. But precision did not mean pedantry, and he had a cheerful appreciation of the follies of mankind and, strange as it may seem to those who only knew him distantly, Finberg saw Finberg as part of mankind.

He married in 1933 Joscelyne Henrietta Prideaux Payne. They had two sons.

November 5, 1974.

Sir Morris Finer, a judge of the Family Division of the High Court and chairman of the Royal Commission on the Press, died in hospital on December 15, 1974. It was only in the previous summer that the committee on the one-parent family, of which he was chairman, reported.

In his death at only 57, the legal world has suffered a most grievous loss.

He was one of the outstanding members of the Bar in the post-war period and achieved a high reputation as an advocate in the heavy commercial cases in which he was engaged before his elevation to the Bench in December 1972.

He will be sadly missed by many friends at the Bar and elsewhere, where his friendly and genial personality endeared him to all.

The son of Charles Finer, he was educated at Kilburn and the London School of Economics, from which he graduated in 1939. He had an abiding interest in the school, becoming a governor in 1964 and vice-chairman in 1970.

He was called to the Bar by Gray's Inn in 1943 and soon acquired a large practice at the common law bar. He became an expert on company law and industry.

After taking silk in 1963 he took part in many leading trade union and industrial cases.

Finer was counsel for the Transport Salaried Staffs' Association when the Court of Appeal sat for the first time on a Sunday in May 1972 to hear appeals from the National Industrial Relations Court in the railway ballot case.

He was made a Bencher of his Inn in 1971, and his appointment as a High Court judge came as no surprise. Assigned as he was to the Family Division, his deep interest in social conditions and wide knowledge of social security legislation proved of great value to him in his work on the Bench.

He was noted for his tireless capacity to work a day of 16 or 17 hours. After his appointment as chairman of the Press Commission he continued as a judge.

Sir Morris obtained first hand knowledge of newspapers in two ways. As a young barrister he did part-time journalism on the London *Evening Standard* mainly as a leader writer.

Later Sir Morris was briefed as counsel in cases involving newspapers and unions in the industry.

He leaves a widow, whom he married in 1943, and two sons.

December 16, 1974.

Bram Fischer, the former Johannesburg Q.C. and head of the South African Communist Party which is banned in that country, died on May 8, 1975.

He was 67.

Fischer, a member of one of the nation's most respected Afrikaner families, was con-victed in 1966 of conspiring to commit sabotage and overthrow the government violently, and of 14 subsidiary charges of furthering the aims of the Communist Party. He was sentenced to life imprisonment.

The quality of mercy was strained when at the age of 65 he was taken from prison to a Pretoria hospital suffering from terminal cancer. Although visiting restrictions were lifted so that his immediate family could see him, a police guard remained close by. He was still technically a prisoner.

He died at his brother's home in Bloemfontein, where he was transferred from a prison hospital in March, a statement issued by the Commissioner of Prisons said.

He was cared for by his family after the mounting of a prolonged campaign for his release from the restriction of the hospital. But he was still classified as a prisoner and under the conditions laid down by the Government was due to return to the prison on June 10.

Fischer was born on April 23, 1908 in Bloemfontein. His grandfather, Abraham Fischer, was a member of the Cabinet in the first Union government and his father, Pieter Fischer, a Judge President of the Orange Free State. Fischer grew up in the strong Calvinistic, Afrikaner tradition and followed the family footsteps into law. He studied at the University College of the Orange Free State for his B.A. and LL.B. In 1932, he was awarded a Rhodes Scholarship to Oxford. He spent five years there and it was at Oxford that his views began to change.

During the 1940s and early postwar years he quietly practised his profession without attracting too much attention.

In the early 1960s he entered the limelight as leading defence counsel in the Rivonia sabotage trial, at which Nelson Mandela, leader of the African National Council in South Africa, and Walter Sisulu, head of the "spear of the nation" organization, were imprisoned for life.

A few months later Fischer found himself in the same dock at the Pretoria Supreme Court, accused with 12 other whites of being a member of the Communist Party and of taking part in acts to further the party's aims.

At the end of 1964, Fischer was granted £5,000 bail to appear in a case in London before the Privy Council. He returned to the country the following January but absconded until the following November when he was arrested in Johannesburg heavily disguised.

He had been one of South Africa's most wanted men. His subsequent trial lasted four months.

Fischer was awarded a Lenin Peace Prize in 1966.

His wife Molly died in a car crash in 1965 and his son, Paul, from an illness in April 1971.

May 9, 1975.

Archbishop Lord Fisher of Lambeth, who died on September 15, 1972 at the age of 85, was little known to the general public when in 1945 he succeeded William Temple as Archbishop of Canterbury.

It soon became apparent that his primacy was to be distinguished by essentially different qualities from those of his predecessor: Temple's great contribution had been moral and intellectual leadership, the influence of which extended far beyond the domain of the Church of England; Fisher's was first-class administration. He brought to his office the temperament and gifts of a great headmaster; he combined generous humanity and a completely unaffected manner with a passion for order and efficiency.

At Fisher's accession, the Church of England, which had received at Temple's hands the ministrations of a prophet, was in urgent need of a thorough-going practical reform and it was this need that the new Primate set out to supply. During his tenure of office, Fisher raised the stipends of the clergy, eliminating extreme inequalities in the process; he inaugurated an elaborate revision of the Canon Law designed to clarify and strengthen the legal foundations of the Church of England's unity; he threw himself with zeal into the ecumenical movement, concentrating his attention at first on limited and specific plans for bringing the Church of England and the Free Churches into union by a gradual process of coalescence.

Later, he directed his attention increasingly to improving relations with Protestant and Orthodox Churches abroad, and one of the last acts of his Archbishopric was a visit to the Pope in December 1960 which has had a marked and beneficial effect on relations with the Roman Catholic communion. His pronouncements on social and political matters were comparatively rare and often open to the charge of being gravely misjudged. The price of his wholesome disapproval of slackness or eccentricity in the clergy was a tendency to favour docile subordinates, a tendency from which the Church suffered in proportion as the Archbishop's influence on ecclesiastical appointments grew. The good-natured firmness with which he exerted power won him many admirers but also caused intense irritation to men with more introverted dispositions than his own. His achievements were solid and are likely to endure.

Geoffrey Francis Fisher, who was born on May 5, 1887, was the youngest son of the Rev. H. Fisher, Rector of Higham-on-the-Hill, Nuneaton; thus he was brought up in a rectory, although he never became an incumbent himself. He was educated at Marlborough, and Exeter College, Oxford, where he won an open scholarship. He gained three first classes, in Moderations, Greats, and Theology, and was Liddon Scholar in 1911. He was also captain of his college boat club, and in 1908 rowed in the trial eights. After a year at Wells Theological College, he was ordained and returned to Marlborough as an assistant master. In 1914, at the early age of 27, he was appointed headmaster of Repton, succeeding Temple, whom he was also destined to succeed at Lambeth 40 years later.

Fisher had never courted public notice at Repton and much surprise was felt at his appointment in 1932 to the Bishopric of Chester. He was well liked in that diocese, however, and the close personal interest which he showed in the clergy under his care combined with his administrative prowess to make it clear that he was cut out for the role of pastor pastorum. In 1926 he already showed his preoccupation with clerical remuneration by telling his diocesan conference that, if he were dictator, he would make every benefice carry the same stipend, with additional allowances for length of service and special claims. Men who saw Fisher at work soon began to say that he was marked out for substantial preferment.

This came in 1939 when he was appointed Bishop of London in succession to Dr. Winnington-Ingram. London has its own problems of which, notoriously, the chief is clerical dissent from the provisions of the Book of Common Prayer. The diocese has a tradition of ritualism which largely explains the humorous description of Anglo-Catholicism as the "London, Brighton and South-Coast religion". Winnington-Ingram had been a mild man, and there was leeway for a zealous devotee of the principle of apostolic authority to make up.

More formidable still, however, were the tasks presented by the war and the aerial bombardment of London. The bishop went about his duties with a calm diligence which won general respect, and returned each night to sleep in the cellar at Fulham Palace. He welcomed that improvement in inter-Church relations in Britain which the war and the energetic leadership of Archbishop Temple were bringing about and acted as chairman of the joint standing committee in which the Anglican and Free Church "Religion and Life" movement cooperated with the Roman Catholic "Sword of the Spirit" in the cause of moral regeneration and social reform.

It is no secret that on the sudden death of Temple in 1945 the vacancy of Canterbury was offered, almost as a matter of course, to Garbett, the incumbent of York, but that, for reasons of age, the offer was declined. Fisher, with his record of outstanding success in the episcopal office, was in these circumstances the natural choice. In the years that followed he and his brother at York cooperated in the government of the Church in an unusually close manner made possible by strong mutual regard. Garbett had a wider knowledge of social affairs and was more at home than Fisher in the disputed territory which lies between religion and politics. Fisher was happy to have his hands free for the task of refurbishing the administrative structure of the Church.

Apart from his universally admitted success in grappling with the problem of clerical stipends, he had one other achievement which few contested to his credit; he was a perfect ambassador of the Church of England and indeed of the English nation during his numerous travels abroad.

The bitter controversy which was provoked by his policy of Canon Law revision and his support for the recognition (subject to safeguards) of the Church of South India is only to be understood by considering the general strategy in Church affairs which his critics attributed to him. In 1946 he preached a university sermon at Cambridge on the theme that union between the Church of England and the Free Churches was possible and ought to be pursued, and he invited the Free Churches to take episcopacy into their system. The blessings which, after much reserve, he gave to the new Church of South India founded on a coalition between Anglican and Free Church missionaries pointed in the same direction, and so did his zealous support of the World Council of Churches.

All this invited from Anglo-Catholics the charges of pan-Protestantism, and the vigour with which the Archbishop criticized the exclusiveness of the Church of Rome seemed to confirm this. Accordingly the right-wing of the Church of England was from the first suspicious. Ritualists were further disturbed by the laborious and detailed revision of Canon Law to which Fisher devoted so much energy. They thought that he was permitting, under a guise of liberalism, certain modest deviations from the Book of Common Prayer merely in order to get an excuse for enforcing conformity more vigorously than before. In the name of the middle way, they said, he was plotting the destruction of the Anglo-Catholic movement as a prelude to the creation of an unequivocally Protestant National Church and its absorption in a loose federation of Churches without even the common bond of episcopacy.

Liberals in the Church found equal cause for complaint; to them the Canon Law reforms were an instance of bureaucracy run riot. They thought that a regime of prosecutions and petty persecutions was about to be instituted.

Fisher had excellent answers to both kinds of critic, answers which satisfied the overwhelming majority of churchmen. As an adherent of the ecumenical movement it was his duty to seek unity with all who were willing to unite. When at length he thought the time was ripe, he took the dramatic step of visiting the Pope, and the moving manner in which he described his reception left no doubt of the sincerity of his wish to heal the breach with Rome. It is not too much to say that the whole atmosphere of relations between the two Churches was revolutionized by Fisher's visit.

To the charge of authoritarianism in his approach to Church government Fisher could reply that a measure of order is inseparable from the nature of a Church and that to want to define laws clearly is not the same thing as wanting to enforce them fanatically. A state of affairs in which the Anglican worshipper on holiday can find the Holy Communion being celebrated in a parish church in a largely unfamiliar manner is a grave handicap to the Church's mission. By allowing regulated experiments in liturgical reform, Fisher hoped to bring the Church's practice back to that degree of uniformity which is an essential feature of the true Anglican tradition. Nevertheless there were those who felt that his good-natured candour and his benign authoritarianism were better suited to a headmaster then to an Archbishop.

Fisher carried out the ceremonies of the Coronation with a dignity which impressed all. In the later years of his episcopacy, however, his public pronouncements often caused controversy and some regretted the disappearance of the stabilizing influence of Garbett's political experience.

The popular verdict might be "a good-natured, somewhat bossy man" and such a judgment would certainly have won an appreciative smile from Fisher himself. There were those who thought he had the qualities of Martha rather than Mary, yet a Church needs its administrators no less than its prophets and its mystics. None could doubt that the self-assured manner, the capacity for calm leadership and the almost incredible industry of the late Archbishop sprang from a strong personal faith, a faith which had never for a second been disturbed by doubt.

On his retirement, which took place on May 31, 1961, Fisher was appointed to a life peerage. He went to live at the village of Trent in Dorset, in the rectory. He was not rector but shared the ministrations with the incumbent. He slipped easily and happily into country life. But his interest in church matters in general and in public affairs remained keen, and his interventions were often controversial.

This was particularly the case with what some took to be his change of position over church unity (although his quarrel was really with the turn taken by Anglican-Methodist negotiations.) As early as 1964 he issued a pamphlet in which he argued that it would be a mistake to proceed to stage II of the Anglican-Methodist scheme for unity, the stage of "organic union". Full communion without merging was goal enough. And he drew a distinction on which he was to continue to insist between union, which he thought a mistake, and unity, which he sought.

Speaking a little later before a Methodist synod Fisher's successor, Dr. Ramsey, expressed surprise at his view that intercommunion was sufficient goal in itself; and he quoted opposition to that opinion from a report of the 1958 Lambeth Conference over which Fisher had presided.

Fisher, however, was undeterred by this rebuke; and a little later he produced another pamphlet in which he described the projected Service of Reconciliation between Anglicans and Methodists as a "pious subterfuge: pious and sincere, but still a subterfuge".

He remained fully ecumenical in outlook, but stuck firmly to his view of the correct means of seeking church unity. It was a position towards which opinion in the Church of England has tended to move.

In 1917 Fisher married Rosamund Forman, daughter of a Repton master and granddaughter of a former headmaster. There were six sons of the marriage.

September 16, 1972.

The Rt. Rev. J. E. Fison, Bishop of Salisbury since 1963, died on July 2, 1972 at the age of 66.

Joseph Edward Fison was born on March 18, 1906, the son of F. F. Fison, and educated at Orley Farm Preparatory School, Shrewsbury, and Queen's College, Oxford, to which he won a scholarship. Leaving with a second in Greats and a first in Theology, he taught for a time at the English Missionary College in Cairo; returned to Oxford to be ordained in 1934; and spent the next six years there, on the staff of Wycliffe Hall and St. Aldate's. There followed a period of war service as an Army Chaplain in the Middle East; and as senior Chaplain in Jerusalem he acted as guide to the Holy Places to thousands of serving soldiers and airmen.

During these years he had been outgrowing the older-fashioned evangelicalism in which he had been brought up, and he gradually fused in his own person the prophet and the mystic, the evangelical and the catholic.

For seven years after the war he was a Canon Residentiary of Rochester Cathedral, and then moved into the west country to become Sub-Dean of Truro Cathedral, where he enjoyed the Cornish as much as they enjoyed him.

In 1959, after being offered and having accepted the chancellorship of Lincoln Cathedral, he was "hi-jacked" by authority to Cambridge to succeed Mervyn Stockwood at Great St. Mary's. This was a move which accorded with his genius, and he did the job with distinction.

When his appointment to the See of Salisbury was announced many of his friends thought that a racehorse was being harnessed to the shafts of a farm wagon. But he shouldered the burden of a large rural diocese with dogged devotion. He was indeed apt to punctuate his sermons to country congregations with impish allusions which left them mystified, but after the service would win all hearts at a social gathering in the village hall. He would greet a Salvation Army guest to the Diocesan Conference with shouts of "Alleluia"; and rely upon his friends to pacify bemused and indignant parents after a public school confirmation. Embarrassing to his detrac-

tors, his sallies were endearing to those who understood and loved him.

He suffered agonies as much from his own "gaffes" as from the quarrels and tragedies which beset a bishop's path. He was literally prostrated by international incidents such as the Suez crisis.

When it was proposed to give him an Honorary Doctorate at Aberdeen, some Scottish Divines feared that they might be honouring a lightweight, but in the event were captivated not only by his wit and charm, but because they found themselves in the presence of a prophet.

He was in demand as a speaker at clergy gatherings and had a way of leading his hearers on to believe that he was in full sympathy with their favourite notions or cherished prejudices and then shooting them down with a barbed arrow, not from spite, but because he knew that all fall short of the fullness of truth.

His knowledge of the Bible was profound, and he continually pleaded for a full-orbed biblical perspective as against the flatness of favourite texts and wrested meanings.

His books were an original contribution to imaginative theology. Beneath the surface of *The Blessing of the Holy Spirit* can be discerned the course of his own spiritual and intellectual pilgrimage. *The Christian Hope* is a study of the Second Coming of Christ and its implications for the individual and society, its *leit motif* characteristically drawn from Feste's song—"Journeys end in lovers' meeting".

His paper-back *The Faith of the Bible* is a fine piece of exposition, and received praise from the most fastidious critics.

Fison was in the happiest sense a family man. In 1944 he married Monica Irene Stober. They had two daughters and two sons.

July 3, 1972.

Bernard Fitzalan-Howard, 16th Duke of Norfolk—See Norfolk.

Allan Flanders, C.B.E., who died on September 29, 1973, at the age of 63, was an outstanding authority on trade unions and industrial relations.

His writings, which were stamped by a controlled clarity of argument, and his teaching, which inspired other entrants to this expanding field of study, were highly influential. He made seminal contributions to theoretical analysis of the British system of industrial relations and to the debate about policy proposals for its reform.

Political as well as academic commitments featured prominently in Flanders's life, and he served as chairman of the editorial board of *Socialist Commentary*, the influential monthly of moderate Labour Party opinion from 1950 until his death. In that capacity he worked closely with Rita

Hinden (the journal's editor for many years), editorials of their joint composition often achieving a rare fusion of penetrating analysis and passionate conviction.

He was Reader in Industrial Relations, Warwick University from 1971. Earlier he was Senior Lecturer in Industrial Relations at Oxford (1949-69); Faculty Fellow, Nuffield College (1964-69) and Visiting Professor of Industrial Relations, Manchester University (1969-71).

Allan David Flanders was born of working class parents on July 27, 1910; he followed a conventional path of elementary and secondary education up to the age of 18, culminating in two years at the Latymer School, Hammersmith, and an Intermediate B.Sc.

He spent two years studying philosophy, political history and economics at an international adult college near Kassel, set up by the German philosopher and educationalist, Leonard Nelson, as an experiment in a particularly free type of educational method. The ethical convictions and the socratic method of instruction which he brought away from the "Walkemuehle", as it was called, thenceforward determined his social and political beliefs and his rigorous analytical approach to them.

For a period Flanders earned his living as an engineering draughtsman and designer and was active in the Association of Engineering and Shipbuilding Draughtsmen. In 1943 came his appointment as Research Assistant to the T.U.C., and in this capacity he drafted the greater part of the 1944 T.U.C. Report on Post War Reconstruction, together with some of the more detailed statements in 1945. After three years at the T.U.C. he spent eighteen months as Director of the German Political Branch of the British Control Commission, going from there to the U.S.A. on a Whitney Foundation Fellowship to study research and education in American unions. In 1949 he took up a Senior Lectureship in Industrial Relations at Oxford University.

For Flanders himself, writing was a slow and arduous task (partly because of the extreme logical rigour which he brought to it) and his publications do not really reflect his influence. They include *Trade Unions,* joint editorship with H. A. Clegg and a contributing chapter to *The System of Industrial Relations in Britain;* contribution to *Comparative Labour Movements* (ed. by W. Galenson); *Contemporary Collective Bargaining,* (ed. by W. Sturmthal); and *The Fawley Productivity Agreements.*

This work crystallized much of Flanders's thought and ensured its wider recognition. Its concluding chapter on the wider lessons of productivity bargaining has been described as a classic in the industrial relations literature.

Two of its leading themes—(a) the importance of work-place bargaining and (b) the responsibility of management to secure the consent of unions to proposed changes in working practices—were taken up by the Donovan Commission Report on Trade

Unions and Employers' Associations in 1968.

In his own evidence to Donovan, Flanders outlined the case for creating a public agency to stimulate, without imposing, essential reforms of collective bargaining procedures. This eventually became the task of the Commission on Industrial Relations, on which Flanders served as a full-time member from 1969 to 1971. His imprint there was formative, both in setting the commission's objectives and the methods of work and in shaping its organization. Other books to appear in this period included *Experiment in Industrial Democracy: A Study of the John Lewis Partnership* (with Ruth Pomeranz and Joan Woodward), *Management and Unions,* and a Penguin collection of readings on Collective Bargaining.

Suddenly struck down by paraplegic disablement in 1970, Allan Flanders bore the many ensuing tribulations, including pain of intense severity, with fortitude and hope. In this he was sustained by the devoted care of his wife, Anne Marie.

Flanders was a man of massive integrity whose unshakable principles nevertheless remained rooted in a strong practical sense. Although not a man readily to reveal himself, he set the highest value on friendship and in the course of his life was a strong personal influence in the lives of many people. The nature of his experience and the quality of his mind, which moved with power and deliberation to produce results of sometimes deceptive simplicity, made him in some ways one of the most unusual factors at work in the background of the postwar labour movement scene.

October 2, 1973.

Michael Flanders, the actor and lyricwriter, who died on April 14, 1975 at the age of 53, was long familar on the London stage, particularly in the two-man entertainment with Donald Swann, where he described himself as "the big one with the beard who writes all the words and does most of the talking" (both of them, he said, "for want of a better word", sang). Since a severe attack of poliomyelitis while serving in the R.N.V.R. during 1943, he had been confined permanently to a wheelchair.

Born in London in March 1922 and educated at Westminster School and Christ Church, Oxford, (where he read History), he directed and acted for University societies and began as a professional at the Oxford Playhouse in 1941 as Valentine in *You Never Can Tell.* Later he served as an able seaman in a destroyer on convoys to Russia and Malta, and—after his ship was torpedoed during the African landings —as an officer in Coastal Forces. Now, he contracted polio; at last, when out of hospital, he became a writer, and later a broadcaster.

Donald Swann, a light composer and accompanist, had been with Flanders at Westminster (they put on a revue there in 1940) and the pair started a professional collaboration with material for various intimate revues, particularly for three devised by Laurier Lister: *Penny Plain* (St. Martin's, 1951), to which, among other things, they contributed "Surly Girls" with decor by Ronald Searle, and "Prehistoric Complaint"; *Airs on a Shoestring* (Royal Court, 1953), for which they were the principal writers (and in which Max Adrian sang "Excelsior" and the company joined in "Guide To Britten"); and *Fresh Airs* (Comedy, 1956), where again, most of the work was their own.

Presently—and this was the zenith of their association—they became performers themselves. On New Year's Eve, 1956, they put on a new show *At The Drop of a Hat,* described as an "after-dinner farrago", and modestly presented and wittily filled out; it opened on the bare stage of the little New Lindsey Theatre at Notting Hill Gate but went on at once to the West End and a run of 759 performances. It was then that London heard "Tried by the Centre Court", "The Hippopotamus" ("Mud, mud, glorious mud"), and "The Honeysuckle and Bindweed", "Misalliance", and other songs that enabled Flanders and Swann to hold a theatre on their own.

They would sustain the entertainment, in various forms and in many places. Thus, they played, for example, throughout the United States (New York, 1959) and in Australia and New Zealand (1964); Flanders was married in New York to an American girl, Claudia Davis. The show developed into its second programme *At The Drop of Another Hat,* in 1963; this had two London scenes—at the Haymarket and the Globe—and from it came such things as "Slow Train", "Armadillo Idyll", and what a critic called the celebration of old brass bedsteads in any normal English pond.

Flanders, in his difficult circumstances, kept an unchallenged warmth and urbanity. During his career he made innumerable broadcasts of all kinds on radio and television; at one stage he was chairman of The Brains Trust. He wrote the libretti of two operas; translated (with Kitty Black) Stravinsky's *The Soldier's Tale;* and in 1962 appeared as The Storyteller in the Royal Shakespeare Company's production of Brecht's *The Caucasian Chalk Circle* at the Aldwych, London. In 1964 he received the O.B.E.

April 16, 1975.

Leslie O'Brien Fleetwood-Smith, who died in Melbourne on March 16, 1971 at the age of 60, played cricket 10 times for Australia during the 1930s.

Because of a broken arm "Chuck" Fleetwood-Smith changed from being a right to a left-hand bowler. Having done so he developed prodigious powers of unorthodox spin (Chinamen and googlies) and on his day he could bamboozle the greatest of batsmen. When the M.C.C. team landed in Australia in 1932-33 he was being hailed as the most dangerous bowler to have appeared on the Australian scene for many years. In the match against Victoria Wally Hammond* was urged by his captain, D. R. Jardine, to set about him, and to the Englishman's relief he did so to the tune of a double-hundred. It was therefore not until 1935 that Fleetwood-Smith played in his first Test match.

With 4 for 129 and 6 for 110 he was largely responsible for Australia winning the fourth Test match against England in 1936-37 and thus levelling a series which they went on to win. At the Oval in 1938 he had a very different experience, his one wicket costing him 298 runs from 87 overs. This was typical of one of the most mercurial bowlers of his time.

With a more dedicated approach to his cricket Fleetwood-Smith would no doubt have taken more wickets than he did, though in the process he might have enjoyed himself less. When Len Hutton made 364 in that match at the Oval he should have been stumped when he was 40—off Fleetwood-Smith. This was one of the most celebrated mistakes in cricket history, but it afforded Fleetwood-Smith much amusement.

March 17, 1971.

Colonel Peter Fleming, O.B.E., the author and explorer, brother of Ian Fleming*, the creator of James Bond, died on August 18, 1971 while grouse shooting in Black Mount, Argyllshire. He was 64.

Peter Fleming made a name for himself before he was 25, and by the time he was 30 he had a world-wide reputation. On his father's side he was the second generation in England of solid Aberdeen stock, and was himself nurtured in the rich loam of Oxfordshire. He combined with an intense love of his home and family an insatiable thirst for adventure and excitement. He wrote prolifically, but never sloppily, and always with wit. As a stylist he was in the top flight; as a traveller he was *sui generis,* for his journeys and his manner of recounting them belonged to a school of his own devising. His light-hearted attitude to life and his refusal even to contemplate a more orthodox career caused some to think that he had made too little use of his comfortable circumstances and his considerable endowments of character; but those who knew him well would rebut such a view with force.

Robert Peter Fleming was born in 1907, the eldest of the four sons of Major Valentine Fleming, a Yeomanry officer who was for some years M.P. for Henley, and who was killed after winning the D.S.O. in the First World War. Val Fleming, a gay and widely popular figure, was the son of

Robert Fleming, who came from Aberdeen to the City of London in the closing years of the past century, and amassed a great fortune as a merchant banker. Peter Fleming was an Oppidan Scholar and Captain of the Oppidans at Eton, where he edited the *Eton College Chronicle,* and subsequently took a first in English Literature at Oxford, where he was at Christ Church. As soon as he went down, brimming with promise, he joined both the staff of the *Spectator* and the Supplementary Reserve of the Grenadier Guards.

His infectious and rather irreverent gaiety did not conceal, even then, his resolution and considerable public spirit. His powerful build and superb physical fitness always made him look like a visitor to, rather than a denizen of, Gower Street, where the *Spectator* offices were, the Garrick Club, which he frequented, and Printing House Square, for he was already linked with *The Times.* He continued to spend much of his time at home in Oxfordshire, where he showed himself a determined though not a skilful rider, a fine shot and a good naturalist. In 1933, with the publication of *Brazilian Adventure,* he became famous overnight.

Brazilian Adventure, which remains a classic, is a ludicrous account of a tough journey. Colonel P. H. Fawcett had disappeared with two companions in the Matto Grosso region of Brazil in 1925. An advertisement appeared in the Agony Column of *The Times* inviting applications to join a search party. Fleming answered it and was accepted. He was unimpressed by his fellow-members, and persuaded his close friend Roger Pettiward (afterwards killed in the Second World War) to join him. The locally domiciled leader of the expedition showed no taste for personal risk and turned back on the fringe of the unknown, accompanied by most of the party. Fleming and Pettiward pressed on, though deprived of most of their needs and with no real prospect of success, into circumstances of some danger; they were eventually obliged to return also, and indeed reached civilization before their rivals.

The resulting book set the world laughing. Fleming chose to portray himself and Pettiward as the deserters, and scrupulously described the others as "the loyalists". The book as a whole was a parody of all adventure stories; water, for instance, became the "precious fluid." It was a young man's book, but very funny; it administered the *coup de grace* to a boastful type of travel book then fashionable; it was translated into many languages, and is still selling today.

Other journeys followed, chiefly in Russia and in Central and Eastern Asia. He reported these in the same light style in *One's Company* and *News from Tartary.* In 1935 he married Celia Johnson, the distinguished actress, who had just made her name in Merton Hodge's *The Wind and the Rain*; and shortly before the war he went back to China, accompanied by his wife and travelling up the Burma Road through Lashio.

On the outbreak of war he was mobilized as a Grenadier, but was soon in demand for unconventional jobs. In April 1940 he was on General Carton de Wiart's* staff for the short-lived campaign in Norway. After the British withdrawal he remained to organize "stay-behind" parties, to harass the occupying forces, returning to Britain eventually through Sweden and by air. He arrived in an England stolidly awaiting invasion, and was set to organize similar parties in the south-eastern counties, burying arms and explosives for use behind the German lines in case the enemy should succeed in getting ashore. When Germany invaded Greece in 1941, Fleming was sent there in a similar role, and was once again left behind. He escaped in a caique with Mr. and Mrs. (afterwards Sir Harold and Lady) Caccia from the British Embassy, and Mrs. Caccia's brother. While lying up for daylight in the shadow of a Greek island they were bombed and sunk and Mrs. Caccia's brother was killed. The survivors eventually reached Egypt in another vessel.

By this time Fleming had attracted the notice and friendship of General Wavell. Less than a year later Wavell, now Commander-in-Chief in India, was faced with the problem of getting his forces out of Burma, and decided to resort to those techniques of deception which he had witnessed under Allenby before the victory of Megiddo in 1918. He sent for Fleming, and set him up in Delhi with a carefully-selected staff of Fleming's own choosing. From this cell developed the whole complicated deception organization, carefully integrated with that of Brigadier Dudley Clark (another of Wavell's choices) in England, whose most spectacular success was that of D-day in Normandy. For this work Fleming's imagination and impish humour was particularly suited; and at the end of the war it was discovered that the Japanese version of the British Order of Battle in India and Burma was that which Fleming had been deftly building up and selling to them over the past three years.

It was never easy to keep him in his office, and not the least remarkable of his adventures occurred when he broke away into Burma, to fly in a towed glider with Wingate's airborne invasion in March 1944. The tow-rope parted, and the glider landed at a point in Burma which has never been identified. Its crew and passengers were a mixture of British, American and Gurkhas. Fleming took command, and, map-less, set a course due west for India, which he duly reached with the majority of his party after a march lasting over a month, and several brushes with the Japanese. He succeeded in visiting the Chindits inside Burma on two subsequent occasions.

After the war Fleming, now aged 38, returned to his home near Henley. He had sold Joyce Grove, his grandfather's enormous mansion, and was living in a smaller house which he had built on the estate just before the war. He farmed his acres and

shot over them; he joined the County Council, and commanded the local Territorial battalion; he was High Sheriff of Oxfordshire in 1952. He wrote Fourth Leaders for *The Times* and contributed for many years a weekly column for the *Spectator* under the pseudonym of *Strix.* From time to time he went off on a journey, participating, for example, in the operation in Oman in 1955 as a Special Correspondent for *The Times.*

A week before he died he wrote to *The Times* on the proposed boundary changes in South Oxfordshire. His style of writing remained highly individual: one critic described it as "countrified Max Beerbohm." His *Spectator* essays were gathered up in various volumes and remain models of their kind. In 1970 he became a Deputy Lieutenant for Oxfordshire.

During the war, he had published, in 1941, *The Flying Visit,* a satirical account of Hitler making an inadvertent parachute descent on Britain; the arrival of Rudolf Hess by air in Scotland a week after its publication was a startling coincidence. After the war, he turned to serious history with *Invasion 1940,* an account of Hitler's plans for the invasion of Britain, and the British counter-measures in which he handled admirably a great deal of abstruse material. Thereafter, while his younger brother Ian was annually producing a fresh episode in the career of James Bond, secret agent, Fleming was quarrying in those periods of history where much of the evidence was documentary, but where a few aged survivors were still available for their memories to be cudgelled in interviews. The result was in three excellent books: *The Siege of Peking; Bayonets to Lhasa,* an account of the Younghusband Expedition; and *The Fate of Admiral Kolchak.* All these involved solid research; but in all he maintained his lightness of touch without ever lapsing into facetiousness.

Despite his fame as a young man, Fleming never sought the limelight; and was more than content to hide his own light under a bushel. He pulled more than his weight in his own county, was an enlightened and progressive landowner, and moved happily and contentedly in a wide circle of friends. He surreptitiously smoothed the path for many people who were going through a bad patch. He remained superbly fit physically, and was completely impervious to discomfort or privation.

It has been said of him that he should have spread his wings more widely; should have accepted the Governorship which was once offered him. Certainly, if he had wished, he could have had a dazzling career, fully in the public eye, but he preferred a role less familiar to his own generation than it was 50 years earlier, that of an English country gentleman, cultured and enterprising, whose first concern was with his own estate and countryside, but who remained acutely interested in what was astir in the world beyond. He was a gay and gallant figure, without any peer in the various fields which he made his own.

He is survived by his wife, a son and two daughters. He was made an O.B.E. in 1945.

August 20, 1971.

Friedrich Flick, the German multi-millionaire industrialist, died on July 20, 1972 at the age of 89. In the years between the world wars Flick built up one of Germany's largest iron, steel and coal concerns. He lost most of his company through the war and the partition of Germany, but in his last 20 years he established a new and even larger giant concern.

The full extent of Flick's fortunes has never been ascertained, but he has often been regarded as the wealthiest man in West Germany. His company has major interests in steel, paper, chemicals and motor-cars; excluding Flick's 40 per cent holding in Daimler-Benz A.G., his other companies currently have annual sales of around £670m.

Friedrich Flick was born in Ernsdorf in the Siegen area on July 10, 1883. He was the second son of Ernst Flick, a farmer. Friedrich Flick studied at the technical high school in Cologne and after a couple of years in the infantry in 1904 and 1905 he went into the steel industry as a junior executive.

He joined the A.G. Charlottenhuette in Lower Saxony, became a director of this company in 1915, and four years later managing director. From then on he invested in various enterprises concerned with the steel industry and rapidly built up a huge empire. In the 1930s Friedrich Flick was owner of companies that, combined, amounted to the second largest steel firm in Germany with output annually of 2 million tons, as well as being one of the largest owners of the German coal industry.

Friedrich Flick lost about 80 per cent of his industrial empire with the partition of Germany. He was interned by the Allies in 1945 and went on trial at Nuremberg in 1947 in the major war crimes case against German industrialists. Friedrich Flick was sentenced to seven years in prison, but was released from Landsberg in August 1950, and then at the age of 68 he started to build up another huge industrial empire.

The allies forced Flick to sell most of his coal and steel interests, which turned out to be a blessing in disguise, for he invested heavily in new growth industries in the 1950s with the money he received for the forced sale of some of his interests. His major acquisition was a large block of shares in Daimler-Benz and today the Flick family has the largest single block of shares in this company.

Flick continued to the end to rule his empire with a firm grip. In recent years he rarely left home in Lindau on the Bodensee and his continued dominance over his industrial holdings led to a major split with his eldest son, Otto-Ernest Flick. The son tried to gain greater control of the family empire through the courts in 1963 and three years later a final settlement was reached with a large cash payment and the son relinquishing all claims on the family fortunes.

Friedrich Flick lost his second son in the last war; and his youngest son, Friedrich-Karl (who is 45) has been in the family company for 15 years and is now to shoulder the major burden of running the massive industrial empire. Friedrich Flick lost his wife after 50 years of marriage in 1966 and recently he made the two sons of Otto-Ernst Flick co-owners of the Flick holding companies. These grandchildren, Gert Flick (who is 29) and Friedrich Christian Flick (who is 28) will now have major responsibility for the family fortunes alongside their uncle and Friedrich Flick's old chief managers, Otto Friedrich and Konrad Kaletsch.

Friedrich Flick was a quiet person, something of a recluse. He was famed for his exceptional modesty; he was once photographed driving himself in a Volkswagen. But he was also a strong-willed, autocratic individual. He created a charitable foundation; and he gave a great deal to charities and received honorary degrees from many universities both in Germany and abroad. On his 80th birthday Ludwig Erhard presented Friedrich Flick with one of the highest German honours, the Federal Garter with star.

July 22, 1972.

Air Chief Commandant Dame Katherine Trefusis-Forbes—See Dame Katherine Watson-Watt (Lady Watson-Watt).

John Ford, who died on August 31, 1973, came as near as possible to embodying in one personality and one career the classic image of the American cinema. His speciality as a film-maker was Americana, and in the open air cinema of the Western, especially, there was none to touch him.

He was born at Cape Elizabeth, Maine, on February 1, 1895; his real name was Sean O'Feeney. When he graduated from Portland High School in 1913, his older brother Francis was already working in Hollywood as a director, writer and actor at Universal Studios. He had taken the name of Ford; and when Sean went out to join him he called himself Jack Ford.

For three or four years he did any sort of odd job around the studio as assistant to his brother; he seems to have directed four shorts called *Lucile Love—The Girl of Mystery* in 1914, but no trace now survives. The first film he could remember directing was a two-reeler, *Cactus My Pal,* starring Harry Carey in 1917.

During the next six years he directed some 40 or 50 shorts, mainly Westerns, with such favourites as Tom Mix and Buck Jones, before graduating to full-length features with *Cameo Kirby,* starring John Gilbert, in 1923. The next year saw one of his most famous films, and the best of his silents, *The Iron Horse,* an epic story of trans-continental railroad building.

None of his subsequent films markedly advanced his reputation until 1931, when he was employed by Samuel Goldwyn to direct Sidney Howard's adaptation of *Arrowsmith,* by Sinclair Lewis. This film, dealing as it does primarily with a conflict of ideas in scientific research, was very unusual in the work of a director who preferred on the whole to work in the open air on films about simple people. But it was highly praised and a popular success.

During the 1930s Ford turned his hand to almost every kind of subject, some of them rather unlikely, such as *Mary of Scotland* with Katharine Hepburn, and *Wee Willie Winkie* with Shirley Temple (though this latter is in fact a characteristic Ford film and it seems he enjoyed working with Shirley Temple). More indicative of his mature interests, though, were his first films dealing with the South (*Judge Priest,* 1934) and with Ireland (*The Informer,* 1935), both themes which were to run alongside the old West throughout his career.

They recur almost immediately in two of his best films of the time, respectively *Steamboat Round the Bend* (1935) and *The Plough and the Stars* (1936). In 1939 appeared two of his most famous films, *Stagecoach,* a classic Western and the first in which he used the spectacular terrain of Monument Valley, which was to become a hallmark of his films (not to mention a star who was to become equally inseparable from the idea of a Ford film, John Wayne); and *Young Mr. Lincoln,* with another star who was for long to be a favourite of his, Henry Fonda.

The years immediately before America's entry into the Second World War were particularly rich for Ford. He made a succession of outstanding films in a variety of different genres, from *Stagecoach* to *How Green Was My Valley* (1941), seven classics in three years. *Drums Along the Mohawk, The Grapes of Wrath, The Long Voyage Home, Tobacco Road* and *How Green Was My Valley* would be a remarkable sequence of films from any director.

During the war Ford joined the Navy, as chief of the Field Photographic Branch, and made several war documentaries, among them one of the most famous, *The Battle of Midway.* His first job after the war was a large-scale war film based on a field of combat with which he had been closely associated, *They Were Expendable.* Then in 1946 he began a cycle of classic Westerns with *My Darling Clementine,* the story of Wyatt Earp and Doc Holliday. Later ones in the series included *Fort Apache* (1948), *She Wore a Yellow Ribbon* (1949), *Wagon Master* (1950), perhaps the best of them all, *Rio Grande* (1950), *The Searchers* (1956), *The Horse Soldiers* (1959),

Two Rode Together (1961), and *The Man Who Shot Liberty Valance* (1962).

Taken all together they make up a view of the old West which comes close to the definitive, not so much from a greater degree of documentary authenticity—Ford was always a romantic—but from the intensity and completeness of the vision, a man's world where simple values obtained, simple codes of honour still applied.

Though most of the outstanding films of Ford's latter years were Westerns, he made many other sorts of film during that time. Comedies like a new version of the old First World War play *What Price Glory;* the piece of curiously appealing stage-Irishry *The Quiet Man,* and *Donovan's Reef;* the political drama *The Last Hurrah;* the romantic drama *Mogambo.*

His two last films were *Cheyenne Autumn,* a spectacular return to the Western, and *Seven Women* (1966), a surprising departure in that it was almost entirely an intimate, indoor picture with a largely feminine cast.

In his later years John Ford was widely recognized as one of the great poets of the cinema, and few would deny him that title. He was always a practical filmmaker first and foremost, willing if need be to make commercial pot-boilers, if they would secure him the freedom to do what he wanted as well.

He was indeed basically a simple man, with simple, old-fashioned values which sometimes betrayed him into excesses of sentimentality. But on his home ground, the Wild West or the Deep South, his mastery was complete and his acute visual sense never betrayed him, whatever the faults of his script.

Ford won Academy Awards with four of his feature films, *The Informer, The Grapes of Wrath, How Green Was My Valley* and *The Quiet Man.* Two wartime documentaries also won Oscars.

September 3, 1973.

Air Chief Marshal Sir Robert Foster, K.C.B., C.B.E., D.F.C., who was C.-in-C. 2nd (British) Tactical Air Force 1951-53 and 2nd Allied T.A.F. 1952-53, died at the age of 75 on October 22, 1973.

Robert Mordaunt Foster was born on September 3, 1898, the third son of Colonel M. G. Foster. He was a brilliant scholar at Winchester and might have gone on to a career of academic distinction if the First World War had not broken out. Instead he entered the Royal Military College, Camberley, and was later commissioned in the Royal Fusiliers. Less than three months after leaving the Royal Military College he transferred to the Royal Flying Corps and before the end of the year was in France with the redoubtable No. 54 Squadron. He won a D.F.C. in 1918, and was twice mentioned in dispatches.

After being granted a permanent commission in the R.A.F. he went to India in 1919 and served with No. 20 Squadron. Early in 1923 he force-landed in enemy territory in operations in Waziristan and was taken prisoner. He spent a fortnight in captivity before he was able to get back.

He went to No. 2 Group Bomber Command, in September 1939, and before the end of the year was commanding No. 110 Squadron. The following year he was appointed to command the bomber base at Wyton but a year later, to his great satisfaction, he went back to the Middle East and commanded successively in 1942 No. 214 Group in Iraq and No. 213 Group in the Levant.

In 1944 he was briefly A.O.C., Malta and then went to Italy to succeed Air Marshal Dickson as A.O.C., Desert Air Force, the tactical formation which maintained its name rather incongruously through its advance across the Mediterranean and through Italian countryside.

Soon after V.E. Day he went to Vienna as Chief of the Air Division in the Control Commission of Austria. He returned home in July 1946 to command No. 3 Group, Bomber Command, The following February he went to the Air Ministry as Assistant Chief of Air Staff (Policy). In 1949 he succeeded Sir Alan Lees as the second postwar A.O.C.-in-C. of Reserve Command, with the rank of Air Marshal.

He was a keen sportsman and as well as riding, shooting, sailing and squash rackets, he took part in winter sports when he could. He was Deputy Lieutenant for Suffolk.

He married in 1940 Ruth Elliott, and they had a son and a daughter.

October 24, 1973.

Christian Fouchet, the French diplomatist, former Gaullist minister and author of the Fouchet Plan, died in Geneva on August 11, 1974 at the age of 62.

Fouchet was one of the first Gaullists, arriving in London on June 17, 1940 concealed in an R.A.F. aircraft, and making his way, after witnessing the confusion at the French Embassy, to the building where de Gaulle* had just taken up his residence. "De Gaulle", he records, "did not exactly throw his arms around me—indeed he was pretty brusque—but his determination to fight on impressed me and I volunteered at once." Fouchet was then 29. For the rest of his life, while the General was in power, he was at de Gaulle's disposal and was given some of the toughest tasks. He came to belong to the inner circle of Gaullists and was, as the French say, a "baron" of the regime.

His name first became widely known in 1961 when, as ambassador to Denmark, de Gaulle made him chairman of a six-man committee of E.E.C. members who were to draw up a plan for European political unity which would reconcile the believers in a "Europe of States" with the believers in a supra-national federation. The first Fouchet Plan advocated a confederal Cabinet for foreign affairs and defence but suggested that the institutions of the Community should be subordinated to an elected European Parliament. If this did not altogether satisfy the federalists, they would probably have accepted it as a first step. However, during the summer of 1961 de Gaulle's attitude hardened towards the Community, the draft Fouchet Plan came to nothing, as did progress to political unity.

A distinction is often made, first perhaps by Soustelle, between Gaullists by faith and Gaullists by reason, the former accepting de Gaulle and all his policies *en bloc.* Fouchet was maybe in a different category —that of Gaullist by nature. The son of a cavalry officer, he came from a similar social milieu. He belonged, as did de Gaulle in his youth, to the Right but, though he believed in the need for authority in government, he did not share the political prejudices or social views of the conservative classes. He was basically anti-colonialist and in the early 1950s, when he was President of the R.P.F. (Gaullist) Deputies in the Assembly, he referred to France's involvement in Indo-China as France's "Mexican" expedition, a reference to Napoleon the Third's ill-fated expedition. He did not belong to the left-wing Gaullists but believed strongly in worker participation.

Tall, taciturn and energetic, he was a man of action, attracted by intellectual conceptions of politics and history. A "natural" Gaullist, Fouchet was not an "unconditional" one. He was a "European", and under the Pompidou regime he criticized the President for failing to take steps to secure an elected European parliament. He told de Gaulle in 1969, looking back at the past, that he thought he had been wrong to torpedo the Fouchet Plan as it would have been an irreversible step to European unity.

Born at St. Germaine en Laye in 1911, Fouchet studied law and then passed through the École des Sciences Politiques and, like his friend Geoffroy de Courcel, had embarked on a diplomatic career before the war. De Gaulle sent him to Chad in 1940, and he then served under General Leclerc in the Fezzan and Libya campaigns.

Later, after some missions to the Resistance in France, he was sent on diplomatic service to Italy and then to the Soviet Union. He became, as Major Fouchet, the French representative with the Polish Lublin Committee. From 1945 to 1947 he returned to diplomacy and went as Consul General to Calcutta. In 1947 de Gaulle called him out for the Rassemblement du Peuple Français and he became the star organizer for the Paris region, being returned as one of the R.P.F. Deputies for Paris in 1951.

With de Gaulle's permission, he joined the Mendès-France Government in 1954 as Minister for Tunisian and Moroccan affairs, accompanying the Prime Minister and General Juin* on the visit to Tunisia which set that country on the road to independence. From 1958 to 1962 he was ambassador to Denmark during which time he was occupied with the Fouchet Plan.

In March 1962, following the Evian agreements which ended the war with the Algerian F.L.N., he left normal diplomacy for good and was sent to Algeria as High Commissioner, his task being to maintain French authority until independence in July. He carried out this dangerous duty in an impressive manner. Minister for Information in 1965, then of Education, he was Minister of the Interior in 1967. In charge of the police and the C.R.S., though not of general policy nor of the University, Fouchet who had done his best to avoid escalation became the students' bête noire.

Fouchet had little sympathy for the Pompidou regime and in 1971 resigned from the Gaullist party. He reproached France's foreign policy for being that of an affluent and conservative country and in March 1974 he gave a press conference in which he advocated the creation of a European Parliament after a referendum, a parliament which should have power to draw up lines for European integration.

After the death of Pompidou he stood for the Presidency, but on the advice of Malraux he stood down so as not to split the vote for Chaban-Delmas.

He published chez Plon in 1971 *Au Service du Général de Gaulle* and in 1973 *Les Lauriers sont Coupés*. Both revealed a great deal about de Gaulle "unbuttoned", and the last indicates how in his old age he still had the power not only to stand firm—but also to have a new vision of French society and its needs. They both add greatly to the study of this great man. Fouchet married Mlle. Colette Vautrin, by whom he had a daughter.

August 13, 1974.

Uffa Fox, C.B.E., died on October 26, 1972 at the age of 74.

His name was for many years almost synonymous with yachting. This in itself is something of a paradox since few sailing personalities ever become known to the general public. An atmosphere of deliberate mystery that surrounds the world of small boats tends to inhibit the mass media.

That he was able to surmount this barrier is largely due to his long association with the Royal Family. For many years not a season went by without newspaper pictures of him sailing with the Duke of Edinburgh, often with Prince Charles or Princess Anne at his side. Visitors to Cowes soon learnt to recognize the stocky figure with the broad Hampshire accent and ready laugh.

But he deserves to be remembered more for his achievements as a designer. Chief among these was the concept of the planing dinghy which transformed sailing from a rich man's pastime into a popular sport enjoyed by millions. Realizing that a V-shaped hull, as opposed to the then conventional round section, would enable a boat to ride up over its own bow wave and so double or treble its speed, he designed and built the 14ft. Avenger. In 1928 she gained 52 victories, two second places and three thirds in 57 starts, astonished the yachting world, and is recognized now as the prototype modern racing dinghy.

In the following years he designed dozens of boats from dinghies and day-sailers to cruisers and ocean-racers, and achieved a high place among the world's leading marine architects. Among the most popular were the Firefly, National Redwing, Albacore, and Flying Fifteen, still flourishing classes which alone bear ample testimony to his creative ideas.

He did not, however, restrict himself solely to racing craft and in the Second World War he was responsible for the parachuted airborne lifeboat which saved hundreds of lives of airmen shot down at sea. Realizing that rubber dinghies were of little use unless the occupants were quickly rescued, he designed a 20ft. plywood boat which could be carried folded but which would be automatically unfolded by the parachutes. It was self-righting and self-bailing, carried food and clothing, protected the men from exposure, and could be motored, rowed or sailed to safety.

He was born in Cowes in January 1898 and from childhood acquired a deep love of the Isle of Wight where he lived nearly all his life. At the age of 14 he was apprenticed to the boatbuilder S. E. Saunders but left to join the Royal Naval Air Service during the First World War, when he worked on flying boats and seaplanes. After completing his apprenticeship he started his own firm and quickly acquired a high reputation.

Although his life was closely bound up with sailing, his other sporting enthusiasm embraced cricket, rowing, riding and shooting. To all these activities he brought a zest and an ability as a raconteur that won him many friends. In 1956 he married Madame Yvonne Bernard of Paris and lived part of his later years in France.

He was also the author of several books, including *Sailing, Seamanship and Yacht Construction, Sail and Power, Racing, Cruising and Design* and *Sailing Boats.*

October 27, 1972.

Gilbert Foyle, who died on October 28, 1971 at the age of 85, with his brother William built up the firm of W. & G. Foyle, of Charing Cross Road, the biggest bookselling business in Great Britain and, perhaps, in the world.

Gilbert Samuel Foyle was born on March 9, 1886, one of seven children of William Henry Foyle, a Shoreditch wholesale grocer. He was educated at Owen's School, Islington, and at 15 took a short course at King's College, London, afterwards working for about a year in the offices of the Shoreditch Borough Council. In 1900 both Gilbert and William sat for, and failed, the Civil Service entrance examination. By an odd quirk of fate this initial rebuff became the foundation of the fortunes.

Deciding to sell their examination text books, the brothers received so many replies to their advertisement that they began to see possibilities in bookselling as a vocation. The family kitchen at Shoreditch soon became cluttered with books and in 1903 a little shop was rented in Islington. From there the Foyles conducted their small business, wrote out catalogues by hand, cooked their own meals, and worked late into the evenings. Within a year they had moved to the bookselling region of Charing Cross Road; and in 1912 they were able to take far larger premises in the same road. In 1929, after 26 years of trading, they had added an annexe in Manette Street, which was opened by the Lord Mayor of London.

The career of the Foyle brothers followed a course of expansion, conservation and back-ploughing of profits. The first year's turnover in Islington was £10; but by the jubilee year, 1954, it had reached some £2m., and from an initial staff of one assistant the number of employees had reached the neighbourhood of 600. Bookselling was by no means the sole activity of the firm. In 1920 there was started Foyles Educational, Ltd., school suppliers, and in 1929 three new departments came into being—one devoted to the sale of gramophone records, a second setting up a chain of small lending libraries all over the country, and the third consisting of an art gallery, which has housed one-man exhibitions of work by some artists of note.

The Foyle Literary Luncheons, started in 1930, attracted a good deal of public attention. In 1937 again three new ventures began: a book club, a publishing house, and a literary agency. In 1944 the brothers took over the Lecture Agency (founded in 1879), and so became agents for such notable lecturers as Neville Cardus, Sir Adrian Boult and Sir Arthur Bryant.

Gilbert Foyle served in the 1914-18 War as a private in the Royal Army Service Corps. In 1951 he lodged with the London County Council securities worth £20,000 to form the Gilbert Foyle Educational Trust, with the object of helping worthy but needy students through their university careers. He lived in Eastbourne, where he took a great interest in municipal affairs, serving on the borough council. He was also a generous benefactor of the town, giving the money to buy 95 acres of land on the downs near Beachy Head in 1957. Some years later he gave over £36,000 to provide Eastbourne with a new sun lounge and café on the front as a tribute to the courage and endurance of the town during the bombing in the Second World War.

He married in 1911 Ethel Ellen Cook and had two sons, both of whom entered the family business.

October 29, 1971.

General Franco—Francisco Franco Bahamonde—who ruled Spain for more than a third of a century after the Nationalist armies under his command had finally defeated the Republic in April 1939, died on November 20, 1975 at the age of 82.

Doubtless his greatest achievement was to have ensured Spain a long period of order and political stability, which last the country had not enjoyed since the early nineteenth century. This made possible the economic advance of Spain which has rescued the country from its former backwardness and apathy, By financial reforms and a programme of modernization of the administration and of industry which Franco set going around 1959, Spain today is relatively prosperous, and this has affected the living standard of a large section of the urban working class and, though more patchily, the conditions of the agricultural workers. Industrial development is no longer confined to the northern provinces and Catalonia. Economically, Spain's entry into the E.E.C., the avowed aim of the government dominated by technocrats which Franco formed in October 1969, is feasible.

But as regards the political condition of the country, in which political parties are banned, free trade unions forbidden, and military courts still play a part in maintaining public order, the Pyrenees still stand between Spain and Western Europe. During the sixties, it looked as though Franco was willing to allow a cautious political and social liberalism. But this went into reverse in 1970 most markedly after the uproar in Spain and abroad caused by the trial by a military court at Burgos of 16 Basques arrested in 1968. By the end of 1971, Franco said at a public rally in Madrid that so long as he lived there would be no deep-seated political reforms, and added that his designated successor as Head of State, Prince Juan Carlos, would maintain the same attitude.

While Franco lived, the majority of Spaniards continued to put their trust in him. Nevertheless the Franco consensus became frayed, with workers more rebellious and the professional classes more critical. Above all the Church, from the highest levels to the parish priests, though there were of course exceptions, had become openly opposed to the regime.

Without the advantages of birth, influence or wealth, without that of physical prestige, for he was short, inclined to be plump even in youth, and spoke with a slightly high voice, Franco became Spain's youngest major and youngest general. During the Moroccan wars he showed exceptional courage, ability to lead men and, as a more senior officer, tactical skill. The Second Republic, which came to power after King Alfonso XIII had gone into voluntary exile, employed him in the suppression of the revolt in the Asturias. He was Spain's most capable general.

When the nationalist revolt broke out in 1936, and after General Sanjurjos's death

in an aeroplane accident, there was little doubt that Franco would inevitably become leader of the nationalist cause. This happened at Burgos in October 1936, Franco becoming Generalissimo and also Head of State. The nationalists were as divided as the Republicans and their unity was as liable to crack in adversity. The military leaders who knew him were well aware that he was the only man who could deal with rivalries between generals and intrigues between monarchists, Falangists and the traditionist volunteers from the north. He proved adept at keeping the overbearing Italian and German commanders in their place and also at giving the fewest economic concessions to Hitler, while getting nearly all the aid he needed.

In 1937 the nationalists might have been defeated but for German and Italian aid. That is a hypothesis. What is certain is that Franco's ability to impose unity on his supporters was the essential condition of victory—the Republic's disunity being the major factor in its defeat. The nationalist call to revolt in 1936 had been less widely followed than expected and Franco had with him only just more than half the army and the police forces—though the most convinced and active part. The support of the Falange, the Spanish fascist movement, one million strong, was vital. But the Falange with its anti-religious and radical social doctrine was bound to be at odds with the monarchists at Burgos and with the popular traditionist forces from northern Spain with their own militia.

Aware that the Germans were actively encouraging the Falange, Franco forced a shotgun marriage between the Falange and the traditionist popular forces, not without drastic treatment of recalcitrant leaders from both sides. They were amalgamated into the National Movement which was to become, after the civil war, the only legitimate political party in Spain. The future of Spanish fascism was therefore to become only one of the several forces, at times far the most troublesome, which were allowed to exert pressure on a dictatorship which, though it remained fundamentally ultra-conservative and nationalist, listened, when expedient, to more liberal voices.

Franco's absolute mastery of the nationalist movement, and particularly of the fascists, stood him in good stead in 1940. His decision not to honour his debt to the Dictators and to keep Spain out of the Second World War was, as Winston Churchill* acknowledged in 1944, of immense importance to Britain and to ultimate allied victory. Like de Gaulle, Franco foresaw that Hitler had not won after the Battle of France. The Franco-Hitler debate was not ended by the dramatic interview at Hendaye in 1940, which so infuriated Hitler. Franco had said neither yes nor no. Many of Franco's most important advisers, including the then Foreign Minister, Serrano Suñer, were for entry into the war and Franco had constantly to keep them in check. Spain's neutrality was benevolent

towards the Axis powers. It was not until 1942, when Franco made the pro-British Jordana Foreign Minister, that the Falange generals and personalities were finally put in their place.

Born on December 4, 1892, at El Ferrol, in Galicia, he was the second son of a naval paymaster. It was originally intended that he should enter the Navy, but owing to retrenchment in this service he instead entered the Infantry Academy at Toledo in 1907. He volunteered for service in North Africa, where war had broken out in Morocco against the rebellious Riffs. From 1912 he saw bitter and costly fighting in command of Moorish troops and earned a reputation for great bravery and a charmed life. In 1916 he was seriously wounded in the stomach and invalided home.

After a four-year spell of garrison duty at home he returned to Morocco as secondin-command of the Foreign Legion, and in 1923 was appointed to its command. Under him the Legion played a leading part in the final operation against Abd el Krim, the Riff leader. During the dictatorship of Primo de Rivera he became director of the Military Academy at Saragosa, but with the advent of the Republican Government the academy was abolished, and Franco found himself posted to the Balearic Islands, out of harm's way. In 1934 the Republic called him to suppress a revolt by the Asturian miners, which he accomplished with ruthless severity, and later filled the post of Chief of General Staff.

By 1936 internal conditions in Spain had seriously deteriorated and before once more being sent out of temptation's way, this time to the Canary Islands, Franco had succeeded in laying his plans for the subsequent revolt by making arrangements to keep in touch with generals in command of those divisions which he felt could be relied on for his purpose. Virtually a prisoner in Santa Cruz de Teneriffe, Franco managed to obtain permission from the Government to attend the funeral of a comrade in Las Palmas. Here word reached him that the murder of Calvo Sotelo, a leading Monarchist, had precipitated the revolt and, as arranged, he immediately took command of the rebel forces in North Africa. From there he invaded the Spanish mainland with the help of Italian transport aircraft. His army, largely composed of Moorish troops, began the slow conquest through Estremadura, Salamanca and Burgos that was to end in victory in Madrid and Barcelona three years later.

Colonel Ritter von Thoma, in charge of the Condor Legion, considered Franco a sound but old-fashioned commander; Mussolini, despite the conspicuous failures of Italian troops in Spain, often reproached the nationalists with going too slowly. Franco was actually a student of Liddell Hart* and Fuller*, and his own officers, whom he had weaned from tactics used in the Moroccan wars, considered him overdaring. Franco did not himself command in the field though he frequently visited the battle fronts and caused anxiety by exposing himself to risks. His overall strategic plan was sound though inevitably cautious; the army was not equipped with transport for motorized infantry and not capable therefore of dynamic tactical movements. He constantly stressed the need for training at all levels. Contrary to what was once believed, more senior officers served the Republic, or abstained altogether, than joined the nationalists.

At the end of the Second World War, Franco managed to maintain his hold on power in face of the hostile opinion of the victorious Allies. Spain was debarred from membership of the United Nations, which in December 1946 adopted a resolution recommending the withdrawal of diplomatic representatives from Spain. To this challenge Franco responded with characteristic courage. In fact hostile attitudes abroad helped to rally Spanish opinion behind him.

By skilful planning and exceptional patience in execution, combined with an excellent sense of timing, he succeeded in restoring Spain to respectable diplomatic society. Spain became a member of the United Nations in 1955. This success had been achieved by a systematic plan to woo the countries of Latin America and of the Middle East and thus secure their votes in the United Nations.

As part of his plan to gain respectability for Spain, Franco was determined to conclude a Concordat with the Vatican. Despite the favourable treatment accorded the Church under Franco, the Pope showed reluctance to associate himself too closely with the Falangist regime. It was not until 1953 that Franco's patience was rewarded and the Concordat signed. Even so his relations with the Church were seldom much more than businesslike.

Another major aim of Franco's foreign policy was to secure a share in United States aid. In this he was greatly helped by the cold war, more particularly when its temperature was raised by the conflict in Korea. The United States military need for strategic bases proved greater than its political reluctance to be associated with the Franco regime; and after protracted negotiations which lasted for nearly three years, agreement was reached on September 26, 1953 for United States aid to be given to Spain in exchange for the use of military bases. Franco had proved himself a tough bargainer and the United States found itself forced to agree that the Spanish flag should fly over all United States bases and that American personnel should not wear uniform outside the bases themselves, provisions which were of psychological importance to Spain.

When, in December 1959, General Eisenhower*, then President of the United States, publicly embraced Franco while on a visit to the country, a seal of success was set on the Caudillo's foreign policy. Only membership of Nato still eluded Spain.

Two constants in Spanish foreign policy were the maintenance of good relations with the Arab world and particularly with Morocco and Algeria, and the return of Gibraltar. In the last, Franco had the support of virtually all Spaniards, including that of the Republican government in exile in Mexico. Having received King Abdullah, the King of Libya and other Arab potentates after the war, his relations with the new revolutionary regimes in the Arab world were carefully fostered. During Morocco's struggle for independence from France, the Spanish zone was quiet, and it was returned to Sultan Mohamed V in 1956 when Morocco became independent.

He ceded the enclave of Ifni to Morocco and in 1968 Equatorial Guinea came into existence as a state. However, Franco kept the Rio de Oro, with its huge phosphate deposits, sending troops and warships to reinforce the garrison in 1970 when Algeria, Morocco and Mauritania were most vigorously pressing for Spain to withdraw. Franco offered a referendum but insisted that it should be held by the Spanish authorities. In spite of tension and Arab threats to demand a withdrawal from Ceuta and Melilla, Spanish trade with Algeria and Morocco continued, though North African support for Spain's efforts to get Britain to "decolonize" Gibraltar became less wholehearted.

In the late fifties, Franco began to demand the return of Gibraltar with increasing vigour, and the policy of blockading the Rock began. By 1970 Gibraltar was completely cut off from the mainland. In 1966 Britain had accepted the United Nations request to open negotiations with Spain. After a number of sessions in London and in Madrid, with both sides putting forward conditions, these proved useless; the British could not accept Spain's demand for a return of sovereignty as an indispensable preliminary. Thanks to Arab and Latin American votes at the United Nations, there was a majority for a resolution that Britain should decolonize the Rock. This was rejected by the British so long as the Gibraltarians wished to remain under the British flag, as they had shown by a nearly unanimous vote that they did in a referendum in 1967.

Franco conducted his Gibraltar policy without bluster, stating that Gibraltar was not worth a war but that the problem, vital to Spain, destroyed the sincerity of Anglo-Spanish good relations. He showed himself slow to adopt a friendly policy towards the Gibraltarians, which might have made them change their attitude to Spanish sovereignty. In 1973 when Lopez Rodo became Foreign Minister in the Carrero Blanco government, there were indications that the Spanish Government had realized this and was beginning to woo the Gibraltarians.

In 1959 Franco appointed a number of technocratic Ministers, some of them belonging to the Catholic lay movement Opus Dei, and their effect was to add impetus to industrial planning and to accelerate much needed reforms in the administration. Spain joined O.E.C.D. in 1960. In a government reshuffle in 1969, the technocrats and their sympathizers formed a majority of the Cabinet, with Lopez Bravo as Foreign Minister. The aim was to enable Spain to join the E.E.C. and this programme, unpopular with the Falange, was welcomed by the increasingly wealthy industrial and professional classes. The benefits of growing economic strength spread downwards and affected even the impoverished rural workers of Andalucia. By 1973, Spain had become one of the relatively "affluent" nations of Europe and inflation began to be a serious problem.

During the 1960s various liberal reforms sponsored by independent members of the government such as Fernando Castiella, the former Foreign Minister, Fraga Iribarne and Ruiz Jimenez gave a measure of religious toleration, abolished rigorous aspects of the press censorship and relaxed many bans on publishing, film making and public entertainment. Some trials for political offences were carried out in public and with remarkable fairness to the accused. Opposition groups of monarchists, Catholic Action and Socialists were tolerated though remaining illegal. But for every two steps forward there seemed to be one backward. From the middle 1960s, the movement of protest from regime supporters as well as opponents became more intense. The student movement in 1965 and 1966 became increasingly violent and anti-regime. Franco was more concerned by a petition signed by 1,500 persons well known in all the main professions, including an old friend, Alonso Vega, calling for an independent inquiry into the torture of political prisoners. A general meeting of the Council of Lawyers passed with a huge majority a resolution which called for the abolition of the Special Tribunals and the limitation of the use of military courts to purely military offences. Shortly after this, and following disorders in the Basque provinces in 1968-69, and student riots, Franco proclaimed a three months' "state of exception" which gave the police and the army additional powers.

In December 1970 Franco faced the gravest test for the regime. The trial by a military court of 16 Basque activists who included two priests and two women, opened at Burgos. All the defendants were accused of seditious activities committed in 1968, and some, for whom the military prosecutor asked for the death sentence, of killing a police inspector. Spanish opinion as a whole had little sympathy for the Basque demand for autonomy and still less for the Basque revolutionary movement E.T.A., to which most of the defendants belonged. But progressive opinion was revolted by the image which this military trial gave Spain. The Vatican asked for clemency, as did other friendly governments. Even some high-ranking officers were known to dislike the fact that the Army was being given a repressive role. Although Franco commuted the death sentence to life imprisonment, the regime did not bow to the storm and a number of reactionary generals, with Franco's approval, organized Falange demonstrations all over the country against the Basques, the intellectuals, the European-minded technocrats in the government, and interfering foreigners.

1971 and early 1972 showed the dictator and his deputy, Admiral Carrero Blanco, resolutely supporting the foreign policy of Lopez Bravo in favour of Spain entering Europe and of a less intransigent attitude to the United Kingdom over Gibraltar, but, in face of social problems, putting the clock back by 10 years. If, after Burgos, there was a hush for a while, opposition continued in forms which were more dangerous than protests from the progressives and professional classes. In November 1971 the first National Assembly of Bishops and Priests, preparations for which had been made in every diocese in Spain, called for faster social and political progress and for the ending of the Concordat. This was followed by a statement by the Justice and Peace Commission of the Church, to be read in all churches, which called for a fight against the existing social structures, and dismissed the claim that prosperity was creating social harmony. Failure to create a dialogue between the regime and the people could, said the commission, result in civil war.

Reforms of the law governing the *sindicatos* or labour unions allowed strikes, before totally forbidden, provided their causes were purely economic. The strikes, more than usually violent ones, which broke out in the mining region of the Asturias in early 1972 and in a number of industrial towns of north-western Spain, all had in common a will to contest the way the state imposed wage contracts in the public and private sectors through the national trade union organization in which workers and management were grouped together. At El Ferrol, the naval base in Galicia, the birthplace of Franco, troops opened fire on strikers, killing two men and injuring many. The police made a large round-up of communist agitators. But, as the Madrid newspaper *YA* boldly pointed out, communists had virtually nothing to do with the strikes.

During Franco's later years he was preoccupied with the question of the form of government that should control Spain after his death. He had in 1947 declared Spain to be a kingdom, and the following year came to an arrangement with the exiled Pretender to the throne, Don Juan, that his son, Juan Carlos, should be educated in Spain with a view to being made king. Control over the extent of his powers was to be maintained through a Council of the Realm and he was to accept the fundamental principles of the existing regime. Don Juan, however never relinquished his claim to the throne.

When Franco eventually announced his decision on the monarchy in July 1969, he proposed Prince Juan Carlos of Bourbon

as his heir, and Juan Carlos took the oath as future King of Spain during a ceremony in the Cortes (Parliament). He swore loyalty to the principles of the National Movement, the only legal political organization in Spain. Franco passed over the claims of Don Juan.

In November 1966 he presented to the Cortes a new "Organic Law" of the state, providing for a Prime Minister to be appointed by the head of state from a list of three proposed by the Council of the Realm. Political parties remained forbidden but the law introduced elections for some deputies to the Cortes. In December 1966 the law received a huge favourable vote on a referendum.

In June 1973 Franco implemented the most important clause of the 1966 Organic Law—the separation of head of state from head of government. Thus, for the first time since Burgos in 1936, the Caudillo shed a part of his absolute power. The Prime Minister was Admiral Carrero Blanco, aged 70, who had long been Franco's closest political associate, and who could be guaranteed to keep "Francoism" going. The new government had fewer technocratic ministers, Lopez Bravo was retired, but the European policy was to be kept going at full steam. A degree of political participation through "associations" inside the National Movement, which would enable criticism of government policy to be expressed, was to be encouraged.

Admiral Carrero Blanco, and his car, were blown over a six-storey building in central Madrid on December 20 by an explosion engineered by Basque separatists.

Franco took the death of his life-long friend remarkably calmly. As Prime Minister in succession to Carrero he chose Carlos Arias Navarro, a man of proven administrative ability but even more renowned as an uncompromising upholder of the law. He allowed Arias to form his own Cabinet and to include in it men committed to liberalization. On February 12, 1974 Arias announced his intention to put before the Cortes Bills to reform local authorities on more democratic lines and to legalize political associations—the term parties had been anathema to Franco since 1939. Censorship of the printed word became little more than a formality immediately. The proposals met with determined opposition from a small body of Falangists of the old school known as the *Ultras*. When it appeared that Prince Juan Carlos favoured even greater liberalization they sought to persuade Franco to dismiss Arias and to change the succession.

On July 9, however, Franco developed thrombo-phlebitis and 10 days later suffered a very severe haemorrhage from which he was not expected by his doctors to recover. Franco thereupon assented after some persuasion to the temporary assumption by the Prince of the powers of Head of State, powers which he withdrew on September 1, the moment his doctors declared him "as fit as could be expected in a

man of his age".

During his convalescence Franco had turned to the friends of his earlier years who were principally *Ultras*, civilian and military. They failed to persuade him to change the succession or dismiss Arias after his reassumption of the headship of State, but they did obtain a minor victory when Franco dismissed Arias's liberal Minister of Information, Pio Cabanillas; and a greater one when, in December, Franco personally rejected Arias's proposals for a liberal statute of political associations and imposed on him a statute prepared by the *Ultras* which proved totally unacceptable even to the most moderate of would-be reformers of the regime. In all this, and in increasing their power over Franco during 1975, nothing helped the *Ultras* more than the acts of terrorism which occurred during the period in the Basque provinces, Madrid, Barcelona and elsewhere. Each act was presented to the ever more aging Franco as proof that any liberalization would end only in anarchy similar to that against which he claimed to have risen in 1936. He insisted to the last on the persecution of dissidents, and turned a deaf ear to appeals from the Church for mercy and amnesty for the political prisoners and detainees who came to number, during 1975, more than at any time over the previous 25 years.

Public opinion polls in Spain on political questions are rare. One, however, held in 1971 showed how ordinary Spaniards thought about Franco and the regime. Nine Spaniards out of 10 said they wanted Spain to join the E.E.C. and no less than 91 per cent approved of Franco's recent efforts to improve relations with Eastern Europe. More than 70 per cent believed that Spain's political structure was bound to change fundamentally over the next few years, and 62 per cent expected trouble when Franco went.

Franco gave Spain a period of law and order which was not merely the result of exhaustion from the ferocious civil war. In terms of Spain's past, it was no mean achievement. Between 1836 and 1936, three Spanish Kings had been dethroned, two Regents exiled, four Prime Ministers assassinated. There had been 24 major Army revolts, and three civil wars. Spain had had two dictatorships and two Republics. Further, Franco and his advisers, most notably after 1959, encouraged the forces which turned Spain into a modern industrial country rather than one in which the interests of the great landowners predominated. Spain caught up with the rest of Western and Southern Europe so far as economic development was concerned. The level of literacy rose, as did the standard of living.

Franco maintained a personal consensus which in the seventies was the stronger because of material progress. Yet the Franco regime itself was accepted with increasing reluctance by the Spanish people because of the restrictions which it maintained on elementary political liberty.

Franco governed by treating politics as a branch of military science. He prevented Spain from becoming a totalitarian fascist state (though it is still mistakenly called one), but he did not create a country in which the majority of its inhabitants felt reasonably free. Posterity is likely to judge his achievement by whether or not, under his trained and chosen successor, Spain evolves into a democracy which, though it will be a distinctively Spanish form of democracy, will allow free political expression and free trade unions. Apart from these fundamentals, it is probable that an understanding policy towards Basque and Catalan desires for autonomy will have to be adopted—and on this road, Franco did not take even a few timid steps. It is unlikely that the new regime, in which no one will have the kind of consensus Franco enjoyed, will be able to maintain the existing structures and methods without using intolerable repression and violence. Spain must go another way, and not that which the Caudillo indicated.

This "clever, harsh, patient, unimaginative General" (Hugh Thomas's phrase) had none of the meretricious qualities of many political leaders. He was not vain. He was not, except for *raisons d'état,* an inhumane man. His character aroused general respect and, among his supporters, admiration. He was personally uninterested in money, worked exceptionally long hours until the last, and lived frugally, at the Pardo palace on the outskirts of Madrid which, though built by the Bourbons as a hunting lodge, had all the suitable grandeur of a royal palace. Franco's intimate friends were mainly military men, some of whom were friends from Moroccan days, and not all great figures in the regime.

Franco liked shooting and spent much of his holidays deep-sea fishing. His private life was exemplary. He married in October 1923, with a representative of King Alfonso at his wedding, Carmen Polo y Martinez Valdes, of an aristocratic and learned family of Oviedo. The only child of this marriage, a daughter, married the Marquis of Villaverde and has seven offspring. One of Franco's grand-daughters married in 1972 Alfonso de Borbon y Dampierre, a grandson of King Alfonso and therefore a cousin of Prince Juan Carlos.

November 21, 1975.

Benjamin Frankel, the distinguished composer, died on February 12, 1973. He was 67.

He was born in London on January 31, 1906, and studied the piano in his youth before being apprenticed to the watchmaking trade. However in 1922 he managed to get to Germany to study the piano and violin. On returning he combined study at the Guildhall School of Music with earning his living as a jazz violinist in clubs and cafés.

Although he had already begun serious composition by the 1930s, most of his work at this time was in the more mundane field of orchestration, particularly for West End musicals and revues, including Coward's *Operette.* He gave up that work in 1944 but continued to write highly accomplished film scores, upwards of 120 of them, the most recent being for *The Battle of the Bulge.*

During and after the war his serious compositions gradually began to gain the reputation they deserved. The violin concerto, written for the Festival of Britain in 1951, was the true breakthrough, and was followed by a fairly prolific output of chamber and orchestral music. However all his eight symphonies had been composed since 1958, and he was already engaged on a ninth, a choral one, as a Prom commission. In these symphonies (all of which were broadcast in 1972 on Radio Three) he tried to show that 12-note serialism could be reconciled with tonality, and in this attempt he achieved a welcome directness and accessibility of expression in a very personal, rather introspective idiom.

He wrote four quartets up to 1952, adding only one other in 1965 during the period of late maturity. He also wrote further concertos for different instruments and combinations.

He had completed the short score for his opera *Marching Song,* to a libretto by Hans Keller based on John Whiting's play of that name.

The work had been accepted by Sadler's Wells opera, and it is to be hoped that with the cooperation of Frankel's pupil, the composer Buxton Orr, the work can be prepared for stage performance.

February 13, 1973.

David Franklin, the noted bass singer, who later made a career as a television and radio performer, died at the age of 65 on October 22, 1973.

Franklin was born in London on May 17, 1908. He was educated at Alleyn's College, Dulwich, and St. Catharine's College, Cambridge, and worked as a schoolmaster from 1930 to 1935, singing only as a pastime. In December of the latter year he was heard by Fritz Busch at a London audition and immediately invited to sing the Commendatore in *Don Giovanni* at the 1936 Glyndebourne Festival, where the following year he also sang Sarastro. In 1938 he again sang the Commendatore and added Banquo in *Macbeth.* At the same time he established himself as one of Britain's leading oratorio basses.

In 1946, after war service, he joined the new resident company at Covent Garden as principal bass and from then, until struck down by illness in 1951, he sang the following parts: Mars (in the premiere of Bliss's *The Olympians*), Rocco, Sarasto, Bartolo, Pimen, King Mark, Hunding, Faf-

ner, Pogner, Sparafucile and Baron Ochs. In all these parts his resonant, deep bass of uncommon range and his height and dignity of bearing were great assets.

While at the top of his profession, he lost his singing voice as a result of an operation. He had to build a new career. Making a virtue of necessity, he began to lecture and broadcast. Gradually his speaking voice, full, fruity and a little lugubrious, became well-known to millions of listeners through music talks, contributions to magazine programmes, and above all, panel games and quizzes, most successfully in *My Music* and as chairman of *Twenty Questions.*

As he said in his amusing, instructive autobiography, *Basso Cantante* (1969), "Although the change in my life had been a bit brutal and painful, it was the best thing that could have happened to me." That book, and some of his talks, tended at times to over-revere Glyndebourne and there was an element of schoolmasterly facetiousness in his spoken and written style that could annoy the fastidious. But his lively personality and friendly delivery won many new friends for music, and especially for opera, and his book contains much good advice about the teaching of young singers. He will be sorely missed in many circles.

October 23, 1973.

Lord Fraser of Lonsdale, C.H., C.B.E., who died in a London hospital on December 19, 1974, aged 77, was made a life peer in July 1958 but to the general public he will always be remembered as Sir Ian Fraser for the great work he did on behalf of St. Dunstan's and the British Legion.

Few men can have rendered greater service to the blind. As chairman of the Executive Council of St. Dunstan's, a Member of the House of Commons, President of the British Legion, a former Governor of the British Broadcasting Corporation, a director of a family business in South Africa and of many public companies, he overcame with great courage and determination the grave handicap of blindness. In St. Dunstan's he leaves behind an institution which will always be a memorial to two men, Sir Arthur Pearson, its founder, and Sir Ian Fraser, his lieutenant and successor.

William Jocelyn Ian Fraser was born at Eastbourne in 1897, and educated at Marlborough and the Royal Military College, Sandhurst, where he was senior cadet officer in 1915. In the 1914-18 War he served with the 1st Battalion, The King's (Shropshire) Light Infantry and was attached to the 1/4th Glosters. He had been in France only a few weeks when he was blinded at the Battle of the Somme, and on his retirement from the Army in 1917 was promoted captain.

He told in his autobiography, *Whereas I Was Blind,* how his whole life was changed while he was in hospital. He was visited by a V.A.D., who worked at St. Dunstan's as Sir Arthur Pearson's personal assistant and guide, and "who wore the smoothest and most beautiful kid gloves that I had ever felt".

She brought with her a letter from Sir Arthur telling how he had established St. Dunstan's to train blinded officers and men, and inviting him to go there. As a result Sir Ian's long association with St. Dunstan's began; he married the girl with the kid gloves, Irene Gladys, C.B.E., the daughter of George Mace, of Chipping Norton, and to quote his book again, "they both lived happily ever after".

In 1917 he started work as Pearson's assistant at St. Dunstan's. By 1921 he had become his second in command and when Pearson died at the end of that year Fraser was appointed, at the age of 24, chairman of St. Dunstan's. At first the centre of the organization was at St. Dunstan's Lodge in Regent's Park, but as the work increased the accommodation became inadequate and new headquarters were obtained in Marylebone Road as well as offices in South Audley Street. A convalescent home was established at Ovingdean, near Brighton, and during the 1939-45 War a large amount of the work was transferred to Church Stretton.

In all these changes Fraser was the moving spirit in spite of much other public work. Even before Pearson's death, he had decided that he must seek a wider outlet for his activities. He entered the London County Council in 1922 and served for three years as a Conservative member for North St. Pancras. From 1924 to 1929 he represented the same constituency in the House of Commons.

He lost the seat in 1929 but won it back two years later with a substantial majority and retained it in 1935. In the following year he retired temporarily from the House of Commons. He had been a member of the Broadcasting Committee of Inquiry which sat in 1925-26 and in 1936 he was invited to become a Governor of the B.B.C. He accepted and decided to retire from the House of Commons. In 1939, because of the war the number of governors of the B.B.C. was drastically reduced and Fraser, among others, resigned.

This left him free to return to the House of Commons. In 1940 he was elected unopposed for the Lonsdale Division of Lancaster, and was returned for Morecambe and Langdale in 1950 after the reorganization of constituencies. In 1941 the number of B.B.C. governors was increased and Fraser was reappointed. He continued to act as a B.B.C. governor until 1946. He enjoyed the work immensely and brought to it a special and invaluable knowledge of the needs of the blind listener.

In the House he was popular with members of all parties. He fought vigorously the battle for increased pensions for disabled former servicemen and women, and on many occasions with considerable suc-

cess.

In 1947 Fraser was appointed national president of the British Legion. He threw himself into the work with all his accustomed energy, and the legion could have had no finer advocate in the House of Commons. There were a few legion members, however, who felt that the president should not be attached to any political party, but when a vote of censure was moved on Fraser at the 1952 conference for his attitude in the House to the legion's demand for a weekly pension of £4 10s., only five out of the 650 delegates voted for it, and he was reelected president unopposed.

He retired from the national presidency at the Whitsun conference in 1958. When presentations were made to him and his wife, he announced that he would use the balance of the presentation fund, about £2,000, to establish a "Fraser Trust" to help the orphan of a former service man or the child of a 100 per cent disabled pensioner to gain something more from his or her education than would otherwise have been possible.

He was made a Companion of Honour in 1953. He had been knighted in 1934 and he always regarded these honours as a tribute to the blind community rather than to himself. As a director of a family business he went on a number of occasions to South Africa. He also visited the United States, Canada, Southern Rhodesia, Australia and New Zealand as well as other parts of the world to tell the story of St. Dunstan's.

He was a director of a number of English companies and whatever he took up he worked for indefatigably. In spite of all this he found time for recreation. He liked to visit the theatre or the cinema as well as to go boating and swimming and in his later years he became a keen fisherman. With the help of his retentive memory and Braille cards, he was a good bridge player.

But probably his greatest recreation of all was when he and his wife entertained some of their large circle of friends, either at the House of Commons or in their home, St. John's Lodge, in Regent's Park.

He is survived by Lady Fraser and the daughter of the marriage.

December 21, 1974.

Sir Ronald Fraser, K.B.E., C.M.G., diplomat and author, died on September 12, 1974 at the age of 85.

Born on November 3, 1888, the son of John and Louise Fraser, Arthur Ronald Fraser was educated at St. Paul's School. He enlisted in 1914, served in Flanders and in France, was wounded and disabled for further service and in 1917 joined the Foreign Trade department of the Foreign Office. His abilities soon became evident and his promotion in the Civil Service was rapid.

He served as British representative on the Inter-Allied Black List Committee in 1918, was assistant secretary to the Imperial Economic Conference in 1923, assistant secretary to the Balfour Committee on Industry and Trade during 1924-29, and Board of Trade adviser to H.M. Ambassador in Buenos Aires during the Anglo-Argentine negotiations of 1933. Then, while an assistant secretary at the Board of Trade, he was appointed Minister (Commercial) at the Embassy in Paris in September 1944. His appointment as resident-director of the Suez Canal Company gave further recognition to his practical and administrative abilities. Not, perhaps, an outstanding civil servant, he had nevertheless qualities of address and reasonableness and a knowledge of commercial policy that made him extremely valuable in the posts he filled.

As a novelist Fraser exhibited an entertaining gift of fantasy and a marked concern for his own carefully modulated prose style. The beauty which he cultivated so strenuously takes rather conventional forms; his imagery, indeed, is always inclined to be a little shopworn. But at his best, as in some of his earlier books, he attains a nice level of fantastic comedy, while the delicacy of his diction is kept more or less within the bounds of the intelligible and unaffected.

His first novel, *The Flying Draper,* appeared in 1924, and was followed, in successive years, by *Landscape with Figures* and *Flower Phantoms.* All have their engaging qualities, though the fantasy is streaked with crude colour and the vaguely mystical intimations seem rather forced; the last of these novels, which unfolds the dreams and sensibilities of a botanical student at Kew Gardens, pursues a not very confident hint of allegory. It was with *Rose Anstey* (1930) that Fraser made an impression. There are some very charming touches in this story of the lovely Rose's irruption into a London house filled with the trappings of an old family country house.

After that work came books such as *The Ninth of July, Surprising Results, A House in the Park, Bird under Glass,* and *Miss Lucifer.*

His literary output continued until the end of his life—his last books being *Trout's Testament, City of the Sun* and *The Pueblo.*

Fraser was a person of elegant and indeed fastidious taste, an excellent host—he gave his individual attention to the minutest details of the preparation and serving of a meal—and a most companionable *bon viveur.*

Fraser married, in 1915, Sylvia Blanche Powell. There were two sons and two daughters of the marriage.

September 13, 1974.

King Frederik IX of Denmark—See Denmark.

Professor Maurice Freedman, Professor of Social Anthropology at Oxford University, died on July 14, 1975 at the age of 54. He followed a distinguished career in London by becoming head of the Institute of Social Anthropology at Oxford and a Fellow of All Souls; he played an important role in the organization of anthropological research in Britain and abroad; he was a true scholar whose high standards of work were demonstrated in numerous publications; and he had an international reputation for his pioneering studies in southeast Asia, especially of Chinese institutions.

Freedman's university education was interrupted by the war. As a Henry Neville Gladstone scholar at King's College, London, he read English and was expected to get a first class, but took his degree hurriedly in two years in order to enter the army, and did not do well. But his academic recovery was spectacular. He served in the Royal Artillery from 1941 to 1945. More than three years of this military service was spent in India, and his Asian experiences turned him towards the study of "race relations".

His interests were crystallized by his entry in 1946 into the department of anthropology of the London School of Economics. His first graduate work was done on racial and cultural relations in Malaya. But for a man of his intellectual power a main challenge to thought lay in the theory of social anthropology itself. He was soon handling its most sophisticated problems with skill and critical acumen. He was then gravitating towards his major field of interest, the study of Chinese society.

In 1949-50 he spent nearly two years in field research among Hokkien-speaking Chinese of Singapore, speaking the vernacular and living in a variety of rural and urban settlements. A notable result of this study, carried out in difficult conditions, was the path-breaking *Chinese Family and Marriage in Singapore* (1957), first presented as a report to the Colonial Social Science Research Council, which had sponsored the research. (At the same time his wife Judith Djamour, whom he married in 1946, an anthropologist in her own right, carried out parallel studies among the Malays of Singapore, while also helping her husband in his own work, as she did throughout his career.)

For the next quarter of a century Freedman built on these foundations. He obtained almost encyclopaedic knowledge of material on the overseas Chinese and deepened his understanding of basic Chinese concepts and institutions. Despite the handicap of not having entered Chinese studies through the orthodox gate of classical Chinese language and literature, his command of contemporary Chinese thought and behaviour and his analytical and integrative strength were such as to gain him the respect and trust of his sinological colleagues, in southeast Asia itself as well as in the western hemisphere.

His contribution included clarification of issues in three related fields of major importance: the structure of lineage and kinship in southeastern Chinese society; the nature of ancestor-worship; and the significance of geomancy—the art of relating a site, especially for burial, to the good fortune of men. In each of these topics Freedman's work has laid new foundations.

He never visited the People's Republic of China—though he was able to visit the New Territories of Hongkong—but, building on the work of early scholars such as de Groot and Granet, he was helping towards a re-interpretation of Chinese traditional society. Here he did much to dispel any constraint which may formerly have marked relations between anthropologists and sinologists.

But his interests were not restricted to Chinese studies. As organizing secretary and then chairman of the London Committee of the London–Cornell Project for research in south and southeast Asia, he was between 1962 and 1970 a central figure in an unusual experiment in international academic cooperation which produced a series of important studies over a range of societies in those regions. And one of his most recent inquiries, in 1971, on behalf of the British Academy, was in preparation for the establishment of a British Institute in South-East Asia, based on Singapore.

A very special place in Freedman's academic life was held by Jewish studies, about which he felt deeply. He had developed many contacts with Israel, which he described on his first visit in 1956 as "the disturbingly interesting land of my forefathers". But as a sophisticated scholar of cosmopolitan tastes, not a ritualist in any very overt way, it was with general Jewish culture and ideas that he had strong bonds and in which he had great belief for their significance for the world of learning.

As early as 1955, as editor of a book *A Minority in Britain*, he argued stoutly for a scientific study of Jewish social life in Britain. It would help to illumine the workings of British society; and "a dispassionate study of Jews is good for Jews" in setting their problems in a wider perspective and in helping Gentiles to understand these problems better.

In 1957, in the Noah Barou memorial lecture delivered at University College London, he examined aspects of changing Jewish life in the Diaspora more generally. And in 1959, with Morris Ginsberg* as colleague, he began his long service as managing editor of the new *Jewish Journal of Sociology*, which was founded to provide an international vehicle for serious writing on Jewish social affairs.

For the most part Freedman's academic career was one of steady progression. Appointed to a lectureship in anthropology at the London School of Economics in 1950, he became Reader in Anthropology in the University of London in 1957, and was elected to a personal chair of anthropology in 1965—moving in 1968 to an established post in the subject.

He also held visiting appointments at Yale, Cornell and the University of Malaya. In 1961 he was offered a new chair in Asian anthropology at Yale, but decided against it. In 1970, however, after he had been actively involved as a governor of the London School of Economics in the disturbances of the previous year, he became disenchanted with the atmosphere. Doubtless this played a part in his acceptance of the chair of social anthropology at Oxford, left vacant by the retirement of Sir Edward Evans-Pritchard.

To succeed Evans-Pritchard, from whom he differed greatly in intellectual background, sphere of work and personal temperament, could not have been easy. Freedman respected the work being done at the Institute, but perhaps enjoyed the fellowship of All Souls even more. He had begun to develop his own body of teaching, including joint seminars with colleagues in Chinese literary and historical studies working within the University and coming from elsewhere.

On the more personal side Maurice Freedman sometimes presented a paradox. He could be blunt, even brusque in his reactions; rigid, even dogmatic in the expression of his opinions; harsh, even tactless in criticism of ideas or behaviour of which he disapproved.

Yet he was an elegant writer and a good conversationalist, with graphic power of narrative and pungent wit.

July 22, 1975.

Pierre Fresnay, the distinguished French actor, who was conspicuous throughout his career in the theatre and films for the scrupulous, almost ruthless, integrity of his performances, died in Paris on January 9, 1975 at the age of 77.

As a young man he often acted in England both in French and in English, and he remained a familiar figure to British audiences through the showing of such films as *Monsieur Vincent* and *La Grande Illusion*. Many filmgoers will recall with a particular pleasure his playing in the famous trilogy, *Marius; Fanny;* and *César.*

Fresnay came of an Alsatian family, by name Laudenbach. He, Pierre-Jules Laudenbach, the son of a *professeur*, was born on April 4, 1897 in Paris, was educated there at the Lycée Henri IV, and trained for the stage under his uncle, Charles Garry. Just before the First World War he joined Mme. Réjane's company at what became the Théâtre de Paris, but he was accepted some months later as a pupil at the Conservatoire National and became a *Pensionnaire* of the Comédie Française early in 1915.

Between 1919, when he returned to it after three years' service with the French Army, and 1926, Fresnay once visited London with the company and frequently gave recitals in French in the English provinces, in addition to taking 80 parts in Paris, in some of which, especially those in the plays of Alfred de Musset, he was considered to have excelled all other actors in living memory. None the less, he was dissatisfied with the Comédie Française and he left it, not without being sued for breach of contract and fined 200,000 francs, to make a new career in the theatres of the boulevards and in the cinema.

With the Compagnie des Quinze he was seen in the title parts of two plays by André Obey, Noë in Paris and Don Juan in London, where he also succeeded Noël Coward as leading man to Yvonne Printemps in Conversation Piece. Coward had written this operetta, in English, specially for Mme. Printemps, but since she did not speak the language at that time, Fresnay had had to teach the part to her word by word.

Mme. Printemps and Fresnay appeared together in Conversation Piece in New York, and again in London (more briefly) in a comedy by Ben Travers; and in 1937, after the long run in Paris of the operetta Trois Valses—here, too, Fresnay's part was necessarily a non-singing one—they acquired a standing professional address at the Théâtre de la Michodière. Henceforward they worked there exclusively, except when making films. They were associated in the management of it first, till his death in 1942, with Victor Boucher, later with François Périer. Fresnay there acted in and directed, among other plays, Léocadia (Time Remembered) and Le Voyageur sans Bagage by Jean Anouilh, whose first play L'Hermine he had put on elsewhere in 1932, Marcel Achard's Auprès de ma Blonde and André Roussin's Les Oeufs de l'Autriche.

In the cinema Pierre Fresnay's work was cast in an intelligent, sometimes aesthetic, mould. It was ultimately powerful, though, because he was able to suggest the torment that tried to claw its way through to the composed exterior. This was never demonstrated better than in Maurice Cloche's Monsieur Vincent, the lustrous film about the French priest and philanthropist made in 1947. Professionally Fresnay found it difficult to rid himself of the saintly trappings of that role, and it is a measure of his success in Cloche's film that film-goers who saw him in subsequent films still fancied they saw traces of a halo round his head.

Fresnay's screen debut was in 1931, playing the title role in Marius. This was the first film of Marcel Pagnol's famed trilogy about life in the Marseilles docks in the 1920s. The following year he appeared—again with Raimu, Orane Demazis, Charpin and Maupi—in the sequel Fanny and, two years later, came the film that completed the trilogy, César. Conversation pieces though the films undoubtedly were, they achieved considerable commercial success and artistically they gave discriminating film-goers the world over a taste for provincial French fare.

Fresnay appeared briefly in Alfred Hitchcock's The Man Who Knew Too Much, made in Britain in 1934. But it was not until three years later, in Jean Renoir's La Grande Illusion, that he again made an impact on the film scene. He played the French officer, a First World War prisoner, whose civilized outlook erected a bridge between himself and his captor, the aristocratic camp commandant played by Eric von Stroheim. This was Fresnay in typical mood, controlled, and yet inwardly coiled; it was a devastatingly attractive performance, made even more effective by the underlying intellectualism that was sometimes to be the despair of his fellow actors.

Jean Gabin, who appeared with Fresnay in La Grande Illusion, is reported to have said of him: "He's a marvellous actor, but he always makes you feel you are using the wrong spoon." Fresnay will also be remembered for his enigmatic contribution to Clouzot's frightening Le Corbeau, made in 1943, and for his relaxed impersonation of Offenbach in the enjoyable soufflé La Valse de Paris in 1949. Few of the films which he made in more recent years did anything to enhance his enviable reputation.

Fresnay was married three times, the marriage with Yvonne Printemps being the third. His previous marriages with respectively Rachel Berendt and Berthe Bovy of the Comédie Française were dissolved.

January 11, 1975.

Rudolf Friml, who composed the music and words for the light operas Rose Marie, The Vagabond King and many others, died in Hollywood on November 12, 1972 at the age of 92. He was the last of a generation of composer-writers in Hollywood which included Sigmund Romberg and Victor Herbert.

Rudolf Friml, the American-Czech composer, was born in Prague in December 1879. As a pupil of the Prague Conservatoire he studied piano with Jiránek and theory and composition with Foerster. He also pursued a further course of study in composition with Dvořák.

After graduating, he toured Austria, England, Germany, Russia and the United States of America for five years as accompanist to the great violinist Jan Kubelik, father of the distinguished conductor Rafael Kubelik. In 1904 Kubelik and Friml visited the United States for the second time and Friml decided to settle there. In America he started as a concert soloist, giving innumerable piano recitals and appearing with several of the large symphony orchestras. He played his piano concerto with The New York Symphony Orchestra and composed assiduously.

Friml's entrance into the popular field was made in 1912 when an emergency substitute was needed to create an operetta for Emma Trentini. What happened was that Victor Herbert had been contracted to write the music of The Firefly for Emma Trentini as a follow-up to Naughty Marietta, which had been a big success. During the run of Naughty Marietta, Herbert and Mme. Trentini became embroiled in a bitter quarrel in which each refused to communicate with the other. Herbert now refused to write any more music for her and she refused to appear in anything Herbert wrote. Since The Firefly was scheduled for early production, Arthur Hammerstein, the producer, had to find another composer. G. Schirmer, Friml's publisher, suggested to Hammerstein he take a chance on the young and untried Friml. Speed was essential. With no experienced composer available Hammerstein yielded to persuasion.

Hammerstein was rewarded for his gamble on a novice with one of the most remarkable operetta scores of that period; the melodies fresh and expressive and beautifully written for the voice. They include "Giannina Mia", "Love is like a Firefly", "The Dawn of Love", "When a Maid comes knocking at your Heart" and the duet "Sympathy". There is still one more number associated with The Firefly, "Donkey Serenade", without which no revival of the operetta is complete. This song was not in Friml's original stage score. He wrote it in 1937 in collaboration with Herbert Stothart for the film adaptation of The Firefly. The melody started life as a piano solo called "Chanson". In 1924 it was turned into a foxtrot "Chansonette", and introduced by Paul Whiteman* and his Orchestra at the same concert at which Gershwin's "Rhapsody in Blue" was first heard.

In 1924 Friml scored a sensational success with Rose Marie, a romance of the Canadian Rockies. In New York the stars were Dennis King and Mary Ellis and at Drury Lane Derek Oldham* and Edith Day. The best remembered songs are the title number, "Indian Love Call", "The Mounties", "Door of my Dreams" and "Totem Tom Tom". In 1925 came The Vagabond King, a dramatic day in the life of François Villon with effective numbers like "Song of the Vagabonds", "Only a Rose", "Someday".

Friml's last success was The Three Musketeers (1928), produced with splendour by Florenz Ziegfeld. Alexander Woolcott wrote in his first night notice: "I did greatly enjoy the first few years of Act I". Other shows of Friml's to come to London were Katinka, The Little Whopper, The Blue Kitten and High Jinks.

Friml possessed a spontaneous gift for writing operetta tunes with a little more substance than the ordinary musical-comedy song and his sensitive feeling for the voice made his tunes grateful to singers without taxing their resources. He set a pattern for musical plays which endured until the "new style" of Oklahoma ushered in a different style of musical show.

November 14, 1972.

Wing Commander David Fryer, an authority on aviation medicine, died in a car accident on March 16, 1971. He was 43.

David Fryer was born on July 4, 1927 and was educated at Woking Grammar School, at University College and University College Hospital, graduating B.Sc. in Physiology in 1947, M.B., B.S. in 1950 and M.D. in 1968.

He entered the R.A.F. in 1952, and after brief service in Fighter Command, he joined the research staff of the R.A.F. Institute of Aviation Medicine later that year. Except for a period from 1967-1969, when he was the aero-medical staff officer at the Embassy in Washington, he remained at the Institute till his death. He was made O.B.E. in 1961, and elected an associate fellow of the Royal Aeronautical Society in 1967. He was appointed an R.A.F. Consultant in Aviation Medicine in 1968.

He worked initially on the effects of rapid decompression, and it was his experience here which involved him in the investigations carried out by Armstrong, Fryer, Stewart and Whittingham into the interpretation of the injuries suffered by passengers in the Comet disasters of 1954. From this work Fryer developed an interest in the pathological aspects of aircraft accidents and deductions from them on matters concerning flight safety; and he became one of the original crash injury pathologists. As a result of these studies he was able to make various recommendations with the aim of improving flight safety and survival. His interest in the effects of ram pressure and high wind velocities on man, such as occur during escape from aircraft, led to experiments in which air velocities up to nearly 600 miles per hour were simulated at much lower speeds by immersion in water.

These experiments established certain physiological criteria regarding the effects of differential pressures acting over the surface of man. They were complex, difficult and not without danger. They were carried out on himself as the only subject, and truly established a limit of human endurance.

His principal abiding interest was probably decompression sickness and in this field he was extremely widely read. He sought every opportunity to search through the literature of the problem and seek original sources. He served on the Medical Research Council's Panel on Decompression Sickness, and his monograph on *Subatmospheric Decompression Sickness in Man* is the standard work in its field, and is likely to remain so for many years.

He was a man at home among books, and was an enthusiastic collector of items of historical significance in aviation medicine; in particular he had been undertaking a survey of the history of the pressure cabin.

Fryer was an excellent and enthusiastic educationist, and when in 1966, the R.A.F., in association with the Royal Colleges, founded a Diploma in Aviation Medicine, it was Fryer who undertook much of the spade work for the Professor in the preparation of a syllabus, and he was soon appointed an examiner for this new subject.

At the time of his death he had been engaged in the preparation of a textbook in aviation medicine.

April 12, 1971.

The Ruler of Fujairah, Sheikh Mohammed Bin Hamed Al Sharqi, who died in a London hospital on September 17, 1974, was one of the last independent tribal Sheikhs of Arabia. He ruled his mountain people for over 40 years.

In the early days of his power Trucial Oman was virtually unknown to the outside world, a wild and turbulent land of which Fujairah, tucked away in the mountains along the Gulf of Oman, was the most inaccessible part. In those days there was doubt that Fujairah could maintain a separate identity, and it was solely due to her ruler's skill and diplomacy that in 1952 Britain and the other six Trucial States formally recognized Fujairah as an independent Sheikhdom.

This spirit of independence never deserted Sheikh Mohammed, who encompassed in his lifetime the modern and the medieval; the age of oil and the age of tribal blood feud; a time of immense wealth and a time of great poverty. Throughout the negotiations leading up to British withdrawal from the Gulf, the emergence of Fujairah as a member of the United Arab Emirates, and latterly when Fujairah alone of the states did not benefit from the revenues of oil, he maintained his position with firmness and dignity.

With the passing of Sheikh Mohammed the Gulf lost one of its most colourful characters. Small in stature, his eyes twinkling behind a great bushy beard, and dressed in the cloak and robes of the desert, he swept through life leaving an impression that was piratical and romantic but wholly attractive. Renowned as a warrior, he mellowed in later years, devoting his energies to modernizing and developing the state, a task in which he was assisted by a lifelong friendship with Sheikh Zaid bin Sultan of Abu Dhabi.

His hospitality and keen sense of humour were famous. A strict but tolerant Muslim, he expended much time and patience as a judge and lawgiver to his people and it is in this role that perhaps he will be best remembered.

September 25, 1974.

Anne Furlonge (Lady Furlonge), who died on March 28, 1975 after a long illness, was one of the most prominent British women lawn tennis players between the two world wars, first as Miss E. A. Goldsack and later as Mrs. J. B. Pittman.

She first achieved fame in 1925 when, on her first appearance at Wimbledon, she won from Suzanne Lenglen one of the five games which that redoubtable player lost throughout the tournament.

During the next 10 years, a full social life prevented that dedication to the game which could have brought her the highest honours, but she won numerous tournaments in both Great Britain and the United States, notably the women's singles and doubles at the Bournemouth hard court championships; she also reached the final of the ladies' doubles at Wimbledon (1937) and the semi-finals of the singles at both Wimbledon (1929) and Forest Hills (1932), on both occasions losing to Helen Wills.

She gave up competitive tennis in 1939, and in 1952 entered diplomatic life by marrying Mr. (later Sir Geoffrey) Furlonge, whom she partnered at his successive Heads of Mission posts at Amman, Sofia and Addis Ababa; in all these countries her exceptionally friendly and sympathetic nature brought her innumerable friends among local people and diplomatic colleagues alike.

April 1, 1975.

Major Sir Ralph Furse, K.C.M.G., D.S.O., who died on October 1, 1973 at the age of 86, made a unique personal contribution to the history of the British Colonial Service.

Born in September 1887, the son of J. H. M. Furse, he was educated at Eton and Balliol College. In 1909 he was brought into touch with the Secretary of State for the Colonies, Lewis Harcourt, who was looking for an additional Assistant Private Secretary, to help his so-called "patronage" work. Up to that time apart from the Eastern Cadetships, which were filled by competitive examination, recruitment for the Colonial Service had been sporadic and not on such a scale as to call for any special organization. The rapid development, from 1900 onwards, of the hitherto unadministered inland territories of Tropical Africa changed all that.

When Furse went to the Colonial Office in 1910 the administrative staffs alone of the Tropical African Dependencies had increased from a mere handful to a total of nearly 500. To deal with this situation was the task offered to Ralph Furse; he undertook it with alacrity. Though in form a personal Private Secretary to the Minister, and liable to discharge on a change in the incumbency, he was too good to lose, and he was kept on until 1914, by which time he had established a close relationship with University Appointments Boards and other sources of supply and had built up a system of selection based on the candidate's personal record and the impression made by him at interview.

After his service in King Edward's Horse in the First World War, in which he won the D.S.O. and bar, the Colonial Office again turned to Furse, and in 1919 he was once more installed as Assistant Private

Secretary (appointments). From 1919 onwards, Furse, though still holding no official position and still nominally a member of the personal entourage of the Secretary of State, was in practice the head of an efficient and growing Recruitment Department.

The separation of the Dominions Office from the Colonial Office in 1925, and the appointment of a Colonial Governor, Sir Samuel Wilson, as Permanent Under-Secretary of State, enabled attention to be given to the need for reorganization of the office. Furse felt that satisfactory recruitment would be made possible only if the Colonial public services could be unified on a functional basis instead of being regarded as entirely separate territorial organizations. Largely as a result of Furse's representations, Leo Amery, as Secretary of State, decided in 1929 to set up a committee, under the chairmanship of Sir Warren Fisher, to go into the question of recruitment.

As a result of this committee's recommendation, the policy of unification was accepted by the succeeding Secretary of State, Lord Passfield; a Personnel Division was set up in the Colonial Office and Furse, along with his team of assistants, was admitted by special dispensation to the established Civil Service to form that half of the new division which was to be responsible for recruitment and training.

Furse took a full share in the subsequent working out of the unification policy, and under his direction (he was now styled Director of Recruitment) the staffing of the Colonial Service went ahead until the outbreak of war in 1939.

One of Furse's major concerns was the establishment of Colonial Administrative Service courses at Oxford and Cambridge, and also, subsequently, at London University. During the Second World War he initiated further study of the problem which was undertaken by a committee under the chairmanship of the late Duke of Devonshire when Parliamentary Under-Secretary of State. As a result the well-known "Devonshire" courses were established after the war.

Furse retired officially in 1948 but continued until 1950 to act as part-time adviser to the Colonial Office on training questions.

But his main and unique contribution was the system of recruitment, which was almost entirely his personal creation and which stood every test to which it was subjected in a period of bewildering changes. His own flair for selecting the right man for a job amounted to genius; but he was able to translate it into a technique which could be used by others with little if any less success. Though handicapped by deafness, which increased with advancing years, he triumphed over this disability and could even, on occasion, turn it to advantage in a discussion which seemed to be going the wrong way.

He was a man of great personal charm, an inspiring leader in peace as in war. His penetrating gaze seemed to miss little, but his gentle courtesy won the heart.

By his marriage to Margaret Newbolt, daughter of Sir Henry Newbolt, he had two sons and two daughters. The elder daughter, Jill, was an actress of distinction and was married to Laurence Whistler, O.B.E. She died in 1944. Her younger sister, Theresa, was married to Mr. Whistler in 1950.

October 5, 1973.

Ekaterina Furtseva, the Russian Minister of Culture, and the only woman ever to rise to the Kremlin inner circle, died on October 25, 1974. She was 63. She was dropped from the Politburo, as the party praesidium became known, in 1961, but retained considerable influence as a Minister.

She had been excluded from the Supreme Soviet (Parliament) since June 1974 when her name had not appeared among the 1,517 candidates for the two houses, and it had been forecast that she would be replaced in her ministerial post, but in July, when Kosygin read out the entire list of nominees to senior government posts, Mrs. Furtseva's was still among them.

Her dismissal had been expected because there had been stories that she had been reprimanded by her superiors for using her position to build a luxurious *dacha*, a country house, near Moscow.

In her day she was the most prominent and politically important woman in the Soviet Union. While her sex undoubtedly played some part in securing a place for her in the praesidium of the party central committee, her demotion from this supreme policy-making body in the Soviet Union showed that her role in the highest echelons of the party had been more than that of a mere figurehead representing Soviet womanhood.

Born in December 1910 in the textile manufacturing town of Vyshniy Volochek, about 150 miles north of Moscow, Ekaterina attended a few grades of school, and after training in a trade school she followed in her parents' footsteps and became a weaver in the *Bolshevichha* ("Bolshevik Woman") Textile Mill. Although most children do not enter the *Komsomol*, the Young Communists League, until the age of 17, the energetic Ekaterina was admitted at the age of 14.

By the time she was 20 years old, in 1930, she was admitted to membership in the Communist Party. Her rise in the party ranks was steady and sure due to hard work, organizational ability, a talent for public speaking, and a persistent, ambitious nature. She served as a secretary of *Komsomol* organizations in the cities of Kursk and Feodosia, and finally in the Crimea area committee.

In 1937, at the age of 27, she resumed her education; entering the Moscow Institute of Chemical Technology, where five years later she took her degree as a chemical engineer.

Upon graduation, with full time again to devote to the party, she became secretary of the Frunze District Party Committee. It was during this period that she first caught the eye of Nikita Khrushchev who was first secretary of the Moscow Party organization. After Stalin's death, when Khrushchev's star began to climb, it was no coincidence that Furtseva's rose, too.

In 1950 Furtseva was elected second secretary of the Central Committee of the Party's organization for all of Moscow— the most important party unit outside the national apparatus. Four years later she was first secretary (or chairman) of the Moscow Party organization, and by that time had climbed the ladder to the national level. At the 19th Congress of the Communist Party in October 1952 she was elected a candidate (or second-rank) member of the Central Committee of the Communist Party of the U.S.S.R. The full-fledged members of the Party's Central Committee numbered 133, of whom only three were women.

It was in 1956 at the Twentieth Congress of the Party which was dominated by Khrushchev's speeches initiating a new post-Stalin order in the Soviet Union, that Furtseva attained the triple distinction of becoming a candidate member of the Praesidium.

With the expulsion of the "anti-party group" from the 11-member Praesidium, Furtseva rose to the level of a full member in a newly formed 15-member Praesidium under the undisputed leadership of Khrushchev, becoming the first woman to attain this pinnacle of Soviet prominence.

In the late 1950s she came to exercise a more important role in Moscow's cultural life and education and in May 1960 she became U.S.S.R. Minister of Culture. In the era of Boris Pasternak and greater contact with the "contaminating" influences of the non-communist world, this was an especially important assignment for a person with the qualities of Furtseva.

The decline in Furtseva's political position began with her departure from the C.C.'s secretariat with its control of the executive apparatus in the summer of 1960 and culminated with her demotion from the Praesidium in 1961. The factors in her fall were multiple but among the more important is the fact that it was a part of Khrushchev's policy to remove from the Praesidium as many as possible of those who witnessed his difficulties in 1952 or assisted him in the consolidation of his position. Another factor is that pressure existed within the Moscow party organization, which is one of the most important in the country, that it be represented by a man.

As Minister of Culture she led an active public life in frequent contact with western impresarios and artists and clearly enjoyed introducing foreign companies to the Russian public. She had latterly attended the first Moscow performance of an American country music show.

She announced that she would visit Mexico in November 1974 to attend a film festival. This was taken as further evidence that she had emerged unscathed from the *dacha* building affair.

She was a stern opponent of modern art ("which does not serve the people") and attacked Alexander Solzhenitsyn, the writer, as an "active opponent of Soviet reality".

She visited Great Britain with a Russian parliamentary delegation in 1956; in 1961 when Minister of Culture; and four years later again as a guest of Miss Jennie Lee (as she then was), Minister with special responsibility for the arts.

She was married to Nikolai Firyubin, for many years a deputy Foreign Minister. She leaves a daughter, Svetlana, who visited Britain with her mother in 1961.

October 26, 1974.

Fu Tso-yi, the Nationalist general who surrendered Peking to the investing communist forces in January 1949, died on April 19, 1974 aged 79. It was not only a recognition of this action but a tribute to Fu's energy and ability that he served for 14 years thereafter as Minister of Water Conservancy in the government under Chou En-lai.

Fu belonged to that generation that matured after the old civil service examinations had been abolished, when the new nationalism seemed to make the army a worthy career. He was a Shansi man and he was associated with the reforming but independent Shansi warlord Yen Hsi-shan. He won a reputation in 1927 when his army—then nominally allied to those of Chiang Kai-shek—was surrounded in the walled city of Chochow in north China by forces of the Manchurian warlord Chang Tso-lin. Fu's tenacity and hold over his troops enabled him to survive for three months in hopes of relief by the Nationalist forces.

No relief came and Fu surrendered with his starving garrison in January 1928. A year later he was active in the new warlord alliance against Chiang Kai-shek of Yen Hsi-shan and Feng Yu-hsiang.

When the war against Japan brought all the warlord forces under Chiang Kai-shek's command, Fu Tso-yi held the Inner Mongolian provinces of Suiyuan and Chahar. Thereafter as nationalist commander in north China during the civil war he complained of being starved of weapons and supplies by Chiang, who probably had never trusted him. Fu sought direct aid from foreign powers including Britain but without success.

After Tsinan, capital of Shantung province, fell in September 1948, Fu's position in Tientsin and Peking became untenable. By a typical Chinese arrangement Dr. Chi Ch'ao-ting, a distinguished economist then serving as an adviser to the Nationalist Bank of China in Shanghai, flew north to serve as economic adviser to Fu Tso-yi. Chi was a secret communist but also a Shansi man.

Tientsin fell to the communists on January 15, 1949 and on January 22 a couple of mortar rounds fired by each side served as a symbolical battle after which Peking could be surrendered to the communist forces then under Lin Piao. On January 31 the P.L.A. marched into what was to be their new and undamaged capital.

April 25, 1974.

Sir Hudson Fysh, K.B.E., D.F.C., a pioneer of civil aviation in the Commonwealth, who died in Sydney on April 6, 1974 at the age of 79, was chairman of Qantas Empire Airways Ltd, from 1947 to 1966.

After the First World War he and a few friends founded in the Australian outback a company which they called Queensland and Northern Territory Aerial Services Ltd. (the source, later, of the name Qantas), with a paid-up capital of £A6,700 (£5,360 sterling), and thereafter the story of his life is largely the story of this company's development into one of the world's great international airlines. "We took up civil aviation not sure where it would lead us", Fysh once confessed, but others would say that civil aviation was led not a little by the man himself. His services to aviation were recognized in 1954 when he was knighted.

Fysh was born on January 7, 1895, at Launceston, Tasmania, and educated at Launceston Grammar School and Geelong Grammar School, Victoria. He left to become a wool classer, but the war broke out and he volunteered for service overseas with the first A.I.F. He began as a trooper in the 3rd Regiment of the 1st Australian Light Horse Brigade and was at Gallipoli and in Palestine. In 1916 he was commissioned in the brigade's machinegun squadron, before transferring to the Australian Flying Corps as an observer. He won the D.F.C. and graduated as a scout pilot in 1918.

Early in 1919 Fysh, Pat McGuinness, also an ex-service airman, and an engineer called Arthur Baird decided to try to win the Australian government's prize of £A10,000 (£8,000 sterling) for the first flight from England to Australia. But their financial backer, Sir Samuel McCaughey, died and they had to give up. Instead they were commissioned by the Australian government to survey the Longreach (Queensland)/Darwin section of the England/Australia route. They travelled in a T-model Ford, which was the first car to reach the shores of the Gulf of Carpentaria, and met a rich western grazier, Fergus McMaster, who was later knighted as the first chairman of Qantas.

One year later Fysh, McMaster and McGuinness and two other graziers, Ainsley Templeton and Alan Campbell, sat round a table in the Gresham Hotel, Brisbane, and decided to form Queensland and Northern Territory Aerial Services Ltd. Fysh invested £A500 (£400 sterling) of his £A600 (£480 sterling) savings in the venture. The company's first head office was at Winton and it began with two old planes with maximum payloads of 400lb. and an average ground speed of 67 mph. Fysh wanted to bring all the benefits of aerial transport to the great distances of the outback, where often in the wet season the land is too bogged for movement and people would sometimes die before they could reach hospital. But first he had to interest the west in flying and convince the people of its safety.

The company moved its head office to Longreach in 1921 and advertised joy-rides at 50s. a time (looping the loop £A5). Within two years 871 joy-riders had been taken up, but the company was £A8,000 £6,400 sterling) in debt. However, Fysh had carried Australia's first maternity case to hospital by air and organized the first aerial shoot of wild bush turkeys. He had also carried a body from Longreach to Brisbane, after removing the aircraft's second seat to get the business.

On November 2, 1922 Qantas opened its first service, which was only the second regular service in Australia. The first Qantas service, for which the company receive an invaluable mail subsidy, was between Charleville and Cloncurry—577 miles flown in two stages, with an overnight stop. McGuinness flew the Charleville/Longreach section, Fysh the Longreach/Cloncurry section. They used two aircraft, an Armstrong Whitworth FK8 and a De Havilland 4.

Fysh took his wife to live in Longreach, in a weather-board house with a kitchen of corrugated iron and a stove that burned wood. Years afterwards, describing the life, Lady Fysh said: "With the heat, no refrigerators and no wirelesses, we had trouble keeping pilots once they were married. When I was in hospital after my son was born the temperature was 117 degrees." Once she was asked on the telephone by one of the pilots to put on her high-heeled shoes, go to the airfield and tell him how far the heels sank in after the rain, "so I'll know if it is safe to land".

In 1923 Fysh became managing director of Qantas and remained, of course, one of its pilots. On November 30 he flew S. M. Bruce, the Prime Minister, who was later to be Lord Bruce of Melbourne*, from Winton to Longreach on an election tour. Next year Qantas received its first plane with a cabin, the DH50. In 1926 Qantas built its own first aircraft, the DH50a, which was a remarkable achievement in a little place like Longreach.

By 1928 Qantas had started flying schools in Longreach and Brisbane, and that year the Australian Inland Mission began its flying doctor service, with headquarters in Cloncurry and planes provided by Qantas. The company also began to operate, between Brisbane and Toowoomba, Australia's first daily air service. In 1929 it received its first DH61 which, said Fysh years later, "had a lavatory aboard". In 1930 Qantas registered its first million miles and moved its head office to Brisbane.

Next year Fysh on behalf of Qantas, flew the Bisbane/Darwin section of the first experimental air mail service between Australia and England. Imperial Airways flew the main Darwin/London section. In 1933 Qantas become interested in tendering for the Brisbane/Singapore section of the proposed Kangaroo route between Sydney and London, and Fysh flew to London for consultations with Imperial Airways. These led to the formation of Qantas Empire Airways Ltd. which flew the Brisbane/Singapore section when the service was officially opened by the Duke of Gloucester.

In 1937 and again in 1938 Fysh went to London and the continent to arrange for the opening of the England/Australia flying-boat service. The Australian terminus was to be in Sydney and so, in 1938, Qantas Empire Airways Ltd. moved its headquarters from Brisbane to Sydney.

Within three weeks of the outbreak of war in 1939 the R.A.A.F. requisitioned two Qantas flying-boats, but in October Qantas was still in a position to relieve the hardpressed Imperial Airways of its responsibility for the Sydney/London route as far as Karachi. In 1940 the first air service to New Zealand from Australia was inaugurated and Tasman Empire Airways Ltd. (T.E.A.L.) was established, with Fysh as a founder director. In 1941 Qantas ferried the first of 19 Catalina flying-boats from California on behalf of the Australian government, and in 1942 it lost five flying-boats in action against the Japanese, for Fysh, who was in Singapore when Japan attacked Pearl Harbor, had thrown his company's resources into the fight.

In 1943 Qantas flying-boats made 765 flights to New Guinea with 24,167 troops and much equipment, evacuating casualties on their return trips. In July that year it reopened the Middle East air route to England, which had been cut since the fall of Singapore and Java, by routing its Catalina flying-boats from Perth to Ceylon—a distance of 3,513 miles and the longest non-stop regular air service ever established. It took 27 hours.

Soon after the war the Australian government acquired B.O.A.C.'s half interest in Qantas and later became the company's sole owner. When this happened, in 1947, Fysh, who had been managing director since 1923, became, in addition, chairman of the company, in succession to Sir Fergus McMaster. He stayed as managing director until 1955.

In 1959, Qantas took delivery of the first American jet airliners to be exported, the Boeing 707-138.

Fysh leaves a widow, a son and a daughter.

April 9, 1974.

G

Lieutenant-General Sir Humfrey Gale, K.B.E., C.B., C.V.O., M.C., who was Chief Administrative Officer and Deputy Chief of Staff to General Eisenhower during the campaigns in North Africa and Western Europe, died on April 8, 1971 at La Tour-de-Peilz, Switzerland, at the age of 80.

He was a specialist of outstanding reputation in problems of supply and transport. He had a gift for getting on well with foreigners, and his sympathetic nature and keen sense of humour endeared him to his subordinates.

Humfrey Myddleton Gale was born on October 4, 1890, the eldest son of Ernest Gale of Liphook. He was educated at St. Paul's School and the Royal Military College, and was commissioned in the Army Service Corps in 1911. In the 1914-18 War he served on the Western Front for four years at regimental duty and in the transport directorate. He won the Military Cross and was twice mentioned in dispatches. Between the wars he held a number of staff appointments at the War Office, graduated at both the Army and Naval Staff Colleges, and was for three years an instructor at Camberley.

At the beginning of the Second World War he was assistant director of supplies and transport at the War Office. Next he served as head of the administrative staffs of the 2nd and 3rd Army Corps, for part of the time in France. In 1941 he went to the Scottish Command as major-general in charge of administration, Scottish Command, and a year later he became chief administrative officer to Sir Alan Brooke (later F.-M. Lord Alanbrooke*) at G.H.Q., Home Forces.

When General Eisenhower* took over the command of the forces preparing for the landing in North Africa, Gale was selected to be his chief administrative officer and deputy chief of staff. This was the beginning of an association which lasted till the end of the war.

When the North African campaign was over, Eisenhower took Gale with him to England as his chief administrative officer for the campaign in Western Europe. He declared that he would be unwilling to undertake another large allied command without his administrative assistance, saying, "He has that irreplaceable quality of being able to handle British-American supply problems with tact and judgment, and he is almost as familiar with the American system of supply as with the British." When the plans for the landing in Normandy were being explained to Churchill* it fell to Gale to describe the administrative arrangements.

At the end of the war he became the personal representative in Europe of Herbert Lehman,* the Director General of Unrra. In this post, which he held until Unrra was dissolved in 1947, he was head of a staff of some 2,000 in the regional office, and responsible for the work of missions in 17 countries.

From 1954 to 1964 he was chairman of the Basildon New Town Development Corporation.

He was Colonel Commandant of the R.A.S.C., from 1944 to 1954 and of the Army Catering Corps from 1946 to 1958.

He married in 1917 Winifred, second daughter of William Cross, and they had two daughters. She died in 1936, and in 1945 he married, secondly, Minnie Grace, daughter of Count Gregorini-Bingham.

April 10, 1971.

Gaston Gallimard, perhaps the most influential Paris publisher of this century, whose sober volumes of Gide, Claudel, Valéry, Apollinaire, Saint Exupéry, Camus, Malraux and Sartre took the fame of French literature round the world, died in Paris on December 25, 1975 at the age of 94.

Gallimard today is one of the most powerful French publishing houses, reckoning to put out some 250 titles a year from the 5,000-odd manuscripts received. But its creator, who became president and director-general of the group, began as a dilettante of the epoch, brought up in a Paris artistic home where the Impressionist painters were collected. "I grew up amidst Renoirs, Van Goghs, and Cézannes," Gallimard recounted in later life. He was the grandson of an industrialist who had made a fortune under Louis-Philippe.

It was only in 1911 that, with the writer André Gide and another friend, Gallimard timidly turned the review they had been running into a publishing house, the future Librairie Gallimard, intended for friends' books. Gallimard had to borrow the 6,000 francs put up as his share from an uncle, his father having refused him the cash.

Though a friend of Marcel Proust, Gallimard first missed *Du Côté de Chez Swann* (1913) but bought it from Grasset three years later and went on to win his first Priz Goncourt with the publication of the second volume of Proust's masterpiece, *À L'Ombre des Jeunes Filles en Fleurs.* That was to be the first of 25 Goncourts, 16 Feminas, and 12 Interalliée Prizes won by Gallimard over the years.

From then on nothing could touch Gallimard's judgment with good young authors or his business success. Besides the new generation of French novelists of the inter-war years, Gallimard brought out in France foreign writers like Kafka and Hemingway.*

"If I could have my life over again," Gallimard remarked playfully late in his long life, "I would choose as a first occupation something having nothing to do with publishing—say a pharmacist's or plumber's business. There the income would allow me to publish on the side only all that pleased me, without having to think in the slightest about the commercial side."

December 29, 1975.

Sir Leslie Gamage, M.C., F.C.I.S., chairman and managing director of the General Electric Co. from 1957 to 1960, died on October 17, 1972. He was 85.

Although he was for a short time himself associated with the enterprise whose name he bore, his career was almost entirely linked with productive industry and essential services. In particular he will always be remembered for an almost lifetime of association with the General Electric Company into which he went having married a daughter of one of its founders, Hugo (afterwards Lord) Hirst, but he was also on the boards of many of its associated companies, and others engaged in the production of cables and tubes, engineering and mining.

Leslie Gamage was born on May 5, 1887, the second son of A. W. Gamage, founder of the store, and was educated at Marlborough, and Exeter College, Oxford, where he was senior scholar and graduated with honours. He was originally intended for the law, and in fact sat for the solicitors' final examination which he passed with honours in 1914. He joined the Army and was captain and adjutant in the 24th London Regiment with which he served, being twice wounded and awarded the M.C. before being taken prisoner.

After his release and demobilization, he went to the General Electric Company first in the secretarial department, where his legal knowledge proved to be of considerable value. Within a few years he was appointed to the board, and later became general manager, before succeeding to the post of joint managing director and vice-chairman.

Almost from the start he specialized in the company's constructional department and export sales, and in these capacities he travelled for many years practically all over the world, but especially within the Commonwealth, where the company had already established widespread connexions. This department of commerce remained one of his principal interests for the rest of his life and for some years he was president of the Institute of Export which owes much to his energy, foresight, and service.

He had been president of the Chartered Institute of Secretaries in 1941—its jubilee year—and also of the Royal Commercial Travellers' Schools from 1950 to 1954. He was a former Master of the Glaziers Company, and for some years was chief business adviser to the Ministry of Civil Aviation.

In 1919 he married the Hon. Muriel Elsie, elder daughter of Lord Hirst. She died in 1969.

October 18, 1972.

Carlos Garcia, former President of the Philippines, died in Manila on June 14, 1971, three days after he had been elected president of the country's constitutional convention. He was 74 and was Chief of State from 1957 to 1961.

A former teacher, he became Vice-President in 1953 and Minister for Foreign Affairs the following year.

He took office as President after the death of the powerful president Ramon Magsaysay, who was killed in an aircraft crash.

With 46 years in politics—first as representative of his home island Bohol, then governor of the island and senator—Garcia's greatest claim to fame was his championing of the nationalistic "Filipino first" policy, which sought to transfer control of the country's economy from foreign to Filipino hands.

As Foreign Minister, he presided over the Manila Conference of 1954, which produced the South East Asia Treaty Organization, and later led the Filipino delegation to three succeeding Seato meetings in Bangkok, Karachi and Canberra before becoming President.

Born on November 4, 1896, he studied law and taught in a state school for two years before entering politics. During the Japanese occupation of the Philippines in the Second World War, he became a guerrilla leader, hunted for three years with a price on his head. He managed to escape capture, though he was cornered three times and shipwrecked once.

He was known as a poet in the Visayan dialect.

June 15, 1971.

Philip Clarke Garratt, former vice-president and managing director of de Havilland Aircraft of Canada, Ltd, died on November 16, 1974 aged 80. He retired in 1966 after nearly 30 years with the company but retained a seat on the board until 1971, when he severed his last official ties with the company.

During these years he guided de Havilland from a small aircraft assembly operation to an international leader in S.T.O.L. (short takeoff and landing) aircraft design and production. He was awarded the McKee Trophy for meritorious service in the advancement of Canadian aviation in 1951 and the McCurdy Medal for his contribution to aviation in Canada in 1960, and was again awarded the McKee Trophy in 1965.

In 1971 he was awarded the Canada Medal. In April 1974, by Order-in-Council, the federal Government presented him with a lifetime pilot licence and in July he was elected to the Canadian Aviation Hall of Fame.

Garratt began his flying career as a student pilot at Curtiss Aviation School, Toronto, in 1915. Like many enthusiastic young Canadians anxious to get into the air war over Europe, he had to learn to fly before he could join the allied forces.

In 1916 he joined the Royal Flying Corps, served as a fighter pilot on the Western Front and was awarded the A.F.C. For the next 50 years he continued to fly.

In 1920 he flew as a pilot with Bishop Barker Airplanes on "barnstorming" tours, and in 1921 served as an Air Force instructor at Camp Borden. By 1928, when de Havilland began its Canadian operation, he was managing his own chemical business.

However, he quickly saw an opportunity to renew his great love for flying and offered his services on a part-time basis to de Havilland to test and ferry their aircraft. In 1936 flying won, and he ended his own business to become managing director of de Havilland, Canada.

In 1946, after the peak production years of the Second World War, he initiated the first "all Canadian" design, the highly successful DHC-1 Chipmunk trainer. This was followed by what is perhaps the best known of all de Havilland Canada aircraft, the DHC-2 Beaver. The Beaver, designed for operation in the Canadian North, was the first of a series of five successful S.T.O.L. aircraft which have earned for de Havilland a worldwide reputation as manufacturers of S.T.O.L. aircraft.

Under Garratt's unique leadership de Havilland Canada continued to grow and the DHC team went on to design and produce the DHC-3 Otter, the DHC-4 Caribou, the Turbo-Beaver, the DHC-5 Buffalo and the universally popular DHC-6 Twin Otter. The experience gained from his family of S.T.O.L. Aircraft led to the development of the Dash 7 Quiet S.T.O.L. Airliner, de Havilland's latest project.

The growth and success of de Havilland Canada was profoundly influenced by Garratt's devotion to aviation, the foresight and skill of this great Canadian and the unique way in which he attracted the staunch loyalty and affection of the people who worked with him.

December 2, 1974.

Robert Gascoyne-Cecil, 5th Marquess of Salisbury—See Salisbury.

Lord Geddes, K.B.E., for many years a prominent figure in United Kingdom tanker shipping and tourism, died at sea on February 2, 1975 while on a cruise. He was 67.

Ross Geddes was one of those people who seem larger than life. His big, bulky figure and resounding voice went with a strong, forceful personality. He was a man of enthusiasm and determination; a powerful advocate for British shipping in the House of Lords and elsewhere.

The son of Sir Auckland Geddes, later first Lord Geddes, sometime President of the Board of Trade and Ambassador to Washington, Ross Campbell Geddes was born on July 20, 1907 and educated at Rugby and Gonville and Caius College, Cambridge, (Mechanical Engineering Tripos 1929). He joined the Shell group of oil companies in 1931, remaining with them until 1946. From 1942 to 1944 he was a member of the British Merchant Shipping Mission in Washington and Deputy Director, Tanker Division, Ministry of War Transport (1944-1945).

He was appointed tanker adviser to the P. & O. Group in 1956 and was elected to the P. & O. board in 1957. He was appointed chairman of the former Trident Tankers—now integrated within the P. & O. Bulk Shipping Division—on its foundation in 1962. He served as president of the Chamber of Shipping of the United Kingdom for the year 1968-69, and was from 1965 to 1972 chairman of the tanker committee of the International Chamber of Shipping.

From 1964 he was chairman of the British Travel Association until its responsibilities were transferred to the British Tourist Authority in January 1970. Lord Geddes was also chairman of the Clerical, Medical and General Life Assurance Society, and Monks Investment Trust Limited, and a director of Electronics Trust Limited, Foseco Minsep Limited and Brixton Estate Limited. He was a former chairman of the council of the Westminster Medical School and a member of the governing body of Westminster Hospital.

From October 1971 until January 1972 he was Chief Executive of the P. & O. European and Air Transport Division. He was a past president of the Institute of Petroleum, a former chairman of the Navy Department Fuels and Lubricants Advisory Committee, a member of the Molony Committee on Consumer Protection (1959-1962) and chairman Ministry of Transport Committee of Enquiry into Carriers' Licensing (1963-1965). Lord Geddes, who retired in July 1972, was created C.B.E. in 1958 and on January 1, 1970 was advanced to K.B.E. for his services to tourism and shipping.

He is survived by Lady Geddes, a son and a daughter.

February 4, 1975.

Göran Gentele, general manager of the Metropolitan Opera, New York, died in a car accident on July 18, 1972 at Olbia, Sardinia. He was 54. Two of his daughters were also reported to have lost their lives.

He was born in September 1917, the son of a Swedish army officer. He studied languages in Paris, and then took a master's degree in economics, political science and languages at Stockholm University, graduating in 1939. From 1941 to 1944 he was a pupil at the School of Dramatic Theatre in Stockholm. After serving in the army, his early career was spent as an actor in films and on the stage. He appeared frequently at Sweden's Royal Dramatic Theatre, where

he also gained his first experience in producing from 1946 to 1952 before moving to the Royal Opera, where he first worked in 1952. Between then and 1959 he established an enviable reputation as a producer, in close collaboration with that house's musical director Sixtus Ehrling. In 1963 he was appointed administrator of the Royal Opera and remained in that post until his appointment to the Metropolitan in 1972.

While at the Stockholm Opera, he had been responsible for a consistently enterprising programme liberally sprinkling the repertory with modern works, including those of Swedish composers such as Hilding, Rosenberg and Karl-Birger Blomdahl, whose *Aniara,* a space age opera, was taken by the company to Edinburgh in 1959 and Covent Garden the following year, together with his historically accurate production of Verdi's *Un ballo in Maschera,* depicting King Gustavus as a homosexual. On the strength of these productions, Gentele was invited to Covent Garden to produce Gluck's *Iphigenia in Tauris,* the first production of the Solti regime, in 1961; it was first seen in Edinburgh before moving to London. Unfortunately it was not considered an unqualified success and he never returned to the House. His last production in Sweden was a notable *Pelléas et Mélisande,* in 1971.

Gentele's appointment to the Metropolitan, considered rather revolutionary by regular subscribers used to the Bing regime, had certainly been destined to disturb the conservative thinking of the house and its patrons. In this he would have had the full cooperation of Rafael Kubelik, the new musical director. Among their plans were productions of work new to the house such as Berlioz's *The Trojans* and Busoni's *Doktor Faustus.* Gentele was also planning a "piccolo Met.", at a smaller auditorium in Lincoln Centre with the aim of changing the house's image by the introduction of contemporary works at a price a younger public could afford to pay.

The first production of the new regime was to have been *Carmen,* conducted by Leonard Bernstein and produced by Gentele himself, who was thereby staking his reputation as a producer as well as an administrator from the very beginning. To all who met him Gentele was a man of great charm, imagination and industry.

July 20, 1972.

Dr. M. Dorothy George (Mrs. Eric George), O.B.E., the social and economic historian, died on September 13, 1971 at the age of 93.

She was the daughter of Alexander Gordon, barrister at law, and was born on July 14, 1878. By her own account, she never had a career, everything in her life having happened by chance, not design. When she was nine, her father, a Cambridge graduate, seeing the *Punch* cartoon "First Class,

Ladies only", which celebrated Agnata Ramsay's monopoly of the First Class of the Classical Tripos in 1887, declared that Dorothy must go St. Leonard's, Miss Ramsay's school, and to Girton, Miss Ramsay's college. He died six months later, but his widow carried out his plans and Dorothy Gordon entered Girton from St. Andrews in 1896 to read history.

Though attending the lectures of Acton, Cunningham and Tanner, she was left very much to her own devices by the redoubtable Ellen McArthur, whose energies, apart from the research she was doing with Dr. Cunningham, were devoted to the students working for the revised Tripos with its two parts. Miss Gordon's first class in 1899 under the old regulations was a complete and not altogether welcome surprise to her don. Research was not then the natural sequel to a first class and Miss Gordon spent the next nine years abroad with her family (except for one year when Miss Dove persuaded her to teach history at Wycombe Abbey) and only in 1909, at a friend's suggestion, did she enter the London School of Economics for post-graduate study under Lilian Knowles. She had almost completed a thesis on early Stuart finance when she became engaged to Eric George the painter, and during her honeymoon the manuscript disappeared, her mother having unwarily described it as the most valuable thing in the house.

Two articles in the *English Historical Review* on the seventeenth century Exchequer survived the wreck, but the accident in effect had shifted her field of interest. From 1915-19, however, she was mainly occupied with intelligence work for the War Office (MI5) where she became responsible for the counter-espionage list. Her services were officially described as valuable.

After the war she concentrated on the social and economic history of the eighteenth century, and she published a number of articles and books, of which the most widely appreciated have probably been the *London Life in the Eighteenth Century* (1925), as readable as it is learned, and the paper *Foxe's Martyrs,* read to the Royal Society in 1930, in which she effectively counteracted Laprade's interpretation of the election of 1780.

In 1931 the Cambridge Litt.D. set the seal on her scholarly achievements. By this time, however, she had been almost fortuitously committed to what was to be her *chef-d'oeuvre*—the continuation of the *Catalogue of Political and Personal Caricatures in the Print Room of the British Museum.* The seven volumes for which she was responsible, appearing from 1935 to 1954, cover 12,000 prints of the period 1771 to 1832. They are, in effect, a calendar of original material for a history of contemporary opinion. Dr. George's comprehensive introductions, her exact elucidations of all allusions, and her indexes of persons, titles, subjects, artists and printsellers make the volumes a mine to dig in, while her lively and detailed descriptions of the prints enable the reader to visualize these ebullitions of party and patriotic feeling. She was able, however, to reproduce a wide selection of the caricatures in her book *English Political Caricature 1793-1832* (1959) which is not only a study of opinion and propaganda, but also traces the evolution of the art from the "Emblem" style of the sixteenth century, through the "classic age" of Gillray and Rowlandson to the gentlemanly cartoons of H.B., a theme well illustrated by the pictorial evolution of John Bull himself.

In 1955 she was elected an Honorary Fellow of Girton College, and during the 1960s her work became known to a wider public through the Penguin series, for which in 1967, when she was 89, she wrote *Hogarth to Cruikshank, Social Change in Graphic Satire*.

Mrs. George had the modesty of the true scholar. The Girton contemporaries who penetrated her retiring personality recognized the acuteness of her critical faculty and the extreme fastidiousness of her taste. Her marriage, though childless, was entirely happy; after the death of her husband in 1961, she returned to her studies—which had been set aside during his last illness—and in the centenary year of the college, 1969, she contributed some vivacious reminiscences of her undergraduate days.

September 15, 1971.

Geraldo—Gerald Bright—one of the most famous dance band leaders of the 1930s and 1940s—died while on holiday in Switzerland on May 4, 1974. He was 69.

Born, the son of a City master tailor, in August 1904, Geraldo began broadcasting in the early thirties with a light orchestra in Blackpool. Like his pianist brother Sidney, he was musical from an early age, became a cinema pianist accompanying silent films, and played the organ in a restaurant.

After a South American tour to study Latin-American rhythms, he returned as Geraldo and with his Gaucho Tango Orchestra made over 2,000 broadcasts from the Savoy Hotel in London.

During the war he took orchestras through the Middle East, North Africa and Europe, giving troop concerts, and since the war had been more concerned with the business side, having orchestras playing in provincial theatres and on Cunard and other liners, and promoting concerts and cabaret throughout the world.

He was a founder director of Harlech Television and a former musical director of Scottish Television. He last appeared in public at Eastbourne a few weeks before he died.

A series of Festival Hall concerts in 1969 led to a networked television series recalling the heyday of swing music.

Geraldo and his wife lived in Sussex.

May 6, 1974.

Therese Giehse, one of the few truly great actresses of the German stage, died in Munich on March 3, 1975, three days before her 77th birthday. Miss Giehse's real name was Gift.

Friedrich Luft, drama critic of *Die Welt,* wrote in his obituary notice that she was born in the United States, a second-generation American of German-Jewish stock, and was brought by her returning parents to Munich at the age of 12.

Determined to be an actress, the plump and plain-looking Therese got her first engagement in the Bavarian City theatre in *Landshut*, in spite of failing to get into drama school. Condemned by her appearance, and her Bavarian accent, to play character roles from the outset, she made a virtue of necessity and for half a century decorated the stage, mostly in Zurich, and in Munich, but also in Berlin, Salzburg, and Vienna, as well as the cinema and television screens, with a series of unforgettable performances of portly or matronly, mostly comic old women, ranging from Marthe Schwerdtlein in *Faust* in her 20s to the heroine of Franz Xaver Kroetz's television monodrama *Further Outlook*, in winter 1974, of a crone who is shipped off to an old people's home to die. While at the Munich Kammerspiele from 1925 to 1933, she played Mrs. Peachum in the Munich premiere of *The Threepenny Opera* in 1929.

Zurich, where the flower of the German theatre had assembled during the Nazi interregnum, became her third home in 1933. Some of her finest creations that include Queen Margaret in *Richard III,* and the Nurse in *Romeo and Juliet* belong to her Schauspielhaus period. She created the title-role in Brecht's *Mother Courage* in 1941 and when she later acted the part in Brecht's own revival in Munich in 1950, he dubbed her "the extraordinary Miss Giehse". He based the definitive "model-version" of the published text on uniquely instructive comparisons between her performance and Helene Weigel's at the Berliner Ensemble. Here Miss Giehse also worked, under Brecht, for two productive years from 1949.

In 1936 Miss Giehse had married John Hampson, the writer, and acquired British citizenship, retaining her United Kingdom passport and domicile until her death. In 1957 she visited London with the Kurfürstendamm Theatre company, playing Martha Rull in Kleist's *The Broken Jug* alongside Brecht's daughter Hanne Hiob, and the Grandmother in Büchner's *Wozzeck*. In 1953 she had created the role of Celestina in Frisch's *Don Juan* in Zurich; and in 1961 Dürrenmatt rewrote the role of the sinister owner of a mental home, Dr. von Zahndt, in *The Physicists* specially for her, changing it from a male doctor into a female.

In the late 1960s she returned to the Schauspielhaus and gave yet a third and infinitely maturer performance as the stricken Courage in Brecht's drama. In 1970 she threw in her lot with the youngsters who, under Peter Stein, were to make the Berlin Schaubühne am Halleschen Ufer

Germany's outstanding theatre today, and played the title role in Gorki's *Mother* for him. In recent years her recitals of Brecht were much in demand. Her films include the Swiss film *The Last Chance* (1945) for Leopold Lindtberg, *Anna Karenina* (1948) for Duvivier*, and *Lucien Lacombe*, which she made for Louis Malle in 1974.

March 11, 1975.

Dr. Hans Globke, the "eminence grise" of Germany after the Second World War, died on February 13, 1973 in Bonn, at the age of 74.

Globke was born in Düsseldorf on September 10, 1898 and studied law in Bonn and Cologne and joined the civil service in 1929. As a member of the Ministry of the Interior in the Nazi period he wrote the commentary to the Nuremberg racial laws, the basis for Hitler's anti-Jewish race legislation.

This fact made him one of the most controversial figures after the Second World War, when Dr. Konrad Adenauer* the Federal Chancellor appointed him Secretary of State in his Chancellory. Unmoved by attacks against his right-hand man, Adenauer stood by Globke, and he held this position from 1953 until 1963 when he—together with Adenauer—retired, decorated with the highest order of the Federal Republic of Germany.

Though Globke (whose health had suffered by the various campaigns against him) repeatedly tendered his resignation, Adenauer would not part with his confidant. The quiet, unobtrusive man, who kept very much in the background and of whom Adenauer said that he had all the virtues of the old Prussian Civil Service—industriousness, loyalty, discretion, complete integrity—became the target of severe attacks by the East and also by leading Western politicians of his time. If nothing else was held against him by the latter, then at least a man who wrote the commentary to the Nuremberg laws should not have a powerful position in the new Democratic state and should not in fact be the second most important man.

Other prominent personalities stood up in defence of Globke and said, contrary to his opponents, that he did his best to modify the impact of the Nuremberg laws. Also, Jews or people of Jewish descent spoke in his favour. It was reliably reported that he, thereby risking his life, kept the Catholic Church informed during the war on measures planned by the Hitler regime.

The campaign against Globke reached a new climax during the time of the Eichmann trial. But no evidence was established that he personally had anything to do with the persecution of Jews or with Eichmann and the Jewish Department.

February 14, 1973.

The Duke of Gloucester, who died on June 10, 1974, was the last surviving son of King George V and an uncle of the Queen. He was 74.

Prince Henry William Frederick Albert, the third son of King George V and Queen Mary, was born on March 31, 1900 at York Cottage, Sandringham. Two of his godparents marked the moment of history at which he was born. One was Lord Roberts—the hero of the hour, who had lately arrived in South Africa and relieved Ladysmith. The other was the German Emperor, emerging from a period of estrangement from the English Royal Family after his telegram to Kruger. In his ebullient, not wholly sincere style he wrote to Queen Victoria to congratulate her on the birth of Prince Henry: "I hope that May and her boy will prosper, and that he may add a new ray of sunshine in the pretty lodge (York Cottage)."

But in spite of these illustrious sponsors, Prince Henry moved into a childhood which was secluded and perhaps not greatly different from that of his well-to-do East Anglian contemporaries.

He was the first son of a reigning sovereign to go to a private school—at Broadstairs—and then on to Eton. He was in fact the only son of an English King or Queen to go to that school and he was treated without privilege except that he was met by a royal brougham at Slough on arriving for his first term. He was in Mr. S. Lubbock's house, where was also King Leopold of the Belgians, a chance which was not without importance in the dire days of 1940.

In October 1919, Prince Henry went up to Cambridge with Prince Albert—the future George VI. The brothers were only to stay for a year and while the high spirits and gaiety of university life, immediately after the victory of 1918, found a ready response in them the influence of Cambridge did not perhaps cut very deep. Prince Henry does not appear to have formed lasting college friendships—possibly because of his father's insistence that he should not live in college but in an ugly little house off the Trumpington Road.

The Army was Prince Henry's choice of career, and with two elder brothers between him and the succession he was able—at any rate until the Abdication of 1936—to follow his career with professional assiduity. He was to prove far more than a mere ceremonial soldier. On coming down from Cambridge in 1919 he was gazetted a second lieutenant in the K.R.R.C., later being transferred to the 10th Royal Hussars—formerly the Prince of Wales's. He was promoted captain in 1929—and this rather leisurely step upwards emphasizes that his Army career was more professional than royal. In 1928 he was created Baron Culloden, Earl of Ulster and Duke of Gloucester—titles which were all closely linked with the Hanoverian family to whose members the Duke bore some physical likeness.

In the 1920s an Army career had lost some of its pre-1914 glamour; indeed it was dismissed as an irrelevance among those intellectual circles which were beginning to shape the thinking of that wild decade. Such thinking, together with the Duke's absorption in his profession, made him a decidedly less familiar personality to the public than were his brothers and sisters.

But with the serious illness of King George V in 1928 the Duke had to interrupt his Service career to take his place in the work of the Royal Family. In 1929 he headed a Garter Mission to invest the Emperor of Japan with the order of the Garter. The ceremony took place in May in the Imperial Palace of Tokyo, and the Duke was presented afterwards with the Grand Order of the Chrysanthemum. He had the blunt, forthright humour of the Royal Family and when, 12 years afterwards, he heard the news of Pearl Harbour he exclaimed to a friend: "And to think they made me travel 10,000 miles to give the Garter to that damned Mikado."

In the following year the Duke represented his father at the coronation of the Emperor Haile Selassie at Addis Ababa. The Duke's presence lent authority to the negus negusti although some aspects of the occasion are believed to have inspired Waugh's* delightful book *Black Mischief*. On getting home the Duke was again allowed to resume his professional career, becoming a staff captain with the 2nd Cavalry Brigade at Tidworth. In 1934 he rejoined the 10th Hussars as major, and joined the staff college two years later.

The events of 1936 immediately affected the Duke's position in the Royal Family. From being very much the younger son he became the next brother to the King, and in fact only three lives were between him and the succession. King Edward had perhaps less in common with the Duke than with the others of his immediate family and when he told him that he was going to abdicate the Duke accepted the news undemonstratively. "All the same, I sensed that he was disappointed." And possibly the disappointment was not only that it meant the end of the Duke's professional career but also that he felt the removal from the kingship of his brother's gifted personality.

The representation side of the Royal Family's work came to him far less naturally than it did to either the oldest or the youngest of George V's sons. He shone in the mess, the hunting field, the covert, and the big-game reserves; by nature he was a countryman, reluctantly drawn from his favourite pursuits to lay a foundation-stone, make speeches, or form the centre of a crowd.

These natural predilections were strengthened by a happy marriage. He had become engaged in the summer of 1935 to Lady Alice Montagu-Douglas-Scott, the daughter of George V's close friend, the 7th Duke of Buccleuch. The wedding would have been held in Westminster Abbey, but

owing to the death of the bride's father it took place privately in the chapel of Buckingham Palace on November 6, 1935. During the early days of their married life the Duke and Duchess lived in the Pavilion at Aldershot which had been built by Queen Victoria and the Prince Consort during the Crimean War.

The Duke was a discriminating collector, and he enjoyed decorating the Pavilion with souvenirs of its former owners. He had also a splendid collection of Chinese porcelain, and he collected sporting books and drawings. He had the royal characteristic of careful observation, together with an unexpected shaft of humour. These are shown in the account which he wrote for the Lonsdale Library of a shooting expedition which he was able to make from Addis Ababa to the interior in 1930.

He was 36 when George VI came to the throne, and the change in his position was immediately marked by his being made major-general—the first Army promotion which he had received on account of the blood-royal. Within two-and-a-half years war followed, and for princes in the modern world war brings peculiar difficulties. Those remote from the throne—members of the Battenberg family illustrate the point—have gone with gallantry into the fighting, but this is not possible for the immediate supporters of the Sovereign; if such men were given an active command there would be an immediate outcry as to their unsuitability, as has, of course, happened in former times. The Duke, though trained for action, was made chief liaison officer between Lord Gort and the B.E.F. He served throughout the disastrous Battle of Flanders, becoming chief liaison officer to G.H.Q. Home Forces in August 1940.

Possibly the most important task of his public life came with the end of the war, when it was announced that he was to be the first royal Governor-General of Australia—a position originally destined for his brother the Duke of Kent. Accompanied by the Duchess and their two sons—Prince William, who was born in 1941, and Prince Richard, who was born in 1944—they were given an uproarious welcome at Sydney, their arrival coinciding with Australia Day. For all representing established authority the transition from the exaltations of war to the more humdrum days of peace which follow is inevitably a test. To an extent, the Duke experienced this in Australia, but his straightforward character and unflagging hard work made his term of office conspicuously successful.

If he was the first royal Governor-General he was also the most mobile Governor-General. There was scarcely a nook or cranny of the country which he had not visited or flown over. As he was obliged to spend much time in Canberra on the official business of the Government, he decided to have a specially equipped Avro York to enable him and the Duchess to move freely round the country. This aircraft was named Endeavour—a reminder of the ship in which Captain Cook went to Australia. During their two years in Australia the Duke and Duchess covered 76,000 miles (the equivalent of three times round the world) in Endeavour.

His appointment was for only two years and this was strictly adhered to so that he could be in England when the King was in South Africa. The need to help his brother grew less with the marriage of the present Queen and by degrees it was possible for him to take a rather less active part, but his visits overseas during George VI's reign were constant. In 1948 he opened the Dominion Parliament in Ceylon on behalf of the King, and two years later he went to Kenya with letters-patent from his brother creating Nairobi a city of which he became the first freeman. In 1957 he represented the Queen at the ceremonies inaugurating the independence of Malaya. In the following year he spent 12 days in Abyssinia—reflecting no doubt on the astonishing changes in the fortunes of the Emperor since he watched his coronation nearly three decades earlier. In 1955 the Queen presented him with his field-marshal's baton.

The Duke and Duchess, when they were in London, lived in York House, St. James's Palace. But their true home was a delightful stone manor house, Barnwell, in Northamptonshire, formerly in the possession of the family of Lord Huntly. Here in later years farming and gardening had absorbed the Duke's leisure; he could rightly claim, through his interest in the science of farming, to be an agriculturist—a true descendant of George III.

Physically he looked robust, and he had the stamina of Queen Mary and her family: it was always recognized as something of an ordeal when he visited an officers' mess, because of his habit of perpetually standing, glass in hand, before the fire. Gallant officers were known to disappear in order to rest their aching feet. But in spite of the outward appearance of health and vigour, the Duke was troubled by illness; for one who loved horses and hunting it was noticed that he gave up hunting at a comparatively early age.

His elder son, Prince William of Gloucester, lost his life in a flying accident in 1972 and his heir was his younger son, Prince Richard of Gloucester.

June 11, 1974.

Prince William of Gloucester, who was ninth in succession to the throne, was killed on August 28, 1972 in an air crash. He was 30.

Prince William was first appointed a Counsellor of State in January 1963 and had since acted as such on other occasions during the Queen's absence from Britain.

Prince William was born on December 18, 1941 at a nursing home in Barnet—the elder son of the Duke and Duchess of Gloucester. He was christened William Henry Andrew Frederick in the private chapel of Windsor Castle on February 22 the following year, though the place of the christening was not announced owing to the war. His father, brother of King George VI, had been appointed chief liaison officer to G.H.Q. Home Forces in 1940. His parents had been married privately in the Chapel of Buckingham Palace in 1935 and not in Westminster Abbey owing to the death of the bride's father. His mother before her marriage was Lady Alice Montagu-Douglas-Scott, the daughter of King George V's close friend, the 7th Duke of Buccleuch.

As soon as the war was over, the Duke of Gloucester became the first royal Governor-General of Australia, a position originally destined for his brother, the Duke of Kent. The Duke, accompanied by the Duchess, Prince William and Prince Richard, their second son, arrived in Sydney and were given a tremendous welcome.

When he was five Prince William and Prince Michael of Kent were pages at the wedding of Princess Elizabeth (now the Queen) and the then Lieutenant Philip Mountbatten. The two small pages had some trouble with the very long bridal train, almost causing King George VI to lean forward and disentangle them, but in the end they managed all right. Prince William and his brother were brought up by Miss Lightbody, who later came to public notice as governess to the Queen's children.

Prince William was educated at Wellesley House Preparatory School, where he was an unassuming child and became a keen footballer and cricketer. At the age of 12 Prince William went to Eton, where he was an average-to-good scholar. He was a house prefect and n.c.o. in the Junior Training Corps.

Prince William went to Cambridge in October 1960 to read history at Magdalene College. He was very popular and took part in university life. He became a member of the Officers' Training Corps, and rowed for his college. In his third year at Cambridge he learnt to fly, like Prince Philip and his cousins the Kents.

In 1963 Prince William left Cambridge with an honours degree in history. He went home to a party at Barnwell Manor and set off next morning on a Land-Rover safari to Africa with seven Cambridge friends. He made a film record of the journey, and the B.B.C. were so impressed that the next year some of his Ethiopian shots were included in the "Travellers' Tales" series.

In September 1963 Prince William went to San Francisco, where he was to spend a post-graduate year at Stanford University, studying economics and political science. Earlier that year the Queen had assigned arms to Prince William: the coat of arms was a differenced version of the Royal Arms and had a label of five points argent charged with three lions passant guardant gules and two St. George's crosses alternately. On his return in 1964 he joined Lazards, the City merchant banking firm, for six months.

In June 1965 Prince William was successful in his ambition to join the Commonwealth Relations Office when he was accepted on a three-year contract under a temporary officers' scheme. He had twice failed his Civil Service examinations for a permanent appointment in the C.R.O. Prince William was appointed Third Secretary at the British High Commission at Lagos.

As the first Royal career diplomat, he began on the lowest rung; it was to prove a challenging appointment as a diplomat, as civil war broke out in Nigeria, but he made a wide range of friends. In 1968 Prince William was promoted to Second Secretary (Commercial) at the British Embassy in Tokyo; he left Lagos in a twin-engined Piper Comanche aircraft to fly across the Sahara to London, and later to Tokyo. The 10,000-mile journey to Japan took Prince William and his co-pilot, Vyrell Mitchell, slightly more than two weeks, with stops at Cannes, Amman, Karachi, Bangkok, Singapore and Okinawa. He was admitted as a freeman of the Guild of Air Pilots and Air Navigators.

In 1970 the Prince resigned "at his own wish" from the diplomatic service and since then spent much of his time at Barnwell Manor, where he had extensive farming interests.

While he was in Tokyo, Prince William, an experienced flyer, helped to start the negotiations that led to a scheme whereby Britain was to train 150 Japanese pilots. He flew his speedy Piper Cherokee light aircraft in several international air races in early 1972.

He was also training for his balloonist's licence. In 1971 Prince William competed in the Welsh Air Derby, finishing fourth in his Piper Cherokee. In May 1972, together with Princess Margaret, Lord Snowdon and the Duke of Kent, Prince William made a supersonic trip in Concorde. He flew in the *Daily Express* National Air Race that month. In 1969 he became president of the British Light Aviation Centre.

Prince William, a bachelor, was best man to his brother, Prince Richard, when he was married at Barnwell in July 1972.

August 29, 1972.

Professor Max Gluckman, Nuffield Research Professor of Social Anthropology in the University of Manchester, died in Jerusalem on April 13, 1975 during the tenure of a visiting professorship at the Hebrew University of Jerusalem. He was 64.

Gluckman was born in 1911 in Johannesburg as the second son of Emmanuel and Kate Gluckman, who had gone to South Africa from eastern Europe as children. They settled in Israel after the establishment of the state. Max Gluckman went to the university of the Witwatersrand to read law, but switched to anthropology.

The law however was in the blood, and it was through his researches in anthropological jurisprudence that Gluckman later made his unique contribution to modern social anthropology.

A brilliant academic career and a fine record as a sportsman and student leader gained him the Transvaal Rhodes scholarship. This took him in 1934 to Exeter College, Oxford. There a close friendship with Evans-Pritchard and Radcliffe-Brown decisively influenced his intellectual development.

Gluckman was engaged in fieldwork in Zululand during 1936 to 1938. In 1939, having gained his Oxford doctorate, he joined the staff of the Rhodes-Livingstone Institute of Northern Rhodesia. There Gluckman embarked on the field research in Barotseland which later formed the basis of his path-breaking studies in anthropological jurisprudence. But it was as director of the Institute from 1941 to 1947 that he laid the foundations of what eventually became the Manchester School of Theory and Research in Social Anthropology.

He expanded the Institute's publication to reach both a lay and academic public, drawing on colonial service and other local personnel, as well as professional researchers, for contributions that covered the whole range of central African social and anthropological problems. It was in part the prospect of new developments in what was emerging as British structural theory that induced Gluckman to accept a lectureship at Oxford in 1947, but he had hardly the time to show what an inspiring teacher he was when he was invited to accept the chair of social anthropology specially created for him at Manchester University in 1949.

From the outset he decided to concentrate on establishing a research school. He began by making his department the home base for his Rhodes-Livingstone team. New recruits to central African research started to come forward and continued to do so for 20 years. They were steered to work in the urban areas, in industrial undertakings and among sectarian groups as well as in traditional societies, the aim being to explore the stress and strains of what is now called modernization, as well as tribal custom and law.

By the late 1950s the Manchester department had extended its research interests to India and the Middle East. With the help of grants from Mr. (now Lord) Bernstein of Granada Television, Gluckman planned an extensive and still continuing programme of collaboration in research and teaching with the Israeli universities, among whose first projects were field studies by Israeli students in Beduin communities.

Endowed with exceptional powers of work, drive which his critics sometimes labelled egocentricity and a streak of authoritarian assurance, Gluckman saw to it that the results of these researches were quickly published. But what mainly brought the Manchester school into the anthropological limelight was the celebrated Gluckman seminar. He dominated it but with such insistence on the pursuit of truth and on respect for the opinions of others that no one felt inhibited.

Important also was the circle of outstanding contemporaries in other departments and many distinguished foreign visitors with whom he became intimately linked. The crossfertilization was invaluable. The analysis of the concept of "The Reasonable Man" in African jurisprudence in Gluckman's book, *The Judicial Process among the Barotse of Northern Rhodesia,* which put him immediately in the front ranks of contemporary social anthropologists, owes much to discussion in this circle; and these influences can also be detected in his other writings on politics, law and ritual.

A notable feature of the 20 years before Gluckman relinquished the headship of his department to accept a research professorship was that he found time and energy for a host of extramural activities. As chairman of the Association of Social Anthropologists, he made anthropological history by organizing in 1963 the first Anglo-American conference on new trends in the discipline. Among the lectures he gave at universities in Britain and America, his Frazer lecture on "Rituals of Rebellion" threw out a bold hypothesis that continues to provoke controversy.

As a member of sundry governmental and academic advisory bodies, he was specially valued for his strict adherence to high scholarly standards without the sacrifice of common sense. He believed in taking risks with young scholars even if this meant that there would be some failures. He was a keen golfer, and became an authority on soccer as a devoted supporter of Manchester United. After the air crash in Germany which nearly wiped out the team, it was Gluckman who was chosen to deliver the requiem address for them on the radio.

Academic honours were lavished on him. He was elected a Fellow of the British Academy in 1969, and a foreign honorary member of the American Academy of Arts and Sciences in 1970. After serving for many years on the executive of the International African Institute, he became one of its consultative directors in 1968. His wife, Mary, and three sons survive him.

April 21, 1975.

Lord Goddard, P.C., G.C.B., former Lord Chief Justice of England, died on May 29, 1971 at the age of 94.

With his death there passed from the scene a great judicial figure, whose strong personality was made familiar far beyond legal circles by his fearless, independent, and often controversial expressions of opinion. He held high judicial office for more than a quarter of a century; for 12 years, from 1946 to 1958, he was Lord Chief Justice of England.

Rayner Goddard, G.C.B., Baron Goddard of Aldbourne, was born on April 10, 1877, the son of Charles Goddard, of Peacock and Goddard, the well-known firm of solicitors. At Marlborough he became captain of the rifle corps and Victor Ludorum; at Trinity College, Oxford, he obtained 2nd class honours in Law and was awarded an Athletics Blue as a sprinter. He won the 100 yards at Oxford in 1898 in 10 3-5 sec.

He was called to the Bar by the Inner Temple in 1899. He joined the Western Circuit, and it was in the western counties that he first began to obtain work. Although, as the quantity and the weight of his briefs increased, his practice kept him more and more in London, he retained a life-long affection for this most sociable of circuits. While at the Bar he never lost touch with it as he became successively Recorder of Poole (in 1917), of Bath (in 1925) and of Plymouth (in 1928); his experience, gained in those agreeable towns, of the working of the middle levels of criminal justice, was invaluable to him when, as Lord Chief Justice, he had to decide innumerable appeals from Quarter Sessions.

Having built up an excellent junior practice Goddard took silk in 1923, and was much in demand in the best class of litigation, particularly commercial cases. He revelled in hard work, and had little in common with those barristers who pride themselves on their ability to pick up the details of a case as they go along. One result of this unremitting industry was that he acquired a remarkable mastery of case and statute law, and also an almost unrivalled knowledge of legal history; when on the Bench his unfailing ability to produce, from the recesses of a capacious and retentive memory, an apposite reference or quotation from any authority from Bracton to Hewart, never failed to astonish and fascinate the Bar.

By conviction and temperament Goddard was a strong Conservative, but his only active intervention in politics began strangely, and ended in something like disaster. Shortly before the general election of 1929, the sitting member for the impregnable Conservative stronghold of South Kensington had been divorced, and some disapproving constituents decided to find a more congenial rival candidate. In an unlucky moment Goddard was persuaded to stand as an Independent Conservative. He came bottom of the poll, in a three-cornered fight, with some 6,000 votes, while the retiring member, whose character was by implication under attack, was triumphantly re-elected with a score of 28,000. This episode inevitably (but temporarily) earned the loser the soubriquet of "Purity Goddard", though no one could have been less prudish or sanctimonious than he.

In the same year as this solitary electoral foray, Goddard was made a Bencher of his Inn, and he was by now clearly in line for promotion. When, in 1932, he was appointed a Judge of the King's Bench Division, there was no surprise and a wide measure of approval. From the first he showed himself to be a strong Judge, who exercised complete control over his court. He was quick to see the point, and to make up his mind, and equally intolerant of dilatory counsel and of evasive witnesses. He made an especially favourable impression in his handling of commercial cases.

In 1938 the Court of Appeal was enlarged, and Goddard was promoted to fill one of the additional posts. In this role, too, he was a great success. The Second World War was raging during five of his six years as a Lord Justice, and for much of the time he sat with his colleagues in a sandbagged cellar in the Law Courts. It was a period of continuous discomfort and intermittent danger, but he was not in the least worried by these impediments to judicial calm; his only concern was that there was not sufficient work to keep him fully occupied. This slightly unusual complaint was met by the Lord Chancellor appointing him to sit, in addition to his normal duties, as an extra Judge in the King's Bench Division.

In July 1944 Goddard went to the House of Lords as a Lord of Appeal in Ordinary. This further upward step, at the age of 67, must have seemed the climax of a highly successful career; for 45 years he had given distinguished service to his profession and to the community. But within 18 months a completely new vista of activity opened up before him. The Lord Chief Justice (Lord Caldecote) was in failing health, and it was apparent that a successor would soon have to be found. Over recent years a tradition had grown up (not without criticism) that this high office was a political appointment to be filled, almost automatically, by the Attorney General of the day.

On this occasion the new Labour Government had just taken office, as a result of the dramatic general election of 1945. In the circumstances it would hardly have been appropriate to promote the brilliant young Attorney General (Sir Hartley Shawcross); in any case, the Prime Minister (Mr.—later Lord—Attlee*) may well have thought it time that this outmoded method of selection should be changed. When, in January 1946, Caldecote resigned, precedent was broken, and Goddard was appointed to succeed him.

He was frankly delighted by his final promotion. Although he had been happy as a Lord Justice and as a Law Lord, his new position was in general more suited to his taste and temperament. He was glad to be able to go on circuit again—especially on his own circuit. And for the rest of his active career he never again needed to fear under-employment; quite apart from his many and varied judicial duties there were formidable administrative problems, partly connected with the aftermath of the war, which required urgent attention.

Goddard set about his task with enthusiasm and immense industry. He told a friend that there were a thousand things he wanted to do and that he had no more than three years in which to do them. Here he greatly underestimated his strength and staying power; when he retired, after 12 arduous years, at the age of 81, his physical fitness and mental alertness remained remarkable. On the administrative side of his work (little seen by the public but none the less important) he proved to be a first-class organizer. It was largely due to his initiative that the delays in the cause lists, manifest when he first took office, were reduced to manageable proportions. At his instigation the successful scheme of fixing dates for trials was launched. The establishment of the Crown Courts in Manchester and Liverpool, which has done much to reduce the congestion of criminal business in those conurbations, owed a great deal to his advocacy.

Although Goddard tried, as Lord Chief Justice, a large number of civil causes, it was in relation to the criminal law that he made his real impact. In this field his activity and influence were ubiquitous. In April 1948 he made a remarkable maiden speech in the House of Lords, intervening in the debate on the Criminal Justice Bill, "because I suppose I am the head of the criminal judiciary". He ranged widely over his subject, discussing matters as various as the duties of magistrates' clerks and the uses of probation. But it was on his views about punishment that attention was focused; these made him a widely known and highly controversial figure. He was a strong supporter of both corporal and capital punishment, and remained so long after the weight of legal and political (though not necessarily of popular) opinion had gone the other way. While opposed to the "cat", he thought that birching should be permitted in all cases of felonious violence; he maintained that a short sentence and a whipping was a more effective penalty than a long term of imprisonment. And he argued that to abolish the death penalty would be to dispense with a unique deterrent, and to gamble with the lives of the police.

His attitude was often described as reactionary. In one sense of that imprecise and emotive word the charge was true; he led the reaction (perhaps a timely one) against the view that all crime is a symptom of disease, and that the idea of punishment is an irrelevant or immoral anachronism. Much of the criticism to which he was subjected was ill-informed. There were those who suggested that he was a cruel man. And he himself admitted that many people regarded him as a bewigged obscurantist— a latter-day Ellenborough (his nineteenth-century predecessor, who thought that children who stole ought to be hanged). The suggestion and the comparison were equally ridiculous. In so far as he favoured severe penalties, it was not because of his inhumanity but because of his humanity. He was profoundly disturbed by the prevalence of violent crime and he felt deeply and personally involved in the tragedy of the men and women who had lost their lives or their health because of it.

There was another side to the popular conception of him as a stern figure of retributive justice. On innumerable occasions he and his colleagues in the court of Criminal Appeal set aside sentences of imprisonment, and substituted probation orders, especially when young offenders were concerned, where there seemed to be a chance that they would respond to lenient treatment. This attitude on the Bench was matched by countless acts of unostentatious and almost surreptitious kindness out of court; his former clerk recalls him buying new boots for ragged young burglars, and giving many other prisoners money to help them to make a fresh start.

His consideration and generosity to his staff were well known: those who had served under him held him in the highest affection and regard. As for the charge of obscurantism, it was sometimes forgotten, in the heat of controversy, that on many subjects he was a vigorous champion of reform. He urged the need for a speedy simplification and clarification of the law of larceny; he advocated a complete revision of the time-honoured (and time-wasting) method of taking depositions; he brought about an almost revolutionary change in sentencing procedure by ruling that it was not improper for a probation officer to recommend how the court should deal with a prisoner.

On the Bench Goddard was the embodiment of authority and power. Although below medium height, he was an impressive figure, with his massive head and his rugged and expressive features, which clearly showed how his mind was working before he gave utterance to his thoughts (for which those addressing him did not usually have to wait very long). Young counsel appearing before him found the experience at once daunting and exhilarating. He was often impatient and sometimes irascible, and he could destroy a bad point or a specious argument in a single crushing sentence. But he respected an advocate who stood firm, in the interest of his client, in the face of a verbal barrage, and if he could be persuaded that his original view was wrong, he would not hesitate to change his mind; in this he was never inhibited by any false pride. In spite of his great knowledge of the law, he had no particular love for over-subtle or sophisticated argument; his approach to the problems before him was basically a practical one. His capacity for delivering a lucid judgment, without taking time for consideration, at the end of a long and involved case, was extraordinary. Occasionally this procedure led him to say something inconsistent with the law as he had previously expounded it; on such occasions he always admitted, with disarming frankness, that he had spoken too hastily.

In academic circles he was never regarded as one of the great moulders or interpreters of the law. But he was a man of immense ability who brought to his great office the qualities of high courage, absolute sincerity, wide knowledge, and robust common sense.

He will be remembered with affection as well as respect because of his complete absence of conceit or pomposity: not far below the rather gruff image which he presented in public his basic character was friendly, uncomplicated and even humble.

His old college, Trinity, Oxford, made him an Honorary Fellow in 1940, and the university gave him an Honorary D.C.L. in 1947. The universities of Montreal and New York also conferred that degree upon him, and he was an honorary LL.D. of Cambridge and of Sheffield.

Goddard's love of the law, and of everything to do with it, extended to the social side of the profession. He never missed a Western Circuit dinner if it was humanly possible for him to attend: when, in 1957, his old circuit entertained him to dinner in honour of his eightieth birthday, this event gave him greater pleasure than many more formal tributes to his achievements. He was a frequent and welcome guest at countless other social occasions; his unlimited store of legal stories and anecdotes caused him to be much in demand as a speaker. His repertoire included a recitation of "Albert and the Lion" which was much admired.

He married in 1906 Mary Linda, daughter of the late Sir Felix Schuster, Bt. She died in 1928. He is survived by three daughters, the second of whom is the wife of Lord Justice Sachs.

May 31, 1971.

Admiral John H. Godfrey, C.B., who died on August 29, 1971 at the age of 83, was Director of Naval Intelligence during the most critical years of the Second World War, and afterwards commanded the Royal Indian Navy.

If Godfrey fell a little short of the achievement of his great naval intelligence forerunner in Naval Intelligence, Admiral Sir Reginald "Blinker" Hall, it was for reasons which he himself would readily admit. Between the two German wars much had changed in Whitehall and at the Admiralty. The latter's monopoly of signal intelligence and code-breaking between 1914-18 had been broken when the Foreign Office took control in the early twenties; and from 1940 onward the study and appreciation of all intelligence about the enemy was increasingly organized on inter-Service lines. The day of the swashbuckling, independent D.N.I. was past. This was the time when the first Joint Intelligence Committee, later with its first Joint Intelligence Staff, began to establish itself in the Chiefs of Staff organization.

There was, none the less, pioneer work to be done when Godfrey took over in February 1939, as a Rear-Admiral, strongly recommended for the post of Director by Admiral Sir Dudley Pound, under whom in the Mediterranean Fleet (1936-38) he commanded the battle-cruiser Repulse.

There was just time before war broke out to ensure that the Admiralty recalled one lesson learnt in Hall's Room 40—and disastrously ignored during the Jutland Battle—that Operations and Intelligence must work side by side without hiding secrets from one another. So the navy, thanks to the initiative of Admiral James, as Deputy Chief of Naval Staff, began hostilities with a fully staffed and already exercised Operational Intelligence Centre, which played a decisive part in the struggle against the U-boats and in the watch on the German and Italian surface fleets. Likewise, Godfrey followed the example of Hall—still available for advice—by recruiting for his personal staff and some geographical sections of N.I.D. a brilliant company of lawyers, writers, scholars, journalists—not least of them the young stockbroker Ian Fleming,* who was later to write the famous Bond novels.

Because the Navy was inevitably first in action with the enemy, Godfrey saw more quickly than some in Whitehall the need for new inter-Service organizations in the intelligence field; for the collection of detailed topographical information on which future combined operations, like the return to Europe or South-East Asia, must be based; for elaborate deception of enemy intelligence; for psychological warfare; for keeping the Fleet informed by a weekly report of the course and purposes of the war. For one who was sometimes accused of empire-building—an unfair charge which damaged his career—Godfrey was a conspicious advocate of cooperation between the Services, lack of which he had seen causing disaster years previously at the Dardanelles. With his decisive and brilliant mind, great energy and at times irascible temper, Godfrey did not suffer mediocrity gladly, but from most of his staff he won enduring respect and affection. Nor did he perhaps appreciate the advantages over other Directors of Intelligence that he enjoyed: wide overseas experience, an unusually thorough staff training in Plans Division and at Greenwich, a spell of study on his own at Cambridge, and a home background of exceptional stability and quality. His wife Margaret, who survives him, was recognized by all in the N.I.D.—of which she was a member—to be as skilled in organization as Godfrey himself —and a person of tact and grace. The great Inter-Services Topographical Department, numbering hundreds of men and women, established at Oxford when the raids on London began, was their joint creation.

Godfrey, who would often criticize the narrow education given to his generation of naval officers, enjoyed greatly the company of scholars and artists, men of affairs and journalists. He was runner-up to Captain Cyril Falls in 1946 for the Chichele Professorship of the History of War at Oxford. Indeed, there was about Godfrey a touch of the academic manqué, although he was appalled at any suggestion that he was (even by naval standards) an "intellectual" and set greater store by his success as a handler of ships and leader of men at sea.

The early days of the war were marked by some costly intelligence failures (the result of peacetime parsimony), for which Godfrey took the blame: the fiasco of the Norwegian landings; the underrating of the speed and power of the Bismarck over which the Germans had cheated; the appalling insecurity of many of our convoy and naval signals in the early part of the war (much more the fault of the Foreign Office than of the Admiralty). But when Godfrey handed over to Edmund Rushbrooke at the end of 1942 there had been a transformation and his division had reached a high level of efficiency. Rushbrooke's inheritance was brilliant and Godfrey's had been sparse.

Godfrey's period as Flag Officer Commanding the Royal Indian Navy (1942-45) was creative but embarrassed by the uncertainties and disloyalties in India at that time. When the time came for demobilization, there were demonstrations in the R.I.N. which Godfrey insisted on calling, and treating as, a mutiny, with the result that they came quickly to an end. His drastic action was not approved because of the possible political repercussions. It was doubtless because of that episode that Godfrey was the only naval officer of his seniority and rank to receive no recognition at all of his distinguished war service.

August 31, 1971.

John Goffage—See Rafferty.

E. Anne Goldsack—See Furlonge.

Samuel Goldwyn, one of the last survivors from the first generation of American movie magnates, and judged by his work easily the most distinguished of them, died on January 31, 1974 in Los Angeles. He was **91.**

In his lifetime he became something of a Hollywood legend, for his malapropisms, and his exuberant but often immature enthusiasm, were often held up for ridicule. Yet he was a born showman, with all the showman's instinctive appreciation of what the public wanted, and his admiration for the classics was genuine, even though it was often naïve. He entered the film industry when it was in its infancy, and became one of its pioneers, helping to transform it from a childish novelty into one of the most popular mediums of story-telling in the 20th century. He also had a flair for discovering star players.

He was born in Poland on August 27, 1882; his real name was Samuel Goldfish. He emigrated early to the United States and entered the clothing business, where he achieved some success through his business acumen. His entry into the film business was largely accidental; he married Blanche Lasky, sister of Jesse L. Lasky, who was at that time a theatrical impresario. Lasky had become interested in the commercial potentialities of the film and, when he and an aspiring young actor and dramatist, Cecil B. de Mille, decided to try their hand at film-making, it was only natural that Goldwyn should be enlisted to take charge of the financial side of the venture. He became treasurer and general manager of the Jesse L. Lasky Motion Picture Company in 1913, was briefly associated with its successor, Famous Players-Lasky, and later the Goldwyn Company, formed in 1916 (the name was a composite of Goldfish and Selwyn, the name of the company's two vice-presidents; it was not till 1918 that Samuel Goldfish legally became Goldwyn). Goldwyn soon realized that to make films the way he wanted he had to have complete control of them. His first personal production was *The Eternal City* (1923), a tale of the early days of fascism, but the fortune of his company was based for several years on the outstanding popularity of his *Potash and Perlmutter* and its two sequels.

From the first he persevered in his policy of hiring the leading talents of the time; among his stars were the Talmadge sisters, Constance Bennett,* Vilma Banky, and, in film after film, Ronald Colman. Indeed, most of Ronald Colman's most notable films in the 1920s were made under Goldwyn's guidance: *Tarnish, A Thief in Paradise, His Supreme Moment,* and a long series in which he starred with Vilma Banky, such as *The Dark Angel, The Winning of Barbara Worth* (which also marked the debut of Gary Cooper*), *The Night of Love, The Magic Flame, Two Lovers,* and others. All of these were outstanding commercial successes, but it could not be claimed that any of them offered a notable contribution to creative film-making, with the possible exception of *Stella Dallas* (1926).

With the coming of sound, Goldwyn was able to show his full stature as a producer. At first, understandably, he played safe with Ronald Colman as an impeccably suave *Bulldog Drummond* (1929) and *Raffles* (1930), or musicals with Eddie Cantor* (*Whoopee, Roman Scandals, The Kid from Spain*) or Evelyn Laye (*One Heavenly Night*). But in 1931 he produced *Street Scene*, adapted by Elmer Rice* from his play, and directed by King Vidor with a realization, remarkable for its time, how to convert a fairly talkative and static stage play into strong cinema.

This film first signalled Goldwyn's readiness to interest himself in current problems and serious social analysis within the framework of the commercial film. At this time also there appeared for the first time on the credits of his films some of the distinguished names associated with Goldwyn's greatest achievements: Gregg Toland, the brilliant photographer whose experiments he encouraged and exploited; writers such

as Preston Sturges, Lillian Hellman, Ben Hecht,* Robert Sherwood and Maxwell Anderson; directors like Vidor, Ford, Hawks, Mamoulian and above all Wyler.

Wyler's first film for Goldwyn was *Dodsworth* (1936) from another of Sinclair Lewis's novels—John Ford had made *Arrowsmith* in 1931. In 1936 also, Toland joined the partnership for *These Three*, a neatly-tailored version by Lillian Hellman of her play *The Children's Hour;* and in subsequent years the three talents were re-united in *Dead End, Wuthering Heights, The Westerner, The Little Foxes* (which contained one of Bette Davis's best performances and some of Toland's most masterly photography), and, finally, after the war, in *The Best Years of Our Lives*, the best-loved of all Goldwyn films. Though these films represent the crown of Goldwyn's achievement during those years, they were not the only notable films he made by any means. In 1937 Ford's *Hurricane* included some of the finest storm scenes on film, and Vidor directed a new version of *Stella Dallas* with a striking performance by Barbara Stanwyck. Goldwyn moved Balanchine to Hollywood to direct the ballet sequences in *The Goldwyn Follies,* otherwise, despite two of Gershwin's best songs, an interesting misfire; and in 1941 Howard Hawks directed for him one of the most intelligent films ever made about popular music, *Ball of Fire*.

During the war Goldwyn contributed to international understanding with Milestone's *North Star*, a rather rose-tinted view of Russian life with some fine battle-scenes, and to national morale with two good Bob Hope films, *They Got Me Covered* and *The Princess and the Pirate*, and several films starring a new discovery of his, Danny Kaye. His first post-war production was *The Best Years of Our Lives*, but unfortunately after this peak his films began to show a decided decline: *The Secret Life of Walter Mitty* provided Danny Kaye with one of his aptest vehicles, but the "serious" films offered little of interest except *A Song is Born*, a diluted remake of *Ball of Fire*, and *Edge of Doom*, a dark but powerful film ruined by reshooting with an eye to general popularity (one of Goldwyn's very few remarkable concessions to public taste). In 1952 he imported Roland Petit to provide a ballet for *Hans Christian Andersen*, and from that time on produced only a small number of very expensive films, starting with *Guys and Dolls*, and a wide-screen version of the Gershwin opera *Porgy and Bess*.

Samuel Goldwyn made his mistakes, like any other film-maker—though fewer than any comparable figure—but his record is quite without parallel for its determined seeking of the best in all fields connected with film-making; the best writers, the best directors, the best actors, the best technicians. From his earliest days he sought to make films of style and intelligence, and along the way he acquired, as well as a formidable knowledge of the film medium,

a wide and varied background of culture, which helped him to deal with collaborators of the greatest distinction in their own fields. His fractured English was legendary, although most of the famous examples were apocryphal, and the genuine ones, such as "a verbal contract isn't worth the paper it's written on", contain a measure of shrewd comment. He once said "I make my pictures to please myself", and that might serve as his most fitting epitaph.

February 1, 1974.

Buzz Goodbody, whose death at the age of 28 was discovered on April 12, 1975, was the first and only woman director on the staff of the Royal Shakespeare Company.

Miss Goodbody, whose real name was Mary Ann, was the daughter of a barrister, D. M. Goodbody. Educated at Roedean she went to Sussex University where she caught the attention of the R.S.C. director, John Barton, through an adaptation of Dostoevsky's *Notes from the Underground* which she wrote, directed and won a prize for, in the 1966-67 National Student Drama Festival.

This monodrama was a natural companion piece to Gogol's *The Diary of a Madman* and lingers in the memory as a far more powerful production than either of the professional versions of the Gogol text. When the show briefly appeared at the Garrick its quality was recognized and its director was invited into the company in which she spent the brief remainder of her career, as Barton's assistant.

Her first involvement with the company was with the R.S.C.'s touring Theatregoround company for which she directed two productions including *King John*. Her first main stage production for the company was *As You Like It* in 1973 and she was assistant to Trevor Nunn for his Roman season of 1973-74.

In 1974 she was appointed Artistic Director of The Other Place, the R.S.C.'s smaller theatre in Stratford and it was here that she made her most creative contributions to the company as a director. Her last season at The Other Place was considered an outstanding success. It included Trevor Griffiths's *Occupations* and continued with her very well received production of *King Lear*. The latter was subsequently seen at The Place in London and went to New York, where it was performed at the Brooklyn Academy in early 1975.

There was a general feeling in the theatre world that she was a director of enormous potential. Certainly from these productions in conjunction with her Dostoevskian debut emerges the feeling that she valued the theatre as a precision instrument for analysing and judging human action.

In Griffiths's political fable, based on a key episode in the history of Italian trade unionism, the need to place personal emotion in a broad social perspective cer-

o

tainly lay as much in the text as in the production. But in *Lear* she was on her own; and the result was the most dispassionate reexamination of the play since Peter Brook's 1962 version.

At one extreme, the production was anchored in human credibility; everything was done to show how much the two sisters had to put up with before turning against the King. At the other extreme, the Fool emerged as a moral commentator, released from dependence on Lear and addressing the house directly. In short, the production emphasized all the possible extenuating circumstances and excuses, and then went on to deliver judgment. Coming when it did, in the midst of the financial crisis, the spectacle this production achieved with the aid of a few banners on a bare floor also contrasted favourably with the R.S.C.'s grandiose Stratford revivals.

Her death closely follows the announcement that her production of *Hamlet* was due to open in May 1975 at The Other Place.

April 15, 1975.

Betty Grable, the Hollywood song-and-dance star renowned for her "million dollar legs", died in Santa Monica, California, on July 2, 1973. She was 56.

For most of the 1940s she was one of the top box office attractions in the United States and it was estimated that over a period of ten years her films made a profit of £6m. She was well rewarded for this enormous popularity; in 1949 she earned £115,000 and was said to be the highest paid woman in the world. Yet her talents, as she was the first to admit, were modest and most of her films are now forgotten. She did not dance as well as Ginger Rogers, had an ordinary singing voice and once confessed "I am no actress and I know it". She was a small shapely blonde, who wore a lot of lipstick, and her greatest asset was her legs, which were once insured by Lloyd's for £250,000.

Perhaps the key to her success was that unlike Dietrich or Garbo she was not some unattainable goddess but an ordinary girl who happened to lead a rather glamorous existence on the screen—the small town waitress, who in one picture manages to grab herself a millionaire husband. She might have been the G.I.'s favourite pin-up during the Second World War but she was also someone that millions of girls leading humdrum lives loved to identify with.

She was a likable actress with a talent for putting over a droll line that not all her directors sensed.

Betty Grable—her real name, though curiously enough she began her career as Frances Dean—was born in St. Louis, Missouri, on December 18, 1916 of a stockbroker father and a mother who was determined to put her into show business. When she was five she was learning to sing and

dance and play the piano, at 12 she went with her mother to Los Angeles for further dance tuition, and in 1930 made her first film appearance at 14 blacked up in a chorus line. Her career took a long time, however, to get underway. Sam Goldwyn signed her up and dropped her and R.K.O. did the same, despite her considerable success in *The Gay Divorce* in 1934. She made a third false start with Paramount, was briefly married to the former child star Jackie Coogan, and finally made it with Twentieth Century Fox. They signed her up in 1940, put her in *Down Argentine Way* when Alice Faye was taken ill, and she went on to make nearly 30 films in the next 14 years. They were nearly all musicals, with formula plots and little artistry—and they were unfailingly popular.

Sweet Rosie O'Grady, Pin Up Girl, The Dolly Sisters (with June Haver), *Diamond Horsehoe* and *Mother Wore Tights* were just a few of them. But towards the end of the forties, with Grable getting older, busts taking over from legs and musicals slipping out of vogue, Hollywood demanded new stars. In 1951 Betty Grable was suspended by the studio for refusing a part and the same thing was to happen twice more. Finally, in 1953 Fox's leading female star had her contract ended after 13 years, and her appearance that year in *How to Marry a Millionaire* with the girl who was to supersede her, Marilyn Monroe*, marked the effective end of the Betty Grable era.

She continued in films for a little while more but after the ironically titled *How to be Very Very Popular* in 1955 she decided that the cinema had nothing more to offer and she went into semi-retirement in Las Vegas with her second husband, the band leader Harry James, and their two daughters. In 1965, to general surprise, her 22-year-old marriage to James ended in divorce and Grable, nearly 50 and soon to be a grandmother, started a come-back on the stage.

She did *Guys and Dolls* and *Born Yesterday* and in 1967 turned up as the leading lady in *Hello, Dolly!* on Broadway. Two years later she went to London, her legs and her legend intact, to play *Belle Starr* in a musical of that name, but the show was savaged by the critics and taken off after less than three weeks. At the time of her death she was due to appear in a revival of *No, No, Nanette* in Australia.

July 4, 1973

Stephen Graham, who died on March 15, 1975 in London at the age of 90, was an author who had travelled on foot in many parts of the world and most of whose books were a direct account, at once thoughtful and picturesque in style, of his travel experiences.

The foreign country he knew best was Russia—pre-revolutionary Russia—of which he was a popular and enthusiastic English

interpreter, although a somewhat idiosyncratic and misleading one. It was Stephen Graham who was probably more responsible than anyone else in Britain for the cult of Holy Russia and the idealization of the Russian peasant that were beginning to make headway there before 1914 and during the years immediately after.

Born in 1884, the son of P. Anderson Graham, he began to write at the first opportunity, was encouraged by Austin Harrison when the latter took over the *English Review*, and then, in his own words, "attracted to Russia by the spirit in Russian literature, gave up life in London and took his chances with Russian peasants and students".

With little or no money in his pocket he wandered about the Ukraine, lived in Moscow, tramped through the Crimea and large parts of the Northern Caucasus, travelled to the Urals, discovered the Siberian *taiga*. Contact in these circumstances with "the broad Russian nature" induced in Graham an essentially romantic view of the Russian peasant and a not less romantic view of the Orthodox Church. Something of Tolstoyan teaching mingled with his conception of the one, something of Slavophil mysticism with the other.

At a time when Russia was a remote and unknown land to the majority of Englishmen, Graham's vivid and intimate sketches did not lack illumination. They were, nevertheless, over-coloured in style and often naïve in historical argument.

Always an extremely fluent writer, in the years before the First World War he produced, in rapid succession, *A Vagabond in the Caucasus; Undiscovered Russia* (the northern forests); *A Tramp's Sketches* (the shores of the Black Sea); *Changing Russia; With the Russian Pilgrims to Jerusalem.*

In *Russia and the World* (1915), which incorporated the substance of a series of special articles he wrote for *The Times*, and which reflected the common wartime mood and sentiment regarding Russia, he sought to give more formal shape to his interpretation of the Russian soul; while in *The Way of Martha and the Way of Mary*, published in the same year, he contrasted the practical temper of Western society with what he felt to be the simplicity, asceticism and mystical faith of the Russian temperament as it had been nurtured by the Eastern Church. *Through Russian Central Asia* (1916) was a more valuable book and gave evidence of his real gift for descriptive narrative.

The Russian Revolution necessarily brought a sharp change in Graham's attitude. He maintained his belief in the essential goodness, purity of heart and deep-rooted religious instinct of the Russian peasant, but his anti-Bolshevist bias was all the more unanswered in consequence, and led him in time to abandon in silence his more facile assumptions.

Although he continued to write of Russia, other subjects and travel experiences were always at hand. He had made a book,

With Poor Emigrants to America (1914), out of a steerage crossing of the Atlantic, and books now appeared on his experiences as a private in the 2nd Battalion of the Scots Guards in 1917-18, on the Negro question in America as it impressed him during a tramping tour of Georgia, on a tour of the battlefields of France, on another tramping tour, with the poet Vachel Lindsay, in the Rockies, on London, on New York, on tramping generally.

He was, indeed, an indefatigable traveller and an indefatigable recorder of his travels. Mexico, which he visited with his friend Wilfred Ewart, most of the European frontier of Soviet Russia in 1924, from Lake Ladoga to the Black Sea, Dalmatia and various parts of the Balkans, Carpathian Poland, Bosnia, Macedonia, Swaziland and Transvaal—these all served for the writing of books.

He edited *The Tramp's Anthology;* he wrote a series of picturesque but not very profound Russian historical volumes—on Peter the Great, Ivan the Terrible, Boris Godunov and Alexander II—and also a book on Stalin and another on Alexander of Yugoslavia; he turned his hand to fiction of a semi-documentary character, the most notable of such works being *St. Vitus' Day*, a study of the mind and personality behind the fatal act of assassination at Sarajevo in 1914. From 1941 to 1965 he worked for the B.B.C. Foreign Service. He was made F.R.S.L. in 1950. In 1965 he published *Part of the Wonderful Scene*, an autobiography.

Graham was a man of striking appearance, tall, handsome, heavily moustached and with a clear and candid gaze. He lived for many years in Frith Street, Soho, and had a fond and possessive feeling for that part of London. He married in 1909 Miss Rose Savory; she died in 1956 and he married secondly Vera Mitrinovic.

March 20, 1975.

Professor Sir James Gray, C.B.E., M.C., F.R.S., died at Cambridge on December 14, 1975 at the age of 84. For the last 10 years of his life he had been sadly incapacitated as the result of an accident. He was Professor of Zoology in the University of Cambridge from 1937 to 1959.

James Gray was born in October 1891 of Scottish parents. He was educated at Merchant Taylors' School, and from there won a scholarship to King's College, Cambridge. He began research immediately after taking his degree, and was elected a Fellow of King's College in 1914. But his career was soon interrupted by the war during which he served as a captain in The Queen's Royal West Surrey Regiment from 1914-1918, and was awarded the Military Cross. What he was most proud of, however, was the Croix de Guerre with palms conferred upon him on the field of battle by Marshal Foch.

Returning to Cambridge after the War he was successively Balfour student, lecturer in the Department of Zoology, and Reader in Experimental Zoology. It was during this time that he produced the research for which he will principally be remembered: on the division of cells, on growth, and on ciliary movement. This work, meticulously carried out and beautifully described, established him as one of the leaders in the field of cell biology, and he was elected to a Fellowship of The Royal Society in 1929. He also wrote a monograph on ciliary movement, and a text book, *Experimental Cytology*, which was a classic in its day, and even now is still consulted.

After the publication of *Experimental Cytology*, Gray gave up cell biology completely, and turned to the study of animal locomotion. Just why he made this change is not clear. Perhaps he felt that the great reorientation in cell biology which followed the discoveries of the biochemists and biophysicists left no room for his own, more biological, sort of approach. But his new field of research proved equally rewarding, and led to a further series of important papers on the mechanics of swimming in fishes, on the nervous control of movement, and on ciliary and flagellate movement in spermatozoa and micro-organisms.

Whether this research ever satisfied him, as his earlier work did, is doubtful. Perhaps it was this quantum of dissatisfaction that led him, towards the end of his life, to return once more to his first love, and to examine again some of the problems of cell division. James Gray once said that if anyone were ever to tell him how a cell divides, he would die contented. This particular joy was denied him, but perhaps he derived some consolation from the fact that several of his own students continued his work on this problem.

He never let his research slip from first to second place. He managed, nevertheless, to be a superb lecturer—his Royal Institution Christmas lectures for children, in particular, were magnificent—and he carried a great weight of administration. He was largely responsible for the planning and building in the early thirties of the new Zoology Department at Cambridge. Then in 1937 he became Professor of Zoology at Cambridge, and gradually built up one of the largest, and certainly one of the foremost of Zoology Departments in the country.

During and after the 1939-45 War he served on the Agricultural Research Council. He was also president of the Marine Biological Association, a trustee of the British Museum, and a Development Commissioner. Honorary doctorates were conferred on him by Durham, Edinburgh and other Universities, and for his public work he was made C.B.E. in 1946, and was knighted in 1954.

It was not for his public work that he would most wish to be remembered. He was happiest in private, with his wife and

adopted son and daughter at home in Cambridge or on holiday in Scotland, and with his colleagues in the laboratory, or at the Marine Station on the Isle of Cumbrae in the Clyde, where he did so much of his research. The best testimony to him, both as a scientist and as a man, is indeed a private one: it comes from the great body of Cambridge men, many of them now in Chairs all over the world, who began their work under him, and who held him in great affection.

He married in 1920 Norah Christine King.

December 16, 1975.

"Henry Green", the pseudonym of **Henry Vincent Yorke,** died on December 13, 1973, at the age of 68. He was the author of nine novels that comprise one of the most original contributions to English fiction in our time.

Born near Tewkesbury on October 29, 1905, the son of Vincent Wodehouse Yorke, he was educated at Eton, where he was a member of the brilliant generation that included Robert Byron, Cyril Connolly, Harold Acton, Orwell and Anthony Powell. It was at Eton that he began his first novel, *Blindness*, published in 1926 when he was barely 22.

From Eton he went to Oxford, but left at the end of his second year in order to go into the family business in Birmingham, H. Pontifex & Sons, manufacturers of brewing equipment. As H. V. Yorke, he was to become the firm's managing director and chairman of the British Chemical Plant Manufacturers' Association; but he entered the business as a labourer in the family, living in lodgings in working-class Birmingham. The fruit of that experience was *Living* (1929), a novel that is still unique, because of its freshness and vividness, as an evocation of life among industrial workers both in the factory and at play.

At that time, Green's identity was unknown to the literary world generally, and he was very much a mystery figure. It was inevitable, given the social and political preoccupations of the young writers of the period, that *Living* should have been accepted as primarily a realistic work, a document of working-class life, and for a time Green was thought of as the counterpart in the novel of Auden and Spender in poetry. It was equally inevitable in these circumstances that his next novel, *Party Going* (1939), should have proved disconcerting to many of his admirers, for in content at any rate it was at the furthest possible remove from *Living*. A party of rich, idle young people, who might have stepped out of the pages of Evelyn Waugh, assemble at Victoria to catch the boat train to France. Fog descends, all train services are suspended, and the young people are marooned in the upper rooms of the station hotel while hordes of frustrated commuters fill up the platforms below and threaten by sheer pressure of numbers to pour into the hotel itself. That is all, but it was enough to enable Green to produce a most unusual comic novel.

One effect of *Party Going* was to reveal *Living* as an altogether richer novel than had first been thought, a novel in which exact social observation went hand in hand with a haunting symbolism and in which its author's idiosyncratic way with language, suggestive at once of Gertrude Stein and the *Anglo-Saxon Chronicle*, was seen as serving poetic ends. Green suddenly appeared, in fact, as essentially a poetic novelist; this was confirmed in his autobiography, *Pack My Bag*, in 1940.

During the war Green served as a fireman in the Auxiliary Fire Service, and his novel *Caught* (1943) is a memorable rendering of the mood of London during the "phoney war" and of the air raids on the docks that heralded the Battle of Britain. But it is also a complex tragi-comedy of suspicion and misunderstanding between the classes. His next novel, *Loving* (1945), was, on the face of it, as different again: a comedy of life among the servants, most of them English and uneasy refugees from the war, in a great country house in neutral Ireland. In this novel, which contains what is probably his most brilliantly realized character, the butler Raunce, the two sides of Green's talent are in perfect balance, his uncannily accurate ear for the patterns, repetitions and nuances of colloquial speech and his intense visual sense.

In the novels that followed Green seemed deliberately to divorce these two sides of his talent one from the other. *Back* (1946), on a soldier returning from the war, in a condition of shock, and *Concluding* (1948), a novel at once about old age and about the future, appear almost as fictional equivalents of late Impressionist paintings; it is as though character, action, plot are dissolved in the surface play of light and colour, sacrificed, it is difficult not to think, to the quest for visual beauty. Then, in his last novels, *Nothing* (1950) and *Doting* (1952), both comedies of upper-class life in London during the years of post-war austerity, he seemed to suppress his visual sense altogether and rely entirely on his remarkable ear for speech, producing novels conducted almost wholly in dialogue.

Yet despite his sophisticated techniques, which were those of a virtuoso, Green was much closer in fundamentals to the experience and aspirations of common humanity than many novelists whose works appear to be much more homespun. His art, it has been truly said, is one of acceptance. In his novels the human lot is presented as sad but comic; and objectivity never precludes sympathetic understanding.

He married in 1929 the Hon. Adelaide Biddulph, by whom he had one son.

December 15, 1973.

Martyn Green, one of the most distinguished of Savoyard singers, died on February 8, 1975 in hospital in Hollywood, where he had been working for two years as an actor. He was 75. Green was in the royal line of D'Oyly Carte singing-actors that began with George Grossmith and progressed through Sir Henry Lytton to him.

He was born William Martyn-Green in London on April 22, 1899 and studied singing with his father. Then he went to Gustav Garcia at the Royal College of Music from 1919 to 1921, the year he made his London debut at the Palladium in *Thirty Minutes of Melody*. He first appeared with the D'Oyly Carte Company in the small part of Luiz in *The Gondoliers*. After a thorough grounding in the G. & S. works in small parts and as an understudy, a customary apprenticeship in those days, he took over the leading roles from Lytton in 1934 and continued successfully to fill them until 1951. In 1938 he appeared in a film version of *The Mikado*.

After retiring from the D'Oyly Carte Company he took up a new career as a straight actor in the United States. In 1959 he lost a leg after a lift accident. With great resolution he began to remake his career, using an artificial limb. About that time he commented that it was a bit like a baby learning to walk, falling down and picking himself up again. He was a regular performer on the New York stage and was last seen in a film of Eugene O'Neill's, *The Iceman Cometh*.

Many of those who today enjoy the Savoy operas remember Green's performances with affection, and still judge the interpretations of his successors by the high standard in enunciation and characterization that he set. His Bunthorne had a sneering, lazy hauteur, his Major-General in *Pirates* was properly preposterous, and his Lord Chancellor in *Iolanthe* was tetchily amusing, but he was just as able to bring out the pathos of Ko-Ko's "Tit Willow" or Jack Point's "I have a song to sing O".

His voice could be politely termed a light baritone. All the projection came from his inimitable way with a text, his perfect timing and his light-footed acting. In brief he had an exemplary sense of style. In the early days of L.P. he happily left a memento of his art in complete recordings of his chief roles.

February 11, 1975.

Walter Greenwood, the novelist and playwright, died on September 13, 1974 at the age of 70.

Born into a working class family in Salford, Lancashire, on December 17, 1903, he inherited a family tradition of determined radicalism, enthusiasm for books and love of music. His elementary school education was thus supplemented by the respect of his parents and grandparents for learning and by his own ambition to escape from the life of the industrial slum which became the background to his best books.

Thirty years of struggle in which unemployment alternated with menial, unrewarding work preceded Greenwood's success. His father died while he was still a schoolboy, and when he was 12 years old he worked outside school hours as a pawnbroker's clerk. Leaving school at the age of 13, he worked as an office boy until the urge to escape turned him for a short time into a stable lad. The escape was shortlived, as the car supplanted the horse as a means of transport within cities and the years of depression crushed the cotton industry. By the time he was 30, with spells of unemployment between posts, Greenwood had been a box-maker, a signwriter, a driver, a warehouseman and a salesman, but he had never succeeded in earning more than 35 shillings a week.

During these years, however, he had been turning himself into a writer, an observant recorder of the life he knew, the type of people with whom he lived, their response to the grim age through which they were passing. His materials were the decaying slums of the Industrial Revolution, the ways of escape offered by books, plays and music, and the delight of cheap day excursions to the Pennine moorlands or the Peak District. These were materials of his first novel, *Love on the Dole*, published in 1933.

Love on the Dole is simply and directly written, eloquent by virtue of honesty, compassion and anger rather than through any attempt to paint poverty and the degrading effects of unemployment in vivid colours. There are many novels and as many or more documentaries, studies of the Great Slump, but Greenwood's unaffected backstreet tragedy has become the standard classic of the period. Dramatized in 1934 in collaboration with Ronald Gow, filmed in 1941, its classic status was confirmed when, in 1970, it reappeared as a musical.

Nine novels and a book of short stories followed, all written with the same unaffected directness and honesty, and they showed that Greenwood's range was not limited by slum streets and the gloom of industrial breakdown; he handled humorous situations precisely as he had made his *cri de coeur*, simply and sincerely. *Only Mugs Work*, written in 1938, followed *Love on the Dole* to the stage, and among his other books *His Worship The Mayor* (1934) and *What Everybody Wants* (1953) were particularly successful. His plays seemed to retain much of the attacking vigour of his first novel as well as a growing mastery of the mechanics of stage writing. *My Son's My Son*, in 1935, *The Cure for Love*, in 1951 and *Saturday Night at the Crown*, in 1953, were perhaps his most successful and valuable work for the stage; within an entirely conventional view of the theatre and its purposes he succeeded in presenting lively situations and unusual characters. *Saturday Night at the Crown* reversed the direction of his earlier plays by being converted into a novel (published in 1959) instead of being a play formed from a published story.

Greenwood began a secondary career as a film script writer in 1935, when he wrote the film *No Limit*, for the comedian George Formby*. He followed this with *Six Men of Dorset*, a dramatization of the career of the "Tolpuddle Martyrs" in 1944; and in 1947, in *Chance of a Lifetime* he managed, in a light and gently told story, to tell a cautionary tale for a time of industrial unrest. The workers of a factory, striking against inefficient management, accept their employers' challenge to run the factory themselves, and find themselves ultimately convinced of the need for cooperation with their boss. Greenwood also wrote a B.B.C. television serial, *The Secret Kingdom*, in 1960. In *There was a Time*, published in 1967, he told the story of his first 30 years and returned to the place and situation of *Love on the Dole*. Vividly written to read like a novel, crowded with people of unchallengeable authenticity, it was dramatized as *Hanky Park* (the name he gave to his archetypal Salford slum) and was produced with some success in London in 1970.

Greenwood was a widely read and vigorous-minded man whose plays and novels owe nothing to modern, or any other, theories of literature and drama. The stories he told, he convinced both readers and theatre audiences, were the inevitable result of the situations which faced the people he created. He was, in reality, a primitive, a literary equivalent to L. S. Lowry, who painted the scenes in which Greenwood's work is set. Simplicity of statement, a sense of proportion, direction of approach and honesty of purpose rather than literary finesse were his weapons, and he used them powerfully.

September 16, 1974.

The Rt. Rev. W. D. L. Greer, Bishop of Manchester from 1947 to 1970, died on October 30, 1972. He was 70.

William Derrick Lindsay Greer was born on February 28, 1902, the son of the Rev. Richard Usher Greer, a clergyman of the Church of Ireland. To his parents he owed the inestimable boon of a Christian home and upbringing; to his Ulster environment the suspicion of an Irish brogue which never quite left him and which he could and did turn on when it suited him. In his background, religion and life were closely intertwined with politics and prejudices, religious and secular. It is not fanciful to think that in a lesser character these might have been a handicap; but in William Greer they became assets.

He too could not separate religion from life, and the strains and stresses of the Irish conflicts taught him not bigotry but tolerance and an understanding of the other man's opinion essential for an Anglican bishop.

Indeed he developed a temperament that might have been described as typically British rather than Irish, extremely reserved and unemotional (though the emotions within were strong enough), a man whose heart was never on his sleeve and who cared nothing for appearances.

After schooling at St. Columba's College, Dublin, he went in 1920 with a scholarship to Trinity College, Dublin, where he read classics and theology with his vocation in view. Without being a scholar of the first rank he had a first-class mind and carried off the Vice-Chancellor's Prose Prize and several others before taking a "first" in his degree.

On leaving Trinity he became a civil servant because he wished to experience the strains and stresses of life as a layman before he took holy orders. Four years in the service of the Northern Ireland Government as assistant principal in the Ministry of Home Affairs enabled him to observe the workings of government administration and the personal methods of government leaders, as well as giving him an insight into the political world which was useful to him in after years.

When the time seemed ripe to follow his calling, he was not one to be confined to the rather narrow orbit of the Church of Ireland, and went to Westcott House, Cambridge, intending to give himself to the Church of England. The Principal of Westcott House was at that time Canon B. K. Cunningham, revered and respected both as teacher and example of a comprehensive Anglicanism.

Greer had only three short terms there, but B.K. (as he was affectionately called) gave him just what he needed and when he was ordained deacon at Newcastle in 1929 he had lived with and had learnt to understand both the Anglo-Catholic and the modernist. The third element in Anglicanism, the Evangelical, was his already from his Ulster-Protestant youth, and it never left him, though further on he combined it with Catholicism in the deepest and best sense of that word.

For the minutiae of ceremonial or ritual he cared nothing at all, but for the ordered, dignified and homely liturgy of the Book of Common Prayer he learnt to care enormously and to hate untidiness and carelessness and anything that erected a barrier (so it seemed to him) between the worshipper and God.

He was ordained deacon four years later than usual and was already at 27 mature beyond his years when he became assistant curate in the parish of St. Luke the Evangelist, Newcastle upon Tyne. Tyneside in the years of terrible depression was an education indeed. He threw himself into parochial life with the ordered thoroughness with which he did everything and learnt to love and understand the British working man. At the same time he became a student of the economic order and gained a remarkable knowledge of industry and trade. His understanding of and critical

sympathy with the business world was in later years made very clear when, as president of the Manchester and Salford Savings Bank, he used to deliver himself, at the annual meeting, of a chairman's speech which was remarkable not only for its Christian insight (which was to be expected) but for its shrewd business acumen.

After two years as curate he became vicar of the parish—an uncommon promotion—and endeared himself to his parishioners (both those who came to church and those who did not) when they discovered that in their rather austere and extremely efficient vicar they had a friend with a most pastoral heart.

After six years on Tyneside, he became general secretary of the Student Christian Movement. This post he held for nine years of almost continuous strain and crisis. It was a task that suited his many gifts and took him back into the university world where he was more at home than in a parish.

In 1944 B. K. Cunningham resigned the principalship of Westcott House, which he had held since the house was founded in 1919, and William Greer succeeded him. Greer had to steer the college through the impatient first year of release; he had to adapt the course to men who had been through the fire, mature in mind as well as years, and mostly already married.

All this he did with no fuss and with quiet sagacity. It was no small tribute to him that he won so soon and so completely the trust and admiration of those who came from the forces full of suspicion of the civilian church and of academic life. In 1946 he took to himself a wife and turned the old Principal's rooms into married quarters. Marigold Stogdon was just the wife he needed and threw herself heart and soul into caring for the wives of the married students.

But college life was not allowed to claim him for long. To the surprise of many, to the chagrin of some but to the great credit of his Majesty's advisers, Greer was appointed Bishop of Manchester and consecrated in York Minster on Michaelmas Day, 1947.

The difficulties before any bishop called to any urban diocese in the post-war years were great enough. Spiritual life was at a low ebb, manpower was sadly depleted, and the material ravages of the war years had to be repaired. On these two great tasks Greer brought an almost superhuman energy to bear.

The staffing of his 372 parishes became at once and remained his chief personal task. Indeed he used sometimes to complain—the only complaint he ever made—that he was an employment agency rather than a bishop. It may justly be claimed for him that he put the North on the map for young men seeking a title or a parish and a steady and increasing stream of them began to find their way as curates and incumbents into the diocese of Manchester. With the recruiting of men, and with the changing temper of the times, spiritual life began to revive. For the third great problem of bricks and mortar he found a diocese already well organized and he encouraged, stimulated and trusted his diocesan committees, largely composed of Manchester business men.

He had strong views on disarmament and on many occasions spoke out in favour of the unilateral renunciation of atomic weapons by Britain.

He is survived by his widow, a son and two daughters.

November 1, 1972.

J. M. Gregory, the Australian fast bowler and hard-hitting batsman, died on August 7, 1973 in Bega District Hospital, about 100 miles south of Sydney. He was 77.

In all he played in 24 Test matches, taking 85 wickets for 2,648 runs. His average was 31.15. He scored 1,146 runs in Test cricket with a highest score of 119.

He was born on August 14, 1895. He bore a name already well known in Australian cricket, for he was the nephew of David Gregory, who in 1878 captained the first team from Australia to visit England. S. E. Gregory, who figured in many Test matches, was his cousin.

During the first World War J. M. Gregory served as a cadet in the Royal Artillery. He came into notice in 1919, when he toured England as a member of the Australian Imperial Forces eleven. He showed himself good all round, as a hard-hitting left-hand batsman, and a right-hand bowler of exceptional pace. He scored nearly 1,000 runs for the side and took 131 wickets. His success caused him to be chosen for Australia in the campaign of 1920-21, when the visiting tourists from England, under the captaincy of J. W. H. T. Douglas, had the unprecedented experience of losing all five Test matches. Gregory as an all-round man had a good deal to do with the success of the side, but, though he took 23 wickets, it was as a batsman that he shone most. His aggregate came to 442, and his average to 73, with 100 in the second Test, and other good scores.

When a month or two later the Australians visited England under the captaincy of W. W. Armstrong, they proceeded to win the three first Test matches of the tour, which meant that they had won eight of these contests in succession. They did not win by making their usual huge scores, but by the failure of England batsmen. Gregory was now partnered in the attack by Macdonald, who was nearly as fast, and, as some said, a better bowler. But Gregory was considered the more alarming of the pair. A tall, strongly-built man, with a long run—it ended with a huge bound of some nine feet—and waving arms, he pounded down his deliveries, which scattered the stumps, or whistled about the ears of the English batsmen with a most intimidating

effect. In the first three games of the rubber England could make no headway at all, and by some of the critics Gregory was hailed as the greatest match-winner to be found anywhere.

But Gregory, against England, seems never to have regained his bowling form. He got some wickets, though very expensively, against Gilligan's team in 1924-25, but when he visited again in 1926 he was not a force to be reckoned with.

In 1928-29 he was back in the field, played at Brisbane in the first Test and broke down in the first innings, during which he bowled 41 overs and took three wickets for 142 runs.

He was in his day a superb match-winning cricketer who excelled in all departments of the game for in addition to his prowess with bat and ball he was a spectacular slip-field, "a tumbler and conjuror combined", as A. G. Moyes put it, adding, "as a box-office attraction he was on the top rung of the ladder".

August 8, 1973.

John Gregson, star of many popular British films, collapsed and died on January 8, 1975 while on holiday with his family in Somerset. He was 55 and had suffered from heart trouble.

Starting his film career just after the war, Gregson became one of the leading British screen actors of the 1950s. He appeared with equal success in comedies and war films, and his easy charm and dark good looks brought him a large following. When, later, the British cinema demanded a less glamorous type of hero, Gregson turned increasingly to the theatre and television.

He was born in Liverpool on March 15, 1919 and started acting as an amateur before training professionally at the Liverpool Old Vic and Perth Repertory Company. He entered films in 1948, at a boom period for the British cinema, and worked for Ealing studios in celebrated pictures like *Scott of the Antarctic, Whisky Galore, The Lavender Hill Mob* and *The Titfield Thunderbolt.*

His greatest success came in 1953 when he appeared with Kenneth More, Kay Kendall and Dinah Sheridan in *Genevieve,* a comedy about the London to Brighton veteran car run. The film was an enormous hit and launched Gregson as a star.

By the late 1950s he had made 23 films in 10 years, alternating comedies like *The Captain's Table* with war pictures (*Above Us the Waves* and *The Battle of the River Plate*).

With the arrival of films like *Room at the Top* and a new realism in the British cinema, Gregson's popularity declined and his film appearances became rarer. He was seen in character roles in *The Longest Day, Live Now Pay Later* and *The Night of the Generals* but his career then switched.

In 1965 he starred as Commander Gideon

in the television police series based on the John Creasey novels, and four years later took over the leading role (from Kenneth More) in the William Douglas-Home comedy, *The Secretary Bird,* on the London stage. In 1971 he starred in another television series, *Shirley's World,* with Shirley Maclaine.

Gregson was married and had six children. The family lived in an eighteenth-century mansion, once the home of Charles Dickens, at Shepperton, Middlesex.

January 10, 1975.

Mary Grey, the actress, who died in her 97th year, in October 1974, is remembered for her witty versatility during the seasons in which her second husband, James Bernard Fagan, directed the Court Theatre. She was also (1925) Madame Ranevsky in *The Cherry Orchard* at Hammersmith, the most successful production, to that time, of Chekhov in England.

Welsh by birth (Ada Bevan ap Rees Bryant), she was a sister of the actor, Charles Bryant. Always a poised and handsome woman, she worked in her youth with Frank Benson's Shakespeare company, and later (1908-9), as an accomplished singer, in operetta at the Hicks Theatre and at Daly's. She went (1911) into Alexander's St. James's production of *Bella Donna,* adapted by Fagan from the Robert Hichens novel.

Although during 1917 she had exacting parts in *Damaged Goods* and *Rosmersholm* (Rebecca) at the St. Martin's, her fullest chances came under her husband's direction at the Court between the autumn of 1918 and 1921.

This was a fruitful period in the record of a theatre that, again and again, has added to stage history. Beginning as Olivia in *Twelfth Night,* Mary Grey went on to Lady Teazle, Portia, Oberon—there was argument here about the singing of certain speeches that should have been spoken—Emilia to Godfrey Tearle's first Othello, and a precisely-keyed Hesione in the English production (1921) of Shaw's *Heartbreak House*: she repeated this in 1937 at the Westminster.

In the West End, and elsewhere, she played numerous parts, notably—in London and New York—Mrs. Knight in her husband's Pepysian comedy, *And So To Bed.* But her highest achievement was Madame Ranevsky in Fagan's production of *The Cherry Orchard,* from Oxford, when Chekhov at last became acclimatized. This ran at the Lyric, Hammersmith, and the old Royalty (John Gielgud was Trofimov, the "perpetual student"); and James Agate spoke in his notice, influential at the time, of the beauty of Mary Grey's "pose in the second act and dumb grief in the third".

October 12, 1974.

John Grierson, O.B.E., the film producer, died on February 19, 1972 in Bath. He was 73. Grierson, as founder of the documentary film movement, had a profound and world-wide influence not only on developments in the realm of film but also on the whole conception of the use of mass-media in the public service.

A small, wiry man with piercing eyes and an aggressive stance, Grierson pushed forward his plans with an energy which often left his colleagues far behind. He had a reputation for ruthlessness; but he was in fact only ruthless when all other courses failed. His bristling exterior camouflaged an affectionate and sympathetic nature, as those comparatively few who came close to him very soon discovered. He was regarded by film-makers as a hard taskmaster, but he rewarded hard work with a complete loyalty. As a producer he was brilliant. He never imposed his own ideas, but compelled each director to extract from his own inner resources the solutions to his problems.

He was born at Kilmadock, in Stirlingshire, in 1898, the son of Robert Morrison Grierson, a schoolmaster. From 1915 to 1919 he served with the R.N.V.R. In 1923 he took his M.A. degree at Glasgow University with distinctions in English and moral philosophy. In the following year he won a Rockefeller Research Fellowship in social science and spent the next three years in the United States studying what later came to be called the mass-media of communication.

During his stay in America he was particularly influenced by two events—the premiere in New York of Eisenstein's *Battlecruiser Potemkin* (a film which he analysed in minute detail), and his meeting with Robert Flaherty, in writing of whose films he first coined the word "documentary". Both *Nanook* and *Moana* had a strong effect on Grierson, and although he subsequently differed from Flaherty's somewhat romantic conception of documentary, he never ceased to respect what he once called "the finest eyes in cinema".

His experiences in America led Grierson to the conclusion that the film was the most powerful as well as the most universal medium of public persuasion and information the world had ever known. It was, he felt, of vital importance that it should be used as such.

On his return to England in 1927 he succeeded in getting an introduction to Sir Stephen Tallents, head of the Empire Marketing Board. Tallents, a public servant of rare vision, realized the importance of Grierson's ideas and arranged for him to be appointed Films Officer of the Board. In this capacity he bombarded the members of the E.M.B. with memoranda on the use of films in other countries and with specially arranged showings of films from many parts of the world, including the Soviet Union. Eventually the point was reached when it was felt the E.M.B. might embark on the production of a film of its own. The board, however, was split between two propositions. One, based on an idea by Rudyard Kipling, concerned a small boy's dream about the dominions and colonies bringing to Buckingham Palace the ingredients for the King's Christmas pudding. The other was to be a wholly realistic film about the North Sea herring fleets. In the event both films were made, but only *Drifters* (by far the less costly of the two) was a success. In this film Grierson put to good use his intensive studies of film techniques—and especially those newly developed in Russia—and by imaginative cutting, no less than by fine photography, created something which, in the context of the uninspired and overconventional British films of the day, was nothing less than sensational.

The success of *Drifters* gave Grierson and Tallents the chance to expand the E.M.B.'s film activities. At this point Grierson took the most important and far-reaching decision of his career. He decided to give up film-directing and to devote all his energies to producing. Thus in the last two months of 1929 there appeared the nucleus of a film unit, and within a couple of years this unit had become a force to reckon with. Grierson was joined by enthusiastic youngsters like Basil Wright, Arthur Elton, Stuart Legg, Edgar Anstey, John Taylor and others. Their tyro work under Grierson's control represented a combination of public service and aesthetic experiment which, when successful, was received with enthusiasm by cinéastes and educationists alike.

With the demise of the E.M.B. in 1933 Tallents too the unit with him to the G.P.O., to which he had been appointed public relations officer. Here the unit continued to flourish and expand. More youngsters, including Harry Watt, Humphrey Jennings and Pat Jackson came to serve their apprenticeship. All the unit's directors were encouraged to experiment and to see (to use Grierson's words) "the gale-warning behind the Central Telegraph Office, the paradox of nationalism and internationalism behind the cable service, the choral beauty of the night mail, and the drama tucked away in the files of the ship-to-shore radio service." The great Flaherty had already made his contribution by directing *Industrial Britain* for the E.M.B.; now Grierson invited Cavalcanti to come over from France and experiment in the still new techniques of the sound film. This period produced such works as *Coalface, Song of Ceylon, Weather Forecast, Night Mail* and *We Live in Two Worlds*. To these young artists from other fields made their own contributions— W. H. Auden, Benjamin Britten, William Coldstream, Walter Leigh—to name but a few.

By this time Grierson's influence was reaching far beyond the confines of government departments. Various practitioners in the comparatively new profession of public relations began to sense the potentialities of the documentary idea. Grierson therefore encouraged some of his colleagues to move out of the G.P.O. Film Unit and set up their own production companies to serve the film needs of sponsors like the oil and gas industries and similar organizations.

In 1937 Grierson was invited to Canada to prepare plans for the development of government film production. The report he wrote resulted in being asked to draft a Bill to be placed before the Dominion Parliament; and in 1939 the National Film Act became law. It provided for the creation of a National Film Board through which all Government production and distribution should be channelled.

While Grierson was visiting Australia and New Zealand for the Imperial Relations Trust, and in fact laying the foundations for new government film organizations there, the Second World War began. The Canadian Government immediately invited him to become the first Film Commissioner under the new Act. This post he accepted, for a trial period of six months. In the event he remained in Canada until the end of the war, by which time he was effectively in charge of all Canadian Information Services, while the National Film Board had become one of the most influential film-making centres in the world.

At the end of the war Grierson resigned from the Film Board and with Legg and Raymond Spottiswoode went to New York. Here they formed International Film Associates, a body designed to produce on a world basis, and with allied companies in Europe and elsewhere, a series of films of international interest and validity on scientific, technological, and artistic developments as well as on human skills and excellencies in general, wherever they might be found. Unfortunately the distribution negotiations with United Artists could not be brought to a satisfactory conclusion. Moreover the beginnings of the anti-Red panic which ended in McCarthyism did not leave Grierson unscathed. An ex-secretary at the Film Board was involved in the Canadian spy trial and on both sides of the border Grierson found himself (quite unjustifiably) smeared.

In 1947 he was back in Europe at the headquarters of the newly formed Unesco in Paris where, at the invitation of its first Director-General, Julian Huxley, he became Director of Mass Communications and Public Information. He flung himself into this new job with his usual intensity. The trouble was, however, that there was money for planning but not for production.

In 1948 he returned to Britain to become Film Controller at the Central Office of Information. Here was another disappointment. The war-time Ministry of Information, which had considerable powers of initiative, had been abolished and the Central Office set up in its place. The C.O.I., being only an agency, was in effect deprived of initiative. Faced by interdepartmental skirmishes on the one hand and a certain post-war lassitude on the part of the film-makers on the other, Grierson experienced a period of frustration.

With the setting up of the National Film Finance Corporation in 1949, came the creation of a production company named Group Three designed as a training ground where young feature film directors could be tried out on low-budget productions. There could be no doubt that a number of these would be documentary in style, if only for purposes of economy, and the direction of the new company was entrusted jointly to Grierson and to John Baxter, an established feature director who had made *Love on the Dole*.

Although for a number of reasons, mostly relating to government and film trade politics, the Group Three project was not a financial success, Grierson's invigorating approach to the experiment was of no small value. It brought to the fore young filmmakers like Philip Leacock, Pennington Richards, Cyril Frankel and John Eldridge; and actors such as Peter Finch, Kenneth More, Peter Sellers and Tony Hancock* had their first chances at Group Three.

With the demise of Group Three in 1955 Grierson found himself, for the first time in his life, in the doldrums.

In 1957 he met Roy (now Lord) Thomson and put forward a plan to put out on Scottish Television a programme entitled *This Wonderful World*. This was agreed. The programme was an immediate success and was soon networked through the British Isles. In *This Wonderful World* Grierson personally introduced, with comments of his own, films, or extracts of films from all over the world.

It was a programme which, towards the end of his career, vindicated the saying with which he began his documentary work —"The motion picture can open for us a window on the world." From 1957 the series continued until 1968 when a severe illness caused him to give up the programme. Subsequently, however, he accepted a professorship of mass communication at McGill University, Montreal; and from here in 1970 he made a sabbatical visit to India where he combined his advice to the Government on the use of the mass media with a penetrating aesthetic study of the relations between Indian dance movements and those of the motion picture.

He married Margaret Taylor in 1930.

February 21, 1972.

James Griffiths, C.H., P.C., one of the Labour Party's most influential and best-loved figures, died on August 7, 1975 aged 84, at his home at Teddington. He was M.P. for Llanelly from 1936 until he retired at the 1970 general election.

Griffiths was Minister of National Insurance from 1945 to 1950, Colonial Secretary from 1950 to 1951, and Deputy Leader of the Parliamentary Labour Party from 1955 to 1959.

The crown of his political career was his appointment (1964-66) as the first Secretary of State for Wales with a seat in the Cabinet and a department to which Whitehall had transferred the most important Welsh responsibilities.

Griffiths brought to the Labour movement's service the endowment of a warm and generous personality. He stood in the true line of those working class leaders whose social ideal nourished the roots from which the party drew its political strength. Griffiths never lost the sense of mission of that radical-nonconformist tradition in which he was bred. It gave something of a prophetic quality to his passion for social justice and lifted him above the striving of rival factions. He stood for something stable and enduring which gave him unique authority as an influence for peace and reconciliation.

When the opportunity came for him to translate that faith into political action he rejoiced in being the chosen instrument, as Minister of National Insurance, to build into the fabric of the welfare state a comprehensive measure of social insurance against sickness, unemployment and old age. Later, as Colonial Secretary, he strove to apply the same broad principles to the conduct of his responsibilities in overseas territories. His simple duty, as he conceived it, was to apply on a world-wide scale the liberalizing benefits of the welfare state. If, in the eyes of his critics, he strayed into errors of judgment in Colonial policy, his mistakes were those of a man whose heart ruled his head.

His early experiences as a trade union leader in the harshest periods of the working-class struggle never embittered him. He fought hard but without rancour. He could kindle the ardour of an audience but he never sought to inflame it. If he was a sentimentalist, the sentiments were deep and genuine. Cynics might sneer when Jim Griffiths, hand on heart in that familiar gesture, poured out a flood of Celtic emotion. In his highest flights of Welsh fervour he could be prolix, repetitive, often obscure, but real sincerity shone through the welter of words. He beguiled by lack of guile. Much more than by what he said—and he said a great deal—Jim Griffiths commanded respect and affection by what he was, a man who enriched and sweetened political life with rare qualities of heart and mind.

James Griffiths was born at Ammanford, South Wales, in 1890, the youngest of 10 children of the local blacksmith. Until he was five he spoke not a word of English. From the Bettws council school he went to work at the local anthracite colliery at the age of 13. Four years later he joined the Ammanford branch of the I.L.P. and soon became its secretary. In 1919 he won a scholarship to the Labour College in London and was there for two years while his wife helped to supplement their small allowance by waiting in a tea-shop. He returned to the coal face and spent four nights a week giving classes in economics and industrial history. He became chairman of the miners' lodge and secretary of the local trades council. In 1922 he went to his first full-time political post, as agent of the Llanelly Labour Party, and three years later he became miners' agent in the Anthracite Mines Association. This was the period of the great miners' strike which preceded and outlasted the General Strike of 1926.

Griffiths worked hard to help rebuild the South Wales Miners' Federation. He became known as a skilful and patient negotiator and one of his fondest memories was of announcing to the stay-down striking miners, to the singing of "Cwm Rhondda", that he had secured a victorious settlement. In 1934 he became president of the federation and also was elected to the executive of the Miners' Federation of Great Britain. It was a time of bitter struggle which left Griffiths with burning memories of the unemployment and hunger marches of those days.

A by-election at Llanelly sent him to Parliament in 1936 and he was soon making his voice heard in denouncing the means test, attacking the mine-owners and advocating the extension of social insurance. He rose steadily to prominence as a fervent and forceful debater, and in 1939 he was elected to the National Executive, a remarkably rapid move. After Labour's victory at the polls in 1945, Griffiths was an obvious choice for office and he became a Privy Councillor and Minister of National Insurance, charged with the task of implementing the substance of the Beveridge* proposals and the Coalition White Paper.

It was a complex task, but he eventually presented a measure of wide comprehension which knit together all the previous schemes of insurance against sickness, unemployment and old age. Apart from raising the general level of benefits and contributions from worker, employer, and the state, the Act introduced important new principles. The scheme was to be universal in its application, based on the simple axiom of "one fund, one card, one stamp", and its administration amounted to a major undertaking. It provided the most extensive system of benefits the nation had ever known. When it had come into operation, Griffiths developed it and removed many anomalies, working hard to ensure its smooth running.

He was elected chairman of the party in 1948-1949. At the General Election of 1950 he held his seat at Llanelly by a majority of 31,626, the fourth biggest in the election and the highest in Wales. In the new Labour Government, Clement Attlee* transferred Griffiths to the Colonial Office. Many found it a surprising choice, but Griffiths threw himself with the zeal of a Welsh revivalist into the task of increasing native participation in territorial government. He travelled widely, visiting Malaya, Hongkong and many other places in 1950 and East and Central Africa the next year. This was before the Mau Mau threat had fully emerged, and Griffiths was keen to press forward with plans for constitutional development in Kenya. In August 1951 he went to Nyasaland and Northern Rhodesia to find out for himself the reactions of the various communities to proposals for Central African federation. He believed passionately in the right of the people to determine their own future. At the subsequent Victoria Falls conference he found the African representatives hostile to the federal scheme, and was later accused by the leader of the opposition in Southern Rhodesia of having given the African delegates a false idea of their own importance. This was typical of the criticism he encountered in some quarters. It sprang from the eagerness he showed in enabling native communities to take a wider share in the government of their own territories. He achieved much in furtherance of this aim and it was his proud boast that twelve new constitutions were adopted while he was Colonial Secretary.

He much regretted having to leave the Colonial Office with the fall of the Labour Government in 1951 and he was outspoken in his criticism of some aspects of Conservative policy in that field as in many others. His popularity in his party grew rapidly, and he was elected at the top of the poll among the candidates for the Shadow Cabinet in 1955. In the contest for the Deputy Leadership of the Parliamentary Labour Party that year he defeated Bevan by 141 votes to 111 and continued to be reelected until he retired from it in 1959. He had been a member of the National Executive for 20 years, having been reelected repeatedly by the constituency section. He survived the acutest phase of the Bevanite crisis precisely because he was so deeply respected by all sections of the party as a man who transcended all the warring feuds, one whose integrity recalled the Labour movement to its best self. This was his greatest service to it and his enduring memorial. In May 1967 he announced that he would not stand again for Parliament.

Griffiths was made an hon. LL.D. of the University of Wales in 1946. In 1966 he was made a Companion of Honour. In December 1953 he suffered a grievous personal loss by the death of his brother, David Rhys Griffiths, the well-known poet and bard. His autobiography, *Pages from Memory,* was published in 1969.

He married in 1918 Winnie Rutley, of Overton, Hampshire. They had two sons and two daughters.

August 8, 1975.

General George Grivas, leader of the Greek-Cypriot movement for *enosis*, the union of Cyprus with Greece, died in Cyprus on January 27, 1974. He was 75. He fought the British colonial rule from 1955 to 1959, then resumed his underground struggle in 1971, one decade after the island was proclaimed independent.

During four tragic years in the late 1950s, Grivas, with £10,000 on his head, eluded the search of 30,000 British troops. To the British he was an "arch-terrorist and a killer"; to the Greeks he was the "liberator" and a national hero. Whichever opinion may ultimately prevail among later historians, it can hardly be disputed that Grivas was, above all, an idealist and that his presence in Cyprus had been a direct consequence of a basically unwise British policy in that former Crown Colony.

Grivas was born at Trikomo, a village in Cyprus, on May 23, 1898. Soon after completing his studies he realized, with much disgust, that his father intended him to be a physician. So he fled to Athens and joined the Officers' Cadet School. He was commissioned in 1919 and completed his military studies at the Ecole de Guerre, in Paris. The system of slow promotion which then prevailed in the Greek Army delayed his ascent. It took him 22 years to reach the rank of lieutenant-colonel in 1941.

Grivas did not display any exceptional qualities in the course of his army career. He took part in the Asia Minor campaign as a junior officer, and in the Greek-Italian war he served as chief of staff in the 3rd Division. His personality was given a chance to emerge in those desolate days of the Nazi occupation of Greece. It is, perhaps, to his credit that he was among the first to realize that the Greek communists, by assuming the leadership of the main resistance movement in Greece, were hoping to seize political power after the war. In 1943 he organized a militant royalist group to fight the communists. He named his organization "X" (from the symbolic monogram of King George II). Rumours that he had accepted arms and assistance from the German authorities to combat the communists, though never proved, wrecked his reputation as a *bona fide* resistance leader. None the less, during the bloody communist uprising in Athens in December 1944, Grivas and his men fought side by side with the British troops against the red insurgents.

With the return of normal conditions in Greece, and the restoration of monarchy, Grivas, who had been retired with the rank of lieutenant-colonel in 1944, developed political ambitions. He reshaped his militant organization into a political party and campaigned in the first postwar elections, in 1946. His failure was total and even official election statistics did not deign to name his group separately, but classified it among the dishonoured "Other Parties", which had polled a total of 15,000 votes throughout the country.

In the 1950 elections he tried again, after re-christening his party "National Agrarian Party 'X'", but was again unsuccessful.

None the less Grivas persevered. In the 1951 elections he tried to make a safe gamble by standing as a simple candidate for the then largest right-wing party, the Populists of ex-Premier Constantine Tsaldaris,* but he was a third time unlucky.

A restless character, Grivas could not be satisfied with the pensioner's sedentary life to which he had been forced by the advent of political stability in Greece. Persons who had met him spoke of him with some respect. His personality was not likable, but he had a good reputation as an honest and incorruptible idealist. He also possessed a powerful inner drive and a quality of commanding devotion and loyalty from those close to him.

It was, probably, these radiating qualities rather than any political wisdom which helped him build up a resistance movement in Cyprus, aimed at uniting the island with Greece. It is not yet entirely clear who first conceived the idea of organizing an armed uprising in Cyprus. What is known, however, is that Grivas was chosen to lead this expedition.

He left his modest home, near the Acropolis of Athens, in great secrecy on October 26, 1954. He reached Rhodes and, embarking in a caique, made for Cyprus, landing on an isolated beach, near Khlorakas village, on the Paphos coast on November 7. Within six months, helped by arms shipments from Greece (of which one was captured by the Royal Navy), Grivas organized highly effective terrorist and sabotage groups which he named E.O.K.A. from the Greek initials for "National Organization of Cypriot Fighters". His first operation was sabotage against the power station, which plunged Nicosia into darkness. He operated under the assumed name of "Dighenis".

Almost four years later in 1959, Grivas returned in triumph to Athens. With the settlement of the Cyprus issue he was allowed an honourable retreat. He did not, however, agree entirely with the solution which gave Cyprus independence, while he had fought for the island's union with Greece (*enosis*). He accepted the Cyprus agreements as a *fait accompli*. In Athens, Grivas was showered with honours.

Grivas had become a hero. He was regarded by the Greeks as the epitome of all the virtues which lent so much glory to the men who made history in Greece. And this popularity evidently rekindled his erstwhile political ambitions. Prodded by many politicians who were in search of a protective wing to regain the power which had been denied them by the advent of political stability, Grivas embarked on a campaign of political verbosity which reduced him to ridicule. The idol had fallen. After this initial skirmish with the politicians he was no longer a national hero, he had become a politician himself.

In May 1960 he launched his "National Regeneration Movement" which promised to turn Greece into a land where "the division between hungry and glutted" would disappear. Some of his speeches were so crudely outspoken that his supporters took fright. Those who had encouraged him soon deserted him in September 1961, to join George Papandreou's* newly founded party, the Centre Union.

Disgusted, the General gave up politics and retired in a small rented villa in Halandri, an Athens suburb.

The intercommunal clashes which erupted in Cyprus late in 1963 vindicated his erstwhile opposition to the agreements. He decided to interfere once again in the hope of leading Cyprus towards *enosis* which, he believed, was the only pragmatic and permanent solution.

As the island's Turkish minority barricaded itself in fortified pockets throughout Cyprus, private armies of gunmen sprang up on the Greek-Cypriot side, and Turkey renewed threats of intervention. The popular demand in Cyprus for Grivas's return grew. He went to the island in the middle of 1964 to restore discipline within the Greek camp and organize the island's defences with the Greek Government's blessing in the shape of one division of Greek troops clandestinely despatched to Cyprus under the guise of volunteers.

While the physical separation of the two communities tended to become a status quo by the end of 1967, Grivas suddenly authorized raids against two Turkish villages. His action (he claimed he was obeying orders from Athens) unleashed one of the most serious crises yet between Greece and Turkey. War was averted by the combined efforts of the United States, the United Nations and Nato; but Greece, which had been taken over by a military junta, under the peace terms, had to suffer the humiliation of recalling Grivas and repatriating the army of mainland "volunteers". Grivas returned to his suburban retreat in Athens at the end of 1967, and as the island's two communities tried to find a *modus vivendi* at the conference table, his overall appeal waned.

Grivas had always accused Makarios of forsaking the "sacred aspiration of *enosis*" in favour of the island's independence in order to wallow in temporal power. In the autumn of 1971, as the first reports came that the long-drawn-out inter-communal negotiations were reaching agreement which would consolidate Cyprus's independence and, above all, rule out *enosis* for ever, Grivas, although 74, returned clandestinely to Cyprus to "prevent a betrayal of *enosis*".

The general was clearly obsessed by the idea that he should achieve *enosis* before dying. He even declared his readiness to accept some settlement involving temporary territorial concessions to Turkey in exchange for the island's union with Greece. He soon organized armed bands, raided police stations and mines to seize weapons, explosives and wireless sets. His campaign of terrorism reached its climax early in August 1973 with the kidnapping of the Cypriot Minister of Justice. Grivas's terms to President Makarios were for a referendum on *enosis* and for Makarios's resignation either from his leadership of the Cyprus Church or the Presidency of the Republic. The terms were rejected and the minister was released a month later.

January 29, 1974.

Vittorio Gui, doyen of Italian conductors, died on October 16, 1975 in Florence. He was 90.

Gui's reputation rested not only on his complete understanding of the operatic repertory ranging from Gluck to modern works but also on his knowledge of a vast range of orchestral music. He is mainly remembered in Britain for his work at Glyndebourne from 1952 to 1963.

Gui was born on September 14, 1885 at Rome. After studying at the Santa Cecilia Academy in that city with the intention of becoming a composer, he made his début as a conductor quite by chance. A colleague fell ill, and he was asked to take charge of *La Gioconda* at the Teatro Adriano at Rome on December 7, 1907. The result was a triumph, and from then on the course of his career was determined. That début was followed shortly by a performance of the rarely heard Donizetti opera, *Maria di Rohan,* with Battistini in the cast, at Turin.

For some years he divided his time between the concert halls and opera houses of those two cities, on one occasion being chosen specially by Debussy to direct a performance of his music at Rome. The young conductor was also a devoted disciple and friend of his contemporaries, among them Puccini, Stravinsky, Strauss, Pizzetti and Elgar. He also began during those years one of his lifetime's loving tasks, the revival of neglected masterpieces in the operatic repertory.

After service as a soldier in the First World War he resumed his career for a time in Portugal until he was called by Toscanini to La Scala in 1923, from where he returned to Turin to form a notable ensemble which revived such works as *L'Italiana in Algeri, Cosi fan tutte,* and Gluck's *Alceste* that were then quite neglected.

In 1928 he moved to Florence to form the orchestra Stabile, and was one of the founders of the Maggio Musicale there in 1933, continuing to conduct at that festival up to the late 1960s, but he returned to La Scala in 1933 to open the season with Verdi's *Nabucco,* then a considerable rarity.

He first appeared at Covent Garden in 1938, when he conducted the Italian repertory, and returned the following year for *Otello* (with Melchior) and *Trovatore* (with Bjoerling). His only post-war appearance at the Royal Opera House came in 1952 when he conducted *Norma* on the occasion of Callas's début at the House.

His closest and happiest time in Britain was his 11-year association with Glyndebourne. He first appeared with that company in 1948 at the Edinburgh Festival conducting *Cosi fan tutte,* adding *Ballo in Maschera* in 1949. He went to Glyndebourne itself in 1952 when he was in charge of *Macbeth* and *Cenerentola,* the first of several highly successful Rossini revivals, notable among them *Le Comte Ory,* which he later recorded. He was just as at home there in Mozart, in Verdi's *Falstaff* and in

Fidelio. His last, and memorable, performances at the House were of his beloved Debussy's *Pelléas et Mélisande,* 1962-63. Another of his Glyndebourne works was *Alceste,* of which he made an intelligent conflation from the French and Italian versions for the Maggio Musicale in 1968. He was still fighting seemingly lost causes in 1972, when he revived Rossini's *L'Occasione fa il ladro* at Turin. He continued to conduct, particularly concerts, right up to he time of his death.

His interpretations were distinguished by a wonderful buoyancy and attack and by a human warmth, which came from the heart of this much-loved and much-admired maestro. He had many wise sayings about opera, one of which was, "There are no small parts, only small artists".

He was also a noted composer, his works including the opera *Fata Malerba,* given at Turin in 1927.

October 18, 1975.

Dr. Jose Maria Guido, the former provisional President of Argentina, who ruled the country for 19 months during a period of turmoil in the early 60s, died on June 13, 1975. He was 64.

Guido was provisional chairman of the Senate before being sworn in as President of Argentina in March 1962, after President Arturo Frondizi had been overthrown by the armed forces.

The military were the real power behind Guido, but he managed to keep his post despite a virtual civil war between rival army factions.

He presided over the general elections of July 1963 and handed power to the winner, Radical Party candidate Arturo Illia, three months later. Illia was himself overthrown by the armed forces in 1966.

Guido was appointed by the present Perónist Government to a high post in a corporation entrusted with the development of the southern Patagonia region. He resigned shortly afterwards.

June 14, 1975.

Claude Guillebaud, C.B.E., economist, arbitrator in many wage disputes, for many years Tutor of St. John's College, Cambridge, died on August 22, 1971. He was 81. Guillebaud was Emeritus University Reader in Economics at Cambridge.

Claude Guillebaud, born on July 2, 1890, one of twin sons of the Rev. E. D. Guillebaud, was educated at Repton School and after a brief period at Manchester, at St. John's College, Cambridge. A nephew of Mary Marshall, one of the earliest students of Newnham College and wife of the great Alfred Marshall, it was natural that he should turn to economics. He was in the first class in the tripos of 1913; he won the

Adam Smith Prize in 1914 and was elected to a fellowship in 1915. After a period of work in the Civil Service during the First World War, ending on the staff of the Supreme Economic Council in Paris in 1919, he returned to Cambridge and from then onwards, until his retirement, he was continuously engaged in teaching and in the running of his college.

Guillebaud was much too modest a man ever to think of himself as among the foremost economists of his generation. He was too diffident to be an outstandingly good lecturer. He was at his best in the quiet friendliness of college supervision. Possessed of a strong sense of justice, he was an excellent examiner. In his faculty he could always be counted on to fill a gap or to come to the rescue in an emergency. He served for some years as chairman of the Faculty of Economics and Politics at a time when Cambridge economics was deeply divided between Keynesians and anti-Keynesians.

His power of seeing the best in people sometimes betrayed him; for a short period before 1939 he was able to see more good in the economic adventures of the Nazis than most of his colleagues and published a study called *The Economic Recovery of Germany*. Most of his other writings were in the field of labour relations. But his great contribution to economic scholarship was completed when he was over 70. He had worked for a quarter of a century with all the devotion of a nephew on the textual development of Alfred Marshall's *Principles of Economics* from the first edition to the last; the Royal Economic Society, on whose council he served for many years, published the two great volumes of his monumental *Variorum Edition* in 1961. They traced the progress of Marshall's thought and exposition with a care and understanding that was possible only to a real scholar after a life-time of study.

Claude Guillebaud's great gift was the gift of friendship. In Cambridge and outside it, he was rich in friends. He was a person to whom one instinctively turned for advice. And it was this gift of patient, courteous, unhurried impartiality which made him an outstandingly good chairman of any wage-negotiating body. He served his apprenticeship on wages boards. He was over many years successively member and chairman of a large number of boards covering industries as varied as baking, road haulage and bespoke tailoring, to mention only a few. In addition he was independent member of agricultural wages boards in Great Britain and adviser or arbitrator in disputes in the Rhodesias and Tanganyika.

His main titles to fame in this sphere came from his successive chairmanships of the Guillebaud Committees on the National Health Service and on Railway Wages. In both cases he produced a report which achieved a settlement in most difficult circumstances. In both cases he came in for much criticism from economic colleagues

who thought that he had made too great concessions in circumstances in which they themselves would have wished to see intransigence. But in many respects these and other settlements reflected Guillebaud's character at its best. He cared more about justice and equity than about enforcing anti-inflationary policies.

Guillebaud was one of those men, few in any generation, on whose unstinted work a Cambridge college must depend for its well being. As Tutor for many years, and finally as Senior Tutor, he was kind and shrewd in his dealings with individuals. He managed to the end to retain a real interest in young people which brought him many friends, especially among research students and young fellows. There was no trace of pomposity about him and he was an enemy of cant. He never allowed administrative tidiness to come between him and personal problems. Always prepared to admit his own mistakes, he never shirked a difficult interview and because his plain speaking was so courteous, he made few enemies. Cultivated as well as humane, he acted for years as Director of Studies in Modern Languages and showed discriminating judgment whether in pictures or in wine.

He married in 1918 Marie-Thérèse Prunner, much better known to many generations of their friends as Pauline, and they had two daughters.

August 23, 1971.

Nubar Gulbenkian, only son of oil millionaire Calouste Gulbenkian, died in Cannes on January 10, 1972. He was 75.

Unlike his father, Gulbenkian was no recluse: he enjoyed sporting his eccentricities and family differences publicly. The fresh orchid in his buttonhole each day (except on French territory, and blue for the Harrow and Eton match at Lord's) was one of his proudest boasts. A legal action against his father was his way of settling a row started by a disagreement over a chicken he bought out of the office petty cash. His costs of £30,000 were eventually settled by his adversary.

Gulbenkian was an Armenian (though he later assumed Turkish nationality) who delighted in following English pursuits with a full oriental flourish. In scarlet, with silk top hat and orchid, he enjoyed hunting with the Old Berkeley and Whaddon Chase.

His bearded face, with a monocle, was well known at the tables of the Ritz in London, the Aviz in Lisbon, the Georges Cinq in Paris, and many other hotels. His entertaining was in inverse proportion to his station as a minor diplomat (commercial attaché to the Iranian Embassy from 1926-51 and 1956-65): lavish dinner parties at the Ritz and elsewhere. In London, at the conclusion of film premieres, memorial services, or receptions, he could always easily pick out his own car—with its special basketwork body.

Gulbenkian worked for most of his life under his father as a negotiator in oil dealings, and a defender of the Gulbenkian interests. He was a director of the Iraq Petroleum Company in which his father had his famous five per cent share, but was displaced for a time after he had silenced a fellow director with "Hold your tongue!" For a brief time he worked for the Royal Dutch Shell group. Towards the end of his father's life there were more differences. They ranged from stormy rows about the site of the grave of Nubar's mother to bitter quarrels about his exclusion as an original trustee of the charitable foundation his father wished to create.

When his father died, Gulbenkian had not been named as a trustee of the Foundation with an income running into millions each year. Soon, in April 1956, he was offered a trusteeship on a board composed of a majority of Portuguese members. He dithered, then accepted—but too late as the offer had expired the previous day. He refused to become honorary president of the Gulbenkian Foundation. Instead he turned public critic. In 1962 he sued the B.B.C. for a tape-recording promised him of the "Face to Face" programme he appeared in with John Freeman. He was awarded a public platform for his grievances—and forty shillings damages. It cost him on his own reckoning £10,000 in lawyers' bills.

Nubar Sarkis Gulbenkian was born at Kadi Keui, near Constantinople, on June 2, 1896, the year of the Armenian massacres. Three months later, the Gulbenkians fled with the young baby—according to family legend—in a Gladstone portmanteau. Gulbenkian was educated at Harrow, Bonn University, and Trinity College, Cambridge, where he took a degree in law.

His education and working life were to be dominated by his father. He started work as a clerk—in his father's office. From 1917 to 1921 he was attached to the French Ministry of Supply to facilitate the working of various contracts between the Royal Dutch Shell and the French Commissariat aux Essences.

It was a few years before Nubar seriously defied his father. Gulbenkian senior threatened to put him out of a job if he married the Spanish beauty Señorita Herminia Elena Josefa Rodriguez Feijóo. He did in 1922—and although the marriage was finally solemnized with full Armenian rites and the family's blessing in the Ritz Hotel, he had lost his job. Meanwhile he had successfully asked the chairman of the Royal Dutch Shell group, Henri Deterding, for one. Only later did he discover that, even in this, his father had had a hand. He was placed in the Mexican department—being to an extent a buffer between the two oil kings—and for a time acted as Deterding's personal assistant. When relations worsened between the Royal Dutch Shell group and Gulbenkian senior, Deterding offered Nubar the post of general manager in Spain. Gulbenkian senior would not hear of his son being "banished" to Spain, so Nubar declined the post, and was dismissed. Then he returned to work for his father. For the rest of his life until his father's death, he was concerned with the Gulbenkian oil and financial interests.

Gulbenkian was brought up in the orthodox Armenian faith, but could not describe himself "truthfully as a believer", though adhering to the outward forms. In Lent he brushed his bushy beard, dark eyebrows and moustache downwards—and on Easter morning, upwards. He showed a devout filial devotion in mourning his parents —visiting his mother's grave in Nice twice a year. The church was for him, as for many Armenians, an embodiment of their independent traditions. From 1955 he served as honorary president of the church built and endowed by his father in London. In 1967, Gulbenkian spoke out against the proposed sale of Armenian manuscripts. They were later withdrawn.

He published his autobiography *Pantaraxia* in 1965. A year later he was created an Honorary Counsellor to the Turkish Embassy in London. In 1967 he won an appeal against a High Court decision that two settlements made by his father were "void for uncertainty". As a result he was richer by more than £80,000.

Gulbenkian went to extraordinary lengths over the years to get a sight of his obituary kept at *The Times*, approaching and entertaining directors and senior members of the editorial staff in the hope of achieving his aim which would, of course, have been directly contrary to the paper's practice. He was not successful.

He was three times married: firstly, in 1922 to Señorita Herminia Rodriguez Feijóo, and the marriage was dissolved in 1928; secondly, in 1928, to Doré Freeland, and this marriage was dissolved in 1937; thirdly, in 1948 to Mrs. Marie Berthe Edmée.

January 12, 1972.

Sir Tyrone Guthrie, who died on May 15, 1971, at his home in Newbliss, co. Monaghan, Eire, at the age of 70, was a director of plays and of opera and a planner of playhouses whose influence came to be felt in practically every country in which the theatre exists. In many he himself tested his ideas for the development of a close, reciprocal relationship between actors and the audience, on which, in his view, the meaning and value of a theatrical performance depends.

The antecedents of this much-travelled man, who was in his own words "a great getter-out", a passer-on from one experiment to the launching of another, were Irish, predominantly Scots-Irish, Ulster-Irish. Perhaps Belfast or Edinburgh, Dublin or Glasgow were the cities with whose life he would most have liked to identify himself, but circumstances and events steered him rather towards the acknowledged theatrical capitals of the western world.

William Tyrone Guthrie was born in England at Tunbridge Wells on July 2, 1900, the son of Thomas Clement Guthrie, doctor and surgeon, and of his wife Norah, whose grandfather, Tyrone Power, was the first of the line of actors of that name. Tyrone ("Tony") Guthrie went to Wellington College and as a history scholar to St. John's College, Oxford, and in 1923, because he was stage-struck and acting seemed to offer an escape from the unwelcome notice attracted to him in everyday life by his tallness and rather small head—together they reminded one observer of an alert-looking heron—he accepted J. B. Fagan's invitation to join the original stock-company at the Oxford Playhouse; but he remained there a few months only.

In the new medium of radio he found more scope; first, at Belfast; then, after two years at Glasgow as director of the Scottish National Theatre Society; with the B.B.C. in London; and again, having worked for a year at the Festival Theatre, Cambridge, as director of Anmer Hall's repertory company; with the Canadian Broadcasting Corporation. At the Westminster Theatre in London, opened by Anmer Hall in 1931, he directed the inaugural production of Bridie's *The Anatomist* and later a production of *Love's Labour's Lost* that led to his engagement by Lilian Baylis as play-director at the Old Vic and Sadler's Wells in 1933.

He stayed for one season, but it was the beginning of a long and historic association. In the first season, for which he raised a company headed by Flora Robson, Charles Laughton* and Athene Seyler, he succeeded in improving the costuming and general look of the productions, but not entirely in winning the confidence of the manager and her regular following. However, at the end of two years' work in the West End and on Broadway, realizing that to make a career was less important to him than to help build up an institution, Guthrie was back in the Waterloo Road, to which he introduced Laurence Olivier, for the first time, as Hamlet.

After Lilian Baylis's death in 1937, Guthrie was appointed administrator of the two theatres, work of which had come to include that of the ballet founded by Ninette de Valois. He retained that position, sharing it for some of the war years with Bronson Albery, till the end of the Second World War. During that period, for all the prestige that now attached to the Old Vic, reaching its height in the West End season at the New in 1944-45, when Ralph Richardson, Olivier, Sybil Thorndike and Nicholas Hannen led the company, the drama, opera and ballet companies began to diverge in their courses. For this Guthrie blamed himself as for the most serious failure of his professional life, and the conviction grew in him that on proscenium stages such as these, with the acting-area sharply divided from the auditorium, completely satisfactory performances of Shakespeare were not possible.

His engagement at the Edinburgh Festival in 1948 revealed to him a practical alternative. His audience in the Assembly Hall of the Church of Scotland, which he used for David Lyndsay's satire *The Three Estates*, seated on three sides of an arena, were, it seemed to him, "assisting in" the performance instead of merely watching it, and were participating jointly with the actors in what he later designated a ritual. To provide the conditions in which, whatever the locale or the play, an experience of ritual might be shared by the two parties would be to serve the true aim of the theatre, as Guthrie now saw it.

He did not believe that the meaning of any play was what the author originally supposed, or that a play had a meaning that could be described as an objective meaning. A play existed, he said, in order to suggest many ways in which an undefined truth might be approached. The criticism that all his own productions save the very best were unequal, that they proliferated, lost and found themselves again many times over before the end, was one that he himself would probably have accepted, but would not have regarded as disproving his contention that a director's interpretation ought to be subjective.

Guthrie returned to the Old Vic, whose structure was unalterable beyond a certain point, for the 1951-52 season, and immediately afterwards was invited to Canada to advise on organizing a Shakespeare Festival at Stratford, Ontario. A year later a provisional tent theatre with an arena stage from which none of the 2,000 seats was further removed than from Row M., designed by Tanya Moiseiwitsch, opened with *Richard III;* but, though Alec Guinness and Irene Worth headed the cast, Guthrie from the beginning envisaged this as a Canadian project, with Canadian actors presented to a Canadian audience. Accordingly, he made way after three seasons for Michael Langham as Artistic Director. Guthrie once wrote that his *Tamburlaine the Great,* which opened in Canada, with many Canadians in a cast led by Anthony Quayle, and later transferred to the Winter Garden, New York, was the best production of his career, though it was not in fact designed for an "open" stage.

Other plays directed by him on proscenium stages in the 1950s and early 1960s included Thornton Wilder's *The Matchmaker,* O'Casey's* *The Bishop's Bonfire,* Paddy Chayevsky's *The Tenth Man,* two of Gilbert and Sullivan's Savoy operas, and in 1962 *The Alchemist* at the Old Vic. The following year saw the opening of the Tyrone Guthrie Theatre and Repertory centre at Minneapolis, United States, of which he, Oliver Read and Peter Zeisler were the founders, and where Shakespeare, Chekhov and Jonson were among the authors produced by him on an apron-stage surrounded on three sides. Guthrie again retired at the end of three seasons, being succeeded by Douglas Campbell as artistic director, and he declined on grounds of age an invitation from Gregory Peck to found a repertory theatre in South Carolina, referring Peck for advice to his recently published book *A New Theatre*. Later he was a guest director at Minneapolis for the *Oresteia* trilogy and at the National Theatre, London, for *Tartuffe*, with Gielgud in the cast, and for *Volpone*, both during the 1967-68 season.

Knighted in 1961, Guthrie became Chancellor of Queen's University, Belfast, in 1963 (retiring in 1970). In a speech at City Hall he urged students of that university and of Trinity College, Dublin, to work for the abolition of "the senseless line which separates our countries", but had to explain subsequently that he was not speaking in his capacity as head of a non-party institution. In 1965 he became chairman of the Ulster Council for raising funds for a national theatre complex. He received honorary degrees, as well as those from Queen's University, Trinity College, Dublin, from St. Andrews, from Franklyn and Marshall University, Pennsylvania, from Western Ontario, from Ripon College, Wisconsin, and from Citadel Military College, Charleston.

Guthrie published several of his microphone plays, an acted stage-play *Top of the Ladder*, an autobiography (in 1960) entitled *A Life in the Theatre* and a miscellany (in 1965) entitled *In Several Directions,* two substantial books on the performing arts, their origins and their scope, which are also monuments to his humour and wit.

He married in 1931 Judith Bretherton, whose adaptation of Andreyev's *He Who Gets Slapped* he produced in New York and London in the late 1940's. There were no children of the marriage.

May 17, 1971.

Barbara Gwyer, Principal of St. Hugh's College, Oxford, from 1924 to 1946, died on February 16, 1974.

She was born in 1881, the daughter of J. E. Gwyer. She was educated at the Grove School, Highgate, and was a scholar of Lady Margaret Hall, where she read Literae Humaniores.

Her first posts were secretarial, after which she became educational organizer under West Riding County Council. From 1911-13 she was Vice-Warden of Ashbourne Hall, the university women's hostel at Manchester. She had now found her proper work; and from Manchester she went on to Leeds as Warden of University Hall, where she worked in her own unobtrusive, thorough way for seven years under somewhat difficult conditions. Those at Leeds who knew her well remember her with affection.

Her appointment as Principal of St. Hugh's College was upon no ordinary occasion. The college's fortunes had been marred by a serious internal conflict: there had been an almost complete breach in the continuity of its life and organization; and it had lost in reputation and become the subject of widespread debate and partisanship. Barbara Gwyer was now able to show her qualities, and it seemed as if they had been a special endowment for the college's needs which were not for the stimulus of some dominating personality, but for a quiet and healing influence which would allow confidence and trust to grow.

The new principal showed herself a Christian and a true liberal, and her success was due as much to what she refrained from doing as from what she did. In her company others could rise to their full stature: she offered them not leadership, but respect, tolerance and appreciation. Her life was wholly dedicated to her religion, but she never sought to impose her standards and beliefs upon others. Some, indeed, may have criticized her for an attitude that was almost too retiring for a principal; it was only those undergraduates who had the qualities which enabled them to recognize hers, and who themselves had reached out towards the real woman behind a rather severe manner and appearance, who were able to establish a relationship with her that sometimes became profound friendship.

Her humility and sincerity, untouched by any strain of false sentiment, marked her addresses in chapel. Their highly individual flavour was salty rather than sweet; and that came from her downright honesty, her almost severe classicism and her rather dry sense of humour.

Some of her addresses were published in 1928 under the title of *Exhortations and Addresses in St. Hugh's College Chapel.* The same bracing, astringent flavour marked her introductory memoir to the book *Degrees by Degrees,* which her friend Miss Rogers wrote about the campaign to win for women their present status at Oxford.

Retirement from the principalship merely meant that she extended her many interests and services as an educationist. It might be said that she "specialized in prize giving" at schools because she felt, for all the diffidence that clung to her, that she had something real to say at them.

Two of her main interests were the St. Margaret's House Settlement, Bethnal Green, where she was for some years chairman of the council, and the Institute of Christian Education which she helped to found. In the war she represented Oxford University on the Southern Region Tribunal for Conscientious Objectors.

She will be remembered not as a great figure impressing a brilliant picture of herself upon her generation, but as one who cared nothing for the usual success standards of the world, but knew how to serve and to wait, to do small as well as big things, and who, simply by the quiet manifestation of her own qualities, gave a fuller meaning to the words integrity and sincerity in the field of education.

February 19, 1974.

Aklilou Habte-Wold, who was executed in Ethiopia on November 24, 1974 during the rising, was for many years head of the Ethiopian Government and the closest adherent of the former Emperor Haile Selassie.

Born in 1908 in Addis Ababa of a family renowned for its loyalty to the Emperor, he was educated at the Menelik School in Addis Ababa and then read law in Paris before entering the Ethiopian Foreign Service. After the Italian occupation of Ethiopia in 1936 he remained in charge of the Ethiopian Legation in Paris, but in 1940, when the Germans occupied the city, he escaped and joined the Emperor in exile.

He returned to his own country after its liberation and in 1943 was appointed Vice-Minister for Foreign Affairs. For the next 30 years he was the Emperor's principal adviser in that field. His ability and growing powers of advocacy were of particular service in 1950, when he was largely responsible for securing the adoption in the United Nations Assembly, against strong opposition, of a proposal that the former Italian colony of Eritrea should be federated into Ethiopia.

In 1954 he was awarded an honorary G.C.V.O. when he accompanied the Emperor on a state visit to Britain. In 1956 he took a prominent part in the discussions which followed Nasser's nationalization of the Suez Canal and was a member of the abortive Menzies Mission to Cairo.

In 1957, on the retirement of the Ethiopian Prime Minister, the Emperor left his post vacant but appointed Habte-Wold Deputy Prime Minister and retained him at the head of the Ministry of Foreign Affairs. In 1958 he asked to be relieved of this latter burden and was put in charge of the Royal Secretariat. But in 1960 he reverted to the Ministry of Foreign Affairs while remaining Deputy Prime Minister.

Later in 1960 he was fortunate to be touring South America in the suite of the Emperor when a revolt of the Imperial Guard broke out in Addis Ababa. Although it was speedily crushed, his elder brother and several ministerial colleagues were put to death by the insurgents.

In the Cabinet reshuffle thus necessitated, the Emperor at last made him substantive Prime Minister, although his influence on foreign affairs remained predominant.

For the next 12 years he continued to serve the Emperor with the same complete devotion that he had always shown. He had to contend with many difficulties. Externally, there was constant tension on the frontier with Somalia, and unrest, incited and supported from outside, among the Muslims of Eritrea.

Internally, there was the resentment of the numerous Ethiopians who had been educated abroad but failed to find responsible posts on their return, and increasing accusations of inefficiency and corruption in his administration. This unrest, which had also been at the root of the 1960 revolt, was brought to a head by disastrous famine in 1974.

Unrest spread and the Prime Minister, not altogether fairly, was blamed for the country's ills. He was forced to resign and was later arrested.

November 25, 1974.

Messali Hadj—See Messali.

Dr. Kurt Hahn, C.B.E., a great innovator in education, and the schoolmaster of the Duke of Edinburgh at Salem and Gordonstoun, who died on December 14, 1974, was born in Berlin on June 5, 1886, the son of a Jewish family with industrial, medical and musical connexions.

In his headship of Salem on Lake Constance, and Gordonstoun, in the County Badge scheme before the Second World War, a precursor of the Duke of Edinburgh's Award, and in the foundation of the Outward Bound schools, Kurt Hahn worked to the theory that the first condition of good citizenship was self-reliance and self-confidence, qualities in their turn dependent on a sound body and the development and realization of its capabilities.

He went to school at the Wilhelmgymnasium in Berlin but in 1904 his father, who had also been educated in England, sent Hahn to Christ Church, Oxford, to read classics. It was there that he gained an admiration, which never left him, for the characteristic qualities of the best products of the English public schools.

He returned in 1906 to study in Berlin, Heidelberg, Freiberg and Göttingen, going back to Oxford in 1910 to work under J. A. Stewart, the Platonist, with whom he discussed plans for founding a school.

In August 1914 the war found him attached to the German Foreign Office. He became closely associated with Prince Max of Baden, the last Imperial Chancellor, and, when he took up residence in Salem in 1919, Hahn went with him to assist not only in preparing his memoirs but in establishing the famous Schloss Salem School, which opened with a few pupils in 1920. Hahn began as master of the boarding school, but later became head.

By the early 1930s he was getting at cross purposes with the Nazis, and after Potempa's murder in 1932 he urged Salem old boys in the S.S. or S.A. to relinquish either their loyalty to Hitler or to Salem. In 1933 he was imprisoned, but was released partially through the intervention of Ramsay MacDonald, the British Prime Minister, and emigrated to England.

In November of that year Gordonstoun was founded by a company called British Salem Schools, with William Temple, John Buchan and George Trevelyan among the directors. Gordonstoun was deeply influenced by Salem, but Salem itself had English influences.

In boyhood Hahn had come across two pupils of Cecil Reddie's school at Abbotsholme, in Derbyshire, who had given him *Emlohstobba, Fact or Fiction,* an enthusiastic account of the school by the German, Hermann Lietz.

Reddie's central idea was the harmonious development of all a boy's powers, and the book by Lietz, who founded a number of schools in Germany on the model of Abbotsholme, first gave Hahn the idea of starting a school of his own.

At Salem, which was a mixed school, and at Gordonstoun, bodies were developed less by competitive games than by the gradual achievement of athletic standards within the reach of all who tried and trained.

Service to the surrounding community was another of Hahn's principles and the school fire brigades at Salem and Gordonstoun, the mountain rescue and coastguard service at Gordonstoun, were aimed as much at cooperation with communities round the schools as at teaching young people a reverence for human life.

The Outward Bound Sea School, founded at Aberdovey by Hahn in 1941, attempted in its rigorous four-week courses to foster the same qualities of self-reliance, fellowship and service. By 1966 there were 19 such schools: six in Britain, four in the U.S.A., three in Africa, the rest in Europe and the Commonwealth.

A firm believer also in intellectual studies, Hahn was nevertheless a firm opponent of the over-specialization whose demands stood in the way, as he saw it, of care for a boy's moral and physical growth. He had a part in the creation of the Trevelyan* Scholarships to Oxford and Cambridge, because of his concern for a broader emphasis in the English sixth form.

He retired from Gordonstoun in 1953 and settled in the Hermansburg, one of Salem's junior schools. He remained active, flying between Germany and Britain each month, and worked closely with Air Marshal Sir Lawrence Darvall on a project for "Atlantic Colleges", international sixth form boarding schools for the children of the free world. The first, at St. Donat's in South Wales, became the model for the United World Colleges.

December 16, 1974.

Haile Selassie—See Ethiopia.

Lord Hailes, who died on November 5, 1974, will be remembered chiefly as a Tory Whip of high quality. His period of service as Governor-General of the abortive West Indian Federation was merely the last chapter in a long and highly creditable record of political service.

Patrick George Thomas Buchan-Hepburn was born on April 2, 1901. He was the third son of Sir Archibald Buchan-Hepburn, fourth baronet of Smeaton-Hepburn, co. Haddington. His mother was the daughter of the late Edward Kent Karslake, K.C.

Educated at Harrow and Trinity, Cambridge, he spent much of his youth travelling and at the age of 25 he became for a while honorary attaché at the British Embassy in Constantinople. He had already developed a deep interest in politics and on his return to England was appointed to a post which was to prove of decisive influence on his future.

He became private secretary to Winston Churchill,* and there then began an association which was to last until Churchill's retirement from politics. Those who watched it closely paid Buchan-Hepburn the compliment of judging that his master derived almost as much benefit from the connexion as he did himself.

Churchill's robust, masculine mind sometimes proved deficient in personal sensitivity and in the intuitive grasp of human situations; his young adjutant had an almost preternatural flair for estimating people, managing their foibles and penetrating their motives.

An unsuccessful contest as Conservative candidate for Wolverhampton in 1929 and service on the London County Council were the next stepping stones towards Westminster, and in 1931 Buchan-Hepburn was elected by a substantial majority to the safe Toxteth East division of Liverpool. As a young M.P. he displayed no outstanding oratorical gifts and was not among those who sought to revolutionize the policies of the Conservative Party; but he soon gave evidence of an outstanding flair for backroom work and of a remarkable facility for personal relationships.

At this stage, another association which was to have profound importance developed. Buchan-Hepburn became attached as Parliamentary Private Secretary to Oliver Stanley and accompanied him on a long perambulation through Government departments which, according to the political prognosticators of the day, was intended to end in Stanley's appointment to the Premiership.

This gave him inside experience of the Home Office, the Ministry of Labour, the Ministry of Transport, the Board of Education and the Board of Trade. Again, the contrast between the qualities of the partners was striking.

All this clearly pointed to a place in the Whip's office, and in 1939 he became an unpaid Whip and shortly afterwards a Lord Commissioner of the Treasury. After an interval of war service, in the course of which he attained the rank of brigade major in the Royal Artillery, he was summoned back by Churchill to act as a junior Whip.

In 1945 he became Deputy Chief Whip of the Conservative Party in opposition and in 1948 Chief Whip in succession to James Stuart. This office he held until 1955.

Buchan-Hepburn could claim to have inaugurated a new tradition in the office of Tory Chief Whip. Former occupants had generally been military men with a strictly military view of their functions, the transmission of orders and the imposition of suitable penalties for their breach. The new Chief Whip was a man of a subtler kind, although his displeasure normally proved no less deadly than that of his predecessors.

Tall, handsome and well dressed, his manner was urbane, his resolution unshakable. His shrewd insight into motives led him to conclusions in which some felt that he reposed too much confidence. Some also felt that his extraordinary talent for describing these conclusions in conversation was from time to time over-indulged.

His unaffected charm, however, enabled him to occupy a necessarily unpopular post while making comparatively few permanent enemies, and his political chiefs formed the impression that he was usually right. The unifying effect of the 1945 defeat and the small Tory majority between 1951 and 1955 spared the new Chief Whip some of the problems which were to afflict his successors, but his task was never easy and those most closely concerned hold that it was performed with distinction.

Certainly, the experiment of substituting an artistic temperament (Buchan-Hepburn was an enthusiastic amateur painter) for the bluff soldierly qualities which the office had been held to demand in the past, seemed to have proved successful enough to justify its repetition in the appointment of Edward Heath as Chief Whip.

In 1950 Buchan-Hepburn had moved from East Toxteth to Beckenham which he continued to represent until his elevation to the peerage in 1957.

In 1957 Buchan-Hepburn intimated to Harold Macmillan a wish to retire, and was created a baron. Within a few months, however, his talents were again in demand, this time as Governor-General of the new West Indian Federation. His appointment was widely attacked on the ground that West Indian politicians had not been adequately consulted in its making, and on the grounds that a man with local experience would have been better suited.

Unhappily, the federation was foredoomed to fail. A product of the current Colonial Office preoccupation with the importance of "viability", which led to the view that small adjacent territories under British rule should be parcelled together into administratively convenient bundles, it foundered on the almost total incompatibility of interest between its member states.

On the dissolution of the federation in 1962, Hailes was appointed a Companion of Honour and retired to an inconspicuous private life, devoted largely to his cherished cause: the preservation of historic monuments. In 1945, Hailes had married Mrs. W. H. Williamson. There were no children of the marriage.

November 6, 1974.

Generaloberst Franz Halder, Hitler's Army Chief of Staff during the opening years of the Second World War, died in West Germany on April 2, 1972. He was 87 years of age.

Halder was Chief of the German General Staff for the crucial period, August 1938 to September 1942. In this position, he was responsible for the preparation and planning of the military operations connected with the annexation of the Sudetenland to Germany, in 1938, and with the entry into Czechoslovakia in 1939. The first four major German campaigns of the Second World War, Poland in 1939, France in 1940, the Balkans and Russia both in 1941, were all prepared under his direction. His removal by Hitler followed the turn of German fortunes in Russia. During his first two years of office Halder had also been actively plotting to overthrow Hitler and the Nazi regime.

This was a period of intense conflict of loyalties for Halder. His family had an unbroken tradition of 300 years of military service to the rulers of Bavaria and he was educated in the spirit of military obedience to his government. Yet his appreciation of the nature of Nazism led him to become, in 1938, the first Chief of the German General Staff to engage in plotting against a German government. The plot which aimed at sweeping the Nazis from power and at bringing Hitler to trial, in early October 1938, came to nothing. The action due to take place was cancelled on September 28, when it was announced that Chamberlain was going to Munich for talks with Hitler. Halder feared that Chamberlain's gesture had strengthened the popularity of Hitler with the German people too much for the success of a putsch, which had to be borne on the bayonets of large numbers of young conscripts.

He has been criticized by some for overemphasizing the effect of appeasement, and for a lack of decisiveness and willingness to stake all on a single throw.

More of this planned putsch was heard in the summer of 1970 when, following the publication of *The Diplomatic Diaries of Oliver Harvey 1937-40*, a series of letters discussing the management of prewar British foreign policy was published in *The Times*. One of these was from Professor Nicholas Kaldor, who recalled two interviews he had had in June 1945 with Halder while he (Kaldor) was working for an Allied intelligence agency. Halder had expressed the conviction that but for the unfortunate coincidence of the announcement of Chamberlain's journey to Munich on the critical day, the Second World War would not have taken place—after the Munich agreement the political and psychological conditions for a military putsch were no longer present.

The Polish campaign was a demonstration of the superiority of armoured mobility against cavalry and foot. By long penetrating drives and sweeping hook movements, the resistance of the Polish forces was speedily overcome. Communications and supplies were cut off and headquarters were put out of action, thus obtaining rapid victory at very small cost in casualties. Between the Polish and French campaigns, Halder attempted to organize another plot —the "Zossen Putsch". One of Halder's difficulties was that, as Chief of the German General Staff, he had no troops under command. This necessitated the spreading of the conspiracy. The Commander in Chief of the Army, Field Marshal von Brauchitsch, found it very difficult to resist Hitler. When the moment came for Brauchitsch to present Hitler with a clear statement of military resistance to his policies, Brauchitsch withered before the torrent of anger poured on him by the Führer.

The collapse of Brauchitsch's resistance on this occasion meant the collapse of the plot, and opened the way for the next stage of Hitler's march to catastrophe.

The planning of all three of the following campaigns, in France, the Balkans, and Russia, was done in the greatest of haste. A decisive role in the preparations for the drive to the Channel Coast was played by von Manstein, who suggested that the breakthrough should be made at the point of the hinge of the French defence system. Accordingly, Halder prepared the drive through the Ardennes and the thrust across the Meuse, which ended with the sudden halting of the Panzer divisions on Hitler's orders, while the glory of preventing the British Army from being evacuated from Dunkirk was assigned to Göring and his Luftwaffe.

Between the French and Balkan campaigns, Halder was also occupied by the preparation of plans for Operation Sea Lion, the conquest of Britain. Complete lack of facilities to move the German Army across the Channel frustrated progress and Hitler's impatience caused it to be deferred indefinitely.

The Balkan Campaign was improvised at short notice, but was marked by a daring use of German air superiority. However, the paratroop casualties were sufficiently high to make the German High Command very diffident about ever using them again. The Russian Campaign opened with huge successes, which were the result of the application of the Blitzkrieg technique on a vast scale. Halder designed huge pincer movements which placed the German Army before Moscow by the winter of 1941-1942. Once again the fateful interference of Hitler impeded a German victory. Instead of the attacks on Moscow being forced home with all available strength, new attacks on Leningrad and Kiev were ordered. The bitter argument which then arose, between Hitler on the one hand and Halder and Brauchitsch on the other, led to Hitler taking over the command of the Army himself. Halder endured throughout the summer of 1942, but increasing friction, culminating in the difficulties of Stalingrad, caused Hitler to dismiss him.

He was awarded the Knight's Cross in

1940 for his planning work.

Halder then lived in retirement until July 20, 1944. He was arrested for suspected complicity in the Bomb Plot and flung into a concentration camp, from which he was released by the German Army, just prior to the collapse in May 1945. His diaries covering his period of office as Chief of the German General Staff are a most valuable historical source for the period. They were published between 1962 and 1964.

Franz Halder was born on June 30, 1884 in Würzburg. On his eighteenth birthday he entered the Royal Bavarian Field Artillery No. 3, the "Queen Mother's Regiment". Here he developed his liking for horsemanship, which became one of his major relaxations. In 1911 he was admitted to the Bavarian Kriegsakademie and in 1914 received the coveted admission to the General Staff. His service in the First World War was in staff appointments, from Divisional to Army Group level. In the Reichswehr he was a tactics instructor in Munich and commanded a battery of Mountain Artillery. In February 1933 he was appointed Artillery Commander of 7 Division in Munich. This was a code name for the commander of a clandestine division. He was promoted to Generalmajor in July 1934. He commanded 7 Division, Munich, from October 1935 to October 1936, and was promoted Generalleutnant in August 1936.

He then began his long period in Berlin, initially as the head of a number of departments in the General Staff. In February 1938, he became General der Artillerie and in March Director of Operations and deputy to Beck, the then Chief of the General Staff. After Beck's resignation over Hitler's plans for Czechoslovakia, Halder became his successor on August 22, 1938. He was promoted to Generaloberst on July 19, 1940.

Halder's activities after the end of the war were mainly directed towards the writing of official histories, in conjunction with the American Army in Karlsruhe. He was acquitted at the Nuremberg Trials of planning an aggressive war. In 1958 he retired from historical activity and moved back to his beloved Bavarian mountains, in the village of Hohenaschau, where in his green waistcoat, Bavarian jacket and hat, he was perfectly at home.

Halder had a most lively personality. He was quick and witty, and his sense of humour remained with him to the last. His conversations and letters were full of entertainment. The size of his correspondence in later life was surprisingly large, and it was well matched by the quality of its content. His comments were usually penetrating, direct, and showed much wisdom. Some of his comments are preserved in Peter Bor's *Conversations with Halder*. In 1949 he wrote *Hitler as the Commander*, out of his war experiences.

He was married.

April 4, 1972.

Nim Hall, the former Richmond and England Rugby Union captain, died in London on June 26, 1972 at the age of 46. He had been ill for six months,

Nim Hall was England's first stand-off half after the last war, and played an invaluable part in re-establishing the game at that time. The first of his 17 England caps was won against Wales in 1947, and the last against Ireland in 1955, during which span he had been captain 13 times either at stand-off half or at full-back, leading the unbeaten team of 1953.

He also captained Richmond, and played for the Army and Huddersfield. He captained England against South Africa in 1952, and in that year Richmond had another national captain as well in P. W. Kininmonth of Scotland, a rare distinction for any club. He was also a notable seven a side player.

Hall was a famous kicker, especially of dropped goals, but there was an inclination to criticize his lack of speed. It was true that he was not fast, but he was such a natural player, with such fine balance allied to an eye for an opening, that it was not unusual to see him literally walking through a team to score. His name was already a byword when he joined Richmond, for whom he started at stand-off, moved to centre-three-quarter, when T. A. Kemp the present president of the R.F.U. returned, and later to full-back. He sometimes looked too casual on the field, but it was most unwise for opponents to fall for this.

Nim, with his exceptional rugby background, was one of the most modest men on earth, always the last man, almost apologetically, on to the field, and always, with his vast experience, at the disposal of young players. Nobody ever heard him of his own accord refer to any of his many successes, and he never said an unpleasant word about anyone. He was as rare a man off the field as on.

He leaves a widow, Penny, and a son.

June 27, 1972.

Sir Edmund Hall-Patch, G.C.M.G., died on June 1, 1975 after a career as strange as it was distinguished.

He was born in Petersburg in 1896, the son of W. F. McD. Hall-Patch, an English solicitor who practised there, but later moved to Paris, where his son Edmund was brought up bilingual and at heart a Parisian. When he left school he determined to become a professional musician, His father declined to support him if he held to this; so he supported himself in Paris by innumerable means.

He played in orchestras (thus winning a union card which stood him in good stead later on); he wrote sometimes the words and sometimes the music for an avant-garde revue which changed both fortnightly; he even wrote a book whose only purpose was to sell—*Deux Maîtresses*, by "Henri de Beaurivoire". However, by the time the First World War broke out, he had satisfied himself that his musical talent was insufficient and that he must find another career.

He fought throughout the war in the Royal Artillery. After it he joined the Reparations Commission, and found himself in its financial section, where he rapidly became an expert and gained a name: so much so that, by the time the job came to an end, he was appointed Financial Adviser to the Siamese Government. There he enjoyed himself immensely, with typical caginess learning Siamese secretly from a missionary priest (he was a Catholic from birth, and was everywhere usefully in touch with the hierarchy), without disclosing that he could understand all that was said. But Siam, in those pre-Thailand days, was not a place where a man of principle could stay very long. Hall-Patch found himself equally opposed to corruption in Bangkok and to pressure from Europe, with the result that when the former made him resign he was in the middle of a quarrel on Siam's behalf with Montagu Norman, and all doors were closed to him in London.

He went to New York, where he had many friends, in search of employment, apparently with infinite leisure and at a good address, but without enough money to eat. He made out by spending his nights playing the saxophone in a night club, thanks to his union card.

Then, in London, he was an efficient instructor in a riding school, as a few of his pupils remember. Luck turned, and for some time he acted as a freelance financial adviser, usually under the League of Nations, in Romania and elsewhere.

But his new life started when Sir Frederick Leith-Ross took him into the Treasury, as an Assistant Secretary, in 1935. He went out to China with Leith-Ross and stayed as Treasury representative. With some intervals spent at home, he was in China and Japan till the Far East was closed. His knowledge of Chinese financial affairs was immense, and he had very varied Chinese friends. He was godfather to one of the children of T. V. Soong, and he shared a shelter in Chungking with Chou En-lai and Syngman Rhee.*

In 1944 he was transferred from the Treasury to the Foreign Office as Assistant Under-Secretary of State; in 1946 he was promoted to Deputy Under-Secretary. There he built up with skill and energy the economic side of the Foreign Office's work. In 1948 he was made head of the British mission to the newly-founded O.E.E.C., of whose executive committee he was chairman; in 1952 he became British Executive Director of the International Monetary Fund and of the International Bank for Reconstruction and Development. In these assignments he had the personal rank of ambassador. In 1954 he retired from the service and shortly afterwards followed his friend Leith-Ross on the board of the Standard Bank, of which he was chairman from

1957 to 1962.

Hall-Patch was a unique character, who inspired deep affection. There was something almost mythical about his life; fascinating stories abounded; nothing was finally confirmed or denied, and one vaguely felt that the half was not told. To take a small example: there were those who believed that he was the composer of that sensuous waltz in *L'Extase*; was he or was he not? He denied it, but admitted to playing a part, ill-defined, in producing the music for the film.

What shone out was the kindest of natures. He combined a great love of his friends, and of children, to whom he was a delight, with a brilliant and somewhat tortuous intellect of French cast, and a fundamental pessimism about human affairs (he had had more than his share of trials, disappointments and personal tragedy). "Send for 'All-Patch," Ernest Bevin once said to an optimist; " 'e'll make your flesh creep." He did, but so charmingly that one survived it.

He was unmarried.

June 4, 1975.

Group Captain the Duke of Hamilton and Brandon, K.T., P.C., G.C.V.O., A.F.C., died on March 30, 1973 in Edinburgh at the age of 70.

His death recalls the extraordinary flight to Scotland of Rudolf Hess, Hitler's Deputy, in 1941. Believing he might arrange a peace settlement between Britain and Germany, Hess sought to get in touch with the Duke of Hamilton through whom he thought he might arrange a link with Winston Churchill*. The Duke had never met Hess.

He was Hereditary Keeper of Holyroodhouse and also hereditary bearer of the Crown of Scotland (which the kilted duke carried before the Queen to St. Giles' Cathedral in Coronation Year). He was ceremonial head "below stairs" of the royal palaces as Lord Steward of the Household 1940-1964, being awarded by the Queen the Royal Victorian Chain. From 1948 he was Chancellor of St. Andrews University.

He was an active elder of the Church of Scotland and was Lord High Commissioner to the General Assembly in 1953, 1954, 1955 and 1958.

The duke was kind and gentle in nature, with immense stamina. His sometimes apparently vague manner usually meant that he was keeping his own counsel until he had thought things over and discussed them with his talented duchess, who unobtrusively helped him in directing the driving-force behind the wise and good influence that emanated from them in the home they acquired and established in the old Scottish castle of Lennoxlove.

After a formal sitting of Lyon Court (in which the Duke sat as one of Lyon's two hereditary Lords Assessors), a foreign prince observed of the duke: "only a true *grand seigneur* could look so naturally distinguished while wearing a soft collar under his state robes".

But he overcame his inborn modesty only to help other people and to carry out the many duties—both ceremonial and in business, but more particularly in social welfare and in setting a public example—that his historic role and personal aptitude properly fulfilled in contemporary Scotland. He cared very much about everything to do with Scotland; both in the preservation of her past traditions and continuing identity, but more especially in the building of her future as a meaningful country in the modern world.

He was born on February 3, 1903, eldest son of the thirteenth Duke, and was educated at Eton and Balliol College, Oxford. Styled Marquess of Douglas and Clydesdale, he became a national figure as "the boxing Marquess", winning many amateur contests. After Oxford, where he captained the university boxing team, he went round the world with Eddy Egan, an American friend, challenging all comers; and had an alarming bout with a gigantic stoker whom he managed to knock out just in time.

But his chief interest was already in social welfare, youth clubs (he was for many years treasurer of the Boy's Brigade in Scotland and was later made honorary president) and housing in the Glasgow and Lanarkshire areas; and he worked incognito as "Mr. Hamilton" at the coal-face down one of the family mines, where he learnt working-class problems at first hand and got his trade union card.

From 1930 until his succession to the dukedoms in 1940, he was M.P. for East Renfrew, greatly increasing the Unionist majority. But, filled with the zest for daring and adventure of his forefathers, the mighty Red Douglases, he had become one of the earliest private owners of an aeroplane, had made himself an exceptionally expert pilot, and rose to command 602 Squadron of the Auxiliary Air Force. In 1932 a meeting of his constituents unanimously gave him leave of absence to act as chief pilot in the Houston Mount Everest Expedition, which he called "the only one original flight worth while". The flight story is told fully in *First Over Everest* (1933), to which the Duke and his second-in-command added their individual experiences in *The Pilot's Book of Everest* (1936). Overcoming great difficulties and hazards, he was the first man to fly over Everest, clearing the summit by a narrow margin. On his return, he received the Freedom of the Burgh of Hamilton, and was later awarded the A.F.C.

He played a large part in the foundation of Scottish Aviation Limited at Prestwick Airport, which now employs several thousand people in the West of Scotland. It was mainly due to his vision that Prestwick airport was established at a site which is practically fog-free. During the war he was a controller with 11 Group, Fighter Command, and was mentioned in dispatches for his services in France. During the Battle of Britain he commanded the Turnhouse Air Sector, and afterwards he commanded the Air Training Corps in Scotland.

In 1964 he chaired a government committee on pilot training and he was for many years president of the Air League. He was associated with the Air Cadet Council, the Air Training Corps, the Guild of Air Pilots and Air Navigators, and was president of the British Air Line Pilots Association.

In 1941 Hitler's Deputy, Rudolf Hess, parachuted into Scotland with the idea of personally negotiating peace between Britain and Germany using Hamilton as an intermediary. He landed near the Duke's home but was at once arrested. He asked to see Hamilton, who had never seen him before. Hamilton met him at Maryhill Barracks. The Duke's account of what followed, which he gave to Prime Minister Churchill, was published in *Motive for a Mission* by James Douglas-Hamilton which was serialized in *The Times* in 1971. The Duke flew in a Hurricane to Northolt and was then driven to Ditchley Park in Oxfordshire, where he was seen by the Prime Minister and Sir Archibald Sinclair [Lord Thurso*], Air Minister. Churchill found the tale improbable, saying : "Well, Hess or no Hess, I am going to see the Marx Brothers." Later that night, however, he had a long and detailed talk with the duke, going over again every detail of what the duke had told him earlier.

He married in 1937 Lady Elizabeth Percy, elder daughter of the eighth Duke of Northumberland, K.G. They had five sons of whom the eldest, the Marquess of Clydesdale, succeeds.

April 2, 1973.

Admiral Sir Frederick Dalrymple-Hamilton —See Dalrymple.

Therese Hampson—See Giehse.

Dame Florence Hancock, the trade union organizer and a former president of the T.U.C., died on April 14, 1974 at the age of 81.

She was born on February 25, 1893 at Chippenham, Wiltshire, one of a family of 14.

Her father, a weaver, was politically-minded, and often discussed the news with his family. Dame Florence went to work at the age of 12, and had a hard and miserably-paid adolescence, first as a café hand and then in a condensed milk factory. Her mother died when she was 17, so that in addition to her hard work outside the home she had to take a large share in looking after the family. In 1913 the Workers' Union began activities in the factory in which she worked. She joined, brought 20 more members in, and became first collector and then branch secretary.

So evident were her enthusiasm and ability that in 1917 she was made a full-time union official, acting as district officer, first for Wiltshire and later for Gloucestershire. When in 1929 the Workers' Union was merged with the Transport and General Workers' Union, she was sent to Bristol as woman's officer, serving in that post until 1942. Meanwhile she was nominated in 1935 to the general council of the T.U.C., and in due course served as its nominee to the International Labour Office, travelling as a delegate to France, Canada and the United States. In the years 1941-45 she was a member of a women's consultative committee advising the Minister of Labour on the utilization of women's labour for war work.

In 1942 there came her major promotion, to be Chief Woman Officer of the T.G.W.U., supervising the industrial affairs of some 200,000 women. The T.U.C. elected her President in September 1947.

Dame Florence belonged to the old-fashioned type of trade unionist, being by no means a theorist but approaching the problems of industrial organization from the personal and human side. She was by nature brisk, cheerful and good-natured, and her own early years of poverty and struggle gave her a close insight into the lives of the unskilled or semi-skilled workers with whom she mostly dealt. Equal pay for women in the engineering and other industries was one of the causes to which she gave whole-hearted support. A member of the executive committee of the National Union of Domestic Workers, she campaigned on their behalf for shorter hours, overtime and holiday pay, and a better social status. She was also a member of the National Advisory Council for Juvenile Employment, and took a keen interest in the provision of day nurseries for the children of married women working outside the home.

Created D.B.E. in 1951, Dame Florence retired from her post as Chief Woman Officer of the T.G.W.U. in 1958. In the same year she left the T.U.C. General Council.

In 1953 she was appointed to the Piercy Committee which reviewed the provisions for the rehabilitation, training and resettlement of the disabled. In 1955 she was made a member of the Franks Committee to review the constitution and working of administrative tribunals.

She was a director of Remploy Ltd. from 1958 to 1966, a director of *The Daily Herald* from 1955 to 1957 and a governor of the B.B.C. from 1956 to 1962.

She married in 1964 Mr. John Donovan, a former national secretary of the dockers' section of the Transport and General Workers' Union.

April 16, 1974.

Latife Hanim, who was married for two years to Mustafa Kemal Ataturk, founder of modern Turkey, and who played a symbolic role in the emancipation of Turkish womanhood, died on July 12, 1975 in Istanbul at the age of 76.

Born in 1898, the daughter of a wealthy family in Izmir (then Smyrna), Latife Hanim met the conquering Turkish commander after he rode triumphantly into Izmir following the Turkish rout of invading Greek troops in 1922. When a fire burnt much of Izmir she invited Ataturk to stay at her family's villa in suburban Bornova while he directed negotiations with the First World War allies on Turkey's independence and new frontiers. Educated in France, she served as secretary and translator of French and English diplomatic correspondence for Ataturk. He stayed there for 20 days and then returned to Ankara, the new capital.

She wrote to him a (recently published) letter in October 1922, in which she said: "My whole happiness lies in serving your excellency. My only wish is that my loyalty be a weapon at your side. How many people are there actually who love your excellency and are free from every sort of personal ambition?"

Latife proved her loyalty later, even though their marriage ended in divorce, by refusing ever, as one Turkish writer put it, "to exploit that great name for sensation or politics."

Ataturk went to Izmir in January 1923, and married Latife. She was 24 and he was 42. Ataturk used Latife to show Turkish women how he expected them to act after the Republic was declared in 1923. As President he took her unveiled around the country with him, to the discomfort of local officials who had to break tradition and bring their own wives into public. She was a symbol of the new Turkish women to be freed from the Muslim restrictions of the harem and veil, under Ataturk's reforms.

Friction between Ataturk and Latife developed over his late nights and heavy drinking on top of a crushing work schedule. She attempted to put a rein on him to conserve his energy. Ataturk grew restive as she tried to order his regime and on August 5, 1925, he divorced her by the simple declaration which was all that was necessary. Shortly thereafter the Turkish laws were changed, including civil divorce, giving women equal rights.

In her later years Latife Hanim lived a secluded life in a house in Istanbul's Ayazpasha district overlooking the Bosphorus. She refused to the end to give press interviews or relate her memoirs which would have been a blockbusting sensation in view of the idolization of Ataturk in Turkey. Sevket Sureyya Aydemir, a close associate of Ataturk, wrote recently that her seclusion and silence "showed the signs of dignity and a sensitive and touching character."

July 17, 1975.

Nicholas James Hannen, O.B.E. (MIL.), the actor, died on June 25, 1972. He was 91.

He will be remembered for the high standard of his work over a long period during which the theatre in England was fighting for official recognition as a serious art-form and a constructive force in the life of the community. By the time the battle could be considered as won, early in the 1960s, Hannen was tired and, by the irony of things, out of sympathy with the England that had set up and was enjoying the kind of theatre he had striven for. When he saw his ideal, he no longer recognized it. Too much else that he disapproved of was going on in the "entertainment industry", as he hated his vocation to be called. In his retirement he had the resource of laughter and of the happiness which his second marriage to Miss Athene Seyler, the actress, brought him.

The son of Sir Nicholas John Hannen, "Beau" Hannen was born on May 1, 1881 and educated at Radley, Heidelberg and Rouen. He was an architect in Edwin Lutyens's office before going on the stage in 1910 in a musical comedy, and it was not until after four years' work in that branch of the theatre under George Edwardes, and an engagement with the Glasgow Repertory Theatre, that Hannen, who had had to turn down Feste in Granville Barker's *Twelfth Night*, joined Barker's company and came under his enduring influence.

Hannen's association with him in London (in Hardy's *The Dynasts*) and in the United States (in Shaw and Shakespeare) ended when Hannen joined the Army in June 1915.

On his return to a theatre in which Barker was not regularly active, Hannen worked for the Phoenix Society in their first two productions of Webster and Dryden; for Lewis Casson* and Bruce Winston in a season at the Holborn Empire which established Casson's wife, Sybil Thorndike, as an interpreter of Greek tragedy; and at a new little theatre in north London, namely the Everyman, Hampstead.

Meanwhile West End managements came to regard him as a possible leading man, certainly as a first-class player of "seconds", and were prepared to try him out accordingly.

In the latter capacity he appeared in Pinero's new play *The Enchanted Cottage*, in Milne's *The Dover Road* at the Haymarket, in a revival of Pinero's *The Gay Lord Quex* and, after a Shakespearian season under Donald Calthrop, in Galsworthy's *The Forest*, both plays directed by Basil Dean. As a leading man he was perfectly cast in *The Conquering Hero*, Allan Monkhouse's play about a reluctant soldier of the First World War, and in 1925 Barker, who had recently seen Hannen play two characters in the same evening and had paid him the compliment of thinking that they were played by different actors, chose him for the part originally taken by Dennis Eadie in a revival of Barker's 15-year-old *The*

HARLAN

Madras House.

At the Ambassadors this was followed by several plays of note in which the integrity and distinction of his work was recognized: Clemence Dane's* *Granite* (with the Cassons), Galsworthy's *Escape* (with Hannen making perhaps the most conspicuous success of his whole career as a convict on the run), Miles Malleson's* *The Fanatics*, and Monckton Hoffe's *Many Waters*, which was one of several plays directed by Hannen. A South African tour was followed by his taking over from John Gielgud in Nigel Playfair's revival of *The Importance of Being Earnest,* and a tour of Egypt and Australia by his exceedingly funny performance as the "square" but shrewd Prime Minister of a National Government in Shaw's *On The Rocks.*

In Tyrone Guthrie's wartime production of *The Cherry Orchard* Hannen played Gaev to Athene Seyler's Mme. Ranevsky, and three years later, still during the Second World War, when Guthrie, Richardson and Olivier were forming an Old Vic Company to open in the West End Hannen was invited to join it: "Ralph Richardson, Laurence Olivier, Sybil Thorndike, Nicholas Hannen in repertory" was the announcement in the restricted press-advertisements of those days. He remained with the company for the first three seasons: Henry IV and Kent in Shakespeare, Sir Epicure Mammon in Jonson were among his characters. After leaving in 1947, he was seen over the next 10 years in such roles as the Doctor in two different revivals of *The Seagull*, King Priam in Christopher Fry's adaptation of Giraudoux's play about Troy, the Colonel in *Pygmalion* with John Clements and Kay Hammond, and the Bishop of Ely in Olivier's film of *Richard III.* His last stage appearance was with the Cassons in Hugh Ross Williamson's play about St. Teresa of Avila in 1961.

He married first in 1907 Muriel Melbourne Victoria Morland (who died in 1960) and they had two daughters and one son; and secondly Athene Seyler.

June 27, 1972.

William Hardcastle, the presenter of the popular B.B.C. Radio news programme *The World at One,* died on November 10, 1975 following a heart attack he sustained on November 7. He was 57.

William Hardcastle's was a comprehensive journalistic career which saw him in a multitude of roles from crack reporter to national newspaper editor. But none of his achievements brought him the wide audience—by the end four million—who daily tuned in to Radio 4 to listen to his compulsive handling of the news on *The World at One.* Hardcastle was in essence a newspaper journalist and when he made the switch to broadcasting he seemed to bring some of the urgency and heat of Fleet Street on to the air with him.

From the outset *The World at One,* which he presented for 10 years, was a programme concerned with the hard commodity of what has just happened—a far cry from the ruminative news magazines which it superseded. Hardcastle's compulsion was with news and it was the sense of his relentless pursuit of it that communicated itself even to the lay listener. Certainly he gave style to the programme. But it was not a style which had anything to do with the use of words—he early learnt that these were prone to expendability in the service of packing in as much relevant information as possible. For his four million lunchtime listeners the Hardcastle style was, rather, an ability to make the process of getting hold of the news itself sound an exciting one.

William Hardcastle was born on March 26, 1918, the son of a Newcastle doctor who died when he was five. He himself hoped to enter medicine but contracted osteomyelitis at the age of 15 and spent five years as an invalid. In 1938 he joined the *North Shields Evening News* as a reporter. Unfit for military service at the outbreak of war, he went to the staff of the *Sheffield Telegraph*, progressed to the Kemsley Newspapers London bureau and then joined Reuters. He became their correspondent at Supreme Allied Headquarters in 1944 and later served in New York and Washington.

In 1952 he returned to London as assistant editor of the *Daily Mail.* After a brief interlude of six weeks in which he edited the *Sunday Dispatch,* he became the *Daily Mail's* editor in 1959.

Sacked like many before him, after three and a half years in the chair, he moved over to broadcasting in 1963 to begin a completely new career. Initially he made contributions to a number of programmes, was an adviser to *This Week* and appeared and spoke on several sound and T.V. spots. When *The World at One* was launched in 1965 Andrew Boyle invited Hardcastle to join it.

From that point, despite division of responsibilities, it became progressively the Hardcastle show. And the famous pregnant enunciation of the programme's title was to usher the daily half hour and remain with us for ten years. Though he remained an astute and pungent commentator, especially on press and media affairs—notably in the B.B.C. T.V. programme *The Editors*, but also in print—the programme was the metier in which his particular talents were best displayed.

He might be—and frequently was—accused of stripping bare the English language, of an obsession with facts at the expense of comment. Yet his large captive audience was always an indication that media news gained from a return to these virtues.

November 11, 1975.

Justice John Marshall Harlan died in Washington on December 29, 1971. The Justice, who had resigned from the Supreme Court on September 23, was 72.

Harlan, a former Rhodes Scholar who was a superb legal authority and constant critic of the activist judicial role of the Warren Court, won wide respect as the "conservative conscience" of the court.

In recent years he and Justice Hugo Black, who resigned six days before him, were regarded as the court's twin intellectual pillars, maintaining reputations for judicial integrity, dignity and closely argued decisions through some of the court's most difficult years.

The two judicial experts, although close friends off the bench, found themselves taking diametrically opposed positions as the court began to tackle new problems of government surveillance, police powers and the civil rights of criminal defendants. While Black was hailed as a champion of civil liberties, Harlan came under fire from liberal critics who wanted the court to play an ever more energetic role in eliminating racial and economic inequities and implementing the more far-reaching provisions of the Bill of Rights.

The critics challenged him for adhering to precedent in an age when all precedents were being overturned; for insisting that the Court should play a limited role at a time when it was interpreting the laws with increasing zeal; and for upholding the "integrity" of the Federal system and States' rights at a time when many considered the inherited system of government was in many respects outmoded in the modern world.

Harlan's most powerful dissents were expressed against decisions imposing "one man—one vote" rules for State legislative reapportionment, which he considered were not called for under the constitution. He also dissented against rulings requiring the police to inform all suspects of their right to counsel and to remain silent under questioning, and allowing all convicted indigent offenders to have free lawyers in their appeals.

However, he voted in 1955 to proceed with "all deliberate speed" in carrying out school desegregation edicts, concurred in 1963 with a ruling giving free legal counsel to indigents convicted of major crimes, and in one of the most significant decisions ever written in the field of freedom of expression, ruled in June that a jacket emblazoned with an obscene reference to the military conscription law was constitutionally protected free speech.

Had he lived, there is little indication that Harlan would have been the obedient instrument of the Nixon administration's judicial philosophy that his critics feared.

Born in Chicago on May 20, 1899, to John Maynard Harlan, a lawyer and city alderman, and Elizabeth Palmer Harlan, the young John Harlan went to the Appleby School, in Oakville, Ontario, and the Lake Placid school in New York. He then entered Princeton University in 1916, where he was president of his class for three years and editor of the *Daily Princetonian*.

After receiving a Princeton degree he took a Rhodes scholarship to Oxford. At Balliol College he won first class honours in jurisprudence. In 1923 he joined the New York law firm of Root, Clark, Buckner and Howland. After further studies at New York law school he was admitted to the New York bar in 1925.

When Emory Buckner, the law firm's senior partner, was appointed as an assistant federal prosecutor in Manhattan, Harlan became chief of the Prohibition Unit, even though he considered the Prohibition laws were foolish.

During the Second World War he was chief of the operational analysis section of the Eighth Air Force, winning the Legion of Merit and the Croix de Guerre of France and Belgium. After the war most of his work was with his law firm, though he did serve as Chief Counsel of the Crime Commission established by Governor Thomas Dewey, investigating gambling.

His most famous corporate service was to the Dupont Family Corporation, assuring their eventual victory in 1954 over a government charge that they improperly invested in General Motors Stock. In early 1954 he was nominated to the Court of Appeals for the Second Circuit (New York). A few months later Justice Robert Jackson died and President Eisenhower* nominated Harlan to succeed him.

Confirmation was delayed as Southern Democrats, angered over the 1954 school desegregation decision, assailed him as an "internationalist" and a New York "one-worlder" who wanted to substitute the United Nations charter for the constitution. As it turned out, of course, his performance on the court was sharply different.

During his last seven years Harlan's eyesight became steadily worse and he could read only with the aid of a strong eyeglass and bright light. In September he announced that he had become stricken with spinal cancer and had decided to retire.

He is survived by his widow, daughter, and grandchildren.

December 31, 1971.

Dr. Harley Williams—See Williams.

Sir George Harriman, C.B.E., who became president in 1968 of the British Leyland Motor Corporation and was formerly chairman and managing director of the British Motor Corporation Ltd., died on May 29, 1973. He was 65. Harriman dedicated much of his life and exceptional abilities to the development and progress of the British Motor Corporation.

George William Harriman was born on March 3, 1908, at Coventry and began his apprenticeship in 1923 at the Hotchkiss fac-tory at Coventry. This was bought by Lord Nuffield* (then W. R. Morris) to become the engine factory of Morris Motors Ltd., at which Leonard Lord (later Lord Lambury*) was already making his mark. In 1938 Harriman was promoted to assistant works superintendent, with the responsibilities of production and planning control at the Morris factories at Cowley as well as in Coventry.

It was early in the war, in 1940, that Lord, who had joined the Austin Motor Company Ltd. two years before as works director, sought and obtained his services as production superintendent of the Austin engine machine shops. In addition to his Austin duties he worked closely with Leonard Lord, who had been appointed as Government controller of Boulton Paul Ltd. to expedite production of Defiant night fighters.

Harriman was awarded the O.B.E. in 1943. In 1954 he became production manager at Longbridge and a year later was promoted to the Austin board as director and general works manager. He became deputy managing director in 1950 and deputy chairman in 1952. He was awarded the C.B.E. in 1951.

Following the formation of the British Motor Corporation in 1952 by the amalgamation of the Austin and Nuffield concerns—one of Britain's largest commercial organizations—Harriman was appointed deputy managing director of the vast new industrial giant. In 1956 he was promoted to deputy chairman and joint managing director and five years later, in 1961, he became B.M.C.'s chairman and managing director on Sir Leonard Lord's retirement. In the 1965 Birthday Honours List Harriman was knighted for his services to export.

When Harriman took over his onerous duties in 1961 at the age of 53, he accepted probably the most challenging task in the whole country. His career was always very closely associated with that of Sir Leonard Lord, who early recognized his promise for high responsibility, and when Sir Leonard gave up the reins he knew that his successor was cast in the same die as himself. With the passing of each year from 1961, Harriman showed increasing statesmanship and under his direction the destiny of B.M.C. prospered.

All who met Harriman in the course of business knew him for his drive and attack on the immediate problem of the moment, his quick appreciation of essentials and his unfailing enthusiasm and cheerfulness. He brought warmth and understanding of human relationship to every aspect of each day's work, was always accessible to any executive requiring help or guidance and retained great popularity with the men and women on the workshop floor. Having started from ground level in 1923, he never forgot that teamwork was essential in producing first class products at the lowest possible price.

In the early 1930s George Harriman was a leading rugby player and captained both Coventry and Warwickshire County XVs. In 1933 he played for England v. The Rest. In his latter days he found relaxation in golf and trout fishing.

May 30, 1973.

Sir Eric Harrison, P.C., K.C.M.G., K.C.V.O., who was Deputy Leader of the Australian Liberal Party from 1944 to 1956, died in Sydney on September 26, 1974 aged 82.

He began his long career in Australian politics by being elected the Liberal member for Wentworth in New South Wales in 1931—a seat he held without a break until 1956. He held many different ministerial posts in different governments; he was Minister of Trade and Customs in Menzies's first wartime Government, Minister for Defence from 1949 to 1950, and Minister for Defence Production from 1951 to 1956.

But his greatest value to Menzies during these years was not as an administrator but as a tough, resourceful politician and loyal deputy. In many ways he complemented Menzies perfectly. He was popular in New South Wales, where support for Menzies was always weakest. He was a good mixer whereas Menzies often seemed arrogant and aloof. He understood the ways of businessmen—he had himself started life in a Sydney store—while Menzies was happier with members of the Bar and other professional men. He had none of Menzies's eloquence but could hold his own in the rough-and-tumble of debate.

He was also unfailingly loyal. When the Menzies-Fadden coalition was most unpopular with business circles—and it was sometimes very unpopular indeed—Harrison would be sent to Sydney to appease the critics, taking cheerfully whatever insults were thrown at him and giving as good as he got in return.

He was drafted for any odd or awkward job that was going. Sometimes these were pleasant as well as difficult—he was Minister in Charge of the Royal Tour in 1954; sometimes they were simply onerous as when he acted as Prime Minister and Treasurer in June 1956, when Menzies was occupied in the Suez crisis of that year. But whatever the task, he never flinched and his common sense and political shrewdness carried him safely through. He was appointed High Commissioner in London in 1956 and remained there until 1964.

He married Mary McCall in 1920 and they had three daughters. He married secondly Linda Fullerton in 1944.

September 27, 1974.

Brigadier-General Sir Harold Hartley, G.C.V.O., C.H., C.B.E., F.R.S., M.C., who died on September 9, 1972 at the age of 94, was one of the most prominent and practically minded scientists of his day. He was created

C.H. in 1967 for services in scientific and public affairs.

Having attained to an assured position in the academic world of Oxford, he left it when over 50 in order to begin a fresh career as a vice-president of the L.M.S. Railway. Just as he had brought to his activities as a university tutor the invigoration of his many contacts with outside interests, so to the public and official concerns of his later life he contributed the clarifying and liberalizing influence of a precise and disinterested scholarship.

He was indeed a link between two worlds and, both by example and endeavour, did much to strengthen the cooperation which he always felt should exist between them. Hartley stood for scientific principle, humane values and long-sighted policy in practical affairs, and in academic ones for common sense and efficiency. He could inspire confidence in the most varied circles, and his support was a pillar of strength in the most diverse circumstances. He was a most valued member of the board of The Times Publishing Company from 1936 to 1960 and contributor upon occasion to the columns of the paper.

Only a week before he died he acted as host from his sick bed to over 100 relations and friends, young and old, to celebrate his 94th birthday.

Harold Hartley was born on September 3, 1878. The son of Harold T. Hartley, a partner in the publishing firm of Emmott, Hartley & Co., he was educated at Dulwich College and went up to Balliol as a Brackenbury Scholar. At Oxford he read chemistry and obtained a First in the Schools in 1901. In the same year, before actually taking his degree, he was elected to a Fellowship at Balliol. His connexion with the college was never to be interrupted; he was in unbroken succession tutorial fellow, senior research fellow and honorary fellow, and Balliol remained one of the major interests of his life.

His earlier scientific occupations were largely in crystallography, to which he had been introduced by Miers, but after a time he began to interest himself in the problems of the physical chemistry of electrolytic sections, which were to form the subject of his main contribution to scientific research. At this period of his life he married Gertrude, the eldest daughter of A. L. Smith, subsequently Master of Balliol. They had one son, Air Marshal Sir Christopher Hartley, and one daughter. His wife died in 1971.

In 1914 Hartley joined the Army, and served until 1915 in the 7th Battalion The Leicestershire Regiment. Then he was appointed chemical adviser to the Third Army. In 1917 he became Assistant Director of Gas Services in France, and was transferred in the following year to the Ministry of Munitions as Controller of the Chemical Warfare Department. He rose to the rank of brigadier-general, a matter in later years of some mystification to the Germans, for the famous Haber, who might have been deemed his opposite number, was only a captain. He was awarded the M.C., and was thrice mentioned in dispatches. In 1919 he was created C.B.E.

The wide experience and heavy responsibilities of the war years had matured and strengthened him and it was a somewhat different Hartley who returned to Balliol. He reduced direct formal instruction to a minimum, but he imparted a great deal of wisdom and experience and even more of stimulus and advice. No pains were too great for him in helping in the solution of personal problems. He had a keen sense of form and was fastidious in matters of literary presentation. Although it made him an exacting critic of papers, he was quick to discern essential merit and very generous in recognizing it. Serious though he was in important matters, he had a light-hearted sense of humour, which found expression in *obiter dicta* of a special flavour.

In the decade after the war Hartley developed the work on the conductivity of electrolytes which he had suspended during the years of conflict. In spite of many other claims upon him, he gathered together a small school of researchers who made what is probably the most precise of all contributions to experimental knowledge of the electrolytic properties of non-aqueous solutions. It acquired a special relevance and importance with the advent of the Debye-Hückle theory of electrolytes. In 1926 he was elected a Fellow of the Royal Society.

During these years his activities widened steadily, and Government committees, directorships and universities made increasing inroads upon his time. To all matters, however, whether great or small he gave of his best, and brought to bear on each of them a fair and clear perception, a shrewd and humorous judgment of personalities, a realism which could be hard-headed without compromise in regard to ultimate ideals, and above all an intense desire that the right thing should always be done.

In 1928 Hartley was knighted and in 1930 left Oxford to become vice-president and director of scientific research of the L.M.S. Railway. It was a wrench to say goodbye to the university and his work there.

His primary task for the railway was to unify and extend the facilities for research which had been taken over some years previously from its constituent companies. The result was a competent job of reorganization, but hardly the worthiest of his monuments, and it was not long before his versatility and energy found further outlets. In 1932 he became chairman of the Fuel Research Board of the Department of Scientific and Industrial Research and later adviser to the Mines Department. He had been interested from the beginning in air transport, and in 1934 he became chairman of Railway Air Services, Ltd. From 1935 onwards he was chairman of the British national committee and the international executive council of the World Power Conference, an organization which held a special place in his affections. As he was so often to do himself, it sought to view the problems of energy resources and use as a whole.

As chairman of the Fuel Research Board he had foreseen well before the Second World War that aviation spirit would be needed in vast quantities, and had begun to think and plan accordingly. In 1939 he was made chairman of the Government factory for the production of 100-octane fuel.

As the adviser to the Ministry of Fuel and Power, he became a national advocate of fuel economy. As chairman, from 1941 onwards, of the committee that estimated the production and consumption of oil by the Axis powers and advised on the choice of fuel targets for bombing, he influenced the other, and in the end more important, side of the reckoning. It was, for him, a war of energy resources. But he was concerned also with gas defence, was chairman both of the Fido Scientific Committee and of the committee responsible for internal air services, and helped to turn over the workshops of his railway to aircraft and tanks.

His position as chairman of Railway Air Services Ltd., which he retained through the war, led to his appointment in 1945 to the board of the British Overseas Airways Corporation, and his connexion with railways came to an end. A year later, when British European Airways was established as a separate corporation, he was its first and already designated chairman. In 1947 he became chairman of B.O.A.C. He saw the corporation through two difficult years, pending delivery of its first postwar fleet of aircraft.

After the interruption imposed by war on the work of the World Power Conference, he did much to promote its return to full activity. His position in this body, his broad outlook and his many contacts both with universities and in industry made him a natural appointment as first chairman of the Electricity Supply Research Council when he left B.O.A.C. in 1949. He was chairman of the fourth World Power Conference when it met in London in the summer of the next year, and contributed substantially to its success. In the same year he was president of the British Association —an office by no means free from work. He had been elected President of the World Power Conference at the London session, and continued in office until 1956.

Hartley left the Electricity Supply Research Council in 1952, when he was already 73, and it might have been thought that the time had come for retirement. Instead, he found a succession of new offices to work from, together with new jobs and interests. He could be of use, and was determined to be.

One of his new and, as it was to prove, major interests had begun already. He had been impressed with the importance of chemical engineering in postwar industry, and accepted the presidency of the Institution of Chemical Engineers for the year 1951-52 and again in 1954-55.

In the middle eighties he became very active again as a consultant to the Central Electricity Generating Board. In 1966 he received the Kelvin medal in recognition of his great services in furthering the fruitful union of science and technology.

As president of the British Association he had been the immediate predecessor of the Duke of Edinburgh, and from 1954 to 1956 he was chairman of council of the Duke's study conference on human problems of industrial communities. In 1955 he took on another new job as chairman of the Energy Commission of the Office of European Economic Co-operation. In 1957 he accepted the presidency of the Society of Instrument Technology: he backed with his authority the claim that control engineering should be recognized as a primary technology, and added once again to his range of contacts and experience.

In 1964 he delivered the Romanes lecture in Oxford.

He worked, wrote, talked, and intervened on behalf of anyone whom he thought he could help almost to the last.

Hartley had a way of making a person to whom he was talking feel that there was nobody he had been more anxious to meet at that moment or to whose views he attached greater importance. Some people occasionally wondered if this trait could be genuine; the fact that it was entirely so was one of the secrets of his influence. In this way he made hosts of friends, but it was the deep sincerity and kindness of his nature which enabled him to keep them.

As a chemist, he aspired to be no Lavoisier. But some words that he wrote of Lavoisier might have been written as an epitaph, in part, on himself: "Ambition, curiosity, humanity, and love of action took him into many fields, and in each his creative mind saw an opportunity for constructive work."

September 11, 1972.

L. P. Hartley, C.B.E., the distinguished English novelist, died on December 13, 1972 at the age of 76.

Leslie Poles Hartley, the son of H. B. Hartley, was born on December 30, 1895, at Whittlesea and brought up at the family house, Fletton Towers, near Peterborough. His father was a solicitor who retired early and took over the chairmanship and direction of a brickworks.

Educated at Harrow and Balliol, he was in France during the First World War as a junior officer in the British Army. For more than 20 years from 1923 he was an indefatigable fiction reviewer for such periodicals as the *Spectator, Saturday Review, Week-end Review, Sketch, Observer* and *Time and Tide*, often writing his notices from Venice, where he lived for part of each year until the Second World War. His

first reputation was as a short-story writer: *Night Fears* was published in 1924, *Simonetta Perkins,* a novella in the manner of Henry James set in Venice, in 1925, and *The Killing Bottle* in 1932.

The Shrimp and the Anemone, his first novel, did not appear until 1944, when he was living outside Bath in a house on the bank of the Avon. The first volume of a trilogy, it was followed by *The Sixth Heaven* (1946) and *Eustace and Hilda* (1947), the title by which the whole work is generally known. It was recognized immediately as a major contribution to contemporary English fiction. *The Boat*, a novel which captured many aspects of Hartley himself, of his life in Bath and of his love of the Avon—for many years he was a familiar figure rowing on the river in the late afternoon—was published in 1950, and thereafter he was a surprisingly prolific writer with *The Travelling Grave* (1951), *My Fellow Devils* (1951), *The Go-Between* (1953), *The White Wand*, a book of stories (1954), *A Perfect Woman* (1955), *The Hireling* (1957), *Facial Justice*, a fictional view of the future (1960), *Two for the River,* short stories (1961), *The Brickfield* (1964), *The Betrayal* (1966), *Poor Clare* (1968), *The Love-Adept* (1969), *My Sisters' Keeper* (1970), *The Harness Room* (1971), and *The Collections* (1972).

In 1968 he delivered the Clark Lectures at Trinity College, Cambridge, taking as his subject Nathaniel Hawthorne, the writer for whom, together with Emily Brontë, he felt an especial love and affinity. In 1967 he published *The Novelists' Responsibility*, a collection of critical essays.

Hartley's range as a novelist was narrow, and when he strayed outside it his admirers were sometimes embarrassed. Within his limits, however, he was a consummate artist, and the apparent narrowness of his rendering of life was more than compensated for by its depth. He is seen at his best in the *Eustace and Hilda* volumes and *The Go-Between*, works which, it is impossible not to think, will be read for many years to come. Thinking of them, some names come irresistibly to the mind as defining their scope and quality, Jane Austen, Hawthorne, Henry James, Forrest Reid. The *Eustace and Hilda* books trace the relationship through something like twenty years between a boy and his slightly older sister, a relationship beautifully symbolized in the description of the small boy Eustace's indecision and agony of conscience when faced with the spectacle of an anemone about to devour a shrimp in a rock pool. The work is one of the finest and most accurate evocations of boyhood and young manhood in our fiction; it is throughout executed with the most delicate and subtle humour; at the same time it is tragic in its implications.

So too is *The Go-Between*, which records the arrested emotional development of a man owing to a too-early involvement, as a go-between, in the fierceness and catastrophic consequences of sexual passion. The action

is set in a country house in Edwardian England during a summer of great heat, and never has one aspect of the period been caught more richly or with greater intensity. There is the same quality of humour, unemphatic and delightful, as in the account of the village cricket match. *The Go-Between* was made into a highly-successful film a few years ago.

As in the *Eustace and Hilda* books, Hartley delineates the small things of life, the small pleasures and the small miseries, with such affectionate precision that one trusts implicitly the vision of the darker things that he sees as lying below, but only just below the surface of the ordinary.

In his way of life, Hartley was essentially a private man, but he had great charm and a quality of generosity that expressed itself in many ways. Without, one would think, an enemy in the world, he had a large circle of friends who delighted in him and whom he delighted to entertain at Bath and his London flat. A very well-known figure in the London literary scene, he was always at the service of his fellow-authors, for several years as a member of the management committee of the Society of Authors and, later, as the president of the English section of the P.E.N. Club.

December 14, 1972.

Laurence Harvey, who died on November 25, 1973 aged 45, had a long and in many respects successful career as a leading man, both in Britain and in Hollywood. But he suffered almost always from falling somewhere uncomfortably between the actor and the star.

He was born in Lithuania on October 1, 1928, his real name being Skikne, and moved to South Africa with his family when a child. He was educated in Johannesburg and began his professional career there at the local repertory theatre in 1943 with an appearance in *Cottage to Let*.

After military service in the South African Army he went to London in 1946 and studied briefly at R.A.D.A. before joining the Manchester Library Theatre company for a year. He was rapidly discovered as a potential film star and from 1947 on was occupied largely, and for many periods of his life completely, with the cinema, returning only occasionally to the stage.

During his first period as an up-and-coming star of British films he was seldom given anything very substantial to do: mostly a succession of spiv and wide boy roles with, at that time, a blond quiff much in evidence, in such films as *Women of Twilight* and *The Good Die Young*.

In the theatre he sometimes had better opportunities, especially at Stratford, where he played the 1952 season and returned in 1954 with greater notice, playing Romeo in a famous production, and Troilus. He had already played Romeo on screen the previous year in Castellani's visually exquisite but otherwise ill-fated Anglo-Italian film version.

In 1955 Harvey had another chance at a solid film role in *I am a Camera*. In 1958 he achieved his major breakthrough as a screen actor by playing Joe Lampton in Jack Clayton's film of *Room at the Top*, suitably disguised with a crewcut and a Northern accent, which alleviated a certain tendency he had at that period to fall back when in doubt on a "Shakespeare poetry voice".

Meanwhile he had made his New York stage debut in Ugo Betti's *The Island of Goats*; and had shown unsuspected comic gifts in the Royal Court revival of *The Country Wife* (1956), which he later took to the West End and New York. In 1958-59 he toured the United States with the Old Vic company. But during those years he was very fully occupied with films, few of them, it must be confessed, of much note from any point of view. Some, like *Spinster*, with Shirley Maclaine, were at least bizarre; others, like *The Alamo*, were big or, like *Butterfield 8*, with Elizabeth Taylor, extremely popular. In 1965 he repeated the Joe Lampton role, with less success, in *Life at the Top*.

He took up direction with *The Ceremony* (which he also starred in and co-produced), a pretentious semi-allegorical political piece set somewhere on the Mediterranean which nevertheless has the courage of its own oddity and remains, after a fashion, compulsive. He completed Anthony Mann's film *A Dandy in Aspic*, in which he was starring, when the director died suddenly in the middle of shooting.

He gave what is arguably his best performance in 1962 in John Frankenheimer's *The Manchurian Candidate*, in which he played a pawn in the hands of his politically ambitious mother, a weirdly cast Angela Lansbury.

Later stage roles included a spell as King Arthur in the London production of the musical *Camelot* (1964), a return to Shakespeare two years later as Leontes in *The Winter's Tale*, which was also filmed, and a season at Chichester in 1970 where he played Sergius in *Arms and the Man*. He also made a film under the direction of Orson Welles which might perhaps show some new facets of his talents, but which unfortunately has remained up to now unreleased.

In general one has the feeling that his career was never quite clinched. He was always on the point of doing better, appearing in better films, than he ever actually did. On the other hand, he probably made the very most of what he was given in the way of talent, and remained somehow a figure to be reckoned with, even if it was often hard to say quite why.

He was married to Paulene Stone, a model; earlier marriages, to Margaret Leighton and Joan Cohn, were dissolved.

November 27, 1973.

Eva Hasell, M.B.E., who died on May 3, 1974, was the founder of the Canadian Caravan Sunday School Mission, to which for over 50 years she devoted every moment of her life.

Frances Hatton Eva Hasell was born in 1887, the younger daughter of John and Maud Hasell of Dalemain, Penrith. She trained at St. Christopher's College and, inspired by two friends there, she started her missionary work for the Church of England in 1920 in the van "Pioneer" with a 400-mile trip to Regina. What is now a five-hour drive on the paved Trans-Canada Highway in 1920 took six days over potholed prairie trails.

She and her companion started Sunday Schools, taught in day schools and farmyards, led services, visited remote homes and enrolled members in a greatly revived Sunday School by Post. This was to be the pattern for many years to come. For her caravan idea created enthusiasm among the frontier bishops who were desperate to supplement the ministry to scattered English and Anglican families pouring into their dioceses and Eva Hasell pioneered the work in each diocese: 1923 Edmonton, 1924 Cariboo, 1925 Brandon, 1926 Kootenay. By 1928 there were nine vans on the road and, because one of them was not ready, she and her faithful friend Iris Sayle became the first white women to walk the 60-mile pack trail into the Peace River Block in Northern Alberta. For two months they penetrated an area of 10,000 square miles where there was one Anglican church and no clergyman. They covered 15 to 20 miles a day and during the season walked over 900 miles.

In 1935 Miss Hasell was created M.B.E. and the work reached a peak in the early 1950s when there were 32 vans on the road; and so for over 50 years her devotion to the cause continued, with lectures in the autumn and winter to recruit workers and to raise funds, and without a holiday.

In 1965 Eva Hasell became the first woman to be awarded the degree of Doctor of Divinity by the College of St. Emmanuel and St. Chad, Saskatoon, and in 1969 she was invested as an Officer of the Order of Canada.

She started something entirely new; she overcame every obstacle to meet the needs of children and lonely people and took modern teaching methods to places which had never experienced them.

May 6, 1974.

Dame Sibyl Hathaway, the Dame of Sark, died on July 14, 1974 at her home, **La Seigneurie**, Sark, at the age of 90.

Dame Sibyl became *seigneur* of Sark in 1927 on the death of her father, William Collings, and governed the island with almost feudal powers by the force of her personality. The twenty-first ruler of the tiny Channel Island, which is 3½ miles long and 1½ miles wide, and has about 570 inhabitants, she held her powers from a charter granted by Elizabeth I to Helier de Carteret, who arrived in Sark with other settlers from Jersey.

She was, to use her own words, "feudal chief and owner of the last bastion of feudalism in the world". On the island there was no divorce, no income tax (or death duties, estate duties or capital gains tax), no trade unions, no cars, and no bitches except, as she explains in her autobiography, *Dame of Sark*, published in 1961, those kept by herself.

Born in 1884, she was brought up by an eccentric father who taught her to shoot straight, who threw books at her head, and who instructed her never to mention personal worries or pains. "Father came into my room about midnight," she wrote, "dragged me out of bed and downstairs in my nightgown and, without saying a word, opened the front door and threw me out of the house." This was the treatment meted out when she was rebellious.

She married in 1901 Dudley Beaumont, and they had three sons and three daughters. Widowed in 1918 and in financial difficulties, she went to her father, who merely remarked, "You are perfectly capable of taking care of yourself and your children. I brought you up to be independent and I refuse to allow you to come to me for help."

She remarried in 1929 Robert Hathaway, an American who became a naturalized British subject. During the war, when Sark was occupied by the Germans, he was deported to Germany while she and the islanders refused to move even though they were close to starvation. He died in 1954.

Some reforms were introduced by Dame Sibyl, but only those that "did not threaten the island's peace. Sark people have always been very intelligent about reforms", she said. "We were quite ready to have telephones, for instance." Her aim, realizing that a thriving tourist trade was the mainstay of the island's economy, was to bring Sark into the twentieth century by accepting the good things of technological progress while rejecting what she considered the bad and the unnecessary. The ban on cars remained and the island's parliament, Chief Pleas, passed a resolution in 1971 forbidding any aircraft to land except in emergency. Two years earlier she had threatened to abdicate because, she claimed, members of the parliament were breaking the laws they themselves had passed, and she suggested that the administration should be handed over to Guernsey. Six months later she retracted that decision and part of her duties was given to a three-man advisory committee.

Her heir is her grandson, Michael Beaumont, who works for the Bristol Aircraft Corporation in Bristol. He is the son of her eldest son, who was killed in the war.

July 15, 1974.

Elisabeth Hauptmann, who died in East Berlin on April 20, 1973, was for many years Bertolt Brecht's principal collaborator and editor and served as the chief intermediary between him and the literature of the English-speaking world.

It was she who translated the *Beggar's Opera* for Brecht in 1928 as a basis for the *Threepenny Opera*, and introduced him a year or two later to the translations of Arthur Waley, whose *The No Plays of Japan* not only provided him with his "school opera" *Der Jasager* (again to Kurt Weill's music) but helped form his ideas of the "Lehrstück", or didactic cantata, a genre which he made distinctively his own. She shared his enthusiasm for Kipling, whom he was at last about to approach in the original with her aid; helped him to transmute this into the play *A Man's a Man* (with its annex *The Elephant Calf*); and herself wrote some of the English-language passages in *Mahagonny*, notably the "Alabama Song" which starts "O show us the way to the next whisky-bar".

Born at Paderborn in 1897, the daughter of a doctor, she studied English and for a time taught it in schools. In 1924 she was working as a reader for the publisher Kiepenheuer in Potsdam when she was delegated to work with Brecht on the completion of his first book of poems, then some two years overdue. Though Brecht changed publishers when one of Kiepenheuer's backers wanted a poem excluded, Miss Hauptmann stayed on to have a hand in virtually all his writings until he left Germany in 1933. At that moment she had as tenants in her Berlin flat Lili Brik (Mayakovsky's close friend and Elsa Triolet's sister) and her then husband, a senior Red Army officer on detachment to the Wehrmacht, who was able to preserve Brecht's papers from the Gestapo.

She herself left the country the same year after a short period of underground political work, and went to join her sister in America. For some years she taught there in a girls' high school in St. Louis, before the arrival of the Brechts themselves in 1941. She then again did some work with Brecht both in Santa Monica and in New York, subsequently abandoning her teaching job and returning to East Berlin after the foundation of the Berliner Ensemble, one of whose artistic directors she became.

She was put to work editing all Brecht's publications, first of all in the revived "Versuche" series which she had edited between 1930-33, and then in the East and West German collected editions. She was also involved in some of the Ensemble's adaptations, notably of "Don Juan" and "The Recruiting Officer", but since Brecht's death in 1956 her principal job has been the editing of his poems, on which she spent most of her energies during her last few years of ill-health.

Her exact share in Brecht's work remains to be determined, but it was certainly greater than most people realized, even within the circle of the Berliner Ensemble. She was herself an unusually gifted writer— a short story by her in Wieland Herzfelde's volume *30 Neue Erzähler* (c. 1931) is in the special vein normally identified with Brecht, and she also wrote some radio plays and adapted Ferdinand Reyher's *Don't bet on fights* for the Prussian State theatre (boxing, like the Salvation Army, was among the interests she and Brecht shared).

The one collaboration for which Brecht allowed her to take full responsibility was *Happy End,* the successor to the *Threepenny Opera,* for which she wrote the book on the basis of a supposed story by one "Dorothy Lane"—this is in fact oddly close to the Runyon story which later served for *Guys and Dolls*—with Brecht supplying the songs and Kurt Weill the music. Though this failed at the time (1929) it has been much more successful in recent revivals; none the less, Brecht in effect washed his hands of it, using some of the material for his play *St. Joan of the Stockyards.*

April 27, 1973.

Jack Hawkins, C.B.E., the actor, who died on July 18, 1973 at the age of 62, will probably be remembered best as having played the leading part in some notable British films concerned with life in the Services during the Second World War.

He began his career, however, in the "live" theatre, where he gave distinguished performances in several classical parts, and he would no doubt have spent more time there in later years if his freedom had not been restricted by commitments arising out of his great success in films and more recently by ill health.

John Edward Hawkins, the son of a public works contractor in north London, was born on September 14, 1910, was trained for the stage by Italia Conti, and while still one of her pupils made his first professional appearance during the Christmas season of 1923 in *Where the Rainbow Ends.* Bernard Shaw picked him some weeks later for the part of Dunois's page in the original production by Sir Lewis Casson of *Saint Joan,* and Sir Lewis and Dame Sybil Thorndike continued to employ him over the next two years, James Agate publicly referring to Hawkins on one occasion as the most promising boy player he had ever seen.

He gained further experience under Basil Dean; in the latter's production of *Young Woodley* he was the hero's best (schoolboy) friend; and in Dodie Smith's *Autumn Crocus* he played opposite Jessica Tandy, whom he married. Meanwhile he had made his debut in New York as the malingering subaltern in the First World War play *Journey's End*—a strange role for Jack Hawkins whom the public came to associate with stalwarts in Second World War films— and had had his first experience of filming in England, in Maurice Elvey's *The Lodger,* in which the star was Ivor Novello, in 1932. He played leading parts in Shakespeare and Milton (*Comus*) for Robert Atkins in Regent's Park, but what probably helped him most to find his feet in the theatre was the opportunity of working frequently, when they were stage brothers in Ronald Mackenzie's *The Maitlands,* with Sir John Gielgud. Between 1934 and 1940 Hawkins was first Horatio and later Claudius and the Ghost to Sir John's Hamlet, Algy to his John Worthing in *The Importance of Being Earnest,* Edmund to his King Lear and Caliban to his Prospero.

Hawkins joined The Royal Welch Fusiliers in 1940, was commissioned and served with the Second British Division in India. In 1944 he was seconded to G.H.Q. India and soon afterwards succeeded to the command, as a colonel, of Ensa administration in India and south-east Asia.

Demobilized in 1946, he returned to the theatre and to the cinema. In the one he earned praise at home and in Europe by his Othello and his Morel in *Candida,* in the other his success in British films dealing with the late war conferred on him an altogether new status in his profession. Here was an actor of romantically rugged aspect whom, since he could suggest an inflexible devotion to duty joined with a humane disposition, British cinema audiences in the early 1950s were prepared to accept in the part of a war hero.

Angels One Five, a film about the Battle of Britain, established this; *The Cruel Sea* and *Malta Story* confirmed it. He was declared to be the most popular British film star of the day after polls had been taken in 1953, 1954, and again in 1957.

It had become necessary for him to get away from the late war, and he did so more or less successfully in such films as *The Prisoner, Fortune is a Woman,* and William Wyler's *Ben Hur.* The problem how to return to the theatre was more complicated; Hawkins could not now afford the financial sacrifice of joining the company at the Shakespeare Memorial Theatre, Stratford-on-Avon, and after 1951, when he appeared in Christopher Fry's *Thor, with Angels,* he found no opportunity of working in a suitable play by a contemporary author till 1960. No sooner had he begun rehearsals of John Hall's *The Lizard and the Rock* in that year than trouble with his vocal chords compelled him to break off and rest completely. On his recovery he decided to spare his voice still further by next making a film, and tempted by the part offered him in *Two Loves* (shown in England as *The Spinster*) he went to work in Hollywood for the first time. When John Hall's play was eventually produced in London, Hawkins's intended role of an Australian senator and pioneer was taken by Harry Andrews.

Hawkins went on to make other films, including Columbia Pictures' *Five Finger Exercise,* in which he co-starred with Rosalind Russell, David Lean's *Lawrence of Arabia,* in which he played General Allenby, and Richard Brooks's version of Conrad's *Lord Jim*.

On television in Britain he was seen as King Magnus in Shaw's *The Apple Cart*, in *The Four Just Men* series and, late in 1965, in the name part of Alan Seymour's *The Trial and Torture of Sir John Rampayne*. Trial and (mental) torture were an exacting assignment for an actor the state of whose throat was once more causing him grave anxiety, and Hawkins came through the ordeal with credit. The strain under which he worked was hardly perceptible to the audience at large. He showed as much integrity in his performance as Rampayne, a soldier and empire builder placed at the receiving end—he is kidnapped and put on trial by the younger generation—as in his performances in more grateful roles during the 1950s, when the accent was all on the virtues and leader-like qualities of men not essentially different from Rampayne himself. The play was a challenge to him, and Hawkins met it. Less than three months after it was screened, he underwent an operation for the removal of a malignant growth in his throat.

He made a good recovery and even achieved a form of speech by gulping air into his stomach and then ejecting it. He was determined not to give up his professional career and managed to appear in several films including *Great Catherine* and *Shalako* but it was necessary to dub his voice. Earlier in 1973 he underwent an operation in America and an attempt was made to fit him with an artificial voice box, but it had to be abandoned.

Hawkins's marriage to Jessica Tandy was dissolved. In 1947 he married Doreen Lawrence, whom he had first met when she was touring India with an Ensa company during the war. He had a daughter by his first marriage, and two sons and a daughter by his second. He was appointed C.B.E., in 1958.

July 19, 1973.

Sir Ralph Hawtrey, C.B., the economist, died on March 21, 1971 in his 96th year.

He was born in 1879, the son of George Procter Hawtrey, and was educated at Eton and Trinity College, Cambridge, where he read mathematics and was nineteenth Wrangler. He entered the Admiralty in 1903; but was transferred to the Treasury in 1904, where he remained until his retirement in 1945.

He was the recipient of many honours: a Fellow of the British Academy; honorary D.Sc. (Econ.) of London University; an honorary Fellow of Trinity College, Cambridge; president of the Royal Economic Society, 1946-48. He was awarded the C.B. in 1941, and was knighted in 1956.

Hawtrey was first and foremost a monetary economist, and he made important contributions in this field. He was one of the English pioneers of what is now termed the "income approach", which was to prove so fruitful in integrating monetary theory with the main corpus of economic thought; while the emphasis he laid on money itself as being something abstract, although capable of numeration—a unit of account, divorced from any necessary link with a metallic or other substance—made a marked impact on the minds of a generation of economists who had grown up under the nineteenth century gold standard.

His name is associated in the minds of most economists with the doctrine that the trade cycle is essentially a monetary phenomenon. He based this primarily upon the inherent instability of credit due to the working of the banking system, and the way that affected in particular the holders of stocks—merchants, wholesalers and retailers.

It was chiefly because of the importance which he attached to the role of dealers that Hawtrey, unlike Keynes and most other economists of recent times, always maintained that the operative instrument for credit regulation was the short and not the long-term rate of interest. In his earlier books he was an opponent of the policy of using public works as a counter-cyclical device.

But he later modified his position to the extent of admitting that in a really deep depression public works could make a contribution to recovery which could not be achieved by monetary policy alone.

He suffered a good deal from inadequate statements of his views: he had been apt to be regarded as having taken up an extreme position from the outset and maintained this regardless of all the changes of the past 40 years. Although he adhered in general to his fundamental tenets, he modified their expression so as to take into account both historical developments and the evolution of contemporary economic thought. It is indeed by his later writings, including new editions of his earlier books, that his work as a whole should be assessed.

Hawtrey's place in the ranks of monetary theorists depends not so much on the validity or otherwise of his views on the causation and control of the trade cycle as upon the clearer understanding which he undoubtedly wrought of the operation of the banking system and of the role of money in a modern economy.

A high point of his official career was the contribution he made at the International Conference held at Genoa (but without the participation of the United States) in April 1922. He was one of the representatives of the British Treasury, and it was largely because of his influence that agreement was reached on the need for cooperation between the central banks in the regulation of credit in order to prevent undue fluctuations in the purchasing power of gold.

Nothing came of this, however, and the Genoa resolutions were never put into effect; but Hawtrey never tired of urging that the *primary* objective of monetary policy should be to stabilize as much as possible the wealth value of the money unit.

Throughout his life he held only two academic, or quasi-academic appointments. In 1928-29 he was given special leave by the Treasury to lecture in economics at Harvard University; and after his official retirement he was elected Price Professor of International Economics at Chatham House, a post which he held from 1947 to 1952.

He has often been regarded, quite incorrectly, as one of the Cambridge academic economists, and grouped with Pigou, Keynes, Robertson and other pupils of Alfred Marshall. But he acquired his knowledge of economics, not at Cambridge (being a mathematician he never attended any of Marshall's lectures), but at the Treasury, where he came under the stimulating influence of Sir John (later Lord) Bradbury, Permanent Secretary of the Treasury.

Hawtrey was a prolific writer on many branches of economics. His three most important books in the monetary field were *Currency and Credit* (4th Edition, 1950); *Capital and Employment* (2nd Edition, 1952); and *The Art of Central Banking* (2nd Edition, 1962). On other topics, *The Economic Problem* (1926), and *Economic Destiny* (1944), were among his main works, although they have not received as much recognition as they merited.

Personally he was one of the kindest and friendliest of men; but he could be exasperating when, as a member of a committee, he would drag in by hook or by crook whatever was his particular King Charles's head of the moment, the most recent being the "under-valuation" of the pound in 1949, to which he attributed most of the subsequent difficulties of the British economy.

He married in 1915 Hortense Emilia d'Aranyi, one of three Hungarian sisters, who were all talented musicians. There were no children of the marriage.

March 22, 1971.

Lady Margaret Hay died on May 24, 1975 at the age of 57.

Margaret Seymour was born in 1918, the only daughter of Brigadier General Lord Henry Seymour and Lady Helen Grosvenor, daughter of the first Duke of Westminster.

After wartime service as a nurse, her interest in pictures and works of art led her to take a job with Spinks where she met her future husband, Alan Philip Hay, later Sir Philip Hay. They were married in 1948 and had three sons.

In 1947 she accepted a post as Lady-in-Waiting to Princess Elizabeth. She continued as Woman of the Bedchamber to the new Queen. She was thus by far the longest serving member of the Queen's Household and one whose conscientiousness, experience and sound common sense were of constant value to her Sovereign. She was made a C.V.O. in 1953 and a D.C.V.O. in 1971.

Margaret Hay never lost her head, her temper or her agreeably sardonic sense of humour. She had a caustic wit with which she could deflate any balloon, and an instantaneously wholesome reaction to nonsensical views and impractical proposals. Yet she was compassionate rather than censorious, and no trouble was too great for her, however tired or ill she might be, to meet the calls both of duty and of friendship.

The daughter of a gallant Grenadier, and of a mother whose personal charm was matched by her firmness of purpose, Margaret was deeply imbued with the values of her parents' generation, and nothing in a changing and, for her personally, much less affluent world induced her to lower the standards in which she was brought up to believe.

Among them was total intellectual honesty, physical courage, a disregard for unimportant luxuries and an unemotional acceptance of the pleasant and the unpleasant without pride and complacency in the one case or envy and complaint in the other.

May 26, 1975.

Susan Hayward, the red-haired American film actress who specialized in fiery heroines, and who died on March 14, 1975 at her home at Beverly Hills, had suffered for two years from an inoperable brain tumour.

She followed in the tradition of Joan Crawford and Bette Davis, though never quite achieving their magnetism on the screen, and her career suffered from too many indifferent pictures. But she was a popular star for more than 30 years, achieving her peak in the early 1950s when she was among America's top 10 box-office stars two years running; and she was back in the list in 1959 following her Oscar-winning performance in *I Want To Live.*

Susan Hayward was born Edythe Marriner in Brooklyn in 1918, left school to become a model and was spotted by the Selznick studio on the cover of the *Saturday Evening Post.* She was tested for the part of Scarlett O'Hara in *Gone With the Wind* and, although she was unsuccessful, the publicity helped her to get a start in films. It was, however, some years before her first success with critics, in *The Hairy Ape* (1944) opposite William Bendix.

During the forties she was often cast as an alcoholic, notably in *My Foolish Heart,* with Dana Andrews, and this turned out to be useful practice for one of her best performances in *I'll Cry Tomorrow.* Before this she had had a string of successes with *David and Bathsheba, The Snows of Kilimanjaro* (both opposite Gregory Peck) and the enormously popular *With a Song in My*

Heart. In the last, Hayward played Jane Froman, a singer crippled by an air crash in the Second World War (though Froman herself provided the singing voice).

Hayward's other major film parts were also portrayals of real people. In *I'll Cry Tomorrow,* she was Lillian Roth, another singer and an alcoholic; it was a convincing performance, though overshadowed in some eyes by that of Jo Van Fleet, who played Hayward's mother. Two years later came the film for which Hayward is best remembered, *I Want to Live,* the story of a prostitute charged with murder who in a final, chilling sequence is led off to the gas chamber. Hayward owed a lot to the taut direction of Robert Wise but her Oscar was well earned.

After this peak, her career seemed to lose direction, though she was the producer Walter Wanger's original choice for the 1962 *Cleopatra* (a part eventually taken by Elizabeth Taylor). Hayward's later films included *Where Love Has Gone,* in which Bette Davis played her mother, *The Honeypot,* a modern Volpone with Rex Harrison, *Valley of the Dolls* and *The Revengers.* Her first marriage, which produced twins, broke up in 1953. She remarried but her second husband died in 1966.

March 17, 1975.

Cardinal William Theodore Heard, D.D., PH.D., D.C.L., the first Scottish convert to be made a cardinal, died in Rome on September 16, 1973 at the age of 89. Before entering the Sacred College he was Dean of the Sacred Roman Rota, the Holy See's high court which deals with matrimonial cases and appeals.

Cardinal Heard practised for two years in London as a solicitor before deciding to study for the priesthood. He obtained a triple doctorate in Rome, in each instance *summa cum laude,* and was recalled to Rome in 1927 on appointment as Auditor for the English language of the Sacred Roman Rota. He worked also for the Sacred Congregation of Rites for causes of beatification and canonization.

The son of the Rev. W. A. Heard, LL.D., the second Headmaster of Fettes College, Edinburgh, he was born on February 24, 1884, and educated at Fettes and at Balliol College, Oxford. He rowed in 1907 in the Oxford eight. He was admitted a solicitor in 1910 and in the same year was received into the Roman Catholic Church. In 1913 he entered the English College, Rome, where he was ordained to the priesthood in 1918.

After his return to England in 1921 he was appointed curate of the parish of the Most Holy Trinity, Dockhead, Bermondsey, London, where he had once taken part in the running of a boys' club. He was later appointed administrator of the parish, where he remained until 1927, when his appointment to the Sacred Roman Rota

followed his recall to Rome. In the same year Pope Pius XI conferred a domestic prelacy on him with the title of Right Reverend Monsignor.

The canonization of St. Thomas More and St. John Fisher and the beatification of the English Martyrs occurred while he worked for the Sacred Congregation of Rites. He became Dean of the Sacred Roman Rota in 1958.

He was named Cardinal by Pope John XXIII* in 1959 and was consecrated Archbishop by the same Pope in St. John Lateran, Rome, in 1962.

He was one of three consultants named by Pope John to the Pontifical Commission for the Interpretation of the Code of Canon Law. In 1962 he was appointed Cardinal Protector of the English College, Rome; and in November of that year was nominated to the central administrative committee of the Vatican Council.

He was elected an honorary Fellow of Balliol and he gave to the college in 1964 a portrait of himself commissioned by a group of Balliol men and painted by Derek Hill. He received an honorary Doctor of Laws degree from Edinburgh University in October 1968.

Cardinal Heard had the affectionate regard of many friends. He was a man of the most positive personality, with a sardonic sense of humour. Hundreds of priests who studied in Rome and now work in Britain knew him well, not only as a Rota judge but also as an outstanding confessor.

September 17, 1973.

Cardinal Heenan, Archbishop of Westminster and leader of the four million Roman Catholics in England and Wales, died on November 7, 1975 at the age of 70.

The twelve years during which he presided over the Roman Catholic hierarchy in England and Wales were years of exceptional change and stress. He attended the later sessions of the Second Vatican Council, in which he intervened notably for the causes of religious liberty and reconciliation with the Jews. And he had to manage the consequences of the impact of that council on a rather conservative Catholic community at home. He was at his most successful in this respect as an embodiment of the ecumenical spirit of courtesy and mutual respect among the Christian churches. He was already practised in the art of good-tempered argument, and his natural good will responded happily to new opportunities for expression.

In face of the theological ferment stimulated by the Vatican Council, and the public controversy and factions that broke out within the Roman Catholic Church, Heenan sometimes seemed to have lost direction. But one constant priority for him was the unity of his church in England and Wales. A serious threat to that unity was posed by the publication of the papal encyclical

Humanae Vitae on the subject of contraception. He had been a vice-president of the commission advising the Pope on birth control, a majority of which advocated change in the church's position. When the Pope adhered to the other view Heenan was placed in an embarrassing position. Furthermore, in no Roman Catholic community was controversy over this teaching more intense than among English Catholics. Heenan managed the crisis with skill, recognizing the relevance of the principle of individual conscience without appearing to detract from the substance of the encyclical.

The liturgical changes dependent on the introduction of the vernacular into the Mass were less well managed, the new liturgy being neither stable nor distinguished by style. The virtual abolition of the Tridentine rite—contrary, critics held, to assurances given in Rome—was deeply regretted by conservative Catholics.

He was an incisive administrator and excellent public speaker, forthright and communicative. His pastoral letters contained an unusually high proportion of matter to circumlocution. He was always evidently a priest as well as a public man. His pronouncements on social questions were neither memorable nor sustained, but they were invariably liberal. As the leader of his community he had the important attribute of being a publicly recognizable character rather than an episcopal type.

The Most Rev. John Carmel Heenan was the eighth Cardinal Archbishop of Westminster in the restored Roman Catholic hierarchy, and the fifth to come from the English College in Rome. He was born at Ilford on January 26, 1905, of Irish parents, and was named after a great-grandfather who was a famous pugilist. His father was in the Civil Service, but sufficiently low down in the scale for his son afterwards to claim on occasion to be the son of a working man. His father, however, was able to send him to the day school of the Jesuits at Stamford Hill, where he soon manifested both his intellectual brightness and his ardent Catholic piety.

By the time he was 16 he was already speaking in Hyde Park for the Catholic Evidence Guild under Dr. Frank Sheed. The story is told how in one of his first attempts, when he was being boisterously heckled, a man in the crowd continually prompted him, and supplied or improved his answers, till the irritated chairman asked the boy if he could not get the person in the crowd to stop. "How can I?" replied young Heenan. "He is my father."

It was not surprising when he expressed his desire to go on for the priesthood, and he was accepted for Brentwood and sent to Ushaw College in the north. There he attracted the attention of one of the professors, William Godfrey,* afterwards to be his lifelong friend and supporter and his predecessor at Liverpool and Westminster. The young student was sent to the English College in Rome, where he finished his studies with two doctorates in Philosophy

and Theology, and was ordained in 1930. In the Rector of the English College, the future Cardinal Hinsley, the young Heenan had made another lifelong friend.

Returning to England, to the diocese of Brentwood, he was for some years curate in the East End of London. It was in these years that he showed his versatility and originality by visiting the Soviet Union under the guise of a student of engineering, and he used to relate afterwards how he had received three invitations to marriage on that trip. It gave him a great advantage in the many subsequent debates he had with Communists that he had seen the Soviet Union for himself in those dramatic years of the early 1930s.

He was given his own parish at Manor Park after only seven years as a curate and threw himself into the pastoral work of the East End during the years of the war and the blitz.

It was also in these years that he first became nationally known. He wrote to the B.B.C. to criticize British broadcasts to America, saying "you are spending too much time telling the Americans what the British are doing and not enough in telling them why the British are doing it". There followed an invitation to come and take part himself, and this he did so effectively that the B.B.C. continued to employ him for the rest of the war to broadcast not only to America but to the British Forces overseas, and he became known as the Radio Priest. He was also well known as a platform speaker and he soon had several books to his credit of a pastoral kind: *Priest and Penitent*, about confession, *The Layman's Priest*, and a memoir of Cardinal Hinsley. So it was not surprising that the hierarchy selected him to revive the Catholic Missionary Society, a society of priests dedicated to the conversion of England, which had been dormant during the war years.

Father Heenan prepared himself for this new work by a prolonged visit to the United States to study new forms of the apostolate. On his return he acquired a new home on Hampstead Heath for the Missionary Society, and from that base began four years of intense activity in all parts of the country which gave him an exceedingly wide acquaintance with his fellow countrymen. He enlarged the society, drawing in priests with an aptitude for the work from many dioceses, and did not neglect the small towns and the villages as well as the large cities in which the Missionary Society Fathers would give a week of conferences. Heenan's old professor, now Archbishop Godfrey and Apostolic Delegate, with the ear of Rome for the appointment of Bishops to England, recommended him, and at the age of 46 he was nominated Bishop of Leeds in 1951. He here showed a disconcerting fondness for making great changes in what had been under the previous Bishop a quiescent and easy-going diocese, and it earned among the clergy of the North the nickname of "the cruel See", so many and abrupt were the orders

moving the clergy of the diocese from one position to another.

The new Bishop showed himself tremendously hard-working, and at the beginning left the Bishop's residence to live in the middle of Leeds by the Cathedral. But he recognized afterwards that this was a mistake, that he became too much a parish priest in the city of Leeds, to the detriment of the outlying parts of a large diocese.

So ready a speaker and writer with a gift for catching the headlines might occasionally still be a little brash, in a way that mattered more for a Bishop than it had mattered for a missionary priest. He was rather addicted to sweeping judgments, as that Oxford and Cambridge were finished or that England was finished if the nation did not return to the Roman Catholic Faith. But all this was done so naturally and artlessly that his gaffes were not held against him, by comparison with the ardent charity and good will that so plainly radiated from him and made him a popular figure in the north of England far beyond the ranks of his own flock.

After five years he was translated to Liverpool, to succeed Archbishop Godfrey who had been brought to Westminster in the summer of 1956. For the next six years Archbishop Heenan devoted to the Archdiocese of Liverpool the same unremitting labours that he had performed in Leeds; but he was a little gentler in moving round the clergy. His Irish blood made him particularly at home with the Liverpool Irish Catholic population, and he showed himself keenly interested in all sides of civic life.

The most memorable event of his six years in Liverpool was the open competition and the selection of a design for an ultra-modern Liverpool Cathedral. The Cathedral project had been started by Archbishop Downey before the Second World War, with Lutyens as architect, on a scale always over-ambitious and soon out of the question with the increased costs of the postwar period. Archbishop Godfrey had revised the plans downward, to be content with a much smaller building, but in the line of the original Lutyens design. Heenan scrapped this altogether. The project was put to competition and of nearly 300 submitted Frederick Gibberd's remarkable circular design with central lantern and cross was chosen. It was consecrated in May 1975.

Although he had been a Bishop in the north of England for over 10 years, he belonged to the south and to London and was always in constant demand as a speaker, especially on great occasions at the Albert Hall, as at the rally in defence and support of the Hungarian Rising in 1956, and on similar occasions. It was generally expected that he would be the most likely successor when Cardinal Godfrey died in 1963; and so it proved. Heenan was told that he had been the selection of Pope John, who had died before the decision could be made public, and was then again the choice of Pope Paul. He was appointed to Westminster and in 1965 was created Cardinal.

At the second Vatican Council he made a number of interventions—sometimes, "for the record", to put the English Hierarchy on the record with their American counterparts as protagonists of religious liberty and as champions of the "Degree on the Jews", for he was specially connected with the Council of Christians and Jews in England. He was also made a vice-president of Cardinal Bea's Secretariat for Christian Unity, and as such was drawn into the ecumenical movement. He made a number of appearances on television and elsewhere to mark the new friendliness with the leaders of the Church of England and other Christians, and took very happily to this new climate of opinion, very different from that which he had encountered in his years at the head of the Catholic Missionary Society. Just as then he had always been a good-tempered controversialist, who fully recognized the good faith of those who did not agree with him, so it became very easy for him to represent the Catholic side of the new friendliness which had come in with Pope John.

He was less happy with some other manifestations of the new winds blowing through the Church, for he was by predisposition theologically rather conservative, though not so conservative as his immediate predecessor. He was a man full of the conception of the priesthood as a paternal relationship, the priest as the father of his people, sacrificing himself cheerfully for them, but also having his injunctions heeded and his lead loyally followed. The new spirit of criticism from the laity was accepted by him, but without any belief that he was witnessing a new and fruitful development in the life of his communion.

He was very ready to emphasize that in many fields like the economics of aid to developing countries bishops should show a public readiness to let lay people who had specialized in such questions instruct them. While he kept himself readily accessible and responded to the constant invitations to speak or write, he coped with a large correspondence and got through an enormous amount of current business. If anything the criticism was that he was rather too prompt with his decisions, and he effected many changes in the residences and duties of the Westminster clergy, changes which were sometimes found hard to understand by those involved in them.

He appointed two auxiliaries to the Westminster Archdiocese, Bishop Casey, who also became his Vicar-General, and Bishop Butler, better known as the Abbot of Downside, who was brought in with a special responsibility for Hertfordshire, to strengthen the theological resources of the Archdiocesan seminary at St. Edmund's, Ware, and to be chairman of an editorial board for the *Clergy Review* following the defection of its editor, the Rev. Charles Davis, in December 1966. On that occasion Cardinal Heenan set the key-note—which was generally followed—that Father Davis's decision, deeply regretted, was to be treated as a personal decision without recriminations and with the minimum of controversy.

Cardinal Heenan was made one of the vice-presidents of the special Papal Commission on contraceptive practices and the newly developed Pill, a topic which loomed large in the voluminous post that reaches Archbishop's House. Here, as in other matters, he was particularly concerned to demonstrate a paternal understanding of the trials and difficulties of lay people, and he found very wounding and unjust the criticism that he embodied a legalistic diocesan structure, lacking in understanding or compassion. Certainly he himself was lacking in neither, and the chief memory he leaves behind is that, through all the increasing responsibilities which were placed on his shoulders, he remained essentially what he had set out to be as a young man, a priest and a pastor, and this was the burden of the book he published in 1966, an explanation and commentary of the Conciliar decree on the priesthood.

In the summer of 1968 there came the sudden publication of the long-awaited Papal ruling on contraception in the Encyclical *Humanae Vitae*. Although the Cardinal had been with the Archbishop of Munich, Cardinal Doepfner, vice-president of the commission, he had only a few days' warning of the decision. To judge from an article he had contributed to *The Tablet* a few months previously, he had seemed to expect a modification of the traditional Catholic teaching; the Encyclical was a surprise. So, too, was the "furore" created. Cardinal Heenan was on holiday at the time, and did not take part in the discussions through August. He issued a Pastoral Letter, in which, while expressing the natural necessity for Catholics to accept papal rulings on such matters, he recognized that there could be conscientious objections. It was not until the end of October, after the bishops' October meetings, that a rather firmer statement was issued by each bishop to his own clergy, telling them that they must not publicly oppose the Encyclical whatever their private feelings might be. At the same time it was made clear that the bishops wanted to make things as easy as possible for priests who were distressed in mind, and no priests in the Cardinal's own diocese were removed from their parishes.

In television appearances to discuss the papal ruling, Cardinal Heenan was not always happy, and eyebrows were raised when, in an interview with David Frost, he committed himself to saying that a confessor confronted with a penitent who said he or she could not conscientiously obey the Church's teaching, could only say to them "God bless you". The Cardinal found less difficulty in giving wholehearted support to the Pope when the issue of clerical celibacy was raised by the Dutch hierarchy, because that issue never became a live issue among the priests in Great Britain.

He attended the episcopal Synod of 1969, expecting that there would be greater relaxations coming from it in the discipline of mixed marriages. He committed himself publicly to the view that the Pope would himself retire at the age of 75, on the ground that diocesan bishops were being encouraged to offer their resignation at that age, and that he did not think the Pope would fail to follow the example he recommended to others. It was one of several remarks which did not read too happily when copied into the Italian press.

Cardinal Heenan became increasingly anxious to see the next generation of clergy equipped with university degrees, as the number of graduates in the country was being rapidly increased all the time. This was the basic reason why, although he was the first Chancellor of the newly created Pontifical Athenaeum established at Heythrop College in Oxfordshire, he sided with those who argued that instead of collecting church students in a place apart, it would be much better to arrange for them to pursue their studies for the priesthood in great cities and in connexion with established secular universities. In 1969 the buildings of Heythrop were sold to the National Provincial and Westminster Bank, and the College was moved to London. In connexion with this rearrangement, Cardinal Heenan appointed in 1970 a new auxiliary Bishop, Father Mahon of the Mill Hill Fathers, to give special attention to ecclesiastical education, while Canon Guazzelli, the Vicar General, also became an auxiliary at the same time, to reside in the East End.

In September 1971, Cardinal Heenan circulated all the clergy in his diocese with a request for nominations for his successor. The move led to speculation that he might be considering resigning on the ground of ill-health. But it was explained as part of the process of consultation he was anxious to foster within the church.

He criticized the concept of a part-time priesthood. Priests should accept outside jobs only as a last resort. Later he proposed that the Pope should encourage Roman Catholic churches to sell their treasures and possessions to help the world's poor and needy. The Vatican could take the lead by selling some of its art masterpieces and properties in various parts of the world, he said.

In November 1971 he published *Not the Whole Truth,* the first volume of his autobiography, covering his life until his consecration as Bishop of Leeds. A second volume *Crown of Thorns* came out in 1974.

Early in 1972 the academic staff of Corpus Christi College, the Roman Catholic study centre for mature students in London, resigned *en bloc* in protest against Cardinal Heenan's intervention in the selection of visiting lecturers. The cardinal, the college's founder, had sought the withdrawal of invitations to five distinguished scholars; he said he proposed to appoint priests to lecture in their place. He told students at the college that the issue "is not, in fact, one of academic freedom but of responsibility". In the beginning the chief (and probably inevitable) mistake had lain in the choice of students: nobody had foreseen that candidates who were unstable elements in their own religious communities would be sent to Corpus Christi.

He spoke at various times on most of the social-medical-moral questions agitating the public. He was highly critical of a liberal abortion law, and later regretted that he had not converted his church's opposition to the Abortion Bill into a campaign against it. And he issued warnings against the approach of legalized voluntary euthanasia, which he strenuously condemned.

He was held in high esteem by the Jewish community in Britain and, in particular, had a close relationship with the Chief Rabbi, Dr. Immanuel Jakobovits, with whom he shared a platform on many occasions. This was very largely a result of the important part he played in drafting the Vatican Council's Declaration on non-Christian Religions—in effect a declaration against anti-semitism—as well as the tirelessness of his lobbying in the cause of getting the Vatican Council to adopt the resolution on the Declaration.

November 8, 1975.

Professor H. A. Heilbronn, F.R.S., who died on May 28, 1975, was Henry Overton Wills Professor of Mathematics, University of Bristol 1949-64, and since 1964 Professor of Mathematics in the University of Toronto.

Hans Arnold Heilbronn was born in Berlin on October 8, 1908. In 1926 he entered university to study mathematics and, as is usual in Germany, he moved around, studying first in Berlin, then in Freiburg and finally in Göttingen, in those days the centre of German mathematics. There he became an assistant in 1930, working with E. Landau, one of the leaders in the flourishing school of number theory in pre-Hitler Germany. Throughout Heilbronn's life his principal research interest remained with number theory and he was to make many significant contributions, mainly in algebraic number theory and in the application of analytic methods.

After Hitler's rise to power, Heilbronn left Germany for Bristol, where he held a research scholarship from 1933 to 1935. It was during these years that Heilbronn sprang into prominence in the world of mathematics with a proof of a famous conjecture of Gauss on the class number of definite binary quadratic forms, which had withstood all attempts since the early nineteenth century. This work was a milestone in a line of research which still continues.

After a brief stay in Manchester, Heilbronn was elected to a Bevan Fellowship at Trinity College, Cambridge, 1935 to 1940. This period saw the beginning of a

life-long friendship and a close collaboration with Harold Davenport*, which led to a remarkable series of joint papers, the first published in 1936 and the last in 1971, after Professor Davenport's death.

Heilbronn served in the British Army from 1940 to 1945 and then, after a year at University College London, he returned to Bristol University in 1946 first as a Reader and from 1949 as Professor and Head of Department. He succeeded in building up a department with an excellent reputation. During these years his influence on mathematicians of the younger generation was most marked. Perhaps some measure of his success may be gauged by the number of former colleagues or students who hold senior appointments.

Heilbronn was always a vigorous champion of his department and a man of strong convictions. Those closest to him were not surprised when, by 1964, he had decided that he must uproot himself once more. He was clearly out of sympathy with post-Robbins university policy, and one might say that developments in recent years have gone far to justify his judgment.

In 1964 Heilbronn married Mrs. Dorothy Greaves and the couple settled in Toronto where Heilbronn held a chair until his death. His influence was soon felt in Canadian mathematics. In particular he played a crucial part in the preparation for the International Congress of Mathematicians in Vancouver, 1974.

Heilbronn was elected F.R.S. in 1951; he was president of the London Mathematical Society 1959-61 and a member of the council of the Royal Society of Canada 1971-73. All those who knew Heilbronn will remember him above all as a man of principle and great sincerity.

May 30, 1975.

Professor Rudolf Heinrich, the German stage designer, died in London on December 1, 1975. He was 49. He had been attending rehearsals for the past month and had spent the whole of the previous day lighting the English National Opera's forthcoming production of *Salome* at the Coliseum.

One of the world's most prolific, inventive, and hard-working theatrical designers, it can be said of him that he died as he would have wished, in harness.

Born in Halle on February 10, 1926, Professor Heinrich studied art there, after the war becoming first assistant designer and then, after making his debut with *Hansel and Gretel* in 1949, principal designer in Leipzig. He designed several Handel operas in Halle but first tasted international fame when two of Walter Felsenstein's celebrated productions at the East Berlin Komische Oper, whose chief designer he was from 1954 to 1961, visited the Theatre of the Nations in Paris. These were *The Cunning Little Vixen* (1956) and *The Tales of Hoff-*

mann (1958), noted—as was all his work—for stylized realism and suggestiveness.

After leaving East Berlin in 1961 he worked as a freelance from his new home in Munich, where he became professor of stage design at the Academy of Fine Arts, and where his American-born wife, the former singer Joan Carroll, also taught. He was a member of the Berlin Academy of Arts.

His subsequent work, which began increasingly to depart from his early realistic approach, included *The Master Builder* (at the Old Vic, 1964), *Salome* (New York, 1965), *Figaro* (Salzburg, 1966), *Moses and Aaron* (Vienna, 1972) and *Lohengrin* (Vienna, 1974), with Joachim Herz, with whom he had been working on the London *Salome*. He was much in demand the world over.

After his long absence from Eastern Germany, Herz persuaded him to return to Leipzig in 1973 as a guest-designer for a new, politically-orientated—it was inspired by the writings of Shaw and Thomas Mann —version of Wagner's *Ring*, of which only *The Twilight of the Gods* remained uncompleted. He had also been working on designs for *Tosca* in Hamburg and the world première of Josef Tal's *The Temptation* in Munich, both with Götz Friedrich.

December 3, 1975.

James Pope-Hennessy—See Pope-.

Lady Henriques, widow of the well-known social worker and children's magistrate, Sir Basil Henriques,* died on December 21, 1972.

She was born in London on August 17, 1889, the only daughter of James Loewe, well known in his day in London Jewry as an active worker in Jewish causes, and perhaps still better as one of the sons of Dr. Louis Loewe, the orientalist and travelling companion, on most of his missions of mercy, of Sir Moses Montefiore, a name very prominent in the annals of philanthropy a century ago.

One of Lady Henriques's two brothers was Herbert Loewe, also an orientalist and a great spiritual influence among the younger Jewish men at both of the leading universities. With such a background it was not surprising that Rose Louise Henriques threw herself also into social work and this form of public service was almost her chief interest throughout her married life and earlier.

Together with her husband, whom she married in 1916, she directed and watched over the fortunes of the Bernhard Baron and St. George's Jewish Settlement and of the many activities that radiated from it. Basil Henriques had founded this institution in 1914 as the Oxford and St. George's Club and remained as its Warden until 1947, when he retired from office but not from residence in east London nor from his other activities there. Lady Henriques of course remained with him and continued her East End and other work as before. These activities, where they could be defined by title, included the vice-presidency of the St. George's Settlement Synagogue, a trusteeship of the Whitechapel Art Gallery and membership of the Council and Executive Committee of the League of Jewish Women. These were all English activities.

The plight of the survivors on the Continent of the victims of Nazi persecution at the end of the Second World War opened a new field for her, which she entered wholeheartedly at once. She paid frequent visits to the Continent to learn at first hand of conditions there and the reports she brought back had considerable influence on the policy of those in England who were striving to afford constructive relief. These visits were not merely for a day or two. Some of them extended over weeks and at first even months. To these activities belongs her chairmanship of the Germany Department of the Jewish Committee for Relief Abroad.

December 28, 1972.

Patrick Buchan-Hepburn, 1st Baron Hailes
—See Hailes.

Dame Barbara Hepworth, who died in a fire at her home in Cornwall on May 20, 1975, aged 72, was a sculptor of abstract and monumental works in stone, wood and bronze of a quality which gained her an amount of international recognition which few English artists have received.

In some ways her work might be compared with that of Henry Moore and it is by no means irrelevant to recall that they came from the same district of Yorkshire, she from Wakefield and Moore from Castleford, a few miles away; that they were students at the same time at the Leeds College of Art and the Royal College of Art. Later in London they had artist friends and ideas in common.

She seems to have developed, somewhat earlier than Moore, the relation of solids and hollows, of exterior and interior forms which they both used to striking effect, though with less of the energy with which he drew forms out of the material. In the comparatively passive shapes she treated with great refinement she might be said to show a feminine quality in contrast with his essentially masculine expression though there is also the difference between her "classic" and his more romantic sense of form.

The formative influences on her art included those of nature. She was responsive in youth to the landscape of the industrial West Riding and the Pennines. Cornwall, where she worked in later life, also evoked

an uplift of mood akin to that she derived from Greece. She wrote of the carving in yew, "Nanjizal", now in the Tate Gallery, as "really my sensations *within* myself", when resting in a Cornish cove with archways through the cliffs. In sculpture the revival of carving found in her a devoted adherent, the texture of surface obtained by this means being one of her main preoccupations. Carving, she defined, in a statement in *Unit One*, 1934, as "a perfect relationship between the mind and the colour, light and weight which is the stone, made by the hand which feels".

From early stylized figures (which found an appreciative buyer in the collector George Eumorfopoulos) she turned towards the abstract in the 1930s. Her ideas in this respect were parallel with those of her second husband, Ben Nicholson. There was much in her work at this period that shows the influence of Brancusi in the simplicity of ovoid shape. Visits to his studio and those of Arp,* Picasso, Braque* and Mondrian made for a great sympathy with the trend of art on the continent. In the highly productive postwar years, when she also pursued the study of anatomy and structure in drawings and added proficiency in bronze casting to her accomplishment in carving, she showed most conclusively her ability to conceive a formal and geometrical completeness in harmony with natural surroundings.

Jocelyn Barbara Hepworth was born at Wakefield on January 10, 1903, the daughter of H. R. Hepworth, C.B.E., county surveyor, and Gertrude A. Hepworth. After study at the Leeds College of Art, 1920-21, she went to the Royal College of Art, 1921-24, competing for the Prix de Rome in sculpture, which she missed winning by a narrow margin. A West Riding travelling scholarship enabled her to go to Italy, where she met John Skeaping, the sculptor, who had won the Rome competition. They were married in Florence in 1925 and exhibited together. For some years thereafter they were members of the mildly avant-garde "Seven and Five" Society and contributed to its exhibitions, but their first exhibition was held at the Beaux Arts Gallery in 1928.

Both by this time were enthusiasts for direct carving, giving much attention to the different qualities of the marble stone and wood they employed. At a second joint exhibition at Tooth's gallery in 1930 Miss Hepworth was especially praised for her "Mother and Child" in Honiton stone, her work at this stage being more of note for its sensitive treatment of material and craftsmanship than for new departure in style.

From 1931 she worked in association with Ben Nicholson, whom she married after divorce from Skeaping in 1933. They exhibited together at the Lefevre Gallery, where a number of Barbara Hepworth's later exhibitions were held (1933-54) and became jointly active in the groups promoting abstract art, "Unit One", 1933-34, and

in Paris "Abstraction-Création", 1933-35. London remained her headquarters until 1939, when she moved to St. Ives, Cornwall. This remained her home and place of work. In 1960 she bought the building that had formerly been the "Palais de Danse" and made it into a studio. In the church near by is the "Madonna and Child" which she carved in memory of her son Paul, who was killed in action while serving with the R.A.F. in Malaya in 1953.

An increasing interest in modern sculpture brought her work prominently into notice at home and abroad in the 1950s. Monumental commissions included the "Single Form" (bronze) for United Nations, New York, 1963, the Dag Hammarskjöld* memorial and the 15ft bronze for the office building in Holborn, State House, a dynamic system of curves.

Perhaps her culminating achievement was the completion in 1972 of the monumental nine-piece group "Family of Man" which she designed to occupy a special hillside setting in Cornwall.

She was the recipient of many awards and honours and was created C.B.E. in 1958 and Dame Commander of the Order of the British Empire in 1965. Her works are widely distributed about the world in museums and private collections. There are monographs by William Gibson, 1946, Sir Herbert Read,* 1952, Professor A. M. Hammacher, 1959, Dr. J. P. Hodin, 1961, and Michael Shepherd, 1963. A film about her work, *Figures in a Landscape*, was made in 1952-53.

In person she was broad of brow, firm and precise in speech, neat in habits of dress and with a fondness for the outdoors which extended to carving in the open.

The abstract nature of her art implied no coldness of feeling. She was as sensitive to beauty in any form as she was bitter against ugliness, the ugliness she found, for example, in much modern architecture. Undertaking drawings in a hospital in 1947, she feared she might not be able to bear the sight of an operation but in fact found herself absorbed, as she put it in her own words, by "the extraordinary beauty of purpose and coordination between human beings dedicated to the saving of life". She dated her sculpture, it was noted, from intimate and emotional circumstances, a change of style for instance from the birth of her children. Domestic life and children were as important to her as any woman. She spoke of "this wonderful business of having children" and the care they needed as something that "flowed back" into her work.

Sensitiveness was combined with a strong will and fighting spirit that supported her during the lean years of unpopularity. She was never intimidated by the idea of competing with men in sculpture. The woman's approach, she said, had a different emphasis and a special range of perception. She thought of "the sensation of being a woman" as "another facet of the sculptural idea".

She had four children, the first by her marriage to John Skeaping, and triplet children, a son and two daughters, born in 1934 by her marriage to Ben Nicholson. Their marriage was dissolved in 1951. She herself designed a tombstone for her grave, though it was reported in 1967 to be a problem for local officials as it was 3ft. over the permitted height.

May 22, 1975.

Sir Alan Herbert, C.H., who died on November 11, 1971 at the age of 81, did more than any man of his day to add to the gaiety of the nation. His wit, lighthearted or biting, played on a variety of themes and was expressed through many channels.

Some 50 books, musical plays and revues, light verse and articles, were proof of his energy and versatility. He was a humorist quickly roused to satire, and always ready to tilt—even sometimes at windmills. Beneath his gaiety was a tough core of earnestness. He hated injustice, cant, humbug and stupidity, and attacked them with scorn and mockery. There never was a jester who suffered fools less gladly. Ashore or afloat, he gathered many friends in all walks of life, and they invariably came away feeling more cheerful for having been in his company. There were many more who, knowing him only on paper or across the footlights, were in debt to him for laughter—and for being made to think.

His tall figure, expressive features (glasses could not hide the darting perceptiveness of those eyes), his delight in the simple pleasures of life, all added up to a rich personality. Whether he was championing a minority cause or extemporizing rhymes, playing the organ or skittles, explaining how to handle a sextant, performing strenuously on a lawn tennis court, or refusing to let his fellow members in the House of Commons brush him off as a light-weight, he was always enjoying himself.

At the height of his popularity he had become a national figure. On the first night of *Big Ben* in 1946 a row of stalls looked like the Treasury Bench and, if an emergency Cabinet meeting had been held in the interval, Ministers would not have lacked the very highest military advice. As river guides on the Thames tideway passed his Hammersmith home their megaphone voices used to be heard pointing out a famous public house and an island with "There between them, him without his shirt, is the famous writer, A. P. Herbert".

Alan Patrick Herbert was born at Elstead on September 24, 1890, son of P. H. Herbert, an Irishman who served in the India Office, and his wife Beatrice Selwyn. He went to school at Winchester, where Sir Stafford Cripps gave him his football colours, and he wrote his first contributions for *Punch*. Going up to New College, Oxford, he got a first in Jurisprudence in 1914 and at once joined the Royal Naval Division (Hawke Battalion) being mentioned in dispatches in Gallipoli and wounded in France.

Before he went overseas he had married, in bell-bottom trousers, Gwendolen, daughter of the artist Harry Quilter; their partnership was a strength and comfort to him all through his life. In 1918 he was called to the Bar but never practised, to his later regret, as he felt that it would have helped him in writing on legal matters. For two years he was Private Secretary to Sir Leslie Scott, K.C., M.P., who gave him some insight into the workings of Parliament. In 1924 he joined the *Punch* table and next year represented the magazine at the third Imperial Press Conference.

Thanks to a scintillating address, the help of his agent, Lord Longford*, and enthusiastic canvassers, he got elected, to his undisguised surprise and delight, as Independent member for Oxford University in 1935, and he held the seat until 1950 when it was abolished. He had advocated reform of the divorce laws in his address and in 1937, by a memorable parliamentary performance marked by tact, energy and public spirit, he steered the Matrimonial Causes Bill through the House of Commons on its way to the Statute Book. During the second war he joined the River Emergency Service on the Thames on September 3, 1939, and the Naval Auxiliary Patrol in June 1940, serving as a Petty Officer and gaining two good conduct badges.

As an author he scored his first success with *The Secret Battle* in 1919, in which he combined a grim, realistic description of the horrors of Gallipoli with a moving human study of the breakdown on the Western Front of a brave, highly strung young officer. This is one of the best and truest novels of the first war and it led to some improvement in court-martial procedure—the earliest reform achieved by his pen. Field-Marshal Lord Montgomery called it: "The best story of front-line war I have read": and Sir Winston Churchill,* in an introduction to it, wrote that it was "first and foremost a chronicle valued for the sober truth of its descriptions and its narration of what might happen to a gallant soldier borne down by stresses incredible to those who have not endured them, and caught in the steel teeth of the military machine".

Among his other novels *The Water Gipsies* (1930) stands out for Dickensian delight in and sympathy for simple people, and for his inside knowledge of the Thames and those who live by it. In contrast, *Holy Deadlock* (1934) was an undisguisedly propagandist story. Prolific though he was as a novelist and journalist, Herbert most enjoyed writing comic opera. Here he had the help and encouragement of that great man of the theatre, Nigel Playfair, who made the Lyric, Hammersmith, the magnet of playgoers in the twenties. Having started with children's plays, *King of the Castle* and *Fat King Melon*, he moved on to prove himself a master of musical shows, first with Playfair and then with C. B. Cochran in the heyday of the revue. More at home at the Lyric than under Cochran's impresario direction, he still brought off some triumphs that drew packed houses in the West End. His lyrics were witty far beyond the common run of such shows and the casts included George Robey, W. H. Berry and other top comedians, and a galaxy of leading ladies supported by choruses that could sing and dance. A new Herbert musical was always a happy event, quickening the pleasures of the season. *Riverside Nights, La Vie Parisienne, Tantivy Towers, Helen, Derby Day, Mother of Pearl, Paganini, Big Ben, Bless the Bride, Tough at the Top, The Water Gipsies, Streamline* and *Home and Beauty* are the names to revive memories of some of the brightest entertainments staged between the wars and later.

However busy Herbert was with book or play, he always had some cause on hand. David Low* once did a caricature of him "Sticking out his neck as usual;" it hit the mark. As a pleader, invariably persuasive, even when he did not quite carry his point, Herbert campaigned for water buses on the Thames, freedom from D.O.R.A. (the hatefully unpermissive Defence of the Realm Act), reform of betting laws, spelling, taxation of authors and the theatre, and the law of obscenity. He pitched into jargon, especially the Whitehall brand. The Buchmanites came under his stinging lash for the use of Oxford in the name of their movement and on the charge of being pro-Hitler. He fought an action to bring the House of Commons bars into line with the licensing laws and only lost on appeal with the court complimenting him and refusing to grant his opponents' costs. He demanded vehemently that authors of books, like authors of songs, should receive a fee "for the repeated enjoyment of their books".

In 1958 he announced that he was going to stand as an Independent at a by-election in Harrow East to further his attacks on the law of obscenity; but he contented himself with lively pamphleteering. Two years earlier he had torn up the Copyright Bill and put a match to the pieces (it only smouldered) in a B.B.C. programme. Much of his advocacy was conducted in the correspondence columns of *The Times*. He claimed that, had he been paid for all the letters he had written to the paper, he would have been able to buy the yacht of his old friend the late Lord Astor of Hever, in which he had sailed on many holiday cruises. In *Independent Member* (1950) he gave a racy account of his exploits in Parliament and on the wartime Thames. In September 1970 when he celebrated his eightieth birthday he published *A.P.H., His Life and Times*.

Herbert was knighted in 1945. In January 1970 he was made a Companion of Honour. He held a number of offices—Trustee of the National Maritime Museum, President of the London Corinthian Sailing

Club, The Black Lion Skittles Club and the Inland Waterways Association. Queen's University, Kingston, Ontario made him a Doctor of Laws in 1957 and Oxford a D.C.L. in the next year. His widow survives him with their son and three daughters.

November 12, 1971.

Lieutenant-Colonel Richard Heslop, D.S.O., an outstanding secret agent of the Second World War, died on January 17, 1973 at the age of 63.

Under the code name of Xavier, he was the inspiration of several large Maquis in the Ain and in Haute Savoie. Thoroughly English in upbringing and manner, he happened to acquire bilingual French in childhood; a fact which led him, as a subaltern in the Devon Regiment, into S.O.E., where he rose to be lieutenant-colonel. He went to the Riviera by sailing boat in July 1942.

A month later, in a routine French police check at Limoges, accident cast suspicion on him; and he spent three months behind bars. The prison commandant released him in November, when the Germans overran southern France. Heslop worked unobtrusively for some months round Angers, and returned to England secretly by air in June 1943.

In September he went back by a Hudson pickup, with a French friend Jean Rosenthal (now a leading dealer in precious stones in Paris), who knew the area where they were to work, west and south of Geneva. Reconnaissance showed plenty of opportunities. They spent a couple of days in London in October—travelling each way again by Hudson—and settled down to organize resistance systematically.

Heslop had mesmeric, almost magical, qualities of leadership, that now unfashionable virtue; Rosenthal's local knowledge, their joint courage, and their clandestine skill enabled them to raise sizable hidden armies, one of which repulsed an attack by some 4,500 Vichy *milice* in the Ain in February 1944. The German onslaught on the Glières plateau followed, intended to catch Heslop; it was disastrous to the *maquisards* who stayed and fought, but he was not there.

After the Normandy landings, his mission seized control of the countryside in both Departments, and harassed German reinforcements with success; when the allied armies arrived, they found the area already liberated. Heslop, the most loyal of men to his own flag, tried to keep out of politics but got embroiled unintentionally.

After the war he was reduced for a time to working as a Cook's tour guide. His recent autobiography, *Xavier*, is still on sale as a mark of what he was; in the Ain, he will not soon be forgotten.

He leaves a widow, a son and a daughter.

January 18, 1973.

Georgette Heyer, who died on July 5, 1974 at the age of 71, was born in London in August 1902. Her first historical novel, *The Black Moth: A Romance of the Eighteenth Century,* was written when she was 17, as an entertainment for an elder brother who was recovering from a serious illness. It was published in 1921 (and is still in print). It proved to be the start of a long career as a popular and prolific novelist. There were more than 50 books, many of which have been translated and sold all over the world.

Educated privately, Georgette Heyer married George R. Rougier in 1925. He was then a mining engineer, and the next six years were spent in London, Tanganyika, and Macedonia. Later they returned to England, and she persuaded her husband to give up mining and read for the Bar. He was called to the Bar in 1939, took silk in 1959, and was chairman of Cambridge and Isle of Ely Quarter Sessions at his retirement in 1971. Their only son, Richard, was born in 1932.

For 25 years the Rougiers lived in Albany. "I have no hobbies, play no games. I belong to no societies, and make no personal appearances", Georgette Heyer would say. She refused all personal publicity, regarding her fame with a certain amount of sardonic amusement, saying that her readers would find all they needed to know about her through reading her books. She never interviewed, though *The Times* did persuade her to be photographed in 1970.

She was witty, amusing, charming, generous, delighting in the grand manner, a "lady of quality" to quote the title of her last book. The almost annual novel which appeared regularly from 1921 until 1972 came in several forms: the historical —(as in *An Infamous Army*, a story of the year of Waterloo); the detective story— there were 11 of these, and she relied on her husband for plots and details of police procedure; and the always popular "Regency" romances.

Popular her novels were, but there was also a firm core of scholarship and expert knowledge of the Regency period, its fashions, politics, military and social history, modes of speech, even agricultural policy, on which to hang the slender stories of love or hate at first sight, elopements, abductions, duels, gambling debts and happy endings. She kept notebooks of the turns of phrase and slang current for the particular year she was writing about, and a glimpse of her methods may be obtained from the author's note to *The Spanish Bride*, the story of the courtship of Harry and Juana Smith during the Peninsular War. There is not a complete list of authorities, but a number of sources— Harry Smith's own autobiography, Napier and Sir Charles Oman on the War, and "I have not, to my knowledge, left any of the Diarists of the Light Division unread". These include Kincaid, George Simmons, Edward Costello, Rifleman Harris and Quartermaster Surtees, and reference is also

made to regimental histories, journals and lives of the commanders, and the dispatches of Wellington himself.

Her plots were seldom original, and indeed there was more than a little duplication in the rakes and Regency bucks, the eloping 17-year-olds, the ladies of Bath, highwaymen and Bow Street Runners. The excellent, easy style developed early— *Devil's Cub*, one of her best, was published in 1932. There were historical novels of other periods—notably the Elizabethan *Beauvallet* and the Stuart *Royal Escape,* but somehow the result was not quite so happy.

"Another Georgette Heyer" was greeted by her readers with joy and phenomenal sales. She gave her name to a recognizable genre of fiction, but no rival managed to achieve the touch which charmed both men and women from all levels of society. It was rumoured, at one time, that a group of Oxford dons met regularly to discuss her novels, and though it may be an apocryphal story it is not totally unlikely. Her family and many friends, together with her devoted readers, will be saddened to know that there can never be another Georgette Heyer to delight us.

July 6, 1974.

Lord Heyworth, who died on June 15, 1974 at the age of 79, was one of the outstanding figures of British industry in the twentieth century.

Throughout two decades that witnessed a revolution in the nature of industry and its relations with government and society, few men did more than he to strengthen public confidence in business, to increase the understanding of its problems in the outside world, and to link industry itself to that world through closer links with the universities and a flow of graduates into industrial management.

One of the sons of Thomas Blackwell Heyworth, a Liverpool businessman, he was born on October 18, 1894, at Oxton near Birkenhead. After being educated at the Dollar Academy he joined Lever Brothers Limited in September 1912 as a clerk at 15 shillings a week. In a few weeks he was employed in the accounts department at Liverpool. The following year he went to Canada to work under J. E. Ganong. Ganong was the president of the Lever Group in Canada which had interests that stretched from Vancouver and Victoria through Calgary, Winnipeg and Toronto to New Brunswick. This was the most profitable of all the growing overseas enterprises established by William Lever, but it bristled with problems.

Distances were enormous, competition strong. Canada not only gave Heyworth his first ideas about industrial rationalization but also his first opportunity to observe the methods of the efficient and highly competitive American industry over the border. It was an experience he never forgot, and he retained to the end his admiration for the energy and flexibility of the American businessman.

From 1915 to 1918 he served with the 48th Highlanders in the Canadian Army because (as he said) "the Highlanders needed an Englishman's help". In the course of active service he received a leg wound which left him lame and troubled him for the rest of his life. When the war ended he went back to Canada, being recalled in 1924 to London to help to look after Lever Brothers' export trade. There followed four years at Port Sunlight, the traditional *domus* of the Lever business, in charge of sales of soap in the United Kingdom. In 1929 he became chairman of Joseph Crosfields of Warrington, the acknowledged technical heart of the Lever Organisation.

Then in 1931 he was recalled to London to become one of the youngest directors in the history of Lever Brothers, and a member of the triumvirate set up to reorganize the Lever soap trade in the British market. Here the breathless pace of the first Lord Leverhulme's expansion had left a daunting legacy of problems. Forty-nine manufacturing companies and 48 selling companies were making and selling a vast and uneconomic range of competing products and employing an unnecessary army of salesmen. Economy and reorganization were urgently needed and Heyworth provided both.

In 1931 he read to a conference of Lever managers a paper which remains one of the most penetrating essays in the practice of industrial rationalization on record. Its principles, reflecting his experience in North America and at home, were characteristically simple and direct. They were the inspiration of the programme of reform which occupied the Lever management during the next five or six years.

When D'Arcy Cooper, who had succeeded the first Lord Leverhulme as chairman of Lever Brothers in 1926, died in 1941, Heyworth was clearly marked out for the succession. Indeed, it was widely believed that he had long been Cooper's candidate for the succession. It was no ordinary task to follow a man who had come to be recognized not only as the unquestioned master of a vast industry but one who had established a unique reputation in the outside world as a thinker and leader on industrial and economic problems generally.

Heyworth quickly proved himself a worthy successor in all respects. His natural talents were buoyant, his experience wide, he had courage, great clarity of mind and complete honesty of purpose. Moreover Canada had encouraged a natural informality of manner which never left him and which was an enormous asset in dealing with men of every kind. He talked to the commissionaire at the door in exactly the same way as he talked to his colleagues on the board.

From the start he dedicated himself within the business to the same task as his predecessor: to weld a partnership of two nations—for since 1929 Unilever had been half Dutch and half British—into a genuine unity. As he himself put it later, to form " . . . an Anglo-Dutch team and not two nearly balancing factions." In the wider field his policy was essentially simple: to choose the right man for the job and let him get on with it. In a business that was now world-wide in its scope, he regarded delegation and decentralization as fundamentals, not merely as slogans.

Increasingly, his breadth of mind and vision became a byword not only in Unilever but in the outside world too. Increasingly, other institutions demanded a share of his talents. After the war ended in 1945 he was increasingly drawn into Government and academic circles as adviser and friend. But his generosity in these respects did not in any way detract from his concentration on what he regarded as his principal duty, and the astonishing success of Unilever in his later years as chairman owed much to his firm and courageous direction.

Few public men can ever have been less pompous. He was singularly unselfconscious and singularly selfless. He had a remarkable gift for concentrating on the issue in hand and it often seemed that the physical restrictions placed on him by his war wound added to rather than detracted from his immense power of mental concentration. Always, even throughout periods of agonizing pain, and longish spells in hospital, he remained sturdily resilient and cheerful.

But Geoffrey Heyworth was no mere empiricist. There was in him a deep vein of philosophy. He never ceased to be fascinated by the problem of why things were as they were; conversely his remarkable powers of generalization never extinguished his mastery of detail. And if to slower minds his discourse sometimes seemed disjointed it was because his imagination worked at a pace that assumed a quicker understanding in his listeners than they sometimes possessed. Affectation, arrogance, pedantry and conscious charm were all alike utterly foreign to him, but a natural and unceasing intellectual curiosity, a fundamental tolerance and a genuine interest in humanity gave a rare warmth to his conversation.

Like his predecessor, he was not at the start of his public career a fluent speaker. On the contrary, he was uncertain and halting. But sheer sincerity, conviction and a natural fund of humour turned his weaknesses to strengths, and his public speeches, though unorthodox, were always stimulating.

He was chairman of the Court of Governors, Administrative Staff College; of the Gas Industry Committee and of the Advisory Committee of D.S.I.R. He had sat on the Royal Commission on the Taxation of Profits and Income, 1951; the Company Law Amendment Committee, Board of Trade, 1943; the board of London Passenger Transport Board, 1942 to 1947; the Commonwealth Development Finance Co., Ltd.; the University Grants Committee, 1954 to 1958; and the governing bodies of Queen Elizabeth House, Oxford, and of his old school, Dollar Academy.

In August 1947 he became a visiting fellow of Nuffield College, Oxford, and at once entered fully into the life of the college. Geoffrey Heyworth was at his best sitting with men of like mind exploring any subject under the sun. At Nuffield he was at last able to enjoy to the full a range of intellectual stimuli which he had often had to forgo. He was never happier than on those Oxford evenings. But he repaid his debts in full, as a valued member of Nuffield's Governing Body and Investment Committee. In 1961 the college recognized his special services by electing him to an honorary fellowship.

He was an Hon. LL.D. of St. Andrews and Manchester universities and an Hon. D.C.L. of Oxford. He was created a Baron in 1955, taking the title of Lord Heyworth of Oxton. For his special services in helping to organize assistance for the Netherlands after the war, he was created Grand Officer of the Order of Oranje Nassau by the Queen of the Netherlands in 1947.

After his retirement from Unilever he was appointed a member of the Court of Governors of the Hudsons Bay Company, from which he resigned in 1962. In May 1960 he succeeded Lord Cohen as chairman of the Government's Council on Productivity, Prices and Incomes. From 1963 to 1965 he was a member of the Board of Governors of the London School of Hygiene and Tropical Medicine; and from 1964 to 1970 president of the National Council of Social Services.

In 1924 he married Lois Dunlop, of Woodstock, Ontario, Canada. They had no children.

June 17, 1974.

Lady Hicks—See Terriss.

Thomas Farrant Higham, Emeritus Fellow, Trinity College, Oxford, and Public Orator of Oxford University from 1939 to 1958, died on January 29, 1975 at the age of 84.

A son of Sir Thomas Higham, K.C.I.E., he was born on September 20, 1890, and educated at Clifton and Trinity College, Oxford, of which he was elected a Fellow in 1914 after gaining a First Class in Honour Moderations, and the Gaisford Prize for Greek Verse.

He married in 1915 Mary Elizabeth Rogers and had one son and one daughter. From 1916 to 1919 he served with the British Forces in Salonika, being mentioned in dispatches and being awarded the Greek Medal for military merit. From 1940 to 1945 he was attached to the Foreign Office.

Higham was first and foremost a classical

scholar, accurate, graceful and, in the proper sense of the word, meticulous. Had he not been a "perfectionist", he would have published more, but all that he wrote bears the mark of his elegant scholarship —his contributions to the book of *Oxford Compositions*, for which he also wrote an admirable introduction, and his articles in the *Classical Review*, full of curious learning and scholarly humour.

He was one of the editors of the *Oxford Book of Greek Verse*, and joint editor with Sir Maurice Bowra of its counterpart in translation. As a critic and as a composer he had special sympathy with Ovid.

He was just the man to be Public Orator, a post he held for 19 years with a break for war service. No one was more skilful in the art of dealing with intractable modern ideas in elegant classical Latin, and over the years he compiled what almost amounted to a lexicon of Latin equivalents for honorary titles, and technical terms of an academic or scientific kind.

Television he boldly christened *Dido* because Virgil says of her, as she broods on Aeneas, "absentem auditque videtque". W. H. Auden, as Professor of Poetry, mentioned with admiration the Public Orator's "curious wit and felicity of phrase". On retirement from the post of Public Orator in 1959, he published a selection of his Latin speeches, a delectable anthology for those who still enjoy such things.

As an after-dinner speaker he was naturally in much demand, and was often asked to compose Latin inscriptions, of which perhaps the most felicitous is the epitaph for Gilbert Murray in Westminster Abbey.

He was an admirable lecturer and tutor and devoted to his college, of which he was an active member as undergraduate, Fellow, Dean and Senior Tutor, for 49 years except during the two wars. He had been a governor of Clifton and of St. Paul's.

January 30, 1975.

Graham Hill, O.B.E., died on November 29, 1975 in an air crash near Elstree at the age of 46. His death robbed Britain not only of one of its finest racing drivers of any era, but of a person who did much to enhance the prestige and popularity of his sport.

Graham Hill was not merely a double world champion (he took the title with a B.R.M. in 1962 and again with a Lotus following the death of his team mate, Jim Clark,* in 1968) but also the sport's No. 1 ambassador. He was, too, a driver who offered star glamour at a time when motor racing was becoming a highly technical business. His status, both in and away from a racing car cockpit, received official recognition in 1968 when he was awarded the O.B.E.

It is ironical that, like Britain's first world champion driver, Mike Hawthorn, Graham Hill should have been killed within a few months of his retirement from the race track. It had been thought by many that his final race would have been the 1969 United States Grand Prix, in which he suffered severe leg injuries when his car crashed at 150 m.p.h.

The tenacity with which he fought back to partial fitness during the ensuing weeks made him the subject of astonished admiration throughout the motor racing world. Determined to prove his ability to drive a Grand Prix car again, he went to South Africa for the start of the 1970 season still in considerable pain.

He had to be lifted in and out of the Lotus-Ford which the wealthy private entrant Rob Walker had prepared for him, but in the race he paced himself with expert care and the crowd rose to him as he finished, exhausted, in sixth place to earn a world championship point.

Many still wanted that characteristic piece of courage to be the end of it. But Graham Hill loved motor racing too much to leave it with a mere demonstration of self assertion. The single mindedness which had enabled him to make what had seemed to be an impossible recovery now kept him going as a driver and shielded him from the growing opinion that it was time for him to give up.

Certainly some of the former fire had disappeared, but the career was far from over. He went on to add victory in the Le Mans 24 hours race to his titles which, with his world championship and Indianapolis 500 victories, completed a treble which is thus far unique in motor racing history.

He decided to retain his links with motor racing by making a gradual transition from the cockpit to team management, and he formed the nucleus of his own racing team in 1973. But it was not until halfway his last season (1975)—when he realized that in his protégé, Tony Brise (also tragically killed in the same accident), he had another world champion in the making —that he felt able formally to announce the end of his own 22-year driving career.

Graham Hill was born in Hampstead, London, on February 15, 1929, the elder son of a stockbroker's clerk. On leaving a Hampstead secondary school he went to Hendon Technical College in 1942 and studied engineering for three years. His rise to the top in motor racing was an object lesson in skill, dogged determination and mechanical excellence, for he got there after years of trying. Once he made the highest echelon he never looked back, and in spite of a heart-breaking period of mechanical failure gained the reputation of being a calculating and relentless perfectionist.

After technical college at Hendon, he served a five-year apprenticeship with S. Smith and Sons Ltd., and in 1950 was called up for national service, serving for two years as an engine room artificer petty officer in the Royal Navy. He then re-turned to Smith's as a technical assistant and seemed set for an engineering career.

In 1953 an incident occurred which changed his future, for at that time he was an active member of the London Rowing Club—stroking the first eight to victory in the Grand Challenge Cup at Henley. It was while waiting for the rowing season that he was shown a magazine advertisement inserted by the Universal Motor Racing Club. Hill paid his six guineas entitling him to drive a racing car at Brands Hatch, completed four laps, and soon afterwards was giving his free time as an unpaid mechanic. Hill then heard of a man who wanted a mechanic at a new racing drivers' school and applied for the job—on the ground of his previous experience. At that time he resigned from Smith's and went on the dole to take up the new job, which proved to be the first rung of the ladder.

Hill took part in his first race in April 1954, and a few months later was introduced to Colin Chapman of Team Lotus. He then became a mechanic with Lotus, preparing cars for private owners—often operating on a shoestring budget and sometimes sleeping in haystacks beside the road to save on expenses—and managed to get occasional drives himself. He left Lotus in 1957 and joined Speedwell Conversions Ltd., becoming a director and later chairman, and, in 1958, Chapman offered his former mechanic a works drive. After two trouble-fraught years, Hill switched to B.R.M. at Bourne as a Formula 1 driver, and stayed with them for several seasons. Hill's mechanical knowledge always stood him in good stead and although the B.R.M. team did not shine in 1960 and 1961 he persevered both in races and in private testing.

Hill scored his first world championship race victory in the 1962 Dutch Grand Prix and went on to win the German, Italian and South African events that year. These were followed by successive victories in 1963, 1964 and 1965 in both the Monaco and United States Grands Prix—giving him two unique hat-tricks and a total of 10 grand prix wins to date.

As a racing driver Hill showed his talent by his ability to switch from car to car in every category of the sport with consummate ease. He excelled in Formula 2, saloon cars, G.T. and prototype cars, and worked wonders with the Rover-B.R.M. in the Le Mans 24-hour race. Perhaps Hill's finest drive of his career came in winning the Indianapolis 500-mile classic on May 30, 1966, in a Lola 90-Ford. After threading his way through a multiple pile-up in the opening lap, he methodically bided his time in the restarted race and became the first "rookie" since 1927 to win the world's most prestige-carrying motor race at his first appearance.

The year 1967 saw both Hill and Jim Clark driving new Lotus-Fords. Hill had much bad luck, mechanical problems beset his car and it was not until May 1968 that he again scored a Grand Prix success, driving a trouble-free race to win the Spanish event on the Jarama circuit. In May, also, he won the Monaco Grand Prix for the fourth time. He was second in the European Grand Prix to Jackie Stewart and ended the season with a convincing win over Bruce McLaren in the Mexican Grand Prix. Though it had been a mixed year for him he had amassed enough points to win the Formula 1 championship which he had last held in 1962. He crashed in the Spanish Grand Prix at Barcelona in May 1969, but at Monte Carlo later in the month he won his fifth Monaco Grand Prix after Jackie Stewart had led the field in the opening stages of the race.

His total of 176 Grand Prix drives was the highest achieved by any driver, while his total points score of 289 was beaten only by Jackie Stewart, who became his team mate during his years with B.R.M. He won 14 individual Grands Prix, no fewer than five of them at Monaco, where he was considered to be the undisputed master in the 1960s.

Graham Hill will be mourned throughout the motor racing world as well as by many people far removed from the track. His interests and activities extended far and wide into other fields. He was a vigorous campaigner for higher standards of road driving; he was a driving force behind the move to ban three-wheeled invalid carriages, which he felt to be dangerous; he was a dedicated supporter of charities and in particular of the Springfield Boys' Club in the East End of London; he was an eloquent and amusing public speaker; and he emerged as something of a television personality. But above all he will be remembered for his great contribution to motor racing in the role of driver statesman.

He leaves a wife, Bette, and three children.

December 1, 1975.

Professor Kenneth Hill, Professor of Pathology in the University of London at the Royal Free Hospital School of Medicine, and lately Vice-Chancellor of the University of Benin, died in hospital on February 19, 1973. He was 61.

Professor Hill qualified first as a chemist and then as a doctor at King's College London and the Westminster Hospital Medical School. After service throughout the war in the R.A.M.C. he entered a career in pathology which led him to the University of Durham as Lecturer, to Johns Hopkins as Rockefeller Research Fellow, to the University College of the West Indies as Professor of Pathology, and finally to the Royal Free Hospital School of Medicine. His interests in pathology were broadly based and he was an acknowledged authority and, for many years, an adviser to the World Health Organization on many aspects of treponemal and venereal diseases.

Professor Hill's main contribution was in the field of medical education in Britain and the developing countries. He was an enthusiastic teacher of students, fully believing in a broadly based education and the apprenticeship form of medical training, rather than the more rigid "ivory tower" regime which is practised in some academic units. His interest in developing countries may have been aroused by his war services in Accra as a Medical Officer in charge of a medical research team with the West African Forces. During his tenure of the Chair at the University College of the West Indies, he built up a magnificent department, while the college was in special relation with the University of London, and laid firm foundations for the future independent University of the West Indies.

In recent years his major interest had been in helping to establish medical schools overseas, particularly in Nigeria, and in providing teaching aids for the small numbers of trained teachers at these schools. He set up, with the help of the Overseas Development Administration, the International Museum Exchange—an imaginative idea for providing teaching material in pathology in countries where autopsies are rare, and the Overseas Audiovisual Aids scheme in which teaching tapes were made for medical schools all over the world, and he instituted the Overseas Medical Laboratory Technician Tutor Courses in which technicians from many countries were trained to teach.

Professor Hill's work for the third world was fittingly crowned when in 1971 the Government of Nigeria invited him to accept the Vice-Chancellorship of the University of Benin. This was an especially appropriate appointment, because the new university is about to establish a medical school, and it was a matter of particular sadness to his friends and colleagues when ill-health forced him to resign after only four months in Benin.

Professor Hill was a great believer in the British way of life and was much concerned with the maintenance of the prestige of British medicine overseas. His firm belief that British aid in the medical field was acceptable and not suspect politically was confirmed by the high regard in which he himself was held in many developing countries, and more especially in Nigeria. His ideas for training in medicine and the professions supplementary to medicine are bound to have an impact for good for many years to come.

He married in 1938 Elsie Wade. They had one son and one daughter.

February 24, 1973.

William Hill, founder of the bookmaking firm which bore his name, died on October 15, 1971 in Newmarket, where he was attending the yearling sales. He was 68.

Hill, thought to be the world's first multi-millionaire bookie, retired from active participation in the bookmaking business to devote his time to thoroughbred breeding. He owned studs at Whitsbury Manor, near Fordingbridge, Hampshire, and at Moreton-in-the-Marsh, Gloucestershire, and among the famous horses bred by him was Nimbus, winner of the Derby and the 2,000 Guineas in 1949.

It was as a teenage factory worker in Birmingham that he first collected racing bets and from these humble beginnings he built a vast bookmaking empire with headquarters first in the West End of London and then at Hill House in Southwark. Strongly opposed to betting shops, he was a pioneer in the field of fixed odds betting on football until taxation brought an end to this side of a huge business. During some 50 years of turf activity he won many races including the 1959 St. Leger with Cantelo and the Gimcrack Stakes and Champagne Stakes in 1958 with Be Careful.

His interests in recent years had been concentrated on the breeding of thoroughbreds at Whitsbury Manor and Sezencote studs. It was to the former that the American classic winner Celtic Ash came in 1964. It was here too at Whitsbury that Sir Gordon Richards trained in stables leased by him until the end of 1970, when he became racing manager to Lady Beaverbrook and Michael Sobell.

Hill's name will also long be associated with Ballymoss, Europe's champion horse of 1958 and winner of the Prix de l'Arc de Triomphe. He was chairman of the syndicate interested in this sire who in 1967 was at the Banstead Manor stud, Cheveley, Newmarket. Then one October afternoon that year a horse box accompanied by Brigadier Watson, the manager of the William Hill studs, called there with instructions to remove the horse. This was done and a sensation caused in racing circles led to the resignation of trainer Noel Murless from the Ballymoss management committee. A statement was issued later that the move had been made "in the interests of both horse and shareholders".

He was a lavish supporter of the British turf. He sponsored prizes, such as the William Hill Gold Cup, sat on innumerable committees and was never shy of supporting any worthy cause connected with the welfare of racing and those employed in it. He refused to sell Ballymoss when princely offers from abroad abounded. As Lord Wigg, the chairman of the Levy Board, so aptly summed it up "he was always seeking to put back more than he took out".

October 16, 1971.

Professor Edward Hindle, F.R.S., died on January 22, 1973 at the age of 86. He was Scientific Director of the Zoological Society of London (1944-1951) and Honorary Secretary of the Royal Geographical Society from 1951 to 1961.

Hindle, a versatile scientific worker, with an inherent attraction to medical parasitology, filled several niches in allied sciences, so that he has left his mark in many directions. By many he will be remembered as a valuable asset in managing the affairs of the great scientific societies, and in promoting their social activities, and, in so doing, he inevitably became a prominent figure at the Athenaeum.

Hindle was born in Sheffield on March 21, 1886, the son of Edward James Hindle. He was educated locally and at Magdalene College, Cambridge, where he came into contact with Professor G. H. F. Nuttall, F.R.S., the Quick Professor of Biology and a fellow of his college. This association exerted a profound influence on his career, so that he was subsequently able to assist him in founding the Molteno Institute of Parasitology in Cambridge. After taking his degree in the Natural Science Tripos, he worked at the Royal College of Science, later at King's College, London, the Institut Pasteur, and California University. It may be justly claimed that he received a catholic education.

During his student days at Cambridge he made connexions with Dr. Graham Smith, F.R.S., who was conducting experiments on flies as vectors of disease, and afterwards collaborated with him in the first book on this subject (1914). In 1913 Hindle was recalled to his Alma Mater to become Charles Kingsley Lecturer and Bye Fellow of Magdalene College.

Being always interested in military affairs, he served in the Territorials and, at the outbreak of the 1914-18 War, as captain in the Royal Corps of Signals in France, Egypt and Palestine. Subsequently he rose to the rank of lieutenant-colonel (1936-43).

At the end of the First World War he was in Egypt when he became Professor of Biology at the School of Medicine, Cairo, from 1919 to 1924 and, at the termination of his appointment, Milner Research Fellow at the London School of Hygiene and Tropical Medicine (1924-27) and from 1927 to 1933 Beit Memorial Fellow in Tropical Medicine. He next migrated to Scotland and became Regius Professor of Zoology at the University of Glasgow, where he also commanded the University O.T.C. and later the Glasgow Home Guard Battalions (1935-43).

Hindle received many honours in addition to the F.R.S. (1941). He was William Withering Lecturer in 1935, general secretary of the British Association for the Advancement of Science (1946-51), president of the Institute of the Biology and Zoology Section of the International Union of Biological Sciences, as well as of the Universities Federation of Animal Welfare, and hon. vice-president of the Zoological and Philosophical Societies of Glasgow during his professorship.

He did valuable work on parasitology when he worked for two years (1925-27) for the Royal Society's kala-azar commission to China. This disease was specially prevalent in the Yangtse River region and he investigated the Chinese form of the parasite (*deishmania clonovani*) and traced its development through the local species of sandfly and, with the late W. S. Patton, discovered that the Chinese striped hamster (*Cricetulus griseus*) was the reservoir of the disease.

Later he had even greater success with these rodents, which proved to be easy to breed in captivity, so that golden hamsters have become most popular domestic pets and most valuable laboratory animals. The myriads which exist nowadays are descended from two original captive pairs.

From 1927 to 1933 he worked intermittently on yellow fever in West Africa. With the help of the late A. H. Sellard from the Rockefeller Institute, he took back to London from Senegal the frozen liver of a rhesus monkey infected with the yellow fever virus, and established the strain at the Wellcome Research Institution in London. With this virus the first yellow fever vaccine was prepared, and protected monkeys from fatal infection, and subsequently it was used on a large scale to control epidemics in Brazil and in the Congo. Hindle also did valuable work on the spirochaetes of relapsing fever, on which he was an acknowledged authority, and which subject he had for many years reviewed for the *Tropical Diseases Bulletin*. He received the Belgian Croix Civique (1st class) in 1931. Besides his parasitological work Hindle contributed many papers on zoology and allied subjects.

Wherever he went Hindle was a favourite, well known for his affability and helpfulness. He was indeed a man of many friends and the good work he performed in so many directions will live after him.

Hindle married in 1919 Irene Margaret, daughter of John Twist, of Prescot, Lancashire. She died in 1933.

January 24, 1973.

Ho Hsiang-ning (Mrs. Ho), whose death at the age of 93 was reported on September 7, 1972 by the New China News Agency, was one of the first Chinese women to cut her hair short and speak out boldly for nationalism, revolution and the liberation of her sex.

A Cantonese, part-educated in Hongkong, she married a fellow-revolutionary, Liao Chung-k'ai, in Canton in 1897. The two went to Japan as students, met Sun Yat-sen, and joined his T'ung Meng Hui in 1905. In the Kuomintang Liao was an advocate of the link with the Communists and with Russia. After Sun's death in 1925 he was assassinated.

In 1927 when Chiang Kai-shek broke with the Communists, Ho Hsiang-ning resigned her job running the women's department of the Kuomintang, and retreated to Hongkong, where she, together with Soong Ch'ing-ling, Sun's widow, were outspoken critics of Chiang Kai-shek's leadership.

She returned to Peking in 1949 and was active as head of the Overseas Chinese Affairs Commission. Despite her revolutionary ideas, she was a poet and painter in the classical Chinese style.

September 8, 1972.

Lady Hoare, O.B.E., founder of the Lady Hoare Trust for thalidomide and other physically handicapped children, and wife of Sir Frederick Hoare, Lord Mayor of London, 1961-62, died on September 21, 1973.

She was a lifelong voluntary worker, noted for her devotion to the causes she adopted, whose name became synonymous with the struggle to aid children who were the victims of the thalidomide tragedy.

Her campaign list was impressive. She started at 17 with the Invalid Children's Aid Society in Fulham and Poplar. She went on to hold office in the Red Cross; the Royal National Lifeboat Institution; Find Your Feet, a refugee rehabilitation organization; and the Commonwealth Society for the Deaf. She gave her time freely to them.

Her appeal for the thalidomide children, when she was Lady Mayoress, had little success. She said later that people found the situation too horrific; they thought the Distillers' Company would pay and all the children would be put in homes and looked after by the National Health Service.

Her trust got a workshop and artificial limbs research centre started at Oxford and built up a team of medically and socially trained home visitors.

In 10 years the trust collected £750,000; in 1973 there were 900 children on its list, about half of them thalidomide victims. Thanks to the trust's work nine-tenths of the children live permanently at home and three-quarters go to ordinary schools.

But Lady Hoare was anxious that the work should go on and up to the time of her death was hopeful that much more money would be given.

She was Norah Mary, daughter of A.J. Wheeler, and she was married in 1939. She was the mother of two daughters. She worked for 20 years in Hoare's Bank, chiefly in securities. She was made O.B.E. in 1972.

September 25, 1973.

Professor Sir William Hodge, F.R.S., SC.D., F.R.S.E., who was Lowndean Professor of Astronomy and Geometry and Master of Pembroke College, Cambridge, from 1958 to 1970, died on July 7, 1975 at the age of 72.

One of the leading mathematicians of his time, he also played a prominent part both nationally and internationally in the mathematical and scientific world.

William Vallance Douglas Hodge was born in Edinburgh in 1903. He was educated at George Watson's College and Edinburgh University before going on to St. John's College, Cambridge. There he took the Mathematical Tripos and a few years later won the Smith's Prize. With the exception of five years as a lecturer at Bristol and a year at Princeton, the rest of his working life was spent in Cambridge. After holding a research Fellowship at St. John's he became a staff Fellow of Pembroke, until in 1936 he succeeded H. F. Baker as Lowndean Professor. He remained a Fellow of Pembroke and in 1958 he was elected Master.

The title of Astronomy in Hodge's Chair had been nominal for some time and his mathematical contributions were in the field of algebraic geometry. His work here was of a genuine pioneering kind and the theory of harmonic integrals, which was his main contribution to mathematics, has had a profound influence on the development of geometry in the past 30 years. When Hodge first went to Cambridge, geometry, as practised by the Baker school, was in danger of becoming fossilized and cut off from the rest of mathematics. Hodge revitalized the subject by emphasizing and developing its relationship with analysis and topology. In doing this he helped to steer British mathematics back into the mainstream.

Hodge's work was in the great tradition of Riemann and Poincaré, but his more immediate inspiration came from the work of Lefschetz, for whom he had a tremendous admiration. He went to Princeton in 1931, primarily because Lefschetz was there, and he was greatly influenced by Lefschetz's ideas.

As might be expected from his work, there was nothing parochial in Hodge's mathematical outlook. He was very much aware of the importance of maintaining contact with mathematicians abroad and after the war he played a leading part in the formation of the International Mathematical Union, serving as vice-president from 1954 to 1958. He presided over the International Congress of Mathematicians at Edinburgh in 1958 and was responsible for the organization that went with it. He was also one of the prime movers in starting the British Mathematical Colloquium, whose annual meetings since the war have done much to stimulate mathematical activity in Britain. He was president of the London Mathematical Society (1947-49), the Mathematical Association (1955) and the Cambridge Philosophical Society (1947-49).

Hodge was very unlike the conventional picture of a mathematician. Jovial, informal and down-to-earth, he could easily have passed for a successful businessman. In fact he had a considerable interest in the practical matters of university life and was not in the least worried by administrative burdens. He served for many years on important university bodies and for a number of years acted as college bursar. When the Faculty of Mathematics divided into two departments—something which Hodge deplored—he inevitably became Head of the Department of Pure Mathematics.

His scientific eminence and practical experience combined to make him the obvious choice for the Mastership of Pembroke when S. C. Roberts* retired in 1958. As Master he took his duties seriously and always had the best interests of Pembroke very much at heart. Together with Lady Hodge he did much to preserve a friendly atmosphere in the college. His college loyalties, however, did not blind him to the wider needs of the university, and he took a liberal view about the need for colleges to elect more Fellows.

Hodge held very strongly that the place of mathematics was firmly in the sciences. As a result he took a keen interest in the Royal Society. He was elected a Fellow at the early age of 35 and from 1957-65 held the important office of Physical Secretary. He was also a Vice-President from 1959 to 1965.

Honours and medals were showered on him in his later years. He received recognition for his public services by being knighted in 1959. The Royal Society awarded him its Royal Medal in 1957 and the London Mathematical Society gave him the de Morgan Medal in 1959. He held honorary degrees from the Universities of Bristol, Edinburgh, Leicester, Sheffield, Exeter, Wales and Liverpool, and he was a Foreign Associate of the American National Academy of Sciences.

He married Kathleen Cameron in 1929 and had a son and daughter.

July 9, 1975.

Wing Commander Sir John Hodsoll, C.B., who was Inspector-General of A.R.P. Services from 1938 to 1948, died on March 14, 1971 at the age of 76. He was a key-figure in the setting up of air raid precautions before and during the war.

Eric John Hodsoll was born in 1894. From Christ's Hospital he went to the Great Western Railway works at Swindon to train in engineering. On the outbreak of war in 1914 he joined the Royal Naval Air Service, from which in 1918 he transferred to the Royal Air Force. After the war he served at the Air Ministry for three years and then did a course at the Staff College at Camberley.

He was posted in 1924 to the Royal Air Force Staff in India. He was appointed an Assistant Secretary to the Committee of Imperial Defence in 1929, where he remained until his retirement from the Royal Air Force as a Wing Commander and his appointment as Assistant Under-Secretary of State at the Home Office in charge of the newly created A.R.P. Department in 1935. For the rest of his working life he was to be associated with what we now call Civil Defence.

Though he had no experience of departmental administration, he possessed in full measure gifts of enthusiasm and imagination and he found, on taking up his new work, that the Home Office had been able to maintain some degree of active continuity in his field, based on its responsibilities during the First World War.

It was therefore possible for him, with some able assistance from within the Home Office, and from other departments, to make within the next three years substantial progress in the development of plans covering a wide range of matters which did not, however, include police or fire. In the conditions of the time it was inevitable that much of the activity of his organization should be directed to precautions against gas attack. As it proved, this was, on a narrow view, wasted labour for when war came neither side used gas. But there is good reason for thinking that the knowledge that our preparations against gas were far in advance of those in Germany had a decisive effect on Hitler's mind.

By the time of the Munich crisis in September 1938 it had become clear that the A.R.P. drive must be intensified and widened, and that a major reorganization was needed. Some senior men were brought in from other offices and A.R.P. began to assume the shape and size of a major Department, although still a part of the Home Office. Under the new regime administration passed to other hands and Hodsoll was made Inspector-General of A.R.P. Services.

It was in this capacity that Hodsoll was able to give of his best. He was genuinely fond of meeting people, of talking to them, of being known to them and of trying to inspire them with his own enthusiasm; and when heavy bombing began in the autumn of 1940 his quick and manifest sympathy must have heartened many an exhausted Civil Defence worker. He served as Inspector-General for the rest of the war. After the allies had landed in North Africa in 1943 he went on a mission to Allied Headquarters, where he cooperated with the French in planning a civil defence organization.

In 1948, following a full reassessment of the needs of Civil Defence in the light of the imminent probability (as it then appeared) of atomic warfare, the Civil Defence Services which had been stood down in 1945 were reconstituted in a revised form and Hodsoll was appointed Director-General of Civil Defence training. Once more he was in his element: he devoted himself wholeheartedly to touring the country, meeting local authorities and both sides of industry and commerce, in an effort to bring home to his hearers the need for building a framework of Civil Defence which would be capable of standing up to the worst attack. The keen Civil Defence workers of the war responded to Hodsoll's appeals and formed the cadres of the new Civil Defence Corps throughout the country.

When in 1954 he was due to retire from the Civil Service, Hodsoll was offered, and accepted, the post of Civil Defence Adviser to the North Atlantic Treaty Organization and the charge of its Civil Emergency Planning Section.

He was twice married.

March 17, 1971.

Paul Hoffman, who was the first administrator of the Marshall Plan, died on October 8, 1974 at the age of 83.

Appointed by President Truman in 1948 as head of the Marshall Plan organization, Hoffman probably did more than any other person to lift the economies of western Europe out of their depressed state and create a basis for the prosperity that followed. A shortish, likeable and very confident man, Hoffman created the framework for American aid to be channelled to western Europe, travelled continuously, persuading the Europeans to cooperate with one another, and tirelessly needled away at Congress to vote billions of dollars for aid.

The President had told him that his task was "to sustain and strengthen principles of individual liberty, free institutions and genuine independence in Europe", and Hoffman urged the politicians of western Europe to achieve economic unification "without undue delay". If Europe became strong and prosperous, he argued in 1949, then it could work together with Canada and the United States to stop the "ruthless drive" for power of Russian Communism. Later, however, when he was managing director of the United Nations Special Fund, he said that aid must be independent of political considerations and that the underdeveloped countries had to advance through their own efforts; external aid, although vital, was limited. The Marshall Plan, he argued in 1961, had been given too much credit for the postwar recovery of western Europe and he said "it was the Europeans who saved Europe".

Hoffman was born in Chicago in 1891 and became a car salesman with the Studebaker Corporation. He was to make a million dollars before he was 35 and he became president of Studebaker from 1935 to 1948 and chairman from 1953 to 1956. His gift for salesmanship, coupled with idealism, warmth and a natural helpfulness, brought him to the attention of President Truman in the postwar era. For organizing Marshall Plan aid, Hoffman was awarded the Medal of Freedom in 1973.

Resigning from federal service in 1950, Hoffman became president of the Ford Foundation for three years and then went back to industry with Studebaker. He published in 1951 a book called *Peace Can be Won*, in which he urged a halt to all the talk about the cold war and, praising the leadership that Britain had given to the world since the Spanish Armada, hoped that the United States would use its leadership in the same way now that power had passed from the British to the American Common-

wealth.

But Hoffman's work was still not finished. What he had accomplished in Europe was only half the job and in 1959 he dropped his business posts and went to the United Nations as head of the Special Fund, where he stayed until 1965, when he became administrator of the United Nations Development Programme.

There his task was to travel round the world trying to persuade the richer governments to contribute aid for the poorer nations. Again he made known his distaste for cold war politics. It was not possible to win friends with aid, he said. The most compelling reason for giving aid was "that we are living in an unsafe world and our greatest problem today is to prevent its blowing up . . . one of the resasons our world is unsafe is that hundreds of millions of people in the less developed countries are refusing to accept their present position as inevitable". A modest man, Hoffman summed up his United Nations work when he stepped down in 1972 with the remark: "We have made only a feeble start."

He married Dorothy Brown in 1915 and they had seven children. She died in 1961 and he married Mrs. Anna Rosenberg.

October 10, 1974.

Hugh Hogarth, a well-known shipping personality, chairman of H. Hogarth & Sons Ltd., Glasgow, died on August 12, 1973 at his home in Helensburgh, Dunbartonshire. He was 64.

The elder son of S. Crawford Hogarth and the grandson of Hugh Hogarth, the founder of the family firm of tramp shipowners, he was educated at Fettes College, Edinburgh, and Magdalen College, Oxford, where he took a B.A. Afterwards, in 1930, he joined the family firm and in 1935 became a partner. In 1968 his company and the Lyle Shipping Company of Glasgow together formed a new management company called Scottish Ship Management.

Hugh Hogarth played a considerable part in local and national shipping affairs, culminating in 1960 when he was elected president of the Chamber of Shipping of the United Kingdom. He was president of the Glasgow Shipowners' and Shipbrokers' Benevolent Association in 1954 and in 1959 was a joint vice-chairman of the former General Council of British Shipping. He had been a member of the council of the Chamber of Shipping since 1948 and was chairman of the Deep Sea Tramp Section in 1956-57 and in 1958-59, and of the Documentary Committee from 1948 to 1959, and 1961 to 1963. He was also chairman of the Shipowners' Panel Northern Lights Conference from 1966 to 1969.

He is survived by his widow, one son and one daughter.

August 14, 1973.

William Hogarth, who rose from being a fifty-shilling a month deck-boy to be general secretary of the National Union of Seamen and a widely-respected member of the T.U.C. General Council, died on May 13, 1973 after a short illness. He was 61.

"Bill" Hogarth, leader of the N.U.S. for more than ten years, led the union through a difficult decade during which the role of British ships and their crews went through great changes. He also faced, and conquered, a fierce militant challenge to his leadership which culminated in the 1966 seamen's strike.

A short, neat Glaswegian with what has been described as a "long quizzical nose", he began his seafaring career at the age of 16, and being the son of an ardent trade unionist he soon felt the injustice of low pay at sea. He was discharged from his ship as an agitator, and spent the next five years on tankers and tramp ships before rejoining his old firm which was by then unionized.

After Second World War service as a boatswain in troopships, he became a full-time official of the N.U.S., and gradually worked his way up the ladder to London district secretaryship in 1960. Two years later, he was general secretary, successor to Jim Scott by a landslide vote of 68 per cent of votes cast in a secret ballot.

His style of leadership, determined but politically moderate, was the target of constant attack from the Left, which was brought to a head when his executive and annual conference decided to strike in the summer of his fifth year of office.

Though he personally disagreed with the strike, he subordinated his private doubts to the wishes of the majority and led what was then a record-breaking stoppage, the longest since the last war. By doing so, he reasserted his position, and the opposition to his leadership eventually petered out.

After joining the T.U.C. General Council in April 1962, he became a member of the influential Economic Committee and the Nationalized Industries Committee, taking part in key discussions with successive governments on economic affairs.

The last year was not a happy one for relations between the seamen's union and the T.U.C., whose annual Congress had voted to "instruct" affiliated unions not to register under the Government's Industrial Relations Act, and not to have anything to do with the machinery created to carry out the legislation.

The N.U.S., anxious about what would happen to its 50,000 membership if its closed shop in British merchant shipping was nullified by boycotting the Act, defied T.U.C. policy and obtained through the National Industrial Relations Court a legally-valid closed shop.

For so flagrantly breaching T.U.C. policy, the seamen were suspended from the T.U.C. in March 1972, and despite a moving plea at the annual Congress, the suspension is still operative and is likely to be extended to outright expulsion in September 1973.

It was not the outcome of a general secretaryship that Hogarth would have liked. By nature unauthoritarian, he was opposed to dictatorial methods and sought instead to do the best, as he and his executive saw it, for his members. He was appointed C.B.E. in June 1972.

May 14, 1973.

Professor Lancelot Hogben, F.R.S., died on August 22, 1975 at the age of 79.

Lancelot Hogben, born on December 9, 1895, son of Thomas Hogben, a Southsea drysalter and lay missionary, was one of the first contingent of county school scholarship boys to go to Cambridge. As Senior Scholar and Prizeman of Trinity College, he emerged with the equipment of an outstanding experimental biologist but with an ebullient intellect and restless temperament which diversified his career.

He will be remembered especially as a brilliant and persuasive popularizer, author of the best-seller *Mathematics for the Million.*

His laboratory work, always of high order, in genetics and endocrinology (including the Hogben Test for pregnancy) was recognized by his election to a Fellowship of the Royal Society at the age of 41. He became a world best-seller, as a popularizer of mathematics and science. He abandoned zoology for medical statistics. He became fascinated by philology and adventured in linguistic innovation (including methods of conversing with extra-terrestrial beings). After his retirement from Birmingham University he was appointed Vice-Chancellor of the emergent university of Guyana, at the age of 68. This was in 1963 and he held the appointment for two years.

Hogben was one of the most controversial figures in scientific and academic life. He wrote in his introduction to *Science for the Citizen* that he had a "sheer genius for making enemies". That was not true. Rather, as one of his closest associates said, "Lancelot's world was a graveyard of unburied friendships". For many years H. G. Wells, who had a great admiration and affection for Hogben, would ask pathetically "What have I done to offend Lancelot?" and Hogben would be asking "What have I done to offend Wells?" Neither would remember the offending occasion nor the fancied insult and would be lamenting a friendship which had not been lost, just mislaid.

Hogben, one of the most mentally stimulating men in the world, made friends as easily as he thought he lost them. His students and junior staff found, in him, a boon companion with a deep personal interest in their studies, their careers and their personal affairs. Two of his laboratory assistants at the London School of Econo-

mics, whom he encouraged and coached for night classes and a university career, achieved high distinction. His junior academic colleagues never had to fear a predatory professor. He never stood in their way. He was as excited about their ideas as he was about his own. He did not so much direct research as explode firecrackers which made even routine exciting. As one of his now eminent students said, "Three years of Hogben was worth thirty years of anyone else." As he himself wrote, "I had the astonishing good luck to get myself liked by young men of promise and with more social gifts than I possessed."

His quarrels, if they were quarrels, were with his own contemporaries. They were always subjective, and unscientific. In the self-criticism to which he was addicted he attributed his "unmateyness" to two things, to his upbringing and to his experience as an "outsider" at Cambridge. There was a third reason, in later years—self-experimentation, by which he tried to treat a thyroid complaint.

His father was a fundamentalist preacher, who brought up in the fear of hellfire a son who rejected religion for scientific humanism. At Cambridge, as the first of the county scholarship boys, Hogben developed a resentment, which lasted a lifetime, of the social condescension with which he felt he was treated. He picked his quarrels rather on that basis.

In the 1914-18 War he went to prison as a conscientious objector. After the war, when he was a lecturer in zoology at Imperial College, he was active as a Labour Party campaigner in the East End of London. From Imperial College he went to Edinburgh as lecturer in experimental physiology. After two years there he became assistant professor of Zoology at McGill University, Montreal. From 1927 to 1930 he was Professor of Zoology at the University of Cape Town, where he got involved at considerable personal as well as professional risk in the battle for the Blacks and the Coloureds, in the anticipation of what became apartheid.

In 1930 the London School of Economics made a surprising departure by the creation, for him, of the Chair of Social Biology. The new professor brought actual living experiments, and his own disturbing personality, into that institution.

He continued his zoological and physiological research but his social science group, Enid Charles (his wife), Kuczynski, J. L. Gray and D. V. Glass, profoundly influenced the thinking on demography and on the trends in population.

His F.R.S. in 1936 made his scientific status unimpeachable and his appointment in 1937 as Regius Professor of Natural History at the University of Aberdeen, a Chair which had been occupied by that other great popularizer, Sir J. Arthur Thomson, gave him a secure base both for his research and as a writer. He had written *Mathematics for the Million* as "one who had been frightened by mathematics at

school" while he was in hospital, and he had written *Science for the Citizen* while travelling at the weekends in a Southern Railways buffet car between London and Devon. He was now in a Chair which, in terms of research and popularization, was secure for life.

He resigned from Aberdeen in 1941 after an unnecessary dispute with the authorities and was appointed Mason Professor of Zoology at Birmingham. He was an absentee professor because the conscientious objector of the 1914-18 War became, under Brigadier Frank Crew, his former Professor in Edinburgh, a colonel on the staff of the War Office. He had discovered that the military organization gave him full opportunities for his new-found enthusiasm for medical statistics and, to resolve a clash of eminent personalities, Birmingham University created the Chair to fit his new subject. This he occupied from 1947 to 1961.

His postwar activities as an earnest popular educator included an international language "Interglossa", as well as a series of simplified books of great merit and international success, such as *Signs of Civilization* and *Mathematics in the Making.* Through them he had enormous readership in many languages and in every part of the world. They are not tomes like his Primers for the Age of Plenty, in which he could claim succession to the French Encyclopaedists, but they have profoundly influenced the younger generation. Science is the simpler, and the richer, for his efforts at popularization.

His marriage to Enid Charles, the demographer, by whom he had two sons and two daughters, ended in divorce in 1957; and he married Sarah Jane Evans, who died in 1974.

August 23, 1975.

Lord Holford, R.A., F.R.I.B.A., F.R.T.P.I., Emeritus Professor of Town Planning at University College London, died on October 17, 1975 aged 68.

He was the most influential figure in town planning throughout the period during which town and country planning in Britain became transformed from a minor official regulatory activity into a major activity of central and local government departments, employing thousands of people and affecting the national life in innumerable ways.

Holford's work was less important as a practitioner of town planning than as a teacher, a consultant who helped to spread British planning principles all over the world, and a moulder of policies and opinions. He also practised as an architect, and he exerted a powerful influence through his membership—and in many instances his chairmanship—of Government committees and councils, for which his gifts of clear thought and diplomacy were particularly well suited.

William Graham Holford was born in

South Africa on March 22, 1907 and educated at the Diocesan College, Cape Town. He went to England to study architecture at Liverpool University under the late Sir Charles Reilly, and became one of the latter's most brilliant students, taking a first-class honours degree and winning a succession of prizes, culminating, in 1930, in the Rome Scholarship in Architecture. While in Rome he met, and in 1933 married, Marjorie Brooks who was there as holder of the Rome Scholarship in mural painting.

On his return from Rome (where his scholarship was extended to allow him to complete a study of Italian town plans and piazzas), and after a visit to America made possible by another prize gained at Liverpool, Holford practised as an architect and town planner until, at the very youthful age of 30, he was appointed to the chair of Civic Design at Liverpool University in 1937 as the successor of Sir Patrick Abercrombie.

It was also as Abercrombie's successor that, in 1948, he became Professor of Town Planning at University College London, a post he occupied until 1970, when he retired and was created professor emeritus. During the early years of the war he was the leader of a team of Government architects designing ordnance depots, camps and factories, and in 1944, when plans were being made for postwar reconstruction, he became adviser to the newly formed Ministry of Town and Country Planning. Holford was largely responsible, under the then Minister, Lewis (later Lord) Silkin, for drawing up the 1947 Town and Country Planning Act, which, with its subsequent amendments, is the basis of British planning law today.

On leaving the ministry Holford set up his own practice and was much in demand as a planning consultant, travelling to many parts of the world. He was adviser to the city of Canberra, Australia, and made, in 1968, a regional plan for Durban, South Africa. He was also kept busy preparing plans for British local authorities, notably for Cambridge in 1950 and, jointly with the late Charles Holden, for the City of London in 1950-51. He made a separate report on the replanning of the precincts of St. Paul's Cathedral in 1956, commissioned by the Dean and Chapter. This was partially implemented, though the new buildings erected as part of it were less distinguished than Holford must have hoped; the remainder is not likely to be implemented since it placed more emphasis on traffic flow than the public and official attitudes nowadays demand and less on conserving the existing townscape.

Holford next came prominently into the public eye with two successive plans for the rebuilding of Piccadilly Circus. These have likewise been superseded—he was given an unsatisfactory official brief, again with too great an emphasis on traffic movement—but his proposals were a marked improvement on those that had gone before as well as on those subsequently put forward by Westminster City Council to tempt developers to invest their capital.

As an architect Holford was less successful. He was a good critic and judge of architecture; his building probably best known to the public is the Army Museum in Royal Hospital Road, London.

Holford was constantly engaged in a multitude of activities besides teaching and practising as a town planner and architect. He was a member of the Royal Fine Art Commission from 1943 to 1969 and of the Historic Buildings Council from 1953. He was Romanes Lecturer at Oxford in 1969 and served at different times as a Trustee of the British Museum, as a governor of Wye College and as Prime Warden of the Goldsmiths' Company. He was awarded honorary degrees by several British universities. In 1961 he received the Gold Medal of the Town Planning Institute and in 1963 the Royal Gold Medal for Architecture. He was elected A.R.A. in 1961 and R.A. in 1968, was knighted in 1953 and was made a life peer in 1965—the first architect or town planner to be thus honoured.

Among all these activities he found time to serve, from 1960 to 1962, as President of the Royal Institute of British Architects, a task he performed with outstanding success, being wise in professional politics, a born diplomat and a firm chairman who wasted no words. The same personal qualities emerged strikingly on the many occasions when he appeared as an expert witness at planning inquiries. He spoke well and clearly and was imperturbable under cross-examination.

He was the least pompous of men, yet those who saw him only in one of his public capacities, carrying out official duties with suitable gravity and decorum, can have had no conception of his ability to unbend when these were over, or of the gaiety and humour which made him excellent company.

Holford's life from the early 1960s onwards was dominated by the tragic illness, and the consequent invalid state, of his wife Marjorie. He nursed her devotedly and his care for her made the first call on his time and emotions. In 1972 he accepted the part-time post of director of the Leverhulme Trust Fund. He also served from 1974 as chairman of the joint committee, set up by the Department of the Environment, on the planning of Bath.

His wife survives him. They had no children.

October 20, 1975.

Stanley Hollis, v.c., of Middlesbrough, who won a Victoria Cross for bravery on the Normandy beaches on D-Day 1944, died on February 8, 1972 at the age of 59. His was the first V.C. of the land invasion.

He was a company sergeant major serving with The Green Howards and, during the assault on the beaches and the Mont Fleury battery, C.S.M. Hollis's company commander noticed that two pill-boxes had been by-passed and with the C.S.M. approached them. When 20 yards away from one they were fired on. C.S.M. Hollis rushed the pill-box firing his Sten gun, leapt on the top, recharged his magazine, and threw a grenade in the pill-box. He killed two Germans and made others prisoner.

Later the same day in the village of Crepon the company met a field-gun and its crew armed with Spandaus at 100 yards range. C.S.M. Hollis was put in charge of a party to cover an attack on the gun but the movement was held up. Seeing this, C.S.M. Hollis pushed forward to engage the field gun with a P.I.A.T. from a house 50 yards away. A sniper's bullet grazed his face and, all of a sudden, the gun swung round and was fired at point-blank range into the house. To avoid the fallen masonry, C.S.M. Hollis moved his party. By this time two of the enemy gun crew had been killed and the gun was destroyed soon after.

Hearing that two of his men were still in the house, C.S.M. Hollis went to get them out. In full view of the enemy, who were continually firing at him, he went forward alone, with a Bren gun to distract the enemy's attention. Under cover of his diversion the two men in the house were able to get back.

In the citation of his V.C. it was stated that wherever fighting was heaviest C.S.M. Hollis appeared; on two separate occasions his courage and initiative prevented the enemy holding up the advance at a critical stage. "It was largely through his heroism and resource that the company's objectives were gained and casualties not heavier. By his own bravery he saved the lives of many of his men."

Earlier in the Second World War Hollis came through the Dunkirk evacuation and later saw service in North Africa, Tunisia and Sicily. He was mentioned in dispatches for the part he played in capturing a German gun position in Sicily.

February 10, 1972.

Professor H. A. Hollond, D.S.O., O.B.E., Emeritus Professor of English Law in the University of Cambridge, died on October 20, 1974 at the age of 90.

He was a Reader and Professor in the University for 30 years, Dean and Vice-Master of Trinity College for 33 years and an Honorary Bencher of Lincoln's Inn since 1935.

Henry Arthur Hollond was born on October 14, 1884. He was Head of the School at Rugby, and a Classical Scholar of Trinity College, Cambridge, getting First Classes in Part 1 of the Classical Tripos and both parts of the Law Tripos, and becoming President of the Union. He was elected a Fellow of Trinity in 1909, was called to the Bar in 1911, and studied at the Harvard Law School in 1913-14. He served in the Army from 1914 to 1920, and was appointed D.S.O. and O.B.E. for his services as D.A.A.G. at Haig's headquarters.

After the war, Hollond was a leader of reconstruction in college and university. He was appointed in 1919 to the Readership in English Law, which was endowed by Henry Sidgwick for F. W. Maitland, and held successively by C. S. Kenny and H. D. Hazeltine till they were in turn elected to the Downing Professorship.

He then devoted much of his energy to writing a textbook on the new law of real property; but this was laid aside when he became Secretary in 1923 of the Statutory Commission charged with making new statutes for the university. He and Sir Hugh Anderson were the chief architects of the faculty system and other innovations, which enabled Cambridge to conserve what was of most value and yet meet a changing world with flexible resilience. He never finished his book, or wrote another, but he played an active and important part in making the new statutes work.

Although he served for many years on the Council of the Senate and other University bodies, his main influence was felt in the organization of the fast-expanding Faculty of Law. Here he played a part not merely active but devoted, and for many years dominating. Before 1914, law did not attract many undergraduates, whereas in 1950 there were some 500 undergraduate and graduate students and a teaching staff of nearly 30, most of whom owed their appointment largely to Hollond's indefatigable efforts to recruit good men. He was elected in 1943 to succeed his close friend P. H. Winfield in the Rouse Ball Professorship of English Law, founded by his former tutor, and held the chair till he reached the retiring age in 1950. He was a first-rate property lawyer and legal historian, and his lectures were prepared and delivered with meticulous care. Nevertheless his main contribution to the Faculty and the University lay in the sphere of administration.

Hollond always kept in touch with Lincoln's Inn, and in 1935 he was elected an Honorary Bencher. From that time onwards he took a keen and assiduous part in the life of the Bench and in all the activities of the Inn. In this way, and by his untiring efforts to bridge the gap between the study and practice of the law, and his wise counsel in matters academic, he sustained and strengthened the ties between the University of Cambridge and his Inn of Court. In 1946 he was, with the approval of the University authorities, appointed by the Council of Legal Education one of the two Readers in Constitutional Law and Legal History in the Inns of Court, Legal History being allotted to him.

Hollond's services to Trinity, as Fellow, Director of Studies, Dean, Member of Council, and Vice-Master, culminated in 1951, when it fell to him to preside as Vice-Master over the change of Master, the retirement of G. M. Trevelyan* and the installation of Lord Adrian. This occasion made a strong appeal to Hollond's sense of responsibility and devotion, and his handling of it in all its details was admirable.

It was also as Vice-Master that he found most scope for his gifts of hospitality. He enjoyed entertaining, whether his guests were Fellows and their wives, old pupils, or old friends of undergraduate and Harvard days. Although he was abstemious by temperament he was particular about the food and wine served at his table and he prided himself on the coffee he made in a copper saucepan. In the summer of 1966 he moved out of college into a stone house on the Madingley Road, beautifully redecorated and largely rebuilt in accordance with the fastidious taste of his wife; and there they entertained even more hospitably than in the past.

He married in 1929 Marjorie Tappan, formerly of Gloucester, Massachusetts, a distinguished economist and Fellow of Girton.

October 22, 1974.

James Holloway—See Nervo.

Percy Holmes, one of Yorkshire's greatest opening batsmen, died at his home in Huddersfield on September 3, 1971 at the age of 84. With Herbert Sutcliffe he held until 1945 the record for an opening partnership in first-class cricket.

Percy Holmes, who was born in 1886, played his early cricket in the Huddersfield League. In a first class career which lasted from 1913, excluding the war years, till 1933, he scored 30,574, made a thousand runs in a season fifteen times, and hit 67 centuries, including two not-out totals of over 300. With Sutcliffe he shared 74 century stands 69 of them for Yorkshire. Of these, nineteen exceeded 200 runs and four exceeded 300. It was against Essex in 1932 at Leyton that he helped Sutcliffe to score 555 for the first wicket, thus breaking the record of 554, set up by their fellow Yorkshiremen, Brown and Tunnicliffe, at Chesterfield 34 years before.

Holmes's figures, impressive as they are, convey little of the true quality of his batting, which had the authentic sparkle of champagne. For his county he took on the mantle of David Denton, the gay cavalier of Yorkshire batting, and what was said of Denton could have been said even more fittingly of Holmes: "You might get him out, but you could never tie him up." He was wholly free from the characteristic dourness with which Yorkshire batting is, perhaps unfairly, debited; and even when he scored 300, his innings, though long, was devoid of *longueurs*. His off-driving and late cutting had a charm and grace of their own and he could hook a fast ball "off his eyebrows" with an air of innocent impertinence. In the field, especially in the deep, he was not only safe, but exceptionally quick.

Playing in the shadow of Sutcliffe, as Sandham played in the shadow of Hobbs*, Holmes was an idea foil in county games to his more monumental partner, but the presence of England's greatest opening pair prevented him from receiving what would in other times have been his rightful share of Test honours. His appearances for England were limited to seven: once against Armstrong's overwhelming Australian eleven of 1921, when he made top score in the first game and was unaccountably dropped; once in a single unproductive reappearance against India 11 years later; and, in between, in a highly successful tour of South Africa in 1927-28.

A popular figure on all county grounds, he had the happy reputation of playing to please. His was a blithe spirit, like that of a minor, but not very minor, Macartney; and his alert, cheerful manner disguised the pain of a physical disability. Over frequent periods, he suffered from that form of backache which, whatever the medical profession may call it at the time, is perennially painful to the games-player. To the end of his playing career he retained his confident approach and his exuberantly attacking spirit. It was once said that, with his brisk light-infantry step towards the wicket, he looked like a man going off for a day at the races.

At the end of their historic stand of 555, Charles Bray, the Essex captain, came along and sportingly congratulated the two Yorkshiremen on this massive record. Sutcliffe gravely acknowledged the courtesy and Holmes with his customary impish smile and honest West Riding vernacular, declared: "Nay, Mr. Bray, if I hadn't had lumbago, I'd have brayed [buttered] you properly."

September 4, 1971.

Dr. J. S. M. Hooper, who died on May 2, 1974 at the age of 92, had two creative achievements to his credit in the foundation of the Bible Society of India and Ceylon and the leading part which he played in the completion and fulfilment of the Church Union Scheme in South India. On both counts the Christian Church in India will long have cause to be grateful for his clear thinking and for his devoted and effective work.

Born at Stirling in April 1882, son of a Wesleyan Methodist Minister, John Stirling Morley Hooper was educated at Kingswood School, Bath, from which he won an Open Scholarship at Corpus Christi College, Oxford. He graduated with First Class Honours in Modern History in 1905, was ordained into the Wesleyan Methodist Ministry, and sailed in the same year to work as a missionary in the Madras District, South India, where for 27 years he served in country areas and in the city.

In 1910 he married Sarah Rosalind

Cooling. Their one child, Jean, born in 1924, died suddenly at the age of two, and in her memory the Hoopers built a chapel for the Girls' Boarding School at Ikkadu, where she was born.

A considerable part of Hooper's service as a missionary was spent in college and high school work, and he was Principal of Wesley College, Madras, from 1926 to 1932, when he was called to become the first general secretary of the British and Foreign Bible Society in India, Burma and Ceylon, with his headquarters at Nagpur. His responsibilities included the very important one of bringing into being the independent Bible Society of India and Ceylon.

But probably Hooper will be best remembered as one of the main architects of the Church of South India, and as the secretary of the Joint Committee on Church Union for the last dozen years of its work before the union was accomplished in 1947. He was chosen to preach the sermon at the great Service of Inauguration in St. George's Cathedral, Madras, in September of that year. He and his wife returned to England in 1950, and lived at Stratford-on-Avon, where Mrs. Hooper died in 1955.

May 6, 1974.

J. Edgar Hoover, Director of the F.B.I., who served under eight presidents and many more attorneys general, died on May 2, 1972. He was 77.

Not even Kennedy's new wave of youthful administrators could dislodge Hoover from the directorship of the Federal Bureau of Investigation; he held on to the office he was first given at the age of 29. Then, in 1924, President Coolidge had appointed him, initially as acting director of the F.B.I. Later, in 1964, when he was approaching the age of 70, President Johnson exempted him from the Civil Service retirement provision "for an indefinite period of time".

There was no doubt of his value to the American nation as the highest law-enforcement officer—or "top cop". He became, as President Johnson put it, "a household word, a hero to millions of citizens and anathema to evil men". If there was any one man in the United States who was in possession of all the facts on espionage and subversive activities in the country, that man was Hoover.

Hoover's term of office spanned the gangsterism of the twenties to the civil rights disturbances of the sixties; the Prohibition days of the early thirties to McCarthyism of the fifties. His name was already legendary in the thirties when his special agents cornered and shot the Public Enemies No. 1. His national force was at a disadvantage in dealing with the disregard of Prohibition laws abetted by local connivance and corruption. But after the kidnapping of Lindbergh's 20-month-old son 21 Bills strengthened Hoover's bureau's

authority. Kidnapping became a Federal offence. Robberies of national banks were now investigated by the F.B.I. Its role became a strong one.

During the Second World War under Hoover's direction more than 16,000 enemy aliens were rounded up, ten German saboteurs were caught, and a 33-man spy ring in New York was broken up by using hidden film cameras and a "look-through" trick mirror. In the cold war aftermath Hoover was much concerned with combating communism in America—his bureau helped convict top Communist agents, and also screened millions of Government employees for their loyalty to the state. In 1964, his bureau made 21 arrests after the killing of three civil rights workers in Mississippi.

In his more than 40 years of office, Hoover created a ruthlessly efficient law-enforcing machine in the F.B.I. The first move the new head of the "G" or "Government" men made after his appointment was to rid the F.B.I. of political appointees. His special agents—to number some 7,000 in time—were picked for their competency in the fight against criminals ranging from gangsters to racketeers. Hoover took on men who had a law or accountancy training, passed a stringent physical test and were given a further schooling in the use of firearms, wrestling and boxing and other defence methods. In time, as crime became more sophisticated so did the techniques of the F.B.I.; Hoover used espionage penetration methods in his campaigns against secret organizations such as Cosa Nostra (the American Mafia) and the Ku-Klux-Klan. Hoover established a national fingerprint records division to ease identification, and later an international exchange of fingerprints was set up. In 1932, an enlarged technical laboratory was created to employ scientific crime-detecting techniques to the full.

Hoover's immense prestige rested partly on the fact that he remained as much as he could an apolitical figure. His name was brought into political controversies but rarely as a partisan. He never had any difficulty in getting the F.B.I. appropriations approved on Capitol Hill. Yet he was quick to defend the F.B.I. against critics: the gentle strictures of the Warren Commission's report on the assassination of President Kennedy* led to an immediate and angry denunciation of that respected body; later, before the publication of William Manchester's book on the assassination, Hoover told critics that not one shred of evidence had been developed to link any other person with Oswald in the conspiracy. He hit back strongly at Dr. Martin Luther King,* the Negro leader, when he turned critic.

His anti-Communist views were soundly American—he appealed once to American doctors to help wipe out "Communist germs trying to infect the bloodstream of American life". A book he wrote on communism in America—*Masters of Deceit* (1958)—

headed the best seller list for some weeks. He always regarded the Communist Party as "a formidable domestic threat" to the United States. He constantly warned against the dangers of communist diplomatists. His alertness on communist infiltration extended to college students and the impact of the New Left movement in the sixties in particular—"The Communist Party, U.S.A., as well as other subversive groups, is jubilant over these new rebellious activities", he wrote in the *Law Enforcement Bulletin.* Even so, Hoover stressed that his agency was primarily an investigative agency—he himself was against the creation of a national police force.

A heavy-set bachelor, Hoover was dedicated to the bureau he headed. Of his personal courage there was no doubt: once when a Senator implied that he was afraid to make an arrest himself, Hoover proved he was as good as any of his agents. A few days afterwards a group of F.B.I. agents surrounded a house in New Orleans, Louisiana, waiting for the dangerous criminal, Alvin Karpis, to appear. When he finally emerged, J. Edgar Hoover sprang from his car and overpowered him. Hoover also had a fondness for practical jokes; once he told a friend he could play a small part in a film about the F.B.I. providing he reported at F.B.I. headquarters with three complete suits of clothes; only when the friend had changed his clothes five or six times at F.B.I. headquarters did he realise that Hoover was joking.

Hoover was born on New Year's Day, 1895, in Washington, the son of a civil servant. He took a job as a messenger at the Library of Congress to help support his family after his father died, and studied at night for a law degree at George Washington University. After graduating, he went to work as an attorney in the Department of Justice; there he later became special assistant to the Attorney-General in 1919; and two years later Assistant Director of the then Bureau of Investigation.

Hoover held numerous honorary degrees and was a mason. He was awarded an honorary K.B.E. in 1947, and the Medal of Merit (U.S.) in 1946. He also published *Persons in Hiding* (1938), *A Study of Communism* (1962), and *J. Edgar Hoover on Communism* (1969).

May 3, 1972.

F. R. Horne, C.B.E., F.I.BIOL., who was an influential agriculturalist, died on June 27, 1975 at the age of 71.

He was Director of the National Institute of Agricultural Botany, Cambridge, from 1945 to 1970 and largley instrumental in shaping seed legislation nationally and internationally.

Born in 1904, Frank Robert Horne was educated at Hele's School, Exeter, going on to Seale Hayne Agricultural College, Christ's College, Cambridge, and the West of Scotland Agricultural College, where he was Stevens Memorial Prizeman. After a short spell of teaching at Gresham's School, Holt, he returned to Seale Hayne as Head of the Botanical Department, whose work was considerably expanded by a research grant for plant breeding in 1944.

His record in Devon, not only as an agricultural botanist with a special interest in herbage crops, but also as a persuasive and lucid adviser to farmers, made him an obvious choice to head the rapidly expanding Cambridge Institute. It would be no exaggeration to say that his work there transformed the seed trade in Britain and raised its standards to an extent that would have seemed incredible to an earlier generation.

The institute, whose governing body was drawn from farmers and the seed trade, had several functions. It operated for the Ministry of Agriculture an official seed testing service, it carried out comparative trials of new crop varieties submitted on a voluntary basis, was responsible for maintaining and multiplying certain crop varieties, and also undertook the training of field inspectors for the trade.

What brought the institute to wider notice was the flood of new cereal varieties which followed the revival of international trade after the war. From the genesis of a new variety to availability on the farm would take about 15 years and the work of breeders in the late 1930s came to fruition in the early 1950s. New wheats, barleys and oats successively pushed up average yields. Some were of British origin, others from France, Scandinavia, the Netherlands and, later, Germany. Their evaluation as material for English and Welsh growers necessitated rigorously controlled trials, over not less than three years and in a wide range of environments. Account had to be taken of susceptibility to disease and suitability for brewing. Over the years the Institute's recommended lists became an increasingly sensitive guide on these factors.

Horne and his staff had developed very wide contacts in Europe and further afield. When legislation was finally formulated and international conventions agreed, it was obvious that N.I.A.B. was one of the key organizations in their working.

The regard in which the institute was now held by breeders, seedsmen and farmers alike was shown by their fierce reaction to what they saw as an attempted take-over by the Ministry, consequent upon the splitting off of routine seed testing from its other functions. There were some obvious advantages for the staff if they became civil servants but many felt that independence and impartiality weighed heavier in the scale. Characteristically, Horne played a quiet role throughout the controversy but had a large hand in its final happy solution.

He was president of the British Grassland Society in 1957-58 and of the World Seed Year meeting of F.A.O. in 1962.

The Swedish Seed Research Association made him a life member in 1961 and in 1968 the Royal Swedish Academy of Agriculture and Forestry also elected him to membership.

He was Commodore of the Cambridge University Cruising Club from 1961 to 1963.

He married, in 1929, Marjorie Bannister. They had a son and three daughters.

July 1, 1975.

Bernard Fitzalan-Howard, 16th Duke of Norfolk—See Norfolk.

Michael S. Howard, only son of G. Wren Howard, one of the founding partners of the publishing house of Jonathan Cape, died suddenly at his home in Brecon on December 10, 1974. He was 51.

Although he had spent nine months at the Cambridge University Press in 1941 while waiting to begin training as a pilot with the R.A.F., he first became fully engaged in publishing when he entered his father's firm after demobilization in 1946. With modesty and wit he described in his book, *Jonathan Cape Publisher*, his initiation at the hands of his two knowledgeable but not always very communicative mentors and his appointment to the board in 1950. The book was intended primarily for circulation in the book trade in 1971 as a celebration of the company's half-century. Yet, in John Raymond's words, "the reader emerges rubbing his eyes with astonishment, realizing that this excellent book is also a piece of economic and social history".

Having succeeded to the managing directorship in 1960, when his father moved to the chair upon Jonathan Cape's death at the age of 80 he then established himself as a writer of distinction and style with the kind of book few might expect to gain any great attention in the press, much less the critical acclaim it actually received. "The most remarkable book that has ever been written about the business of publishing", began one of the first major reviews to appear, while Michael Holroyd wrote in *The Times* that he had achieved a portrait of Jonathan Cape "comparable to Arnold Bennett's bookseller in *Riceyman Steps*".

Michael Howard's own achievements at Cape lay as much in the enrichment of the renowned Cape style in book design as in the encouragement of authors. He formed close and lasting friendships with those authors whom he advised and published— notably with T. H. White, Ian Fleming*, David Garnett, Elizabeth Jane Howard, John Aiken, and latterly with T. H. White's biographer, Sylvia Townsend Warner. But it was his insistence on style that left an indelible mark on all that he accomplished, not least on his building of a talented team which would restore the House of Cape in the 1960s to its former fortunes.

In April 1965, having spent what he called in his book "an emotionally stren-

uous" five years, maintaining calm and unity in the firm through a period of radical change, he fell seriously ill with hepatitis. It was while recuperating after several months in hospital that he came to the decision to withdraw gradually from the successful business which his father had created so as to be free to set about a new venture of his own. He wanted to establish a retreat where writers and painters could disengage for a while from the domestic round in order to work or find artistic refreshment in conducive and peaceful surroundings. With consideration and enormous care, he went ahead with arrangements that would secure the firm for his successors.

His plans were temporarily stayed when he was pressed to take the chair at Cape after his father's death in 1968. By 1970, he had withdrawn altogether from active participation in publishing and begun restoration on the early Victorian house on the Welsh borders which he had chosen for his new endeavour.

It was there that he died, leaving a wife and three sons.

December 17, 1974.

Professor W. G. Howell, D.F.C., A.R.A., F.R.I.B.A., who died in a motorcar accident on November 29, 1974, was an architect and a teacher of architects of unusual talent and force of character, and a man the profession can ill afford to lose since he still—he was only 52—had clearly much to give it.

He belonged to the generation that made British architecture, in the years after the war, respected all over the world for its close integration of building programmes and social needs, especially in schools and housing. He himself worked during that period in the architect's department of the London County Council, then one of the centres of architectural enlightenment.

Howell was one the group responsible for the Roehampton Estate, which was outstanding among the products of the L.C.C.'s housing programme, and a few years later it was in partnership with three others of the same group that Howell set up in independent practice.

William Gough Howell was born in 1922 and educated at Marlborough, Caius College, Cambridge (where he took his M.A.) and the Architectural Association School in London. Before Cambridge he served with the R.A.F. and had a distinguished war career, flying nightfighters and earning a D.F.C.

Howell qualified as an architect in 1952 when he was already involved in his responsible work on L.C.C. housing. He left the L.C.C. in 1956 to practise architecture privately and at the same time to teach at the Regent Street Polytechnic.

In 1959 he and his L.C.C. colleagues set up the partnership of Howell, Killick, Partridge and Amis, which has continued fruitfully ever since, though with the loss of John Killick who died in the 1972. The partners' first notable effort was to enter for the Churchill College competition, and theirs was one of four designs chosen for the final stage. They were not the eventual winners, but their success brought them other university work, and threequarters of the firm's work over the years has been for universities.

It has included buildings at Oxford and Cambridge: St. Anne's and St. Antony's Colleges at the former and additions to Downing and Darwin Colleges at the latter, as well as the University Centre near Silver Street Bridge; also buildings at Birmingham and Reading. The work at Cambridge was Howell's special responsibility, as were some distinguished mathematicians' houses at Warwick University. Just before his death he had completed an arts centre for Christ's Hospital at Horsham.

Though an equal partner, Howell was in many ways the driving force of the firm. The boldly rectilinear style of its work was unmistakable, but in spite of its uncompromising nature it remained sensitive about the relation of new buildings to old; witness Howell's distinctive but sympathetic addition of a new combination room wing to Downing College, Cambridge.

In 1973 Howell moved to Cambridge on being appointed to the chair of architecture at the university, a challenge he responded to in his usual wholehearted and extrovert manner. Though he had only a little more than a year to establish himself there, he showed promise of becoming a highly successful professor and a useful influence at Cambridge.

For such a position his personal qualities were well fitted. Bill Howell, as he was always known to his friends and fellow-architects, had a relaxed and sociable nature, but strong convictions and the ability to express them persuasively. His stocky figure, bushy moustache and genial personality were familiar on many architectural occasions, for he gave much to the profession besides his buildings and his teaching. He was for several years on the council of the R.I.B.A. and a vice-president in 1965-67. He was elected A.R.A. in 1974. He had a number of other, typically idiosyncratic, pursuits and interests: horsemanship; his collection (before the subject became fashionable) of objects connected with the 1914 War, which was the source of a book entitled *Popular Art of the First World War*, produced in collaboration with Barbara Jones and published in 1972; and his weekend home near Savernake Forest which he converted with zest and wit from a lofty Victorian chapel.

Howell leaves a widow, Gillian, who had been with him in the L.C.C. architect's department and to whom he had been married for 23 years, and four children.

December 3, 1974.

Bobby Howes, the comedian, died in London at the age of 76 on April 27, 1972.

He will be remembered chiefly as a comedian whose personality, humble but hopeful as it was once described, had, provided with a suitable foil and support, been the centre-piece of successful British musical comedies of the 1930s.

Born in London on August 4, 1895, Howes joined at the age of 14 a company known as "Sally Fern and her Boy Scouts". Having been trained in acrobatics and dancing and in the use of his light baritone voice, he entered the field of concert party work and remained there until the First World War.

Jack Hylton* gave him his first postwar job in variety; Jack Hulbert introduced him to the West End in an intimate revue; and in 1927 Philip Ridgeway, by engaging him for a musical comedy with a story and with plenty of sentiment entitled *The Blue Train,* enabled him to prove himself, in the words of *The Times* critic, a born entertainer, expressive of foot and face.

Of his performance in *Mr. Cinders* in 1929 as a poor relation who goes to a ball posing as somebody else, Charles Morgan in the same columns used the word Chaplinesque. In notices of subsequent musical comedies it was not suggested that Howes had gone further on lines laid down by himself, in that direction. He remained not so much a Little Man who is put upon as a Nice Normal Man who finds himself in that position, and whose refuge is in dreaming of a better world and in dancing, when he has the right companion in the one thing and the right partner in the other.

His playmates included Binnie Hale, the leading lady of *Mr. Cinders* and *Yes, Madam?*; Peter Haddon; and three performers who were so often with him during the 1930s that they almost formed a repertory company in his support—Wylie Watson, Bertha Belmore and Vera Pearce. The contrasted sizes and personalities of Vera Pearce and Howes—she big and aggressive, he small and modest—were a feature of two shows that ran for over 300 performances each.

He rejoined Vera Pearce in 1941, when *Shepherd's Pie* reopened after being forced out of London by the Blitz. Later in the war he became yet another Little Man who saves the situation in Stanley Lupino's *Lady Behave* and an American soldier in Cole Porter's* *Let's Face It*: and on his first postwar appearance he shared the honours of a revue *Here come the Boys* with his old benefactor Jack Hulbert.

After an experience of straight acting at the St. James's, where he took the leading part in *The Man in The Street* with Basil Dean's direction, he returned to the musical theatre, and for many months played the founder of a Californian boom town in *Paint your Wagon,* in which he also had the satisfaction of seeing his daughter Sally Ann Howes make a success. He toured as Archie Rice's father in Osborne's *The Entertainer*, and as an Irishman who stole the leprechaun's pot of gold in the musical *Finian's Rainbow,* a part that he had already played in a revival in New York and which he returned to, having completed an Australian tour of *How to Succeed in Business without really Trying*, at Melbourne.

Before the Second World War he had made films of three of his musical comedies, and after the war he was seen on the screen as one of a music-hall act in *The Trojan Brothers,* as a stage manager in *Happy Go Lovely* and in a remake of *The Good Companions*, films all dealing with aspects of show business.

By his marriage to Patricia Malon Clark, which was dissolved, he had a son and a daughter.

April 28, 1972.

Frank Howes, music critic of *The Times* from 1943 to 1960 and a musician active in many fields as writer, lecturer, organizer and administrator, died on September 28, 1974 at the age of 83.

While it is natural to disagree with the views of any critic whom one reads frequently, disagreement with the writings of Frank Howes was of the stimulating sort which compels the protester to examine the grounds of disagreement before he embarks upon argument. Howes was a writer of great authority based upon wide tastes and a vigorous, analytical intelligence.

Frank Stewart Howes was born in Oxford on April 2, 1891 and educated at Oxford High School and St. John's College, which he left as M.A. in 1914. As an undergraduate in the vigorous pioneering days of Sir Hugh Percy Allen, he sang both in the Bach Choir and as a member of the chorus in Allen's productions of Beethoven's *Fidelio* and Weber's *Der Freischutz*. He was, too, an accomplished pianist.

After the First World War he spent the years from 1920 to 1922 at the Royal College of Music, where, as a member of the Critic's Class conducted by H. C. Colles, then music critic of *The Times,* he came under Colles's influence. In 1925 Howes himself joined the staff of *The Times* as assistant music critic and succeeded to the post of principal critic after Colles's death in 1943. From 1938 onwards he was a lecturer at the Royal College of Music; he was at various times an extra-mural lecturer for Oxford University; he delivered the Cramb Lectures at Glasgow University in 1947, and in 1950 he was first Crees Lecturer at the Royal College of Music.

Throughout all this activity as lecturer and critic—the latter with the duty of regular almost weekly articles as well as almost nightly concert or opera notices—Howes, who confessed that he "liked to have a finger in every pie," involved himself deeply in a number of other musical activities. A scholarly enthusiast for English folk song, he became editor of the *Folk Song Journal* in 1927, and remained editor of its larger successor, *The Journal of the English Folk Song and Dance Society*, until 1945. Under his control the *Journal* maintained high standards both of scholarship and of style. From 1938 to 1956 he was chairman of the Musicians' Benevolent Fund, from 1938 to 1945 of the English Folk Song and Dance Society, and from 1948 to 1958 president of the Royal Musical Association, taking the chair at most of its meetings during his term of office—a fact which in itself is enough to show the range of his scholarship and his interests.

At various times he engaged in other musical tasks. He held the chairmanship of the Council for Music in Hospitals; of the working committee of the Institute of Recorded Sound; and, from 1950 to 1955, of the B.B.C. Central Music Advisory Committee. He served on the music panel of the Arts Council. An Honorary Fellow of the Royal College of Music, on his retirement from *The Times* he was made an Honorary Freeman of the Worshipful Company of Musicians.

So full a career would have left most men with little time in which to create a body of critical and scholarly writing, some of which can still be seen as valuable pioneering work. An instructed interest in psychology prompted his first book *The Borderland of Music and Psychology*, published in 1926; its successor, which appeared two years later, was *The Appreciation of Music*, which handled some of his new material in a more popular way. *A Key to the Art of Music* (*1935*) and its successor, *A Key to Opera* (in which Howes collaborated with Philip Hope-Wallace in 1938), with *Full Orchestra*, applied to writing his skill as a lecturer and his fluent clarity of style. *Music and Meanings* developed trains of thought from his earliest writings.

His enthusiasm for English music resulted, in 1928, in his critical biography of Byrd and in two studies for the *Musical Pilgrim* series—*The Music of Vaughan Williams* and *The Music of William Walton*— which grew into major studies of these composers in 1954 and 1965. Together with a British Council publication, *Music: 1945-50,* they were preliminary to another major book *The English Musical Renaissance,* published in 1966, in which detailed history and sympathetic analysis worked together to explain a development in the later stages of which Howes himself had played a not inconsiderable part. This book was, perhaps, the one which lay closest to his heart; at any rate, though Howes was never a writer who paraded facile enthusiasms, its quiet lucidity does not hide his intense sympathy with the subject. He published a history of the Cheltenham Music Festival during the period from 1960 to 1972 when he was chairman of the management committee and had steered it towards international status.

His day to day writings as a critic were all marked by scholarship and intellectual vigour. He was always, in the phrase of E. J. Dent, "on the side of the performer."

His purpose was to discover and evaluate the intention behind a performance and the attitude of the performer to the music he played. He wrote with a seriousness and an innate courtesy which prevented him from succumbing to the critic's occupational temptation of writing to demonstrate his own wit and cleverness at the expense of performers. Humour was not a quality he lacked, but he did not regard it as one of the essential tools of the critic.

A similar courtesy marked not only his treatment of people but also of the music which failed to engage his sympathies. To new music, even when it obviously followed styles which he rejected, he brought an informed interest and a keen analytical sense sharpened by intellectual curiosity; these qualities enabled him to write always informatively, sometimes very penetratingly, of works he cordially disliked.

He was not, however, one of those who grow into a conservative dislike of anything new. It is easy to remember his enthusiasm, even after his retirement, for music which made few concessions to tastes formed in the first 30 years of the century. His views were positive and decisively expressed, supported always by reason and knowledge; if his intuitions were not equally alive to every style of music or to the works of all composers, he regarded it as a duty to write fairly of what was on the paper and what emerged from the instruments playing it. If not all music aroused emotions, the task of criticism was one which he regarded as a discipline compelling him to write honestly not only of his own attitudes but of the work before him. He was created C.B.E. in 1954.

In 1929 Howes married Barbara Tidd Pratt. They had a son and three daughters.

September 30, 1974.

Lord Howick of Glendale, K.G., G.C.M.G., K.C.V.O., who as Governor of Kenya helped crush the Mau Mau, died in Alnwick on March 10, 1973. He was 69.

Evelyn Baring was born on September 29, 1903, being the only child of the First Earl of Cromer by his second wife, Lady Katharine Thynne, daughter of the fourth Marquess of Bath, He may be said to have been born in the proconsular purple, and at the same time he inherited the Baring tradition of business ability.

Educated at Winchester and New College, Oxford, where he graduated with first class honours in history in 1924, it was his ambition to enter the Indian Civil Service, which he joined in 1926. But his destiny lay in Africa, and after only three years service in India he found himself assigned as Secretary to the Indian Agent-General in South Africa. Here he remained until 1934, when his overseas career appeared to be cut short in its prime by ill-health which forced him to resign. Returning to England, he entered the family firm of Baring Brothers, but kept

up some contact with Africa by serving on the London Board of the Sudan Gezira Cotton Syndicate. In 1935 he married Lady Mary Cecil Grey, elder daughter of the fifth Earl Grey.

On the outbreak of the Second World War, Baring took up a temporary appointment in the Foreign Office, and in 1942 he was offered and accepted the Governorship of Southern Rhodesia. In his discharge of the duties of the office, he was noted—and, in some quarters, criticized—for his liberal attitude towards Africans. He was not there for long, however; in 1944 he was appointed United Kingdom High Commissioner in South Africa, a post which, for the next seven years, was to tax all his resources of diplomacy and administrative ability. The High Commissioner was not only the diplomatic representative of his government to the Government of the Union but was also, in relation to the three "High Commission" territories (Basutoland, the Bechuanaland Protectorate and Swaziland), the equivalent of a colonial Governor, directly responsible to the United Kingdom Government for their administration.

During the earlier years of Baring's tenure of office, Smuts was still Prime Minister of the Union, and relations between the Union and the British Governments were untroubled. With the advent of the Nationalist Party to power in 1948, the task of the High Commissioner became far more difficult and delicate, especially as the racial policy of the Union Government moved in a direction unpalatable to the British public opinion and incompatible with the prevailing trend in Commonwealth development. This would in any event have created an awkward situation, but the anomalous position of the High Commission territories added to the tension. The problems were administrative as well as diplomatic. In 1948 a wave of ritual murders swept through Basutoland, even some of the Senior Chiefs being involved. Then followed the long-drawn controversy over the marriage of Seretse Khama and the repercussions which ensued. It is significant that, in the painful dilemma in which he was placed, Baring managed to retain the personal friendship of both Seretse and Tshekedi.

Baring's term of office in South Africa was due to expire in 1949, but was twice extended for a year; and then, after a short interval, he was appointed Governor of Kenya in 1952.

Years later, in an article contributed to *The Times*, he described Kenya as "a land of both danger and hope". It may be said that he found it a land of danger and left it one of hope. He took over when the Mau Mau terror was rising to its peak, and, whereas his real interest was in promoting agricultural and economic development, he was obliged to concentrate his efforts for the time being on the problem of restoring law and order. In this uncongenial task he succeeded in combining firmness with a liberal attitude towards African aspirations. Inevitably this led to his policies coming under attack from many sides, but he continued steadfast in his belief that the problems of Kenya could be solved only by the cooperation of all races, and in his determination to bring this cooperation about.

The strain told on his never robust health, and he was forced to take sick leave in 1954. He returned refreshed to an improving local situation. By 1956 he was able to say: "The worst is very much over. Most of our efforts now are turned towards peaceful development". In 1957 his term of office was extended to March 1959 and then again to September of that year.

During that September, while on a farewell tour of the Colony, he was resting on a beach at Malindi when he was asked to go to the help of two Indian girls in difficulties in the sea. He dashed into the waves and succeeded in saving one of the girls at the serious risk of his own life. For this gallant rescue he was awarded the Queen's Commendation for Brave Conduct.

The closing months of his Governorship were overshadowed by the Hola incident. But, taking as a whole the seven years during which he filled what, even in favourable circumstances, was one of the most difficult of colonial Governorships, there can be no doubt of his claim to be accounted a great Governor of Kenya. If his personal aloofness at times made his relations with Europeans uneasy, he showed great insight in his dealings with Africans. "His methods", said *The Times* in a valedictory leading article on his retirement from the Governorship, "could be infuriating to subordinates, but his high intelligence, his capacity for political manoeuvre, and his fundamental strength of character won through. Nobody could take longer to arrive at a decision and nobody could be more ruthless in carrying it out, once arrived at. He was excessively flexible, but those who mistook flexibility for weakness were wrong."

Baring had been created K.C.M.G. in 1942 and K.C.V.O. in 1947. In 1955 he was promoted to G.C.M.G. and he was elevated to a barony in the New Year honours list of 1960, taking the title of Howick of Glendale. He was appointed a Knight of the Garter in 1972.

In April 1960 he became deputy chairman of the Colonial Development Corporation and he succeeded to the chairmanship in December of the same year. Howick became chairman when C.D.C. was faced with contraction of its original (colonial) area of operations while its investment resources were almost fully committed. Building on the sound foundation established under Lord Reith, Howick used his persuasive powers and great personal prestige in Whitehall to obtain additional finance from the British Government and reinstatement in the newly independent Commonwealth countries (involving a corresponding change of name). Before his retirement in June 1972 C.D.C. had been authorized to invest

also in non-Commonwealth developing countries and its borrowing powers were raised to £225m in recognition of its outstanding success.

Howick's earlier experience had convinced him of the importance of agriculture to the mass of the people in the poorer countries. At C.D.C. he did everything he could to expand agricultural operations including the fostering of cooperation between C.D.C. and the World Bank. He toured regularly overseas, taking a personal and detailed interest in everyone and everything; his little black notebooks were universally and affectionately known. He took particular pride in the success of the Kenya Tea Smallholders' scheme and Usutu Forests in Swaziland, both of which he had helped at the start in his proconsular days before joining C.D.C.

By his marriage he had one son and two daughters.

March 12, 1973.

Godfrey Huggins, 1st Viscount Malvern—See Malvern.

Vice-Admiral John Hughes Hallett, C.B., D.S.O., who died on April 5, 1972 at the age of 70, was naval commander for the Dieppe raid of 1942 and later served as Commodore Commanding the Channel Assault Force and Naval Chief of Staff. He was awarded a D.S.O. for daring and resolution in the Dieppe raid. He played an important part in the planning of the invasion of Normandy in June 1944—for his work he was created C.B. He was Flag Officer, Heavy Squadron, Home Fleet, 1952-53.

In December 1944 the First Lord of the Admiralty, Mr. A. V. Alexander (later Lord Alexander of Hillsborough*), said in a parliamentary answer that it was Hughes Hallett who was the first to suggest the use of an artificial harbour for the landings in Normandy.

He sat as Conservative M.P. for East Croydon in 1954-55 and for North East Croydon from 1955 to 1964. He was Parliamentary Secretary to the Ministry of Transport for Shipping and Shipbuilding from 1961 to 1964.

From 1957 to 1960 he was a governor of Westminster Hospital.

Born in 1901 Hughes Hallett, the son of Colonel Wyndham Hughes Hallett, was educated at Bedford School, Osborne and Dartmouth and Gonville and Caius College, Cambridge. He served in H.M.S. Lion, flagship of the Battle Cruiser Force, towards the end of World War 1.

For many years Admiral Hughes Hallett specialized in torpedoes, having a special interest in torpedo propulsion. This knowledge led to his appointment in command of H.M.S. Vernon, the Navy's Torpedo and Anti-Submarine School in 1946. He was

also an officer with considerable knowledge and experience of naval aviation. He held a civil flying "A" licence, and while serving in H.M.S. Courageous between the wars was jointly responsible with another officer, since killed, for producing the first lighting system for night landing on aircraft carriers which did not depend on flood-lights.

While serving as a captain in 1941 he was mentioned in dispatches for services at the evacuation of Namsos, Central Norway, when in H.M.S. Devonshire. He left the Devonshire towards the end of that year on being appointed Naval Adviser to Combined Operations, in which appointment he acted as Chairman of the Raid Planning Committee for the St. Nazaire and Dieppe raids.

In December 1943 he took command of the cruiser Jamaica, being present at the sinking of the German battleship Scharnhorst, an operation during which he earned another mention in dispatches.

In June 1948 Hughes Hallett took command of the aircraft carrier Illustrious, and following promotion to Rear-Admiral in January 1950, he was chairman of the board of enquiry set up to investigate the loss of the submarine H.M.S. Truculent.

April 6, 1972.

Sir David Hughes Parry—See Parry.

Lieutenant-Colonel Sir Francis Humphrys G.C.M.G., G.C.V.O., K.B.E., C.I.E., who died on August 28, 1971 at the age of 92, had a versatile career of marked distinction in the diplomatic field, especially as British Minister in Afghanistan during the prolonged tribal unrest in the late 1920s leading to the deposition of King Amanullah.

Humphrys had previously shared in the work of transforming the Mesopotamia of the First World War under British occupation into the self-governing kingdom of Iraq. In the years of City activity after retirement his many interests included the chairmanship of the Iraq Petroleum Co. His coolness of judgment was linked with a strong personality and, combined with his charm of manner, inspired the complete confidence of those with whom he was brought into close contact.

Francis Henry Humphrys was born on April 24, 1879, the eldest son of the Rev. Walter Humphrys. His mother also came from a clerical family, being the daughter of the Rev. A. F. Boucher. Francis was educated at Shrewsbury and Christ Church, Oxford. In 1900 he was gazetted to the 2nd Worcestershire Regiment, and served in the South African war in that year and 1901, being awarded the Queen's Medal with three clasps. He continued in military employment until 1902 when he was appointed an Assistant Commissioner in India, as the prelude to his selection to be Personal Assistant to the Chief Commissioner of the newly created North West Frontier Province, the late Colonel Sir Harold Deane, whose daughter Gertrude Mary he married in 1907. A son and two daughters were born to them, and Lady Humphrys was created a D.B.E. in 1929 for her services in Kabul during the crisis. In 1907 Humphrys was appointed an Assistant Commissioner serving successively in Hazara and Charsadda. Later as a Deputy Commissioner he had experience in most other parts of the N.W.F.

Humphrys's early experience as an Army Officer was supplemented in the 1914-18 War by holding a temporary commission as a pilot in the R.A.F. in 1918. There was much unrest on the frontier, and in 1917 he served with the Waziristan Field Force as Political Officer. In the autumn of 1919 he was made Political Agent in the Khyber. Later he had a short experience at Delhi as Officiating Deputy Secretary in the Foreign and Political Department.

In 1922 Humphrys was selected to be Minister in Afghanistan, and was soon concerned with the reforming zeal of the young King Amanullah, who, in order to gain new ideas for the transformation he had in mind, planned, in consultation with the British Representative at Kabul, an extensive tour of foreign lands and especially of Europe. In a farewell speech in December 1927 Amanullah spoke of his country as having said goodbye forever to her stationary position, and having joined the social, living nations of the age. He was accompanied by his wife and, after visits to Italy, Belgium, Switzerland, France and Germany, he went to Britain in 1928. Humphrys had gone to London three months earlier to plan the itinerary of the royal pair in visiting various institutions and manufacturing centres.

In effect the Ambassador had temporarily turned courier. During the seven months of the absence of the King there was increasing discontent among the tribesmen. The King was more determined than ever to follow the example of Mustafa Kemal in his modernization of Turkish life, but the opposition to his policy had developed and he was soon forced to abdicate. The Legation was subjected to heavy fire from the revolutionaries, and the spirit in which Humphrys confronted the perils and responsibilities imposed upon him was warmly commended in the House of Commons by Government speakers. It was decided to use aircraft for the evacuation of British, Indian and other foreigners, and Humphrys, with a small staff, was the last to leave Kabul.

Humphrys arrived in Baghdad as High Commissioner late in 1929 at a time of great political tension and unrest when the Iraqis were pressing hard for immediate independence.

Wisdom and coolness of judgment were required of H.M.'s representative at such a time. These he had as well as a strong personality which with his charm of manner inspired complete confidence among British and Iraqis alike. Within a year with great skill and patience he negotiated a treaty with Iraq and there followed in due course the termination of the Mandate and Iraq's entry into the League of Nations in 1932.

This marked the beginning of a new era and in 1932 he became Britain's first Ambassador to Iraq. There were many knotty problems to solve with the handing over of responsibility and until he left, in 1935, he handled them all with unruffled skill and serenity. He took infinite trouble in finding new work for those British officials in Iraq whose contracts were prematurely terminated through no fault of their own. His tour of service in Iraq was one of great distinction and is still remembered in that country.

Humphrys retired from public service in 1935, and became a prominent figure in the City. For some years he was Chairman of the British Sugar Corporation Limited, and held a similar appointment with the Clerical Medical and General Life Assurance Society, General Reversionary and Investment Co. and Brixton Estates Ltd.

September 1, 1971.

Former Primate of Hungary—See Mindszenty.

Haroldson Lafayette Hunt, the oil magnate, who died in Dallas, Texas, on November 29, 1974, was one of the ten richest men in the world. He was 85.

A virulent rightwinger, health food and yoga addict, he had simple tastes by the standards of the typical tycoon, owning no private jet or yacht and carrying his lunch to work with him in a brown paper bag.

After leaving school at the age of ten, Hunt built up a personal fortune estimated at about $5,000m (about £2,200m), making him perhaps one of the three richest men in the United States. He was one of the original Texas "wildcatters", or freelance oil prospectors in the oil boom days of the early part of this century, and later invested widely. He shunned publicity and liked to think of himself as a man of the people.

Hunt started life as a farm boy in Illinois, and was successively a hobo, lumberjack and dishwasher. Although he made his money in oil he considered that his other enterprises, from cattle ranches to electronics, canned chickens, asphalt and roses brought him in more money. Unlike Carnegie, Rockefeller, Ford and the rest, he did not spend his money on philanthropy.

"I'm more interested in the accumulation of properties than in their liquidation and distribution," he once said. How did he justify his duty to the community? "By furnishing gainful employment. I think that is one of the most important things anyone can do."

Hunt reckoned he could have made three or more times as much if he had not devoted so much of his time to political education. His Lifeline Foundation sponsored a daily 15-minute programme over 384 radio stations and brought out a newsletter reflecting the views of the extreme right wing in American politics.

December 2, 1974.

Professor Herbert James Hunt, Emeritus Professor in the University of London, Fellow Emeritus of St. Edmund Hall, Oxford, and formerly Senior Fellow in French at the University of Warwick, from 1966 to 1970, died on November 2, 1973. He was 74.

Herbert Hunt was born at Lichfield on August 2, 1899, and he was educated there, at King Edward VI School and at Magdalen College, Oxford. After teaching for four years at Imperial Service College and at Durham School he returned to Oxford as Fellow and Tutor of St. Edmund Hall (1927-44), and as lecturer at Exeter and Jesus Colleges. He went to the University of London as Professor of French and Head of the French Department at Royal Holloway College in 1944, and played an active part in the affairs of the college, and as Chairman of the University Board of Studies in Romance Languages and Literatures over a number of years. He retired from London in 1966.

His contribution to French studies was in the field of the French novel and epic in the nineteenth century; everything he wrote gave evidence of meticulous research and was propounded with clarity of exposition and—in English and French alike—elegance of style.

In his first book, *Le Socialisme et le Romantisme en France* (1935), he based upon a detailed examination of the French socialist press between 1830 and 1848 an investigation into the attempts of leading Saint-Simoniens and other politically-minded "sectarians" to proselytize great French authors of the time, whose reactions he then traced. *The Epic in Nineteenth-Century France* (1941) shows a related preoccupation, among both great and lesser writers of the age, with the question eternally asked of poets by nineteenth century seekers after truth: "Poète, d'où vient l'humanité, et où va-t-elle?". His qualities as editor and commentator of texts appear in his edition of selections from *La Légende des Siècles* (1945), where he provides an exposition of Hugo's elusive and often self-contradictory metaphysical doctrines. He wrote many articles and reviews, and was a valued member of the editorial board of *French Studies*.

But his major achievement lies in the two volumes on Balzac, of which the first, *Honoré de Balzac: a Biography*, appeared in 1957 as a biographical prelude to the second book, *Balzac's 'Comédie Humaine'* (1959), which comprised a survey of the complex of novels forming the *Comédie*.

Here the pattern of the historical development of the whole gigantic project is brought out very clearly, and Balzac's own increasing awareness of the interrelationships of its parts. Although, with characteristic modesty, Hunt disclaimed any intention of providing a general assessment of Balzac's work, he does in fact do so, by implication.

The merits of this major study give a particular interest and authority to his subsequent contributions, as editor (*Eugénie Grandet*, 1967) and as translator (*Cousin Pons*, 1968 etc.) of Balzac; in both capacities Hunt shows an exceptionally fine sense of style and meaning; he was stimulated too by the challenge presented by Balzac's vast range of allusions, sometimes misunderstood by previous translators, not surprisingly.

Herbert Hunt was a loyal and kindly man, hospitable and affectionate to his friends, but impatient of pretentiousness in any form. His was a robust religious faith, characteristically supported by an impressive knowledge of Christian doctrine. A fitting acknowledgement of his fine qualities and achievements was made in 1972, with the publication of the volume *Balzac and the Nineteenth Century: Studies in French Literature*, presented by pupils, colleagues and friends, and edited by D. G. Charlton, J. Gaudon and Anthony Pugh (Leicester University Press).

He was twice married and is survived by his second wife and by two sons and three daughters of his first marriage.

November 6, 1973.

Norman C. Hunter, the playwright and novelist, who died on April 19, 1971 at the age of 62, was a man who in the previous 20 years brought a new sensitivity into the conventional commercial theatre. While the theatrical revolution of the late 1950s exploded round him, Hunter, who had been writing for 17 years before success greeted his tenth play in 1951, continued undisturbed to write within the tradition he had managed to extend.

Norman Charles Hunter was born on September 18, 1908, in Derbyshire. He was educated at Repton and Sandhurst before serving for three years in the Dragoon Guards. His first play, *The Merciless Lady,* was written in collaboration with John Ferguson in 1934, and he followed it with *All Rights Reserved, Ladies and Gentlemen, The Little Stranger, Party for Christmas, Galleons Gold* and *Smith in Arcady* before the outbreak of war in 1939. He was, too, on the staff of the B.B.C. in the years immediately before the war.

Although none of his pre-war plays had made a deep impression Hunter returned to drama in 1947, after war service in the Royal Artillery, but it was not until 1951, after two more unregarded plays, that *Waters of the Moon* established him as a writer who brought a new tone and unfamiliar nuances into the English theatre. The play was given a prestige production worthy of the year of the Festival of Britain and a splendid cast headed by Dame Sybil Thorndike and Dame Edith Evans. *A Day by the Sea,* two years later, was a further exploration of the vein of experience Hunter had begun to work in *Waters of the Moon,* and it, too, was given a cast capable of exploiting its ambiguities and subtleness of feeling: Dame Sybil Thorndike, Sir John Gielgud and Sir Ralph Richardson found in it the material for quiet, sensitive and moving playing. *A Touch of the Sun,* in 1958, offered the same opportunities to Sir Michael Redgrave, Diana Wynyard* and Vanessa Redgrave.

The Tulip Tree, which followed in 1962, after *A Piece of Silver,* was possibly an advance on Hunter's earlier successes in the range and variety of material it involved, but without a star-studded cast it made less impression than it should, and Hunter's final plays, *The Excursion* and *The Adventures of Tom Random,* did not rival his three big successes of the 1950s.

Waters of the Moon and its successors were immediately described by audiences and critics as "Chekovian". There is a good deal of truth in that adjective, for their characters are occupied with living, rather than in acting out a critical situation. The plays established them as characters by revealing what in their personalities and past experiences has conditioned them into varied states of regret and ineffectualness. But Hunter lacked the ruthlessness of the Russian master, displaying the weakness and futility of his characters not simply as an act of dramatic analysis but in order to induce audiences to understand and pity them. Nevertheless, the plays offered the West End theatre an alternative way to that of the revolutionary dramatists of the fifties out of a tradition which had become an impasse.

N. C. Hunter was also a novelist. *The Ascension of Mr. Judson,* in 1949, and *The Losing Hazard,* in 1950, were his works in this form which attracted most attention.

April 20, 1971.

Sir Percy Hunting, who was chairman of the Hunting Group of Companies from 1927 to 1960, died on January 2, 1973.

The family fortunes were founded on the land, but later they were transferred to shipping, and still later, under his guidance, what has become known as the Hunting Group developed into one of the most diversified commercial undertakings under British control, including one of the largest networks of aerial survey and mapping organizations in the world. Its investigations revealed, and led to the development of, some of the largest natural resources in at least three continents during this century, and, in one respect at least, Hunting's efforts made history when they resulted in a new strike of oil in Texas.

Percy Llewellyn Hunting was born on March 6, 1885, the elder son of Charles S. Hunting. Hunting was educated at Loretto, and afterwards Paris, and finally Armstrong College at Newcastle upon Tyne, where he studied Marine Engineering. In order to gain practical experience, Hunting went into the workshops of the North-Eastern Marine Engineering Co. During the First World War, he was commissioned in the 4th Territorial Battalion of The Northumberland Fusiliers, with whom he served for some time, but it was his seconding to the Royal Flying Corps, in which his younger brother, Lindsay Hunting, also served, that had decisive results upon the future careers of both of them in the world of commerce.

After the end of hostilities they decided to expand the interest of the family concern into aviation, and as a result there was added to the company's operations a chain of companies involved not only in prospecting for and investigating the world's natural resources, but also a series of aircraft repair and servicing companies in Britain, Canada and Africa. To all this was subsequently added the manufacture of light engineering and equipment, paint manufacturing and oil broking in the City of London, so that eventually there was scarcely any branch of these various enterprises into which the Huntings had not penetrated.

For the greater part of his life Hunting was associated with various organizations connected with the industries in which he was concerned. These included the International Tanker Owners Association, of which from 1934 to 1950 he was deputy chairman; the British Chamber of Shipping Oil Tanker Committee, of which he had been both vice-chairman and then chairman; and the Tramp Tanker Committee, of which he was chairman from 1940 to 1943. He was knighted in 1960.

In 1910, he married Dorothy, eldest daughter of Daniel Birkett of Bexhill-on-Sea, by whom he had two sons, one of whom was lost on active service in H.M.S. Repulse in 1941. His wife died in 1958, and he married secondly, in 1960, Evelyn Marion Birkett.

January 3, 1973.

Lord Hurcomb, G.C.B, K.B.E., wartime Director-General of the Ministry of Shipping and of the Ministry of War Transport, died on August 7, 1975 at the age of 92. His magnificent service during the 1939-45 war was undoubtedly the outstanding peak of his long career.

Cyril William Hurcomb was educated at Oxford High School and St. John's College, Oxford, of which he was made an honorary Fellow in 1938. He entered the Civil Service in 1906 and was appointed to the G.P.O., where, from 1911 onwards, he was private secretary to successive P.M.Gs., among them Lord Samuel*.

He first entered the transport field, in which he spent most of his official life, in 1915, when the Ministry of Shipping was formed and housed in the hideous temporary buildings on the bed of the dried-up St. James's Park lake. There he joined a brilliant team which included John Anderson, afterwards Lord Waverley, and Arthur Salter, later Lord Salter, and worked as Deputy Director of Commercial Services under Sir Percy Bates, of the Cunard Line, with whom he formed a close and lasting friendship. Later, he succeeded Sir Percy as Director of Commercial Services with the responsibility for planning the civil import programme for the country.

After the war he went to the newly-formed Ministry of Transport and remained in that turbulent Ministry, first as Director of Finance, and later in higher positions—he became Permanent Secretary in 1927—suffering rapid changes of Minister and living under the continual threat of abolition, until he was appointed Chairman of the Electricity Commission in 1937.

His experience in the First World War made him the obvious choice to take charge when, at the outbreak of war in 1939, the new Ministry of Shipping was set up to control the operation of shipping and to ensure its most advantageous use in the war effort. This time the Ministry took over also the Marine functions of the Board of Trade, which had not happened in the First World War.

He realized at once that the shipping shortage which was bound to show itself very soon would call for the complete control of all British ships, of their voyages and of their cargoes, and the chartering of as much foreign tonnage as possible. Later, when most of Europe had been overrun, comprehensive agreements were made with the free governments of the main maritime nations, who had then become allies, for the chartering of practically all their ships.

Representatives of those governments were brought into the ministry and assisted in deciding what individual ships—particularly those of their own flag—were to do. They knew they could count on him, with the full support of his colleagues, to see that, even in exile, their views really counted. Thus Hurcomb brought about a happy cooperation of all those countries in this vital and difficult task.

While the Ministry of Shipping thus gained control of the bulk of the tonnage of the free world, except that of the United States, the Ministries of Food and of Supply and the Board of Trade determined the nature of the imports required, and the extremely complicated task of drawing up shipping programmes was carried out by these Departments working together with the ministry. That Britain during war received the supplies of food and materials necessary to sustain the population and to mobilize, transport and supply the fighting forces was due in no small measure to the foresight and driving energy of Cyril Hurcomb.

He foresaw the severity of the coming shortage of shipping long before it made itself felt, and insisted that the planning machinery should be devised and put into operation in proper time. He also saw that shipping must be controlled by an independent department which itself made no claims on shipping services.

It was largely his stout resistance that averted the disaster which would inevitably have overtaken the war effort as a whole had any of the opinionated groups, civil or military, who were so vocal from time to time, succeeded in wresting control of any part of the merchant fleet from the Ministry. Publications some while ago about Lord Cherwell have revealed something of what he had constantly to contend with—quite apart from the activities of the King's enemies. It was said of him once by a man who worked closely with him, but had no great personal liking for him, that he was one of the foremost among the men whose foresight, capacity and energy had saved us from losing the war. This was a just tribute.

When, in May 1941, Churchill* became Prime Minister and amalgamated the old Ministry of Transport with the Ministry of Shipping to form the Ministry of War Transport under Lord Leathers,* Hurcomb took charge of the new Ministry. His responsibilities were widened but his main preoccupation was still the maintenance of our supplies from overseas, vital to our ability to continue to fight the war and, indeed, to our very existence, and the main target of Hitler's effort at sea.

The entry of the United States into the war introduced a new factor promising great and growing military assistance but at the same time increasing the demands upon the already inadequate supply of ships. Clearly the Americans must retain control of their own ships and of many other ships operating in or from the western hemisphere and, equally clearly, the use of all the ships of the free world must be coordinated. The solution, for which Hurcomb was again largely responsible, was to set up an Anglo-American organization, the Combined Shipping Adjustment Board, to control the joint fleets. All ships were regarded as being in a single pool, controlled from two centres, London and Washington. The working of this machine, and the difficulties it encountered, have been well described in the Official History.

Hurcomb's major tasks remained the same, to prevent the starving of this country of food and materials in spite of sinkings and delays, to provide for the continually rising demands for shipping services for military purposes, and to send food and other supplies to countries overseas, particularly in emergencies such as droughts in India and East Africa. Subsidiary problems there were in plenty, for example that of overcoming the strain on inland transport due to the virtual closing of the East Coast ports, particularly London.

When the war ended Hurcomb remained in charge of the Ministry, which dropped the word "War" from its title, and was involved almost at once in the task of devising legislation to "integrate" inland transport, as the political watchword of the day had it, which meant to nationalize the major part of the inland transport of the country. When the Transport Act, 1947, came into force it was Hurcomb who was chosen for the not altogether enviable task of operating the machine which he had been required to play a major part in devising, for he was appointed Chairman of the British Transport Commission when it was set up in 1947.

He applied himself with his usual energy to the supervision of the complex tasks of transferring control of the railways from the Railway Companies to the new Railway Executive, and of the canals and the railway-owned docks to the Docks and Inland Waterways Executive, the acquiring of long-distance road haulage and the initiation of draft area schemes (which were not put into effect) for the control of passenger road transport and the coordination of the operation of docks. He retired in 1953 with some relief soon after the passing of the Conservative Government's amending Transport Act of that year.

From that time he was able to devote himself to ornithology, nature conservation and fishing, which had always been his main interests outside the office.

Fishing had been a lifelong passion, so much so that even during the most severe crises his punctiliousness for duty was apt to waver when the mayfly were due to rise. Like many keen fishermen he gradually became more and more absorbed in the wild creatures around him, above all in the birds, and his experience as Chairman of the Electricity Commission brought him into contact with large civil engineering projects which were often opposed by local interests and which turned his attention ever more keenly towards the immense problems of conservation of nature in a technically developing civilization.

While Chairman of the British Transport Commission he took on the Chairmanship of the Committee on Bird Sanctuaries in the Royal Parks and the Presidency of the Society for the Promotion of Nature Reserves, and later his international friendships and interests led to his appointment in 1954 as Vice-President of the International Union for the Conservation of Nature and Natural Resources. His unfailing support and wise guidance played a decisive part in steering this young international body to success, and culminated in a memorable speech at Cracow in 1960 when he succeeded against long odds in securing a unanimous resolution for drastic reorganization, involving a move of the headquarters from Belgium to Switzerland. The confidence felt in his integrity and disinterestedness by so many foreign representatives of widely differing temperaments was most impressive.

R

Evidence of similar confidence at home was afforded by the many leading positions which he was persuaded to accept in his nominal retirement—chairman of the Council, and later President, of the Royal Society for the Protection of Birds, President of the Field Studies Council, Founder President of the council for Nature, Chairman of the Committee for England of the Nature Conservancy and, from April 1961 to April 1962 of the Conservancy itself.

In accepting one of these offices he specifically stipulated that he would do so only on the understanding that he should have a mandate to promote closer relations between the different bodies in the same field. He was tireless, even in his late seventies, in journeying to address and encourage Naturalists' Trusts all over England, and took pride in serving in 1961 as the Centenary President of the Yorkshire Naturalists' Union. He was also active as a British Trustee of the World Wildlife Fund.

The menace to bird life from the discharge into the sea of oil residues concerned him always.

Hurcomb's character was complex and even contradictory. In administration he was quick to make up his mind, stubborn and unyielding in argument and often apparently blind to points of view other than his own. As a Chairman, however, he often tended to be almost too tolerant for the quick dispatch of business and he had a quizzical, almost a connoisseur's, appreciation of unorthodox or rebellious persons and opinions.

On formal occasions he was impressively objective and judicial with a felicitous command of English and a rare dry humour—on paper also he had a beautiful prose style.

He did not inspire affection in his official life except among the few who knew him well—and probably he had no wish to do so—but no one who knew him could doubt his profound integrity, his outstanding ability, his energy and his devotion to any cause in which he believed, whether it was the preservation of wild life and our heritage of natural beauty or the winning of a war. His country and the free world owe more to him than those outside a small circle who were close to him can ever know.

Hurcomb, who was elevated to the peerage in 1950, married Dorothy Brooke in 1911—she died in 1947—and had two daughters.

August 8, 1975.

Sol Hurok, the American impresario, died early in March 1974.

Hurok landed in the United States in 1906 with $1.50, as a Russian immigrant from the small town of Pogar.

He became one of the world's showmen, dedicated to bringing music and dance to the American people.

During his career he presented Marian Anderson, Artur Rubinstein, Isaac Stern, Anna Pavlova, Isadora Duncan, Margot Fonteyn, the Oistrakhs, Victoria de los Angeles, Fedor Chaliapin, Galina Ulanova and many others.

He organized the appearances of the Royal Ballet and the Bolshoi Ballet, after which he became a leading American agent for artistic exchanges with the Soviet Government, as well as with companies from the Old Vic and the Comédie Française.

Hurok was filled with boundless self-confidence, curiosity and a belief in the qualities of youth; and he turned his obsession for music and dancing into a personal fortune while at the same time promoting international understanding.

In 1969 Hurok sold S. Hurok Concerts Inc., which was making between £3m. and £4m. a year, to the Transcontinental Investing Corporation.

By the first of his two marriages he had one child.

March 7, 1974.

A. S. M. Hutchinson, the novelist and author of *If Winter Comes,* the prewar best-seller, and 15 other books, died on March 13, 1971. He was 91. Hutchinson was editor of *The Daily Graphic* from 1912 to 1916.

Hutchinson published his best-selling *If Winter Comes* in 1921—it sold some half a million copies in America and a quarter-million in Britain. The secret of its popularity led to a correspondence in *The Times* —Margot Asquith (who had confessed to crying herself to sleep over the hero's misfortunes) wrote that "in Mark Sabre the author has brought out the highest qualities of man, and those generally associated with Christ—tenderness, patience and compassion". Other correspondents agreed that Mark Sabre typifies the Christian virtues. The book's American publisher reported that more than a thousand clergymen of different denominations had preached sermons about him. A High Court judge thought that he provided a moral bulwark against social and industrial unrest. One critic, however, observed that "to the majority Mark Sabre must be what most sentimental good fools, living a dull business life, think they resemble".

Mark Sabre, another critic commented, is a good dull man, cheated by his hypocritical business partners, ostracized by his neighbours and tortured by the law. He is painfully honest, and afflicted with the ability to see the other fellow's point of view.

Arthur Stuart Menteth Hutchinson was born on June 2, 1879, in India, the son of General H. D. Hutchinson, a distinguished soldier of the British Indian Army; his mother was a Stuart-Menteth. His father was the writer of several military textbooks. Debarred by deficient eyesight from going with his two brothers into the army, Hutchinson became a medical student at St. Thomas's Hospital, and after a few years abandoned a medical career to be a journalist and author.

His first novel, *Once Aboard the Lugger,* was published in 1908 when he was night editor of *The Daily Graphic; The Happy Warrior* and *The Clean Heart* followed before *If Winter Comes.* He served in the First World War and wrote other novels; *It Happened Like This* appeared in 1942 and *Bring Back the Days* in 1958.

March 15, 1971.

R. C. Hutchinson, an accomplished novelist, died on July 3, 1975 at the age of 68.

His work combined narrative skill with a sympathetic insight into human character and he had a high reputation among a discerning public. He was entirely at ease with a large subject and won the *Sunday Times* Gold Medal for fiction in 1938 with *Testament*, a grandly-conceived novel about the Russian Revolution.

Contemporary European history and the European condition were prominent both in his mind and in his work. Committed writing, required of authors under some political regimes was, in his view, foreign to the novelist's art but he thought that, broadly speaking, a story lacked artistic shape if it did not imply some moral assumptions. His own philosophy was a Christian one, but he was too sound a craftsman to fall into the trap of engaging himself in didactic writing.

He was made a Fellow of the Royal Society of Literature in 1962 and in 1966 won the W. H. Smith Annual Literary Award for his book *A Child Possessed,* the story of the love of a Russian émigré, Stepan Lopuchine, now a long-distance lorry driver in France, for his retarded daughter Eugénie. The book had been published in 1964.

His other published books included *Thou Hast a Devil* (1930); *The Unforgotten Prisoner* (1933); *One Light Burning* (1935); *Shining Scabbard* (1936); *The Fire and the Wood* (1940); *Interim* (1945); *Elephant and Castle* (1949); *Recollection of a Journey* (1952); *March the Ninth* (1957); *Image of my Father* (1961); *Johanna at Daybreak* (1969); and *Origins of Cathleen* (1971).

Ray Coryton Hutchinson was born on January 23, 1907, the son of Harry Hutchinson, of Watford, and educated at Monkton Combe and Oriel College, Oxford. After coming down he worked in the advertising department of J. & J. Colman, of Norwich, mustard manufacturers. He had written from childhood and finished a 20,000 word novel while at school. He also wrote and published short stories—some appeared in the *English Review*—and his first novels were written after office hours. *Testament*, which brought him a measure of esteem, was translated into five languages.

In 1940 he was commissioned into the Army and put in command of a company of a newly formed battalion of The Buffs. Later he was a major in the War Office in London and early in 1945 was sent on a journey through Egypt, Palestine, Persia and Iraq in order to write an account of "Paiforce", the Persia and Iraq command.

He married in 1929 Margaret, daughter of Captain Owen Jones, C.B.E. They had two sons and two daughters.

July 5, 1975.

Sir Julian Huxley, F.R.S., who died on February 14, 1975 at the age of 87, was one of the best-known scientific personalities of our day. He set a seal on his age for the same qualities of mind, and for the same reasons, as did his famous grandfather, Thomas Henry Huxley, before him—insatiable curiosity in almost all intellectual fields; an irrepressible creative urge; a powerful memory; an inexhaustible capacity for work; and an unfaltering courage in stating views on social matters, regardless of their controversial nature or of their likely popularity or unpopularity.

Mostly interested in problems of evolution, he wrote on dozens of other subjects as well, and he wrote from his earliest days to his last. As was said of him on an occasion when he received an honorary degree, he was the brother of an imaginative writer who nearly became a scientist—the reference was to Aldous Huxley*, his younger brother—and was himself a scientist who might have developed as a poet.

Descended on his father's side from T. H. Huxley, and from Dr. Thomas Arnold of Rugby on his mother's, Julian Sorell Huxley was born on June 22, 1887, the eldest son of Leonard Huxley, editor of the *Cornhill Magazine*. He went to Eton as a King's Scholar, and later, as Brackenbury Scholar, to Balliol, in 1909 gaining both a first in his Zoology Schools and a Scholarship which permitted him to spend a year in the celebrated marine biological laboratory that had been founded in Naples by Dr. Dohrn. As an undergraduate he also won the Newdigate Prize for Poetry. After Naples, Huxley spent two more years at Balliol, as Lecturer in Zoology, and then went as assistant professor to the Rice Institute in Texas where he stayed from 1912 to 1916. It was there that he met the distinguished American geneticist, Hermann Muller,* the discoverer of the effects of radiations on heredity, and where he first appreciated the importance of genetics as a discipline basic to any understanding of the processes of selection and evolution.

After a period of war service in Italy, Huxley returned to Oxford in 1919 as Fellow of New College and Senior Demonstrator in Zoology. In 1925 he was appointed Professor of Zoology in King's College London, a post from which he resigned in 1927 in order to devote all his time to writing and research, and to the spread of scientific knowledge. Although he held the office of Fullerian Professor of Physiology at the Royal Institution from 1926 to 1929, the Professorship at King's was Huxley last academic post.

In the space of a paragraph or two it is impossible to give an idea of the scope of the scores of scientific papers and books which Julian Huxley published over the course of more than half a century. He was a pioneer in the scientific field-study of animal behaviour, and was an ardent ornithologist all his life. His paper on the courtship of the great crested grebe, published in 1914, remains a classic in its field. His work on the effect of genetic changes on the time relations of developmental processes in the freshwater shrimp was outstanding in its time. He studied the hormonal reactions of invertebrates, and was among the first to demonstrate the importance of thyroid hormone in the metamorphosis of tadpoles into frogs. He turned his attention to the differential growth of the parts of the body, and in 1932 published a book, *Problems of Relative Growth*, which, too, was a turning point in the study of this subject.

But his main claim to scientific fame derives not from all this but from a capacity for synthesis which gave him a special place among exponents of the theory of evolution. In 1940 he edited an important work called *The New Systematics,* to which he contributed an outstanding chapter on the relation of newer discoveries in genetics to animal classification. His *Evolution, the Modern Synthesis,* first published in 1948, remains the most comprehensive modern work on this subject, bringing together, as it does, the fruits of a wide range of naturalistic, genetical, and mathematical studies. In shorter books published in 1952 and 1953 Huxley elaborated an idea, first developed in the *Modern Synthesis,* that because of his mastery of the environment of the world, man had become "the *de facto* agent for further evolution on this planet", and alone possessed any further potentiality for significant evolutionary progress.

All this work was recognized by the award of the Darwin Medal of the Royal Society, to which he had been elected in 1938, and by a Festschrift published in his honour by a group of his colleagues in 1953, under the title of "Evolution as a Process". It was to Julian Huxley, too, that the honour was accorded of delivering the main address at the International Zoological Congress held in London in 1958 to mark the centenary of the joint publication by the Linnaean Society of Darwin's and Wallace's papers on the theory of evolution.

Julian Huxley's concern about man's dominant influence as a selective force in the world made him deeply interested in demographic studies, and in particular in the dangers inherent in the unrestricted growth of human population when unassociated with economic expansion. On this subject he wrote a great deal too. Much of his knowledge about conditions in underdeveloped countries came from travel. *Africa View,* published in 1931, was based on a visit paid to East Africa in 1929 to advise on native education. Huxley later became a member of the General Committee for Lord Hailey's* "African Survey", and also a member of the 1944 Commission set up to study the problem of higher education in West Africa.

Because of his experience and powerful interest in these questions, as well as his imaginative qualities as a scientist interested in public education, the British Government persuaded him, as a matter of urgency, to become the Secretary-General of the preparatory commission for Unesco. When this international institution was set up in 1946, he became its first Director-General. His awareness of the widespread need to conquer illiteracy in the world, coupled with his achievements as a general writer on scientific matters, provided just those qualities necessary to launch a project as grand as Unesco, even if his experience had failed to prepare him for the many administrative frustrations by which he was soon beset.

Julian Huxley's most influential work in the field of popular science should undoubtedly have been the ambitious *Science of Life,* which appeared in 1929 under the joint authorship of himself, H. G. Wells, and Professor G. P. Wells, F.R.S. But for some inexplicable reason this work did not appeal to the public as did many of his other exercises in popular education and particularly, perhaps, his association with the famed B.B.C. "Brains Trust", which weekly beguiled a vast radio audience during the 1939-45 World War.

From 1935 to 1942, when he resigned the office, Huxley was secretary of the Zoological Society of London. His many efforts to improve the society's educational activities were also not as much appreciated at the time as they were later. The outbreak of the war disrupted an imaginative programme of building which he had instituted, and which the great increase in costs since then has made difficult to resume on the scale he envisaged. For many years he gave powerful support to the work of the Nature Conservancy, and was greatly concerned about problems of conservation throughout the world.

Julian Huxley was always ready to believe the best of his fellow-creatures, and was usually successful in making them show themselves at their best. In the foreword to the volume published in his honour in 1953 appeared these words: "Few other living scientists have so freely given their encouragement, help and criticism to research workers in biology."

Huxley was knighted in 1958, and was the recipient of many foreign academic honours. In 1919 he married Marie Juliette Baillot. They had two sons.

February 17, 1975.

I

William Harold Ingrams, C.M.G., O.B.E., who died on December 9, 1973 at the age of 76, had a varied and distinguished career as colonial administrator, civil servant, expert on Arabian affairs and author.

Ingrams was born on February 3, 1897, the son of the Rev. W. S. Ingrams, of The Schools, Shrewsbury. He was educated at Shrewsbury, and then served as an officer in the King's Shropshire Light Infantry from 1914 to 1918. He received a wound which left him permanently lame, though he made light of his disability and did not allow it to prevent him from leading an exceptionally active life.

In 1919 he was appointed to the Colonial Service in Zanzibar, where he made his first contact with the Arab world and acquired an interest in it which he was never to lose. His service in Zanzibar did not, however, lead at once to Arabia, for from 1927 to 1933 he was Assistant Colonial Secretary in Mauritius.

Then came his appointment to the Political Service in Aden Protectorate. Accompanied by his wife Doreen, youngest daughter of the Right Hon. Edward Shortt, K.C., whom he had married in 1930, he carried out, from 1934 onwards, a notable series of explorations in the Hadhramaut, including regions which had never before been visited by Europeans. By entering into the lives of the people and securing their confidence, he succeeded in establishing the "Ingrams peace", by which the tribes bound themselves to abandon the traditional internecine warfare which had made social and economic progress impossible.

Apart from this administrative achievement, Mr. and Mrs. Ingrams's work added greatly to the store of knowledge about the country and its people. This was recognized by the award to them, jointly, in 1939 of the Lawrence Memorial Medal of the Royal Central Asian Society, and in 1940 of the Founder's Medal of the Royal Geographical Society.

Ingrams continued to serve in Aden Colony and Protectorate in various senior offices until 1945, when he was seconded for two years as Assistant Secretary in the Allied Control Commission for Germany (British Element). In 1947 he returned to the Colonial Service as Chief Commissioner of the Northern Territories of the Gold Coast. Characteristically, he elected to reach his new post by transporting his family overland, an adventurous journey which he commemorated in his book *Seven Across the Sahara*. He was not, however, altogether happy in that job, and he decided to retire from the Colonial Service in 1948.

"Retirement" was not, however, a synonym for inactivity. During 1949 and 1950 he continued to work for the Colonial Office as a freelance, undertaking an inquiry into local government in Gibraltar and a visit to Hongkong for the purpose of writing the first volume of the "Corona Library" series.

Meanwhile he had for some years a roving commission as Adviser to the Colonial Office on Overseas Information Services, in which capacity he visited many of the colonial territories to study and advise on the local public relations organizations.

Ingrams's prolific pen was indeed in constant use both for official and unofficial purposes over a long stretch of years. Some of his books have already been mentioned. In 1931 he published a standard history of Zanzibar and its people, and in 1935 a series of official reports on the social, economic and political conditions of the Hadhramaut. A more personal account of his doings appeared in 1942 under the title of *Arabia and the Isles*.

He had also written school text books for Mauritius and a very large number of pamphlets and articles, both in his own name and under the cloak of official anonymity. His writings are not only picturesque but display an unusual insight into the deeper issues that underlie the history of his times.

Ingrams was a man of great personal charm, with a lively interest in his fellow creatures, a strong sense of humour, and a touch of that genial eccentricity that goes to make a "character". In his Hadhramaut days he took to wearing Arab dress, and even grew a beard so as to merge into the landscape; but nothing could in fact have been more English than the burly figure and the quizzical blue eyes under a shock of white hair.

Ingrams was made O.B.E. in 1933 and C.M.G. in 1939.

His marriage was dissolved and he later married Henrietta Box, who survives him.

December 12, 1973.

Sir Thomas Innes of Learney, G.C.V.O., who was Lord Lyon King of Arms, Secretary to the Order of the Thistle (1945-69) and Marchmont Herald since 1969, died on October 16, 1971. He was 78.

He was one of the most remarkable figures of the present Scottish renaissance. He believed in the lasting value of his office as a centre of Scottish sentiment, and realized its vast potential for unifying the goodwill of Scots at home and overseas.

But his zeal for his office was tempered by a deep personal modesty that was the secret of his good relations with the press, who summed him up with its usual shrewdness as a selfless man and a genuine scholar with an incomparable knowledge of Scottish lore. He had that childlike quality that characterizes the truly great; and he combined instinctive kindness and good sense with an eldritch sense of humour that made him coveted as an after-dinner speaker.

In his mode of dress he was completely unselfconscious, and it is said that he even appeared at the Parliament House in Edinburgh wearing his wig and gown over tartan cycling breeches. He was perhaps the last to speak naturally in the aristocratic but homely Doric now being revived as literary Lallans, and he loved his country simply and completely. But he was far-seeing, and perhaps his greatest achievements lay in adapting Scottish traditional modes to fit the coming requirements of an age of transition.

He was very conscious that his own pre-Union royal household office was one of the modern British monarchy's most active links with the truly Scottish part of its background. This feeling was perhaps best expressed by the State Service at St. Giles' in Coronation Year, for the ceremonial organization of which the Lord Lyon was largely responsible, when the Honours of Scotland were borne in public for only the second time since the Union, and the British sovereign was ritually associated with the Scottish element in her United Kingdom.

Innes was born in 1893, and succeeded his grandfather as Laird of Learney at the age of 17. His family were cadets of the Innes baronets of Innermarkie, themselves a branch of the historic Innes house who gave a cardinal to medieval Scotland and of whom the Duke of Roxburghe as Earl Innes is the head: their founder, Berowald the Fleming, was granted the barony of Innes in Moray by King Malcolm the Maiden in 1160. A Knight of St. John of Jerusalem and an Archer of the Queen's Body Guard for Scotland, Innes himself held the old territorial baronies of Learney, Kinnairdy and Yeuchrie, was Superior of the town of Torphins, and restored Kinnairdy Castle, home of his ancestors, the thanes of Aberchirder. In 1928 he married Lady Lucy Buchan, sister of the heiress of Auchmacoy and daughter of the 18th Earl of Caithness.

He was senior vice-president of the Scottish Genealogy Society, a member of the Councils of the Scottish History Society, the Scottish Record Society and the Scottish Ecclesiological Society (president 1957-60), and member of the National Buildings Record (Scotland).

Educated at Edinburgh Academy and University, he was called to the Scots bar in 1922, and practiced as an advocate for many years. Numerous affectionate tales became attached to him at that period, so that he is now reputed to have secured the acquittal of an accused criminal by assuring the jury: "My client must be innocent. He tells me so himself."

His main interest always lay in heraldry in its widest sense, in armory and genealogy and ritual, and he soon became established as a leading peerage and heraldic counsel. In 1928, he became a royal officer-of-arms as Carrick Pursuivant. In 1934 he published *Scots Heraldry*, and his revised edition will long remain the authoritative text-book of this subject. This book, together with his numerous other works, principally on clans and tartans, undoubtedly assisted in the tremendous revival of public interest in heraldry that has marked the rest of his lifetime; within the next two decades more new coats of arms had been recorded in Lyon Register than throughout the whole of the previous three hundred years put together.

In 1929 and again during 1939-40 he gained practical experience of the everyday work of Lyon Court, by acting as interim Lyon Clerk. In 1935 he was promoted to be Albany Herald, and in 1945 he succeeded Sir Francis Grant as Secretary of the Order of the Thistle and Lord Lyon King of Arms. He was installed as Lyon and knighted by King George VI at Holyroodhouse the following year.

As Lord Lyon, he set about putting his office in order, although his vast erudition and timeless view of history and law sometimes set him at cross purposes with narrower specialists who perhaps could not see the general wood for their cherished period trees. In Lyon Court, he took care to lay down a body of heraldic law for posterity by considered judgments, duly reported in the *Scots Law Times*, and he distinguished carefully between his judicial and his ministerial capacities.

In applying the law, he was as firm with ancient peers and modern councils as with ordinary folk. He refused to allow anything that in his view would adulterate Scots heraldry, which is based on carefully established legal principles and which he believed to be today the purest in the world. All the same, his approach to heraldry was essentially practical and his application of the law was flexible to meet the changing circumstances of the modern world. He differentiated very clearly between stuffy protocol and popular pageantry. His professional advice was deferred to by the nationalized industrial boards. When Scotland developed her valuable tourist trade he was appealed to by the harassed commercial world as the arbiter in matters of tartan; and his guidance was sought by public societies in the niceties of national costume.

He removed the fear of snobbery from heraldry, and showed instead that it was fun. His encouragement restored much colour to everyday life, from the embroidered badges and heraldic jewelry that infuse all classes with pride in their name, to the gay armorial banners that now fly at gatherings and over many of even the smallest Scottish country houses and urban public buildings. He saw the merit of clan societies, cutting across social barriers in the modern world, and was ever ready to guide them with his expert advice.

His jurisdiction was invoked to settle numerous claims to chiefship, about which he clarified the law—Clan Donald was a famous example—and he encouraged the chiefs, who regularly consulted him through their Standing Council, to play their part in giving their world-scattered clansmen the sense of sharing in a special tradition. As the judge of first instance in Scottish peerage cases, his most recent task was to give judgment in the intricate Ruthven Peerage Case. Always accessible, his output of

work was as prodigious as his accumulation of knowledge is irreplaceable. He sought for no material reward, and to retain his judicial impartiality insisted that the Lyon Court fees should continue to be paid over to the Treasury even though they made a profit out of his office. His countrymen recognized his work on their behalf, when at Dundee the University of St. Andrews conferred on him *honoris causa* a doctorate of laws. In 1967 the Queen specially promoted him G.C.V.O.

His eldest son, Thomas, succeeds him as 8th Laird of Learney, Berowald Innes of Inverisla.

October 18, 1971.

General Ismet Inönü, after Atatürk the founding father of modern Turkey, and a former President, died on Christmas Day, 1973 at the age of 89.

Except for an interregnum between 1950 and 1961, and during the period since the 1965 general election, Inönü was almost continuously at the head of his country's affairs from the founding of the Turkish Republic by Atatürk in 1923 until extreme old age. His long and active career falls into three main phases: his close association with Atatürk in the Turkish War of Independence and the Kemalist reforms of the 1920s and 30s; his leadership of Turkey during the Second World War, during which he kept his country neutral; and after 1945 the attempt, with which he more than any other statesman was associated, to establish democratic institutions in Turkey.

When Mustafa Kemal (Atatürk) died in 1938 Inönü was left carrying on the work of a great reformer whose reforms had never been particularly popular with a large proportion of the Turkish people still strongly attached to the faith and traditions of their ancestors. Inönü seems never to have wavered in his belief that Atatürk's vision was right. But his apparently equal conviction that democratic institutions on the western model were the regime most suited to Turkey raised acute problems of how to reconcile this type of regime with the need to push on with the revolution Atatürk had started.

Amid many conflicting pressures, ranging from reactionary currents among the people to extreme radicalism among the army officers and the educated classes, Inönü held the balance with consummate political skill. He preserved a measure of real stability in Turkish affairs during his lifetime, though most observers realized it was a stability which could only delay further profound economic and social changes which sooner or later were bound to come in Turkey.

He retired from the chairmanship of the Republican People's Party in 1972.

Inönü was born on September 24, 1884, in Izmir (Smyrna), though his parents came

from the eastern provinces of Turkey. His education was entirely military, and in 1903 he entered the Turkish Army. Having played an active though subordinate part in the movement that put the Party of Union and Progress in power, he was at the age of 25 appointed Chief of Staff of the Army operating in the Yemen, then in revolt against Constantinople. He saw service in the First World War and was in command of the Third Army Corps when it was attacked and overwhelmed by the British forces at Beersheba on October 31, 1917.

When the Turks surrendered in 1918 Inönü, who was in Constantinople (then under allied occupation), was employed in the Ministry of War, and was believed to have been chiefly responsible for the appointment of Mustafa Kemal to the command of the East. Ismet Pasha (as he was then known) did not join the Nationalist movement at once, but kept them well supplied with information. When the time was ripe, he slipped out of Constantinople.

Ismet played a leading part under Mustafa Kemal in the Turkish War of Independence. Soon after the National Pact of Erzurum he was appointed Chief of Staff of Atatürk's army. During the terrible struggle of the Greek invasion of Anatolia, he twice stopped the Greek advance at the first and second battles of Inönü in Western Anatolia (from which he later took his name), in January and March 1921. In 1922 he took a leading part in the final Turkish offensive against the Greeks and in October of that year signed the Treaty of Mudanya with General Harington, the British commander. He then retired from the army and was appointed Minister of Foreign Affairs. He represented Turkey at the conference of Lausanne where, in spite of his deafness, he proved himself as able a diplomat as he had been a soldier. His famous duel with Lord Curzon resulted in the Treaty of Lausanne, which restored to Turkey most of the territories taken away from her by the earlier Treaty of Sèvres, and was a major diplomatic victory for the Turks.

In July 1923 he returned to Ankara and became Prime Minister. Under his government were carried out the extraordinary series of reforms by which Atatürk aimed to transform Turkey into a modern western nation. Inönü was Atatürk's right-hand man, but he was more than a mere chief of staff who took orders. He had a steadying influence on the Ghazi, whom he knew not only how to guide but at times also how to inspire. He remained Prime Minister until 1937 when, due to a cooling off of relations between him and Atatürk, he was dropped in favour of Celal Bayar. On Atatürk's death a year later, however, he was unanimously elected President of the Republic.

The Second World War broke out almost immediately after this, and Inönü was at once plunged into the severest possible test of statesmanship. His success in maintaining Turkish neutrality throughout the long-drawn struggle, in spite of the strongest pressures from both Allied and Axis powers, must be regarded as one of the most skilful operations of its kind, and one which is generally regarded as having proved, at least in a material sense, highly beneficial to Turkey. Throughout the war Inönü maintained friendly relations with Britain. In February 1943 he had a secret meeting with Churchill* in Adana, in the south of Turkey, where he successfully resisted the British Prime Minister's efforts to bring Turkey into the war. In December of the same year, with a shrewd sense of timing, he broke off diplomatic relations with Germany and attended a conference in Cairo with Churchill and Roosevelt. In February 1945 Turkey decided to declare war against Germany and Japan, a decision which qualified her for a seat in the United Nations.

Now began the third, and what some people find the most controversial, period of Inönü's life: his attempt to establish western democratic institutions in Turkey. In 1945, by a historic decision, Inönü ended the long monopoly of power enjoyed by Atatürk's Republican People's Party; the Democratic Party, led by Celal Bayar and Adnan Menderes,* was created. The first election under the new regime, held in 1946, was very imperfect; but the 1950 elections under Inönü's presidency were without blemish. They resulted in an overwhelming victory for the Democratic Party, and the Republican Party, after holding office for 27 years, was swept from power. This event, the first time the Turkish people by a free and fair vote had turned an established government out of office, has been rightly regarded as one of the great milestones of Turkish history.

It may never be known to what extent Inönü was privy to the 1960 coup. There is little doubt that, with his great authority and influence in the Army, he could have prevented it had he wished. Following the change of power Inönü withdrew into almost too conspicuous retirement, but his dominant personality never ceased to be felt behind the scenes. Many believe his influence to have been behind the expulsion from the Junta, in November 1960, of the 14 "radical" officers led by Colonel Turkesh. Finally, after the elections of October 1961, when the Army transferred power to a civilian Government, Inönü took over as Prime Minister, and formed a coalition with the newly created Justice Party.

Once again, this time at the age of 77, the old statesman was at the helm. But his task was not easy. The Government narrowly survived an Army putsch in February 1962. In May of the same year, after a violent crisis over the question of a possible amnesty for imprisoned leaders of the deposed Menderes regime, Inönü resigned; but was promptly recalled by President Gürsel* to lead a further coalition, this time of three parties. In March 1963 his Government launched the Turkish five-year plan,

the first of its kind since the 1930s.

His most dangerous opponents now were less the politicians than the radical extremists inside the armed forces, who felt the cumbersome parliamentary system was a hopeless proposition for a country needing so many urgent reforms. In May 1963 there was another violent attempt to seize power, again by the leader of the 1962 putsch, retired Colonel Talat Aydemir. The revolt was crushed, martial law imposed, and the leaders imprisoned and later tried. After a long struggle inside the armed forces, during which their fate was in doubt, Colonel Aydemir and the other ringleader, Major Gurcan, were hanged.

With martial law in Ankara and Istanbul, Turkey during this period was governed effectively by Inönü working in smooth co-operation with the chiefs of staff. In December 1963 the three-party coalition government fell to pieces, and there was a political crisis during which the opposition Justice Party, suspected by the Army of having counter-revolutionary tendencies, nearly, but not quite, came to power. Once again Inönü, now in his eightieth year, formed the Cabinet, this time a minority government composed of the Republican Party with the support of a few independent deputies in the Grand National Assembly, but with the all-important backing of the Turkish Army.

In June 1964 at the invitation of President Johnson Inönü visited the United States for talks on Cyprus, and on his return journey also saw the British Prime Minister, Sir Alec Douglas-Home, and President de Gaulle.* It was generally agreed that nobody could have put Turkey's point of view on Cyprus with more force and urgency than the old statesman of the Lausanne conference 40 years before, where so many similar questions of the territorial balance between the Hellenic and Turkish worlds had come up. Inönü succeeded in these talks in getting the western capitals to admit the legal validity of the 1960 Cyprus treaties, an important point for Turkey.

The main issue on Cyprus was whether the Greeks and Greek Cypriots would achieve enosis. With much world opinion tending to favour it, Turkey, under Inönü's guidance, began to seek support from quarters outside the Atlantic alliance. In July 1964 Inönü met with the Shah of Persia and President Ayub Khan of Pakistan in Istanbul, and together the three heads of state launched a new close collaboration between the three countries.

On February 13, 1965, Inönü's frail coalition of Republicans and Independents lost a vote of confidence over budget proposals; Inönü stepped down for the last time. During the years of opposition to Demirel's Justice Party government, Inönü made a point of working closely with Demirel and moderating his criticism. He was in effect telling his more extreme supporters and any who entertained ideas of another coup to overthrow the Justice Party "successors" to Menderes' Democratic Party, that Demirel

was not another Menderes. He seemed determined to set an example of a "loyal opposition".

December 27, 1973.

Lieutenant-General Noel Irwin, C.B., D.S.O., M.C., who died on December 21, 1972 at the age of 79, was a courageous officer of considerable talent and wide experience who might well have reached the peak of his profession. His misfortune was to be twice associated with failure, and luck forsook him at a critical moment in Arakan.

He was born in India in 1892, and educated at Marlborough and Sandhurst. Joining The Essex Regiment in 1912, he was commanding a battalion of Lincolns in the field before he was 25, and finished the First World War with the D.S.O. and two bars, the M.C., the Croix de Guerre and five mentions in dispatches.

He took the 6th Brigade to France in 1939, and was commanding the 2nd Division in England when, in August 1940, he was selected to command the Dakar expedition, one of the most ill-conceived ever to sail from British shores. His troops consisted of four battalions of Royal Marines, with whom he was able to spend only one day before sailing, and 2,500 Free French; General de Gaulle* was in a different ship. Irwin sailed with Admiral Cunningham* in H.M.S. Devonshire; but the Devonshire was suddenly diverted by the Admiralty to chase a French naval squadron which had slipped undetected through the Straits of Gibraltar. The expedition without either its Admiral or its General went on past Dakar to Freetown, while the hapless Admiral and General were heading back northward; but the French squadron gave them the slip and reached Dakar, to put new heart into the defenders.

The War Cabinet now suggested that the operation should be cancelled; but de Gaulle, buoyed up by a false belief that he had internal support in Dakar, begged to be allowed to make his attempt. Irwin and Cunningham backed him; the attempt was made, but called off after two British battleships were damaged by shellfire. Irwin was not blamed: indeed, Churchill* wrote about him to Dill, the C.I.G.S.: "Any error towards the enemy, and any evidence of a sincere desire to engage, must always be generously judged."

Irwin himself wrote an invaluable report on the lessons learnt; and in his paper were the seeds of the idea of the Headquarters Ship, with its elaborate signals system and accommodation for inter-Service staff, which was to prove a winning card for amphibious operations for the rest of the war.

In 1942 Irwin found himself on the Burma front, commanding initially IV Corps and from July onwards Eastern Army. This was a thankless task indeed. He was short of troops; many of those he had were of poor quality; morale was at rock bottom after the ignominious withdrawal from Burma in the spring; and the Japanese were being credited with almost supernatural qualities. The Chindwin front was comparatively stable, and Wavell was urging him to mount an offensive early in 1943, when Wingate's Long Range Penetration Brigade would be available to disrupt the Japanese supply lines; but Irwin was able to persuade him, reluctant though Wavell was, that the single line of communication that then existed through Kohima could not possibly support a major campaign, and that it must be postponed until after the 1943 monsoon, by which time alternatives would exist.

The Arakan front was a different matter. Here the situation was far from stable; the grain of the country and indeed the whole terrain favoured the Japanese. They missed no opportunity of thrusting in from the flank and cutting supply lines which were already tenuous. There was in those unhappy days no air supply, even in emergency; not until much later was it to become the normal system. There were also great difficulties in keeping abreast of the situation. Orders were reaching the commanders of formations and units and subunits which were wholly impracticable when translated into terms of reality on the ground. On several occasions Irwin intervened personally, and on one he relieved the divisional commander and took personal command until the successor arrived. But luck was not with him, and he was himself relieved temporarily by Giffard and ultimately by Slim.*

Thereafter, Irwin's final employment was as Commander-in-Chief in West Africa, from which he retired to Kenya in 1948, returning to England some 15 years later, where he settled in Somerset.

Irwin was not always easy to serve. He had a rough tongue on occasion, and his standards were high. But he was a soldier to his finger-tips, and he deserves to be remembered for his staunchness and resolution in the dark days of the war before the sun broke through.

December 30, 1972.

Tanzan Ishibashi, Prime Minister of Japan for a short period in 1956-57, died on April 25, 1973. He was 88.

In December 1956, against the favourite and strongly backed candidate, Kishi, Ishibashi was elected President of the Liberal Democratic Party, and became Prime Minister shortly after on the resignation of Hatoyama.

From the start he announced bold policies, in line with the advocacy of a lifetime—extensive public works, social welfare, industrial investment, commercial expansion.

But Ishibashi came up against the unpleasant realities of the political situation. His difficulty in forming a cabinet had demonstrated glaringly the dissensions in conservative ranks, and he clashed headlong with the factionalism from which he had remained a comparative stranger. It forced upon him compromises which ill fitted his beliefs or his temperament.

It would be too much to ascribe to him the phenomenal expansion of Japanese exports after 1954—they doubled in three years—but his bold and imaginative views enabled him to make the best of the favourable conditions created by the world economic boom. He had already, by the creation of the Rehabilitation Loan Bank, his "brainchild", just after the war, helped to put Japanese industry back on its feet so that, by 1949, 80 per cent of the country's production facilities were restored.

Originally destined to become a Buddhist priest—his father was one of the leaders of the Nichiren sect—he changed his mind, read philosophy at Waseda University and then entered journalism, joining the Tokyo *Mainichi Shimbun*. After a spell of conscription, he went in 1911 to the Tokyo *Keizai Shimpo Sha*, which published an economic journal, ascending every rung in the ladder of promotion to managing director in 1924, and president of the company in 1939.

In 1934 Ishibashi founded *Oriental Economist*, a monthly published in English, regarded as the most authoritative source of economic and financial information on Japan for the foreign community.

He entered politics in 1945, after the surrender of Japan, later becoming Finance Minister in Yoshida's* first Cabinet. His responsibilities brought him into headlong opposition with the Occupation authorities, of whose economic policies he disapproved, and he was purged from office.

In 1952 Ishibashi was "depurged" and returned to the Liberal Party, sticking to Hatoyama in the party troubles which followed.

When Hatoyama joined the Progressive Party in November 1954, to form the new Democratic Party, Ishibashi, together with Kishi and other Liberal dissidents, followed him, and were expelled from the Liberal fold.

Ishibashi became one of the leaders of the Democratic Party, and, on the formation of the first Hatoyama Cabinet, was given the portfolio of International Trade and Industry, which he retained until he in turn became Prime Minister in December 1956.

As Minister of International Trade, he was active in promoting a more aggressive export policy, and did much to dismantle the edifice of controls which had been erected during the preceding years of deflation.

April 26, 1973.

Tun Ismail bin Dato Abdul Rahman—See Rahman.

Mahalia Jackson, the American gospel singer, died in Chicago on January 27, 1972 aged 60. Her rich-voiced gospel singing made her famous throughout the world.

Born in New Orleans, the home of blues and jazz, on October 26, 1911, her own songs, and also the style in which she delivered them, were in the tradition of the hymns sung by past and present generations of America's black people.

The grand-daughter of a slave, Mahalia Jackson was a deeply religious woman, and she refused to sing in either night clubs or bars. 'I can't be bothered with folks talking and drinking and only listening to themselves," she once said.

Her father worked variously as a stevedore and as a barber, and on Sundays he was the minister at a small local church where Mahalia sang in the choir. Her mother died when she was a child of five.

Mahalia Jackson said in her autobiography, *Moving On Up*, that although several of her aunts were in the theatre and in vaudeville, her father discouraged her and her five brothers and sisters from becoming entertainers.

At home the Jackson family was allowed to listen only to religious music, although at the homes of friends and neighbours Mahalia heard recordings of Bessie Smith and Ida Cox, the blues singers, as well as the operatic recordings of Enrico Caruso.

Later she adapted the style of the great blues singers to her religious music. But she refused to sing the blues themselves.

January 28, 1972.

Sir Richard Jackson, C.B.E., who died on February 17, 1975 at the age of 72, was assistant commissioner of the Metropolitan Police, in charge of the C.I.D. and the Special Branch, and president of Interpol. He was, by training and temperament, a criminal lawyer, not a policeman; and he brought to both offices a quality of common sense and geniality which not only enriched them but gave them more influence than mere professionalism could have achieved.

Richard Leofric Jackson was born in India in July 1902, the third son of William ("Tiger") Jackson, the leader of the Calcutta Bar, and a grandson of Sir Thomas Turton, who had been Advocate-General of Bengal. His father was already 61 when he was born, but lived and continued in practice for another 30 years.

At Eton he acquired the name "Joe", which stuck to him for the rest of his life, when a sportswriter, watching him in the finals of the Public Schools boxing championship, compared him with Joe Beckett,* the current heavyweight champion of England. He subsequently gained a half Blue for boxing at Trinity, Cambridge. In 1927 he was called to the Bar, and six years later joined the staff of the director of public prosecutions.

In 1930 he had married Mary Elizabeth Pooley, whom he met in India, where her father was a civil engineer.

He moved to Scotland Yard in 1946, as secretary to the Metropolitan Police Office, an obscure, but not unimportant, administrative job, which ranks with that of an assistant commissioner. In 1949 he toured Malaya as a member of the Police Mission to advise the Government of the Federation on problems mainly arising from the Emergency.

Then, in 1953, he succeeded his friend, Sir Ronald Howe, as Assistant Commissioner (C.). He also shared Howe's keen interest in the development of Interpol, becoming first the British representative, in 1958 a member of the executive committee, and finally, in 1960, its President.

An extremely clubable and approachable man, and an excellent raconteur, he believed firmly in establishing a relationship of mutual trust with the press. He was, he said, very rarely let down, and it was a policy which paid off handsomely. He applied the same friendliness and genuine interest in people to the delicate problems of Interpol, where the politics which would have divided its members had to be rigorously excluded and a feeling of professional comradeship encouraged.

On his retirement in 1963, he received a knighthood, and became a director and joint vice-chairman of Securicor. He had already edited a new editon of Hans Gross's famous book *Criminal Investigation* and he wrote his memoirs, *Occupied with Crime*. He held and expressed strong views on many subjects. The experience of his childhood convinced him that the British Empire was a good thing and its abandonment a loss to the world; his years at the Bar had shown him the cruelty of professional crime, and he believed in tough sentences, especially for violence; his knowledge of police work persuaded him that, sooner or later, and preferably sooner, Britain must have a nationally organized C.I.D. He enjoyed detective stories, detested liberal reformers, admired the efficiency of the men with whom he had worked, and was devoted to his wife and daughter.

February 18, 1975.

Strode Jackson—See Strode.

Professor E. F. Jacob, Fellow and Librarian of All Souls, and former Chichele Professor of Modern History, Oxford, died on October 7, 1971. He was 77.

Ernest Fraser Jacob was born on September 12, 1894, the son of Professor Ernest Henry Jacob and of Emma Fraser of Leeds. After his father's death his uncle, Edgar Jacob, bishop first of Newcastle and later (1903-20) of St. Albans, interested himself in the boy and his education. From Winchester he went as a scholar to New College, Oxford, where the war of 1914-18 interrupted his studies. He fought with the Hampshire Regiment, in which he reached the rank of captain, was twice wounded, and was mentioned in dispatches. Returning to Oxford in 1917 he took his degree in 1918 and turning to history won both the Stanhope and the Gladstone Prizes in the same year (1920). In 1921 he was elected a fellow of All Souls. After two years as a lecturer in King's College, London, he was elected a lecturer in history and a student of Christ Church, where he taught until 1929, when he went to Manchester as professor of medieval history.

During the previous eight years he had earned a high place among the younger historical scholars in Britain. He turned first to the thirteenth century and, under the supervision of Sir Paul Vinogradoff, prepared a dissertation, published in 1925 under the title *Studies in the Period of Baronial Reform and Rebellion, 1258-1267.* In this work he showed that quick perception of the value of neglected material which was the best quality of his searching mind. In 1924 he cooperated with W. R. L. Lowe and Dr. Montague James in a reproduction of the illustrated life of St. Alban attributed to Matthew Paris, and in 1927 he edited with G. C. Crump *The Legacy of the Middle Ages.*

Jacob served the University of Manchester energetically for 15 years. He identified himself wholeheartedly with the numerous interests congenial to an ardent teacher, and natural to a public-spirited man. He did his best to maintain the traditions of a great school of history, spent much time and care upon his pupils, served on the committee of the University Press and other bodies, was a governor of and a frequent public lecturer in the John Rylands Library, and was active in the promotion of the study of local history. His concern for it was timely, for he was able to further enterprises which needed constant and sympathetic attention. He promoted study in and outside the university, took a hand in the organization of the county record office at Preston, and was a mainstay of the Chetham Society, whose president he became in succession to Professor James Tait. Meanwhile he delivered in 1935-37 the Birkbeck lectures in ecclesiastical history at Trinity College, Cambridge; and he served on the Archbishops' Commission on the relations of Church and State.

When war broke out in 1939 he added to his academic activities regular work in the office of the Regional Commissioner. The strain of night duty in underground quarters was severe, too severe even for him. In 1944, he welcomed an opportunity to return to Oxford as domestic bursar and research fellow of All Souls, where his genial and assiduous regime was greatly appreciated by his colleagues. In 1946 he was made a Fellow of the British Academy; in 1950 he was elected Chichele Professor of Modern History. He became chairman of Council in the Canterbury and York Society, and chairman of the British National Committee of the International Historical Congress. He was a member of the Royal Commission on Historical Manuscripts.

Jacob's practical interest in ecclesiastical affairs was welcomed: in 1945 he became a member of the House of Laity, in 1948 a Church Commissioner. To his manifold activities, as to his relaxations as traveller and fisherman, he seemed to impart an air of beneficence. But primarily he was a hardworking scholar, an omnivorous reader and student.

In his later years Jacob's specialized interests turned to the period of the Great Schism and the Conciliar Movement. He found in this field new and interesting themes for his students, undergraduate and graduate alike, and in his own publications he drew together the results of his own work. His *Essays in the Conciliar Epoch* published in 1953 and his edition of the *Register of Archbishop Chichele*, which appeared in four volumes between 1938 and 1947, were the main results of his years in Manchester, and his volume on *The Fifteenth Century* in the Oxford History of England, published within a few months of his retirement in 1961, brought his tenure of the Chichele Chair in Oxford to a fitting conclusion. (He was appointed Professor Emeritus in 1961.) His retirement from his professorship did not, however, bring his connexion with All Souls to an end. He had succeeded Sir Edmund Craster as librarian, and he continued to preside over the Codrington Library until 1970.

As a man, Jacob's most marked characteristic was a wide benevolence. He felt and expressed towards all men an unfailing good will. Perhaps it was in Manchester that his warm-hearted interest in a great variety of people and activities was most widely appreciated. But his deepest devotion was to All Souls. He savoured every detail of the College's history and traditions, and it was both amusing and delightful to watch the mingled pride and self-depreciation with which he would expatiate on its past. He never spoke ill of any man, and a curious look of indignant embarrassment would come into his face when those of whom he could not approve were mentioned.

For learned men he had an unstinted admiration. The international cooperation of scholars was the cause that won his warmest support, and he served on numerous committees for the promotion of active inter-change in the historical field. No one could know him without recognizing a man of unfeigned, uncomplicated goodness of heart and deep humility in his estimate of his own worth.

October 8, 1971.

Professor Arne Jacobsen, who died suddenly on March 24, 1971, was the best known internationally of modern Danish architects. He was 69.

Hans Dissing Andersen, a colleague for many years, said that Jacobsen collapsed and died instantly of a heart attack while the two of them were looking through old sketches for new ideas.

At the time of his death he was working with the building of Mainz town hall and a Hamburg high school, and was completing the designs for the National Bank in Kuwait. He had just finished designing Copenhagen's new National Bank.

Jacobsen was born on February 11, 1902, and trained at the Academy of Arts in Copenhagen, and first acquired a reputation for restrained and classically disciplined private houses. In the late 1920s he encountered the work of Le Corbusier* in France and Mies van der Rohe* in Germany and was largely responsible for introducing their ideas into Denmark where he himself built, in 1933, the revolutionary Bellavista housing estate near Copenhagen and the Bellevue Theatre, notable for its sliding roof which could open the auditorium to the night sky.

He was also much influenced by the Swedish architect Gunnar Asplund, and his more mature works, such as his town halls at Århus (1937) and Søllerød (1940), had much in common with Asplund's. After the war Jacobsen's buildings took on a more industrial character, employing curtain walling in American style. Notable among them were Rødøvre town hall (1955) and the tall S.A.S. building in Copenhagen (1959).

In 1959 also, he was invited by Dr. Alan Bullock to become the architect of the new St. Catherine's College at Oxford. The group of buildings he designed for the college aroused controversy as well as widespread interest. Their highly schematic layout and the severity of the exterior treatment was not liked by everyone, but the quality of the finish, the impeccable taste shown and the craftsmanlike attention Jacobsen gave to every detail were greatly admired. This last quality was characteristic of all Jacobsen's work and explained his success and his international reputation as a furniture-designer as well as an architect. His chairs and other examples of his furniture are found in modern buildings all over the world. He also devoted much study to landscape and garden design.

He won many prizes at international exhibitions. In 1956 he was appointed professor at the Copenhagen Academy of Arts. He was an honorary corresponding member of the Royal Institute of British Architects and an honorary Fellow of the American Institute of Architects. He was made an honorary D.Litt. by Oxford University in 1961 and LL.D. by Strathclyde in 1968.

He leaves a widow and two sons.

March 26, 1971.

Thomas Jamieson, C.B.E., one of the best-known figures in postwar international refugee work, died in Geneva on December 18, 1974 aged 63.

"Jamie", as he was known to everyone, served from 1959 until his retirement in 1972 as director of operations for the United Nations High Commission for Refugees (U.N.H.C.R.). After that he acted as a senior adviser on special operations, his last assignment being as head of the unit coordinating the main relief and repatriation programme in south Sudan in 1972-73.

Under this, about 180,000 Sudanese refugees were repatriated from neighbouring countries and a start was made on reconstruction work after 17 years of civil strife. For this, Jamieson had conferred on him the Sudanese Order of the Two Niles. Earlier in 1973 he had been made a C.B.E. in recognition of almost 30 years of work for refugees.

He was born and educated in Glasgow. His interest in refugee problems dated from the period during the Second World War, when he was national youth secretary of the Scottish Y.M.C.A. in Edinburgh.

In 1945 he joined the United Nations Relief and Rehabilitation Administration (U.N.R.R.A.) in Germany, continuing with its successor body, the International Refugee Organization. In 1952 he was appointed joint representative of U.N.H.C.R. and I.C.E.M. (Inter-Governmental Committee for European Migration) in Hongkong.

He was afterwards with the United Nations Korean Reconstruction Agency. In 1956 he became director of operations of U.N.R.W.A. in Beirut, remaining there until he joined U.N.H.C.R.

It was under his guidance that the camp clearance drive in Europe was carried through to a successful conclusion in the early 1960s and the first response to appeals for assistance from countries in Africa was organized.

In the next decade, as U.N.H.C.R. handled a succession of programmes in many parts of the world, Jamieson travelled extensively throughout Asia and Africa. One of his most challenging assignments was as head of the office set up in Delhi in 1971 after U.N.H.C.R. was appointed as "focal point" for the United Nations emergency relief operation on behalf of millions of Bengali refugees.

He was respected above all for his thoroughly pragmatic approach. His colourful accounts of his missions, delivered in a characteristic accent, were mainstays of many official meetings. Because of his ability to describe in apt terms the human problems of refugees, he was often asked to address groups working for refugees. He had recently been working on his memoirs, which would have been an invaluable contribution to books in this field.

He is survived by a wife and four children, all living in Britain.

December 20, 1974.

Ronald Jeans, the writer, who died on May 16, 1973 at the age of 86, had contributed the greater part of the "book" of many revues and a number of "straight" plays to the West End theatre over a period of nearly fifty years. Before that time he had helped to promote the foundation of repertory in Liverpool, and from 1938 onwards he was for some years a director of the important play-producing organization known as the London Mask Theatre Company.

The younger son of Sir Alexander Jeans, managing director of the *Liverpool Post and Mercury,* Ronald Jeans was born at Birkenhead on May 10, 1887, was educated at Loretto School, and was working, not very happily, in a stockbroker's office when Basil Dean, a former member of Miss Horniman's company in Manchester, went to Liverpool in search of support for a scheme of "doing repertory" there. Jeans saw to it that his father's newspaper publicized both the initial experimental season and the inauguration of regular repertory in Williamson Square in 1911. Four years later, when the Liverpool Commonwealth Company gave its first season in London, the double bill consisted of an original comedy by Jeans and an adaptation by him from Marivaux.

During the First World War he began to provide material for a succession of intimate revues produced by André Charlot, mostly at the Vaudeville, with casts including Nelson Keys, Gertrude Lawrence, Beatrice Lillie and Jack Hulbert. For the same impresario he wrote, together with the young Noel Coward, the "book" of *London Calling,* and, together with Rowland Leigh, that of *Charlot's Masquerade* which opened the Cambridge Theatre, by which time he had also contributed generously to two of Cochran's more spectacular revues at the London Pavilion and to four shows produced by Hulbert.

His *Lean Harvest,* a serious study of a marriage (husband and wife being played by Leslie Banks and Diana Wynyard*) and *Can the Leopard...?,* a comedy with Gertrude Lawrence in the lead at the Haymarket, both made a good impression in 1931.

Jeans turned back thereafter to writing revue material for Cochran, in collaboration now with A. P. Herbert, now with Hastings Turner. It was perhaps from a need to redress the balance of his activities in the theatre that he served, along with J. B. Priestley and Michael Macowan, as a director of the Mask Theatre, which in 1938, in the course of its first season, staged plays by Shakespeare, Priestley and Eugene O'Neill at the Westminster.

During the Second World War he gave up much time to operating his own cinema for the entertainment of the Forces. Of his post-war comedies, *Young Wives' Tale* gave goodish acting opportunities to Joan Greenwood and Naunton Wayne,* while the remainder emerged as undistinguished.

Much of his writing must be considered

ephemeral, but it may be suggested that for him, a younger son without aptitude for the office-work that had made the fortune of his family, his long adventure in the theatre was an act of liberation and of justification of himself, and constituted its own reward.

He is survived by his widow, the former Miss Margaret Wise, and by a daughter of the marriage.

May 17, 1973.

Ursula Jeans (Mrs. Roger Livesey), the actress, who died on April 21, 1973 in a nursing home in Hertfordshire, had for some forty years served the theatre in London with distinction. She was 66. She had done an approximately equal amount of work in contemporary and classical plays, and in the latter had held her own in the same cast with some of the outstanding performers of her generation.

Born in Simla, India in 1906, she was trained at R.A.D.A.

Her first success in small, eye-catching parts in plays by John Galsworthy and Miles Malleson* was consolidated by her performance under Basil Dean's direction, opposite Noel Coward, in S. N. Behrman's *The Second Man.* Supporting Marie Tempest in *The First Mrs. Fraser* was, perhaps, a painful experience—if it was indeed she who received from the star a lesson in stage-manners which is one of the best known stories told of that great lady—but doubtless profitable, since it was followed by her most acclaimed performance up to date, in the role later played on film by Joan Crawford, in *Grand Hotel,* and by Tyrone Guthrie's invitation to join the company of his first season at the Old Vic. The company included Charles Laughton*, Flora Robson, Athene Seyler, Marius Goring and Roger Livesey, whom, after the death of her first husband, the actor Robin Irvine, she married.

She was back at Guthrie's Old Vic in 1936 and, as Kate Hardcastle and the Shrew, in 1939. After much wartime touring and a performance in Priestley's *Ever Since Paradise* described by him as "astonishingly versatile and brilliant", Ursula Jeans was again seen in the Waterloo Road, under Hugh Hunt's direction, as the heroine of *Captain Brassbound's Conversion* and as Mistress Ford in *The Merry Wives* to Peggy Ashcroft's Mistress Page.

She and her husband toured Australia and New Zealand in *The Reluctant Debutante.* They were also together in a revival of Wilde's *An Ideal Husband*—her last appearance in London, this—and on a tour that included South Africa of a play derived from stories by P. G. Wodehouse.

She achieved what Ellen Terry once described as her own ambition, that of being "a useful actress".

April 25, 1973.

Sir Charles Jeffries, K.C.M.G., O.B.E., Joint Deputy Under-Secretary of State, Colonial Office from 1947 to 1956, died on December 11, 1972.

Charles Joseph Jeffries, eldest son of C.D. Jeffries, of Beckenham, was born in 1896 and went from Malvern College up to Magdalen College, Oxford, as a Classical Demy just before the First World War.

Before he went to Malvern he was at the same kindergarten as Enid Blyton* in Beckenham. After her death in 1968 he wrote to *The Times* saying that he could probably claim to be the only person who had played the March Hare to Miss Blyton's Alice.

He was invalided from the Forces in 1917 after being gassed and wounded. (His injuries permanently impaired his voice and in later years he found it difficult to make himself audible.) He joined the Colonial Office in 1917. His main preoccupation from 1929 until his retirement as Deputy Under-Secretary of State in 1956 was the unification and modernization of the Colonial Civil Service, for which he was mainly responsible.

In 1930 following the report of the Warren Fisher Committee appointed by L. S. Amery the previous year, a new Colonial Service division was created with Jeffries (now an Assistant Secretary) in charge of one of its departments. On him fell the main task of bringing about progressively the unification of the several branches of the Colonial service—administrative, legal, medical and so on—culminating in 1954 with complete unification as Her Majesty's Oversea Civil Service (H.M.O.C.S.) with modernized conditions of service anticipating the progress to independence of the various colonies which took place mainly after Jeffries' retirement. Space does not permit a detailed account but his own two books on the subject, *The Colonial Empire and its Civil Service* (1938) and the sequel, *Whitehall and the Colonial Service: an Administrative Memoir* (Institute of Commonwealth Studies, Paper 15) are the best tribute to his work.

Jeffries had many other interests. He was largely responsible for starting the Overseas Service training courses at Farnham Castle and, with Sir Douglas Veale, for the establishment of Queen Elizabeth House as a Commonwealth Centre in Oxford. He was also secretary and a devoted supporter of the Ranfurly library service. A keen churchman, he was a vice president of the U.S.P.G. and had been a member of the governing body of the S.P.C.K. and the general committee of the British and Foreign Bible Society. He was a member of the House of Laity for some years.

He was both a practising and a practical Christian greatly concerned with the problems of unity on which he wrote with cogency and common sense. An article which he wrote on Christian unity for *The Times* in 1967 attracted a large number of letters, and letters and article were reprinted as a pamphlet. In his retirement he was a regu-

lar and valued contributor to the columns of the paper. He was the ideal contributor, brisk, amiable, and accurate; and his pieces were always widely read.

Jeffries married in 1921 Myrtle, daughter of Dr. J. H. Bennett. They had three daughters.

December 13, 1972.

Dr. John Holmes Jellett, O.B.E., consulting engineer, who died on June 17, 1971 at his home in Southampton, aged 66, was the Admiralty Civil Engineer-in-Chief's representative on the staff during the construction and operation of the "Mulberry Harbour" at Arromanches, for the allied invasion of Europe. He was awarded the O.B.E. in 1944 for distinguished services in operations which led to the successful landing of allied forces in Normandy.

Dr. Jellett was the son of Mr. H. H. Jellett, Chief Engineer of the Bengal-Nagpur railway. He was educated at Shrewsbury and Gonville and Caius College, Cambridge. He joined the Civil Engineering division of the Admiralty in 1933, and served as Assistant Engineer at Chatham and Singapore. In 1938 he returned to Whitehall, and in 1940 became Superintending Civil Engineer, and responsible for headquarters administration of many wartime projects. For two years he served in the Eastern Mediterranean and Malta, and in 1944 was commissioned as a Temporary Captain R.N.V.R. (Special) and appointed to the staff of A.N.C.I.F. for work on the Mulberry Harbour project.

After the war he became Deputy Docks Engineer at Southampton, and from then until his retirement in 1966 as Chief Docks Engineer was engaged in the reconstruction and development work there, including the new passenger terminal. He was made President of the Institution of Civil Engineers in 1968-69; and Southampton University, of which he had been a member of the Council since 1947, gave him the honorary degree of D.Sc. in 1968. He leaves a widow and two sons.

June 19, 1971.

The former Mufti of Jerusalem, Haj Amin El Husseini, who led the Palestinian Arabs against the British Mandate authorities, died in Beirut on July 4, 1974 at the age of 77.

He was president of the Higher Arab Committee for Palestine and the Islamic World Congress.

Born in 1897, Amin was educated in Turkish elementary schools. In 1912, he was sent to Egypt to study Muslim law. His brother, father and grandfather had held office as Mufti, and it was therefore traditional to have an Alim in the family. In Cairo he was put in a private school and while a student accompanied his mother on the pilgrimage to Mecca. He returned to Jerusalem in 1914 and was there when war broke out. He went to the military training school in Constantinople, was posted to a regiment and was made A.D.C. to its commander. By 1917 he was back in Jerusalem on sick leave, and was still there at the Occupation. During the following few months he became as a layman a prominent member of a young men's club "The Arab Society".

In 1918 Major Jibrail Haddad Pasha, assistant to Colonel Storrs, then military governor of Jerusalem, made him his personal assistant at £(E)10 a month. Six months later when Haddad Pasha was appointed director of public security in the Emir Feisal's government in Damascus, Amin followed him and was given a post as political agent at £(E)15 a month and as such kept travelling between Palestine, Syria and Transjordan.

In April 1920, when there were troubles between Arabs and Jews, he was accused of having instigated the riots and was sentenced by a military court to 10 years' imprisonment, but escaped to Kerak in Transjordan. He was later pardoned on the intervention of certain Transjordanian notables.

After the death of his brother, Kamil Effendi, the reigning Mufti, Haj Amin, after a good deal of lobbying, was appointed Mufti by the High Commissioner, Sir Herbert (later Lord) Samuel.*

After the serious riots in 1929 the Mufti was called upon to give evidence before the Shaw Commission and gained great prestige in Muslim eyes by insisting upon the privilege of his office, in order to conform with which the commission had to meet in his official residence in the Horam-esn-Sheriff in order to hear his evidence and cross-examination by Sir Boyd Merriman, K.C. Later, in 1931, Haj Amin still further enhanced his prestige, confounded many of his critics and opponents and definitely emerged as acknowledged leader in Islam by the way in which he conducted the business of the Moslem Congress which he had convoked in the December of that year. In 1934, he headed a delegation to the Hejaz, and endeavoured to mediate in the war between Saudi Arabia and the Yemen.

When, on the outbreak of the disorders of 1936, the Arab Higher Committee was formed to take the place of the defunct Palestine Arab Executive, Haj Amin was elected President. In this capacity he was responsible for directing the Arab movement during 1936 and for conducting negotiations with the Administration. He was often regarded as intransigent; but in fact at one time he was probably a restraining influence on the younger men, who were beginning to make their power felt in political affairs. He strongly discouraged all attempts to create dissension between Christians and Muslims, but was a thoroughgoing antagonist of the Zionists who regarded him as their most dangerous enemy and were unceasing in their demand that the Administration should remove from his

control the extensive patronage of which he disposed as Head of the Supreme Moslem Council.

If in the earlier stages of the Arab revolt in Palestine the Mufti had the reputation for restraining the hot heads among his followers, in the later stages he ceased to exercise that moderating influence and was officially described in Parliament by the then Colonial Secretary (Malcolm MacDonald) as "the head of an organization held responsible for the campaign of terrorism and assassination against British and Jews but also the head of a faction which has for many months past pursued persistently a similar campaign against large numbers of Arabs".

The Government of Palestine, in spite of the notoriety of the Mufti's subversive activities in Jerusalem and throughout Palestine, declined to take action against him or remove him from offices.

Under cover of a report that he had taken to his bed, and disguised as a Bedu, Haj Amin walked out of Jerusalem on October 17, 1937, and made his way to Lebanon. There he remained, at Jimeh on the coast, for some time, nominally under French surveillance and theoretically bound by an undertaking not to take part in political activities, a restriction which was very loosely interpreted as he received a great many visitors who came to consult the oracle on matters which very closely touched on current politics in Palestine, Syria and Egypt.

On October 17, 1939, having evaded the French surveillance, Haj Amin appeared quite unexpectedly, and without passport or visa, in Baghdad. Here he was allowed to remain. Later however he was in such close touch with German and Italian agents that he considered it wise to anticipate the collapse of the pro-Axis Rashid Ali cabinet, which was at the time engaged in hostilities with the British, by leaving for Iran.

Eventually he found his way to Italy and placed himself under the protection of Nazi Germany where he advised and aided the Germans in their subversive work in the Near and Middle East. Winston Churchill once referred to him as the deadliest enemy of the British Empire.

After the collapse of Germany he was interned in a Paris hotel, but he escaped and made his way to Egypt, eventually settling in the Lebanon where he kept up a propaganda war against Israel.

July 6, 1974.

B. S. Johnson, who was found dead at his home in Islington, London, on November 13, 1973, was one of the most naturally gifted writers of his generation. He was also one of the very small number to commit himself whole-heartedly to the experimental presentation of fiction. His *Albert Angelo* (1964) included carefully holed pages in order that readers might

choose for themselves the order in which they received the writer's words; *The Unfortunates* (1969) carried the pursuit of disintegration further by being printed, and boxed, in interchangeable sections. Throughout his career he believed that to adhere to the disciplines of conventional form was to risk the distortion of truth.

Brian Stanley Johnson was born in 1933, educated at King's College, London, published his first novel *Travelling People* in 1963 and his first collection of poetry a year later. Over the next decade he produced a prolific and vigorous body of work, including six further fictions, three films for the cinema and eight for television. His third, *Trawl,* won the Somerset Maugham* Award for 1967; his film *You're Human Like the Rest of Them* won the Grand Prix at both the Tours and Melbourne Festivals in 1968. In the teeth of distinguished competition, he was appointed First Gregynog Arts Fellow at the University of Wales in 1970.

He was a combative but immensely likeable man. To meet him was to feel, as did most of his English admirers, that his natural gifts and his chosen method of using them were in perpetual conflict with one another; his sensibility remained a traditional one, and the influences that shaped him and recur in his work—a wartime childhood, a passion for football, an acute sense of the working life—were those that shaped many of his English contemporaries.

He was interested in and always concerned to communicate the common experience, editing two anthologies—*The Evacuees* (1968) and *All Bull: the National Serviceman* (1973). The descriptions of fishgutting in *Trawl,* of teaching in *Albert Angelo,* and the factory scenes in *Christy Malry's Own Double Entry* (1973) achieve a high quality of observation and poetic immediacy; but the devices by which he seeks to defuse and intellectualize their impact produce a sense of irresolution and leave the reader hungry for more.

His later books, *Christy Malry* and *House Mother Normal* (1971) were as good and funny as anything he wrote, and one could say of him, as of few writers at 40, that his talents might still have taken him anywhere.

November 15, 1973.

Cecily Johnson—See Arnold.

Major-General Dudley Graham Johnson, V.C., C.B., D.S.O., M.C., died on December 21, 1975 at the age of 91. He won his V.C., one of the last of the First World War, for bravery on November 4, 1918 at the forcing of the Sambre Canal.

Johnson, then a Lieutenant-Colonel, commanded the 2nd Battalion Royal Sussex Regiment, itself part of the 2nd Infantry Brigade which was detailed to cross the canal lock south of Castillon as the spear-head of the forcing operation.

The terrain leading to the lock was extremely difficult to negotiate in the face of the heavy barrage the Germans had laid down, including as it did a secondary waterway between the attacking forces and their objective. Royal Engineers who were attempting to perform the bridging operation were in total confusion and the whole assault was in danger of breaking down when Johnson arrived on the scene.

He rallied the forces to the attack and, in spite of the fact that his first fresh assault was again disrupted by heavy fire, succeeded on a second attempt at crossing the lock. From that point the practical problems involved in that sector of the British advance took on a different complexion, in spite of the heavy casualties sustained by the attacking forces.

Born in 1884 and educated at Bradfield College, Johnson was already a well-decorated man by this stage in the war. He won a D.S.O. fighting against the Germans at Tsing-Tau in 1914, an M.C. in France in January 1918, and a bar to his D.S.O. for services at Pontruet in September that year. He also served at Gallipoli.

After the war he was successively Chief Inspector at the Small Arms School and the Machine Gun School, and his appointments included commands of the 12 (Secunderabad) Infantry Brigade and, between 1938 and 1940, of the 4th Division. He was G.O.C. Aldershot Command in 1940 and Inspector of Infantry in 1941. He retired in 1944 and was Colonel of the South Wales Borderers, with whom he had served both at Gallipoli and in France, from 1944 to 1949. He was made a C.B. in 1939.

He married Marjorie Grisewood, who died in 1950, and had one son and two daughters.

December 23, 1975.

Lyndon Baines Johnson, former President of the United States of America, who died on January 22, 1973 after a heart attack at his ranch in Texas, had succeeded automatically to the presidency when President Kennedy* was assassinated on November 22, 1963. A year later he was elected in his own right by an overwhelming landslide against the right-wing conservative Senator Goldwater.

With his technical mastery of the American political system, acquired through long service in Congress, Johnson achieved a breakthrough in domestic legislation that will give his Administration a lasting place in American history. Much of the programme had been drawn up by his predecessor, President Kennedy; many of the basic ideas went back to the New Deal; some of the new laws would have passed anyway, for public opinion and the power structure of the country were changing; but Johnson was able to provide the impetus

that made the difference between evolution and revolution. He cleared the decks of a vast backlog of overdue reforms and was able to look ahead to new horizons.

It was Johnson's misfortune to be saddled with a commitment in Vietnam that was not of his own choosing and where the balance of advantage was turning against him. It gradually broke his Administration and his own confidence until, at the end of March 1968, he announced that he would not stand for reelection. The indecisive war had divided the American people. It had made President Johnson fiercely hated by many of the young. It diverted money and attention from domestic problems and thus increased the anger of the Negroes. It put inflationary pressures on the economy. Above all, it set off a searching appraisal of the moral and political purpose of the United States, its role in the world, its power and its impotence.

President Johnson, enmeshed in vain efforts to win the war, proved incapable of mastering this debate. He saw the Vietnam war in simple terms as an American commitment that had to be honoured, a battle that had to be won. He felt the dissenters were helping the enemy.

As a man he was a curious combination of simple country virtues, uncanny political skill, tremendous egocentricity and almost religious patriotism. Many people found him difficult to define as a person, yet in some way reassuring as a President though the myth of the unprincipled Texan "wheeler-dealer" died hard. He brought a folksy, Jacksonian atmosphere to the White House which contrasted sharply with the patrician elegance and intellectual polish that were the hallmarks of his predecessor's term. Businessmen and Congressmen became more frequent visitors to the White House. Stetsons appeared on the hat racks. Harvard professors, artists, musicians and entertainers were edged out of the limelight. It seemed the end of President and Mrs. Kennedy's efforts to make the White House a cultural and intellectual centre. In compensation, it became still more active and aggressive politically, and although the new style jarred finer susceptibilities it became generally acknowledged, even by Liberals, that Johnson was getting results and getting them fast.

It was impossible to fit Johnson's personality into any neat definitions. He was a vain man who delighted in the money that came to him in adult life. Until the Vice-Presidency restrained him, he wore expensive suits with cowboy trappings and loud shirts. He liked to see his initials everywhere, even flaunted by his wife (nicknamed Lady Bird), his children (Lynda Bird and Lucy Baines) and his dog (Little Beagle Johnson). He was very sensitive to criticism and could be deeply wounded by hostile references to him in the press. One reason for this was that he believed so passionately in his own good intentions that criticism could derive only from pure malevolence or

misunderstanding. But he was also a humble and religious man. When he stepped from the aircraft that brought him from Dallas to Washington with the body of President Kennedy, he spoke his first public words as President with utter simplicity and humility. "I will do my best," he said. "This is all I can do. I ask for your help and God's."

At other times he could be the epitome of earthy Americanism, slapping backs, squeezing elbows, pumping hands and uttering the corniest social platitudes with devastating sincerity. In this mood he could seem very much the country boy grown rich. In the upper reaches of diplomatic and international life he could be out of his depth and often embarrassing.

Less than a year after he left office he stated, in a remarkable television interview, not only that he had not wanted to be president, but that he had never felt adequate to the responsibilities of office, either by experience or training, and that he took his wife's advice about running in 1964, on the basis that it would only be for one term. He repeated his reasons for not running in 1968—that his candidacy would have added to the divisions in the country and distracted him from the pursuit of peace—but characteristically insisted that if he had run, he would have won: and he blamed the maladroitness of Vice-president Humphrey for losing the election for the Democratic Party.

Applied to domestic politics, to wooing reluctant politicians or rousing a crowd, the "Johnson treatment" was pure magic. Hardly anyone or anything could withstand it. He had a shrewd instinctive feel for the nerve centres and weak spots of those he dealt with. He knew when to intimidate them, when to appeal to their pride and their patriotism, their gratitude and their self-interest. He seldom believed that any dispute could not be reconciled, and he was a master at finding how to do it. "Come let us reason together" was one of the guiding principles of his life.

His background throws some light on the complexities of his character. On his mother's side were not only politicians but Baptist preachers and teachers, modest conservative pioneer types, who perhaps passed to him his rugged individuality and religious sincerity. The main political influence came from his father and grandfather, both of whom sat in the Texas Legislature. Geographically there were also mixed influences. Texas is commonly thought of as the land of newly rich oil men, brash, vulgar and unscrupulous. As a senator Johnson could represent these men, and to some extent the whole southern ethos as well. But his own part of Texas was an unusual bit of hill country settled largely by liberal Germans after 1848. This was farming and cattle country and in some ways worlds apart from oil and industry. His grandfather was a Populist who saw himself representing the people against the economic power groups. His father fought the Ku-

Klux-Klan.

Hence, perhaps, the paradox which Johnson represented—a southerner who could champion civil rights for the Negroes, a Texan who could idolize Roosevelt and the New Deal, a conservative by temperament who could yet battle for liberal causes, a New Dealer who could speak the language of the south and enjoy the close friendship of people like Senator Russell of Georgia. But above all it was his fervent, almost childlike belief in the greatness and goodness of the United States that made him feel that all the diverse and conflicting interests that make it up must somewhere, somehow, be capable of resolution.

Lyndon Baines Johnson was born on August 27, 1908, in a three-room farmhouse near Johnson City. It is said that his grandfather rode among his neighbours on horseback telling them "a United States senator was born this morning". Politics was certainly the obvious destination for the child. His maternal grandmother was the niece of the man who signed the Texas Declaration of Independence from Mexico. His maternal grandfather served in the Texas Legislature. His father was a teacher, farmer, and state legislator, first elected in 1904, who campaigned for better roads and help for farmers hit by drought.

The future President was a bright and active child but tended to resist education. His mother pressed him hard, and by the age of three he could recite all the Mother Goose rhymes, and a good deal of Longfellow and Tennyson. He could read at four. Persistent maternal pressure was applied throughout his schooling, and he got reasonably good grades, but when he graduated from high school he refused to go to college and worked his way to California, taking odd jobs such as dish-washer and labourer. Eventually he returned home but continued to work as a labourer building roads. His parents went on pressing him to go to college and he finally gave in, three years after leaving school. He entered the Texas State Teachers' College at San Marcos, where he applied himself while earning most of his keep in his spare time. He also became a star debater and editor of the college newspaper. Graduating after three and a half years he took a job teaching public speaking and debating at a high school in Houston.

He entered politics by assisting the wealthy rancher Richard Kleberg to win election to Congress in 1931. Kleberg took him to Washington the following year. Johnson took to the life like a duck to water, and was seen as a fast worker and tireless arguer. He was helped by his father's friendship with Congressman Sam Rayburn,* later to become Speaker of the House and sponsor of Johnson's bid for the presidential nomination in 1960. Franklin Roosevelt had just become President, and Johnson became an ardent admirer and supporter of the New Deal. On one of his visits home during this period Johnson met Claudia Taylor, daughter of a prosperous Texas landowner and businessman. Typically, Johnson made up his mind immediately, and within six weeks they were married. She proved herself an ideal politician's wife and an accomplished businesswoman, gradually accumulating substantial wealth based mainly on a number of local radio stations.

In 1935 Roosevelt, who had spotted the newcomer's potentialities, appointed Johnson Administrator of the National Youth Administration in Texas. It was an important job, vital to the New Deal's efforts to get young people into useful employment. Johnson tackled it with characteristic vigour and gained not only the special praise of the national director but also the undying gratitude of thousands of young Texans.

After serving for only two years Johnson was elected to Congress in 1937 on a platform of unqualified support for Roosevelt's plan to pack the Supreme Court. Roosevelt took him on his special train through Texas, and the relationship, based on mutual admiration, was firmly established. However, a few weeks after taking his seat in Congress, Johnson voted against both the President and Rayburn in favour of low interest loans to farmers. Like all good Congressmen he had the interests of his own district at heart, and he proved this again and again by securing for it a quite remarkable number of Federal projects. As early as that he had got straight to the heart of a Congressman's job, and was becoming known as a tough negotiator and sharp trader, a master of the mechanics and power patterns of Congress.

One hour after voting for the declaration of war in 1941, Johnson, already in the reserve, volunteered for active service. Within three days he was a Lieutenant-Commander and the first member of the House in uniform. He won the Silver Star for gallantry in a flight over New Guinea, and served as the President's special emissary to Australia and New Zealand. But he had to return to his seat in the House in 1942, when the President decided that members should not serve in the forces.

In 1941 Johnson had narrowly missed being elected to the Senate. In 1948 he tried again and won, after a typically vigorous campaign in which he chartered a helicopter equipped with a loudspeaker and hovered over remote villages bellowing down at them the glad news of his candidacy. Most of them had never before seen either a helicopter or a candidate for the Senate. Certainly they had never seen anyone like Johnson. But it was an extremely tough campaign and he squeezed in by a narrow margin.

Once in the Senate, he applied the same recipe that had served him so well in the House. "Almost half the people who voted in the Democratic Primary did not want me for their senator", he said. "My big job is to get them to change their minds about me". He gathered a large staff around him and proceeded to serve Texas and the Texans in every way he knew. After two years he became Democratic Whip, and two years after that, when the Democrats lost their majority, floor leader. At 44 he was the youngest in American history. He was now approaching the first peak of his career, but in July 1955 he was struck by a very severe heart attack. He organized his recovery with the same systematic thoroughness that he applied to everything else. Among other things he stopped smoking. But he could not stop work. Before long the entire seventeenth floor of the hospital was occupied by typewriters, duplicators, telephones, and members of Johnson's staff. Work continued when he went back to his ranch to convalesce. By December the doctors allowed him to return to Washington.

In the election of 1956 the Democrats regained control of both houses of Congress, and Senator Johnson found himself Majority Leader—a position of great power, especially with a Republican President in the White House. It was in this job that Johnson really came into his own. In spite of liberal Democrats who wanted to establish a record of opposition to the President, Johnson kept tight control of the party and insisted on a sensible and constructive degree of cooperation with the White House. He commanded a company of highly individualistic and temperamental men whom he had to control largely by the force and subtlety of his personality. And he had to preserve a working relationship not only with the White House but between the northern and southern wings of his party. His liberal critics became more vocal in the second Eisenhower* Administration, when they claimed that he was disregarding the liberal mandate received by the Democratic Party in three successive elections. But he continued to tailor his objectives to what he thought a Republican President would accept, instead of fighting for ambitious lost causes. To him half a loaf was always better than no bread. Not that his desire for compromise was purely tactical. He was concerned mainly to keep the government running. But his character also combined liberal and conservative elements in a way that made it possible for him to be quite sincerely in both camps at the same time. It might almost be said that his friendships were in the southern camp but most of his votes with the liberals. He was a constant supporter of foreign aid, and his skilled management was largely responsible for the passage of the Civil Rights Bill of 1957.

In the day-to-day business of the Senate he possessed sensitive antennae that registered every nuance of feeling in his own party and in the opposition. He used to remember a remark of his father's: "If you can't come into a room full of people and tell right away who's for you and who's against you, you have no business being in politics". He established a formidable reputation for counting votes before they were cast. He also had a bag full of procedural tricks, with an instinct for using them at the right time. Probably his greatest gift was

269

for establishing personal relationships with people of widely varying views and temperaments.

Perhaps he was not quite discriminating enough, for it was during this period that the seeds were sown of a scandal that cast an uncomfortable shadow on his presidency. Johnson's right-hand man in the Senate was Bobby Baker, Secretary to the Majority Leader. Baker was described as Johnson's "bluntest instrument in running the show". He was an extra pair of eyes and ears, a rounder up of votes and a twister of arms. Johnson thought the world of him and made absolutely no secret of it. Baker became known as "Little Lyndon".

Late in 1963 Baker suddenly resigned amid a flood of rumours. It was alleged that he had used his position to engage in a wide range of dubious and unscrupulous business activities in the course of which he had amassed a considerable fortune. Johnson was directly involved in only two minor aspects. He was said to have received the gift of a stereophonic radiogram in connexion with some life insurance he had taken out through an agency in which Baker had an interest. And the same agency was said to have purchased advertising time on one of Mrs. Johnson's radio stations in gratitude for having got Johnson's business. These were minor and unsubstantiated accusations, but there is no doubt that the affair as a whole shocked many people and did not leave Johnson unscathed. However, Republican as well as Democratic senators were involved in the accusations, so that it did not become a party issue and the investigating committees limited their action.

Johnson often said that he had no ambition to be President. Probably he was sincere. In any case he was realist enough to see that his Southern background made it impossible for him to be nominated and elected in the usual way. He was not a national figure and was little known outside Washington. If this rankled he seemed to accept it as inevitable. But as the Democratic convention of 1960 approached, his ambition was kindled. His friends in the Senate, particularly old Sam Rayburn, resented the rise of the young and inexperienced Senator Kennedy. They gradually persuaded Johnson that he had a chance, perhaps even a duty to beat this immodest upstart.

In the ensuing rivalry acrimony developed between the two men. It was therefore a great surprise when Kennedy asked Johnson to be his running mate and an even greater surprise when Johnson accepted. Kennedy's reasons were simple. He respected Johnson's abilities and he needed someone to carry the South, where he himself was weak. And he was not a man to bear grudges. Johnson's reasons for accepting were more obscure but they included genuine patriotism, loyalty, and his own ambition to become President one day.

Once in the Vice-Presidency Johnson almost disappeared from view. Deprived of his power and his platform he became a bit of a mystery. But he remained very active behind the scenes. President Kennedy gave him special responsibilities in connexion with the space effort and with winning equal employment opportunities for Negroes. He also kept him fully informed and closely involved with all the major decisions, so that when he took over after the assassination he was probably better equipped than any previous Vice-President. He represented the President abroad on a number of occasions, notably in Berlin and in Pakistan, where he exuberantly invited a camel driver to visit the United States. To everyone's surprise and consternation the invitation was taken up, and Johnson came in for a certain amount of mockery. But he—and the camel driver—rose to the occasion, and the visit was a resounding success in both countries. It was a typically Johnsonian gesture—spontaneous, crude, warm-hearted unconventional, risky, and in the end successful. Hardly anyone else could have brought it off.

When President Kennedy was assassinated on November 22, 1963, Johnson succeeded automatically to the Presidency. He plunged into the Presidency with the same vigour, skill and devotion that he had shown throughout his political career. His determination to maintain the momentum and direction of the Kennedy Administration did much to reassure a world badly shaken by the assassination. He quickly won the confidence of many who had previously doubted his capacity for the job. In particular he dedicated himself to passing the Civil Rights Bill and to continuing efforts to negotiate with Russia.

He also performed with such overwhelming energy that people worried whether his health could stand it. In one memorable week in April 1964 he travelled 3,000 miles, made more than 20 speeches, held three press conferences, appeared several times on national television, opened the New York World's Fair, announced a settlement of a four-year-old railway dispute, disclosed a new understanding with the Soviet Union on reducing production of fissile material for nuclear bombs, and shook so many hands that his own right hand began to bleed.

As he took office, relations with Russia had reached a stage of cautious equilibrium since the confrontation over the missiles in Cuba. Both powers were anxious not to rock the boat, and as the hypnotic fascination of the cold war lessened it became easier to face up to the blemishes in American society, such as racial discrimination, urban squalor, pollution, poverty, the medical needs of the aged, and the lack of federal money in education.

President Kennedy's programme for dealing with these problems was still bottled up in a stubbornly conservative Congress, but the time seemed ripe for change. The evolution of communism and the lessening threat from Russia made it more difficult for conservatives to equate social legislation with socialism. The southern oligarchy in Congress was beginning to age and weaken, while the redrawing of constituency boundaries ordered by the Supreme Court was slowly giving the urban areas their proper voice. The resounding defeat of Senator Goldwater helped to put the right wing in perspective.

Above all, President Johnson himself seemed perfectly equipped for breaking the deadlock and gathering the country around him for a move towards a juster and better balanced society. As the first southern President since the Civil War he could begin to heal the rift between north and south and urge better treatment for the Negroes without entirely alienating the white conservatives. He openly admitted that he was a late comer to the cause of civil rights but this probably helped him by showing that he was not a doctrinal liberal. Nor was he a doctrinal conservative. Early poverty had given him a strong social conscience that was later nurtured by his devotion to President Roosevelt and the New Deal. It survived his rise to a position of enormous power in the senate, where he was Democratic Leader for eight years. His ability to handle this fractious body stood him in good stead as President.

He seemed able to be all things to all men without losing his personal integrity. He spoke to southerners as one of them yet persuaded the Negroes that he was dedicated to their interests. He promised to reduce government spending and at the same time to fight poverty and improve social services. In a very short time he had gained a substantial measure of support from liberals and conservatives, business and labour, Negroes and whites, northerners and southerners. He seemed, in fact, to be on the way to building the consensus of opinion that is essential to the proper working of the American presidency.

President Johnson's first year of office was devoted to consolidating his support, driving through domestic legislation, and fighting his election campaign. In his State of the Union message in January 1964 he called in particular for passage of the Civil Rights Bill and for an "all-out war on human poverty and unemployment in these United States". In his subsequent budget he announced a cut in defence spending (which involved braving the protests of congressmen from districts where bases would be closed). Some of the money would be diverted into a whole series of legislative proposals designed to increase opportunities, improve education, reduce poverty and unemployment. Much of this he was able to see passed before the election campaign.

In July he signed the historic Civil Rights Bill, considerably modified and strengthened since President Kennedy first introduced it more than a year earlier. Then, having chosen Senator Hubert Humphrey as his running mate, thus consolidating his liberal support, he embarked on the colourful and, as it turned out, easy task of defeating Senator Goldwater in the presidential election. Running on a platform that stressed domestic reform and moderation and responsibility abroad, he had no difficulty in persuading an overwhelming majority of the electorate that his opponent was dangerously impulsive in foreign policy and completely out of touch with the social and material problems of the country. Senator Goldwater, in return, concentrated on the question of moral corruption and "violence in the streets", a thin disguise for the racial problem. The arrest of Walter Jenkins, one of President Johnson's closest friends and assistants, for a homosexual offence seemed for a while a godsend to the Republicans, but failed to make much impact. In the end Senator Barry Goldwater carried only six states, mostly by winning the white Southern vote on the racial issue.

Buoyed up by his success, President Johnson delivered a State of the Union message outlining his concept of the Great Society—"Ahead now is a summit where freedom from the wants of the body can help fulfil the needs of the spirit. . . . We do not intend to live—in the midst of abundance—isolated from neighbours and nature, confined by blighted cities and bleak suburbs, stunted by a poverty of learning and an emptiness of leisure." This was followed by an inspirational Inaugural Speech reflecting Johnson's vision of a country from which poverty and inequality are banished. It reflected the idealism of the New Deal heightened by religious fervour and backed by the belief that the technological revolution would make all things possible. There were critics who felt the problems were greater than the President realized, and that the legislation he proposed fell far short of the requirements, but no one doubted the sincerity of his ideals.

Congress was deluged with new legislation but foreign affairs were not forgotten. In January 1965 President Johnson invited the new Soviet leaders, Kosygin and Brezhnev, to visit the United States. He also promised to intensify efforts to reach further disarmament agreements. President Johnson was determined to pursue good relations with Russia, partly in order to give as much attention and money as possible to domestic problems but also because it was his nature to believe in peaceful coexistence.

But the deepening involvement in Vietnam and the impulsive intervention in the Dominican Republic pushed him into the relatively unfamiliar world of foreign affairs. The fragile détente with Russia began to wobble, and allies became restive. By the summer of 1965 Washington was in a state of almost constant crisis, and criticism was growing on both left and right. The domestic programme was still moving but the President could no longer be sure of getting everything he wanted. The consensus was breaking up. He worked harder and harder, ageing visibly as he supervised practically every detail of the operations in Vietnam. He was as deeply involved in his foreign commitments as he had been in domestic reform but his touch

was less sure and his power more restricted.

As the communists began to gain strength in South Vietnam at the expense of the Americans and a series of tottering governments, President Johnson began to be faced with the choice of accepting defeat or increasing American help.

Although as a senator he had been against committing American troops to the mainland of Asia he now decided that the only way to prevent a Vietcong victory was to send the Americans into action as combat units instead of merely as advisers to the South Vietnamese. From this moment the war became an American war and an irrevocable American commitment. American troops poured steadily into Vietnam until by October 1966 there were 319,000 of them. The tide of Vietcong success was halted but not reversed. Predictions of an early victory proved false. Each increase in American troops was balanced by reinforcements from North Vietnam, and the President came under increasing pressure to carry the bombing across the border. Eventually in February 1965 he gave in. Once again Pentagon predictions proved false. The bombing of the north had no more than a marginal effect on the North Vietnamese war effort and appeared to stiffen political resistance to negotiations.

At the end of April 1965 President Johnson sent the marines into Santo Domingo. The first explanation was that they were there to protect American lives and property from the fighting that had broken out between rival factions but they stayed on to keep the factions apart and bring about a political settlement. They became involved in the political dispute—neutral, as it was said, first on one side and then on the other. The President had been convinced that communists had infiltrated one of the factions and were about to take over, but many felt his decision was taken without full information and primarily with an eye on the domestic repercussions should another close neighbour follow Cuba into the communist camp. In any case it revived all the familiar Latin American fears of United States interventionism.

The episode shook many people's faith in Johnson's judgment and lost him a lot of credit in Latin America. Among other things it seemed to reverse the Kennedy policy of trying to encourage left-wing reform movements as the best defence against communism. In the end, however, the worst fears of his critics were not realized. The intervention was precariously legitimized by the Organization of American States and an inter-American force was formed that supervised elections in the summer of 1966. Dr. Balaguer, the candidate preferred by Washington, was elected and took office peacefully. The last American troops departed quietly in September.

Meanwhile, Vietnam continued to dominate domestic and foreign affairs. While preparing the United States for a long test of wills, President Johnson began to hope that the Russians, benefiting from the in-

creasing isolation of China, might gather sufficient support and influence to bring Hanoi to the conference table. Partly to encourage them, and partly to counteract the influence of General de Gaulle* in Europe, he delivered an important speech on October 7, 1966. He emphasized his desire for east-west cooperation in Europe and offered a number of concessions. He suggested that the two alliances should work together on security and economic relations. It was a far cry from the old talk of rolling back or breaking up the Russian sphere of influence in Europe. It was also a new departure in that it put German reunification at the end of a process of reconciliation instead of at the beginning. It was clear that the President had decided not to allow west Germany to stand in the way of a détente. Quietly he dropped all talk of a multilateral nuclear force designed to give west Germany a share in nuclear strategy.

Meanwhile, as the November elections for Congress approached, Johnson was steadily losing popularity at home. Much of the decline was attributed to his handling of the war in Vietnam. At first the main source of criticism was the academic community, which debated the whole basis of the American commitment. Gradually, as more and more American troops became involved, the unease spread through the country and covered the whole political spectrum from a small minority that called for complete withdrawal to another minority that wanted an all-out war. Between these extremes the majority disliked the war without clearly espousing any alternative. Most people broadly supported the commitment but felt that Johnson was handling it badly.

One of the sensations of the summer of 1966 was the rising popularity of Senator Robert Kennedy, brother of President John Kennedy. On Vietnam he took a position slightly to the left of Johnson. He seemed to arouse a widespread nostalgia for the presidency of his dead brother, and a lot of support for his own hopes of one day taking up the succession.

In domestic affairs some of Johnson's magic was also deserting him. He failed to persuade Congress to pass a labour Bill that he had promised to the unions. He also failed to get through a new Civil Rights Bill that would have made it an offence in many cases to refuse to sell a house to a Negro. Public opinion was clearly not ready for such a measure and was hardening against the pressure of Negro demands. Street riots and the extremism of some of the Negro leaders began to alarm city and suburban dwellers and to alienate even liberals.

Another boost for Johnson's more conservative opponents was provided by the increasing signs of inflation and over-heating in the economy, partly caused by the war in Vietnam. The cost of living was increasing noticeably and becoming an election issue. At the same time liberal opinion was more and more dismayed by the way in which Vietnam was taking money from domestic needs such as education, urban renewal, and other aspects of the war on poverty.

In the congressional election campaign of 1966 Johnson could no longer appeal to the broad consensus that gave him his huge victory over Senator Goldwater. Supporting the Democratic candidates across the country he was forced into a more defensive and partisan role and some candidates were even reluctant to receive his help.

In October Johnson attended a conference in Manila of seven nations fighting as allies in South Vietnam. He also became the first American head of state to visit Australia and New Zealand. His visits emphasized the involvement of these two territories with the United States in Vietnam where British troops had not been taking part. Johnson also made an unannounced visit to American troops in Vietnam.

On his return to the United States just before the mid-term Congressional elections, Johnson pointedly warned Americans against voting for white "back-lash" candidates, even though many Southern Democrats were running on racist platforms. The Republicans made gains in the Senate and the House, leaving Democrats the majority party in both. Johnson said the shift might threaten advance to the Great Society, but would not affect national security policy or the war in Vietnam. Particularly significant were Republican gains of state governorships which produced new rivals to Johnson for the 1968 presidential election.

His 1967 State of the Union message reflected the shift in Congress, and though Johnson asked for a six per cent surcharge on personal and corporate income tax for the Vietnam war and for consolidation of domestic programmes already enacted, he said his proposals would not lead to large increases of federal spending. He warned that the Vietnam war would continue to be a long and costly struggle.

The war which provided some of Johnson's most delicate diplomatic problems in 1967 was that between Israel and Egypt, Jordan, and Syria in June. Johnson condemned the Arab blockade of Israel shipping in the Gulf of Aqaba, and moved the United States Sixth Fleet to the eastern Mediterranean.

He had to balance America's general policy of cooperation with all Middle Eastern countries against an important Jewish vote in the United States in the run-up to election year, and the Soviet Union's clear alignment with the Arab cause. Johnson tried to persuade Israel to wait for a great power solution to the dispute. The great powers were unable to prevent the outbreak of war, but their forces were not involved. Arab allegations of British and American military intervention on Israel's side were later discredited.

The war brought into use for the first time the "hot line" teleprinter link between the American President and the Soviet Prime Minister, first for assurances of non-belligerency and secondly when Israeli torpedo boats damaged an American intelligence ship and American aircraft went to aid the Liberty. Johnson told Kosygin, the Soviet Prime Minister, that his aircraft were not going to help Israel.

Johnson took the opportunity of Kosygin's visit to the United Nations after the Middle East war to have a summit meeting, the first American-Soviet summit for six years, from which the firmest commitment to emerge was agreement on the need for steps to prevent nuclear proliferation, and a promise that a dialogue would be maintained between Moscow and Washington.

After Britain devalued the pound in November 1967 Johnson was faced with additional pressure on the dollar as a reserve currency. He reacted by ordering cuts in the United States capital investment overseas and reductions of United States tourism. In his State of the Union message in January 1968 he confirmed that the Vietnam struggle would go on but was careful to say that any moves towards peace negotiations would be examined. He urged Congress to continue the war against poverty in the cities.

Johnson entered the presidential election year faced with these fundamental problems, Vietnam and violence in the streets, both of which threatened his position as President. Though the American mood favoured Johnson's continuing in a difficult task, some observers felt that if the United States was to extricate herself from the Vietnam involvement it would have to be under the leadership of someone who was not so clearly committed to the war as Johnson. Conflicting attitudes to the Vietnam issue were disrupting traditional political loyalties. Similarly the struggle within the United States for Negro rights had moved into a phase of violence where separatist black power movements grew up in some sectors of the Negro communities, and ordinary white people were alienated from sympathy by reports of crime and race riots.

According to Johnson's later account he gave his Union message early in 1968 with a statement in his pocket of his intention not to run again. However that may be, he certainly entered presidential election year knowing that he had lost support very badly. He could perhaps have weathered growing economic difficulties and the surge in ghetto violence—which actually reached its peak at the time of Luther King's* assassination in March—but the war was another matter.

Disillusion in the prowess of the Pentagon had gone deep and with it any real expectation that Johnson could extricate the country. The attack on him for the Gulf of Tongking decision was mounting. Senator Eugene McCarthy stepped forward and put himself ahead of the anti-war forces—which some interpreted, wrongly, as the head of all radical causes too. Senator Robert Kennedy, however, was still backing Johnson in January, but the New Hampshire primary suddenly revealed just how unpopular the President had become. McCarthy won 42 per cent of the Democratic vote and Kennedy promptly changed his position on running for nomination. Both he and McCarthy attacked Johnson's policy with new assurance, and on March 30 the President ordered a partial halt to the bombing of North Vietnam and asked Ho Chi Minh* for a "positive response". The following day he announced that he would not seek, or accept, renomination, in order to put the unity of the people and work for peace first. He thus opened the way to the contest between Kennedy, McCarthy and Humphrey which was to lead to the assassination of the first, the rejection of the second at the disastrous Democratic convention in Chicago, which Johnson carefully did not attend, and Humphrey's narrow defeat by Nixon in November.

During the presidential struggle, Humphrey, as vice-president, seemed to be hampered by his loyalty to the president in his pronouncements on the war, which were derided by the liberal wing of his party. It seemed to some observers that Johnson, having renounced office himself, was not prepared to back his vice-president for it, and there were many reports of Humphrey's unhappiness in his position. He broke through only after nomination, and only then got Johnson's full blessing.

Johnson, who on November 1 announced a total halt on bombing as peace prospects were improving, was earlier disappointed by the North Vietnamese reaction to plans for a peace conference; and the wrangling over the location of it, and the admission of Saigon, went on through the summer. The extravagant statements by McCarthy and Kennedy hardly encouraged Hanoi to start serious negotiations. He visited President Thieu in July and promised him full support.

His hopes of closer contacts with Russia over disarmament were set back by the invasion of Czechoslovakia in August—he had hoped that he might yet round off his term of office with such a breakthrough, but disappointment in foreign and domestic policy now dogged him to the end, as he was defeated on tax and price proposals, on his gun restriction law, and finally on his nomination of Abe Fortas to the Supreme Court.

It is fair to say that Johnson was always ill at ease in foreign affairs and with foreign leaders. He lacked a sensitive appreciation of the needs of uncommitted nations, feeling that everyone should line up and vote on one side or the other. Nor was he comfortable with the view taken by President Kennedy that in many countries, and especially in Latin America, the democratic left may be a better antidote to communism than the right wing forces on which American policy had relied so much in the past.

He did, however, have a genuine sympathy for the poor and under-privileged both at home and abroad, and a deep belief in America's duty to help them. There was always a danger that this missionary spirit could lead him into over-extended and clumsy commitments round the world, especially in Asia, but without the crippling entanglement of Vietnam he might have gone on to become one of his country's great domestic reformers.

In 1971 he gave an account of his stewardship in *The Vantage Point: Perspectives of the Presidency, 1963-69*.

January 23, 1973.

Franz Jonas, the Federal President of Austria, died on April 23, 1974 at the age of 74.

Born on October 4, 1899, Jonas was one of eight children of working-class parents. After attending primary and secondary schools he went to a printers' school of graphic arts. In 1917, he was called up for military service in the Austro-Hungarian Army and saw active service on both the Russian and the Italian fronts during the First World War. After the war he served in the National Defence Force and took part in the defence of Carinthia's southern frontier in the Lavant valley.

From 1919 till 1932 he was employed as a typesetter and at the same time he served as an official of the printers' union, and as a representative of the socialist youth movement within the Social Democratic Party. He also attended the Workers' Educational Centre in Vienna where Dr. Karl Renner instructed him in political science, Dr. Adolf Schärf* taught him constitutional law, and General Theodor Körner military science. All three of them were later, like Jonas himself, to become Federal Presidents of Austria. In addition, the industrious young typesetter attended evening classes in economics at the Vienna Adult Education Centre and studied English and Italian.

From 1932 until the political disturbances of February 1934 Jonas was secretary of the Floridsdorf branch of the Social Democratic Party in the industrial suburbs of Vienna. Early in 1935 he was arrested and accused of high treason after taking part in the illegal conference of revolutionary socialists at Brünn in Czechoslovakia, but during the mass trials of socialists in 1936 he was acquitted owing to lack of evidence. It was not, however, until 1938 that he could resume his work as a linotype operator. Later he worked as a clerk in an engine factory.

Following the liberation of Vienna in April 1945, Jonas was appointed to the local council of Floridsdorf. It was here that he first demonstrated his qualities as an organizer and administrator. Floridsdorf suburb lies north of the Danube and was completely cut off from the rest of the city at the time, as the retreating Germans had blown up all but one of the Danube bridges. Almost single-handed, Jonas proceeded to build up a local civil administration and to organize supplies for the population. In February 1946 he was appointed chairman of the Floridsdorf local council by the Mayor of Vienna, Theodor Körner. In June 1948 Jonas became a city councillor with responsibility for the city's food supplies, and in December 1949 he took over housing, at a time when the Vienna Municipality was launching a big housing programme to make good the severe war damage to the city.

On Körner's election as Federal President, in 1951, Jonas succeeded him as Mayor and Governor of Vienna. During his 14 years as mayor of the city, Jonas concerned himself mainly with housing, schools, hospitals, kindergarten and domestic policy in general. He broadcast regularly to the population on the municipality's problems and activities, and strongly advocated the strengthening of Vienna's position in Europe and cooperation in bringing about a united Europe. It was his ambition to make the Austrian capital a popular congress centre, a wish which has since been fulfilled.

Only four of the 170 mayors of Vienna since 1282 have been able to boast of a longer tenure of office than Jonas. During the 14 years he was mayor Jonas travelled extensively abroad to see other major cities, not only in Europe, but in the Soviet Union, the United States, the Middle and Far East.

From 1951 until 1953 he was a member of the Upper Chamber of the Federal Parliament, and was afterwards a member of the Lower House. On May 23, 1965 he was elected Federal President of Austria, and on April 25, 1971 he was re-elected for a further term of six years.

In 1966, President Jonas paid a state visit to Britain, and three years later, in May 1969, he received the Queen on a state visit to Austria.

In private life, Jonas was a most modest and a likable personality. For most of his life he lived in a two-room flat with his wife Grete, whom he married in 1922. He was a keen nature-lover, and liked nothing better than a stroll in the Vienna woods. He was also a music-lover with a special preference for Mozart, Beethoven, Schubert and Richard Strauss.

April 25, 1974.

Bobby Jones—See Robert Tyre Jones.

David Jones, C.H., C.B.E., the writer and painter, died on October 28, 1974 at the age of 78.

David Jones has often been compared with William Blake—inevitably, no doubt, for anyone who is ranked equally highly as painter and poet. They are akin, too, in the intensity of their personal vision of man and his destiny—so personal that many who have admired the paintings feel themselves, on first contact with the writings, to some extent shut out or even repelled. Neither is an easy poet to get on terms with; neither, once the association has been made, can ever be again neglected.

It was not until he was about 32 that David Jones began writing at all, and it was not until 1937, when he was over 40, that anything from his pen appeared in print. This was *In Parenthesis*, based on his experiences on the Western Front. In 1952 came *The Anathemata*, and at sporadic intervals and in various forms the last 20 years have seen fragments published from a third work in progress. Here is none of the usual apparatus of a poet—no lyrics, no fragments for the anthologies; instead two, perhaps eventually three, intricately fashioned pieces of writing which, either in whole or in part, may hardly seem to rank as poetry at all. Even to the poetry-reading public (if there is such a thing) David Jones remains little known. Yet T.S. Eliot* was to call *In Parenthesis* "a work of genius", and W. H. Auden to describe *The Anathemata* as "probably the finest long poem written in English in this century". And it was to the poet's suburban cell, stacked with books, paintings, teacups, and the "deposits" (to use a favourite word) of an accumulative but unacquisitive life that the octogenarian Stravinsky made pilgrimage the last time he was in England.

David Jones's slow production of words for publication is in strong contrast to his output in paintings, at least during the years before he began to write. "I painted all the time; I never seemed to stop painting in those days", he said, speaking of the time between 1927 and 1933—the period to which most of his surviving watercolours belong. Anyone who saw the 1955 Arts Council exhibition at the Tate Gallery or in Wales or Edinburgh must have been amazed by the extent and variety of the harvest of these fertile years, which gave the art of Britain a legacy unlike anything else.

It would be wrong to set the two aspects of David Jones's work, writing and the visual arts, in any sense in opposition—or even in contrast—to each other. Few recent practitioners have thought so much about what they were trying to do (in whatever medium) or—though he found exposition "excruciatingly difficult"—tried more helpfully to explain what they were up to. In a number of essays, comments and letters, David Jones elaborated his ideas about the inevitable purpose of an artist—ideas which, he was the first to concede, owed a great deal to Maritain and Eric Gill, though developed in a practical and individual way.

In crude summary these ideas were that the chief mark of man is his capacity to do gratuitous acts, that gratuitous acts partake of the nature of art, and that things so made are signs of something or other. Further, a sign "must be significant of something, hence of some 'reality', so of something 'good', so of something that is 'sacred' ".

The signs David Jones was in the habit of using, particularly in his poems, were sometimes such—for example those drawn from Welsh language and legend—that his audience could hardly be expected to recognize. But others—from Rome or Troy or Mallory or music-halls, or, above all, from the Mass—he might well feel should be comprehensible were this not an evil generation which does not know a sign when offered one. The truth is not so much that David Jones speaks a private language as that he speaks a language which is historically public but now forgotten. How to reconcile "man the artist, man the signmaker" with the modern world was a riddle that increasingly worried him and to which he never found an answer, probably because there is none.

David Jones was born on November 1, 1895 in a small suburban house in Brockley, Kent. His father's family was Welsh-speaking from Flintshire, but his father, who had been apprenticed to a printer in Liverpool, moved to London in the eighties. There he married Alice Ann Bradshaw, daughter of a Rotherhithe mast and block-maker. David Jones was very happy with, and proud of, both sides of his ancestry, the Welsh and the Cockney. They came together again in his wartime companionship and they are inextricably linked in all his subsequent thought.

"I cannot recall", he said, "a time when drawing was not a preoccupation." When he was 14 he entered the Camberwell School of Art, under A. S. Hartrick, who no doubt encouraged his freedom of drawing, and Reginald Savage. In 1915 he enlisted as a private in The Royal Welch Fusiliers and served with them in France until, after being wounded, he was finally invalided home in 1918.

The war loomed over David Jones for the rest of his life—as much, in a way, a flaming light as a shadow. The imagery of the trenches coloured his writings, his designs, his conversation. The comradeship of his section, platoon, and company had a value for him apart from anything that came later, even in a life singularly rich in friendships.

When he was demobilized David Jones spent three years at the Westminster School of Art under Walter Bayes, Bernard Meninsky, and Randolph Schwabe. In 1921 he was received into the Roman Catholic Church. Although, as he said later, "there are . . . no such things as the Catholic arts of painting or engraving or the Catholic art of writing proses or poems" there is equally no part of his work from which the Catholic content can be separated.

At about this time David Jones met Eric Gill, and in 1922 joined his Guild of St. Joseph and St. Dominic at Ditchling. Gill was to become one of the great influences in his life. The remarkable thing is that he should have been able to pursue his own course in spite of the closeness of this strong personality which duplicated at so many points his own interests—Catholic, engraver, letterer.

He had learned engraving from Fr. Desmond Chute, and eventually became one of the most accomplished exponents of an art which was then enjoying a vigorous renascence in Britain. After some early undistinguished work for the St. Dominic's Press at Ditchling he rose magnificently to the opportunity given him by commissions for Robert Gibbings's Golden Cockerel Press. Illustrations to *Gulliver* in 1925 were followed by *The Book of Jonah* in 1926, the *Chester Play of The Deluge* in 1927, and—in the opinion of many his finest work as an illustrator—10 engravings on copper for Douglas Cleverdon's 1929 edition of *The Rime of the Ancient Mariner.*

Then followed the painting years. Perhaps the most characteristic David Jones water-colour is looking out of a window—at the sea, at a park, at a tree; or towards a window by way of a bowl of flowers, a table, a printing-press, a cat. "I like the indoors outdoors, contained yet limitless feeling of windows and doors." Yet he painted much else, including quite a few portraits and some oils (among which "Portrait of a Human Being"—a self-portrait—is perhaps the most outstanding).

The full years were followed by a complete breakdown in health, leaving a miserable legacy of neurasthenia which plagued him on and off for the rest of his life. It was as an alternative form of expression (certainly not as therapeutic relief) that he began to put into shape his disjointed writings about the war. The result was *In Parenthesis.* Acclaimed by critics at the time (it was awarded the Hawthornden Prize in 1938), *In Parenthesis* has always been more easily described by what it is not than by what it is. It is not a "war book"; it is not autobiographical; it is not, by any usual standards, a poem. On the other hand it can reasonably be called an epic based on David Jones's experiences as a private in the trenches. Again, it is about all wars; yet, as in the paintings, it is details that compel attention—the fragmentary portraits of real people in a particular war.

When, two years later, Britain was at war again, David Jones seemed in a way back on familiar though terrible ground. In central London, and then in Harrow-on-the-Hill—where he was to spend the rest of his life, increasingly reluctant to move even a short distance—he began painting again. Many of these later paintings have an intricacy of detail and symbolism which marks them off from the lyrical spontaneity of the earlier water-colours. Yet they include such works as "The Annunciation", "Trystan ac Essyllt", "Guenever", "Vexilla Regis", "The Four Queens", which in spite of their very sparing use of colour, are more immediately impressive than almost any of his other paintings.

In these post-war years, too, David Jones developed an art form which he made specially his own—the painting of inscriptions. Calligraphy in his hand achieved a Chinese sensitivity. Reproductions of some of these inscriptions are to be seen in *The Anathemata* and later publications and form adornments for the books of other writers.

The Anathemata, which appeared in 1952, is an awe-inspiring but demanding work. If read (preferably aloud) four or five times by a person of scholarly attainments the reason for the enthusiastic superlatives it has evoked will be understood. This, of course, is asking a lot. But the difference between *The Anathemata* and another twentieth-century masterpiece with which it is sometimes compared, Ezra Pound's *Cantos,* is that David Jones is never deliberately obscure in his language or recondite in his imagery. Indeed, he always manifested an almost exaggerated humility towards learning in others. He regarded himself as a self-taught monoglot; called his writing "meandering", and compared it, in *The Anathemata,* to "a longish conversation between two friends, where one thing leads to another". But the fact is that he had absorbed from his wide reading more than 99 per cent of scholars get out of theirs, and that the inheritance of Britain from pre-history onwards, which is the "theme" of *The Anathemata,* is not easily put in a simple mould.

David Jones was a singularly dignified, gentle, and warm spirit, amused and amusing. He was unmarried. He was made a C.B.E. in 1955 and a C.H. in June 1974.

October 29, 1974.

Sir Melvill Jones, C.B.E., A.F.C., F.R.S., Francis Mond Professor of Aeronautical Engineering at Cambridge University from 1919 to 1952, died on October 31, 1975 at the age of 88.

The son of a Liverpool barrister, Bennett Melvill Jones went to Emmanuel College, Cambridge from Birkenhead School, graduating with First Class Honours in the Mechanical Sciences Tripos.

In 1910 he went to the National Physical Laboratory. For the first two years of the First World War he was at the Royal Aircraft Establishment, at Farnborough, moving in 1916 to Orford Ness, where he started work on aerial gunnery and also learned to fly. He made important contributions in this field, and to ensure that he understood the practical implications of his work he flew as an observer with No. 48 squadron of the R.A.F. and was awarded the A.F.C. in 1918.

In 1919 Jones was elected to the Professorship of Aeronautical Engineering which had been endowed at Cambridge University by Emile and Angela Mond in memory of their son, Francis Mond, who had been killed in action while serving with the R.A.F. Initially he devoted himself to the study of aerial surveying, using aircraft provided by the R.A.F.

He then studied in detail processes occurring when an aeroplane stalled; this led to a major advance in understanding and contributed to a reduction in flying accidents. In 1929 he presented a paper to the Royal Aeronautical Society on the streamline aeroplane. In this he showed with clarity that, by streamlining, the power required to propel an aeroplane could be greatly reduced. This paper was in advance of its time and had a great influence on the development of the clean monoplane during the next ten years.

From 1919 to 1935 Jones and his team worked on the development in flight of a direct and elegant method of measuring the drag of a section of a wing. This led to further study of the nature of the flow in the boundary layer and the possibility of reducing drag by maintaining the layer in the laminar state.

With the start of the Second World War, Jones was asked by the Air Ministry to return to his work on aerial gunnery which had been so successful in the First World War. He worked in this field until 1943, laying the foundations for the gyro gunsight. He then moved to the Ministry of Aircraft production in London and became Chairman of the Aeronautical Research Council. When he returned to Cambridge after the war he was determined to reduce the drag of aeroplanes still further. He realized that this could be done by sucking air in through the surface so as to maintain the boundary layer in a laminar state. By experiments in flight he and his team showed that it was indeed possible to obtain a substantial reduction of drag in this way.

After his retirement from the professorship in 1952, Jones worked for a number of years as a consultant at the Royal Aircraft Establishment, where his wisdom and experience were of great value to young research workers.

Jones established at Cambridge a formidable school of aeronautics which attracted students of the highest quality. He is remembered with affection by his students and colleagues as an inspired teacher and the kindest and friendliest of men, always modest and ready to give credit to others.

He was elected F.R.S. in 1939 and knighted in 1942. He married Dorothy Laxton Jotham, who died in 1955. They had two sons, one of whom was killed in action while serving with the R.A.F., and one daughter.

November 6, 1975.

Sir Reginald Watson-Jones—See Watson-.

Robert Tyre Jones—Bob Jones to his fellow golfers in America but to the British for ever Bobby Jones—died on December 18, 1971 at the age of 69.

Jones gave up public golf in 1930, seven years before Vardon died. Most of those who play today never saw him, yet in the intervening years his name became legendary as the man in whom all golfing virtues came together—natural ability, determination, intelligence, concentration, humility and courage. Through the medium of the Masters, the legend was kept fresh; through it, also, his joy in the game and his flawless sportsmanship continued to exert an influence which is perhaps his greatest contribution to golf.

"A golfer matchless in skill and chivalrous in spirit" reads the inscription on the plaque presented to him by the Royal and Ancient golf club after he had completed the greatest feat in golf by winning the Open and Amateur titles of Britain and America in one year, 1930. The tribute embraces not only the supreme moment in his career, but the achievements that preceded it, the brilliance of which it sometimes obscures. The question is often asked: "How good was he?", to which no better answer has been found than that given by his distinguished contemporary, Francis Ouimet. "Look at the record!"

In the nine years between 1922 and 1930 which make up most of his career, he played in 11 British and American Open championships and never finished lower than second. He finished first in nine of them, but lost the play-off for two of them. He also won in the same time five American Amateur titles, and at last, in 1930, the one that had hitherto eluded him, the British Amateur: a total of 13 major championships. An amateur competing against the best professionals in the world, yet he devoted no more than three months out of 12 to golf, including travel. In the opinion of his chronicler and constant companion, O. B. Keeler, Jones emphatically played less golf in the eight years of his championship victories than any other first-class golfer. There were defeats, for no one can remain always at his peak, but in what mattered he stood supreme; thus it was that he won all six of his Walker Cup singles, always against Britain's best, and sometimes by a huge margin.

Yet, as in the case of other geniuses, success did not come easily to him. The ostensible cause of his retirement at the age of of 28 was that he decided to make an instructional film, and he thought that this might be held contrary to the spirit of amateurism. But as Bernard Darwin,* who was present at all his triumphs in Britain noted: "It was in any case a wise decision, for no man ever felt more keenly the strain of competition. He subdued a naturally fiery temper, but he could not subdue his silent sufferings; he lost sometimes a stone in weight during a championship and often dare not wear a tie lest it should make him physically sick."

Even at an early age he was so obviously a great golfer that many of his friends were in despair because he did not instantly win everything. At 11 years of age he went round a full-length course in his native Atlanta in 80. At the age of 14 he went three rounds in the American Amateur championship. Yet because at the age of 20 he still had

not won a major championship there were murmurings that for all his great talent he lacked the punch. In 1921 he visited Britain and encountered for the first time seaside winds and parched greens. He was beaten in the fourth round of the Amateur, and in the Open at St. Andrews he tore up his card in the third round, having reached the turn in 46 and started back with a six.

At first he hated the Old course, and the fiery gesture echoed his schoolboy days, when he would throw his club after a bad shot; but he came to love that course with a greater intensity than any foreigner before or since has shown. St. Andrews responded to that feeling, taking him to her heart when he won his second Open there in 1927 with a score of 285, a record for the course and the Open, which was to stand for 25 years. That bond was sealed in 1958 when, on the occasion of his visit to launch the first Eisenhower Trophy world tournament, the freedom of the burgh was conferred on him in a ceremony which unmanned even the hardest-bitten American journalist present.

In 1922 Jones was defeated 8 and 7 by Jesse Sweetser in the third round of the American Amateur, but a year later, after obtaining a first-class science degree at Harvard, whence he had graduated with honours from Georgia Technical College, he fashioned the victory, in the national Open, from which all others flowed. At last, Keeler could say what he had wanted to say all through the years of waiting: that the frustration had been due not to a faint heart, no stouter heart beat in any golfer, but because he had been the victim of too keen a mind and too fine an imagination.

The run of championship titles now began, until in 1926 he renewed his brief acquaintance with British golf. Unexpected defeat in an early round of the Amateur at Muirfield stung him into staying on for the Open at Royal Lytham. He qualified with rounds of 66 and 68 at Sunningdale, the first of them known as his perfect round, because he missed only one green and found 10 of them with a two iron or with wood. It was during these years that Bernard Darwin came to admire his game as he admired that of no other player: "Bobby was not only in his time an incomparably great player, but his style, so lithe and smooth, with a full turn of the shoulders and a drowsy, rhythmic grace, remains a model in memory of all who ever saw it. He was not only a delightful and friendly creature but an extremely intelligent one who bore a long, painful and disabling illness with admirable courage."

At Royal Lytham his victory by two strokes from his fellow American, Al Watrous, is remembered chiefly for his second stroke to the 17th in the final round, a full iron from sand to a hidden green 170 yards away. His career is punctuated by such landmarks. The stroke that won him the first of his four American Opens, an iron to within 6ft. of the last hole of the play-off

190 yards away across water; the "lilypad" shot at Interlachen in his third American championship when another giant shot across water skidded on the water's surface and hopped to dry land; the slice of luck that stopped his ball from running on to the road at the 17th at St. Andrews in the crucial match of the 1930 Amateur against Tolley; the seven in the final round of the Open at Hoylake the same year.

This last is an illustration that in completing his greatest triumph in 1930 Jones played below his best. Tolley asked him before his return to America with both British trophies whether he had ever played quite so badly for so long, and Jones replied that he thought not.

There were shining patches, as when he beat Wethered in the final of the Amateur, and his scores in both Opens were good; but it was only by bolstering his varying form with vast experience, philosophy and courage, that he completed the "grand slam".

That was, historically speaking, the end of his golf, but the great course he created with a few friends near the small town of Augusta now stages a world-famous event bigger than anything he dreamt of when professionals were first invited to a tournament there in which Jones also took part. For years the world's best golfers have competed there annually, coming under his influence until it became true that no man has stamped his character so deeply on the game.

His appearances in Britain became rare and the prospect of them even rarer once his crippling illness of the spine confined him to a wheelchair. During the war, while in Britain as a colonel in the United States Air Force, he exercised his right as a member of the Royal and Ancient golf club to return to the course at St. Andrews he loved above all others. To the club he made a unique present, a copy of the portrait of Francis Ouimet, the first American captain of the club, made by President Eisenhower.* The failure to honour Jones in the same way as Ouimet now seems quite inexplicable, although it is unlikely he would have accepted once his illness confined him to a wheelchair.

He married Mary Malone, a childhood friend.

December 20, 1971.

The former King of Jordan, Talal ibn Abdullah, father of the present King Hussein, died in Istanbul on July 8, 1972. His death closes a tragic episode in the history of the Hashemite dynasty.

He was born in 1909 in Mecca, where his grandfather Hussein was at that time Sherif under the Turks. By the time Talal came of school age his father Abdullah had become Emir of Transjordan, and he was therefore educated privately in that country; later he went to school in England and also took a course at Sandhurst.

He showed himself to be intelligent, conscientious, and likable, but appears to have been basically antipathetic to his father, by whom he deemed himself neglected, and early developed neuroses generally thought to have been caused by his deep resentment at this real or imagined neglect. His marriage in 1933 to his beautiful cousin Zein, and the happy family life which he lived thereafter with her and their four children, did not improve his mental condition, which on the contrary had by 1951 become sufficiently serious to necessitate his being sent to Switzerland for treatment.

This appeared to have effected so much improvement that when, later in the year, his father was assassinated in Jerusalem, his succession to the throne could not justifiably be opposed. In the early months of his reign he performed his duties impeccably and created a generally favourable impression; but behind the scenes his state gradually relapsed to an extent which aroused acute anxiety, in the minds of the few who were aware of the facts, for the safety of his family who were the immediate victims of his frenzies.

In the spring of 1952 he was induced to return to Europe, accompanied by his Queen, for further treatment, but this had no appreciable effect and by the time he returned to his country it had become clear to his Prime Minister, Taufiq Abul Huda, that he could no longer be permitted to rule. In this crisis the Prime Minister acted both firmly and astutely. Malicious rumours were circulating to the effect that the King was not really ill but that his abdication was being plotted by the British Government because he would not obey their demands, and colour was given to these rumours by Talal's normal behaviour in public.

Taufiq Abul Huda therefore invited two Egyptian mental specialists to Amman and induced the King to submit to their examination. They unhesitantly reported unfavourably on his mental state and chances of recovery, and on the strength of this evidence the Jordan Parliament voted his abdication and the accession of his son Hussein, at that time a cadet at Sandhurst.

Talal left for Egypt accompanied only by a small personal staff, his Queen having no doubt decided that her place lay beside her young son and her other children. Later he was transferred to an island in the Bosporus, where he remained under medical supervision, pursuing his religious devotions and seeing no one, until his death.

July 10, 1972.

Hans Peter Juda, C.B.E., who died on February 3, 1975 at the age of 70, was the founder (in 1935) and then editor and publisher of the British export magazine *The Ambassador* until 1964.

He became director of Thomson Publications in that year.

His career was devoted to the fostering of British exports. He was convinced that the arts must be closely allied to industry—in fact, cross-fertilization was one of his favourite concepts. It was he who originated the "British events in Overseas Markets", starting in 1949, by linking industry with the sponsoring of the visit of the Royal Ballet, then the Sadlers Wells Ballet, to America.

After that success the message spread to Canada, Australia, New Zealand, and all over Europe and now British Weeks are a recognized vehicle for British trade promotion.

In 1961 he created the annual Ambassador Awards for achievement, a permanent form of recognition to firms or personalities in differing fields whose achievements were outstanding, such as design policy, contribution to export, the fine and applied arts. The unlikely combination of Wedgwood and the Amadaeus Quartet, Graham Sutherland and Alex Moulton, Sotheby's and Nieman Marcus gives some idea of the concept's breadth. He was created O.B.E. in 1955 and advanced to C.B.E. in 1970.

Born in Trier on the Moselle on September 25, 1904, of a French mother and German father, from the start he was seen to be a boy of great gifts and originality.

He studied economics, law and sociology in the Universities of Munich, Freiburg, Paris and Frankfurt, and in 1927, when in his early 20s, he was appointed Financial Editor of the *Berliner Tageblatt*.

In 1931 he married Elsbeth, daughter of a philosophy professor—a lifelong family friend. They left Germany in 1933 to make a new life in England. Juda became passionately committed to the country of his adoption, and never ceased to be grateful to it.

The Royal Society of Arts awarded him its Bicentenary Medal for 1965. He was a member of the council of the Royal College of Art, and was appointed an honorary Fellow by the College in 1959. He received a similar honour from the Society of Industrial Artists and Designers for his services to industrial design in 1956. He was appointed a governor of the Central School of Arts and Crafts, now the Central School of Art and Design, in 1957 and was chairman from 1965 to 1973.

In his fostering of the arts, he devoted much of his time to the cause of contemporary art and gave considerable practical help to young artists of promise and fame, culminating in the sale of his own collection of modern works of art at Sotheby's in 1967, the proceeds of which were devoted entirely to the creation of a fund to enable artists to travel and widen their experience.

February 6, 1975.

James Robertson-Justice—See Robertson-.

K

Louis Kahn, who died in New York on March 17, 1974 while on his way home to Philadelphia from a visit of inspection to one of his building projects in India, was probably the American architect with the greatest world-wide influence since the death in recent years of such pioneers as Walter Gropius* and Mies van der Rohe.* He was 73.

Kahn's influence was especially strong among the young, to whom his clear grasp of the essentials of a building programme, and his equally clear articulation of the forms each programme logically determined, came as a revelation in the 1960s, at a time when the glass-clad, frame-constructed modern building appeared to be degenerating into a formula. Kahn's original mode of thinking, and the expressive and highly personal style of design that emerged from it, were first widely noticed in his medical research building (1958-60) for the University of Pennsylvania which was dominated by a cluster of brick towers housing the stairways and the scientific and ventilation services independently of the laboratory spaces.

A similar clear separation of functions characterized his next important buildings: a Unitarian church at Rochester, New York (1964) and—even more strikingly—the laboratories for the Salk Institute in California (1965). Thereafter his every building was eagerly studied and analysed by students all over the world, and the reputation he acquired brought him many commissions outside America. The most important of these were the Institute of Management at Ahmedabad, India—the building he had just been visiting when he died—and the Assembly building at Dacca, Bangladesh, which was part of a new capital complex he had planned in 1962.

Both these buildings are still unfinished, but that at Ahmedabad, which has been under construction for several years, is nearly enough complete to show the monumental power of which Kahn was capable and also the somewhat mannered idiom he employed in his last years. It is a vast complex of teaching, library and residential buildings, almost wholly in brick with a dramatic use of arches and buttresses and of circular openings admitting light into the depths of a sequence of courtyard spaces.

Kahn's massive use of red brick, here and at Bangladesh, refers back to some of the early work of Frank Lloyd Wright but also—which perhaps partly explains his immediate appeal to this generation—to the work of mid-Victorian architect-engineers. Yet he was consciously an architectural philosopher rather than one to bury himself in a vernacular style. His influence was reinforced by his outstanding talents as a teacher (he had been Professor of Architecture at the University of Pennsyl-

vania since 1957) and his ability to express ideas in succinct, memorable aphorisms.

Louis I. Kahn was born on the Island of Ösel, Estonia, in 1901. He went to the United States when four years old and had a traditional architectural training at the University of Pennsylvania, graduating in 1924. During the depression of the 1930s he organized a fruitful housing and planning research group. His first involvement with the modern movement in architecture was his association, in 1941, with George Howe, partner in the pioneering firm of Howe and Lescaze. In 1947 he was appointed design critic at Yale University, and from 1948 to 1957 was Professor of Architecture at Yale. From 1950 to 1951 he was also resident architect at the American Academy in Rome. In 1971 he was awarded the Gold Medal of the American Institute of Architects, and he received many other honours and awards including, in 1973, the Royal Gold Medal of the Royal Institute of British Architects.

March 22, 1974.

Chester Kallman, the poet and librettist, and a close friend of the late W. H. Auden, died in Athens at the age of 54 on January 17, 1975.

The son of a dentist who survives him, he was born in Brooklyn and educated at Brooklyn College and the University of Michigan. He wrote three books of poetry, *Absent and Present* (1953), *Storm at Castelfranco* (1956) and *Sense of Occasion* (1971). He also wrote the libretto for Carlos Chavez's opera *The Tuscan Players*, and with W. H. Auden the libretto for Stravinsky's *The Rake's Progress* (1951).

He and Auden also collaborated in preparing a new English version of *The Magic Flute*; in editing *An Elizabethan Song Book;* and in writing the libretti for Hans Werner Henze's operas *Elegy for Young Lovers* and *Die Bassariden*. One of their last collaborations was in the libretto of an opera by Nicolas Nabokov based on *Love's Labour's Lost*.

Kallman had an extraordinary love of opera. From the age of 10 he went to every opera performance at the Metropolitan or elsewhere in New York. He became friends with performers and singers and in a sense it was he who guided Auden into the world of opera.

In addition to the libretto for Chavez's opera Kallman translated into English libretti of *Falstaff, Anne Boleyn,* and *Die Entführung aus dem Serail*.

After the Second World War he lived on the island of Ischia, but then Auden won a generous Italian literary prize and the money went to buy a house outside Vienna, near Kirchstetten, where Auden is now buried.

January 21, 1975.

Dr. Alfred Kalmus, who died in London on September 24, 1972 at the age of 83, was a valiant champion of new music, first in his native Austria, then, after removing to England, of the postwar avant garde in Britain and abroad. His life-work as music publisher began while Mahler was still submitting new works to the firm of which Kalmus became the senior director. He retained his youthful enthusiasm for fresh, challenging music into his octogenarian years. To honour his eightieth birthday 11 composers wrote musical tributes which were performed at a birthday concert in London; significantly they were all composers well below middle age.

Alfred August Ulrich Kalmus was born in Vienna on May 16, 1889. He graduated in law at Vienna University, obtaining his Doctorate of Letters, but he also studied music there under the great scholar Guido Adler. In 1909 he joined the young music-publishing firm of Universal Edition which, under Emil Hertzger, was placing its faith, notwithstanding reactionary scorn, in the new pioneer composers of the twentieth-century—Mahler, Janácek, Bartok, Schoenberg, Berg, Webern, Weill.

Kalmus, ideally qualified in law as well as music, learnt his trade during these heady years. In 1922 he left Universal to found his own Philharmonia edition of pocket scores with their now familiar grey and black paper covers and excellent print. He returned eventually to Universal, bringing his edition with him, and augmenting its catalogue ever after. The menace of National Socialism took him fortunately to England where he was employed to inaugurate a London branch of Universal Edition. (His brother Edwin likewise emigrated to the United States and founded the American Kalmus edition.)

During the war Universal Edition's London branch was taken under the wing of Boosey and Hawkes. Here Kalmus not only kept his catalogue alive but added a new enterprise, the Anglo-Soviet Press, which made much new Russian music publicly available, notably works by Prokofiev. Shostakovich and Khachaturian. He was also actively involved in the valuable series of Boosey and Hawkes concerts where contemporary music, elsewhere largely shelved in favour of favourite classics, found a regular hearing. Kalmus was especially proud of the concerts in which all six string quartets by Bartók were played in a series.

In 1949 he was able to reopen his own Universal publishing firm in London, as well as the Alfred A. Kalmus edition which acted as agents for foreign firms and for Universal abroad. From his office in Soho he promoted the modern classics with which he had been connected during his Viennese youth, and gradually he accumulated a handful of leading young composers, among them Berio, Boulez, Stockhausen, Bennett, Birtwistle and Kagel.

Kalmus knew from his apprentice years that a music publisher who cashes in on success may gain a quick pound or so, but not prestige or self-fulfilment. He lived to see the international popularity of Mahler, and to bring out from studentship, inspire and publicly promote into celebrity, composers born almost three quarters of a century later. The modern concept of a music publisher as friend, mentor, muse and P.R.O., not to to mention music purveyor and financial adviser (Kalmus was proud to be a director of the P.R.S.) owes much to Kalmus's successful example.

Kalmus leaves his widow, born Marianne Blau, and two daughters. He will be remembered for his kindliness, disinterested generosity, engaging, witty conversation, and regular attendance at musical occasions everywhere, by many who knew his smile and his benign, bearded presence, but never, perhaps, had the pleasure of making his acquaintance.

September 27, 1972.

Um Kalthoum, the celebrated Egyptian singer whose voice entranced an entire generation in the Middle East, died on February 3, 1975 in a Cairo hospital, after lying in a coma for five days. Her exact age was uncertain, but she was reportedly nearly 80.

Loved and revered by millions, affectionately nicknamed the "Star of the East", and "Nightingale of the Nile", Um Kalthoum became a legend in her lifetime. For more than 50 years her haunting voice inspired audiences from Morocco to the Gulf, rich and poor alike. Her emotional impact rivalled Edith Piaf*, her fame outshone that of any opera singer, her repertoire included songs specially composed for her by the best poets and writers of her generation. Possibly with the exception of Nasser* she was the greatest embodiment of pan-Arab feeling in the modern Middle East; undoubtedly she united the Arabs in admiration for her more than any other artist.

Um Kalthoum was born into a poor farmer's family in the Nile Delta. She began as a reciter of the Koran, but the strength and quality of her voice soon established her as a singer in her own right. Her concerts were already drawing vast audiences by the 1920s.

Her style of singing was typically Arab. Her theme was usually lost love, or some tale of bravery and sadness, but she widened her range to include political panegyrics, battle hymns and rousing nationalist songs. Above all, however, it is the traditional love ballad with which she was associated.

Alone on the stage with a small orchestra, her performances had a mesmerizing effect. They would last for hours; her stamina was immense, even as she grew old. She was far from beautiful and moved little while singing, except to wave a silk scarf she always held in one hand. But her towering personality instantly communicated itself: a personality that seemed to grow in force as she grew older. This came over

equally well on radio, and until she became ill Cairo radio regularly devoted the first Thursday of every month to her concerts. On these days no statesman could take action, no major cultural event could take place; there were no rivals to her singing. Throughout her life, especially in the late sixties when she joined forces with some famous composers, she made many records, and travelled extensively in the Middle East and beyond. She became immensely rich, reportedly receiving £14,000 for two recitals in Paris in 1966.

To the Arabs she was more than just a singer. Appealing to what is still an oral culture in many places, she reinforced traditional cultural values at a time when the Arabs were searching for a truly Arab cultural identity. She made no compromise with Western pop or folk music, which may partly explain why this had had so little impact in the Middle East. To the end, she remained the most "Arab" of the many singers who have achieved fame.

February 4, 1975.

Kumaraswamy Kamaraj, who was a link figure in Indian political history, died on October 2, 1975 at the age of 72.

He was a regional politician, for 10 years chief minister of Madras and a potent practitioner in the politics of caste and region; then briefly he played a crucial role in national politics when, as president of the Congress Party, his influence was decisive in the choice of two prime ministers, Lal Bahadur Shastri* and Mrs. Indira Gandhi; finally he was left behind by the forces of regional nationalism with which he had at first partially been able to identify himself, and lost all power and most of his influence.

Kamaraj became chief minister of Madras in 1954, displacing C. Rajagopalachari, who was a nationally respected Congress leader—and former governor-general—but also a Brahmin. Kamaraj was of low caste (in deference to his party's secular posture he did not use his caste name, Nadar), and his elevation to the leadership of the state Congress Party marked the relegation of the Brahmins who had hitherto dominated Madras politics—there were no Brahmins in his first cabinets. Anti-Brahminism in Madras was twinned with hostility to what was seen as north Indian domination; and Kamaraj saw that if the Congress were to retain its position in the state it could not allow itself to be outflanked by the two parties, the D.K. and the D.M.K., which expressed and encouraged the demand for a separate, sovereign Dravidian state in south India.

Coupling firm repression of the Dravidian parties' various campaigns of agitation in the 1950s with efficient governance, a tight grip on the Congress organization, and personal reputation unstained by charges of self-indulgence or favouritism, Kamaraj

made his state a Congress model in his decade in office.

In 1963 Kamaraj was elected president of the party and relinquished the chief ministership. The presidency was then much shrunken from its pre-independence stature but Kamaraj, in spite of the severe limitation of his knowing no Hindi and little English, made it again, if briefly, an office of power. Kamaraj's reputation inside the Congress Party was such that, even before he became president, Nehru* gave his name to a plan for revitalizing the party by shifting certain leaders from legislative to organizational roles (in fact the "Kamaraj Plan" was not conceived by Kamaraj), thus incidentally getting rid of sundry of Nehru's opponents. As president Kamaraj's hour came in May 1964, when Nehru died suddenly.

Lending his own weight—great not only because of his personal standing but more because he was a southerner—to the cause of those who were backing Lal Bahadur Shastri for the succession, Kamaraj so manoeuvred as to create a consensus, nullifying the rival claim of Morarji Desai. Shastri, as a unifying figure, was undoubtedly the party's best choice, and his record during his brief prime ministership fully justified Kamaraj and the others who had supported him.

The death of Shastri in Tashkent early in 1966 saw the play re-enacted, Kamaraj again deploying his power to head off the claim of Morarji Desai, this time in favour of Indira Gandhi, Nehru's daughter. His instinct was for the unifying figure, for the candidate of maximum acceptability in the party; and this rather than personal regard (he and Mrs. Gandhi were never on good terms) led him to support her candidacy. In 1965 the contest went to an election, which saw Mrs. Gandhi handily the victor.

For the third time after Nehru's death the party chose a leader in March 1967. Kamaraj was still Congress president. Again, though much more reservedly, he backed Mrs. Gandhi—but the political landscape in India had been much changed by the earthquake of the 1967 election, and Kamaraj himself was a casualty. The popular swing against the Congress Party had not been dramatically great, but the consequences were. By the end of 1967 six of the states were lost to Congress. Some were to be regained, but plainly the period of Congress Raj, of the party's almost unchallenged domination of Indian politics, was over.

In Madras the Dravida Munnetra Kazhagam (D.M.K.), now the prime vehicle of Tamil nationalism, swept the Congress from power, and a student leader defeated Kamaraj, who had stood for the state assembly in his old rural constituency. With his base of political power lost, and the added humiliation of personal defeat, Kamaraj's influence in the party was sharply reduced. Beyond his adroit ring-mastering of the leadership elections he had not made any mark on the party organization during his tenure, and after he ended his second term in 1968 his role was little more than that of a member of one of the party's several cabals. The general elections of 1971 resulted in a further setback to his prestige and authority and he vacated the limelight.

Kamaraj had worked his way up in the Congress, serving nearly eight years in British gaols, beginning with participation in Gandhi's salt march in 1921. His formal education did not go beyond school, and his rise in the party must be traced to his quietly powerful personality, his innate political grasp, and low caste background —paradoxically, had he been of higher caste, it is probable that he could not have reached such positions of power. Kamaraj never married, a rarity in India, and his bachelorhood confirmed his reputation for personal austerity and single-minded concentration on politics and government.

October 3, 1975.

Shaikh Abeid Amani Karume—See Zanzibar.

Erich Kästner, the German writer, died in a clinic in Munich on July 29, 1974 at the age of 75.

Kästner made a worldwide and lasting reputation with one of his earliest books. This was a story for children entitled *Emil and the Detectives*, published in the original German in 1929, and soon translated into several languages. It was also turned into a play and into a film, with the script by Emerich Pressburger, which made its triumphant way all over the world. Later Kästner wrote several other books, more stories for children, novels for adults—of a very different kind—poetry and autobiography. But none equalled in popularity his children's masterpiece.

He was born in Dresden on February 23, 1899. He was a schoolboy when the First World War broke out, but before its end he was, in spite of indifferent health, called up. Though the war ended before he could be sent to the front, his experiences embittered him, and gave a twist of cynicism and disillusionment which marked almost all of his writing for adults. It certainly marked his early poems, with their bitter, anti-militarist satire. Thornton Wilder, when he met Kästner many years later, told him he was "six Kästners", and certainly it was an entirely different character that found expression in *Emil and the Detectives*. The hero is robbed of his pocketmoney by a sinister man in a bowler hat and forms, with his school-fellows, a detective squad to track down the thief. It has a simplicity, spontaneity and naturalness, spiced with adventure and delightful humour, that at once ensured its success. Before long it was a favourite German reader for young students of that language. As a play it was kept in many a theatrical repertory into the 1960s.

In 1931 Kästner published a novel, *Fabian*, which contained the essence of his disgust, tempered by a kind of Swiftian humour, with the futility and corruption into which he conceived his country had descended in the closing years of the Weimar Republic. But Kästner did not want the Nazi regime as an alternative. His books were among those of other anti-militarist writers which were publicly burnt in the early days of Hitlerism on May 10, 1933. He was forbidden to publish in Germany, but allowed to issue certain of his books abroad. So in 1933 he issued, in Zurich, another successful children's book, *The Flying Schoolroom*, and next year a comic novel, *Three Men in the Snow*. In 1935 a delightful successor to *Emil* was published, *Emil and the Three Twins*. Kästner was twice arrested by the Gestapo, but released after questioning.

In 1938 he visited London and made contact with English writers whom he had come to know as members of the P.E.N. Club. He returned to Germany before the outbreak of war. He was still forbidden to publish but was allowed, anonymously, to write the script and help in the production of the Ufa film, *Münchhausen*. In 1942 his death was reported, and appreciations of his work appeared in many papers. In fact one of his friends was executed for "defeatism" and another committed suicide. Kästner eluded arrest and continued to write satirical sketches and poems which were published after the war. In the calamitous air-raid on Dresden in February 1945 his home was destroyed.

Although he was a friend of writers of the extreme left such as Brecht he chose not to live in the Soviet Zone, but made his home in Munich. Here he continued to produce plays and poems, wrote for a cabaret as some gaiety returned to the city, and made fresh film-versions of his early successes. In 1951 he was elected president of the West German branch of the P.E.N. Club. In 1957 he published a bitter satirical comedy, *The Three Dictators*, which he considered one of his best works. A German critic compared it with George Orwell's *1984*, but it lacked originality. The same year Kästner received the Büchner prize, named after the nineteenth-century revolutionary German dramatist whose work was rediscovered in 1918. In 1960 came another award, that of the Hans Andersen prize for children's books, a testimony to the more genial side of his talent.

Kästner gave, in two or three autobiographical works, a picture of the Germany he knew as a young man and the Germany that collapsed in 1945. After the war some correspondents asked Kästner why he had ever returned to that Germany, and he replied that he wanted to look not behind the scenes but "at the drama due to be played in front of the audience". It was apparently his intention to gather the material for a big *comédie humaine* about the rise and fall of the Third Reich, and in 1960 he published in *Notabene, 1945,* what were evidently notes for such a work. But it proved impossible; he did not find, he said, that tragedy and horror on such a scale as he had witnessed could be turned into fiction. It may be doubted whether his powers as a writer would have been equal to such a task. His abilities lay in one volume novels, satirical sketches and poems; in his writing for children his ability was raised to something like genius.

July 30, 1974.

General Sir Charles Keightley, G.C.B., G.B.E., D.S.O., who died on June 17, 1974 at the age of 72, had a distinguished career in the Second World War as a divisional and corps commander in the Tunisian and Italian campaigns, held the three chief commands in the Army after the war, and was Governor of Gibraltar for four years. But it is as the Army Commander-in-Chief in the ill-fated Suez operations of 1957 that he was best known to the public.

Keightley was a tall, broad-shouldered man, with a fine presence. He was one of the cavalrymen who emerged early in the war as an outstanding trainer and leader of armoured troops, and he always strove to exploit their characteristics of speed and surprise. It was sad for him that, in his last operation of all, he was denied the means and the opportunity to put his favourite principles into practice. He was a splendid administrator, and had an exceptional capacity for grasp of detail, which he combined with ability to see the wood as well as the trees. Though he drove his staff and his troops hard, he was a popular commander and was liked for his charm of manner, his cheerfulness, his sense of humour and his approachability. In his youth he excelled as a polo player, and in 1929 he played for the Army in India against Australia.

Charles Frederic Keightley was born on June 24, 1901, the son of the Rev. C. A. Keightley. He was educated at Marlborough, and was commissioned from Sandhurst in 1921 in the 5th Dragoon Guards. He became adjutant to his regiment after its amalgamation with the Inniskilling Dragoons, graduated as staff officer to the Director-General Territorial Army and as brigade major of the Cairo Cavalry Brigade.

In 1939 he was at the Staff College, Camberley, as an instructor, but he was released for a short spell of active service as A.A.Q.M.G. of 1st Armoured Division in France. While holding this appointment he was largely responsible for originating a new system of supply to tanks in the front line which became the model for armoured formations during the war. At the age of 40 he was promoted major-general and put in charge of the Royal Armoured Corps Training Establishments in the United Kingdom.

His next important command was the

6th Armoured Division, which he led with distinction in the North African landings and throughout the Tunisian campaign. His division played a notable part in the battle of Hamman Lif and, later, in the capture of Tunis and Cape Bon. He continued to command the 6th Armoured Division in the Sicily campaign and in Italy until the end of 1943. He was then transferred to the 78th Infantry Division, and took part in the fighting round Cassino and in the subsequent advance of the 8th Army. In 1944 he was given command of the 5th Army Corps as lieutenant-general, and he commanded this corps with outstanding success until the end of the Italian campaign.

After the war he served at home for two years as Director of Military Training at the War Office, and then as Military Secretary to the Secretary of State, Mr. Shinwell. His tenure of the latter appointment was cut short when he succeeded General Sir Brian Horrocks, who had fallen ill soon after assuming duty as G.O.C.-in-C. of the British Army of the Rhine. After three years in Germany he was appointed C.-in-C. Far East Land Forces in 1951, and was promoted general.

In 1953 he took over his last active appointment, as C.-in-C. Middle East Land Forces. His command was transferred to Cyprus in December 1954, when the Suez bases were handed over to Egypt. Two years later, by a strange irony of fate, it was he who was ordered to reoccupy them, surely one of the most unenviable military tasks of modern times. The crisis came at the moment when his normal tenure of command had expired, but his great experience was considered indispensable, and he was appointed Commander-in-Chief of the British and French forces which were to intervene in the Canal Zone.

In all the controversy over the different aspects of the Suez affair, there has been none over the part he played. His dispatch throws little light on the political intervention in the execution of the military plan, which must have taxed even his imperturbability, as the stream of confusing and contradictory instructions, which he received from the Government at every stage, must have sorely tried his remarkable capacity for flexibility. Keightley claimed that the operations were a "straight military success", and there is certainly little doubt that, had they not been called off two days after the troops had landed, he could have reoccupied the whole canal down to the Red Sea in a few days more.

The complexities of his task were great. The forces assigned to the operation had to be collected from places as far apart as Cyprus, Malta, Algeria and the United Kingdom. He was given only 10 hours notice to put his plan into operation instead of the promised 10 days, and, in addition to the obvious need for great speed of movement, there was the difficulty of avoiding unnecessary casualties to civilians and damage to property.

When the British Government issued their ultimatum to Israel and Egypt, and Egypt refused to accept the conditions, Keightley was ordered to go ahead immediately. One consequence of this was that he was instructed to begin the bombing of the Egyptian airfields six days before the assault troops could arrive at Port Said from Malta, over 900 miles away, thus introducing the agonizing and protracted pause in the operations during which international tension mounted so dangerously. A British and French airborne force was launched from Cyprus on November 5, and captured Port Fuad with few casualties. On the following day the seaborne assault went in and occupied Port Said, and by that evening the allied troops were 23 miles down the canal. This was the point at which the operations were called off on orders from London that a United Nations force would take over.

Keightley was retired from the Army two months later at the age of 56, and his retirement caused much comment in his own country and in France. The truth was that, in the ordinary course, he would have retired a year earlier on completion of his tenure of command in the Middle East. He was made G.B.E. and appointed Governor and Commander-in-Chief Gibraltar, rewards which were generally accepted as sufficient acknowledgment that, within the resources provided for him, his operations at Suez had been successful until they were stopped on political grounds.

He was Colonel Commandant of the Royal Armoured Corps from 1950 to 1958, Colonel Commandant of the Royal Armoured Corps Cavalry Wing from 1958 to 1968, and Colonel of the 5th Royal Inniskilling Dragoons from 1947 to 1957. He was A.D.C. to the Queen from 1953 to 1956. He was a Grand Officer of the French Legion of Honour and had the Croix de Guerre and the American Legion of Merit.

He married, in 1932, Joan, daughter of Brigadier-General G. N. T. Smyth Osbourne of Iddesleigh, and had two sons.

June 19, 1974.

Sir David Lindsay Keir, Master of Balliol College, Oxford, from 1949 to 1965, died suddenly at his home at Boar's Hill, Oxford, on October 2, 1973. He was 78.

Like so many Scots who have made a name for themselves in their chosen walk of life, Keir was a son of the manse. Educated at Glasgow Academy and Glasgow University, serving with the K.O.S.B. from 1915 to 1919, he went up to New College after demobilization, and was placed in the First Class in the School of Modern History in 1921, his examiners ranking his performance as the best of his year.

University College at once elected him to a Fellowship in History, which he held until 1939. He was a stimulating and successful tutor, and outside his work in the pupil-room and as a writer he found time to be Dean of his College, and an admirable Estates Bursar, as well as honorary treasurer of the O.U.R.F.C.

For 10 years after 1939 he was President and Vice-Chancellor of The Queen's University, Belfast. When he took up office there the programme of expansion contemplated by the University was at once frustrated by the war, and, instead of presiding over a rapidly expanding institution, Keir was faced by the difficulties and problems that the war brought with it. He was determined, however, that these developments should only be postponed, and that in the meantime it was the plain duty of Queen's to maintain its work at the highest possible level of efficiency. This, despite an increase in the number of undergraduates and a diminished teaching staff he was able in full measure to achieve largely through his own enthusiasm and wise leadership.

From the end of the war Keir was able to induce both the Government of Northern Ireland and the U.G.C. to make substantial new grants to his university, both for capital and for recurrent expenditure, and before he laid down office in 1949 he had seen Queen's enjoy the first fruits of the revised programme which he had so carefully planned and which he had done so much to bring about.

New sites were acquired, new science buildings erected, houses were provided for the staff, and their conditions of pay and service adjusted up to those enjoyed by their fellows in Great Britain. Under him Queen's successfully completed the first major phase in its post-war development, and he left the University strong in its staff, in the number of its students, in its wealth and prestige, and in that corporate spirit which means so much to a place of learning, an inheritance in no small measure due to his vision, initiative, and guidance.

When Lord Lindsay went to be the first head of the new University College of North Staffordshire, Balliol asked Keir to follow him as Master. Under Lindsay the college had successfully re-adjusted itself to the demands of the post-war world, and Keir was not asked to undertake the sort of creative work that he had done for Queen's. He regarded with suspicion the increasing influence of the University, the University Grants Committee and the Ministry of Education in college affairs, and was not in sympathy with some recent trends in Oxford education, for example, the growing emphasis on post-graduate training, and the proposals (both in Balliol and in New College) to introduce some form of co-education.

But, if he was content on the whole to preside over a college developing along lines already in principle laid down, he did much to maintain its high reputation. Perhaps the greatest single contribution he made to its life was in his revival of the admirable tradition, so strong under Jowett and Strachan-Davidson, that made the college, and especially the Master's Lodgings, a port of call not only for all old Balliol men but for others of distinction in every walk of life, a task in which the charm and devotion of his wife helped him in ways which only those who knew them both can fully appreciate.

This generous interest he extended in full measure to his undergraduates whom, despite the increased size of the college, he made it his business to know personally, to the enormous benefit of Balliol. The intimate knowledge of their problems and progress, and the shrewd appositeness of his criticism and advice which he showed at the terminal "hand-shakings", was a constant surprise to many of them, as it was, indeed, at times to their tutors.

At a time when the college had to undertake a good deal of building, both of college houses and in the reconstruction of the library, and when financial problems were ever present, his sound business head and his intimate knowledge of architects and of architecture were invaluable. Able, devoted, a man of transcendant honesty of purpose, he was unsparing of himself in the performance of his duties as Master, and to him Balliol must always owe much.

This was particularly evident in connexion with the college's 700th anniversary, celebrated in 1963, and the associated appeal fund.

He was an able historian, who, had he not given up so much of his time to administration, would have written much more than he did. In scholarship his interests lay chiefly in the field of constitutional history and law, and despite his many other activities he found time to write two books which will remain standard works in their respective subjects: his *Constitutional History of Modern Britain*, which ran into editions, and, with Professor Lawson, *Cases in Constitutional Law.*

He married in 1930 Anna Clunie, daughter of R. J. Dale, of Montreal, and had one son and one daughter.

October 4, 1973.

Professor Alan Kekwick, who died on April 5, 1974 at the age of 64, was one of the pioneers of blood transfusion and also a recognized authority on nutritional problems.

He was one the prominent members of the younger generation of physicians who qualified in the 1930s and decided that a rationalization of the practice of medicine was essential if clinical medicine was to keep pace with the advances of biochemistry, physiology and pharmacology. Problems such as blood transfusion, wound shock and nutritional disturbances, particularly obesity, therefore appealed to him and gave him scope to harness to his teaching, which was always clinically sound, a scientific and research approach which was as stimulating to his students as it was invaluable to the rapidly changing face of medicine.

Fundamentally a physiologist, he integrated the scientific study of the functions of the body with the practice of medicine in a way which, while it may now be commonplace, was in his early professional days far from common.

Alan Kekwick was born on April 12, 1909, and educated at Charterhouse, Emmanuel College, Cambridge, and the Middlesex Hospital Medical School. He graduated in 1933. A three years' spell as resident medical officer at the Middlesex Hospital followed by a two-year spell holding a Leverhulme Research Scholarship capped his post-graduate career and gave him that breadth of outlook, clinical and scientific, that were to mark the rest of his career. After a spell in the R.A.M.C. during the 1939 war he returned to the Middlesex Hospital and its medical school where he was to spend the rest of his professional career as professor of medicine, physician and director of the Institute of Clinical Research.

To a certain extent he was a lone worker, though he made an excellent chief, teacher and colleague. A quiet, unassuming character, he yet knew his own mind and had seldom any hesitation in following out any idea which he considered reasonable, even though some might consider it somewhat unorthodox or premature. In some ways he was more successful as director of the Institute of Clinical Research than as a physician. Here he obviously felt at home, but his undergraduate teaching duties were never overlooked.

Although the Middlesex Hospital and its medical school were his professional home he played his part in the wider medical field, serving at different times as a member of the Senate and the Academic Council of London University, senior censor of the Royal College of Physicians of London, of which he was a Fellow, and chairman of the Pharmacological subcommittee of the Ministry of Health. He also served as an external examiner in medicine and physiology at Makerere College, Kampala; University College, Ibadan; the University College of the West Indies; and the University of Baghdad.

April 10, 1974.

Sir Gerald Kelly, K.C.V.O., P.P.R.A., portrait painter and President of the Royal Academy from 1949 to 1954, died on January 5, 1972 at the age of 92.

Gerald Festus Kelly was born in London on April 9, 1879, the only son of the Rev. Frederic Festus Kelly, sometime vicar of Camberwell. He was educated at Eton, where he contracted liver trouble and left school at the end of his third year in order to go to South Africa for his health. On the way out he shared a cabin with an architect named Masey, who praised some of his water colour paintings and inspired him

with a desire to go and live in Paris. His father at first opposed the idea, but gave way on condition that Kelly also went to Cambridge. At Trinity Hall he did no work but managed to win the Winchester Reading Prize. His elocution was always as excellent as his literary style.

After leaving Cambridge Kelly wanted to go on the stage, but his father insisted that he must be a painter or nothing, and in the autumn of 1901 he became a student in Paris. He regarded himself as extraordinarily lucky, for the very first painting he completed was hung on the line in the Salon des Artistes Français in the spring of 1902, and he had quite a little success, though he regarded his pictures of that period as little better than dingy imitations of Whistler.

In France he met Somerset Maugham*, who became a close friend and whom he painted on more than one occasion. Maugham was living in Montparnasse, Kelly had a studio nearby and they dined each evening with other painters and writers in a small restaurant in the rue d'Odessa. Kelly met Renoir and Monet ("a lovely man") and visited a rather tetchy Cézanne in Provence. He recalled in 1969 that he used to knock humbly on Degas's door: "sometimes he would say 'come in' and sometimes he would tell me to go away."

In 1903 the French Government bought a picture out of the Autumn Salon of which he was made a Sociétaire, and his pictures were regularly hung in the Salon de Champs de Mars and the Autumn Salons. He was made Commander of the Legion of Honour in 1950.

In 1904 he was invited by Hugh Lane to exhibit in an exhibition of Irish painting at the Guildhall, and in the autumn of 1907 when he left Paris and brought some pictures to London, Lane bought the "Mrs. Harrison" for his Municipal Gallery in Dublin. Lane saw to it that Kelly never wanted work from that time onwards, and through him Kelly found his way smoothed in London. His pictures were rejected from the Royal Academy in 1905, 1906 and 1908; but from 1909 onwards he exhibited there constantly. From 1909 he exhibited at the International Society, of which he was soon made a member.

In 1907 he joined the Modern Society of Portrait Painters and exhibited there five pictures every year until 1914. It was probably in this exhibition more than in any other that he became known. He also exhibited in the Royal Society of Portrait Painters from 1904 to 1909 and in the National Portrait Society from its foundation in 1909 until the 1914-18 War.

In 1908 he went to Burma, where he remained about nine months. He did an enormous amount of work, and if it was not very good it certainly gave him a great thrill. Subsequently Burmese dances were often his subject. In 1911 he went to Seville with the intention of staying there five or six months, but stayed on until 1914. He went there again in 1917 under the Intelligence Department of the Admiralty. In 1908 he was elected an Associate of the Royal Hibernian Academy and a full member in 1914. In 1922 he was elected an Associate of the Royal Academy in London, and a full member in 1930.

In 1938 Kelly was appointed a member of the Royal Fine Art Commission, a position he held until 1943, in succession to Sir William Rothenstein, who had retired. He was commissioned to paint the state portraits of the King and Queen in 1938, though these were not completed until 1945, when they were shown in the summer exhibition of the Academy. He was knighted in that year.

At the age of 70, in 1949, Kelly was elected president of the Royal Academy in succession to Sir Alfred Munnings, who had retired because he wanted to live in the country and thought that the president ought to remain in London where he could be consulted at any time. In view of Munnings's violent attack on modern art at the Academy banquet that year, Kelly was asked by a journalist his opinion on the subject. He said: "No two men ever had the same opinion about art. I think that modern art, like every other art, has in it some good, some bad, and some indifferent, and some of it is danged bad."

Kelly married, in 1920, Jane, the fifth daughter of S. Ryan. It was a very happy marriage, and Kelly painted his wife no fewer than 50 times. Year after year a portrait of her would appear at the Academy with the simple title of "Jane I", "Jane II", "Jane III", and so on, as the numbers mounted up. When asked why he painted so many portraits of his wife, Kelly said: "I paint my wife because I think nobody has a prettier wife than I."

Kelly is represented at the Tate Gallery by two oil paintings: "Ma Si Gyaw, Dancer", presented by the National Loan Exhibitions Fund Committee in 1914, and "The Jester (W. S. Maugham, 1911)", a Chantrey Bequest purchase of 1933.

In 1957 some 300 of his paintings were shown in an exhibition at Burlington House where those who had only seen his work in the crowded and sometimes clamorous surroundings of a Summer Exhibition at the Academy were able to see his consistent level of achievement; his industry; his craftsmanship; and his unexceptionable accomplishment as a literal draughtsman.

He had a versatile mind and was a most lively talker—always at his best with intimates like Somerset Maugham. He gave dinners at which the food and wine well matched the talk. He maintained that any man of natural ability could master the technique of almost any art but music. He was entirely unpretentious, though his wit sometimes ruffled the subjects of it. A characteristic understatement was the postscript he added to his preface in the catalogue of the Flemish Art exhibition at the Academy, 1953-54. After a long list of acknowledgements came the remark "P.S.— Some credit is due to the painters who

produced these lovely things!" He was a loyal and delightful friend, and his death will be regretted in many different circles.

January 6, 1972.

Sean Kenny, the stage designer, died in London on June 11, 1973. He was 40.

Kenny was responsible for the spectacular stage sets for shows like *Oliver, Blitz, Pickwick* and *Lock Up Your Daughters.* His successes included the design of the Gyroton, a huge thrill ride for Expo 67 in Canada, that of an all-glass underwater restaurant in Nassau and a mechanized, multi-layer stage for a Las Vegas nightspot.

In 1968 he was concerned with the problems of dimension and proportion with *Gulliver* for the Mermaid Theatre in London. Kenny's ideas were projected on to three elastic film sequence backgrounds so that the audience had the illusion of Gulliver wading into the ocean to oblige the Lilliputians to pull back the midget ships of the enemy's navy and the hero appeared to be soaked in the real thing.

Sean Kenny, the eldest of nine brothers, was born in Tipperary, Ireland, on December 23, 1932 and started his theatrical career in London in 1957 and quickly became an established member of the London theatrical scene. Between 1960 and 1970 he designed sets for 32 major West End productions. Starting with plays like the rumbustious *Hostage* and moving through satirical *Lily White Boys* and Dunkirkian *Henry V*, he went full-size with the five-encores-a-night *Oliver.* The set for *Oliver,* which was one unit of robust timber baulks, revolved, moved in and out and up and down to present a picture of murky old London Bridge, a ghastly workhouse, a people-packed street or an elegant Regency town-house.

To get to America, where Kenny studied under Frank Lloyd Wright in his Wisconsin school, Kenny sailed a small boat across the Atlantic with two companions. Wright taught him that "to be an architect meant being in love with architecture". He practised for a time as an architect in Dublin, but his one success was a house he built in Donegal where he adapted his modern thinking to the romantic lore of a tranquil country site.

Among his designs were those for Michael Tippett's new opera *King Priam* which appeared at Covent Garden in 1962. The previous year he had designed I.T.V.'s production of *The Plough and the Stars,* and *The Devils* for Stratford-on-Avon. Other successes were *Maggie May* and *Blitz.*

The unexpected death of Sean Kenny at such a young age robs us of one of the outstanding talents which had helped to usher the theatre into a period in which the conventional barriers were being broken down.

The abolition of the old dividing line

between architecture and design was one of the most important steps that had to be taken; and Sean Kenny, with his architectural training, his originality as a designer, his forceful personality, his prodigious energy and his capacity for thinking in three-dimensional and kinetic terms about how to fill theatrical space, was ideally equipped to play an extremely important part in exploring the new possibilities.

He was also interested in breaking across the frontier between directing and designing. It is a cruel irony that has prevented him from making his London debut as a director, as he would have done at the beginning of July 1973 at the Mermaid Theatre, with which he had been associated from the time it was being planned, and where he designed the extremely successful production, *Lock Up Your Daughters.*

For the National Theatre, too, he not only designed the opening production, *Hamlet,* but redesigned the Old Vic Theatre to make the proscenium less constricting for the new company.

In the original souvenir book for the Mermaid he wrote a piece called "Let's get the Theatre out of its Coffin". He said: "Let us rebel, fight, break down, invent and reconstruct a new theatre. Let us destroy and liberate. Let us free the theatre from the cumbersome shackles of outmoded traditions."

It can be claimed for him without exaggeration that he did as much as, if not more than, any other architect or designer towards that end. He loved movement and hated rigidity, and his famous and ingenious set for *Oliver* demonstrated that decor could consist of a piece of moving architecture.

June 12, 1973.

Paul Keres, the great Soviet chess grandmaster, died in Helsinki on June 5, 1975 at the age of 59.

Keres, three times champion of the Soviet Union, four times winner of world chess olympiads and three times champion of Europe was, arguably, one of the greatest chess players never to win the world championship. During his career many world champions became his victims during international tournaments.

An Estonian, he early came to prominence when he won the schoolboy's championship of Estonia in his early teens. From that point his dashing, individual style of play quickly established him as one of the world's leading players. The outstanding technique with which he overwhelmed Winter's Sicilian Defence, as a 19-year-old, foreshadowed the genius with which he was later to defeat great players like Capablanca and Alekhine in the 1930s and, after the Second World War which effectively intervened in his career when he was at the height of his powers, to beat Botvinnik, Petrosian and Spassky in major tournaments.

The romantic flair of the young Keres seemed particularly effective against a Sicilian defence and it was at the age of only 22 that he met and prevailed against the cool, classical style of the great Capablanca in 1938.

The outbreak of the Second World War saw Keres at his best and a challenger for the world championship, but international chess was virtually in abeyance for the next six years. These were the wasted years for Keres and though he returned to the international arena to play with great distinction thereafter, the physical and intellectual rigours of qualifying for a challenge to the world title possibly proved a little too much for a man fractionally past his peak.

Nevertheless he continued to record international victories. He triumphed over Botvinnik, by then an ex-world champion, at the Alekhine Memorial Tournament of 1956. In 1958 he won first prize in the premier tournament in Hastings and in 1968 easily outdistanced Petrosian, then world champion, at the strongly contested Bamberg tournament.

He was returning from another victorious tournament in Canada when he died of a heart attack in Finland.

Keres's career was one of remarkable development from a dazzling addiction to gambits which overthrew many fine classical defences to a steadily deepening grasp of the strategy of positional play. His maturity was one of mastery in every phase of the game, but through circumstances he remains, along with Akiba Rubenstein, a great player who was denied the supreme prize in chess.

June 6, 1975.

Field-Marshal Ayub Khan —See **Ayub.**

Nikita Khrushchev, who died on September 11, 1971, will be remembered principally as the man who reversed the Stalinist trend of Russian communism. Under his control as the supreme figure in the Soviet Union for over a decade, several historic lines of policy were changed. Not only were the bonds loosened at home, but abroad he accepted the logic of the nuclear age.

Tough and canny as he was, ever ready to take advantage of an opponent, utterly ruthless on occasion and frequently unpredictable in action, he nevertheless managed over a period to convince the leaders of the western world that his desire for peace was sincere and that he would pursue his initiatives always within that limit.

He brought the Soviet Union back more into the mainstream of international affairs —though at the expense of the unity of the communist bloc, in Europe as well as in Asia. Where Stalin was a sinister figure of mystery—almost it seemed a living myth —Khrushchev was very much a creature of

flesh and blood. His outrageous ebullience, his earthy humour, the loquacity generated within that pugnacious bald head, even his tempestuous moods—all came ultimately to be regarded with something nearly approaching affectionate tolerance. It was a mark of the extent to which he changed the image of Russia in the outside world that, in spite of the unsavoury aspects of his record, his swift departure from office on October 15, 1964 was greeted with regret: it was felt that in the most basic sense he was a force of stability.

It may have been his over-confidence, based on this extreme concentration of power, which proved to be the cause of his undoing. High-handed actions and failure to consult with his colleagues were among the reasons for his removal hinted at by the Russian press in the weeks following his fall. His conduct during his last few weeks in power certainly suggests that he considered a serious threat to his position unthinkable.

After his fall from power he was seen in public on infrequent occasions, usually about to cast his vote in some election. He was invariably asked what he had to say about current international problems, and invariably was at pains to point out that as a "mere pensioner" he was not in a position to offer any comment.

Then, in the autumn of 1970, the world was startled by the publication of the book, *Khrushchev Remembers*, a collection of reminiscences which were apparently partly recorded by Khrushchev on tape, partly dictated to members of his family, and partly collected by other hands. Although the publication in the West was denounced by the Soviet authorities, and caused a great deal of argument among Soviet experts in the West, the general consensus was that the book was based mainly on Khrushchev's own words.

It certainly was in character. Krushchev showed himself to be passionately against Stalin and to be searching for some checks and balances that might operate with the Soviet system to forestall a new attempt at personal tyranny. In his reminiscences he spoke as he always had done—with little logical order, with not much ideological depth, with many exaggerations and some plain lies, but always compellingly and usually with a vein of hard common sense.

Once again he revealed himself as shrewd, undisciplined in thought, imaginative in many of his plans, intuitive, suspicious, seeking to improve the working conditions of ordinary people, proud of Russian might— in fact very much a Russian of the Russians. In actual substance the reminiscences did not change much of what was known of Soviet life and Soviet policy, but they were full of illuminating sidelights on persons and events.

Krushchev was a strong, short, stocky man with a powerful, pleasantly ugly face. He was a vivid talker, and his wit was quick, though apt to be brutal when inflicted on his subordinates. He was a man

of the people and proud of it, claiming to have no use for diplomatic or academic subtleties. Even at official receptions he was bluff and jovial—"the life and soul of the party"—though quick-tempered if insulted or answered back. He had a tremendous capacity for hard work and took a personal interest in many problems, especially in agriculture, that other men would have left to specialists. Unlike his predecessors, he enjoyed his public appearances, and liked making personal contact with the man in the street in his own, and other, countries. Above all, he was as shrewd as one of his own peasant proverbs.

Khrushchev was the first of the great Soviet leaders to have had no part in the making of the revolution; he did not become a member of the Communist Party until 1918. He gained his experience not in the underground struggle but entirely in the complex and often confused effort to organize the young Soviet Union. As a statesman he was a frank and genial opportunist, without the intellectual capacity of Lenin or the sly brutality of Stalin. His decisions were usually dictated by the immediate needs of the moment rather than by the doctrines of Marxism-Leninism— or even by his own pronouncements. He left it to others to provide the theoretical justification for his works, while he himself pressed on with the reforms in hand.

It was under his leadership that the industrial capacity of the Soviet Union reached the point where the living standards of the people could be improved.

With his stress on material incentives and the promise of a better life today rather than in some future millennium, he harnessed to his cause the popular reaction against the austerities of Stalinism. Under his leadership greater resources were devoted to the production of consumer goods, and the face of Russia was changed not only by power stations and massive new blocks of flats but by some private cars and television aerials. He maintained the emphasis on heavy industry, however, in spite of pressures in favour of a diversion from this priority. In agriculture, which had always been a special preoccupation of his, he tried to compensate for the low production in the European part of the country by expanding the arable area into the virgin lands of Kazakhstan. However, it was one of his greatest failures that the high hopes held out for farming in this area came to little, and the emphasis was shifted back to intensive cultivation of the traditional areas.

The tension in the atmosphere of the country was relaxed, and the traditional friendliness of the Russian people was released. He himself, by his racy speeches laced with folk proverbs (traditional or invented for the occasion), earned popularity among them. But he never inspired the reverence shown to his predecessors, and probably never aspired to it. For he was not so much interested in titles and applause as in having his own way as quickly as possible.

He came late to international affairs, making the first of his diplomatic trips at the age of 60. In them his chief aim was to relax tension abroad, as he had at home, and thus to release Russia's vast resources from armaments for the use of her own citizens. To this end he immediately embarked on an effort to make the Soviet Union accepted as a negotiating partner by the other nations. His slogan of "peaceful coexistence" was backed first by ceremonial tours of India and Burma, followed by Britain. After the Cuban confrontation with the United States in the Caribbean in the autumn of 1962 his policy was aimed at consolidating the uneasy balance between the two super powers. It was to a great extent this special relationship with the United States which strained the Sino-Soviet alliance to the point of open rupture.

Nikita Sergeyevich Khrushchev was born on April 17, 1894 at Kalmkova, a small village in the Kursk region on the borders between Russia and the Ukraine. He was the son of a miner, and spent his early years as a shepherd boy. Later he became a fitter and metalworker, moving between the industrial towns of the Ukraine, including Kharkov.

Like most industrial workers of the time, he was vaguely involved in revolutionary activity, but it was not until 1918, after the October Revolution, that he made his final choice between the variety of socialist parties and joined the Bolsheviks. He went off immediately to take part in the Civil War and fought for the next two years, first against the Germans and the Ukranian Republic which they sponsored, and then against the White Army of General Denikin. In 1920 he was demobilized and went back to work in the mines of the Donetz Basin. He was soon sent to one of the new party technical colleges. In 1925 he emerged as a full-time political leader, first in Stalino and then in Kiev, where he worked under Kaganovich, who was to be his first patron in the party hierarchy.

In the late 1920s his career in the Ukraine was checked by his poor knowledge of the Ukrainian language, for at this time great value was attached to the cultural autonomy of the various national republics. However, he was transferred in 1929 to the Moscow Industrial Academy. In 1931, when he graduated, he was directed to political work in the Moscow Region. By 1934 he was Second Secretary of the Regional Party Committee and a member of the Central Committee of the Communist Party of the Soviet Union, and in 1935 he became First Secretary of the region. Here he first became famous for his work in the building of the Moscow Metro, which he organized under the guidance of Kaganovich and with the help of Bulganin. For this he was awarded the Order of Lenin.

He was transferred back to the Ukraine in 1938 as First Secretary of the party there, and as a candidate member of the Politburo. The next year, at the eighteenth Party Congress, he became a full member of the Politburo, and was awarded the Order of the Red Banner of Labour for his successes with Ukrainian agriculture. In 1941, when the Germans again invaded Russia, he directed guerrilla warfare behind the German lines for a year and was then transferred to act (with Malenkov) as party representative on the southern front at Stalingrad, with the rank of Lieutenant-General. In 1944, when the Germans retreated, he returned to the Ukraine as First Party Secretary and Chairman of the Council of Ministers, and conducted the purge of collaborators. He remained in these posts for five years, except for an interval in 1947 when he gave up his party post for nine months.

In his later years, after the congress of 1956, a rejection of the extreme repressive measures used by Stalin became one of the principal planks of his platform. For this reason his activities as the old dictator's henchman in wiping out Ukrainian resistance have often been passed over in silence in Soviet biographies. In fact, it has been estimated that several thousand party officials disappeared in the purges which he directed. The zeal which he brought to this gruesome work cannot be overlooked in an assessment of his career. In 1938 he called for a "merciless" campaign against the enemies of the world. "Our work is holy", he said. "He whose hand will shake or who will falter half-way—the person whose knees give way beneath him when he has to kill ten or a hundred enemies—that person exposes the revolution to danger."

In 1949 he was again appointed First Secretary of the Moscow Region Party Committee, and at the same time Second Secretary of the Party Central Committee. He still took a particular interest in agriculture and advocated the idea of "agro-towns," in which the peasants, though working in the fields, would live in urban conditions. Apart from one or two show-pieces these were hardly a success.

At the Nineteenth Party Congress in 1952 he was entrusted by Stalin with the task of drawing up new party statutes. It was at this congress that the Politburo was abolished and replaced by the Praesidium of the Central Committee, leaving more power in the hands of the committee secretariat, of which Khrushchev was a leading member.

But the death of Stalin in March 1953 threw the whole party organization into turmoil. Malenkov resigned his post as First Secretary, while remaining Chairman of the Council of Ministers, and Khrushchev was the first-named member of the new secretariat. Six months later he was given the official title of First Secretary of the Communist Party.

Meanwhile the new principle of "equality among colleagues" was already under strain, and Beria had been declared a "hireling of imperialist forces" and executed. The immediate policy of Stalin's successors was a slackening of the regime's severity, and Khrushchev's own contribution was to ad-vocate more resources for agriculture and more incentives for the collective farmers, and to start a massive campaign for the colonization of the "virgin lands" of Central Asia.

From the end of 1954 policy differences began to crystallize on the issue of centralization as against greater local responsibilities, and on the issue of the priority of heavy as opposed to light industry. A group of managerial experts headed by Malenkov, who were in favour of increased emphasis on consumer goods, and another chiefly representing the party and the army, wished to reassert the primacy of heavy industry. In February 1955, at a party Plenum devoted to the Budget, Malenkov was induced to resign as chairman, and on Khrushchev's proposal his old colleague Marshal Bulganin was appointed to the post.

Meanwhile Khrushchev had started his international career with visits to Poland and China in 1954. In May 1955 he went with a Soviet delegation to Belgrade which patched up the quarrel between Yugoslavia and the Soviet Union. It was noticeable that he took the chief part in the talks, although Marshal Bulganin, the official head of the Government, was also present. He was also part of the Russian delegation to the "Big Four" conference in Geneva in July of that year, though there he was less prominent. He and Marshal Bulganin finished the year with a highly garlanded tour of India and Burma, and in April 1956 the two travellers visited Britain for pleasant but not very productive talks with Sir Anthony Eden.

The Twentieth Congress of the Party, in February 1956, marked his final break with Stalin's heritage. At the end of the Congress he delivered to a secret session a merciless attack on the abuses of Stalin's later years. The cult of Stalin's personality, he said, had distorted the internal development of the Soviet Union and enabled the dictator himself to torture and murder many innocent people. No one knew who would be the next to suffer. The effect of this denunciation filtered through eastern Europe and encouraged the Poles and Hungarians in particular to rise against the nominees of Stalin who still ruled them. After the abortive Poznan riots of June 1956, a bloodless revolution in Poland in October brought back the moderate Gomulka back to power, with Khrushchev's grudging acceptance. But in Hungary the revolt threatened to remove the country from the Soviet orbit, and the Red Army moved in to put it down, in spite of the protests of the rest of the world.

In his speeches Khrushchev still avoided extreme anti-Stalinism, denouncing Stalin's "mistakes" while praising his attitude to imperialism and the class struggle. In his policy, however, he continued to change and loosen the machine that had ruled Russia under his predecessor. In early 1957 he decided to reorganize industry by abolishing the central ministries which had controlled it and by splitting their powers among over 100 Regional Economic Committees.

This move was heavily opposed inside the Praesidium, where Khrushchev found himself in a minority against the bureaucrats and economic experts led by Molotov, Kaganovich and Malenkov. However, he appealed to a hastily-summoned meeting of the Party Central Committee, which supported him and expelled the three ringleaders of the so-called "anti-party group", together with Shepilov, "who joined them". In this controversy he was supported by Marshal Zhukov, the representative of the Army, but in the autumn the latter also was dismissed for setting up the Army in independence of the Party. The Party, in the person of Khrushchev, now held complete control over political, economic and military affairs.

The seal was set on his triumph by the resignation in March 1958 of Marshal Bulganin, who was accused of wavering in the struggle of the previous year. Khrushchev now became Chairman of the Council of Ministers as well as First Secretary of the Party. He continued his reform of the Stalinist system, abolishing the machine-tractor stations, the state-owned watchdogs of the collective farms, and allowing the latter to buy up their machinery. Compulsory deliveries were also abolished, and the prices for sales of food to the state were raised.

His chief interest, however, was now in foreign affairs. Throughout 1958 he appealed for a summit meeting, first on general topics and then, during the Middle East crisis, on the Middle East. He even seemed prepared for a summit within the United Nations Security Council, but withdrew from this position and hastily visited Peking. In November he challenged the Western right in Berlin, and threatened to conclude a separate peace treaty with East Germany. At first this merely produced a deadlock, but a visit to Moscow by Harold Macmillan in February 1959 gave a chance for frank discussions, and in May 1959 the Foreign Ministers met in Geneva to discuss the whole problem of Germany. The chief result of this conference was an invitation from President Eisenhower* for Khrushchev to visit the United States in September, to be followed by a return visit by the President to Moscow in the spring.

The emphasis on coexistence during his talks with President Eisenhower at Camp David produced a sharp reaction in Peking, where such a "soft" policy to the "imperialists," as well as the attacks on Stalin, was viewed with mistrust. Returning from the United States, Khrushchev faced the main critics of his policy of coexistence when he attended the tenth anniversary celebrations of the Chinese People's Republic. His speech about the wrongfulness of "testing the stability of capitalist society by force" was understood to be a criticism not only of Chinese action on the Indian border but more widely of the revolutionary policies advocated by China. The theoretical dispute about the inevitability of war was only one aspect of the profound clash of national interests and the policies to be followed by the communist powers in their relations with the outside world.

The destruction of an American U2 reconnaissance plane over Soviet territory on May 1, 1960 appears to have added weight to the arguments of those who opposed the relaxation of relations with the west, and Khrushchev's behaviour at the abortive Paris summit meeting was strikingly at variance with his attitude during the American visit. Once President Eisenhower had shouldered the responsibility for the flight—which perhaps made it impossible for Khrushchev to draw a distinction between the President and the aggressive "Pentagon clique"—it is clear that he decided that the top level meeting should not even begin. The invitation that President Eisenhower visit the Soviet Union was withdrawn, and Soviet-American contacts dwindled during the six months before the inauguration of President Kennedy*.

Hopes that a meeting between Khrushchev and the American President might take place during the fifteenth session of the United Nations General Assembly, which Khrushchev attended, were not realized. The session was characterized by Khrushchev's attack on Dag Hammarskjöld*, and his formulation of the so-called "troika" doctrine, under which the office of a single secretary-general would be replaced by a triumvirate drawn from the west, the communist block, and the neutral states.

Evidence of strain in Sino-Soviet relations continued to accumulate during the second half of 1959 and 1960. The Chinese later revealed that a major factor in the deterioration of relations was Khrushchev's decision in June 1959 not to pass Peking information on the manufacture of nuclear armaments. A Sino-Soviet treaty of October 15, 1957 bound Russia to provide China with a prototype nuclear weapon as well as technical assistance for its development. One of the reasons for Khrushchev's *volte face* must have been Mao Tse-tung's increasingly independent conduct of foreign policy, such as his attack on President Tito, precisely at a time when Khrushchev was improving relations with Belgrade. Likewise the bombardment of the off-shore islands of Quemoy and Matsu must have alerted Khrushchev to the danger of a nuclear collision between China and America. The withdrawal of some 1,300 Soviet technicians from China in the summer of 1960 was an unmistakable sign of deteriorating relations.

Khrushchev made a direct attack on Chinese insubordination at a meeting in Bucharest attended by representatives of 45 communist countries. His denunciation of dogmatism at this meeting was particularly revealing of his political philosophy. He argued that the changes which had occurred in the world since Lenin's day meant that communism would be victorious without war. "It should not be forgotten that Lenin's propositions on imperialism were advanced and developed many years ago, when the world did not know many things that are now decisive for historical development." Foremost among these changes was the tremendous development in the destructive power of atomic weapons, which made war suicidal. This theme recurred frequently in Khrushchev's speeches during this period.

As a further attempt to restore unity in the communist block Khrushchev called a meeting of 81 communist parties in Moscow in November. He achieved little more than the adoption of a formula which papered over the cracks in his relations with China. Throughout 1960 Khrushchev practised his brand of personal diplomacy assiduously. Apart from the journeys to France and New York he visited India, Indonesia, Burma and Afghanistan in February, east Berlin on his way back from summit meetings in May, Romania in June, Austria in July, and Finland in September.

In the face of the many failures in his own preferred field of agriculture, particularly in the production of meat, Khrushchev turned resolutely at the beginning of 1961 to the task of increasing farming efficiency. Never, however, did he risk any fundamental change in the system which deprived the peasant of a sufficient plot of land. His measures were directed at improving party control over the existing organization of state and collective farms, and to secure greater investment in artificial fertilizers. However, the appreciable increase in grain production under his direction was achieved mainly as a result of increasing the area under cultivation and it was only in 1963 that an appreciable increase in the production of artificial fertilizers was decided on.

While stumping the country addressing meetings of farmers and secretaries in the first part of 1961 he became increasingly preoccupied with the continued exodus of refugees through Berlin, and the growing dis-equilibrium between the two Germanies. Probably because he was wanting to test the qualities of his young opponent in the White House, he used the meeting with Kennedy in Vienna in June 1961 to insist that unless a peace treaty was signed within six months the Soviet Union would do so unilaterally.

The construction of the wall dividing east from west Berlin in August was effective in stopping the drain of manpower from East Germany. This doubtless made the German problem less urgent for Khrushchev and he was able to withdraw his deadline for the signature of a German peace treaty at the twenty-second Congress of the Soviet Communist Party in November. That he did not accomplish this switch in policy without opposition was evident from the fact that he needed to devote almost the whole of his meeting to a renewed attack on his opponents in the "anti-party group." Adding Marshal Voroshilov* to the group, he pilloried it for its complicity in Stalin's crimes. Naturally, no reference was made at the Congress to his own role as the old dictator's henchman in the Ukraine or during the purges of 1951 to 1953.

Visits to East Germany, to Bulgaria and Romania, and lengthy talks with President Tito in the autumn clearly displayed Khrushchev's efforts to consolidate his support in the face of China. A turning point, however, in his conduct of foreign policy came in the autumn, when his attempt to install nuclear-tipped rockets in Cuba was met by President Kennedy's blockade. The resolute American stand on this issue, which faced Khrushchev with the prospect of nuclear war, must have convinced him painfully about the truth of his own theories that in the nuclear age war was no longer an instrument of policy. An exchange of letters with Kennedy led to Khrushchev's agreement to withdraw the rockets, but he was quick to hail this retreat as a diplomatic triumph which deterred an American invasion of the "Island of Freedom". The Chinese denunciation of the installation of Russian rockets in Cuba as "adventurist", and their withdrawal as "capitulationist." produced such tension that at a series of foreign communist party congresses at the end of the year it became impossible to conceal the quarrel from the public.

The rapport which developed between Khrushchev and Kennedy after the Cuba crisis and the American avoidance of any kind of gloating over Khrushchev's defeat led to a marked improvement in Soviet-American relations during 1963. Khrushchev saw in the test ban agreement which was signed in Moscow a possibility of further agreements; and the establishment of a "hot line" between the Kremlin and the White House was one more symptom of the improved atmosphere which lasted until the assassination of President Kennedy.

A large portion of Khrushchev's last year in office was spent outside Moscow. In the spring he visited the United Arab Republic, passing several days in the gruelling heat of Aswan. After a few weeks at home he embarked for Scandinavia, where he spent three weeks on what was essentially a goodwill trip, looking at intensive farming methods and inspecting shipyards. Trips to Czechoslovakia and East Germany followed, and then a lengthy journey across the Asian farmlands of the Soviet Union.

Khrushchev was closely observed by foreigners during his foreign missions, and his resilience and apparent good health were noted repeatedly. Many analysts believe, however, that his position had already been shaken by his Cuban fiasco and that Brezhnev's assumption of full-time duties in the secretariat of the Central Committee marked a shift of power which was consolidated during Khrushchev's prolonged absence.

The suddenness of his removal from the supreme positions in the party and state was in keeping with Russian political tradition. On the evening of October 15, 1964 Tass briefly announced that his resignation had been accepted for reasons of ill-health. From the first this explanation was greeted with utter disbelief, and a number of influential foreign communist parties demanded further explanations. Even after missions of inquiry had been sent to Moscow certain parties—such as the Italian—declared themselves dissatisfied with the answers they had received in Moscow. Many different accounts of the real reasons for his removal circulated for some time after he fell, but the new leaders preferred to issue no official indictment. Moscow insisted that there would be no change in policy, and *Pravda* hinted that only his manner—"hare-brained schemes" and failure to consult with his colleagues—had caused offence.

In fact many mistakes over the years had brought his downfall, and his colleagues distrusted his tactics over China. In July he had called for a meeting of communist parties with the thinly-veiled purpose of condemning China. By the time of his fall only 13 of the 26 parties invited to attend the preparatory conference had signified that they would come, and China had stated that if the meeting took place this would mark a permanent schism. Any kind of accommodation with China was seen to be difficult for so long as he remained in charge of Russian policy.

Also, alongside the widening breach with China, his new policy of rapprochement with Bonn and his son-in-law's talks about a "new Rapallo" must have aroused serious opposition and had the effect of welding together some very different pressure groups opposed to various aspects of his policy.

September 13, 1971.

King Edward VIII—See Windsor.
Kings of Bhutan, Denmark, Nepal, Saudi Arabia and Sweden, and former King of Jordan—See names of those states, etc.

Hetty King, one of the truly great artists of the music hall in its golden Edwardian era, died at the age of 89 on September 28, 1972.

She belonged to the age of Harry Tate, Dan Leno, Albert Chevalier, George Robey, Harry Lauder, Eugene Stratton, and Marie Lloyd—unforgettable names among which hers took an honourable place. Her home was the Tivoli in the Strand, and her line was that of male impersonator.

To the connoisseurs of the music hall there have been only two great male impersonators, one of whom was Vesta Tilley, the other Hetty King. Vesta Tilley, slim, dark and petite, was the more delicate and the more subdued in her approach; Hetty King, larger of build, broader in style and almost her equal, although never her superior. Both presented the "toff", and Hetty King specialized in the guardsman, the swell and the drunk. They never appeared together on the same bill because of the similarity between their two acts, but one never imitated the other. This was the era when 20 or more top stars would appear on the Tivoli bill, seldom earning more than £10 a week there but also appearing at the same time at several other halls as well. To maintain a position of pre-eminence when so many were so good was in itself a hallmark of her quality.

The type of act she presented, the art of which she was a master—a half-and-half combination of highly trained professional expertise with a warm, flamboyant and vigorous personality—and even the songs she sang satisfied an incurable nostalgia for the good old days. She had the power, in her later years, of convincing those born into a less colourful age not only that the old days had been good but that we too really belonged to them.

Her career continued almost to the day before yesterday, through summer seasons at holiday resorts, occasional appearances in London and sporadic descents to television studios: she needed no new songs, new tricks or gimmicks. She was, in these later years, simply herself, offering us the illusion that we too belonged to a more spacious, simpler and essentially happier age.

September 29, 1972.

Norman Kirk, the Prime Minister of New Zealand, died suddenly in hospital in Wellington on August 31, 1974. He was 51.

A man with impressive qualities of leadership, Kirk was able both to develop and to exploit the mood of nationhood in a country which has been reluctant to forgo its British identity. He succeeded in making New Zealanders aware of their country's place and influence in the Southern Pacific and in South-East Asia. British membership of the E.E.C. was sealed just as Kirk came to power at the head of New Zealand's third Labour Government and at the same time the United States was in retreat from its Vietnam entanglements. These two events thrust New Zealand into a role of greater self-reliance.

At home, at the Commonwealth Conference in Canada and in visits to South-East Asian capitals, Kirk was able to fashion a more independent stance for New Zealand. He probably succeeded in making more of an impact in foreign relations (he was also Minister of Foreign Affairs) than on the domestic front, where steep inflation bedevilled much of his government's attempts to implement economic and social reforms.

Kirk was of working-class origin. The hardships of the depression years committed him early to Labour philosophies and the championship of the underdog. He was born in 1923 in Waimate, a small South Island town, the son of a cabinet-maker. The family moved to Christchurch in search of work when Kirk was five. His job was cleaning guttering at 77 cents a week. As a boy he joined the state-run railways as a cleaner before earning his fireman's ticket. He subsequently worked in various parts of New Zealand as a stationary engine driver on mining sites. He became active in party work in the early forties.

As a self-taught man, Kirk had a distrust of intellectuals. Though he was no cloth-cap traditionalist, he retained other conservative traits held by many manual workers. He was opposed to long hair, the New Left and demonstrators; he was strong on law and order and stood for the *status quo* on such moral issues as abortion and homosexual reform. For all that, he possessed a remarkable grasp of wide-range subjects and won respect for his warmth and for the sincerity of his feeling for the under-privileged everywhere. Kirk once recalled turning down an invitation to stand for Labour in 1951: "For one thing I did not have a suit", he said, "and I could not afford to buy one. We had three small kids and I was building a house." But he won the mayoralty of a small town near Christchurch that year. Six years later he entered Parliament, representing Christchurch's port district of Lyttelton.

The Labour Party at that time tended to be overburdened with old-guard factions inclined to look nostalgically back on the achievements of Labour's long, first reign from 1935 to 1949 rather than forward with new ideas. Arnold Nordmeyer, Labour leader, was turned out by a caucus vote in favour of Kirk in 1965. At 42 Kirk was the youngest leader in the party's 55-year history. He succeeded in his third attempt in 1972 to lead Labour back to the Treasury benches.

His short period as Prime Minister was marked by some radical policies in a country that had been known for its conservatism. He opposed the French nuclear tests in the Pacific and, with Gough Whitlam, the Labour Prime Minister of Australia, took the issue to the World Court at The Hague. He banned all visiting sports teams from South Africa until, as he said, there was "clear, irrefutable evidence that sport in South Africa was no longer organized on a racial basis".

He often expressed his disappointment with the special arrangement for New Zealand concluded by Britain at the negotiations to join the E.E.C., and in 1974 Britons who wished to emigrate to New Zealand had for the first time to obtain entry permits. The time had come, he believed, for New Zealand to control its flow of immigrants to ensure that only those with the skills the country needed were admitted. To emphasize the country's new independence, Kirk wanted to extend diplomatic and political influence in Eastern Asia, but at the same time he saw the need to keep strong links with Australia, Canada and the United States.

Kirk's reputation for brashness, rather undeserved as it turned out, worked against

him at the start. As Prime Minister he proved himself no radical but a leader more cautious than some of his campaigning colleagues would have wished.

He married Ruth Miller in 1941 and they had three sons and two daughters.

September 2, 1974.

Dr. G. S. R. Kitson Clark, Reader in Constitutional History, University of Cambridge, from 1954 to 1967, died on December 8, 1975 at the age of 75.

By his death the historical faculty at Cambridge lost one of its most active and colourful personalities. A leading authority on nineteenth century England, he did much to promote and guide research on that subject.

George Sidney Roberts Kitson Clark was born at Leeds on June 14, 1900. The younger son of Lieutenant-Colonel Edwin Kitson Clark and Georgina Bidder he came of solid Yorkshire stock on both sides. His grandfather, E. C. Clark, was Regius Professor of Civil Law at Cambridge, and G. E. Bidder, the zoologist, was his uncle. He followed his father to Shrewsbury and went up to Trinity College, Cambridge, as an exhibitioner in 1919. He won a Trinity Research Fellowship in 1922, only one year after taking his degree with a First in Part Two of the Historical Tripos. He became a college lecturer in 1928, a university lecturer in 1929, and a college tutor in 1933, holding this last office beyond the normal span of 10 years until 1945. In 1954 he was made Reader in English Constitutional History.

He played a leading part in the introduction of United States History and the "Expansion of Europe" paper into the Historical Tripos; in the establishment of the visiting American History professorship; and in a postgraduate Certificate in Historical Studies, all of which he regarded as in some degree his children. In 1953-54 he was visiting lecturer at the University of Pennsylvania and in 1964 at that of Melbourne. His forceful, outspoken personality and strongly-held views made him a highly successful lecturer in Cambridge, America and Australia alike, and he wrote an interesting pamphlet on *The Art of Lecturing*. He also lectured widely on a variety of topics to educational and cultural institutions. He was interested in Commonwealth affairs and was chairman of the Cambridge branch of the Commonwealth Association. He was among the most active of those concerned with the establishment of New Hall, the third women's college to be founded in Cambridge.

Kitson Clark's main interests came to centre on nineteenth century England. His work in guiding research students, with whom he took infinite pains, towards important results was among the most valuable of his activities, and many established scholars look back to his inspiration with affectionate gratitude. His *Guide to Re-*

search Students in History was a timely publication which achieved a wide circulation.

His first book was *Sir Robert Peel and the Conservative Party* (1929; reprinted in 1964), and he published a short *Life of Peel* in 1936. *The English Inheritance* (1950) and *The Kingdom of Free Men* (1957) dealt with wider themes but in 1962 *The Making of Victorian England,* based on his Ford Lectures at Oxford, marked a return to nineteenth century English history, summing up work recently done by himself and his pupils, and pointing to many areas which needed further exploration.

His retirement in 1967 was marked by a volume of essays in the form *Ideas and Institutions of Victorian Britain,* and in the same year he published *The Critical Historian,* dealing with many of the general problems of the historian's trade, and *An Expanding Society,* based on lectures given as the first George Scott Visiting Fellow at Ormond College, Melbourne.

Churchmen and the Condition of England (1973) was also based on lectures given in Cambridge, Leicester and London. His latest work was the preparation of an edition of G. M. Young's *Portrait of an Age,* annotating (and often correcting) that brilliantly impressionistic account of Victorian England.

Writing did not come easily to Kitson Clark though he took enormous pains over his books and articles. Talk was his natural medium. He was an untiring, amusing and whimsical talker, if often somewhat boisterous or inclined to dwell upon his own immediate concerns. He delighted in the role of the jovial rubicund Yorkshireman, seeking to draw people out or put them at ease with rumbustious banter. But like many other ebullient people he had his moody and difficult times. He was quick to make up his mind, and on committees could be impetuous as well as forceful. But he had a high degree of moral courage, never attempting to hide his meaning or refraining from intervention when he thought it desirable.

He took a Cambridge Litt.D. in 1954 and his honorary degrees from Durham, East Anglia, Glasgow, and Leeds gave him great pleasure. He was unmarried.

December 11, 1975.

During the last years of his long and eventful life **Dr. Otto Klemperer,** who died on July 6, 1973 in Zurich, was revered, in Britain at least, as the greatest of living conductors. He was 88.

This renown was the reward of uncompromising honesty and limitless determination. The honesty drove him to seek only, in his performances, for a strictly truthful and just representation of the composer's instructions (not merely his intentions); the determination enabled him to survive and continue conducting after fate had struck him down again and again.

Klemperer was born in Breslau on May 14, 1885. He spent his schooldays in Hamburg, then studied music at the Hoch Conservatory in Frankfurt-am-Main and in Berlin, specializing in composition, under Pfitzner, and the piano. In 1905 he met Mahler in Berlin and, being passionately desirous of joining the great man's musical staff at the Vienna Court Opera, made a piano transcription of Mahler's Second Symphony; early in 1907, while visiting Vienna for a recital at which he was the accompanist, Klemperer called on Mahler, presented him with the transcription and played the scherzo from memory. Mahler advised him to continue as a pianist, but gave him an open letter of recommendation as a conductor.

An overheard remark led him to apply for a post at the German Opera in Prague; Angelo Neumann gave Klemperer the post simply on Mahler's recommendation, and in the autumn of 1907 Klemperer made his debut as a conductor; the opera was Der Freischütz. Three years later he was appointed chief conductor at Hamburg Municipal Opera (where Lotte Lehmann and Elisabeth Schumann made their joint debuts as Pages in Lohengrin under his baton), and he remained there until 1914; he conducted his first important symphony concerts during this period.

In 1917 he moved from Strasbourg to Cologne and made his name as a champion of modern music with a repertory, symphonic and operatic, that included the newest and most progressive works; soon after the First World War ended he was in demand internationally as an opera conductor. In 1924 he was offered a post at Berlin State Opera but he turned it down in favour of the musical directorship at Wiesbaden.

A Berlin musical directorship was forthcoming in 1927, at the Kroll Opera, which had been opened three years earlier. During Klemperer's four years in office there the Kroll Opera was rated the leading experimental opera house in Europe, some said in history. The repertory included Schoenberg's Die glückliche Hand and Ewartung, Stravinsky's Mavra and Oedipus Rex, Janácek's From the House of the Dead, Hindemith's Cardillac, Hin und zurück, and Neues von Tage.

Productions and scenic designs, not only in these but in the whole repertory of 44 operas ranging from Gluck to Offenbach, were in the hands of the most brilliant progressive artists of the German theatre.

During these years too Klemperer's symphony concerts in Berlin included new works by Bartok, Webern, Krenek and Weill, as well as by the composers already mentioned. In 1928 he re-formed and built up the Berlin Philharmonic Choir.

Klemperer's activities at the Kroll caused much displeasure to the more conservative music critics and politicians as well. In 1931 the Kroll Opera was closed down, but Klemperer continued to conduct in Berlin at the State Opera. In January 1933 President Hindenburg presented him with the Goethe Medal for his services to German culture. Two months later German culture acquired other significance. Klemperer's contract was abruptly terminated (even if his artistic policies had been less controversial, he was by birth a Jew—though by faith a Roman Catholic convert) and he took refuge in Switzerland.

The New World claimed him, like many of his German colleagues. In the same year he was made musical director of the Los Angeles Symphony Orchestra and now his secondary career as a symphonic conductor became his principal activity. Honours were conferred upon him; in 1937 he formed the Pittsburgh Symphony Orchestra; he conducted frequently in New York. The new life seemed as promising as the old one. Then fate struck its first hard blow. Klemperer was found to be suffering from a brain tumour (caused, it was thought, by a fall from the rostrum in Leipzig in 1933) and the treatment for this, though successful, left him lame and partly paralysed.

After some fruitful years at the Budapest Opera in the early post-war years he began once again to appear in concert halls all over Europe, and in 1951 contributed two splendid concerts to the Festival Hall's inaugural season. They were given with the Philharmonia Orchestra, a body with which he was henceforth to be particularly associated.

But not at once. At Montreal Airport, later in 1951, he fell and fractured the femur of his unparalysed leg, and was obliged to walk on crutches and to conduct sitting down. Further operations retarded his recovery, but in May 1955, during a broadcast performance of Don Giovanni at Cologne, he involuntarily rose to his feet to bring in the trombones at the Commendatore's arrival in Don Juan's house. He remained standing.

Klemperer began a period of intense activity in London. His repertory was no longer the challenging progressive one of his younger days, but centred firmly on the German classics and romantics from Bach to Richard Strauss, with Beethoven as its centre and crown. Klemperer's fingers could not hold a baton but his arm movements were sure and expressive, his personality and willpower ample to communicate all that he wished to an orchestra.

The Philharmonia Orchestra's founder, Walter Legge, was also artistic director of Columbia Records, and Klemperer was able to prepare many of his performances in the unhurried calm of the recording studio, committing an interpretation to disc and then repeating the finished performance in the concert hall. So it was that London heard the superb, heaven-storming Beethoven cycles conducted by Klemperer in the 1950s, a series memorable particularly for spacious, perfectly proportioned architecture, strength and intensity and inner radiance of sonority, majesty of line, qualities signally favourable to the Eroica and Seventh Symphonies, above all to the Ninth Symphony and the Missa Solemnis. In these, Klemperer had the collaboration of the magnificent Philharmonia Chorus, whose debut in a performance of the Choral Symphony under him was a musical high-point of the decade.

There were superb series of Brahms concerts, too, and Mozart cycles—Klemperer's reading of Mozart was idiosyncratic, too heavy and earnest for some tastes, but undeniably illuminating. For the season 1958-59 Legge had planned a series of 21 Klemperer concerts in London comprising a tremendous repertory. Yet a third time misfortune fell upon him: recuperating from bronchitis he fell asleep while smoking his pipe, woke to find the bedclothes alight, and seized the nearest liquid to douse the flames—it was spirits of camphor, and he was grievously burned.

But Klemperer triumphed yet again to conduct. His concerts in the 1960s and after included further excursions outside the German classics and romantics: Bartók's Divertimento, Tchaikovsky, Dvorák, Berlioz (a glorious interpretation of the Fantastic Symphony). He conducted and recorded much of Bruckner, some Mahler (notably the Resurrection Symphony), and a deeply moving account of Bach's St. Matthew Passion. In 1961 he turned once again to opera and made his Covent Garden debut in his own production of Fidelio, which was traditional, unfussy, grandly conceived, and profoundly revealing.

Klemperer had been appointed principal conductor for life of the Philharmonia Orchestra when he returned to conducting in 1959 after recovery from his burns. In 1964 Legge dissolved his orchestra, and Klemperer's last appearances with it were in a recording of The Messiah and in two Mozart concerts for the City of London Festival. But the players had reconstituted themselves as the New Philharmonia Orchestra, and Klemperer at once accepted the honorary presidency.

His physical stature was huge, and he remained erect and unbowed by calamity. In this he was like his interpretations, as in his fearless honesty which often caused offence in his younger days. During the last days of romantic interpretation he was, as we have seen, a modernist. When he turned to the classics the trend of the times was favouring extreme virtuosity and high polish. Klemperer again swam against the tide; having established the balance he favoured, as the "Klemperer sound", he concentrated entirely on the structure and inner content of the music, resisting any fashionable desire for glamour or high speed. It was the plain truth alone that guided his work.

He married in 1919 Johanna Geissler. They had one son and one daughter. She died in 1956.

July 9, 1973.

Sir Hughe Knatchbull-Hugessen, K.C.M.G., who died on March 21, 1971 at the age of 84, was British Ambassador to Turkey for much of the Second World War.

The son of the Rev. R. B. Knatchbull-Hugessen, he was born on March 26, 1886 and was educated in college at Eton and at Balliol. He passed into the Foreign Office, then separate from the Diplomatic service, in 1908. During the First World War he was in the Contraband Department of the Foreign Office and in 1919 served on the British Delegation to the Peace Conference. When in 1918 the Foreign Office and Diplomatic service were amalgamated, Hugessen became eligible for posting abroad and seized the opportunity of going to The Hague, where Sir Ronald Graham was Ambassador.

Hugessen spent four years at The Hague followed by a year in the Embassy at Paris under Lord Crewe and then three and a half years in Brussels, first under Sir George Grahame and then Lord Granville. The heads of all these posts were men of the world, well versed in the old diplomacy, and Hugessen had an opportunity, of which he took full advantage, of learning the technique of his profession from a series of highly skilled practitioners.

In 1930 he was sent as Minister to the three Baltic states, Latvia, Esthonia and Lithuania, living in Riga and superintending the posts in Tallinn and Kovno which were occupied by members of the Consular service.

In 1934 the British Legation at Teheran fell vacant and Hugessen, by now regarded in the Foreign Office as a safe man, was sent there.

In 1936 Sir Alexander Cadogan* was recalled from the post of Ambassador in China to the Foreign Office and Hugessen took his place. It was at the time of the Japanese aggression, the so-called "Incident", and the situation swiftly reached a stage where Hugessen could be little more than an interested and sympathetic spectator.

But his service in China came to an abrupt end when a car in which he was travelling was machine-gunned by a Japanese airman and Hugessen was shot, narrowly escaping paralysis if not death. He had to return to England and it was more than a year before he was again fit for service.

In 1939 he was chosen to succeed Sir Percy Loraine* as Ambassador to Turkey and he stayed there until 1944. It was a period of intensive diplomatic activity, with Hugessen and his German opposite number, von Papen, pulling different ways. Hugessen played his cards skilfully and established the friendliest relations with the leading personalities in the Turkish Government, whom he both liked and admired, but, as he was always the first to recognize, the attitude of the Turks, realists to the core, towards such (for us) crucial questions as the supply of chrome and their neutrality or belligerency depended on factors outside the range of any diplomacy, however persuasive.

No account of Hugessen's life would be complete without mention of the famous spy case known as "Operation Cicero".* During the war it was the practice of the Foreign Office to keep certain Embassies fully posted about the Allied plans. Ankara, owing to the key position held by Turkey, was one of those which was regularly informed in detail of some of the most closely guarded political secrets of the war, such as the transactions of the allied meeting at Casablanca and of the Moscow, Cairo and Teheran conferences. For some six months, from October 1943 until April 1944, these top secret documents and many others were almost daily photographed by Hugessen's Albanian valet, who had managed, by means of a false key, to obtain access to the despatch box where Hugessen kept them, and were passed by him to the German Embassy. The whole almost incredible story has been told by a German attaché at Ankara who dealt with the case in his book *Operation Cicero*.

Providentially, owing partly to jealousies between Ribbentrop and Kaltenbrunner, little use was made by the Germans of these documents, for which the valet, christened "Cicero" by von Papen*, the German Ambassador at Ankara, owing to the eloquence of the documents he produced, was said to have received from the German Government no less than £300,000, of which, however, all but the first £20,000 was in forged sterling notes.

It is proof of the high regard felt in the Foreign Office for Hugessen that this strange affair did not affect his career.

In 1944, the tide of events made it necessary to find an Ambassador to the Belgian Government on their return to a liberated Belgium, and Hugessen was recalled from Ankara and sent to Brussels, where he had served some 20 years before, and remained there until his retirement in 1947.

Hugessen's career was a successful one and he was fortunate in never having had to meet a situation demanding more of him than he had to offer; for he had his limitations, of which he was charmingly conscious and which he openly admitted. He had not, for instance, the kind of compelling personality which can influence men or events. Indeed, there was something boyish, almost ungrown-up, about him; not for nothing did the nickname "Snatch", conferred on him at school, stick to him all his life.

His strength lay elsewhere. He was a smooth transactor of business, for his early training had made him a master of the minor but necessary tricks of his trade. He was excellent with subordinates and got the best out of them. In Persia, China and Turkey, for instance, he necessarily had to rely on his local experts and was always well served by them for he was never afraid to ask for or accept advice and was generous in giving praise and credit. He had, too, the immense and sustaining virtue of seeing the humorous side of things; of not taking himself too seriously and—endearing trait in the highly placed—of being able to laugh at himself. It was also a definite advantage that he had a mind which, while agile and resourceful, instinctively eschewed complexities and so saved him from the pitfalls which, especially in dealings with clever foreigners, beset the path of the over-ingenious intellectual.

Above all, he thoroughly and unashamedly enjoyed diplomatic life, with its parties and pageantry, and brought to that enjoyment a tact, friendliness and social flair which smoothed his path and enabled him to cope more than adequately with a wide range of problems and a succession of unusually variegated personalities.

He played the piano more than adequately, though without any strong feeling for music, and could make pleasant sketches in pencil, pen and watercolours. He had a ready pen (an aunt on his mother's side was the author of that Victorian best-seller *Little Lord Fauntleroy*) and was fond of writing light humorous verse, less unamusing to the uninitiated than such productions usually are. A number of specimens can be found in his autobiographical *Diplomat in Peace and War*.

He married in 1912 Mary, daughter of Brigadier-General Sir R. G. Gordon-Gilmour. They had two daughters.

March 23, 1971.

Professor the Rev. David Knowles, O.S.B., Regius Professor of Modern History in the University of Cambridge, 1954-63, died on November 21, 1974.

Michael Clive Knowles (in religion David) was born in 1896, the only son of H. H. and Carrie Knowles. He attended the Benedictine School at Downside, and was afterwards at Christ's College, Cambridge, and the Collegio Sant'Anselmo, Rome. In 1914 he entered the noviciate at Downside Abbey. In 1922 he was ordained priest.

For some years he taught classics in the school. His appointment as temporary Novice Master in 1928, and as Junior Master in the following year, heralded a change in his interests, and he seemed to be moving away from the humane subjects to concentrate on theology, and particularly on ascetical and mystical theology. Also, what might be called his purely monastic interest was seen to increase. At this time Father David developed a deep, vivid sense of the claims of the contemplative life. It has to be remembered that the monks of Downside had the responsibility of running a large modern public school. In Father David's mind, the conviction emerged that these responsibilities implied too many distractions, and that their impact brought about a diminution of the Benedictine norm of regular life and prayer.

Fr. David was an inspiration to many under his charge, but his intensifying sense of mission was soon to make a problem for his community, and to change the course of his own life. The situation which now presented itself followed a familiar pattern: on the one hand, the obligation of religious obedience to a superior, on the other, the reformer's sense of obligation to his vision, albeit no stricter or more orthodox Catholic than Fr. David could be imagined.

The matter was brought to a head when Abbot Chapman succeeded Abbot Ramsey in the spring of 1929, and when the project was formed of making a new foundation in another part of the country to carry the junior school. Fr. David threw down the gauntlet, not only opposing, but also denouncing the plan. He had a number of sympathizers, but did not succeed in imposing his views on the community.

Shortly before Abbot Chapman died, he thought it necessary to send Fr. David to live at Ealing Priory. Fr. David, for his part, felt impelled to carry the dispute to Rome. He pleaded that his little group be allowed to make a new foundation which should follow a stricter monastic observance. The ruling of the Sacred Congregation rejected the plea. It did not condemn his aspirations, but instructed Fr. David and his sympathizers to seek to put these into practice in their own monastery. It seems almost certain that, unlike the others, Fr. David was never able to give interior acceptance to Rome's verdict.

Moreover, when Fr. Trafford, who had been Head Master of the school, became Abbot in 1938, in Fr. David's eyes it was a case of the school triumphing over the monastery yet more decisively than before. Fr. David was preserving exterior obedience, and living withdrawn and austerely at Ealing. The strain told in the end. The succeeding phase, when he left, and declined to return to Ealing, was unhappy. The rights and wrongs of it are impenetrable. Nor do they need to be penetrated. But perhaps it is not unfair to say that a presiding difficulty lay in the fact that neither Fr. David nor Abbot Trafford was a man who found it easy to believe he might be wrong.

In 1944 Fr. David's life took an entirely new turn. The repute accruing from his book *The Monastic Order in England* led to a Fellowship at Peterhouse, Cambridge. The academic career upon which he now embarked was of great distinction. University Lecturer in History in 1946, he was elected Professor of Medieval History in 1947. In 1954 he became Regius Professor of Modern History. Thus it was that the Whig chair established in the reign of George I to promote the Protestant Succession, found itself occupied by a Benedictine monk. He was Ford's Lecturer in English History at Oxford from 1948 to 1949, and in the latter year British Academy Lecturer. Oxford gave him an honorary D.Litt. in 1952, he became an honorary member of the Royal Irish Academy in 1955, and he became a Litt.D. of Bristol in 1956; honorary degrees from other universities were to follow. He was made an honorary Fellow of Christ's College in 1958. He was Creighton Lecturer at London in 1956 and in that year was elected president of the Royal Historical Society.

In the meantime, the efforts of Trafford's successor, Abbot Butler, to disentangle at Rome Professor Knowles's anomalous ecclesiastical position were brought to a conclusion. Professor Knowles was exclaustrated; that is, he was relieved of his monastic obligations and removed from the jurisdiction of the Abbot of Downside. The effect of this was to put Professor Knowles once more *en règle* with the Church.

In losing what might have been a monastic reformer of note, the world unquestionably gained a scholar of renown. The strange course of Knowles's life had carried him back to those humane studies with which he had started out, but the historical work with which he had made his name grew out of the spiritual preoccupations of his campaign for an intenser monastic observance. It was precisely that struggle which transfigured the youthful historian of the American Civil War into the great historian of the English Religious. When he presented a copy of his concluding volume (the one which described the Dissolution under Henry VIII) to the son of a colleague, he wrote, "In this volume there is more of myself than in any other".

Knowles's publications include: *The American Civil War* (1926); *The English Mystics* (1927); *The Monastic Order in England* (1940); *The Religious Houses of Medieval England* (1940); *The Religious Orders in England* (1948-59); *The Monastic Constitutions of Lanfranc* (1951); *The Episcopal Colleagues of Archbishop Thomas Becket* (1951); *Monastic Sites* (1952); *Charterhouse* (with W. F. Grimes, 1954). He also contributed many articles to the *Downside Review* (of which he was Editor from 1930 to 1934), to the *English Historical Review* and the *Cambridge Historical Journal*.

Perhaps Dom David's greatest contribution to the study of European history was his masterly summary of the controversy on the *Regula Magistri* and the Rule of St. Benedict. No better assessment of the problem exists: and this work (published alongside his *Great Historical Enterprises*) reveals all that one had come to expect in the way of judgment, learning, wit and style.

Knowles was a man of the widest historical and literary learning, classical, medieval and modern. He was a brilliant lecturer and wrote a fine style of English, and he combined these gifts with a grasp of practical affairs; he was, for instance, an admirable chairman. The charm and range of his conversation will be remembered. But the shy, gentle manner belied an iron will, and one was easily aware of the intensity of his inner life.

November 26, 1974.

Professor Sir Francis Knowles, BT., F.R.S., Professor of Anatomy at King's College, London, who died on July 13, 1974 at the age of 59, was a distinguished biologist and neuroendocrinologist.

Born in Canada on March 9, 1915, he became the sixth baronet in 1953, succeeding his father, Sir Francis Howe Seymour Knowles, fifth baronet, formerly Physical Anthropologist to the Zoological Survey of Canada.

He was educated at Radley and Oriel College, Oxford. He was granted the Oxford University Naples Scholarship in 1937 and obtained his D.Phil. in 1939. At this time he was appointed to the Biology Department of Marlborough College, and later became Head of the Department. During his time at Marlborough he showed himself to be a fundamental scientist of outstanding calibre, greatly extending his work on colour change in crustaceans and becoming the leading authority in this field. He was awarded the Royal Society Browne Fund Scholarship in 1949 to do research in Bermuda and received a Nuffield Foundation Scholarship in 1958.

In the mid-1950s he carried out pioneering work into the ultrastructure of neurosecretory systems and came to the notice of Sir Solly (now Lord) Zuckerman, who took him to his Department of Anatomy in Birmingham in 1958. In 1963 he was appointed Reader and in the same year was awarded the D.Sc.(Oxon). In 1966 he was elected Fellow of the Royal Society and in 1967 was appointed to a Professorship of Comparative Endocrinology at the University of Birmingham. Later in the same year he became Professor of Anatomy in the University of London and Head of the Department of Anatomy at King's College, London.

He was a leading figure in propounding the modern concept of neurosecretion and the role of neurosecretion as a major mechanism for neural control of endocrinesystems. He did a great deal of the pioneering work in this field. Until his death he was active in establishing the role played by specialized ependymal cells in neuroendocrine control. One of his main aims was to further research links between Britain and other European countries. He instituted and took an active interest in research groups where many younger European scientists were brought together. Recently he had the great satisfaction of being the organizer and host in London who drew together some 200 scientists from all parts of the world.

He was a member of the editorial boards of several learned journals and an author of many books, including the well-known *Man and Other Living Things*. He was chairman of the Biological Sciences Committee of the Science Research Council and served on a number of committees of the University of London. He was a member of the council of the Marine Biological Association of the United Kingdom. In all these he was greatly admired for his remarkable power of succinct summary of conference and committee material.

Those who had the privilege and pleasure of working closely with Sir Francis Knowles found a humble, yet highly inspiring and loyal companion. His wise judgment will be greatly missed in King's College.

In 1955 he acquired Avebury Manor. Its restoration became one of his personal pleasures and favourite pastimes. The success of his efforts is reflected in the large number of visitors attracted since he opened his house to the public.

In 1948 he was married to Ruth, widow of Pilot Officer R. G. Hulse, R.A.F., and daughter of the Rev. Arthur Brooke-Smith. He also leaves one son, Charles Francis Knowles, who succeeds to the baronetcy, three daughters and a step-daughter.

July 18, 1974.

Prof. the Rev. Michael Clive Knowles— See Prof. the Rev. David Knowles.

E. V. Knox, who died on January 2, 1971, at the age of 89, was editor of *Punch* from 1932 to 1949, a member of the famous "Table" from 1921 onwards, and a regular contributor over the pen-name Evoe for more than fifty years.

Edmund George Valpy Knox was born on May 10, 1881, at Oxford. His father was for many years Bishop of Manchester; his mother was the daughter of Dr. Valpy French, Bishop of Lahore; his first wife, Christina, whom he married in 1912, was the youngest daughter of Dr. E. L. Hicks, Bishop of Lincoln; two of his three brothers took holy orders, one of them, Ronald, to become eventually Monsignor in the Church of Rome.

But E. V. Knox (he never used the "G") had no clerical leanings. There was always a kind of diffidence about him, a sensitive distaste for putting other people right or "interfering", that made him the last man to want to preach, or teach. He had, indeed, after being educated at Rugby and Corpus Christi College, Oxford, a period of schoolmastering in Manchester, but it was very brief, and his early twenties saw him launched on the career of humorous writing to which his quick, irrelevant mind, detached and sardonic but rarely bitter outlook, and fastidious feeling for words were so admirably suited. *Punch* was his natural home, and to it—with a break during the First World War, when he served with the Lincolnshire Regiment and was wounded at Passchendaele—he devoted all his working life.

As a writer "Evoe" was a miniaturist, with the careful craftsmanship that small-scale work demands. His prose pieces rarely exceeded a thousand words, and he never seems to have felt the need for self-expression or communication that drives authors to the labour of full-length novels and plays.

It was not that he had nothing to say—his conversation was full of "things counter, original, spare, strange"—but that he did not care to say them to strangers. Few men, writing so regularly for so long a period, have revealed so little of themselves in print. He regarded his writing as something altogether remote from his private and personal life, as words that you manipulated, with all the skill at your command, to produce particular effects, to give a particular kind of pleasure, not as a credo. Only when strongly moved to anger or contempt—as he was by the prewar antics of Hitler and Mussolini, at a time when so many still thought the dictators meant well—did he allow a glimpse of his own deeper feelings and beliefs.

Despite, or perhaps because of, this detachment he had a subtly individual style difficult to pin down in words and impossible, hard though many humorous aspirants tried, to imitate. His verse at its best is brilliant: accomplished, scholarly, metrically interesting and rich in echoes, with a humour that ranges from inspired lunacy to strong satire. As a parodist he was the peer of Calverley and J. K. Stephen, writing verses that were not merely masterly as parody but very funny in themselves, and his Masefield "The Everlasting Percy" is a connoisseur's piece.

When Sir Owen Seaman retired in 1932, after 26 years in the chair, E. V. Knox was his natural successor as editor of *Punch*. He had no easy task. He had to clear away the cobwebs, the archaisms, the out-of-date targets, the rigid traditionalism to which Seaman in his later years had increasingly succumbed. And he was not by nature an editor, not "dynamic" or a born innovator and planner. He used to say, when his 16-year term was running out, that he had what he had to do, and in his own quiet, undramatic, almost haphazard way, he did it. He shortened and speeded up the pictorial jokes, weeded out by stages the mass of explanatory matter in brackets so dear to Owen Seaman (who always feared that somebody, somewhere, might miss the point); he found new writers, greatly widened the paper's range, modernized its layout and in general, without attempting to do violence to the middlebrow respectability into which it had long ago settled, made *Punch* into a humorous magazine of its own time.

In all that is meant by public relations Knox could never bring himself to take the slightest interest. His dislike of the limelight and that characteristic distaste for instructing or interfering made him reluctant to meet people in his official capacity, and even to contributors he gave little in the way of praise or criticism. "What on earth", he was known to ask, when some contributor of 10 years' standing sent up his card, "can the man want?" He was so severe a critic of his own writing, always giving of his very best without prompting, that it scarcely occurred to him that others might do better with a word of praise or an occasional jolt. To many who drew and wrote for him in those days he must have seemed a cold and inaccessible man.

In those who came to know him—in the members of his editorial staff and of the Table, and in the many friends he made in Hampstead, where in his later years he took a lively interest in local affairs—he inspired a quite extraordinary affection and respect. It was not only that he was so unassuming, so utterly free from pomposity or self-importance; it wasn't his incorruptibility or his casual courage (he took to wandering about, during the Second World War, wherever the bombs fell thickest with a bottle of whisky in his overcoat pocket, looking for people who needed it); it wasn't simply that his mind was so full of invention and interest or that he said good things (though he said plenty: his dismissal of Piccadilly Circus, seen at night through the windows of the old Criterion Restaurant, as a place "where every prospect pleases and only Beans are Bile" was typical of his wilder flights); it was something more than the sum of these things.

There was an intangible equality about him, whether he happened to be talking or just listening with that strange lop-sided smile, that could not be overlooked. Once, after some literary dinner, he went with four or five friends into a bar for a good-night whisky, and there the group fell into conversation with a stranger, who was blind. The talk was desultory, and Evoe spoke if anything less than the rest. Yet after a few minutes the blind man turned his face towards him, and nodded, and said apropos nothing in particular, "This is the one! This is the best of the lot of you". No one in that company, nor in any other company of Evoe's friends would have dreamed of denying it.

After the death of his first wife in 1935 E. V. Knox married Mary Shepard, daughter of E. H. Shepard the artist, who survives him, as do his two children by his first marriage.

January 4, 1971.

General Sir Harry Knox, K.C.B., D.S.O., who was Adjutant-General to the Forces from 1935 to 1937 and Governor of the Royal Hospital, Chelsea, from 1938 to 1943, died on June 10, 1971. He was 97.

Knox was a man of strong and lovable character, devoted to his profession, and inspired throughout his long service by a remarkable sense of duty. He was immensely popular in the Army. He endeared himself to all who knew him by his humanity and his delightful sense of humour. He had a gift for bringing out the best in everyone who worked with him.

He lived through a period of revolutionary change in military organization and tactical methods, and many of the new ideas caused him genuine distress. He believed them to be wrong and it was his inability to accept them that brought him into conflict with Hore-Belisha before the war and caused the premature termination of his term of office as Adjutant-General.

Harry Hugh Sidney Knox was born on November 5, 1873, educated at St. Columbia's College, Dublin and commissioned in the 5th Royal Irish Rifles (Royal South Down Militia) at the unusually early age of seventeen. He later transferred to the Northamptonshire Regiment.

When the 1914-18 War broke out he had reached the rank of major. In 1915 he was posted to the Western Front, and there he joined the headquarters of the 5th Army Corps in time for the second battle of Ypres in 1915. His qualities as a staff officer were valued so highly that he was retained on the general staff for the rest of the war. At the end of 1915 he became G.S.O.1 of the 15th Scottish Division and in this capacity he served in the battle of the Somme in 1916 and in the battle of Arras in 1917. After Arras he was appointed Brigadier-General Staff of the 15th Army Corps and he remained with this corps until the armistice, distinguishing himself particularly in the German Flanders offensive in the spring of 1918 and in the subsequent victorious advance into Belgium. During the August fighting he was in temporary command of the 29th Division, and after the armistice he was for a short time acting major-general, general staff of the 1st Army.

In 1932 Knox was promoted lieutenant-general and in the following year was appointed Lieutenant of the Tower of London. In 1935 he was brought back to active employment as Adjutant-General to the Forces and 2nd military member of the Army Council. At that time the post of Adjutant-General was usually given to a very senior general, and it was a mark of the esteem in which he was held that he was appointed over the heads of 13 generals and lieutenant-generals who were senior to him.

In the summer of 1937 Hore-Belisha became Secretary of State for War and at once set about making drastic changes in obsolete and traditional methods, many of which had come to be regarded as sacrosanct. In his efforts to modernize and popularize the Army he soon came into collision with Knox. The first encounter, in which Knox was worsted, was over a new scheme for recruitment. The next clashes were over the expansion of the anti-aircraft units and the methods to be adopted to accelerate mechanization. The conflict with the military authorities became so intense that Hore-Belisha resolved that changes must be made at once in the Army Council, and in November 1937 he obtained the approval of the King and Neville Chamberlain, the Prime Minister, to the removal of the C.I.G.S. and the Adjutant-General.

Knox accepted the decision with good grace, but it must have been a bitter blow to an officer so devoted to the service as he

was. Hore-Belisha, for his part, acted with magnanimity, and, when a vacancy occurred in two months for the governorship of the Royal Hospital in Chelsea, he offered it to Knox. Knox accepted gratefully and wrote to Hore-Belisha, "I'll love the place and the work with those old men".

Some of the pensioners and staff were evacuated to the country when the war began, but most of them remained at Chelsea. The hospital was heavily bombed more than once and the pensioners suffered casualties. Knox found a task after his own heart in caring for them and keeping up their morale and, when his governorship came to an end in 1943, his departure was deeply regretted by them all.

He was created K.C.B. in 1935. He was A.D.C. to the King from 1925 to 1926 and was Colonel of The Northamptonshire Regiment from 1931 to 1943.

He married Grace Una, daughter of the Reverend R. A. Storrs, in 1904. She died in 1954. They had one daughter, Lady Nye, the wife of Lieutenant-General Sir Archibald Nye*.

June 11, 1971.

Teddy Knox, the comedian, died in a Devon hospital at the age of 78 on December 1, 1974.

He was the second half of Nervo and Knox who appeared for over 30 years with the Crazy Gang at the Victoria Palace Theatre, London. Knox, who had been ill for some time, lived in retirement in Salcombe, Devon.

His real name was Albert Edward Cromwell-Knox and his partnership with Jimmy Nervo (James Holloway) was a long-standing one. Many years ago when looking back over what was already a 41-year partnership, they reckoned they had broken about 60,000 eggs over each other's heads. They had played in America where they were with Flo Ziegfeld's Follies for two years, and in other parts of the world, sharing a dressing room and rarely apart at other times.

The early 1930s saw the arrival of the Crazy Gang which added a new dimension to comedy in the variety theatre. Chesney Allen, Bud Flanagan's* old partner, in a newspaper interview which appeared in the *Guardian* in 1972, stated that it was Nervo and Knox who started the Crazy Gang with "Young Bloods of Variety," incorporating features which had not been done before, such as interruptions from the boxes, and artists walking round the auditorium.

After a successful week at the London Palladium George Black, senior, had decided to run a "crazy month" and, according to Allen, it was then that Bud Flanagan and himself and Naughton and Gold joined the shows, not forgetting "Monsewer" Eddie Gray. It was not until 1962 that the Crazy Gang gave their farewell performance.

The "interruption" gag which Nervo and Knox did so expertly was said to have originated when they butted in unannounced into a Jack Hylton* band programme; it was not even playing in the same theatre as the comedians.

December 4, 1974.

Ludwig Koch, M.B.E., who died on May 4, 1974 at the age of 92, was the pioneer of the mechanical recording of the voices of animals.

He was born in Germany on November 13, 1881, and what was to become the obsession of a long lifetime seems to have begun in 1889 when, as a boy of eight in his native town of Frankfurt-am-Main, he was presented by his father with an early Edison phonograph and a set of cylinders. With this apparatus he made a recording (still extant) of one of his numerous pets, an Indian shama. It is highly likely that this is the earliest animal sound-recording to have been made. Koch's youth was devoted primarily to music, which he intended to embrace as a career and for some time did. He studied the violin, at first under Eduard Bröckl and later under Hugo Heermann. Later he studied singing under Clara Sohn, under Johannes Messchaert (who developed his capacity to sing *Lieder*) and under Jean de Reszke.

His career as a concert singer lasted from about 1905 to the outbreak of the First World War. After the war he did not return to the concert platform but became a musical impresario in Frankfurt. This work culminated in the international music festival and exhibition, "Music in the Life of Nations", in that city, which Koch himself designed and organized as a 10-week musical festival. It was at this time that his chronic interest in animals appears to have revived, for while his connexion with music continued in a new post in the principal German record-manufacturing company, he began seriously to devote much of his energy to recording, with improved apparatus, the voices of animals—and in particular the voices of wild birds.

An outspoken critic of the Nazi party, Koch found it necessary to leave Germany in January 1936 and arrived on February 17 in London, the city that became his home for the rest of his life. In collaboration with the distinguished German ornithologist, Dr. Oscar Heinroth, Koch had already published what is believed to be the world's first "sound-book" which embraced the disc-recorded voices of 25 wild song birds; its title, *Gefiederte Meistersänger.* This collection of records, and some others made by Koch in the decade beginning in 1927, survive; but many more appear to have been destroyed in Germany after Koch's departure.

In Britain Koch got quickly to work on the rebuilding of his collection of recorded sound, with the help of H. F. Witherby,

Sir Julian Huxley, E. M. Nicholson and other prominent British naturalists. Before 1936 was out he had published *Songs of Wild Birds* with E. M. Nicholson, which was followed by another sound book, *More Songs of Wild Birds*, in 1937; and by *Animal Language* in 1938, a collaboration with Julian Huxley. During the Second World War, Koch worked with the European Service of the B.B.C., and then with the Home Services, and continued to build up his collection of records; and it was at about this time that he began to emerge in his own right as a radio personality. His singer's voice never lost its German accent; indeed, some have compared it with that of an Englishman imitating a German talking broken English. That Koch could have cultivated this as part of his radio personality seems highly probable, for he was, in fact, an accomplished linguist, with a faultless French accent and Parisian vocabulary that was of great service to German Intelligence in the First World War.

Koch continued to make new records in the field and to broadcast frequently until the end of his life, making trips as far as the Scilly Isles, the Channel Islands, Shetland and Iceland. Throughout his career he remained wedded to the wax disc and its heavy machinery, which he used long after those whom he had inspired had begun to get more abundant and sometimes better results with the use of tape and parabolic reflectors.

In his distinguished career he made records of first-class quality of the sounds of at least 200 species of birds and nearly 100 other kinds of animals. His magnificent collection is now the backbone of the natural history section of the Recorded Programmes Permanent Library of the British Broadcasting Corporation, where it is widely used for research purposes by ornithologists. Indeed, its scientific value only began seriously to be exploited by the zoological world in the early 1950s, much to Koch's own disappointment.

Koch himself could never have been described as a conventional scientist. He had no zoological training and very little understanding, or even knowledge, of the general principles of ornithology.

On location he relied largely on companions to find his material. But once at work with recording van, cables and microphones, he became a sleepless obsessive, capable of spending a week or more on one subject. Koch was always innocently pleased to boast about his overtime to friends and colleagues and to his vast radio public, who held in affection someone whom they rightly believed to be the master of nature's music.

In 1955 he published *Memoirs of a Birdman*. He was made M.B.E. in 1960.

In 1912 Ludwig Koch married Nellie Sylvia Herz. They had a son and a daughter.

May 7, 1974.

Alexander Komissarov, a leading actor of the Moscow Arts Theatre, died in Moscow on August 7, 1975 aged 71.

Komissarov was born on February 27, 1904, and studied for the stage at Stanislavsky's Second Moscow Arts Theatre Studio before joining the parent company in 1924. He remained with it all his life.

Komissarov specialized in comic roles and these were characterized by their irresistible charm and liveliness. By sticking to one type of part he did not always have a chance to shine in the lead, being usually cast in subsidiary roles. But he proved time and again the truth of Stanislavsky's dictum that "there are no small roles, only small actors".

His Cherubino in Beaumarchais's *The Marriage of Figaro* (1927) was remarkable for the infectiousness of its manly grace. Thereafter he excelled in simpleton types.

Outstanding interpretations of character parts in recent years included Alyosha, the Cobbler in *The Lower Depths*, Count Aubespine, the French Ambassador, in *Mary Stuart*, Golotvin in *The Diary of a Scoundrel*, Bobchinski in *The Government Inspector* and Yepikhodov, alias "22 Misfortunes", in *The Cherry Orchard*. In the last-named role he was seen in Sir Peter Daubeny's first World Theatre Season in 1964, in which he also played Koukou in *Dead Souls* and The Man with Boots in *Kremlin Chimes*.

On returning to Moscow he was to become equally celebrated as Chichikov, the protagonist of *Dead Souls*, a role he was playing until quite recently.

A People's Artist since 1948, Komissarov was also a teacher at the Moscow Art Theatre Drama School.

August 9, 1975.

Marshal of the Soviet Union Ivan Konev, one of the great Russian generals of the Second World War and later Commander-in-Chief of the Warsaw Pact forces, died on May 21, 1973 at the age of 75.

As an Army commander he was an outstanding exponent of what was known in the Red Army as Stalin's strategy of manoeuvre, of flank attack and indirect approach to an objective. He was also closer to the party than many Russian generals, displacing Marshal Zhukov, his former chief, after the end of the war, and finally denouncing him as a braggart and in some respects a bungler.

Ivan Stepanovich Konev was born in 1897, the son of a Siberian peasant. He received an elementary education and served in the ranks of the Tsarist Army. Having joined the Communist Party in 1918 he formed a company of volunteers and put them at the disposal of the revolutionary military soviet. He spent the civil war as commissar of an armoured train which operated against Admiral Kolchak and Japanese occupation troops in the east. In

1926 he was posted to the Frunze Military Academy, where he began his profound study of military theory. He was read in German and English works of strategy, and his library on the subject became renowned.

When the Germans invaded Russia Konev was no more than an untried product of the Soviet military academies with early experience of guerrilla warfare. He was given a command under Zhukov in the defences of Moscow and was selected to command a counter offensive in the autumn of 1941. His objective was Smolensk. This he failed to gain, partly on account of the unexpectedly early onset of winter; but coordinating his attack with partisans behind the German lines, he drove the enemy back to Yelnia and they were forced to retire to Smolensk.

In 1942 his armies on the central front captured Klin and Karlinin and drove on to Rzhev and Toropetz, where his attack during a snowstorm in the winter of 1942 gave a foretaste of his ability to turn to his advantage elements which most would consider obstacles to success. It was only, however, when in the following summer he was placed in command of the Steppe Front south of Kursk, later renamed the Second Ukrainian Front, that his powers as a commander in mobile warfare were given full rein. The bare, rolling country, the short winter and long spells of fickle weather in spring and autumn, the wide rivers, Donetz, Vorskla, Dnieper, Bug, suited his audacity. His campaigns were characterized by swift, oblique movements, flanking attacks, and a skilful use of the element of surprise.

To cross the Donetz he selected the Liubotin marshes. On reaching the Dnieper, where the Germans expected him to concentrate his forces for the crossing, he ordered the establishment of 18 separate bridgeheads along a front of 60 miles. Without waiting for pontoon bridges, his men crossed the river on tree-trunks, barrels, cottage tables, straw-stuffed capes, anything that could be improvised. Thirteen of the bridgeheads were held until they flowed into each other. The main supply base of the German Army group was taken with 5,000 lorries, and in a concise campaign lasting only three days Kirovograd was liberated almost intact.

Konev's greatest exploit, the liquidation of the Korsun salient, followed swiftly. There 10 divisions of Manstein's Eighth Army were encircled and defeated with vast loss of men and material. Two months later Konev forced a passage of the river Pruth into Romania and was the first to carry the fighting out of Russian territory. In the offensive of 1945 he advanced from the Vistula to the Oder, forcing a passage at Breslau and entering Prague.

It was his custom to direct his battles from an advanced position—he was several times lightly wounded—and he coordinated all arms at his disposal with precision. He was of a rather morose temperament and of few words, with a passion for accuracy—"You go about things like Pierre Bazukov", he would say to subordinates whose work he found slipshod. He calculated long, smoking heavily and pacing the room with hands behind his back. Over his uniform in the field he wore a plain greatcoat, and throughout his armies the tale was told how, going forward in a tank during the Korsun battle, he came across a column of supply lorries bogged down by the side of the road; unrecognized by his men he took a shovel and helped to dig them out.

After the defeat of Germany Konev commanded the Russian armies of occupation in Austria and Hungary. In 1946 he took Marshal Zhukov's place as Commander-in-Chief of the Soviet Army. To his professional suitability for the post was added his claims, which were superior to Zhukov's, as a trusted party enthusiast.

Thereafter the fortunes of his career reflected the struggle for power in the Kremlin. He was out of favour during Stalin's last years but his star rose again under Khrushchev, and in 1955 he was made Commander-in-Chief of the Warsaw Pact forces. In 1957 Konev was foremost among the senior officers who added to Marshal Zhukov's public confession of errors their own denunciations.

Konev resigned from command of the Warsaw Pact forces because of ill health in 1960, but in August the following year he was recalled from retirement to the post of Supreme Commander of Soviet forces in East Germany. The appointment was widely regarded as an indication of the seriousness of Russian intentions over Berlin, but eight months later he returned to Moscow to take up duties at the Defence Ministry.

May 22, 1973.

Josef Krips, the distinguished Viennese operatic and concert conductor, died in Geneva on October 13, 1974 at the age of 72. He was particularly noted for his interpretations of the Viennese classics from Mozart to Brückner.

Krips was born in Vienna on April 8, 1902, and studied at the Music Academy there, concentrating on conducting, for which his teacher was Weingartner, with whose warmhearted readings of Mozart and Beethoven his own could later be compared. His first engagement was at the Vienna Volksoper in 1921. From there he moved to Dortmund and then to Karlsruhe, where he was music director of the opera from 1926 to 1933. In the latter year he returned to Vienna and to the State Opera, where he was to spend much of the rest of his life, apart from an interruption between 1938 and 1945, when he was kept out of Vienna's musical life by the Nazis.

In 1945 he conducted the first opera performance in Vienna after the war, and was instrumental in getting the Salzburg Festival restarted. He went to Covent Garden with the State Opera in 1947, and conducted *Cosi fan tutte, Figaro*, and *Don Giovanni*. This led directly to his appointment as principal conductor of the London Symphony Orchestra in 1950, a post he retained for four years. From 1954 until 1963 he was principal conductor of the Buffalo Symphony and held a similar post with the San Francisco Symphony from 1963 until 1970.

Krips returned to Covent Garden in the 1962-63 season to conduct *Don Giovanni,* in 1971 for a much-commended revival of *Der Rosenkavalier*, and in 1973 for *Fidelio*. In these latter years he also struck up a sound relationship with the London Philharmonic Orchestra, with whom his Brückner and Mahler interpretations were notable.

His *gemütlich* appearance and firm, nononsense approach were always welcome in London. His interpretations were sane and well-tailored, attentive to internal balance and to structure. His genial presence will be missed in more than one musical centre.

He married firstly Mitzi Wilheim in 1947, and secondly Harrietta Freün von Prochazka in 1969.

October 14, 1974.

Krishna Menon, the former Indian Minister for Defence, who was one of the leaders in the fight for independence against Britain, died in New Delhi at the age of 77 on October 5, 1974.

"A lone wolf": the trite phrase fits this remarkable yet unlikable man who worked untiringly all his life for his country, yet never received a nation's gratitude, or even acceptance. His career falls into four main phases. There were 28 years in England, mostly as an unknown partisan for Indian freedom, but later as India's High Commissioner. Then a period of world travel as his country's representative at international gatherings; a return to India and Cabinet office and, finally, political defeat.

In obscurity, and as an international celebrity, Krishna Menon always stood apart, alone. This isolation was almost always ascribed to his peculiarly irascible temperament, which made him a man of few friends (though among these few was Jawarhalal Nehru*), but aloofness was in part forced upon him by his solitary role as a protagonist of India. "He was ever a fighter", and he fought to win; using every weapon that his trenchant brain and withering personality could command.

The Menons (it is a caste name) come from Malabar, or Kerala. Vengalil Krishnan Krishna Menon was born at Calicut (Kozhikode) on May 3, 1897. He graduated B.A. from Presidency College, Madras, and as a young man he joined the Theosophical Society. He became a member of Mrs. Annie Besant's own circle and was a volunteer in her Indian Home Rule campaign. In 1924, Mrs. Besant took him to England for a visit which was to become a long sojourn. While teaching at a theosophical school at Letchworth, St. Christopher's, he attended evening classes at the London School of Economics. He was placed in the First Class of the B.Sc. (Econ.), gained the University Diploma for Education, an M.A. (for research in the Physiological Laboratory at University College) and the M.Sc. (Econ.), back at the L.S.E. He also studied law, and was called to the Bar by the Middle Temple.

In 1929 he was elected general secretary of the India League, which had hitherto been little more than a debating club of Indian students and other sympathizers of the Indian National Congress. Krishna Menon soon made it into a real political force, and the Congress leaders' chief instrument of propaganda in Britain.

A bachelor, vegetarian, non-smoker, and total abstainer, he lodged in rooms in Camden Town, and was reputed to live mostly on toast and tea.

For more than a dozen years he was a member of the St. Pancras Borough Council, being elected chairman of the Library Committee. It was during this period as a leader of the minority Socialist group on the council that he developed his technique of political encounter. One of his most effective, though least endearing, tactics was the searing contempt he would display for dim argument or slipshod action. No opponent could afford to nod—but no comrade could either.

Krishna Menon's activities were not exclusively political. He edited the "Twentieth Century Library" issued by Bodley Head, and he was the first editor of Pelican Books. A new standard in popular education was established: he was not concerned to "improve" the minds of earnest clerks and working men, but to illumine and ignite the thoughts of thoughtful men adrift in the time of Munich. There is still an intellectual thrill in going down the list of his first 20 magnificent authors.

While still at L.S.E. he joined the Labour Party, and he became well known to many of its leaders. He helped to strengthen the link between Labour and the Congress which was to be a constant (though dwindling) factor in the British-Indian relations down into the 1960s. He had leanings towards communism in the 1930s, but early in the war he was chosen as Labour candidate for Dundee. For speaking at a communist-inspired meeting in 1941 he was removed from the list of candidates. He thereupon resigned from the Labour Party, bitterly complaining of its alleged apathy towards Indian claims. He rejoined the party at the end of the war, and soon many of his old Labour colleagues were in high ministerial office.

Following the transfer of power in August 1947, Krishna Menon was appointed High Comissioner to the United Kingdom, contrary, it was understood, to the wishes of officials in Whitehall, and also of most members of the

Indian Cabinet. His position, then and subsequently, derived from his close relationship with Nehru, with whom he had been an intimate friend since 1936.

The years at India House (1947-52) were not smooth. Krishna Menon appeared to regard his role as still that of spokesman of a people struggling against imperialist oppression. However, one major achievement must be ascribed to him: next to Nehru, Lord Mountbatten, and perhaps Sir Benegal Rau, he more than anyone was responsible for influencing events so as to keep India within the Commonwealth family. Krishna Menon was to find a more congenial role as India's chief representative at the General Assembly of the United Nations and in other international gatherings.

In 1953 Krishna Menon was elected to the Upper House of the Indian Parliament. He entered the Cabinet in February 1956 as Minister without Portfolio, acting as the Prime Minister's adviser on foreign affairs. When, in July, President Nasser* nationalized the Suez Canal, he took a leading part in the negotiations which followed. In retrospect it is clear that India had as great an interest as Britain in reaching a reasonable settlement, and the plan presented by Krishna Menon in August would have salvaged more for British interests than was eventually gained (or lost) by force.

In April 1957 he was made Minister of Defence. Krishna Menon, like Nehru, believed that the main, indeed probably the only, military threat to India came from Pakistan, and found no reason to change that belief in the context of the border dispute with China. Though it was Nehru who made a negotiated settlement of that dispute impossible (Krishna Menon's instinct was to settle) he held as unshakably as Nehru that no real attack from China was possible, *no matter what India did*. As domestic attacks on the Government's defence and foreign policies mounted in the late 1950s, Krishna Menon and the Prime Minister countered misleadingly by affirming and reaffirming that India's defence services were well up to the mark and fully capable of any task given to them.

The folly of the assumption that China would never attack and the falseness of the assurances that the Indian Army could take care of any eventuality were brutally exposed in 1962, when the army, undersupplied, outnumbered and badly led, was broken and routed by Chinese troops in the North-East Frontier Agency. All of the political anger in India against the Government was focused first on Krishna Menon. Nehru tried to stand by him, but it soon became apparent that unless he went the attacks would turn against the Prime Minister personally, and Nehru then accepted Khrishna Menon's resignation as Defence Minister. It was typical of the Prime Minister that he attempted to save his colleague's (and his own) face by keeping him on in the Cabinet as Minister of Defence Production, a gesture that simply condemned

Krishna Menon to two humiliating resignations rather than one. It took only another week for him to be forced right out of the Government.

After a series of savage rows with the Congress Party leadership he resigned from the party in 1967 and went down to defeat twice as an independent. But by 1969 he was back in Parliament after strong Communist Party backing had helped him to a big victory in West Bengal.

Much can be said in praise of Krishna Menon, and praise that in the Indian context is by no means common. He was honest, dedicated, hard working; modern-minded, he had no time for the astrologers and sadhus who were patronized with varying degrees of furtiveness by most of his party colleagues. He was wholly loyal to Nehru, neither in his lifetime nor after his death standing apart from or criticizing his old friend and patron. But his qualities as much as his failings of personality set him apart from the mainstream of Indian political life—a mainstream that was an underground river during Nehru's prime—and made him a peripheral figure, magnified by the communist-hunting demonology of American journalism as much as by the attacks of those in India who turned on Krishna Menon when they dared not tackle Nehru.

October 7, 1974.

Gene Krupa, who died on October 16, 1973, at the age of 64, was one of the most famous drummers in the history of American music. He was one of the first jazz musicians ever to receive the dubious honour of a Hollywood screen biography, which reflects as well as anything the way he combined the status of a respected jazz musician and the image of a popular showman.

Only an exhibitionist drummer could ever have won Hollywood tinsel affection; only a fine musician could have fought his way through in the first place. The first place, for him, was Chicago of the 1920s, where he matured as a drummer in the first white generation of genuine jazz musicians, mostly of college background, who will always be associated with the name of Eddie Condon. But, unlike the majority, he comfortably made the transition in the 1930s to the swing band world, and by 1935 had emerged as a star drummer with Benny Goodman (another Chicago graduate).

He was not a particularly subtle drummer, but subtle drummers have never become famous, and Krupa was fortunate to have just the right instinct for the kind of musicianship that was needed to propel a band like Goodman's. Quite apart from the flashing smile and unruly locks, he had exactly the right drive and uninhibited rhythmic power to turn him into a star at a time when no drummer had been a solo attraction before. That he was not just a

power-house performer is amply proved by the many small group recordings he made with Goodman, Teddy Wilson, and Lionel Hampton.

But it was as a big band performer that he was fated to be cast, and during the 1940s he led his own orchestra as a showcase drummer, and, to his credit, as the patron of some of the newer trends in jazz.

Although active right to the end, as a leader of small groups and as a teacher, Krupa may well be remembered as the man who first made drum solos acceptable to the public. Whether that makes him a hero or a villain, it is undeniable that jazz followers will always have a soft spot for him.

Loud, limited, yet immensely talented in the role he found himself in, he was one of the first jazz musicians to combine public appeal with a solid talent. Jazz might be more popular today if there were more men with the same combination of apparently irreconcilable gifts.

October 19, 1973.

Vladimir Kuts, one of the world's great 5,000 and 10,000 metres runners, died of a heart attack in Moscow on August 16, 1975 at the age of 48.

The winner of the 5,000 and 10,000 metres at the Melbourne Olympic Games of 1956, he repeatedly broke the world records for these two distances and succeeded the great Emil Zatopek as the world's best middle distance runner of his time.

It was at the European games of 1954 that he announced this supremacy and his unique tactics of astonishingly fast starting, front running and punishing pace variation, when he spreadeagled an international 5,000 metres field from the gun and went on to lead Zatopek and Chataway throughout the race, finishing in the lead by a wide margin, in the world record time of 13min. 56.6sec.

Two months later in a memorable 5,000 metres classic at the White City, Chataway rose to these tactics and hung on to beat the Russian in the final yards of the race in another world record of 13min. 51.6sec. Kuts, whose "total" training techniques were instrumental in fostering a whole new approach to athletics training in the West, lowered this mark again only weeks later.

Just prior to the Melbourne Olympics he established a world 10,000 metres record of 28min. 30.4sec. and in the Olympics themselves he was master of the fields at both distances, leaving Gordon Pirie a distant second in the 10,000 metres.

His 5,000 metres world record of 13min. 35sec., set in 1957, survived for seven years.

After his retirement in 1959, he became a prominent coach in Russia. He was awarded the Order of Lenin for his services to athletics.

August 18, 1975.

L

Dr. David Lamber Lack, F.R.S., who died in Oxford on March 12, 1973, was one of the most outstanding among world ornithologists.

He was born in July 1910, the son of H. Lambert Lack, a surgeon and himself a keen ornithologist, and was educated at Gresham's, Holt, and Magdalene College, Cambridge. His interest in birds dated from his early days and was encouraged at school. While still an undergraduate he wrote the greater part of his book *The Birds of Cambridgeshire*, published the year after he went down. After taking his degree he became biology master at Dartington Hall, where he remained for seven years. During this time he had the opportunity to carry out his studies of the biology and behaviour of the robin which resulted in important papers and a little book of wide popularity, *The Life of the Robin* (1943). Would that schoolmasters generally were treated so well and able to use their leisure to such good advantage!

From Dartington, shortly before the war, David Lack made an expedition to the Galapagos Islands. His subsequent interpretation of the geographical variation of the small finches of those islands, which 100 years earlier had stimulated Darwin's earliest ideas about evolution, led to great advances in the understanding of species-formation, competition between species, and the evolution of island faunas which subsequent workers are still exploiting. The book in which Lack expounded his general ideas on these topics, *Darwin's Finches* (1947), has become a classic of evolutionary literature. Twenty years later he returned to the subject of island biology, and his last work, the result of a sabbatical year in Jamaica, was concerned with the evolution of the West Indian avifauna.

It was characteristic of David Lack that no duties, however arduous, not even his wartime services in the Army Operational Research Group, were able to stop him working and writing on birds. All was grist to his mill; and his wartime expertise in the development of radar tracking led directly to his outstanding later work on the use of radar methods for the study of migration.

At the end of the war he was appointed Director of the Edward Grey Institute of Field Ornithology at Oxford and all his later studies have been linked with his work there. His influence rapidly became paramount in British ornithology, and the Edward Grey Institute became a foremost centre for bird research and received students from all over the world. Many look back with pleasure at the annual student conferences in bird biology which he held every January, at his brilliantly clear and stimulating lectures and the encouragement which he gave to young ornithologists.

David Lack's remarkable originality of approach and the breadth of his interests led him to make advances in several different fields of research, all of them of importance not to birds only, but for the light that they threw on wider aspects of biological theory. He began to investigate the reproductive rates of birds, and developed a theory of the natural selection of family size the validity (or otherwise) of which is basic to an understanding of the natural control of animal populations. His ideas on this subject were expounded in *The Natural Regulation of Animal Numbers* (1954), in which he also summarized his extensive analyses of ringing returns, thus providing information about the survival of young and adult birds under various conditions.

Meanwhile, at first as a sideline, migration began to interest him increasingly. Some chance observations suggested that it might be much easier to observe birds in their migratory flights than had been realized; he followed this up with systematic watches along inland escarpments, on the south coast of England, and in Pyrenean passes, and was able to throw much new light on the movements of birds to and through Britain, and through mountains, and on their reactions to topographical features and to weather. Later, when it became clear that such observations of "visible migration" covered only a fraction of the total movements involved, he switched to radar as his primary method of study and made quantitative studies of the volume and direction of migration reaching Britain from the European mainland.

Lack also produced many distinguished studies on the biology of individual species. His work on the Great Tit in Wytham Wood near Oxford, carried on for many years by a succession of students under his direction, is one of the most remarkable long-term studies of a single bird population. His study of swifts, published in semi-popular form in *Swifts in a Tower* (1956), ranks with *The Life of the Robin* as a model of how to present scientific work for the enjoyment of the intelligent layman.

Lack was elected a Fellow of the Royal Society in 1951 and president of the International Ornithological Congress for 1966: but although he so greatly influenced the course of ornithological studies and by his friendly and enthusiastic nature inspired many students to take up the study of birds, he did not engage widely in public affairs. He was essentially an individualist, with only a few really intimate friends. Moreover, his standards were so high that he was apt unwittingly to offend the amateur ornithologist.

Lack was a devout Anglican, much concerned with the implications of certain kinds of scientific theory on religion. He wrote a book, *Evolution and Christian Belief: the Continuing Conflict*, which was in some ways a reaction against the tendency at the time to imply that the much discussed antagonism between religion and science was all a mistake. The book encountered a good deal of critical comment as books on such subjects are bound to do; but it undoubtedly played a useful role in clearing the air and pointing some of the issues afresh. His writing was simple and clear, and almost everything he wrote was a delight to read. He delighted in music and in English literature.

In 1949 he married Elizabeth Silva, with whom he collaborated in a number of papers. He had four children, three boys and a girl.

March 13, 1973.

Pär Lagerkvist, the Swedish novelist, dramatist and poet, died in Stockholm on July 11, 1974. He was 83. He was awarded the Nobel Prize for Literature in 1951. In all he wrote some 40 novels, plays and collections of essays.

He became a significant figure on the Scandinavian literary scene towards the end of the First World War; his early work reflected an extremely sensitive personality at odds with his own war generation and yet mirroring the brutality of that generation. It was some time before he achieved a wider than local reputation.

Friends and critics described Lagerkvist as "a believer without a faith, a religious atheist", and throughout his life he fought for humanity, culture and human values. He felt deeply the tragedy of World War I —his works from this period were *Anguish* and *Chaos*, and he reacted to the rise of Nazism in the 30s with equal vigour.

His drama *The Hangman* in 1933 warned of the impending collapse of culture, and his novel *The Dwarf* in 1944 gave a brilliant analysis of the problem of evil apparent in every man, the will to hate and destroy. *The Hangman* was staged in London in 1935 with Frank Vosper as the hangman.

Barabbas, a fictional account of the thoughts of the condemned robber who was set free while Jesus Christ was crucified, was translated into English in 1952 and was also translated into some 30 other languages. It was filmed in Sweden in 1953 under the direction of Alf Sjoberg, and another version, directed by Richard Fleischer with a cast including Katy Jurado, Jack Palance, Arthur Kennedy and Silvana Mangano, was made in 1961-62.

July 12, 1974.

Professor Imre Lakatos died suddenly on February 2, 1974 at the age of 51.

He was the foremost philosopher of mathematics in his generation, and a gifted and original philosopher of empirical science, and a forceful and colourful personality.

He was born in Hungary on November 9, 1922. After a brilliant school and university career he graduated from Debrecen in

Mathematics, Physics and Philosophy in 1944. Under the Nazi occupation he joined the underground resistance. He avoided capture, but his mother and grandmother, who had brought him up, were deported and perished in Auschwitz.

After the war he became a research student at Budapest University. He was briefly associated with Lukács. At this period he was a convinced communist. In 1947 he had the post of "Secretary" in the Ministry of Education and was virtually in charge of the democratic reform of higher education in Hungary. He spent 1949 at Moscow University.

His political prominence soon got him into trouble. He was arrested in the spring of 1950. He used to say afterwards that two factors helped him to survive: his unwavering communist faith and his resolve not to fabricate evidence. (He also said, and one believes it, that the strain of interrogation proved too much—for one of his interrogators!)

He was released late in 1953. He had no job and had been deprived of every material possession (with the exception of his watch, which was returned to him and which he wore until his death). In 1954, the mathematician Rényi got him a job in the Mathematical Research Institute of the Hungarian Academy of Science translating mathematical works. One of these was Polya's How to Solve It, which introduced him to the subject in which he later became preeminent, the logic of mathematical discovery. He now had access to a library containing books, not publicly available, by western thinkers, including Hayek and Popper. This opened his eyes to the possibility of an approach to social and political questions that was non-Marxist yet scientific. His communist certainties began to dissolve.

After the Hungarian uprising he escaped to Vienna on Victor Kraft's advice, and, with the help of a Rockefeller fellowship, he went to Cambridge to study under Braithwaite and Smiley.

Some years afterwards, when he feared that the principle of academic autonomy was in danger in Britain, he wrote: "As an undergraduate I witnessed the demands of Nazi students at my University to suppress 'Jewish-Liberal-Marxist influence' expressed in the syllabuses. I saw how they, in concord with outside political forces, tried for many years—not without some success—to influence appointments and have teachers sacked who resisted their bandwagon. Later I was a graduate student at Moscow University when resolutions of the Central Committee of the Communist Party determined syllabuses in genetics and sent the dissenters to death. I also remember when students demanded that Einstein's 'bourgeois relativism' (i.e. his relativity theory) should not be taught."

When he reached England he could speak German and Russian, and read French and English. Now he began to master spoken English. If he never succeeded quite per-

fectly ("thinking aloud" became "thinking loudly") he did enrich the language with his "body scientific", "monster-barring", "book-act", etc.

In 1958 he met Polya, who put him on to the history of the "Descartes-Euler conjecture" for his doctorate. This grew into his "Proofs and Refutations" (1963-64), a brilliant imaginary dialogue that recapitulates the historical development. It is full of originality, wit, and scholarship. It founded a new, quasi-empiricist philosophy of mathematics.

In England the man whose ideas came to attract him most was Professor (now Sir Karl) Popper, whom he joined at L.S.E. in 1960. (There he rose rapidly, becoming Professor of Logic in 1969).

His interests now turned increasingly to the methodology of the physical sciences. In 1965 he organized a famous colloquium in London, which brought together from all over the world outstanding thinkers in logic and methodology.

Its proceedings, in four volumes, contained two major papers of his, each constructively critical of the philosophies of science of Carnap* and of Popper. He accepted many of Popper's ideas, but he felt that Popper's critical philosophy must itself be subjected to searching criticism; and he now developed a distinctive methodology —his "methodology of scientific research programmes"—in which philosophy of science is more intimately related to the actual history of scientific discovery.

When he lectured, the room would be crowded, the atmosphere electric, and from time to time there would be a gale of laughter. He inspired a group of young scholars to do original research; he would often spend days with them on their manuscripts before publication. With his sharp tongue and strong opinions he sometimes seemed authoritarian; but he was "Imre" to everyone; and he invited searching criticism of his ideas, and of his writings over which he took endless trouble before they were finally allowed to appear in print.

From 1964 on he was a frequent visitor to the U.S.A. He kept up a huge correspondence. He was not without enemies; for he was a fighter and went for the things he believed in fearlessly and tirelessly. But he had friends all over the world who will be deeply shocked by his untimely death.

February 6, 1974.

Veronica Lake, who died in Vermont on July 7, 1973 aged 53, was an emblematic film star of the early 1940s. At the height of her fairly brief popularity she received 1,000 fan letters a week. Her "peek-a-boo bang"—long blonde hair falling over one eye—was widely copied by American girls. But after several accidents in munitions factories, caused by hair catching in machines, the United States Government asked her to adopt a shorter style.

Born Constance Ockelman in New York in 1919, she made her first three pictures under the name of Constance Keane before winning sudden fame, and a seven-year contract with Paramount, in the aviation film, *I Wanted Wings,* in 1941.

Her next film, and arguably her best, was Preston Sturges's satire *Sullivan's Travels,* shown on B.B.C. television after her death. But the box office preferred her thrillers with Alan Ladd,* *This Gun for Hire,* based on a Graham Greene novel, and Dashiell Hammett's* *The Glass Key.* She was excellent in the René Clair comedy *I Married a Witch.*

In 1946 another thriller with Ladd, *The Blue Dahlia* (and screenplay by Raymond Chandler), saw a partial revival. But by 1951 her film career was virtually over. She returned to the theatre for a time and then disappeared until she was discovered years later working in a cocktail lounge. She returned to acting, made a film in Canada, and in 1968 published an autobiography, *Veronica,* in which she looked back on her rise and fall with considerable bitterness.

In the same year she made two stage appearances in Britain. Her performance as Blanche in *A Streetcar Named Desire* suggested that she might have become a considerable mature actress. She was married four times.

July 9, 1973.

Joseph Laniel, who died on April 8, 1975 at the age of 85, was Prime Minister of France from June 1953 to June 1954, a bad period for France and for French political institutions.

His right-wing government which had the support of the Radicals and some Gaullists, was elected after a five-week parliamentary crisis during which Paul Reynaud* called France the "Sick Man of Europe". It was a period in which events in Indo-China and North Africa were demanding bold and liberal policies and when London and Washington were becoming increasingly insistent that France should sign the European Defence Community Treaty and so make possible a German contribution to the defence of Europe. It was Laniel's misfortune not to have a clear majority for any of these things.

At the Bermuda conference with Eisenhower* and Churchill,* no great politeness was shown to the French Prime Minister and this, though it made French opinion indignant, did not make Laniel popular. Events in Indo-China moved fast towards disaster and though the Geneva conference opened in 1954 little progress was made and the Laniel government was overthrown three days after the fall of Dien Bien Phu. The election of the second President of the Fourth Republic, René Coty,* took place during the Laniel Government and the 13 ballots and the six days of manoeuvring at Versailles did not resound to the credit of the system—or to that of Laniel who was an unsuccessful candidate.

Born at Vimoutiers on October 12, 1889, Laniel directed the old established family textile business with great skill and was one of the richest men in parliament. He entered the Assembly in 1932 as Deputy for Calvados and served in the Reynaud government from June 1940 as Under-Secretary for Finance.

During the war, this placid stocky Norman businessman was one of the few right-wing politicians to side with the Resistance. He was a vice-President of the Conseil National de la Résistance and walked with General de Gaulle* down the Champs Élysées in the victory march after the liberation of Paris. Though Laniel lacked imagination and perhaps force of character in dealing with foreign affairs (he was in many ways ill-served by his Foreign Minister, Bidault), he was no reactionary bigot.

Unsuccessful abroad, his government stabilized the franc and kept prices down in France and encouraged the modernization of French industry. Indeed Laniel and his Finance Minister, Edgar Faure, played a major part in making possible the long period of French economic prosperity.

He published *Jours de Gloire et Jours Cruels (1908-1958)* in 1971.

April 12, 1975.

Latife Hanim—See Hanim.

James Laver, C.B.E., F.R.S.A., F.R.S.L., who died on June 3, 1975 at the age of 76, was one of those formidable polymaths who, by applying a versatility of talent to several subjects, give each of them a new dimension. He had a mind so alive, so apt to dance vivaciously from one topic to any other which seemed germane, that critics were tempted to dismiss him as merely a polished stylist. Certainly his work as poet, novelist, dramatist, biographer and art historian was never on the most profound level; but the understanding of other classes and countries that his dynamic dilettantism gave him was of great value in the discipline he made his own: the psychology of taste, especially of fashion in costume.

For him, the hemline was a seismograph, in which he saw the rise and waning of civilizations. He read omens in overcoats, portents in petticoats, sermons in stoles. He delimited erogenous zones with the ruthless nicety of a Versailles diplomatist. His thesis was that "fashion is never arbitrary. It has its roots in the unconscious, the Collective Unconscious if you will, and the hopes and fears of a whole society are reflected in the cut of a dress".

Laver was born in Liverpool on March 14, 1899, the son of a printer.

At 12 he won a scholarship to the Liverpool Institute. A member of one of the great Liverpool shipowning families saw promise in him and gave him £1,000 to go to Oxford. He was accepted by New College as a Commoner. Matriculating in 1917, he was immediately afterwards gazetted to the King's Own (Royal Lancaster) Regiment. As he did not arrive in France until two days before the Armistice, he saw no fighting ("I am probably the only soldier in the First World War", he later wrote, "to have received a medal for *every day* of active service").

At Oxford there were aesthetes and hearties, and Laver tended to side with the latter, although he horrified his rowing friends in 1921 by winning the Newdigate prize for a poem on Cervantes.

In 1922 he was appointed an assistant keeper in the Department of Engraving, Illustration and Design at the Victoria and Albert Museum, where he was to remain for 37 years. Martin Hardie was then Keeper, a position Laver succeeded to in 1938. The other young officials included Herbert Read,* William King and Leigh Ashton. One of his most interesting assignments was organizing an exhibition of Samuel Palmer's works owned by his irascible son A. H. Palmer. Laver established the states of all the Palmer etchings, which are still known as "L.58, state 3" or whatever it may be.

Meanwhile, writing in the evenings, he kept up a prolific literary output. His studies of living artists, *Portraits in Oil and Vinegar* (1925), which began with a spurious Sainte-Beuve epigraph mischievously invented by Laver himself, was generally well received, although slated by Clive Bell in *The Athenaeum*.

But he sprang into real prominence in 1927, with the publication by the Nonesuch Press of his poem *A Stitch in Time*. It was a frank pastiche of *The Rape of the Lock*, transposed into modern times.

Desmond MacCarthy and other critics praised it exorbitantly and the *Financial Times* spoke admiringly of the bullish qualities of a publication which rose in price, in two weeks, from 3s. 9d. to £1 15s. Saucy, satirical, slightly scandalous, the poem made Laver's name and gave him the *entrée* into the popular Press. There was a sequel in 1929, *Love's Progress*, and in 1933 the two were published together as *Ladies' Mistakes*. All of these volumes are now collectors' pieces.

Perhaps by reaction to his Puritan upbringing, Laver developed a passion for the theatre. He arrived at the Victoria and Albert Museum at a fortunate moment. The International Theatre Exhibition had been transferred there from Amsterdam and was shown in his department. It contained work by all the leading Continental and English designers. The Museum bought a large number of designs and models, including Edward Gordon Craig's*, and it was decided to make these the nucleus of a collection of the Art of the Theatre. Laver was put in charge, and stage design became one of his special interests.

He also did some amateur production, and translated several plays from the French and German, notably Klabund's *The Circle of Chalk*. A play for children, *The House that Went to Sea*, was produced at the Liverpool Playhouse in 1936. But Laver's biggest stage success was the dramatization of his novel, *Nymph Errant*, which ran during the 1933-34 season.

Nymph Errant, which appeared in 1932, was the longest and best of Laver's novels. It related the adventures of a Lancashire girl travelling across Europe, who eventually finds herself in a Turkish harem. Sir Charles Cochran had it turned into a musical with lyrics by Cole Porter* and Gertrude Lawrence as the leading lady.

Laver began to feel he was leading a double life. As he put it himself, with characteristic comedy: "To my colleagues at South Kensington I had become a cigar-smoking, Savoy-supping, enviable but slightly disreputable character, hobnobbing with chorus girls and hanging round stage doors. To Gertrude Lawrence and her friends I was something 'in a museum', engaged in mysterious and apparently useless activities quite outside their comprehension; a character out of *The Old Curiosity Shop*, hardly fit to be let out alone."

But Laver seemed to be able to manage two lives very well. There was nothing amateurish in his contributions to art history. *French Painting and the Nineteenth Century* (1937) was a judicial assessment with a new psychological approach. *Adventures in Monochrome* (1941) surveyed the popular graphic arts. Two works of 1930, *A Complete Catalogue of the Etchings and Drypoints of Arthur Briscoe* and *A History of British and American Etching*, showed how entirely seriously he took the subjects that he was paid by the state to know about. His admirable pioneer book on the French painter, James Tissot, was published in 1936.

Laver's interest in the history and psychology of costume began through his wanting to date paintings by the costumes. It was now that he began to develop the theories for which he will be best remembered—about the so-called "cycles" of fashion, the relationship between dress design and the other applied arts, and the economic and social factors controlling the evolution of taste. He published several important books on these topics.

Just before the Second World War, Laver was concerned in the removing and packing away of the Victoria and Albert Museum's treasures; part of one wall had to be pulled down to get out the Raphael Cartoons. Three days after the outbreak of war he was installed in the Treasury, where his reputation became that of an unorthodox official.

He was then invited by Sir Robert Kindersley to become a national lecturer on the National Savings Committee. He talked to Irish labourers on muddy airfields, to miners in the pithead baths, to men puddling steel and girls filling detonators. In the course of this valuable war work he became slightly alarmed at the power he was experiencing as a demagogue. "The trouble about all public speaking", he later wrote, "is that one begins to evoke emotions one no longer feels—and that might almost be the definition of a prostitute."

Laver's mind remained one of darting intelligence. It was absolutely typical of him to decide that on his long train journeys up and down the country he would "read all the books in the London Library under the rubric 'Occultism' ". He became an expert in this field and wrote a book on the sixteenth-century prophet Nostradamus.

In his 1963 autobiography, *Museum Piece* (of which *The Times Literary Supplement* unkindly remarked that it reminded one of the man who came to tea and stayed for a month), Laver interrupted his cosy recollections to wonder whether, with all his varied and sprightly achievements, he was not after all a failure. "Instead of proceeding, in however pedestrian a fashion, along the highways of literature, "I had been diverted into the bypaths of expertise." He was a natural dilettante. But he was no fribble. His works on fashion will stand as minor classics; and he must also be credited with the valuable service of cross-pollination between subjects which is the dilettante's special office and virtue.

In 1928 Laver married the actress Veronica Turleigh (Bridget Veronica Turley); a son and a daughter were born of the marriage. His wife died in 1971.

June 4, 1975.

Veronica Laver—See Turleigh.

Lord Justice Lawrence—See Oaksey.

Jack Leach, the former Newmarket trainer and a well-known flat-race jockey, died on January 29, 1972 at the age of 70.

Jack, son of the trainer Felix Leach, was the brother of "Chubb" Leach and Felix Leach junior. He rode some 500 winners, his greatest success coming in the 2,000 guineas of 1927, which he won on 20-1 chance Adam's Apple.

His family was connected with racing to such an extent that on one afternoon at Yarmouth four Leachs were connected with the first four winners. Jack rode the first winner, trained by his brother Felix. He also won the second. "Chubb" rode the winner of the third, also trained by Felix jun., and their father trained the winner of the fourth.

When he gave up riding, Jack took up training at Graham Place, Newmarket. After the First World War, in which he served as a captain with The York and Lancaster Regiment, he had under his care that good sprinter Delirium who won one of France's top juvenile prizes, the Prix Morny at Deauville. He also owned and trained Figaro, winner of the 1934 Stewards Cup.

He wrote about racing for both the *Observer* and the *Sporting Life*. He had a highly individual and colourful style. A book of his reminiscences called *Sods I have cut on the Turf*, which had a foreword by Sir Gordon Richards, appeared in 1961.

January 31, 1972.

Group Captain John Leacroft, M.C., who died at Bexhill-on-Sea on August 26, 1971 at the age of 82, was an outstanding fighter pilot of the First World War who was twice decorated in the field "for conspicuous gallantry" in the great air battles on the Western Front in 1917 and 1918.

In 11 months, in two tours of duty, he destroyed or brought down 21 German aircraft as a patrol leader with 19 Squadron, then in constant combat with von Richthofen's newly-formed "circus" of multi-coloured Albatros Scouts and Fokker triplanes.

His score included seven of the formidable Albatros fighters, armed with twin Spandau machine-guns, and he accounted for six while flying the French Spad fighter, armed with only a single machine-gun firing through the airscrew, with which the squadron was equipped in 1917.

In one dogfight over Flanders the following year, when the Spads had been replaced by single-seat Sopwith 5 F1 Dolphin biplanes, with a top speed of 131 m.p.h. his formation of three fighters destroyed six German aircraft and forced another down without suffering damage or casualties itself.

Major E. R. "Toby" Pretyman, the squadron commander in 1918, described him as "a most outstanding pilot and the best flight commander on the Western Front in his time".

Joining the squadron in May 1917, when low-level attacks on enemy ground forces were introduced for the first time before the Battle of Messines, he quickly won note for the "vigour and dash" of his hedge-hopping sorties across the German lines, often in bad weather.

With a box of 25lb. bombs in the cockpit because the Spad could not be fitted with racks, he carried out several low-flying special attack missions against enemy troops and guns during the Third Battle of Ypres, winning the Military Cross in October 1917.

Later he was one of the pilots whose daring low-level attacks were crucial in helping to smash the German advance when the Allied front was crumbling beneath the weight of Ludendorff's offensive with 68 divisions and 730 aircraft in March 1918.

His attack on the Albert Road on March 27, when the Fifth Army had been forced back to the Somme, won him a Bar to his Military Cross and is reported in the official history, *The War in the Air*, as an illustration of the tactics used to meet the

desperate situation.

Joining the Army in 1914, he transferred to the R.F.C. as a captain in 1915 after serving with the R.A.S.C. in France and Egypt, and flew as an observer during the Senussi Campaign and the Second Turkish attack on the Suez Canal before qualifying as a pilot in 1917.

He was given a permanent commission in the R.A.F. on its formation in 1918, and was in action against rebel Kurdish tribesmen in Iraq in 1922-24. He later held various home appointments, including the command of 17 Squadron, 1924-28, and spent seven years at Halton from 1930 to 1937, four of them in command of No. 1 Wing.

As a flying instructor at the R.A.F. College, Cranwell, 1920-22, and as chief flying instructor at No. 3 Flying Training School, Grantham, in 1928-30, he trained many of the pilots who flew in the 1939-45 War.

He retired at his own request as a group captain in 1937, when commanding the Coastal Command station at Thornaby, Yorks, but rejoined in June 1939. In 1942, he became president of the Air Crew Selection Board at Cardington, Bedfordshire.

The son of Dr. John William Leacroft, he was educated at Aldenham and at Pembroke College, Cambridge. A keen sportsman, he was a prewar member of the Belvoir and other hunts, and represented the R.A.F. at cricket and polo and at Bisley between the wars.

He married, in 1926, Gladys, daughter of George Underhill Cuddon, who survives him with one daughter.

August 31, 1971.

Sir Eric Leadbitter, K.C.V.O., who died on February 25, 1971, was Clerk of the Privy Council from 1942 to 1951. He had previously served in the Public Trustee Office and in the Treasury.

Somewhat in the tradition of an office several of whose holders had enjoyed repute in various branches of literature, he had in his younger days written some half-dozen novels, whose merits had attracted the attention of fastidious readers of fiction.

Eric Cyril Egerton Leadbitter was the youngest son of T. F. Leadbitter, of Warden, Northumberland, and was born on June 8, 1891. He was educated at Shrewsbury School, and he entered the Public Trustee Office in 1910. In the war of 1914-18 he served in the Royal Navy Reserve. The war put a strain upon his health and he was awarded a 50 per cent disability pension.

In 1919 an expanded Treasury was combing the departments for able additions to its staff, and Leadbitter was selected and transferred there with the rank of an Assistant Principal, and he was shortly afterwards appointed Private Secretary to Sir Malcolm Ramsay, the Director of Establishments. Two years later, he became Private Secretary to the Permanent Secretary,

Sir Warren Fisher. This post he held for some years, at the end of which, on the retirement of Sir Charles Dalrymple Hay from the post of Senior Clerk in the Privy Council Office, Leadbitter was chosen to fill it.

In 1934 he was made Deputy Clerk of the Privy Council. At that time the Clerk of the Council was Sir Maurice (afterwards Lord) Hankey,* who combined the office with that of the Secretaryship of the Cabinet, which latter post was a full-time office in itself, so during those years Leadbitter was virtually the active head of the Privy Council Office. When, in 1938, Sir Rupert Howorth* succeeded Lord Hankey as Clerk of the Council, the two offices were divided again. In 1942 Howorth retired and on the recommendation of the Lord President of the Council, Sir John Anderson, Leadbitter was appointed to succeed him. Throughout the service Leadbitter was recognized as a man of outstanding ability, and of the varied and often highly technical work of the Privy Council Office he had a complete mastery. He had been trained in the hard school of the Treasury under a brilliant and none too easy a chief, and he had thus acquired an all-round knowledge of the Civil Service invaluable in an office like the Privy Council, which is in daily contact with every department, as well as with the Court.

Behind a singularly modest, and even retiring, manner was concealed a remarkably clear and critical mind with a sense of dry humour that could never be side-tracked by either irrelevance or sentimentality, and the essential kindliness of his nature had made him popular throughout his career with both colleagues and subordinates.

Leadbitter was a man of wide culture, and his minutes were models of clear thinking presented in an admirable style. Indifferent health throughout his career had limited outdoor pursuits, and literature was his principal recreation. Between 1915 and 1928, he published six novels: *Rain before Seven, The Road to Nowhere, Perpetual Fires, Shepherd's Warning, Dead Reckoning,* and *The Evil that Men Do.*

He married in 1918, Irene, daughter of Frederick Lloyd.

March 6, 1971.

Harvey Leader, or "Jack" as he was affectionately known to a multitude of friends in and outside Newmarket, died on January 30, 1972 at the age of 78.

He gave up training racehorses only in the previous November at the end of the flat-race season. He had held a licence since 1918. The fourth son of "old Tom Leader" who saddled George Frederick to win the 1874 Derby, he was born into a family which for a century brought widespread fame and distinction to the British turf.

Like his brothers, Tom, Fred and Col-

ledge, he became a trainer after experience as a jockey and he rode his first winner at the age of 12. It was at Newmarket, the headquarters of racing, that the Leaders settled in 1888, and after the early and unexpected deaths of Fred and Colledge in the 1930s the responsibilities of carrying on the family tradition fell on him and his nephew, Ted Leader.

His first important win came in 1920, when Caligula triumphed in the St. Leger. Few Newmarket trainers nowadays take an active interest in the National Hunt side of racing, but with him it was very different. Increasing weight had led to him riding "over the sticks", and it was natural enough that, in later years, he should be a keen supporter of the local hunts and of polo. In the meantime he had won the 1926 Grand National with Jack Horner.

He won a "Lincoln" with the 100-1 chance Elton, and three Cambridgeshire Handicaps with Hidden Meaning, Dites and Gyroscope. The two horses, however, which older racegoers will never forget were the brilliant sprinters Diomedes and Shalfleet. The former he picked up for only 240 guineas and the colt won 17 of his 19 races. Shalfleet was an even more popular favourite with prewar racegoers and his score ran to 16 victories, including Doncaster's much-coveted Portland Handicap two years in succession.

He was never short of owners or of horses. Lord Willoughby de Broke, Lady Bullough and Lady Durham, Lord Cadogan and the well-known Milan breeder Dr. Carlo Vittadini were among his distinguished patrons. He was an attentive and generous host and he never lost a friend. He was patient and courteous to those around him, and the scribes who write on turf matters will long remember his understanding and cooperation when answering their innumerable questions.

He married Miriam Gardner, by whom he had two daughters.

February 1, 1972.

Louis Seymour Bazett Leakey, M.A., PH.D., D.SC., F.G.S., F.B.A., who died in London on October 1, 1972, will chiefly be remembered as a prehistoric archaeologist, palaeontologist and physical anthropologist. In all these fields he was one of the foremost authorities of his day; but such was his versatility that he was also an expert on the Kikuyu tribe, on handwriting, and on animal life. His keen powers of observation and of criticism, together with his intense interest in anything at all out of the ordinary, made him an ideal museum curator and a successful writer and lecturer.

Leakey was born on August 7, 1903 at Kabete, Kenya. He was the elder son of Harry and Mary Leakey of the Church Missionary Society, both of whom were working among the Kikuyu. His playmates

were boys of this tribe and he very seldom saw white children other than his brothers and sisters. He received his early education from his father and from a governess, and the outbreak of war in 1914 prevented him from going to school in England as planned. From 1917 until the end of the war he helped recruit Kikuyu volunteers for the Volunteer Carrier Corps, which had been organized mainly by missionaries to take the place of the conscripted carrier corps of the early war years. Early in 1920, at the age of 16, Leakey went to his first school, Weymouth College, where he found himself fag to a prefect younger than himself.

In October 1922 he gained entry to St. John's College, Cambridge, as a Sizar. As his subjects for Part I of the Tripos he chose Modern and Medieval French and Kikuyu, a subject which caused some difficulties owing to the absence of competent examiners: Leakey, in fact, had to teach the language to his examiners! A year later, while playing rugger, he was badly concussed and his medical adviser recommended a year in the open air. Leakey obtained a job as assistant to W. Cutler, a Canadian, who was about to leave for Tanganyika to excavate for dinosaurs on behalf of the British Museum (Natural History). From Cutler, Leakey learned many invaluable techniques in connexion with fossil collecting and preserving.

After obtaining a first class in the Modern Languages Tripos, he went on to take another first in Archaeology and Anthropology in May 1926. The following month he was leading the first of four very successful East African Archaeological Expeditions, having been awarded an 1851 Exhibition research studentship. In 1929 he was made a Research Fellow of St. John's and obtained his Ph.D. The fourth archaeological expedition to East Africa under Leakey's leadership ended in 1935. During these expeditions he worked out the main sequence of prehistoric cultures in Kenya, basing their relative dating on climatic changes during the Pleistocene. Leakey's early discoveries included the Kanam jaw and the Kanjera skulls, probably dating from the Middle Pleistocene. He also excavated the rock shelter known as Gamble's Cave, recovering skeletons of the makers of the Upper Kenya Capsian culture, and began his work in Olduvai gorge, northern Tanganyika, one of the most important early Palaeolithic sites in the world.

In 1937 Leakey returned to Kenya to make a two and a half years' study of the Kikuyu tribe, whose customs he felt should be recorded. He was recognized as a member of the tribe and was admitted as a second-grade elder. The manuscript of his lengthy work on the Kikuyu was just completed when the Second World War broke out. Leakey was put in charge of the African section of Special Branch C.I.D. headquarters, a post he held until the end of the war.

It was in the course of his work with the C.I.D. in Nairobi that Leakey was called upon to investigate and give evidence on handwriting cases. At Cambridge he had taken a special interest in calligraphy in so far as it affected the determination of the authorship of emendations in medieval manuscripts. This led to his becoming handwriting expert to the C.I.D., a work which he continued in his spare time for many years after the war. He became one of the leading authorities in this field and gave evidence in court on several hundred occasions.

During the war Leakey became a trustee of the Coryndon Museum, Nairobi, and later took on the running of the museum in his spare time. In 1945 he became full-time curator and set to work to reorganize the museum and build it up as a research centre for east and central Africa.

On periods of leave during the war, Leakey and his wife discovered the famous Acheulian site of Olorgesatlie in the Rift Valley. They also did field work on Rusinga Island in Lake Victoria, where they found the remains of Miocene apes and other fauna. Leakey organized the first Pan African Congress on Prehistory in Nairobi in 1947 and, as a result, he obtained funds to continue his researches into the Miocene deposits of western Kenya. The most important find was an almost complete skull of *Proconsul africanus*, the earliest ape skull yet known.

During the Mau Mau troubles, Leakey's unique knowledge of the Kikuyu and their language was made use of by the Government. He was official interpreter during part of the trial of Jomo Kenyatta. Oxford University paid tribute to his work on physical anthropology by awarding him a D.Sc. *honoris causa*. His scientific medals included the Swedish Vega medal, the Pitt-Rivers memorial medal of the Royal Anthropological Institute, the Henry Stopes medal of the Geological Association, and the Cuthbert Peck medal of the Royal Geographical Society.

As a result of substantial grants, mainly from the National Geographical Society of Washington, Leakey was able to undertake excavations on a large scale at Olduvai from 1959 onwards. In order to be able to devote more time to research he gave up the curatorship of the Coryndon Museum, but founded the National Museums Centre for Palaeontology and Prehistory adjoining the Museum. It was at Olduvai that Leakey and his family made their most important discoveries of early hominids. In 1959 Mrs. Leakey found the skull of *Australopithecus* (*Zinjanthropus*) *boisei*, and the following year their son Jonathan found the first remains of another hominid closer to the human line which was later named *Homo habilis*. These remains were dated by the potassium argon method to 1.7 million years ago. In 1960 Leakey also discovered the skull of one of the makers of the early Acheulian hand-axe culture *Homo erectus* at Olduvai.

In the following year at Fort Ternan in western Kenya he found the upper jaw of

Kenyapithecus wickeri—14 million years old and considered to be one of the earliest hominids—as well as other later Miocene fauna. For these discoveries he was awarded the Wenner-Gren Viking Medal for Anthropological Research in 1962.

Leakey was a great lover of animals, both wild and domestic. He became a trustee of the National Parks of Kenya and of the Kenya Wild Life Society, and Vice-President of the East African Kennel Club. As a teacher, he had a wonderful gift of inspiring enthusiasm. He started experimenting on flint-knapping while still at Cambridge and later he often demonstrated the art of making "prehistoric" stone tools. He always tried to put theories to practical test, for instance by living on the game he could kill with his hands or with stone tools in the manner of Stone Age hunters. He gave hundreds of public lectures in schools and colleges and was a frequent contributor to the *Illustrated London News* and other papers in an attempt to make the subject of man's past more widely understood. His publications included *The Stone Age Cultures of Kenya Colony; The Stone Age Races of Kenya; Adam's Ancestors; Stone Age Africa; Mau Mau and the Kikuyu; Defeating Mau Mau; Olduvai Gorge; and Olduvai Gorge 1951-1961.*

In 1928 he married Henrietta Wilfreda Avern, by whom he had a son and a daughter. This marriage was dissolved and in 1936 he married Mary Douglas Nicol, by whom he had three sons. She was closely associated with his scientific work, particularly in connexion with the archaeology of Olduvai.

October 2, 1972.

Lord Leconfield—See Egremont.

Sir Frank Lee, P.C., G.C.M.G., K.C.B., who died on April 28, 1971 at the age of 67, had been Permanent Secretary, Ministry of Food and Board of Trade, and from 1960 to 1962 Joint Permanent Secretary of the Treasury. Since 1962 he had been Master of Corpus Christi College, Cambridge. He was by any reckoning a public servant of altogether exceptional ability. A mere catalogue of his many and various official positions is enough to prove the point—though not to appraise the man.

Frank Godbould Lee was born in 1903 in Essex, the son of Joseph Godbould Lee, a schoolmaster. After a period in Warley Elementary School he went to Brentwood School. From there at the age of 18 he went to Downing. He read two triposes, English and History, and took firsts in both. He had thoughts of an academic career but chose (in response, one imagines, to a natural bent towards the life of affairs) to go for class I of the Civil Service, and entered the Colonial Office in 1926. He was

in Nyasaland for two years, visited several colonial territories, and spent the year 1938 at the Imperial Defence College (an experience which stood him in good stead later on).

In January 1940 he was transferred to the Treasury, as a principal, and was posted to the defence material division. The division was, in effect, the war division of the Treasury dealing with the requirements of the Service and supply departments, the raw material programmes, the general principles of Government contracting in war and, for good measure, oil. It was here that Frank Lee made his mark, and an indelible one. His parish was the War Office and the Ministry of Supply in all its aspects, including raw materials and the associated controls. He dealt with this mass of work very largely on his own (he always welcomed responsibility); he made it his business to know everybody concerned in the departments and in the control; he mastered the job, and gained the full confidence of the people concerned with it. Here, clearly, was an administrator of high quality. In 1943 he succeeded to the headship of the division, but not for long. He was by now earmarked for higher things.

In 1944 he went to Washington as deputy to Lord Brand*, head of the Treasury delegation. Here he became associated with Maynard Keynes (whom he had already met in London at the Treasury) in the negotiations for the loan agreement and winding up the lend-lease arrangements. He would not have claimed to be Keynes's equal in imagination, or in presentation of argument, but he had perhaps a clearer view of what was practicable. Certainly he was one of the few people who could and did argue on equal terms with the redoubtable Keynes.

Thereafter his progress was rapid and varied. In 1946 he became deputy secretary to the Ministry of Supply dealing with iron and steel and particularly the problems of nationalization. In 1948 he returned to Washington with the rank of Minister, being much concerned with the distribution of Marshall Aid. In 1949 he became permanent secretary of the Ministry of Food, and in 1951 secretary to the Board of Trade.

In 1956 he succeeded Sir Roger Makins as joint permanent secretary to the Treasury, taking charge of the whole of the financial and economic work of the Treasury, and becoming the chief official adviser directly responsible to the Chancellor of the Exchequer. This was, and is, probably the most responsible and exacting job in the Civil Service. It comprises the whole complex of questions, external and internal, which affect the economy of the country. It is at this point that the Treasury is the target of every sharpshooter—informed or uninformed; and it needs a cool head and a tough carapace to withstand the bombardment.

Both of these characteristics Frank Lee had; but also much more. He had no particular advantages of presence of manner. He was short of stature and not impressive in appearance. He was easily caricatured— as for example, rushing into a room, hands ruffling his short black hair, a pencil between his teeth; and then (disposing somehow of the pencil) bursting into excited but coherent speech. Such things mattered not at all when the power of his mind was deployed. It was, to begin with, essentially inquisitive. He could penetrate into and absorb the relevant detail; but equally could extract from the detail what was at the heart of the matter. It was, moreover, a positive mind, one capable of decision, quick, always ready to wait if the practical situation needed patience. "Quick, apprehensive, forgetive" fits the man.

His power of oral exposition of a line of argument, if not dazzling in the Keynes manner, was extraordinarily lucid and persuasive. It was the marshalling of solid argument, and so the listener realized.

Finally he was indefatigable, whether mentally or physically. His output of work —all at the same high level of quality— was phenomenal, for he worked fast, and he worked long hours. Indeed he may have presumed too much on his stamina.

If he is to be faulted as an administrator it is on the ground that he delegated too little, preferring to do all the work himself without much regard for its inherent importance or interest. As one of his colleagues put it—"The curious thing about Frank is that he has never become aware of the fact that there is such a thing as uninteresting work".

He was an ardent globe-trotter. As Secretary to the Board of Trade he broke all records in the number of visits he paid abroad, largely, but not exclusively, in the Commonwealth and the United States of America. He liked to see for himself on the spot; and he liked meeting everybody at home or abroad who was significantly concerned with the job in hand.

It would be wrong to recall merely the man at work. He pursued his relaxations with an equal zest. Married to an accomplished pianist, he greatly enjoyed music, and especially music in the home. He loved most ball games (for an Englishman he was knowledgeable about baseball); but cricket was his dearest love, and he played it when he could.

Frank Lee was never far from the roots of his community in Essex, the county of his birth. He would spend a week of his holiday hay-making and not in any halfhearted, amateurish way. He enjoyed good food, good wine and, above all, good company and good conversation. Behind the hard working official was a very human, very friendly and widely interested man; and to those who knew him well—and they were many—a lovable one.

In 1960 he was elected an honorary Fellow of his old Cambridge college, Downing.

Two years later he became Master of Corpus Christi and threw himself ener-getically and conscientiously into the work of the college. He took a special interest in undergraduates and their sporting activities, and also in the college's new graduate colony of Leckhampton, to which he presented a piece of sculpture of Henry Moore. But his experience was of even greater value to the university, and he soon found himself engaged in some of its most important activities.

Within a year of returning to Cambridge he was elected to the Press Syndicate, and soon afterwards, on the retirement of Stanley Bennett, he became its chairman. In 1963 he was appointed a member of the Financial Board of the university; and his wide knowledge of men and affairs outside Cambridge made him a natural, and admirable, chairman of the Faculty Board of Engineering and, as deputy for successive Vice-Chancellors, of the University Appointments Board.

He married in 1937 Kathleen Mary Harris. They had three daughters.

April 29, 1971.

Manfred B. Lee, who collaborated with his cousin, Frederic Dannay, to create one of the most famous names in detective fiction, Ellery Queen, died on April 3, 1971 of a heart attack.

The name was used both for the hero of their books and as a pseudonym for the author. Lee and Dannay in their long partnership probably did more than anybody else to raise the standard of the best American mystery stories to a very high level of literacy and ingenuity.

Lee was born in Brooklyn in 1905. At New York University his chief interest was in music; he was a talented violinist and ran his own orchestra. He had embarked on a career as copywriter in the advertisement department of a film company when in 1928 he and his cousin, who lived near him and had been his friend since childhood, decided to write a detective story for a magazine competition. They won the competition but the magazine went bankrupt.

The story appeared in book form the following year, called *The Roman Hat Mystery*, and it scored such a resounding success that both men gave up their jobs and settled down to a serious collaboration as authors.

It proved a wise decision. A succession of Ellery Queen stories, from *The French Powder Mystery* (1930) to *The Spanish Cape Mystery* (1935), established them in the front rank of mystery writers at a time when the classic detective story was at the height of its popularity. Several of those early books were sub-titled "A Problem in Deduction" and they lived up to the claim: they were scrupulously fair and rigorously conventional.

The later books certainly became more idiosyncratic and perhaps less classically satisfying; but *Calamity Town* (1942), for instance, and *Cat of Many Tails* (1949) show the Queen technique at its most dazzlingly artful.

Under the name "Barnaby Ross", Lee and Dannay tried a second series, this time about an actor detective called Drury Lane. It had only moderate success and ended with the fourth volume, *Drury Lane's Last Case* (1933). The collaboration remained a close secret until 1938. Lee once lectured in a mask at Columbia University, and the two men staged a masked debate on a public platform as "Queen" and "Ross".

The failure of a trick anthology called *Challenge to the Reader* (1938) persuaded Lee and Dannay to start what became a unique collection of high quality, short detective stories. They put this collection to good use when in 1941 they were invited to edit a new periodical, *Ellery Queen's Mystery Magazine*. This magazine and the series of annual volumes culled from it, *The Queen's Awards*, gave most valuable encouragement to detective story writers not only in America but all over the world.

Lee and Dannay produced numerous anthologies of detective fiction linked by particular themes. They wrote excellent short stories themselves and, under the name "Ellery Queen, Jr.", a series of mystery novels for children. As senior members of the crime writing profession, they insisted on, and themselves maintained an admirable standard of writing and construction.

Lee married Kaye Brinker in 1942 and had eight children.

April 5, 1971.

Théo Lefèvre, who died in Brussels on September 18, 1973 at the age of 59, was Belgium's Prime Minister from 1961 to 1965 and one of the country's most colourful, courageous and controversial politicians. He was national president of the Social Christian Party from 1950 to 1961, president of the European Union of Christian Democrats during his premiership; and was responsible for scientific affairs in the Eyskens governments of 1968 and 1972.

Théodore Joseph Albéric Lefèvre was born in Ghent on January 17, 1914. His father died in 1920 from wartime gas poisoning.

Lefèvre, described by his professors at Ghent University as "mediocre and ambitious", was called to the Bar of the Court of Appeal in Ghent in 1940. During the war he was a sergeant in the 18 days' campaign of 1940 and became a member of the underground movement. He was active in the Mouvement Royaliste Belge and wrote for the clandestine press.

Lefèvre entered Parliament in 1946 and played an active part in re-animating Christian Democracy in Western Europe. He regarded politics as a vocation, and his deep convictions, coupled with a rare gift for sharp formulation, soon brought him to the top.

Either as president of his party or as Prime Minister, Lefèvre was involved in most of the bitter disputes which have riven Belgium since the Second World War. In the coalition with the Socialists which he formed in 1961, which represented the first serious opening to the left of the Social Christians, he showed a readiness rare among Belgian politicians to grapple with grave issues.

Théo Lefèvre's determination and courage reflected his compassion for the poor and underprivileged, derived in part from observing his father's work as a lawyer defending the poorest seasonal agricultural workers of Flanders.

Determined to grasp the political nettles, Lefèvre's government tackled the reform of the tax and social security systems, fixed the bitterly contested linguistic frontiers which also put limits to the expansion of Brussels, settled the almost equally vexed problem of the teaching of languages in schools and use of the Dutch and French languages in the public service, and at the same time set in train the revision of the constitution.

It was his hope that these steps would clear away the festering linguistic problem and preserve the unity of the nation. Although intensely proud of Flemish culture and his native city of Ghent, Lefèvre was a unitarist, and derived little pleasure from Belgium's gradual progress towards "regionalism", a muted form of federalism between Flanders, Wallonia and the Brussels agglomeration.

But political courage is not always rewarded, and Lefèvre made many enemies. Not least among these were the doctors, who reacted to his reforms by going on strike in April 1964.

His government survived the four-year course—a rare feat—but was badly mauled in the 1965 elections, when the Liberals doubled their representation. Lefèvre had paid the price for his outspokenness and indifference to the views of those he considered wrong.

General de Gaulle* was among those who felt the lash of his tongue. As a convinced European, Gaullist policy was among his bêtes-noires. Lefèvre caused a furore after a particularly abortive meeting of European science ministers in 1969 by recommending that de Gaulle should be buried alongside Pétain.

It was a tribute to Lefèvre's personality and stature in Europe that he should have been entrusted for five years with the presidency of the European Space Conference. He was undoubtedly hurt when he was demoted from ministerial to state secretary rank in the Eyskens government of 1972, and had hoped to find a place in the three-party coalition government formed by the Socialist Edmond Leburton in January 1973.

In private life Lefèvre was a man of immense charm and exceptional erudition; in any country politicians with such a broad cultural base are rare. He read voraciously in French, German, Dutch and English literature, and to the end set aside an hour a day to read a non-political book. His choice was often guided by *The Times Literary Supplement*, to which he was firmly addicted. He leaves a widow and two children.

September 19, 1973.

M. St. L. Léger—See Perse.

Sir Harry Legge-Bourke, Conservative M.P. for the Isle of Ely and chairman of the 1922 Committee until ill-health obliged him to resign in the autumn of 1972, died on May 21, 1973. He was 59.

He had represented the constituency since 1945. As one of the most senior, most independent and most respected Conservative members, his election to the chairmanship of the 1922 Committee in 1970 was both appropriate and deserved. His open, direct and constructive way of going about things (for he was a man of shining candour and faultless standards of personal conduct) amply confirmed the rightness of the choice, and his retirement from the chairmanship was regretted throughout the Conservative Party in Parliament.

His death is a loss not only to his party, however, but to the House. He was one of the last of the English country gentlemen who chose a life of public service from a conviction of duty and obligation, seeking nothing more for himself, certainly not office; but modestly and very effectively doing his best for his constituents and for the national interest as he saw it. Beneath the bearing of the Brigade of Guards lay a sensitive nature (a quality not uncommon in that body) which found part of its expression, when he was younger, in the writing of poetry.

Originally a professional soldier, he often found himself at odds with his party leaders, notably on issues of defence and foreign policy. During the negotiations which led to the Anglo-Egyptian Agreement for the withdrawal of British troops from the Suez Canal Zone he was one of the 40 Conservatives with Captain Charles Waterhouse —known as "the Suez rebels"—who bitterly opposed this policy. So strongly did Legge-Bourke feel about this at the time that he resigned the Conservative whip in 1954 and elected to sit in the Commons as an Independent Conservative. Despite this gesture the party whip was restored to him, at his own request, a few months later.

Himself a farmer, he was a diligent representative of his Fenland constituents and apart from his quixotic forays into foreign affairs he frequently spoke in the House on such subjects as agriculture and land drainage.

Legge-Bourke was created K.B.E. in 1960 for political and public services. He was a member of the House of Commons Chairmen's Panel for many years, and in the 1964-66 Parliament he served as an additional Deputy Chairman of Ways and Means during the absence through illness of the Speaker. He was much liked on both sides of the House.

Edward Alexander Henry Legge-Bourke was born on May 16, 1914, the son of N. W. H. Legge-Bourke, Coldstream Guards, and Lady Victoria Forester. Educated at Eton, he was for six years a Page of Honour to King George V. From Eton he went to the Royal Military College, Sandhurst and in 1934 he was commissioned in the Royal Horse Guards. During the war he was wounded while serving in Greece, in 1941, and afterwards spent a year as A.D.C. to the British Ambassador in Cairo. He described some of his experiences while serving Lord Killearn* at this time in an article in *The Times* in March 1973. He later served with the 7th Armoured Division in the North African campaign.

When the European war ended Major Legge-Bourke was released from the Army to stand as a Conservative candidate and was nominated for the Isle of Ely, a seat which had been held for 16 years by a Liberal, Mr. James de Rothschild. In a three-cornered fight Legge-Bourke wrested the seat from de Rothschild by a majority of over 2,000 votes, remaining there ever after.

That he never achieved promotion under Conservative governments was probably due to the uncompromising nature of his views and to his suspicion that many if not most moves in overseas policy involved some abdication of British interests.

In 1962 Legge-Bourke indulged in some public criticism of the party leadership and suggested that the time had come for the Prime Minister (Harold Macmillan) to resign. Holding these views, he thought it necessary to resign the chairmanship of the Conservative Party's Parliamentary Defence Committee, to which he had been elected only a few months before. He had previously been secretary of the committee and was also a member of the executive of the 1922 Committee. He had served as chairman of the party's Science and Technology Committee and was chairman of a sub-committee of the Select Committee on Science and Technology which presented a report on coastal pollution after the Torrey Canyon disaster.

Legge-Bourke was married in 1938 to Catherine Jean, daughter of Colonel Sir Arthur Grant, D.S.O., 10th Baronet of Monymusk, and they had two sons and one daughter.

May 22, 1973.

Le Gros Clark—See Clark.

Frida Leider, the great Wagnerian soprano, died on June 4, 1975 at the age of 87.

She was born, the daughter of a carpenter, in Berlin on April 18, 1888. After studying in Berlin and Milan, she made her debut at Halle as Venus in *Tannhäuser* in 1915. After singing for some years in minor German opera houses, learning her art thoroughly in the old-fashioned, solid way, she went to Hamburg in 1919, staying there for four years.

She then moved to the Berlin State Opera, which remained her base for the rest of her active career, that is until the Second World War.

Until Hamburg she had sung mostly the Mozartian and Italian *spinto* repertory, and her early records demonstrate that she was as accomplished in this field as she was later to become in the heavy Wagnerian repertory.

Leider's international career began when she went to Covent Garden, under the auspices of Bruno Walter,* to sing Isolde and Brünnhilde in 1924. She immediately established herself as London's favourite Wagnerian soprano, and returned there regularly until 1938.

She also appeared as Donna Anna in the famous 1926 revival of *Don Giovanni,* appearing with Lotte Lehmann, Elisabeth Schumann and Mariano Stabile under Bruno Walter. Her other Covent Garden roles were Leonora (*Trovatore*), Gluck's *Armide*, both arresting portrayals, Venus and Kundry.

Leider's association with Bayreuth lasted from 1928 until 1938, and in 1928 she also made her American debut in Chicago, as Brünnhilde. After four years there in a variety of parts, including Rachel in *La Juive* and the Marschallin, she moved to the Metropolitan in 1933 and sang the Wagnerian "heavies" there for two seasons.

Among other roles she sang with success in Berlin were the Countess, Ariadne, Amelia (*Ballo in Maschera*), Dido (*Les Troyens*) and Leonore (*Fidelio*). After the war, she sang in a few concerts, then devoted herself to production and teaching, first as a director in East Berlin and from 1948 to 1958 as a voice teacher in the West Berlin Conservatory.

Her rich, beautiful voice was allied to a strong dramatic instinct and a keen intelligence. She always laid stress on pure tone and eloquence of phrasing, never indulging in histrionic or vocal excess. She always maintained that her long years of apprenticeship enabled her to achieve her long, successful and rewarding career, and she was right. Fortunately, substantial extracts of her incomparable Isolde and Brünnhilde remain on record as object-lessons for future generations of Wagnerian sopranos.

Her other discs are no less enjoyable and instructive. All are proof of the penetration of her interpretations, and of their musical accuracy.

June 5, 1975.

C. A. Lejeune, the doyen of English film critics, died on April 1, 1973 at the age of 76.

When she retired from *The Observer* in 1960, she had been reviewing films for 40 years. Her career spanned the rise, the great days and the beginning of the decline of the film industry, and the start of the television age. Her column was eagerly read, because of its wit, its percipience, its kindliness and its sheer good writing, by people who never went to films at all.

Caroline Alice Lejeune was born in Manchester in 1897, the youngest of a large Victorian family. Her father was a cotton merchant who had gone to England from Frankfurt.

Her mother was the daughter of a well-known non-conformist minister, Dr. Alexander Maclaren. She was educated at Withington girls' school and, having refused to follow her sisters to Oxford, at Manchester University. C. P. Scott was a close friend of her mother, and, with his help, she began writing pieces for the *Manchester Guardian.*

Gilbert and Sullivan, Verdi and Puccini were her particular passions but she also enjoyed the new, and not quite respectable, medium of the cinema, and saw in it the possibility of creating a novel career. She went to London, accompanied by her mother, and, in 1922, succeeded in persuading the *Guardian* to let her write a regular column called "The Week on the Screen". In 1925 she married Edward Roffe Thompson, who at one time was editor of *John Bull.* Three years later J. L. Garvin invited her, with C. P. Scott's blessing, to move to *The Observer*, where, though she wrote also for many other journals, ranging from *The New York Times* to the *Farmers' Weekly,* she stayed for the rest of her career.

After the war, for a little while, she reviewed television as well, and subsequently adapted several of her favourite books—the Sherlock Holmes stories, *Clementina, The Three Hostages* as television serials. Postwar trends in the cinema—towards politics, pretentiousness and pornography—left her increasingly disenchanted. Her interest in films diminished. After leaving *The Observer* in 1960 she never went to the cinema again. The things she cared about were at home—roses, dogs, detective stories and her family. In 1964 she published a delightful autobiography called *Thank You for Having Me.* Her other books were *Cinema* (1931), *Chestnuts in Her Lap* (1947), which was a collection of reviews, and *Three Score Years and Ten* (1961), an unfinished novel by Angela Thirkell* which she completed.

Peter Sellers once summed up her career: "Her kindness, her complete integrity and her qualities as an observer and a commentator have gained her the unqualified admiration of my profession. She respects integrity in others and has no harsh word for anyone whose honest efforts end in failure. Everything she has written, I am sure, has come as much from her heart as

her head, and the high quality of her writing, and the standard of film-making she encourages, have made her work a part of cinema history."

She is survived by her husband and her son, Anthony Lejeune.

April 2, 1973.

Sean Francis Lemass, who was the last premier of the Irish Republic to be chosen unanimously for the position by his party, died at the age of 71 on May 11, 1971.

Lemass was the prime mover on the Irish side in the establishment of the Free Trade Area between Britain and Ireland and he initiated, with Captain Terence O'Neill, the Eire-Northern Ireland dialogue of better relations.

Lemass resigned from the premiership and from the leadership of the Fianna Fail Party in the autumn of 1966 and his departure led to a struggle for the succession within the party which was eventually resolved by the election of Jack Lynch. Sean Lemass remained in politics for a time after he went to the back benches but in 1969 he left the political scene for good.

Lemass became premier of the Republic in 1959 after Eamon de Valera, the founder of the Fianna Fail party, had relinquished the post to become the country's third president.

Under the Lemass leadership the country took on a more outward-looking approach. Economic problems became the priority and he strove diligently to get Ireland into the European Community as he saw in it the greatest prospect for the advancement of agriculture and industry. Departing sharply from the de Valera attitude towards Northern Ireland he travelled to Belfast in 1965, passed through the gates of Stormont, the Northern Ireland Parliament, to exchange greetings with Captain Terence O'Neill. It was the most dramatic event in Irish politics since the advent of Fianna Fail to power and it might have led to a better understanding between North and South had the process not broken down in the northern turmoil of later years.

Lemass also had a cordial relationship with Harold Wilson and was instrumental in having the remains of Roger Casement returned to Ireland, thereby ending another 40-year-old controversy.

The working out of the Free Trade Area Agreement, which occurred about the same time (1965) brought the two prime ministers to a very close understanding, and the two countries to closer ties than had existed since the Treaty of 1921.

Lemass, who had been Minister for Industry and Commerce in successive Fianna Fail governments since 1932, was born in July 1899, and became identified with the Irish revolutionary movement at an early age. In the Easter Week Rising of 1916, not yet 17, he served in the garrison at the General Post Office in Dublin. When caught by British soldiers, the story goes that, struck by his boyish looks, they told him to "go back to mother". This did not please him; he had already seen action, and no longer looked on himself as a boy.

His enthusiasm for the cause burned fiercely, and later he rejoined the Irish Republican Army. After the Anglo-Irish Treaty he threw in his lot with the opponents of the Treaty under de Valera and was captured and imprisoned when the Four Courts fell at the beginning of the Civil War.

He was elected to the Dail in 1924, but like other members of the Anti-Treaty block did not take his seat. A year later he proposed to de Valera the formation of a new party, Fianna Fail, which would take over the policies of Sinn Fein and apply them constitutionally.

Fianna Fail came to government in 1932 and Lemass became the youngest minister in the new Government, and incidentally the youngest Cabinet minister in Europe.

De Valera, with whom he was on the terms of closest friendship, although the two men differed radically in character and temperament, called him the Benjamin of the Government. As Minister for Industry and Commerce, his uncommon grasp of practical matters served the country well, acting as a counter-balance to the visionary qualities of his leader. Under him the concept of state enterprise, which has successfully taken on tasks which are too risky to attract private capital without encroaching on the preserves of private enterprise, was worked out, at first in the development and extension of electricity supplies and the establishment of air companies.

The narrow ideas of economic self-sufficiency fostered by Sinn Fein which were responsible for the period of economic war that embittered relations with Britain in the first part of the 1930s were thrown overboard when he negotiated the Anglo-Irish trade agreement in 1938.

In a country where ideology of any sort is frowned on, and Lemass himself was an avowed pragmatist, he saw the need for a shift to the left, embracing better social services and educational facilities.

What may be counted as one of the first fruits of this policy of moderate direction by the state, the national wages agreement worked out by employers and unions under the aegis of the Government in 1964, was not an unmitigated success. The unions, having won a general rise in wages of 12 per cent, proceeded to press for a reduction of working hours. Economic troubles followed and there was not to be a repeat of the experiment for a number of years.

Lemass was the prime mover and architect of the Republic's economic programmes. These were launched under his direction and those which ran through his period of office were largely successful.

He was intimately associated with the difficult period when the state was founded, when emotions dominated men's actions, but nevertheless Lemass attended primarily to the business end of politics and looked to the future. He eschewed the way of easy popularity to be won by advocating the aims of self-conscious nationalism. Therefore, when the time came to replace the older men of the revolutionary period, he was the bridge by which young men of ability came into the Cabinet.

He is survived by his wife, a son and three daughters.

May 12, 1971.

Jozsef Lengyel, the Hungarian author who spent 18 years in Stalin's Siberian labour camps, died in Budapest on July 14, 1975 at the age of 79.

Born in 1896 in the Hungarian province of Somogony, Lengyel gained recognition as an avant garde poet in his twenties, though it was as a novelist that he made his international reputation.

A founder member of the Hungarian Communist Party, he played an important role in the brief post-First World War communist republic of Hungary. When it collapsed in 1919 he fled, first to Austria and later to Moscow, where he edited a Hungarian newspaper.

He was arrested in 1937 and spent the next 18 years in prison camps and in exile in Siberia. After his return to Hungary his first novels started appearing in the West. *Prenn Drifting*, which is set in the Budapest of 1919, was published in English in 1966.

But it was the two stories in the volume entitled *From Beginning to End*, published in Britain in the same year, which extended his reputation. And their unsparing relation of conditions in Stalin's labour camps led to perhaps inevitable comparisons with Solzhenitsyn.

Subsequent novels and stories, *The Judge's Chair* (1968), *Acta Sanctorum* (1970), and *Confrontation* (1972), all found their way to publication in the West in spite of their themes, substantially condemnatory of Stalin's communism.

Lengyel himself gained several literary awards, including the Kossuth Prize.

Protected by his international reputation and a Hungarian acquiescence in the publication of his work, albeit in a strictly limited form, he escaped in the latter years of his life the consequences of literary outspokenness which befell Solzhenitsyn.

July 16, 1975.

Sir Shane Leslie, author, poet, and notable Anglo-Irish personality, died on August 13, 1971 at his home in Hove. He was 85. He was a member of the Irish Academy.

His Anglo-Irishry, which prompted him as a young man to assume for the name of John the Irish form "Shane", while continuing for the most part to live in England, was a principal key to the man and writer. A wit, an engaging figure in the society he knew best, an active convert to the Roman Catholic Church, Sir Shane Leslie brought a buoyant and nostalgic temperament to his experience of life and to his busy career as a man of letters. He was poet, novelist, travel writer, biographer, student of history and Catholic apologist, and in all these capacities he managed as a rule to offer both pleasure and instruction. His work, which exhibits a remarkable fluency, lacks the highest distinction and is at times both untidy and epigrammatically laboured, but there is much to reward the reader in his volumes of reminiscences and in the best of his studies and portraits of the eminent.

Born in 1885, John Randolph Leslie was the eldest son of Colonel Sir John Leslie, second baronet, of Glaslough, County Monaghan, and succeeded to the title in 1944. His mother was Léonie, the second of the three daughters of Leonard Jerome, of New York, owner of newspapers and racehorses. The eldest daughter married Lord Randolph Churchill; the youngest married Moreton Frewen and became the mother of Clare Sheridan*. John Randolph Leslie (he was named after Lord Randolph) went to Eton, where he was noted for his wit and literary taste, and to King's College, Cambridge.

Two great figures at King's in his day were Robert Hugh Benson and "Mugger" Barnes, both Etonians and both fervent converts to the Roman Catholic faith. Leslie was received into the Church of Rome while still an undergraduate, shortly afterwards assumed the Christian name of Shane and—this marked another departure from the family tradition—stood in 1910 as a Nationalist for Derry. He took a degree in 1907 and went that winter to Russia where he became a friend of Tolstoy and adopted his social opinions.

He had published two books of verse before he made an impression in 1916 with *The End of a Chapter*, begun while he was in hospital, invalided in the war. Brilliant, candid, nostalgic, these memories of youth and of the glamour and security of the world before 1914 project the character and style of much of his most successful writing. A mood of autobiography was seldom wholly absent from his work. In 1922, the year in which he published a *Life of Cardinal Manning*, designed to counter the effect of Lytton Strachey's essay, and a biographical portrait of his friend Mark Sykes, Leslie also brought out a novel about Eton, *The Oppidan*. This provoked some controversy and seemed to be very much a novel for Etonians only. Next year came *Doomsland*, a semi-autobiographical novel with an Irish setting; then a volume of short stories *Masquerades*, dedicated to Frederick Rolfe (Leslie had been one of the earliest admirers of that strange figure, the author of *Hadrian the Seventh*); and after that *The Cantab* (1924), an entertaining if somewhat exaggeratedly satirical novel which was banned by Rome and which the author withdrew from circulation after complaints had been made against it on the score of indecency.

The list of Sir Shane Leslie's published works is long. The more important include what at the time was perhaps a too fashionable defence of the character of *George the Fourth* (1926); *The Skull of Swift* (1928); a selection of prose renderings from the Greek Anthology (1929); a memoir of J. E. C. Bodley (1930); a narrative poem in alexandrine couplets, which follows very faithfully the official narratives, on the Battle of Jutland (1930); a study, from a conspicuously Roman Catholic point of view, of the Oxford Movement (1933); *The Passing Chapter* (1934), at once a breathless review of current topics and in some sort a sequel to *The End of a Chapter;* an entertaining volume of studies in late-Victorian biography, *Men were Different* (1937); *The Film of Memory* (1938), in which he returned once more to the shining period of his youth; the two somewhat diffuse but highly instructive volumes of his portrait of Mrs. Fitzherbert (1939-40), in the writing of which he had had access to important new material; and *The Irish Tangle* (1946), in which his historical generalizations were not seldom inexact or a little extravagant but characteristically pointed with epigram.

In 1954 he published a memoir of Cardinal Gasquet. *Shane Leslie's Ghost Book*, a collection of stories about ghosts, followed in 1955; and his last book *Long Shadows*, a memoir, appeared in 1966. An unflagging verbal address and animation marked, indeed, almost everything that Shane Leslie wrote.

He married first in 1912 Marjorie (who died in 1951), youngest daughter of Henry C. Ide, of Vermont, who had been Governor-General of the Philippines and United States Ambassador to Spain. They had two sons and a daughter. He married secondly in 1958 Iris, daughter of C. M. Laing. His son John Norman Ide succeeds to the baronetcy.

August 16, 1971.

Benn W. Levy, M.B.E., who died on December 7, 1973 in Oxford at the age of 73, was for many years active as a playwright and as a director of his own and other people's plays. For nearly five years, from 1945 to 1950, he was Labour M.P. for the Eton and Slough Division of Buckinghamshire.

The son of Octave Levy and the grandson of the Hon. J. Levy of Sydney, New South Wales, Benn Wolfe Levy was born on March 7, 1900, in London. Educated at Repton and, after service in the R.A.F., at University College, Oxford, he started publishing in 1923 and became managing director of Jarrolds. But a new career began for him in 1926 when his comedy *This Woman Business*, which had been tried out on a Sunday night, received a production at the Haymarket, with Fay Compton and Leon Quartermaine* in the cast, followed, if only for a short run, by a production from an American management in New York.

In the years 1928 to 1930 English managements presented two adaptations by him and several original straight plays. The latter, consisting of one of those pro- and anti-Labour harangues as Tallulah Bankhead* called it, a fantasy, a comedy and a reworking of the theme of *The Hound of Heaven*, were generally thought to be as uneven in quality as they were various in kind.

However, with the coming of sound he was in demand as a writer of dialogue for films. He worked in that capacity on Alfred Hitchcock's *Blackmail*, usually accounted the first of British talking films, and for U.F.A. in pre-Hitler Germany. While in Berlin he conferred with C. B. Cochran and Lorenz Hart, the lyricist, on the project of a musical for Jessie Matthews and Sonnie Hale, and the end-product, *Evergreen*, with music by Richard Rodgers gave Levy as librettist his longest run up to date.

His next two original plays, *Hollywood Holiday*, written in collaboration with John Van Druten, and *Springtime for Henry*, a four-handed farce, were directed by Levy himself. Cochran fostered this new interest of his by engaging him to direct a very strong cast in Clemence Dane's* play about the Brontës. Meanwhile, Levy had added to his credits the direction of an English film for Hitchcock and the dialogue to be spoken by Tallulah Bankhead, Gary Cooper* and Charles Laughton* in a film for Paramount. "What's my part like?" Laughton had asked of him by cable. "Even if I played it, it would steal the picture", Levy replied.

In 1933 he married the American actress Constance Cummings, who was already established in the United States in plays and films. The following year he directed her on her first stage appearance in London. He directed her again in New York in his adaptation of *Madame Bovary*, and in London, in conjunction with William Armstrong, in the American comedy *Skylark*. During the Second World War he served for three years in the Royal Navy, first as an ordinary seaman, later with the rank of lieutenant. He was wounded in the Adriatic and made M.B.E.

In the general election of 1945, which placed his party securely in power for the first time, Levy won the new constituency of Eton and Slough for Labour by a majority of 2,424.

During the life of that parliament he had the satisfaction of seeing his comedy *Clutterbuck*, which he directed in London and which also did very well in New York, run for 366 performances at Wyndhams with his wife in the cast. He also directed her in an adaptation of a short story by Maugham* and after his decision not to seek reelection to Parliament had taken effect, in a drama of his own, *Return to Tyassi*, which might in the general opinion have turned out admirably if he had been willing to rewrite certain scenes after the try-out.

He did not direct his later plays. His comedy on the subject of the ninth labour of Hercules, directed by John Clements, had a deservedly long run towards the end of the 1950s, with Kay Hammond and Constance Cummings in the roles of the two Queens of the Amazons; but *The Tumbler*, staged in New York under Laurence Olivier's direction, was a failure in 1960. *Public and Confidential*, dealing with a crisis in the affairs of a man in public life in contemporary England, produced after a long period of inactivity imposed upon Levy by ill health, came somewhere between the two extremes in 1966.

In public debate on matters connected with the theatre and the arts in general, Levy was, on the platform and on radio, a persuasive speaker. From 1953 to 1960, he was an executive of the Arts Council. He is survived by his wife and by a son and a daughter.

December 8, 1973.

Professor Hyman Levy, Emeritus Professor of Mathematics, University of London, Imperial College, who died on February 27, 1975 aged 85, was born in Edinburgh and was educated at George Heriot's school and at the universities of Edinburgh, Oxford and Göttingen.

After serving for four years as a member of the Aerodynamics Research staff at the National Physical Laboratory, he joined the Department of Mathematics at Imperial College in 1920 as assistant professor. He remained there for 34 years until his retirement in 1954. He was appointed full professor in 1923 and became head of the department in 1946.

His presence in the council chamber will be remembered by many colleagues for his remarkable gift of quick appreciation and sensible comment; and his regular attendance at student gatherings, either as lecturer or after dinner speaker, an art at which he excelled, will also be long remembered with affection by generations of students.

The governing body of the college showed its appreciation of his abilities by electing him to be one of its members, and by appointing him Dean of the Royal College of Science in 1946, an office which he held for the unusually long period of six years. In 1957, after his retirement, the highest honour which the college can bestow, its Fellowship, was conferred upon him.

Levy's most significant contributions to mathematics, and the development of mathematical teaching, arose from his interests in numerical methods. This, and the related subject of statistics, remained his favourite field of mathematics throughout his life.

One of his earliest books, written in 1934, dealt with the numerical solution of differential equations; and another, written 24 years later, after his retirement, dealt with the related subject of finite difference equations. Both books were written in collaboration with former students.

No notice of Hyman Levy would be complete without some reference to his lifelong interests in Marxism. To those who knew him well it was clear that his philosophy and political theory stemmed from a deep humanitarianism. Late in life, after a visit to Russia, he lost some of his fervour for the practices of communism.

Levy was a member of a delegation from the British Communist Party which visited Russia in October 1956. He was given the specific task of investigating reports that Jewish writers, artists and intellectuals had been tortured and killed and Jewish culture suppressed. His findings appalled him and he wrote an exposure of the persecution between 1948 and 1952 of the Russian Jews. This was printed in the communist weekly *World News* in January 1957.

Levy, for long one of the admired intellectuals of the British Communist Party, pursued his theme in an impassioned speech at the party's Easter congress at Hammersmith in April. How much of the persecution, he demanded, had been known to the leaders of the British Communist Party?

Later, a highly critical review by R. Palme Dutt, the British Communist Party's *eminence grise*, of Levy's book *Jews and the National Question*, contained the ominous words: "With this book Levy finally parts company with Marxism."

In April 1958 Levy wrote to the *New Statesman* saying "... the official journal of the British C.P., horrified that I presume to criticize the Soviet Union in any way at all, devoted seven columns to what is in effect personal vilification and misrepresentation of my views. My expulsion follows inevitably."

The titles of some of his books are characteristic of the thoughts which, with mathematics, dominated his life: *Science, Curse or Blessing?*; *Social Thinking*; or, *Science in an Irrational Society*. In this aspect of his life he was not only a thinker and a writer, but also, in a certain sense, a man of action. He was, for example, chairman of the Scientific Advisory Committee of the Labour Party from 1924 to 1930.

Neither in his mathematics nor in his political interests was Levy content merely to study and write; he strove to express his views wherever possible in speech and action. He will be be sadly missed by a wide circle of friends and acquaintances. In 1918 he married M. A. Fraser. There were two sons and one daughter of the marriage.

March 1, 1975.

Sir Aubrey Lewis, F.R.C.P., Emeritus Professor of Psychiatry in London University, the outstanding psychiatrist of his time, died on January 21, 1975 at the age of 74. His contributions to academic psychiatry were profound and will be long lasting.

Aubrey Julian Lewis, who was born in Adelaide, South Australia, obtained his primary medical qualification in his home university in 1923. After postgraduate medical experience in Adelaide, during which he became engaged in anthropological research on aborigines, he was awarded a Rockefeller Travelling Fellowship, and visited the famous Phipps Clinic at Johns Hopkins, the Boston psychopathic hospital, the National Hospital, Queen Square, and the University Clinic at Heidelberg.

Exposed to American psychiatry, then greatly influenced by the teaching of Adolf Meyer and of Freud, and to European psychiatry which followed the medical model of mental illness laid out by Emil Kraepelin, Lewis found himself more attracted to the latter, no doubt because of its hard empiricism and the scientific rigour of its observations.

Nevertheless, throughout his career he retained a discriminating eclecticism, his judgments on the theory of psychoanalysis being reserved. In 1928 he was appointed to the Maudsley Hospital. His immense erudition, his powerful intellect and his acute critical faculties made an immediate impression.

His delight in controversy and the sceptical aggressive challenge which he brought to it were sometimes painful to his opponents who were less well versed, but he always earned their respect. His rise to intellectual preeminence in the Maudsley was very rapid.

By 1936 he was made Clinical Director of the hospital, and it was clear that he was the obvious choice to succeed Edward Mapother to the Chair of Psychiatry, after Mapother's death in 1940. Nevertheless, because of the disorganization caused by the war, the closure of the hospital and the medical school, he did not succeed until 1946.

During the war Lewis gave academic leadership to the group of Maudsley psychiatrists who staffed the emergency hospital set up in Mill Hill School. Being also the Consultant in Psychological Medicine at the British Postgraduate Medical School, he came into close contact with Sir Francis Fraser, then in charge of the emergency medical services, a relationship which was to serve a great purpose after the war when the Maudsley medical school was to become the Institute of Psychiatry, a constituent member of the British Postgraduate Medical Federation, of which Fraser was the first Director.

During the 20 years of Lewis's leadership the hospital and institute won a unique position in the country and became one of the main postgraduate centres for teaching and research in psychiatry in the world. Under his tutelage, which was often severe

and uncompromising, a new generation of British psychiatrists emerged who were to fill many of the important positions in academic departments to be created not only in Britain but also in the Commonwealth.

Lewis's personal interests gradually turned to social and psychological research, but he also established departments of neuroscience in the institute. In 1948 the M.R.C. founded the Social Psychiatry Research Unit under his honorary directorship, a development which was to have far-reaching consequences. Lewis and his pupils laid the foundations of psychiatric epidemiology in Britain, which has given the subject in Britain its particular social slant. In 1952 he became a member of the Medical Research Council, the first psychiatrist to hold this position.

Lewis's approach to psychiatry was that of a scholar with a deeply ingrained critical scepticism. His Bradshaw lecture before the Royal College of Physicians in 1957, "Between Guesswork and Certainty in Psychiatry", expressed his own dilemma. He was profoundly critical of a psychiatry which suffered too much from "hopeful illusions and clichés used as incantations". He trusted the scientific method, but was for ever seeking to challenge the research done by others.

He disliked loose thinking, ill-defined terms, inadequately supported conclusions. As a teacher he was a remorseless scourge to students who could not rise to his own high intellectual standards. Throughout the formative period of psychiatry after the war, Lewis had to accept much hostile criticism which he largely ignored. He had great determination and courage, but he rarely defended his position.

His main endeavour was to promote the academic status of psychiatry, to train and educate the future teachers and research workers whom he knew the country would need. He had less sympathy with those who dedicated themselves to relieve the plight of sick individuals than with those who, standing back from the clinical struggle as he did, tried to advance knowledge of the subject.

His output of clinical writing was not great. His studies of melancholia and of obsessional illness, carried out in 1934-1936, are the best known. His scholarship was at its best in his historical writing, whether in commentary on significant figures of the past, or in reflection on the scientific status of psychiatry as in his Harveian Oration of 1963, "Medicine and Afflictions of the Mind".

Lewis promulgated his ideas about the education of psychiatrists, ideas which he and his pupils have largely put into effect. On his retirement in 1966 the postgraduate clinical students, then at the institute, published two volumes of his selected papers, *Studies in Psychiatry*.

Lewis had unusual literary gifts. He had a felicitous sense for the rightness of words, an economy of phrase and in later years a lightness of touch which permitted a lyrical quality and warmth not evident earlier. His style identified him even in reviews which he occasionally undertook for *The Times Literary Supplement*.

He was knighted in 1959. In 1966 he was awarded an Hon. LL.D. of the University of Toronto and an Hon. D.Sc. of Queen's University, Belfast, in 1967. He was honoured by many foreign societies and, an unusual distinction for a psychiatrist, he was an elected member of the American Philosophical Society.

In 1934 he married Hilda Stoessiger, M.D., and they had two sons and two daughters. Lady Lewis died in 1966.

January 22, 1975.

Cecil Day-Lewis—See Day-.

Cardinal Achille Liénart, former Bishop of Lille and a leading figure in the reorganization of the priest-worker movement in France, died on February 15, 1973. He was 89.

Raised to the Sacred College at the early age of 46, Liénart was known from the beginning of his life as a priest for his intense interest in the application of the social principles of the Church and in the coordination of activities for the betterment of the workers in French industry. His exceptional bravery as a chaplain in the 1914-18 War had made him a public figure before he was appointed to his first parish, and within two years he had become Bishop of Lille, where he began immediately to play an active part, using his influence to the full, in the serious disputes that then were antagonizing employers and employed.

When later Cardinal Sunard set up the priest-worker movement, giving priests the care of factories rather than parishes and working themselves as factory employees, Liénart welcomed the innovation in his own diocese, while seeing clearly the problems that confronted it. These problems affecting the spiritual duties of the priest-workers led to the condemnation of the movement by the Holy See; but Liénart drew up plans for similar work on a different basis.

In 1954 his proposals were sanctioned by the Holy See in the setting up of the Mission de France de Pontigny, with Liénart at its head. The Cardinal had begun from the premise that there was no way of combining the functions of a priest and a factory worker in one person, without risking too close an identification between spiritual and temporal duties. Consequently his organization brought priests and laymen together in a form of secular institute, all the members of which were devoted to the social apostolate. Its development in the years that followed represented, probably, the outstanding achievement of the Cardinal's career.

Born in Lille, he went from St. Joseph's College, Lille, to St. Sulpice, Paris, where he was ordained to the priesthood in 1907. After further study at the Institut Catholique in Paris he went to Rome, where he gained a doctorate in Sacred Scripture at the Pontifical Biblical Institute.

Until the outbreak of war in 1914 he taught Sacred Scripture at the diocesan seminary at Cambrai. Then he volunteered for service as an army chaplain. During the war he was awarded the Legion of Honour Croix de Guerre, the principal of six citations describing an incident near Soissons when the French evacuated a post on the Aisne, withdrew to the other side of the river before destroying the bridge, and were obliged to leave behind a number of wounded soldiers. Liénart found a rowing boat in which he crossed the river several times under heavy enemy fire and thus brought back all the wounded.

After the war he returned to seminary duties, was appointed in 1926 to a parish near Lille and in 1928, on appointment to the diocese of Lille, he became the youngest bishop in France. He resigned in 1968 from his appointment as Bishop of Lille, owing to ill health.

The Liénart family had been manufacturing in Lille for several generations and the young bishop had special means of knowing of conditions in factories throughout his diocese. On several occasions he intervened as mediator during strikes. Once, when employers refused to negotiate, he published an open letter stating the case for the workers, with the result that a meeting between the parties at the Bishop's Palace was agreed to, and a conciliation board was established.

He was elevated to the Sacred College of Cardinals with the title of St. Sisto by Pope Pius XI in 1930, continuing, by a series of pastorals and the formation of coordinating diocesan societies, his work to bring employers and workers together as partners in Christian enterprise.

February 16, 1973.

Colonel Charles Lindbergh, the American flier, who made the first solo transatlantic non-stop flight from New York to Paris in 1927, died at the age of 72, on August 26, 1974.

Lindbergh came of Scandinavian stock. He was born on February 4, 1902, in Detroit but, while he was a child, the family moved into Minnesota and his father was elected to the House of Representatives, where he opposed the entry of the United States into the war in 1917. On his death, Mrs. Lindbergh returned to Detroit, and Charles Augustus grew up in the developing world of motor engines. He soon turned to flying and ground his way forward from wing-walking and parachuting to piloting through a flying school at Lincoln, Nebraska, and into the struggling

air line at St. Louis.

One night, while ploughing through a storm, he decided he would try to win the $25,000 offered by a French hotel proprietor for a direct flight from New York to Paris. He planned his flight from the start, persuaded his backers in St. Louis to support him, did his own negotiating with the Ryan company and almost his own designing, laid down in the most precise terms what he wanted, and lived on the construction job to make sure he got it, worked out his own navigation scheme, finally did his own interpreting of a dubious weather report, and at last asked permission of Admiral Byrd to make use of the runway he had prepared for himself. To all this meticulous planning he brought his own skill and peculiar accomplishment in estimating risks and playing them not foolhardily yet up to the limit. In his air mail days he had twice stepped out and used his parachute. This time he had no parachute.

On May 20, 1927 Spirit of St. Louis, with nearly one and a half tons of petrol on board, staggered off the runway at Roosevelt Field, New York, narrowly missing some trees and telephone wires.

With a single engine, no radio aids and no forward view from his cockpit, he appears now (as he did then) to have been accepting ridiculous odds. His compatriots indeed promptly named him the "flying fool" and nobody believed he could pull off so enormous a hazard. When he did, the achievement stood out so much the more brightly among the series of other and bigger projects he beat to the post, especially as his adventure in comparison had been financed on the proverbial shoestring.

Lindbergh's great flight lifted him at one spectacular stroke out of obscurity to a position of popular interest which shocked and embarrassed him then and was to lead him into difficult situations thereafter. He had a powerful sense of personal rectitude and no sense at all of the effects his fame, allied with his intense seriousness and honesty, might have in the wider field of public affairs. He was a fine pilot and navigator and at least as able an engineer. His clear mind, thrusting initiative, love of achievement, persistence and transparent honesty guaranteed him success in his chosen line; but when, in a brief $33\frac{1}{2}$ hours over the ocean, success came to him, it was of a nature and quality that were wholly outside his experience.

At the Paris airport he was virtually mobbed. At Croydon later his arrival was greeted by an enormous crowd. He shrank from these unbridled manifestations of public favour as something indecent and dangerously intemperate. He was almost as startled by the attention he received from the press and soon was as hard for a reporter to get hold of as a crowned head. Having been received and decorated by the heads of states, having been fêted and congratulated by important societies, he was so impressed by his new status that, like Agag, he trod delicately wherever he went and retired into the natural reserve which, hitherto, only his fellow-pilots had penetrated when they nicknamed him "Slim" on his little air mail line centred on St. Louis.

This betokened no lack of courage. It marked rather bemusement, distrust, fear and distaste, together with an obstinate resolution not to be made use of in projects he did not understand and could not fully control.

His feat, which blazed the trail for the massive air traffic of today, fired the imagination of the world. Lindbergh was an instant legend; babies, streets, even a town were named after him. In 1932 his child was taken from his crib at Lindbergh's New Jersey home and a note asking for a ransom of $50,000 left on the window sill. Although the ransom was paid the child was found murdered. Bruno Hauptman, tried and convicted of the crime, was not executed until 1936. The case attracted enormous publicity, and Lindbergh paid dearly for his fame both then and later, when in 1940 he brought a hornet's nest about his ears by his intervention in world politics as an outspoken isolationist.

He was heavily handled by members of Roosevelt's Government, taunted by Harold Ickes, then Secretary of the Interior, with being "a knight of the Golden Eagle" and, having retorted that he had accepted his German decoration on the advice of the United States Ambassador in Berlin, he resigned his commission in the United States Army Air Corps Reserve, stepped down from his isolationist platform and out of the limelight.

Yet, true to type again, he did not step out of his chosen profession or sidestep his duty as a citizen. Throughout the war he was engaged on work he could do well, on testing new aircraft, trying them on active service, sometimes in combat, advising on technical and tactical matters, all under his chosen shroud of deep secrecy. Not until long after the end of the war was he commissioned again. He published his autobiography (*The Spirit of St. Louis*) in 1953. A film of his first epic flight, called by the same name, appeared in 1957 with James Stewart in the title role.

Many years before, on a flight to Mexico City, he had made the acquaintance of Dwight Morrow, the United States Ambassador and a former banker. In 1929 he married Morrow's daughter, Anne, and settled in New Jersey, not far from New York. After their domestic disaster, the Lindberghs secretly left the United States and stayed first in South Wales and later in Kent, where they enjoyed a welcome freedom from the attentions of the press. Eventually they returned to the United States.

Earlier in their married life they had flown on long journeys together. One of the first was to China by way of the Arctic. Other long flights were made after their return from England, most of them in a single-engined float seaplane. These trips yielded material for Mrs. Lindbergh's books, in which some of the best writing on flying is to be found.

August 27, 1974.

Lord Lindgren, trade unionist, local councillor, and one of a band of Labour M.P.s who entered the House of Commons in the 1945 general election and were immediately appointed to office in the Attlee Government, died on September 8, 1971 in hospital while on holiday in Majorca, aged 70. He represented Wellingborough from 1945 to 1959 and was one of five life peers created in January 1961 to strengthen the Labour front bench in the House of Lords.

George Samuel Lindgren was born on November 11, 1900, the son of George William Lindgren, and was educated at an L.C.C. elementary school. He became interested in politics at an early age, and at 22 was secretary of the St. Pancras branch of the Independent Labour Party. Soon afterwards he moved out to Hertfordshire and, transferring to the Labour Party, took an active part in local affairs. He served as leader of the Labour group and for a while as chairman of the Welwyn Garden City urban district council, and later became the first Labour alderman on the Hertfordshire County Council.

He started as a railway clerk on the L.N.E.R., became a member of the union's national executive committee and vice-chairman of its London political council, and was chairman for four years from 1938 of the London Trades Council. From 1942 until the end of the war he was Deputy Regional Commissioner for Civil Defence in the Midlands.

He first stood for Parliament in 1933 as Labour candidate at Hitchin, but was unsuccessful. In the 1945 administration he was appointed successively as Parliamentary Secretary to the Ministries of National Insurance and Civil Aviation, and in the following Parliament went to Town and Country Planning and then to Housing and Local Government. He returned to office again with the Labour Government in 1964, in which he served in the House of Lords as Parliamentary Secretary to the Ministry of Transport and subsequently at the Ministry of Power. He resumed his active trade union work in 1956 as treasurer of the Transport Salaried Staffs Association, retiring in 1961.

For 35 years he had been a magistrate at Welwyn, and in 1969, as chairman of the bench, he became involved in a dispute with three local solicitors which ended in the High Court. As a result, he and two fellow magistrates were banned from hearing the remainder of a court case which, it was claimed, he had constantly interrupted.

Lord Lindgren had represented England and Hertfordshire at bowls, and until recently he used to run the threequarters of a mile from his home to Welwyn Garden swimming pool for an early morning swim.

He married, in 1926, Elsie Olive Reid and they had one son.

September 10, 1971.

David Lindsay, 28th Earl of Crawford and 11th Earl of Balcarres—See Crawford.

Walter Lines, the toy manufacturer, who was president of Lines Brothers Ltd, died on November 23, 1972 at the age of 90.

He spent some 40 years as chairman of the firm which makes Tri-ang toys. The trademark was derived from the word triangle and chosen in 1919 by the three Lines brothers. They had broken away from their father's toy business on returning from the First World War. Walter Lines, who was managing director at the time, worked for £5 a week; his father thought that rocking horses were the end of the toy business and would not increase their salaries. Walter Lines built the company up until in the sixties it had more than a third of the toy trade.

After leaving Owen's School at the age of 14, Walter Lines carved rocking horses in the family factory. He opened the factory at 7.30 a.m. and after a working day until 7.30 p.m. attended classes in design, building, carpentry and cabinet making. The new factory which he opened with his brothers was based on a wooden scale model made by Walter.

He later designed factories in Australia, New Zealand, Margate and Merton for Lines Brothers Ltd. Many of the youths who joined the brothers in the early days at their factory off the Old Kent Road later became foremen and managers in the company. Later the brothers bought 20 acres at Merton and built a factory there.

Walter Lines used to deliver toys to Hamleys in his father's horse-drawn van. He made a dolls' house for Mr. Hamley for which he charged him about £30. A Rothschild bought it furnished for £120. It was a gift for the Queen of Spain. When Hamleys toyshop nearly closed in 1931 Lines Brothers bought it.

He married in 1922 Henriette Katherine Hendrey (who died in 1970) and they had two sons and two daughters.

November 24, 1972.

Eric Linklater, C.B.E., novelist, playwright and biographer, died on November 7, 1974 in St. John's Nursing Home, Aberdeen, aged 75. He was admitted to the nursing home several weeks earlier with thrombosis.

Eric Linklater never quite achieved the critical recognition that would seem due to an author who possessed such powers of wit and comic invention and so lucid and elegant a prose style. No doubt his versatility was partially responsible for this, but there is also the fact that his work, for all its distinction, fell only uneasily into the normal literary categories.

Although he had his affinities with Peacock, and with other Scots writers such as Urquhart, Norman Douglas and perhaps Stevenson, he was very much his own kind of writer.

Eric Robert Linklater was born in 1899 at Dounby, Orkney, of the Norse stock of the island on his father's side, and on his mother's of mixed English and Swedish descent. Both his father and his mother's father were sea captains. He was educated at Aberdeen Grammar School, and in 1917, after a term or two as a medical student at Aberdeen University, he went into the Army.

He saw the war through as a private in the Black Watch, was wounded, and after the war went back to Aberdeen University to study medicine, which he abandoned later to read English. "English" included Anglo-Saxon, which led him by stages to Icelandic and to an absorbed interest in the Norse sagas. On graduating in 1925, he went to Bombay as an assistant editor on *The Times of India.*

Two years later he was appointed assistant to the Professor of English at Aberdeen, and from 1928 to 1930 he was in the United States as a Commonwealth Fellow, ostensibly to work on a book on Ben Jonson, which did indeed appear in 1931 as *Ben Jonson and King James* but, more significantly, to gather material for his satirical novel, *Juan in America* which, also published in 1931, brought him immediate fame.

Thereupon he settled down to a life of professional and prolific authorship combined with much travelling—to India again and to China, for material for *Juan in China*, which appeared in 1937—a life interrupted in 1932 by an incursion into politics as Scottish Nationalist candidate in the East Fife by-election.

Before the Second World War he was an officer in the Territorial Army, and from 1939 to 1941 he was a major in the Royal Engineers commanding Orkney Fortress. The rest of the war he spent in the Directorate of Public Relations at the War Office. He was Rector of Aberdeen University from 1945 to 1948. During the Korean War he was a temporary lieutenant-colonel in Korea.

In his admirable and wholly characteristic autobiography, *The Man on My Back* (1941), Linklater observed that "few authors can spare for their own lives much of the colour, the adventuring and vivacity of their work". Linklater was one who did. The panache of his books he wore in his own life.

No author, to meet, was more like his work. He looked, and often sounded, with his barking voice (although there was a conscious irony in his presentation of himself) very much like the conventional notion of a professional soldier, but a professional soldier who bubbled with wit and high spirits, was a brilliant talker and had a vast and exuberant knowledge of literature.

He held strong views about the virtues of the British soldier, and for the rest of his life bore evidence of the ardours of service in the front line. His skull was deeply indented as a result of his First World War wound.

As his work shows, he was a combination of what are usually regarded as opposed types, the romantic and the satirist. Novels as widely apart in the time of their writing as *Poet's Pub* (1929) and *Position at Noon* (1958), reveal that his kinship with Peacock was a real one.

At the same time, the correlation indicates both his strength and his weakness as a writer. He wrote one of the best prose styles of our time, a prose firmly based in the eighteenth century, at once sonorous and sharp, masculine and mannered to the point of dandyism.

But with few exceptions in his books—the most obvious being the delightful *Private Angelo* (1946), his novel of the campaign in Italy—his approach to life was through literature. This was apparent from the beginning, in *Juan in America*, the first of a series of brilliant *tours de force.*

Although there were times, as in *Men of Ness*, when it resulted in something close to literary archaeology, it never precluded wit; far from it. Nor did it preclude imagination. Rather, it seemed that Linklater needed a story or a fable of the past in order to focus his imagination, as, for example, in his remarkably sympathetic recreation of the Samson story, *Husband of Delilah* (1962).

Linklater called himself a carpenter, not an artist. He was in fact a fine and fastidious artist, but his art often demanded a considerable connoisseurship of literature before it could be appreciated at its real value, which, although admittedly not of the highest kind, was one that has never been common, and was much less than common in the period in which he wrote.

In recent years his works included *The Voyage of the Challenger, Fanfare for a Tin Hat,* and *The Corpse on Clapham Common.* Linklater was married to Marjorie, younger daughter of the late Ian MacIntyre, by whom he had two sons and two daughters.

November 8, 1974.

Professor J. W. Linnett, F.R.S., Master of Sidney Sussex College, Cambridge, died suddenly of a heart attack in the Athenaeum on November 7, 1975, only five weeks after ceasing to be Vice-Chancellor of the university. He was 62.

John Wilfrid Linnett was born on August 3, 1913. He was educated at King Edward VIII School, Coventry, and won an open scholarship to St. John's College, Oxford. In 1935 he was awarded a 1st in the Honours School of Chemistry, and three years later he obtained his D.Phil. He was a Henry Fellow at Harvard in 1937-38. Balliol College elected him to a Junior Research Fellowship in 1939, a post which he held until he was elected a Fellow and Praelector in Chemistry at The Queen's College in 1945. He was a lecturer at Brasenose College from 1943 to 1945 and first a departmental demonstrator from 1939 to 1944, then university demonstrator from 1944 to 1962, and finally Reader from 1962 to 1965 in the Inorganic Chemistry Laboratory, Oxford.

In 1965 he was appointed Professor of Physical Chemistry at Cambridge and became a Professorial Fellow of Emmanuel College. In 1970 he was elected to the Mastership of Sidney Sussex College. Among the honours that he received were Fellowship of the New York Academy of Sciences (1965), the Coventry Award of Merit (1966), and an Honorary Fellowship of St. John's College, Oxford (1968).

Linnett's scientific research interests covered almost the whole field of physical and theoretical chemistry, and he published monographs, textbooks, and a multitude of papers in these areas. In recent years he also took an avid interest in scientific education as a whole. The Royal Society elected him a Fellow in 1955, and he served as a member of Council of the Royal Institute of Chemistry, as a Vice-President of the Chemical Society, and as President of the Faraday Society.

He became Vice Chancellor of Cambridge in October 1973, on the same day that a Cambridge graduate, H. J. Habbakuk, became Vice Chancellor of Oxford, and he was always interested in making comparisons between his two universities. He regretted that the short term of Oxbridge Vice Chancellors made it difficult for them to play a full part in the affairs of the Vice Chancellors' Committee, and he lost no opportunity of taking on as much as possible. He was chairman of one of the committees dealing with common market affairs, and he attended several meetings of the Rectors of European Universities.

In Cambridge he was particularly concerned that the growth of the university had outstripped internal communication, and he was always striving to keep as many people as possible in the picture, particularly by frequent working lunches.

The experimental correspondence column in the *Cambridge Reporter* was his idea, and aimed in the same direction. Despite the very heavy commitment which he took on, he had a remarkable capacity for always being available when his guidance was needed. He was particularly concerned with the remarkable benefaction of £10m. for the founding of a new college. He alone had all the initial discussions with David Robinson, and it gave him great pleasure to see the last major hurdle surmounted.

Cricket and travel were his main non-scientific interests, though he could and did play most games with skill and competence. As a cricketer he was one of the few people who have played county cricket as a batsman, a bowler, and a wicket-keeper.

Lecture tours and scientific meetings enabled him to travel to most parts of the world. He paid many visits to the United States and Canada, and he had particularly close ties with the University of California at Berkeley.

He married, in 1947, Rae Ellen Libgott. They had one son and one daughter.

November 10, 1975.

Lin Piao, whose reported death on September 12, 1971 was confirmed by two Chinese Embassies on July 28, 1972, had been the designated successor of Mao Tse-tung as leader of the Chinese people, Vice-chairman of the party and Minister of Defence, the army's supreme authority.

As Chairman Mao's "close-comrade in arms" and designated successor, Lin Piao was the person second in importance to China's leader. In the exercise of his functions, in the role he played in party or army, in his public appearances which were even more rare than Mao's, in the impression he created in public, and probably also among his closer colleagues, he fell very far short of the stature required as Mao's deputy.

Yet of his brilliance in some spheres there can be no doubt. He was a graduate of the Whampao military academy in Canton (where Chou En-lai was a political instructor) in the days before the Kuomintang-Communist split. He commanded a battalion at 21. He showed himself to be an able military leader and skilled tactician in operations against the Japanese. After the war as commander of the communist forces who out-manoeuvred the Nationalists in Manchuria Lin laid the foundations for the communist victory in the civil war.

But whatever the qualities that had marked his career before the new China came into being in 1949, ill-health effectively removed Lin from active influence for many years thereafter. And when he was finally elevated to a much greater eminence by Mao Tse-tung his personality made little effect.

The gradual takeover of authority throughout China by the army in 1968 and 1969 and the continuing authority exercised by military men at the head of most party committees may have been arranged by Lin out of disenchantment at the course of events. He may also have been under pressure by many provincial commanders who were themselves urging moderation.

He first acquired fame in the 1930s, when he emerged as one of the most successful of the Communist Party's guerrilla generals. He led the vanguard of Mao Tse-tung's forces on their legendary Long March in the Chinese interior, and later, in the Sino-Japanese War, he scored a remarkable victory over the Japanese army in 1937, using the so-called "short attack" which he had pioneered.

Illness interrupted his career several times thereafter, but in 1958 he became more active and was elected to the Standing Committee of the Party's Politburo, to rank sixth in the hierarchy of power. The following year, when Peng Teh-huai was dismissed for advocating a truce in the ideological dispute with the Soviet Union (China's chief source until then of advanced military weapons and technology), Lin succeeded him as Minister of National Defence.

He now began a programme of political reform in the army with the aim of rendering it ideologically loyal to Mao Tse-tung and free from the influence of those "professional" officers who placed more faith in modern weapons than in revolutionary morale. Mao had apparently found that the party establishment had grown too conservative in its ways, especially after the failure of the Great Leap Forward of 1958-59, and chose the army as an instrument for its chastisement and rectification.

Lin Piao gradually built himself up as a spokesman not only for the army but also for Mao himself. In September 1965, his 30,000-character article on the twentieth anniversary of V.J. Day, entitled *Long Live the Victory of the People's War*, was published.

His article attracted enormous interest abroad for its global application of Mao's strategic principle of encircling the towns from a rural base. This had been unorthodox Marxism when Mao made it succeed in China in the 1930s; the prospect of its imitation in the 1960s and 1970s throughout the underdeveloped lands of Asia, Africa and Latin America (the world's "villages", which would eventually defeat the "cities" of the industrialized, economically advanced North America and Europe) disturbed Soviet and Eastern European opinion almost as much as it did Western. In fact Lin's thesis had little originality and contained as much cautionary advice as it did encouragement for foreign revolutionaries.

Lin had now established himself as the chief interpreter of Mao's thought, and in August 1966 at the first parade in Peking of the Red Guard (the new youth organization formed to prosecute the prolitarian cultural revolution, Mao's last bid for the preservation of revolutionary fervour in China) Lin appeared as second only to Mao.

He was described as Mao's "close comrade-in-arms" and took precedence over Liu Shao-chi, then head of state, and Chou En-lai, the Prime Minister. The draft constitution of the newly-rectified Communist Party circulated at the end of 1968 named him as Mao's official heir and next chairman.

July 29, 1972.

Jacques Lipchitz. whose works of art rank him among the greatest of twentieth century sculptors, died in Capri, where he was on holiday, in May 1973. He was 81.

Lipchitz was among the first to use the principles of Cubism in sculpture, but became most famous for the heroic themes with which he infused his work after emigrating to the United States in 1941.

He was born Chiam Jacob Lipchitz, on August 22, 1891, in Druskieniki, Lithuania. His father Abraham opposed his early interest in sculpture and sent him to engineering school in the capital city of Vilna in 1906. But in 1909 Lipchitz's mother Rachel sent her son to study in Paris, without the knowledge of his father. Tuberculosis and the financial reverses of his father—who eventually agreed to his son's chosen career—interrupted Lipchitz's studies in 1911, as did military service in Russia in 1912.

Lipchitz returned to Paris in 1913 and remained there until the outbreak of the Second World War. During this time he became one of the leaders in what was to be called the School of Paris. Among his friends were Pablo Picasso, Gertrude Stein and the Italian painter Modigliani.

He became a French citizen in 1924 and in the same year married the Russian poet Bertha Kitrossky.

One of his most famous works, "Prometheus Strangling the Vulture", was prepared for the international exhibition of 1937 in Paris. The approach of war drove the artist from France to the United States, where he transformed his art into an eloquent statement on the great and heroic in man. Among Lipchitz's most famous works are the sculptures "Joie de Vivre", "Figure", "Man with Guitar", and "Return of the Prodigal".

He returned to France after the war, then went back to the United States. His wife remained in France and they were subsequently divorced. In 1948 he married Yulla Halberstadt. They have one daughter, Lola.

May 29, 1973.

Walter Lippmann, the columnist, editor and author, who occupied a unique position in political journalism for some decades, died on December 14, 1974 at the age of 85.

He will be remembered most for his regular columns, first syndicated by the *New York Herald Tribune* and later by the *Washington Post*. They established in American journalism new and high standards of detached and well-informed comment: and if it can be said that the limitations of the provincial American press made his success possible, it was his considerable talents that often transferred a syndicated column into a platform of international debate.

Widely travelled and widely published, he was received everywhere with the respect and attention normally reserved for those in high office. Distinguished visitors to Washington sought him out in the old rectory in Woodley Road, which was long his home, and when he called on Khrushchev the entire diplomatic world seemed to wait upon his pronouncements.

He was a constant advocate and defender of the postwar special relationship between the United States and Britain. Above all, he sought to improve the channels of communication, not only between government and the press, and the press and the reader, but also in diplomacy. In a way he became an integral part of the political and diplomatic world, especially in the traffic of ideas.

Walter Lippmann was born on September 23, 1889, of a comfortably situated New York family, and even in his early days at a private school he was something of a prodigy. Much was expected of him before he went down from Harvard, and the Fates dealt kindly with him in opening many doors and providing opportunity.

Looking back over his long career—he was born in Victoria's reign and yet remained a powerful influence well into the nuclear age—it seemed always attended by success. This was not the case; he was never completely effective until he withdrew from active participation in political affairs. His essays into politics always ended in disillusionment, an indulgence he did not permit himself in later life.

To many friends at the time it also seemed that he had followed the well-trodden path from the left to the right. He had been president of the Harvard Socialist Club, but his early enthusiasm was quickly restrained. His political development was apparent in his first two books, *A Preface to Politics* and *Drift and Mastery,* in which he rejected Socialist doctrine as sterile and Marx as an empty theorist.

This was to have been expected, but he later attacked many of the policies of the New Deal, and supported Landon for president. Roosevelt, whom he had earlier admired in New York, was dismissed as a pleasant man but too eager to please, and without any important qualifications for the presidency. The National Recovery Administration was opposed, as well as the packing of the Supreme Court, and he suggested that beneficiaries under the Works Progress Administration should be disenfranchised. He repeatedly encouraged Congress to resist the extension of executive authority.

This apparent swing to the right was accompanied over the years by a similar progression from a liberal periodical to a Republican newspaper. From an associate editorship of the *New Republic* he went to the editorial chair of the now defunct *New York World*, and then to the *New York Herald Tribune* as columnist.

In the fifties and sixties, when most men of his generation had retired, Lippmann's reputation and influence continued to grow. The strict discipline he imposed upon himself, together with his long political memory,

and his continuing interest in the world around him, gave him an enviable authority and an astonishing freshness. When he was met at dinner parties and functions, it was difficult to realize that this quiet elderly man was the author of political and social comment that often made his younger imitators appear to be both incompetent and dusty.

He shone best in foreign affairs. In his earlier years he always had been intellectually superior to what was then essentially provincial America, and when his country assumed the responsibilities of a world power he was well equipped to influence—and occasionally lead—its leaders. He was a linguist, a constant reader of foreign newspapers, and a traveller for whom the outside world was neither strange nor inferior.

It was this that raised him well above his competitors, and made his comment and suggestions acceptable abroad, but there was more to it than that. Lippmann was a journalist who believed that the press had an important role in political affairs, not only in informing but also discussing, exchanging, refining and indeed initiating ideas.

Lippmann became seriously critical of President Johnson's policies in Vietnam, though supporting his domestic programmes. He argued that the United States had no business fighting wars on the mainland of Asia, which was not in its legitimate sphere of influence. He did not advocate immediate withdrawal but suggested that America would have to be content with limited objectives and an unsatisfactory compromise. He fought ceaselessly against the view that the United States had an obligation to fight communism under any conditions in any part of the world.

Alas, he could not move Johnson, and eventually Lippmann decided there was no point in living and working in Washington any more. His abrupt departure to New York also brought to an end the columns he had written over the decades. He afterwards made occasional contributions to *Newsweek*, before accepting retirement with his usual good sense and grace.

Lippmann was twice married; first, in 1917 to Faye Albertson and, secondly, in 1938 to Helen Byrne Armstrong who died in 1974.

December 16, 1974.

Sonny Liston, former world heavyweight champion, was found dead at his home in Las Vegas on January 5, 1971.

Hailed briefly for knocking out Floyd Patterson in the first round in successive fights in 1962 and 1963 to become world heavyweight champion, the "Big Bear" received far more and far worse publicity for his defeats by his successor, Cassius Clay (Muhammad Ali). He learnt his boxing while in gaol serving a term for robbery

with violence, and was involved in scrapes with the law throughout his boxing career.

Charles Liston was born in St. Francis County, Arkansas, (by some reports on May 8, 1932). Life was hard on him, and at 13 he ran away from his family. He was one of 25 brothers and sisters—his father married twice. There followed frequent clashes with authority culminating in a five-year gaol sentence in the Missouri State Penitentiary, where the chaplain taught him to box.

By 1953, after being amateur heavyweight champion of the United States, he turned professional. In his early years in the ring, Liston struck terror into his opponents, looking every inch the tough executioner, with enormous neck, a phenomenally strong jaw, and a baleful look in his eyes. The only fight he lost before Clay beat him was against Marty Marshall, who outscored him in 1954.

The Patterson and Clay fights were reported to have brought him nearly £1m. for less than 24 minutes boxing, but a year later he was back in the ring. Tax and manager's fees had eaten up most of his money. Over the last four years his career was a mixture of ring victories against mediocre opponents and newspaper headlines for various charges of drunken driving and of carrying offensive weapons. By the end of 1969 he was back to number three in the world heavyweight rankings and was living with his wife Geraldine in a luxurious house in Las Vegas. But his championship comeback hopes ended then with a knockout by Leotis Martin.

Charles "Sonny" Liston was not a great world champion. His main assets were brute strength and an image of invincibility created by astute publicity men. There is no doubt that his massively-muscled ebony frame, topped by a weather beaten face which wore a permanent brooding scowl induced, at the least, apprehension in most of the men he fought. In some cases, apprehension became plain, old fashioned fear, so that many of his opponents were beaten before a punch was thrown.

Such was the terrifying picture conjured up by this huge Negro of indeterminate age who mowed down a succession of mediocrities and a few semi-skilled boxers, culminating in the quick destruction of a blond German called Albert Westphal.

This latest triumph over a boxer of strictly limited ability precipitated Liston into a world title fight against Floyd Patterson, the then champion. Patterson, far more skilled than Liston, though by no means an outstanding champion himself, was clearly awed by the challenger's reputation. His tactics were those of a man who felt himself doomed to defeat from the start and he was knocked out in the first round.

Liston gave a repeat performance against the same boxer ten months later and it was not until he met Cassius Clay (Muhammad Ali, if you like) that his limitations were exposed. Clay's speed was too much for the lumbering Liston who, complaining of a back injury, retired on his stool at the end of the sixth round.

In a return match Liston was knocked out in the first round by a blow which, it seemed, would not have inconvenienced an elderly maiden aunt.

Whatever the rights and wrongs of that controversial affair, it appeared clear that Liston had realized his shortcomings as a boxer and had opted for a quick well-paid exit.

Liston subsequently fought his way back into the world ratings but the bubble had been burst, the aura of indestructibility shattered.

It is fair to say that at a time when good heavyweights were few, Liston was no more than a slow-thinking, slow-moving plodder with sufficient native strength to overcome most men.

He had a reasonable left jab with which he would probe for an opening for an extremely powerful right hand punch. This was his only tactic and when it failed he was reduced to little more than a groping novice. He would come very low in a list of world heavyweight champions.

January 7, 1971.

Admiral Sir Charles J. C. Little, G.C.B., G.B.E., who died on June 20, 1973 at the age of 91, had a distinguished career of some 48 years in the Navy (1897-1945), culminating in the post of Commander-in-Chief at Portsmouth during the invasion of Normandy.

In his early career, Little was a pioneer in submarines. He commanded the flotillas in the Dover Patrol and in the Grand Fleet in the war of 1914-18, and as a rear-admiral was head of the branch at Gosport. He also had considerable staff and administrative experience, both afloat and at the Admiralty.

At the outbreak of war in 1914 he was appointed to command the Arrogant and the submarines of the Dover Patrol, but in 1915 was selected to be assistant to the Commodore (S) at Gosport. In 1916, he went north to command the Fearless and the flotilla of large "K-class" fleet submarines in the Grand Fleet, serving there for two and a half years until after the war ended, during which period he was promoted to captain in 1917, again the first of his team.

In 1933 he went to the Admiralty Board as Deputy Chief of Naval Staff, remaining there until 1935. It was an important period, which saw the birth of rearmament and the conclusion of the Anglo-German naval agreement. Little left the Admiralty to become Commander-in-Chief in China from 1936 to 1938. Here he had an anxious and strenuous time owing to the Japanese attack on China, and supervised the measures taken at Shanghai and elsewhere for the protection of British nationals.

In September 1938 he returned to the Board of Admiralty as Second Sea Lord and Chief of Naval Personnel. It was the time of the Munich conference, and two days earlier a mobilization of the Fleet had been ordered. Before this was completed the Munich agreement had been signed and the immediate need had passed, but the mobilization provided valuable experience of the machinery which 11 months later had to be used again. Little was responsible for the personnel of the Navy during the first two critical years of the war, during which his administration had to provide for immense expansion in all branches.

After nearly three years in that capacity he was appointed Head of the British Admiralty Delegation in Washington, a post which he held until he was relieved in 1942 by Admiral Sir Andrew Cunningham [Lord Cunningham of Hyndhope*]. He left Washington to become Commander-in-Chief at Portsmouth, where he flew his flag from 1942 to 1945, and thus the chief administrative authority in the naval side of the organization behind the Allied invasion of Normandy of June 1944.

June 22, 1973.

Prince Littler, C.B.E., the theatre proprietor and producing manager, died on September 13, 1973 at the age of 72.

The son of Frank R. and Agnes Littler, lessees of the Royal Artillery Theatre, Woolwich, Prince was the younger brother of Blanche and the elder brother of Emile, and of all the Littlers he it was whose influence on the "live" theatre, measured in terms of the theatrical bricks and mortar directly or indirectly controlled, and of the number of productions sponsored by him, was the most considerable and widespread.

Prince Littler, born on July 25, 1901, at Ramsgate and educated at Stratford-on-Avon, was for some years resident manager at his parents' theatre, but in 1927 he began jointly with his sister Blanche to send out companies on tours of London successes, and in 1931 he became a theatre proprietor, buying two playhouses in Leicester which he proceeded to manage. During the decade of the 1930s he bought two theatres in Cardiff, acquired the leases of two more in Manchester and Norwich and made a start in London. This he did by presenting revivals of George Robey and Violet Loraine's wartime hit *The Bing Boys Are Here*—this in conjunction with Blanche, who was Robey's manager and was later to be his second wife—and of Ivor Novello's *Glamorous Night;* also with pantomimes, two of them in association with Blanche, at successively Drury Lane, the Coliseum and Princes'.

During the Second World War Prince Littler was appointed chairman and managing director first of Stoll Theatres Corporation Ltd., secondly of Associated Theatre Properties (London) Ltd., which in later years bought the leases of the Globe and the Queen's, and thirdly of Drury Lane. There he reopened after its wartime occupation by E.N.S.A. with a musical by Noel Coward, one of "the Master's" few failures in that line, in which, however, Mary Martin made her English debut. By 1947 Littler was also a director of Howard and Wyndham Ltd., whose field of operations was Northern England and Scotland, and chairman of Moss Empires Ltd. The productions presented or co-presented by him in the West End during the 1950s included *Carousel* at Drury Lane, *Guys and Dolls* and *Can-Can* at the Coliseum, and *Teahouse of the August Moon* and *No Time for Sergeants*, two straight plays, at Her Majesty's, all of them entertainments that had first been produced in the American theatre.

His wish to bring about a merging of his interests in Stoll Theatres and Moss Empires was realized in 1960 when he successfully countered an attempt by Charles Clore, Jack Cotton* and Bernard Delfont to gain control of Moss, which at that time owned 16 London and provincial play-houses, among them the Palladium and the Victoria Palace, and which had also a substantial holding in Associated Television.

Some years later Littler, a director since its formation and for a time chairman of Associated Television, negotiated an arrangement by which it gained financial control of the Stoll-Moss Empires group, while he himself remained chairman and managing director of Stoll and might have been described as the chief executive of the theatre division of the expanded enterprise. As such he was a plaintiff in an action for libel brought against his brother Emile after the latter alleged in 1965 that a plan had been made to ensure the withdrawal of a production of Emile's from a theatre owned by a subsidiary of A.T.V. The plaintiffs won, and Emile's subsequent appeal was dismissed in 1968, at a time when Prince, who had not become personally estranged from his brother, was directly interested, either as company chairman or as licensee, in three of the most prosperous of the contemporary productions on the London stage, two of them British in origin and one American: *The Black and White Minstrel Show* at the Victoria Palace, Terence Frisby's *There's A Girl in my Soup* at the Globe, and *Fiddler on the Roof*, the musical based on the stories of Sholom Aleichem, at Her Majesty's.

Prince Littler married Miss Nora Delany in 1932.

Of the handful of men and companies whose empires were said to dominate Britain's entertainment industry at the time of the libel action in the 1960s, Prince Littler was probably the man least accessible to photographers and interviewers. When he contributed a foreword to the playbill of Drury Lane on its postwar reopening, he subscribed to the familiar lines of Dr. Johnson's, spoken from that stage by Garrick not quite 200 years previously:

"The drama's laws, the drama's patrons
    give,
For we, that live to please, must please
    to live".

Some years later he was quoted as having put the matter in somewhat different terms: "I am not in this business for fun, but only as long as the shareholders are happy". Fun or not, there can be no doubt that the theatre was a business to which he was dedicated. He was past president of Denville Home for aged actors and actresses, vice-president of the Variety Artistes' Benevolent Fund, and of the Society of West End Theatre Managers, and a member of the South Bank Theatre and Opera House Board. One of his hobbies was the breeding of Guernsey dairy cattle and Sussex cattle. He was appointed C.B.E. in 1957.

September 14, 1973.

Anatole Litvak, the film director, died in Paris on December 15, 1974 at the age of 72.

Russian by birth, he worked in most of the major film-producing countries, including France, Germany, Britain and America, and his pictures often drew on recent European history. At his best, he was a superbly efficient story-teller, with a flair for melodrama; but his output was uneven and some of his later films, particularly, cried out for less ponderous treatment.

He was born in Kiev, the son of a bank manager, studied philosophy at the University of St. Petersburg and later worked as an assistant director and set designer. In 1925 he left Russia for Berlin where he was assistant editor on Pabst's *The Joyless Street*, one of the early films of Greta Garbo. He stayed in Germany until 1932, moved briefly to London and then to Paris, where in 1936 he made a film of the nineteenth century Habsburg tragedy, *Mayerling* with Charles Boyer and Danielle Darrieux in the leading parts.

Soon afterwards he went to Hollywood where his early successes included a rare comedy, *Tovarich, The Amazing Dr. Clitterhouse, Confessions of a Nazi Spy* and *All This and Heaven, Too.* In 1940 he became an American citizen and he served with the American Air Force during the war, rising to the rank of lieutenant-colonel and working with Frank Capra on the *Why We Fight* series.

He returned to Hollywood for a controversial re-make of the pre-war French classic, *Le Jour se Lève*, which was called *The Long Night*, and then directed perhaps his two most famous films, *The Snake Pit* and *Sorry, Wrong Number.* The first, which starred Olivia de Havilland, was a study of the treatment of mental illness which had such an impact that it influenced changes in the law; the second was a thriller with Barbara Stanwyck.

Litvak's later career was less distinguished. In 1955 he went to Britain for the film version of Terence Rattigan's play *The Deep Blue Sea*, and thereafter worked mainly in Europe. There was another version of *Mayerling, Anastasia*, about the supposed survivor of the Russian royal family, *The Journey*, which was inspired by the 1956 Hungarian uprising, and a version of Françoise Sagan's *Aimez-Vous Brahms?* entitled *Goodbye Again.* More recent films included *The Night of the Generals* (1966), a Nazi piece with Peter O'Toole, and a thriller, *The Lady in the Car With Glasses and a Gun,* in 1970.

He was married twice, his first wife being the Hollywood actress, Miriam Hopkins.

December 17, 1974.

Liu Shao-chi, the former Chinese head of state, who was disgraced during the cultural revolution in 1966, was reported dead in the communist-backed newspaper *Ta Kung Pao* in Hongkong at the end of October 1974.

Though he was reported dead more than once in past years, the current report of Liu's death probably emanated from official Peking sources and can be taken to be true. He was 76.

Liu Shao-chi's career and outlook might be regarded as the antithesis in the Chinese Communist Party to that of its leader, Mao Tse-tung. That he had gained a position second only to Mao even before the Communists took power in 1949, and that he should have been naturally regarded as Mao's probable successor until at least as late as 1962, perhaps made inevitable the clash between the two men in the cultural revolution. To Mao Tse-tung, at least, Liu Shao-chi was the "top party person in authority taking the capitalist road"; he was dubbed "China's Khrushchev"; he was the subject of endless mass rallies and denunciations in the press; and his whole career was raked over to show how he had been a traitor to the cause from the beginning.

The profound difference in temperament between the two men only emphasized the parting of the ways that follows all revolutions, the parting between those whose *métier* has been the barricades and the organization of struggle, and those for whom victory offers the opportunity for order, discipline, constitutional procedures, and the evolution of authority in all its forms. Here lay the cast of Liu's orderly temperament. To him as much as to Mao could be attributed the building up of the party so that it could maintain its grasp on China. For Liu, therefore, even discounting the differences of personality and policy that divided him from Mao, the open attack on the party as such, in which ad hoc bodies such as the Red Guards engaged, was reason enough for Liu's outright hostility to the course of Mao's cultural revolution.

The contrast between the two men arose at many points in their different careers. As a young man Liu went as a student to Moscow in 1921 and never quite lost some sense of attachment to the international communist movement. Liu's early years as a party worker were devoted to the organization of trade unions and thus kept him in urban surroundings. Although he came to Mao's liberated area of Kiangsi province in 1932 along with other members of the central committee from Shanghai, Liu was left behind when the Red Army set out on its Long March to the north-west. He went on working in what were known as the "white areas" under Nationalist Government control, being responsible especially for the organization of the December 9, 1935 student outbreak in Peking. Not least, in the contrast to Mao's deep attachment to the army as the truly revolutionary body, and to Mao's romantic militarism as a means to revolution, was Liu's distaste for the army and his natural preference for the party.

From these differences of temperament and experience Liu's distinctive position developed. But there was no reason to think that Liu was opposed to Mao from the beginning; the differences only developed when Mao pushed his personal policy to extremes, internally as in the great leap forward, externally in his quarrel with the Russians. At the seventh congress of the party held at Yenan in 1945—the first to be held after the remaking of the party under Mao's leadership—Liu made the standard report and referred then to the necessity of learning from the "thoughts of Mao Tse-tung". As one of the three vice-chairmen of the new People's Republic and senior vice-chairman of the party's central committee when the new government was formed in 1949, Liu's position seemed as much accepted by Mao as Mao's was by Liu.

The change came in the next two years with the growth of the Sino-Soviet rift and the imposition of Mao's great leap forward in the autumn of 1958. A crisis soon developed in the party and Mao was evidently worsted. As a result he gave up the chairmanship of the People's Republic on the plea of devoting himself to party affairs and Liu Shao-chi took his place in 1959. For some time the situation remained equivocal, an "anti-rightist" campaign in the party at the end of that year seeming to be aimed at precisely those leaders whose opposition to Mao's great leap forward had triumphed.

Nevertheless, according to the charges later made against Liu during the cultural revolution, it was in the years of recovery from the great leap, 1960-62, that Liu was in the ascendancy and was blamed for the liberal policies he initiated.

Incentives were introduced in agriculture —one of the charges against Liu was of his opposition to Mao's collectivist policies as far back as 1955—private plots were restored or increased, a liberal wind blew through the arts, and against the Maoist slogans of "red and expert" or "politics takes command" a much greater tolerance crept in.

The first plain sign of Liu's fall from grace did not come until after the extraordinary meeting of the Central Committee at the beginning of August 1966.

At the first rally at which Red Guards appeared, those present were listed in a new order and Liu had unaccountably dropped to seventh place. For three months he still appeared in public but wall posters began to multiply in their attacks. He was said to have made a confession which did not pass muster—though he later retracted it. By December his public appearances had ended and on more than one occasion he and his wife were subjected to Red Guard "struggle meetings" at which they were humiliated.

Yet Liu continued to live in the reserved area of Chung Nan Hai near the Forbidden City. Though said to have been sacked from his party posts he could not officially be denounced without a vote of the National People's Congress which Mao was plainly unwilling to call. In the spring of 1967 the cultural revolution took a new turn with a spate of attacks on Liu in vast demonstrations all over China. For two months they went on while his short book *How to be a Good Communist* was attacked in article after article. All this was done without Liu being named in the official press, though he was shouted down by demonstrators.

In 1968 Peking radio said that Liu had been deprived of all his powers and ranks and expelled from the Communist Party.

Born in 1898 in Ninghsiang, Huan province (not far from Mao Tse-tung), of a moderately well-off peasant family, Liu was educated—again like Mao—in Changsha and then moved to Shanghai where he joined the Socialist Youth League founded by the Comintern agent Voitinsky. Liu was sent to Moscow to the University of Toilers of the East. After a year he returned to China and soon made his mark in the Communist Party as a labour organizer among coal miners, railwaymen and in the anti-British agitation in Shangai in 1925. He was elected to the party's central committee in 1927, graduated to the political bureau in 1932 and was made head of the North China bureau in 1937. Apart from a brief spell as political commissar of the New Fourth Army Liu was busy in Yenan in party organization.

November 4, 1974.

Ursula Livesey—See Ursula Jeans.

Harold Lloyd, one of the most popular and successful comedians of the silent screen, died on March 8, 1971 in Beverley Hills, California. He was 77 and lived to the last in his 40-room house standing in 20 acres of extremely valuable Beverley Hills land.

Of him it may be said that he was born into an era that was rich in comedians and yet held his place by the individuality of his style and by comic invention of unfailing gusto and vigour. He lacked the pathos which distinguishes the great clowns of film history, and was neither forlorn and undersized like Chaplin, nor large and ridiculous like Oliver Hardy. Indeed he was cast physically more in the mould of a film hero, for he was good-looking and presentable, even in his horn-rimmed glasses. Perhaps this was why he favoured the daredevil style of comedy which found him precariously suspended high above city streets or clinging agonisingly to some flimsy support.

The hair-raising scenes were not faked for Lloyd used no double. He was protected from a possible fall by mattress-piled platform some way beneath; from where he was acting the platform did not look over-large.

He belonged essentially to the silent screen, with all its energy, mime and movement, and, like so many of his contemporaries, he was unable to hold his preeminent position after the coming of sound; but by then he had enjoyed a decade of unqualified success.

His career followed the standard pattern of the silent comedian, for he was the product of both the Mack Sennett and the Hal Roach schools of comedy. He was born on April 20, 1893, in Burchard, a small village in Nebraska, where his father was a salesman. As a boy of 12 he met John Lane Connor, an actor who ran a dramatic school, and for him made his debut on the stage as Little Abe in *Tess of the D'Urbervilles*. His father was delighted, and later sent Harold to the San Diego Dramatic School, where he yearned to become a great dramatic actor, but was advised to try comedy instead.

He drifted to Hollywood, where he became friendly with an extra player named Hal Roach. Roach inherited a small sum of money and started making short comedies, and Lloyd was put to work as a comedian. Everyone was imitating Chaplin at that time, and Lloyd did the same. He left Roach for a time to try his hand with Mack Sennett and his Keystone Cops, but later returned to Roach, this time as a character in the Chaplin style called "Lonesome Luke" and with a 15-year-old "leading lady" named Bebe Daniels.

It was in 1917 that the chance purchase of a pair of spectacles altered his career. He bought them in Los Angeles with the idea that they might fit in well with the rather earnest, simple type of character in which he specialized. The effect was to provide him with originality. He ceased to imitate the Chaplin style of comedy and struck out on his own, and it was not long before he had made such a name for himself that he was even being considered as a serious rival to Chaplin. He represented a serious, well-intentioned and rather humourless young man in a world of crooks and city slickers,

and therefore appealed strongly to the teenage members of his audiences as well as to the older ones. His comedy was always wholesome, and a Harold Lloyd film was essentially something for the family as a whole.

Although the coming of sound was a handicap to him, he experienced no difficulty in the change from short films to longer ones, and *Grandma's Boy*, one of his early silent films which ran for nearly an hour, was so good that Chaplin wrote to thank him for the inspiration he had found in it. Lloyd's silent films are too numerous to mention, but they included *Doctor's Orders, Safety Last, Why Worry?, College Days, The Kid Brother, For Heaven's Sake, Speedy, Girl Shy*, and many others.

His last silent film was *Welcome Danger*, made in 1929. He realized at once that sound had come to stay, and that he must try to adapt himself to it. But he also realized that sound, especially as it was used in the early days, could only have the effect of slowing down the pace of comedy. His first sound picture was *Feet First*, made for Paramount in 1932, and this was followed by *Movie Crazy, The Cat's Paw, The Milky Way*, and, in 1938, *Professor Beware*. During the war he turned producer, and it was not until 1947 that he decided to return once again to the screen as a comedian. *Mad Wednesday* (known also as *The Sin of Harold Diddlebock*) was a return to the material of his youth, and showed the hero as a college boy scoring the winning try in a big football game. It was written and directed by Preston Sturges, but was not shown until 1951. It was only moderately successful, and was handicapped by the fact that one of the best of his prewar comedies, *Movie Crazy*, had been revived only the year before. Moreover the choice of subject in *Mad Wednesday* revealed an inherent weakness in Lloyd's style.

Lloyd was never one of the truly great comedians of the screen. His comedy sprang largely from ingenious "gags" and "props", and the central character, though lovable, was superficial. Hal Roach, who produced so many of his films, said of him that he had not a funny bone in his body, but was such a good actor that he could always be relied upon to get the maximum number of laughs from a good script. The agility, zest and tremendous pace which he revealed in his pictures made him outstandingly successful in the golden era of film comedy which lasted from 1920 until the coming of sound. The comment that he was for long a serious rival to Chaplin is, in itself, the highest compliment that can be paid to him.

He married Mildred Davis, who had acted with him. She died in 1969.

March 10, 1971.

Lloyd-Greame—See Swinton.

Dr. William Ernest Lloyd, M.D., F.R.C.P., who died on May 26, 1975, was one of a trio of Welshmen who brought international fame to the Westminster Hospital as a centre for the surgical treatment of diseases of the chest. He was the physician; the other two were the outstanding chest surgeons, Tudor Edwards and Sir Clement Price Thomas. All three were also on the staff of the Brompton Hospital for Diseases of the Chest.

It was Tudor Edwards and later Sir Clement Price Thomas and their surgical colleagues at the Brompton Hospital who pioneered lung surgery in Britain and the excellent results now obtained with such operations are largely due to their efforts. To achieve such excellent results they were dependent to a large extent upon the clinical skills of their physician colleagues including Dr. Lloyd.

Not only was he a skilled general physician as well as a chest physician; he had also a sympathetic understanding of his patients which, combined with his inherent modesty (as exemplified, for example, by the brevity of his entry in *Who's Who*) endeared him to all who came to him for advice. Indeed, he would probably be happiest if he felt that his memory was enshrined in the respect and affection of his patients rather than his professional reputation among his colleagues. All, however, who came in contact with Ernest Lloyd, whether patients, colleagues or students, had the greatest respect and affection for him, and he fully earned the title of "much loved physician" bestowed on him in the history of the Westminster Hospital published in 1966.

Dr. Lloyd qualified from St. Bartholomew's Hospital in 1921, proceeding to his M.D. (with gold medal) of London University in 1925. He was elected a Fellow of the Royal College of Physicians of London in 1934, and in 1951 he delivered the Mitchell Lecture before the college.

May 30, 1975.

Frances, Lady Lloyd George of Dwyfor, C.B.E., who died on December 5, 1972, was the second wife of the war-time leader and Liberal statesman, whom she married at Guildford register office in 1943; but, in her own words, "our real marriage had taken place 30 years before".

As a young school teacher she joined Lloyd George's household to coach his daughter Megan* and, flat against the promptings of her Victorian upbringing and wish for a conventional married life, she fell for him at their first interview feeling a "magnetism which made my heart leap and swept aside my judgment, producing an excitement which seemed to permeate my entire being. I was strung to the utmost point of awareness by this strange encounter which meant so much to me then and for ever after. I was enslaved for the rest of my life."

She had been born in the year of his first marriage, but disparity of age proved no barrier to their long unbroken intimacy. Attraction was mutal. From the start, however, he made no bones about wanting her as mistress and secretary—not as wife. He gave her a copy of Kitty O'Shea's book on Parnell, the Irish leader whose political career had been ruined in the "stench of the divorce courts," and told her bluntly that she must not hope for marriage until he became a widower. On these terms she was installed as private secretary and had an active share in the ups and downs of his fortunes through peace and war and in and out of office.

Temperamentally they were on the same wavelength. He relied on her for solace in adversity and, when making decisions, turned to her, on occasion, for advice. As Miss Stevenson, the ever-present background figure in 10 Downing Street during his years as Prime Minister, she quickly grew to be familiar to callers from cabinet ministers downwards and even the most influential were glad to win her ear. There has been no obvious parallel case in British life of such an *éminence grise* on the distaff side. Thanks to her unswerving discretion—and to his lucky star—scandal was avoided, although the truth about this unusual relationship was common knowledge in and beyond the Westminster Square Mile and bitterly resented by members of Lloyd George's family, especially by Megan.

Frances Louise Stevenson was born in London in 1888 of mixed parentage. Her father came of sternly religious stock of old established Lanarkshire farmers. Her mother was the child of a Genoese artist who had broken away from the family business of producing playing cards in the Latin Quarter of Paris, married a French woman and settled in London. So Puritan and Bohemian strains mingled in Frances. Staying with her paternal grandmother she was forbidden to touch the piano on a Sunday except to play hymns. But by a precocious exercise of resourcefulness she evaded this prohibition, finding a cake-walk called *Stepping Heavenward* which was deemed to be permissible. Although her happy home life in South London was less strait-laced she got no encouragement from either parent for deviation from conventional social behaviour. In vain she defended herself when the Lloyd George affair was brewing; her mother's reaction to the confession was "I would rather see you dead at my feet".

By that stage she had already caused domestic distress by being an ardent, though not a militant, suffragist and avidly reading *Ann Veronica, The New Machiavelli* and other books by H. G. Wells, of which her mother strongly disapproved as unsuitable for the education of a young woman. An early passion for the Greek and Latin classics fired her with ambition to get a scholarship at Newnham or Girton. This was not to be achieved; instead she went from Clapham High School with a London scholarship to Royal Holloway College.

After taking her degree she taught at a Wimbledon girls' boarding school where she got into hot water for the rash remark, made in the presence of a pupil whose father was a canon, that "no one really believes in the Thirty Nine Articles nowadays". It was from this post that, in 1911, she was recommended as a suitable person to take charge of the Chancellor of the Exchequer's youngest daughter, Megan, who was backward in elementary subjects. Thus began the historic liaison.

Soon after she received an offer of marriage from a rising civil servant and Lloyd George, being consulted, replied that she must do as she thought right. Almost immediately, however, he sent her an urgent letter telling her that something terrible had happened and that he needed her at once in London. She went and heard that the Marconi scandal was about to break. She stayed and saw him through it, as she was to do in so many later crises of his career. The Welsh wizard who could charm a bird off a tree in politics was no less a practised hand in the affairs of the heart. When Frances found him with red-rimmed eyes saying "I have to flog myself, otherwise I could not go on", he had her where he wanted her—and "I wanted more than anything to help him".

Thereafter she was always at his side. She had the stamina to keep up with his dynamic vitality during the war years, being a power in her own right behind the scenes at home and accompanying him to Italy in 1917 after the Caporetto disaster. If things looked black for him, as in the parliamentary battle caused by General Maurice's challenge to his figures on manpower in the army, she had no scruple over helping him out of tight corners, even involving suppression of a key document.

Always assiduous in guarding Lloyd George's health, she prospected the Surrey site on which he built Bron-y-de, the country home he came to delight in, with Beaverbrook* as their near neighbour. When he was bored she cheered him with a supply of "shilling shockers" (as he called them) and American wild west stories. Her faith in him did not flag in the long out-of-power period and, when war came, she tried to get him back in office under Churchill,* although he was visibly failing. Before this she had tackled the mammoth task of assembling the mass of documents, personal and official, used in his memoirs, and handled them as efficiently as, earlier, she organized a filing system of newspaper cuttings and quotations from opponents to provide deadly ammunition for his speeches.

She was made C.B.E. in 1918 and published in 1967 her volume of revealing recollections, *The Years that are Past*. In 1971 she published *Lloyd George: A Diary;* this was edited by A. J. P. Taylor.

December 7, 1972.

Marie Löhr, the actress, who died on January 21, 1975 in Brighton, at the age of 84, made her debut as a child of four and continued acting until she passed the age of 75. As leading lady and actress-manageress she had more than her share of vicissitudes, but in later years she was the object of that special kind of affection which players and audiences reserve for the good trouper.

Marie Löhr, the daughter of Lewis J. Löhr, a former treasurer of the Opera House, Melbourne, and of his wife Kate Bishop, a member of a well known English theatrical family, was born in Sydney, New South Wales, on July 28, 1890 and first appeared as a child actress in that city.

She was 11 when she first played in London, and 12 when William and Madge Kendal, her godparents, first took her with them on tour. She returned to the Kendals after some experience of musical comedy and again after an engagement with Tree at His Majesty's.

Even when she had made a real success at the Haymarket in 1907, her godmother insisted on her rejoining the Kendal company for their autumn tour: "Yes, you must come back, you can still learn some more from me."

In 1908 she was in the original production of Shaw's *Getting Married,* but was then re-engaged for His Majesty's where she played Margaret in a new adaptation of *Faust,* Hannele in Gerhart Hauptmann's play of that name, Lydia in Shaw's *The Admirable Bashville,* Lady Teazle to Tree's Sir Peter Teazle, without a rehearsal, because Tree had done the play so often that he could not bear to rehearse her in it, and Ophelia to his Hamlet.

In *Smith* Somerset Maugham* wrote for her the part of a parlour maid, country bred, who struck her mistress's brother as being a suitable wife for a farmer and empire builder. To be what A. B. Walkley in *The Times* called a sugar sprite or else (a word much favoured by him) a "roguey-poguey", was continually required of her, not in her best interests as an actress, although the plays included old and new examples of the work of such highly esteemed writers as Pinero and Barrie.

In 1911 she had married Anthony Prinsep, son of the late Val Prinsep, R.A., and in 1918 her position in the theatre seemed to warrant their entering into management at the Globe, their first production being a new play by Maugham.

Several comedies presented by her, including Lonsdale's *Aren't We All?* were acknowledged to have merit, but her failures came to be more remarked upon than her successes, and the Löhr-Prinsep management acquired the reputation of being unlucky.

Maugham's *Our Betters* in 1923 was an enormous success, but Marie Löhr did not appear in it or in any of the plays subsequently presented by Prinsep at the Globe, another actress having replaced her as that theatre's permanent leading lady.

She took engagements elsewhere, and, thanks to a talent for light comedy which she revealed in Maugham's *Caroline* two years before her marriage was dissolved, and to the authority that she could bring into play at will, she made a success of the second half of her career.

She had fresh opportunities, appropriate to her age, of interpreting some of her old authors: Barrie, in revivals of *Peter Pan,* as Mrs. Darling; Pinero in revivals of *Dandy Dick* and *The Benefit of the Doubt;* Maugham in *The Breadwinner* in London and in New York; and Lonsdale, in revivals of *Aren't We All?* She was also seen in the comedies of younger playwrights such as Dodie Smith and Esther McCracken and in musical plays ranging from Clemence Dane* and Richard Addinsell's *Adam's Opera* at the Old Vic to Ivor Novello's *Crest of the Wave* at Drury Lane.

After the Second World War her presence and sonorous tones helped to make outstanding figures of the doyenne of the company in Rattigan's comedy of life in the English theatre, *Harlequinade,* and of the Amazonian sergeant-major in John Whiting's comedy of life in England during the Napoleonic wars, *A Penny for a Song.*

She served Noël Coward equally well in 1960—in *Waiting in the Wings* after falling down and breaking her wrist on the very day of the London opening—as a super-annuated classical actress not at all reconciled to her retirement.

In her film career, which began in 1932, two of her best roles were Shavian: Mrs. Higgins in Asquith's* *Pygmalion* and Lady Britomart in Pascal's *Major Barbara.* Her last stage appearance in the West End, in 1965-66, was, again, as a Shavian mother, namely Mrs. Whitefield (to Sian Phillips's Ann Whitefield) in *Man and Superman.*

Anthony Prinsep, her former husband, died in 1942. There was a daughter of the marriage.

January 24, 1975.

Mark Longman, one of the most able and popular figures in the world of publishing, died on September 6, 1972 at the age of 55.

He was president and former chairman of the Longman Group of Publishing Companies, a director of Pearson Longman Ltd., and vice-chairman of the Penguin Publishing Company.

Mark Frederic Kerr Longman was born on November 12, 1916, the son of Henry Kerr Longman and Margot Amy Cecil Russell. Educated at Eton and Trinity College, Cambridge, he joined the staff of Longmans Green in 1938 and went through a thorough and realistic apprenticeship up to the outbreak of war. Then he served as a captain in the City of London Yeomanry in Africa and Europe.

He returned to the family firm in 1946, when he took over and built up the general publishing list from his uncle Robert Long-

man, becoming a director the next year.

In 1968 he initiated and handled the negotiations which resulted in the take-over of Longmans Green by S. Pearson and Son, leading to the formation of Pearson Longman Ltd. He also took the major part in the Penguin merger after Sir Allen Lane's* death.

As president of the Publishers' Association (1969 to 1971) he was an outstanding success. He helped to overcome the threat of S.E.T. and became an expert on the complex problems arising out of new international copyright proposals. His unstinting efforts gained him widespread admiration and sympathy at a time of illness and pain. The Longman family link with the Publishers' Association goes back to 1896, when C. J. Longman was the first president.

Longman's work as chairman of the National Book League did more than simply tide it over a difficult period. He gained enough support to enable the league to continue and to expand. At the same time he was treasurer of the English-Speaking Union and chairman of the Fine Arts Society.

He had many friends in American publishing circles and much enjoyed his frequent visits to New York. His energetic diplomacy and instant grasp of local difficulties overseas enabled him to further the interests of British publishing and of his own firm most advantageously. He visited most of the countries which were developing new publishing ventures especially in the field of education. In particular, few other publishers so well understood the implications of the wind of change in Africa in relation to the need for revolutionary publishing policies based on local organization and control.

The quality of his personality stood out in the concern he showed for people and for publishing causes. Devoid of all conceit or pomposity, he was readily accessible to everyone, while his genuine charm and friendliness were combined with considerable business acumen.

When Mark Longman chaired a meeting or made a speech it was usually a lively affair as he made judicious and well-timed use of a slightly eccentric vocabulary which nicely embellished and brightened such occasions. His death breaks the continuous connexion of seven generations of the Longman family with the firm since it was founded by Thomas Longman in 1724.

In 1949 he married Lady Elizabeth Lambart, daughter of the tenth Earl of Cavan, and they had three daughters.

September 7, 1972.

Dame Kathleen Lonsdale, D.B.E., F.R.S., Professor of Chemistry and Head of Department of Crystallography, University College London from 1949 to 1968, died on April 1, 1971 at the age of 68.

Crystallographer, Quaker and pacifist, she

was the first woman President of the British Association for the Advancement of Science. Her presidential address delivered in 1968 was a characteristic utterance aiming darts at a variety of targets: the uses of science and technology; the sale of arms; the narrowness of many scientists; and responsibility of scientists as a whole for the use made of their discoveries.

Born January 28, 1903, Kathleen Yardley was the youngest of a large family which had a distant connexion with the makers of perfume. Certainly in later life her appearance was more suggestive of lavender than of the professor, Dame of the British Empire, vice-president of the Royal Society. The camera could catch her, when she was serious, to give a typical slightly grim look, partly attributable to a depth of eyes exaggerated by lenses, but normally she looked quietly happy. Simply dressed, she was in no way unfeminine. Her hair was usually allowed to blow in the wind and could take on a slightly golliwog form. When she was summoned to Buckingham Palace, on the same day as the leading ballerina, she made herself a neat hat for a few shillings.

After taking her first London degree from Bedford College for Women she became research assistant to Sir William Bragg at the Royal Institution in 1922. At that time X-ray diffraction methods, pioneered by the Braggs, had been applied to determine the arrangement of atoms in the crystalline forms of a few fairly simple chemical substances. The possibility of determining almost any crystal structure, however complex, could be seen, but the practical difficulties seemed very great. The relative position of a few atoms could be found; no one yet thought of tackling the detailed structure of a protein containing thousands of atoms though the possible revolutionary effects on the biological sciences could be foreseen.

In fact the general forms but not the dimensions and structural details of the simplest molecules of organic compounds were still known almost entirely from chemists' inferences. In particular the form of the benzene ring, a group of six carbon atoms, the basis of "aromatic" chemistry and perhaps the most disputed of all molecular structures, had not been determined. Kathleen Lonsdale investigated some other organic substances, and years later recalled with glee that her doctorate was awarded for a structure that later was found to have errors, but her first outstanding achievement was to find the structure of the hexamethylbenzene molecule. This showed that the benzene ring consisted of a flat regular hexagon of the six carbon atoms with the other six carbon atoms of attached methyl groups coplanar with the ring. Previously there was no certainty that it was not a puckered non-planar ring and though it was expected by many that all the sides would be equal there were as many who would not have been surprised had it been otherwise. Even today the aromatic ring is for convenience often represented by a drawing suggestive of alternate longer and shorter sides though this first aromatic crystal structure, and a host of others that came after it from the Royal Institution and elsewhere, established the essential equivalence of many carbon-to-carbon bonds which, in a single graphic formula of the molecule, are misrepresented. Much theoretical work on the nature of aromatic compounds followed this demonstration.

She held research appointments as Amy Lady Tate Scholar at Leeds University 1927-29, Leverhulme Research Fellow 1935-37, Dewar Fellow at the Royal Institution 1944-46, Special Fellow of the United States Federal Health Service 1947, and in 1949 became Professor of Chemistry and Head of the Department of Crystallography at University College London. In all these posts she was active in research. Her interest was not in the determination of great numbers of crystal structures or in the unravelling of those of the greatest novelty or complexity. She dealt rather with some aspects of the physics of crystals, the fundamentals of structure determination and some key structures.

Her work included extensive investigations of diamonds, both natural and synthetic—by no means the simple matter that a first examination of this form of elementary carbon might suggest. This work was partly linked with the study of diffuse scattering of X-rays by crystals, which is often related to the movements of atoms in crystal lattices and so may be exploited as an aid to structure determination. She also made detailed studies of thermal movements of atoms in selected lattices at room temperature and at much lower temperatures. One series of investigations contained fundamental work on the magnetic susceptibilities of crystals. From magnetic measurements alone it was possible to calculate the orientations of aromatic molecules in crystals and independent proof of the nature of the complex atomic ring system in the phthalocyanine molecule was obtained.

She also played a great part in the development of her subject, stimulating and in a remarkable way assisting others engaged in it. She wrote a book on crystals and X-rays but is better known for a number of invaluable aids to crystal structure determination. With Astbury, early in her career she put out fault-free descriptions of the 230 Fedorov space groups, a tiresome and difficult feat. In 1936, when the need was felt, she published the first simplified and practical forms of tabulated mathematical formulae for X-ray crystal structure analysis, first working them out and then, in her own neat script, writing nearly two hundred pages of them so that they could be reproduced without the possibility of printer's errors. Later she was general editor for the International Union of Crystallography of the several massive volumes of its International Tables. She served on national and international committees which foster the subject. Her work can be seen in great numbers of scientific communications which do not bear her name.

Many honours came to her from universities and scientific societies at home and throughout the world and she visited many countries to lecture on her work. In 1945 she was elected Fellow of the Royal Society, one of the first women to join it. She was awarded the society's Davy medal in 1957.

It is quite clear where the pursuit of scientific knowledge stood in relation to her adherence to Quaker principles. "We utterly deny all outward wars and strife, and fightings with outward weapons, for any end, or under any pretence whatever; this is our testimony to the whole world." These are the words of Declaration to Charles II, 1660, which she repeats as preface to *Quakers Visit Russia*.

Once, as a result of her writing to *The Times* complaining about the difficulty of getting funds for certain scientific purposes, a military organization offered support in the form of research contracts. Her reply must have been polite, powerful, and final. When asked, for purposes of obtaining an entry visa, whether she belonged to any peace societies she replied "as many as I can afford". When similarly asked to state her race she said "human". The visit of seven Quakers to Russia in 1951 was made to explain the methods which they believed essential if peace was to be achieved. They did not succeed in seeing Stalin, Gromyko or Vyshinsky but were received by Malik at the Foreign Office and talked for some hours. The talk seems to have been straight and followed lines that might have been predicted. They met representatives of the Soviet press, the Soviet Peace Committee, and leaders of the Baptist and of the Eastern Orthodox Churches. Kathleen Lonsdale said that the party and those they represented may have been idealists but not simpletons. They were not being "used" by others. What the effect was or may be is not for those of limited knowledge to conjecture. Her other public contributions to peace causes include the Swarthmore Lecture (1953) on "Removing the Causes of War" and the Penguin Special *Is Peace Possible?* in 1957.

To the Quaker, conscription for military training is an offence against the human spirit. What service the individual may voluntarily undertake is a matter of conscience. When compulsory firewatching for civilians was introduced after some of the great air raids in Britain no one bothered about a conscience clause similar to that applicable to ordinary military service. Men and women were called upon to register. Kathleen Lonsdale responded in a way that was inevitable. She did not object to fire-watching—in fact was already doing it —but the Act, without the clause, was contrary to principle. She knew that her three small children would exempt her but she failed to register. Authority could not budge so eventually she refused to pay the fine and went to Holloway. Someone else paid the fine so her stay was short, but she learnt a lot, including the reason for the temporarily assumed religious adherence of the more knowing ladies in detention. It has something to do with lipstick-substitutes and she must have learnt it when they heard, probably for the first time, of the Quaker way of things. She would not wish this incident to be suppressed, though she certainly never used it in any boastful way.

Aggressiveness had to show somewhere. She was forthright in committee and inclined, with the best intentions, to stick to rules sometimes to the extent of blocking action. Sessions of the Assembly of the International Union of Crystallography, over which she presided, in Moscow in 1966, were prolonged until she was satisfied that the right things were done and were done in the right way. Walking down the staircase at the British Embassy from a pleasant party, broken off too soon for him, her successor, Professor Belov, as she dragged him on to another committee meeting, was heard to say "Kathleen, you are a martinet".

In 1927 she married Dr. T. J. Lonsdale, physicist (and Quaker) like herself. She had a son and two daughters.

April 2, 1971.

Fyodor Lopukhov, the distinguished Russian choreographer and ballet director, died in Leningrad on January 28, 1973. He was 86.

He was born in that city, then St. Petersburg, in October 1886, one of the five children of an usher at the Imperial Alexandrinsky Theatre and his German-Scottish wife. All but one of the children became dancers; Fyodor entered the Maryinsky school in 1896 and graduated in 1905, having for his examination performance the role of Acis in the premiere of Fokine's first ballet, *Acis and Galatea.*

In spite of this promising start, his dancing career appears to have been less notable than that of his sister Eugenia and brother Andrei, both greatly admired as character dancers in their native land, or of his other sister who, as Lydia Lopokova, was one of Diaghilev's stars and later settled in England as the wife of Maynard Keynes. However, Fyodor soon showed an interest in choreography, where his earliest achievements included solos in a pastiche of Petipa's style, one of which, for the Lilac Fairy in *The Sleeping Beauty*, has been accepted in all subsequent productions.

As early as 1916 Lopukhov wrote a book (published in 1925) entitled *Paths of the Ballet Master* in which he developed comprehensive theories of a symphonic ballet, an idea which caused great controversy in the west two decades later. He used his ideas in *Dance Symphony*, to Beethoven's *Fourth Symphony*, at the Maly Theatre in 1923. The extent of his range was shown by *The Red Whirlwind* the following year, the first attempt at a specifically Soviet revolutionary ballet, with speech, song, acrobatics and dancing.

In the course of a long career Lopukhov had periods out of favour but for many years he directed, successively, the Kirov and Maly companies in Leningrad and staged ballets also for many others. He could be revolutionary in his inventions, for instance in a staging of *The Nutcracker* where the ballerina was carried on stage upside down doing the splits, but he could be lightly humorous or charming too, and had a genuine concern to preserve the classical tradition, manifested in his careful revivals of *Sleeping Beauty* and *Swan Lake.* One of his innovations, the trick of carrying a ballerina high above her partner's head, has passed into general usage, first in Russian ballet and subsequently in the west.

Besides his early treatise, Lopukhov published an autobiography, *Sixty Years of Ballet* (1966) and *Choreographic Confessions* (1971). He was awarded the titles People's Artist of the R.S.F.S.R. and also, uniquely, Honoured Ballet Master. His wife Maya was a dancer and their son Vladimir entered the Kirov Ballet in 1965.

February 8, 1973.

Tilly Losch, the dancer and actress, died in New York on December 24, 1975 at the age of 68.

Ottilie Ethel Losch was born in Vienna on November 15, 1907 and made her first stage appearance in 1912 at the Stadt Opera House, Vienna, as a child dancer in *Wiener Wältzer.* She appeared later in Korngold's ballet *Das Schneemädchen* and became première danseuse of the opera house. She was associated with Max Reinhardt's company in Vienna and Berlin, and went with it to the United States in 1927, dancing in a number of productions in New York.

Her first visit to London, where she was to captivate audiences of the 1930s, was in 1928, when she appeared at the London Pavilion in Cochran's *This Year of Grace.* She danced for Reinhardt again at the Salzburg Festival later that year, but returned to London in 1929 to appear in *Wake Up and Dream.*

After two more years in the United States she returned to London for a longer period, forming her own company, Les Ballets, in 1933, and appearing at the Savoy Theatre, the Palace and the Ambassadors.

Besides being a dancer she appeared in films and was also an artist of some note. Exhibitions of her work were held in London, New York, Philadelphia and San Francisco.

She was twice married, first in 1931, to Mr. Edward Francis Willis James, from whom she was divorced in 1934. Her second marriage, in 1939, was to the Earl of Carnarvon. This marriage ended in divorce in 1947.

December 27, 1975.

Sir Francis Low, for nearly 15 years editor of *The Times of India*, Bombay, and later its London representative, died at the age of 78 on September 18, 1972.

He was born on November 19, 1893, son of Francis Low, of Finzean, Aberdeenshire. He was educated at the Robert Gordon College, Aberdeen. In 1910 he began as a reporter on the staff of the Aberdeen Free Press. He served in the First World War, being commissioned to the 4th Battalion Gordon Highlanders in 1916, and later was attached to the 6th Battalion Hampshire Regiment. He was in the Mesopotamian campaign during which he was appointed to the Intelligence Staff I Corps in 1918; in the following year, he was a Special Staff Officer at the G.H.Q. there. In 1920, he returned to his paper in Aberdeen as chief reporter.

Two years later, in 1922, Low went out to Bombay as a sub-editor on *The Times of India*, then under the virile charge of Sir Stanley Reed*. In 1923, he was made editor of *The Evening News of India*, but within two years was back on the morning daily in the capacity of news editor. Three years later, he was selected to be assistant editor, and in 1932 he succeeded "Sammy" Sheppard in editorial charge.

Low was to guide *The Times of India* through the most tempestuous years of India's modern history. Clear-sighted, able to establish easy communications with the rising leadership of the nationalist movement, enjoying the confidence and respect of his staff, he helped *The Times of India* grow into a major forum of opinion. During his tenure as editor, he had to pilot his great paper through the heavy seas of the war period. He preserved his remarkable sense of fair play during the anxious, tension-charged years which were to come to a climax with the transfer of power. His knighthood, bestowed in 1943, was richly deserved.

Trained in all the departments of a newspaper, and more than ordinarily conscious of the threat which advertising columns posed to news columns, he was able to widen the coverage of *The Times of India* and to improve the quality and content of reporting. As a result, the sales of the paper were soon larger than any other in India. A diligent worker, he never lost touch with his craft; he tracked down proofing errors, checked sloppy displays and had a critical eye for printing deficiencies. In addition, he maintained a considerable correspondence with readers, or what he used to describe as his one-man public relations effort. This desire to build a living contact with India was best seen at the question-and-answer meetings popularized through the Y.M.C.A. in Bombay during the explosive war years.

Low was sometime chairman of the Indian branch of what is now the Commonwealth Press Union, and led the delegations from that country to the conference of the Union held in London in 1946. His anxieties were much increased when the paper and its great printing business were sold at high prices to the Dalmia group. On retiring from the editorship in 1948 he became the London representative of the paper, which was no easy post in the circumstances.

He married in 1926 Margaret H. Adams, and they had two sons and a daughter.

September 20, 1972.

Sir Denys Lowson, BT., financier and former Lord Mayor of London, died on September 10, 1975 at the age of 69.

Born in 1906, Lowson was educated at Winchester and Christ Church, Oxford, and was called to the Bar in 1930. He began rapidly to establish a position in the City in the field of unit trusts and, during the 1940s, gained control of the National Group of Unit Trusts, which was to be the centre of his post-war financial empire. He became the youngest Lord Mayor of modern times in 1950-51, the year of the Festival of Britain, at the age of 44. As Lord Mayor he showed a flair for publicity.

In his personal affairs, however, he shunned such exposure. His empire was a tangle of cross-shareholdings, based on some 100 trading and industrial companies throughout the world, owned and controlled, at the end, through 14 often interrelated investment trusts.

In 1974, following exposures in the *Investors' Chronicle*, inspectors appointed by the Secretary of State for Trade and Industry accused Sir Denys of grave mismanagement of companies in his control. They concluded that his motive was "to obtain very substantial gain for himself and his family". These charges arose out of an episode in 1972 when Sir Denys bought shares from the National Group, which he controlled, for about 62p. each, selling them again within a few months for £8.67 each. It was estimated that this personal transaction netted Sir Denys a profit of some £5m. The inspectors' interim report charged him with putting personal gain before his duty to the companies of which he was a director and to their shareholders.

Sir Denys admitted error and undertook to make substantial repayments. His counsel attributed his mistake to age, ill-health, obstinacy and secretiveness rather than to any intent to deceive. The inspectors rejected this defence, concluding that throughout his evidence to them he had demonstrated "a firm grasp of the points at issue".

Within a matter of weeks of the publication of that report in July 1974, Lowson had resigned from executive positions in the web of companies and trusts which he had totally and personally controlled in many cases for a quarter of a century and more. In rapidly failing health, he went on a round-the-world cruise in the QE2.

Lowson began his career in the City before the war, when the standards of financial morality and duty to shareholders were less developed than they are today. He showed consistently that he was more concerned to turn situations to the advantage of himself and the interests he controlled than with his fiduciary duty to the companies of which he was a director. His reputation in this respect was established with the more respected leaders of the City early in his career and his methods never represented the best City practice. In the quarter century since the war, however, the ethics of the City generally advanced in a way which placed Sir Denys increasingly out of tune with the City establishment.

Lowson, who became a baronet in 1951, was for many years closely involved in public affairs ranging over a wide field: a governor of well-known London hospitals; a former Master of City Livery Companies; a former member of the L.C.C. for the Cities of London and Westminster; and a president and vice-president of many national and Commonwealth organizations concerned with commerce and with philanthropy.

He married in 1936 the Hon. Anne Patricia Macpherson, younger daughter of the 1st Baron Strathcarron. They had a son, Mr. Ian Patrick Lowson, who succeeds his father, and two daughters.

September 11, 1975.

General Sir Henry Loyd, G.C.V.O., K.C.B., who died on November 11, 1973, had a distinguished career in the Army. He was Colonel of the Coldstream Guards from 1945 to 1966.

Henry Charles "Budget" Loyd was a man of strong and delightful personality. He had a good sense of humour, an uncommon degree of shrewd common sense combined with an imperturbable calm; and his considerable ability marked him as a leader from an early age. Above all he was a great Guardsman.

Loyd was born on February 21, 1891, the second son of Edward Loyd of Langleybury, Hertfordshire. He was educated at Eton and the Royal Military College, from which he was commissioned in the Coldstream Guards in 1910.

In the First World War he distinguished himself as a regimental officer and as a junior staff officer. He just missed a V.C. in the Battle of the Marne, but won the D.S.O., the M.C., and the French Croix de Guerre, and was three times mentioned in dispatches. By the end of the war, at the age of 27, he was an acting lieutenant-colonel in command of a battalion, and had been wounded four times.

Loyd was selected after the war for entry without examination to the staff college. He returned to Camberley as an instructor in 1925. Between the wars he held staff appointments at London District, in the War Office and at Aldershot, and he commanded, in succession, the 3rd Battalion the Coldstream Guards and the Regiment and Regimental District.

In 1936 he was promoted to brigadier and appointed Chief of Staff at Army Headquarters in Cairo, where he served for three years. On his return to England he was given command of the 1st Infantry Brigade. In 1939 he was selected to command the 2nd Division at Aldershot.

When the Second World War broke out it seemed certain that he was destined for high command in the field. But that was not to be.

He took his division to France with the B.E.F. and commanded it in the frontier defences south of Lille through the winter and spring of 1939-40. When the Germans invaded Belgium, his division took part in the advance to the river Dyle. A few days later, as the allied armies were beginning their withdrawal, he fell ill. He fainted during a discussion of plans for the retreat to the Escaut, and was sent back to England.

Many felt he should have been given another active command, but he never served again in a theatre of war.

He was back at duty in England almost at once, reorganizing and inspecting troops as they arrived from Dunkirk. When Lord Alanbrooke* became Commander-in-Chief, Home Forces, at the time when invasion seemed possible, he asked for Loyd as his Chief of Staff.

When that appointment ended in 1942, Loyd became Commander-in-Chief Southern Command, gaining a notable reputation as a trainer of troops. In 1944 he was transferred to London District and he held that command until his retirement in 1947.

He was made K.C.B. in 1943 and G.C.V.O. in 1965. He was A.D.C. General to King George VI 1946-47. He was a justice of the peace and a Deputy Lieutenant of Norfolk.

He married in 1922 Lady Moyra Brodrick, youngest daughter of the first Earl of Midleton; they had a son and a daughter.

November 12, 1973.

Dr. Heinrich Lübke, who died on April 6, 1972 at the age of 77, was under the double disadvantage on July 1, 1959, when he became second President of the West German Republic, of being the successor of Professor Theodor Heuss* and a stop-gap for Dr. Konrad Adenauer.*

Professor Heuss had been outstandingly successful in the office and had embodied to perfection the concept of "scholar and gentleman" in the exceptionally difficult circumstances in which Germany found itself after defeat in Hitler's war of aggression. He did as much as any one man could as ceremonial head of state to restore his country's image as one of poets, philosophers and musicians.

But Lübke was made of quite other clay. He was born in a Westphalian village as the fourth child of a shoemaker and small farmer and eventually became Minister of Food and Agriculture in one of Dr. Adenauer's governments. He was liked for his solid qualities of honesty and dependability but had none of the mind and personality that had made Professor Heuss admired and respected as well as loved, and he was also hampered by having been chosen as a stop-gap after Dr. Adenauer suddenly declined the honour on finding it did not carry as much power as he thought.

Dr. Lübke's lack of enemies became suddenly valuable. In the midst of the row that surrounded his election the stop-gap candidate himself remained supremely unconcerned. Indeed he was quoted as saying only 24 hours before the election that "as the day of execution approaches the better I feel".

As soon as it was all over the new President began to show not only that he meant to enjoy his office but that he was capable of making a better job of it than most of those who had voted for him would have thought possible.

During the nearly 10 years of his presidency (he was re-elected in 1964) he represented his country as head of state in most parts of the world. He did so with dignity, even though there were always some to poke fun at the simplicity of his speech and his linguistic lapses, especially in English, some of which were published in a book.

Although without Dr. Adenauer's ambition, Lübke showed from time to time at least a desire to exploit such possibilities as his office offered. The constitution allowed him to keep himself informed and this he did at times when governments were being formed. He went farther on one or two occasions and was criticized for lacking impartiality, especially at the time of the government crisis of 1966, when he worked almost openly for a "grand coalition" of Christian Democrats and Social Democrats. His reason for preferring this to a revised version of Dr. Erhard's out-going Christian Democrat-Free Democrat alliance may have been that the Free Democrats had voted against him at the time of his reelection in 1964. As it happened, the Grand Coalition did come about, though without any part being played by the president's views.

When Dr. Lübke (honoris causa Bonn University) first became president, journalists asking for material about his early life were told by his own staff that they knew very little about it. They, too, had been taken by surprise. They later made known that the new president had been born in 1894 in the village of Enkhausen and had attended the local grammar school. He had studied architecture and engineering, community development and agriculture in the universities of Bonn, Berlin and Münster. He had been a lieutenant in the First World War and had then settled down from 1922 as manager of the Combined Farmers' Federation. He was a Centre Party member of the Prussian Landtag (parliament) until expelled by the Nazis in

1933 and imprisoned by them for 20 months. From 1935 to 1944 he worked for a building construction firm. Later he was accused by the east German communists of having constructed concentration camps during this period.

Suspicion was never quite dispelled, and after allegations in a west German magazine in 1968 a political storm brewed up and Dr. Lübke appeared on television to say that he had worked only on living quarters and could not remember every piece of paper he had signed. It was not, he said, part of his duties to sign blueprints for wooden barracks.

After a period in the *Land* parliament of North Rhine-Westphalia after the war, he became a Christian Democratic deputy in Bonn. In 1953 he became Minister of Food and Agriculture and was a special friend of small farmers during the difficult period when German agriculture was being modernized. He was praised by the Social Democrats as a "man without enemies," although some of the larger farmers complained that their interests were neglected.

He leaves a widow.

April 7, 1972.

___

Admiral Sir David Luce, G.C.B., D.S.O., O.B.E., who retired as First Sea Lord in 1966 in protest against the Government's abandoning of the aircraft carrier programme, died on January 6, 1971. He was 64.

Luce, who was appointed Chief of Naval Staff and First Sea Lord in 1963, retired when the Government's Defence White Paper was published, outlining cuts by a third in overseas defence. Christopher Mayhew, Minister of Defence for the Navy, resigned shortly before.

Luce was head of the three-Service command established in the Far East from 1962 to 1963, where, in initiating this new type of command in the Far East, he exercised a tact and diplomacy that provided a blueprint for such establishments. He was a submarine specialist.

Luce's wartime service—apart from submarines—was with Combined Operations with Admiral of the Fleet Lord Mountbatten, and he was Chief Staff Officer to the naval forces at the invasion of Normandy.

After the war he was Deputy Director of Plans in the Admiralty, in command of the cruisers Liverpool and Birmingham, and, upon his promotion to flag rank, he served as naval secretary to J. P. L. Thomas (afterwards Lord Cilcenin), and was Flag Officer Flotillas Home Fleet. In 1958 he was promoted Vice-Admiral and appointed Flag Officer, Scotland.

Luce entered the Navy in 1911; he won his D.S.O., early in the Second World War for good services during successful submarine patrols and operations against the enemy. He was awarded the O.B.E., in 1942

for skill and resource displayed during the amphibious attack on Dieppe.

From 1960 to 1962 he was C.-in-C. Far East Station; and later United Kingdom Military Adviser to Seato.

Luce married in 1935 Mary Adelaide Norah Whitham, and they had two sons.

January 7, 1971,

___

Frank Ludlow, O.B.E., a notable traveller in the Western and Eastern Himalayas, and more particularly in south-eastern Tibet, died on March 25, 1972. His name is best known in horticultural circles for the rich influx of hardy plants to Britain from expeditions undertaken jointly with Major George Sherriff and a few other companions.

Ludlow was born in Chelsea on August 10, 1885 and graduated at Cambridge in 1908. During the First World War he was commissioned with the 97th India Infantry and served for some time in Mesopotamia.

It was while Ludlow was in the Indian Educational Service that he was asked to recommend someone to open a school in Gyantse in Tibet, to teach Tibetans of good family the rudiments of western education. The remuneration offered was not high but Ludlow, sensing a challenge to his adventuresome nature, proposed himself for the job and was appointed. He went to Gyantse in October 1923 and remained until October 1926 when the school was closed because the Lama element was too antagonistic towards, and feared Ludlow's influence on, the young, impressionable Tibetans. Nevertheless, Ludlow remained *persona grata* with the Tibetan Government and was allowed access to the country over a period of years with chosen companions—a privilege which was almost unique. Most of Ludlow's pupils rose to high office in the Tibetan Government.

In 1927, the year in which he was given the O.B.E., he retired to Srinagar in Kashmir, and from this date he started travelling extensively, collecting birds and plants for the British Museum of Natural History. In 1928 Ludlow went on a shooting and collecting expedition to Turkistan, and in Kashgar met Sherriff, and thus started a friendship which led to a series of extremely rewarding expeditions to the eastern Himalayas and to south-east Tibet.

It was while on his way to Kashgar in 1928 that Ludlow gained the impression that the Shyok Dam, which impounded a lake 14 miles long, was unsafe and he predicted its collapse if it was not strengthened. The Punjab Government got to know of this premonition and invited Ludlow in the spring of 1929 to accompany the surveying party to inspect the wall of the dam and estimate the volume of water, but before reinforcements could be made, the barrier collapsed, fortunately without loss of life.

He several times went to Kashgar and Tibet to collect birds and plants.

Ludlow became Joint Commissioner in Ladakh in 1940, but in March 1942 he was sent to Lhasa to persuade the Tibetan Government to allow supplies to pass through Tibet to China. He remained in charge of the British Mission until 1943, and he then returned to Ladakh where he served until 1946 as Joint Commissioner.

Ludlow was a most retiring, modest man who shunned publicity. He returned to Britain in 1947 to work on his plant collections at the Natural History Museum.

March 27, 1972.

Air Chief Marshal Sir Edgar R. Ludlow-Hewitt, G.C.B., G.B.E., C.M.G., D.S.O., M.C., who died on August 15, 1973 at the age of 87, was a gifted and zealous officer whose service in the Army, R.F.C. and R.A.F. extended over 40 years.

After distinguished service in France during the First World War, when he rose to the rank of brigadier-general at the age of 31, he held a number of staff and command posts with success. As head of the Staff College from 1926 to 1930 he helped to lay the foundations of the successful conduct of the war in the air a decade later. As Deputy Chief of the Air Staff he was responsible for dealing with many complex problems arising out of the first expansion programme and the introduction of new types of aircraft and equipment. As Commander-in-Chief Bomber Command, in 1939-40 he planned the first bombing raids on Germany and the successful reconnaissances and leaflet raids across Germany, Austria, Czechoslavakia and Poland.

Edgar Rainey Ludlow-Hewitt was born on June 9, 1886, the second son of the Rev. Thomas A. Ludlow-Hewitt. He was educated at Radley and Sandhurst, and in August 1905 was commissioned to The Royal Irish Rifles, with which he served until 1914. In that year, before war began, he learnt to fly at Upavon. He was appointed to the Royal Flying Corps on probation in August 1914.

In 1915 he joined No. 1 Squadron in France, where he took part in some successful bombing raids during the Battle of Neuve Chapelle and reconnaissance work before and during the fighting at Hill 60. Later he commanded No. 3 Squadron, and in February 1916 he was promoted wing-commander and temporary lieutenant-colonel to command the Third Corps Wing at Bertangles. He was awarded the Military Cross in 1916 and the Croix de Chevalier, Legion of Honour, in 1917.

Between the wars he was Commandant of the R.A.F. Staff College, Andover (1926-30); Director of Operations and Intelligence, Air Ministry, and Deputy Chief of Staff (1933-35); A.O.C. India (1935-37); and then A.O.C.-in-C., Bomber Command, a post which he held when war broke out in 1939. From 1940 to 1945 he was Inspector-General of the R.A.F.

When in 1945 the Government decided to establish a College of Aeronautics for the engineering, technical and scientific training of students for leadership in the aricraft industry, civil aviation, and the Services, Ludlow-Hewitt was the obvious choice for the post of chairman of the board of governors.

He was appointed a Deputy Lieutenant for Wiltshire in 1953.

He married, in 1923, Albinia Mary, daughter of Major Edward Henry Evans-Lombe and widow of Francis William Talbot Clerke, Coldstream Guards. She died in 1972.

August 17, 1973.

György Lukács, the eminent Hungarian philosopher and critic, who was born in Budapest on April 13, 1885, son of a wealthy Jewish financier, died on June 4, 1971 at the age of 86.

Lukács became one of the leading figures in the history of Marxist thought, and although he was often at variance with the party leadership he not only remained a convinced Marxist but continued to live under a Communist regime.

After a brilliant academic career in Budapest, Berlin and Heidelberg, Lukács joined the newly-formed Hungarian Communist Party in December 1918, and in 1919 he was Commissar for Education in Bélar Kun's communist government. After Kun's overthrow Lukács went to Vienna, where he continued to be active in Party affairs and where he worked on his most famous book, *History and Class-Consciousness* (1923). The book was severely criticized at the Comintern Congress of 1924; Lukács later joined in the denunciation of his own work, and it was many years before he allowed it to be republished (1968).

On Hitler's rise to power Lukács took refuge in the Soviet Union, staying there from 1933 to 1944. In 1944 he returned to Hungary and was made Professor of Aesthetics at the University of Budapest. His writings again led him into trouble with the authorities in 1949, the year of the Rajk trial, and in 1951 Lukács decided to withdraw from public life. He emerged again, briefly, in 1956, when he was Minister of Culture in Imre Nagy's government. After the suppression of the Hungarian Revolution, Lukács was deported to Romania. He was allowed to return in 1957, but lost his university post and was expelled from the party. After a long period of disgrace he was taken into favour, and was readmitted to the party in 1967.

The Marxism expressed in Lukács's voluminous writings is of a very individual kind. It rests on three fundamental concepts, those of history, totality and class.

Lukács knew well that the first two of these are also important concepts in Hegel, and he always stressed the connexions between Hegelianism and Marxism. These two concepts appear in his pre-Marxist works: that of totality is present in his first important work, *The Soul and the Forms* (1910-11), which has been seen as a stage in the development of existentialism; and both totality and history are present in *The Theory of the Novel* (1916), in which Lukács applied history to aesthetic categories, regarding the novel as an epic form which arises under certain historical conditions. All three appear in *History and Class-Consciousness*. Here, totality is declared to be the fundamental category of reality, the recognition of which distinguishes Marxism from bourgeois science. Lukács means that every advance in knowledge is a move from a part towards the whole; it is also (another borrowing from Hegel) a move towards the identity of knowing subject and known object. But whereas Hegel could not find in history the totality which he sought, Lukács argued that the identical subject-object is to be found there—in the shape of the class-conscious proletariat. Lukács adds that the proletariat is also able to overcome the "reification" which is typical of bourgeois thought, and it was perhaps to what it said about reification (which is related to alienation, a concept which was to become so important in twentieth century Marxism) that the book owed much of its influence.

As a literary critic, Lukács worked within the established Marxist canons in taking "realism" to be the standard of artistic excellence. What made him distinctive as a critic were his attempts to deepen the concept of realism by distinguishing it from the merely representative, the skill and learning with which he related the work of art to its social context, and the range of his knowledge, which covered almost the whole of European literature.

Lukács also made solid contributions to the study of the history of philosophy. *The Young Hegel* (1948) stressed the importance of Hegel's study of the political economy; while *The Destruction of Reason* (1954) was a bitter but often shrewd indictment of post-Hegelian German philosophy.

Lukács's chief philosophical work, however, was in the field of aesthetics. *The Specific Nature of the Aesthetic* (1963) was intended to form part of a still larger work, but is in effect a kind of truncated *Summa* of Lukács aesthetic theory. The work tries to do justice to what is valid in non-Marxist thought; it also displays another aspect of Lukács, his humanism. Lukács asserts that art is man-centred and "this-worldly," and that "in its objective intention art is as hostile to religion as science is."

In his last years, Lukács struggled to complete an *Ontology of Social Being;* he also planned a work on Marxist ethics. He was a great rationalist and a great humanist, and in the encyclopaedic range of his work he bears comparison with those from whom he drew most, Marx and Hegel.

June 5, 1971.

Sir Arnold Lunn, author, controversialist, Catholic apologist, and guide to Switzerland, who was the leading English authority on skiing and the inventor of the slalom, died on June 2, 1974 at the age of 86.

The son of Sir Henry Lunn, who abandoned a promising business career to become a Methodist missionary in India and who then became head of the prosperous travel agency that bears his name, Arnold Lunn was born in Madras on April 18, 1888. From Harrow he went up to Balliol, where the versatility of his interests and his energy of body and mind might have seemed a shade unusual even to his Balliol contemporaries. He was, among other things, secretary of the Union, editor of *Isis*, and founder of the Oxford University Mountaineering Club. Switzerland was not simply a playground for him. He had known Grindelwald since childhood, while the *Alpine Journal*, in his own phrase, was his Bible at Harrow, and as a boy his pleasure in the scenery of the Swiss Alps went with strong feelings of attachment to the country and its people; it might fairly have been said that the Oberland was his second home.

The British addiction to winter sports in the Alps owes much to Lunn's enthusiasm and knowledge, and his many achievements in the world of skiing made him internationally famous.

Lunn first skied in 1898 in Chamonix. In 1908 he founded the Alpine Ski Club. In 1920 he became editor of the *British Ski Year Book* and achieved an unbroken series of over 50 productions—volumes of such high standard of content that they have done much to establish and maintain the reputation of the Ski Club of Great Britain all round the world. In spite of the fact that, in 1909, a bad fall climbing on Cader Idris in Wales left him with one game leg inches shorter than the other, Lunn never thought of abandoning skiing.

He caused Mürren to become a national, and international, centre for the new sport of ski racing—a sport in which his was the major guiding hand. He invented and set the first modern slalom on Mürren's practice slopes in 1922. In 1924 he founded the Kandahar Ski Club—the world's senior ski-racing club. In 1925 he introduced the Anglo-Swiss University Race and, with Hannes Schneider, founded the internationally famous Arlberg-Kandahar in 1928. He was responsible for drafting the Downhill/Slalom Racing Rules and got these accepted by the Federation Internationale de Ski in 1930 at Oslo—and he represented Great Britain on the F.I.S. from 1928 to 1949. Lunn organized the first World Championship in Downhill and Slalom racing in 1931 at Mürren and introduced these races into the Olympic Games in 1936 at Garmisch Partenkirchen. Among his most important innovations was the establishment of the Duke of Kent's Cup—the first of the "Citadin" Races—in 1937, and the inauguration of the first "Lowlander" Championship in 1948.

Perhaps his greatest love was for ski-touring and ski-mountaineering. Had he had no physical handicap his list of triumphs would have been immensely long, but few skiers, with two good legs, could have achieved the first ski ascent of the Eiger, which he did, with Dr. Walter Amstutz, in 1924.

At various times he was president of the Ski Club of Great Britain, of the Alpine Ski Club and of the Kandahar Ski Club.

At Oxford he read history, then philosophy, but failed to take a degree. It was chiefly his undergraduate experience of Switzerland which provided the subject of his earliest books. He edited a volume of *Oxford Mountaineering Essays* (1912) and in the same year published *The Englishman in the Alps*. Then came, in the following year, a novel, *The Harrovians*, which followed and stimulated the then prevailing fashion of adolescent rebellion against the public schools and especially against the compulsory games system, and the first of his numerous descriptive, analytical, instructional, and impassioned works on *Skiing*. In 1914 he produced a volume on *The Alps* in the Home University Library. Even in these early books Lunn proved himself a writer of uncommon ease and naturalness, always vigorous and always unfettered. He had a genuine love of poetry and literature, an inquiring and resourceful turn of mind, and the crowning gift of enthusiasm. At his best he wrote with great liveliness and pungency. He went to France in 1915 with a Quaker ambulance unit and, after returning home and being medically rejected for military service, found work at Mürren on behalf of British and French internees.

The changing direction of his intellectual interests became apparent only slowly. He continued to write books about skiing (*Cross Country Skiing, Alpine Skiing, Skiing for Beginners, A History of Skiing*); about mountaineering, notably *The Mountains of Youth* (1925); and about Switzerland—there was a volume, in 1928, on "topographical, historical and literary landmarks".

But in between came other volumes of a very different character. Lunn had been brought up in an actively Methodist household and in his nonconformist sympathies had inclined towards a vigorous radicalism. In a volume on *Roman Converts*, published in 1924, his intellectual point of view is one of mere indulgence towards Roman Catholicism. A study of John Wesley, which appeared in 1928, seems to bear witness to an unaltered view of religious matters.

But in *The Flight from Reason*, two years later, which attempts a broad and perhaps too dashing criticism of the claims of science, a leaven of inward unrest and dissatisfaction is plainly at work. Controversy with the Rev. Ronald Knox (as he then was), published under the title of *Difficulties* (1932), and another published debate in the year following with C. E. M. Joad on *Is Christianity True?* gave clear indications of the turn that Lunn's mind was taking. In the latter year he was received into the Roman Catholic Church, and in *Now I See* composed an apologia for the faith in terms, as he conceived them, of strict reason that was expressly approved in Rome itself.

The controversial and dialectician in Lunn now took charge. His standpoint henceforth was militantly Roman Catholic, Tory (with a romantic admixture of Chester-Bellocian "distributism"), and patriotic, for instance in his support for General Franco and an impartial condemnation of Nazism and communism.

His published work up to 1939 included a debate with Professor J. B. S. Haldane* on *Science and the Supernatural* and a combative volume on *Communism and Socialism*. The war itself drew from him a lengthy essay on *Whither Europe?* (1940), and in the same year he published an essay in autobiography, *Come What May*, which was very much the work of a convert to Rome.

As he grew older Lunn appeared to grow more untiring. He published his fiftieth book in 1958 and during the previous 10 years brought out more guidebooks of Switzerland, more medleys of guidebooks and history, more works of mingled argument and personal reminiscence, more ventures in philosophy and theology.

At the age of 67 only a sudden change in the weather defeated him on the last lap of an attempt to climb Mont Blanc once more, but he put this right by being taken to the summit by helicopter in 1963 at the age of 75. He was still able to put on skis in 1972.

He was knighted—"for services to skiing and Anglo-Swiss relations"—in 1952, in which year he also became Citoyen d'honneur of Chamonix.

He married in 1913 Lady Mabel, daughter of the Rev. John Stafford Northcote. She died in 1959. There were two sons and a daughter of the marriage. The elder son, Peter Lunn, C.M.G., O.B.E., became in his turn a leading skier in the Olympic team. In 1961 Sir Arnold married Phyllis Holt-Needham, who looked after him, and prolonged his life and energies by her care.

June 3, 1974.

Oliver Lyttelton, 1st Viscount Chandos—
See **Chandos.**

M

Sir Ivison Macadam, K.C.V.O., C.B.E., Secretary and Director-General of the Royal Institute of International Affairs, 1929-55, died on December 22, 1974 at the age of 80. He was editor of the *Annual Register of World Events* 1947-73, and founder president and trustee of the National Union of Students.

He put the *Annual Register* on a sound financial footing and strengthened its worldwide reputation by bringing in a wide range of specialist contributors. Sales expanded considerably, particularly in the United States.

At Chatham House (the Royal Institute of International Affairs) he is remembered for his Scottish drive and application in pure "admin". matters. He organized persons, events, and work with equal stern objectivity, and got a lot done accordingly, though sometimes making opponents by his singlemindedness on behalf of Chatham House. He worked early, late and continuously, and he never shunned unpleasantnesses which fell to him to handle: of which, in the troubled decade 1929-39, and with a smaller but perhaps keener R.I.I.A. membership, there were quite a few notably during the so-called "appeasement" period.

The second son of Colonel W. Ivison Macadam, Professor of Chemistry, Edinburgh, he was educated at Melville College, Edinburgh, King's College London, and Christ's College, Cambridge. In the First World War he saw service with the City of Edinburgh (Fortress) Royal Engineers and had a searching experience as O.C. the Royal Engineers in the Archangel, North Russian Expeditionary Force. He was three times mentioned in dispatches.

For a period in the Second World War he was Assistant Director-General and Principal Assistant Secretary, Ministry of Information.

A former colleague remembers him about the year 1925 when he was "bringing to administrative perfection" the National Union of Students, which was then in Endsleigh Gardens off Endsleigh Street, Bloomsbury.

He put in very hard work at establishing, developing, and dovetailing into the International Union the new N.U.S., and his tall, lean, blond-capped figure was a familiar sight round Gordon Square and parts of the emergent new campus of the University of London.

The University Union was an old wartime hut in Malet Street which lasted up to the Second War; and in its early days the fellows back from the First War forgathered there, Ivison coming occasionally among them, and all of them prematurely matured by their wartime experiences. He was a remarkably good public debater, speaking with a soft Edinburgh burr which he never lost.

He married in 1934 Caroline Ladd, daughter of Elliott Corbett, of Portland, Oregon. They had two sons and two daughters.

December 24, 1974.

Ida Macalpine, M.D., F.R.C.P., who died on May 2, 1974 at the age of 74, had a rare combination of gifts of intellect, humanity, strength of character and capacity for hard work. Three times fate changed the direction of her life and each time she responded by carving out a new career. To observe her courage during her last illness—about which, alas, she was allowed to know too much—was a humbling experience. The contributions to psychiatry which made her internationally known came at an age when most are planning or enjoying retirement.

She was born on June 19, 1899, the fourth of five children of Sigmund Wertheimer, merchant and town councillor of Nuremberg, and his wife Mathilde (*née* Lust). As a schoolgirl she helped to tend the injured of World War I and determined to become a doctor. Her studies, during which she worked to support herself, were interrupted by marriage. In 1927 she graduated M.D. Erlangen, and the following year settled in Berlin as a physician and medical officer to the Pestalozzi-Froebel Haus.

Early in 1933, when she foresaw the way things were going in Germany, she took her two young sons and ageing mother to England where there were family ties. She requalified at Edinburgh in 1934 on the Scottish triple conjoint, and practised in London until World War II. In 1941 she married George Lawson Macalpine of Accrington, Lancs., who died in 1948. She returned to London and devoted the rest of her life to psychological medicine.

At first she interested herself in psychoanalysis and her papers on the development of transference and on the Schreber case challenged many of its basic tenets. She specialized in psychosomatic medicine and for a dozen years worked as psychiatrist to the skin department of St. Bartholomew's Hospital. She made herself expert in the history and literature of psychiatry and published in 1963 a book of annotated selected readings, *Three Hundred Years of Psychiatry, 1535-1860,* which became a standard work of reference. Like all her later writings it was the product of a possibly unique professional partnership with her son Dr. Richard Hunter. A companion volume bringing the history of psychiatry—as exemplified by developments at a famous old mental hospital in North London—up to date, so to speak, *Psychiatry for the Poor*, was timed to appear in June 1974 on her 75th birthday, and she corrected proofs and made the index on her sick bed.

Growing experience of the whole range of acute and chronic psychiatric disorders convinced her that psychosocial factors cause distress but not disease, and her orientation shifted from the psychological to the neurological, from mind to brain. This was the essence of her studies of the royal malady which began to appear in the medical press in 1966 and which culminated in an acknowledged classic of historical pathography, *George III and the Mad-Business*, published in 1969. Her conclusions caused a fundamental revision of that "much maligned monarch's" life and reign as every subsequent history and biography testifies.

She was elected Member of the Royal College of Physicians of London under the by-laws in 1959, and Fellow one week before she died.

May 18, 1974.

Jock McAvoy, who died at Partington, Cheshire, on November 20, 1971 (his sixty-third birthday), was pound for pound one of the outstanding British boxers of the 1930s. He held both the British middleweight and light-heavyweight professional titles and challenged valiantly though unsuccessfully for the world light-heavyweight and the British heavyweight championships.

McAvoy's real name was Joseph Bamford, but he earned the nickname of "the Rochdale Thunderbolt" after he had gained a series of victories with two-handed attacks which left his opponents helpless.

McAvoy had 10 contests for British professional championships, beginning in 1932 when he challenged unsuccessfully the brilliant Len Harvey for the middleweight title. The next year McAvoy took the title from Harvey and he defended it successfully four times before moving up to light-heavyweight.

He won the light-heavyweight championship in 1935 but was beaten in this new division twice by his old rival, Harvey, and failed with a bid for the world's title when he was outpointed by the American John Henry Lewis in 1936.

McAvoy was always ready to concede many pounds to heavier opponents and it was surprising that one of his few thorough defeats came at the hands of another middleweight, the Frenchman Marcel Thil. Internationally, McAvoy's most explosive performance came when he knocked out the American world middleweight champion, Babe Risko, in the first round of a non-title contest.

McAvoy was never knocked out in well over 100 professional bouts, but shortly after the war he was reduced to a wheelchair for the rest of his life by an attack of polio. In recent years he was often a spectator of the promotions at Belle Vue, Manchester, and was still pugnacious enough to strike a reporter who had annoyed him, even from his handicapped position.

November 22, 1971.

R. B. McCallum, Master of Pembroke College, Oxford, from 1955 to 1967, died on May 18, 1973 at the age of 74. From 1967 to 1971 he was Principal of St. Catharine's, Cumberland Lodge, Windsor Great Park.

Though Ronald McCallum was born (on August 28, 1898) in Paisley of a family of well-to-do West of Scotland dyers, his physical appearance as well as a special style of courtesy which was characteristic of him showed clearly enough the Highland inheritance from the grandfather who had come from Skipness in Kintyre. He was sent to school at Glenalmond, where he disliked the cold baths but admitted to having been excellently taught, especially by one of his masters, P. E. Roberts, whom he later found waiting for him as his tutor in modern history at Worcester College. There (after two years with the Labour Corps of the B.E.F. in France) he read modern history and obtained a First in 1922.

This was followed by a year at Princeton, a year's lecturing at the University of Glasgow, and then election to a Fellowship at Pembroke College, Oxford. Seven years later he resigned his Fellowship on marriage—the last Pembroke Fellow to fall in this way under the rule of the old Statutes—was reelected and remained in the service of his College until he retired from the Mastership in 1967.

Born and brought up in a great radical constituency, McCallum, whose first published book was a life of Asquith, early developed the traits and predilections of the Liberal intellectual. In his last book, published in 1963, *The Liberal Party from Earl Grey to Asquith*, he showed himself a masterly exponent of the history and philosophy of the Liberal tradition and a writer fitted by natural endowment and by training to express its spirit. His conversation on these topics was a political education.

With neither taste nor talent for philosophical exercise, he had to an outstanding degree the social and political historian's ability to "place" a movement or idea in the intellectual history of its period. He was a born historian and a brilliant connoisseur of opinion. These qualities emerge at their clearest in the book *Public Opinion and the Last Peace*, (1944).

As a tutor he taught widely in both the Schools of Modern History and P.P.E., making a special contribution in the modern history of Parliament and its procedure. An acute observer of the undergraduate, there was very little about students or tutorials he did not know.

With his friend, C. H. Wilson, of Corpus, he produced at that time the Blackwell's series of Political Texts, characteristically taking John Stuart Mill as his own volume. He had a devastatingly accurate ear for academic nonsense, whether from his seniors or his juniors, and a remarkable series of contributions to the *Oxford Magazine* bears witness to this gift.

He was one of the earliest supporters of Nuffield College, and for them he produced the first of those studies of general elections which have become an established part of modern political science. With Alison Readman, and using the help of graduate students such as David Butler, he brought his flair for the analysis of political opinion and the analysis of parliamentary history to bear on the election of 1945.

He served the university in a very large variety of ways as Senior Proctor, as Pro-Vice-Chancellor, as a university member of the City Council, and as Senior Treasurer of the Union. In his younger days he was Editor of the *Oxford Magazine*, and after the war it was mainly due to his efforts that this organ of senior opinion in the University survived many serious difficulties. Yet it is as a College, and a Pembroke man, he would have wished first to be remembered.

In 1955 he succeeded Dr. Homes Dudden as Master of the College which he had served in most of its offices for 30 years, the first lay Master since its foundation.

He was well qualified to know just what the college needed. It needed money for building and development. And it needed to modify the conservatism which had earned it the reputation of being a solid, middle-of-the-road, but academically unexciting, place.

Within a few years he had achieved a truly remarkable transformation. The number of Tutorial Fellows had been trebled and reinforced by a substantial leavening of scientists not one of whom had been appointed prior to his Mastership. A rapidly lengthening list of scholarships and exhibitions and examination successes contributed to raise the whole standard of the college's academic reputation. Its buildings were embellished and amenities improved, while in 1962 a new quadrangle was added by the skilful adaptation of a row of historic houses and their inclusion within the precincts of the college.

The funds for this rapid academic and material expansion were provided by a progressive investment policy which McCallum fostered and encouraged at every stage, and by the generosity of Pembroke *alumni* whose loyalty to the college his interest and friendship had always done so much to ensure.

In all this he won and retained the confidence and vigorous support of a Governing Body whose unity and enthusiasm owed much to his inspiration and leadership.

McCallum was twice happily married. By his first wife, Ischar Bradley, who died in 1944, he had two daughters. In 1950 he married Margaret Veale, daughter of Sir Douglas Veale, Registrar of the University. By this marriage, there were a daughter and two sons.

May 19, 1973.

Sir Andrew McFadyean, diplomat, economist, Treasury official, man of business and Liberal politician, publicist and philosopher, died on October 2, 1974 at the age of 87.

The son of Sir John McFadyean, he was born on St. George's Day, 1887. His gifts of intellect and character were such that he might well have come to the front in any one of six or seven professions. After a distinguished performance at University College School, of which he was later a governor, and at University College, Oxford, where in 1909 he won his first in *litterae humaniores*, he entered the Treasury by open competition in 1910, three years before his marriage to Dorothea Emily, younger daughter of the late Charles Keane Chute.

He rapidly made his mark in the Civil Service, becoming private secretary successively to Charles Masterman, Edwin Montagu, Francis Acland and T. McKinnon Wood, all ministers in the Asquith Administration, Sir John Bradbury, Sir Hardman Lever—whom he accompanied in 1917 on a special financial mission to the United States—and Stanley Baldwin, Financial Secretary to the Treasury in the Lloyd George combination.

McFadyean then served for four months as the Treasury representative in Paris. It was as the leading Treasury specialist on reparations and war debts during the Versailles era that McFadyean established his reputation in the European capitals. He served as secretary to the British delegation to the Reparation Commission from 1920 until 1922; general secretary to the Commission itself from 1922 until 1924; secretary to the Dawes Committee; and afterwards as Chief Commissioner of Revenue in Berlin until his departure from this sphere in 1930.

In 1919 John Maynard Keynes, in *The Economic Consequences of the Peace*, had struck the first blow for reasonableness towards Weimar Germany. "Mr. Lloyd George", wrote McFadyean, "watched the cat jump, and jumped after it—almost as quickly but not quite so far". On April 9, 1924, the year after Poincaré's ill-advised occupation of the Ruhr and the tumultuous collapse of the mark, the Report of the Principal Committee of Experts, headed by General Charles C. Dawes, afterwards President Hoover's* Ambassador in London, was published.

This unanimous Report is usually concluded to be the work of Sir Josiah (later Lord) Stamp; future economic historians may well interpret it as almost equally the work of McFadyean. Its major recommendations were that Germany's currency be stabilized on a gold basis, that Germany pay an annual sum for reparations rising from 1,000 million marks in the first year to 2,500 million marks in the fifth and subsequent years, and that such revenues be obtained by three means, from ordinary budgetary taxation (more specifically customs and excise revenue), from certain specified industrial debentures, and from bonds issued against the German Railways.

These terms heralded a very different atmosphere from that which had prevailed during the "Hang the Kaiser" coupon election campaign of 1918; McFadyean was an influence for magnanimity. In May 1924 the political climate further improved when the French elections replaced Poincaré as Prime Minister by Herriot, the Radical leader. Next came the Young plan, a new settlement of German reparation in 1929, and the Rhineland evacuation in 1930. "If the world has to adapt itself to anything like the present level of prices", opined McFadyean in 1930, "I incline to the belief that from the reparation standpoint the most important fact which emerges from a consideration of the economic phenomena of the last 12 months is that the real burden on Germany, as determined by the Young plan, may well prove, owing to the change in the value of gold, to be heavier, and not lighter, than the obligations of the Dawes plan, which were adjustable to such a change".

However, the death of Stresemann on October 3, 1929, proved to be a vital factor in the transition from the Weimar Republic to the Third Reich; the economic blizzard, wrecking the work of conciliation, reinforced and consolidated the propaganda of the Nazis whose representation in the Reichstag rose in September 1930 from 12 seats to 107 seats.

It was in that year that McFadyean's career took a new turn and assumed different dimensions. Still only 43, he had already completed 19 years of distinguished service in a sphere which partly involved the Treasury and partly concerned diplomacy. He turned to the City and to politics.

At the general election of 1945, he stood as Liberal and Free Trade candidate for the City of London, then a two-member constituency. S. W. Alexander flanked him as Independent Free Trade candidate; they polled a quarter of the votes in that Tory stronghold. In 1949 he succeeded Elliott Dodds as party president, and, after a year's heavy campaigning, fought at Finchley in the general election of 1950, polling well in that constituency, despite the fiercely anti-Liberal mood of most English electors at that time. For the subsequent decade, from 1950 until 1960, he held office as Vice-President of the Liberal Party.

Meanwhile, in 1948, on the death of his friend, Walter, first Lord Rea, McFadyean became President of the old Free Trade Union, which was then renewing its activities and crusading for what it termed "Free Trade in Modern Dress". He served in that capacity for eleven years.

After the Second World War, McFadyean, together with a close friend, John MacCallum Scott, was the foremost British architect of the Liberal International, modern successor of the interwar Entente Internationale des Partis Radicaux et Démocratiques. Founded at Wadham College, Oxford, in 1947, the body could count the presidents of the Italian and Federal German Republics as well as Herriot, Plevens, and Queuille,* and Judge Learned Hand* among its patrons. McFadyean became a Vice-President and played a significant part in successive European Conferences, notably the Stuttgart Congress of August 1950. The cause of the Common Market and of a United States of Europe found in him a persistent and resourceful advocate.

He and Lady McFadyean had three daughters and one son.

October 3, 1974.

Dr. Marjorie Giffen Macfarlane died suddenly on July 17, 1973 in West Hartlepool, the town in which she was born in 1904.

She was a student in physiology at St. Andrews University and graduated with honours in 1926. A year later she went to work in the Biochemistry Department at the Lister Institute of Preventive Medicine in London, first as a research student with Professor Sir Arthur Harden and then as a Carnegie Fellow with Professor Robert Robison, who succeeded Harden as Professor of Biochemistry in 1929. She obtained the degrees of Ph.D. and D.Sc. of London University and in 1935 became a permanent member of the institute's staff, a post she retained until her retirement in 1965.

During her earlier years at the institute she worked on the occurrence of phosphorylation in intact yeast cells. Just before the 1939-45 War, she took up the study of the enzyme content of vaccinia virus and later, with her colleague Dr. B. C. J. G. Knight, demonstrated the enzymic nature of a lethal bacterial toxin. This discovery was of great importance and it opened up a whole field of chemical investigation concerning the enzymic action of toxins on tissue components.

During the latter part of the war, because of her specialized knowledge of the gas-gangrene group of organisms, Dr. Macfarlane acted as secretary of the Medical Research Council's subcommittee on anaerobic wound infections. In 1948 she again resumed her academic studies on fatty substances in animal and bacterial cells and, with a small group of co-workers, discovered several new compounds of importance as components of cellular membranes.

She had a modest view of her own contributions to science, and retired at 60 when her work was still receiving full international recognition.

Marjorie Macfarlane established a position for herself in the biochemical life of Britain when the numbers of women scientists were still relatively few. She at all times showed a fearless integrity and was forthright and unyielding in many of her opinions. Nevertheless her friends were delighted with the charming gaiety and wit of her conversation, and her powerful intelligence and wide interests allowed her to contribute usefully and entertainingly on subjects far from her own speciality.

Marjorie Macfarlane was an excellent hostess and her hospitality was extended alike to fleeting visitors to Britain, nervous newcomers to the Lister Institute and friends of long standing. She was always interested in her younger colleagues and, while generous in her acknowledgment of their achievements, urged them to retain a sense of humour and to guard against taking themselves too seriously. Her retirement had altered the direction of her energies but not lessened her zest for life or the vigour with which she pursued her goals. She will be sadly missed.

July 23, 1973.

Denis Mackail, writer of sophisticated novels in the lighter vein, died on August 4, 1971 at the age of 79.

His mildly satirical style and the frivolity of the characters he portrayed was in contrast to the atmosphere of high endeavour and serious accomplishment in which he had been brought up. His father, J. W. Mackail, O.M., was Professor of Poetry at Oxford and a distinguished man of letters. By his marriage to Margaret Burne-Jones, Professor Mackail was brought into the pre-Raphaelite circle, and their London home became famous for witty and learned conversation. Into this home Denis George Mackail was born two years after a sister who, as Angela Thirkell,* was also to gain distinction in the literary field.

From St. Paul's School he went up to Balliol, of which college his father had been a distinguished scholar. As his own talent developed it was as though he turned it deliberately—even defiantly—to frivolous subjects. His first work, *What Next?* appeared in 1920. In *Bill The Bachelor*, a robust light novel which was published two years later, there were signs of a stronger ability and a wider range than were to show in his later, more assured works.

Throughout the twenties and thirties he wrote busily and with continuous success, and hardly a year passed in which at least one work from his pen did not appear. The best known, *Greenery Street*, which came out in 1925, won immediate popularity. In this and later books on the same theme, such as *Tales of Greenery Street*, *The Livingstones*, and *Ian and Felicity*, he became the official chronicler of the domestic preoccupations of the upper-middle-class in London. The lives of the nice young men with their public school education, and of the charming young women who took presentation at Court as a matter of course, may not have been very eventful, but the author found so much that was interesting, ridiculous, and above all pleasant in what happened to them that mere plot frequently became no more than a formality.

It was typical that when he dealt with murder, as in *The Majestic Mystery,* one of his characters should remark that he doubted whether anyone would trouble to mention the matter on Judgment Day. Even so, it is unlikely that his popularity would have remained as secure as it did over such a long period, if his writing had not also shown other qualities—a genuine sympathy with the exuberance of youth, a clear-sighted but tolerant irony, and a philosophical reflection underlying the gaiety and charm.

Not all his publications were novels. Some of them, *The Fortunes of Hugo* (1926) and *How Amusing!* (1929), to name two examples, were collections of short stories, for which form of writing he also showed great facility. He contributed frequently to *The Strand* and to other literary magazines, and the editor of one of them once remarked that Mackail was the only author from whom he would accept a story simply on the charm of his writing. Book reviewers were not always so accommodating, and in the irritation to which they sometimes gave expression was reflected the suggestion that they discerned in him possibilities to which, it seemed, he perversely denied any outlet.

It was not until 1941 that his first and only truly serious work appeared, *The Story of J.M.B.* His affection for the man and his intimate knowledge of the Barrie circle gave him special qualifications for the work, and he made full use of the material and help given to him by Barrie's executors, Lady Cynthia Asquith and Peter Davies. In this voluminous work, consisting of more than 700 pages, no detail of Barrie's life was overlooked, and every recess of a complicated nature was visited in the author's urbane and conversational style. Even so, there were those who felt that the lightness of touch which had carried him to success elsewhere was not best suited to this kind of work. Some works in lighter vein continued to appear at intervals during the war, but the gaiety had lost some of its freshness and the ready public which he had entertained for so long was no longer in the mood for such frivolity. With the death of his wife in 1949 he stopped writing altogether.

He married in 1917 Diana, only child of the late Sir Guy Granet, G.B.E. They are survived by two daughters.

August 5, 1971.

Sir Compton Mackenzie, O.B.E., who died in Edinburgh on November 30, 1972 at the age of 89, began as an infant prodigy and ended as an octogenarian with the gaiety and undimmed zest for life of a teenager.

The ups and downs of fortune in his long pilgrimage were dramatic. By 1914 he had established himself in the first flight of daring young novelists; Henry James hailed him as a rising hope of English fiction. American publishers bowdlerized him (cutting out such wicked words as "tart" and "bitch") and he was attacked for corrupting youth. By 1924 he had been dropped by the high-brows, but continued to be a best-seller. By 1934 his position was unchanged, except that his output of novels and other work had flowed on unceasingly in a Balzacian spate of words. By 1954, thanks to broadcasting and the cinema, as well as to his unflagging output, he had become a popular figure on a national scale and he remained one to the last. As he grew aged—though never venerable—the critics began to scrutinize him again, first with curiosity and then with growing respect.

Through all these fluctuations "Monty" Mackenzie remained his cheerful, egotistic, ebullient, pugnacious self. The incense of the pundits in his youth did not go to his head. Critical neglect between the wars left him unsoured. At the nadir of his reputation, when he was often dismissed as a pot-boiling hack, he said that the theatre was in his blood, and he asked nothing better than to succeed as an entertainer. A microscopic memory served him well as novelist and autobiographer. He retained a practically continuous recollection of his life from before he was two, and not merely of incidents but of what he thought about them at the time. He taught himself to read at 22 months.

His hundred books were far from absorbing all his energies. He threw himself with zest into Scottish Nationalism and the championing of Greece. His connoisseurship embraced music (he edited *The Gramophone*), gardening, the collecting of islands and the cultivation by day and night of the art of good talk; to have heard him, Max Beerbohm and Ronald Knox reminiscing together was a delight never to be forgotten. His friends of both sexes were drawn from all classes and many countries.

Edward Montague Compton Mackenzie was born on January 17, 1883, at West Hartlepool (where his parents were on tour), the eldest son of Edward Compton, the actor-manager, and his American wife, Virginia Bateman, daughter of another stalwart Victorian man of the theatre, Hezekiah Linthicum Bateman, who launched Irving at the Lyceum. His paternal grandfather, Charles Mackenzie, had taken the stage name of Henry Compton. This family background brought him into contact while still a preparatory school boy with many stage and literary celebrities. Educated at St. Paul's, he disappointed his High Master, the great Dr. Walker, who saw in him a Balliol classical scholar, by preferring to go up to Magdalen as a commoner and reading History. The atmosphere of late Victorian and Edwardian London and Oxford was exquisitely caught in his early novels *Carnival* and *Sinister Street;* in them he showed himself a master of Cockney idiom and humour. They had been preceded by some pleasant conventional poetry and a first novel *The Passionate Elopement,* a graceful eighteenth-century pastiche for which he had much difficulty in finding a publisher, until Martin Secker came to the rescue.

During the 1914-18 War he served on Ian Hamilton's staff in the Royal Marines at Gallipoli, and then as an intelligence officer in the Aegean. These experiences were used in a series of novels and memoirs, including *Greek Memories,* which led him to be prosecuted under the Official Secrets Act. He hit back at what he regarded as a frivolous and spiteful action in *Water on the Brain,* satirizing the Secret Service. The offending *Greek Memories* was accident-prone in encounters with the law; having sold the copyright of his first twenty books for £10,000 in 1943, believing this would be a capital transaction, he had to pay income tax in the year of sale.

His output of novels never stopped. *Guy and Pauline* (1915), *Sylvia Scarlett* (1918), and *Sylvia and Michael* (1919) were linked with those of his school and Oxford days. During the twenties and thirties he poured out light comedy, including *Poor Relations* and *Rich Relatives* and *Vestal Fire* and *Extraordinary Women* in which he revealed a humorous, sympathetic understanding of male homosexuals and lesbians, which was considerably in advance of the times. His absorption in questions of faith and ritual, dating from school days, went into a trilogy on clerical life beginning with *The Altar Steps.* As in so much of his work, these were partly autobiographical, and helped to show how he followed the path to conversion, in the spring of 1914, to the Roman Catholic Church. Between 1937 and 1945 he produced *The Four Winds of Love* in which he spread himself, again to some extent autobiographically. By then, he was deeply committed to Scottish Nationalism, and had found a home in the Hebridean island of Barra, where he commanded the wartime Home Guard. Scotland gave him material for exploiting his genius for high spirited fun in, among others, *Whisky Galore* and *The Monarch of the Glen.*

Novels did not exhaust his powers. The Abdication brought him into the ring with *The Windsor Tapestry.* He did biographical sketches of Roosevelt, Benes, Pericles and Prince Charlie. At the end of the war he visited the battlefields in India as a guest of the Indian Government, and described it in *Eastern Epic.* In 1963 he brought out "Octave I" of *My Life and Times* and thereafter new volumes appeared each year until 1971, which saw the publication of Octave Ten. Here that microscopic memory, helped by the hoarding of letters, served to make this a unique *tour de force;* no detail, no small change had got through the net from earliest childhood. The tabby cat which, at two, impressed him as "large as a lion" was by no means his first memory.

Although he had been so closely linked from the start with the theatrical world, he never succeeded as a dramatist on a scale at all comparable to his achievements in other kinds of writing. He made a few appearances on the stage and might have had a career as an actor. But he preferred authorship. Soon after coming down from Oxford, he made some gay contributions to the lighter stage and was associated with that most famous of troupers, Pélissier of the Follies, who married his sister, Fay. His plays included *The Gentleman in Grey, Carnival, Columbine* and *The Lost Cause*. As an amateur, he once played Hamlet at Fowey in Cornwall under the auspices of "Q", Sir Arthur Quiller-Couch, the novelist and Cambridge Professor of English Literature, who was among his most enthusiastic early admirers.

Passionately though he identified himself with places, he had a restless temperament and would turn his back without regret from a beloved spot where he had grown roots. For years the London he had known so well and with such deep affection scarcely saw him except in brief visits to the Savile Club. He divided his time in old age between Edinburgh and Pradelles, Les Arques, Lot, the French house which he found so conducive to recollecting times past.

Many honours and distinctions came his way. He was Rector of Glasgow University in the 1930s; Governor-General of the Royal Stuart Society; an honorary LL.D. of Glasgow; a C.Lit. of the Royal Society of Literature; and a former president of the Croquet Association.

He married three times, first in 1905 Faith, younger daughter of the Rev. E. D. Stone, of Eton, and sister of Christopher Stone*; she died in 1960. His second wife, Christina, whom he married in 1962, was the daughter of Malcolm MacSween, of Tarbert, Harris. She died in the next year, and in 1965 he married her sister Lilian.

December 1, 1972.

Lord McNair, C.B.E., Q.C., died on May 22, 1975 in Cambridge at the age of 90.

Arnold Duncan McNair was born on March 4, 1885, and educated at Aldenham School and Caius College, Cambridge. There was early evidence of his remarkable intellectual versatility in his University career, for besides the distinction he attained in the Law Tripos, he was President of the Union in 1909. He took his degree in that year and practised as a solicitor in the City of London until 1913 when he returned to Cambridge as a Fellow of his College, of which he was for some years the Senior Tutor.

He changed his professional qualification by joining Gray's Inn, and his legal ability was recognized in his being made a Bencher of his Inn and in his election to the Treasurership of it in 1947. He was also appointed a King's Counsel. He held

a Readership of International Law in London University 1926-27, and in 1935 was elected Whewell Professor of International Law at Cambridge. He had already occupied Chairs abroad—the Tagore Professorship at Calcutta and a Chair of International Law at The Hague Academy. After two years' tenure of the Whewell Chair, he resigned it on his apppointment to the Vice-Chancellorship of Liverpool University in 1937.

After the war he gave up the Vice-Chancellorship in order to return to Cambridge as Professor of Comparative Law in succession to Professor Gutteridge. Here, again, his tenure of the Chair was brief owing to his selection as British member of the Permanent Court of Arbitration at The Hague. This was quickly followed by his election to a Judgeship of the International Court of Justice on its creation early in 1946 as successor to the Permanent Court of International Justice.

Lord McNair's tenure of this high office lasted until 1955; from 1952 he was the President of the Court.

Among his more notable judgments will be remembered that in the Norwegian Fisheries Case, where he dissented from the majority opinion, and his independent, though assenting, judgment, in the Anglo-Iranian Oil Case. On his retirement from the Court, McNair received the honour of a peerage. He had been knighted in 1943. He at once resumed his activities as a much-sought-after consultant in international law and other public matters. In 1959 he was elected the first President of the European Court of Human Rights at Strasbourg, holding that post until 1965. He had long been a member of the Institute of International Law, of which he was President in the year 1949-50.

Few university dons can have had wider experience in the sphere of public work. He was secretary of the Coal Conservation Committee, 1916-18, the Imperial Mineral Resources Bureau, 1918-19, and the Sankey Coal Commission, 1919. For these services he was made C.B.E. The reputation that McNair acquired as a result in particular of his services to the Coal Commission was enhanced in the Second World War by his chairmanship of the Committee on Supply and Training of Teachers and of the Palestine Jewish Education Committee and his membership of the Board of Investigation into Miners' Wages. After the war he was Chairman of the Department Committee which inquired into the supply of dentists, and from 1956 to 1958 was Chairman of the Burnham Committee on Teachers' Salaries.

His contributions to legal literature—mostly in connexion with international law—are notable for their profound learning, clarity of expression and practical approach to the solution of problems. His principal books were *The Legal Effects of War*, 1920, which was greatly enlarged in the second and third editions after the Second World War, *The Law of Treaties*, 1938,

and again in greatly enlarged form, 1961, *The Law of the Air*, 1932, second edition 1953, *International Law Opinions* (three volumes), 1956. These volumes, with the author's valuable annotations, are a collection of the opinions of the law officers of the United Kingdom on international law matters. With the late Professor W. W. Buckland there appeared in 1936 *Roman Law and Common Law* (second edition, 1952). In another field McNair published in 1949 *Dr. Johnson and the Law*.

McNair's personality was as attractive and impressive as his intellect. His inborn sympathy with all those who came in contact with him, whether professionally or socially, made them anxious to keep in touch with him for the rest of their lives. He was always keen on understanding points of view that differed from his own and it was characteristic of him that he looked upon all meetings that he attended as useful in forming his final decision on any point under discussion, whatever may have been his own opinion before the discussion opened. Not unnaturally, that opinion was often the one that was adopted by the meeting. Former pupils of his constantly relied on him for advice and help in their careers after they had left his tuition. The amount of social entertainment that he and Lady McNair gave to so many will remain a golden memory.

His record in academic and in public life will stand as a monument not only of the success that he achieved in both spheres but also of the way in which he achieved it.

No appreciation of his life would be complete without some reference to his college and his standing as a teacher of law. It is no exaggeration to say that his colleagues at Caius and in the Cambridge Law Faculty admired and respected him to a degree which can seldom have been equalled. This admiration ripened into warm affection on the part of those who were privileged to be his close friends.

McNair married in 1912 Marjorie, the younger daughter of the Hon. Sir Clement Bailhache. She died in 1971. He is succeeded by his son, the Hon. John McNair, and also leaves three daughters.

May 24, 1975.

Sir John Macpherson, G.C.M.G., Permanent Under-Secretary of State for the Colonies from 1956 to 1959, died on November 5, 1971 at the age of 73.

He was a devoted servant of the Commonwealth who won the admiration of many thousands who barely knew him. He attained to high posts: Governor (and later Governor-General) of Nigeria in 1948, and Permanent Under-Secretary of State for the Colonies—an almost unprecedented appointment for a man whose life's work had been overseas. To his friends of all colours and creeds he remained "Jock".

Beneath a debonair manner, and though

he spoke with only the faintest trace of a Scottish accent, Macpherson was a Scot of Scots—a man of precise and powerful mind, endowed with all the toughness and tenacity of the best of his race.

John Stuart Macpherson was born on August 25, 1898, in Edinburgh, where his grandfather and father, who was in the hotel business, were prominent in civic life, and was educated at George Watson's College and Edinburgh University. His war service with the Argylls brought him a spinal injury which, from time to time throughout his whole career, caused him great pain and made it necessary for him to wear always a steel brace or corset—in itself a serious incubus in the tropics. But only a few of his most intimate friends were aware of its existence. He also concealed with great skill the fact that, as a result of the same war wound, he was completely deaf in one ear.

From the start of his Malayan days Macpherson displayed high ability in the varied work of a district. He spent two years, from 1933 to 1935, in the Colonial Office in London, returned to Malaya, and went to Nigeria as Principal Assistant Secretary in 1937. By this time—in 1928—he had married Joan Fry, who was to bring him incalculable help and happiness. They had one son, who in due course followed his father into the colonial service.

In 1939 Macpherson was made Chief Secretary of Palestine. This, in the troubled days of the British Mandate, was a thorny post, but Macpherson found one great satisfaction in it. The High Commissioner, Sir Harold MacMichael, was a man with as keen a sense of humour as his own, and for him Macpherson came to feel the same respect and affection that he himself inspired in his subordinates.

After two years in Washington as head of a wartime body, the British Colonies Supply Mission, Macpherson was created K.C.M.G. in 1945, and took up the dual role of Comptroller for Development and Welfare in the West Indies and British Co-Chairman of the Anglo-American Caribbean Commission. The first Comptroller, Sir Frank Stockdale, had laid some solid foundations; Macpherson built on them to such effect that in three years the Development and Welfare Organization was shedding a powerful influence throughout the region from its headquarters in Barbados, and was becoming a major factor in the progress towards the short-lived West Indian Federation.

In 1948 Macpherson was appointed to the governorship of Nigeria—a surprising appointment for one who had never served even as an acting governor elsewhere. Though surprising, however, the appointment was successful, both in personal terms —Macpherson was widely liked and respected in Nigeria—and in terms of political judgment.

In 1948 Nigeria had just received a new constitution, the first for over 20 years, usually known as the Richards constitution after the Governor, Sir Arthur Richards (later Lord Milverton). It had established a central legislative council and regional assemblies, but it had failed to take account of the rapidly developing nationalist forces that were currently sweeping West Africa. Macpherson's great merit lay in his recognition, within a short period, that the Richards constitution must be replaced and not allowed to run its full term. At once he instituted a series of discussions at local and then at national levels to discover the views of Nigerians on the type of constitution that should be drawn up.

The results emerged in 1951. The 1951 constitution gave considerable powers to the centre but was designed to prevent nationalist politicians from controlling the legislature by placing in the hands of regions a kind of "braking power". But the degree of power placed in Nigerian hands, at the centre and in the regions, did not satisfy ambitious politicians, and the constitution had to be changed. For this, however, Macpherson can hardly be blamed, since at this period the sense of nationhood in Nigeria was embryonic, although the demand for African control was vociferous.

In 1954 the new constitution came into force. It gave to the regions greater autonomy and ability to progress to self government, and reduced the power of the centre to intervene. It formally established Nigeria as a federation. Looking back through the events of early 1966 in Nigeria, one can reasonably suggest that other methods of preventing centre and regions from treading on each other's toes might have been more satisfactory, but in 1954 the era of disenchantment with federal solutions had not begun. Nor would it have been politically possible to have broken up the North into several regions and made it seem less of a threat to the South.

Macpherson can be credited with grasping the essential truth that times were changing, and having the courage, the skill and the energy to change course to meet them—no small achievement at a time when the "wind of change" had not been generally recognized. By his constitution-making, and perhaps still more by his efforts to see that Nigerians were trained to take senior Civil Service posts, he laid the foundations for independence.

Macpherson, to his own considerable surprise and the great pleasure of the colonial service as a whole, was made Permanent Under-Secretary in 1956. He accepted the post for two years, but was persuaded to remain in it for a third.

It has been suggested that it might have been better if he and Lennox-Boyd (later Lord Boyd of Merton), the Secretary of State throughout his term of office, had been less alike in temperament and outlook: that something less of optimism and ardour and imagination in one or the other of them might have made a more effective team of the two. What can be said is that as the administrative head of a great Department of State Macpherson was a huge success, and that the powers of devolution that had always paralleled his immense capacity for work were particularly valuable to him here.

On finally leaving the Colonial Office in 1959 Macpherson still remained active in public life. He was deputy chairman of the Basildon Development Corporation from 1960 to 1964, and chairman from 1964 to 1967. He was chairman of Cable & Wireless from 1962 to 1967. He was also a vice-president of the Royal Commonwealth Society. From 1962 he was vice-chairman of the Advisory Committee on Distinction Awards for Consultants.

November 9, 1971.

Ross McWhirter, who was murdered at his home in Enfield—a victim of the northern Ireland troubles—on the night of November 27, 1975, was perhaps most widely known for his share in the *Guinness Book of Records*, the continuing best-seller which he and his twin brother, Norris McWhirter, created. Yet in his last few years he was becoming increasingly known for his challenges to what he saw as violations of the law and for his campaigns in defence of individual freedom. He was 50.

There was more to McWhirter than a remarkable memory and an insatiable appetite for facts. He had a robust belief in the individual and what the individual, even in days of encroaching bureaucracy, could achieve within the law. He was, and it is curious that it has to be said, a man of unfashionable cut and cast of mind. He felt strongly that what is sometimes called the silent majority was all too often put upon by a vociferous and intimidating minority in more than one sphere of life, and that these were trends which ought to be resisted.

He was not just a talker content to grumble and rail, he was a doer; he acted. Over the years, when he saw occasion, he contested actions which he felt should be contested, leading High Court actions against, for example, a local council's plans for comprehensive education and against the signing of the Treaty of Accession to the Common Market. In 1973 he was successful in getting a temporary ban placed on the showing of a controversial film about the painter and film maker Andy Warhol.

As chairman of Self-Help, he launched an appeal for the raising of £50,000 to establish a reward fund out of which sums would be paid to people who provided information leading to the arrest of terrorist bombers. It was after this stand that many of his friends felt that he was putting his life at risk. He was aware of this but would never have dreamt of withdrawing.

McWhirter's zeal was remarkable; he was the moving spirit in the setting up of the Current Affairs Press which it was hoped would produce a newspaper should Fleet Street be paralysed by a strike. In 1975, he was closely involved in the High Court action to free a car from the car ferry Eagle when, during a dispute, the crew refused to allow car owners to disembark their vehicles.

Early in the summer he signed an advertisement by Current Affairs Press which appeared in *The Guardian* and urged cooperative action by commuters and other travellers in the face of the threatened railway strike. In the advertisement his strong views on trade union powers were firmly stated.

Ross McWhirter was born on August 12, 1925, at 8 p.m.—20 minutes later, he was wont to say, than his twin brother Norris. He was educated at Marlborough College. He saw service in the Royal Navy and like his brother read law at Oxford where both distinguished themselves as athletes. Later they established a reputation as sporting commentators. That special rapport which exists between twins served them brilliantly and they began specializing in a fact and research agency concentrating on sporting achievements.

In October 1955 appeared the first edition of the *Guinness Book of Records*, co-edited by the McWhirters. It was at once apparent that the McWhirters' passion for facts and figures and an urgent need to know was shared by the public at large: in a year five editions were called for and it is now estimated that over 24 million copies have been sold. Ross McWhirter stood unsuccessfully as a Conservative at Edmonton in 1964.

Recently both he and his brother had been seen on B.B.C. televison with Roy Castle in *The Record Breakers*.

He was married and had two sons.

Ross, a sprinter with his twin brother Norris for the Achilles Club, made a considerable impact as a sports journalist in the 1950s. He wrote about rugby football and lawn tennis for the *Star*; edited the monthly magazine *Athletics World;* was co-author of *Get to Your Marks* (1951), a masterly statistical and historical survey of athletics and, together with U. A. Titley of *The Times*, was the author of the official history of the Rugby Football Union. He was a former chairman of the Sports Writers' Association.

Ross had a wide range of interests outside sport which made him the ideal man, with his twin Norris, to compile and edit, back in 1955, the first edition of the *Guinness Book of Records*—a unique collection of superlatives which had really been conceived when they were boys at Marlborough. Medals and decorations, coins and knotty points of law were among the many subjects upon which he could provide an almost omniscient knowledge.

He thought and talked crisply but, even if his firmly-held political views sometimes seemed extreme, he was capable of many private acts of kindness and was always ready to share his knowledge with lazier and less intelligent colleagues. Together with his twin, he brought an increased international awareness to British athletics reporting and a healthy regard for facts which was later to be developed into one of the most remarkable publishing success stories of this century.

November 29, 1975.

Bruno Maderna, the distinguished Italian conductor and composer, died at Darmstadt, West Germany on November 14, 1973.

Maderna was born in Venice in 1920, and studied the violin and theory at the Conservatory there. Then he went to Milan, to study with Pizzetti for a year, and then to Rome, before returning to Venice to work with Malipiero, who gave him his first interest in Stravinsky and Schoenberg. After the war he went to Scherchen in Vienna. There he became more seriously interested in the Second Viennese School. Debussy and, later, Mahler were the other big influences on him.

His own first composition of consequence was his *Musica per due dimensione* in 1952, in which he for the first time combined electronic means with ordinary instruments. He developed these methods in his second work of the same name in 1958, and with *Serenata III* and *IV*. Other works of significance were *Continuo* (a purely electronic work), a piano concerto, string quartet, *Honegrêves*, for flute and piano, oboe concertos, the third of which had its premiere at the Holland Festival in summer 1972 and was performed for the first time in Britain only a month before he died.

He came to stand beside Berio as leader of the avant garde in Italy, and together they founded the experimental studio in Milan.

Maderna was a leading light of the various Darmstadt modern music gatherings and generally in the dissemination of new music through his lectures and his conducting, and he was acknowledged as a complete master of the most difficult score.

Over the past few years Maderna worked often and successfully with the B.B.C. Symphony Orchestra at the instigation of his friend Sir William Glock. His last appearance in Britain was on November 5, 1973 with the London Symphony Orchestra.

Those who worked with Maderna always found him cheerful, amusing and educative without ever being didactic. His music was an expression of that personality, its pointillism never degenerating into mere attenuation, his control of the post-Webernian means always related to solid musical worth and not mere experimentation for its own sake. His command of the orchestra was matched by his feeling for the voice in his few vocal works, and he always rejected mere machine music, realizing that the art must have a human basis.

November 16, 1973.

Anna Magnani, who died on September 26, 1973 at the age of 65, was in every way the most formidable star the Italian cinema has produced. An actress of enormous temperament and volatility, she seemed able to epitomize Italian womanhood in all its various aspects, whether the "Appassionaria" of the occupation years in *Rome, Open City,* or the incorrigible matriarch, indomitable in Visconti's *Bellissima,* or defeated by life in Pasolini's *Mamma Roma.*

She was born on March 7, 1908, in Alexandria, the daughter of an Egyptian father and an Italian mother, and was taken to Rome when she was five. She studied acting at the Eleanora Duse school and began her stage career at 17.

An early success was in the title role of O'Neill's *Anna Christie,* which she subsequently toured with her own company. Her first film appearance was in 1934, and the following year she married the director, Goffredo Alessandrini, who directed her in *Cavalleria* (1936). The actress separated from her husband, by whom she had a son, in 1950.

International stardom came to her with Rossellini's *Rome, Open City,* in which she played the girl friend of a Resistance leader who is shot by the Germans when she incites the women of a popular quarter to stone the soldiers who have taken off her man. She was again directed by Rossellini in *The Miracle,* and in a highly idiosyncratic interpretation of Cocteau's* dramatic solo, *La Voix Humaine.*

Visconti directed one of her most memorable performances in *Bellissima.*

By this time a major international figure, Magnani made three films in Hollywood in the fifties: George Cukor's *Wild is the Wind* and two adaptations from Tennessee Williams, Daniel Mann's *The Rose Tattoo* and Sidney Lumet's *The Fugitive Kind,* from *Orpheus Descending.*

In recent years her screen appearances had become less frequent. In 1962 she played the tart-mother of Pasolini's second film, *Mamma Roma;* and her remarkable last appearance in a major feature film was a brief comic rebuke to the director in Fellini's *Roma.*

Recently she had overcome her mistrust of television to embark on a series of films directed for Italian television by Alfredo Giannetti. The subjects of the episodes promised to add to her gallery of portrayals of Italian womanhood.

September 27, 1973.

King Mahendra—See Nepal.

René Maheu, who was Director General of the United Nations' Educational, Scientific and Cultural Organization (Unesco) for 12 years before he retired in November 1974, died in France on December 19, 1975 at the age of 70.

The son of a family of teachers from South-West France, Maheu spent almost 30 years in Unesco joining it at its beginnings under Julian Huxley, and probably no single official ever personified the Paris-based world body better. Running an international bureaucracy, subject always to member governments' attempts at pressure, Maheu insisted with typical French intellectual stubborness that Unesco must be at the service of a militant humanism, based on the respect of the cultural diversity of all nations.

He led more than anyone the transformation of Unesco from an essentially western organization to one where the emerging "third world" of the 1960s gradually assumed its full place. This he believed would be a long term gain, even if aspects of the change, such as the Arab-Israeli conflict, created serious problems for the organization and soured the original funding countries.

After graduating from the École Normale Supérieure, Maheu first taught philosophy in Cologne and then went to London, where he remained at the French Institute till the Second World War broke out. It was during the war that he first became involved in educational reform, serving in Morocco in the French administration.

In 1965 the World Congress of Education Ministers endorsed Unesco's programme to combat world illiteracy. With characteristic courage and frankness Maheu was later to describe this endeavour as "my greatest defeat", for at the end of a decade's effort with the population increase the absolute number of illiterates in the world had risen. Maheu observed that the reasons were "as much political as financial".

One of his last appeals as Director General was to the newly-rich oil states to help finance fresh programmes.

December 22, 1975.

Ivan Mikhailovich Maisky, who died on September 3, 1975 at the age of 91, will remain one of the central figures in the diplomatic history of Europe of the 1930s; and during the 1939-45 War no man played a greater part than he in the history of Anglo-Soviet relations.

Maisky had, indeed, been Soviet Ambassador in London for a record period of over 11 years—from 1932 to 1943—and there must be few British statesmen, politicians and leading journalists of the older generation who do not remember, with some warmth, "pussy-face" Maisky, who, especially during the second half of his ambassadorship, succeeded in becoming one of the most popular figures in London.

Like other Ambassadors, Maisky was, needless to say, first and foremost his own government's agent: but when he spoke in his quiet, often humorous way, he always seemed to speak as an individual, not as a mere record of his master's voice. He had, indeed, none of the characteristics of the more formal and self-important Stalinist type that was to develop especially after the Second World War. There was nothing forbidding or standoffish about Maisky: like Litvinov and Vmansky, he belonged to that class of Soviet diplomat of the 1920s and 1930s who sought to "make friends and influence people". In this Maisky succeeded admirably. He and Madame Maisky were wonderful hosts, and there is no doubt that they did their utmost to influence British public opinion by a sheer display of friendliness. Conservatives were just as welcome at his luncheon parties as Labourites, and he certainly cultivated a large part of the British press with consummate skill.

He lost few of his British friends even during the most difficult period—during the Soviet-German Pact and the Soviet-Finnish war. He would explain to them *con dolore* how the western powers had brought the "most regrettable" pact with Hitler upon themselves; or why the Finnish war was a hard strategic necessity. Occasionally he gave the impression that he was not entirely in agreement with this or that aspect of Soviet foreign policy; and this was perhaps true.

For if Stalin and Molotov were extremely hardheaded men in their diplomacy, men like Litvinov, Maisky, and Vmansky had a genuine liking for "the West", and were personally devoted to that cause of collective security which they had tried to defend in vain.

Yet for all his apparent geniality and good humour, Maisky was also a man of strong likes and dislikes; if he liked Lloyd George and Eden, he distrusted Simon and Halifax, and was little short of pathological in his hatred of Chamberlain.

Maisky's association with England had been a much longer one than the 11 years of his ambassadorship. He first arrived in Britain in 1912, aged 26, an almost penniless political refugee. He had been born in 1884 near Nizhni-Novgorod, the son of an Army doctor. Although his father, whose real name was Lyakhovetsky, was of Jewish descent, Maisky did not like this mentioned. He was in fact a typical old-time Russian *intelligent*. He spent most of his early youth at Omsk, where he received his secondary education, and later went to St. Petersburg University. Like many other students of his generation he engaged in revolutionary agitation, and was exiled for a short time to Siberia. However, he escaped to Germany and took a degree in economics at Munich University, and then in 1912 went to England, where he met Litvinov and also a number of Labour leaders.

In 1917 he returned to Russia and joined the Mensheviks, but became converted to Bolshevism by 1922. Good linguists with a good knowledge of the outside world were (apart from the former upper classes) scarce in Russia in those days, and Maisky was given his first diplomatic job as a press officer at the Commissariat of Foreign Affairs: a "cosmopolitan" and émigré background was still very common among Soviet diplomats in the 1920s. He made rapid progress; by 1925 he was sent to London as counsellor to Krassin, and stayed two years.

The most memorable episode in which he was personally involved during those years took place at Stratford on Avon. Somebody at Stratford had sent by mistake an invitation to the Soviet Embassy to the Shakespeare Birthday Celebrations in April 1926.

In those days feeling against Russia was running high in official quarters, and, when the Foreign Office learnt that a representative of the Soviets had been invited to Stratford, various clumsy attempts were made to dissuade Maisky from going. He declared, however, that since the invitation had not been withdrawn he would go. Once at Stratford he made a cultured little speech about Shakespeare's popularity in Russia, and left it at that. His hosts were still highly embarrassed by his presence, which, moreover, produced later in the day a street demonstration in his favour on the part of numerous workers, who had specially come from Birmingham. The organizers of the celebrations whisked him away in a car to a remote railway station where he was put on the London train. This was Maisky's first experiment in "public relations" in Britain.

Worse was to come. After the Arcos raid, which, needless to say, he thought wholly unjustified, Maisky found himself forced to leave London. He saw in the Arcos raid the temporary triumph of the "die-hards" (Birkenhead, Churchill,* Joynson-Hicks) over the "moderates" (Austen Chamberlain and Balfour), and did not think that the breach would last very long. Moreover, he knew that Labour was pro-Russian.

Maisky was seen off at the station by Arthur Henderson, Citrine, Tillett, Lansbury and other prominent leaders. The *Morning Post* was furious.

After a spell in Tokyo and Helsinki, Maisky was appointed Ambassador to London in October 1932, after Sokolnikov's recall to Moscow. British opinion was still sharply divided in its attitude to Russia, and Maisky was faced with a variety of problems ranging from the outcry against "Russian dumping" to the ludicrous "Jesus Christ Safety Matches" affair. A few days after his arrival, he was booed at the Guildhall banquet and his relations with the Foreign Secretary, Sir John Simon, were on the frigid side. Nevertheless Maisky persisted in his efforts to normalize Soviet-British trade relations. New complications arose as a result of the arrest of the Metro-Vickers engineers in Russia in March 1933;

the trade negotiations were suspended, and Simon introduced on April 5 his embargo Bill banning 80 per cent of Soviet imports. It was not till July that the prison sentences on the two remaining Vickers engineers were commuted (the others had been expelled from Russia), and that trade negotiations were resumed. Maisky had handled a highly tricky situation with great tact and skill.

Maisky was fully aware of two conflicting currents in British foreign policy and did his utmost to bring about a top-level *rapprochement* between London and Moscow with the help of the "collective security" and anti-appeasement elements. Although he failed to persuade Simon to go to Moscow, after his Berlin visit, he nevertheless helped to arrange an Eden-Stalin meeting in Moscow. This took place at the end of March 1935 in the presence of both Litvinov and Maisky.

Maisky's line then, as later, was that there were no fundamental differences of interest between Britain and the U.S.S.R., that it was their common interest to maintain peace with the help of the League.

But his task was not easy. After the Abyssinian fiasco and the Rhineland coup came the Spanish war. As the Russian representative on the non-intervention committee Maisky, increasingly exasperated, denounced its activities on October 16, 1937 as "a complete farce". Then came the invasion of Austria, and, soon afterwards, Munich.

On behalf of the Soviet Union Maisky made one desperate appeal after another to "stop aggression". After the Anschluss, Russia proposed, in vain, an international conference; she was excluded from Munich; then, after the German invasion of Czechoslovakia in March 1939 Maisky proposed a six-power conference (Britain, France, Soviet Union, Poland, Romania, Turkey). Chamberlain turned down the proposal as "premature". Instead, Russia was urged to give unilateral guarantees to Poland and Romania similar to those given them by Britain.

On May 3, 1939 Molotov replaced Litvinov as Foreign Commissar; it was a clear sign that something had changed; the "Litvinov-Maisky" policy might yet be given one more chance—but only one. Those who remember Maisky during the summer of 1939 also remember the extreme anxiety with which he viewed the whole situation—complete with the Strange mission to Moscow, followed by the Drax-Heywood mission, which, somehow, ran parallel with certain last-minute appeasement attempts.

After the signing of the Soviet-German Pact and the beginning of the Second World War, Maisky was in an extremely difficult position. He was an unhappy and disillusioned man.

After Molotov's abortive visit to Berlin in November 1940, and after Eden had succeeded Halifax at the Foreign Office a month later, there was a slight improvement in Anglo-Soviet relations; on February 12 1941, Eden, the Foreign Secretary, even lunched at the Soviet Embassy; this was something that had not happened for a very long time.

But it was not till the German invasion of Russia that Maisky came into his own again. Once again he became a highly popular figure in London; but as early as September 22, 1941 he had already made his first "Second Front" speech, a theme he was not to relinquish until the end of his ambassadorship.

During those first two years of the Russo-German war, Maisky was enormously active. He signed mutual assistance pacts with Poland and Czechoslovakia, accompanied Eden on his visit to Moscow in December 1941, and played a leading part in negotiating the Anglo-Soviet alliance during Molotov's visit to London in May 1942. In September that year he was awarded the Order of Lenin to mark the tenth anniversary of his ambassadorship in London.

In 1943 Maisky was recalled to Moscow, where he became one of Molotov's deputies at the Foreign Commissariat. Although he was to play a fairly important role during the next few years (notably as Soviet member of the Reparations Committee) both he and Litvinov began, more and more, to be treated as backnumbers. Both were too "Western" and too "cosmopolitan" to Stalin's taste, and it is common knowledge that neither was wholly in sympathy with some of the harsher aspects of postwar Soviet foreign policy, as personified by Stalin, Molotov and Vyshinsky.

But Maisky was, if anything, luckier than Litvinov, perhaps because he was more tactful and discreet. If Litvinov openly criticized the official Russian post-Yalta policy—which was miles removed from anything he had stood for—Maisky resigned himself to a dull, but honourable old age. He was elected member of the Academy of Sciences, and wrote a number of books, including his memoirs. In Britain they were published by Hutchinson in the years stated. *Journey into the Past* (1962), which described his early years in London, was full of salty reminiscences and was soon followed by the weightier volume, *Who Helped Hitler?* in 1964, which was a highly spiced main course. His version of the events of the years 1938-39 and in particular of the moves and motives which led to the signing of the Soviet-German pact, did not accord with received opinions in the West, and *The Times* review of the book set in train a notable correspondence in which Maisky himself joined.

Further volumes of reminiscence continued to appear. *Spanish Notebooks* was published in the West in 1966 and a year later came *Memoirs of a Soviet Ambassador*. Three extracts from this book were printed in *The Times*.

September 6, 1975.

Endelkatchew Makonnen, a former Ethiopian Prime Minister, who was executed on November 24, 1974, was at one time Ethiopian Ambassador in London.

Born in 1926 of a distinguished father who had been Prime Minister and Ethiopian Ambassador in London, he was educated in England and took a degree at Oriel in 1951. In 1952, having entered the Ethiopian Foreign Service, he was appointed Chief of Protocol in Addis Ababa. In 1954 he went to London in the suite of the Emperor and was made an honorary C.V.O.

In 1955 he led the Ethiopian delegation to the Afro-Asian conference at Bandung, and in 1956 he attended the London conference which followed Nasser's* nationalization of the Suez Canal. After a spell as Vice-Minister of Social Affairs and Education, he was in 1959, to his obvious pleasure, appointed Ambassador to London as his father had been.

In 1961 he was taken back to Addis Aba to become Minister of Commerce and Industry, and next year he led an Ethiopian delegation to a United Nations conference. In 1965 he was awarded an honorary G.C.M.G. on the occasion of the Queen's state visit to Ethiopia, and subsequently he became successively permanent Ethiopian representative at the United Nations and Minister of Communications.

When in 1974 the revolt in Ethiopia led to a popular demand for the resignation of the Cabinet and the impeachment of its members on charges of inefficiency and corruption, the Emperor called on Makonnen to form a new cabinet.

He was confronted by a serious situation, with the armed forces striking for higher pay and unrest throughout the country. But he was relatively well thought of by the younger educated Ethiopians who were the principal malcontents, and by a mixture of firmness and conciliation he succeeded in restoring comparative order.

Within five months, however, it became clear that his moderation was inadequate to satisfy the reformist zeal of the so-called Coordinating Committee of the Armed Forces, a body of comparatively junior officers into whose hands much of the real power had passed. In July he was forced out of office and held in an army camp.

November 25, 1974.

Gian Francesco Malipiero, who died at Treviso, Italy, on August 1, 1973 at the age of 91, was the doyen of Italian musicians, since he was active as a composer into old age, presided for many years over the Venice Conservatoire, and edited Italian classics, in particular the complete works of Monteverdi.

He was a member of the group of Italian composers with Casella at their head who soon after the First World War sought to enlarge the scope of Italian music by breaking through the national obsession with opera. He was himself the composer of a number of operas, but he set himself to pick up the old Italian tradition of chamber music and to write symphonies, concertos and various kinds of symphonic poems that might look France and Germany in the face.

His opera *Sette Canzoni* was performed in Edinburgh in 1969. Performances of his instrumental and choral works have been intermittent in Britain. His aim of achieving a rhapsodic line of extended lyrical melody, which has labelled him "neo-baroque", is realized most successfully in his slow movements. The quick movements of his very varied symphonies have been sometimes criticized as being contrived and lacking in impulse, though withal well contrived and scored with a sense of orchestral colour—for was he not after all a Venetian?

He was born in Venice and had his musical education principally at Bologna, where he was a composition pupil of Enrico Bossi. He taught at Parma and became principal of the Liceo Benedetto Marcello in Venice in 1939. Installed in the Palazzo Pisani, he restored the building and revised the curriculum, soon making it a centre for his own teaching of composition to students from all over the world. His complete edition of Monteverdi occupied him from 1926 to 1942; in the next decade he devoted himself to Vivaldi in his capacity as artistic director of the institute formed for the systematic publication of that earlier Venetian's works.

In his operas he moved away from large-scale dramatic designs in favour of sequences of tableaux on themes from Euripedes, Seneca and Shakespeare. For his choral works he took texts from Virgil (both *Aeneid* and *Georgics*) and Horace. His orchestral works were impressionistic and evocative of places, though they have not gained the wider currency attained by his contemporary Respighi. There are for instance three sets of three tone-poems called *Impressioni dal vero* and seven symphonies with rather less specific programmes.

He wrote a score of piano pieces and a handful of songs. At the Venice festival of the International Society for Contemporary Music in 1957 a whole programme was devoted to Malipiero's larger works, which included two examples from a series of pieces described as *Dialoghi*, one a harpsichord concerto and the other a setting for baritone and orchestra of *La morte di Socrate*, based, like Satie's cantata, on Plato's *Phaedo*.

Malipiero's range was thus wide in subject and medium, but he remained a great Venetian rather than a great Italian or a great international figure. He did, however, contribute much to the restoration of Italian music, other than opera, that is, to the international musical scene.

August 3, 1973.

Lord Malvern, P.C., C.H., K.C.M.G., first Prime Minister of the Federation of Rhodesia and Nyasaland from 1953 to 1956 and earlier for 20 years of Southern Rhodesia, died on May 8, 1971 at the age of 87.

Lord Salisbury, in an appreciation written on Malvern's retirement from the Premiership of the Federation of Rhodesia and Nyasaland in 1956, said: "That he should have held the position of Prime Minister longer than any other man in the history of the British Commonwealth and Empire would in itself entitle him to a high place in our history. But what makes his career more remarkable . . . is that it was not until he was well on in middle age that he came into political life at all . . . until then his whole life had been spent in medicine as a physician and surgeon".

Malvern's years as Prime Minister of Southern Rhodesia were marked by the country's steady development before the war, by its great record during the war and by its leap forward on the path of progress after the war. It was this record of economic development and evidence of political maturity and stability under the leadership of his personality that played a highly important part in bringing about the federation.

The Rt. Hon. Godfrey Martin Huggins, first Viscount Malvern, of Rhodesia and Bexley, was born at Bexley on July 6, 1883, the eldest son of Godfrey Huggins, a member of the Stock Exchange. Huggins was educated at Malvern College. It was there that he developed mastoid trouble which left him with the permanent handicap of deafness which he was so brilliantly to overcome.

At the age of 18, he became a medical student at St. Thomas's Hospital, London. He qualified as a doctor in 1906 and became F.R.C.S. two years later. After 2½ years in post-graduate appointments at St. Thomas's he went to the Hospital for Sick Children in Great Ormond Street, first as house physician and then as medical superintendent. He went to Southern Rhodesia in 1911 "for a rest and a change" and acted as locum for a Salisbury doctor. But he soon grew to like the country and decided to remain, as a general practitioner and surgeon.

In the First World War he joined the Royal Army Medical Corps, became a captain and surgical specialist, and served in England, France, and Malta. One of the books on surgery which he wrote from his wartime experience—on amputation—is still a standard work. In 1921 he gave up general practice to become a consulting surgeon, a branch in which for long he was one of the best-known figures in Southern Africa. His reputation was such that when he became Prime Minister he found it impossible to give up surgical practice altogether. His old patients and their friends were insistent that he should attend to them. He would often operate in the early mornings before going on to his

ministerial duties. It was not until 1950 that he gave up surgery altogether.

Huggins was first elected to represent Salisbury North in the Southern Rhodesia Legislative Assembly in 1923. Although he favoured linking Southern Rhodesia with South Africa, like many other Rhodesians after the referendum of 1922, he loyally accepted the decision of the majority and joined Sir Charles Coghlan's Rhodesia Party to help make a success of self-government.

Huggins was returned again, with the big majority in his constituency which he always commanded, in the general election of 1928 but as time went on he became impatient with the policy of his party.

Then the world depression hit Southern Rhodesia and the Government was forced into strict economies. One measure introduced into the House was to reduce the salaries of civil servants and it was over this that Huggins's break with the Government came. In the end the one vote needed to give the Government its required two-thirds majority was his. He gave it as he was pledged to support the general policy of his party, but with greatest reluctance; and announced at the same time he would leave the party. After a period in the political wilderness he was persuaded to accept the leadership of the Reform Party, in opposition to the Rhodesian (Government) Party, shortly before the general election of 1933.

In this campaign, he showed the drive and gifts of a born political leader, and the Reform Party, with 16 seats, was returned with a clear majority over the Rhodesia Party (nine) and Labour (five) combined. This upset of a long-established order was a surprise and to none more so than Huggins. But having put his hand to the plough, he was not one to abandon it, and that guiding hand remained for 23 years.

The Reform Party proved a difficult team to handle because of the strong individuality of some of its members. The situation came to a head within a year, and the major elements of the party decided to merge with similar elements in the old Rhodesia Party to form a new party under Huggins's leadership. They went to the country in November 1934, and the new United Party was returned with 24 seats to Labour's five and Reform's one.

The next general election was in April 1939, held before the statutory five years elapsed in order to get the country's decision on its Government because of the threat of war. Huggins's United Party was returned, again with a very large majority—23 seats to Labour's seven. War broke out in September, and later the fifth Parliament of Southern Rhodesia, and with it the third Huggins Government, had its life prolonged by Act of Parliament to seven years, which took it through the war period.

For nearly a decade the Liberal Party—formed towards the end of the war—had a big influence in Southern Rhodesian politics, and in the first postwar general election in 1946 nearly defeated the United Party Government. The Liberals won 12 seats to the United Party's 13, while the revived Rhodesia Party gained three and Labour two.

The Government was always at the mercy of a small minority group. Eventually it was defeated in the House on a minor financial issue and again went to the country. By this time—1948—closer union with Northern Rhodesia had become a dominant issue in Southern Rhodesian politics. With this in the forefront Huggins led the United Party with all his old fire, and the result was as overwhelming as that of 1934. The United Party gained 24 seats to the Liberals' five and Labour's one.

This Government was in power during the negotiations which led to the advent of the ill-fated Federation of Rhodesia and Nyasaland in 1953. Huggins then relinquished office as Prime Minister of Southern Rhodesia to assume immediately that of Prime Minister of the new Federation. It was on February 17, 1955, that Huggins set up his record as the Commonwealth Prime Minister with the longest period of service, completing 7,829 days of continuous service from 1933.

In the multitude of affairs in which Lord Malvern had perforce to take an active interest, he would probably have indentified himself most prominently with native affairs, education and the federation. Sympathetic in outlook towards the African and his advancement, he was also a realist —with the not unexpected result that from time to time he was vigorously assailed both by those who would force the pace of African advancement and those who feared that the pace was too fast already.

For many years he held the portfolio of Native Affairs in Southern Rhodesia as well as that of Prime Minister, and under his guidance native education, housing, hospitals and clinics made big strides, while Rhodesia came to the forefront in research into tropical diseases. He was guided by the principle, which he repeatedly expressed, that no modern civilized society can be built up at the expense of any class or any race.

He believed that the economic and social advancement of the African masses was of greater importance than their political advancement, and that economic and social advance would gradually justify and bring political advance. He urged that wise provision must be made for the African's absorption into industry, for the population increase was at a rate that would soon make the old peasant life in the reserves an impossibility for most of them.

He was described as the chief architect of federation. It is certainly very doubtful whether, without his influence with British statesmen and the confidence the people of Southern Rhodesia—whose vote was the deciding factor—had in him, federation would have come about.

He retired on November 1, 1956, the day the British Government, supported by the French, launched the Suez adventure. His successor as Prime Minister of the Federation was Sir Roy Welensky. The question is often asked: would the federation have survived had Malvern remained its leader? His biographers, Dr. L. H. Gann and Dr. M. Gelfand, do not think so. His thinking was not in accord with British thinking, which favoured African nationalist aspirations.

In public life Malvern caused comment and criticism from time to time by habit variously described as impishness, puckishness, and a propensity for saying exactly what he thought irrespective of the place or the occasion. He did this to the exasperation of his political opponents and the anxiety of his friends.

He was awarded honorary degrees by the universities of Oxford, London, Rhodes and Witwatersrand and in April 1955 the Freedom of Salisbury (Rhodesia).

After his retirement he seldom intruded actively into politics, but he quickly assumed the role of elder statesman and his advice was sought by many. He watched anxiously and angrily as the federation ran deeper and deeper into trouble. Like his successor, Sir Roy Welensky, he believed that Britain let the federation down. He made a number of trips to Britain and spoke in the House of Lords on the subject.

But perhaps his saddest disappointment was the defeat in Southern Rhodesia, in the general election of 1962, of Sir Edgar Whitehead and the United Federal Party by the Rhodesian Front. It meant that the Rhodesian electorate, after more than a generation, had turned away from the policies of racial progress which he had initiated. He told his friends it was a victory for those white Rhodesians who had always been anti-everything.

Later, as the Rhodesian Front's policies began to harden and a note of intolerance to creep into Rhodesian politics that had not been there before, he was to tell them that for the first time he was concerned about Rhodesia's future.

He remained pro-British and a dedicated loyalist to the end, emerging from his retirement into the political arena to condemn both Rhodesia's unilateral declaration of independence and the declaration of a republic. One of his few latent public appearances included an attack on the Government for the abolition of the Union Jack and the adoption of the republican flag which he described as "pagan".

In 1921 he married Blanche Elizabeth Slatter, daughter of James Slatter of Pietermaritzburg.

They had two sons—his heir, John Godfrey Huggins, born in 1922, and the Hon. Martin James Huggins, born in 1928.

May 10, 1971.

Former Bishop of Manchester—See Greer.

Constantine Maniadakis, the notorious Minister of Security of the Metaxas dictatorship in Greece from 1936 to 1940, died in an Athens hospital on February 28, 1972 after a brief illness. He was 78.

He acquired a reputation for torturing opponents of the regime with massive doses of castor oil and forcing them to sit on blocks of ice; yet many suspect that these rumours had been put out by himself as a psychological deterrent to subversive activity.

Born of poor peasant stock at Sofikon, near Corinth, in 1893, he claimed he went to grammar school in a neighbouring village by walking barefoot, in order not to wear out his shoes which he would put on outside the classroom. In 1912 he volunteered for service in the Balkan wars, later passing through the army officers' cadet school where he graduated in the class of 1916—the one which gave Greece several of its postwar politicians.

He took part in the Asia Minor campaign in 1919 and kept his men under such tight discipline that, during the Greek Army's debacle there, he was the only battalion commander to return home with his unit intact. He was cashiered in 1923 for his part in the abortive royalist *coup d'état* of General Metaxas.

He made a fortune later as a public works contractor. In 1936 his lucrative career was interrupted when, after the successful Metaxas *coup d'état*, the dictator asked him to become Minister of Public Order. His name soon became a household bogy because of the rumours of tortures he inflicted on those who opposed the regime. Former politicians were banished to provincial cities and he scored major successes by disrupting the entire machinery of the Greek Communist Party. When the Greek-Italian war broke out in 1940 he promptly "bagged in" all Axis agents.

The possibility that he might become Prime Minister was discussed between King George II and the British after the sudden death of Metaxas in 1940, but he himself declined because he felt he was not qualified. After the German invasion in 1941, he fled from Greece to Cairo with the government of Emmanuel Tsouderos, in which he served as Minister of the Interior. He was soon (June 1941) sent on a "mission" to South America, mainly because he was an embarrassment to the Greek statesmen he had persecuted and who were now serving in the same cabinet. He returned to liberated Greece in 1949 and set up the National Revival Party which won 16 seats in the short-lived parliament of 1950. Later he founded the party of "The Principles of Ioannis Metaxas", but he eventually sided with the National Radical Union, the main right wing block, and was elected deputy for Corinth in 1958, 1961, and 1964, the last year that elections were held in Greece.

A thick-set, witty and picturesque character, he managed to restore friendly personal relations with all his former "clients", as he called them, the politicians he had persecuted and exiled. Being a bachelor he had become a "regular" at the open-air cafés of Kolonaki Square in Athens where he revelled in post-midnight political discussions.

February 29, 1972.

Arthur Mann, C.H., who died on July 26, 1972 at the age of 96, edited the *Yorkshire Post* for 20 years with outstanding independence and distinction, particularly in its fight against appeasement before the Second World War. He retired from journalism in November 1939, was made a Companion of Honour in the New Year Honours List, 1941, and was a Governor of the B.B.C. from 1941 to 1946.

The recent death of the Duke of Windsor recalled for many people the initiative he took in writing a strong leader prompted by the Bishop of Bradford's address admonishing the Duke when King Edward VIII.

Arthur Henry Mann was born at Warwick on July 7, 1876, the eldest of the 13 children of Alderman James Wight Mann, who was an honorary freeman and twice mayor.

Arthur was educated at Warwick School where he captained the cricket eleven. His first post was that of a reporter on the *Western Mail*, Cardiff, where he was articled for three years to Lascelles Carr, uncle of Sir Emsley Carr, and was trained by Sir William Davies. He found time to play cricket for Glamorgan until his appointment to the company's evening paper, which he sub-edited mostly single-handed.

After a period on the *Birmingham Mail*, he edited the *Birmingham Despatch*, and next became London editor of the Manchester *Daily Dispatch*, then owned by Sir Edward Hulton. By now it was clear that Mann would rise higher, and in his next editorship, that of the *Evening Standard*, also owned then by Hulton, he showed judgment and ability which had been strengthened by his varied experience. It was he who raised the intellectual level of the paper, and who, during the 1914-18 War, started "The Londoner's Diary", which has been a feature of London evening journalism ever since.

When J. S. R. Phillips died in 1919 Mann was offered the editorship of the *Yorkshire Post*, and until his retirement he edited it brilliantly and fearlessly. His tall figure and seeming air of quiet detachment were apt to create in others an impression of austerity, but behind his manner was penetrating observation combined with shrewd judgment. He wrote little, although his briefs to his leader-writers were sometimes nearly as long as the leading articles themselves, and he was exacting in his demands for a high standard of work from his staff. He himself was at his desk from noon until after midnight. Outside the office his chief personal interests were politics, horse-racing and bridge.

Mann had a deeply rooted belief in the value of independence in newspapers. Although the *Yorkshire Post* was Conservative in politics, he never hesitated to express in it bold criticisms of policy or to deviate from the party line when convinced that it was right to do so. He gave many warnings against the dangers facing Britain, and vigorously opposed the appeasement policy of Neville Chamberlain before and during the Munich crisis of 1938.

Criticisms of Chamberlain which he published displeased many leading Yorkshire Conservatives and some shareholders and directors of the newspaper company. But he was strongly supported by the chairman, Rupert Beckett, who told the shareholders roundly that he would himself resign rather than let criticisms of Arthur Mann be pressed. It was a tense and successful battle for the independence of an editor.

As editor Mann was fearless, and he never wavered from his duty as he conceived it. "I believe", he once said, "that in the long run a newspaper, taking from honest conviction an unpopular line, does not lose influence, and soon, when feeling has cooled down, recovers any circulation it may have lost".

The steep rise in the cost of newspaper production on the eve of war placed the *Yorkshire Post* in a difficulty. Its quality was high, its sales low. Mann resolutely refused to drop the price from two pence to a penny to increase its sales. The board decided that the only possible course was to bring about a merger—discussed for some years previously but staved off—between its companion morning paper the *Leeds Mercury* and the *Post,* and to arrange for Mann to retire. This was done in November 1939.

Mann resigned on this issue alone, and not, as was erroneously believed, because of any resentment of his foreign policy. He was succeeded by William Linton Andrews, who had edited the *Mercury* since 1923, and who was knighted in 1954.

In 1934 the University of Leeds conferred on Mann the honorary degree of LL.D. for his services to journalism. His appointment as a Governor of the B.B.C. was made when the board was reconstituted in 1941. Mann was an honorary trustee of *The Observer* until he resigned in November 1956, because he disagreed with the way in which it had expressed its attitude over the Suez crisis. He was chairman of the Press Association from 1937 to 1938, and became a director of the Argus Press, Ltd., in 1946.

In private life, Mann was a charming host and a lively talker. Politics was only one of his interests. He could range widely with knowledge. Even in his tenth decade he took a lively interest in all about him. His lifelong hobby and closest interest outside his work was horseracing.

July 28, 1972.

Dr. Hermann Mannheim, who died on January 20, 1974 at the age of 84, was often called the father of modern English criminology.

The discipline of criminology is a comparatively recent addition to the British academic scene. Until the establishment of an Institute of Criminology at Cambridge, it had scarcely more than a foothold in the universities. In the long struggle to establish criminology, Mannheim was in the forefront.

Mannheim was born on October 26, 1889, the only child of Wilhelm Mannheim, of Berlin, a merchant in the Baltic trade.

Hermann was educated at the classical *Gymnasium* at Tilsit in East Prussia. From the age of 19 until he was 22 he studied law and political science at the universities of Munich, Freibourg, Strasbourg and Königsberg. From an early age he had been curious about ethics and social justice; and he attended lectures in philosophy, psychology, psychiatry and sociology.

By 1911, when Mannheim began his legal career proper, he found that the social sciences were of immense relevance to the problems of the criminal act, a line of reasoning which was to develop expression in all his published work. In 1912 he was awarded the degree of *Dr. Juris* at Königsberg for a thesis on criminal negligence, and in 1914 he qualified to practise law as a barrister or magistrate.

Between 1914 and 1918 Mannheim was an artilleryman, first on the Russian front and later in France. His legal and criminological talents did not go unnoticed in the army, and in 1917 he was appointed a judge of court martial. The postwar period saw him serving variously as a legal adviser in local government, and as the chairman of several industrial courts and industrial dispute tribunals.

Mannheim still had strong academic interests, and in 1925 he was appointed a lecturer in law at Berlin University, and at the same time became a deputy magistrate. His abilities were soon recognized, and his promotion through the courts was seen to be rapid.

In 1929 he was made *Professor Extraordinarius* and in 1931 was promoted to be a judge of the *Kammergericht*, the highest court in Prussia, where he sat in the criminal division. By 1933, at the age of 44, he had reached a position of judicial and academic eminence; but within a year he became yet one more victim of Nazism. Stripped of his professorship he resigned from the bench before being ignominiously demoted to a minor post in the Rhineland.

In 1934 Mannheim went to England to begin, as an alien, the second, and in many ways greatest, part of his life. The study of crime as a scientific discipline was hardly known there. Apart from the pioneer work of Charles Goring and Sir Cyril Burt, virtually nothing had been done.

His first year as an émigré he spent in humble conditions, patiently mastering

English, in which he was later to write so eloquently, and studying the English penal system and social conditions generally. In 1935 the L.S.E. appointed him an honorary part-time lecturer, and in 1936 he was awarded a Leon Fellowship at London University which enabled him to carry out his first major researches in this country. The results were published in 1940 under the title of *Social Aspects of Crime in England Between the Wars*, and constituted among other things the first, and most important, critique of English criminal statistics since the late nineteenth century. Meanwhile he enriched his knowledge of sociology, and characteristically involved himself in the penal system, by working as a teacher in Pentonville Prison.

In the winter of 1938-39 he delivered an important series of public lectures at the school, subsequently published as *The Dilemma of Penal Reform*. The removal of the school to Cambridge, with Mannheim now on the staff, saw the publication in 1941 of his classic lectures on *War and Crime*, and gave him the chance to study delinquency among evacuees (*Juvenile Delinquency in an English Middletown*, published in 1948).

By this time Mannheim had established criminology as a subject in the academic curriculum, as well as his own position as a researcher of status. Together with Sir Alexander Carr Saunders,* then director of the school, and Professor E. C. Rhodes, the statistician, he undertook a study for the Home Office which appeared in 1946 under the title *Young Offenders*.

In 1946 Mannheim was appointed Reader in Criminology at London University, the first designated reading post in the subject in the country; an appointment which he held until his retirement in 1955.

Two years before the great Criminal Justice Act of 1948, Mannheim published what many believe to have been his most influential—certainly his most widely read —book, *Criminal Justice and Social Reconstruction*.

Changes then made in the London B.Sc.(Econ) degree in 1949, and in the establishment of the degrees of B.A. and B.Sc.(Sociology), introduced criminology as an examination subject for undergraduates for the first time in a British university. Meanwhile graduate students began to arrive to study under him at the L.S.E. in increasing numbers. In response to his suggestion, criminology became a subject for the degree of LL.M., while the university began to award Ph.D. degrees for theses in criminology and penology.

Mannheim never believed in the isolation of the academic criminologist from the practical sphere. From 1940, until ill health compelled him to retire in 1960, he was a member of the executive committee of the Howard League for Penal Reform. His connexions with the Institute for the Study and Treatment of Delinquency (founded in 1932) were of long standing and he was a member of both the council and the executive of the institute. He was one of the small group of criminologists, lawyers and psychiatrists responsible for founding in 1956, under the auspices of the institute, the Scientific Group for the Study of Delinquency Problems, which later became the British Society of Criminology. He was its chairman from 1956 to 1958.

Again, under the auspices of the institute, he founded, with Edward Glover and Emmanuel Miller, the *British Journal of Delinquency* (now the *British Journal of Criminology*), which rapidly achieved distinction as one of the leading international publications in the field of crime and its treatment. Ten years later, in 1960, the same group began the *Library of Criminology*.

In his last year as an academic teacher he produced with Leslie Wilkins one of the most important studies in penology to appear in Britain, *Prediction Methods in Relation to Borstal Training*. The Mannheim-Wilkins scale provided for the first time a scientific means of assessing the prognosis of Borstal boys.

In the same year he published *Group Problems in Crime and Punishment*, a collection of lectures and papers written over some 20 years. After his retirement he continued his association with the L.S.E. as honorary director of the Criminological Research Unit, working on such problems as those of the short prison sentence, sentencing policy in the magistrates' courts, and the sociology of the prison community. He published *Comparative Criminology* in 1965.

The West German Government conferred on him the rank of Retired President of the Court of Appeal in 1951; he was awarded the Coronation Medal in 1953 and an honorary Doctorate in Laws at Utrecht University in 1957; and was made O.B.E. in 1959.

Although perhaps one of the world's truly great scholars, Mannheim was never too busy to read the faltering essay of the most junior student. His German accent never left him, although his command of written English was superb; but it was never a handicap, rather a source of endearment to those who knew him closely. He became a British subject in 1940, together with his wife, Mona Mark, whom he married in 1919 and who was an unfailing support to him throughout his life. He lived a quiet, unostentatious life in a charming little house in Orpington, in the garden of which some of his greatest work was written.

The debt British criminology owes to Mannheim is great indeed. Future historians of the discipline will, without doubt, place him alongside Tarde, von Liszt, and Sutherland as one of the greatest criminological scholars, as one who was, to quote the title of a notable book he edited in 1959, a Pioneer in Criminology.

January 24, 1974.

Field-Marshal Erich von Manstein, one of the outstanding soldiers of the Second World War, died on June 10, 1973 at the age of 85.

His influence and effect came from powers of mind and depth of knowledge rather than by generating an electrifying current among the troops or "putting over" his personality. Ice-cold in manner although with strong emotions underneath, he commanded more in the style of Moltke than Napoleon and those who cultivate the Napoleonic touch. The range and versatility of Manstein's ability was shown in the way that, after being trained as an infantryman, and then becoming preeminent as a staff planner, he proved a brilliant and thrusting armoured corps commander in his first test run with mechanized troops. In his next big test he proved equally successful in directing the siege-attack on a fortress. By the variety of his experience and qualities he was exceptionally well equipped for high command.

Erich von Manstein was born on November 24, 1887, the tenth child of his parents. His original surname was von Lewinski, but his parents agreed to his adoption by a childless aunt who had married a von Manstein. Both families had long-standing military traditions and 16 of the boy's immediate forbears had been generals, in Prussian or Russian service. After leaving a cadet school in 1906, he was commissioned into the 3rd Regiment of Foot Guards. Badly wounded in the autumn of 1914, he was given a staff post on recovery, and made his mark in a series of such appointments on the Eastern, Western and Balkan fronts.

After the war he was taken into the Reichswehr, and by 1935 he had risen to be head of the operations section of the General Staff, while the next year he was advanced to *Oberquartiermeister 1*—the deputy to the Chief of the General Staff, then General Beck.

Early in 1938, when Fritsch was dismissed from the post of Army Commander-in-Chief, Manstein was sent away to command a division, having come to be regarded in Nazi circles as an obstacle to the extension of their influence in the Army. But on mobilization in 1939 he was made Chief of Staff of Rundstedt's Army Group, which played the decisive role in the Polish campaign. He then moved with Rundstedt to the Western Front, and there soon began to advocate a change in the plan for the coming offensive. He urged that the main thrust, with the bulk of the armoured forces, should be shifted from the right wing in the Belgian plain to the hilly and wooded Ardennes—as the line of least expectation. His persistence in pressing for the change of plan deprived him of a hand in directing it, for he was honourably pushed out of the way by promotion to command a reserve corps, of infantry, just before the new plan was adopted under Hitler's pressure—after hearing Manstein's arguments.

In the crucial opening stage of the offensive, which cut off the Allies' left wing and trapped it on the Channel coast, Manstein's corps merely had a follow-on part. But in the second and final stage it played a bigger role. Under his dynamic leadership, his infantry pushed on so fast on foot that they raced the armoured corps in the drive southward across Somme and Seine to the Loire.

When the German plan of invading England was discarded in favour of an attack on Russia, Manstein was given the command of an armoured corps. With it he made one of the quickest and deepest thrusts of the opening stage, from East Prussia to the Dvina, nearly 200 miles, within four days. Promoted to command the Eleventh Army in the south, he forced an entry into the Crimean peninsula by breaking through the fortified Perekop Isthmus, and in the summer of 1942 further proved his mastery of siege warfare technique by capturing the famous fortress of Sebastopol, the key centre of the Crimea—being Russia's main naval base on the Black Sea.

He was then sent north again to command the intended attack on Leningrad, but called away by an emergency summons to conduct the efforts to relieve Paulus's Sixth Army, trapped that winter at Stalingrad, after the failure of the main German offensive of 1942. The effort failed because Hitler, forbidding any withdrawal, refused to agree to Manstein's insistence that Paulus should be told to break out westward and meet the relieving forces. Following Paulus's surrender, a widespread collapse developed on the Germans' southern front under pressure of advancing Russian armies, but Manstein saved the situation by a brilliant flank counterstroke which recaptured Kharkov and rolled back the Russians in confusion.

Then in the Germans' last great offensive of the war in the East, "Operation Citadel", launched in July 1943 against the Kursk salient, Manstein's "Southern Army Group" formed the right pincer. It achieved a considerable measure of success, but the effect was nullified by the failure of the left pincer, provided by the "Central Army Group". Having checked the German offensive, the Russians now launched their own on a larger scale along a wider front, and with growing strength.

From that time onwards the Germans were thrown on the defensive, strategically, and with the turn of the tide Manstein was henceforth called on to meet, repeatedly, what has always been judged the hardest task of generalship—that of conducting a fighting withdrawal in face of much superior forces. His concept of the strategic defensive gave strong emphasis to offensive action in fulfilling it, and he constantly looked for opportunities of delivering a riposte, while often ably exploiting those which arose. But when he urged that a longer step back should be made—a *strategic* withdrawal—in order to develop the full recoil-spring effect of a counter-offensive against an over-stretched enemy advance Hitler would not heed his arguments.

Unlike many of his fellows, Manstein maintained the old Prussian tradition of speaking frankly, and expressed his criticism forcibly both to Hitler in private and at conferences, in a way that staggered others who were present. That Hitler bore it so long is remarkable evidence of the profound respect he had for Manstein's ability, and a contrast with his attitude to most of his generals, and to the General Staff as a body. In March 1944 Hitler removed Manstein from command and thereby removed from the path of the Russians and their allies the most formidable individual obstacle in their advance to victory.

Manstein moved westward when the Russian tide of advance swept over Eastern Germany, and surrendered himself to the British in May 1945. The Russians demanded that he, along with other generals who had served on the Eastern Front, should be handed over to them as war criminals. The British and Americans refused, but agreed to put them on trial in special military courts. Many questions were raised in England about the legality or justice of the procedure adopted, while a long delay occurred, during which most of the other British-held prisoners of war were released. But Manstein was eventually put on trial, at Hamburg, in August 1949—four years after the end of the war. A subscription list was opened in England, on the initiative of Lord De L'Isle, V.C., and Major-General Lord Bridgeman, to provide funds necessary for an adequate defence and Winston Churchill* was one of the first subscribers. R. T. Paget, Q.C., offered to lead the defence without fee. The trial continued, with intervals, until the week before Christmas.

In the end, Manstein was acquitted on the eight most serious charges, and convicted only on a number of lesser or modified charges. The decision of the court followed Nuremberg Trial precedents, and he was sentenced to 18 years' imprisonment, but this was later reduced, and in 1953 he was released. In a deeper sense, however, that period of imprisonment was penalty and retribution for his failure, in common with most of his fellow generals, to make a firm and timely stand against the Nazi regime and its abuses, despite the disapproval he early and often showed.

In 1955-56 he was chairman of a Military Sub-Committee appointed to advise the Bundestag Defence Committee on the organization, service basis, and operational doctrine of the new German forces of the Federal Republic.

In 1920 Manstein married Jutta Sibylle von Loesch, daughter of a Silesian landowner, and had two sons, the elder of whom was killed in the war.

June 13, 1973.

Gabriel Marcel, who died on October 8, 1973, was a notable French writer, especially celebrated outside France for his philosophical writings and a few out of his many plays. He was also a much-esteemed dramatic critic for many years in Paris.

Although he himself disclaimed the title, he was known as the exponent of a Christian form of existentialism, in opposition to the existentialism of Jean-Paul Sartre. He gave the essence of his thought and experience in a succession of books published in English from 1948 onwards. In them he expressly refuted Sartre's pessimism and atheism; and of Marxism he said it could only numb the disquiet that everyone comes to experience, especially when confronting the problem of death.

To his attachment to Christian values Marcel had come by a long and winding path, as he later described it.

He was born in Paris on December 12, 1889. His father was a distinguished public servant.

Marcel began, in 1914, to write plays of a philosophical kind. He taught philosophy at various lycées, but worked mainly as a freelance critic and philosophical writer. His doctoral dissertation was on Coleridge as compared with Schelling.

Among the chief influences on his development as a thinker were Nietzsche, Kierkegaard, Bergson, and the English and American idealists, Bradley, Bosanquet and Royce. Gradually he emancipated himself from them, and slowly drew nearer to traditional Christianity. At first he inclined to Protestantism, but was converted to Roman Catholicism in 1929, when he was 40.

His philosophic writing now took on a remarkable depth and fervour; but he was never a systematic philosopher, not even primarily a Catholic philosopher. Profoundly attached to his faith, he had a singular openness and tolerance. Most of his writing may be called a self exploration.

His first work to be published in English was *The Philosophy of Existence*, in 1948. The next year, and in 1950, he delivered the Gifford lectures in Aberdeen. They were published in 1951 under the title *The Mystery of Being*. Several other translations followed, and in 1955 one of his plays, Ariadne (French title *Le Chemin de Crète*) was given at Cambridge, and produced at the Arts Theatre in London three years later.

Another play, *Man of God*, the last he wrote before his conversion, toured the Midlands in 1953, and the B.B.C. Third Programme gave the play *Increase and Multiply* in 1955. All these productions received favourable notices. His best and most characteristic play, *Le Monde Cassé* (Broken World) had been first produced in Paris in 1930.

Of his plays in general, he said they were about the soul in exile, the soul suffering from failure to attain communion with itself and its fellows.

The name Marcel himself gave to his philosophy was "concrete"; he was also called a Socratic Christian. Although his language was often difficult, he was not an abstract thinker. Widely acquainted with foreign literature—he quotes E. M. Forster,* T. S. Eliot* and Thomas Hardy, among others—he may, in brief, be said to have discovered for himself that goodness and holiness could not be separated from an acknowledgment of the all-embracing mystery of God.

As he modestly said, his philosophy was more an aid to discovery than a matter of strict demonstration. He was nevertheless found by an increasing number of readers to offer an inspiring answer to materialist frustrations. He was an eloquent advocate of human values in a world more and more dominated by the mechanical and technical. "Master your master", he said.

Apart from the invitation to deliver the Gifford lectures, Marcel received many other marks of esteem; the Grand Prix of Literature of the French Academy in 1948, the Goethe Prize in 1955; he was William James lecturer at Harvard in 1961.

October 10, 1973.

Fredric March, who died on April 14, 1975, at the age of 77, was one of those rare Hollywood performers who maintained throughout his career the respect of critics and public for his acting abilities in spite of his enormous success as a star personality.

Born at Racine, Wisconsin, in 1897, Fredric March, whose real name was Frederich McIntyre Bickel, began his career as a banker after studying at Wisconsin University, but after a spell of war service in the First World War he decided to become an actor instead.

From 1920 he was appearing on the New York stage in such plays as *Your Obedient Husband* and *The American Way*, and even after he had become a prominent film star he continued to return to the stage from time to time. His first film was *The Dummy* (1928) and his first notable one *The Royal Family of Broadway,* Cukor's version of a famous stage skit on the Barrymores. In the next year, 1931, he consolidated his success and won an Academy Award with his brilliant performance in Mamoulian's film of *Doctor Jekyll and Mr. Hyde,* later remade less successfully with Spencer Tracy.*

From this time he starred in a long succession of lavish productions which gave him ample opportunity to show his immense versatility as well as to appear opposite many leading stars under a number of major directors. His range included light comedy as well as heavy drama, and costume roles of all periods and styles. In 1932, for instance, he appeared in de Mille's *Sign of the Cross* and that classic "woman's picture" *Smilin' Through.*

The next year saw him in *Death Takes a Holiday* and the Lubitsch comedy *Design for Living,* and in 1934 he made *We Live Again,* a sombre version of Tolstoy's *Resurrection* with Anna Sten, the more lighthearted *Affairs of Cellini* and *The Barretts of Wimpole Street,* in which he played Browning to Charles Laughton's* Mr. Barrett and Norma Shearer's Elizabeth Barrett. This ability to play a remarkable variety of roles enabled him to remain an actor even when, as a leading star, he would have found it easy to settle into a routine of sterotyped parts. It also explains why he has never been too easy to pin down with a simple public personality, a sort of professional trade-mark.

During the remainder of the 1930s, he was seen mainly in costume dramas and comedies including, of the former, *Les Misérables, Anna Karenina,* with Garbo, *Anthony Adverse* and *Mary of Scotland,* with Katherine Hepburn, and of the latter most notably Ben Hecht's* acid *Nothing Sacred.* Among his other films *A Star is Born,* with Janet Gaynor, de Mille's *The Buccaneer* and Cukor's *Susan and God,* with Joan Crawford, deserve mention. During the war years his only interesting film was Clair's elegant comedy *I Married a Witch,* with Veronica Lake, and in 1945 he returned to the Broadway stage to appear in John Hersey's *A Bell for Adano.*

The next year, however, he went back to Hollywood to make one of his most successful films, *The Best Years of Our Lives.* In this long study of a group of men adjusting themselves to civilian life after war service he gave a beautifully controlled performance as an officer who takes up his old job in a bank with his ideas much changed by his wartime experiences, and it brought him his second Academy Award. There followed the unfortunate *Christopher Columbus,* made in this country with his wife, Florence Eldridge, as Isabella of Spain, and another film in which he appeared with his wife, *Another Part of the Forest,* based on Lillian Hellmann's stage play. He also played Willie Loman in the film of Arthur Miller's *Death of A Salesman,* and despite a certain stagey quality in the conception of the film as a whole, gave one of his most interesting performances.

After another Broadway play in 1951, *Autumn Garden,* he made several films of some quality, among them Kazan's *Man on a Tightrope, Executive Suite, The Desperate Hours* and *Alexander the Great,* in which he played Phillip of Macedon, before scoring perhaps his greatest stage triumph in 1956 with a superb performance as James Tyrone in O'Neill's *Long Day's Journey into Night,* in which he was again partnered by his wife. For this performance he received the New York Drama Critics' Award for the Best Actor in a Straight Play.

After this his films were fewer and farther between, but they included some of his best performances, such as that he gave as a middle-aged businessman hopefully in love with a young girl in *Middle of the Night,* and his bravura performance opposite Spencer Tracy in the screen version of *Inherit the Wind.* Other films he played in at this time included de Sica's *The Condemned of Altona* (some way after Sartre), *Seven Days in May* and *Hombre.*

Fredric March was one of the very few performers who could legitimately lay claim to being a top film star with a considerable film following, and yet remaining first and foremost an actor. His refusal to be typecast in conventional star vehicles seems to have done little harm to his enduring popularity, while it certainly did him nothing but good as an actor.

As a dramatic actor it would be difficult to find his equal in Hollywood, but one should also remember his distinct comic talent, little exercized in recent years, and his ability in his early films to play a fairly conventional romantic lead and endue it with depth and individuality.

He married in 1927 Florence Eldridge and they had a son and a daughter.

April 16, 1975.

André Marie, who was Prime Minister of France for a month in 1948, died on June 12, 1974 in Barentin, of which town he had been Mayor since 1945.

In 1953 he made an unsuccessful attempt to form a second administration.

Of Norman stock, the son and grandson of school teachers, he was born at Honfleur on December 3, 1897. He was called up, a schoolboy finishing his studies in Rouen, in 1915, served as a lieutenant in the artillery, and was awarded the Croix de Guerre.

After the armistice he took up law and was called to the Bar in Rouen. In 1928 he was elected a Socialist-Radical deputy for one of the Seine-Inférieure constituencies. In 1933 he was appointed Under-Secretary of State for Alsace and Lorraine in the Sarraut* Cabinet (he retained in later years the standing of an expert on the two provinces), and a year afterwards was Under-Secretary of State for Foreign Affairs in the Daladier* Government. One of the small distinctions that fell to him in these years of doubtful peace was the introduction in the Chamber in 1936 of the Bill providing paid holidays.

A volunteer at the outbreak of war in 1939, he served as an artillery captain until he was taken prisoner in June 1940. Released as a veteran of the earlier war, he joined the Resistance and was eventually seized by the Gestapo, and imprisoned in Buchenwald, where he remained for a year and a half until release came with the American Third Army. He was in bad physical condition by that time, much reduced in weight and suffering from lung trouble, but he had the right temperament for recovery and came back with relatively little delay to political life. He was elected to both Constituent Assemblies and then to the National Assembly, becoming president of the Socialist-Radical group in the Chamber Minister of Justice in Ramadier's* administration, he held the same portfolio under Schuman*.

It had scarcely been expected that a Socialist-Radical would again lead a French Ministry, at least within little more than three years since the liberation. But the manoeuvres of the parties in the summer of 1948 gave Marie an unexpected opportunity. In his favour, his personal record apart, was the fact that from the first he had been strongly in favour of the Marshall Plan.

Marie, on accepting the President's invitation, announced that he sought a union of all Republicans without exception, but his was in fact the first mainly Conservative French Government since the war. His administration, formed in July, ended in late August after divergencies in the Cabinet were found to be irreconcilable. He was Minister of Justice and Vice-Premier in the succeeding Queuille* Cabinet and later Minister of Education in the Cabinets of Pleven, Faure, Pinay, Mayer and Laniel.

June 14, 1974.

Professor Spyrhidon Marinatos, one of the most renowned, if controversial, Greek archaeologists, was killed on October 1, 1974 in an accident while exploring his most spectacular discovery, the Minoan city buried by the gigantic volcanic eruption that destroyed the Aegean island of Thera about 3,600 years ago.

He was born at Lixouri on the island of Cephalonia, on November 4, 1901, and studied archaeology and philology at Athens, Berlin, and Halle universities. His archaeological career began when he was appointed Caretaker of Antiquities. At that time the archaeological department was a section of the Ministry of Education.

He spent 20 years in Crete, becoming a director of the Archaeological Museum of Herakleion, which contains the richest collection of Minoan art and artifacts in the world.

In 1937 he became Director of the Archaeological Division of the Education Ministry and two years later he was given the chair of Archaeology at the University of Athens. Two generations of Greek archaeologists were reared by him.

His main excavations were in Crete and at Pylos. He located the actual battleground of Thermopylae where the 300 Spartans of King Leonidas fell in 480 B.C. and did extensive research on the battleground of Marathon.

He used to tell friends: "An excavation is like opening a book written in the language that the centuries have spoken to the earth. But it is a language you can only read once—at the time of digging". For the past 50 years, he had tried to decipher this language in order to fill in the vast gaps which remain in the knowledge of Greek history and prehistory.

He had an exceptional knack for translating the most complex archaeological puzzles into lay language, a virtue which ensured him great publicity for his discoveries, especially in Thera.

It was in 1966 that he decided that if there had been a pre-eruption civilization on Thera, its relics would have been on the southern shore facing Crete, the seat of a vast and rich empire. He struck and found the first evidence of what may turn out to be the largest Minoan city in Greece. Its houses, two and three storeys high, were decorated with remarkable wall paintings.

It was he who, in 1939, first advanced the theory that the Thera volcanic eruption about 1500 B.C. could have been the cause of the destruction of the Minoan civilization in the Aegean.

When the military junta seized power in 1967, he was appointed Inspector-General of the Archaeological Services. Quite naturally there was criticism, rivalry, and hostility. He himself rejected any part in the purge of his own colleagues, claiming that he was not a politician.

He was elected a member of the Athens Academy in 1955 and that was the forum he preferred in order to make his most fascinating discoveries known. The second military coup relieved him of his duties.

He was then a very embittered man, but he still had Thera.

The results of 1974 excavations were so striking that he decided to prolong the season. On the last day he was standing on an ancient wall, giving instructions on the latest discoveries. The wall collapsed and buried him under the prehistoric debris.

October 3, 1974.

Edythe Mariner—See Hayward.

Jacques Maritain, without doubt the most outstanding exponent of twentieth-century neo-Thomism, died in Toulouse on April 28, 1973. He was 90.

When an intellectual lives to such an advanced age, he is almost bound to be overtaken by changed attitudes and shifts of interest. There is a sense in which Maritain was overtaken, in the last two decades, by religious thinkers as diverse as Bonhoeffer and Teilhard de Chardin, Bultmann and Simone Weil. Nevertheless, he left an indelible impression on his times. He had a striking influence across the whole range of the arts—Stravinsky, Rouault, T. S. Eliot*, etc—and also made a unique contribution to that fascinating and often neglected area of inquiry lying between philosophical questioning and religious belief.

Like some of his most notable contemporaries such as Berdyaev and Buber*, Maritain was more a religious philosopher than a strict theologian. While he did much to make theology more philosophical, he also gave philosophy a more distinct sense of the religious dimension in life. He went on to apply this dual approach in the spheres of poetry and art, psychology and politics, earning the right to be included in that category of thinkers described by Tillich as "theologians of culture".

Jacques Maritain was born in Paris on November 18, 1882. The family was nominally Protestant, but in practice fairly indifferent to religion. He attended school at the Lycée Henri IV and went on to the Sorbonne where he displayed outstanding gifts in the study of philosophy and natural science. In 1904, while still at the Sorbonne, he married a fellow-student of Russian Jewish origin, Raissa Oumansoff, and thus began a remarkable domestic and intellectual partnership. The couple had already been attracted, like so many of their generation, by the personality and ideas of Péguy. At the latter's suggestion they attended Bergson's famous Collège de France lectures. They were already dissatisfied, at a purely secular level, with late nineteenth-century materialism and pseudo-science, and found much to admire in Bergsonism. Nevertheless they could not accept the substitution of subjective intuitionism for rationalism. In his *L'Évolutionnisme de M. Bergson* of 1911, Maritain was to formulate the essence of his position by saying that "a philosophy which blasphemes against reason will never be a Catholic philosophy". In fact, his criticism of positivism was not an objection to rationalism but to what he considered to be a misuse of reason.

The two most crucial events in Maritain's life were his own conversion to Roman Catholicism and his discovery of St. Thomas Aquinas. In 1906 he and his wife were baptized into the Church, largely through the instrumentality of Léon Bloy. Maritain initially equated conversion with an end to philosophical training, and spent the next two years working on mathematics and biology under Hans Driesch in Heidelberg. Nevertheless, on his return to France in 1908, and with encouragement from his spiritual adviser Father Clérissac, he turned to the study of Aquinas and discovered, as he later explained in *La Philosophie bergsonienne* (1914), that he was a Thomist without realizing it.

Maritain expounded Thomism on his appointment to the Collège Stanislaus in 1912 and in 1914 was elected to the Chair of Philosophy in the Institut Catholique in Paris, where he gave a series of influential lectures. He had already embarked on one of his most distinctive achievements by drawing Thomism out of the confines of theological scholarship and locating it in a much wider cultural context—e.g. *Art et scolastique* (1920) and *Scholasticism and*

Politics (1940). In fact, he made a major contribution to the Catholic renewal in France after the First World War.

Part of this contribution took the form of an increasing concern with politics, in the broadest sense of the term. For a period during the 1920s Maritain was loosely associated with the right-wing Action Française, sharing its intellectual and classical assumptions, but wholly opposed to its anti-semitism. His position in the movement was basically a false one, however, and he had disengaged from it before its official condemnation by Rome in 1926. Significantly, he followed his break with a movement which took as its motto "la politique d'abord" by publishing *La Primauté du spirituel* (1927). On the other hand, throughout the thirties, he was associated with liberal political causes but also published some important works of Thomist exegesis including *Distinguer pour unir, ou les Degrés du savoir* (1932) and *Humanisme intégral* (1936).

When France fell in 1940 Jacques Maritain was lecturing in the United States. He remained there throughout the war, contributing to the intellectual Resistance and teaching at Columbia, Princeton and the Pontifical Institute of Medieval Studies in Toronto. His dismay at the general direction in which civilization seemed to be moving and his conception of a truly Christian democracy are reflected in such works as *Crépuscule des civilisations* (1941) and in his attempts to found the whole concept of human rights on Natural Law. By now he had a wide following in North America also, and English-speaking readers will be particularly familiar with such works as *Education at the Crossroads* (1943), *Christianity and Democracy* (1944), *The Person and the Common Good* (1947), *Existence and the Existent* (1948). It was in the latter work, incidentally, that he described Thomism as "the only authentic existentialism".

In 1945 Maritain was appointed French Ambassador to the Vatican by General de Gaulle*. He occupied this post for three years and then accepted a Chair of Philosophy at Princeton. He retired in 1952 but continued to live in Princeton with the title of Professor Emeritus until his wife's death in 1960. A year later he received the Grand Prix de Littérature de l'Académie Française and the Grand Prix National des Lettres in 1963.

Towards the end of his life Maritain was particularly associated with trenchant opposition to the Second Vatican Council and "neo-modernism" or what, judging from *Le Paysan de la Garonne* (1967), might more accurately be termed "neo-clericalism". This same book contained a fierce and uncompromising polemic against the ideas of Teilhard de Chardin.

In terms of both the affection which he inspired and the intellectual influence which he wielded, Maritain appealed to a wide and varied circle. He was personally admired, and his works have been read, by Protestants, Jews and agnostics as much as by Roman Catholics. Though he spoke with authoritative conviction, he understood doubt and hesitation. His scholasticism was accompanied by a distinct and personal faith. He continually sought to show the importance and relevance of his faith in a predominantly secular, yet dissatisfied, age. Scholarship and wisdom, spirituality and charity, were the hall-marks of his writing.

April 30, 1973.

The Duke of Marlborough died on March 11, 1972 in a London hospital. He was 74.

He was the tenth Duke, a kinsman of Sir Winston Churchill* and, like him, a descendant of the famous first Duke of Marlborough who won the battle of Blenheim in 1704.

The Duke, who succeeded his father in 1934, was responsible, with the aid of Government grants, for the restoration of his home, Blenheim Palace, birthplace of Sir Winston Churchill.

He was born in September 1897. His mother was Consuelo, daughter of W. K. Vanderbilt, possessor of a fortune made in American railroads. She was 18 when she married the ninth Duke.

The Duke and Duchess were subsequently divorced and in 1921 the Duchess married Lieutenant-Colonel Jacques Balsan. She published an autobiography entitled *The Glitter and the Gold* and died in 1964.

Educated at Eton, the tenth Duke served in the First World War as a captain in the 1st Life Guards, and retired from the Guards in 1927. In the Second World War he was military liaison officer to the Southern Region commander. From 1942 to 1945 he served as liaison officer to the United States forces. He was a former mayor of Woodstock, the Oxfordshire country town next to Blenheim Palace.

His first wife, daughter of the late Viscount Chelsea, died in 1961. She was the Hon. Alexandra Mary Cadogan, C.B.E., and married the tenth Duke in 1920. They were married at St. Margaret's, Westminster, in the presence of King George V, Queen Mary, and other members of the Royal Family. Both Winston and A. J. Balfour signed the register in company with the King and Queen.

The Duke was one of the first to enter the "stately homes league". In 1950 he opened Blenheim Palace to the public at a charge of 2s. 6d. a head and himself stood at the door selling guide books. He later allowed a steam boat on the lake and a miniature railway. But he did not admire the methods employed by some owners of stately homes to draw bigger crowds.

The Palace was built for the first Duke by Queen Anne in gratitude for his victory at Blenheim. The tenth Duke created a wild, romantic English garden with influences drawn from the eighteenth-century Italian gardens; it consisted of small lakes with mossy stones, shrubs and winding walks. In 1964 he bought a house at Montego Bay, Jamaica. In 1966 a grant of £55,000 towards the restoration of Blenheim Palace was made by the Ministry of Public Building and Works. The Duke contributed a similar amount.

Malvern College, followed by MI5 and others, was evacuated to the Palace during the Second World War. At the end of the war the Office of Works spent a year restoring it.

The Duke married for the second time in January 1972. His new wife, Mrs. Laura Canfield, widow of an American publisher, was an old friend and a well-known figure in society. She was born Laura Charteris, daughter of the Hon. Guy Charteris, son of the 11th Earl of Wemyss, and she was married first to Lord Long, secondly to the third Earl of Dudley, and thirdly to the late Mr. Canfield.

By his first wife the Duke had two sons and three daughters. He is succeeded by his elder son, the Marquess of Blandford, to whom Winston Churchill was a godparent. He married in 1951 Susan, daughter of Michael Hornby, by whom he had two sons and a daughter, of whom one son and a daughter survive. The marriage was dissolved in 1960 and he married secondly, in 1961, Athina Mary (Tina) daughter of Stavros Livanos and formerly wife of Aristotle Onassis. In December 1971 Lord Blandford was granted a declaration by the High Court Family Division that his wife had validly ended their marriage by a French divorce decree made final in June 1971.

March 13, 1972.

Terence de Marney—See **de Marney.**

Hilary Marquand, P.C., former deputy chairman of the National Board for Prices and Incomes, and a former Minister of Health, died on November 6, 1972. He was 70.

Before he entered national politics in 1945 Marquand had been Professor of Industrial Relations at University College, Cardiff, for 15 years and during the industrial depression of the thirties he played a leading part in diagnosing the economic ills of South Wales and formulating plans for the region's industrial recovery.

He entered the House of Commons in 1945 as Labour member for East Cardiff after defeating Sir James Grigg*, who was then Secretary of State for War in the Churchill "Caretaker Government" which followed the break-up of the war-time coalition. When the constituency of East Cardiff disappeared in 1950 in a redistribution of parliamentary seats Marquand transferred his candidature to East Middlesbrough where he was duly elected again. He continued to represent East Middlesbrough until 1961, when he resigned the seat on being appointed Director of the International Labour Organization's new International Institute for Labour Studies, at Geneva.

During his 16 years in the House of Commons, whether as minister or private member, Marquand worked diligently for the causes in which he believed. He was interested not only in industrial and economic affairs but also in social welfare, and both as Minister of Health and when he served for three years earlier as Minister of Pensions he proved both a humane and able administrator. Quiet and sedate in manner, he was an academic without arrogance who brought a calm and detached approach to the coarse hurly-burly of politics. He had a dull and slightly pedantic style at the dispatch box but even if he was no orator he was well-liked in the House and was always listened to with respect.

Hilary Adair Marquand was born in Cardiff on December 24, 1901. His father, who had come from Guernsey and married a Scotswoman, was a clerk in a coal-exporting firm but his grandfather and an uncle were shipowners in Cardiff. From Cardiff High School Marquand went on a state scholarship to University College, Cardiff and there graduated with first-class honours in history and economics. After spending two years in the United States as a Rockefeller Fellow in social studies he was appointed in 1926 Lecturer in Economics at Birmingham University. Four years later he went back to his old University College as Professor of Industrial Relations. At that time he was 29 and the youngest university professor in Britain.

During the next decade he made an intensive study of industrial and economic conditions in South Wales and became a recognized authority on the subject. He made one industrial survey of the area for the Board of Trade in 1931 and another for the Commissioner for Special Areas in 1937. These surveys were published in book form and the second was in three volumes. In these studies Marquand dealt in great detail with the reasons for the abrupt decline of the basic coal and steel industries, the effect of this on the region's economy and the new pattern of industry needed for recovery. In 1936 he wrote a book entitled *South Wales Needs a Plan*, in which he expounded his views in more popular language. He also wrote in *The Times* on the subject. In 1939 he spent another year in the United States as visiting Professor of Economics at the University of Wisconsin.

During the war years Marquand worked as a civil servant. In 1940 he was at the Board of Trade, where he helped to organize the war-time concentration of industry. The following year, at the request of the then Sir William (later Lord) Beveridge,* he was transferred to the Ministry of Labour and put in charge of

national service organization in Wales. He took over the chairmanship of the Cardiff manpower board. In 1943 he was appointed Labour Adviser to the Ministry of Production, where he was again concerned with the allocation of industrial manpower.

Marquand had been a member of the Labour Party since his undergraduate days, and when the war ended he decided to become an active politician. By defeating the Secretary of State for War in the postwar Labour landslide he was fortunate enough to secure election to Parliament at the first attempt. He was also fortunate enough to be given a Government appointment as soon as he took his seat.

Attlee* appointed him Secretary of the Department of Overseas Trade at the age of 43. Soon afterwards this Department was merged in the Board of Trade and Marquand then became Secretary for Overseas Trade. During the next two years he conducted trade negotiations with many European countries and also made the first postwar trade agreement with the Soviet Government, for the supply of timber. He travelled extensively and in the autumn of 1946 he led the British delegation at the international conference on trade and employment.

In March 1947 Marquand was appointed Paymaster-General (and Harold Wilson was appointed to succeed him as Secretary for Overseas Trade). In this new office, carrying no departmental responsibilities, Marquand was free to undertake special duties. He was sent by the Government on an important trade promotion mission to the African colonial governments and to the governments of Rhodesia and the Union of South Africa. He made a six weeks' tour in Africa and did some 18,000 miles of air travel. After having held the office of Paymaster-General for little more than a year he was appointed in 1948 to succeed George Buchanan as Minister of Pensions. While serving in this post Marquand visited Canada and the United States, to study the problems of the 15,000 British pensioners living in North America and the methods of pensions administration in those countries.

Then, in January 1951, when Aneurin Bevan left the Ministry of Health to become Minister of Labour and National Service, Marquand was appointed to succeed him as Minister of Health. But at that time of the change-over the Ministry of Health was shorn of its important functions relating to housing and planning and the new Minister was not included in the Cabinet. Marquand was destined to hold this new office for only nine months. In October 1951 came the general election which brought the Conservative Party back to power, although Marquand retained his own seat at East Middlesbrough with his big majority little diminished. During the years in Opposition he was an active front bencher and in 1959 he was chosen as the leading Opposition spokesman on Commonwealth Affairs. He resigned his seat on

taking up the I.L.O. appointment at Geneva in 1961. He was deputy chairman of the Prices and Incomes Board from 1965 to 1968.

Marquand was married in 1929 to Miss Rachel Rees and they have two sons and one daughter.

November 8, 1972.

Sir Alec Martin, K.B.E., managing director of Christie's from 1940 to 1958, died on April 15, 1971 at his home in Roehampton. He was 86.

Alec Martin was born on November 25, 1884, in Yeomans Row, Brompton Road. A month before his 13th birthday he joined Christie's as office boy on the assurance that if he attended to his duties he might easily rise in the hierarchy to be one of the porters.

For three months in the year the sale rooms were shut and Martin, as a junior employee, was stood off. Work had to be found and on one occasion he washed dishes in a café in Montmartre.

Before joining Christie's he was already a person with business experience behind him, for while still at All Saints' Church School, Knightsbridge, he assisted the Brompton Road local newsagent, a Mr. Roberts, in the shop and delivered papers around the neighbourhood. He was fond of telling how, on one occasion, he was offered a vacancy as boot-boy in a house in Ennismore Gardens and very nearly accepted the job; his schoolmaster however dissuaded him "and so", he would say, "I ended up as managing director of Christie's and not as a gentleman's gentleman".

As he grew up in daily proximity to works of art of all kinds his natural capacity, aided by a sensitive eye, gradually made him indispensable as the firm's picture expert, while a gift for making friends brought him into close contact with innumerable people in all walks of life. Among connoisseurs of the past he valued greatly his friendship with Hugh Lane and Robert Witt, each of whom taught him much. He accompanied the former to Liverpool in 1915 to bid him farewell before he embarked on what was to prove his last voyage in the Lusitania, and he succeeded the latter as hon. secretary of the National Art Collections Fund.

In 1924 he was appointed a Governor of the National Gallery of Ireland, and in 1929 succeeded the fifth Lord Rosebery as a trustee of the The Wallace Collection, later becoming chairman. He became a partner in Christie's in 1931, was knighted in 1934, and created K.B.E. in 1959. In his younger days he was a member of the London Scottish and had been an elder of the Church in Pont Street for many years.

During the 1939 war he was left to carry on Christie's alone while his partners were on war service; undeterred by the destruction of the King Street building in

1941 he was holding sales at Derby House a month later with the aid of a borrowed typewriter and a few tables.

He always considered that the crown of his business career was the successful outcome of the lengthy negotiations for the acquisition by the nation of the chief works of art at Chatsworth—negotiations which earned him the thanks of both parties to the agreement.

If so busy a man can be said to have had a hobby, it can perhaps be best defined as a determination, as far as was reasonable and possible, to enrich the national collections with fine works of art, and it may be that the results of his long years of work on behalf of the National Art-Collections Fund will remain his most lasting memorial.

Smallish, roundish, indefatigable, bright of eye, he will be long remembered as adviser to many and as good and faithful friend to more—one who retained to the last a sense of adventure.

He married in 1909 Ada Mary Fell and there were three sons and two daughters of the marriage.

April 17, 1971.

Frank Martin, the distinguished Swiss composer, resident in Holland since 1946, died at Naarden on November 21, 1974 at the age of 84. He wrote in a style that was convincingly individual, and wholly fastidious. His most notable works, the dramatic oratorio *Le Vin herbé* on the Tristan legend, and several concertos are imaginative enough to place him high in the ranks of twentieth-century composers.

He was born on September 15, 1890 at Geneva, and studied there with Joseph Lauber. After a period of further study in Paris, Rome and Zurich, he returned to his home city to found and become the keyboard player with the Societé de Musique de Chambre. From 1928 until 1938 he taught at the Dalcroze Institute, and from 1950 to 1955 at the Cologne Conservatory.

Martin began composing at an early age, mostly chamber works and songs, strongly influenced by Ravel and Fauré. Later, he began to take note of the Schoenbergian revolution, and, without fully subscribing to the full implications of the 12-note school's aesthetics, applied them to his own music in several works written during the 1930s. His style became really marked and individual with *Le Vin herbé* (1942), which combines 12-note technique with conventional harmony and employs for the first time Martin's method of sub-dividing his vocal forces to represent different characters and concepts.

His sensitivity in setting texts was further shown in his Six Monologues from Hofmannsthal's *Jedermann* (1943). Then came *Der Sturm*, his only opera, in Schlegel's translation of Shakespeare, which shows great respect for the play while maintain-

ing musical continuity. The oratorios, *Golgotha* (1948), and *Le mystère de la Nativité* (1959) are eclectic in style, the latter giving different idioms to the representation of heaven, earth, and hell. The *Maria Triptychon* of 1969 was specially written for the soprano Irmgard Seefried and her husband Wolfgang Schneiderhan. The impressive Requiem (1972) was one of his last works.

Of his many concertos, the *Petite Symphonie Concertante* (1945) for harp, harpsichord, piano and double string orchestra, is probably the most significant for its combination and contrast of sonorities and instruments, but later works such as the violin concerto (1951), concerto for harpsichord and orchestra (1952), written for Isabelle Nef, and the *Trois Danses* (1970) for oboe, harp and strings, composed for the Holligers, continue to show his facility in this field.

November 23, 1974.

Edward J. Mason, who died on February 3, 1971 at the age of 58, was the chief script writer of the B.B.C.'s apparently indestructible radio serial *The Archers*. For 20 years he dramatized the life of a Midland farming family, the community that surrounds it and the problems which it encounters. The 3,000th script in which he was concerned was recorded only a few hours before his death.

Edward J. Mason was the son of working-class parents in Birmingham. He left school at the age of 15, worked for many years at Bournville, and did not begin to write for radio—a medium to which he remained faithful in spite of temptations from television—until after the war. His first radio work was to write the lyrics for a revue produced by Martyn C. Webster. *Dick Barton, Special Agent*, the thriller serial which won great popularity through carrying on the tradition of boys' adventure stories, brought him into collaboration with the late Geoffrey Webb and to his own special field of action.

At 6.45 each evening, practically the whole nation switched on the Light Programme to hear the latest breathless adventure of Dick and Snowy and Jock, introduced by the rousing signature tune "The Devil's Gallop".

In 1951, shortly before his collaborator's death, the two were asked to work on what was described as "a farming Dick Barton" and thus *The Archers* came into being.

Though a townsman by birth and, it seems taste, it was never possible to find serious fault with *The Archers* on factual grounds; it was part of Mason's brief to give information and instruction, and the Archers found their lives complicated by changes not only in farming techniques and scientific progress but also in the regulations made for them by governments. If there are simplifications of character and

situation inherent in the form of soap opera, the Archers remained honest within the terms they dictate.

Its characters age, time does not stand still with their environment, and as long ago as 1955 the death of Grace Archer in a stable fire provided a traumatic shock for the serial's innumerable fans; such intrusions of harsh reality, Mason and the B.B.C. were told, have no place in soap opera. Some listeners rang up for assurance that the actress who played the part of Grace was unhurt.

For all that, the Archers and their neighbourhood became a cosy reality to listeners who hoped to buy Christmas turkeys from them and who entered with complete conviction into all their necessary vicissitudes. In so far as the art of the writer of such a serial is to set his characters off on an apparently inevitable course and never be seen to manipulate them, Mason was magnificently successful.

As well as *The Archers*, Edward Mason was responsible, with Tony Shryane, for *My Word*, arguably the radio parlour game which most successfully demands wit and ingenuity from its participants, and for the almost equally clever and hilarious *My Music*. One of his sons is at present heard in *The Archers* in the part of Roger Travers-Macy.

February 4, 1971.

The Most Rev. David Mathew, F.B.A., F.R.S.L., Archbishop of Apamea, who died on December 13, 1975 at the age of 73, made his mark in two different and difficult fields of activity, as an ecclesiastic and as an historian.

Born on January 15, 1902, he was a great nephew of Lord Justice Mathew; his mother was a sister of Sir John Woodroffe, and daughter of James Tisdall Woodroffe, sometime Advocate General of Bengal.

But David Mathew was educated not for the law but at Osborne and Dartmouth for the Royal Navy, and served as a midshipman in the second part of the 1914-18 War. He never lost his affection for the Navy, but it was not his calling, and after a year in which he tried his vocation as a Carthusian, he made his way to Balliol College, Oxford, took a first in history, and continued as a research scholar before going to the Beda College in Rome. He was ordained in 1929.

David Mathew started his priestly life as a curate at Cardiff Cathedral, but because of his academic attainments, he was soon moved to London as chaplain to the Catholics of the University of London. It was here that he produced his first serious book on the Celtic peoples and Renaissance Europe. He was breaking new ground, where his special strength, a genealogical interest in families, their continuity and their ramifications, found plenty of scope.

His younger brother and lifelong intimate,

the Dominican Father Gervase Mathew, was also a scholar, and the brothers produced jointly a study of the contemplative life at the time of the Reformation; and from the thirties on, David Mathew's historical writing stayed within the limits of the Tudors and the Stuarts.

In 1945 he gave the Ford Lectures at Oxford on the Social Structure in Caroline England. He continued his historical writing throughout his life, but it would be misleading not to add that he ranged widely. He produced a study of Catholicism in England, particularly strong on the early centuries following the Reformation, and perhaps perfunctory for the twentieth century; books on our naval heritage and British seamen; and two books on Lord Acton.

He also tried his hand as an imaginative writer with novels whose elusive and elliptical character puzzled many readers.

This was unfortunate for his ecclesiastical career, because David Mathew was a sagacious and severely practical priest, with a great sense of the possible, and while chaplain in London he attracted the attention of the new Archbishop of Westminster, Cardinal Hinsley. He was selected to be an auxiliary bishop in his middle thirties, and *The Tablet* acclaimed his appointment as the beginning of a great ecclesiastical career. To the aging Cardinal Hinsley he was invaluable, and when the war came he showed himself capable and ready to take on more and more responsibility, as well as showing great intrepidity in giving the Last Sacraments in the blitz. But Cardinal Hinsley died in March 1943, long before the young Bishop Mathew had had any opportunity to make his mark in Rome. When, after many months, the new Archbishop of Westminster was announced, it was not the young Auxiliary of Westminster but the equally young Auxiliary of Birmingham, Bernard Griffin.

As auxiliaries are the personal appointments of archbishops, it was quickly understood on both sides that Bishop Mathew would be found another sphere for his gifts.

He went to Africa as Apostolic Delegate to the British Colonies both East and West, a position his patron, Cardinal Hinsley, had filled with distinction 15 years before. He threw himself into this new and unexpected field with great enthusiasm, travelling between East and West in light aeroplanes, and building up a native hierarchy to meet the increased tempo of African impatience. He did a great work, and he quickly learnt the ways of the Holy See which takes its own decisions and expects its agents in the field to report all the facts, but then to await instructions.

How much confidence he inspired by labours which, incidentally, greatly impaired his health, was shown when Pius XII offered him, on his return in 1953, the Nunciature at Berne. This is an important Nunciature because of Geneva and all the United Nations agencies, and one that generally leads to the Curia and a Car-

dinal's hat. Pius XII did not like to have his offers refused, but David Mathew ventured to decline, saying his ambitions were pastoral and in his own country. Unfortunately for him, while he was admired at home, he was also thought to be out of touch with the common man, and especially out of touch in postwar Britain. He was not recommended for different archiepiscopal sees as they fell vacant.

After he had refused Berne, the Pro-Secretary of State, Monsignor Montini, now Pope Paul VI, said the Holy See had offered him the best they could. Now it was a question of what the English hierarchy could do for him. The answer came the next year. Remembering that he had served in the Navy, the Apostolic Delegate and the bishops recommended him as Bishop-in-Ordinary to the Forces. He accepted the appointment, though it was not what he would have chosen, and there were several respects in which he was not particularly well suited for it. He held it, however, for some eight years, and it enabled him to continue his literary work.

He suffered a further disappointment when, having been an obvious selection for the Preparatory Commission on the Missions for the Second Vatican Council, he was dropped from the council itself. The pace of development had been so fast in Africa that the native bishops regarded him as belonging to a bygone colonial age. After a brief appearance, he dropped out of the council's sessions, accepting this, like other disappointments, with a large serenity which he attributed to the invaluable year he had spent as a Carthusian postulant which had given him a correct sense of proportion about all sublunary things. He also had a rich and unfailing sense of humour.

In the last decade of his life he was fortunate in being invited to make his home with Lord and Lady Camoys at the historic Stonor Park, near Henley, and undoubtedly the quiet and regular life and congenial society gave him just what he wanted for the placid and tranquil old age in which he all the same continued quietly a further output of historical writing, with studies of James I, the Courtiers of Henry VIII, and Lady Jane Grey.

December 17, 1975.

Muir Mathieson, a distinguished figure in British film music, died in hospital at Oxford on August 2, 1975 at the age of 64. As arranger and conductor he worked on more than 600 films and helped to bring to the cinema composers of the stature of Sir Arthur Bliss and Ralph Vaughan Williams.

Born in Stirling, Scotland, Mathieson won a scholarship to the Royal College of Music and conducted a major concert at the Royal Albert Hall when he was only 24. He was first associated with film music on Sir Alexander Korda's *Private Life of*

Don Juan in 1934 and he stayed with Korda up to the war, working on such pictures as *The Ghost Goes West, Rembrandt, Elephant Boy, Fire Over England* and *The Four Feathers*.

But his most influential collaboration was with Arthur Bliss on the score for the H. G. Wells film, *Things to Come*, in 1935. This was one of the first occasions on which a composer worked with the film-makers from the scripting to the final editing. Later performed as a concert suite, the score did much to further the status of film music and encourage other leading composers into the cinema, among them Walton, Walter Leigh, Britten and William Alwyn. In the early part of the war Mathieson introduced Vaughan Williams to film music for *49th Parallel*, launching the composer, who was then nearly 70, on a fruitful new career culminating in his *Scott of the Antarctic* score which became the Antarctica Symphony.

During the wartime and post-war renaissance in the British cinema, Mathieson contributed to several notable films including *The First of the Few, In Which We Serve, This Happy Breed, Henry V, The Seventh Veil, Brief Encounter, Hamlet* and *Oliver Twist*. He also directed several musical documentaries of which the best known is *Instruments of the Orchestra*, featuring Britten's *Variations and Fugue on a Theme of Purcell*.

In an article written in 1947 Mathieson wrote that "a good score can enormously enhance a picture, it can give added dramatic content, it can create humour or pathos; above all, music has the power of appealing to the emotions in a manner that no element in a film can". But he added the important qualification that "music must obtain its effect subconsciously".

Mathieson often conducted film music at public concerts, both in Britain and abroad; he appeared as conductor with most of the major orchestras and was principal conductor of the Sinfonia of London, He gave particular encouragement to youth orchestras and was a popular broadcaster. He was married, with a son and three daughters.

August 5, 1975.

Professor Sir Robert Matthew, C.B.E., P.P.R.I.B.A., F.R.T.P.I., F.R.I.A.S., A.R.S.A., who died on June 21, 1975 aged 68, was for seven years architect to London County Council and then for 15 years Professor of Architecture at the University of Edinburgh.

He was also senior partner in a firm of architects with a quantity of notable work to its credit and was much in demand as a town-planning consultant. But more than all this he was one of those men which every profession throws up from time to time who, by virtue of unusual qualities of character and leadership, exert an influence far beyond that which their professional attainments suggest.

His clear-sightedness and intellectual probity set him apart from the often conflicting factions created in the architectural profession by differences in age and fashion and from alliance with one section of the profession or another. The respect with which he was held, moreover, extended far overseas, largely because of his work for the International Union of Architects (whose President he was from 1961 to 1965) and for the Commonwealth Association of Architects. Both these bodies will find him hard to replace; in fact it may be said that without his leadership and continuous labour behind the scenes neither would have achieved the position and influence it has.

Robert Hogg Matthew was born on December 12, 1906, the son of John Matthew, himself a noted Edinburgh architect. He was educated at Melville College, Edinburgh, and at Edinburgh College of Art. He was an able and industrious student, winning a succession of prizes: the Pugin studentship of the R.I.B.A. in 1929, the Soane Medallion in 1932 and the Bossom gold medal in 1936. His long career of public service began in 1936 when he joined the Department of Health for Scotland. By 1945 he had become the department's chief architect and planning officer.

The following year he went south on being appointed architect to the L.C.C. This was at a time when the L.C.C. architect's department had vast responsibilities but an internal structure ill suited to making the best of them and a reputation for work that was unprogressive and uninspired. Its responsibilities were increased in 1950 when housing, hitherto designed in a separate department under the valuer, was transferred to the architect's department after much criticism of the quality of work being produced.

Matthew set to work reorganizing the department, and in particular giving small groups of architects the responsibility for building projects from start to finish so that they acquired a sense of personal involvement instead of being mere cogs in a machine. The result was that the department changed almost overnight from an inert bureaucracy to one of the liveliest offices in the country, in which ambitious young architects were eager to work. L.C.C. architecture earned admiration all over the world and, by its example, transformed the image of local authority architects throughout Britain. Many of the young architects who worked under Matthew at the L.C.C. subsequently became the leaders of a new generation.

While at the L.C.C. Matthew was responsible for the Royal Festival Hall. He brought into the department, as his deputy, to take direct charge of the project, Leslie Martin (now Sir Leslie and his eventual successor as architect to the council). One

of Matthew's qualities was his ability to delegate work and still retain a sufficient degree of control.

In 1953 he left the L.C.C. and returned to his native Scotland to occupy the chair of architecture at Edinburgh, a post he held for 15 years, giving it a new authority and broadening the scope of the department to include other environmental disciplines. He combined this with a remarkable variety of other work: lecturing, committee work, consultancy and architectural practice. These required incessant travelling. Matthew used to acknowledge, not without pride, that at times he spent more nights in the train between Edinburgh and London than in his own home.

Such an existence demanded unusual stamina and would have been impossible if he had not had a devoted wife. In 1931 he had married Lorna Louise Pilcher, who survives him with one son and two daughters. She ministered to and organized his daily life, entertained for him in their houses in Regent's Park and East Lothian and accompanied him on many of his exhausting excursions overseas.

His activities after 1953 included private architectural practice in Edinburgh and, from 1956, a leading part in the firm of Robert Matthew, Johnson-Marshall and Partners. He took a considerable share in the design of some of their largest projects. One of these was New Zealand House, London. At the same time he acted as a planning consultant in many parts of the world and as a judge in many architectural competitions. This was a role for which his analytical mind and his refusal to allow details to obscure principles equipped him well. He was an excellent chairman. The same attributes were evident in his tireless efforts on behalf of the International Union of Architects and the Commonwealth Association of Architects. At their conferences he was always the most authoritative figure, handling difficult situations with common sense and courage. He played a central part in the I.U.A. conference at Madrid in May 1975 while already afflicted by his final illness.

Matthew served on the Royal Fine Art Commission for Scotland and the Historic Buildings Council for Scotland and, from 1970, was adviser on building conservation policy to the Secretary of State for Scotland. From 1962-64 he was a notably wise and far-sighted president of the R.I.B.A. From 1963-67 he was a member of the B.B.C.'s general advisory council. He was also president of the Saltire Society. After his retirement from the chair of architecture at Edinburgh in 1968 he was made chairman of the University's School of the Built Environment, which enabled him to continue the process he had himself begun of moulding it to suit contemporary needs and his life-long service to architectural education. In 1974 he was made professor emeritus.

In 1972 Matthew was appointed by the Government to advise (with Mr. W. P. D.

Skillington, of the Department of the Environment) on standards of design in Government buildings. The resulting report was welcomed by all those concerned with improving official architecture and attracting better architects into government service, and it was a disappointment to him that the action he had recommended was not taken.

During all Robert Matthew's years in London and his later years as an international figure he remained essentially a Scot. Rather than the conventional, though distinguished, personality his official and academic record might suggest, he was a true original. A quiet but persuasive way of speaking concealed an acutely analytical brain which enabled him to marshal facts and promptly come to sensible conclusions about them; yet it was his personal simplicity—one might even say his innocence—that inspired so much trust in him as well as so much affection from his friends. He had an endearing vagueness in his manner, though he liked his own way and expected his household to revolve round him. He unaffectedly enjoyed the fame his achievements brought him.

His services to architecture were honoured in many ways. He was accorded the R.I.B.A.'s distinction in town-planning in 1949, made an honorary Fellow of the American Institute of Architects in 1951 and a C.B.E. in 1952, knighted in 1962, made an Hon. LL.D. of Sheffield University in 1963 and given the gold medal of the Danish Architectural Association in 1965. In 1970 he received the highest award that British architecture has to bestow: the R.I.B.A.'s Royal Gold Medal.

June 23, 1975.

Sir Arthur Matthews, O.B.E., who died on May 1, 1971 at the age of 84, had a long and distinguished career in heavy industry.

His grandfather was Humphrey Matthews, millwright, a specialist in agricultural machinery. His father was Robert Matthews who was for many years head of the engineering branch of Sir W. G. Armstrong Whitworth.

Arthur was born at Hyde in 1886, and educated at the Leys School and Jesus College, Cambridge, where he took an Engineering Degree. He was apprenticed in 1907 to Armstrong Whitworth, Openshaw, and rose to be Works Manager, Steelworks Engineering and Ordnance, and he received the O.B.E. in the 1914-18 War for acceleration of gun production at that works.

He joined Thos. Firth & Sons Limited, Sheffield, in 1922 as Works Manager and Local Director, becoming works general manager on the fusion of Firth's interests with John Brown & Company Limited in 1930, and a director of Firth-Brown's in 1934. He was appointed assistant managing director in 1938 and managing director in

November 1944.

He was knighted in 1941 for vital work on Special and Alloy Steel Production to meet the critical aircraft needs of 1940, and was chairman under the late Lord Beaverbrook* at the Ministry of Aircraft Production. He was chairman of the Advisory Committee on Special and Alloy Steels under Sir Charles Wright, the Iron & Steel Controller.

On retirement as executive managing director of Firth-Brown's in July 1951 he continued his close connections with industry by serving as director on the boards of 15 companies, including those of the Staveley Group where his technical engineering knowledge was invaluable in building up the initial successful expansion of their interests. These activities he progressively relinquished, refusing to serve any longer after reaching the age of 75.

He was twice married, and is survived by Lady Matthews, and the two children of his first marriage, Mrs. Christopher Gegg and the Rev. John Matthews, Vicar of Great Dunmow, Essex.

May 5, 1971.

Dr. W. R. Matthews, K.C.V.O., C.H., D.D., Dean of St. Paul's from 1934 to 1967 and subsequently Dean Emeritus, died on December 4, 1973 at the age of 92.

By his death the Church in England loses one of the small company of philosophical theologians of outstanding quality who have enriched its life during the last half-century. But he was more than that. The picture that remains is that of a full life at many levels; the life of a thinker, a convinced churchman and a citizen of the world. He was made C.H. in 1962.

Walter Robert Matthews, the son of P. W. Matthews, sometime Chief Inspector, Bankers' Clearing House, was born in Camberwell in September 1881. From Wilson's Grammar School, Camberwell, he entered the Westminster Bank, remaining a clerk for five years until he was able with help from his father and his own savings to enter King's College London as an undergraduate. He soon became a distinguished student and a frequent prize-winner.

He took his B.D. degree in 1907, gained a first-class in the philosophy of religion in the following year, and afterwards proceeded to the degrees of M.A. in 1912, D.D. in 1922, and D.Litt. in 1934. St. Andrews, Glasgow, Trinity College, Dublin, Columbia, Toronto, Winnipeg, Manitoba, and Cambridge conferred upon him the honorary degree of D.D. Although he was well read in English literature and was a lively member of many cultural societies, intensive study of his special subject, aided by natural ability, had given him a remarkable mastery of it.

He was ordained in 1907, and beginning at St. Mary Abbot's, held in rapid succession a number of London curacies, and, from 1916 to 1918, the benefice of Christ Church, Hornsey. These posts he combined with the work at King's College which, for 23 years, was to be the main business of his life. He began (in the year of his ordination to the priesthood) as lecturer in philosophy, and added to this the lectureship in dogmatic theology 12 months afterwards.

In 1918 he became Dean of King's College and Professor of the Philosophy of Religion, both of which posts he retained until his transference to Exeter in 1931. With these he held at various times a large number of external lectureships, including the Boyle lectureship in London, the Wilde lectureship at Oxford, and the Noble lectureship at Harvard. He was also Chaplain to Gray's Inn from 1920 to 1930 and Preacher for a year afterwards. In 1937 he was appointed Warburton Lecturer at Lincoln's Inn. He was appointed Chaplain to the King in 1928, and for a year from 1931 he was Canon-Theologian of Liverpool Cathedral. After King George V's Jubilee service he was created a K.C.V.O. and was made Dean of the Order of the British Empire in 1957. He held the post until 1967.

In 1931 Matthews was appointed Dean of Exeter. His stay at Exeter, which lasted for three years only, made its mark on the life of the cathedral, and the clergy of the diocese found the Dean very accessible and most willing to help them by preaching in their churches. His lectures, too, were welcomed by the studious.

When Dr. Inge retired from St. Paul's the task of following so conspicuous and brilliant a Dean was not easy. Yet Dr. Matthews's intellectual qualifications seemed to fit him for the post; his nomination to it was generally applauded, and by none more warmly than by Dr. Inge.

Matthews became a great St. Paul's man. He was devoted to the building, which he, with the "Watch" gathered around him, was largely instrumental in saving from destruction in the Second World War. His proudest monument is the splendid restoration carried out in the postwar years. He was devoted also to the life of the place. He attended its services regularly, never refused an invitation from his colleagues to preach in it on occasions beyond his statutory duties, and took the liveliest interest in every detail of its multifarious business. Since, as Dean of a cathedral of the "old foundation", he was *primus inter pares* but had no arbitrary powers, it was specially important that he should keep on good terms with his Chapter; and that he did with considerable success through the many changes of personnel during his long reign. Not only the members of Chapter but the whole *familia* of the cathedral regarded him as a friend. The result was seen in the great outburst of affection when all its members from the Lord Bishop of the diocese to the youngest chorister assembled to entertain him on the twenty-fifth anniversary of his installation.

In 1945, on the retirement of Dr. Cranage, Matthews was elected Prolocutor of the Lower House of Convocation, a post in which he was not particularly happy and which he relinquished five later years later.

The Dean was a familiar and much loved figure in the City. He was a frequent diner-out and was a welcome guest not only on account of his lively and well-informed conversation, but also as a first-rate after-dinner speaker. For a cathedral dignitary he was also uncommonly well known in the diocese, not because he sat on diocesan committees—a hobby for which he had no taste—but because he was so ready to appear in the pulpits of hard-pressed parochial clergy.

He was an exceptionally interesting preacher, understanding all the doubts and anxieties of modern man, and delighting to reason them out without ever claiming too much for the traditional faith. This habit, which was invaluable on normal occasions, still clung to him on the great festivals, and was a little chilling to those who were longing for some ringing affirmation of the lessons of Christmas and Easter.

He insisted on claiming the name of Modernist, but in tone of mind was much nearer the Cambridge Platonists. Actually in all the fundamentals of the creed he was intensely orthodox. As a compensation he demanded the utmost freedom in dealing with all outlying subjects. He was of a whimsical, not to say puckish, temperament and would sacrifice a good deal for a *bon mot*. He delighted in writing a minority report, and in taking the unexpected view in a discussion. Artificial insemination, new credal definitions, revised articles, women priests, euthanasia, psychical research, all at one time or another received his support. But this commendation did not go much beyond the sphere of argument. If the practical results of his proposals were pointed out his reply might well be: "But you must not carry things too far!"

His greatest contribution to theology is to be found in his *God in Christian Thought and Experience*, which ran into nine editions. Another book in the same genre was his *Purpose of God*. Of a different type was the *History of St. Paul's Cathedral*, of which he was co-editor and in which he incorporated interesting reminiscences of his own past connexion with the church. He rendered good service to theological studies by his general editorship of the Library of Constructive Theology. Many small volumes reveal his insight into the relations of philosophy and doctrine, and many others reveal his interest in humanity and his strong pastoral sense.

He followed the example of his predecessor in using the press as a means of reaching a wider public than he could hope to influence from the pulpit. These more popular and homiletical efforts no doubt prevented the appearance of any further *magnum opus* (although he was known to be engaged upon an important volume on

Faith), but the loss to scholarship was balanced by the immense gain to a very large circle of average folk. He published *Memories and Meanings* in 1969.

What those who knew him will chiefly miss is not, perhaps, the guidance of his erudition, valuable though that was, but his kindness, his simple goodness, his transparent sincerity.

Matthews married in 1912 Margaret Bryan. They had a son (who was killed in action in 1940) and a daughter. His wife died in 1963.

December 5, 1973.

Sir Edward Maufe, R.A., F.R.I.B.A., architect of Guildford Cathedral, who died on December 12, 1974, aged 91, may be described as a designer of churches by conviction, aiming directly at the creation of a religious atmosphere.

In past centuries the designer of churches worked to explicit terms of reference, determined by the spirit of the age. The idea that the architect himself can, so to speak, put the religion into the church is comparatively modern. Maufe contributed much to the realization of this idea, which must be borne in mind if his work, with its merits and defects, is to be properly appreciated.

The merits are those of extreme sensibility and refined taste in the designer, coupled with a clear view of practical requirements. The defects can be summed up by saying that Maufe's churches are apt to look a little self-consciously religious—the architectural equivalent of the "parsonical voice". Maufe was, nevertheless, aware of risks attending the responsibility of the contemporary church architect. He once said that the churches of the Gothic Revival, although he recognized the great merits of some of them, were "rather like museum specimens". "Our danger now", he added, "is not one of dead replicas, but of forms built merely in revolt, of stunt architecture, of building primarily to surprise".

Both these dangers he avoided in his own work, which rose in quality in proportion as the requirements were definite. Good examples are the two churches he designed for the Royal Association in Aid of the Deaf and Dumb: St. Saviour's, East Acton, and St. Bede's, Clapham. In these everything is considered with regard to the needs of a congregation that can see but cannot hear. The East window is eliminated, artificial lights are screened from the congregation so as to throw their light forward, the floor is raked as in a theatre. It would seem that in his preoccupation with these practical requirements all that the architect had of religious feeling and artistic taste was released to operate unconsciously, and the result is singularly impressive. On the other hand the studio for religious services which

Maufe designed at Broadcasting House can only be called embarrassing in its conscious holiness.

Maufe was born at Ilkley in 1883 and educated at Wharfedale School and St. John's College, Oxford, where he took his degree of M.A. He was articled to William Pite and also studied at the Architectural Association. During the 1914-18 War he served as lieutenant in the Royal Artillery in Salonika. His earlier works include several country houses and gardens—Kelling Hall, Norfolk; Far Scar, Grassington, Yorkshire; and Little Roothing, Essex, among them; monuments to Joseph Chamberlain in the crypt of Westminster Abbey; the third Lord Chesham, at Aylesbury; Sidney Ball at St. John's, Buntingford; and several buildings for Lloyds Bank.

His earlier work in churches was mainly in the way of alterations and redecorations, as at St. Martin-in-the-Fields, All Saints', Southampton, and St. John's, Hackney. In addition to the churches for the deaf and dumb at Acton and Clapham already mentioned, he designed the Wesleyan Methodist Church at Walworth. His most important postwar church was the rebuilding after bombing of St. Columba's, Pont Street, but this was not one of his happiest efforts.

It was in 1932 that Maufe won the competition for Guildford Cathedral. Cruciform in plan, with shallow transepts providing for a great open space at the crossing under the central tower, and with the roof lines of nave and chancel at the same level, Guildford bears some resemblance to Liverpool, in that it is symmetrical in side as well as in end view, but it carries the simplification of Gothic, with the substitution of modelled for linear treatment, still farther than Sir Giles Scott's building. Of concrete construction, it is faced with brick and stone. The nave, of seven bays, has tall two-light windows of the lancet type, and the aisles are for circulation only, to the gain of seating space. The cathedral stands on a green mound about 50ft high, and the approach from Guildford is a walking-way only, with steps at intervals and flanking avenues. From these approaches it builds up to the central tower with an effect of monumental and slightly austere simplicity, thoroughly characteristic of the architect.

Later works by Maufe include buildings for Trinity and St. John's Colleges, Cambridge, and Balliol and St. John's Colleges, Oxford (of which last he was an honorary Fellow), the Festival Theatre, Cambridge, the Playhouse, Oxford, the rebuilding in a scholarly neo-Georgian style of the war-damaged Middle Temple and of Gray's Inn (who made him an honorary Master of the Bench), and memorials at Tower Hill (an extension of the earlier memorial by Lutyens) and at Runnymede.

He was chief architect and artistic adviser to the Imperial War Graves Commission. Although he belonged to the old school of historical reminiscence he was always open minded, being, for example,

one of the judges who gave first prize to Sir Basil Spence's design in the competition for Coventry Cathedral.

He was elected A.R.A. in 1938, R.A. in 1947, and was knighted in 1954. He received the Royal Gold Medal for architecture in 1944.

Maufe was a tall, remarkably handsome man of almost episcopal appearance with charming manners. In his youth he was an exceedingly graceful dancer, and when he and his wife took the floor there was always a circle of admirers.

He married Gladys Prudence, daughter of Edward Stutchbury of the Geological Survey of India, and had one son. Lady Maufe, who is an experienced interior decorator, often assisted her husband in his work.

December 14, 1974.

René Mayer, the former French Prime Minister, died in Paris on December 13, 1972. He was 77. Mayer was Prime Minister for a brief period in 1953.

Half technocrat, half politician, René Mayer belonged to the small group of Frenchmen largely responsible for the modernization of France's economic life during the past half-century. Born on May 4, 1895, Mayer, in the thirties, held a number of railway directorships, a fact which made his advocacy of railway nationalization the more effective. He took a leading part in the creation of the S.N.C.F., the national railway company formed in 1937, of which he was on the Board. He was also concerned with the merger of private French air-lines into Air-France.

Like Jean Monnet, Mayer was an advocate of a united Europe and an Atlanticist. Whilst Monnet, with whom his career criss-crossed, always remained detached from French internal political life, Mayer went into politics after the war, joining the Radical party which was much discredited for the support it had given to Vichy, rightly seeing that the Radicals would inevitably provide a large share of Ministers and Prime Ministers when the war-time alliance of Communists, Socialists and progressive Catholics (the M.R.P.) had broken down. He held a number of posts in the late forties, and in 1951, as Finance Minister, presented the Coal and Steel Community Treaty to the Assembly.

He was Prime Minister from January to May 1953 and his government was the last which might have steered the E.D.C. Treaty, which aimed at creating a European army with a German contribution, through the French Parliament. But Mayer had to rely on Gaullist votes in the Assembly and he could never convince them that he could obtain sufficient safeguards from the Americans and British to make the Treaty palatable.

In 1955 Mayer succeeded Jean Monnet

as President of the High Authority of the Coal and Steel Community, resigning in 1957 when the Common Market was coming into being and a reshuffle of post was necessary.

Mayer was of Jewish ancestry on both sides, his grandfather having been the Rabbi of Paris. His mother was connected with the Rothschilds by marriage. In spite of this, Mayer returned to France in June 1940 from London where he had been head of the French armaments purchasing mission. Jean Monnet, on the same mission, left London for the United States. In 1942 Mayer escaped from France to Algeria where he joined General Giraud. Monnet was also attached to Giraud. The two made their peace with General de Gaulle* and Mayer became Minister of Works in the Provisional government after liberation.

Tall, always carefully dressed, reserved with a touch of hauteur, Mayer's opponents often accused him of being a stooge for reactionary banking interests. He was certainly a very conservative Radical but would better be described as an enlightened neo-capitalist and an internationalist.

He had many connexions with Britain, and his wife was the translator of a number of English books. Mayer was a good pianist and a great lover of music.

December 15, 1972.

Lord Melchett, chairman of the British Steel Corporation since 1967, died suddenly in Majorca on June 15, 1973. He was 48.

Julian Edward Alfred Mond was born on January 9, 1925, the second son of the second Baron Melchett, and grandson of Sir Alfred Mond, founder of Imperial Chemical Industries. Educated at Eton, he joined the Royal Navy in 1942 and served as a Fleet Air Arm pilot.

At the end of the Second World War he turned to farming in Bedfordshire, and maintained a lively interest in agriculture.

Melchett's direct links with the City were forged in 1947, when he joined an associated company of M. Samuel and Co., the merchant bankers. Six years later he was appointed a managing director of the parent company, which became Hill, Samuel and Co.

He became actively involved with the development of the international business and was placed in executive charge of the organization's banking and overseas department. There were during this period reports of unhappy personal relationships with the Philip Hill side of the merged bank.

Membership from 1963 to 1966 of the British Transport Docks Board gave him his first practical experience of the workings of a nationalized industry. Over roughly the same period he was a member of the Advisory Council of the Export Credits Guarantee Department and served on the Council of Administration of Malta Dock-

yard.

In 1966 Mr. Richard Marsh, then Minister of Power, persuaded Melchett to accept the post of chairman of the organizing committee established in September of that year to plan the transfer of the bulk of the British steel industry to public ownership. The appointment caused consternation among some Conservatives. But Melchett and Marsh remained calm.

Formal establishment of the steel organizing committee in September 1966, gave Melchett little more than six months in which to arrange the takeover and create the British Steel Corporation, which was due to come into being in April 1967. Melchett had few illusions about the magnitude of his task and was acutely conscious of his own lack of knowledge of the basic industry.

A seemingly endless round of discussions began. Melchett had somehow to integrate a collection of medium to large steel companies, scattered throughout the country, employing roughly a quarter of a million men, and engaged in a business with a turnover of about £1,500m. a year. Many of the works to be acquired were old and poorly sited. Morale was low, and the overall return on capital employed had slumped from 15-16 per cent to a derisory 2 per cent or less.

From the start, Melchett showed a determination in dealing with Whitehall and Westminster that was to characterize most of his years at the head of the corporation. His admirers described this quality as tenacity, his critics said it was stubborness.

Before Vesting Day, Melchett made several largely unpublicized visits to I.C.I.'s headquarters on Millbank, where he studied the structure of the undertaking his grandfather had created. But in the event, lack of time forced a structural decision upon him. The state sector would begin life on a four-division, geographical basis: an arrangement, it was thought, that would minimize the dislocation likely to be caused by the takeover and enable home and overseas trading to proceed in the early months much as before.

Like Lord Robens, his Socialist opposite number at the National Coal Board, Melchett was convinced that the salary levels of corporation board members should be considerably higher than those then prevalent in the public sector. Eventual Cabinet acceptance of that, although on a smaller scale than advocated, was the first major victory scored by the chairman-designate in what was to prove a series of running battles with politicians and civil servants.

The obvious sincerity with which Melchett discussed the need to turn state steel into an efficient, profit-making concern, coupled with his considerable charm, won him a large measure of support at works level. But at headquarters the going was more difficult. Many of the chairman's senior colleagues were former chief executives of the privately-owned steel companies. Only one or two had faith in nationaliza-

tion; most accepted with reluctance the reality of the takeover, and a few still looked forward hopefully to the possibility of persuading a future Conservative administration to return the larger companies to private ownership.

In the second week of January 1968, while an internal argument over the merits of centralization and decentralization of control was building up, Melchett suffered a coronary thrombosis. The nature of the illness and reports of internal differences over the corporation's future structure led to rumours of the chairman's impending resignation. But Melchett refused to take the easy way out.

Gradually the corporation assumed an identity of its own. A change of government, and the eventual realization that further political interference with the industry's ownership was not contemplated, helped to stabilize the internal situation.

Increasingly Melchett was able to concentrate on running the industry and guiding its policymakers.

He had already achieved notable success in persuading the Government to accept the idea of a measure of public dividend capital in the management of the corporation's financial affairs, enabling it to pay dividends to the Treasury in good years and to waive them in bad ones.

Much less successful, however, were his attempts to win the right to run his organization on what he described as "a commercial basis". More than once he vigorously demanded permission to raise prices and more than once ministers, fearful of the repercussions on the economy as a whole, said no.

Melchett scornfully rejected suggestions that steel sought to abuse its "monopoly" position in putting forward pleas for higher returns. "What monopoly?" he asked.

With prices pegged while costs continued to mount, the familiar state industry pattern of large potential losses began to emerge. The corporation's financial forecasts were repeatedly thrown out of gear, and criticism grew. But Melchett, too, had grown in stature. With increasing confidence came a readiness to speak even more bluntly to ministers in private and to complain, more publicly, about what he regarded as the delays and changes of course imposed upon him by the Government machine.

Despite the difficulties, some progress was made. From the outset, Melchett had realized that the industry was heavily overmanned by international standards. He had watched Lord Robens's skilful rundown of the coal industry with admiration, and he launched his own campaign of quiet, and, where possible, painless, closures and rationalization.

Eventually he switched the corporation's structure from a geographical to a product basis, ending the period of "separatism" among the old steel companies and making the prospect of eventual denationalization even more remote. Work was started, too, on the complex business of straightening the "ragged frontiers" which the nationalization Act had drawn between the state and private sectors of steel.

With the beginning of a new financial year in April 1971, it was decided that executive responsibility for the operational activities in the corporation's product divisions and head office should be delegated by Melchett, as chairman. to Dr. H. M. Finniston, who became chief executive and deputy chairman. Melchett retained direct control of the development and initiation of policy, future planning, and the vitally important external relations with the Government and steel industry leaders abroad.

The reward for Melchett's leadership of the B.S.C. came in December 1972 with the Government's agreement to the biggest modernization and expansion programme in the steel industry's history. Involving the investment of £3,000m. over the next 10 years, it aims to concentrate bulk steel production at five major steelworks around Britain.

Although Melchett had attempted to reduce his work load and to delegate more of his functions after his illness, he proved unable to divest himself of much work. Relaxation took the form of weekend visits, whenever possible, to his 800-acre farm in Norfolk, the maintenance of his interest in flying, holidays at his villa in Majorca and collecting modern paintings.

Melchett joined the steel industry at a time when its fortunes were at a low ebb. Not until several years have passed will it be possible fully to evaluate his work. He will, however, be remembered as a tough and courageous fighter, who sought neither to capitalize on his family's name and prestige nor to retire when the going became difficult.

He had a strong sense of public duty and an abiding faith in Britain's future as a major industrial nation. If his public image was that of a mild-mannered, unforceful man, it was belied in his private contacts with ministers, civil servants and staff, who undoubtedly regarded him as one of the most effective of the state board chairmen.

He married in 1947 Sonia Elizabeth, daughter of Lieutenant-Colonel R. H. Graham. They had one son and two daughters. His heir is the Hon. Peter Robert Henry Mond, who was born in 1948.

June 16, 1973.

Lauritz Melchior, whom English opera goers remember as the greatest Wagnerian *Heldentenor* of his generation between the wars, died in Santa Monica, California, on March 18, 1973. He was 82.

His great powers of endurance enabled him to sing through a *Ring* cycle as Siegmund and Siegfried without tiring, and his performance of Siegfried's final narra-

tion was generally remarkable for its freshness.

Born in Copenhagen on March 20, 1890, he studied at the Royal Opera School there and made his début in 1913. His first appearance at Covent Garden was in 1924 as Siegmund, and from then till the outbreak of war he sang regularly in *The Ring* and *Tristan*. He also sang Wagnerian roles at Bayreuth and at the other chief German opera houses. He was a leading tenor with a large following at the Metropolitan in New York for over 20 years. He was a singer with a powerful physique and a big voice that never seemed to tire, so that he made an ideal Siegfried.

He was also a notable Tristan, perhaps one of the best interpreters of the part of his generation from the vocal if not always from the histrionic point of view. His voice, though robust, was a true tenor of ringing yet seductive quality. He sang from time to time Italian roles, notably Otello in Verdi's opera, but it is as a Wagnerian that he is remembered, and when after the Second World War he no longer appeared at Covent Garden—though he continued to do so at the Metropolitan—it cost London some pains to identify another singer with the characters of Siegfried and Tristan. Melchior also sang the other Wagner roles, Lohengrin and Parsifal. He was honoured at home with an official appointment at the Danish court and the title of Knight of Dannebrog and abroad with that of Chevalier of the Legion of Honour.

He was seen in several Hollywood films including *Thrill of a Romance; Two Sisters from Boston; This Time for Keeps; Luxury Liner;* and *The Stars are Singing.*

March 20, 1973.

Jean-Pierre Melville, who died of a heart attack at the age of 55 on August 2, 1973, was not only a distinguished film maker in his own right but an important influence on the group of young directors who emerged during the French "new wave" of the late 1950s.

Melville's career presented an apparent contradiction. While he was a great admirer of the popular Hollywood cinema, to which he paid homage in a series of gangster films, his own work was done outside the commercial sphere. He had his own production company and studio (which he had to rebuild after a fire in 1967) and exercised maximum artistic control over his films, writing as well as directing, and having an obvious influence on the camerawork.

One of his early films was an excellent adaptation of Jean Cocteau's* *Les Enfants Terribles*. But he was equally at home with traditional Hollywood directors like John Ford and Howard Hawks. Melville provided an important bridge between the classic Hollywood genres and the work of younger French directors like Truffaut,

Chabrol and Godard.

He was born Jean-Pierre Grumbach in Paris on October 20, 1917, later adopting the name of the nineteenth-century American novelist, Herman Melville (yet another gesture to America was his habit of wearing a cowboy hat and dark glasses when he was directing films).

Though a keen amateur film maker as a young man, he went through a number of jobs, including travelling salesman, before settling on the cinema as a career. During the war he served in the Free French Army and while stationed in England had the chance to see Welles's *Citizen Kane,* which profoundly impressed him.

Melville's first film was a short, *24 Hours in the Life of a Clown,* made in 1946 and followed a year later by his feature début with *Le Silence de la Mer.* Both that film and *L'Armée des Ombres* (1969) reflected Melville's experiences with the wartime Resistance. His early films established his meticulous, leisured approach to film making: his quest for perfection limited his output to a fairly modest dozen films in nearly 25 years.

The six-part gangster series began with *Bob le Flambeur* in 1955, a beautifully realized story of a compulsive gambler whose planned robbery of the Deauville casino ends, as so often with Melville, in betrayal. It was followed by *Deux Hommes Dans Manhattan, Le Doulos, Le Deuxième Souffle, L'Aîné de Ferchaux* (after a Simenon story), *Le Samourai* and *Le Cercle Rouge.* The last, which appeared in 1970, was Melville's biggest commercial success. The films are notable for the acting performances of players like Jean-Paul Belmondo, Lino Ventura and Yves Montand.

Belmondo was less convincing in a film of an entirely different type, *Leon Morin Prêtre.* Made in 1961, it was the story, again with the background of occupied France, of a young girl who falls in love with a priest.

Melville was an occasional actor; he appeared in Cocteau's *Orphée,* Godard's *Breathless* and Chabrol's *Bluebeard.*

August 4, 1973.

Menon—See Krishna Menon.

Messali Hadj, sometimes known as the Patriarch of Algerian Nationalism, died in France on June 3, 1974 at the age of 76.

It was calculated that he had spent over 30 years in prison, in internment, or under house arrest. In 1962 he was freed after the signing of the Evian Agreement.

In the years after the First World War when political discontent was awakening in Algeria, the main trends in Muslim thinking sought to explore all possibilities of integration with France. Messali Hadj was opposed to all such policies. As early as 1925 he founded L'Étoile Nord-Africaine which demanded complete independence, withdrawal of all occupying troops, and the creation of a national army.

Born in 1898 of working class parents at Tlemcen, he saw service in the French Army in the First World War and stayed on in France at the end of hostilities, marrying a Frenchwoman. He was for a time a member of the Communist Party and the training the party gave him left its imprint on him. He later founded *Al Oumma*, a nationalist paper and in 1929 was imprisoned for the first time and the paper banned.

After further brushes with authority, he spent some time in Switzerland, returning to France under an amnesty granted by the Popular Front government, although his nationalistic movement was still banned.

In 1936 he founded at Nanterre the Algerian People's Party which gained great support from poorer Muslims, whose enthusiasm led to disorders which were serious enough to land Messali Hadj once more in prison. He was in the toils of the Vichy Government in the Second World War but in 1943 was pardoned by General Giraud. At the end of the war he was restored in triumph as principal nationalist leader, but in the aftermath of the Setif rising was yet again arrested together with most other Algerian leaders and deported to Brazzaville. By the time he was released in 1947 other younger men had come to the fore to lay the foundations of a seizure of independence through rebellion.

In the year of his release he founded the movement for the Triumph of Democratic Liberties (M.T.L.D.) from which both the Algerian Nationalist Movement (M.N.A.) and the F.L.N. were to emerge. The irrepressible Messali Hadj was arrested for the last time in 1952 and taken to France, where his movements were restricted until 1962, when Algerian independence was finally achieved.

June 6, 1974.

General Sir Frank Messervy, K.C.S.I., K.B.E., C.B., D.S.O., died on February 2, 1974 at the age of 80.

He had a distinguished and adventurous military career. In the Second World War he commanded five different divisions, which must be something of a record, and in the closing stages of the Burma campaign he was a corps commander. After the war he held three posts in succession as commander-in-chief.

A soldier by instinct, and certainly by inclination, the Army was the service he deliberately chose for a career. He never wavered in his allegiance to it.

He was an inspiring leader. In battle he was constantly up at the front in the thick of the fighting, and in the Western Desert, where he served for two years, he was a bizarre figure as he moved among the foremost troops with his straggling beard, balaclava helmet and long scarf. He was devoted to his men and his name became a legend.

He had his ups and downs in the desert, and his experience in that hard school stood him in good stead in Burma, where he earned well merited fame by the part he played in the defeat of the Japanese in the Arakan and at Kohima, and by his brilliant conduct of the drive of the IV Corps on Rangoon.

Messervy was tall and thin, and had a quiet, detached manner. He was a man of immense will power and staunch religious faith.

Frank Walter Messervy was born on December 9, 1893, the son of Walter Messervy of Bletchingley and Myra de Boissiere. He was educated at Eton and commissioned from Sandhurst in the Indian Army in 1913. He served with Hodson's Horse in the First World War in France, Palestine, Syria and Kurdistan and was with his regiment when it took part in Allenby's great cavalry drive on Damascus in 1918.

Between the wars, except for two years at the Staff College, Camberley, he served in India at regimental duty, as Brigade Major of the 1st Risalpur Cavalry Brigade, as an instructor at the Quetta Staff College, and as Commander of the 13th Duke of Connaught's Own Lancers, which was mechanized during his command.

In the Second World War he went to the Sudan with the 5 Indian Division as G.S.O. 1st Grade, but was soon given command of a small raiding force known as "Gazelle Force" and made a name for hunting the Italians. When General Platt advanced into Ethiopia, he commanded the 9th Infantry Brigade which captured the fort at the battle of Keren.

After Keren, Messervy was appointed to command the 4 Indian Division in the Western Desert. He distinguished himself in the battle at Sidi Omar in November 1941, when his headquarters and one of his brigades were surrounded for seven days. By his staunch and skilful defence he held and finally drove back the enemy, thus checking Rommel's offensive over the Egyptian frontier.

His division took part in Auchinleck's advance to Benghazi in the winter of 1941. In the retreat which followed, Messervy was transferred to command the 1st British Armoured Division, whose commander had been wounded. Now his luck deserted him. The division was eliminated as a fighting force within 96 hours of its first contact with the enemy. He was sent back to India; but no sooner had he arrived there than he was ordered to return to the Middle East.

General Jock Campbell, V.C., commander of the 7 Armoured Division (the "Desert Rats"), had been killed and Messervy succeeded him. He commanded the division with courage and dash, through many tribulations and grievous losses, during Rommel's push on Tobruk. But he did not see the end of the battle, for, at General Ritchie's request, Auchinleck relieved him of his command a few days before Ritchie himself was removed. While he was with the 7 Armoured Division his headquarters had been surprised and overrun by one of Rommel's battle groups. He tore off his badges of rank and told his captors he was the general's batman. Eighteen hours later he escaped through the German lines and rejoined his division.

After a short spell as D.C.G.S. at G.H.Q., Cairo, he was posted again to India, where he commanded the 43 Indian Armoured Division for a time and then joined G.H.Q., Delhi, as Director of Armoured Fighting Vehicles.

In 1943 he was given command of the 7 Indian Division, which was holding the line in the Arakan. When the Japanese launched their offensive there early in 1944, his division was at first cut off. But he counterattacked successfully and conducted a skilful and resolute defensive action in the battle of the "Admin. Box". In three weeks, as a result of a counter-offensive in which Messervy's troops played a leading part, the Japanese force disintegrated and was almost completely destroyed. For his share in those operations Messervy was awarded a bar to his D.S.O.

His division was next engaged in the battles at Kohima and Imphal, but in October he left it to take over the command of the IV Corps.

After the end of the Burma campaign he was appointed in 1945 to be G.O.C.-in-C. Malaya, and the following year he returned to India as G.O.C.-in-C. Northern Command. In 1947, on the partition of India, he was selected by the Government of Pakistan to be their first Commander-in-Chief.

He retired in 1948 with the honorary rank of general. He was made C.B. in 1942 and was created K.B.E. in 1945 and K.C.S.I. in 1947. He was Colonel of the 16th Light Cavalry from 1946 to 1949 and Colonel of the Jat Regiment from 1947 to 1955.

He was keenly interested in the Boy Scout movement, and was Deputy Chief Scout from 1949 to 1950.

He married in 1927 Patricia, daughter of Colonel E. Waldegrave Courtney. They had two sons and a daughter.

February 4, 1974.

Perle Mesta, formerly American Ambassador to Luxembourg, and a well-known Washington hostess for many years died in Oklahoma City on March 16, 1975. She was believed to be 85.

She was known, however, far outside the world of Washington, because Sally Adams, "the hostess with the mostest" in Irving Berlin's musical show *Call Me Madam*, was said to be modelled on her.

Except for the Kennedy era, when she was out of favour, Mrs. Mesta, a widow since 1925, entertained presidents, diplomats and American rank and fashion in her

Washington salon.

Her father, W. B. Skirvin, at one time a farm-implement salesman and real estate dealer, struck oil on an acre of land in Texas. Later the family moved to Oklahoma City where Skirvin established an oil company and also built the Skirvin Hotel.

In 1917 Perle Skirvin married George Mesta, who was president of the Mesta Machine Company in Pittsburgh. The Mestas travelled extensively. Mrs. Mesta visited nearly every country in Europe with her husband. Several years after her husband's death Mrs. Mesta lived for six months in London and was presented at Court. She frequently went to Washington in connexion with the work of the National Woman's Party.

She began going to national political conventions with her father when she was a girl. For many years a member of the Republican Party, she changed to the Democratic Party early in the Second World War, and in 1944 she was a delegate from Arizona to the Democratic National Convention. Four years later she was a delegate from Rhode Island.

Mrs. Mesta and her husband were frequent guests at the White House during the Calvin Coolidge Administration (1923-28). She met Harry Truman when he was still a Senator from the State of Missouri, and she and the Truman family became close friends. She gave Margaret Truman, the President's daughter, her first big Washington party in the spring of 1946.

Astute in business matters, she has kept the fortunes left to her by her father and husband. She proved to be an excellent fund raiser and organizer for the Democratic Party in the 1948 Presidential election.

Mrs. Mesta was appointed American Ambassador to Luxembourg in 1949. Although some said she lacked qualifications for the job, she proved popular.

After four years she returned to Washington and the new Eisenhower Administration.

Her success as a hostess owed something to her gift for providing excellent food and drink but something also to her socio-political instinct. She also succeeded in creating an atmosphere in which guests felt inclined to entertain each other. President Truman on occasions played the piano; General Eisenhower* had been known to sing "Drink to me only with thine eyes"; and it was put about that Mrs. Cornelius Vanderbilt had whistled in a duet.

In 1972 she broke a hip and in 1974 left Washington to resettle in Oklahoma.

March 18, 1975.

Lord Methuen, R.A., R.W.S., died on January 7, 1974 at the age of 87.

A prolific and talented painter he had been a member of the Royal Fine Art Commission, a trustee of the National Gallery and of the Tate Gallery.

Paul Ayshford Methuen, fourth Baron Methuen, was the eldest son of Field-Marshal Lord Methuen, whom he succeeded in 1932. He was born in 1886 and educated at Eton and New College, Oxford, taking second class honours in Natural Science in 1910. From then he was assistant at the Transvaal Museum, Pretoria, until the outbreak of the First World War, during which he saw active service in France as lieutenant in the Scots Guards. After the war he was appointed firstly Live Stock Officer and later Marketing officer to the Ministry of Agriculture, holding the post until 1932. In 1940 he rejoined the Army.

All his life, however, at Eton and Oxford and in the intervals of zoological studies and farming, Methuen had painted when he had the opportunity. While he was working at the Ministry of Agriculture he became a pupil of Sickert, having previously studied at Oxford under Sir Charles Holmes, who was then Slade Professor at the University. Under Sickert's encouragement Methuen gave up his post at the Ministry to become a whole-time artist, and it was in that capacity that he was known.

With a distinct talent of his own, Methuen may be said to have reflected something of both of his mentors. From Sickert he learnt to plan a picture in a limited scale of broad tones of colour, and the influence of Holmes was to be seen in a late Italian mannerism, particularly in architectural drawings. Methuen began to exhibit at the Royal Academy in 1929. From then onwards he was a regular exhibitor of landscapes, portraits and flower paintings. In landscape he often made a feature of buildings, having a special feeling for the spirit of place as expressed in architecture. The warm grey stone buildings of the West of England, such as Corsham Court, the family seat, which he painted more than once, lent themselves admirably to his purpose.

Corsham Court housed his family's splendid art collection and in 1969 Methuen announced that he had negotiated for Bath City Council and the National Trust to be responsible for the building. The council uses a large part of the house for its academy of art.

Methuen exhibited regularly at the New English Art Club and at the London Group and held many one-man shows in London.

A good-looking man of pleasant manners, unconventional in his dress, Methuen was a true countryman, interested alike in scientific farming and in the care of the relics of the past. He took an active part in the cultural life of the West of England, his sympathies embracing both ancient and modern art. Both Bristol and Bath awarded him honorary degrees.

He married in 1915 Miss Eleanor Hennessy, daughter of W. J. Hennessy. She died in 1958. The heir is Lord Methuen's brother, Captain the Hon. A. P. Methuen.

January 8, 1974.

Sir Francis Meynell, R.D.I., died on July 9, 1975 at the age of 84.

Youngest of the eight children of Wilfrid Meynell, man of letters, and his wife Alice, the poet and novelist, Francis Meredith Wilfrid Meynell "was born with a silver pen in his mouth". His parents named him after their *protégé* Francis Thompson, and their favourite novelist George Meredith.

Born on May 12, 1891, at a house in Palace Gate built for his parents by Leonard Stokes, he was allowed as a small boy to sit under the library table while his parents corrected proofs with their literary friends. His education was completed at Downside and Trinity College Dublin.

As managing director of Burns & Oates, his father initiated him into book design and in 1913 provided him with an assistant, Stanley Morison.* Both young men shared a devotion to religion, socialist politics, seventeenth century Fell types, and cricket. Together they planned many fine books for Burns & Oates, notably the *Ordo Administrandi Sacramenta* (1915).

In 1913 Meynell began a close friendship with George Lansbury, and a deep involvement with political life. He joined his mother and sisters in support of the Suffragists (not to be confused with the militant Suffragettes). Shortly after the outbreak of war in 1914, he joined Bertrand Russell* in The Union of Democratic Control, an anti-war body, and wrote articles in the *Herald* violently denouncing the war. In 1916 he set up the Pelican Press, from which soon flowed a stream of elegantly designed anti-war propaganda, some of it instigated by the Guild of the Pope's Peace which Meynell founded with Morison in 1916. But in the same year Meynell was called up; he went to the length of a painful thirst strike before the army released him.

He helped to found the Anglo-Russian Democratic Alliance in March, 1917, and joined the staff of the *Daily Herald*. After the Russian Government offered a subsidy to the new daily newspaper, he was involved in an absurd jewel-smuggling affair. He edited *The Communist* but resigned when J. H. Thomas brought a libel action against the paper.

In 1921 he returned to the Pelican Press where Morison had deputized for him since 1918. With Morison's help an exceptional array of types was installed, including a fine poster type which Meynell commissioned from the great American typographer Bruce Rogers, whose work had a strong influence on Meynell's adventures in book design.

With the creation of the Nonesuch Press in 1923, Meynell "made book production an entertainment as well as an adventure" as Holbrook Jackson later observed. Meynell showed that, with mechanical composition and presswork, he could make books which carried on the traditions of the English Private Press Movement. But his books had a wit, charm and grace which stemmed entirely from his own taste and style. He commissioned illustrations from a diversity of artists, among them Georg Grosz, Stephen Gooden, E. McKnight Kauffer, Rudolf Koch, Paul Nash, and Reynolds Stone. He used many of the types introduced by the Monotype Corporation, following the advice given to them by Stanley Morison.

Nonesuch books were designed to be read with enjoyment, not merely to impress. Meynell was especially proud of his modestly priced compendious series of British writers. He published much of Donne (whose *Love Poems* were chosen as the first Nonesuch book). And he produced a splendid set of Restoration dramatists in quarto. Formats varied from small folios to duodecimos, and it was a characteristic of all Nonesuch books that they were a pleasure in the hand.

The market for private press books was affected by economic conditions in the 1930s. Consequently Meynell welcomed proposals in 1935 for a takeover by The Limited Editions Club of New York. In the same year he became a columnist with the *News Chronicle*. His journalism came to the attention of United Artists who engaged him to design their advertising (he had written a useful book in 1929, *The Typography of Newspaper Advertisements*). After further work in the film industry for the Gaumont-British Picture Corporation, he joined the advertising agency of Mather & Crowther, who loaned him during the Second World War to the Board of Trade, where he became a persuasive and skilful adviser on consumer needs. His duties connected with rationing led an evening newspaper to comment that he was going "from limited editions to limited clothing".

A shower of honours began to fall on him from 1945, in which year he was appointed Royal Designer for Industry, and Honorary Typographical Adviser to His Majesty's Stationery Office. He was knighted in 1946, when he was also invited to join the Cement and Concrete Association, of which he became a highly successful Director-General. He was made a member of the Advisory Council of the Victoria & Albert Museum, the Royal Mint Advisory Committee, and served on the council of the Royal College of Art and on the Council of Industrial Design.

In the midst of a busy public life, he was delighted when the Nonesuch Press was given back to him in 1951. He found time to design new editions of Shakespeare in four volumes and the Bible in three; a collection of Belloc; a series of Nonesuch Cygnets for children; and many others.

His varied public posts gave full play to his qualities of discrimination and resourcefulness: and also to his skill with the written word. That skill was shown not only in prose but in the small output of his poetry, gathered in his *Poems and Places* of 1961. He owed not a little to the confluence of Alice Meynell's serious wit with the playful humour of Wilfrid. The fancy is sometimes strained, but there is an acute feeling for the beauty of language and several pieces are memorable for subtlety and point.

Meynell was more complex in nature than his grace of appearance and manner might suggest. A man of keen interests, he was apt to pursue them to the point of self-centredness, yet his impulses were sympathetic and generous. There was much in him of the rebel, yet in literary matters he was conservative. In his autobiography *My Lives* published in 1971, a few days after his eightieth birthday, he took a contented look back over a richly varied life.

He was married three times: first in 1914 to Hilda Saxe, by whom he had a daughter; second in 1925 to Vera Mendel by whom he had a son; and third in 1946 to Alix Hester Marie Kilroy (Dame Alix Meynell).

July 11, 1975.

Sir Eric Miéville, G.C.I.E., K.C.V.O., C.S.I., C.M.G., who was Assistant Private Secretary to King George VI from 1937 to 1945, died on September 16, 1971 at the age of 75.

In 1936 he became Private Secretary to the King when he was Duke of York. He was with him during the crisis of the Abdication. In addition to his duties as Assistant Private Secretary to the King, Miéville was also for some time in charge of press matters at the Palace.

Eric Charles Miéville was born on January 31, 1896, and educated at St. Paul's School, London.

After serving in the First World War, he joined the Far Eastern Consular Service in 1919 and served as private secretary to successive British Ministers in Peking from 1920 to 1927.

From there Miéville went as secretary to Lord Willingdon, Governor-General of Canada, until 1931; and when the latter was appointed Viceroy of India, Miéville accompanied him as private secretary. There were some heartburnings that this plum, to which the Indian Civil Service claimed an almost proprietary right, should be given to a man who had never been in India before, but Miéville soon won the confidence and esteem of everyone from the highest to the lowest.

In 1945 he resigned his post as Assistant Private Secretary to the King and was elected to various directorships, including the Westminster Bank. But in 1947 Lord Mountbatten asked him if he would join his friend Lord Ismay* on the high-powered staff which he was taking to India to carry out the instructions of his Majesty's Government that power in India should be transferred to Indian hands by June 1948 at the latest. Miéville, despite the sacrifices involved, accepted without a moment's hesitation and left England in April. He returned to England after India and Pakistan had been given independence in August.

Miéville's knowledge of the world and his experience of affairs made him a valuable member of a board of directors and this was recognized in many quarters. His understanding of people and his cheerful and sympathetic personality enabled him to contribute much to the handling of staff matters. He was a man of many and lasting friendships, which included conspicuously those with the distinguished personalities whom he had served so well and always so devotedly.

September 17, 1971.

Captain Einar Mikkelsen, who died in Copenhagen at the age of 90 on May 3, 1971, was internationally famous as an Arctic explorer. Almost all his long life was devoted to seafaring, exploration and writing about his exciting adventures and notable discoveries.

Mikkelsen was one of the men who were hard up against the elemental problem of survival. They accepted an incalculable risk and the certainty of loneliness and extreme privation if things went wrong.

He was born in Copenhagen in December 1880 and went to sea in the merchant service when he was only fourteen. Six years later he served in G. C. Amdrup's Danish expedition to Eastern Greenland and, although he later made voyages to many other parts of the world, it was on this region that he became the foremost authority.

In 1901 an American expedition which he accompanied failed in its attempt to reach the North Pole from Franz Josef Land, but gave Mikkelsen such valuable experience that, after a spell with the Danish Hydrographical Service, he was appointed joint leader with his comrade, Ernest Leffingwell, of an expedition which set out to find, north of Alaska, undiscovered land which Mikkelsen and many others believed to exist.

Mikkelsen set to work to raise the necessary funds to supplement the original contribution from Leffingwell's father. In London he was received by his fellow countrywoman, Queen Alexandra, who would have contributed but for the fact that she felt that she could not help an undertaking which involved the killing and eating of sledge-dogs if necessary! The Royal Geographical Society made a donation, but the greater part of the funds came from the Duchess of Bedford, after whom the expedition ship was named, or from the United States. The supposed "land" was found to be a gigantic "ice-island" on which, after the Second World War, the Americans were able to set up an air-base. The bay near where Mikkelsen and his companions wintered in 1906-1908 was later given his name.

Perhaps his most famous exploit belongs to the expedition of 1909-12 to north-east Greenland which he led to look for the diaries and reports left by Mylivs-Erichsen, leader of the Danmark expedition, 1906-8.

Some of the diaries and maps had already been recovered and Mikkelsen found others, but his journey with I. P. Iversen turned into a nightmare. They ate their dogs; abandoned their sledges; cached the diaries; and staggered on in the hallucinating stages of hunger and exhaustion. They found an abandoned ship and a hut containing provisions but, knowing themselves overdue, wondered if any rescue vessel would ever come. They survived two further winters in Greenland suffering fearful physical and mental hardships before they were found.

In 1913 Mikkelsen published *Lost in the Arctic*.

The Danish Government now took Mikkelsen into its service. He was attached to the Danish delegation that went to The Hague in 1932 to discuss Denmark's sovereignty over Greenland. The Danish claim received international recognition and for the next eighteen years Mikkelsen served as Inspector-General of East Greenland. In this he displayed his deep sympathy with and understanding of the Greenlanders, and this influenced in no small way the development of Danish policy towards their enormous "colony". After the German occupation of Denmark in 1940 the Danish Minister in Washington, Henrik Kauffman, made an epoch-making agreement with the United States government permitting the establishment of American bases in Greenland, and in 1944 Mikkelsen was attached to the Danish Legation as an adviser on Greenland questions. In fact he never ceased to concern himself with the welfare of Greenlanders.

His exploits brought honours from several governments and scientific societies. The Royal Geographical Society gave him the Patron's Gold Medal in 1934, and the Livingstone Gold Medal in 1948.

Mikkelsen was a talented writer, and in addition to many special memoranda on Arctic matters published several books of more popular appeal. "Miki", as he was affectionately called in Denmark, was a well-loved figure in his own country, and his genial character gained him many friends in other lands.

On his 90th birthday in December 1970, a national tribute was paid to him in Denmark. One comment made was that, like Nansen, he had passed from the work of Polar exploration to the task of humanitarianism, the raising of the standard of living of the Greenlanders. His most important book *Lost in the Arctic* was on this occasion published in a new edition.

May 5, 1971.

Erhard Milch, formerly a German Field-Marshal and sometime Inspector-General of the Luftwaffe, died in the last week of January 1972 at the age of 79 and was buried on January 28.

He was brought to the front by Hermann Goering after Hitler came to power, and became his right-hand man during the building of the Luftwaffe.

A pilot in the First World War, which saw the beginning of his acquaintance with Goering, he is believed to have gone back to take up university studies when the war ended but he was passionately interested in aviation and is thought to have been involved in the foundation of air ventures in Sweden, Hungary and Austria. He was in at the birth of the great German civil airline, Lufthansa, in the 1920's and soon made his way to the top.

When the Nazis came to power Goering made him Under Secretary for Air. His rise continued as the Nazis began to spread their wings, being made lieutenant-general in 1935, general a year later, chief of staff in 1938 and subsequently Inspector-General of the Luftwaffe. His position was inevitably weakened later in the war as German air power was not seen to be in the ascendant, and he lost further ground after a dispute with Hitler over the employment of the German Me 262 jet fighter, a dispute in which it may well be that the right lay with Milch.

He is described in Goebbels's diaries as being sharply critical of his former chief (Goering) in 1943 but at the Nuremburg trial gave evidence for him.

Milch himself stood trial in 1947 and was found guilty by an American court of war crimes against humanity in recruiting slave labour for aircraft plants and in his treatment of such labour. He was sentenced to life imprisonment, which was later reduced to a term of 15 years. During the last years of his life he had worked as an industrial adviser.

January 29, 1972.

Darius Milhaud, the French composer, died in Geneva on June 22, 1974 after a long illness, at the age of 81.

No other composer of the twentieth century worked in so wide a variety of forms and style. His vast catalogue of works—operas, ballets, incidental music, symphonies, concertos, choral works, chamber music and songs seemed to come from him in a continuous stream—is notable not only for its extent but also for the freedom with which he adopted whatever style seemed to him to be suitable for the task which occupied him at the moment, and for the elaborate problems in harmony, orchestration, rhythm and form which he chose to set himself, often in the context of some otherwise unambitious functional task.

Darius Milhaud was born on September 4, 1892, in Aix-en-Provence. His parents were Jewish, prosperous members of the commercial class, and closely in touch with the musical and cultural life of their region. Their son began to show his unusual musical gifts very early in childhood, but his ill-health deterred them from allowing him to learn an instrument until, at the age of seven, he began to study the violin and, with their approval, planned a career as an instrumentalist.

During his studies at the Paris Conservatoire, however, he discovered that his destiny was to become a composer, and Paris, in the years before the First World War, formed his tastes and created the foundations upon which his own works were created. The music of Wagner and the later German composers became objects of his intense dislike, while his imagination was stimulated by the music of Debussy and Mussorgsky; the conservative academic training provided by the Conservatoire helped him less than his wide friendships among musicians, artists and writers, especially his eventually fruitful association with the writers Francis Jammes and Paul Claudel. The outbreak of war in 1914 interrupted his studies, and in 1916 Jammes, at that time a diplomat, was appointed French Minister in Brazil, and invited Milhaud to accompany him as his secretary. Two years in Rio de Janeiro gave the composer a delight in Brazilian folk music and the life of the country, which showed itself in his later music, particularly in the ballet *Le Boeuf sur le Toit* and the dance suite *Saudades do Brazil*.

When he returned to Paris in 1918, he found that his own rebellion against German musical ideals was widely shared by other musicians, and he was drawn into the group of artists, writers and composers—Georges Auric, Louis Durey, Francis Poulenc,* Germaine Tailleferre and the Swiss Artur Honegger were the composers of the group—surrounding the veteran composer Erik Satie and the writer Jean Cocteau, who for a time was their cultural law-giver. For a time there was sufficient unanimity in the attitudes and aims of the composers to justify the collective name *"Les Six"* which was given to them in the early 1920s and has clung to them ever since, although it was not long before the composers' roads diverged, even if many of their principles remained unchanged. From the start Milhaud was the most intrepid of them in breaking new ground.

Although as early as 1915, in his music for a production of Claudel's translation of the *Choephori*, Milhaud had constructed an entirely revolutionary score in which percussion instruments accompanied human voices uttering cries of grief and moans of anguish, together with natural sounds like those of the wind, it was his association with Jean Cocteau* and *Les Six* which brought him into almost scandalous prominence. There was a sense in which he feared that his associates seemed to be manoeuvring themselves into an aesthetic which would make their work no more than frivolously decorative, and in 1920 the sensation created by his ballet, to a scenario by Cocteau, *Le Boeuf sur le Toit* (anglicized as *The Nothing Doing Bar*)—a sensation as much scandalous as artistic in its treatment, to South American rhythms, of strange events in a North American speakeasy during the days of prohibition—gave him the reputation of an ingenious jester.

His songs, lyrical, often light and gracefully charming, his instrumental music and the scores of incidental music for a variety of plays—those for Claudel's translation of Aeschylus all as vigorously experimental as that for the *Choephori*, that for his *Protée* yielding an orchestral suite which was virtually howled down at its first performance in 1922—naturally seemed to contribute less to the general idea of Milhaud's aims, principles and gifts than did, for example, *Machines Agricoles*, a setting for voice and seven instruments of a trade catalogue composed in 1919.

His first opera, *La Brebis Égarée*, composed between 1910 and 1915 to a text by Jammes, was given its first performance at Opéra-Comique, Paris, in 1923. The negro ballet, *La Création du Monde*, inspired by the music of negro jazz musicians heard during a visit to New York and one of the most successful pieces of "symphonic jazz" was seen in the same year, and it was followed in 1924 by the ballets *Salade* and *Le Train Bleu*, which were taken into the repertoire of Diaghilev's Russian Ballet. His complex opera, *Christophe Colomb*, which made use of such diverse styles and techniques as those of a quasi-Greek chorus, the miracle play, the *leit-motif* of Wagnerian music drama, and cinematically projected scenes, was produced at the Berlin State Opera in 1930, and the decade that followed saw the composition of three more operas hardly ambitious in style, more than 20 scores for plays, and almost as much film music. Taken in conjunction with an enormous list of choral, orchestral and chamber works, and songs with orchestral or piano accompaniment, the mere bulk of his output in these years becomes staggering.

After the fall of France in 1940, Milhaud made his way to the United States, where he was Professor of Composition at Mills College, Oakland, California, and where he stayed until 1947. After his return to France, although he was occupied not only with composition but also with the Professorship of Composition at the Paris Conservatoire, he returned regularly to Mills College for some part of each year.

It was not until 1939, after five symphonies for small orchestra, that Milhaud committed himself to a symphony on a full orchestral scale, the first of four symphonies written in less than 10 years, the Third being a choral and orchestral work celebrating the liberation of France in the Second World War and ending in a setting of the *Te Deum*. Unlike many composers, he did not, as time passed, settle into a single style, lose interest in new forms or find his appetite for experiment diminished; even the use of the term "experiment" is justified, for unlike many composers Milhaud attempted to do new things, often at unexpected points in a composition, less from a sense that they were expressively right in their context than from the sense that they were interesting.

Time alone will be able to sift the works of lasting value from those of merely transitory interest in his huge output, and time's task in this will not be entirely easy, for Milhaud was never less than a scrupulously exact and remarkably inventive craftsman with an enviable gift for the creation of memorable melodies. It was his determination never to pour music into any given mould but always to find styles, forms and materials appropriate to the work in hand which gives even the slightest of his works a certain interest, refinement, and an undeniable freshness. In a sense, he was the Telemann of twentieth-century music, never at a loss for music whatever the specifications of the work demanded from him.

In 1925 Milhaud married his cousin, Madeleine Milhaud.

June 26, 1974.

John Millar Watt, one of the finest artists to devote himself to a strip cartoon, died on December 13, 1975 at the age of 80.

His popular creation, "POP", the rotund, bald, bespatted figure, sporting top hat, cravat and tail coat, will go down in newspaper history as one of the earliest and best strip cartoons to appear in England and was one of the longest running.

Millar Watt was born in 1895 in Gourock on the Clyde. Educated in Ilford and at the Cass Art Institute in London, he joined the advertising agency of Mather & Crowther at three shillings a week, eventually succeeding Tom Purvis, the poster designer.

He joined the Artists Rifles in 1915 and was commissioned in 1916 in the Essex Regiment. After the war he went to the Slade School and while there drew some sports cartoons for the *Daily Chronicle*.

Answering an advertisement in *The Times* for an artist for the *Daily Sketch*, he thought up a number of ideas from which was born the prototype of "POP" in 1921. The final figure to emerge had a "figure eight" head with tiny eyes and button nose. No mouth was visible except when emitting a cry.

Later to join the cast were the Colonel, a tall tail-coated figure with white moustache, "Ma" and daughter Phoebe. Millar Watt's feeling for drawing children was surpassed by that of Ernest Shepard only.

Once launched, "POP" achieved an increasing popularity, appearing every day in the *Daily Sketch* for over 25 years, despite tempting offers from the rival *Daily Mirror* to lure him away. "POP" was syndicated throughout the world, and annual collections (now collectors' items) were published by the *Daily Sketch* at one shilling per copy.

A tall alert figure with aquiline nose, he lived in active retirement, in a spacious early Tudor house with Georgian frontage, in the medieval wool town of Lavenham, Suffolk.

His chief hobby was buying antiques and period houses and restoring them.

He was also an expert on painting materials and methods of painting by the old masters, especially Titian and Rubens. An imposing copy of "Bacchus and Ariadne" by Millar Watt was a prominent feature in his hall at Lavenham.

During the Second World War, he volunteered to do war work—he wanted to design in an aircraft factory. "POP", however, was considered a national asset to morale; King George VI and Churchill* were known to be devoted followers. Millar Watt went back to the drawing board and "POP" exchanged top hat for tin helmet and joined the Home Guard.

After the war, Millar Watt wanted to stop drawing "POP", and so an arrangement was made whereby the *Daily Sketch* kept the copyright and the strip was continued by another artist. He resumed painting and illustration at his leisure; the magazine *Everybodys* commissioned several series of historical illustrations, and "POP"-like figures with a wooden leg appeared on the hoardings advertising beer.

Millar Watt's reputation is secure in his creation of one of the first and most original comic strips of this century.

He married a fellow artist, Amy Maulby Biggs, a painter who herself exhibited for 14 years at the Royal Academy.

December 17, 1975.

Ernest Milton, the actor, died on July 24, 1974 at the age of 84.

He achieved theatrical success the hard way, for he had played a wide range of parts both in America and in Britain before he had his first notable triumph in John Galsworthy's gripping play *Loyalties* in March 1922.

Born in San Francisco on January 10, 1890, he made his first appearance on the New York stage in 1913 as the first camel driver in *Joseph and his Brethren*, and thereafter he played in repertory companies in the New England states. His first appearance in London was in a small part in the production of *Potash and Perlmutter*, and two years later he played the same character, though considerably developed, in a sequel *Potash and Perlmutter in Society*.

In 1917 he toured the camp theatres and just before the end of the First World War he joined the Old Vic Company and played many of the principal Shakespearean characters, including Hamlet, and a Shylock which in later years was to stamp him as one of the leading tragic actors in the London theatre. One recalls his performance at the Old Vic in *Wat Tyler* in which he had one speech, a soliloquy in prison which took about 20 minutes to deliver and in which his fine diction held his audience spellbound.

Then came the production in 1922 of *Loyalties* which ran for 400 performances at the St. Martin's. His part was that of a Jewish guest at a country house whose special loyalty was to his race, to his pride in it and to his defiant scorn of the anti-Semitism that in "society" oppressed him. He is robbed of his note-case by a fellow guest, an army captain, and when the accusation of theft is made the captain and the Jew fight the matter out in the courts.

Although audiences of the time were inclined to think that both the racial and the "anti" feeling were latent in actual life rather than warring openly as they did in the play, Milton played the part with a tense emotion which enabled him to retain fully the sympathy and possibly the admiration of the onlooker.

Another of Milton's performances which will be remembered was his *Henry IV* in the play of that name by Pirandello, first at the Everyman in 1925 and again under his own management at the Queen's in 1929. It was a remarkable picture of a madman who, being secretly cured, feigns madness in order that he may continue in his isolation from the world that has outgrown him. Before the eyes of his audience he confesses his sanity; in an astonishing ecstasy he kills the man who has most deeply injured him; then with infinite weariness he sinks back upon his mock throne and slips again into his protective madness.

Milton moved with a beautiful sensitiveness to truth and to pretence. His mood looked from his eyes. His imagination rang and whispered in his voice. His secret prayers spoke in his silences. His performance was a remarkable piece of lucidity and many flashes of drama added force to a brilliant characterization.

Many other successes followed—his sketch of the cynical doctor in *Grand Hotel* analysing the crowds passing and repassing through the lounge as a crowd in a civilized madhouse; his performance in a revival of Granville Barker's *The Madras House*; his appearance as Pierrot in *Prunella* at the Everyman; his vivid portrait of Disraeli in Laurence Housman's *Victoria Regina*, which fully suggested his influence on the Queen and the extravagance of his genius.

The two contributions which he made to the contemporary theatre in 1932 must be mentioned. In April of that year he went into management at the St. James's Theatre and appeared as Othello and Shylock. He himself produced *Othello*, which was vital and ardent.

Being at heart an artist, he took many risks and invited many challenging comparisons. The praise for his production was unanimous; about his acting the critics were divided and certain extravagances of gesture, manner and voice did possibly prejudice the splendours of his performance. But those who thought that an actor of his elaborate sensitiveness must fail in the soldierly splendours of the Moor were mistaken. When he was still, when dignity was his quest, when he was defending himself in Venice or reproving Cassio's outbreak

on the night of triumph, he was magnificent. But it was felt that if he would moderate some of his rage and jealousy, the fire, the emotional brilliance and the imaginative range of his performance would not be impaired.

For his Shylock there was nothing but praise. He was deliberately light at the outset, so that his discovery that Jessica had gone had the effect of a thunder-clap on a summer evening. He held himself back from extravagance and, even in the trial scene, Shylock's emotion, whether of triumph or despair, was controlled. Although he made no openly spectacular or self-conscious demands upon his audience, no eye could leave him. He was neither a whining usurer at one extreme nor a tragic prophet at the other, but a man betrayed, stung, perverted towards cruelty, and at last forced by defeat to an acceptance that had splendour in it. "Not a whirlwind; not a 'sensational' Shylock", wrote the dramatic critic of *The Times*, "but a recognizable and a memorable one".

His Hamlet was a performance of striking personality and intensity, and his Shylock and Othello were outstanding, but the theatre is under a debt of gratitude to him for the careful thought and attention to detail which he gave to every part entrusted to him. To each of them he brought an intensity of imagination and originality of vision which, however startling they were, seemed never to impose anything upon a play extraneous to its own nature.

He was last seen on the London stage in 1967 in Dürrenmatt's *The Deadly Game* at the Savoy Theatre. A play written by Milton, *Christopher Marlowe*, was published in 1924 and acted at East London College in 1931. He was also author of a play about Paganini, and a novel, *To Kiss the Crocodile*, published in 1928.

Ernest Milton appeared in a number of British films, among them *The Scarlet Pimpernel*. He was seen occasionally on television, notably as Archbishop Temple in Housman's *Victoria Regina* in 1964, and viewers saw him speaking with depth and enthusiasm in a discussion of *Hamlet* and, in another theatre discussion programme, playing scenes from *King Lear*. He was a naturalized British subject and in 1926 he married Miss Naomi Royde Smith, the novelist. She died in 1964.

July 29, 1974.

Cardinal Jozsef Mindszenty, former Archbishop of Esztergom and Primate of Hungary, died on May 6, 1975 at the age of 83.

The Cardinal's episcopacy was marked by two imprisonments: during the German occupation as an anti-Fascist, and after 1948 as an opponent of the Communist-controlled government in Hungary. His courage before each arrest was undoubted, but there was considerable speculation about the extent of his involvement in pure-

ly political matters.

After his brief reappearance in public life, during the abortive Hungarian rising, he lived, practically incommunicado, in the American legation.

Several times there were signs that both the Vatican and the Hungarian Government were anxious to find a solution which would enable the Cardinal to leave Hungary; one of the most promising signs was the agreement of 1964 between the two authorities on the appointment of five bishops, the first such agreement to be reached by the Holy See and a communist government. However the years went by and Mindszenty, though occasionally reported to be about to leave, remained in the legation. He was several times visited by Cardinal Koenig, Primate of Austria, who sought to find ways of persuading Mindszenty to end his self-imposed exile. Finally, rumour became fact and in September 1971, he arrived in Rome. After a short stay in the Vatican he left Rome for Vienna where he took up residence at the Pazmaneum, a hostel for priests and founded by a former Primate of Hungary.

A slight, intense-eyed churchman, he fought both the Nazis and the Communists with a spiritual weapon, the pastoral letter, sharpened by his gift of expression. He was of peasant origin and was born in 1892 at Csehimindszenty, in west Hungary, but his forebears had come from Suabia. Ordained to the priesthood at the age of 22, he spent some time as a parish priest, but his ability led quickly to preferment and he was successively teacher, dean and domestic prelate. His writings and his sermons during the 1939-45 War earned him wide recognition, and in 1944 he became Bishop of Veszprem, but a very short time afterwards was imprisoned for his uncompromising opposition to the Germans who were then in control of Hungary.

It was during the German occupation that he changed his name from Pehm to Mindszenty, which he took from his native village.

Released in the spring of 1945, he succeeded Cardinal Seredi as Archbishop of Esztergom and Primate of Hungary a short time afterwards. At once he began to combat both the policy and the doctrines of the Communists. Elevated to the Sacred College in February 1946, he arrived a week late for the Consistory owing to delay in the grant of his exit permit from Hungary. For the remainder of his time at liberty he continued on his uncompromising course. With Russian influence in the country becoming ever stronger, there could be but one end and the Cardinal was arrested the day after Christmas Day 1948, St. Stephen's Day. The arrest raised a storm of protest, which was by no means confined to members of the Roman Catholic Church.

The protracted struggle between the hierarchy and the Hungarian Government reached its climax in 1949 with the public trial of the Cardinal on charges of illegal dealings in currency, conspiracy against the state, and espionage. He pleaded guilty and was sentenced to life imprisonment. In July 1955 the Hungarian Ministry of Justice announced that the sentence had been suspended because of his bad health and age—he was 63—and that he was living in a "church-owned building", the location of which was not revealed.

A year later, during the brief revolt in Hungary, crushed by Russian troops and tanks, the Cardinal was liberated and returned to Budapest. He was reticent about his treatment during and after the trial, his few public statements including, instead, an appeal to the United Nations on behalf of his country and another to the people of other nations to send food and medical supplies.

As the Soviet tanks moved into Budapest to suppress the rising, Cardinal Mindszenty sought asylum in the American Legation there. In accordance with international law he became a voluntary prisoner unable to communicate with anyone outside the legation and sharing the conviction of others that, even if offered a safe conduct, he would face the prospect of arrest if he left its shelter.

The circumstances of the trial and the events that had preceded it gave rise to many theories as to the methods by which the confession had been obtained. Throughout 1948 he had expected to be arrested and in November of that year, when issuing a pastoral letter sharply critical of the regime, he had added a brief letter *ad clerum* stating that if he resigned or confessed to crimes it would be due to human frailty and his declarations would be null and void. This letter was referred to during the trial when the Cardinal stated that his confession was quite voluntary and came from a better understanding of conditions than he possessed when the letter was written. Nevertheless the contrast between the uncompromising and certainly brave Primate of earlier years and the abject penitent who appeared in court was so striking that few foreign observers accepted his testimony as being likely to be true. There was considerable speculation as to the possible use of drugs or hypnosis to unseat the will, and make the man a pliant political instrument; it was more widely believed that known methods of sapping resistance by remorseless questioning, enforced fatigue, and deprivation of ordinary human dignity had been responsible for the effect at which his accusers arrived. This was later borne out when the Cardinal left Hungary in 1971; he was shamefully used by his communist interrogators, who beat him on many occasions and made him run naked round a cellar for over three hours.

The Cardinal accepted responsibility for transactions in currency made by members of his household and agreed also that he had conspired for the restoration of the monarchy and, on other occasions, to prevent the return to Hungary of the historic Crown of St. Stephen. But against his own evidence at the trial was the fact that on the date when he was alleged to have attended a secret meeting with the Archduke Otto, he was actually in Canada attending an international congress. It was true, however, that he had approached Cardinal Spellman,* Archbishop of New York, with regard to the safe keeping of the Crown of St. Stephen, which had been recovered by the American forces after its removal from Hungary by the German Army. Cardinal Mindszenty feared for the future of the relic should it come into the possession of a Communist regime and hoped that it might be transferred temporarily to the custody of the Holy See. The motives for his conduct in this particular were honourable therefore and patriotic, if they were not wise.

The most difficult aspect of the trial to accept in view of his previous actions was the Cardinal's public repudiation of the warning to his clergy that any future confession would be due to human frailty. He was, indeed, the man least likely to be ignorant of the methods by which confessions can be extorted; for he had been a victim, in prison, of terrorism during the brief regime of Bela Kun and suffered also during the Nazi occupation, when after his arrest he insisted on walking to prison in his robes, blessing the people as he went. Moreover, the pastoral letter of November 1948, which the warning accompanied, was almost prophetic in its statement of the persecution that he faced.

As Primate, and after his elevation to the Sacred College in 1946, Cardinal Mindszenty had expressed willingness on behalf of the hierarchy to negotiate a concordat with the *de facto* Government of Hungary. But as he pointed out in the pastoral of 1948, while the Government expressed willingness to settle by negotiation any questions that involved Church interest, it settled unilaterally the most important question of all by nationalizing the schools and thus preventing the continuance of Christian education.

Mindszenty was to spend 15 years in seclusion in the American Legation, towards the latter end of which time he received several Vatican emissaries in an attempt to get him to change his mind and leave Hungary.

At last in 1971 as a result of Vatican determination to press ahead with better formal relations with the Communists he was persuaded to leave Budapest.

But his assent was only obtained as a result of considerable pressure from Pope Paul VI and in the light of more progressive Vatican thinking that his patriotic stance had become symbolical, of no further practical value in the context of the realities of the situation of the Church in Hungary.

The Hungarian Government remitted the rest of his sentence and in September 1971, amid delicate security, he was flown to Rome. The following month he went to Vienna, as the nearest Western centre to his homeland and spent the rest of his life, punctuated by visits to other Roman Catholic communities throughout the world, in a Hungarian religious community in the city.

In 1974 the Pope retired him, again against his will, from his position as Archbishop of Esztergom and Primate of Hungary. At this he felt free to publish his *Memoirs* which also appeared in 1974. Controversial and unsparingly honest, their relation of the struggle of a man totally devoted to the Church he had served all his life, evoked wide response.

Whether or not Mindszenty's stance was practical political behaviour in the turbulent age he found himself born into, it emerges clearly from the *Memoirs* that he regarded the Church and spiritual truth as things which ought to be above policy and exigency. Nothing finally hurt him more than the quarrel he was forced to have with the Church and Vatican which he believed in and so faithfully served.

May 7, 1975.

Dr. José Miró Cardona, the first prime minister in Castro's revolutionary government, who later defected to become leader of the Cuban exiles in the United States, died in Puerto Rico on August 10, 1974 at the age of 71.

Miró, a small but heavy-looking man, was an able and passionate orator. Born in Havana, he took a degree in political, social and economic sciences at Havana University in 1937, became a doctor of law and then studied at Rome University. Although more an academic than a politician, more idealistic than rebellious, he became active in the struggle against the harsh regime of Batista. Appalled by its excesses, he spent years outside the island organizing the movement that finally brought down the Government. After the revolution, Miró became prime minister, but Castro pushed him aside to take that post for himself after only 45 days. Miró was sent to Madrid as ambassador until Castro curtailed diplomatic relations with Spain, and was then appointed as ambassador to Washington.

But he was never to take up that position. He fled into the Argentine embassy in Havana, left for exile in Miami, and bitterly denounced Castro for failing to establish democracy in Cuba.

As leader of the Cuban National Revolutionary Council, he called for an uprising against Castro and the end of "international communism's cruel oppression". If his movement had succeeded he would have become provisional president until the calling of elections. Although the council did not represent all the 200,000 Cuban exiles then in the United States, Washington saw it as the leading movement and Miró was in the forefront of the organization of the Bay of Pigs invasion. After the failure of that extraordinary operation, Miró attacked the United States for not giving the invaders proper backing, and in 1963 he resigned his office. He accused the United States of having decided to coexist with Castro and of betraying its promise that there would be a second invasion of Cuba. Moving to Puerto Rico with his family, Miró became a professor of law.

August 12, 1974.

Sir Eustace Missenden, O.B.E., Chairman of the Railway Executive from the time of nationalization of British railways until 1951, died on January 10, 1973 at the age of 86.

Eustace Missenden was a career railwayman of the best type. He had risen by merit from being a booking clerk at 13 years of age at a country station to the head of his profession. By the time he was 37 he was operating superintendent of the South Eastern and Chatham Railway, the toughest task to serve the toughest commuters.

The Southern Railway, under Sir Herbert Walker, absorbed the S.E. & C.R. in 1923 and recognized Missenden's quality not only in his own operating field. He became Docks Manager at Southampton at a time when the great expansion of the Ocean Terminal was planned and carried through. After a time as Traffic Manager he became General Manager of the Southern in 1939 and almost simultaneously succeeded Gilbert Szlumper as a member of the wartime Railway Executive.

He was intimately concerned with the transportation of the British Expeditionary Force to France in 1939 and with the reception and dispersal of the troops after the evacuation from Dunkirk. Later in the war he played a vital part in planning the flow of railway traffic before D-day in 1944.

After the war, when nationalization came, Missenden was the natural choice to head the railways, which became part of Lord Hurcomb's British Transport Commission. The task of welding together four railways that had been historic rivals called for a phase of centralized management. The Railway Executive was a committee of strong-willed professional departmental chiefs. It was hard going, especially for its chairman, Missenden. He succeeded in standardizing most of the procedures for the national railways, if not their thinking. In 1950, at the age of 64, he had had enough, and retired with the goodwill of all his colleagues.

Eustace James Missenden was born in 1886. He entered the service of the South Eastern and Chatham Railway in 1899 and was promoted successively District Traffic Superintendent 1920, Divisional Operating Superintendent 1923, Assistant Superintendent of Operations 1930, Docks and Marine Manager, Southampton 1933, Traffic Manager 1936, and General Manager Southern Railway 1939.

He was knighted in 1944. From 1949 to 1951 he was Colonel-Commandant of the Engineer and Railway Staff Corps R.E. (T.A.).

He married in 1912 Lilian Adeline, daughter of Henry Gent. There were no children of the marriage and his wife died in 1959.

February 2, 1973.

Nancy Mitford, C.B.E., who died on June 30, 1973, thoroughly deserved her wide popularity as a writer and also the devotion she inspired in her many friends.

She was born in November 1904, of exceptionally gifted stock. Her paternal grandfather (ennobled as Lord Redesdale) was a man of cosmopolitan culture and one of the first English experts upon Japan. From his wife, a daughter of the seventh Earl of Airlie, she inherited the brilliant blood of the Stanleys of Alderley, and was thus a cousin of Bertrand Russell* and Lady Spencer-Churchill. Her maternal grandfather, Thomas Gibson Bowles, was uncommonly clever, made a fortune by founding magazines, and became backbencher with independent opinions.

Her father, the second Lord Redesdale (whom she caricatured in her fiction as "Uncle Matthew"), allowed his daughters the run of his large library, but no formal education. She never learnt to spell or to punctuate; she spoke French fluently but with an aggressively English accent, and knew no other foreign language. Her style with its paucity of clauses has been described as a schoolgirl burble. By pertinacity and tireless rewriting she made it, however, finely economical and easy to read.

Her sister Jessica in *Hons and Rebels* recalls *Highland Fling* being written in a school exercise book at Swinbrook, the family home. It marked the debut of their father Lord Redesdale "... there, larger than life-size, felicitously named 'General Murgatroyd', was Farve."

Her earliest novels, *Christmas Pudding, Wigs on the Green, Highland Fling,* and *Pigeon Pie,* no longer included in the canon of her work, were amusing and had no aim other than to amuse. She first won the great public with *The Pursuit of Love,* which sold over one million copies. The best of the novels is *Love in a Cold Climate.* Her leading characters were usually based upon her relations and friends; and she devised ingenious plots and situations to display their idiosyncrasies. Her wit may well ensure the survival of her fiction (like E. F. Benson's "Lucia" books) when the society it portrays has vanished. In her sense of comedy, though not in her style, she can be compared with Evelyn Waugh.*

Her studies of the French past, *Voltaire in Love, Madame de Pompadour* and *The Sun King* (less valuable) were founded on wide and careful reading. They won the applause of scholars as well as of the general reader. Shrewd judgment of charac-

ter was her forte, even if love for Louis XV and the Pompadour blinkered her sometimes to their limitations and defects. Her *Frederick the Great* would have been continuously enjoyable, if she had concentrated upon his personal relationships; but she liked writing about battles, because there was nothing, she felt, that she would have enjoyed more keenly than leading a cavalry charge. A good horsewoman in her youth, she was always conspicuous for courage—one of the few Londoners who positively relished the air-raids. Later she endured the acute pains of a long illness with exemplary stoicism, avoiding sedatives for as long as possible because they dulled her intelligence. "Never," she wrote at the peak of her suffering, "never has the world seemed more beautiful than it does now."

She edited two books about her ancestors based upon their correspondence, *The Ladies of Alderley* and *The Stanleys of Alderley*, which make delightful reading, and reveal also the traits that she and her sisters inherited from ancestors with powerful personalities.

She wrote, also in a light-hearted way, about current class distinctions in which, like all our comic novelists, she took an amused interest, though her friendships were never confined to members of her own class. Some of her remarks about "U" and "non-U" are questionable; she deplored, for instance, the use of the word "mantelpiece", although the letters of her great-grandmother, Lady Airlie, reveal that this was the old Tory term for what the Whigs called a "fireplace". Her talk of such distinctions must not be taken too seriously; it was part of her love for teasing; and she was enchanted when her friends teased her in return. She wrote longer and more frequent letters than most of her contemporaries. When these are published, they may place her among the liveliest epistolaries of her time.

In 1933 she married the handsome and energetic Peter Rodd, second son of the first Lord Rennell; but to her profound regret they had no children, and the marriage was dissolved in 1958, nor did she remarry. Her devotion to her family was intense. The only brother, Tom, was killed on active service. She was the eldest of six sisters, four of whom have survived her, and to whom, despite strong political differences with three of them, she was deeply attached. The eldest of these, Pamela (who married Wing Commander Derek Jackson, F.R.S.), was her companion and interpreter when, already an invalid, she visited Potsdam, Dresden, and Prague to study the background of Frederick the Great. The third daughter, Diana, married first the present Lord Moyne and then Sir Oswald Mosley. The fourth, Unity, became an enthusiastic admirer of Hitler, and died in 1948. The fifth, Jessica, married first Esmond Romilly, and after his death an American academic, who shared her left-wing convictions. She has earned great success as an author. The youngest, Deborah, is the beautiful Duchess of Devonshire.

Nancy Mitford's features, eyes, skin and dark hair made her no less attractive than her blonde sisters; and she always retained her elegant wasp-waisted figure.

After the Spanish civil war she worked in a French camp for refugee republicans; and she always hated dictatorships, whether of the Right or the Left. During the German occupation of France she welcomed to her London house a number of the French who had rallied to General de Gaulle*, and henceforward was one of his most ardent supporters. When the war ended, she decided to settle in France, where she became increasingly attached to everything and everyone French, including the General, although she never met him, except once or twice at parties. Any criticism of him, however mild, was dismissed as either reactionary or communist.

She lived first in a charming flat *entre cour et jardin* in the serene heart of the Faubourg St. Germain, then in a small quiet *Louis Seize* house at Versailles. Her fine French furniture and Italian pictures were 18th century: she disliked almost all modern artifacts, apart from the latest Parisian clothes. Nor did she ever travel much, except for one venture to what she called the "English" Embassy in Moscow, several visits to Greece and a month or more every summer with an Italian friend in Venice. In France she found almost all she needed for her happiness, including the company of her sister, Lady Mosley.

Though nobody could be quicker to seize the comic aspect of everyone and everything, her warmth of heart made her sympathize with the sorrows as well as with the gaieties of her friends. These had included Evelyn Waugh* and Robert Byron. To start naming those who have survived her would be invidious: they are so many, including French, Italians and Austrians. Today they find their world colder and less merry: like Beatrice in *Much Ado*, she was born under a star that danced.

July 2, 1973

Sir Walter Moberly, G.B.E., K.C.B., D.S.O., died on January 31, 1974 at the age of 92.

By his death the country loses a valued educational statesman who made his name in university life as a Vice-Chancellor and as Chairman of the University Grants Committee. Among Anglicans he had a reputation as a liberal churchman.

Walter Hamilton Moberly was born on October 20, 1881, the eldest son of Robert Campbell Moberly, Canon of Christ Church. He inherited the interests of his father, the author of *Atonement and Personality* (1901). He was largely responsible for the well-known volume *Foundations* (1912), himself contributing two important chapters, the second of which, "God and the Absolute" was the target for Father Ronald Knox's raillery in the poem *Absolute and Abitofhell.*

From Winchester Moberly took a Scholarship at New College and after a First in Greats and the Aubrey Moore Studentship in Divinity was elected a Fellow of Merton in 1904. Then, after a brief interval at Aberdeen, he became Fellow and Lecturer in Philosophy at Lincoln College (1906). During the 1914-18 War he served in the Oxford and Bucks Light Infantry, winning the D.S.O. and being twice mentioned in dispatches.

The war over, Moberly, now tutor and Dean of Lincoln, gave a series of lectures on the history of political thought which were memorable for their emphasis on the thinkers of the long period between Aristotle and Hobbes, a period unfamiliar to many teachers of Literae Humaniores. In his energy, zest and resourcefulness he was becoming one of the leading Greats dons, but in 1921 he was made Professor of Philosophy at Birmingham: three years later, owing in no small degree to the promptings of Charles Grant Robertson, he went as Principal of University College, Exeter. Having graduated, so to speak, in two centres of learning where great changes were either being planned or were in progress, Moberly took the important step in 1928, on the death of Sir Henry Miers, of accepting the Vice-Chancellorship of Manchester University.

Here he was to spend eight strenuous and formative years. The university, once a member of the tripartite Victoria University of Leeds, Manchester and Liverpool, was renowned for its enterprise in research and for the distinction of its scholars. Its independence and integrity were respected in the area: but its aims were not always appreciated nor was it as yet fully integrated in the industrial and business community surrounding it. Moberly's vice-chancellorship played an indispensable part, the prelude to Lord Stopford's* regime, in bringing about an atmosphere of confidence and making the people of Manchester look upon it as their own university.

In 1934 he was knighted, a recognition of his leading position in university direction.

After the death that year of Sir Walter Buchanan-Riddell he became the first full-time chairman of the University Grants Committee, and he remained in that office throughout the next fifteen years. The early years of his chairmanship may perhaps be best regarded as a preparation for the exercise of the new and wider responsibilities which awaited the committee after the war. At the end of 1943, the committee was reconstructed and enlarged: two only of its pre-war members remained in office, and it rested almost entirely with the chairman to achieve continuity between past and future practice. The universities (and perhaps the Treasury too) owe much to him for the wisdom and insight which he displayed in the conduct of the business of the committee during that critical period.

His experiences and reflections on university policy lie behind his striking book, *The Crisis in the University* (1949). That year he became Principal of St. Catherine's College, Cumberland Lodge, Windsor, a theological college for women; a heavier responsibility was his chairmanship of the Commission appointed in 1949 by the archbishops, to consider the relations of Church and State.

Moberley married in 1921 Gwendolen Gardner who, while at St. Hugh's College, had been his pupil in Political Philosophy. Her help to him at Manchester and elsewhere was notable. There were four sons of the marriage.

February 2, 1974.

General Mohamad Oufkir—See Oufkir.

Guy Mollet, who died on October 3, 1975 at the age of 69, was Secretary-General of the French Socialist Party, S.F.I.O., from 1946 to 1948. No one played a more influential part in the Fourth Republic than he did.

Mollet was Prime Minister of the longest-lasting government of the Fourth Republic, the Socialist-Radical coalition which was in power from January 1956 until May 1957. He was also a Minister of State in de Gaulle's emergency government which prepared the Fifth Republic after June 1958. His influence as Secretary-General of the Socialist Party was great because of the key position held by the Socialists throughout the post-war period; it was supplemented by his close friendship with the first President of the Republic, Vincent Auriol,* and with the second, René Coty,* who considered Mollet one of the bulwarks of the republic.

Few political leaders, however, were more bitterly criticized at times by members of their own party; his ability to get his policies accepted was therefore a tribute to his sturdy and unyielding character and to an understanding of the mechanism of political power in the Fourth Republic which had no parallel. "I would rather", he said early in his political career, "be Secretary-General of S.F.I.O. than Prime Minister".

Born in 1905, in Northern France, Guy Alcide Mollet was the son of a textile worker and a concierge. Part-time jobs as a youth, including selling sheet music, were necessary to supplement scholarships and grants and to earn him a degree in English. He spent some time in England, a happy period of his life, near Oxford and in Canterbury. He became a Professor of English at the lycée at Arras, the birthplace of Robespierre, with whom Mollet has some similarities. At this time he wrote an English grammar in French phonetics, took a part in local politics, becoming secretary of the teachers' union. Mobilized in 1940, he was taken prisoner and later released on a prisoner exchange. He worked in the Resistance network, Liberation-Nord, was arrested by the Gestapo three times, and emerged in 1944 as *responsable civil et militaire* for the Pas de Calais department.

One of the new men in politics, he was elected Mayor of Arras in 1945 and, in October of that year, Deputy for the Pas de Calais. He became the Secretary-General of the Socialist Party in 1946, representing the Marxist working-class trend in the party, which opposed collaboration with the bourgeois parties and was hostile to the dominant intellectual influences in the party represented by Léon Blum and by Daniel Mayer, whom Mollet defeated in the election for secretary-general. Though his influence in the party was directed against "Bourgeois and Bolshevik" he spent most of his time fighting the Communists whom he described as "not left but East".

As head of the government in January 1956, Mollet's principal task was to secure peace in Algeria where the civil war had been raging since November 1954. He appointed General Catroux,* a well-known liberal in colonial affairs, as Governor-General of Algeria, and this seemed to mean business. He went himself, for the first time, to Algeria, "to install the General" as he said. But, after being pelted with tomatoes when he paid the traditional homage to the dead at the War Memorial in the centre of Algiers, he realized the strong hostility of the French Algerians to Catroux, bowed to *force majeure* and accepted Catroux's resignation.

French public opinion was not yet ready to support radical action in Algeria; and Mollet won the tolerance and respect of the Centre parties and Conservative leaders, such as Antoine Pinay, who, without being ready for bold measures, were prepared to move slowly towards a liberal settlement. Mollet's programme for Algeria was similar to that of General de Gaulle* in the first stage; it was to secure a cease-fire, to begin large-scale reforms in favour of Muslims and, through negotiations later, to accept what Mollet called "the personality of Algeria". In fact, however, the Mollet policy became increasingly one of repression and reliance on military victory over the F.L.N. and on military administration. His Governor-General, Robert Lacoste, was won over increasingly to the diehard positions of the settlers.

It was mainly on account of the support given by Nasser* to the F.L.N. that Mollet allowed himself to be led into the Suez adventure by his military advisers. The failure did not damage his prestige in the eyes of the nation as it did that of Eden in Britain. His Government was defeated on a financial issue and with it went the last chance of a stable government in the Fourth Republic. "The French", he said at the time, "have the most stupid Right in the world". Nevertheless, he was adept at collaborating with its more moderate leaders.

In May 1958 Mollet persuaded half the Socialists in the Assembly to vote for the return of General de Gaulle. When the first government of the Fifth Republic under Debré went into office in 1959, Mollet took the Socialists into opposition, but he continued to support de Gaulle on Algeria. De Gaulle kept up frequent contacts with Mollet until 1962. When de Gaulle decided to appoint Pompidou as Prime Minister in that year, Mollet said it was unwise to appoint a man without experience of the Assembly and that to do so was a sign that de Gaulle was forsaking the role of arbiter in politics, to which he was pledged by the constitution he had made himself. "You have two good chapters in your life" he is reported as saying, "1940-45, and then the decolonization of Algeria. You should take care to see that the third isn't a bad one and that will depend on what appears after you. I admit I am anxious".

When, in 1964, Gaston Defferre, Mayor of Marseilles, announced his candidature for the presidency, the Socialist Party reluctantly endorsed it, and the reluctance was shared by its secretary-general. It was, if not Mollet, at least "Molletism", and in particular the anti-Catholic prejudices of the Socialists, which helped to make impossible the democratic coalition between progressive Catholics, Radicals and Socialists that Defferre was seeking. When Deffere withdrew, the Socialist Party decided to support François Mitterrand in November 1965, and so, having previously rejected Communist demands for a common Socialist-Communist programme against Gaullism, entered into an electoral alliance with the Communists.

Mollet had no strong liking for this either but was in favour of forming the Federation of the Left with the Radicals. He had a general mistrust for non-affiliated politicians of the Left. Towards the end of the events of May-June 1968 when, with a regime which appeared to be falling before the students and the strikers, Mitterrand and Mendès-France were preparing to step forward with an alternative government and President, Mollet, thinking of the Communist party, is reported as saying "Take care. At best we may do a Wilson. At worst we are making possible a *coup de Prague*".

In November 1968 he announced he was not contesting the leadership of the about-to-be reformed Socialist party. In 1969, still a member of the Socialist executive committee, Mollet was not in favour of Gaston Defferre standing against Pompidou in the Presidential election and would have preferred the party to support Alain Poher. Defferre's failure, in spite of Mendès-France's backing, showed Mollet's political insight. None the less this strong, clear-headed man had not succeeded in creating a unified opposition to Gaullism. Did his strict Socialist principles make the task impossible?

After June 1971, when a new Socialist party was formed with François Mitterrand at its head, **Guy Mollet** took a back seat. He was critical of much of the policy of the united Left, the alliance between the Socialists, Communists and left-wing Radicals created in 1972, and was known to favour outright opposition to the institutions of the Vth Republic. He wanted the Socialist party to fight for a return to a more parliamentary system on the lines of the IVth Republic.

In 1930, Mollet married Mlle Odette Fraigneau, by whom he had two daughters. His wife died in November 1973. From the 1940 War, he earned the Croix de Guerre and the Médaille de la Résistance.

October 4, 1975.

Captain Edward Molyneux, M.C., the English-born Paris dressmaker who dressed some of the world's most elegant women between the two world wars, died on March 22, 1974 at his home in Monte Carlo at the age of 82.

He was born in London of Irish parents on September 5, 1891, and was educated at Beaumont College, but on the death of his father when the young Edward was only 16, his formal education came to an end. He had wanted to be a painter, but a living had to be made and with some experience in fashion drawing he was taken into the famous London house of Lucille where, according to Cecil Beaton, he started his career "drawing on a landing at the turn of the great staircase in the Hanover Square establishment".

This career was interrupted by the First World War in which he served with distinction with The Duke of Wellington's Regiment. He was twice mentioned in dispatches and received the Military Cross. He was wounded three times with the ultimate loss of the sight of the left eye due to shifting shrapnel.

After the war and on borrowed capital he opened his own house in Paris at No. 14 rue Royale—almost exactly opposite No. 5 rue Royale which, a little more than two years later, was in a fair way to becoming one of the world's greatest dressmaking houses.

The secret of Molyneux's almost immediate success—a success which was to continue through the next 25 years—was seen in the discreet, well-bred distinction which characterized everything he made; and while it can be said that his genius lay rather in his power to establish trends than to set them, his clothes had a unique style that put him in a class apart as a designer. "Clothes", he was once heard to say, "must avoid the overdressed, the obvious, the showy; also they must wear well".

At the height of his success the world's most elegant women passed through the famous pearl-grey salons of the rue Royale, where there reigned a quiet, efficient, well-bred atmosphere that contrasted strongly with the noise, bustle and apparent confusion that is traditional in the couture salons of Paris. Among famous Molyneux bridal dresses were those of the Princess Royal* and Princess Marina, Duchess of Kent*. Gertrude Lawrence was considered by Molyneux the ideal woman to dress.

In 1925 Molyneux opened a branch in Monte Carlo, followed two years later by one in Cannes. His London house was opened in 1933.

A few days before Paris fell, Molyneux left Bordeaux in a coal boat for England, where he at once took over the management of the London establishment. In spite of the war, business boomed; and so important as a dollar-earner did the London branch become ($2m. worth of fashion was exported by the house to the United States between June 1940 and April 1941) that the Overseas Board of Trade decided to send Molyneux to the United States with the mission of surveying American markets. His mission completed, he returned to the United Kingdom with something like $16,000 raised by lecture tours in aid of Britain's Refugee Committee.

Edward Molyneux was one of the first British civilians to return to France after the Liberation. He set about reorganizing his Paris house which his French staff had kept going under the Occupation; but because of ill-health and the threatened loss of his "good" eye he decided to retire.

He closed his Paris house in 1950, but, becoming bored with social life, reopened it in 1964 with the designing under the direction of John Tullis. He lived in his various homes in New York, Jamaica and at Biot on the Côte d'Azur where he cultivated flowers on a commercial basis. As well as being a painter of distinction himself, he had been a collector of paintings over a period of many years and was the owner of a very fine collection of French Impressionists.

March 25, 1974.

Hugh Molyneux, 7th Earl of Sefton—See Sefton.

Sir Alan Moncrieff, C.B.E., M.D., who died on July 24, 1971 at the age of 69, will be remembered for his work with children and particularly as the first Professor of Child Health in the University of London, a post which he held at the Hospital for Sick Children, Great Ormond Street, and from which he retired in 1964. He was for many years Medical Correspondent of *The Times*.

Alan Aird Moncrieff, the eldest surviving son of the Rev. William Moncrieff, was born in October 1901, and educated at Caterham School. He trained in medicine at the Middlesex Hospital qualifying in 1922, obtaining distinctions in medicine and surgery and the London University Medal. In 1923-24 he studied in Paris while working in the Health Division of the League

of Red Cross Societies. He held resident posts both at the Middlesex Hospital and the Hospital for Sick Children, Great Ormond Street, and was appointed to the consultant staffs of both hospitals in 1934. From this time until the beginning of the War in 1939, his qualities led to the rapid build-up of a large private consulting practice in addition to his hospital work. The war ended this when his help was required by the Emergency Medical Service for the wider care of sick children. His talents were also used in the organization of the arrangements for sick children in other countries when the war ended.

In 1946 the Institute of Child Health was founded at the Hospital for Sick Children and he was appointed there as the first Nuffield Professor of Child Health, retiring at the end of 1964. During this time he built up the national and international reputation for the institute and he was continually in demand at home and overseas in the organization of services for sick children and the education of doctors and others engaged in their care.

In the international field, he was a member of the council of administration of the International Children's Centre in Paris, being also chairman of this body's working party on the Physically Handicapped Child. He founded the Study on Growth and Development at his Institute of Child Health and this has now been integrated into the international study organized by the International Children's Centre.

He was always deeply interested in the social aspect of child health and this led him to become chairman of the Central Midwives Board, chairman of the British Committee of the National Council of Social Service and chairman of the National Survey of Child Health and Development. He was also chairman of the Paediatric Committee of the Royal College of Physicians of London and a member of the Technical Advisory Committee of the National Birthday Trust.

For many years, he was a Justice of the Peace, working in the Juvenile Courts in the County of London. He was always interested in the problems of juvenile delinquency and continued this work after his retirement from the hospital.

He was created C.B.E. in 1952 and elected F.R.C.O.G. in 1958—a well-deserved recognition of his services in the field of obstetrics and midwifery. In 1961 he was the first recipient of the James Spence medal of the British Paediatric Association which is awarded for outstanding contributions to paediatric knowledge. In 1964 he was knighted.

He was an excellent speaker and broadcaster and a superb chairman. He would spend hours in preparation for his committees, which he ran with a smooth efficiency so that it was always a pleasure to serve under him.

He was very much the family man. He was desolated in 1954 by the loss of his

first wife, Honor, the only daughter of Cecil Wedmore, by whom he had his three children, one of whom is a doctor specializing in paediatrics. The following year, he married Mary Katherine, the eldest daughter of Ralph Wedmore and cousin of his first wife. His second marriage was equally happy and helped him to recover from the loss he had suffered.

As skilled in writing as in talking, he contributed to many medical publications and both edited and wrote a number of textbooks on diseases of children and their nursing care.

Modest, shrewd and thoughtful, Alan Moncrieff was a man of simple tastes with an immense capacity for work. He was fearlessly outspoken in support of causes in which he believed, thereby sometimes becoming the centre of controversy. An enthusiastic advocate, indeed a pioneer, of visiting in children's hospitals, he started a heated correspondence in *The Times* in 1966 when, in an article published in *Family Doctor*, he suggested that increased facilities for parents to see their children in hospital might not be a good thing in certain cases.

Alan Moncrieff will be widely mourned, and paediatrics in Britain has lost one who played so large a part in its development.

July 26, 1971.

Julian Mond, 3rd Baron Melchett—See Melchett.

Walter Montagu-Douglas-Scott, 8th Duke of Buccleuch—See Buccleuch.

Toti dal Monte, one of the foremost lyric and coloratura sopranos of her generation, died on January 26, 1975 at Treviso. Her purity of style exhibited to a clear, bell-like tone was a constant delight in a period when heavier, more thrusting voices largely dominated the operatic stage.

She was born near Venice in 1893 (some reference books give 1898), and studied with Barbara Marchisio before making her debut at La Scala as Biancafiore in Zandonai's *Francesca da Rimini* in 1916. After a period in the Italian provinces, she returned to La Scala at Toscanini's behest to sing Gilda, and after that decided to concentrate on the *leggiero* roles. She made her American debut at Chicago in 1924 and in the same year appeared at the Metropolitan.

Her sole Covent Garden season was 1925, when she appeared in two of her best parts, Rosina and Lucia. Of the latter, *The Times* commented that she "enchanted her listeners by her soft, diatonic scales, which came into the *cantabile* melodies like little ripples on the surface of an otherwise calm water". In spite of her success, she was never re-engaged by the somewhat erratic managements of those days at the Royal Opera. Her international career flourished until the early 1930s, but as the years went by she devoted herself more and more to the kind of celebrity recital now almost defunct.

In 1939 she made a famous recording of *Madama Butterfly* with Gigli who, in his memoirs, recalled that earlier in her career she had been a lyric soprano of great charm. That quality combined with pathos makes her Cio-Cio-San still one of the most moving on disc. Her Lucia apparently had a similar ability to touch the heart, in spite of a certain whiteness in her tone at the top of her register. She made a few appearances after the war, but devoted most of her later years to a fruitful teaching career. She was married to the tenor Enzo de Muro Lomanto.

January 28, 1975.

Henri de Montherlant—See de Montherlant.

Marianne Moore, the poet, died in New York on February 5, 1972. She was 84.

Marianne Moore was one of the last of the great American poets in the generation of Pound, William Carlos Williams and Frost*. Born in St. Louis, Missouri, on November 15, 1887, she was brought up in the home of her grandfather, a Presbyterian minister, to whose example she owed her initial strong sense of moral values and her lifelong feeling for the importance of the individual, the family and social responsibility, and her love of freedom. She once paid tribute to her mother's thinking and phrasing as the origin of her own "thought or pith". After formal education at Metzger Institute in Carlisle, Pa., and at Bryn Mawr College (B.A. in 1909), she took courses at the Carlisle Commercial College and then taught stenography.

From 1921 to 1925 she worked as assistant in the New York Public Library, but she had already met Pound and Williams and had been contributing poems to the *Egoist* since 1915. Her work had appeared in *Poetry* and Alfred Kreymborg's *Others*, and in 1921 her first book of poetry, *Poems*, was published without her knowledge by HD, Robert McAlmon and Bryher. In 1924 these 24 already published poems were reprinted with additions, as *Observations*.

Between 1926 and 1929 Marianne Moore served as acting editor of the *Dial*, making it one of the most vigorously necessary little magazines of its time. In 1924 she won the *Dial* award, in 1932 *Poetry's* Levinson prize, in 1935 the Hartsock prize, in 1951 the Bollingen prize, and the Pulitzer prize in 1952. T. S. Eliot* arranged and introduced her *Selected Poems* (1935) and there followed *The Pangolin and Other Verse* (1936), *What Are Years?* (1941), *Nevertheless* (1944), and *Collected Poems* (1951), which Eliot again introduced. The

National Institute of Arts and Letters awarded her its Gold Medal for Poetry in 1953, and in 1955 she published her essays in *Predilections*. Her nine years work of translating appeared finally in the brilliant *Fables of La Fontaine* in 1954, and further volumes of poetry included *Like a Bulwark* (1956), *O To Be A Dragon* (1959), and *The Arctic Ox* (1964).

Throughout this long and prolific career, the Marianne Moore poem developed comparatively little as a form: it would be a composition of varying line and stanza lengths controlled by a syllabic count or some kind of linear quantity judged by her impeccable ear, with additional controls from rhyme schemes. The forward movement is a logic of details whose range draws in practically every field of her interest or her chance acquaintance: plant and animal life, newspapers, painting, films, scholarly works, and anything her wide reading offered.

The references are made into images within a lyrical structure, considerable skill and quiet joy, not to speak of a frequent silent hilarity. Her famous precision occasionally grew finicky but never careless. At its finest it could reveal relationships between facts which were themselves insights. The individualist morality and social responsibility of Marianne Moore's poems did not descend to preaching, and her even rhetoric completely dramatized her formidable irony. The sharp observation of some relevant fact, movement, sight of colour or shape, is enclosed in a firm, whole argument whose dry, athletic and sometimes grotesque pattern grew increasingly sure as her genius matured, only occasionally seeming to be intolerably whimsical. The La Fontaine translations are exactly her line of business: the witty dramatization of moral circumspection and adult sophistication. As Eliot, who criticized her work favourably as early as 1923, observed: "Her poems form part of the small body of durable poetry written in our time", and his judgment has been supported by such distinguished critics as Yvor Winters, R. P. Blackmur, Morton Zabel and Randall Jarrell.

Marianne Moore's poetry was never modernly difficult or overtly right or left in its social consciousness. One was careful what one said in her presence because she listened and then commented from a mind trained to accuracy. Her conversations were like her poems—in her own words: "imaginary gardens with real toads in them". Sometimes she would sound like a poetic Dubuffot, with her elephant as 'black earth preceded by a tendril", and only perhaps D. H. Lawrence came near her imagist impressions of plants and animals. For her early poetry was Imagist and her associates the Imagists of the movement who stressed impersonality and the making of a poem as an object.

But she was a city poet basically, living in New York most of her life, in a Greenwich Village apartment, a Brooklyn flat

(with her naval chaplain brother to be near the old Navy Yard where he was stationed), and finally back again to lower Manhattan. When she was young she wanted to be a painter and to study medicine, but she settled for language and the morality of poetry. She once said: "I feel that unselfish behaviour of individual to individual is the basis for world peace", and in her poetry this became the practice she described to Donald Hall (for the *Paris Review*): "Precision, economy of statement, logic employed to ends that are disinterested, drawing and identifying, liberate—at least have some bearing on—the imagination, it seems to me". But William Carlos Williams called one of her poems "an anthology of transits" and it is their connective flow of definitions which separates them from Imagism, their forms which, in the words of John Fuller, "allow the conversational flow of thought to proceed without prosodic check or ordering . . . and to test and explore the unity of Nature".

Her poetry concerns the dangers to that unity and to the developed life within it, how to maintain a measure of heroic dignity by being, as she and her poems were, alert, discriminating, pliant and surprising, enjoying the particular person or thing or scene for its specialness, and taking it with joy, like the scene with which she opens "The Steeple-Jack": "Dürer would have seen a reason for living/in a town like this, with eight stranded whales/to look at; with the sweet sea air coming into your house/on a fine day". Marianne Moore did not like diamonds or the smell of gardenias because she liked understatement; Randall Jarrell remarked on "her restraint, her lack—her wonderful lack—of arbitrary intensity or violence, of sweep and overwhelmingness and size, of cant, of sociological significance".

This is true, but social criticism is everywhere in her poems—in "The Icosasphere", where she calmly excoriates pseudo-heroes who "paid fines for risks they'd run" and thereby break the first rule of her concept of "integration", and in her World War II poems, "In Distrust of Merits": "They're fighting that I/may yet recover from the disease My/Self". Marianne Moore's work was a lifelong dramatization of that informed economy and precision from which profound emotions are generated.

February 7, 1972.

Agnes Moorehead, the American stage and screen actress of severe countenance, whose career spanned nearly half a century, died on April 30, 1974 at the age of 67. In recent years she had added a new dimension to her work, playing the razor-tongued witch in the television series *Bewitched*.

Miss Moorehead, the daughter of a Presbyterian minister, studied at the American Academy of Dramatic Art. During the 1920s she appeared in many Broadway productions including *All the King's Men* and, with Gertrude Lawrence, *Candlelight*.

Her screen debut was in Orson Welles's *Citizen Kane* in 1941, and it was for her performance in Welles's second film *The Magnificent Ambersons* that she received the first of her five nominations for an Academy Award. The other nominations were for her portrayals in *Mrs. Parkington*, *Johnny Belinda*, *All that Heaven Allows* and *Hush, Hush, Sweet Charlotte*.

Other films to which she brought distinction, usually in supporting roles as embittered women, were *Journey into Fear*, *Jane Eyre*, and *Since You Went Away*. In *The Last Moment* she played a 100-year-old woman; it was a triumph of artistry over make-up.

In the early 1950s she went to Britain to make a provincial tour in Charles Laughton's* production of the "Don Juan in Hell" scene from Bernard Shaw's *Man and Superman*.

May 2, 1974.

Yvon Morandat, an important figure in French wartime resistance, died on November 8, 1972 at the age of 58.

He was the second of three sons of a peasant in the Ain; and before the war began had already made his name as a trade union youth leader in Savoy. After the catastrophe of 1940 he was able to reach England, where he took service under General de Gaulle*, that remote and then little-regarded eminence. Morandat matched him in the austerity of his devotion to France. He was a short, stocky man, with the gift for passing unnoticed in a crowd, nerves of steel, and the countryman's gift of silence.

As early as the night of November 6/7, 1941, he was parachuted into France on a civil mission from the Gaullist Commissariat of the Interior. His work lay primarily among the trade unions of the C.F.T.C. (Confédération Française de Travailleurs Chrétiens), the second largest labour organization of the dying Third Republic. He carried it out quietly, shrewdly and safely, and did a great deal besides towards the organization of resistance.

Before he left England he had been trained at S.O.E.'s secret school in the New Forest in the techniques of undercover existence, and he took his lessons seriously. Inconspicuous but enterprising, careful but not to the point of being ineffectual, he travelled widely, but never without a valid excuse; did nothing to attract hostile attention; and made the force of his personality felt where it mattered. The widespread demonstrations of the first of May 1942, owed much to his initiative. He complemented the work of Jean Moulin, with whom he cooperated freely; between them they unified the diverse movements of protest they had found on arrival.

After a year Morandat was withdrawn

by a clandestine light aircraft of the R.A.F. for a rest. He was back in France by the late spring of 1944 as one of de Gaulle's senior emissaries. During the Paris insurrection, he and a girl friend cycled to the Hotel Matignon, the French Prime Minister's official residence. They told the sentry they had come in the name of General de Gaulle; the guard turned out and presented arms.

After the war, Morandat worked in the French nationalized coal industry, of which he rose to head the Northern and most important sector. He was Secretary for Social Affairs in Pompidou's government of 1968; and his early death is a loss to the European Community, as well as to his widow and children.

November 11, 1972.

Horace Denton Morgan, senior partner in the firm of Sir William Halcrow and Partners, consulting engineers, of London, died on February 25, 1971 after a brief illness while on a skiing holiday in Austria.

Morgan, who was 66, was a world authority on tunnelling and hydraulics and was closely associated with the Channel Tunnel Studies. Among major engineering works, in the design and construction of which he had lately been involved in the United Kingdom, were the Victoria Line and the Royal Sovereign Light Tower.

Educated at St. Paul's School and the City and Guilds College, London University, he commenced his career in 1926 as a contractor's engineer on the Lochaber Water Power Scheme. Subsequently he was sent to Beira to participate there in harbour development works, and then to Mutarara, in Portuguese East Africa, as engineer-in-charge of borings for the Zambezi Bridge.

In 1936 he was appointed chief design engineer in C. S. Meik & Halcrow, having joined that firm seven years earlier; in this capacity he became responsible for the design and construction of hydraulic works, underground railways, and water supply systems. He made a special study of arch, gravity, and earth dams in connexion with the design of the Laggan, Treig, and Spey Dams on the Lochaber Water Power Scheme, the St. Saviour's Dam in Guernsey, the Alto Ceira arch Dam in Portugal and, more recently, the Claerwen Dam in Wales. He was taken into partnership in 1941.

During the 1939-45 War he was engaged on the design of military ports and the Mulberry Harbour for the Army Council, and worked closely with the Ministry of Defence and the Home Office on the design of deep tunnel shelters; he was also concerned, among other works of national importance, with the design and construction of flood gates for London Passenger Transport Board.

Since 1945 he had been concerned with many power-production and tunnelling developments in the United Kingdom and

overseas, and had also taken a particular interest in coast protection works and in the design of light-towers.

He was the author of many papers presented to the Institution of Civil Engineers or read at international conferences, and for these had received numerous awards. He was a past member of the councils of the Institution of Civil Engineers, and the Association of Consulting Engineers, and of the Société des Ingénieurs Civils de France; he was also a Member of the Smeatonian Society of Civil Engineers.

He leaves a widow, a son and a daughter.

March 2, 1971.

Kay Summersby Morgan, who was secretary, driver and occasionally hostess to General Eisenhower* during the Second World War, died on January 20, 1975 in Southampton, Long Island. She was 66.

By her own account she was born in Ireland, the daughter of an Army officer, and in the 1930s worked as a mannequin and a film extra. She drove in the M.T.C. during the London blitz and in 1942 was chosen to be Eisenhower's driver. The association flourished; her duties were extended to those of a secretary and she made up a fourth when Eisenhower played bridge in the evenings with his two aides.

She set her course by the General's stars, went nearly everywhere, met nearly everyone and was always introduced by Eisenhower to the great as his British driver. She always denied recurring reports that the association between Eisenhower and herself had become a romantic one.

Her memoirs, *Eisenhower was my Boss*, published in 1948, were both arch and pretentiously frank. The *Times Literary Supplement*, reviewing the book in 1949, thought it, to date, the least attractive book written about the war.

A previous marriage had ended many years earlier and in 1952 she married Reginald H. Morgan, a Wall Street stockbroker. They were divorced in 1958. In recent years Kay Summersby had worked as a fashion coordinator and set and costume designer for television and stage productions in New York.

January 22, 1975.

Dermot Morrah, Arundel Herald Extraordinary and for many years a member of the editorial staff of *The Times*, died on September 30, 1974, at the age of 78.

He was a journalist and writer of exceptional intellectual range, a polymath, gifted with an exceptional memory, and a passionate curiosity that led him into many fields of knowledge.

Dermot Michael Macgregor Morrah, who was born on April 26, 1896, was the elder son of Herbert Arthur Morrah, a journalist and in his time president of the Oxford Union. He showed his intellectual promise very early, when he went to Winchester as a classical exhibitioner in 1909 and had won various prizes there before ending his Winchester days with a mathematical scholarship at New College in 1914. The war intervened, and he served with the Royal Engineers through the Palestinian campaign, in which he was wounded. When he returned to Oxford in 1919, he did not continue with his mathematical studies, but switched to modern history, and in two years took a first, and in November of 1921 was elected a Fellow of All Souls.

All Souls was henceforward to mean a great deal to him, and he became a master of its traditions, ancient and modern; few can have appreciated more than he did the intellectual companionship that the college offered. He married in the following year Ruth Houselander, and they had two daughters. His wife later became well known as chairman of the Metropolitan Juvenile Courts. Marriage involved leaving the fields of academic scholarship which he found so congenial, and he entered the Civil Service, and spent six years in the Mines Department. The Civil Service was not very suited to his temperament, and in 1928 he joined the editorial staff of the Daily Mail. A few years later he was very glad to receive an invitation from Geoffrey Dawson, also a Fellow of All Souls, to Printing House Square, where he was to remain for 30 years. The invitation was to be partly an editorial writer, but partly to busy himself with the projected History of The Times.

As a leader writer, he soon made his all that important side of the national life that was concerned with constitutional questions and the monarchy. Morrah was by birth a member of one of the old Irish families who trace their descent back to the clans and kings, and he would in fancy dress have looked just like the illustrations of Irish chieftains of 1,000 years ago. He had a deep and passionate loyalty to the Crown, and much of his best writing was concerned with the events in which George V, George VI, and Queen Elizabeth II were the leading figures. He covered the royal tour of South Africa in 1947 for The Times.

Like many highly intellectual men, Morrah was not naturally endowed with great industry, and he was singularly free from vanity or any desire to make a name for himself. So his published works are relatively few, but mention should be made of his play Caesar's Friend, written in conjunction with Campbell Dixon, which had a certain success, and a book which shows his great historical knowledge, and a lively approach to history, If It Had Happened Yesterday, a book in the tradition first established by E. V. Lucas.

His other books dealt with the Royal Family in time of war in 1945, a short life of Princess Elizabeth in 1947, a biography of Prince Charles (To Be a King),

and other writings on the Royal Family. He had a minute knowledge of heraldry and the office of Arundel Herald Extraordinary was revived for him in 1953. His All Souls connexion brought him the friendship of many of the surviving members of Milner's Kindergarten; and he was appointed editor of The Round Table in 1944, and continued to edit that quarterly, maintaining its high standards for the next 20 years.

He was a member of the council of the Commonwealth Press Union for many years and became chairman of the Press Freedom Committee in 1956.

In 1961, on reaching the age of 65, he left the staff of The Times but he continued to be active in journalism, and joined The Daily Telegraph. Among his many interests a high place must be given to his knowledge of and appreciation of wine, which brought him the chairmanship of the International Exhibition Cooperative Wine Society, for whom he did a great deal in his term of office. He had been a chess blue at Oxford, and he was also no mean player of lawn tennis. He was received into the Roman Catholic Church in 1922, and continued all his life to take a keen interest, particularly in the medieval history of England, in its bearing on the Church of his adoption.

Morrah was a singularly agreeable companion, vivacious, courteous with an old-world charm, lively and, though his stores of knowledge continually surprised his friends, he was no monopolizer of the conversation, and he managed to make the corrections of fact which less exact minds sometimes invited in a very undidactic, and almost diffident, way. On his side he was never put out when his own somewhat free attitude towards some historical dates had to be corrected. In his various London homes he somehow managed to bring with him the sense of a Common Room.

October 1, 1974.

The Most Reverend Dr. A. E. Morris, Archbishop of Wales from 1957 to 1967, died on October 19, 1971. He was 77.

Morris was a prelate who won general respect by the lead he gave on controversial questions. Though an Englishman by birth, who never acquired the ability to speak Welsh, he devoted all his ministerial life to the Church in Wales and by his sincerity of purpose disarmed linguistic critics of his election to the archiepiscopal throne.

Alfred Edwin Morris was born at Lye, Stourbridge, on May 8, 1894. His father, Alfred Morris, was in business for 60 years at Stourbridge as a jeweller. The name Morris is not uncommon in Wales, and it may be that in proceeding, after local schooling, to St. David's College, Lampeter, he was obeying a call from the land of his fathers. He passed into Lampeter as senior scholar, but his career was interrupted by the First World War, during which he served in France with the

R.A.M.C.

On returning to Lampeter, Morris won the Bates prize, the Hebrew prize (twice) and the Theological prize, and gained an exhibition at St. John's College, Oxford, where he was elected in later life to an honorary fellowship. He won the Junior Septuagint prize in 1923 and the Junior Greek Testament prize in 1924, and in this latter year he took a first in theology.

Morris returned immediately to Lampeter as Professor of Hebrew and Theology and was there for the next 21 years—until shortly after the outbreak of the Second World War. He was examining chaplain to the Bishop of Bangor from 1925 to 1928 and to the Bishop of Llandaff from 1931 to 1939. In 1931, while continuing to occupy his chair, he was made the Lloyd Williams Fellow, Lampeter provides a high proportion of the Welsh clergy, and by emigration not a few priests for the Church of England, and this important task fully occupied Morris's energies while he was there.

In 1945 the see of Monmouth became vacant by the death of Dr. A. E. Monahan. It was the only see in Wales to which a priest not fluent in Welsh could prudently be elected since disestablishment, and it provided the opportunity to strengthen the episcopal bench with Morris's talents. At Newport he found, despite the competing claims of the industrial and rural halves of his diocese, the opportunity to write the books for which his work at Lampeter had prepared him; and there appeared in quick succession The Church in Wales and Nonconformity (1949), The Problem of Life and Death (1950), and The Catholicity of the Book of Common Prayer (1952). They revealed him as a sound though not perhaps a penetrating scholar, and a churchman with a keen sense of the Church's historical continuity. He also found leisure to pursue his favourite recreations of gardening and painting in oils.

Two incidents in his time as Bishop of Monmouth showed the strength of his central churchmanship. On finding the service of benediction in use at the church of St. Thomas-over-Monnow, he withdrew the permission given by his predecessor and required the incumbent to discontinue it. The incumbent obeyed, but soon made his submission to the see of Rome. Some who applauded the bishop's stand in this matter were less happy in 1952, when, preaching in Westminster Abbey, he said that the oath which the Queen would take at her coronation was a state document and it did not follow that members of the Church of England ought to accept the phrase "the Protestant reformed religion established by law" as a description of their own faith.

When Dr. John Morgan died in 1957, Morris was his obvious successor as Archbishop of Wales on the score of intellectual and administrative ability no less than that of seniority, but his inability to speak the Welsh language was thought by many to be an impediment. The electoral college of

41 members was not deterred, and Morris was duly enthroned at St. Woollos as the fifth Archbishop. Though it might have been tactful for him to have learnt Welsh, as his predecessor, Dr. C. A. H. Green, had done, the Church in Wales never had cause to regret the decision.

His fearlessness was shown in 1960 when, cutting through the cant that had enveloped so much Welsh thinking on the subject, he said he could not understand how anyone who acknowledged the Lordship of Christ could say that it was morally wrong to drink alcoholic beverages; and in relation to the Government's licensing bill he declared that he could not see how drinking could be right in principle on weekdays but wrong in principle on Sundays. Later he developed these views in a booklet, and although he felt obliged to resign his vice-presidency of the Fellowship of the Lord's Day in Wales, and was criticized for a "bee in his bonnet", there was much silent approval of his stand. In a widely-reported address to the Governing Body in 1961 he demolished the argument for unilateral disarmament, and said: "There is at least the possibility that the nuclear bomb may eventually be a schoolmaster leading men to Christ".

In 1925 Morris married Miss E. L. Davis (who died in 1968) and they had four sons and one daughter.

October 20, 1971.

Sir Parker Morris, who was Town Clerk of Westminster from 1929 to 1956, died on January 22, 1972.

Parker Morris will be best remembered by the report on housing standards which bears his name. This report, *Homes for Today and Tomorrow*, was prepared by the Housing Standards sub-committee of the Central Housing Committee, a body set up to keep successive Ministers of Housing and Local Government informed of trends in the planning and construction of local authority housing.

Parker Morris in 1959 became chairman of this sub-committee, which drew on some of the best architectural and other technical brains in the country. Its report of two years later pressed the case for higher standards in house building—of floor space, ceiling height, electrics and, not least, optimum sequence of space. The report recommended that housing authorities should not only submit their housing plans for ministry approval but should indicate how the furniture should be planned.

Morris, who was 70 when the report was published in 1961, may not have had the incisiveness of earlier years but he got the very best out of his committee and so played a major part in the production of a landmark in the planning of houses which is likely to influence both public and private house building for decades to come. In nothing was he more prescient than in forecasting a growing national affluence which made higher house standards not only socially desirable but likely to be economically possible. It is to the credit of successive governments that the recommendations of his report have been safely held.

Morris began his work in local government as Deputy Town Clerk of Salford and then became Town Clerk of Chesterfield. During the First World War he served in France with the Manchester Regiment and was wounded in 1917. Morris's main interest was always housing. Chesterfield under his guidance was the first municipality to employ women house property managers.

From 1929 to 1956 Morris was Honorary Clerk to the Metropolitan Boroughs Standing Joint Committee. He was a member of the Central Valuation Committee for England and Wales from 1937 to 1949; and of the Royal Commission on the Location of Industry from 1937 to 1939.

Morris was chairman of the National Federation of Housing Societies from 1956 to 1961; and of the Greater London Citizen's Advice Bureaux Advisory Committee from 1957 to 1967.

Morris was knighted in 1941 for his organization of civil defence; he became an honorary F.R.I.B.A. in 1970; and was decorated by several governments.

He married in 1918 Dorothy Aylmer Hale, and they had one son and one daughter.

January 24, 1972.

Wayne Morse, who died on July 22, 1974 in Portland, Oregon, at the age of 73, represented the state of Oregon in the Senate of the United States from 1945 to 1969 as a Republican, an Independent and then as a Democrat.

Known early in his career as the "maverick of Capitol Hill", Morse was a supreme individualist; he was wont to explain that he had been taught as a boy that unpaid obligations were a source of embarrassment and that one should be never in debt—which might have been the key to his independent political career. He was among the original Senate advocates of Eisenhower* as the Republican presidential nominee in 1952 but deserted the cause, supported Adlai Stevenson* and became an "independent". It was said that his reason was because of repugnance to Eisenhower's attitude to McCarthyism but there was also a whispered suggestion that he was upset at not being nominated for Vice-President.

By 1954 he had been welcomed into the folds of the Democrats. But this did not stop his attacks on John F. Kennedy* for proposing a government-regulated corporation to run the United States share of a satellite communications system, or calling Johnson's Vietnam policy "unconstitutional".

Wayne Lyman Morse was born at Madison, Wisconsin, on October 20, 1900; an ancestor, John Morse, or Moss, had settled in America as early as 1639 and had helped to establish New Haven, Connecticut. After taking his master's degree he left for Minneapolis, where he had obtained a teaching position (in "argumentation") at the University of Missouri.

He went to the University of Oregon to teach law and by 1931 he had become a full professor and Dean of the School of Law. He came into prominence two years later when he led a rebellion of the teachers of the university against its autocratic President, W. J. Kerr, and ultimately forced him to resign.

In 1936 Morse went to Washington to act as an assistant to the Attorney-General of the United States who needed his help in directing a survey of the criminal law. Shortly afterwards he began to serve as an arbitrator in labour disputes on the West coast, a field in which he made a first class reputation. From 1942-1945 he served as a member of the National War Labour Board. Morse became regarded as one of America's greatest experts in labour-management relations.

A persistent talker from his early youth, Morse led a "filibuster" in the Senate against a Bill dealing with the peaceful use of atomic energy, himself speaking (on three occasions) for 26 hours and 15 minutes. He attacked the Bill as a "give away to big business", and though it was passed, amendments secured for public bodies a share in the electrical energy to be produced by atomic power.

He married Mildred Downie in 1924 and they had three daughters.

July 23, 1974.

Lord Morton of Henryton, M.C., who died on July 18, 1973, was a Lord of Appeal in Ordinary from 1947 to 1959. He was appointed under the Appellate Jurisdiction Act of 1947 which authorized the increase of the number of Lords of Appeal from seven to nine. He had been a Judge of the Chancery Division from 1938 until 1944, when he succeeded Lord Justice Luxmoore as a Lord Justice. During the Second World War he was deputy chairman of the contraband committee set up by the Ministry of Economic Warfare.

Fergus Dunlop Morton was the son of the late George Morton of Lochgreen, Troon, Ayrshire. He was born on October 17, 1887. He was educated at Kelvinside Academy and St. John's College, Cambridge, where he won an open classical exhibition.

In his first year he was awarded a college prize in classics and later a college classical scholarship. In 1909 he was in the first division of Class 2 of the Classical Tripos, and in 1910 he took a first in Part 2 of the Law Tripos and was awarded the McMahon Law Studentship by his college and took his LL.B.

With these academic distinctions to his credit, he was called to the Bar by the Inner Temple in 1912, and by Lincoln's Inn in 1914. He had hardly begun to practice when war broke out, and within a month he had obtained a commission in the Highland Light Infantry. He attained the rank of captain and was awarded the Military Cross.

At the close of the war, Morton decided to settle in Lincoln's Inn and to practise in the Chancery Division. In the chambers of Tomlin, afterwards the famous judge, for whom he devilled, he saw the best class of equity business.

To a sound knowledge of law, Morton added a particularly attractive manner and address, and his success could never have been in doubt. He took silk in 1929, at the age of 42. As a leader his progress was continuous and he was frequently briefed in the House of Lords and before the Judicial Committee of the Privy Council.

His nomination to the Bench in January 1938, by Lord Chancellor Hailsham, at the age of 50, was received by the Bar with great satisfaction. From the Chancery Division to the Court of Appeal and to the Lords was a matter of but nine years, a record it would be hard to beat.

He was an honorary fellow of his old college, St. John's. In 1950 he was appointed chairman of the Committee on the Law of Intestate Succession, which issued a valuable report in July 1951. In the following month he was made chairman of the Royal Commission on Divorce, which reported in 1956.

He married in December 1914 Margaret Greenless, elder daughter of James Bigg. He leaves a daughter.

In the world of golf he was "Fergus" to many, even to the young when he was a distinguished judge. He went out of his way to put newcomers to the Oxford and Cambridge Golfing Society at their ease. He was for some years the society's president, but at all times his advice was sought, for in the affairs of the society none showed more wisdom or common sense than he. He was elected captain of the Royal and Ancient Golf Club in 1958.

Lord Morton was a regular member of touring society teams.

To old and new friends he was a lovable figure, gentle, courteous, steeped in the humour and fellowship of the game he had played since childhood.

July 19, 1973.

R. H. Mottram, the novelist, who wrote one of the most impressive novels of the War of 1914-18, *The Spanish Farm*, died on April 15, 1971. He was 87.

The Spanish Farm was his first novel and much the best book he wrote. Although for 20 years before he had been helped and encouraged in his literary ambitions by John Galsworthy, he discovered himself as a writer, or at least as a novelist, only in the attempt to convey the reality of his experience of the fighting in France.

Ralph Hale Mottram, who came of a family that for three generations had served in Gurney's Bank, Norwich, was born in the bank house, in the heart of that city, on October 30, 1883. He was educated at Norwich and Lausanne. It seemed natural and inevitable that a Mottram should go into the bank, and he duly followed his father and his grandfather there.

When war broke out in 1914, however, Mottram, though of Quaker stock, promptly enlisted in the ranks, was commissioned in the following year, and served in France, in his own words, "partly as a troop commander, partly as a sort of military diplomat".

He returned in 1919 to his post in Gurney's Bank. *The Spanish Farm* appeared in 1924. It got off to a fairly slow start, but secured wide public recognition after it had been awarded the Hawthornden Prize for that year. Its successors, *Sixty-four, Ninety-four* (1925) and *The Crime at Vanderlynden's* (1926), dealt with other phases of the fighting in France and Flanders, and the three parts were reissued together in 1927 as *The Spanish Farm Trilogy*. In the same year Mottram published his first "civilian" novel, *Our Mr. Dormer*, which dealt quietly—and well—with the life of a provincial businessman. Then, having disposed of the film rights of *The Spanish Farm*, he gave up his work as a bank clerk and at the age of forty-four set out on a professional literary career. *The Spanish Farm* was shown on B.B.C. Television in 1968.

He maintained a steady output of work, including a deal of journalism of one sort or another. *The English Miss* (1928), *Europa's Beast* (1930), *Flower Pot End* (1935), *Success to the Mayor* (1937), *The Ghost and the Maiden* (1941), *The World Turns Slowly Round* (1942) were some of his pleasantly readable if unassuming works of fiction. His works of non-fiction include *A History of Financial Speculation* (1929), a study of *John Crome of Norwich* (1931), and a biography of *Buxton the Liberator* (1946).

In 1953 he published, under the title of *If Stones Could Speak*, a social history of his native city of Norwich.

Together with Sir Colin Coote, Mottram wrote a history of the Butterley Company on the borders of Derbyshire and Nottinghamshire during the century and a half in which it had progressed from small-scale coal mining to large-scale steel production —*Through Five Generations* (1950). He continued to produce almost every year a new volume of fiction, but his chief efforts towards the end went into three volumes of autobiography, *The Window Seat* (1954), *Another Window Seat* (1957), and *Vanities and Verities* (1958), all of them gossipy, unaffected and a little artless, and *For Some We Loved* (1956). His last book, *The Twentieth Century: A Personal Record,* appeared in 1969.

April 17, 1971.

Elijah Muhammad, who died in Chicago on February 25, 1975 aged 77, was one of the most bizarre and mystical leaders of the black American community.

A strong opponent of the notion of racial integration, he was the leader for many years of the Black Muslims, or "Nation of Islam", which believes that black Americans should withdraw from the United States and set up their own nation. He, himself, he said, was the "Messenger" of Allah.

Elijah Muhammad was born Elijah (or Robert) Poole on October 7, 1897. His parents were both former slaves, and they lived on a small piece of cotton land near Sandersville, Georgia, which his father worked as a sharecropper. Elijah left school at the age of nine, left home at 16, and eventually found his way to Detroit, where he worked on a car assembly line.

It was in Detroit that he met a pedlar, W. D. Fard, whom he recognized, he said later, as Allah. This was the beginning of a career which took him to the head of the Black Muslims, and to a position of both religious and political power.

It was not easy, however. First he had power struggles with other members of the movement, and during the Second World War he was sentenced to four years' imprisonment for openly sympathizing with the Japanese.

He was released in 1946 and from then on he became the undisputed leader of the Black Muslims. The group grew slowly for a time, but picked up strength in the 1950s. Elijah Muhammad was consistently critical of the attempts of other black leaders to achieve racial integration. Inside the Nation of Islam he insisted on very strict moral rules and on members setting up and running their own businesses.

Under Elijah's direction, the Chicago Muslims acquired a flourishing economic base, apartment houses were bought, as well as grocers' shops, restaurants, farms and all manner of small businesses.

The pattern was repeated in other large cities where the cult spread among black communities, amassing assets estimated in 1974 at more than $60m. (about £24m.). The cult attracted several hundred thousand members. Its newspaper, *Muhammad Speaks*, continues to be widely read.

The two best known converts were Malcolm X and Muhammad Ali, the former Cassius Clay, the boxer, who poured thousands of dollars into the movement. For a time Malcolm X was the Black Muslims' best known speaker, but he broke with the group in 1965, and was subsequently murdered.

The two men convicted of the murder were said to have connexions with the

Black Muslims, but Elijah Muhammad consistently denied any official participation of the group in the murder.

Elijah Muhammad was a compelling speaker, and under him the Black Muslims became a tightly disciplined and secretive group, with considerable economic power. He himself had six sons and two daughters, who are active in the group.

February 26, 1975.

Sir Edward Muir, Sergeant Surgeon to the Queen and President of the Royal College of Surgeons of England, died suddenly on October 14, 1973. He was 67.

His small, unassuming figure was a façade behind which lay one of the most penetrating minds in surgery. To the public and indeed to many doctors outside surgery, he was probably the least well known of recent Presidents of the Royal College of Surgeons of England. The most unostentatious of men over the years, he quietly acquired a position of authority in surgery culminating in his election as president of his college in 1972. This, the highest honour that surgeons can bestow on one of their colleagues, was a fitting tribute to the status he had acquired both as surgeon and as administrator.

The son of Dr. D. D. Muir, he was born on February 18, 1906, and was educated at Eltham College and the Middlesex Hospital Medical School. He graduated M.B., B.S., London in 1928, proceeding to his M.S. (with Gold Medal) in 1932. The previous year he had been elected F.R.C.S. In due course he was elected to the staff of King's College Hospital, where he rapidly achieved a high reputation both as surgeon and teacher. He was in the R.A.M.C. from 1940 to 1945, impressing all with whom he came in contact—both senior and junior —with his technical skill and diagnostic acumen, and it was largely as a result of this wider experience that he became known to surgeons throughout the United Kingdom.

When he returned to civilian practice he rapidly established himself as one of the leading surgeons in London, and from 1964 until his appointment as Sergeant Surgeon to the Queen he was Surgeon to the Household and the Queen.

In his own college he was a member of the Court of Examiners and of the council, and he had served a term as vice-president. In addition he had been dean of the Institute of Basic Medical Science and he had examined in surgery in the University of Cambridge, Oxford and London. He was a consultant surgeon to the Army and had been president of the Medical Society of London.

He married in 1929 Estelle Russell. They had two sons.

October 16, 1973.

Shaikh Mujibur Rahman, President of Bangladesh, was overthrown and killed in the Army takeover of the country on August 15, 1975. He was 55.

Shaikh Mujib was primarily responsible for introducing the prime ministerial system of parliamentary democracy when Bangladesh became newly independent, just as he was primarily responsible for scrapping that system in favour of a one-party presidential regime earlier in 1975.

He dominated Bangladesh politics, and his personal popularity appeared to survive the most difficult economic circumstances and widespread criticism of the inefficiency and corruption of his administration. He met criticism by increasingly concentrating power in his own hands, and resorting to authoritarian methods in an attempt to achieve more effective government.

Press criticism in Bangladesh was muzzled, and it was not clear how much opposition to him had built up within the ruling party and other institutions which contributed to his downfall.

But in spite of all this Shaikh Mujib will be remembered as the man without whom Bangladesh would never have existed.

Born on March 17, 1920 in a village west of Dacca in what was then undivided Bengal, he came from a family of middle-class landowners. After matriculating from the mission school he attended the Islamia College at Calcutta and later studied law at Dacca. By this time the state of Pakistan had come into existence. Shaikh Mujib, with his strong sense of Bengali nationalism, organized student demonstrations against the imposition of Urdu as the official language of the new state. For these activities he was sentenced to six days in jail, but on his release discovered that he had been expelled from the university. Undaunted by official disapproval, he then organized a strike of menial workers at the university and was again arrested and sentenced to two-and-a-half years' imprisonment.

While still in jail, Shaikh Mujib was elected secretary of a new political party, the Awami League, founded by the veteran politician H. S. Suhrawardy* after his withdrawal from the then dominant all-Pakistan party, the Muslim League. Though in 1954 Shaikh Mujib held the portfolio of industry in the provincial government and was in charge of the fight against corruption, his talents lay in party organization. He was mainly responsible for the resolution passed in the East Pakistan assembly in 1956 which outlined demands for provincial autonomy. Convinced that East Pakistan was continually exploited by the western half of the country, he dedicated himself openly to the liberation of East Bengal. When the Pakistan army seized power in 1958, Mujib was one of the first to be jailed under the new regime's Public Safety Ordinance, and was held without trial for a year and a half. In 1962 he refused to give an undertaking that he would not take part in politics for five years, and this time

spent six months in jail.

During his periods of liberty, Shaikh Mujib continued to make inflammatory and "seditious" speeches calling for the end of "colonialist domination" by the Western Wing. The war with India in 1965, during which East Pakistan was left undefended by the predominantly West Pakistani army, appalled many East Pakistanis, increasing their support for Shaikh Mujib. The following year, he propounded a six-point programme which was, in effect, a detailed elaboration of the autonomy resolution of 1954. The response of the Pakistan government was to arrest him once again.

Emerging from a period of detention in January 1968, Shaikh Mujib was seized by military police and held in solitary confinement for five months. He was then brought to trial with thirty-five others before a military court in what became known as the Argatala Conspiracy Case. It was alleged that he and the other defendants had been involved in a secessionist plot with Indian accomplices. The trial increased Mujib's popularity with the masses of East Bengal and turned him into a national hero. The students, whose rioting led to the downfall of President Ayub Khan in 1969, made it one of their principal demands that Shaikh Mujib should be released, and the trial was abandoned. On his return to Dacca he was greeted by a vast crowd, said to number more than a million people.

The extent of Shaikh Mujib's popularity was revealed when, in the elections held for a new constituent assembly in December 1970, his party won 167 of the 169 seats allotted to the Eastern Wing—giving it a majority in the whole country. Faced by the probability of a Prime Minister from the East and a constitution fashioned by an Eastern majority, both the Pakistan army and the leader of the new majority party in the Western Wing, Zulfikar Ali Bhutto, began to intrigue against Mujib. His insistence on the six points, by then famous, protracted negotiations between him and the President and serious civil disturbances took place in East Pakistan. Finally, under pressure from Bhutto and others, President Yahya ordered the army to suppress the Awami League and bring the people of East Pakistan to heel. Shaikh Mujib was arrested and removed to West Pakistan.

The violence with which the army reasserted control over East Pakistan—a violence which resulted in many atrocities and the flight of millions of refugees to India —outraged world opinion and finally led to the Indian invasion of East Bengal and the subsequent defeat of the Pakistani army in December 1971. During these events, Shaikh Mujib was held in a fortress in West Pakistan. On the declaration of the independence of East Pakistan as the new state of Bangladesh, Shaikh Mujib was elected President in his absence. When Bhutto took over the Presidency of West Pakistan from Yahya after the ceasefire with India in December 1971, Shaikh Mujib was released into house arrest, and unsuccessful attempts were made by President Bhutto to persuade him to keep East Bengal within the state of Pakistan. Shaikh Mujib later said that he was to have been hanged after a secret trial and condemnation for treason, but was saved by a kindly jailer while his grave was being dug.

In January 1972 Shaikh Mujib was put on a plane for London and from there returned to a tumultuous welcome in Dacca, the capital of the new state of Bangladesh.

Within a few days of his return, Shaikh Mujib relinquished the Presidency for the office of Prime Minister. He found a country ravaged by war, in economic chaos, and with the threat of starvation hanging over millions. The new state was virtually without an administration and there were large numbers of guerrillas roaming the countryside. To the task of creating a nation, Shaikh Mujib brought vast popularity but little practical experience. His political philosophy was a gentle democratic socialism on the pattern of the British Labour party, for which he professed admiration.

Even in the first few months of his premiership, Shaikh Mujib met acute problems of staving off starvation of his people and at the same time making a Government machine work satisfactorily. The latter task was all the harder for insistence on use of the nationalists' own language—there were even complaints of the lack of typewriters to cope with it, and failure to accept technical and managerial assistance from outside.

However, in March 1973 the ruling Awami League, enjoying the only party organization that could be called effective, won a landslide victory in the nation's first general election.

Apart from a handful of seats, the League triumphed everywhere, winning more seats than at the last provincial assembly election. The Opposition was wiped out as a political force.

One more triumph remained for Shaikh Mujib when, in February 1974, he and Bhutto, once his bitter rival for power, embraced in a scene of reconciliation in Lahore, brought together by President Boumedienne of Algeria.

The happy effects of this spectacular triumph were not lasting. In the following month, Shaikh Mujib flew to Moscow to consult Russian doctors, and entered hospital there suffering from bronchitis.

By October there were calls in Bangladesh for an all-party Government to take the country through a further crisis, and before the year ended a state of emergency had to be proclaimed to meet ever-increasing acts of violence. Allegations of corruption, right through the administrative line, persisted.

All fundamental rights conferred by the constitution, such as free speech and *habeas corpus* were suspended, and from this time

on there could be no other view than that the country was in the total grip of dictatorship.

The Times correspondent in Delhi described the moves as "the extinction of Shaikh Mujib's over-ambitious experiment in democracy".

Law and order had never really been established, and although some 3,000 members of the ruling Awami League had been estimated as losing their lives, in political and personal feuds, the security forces were also blamed for a share of the killing.

Shaikh Mujib leaves a widow and five children.

August 16, 1975.

Dr. A. N. L. Munby, who died on December 26, 1974, was a well-known authority and personality in the bibliographical world.

"Tim" to his innumerable friends, he was universally loved for his warm and generous nature and his incomparable sense of humour. For them, and for King's College, Cambridge, where he was an undergraduate, and since 1948 a Fellow, his loss is irreparable. He served the college with the utmost efficiency and devotion as Librarian from 1947, as Praelector from 1951 to 1960, and as Domus Bursar from 1964 to 1967 during the construction of the Keynes building and the reconstruction of the Hall.

As an historian of the antiquarian book trade and of book collecting in England his knowledge was unrivalled, and he put it generously at the disposal of countless inquirers. In 1974 he became president of the Bibliographical Society, as he was already of the Cambridge Bibliographical Society. In the national dimension he was a trustee of the British Museum from 1969 and a member of the British Library Board from 1974.

Alan Noel Latimer Munby was born on Christmas Day, 1913, the son of A. E. Munby, an architect. His passion for books developed when, as a schoolboy at Clifton, he frequented the bookshops in the old harbour quarter of Bristol. At Cambridge he read Classics and English, and on graduating went to work in Quaritch's bookshop. Three years before war broke out he joined the Queen Victoria's Rifles as a Territorial; and in the crisis of 1940 he was among those from the K.R.R.C. sent over to hold Calais for as long as possible while the main expeditionary force was evacuated from Dunkirk. He was mentioned in dispatches, and subsequently awarded the Territorial Decoration.

Nearly five years of dreary imprisonment followed; but he made the best of them; besides keeping up with his bibliographical knowledge from sales catalogues he made lifelong friends, thought out ingenious ways of baiting their captors and composed admirable ghost stories in the manner of M. R. James, naturally one of his heroes,

which were published in 1949 under the title *The Alabaster Hand* and later reissued in paperback. Of his sardonically amusing poems, *Lyra Catenata*, only 35 copies were printed.

He returned after liberation to learn that his wife, whom as Joan Edelsten he had married in 1939, had just died; but fortunately he soon refound happiness in marriage to Sheila Crowther-Smith, who survives him with their son Giles. He had scarcely moved from Quaritch's to Sotheby's when King's, now needing a full-time Librarian because of the accession of Lord Keynes' library, invited him back to Cambridge. Despite his many college preoccupations (which included dispensing delightful hospitality to a ceaseless succession of members, senior and junior) he was prolific of writing. His major work was on a subject ideally suited to him, the book-collecting activities of that extraordinary eccentric Sir Thomas Phillipps. The five volumes of *Phillipps Studies* (1951-60), which earned him his Litt.D., are so full of biographical as well as bibliographical interest that a successful radio programme was extracted from them, the essence of which he preserved in book form in *Sir Thomas Phillipps, Portrait of an Obsession* (with N. Barker, 1967).

Wide recognition followed. He was Lyall Reader in Bibliography at Oxford (1962-63) and Sandars Reader at Cambridge (1969-70), Arundell Esdaile Lecturer for 1964, and David Murray Lecturer at Glasgow for 1965, besides being a Visiting Fellow of All Souls in 1968. As much as anything, perhaps, he relished his election to the Roxburghe Club. Meanwhile he was producing a series of shorter works, including a most useful guide for research students to the libraries of Cambridge, *The Cult of the Autograph Letter in England, The Libraries of English Men of Letters, Macaulay's Library,* and *Connoisseurs and Medieval Miniatures, 1750-1850.* And he was General Editor of *Sales Catalogues and Libraries of Eminent Persons.* On one occasion he was flown to America to give a half-hour lecture; and he was honorary Fellow of the Pierpont Morgan Library at New York.

December 27, 1974.

Claude Muncaster, R.B.A., R.W.S., R.O.I., P.S.M.A., died on November 30, 1974 at the age of 71.

Landscape and marine painter, author and lecturer, Claude Muncaster was the son of Oliver Hall, R.A., R.W.S., but changed his name to Muncaster to avoid confusion with his father.

He first exhibited at the Royal Academy in 1919, when he was 16, and held his first one-man show in 1926. Subsequent one-man exhibitions were held in London, the provinces, Cape Town and New York. His works have been bought by the Tate

Gallery and the civic galleries of Birmingham, Glasgow, Sheffield, Brighton, Worthing, Eastbourne, Plymouth and Hull, also galleries overseas. His oil painting "Shipyard in Majorca" was bought in 1946 by the Royal Academy (Edward Stott Fund).

During the Second World War, with the rank of Lieut.-Commander, R.N.V.R., Claude Muncaster—as Grahame Hall—was an adviser to the Admiralty on camouflage of ships at sea. He was president of the Royal Water Colour Society Art Club from 1951 to 1960, and president of the St. Ives Society of Artists from 1955 to 1963. He became president of the Society of Marine Artists in 1957.

He was commissioned by the Queen Mother during 1946-8 to execute a series of water colours of Windsor, Sandringham and Balmoral landscapes.

Muncaster was an "outdoor" man, and in his younger days he played cricket, tennis, golf and football, interests which were recalled in an oil painting of "The Village Cricket Match", in the Academy of 1936. He made several deep-sea voyages, and in 1933 he published *Rolling Round the Horn*. This was an account of a four months' voyage in the "Olive-bank", a four-masted Finnish barque carrying grain from Australia, for which Muncaster signed on as deck hand at two pounds a month, feeling that in order to paint the ship's voyage in all its aspects he ought to have lived a seaman's life and seen the whole thing from the inside.

In 1933 Muncaster married the Hon. Primrose Keighley, youngest daughter of the first Baron Riverdale. They had two sons.

December 3, 1974.

Hilda Munnings—See Sokolova.

Sir Leslie Munro, K.C.M.G., K.C.V.O., a former president of the United Nations General Assembly, died suddenly on February 13, 1974 in Hamilton, New Zealand, at the age of 72. A man of outstanding intellectual energy, his career embraced politics, diplomacy, law and journalism.

He was born in Auckland on February 26, 1901, subsequently practising law there and lecturing at Auckland University College in jurisprudence, Roman law, constitutional law and history. In 1942 he became editor of the *New Zealand Herald,* the country's largest circulation daily newspaper.

He served as New Zealand's ambassador to the United States from 1952 to 1958 and was the Permanent Representative for his country at the United Nations during the same period. He served on the Trusteeship Council, the Security Council and was elected in 1957 President of the Twelfth Regular Session of the General Assembly.

In 1958 he was president of the Third Emergency Special Session of the General Assembly dealing with the crisis in Lebanon and Jordan. After relinquishing office as Ambassador to Washington and as Permanent Representative at the United Nations, he was appointed in December 1958 the General Assembly's watchdog in Hungary to report on the implementation of United Nations resolutions there. This was to prove a frustrating assignment.

Subsequently Sir Leslie became secretary-general of the International Commission of Jurists before returning to New Zealand to enter political life. He was first elected to Parliament as a member of the then ruling National Party in 1963. His credentials seemed a natural passport to Cabinet rank but, to the surprise of many and his own expressed disappointment, he was relegated to the back-bench where he remained until his retirement in 1972. He said then he felt he had ruined his chances of promotion to the Cabinet when several years before he had crossed the floor of the House of Representatives to vote against his Government's legislation restricting foreign shareholding in newspapers. He once declared that if there were to be any liberty in party politics somebody had to be willing to express himself freely, succinctly, with candour and with intellectual honesty. To many that was his contribution to New Zealand's political life.

If parliamentary life did not fulfil all his hopes he nevertheless left his mark as a formidable debater with a streak of independence rarely encountered in the highly disciplined party structure of New Zealand politics. Jack Marshall, the former National Party Prime Minister and now Leader of the Opposition, described Sir Leslie as one of New Zealand's most brilliant and colourful figures in modern times, but he added: "He came too late to Parliament to secure advancement which in other circumstances his qualities would have gained for him". Norman Kirk, the Prime Minister, said that Sir Leslie was a man "for whom life represented a continuing and exciting challenge".

Sir Leslie received many academic honours including honorary LL.D. degrees from the universities of Harvard and Michigan as well as honorary membership of the New York Bar Association. In 1960 he published *United Nations: Hope for a Divided World*, and he had almost completed a book on his experiences. He is survived by his wife and two daughters.

February 14, 1974.

Dr. K. M. Munshi who, after playing an important part in the Indian National Congress Movement, was a member of the Assembly which framed the Constitution of the Republic, died in Bombay on February 8, 1971. He was 83.

Munshi was founder president of Bharatiya Vidya Bhavan, India's largest educational and cultural organization.

He was Agent-General for India in Hyderabad during the prolonged negotiations between the Delhi Government and the Nizam, culminating in armed intervention and the ending of the Nizam's rule. Later he was in Nehru's* government as Minister of Food and Agriculture, and in 1952 was appointed Governor of Uttar Pradesh. He was an outstanding author, especially in his mother tongue, Gujarati, though there were also many English works by him.

Kanialal Maneklal Munshi was born on December 30, 1887 and was educated at Baroda College. He was enrolled as an advocate of the Bombay High Court in 1913. He did a considerable amount of journalistic work in support of the Congress movement and was joint editor of *Young India* for two years from 1915. For nine years from 1922 he edited *The Gujarat* and in 1940-46 he edited *Social Welfare*. Both in journalism and in authorship he had the skilful partnership of his wife, Srimati Lilawati, the best known authoress in Gujarati literature of her day. They both became devoted followers of their eminent Gujarati Elder, Mahatma Gandhi.

Munshi had been Secretary of the Bombay Home Rule League in 1919-20 under the aegis of Mrs. Annie Besant. At an early date Munshi followed the example of Mahatma Gandhi in the matter of dress. He joined that great leader in 1930 in a 200 mile trek to the seaside for the purpose of collecting salt in breach of the law regarding the salt duties. He was arrested and sentenced to six months' imprisonment. In the same year he became a member of the Working Committee of the National Congress, and also of the All India Congress Committee. In connexion with the Civil Disobedience Movement of the Mahatma, Munshi in 1932 was imprisoned for two years. After release he was Secretary of the Congress Parliamentary Board.

When Provincial Autonomy was introduced in April 1937, Munshi became the Home Member of the Bombay Government, and he gained the friendship of Lord Scarbrough,* the Governor. Shortly before the outbreak of war in 1939 the Provincial Congress Ministries resigned. In 1940 it fell to Lord Scarbrough to arrange for Munshi's arrest and detention for six months.

Munshi was a member of the Constituent Assembly set up to prepare the way for the transfer of power in August 1947. He had an important part to play in the long drawn out negotiations of the Nehru Ministry with the Hyderabad Government following on a stand-still agreement entered into by the Nizam. Munshi was appointed Agent-General for the Delhi Government. A prolonged blockade of the land-locked state did not solve the crisis. Indian troops moved into the state, and the Nizam's authority was replaced in the first instance by that of a quasi-military regime. Nehru* selected Munshi to be Food and Agriculture Minister in 1950. Two years later he was moved to Lucknow to be Governor of Uttar Pradesh, known in British days as the United Provinces of Agra and Oudh.

In 1925 Munshi was made a Fellow of the then newly-created Baroda University, as well as of the Bombay University. He was a member of the Commission relating to Baroda University in 1926 and for no less than 19 years he was the representative of the Bombay University in the Provincial Legislature. A man of great versatility and alertness of mind Munshi did not allow official duties to deter him from his beloved authorship. From 1951 he was chairman of the Sanskrit Vishva Parishad. His many contributions to Gujarati literature were recognized by his presidentship of the Golden Jubilee Session of Gujarati Sahitya Parishad Nadiad in 1955. His many English works included *Gujarat and its Literature, I Follow the Mahatma,* and the *Bhagwad Gild and Modern Life.* His boundless stores of knowledge and his powers of adaptation to his audience were reflected on a brief visit to Britain in the summer of 1958. He lectured to the Ramakrishna Vedanta Centre on India's spiritual conceptions of values and democracy, and a few days later to the East India Association on the great international importance of the Commonwealth. On both occasions he was skilful in his replies to questioners.

February 9, 1971.

Sir Ernest H. Murrant, K.C.M.G., M.B.E., a former chairman of Furness Withy & Co. Ltd. and, for many years, a leading figure in British shipping, died on March 29, 1974 at the age of 84. He had been in poor health.

It was in 1902 that 13-year-old Ernest Murrant joined the staff of Furness Withy & Co. Ltd., at an annual salary of £20. He was appointed to the company's chartering department, where work started at 8.45 a.m. and generally finished at around 7 p.m. Young Ernest Murrant subsequently was employed in various departments of the company and during the 1914-18 War was responsible for many foreign ships chartered for service with the British Government. For his work on these duties he was appointed an M.B.E.

In the inter-war years he was heavily involved with Furness Withy interests in the Near East which resulted in him making many journeys to Eastern Europe. In 1924 he was elected a director of Furness Withy, just over 20 years after joining the company, and in 1935 he became deputy chairman.

Following the outbreak of war in 1939 Murrant was appointed by the Minister of War Transport as his Special Representative in the Middle East and he left in August 1941 to take up these duties. He was responsible for the supervision of all Allied shipping in an area ranging from Turkey to Aden.

Three years later, in June 1944, the then chairman of Furness Withy, Lord Essendon, died. Murrant was in Palestine at the time but he returned to the United Kingdom and was elected chairman of the company. For his services in the Middle East during the war he was appointed K.C.M.G.

On his return to the United Kingdom Sir Ernest quickly took up the reins of chairmanship of one of the major British shipping companies and also became closely involved in general shipping matters. In 1946-47 he was elected vice-president of the Chamber of Shipping and in the following year became president of the chamber. He also served on several government committees associated with shipping. At the time of his retirement in 1959 he was chairman or director of 15 shipping companies, three insurance companies, a bank and several other allied undertakings.

He also took a close interest in social and welfare work associated with seafarers, being at various times chairman of the committee of management of the Seamen's Hospital Society, treasurer of the Royal Alfred Merchant Seamen's Society, vice-chairman of the committee of management of the Thames Nautical Training College, H.M.S. Worcester, a governor of Christ's Hospital, and a member of the Court of Assistants of the Worshipful Company of Shipwrights. He was Prime Warden in 1957-58.

He leaves one son, Geoffrey Murrant, who is deputy chairman of Furness Withy. Lady Murrant died in 1973.

March 30, 1974.

Sultan of Muscat and Oman from 1932 until his deposition in 1970, **H.H. Saivid Said bin Taimur** died on October 19, 1972 in London at the age of 62.

Born in 1910 and educated in Baghdad and at Mayo College in Ajmer, he succeeded in 1932 to the throne of Muscat, which included sovereignty over the neighbouring provinces of Oman and Dhofar. His state, unlike other Persian Gulf shaikhdoms, had never been under British protection, but was linked to Great Britain by a long-standing treaty of alliance, by virtue of which the Sultan entrusted the British Government with the conduct of his external affairs, employed British subjects in important administrative posts, and later obtained British economic aid and British officers, equipment, and training for his armed forces.

The Sultan held loyally by the treaty, and British support enabled him to avert a series of threats to his sovereignty: in 1953 the British Government rejected on his behalf a claim to part of Oman advanced by Saudi Arabia, and in 1957 British units flown in for the purpose assisted his forces to put down a Saudi and Egyptian-backed separatist movement in Oman, which had hitherto been autonomous, and to establish

his authority over the whole of it. For this action 10 Arab states attempted to arraign Great Britain before the Security Council, on whose agenda "the Oman question" remained for some time.

Meanwhile the grant of a profitable oil concession to an international consortium assured the Sultan of ample resources for the needs of his remote and backward realm. Unhappily, being a deeply religious man of a retiring and somewhat parsimonious disposition, he appeared chiefly concerned to conserve these resources and to keep his people insulated against the spread of modern ideas and developments. He spent most of his time shut up in his distant palace at Salaleh, surrounded by his family and retainers, whom he kept in complete subservience, and he failed to provide adequate funds for administration, for even minimal social services, for the creation of employment, or for modernizing his armed forces.

Discontent with his rule gradually developed and was fanned by radio propaganda, received through the ubiquitous transistor radio, from left-wing Arab states, who disliked his traditionalism and his dependence on Great Britain.

In 1965 a revolt broke out in Dhofar, his westerly province. It could probably have been suppressed with comparative ease by firm military action followed by a redress of administrative shortcomings, but the Sultan still refused to provide the resources needed. In 1966 he narrowly escaped assassination at the hands of a rebel; and in 1968 the revolt took on a new aspect with the arrival of some 30 Dhofaris who had been trained as revolutionaries in Communist China. In the next two years Communist-trained and led groups, stiffened by Chinese instructors and supplied with arms and money by the newly independent state of Southern Yemen, extended their control over most of Dhofar, up to the very gates of Salaleh.

At this critical point the Sultan's only son, Sayid Qabus, who since his return from education abroad had been kept in enforced idleness in Salaleh, intervened decisively to save the state: in July 1970 he engineered a palace coup d'état which was completely successful, and his father, who was wounded in the operation, was deposed and flown to exile in London.

October 23, 1972.

The former Maharaja of Mysore, Jaya Chamarajendra Wadiyar, G.C.B., G.C.S.I., the last ruling member of a dynasty which was established in the state of Mysore at the close of the 14th century, died on September 23, 1974 in his palace at Bangalore.

There were two breaks in this personal rule, the first when Tippu Sultan was winning his short-lived victories at the close of the eighteenth century before being defeated by the future first Duke of Wellington; and the second during the 50 years of British administration of the State ending in 1881 with Lord Ripon's rendition of the State to the Wadiyar family.

The progress made in the second interregnum was well maintained and developed by the two succeeding Maharajas. The second of these rulers, Maharaja Sri Krishmaraja Wadiyar (1884-1940), was an orthodox Hindu who was held in the highest esteem and was served by a succession of able prime ministers, notably Sir Mirza Ismail, a gifted and farsighted administrator. The Maharaja had no issue and his younger brother was the Yuvaraja (or heir apparent). This brother pre-deceased the Maharaja and the succession fell to his nephew, His Highness Maharaja Sri Jaya Chamarajendra Wadiyar Bahadur.

Born on July 18, 1919, he succeeded in 1940 to the rulership and followed the example of his uncle in giving strong support to the cause of the Allies. He maintained a Mysore squadron of the R.A.F. which had as its emblem a two-headed bird, the Gunda Bharunda of Indian mythology, a symbol of might, majesty and victory. In the later stages of the war the Mysore state provided great facilities for the massing and preparation of troops for the expulsion of the Japanese from Burma.

The Maharaja was a man of much culture and was especially interested in music. Purchases were made for him in Britain for the formation of a great library of gramophone records. He travelled extensively in the Far East and Europe. His various studies and researches reproduced in printed form included a treatise on *Ecological Surveys to Precede Large Irrigation Projects*. He also wrote *African Survey*, with particular reference to the relationship between India and the African continent (other than in South Africa) and urged the need for fostering closer economic, cultural and political relations.

After the withdrawal of the British in 1947 the Maharaja signed both an Instrument of Accession to the Indian Union and what was known as the Standstill Agreement. In 1949 with his active cooperation there came full responsible government on the democratic pattern, soon after adopted in the Constitution of the Union with the Maharaja as Rajpramuk or Governor.

Until 1971 the Maharaja was allowed to retain his title and received annually a tax-free privy purse equivalent to £140,000 at the present rate of exchange. In that year Mrs. Gandhi, the Prime Minister, "de-recognized" the Princely Order and abolished their purses.

As plain Mr. Wadiyar, the former Maharaja continued in the remaining years of his life to be revered by many of his old subjects. A noted philosopher and Sanskrit scholar, he is survived by two wives, one son and four daughters.

September 24, 1974.

N

Sir Gerald Nabarro, Conservative M.P. for South Worcestershire since 1966, and for Kidderminster from 1950 to 1964, died on November 18, 1973 at the age of 60.

In the Commons Nabarro cut a dash as a backbencher whose opinions might be ignored—for a time—but whose panache could never be. With Falstaffian aplomb he played a buffoon-like propagandist; the handlebar moustache, resonant voice, and silk topper were part of an idiosyncratic presence easily recognizable to the populace at large. With his fleet of "NAB" registration lettered cars, country house in Worcestershire, and knighthood, he endeared himself still more as a squire-like champion whose bounder characteristics were more often than not overlooked.

Countless constituents, letter writers and listeners to *Any Questions* admired him for his response to their worries. As a self-made man, he kept the common touch and used it with a flair for publicity. Those who jibed at his faddish views forgot that his energetic pursuit of the seemingly ridiculous did help to bring about some real reforms.

The most important was the simplification and rationalization of the purchase tax system after Nabarro spent years campaigning against its anomalies and absurdities with his skilful use of parliamentary questions. He exploited Private Members' Bills to persuade the Government to pass the Clean Air Act in 1955, and to legislate on health warnings on cigarette packets in 1971.

Nabarro's across-the-floor alliance with Wedgwood Benn in his fight to remain a commoner led eventually to a law allowing the renunciation of peerages. His tenacity on the Conservative side in battling for that cause was ironically a link in the process which ultimately led to Sir Alec Douglas-Home becoming Prime Minister.

Nabarro's political viewpoint was very much that of an independent backbencher. He was pro-Powell; supported Rhodesia; advocated withdrawal of grants from unruly students; was anti-pornography; supported tax reductions, particularly for pensioners and motorists.

His contrariwise actions made him an *enfant terrible* in the eyes of the Conservative whips, who could not always be certain which way he would vote. Nor did his rebelliousness end when he was knighted in 1963. In 1971, for instance, in his opposition to hiving off National Coal Board assets, he supported an Opposition amendment.

Nabarro's exhibitionism came close to simple irresponsibility at times. His naivety in his allegations that there had been a pre-Budget leak on increased road taxes in 1969 was exposed by an all-party select committee investigation. Nabarro had campaigned against the sharp increase in road tax on rumours which the committee

found had no basis in fact. Despite that conclusion, Nabarro insisted that he had "won" a victory, since the tax had not been increased. He told the committee that "when one is propagating views and ideas one does not determine too closely what is fact and what is supposition".

Nabarro championed the interest of motorists. He was a member of every major motor club in Europe and former chairman of the House of Commons club.

In 1972 Nabarro was convicted of dangerous driving. After the Court of Appeal had heard six new witnesses, a new trial was ordered. It was held in October 1972 and Nabarro was acquitted by unanimous verdict of an all-male jury.

Gerald David Nunes Nabarro was born in London on June 29, 1913. He attended a primary school until he was 14 and then went to sea for a short time. When he was 15 he joined the Army as a boy soldier. He rose to the rank of staff sergeant instructor.

On leaving the regular Army in 1937 he joined the Territorial Army. He was commissioned the following year, in the Royal Artillery. During the Second World War he was engaged on special duties.

After the war he went into industry. He described himself as having worked in all grades of employment, mainly in engineering and sawmilling, from labourer and machine-hand to factory manager and managing director. He worked as a factory manager in London and on Merseyside and later became managing director of two engineering companies in the Midlands.

He first attempted to enter Parliament in 1945, as Conservative candidate for West Bromwich, but was heavily defeated by the Labour candidate. In 1950 he tried again and was returned as Conservative M.P. for Kidderminster, a seat he won from the Labour Party.

He was a diligent constituency member and continued to represent Kidderminster, with increased majorities at each succeeding election, until 1964. Because of ill-health he then had to give up his political work for a time.

In 1966 he was back again in the Commons as Conservative M.P. for South Worcestershire, with a majority of more than 11,000.

Conspicuous among his freelance activities as a backbencher was his jostling of the Conservative Government in 1955 to legislate for the abatement of air pollution. Nabarro introduced his Clean Air Bill, to implement the recommendations of the Beaver Committee's report. He was backed by other Conservatives and by six Labour M.P.s, including three former ministers.

For financial and other reasons it obviously had to be a government rather than a private member's measure; but it was not until the Government gave a firm promise of legislation that session that Nabarro agreed to withdraw his Bill. As a complementary measure he later introduced, and got passed into law—with government backing—the Thermal Insulation (Industrial Buildings) Act.

He was also the author of the Coroners Act, 1950, and the Oil Burners (Standards) Act 1960.

Nabarro always took a keen interest in the fuel and power industries. He was an unremitting critic of various aspects of nationalization in the field. In 1952 he set out his own views on a national fuel and power policy in a pamphlet entitled *Ten Steps to Power*. He was joint secretary of the Conservative Fuel and Power Committee but resigned in 1955 because he found himself in conflict with the policy of the Minister of Fuel and Power, Geoffrey Lloyd. Nabarro was also chairman of the Council for Independent Education and vice-chairman of the Conservative Atomic Energy Committee.

His other most assiduous campaign from the backbenches was against purchase-tax anomalies. He ferreted out all the more grotesque examples of the unequal incidence of the tax and plagued the Chancellor of the Exchequer with three questions on every day that Treasury questions were answered in the House. He had a pretty sense of humour and on this theme ridicule was his chief weapon.

When Lord Amory was Chancellor of the Exchequer he retorted to one of Nabarro's jibes by a reference to electric moustache curlers as a "domestic heating appliance" chargeable at a steep rate of tax, which did not at all deter his inquisitor. Nabarro's purchase tax questions, followed by skirmishes on successive Finance Bills, were numbered in hundreds and went on for years.

He later applied himself busily to other tax anomalies. Sometimes his ready tongue got him into trouble and some ill-judged observations which he made outside the House about Randolph Churchill* in 1958 led to a long High Court action for slander, which cost Nabarro £1,500 damages and costs.

Nabarro was a governor of Birmingham University. He was a former president of the Road Passenger and Transport Association.

He married in 1943, Joan Maud Violet im Thurn, daughter of Colonel B. B. von B. im Thurn, and they had two sons and two daughters.

November 19, 1973.

Ogden Nash, the humorist and writer, died on May 19, 1971 at the age of 68.

Ogden Nash introduced the collected edition of his verse published in 1961 with an epigraph from John Aubrey: "How these curiosities would be quite forgot, did not such idle fellows as I putt them downe". Nash might modestly choose to describe himself as an idle fellow, but his many admirers will grieve, on learning of his death, that they can no longer count on his industrious idleness for yet another volume of delightful and topical verse.

Ogden Nash was born on August 19, 1902 at Rye, New York. He spent a year at Harvard (1920-21), and, after a brief period as a salesman, entered the advertising department of Doubleday, Page, the publishers, in 1925. He joined the editorial staff of *The New Yorker* in 1931. He later became associated with the house of Rinehart and Farrar, but shortly resigned to devote himself to writing. He married Frances Rider Leonard in 1931. There were two daughters, one of whom, Linell, illustrated some of his books for children.

His resignation from publishing shows how successful he was as a popular writer: as he himself said, with his usual modesty, his verse, whatever its weaknesses, enabled him "to support a family." He contributed to many of the better-known American magazines and, beginning with *Hard Lines* (1931), regularly gathered up his scattered verses into books which were, in their turn, brought together in several collected editions.

He collaborated with S. J. Perelman in the musical *One touch of Venus* (1947).

Many of his admirers called his mangled verse an emancipation proclamation for all would-be poets who had the illusion that poetry had to follow some strict law of rhyme and metre. Actually, the man who could blithely rhyme "petunia" with "Pennsylvania," and deprecate a hated herb with the lines:

> parsley
> is gharsley

was a careful craftsman.

Much of his reputation was based on his long, straggling lines of wildly irregular length, often capped with extravagantly mis-spelt words to create weird rhymes, but they were lines that, on close examination, revealed a carefully thought-out metrical scheme and a kind of relentless logic.

In addition to being a writer of droll and witty verse, however, Nash was an ingenious critic of frailty and absurdity, whose targets ranged from animals to the income tax.

As one critic put it, Ogden Nash was "a philosopher, albeit a laughing one," who wrote of the "vicissitudes and eccentricitudes" of domestic life as they affected an apparently gentle, somewhat bewildered man.

Nash said he never crossed out words, but simply erased a wrong word and searched for the right one. "Sometimes a poem is suggested by some human foible," he said, "and sometimes by the play on words. I'm very fond of the English language. I tease it, and you tease only the things you love."

He could be extraordinarily teasing when he rhymed "lullaby" with a "gullaby" in a poem about birds, and "lioness" with "your hioness." One of his most hilarious verses concerned a Mr. Schwellenbach, an extremely careful driver, who was hit by another car and "knocked from here to Hellenbach."

Nash was America's best-known writer of limericks. In 1931 he wrote:

> Candy
> Is dandy,
> But liquor
> Is quicker;

In the nineteen-sixties he added the line:

> Pot is not.

The idiomatic and word-fracturing quality of his work has not daunted the translators. Nash has been translated into some dozen languages, including Dutch and Yugoslav.

His posed and sophisticated attitude, his keen observations of contemporary follies, foibles and assumptions, his tolerant wit, his unpretentious manner, and his occasional touch of genuinely poetic sentiment, made him one of the most effective, as he was certainly the most popular, of the writers of his kind and day. The social historian of the future may thank him for his "curiosities," and the general reader will expect his best pieces to keep their place in the anthologies.

May 20, 1971.

Sir John Neale, the distinguished Elizabethan scholar, died on September 2, 1975 at the age of 84.

J. E. Neale was a great scholar whose life was dedicated to two causes: Elizabethan research and University College London. He served them both with utter devotion and great distinction.

John Ernest Neale was born in Liverpool on December 7, 1890, and educated in the schools and university of that city. Having obtained a second class degree in history, he started research on the nineteenth century; but he shortly after moved into the sixteenth, when he began work under the late Professor A. F. Pollard at University College London, a little before the First World War. This marked the opening of Neale's association with the London school of history, an association which was to endure throughout his life.

Soon after the war he was appointed, at the age of 29, to his first post as assistant in history at University College; and for the next six years he served a rigorous apprenticeship under the stern governance of Pollard, then ruling the history department with a rod of iron. Soon Neale was writing distinguished articles, marked equally by meticulous scholarship and an attractive prose, at a time when most contributions to learned periodicals were notable for their weight of learning rather than their engaging style. Neale's high promise was quickly recognized by his master with whose strong recommendation he was appointed in 1925 to the Chair of Modern History at the University of Manchester. His stay was brief: two years afterwards he was invited back to University College to the Astor Chair in English History, which he held until his retirement 29 years later. With his return to London there followed a steady stream of articles and reviews until, in 1934, appeared his eagerly awaited biography of Queen Elizabeth I.

It came when the scene was still dominated, either by the views of Froude that Elizabeth was a wayward shrew who ruined every policy on which she laid her hands, or by those of Lytton Strachey, who had formed an equally jaundiced opinion of the queen but injected into it a little of the Freudian psychology, then making its first incursions into historical writing. In such an atmosphere Neale's book came like a breath of fresh air. Exploring every source that he could find, he yet produced an extremely human portrait of a woman who, with skill and patience, sometimes stood alone for her ideals when others urged religious persecution or aggressive diplomacy. The book showed Neale's style at its best and it won immediate acclaim in the historical literary world.

In a section of the academic world things were different. For Neale had taken a step, unprecedented in modern historiography, of publishing the work entirely without footnotes or other critical apparatus. Believing that a work of scholarship could, and should, reach the general reader, Neale agreed to jettison all the formal historical evidence upon which his biography rested. To some of his colleagues this seemed an indefensible decision. "Neale has sold the pass", said one of them to the late Eileen Power; to which she replied; "He has also sold 20,000 copies." The story got back to Neale, and he loved to repeat it, roaring with laughter. He may have been acting on the advice of his close friend and publisher, Jonathan Cape. Yet he would himself say that if he had been writing in the 1950s or 1960s the full documentary references would have been given.

There was also another paradox in his remarkable book. Impervious as he was in the early days to the modern views about the equality of women, Neale argued throughout the biography, and in his later books, that Elizabeth I, a woman ruler, outstripped every one of her ministers in all the arts of a statesman. To some historians, indeed, it seemed that he exaggerated the role of the queen, and had not stopped short this side of idolatry. He himself used to comment: "They say that I am in love with Elizabeth I. How absurd!"

Yet there was some truth in the criticism. In seeking to redress the balance, Neale tipped the scale too heavily towards the Queen. Statesman he showed her to be, but there was little to indicate her waywardness, her inordinate vanity, her failure as a ruler in the last years of her reign. The same imbalance was to some extent present in the major works which followed.

Neale had now won himself a literary reputation far beyond university circles. But he did nothing to exploit it. He never became a "personality" in the current sense of the word, and resisted a number of tempting offers to enlarge his fame and his income in the press and elsewhere. Indeed, he devoted long hours to his work on the Elizabethan Parliament. The first volume of his trilogy, *The Elizabethan House of Commons*, appeared in 1949, to be followed by *Elizabeth I and Her Parliaments*, issued in two parts in 1953 and 1957. He had, earlier, written a short book on *The Age of Catherine de Medici* and a collected edition of his papers was published in 1958. Neale's interests were almost wholly restricted to the Elizabethan age; he never showed any serious desire to research into other periods. But, in his chosen field, he was the acknowledged master.

With the appearance of *The Elizabethan House of Commons*, full academic recognition, which had tarried for so long, came speedily. He was elected a Fellow of the British Academy in 1949, and awarded honorary doctorates by a number of universities. In 1954 the leading biographer of the first Queen Elizabeth was, appropriately enough, knighted by the second. In 1958, the fourth centenary year of the accession of Elizabeth I, he at last agreed to deliver a series of lectures in the United States, where his fame had long preceded him. His triumphal tour had in it something of a royal progress worthy of the great queen herself.

After his retirement, Neale devoted himself to his work on the History of Parliament, sponsored by both Houses, and to his other historical studies. He also continued, as he had done for three decades, to preside over a postgraduate seminar at the Institute of Historical Research, to which he attracted scholars and students from both sides of the Atlantic. He had, meanwhile, collected a fine library of books on Elizabethan history; and to be shown round it was a memorable delight. To his wife, Elfreda Skelton, whom he married in 1932 and by whom he had a daughter, Neale always recognized that he owed a considerable debt for her scholarly criticism of all he wrote.

In appearance, Neale was below medium height, rotund and Pickwickian, with a sunny countenance and a happy smile, which made him known as "Jimmy" Neale from almost the beginning of his career. Behind the warm genial personality was a tough, conscientious scholar, who had no patience or use for the second rate. As administrator and scholar, he would call upon his immense vitality to the last ounce; and he would expect his pupils and colleagues to do the same. In his middle age Neale had aroused some hostility by his Lancastrian bluntness and moments of supreme tactlessness. But beneath it all was a profound humility in the presence of historical scholarship; and those who knew Neale well spoke of the mellow generosity of a great scholar. The corridors of University College, which he loved deeply and proudly, will long echo with the warm speech and the gusty laughter of this outstanding Elizabethan historian.

Queen Elizabeth is the greatest biography of the queen that this century has produced; and his parliamentary studies are masterpieces of Tudor scholarship.

September 4, 1975.

Lady Neame—See Desmond.

Sir Victor Negus, M.S., F.R.C.S., the distinguished laryngologist, died on July 16, 1974 at the age of 87.

Victor Ewings Negus was born in February 1887, the son of William Negus, who was Lieutenant for the County of Surrey. He was educated at King's College School, which was later removed from the Strand to Wimbledon. From the school he passed to King's College in the Strand where he studied the premedical and preclinical subjects. After passing the second medical examination he began his clinical studies at the old King's College Hospital in the Strand and worked under Watson Cheyne with thereby an indirect connexion with Lister.

He qualified in 1912 and at an early stage took an interest in laryngology. He acted as clinical assistant to Charles Hope and Lionel Colledge at the Hospital for Diseases of the Throat in Golden Square before the outbreak of the First World War. He immediately joined the R.A.M.C. in 1914 and went out to France with the original expeditionary force. He spent a very active eighteen months in this theatre of war and was blown up during the trench warfare of that period. This led to a tinnitus that persisted throughout his life, which provided him with some scientific interest but which he did not allow to inconvenience him in any way.

Back in London in 1919 he set about preparing himself for his future career as a laryngologist with great energy. Acting on the advice of Sir St. Clair Thomson, he obtained the F.R.C.S. diploma, acted as house surgeon at the Hospital for Diseases of the Throat, studied in Bordeaux at the Clinic of Moure and Portmann, and also at that of Chevalier Jackson in Philadelphia, and then joined St. Clair Thomson at King's College Hospital first as Clinical Assistant, then as Assistant Surgeon. At that time the Departments of Otology and Laryngology were separate, and though on the retirement of Gilbert Jenkins and St. Clair Thomson they were merged, Negus was always a laryngologist and rhinologist and never interested himself unduly with otological problems. At an early stage, however, he became immersed in scientific problems and carried out in the laboratories of the Royal College of Surgeons a series of dissections of the larynx in a very large number of animals of every kind and traced the stages of evolution and development of that organ. This work was published in a book—*The Mechanism of the Larynx*—the first part of which had been submitted to the University of London as a thesis for the degree of Master of Surgery. To the award of the degree was added a Gold Medal.

At the same time laryngology was being studied and practised at King's College Hospital, new ideas were born, new techniques developed and new instruments devised and perfected—a whole new range of endoscopic tubes and forceps introduced with the assistance of Mr. Schranz of the Genito-Urinary Manufacturing Company. These, with their improved double lighting and many practical improvements in construction, made them the most popular of available types. He devised the so-called King's College table which delivered electric current for all types of lamps, and incorporated a suction pump and a diathermy generator. He also devised and had constructed the speaking valve for use in a tracheotomy tube, which enabled tracheotomized patients to talk.

He was awarded a Hunterian Professorship, the Lister Medal of the Royal College of Surgeons of England, and the Semon Lectureship of the University of London, and was widely honoured by other awards. He was knighted in 1956.

He retired from King's College Hospital in 1952 and spent the next four years as Curator of the Ferens Institute. He published *The Biology of Respiration* in 1965.

Negus was a tireless worker, strove to keep laryngology a strict surgical science, and did much to enhance the status of that speciality. He may be described as having, in this respect, made a worthy fourth to Morell MacKenzie, Felix Semon and St. Clair Thomson, who in Britain organized the speciality of laryngology.

Negus married in 1929 Gladys Rennie Negus who, known always as Eve, gained the affection of her husband's innumerable colleagues and friends at home and abroad. They had two sons, one a surgeon.

July 17, 1974.

A. S. Neill, the educationist, died on September 23, 1973 at Aldeburgh at the age of 89.

If children anywhere are happier nowadays in school than their elders sometimes were it is due in no small measure to this craggy, lovable Scot. For much of his career he himself supposed that the best contribution he could make to education was to champion Freudian psychology. That opinion he later modified. In reality his chief value always lay in the ceaseless challenge he presented to accepted notions about children and their schooling.

He believed passionately that they should be left free to develop in their own way. To that end he seized every chance of making his fellow adults rethink their ideas. His iconoclasm was displayed in numerous books and in a lifetime of lecturing up and down the world. It was displayed, too, at Summerhill, his own famous, or, as he gleefully acknowledged, notorious school.

Alexander Sutherland Neill was born on October 17, 1883, in Angus. He was educated at his father's village school. Leaving school at 14 to be a clerk he subsequently qualified as a teacher and then went to Edinburgh University where he took second-class honours in English.

The outbreak of the First World War found him in publishing. A leg injury at first kept him out of the Army; and before he was called up he returned to teaching, became headmaster of Gretna Green School, and wrote in 1915 *The Dominie's Log,* the first of his controversial books. ("I was beginning to get into trouble with parents; you know: 'I send my Tommie to school to learn, not to dig in the garden'.") At that time he was much influenced by Homer Lane, the American school reformer.

After army service Neill taught for a time at King Alfred School in Hampstead. But in 1921 he went to Dresden to run the international department of a school there.

Soon he had moved to Austria to start his own school. That school he moved to England in 1924, establishing it first at Lyme Regis and subsequently at Leiston in Suffolk. That was Summerhill School. There he allowed his pupils to govern themselves. He encouraged an easy familiarity with the staff. Attendance at lessons was optional.

Neill's unorthodox methods and the many anecdotes he told about them led the public to regard him as a crank. In fact he was astonishingly successful with difficult children, often when other schools had despaired of them. As he was not a man to hide that, the teaching profession was forced against its better judgment to take him seriously, and even to adopt many of his less extravagant ideas.

In the end, therefore, he was no longer quite the rebel he liked to be, though the publication of *Summerhill* in 1962 brought him fresh attention on both sides of the Atlantic.

An influx of American students kept the school on its feet financially, although they tended to arrive older than English children and did not always fit in. Children also arrived from Germany.

In 1966 Neill was made an honorary M.Ed. of Newcastle University. In 1968 he received Exeter University's honorary degree of Doctor of Laws as "perhaps the most distinguished figure in progressive education".

Summerhill became so famous that the pupils eventually banned sightseers.

Neill was twice married and had a daughter. He soldiered on at Summerhill to the end, having no money to retire.

September 25, 1973.

King Mahendra of Nepal died on January 31, 1972 after suffering a heart attack on the previous day. The King, who was 51, died at his winter home at Bharatpur.

When he ascended the throne of Nepal in 1955 the Nepali monarchy had already escaped from its long servitude to the Ranas, the line of hereditary prime ministers who had been for more than a century the real rulers of the Himalayan kingdom, but it remained for Mahendra to restore the throne to full power. He did that in 1960 by aborting the process toward democratic forms and constitutional monarchy that was then nearly a decade old and assuming autocratic powers himself.

Mahendra had no difficulty in staging his royal coup, dissolving the national assembly, imprisoning the political leaders and abrogating the constitution. He not only had the Army at his disposal, but Nepal was still a primitive polity outside the narrow Katmandu valley and the throne had a deeper claim to legitimacy than had the stripling democratic forms which he brushed aside. The middle class, with some backing in the streets of Katmandu, was too small and shallow an overlay on the traditional ways of Nepal to present any serious threat to the King.

Mahendra explained his action by citing the corruption and inefficiency of the government he had dismissed. His complaints were well founded—although the experience of his own government showed that he failed to eradicate those failings—but at least as much as disapproval of a form of governance he judged unsuitable for the kingdom the recognition that his own powers were shrinking seems to have driven him to action.

Sandwiched between India and China, Nepal's foreign policy is more or less prescribed by its geography, but Mahendra gave the almost mandatory non-alignment sound expression. Finding his country overcommitted to India, which had supported the Nepali Congress and his father against the Ranas, Mahendra opened cordial relations with China—the fact that the Indian Government strongly disapproved of his *coup* and for two years or so connived at attempts by Nepali emigrés in India to overthrow him, also encouraged him to lean back from India. After delimiting their boundary, China and Nepal entered into treaties of trade and friendship, and China provided economic assistance in road-building and other development projects. The strategic Lhasa-Katmandu road alarmed westerners and India, but the Nepalis found no reason to complain about the attitude or action of the northern neighbours. Mahendra succeeded in retaining the friendly support of the United States as well as China, and after 1962 India too did all she could to support him. His foreign policy must be counted a success.

In November 1967 he addressed the United Nations General Assembly, calling for a speedy end to the war in Vietnam and the admission of China to the United

Nations.

In April 1970 he named a new cabinet under his own chairmanship, comprising five ministers and five assistant ministers, but 12 months later he gave up the post of Premier.

Mahendra Bir Bikram Shah Deva was born in 1920 and his education was such as the Ranas prescribed for the royal heirs —that is, scanty, shallow and strait, lest the Ranas be troubled by the presence on the throne of anyone with ideas above his station. But if they succeeded in limiting his knowledge, they plainly failed to crimp his independence of will, which he demonstrated at the age of 20 in insisting on a monogamous marriage. By custom, royal princes of Nepal had taken two wives in Hindu marriage, the better to assure the line, but Prince Mahendra refused. His first wife died in 1950, after she had borne him five children, and two years later he married her younger sister, Queen Ratna.

Mahendra travelled widely, making up for the years of his youth when the Ranas kept him hobbled, not only abroad, with frequent state visits and private tours (he and the Queen were in London in the autumn of 1971) but also within Nepal, making the monarchy visible in remote parts of the kingdom where it had been only a vague concept.

February 1, 1972.

Pablo Neruda, the Chilean poet, died on September 23, 1973 in a Santiago hospital. He was 69. In 1971 he won the Nobel Prize for Literature.

A member of the central committee of the Chilean Communist Party, Neruda was the party's nominee for the presidency in 1970. He withdrew, however, in favour of an old friend Dr. Allende. Allende won and, immediately after the election, Neruda was appointed ambassador to France, a post he held until his return to Chile in 1972, when he became ill.

The most prolific and conspicuous of Latin American poets, he was born Ricardo Neftali Elizier Reyes Bascalto on July 12, 1904, in Parral, a small agricultural community in the grape-growing region of southern Chile.

His father, a railroad worker, was killed in a train accident before Neruda reached adulthood. His mother, a schoolteacher, died of tuberculosis when he was about three.

When Neruda was about a year old, the family moved to Temuci, in a rainy and densely forested area, and his memories of the unspoilt natural beauty of this Chile of his childhood later dominated his poetry.

When he was 15 he sent his first poems to a magazine and signed himaelf "Pablo Neruda", taking the surname of a short story writer, Jan Neruda, whom he admired, as his pseudonym.

Neruda was sent to Santiago when he was 16 and entered the leading Chilean teachers' training college where he specialized in French. An indifferent student, he spent much of his time in the Bohemian atmosphere of cafés, discussing literary topics.

At the age of 20 Neruda won recognition with his *Veinte poemas de amor y una cancion desesperada* (Twenty poems of Love and one song of Despair).

In 1927, in keeping with Latin American tradition, the Chilean Government gave official recognition to Neruda's poetic achievements by appointing him to the Consular Service.

In 1934 he was sent to Spain, where he served as consul first in Barcelona and then Madrid. During this time he collaborated with Lorca and other Spanish poets in editing a poetry magazine.

The outbreak of the Spanish Civil War in 1936 marked a turning point in Neruda's life. Without waiting for orders from Santiago, Neruda used his office as consul to declare Chile on the side of the Spanish Republic.

At the same time he wrote his *España en el corazón* (Spain in the heart), an impassioned verse tribute to the republican loyalists.

He was recalled to Chile for overstepping his authority but later the government sent him to Paris to organize the safe passage of republican refugees to Chile.

Elected to the Senate in 1947, Neruda published letters in Mexican and Venezuelan newspapers claiming that the president of Chile, Gabriel Videla, had sold out the national interest to the United States. He was charged with treason and, stripped of his senatorial immunity, went into hiding and eventually fled to Mexico. He did not return home until 1953.

In 1965 Oxford University made him an honorary D.Litt. He was awarded an International Peace Prize in 1950 and also Lenin and Stalin Peace Prizes.

It is hard to generalize about Neruda's work, for at first sight it would appear that few poets had undergone such radical developments and shifts of ground. He was a Romantic lover in his vastly popular *Viente poemas* (1924); an often hermetic and tormented Surrealist in *Residencia en la tierra* (Residence on Earth, two volumes 1933-35); an aggressively declamatory denouncer of fascists and oligarchs in *España en el corazón*, and *Canto General* (1950); and ultimately, from the publication of *Odas elementales* (1954) until his death, the deployer of a mature, autumnal benignity and compassion, of a sense that he had found himself and could now observe the world with amused and relaxed wonder.

Like Picasso, Neruda would appear therefore to have been many men, but like Picasso's his prolific career had a fundamental continuity.

Throughout his poetry, whether as a tormented surrealist or as a militant communist, Neruda indeed searched for an Edenic telluric past, for a lost origin in a maternal nature from whose "green uterus" man had been tragically torn.

Like Aragon and like many poets of his generation, Neruda was a Stalinist rather later than is normally considered respectable. But his relentless political orthodoxy and his blind adherence to the latest vicissitudes of the Moscow line are not hard to explain. Neruda was never an intellectual. He was fundamentally an intuitive man who instinctively put his faith in the Communist Party. He genuinely believed that his party, not he, was competent to assess the practical necessities of society. His own final period of maturity no doubt corresponds to the era of respectability which the Chilean Communist Party later found itself in. Whereas in the Cold War period it was correct for a poet to denounce American imperialism and its local Latin American "lackeys", in the past two decades it became increasingly natural for Neruda casually to contemplate the architecture of an onion, or to write unforgettably on the terrible problem of getting up in the morning.

When Allende was elected to the Chilean Presidency in 1970, Neruda was appointed Ambassador in Paris. *The Times* was quick to quote a poem from the *Canto General* in which Neruda had asserted that all Chilean ambassadors were idiots by definition, indeed that all Chilean idiots were made ambassadors. Neruda was no doubt able to laugh heartily at the joke. No poet can ever reach greatness until he learns to laugh at himself. There was a pious, sanctimonious side to the more political Neruda which he mercifully jettisoned. He died a complete man, incurably still a Romantic, yet able to subject his Romanticism to ironical contemplation.

He was three times married.

September 25, 1973.

Jimmy Nervo, remembered as a member of the Crazy Gang, died on December, 5, 1975 in a London hospital. He was 78 and had been ill for some time.

Nervo (real name James Holloway) was associated with the Gang from the 1930s with his friend Teddy Knox (real name Albert Edward Cromwell-Knox), who died just a year ago, also aged 78.

Nervo's father was one of the Four Holloways, a circus acrobatic turn. His great-grandfather had been a clown, so he was born to a life of buffoonery and balancing. One of his earliest memories was being given a reward of sixpence for his first somersault on a wire.

The comedy team of Nervo and Knox was born in 1918 when the two men met in a London street. The partnership thrived and in 1937 they took out an insurance policy for £20,000 against having a tiff. Nervo suffered a series of fractures during years of comic falling that delighted millions.

Chesney Allen, the partner of Bud Flanagan, stated in an interview in 1972 that it was Nervo and Knox who originated the Crazy Gang with their "Young Bloods of Variety", which introduced features such as the interruptions emanating from boxes and artists roaming round the auditorium. After a successful week at the London Palladium, George Black senior, the impresario, plumped for "a crazy month" and, according to Chesney Allen, it was then that Bud Flanagan and himself and Naughton and Gold joined the shows.

It was not until 1962 that the Crazy Gang gave their farewell performance.

December 6, 1975.

Lieutenant-Colonel Augustus Charles Newman, V.C., O.B.E., formerly of the Essex Regiment, who died on April 26, 1972 at the age of 67, commanded the military force which took part in the heroic raid on the French port of St. Nazaire in March, 1942.

St. Nazaire was a port of high significance, the only one on the French coast capable of providing a base for the German battleship Tirpitz. If the dock could be destroyed, a sortie by the Tirpitz from Trondheim into the Atlantic would become most hazardous. The main objective of the raid was to block the great dry dock known as the Forme Écluse which had been specially constructed in 1932 to berth the liner Normandie. Newman and his men, mainly drawn from No. 2 Commando, were detailed to destroy dock installations, swing bridges and two flak towers. The naval force was commanded by Commander R. E. D. Ryder, also awarded the Victoria Cross for his part in the raid. The destroyer H.M.S. Campbeltown (Lieutenant-Commander S. H. Beattie), with specially stiffened bows filled with high explosive, accompanied by other naval vessels, sailed undetected up the Loire estuary until nearing her goal when all came under fierce fire of all kinds. She rammed the main dry dock "with a grinding crash" and became firmly wedged.

Newman was in the leading craft (MGB 314, Commander Ryder), steaming up the estuary and stood "coolly and calmly" on the bridge though caught in the glare of searchlights and murderous crossfire, which caused many casualties. Although he did not have to land himself he was one of the first ashore and during the ensuing fighting personally entered several houses and shot up the occupants and supervised the operations in the town regardless of his own safety. He directed fire to put out of action enemy gun positions and to compel an armed trawler in the harbour to withdraw. Under Newman's brilliant leadership the troops held superior enemy forces at bay while the demolition parties got to work.

By this time, however, most of the landing craft had been sunk or set on fire and evacuation by sea was no longer possible. Although the main objective had been achieved, Newman nevertheless was now determined to try to fight his way out into open country and so give all survivors a chance to escape.

The only way out of the harbour area lay across a narrow iron bridge covered by enemy machine-guns and although severely shaken by a German hand grenade, which had burst at his feet, Newman personally led the charge which stormed the position and under his inspiring leadership the small force fought its way through the streets to a point near the open country, when, all ammunition expended, he and his men were finally overpowered by the enemy.

Colonel Newman was born on August 19, 1904, and educated at Bancroft's School, Essex. He joined W. and G. French Ltd., civil engineering and public works contractors, in 1922 and retired as managing director of the firm in 1969.

April 28, 1972.

Sir John Newsom, C.B.E., the educationist who was chairman of two "Newsom" commissions (one on the education of average and below-average children, the other on public schools), died on May 23, 1971 at the age of 60.

John Hubert Newsom was born in Glasgow on June 8, 1910, the son of Hubert and Dorothy Newsom. He was educated at the Imperial Service College and Queen's College, Oxford, where he was awarded a scholarship in 1928. Much of his later life was influenced by his years at Oxford. He had no financial support except his scholarship and maintained himself during the vacations by taking unskilled work in the East End of London. He lodged in common lodging houses and gained a knowledge of life among the poor and unemployed which he came later to regard as an integral part of his education.

Largely as a result of these vacation experiences, when he came down from Oxford in 1931 and until 1938, he held various posts in the social and community service. He considered taking Anglican orders at one time but lost his faith and remained an agnostic for many years, until he was received into the Roman Catholic Church in 1946.

Having married immediately on coming down from Oxford, he needed an income to support a home, and combined lecturing in philosophy at King's College, London, with part-time social work on an L.C.C. housing estate at St. Helier, Surrey. For a short time he served as licensee of a public house as part of an experiment in community development—a brief excursion which enabled him to derive pleasure from including licensed victualling among his various careers in *Who's Who*.

After helping to run a training centre for unemployed miners in the Midlands for the National Council of Social Service, he was appointed by the council as first director of the Community Service Association for the city of Durham. In 1938 he went with Lionel Ellis, secretary to the National Council of Social Service, to join the original staff of the short-lived National Fitness Council under the Board of Education. (Others included the present Lady White and Lord Greenwood.

After Munich in 1938 he was sent to Hertford, under the emergency regulations, to consult with the Hertfordshire County Council about evacuation preparations. During this time he evidently impressed the county authorities, who invited him to apply for the post of deputy chief education officer with the prospect of the early succession to the chief position. This he did, was appointed, and the following year became chief education officer at the age of 30. He held the post from 1940 to 1957. He was a brilliant and unorthodox administrator. Not by any means an administrator's administrator, his achievements lay in the field of altering attitudes and creating the circumstances in which good education could flourish by releasing initiative in others.

His most obvious contributions were in school building and in the devolution of control over detail from the education office to the heads of schools. Under his administration and by a most fruitful partnership with C. H. Aslin (then county architect) immediately after the Second World War, Hertfordshire became the leading exponent of modern school architecture, and pointed the way to many of the developments in the Ministry of Education (as it then was) which helped to spread the best practice throughout the county. This was only possible because of the skill with which Newsom educated the members of his own education committee.

Hertfordshire before 1939 had not been a county which was rated particularly highly as an education authority. After 1945 there was a rapid influx of population and an immediate demand for many new schools, at a time when everything needed for school building was scarce. Newsom and Aslin, with Aslin's deputy, Stirrat Johnson-Marshall, later joint head of the Architect and Buildings Branch at the Ministry of Education, pioneered the close cooperation between architects, educators and administrators which opened up the way for distinguished as well as rapid building and promoted the systematic study of school needs and their translation into modern design. In particular, they pressed ahead with prefabrication and modular construction methods.

Newsom was a man of genuine originality who stimulated originality in others. He disliked the conventional attitude of organized distrust which characterized the financial relationship between the county council and its head teachers. Working closely with R. S. McDougall, the county treasurer, who had similar unorthodox views, Newsom was determined to trust the teachers. A scheme was devised which transferred the purchase of many items of school supplies from the county administrative staff to the head teachers themselves. The heads responded to the responsibility which they had been given; signing the cheques themselves was a psychological tonic. The side-effects were to save the county £6,000-£7,000 a year in clerical expenses, but this was not the prime object of the scheme, which was to build up and sustain the morale of the teachers.

Another achievement of Newsom's administration was in persuading Hertfordshire to collect original works of art, pictures and sculptures, to adorn the new schools. The work of artists such as Henry Moore and Barbara Hepworth was purchased for this purpose, but the education committee did not appreciate the taste of the distinguished connoisseurs, Sir Kenneth Clark among them, who chose the *objets d'art*. The straw which broke the camel's back came when the Duke of Edinburgh, while opening a new technical college, was confronted by a modern piece of sculpture; "Good God, what's that?" was the Duke's reported comment, and shortly afterwards the education committee struck out the item for the purchase of original works of art from their estimates.

Newsom resigned as chief education officer in 1957 as a result of ill-health, and became a director of Longmans Green & Co. Ltd. The unexpected death of another director resulted in his soon becoming a managing director, in spite of his health, and in this capacity he began to apply to publishing some of the administrative techniques he had learnt in local government—a school of efficiency which he always maintained was more cost-conscious than business.

As an ex-chief education officer still under 50 but with many years of experience behind him, he became an obvious figure to be used by the Ministry of Education. Sir David (later Lord) Eccles appointed him to the Central Advisory Council in 1961 as an expert deputy to Lord Amory, who was to be chairman of an inquiry into the education of children of average and below average ability. On Lord Amory's appointment as U.K. High Commissioner in Canada, Newsom became chairman and gave his name to the report which emerged in 1963—*Half our Future*. He was happy to be identified with a section of the school population, known as "Newsom children", who had received less than their share of attention. He was knighted in 1964. He remained a member of the Central Advisory Council, as deputy to Lady Plowden, for the inquiry into primary education.

In 1965 he was chosen by Anthony Crosland to chair the Public Schools Commission which reported in 1968. Tied closely to terms of reference which ensured that its proposals would please nobody, the commission was largely abortive and proved to

be an unrewarding labour for its chairman.

His other interests were wide. In 1966 he became chairman of the Harlow Development Corporation. He served on the Arts Council, on departmental committees on colonial education, public libraries and charitable trusts. He was a vice-chairman of the National Youth Orchestra of Great Britain, a governor of the Royal College of Art and the British Film Institute. He was an honorary F.R.I.B.A., for his services to schools architecture and, as a result of an obscure and secret incident during the Second World War, during which for a brief while he held the rank of Captain R.N., he was made an Officer of the Legion of Honour.

He wrote various books on educational topics, the best known of which, *The Education of Girls*, 1948, stirred up controversy by challenging the feminist orthodoxy that girls must be educated in exactly the same way as boys. He was an amusing and stimulating speaker, but at his best in private conversation with a gift for outrageous exaggeration and a delight in innocent gossip. He was a man of many friends, and the breadth of his interests and the warmth of his personality made him excellent company.

He married, in 1931, Barbara Joan Day, by whom he had one son and one daughter.

May 24, 1971.

J. D. Newth, C.B.E., who had been until March 1973 joint managing director of the publishing house of A. & C. Black, and who was president of the Publishers Association from 1949 to 1951, died suddenly on December 18, 1973 in his seventy-first year.

Jack Newth was one of the ablest publishers of his generation and one of the most unassuming; it is entirely in character that there is no entry under his name in *Who's Who*, the most famous publication of the firm he served for the whole of his working life.

His knowledge of his chosen profession was deep and wide-ranging; his judgment, sound, decisive and sometimes sharp, was firmly rooted in experience. His advice was readily at the disposal of all who sought it. Many did, publicly and privately, and emerged both wiser and more cheerful. He served on the council of the Publishers Association for 21 years and took on for successive presidents the more difficult and unrewarding chores; his own presidency brought distinction to that office.

He played an active part in the affairs of the National Book League and as treasurer was largely responsible for securing its Albemarle Street premises; he was president of the Book Trade Benevolent Society. He was among the first to establish contact after the war with the book trade of Eastern Europe for the British Council and the Publishers Association.

He was a quiet, unostentatious man, though a sociable one; he was shrewd in business but scrupulous. He had an astringent, sometimes sardonic, wit, which never hid his fundamental kindness or his genuine modesty. He hurt no one, and though he was, properly, held in great respect by his professional colleagues, senior or junior, no one was frightened of him. He was a publisher first and foremost; he never lost touch with the day-to-day conduct of his own business, and had an amused contempt for those who did. He never confused bigness with greatness or thought that efficiency could be achieved at the expense of humanity.

Though everyone in the book trade knew him and many valued him as a counsellor and a friend, he was also a private man. Most of his friends in the trade and in the Garrick Club knew no more than that he obviously enjoyed a happy family life with the wife, three sons and three daughters who survive him.

December 22, 1973.

Nora Nicholson, the actress, who died on September 18, 1973 aged 80, was proudest of being an Old Bensonian of (as she used to say) "the real lineage".

Her eldest brother—born on December 7, 1892, she was the youngest of the long family of a Leamington vicar—was 21 years her senior, the celebrated comedian, H. O. Nicholson ("Nick"), one of the stars Frank Benson created so prodigally. She was at school with the Bensons' daughter Brynhild ("Dick"), who remained her lifelong friend; and, after studying in the Benson dramatic school, she made her debut at Stratford-on-Avon in 1912, not in Shakespeare but as Dolly, the girl twin in *You Never Can Tell*.

More than two years later she was acting, in the original Shakespeare company of the Old Vic, such parts as Titania, Jessica, and Ariel, and meeting there another friend for life, Sybil Thorndike. Thenceforward her career, punctuated by much-enjoyed service in the W.R.N.S. for a year at the end of the First World War, took a long time to develop.

Never meant for the mild drift of drawing-room comedy, she was regarded very soon as a "character" actress; and in those type-ridden days there were few parts that would suit her frail, eager, bright-eyed figure. During her first quarter of a century on the stage, during which she became gradually better known, only a few parts stand out: the governess in *The Cherry Orchard* at the Royalty (1925); the deaf aunt in the American production of Patrick Hamilton's *Rope*, there known as *Rope's End* (1929); and Miss Trafalgar Gower in the Old Vic's *Trelawny of the "Wells"* (1938).

During the Second World War she had five fruitful years as a member of the company at the Playhouse, Oxford (she acted O'Casey's* Juno), but her renown was local, and her late flowering in London had still to come.

Suddenly it did. Its first expression was the spinster in Wynyard Browne's *Dark Summer* at the Lyric, Hammersmith, and St. Martin's (1947). Thereafter she was accepted as one of the most subtly thoughtful of the elder players. She was quietly moving as the persecuted former schoolmistress in Pamela Hansford Johnson's *Corinth House* (New Lindsey, 1948), which did not reach the West End—some years later she acted it on television in Canada —and in May 1949 she found an admired stage part, Margaret in Fry's *The Lady's Not For Burning*, which she created with her special sense of twinkling gravity: "I study such flowers as moon-daisies, and learn to be placid". She acted this again, in New York, during 1950.

The parts would stream in now. A few only: Miss Teresa in the American production of Graham Greene's *The Living Room* (1945); Ivy in *The Family Reunion* revival (Phoenix, London, 1956); another major memory, Coward's Sarita Myrtle, wits awry, in *Waiting in the Wings* (Duke of York's, 1960), touching and beautifully timed; Ardotya Nazarovna in *Ivanov* (with Gielgud, Phoenix, 1965); and the Nurse in *Forty Years On* (again with Gielgud, Apollo, 1968), which she played for 12 months. Her last appearance, in the spring and summer of 1973, was as the Nurse in *A Doll's House* (Criterion).

By now she had long been a star of television. She had played in various films, as well, and would go on to the last, ready for anything in any medium. But the part that established her in the public mind was "the aunt with the dog" in the early instalments of the televised version of *The Forsyte Saga*. For the first time, she said, she found herself greeted by strangers in the street and knew what it was to be "an international face".

She was among the most endeared players in her profession: gently deprecating, externally a trifle timid, but when working immensely professional in style and technique, never cast down, and with a softspoken humour that managed to aerate the dullest exercise on stage or off. She liked to write short stories and poems, and in her last year had finished a quietly witty and generous autobiography. To the end she was the most loyal of Bensonians.

September 20, 1973.

Guy Oliver Nickalls, the oarsman, died on April 26, 1974 in London at the age of 75.

Born on April 4, 1899, the son of Guy Nickalls, he inherited his father's boundless vitality and prowess on the river. He was educated at Eton, and, after service in the Rifle Brigade in Salonica from 1918 to 1919, at Magdalen College, Oxford. He twice rowed head of the river, and twice won the University Fours and Pairs. He rowed for Oxford in the Boat Race for three years and was president of the O.U.B.C. in 1923.

"Gully", as he was affectionately known to all oarsmen, earned a reputation second to none on the river. Between 1920 and 1928 he won the Grand Challenge Cup at Henley seven times. He also rowed in the Silver Goblets in eight successive years, winning twice, and in the Stewards' Four for five successive years, winning once. In 1920 and 1928 he rowed in the British Olympic eight and in 1923 he was in the winning Leander eight at the Toronto International Regatta.

Nickalls several times coached Oxford, including the winning crews of 1937 and 1938. He was a Steward of Henley Regatta, and for many years an umpire and a member of the Committee of Management. From 1946 until 1952 he was honorary secretary of the Amateur Rowing Association, and was chairman from 1952 until 1968.

His interests were not only confined to the river. He joined the advertising firm of Alfred Pemberton Ltd. in 1926, and from 1945 to 1962 was vice-chairman. A man of many abilities, he might have excelled in any of several spheres, had he chosen to concentrate his attention in one direction. He had a number of pictures hung in the Royal Academy, and was able to turn his pen to journalism, the writing of books, of plays, and of lyrics.

He married Violet Rachel Pearce, the daughter of Colonel Serocold in 1929.

April 27, 1974.

Professor Reinhold Niebuhr, probably the best known and most influential American theologian of our time, died at Stockbridge, Massachusetts, on May 31/June 1, 1971. He was 78.

He was greatly esteemed as a Christian moralist, as a political thinker and counsellor, as a university preacher and as an individual of extraordinary vitality and personal authority.

He was born in Wright City, Missouri, in 1892, the son of an Evangelical pastor of German descent. He was himself a minister of the Evangelical and Reformed Church, which has now united with the Congregational Christian Church of the United States. He was trained at Yale Divinity School and his first and only ministerial charge was that of an Evangelical and Reformed church in Detroit, where he took an active part in the social and political struggles of that city. He went to Union Theological Seminary, New York, in 1928, specializing in the teaching of Christian social ethics, and it is from there that his most characteristic work was done. He was Professor of Applied Christianity from 1930 to 1968 and subsequently Professor Emeritus.

He began to be widely known in the early 1930s as a theological writer who stood firmly in the succession of Walter Rauchenbusch and the Social Gospel movement, but who did not share the optimistic and pacifist outlook displayed by many in that movement during that period. Under the influence of the growing revival of the theology of the Reformation he saw new meaning in the doctrine of original sin and, aided by his interpretation of Marx and Freud, he could analyse human motives and moral dilemmas with far greater subtlety and realism than many of his contemporaries displayed. This meant that he was viewed with suspicion by many of his liberal Protestant American colleagues, and in fact his earlier books, *Moral Man and Immoral Society* and *The Interpretation of Christian Ethics* were at the outset more appreciated in Britain than in America.

This made it fitting that his largest and most distinctive book, *The Nature and Destiny of Man*, should have been based on the Gifford Lectures which he delivered in Edinburgh during the early days of the last war. These lectures, which attracted unparalleled interest when they were delivered, established him as one of the leading prophetic spokesmen in the Protestant world.

His later work developed along two lines. On the more technical level, he had been particularly concerned with the nature of history, as exemplified by his books *Faith and History* and *The Self*.

But Niebuhr applied his characteristic insights to the spiritual situation of the democratic countries as they found themselves confronted by Communism. This found more generalized expression in his widely read books *The Children of Light and the Children of Darkness* and *The Irony of American History*. His remarkably detailed understanding of political affairs, especially on the international level, also issued in a constant stream of commentary in the periodicals of which he had been a moving spirit, *Christianity and Society* and *Christianity and Crisis*.

Niebuhr once described himself as "a moralist who has strayed into theology". It is true that he did not contribute very much to the study of directly theological problems in the way in which his distinguished brother, Professor Richard Niebuhr of Yale, did. He was more interested in defining human nature and destiny, in the words of the title of his largest book, in the light of a Christian understanding of God which is presupposed rather than stated. In the process, however, few people have spoken with greater relevance and illumination in the social situation of our time. Niebuhr was one of the first to recognize what could be learnt from the challenge of Communism, as he was one of the first to point out its dangers. If Protestant theology speaks with greater maturity and awareness of the complexities of the human situation than it did a generation ago, it has been due to the work of Reinhold Niebuhr more than to that of any other individual. And he did as much as any other thinker to prepare America for facing responsibly the realities of world power.

This is partly proved by the fact that no theologian in the United States has been listened to with greater respect by the general academic community and by people concerned with political affairs. When he preached, as he frequently did, at American universities, the composition of the congregation was often significantly different from what it was on other Sundays. He was frequently informally consulted by representatives of the government in the U.S.A. and sometimes by British politicians as well. He was awarded the Presidential Medal of Freedom in 1964. He was an active leader of the Liberal Party in New York and of Americans for Democratic Action. He was contributing editor of the *Nation* and had a wide influence among the intellectual leaders of American Jewry. He was deeply attached to England and to English institutions.

His English wife, Ursula Keppel-Compton, among many other distinctions, was the first woman to win a First in theology at Oxford. There were two children of the marriage. Niebuhr was awarded honorary degrees by many universities, including Oxford, Glasgow and Manchester.

Those who heard him speak are never likely to forget the experience. Hawk-nosed and speaking in tortuous sentences with a Mid-West accent, he seemed to be a mass of waving limbs. Yet he was an incandescently brilliant speaker whose eloquence was always controlled by a sharp and humble mind and by his gift of irony. His wisdom and vitality were just as apparent in his personal conversation as in public. Serious illness severely curtailed his activity in later years but his writing lost little of its vigour and relevance. William Temple, Archbishop of Canterbury, said of him, "At last I have found the troubler of my peace". Many others have said the same, and have said it in gratitude and affection for one who, in a time of darkness and confusion, made them more aware of the judgment and mercy of God.

June 3, 1971.

Sir Otto Niemeyer, G.B.E., K.C.B., who for many years was one of the most influential figures in the world of high finance, serving first at the Treasury and thereafter at the Bank of England, died on February 6, 1971. He was 87.

After working for 20 years at the Treasury and reaching the elevated position of Controller of Finance before his fortieth birthday, he joined the Bank of England during the governorship of Montagu Norman and played a major part in national and international financial affairs as a director and executive of the bank for another quarter of a century.

Otto Ernst Niemeyer was born in 1883 at Streatham, the son of F. A. W. Niemeyer, who came of a north German professional family and migrated in 1870 to Britain where he became a naturalized British citizen and married Ethel Rayner, daughter of a Liverpool West African merchant.

Otto Niemeyer was educated at St. Paul's School and won a classical scholarship at Balliol College, Oxford, where he had a most successful academic record. The particular success which pleased him most in retrospect was a *proxime accessit* for the Hertford scholarship. He was defeated by a short head for the latter by Wilfrid (later Lord Justice) Greene. (Legend relates that Greene, who like Niemeyer remained an enthusiastic classicist throughout his life, just tipped the balance by rendering "sticker plaster" into Horatian verse as *medico papyro*).

After gaining first-class honours in Classical Moderations and Lit. Hum., he won first place in the Civil Service examination in 1906—beating Maynard Keynes into second place in the process—and was posted immediately to the Treasury. (It is of some interest to recall that, but for a last-minute change of mind on the advice of a family friend, Niemeyer would have made the India Office his first choice, and thereby presumably he would have gone to the India Office and Keynes to the Treasury—with which ultimate consequences for the two men's lives it is intriguing, if difficult, to guess).

At the Treasury promotion came rapidly. He was in charge of the Finance and Budget Divisions from 1919 to 1921 and was made Deputy Controller of Finance in 1921. In 1922 Sir Basil Blackett, the Controller, was appointed finance member of the Executive Council in India, and Niemeyer succeeded him at the early age of 39 as Controller of Finance, one of the select positions in the rank immediately below that of the Permanent Secretary. In this post he was responsible for all the technical control of the national finances, which in those postwar years involved exceptional operations, problems associated with the management of the National Debt, conversion operations, settlement of war debts, and various currency matters. At the same time he became a member (from 1922) of the Financial Committee of the League of Nations. In the event he was to serve on this committee for over 15 years and was appointed its chairman in 1927.

On the League Committee he threw himself wholeheartedly into the problems of financial and economic reconstruction in Europe. It was a sphere in which there was little practical experience to guide the committee, and in which Sir Otto's powerful and imaginative intellect could make an exceptional contribution. Some of those who were familiar at first hand with his work on the committee in the 1920s were of the opinion that this was one of the most fruitful labours of his whole career, and certainly the committee's plans for the reconstruction of the many bankrupt and disordered national economies of Europe succeeded far beyond most people's expectations. He was created a K.C.B. in 1924 and a G.B.E. in 1927.

After serving with such distinction as Controller of Finance and U.K. member of the League Financial Committee, Sir Otto at the age of 44 was to all appearances a strong candidate in due course for the highest position in the Civil Service. In 1927, however, he left the Treasury to join the Bank of England. Such a transfer was unprecedented. But the position of the Bank of England at that time was unprecedented likewise. Montagu Norman, effectively the first "permanent" governor of the Bank, was busy reorganizing its whole structure and control and was building up a small group of trusted lieutenants, partly taken from outside sources, to cope with the future expansion of the Bank's work and responsibilities as he instinctively foresaw them. Sir Otto, like others of this group, went to the Bank as an official; for at that time there was no provision for executive directors, and the Bank's Court consisted —at any rate in theory and in terms of remuneration—wholly of part-time members. In 1938, however, Norman changed this arrangement, as he had already changed much else, and two of the trusted lieutenants—Sir Otto himself and C. F. Cobbold who was later to become Governor—were immediately elected to the Court.

A wide range of duties fell to Sir Otto during his first few years at the Bank of England, for the Bank's higher administration was then in very few hands and there was nothing resembling the highly organized executive hierarchy that has been established since. Some of the more pressing problems were in the domestic fields, with agriculture and the cotton textile and shipbuilding industries all in a chronically depressed condition, and it was to these industries that the Bank was turning its attention to see whether new financial facilities and organizations could assist them. Niemeyer was especially concerned with agriculture and the cotton textile industry, and he played a leading part in the schemes eventually prepared by the Bank and others to strengthen their position. The plans then laid have on the whole justified themselves well, and in particular the two new organizations which the Bank took a leading part in establishing—the Agricultural Mortgage Corporation and the Lancashire Cotton Corporation, later part of the Courtauld group—remain as solid memorials of Sir Otto's work.

International financial affairs, however, were demanding ever-increasing attention from 1930 onwards. In this field he had already gained much experience at the Treasury, notably in his work on the League Financial Committee. He continued his membership of the League Committee and also became a director of the Bank for International Settlements, which had been set up to deal with reparations and debt payments and in general to promote cooperation between central banks, and he was chairman of the board of the B.I.S. from 1937 to 1940. He retired as a director in 1965.

The activity which brought Sir Otto most prominently into the public limelight, however, and did in fact give him great responsibilities and opportunities, was the series of missions which he undertook at the request of overseas governments to examine the financial situation of the countries concerned and to advise on financial and economic policy. The first and most important of these—important not only because of the country concerned but because of the comprehensive nature of his assignment—was his mission to Australia at the invitation of the Commonwealth government in 1930.

Australia was then in extremely difficult financial and economic straits, and he was asked to examine Australia's whole economic position and to report thereon to the Federal and State governments. His report was one of the most outspoken documents of its kind ever published. He described Australia as being "out of budget equilibrium and out of exchange equilibrium" and pointed out that Australian credit was "lower than that of any of the other dominions" and that the "serious problem" of her financial straits was "not rendered any easier by the natural optimism of the Australian". Criticizing Australian tariff policy and its effect on primary production cost, he urged that "so long as the sheltered trades of Australia insist on taking so large a share of the national dividend and even an increasingly large proportion as the national dividend drops, the difficulties of the unsheltered export trades can only increase". It was a difficult mission, which naturally aroused much controversy. But the Australian people took his diagnosis and his suggested cures in good part, and a detailed programme of retrenchment along the lines he suggested was agreed upon by a conference of Federal and State Premiers and Treasurers. The verdict of most Australians was faithfully reflected in the *Melbourne Argus*, which wrote at the time that he had "fulfilled his mission with conspicuous tact, placing unpleasant facts on record in a manner that left no sting", and that he had left the "abiding impression of a kindly, courteous gentleman who has rendered conspicuous service to the Commonwealth".

At any rate, other governments were sufficiently impressed by his work to follow Australia's example and to invite him to examine their own financial and economic positions and to make recommendations on what policies should be followed. In 1931 he was invited by the Brazilian Government to advise on a plan for reconstituting the Bank of Brazil on monetary reform and exchange stabilization, and on problems connected with the budget and foreign borrowing. Here again the Brazilian Government was well satisfied with the advice which he gave and did its best to implement it. Missions of the same kind varying somewhat in the range and type of subject-matter which he was asked to deal with followed—to Greece and Egypt in 1932, to Argentina in 1933, and to India in 1935.

These important missions had to be fitted in with his ordinary regular responsibilities as an executive director of the Bank, and throughout the 1930s, Sir Otto was active as director and chairman of the Bank for International Settlements, and also as a member of the Council of Foreign Bondholders, the representative body which, with government recognition, was primarily responsible for looking after the interests of British loans to overseas countries.

The Second World War naturally brought a great increase in the weight of the ordinary Bank of England work, particularly as it applied to control of exchange and securities. But in 1941 he was called on to carry out another important mission —this time as head of a mission which went to China at the invitation of General Chiang Kai-shek—to advise on the stabilization of the Chinese currency, on the use of economic and financial aid to China, and on various questions relating to Chinese external trade. This was the last of his major missions, and from then onwards he was chiefly engaged in the more ordinary work of the Bank of England, the burden of which grew enormously during the war and early postwar years. Shortly after his return he became the Bank of England's representative on the Capital Issues Committee, which had been set up under Lord Kennet's chairmanship to advise the Treasury on the control of borrowing and on the raising of new capital. This control was strict during the war and for many years after the war ended, and the committee's work was of the utmost importance.

Like the other executive directors of the Bank of England, he was appointed an executive director of the Bank in its new form when it was nationalized in 1946. He retired from the Court of the Bank of England in 1952, as he would have exceeded the Court's standard age limit if he had served for a further term. He continued to engage actively, however, in the external work which had become of much importance—on the Council of Foreign Bondholders, on the Capital Issues Committee, and on the Bank for International Settlements. Indeed he played an outstanding part in the Anglo-German debt negotiations which led to the International German Debt Agreement of 1952 and which had just got into full swing at the time when he retired from the Bank Court. On his retirement from the Court he joined the boards of several important companies, including the International Nickel Company and the Central Mining and Investment Trust.

He retained his position as vice-chairman of the B.I.S., and also his chairmanship of the Council of Foreign Bondholders until his eightieth birthday. Until then he also had a room at the Bank of England, where his views and advice were always welcome and often invited.

Sir Otto found time for various general activities in addition to his financial work. He was for a period chairman of the Governors of the London School of Economics, and he was chairman of the provisional National Council for Mental Health from 1943 to 1946. He was a governor of St. Paul's School and a Lieutenant of the City of London.

He was a man of outstanding intellect. Probably no finer brain has been applied to the practical detailed complexities of twentieth-century national and international finance. By temperament and character, moreover, he was well suited to practical financial work on the highest plane. With all his brilliance he was—and looked—the embodiment of sturdy common sense. And his intellectual integrity was unshakable. He was not fond of compromising with the truth or of avoiding inconvenient conclusions, and he could be blunt in his speech on occasions. But, as his diplomatic test in Australia showed, the ultimate kindliness of his character and his real charm—charm which was still more apparent on off-duty occasions—enabled him to speak plainly without giving offence.

His abilities were of the highest and there were many who felt that the formal position to which he attained was something rather less than those abilities really justified. But that would perhaps be to under-estimate the true significance of the role that he filled for so many years. If he never occupied the highest position of all, either at the Treasury or at the Bank, it was a sufficient compensation to have achieved so much for so long in both places. It is doubtful, indeed, taking it all in all, whether anybody in his generation had a greater or more beneficial influence on public financial affairs than he.

He married in 1910 Sophia Benedicte, daughter of Theodor Niemeyer, a distant cousin. They had three sons and one daughter. Their second son was killed on active service as a Flight Lieutenant in the Royal Air Force in 1943.

February 8, 1971.

Bronislava Nijinska, sister of the great dancer Vaslav Nijinsky, died at her home in Los Angeles on February 22, 1972. She was 81.

She was born at Minsk on January 8, 1891. Her father and mother were both professional dancers, so it was natural for their children to study ballet also. Bronislava and her older brother Vaslav Nijinsky both showed talent enough to gain admission to the Imperial Theatre school in St. Petersburg, where her teachers included

Cecchetti, Fokine and Nicholas Legat. Graduating with distinction in 1908, she joined the ballet of the Maryinsky Theatre and soon started dancing solos. At the end of her first year, during the summer holidays, Nijinska took part in the inaugural season of Diaghilev's Russian Ballet in Paris. With this company she later danced important roles in *Carnaval Petrushka* and other works.

In 1911 she resigned from the Maryinsky (at the time of her brother's dismissal following a possibly trumped-up scandal) to join Diaghilev permanently. However, the outbreak of war in 1914 found her cut off from Diaghilev in Russia. After an engagement as ballerina of a private company in St. Petersburg, she went to Kiev where she danced, made her first attempt at choreography and also opened a school. In 1921 she was able to leave Russia and rejoined Diaghilev in time for his production of *The Sleeping Princess,* in which she danced the Lilac Fairy (alternating with Lopokova).

For this production she also devised some additional choreography, and the following year she became principal choreographer to the company on Massine's departure. After staging Stravinsky's *Renard,* she went on to produce the two works which have survived in the international repertory to be recognized as masterpieces, *Les Noces* (1923) and *Les Biches* (1924).

In *Les Biches,* to Poulenc's* music, Nijinska produced the ballet which more than any other epitomizes the spirit of the 1920s: chic, sophisticated, with hints of decadence beneath a surface of bubbling wit. *Les Noces,* with music by Stravinsky, was a complete contrast, a timeless expression of a way of life, in terms of a village wedding in old Russia. Other choreographers had always spoken admiringly of Nijinska's exceptional craftsmanship, and although she was never again to equal the inspiration of these two ballets, she always had exceptional ability to show off dances to advantage.

After several more works for Diaghilev, including *Le Train Bleu,* in which Anton Dolin made his name, Nijinska worked at the Colon Theatre, Buenos Aires, and for Ida Rubinstein's Company in Paris, where the productions included another commission from Stravinsky, *Le Baiser de la Fée.* In the 1930s she briefly formed her own company, before staging further new creations and revivals for the de Basil and Markova-Dolin companies. Since 1938 she lived and worked mainly in America with her husband, although she was for a while ballet mistress of the de Cuevas* company in Europe. She arranged the dances for Max Reinhardt's film of *A Midsummer Night's Dream,* made in 1935.

In 1964 Frederick Ashton coaxed Nijinska out of semi-retirement to stage *Les Biches* at Covent Garden and two years later *Les Noces.* He has since said that this is the single action as artistic director

of the Royal Ballet of which he is most proud. A strict disciplinarian, but a woman of outstanding gifts and charm, Nijinska was admired by all who were privileged to work with her. Her brother died in 1950.

February 23, 1972.

Dr. Kwame Nkrumah, former president of Ghana, who died on April 27, 1972 in Conakry, Guinea, had increasingly assumed, after Ghana's independence, the role of a formidable dictator for whom the democratic processes, useful in achieving a position of power, meant increasingly less. It is fair to add that he was under strong pressures. Within his own party there was a fundamental dichotomy between the pro-western old guard—whose pro-westernism could be held against them in newly independent Africa—and the militant left wing. There is no doubt, however, that Nkrumah himself relished the panoply of power, and was as ready to imprison his opponents without trial as the old colonial regime had been to imprison him. Whereas he was released, they often died in jail.

He became a tyrant, and showed many signs of megalomania, not least the cultivation of a belief in his own immortality. It was a sign of the extent to which his reputation had fallen that when he was removed from office in February 1966—in his absence on a visit to Peking—the reaction in Ghana was of spontaneous jubilation.

Nkrumah went into exile in Conakry, Guinea, where President Sekou Touré had initially welcomed him as "co-president". Meanwhile in Ghana the corruption of Nkrumah's regime was examined by a commission of inquiry and various attempted counter-coups were uncovered.

Within hours of his overthrow Nkrumah's picture had been removed from public display, and the statue which he had had built to himself in his own lifetime was demolished. He had undoubtedly become an evil influence, caring nothing for normal decent standards, and his behaviour was exaggerated by his own state of fear. He lived increasingly behind barbed wire, heavily guarded, surrounded by sycophants who told him only what he wanted to know, cut off from the people he claimed to lead.

It was a sad transformation of the man who had been a genuinely popular leader with Ghana at his feet. The charming, compelling personality became a diabolic force. The freedom for which he had fought became a mockery under his leadership. Its roots, fortunately, ran deep, however, and Ghana eventually ousted him.

Perhaps the turning point was his dismissal at the end of 1963 of the Chief Justice of Ghana, Sir Arku Korsah, after a special court over which he had presided had acquitted three leading political figures of treason charges. The dismissal cut away at a stroke the one important independent

safeguard for Ghanaians at a time of increasingly vigorous security measures, and reduced still further individual liberty. On December 31, 1963, Nkrumah announced that a referendum would be held to amend the constitution, making it formally a one-party state, and giving him power to remove judges from the bench, as well as the Chief Justice from his post.

Two days later, an unsuccessful attempt was made on the President's life. Several other attempts had been made previously.

The troubles of the opposition really began when the Constitution (Repeal of Restrictions) Act was passed in December 1958 to remove the need for consulting regional assemblies before changing the constitution. It cut away at one blow the precarious arrangements, decided upon in haste before independence, under which the fears of the regions, notably Ashanti, were allayed by the setting up of five regional assemblies.

In 1960 Ghana became a republic, and Nkrumah its first president. A new constitution provided for a parliament sitting in five year terms, but the sitting Parliament, due to expire in 1961, had its life extended. It later became clear, as opposition leaders were removed to jail and dissident voices within Nkrumah's own party were cast aside, that one-party rule was the President's intention.

In 1961 the President stepped up his campaign against the opposition, and at the same time there were strong hints of unrest in the country and danger to Nkrumah himself.

It was against this unhappy background, exacerbated by an almost total breakdown of understanding between Ghana and Britain, both at government and press level, that the tour of the Queen and the Duke of Edinburgh took place. The royal visit was welcomed by Ghanaians of most political complexions but it was also undoubtedly a feather in Nkrumah's cap. It enabled him for a while to ride above the ugly storms of unrest and the disquiet caused among Ghana's friends by the draconian measures he adopted to deal with it.

In 1962 the Ghana Government took even wider powers of detention without trial in a new Act, but at the same time Nkrumah decided to release a number of the country's political detainees. In the early summer of that year the President was awarded a Lenin Peace Prize.

In 1963 the Preventive Detention Act of 1958 was amended to give the President power to renew detention orders for further periods of five years before the expiry of the original term.

In August 1962 an attempt was made on Nkrumah's life in a bomb incident which killed a child and injured a number of people but left the President unharmed. A few weeks later a second attempt was made.

From obscurity Kwame Nkrumah, whose real name was Francis Nwia Kofi, went straight from jail to become Leader of

Government Business and later first Prime Minister of Ghana. His elevation was partly the result of his inflexible political determination—the liberation of the Gold Coast (Ghana) from foreign rule—and fortuitous circumstances.

In America and Britain Nkrumah tok an interest in political organizations, and in Britain he was actively associated with the West African National Secretariat and the Pan-African Federation, after unsuccessful attempts to enter the Inns of Court and read for the Bar examinations. However, his career as a full-time politician did not actually begin until towards the end of 1947 when he was invited to accept the post of General Secretary of the United Gold Coast Convention, which was a nationalist movement.

Nkrumah returned to his native Gold Coast (Ghana) with his unrepentant political ideologies of the destruction of colonialism and the formation of a Union of West African Soviet Socialist Republics. His ability as an organizer was soon recognized by the leaders of the U.G.C.C. On February 27-28, 1948, certain disturbances culminated in looting and rioting; Nkrumah and five other leaders of the U.G.C.C. were removed to various parts of the country under a Government Order. When the police made a search on Dr. Nkrumah they found among his papers a Communist Party membership card No. 57565 which, however, did not contain his signature. There was also found another document known as "The Circle". This document was a political plan for the implementation of West African unity and national independence. The motto was: "service, sacrifice, suffering", and every member had to make a pledge to accept the leadership of Nkrumah.

After six years of independence, Ghana was increasingly directed along a path of "scientific socialism", and it became ever more evident that the President himself was a believer in the communist ideology, albeit communist ideology with a personal gloss.

Later, it became evident that there was a sharp difference between the political programme of Nkrumah and that of the other leaders of the U.G.C.C., principally Dr. J. B. Danquah*. By skilfully wooing the dissident ex-servicemen and carrying out an intensive campaign of vilification against the leaders of the U.G.C.C. Nkrumah created a chasm of disagreement within the U.G.C.C. and he broke the United Front by resigning from the movement.

On June 12, 1949 he founded his own political party which he named the Convention People's Party (C.P.P.). This event marked the introduction of party politics into the Gold Coast. His programme for his party was based on four principles—organization of the masses, denunciation of imperialism, abolition of political illiteracy, and the establishment of a nationalist press. His policy of "self-government now", as opposed to the U.G.C.C.'s policy of "self-government within the shortest possible time", won a great following for his party.

Because the recommendations of the Coussey Committee fell short of the immediate grant of self-government Nkrumah declared "positive action" on January 8, 1950. He was charged with inciting divers people to participate in an illegal strike by advocating "positive action" and at the end of his trial he was sentenced to 12 months' imprisonment.

While he was in prison the first general elections were held in the Gold Coast, and the results confirmed the claims of Nkrumah's C.P.P. as the most popular political organization in the country. He topped the polls and was consequently released to become the Leader of Government Business. On Friday, March 22, 1952 Nkrumah was, as a result of constitutional changes, elected first Prime Minister of the Gold Coast by the Legislative Assembly. Local Government reforms and a fee-free education scheme were introduced. His over-riding objective was, however, the achievement of self-government for the Gold Coast. In pursuance of this, he moved a motion in the Legislative Assembly in July 1953 calling upon the British Government to grant the Gold Coast independence as soon as the necessary administrative and constitutional arrangements could be made. The slogan of his party at this time was: "We prefer self-government with danger to servitude in tranquillity". The emergence of the National Liberation Movement—principally an Ashanti revolt against the policies of his Government—was one of Nkrumah's toughest problems in his political career.

On March 6, 1957, after a compromise between the Opposition parties and Nkrumah's party had been reached, independence was achieved. Within three months came disillusion and frustration within Nkrumah's own party and in the country; the ex-Service men who were his strong supporters revolted and a political movement known as the *Ga Shifimo Kpe* was formed in his own constituency, Accra, in opposition to his Government. Nkrumah met this challenge by resorting to a tough policy which took the form of deportations and silencing critics and political opponents. He also embarked upon his personality cult.

As a politician, he derived his early success and strength from his popular appeal, his compelling oratory when addressing mass rallies and his methods of rendering his political opponents unpopular. In December 1953 he convened a West African Nationalist Conference in Accra. A great believer in geo-politics, Nkrumah believed that he had two missions in life—the achievement of independence of the Gold Coast (Ghana) and the uniting of African states.

He was born in the village of Nkroful, in Nzimaland, in Ghana, on September 21, 1909. His mother, Nyanibah, was a petty trader and his father a jeweller. He was the only child of his mother and, at the age of six years, he began his education at the Roman Catholic elementary school in Half-Assini. He taught for a year and was later sent to Achimota where he took a course in teacher-training. Inspired by the oratory and journalistic excellence of Dr. Noamdi Azikiwie (then editor of the *African Morning Post* in Accra) and the wisdom of Dr. Kwegyir Aggrey, Nkrumah went to America for higher education. He studied at Lincoln and Pennsylvania Universities and later lectured for a while at Lincoln.

As a politican, he was ruthless and jealous of any of his Cabinet colleagues becoming popular. If he was not occupying the first place, he would not cooperate. But he was also ambivalent in nature and easily gave in to pressure from the "tough boys" in his party. He had a great capacity for laughter and displayed considerable charm. He described himself as a Marxist socialist" and, although he was once a staunch Roman Catholic, he later declared that he was an "undenominational Christian". The impression of mysticism which he gave at times was unreal.

Nkrumah's removal from power could only be counted a blessing for the people of Ghana. History, however, will certainly give him an important place. He was, after all, the galvanic leader who set in motion the rapid progress to independence of black Africa. He could have been, and for a time almost was, the leader of the continent. Within Ghana itself he did a great deal of good. He was a tragic illustration of the corrupting quality of absolute power.

On Monday, December 30, 1957, Nkrumah married Miss Fathia Halen Ritz, an Egyptian. The ceremony took place at Government House, Accra, by special licence but it was kept a secret even from very close friends of his. There were two sons and one daughter of the marriage.

April 28, 1972.

The Duke of Norfolk, K.G., P.C., G.C.V.O., G.B.E., Premier Duke and hereditary Earl Marshal, died on January 31, 1975. He was 66.

Bernard Marmaduke Fitzalan-Howard, 16th Duke of Norfolk, was born on May 30. 1908. His father died in 1917. He therefore succeeded in childhood to the premier Dukedom in England and to the position of hereditary Earl Marshal. During his minority the duties of his post were performed by his uncle, Lord Fitzalan. But the most important functions of the Earl Marshal are concerned with the arrangement of a coronation and it so happened of course that, with George V on the throne, no coronation took place during the years of the Duke's minority.

The leader of the premier Roman Catholic family in the country, he was educated at the Oratory School near Reading and failed thence to obtain entry into Christ Church at Oxford. He made no pretence to scholarship or to an interest in letters. He was a keen cricketer of more than average, if not of first class, ability.

He took—as his father never had—an avid interest in racing, which if it be the sport of kings and highly respectable recreation for middle-aged noblemen, is not always thought on with such favour when the betting in it is indulged in by schoolboys. There were those among his schoolmasters who thought that he had developed his sporting tastes a little too early in life. On leaving school he held for a time a commission in the 4th Royal Sussex Regiment and thence transferred to the Royal Horse Guards. He described life there as "frightful".

When he came of age in 1929 his majority coincided to the day with the election of a Labour Government. He assumed his functions as Earl Marshal and the first duty which he was called on to perform was to inaugurate a Labour Lord Chancellor. His coming of age was celebrated by festivities which lasted for days; there was a ball at the castle; a bonfire was lit on the South Downs; 1,500 children had a free tea; and Arundel had a public holiday and a fête which went on until nightfall.

The Duke was first called upon to exercise his functions in a fully public manner on the death of George V in 1936, on the proclamation of Edward VIII and afterwards of George VI, and at the coronation of George VI. Wisely he put much reliance on the long experience of his uncle. Nevertheless he was able to prove both that he took seriously and performed competently the unique duties which the constitution imposed on him.

The Earl Marshal is the head of the College of Heralds. It falls to him to instruct officials, peers and peeresses on their duties at a coronation, to give the rulings on points of precedence of which there are many and to allot seats in the Abbey. His most important task is to instruct the members of the Royal Family on their part in the ceremony and to supervise at the coronation the procession which is known as the Royal Proceeding. By a typically English anomaly a Roman Catholic is the officer of this most Anglican of all ceremonies. The Duke without difficulty established the most friendly relations with the Anglican bishops who were to take part in the ceremony.

In January 1937 the Duke of Norfolk married in Brompton Oratory Miss Lavinia Strutt, the only daughter of Lord Belper and the Countess of Rosebery. The marriage aroused interest as his wife was not a Roman Catholic. For a time during the war he was Parliamentary Under-Secretary for Agriculture in the Churchill* Administration. A hundred and fifty years ago there were scattered through Britain some dozen magnates who reigned in their different neighbourhoods in almost royal state and enjoyed a prestige that fell only slightly below that of royalty. Today the prestige of the peerage is much diminished and among non-royal peers the Duke of Norfolk alone enjoyed prestige of this order.

Yet the financial problem of maintaining such a role is not easy with modern prices and taxation. The Duke was compelled to make a number of domestic economies and sales. Before the war he sold Norfolk House in St. James's Square and extensive house property in Littlehampton, in Lincolnshire, Sheffield, part of his property in the Strand and elsewhere. After the war he abandoned the attempt to live in Arundel Castle and built for himself a smaller dower house in the grounds. He presented a private Bill in Parliament by which, as originally drafted, it appeared that Arundel Castle would be made into an official residence to be maintained in perpetuity out of public funds for the hereditary Earl Marshal.

Some of the fears suggested were indeed not very well informed and somewhat exaggerated but it was evident that the Bill in its original form would at the best not pass without opposition. The Duke therefore wisely withdrew the controversial clauses and the eventual Act merely freed him from the entail by which his family had been bound since the seventeenth century. To that there was no opposition.

By the time of Queen Elizabeth II's coronation, the Duke, by then a mature and middle aged man, no longer required to lean on the authority of an uncle. He was full of the habit of authority. He brought to his task all that hatred of sloppiness which he had inherited from his father. By general consent his handling of the coronation was of outstanding ability. His command was total and effortless. Without apology he brought his military experience to bear, much as he had disliked it himself when subjected to it, in the ceremony's rehearsals, and conducted them as if he were drilling a squad of soldiers. He was clear-headed, authoritative, unruffled, and, if put to it, corrosive. "If the bishops don't learn to walk in step, we shall be here all night", he said on one occasion.

In January 1965 the Duke was responsible for organizing the State funeral of Sir Winston Churchill.* One of his few regrets in the solemn ceremony in which the nation paid its last respect to its wartime leader was that the procession had been two minutes late in reaching St. Paul's Cathedral—the Duke had allowed two minutes less than was necessary. For the preparations for the funeral, however, the Duke had been flexible—using the Thames for the culminating journey, although it ended at Waterloo and not at Gravesend as had been intended.

The Investiture of the Prince of Wales at Caernarvon in 1969 demanded careful budgeting by the Duke since the Treasury allocated £200,000 for the ceremony —another £100,000 would, the Duke believed, have allowed for a more spectacular pageant. Interviewed shortly before the Investiture, the Duke stated it was his responsibility if anything went wrong to "see that nobody flaps".

In the cricket world he became chairman of the Sussex County Cricket Club and was a keen and very active follower of all its fortunes. He inaugurated the custom of offering to all touring teams from abroad a preliminary one-day practice match against an Eleven of his own selecting, on his private ground at Arundel in the last days of April. When there was some doubt about a suitable manager for the M.C.C. team to visit Australia in 1962 to 1963 the world was astonished to learn that the Duke had accepted the managership, with Alec Bedser as his assistant. The gesture was perhaps more spectacular then successful. Australians may be prepared to cheer for royalty but they do not understand very much about dukes. Some cricket professionals are sometimes awkward—the more eminent, it may often be, the more awkward —and are not prepared to be ordered about as if they were no better than bishops. There are on all cricket tours difficult little incidents when fellow guests in hotels complain that cricketers make too much noise at night and the like, and a man as distant from their ambiences as a premier Duke was probably less well suited for delivering such necessary lectures with tact than would have been some more professional manager who had lived the life of a professional player in his day.

Though the Duke knew a good deal about cricket, some of the professionals were not willing to give him credit for his knowledge, and prognostications from him in the press were sometimes greeted by the players with ridicule. Yet these were domestic matters, sufficient perhaps to make it unlikely that the experiment will be repeated, but not sufficient to prevent the public from deriving the correct impression that the Duke was a man ready to mix himself without side in the amusements of the nation.

The Duke was Lord Lieutenant of Sussex from 1949, and president of the Council for the Preservation of Rural England (as it then was) from 1945 to 1971. From 1956 to 1959 he was chairman of the Territorial Army Council; in January 1966 he withdrew a motion on the future of the Territorial Army in the Lords after he had been reassured by Gerald Reynolds.* Minister of Defence for the Army, about the Government's plans to introduce a home defence force as a second tier to the new reserve army. The same year he was president of the Coordinating Committee for the Commemoration of 1066. He became an Elder Brother, Trinity House, in 1965.

The Duke's father had been, for over half a century, the leading Catholic layman in England, from the time when, as a young man, he had taken an active and successful part in securing the Cardinal's hat for John Henry Newman in 1878. Manning had received his hat only in the previous year, although he had been Archbishop of Westminster since 1865, and had been a conspicuous figure and majority leader in the First Vatican Council. The representations of the laity led by the young Duke, who was himself an old pupil of Newman's Oratory School, had great weight in deciding the new Pope Leo XIII to set the seal of Roman approval on the distinguished Oxford convert. From that time forward the fifteenth Duke had been prominent in Catholic causes, built a number of fine churches, like those at Cambridge and Norwich, and it became an obvious part of his son's inheritance that he should learn to carry the responsibilities towards his religion which he had inherited with so much else. Although he lost his father when he was no more than eleven, his uncle, Lord Fitzalan of Derwent, took the father's place in teaching the young Duke to be conscientious in meeting the claims which his co-religionists were certain to make upon him. He became president of the Catholic Union of Great Britain in succession to his uncle, and faithfully attended its meetings, as he did those of a society with a more restricted scope, the Converts' Aid Society, which was founded at the beginning of the century, primarily to help convert clergy, especially those who were married, and who, under the conditions then prevailing, had often to face great financial hardship, and this charity specially appealed to him for its severely practical character.

He always spoke of "Cartholic" (as though there were an "R" before the "T") in the old English Catholic tradition, and he would not have disowned the appellation of being a "Garden of the Soul Catholic", brought up upon, and all his life using, that prayer-book which for two hundred years nourished the piety of English Catholics since Bishop Challoner compiled it for them.

It need hardly be added that he did not welcome the liturgical changes which followed the Second Vatican Council, and he let it be known that when he was received in Private Audience by Pope Paul VI after the canonization of the Forty Martyrs, he left the Pope in no doubt that the changes were widely unwelcome in England and urged him to make no more changes.

With his family he attended that function as the kinsman of one of the Forty, Philip Howard, Earl of Arundel, who died in the Tower, and he secured, not without some little difficulty, Home Office permission for the re-burial of the Saint's body in the cathedral church at Arundel.

The Duke owned and bred many horses, and although his sky blue and scarlet colours had a big following, especially at Epsom, Brighton, Goodwood and other south country meetings, he never won a classic race. The 1961 Gimcrack Stakes winner, Sovereign Lad, Sound Track and the two-year-old Skymaster were among the best horses to be trained at Arundel, but it is not as an owner or breeder but as an administrator that he will be remembered by those connected with horse-racing. He was elected a member of the Jockey Club in 1933 and of the National Hunt

Committee five years later.

In 1974 his four-year-old Ragstone, trained at Arundel by John Dunlop, won the Ascot Gold Cup. Trainers who worked for him included Charles Chapman, J. F. Bancroft, Willie Smyth, Gordon Smyth and John Dunlop, who took over the Arundel stable in 1966.

He was vice-chairman of the Turf Board set up in 1964 to govern the racing industry. He was also chairman of two committees which played a prominent part in reshaping and streamlining the sport. One of these dealt with the future pattern of racing. The other was concerned with doping and its report led to the testing of winners and a fairer procedure for trainers under suspicion. Many racing people, however, will remember him best for his long association—it lasted from 1945 until 1972—with Ascot as the Queen's representative. It was due to his drive and enthusiasm that vast new stands were built and that a new course was constructed for National Hunt racing. A race has now been named after him at Ascot.

The Duke had four daughters. His heir is his cousin, Major-General Lord Beaumont.

February 1, 1975.

Gwladys, Lady Norton-Griffiths, who died on June 1, 1974 at the age of 101, must be the last to have had personal contacts with the musical giants of the late nineteenth century. Wife, mother-in-law and grandmother of Members of Parliament, she was born during Gladstone's first administration and died during Wilson's third. She lived under six monarchs, through the Boer War and both world wars and travelled in every continent except Australia.

Born in 1873, she never knew gas-lighting—her father, Thomas Wood, head of the engineering firm of Browning, Wood and Fox, refused to have it in his house in Gordon Square and converted from candles to electricity.

Gwladys Wood's first career was in music. Clara Schumann, before whom she often played as a child, took an interest in her and she went to Cologne in 1888, studying under Humperdinck, among others. She received a prize from Brahms and was launched as a *Liedersängerin*. She returned to London in the nineties, sang at the "Pops" at St. James's Hall under Richter and others, was accompanied by Siegfried Wagner and Otto Goldschmidt (who considered her voice second only to that of his beloved Jenny Lind) and was making a successful career, even approved by the music critic, George Bernard Shaw, when a nervous complaint compelled her to abandon it.

In 1898-9 she went with her mother to visit a brother in Johannesburg. On the way back, while waiting ship at Zanzibar,

she met by chance the man she was to marry, John Norton Griffiths, who was also returning to England. They married in 1901 and her second career began, as the wife of an international public works contractor. Between 1901 and 1914 she travelled with her husband throughout Canada, the United States, Latin America and West Africa. She was in San Francisco before the earthquake, crossed the Isthmus of Panama before the canal was built, and the Andes by mule in mid-winter when the Trans-Andean Railway was inoperative.

In Angola in 1905, she was the first European woman to live at Lobito. There was a labour shortage for building the Benguela Railway; it was she who went to South Africa and negotiated with Gandhi the indenturing of 1,500 Indian labourers.

In 1909 her husband was elected to Parliament and her third career began, that of political wife and hostess. The entertaining by "Empire Jack" and his wife at their house in West Halkin Street and, during the first Imperial Conference of 1911, at Temple House, Marlow, was legendary. During the First World War besides her war work, Lady Norton-Griffiths, as she then became, minded her husband's Wednesbury constituency during his absence at the fronts. A snap election in the early twenties found Sir John in Brazil. His wife ran his campaign for Wandsworth Central and he arrived on the eve of polling day to garner yet another electoral victory.

Her husband's death in 1930 and the loss of a son at Dunkirk in 1940 served only to fortify her faith, her courage and her indomitable will. When the bombing of London started she moved back there and worked, until the end of the war when she was 72, at the old Westminster Hospital, then a leave hostel.

After the war she became the matriarch. Not one of her 21 children, grandchildren and great-grandchildren (along with a round dozen of their spouses) escaped her influence. Some of them, at different times, were in the United States, Argentina and the more distant parts of Europe. She travelled to see them all, and indeed only stopped annual visits to the Continent when she was 93.

At the age of 95, though still playing an aggressive game of bridge, she could no longer hold a pen to write. Undaunted, she bought a typewriter and even during her hundredth year hammered out letters with one finger to her descendants and others.

June 3, 1974

Antonin Novotny, President of Czechoslovakia from 1957 to 1968, died in Prague on January 28, 1975 at the age of 70.

Antonin Novotny was born in Prague of working-class parents on December 10, 1904.

After an elementary education he was apprenticed as a locksmith, and at an early age he became a political activist. When the Social Democratic Party split in 1921 the young Novotny was a founder member of the Czech Communist Party, and in 1929 he became a Communist Party functionary.

This was the era of "Stalinization" in the communist movement, and Novotny had many of the qualities which brought Thaelmann to the top in Germany and Thorez* in France. He was conspicuously proletarian, energetic and tough, unswervingly loyal to the Moscow line, impatient of intellectuals and of ideological vacillation.

In 1937 he was promoted to a leading position in the Prague party organization, was sent in the same year to Moravia to take charge of the party organization and newspaper at Hodonin, and after the Munich Agreement returned to Prague as one of the regional secretaries. He helped to build up an underground resistance movement until September 1941, when he was arrested by the Gestapo.

It was of considerable advantage to Novotny at various points in his later career that he spent the remainder of the war years neither in London nor in the Soviet Union, but in Mauthausen concentration camp.

From 1945 until 1951 Novotny served as the Communist Party leading secretary for the Prague region. In 1946 he became a member of the party Central Committee and in September 1951 he was elevated to its secretariat. This appointment was part of a reshuffle in preparation for the purge in which, among others, Rudolf Slansky, the former Secretary General of the party, and Vladimir Clementis, former Foreign Minister, perished.

Novotny took Slansky's place in the Politburo in December 1951, as the most important of the middle generation of party functionaries who now reinforced Gottwald's Muscovites. In September 1953 he succeeded Gottwald as First Secretary of the party.

In November 1957 Novotny became President of the Republic and was to combine this office with the party leadership until his political fall in 1968.

The office of presidency had been held in high esteem ever since its original occupation by T. G. Masaryk and in postwar Czechoslovakia it continued to be given a greater emphasis than is usual in communist political systems.

Novotny, however, was not a popular President. From the time of the Twentieth Party Congress of the Soviet Communist Party and Khrushchev's attack on "Stalinism", he became potentially vulnerable. That he survived so long may be associated with the relatively satisfactory rate of growth of the Czechoslovak economy during the 1950s, with Novotny's power of appointment and ability to manipulate the Communist Party machine, and with the support which he enjoyed from Soviet party leaders.

Novotny's relationship with Khrushchev was particularly close and this helped him to survive the various attacks on "Stalinism" which in Czechoslovakia were frequently veiled attempts to undermine the position of Novotny and the system of arbitrary power which he personified.

From the early 1960s onwards, when the Czechoslovak Communist Party was shaken by an economic crisis, by Slovak resentment of Czech hegemony (which had been made more explicit in the 1960 Constitution), and by the discontent of the intelligentsia, Novotny's position was a difficult one.

Early in 1962 Rudolf Barak, a member of the Politburo and Vice-Premier, was deprived of his party and governmental posts, and subsequently sentenced to 15 years' imprisonment after a secret trial. Although the main charge against him was embezzlement of public funds, in reality he was punished for attempting to depose Novotny and to succeed to his office.

Barak wrote a letter to Khrushchev in which he alleged that Novotny was closer to the Chinese than to the Russians in his opinions. Khrushchev passed the letter on to Novotny and Barak's imprisonment quickly followed.

In 1963 Novotny was forced to respond to national feelings in Slovakia by sacrificing the First Secretary of the Slovak Central Committee, Karol Bacilek, who had been in charge of the security forces during the great purge, and his close colleague, Viliam Siroky, the Prime Minister, who had been attacked for his part in the persecution of Slovak "bourgeois nationalists". The economic crisis forced further concessions from Novotny. By the end of 1964 he had given his blessing in principle to the economic reform proposals of Professor Ota Sik, although he was far from enthusiastic about them.

A new crisis within the party at the end of 1967 led in early January to Novotny's replacement as First Secretary by Alexander Dubcek. Novotny had become increasingly self-confident and opinionated as the years went by, and his brusque manner towards close colleagues had the effect of losing him valuable friends.

In March the National Assembly joined in the attack and the Praesidium of the Central Council of Trade Unions sent a letter to Novotny demanding his resignation. With pressure mounting on him from all sides, Novotny resigned from the presidency on March 22. The final indignity followed in June 1968, when a plenary session of the Central Committee deprived Novotny of membership of the committee and suspended him from the party.

It is an indication of the degree of unpopularity which Novotny had acquired in Czechoslovakia that even in the period after Soviet armed intervention and after the replacement of Dubcek as party First Secretary in April 1969, no serious attempt at the rehabilitation of Novotny was made.

Although Dubcek's removal was quickly followed by the return to leading positions of conservative communists who had been closely associated with Novotny, the former President played no part in these events and lived quietly in retirement, until he was allowed to rejoin the party in 1971.

As a politician, Antonin Novotny possessed neither intellectual power nor oratorical skill. His abilities were those of an organizer, of one who knew how to manipulate the party machine. Finally, however, he became a liability even to the conservative section of the Czechoslovak Communist Party whose views he shared, and the end of his political career was mourned by few.

January 29, 1975.

Lord Nugent, G.C.V.O., M.C., who died on April 27, 1973 at the age of 77, was Comptroller, Lord Chamberlain's Department, 1936-60 and since then a Permanent Lord-in-waiting to the Queen.

He combined the style of an Ouida Guards officer with a spontaneous kindliness and infectious sense of humour that made him welcome in all the many and varied circles in which he moved. "Tim" Nugent's tall, elegant figure passed easily from attendance at Court to the company of music-hall artists, from the Long Room at Lord's to the Turf Club, and wherever he found himself he was among friends. His wide knowledge of the world, capacity for hard work, common sense and tact enabled him to succeed in several difficult roles.

Terence Edmund Gascoigne Nugent was born on August 11, 1895, the second son of Brigadier-General G. C. Nugent. The family had served for some five generations in the Grenadiers and his father transferred to the Irish Guards on their formation in 1900. Tim went from Eton, where he played in the XI, to the Irish Guards in November 1914, was wounded and in 1917 became adjutant of the battalion commanded by the future Lord Alexander of Tunis.

After the war he served as Personal Assistant to the Chief of the Imperial General Staff and went with the Duke and Duchess of York on their tour in 1927 of Australia and New Zealand. From 1937 to 1952 he was Extra-Equerry to George VI, then to the Queen, and from 1936 to 1960 Comptroller of the Lord Chamberlain's Department.

There he managed the delicate and controversial conduct of stage censorship with consummate skill. Harbingers of the permissive society railed against the anomaly of a retired officer of Foot Guards seated in St. James's Palace, blue-pencilling theatrical scripts. But the theatre people liked and trusted him and the B.B.C., over which he had no jurisdiction, often unofficially consulted him. A keen amateur both of straight plays and musical shows, he cut only with reluctance what he knew would be regarded as over the odds by public opinion of the day. Tolerant he was, but hard to fool. When he had passed a script so blameless that it might have been read aloud at a church assembly, he was liable to check on the performance after some weeks when it was being played on a Saturday night in the provinces, remote from St. James's Palace.

His other Palace duties involved the organization of the Buckingham Palace Garden Parties and the courts and levees until they were discontinued. The ordering of all official functions fell to him and the silken ease for which they were renowned owed much to his cool judgment and the affection in which he was held. His letters were models of resourcefulness and tact. He would handle an awkward subject with honesty and candour and his sincerity was so transparent that he never gave offence. His conversation always added to the gaiety of a company, large or small. The love of cricket he had never lost since his Eton days was rewarded when, to his great delight, he was made President of the M.C.C. in 1966.

He married in 1935 Rosalie, daughter of Brigadier-General the Hon. Charles Willoughby, who survives him. She entered into all his activities and they made a perfectly suited pair. They had no children.

April 30, 1973.

Paavo Nurmi, who died on October 2, 1973 at the age of 76, has been often called the greatest runner of all time. The "Flying Finn", as he was dubbed, won no fewer than seven individual Olympic gold medals, and between 1921 and 1931 accounted for more than two dozen world records at distances ranging from 1,500 to 10,000 metres.

Probably Nurmi's greatest contribution to athletics was in showing the world that hard training coupled with an iron will could produce performances undreamt of by previous generations. It is to Nurmi that much of the credit for the present standard of long distance running must be attributed, for it is he who showed the way.

Paavo Johannes Nurmi was born in Turku on June 13, 1897. Paavo took up running at the age of nine and quickly began to beat much older boys at school. His father died in 1910 and so, at the age of 13, Paavo was obliged to start work as an errand boy to help maintain his family.

Like many of his young countrymen, Nurmi was inspired by the news of the three long-distance running victories of the Finn Hannes Kolehmainen, at the 1912 Olympic Games in Stockholm. It was in that year that he embarked on a training routine that was to continue for over 20 years.

He became obsessed by running. His whole existence revolved around it. Because he thought it would help his track career

he became a vegetarian, abstained from drinking tea and coffee, and rarely mixed with people of his own age.

Progress was slow, though, and it was not until 1919, while in the Army, that he started to make a mark for himself in Finnish athletics. The following season he burst on to the international scene, winning both the 10,000 metres track event and the 8,000 metres cross-country, as well as being placed second in the 5,000 metres at the 1920 Olympic Games in Antwerp.

He had become a national hero, yet that defeat in the 5,000 metres rankled. He took to carrying a stopwatch in training and competition in order to perfect his pace judgment. This practice was ridiculed at first but within a short time the uncanny sense of pace that he developed was to pay handsome dividends. He became the complete runner, able to burn off the opposition with his relentless stride or to hold back and win with his devastating final sprint. He was the combined David Bedford and Jim Ryun of his day for in 1923, while holder of the world 10,000 metres record, he became the fastest miler thus far, with a time of 4 minutes 10.4 seconds.

Although more than 30 years were to elapse before Roger Bannister transformed hopes into deeds, Nurmi stated there and then that a four-minute mile was feasible. The very next day he set a world three miles record, but even that double pales in comparison with his feat of June 19, 1924, when in the space of one hour he accomplished world records for both 1,500 and 5,000 metres. Not surprisingly, he won both these events at the Paris Olympics the following month; but, astonishingly (for he had to run seven races in six days) he also won more gold medals in the 3,000 metres team race and 10,000 metres cross-country. He would probably have won the 10,000 metres track race too, had he been selected. It is said that while his countryman, Ville Ritola, was winning the event in the world record time of 30 minutes 23.2 seconds the disgruntled Nurmi was running the distance solo in training in 29 minutes 58 seconds.

He recaptured his 10,000 metres crown at the 1928 Olympics in Amsterdam and might well have climaxed his career with victory in the 1932 Olympic marathon had he not been disqualified just before the Los Angeles games for alleged professionalism.

But it was not quite the end for Nurmi. Reinstated for domestic competition only, he returned in 1933, aged 36, to win the Finnish 1,500 metres final, and in 1952 he was given the honour of carrying the Olympic torch at the opening ceremony of the Helsinki Games.

Nurmi became a successful businessman but remained rather withdrawn and aloof all his life. His long final illness was particularly embittering to a man who once said: "I love to run. It is my life. As long as I can I shall do so".

October 3, 1973.

Lord Trevethin and Oaksey, who died on August 28, 1971 at the age of 90, was the third holder of the Trevethin barony, having succeeded to the title on the death of his brother in 1959. He was also the first Baron Oaksey, the title he took when appointed a Law Lord in 1957, and by which he still wished to be known.

As Lord Justice Lawrence he was British President of the International Tribunal at Nuremberg in 1945.

The youngest son of the first Lord Trevethin, Lord Chief Justice of England from 1921 to 1922, Geoffrey Lawrence was born on December 2, 1880. He was a Judge of the King's Bench Division from 1932 to 1944, when he was appointed a Lord Justice of Appeal. He had proved an excellent Judge throughout his career. Like his father he was careful, patient, and invariably courteous; irrelevancies and facetiousness found no place in his court. Good sense characterized both his summings-up and his judgments, and appeals from him were seldom successful.

In September 1945 he was called on to play in world affairs a part which had never before fallen to a member of the English judiciary, for he was appointed British President of the International Tribunal "unique in the history of the jurisprudence of the world", to use his words in opening the trial of the major war criminals at Nuremberg on November 20, 1945.

Lawrence, or Oaksey as he will be referred to from now on, was educated at Haileybury and at New College, Oxford, of which he was made an hon. Fellow in 1944. He was called to the Bar by the Inner Temple in 1906, and joined the Oxford Circuit. His career at the Bar was an unusual one. He entered the Chambers of Sir Robert (afterwards Lord) Finlay, then at the height of a very large practice, chiefly before the House of Lords and the Judicial Committee of the Privy Council. In the preparation of his cases before the latter tribunal, Finlay relied much on Oaksey as his principal assistant, and in time he came to be briefed as junior to Finlay, as often as not in Canadian appeals, in conjunction with counsel from the Dominion.

The 1914-18 war closed down his legal career for some four years and he served in the Herts R.F.A. during the whole of the war. He was twice mentioned in dispatches, and was awarded the D.S.O. Subsequently he commanded the 86th Brigade R.A. (T.A.) and attained the rank of colonel. He retained his active connexion with the Territorial Army until 1937, when he retired.

On resuming his practice, it continued to flourish chiefly at the Privy Council, but he also obtained work on the Oxford Circuit and in the Law Courts. In 1919 he appeared as junior counsel for Great Britain at the North Atlantic Fisheries arbitration at The Hague. He had in common with his father an interest in horses, and in 1922 he was appointed counsel to the Jockey Club. (He was also a prominent member of the Pegasus Club, and in his earlier years rode in the Bar Point-to-Point Races.) In 1924 he was made Recorder of Oxford and in 1927 he became an Examiner in Ecclesiastical Causes. He was appointed Attorney-General for the Prince of Wales. He held the above offices till he was elevated to the High Court Bench in 1932. In 1927 he had taken silk and was a Commissioner of Assize on the Oxford Circuit in June 1931.

In April 1932, on the promotion of Mr. Justice Wright to be a Lord of Appeal in Ordinary, Oaksey was nominated as a Judge of the King's Bench Division. His father, the former Lord Chief Justice, was present on the Bench at his swearing-in.

Of great personal modesty, he neither magnified nor advertised either himself or his office, and in consequence his name was little known to the general public. When in July 1944 Lord Justice (afterwards Lord Chief Justice) Goddard was appointed a Lord of Appeal in Ordinary, Oaksey was promoted to the Court of Appeal.

In September 1945 in pursuance of Article 2 of the charter of the international military tribunal for the trial of the major war criminals of the European Axis Powers, he was appointed to be the British member of the tribunal with Mr. Justice Birkett* as the alternative member. It was no easy task to preside over a Court composed of British, American, French and Soviet Judges, but Oaksey succeeded and obtained, and retained to the last, the admiration and goodwill of his colleagues. As previously on the Bench at home, he was the embodiment of good sense and good temper, always alive to the point and considerate to the argument on both sides. His authority and reputation grew as the hearings proceeded.

In his book, *Political Adventure*, Lord Kilmuir* (who, as Sir David Maxwell-Fyfe, was Britain's Deputy Chief Prosecutor at Nuremberg) writing of Lawrence said: "The central figure of the trial was Lord Justice Lawrence, afterwards Lord Oaksey. He personified the great tradition of the English Common Law that the judge should hold the ring and not descend into the argumentative area. But he did hold it, insisted on understanding the relevance of each piece of evidence in the complicated pattern of the indictment, and was quick to stop irrelevance or repetition on the part of the prosecution or the defence. One particularly able observer of the trial has justly written that it might easily have fallen into an unintelligible morass of paper without the meticulously ordered mind of Lord Justice Lawrence to guide it. . . . At this focal point of five nations, bent on perhaps the most far-reaching legal inquiry of all time . . . Lawrence stood out with the modest dignity and firm discipline of an English gentleman in the true meaning of the word. . . . Nuremberg was not a pleasant occasion, and there were very few moments when the almost suffocating grimness of the court room was lightened, but Lawrence gave the trial a humanity, which brought it up to the level required by a civilized concept of justice."

In the New Year's Honours List in 1947 he was raised to the peerage under the title of Baron Oaksey of Oaksey, in the County of Wiltshire. When, in 1947, two additional Lords of Appeal in Ordinary were appointed Oaksey was one of them, and he sat as a Law Lord not only in the House of Lords, but sometimes also on the Judicial Committee of the Privy Council, the scene of his earliest success when a very junior member of the Bar.

His chief hobby was farming, and at Malmesbury he specialized in breeding pedigree Guernsey cattle. He also collected pictures and china.

He was for several years chairman of the Quarter Sessions Appeal Committee for Wiltshire. He was Vice-Lieutenant of the county from 1954.

He married in 1921 Marjorie, elder daughter of the late Commander Charles N. Robinson, R.N. and they had one son and three daughters. The son, who succeeds him, is John Lawrence, well known as an amateur jockey and racing journalist.

August 30, 1971.

André Obey, the French writer, died in Montsoreau on April 12, 1975 in his 83rd year. After service in the First World War, during which he was wounded, he worked as a journalist in Paris writing music and drama criticism, sports notices, essays, short stories and several novels.

His last novel, the autobiographical *Le Joueur de Triangle*, won the Theophraste Renaudot prize in 1928. From that point he wrote exclusively for the stage until 1971, when his last play, *Le Jour de Retour*, was first produced at the Comédie Française.

Obey wrote a score of dramas which singled him out as one of France's most imaginative dramatic poets of the day. He also excelled in translations and adaptations from the classics. Among Obey's modern adaptations, *Cat on a Hot Tin Roof*, which Peter Brook staged in Paris, and Reginald Rose's *Twelve Angry Men* proved highly effective.

Obey wrote some of his most durable dramas inspired by biblical or classical themes, as resident writer for the Compagnie des Quinze. *Noé*, produced at the Vieux Colombier in 1931, and notable for the speaking animals in the cast, visited the Arts Theatre in London and the Ambassadors the same year, where it was followed by *Le Vol De Lucrèce*. *Noah*, translated by Arthur Wilmurt, became a starring vehicle for John Gielgud in 1935; it and Thornton Wilder's adaptation of *Lucrèce* were to become firm favourites on both sides of the Atlantic.

La Bataille de la Marne, an anti-war drama, won the Eugène Brieux Prize in 1932, and *Don Juan* had a world premiere at London's Globe Theatre with Pierre Fresnay in the title role in 1934.

Une fille pour du Vent, first seen in France in 1953, was adapted by John Whiting as *Sacrifice to the Wind* for the Arts Theatre in 1955. It was a bitterly-felt pacifist drama, inspired by the tragedy of the Trojan War; and this theme, though treated light heartedly, also informed Obey's last play. *Frost at Midnight (Les Trois Coups de Minuit)* was seen at the Hampstead Theatre Club in 1963. In 1965 Obey was awarded the Pierre de Coubertin Prize. In 1954 he was Head of Drama and Letters in French radio, and in 1945 served as Director of Theatre in the Ministry of Arts and Letters.

Obey belonged to the prewar generation that strongly influenced the direction taken by the postwar French theatre, but more recently he tended to look askance at the open brutality with which the humanitarian topics so dear to his heart were being expressed.

April 25, 1975.

Kate O'Brien, the novelist and playwright, died on August 13, 1974 at the age of 76.

She was Irish and her own people and their land inspired her most remarkable work. In regard to them her touch was unfaltering and her pen incisive. She saw deeply into the psychology of the Irish middle-class and was able to recreate an historical period with unusual conviction. Knowing Spain intimately she could write of it almost as confidently as of Ireland. Her taste was impeccable and she had subtlety, beauty and imagination at her command.

Kate O'Brien was born in 1897 the fourth daughter of Thomas O'Brien of Boru House, Limerick. She was educated at Laurel Hill Convent in that city and went on to University College, Dublin. Then, moving to England, she entered journalism and was for some time in Manchester on the staff of the then *Manchester Guardian*. Also as a young woman she found employment for a year at Bilbao in Spain, a country which she loved and came to know extremely well.

In 1926 her first attempt at drama, *Distinguished Villa*, was produced at the Little Theatre. It was a drab and distressing play; but it was saved by the patience and accuracy of its observation and by the deep sympathy with which several of its persons were treated. It proved that the strength of its authoress lay not in her hatreds but in her affections. The next year The Arts Club Theatre put on *The Bridge*. It too displayed her keen appreciation of character, but it also indicated that she had a deep sense of the sadness of human lives in their varied entanglements. It had, however, some defects of laboriousness which tended to conceal its qualities.

It was not until 1931 that she published *Without My Cloak*. It showed her to be a writer of fine originality who could exert and sustain an unusual power. Her scene was laid in a provincial town in Victorian Ireland and her characters were middle-class Irish people. It was a world which had lasted into her own time and the fidelity and feeling of her presentation made it an exceptional first novel. It won the Hawthornden Prize and the James Tait Black Memorial Prize. J. B. Priestley described it as a "peculiarly beautiful and arresting piece of fiction".

In 1934 *The Ante-Room* returned to the large Victorian family whose saga had occupied its predecessor, though in this case the action was limited to three days. While a mother, worrying to the last about her children, lay dying, Miss O'Brien gathered them together, as it were in the ante-room, in an atmosphere of suspense and hidden conflict. Collaborating with Geoffrey Gomer and W. A. Carot, she turned it into a play. Staged at the Queen's Theatre in 1936, it was a skilful piece of work, for out of the quietude of a remote Ireland a sense of tension grew; but the difficulty of compressing a subtle and slowly-moving study of temperaments within the compass of the stage proved at times too great. There was, a reviewer wrote, nothing to shout about, but much to admire.

Mary Lavelle, which appeared in the same year, was the idyll of an Irish governess in Spain. Deep understanding was again combined with a sharp power of characterization. *The School-room Window* was a play produced in 1937 at the Manuscript Theatre Club, a well written, slightly sentimental study of a cultivated family in an emotional crisis. *Farewell Spain*, a travel book, was timely in so far as the country she made her subject was, when she published it, a centre of world attention. Much of her description possessed high merit; but it was a difficult moment to have chosen for a book of great reflective quality.

Then in *Pray for the Wanderer*, in 1938, Miss O'Brien returned to her familiar Ireland. It had desultory charm, but the theme was slender and conventional. The time was contemporary, and though there was plenty of politics in it, she avoided rancour.

After an interval of two years, *The Last of Summer* was County Clare just before the outbreak of the war. It was high romance; another of her assured and fine-edged pieces of work. She had witten *That Lady* in 1946, and her later books included *My Ireland* in 1962 and *Presentation Parlour* in 1963.

August 14, 1974.

General Manuel Odría, the military strongman who was President of Peru from 1948 to 1956, died in Lima on February 18, 1974 at the age of 76.

A short, forceful man of mixed Spanish and Indian blood, he had the intelligence to realize that the old aristocratic oligarchy in Peru was gradually losing its power and that a leader had to gain the popularity of the people and had to support social progress. After seizing power in 1948 from the democratically elected President Bustamante, he stood for election in 1950 and was returned unopposed after his opponents had their candidatures declared out of order.

His rule was dictatorial and harsh and his political opponents on the left, particularly the members of A.P.R.A., the left-wing socialist movement led by Haya de la Torre, were kept quiet by extremely repressive measures. He did however give Peru a period of stability, built hospitals and schools and gave social benefits to the workers. It was a time of economic advance and relative peacefulness, but at a cost of the complete loss of political liberty.

Odría was born in Tarma, a small, neat town in the Andes on November 26, 1897 and he enrolled as a cadet at the officers' college at Chorrillos where he became a second lieutenant in 1919, eventually attaining the rank of major.

In 1936 he was promoted to lieutenant-colonel and, while he was chief of staff of the First Light Division, his contingent took part in the short frontier conflict with Ecuador in 1941. He rose to become Chief of the Armed General Staff and briefly served as Minister of Government and Police.

After a revolt from both left-wing and right-wing elements, in 1948, Odría began a military operation from the southern town of Arequipa—the traditional launching-place for coups d'états—and President Bustamante, the respected lawyer who had tried to rule with the help of the *Apristas,* was bundled off into exile in Argentina. Immdiately the *Apristas* were wanted men, and Haya de la Torre found refuge in the Colombian embassy in Lima. There he remained for five years during which time his case became a *cause célèbre* and was fought up to the International Court of Justice. The court's decision was unclear and eventually Odría allowed his old political enemy to leave the country.

When his term of office finished in 1956 Odría decided not to stand again. There had been a few abortive military plots and the old Peruvian problem—the fact that the Indians in the *sierra* were inadequately fed and housed and remained outside the economy—had not been tackled. Odría did however nominate a successor to carry on his policies, but he ran well behind in the elections.

Six years later, Odría began to campaign again. Forming the *Union Nacional Odriista* and using the electoral slogan "Deeds not Words", he offered Peruvians his old formula of order, anti-communism and social progress. He came third, while Haya de la Torre topped the poll, but without the necessary one-third lead to be declared outright winner. It looked as if Haya de la Torre would do a deal with Odría, granting him the presidency in return for certain concessions. This strange mixing of right-wing and left-wing forces damaged both of their reputations and the charge of opportunism was laid at both their doors. The army, meanwhile, who had fought for years against allowing the *Apristas* to hold power, moved quickly and took over. In the elections of the following year Odría again came third, and the young Fernando Belaúnde, who offered a moderate left-wing programme, gained the presidency.

Now an old man, Odría joined his forces with that of Haya de la Torre in the congress and blocked many of Belaúnde's reforms. The cartoonists in the Lima newspapers pictured Odría as a feeble has-been suffering from foot trouble, while Haya de la Torre would be seen continually sleeping —his old radicalism supposedly dead. The two fierce enemies were in old age political buddies. Anything is possible in Latin American politics.

Odría's support dwindled steadily although his party leaders could still gain votes, particularly in the slums of Lima, where they would use fireworks to attract attention and remind the poor of the economic advances in the early 1950s.

February 19, 1974.

Sean O'Feeney—See John Ford.

David Oistrakh, the most admired Russian violinist of his generation, died suddenly in Amsterdam on October 24, 1974. He was 66.

One of the first Soviet artists to be able, in the friendlier atmosphere prevailing between Russia and the West after the middle 1950s, to travel widely, the superb technical quality of his playing and the sumptuousness of his tone were admired all over the world. He was the outstanding exponent of a school of violin-playing which is specifically and traditionally Russian.

David Fyodorovich Oistrakh—his mother was an opera-singer and his father an amateur violinist—was born in Odessa on September 30, 1908, and educated at the Musical and Dramatic Institute of his home town. From the age of 18, when he first began to tour Russia as a soloist, his career seemed to be a series of undisputed conquests. He was first heard in both Leningrad and Moscow in 1928; in 1930 he won the first prize in the Ukrainian Violin Competition in Kharkov and, following the Russian custom (jealously preserved by the Soviet Government) of feeding the finest soloists into the academies as teachers of their instruments, he was appointed Lecturer at Moscow Conservatoire. In 1934 he won the Wieniawski prize in Warsaw.

Concerts in Paris and Brussels in 1937 brought him for the first time into the reach of audiences in Western Europe, but another 14 years—those of the Second World War and its politically disturbed aftermath—passed before he was able to play again beyond what had in the meantime come to be known as the "Iron Curtain".

They were years of continued triumph in Russia. In 1939 he was appointed Professor of Violin at Moscow Conservatoire, and in 1942 he was awarded a Stalin Prize. After his appearance at the Florence Festival in 1951, which was his return to the international scene, he paid a second visit to Paris in 1953 and first played in London a year later. Visits to Japan, Germany and the United States followed in 1955. From then onwards, he was the most busily occupied of Russian musicians outside his own country, and his occasional appearances with his son Igor Oistrakh (who by 1960 had proved himself to be a formidably gifted violinist) suggested something of his quality as a teacher, for his son had been one of his pupils in Moscow.

Oistrakh's repertoire was wide, and he gave great vitality, rich breadth of tone and unusual sensitiveness to all the major concertos and to the classical violin and piano sonatas in which he was more rarely heard. He was particularly associated with the first concerto of Shostakovich, which was dedicated to him; its first performance outside Russia took place when Oistrakh played it in London in 1956. Among his favourite works was Elgar's concerto. Oistrakh, however, never exploited these personal gifts as things in themselves worthy of an audience's attention; he was always a musician dedicated to the work he was playing.

Familiarity with London, where he was made an honorary fellow of the Royal Academy of Music in 1959, and friendship with musicians active in Britain, notably with Yehudi Menuhin, led to a fruitful extension of his activities in London, as in the concerts in which he and Menuhin appeared as conductors of each other's concertos. Though a gift for conducting was not among Oistrakh's most striking qualities, his appearances on the rostrum always led to efficient performances entirely in sympathy with the aims of the soloist.

A vigorously tough, genial man with the face of a rather battered Socrates, David Oistrakh was by nature direct, forthright, friendly and interested in the world. An occasion on which he was unable to find a dinner in Kensington—demanded by the exigencies of travel but not available at an unconventional hour in the early evening—became, through his amusement at the situation, something of a comic pilgrimage in search of food. To have met him, if only briefly, was to carry away memories of cheerful, immediate friendliness as well

as of a personality devoted to the art which he served with rare authority and sensitivity.

Shostakovich wrote a second violin concerto for Oistrakh in 1967. Not considered quite the equal of the first, it was nevertheless, in Oistrakh's hands, a work of considerable accomplishment. The composer also wrote a violin sonata for Oistrakh in 1968, to celebrate the violinist's sixtieth birthday. He was also an expert in Prokofiev's violin music and was very friendly with the composer. Chess was Oistrakh's great hobby and he and Prokofiev often played the game together, once taking part in an official match. In 1969 Cambridge University conferred an honorary degree on him.

He leaves a large and varied legacy of recordings, many of them made in Britain for E.M.I., including quite recently a set of all the Mozart violin concertos and a new stereo version of the first Shostakovich. His recordings of the Beethoven and Brahms are considered classics. Oistrakh last played in London in the "Days of Russian music" in November 1972, but was due in Britain for a concert tour as soloist and conductor during the weekend after he died.

October 25, 1974.

Lady O'Malley, who as a novelist wrote under the name of Ann Bridge, died on March 9, 1974.

Born in 1891, the daughter of James Harris Sanders, Mary Dolling Sanders was educated at home and at the London School of Economics. She married Sir Owen O'Malley, [q.v.,] a diplomat, in 1913. It was the scene and social environment of his various diplomatic appointments abroad, beginning with that as Counsellor at the Peking Legation in 1925, that she drew upon for the works she wrote. Her first novel *Peking Picnic*, published in 1932, was a lively commentary on the ways and habits of the foreign legations in Peking, filled in with nicely observed and picturesque Chinese detail. After that, however, although she was almost always graceful and interesting, she was inclined to fall back upon a rather artificial and overromantic animation by way of making up for a want of serious substance in her fiction.

It was again the life of the foreign legations in Peking that she celebrated in *The Ginger Griffin* (1934), which was shrewdly and amusingly done. Then came *Illyrian Spring* (1935), which had the Dalmation coast for its setting; *Enchanter's Nightshade* (1937), with an Italian background; and *Four-Part Setting*, in which once more she returned to China.

In *Frontier Passage* (1942) she surveyed the more romantic aspects of the civil war in Spain from the vantage point of Saint-Jean de Luz, while *Singing Waters* (1945) was a fluent but opulent story with an Albanian background.

Two of her later works, *The Dark Moment* (1952) dealing with Ataturk's national revolution and *The Portuguese Escape* (1958), were Choices of the Literary Guild of America. Her last book was *Permission to Resign* (1971) in which she told of her successful fight to clear her husband's name after he had been asked to resign from the Foreign Office—he had been accused in 1928 of currency speculation.

There were three children of the marriage, a son and two daughters.

March 11, 1974.

Sir Owen O'Malley, K.C.M.G., a former British Ambassador to Poland and Portugal, died on April 16, 1974 at Oxford. He was 86.

The son of Sir Edward O'Malley, he was educated at Radley and Magdalen. He passed first into the Foreign Office in 1911 and started work under Sir Eyre Crowe, whose famous paper on the German menace had been written a few years before and who was to be the one great hero of O'Malley's life. Crowe at once recognized O'Malley's remarkable abilities and allowed him—he needed no encouragement—to think ahead and imaginatively and to put his thoughts on to paper. O'Malley could write brilliantly, but it is doubtful whether on balance Crowe's influence was beneficial to O'Malley's career or not.

Juniors are liable to be judged by the extent to which they save trouble to their seniors by meticulous discharge of humdrum tasks and, once the influence of Crowe, who was a stickler for routine, was removed O'Malley too often allowed himself the luxury of spending time on lengthy if penetrating analyses when he might, with more profit to his own interests, have been making himself indispensable by beavering away at the dull day-to-day stuff. Thus when in 1928 he became involved in the so-called "francs case" (when some members of the foreign service were accused of speculating in francs) and later when he pleaded not to be posted abroad, he had not built up the kind of position in the Foreign Office which would have enabled many a lesser man more devoted to his desk to escape censure or get his own way.

As things turned out, his appointment to Peking in 1925, however unwelcome at the time, was doubly fortunate. O'Malley, essentially a countryman, loved the outdoor life which a diplomat in Peking was then able to enjoy, and Lady O'Malley (he had married Miss Mary Sanders in 1913) found there the material which she embodied, in 1932, in her first successful novel *Peking Picnic,* written under the name of Ann Bridge.

After two happy and successful years in China, O'Malley returned to the Foreign Office and stayed there until 1937, working in the departments which dealt with Germany and Italy. Crowe had died in 1925 and during these critical years O'Malley was always conscious of his figure standing behind him and he was bitterly disappointed, when he became due for promotion, that room was not found for him in the Foreign Office as an Assistant Under-Secretary. Instead he was sent as Minister to Mexico City.

Soon after his arrival, the Mexican Government expropriated the Mexican Eagle Oil Co. and O'Malley was plunged into a first-class crisis which ended with the Mexican Government, stung by a tactless reference to their financial record in a note which O'Malley had been instructed to deliver, withdrawing their Minister from London and the Foreign Office at once followed suit.

On his return to London, O'Malley was for a while without a post (and, incidentally, under the financial regulations then prevailing, without a salary) but after a few months he was sent to St. Jean de Luz to act as Chargé d'Affaires in the British Embassy to Spain. In 1939 he was moved to Budapest as Minister, and in December 1941, when war was declared on Hungary, he became Ambassador to the Polish Government in London. He held this post until 1945 when he succeeded Sir Ronald Campbell as Ambassador in Lisbon, retiring from there in 1947 when he reached the age of 60.

As British ambassador to Poland writing in his temporary embassy in London, he was the author of the brilliant pungently-expressed despatch examining the massacre in 1940 of upwards of 10,000 Polish officers at Katyn Wood. His report was sent to Anthony Eden (Lord Avon), then Foreign Secretary, in May 1943. The Foreign Office was disconcerted by this "brilliant, unorthodox and disquieting despatch" which reconstructed the cold-blooded execution of unarmed men. It established beyond reasonable doubt that the responsibility on the evidence available lay with the Russians.

It was a varied career at an eventful epoch but to O'Malley, conscious as he was of his great talents, a disappointing one; for with the exception of some highly successful negotiations with the Chinese over the British concession in Hankow, he could not look back on any special moment of triumph when he had been able to influence policy or sway events.

The truth is that he was miscast as a diplomat. His powerful intellect was not matched with the kind of warm personality which secures results in a trade where "the ruling few" are seldom influenced, far less guided, by pure reason. Moreover, to use modern jargon, his was a mixed-up personality. The reason for this will be clear to anybody who reads the chapters recording his youth in his enchanting autobiography *The Phantom Caravan*.

He had as a result few men friends and when he was liked it was often in spite of himself. He despised the venial insincerities of polite society and was liable to

show his contempt too openly for the comfort of his associates. He could be embarrassingly and deliberately unfastidious and he could allow his ever-active defence mechanism to manifest itself in a kind of truculent banter which was not always appreciated. Withal, when he felt that the occasion demanded it, he could be a charming and genial host—or guest; and those who knew him well will recall with pleasure the very different and lovable side of his character which was seen when the tides of fortune flowed against him. His self-consciousness fell away, he ceased to dramatize himself and he emerged as a dignified, calm and generous personality.

O'Malley was most genuinely himself in country surroundings and among country people. He was proud of being an autochthonous Irishman, as he called himself, and the happiest days of his life came after his retirement when he removed to Eire and built himself a house on the shores of the Atlantic in County Mayo, labouring there with his own hands and leading a bucolic life in his beloved ancestral homeland. After some years, however, he came to the conclusion that for reasons of health it would be prudent to live in a less remote spot and he decided with sorrow to return to England and settle in Oxford.

Lady O'Malley died a month before Sir Owen.

April 17, 1974.

Sultan of Oman—See Muscat and Oman.

Aristotle Onassis, the Greek shipowner who died in Paris on March 15, 1975 at the age of 69, bequeaths his name, like Croesus, as a household word for riches. A refugee at the age of 17, he set out with a Nansen passport and 60 dollars in his pocket to make his fortune in Argentina.

Half a century later he was one of the wealthiest men in the world. Most of this he owed to that rough, often ruthless, dynamism that has enabled the genius of Greek individualism to thrive abroad.

Born in Izmir, Smyrna, Asia Minor, on January 15, 1906, he was the son of Socrates Onassis, a well-to-do tobacco merchant whose family had lived for generations on the eastern littoral of the Aegean. When Kemal Ataturk defeated the Greeks in 1922, the Onassis family, like millions of other Anatolian Greeks, fled to Greece.

His father and three sisters settled in Athens. He chose to emigrate to Argentina where he found work as a telephone operator for the United River Plate Telephone Company in Buenos Aires.

It was while listening in on international conversations that he managed to learn several foreign languages. At the same time he set out to induce cigarette manufacturers in Argentina to increase their imports of oriental tobacco from Greece and Bulgaria.

Soon he set up his own business and became a reputable tobacco importer. Later he was appointed Greek Consul in Buenos Aires.

This consular post gave him a chance to meet and exchange ideas with many Greek ship captains who aroused his interest in shipping. In 1930 he took advantage of a world slump to buy for $120,000 six Canadian cargo ships which had cost $2m. to build 10 years earlier.

Within one decade he was the owner of a sizable merchant fleet and had taken delivery of his first oil tanker. During the war he rented his ships to the Allies and most of them were lost. However, victory brought its reward: he was allowed to buy from the United States 23 surplus Liberty ships at a low price.

This deal and his marriage in 1946 to Athena, daughter of Stavros Livanos, the leading Greek shipowner, finally confirmed the newcomer in that exclusive maritime club of the "Golden Greeks".

His spectacular ascent was not without tears. The Liberty deal brought him in conflict with the United States Government which insisted that the ships should be under the control of genuinely American companies. He was fined £7m. for this violation, but the charges of criminal conspiracy against him were dropped.

In 1948 he had turned to whale fishing. He set up a fleet of 20 whalers but was soon in trouble with Peru which claimed a 200-mile territorial sea limit. The Peruvians captured some of his whalers and crews. They agreed to release them only after receiving from the shipowner a £3m. fine. This was later defrayed by Lloyd's. He sold his whaling fleet to the Japanese in 1956, at a loss.

Two years later, the international oil companies agreed to boycott his tankers when it was disclosed that he had concluded a secret deal with Saudi Arabia for the exclusive rights of transporting its crude oil. The reprisals were too heavy, so he gave in and the Saudi deal was cancelled.

For all his misadventures, he prospered, mainly thanks to a sixth sense about ordering ships in time for the next cargo boom. In the mid-fifties and the early sixties he placed orders for large oil tankers, at a time when most competitors concentrated on tonnage that could navigate the Suez Canal. When the canal was closed his giant tankers reaped huge profits on their round-the-Cape journeys.

He was a restless financier. In 1953 he managed to buy up the majority shares of the Société des Bains de Mer of Monte Carlo, which controlled the gambling concession and the larger hotels of Monaco. His original plan was to acquire office premises in this tax haven.

However, he disagreed with Prince Rainier over the economic future of the Principality, and this led to a disagreeable feud. Fourteen years later he was forced to sell his shares to Rainier, although at a handsome profit. The head office of his shipping empire remained in Monte Carlo.

In 1956 he won the exclusive concession for the Greek national airlines and founded Olympic Airways, which soon gained an international reputation for efficiency and safety. Through shrewd bargaining and pleading, he managed to extend the concession until the year 2006, and procured significant privileges.

The energy crisis, the Cyprus war, and the Greek political changes in 1974, caused serious losses for Olympic, so he decided to give up the concession and negotiate the handing over with the government.

He first came into the international limelight because of his friendship with Sir Winston Churchill* and Maria Callas, the opera singer, who were frequent guests aboard his luxurious yacht. The Christina, a Canadian frigate converted in 1954 at the cost of $2.5m, eventually became his real home.

During one of the Christina's cruises in 1959, his first marriage with Tina (née Livanos), broke up because of his estranged affections, and led to a divorce the following year. During another Aegean cruise in 1963, he was host to Jacqueline, the wife of President John Kennedy* of America.

In 1963 he purchased the 500-acre islet Skorpios, off the western coast of Greece, which he used more as a home port for the Christina than as a home for himself. It was in the small chapel on Skorpios that he married the widowed Jacqueline Kennedy in October 1968.

While he was on his honeymoon he paid frequent visits to Athens to negotiate with the dictatorial Greek Government a contract for industrial investments worth at least $400m. He was offering to build an oil refinery, a power plant, and an aluminium smelter, in exchange for the exclusive right to produce for Greece all her crude oil requirements.

During these negotiations his rivalry with shipowner Stavros Niarchos, once his brother-in-law, reached a climax. Niarchos undercut him with an offer to the Government and forced him to increase his bid to $600m. He won and the contract was signed in 1969. However, soaring tanker rates and the world wide scarcity of capital forced Onassis to call off the deal.

The Onassis-Niarchos feud, which was touched off when the two men married Livanos's two daughters, was evident through their lives. They vied with each other for the size of their largest tankers, their private yachts, their successive wives, their distinguished friends, their private islands, their Greek contracts, and their paintings. Onassis never forgave Niarchos for taking as his fifth wife Tina, the mother of his two children, Alexander and Christina.

Alexander's death in an air crash in Athens in January 1973, affected his entire outlook in life. Close friends said it had stripped him of the *joie de vivre* which had been such a telling trait in his lifetime. He was proud of Alexander, and had always hoped that when he died his son would have stepped into his shoes to take over and manage the vast financial empire he had built up.

It was an empire that included about 100 companies in a dozen countries, a merchant fleet of 55 ships of 2.5 million tons gross, holdings in banks, shipyards and hotels, as well as Olympic Airways.

Somehow he never wanted to believe that Alexander, who had been an experienced pilot, had died as a result of negligence. On Christmas Day 1974 he put out an announcement offering to pay £360,000 for any conclusive information confirming that Alexander's death was caused by sabotage.

In 1974 he suffered grave muscular illness and later gall bladder trouble.

Earlier in 1974 he had been in hospital in New York for a grave muscular illness. He is survived by his widow Jacqueline and his daughter Christina.

March 17, 1975.

Colette O'Niel—Lady Constance Malleson —actress and writer, who died on October 5, 1975 in her 80th year, was born Lady Constance Annesley, daughter of the 5th Earl of Annesley. At 19 she married Miles Malleson*, the actor, whom she divorced in 1923.

During childhood she lived in the closely-remembered splendour of Castle Wellan, co. Down. There at dinner her father would preside before an enormous window that looks over a three-mile lake to the entire range of the Mourne Mountains.

After education in Europe and at the Royal Academy of Dramatic Art, she began to act during the First World War, when she was also supporting urgently the pacifist beliefs of her husband and their friend Bertrand Russell*.

As intense on the stage as she could be in life, she appeared as Helen, with Sybil Thorndike, in *The Trojan Women* (Old Vic, 1919); in Masefield's* *The Faithful* (Stage Society, 1919); and as the Quaker widow in an *Abraham Lincoln* revival (Lyceum, 1921). In Plymouth she is still recalled for her season—a fresh play weekly—at the Repertory Theatre during autumn 1922.

Later, until retirement in the early 1930s, she had a rich mingling of parts: in a Lyceum drama, *The Orphans*, at the Hull Little Theatre; as Frank Benson's leading lady (Portia, Kate Hardcastle, Lady Teazle) on one of his farewell tours; and abroad with the Cassons.

For a while she lived in Scandinavia. Her published works include a novel, a play and much miscellaneous writing; but the early autobiography, *After Ten Years*, (1931), remains sovereign, a testament of friendship and of a generous, loyal and impulsive nature.

October 8, 1975.

Admiral Sir Richard Onslow, K.C.B., D.S.O., one of the most skilful and successful destroyer escort commanders of the Second World War, died on December 16, 1975 at the age of 71.

His career, which involved him in almost twenty years sea service in destroyers, made him one of the Royal Navy's most distinctive "salt horses" and brought him the remarkable tally of four D.S.O.s during convoy operations in the Arctic and the Mediterranean and, later in the war, in the Far East.

Richard George Onslow was born in 1904 and educated at the Royal Naval Colleges, Osborne and Dartmouth. His career in destroyers began in 1926 and continued, almost without a break, until the end of the Second World War.

It was as commanding officer of the Tribal Class destroyer H.M.S. Ashanti that Onslow, then a Commander, was awarded his first D.S.O. in 1942 for the exceptional skill and judgment he showed in defence of a convoy to Russia. Five months later he got his first bar on the Malta convoy route for resolution and bravery in defence of one of the most important convoys to the beleaguered island.

Before the end of the year he was back with Ashanti on the North Russian convoys, where he gained a second bar for his convoy support work in the face of incessant air and submarine attack. For this feat the Soviet Union awarded him the Order of the Red Banner.

In 1944 Onslow was appointed Captain (D) of the Fourth Destroyer Flotilla and was awarded his third bar for the skill and resolution with which he pressed home an attack on the Japanese naval base at Sabang in the same year.

After the war he was successively Senior Naval Officer Northern Ireland; serving at the Admiralty as Director of Tactical and Staff Duties and commanding the cadet training cruiser, H.M.S. Devonshire. As a Rear-Admiral he was Naval Secretary to the First Lord of the Admiralty in 1952 and as a Vice-Admiral, Flag Officer (Flotillas), Home Fleet, from 1955 to 1956. He was Flag Officer Commanding, Reserve Fleet from 1956 and 1957 and as an Admiral, Commander-in-Chief, Plymouth, from 1958 to 1960 when he retired.

He became a Deputy Lieutenant for Salop in 1960. He was appointed C.B. in 1954 and K.C.B. in 1958. He married, in 1932, Kathleen Meriel Taylor. They had two sons.

December 18, 1975.

Professor Harold Orton, Emeritus Professor of English Language and Medieval English Literature, Leeds University, died in Leeds on March 7, 1975. He was 76.

Harold Orton's death deprives English language studies of an outstanding figure. The English Dialect Survey which he founded and directed in the University of Leeds will surely remain his chief scholarly monument, just as the study of English dialectology was his chief interest; but in the course of a long and active life he made important contributions in several fields, besides winning the admiration and affection of generations of students in three different countries.

Born in Byers Green, co. Durham, Harold Orton went from King James I Grammar School, Bishop Auckland, to Hatfield College, University of Durham. On reaching military age in 1917 he was commissioned in the D.L.I. Wounded in the right arm in 1918, he was invalided out of the army a year later and went up to Merton College, Oxford, still under treatment and resolutely learning to write with his left hand. Under the guidance of H. C. Wyld, he submitted a B.Litt. thesis on his native dialect, one of his examiners being Joseph Wright, editor of *The English Dialect Dictionary*.

From 1924 to 1928 Orton was English Lektor at Uppsala University. He later taught at King's College, Newcastle, where he embarked on a number of tasks—the publication of his book *The Phonology of a South Durham Dialect* (1933); service on the B.B.C.'s advisory committee on spoken English (1934-40); and a detailed survey of Northumberland dialect. In 1939 he moved to Sheffield University as head of the Department of English Language, and was seconded to the British Council from 1942-45, ending up as acting education director. In 1947 he moved to the chair of English Language and Medieval Literature at Leeds where he embarked on his meticulously planned English dialect survey.

Material was collected from 313 localities throughout England and the Isle of Man, mainly in the 1950s. Then followed a publication programme and introduction, and 12 books of basic material between 1962 and 1971.

Harold Orton retired from his chair in 1964; but his retirement was purely notional. From 1965 to 1973 he spent the spring semester each year teaching in the United States of America. In 1972 he began work on the Linguistic Atlas of England which will be brought to its conclusion by his collaborators. His *Word Geography of England* (with Nathalia Wright) was published on February 19, 1975 just before his last illness.

He leaves a wife and one married daughter.

March 11, 1975.

Elise Ottesen-Jensen, a pioneer of the world family planning movement and a founder and former president of the International Planned Parenthood Federation, died in Stockholm at the age of 87 in September 4, 1973.

Born in Höjland, Norway, on January 2, 1886, the daughter of a clergyman, she was the last but one of 18 children, of whom 11 lived to adulthood. She wanted a career in medicine but an accident injured her hands and in 1908 she became a journalist.

As a specialist in women's problems she discovered that the subjects she was most frequently asked about were family planning, the sexual side of life, and maternal and child care. Her growing involvement in that field was spurred by a personal family tragedy: a sister aged 16 became pregnant, with little idea of what had happened to her or what the process of childbearing involved. The child was sent away for adoption; the girl's bewilderment and efforts to recover the baby ended in madness and suicide.

"Ottar" married the Swedish reformer and pacifist Albert Jensen, who was several times imprisoned for anti-military propaganda during and after the First World War.

In 1923 "Ottar" started to make annual tours of the Swedish countryside, staying in rough huts and humble cottages and hearing in the darkness the women confide their troubles and fears. She understood their difficulties; and all the reforms she sought and the programmes she initiated were designed upon that understanding.

In 1933 she founded the Swedish National League for Sex Education and opened the first successful consultation bureau in Sweden. She fought many battles against existing laws and conservative public opinion. Because of her emphasis on the need to involve ordinary people, the working classes, who had always been denied sex education and who recognized their own needs, responded enthusiastically.

Before the Second World War many of her objectives had been achieved. Her new programme aimed towards compulsory sex education in schools; advice centres where guidance would be given on all aspects of sex; reform to prevent illegal abortions; the right to free contraceptives when they were needed for social or medical reasons; and changes in the law on homosexuality. She also called on the Government to promote scientific research and to implement social reforms to use the results of such research.

In August 1946 she called the first post-war meeting of the international family planning movement, which ultimately led to the International Planned Parenthood Federation. She was the federation's second president, following Margaret Sanger*, the American birth control pioneer, and led the movement through a time of major growth.

When she became president in 1959 she was more than 70 years old. But she still gave more than 400 lectures a year; and during that year alone she visited India, Pakistan, Israel, Holland, the U.S.S.R., East and West Germany, Poland and Britain. The questions which had been whispered to her years before were still being asked; but now they were asked openly.

She was nominated for a Nobel Peace Prize in 1972. In 1951 she was decorated with the Illis Quorum by the King of Sweden.

There the Medical Faculty of Uppsala University gave her an honorary degree in medicine in 1958.

Her life and work are described in her two-part autobiography; but her greatest memorials will be the reforms in the lives of women all over the world which she strove for, and largely achieved.

September 7, 1973.

General Mohamad Oufkir, who died on August 17, 1972, had for many years served with distinction in the French Army in France, Germany and Indo-China, being more than once decorated.

In 1960, after Moroccan independence, he was appointed Director-General of National Security, and in 1965 became Minister of the Interior. The following year he was accused in France of being implicated in the disappearance and presumed murder of Ben Barka, a leader of the left-wing Moroccan political party U.N.F.P., and was sentenced by a French court *in absentia* to life imprisonment. He was, however, strongly supported by his King and retained his office.

In 1970 he was mainly responsible for the successful outcome of a referendum on a new Constitution introduced by the King, on which he was able to report a favourable vote of 98.7 per cent; and in 1971 he rendered his sovereign even greater service by foiling an attempted *coup d'état* mounted by a group of officers and cadets; as a result he was entrusted by the King with plenary powers—and in exercising those powers he made many enemies for himself—to crush the revolt, most of whose ringleaders were summarily executed.

August 18, 1972.

Sir Alfred Owen, industrialist and individualist, died on October 29, 1975 at the age of 67.

He was chairman and managing director of the Owen Organization, the largest family business in the country with a turnover of £100m. a year. In addition to the engineering complex at Darlaston, Staffordshire, the firm has factories in Yorkshire and Scotland and subsidiaries in Australia and South Africa.

Owen was a highly individual industrialist. A fervent and articulate Christian, he firmly believed that to be a good Christian one did not have to be a bad businessman. He came of a family of Midland ironmasters and took control of the family firm when his father, Ernest Owen, who had shrewdly geared the firm's products to serve, in turn, the bicycle, car and aviation industries, died in 1930. A. G. B. Owen was then still up at Cambridge. In the years that followed he extended and developed the business organization he had inherited but in the expansion his Christian principles were not discarded. Paternalism in industry may not be fashionable, but his strongest critics could not deny that he was always closely involved in schemes for the well-being of his employees.

Owen had a strong sense of social obligation. For some years he was chairman of Staffordshire County Council and of Darlaston U.D.C.; he was a former president of the National Sunday School Union; chairman of the council of Dr. Barnardo's Homes; a vice-chairman of the National Savings Movement; Pro-Chancellor of Keele University (which made him an honorary D.Sc.) and a member of the council of Birmingham University. Though an Anglican he was willing to support the work of other Christian denominations. He was an early supporter in England of Billy Graham. On most Sundays he could be found preaching, taking a service or helping with a Bible class.

Owen was one of the first businessmen to promise assistance when Raymond Mayes conceived a plan to raise finance to build a British grand prix racing car in 1945, and was eventually destined to play the leading part in the B.R.M. (British Racing Motors) project. Although the first B.R.M. was demonstrated to the press and notabilities of the motoring world at Bourne in 1949 and the British Motor Racing Research Trust was later formed, the new car met severe financial and technical troubles. Its few successes came too late and at the end of 1952 the B.R.M. trust decided to wind up and sell the assets of the company.

But Owen had not lost his initial faith in the B.R.M. project. He purchased the company and from then on B.R.M. became a division of the parent company in Owen Organization, still located at Bourne, Lincolnshire.

It was typical of Alfred Owen that he refused to change the name of the cars to "Owens" and was confident that the previous bad image would be wiped out. In spite of many setbacks, Owen never gave up and it was in 1959 that the Swedish driver, Jo Bonnier, gave a B.R.M. its first major victory by winning the Dutch Grand Prix.

Three years later Owen was present when Graham Hill won the South African Grand Prix in a B.R.M., securing the 1962 drivers' world championship and the manufacturers' cup as well.

His efforts also brought him the Ferodo Gold Trophy and a British Automobile Racing Club gold medal.

Owen was also closely involved in the building of Donald Campbell's* car Bluebird and in Campbell's ultimately successful attempt to beat the world's land speed record.

From 1965 to 1967 he was chairman of the National Road Safety Advisory Council.

He was appointed a Deputy Lieutenant for Warwickshire in 1967 and was a Freeman and former Mayor of Sutton Coldfield.

Born on April 8, 1908 he was educated at Lickey Hills preparatory school and Oundle before going up to Emmanuel College, Cambridge. He married in 1932 Eileen Kathleen Genevieve McMullan by whom he had three sons and two daughters. He was appointed a C.B.E. in 1954 and knighted in 1961.

October 30, 1975.

Harold Owen—See (William) Harold Owen.

Sir Leonard Owen, C.B.E., formerly chairman of the Production Group Board of Management and of the Engineering Group Board of Management, United Kingdom Atomic Energy Authority, died on March 25, 1971.

With Lord Hinton of Bankside, Owen could be regarded as the engineer architect of the industrial development of nuclear energy in the United Kingdom. The design and construction of the atomic energy factories in the north of England was under the supervision of one or other of these two engineers and sometimes of both, and it is not always easy to separate the contribution of each since their qualities were in some measure complementary.

William Leonard Owen was born on May 3, 1897 and was educated at Liverpool Collegiate School and Liverpool University, where he obtained his degree of Master of Engineering.

During the First World War he served in the 6th King's Liverpool Regiment, and afterwards was employed successively by Brunner Mond and Company and I.C.I. Alkali, Limited, where he worked in the engineering department, designing new chemical plant and additions to existing equipment. From 1940 to 1945 he was on loan to the Ministry of Supply as Director of the Royal Filling Factories.

His association with the development of the British atomic energy programme began in 1946, when he was appointed Director of Engineering on the the production side by the Ministry of Supply. In the following year he became Assistant Controller in the Atomic Energy Division's production side. When the United Kingdom Atomic Energy Authority was formed in 1954, his title became Director of Engineering and Deputy Managing Director, and in 1957 he was appointed Managing Director, Industrial Group.

In January 1960 Sir Leonard Owen became member of the Atomic Energy Authority for Production and on April 1, 1961, after changes in the organization of the Atomic Energy Authority, he became member for Production and Engineering.

His appointment as a full-time member of the Atomic Energy Authority ended in

June 1962, and he then served as a part-time member until July 1964. He remained chairman of the boards of management of the Production and Engineering Groups until September 1963.

A recital of Owen's appointments, however, cannot give any indication of the man. During his long association with Hinton, he remained an admirable second in command, maintaining his influence by the quiet advice, often given in private, which was never assertive but respected for its basis in a shrewd judgment and a long experience. He was able to win the respect and friendship of most of the staff working under him whether they were relatively academic in outlook or down-to-earth site engineers engaged in heavy construction.

It is strange therefore that he was never a warm friend of Hinton and when they separated in 1957 it was in an atmosphere which was cool. Left as head of the Industrial Group, Owen was soon seen as a figure in his own right, and although the contributions of Owen and Hinton in the early years can never be separated it was obvious that Owen's was a substantial contribution. The cool relationship persisted but it was always clear later when they met that the two men understood and respected the thoughts and ideas of each other.

When he left the Atomic Energy Authority Owen found many useful outlets for his energies both as a consultant and on the board of United Gas Industries, where he became chairman of three of the company's subsidiaries.

He was created C.B.E. in 1950 and knighted in 1957. Manchester University conferred on him an honorary D.Sc. in 1960.

He married in 1923 Phyllis Condliff. They had two sons.

March 26, 1971.

(William) Harold Owen, artist and author, died at his Oxfordshire home on November 26, 1971. He was 74.

Harold Owen was born in Shrewsbury on September 5, 1897. The childhood he shared with Wilfred the poet, Mary, and Colin he recaptured in *Journey from Obscurity: Memoirs of the Owen Family* with a painter's eye for the detail that gives a picture its true focus, and a range of perception worthy of a major novelist.

In this remarkable trilogy, the second volume of which won him the Royal Society of Literature's W. H. Heinemann Award for 1964, he describes how, uprooted from art school at the age of 16, he joined the Merchant Service in 1913, as apprentice deck-officer, his paintbox in his sea chest. Six months later he almost died from heat apoplexy in Calcutta, incurring damage to his heart that later led doctors to give him little prospect of surviving until he was 30.

He was at sea throughout the war, transferring to the Royal Navy in 1916, and then survived the equally perilous twenties, a penniless ex-officer, his health permanently broken, sustained only by his determination to paint. His stubbornness carried him through; he exhibited, and his paintings and etchings began to sell.

His life entered a calmer, happier phase with his marriage in 1927 to Phyllis de Pass (who survives him). From painting he gradually turned to writing, and with a natural, unforced artistry set down over several years the large work that was first planned as a biography of his brother. A deeply modest man, it worried him later that the title of the work might be taken as referring to his journey, not Wilfred's. These solitary years of remembering and writing were followed by a depressing period in search of a publisher; but when publication of the first volume came in 1963, all was well.

"No one had any right to expect", wrote one reviewer, "that this sailor son, so second a fiddle to Wilfred's promise and pretensions in his youth, would in his age produce a biography of such importance and accomplishment." With the help of his publisher, he now went on to edit *The Collected Letters of Wilfred Owen* (1967), and completed the family history with *Aftermath* (1970), in which he wrote of his life in the twenties.

Devoted, though not uncritically, to Wilfred, he was privately delighted to have demonstrated that there were now two writers in the family. What he had not expected was the warmth of the response to his books. Not many works can have drawn such a tide of admiring, enquiring correspondence, and in his quiet country home, scrupulous in answering every letter, he found the tide almost overwhelming.

Immediately attractive to meet, gentle, chivalrous, sweet-natured, he was at the same time a man of independence and considerable determination. He talked his way back into the Royal Navy in the last war, in spite of his poor health. When he gave up painting he made a bonfire of all his work, a characteristically swift and resolute act that dismayed his friends but was never regretted by him. Meticulous in his person, his studio was equally ordered, like a seaman's cabin. He conducted his correspondence, as he wrote his books, by hand, deliberately and slowly writing everything in capital letters, with the back of the nib. No bank manager or solicitor ever persuaded him to write his signature in any other way.

The man can be seen in his books—delicately truthful, of undaunted spirit. Many who never met him will feel personally bereaved by his death.

December 2, 1971.

Sir (William) Leonard Owen—See **Sir Leonard Owen.**

P

Sir Frank Packer, K.B.E., for many years a powerful and influential figure in Australian newspaper and magazine publishing, died on May 1, 1974. He was 67.

For over 40 years Douglas Frank Hewson Packer was a force to be reckoned with, not only in the world of newspapers but in politics and finance also. An admirer of Sir Robert Menzies, he gave successive Menzies governments unquestioning support for nearly two decades.

He inherited money from his father, Robert Clyde Packer, a successful Sydney journalist who became a newspaper executive and was one of the founders of *Smith's Weekly;* but, the last man to lock up money in a safe place, Frank Packer went on to build the Australian Consolidated Press, which at one time incorporated the immensely successful Australian *Women's Weekly* (Packer was one of its founders in 1933), the *Sydney Daily Telegraph*, and the *Sydney Sunday Telegraph*. The latter two newspapers were later sold to Rupert Murdoch.

Packer had acquired the *Sydney Daily Telegraph* in 1936 from a rival organization and under his ownership it showed a bold initiative in chasing news stories and during the war achieved the largest circulation of a Sydney daily newspaper.

The war saw the appearance of the *Sydney Sunday Telegraph*, which made a profound impression on its rivals. Packer launched magazines with varying success and entered the field of television with Australia's first commercial station. He was a former president of the Australian Newspapers Conference and director of Reuters.

Newspaper proprietors are not often visible public figures; Packer was. He had abounding physical and mental vitality, neither of which could be contained even in the demanding sphere of newspaper production. In his youth he had been a boxer of some distinction and had gone gold prospecting in the dead heart of Australia; later he became a passionate player of polo and headed the syndicate which twice put up a challenge for the America's Cup.

He was a considerable racehorse owner in his day. Variously described as big, brash, ruthless and loyal, around him grew some bizarre stories; for example, during a disagreement on an Australian racecourse he was said to have been bitten in the leg by another newspaper proprietor; and on the occasion of Stalin's death he is said to have written a bill saying: "Stalin's dead: hurrah!". He was in a real sense a colourful figure, but his colours were always primary ones.

He was made C.B.E. in 1951, knighted in 1959 and made K.B.E. in 1971. He was twice married.

May 2, 1974.

The Rt. Rev. Edward Paget, C.B.E., M.C., D.D., who was Archbishop of Central Africa from 1955 to 1957, died near Durban on April 21, 1971. He was 84.

Edward Paget might be said to be the architect of the Anglican Church in Central Africa as it is today. He served his apprenticeship during the 10 years he worked under Bishop Furse in the Transvaal, and, when he was appointed Bishop of Southern Rhodesia, he was one of the youngest bishops in the Church. His new diocese, though so vast in territory, was so small in church membership that for the first four years he was able to fill the offices of both bishop and dean. When he left the country 32 years later, not only had he built up the organization of the church in a remarkable way but he had divided his diocese, formed the new province of Central Africa, and become its first archbishop.

Edward Francis Paget was born in 1886, the son of Francis Paget, Bishop of Oxford. His mother was a daughter of the Very Rev. R. W. Church, Dean of St. Paul's. He was a brother of the late General Sir Bernard Paget* and was a cousin and heir presumptive of Captain Sir James Paget, Bart., of Ballater, Aberdeenshire.

He was educated at Shrewsbury, Christ Church, Oxford and Cuddesdon, and was ordained in 1911. He served for three years as curate at Christ Church and with St. Frideswide's mission, Poplar. Soon after his ordination he had joined a group of 12 young clergymen, friends of Dick Sheppard, who offered themselves to the Church in Western Canada. When this project fell through, Dr. Michael Furse, then Bishop of Pretoria, invited them to his diocese instead, and five of them "of the very best" of whom Paget was one, accepted his invitation and went out to the Transvaal. He was made Vicar of Benoni, a post which he held for 11 years, and there he did splendid work especially in charge of the mines on the far eastern part of the Reef. Bishop Furse used to say that, although Paget was by no means the most intellectual member of his remarkable team, which has been described as an ecclesiastical version of Milner's Kindergarten, he was the man who excelled in getting things done.

During the First World War, which broke out soon after his arrival in Benoni in 1914, he was for two years chaplain to the forces in East Africa and was awarded the Military Cross.

In 1925 he was elected Bishop of Southern Rhodesia. As chaplain-general to the Southern Rhodesian forces he paid several visits to the Middle East during the Second World War. When the diocese was divided in 1952 into the dioceses of Mashonaland and Matabeleland, he became Bishop of Mashonaland. Till 1955 the two dioceses of Southern Rhodesia were under the jurisdiction of the Archbishop of Cape Town, and those of Nyasaland and Northern Rhodesia under that of the Archbishop of Canterbury. This division of control, and very remote control at that, was not conducive to the efficiency of the work of the Anglican Church in Central Africa, and for many years Paget advocated the formation of a new province. When the Federation of Rhodesia and Nyasaland was set up in 1953, the time for the realization of his dream seemed ripe, and the new province of Central Africa was inaugurated in the following year.

Paget retired in 1957 and went to live in Natal. In 1960, when Dr. Ambrose Reeves, Bishop of Johannesburg, was deported, he was appointed Vicar-General of the diocese, but he resigned this post after a few months when it was decided that the diocesan constitution prevented him from presiding over the synod. Since 1961 he has been Assistant Bishop of Natal.

He married in 1932 Rosemary, daughter of Auriol Sealy Allin.

April 23, 1971.

Marcel Pagnol, one of the most individual of French film-makers, died in Paris on April 18, 1974 at the age of 79.

He was born on February 25, 1895, in Aubagne, a suburb of Marseilles. He went to school at the Lycée Thiers, Marseilles, and began to write when he was barely in his teens, founding and editing a local revue, *Fortunio*, at the age of 16 (the magazine survived to become *Les Cahiers du Sud*). He became a teacher, teaching English at Tarascon, Pamiers and finally the Lycée Concordet in Paris, but hankered after a literary career and decided to try his hand at drama.

Two classical pieces, *Catulle* and *Ulysse chez les Phéniciens*, were staged, but his first big success was *Les Marchands de Gloire*, written in collaboration with Paul Nivoix, which opened at the Théâtre de la Madeleine in 1925. Encouraged by the reception of the play, Pagnol resigned his teaching position and the next year saw two plays, *Jazz*, an independent effort, and *Direct au Coeur*, again written in collaboration with Paul Nivoix. After this Pagnol decided to draw on his experience of life in Marseilles for his next work, and wrote *Marius*, which was accepted by a management but shelved until his next play, *Topaze*, had been successfully staged in 1928.

The introduction of the sound film to France found in Pagnol an eager supporter of the new medium. As a playwright he saw at once the possibilities of the sound-film as a means of preserving drama, and wrote a considerable amount of theoretical work on the subject, in a magazine he founded in 1932, *Les Cahiers du Film*, and elsewhere. Though in theory he supported the transformation of theatre into cinema, when he entered the cinema himself his practice tended much more to the straight "canning" of theatre plays with few concessions to the demands of the medium.

His first ventures in the film were as writer and producer: in 1931 he produced a version of his own play *Marius*, directed by Alexander Korda, and followed it in 1932 with the sequel, *Fanny*, this time directed by Marc Allegret (the third in the series, *César*, which concluded the story of the characters, did not appear until 1936, and was directed by Pagnol himself).

The *Marius* trilogy remains in many ways Pagnol's most famous and characteristic work—though he directed only one of them himself, he exerted a strong influence on the way they were shot, and though the technique employed was rather flat and stilted they gained considerably in their excellent location-work in Marseilles and the authenticity of their settings and atmosphere.

After *Fanny* Pagnol supervised the filming of another of his big theatrical successes, *Topaze*, a striking study of a corrupt municipal councillor, with Arnaud; and then himself undertook the direction of *Direct au Coeur*, based on his early play. The success of these films induced him to set up a small studio in Marseilles, where he wrote, produced and often directed films based on his own stories or current stage plays. Most of the films which followed were undistinguished, and such productions as *Le Gendre de M. Poirier* and *Le Voyage de M. Perrichon* suggested to observers that he was embarking on the filming of the entire French theatre repertoire.

Among a series of such productions, however, were *Joffroi* and *Angèle* (1934) and *Merlusse* (1935), all of which presented Pagnol on his home ground in stories of Provençal life. For *Merlusse* he drew on his own experiences as a provincial school-teacher, and in *Joffroi* (directed by his brother René Pagnol) he turned to the work of that other great portrayer of Provençal country life, Giono, for a delightful fable of peasant ways about an old man who sells his field and then tries to hold on both to the field and to the money. *Angèle*, perhaps the best of all Pagnol's films, gave Fernandel one of his few worthwhile parts as a simple labourer who saves a farmer's daughter from prostitution.

During the years immediately prior to the war Pagnol made fewer films: only four between 1935 and 1940, two from his own stores, *César* and *Le Schpountz*, and two from stories by Giono, *Regain* and *La Femme du Boulanger*. *Le Schpountz* and *Regain* both starred Fernandel, the second, with its picture of an abandoned village in Provence, being particularly interesting, and *La Femme du Boulanger*, a rustic comedy with Raimu as a heartbroken baker who refuses to bake his bread when his wife runs away with a handsome shepherd, was one of Pagnol's greatest successes. The war saw only one Pagnol film, *La Fille du Puisatier*, not one of his more successful works, despite the presence of Raimu and Fernandel in the cast: it was begun before the invasion and completed later, but his

next film, *La Prière aux Étoiles*, remained unfinished, and he did not return to production again until 1945, with *Naïs*, adapted from Zola.

Later films include *La Belle Meunière*, starring Pagnol's wife Jacqueline Pagnol and Tino Rossi, a new version of *Topaze*, *Manon des Sources*, a strange and extremely protracted film with sections of authentic poetry, and *Lettres de mon Moulin*, a charming episodic film derived from Daudet. In 1955 Pagnol returned to the theatre, after a long absence, with *Judas*, and the *Marius* trilogy was adapted in America to the demands of a musical, *Fanny*, later filmed. Pagnol's other works included a novel, *La Petite Fille aux Yeux Sombres*, and a book of stories, *Pirouettes*. He was elected to the Académie Française in 1947.

It has always been one of the most cherished principles of *cinéastes* that the true creative artist in films is the director, but Pagnol presented one of the most distinguished exceptions to the rule: as a film-maker he was always writer first even when he directed his own script, and in the films directed by other people from his scripts, his was the dominant personality. Though he was too often content to work to what, wise after the event, we might call the television formula of just setting down the camera and letting something interesting happen in front of it, with a cheerful disregard for the demands of the film medium, there is no denying the enduring interest and power of his best work even years after its creation (the *Marius* trilogy ran into censor trouble and did not receive public showing in Britain until 1950; *Regain* first appeared there in 1957, without any lessening of their impact). These qualities derive from the truth of the character drawing and the careful observation of the characters' milieux. Pagnol was always a man of Marseilles and the south —many of his stars, among them Raimu and Fernandel, came originally from the Marseilles music-hall—and in his films, derived from this rich background, he created something of lasting value.

He married firstly in 1916 and had three children. In 1945 he married the actress Jacqueline Bouvier and they had one child.

April 19, 1974.

Dr. Grace Winifred Pailthorpe, who died on July 19, 1971 at St. Leonard's-on-Sea at the age of 87, gained international repute in the early thirties with her pioneering work on the psychology of criminals.

It was with the publication of her report, *Studies in the Psychology of Delinquency*, by H.M. Stationery Office, the outcome of research sponsored by the British Medical Council, and her book *What We Put in Prison* (1932), that the psychological treatment of criminals was initiated. It was this pioneering research that brought her world-wide acclaim, an unusual happening for such a subject. Not content with this success she initiated the establishment of the world's first clinic for treating, by psychological methods, the unfortunate inmates of our prisons—but outside the prison walls. All schools of psychology were invited to participate. In this way the Institute for the Scientific Treatment of Delinquency was formed. It is now known as the Portman Clinic.

Soon after this she began work on another research project, namely, the investigation of so-called "normal" man. This was begun in 1935 and lasted over 30 years. The success in this research not only brought her into the world of art as one of England's best Surrealist artists (as André Breton,* the father of Surrealism, stated), but it also led her into the realization that behind all psychological patterns of behaviour there existed the world of the Spirit. She evolved a new technique for the release of inner psychological tensions and for the broadening of consciousness. Creative activities were a great part of this technique.

Her own creative work, painting, was always greatly appreciated by the professional painter who saw in her work the freedom of imagination and of technique they themselves wished for. Her painting was always full of richly vital colour. It should be mentioned that she had no professional training, for even though her colleague in the research was a professional painter it had been stipulated from the first that no training was to be given in art. It was the *natural* artist in the person that was being sought. Training would inhibit its emergence.

Although a psychiatrist and psychologist in her later years, she served in the 1914-18 war as a surgeon in charge of what then was called a "flying ambulance" which penetrated into the front lines to attend the wounded. After this military service Dr. Pailthorpe worked her way round the world, acting as doctor wherever opportunity came.

July 22, 1971.

Roundell Palmer, 3rd Earl of Selborne—See Selborne.

Rosetta Pampanini, the distinguished Italian soprano of the inter-war period, died at Corbola on August 2, 1973.

She was born in Milan on September 2, 1900, and made her debut as Micaela in 1920 at Rome. She then retired temporarily for further study before reappearing four years later as Mimi at Biella.

There she was noticed by Toscanini. He invited her to undertake what was to become her most famous part, the title role in *Madama Butterfly* at La Scala in 1925.

She appeared in the same part at her Covent Garden debut in 1928, when her interpretation was described in *The Times* as "sympathetic" and her voice was said to be of "great beauty". Her Nedda and Liu (to Eva Turner's Turandot) in the same season were also favourably received.

She returned the following summer as Mimi and Manon Lescaut, and then, in 1933, again as Mimi and as a fine Desdemona. She also appeared at many other well known opera houses during those years.

She sang regularly at La Scala until the 1937 season, taking on heavier roles in the later years. After retiring from the stage in 1942, she devoted herself to teaching at her own school in Milan. One of her best known pupils was the British soprano Amy Shuard.

Pampanini's voice was a well formed lyric-dramatic soprano, which she used very expressively, as can be heard on her many records.

August 6, 1973.

"Papa-Doc"—See Duvalier.

James Parish, the dramatist, who died in London on December 25, 1973 at the age of 69, was proud of a photograph of the "royal session" in the hall at Blackfriars, a scene from the Casson-Thorndike production of *Henry VIII* at the Empire, London, in December, 1925. In this, as part of the Ricketts scenery—so he used to say—he is a Guard (with pike). Elsewhere, in another non-speaking part, is the young Laurence Olivier.

Parish also remembered the scene because he fainted during a performance and had to be unobtrusively removed. Once he had a foot in the theatre, he never left it, as actor, director, or dramatist, except for his war service, when he became a major in the Intelligence Corps. Even then he was transferred to E.N.S.A., for whom he directed a production of *The Apple Cart* (for troops in Europe), with Barry Jones as King Magnus.

Born on February 15, 1904, in Hampshire, he was educated at King Alfred's School, Wantage, and acted for 10 years before directing plays at the Rusholme Repertory in Manchester and afterwards, at the Prince of Wales, Cardiff. But he became known principally as a dramatist, writing more than a dozen varied plays of substance, some of which had less fortune than they deserved in the pitch-and-toss of the West End.

He had his first sustained success with the murder play, *Distinguished Gathering,* done at the Embassy in the autumn of 1935 and later for a run at the St. Martin's. Soon after that, he had bad luck with *Goodbye to Yesterday,* the renamed version of a piece first called *The Cage;* Gladys Cooper and Philip Merivale acted in it at the Phoenix (1937) in Basil Dean's production. London was under a thick fog, and in spite of some sympathetic notices, the play faded out after four performances.

After the war Parish had five plays (three of which he directed himself) staged within six years. The most important were the moving *Message for Margaret* (Westminster, 1946) which ran for more than 200 performances, with Dame Flora Robson; and *Truant in Park Lane* (St. James's, 1947), a fantastic ghost comedy that, in spite of excellent performances by Clive Brook and Roland Young, failed to survive. Parish's other work included *Mrs. Inspector Jones* (Savoy, 1950); and *The Woman on the Stair* (Westminster, 1959), which was done originally on television. He wrote, too, a novel, *The Hour of the Unicorn.*

Urbane and friendly, Parish was a most professional craftsman and a charming raconteur. He had been ill for some time.

December 29, 1973.

Air Chief Marshal Sir Keith Park, G.C.B., K.B.E., M.C., D.F.C, who died on February 6, 1975 in hospital in Auckland, New Zealand, at the age of 82, had a distinguished career of nearly 36 years with the New Zealand and British armed forces, and was in command of forces which greatly contributed to the defeat of the Axis countries in two principal war theatres. In 1940 he became A.O.C. No. 11 Group, Fighter Command, which bore the brunt of the fighting in the Battle of Britain; later he successfully used his wide knowledge of air defence in Malta.

Keith Rodney Park was born at Thames, New Zealand, on June 15, 1892, the son of Professor J. Park, and was educated at King's College, Auckland, Selwyn Collegiate School, Dunedin, Otago Boys High School and Otago University of Mines.

In 1911-13 he served as a private in the New Zealand Field Artillery (Territorial Force) and in December 1914, joined the N.Z. Expeditionary Force. He was commissioned in the Royal Field Artillery in 1915, and transferred to the R.A. (Regular Army) in 1916, seeing service in Gallipoli and France. A year later he was seconded to the Royal Flying Corps and on the formation of the Royal Air Force in 1918 was promoted captain. Between 1917 and 1919 he served with Nos. 8 and 38 (Reserve) Squadrons and No. 48 Squadron, becoming commanding officer of the last-named on April 10, 1918. He gained the M.C. and bar in 1917, the Croix de Guerre in 1918, and the D.F.C. in 1919.

Between the wars he commanded R.A.F. Northolt, and was chief instructor of the Oxford University Air Squadron. He took the Imperial Defence College course in 1937, became officer commanding R.A.F. Tangmere in January 1938, and later that year, as air commodore, became senior air staff officer at H.Q., Fighter Command.

In April 1940 he was appointed Air

Officer Commanding, No. 11 Group, being confirmed in the rank of air vice-marshal the following July.

No. 11 Group was responsible for the greater part of protective fighter patrols, and, after the German invasion of the Low Countries in May 1940, Park on more than one occasion flew his own Hurricane over Dunkirk to gain first-hand intelligence of the progress of the evacuation.

When the Battle of Britain began Park instructed his Hurricane and Spitfire pilots to split their attacks, half going for the bombers and the others attacking the escort, tactics which resulted in the German formations flying tighter and thus presenting better targets. Towards the end of the Battle, after heavy attacks on No. 11 Group's stations, Park's handling of his fighters, and Dowding's* overall strategy, were the subject of an informal inquiry, instigated primarily by the A.O.C., No. 12 Group (which covered the Midlands), Air Vice-Marshal T. Leigh-Mallory.
stretching from Southampton to Norwich,

Park, with the greatest area to protect, had intelligently used his squadrons, with the help of radar, to place them where the enemy raids were expected, and successfully broke up the formations, even though he had very little warning of their approach. Leigh-Mallory, on the other hand, employed his fighters in larger "wing" formations, concentrating as many as five or even seven squadrons against the raiding bombers, having had time to amass them and in any case having by that time a better idea of the enemy's targets. The differences between the two commanders became so pronounced that eventually the Air Council had to intervene. As it happened, the "wing" tactics were officially more favoured, and Park, along with Dowding, was moved to another post. But the fact remains that the Battle of Britain was won while Park commanded the largest of the fighter groups. While the battle was on he flew 100 hours, mainly in his own fighter.

He had, at the end of July 1940, in cooperation with the Vice-Admiral, Dover, acquired some Lysander aircraft to work in conjunction with launches to retrieve aircrew who had come down in the sea, which may be regarded as the beginning of a comprehensive air/sea rescue organization.

In December 1940 Park became A.O.C., No. 23 Group, Training Command, where his hard-won experience could be passed on to the new generation of pilots. He was appointed A.O.C., Egypt, in January 1942, and in July 1942 became A.O.C., Malta, where his first-hand experience of air defence was immediately put to good use. He introduced new tactics, instructing his pilots (then beginning to receive Spitfires in place of Hurricanes) to intercept enemy raids well out to sea and, besides attaining greater victories, reduced the possibility of bombs falling on the island itself. By the skilful use of his still-limited fighters and bombers he was able to restrict movements of enemy convoys to North Africa. His aircraft supported Tedder's* forces at El Alamein, the advance to Tunisia, and the invasion of Sicily. When supplies began to flow more readily into the Mediterranean, Park, with typical energy, began intensive modernization of the Malta bases.

He became A.O.C.-in-C., R.A.F. Middle East, in January 1944, and—when the emphasis of the war switched from Europe to the Far East—Allied Air Commander, Air Command South East Asia, in February 1945. Here he assumed the immense responsibility of providing a colossal airlift by R.A.F. and American aircraft of materials to support the Allied troops in Burma, besides the overall control of bombers and fighters, which contributed to the successful conclusion of the war in the Far East.

Park retired from the Service in December 1946. In 1947 Oxford University conferred an honorary D.C.L. on him.

He married Dorothy Margarite, daughter of Lieutenant-Colonel Woodbine Parish, C.M.G., C.B.E., in 1918. He had two sons, one of whom was killed on active serivce in 1951. His wife died in 1971.

February 7, 1975.

Lord Parker of Waddington, P.C., who was Lord Chief Justice from 1958 to 1971, died on September 15, 1972 at the age of 72.

Parker, despite his outstanding intellectual gifts and the great office which he held, remained all his life an essentially humble man. He was liked by everyone with whom he came into contact; his quiet humour and his unassuming charm made it equally a pleasure to appear before him in Court and to meet him out of Court. He was especially popular among the J.P.s, the difficulty of whose role at the base of the judicial pyramid he fully appreciated, even if, from time to time in the Divisional Court he found it necessary to criticize the performance of an individual Bench. When he addressed them, or attended their dinners, there was a complete absence of that (sometimes unconscious) *de haut en bas* approach which can so markedly lessen the value of such contacts.

But, although he always seemed to be happy and relaxed on these public occasions, there was a sense in which he was a very private person. While, daily during term-time, his spare and bowler-hatted figure could be seen striding briskly through New Square on his way to a hurried and frugal lunch in Lincoln's Inn Hall, he differed from many great lawyers (and strikingly so from his predecessor, Lord Goddard) in that he took very little interest in the social life of his profession; he was seldom to be seen at any of the guest nights, grand days and other convivial or ceremonial events, which in the Inns of Court form important landmarks throughout the legal year.

Hubert Lister Parker was born on May 28, 1900, the third son of Lord Parker of Waddington, a distinguished Lord of Appeal (1857-1918). There was a strong physical likeness between the two men, and the course of their careers also had much in common. Both, before elevation to the Bench, held the position of Junior Counsel to the Treasury; both became Life Peers, and the son had the satisfaction of taking the same title as that chosen 45 years earlier by his father.

Parker was educated at Rugby; he retained a lasting affection for his school, and served for some years as chairman of its governing body. He went on to Trinity College, Cambridge, where he took a double first in natural sciences. His intention at this time was to make geology his career; many years later he said that the reason that he took to the law was that there was no suitable opening for a geologist at the time he was looking for one.

Parker was called to the Bar by Lincoln's Inn in 1924. In his early years in practice he devilled for Donald (later Lord) Somervell, and his clear and concise pleadings owed something to Somervell's teaching and example. His style of advocacy bore the imprint of a pellucid and logical mind; it was cogent and calm, and unadorned by any rhetorical frills or devices. As an opponent he was at once immensely formidable and completely fair.

In 1945 he became Junior Counsel to the Treasury on the common law side, an appointment which is usually regarded as a stepping-stone to the Bench. It is a position which carries with it an enormous volume of work. Parker dealt with this massive load in a rather novel way; whereas most hard-pressed barristers work deep into the night, Parker preferred to rise at four or five o'clock in the morning, and he was thus able to devote several hours, while his colleagues were still asleep, to preparing himself for the coming day's forensic battles. This habit of early rising and early working persisted, though not always to such an extreme extent, throughout the whole of his professional life.

Parker became a Judge of the King's Bench Division in March, 1950. That he would be a success on the Bench was not open to doubt; but what surprised even his warmest admirers was the ease with which he adapted himself to the unfamiliar hurly-burly of Assize work—a sphere far removed from the more cloistral milieu in which he had carried on his practice for 24 years. He was, in later years, quoted as having said that the first summing-up to a jury he had ever heard had been his own. He had no difficulty in mastering the technique of what was to him a quite novel and different procedure. On all the circuits which he visited, Parker won high praise for his fairness and courtesy, and also for the skill and understanding with which he conducted civil and criminal trials alike.

His time as a puisne Judge was predictably short, and in October 1954 he was promoted to the Court of Appeal. During the next few years he was selected for a number of important and arduous extra-judicial duties, of which the most onerous (and the most celebrated) was as chairman of a tribunal which inquired into an alleged leakage of a change in Bank rate in 1957. This affair has now long been relegated to the lumber-room of forgotten history, but at the time it engendered violent controversy and emotion. The tribunal's report, which firmly and unanimously rejected the allegations of improper disclosure of information, was equally remarkable for the speed with which it was compiled and for the lucidity of its presentation; the skilful guiding hand of Parker was easily detectable throughout the document.

In 1958, Lord Goddard, then 81 years old, had reached the end of his long and memorable tenure of office as Lord Chief Justice. His appointment had broken with precedent, as previously the Attorney-General of the day had almost automatically succeeded to a vacancy. There was a good deal of speculation what would happen on Goddard's retirement, and whether the position would once again be used as a reward for distinguished political services. The widespread satisfaction which greeted Parker's selection represented at once a tribute to his outstanding judicial and personal qualities, and an expression of relief that political considerations were no longer considered relevant when this great office had to be filled. It was in several respects an almost unique appointment. He had never taken part in politics. He had never taken Silk. He was certainly the first Lord Chief Justice to become a Life Peer. He had no children, and he preferred this arrangement (which was made possible by the recently passed Life Peerages Act) to receiving the customary hereditary title.

In 1971 Parker headed an inquiry into the interrogation methods used against internees in Northern Ireland. The recommendations made by the committee of Privy Councillors affecting interrogation in general during internal security operations was published before he died. In the majority proposals Parker concluded that guidelines but not rules should be laid down for Service personnel applying these techniques. The Government decided to abandon some of the methods of interrogation, while allowing questioning in depth to continue.

As Lord Chief Justice, Parker provided a striking contrast to his predecessor. Goddard on the Bench had been the embodiment of massive authority and power—brilliant, impulsive, unpredictable, impatient Parker was invariably quiet, patient and courteous, though he too exercised complete control over his Court. He approached the question of the relationship between the Judiciary and the Government in a manner which attracted some unfavourable criticism. His statement that the Courts "have a positive responsibility to be the handmaiden of administration rather than its governor" did not imply (as some people supposed) that they have now surrendered

their independence, but rather that, in the complex modern world, individual interests have more often to be subordinated to the good of society. Nevertheless, one could not imagine such a phrase being used in any context by a Coke or a Hewart.

It is in connexion with the criminal law that a Lord Chief Justice usually makes his most important contribution. While Goddard had had wide personal experience of the operation of criminal justice at the grass roots, Parker had virtually no first-hand knowledge of the workings of magistrates' courts and quarter sessions, which deal with the vast majority of criminal cases. While there were obvious disadvantages in this, he was able to bring to bear on the complex problems of crime and punishment (never more urgent and baffling than during his period of office) a fresh and flexible mind. In general he was a humane judge; in innumerable cases, when hearing criminal appeals, he and his colleagues substituted probation orders for terms of imprisonment. But where the interests or security of the state were concerned, he himself imposed sentences which were harsh to the point of ferocity; when he sent the spy Blake to prison for 42 years it was said that he was indeed showing himself to be, and to an unjustifiable extent, "the handmaiden of administration".

Parker made an original and important contribution in the field of criminal justice—the organization of conferences on penal policy, at which criminal judges at all levels, with assistance from psychiatrists, probation officers and other persons expert in some branch of the subject, discussed appropriate penalties in specimen cases, and tried to find a way of reducing the disparities in punishments which had often been the subject of adverse comment. This constituted a revolutionary and welcome reversal of the time-honoured assumption that a judge, in passing sentence, was visited by some divine afflatus, which rendered suggestions from anyone else unnecessary and even improper. The fact that sentencing is a difficult subject, and one which demands and deserves serious study, thus for the first time received official recognition.

An ever-rising tide of crime seems to be one of the ineluctable facts of twentieth-century life, and Parker shared the general anxiety about this depressing aspect of modern society. He was especially concerned by the ease with which sophisticated criminals could slip through the meshes of the police and legal nets, and thereby avoid detection or conviction. It followed that he thought that the balance which must always be preserved between the rights of the suspect or the accused, and the needs of the community, had swung too far in favour of the former. And, although no one was more ready and eager to show leniency in a deserving case, he felt that many criminal courts, at all levels, were not nearly stern enough in their approach to crimes of violence, especially when these in-

volved assaults on police officers. During the controversy over the death penalty he had spoken and voted in the House of Lords in favour of abolition, but (after this had come about) he on many occasions expressed his disapproval of the procedures which resulted in convicted murderers being released, after they had served a comparatively short term.

Parker had numerous interests which had nothing to do with the law. He was a keen collector of old books and of antiques. He was an enthusiastic bird-watcher, and he enjoyed working in the garden: in his outdoor activities he preferred challenging constructional tasks, such as the building of walls, to the cultivation of flowers or vegetables. For many years his main recreation was farming; he owned a farm in rural Essex, and made a special study of genetics applied to the breeding of high butter-fat dairy cattle. Later he moved to a small and secluded house in Dorset, where he and his wife spent most weekends and vacations tranquilly and almost in solitude. The fact was that he worked so hard in London that he needed all the rest he could get to recuperate from the ardours of the past week or law-term and to prepare himself for those of the next.

In 1924 Parker married Loryn Bowser, of Kentucky.

September 16, 1972.

Cecil Parker, the comedy actor, died on April 20, 1971. He was 73.

His favourite part was Charles Condamine, the bewildered husband and widower of Coward's improbable farce *Blithe Spirit*. At its first production at the Piccadilly Theatre it ran for 1,997 performances, few of which Parker missed, and it established his position as a leading comedy actor. For any part which called for a certain amount of gentlemanly pomposity, coupled with obtuseness when required, he could not be equalled. He appeared the perfect English gentleman of impeccable manners and rugged commonsense, although he could give the impression that he was not unduly blessed with brains or imagination.

Cecil Parker was born at Hastings on September 3, 1897, and was educated at St. François Xavier College and at Bruges. He was on active service during the First World War and did not make his first stage appearance until 1922 at Devonshire Park Theatre, Eastbourne, with Charles Doran's Shakespearean company, with which he stayed for two years. Engagements with the Huddersfield repertory company, the Abbey Theatre in Dublin and the Liverpool Repertory Theatre followed, and it was with the Liverpool company that he made his first London appearance in Susan Glaspell's play, *Inheritors* at the Everyman at Christmas 1925. In 1929-30 he toured South Africa with Mary Clare* in *The Matriarch* and other plays. Back in London he appeared at the Everyman in a revival of *Lady Windermere's Fan.*

Keith Winter's play *The Rats of Norway* at the Playhouse in 1933 gave him better scope as the headmaster of a preparatory school in Northumberland in which his wife was Gladys Cooper and his masters included Laurence Olivier and Raymond Massey. In a revival of *The Constant Wife* at the Globe in 1937 Parker had all the dryness and control which Somerset Maugham's* comedy demanded and in *Bonnet over the Windmill* in 1937 he made a sparkling irrelevance of the actor-manager who recognizes the talent of the heroine. At this period his reputation was growing steadily and it was finally established with *Blithe Spirit* in 1941, to which he contributed a remarkable sketch of the pompous husband, whose first wife, returning to him after death, causes havoc as a second wife is now installed. In due course he has two disembodied spirits on his hands and one can never forget the roar of laughter which greeted the appearance of Cecil Parker wearing a mourning band on each arm.

It was a richly humorous study of a defective sense of humour and of an intelligence which just fell short of wisdom. Soon afterwards he was seen with Vivien Leigh* in *The Skin of our Teeth*, Thornton Wilder's "history of the world in comic strip". The human race was represented by a family of which Parker was the head, a part he played with skill and tact and drawing genuine pathos from the scene of his final encounter with his blood-maddened son.

He made his first appearance on the New York stage in 1950 in *Daphne Laureola* with Dame Edith Evans, and back in London he made an imposing figure as Menelaus in *The Private Life of Helen.* Parker began a successful film career in 1933 and among his better known pictures are *Caesar and Cleopatra, Captain Boycott, Hungry Hill, Ships with Wings, The First Gentleman, Quartet* and *The Chiltern Hundreds.*

He married Miss Muriel Ann Randall Brown in 1927 and had one daughter.

April 22, 1971.

Dame Nancy Parkinson, D.C.M.G., C.B.E., who died on December 10, 1974, was one of those women, fortunately not uncommon in the history of Britain, who through single-mindedness, a sense of mission, and innate goodness of heart, achieve wonders in their chosen line.

By her dedication to the cause of fostering international friendship, and by bringing the young and the not so young from all parts of the world together, she did as much for comity among nations as any individual could reasonably aspire to.

Nancy Broadfield Parkinson was educated at the College, Harrogate, and at Bedford College, University of London, of which she later became a governor. She read science, and as a young woman she was athletic. Skiing long remained one of her pleasures, and it is one which takes less account of age than many sports.

Dame Nancy first made her mark in work for the National Union of Students. This was recognized in 1938 by her being created O.B.E. She found still more scope when, in 1939, she transferred to the British Council. She was for many years Controller of Home Division and, subject to the guidance of the director general, she was supreme in all the council's activities in Britain.

When she joined it, the council was a young and comparatively untried body, its mandate originating in 1934, its purpose to promote a wider knowledge of Britain and the English language abroad, and to develop closer cultural relations between Britain and other countries.

The war brought pressing and unexpected difficulties, not least being an influx to Britain of people of many nations and of all ages. It was Dame Nancy's business to help absorb them, above all to make them feel at home, and feel that Britain was worth living in, if only for a time. She was as successful as only a tireless and supremely able person could be. Her efforts were recognized in 1946 by promotion to C.B.E.

In January 1965, towards the end of her long career, the Queen created her the first Dame Commander of the Order of St. Michael and St. George, the statutes having been amended to allow for this. This particular order of chivalry, recognizing as it does services abroad, or services to people from overseas, was felt by colleagues, friends and all who had benefited from her work, to be singularly appropriate as a distinction.

In the financial vicissitudes of the post-war years, notably during the 1950s, it was believed that Dame Nancy's division of the British Council suffered least, and this was probably a fair impression. The care of people from overseas was essential. It would have had to be done by some other organization if not by the council, and Dame Nancy had incomparable experience, and a way with her which was hard to resist.

She was subject to disconcerting changes of mood, but there were few stauncher colleagues, and few more generous in responding to an appeal. Her administrative ability, judgment of character and sense of purpose were such that she ruled her extensive domain without challenge.

Her devotion to the young never wavered. She made their interests hers, and although she gave her fuller friendship sparingly, when she did so it was with particular warmth. She enjoyed power, and the battles which go with it.

It helped to give zest to her life, and on any reckoning that was full enough, because she was absorbed by a task which needed doing, and one which she believed must go on if the world is to move towards that unity which can only derive from the fullest possible knowledge between diverse peoples.

Dame Nancy was unmarried.

December 12, 1974.

Val Parnell, who died on September 22, 1972 in London at the age of 78, was a theatre manager and impresario on the grandest scale. For 40 years much that was best in variety and light entertainment passed through his hands to be presented with skill, speed, slickness and panache.

Val Parnell was born in London on February 14, 1894, and educated at Godwin College, Margate. His father, Frederick Thomas Parnell, had begun life as a journalist and, for a time, had edited the *Hackney Gazette*, but in 1896, as Fred Russell, became one of the first professional ventriloquists to make a great success on the music halls.

The colour and excitement of this way of life naturally attracted the child Val Parnell, whose Christmas presents were often toy theatres. At 13 the boy started work in the offices of the De Frece circuit of music halls in the North of England. Later he became assistant booking manager and then booking manager to the Variety Theatre Controlling Company. When, in 1928, the Variety Theatre Controlling Company became part of the General Theatre Corporation, he remained booking manager to the larger group.

In 1931 the General Theatre Corporation was amalgamated with Moss Empires. Val Parnell became general manager of the new organization, Moss Empires Limited, and joined the Board of Directors in 1941. After the death of George Black in 1945, he was appointed managing director. With the coming of commercial television in 1956, he became chief executive of Associated Television, and was its managing director until 1962, when he was succeeded by Lew Grade. He welcomed television, convinced that once its novelty value had evaporated, it would be more likely to attract audiences to the theatre than to keep them away.

There was little about Val Parnell of the traditional idea of a great theatrical manager. Quiet and unobtrusive in dress, his appearance suggested success in banking rather than in the theatre. His work was done conscientiously and with complete efficiency, but his combination of extreme reliability with great sympathy for the artistes with whom he worked won him their complete confidence. This ability to work always on friendly terms, drawing from his wide experience as booking manager, was the foundation of his control over an empire which included the London Palladium, the London Hippodrome and the Prince of Wales Theatre, where, under his rule, pantomime and variety flourished.

For 29 years he was responsible for every act seen at the London Palladium, which he made internationally famous as a place of pilgrimage not to be missed by, for example, visiting Americans, and the dream palace of millions of television viewers through his regular show *Sunday Night at the London Palladium*. For many years he was annually responsible for the "Royal Variety Show", an event which, in his hands, worked with remarkable smoothness in spite of the number of flamboyant personalities it involved and which was always successful.

Val Parnell could not, of course, make stars. He could infallibly recognize the talents and qualities of personality which become stars. He did not create the now-legendary "Crazy Gang", but it was he who, when the individual, already successful comedians who compose that anarchic institution came together, found them the name under which they romped for some 30 years. His international variety shows at the London Palladium attracted the great names of American entertainment—among them Judy Garland*, Frank Sinatra, and Danny Kaye—to London, and by doing so helped to revitalize American vaudeville through the success won by such artistes in Britain.

Val Parnell married Helen Howell in 1938 and this marriage was dissolved in 1963. Three years later he married the singer, Aileen Cochrane.

September 25, 1972.

Sir David Hughes Parry, Q.C., chairman of the Court of London University from 1962 to 1970, Professor of Law in the university from 1930 to 1959 and latterly Professor Emeritus, died on January 8, 1973 at the age of 80. From 1947 to 1959 he was Director of the university's Institute of Advanced Legal Studies, and was formerly President of University College, Aberystwyth.

He was chairman of the committee set up by the Government in 1963 which recommended that the Welsh language should be given the same legal status as English in Wales and Monmouthshire.

If it is true that those who come from small countries leave their hearts behind them, then it may fairly be said of Hughes Parry that, although he spent almost the last 50 years of his life in the legal heart of London, his own heart never ceased to beat in Wales. As a voluntary exile he dedicated himself without reserve to the University of London, yet he always maintained his lines of communication with his homeland. Since 1934, for example, he was a member of the council of the Society of Cymmrodorion, and more recently deputy chairman of Caernarvonshire Quarter Sessions. When, in 1959, he reached the age of retirement as a professor in the university and returned to live in Wales, his dual nationality was so nicely balanced that he still found himself regularly and frequently in the precincts of the university which he had served for so long.

As a university administrator Hughes Parry was outstanding, and it is in this capacity that he will be chiefly remembered. His service on the Senate and the Court of the University of London goes back to 1930 and was crowned in the years immediately after the war by his tenure of the office of Vice Chancellor, followed by a knighthood. This was a very difficult period in the life of the university. For many years its affairs were controlled by a triumvirate (if such a term may include a famous woman), of which Hughes Parry was in many respects the outstanding personality. His administrative ability in the service of universities at home and overseas was recognized throughout the Commonwealth by the conferment of honorary degrees, and in non-academic circles by the part he played on many public committees.

After service with The Royal Welch Fusiliers during the 1914-18 War Hughes Parry practised at the Bar—he was called by the Inner Temple in 1922—from 1924 to 1946. Yet practice was not his main vocation, for during much of this time his chief task was that of building up the Department of Law in the London School of Economics, where he became professor in 1930 and so remained until his retirement in 1959. The early years of this period were a time of struggle among the Law Faculties of the London Colleges. Hughes Parry's efforts were directed strongly to the limiting of competition in law teaching, but the scarcely veiled hostility of that period may be said to have ended in 1951.

One may submit with confidence that Hughes Parry's greatest achievement was the establishment of the Institute of Advanced Legal Studies of the University of London, for this, with the help of money, especially from the Nuffield Foundation, and strong legal support, was largely his idea and his creation. In legal circles, academic or professional, throughout the common law world and beyond, there is no need to explain the importance of this institute of the University of London as the outstanding legal library and research centre of the Commonwealth. Hughes Parry became naturally and properly its first Director, and when after 12 years he retired, he had established an enduring reputation in the history of law teaching. It was in the opinion of some of his friends a mistaken decision on his part later to accept nomination as the chairman of the committee of management of the institute, of which he had so recently ceased to be director.

Not only in the Institute of Advanced Legal Studies but in the University generally Hughes Parry's retirement marked for him the beginning of a new phase of administrative activity. He was now an elder statesman and, as chairman of the University Court, the all-powerful Chancellor of the Academic Exchequer. In his later years he was fortunate to survive two serious illnesses, yet his life seemed to become fuller and fuller. No longer were his administrative talents employed in London alone, for from 1954 to 1964 he was president of University College, Aberystwyth. In the end, perhaps, both his heart and his mind were shared equally by his two countries.

Hughes Parry was born in Caernarvonshire on January 3, 1893, the elder son of John Hughes Parry. From Pwllheli County School he followed a familiar path through the University of Wales—where he took a First in economics—to Peterhouse, Cambridge, where he was placed in Class I of Part II of the Law Tripos. But his distinction as a student at Aberystwyth and Cambridge was not to be allowed to take him far in the direction of academic scholarship. Though an excellent lecturer and an able author and editor in the field of English law, he had preferred the path of academic power, and accordingly had time only on rare occasions, such as his Lionel Cohen Lectures at the Hebrew University of Jerusalem in 1956 and his Hamlyn Lectures in 1958, to allow us a glimpse of what he could have done.

His character was triumphant, filled with determination and inner contentment. He never failed to help those who turned to him for advice. He was never too busy for the many needs of humanity. Yet something about his administration had the taste of tempered steel. He himself seemed quite incapable of believing that he might be mistaken or that the good of the university could be other than he supposed. His tall, dominant and slim figure will be greatly missed.

He married in 1923 Haf, only daughter of Sir Owen Edwards. She died in 1965.

January 10, 1973.

Admiral Sir Edward Parry, K.C.B., who died on August 21, 1972 at the age of 79, sprang to fame when, as Captain of the New Zealand Navy's cruiser Achilles, he took part in the Battle of the River Plate on December 13, 1939.

The first winter of the Second World War was a very difficult period for the Navy, and one of the most serious anxieties was the depredations of the very powerful German pocket battleships, two of which were scouring the remoter trade routes and attacking unescorted merchant ships. A far-sighted appreciation by Commodore H. H. (later Admiral Sir Henry) Harwood, commander of the South American Division, resulted in the concentration of three cruisers off the estuary of the River Plate on December 12; and in the early hours of the following morning they sighted the Graf Spee.

Though his ships were out-gunned and out-ranged Harwood at once engaged her, and after his most powerful ship the Exeter had been put out of action he pursued his adversary with the light cruisers Ajax and Achilles as she sought shelter in the neutral port of Montevideo. Both British ships were damaged, and Parry himself was wounded but continued in command of his ship.

A blockade of the port followed while the Graf Spee sought time to repair her damage. Brilliant British deceptive intelligence convinced her captain, Hans Langsdorff, that far more powerful forces were waiting off the estuary than was actually the case. After anxious consultations with Berlin, on Hitler's personal orders he therefore scuttled his ship on December 17— a success to Britain which was as timely as it was welcome, Langsdorff committed suicide shortly after carrying out the order he had been given, and Parry was made C.B. for his part in the battle.

William Edward Parry was born on April 8, 1893 and came of a family with a very long and distinguished naval tradition. His great-grandfather was Admiral Sir William Parry, the Arctic explorer of the 19th century; and his great-great-grandfather was Admiral Sir Thomas Fremantle, who was captain of the Neptune and third in the line to the Victory at Trafalgar.

W. E. Parry entered Osborne as a naval cadet in September 1905, and passed out of Dartmouth College four years later. He gained five prizes (three firsts and two seconds) in the final examinations and was head of his term.

In the First World War he saw service in the Grand Fleet as torpedo officer of the cruiser Birmingham.

His first command was the anti-submarine school at Portland from 1936 to 1937, after which he attended the course at the Imperial Defence College.

From 1940 to 1942 he was Commodore, Chief of Staff, and First Naval Member of the New Zealand Naval Board. During 1943 he commanded the battle cruiser Renown, which besides war operations conveyed Winston Churchill* to Quebec and Alexandria for conferences of the Allies.

Parry was promoted Rear-Admiral in January 1944, and commanded Force L, one of the two "follow-up" assault forces which launched the invasion of Normandy in June of that year. He afterwards joined the staff of the Allied Naval Commander-in-Chief of the Expeditionary Force, and in 1945 to 1946 was Deputy Head of the Naval Division, Control Commission for Germany at Berlin.

In July 1946 Parry became Director of Naval Intelligence at the Admiralty, at that time still one of the most influential appointments on the Naval Staff. He was promoted to Vice-Admiral in January 1948, and in July was lent to India as Chief of Naval Staff and Flag Officer Commanding, Royal Indian Navy. In this appointment, at a time when the "Indianization" of the R.I.N. was being greatly accelerated, Parry's ability and tact, aided by the con-

stant and sympathetic support of his charming wife, made him as many friends as they had gained in New Zealand. Their departure from India was universally regretted by the naval and political leaders of the newly independent nation. Parry was on particularly friendly terms with Pandit Nehru.* In the New Year honours of 1950 he was advanced to K.C.B. and in the following year was promoted Admiral. He retired in 1952.

Parry married in 1922 Maude Mary Phillips, by whom he had one son and one daughter (twins). Ann Parry, his daughter, has published brilliant biographies of her Parry and Fremantle ancestors. Lady Parry died in 1971.

August 22, 1972.

Sir Thomas Parry-Williams, one of the best-known figures in Welsh literary circles for over 50 years, died at his home in Aberystwyth on March 3, 1975. He was 87.

He had outstanding successes as a poet, being the first Welshman to achieve the double at the National Eisteddfod, winning both the Crown and the Chair competitions at the Wrexham Eisteddfod in 1912, and repeated the performance at the Bangor festival in 1915.

Throughout his life, he had been a leading writer of both verse and prose and had published numerous books. He was a former president of the National Eisteddfod court and for many years had been an adjudicator of the chief literary subjects at the Eisteddfod. He was the first chairman of the B.B.C.'s Welsh regional council and a former president of the National Library of Wales.

He was born at Rhyd-ddu, Caernarvonshire, in 1887, the son of Henry Parry-Williams, the village schoolmaster. He was educated at his father's school, Portmadoc County School, the University College of Wales, Aberystwyth, Jesus College, Oxford, the Sorbonne and the University of Freiburg. In 1911 he became Lecturer in Welsh at the University College of Wales, and in 1920 he was appointed to the Chair of Welsh, which he occupied until his retirement in 1952.

His first contribution to Welsh scholarship was the work entitled *The English Element in Welsh*, published in 1923, an exhaustive survey of borrowing from English in the Welsh language. His researches into the development of Welsh poetry in the free metres produced *Canu Rhydd Cynnar* (1932), a collection of such 16th and 17th century poetry, and also *Hen Benillion* (1940), an anthology of Welsh epigrammatic verse. In 1947 he delivered the Sir John Rhys Memorial Lecture to the British Academy on the subject, "Welsh Poetic Tradition".

Parry-Williams's achievements in scholarship are, however, eclipsed by the eminence of his original contributions to Welsh

literature, both as poet and prose writer. His poetry, of which he published four volumes between 1931 and 1944, is unique for its style and diction. Metrically, it is simple, most of the poems being rhymed couplets, but the forthright expression, embodying words and idioms from the live, colloquial speech of his day, is a definite break with the standard poetic diction of the age.

Equally novel and individual are the short essays, the first volume of which, under the title *Ysgrifau* (1928) gave a powerful incentive to this type of writing in Welsh. Parry-Williams also translated into Welsh a number of well-known libretti such as *Faust, Messiah, Elijah* and *Samson.*

He married in 1942 Amy Thomas of Pontyberem, Carmarthenshire.

March 5, 1975.

Pier Paolo Pasolini, the Italian film maker, was found murdered on November 2, 1975 in the Rome suburban wasteland which had been the background of much of his life and work. His death, which deeply shocked a nation already unnerved by a wave of atrocious crimes, could have been drawn from one of his own films. Pasolini was 53.

Enigmatic and contradictory, a quiet, unobtrusive man who was nevertheless frequently the centre of scandals, who cultivated the company of the criminal or near criminal classes and who, by turns, offended orthodox Marxists and orthodox Catholics, Pier Paolo Pasolini was an outstanding talent in the contemporary Italian cinema.

His father, whom he described as "overbearing, egotistic, egocentric, tyrannical and authoritarian" (though later in life he decided that his hatred for his father was a kind of love), was an army officer and fascist from an old family. His mother, whom he adored, came from a peasant family.

His outlook was formed from the beginning by a passionate emotional identification with the peasantry. He learnt the Friulian dialect in order to write his earliest poetry. The choice was initially a search for "the maximum of irrealism, the maximum hermetic obscurity" (hermeticism was a watchword of Italian writers in the late 1930s) but he quickly discovered that the dialect brought a deeper understanding of the world of the peasant. Later, for the same reasons, he made extensive use of Roman dialect in his novels and films.

This identification with the peasants conditioned his lifelong dedication to Marxism, but he was always ready to admit (and constantly revealed through his work) that his ideas were as much shaped by the legacy of Catholicism which, even as a non-believer, he could not escape or ignore.

He arrived in Rome penniless, existed by teaching, and chose to live in the slum district of Ponte Mammolo. He enjoyed the company of pimps, tarts and petty thieves, which he later recorded in his novels. His first work in films was as an expert on low life themes. He worked as writer on upwards of a dozen pictures including Fellini's *Le Notti Di Cabiria,* Bolognini's *La Notte Brava* and Franco Rossi's *Morte di un Amico.*

In 1961 he made his debut as director with *Accatone,* a portrait of a Roman pimp in which dream sequences and the use of Bach music emphasized a mystical element which was never to be far absent from his films.

An episode in the omnibus film *Rogapag, Laricotta,* about a film maker directing a commercialized life of Christ, offended conservative religious opinion; but Pasolini redeemed himself—and surprised a lot of his Marxist admirers—with his sober and reverent *Il Vangelo Secondo Matteo* (1964). Later he reinterpreted two of the great classical myths, *Edipo Re* (1967), which he packed with selfconscious autobiographical references, and *Medea* (1969).

With *Il Decamerone* Pasolini began his series of entertaining and highly erotic adaptations of medieval story cycles. It was altogether more successful than the *Canterbury Tales* (1972) which betrayed its being mainly shot on a lightning tour across rural England, as well as Pasolini's failure to grasp the Chaucerian style. *Il Fiore delle Mille e Una Notte* (1973) was a film of remarkable visual beauty with a profound understanding of Oriental myths. At the time of his death Pasolini was still at work on *Sato,* or the *120 Days of Sodom.* The film was in the news when the negative was "kidnapped" from a cutting room in Rome.

Pasolini generally chose to work with non-professionals, using his players' natural affinities to the roles in which he cast them —though he did on occasion use major stars like Orson Welles and Maria Callas, who made her screen debut in *Medea.* In the course of 15 years he built up a loyal company of his own repertory players and occasionally played in his own films; he was Giotto in *Il Decamerone* and Chaucer.

November 3, 1975.

The Maharaja of Patiala, Lt.-Gen. Yadavindra Singh, G.C.I.E., died on June 17, 1974 in The Hague at the age of 61. He had been Indian ambassador to Holland since November 1971.

Born on January 7, 1913, he was educated at Aitchison College, Lahore. His father, Maharaja Bhupindra Singh, determined that his eldest son should be trained in leadership, sent him first to the Police School at Phillaur where he underwent a thorough training in police methods. He was then appointed Superintendent of Police, Patiala district, being promoted in 1933 to Inspector-General. In 1935 he was attached to a crack Sikh regiment, helping in rescue and reconstruction work after an earthquake had destroyed the town of Quetta where the regiment was posted.

His father died in 1938 and he succeeded to the "gaddi"; his first acts were to create a public health department, stabilize the state's finances and assure his people that he would bring justice to all communities, irrespective of religion. After the outbreak of the Second World War, he urged all the Sikh community to sink their differences and to unite with the British cause. "I should like to impress on all my countrymen," he said, "that this war is our war no less than Great Britain's. It is a war to save civilization from ruin." He served in Malaya, the Western Desert, Italy and Burma.

At the time of independence he took a leading part in negotiating the settlement concerning the Indian princes and, as chancellor of the Chamber of Princes, he was the main spokesman in discussions with Gandhi, Nehru*, Patel and Mountbatten. After the merger of Patiala with the East Punjab States, he became Rajpramukh from 1948 to 1956.

For many years he was leader of the Indian delegation to F.A.O. conferences and he went to the U.N. as a delegate in 1957. He was ambassador to Italy from 1956 to 1966, and a member of the Punjab legislative assembly from 1967 to 1968.

A keen sportsman—for many years he was one of the leading cricketers in India and he captained the national team in the thirties—he was founder of the Asian Games Federation, president of the Indian Olympic Association and chairman of the All India Council of Sports.

He is survived by the Maharani of Patiala, two sons and two daughters.

June 19, 1974.

Julius Patzak, the great Austrian tenor, died on January 26, 1974 at Rottach-Egern, Germany, at the age of 75. At once the most persuasive Florestan and Evangelist (in the Bach Passions) of his day, he was equally successful as an interpreter of operetta and of Viennese Heurigen songs.

Patzak was born in Vienna in April 1898, and studied to become a conductor. However, in the mid 1920s his voice was suddenly "discovered" and, as he was proud of saying, without a single lesson he began his career as a tenor, making his debut in no lesser role than Radames at Reichenberg in Bohemia in 1926. In the following season he sang at Brno and then in the autumn of 1928 joined the Bavarian State Opera at Munich, where he remained until 1945 as one of the principal lyric tenors, singing every kind of part and appearing more than 1,000 times.

He was probably most famous at this stage in his career as a Mozartian, and among his many appearances at the Munich Festival before the war was one as Belmonte in 1932 in performances of *Entführung* conducted by Beecham*; who invited him to sing Tamino under him in the singer's Covent Garden debut in 1938.

He also sang in Mozart at the Salzburg festivals before the war, and also appeared as a guest at the Berlin State Opera.

Patzak was at the same time building up an enviable reputation as an oratorio and Lieder singer. As early as 1929 he was singing the Evangelist in the St. John Passion and in the 1930s added the same part in the St. Matthew Passion. His Lieder recitals at this time are also well remembered in Munich.

In 1938 he undertook for the first time the title role in Pfitzner's *Palestrina,* which was to be associated with him for the rest of his working life, and he also began to take on heavier parts such as Herod in *Salome.* In 1945 he joined the Vienna State Opera, remaining on the roster there until 1960. When the company went to Covent Garden in 1947, audiences were able to savour for the first time his uniquely moving interpretation of Florestan and his arrestingly characterized Herod.

The same year he returned to Salzburg and sang in the première of von Einem's *Danton's Tod,* and the following year Tristan in Martin's *Le Vin Herbé,* but it was his Florestan under Furtwängler from 1948 to 1950 there that was perhaps the climax of his career. He returned to Covent Garden in the early 1950s to sing that part several times in English with the resident company, and he was also Hoffmann in a new production of Offenbach's opera in 1954.

Hampered by the English text, his performance was only a shadow of what it was in Vienna where it remained a model for years. His last public appearance as a singer in Britain was a memorable Lieder recital at the Festival Hall in 1959.

Patzak's natural, easy, rather reedy tenor was unmistakable in timbre. His vocal intensity matched to clear diction was self-evident in each musical field of which he was master. In opera he always completely identified with the character he was portraying. On the concert platform his eloquent utterance was as notable in Haydn's *Creation* as in Mahler's *Das Lied von der Erde,* and his poignant *Winterreise* remains an ineffaceable memory for all those who heard it. Fortunately he has left a large legacy of records, ranging over the whole gamut of his wide repertory.

He is survived by his widow.

January 29, 1974.

Joseph Paul-Boncour, a notable political figure in France during the last 20 years of the Third Republic, frequently a member of the Cabinet and once Prime Minister, who was distinguished in particular for his devotion to the cause of the League of Nations, died on March 28, 1972 at the age of 98.

A picturesque figure, short, erect, with a noble mane of white hair and gestures that matched the fire of his oratory, Paul-Boncour was for many years second only to Briand in the favours of the French political cartoonist. Although a lesser personality, as a politician he was in outlook and temper not altogether dissimilar from Briand, whom he succeeded, after he had for some years spent almost as much time in Geneva as in Paris, as permanent delegate to the League. Paul-Boncour's was a sincere and reasoned internationalism, supported in domestic issues, at least in the earlier part of his career, by Socialist convictions of a moderate stamp—so moderate, indeed, that at times they seemed scarcely Socialist at all.

Born at St. Aignan-sur-Cher (Loir-et-Cher) on August 4, 1873, Joseph Paul-Boncour began his career as a lawyer. With no other advantages in youth than his intelligence and industry, he became a barrister at the Court of Appeal and in 1899 was appointed *chef de Cabinet*—private secretary—to the then Prime Minister, Waldeck-Rousseau. He served the latter for three years, was private secretary for another three years (1906-09) to Viviani, at that time Minister of Labour, and with this background entered Parliament as a Republican (independent) Socialist for Blois.

Nobody could have made a more striking initial impression in the Chamber. Thereafter Paul-Boncour changed his party, or group, allegiance several times, though maintaining a general position to the left of the Socialist Radicals. In 1911 he received his first portfolio, as Minister of Labour under Monis—a short-lived appointment, marked by his introduction of the earliest French legislation in the sphere of social insurance.

An officer in the Reserve, Paul-Boncour rose to the command of a battalion in the war of 1914-18, during which he was twice decorated. After the war he established a reputation as a member of France's delegation to the League of Nations. As an expert on foreign affairs and military matters he served continuously on both the Council and the assembly from 1924 until 1927 and was specially active in the sub-committees dealing with the question of disarmament.

When, in the latter year, he was made president of the Foreign Affairs committee of the Chamber he was obliged to curtail his visits to Geneva, though not his enthusiasm for League principles. In 1931 he exchanged his seat in the Chamber for one in the Senate, and soon afterwards resigned from the Socialist Party—largely as a protest against the growing sentimental pacifism of one section of the party and the doctrinaire militancy of another.

In the summer of 1932 he served as War Minister under Herriot and in December himself became Premier and Foreign Minister in a Cabinet of brief duration. After that he had no fewer than four more

spells at the Quai d'Orsay, all of them short, the last in the Blum Cabinet of 1938, and filled in the intervals with Ministerial responsibility for League affairs, several missions abroad, and a great deal of other activity.

Paul-Boncour seems to have remained unmolested during the Nazi occupation of France. After the liberation he had no major part to play in French public life; but the experiment that had failed at Geneva still beckoned him and his silvery mane was to be seen and his eloquent phrases to be heard at the first United Nations Assembly in London.

April 1, 1972.

Katina Paxinou, the veteran Greek tragic actress who won an Oscar for her portrayal of Pilar in the film version of Hemingway's *For Whom the Bell Tolls,* died in an Athens hospital on February 22, 1973 after a long illness.

Born in Piraeus in 1904, she studied drama at the Geneva Odeon. Her first stage appearance was in 1920 in the title role of *Beatrice,* an opera by Dimitri Mitropoulos. In 1929 she went over to prose and worked with the Marika Cotopouli company.

In the early 1930s she set up a company with the help of Alexis Minotis who, later, was to become her husband. In the same decade she worked with the Greek National Theatre and in 1939 took part in the National Theatre's tour of England and played Sophocles's *Elektra.* In 1940 she returned to London where she played Ibsen with the Charles Cochran company.

Unable to return to Greece because of the war, she went to the United States. In January 1942 she played Ibsen's *Hedda Gabler* on Broadway. Engaged by Paramount Pictures, she played in *For Whom the Bell Tolls* and in 1946 in the English film *Uncle Silas.*

She returned to Athens in 1953 and helped in the revival of ancient Greek tragedy undertaken by the National Theatre. She and her husband, Alexis Minotis, translated several American plays into Greek.

February 23, 1973.

Lester Pearson, C.C., P.C., O.M., O.B.E., who was Prime Minister of Canada from 1963 to 1968 and a distinguished Canadian statesman who played an important part in the international arena, died on December 27, 1972 at the age of 75. He was awarded a Nobel Peace Prize in 1957.

He was one of the senior advisers at the San Francisco conference of 1945 that drew up the U.N. charter. It was work much to his taste. He grew to be one of the main architects of a distinct Canadian diplomacy which exerted an influence for

peace, compromise and the use of international machinery to deal with disputes that might threaten serious conflict. His views on sovereignty, nationalism and the problems of peace-keeping were lucidly expressed in the Reith Lectures which he gave in the autumn of 1968. In that year he had been honoured as Companion of the Order of Canada, and in 1971 he was given the Order of Merit. In 1970 he had an eye removed. In 1969 he was head of the World Bank Commission on World Economic Development; the Commission published a report which outlined a 10-point economic development strategy for the 1970s.

As Minister of External Affairs in the St. Laurent Liberal Administration, he was a masterful negotiator in the corridors of the United Nations, as was shown during the Suez crisis of 1956. Again during the Vietnam situation in 1965 his voice was heard, not always to President Johnson's liking, in influential forums as he tried to find a formula for bringing about a cease-fire (or at least a temporary halt to the American bombing) between Saigon and Hanoi. Indeed, in spite of some differences of approach, President Johnson did not underestimate his ability, flying to Lake Harrington, Pearson's summer home, in the late spring of 1967 to seek his advice on the Arab-Israeli war. He was a respected diplomatist at home and at the international conference tables and never happier than at some small intellectual gathering where he could expound his ideas for furthering peace in the world, sometimes by sheer "kite flying". Occasionally the ideas bore fruit, although others tended to "scalp" them as their own on both sides of the Atlantic.

However, as a domestic politician, he was unable to show initially in Parliament his undoubted talents for successful negotiation in the hurly-burly of the Commons debate or on the hustings. His whole training in academic life and in the cloistered surroundings of the East Block appeared not to fit him for a career as a political leader.

When he took over the reins of the Liberal Party in the Commons and tried to outmanoeuvre Diefenbaker, then Prime Minister, in the late winter of 1958, he was given such a lesson in political strategy—Diefenbaker gave the "Grits" the worst beating they had had at the polls in Canadian history—that he had to rebuild the whole Liberal Party.

The Diefenbaker Administration, which had started out so successfully in 1957 after 22 years of Liberal government, began to show signs of internal strain in 1959, and in the 1962 summer election the writing was on the wall when they barely scraped back into power. Nine months later there came the abortive palace revolution with the Tory Cabinet. Diefenbaker found his team in disarray and a federal election was called. When Pearson went out on the campaign trails that cold February in 1963 there were few political observers who believed he could not help being returned to power perhaps with a large majority, even campaigning with one hand tied behind his back.

But it was not to be. The Liberal leader could not really recapture the imagination of the electorate. Some saw him still as Minister of External Affairs rather than as a potential national leader. Incredible mistakes were made by his party advisers, what with "Truth Squads" that were ridiculed, pigeons that flew the wrong way with Liberal greetings, and a reliance on the old guard in Quebec that did not reflect the new thinking in *la belle province*. Yet Pearson managed to battle his way doggedly through organized booings and other hostile demonstrations, showing that he was much tougher than was at first generally realized.

Even so, when the polls were counted, Pearson, with everything going for him plus moral support from the United States, could only squeeze back to power with a small minority government.

Pearson's promises of great things during the Sixty Days of Decision did not materialize in quite the way he wanted them to. The first budget was a fiasco and there were demands that the Minister of Finance, Mr. Gordon, be sacked. However, Pearson stuck by him. In the next 18 months, while much legislation was passed, notably the Pension plan and the New Flag, it became obvious that the Government was at best accident-prone. It was beset by scandals in high places involving alleged bribery and corruption, which were examined by the Dorian Royal Commission. Ministers were involved, mostly from Quebec. There were some dismissals but little was done to clean house. The Prime Minister was beset with all kinds of internal problems involving federal provincial relations in which Quebec, now undergoing a quiet revolution, was determined somehow to be *maître chez nous*. Pearson evolved a new relationship between the provinces and Ottawa called Cooperative Federalism but many saw the formula as a move towards disunity at a time when more central control was required in the face of strong economic pressures from south of the border and a steady integration, not only of defence but also of industry, on a continental scale. During his regime there was an increasingly close relationship with Washington and ties with Britain inevitably became more tenuous.

His political reputation was probably at its peak in the summer of 1967. His handling of the de Gaulle* affair (the General, speaking to an enthusiastic gathering in Montreal, could not resist shouting out a slogan favoured by Quebec separatists, thus delighting French-speaking Canadians and gravely offending many of their English-speaking compatriots) was considered masterly. De Gaulle, rebuked publicly by Pearson, flew home without visiting Ottawa.

The main criticism of "Mike", as everyone called him, was the fact that he was not the lonely captain on the bridge. He was accused of being afraid of the sight of blood if there had to be some butchery

among his Cabinet colleagues. He showed great loyalty to his colleagues and would not be stampeded by adverse criticism of them. Yet he was badly let down by some of them who simply on occasions did not let him know what was happening, with disastrous and sometimes humiliating results; one saw this particularly in the affair that led up in 1966 to the Munsinger inquiry.

Lester Bowles Pearson was born in a Methodist parsonage in Newtonbrook, Ontario, on April 23, 1897. The son of the Rev. E. A. Pearson, he received his early education at collegiates in Peterborough and Hamilton, Ontario. He was in his second year at Victoria College in the University of Toronto where an uncle on his mother's side was chancellor and Vincent Massey,* a former Governor-General of Canada, was dean, when the First World War broke out. In March 1915 he enlisted as a private in the Canadian Army and celebrated his eighteenth birthday in England. Later that year he was posted to a Toronto-recruited base hospital in Egypt and was among the first British troops landed in the Balkan theatre. He served on the Salonika front for 18 months and was an acting corporal on his nineteenth birthday. He was then sent on an officers' training course in England.

After being commissioned in the Western Ontario Regiment he was later transferred to the Royal Flying Corps. On an early solo flight he crashed. Later, he was hit by a London bus in the blackout during an air raid and returned to Canada in April 1918.

Returning to Toronto University he graduated in history and entered Osgoode Hall Law School. However, he quickly realized that law was not to be his *métier* and got a job at a meat packing plant, first in Hamilton, Ontario, and then in Chicago. Still restless after the war years, he returned to Canada and received a Massey Foundation scholarship and, with it, two years at St. John's College, Oxford, where he won half blues for ice hockey and lacrosse.

Returning to Toronto University he became a lecturer in modern history and was given an assistant professorship there in 1928. However, in that year, with Canada's diplomatic service expanding, he was persuaded to join the Department of External Affairs and, gaining top marks in the entry examinations, he started his career as a foreign service officer at the age of 32. In 1930 he gained the attention of Lord Bennett, the Conservative Prime Minister and his own Minister of External Affairs. Bennett thought so highly of Pearson's abilities that he gave him a chance to show them in some important duties. He employed him on Canada's delegations to the Imperial Conference in London in 1930, and the famous one in Ottawa two years later.

From his work at these commissions and conferences, including the disarmament gatherings in Geneva, he gained wide experience of domestic and international problems. Bennett, who by this time regarded his protégé as one of his most able

officials, before he left office in 1935, promoted him to the rank of first secretary and sent him to the office of Canada's High Commissioner in London. There he did useful work for six years and was promoted to be Secretary with the rank of Counsellor. He made close contact with the Foreign Office, and with storm signals flying over the continent of Europe he reported to Ottawa on the fast-moving developments which led to the Second World War. During those early war years he was second in command to Vincent Massey, the Canadian High Commissioner, and his work during those tense and difficult days of Dunkirk and the Blitz drew praise from newspapers and respect from everyone who knew him.

In 1941 Mackenzie King called him back to Ottawa to be Assistant Secretary of State for External Affairs. In 1942 he was transferred to Washington as Minister Counsellor, and by 1945 he was his country's ambassador in the United States. His tenure of this office was successful but comparatively short because, when in 1946 Norman Robertson* gave up the Under-Secretaryship for External Affairs to become High Commissioner in London, Pearson was offered the post. It had been always understood that as a condition of his acceptance of it he insisted that, in view of the enormous expansion of the department's work, it should be retained in the hands of the Prime Minister, but at the same time entrusted to a separate Minister. So King, realizing the wisdom of this request, appointed St. Laurent Secretary of External Affairs, and he and Pearson formed an admirable team, cooperating very effectively in enhancing Canada's influence and prestige in the international arena. St. Laurent had not previously shown much interest in foreign affairs and Pearson's influence with his chief had always been credited with the latter's transformation into a Liberal internationalist. As a result, Canada was able to play an increasingly important role at world conferences and made a notable contribution to the organization of Nato.

Just before his retirement in 1948, King decided he would strengthen the Liberal Party by appointing Pearson to the Secretaryship for External Affairs, which his chosen successor, St. Laurent, was due to vacate. Pearson had considerable reluctance about embarking upon the vicissitudes of a political career, but his confidence in St. Laurent induced him to accept office, and he was returned to the House of Commons for the Algoma East division of Ontario in a by-election in October 1948. In the House he was soon recognized as one of the ablest members of the new cabinet, but he concentrated his energies upon international affairs and made only rare contributions to debates on domestic politics. As Canada's representative at international conferences such as the meetings of the United Nations and Nato, he had long spells of absence from Ottawa, but he gradually became one of the dominating figures at these meetings.

His abilities as a negotiator and conciliator, reinforced as they were by a genial bonhomie and gift for friendship, won for him the affectionate admiration of many members of other delegations and the widespread confidence reposed in him was responsible for his election as chairman of the Nato Council in 1951-52 and president of the seventh Session of the General Assembly of U.N.O. in 1952-53.

He negotiated with the United States the final arrangements which enabled a start to be made with the construction of the St. Lawrence Seaway and, while he never wavered in his belief that close cooperation with the United States in the international field must be a governing factor in Canada's foreign policy, he did not hesitate to make sharp criticisms of certain U.S. policies.

He was firmly convinced of the value of the British Commonwealth and Canada's need for close partnership in it. He became sceptical about the merits of some of the British Government's policies which it was pursuing, particularly in the Middle East, and in the summer of 1956 he warned the Eden Ministry that any military intervention in Egypt, which had not the authority of the United Nations, would have dangerous consequences and could not command Canadian approval. So he and St. Laurent were both justifiably indignant when news of the Anglo-French invasion of Egypt reached them without warning. At Ottawa the British action was construed as an indefensible violation of an agreement that no partner in the Commonwealth should undertake any major move in the international field without consultation with the other partners. Pearson immediately bestirred himself to repair the damage which had been done and took a prominent part in persuading the United Nations to express its disapproval of the invasion and to organize an international force, to which Canada sent a contingent, for policing the Gaza strip. He thereby incurred great unpopularity with many pro-British Canadian Tories.

When the Liberal Party was defeated in the election of 1957 St. Laurent retired from its leadership. Not without some opposition Pearson was chosen to succeed him.

He was slow to find his feet and, because Diefenbaker had dragged the Progressive-Conservative Party so far leftward from its traditional moorings, it was difficult for him to evolve for the Liberal Party a distinctive alternative programme, which would not have a Socialist flavour, unpalatable to many of his French-Canadian supporters. Some years elapsed before he acquired a sure touch about domestic problems, but he gradually developed considerable expertise as an assiduous "grass roots" campaigner. He strongly criticized the obstructive attitude adopted by the Diefenbaker Ministry towards Britain's move for admission to the E.E.C., to which he was sympathetic, and resumed his advocacy, begun some years previously, of the idea that Canada should take the lead in the forma-

tion of a broadbased North Atlantic trading community, although he later modified his stand on this matter.

In 1925 he married Maryon Elspeth Moody, of Winnipeg. He is survived by her and a son and daughter.

December 29, 1972.

Donald Peers, the popular singer who had a habit of making "comebacks" after the peak years of his success, the late forties and early fifties, died in Brighton on August 9, 1973 aged 64.

Peers, variously known as the cavalier of song and the grand old man of pop songs, was a former house painter who became the darling of female audiences. They swooned and screamed for him long before rock and roll stars made such behaviour fashionable.

He sold millions of records, appeared in films and on television, and was a regular broadcaster. He wrote a book and contributed articles to women's magazines.

Careful with the money he made, he once said he had no need to achieve again his old popularity. The son of a Welsh colliery worker, he was a debonair man who dressed well. He had great resilience, overcoming illness and injury to keep his career going.

Peers was a master of the "evergreen" song. He made hits of numbers like "Powder your face with sunshine" and "Faraway places". The song that became his signature tune was "By a babbling brook", which he sang on his first radio engagement, to his own ukelele accompaniment.

He first tasted real success in 1949. The year's high points for him were a one-man performance at the Albert Hall and a London Palladium engagement.

He worked in Australia, South Africa and India in the later fifties. When he returned to Britain he had to rebuild his reputation, by way of the northern club circuit. He reached the pop charts once more in 1969 with a revival of romantic ballads.

In 1972, with the aptly named song "Give me one more chance", he returned to the limelight after overcoming a severe back injury sustained on stage in Australia.

Peers parted from his wife Marie in 1953.

August 10, 1973.

Dr. Norah Penston, F.L.S., Principal of Bedford College, University of London, from 1951 to 1964, died on February 1, 1974. She was 70.

The daughter of A. J. Penston, Norah Lillian Penston was born on August 20, 1903. She went up to St. Anne's College, Oxford, from The Bolton School in 1924 and read botany, graduating with First Class Honours in 1927. She found herself attracted to research in plant physiology

and began work under the guidance of Dr. W. O. James on a problem of the potassium nutrition of potatoes. In these first studies she developed valuable techniques for the micro-chemical determination of that element and used this to study its distribution in the developing plant. She was awarded the D.Phil. of Oxford in 1930.

From Oxford she went to the Botany Department of King's College London as a Demonstrator and rose in due course to Assistant Lecturer and Lecturer, and acted as Head of the Department over the period 1940 to 1944, when the College was evacuated to Bristol University.

In 1945 she was appointed Vice-Principal of Wye College in Kent, the School of Agriculture and Horticulture of the University of London. It was the first time that this appointment had been filled by a woman; Dr. Penston's appointment was consequent upon the amalgamation of Wye College, which had been under military occupation during most of the war, with Swanley Horticultural College for Women, which had been rendered homeless as a result of enemy action to buildings. At Wye she combined the office of Vice-Principal of the new joint foundation with that of Head of the Biological Sciences Department and Warden of women students.

To her fell considerable responsibilities for the reorganization of the college administration, in assisting with the planning of the first university hostel to be erected in Britain in the immediate post-war period (Withersdane Hall at Wye) and with the complete recasting of the teaching work of her department.

Perhaps some of her happiest years were those spent at Wye in the pleasant countryside of East Kent. Though not herself a country woman, she readily adapted to country ways and managed to find time, in her full life, to take an active part in village and local affairs. Above all, she was at her best in dealing with students and in the small fully residential community of Wye College she had the opportunity, of which she took the fullest advantage, of knowing them all as individuals.

Even with the very heavy duties as Principal of Bedford College from 1951 to her retirement in 1964, she maintained an active interest in botany and in the early years of her principalship she lectured in the botany department giving short courses to undergraduates on the mineral nutrition of plants and certain aspects of plant anatomy. She was also a keen field botanist, and, when her timetable permitted, took part in field courses run by the botany department. In later years she had to abandon this as the pressure of her duties increased.

She was a member of the Senate of London University from 1951 to 1964 and until late in life sat on the council of several academic institutions. She was a member of more than one educational trust.

February 5, 1974.

Dr. Marguerite Perey, who discovered the element francium in 1939, died on May 13, 1975 at the age of 65. Her death occurred at the end of 15 years of treatment for diseases due to radiation.

Born in 1909, Dr. Perey had originally hoped to study medicine. Her father's early death forced her to abandon this ambition and in 1929 she joined Marie Curie's staff in the humble post of junior laboratory assistant.

At the time she intended simply to work out her three months' notice and leave, so austere and forbidding seemed the conditions of working.

Instead she remained for 20 years in which time she created a career as a celebrated nuclear scientist and became the first woman ever to be elected to the Académie des Sciences, an honour consistently denied to Madame Curie herself.

In her research she was a successor to the great traditions of Pierre and Marie Curie. And only 10 years after joining the laboratory she had discovered actinium K, which she later named francium.

But these feats were only achieved through dedication and hard work from someone who had joined a laboratory replete with highly qualified staff as a minor chemical technician. In her climb up the academic ladder she had the unique distinction of gaining her *licence* and *doctorat des sciences* in the same year.

Thereafter she was graced with many major scholastic honours and posts. She was first head of research and subsequently administrator and a director at the nuclear research centre at Strasbourg. She held a chair there from 1949.

Her decorations included the Legion of Honour, to which she added other distinctions: the Grand Prix Scientifique de la Ville de Paris (1960), Laureate de l'Académie des Sciences, (1950 and 1960) and the Lavoisier Silver Medal of the Chemistry Society of France (1964).

But her crowning honour was election to the French Institute as the first woman member of the Académie des Sciences in its 200-year history.

The last years of her life were spent undergoing treatment for the radiation diseases which prevented her from being well enough to attend her election to the Académie.

May 15, 1975.

Juan Domingo Perón, whose name dominated the recent history of Argentina, died on July 1, 1974 at the age of 78. He was President of his country from 1946 to 1955, when he was deposed in a *coup d'état*, and was called back from exile to be reelected in 1973.

In spite of all the excesses and eccentricities which marked his first period in office, he was undoubtedly one of the most original, talented and versatile leaders ever produced in Latin America. A born leader of men, he had all the qualities needed to appeal to the masses—good looks, personal charm, eloquence, power of oratory, an extraordinary understanding of mass psychology and, what is rare in a dictator, a sense of humour. He created in Argentina a movement that bore his name, whose strength lay in the urbanized working class, which remains the strongest political force in the country.

Few politicians, let alone dictators, even in Latin America have had the experience of being turned violently out of office and then, 18 years later, with all mistakes forgotten, invited back to lead the nation once again. There was a great contrast in his two presidential periods. His great defect, which led him to be deposed in 1955, was his inability to rest on his laurels and govern quietly and peacefully. He seemed to be forever seeking new enemies and he thrived on tumult.

During those first nine years his speeches were those of an agitator rather than a ruler, and Argentina acquired increasingly the characteristics of a police state; all forms of freedom allowed to political opponents gradually disappeared. He had the dictator's lonely temperament and most of his early collaborators incurred displeasure and punishment.

He was intolerant of men who showed personality or brilliance and came to be surrounded by insignificant people. After his return from exile in 1973 he basked in his vindication and, now an old man, was content to govern quietly, delegating responsibility to such a degree that it was constantly asked how much control he actually exercised. In fragile health, his main task became one of trying to stop his Perónist movement, which encompassed diverse shades of political opinion, from splitting apart.

Perón was born at Lobos in the Province of Buenos Aires on October 8, 1895, and educated at the International College of Olivos, a suburb of Buenos Aires, and at the International Polytechnic College. He entered the Military College in 1911 and nearly three years later was commissioned lieutenant in an infantry regiment. He was at the Argentine Staff College (Escuela Superior de Guerra) from 1926 until 1929. In all his military examinations he did well without being brilliant. He was professor of military history at the staff college from 1930 until 1936, when he was appointed military attaché in Chile.

He went on a special mission to Italy to study mountain warfare and was greatly impressed by Mussolini. "We shall create a fascism that is careful to avoid all the errors of Mussolini", he was to say later. He wrote a number of books on military operations, including *The Eastern Front in the World War of 1914*, *The Theory of Military History*, *The Russo-Japanese War* in three volumes, and *Operations in 1870* in two volumes, in collaboration with Colonel Enrique Rottjen of the Argentine General staff.

The Argentine military revolution of June 4, 1943, paved the way for Perón's political career. In November 1943, he was appointed Secretary of Labour and Welfare and began organizing the workers. He was already emerging as the strong man of Argentina, and early in 1944 held simultaneously the three posts of Vice-President, Minister of War, and Secretary of Labour and Welfare. In less than nine months he created his own personal following, and his speeches became steadily more inflammatory. He was still a colonel on October 9, 1945 when military opposition to him came to a head and he was obliged to resign all posts in the Government. Two days later he was arrested and imprisoned in the island fortress of Martin Garcia, in the River Plate.

The political opposition, however, failed to cooperate with the military officers who had overthrown Perón. The Perónists took advantage of their enemies' indecision and spurred on by the oratory of a young actress, Eva Duarte, who was to become his second wife, demonstrated in the streets. Perón was released and addressed the workers from the balcony of Government House on October 17, 1945. He soon announced his intention of standing as candidate for the Presidency in elections fixed for February 24, 1946.

Perón, who by now had been promoted general, won the presidential election with 55 per cent of the votes cast and took office on June 4, 1946. The fairness of this election was not questioned, although there were certain suspicious factors.

After becoming President, Perón accelerated his programme of social reform known as "justicialismo", while his wife, Eva, now idolized by the masses, monopolized the departments of labour and health and dispensed charity through the foundation that bore her name. Perón preached economic emancipation from foreigners, particularly Britain and the United States, and was able to get higher and higher prices for the beef that a war-weary Britain needed. Anglo-Argentine relations reached a low ebb when the British-owned railways were nationalized in 1948.

He was forever putting forward his philosophy of the necessity for Argentina to take a middle way between communism and capitalism, and made various bids to make Argentina the leading nation in South America and in the Third World. He was reelected for a second term in November 1951.

Although undoubtedly improving the position of the working classes and accelerating the industrialization of the nation, his economic policies began to prove unsuccessful. By 1952 there were warnings of bankruptcy; and in that year Eva died of cancer.

In April 1953, while Perón was addressing the workers from the balcony of Government House, two bombs exploded in the Plaza de Mayo, in Buenos Aires, killing six people and wounding 93. The Perónists in reprisal the same night burnt down the Jockey Club of Buenos Aires and the headquarters of the Radical and Socialist parties without interference from the police. A reign of terror followed and about 1,000 people, mostly of the upper class, were arrested.

Even after the first military rising, Perón might have remained President but for two mistakes—his decision to quarrel with the Roman Catholic Church and his grant to an American oil company of a far-reaching and unpopular concession in Southern Patagonia.

His attack on the Church, with whom his relations previously had been cordial, came suddenly in October 1954, and was precipitated by ecclesiastical disapproval of Perón's personal interest in the organization of girl students. After an initial official press campaign, Perón formally denounced three Argentine bishops by name as "open enemies of the Government". A series of violent measures were rapidly taken against the Church. Anti-clerical street demonstrations were organized by the Government, Roman Catholic processions and ceremonies were banned, divorce was legalized, and a Bill was submitted to Congress to amend the Constitution and disestablish the Church. The Catholics fought back in defence of their faith, successfully defied police bans, and demonstrated in the streets of Buenos Aires against the anti-religious policy. Rioting occurred almost daily. In the hope of discrediting the Catholics, Perón's Government committed the enormity of burning the Argentine flag and blaming it on the Catholics.

In April 1955 an agreement was signed between the Argentine Government and the Standard Oil Company of California, whereby the company was to prospect for oil in Patagonia. The concession, which included the right to build airfields, caused such an uproar that even the Perónist Congress failed to ratify it. The armed forces believed that its purpose was to cede military air bases in Argentina to the United States.

A naval and air force rising occurred in and around Buenos Aires on June 16, 1955. Naval aircraft bombed Government House and other strategic points for several hours, while sailors and marines from the Ministry of Marine building attacked Government House by land. The rising failed after about 200 people had been killed and 1,000 wounded. A few hours later the Perónists burnt nine Roman Catholic churches and the archiepiscopal seat in reprisal.

After this second rising Perón was not in complete control of Argentina's destinies, and a third armed rebellion was seen to be only a question of time. He made various efforts to face the gathering storm. He attempted a reconciliation with the Church, sent a telegram to the Pope, appealed for a party truce and promised to rule democratically. When these resorts failed, he made a desperate attempt to save his regime by arming the workers. But it was too late.

On September 16, 1955, simultaneous military, naval, and air force risings occurred in the provinces of Córdoba, Corrientes, Entre Rios, and Buenos Aires. The Navy was solid in the rebel cause and seized the naval bases of Puerto Belgrano and Río Santiago. Troops and aircraft sent to repress the rebellion changed sides, and after nearly four days' fighting the Perónist generals sued for peace. Perón published an ambiguous letter suggesting that he might withdraw from the scene to facilitate a settlement and avoid further bloodshed, and eventually took refuge in a Paraguayan gunboat in Buenos Aires. He went into exile, moving from one republic to another in Latin America; once driven out by a sudden change of government, another time because he had not adhered to the conditions of asylum. Finally, in 1960, Perón, an old friend of General Franco, settled in Spain.

His following in Argentina remained strong and he controlled his party from his opulent home in Madrid. For the next 12 years Perónism—estimated at having the support of about one-third of the nation—bedevilled Argentine politics. The armed forces were anxious to "cleanse the nation of Perónism" and ousted President Frondizi in 1962 when he allowed the Perónists to put forward candidates in the elections.

In 1964 Perón announced to his supporters that he would return to Argentina "within the year". He was to leave his attempted return until December, and some said afterwards that it was only half-heartedly meant. He crossed the South Atlantic, but at Rio de Janeiro the Brazilian authorities turned him back. His dramatic bid to return had fizzled out in humiliation. In Spain the Government demanded stricter assurances from him that he would abstain from political activity. Nevertheless, his third wife, Isabel Martinez de Perón was active on his behalf—and in January 1966 announced, in Buenos Aires, "a high command" of the Perónist movement, dedicated to returning him to power.

The armed forces changed their tactics towards the end of their seven years in power from 1966 to 1973 and General Onganía allowed Perón to make a triumphant return to Buenos Aires in November 1972. In the first elections of 1973 Perón was unable to stand because of residence requirements imposed by the outgoing military regime; so his close colleague, Héctor Cámpora, became the standard bearer for Perónism and was elected with 49 per cent of the vote. He resigned suddenly after only a few months in office and in new elections in September, 61 per cent of the vote went to Perón and his wife, who stood as vice-president.

The majority of Argentinians expected too much. The republic, during this second Perónist age, merely marked time. The fact could not be obscured that the caudillo, despite his broad smile and clear rhetoric, was old and in fragile health. Faced with a dangerous war between the left and right-wings in his movement, he chose the right. The young radicals and guerrilla groups, who had chanted and yelled in the streets for his return in the belief that he would lead them to a new socialist society, were slowly and inevitably becoming disillusioned.

Perón may have died a satisfied man, in his homeland at last and as president once more, but for Argentina it was little more than a short, heady time for nostalgia and illusion.

July 2, 1974.

St.-John Perse, the French poet and Nobel Prize winner, died on September 20, 1975 at Presqu'ile de Giens, in the south of France, at the age of 88.

A curious and in many ways detached figure in European literature, with his birth on a West Indian coral island, his extreme modesty, his career as a diplomat pursued under his real name, Alexis Léger, and his profound yet atheistic optimism, his work ranks among the most important in twentieth-century poetry.

His work was never easily assimilable by the general reader. A poet's poet, though not necessarily thereby regarding himself as a literary one, his admirers and translators included from the outset men like T. S. Eliot* and Rilke. Yet his poems celebrate his perception and conviction of the triumphant nature of human life. Though both he and T. S. Eliot share the early twentieth-century's preoccupation with the rediscovery of the values of the past, St.-John Perse's *Anabase*, with its continuous celebration of the rites of nature, is at a far remove from the literary despair of *The Waste Land*.

Marie-René-August-Alexis Saint-Léger Léger was born on May 31, 1887, on an island near Guadeloupe in the Antilles. The community around him was peopled with Africans, Asians and native Caribbeans besides the French and other Europeans, and the child delighted in the richness and joy of that exotic world, while at the same time belonging to a cultured French family. In 1889 the family returned to France, settling in the town of Pau, and the future poet attended the *lycée*, where he still gave his home town as far-off Pointe-à-Pitre for the prize-day list on which he figured in 1903. The great botanist, Father Düss, gave him his taste for botany, which he developed in the Pyrenees, together with a knowledge of birds and geology—these alongside his philosophic, linguistic, and literary interests, besides music, on which he later wrote a series of articles.

Before going to Bordeaux University in 1904, he had met Francis Jammes; and, soon after, he began a lifelong friendship with Claudel. Alain-Fournier, Odilon Redon and Gide were also of this circle, and the editor of the *Nouvelle Revue Fran-*

çaise, Valéry Larbaud.

After his father's death he entered (on Claudel's advice) the diplomatic corps. In 1914 he joined the diplomatic service as an attaché, and quickly rose in his chosen career. He was posted to the French Legation at Peking and promoted to Secretary. There he spent the next five years. Called in 1921 to an international conference on arms restriction in Washington as political expert on Far Eastern affairs, he was noticed by Aristide Briand, who chose him as his *chef de cabinet*, and with whom he remained in close association until Briand's death in 1932. He played a considerable rôle in the Locarno agreements (1925) and in the 1928 Briand-Kellogg pact outlawing war, and also at the League of Nations. As Sécretaire Générale from 1933, and with the highest civil honours France could bestow, Léger held office and represented his country at conferences where he met all the leaders soon to confront one another as enemies—Stalin, Churchill,* Mussolini, Hitler. In the face of the growing Nazi menace, he constantly opposed the policy of appeasement.

In 1940 France's Prime and Foreign Minister, Paul Reynaud,* influenced by intrigue at an unstable time, unconstitutionally dismissed Léger in May 1940. He refused the sop of a post as Ambassador in Washington, and, without returning to his flat, drove to Arcachon (where his mother was living) and, when in June Reynaud resigned his office to Pétain, left France as Hitler's troops entered Paris. By Hitler, he was a marked man: the Gestapo ransacked his flat in search of State papers, but found instead five complete cycles of poems by "St.-John Perse", a drama and a philosophical essay. None of these has been recovered.

After spending a few weeks in England with his opposite number Lord Vansittart, conferring with Churchill, Halifax and others, he crossed the Atlantic; for personal reasons he did not feel able to work with de Gaulle.* In October the Vichy government deprived him of his nationality, property and civil honours (he was a Grand Officier of the Legion of Honour) all of which were restored only after the Liberation. He proudly refused any work, in the United States, in connexion with government; and, with the help of a modest bursary from the Library of Congress in Washington, D.C., he accepted (as did Thomas Mann) "consultative work".

Although his rights were fully restored to him in 1944, Léger chose to remain *en disponabilité* until his official retirement in 1950. He returned to France only in 1957, for the first time since his exile, to take possession of a house presented to him by American friends and admirers at Presqu'île de Giens, not far from Hyères. At the age of 70 he had married, in Washington, Dorothy Russell, née Milburn; and continued, from that time, to divide his year between France and America.

Honours were heaped upon him, both in America and in France, culminating in the Nobel Prize for Literature awarded in 1960.

The full and rich life of Alexis Léger is an indication of the stature, not an explanation of the work of "St.-John Perse". Beyond a small circle few, before 1940 when his diplomatic career ended, were aware that the poet Perse was the same person as the diplomat Léger. Yet, his knowledge of literature, philosophy and the other arts notwithstanding, he wrote less from an enthusiasm for "letters" than from his experience of the "marvels" of the world. Eliot, he said, owed his rich vocabulary to his knowledge of language and literature; his own (no less rich) he owed to his knowledge of many things—plants and their uses; birds; ships; many lands and their peoples; many seas. Like Joseph Conrad (who had given the young poet his friendship, and whom he supremely admired) he wrote not from books but from direct experience. Through Conrad he had also met the English naturalist W. H. Hudson; it was men like these—naturalists and seafarers—who were his poetic tutors.

His first poems, *Images à Crusoe,* were composed when he was 17; and a few years later, *Pour fêter une enfance,* and *Eloges*—all these memories and celebrations of Guadeloupe and his native Caribbean. His first volume, *Eloges* (published by the help of Gide) was noticed by Proust and mentioned in *À l'Ombre des Jeunes Filles en Fleur.*

Anabase was written in a disused temple near Peking after a journey to Outer Mongolia; *Amitié du Prince* (in praise of a Malayan potentate he had known), on his return voyage from Peking by way of the South China Sea, Samoa, Oceania and the Western Seaboard of the United States.

Although known in England chiefly through T. S. Eliot's fine translation (1931) of *Anabase* (published in French, 1922) the years of his greatest poetic productivity were the years of his exile in Washington; the tragedy of Alexis Léger was the opportunity of the "poet, brother of the prince". He was a man who never looked back; once, in a yacht, he sailed round the coast of his native island, yet would not go on shore. For him, the great horizons of the American continent opened towards the future into which humanity (nature's latest and greatest advancing wave of life) travelled on into ever new fields of experience. *Exil* (1947), although occasioned by his own banishment, was "a poem of the eternity of human exile. A poem born of nothingness and made of nothingness." Yet for him that Oriental "void" was the rich mother of marvels: "La terre enfante des merveilles", he wrote in *Anabase*. His eyes found these marvels everywhere, from the vultures that circle over the city of Washington or the fungi that thrive on poster-glue, to mankind's perpetual migration into the future of the **earth.**

If his work has been more widely known and appreciated in America than in England, this is doubtless because the wide horizons of his forward vision finds there its natural landscape and its natural response. It is also thanks to the admirable translations of his work made by several distinguished poets and men of letters and published, in bilingual editions, by the Bollingen Foundation. These include *Exil* (1945), a tetralogy including *Poème à l'Etrangère* (1942), *Pluies* (1943) and *Neiges* (translated by the Irish poet and ambassador Denis Devlin), *Vents* (1946), *Amers* (1957), translated by Wallace Fowlie, *Chronique,* translated by Robert Fitzgerald (1959), and *Oiseaux* (1962) with illustrations by Braque.* *Anabase* and his later works have been translated into many languages.

Alexis Léger was a wonderful conversationalist, though preferring to speak of the world and its marvels rather than on "literature". To be a poet, he held, is a way of life; he avoided all things academic, never forgetting that "the birth of a book is the death of a tree" and how few books are worth the tree they kill. His only public statement on the theme of poetry was his speech of acceptance of the Nobel Prize for Literature.

After the death of Claudel and of T. S. Eliot, St.-John Perse was unquestionably the greatest poet writing in any Western European language.

September 24, 1975.

Dorothy Peto, O.B.E., who was superintendent of the Metropolitan Women's Police from 1930 to 1946, died on February 26, 1974 at the age of 87.

To Miss Peto belonged the distinction of being the first woman in Britain to command and train an official force of women police. Long before she was appointed, a voluntary organization of women wearing uniforms, exercising some of the functions of the police, had been established by Dame Mary Allen. The attitude of the authorities—and particularly Scotland Yard—to the force was one of toleration rather than approval but gradually developed into an inclination to welcome its cooperation, within carefully defined limits. Dame Mary assumed the title of commandant, however, and using experience gained in organizing one of the most important women's suffrage societies launched a women's police force.

In association with Damer Dawson, who on the outbreak of war in 1914 had persuaded a number of women to undertake what were virtually police duties, Dame Mary became an enthusiastic recruiting agent for the new force, which rapidly grew in numbers and prestige until it could no longer be ignored by the authorities.

It was undoubtedly the work of this voluntary body of women that convinced the authorities of the necessity of adding women to the official police establishment. Scotland Yard, therefore, added a women's section and Miss Peto was appointed, with the rank of Superintendent, to build up the new force. The number aimed at was 150, but from the beginning the task of getting enough women of the right type was beset with difficulties. Some recruits quickly tired of the work, and losses due to marriage and other causes tended to become embarrassing. There were also instances where the women police in their zeal exercised their powers of arrest without taking into account the physical danger to themselves of tackling men inclined to violence. On the other hand, some of the women allotted observation duties displayed such qualities of resource, devotion, and tact that they proved invaluable, and police chiefs realized that they were a great asset in investigations which men detectives found difficult to carry out without arousing the suspicion of those under official scrutiny.

Dorothy Olivia Georgiana Peto was born on December 15, 1886, and was educated at home. In her early twenties she took a keen interest in ambulance work, and when a demand arose during the First World War for women to undertake semi-police duties she first became deputy director of Bristol Training School for Women Patrols and Police, and later director.

After the war she was appointed detective inquiry officer to the Birmingham City Police, relinquishing that post to organize the British Social Hygiene Council in 1925. About two years later, she was selected as director of women police patrols at Liverpool, where she remained until her appointment to take charge of the women's section of the Metropolitan Police in 1930. She was awarded the King's Police Medal in 1945, and retired in 1946.

March 1, 1974.

Edwin Phelps, the senior member of his generation of the famous Putney riverside family, died on March 11, 1974 at the age of 83.

The eldest of seven brothers, he was born on March 22, 1890, within reach of the tidal waters of the Thames in the old Unity Boathouse (now the Ranelagh Sailing Club) where his father, the champion sculler, Charles Phelps, carried on his boat-building business. Ted, as Edwin came to be generally known, would recall in his old age the tideway scene of his childhood. Craven Cottage, now Fulham F.C.'s ground, was farmland and orchard, and at low tide boys from Putney would swim across the water to pick up apples and return by the same route. Although like all his brothers a first-class sculler and waterman, Ted Phelps was preeminently a builder of racing boats, being apprenticed to his relative, the notable Bossy Phelps, in 1906.

In a career of nearly 70 years Ted established himself as a great master craftsman and until well over 80 remained actively associated with the boat-building firm of his son, Edwin junior. Edwin senior was defeated in his attempt for the Doggett's Coat and Badge in 1914 and a source of greatest pride to him was the success of his son in the 1938 race—the tenth member of the Phelps family to win the event.

March 16, 1974.

Sir Henry Phillimore, P.C., O.B.E., a Lord Justice of Appeal from 1968 until April 1974, died at Maplecroft, Berkshire on June 4, 1974. He was 63.

He was the leading junior counsel with the British team at the trial of the major German war criminals at Nuremberg in 1945-46. A Recorder from 1946 to 1959, a High Court judge from 1959 to 1968, a Master of the Bench of the Middle Temple, a Fellow at Eton, he served on committees and commissions of great social and legal importance. *Putting Asunder*, the report of the group appointed by the Archbishop of Canterbury, of which he was a member, presaged the "Divorce Law for Contemporary Society" now in force, and he was chairman of the committee to consider the law relating to contempt of court.

Modest, friendly, forthright, unassuming, with a love for country life and country sports, it might have seemed that it would be hard for him at times to give all the working hours required for such devoted service to his country and his profession. He gave them, and seemed to give them easily, working over weekends and late into the night with the necessary piles of papers.

He was the son of Charles Augustus Phillimore, a partner in Coutts' Bank. His father's cousin was the first Lord Phillimore, who was a Lord Justice of Appeal from 1913 to 1916. Lord Phillimore's father, Sir Robert Phillimore, who died in 1885, was the last judge of the ancient High Court of Admiralty, and Sir Robert Phillimore's father was at one time Regius Professor of Civil Law at Oxford.

Phillimore was an Oppidan at Eton, going on to Christ Church, Oxford, where he took a second in Greats. He was called to the Bar by the Middle Temple in 1934. He was a pupil of Edward Holroyd Pearce, now Lord Pearce, and stayed in those chambers with their clerk, Arthur Smith. He joined the Western Circuit and soon had a wide ranging practice for he was a sensible, thorough, reliable advocate, who saw the essentials in a case. Work came easily to him. His quiet integrity gave confidence.

He joined the Territorial Army as a gunner in July 1939 and was commissioned in December. He served in Norway in 1940 and was afterwards in the Prisoner of War Department at the War Office. In 1944 he attended the Yalta Conference. In 1945 he was a full colonel and was appointed Continental Secretary of the British War Crimes Executive.

In the autumn of 1945 the trial of the German major war criminals began before the International Military Tribunal under the presidency of Lord Justice Lawrence (Lord Oaksey) at Nuremberg. Junior counsel had a great responsibility during the trial. The documentation was immense and had to be mastered.

The trial lasted nearly a year. After it Phillimore resumed practice in his old chambers. In October 1946 he was appointed Recorder of Poole; he took Silk in 1952, and in 1954 he succeeded Sir Reginald Hills as Recorder of Winchester. He was a good Recorder, patient, thorough, penetrating, with an easy authority in his court.

In 1956 he was appointed deputy chairman and was later chairman of Quarter Sessions in his home county of Oxford. In 1957 he reported in his forthright way to the Home Office on the administration and discipline of the Cardiganshire Constabulary. In February 1959, he held a public inquiry into the Viking crash at Southall the previous September.

In April 1959 Phillimore was appointed a High Court judge in the Probate, Divorce and Admiralty Division. In the same month he was elected a Master of the Bench of the Middle Temple.

He was an excellent divorce judge. He had the necessary qualities of common sense, understanding, patience and thoroughness. Sometimes counsel would try to investigate matters that might have occurred before the marriage and would be firmly advised to "start with the marriage". In 1962 he was transferred to the Queen's Bench Division on the retirement of Mr. Justice Hilbery. He was an immensely competent, conscientious judge.

In 1964 he was invited by the Archbishop of Canterbury to serve on the group to review the divorce law of England under the chairmanship of the Bishop of Exeter: "to consider whether any new principle or procedure in the law of the State would be likely to operate (1) more justly and with greater assistance to the stability of marriage and the happiness of all concerned ... and (2) in such a way as to do nothing to undermine the approach of couples to marriage as a lifelong covenant."

The group reported in *Putting Asunder* (S.P.C.K. 1966) that the substitution of the doctrine of the breakdown of the marriage for that of the matrimonial offence would not "affect adversely the status of marriage or the lifelong intention of the marriage covenant" (page 60) and recommended that change. The concept of the irretrievable breakdown of the marriage, embodied in the Divorce Reform Act, 1969, is now the basis of the law of divorce. It was expressed in the judgment of the Court of Appeal of which Lord Justice Phillimore was a member in *Wachtel v Wachtel* ([1973] 2 WLR 366).

In 1967 Phillimore succeeded Mr. Justice Atkinson as a member of the Royal Commission on Assizes and Quarter Sessions, whose chairman was Lord Beeching. The Commission's report in 1969 led to the

Courts Act, 1971, which replaced Assizes and Quarter Sessions by a single Crown Court and unified court administration under the Lord Chancellor.

In August 1968 he was appointed a Lord Justice of Appeal when Lord Diplock went to the House of Lords as a Lord of Appeal in Ordinary. He was a splendid Lord Justice of Appeal: economical in expression; always seeking the heart, the kernel, of the case; in harmony with his fellow Lords Justices; inflexible in integrity; and always happy when the result accorded with what was right and just.

In March 1971 he succeeded Lord Upjohn as fellow of Eton. He was chairman of the committee set up to consider whether any changes were required in the law of contempt of court.

A good fisherman and a good shot, Sir Harry was a born gardener. As Master of the Gardens of the Middle Temple he was a transforming director of work in the gardens, moving the sundial from the shade of the plane trees and surrounding it with roses. In the summer he found relaxation in vigorous croquet. He liked, one felt, to see life as a comedy.

In 1938 he married Katharine Mary, daughter of the late Lieutenant-Commander L. C. Maude-Roxby, R.N. and Mrs. Maude-Roxby. She and two daughters survive him.

June 5, 1974.

Wendell Phillips, archaeologist, explorer, author and a private oil concessionaire, died on December 4, 1975 after a heart attack in Arlington, Virginia. He was 54.

He attracted world-wide attention in 1952 when an archaeological party which he led into Yemen was forced from the country. The expedition sought to uncover the ancient capital of the Queen of Sheba at Marib.

The Government of Yemen later accused Phillips of smuggling a statue of the queen from the country. Phillips denied the charges, describing his adventures in *Qataban and Sheba*, a book he published in 1955.

Phillips's largest treasure, however, was yet to come. He persuaded the Chrysler Corporation to give him specially-built trucks for an expedition into Africa. Another firm gave 50,000 gallons of petrol. During the expedition Phillips met someone who advised him to concentrate his archaeological efforts in Arabia. That led Phillips to Sultan Said bin Taimur of Oman. They became friends and the Sultan appointed Phillips his economic adviser and director of antiquities. He also gave him the oil concession to a large area. Phillips sold the concession for $1m. and 2½ per cent of the realized profits.

His first expedition was in 1950 when, in cooperation with the Library of Congress, his group microfilmed more than two million pages of ancient manuscripts at the Monastery of St. Catherine on the Sinai Peninsula.

Phillips continued to write and explore. During one expedition he was said to have cured sick children, and was made a Shaikh in the Bal-Harith tribe on the Arabian Peninsula. "Not even Lawrence of Arabia was given that honour," he said in an interview in 1975.

In 1972 he lectured at the American Museum of Natural History in conjunction with an exhibition of treasures he had unearthed on his Arabian expeditions.

Phillips was a 1943 graduate of the University of California at Berkeley. He served with the United States Merchant Marine during the Second World War but contracted poliomyelitis.

December 6, 1975.

Pablo Picasso, who died on April 8, 1973, was the most famous, the most controversial, in many ways the most influential, and undoubtedly the richest artist of his age.

He was a draughtsman of genius, and there is probably no single artist, except Giotto or Michelangelo, who can justly compare with him in being responsible for so radically altering the course of art in his time. It was natural to think of him in superlatives. Yet the most pertinent superlative of them all only leads into a maze of, as yet, unanswerable questions. Was he, quite simply, the greatest artist of the first half of the century?

The question poses itself because Picasso bestrode the earlier decades of it with an indisputable authority. His art was always astounding for its diversity, the rate of its production, and its plain ability to surprise. For artists it held, for many years, a sort of bemusing and inescapable glamour. Yet, particularly towards the end of his life, it was seen to lie open to a number of grave charges.

Briefly, these hinged on the fact that Picasso fed, to a degree unprecedented in so eminent an artist, on the stylistic devices of other ages and of other artistic traditions, and that it was only by a peculiar legerdemain, the "transformation" process that was the Picassian hallmark, that he was able to absorb them and, as it were, re-edit them as a personal manner. A museum-bred art of this sort, it was urged, had had all its really serious artistic problems solved for it before it began: Picasso, to whom disguises and transformations were a life-long passion, was in fact only engaged, though with startling brilliance of invention and improvisation, in icing on somebody else's cake.

This charge led to the secondary but almost as damaging criticism that his skill was fatally facile, and it is certainly true that after the 1930s only a handful of his paintings can, individually, be said to escape a certain feeling of triviality engendered by the reckless speed of their execution and a tendency to dissipate the pressures of an extreme emotionalism in a dazzling multiplication of pictures rather than concentrate them in the perfection of the few.

It may, however, be said that much of this is symptomatic of the exasperation, neurosis and tragic despair of the age Picasso's art was reflecting. For as important as the strictures on his methods and achievements, and surely as relevant, are the claims that Picasso mirrored the emotional stresses of his times more compendiously than any of his contemporaries. His vein of savagery drew its power to shock from his Spanish blood, but it was as apt as Goya's and as timely for indicating the worst affronts to humanity of the modern age. For Picasso's art can be more easily interpreted in terms of Mediterranean humanism than most. It can be seen to have encompassed an exceptionally wide range of human emotional experience—horror, cruelty and death on the one hand; fantasy and the love of art, domestic tenderness and the gaiety of living on the other.

"Guernica", the terrible, apocalyptic picture recording the bombing of the little Basque town in 1937 and one of the few indisputable masterpieces of modern painting, is clearly the representative example of the first group. Picasso, indeed, seemed to give his *imprimatur* to this, the "black" side of his work, when he made himself responsible for the selection of paintings shown in an important exhibition in Rome in 1953. It contained many of his most horrifying images, like the almost beastly "Man Sucking a Lollipop" (1938) and the appalling "Nude Dressing her Hair" of 1940, and played down other aspects.

This "black" mood for obvious reasons aroused continuous controversy, and there was a notable outburst of pain and indignation, recorded in a memorable correspondence in *The Times*, when a selection of Picasso's most bitter works, many of them painted during the German occupation of Paris, was exhibited at the Victoria and Albert Museum at the end of 1945.

But the vein of sentiment or of impish gaiety was quite as persistent an element of his art. It accounted for a number of occasions when he disconcertedly reverted, in the middle of some particularly perverse style of distortion, to a simple naturalism in order to record the face of a friend, a mistress or a child. It became predominant in the period of his "antique" arcadian manner after the Second World War, and it was seen in a particularly touching form in a sequence of drawings shown at the Marlborough Gallery in 1953, in which the artist played subtle psychological variations on the themes of the artist and his model, intelligence and sensuality, which had always attracted him.

Pablo Ruiz Picasso was born on October 25, 1881 at Malaga, where his father Jose Ruiz Blasco, a competent painter in an academic tradition, was a teacher at the local school of art and crafts. Picasso was his mother's family name, and there has been some suggestion, as it is uncommon in Spain, that the family was of Italian origin; as far as both branches can be followed with any certainty, however, they were predominantly Andalusian.

The young artist soon gave evidence of the talents proper to prodigy. His father undertook to give him a sound academic training when he was seven, and when he was 13 handed over his paints and brushes to him in token of resignation to his superior powers. At 15, when his father had been promoted to the School of Fine Arts in Barcelona, he completed the competitive entry examination to the school, usually spread over a month, in one day; he was under age, but won first place over all the adult competitors. Two years later he repeated these examination feats for the Academy of San Fernando in Madrid.

While in Barcelona he had been drawn towards a small group of poets and painters who had founded a "revolutionary tavern" called *Els Quarte Gats*, the Four Cats. The prevailing attitude among these young Catalan intellectuals was an anarchic, rebellious bohemianism, not untinged with *fin-de-siècle* decadence. It was in the spirit of this group combined with first-hand observation of the miseries of poverty both in the slums of Barcelona and in the peasant communities of villages like Horta Da Ebro in Catalonia, where he was sent for a long convalescence after an attack of scarlatina, that he formed his first distinctively personal style, known as his "Blue Period".

It was with this style, nervous, highly charged with pathos and with a greater social consciousness even than he showed in his paintings of social outcasts, clowns, beggars, jugglers and harlequins who were the subjects of the ensuing "Rose Period", that Picasso finally arrived in Paris. He had made three unsuccessful attempts on the art citadel of Europe, during one of which he had been reduced to burning his own drawings to keep warm. In 1904 he came to stay, and found himself a studio in a battered Montmartre tenement derisively known as the Bateau Lavoir.

Here he worked for five years, the centre of a growing circle of writers and artists, among whom were his first patrons, Leo and Gertrude Stein, and the first champion of Cubism, Apollinaire. It was to this studio, too, that in the spring of 1907 he invited a few friends to see the large and astonishing canvas, now in the Museum of Modern Art, New York (and never, incidentally, finished) known as the "Demoiselles d'Avignon." It came as a shock even to his most devoted admirers, and no one (Braque*, Derain and Matisse were of the company) pretended to understand what Picasso thought he was doing.

It is nevertheless from this famous picture, with its brutally angular nudes and the savagely scarred faces which reflected Picasso's absorption at that time in Negro art, that Daniel-Henri Kahnweiler, who soon afterwards was to become Picasso's

dealer, has dated the birth of Cubism. Cubism proper, however, is generally regarded nowadays as the joint invention of Picasso and Braque, arrived at independently by both artists while on holiday in the summer of 1908, and made public when the word "cubist" as a term of derision was first used to describe Braque's landscapes in the Salon d'Automne of that year.

From now until 1914, when the outbreak of war permanently disrupted the early Cubist movement, Picasso and Braque worked together in an artistic partnership of extraordinary intimacy and concentration. The two artists submerged their individuality in a common style. The idiom they were working out was partly an excessive application of Cézanne's formulation of the geometry underlying natural appearances, partly an attempt to grasp pictorial space intellectually by presenting simultaneously the various views of an object which would contribute to a full knowledge of its shape and solidity. The first phase was appropriately known as "analytical" cubism, and this style, in which Picasso even executed a few portraits, remains the hardest to "read". But a desire for less involved complexity, and also for a new way of grasping "reality" by actually introducing "real" textures, or *collage*, into the composition, led in 1911 to what is now known as "synthetic" cubism.

In 1917 Jean Cocteau* invited Picasso to go to Rome with him to design for Cocteau's new ballet *Parade*. In this way he was drawn into the creative circle of Diaghilev's Russian Ballet, and the discipline of cubism gave way to less cloistered delights both in his life and in his work. In 1918 he married a dancer from the troupe, Olga Koklova, and in 1919 his travels with the ballet took him to London for the world premiere of *The Three-Cornered Hat* at the Alhambra, for which he produced the most celebrated of his stage designs.

Picasso's styles during the following two decades can only be briefly recorded with a comprehensive remark on their protean variety and their lack of any logic of development. 1920-21 saw the first massive, impassive goddesses of his "neo-classic" period. Between 1923 and 1926 he executed a number of extraordinary, sumptuous and complex still-life subjects which were the final and, as it were, nostalgic flowering of synthetic cubism, but in 1923 there had already begun the series of disquieting disruptions of human anatomy which were to culminate in his most horrifying images.

The element of horror had entered his art with his interest in Surrealism and had broken out in a purely sensational form, in the so-called "bone" styles of 1928-29. In 1935, owing to the disruption of his marriage, he stopped painting for 20 months. But it was in this year that he completed his most elaborate and haunting print, the large etching called the "Minotauromachie". Picasso's print-making was always an activity parallel and complementary to his

painting, and it may even be said that it forms as a whole the most perfectly satisfying achievement of an artist whose talents were essentially linear rather than those of the colourist, and who was more at home with technical invention than with purely painterly sensitivity.

No artist in history lived more in the glare of publicity than Picasso, and after the Second World War he became as good for a *bon mot* in the popular press as his work had ever been for an artistic furore. His uncompromising integrity during the occupation, and the publicity surrounding his attachment to the Communist Party the moment it was over, are the two factors which probably contributed most to the very personal form of attention which was now centred on him and continued till his death. On the other hand, his influence on contemporary art was suddenly seen to have declined, although his own artistic activity, which now branched out into sculpture and especially ceramics as well as painting, drawing and print-making, remained as prolific as ever. It seemed natural that by 1957 a London gallery should mount an exhibition called "Post-Picasso Paris".

The result was a beginning of the embalming process. Documentary information surrounding him had never been in short demand, but now film-records were added to it. The most remarkable of these were one by Lucio Emmer and one by H. G. Clouzot. The first was of Picasso's days at Vallauris, in the south of France, with the artist working at his pottery or executing, clad only in shorts and sandals and perched on a pair of steps, a trial fresco in a matter of minutes across the vault of a deserted chapel. The second concentrated on the stages of development through which Picasso's designs were propelled. In these films a larger public than ever before was introduced not only to the artist's squat, simian but muscular appearance, with the owlishly wise and humorous face and the piercing black eyes, but also to the turbulent inventiveness of his mind; the speed of hand and wit of line, the characteristic *horror vacui*, the creation based on destruction, and the endless process of transformation that made up the characteristic strengths and weaknesses of his art.

In 1960 the Tate mounted the most comprehensive exhibition of his work—and about 450,000 people saw it. Russia was persuaded to send several works from the Hermitage, and every important western gallery lent others to make it a more or less complete illustration of his artistic development.

By now few weeks went by without news of Picasso works changing hands at high prices. In 1964 £90,000 was paid by the Bavarian Government for a single portrait —said to be the largest sum ever paid for a work by a living artist. And early in 1965, not without criticism, the Tate bought "Les Trois Danseuses" for £60,000.

Exhibitions of a large scale, giving a wide survey of Picasso's work, early and late, and accompanied by elaborate catalogues, included "Picasso and Man" (the Art Gallery of Toronto and Montreal Museum of Fine Art, 1964). A salient aspect of his astonishing versatility, his sculpture, was commemorated in the exhibition at the Museum of Modern Art, New York, "The Sculpture of Picasso, 1967", the published record containing an essay by Roland Penrose. His versatility in graphic art and graphic processes was a continuing feature of his later years, as witness a remarkable series of colour linocuts produced in the 1960s, exhibited in London at the Hanover Gallery in 1963.

Of a special note among the many displays and tributes given throughout the world to mark his eighty-fifth anniversary was "Hommage à Picasso", 1966–67, Grand Palais, Paris, a comprehensive exhibition in the catalogue of which Jean Leymarie made the trenchant remark: "Picasso dominates his age as Michelangelo dominated his own."

His first wife, Olga Koklova, had died in 1955, and in 1961, at the age of 79, he married Jacqueline Roque, his model.

Probably the most intimate and in some ways the most unpleasant biographical work about Picasso appeared in 1965. It was written, in collaboration with Carlton Lake, by Françoise Gilot, whom he first met in 1943, who shared his life for seven years, and mothered two of his children. In a series of court actions Picasso attempted, without success, to suppress editions of the book and extracts of it in magazines.

April 9, 1973.

Group Captain J. R. W. Smyth-Pigott—See Smyth.

Geoffrey Langton Pilkington died on January 8, 1972 at the age of 86.

He was, from 1932 until 1949, when he retired, chairman of Pilkington Brothers Ltd., the famous glass manufacturers. But it was as an amateur horticulturist that he was best known, and will be remembered with affection by a great many people.

At his preparatory school, Stone House, Broadstairs, the then headmaster was an enthusiastic gardener and did all he could to inculcate a love of gardening in his charges. Geoffrey Pilkington, apparently, was an apt pupil and was eventually put in charge of the headmaster's garden. From Broadstairs he went to Eton and Magdalen College, Oxford.

He joined the family firm in 1909, became a sub-director in 1910 and a director in 1919. In 1911 he joined the Lancashire Hussars and served in England and in Egypt until 1916 when transferred to the Royal Flying Corps. He raised and commanded 611 (West Lancashire) Squadron, Royal Auxiliary Air Force from 1937 and

was mobilized with it in 1939. Being then 54 years of age, he had to hand over the command of his fighter squadron to younger hands, but he ultimately became its honorary air commodore.

His first love among plants was the genus Iris which he grew and hybridized extensively in his garden at Lower Lee, Woolton, where he was lord of the manor. He was also lord of the manor of Grayswood when he retired to Grayswood Hill. He was president of the Iris Society in 1925-26, 1937, 1938 and 1939. Among the many beautiful bearded irises he raised were Sahara, which won the Dykes medal.

He was an enthusiastic and indefatigable worker for the Royal Horticultural Society and served on its council for many years. There is scarcely any possible honour which he did not receive from the society. He was a vice-president. He received the Victoria Medal of Honour in 1960 and the Veitch Memorial Medal in 1965. The honour of which he was probably the most proud was the dedication in 1970 to him of a volume of the *Botanical Magazine* in recognition of his work for the Royal Horticultural Society, its gardens at Wisley and for the young student gardeners who worked there.

Geoffrey Pilkington was a man of unfailing kindliness and good humour and a great plantsman. When he retired to Grayswood and took on, not without misgivings, the large and beautiful garden at Grayswood Hill, he was by no means expert in the care of trees and shrubs for which the garden is famous. But for over 20 years he and his gardeners have cared for and enriched this garden. His wise counsel and kindly interest in all aspects of horticulture will be greatly missed.

He is survived by his widow, his daughters Cynthia, Barbara and Angela, and his sons Robert and George.

January 10, 1972.

General Rojas Pinilla—See Rojas.

Alberto Pirelli, president of the Pirelli Rubber Company from 1956 to 1965, died on October 19, 1971 at the age of 89. He was the father of the present company president, Leopoldo Pirelli. He had been honorary president of the Italian company and the international Pirelli-Dunlop group since his retirement in 1965.

He was a distinguished member of the family that gave Italy a leading position in the world rubber industry and a well known figure in European diplomacy.

Born in Milan in 1882 he belonged to the second generation of the Pirelli dynasty. The firm had been founded by his father, Giovanni Battista Pirelli, a pioneer of Italian industrialization, in 1872. Two years before, an Italian ship, sunk in the Adriatic, had taken several months to be refloated

because some rubber cables that were needed for the operation had to be bought abroad. Giovanni Battista Pirelli decided that this should not happen again and that Italy must have a rubber industry. He built his first factory in what was then the outskirts of Milan and called it the Sevesetto from a creek, the Seveso, hard by. Now the creek has been covered and what 100 years ago was country has become part of the centre of the town. On the site of the old factory stands the Pirelli skyscraper.

Alberto Pirelli made an early and substantial contribution to the company's growth. He was only 22 when, after studying engineering, economics and law in Milan and Genoa Universities, he was called by his father to share with him and with his elder brother, Piero, the responsibility for the firm's management. In 1921, when it became necessary, because of its size, to transform the family concern into a joint stock company, he was appointed managing director. In 1932, at the death of his father, Piero succeeded him as president and Alberto was appointed vice-president. He became president when Piero died in 1956.

Alberto Pirelli was one of the few Italian industrialists who could show a record of public service. In this also he followed a tradition started by his father, who ran away from home when he was 17 and joined Garibaldi, under whose banners he fought as a volunteer in the 1866 war against Austria and later in the unsuccessful attempt made by the general to conquer Rome in 1867.

Alberto's field was diplomacy. Of his experience as an economic and financial expert with the Italian Foreign Ministry he gave a lively account in a book of memoirs published in 1961 under the title *Dopoguerra 1919-1932 (Aftermath of the war 1919-1932)*, which is also a useful primary source for the historian of the period. After serving in the concluding phase of the war as head of the foreign section in the Ministry of Ammunition, he was one of the leading members of the Italian economic and financial delegation at the Versailles Conference. From 1920 to 1922 he represented Italy at the I.L.O., and from 1923 to 1927 he did the same in the Economic and Social Council of the League of Nations. Between 1922 and 1930 he was a member of the Italian delegations to the Conferences of Cannes and Genoa (1922), London (1924), Paris (1925), The Hague (1929-30). He was in fact the chief negotiator on the Italian side in the settlement of the war debts and reparations. As such he played a significant role in working out the Dawes and Young plans, and at the Conferences of London and Washington the settlement of the Italian war debts.

After the Second World War, apart from participating in the New York negotiations for the American financing of the European industries in 1951, he was no longer active in the diplomatic field. He kept, however, in close contact with the diplomatic world as president of the Milan I.S.P.I. (Institute for the Study of International Politics), of which he was one of the founders in 1935.

Pirelli was a pioneer in sport as well as in industry. He was the first Italian to fly—as a passenger, on Wilbur Wright's biplane, in 1908. He played in the first Milan Association football team. He won several lawn tennis championships. When he was 22 he explored the Amazon river in a canoe.

In politics he was an enlightened conservative. The Pirelli social and welfare services have long been a model. He was the first Italian industrialist to grant his workers paid holidays. He was a staunch supporter of the Common Market—and of Britain's participation in it.

A slender, energetic man with a bright smile and piercing eyes, he sometimes gave the impression, particularly in advanced age, of being a little dry and hard. This was perhaps because he was, for all his social polishing, fundamentally shy—"a shy and patrician cosmopolitan", as he was called by an American magazine. He was a refined *causeur*, with a full command of several languages. His English was flawless. He was above all a shrewd, able, practical negotiator.

October 21, 1971.

Wilhelm Pitz, who from the start trained the New Philharmonia Chorus, died on November 21, 1973. An efficient instrumentalist who became, more or less incidentally, an efficient conductor, he was a choir trainer second to none, indefatigably engaged week by week in Vienna and London, with the *Singverein* of the one and the New Philharmonia Chorus of the other, and occupied year by year with the Bayreuth Festival as well as with the chorus of the Vienna State Opera.

Wilhelm Pitz was born in 1898, and became a violinist in the Opera House at Aachen when he was 15 years old, remaining in the orchestra pit until he was appointed chorus master in 1933. When the Bayreuth Festival was revived in 1951 he undertook the selection and training of the choir, a task he performed at all the succeeding festivals.

When, in 1957, Walter Legge created the Philharmonia Chorus to work with the Philharmonia Orchestra which he had founded 12 years before, he entrusted its training from the start to Pitz, who with apparently boundless energy and enthusiasm seemed to think nothing of weekly journeys from his home in Aachen to Vienna and to London.

In later years Pitz spoke of the creation of the Philharmonia Chorus with a great deal of pride, as one of the best things he had ever done, and he remained with it after its founder had withdrawn from its management and, to preserve itself, it had become an independent body. The results of Pitz's work were heard at its first concert

and have never since been in doubt.

He not only brought a new choir to eminence in a country justly proud of its tradition of choral music, but added new athleticisms and new subtleties of nuance and interpretation to the sturdy wholeheartedness which English choirs seem instinctively to give to music.

His range was wide, from Wagner at Bayreuth to Bach and Handel, to Verdi's *Requiem* and to *Belshazzar's Feast,* taking in all the major choral music of the years between them. His attitude was undoctrinaire, for he rejected the idea that eighteenth-century music should be sung in large modern halls by choirs no larger than those which Bach and Handel would have used. Music to him was essentially dramatic and exciting; mere accuracy, difficult enough to achieve in some music, was only the beginning, and he made it clear that he required not only all the enthusiasm and wholeheartedness of which each singer was capable but also an intelligent and thoughtful awareness of each work's individual demands.

The cruelly high *tessitura* of the soprano part in many passages in the Choral Symphony and the *Missa Solemnis*, which often suggest that Beethoven miscalculated the physical capacities of the human voice, seemed to sound not merely secure but full, unstrained and expressive when sung by a choir which he had trained.

As the Philharmonia's chorus master, he was from time to time seen as a conductor in London, notably in performances of Handel's *Messiah*, a work which he treated in a restrained and classical way but which expressed his vigorous, dramatic attitude in expressive subtleties of choral phrasing and nuance.

The polish and excitement of the choral singing he produced seemed to be the result not of some special technical secrets which he alone could impart but purely a matter of personality.

Would-be singers were auditioned with rigorous exactitude but, at the same time, with a charmingly friendly good nature which won the hearts of his forces no less completely than the unprofessional devotion of the Philharmonia Chorus won his; for he was always stirred by the enthusiasm of men and women who would rehearse exhaustively for mere delight in music after a day's work.

He was appointed an honorary O.B.E. in 1970.

November 23, 1973.

Maurice Platnauer, former Principal of Brasenose College, Oxford, who died on December 19, 1974 at the age of 87, was born at York, the only child of H. M. Platnauer, a member of the museum staff there. He was educated at Shrewsbury, where he was a mathematical scholar, and then at New College, Oxford, where he won first

classes in Classical Honour Moderations and in Literae Humaniores, after being made an honorary scholar of the college.

He then took the B.Litt. degree with a dissertation on Septimus Severus, which was awarded the unusual accolade of praise from a leader writer in *The Times* many years later. He was an assistant master for four years at Winchester, until the First World War, when he volunteered for the Royal Field Artillery.

After three more years at Winchester, where he was exceedingly happy teaching the Senior Division in classics, he was elected a Fellow of Brasenose in 1922. He taught the classics (passmen at first as well as honours), for nearly 35 years, and was a university Lecturer in Classics for most of that time. He was Vice-Principal of the college from 1936 to 1956, Curator of Common Room from 1946 to 1956, and Principal from 1956 to 1960. He was also an Honorary Fellow of New College.

His published works were the monograph on Septimus Severus, a translation of Claudian for the Loeb edition (1921), an edition with commentary of Euripides' *Iphigenia in Tauris* (1937), and *Latin Elegiac Verse*, a most useful book on the linguistic and metrical usage of the Latin Elegiac poets (1951), and he was editor of *Fifty Years of Classical Scholarship* (1954).

He also contributed to the *Classical Quarterly*, which he edited from 1936 to 1947, and to other classical journals at home and abroad. After his retirement in 1960 he was heavily engaged in helping with the revision of Liddell and Scott's lexicon, and produced a new edition, with commentary, of *The Peace* of Aristophanes.

As a scholar he was careful and meticulous. A keen student of language and especially of grammar and syntax, he was one of those rare men who enjoy reading voluminous grammars from beginning to end; and other Oxford dons used to appeal to him as an expert on Greek accentuation. His lectures were exceptionally lucid; he would expound problems in the text of Theocritus without looking at a note, and, in middle age at least, he could cite all the references from memory.

He had a keen taste in classical literature, and was a very good composer in Greek. He was well read, too, in English literature, and was a voracious reader of modern novels.

In his early years at Brasenose his was a notably "civilizing" influence. He was devoted to music, which he also did much to promote in the university, although he would say that he had "a passion" in that sphere "for the second rate".

He was an expert on French wine and food, and would spend months in the summer walking, cycling or canoeing in France. He knew the south of France better than any Englishman or most Frenchmen do.

In later life he inherited a large fortune from his mother, and in 1954 he gave the first of several large benefactions to his college. But his increased wealth made little difference to his habits, except that it enabled him to make large gifts to friends in need, which he did by stealth. He was frugal in his way of life: until old age he rarely took a taxi when he could get a bus.

But his hospitality was proverbial. There can have been few university dons who not only royally entertained so many friends and acquaintances, but also formed such deep and long lasting friendships with members of each generation. He was rather shy, of great modesty, and his gentleness and courtesy won him exceptional affection from the young as well as the old, and not only in the college which he loved so well and served so faithfully.

December 23, 1974.

General Sir William Platt, G.B.E., K.C.B., D.S.O., died on September 28, 1975 at the age of 90. His was a long and distinguished career in the Army, but he was best known to the public as the victor of Keren, the battle which broke the Italian resistance at the outset of the Abyssinian campaign in 1941.

He was a fine tactician, a good administrator and a splendid trainer of troops, and he had the gift of grasping the essentials of a problem and making quick decisions. He was a man of great courage and inexhaustible energy—one of his junior officers once described him as a "stick of dynamite in a hot fire when there was a job to be done".

William Platt was born on June 14, 1885, the son of John Platt of Carnforth. He was educated at Marlborough, and the Royal Military College, Sandhurst, from which he was commissioned in the Northumberland Fusiliers in 1905. His first active service was with his regiment in the Mohmand operations on the North-west Frontier of India in 1908, in the course of which he won the D.S.O., a rare distinction for a junior subaltern.

In the First World War, in which he was wounded, he served in France and Belgium, and was mentioned in dispatches four times and awarded the brevets of Major and Lieutenant-Colonel. He had been a brigade major and a general staff officer, both 1st and 2nd grade, in France, so he already had considerable experience of staff work in the field before he went to the Staff College after the war.

When the Second World War broke out, he had already been a Major-General for a year, and was commanding the troops in the Sudan. Apart from some skirmishes with Italian detachments which crossed the Sudanese border, he was not involved in any serious fighting for the first few months of the war. But his chance to play an active part came when Wavell, having rounded up Graziani's Army in Libya at the end of 1940, turned his attention to the occupation of Abyssinia.

The operations from the North were entrusted to Platt, and he was given two divisions supported by six air squadrons. The opening phase of his advance met with easy success, and the Italians were soon driven back across the frontier. A serious check occurred at Keren. The enemy force outnumbered his by two to one. They stood on an immensely strong mountain position; the flanks could not be turned and there was only a single road, in full view of the defenders.

After several abortive attacks Platt decided to accept the delay necessary to stage a fully prepared assault. When the attack went in, the Italians resisted stubbornly. But after ten days' fighting, in which British troops suffered 3,000 casualties, the defence broke, and Platt pressed the pursuit with vigour.

Then Massawa fell a week later with 10,000 prisoners, and the advance into the interior was continued with complete success.

In the meantime General Alan Cunningham, advancing from Kenya, had reached Addis Ababa. Platt's forces joined hands with his at Amba Alagi, where the Italian Commander, the Duke of Aosta, surrendered on May 18, after his mountain positions had been stormed by British and Indian troops.

On receiving the congratulations of His Majesty's Government upon his conduct of the operations, he described Keren and the other engagements in Abyssinia, with characteristic modesty, as "bows and arrows" battles compared with those which took place in the Western Desert. But, had it not been for his vigorous and competent leadership, the Italian occupation of Abyssinia might have been indefinitely prolonged.

On the conclusion of the campaign he was appointed G.O.C.-in-C. of a new command in East Africa, comprising the territories lying between the southern border of the Sudan and the northern border of Southern Rhodesia. Soon after he had taken over the command, Diego Suarez was occupied by a force sent out from England. The French Governor General refused to capitulate, and it fell to Platt to direct the operations to complete the occupation of Madagascar.

But his duties in this, his last command, were mainly administrative. One of the most important of these was the organization and training of the African troops which played such a notable part in the Burma Campaign, and it was primarily due to him that they achieved such a high standard of efficiency.

After his retirement in 1945, he devoted much of his leisure to the Outward Bound Movement. The theatre became his chief recreation in his latter years, and his delight in it and his warm, infectious interest in every aspect of it opened a new and fascinating world to him. He was for more than eight years an active member of the Drama Panel of the Arts Council of Great Britain.

He was created K.C.B. in 1941 (C.B., 1939) and G.B.E. in 1943. He was A.D.C. to the King from 1937 to 1938, and was Colonel of the Wiltshire Regiment from 1942 to 1954. He was a Commander of the Legion of Honour and a Grand Officer of the Star of Ethiopia, the Order of the Nile and the Belgian Order of the Crown. He was made a Freeman of the Fruiterers' Company, an honour which gave him immense pleasure.

He married in 1921 Mollie, daughter of Dendy Watney of Addlestone and had two sons.

September 29, 1975.

Arpad Plesch, the Hungarian-born lawyer, financier and racehorse owner, died in London on December 16, 1974. He was 85.

At his estate at Beaulieu in the South of France he had assembled a very fine collection of rare plants and a library of botanical books of rare quality. His love of trees and plants was reflected in the names given to his horses.

He was educated at the University of Budapest and other European universities, became a doctor of law and before the Second World War had become a demonstrably successful financier and adviser on investment. Much of his fortune is believed to have come from Cuban sugar but he was never content to confine his business activities to one particular field. After the war he invested in Japanese industry at a time when Japan was still finding her feet after the disasters which had hit her.

In his financial operations Arpad Plesch was a great believer in gold as the best "hedge" against inflation and devaluations. In the 1930s, following the depression and the abandonment of the Gold Standard, he held large numbers of bonds containing "gold clauses" to the effect that the face value and interest were to be redeemable in gold coin or in currency equivalent to the value of gold. In particular, he was the holder of a large block of convertible "gold notes" issued by the British Government in 1917 redeemable in New York or London. However, gold clauses had by then been declared contrary to the public policy of the United States by a resolution of Congress.

In a famous piece of litigation Arpad Plesch (acting through a trustee on behalf of the bond holders) accordingly brought an action against the Crown to pay to him the face value of the bonds and the accumulated interest in London at a rate equal to the value of fine gold prescribed by the law of the United States in 1917.

While this action proceeded through the courts he published two volumes of commentaries and extracts from judgments entitled *The Gold Clause*. However, although the Court of Appeal decided in his favour in 1936 after he had lost at first instance, its decision was in turn reversed by the

House of Lords in 1937 on the ground that the bonds were governed by the law of the United States. In the result the Crown was held liable only to redeem the bonds at their face value. But he never ceased to believe that the decision should have gone the other way, in which case, as he often used to say, he would have been the richest man in the world at the time.

He was a well known breeder and owner of racehorses in Europe and the United States. His greatest success in Britain was with Psidium, who carried his wife's colours in the 1961 Derby.

Her grandfather had won the 1876 Epsom race with Kisper. Psidium's triumph was a memorable occasion, for the first three horses that year were all owned by women and his 66-1 starting price was the longest for a winner of the Derby since the sensational disqualification of Craganour in favour of Aboyeur in 1913.

It was in 1954 that Plesch made his first impact on the racing scene, when he bought several yearlings at the Newmarket sales. Among them was Stephanotis, destined to win six races, among them the Cambridgeshire Handicap. In the following year at the suggestion of Mme. Couturie, the French breeder, he bought from her the Italian brood mare Dinarella and it was from her mating with Pardal at his Dollanstown stud in co. Kildare that he bred Psidium.

At various times he had horses in training with Sir Gordon Richards and Harry Wragg and also with several trainers in Ireland, France, Italy and the United States. In 1962 he announced that his racing interests would be centred in France and 14 yearlings were sent there to François Mathet, whose partnership with Mme. Suzy Volterra had just been dissolved. However, he still kept a few horses in training with Wragg at Newmarket.

He won many big prizes in France with such champions as Sassafras (Prix du Jockey Club and Prix de l'Arc de Triomphe), with Amber Rama (Prix Robert Papin and the Prix Morny) and with Saraca (Prix Vermeille).

December 19, 1974.

William Plomer, C.B.E., F.R.S.L., novelist, poet, discoverer and editor of the Kilvert Diaries, the publisher's reader without whose encouragement Ian Fleming might never have created James Bond, died on September 21, 1973 at the age of 69.

Born of English parents in Pietersberg in the northern Transvaal on December 10, 1903, William Charles Franklyn Plomer travelled to England for his schooling, but after a year at Rugby returned for reasons of health to South Africa, where for a time he was engaged in farming and later as a trader in Zululand. His leanings towards literature brought him into association with Roy Campbell in the production of the review *Voorslag*, a periodical of youth-fully, indeed shockingly, independent and vehement character. The landscape of South Africa—of the whole African continent—stirred Plomer's imagination, and conflicts of race, colour and creed sharpened in him an objective and unconventional habit of mind.

From Africa, he went in 1926 to Japan, where he taught at various colleges but declined the chair of English Literature at Tokyo University. Three years later he travelled to Europe by way of Siberia, took lodgings in London, occupied a position of some detachment on the fringes of "Bloomsbury" literary society, and succeeded Edward Garnett as literary adviser to the firm of Jonathan Cape. It was to Cape's that he introduced Ian Fleming.*

Plomer's quality and purpose as a writer, as he was fully aware, derived largely from never having been rooted in one place. Africa, Japan, Greece, France, Italy all woke in him a personal sense of acclimitization touched by a common affection and a common emotional detachment from the conflicts which they presented. Since he found no deep-rooted conflicts in England, his English themes as an imaginative writer turned chiefly on social distinctions.

Turbott Wolfe, his first novel, published in 1926 when he was 22, was in some sort an angry young man's work. Treating in generous and powerful terms of the problems of race and colour in South Africa, and arguing by implication a case for miscegenation, the book, in Plomer's own phrase, is "a violent ejaculation", which in turn provoked a storm of anger. On its re-publication in 1965 it was acclaimed by liberal South Africans as a pioneer work—and was banned in South Africa.

It was followed a year later by *I Speak of Africa*, a collection of rather formless short stories, but there was promise of a more mature style in a volume of stories about Japan, *Paper Houses* (1929), and two years afterwards the promise was fulfilled in *Sado*. This novel is an essay on contrasting Japanese and European attitudes to life: description is quickened by a lightly dramatic irony and the selection of detail is itself half Japanese. *Paper Houses*, republished as a sixpenny Penguin not long after Japan entered the war, proved the accuracy of the author's appreciation of the character, for good as well as ill, of his former hosts.

Plomer's first English novel, *The Case is Altered*, appeared in 1932. Based upon a real-life murder in a Bayswater boarding house in circumstances in some degree known to him, the story eventually recovers from a hesitating start and makes a strong impression. But in this English setting the author's style seems to lack something of strength or assurance. From now onwards, indeed, Plomer's writing begins to gain in urbanity while losing urgency and power. His next English novel, which was preceded by a small volume of poems, *The Five-Fold Screen*—poems of a restrained romantic quality—and another collection of stories, *The Child of Queen Victoria*, a mixed batch with English, African, Greek and French settings, was *The Invaders* (1934). Here, in a study of working-class life and character transplanted from the country to London, the reporting is sensitive, but the development seems rather too deliberate an exercise.

The diaries of Francis Kilvert, a Victorian country parson remarkable for simplicity, sensibility and humanity, represented a real find; three volumes edited by Plomer appeared in 1938-40, and a single-volume abridgement in 1944. He was president of the Kilvert Society from 1968.

He worked in the Naval Intelligence Division in the Admiralty during the war years, but found time to publish a first volume of autobiography, *Double Lives* (1943) which made very entertaining reading; *The Dorking Thigh* (1945), satires and ballads in an adroit and verbally teasing vein; and *Curious Relations* (1945), ostensibly consisting of the memories of a friend, "William D'Arfey", later revealed as Anthony Butts. This work contributed to the impulse of Plomer's last work of fiction, *Museum Pieces* (1952).

In 1958 came a second volume of autobiography, *At Home*, as engaging as the first and marked by a similar integrity and unobtrusive display of good manners. Of his inner life, however, it revealed almost nothing.

But in his later years it was in poetry that Plomer made, as he would have wished to make, his mark. The *Collected Poems* of 1960, followed by *Taste and Remember*, 1966 and *Celebrations*, 1972, bring into focus his view of life as a mixture of the terrible and the absurd, his sense of character in relation to place and period, his tendency to satire, and a pervading gentleness that more than anything endeared him to a wide disparity of friends. These volumes raised him into the front rank of his poetical generation. A blend of assurance, modesty and cosiness in readings on radio and on public platforms no doubt helped. Already a Fellow of the Royal Society of Literature and an honorary D.Litt. of Durham University, he won the Queen's Gold Medal for Poetry in 1963, and became president of the Poetry Society and was made C.B.E. in 1968.

Of cultivated tastes and a lover of music, Plomer wrote several libretti for Benjamin Britten, notably the coronation year opera, *Gloriana*, and the three "parables for church performance", *Curlew River*, *The Burning Fiery Furnace* and *The Prodigal Son*.

Among his minor writings had been candid yet generous appreciations of such friends as E. M. Forster*, Rose Macaulay, Jonathan Cape, Demetrios Capetanakis and Ian Fleming,* which deserve collecting as much as a tribute to the writer as to the persons written about.

September 22, 1973.

Lord Plunket—Patrick Terence William Span Plunket, the 7th Baron—who died on May 28, 1975, aged 51, will be sadly missed by the Royal Family he served with so much loyalty and devotion, by his colleagues in the Royal Household, and by his many other friends.

Born in 1923, he succeeded to the peerage in 1938 when both his parents tragically lost their lives in an air disaster. He remained unmarried but as head of the family cared for and was devoted to his two brothers and their families. After serving with the Irish Guards he was appointed Equerry to King George VI in 1948, and to the Queen on her Accession in 1952. He became Deputy Master of the Household in 1954, was awarded the M.V.O. in 1955, the C.V.O. in 1963, and the K.C.V.O. in 1974.

In his service to the monarchy, Patrick found fulfilment. The Royal Family, through their love and friendship, gave him security and a sense of belonging. In return he gave them dedicated service which the pain and illness of his last months could not diminish.

He was an aristocrat by birth and inclination and brought elegance, taste, and a detestation of the second rate to all he did. But he was never aloof: with his perfect and easy manners he was able to put people from all countries and from all walks of life who went to the Palace instantly at ease. There are many who will always be grateful to him for this.

He had a genius for entertaining, and in the help he gave the Queen in this he found the perfect outlet for his talents. He was a supreme "Master of the Revels" and understood better than anyone how to mix informality with splendour.

He had a sure sense for decoration and an instinctive appreciation of quality in works of art which led him to form a charming and very personal collection. His good taste was publicly recognized when he was made trustee of the Wallace Collection and the Nati;nal Art-Collections Fund, appointments which gave him intense pleasure. He used this flair in the service of the Queen and was active from the beginning in the inception and development of The Queen's Gallery.

His innumerable friends will miss his gaiety, his humour and his civilized approach to life: those who saw him during his last illness will also be grateful for the example of courage and fortitude he left behind.

He is succeeded by his brother, the Hon. Robin Plunket.

May 29, 1975.

Nikolai Poliakov, who was better known as **"Coco the Clown",** died on September 25, 1974 in a hospital at Peterborough. He was 73.

For years, as Christmas came round, Coco was the herald of Olympian delights. Every December, at Bertram Mills's Circus, before the bandmaster tapped his baton to bring brass and percussion to order for the overture, the spotlights would pick out Coco's bizarre figure, alone in the ring, its sawdust as yet undisturbed by the Grand Parade which was soon to march majestically across the arena.

The moment they saw him the children squealed with delight, for they adored him, from the top of his shock of bright red hair (which unaccountably, but quite literally, suddenly stood on end) to the soles of his gigantic boots (which sometimes made an exit on their own, without his feet inside them). They loved his baggy, check trousers and long, loose coat, from the capacious pockets of which so many strange objects would appear. They revelled in his Belisha Beacon walking stick, and in his make-up, which was never terrifying. After all, how could a rosebud mouth frighten anybody, even if it was black? One felt that he was even more surprised at the turn of events than the audience were. Did not his eyebrows, permanently arched high on his forehead, prove it?

Nikolai Poliakov (or Polakovs—he was not particular about the spelling of his name) was born in a theatre at Besinowitz, Russia, on October 5, 1900. His father was a property-master, who, when "at liberty", turned his hand to cobbling. After appearing on the stage and performing in cafes, Nikolai was apprenticed to Rudolfo Truzzi, a well-known Italian circus proprietor who had settled in Russia. It was he who gave Poliakov his *nom-de-piste,* originally spelt with two "k's", by taking the syllable which occurred in both his surname and first name and repeating it.

In the First World War he served in the 11th Siberian Regiment as an outrider, and in the Revolution he found himself sometimes with the Red Army and sometimes with the White. While in Riga in 1919, he married Valentina, who subsequently presented him with four daughters and two sons. During the twenties he worked in Germany, on stage and screen, before appearing in the ring of the Circus Busch in Berlin. It was while performing here that he received a contract for England.

He arrived in December 1929, and the following spring joined Bertram Mills's Circus. From that moment England became his home, and each year saw him touring the provinces in summer, and at Olympia for the winter season.

In the last war he served in the Pioneer Corps before joining E.N.S.A.; but outside the circus ring, the cause to which he was most dedicated was road safety, and for his efforts he was awarded the O.B.E. He published his autobiography, *Behind my Greasepaint,* in 1950.

If Coco was a flamboyant and slightly outrageous character, seen at his best alone in the ring, then Nikolai Poliakov was almost the antithesis: a simple man who appeared at his best surrounded by his wife, children and grandchildren. In fact, it was Nikolai Poliakov's understanding of the family that made Coco such a deservedly popular star of the circus.

September 26, 1974.

Georges Pompidou, the second President of the Fifth Republic of France, died in Paris on April 2, 1974. He was 62.

He had been Prime Minister from July 1962 when the Algerian war was over, until July 1968, after the May-June "events", a longer period, as de Gaulle* pointed out, than any other French head of government for a century. As President, Georges Pompidou exerted the right of his office—not precisely specified in the constitution of the Fifth Republic—to be the "source of French policy" quite as strongly, though in a different manner, as de Gaulle had done. In some respects he went further than his predecessor, making decisions regarding the choice of minor ministers and important officials which de Gaulle often left to the Prime Minister.

He was elected President in a second ballot on June 15, 1969, against Alain Poher, and received 57.5 per cent of the votes. The smooth succession to de Gaulle engendered euphoria. The Chaban-Delmas government formed on June 21 included members of the Democratic Centre and this opening of the majority was well liked by the electorate and particularly by convinced "Europeans". At the next election, held in March 1973, the government's majority, swollen by the exceptional circumstances of the 1968 election, fell considerably, the majority losing nearly 100 seats. The nation, as regards votes, was evenly divided—as in 1967. It was largely due to Pompidou's election strategy that the Republican Union for Progress (Gaullists and their allies) remained in power.

For the first two years, Pompidou's foreign policy was a blend of continuity and change, with the latter discreetly predominating. The President preserved France's independence from the two superpowers, an independence which the General had seemed to consider, since the 1950s, more seriously threatened by the United States than by the Soviet Union. Pompidou visited Moscow, though after he had been to the United States, and sent his ministers there; there was even an increased volume of technological cooperation between the two countries, but there were no political initiatives. In the Four Power talks on the Middle East during 1970-71 France, on several important issues, drew nearer to the other junior partner, Britain, in opposing the Soviet and American actions.

Pompidou continued to deplore the continued American presence in Vietnam, but the heat was off. In Belgium, after the Anglo-French Summit talks of May 1971, the President explained what France's basic policy towards the United States really was. France was all out to create a European monetary union which would balance the power of the dollar, and help to promote a more humanistic form of civilization than that based on material values. Finally, the President indicated, the time would come when it would be possible to discuss a common defence policy with Washington. A small but not insignificant departure from Gaullism was the mending of fences with the federal Government of Canada. When in 1971 the Head of the provincial government of Quebec visited Paris, the Quebec flag was not flown on official buildings.

Towards the Soviet Union, the President was able to continue to claim that he had not deviated from the policy of his predecessor. In October 1971 Leonid Brezhnev visited Paris for a week and a solemn declaration of Franco-Russian understanding and of scientific and industrial cooperation was signed by the two leaders. Obviously the Ostpolitik of the West German Government and the close binding up of France with the European Economic Community diminished the significance of Paris-Moscow relations for both parties. There was no question of a formal alliance and this was made clear by French official circles before the Brezhnev visit. In June 1973 Pompidou, allegedly at Moscow's request, made an informal visit to Brezhnev in Byelorussia to discuss, among other matters, the European Security Conference. Since this was just before the French general election in March, some people saw in the visit an electoral manoeuvre designed to influence left-wing voters. It was also thought that the Kremlin was not as keen as might have been expected on the prospects of a left-wing victory in France.

With his Mediterranean policy, Pompidou seemed to be following his predecessor, though in a more practical way. Instead of the General's world design, he was concentrating on deepening French influence in a region where she was already a dominant power. Taking shape in 1969, and accompanied by a vigorous campaign to sell arms, the Mediterranean policy aimed at freeing the inland sea from the likelihood of involvement in atomic war. President Boumédienne, who early in 1970 announced his support, saw it as ridding the area of all the fleets and bases of the super-powers. Diplomatic relations between France and Morocco, broken off by de Gaulle on account of the Ben Barka affair, were restored. Eighty Mirage aircraft were sold to Libya, naval vessels to Greece and an important arms and industrial agreement was signed with Spain. Algeria was the cornerstone of the Mediterranean policy.

The "special relationship" with Algeria, which implied some economic sacrifices on the part of France, safeguarded French interests in Saharan oil production and, because of the extent of French aid, had helped to make France, while de Gaulle was in power, the best regarded of all Western nations by the Third World, from China to Chile. The quarrel over oil prices

with Algeria, which finally brought about the unilateral nationalization of French oil and natural gas companies, ended the special relationship though the half a million Algerians who worked in France were allowed to remain. Bridges were not entirely broken with Algeria, but difficulties with Libya over the aircraft contract, a distinct cooling off of Franco-Spanish relations owing to criticism of the Spanish government in the French press and radio during the trial at Burgos of Basque activists at the end of 1970, helped to show that France was not getting much out of the Mediterranean policy.

The President's historic decision was to accept the enlargement of the Community, and with it negotiations for the entry of Britain, and the extension of Community activities towards monetary union and political coordination. It was on his initiative that The Hague Summit of the Six met at Luxembourg in December 1969 to consider carrying out these objectives. This was certainly Gaullism with a difference, even though it was clear that the General himself had realized, by 1968, that the miracle of the Common Market, which served France's interests so well, could not be indefinitely maintained and that sooner or later Britain would have to be admitted. Pompidou's new line was "Europeanism" with a different meaning from that originally given to the idea by de Gasperi, Adenauer* and Robert Schuman*. Pompidou emphasized that he was working towards a European confederation of national states, not a federation, and that he considered European political unity as far away.

But he foresaw the creation in national governments of Ministers charged with European affairs and said that the time would come when these Ministers would meet alone.

Relations between France and Britain improved dramatically after the return to power of a Conservative government, headed by Edward Heath in June 1970. France, it was made clear, welcomed cooperation with Britain in all fields including defence, though Pompidou stated categorically that there could be no question of rejoining the Nato forces. In Brussels the French formed part of an E.E.C. team which had to have a common attitude towards the negotiations with Britain, so there was no question of a French veto. But it was clear that, though the French were not alone in demanding difficult sacrifices from Britain, they were the main protagonists of the most difficult ones. France for a while still seemed the obstacle to Britain joining. The crucial meeting in Paris between the French President and the British Prime Minister took place in May 1971, when the Brussels negotiations had been making slow progress. The talks were not directly concerned with Brussels but the fact that the two leaders made it clear that France and Britain had a common attitude towards the political development of Europe had a marked effect on the negotiations.

After the Paris talks and the successful end of the Common Market negotiations in June 1971, for the first time in history it appeared likely that France and Britain would work together positively in a grand long-term design. The Queen's visit to France in May 1972 seemed to set a seal on a new era in Franco-British relations.

Pompidou had himself proposed a Summit meeting for the enlarged Community, which was to be held in the autumn of 1972. However, in early June of that year, in an unexpectedly frank speech in Paris made at a lunch to the Belgian Prime Minister, Gaston Eyskens, Pompidou expressed doubts whether the Summit would be able to reach effective agreements and stated that if this was the case he did not wish to call it. He had been put out by too much talk, by some of France's partners in the Six, about supra-national issues. He plainly wanted an agreement in advance that European monetary policy should be the main question at the conference. It was not until September, after his visit to Italy for talks with the Italian Prime Minister, Signor Andreotti, that he confirmed that the Summit meeting of the Nine should take place.

The Paris meeting was a success in the sense that it was agreed to accelerate European monetary union and that France accepted the need to pursue at the same time a concerted economic policy. A further fruit of the Summit was a decision to create a fund for backward regions in Community countries, a project which France had opposed but one in which Britain and Italy were vitally interested. Pompidou's declaration that a New Europe must not be a mercantile affair summed up the view, increasingly prevalent after Norway's decision not to join the E.E.C., that there must be a new spirit in the Community.

In a not particularly warm, though eulogistic, summing up of Pompidou, de Gaulle, in the last posthumous volume of memoirs, wrote of Pompidou that "he had a capacity for understanding the most complex matters, a talent for explaining things or remaining silent according to the occasion, the will to solve problems and an ability to gain time". Pompidou's handling of the problems raised in France by Britain's entry showed these political qualities to their fullest extent. In the beginning he said he hoped for success, but stressed some doubts about British willingness to accept inevitable burdens. In 1970 he made a number of more pessimistic and, for the British, disagreeable remarks. He had to be very sure of his ground in his own country. Then in May 1971, not unhelped by the Eurodollar crisis which showed that the West Germans were as liable as anyone else to behave badly and break Community rules to help the Americans, Pompidou made his totally firm declaration of belief in Britain's European vocation. It is true that, between 1968 and 1971, a great many leading Gaullists had realized that the exclusion of Britain would lead to an undue domination, political as well as economic, of the Community by the German Federal Republic. The President always moved with the times, but with the greatest skill in circumventing his critics.

In 1935 Pompidou had married Claude Cahour, a beautiful, intelligent and socially able partner who bore him a son. After the war, the Pompidou menage were prominent members of fashionable "advanced society", friends of Françoise Sagan, collectors of abstract paintings, with a liking for living in the country and also for St. Tropez, where Pompidou was liable to be photographed with Brigitte Bardot and other celebrities. Pompidou's nonchalance, his enjoyment of social and country pleasures, were not put on as a mask. The fact is that he was a very superior individual, perfectly integrated, and could enjoy life as well as exercise power.

Georges Jean Raymond Pompidou was born in 1911 at Montboudif, in Auvergne, the son of a schoolmaster. After the lycée at Albi, he went to Paris and became an agrégé of the École Normale, passing successfully through the École des Sciences Politiques as well. After teaching in Marseilles and Versailles he became a professor at the fashionable lycée Henri IV in Paris shortly before the war. A few months of soldiering and he was demobilized and remained in the lycée Henri IV throughout the war. In 1944, soon after de Gaulle had entered Paris and set up the Provisional Government, a friend, René Brouillet, advised Pompidou to apply for a post in de Gaulle's Secretariat—"an academic who can write" was the requirement. His ability was quickly spotted by de Gaulle who, at that time, frequently complained of the absence of practical men around him. He became a close associate of the General and was virtually the only man without a Resistance record—which Pompidou never claimed—to have won de Gaulle's esteem and confidence.

He never joined de Gaulle's Rassemblement du Peuple Français in the forties nor the Gaullist party, the U.N.R., in later days. He liked to be "on to" things but "in" nothing. This did not displease de Gaulle who, in the early days, used to talk about "the mysterious M. Pompidou" whose discretion and detachment he valued.

After de Gaulle's retirement in 1946, Pompidou joined the Rothschild bank—Rothschild Frères—and became a director. But he was always ready to help de Gaulle when wanted. In 1958, when de Gaulle became Prime Minister, Pompidou was his chef de Cabinet but he returned to Rothschilds when de Gaulle became President of the Republic. In 1961 the General sent him to the secret meeting with the F.L.N.—the Algerian rebels—in Switzerland, a meeting which later bore fruit in the Evian agreements.

If de Gaulle thought Pompidou mysterious, his choice of Pompidou as Prime Minister in succession to Debré in 1962 was a mystery to most Frenchmen. He was se-

lected for the job, without any previous experience of the Assembly, at a critical moment for Gaullism. The Evian Agreements ending the Algerian war had just been signed, and the political parties were about to begin a struggle against the personal power of General de Gaulle, henceforward considered by them unnecessary. The Pompidou government was joined by five M.R.P. ministers but these resigned shortly after when de Gaulle, against the advice of his new Prime Minister, referred to the idea of a supranational Europe as "Volapuk".

More serious trouble was created for the government when de Gaulle decided to hold a referendum on the election of a future President of the Republic by universal suffrage, without having such a project voted on first by the Assembly and the Senate. The Pompidou government was defeated on a confidence motion by 280 votes to 200 and the Assembly was dissolved. The referendum about the election of the President was only a half success; the vote, in October 1962, showed 62 per cent of votes cast in favour but abstentions amounted to 23 per cent of the electorate. At the general election which followed in November, however, the regime won a distinct triumph. The Gaullist U.N.R.-U.D.T. (the left-wing of Gaullism) secured 229 seats which, with a handful of allies, gave them an absolute majority in the Assembly —the first time that such a majority had been obtained in either the Third or the Fourth Republics.

The Presidential elections of November and December 1965 were not an immense success for Gaullism, though their issue was finally satisfactory. But Gaullists noted that the General's remark that chaos would follow if he were not elected was badly received by public opinion. At the general election in 1967, Gaullist strength in the Assembly was greatly reduced. Pompidou had to rely increasingly on the party's allies, the Republican Independents, whose leader Valéry Giscard d'Estaing became increasingly critical of de Gaulle. Pompidou's position became, if anything, stronger because of this.

The student disorders and the workers' strikes in May 1968 shook the regime to its foundations. "The Events" ended with a rallying of public opinion to Gaullism and a general election which gave the Gaullists 284 seats in the Assembly and 63 to their conservative allies. It was the General who, once the opposition leaders appeared on the scene, ended the revolutionary situation by his dramatic 24-hour visit to the French forces in Germany. His prestige took an upward bound, for the moment at least. But, in the eyes of those able to know what had happened on the inside, it was Pompidou who had gained more than his master. The General blundered in making, on May 24, his proposal for a referendum on Participation, had confessed that he found the situation *insaisissable*, and had spoken of retiring. Pompidou, on the other

hand, had, when Ministers were losing their heads, expressed complete confidence as to the impossibility of the "events" resulting in the overthrow of the State. And Pompidou, frequently against the General's injunctions, had insisted on a policy of conciliation towards both the students and the strikers. Although this had not, on its own, succeeded, to have acted otherwise, to have opened fire in the streets of Paris, could have led to real catastrophe.

General de Gaulle praised his Prime Minister for his resolution in warm terms. His decision to relieve Pompidou of office was on the pretext that he needed a rest and that his role should be "in reserve for the Republic". Pompidou calmed the anger of his friends who considered that he had been unfairly treated and remained loyal in word and deed. But he was one of the foremost critics of Edgar Faure's radical reform of the University, which the General backed wholeheartedly. More than ever, Pompidou, the now private Deputy for the Cantal, represented the large part of the majority which was worried by the General's left wing tendencies and also by France's growing isolation from her allies in Western Europe. Most Gaullists voted loyally, but unenthusiastically, on April 27 for the referendum on regionalization which included the abolition of the Senate, the defeat of which resulted in General de Gaulle's retirement.

Pompidou's victory in the Presidential election was only assured after the first round, which he was expected to win, by the Communist Party's decision not to back Poher in the second round but to abstain. Pompidou secured over eleven million votes to the eight million cast for the interim President of the Republic, an authentic enough victory. The common denominator of those who voted for him was the desire to maintain the institutions of the Vth Republic and it was because of this, and fear of the political chaos which could ensue if Poher had won, that many non-Gaullist conservatives and a number of Centre Party leaders backed Pompidou.

It was reasonably clear during the campaign that Pompidou intended to restore the long missing dialogue between government and opposition and also to pursue a more flexible foreign policy, particularly as regards Europe and the enlargement of the E.E.C.

The new government seemed to confirm these promises. It was headed by Chaban-Delmas, a Gaullist of long standing, but not of the inner circle of the former President, who had been President of the Assembly since 1958 and as "Speaker" had consistently shown a more than scrupulous fairness in office. The appointment of Maurice Schumann, a former President of the M.R.P., the once large Christian Democrat party, and a convinced "European", gave reality to the idea of a new policy towards European affairs. Scarcely less important was that of the very conditional ally of Gaullism, Valéry Giscard d'Estaing, as

Finance Minister, an appointment which portended an end to Gaullist financial orthodoxy particularly as regards international monetary policy.

After the student and worker revolt of May 1968, de Gaulle and the new government, headed by Couve de Murville, had emphasized the need for radical changes in French society, changes summed up in the word Participation, which included the idea of worker *interessement* (much more than mere profit sharing) in factories, regional autonomy, administrative and industrial decentralization. Pompidou had no liking for sweeping social reforms, and this was the basic reason why de Gaulle dropped him in 1968. Pompidou, after his election as President, enlarged his first government to include personalities from the liberal Centre party who had supported him in the Presidential campaign but no left-wing Gaullists.

To say that the Chaban-Delmas government turned its back on de Gaulle's social policy would be wrong. The Prime Minister advocated "a New Society" but progress towards regionalism and decentralization was cautious. "I admire your intentions", said a Socialist leader to the Prime Minister, "but with your majority, I doubt your success." He could have said "with your President". A majority of the Gaullist party consisted of hard-headed men who cared little for the idea of creating a society neither communist nor capitalist; they placed greater emphasis on keeping order in the Latin quarter of Paris—which continued to be the scene of student disorders—than on reforms to satisfy the growing generation.

Pompidou's prestige in France and elsewhere had reached maybe its highest point at the end of 1971. The country had been less affected by inflation and labour troubles than most of her partners, and indeed the Prime Minister, Chaban-Delmas, had created far better relations between government and trade unions than had ever been the case in France before. French industrial growth was proceeding apace. Pompidou had enlarged the Community. In December 1971 he had met President Nixon in the Azores and had secured an undoubted triumph in the first dollar devaluation and in the agreement by the American President to work with Europe in the monetary field. It was a personal triumph, though later events showed that the Azores agreements were far from definitive. After 1971, there was no sign of any decline in Pompidou's ability, but he was obliged to be a great deal more on the defensive at home and abroad.

Pompidou's referendum in France on Europe was held in April 1972. The referendum, as might have been expected, received a majority of the votes cast but the abstentions outnumbered the voters. The Socialist party, which was to do well at the March 1973 election, showed that it was gaining popular support in that François Mitterrand had called upon his supporters to abstain not because the party was against Europe, but because it mistrusted Pompidou's policies. The poor result of the referendum appeared to have been the main reason why Pompidou in July changed his Prime Minister and appointed Pièrre Messmer in his place. The President obviously believed that Messmer would exert greater authority on the Gaullist Party than his predecessor had been able to do. Even before 1972 there was a distinct malaise inside the Gaullist Party which was matched by a feeling of discontent with Gaullist social policy in the country as a whole. Neo-Gaullism appeared uncertain of what it stood for, particularly as regards domestic policy. The Gaullist spectrum ran from hard-faced conservatives to the left-wing of the party who had never been enthusiastic about Pompidou and were, as their critics in the party said, more or less socialists. There were resignations. A series of scandals severely damaged the Gaullist image. Messmer succeeded in clamping down on dissension before the election. Long before the end of 1972, the March election campaign had got unofficially under way and a number of opinion polls indicated that the united left—Communists, Socialists and left-wing Radicals who had made an alliance based on a common programme of government in June 1972—were leading the majority by as much as 12 per cent. For some time, Pompidou's only answer to those who asked him what he would do if the united left had a majority in the Assembly was that he would act according to the constitution. This was no doubt exact, in that the President had the right to nominate the government after a general election and, if it were rejected by the Assembly, to call another election. However before the official opening of the election campaign, Pompidou indicated that he would never sanction a government which included Communist Ministers. In the first official T.V. broadcast of the campaign, he intervened directly, saying that a victory for the united Left would wreck France's institutions. Thereafter he played the major part in the campaign, acknowledging that the nation wanted reforms and holding out a hand to the Reformers of the Centre. In a special intervention on T.V. on the eve of the poll he said "The choice is simple—on one side the Communists with their allies; on the other, the rest of the nation".

Although Pompidou had had no political career, nor stood in any kind of an election, when de Gaulle made him Prime Minister in 1962, no one ever showed himself a more consistently smooth and skilful politician, nor a greater adept at winning elections, than did Pompidou. In 1965 he had taken over the tactics of the Presidential election, after de Gaulle had made a mess of the first round. And he had been the organizer of the smashing victory in 1968, by exploiting the groundswell against the Communists. Unquestionably he snatched victory in 1973 and his was the only voice, from the majority, that moderate opinion listened to attentively.

The election, so little won by the Gaullist Party and so decidedly by the President, was followed by Pompidou more openly than ever assuming leadership. It was now his personal policy to back reforms, at which he had previously looked askance. During the week preceding the formation of the second Messmer Government, he came out, in a message to Parliament, for measures which included the checking of the power of the technocrats, reform of the administration, and the participation of workers in factory organization and on boards of management.

Formed early in April, the new government, so far as its personnel was concerned, did not appear to represent the new era which the President and the Prime Minister had promised. It was not Pompidou's fault that it contained no Reformer; Jean Lecanuet had refused a post offered him. It contained many new faces, but mostly Gaullist ones. Changes there were. Debré had refused office, and this in many ways left Pompidou's hands freer. Maurice Schumann had lost his seat.

The new Foreign Minister was Michel Jobert, Pompidou's principal assistant at the Elysée and, as Pompidou had been in 1962, a non-political figure. But the absence of any notably reformist politicians from the new Government—Chaban-Delmas was not offered a post—mattered less because it appeared that the President was going to do the reforming. It was a presidential government and with it France had perhaps moved nearer to a constitution like that of the United States.

The Summit meeting at Reykjavik in May 1973 did not make diplomatic history by paving the way for a future summit between the United States and a European Europe, which would aim at redefining the Atlantic Alliance and reaching agreement on international trade and monetary policies. The Pompidou-Nixon talks were negative on this and Pompidou rejected, for the time being, even the idea of a permanent contact committee composed of American and E.E.C. representatives. Multilateralism was substantially out.

Pompidou accepted the continuation of bilateral talks with the Americans on the subject on which France probably differed the most fundamentally from her European allies, the redefining of the scope of the Atlantic Alliance. This distinctly negative result was probably unavoidable. Pompidou could not claim to speak for Europe whilst President Nixon, on several of the questions uppermost in French minds—nuclear planning and the maintenance of American troops in Europe for example—could make no commitments without consulting Congress—and Congress was in no mood to underwrite whatever the President proposed.

At Reykjavik, Pompidou had shown his usual alertness and wit, but his face was puffy and he showed signs of being physically tired. For some weeks before the Iceland meeting Pompidou's physical indisposition had been the subject of dinner table gossip in Paris. It was after Reykjavik, where he had, inevitably, been constantly photographed by the world's press, that French newspapers, and even the O.R.T.F., began speculating about the state of his health and the political situation which would result if he had to retire before the end of his term in 1976.

Pompidou's frequent indispositions and relatively poor health were not responsible for some loss of prestige which occurred from the autumn of 1973 until the early part of 1974. He was blamed for keeping silent during the Arab-Israel conflict and for leaving, with not altogether happy results, statements about France's attitude to his Foreign Minister, Michel Jobert. But on October 31 Pompidou launched the idea of a Summit of the Nine, exactly at the right moment, to lay the basis of a common Community foreign policy. If the Copenhagen conference was, in the eyes of most people, largely a failure, it was not for any lack of energy on the part of Pompidou.

The decision to float the franc indirectly reflected on the President who had so closely identified himself with the goal of monetary unity: but most Frenchmen considered that he had acted shrewdly. If the Washington conference on energy was realized before the French desire for a prior Euro-Arab meeting, this was not because French diplomacy had lacked initiative, but because of the hard reality of American economic power. By the winter of 1973, the Messmer government seemed less and less to satisfy the nation, its one star being the Finance Minister, Valéry Giscard d'Estaing.

Rumour had it that the President was considering a change of Prime Minister when, on February 7, he had an attack of influenza and was forced to keep to his bed for a few days. This revived rumours that he was suffering from a serious disease.

Succeeding de Gaulle both as the representative of France and as "the source of French policy" required not merely political skill but the ability to impress powerful but critical friends—such as Nixon—and friendly enemies such as Brezhnev. Pompidou never imitated de Gaulle—not even at the solemn Elysée press conferences which de Gaulle had initiated and which Pompidou carried on. Short in stature, inclining to plumpness, with a rugged but agreeable face and bushy eyebrows, Pompidou always had an air of civilized sceptical detachment and of good humour—altogether different from le grand Charles. But he was a master of the political game and, except by his enemies at home, it was widely considered fortunate that such an indisputably able and reasonable man had been there to succeed the heroic but difficult founder of the Fifth Republic.

April 3, 1974.

Elijah (Robert) Poole—See Muhammad.

James Pope-Hennessy, C.V.O., the writer, brother of Sir John Pope-Hennessy, Director of the British Museum, died on January 25, 1974 from injuries he received in an attack upon him in London at the age of 57.

Pope-Hennessy, who was born on November 20, 1916, was the younger son of the late Major-General L. H. R. Pope-Hennessy and the late Dame Una Pope-Hennessy, biographer of Dickens. He became himself a noted biographer, coming to prominence when he was chosen to write Queen Mary's official biography.

Educated at Downside School and Balliol College, Oxford, he was an editorial assistant at Sheed and Ward, the publishers, in 1937-38. He became private secretary to the Governor of Trinidad and Tobago in 1939. He served in the War Office from 1940 to 1944, and was on the British Army Staff in Washington, United States, in 1944-45.

He was literary editor of *The Spectator* from 1947 to 1949, and had worked for *The Times Literary Supplement*. He was made C.V.O. in 1960

With his first book, *London Fabric*, published in 1939, Pope-Hennessy won the Hawthornden Prize. His perambulations round the buildings of London were recounted with charm, knowledge, and, frankly, a good deal of affection. It was a young man's book but such was Pope-Hennessy's talent for winning over critics that even his prejudices were entertaining. It was a timely book, for war was at hand; and one that still bears rereading. With this book behind him he was well prepared to write a commentary for *History under Fire,* a collection of photographs by Cecil Beaton depicting air raid damage to London.

His first full-scale biography was that of Monckton Milnes, first Lord Houghton, one of the more elusively attractive of the less eminent Victorians. To write this work, which came out in two volumes, Pope-Hennessy had the freedom of the muniments of the Marquess of Crewe, the Liberal leader, and the son of Monckton Milnes. Both in this work and in the biography of Lord Crewe, which came out in 1955, Pope-Hennessy showed his skill for capturing a convincing likeness of both the man and his period.

In 1955 it was announced that he had been commissioned to write the official life of Queen Mary. The much-admired old Queen had been a voluminous diarist, which was to the advantage of her biographer, but he was to a certain extent handicapped by the fact that earlier writers, John Gore, Sir Harold Nicolson* and Sir John Wheeler-Bennett, in their lives of George V and George VI, had covered a great deal of the period in which Queen Mary was active. Of her earlier life, which had not always been easy, less was publicly known. This Pope-Hennessy most thoroughly investigated, and from his researches, and the manuscripts placed at his disposal, fashioned an accomplished biography which

was widely read.

The West Indies, where he had served before the Second World War, not always contentedly, provided the background for several of Pope-Hennessy's books. *West Indian Summer* (1939) was concerned with those who had visited the Caribbean in one capacity or another; Cashel, sometime A.D.C. to the Governor of Trinidad; Trollope, Froude, Charles Kingsley and Hans Sloane. It was a different Pope-Hennessy from the biographer, reflective, evocative and critical. *The Baths of Absalom* appeared in 1953; and in 1964 *Verandah.* Sub-titled "Some Episodes in the Crown Colonies 1867-1889", it was a sympathetic and scholarly investigation into the life of his grandfather, the colonial governor, Sir John Pope-Hennessy.

He turned to another part of the globe for *Sins of the Fathers*, a vigorous and well documented study of the Atlantic slave traders between 1441 and 1807. *Half-Crown Colony* was a study of Hongkong and came out in 1969. It was followed by a life of Trollope.

Trollope, fearsomely prolific, presents any biographer with a formidable problem; in spite of his famous autobiography he was an intensely private man; furthermore, there exists Michael Sadleir's *Trollope; a Commentary*, a minor masterpiece of biographical and critical synthesis, and also more modern textual and interpretative offerings. Pope-Hennessy's excursion, though extremely readable and marked by a real feeling both for the author and his period, did not altogether satisfy critical opinion.

After the death of Sir Noël Coward in March 1973, Pope-Hennessy, whose biographies Coward had much admired, was asked by the executors of the Coward estate to write the authorized biography. At the time Pope-Hennessy was still working on his life of Robert Louis Stevenson; but when that was completed in the autumn he began research for the Coward book. At the time of his death he had only recently returned from America, where he had been to interview many of Coward's friends and colleagues.

January 26, 1974.

Marshal of the Royal Air Force Lord Portal of Hungerford, K.G., G.C.B., O.M., D.S.O., M.C., 1st Viscount, died on April 22, 1971.

On him more than on any other R.A.F. officer fell the burden of shaping and directing the policy of the Royal Air Force in the Second World War. He took office as Chief of the Air Staff in October 1940 after spending the first six months of war as Air Member for Personnel and the next seven months as Air Officer Commanding-in-Chief, Bomber Command, and he remained in office until the end of 1945. As a member of the Chiefs of Staff Committee, he played a full part in presenting to the Prime Minister and the War Cabinet the advice of the Chiefs of Staff on allied strategy and on other important matters of military policy. In this capacity he also took part in all the wartime conferences of the allied leaders, culminating in the tripartite meetings at Teheran, Yalta and Potsdam.

All who came into contact with him were impressed by his quick perception, sound judgment, and almost unlimited capacity for hard work. He came to high office early —he was only 47 when appointed Chief of the Air Staff—but with a record of unvarying success and unflagging enthusiasm. He never lost his keenness for flying, and early in the war took a refresher course as a pilot so that he could fly himself on visits to outlying stations. He was an authority on falconry, a first-class shot, and a keen fisherman.

His two outstanding characteristics were, first, his astonishing efficiency in any and every service task which he had to compete with. Probably every inter-service dispute or difficulty which Trenchard had to solve or ride out between the wars was surmounted largely, if not solely, as a result of Portal's backroom boys' work. Then, on the practical side, there were his outstanding skills, ranging from winning a tough motor cycle race to getting a mention in French's first dispatch as a dispatch rider, to his able piloting of any type of aircraft in between his lengthy spells on the staff, and his winning of the Minot trophy as a bomb aimer, against all the picked bomb aimers, when he was a squadron commander. In sum, the general opinion of all who knew him in the service was "Anything I can do he can do better".

Secondly, his extraordinary equanimity under the tremendous burden of work and responsibility which he supported virtually throughout the war. However hot the argument, or urgent the occasion, or pressing the demands upon him, he seemed always the same calm and helpful commander or colleague, with the same even-tempered and wise approach to the multitude of problems with which he was, of course, continually confronted. He was never known to lose his temper and he would invariably go out of his way to avoid hurting anybody's feelings. So much so that on one occasion, when a matter on which he felt particularly strongly came up at a Chiefs of Staff and War Cabinet meeting and argument and counter-argument waxed somewhat stronger than normal, Portal took occasion afterwards to say to Winston Churchill* (who, Winston-fashion, had been goading everyone a bit more than usual!) "I'm sorry if I seemed a bit over-assertive or hot under the collar, Prime Minister", which elicited the typical Churchillian retort: "In war, my boy, you don't have to be sorry—you only have to be Right!"

"Peter" Portal was not only esteemed and admired throughout the service because of his outstanding ability and efficiency; even more so because he was, within the precise meaning of the words, an officer, and a gentleman.

Charles Frederick Algernon Portal was born on May 21, 1893, at Hungerford. He was the son of Edward Robert Portal, of Sulham House, Pangbourne, and an elder brother of Admiral Sir Reginald Portal. The family is of Huguenot origin and arrived in Britain from France in 1695. Educated at Winchester, where he was in the cricket XI, and at Christ Church, Oxford, he won a famous motor-cycle race in 1914 which apparently affected his career, for it was as a dispatch rider in the Motor Cyclist Section, Royal Engineers that he joined the Army on August 6, 1914. As a corporal, he was mentioned in the first dispatch of Sir John French in the following month. By September 27 he was commissioned as second lieutenant in the Motor Cyclist Section. Soon afterwards he had a narrow escape from death when, with a group of whom five were killed by a shell, he was blown through a doorway but was able to help the wounded.

His flying career began as an observer in July 1915, and he was seconded to the R.F.C. in November of that year. In April 1916 he was regarded as a pilot and returned to France. He won an M.C. in January 1917, the D.S.O. six months later, and a Bar to the D.S.O. in 1918 for conspicuous gallantry and devotion to duty—he "always set a magnificent example to the squadron under his command". His promotion was rapid—to flight commander in July 1916, squadron commander in June 1917, and lieutenant colonel, R.A.F. in June 1918, at the age of 25. He had over 1,000 hours of war-time flying, and his prowess became almost legendary.

In 1915, when aerial combat was in a primitive stage, he succeeded in hitting the machine of the famous Immelmann with a Winchester automatic rifle. Later, he crossed the enemy line five times in one night on bombing raids. On another occasion he attacked five enemy aircraft single-handed and destroyed three of them.

In August 1919 he received a permanent postwar commission as squadron leader, and for some time he commanded No. 59 Wing at Cranwell. When the R.A.F. Staff College opened in April 1922 he was one of the first term of students. From 1923 to 1926 he was employed on staff duties at the Air Ministry, receiving promotion to wing commander in 1925, and in 1926-27 he attended the war course for senior officers at the Royal Naval College, Greenwich. From March 1927 he commanded No. 7 (Bomber) Squadron at Worthy Down. The Laurence Minot memorial trophy for competition among bomber squadrons had just been presented to the Air Council, and No. 7 Squadron was the first to win it, the C.O. himself occupying the bomb aimer's position. In 1928 Wing Commander Portal again released the bombs which enabled his squadron to retain the trophy. During 1929 he attended the course at the Imperial Defence College, and in 1930 was employed on special duty in India.

For three years from December 1930 he was again on staff duties at the Air Ministry, during which he became a group captain in July 1931. Then in January 1934 he was appointed Officer Commanding at Aden, where he served two years, the last year as an air commodore. He conducted a two months' blockade of the lawless Quteibi tribe in the Aden hinterland, and later gave an able lecture on Air Force cooperation in policing the Empire at the Royal United Service Institution. In January 1936 he was appointed R.A.F. instructor at the Imperial Defence College, until his promotion to air-vice-marshal in July 1937. His next appointment was as Director of Organization, Air Ministry, in which he served until appointed to the Air Council as Air Member for Personnel in February 1939. He was made a C.B. in the 1939 New Year honours.

On the outbreak of the Second World War he was granted the rank of acting air marshal, and remained on the Air Council until March 1940, when he was chosen to succeed Sir Edgar Ludlow-Hewitt as A.O.C.-in-C., Bomber Command. He was there only seven months, however, as in October 1940 he returned to the Ministry as Chief of the Air Staff, in succession to Sir Cyril Newall (later Lord Newall*) with the acting rank of air chief marshal, and he remained as the professional head of the Force until January 1, 1946, after war had ended.

He was promoted to K.C.B. in the Birthday Honours in 1940, and to G.C.B. in 1942. In April 1942, he received substantive promotion to air chief marshal with seniority of May 26, 1940, and on January 1, 1944 was advanced to the highest rank of Marshal of the Royal Air Force. In the honours announced on the resignation of Churchill's government in August 1945 he was created a baron, and in the New Year honours of 1946 was raised to the dignity of a viscount and also awarded the Order of Merit. On December 3, 1946, he was one of the seven war leaders who were appointed Knights of the Garter.

From 1946 to 1951 he was Controller of Atomic Energy, Ministry of Supply, and in 1960 he was elected chairman of the British Aircraft Corporation. He was president of M.C.C. in 1958-59.

Portal married in 1919 Joan Margaret, younger daughter of Sir Charles Glynne Earle Welby, fifth baronet, and had two daughters. The heir to his barony is the Hon. Rosemary Ann Portal, born in 1923.

April 24, 1971.

Raymond Postgate, who died on March 29, 1971 at the age of 74, was a remarkable instance of a man who, having tried several fields of activity and attained distinction in more than one of them, came to public recognition, in press and broadcast, at an age when most men are looking out their slippers for their retirement. As founder and editor of the *Good Food Guide*, he saw his photograph in the glossy press; but long before that he was known as classical scholar, journalist, Socialist, social historian and even as novelist.

Raymond William Postgate was born on November 6, 1896 at Cambridge, eldest of the four sons of Professor J. P. Postgate, Latin scholar and, with W. H. D. Rouse of the Perse School, a pioneer of the modern pronunciation of Latin and of the teaching of Latin by the "direct method". As instructor to his children, Professor Postgate was a harsh master; but his training helped his son, after attending the Perse School and Liverpool College, to win a scholarship to St. John's, Oxford, and in later years to publish translations of the *Pervigilium Veneris* and the *Agamemnon* of Aeschylus. But the scholar of St. John's never took his degree; for while still at school he had become an ardent Marxian Socialist.

He went up to Oxford in the autumn of 1915, already a strong opponent of the 1914-18 War, and when conscription was brought in he refused to serve and was one of the first undergraduate "conscientious objectors" to go to jail for his convictions. This resulted in estrangement from his father, an extreme right-wing Conservative, and the breach was widened when, just before the Armistice, Postgate married Daisy Lansbury, the daughter of George Lansbury, who was Leader of the Labour Party from 1931 to 1935, and editor of the *Herald* newspaper before, during and after the war.

After the war Postgate endeavoured to support himself for some time by Socialist journalism; he served for eight years in the foreign section of the *Daily Herald*, and subsequently edited various left-wing periodicals, of which may be mentioned the weekly *Tribune*, and the monthly *Fact*, which published a number of quite excellent social studies in the 1930s; he was also, in the mid-twenties, associated with the short-lived Lansbury's *Labour Weekly*. Concurrently—Socialist journalism not being a highly remunerative activity—he had "commenced author". His first book, a brief study of *The International During the War*, appeared in 1918, when he was only 21; it was followed by several books on Labour theory and Labour history, of which *The Builders' History* (1923), commissioned by the building trade unions, is the best-known.

In the late 1920s he took a post as departmental editor for the fourteenth edition of the *Encyclopaedia Britannica;* this drew him to New York, where he made the acquaintance of Alfred Knopf the publisher, for whose firm he became European representative, a connexion which he maintained until 1949. During the whole of the 1930s he continued to work and write vigorously as a Socialist of the Left—not a Communist, for his brief membership of the Communist Party at its foundation had ended in mutual recrimination—and his output of books grew and deepened. He published studies of radicals such as Wilkes

and Robert Emmet, and with his brother-in-law G. D. H. Cole a history, *The Common People* which, revised after the war, was for many years a standard best-seller.

When war came again in Europe he, like the great majority of Socialists, supported it; he early joined the Home Guard, and from 1942 to 1950 he was a temporary civil servant in the Board of Trade, where his main task was to persuade small manufacturers, in the furniture and fur trades, for example, to concentrate their businesses. He found time to write three detective novels one of which, *The Verdict of Twelve*, had considerable success, and a "straight" novel entitled *Every Man is God*.

Very early in life, when still an impecunious journalist, Postgate had made himself, in so far as means permitted, a connoisseur of both wine and cookery; and in the unpropitious circumstances of 1948-49 he conceived the idea of pioneering an amateur guide of the nature of the Club des Sans-Club, by which eager volunteers, working without fee or favour, would visit, sample and report upon British hotels and restaurants and endeavour to shame their keepers into raising their standards.

The first *Good Food Guide*, edited, with a trenchant preface, by the "President of the Good Food Club" (R. W. Postgate) appeared in 1951; the reports—some slightly idiosyncratic—on individual establishments often carried the signatures of well-known gastronomes. If the reports were idiosyncratic, the standard set for their compilers was stiff; no advertisements were allowed to appear in the guide's pages, and reporters were forbidden to accept hospitality of any kind. Recognition came steadily though slowly: in fact, Postgate was first appreciated outside his own country—by the vintners of St. Emilion, who in the mid-fifties conferred on him the status of honorary bourgeois rising later to that of Grand Chancelier d'Ambassade pour la Grande Bretagne.

But as the years passed the sales of the *Guide* and the reputation of its founder grew; his face appeared on television screens showing how spaghetti ought to be eaten; and he published several small books on wine and wine selection. By 1962 the *Guide*'s business, hitherto conducted, as far as compiling and editing was concerned, in his own home with the assistance of his wife and friends, had increased so much as to prompt the Consumers' Association, with its then quarter-of-a-million membership, to take over *Guide*, editor and contributors as a permanent addition to the British gastronomical scene.

Postgate continued to edit it until the autumn of 1968, when advancing years, and a serious operation, from which he made a good recovery, led him to leave London for a country cottage not far from Canterbury, from which, though no longer editor, he continued as "adviser" until the end of 1969. On his final retirement his colleagues presented him with two bottles of wine of every year from 1949 to 1968.

All the while, he maintained that he was a social historian as much as a gastronome; a book called *The Story of a Year, 1848*, appeared in 1955, and was followed in 1969 by *The Story of a Year, 1798*.

Postgate was throughout his life a vigorous personality of wide culture and strong views. In youth a lanky fellow of explosively left-wing temperament and a pen which could be vitriolic upon occasion, he mellowed into a handsome father-figure with a wide circle of friends, who wrote with elegance and individuality on all his wide variety of subjects. He had two sons.

March 30, 1971.

Gillie Potter, whose highly individual humour gave much pleasure to its devotees, died on March 4, 1975 in Bournemouth at the age of 87. He was in his prime as a comedian during the years between the First and Second World Wars, but continued to be heard on the radio long after his stage appearances ceased. He was in the habit of opening his broadcasts by saying, "Hello England, this is Gillie Potter talking to you in English".

He was born Hugh William Peel, the son of the Rev. Brignal Peel, a Wesleyan minister, and from Bedford Modern School went up to Worcester College, Oxford, in 1907. He left without taking a degree.

He began his stage career in the Edwardian decade, appearing at the Lyric Theatre, London, in *The White Man*. Later he toured extensively with H. Hamilton Stewart in *Sherlock Holmes,* and widened his experience by playing in musical comedy, concert parties and pantomime. In 1915 he was George Robey's understudy at the Alhambra.

Whether in music hall, revue, or cabaret (at which he excelled), his costume was always the same. He wore a straw hat (which in certain revues he would raise symbolically "to our manager Archie de Bear"), a blue blazer and light flannel trousers, and he carried a note-book and a cane. He would plant his stocky figure in the centre of the stage and lecture his audience with a genial, bland expression.

The monologue had a literary, historical flavour that had something in common with the humour of "Beachcomber" in the *Daily Express*. It required an educated audience for its full appreciation and might now be deemed slightly "esoteric", like many other good things.

Not that his material lacked popular robustness. He was a favourite with the music hall orchestra because his turn required no music except at the beginning and end. But, as Ernest Irving, the conductor, wrote in his autobiography, "even he had to be watched carefully ... nine times in his 'act' he used the words 'Watney's Brewery', the ninth—or was it the eighth?—time being the cue for the curtain music. At matinees, I believe it was the seventh".

One of Potter's main themes was the impoverished nobility, especially the tribulations and adventures of Lord Marshmallow at Hogsnorton, where the drive gates were tied with string and the entrance was through a gap in the adjoining hedge. Life at Hogsnorton was lived in the spirit of "Olde England", mishaps being plentiful. The pictures included "Lord Marshmallow after Constable"—one wondered, but only for a moment, at this choice of portrait painter—and its companion piece, "Constable after Lord Marshmallow".

Another typical ploy of Gillie Potter's was his parody of abrupt contrasts in *Who's Who* entries, where the hero might be, say: Sub-Postmaster, Chipping Sodbury, 1907; Governor, New South Wales, 1908; Harbourmaster, Watchet, Somerset, 1909. His social material sometimes approached the territory of his namesake Stephen Potter,* the creator of "Gamesmanship".

Gillie Potter was himself an authority on heraldry, which was one of the several subjects on which he wrote regularly to the Editor of *The Times* over the years.

March 5, 1975.

Ezra Pound, the American-born poet who died on November 1, 1972 in a Venice hospital two days after his 87th birthday, was, both as a writer and as a kind of literary impresario, one of the main formative influences behind "modernism" in the Anglo-American literature of this century.

He encouraged Yeats, whom he first met in 1909, towards the sharpening and toughening of his mature style. He helped Joyce to get *Ulysses* published. He arranged for the publication of T. S. Eliot's* earliest poems, and helped him with the recension of a somewhat, originally, inchoate assemblage of verse that ultimately became *The Waste Land.* He had a flair, also, for discovering and promoting talent outside the field of literature; he was one of the earliest admirers of Gaudier-Brzeska and Brancusi and encouraged the young composer Georges Antheil.

The recent publication by Mrs. Valerie Eliot of the original draft of *The Waste Land* with Pound's suggestions for excision and for improvement of the writing of particular passages reveals Pound's extraordinary flair as a physician for other people's sick poems—"There and there thou ailest!"—and his staunchness and loyalty as a friend. It also reveals that Pound, whom one tends to think of as coarse and boisterous where Eliot was refined and reticent, had a kind of essential innocence and fastidiousness that was denied to his friend. The original version of the famous episode of the typist and the carbuncular young man was much longer and, as the final draft is not, nasty. About a couple of particularly nasty lines Pound wrote that they were a bit "beyond the mark". A whole

section in heroic couplets, about a lady of fashion called Fresca, is not only a poor parody of Pope—Pound was right in telling Eliot that you cannot write a parody of Pope unless you can write better than Pope in his own form, which no poet of this century can do—but also peculiarly nasty.

Of the appended short poems in the original draft of *The Waste Land*, one, about Bleistein (who also occurs in Eliot's "Burbank with a Baedeker") is horrifying in its physical anti-Semitism. From Louis Zukofsky to Alfred Alvarez, many of Pound's best friends (to use the horrible old joke-cliché) were Jews. The young Eliot of *The Waste Land* period seems, about Jews, to have had an almost insane physical nausea. If *The Waste Land* had been published in its first draft, it would have been a document of, not exactly madness, but very distressing psychological instability. Pound was the main instrument in turning it into an enigmatic near-masterpiece. His own anti-Jewishness was simplistic and ideological, based on ideas about usury. Jews tend to be open-minded and intelligent, and Pound tended to like individual Jews. Eliot was right to salute him as *il miglior fabbro,* and might also have saluted him as a less obsessed and tormented soul.

In his own poetry, into which he incorporated devices which he had learnt from translating Provençal, Latin, Chinese, and Anglo-Saxon poetry, as well as many words and phrases from these languages, he was a tireless and ruthless technical experimentalist, comparable perhaps to Picasso in the visual arts. Yet his unfortunate political opinions and his personality, which in some ways always remained boyishly immature, and in some ways was radically unstable, made his reputation even at the height of his influence and fame always a distinctly mixed one. Few notable poets have aroused, sometimes in the same critic, a similar combination of whole-hearted admiration and exasperated impatience. His longest work, *The Cantos*, an indefinite-expansion composition on which he was still working when he died, had been seen, by good critics, both as the greatest long poem in English since *Paradise Lost* and as a rag-bag of wilful opinions and pedantic allusions.

To reach one's eightieth year is, for a writer of note, to be forgiven almost everything and the year 1965 saw the publication of one of the most thorough and balanced critical studies devoted to Pound, Professor Donald Davie's *Ezra Pound: Poet as Sculptor.* The aged poet also visited London for the first time in many years to attend T. S. Eliot's memorial service in Westminster Abbey and flew to Dublin to visit the widow of another old friend, Yeats. At Spoleto a ballet was performed, based on an opera he had composed about Villon. There were rumours that he might be asked to attend the Yeats Festival at Sligo in 1966, and he was well enough to pay a short visit to Paris. Friends who saw him closely said, however, that, apart from the

natural fatigue attendant upon old age, Pound suffered from frequent depression, and from worries about whether he had made the best use of his gifts. His old age can be described as stoic but as not wholly serene.

And he leaves behind him a reputation which might perhaps be described as monumental but damaged or incomplete. He had the technical gifts, and some of the gifts of spirit and feeling of a poet of the very first rank, but a certain patience, a certain humility, a certain unpretentiousness were, perhaps, lacking to the last.

But his influence remained vital to the last. Nineteen sixty-five saw the grant of an Arts Council prize to his loyalest English disciple, Basil Bunting, and the publication in the United States of the *Collected Shorter Poems* of one of his loyalest American disciples, Louis Zukofsky. And to the end of his days he remained the modern master from whom young experimental poets, like the Black Mountain group in the United States, were readiest to learn.

Ezra Pound was born in 1885 and was educated at the University of Pennsylvania. He had a short and unfortunate experience as a teacher of Romance languages at a minor American university, and when he was sacked after a term or so for "being too much of a Latin quarter type" he travelled in 1907 to Europe, where he was to remain, apart from one short visit home, until 1945, when he was taken back to the United States to face a charge of treason for broadcasting from Italy during the Second World War. He was declared mentally unfit to plead, and confined to an asylum in Washington until 1958, when he was released and settled in Italy. His daughter was married to a landowner in the Italian Tyrol.

In 1914 he had married Dorothy Shakespear. Dorothy Shakespear was the daughter of Yeats's great friend (briefly, in the 1890s, Yeats's mistress) Olivia Shakespear. Pound's son by Dorothy, Omar, was brought up by Olivia. His daughter Mary by his mistress, Olga Rudge, whom he had met in his Italian years, and who was a distinguished violinist, was brought up by Tirolean peasants till her twelfth year, when she was taken in hand again by Pound and Olga Rudge, who, in spite of her peasant upbringing, expected her to behave with bourgeois propriety at all times (Princess Mary de Rachewiet, as she became, nevertheless shows in her autobiography, *Discretions,* an admirable loyalty towards her father, if more reserved feelings towards her mother). Mrs. Dorothy Pound had been exemplary, as Pound's daughter Mary had also been, in attendance, care, and propaganda for Pound's release during his incarceration in St. Elizabeth's Hospital, Washington. Nevertheless on his release from St. Elizabeth's and his return to Italy, after a short period at his daughter's Tirolean castle, he preferred to set up house with neither his daughter nor his wife but with Miss Rudge, who had also been making strenuous pleas for him in Italy.

All this family history can be known, so far, only from the outside. It is difficult, nevertheless, not to have a sense of the "egotistical sublime" in family and intimate relationships, of an extraordinary impenetrability to the possible sufferings that one may inflict on people close to one. Yet, though clearly a very difficult husband, lover, and father, Pound appears to have received from Mrs. Pound, Miss Rudge, Mary, and Omar, exemplary loyalty. Yet it is possibly just this lack of piety and respect for the feelings of others, or this simple blindness to these feelings, that leaves us feeling that he is a major craftsman but not a major *Human* poet.

This is not a matter of politics. It is a matter of not seeing and feeling and entering into the sufferings and enjoyments of his fellow men. Yeats, equally fantastic in his politics, had a gift of imaginative love and friendship, fully expressed in his poetry, which Pound in his hickory hardness never possessed. He was a good friend practically to many poets in need of help, as to Eliot at the time of *The Waste Land*. But he lacked sympathetic and tactful curiosity, not only about other people but about himself. And he had that wish to impose clear but fundamentally inadequate simplifications on other people, to dogmatize and give over-simple rules, which made Gertrude Stein say: "Ezra is a very good village explainer. But I am not a village."

He had a kind of basic toughness or impenetrability that, in spite of all his years in Europe, made him queerly a symbol of the American provincial Middle West. His life was a long self-education in public. Yet this hard, granitic, impenetrable, (at times innocently and nobly generous, at times intolerably boorish and stupid) bias of character, was the condition of his survival in conditions of extraordinary stress and isolation and of the fragmentary greatness of *The Cantos*. *The Cantos*, as a whole, are not a great poem, as Pound in his later years was at times willing to admit; a great long poem must have unity of design, a coherent vision, and the possibility, at least, of exposition, complication, and resolution.

The Cantos are, however, a very great improvization. And the exasperating form permits the occasional, and in the early *Cantos* and in *The Pisan Cantos*, not so occasional irruption of passages of great poetry, hot and burning lava breaking through the cracks in piles of boiling scree.

Pound will always arouse boredom and fury. He will never cease, at the moments when his pressure is full on, to arouse awed admiration also. No great poet was ever a stranger mixture of the yokel, the salesman and the voice (not so infrequent) that is "something above a mortal mouth". Of all American poets, perhaps only Whitman was so silly, so noble, so eloquent, so touchingly self-convinced and redundant, and, alas, so great.

Pound was in England until 1921, and his shorter poems belong to this period,

including what some critics think his masterpiece, a poem dealing with the isolation of the aesthete in a commercial society, *Hugh Selwyn Mauberley*. He then settled for a year or two in Paris, and then in Rapallo, concentrating on his major effort, *The Cantos*.

Rather paradoxically Pound in his earliest volumes appeared a rather old-fashioned poet, influenced very much by Swinburne, Rossetti, Browning, like the pre-Raphaelites, romanticizing the Middle Ages. His attitude to life remained perhaps to the end a basically late romantic one, and a purely lyrical gift, a faultless sense of cadence, was perhaps his central gift. An urge, however, for technical experiment led him to become, partly under the influence of the Japanese *haiku*, one of the founders of the Imagist movement, and his translation from Chinese classical poetry, *Propertius*, and the Anglo-Saxon *Seafarer* all helped to break the tyranny of the traditional iambic line.

It was from his studies in Chinese poetry and particularly from Ernest Fenollosa's essay on *The Chinese Written Character* that he derived the idea, which is the governing idea behind *The Cantos*, of an ideogrammatic method in poetry, the conveying of general ideas by the juxtaposition of concrete instances: as in Chinese, for instance, an ideogram combining a sketchy symbol for a tree and one for the sun behind a branch conveys the general idea "sunset". In the earlier *Cantos* at least, and in the *Pisan Cantos*, which Pound first drafted during his imprisonment by the American Army in Italy, this method produces occasional extraordinary concentrations of poetry; it seems much less suitable as a vehicle for long mainly didactic passages on economics as illustrated by episodes from Italian, Chinese and American political history, though Pound's denunciations of usury have sometimes a Dantesque grandeur.

Yeats, who greatly admired many of Pound's gifts, deplored the fashion in which political and economic obsessions continually broke down the style of the *Cantos;* he deplored what he called the alternations of style and anti-style. A selected and abridged version of the *Cantos*, concentrating on the passages of visual evocation and lyrical reverie, might be a better monument to Pound than the vast work as it stands.

The later *Cantos*, published after Pound's release from his asylum, are in their digressiveness very much an old man's ramblings. An anti-Semitic bias of a very unpleasant kind disfigures even the moving *Pisan Cantos*. But Pound's politics were the aberration of a man selfless and generous in personal relations (he spent endless time and pains helping some poets, like Eliot, who were worthy of his help, and many who were not). The honourable sincerity of his art is to be found in his devotion to technique, to making rhythm, image, and feeling exactly correspond, rather than the somewhat conventional feelings, or the cranky or wrong-headed opinions, which

the technique was used to convey. His life, for all his great influence, was in some ways a lonely and tragic one. His poetic rank will remain a controversial subject; but he will be somewhere near the centre of any future history of twentieth-century Anglo-American poetry.

November 2, 1972.

Adam Clayton Powell, former Negro Congressman for Harlem, who fought to be reinstated—and won—died in Miami on April 5, 1972. He was 63.

Some thought him a "black Dreyfus"; others argued that he got away with more in the past precisely because he was a Negro. He became a sort of American Parnell, retaining the loyalty of his people more than that of associates who wanted to keep the political process functioning. His struggle in the courts raised constitutional issues; it also became a focal point for the Black Power movement.

After 22 years as a Congressman, Powell, who was chairman of the House Labour and Education Committee, was expelled in March 1967. The House had ignored the recommendation of its special committee which wanted Powell censured and fined. Powell may have done no more than other Congressmen, but he had done it more blatantly.

Powell had misused public funds for his own travel and living expenses. He was also in contempt of New York courts—refusing to pay, in full, damages awarded against him for libelling a woman by calling her a "bag-woman", or collection agent for corrupt policemen.

In April 1967 Harlem reelected him by a popular margin of more than seven to one. The following year the Court of Appeals upheld the ruling of a lower court that Powell could not appeal against his expulsion. Counsel for the House had argued that, under the doctrine of separation of powers, the federal courts had no right to interfere with the internal affairs of Congress.

Meanwhile Powell had been reelected and reseated in the new Congress of 1968. He pursued his appeal, arguing that his seniority and back pay were owing to him. He took the line that the House had no right to exclude a member on the committee's findings and was finally, in 1969, upheld by a ruling of the Supreme Court—one of the last before Chief Justice Warren retired. The Court did not, however, deal with the question of back pay or his loss of seniority. Powell had in the meantime purged his contempt in New York. In 1970 Powell lost his Congressional seat, and went to live in Bimini where he had previously gone in self-imposed exile.

Powell had been an efficient chairman of the Education and Labour Committee in his time; but later his frequent absenteeism destroyed whatever reputation he may have built up. The Democratic caucus soon reduced his authority on the committee.

Powell was born at New Haven, Connecticut, on November 29, 1908. He came to identify himself with the Negro poor in Harlem, and was a pungent columnist on the *Amsterdam News*. The son followed his father in the pulpit of the Abyssinian Baptist Church—which had one of the largest congregations in Harlem—in 1936, a post be held for 34 years.

Powell was elected to the New York City Council at the age of 33. He became a founder, editor-in-chief, and co-publisher of *People's Voice*.

In 1945 he was returned to Congress —with the joint backing of the Democrats, Republicans, the American Labour Party, and the C.I.O. In Washington, his first sally was the tabling of an anti-lynching Bill. He devised the "Powell amendment" system, whereby he tried to tack on a rider against racial discrimination to every piece of social legislation. At the same time he coaxed the Mayor of Harlem into an improvement scheme.

Powell was soon disowned by the Republicans; in 1965 he repudiated the Democrats temporarily. For years he served as deputy chairman on the Education and Labour Committee under North Carolina's Graham Barden. In 1960 he gained the chairmanship of the committee by seniority.

In 1956 his tax position was investigated by a grand jury and he was indicted, but later all counts were dropped. In 1963 a Negro widow had been awarded substantial libel damages against Powell, who failed to pay them and evaded arrest. An inquiry committee of Congress looked into his financial affairs in 1966 after allegations of his "playboy living". He published several books.

April 6, 1972.

Dr. Lawrence Fitzroy Powell, English scholar and sometime librarian of the Taylorian Institution of the University of Oxford, died at the age of 93 on July 17, 1975.

After the death of R. W. Chapman he had become the greatest Johnsonian authority of the older generation.

Powell was born in Oxford on August 9, 1881. He was educated at All Saints' Boys Orphanage, Blackheath. In 1895, after a period in the library of Brasenose College, he joined the staff of the Bodleian Library. Seven years later Sir William Craigie invited him to work on the *Oxford English Dictionary*. Through this employment he met his future wife, Ethelwyn Rebecca Steane. They were married in 1909 and had one son. Mrs. Powell died in 1941. During the war of 1914–18, being in a low medical category, he worked at the Admiralty.

In 1921 he was appointed Librarian of the Taylorian Institution, the centre in Oxford of the study of modern European languages; he held this office until he retired in 1949. During his time the institution enlarged its premises; the library increased greatly in bulk (he was a skilful buyer) and usefulness.

In 1923 Powell was entrusted with the revision of Birkbeck Hill's great edition of Boswell's *Life of Johnson*. The discipline of the *Dictionary* was a good preparation for this work. His primary task was to establish the text, for which some manuscript material had become available. But the work grew under his hand. Four volumes, containing the *Life* proper, appeared in 1934; the fifth and sixth, containing the *Tour to the Hebrides* and the famous index, in 1950. The commentary and the index were greatly improved. The volume containing the *Tour to the Hebrides* was virtually a new work.

Hill's knowledge of eighteenth-century Scotland was imperfect; Powell spent much time in Scotland visiting the scenes of the tour, working in Scottish libraries, and making acquaintance with Scottish scholars. His wife and other scholars also helped him, and not least Dr. R. W. Chapman and Professor F. A. Pottle; but the heart of the work was Powell's unremitting pursuit of accuracy in detail. The edition is the greatest monument of the eighteenth-century scholarship that has flourished in Oxford in our time. It is a model of learning, of accuracy, and of skilful and sometimes witty presentation. As by-products there were a number of articles, notably one on the history of Percy's *Reliques*. In 1958 came a new separate edition of the *Tour to the Hebrides*; in 1963 an edition, in collaboration with Professor W. J. Bate, of *The Adventurer*, forming part of the Yale Edition of Johnson's Works; and in 1964 new editions of the fifth and sixth volumes of the great Boswell.

Powell became first an honorary and later a full Master of Arts of Oxford, and an honorary Doctor of Letters of Durham; he was also a Fellow of the Royal Society of Literature and an honorary member of the Modern Languages Association of America. He was a vice-president of the Bibliographical Society and of other societies. He served on the committees of two great American projects, the Yale editions of Boswell's Private Papers and of Johnson's Works. He visited the United States more than once and was an honoured guest at Johnsonian celebrations there. He was especially pleased when he was granted Senior Common Room rights at Brasenose College. For many years he was a leading member of the Johnson Club.

Powell lived to an unusual degree in the eighteenth century, and especially in Johnson's Oxford. Within that field, and considerably beyond, he was a most clubable man, eager to meet every inhabitant and to welcome every entrant; established scholars who found in him inspiration, information and advice, postgraduate students to whom he was a generous and kindly supervisor, casual aspirants whom he did what he could to guide and encourage.

He was a lively correspondent, and his notes on matters of large interest in Johnsonian scholarship or points of small detail were a joy to receive. His social and scholarly qualities combined to bring him large numbers of friends in Britain and overseas. On his eightieth birthday there was a tribute of spontaneous admiration and affection from both sides of the Atlantic.

July 18, 1975.

General Carlos Prats, who was assassinated in Buenos Aires on September 30, 1974, was the former commander-in-chief of the Chilean army who served in the government of President Allende as Interior Minister. He was 59.

Born in Talcahuano in the south of Chile, Prats graduated from military academy and worked his way through the ranks to become army leader when General Rene Schneider, his predecessor, was murdered in 1970. Prats was an upholder of the tradition—rare in Latin American politics but strong in Chile—whereby military leaders remain outside politics. "The armed forces in Chile", he once said, "are, above all, professional institutions which have not intervened, are not intervening and will not intervene in politics"; and throughout the turbulent three years of Allende's rule he tried to preserve constitutional rule.

Brought into the government as Interior Minister in November 1972, he kept essential supplies moving during the "bosses' strike". When civil order was breaking down in the following year, Prats was brought back as Defence Minister, but by this stage he found that he was too identified with Allende, both politically and personally, although he never publicly pronounced on political issues.

He had attempted to persuade the military hierarchy to cooperate with Allende and had put a number of generals, whom he suspected of plotting a coup, into early retirement. Declaring that he would never divide the armed forces, he resigned all his posts. His successor was General Pinochet, who led the coup against Allende a few weeks later.

After the coup, the junta allowed him to go into exile in Argentina. He and his wife, who also died in the attack, had three daughters.

October 1, 1974.

Dennis Price, a stage and film actor of wide range who was adept at the presentation of both suave villainy and polished comedy, died on October 6, 1973 in Guernsey. He was 58.

He was an intelligent and sensitive performer—at times too sensitive perhaps for the hurly-burly of film-making—who will be remembered with pleasure by a younger generation who never witnessed his style on the stage or in films, for his television appearance as the Wooster manservant, Jeeves, eyeing the peccadillos of the young master with an urbane omniscience—Price was always at his best when displaying emotion tempered with refinement.

There will be many people who, on hearing of Price's death, will feel a pang of regret that an actor of his gifts and potential should, for various reasons, have of late years been seen so little in plays and films.

Dennistoun Franklyn John Rose-Price was born at Twyford, in Berkshire, on June 23, 1915, the son of Brigadier-General T. Rose-Price. He was educated at Radley and at Worcester College, Oxford, and at this time it seemed probable that he would either follow the family tradition of going into the Army, or else might enter the Church. But he became a member of the O.U.D.S. and adopted acting as his profession.

On leaving Oxford he studied at the Embassy Theatre School, and made his stage debut at the Croydon Repertory Theatre in June 1937, as Dick in *Behind Your Back*. He first appeared in the West End in the following autumn, at the Queen's Theatre in John Gielgud's company. A promising career was interrupted by the war, and he served with the Royal Artillery from 1940 until he was invalided out in 1942. He then toured in *This Happy Breed* and *Present Laughter* with Noël Coward; and was seen in *Springtime of Others* at the Arts Theatre, and it was here that he caught the eye of Michael Powell, one of the leading British film directors. As a result his film career began in 1944 when he appeared in Powell's *A Canterbury Tale*, and from then on he was kept busy acting both on the stage and in the cinema.

His cool, sardonic style was never seen to better effect than in Robert Hamer's classic black comedy *Kind Hearts and Coronets* in which he played with Alec Guinness, Valerie Hobson and Joan Greenwood. His other films included *The Bad Lord Byron*, in which he played Byron, *Private's Progress, Caravan, I'm All Right Jack, School for Scoundrels, Don't Panic, Chaps, Tunes of Glory, The Millionairess, Tamahine, Wonderful Life*, and many others. He was also seen frequently in the theatre, nearly always in London, although he appeared in *Bell, Book and Candle* in the United States in 1951. He made his first appearance in South Africa in 1957 in *Table by the Window*, where he also played Major Pollock in *Separate Tables*. In 1959 he made his debut in New York, as Hector Hushabye in *Heartbreak House*. On television he enjoyed an outstanding success in 1965 when playing Jeeves opposite Ian Carmichael as Bertie Wooster.

For some years he had suffered financial embarrassments and had lived in the Channel Islands.

October 8, 1973.

Sir Clement Price Thomas, K.C.V.O., one of the pioneers in Britain of thoracic surgery and the surgeon who operated on King George VI in 1951, died on March 19, 1973 at the age of 79.

He was born at Abercarn, Monmouthshire, on November 22, 1893, and educated at Caterham School and University College of South Wales. He received his medical training at Westminster Hospital Medical School, where he gained an entrance scholarship. During the war of 1914-18 he served in the R.A.M.C. in Gallipoli, Macedonia and Palestine. He qualified in 1921 and took the F.R.C.S. Eng. in 1923. Thereafter he filled resident appointments at Westminster Hospital and for three years acted as surgical registrar to that hospital. His election to the staff of the hospital in 1927 gave him the opportunity to show his great ability. He was also appointed to the surgical staff of the Brompton Hospital for Diseases of the Chest.

At that time thoracic surgery was in process of rapid development; and the Brompton Hospital, with Tudor Edwards in the van, was taking an important part in that major surgical advance. Price Thomas soon became known for his special skill in thoracic surgery and he was appointed Civilian Consultant in Thoracic Surgery to the Army and the Royal Air Force. He also became Consultant to King Edward VII Sanatorium, Midhurst, to the Royal National Hospital, Ventnor, and to the Welsh National Memorial Association, South Wales. He was also Adviser in Thoracic Surgery to the Ministry of Health.

When, in 1951, King George VI had to undergo a serious thoracic operation, Price Thomas was asked to undertake the responsible task. This he did with conspicuous success, bringing the King through his illness with consummate skill. For his services on this occasion he was created K.C.V.O.

His reputation was international, but he was by no means a prophet without honour in his own country. He received honorary degrees from the Universities of Wales, Belfast, Paris, Athens, Lisbon, and Karachi. In his own college he served as Vice-President, and delivered the Bradshaw and Vicary Lectures. He was also president of the Association of Surgeons of Great Britain, the Association of Thoracic Surgeons, the Royal Society of Medicine and the British Medical Association.

The more honours that fell to him, the more did his innate modesty come to the fore. Although proud of what he had accomplished, this was not so much because of the credit it brought him personally but because of the benefit he had been able to bestow on his fellow men and women. He had none of the easy dogmatism and extroversion that tend to characterize the successful surgeon. Rather did he tend to exhibit a rather charming ingenuousness, which seemed to blossom as he matured.

Small of stature, one tended to pick him out in a crowd, not because of any aggressive characteristics, but rather as an attractive-looking man with a sparkle in his eyes and a warmth in his voice that expressed a sympathy and cordiality which must have gone far to commend him to the hundreds, indeed thousands, of patients who had happily placed their lives in his hands.

In 1925 he married Ethel Doris, daughter of Mortimer Ricks, of Paignton, South Devon, and they had two sons.

March 20, 1973.

Sir Raymond Edward Priestley, M.C., the Antarctic explorer and former vice-chancellor of Melbourne and Birmingham Universities, died on June 24, 1974 at the age of 87.

It is told of Priestley that, newly come to Birmingham, he confessed to his undergraduates that it had taken him "16 years and three universities to get his first degree". Thus modestly he epitomized an unusual entry to a successful academic career. The "16 years" included nearly half-a-dozen of Antarctic exploration and as many of active service in the First World War; the three universities were Bristol, Sydney and Cambridge.

He was born in 1886 at Tewkesbury, the second son of the headmaster of Tewkesbury Grammar School. From that school he matriculated at Bristol University. The turning-point in his life came in 1904. Thanks to the good offices of his elder brother, who was professor of botany at Leeds, he was invited to accompany Shackleton's "Nimrod" expedition (1907-1909) as geologist. On his return he was selected for Scott's Northern Party (1910-1913). His work on the first expedition is described in his *Geological Report*. A more popular account of the second is his *Antarctic Adventure*.

The Northern Party carried out important research in glaciology, meteorology and geophysics. They spent the winter of 1911 in a hut on the shore of Lake Adare beset by gales and hurricanes. Later, Priestley, Murray Levick the surgeon, Campbell, who was needed for magnetic observations, two petty officers and a seaman embarked in the Terra Nova for Terra Nova Bay to conduct a six weeks sledging reconnaissance. This was January 1912 and by February the ship should have reembarked them, but by mid-March the ice still stretched 25 miles from the coast; no vessel could have reached them. They therefore wintered in an ice-cave lined with snow and insulated with gravel and dried seaweed.

Bombarded by gales, the six men passed the winter months in these quarters. In September they marched painfully southwards to Cape Evans and by good luck were able to find old food depots. They reached Hut Point in November, there to get the first news of the disaster that had overtaken Scott, Wilson, Bowers and Oates months earlier.

Barely had Priestley become an undergraduate again when the First World War broke out. He served as adjutant to the Wireless Training Centre, was in France with the 46th Divisional Signals and finished active service as C.S.O. with the First Army, being seconded then to the War Office to write the *History of the Signal Service*. From him too, came *Breaking the Hindenburg Line*, the story of the 46th Division.

In 1920 he returned to Clare College, Cambridge, got his degree in 1922 and in 1925 became a Fellow. In 1934 he was made Secretary-General of the Faculties and a year later was appointed Vice-Chancellor of Melbourne. Though the appointment lasted only three years, Priestley proved an able vice-chancellor, admirable in his handling of the Australian undergraduate. Only because his ideas of necessary expansion overtopped the Government's ideas of feasible finance did he resign.

Immediately, Birmingham University appointed him Principal and Vice-Chancellor —the seat occupied earlier by Oliver Lodge and Grant Robertson, and he remained there till he felt, in 1952, that the time had come to retire.

It was no easy task he had undertaken in 1938. Birmingham University was divided geographically into two halves—the Arts side, in the centre of the city, three miles away from the Science and Medical side at Edgbaston. There was also a grave shortage of student hostels, and adequate playing fields were no more than part of a plan.

These problems Priestley hardly had time to ponder when the Second World War was on him, with its stop to development and its transformation of a university of students into an institution devoted mainly to war-time research. After the war there were new complications—a tremendous increase in undergraduate numbers, shortage of staff and funds for expansion. Others might have despaired; Priestley, while he improvized because he must, never lost sight of permanent targets.

For three achievements, at least, he will be remembered gratefully—for his success in making Birmingham and the Midlands feel they and their university were one; for his proving to industry, long before this view became fashionable, that university research and teaching could render it indispensable service; for his relations with the undergraduate body, as he saw clearly the important part undergraduates could play in their university.

His personality was an invaluable asset, inside the university and outside. Quiet, readier to listen than to speak, he spoke always to the point. Slow to take decisions, he was hard to move from decisions taken. Patient, he yet knew when the time for tolerance had passed. His quiet humour helped a lot; his patient sincerity even more. Nor did he reserve these qualities for the university. He was a figure of consequence in the life of the Midlands, notably on the

Advisory Council of the B.B.C. and as a valued governor of King Edward's School.

He seized the opportunities given him by his membership of the Asquith Commission on Higher Education in the Colonies to learn as well as to teach. His work for Malaya and especially for the West Indies will endure. Always he came back a better-equipped vice-chancellor. The knighthood conferred in 1948 was recognition of his many services.

Retirement merely brought different labours. Priestley retained his chairmanship of the Imperial College of Tropical Agriculture in Trinidad; was chairman of the Royal Commission on the Civil Service (1953-1955); was president of the British Association in 1956; and, returning to an old love, became temporary director of the Falkland Islands Scientific Bureau in the absence of Dr. Fuchs during the Geophysical Year, and a member of the Royal Society's Antarctic Committee. To all this he brought both experience and energy.

He was perhaps too busy to do much writing, though the books mentioned earlier show his capacity. Those apart, his literary output was limited to scientific papers and pamphlets and a number of lectures and addresses in which his ideas of and for a modern university are clearly and cogently expounded.

He married in 1915 Phyllis Mary Boyd, a New Zealander by whom he had two daughters. Lady Priestley died in 1961.

June 27, 1974.

Prince William—See Gloucester.
Princes—See names of states concerned.

Princess Marthe Bibesco—See Bibesco.
Princess Patricia—See Ramsay.

Sir Edward Evans-Pritchard—See Evans.

D. N. Pritt, Q.C., who died on May 23, 1972 at the age of 84, was a controversial figure, prominent in law and politics for over half a century. But in the legal world in which he had a highly successful career —he was one of the most formidable advocates of his day—the bright promise which seemed likely to lead him to high office was never fulfilled. He played a part in almost every left-wing cause from the Russian revolution to Vietnam, and from the hunger marchers to the pay freeze.

As his three volumes of autobiography show, he had learnt nothing and forgotten nothing. For him, Marxism of the Soviet variety became as sacred as is the common law to his more orthodox colleagues.

Denis Noel Pritt came of a Lancashire family. The son of the late Walter Harry Pritt, of Billericay, Essex, he was born on September 22, 1887. He won a scholarship to Winchester, but left early to enter his father's business. He studied in Switzerland,

mastered German and French, and later took a pass degree in Law at London University. He entered the Middle Temple in 1906, was called to the Bar in 1909, and became a pupil of A. F. Colam, K.C., to some of whose common law practice he later succeeded. A fine lawyer, Pritt obtained an early footing as a junior in appeals to the Judicial Committee of the Privy Council, and thenceforth for many years the bulk of his work lay in that Court. He took silk in 1927, and in spite of his politics his services were in constant demand by commercial firms in all parts of the Commonwealth.

Before an appeal tribunal, Pritt argued with extreme subtlety and was generally conceded to have few rivals; but in a trial at first instance, and faced with a hostile witness or Court, his patience and tact sometimes failed him. He was strict in upholding professional practice, with one exception—the rule that a barrister must take any brief offered him that is within the normal range of his practice and marked with his normal fee. He resolved at an early age that he would never appear for an employer against a workman, landlord against tenant, or for a political opponent of the working class. His fees were high, but it was known that he was always prepared in a needy case, and especially a political one, to forgo any fee. As a leading figure in the Howard League for Penal Reform, the Bentham Committee for Poor Litigants, the National Council for Civil Liberties, and the Haldane Society, he devoted much time to the giving of free advice.

In the general election of 1910 Pritt worked for the Tories at Bromley. His first political case—for Chief Sekgome of Bechuanaland—was in the same year, and was the first of a long series of defences, on constitutional and other grounds, of outstanding Commonwealth personalities. He joined the Labour Party immediately after the First World War, and was prospective candidate for Sunderland from 1931 to 1935. He was then invited by Jowitt to consider himself as a probable law officer. In 1930 he defended in the Privy Council Ho Chi-minh,* later president of North Vietnam. In 1931 he appeared for the prosecution in the Kylsant case; and the following year he made his first trip to the Soviet Union, and published a report on the Soviet legal system.

In 1933, shortly after the Nazi takeover in Germany, Pritt became Chairman of a Commission of Enquiry into the Reichstag Fire Trial. This holding of a public investigation into an issue which was *sub judice* in the country concerned aroused criticism at the time. Later, however, the findings of the Commission—that the fire had been staged by the Nazi authorities as a pretext for outlawing the communists— were generally accepted.

In 1934 when there were several million unemployed in Britain, Pritt defended Tom Mann, Treasurer of the National Unemployed Workers' Movement, who together with Harry Pollitt was charged with sedition.

Pritt became Labour Member for Hammersmith North in 1935, and was elected to the Party Executive the following year. In 1937, however, he was voted off; and in March 1940, he was expelled from the Party because of his book defending the entry of Russian troops into Finland. In the 1945 election he held Hammersmith North as Labour Independent. He sought readmission to the Party, but in spite of the support of 60 or more Members of Parliament he was unsuccessful. By 1949 four more Labour Members had been expelled, and all five lost their seats in 1950. For nearly two years after his expulsion he was almost boycotted by solicitors.

Out of Parliament, Pritt still found ample scope for political activity, particularly as a sponsor of the World Peace Movement, founded in 1949, and as President of the International Association of Democratic Lawyers. He was awarded a Stalin Peace Prize in 1954.

Political trials took him to many parts of the world. One of his most notable cases was his defence at Kapenguria in 1952 of Jomo Kenyatta and other Africans on charges connected with Mau Mau. Legal history was made in this trial when Pritt was charged with contempt of court in publishing to the *East African Standard* statements contained in a cable which he sent to Labour Members of Parliament, in which he described the conditions in which the trial was being held as amounting "in all to a denial of justice". He was cleared of the charge of contempt.

Pritt's political views did not prevent his election to membership of the Bench of his Inn, but he declined the office of Treasurer. In 1960, at the age of 72, he retired from the Bar, and to some extent from political life. In 1965, however, he became Presidential Professor of Law in the University of Ghana, and he held that post until the deposition of Nkrumah.

In the course of his life Pritt contributed many books and innumerable speeches and letters to controversy on all the main topics of the day. Probably the most remarkable of his books is the three-volume autobiography written after his retirement from the Bar. This work gives a panorama, from personal experience, of every left-wing movement in the 50 years of his political life. One impression left by the book is overwhelmingly of distinguished talents unstintingly devoted to the causes in which he believed, and of the contribution he made in an astonishing variety of fields.

Another impression is that, like the late Dean of Canterbury, Hewlett Johnson,* Pritt seemed able to follow the Communist Party line with a consistency which might be envied by many of the party's own professional leaders. That freedom in Russia had been in far worse condition than in many of the "enslaved" territories that provided settings for the display of his great

forensic skills seems never to have crossed his mind.

Pritt had many friends who appreciated his open-handedness, his generous aid to the underdog (for it was always said that no one ever appealed to him for money in a good cause in vain), and his fearless attacks on injustice and oppression.

He married in 1914 Marie Frances, daughter of Walter Gough, and there was one daughter of the marriage. Mrs. Pritt took a full part in her husband's political life.

May 24, 1972.

Professor Joseph Proudman, C.B.E., F.R.S., who died on June 26, 1975 at the age of 86, was a distinguished mathematician and oceanographer of international repute who gave dedicated service to the University of Liverpool for over forty years.

Having graduated first at Liverpool in 1910, he had a second brilliant undergraduate career at Trinity College, Cambridge, where he became a Wrangler with distinction and started on his studies of the dynamics of tides which were to become his main scientific interest. He returned to Liverpool as a lecturer in 1913, was appointed the first professor of applied mathematics in 1919 and in 1933 transferred to the chair of oceanography, which he held until his retirement in 1954.

In 1916 Horace Lamb asked Proudman to assist him in preparing a report for the British Association on the state of research on ocean tides. This led Proudman to the idea of founding an institute for research into all aspects of tides, an idea which was brought to fruition in 1919 with the financial aid of two Liverpool shipowners.

The Tidal Institute started its work with Proudman as Honorary Director and A. T. Doodson as Secretary, and in a few years acquired a national and international reputation for its tidal prediction services as well as for fundamental research. After several changes of name and status, the Institute is now the Bidston Laboratory of the Institute of Oceanographic Sciences. The Adams prize of the University of Cambridge was awarded to Proudman in 1923 for an essay on tides, which proved to be a remarkable seed-bed of ideas, from which there developed a series of papers, many of them jointly with Doodson, of theoretical and practical importance. Proudman used to say that his partnership with Doodson was so successful because he liked to do the algebra while Doodson preferred the arithmetic.

In addition to his work in developing the departments of applied mathematics and oceanography, Proudman took a full part in University administration and acted as Pro-Vice-Chancellor during the war years 1940-46. Quoting the maxim that "the quickest way to get a lot of things done is to do one thing at a time", he was able to

go straight to the heart of a problem, whether scientific or administrative, with an intuition which matched his intellectual ability. After his retirement the University of Liverpool conferred on him the honorary LL.D. degree. He was a Fellow of the Royal Society, which awarded him the Hughes Medal in 1957, and he served on many scientific and government committees.

Professor Proudman was a well-known figure in international scientific circles and acted as Secretary of the International Association of Physical Oceanography for a number of years before becoming its President in 1951-54. He chose as the subject of his presidential address: "The unknown tides of the oceans", a title which failed to do justice to his own work, and that of other pioneers, but which brought out the limitations of our knowledge at that time. Developments in deep sea instrumentation and computing techniques now make further advances possible, building on the dynamical treatments which Proudman pioneered. His foreign distinctions included membership of the Norwegian Academy of Science and Letters and the Alexander Agassiz Medal of the United States Academy of Sciences.

Professor Proudman was married to Rubina Ormrod in 1916 and there are two sons and a daughter of their marriage. After her death he married Mrs. Beryl Gould, who survives him.

July 3, 1975.

General Sir Harold Pyman, G.B.E., K.C.B., D.S.O., died on October 9, 1971, aged 63.

He was appointed C.-in-C. Allied Forces, Northern Europe in 1961 but in September 1963 suffered a severe stroke and in January 1964 had to relinquish his appointment. Pyman was regarded as one of the army's principal authorities on armoured warfare, especially on the effects of nuclear weapons on strategy. Earlier in 1971 he published *Call to Arms*, a volume of memoirs.

Harold English Pyman, known throughout the Army as "Pete", was born in March 1908, and educated at Fettes and Clare College, Cambridge. He was commissioned into the Royal Tank Regiment in 1929, and after a year with a cavalry regiment returned to the Tanks for the rest of his regimental service. He served in the North-West Frontier Campaign in India in 1937. In 1939 he attended the Staff College at Quetta as a student, and earned the conventional accolade of outstanding ability when he was kept at the Staff College as an instructor at the end of his course.

His war record was distinguished and gave clear promise of the eminence he was later to achieve. In March 1941 he went to the Western Desert as a major, to be second-in-command of an armoured regiment. By 1945 he was a major-general and principal general staff officer of the Allied Land Forces South-East Asia, having been admitted to the Distinguished Service Order in 1942 and been awarded a bar to the decoration at El Alamein in 1943. In 1944, at the age of 37, he was commanding the 1st Armoured Division in the Italian campaign.

After the war Pyman held a succession of important appointments, both in command and on the staff. He returned to England in 1949 from the Middle East, where he had been Chief of Staff, and was appointed General Officer Commanding 56 (London) Armoured Division of the Territorial Army. He then passed effortlessly up the military ladder by way of two senior staff appointments in the War Office —Director General of Fighting Vehicles and Director of Weapons Development— and command of both an armoured division and the 1st British Corps in Germany to a seat on the Army Council as Deputy Chief of the Imperial General Staff. He was appointed to his Nato command in Oslo in July 1961. He had been the Colonel Commandent of both The Royal Tank Regiment and the Royal Armoured Corps.

The Pyman image was one of dedicated professionalism. Technically he was far ahead of most of his contemporaries, having been among the first to detect the changing social and technological patterns of the modern Army. In 1954, while commanding an armoured division, he delivered an important address at the Royal United Service Institution, in which he emphasized the need for mobility as an essential factor in tank warfare under a nuclear threat. He was thus one of the first generals to lead the doctrine of armoured warfare away from the traditional tactics of Normandy and the Western Desert. His positive views were later translated into changes of divisional organization in Germany, and the word "pymanization" passed, not without a good deal of anguish, into the military vocabulary.

Although to many of his subordinates Pyman was remote and autocratic—he was one of the few Army Councillors who could cause major-generals to run in the corridors of the War Office—there was a disarmingly light and genial side to his personality. As Chief of Staff in the Canal Zone of Egypt in 1948 he encouraged the amateur dramatic club at the military headquarters to stage open-air productions in the garden of his official residence at the side of the Bitter Lake. He was even known on one memorable occasion to appear, anonymously but with great panache, in the cast of *Twelfth Night*, alongside another distinguished general more renowned for military science than dramatic art.

The death of Sir Harold Pyman leaves a gap which will be hard to fill in the officer corps of an Army moving not without difficulty into science and technology.

He married in 1933 Elizabeth McArthur, and leaves two sons and a daughter.

October 11, 1971.

R

Dr. Eugene Rabinowitch, who served as senior chemist on the Manhattan Project that led to development of the first atomic bomb, died on May 15, 1973 in a Washington hospital. He was 72.

Since September 1972 he had been a Woodrow Wilson Fellow at the Smithsonian Institution, where he was working on a project dealing with the scientific revolution and its social implications. He was on leave from the state university of New York, where he was a professor of chemistry.

Born in St. Petersburg, Rabinowitch studied in Germany and did post-doctoral work with Niels Bohr* at the Institute of Theoretical Physics in Copenhagen. He went to the United States in 1938 as a research associate at Massachusetts Institute of Technology. In 1945 he and Dr. Hyman H. Goldsmith, a physicist working on the Manhattan Project, founded the *Bulletin of Atomic Scientists* as a forum to explore the implications of the new power they and their fellow scientists had unleashed.

Professor Rabinowitch's scientific research work was mainly concerned with photosynthesis, to which he himself made outstanding contributions, as well as directing a research school during his twenty-one years at the University of Urbana. However, the activities for which he will be most remembered are in an entirely different area, the impact of science on society.

Eugene Rabinowitch was one of the first to recognize the urgent need and duty of scientists to be concerned with the social consequences of the tremendous progress of science and technology, the scientific revolution as he called it. He believed that this revolution demanded a correspondingly radical change in man's attitudes towards many problems, particularly to ways of settling disputes, if the human species was not to perish in a nuclear holocaust.

Rabinowitch not only felt strongly on these issues, but he managed to convert many other scientists to his cause. The foundation of the American Federation of Scientists, and much of the involvement of scientists in the United States in these problems, can be traced back to Rabinowitch's incessant efforts, and his rousing and visionary editorial articles in the *Bulletin of Atomic Scientists*, of which he was editor over many years. Indeed, it would be no exaggeration to say that Rabinowitch was one of the most influential people who shaped the attitudes and policies of the scientific community in the United States.

However, his influence was not confined to America. He realized very early that an international effort is essential, and already in 1951 he convened in Chicago a meeting of scientists from several countries, and pleaded with them the urgency to set up an international movement. When this was finally brought about, at the Conference in Pugwash, Nova Scotia, in 1957, which

started the Pugwash Movement, Rabinowitch was naturally in the lead. His main role in Pugwash was to formulate guidelines and the philosophy of the movement. He drafted the statement of common belief of scientists about their social responsibilities, which was the first to be adopted by scientists from many countries, covering a very wide range of political opinion. He also drafted the so-called Vienna Declaration, which came to be considered as the tenet of the Pugwash Movement, and which was subsequently endorsed by many thousands of scientists all over the world. Rabinowitch attended practically every one of the Pugwash International Conferences, was a member of the Continuing Committee—the governing body of Pugwash—and was president of Pugwash in 1970.

Apart from numerous articles in the *Bulletin of Atomic Scientists* and in Pugwash publications, he also wrote several books about scientists and human affairs. His contribution to educating the scientific community and the public in general received recognition by the award to him in 1964 of the Kalinga prize. His leadership in the new field of science and social affairs was recognized by his appointment as Professor of Political Science in the University of Chicago, and in the setting up at the University of New York, Albany, of a Centre for the Study of Science and Society.

Although an idealist with his head often in the clouds, he had a remarkable ability to assess the political situation realistically, and an uncanny talent to foresee events affecting society. However, the chief characteristic of all his public activities, papers and speeches was his profound concern with, and love of mankind, and his unfailing belief in the competence of scientists to create a better world for all. He had a youthful enthusiasm and the gift of imparting this enthusiasm to others. His teaching and philosophy will long remain as a source of inspiration to the scientific community.

May 17 & 18, 1973.

Dr. Sarvepalli Radhakrishnan, second President of India, died in Madras on April 17, 1975 at the age of 86. Radhakrishnan had earned himself an international reputation as an interpreter of Hinduism to the west before he became Vice-President and then President of India, and his tenure in those offices added to his stature.

Like his friend, Jawaharlal Nehru,* Radhakrishnan was a man of two worlds, as much at home in Oxford, where he was the first Indian to hold a chair, as in Madras, and among the last of a generation of Indians of whom that could be said.

Radhakrishnan's origins were humble. He was born (on September 5, 1888, in Tirutani, near Madras) into a poor family. But he was a Brahmin, and that was some two generations before Brahmin dominance of south India was broken by the foreign weapon of the franchise; his early demonstrated gifts, together with the family's caste tradition of scholarship, assured him an education, which he began at mission school at Tirupati. It is possible that his lifetime dedication to the task of explaining Hinduism, to finding qualities beneath the surface that many foreigners find only quaint, grotesque or repellent, dated from that first experience of western attitudes.

He went on to Madras Christian College and was appointed assistant professor of philosophy at Presidency College, Madras, and six years later became full professor there. His growing academic reputation took him in 1921 to Calcutta, where he held the chair of George V Professor of Philosophy for nearly 20 years. He was knighted in 1931.

He had begun to write while at Presidency College, and characteristically his first work was a study of the philosophy of Tagore (whose Nobel prize had sent a wave of pride and self-confidence through intellectual India) tracing its roots in traditional Hindu thought. A subsequent series of works attracted attention outside India and in 1926 he set out upon his life's task of interpreting Indian philosophical speculation to the western world with the appointment to what was to be the first of three tenures at Oxford University, the Upton Lectureship at Manchester College. In the same year he became Haskell Lecturer in comparative religion at the University of Chicago.

Returning to India in 1927 he published what has been his most popular work, *The Hindu View of Life.*

In 1936 Radhakrishnan was appointed to the Spalding chair of eastern religions and ethics and became a member of All Souls, as the college had linked one of its fellowships with the Spalding chair.

In 1948 Nehru*, by then Prime Minister, made Radhakrishnan chairman of a commission whose report upon the Indian universities had a formative effect upon the new Government's education policies. In the following year he was named Ambassador to the Soviet Union.

Radhakrishnan became Vice-President in 1952 and, in 1962, he was elected President of India.

Dr. Prasad,* India's first President, more than once attempted to assert powers which Nehru denied were properly his and was as often rebuffed; Radhakrishnan took the opposite view, that the President's powers were ultimately no more than the right to be informed and to advise. He was better able to do that because of his affinities with the Prime Minister. He could—and often did—differ from Nehru without his opposition being taken, as was Dr. Prasad's, as the voice of stubborn and often purposeful orthodoxy.

During the border war with China in 1962, when the Government was deeply shaken by the military debacles, politicians began to go to the President to express

their anxieties, to suggest that things were so bad that he must take a stronger role in political affairs—one party of Congressmen even suggested that he should dismiss the Government and assume responsibility himself. Radhakrishnan rejected these temptations; but it was noted that after these events an estrangement developed between him and Nehru.

Another testing time for Radhakrishnan came with the death of Nehru in 1964, when he made what may be seen as a contribution to Indian constitutional practice. He called on the most senior member of the Cabinet, Gulzarilal Nanda, and swore him in as Prime Minister until the Congress Party had elected their new leader.

When the news of Lal Bahadur Shastri's* death in Tashkent reached the Presidential palace in the small hours of January 11, 1966, Radhakrishnan followed the precedent he had himself established. When Gulzarilal Nanda, still the senior member of the Cabinet, went hotfoot to his chambers, the President swore him in as Prime Minister once more; again Nanda exerted all his energies to retain the office chance had given him for the second time; again the Congress Party in Parliament turned away from him, this time electing Mrs. Indira Gandhi their leader.

Radhakrishnan completed his second and final term in 1967.

Radhakrishnan travelled widely and frequently, both as Vice-President and President, his official tours as President including the United States of America, Britain—where in 1963 the Queen crowned the long list of his honours by making him an honorary member of the Order of Merit—the Soviet Union, and many other countries. In 1964 Pope Paul bestowed on him the highest Vatican honour, the Golden Spur.

His calm and friendly bearing, his pure and lucid English (Telegu was his mother tongue, he learnt no Hindi) made him a striking, popular and highly effective ambassador-at-large.

In February 1975 he won the Templeton Prize for Religion valued at £40,000, the first non-Christian to do so.

His wife, Sivakamama Ama, predeceased him in 1956, and he is survived by five daughters and a son, Dr. S. Gopal, an historian and former officer of the Indian Ministry of External Affairs.

April 18, 1975.

Henzie Raeburn, the actress, who died on October 27, 1973 at the age of 72, was familiar in the theatres of Britain and the United States where she seconded her husband, Dr. E. Martin Browne, in his work for poetic and religious drama. She was herself an especially good verse speaker, an accomplished actress, and a dramatist. Except for a gap between 1924 and 1937, when she retired to bring up her two sons, she had been on the stage since 1916.

Born in London on November 2, 1900, and educated at Queen's College, she created an early record as London's first woman assistant stage manager, during the New Theatre run of *The Chinese Puzzle*. Later, for Bridges-Adams, she played such ingénues as Celia and Jessica in the Shakespeare Festival at Stratford (1920). After this she had nearly three years at the Everyman Theatre at Hampstead, working with (among others) Edith Craig, Theodore Komisarjevsky, and Mrs. Patrick Campbell (of whom, not surprisingly, she had some cheerfully crisp memories).

When she returned to the stage in 1937 her husband was recognized on both sides of the Atlantic for his pioneering in the poets' theatre; her New York début (Ritz, 1938) was as the Chorus Leader in *Murder in the Cathedral,* a title she had suggested to T. S. Eliot* before the original production (which Martin Browne directed) in the Canterbury Chapter House.

At the Westminster, London (1939), she was Ivy in Eliot's *The Family Reunion* (eight years later, at the first Edinburgh Festival, she moved to Agatha, among her favourite parts). During the war, 1939-45, she and Martin Browne acted in and ran the Pilgrim Players which toured Britain on an extraordinary variety of stages and in many remote areas; she recorded much of the enterprise in her charming *Pilgrim Story* (1945). Postwar, 1945-49, she appeared in the sequence of poets' plays at the Mercury; and she created Margaret in Jack Hawkins's Arts Theatre production of Fry's *The Lady's Not For Burning* (1948).

Thenceforward her life included such variety as a part in the 18 months' London run of *Harvey* (Prince of Wales from 1949); Mary Magdalen in the Mystery Play at the York Festivals of 1951 and 1954 (in 1966 she was Mary the Mother); and drama recitals with Martin Browne in Australia and New Zealand (1951) and across the United States (1962-65). Annually she aided her husband in his drama programme at the New York Union Theological Seminary.

Latterly she acted a good deal at the Yvonne Arnaud Theatre, Guildford; and in September 1970, she was Leader of the Women in the first production of *Murder in the Cathedral* in Canterbury Cathedral itself.

Henzie Raeburn, with her faith, courage, and generous sympathy, made friends everywhere. She was a natural and good-natured wit. In and out of the theatre she and her husband, who survives her, formed a rare partnership.

October 30, 1973.

Chips Rafferty, M.B.E., one of Australia's best known character actors, collapsed and died in a Sydney street on May 27, 1971 at the age of 62.

In a film career spanning more than 30 years, Rafferty, 6ft. 6in. tall, with a weather-beaten face, came to typify the rugged, good-humoured Australian adventurer.

His real name was John Goffage and he was born in the New South Wales mining town of Broken Hill on March 26, 1909 and went to school in Sydney. His early life was spent in 40 or more different jobs, mainly out of doors, including miner, sheep shearer, drover and airman. He entered films in 1938 and began by playing mostly comic roles: his first picture was called *Ants in his Pants*.

Rafferty served with the Royal Australian Air Force in New Guinea in the early part of the Second World War and went on to appear in some of the few Australian-produced films to reach the international market; among them *Forty Thousand Horsemen* (1940) and *The Rats of Tobruk* (1942), with Peter Finch.

When Ealing Studios under Sir Michael Balcon decided to make a film entirely on Australian locations, Rafferty was chosen for the leading role of the cattle drover in *The Overlanders*, directed by Harry Watt in 1946. He was afterwards taken to England under contract to Ealing, appearing with Googie Withers in *The Loves of Joanna Godden*, but was back in Australia in 1949 for another Harry Watt picture, *Eureka Stockade*.

For the rest of his career he was in steady demand, particularly for films made in Australia by British and American companies. His later pictures included Fred Zinneman's *The Sundowners*, with Robert Mitchum and Deborah Kerr, the remake of *Mutiny on the Bounty*, and Michael Powell's *They're a Weird Mob*.

He was awarded the M.B.E. in January 1971 for his services to the performing arts.

May 29, 1971.

Tun Ismail bin Dato Abdul Rahman, deputy Prime Minister of Malaysia since 1970, died on August 2, 1973 aged 57. A former medical practitioner, he was his country's first Ambassador to the United States.

A courteous and respected politician and diplomat, he had been a leading figure in Malaysia for many years. After the 1969 civil disturbances he played a valuable part in the work of reconstruction, returning from retirement to offer his services to the Prime Minister.

He was a strong opponent of racialism. He said of the 1969 election campaign: "Campaigning on racial lines and racial issues is not democracy; it is licence."

Ismail was much concerned with the policy of neutralization which Malaysia had been following.

The son of Dato Abdul Rahman, who became president of the country's first Senate, Ismail was born at Johore Bahru on November 4, 1915. He was educated at the English College there and at the Medical College in Singapore. He qualified in

medicine at Melbourne in 1945 and practised for six years at Johore before entering local, state and federal politics.

In 1951 he joined the United Malays National Organization and became a vice-president. In time he became the member for lands, mines and communications, and later for natural resources. In 1956 he was appointed Minister for Commerce and Industry.

When Malaya became independent a year later, Ismail went to the United States, with the rank of Minister without Portfolio, to be Ambassador to the United States and also Malaya's representative at the United Nations.

He returned to take over the External Affairs ministry from the Prime Minister; but Tunku Abdul Rahman's foreign bent was so pronounced that there were times when Ismail was overshadowed.

The Tunku took external affairs back into his own hands. Ismail became Minister of Internal Security in 1960.

He flew that year to London to preside over an inquiry into the progress and welfare of the 3,000 Malayan students in Britain and the Republic of Ireland.

In 1964 Ismail became Minister of Home Affairs and Justice. He resigned in 1967 because of ill health, but returned in 1969 after the Chinese-Malay racial rioting which broke out in May after the general election. He was appointed Minister of Home Affairs, and became deputy Prime Minister the following year.

He leaves a widow and six children.

August 4, 1973.

Shailh Mujibur Rhaman—See Mujib.

Professor Harold Raistrick, F.R.S., formerly Professor of Biochemistry at the London School of Hygiene and Tropical Medicine, died on March 8, 1971 in his 81st year. He had a long and distinguished career, and will be remembered mainly for his pioneer work on the biochemistry of moulds. On this subject he published a hundred papers and became not only an authority but *the* authority.

Raistrick was born at Pudsey in Yorkshire on November 26, 1890. Educated at the Central High School at Leeds, he went on to the university and obtained a B.Sc. degree in chemistry with first class honours. After a short period of postgraduate study in the Department of Agriculture, he moved in 1913 to Cambridge, where he worked in the Department of Biochemistry under Professor Gowland Hopkins. Here, assisted by a grant from the Medical Research Council and alongside Dr. Marjory Stephenson, he started his investigations into the metabolism of moulds, while she started her investigations into the metabolism of bacteria. Both of them were destined to open up new fields of inquiry whose later

exploitation was to prove so fruitful.

In 1921 Raistrick left Cambridge to take charge of the biochemical work at Nobel's Explosives Company in Ayrshire. During the eight years he spent there he carried out various investigations, the results of which were published in a series of papers occupying the whole of one volume of the Philosophical Transactions of the Royal Society.

He left in 1929 on his appointment to the Chair of Biochemistry in the newly opened London School of Hygiene and Tropical Medicine. This post he occupied till his retirement in 1956. Without any teaching commitments he was able to spend practically the whole of his time in research. He collected round him a small team of young, able chemists and mycologists and with them continued his work on the biochemistry of moulds.

In collaboration with Professor Topley, he studied the immunizing power of bacterial vaccines and made some progress in elucidating the chemical basis of their efficacy. At Topley's suggestion, he attempted the purification of penicillin, which at that time was chiefly of academic interest but which, as Topley foresaw, had amazing potentialities. Though Raistrick prepared crude penicillin, his attempts at its purification failed, partly because of its instability under the conditions he used to extract it, partly because of insufficient help in animal control work, and partly by sheer bad luck. It was left to [Lord] Florey* and to [Professor Sir Ernst] Chain a year or two later to gain the success that he had been denied.

During the War he acted as Honorary Scientific Adviser on the production of penicillin to the Ministry of Supply. He was elected to the Fellowship of the Royal Society in 1934, appointed Bakerian Lecturer in 1949, and received the Flintoff Medal of the Chemical Society in 1963. He was twice married, having two daughters by his first wife.

March 11, 1971.

Chakravarti Rajagopalachari, first Indian Governor-General after independence from Britain in 1947, died in Madras on December 26, 1972. He was 94.

He succeeded Lord Mountbatten as Governor-General in 1948 and held the position until India became a republic in 1950.

A most devoted follower of Mahatma Gandhi—he was sometimes called the keeper of his conscience—"Rajaji" differed with him seriously over the "quit India movement" launched against the British in 1942.

Early in the century, Rajagopalachari took up the cause of the untouchables in India when as chairman of the Salem Council in Southern India he ordered that they be allowed to use municipal drinking taps.

"C.R." or "Rajaji", as he was variously

known, was born in 1878 in Salem district of Madras, a Brahmin, and educated in law at Madras University. In the early years of the century he built up a practice in Salem but he was one of the many Indian intellectuals drawn to the Congress movement. In 1920 the young south Indian became secretary of the Indian National Congress and later a member of the party's directive body, the working committee.

By the late 1930s C.R. was one of those who swayed the working committee to agree to contesting elections under the India Act of 1935. After the elections in 1937 in which Congress was widely triumphant, C.R. became Prime Minister of Madras.

The Madras Ministry resigned office in 1939, together with all the other Congress ministries, and Gandhi chose C.R. to be one of the first two volunteers to offer individual civil disobedience (the other was Vinoba Bhave), and duly in 1940 C.R. went to jail again—in all he was imprisoned five times. When Japan came into the war a year later his sense of realism led him to the declaration that Gandhi's non-violence needed modification, and he argued again for conditional support being given to the Allies' cause.

After the Congress leaders were released from prison at the end of the war, Rajagopalachari went to Delhi and was a member of the interim government.

When India became a republic and Rajendra Prasad* president, he succeeded Sardar Patel as Home Minister, but stayed in the Cabinet only a year.

C.R. became chief minister of Madras again in 1952, but by then the Brahmin dominance which he could be depicted to represent was beginning to crumble under the impact of universal suffrage. C.R. tried to introduce an educational measure which would have given village children artisans' training—in the crafts of their families. The D.M.K. took the lead in the agitation against the education Bill, but their opposition to it had strong support within the Congress party iself, where the lower castes were beginning to want their day in the sun. Rajagopalachari was forced to resign.

After he resigned the chief ministership in 1954 C.R. moved steadily into opposition. In 1957 he organized the Congress Reforms Group, which was essentially a dissident group within the Madras Congress Party. In the pre-independence period his influence and loyalties in the party had leant towards the right in economic policy and this conservatism emerged in 1959 when C.R. became the leader of the newly formed Swatantra (Freedom) Party, committed to economic laissez-faire and freeing the country from what it denounced as the Congress Government's "permit-raj". The Swatantra Party filled a gap in the Indian political spectrum, offering voters a party that was right-wing without being obscurantist or communal.

December 27, 1972.

Matyás Rákosi, formerly Prime Minister of Hungary and First Secretary of the Hungarian Communist Party, died on February 4, 1971.

One of the most able and ruthless of the Stalinist dictators, Rákosi represented a whole epoch of Russian domination in eastern Europe. Thrown by the First World War into contact with Lenin and the small group of intellectuals who made the Russian revolution, he spent a large portion of his life in prison and then, backed by Stalin's power, he manoeuvred the communists into absolute control in Hungary.

Closely associated with the Russian dictator's policies and methods, his position became difficult alongside the political and economic liberalization which took place in the U.S.S.R. under Khrushchev's influence. After the public denunciation of Stalin at the XXth Congress of the Soviet Communist Party in February 1956, his further retention of power became embarrassing if the policy of de-Stalinization were to be plausible. He resigned during the summer, admitting that the violations of socialist legality perpetrated under his regime had "diminished the attractiveness of People's Democracy". Shortly before the popular explosion in October he managed to flee to the Soviet Union. He remained there for some time and in 1962 was stripped of his membership of the Hungarian Communist Party by Kadar's administration.

The son of a small Jewish shopkeeper by the name of Rosencrantz, his comfortable paunch, bantering humour and constant smile gave him the aspect of a jolly country grocer. Speaking eight languages, including English and Turkish, he impressed many visitors with his erudition.

Winning a scholarship to a Bankers' Association language school, he took up employment in a London bank after graduation. It was here that he became a socialist. He attended an institution called the International Communist Working Men's Club, where he claimed to have met Keir Hardie, Sylvia Pankhurst and Ramsay MacDonald. In 1914 he was forced to leave Britain to avoid being interned as an enemy alien. Commissioned in the same year, he was captured in Russia and interned in the Far East, where he occupied his time learning Russian and Italian. At the outbreak of revolution he made his way to St. Petersburg, where he met Lenin. When he returned home in 1918 he became a Minister—at the age of 26—in the short-lived communist regime of Béla Kun.

After this regime's collapse he displayed considerable courage in returning to Hungary in 1924. Captured and condemned to death, his life was probably saved by an outcry in the western press. Rákosi, however, remained in prison from 1924 until 1940, when, it is said, he was ransomed by Stalin in exchange for the historic flags which the Russians had captured when they crushed the revolution of 1848. Rákosi told an American visitor that "the whole of my youth passed in prison"; the education

he received in a Horthy prison served him well during the terror which he unleashed in his country after Stalin's break with Tito.

Rákosi returned to Hungary with the victorious Red Army, but it was some time before the communists secured absolute control. The manipulations by means of which his followers swallowed the other parties, uniting with the Peasant and Social Democratic parties against the conservatives, only to destroy the Small Holders' Party once it had served his purpose, were ably executed and are reminiscent of the tactics employed by Stalin to deal with the "right" and "left" deviationists in the Soviet Union. When the socialist and communist parties finally "fused" in 1948, Rákosi became secretary-general of the new Hungarian Workers' Party and the leader of the quadrumvirate (Rákosi, Gero, Farkas and Revai) who ruled the country under Russian direction.

Rákosi did not become Prime Minister until August 1952, and at one stage had to cede power to Imre Nagy, but in fact he occupied the position of dictator until the death of Stalin. He remained the dominant influence until 1956.

The darkest pages in Rákosi's biography cover his role as interrogator and persecutor of his opponents. Preparing for some of the rigged trials, he is alleged to have personally supervised the application of torture to his victims. Probably the most renowned of the unjust executions which took place under his administration is that of László Rajk, the former Foreign Minister, who was executed on trumped-up charges of Titoism. It was the rehabilitation and ceremonial reburial of Rajk which sparked off the October rebellion in Budapest.

February 6, 1971.

Lady Patricia Ramsay, one of the surviving grandchildren of Queen Victoria, who lived for more than half a century after divesting herself of the outward signs of royalty and her place in the family, and had in consequence become largely forgotten, died on January 12, 1974, aged 87.

She was the youngest child of Queen Victoria's favourite son—the Duke of Connaught—and was closely connected with the old ruling houses of Europe through her mother, a daughter of the celebrated Red Prince of Prussia. But a conventional royal marriage made no appeal to her, and in 1919 she married a naval officer, Captain Ramsay (later Admiral the Hon. Sir Alexander Ramsay [q.v.]) and lived an unostentatious life, occasionally appearing publicly as an artist. At the time, her work was considered somewhat advanced and her cousin Princess Marie Louise, with faint disapproval, called it "modern, very modern".

Princess Victoria Patricia Helena Elizabeth of Connaught was born at Buckingham Palace on March 17, 1886, St. Patrick's Day. Her father held various army commands abroad, and some of Lady Patricia's very earliest memories were of India. As a teenage girl she spent some years in Dublin when her father was commander-in-chief in Ireland. As child and girl "Patsy"—as she was called in her father's family—was a great favourite of the Queen. She was staying at Balmoral in 1896 when the Emperor and Empress of Russia were staying there and Mr. Downey came to take the first cinematograph film of the Royal family, with the children—in the Queen's words—"jumping about".

Lady Patricia was tall, handsome and intelligent and it was not because of any absence of offers that she did not make a royal marriage. The King of Spain was one suitor, and the then British government, with characteristic subtlety, decreed that it would be all right if the bride became a Roman Catholic but that the King of England must not countenance the conversion by attending the wedding. The prospect did not appeal to Lady Patricia though she always remained on good terms with the King, and her son's Christian names included Alfonso. The Grand Duke Cyril, who was to become the head of the House of Romanoff, was also anxious to marry her, but she remained content with the ordinary English social round, with life in the family home at Bagshot Park, and with accompanying her parents when duty took her father abroad.

Her work as an artist first became noticed in 1910. The subject matter of her paintings was derived largely from travel in tropical countries, particularly the undersea life and vegetation.

She was one of the distinguished royal amateurs of painting. She showed an early taste for the arts in general, was trained in music, like her sister, Princess Margaret (later Crown Princess of Sweden), under Albanesi and had her own painting studio at Clarence House, when it became the home of her father. One of her youthful caricatures was of her uncle, King Edward, seated at the dinner table with a contented smile, the caption being "I *was* hungry". She specialized first in flower paintings, but accompanying the Duke of Connaught on his journeys, as Inspector of the Forces, to Africa and the Far East, developed an interest in tropical marine life and vegetation. Study under A. S. Hartrick, who had known Gauguin and Van Gogh, introduced her to the work of these masters which had some influence on her style. She and her husband opened Hartrick's retrospective exhibition in London in 1936; and his book of reminiscences, *A Painter's Pilgrimage through Fifty Years*, published in 1939, was dedicated "To the Lady Patricia Ramsay, who gave me the title of the book, in homage".

Lady Patricia became a member of the New English Art Club in 1931 and was also an honorary member of the Royal Institute of Painters in Water Colours. She was a regular visitor to the art galleries and gained much affection in the art world by her sympathy with, and encouragement of, contemporary British artists.

In 1911 she went with her parents to Canada where her father was Governor-General. Her mother was in failing health, and in fact died in Canada so that Lady Patricia became her father's official companion and hostess, and made herself not only extremely useful but extremely popular. A strip of territory round Ontario was named in her honour. She was very active in helping to raise Princess Patricia's Canadian Light Infantry in Ottawa, in 1914, and the colour which she worked and presented to them was carried by the battalion through all the battles on the Western Front and is believed to have been the only colour carried by British troops throughout the First World War. Although after her marriage she retired from public duties she always made an exception for the battalion which carried her name. She inspected it in 1940 and visited it in Germany after 1945.

Her marriage in 1919 was a complete break with tradition, and while similarities might be found in some of the reputed marriages of George III's daughters it was probably necessary to go back to the shadowy days of King Edward IV for a comparable precedent. She was married in Westminster Abbey on February 27, 1919, in the presence of all the Royal Family. As she was of royal birth she wore the bride's veil off her face. The relinquishment of her rank had been announced shortly before the wedding in the following terms:

"In accordance with the express wish of H.R.H. Princess Patricia of Connaught, and with the concurrence of H.R.H. the Duke of Connaught, the King has approved that subsequent to Her Royal Highness's marriage she relinquishes the above title, styling and rank, and assumes the name of Lady Patricia Ramsay."

King George V wrote in his diary "No doubt a most popular marriage" and, with that characteristic attention to detail, he added, "She will take precedence before marchionesses".

Thereafter she lived largely in Surrey and was able to be a solace to her father in the loneliness of extreme old age—he lived to be nearly 92 at his home, Bagshot Park.

Her only child, Captain Alexander Ramsay, fought in the Second World War and was severely wounded in North Africa. Her husband died in 1972.

January 14, 1974.

Admiral the Hon. Sir Alexander Ramsay, G.C.V.O., K.G.B., D.S.O., died on October 8, 1972 at the age of 91. He was the husband of Lady Patricia Ramsay, [q.v.] youngest child of the Duke of Connaught, third son of Queen Victoria.

He had a varied and distinguished career in the Royal Navy for 48 years. He was originally a gunnery specialist and was decorated as such for service in the 1914-18 War. From the middle 1920s he took more interest in naval flying, commanded a carrier, and became both Flag Officer Aircraft Carriers and Fifth Sea Lord and Chief of Naval Air Services at the Admiralty. He was in office at the time the Navy reassumed complete control of the Fleet Air Arm in 1939, when the difficulties of transfer were greatly increased by a large programme of expansion.

Alexander Robert Maule Ramsay was the son of the thirteenth Earl of Dalhousie, and was born on May 29, 1881. He entered the Royal Navy as cadet in H.M.S. Britannia in July 1894, and two years later went to sea as midshipman in the Majestic, flagship of Lord Walter Kerr in the Channel Squadron.

In October 1911, he was appointed naval aide-de-camp to the Duke of Connaught, Governor-General of Canada. Eight years later, after the First World War, he married H.R.H. Princess Patricia of Connaught, who surrendered her title, style and rank and assumed the name of Lady Patricia Ramsay. They had one son.

Returning to naval duty in 1913, Ramsay became gunnery officer of the battle cruiser Indefatigable, in the Mediterranean. In her he took part in the first bombardment of the Dardanelles forts in November 1914. Two months later he was promoted to commander and joined the staff of Admiral de Robeck, in the Inflexible and the Lord Nelson. He was awarded the D.S.O. for excellent gunnery work and service in action at Gallipoli. In 1916, he returned home with the admiral and accompanied him to the Grand Fleet as flag commander, Second Battle Squadron.

Promoted to captain in 1919, he was naval attaché in Paris for the next three years. In 1928, he took command of the aircraft carrier Furious, in the Atlantic Fleet and so was brought into direct contact with the Fleet Air Arm. From 1933 to 1936 he was Rear-Admiral, Aircraft Carriers, with his flag in the Courageous. He led the fly-past of naval aircraft at the silver jubilee naval review held by King George V in 1935. From May 1936, he was C.-in-C., East Indies with his flag in the Norfolk.

After two years there he was appointed Fifth Sea Lord and Chief of Naval Air Services from July 1938. It was a momentous period in the development of the Fleet Air Arm as a force separated from the R.A.F. Parliamentary approval had been given in 1937 that the Navy should have administrative as well as operational control of its air forces, and its own shore bases for them. The changeover naturally raised many problems, and it was not until May 1939 that the transfer took effect. Ramsay saw it through and remained in office until November 1939. A month later he was promoted to admiral, and retired at his own request in 1942.

October 10, 1972.

The Rt. Rev. Ian Ramsey, Bishop of Durham, who died on October 6, 1972, was a leading figure on the Episcopal Bench. Forward-looking, scholarly but down to earth, his was a voice always listened to with respect when the current problems of the Church of England in particular and Christianity in general were being debated. He was 57.

He was thought by many to be a likely successor to his namesake, Dr. Michael Ramsey, Archbishop of Canterbury.

He was born in Bolton in January 1915, the only son of Arthur Ramsey, and he went to school there. He went as a Scholar to Christ's College, Cambridge, and was later a student also at Ripon Hall, Oxford. At Cambridge he gained First Classes in Part I of the Mathematical Tripos (in 1936), in Part IIa of the Moral Sciences Tripos (in 1938), and in Part II of the Theological Tripos (in 1939), crowning this remarkable scholastic feat by winning the Burney Prize in 1938 and becoming Burney Student in 1939.

He served as a curate for three years at Headington Quarry, Oxford, and then returned to Cambridge first as Chaplain of Christ's College, and then as Tutor and Fellow and Director of Studies in Theology and Moral Sciences. He left again for Oxford in 1951 to succeed the late L. W. Grensted as Nolloth Professor of the Christian Religion and Fellow of Oriel College.

From his early days at Cambridge he was much in demand as a lecturer. The qualities which made him so attractive a lecturer served him well also in the pulpit. It was no surprise when he became Canon Theologian of Leicester Cathedral in 1944 and he was Hulsean Preacher at Cambridge and many times Select Preacher at Oxford and Cambridge.

As a student Ramsey had been much drawn to Bradley, and this gave his thought a range of interest which saved him from becoming too restricted in outlook when in due course he became much attracted to linguistic philosophy. Just as he moved at ease from Oxford to Cambridge and from academic circles to a world of varied ecclesiastical activity, so he seemed equally at home with the *avant-garde* of empiricist linguistic philosophers and with those who aspired to some sort of metaphysics.

He brought out exceedingly well, in his earlier books like *Religious Language* and *Freedom and Immortality* and in his Inaugural Lecture at Oxford on *Miracles*, the oddity of language which had a transcendent reference; and the homely illustrations with which this was presented were the delight of the lecture halls he filled so easily. *On Being Sure in Religion* sought with the same persistence to be sure in religion itself, in matters ranging from "divine punishment" to "Christian social duty." while being tentative in theology. In this work, as in his subsequent *Models and Mystery,* he made suggestive use of his mathematical and scientific knowledge; and his main attainment, here as in other works,

consisted in the variety of ways in which he exhibited the cautious and qualified way in which we must understand the language we may also speak with confidence in religion. Only by exceptional skill and shrewd sympathetic understanding of religious claims could he sustain this course, through an impressive array of philosophical and theological works, without also conceding more than he should in attenuations of his faith.

In all this Ian Ramsey was helped by a profound and sympathetic social concern in which the warmth and kindliness of his own personality had a prominent place.

Very different duties awaited him on his appointment as Bishop of Durham in 1966. Like most academic theologians he had previously avoided entangling himself in ecclesiastical administration, debate and gossip; he was far more interested in medical ethics than in canon law. At a nobler level of church life, he had little pastoral experience of the normal kind.

In many ways, however, as one of the Church of England's senior bishops, he simply carried on being himself. Apart from his namesake the Archbishop of Canterbury, he was the only outstanding intellectual on the episcopal Bench, and the skills developed at Cambridge and Oxford were obviously needed as Ian Ramsey was called to preach and lecture on many "special" occasions and to guide the discussions of important groups such as the Archbishops' Commission on Doctrine (of which he became chairman when it was established in 1967). His theological contributions to the Lambeth Conference of 1968 were of a rare quality.

He was the leading spirit, and the formulating mind in many—for his health, too many—groups pondering different aspects of the Church's tangled relationship with a secularized England. The most important document to emerge from these discussions was the *Durham Report* on Religious Education, urging a fresh approach to the teaching of Christianity in schools, based more on life-situations than on Bible-stories. He began to make an equally important contribution in an equally vital field when in 1971 he took over as chairman of the Central Religious Advisory Committee, advising both the B.B.C. and Independent Television.

He made good use of his membership of the House of Lords, and of other opportunities, to put into further practice his conviction that theologians ought to converse with men of the world in order that both sides, clerical and lay, might together see more clearly the best approach to current social problems. He called for many more "inter-disciplinary" dialogues, for example between dons and businessmen, in a lecture to the Royal Society of Arts. The approach he wanted was both scholarly and practical, both Christian and humanist; he acknowledged the tensions involved, but always refused to despair of the possibility that good will would reconcile the different

emphases.

His integrity was manifest in his insistence on speaking out when moved by conscience, despite the obvious risks to his career. He was widely viewed as Dr. Michael Ramsey's natural successor at Canterbury, and he could not help being aware of this—and of the dislike politicians have of being "preached at". But the result was that when he received signs of favour from the Labour movement, such as being invited to address the Miners' Gala in Durham, this was regarded by one and all as an honour proper to a man of God, and not as any kind of gimmick.

In his diocesan duties he also developed without altering the gifts which colleagues and pupils had valued in the universities. He stimulated new audiences with popular expositions of his philosophical theology. He invigorated jaded clergy with his vision of the Church cooperating with all men of good will for the benefit of society. He set an example of tireless industry, and he was invariably friendly; whatever the solemnity of the ceremony or the deliberation, he could not help being warmly human. Busy as he always was, he had time for people.

The see of Durham, in medieval times virtually a Prince-Bishopric, has had many distinguished occupants; few have worked harder. None had been so active as a diocesan bishop since the two great Victorians, Lightfoot and Westcott (who had also gone to Durham straight from university chairs). It is scarcely too much to say that Ramsey modernized the diocese in response to the rapid social changes of the time.

His Lancastrian accent and stocky unpretentious figure were definite assets as he moved around the diocese of Durham. He spoke and looked like a North Country vicar, although his quick grasp of any problem and his wit were perhaps not so characteristic of his flock. He won the love and confidence of many in the North, and used to tell his friends that he never regretted leaving Oxford. Characteristically, he would explain that even a professor has too little time for reading, because of his duties.

He married Margretta McKay in 1943. They had two sons.

October 7, 1972.

Major-General Sir Hubert Rance, G.C.M.G., G.B.E., C.B., the last Governor of Burma before that country became an independent republic in 1948, died on January 24, 1974 at the age of 75.

He played an outstanding part in the reconstruction of the administration after the Japanese occupation. From 1950 to 1955 he was Governor and Commander-in-Chief of Trinidad and Tobago. In both these posts he showed himself a strong supporter of the British Government's new approach to the colonies after the Second World War, and in both he won wide praise by his gifts of statesmanship and comprehension.

Hubert Elvin Rance was born on July 17, 1898, the son of Frederick Hubert Rance. He was educated at Wimbledon College and R.M.C., Sandhurst, from which he was commissioned in The Worcestershire Regiment in 1916. In the 1914-1918 War he served on the Western front for five months and was wounded three times. In 1926 he transferred to the Royal Corps of Signals. He went to France with the B.E.F. in 1939, served as commander of divisional signals and on the general staff, and was made O.B.E. and mentioned in dispatches. After Dunkirk he was promoted to Brigadier and was for a time Director of Technical Training at the War Office. The taking of a course at the Civil Affairs Staff College in London proved to be the turning point of his career, for it led to his appointment in 1945 as director of civil affairs in Burma, with the rank of major-general.

He at once applied himself with great diligence to the economic and social problems of the war-ravaged country. He travelled extensively and got to know the people, and made his junior officers do the same. He was a strong supporter of Mountbatten's policy of moving with the rising tide of Asiatic nationalism, a task of considerable delicacy. Rance showed himself a firm and successful administrator.

When the civil government, headed by Sir Reginald Dorman-Smith, was taken back to Rangoon from its wartime headquarters in India, Rance was transferred to England where he took over the command of a military district. But his achievement in Burma was not forgotten. In August 1946, Dorman-Smith was invalided home, and Rance succeeded him. He returned to his uncompleted task, this time with full authority. He found an explosive situation, with widespread strikes and riots. He solved it by coming to terms with Aung San and his powerful Anti-Fascist People's League, and by securing the cooperation of the main political parties in setting up a coalition government. This was a great diplomatic triumph.

Rance gained the full confidence of the Burmese leaders, and, under his administration, considerable progress had been made in restoring the country to an orderly state when the time came for the transfer of power to Burma as a republic in January 1948. He and his wife left on a wave of immense popularity, and, nine years later, they received a great welcome when they went back, on the invitation of the Burmese Government, to share in the Independence Day celebrations.

Soon after his return, to England, Rance was appointed chairman of the Standing Closer Association Committee for the British West Indies and British co-chairman of the international Caribbean Commission. In 1950, he became Governor and C.-in-C. of Trinidad and Tobago, in which capacity he continued to play an active part in the setting up of the West Indian Federation.

Rance played a great part in steering through the complications, but, as events were to prove, the structure, of which he was one of the chief architects, proved too ramshackle to last.

Rance was Colonel Commandant of the Royal Corps of Signals from 1953 to 1962. He married in 1927 Mary Noel, daughter of C. A. Guy, and they had a son and a daughter.

January 25, 1974.

Lord Rank, who died on March 29, 1972 aged 83, was one of the principal architects of the British film industry, and a man who played a leading part in its control and development from the moment when he turned from religious films to the far wider commercial sphere.

He was created a peer in 1957.

Joseph Arthur Rank was not born into the world of entertainment. On the contrary, he was by birth, heritage and tradition a miller, a Methodist and a Victorian. His father, Joseph Rank, made an immense fortune out of his mills and was still leading an active life shortly before his death in 1943 at the age of 89. He was a shrewd business man and a devout Christian and his son, J. Arthur Rank, went into the film business as founder of the Religious Film Society. Thus J. Arthur Rank was not a born showman, as nearly all great film producers are, nor had he the showman's flair for knowing what the public wanted. His strength lay in his business acumen, his Yorkshire solidarity in an entertainment world prone to emotional instability and excesses of alternating optimism and pessimism, and his ability to choose shrewd and reliable lieutenants to implement his policies.

J. Arthur Rank was born in Hull on December 23, 1888, the youngest of Joseph's seven children. He was educated at The Leys School, Cambridge, and was then sent straight into apprenticeship in the flour business. Shortly afterwards he was moved south by his father to work in London. He married Ellen Marshall in 1917 and her sound judgment was to be of great help to him in the years to come. He served in France during the first war, where he differed from the average young soldier only in his resolute teetotalism.

Throughout his youth, and even in middle age, he probably remained under the domination of his father, and continued to work as a miller. It is perhaps significant that his film empire was not fully developed until after his father's death. He lived quietly in Reigate, where he taught regularly in the Sunday school of the local Methodist church. It is said that his interest in the cinema was first aroused by listening to a dull, routine sermon, when the thought came to him that the cinema might well be used to bring the teachings of Christ more vividly to life. The films

available were of poor quality—so in 1933 he founded the Religious Film Society.

What prompted him to leave this small and secluded field and to launch out into the far more worldly sphere of commercial film production? It was a question often asked in his lifetime. The answer was probably no more than that he was the son of his father. He therefore enjoyed expanding a business and running it on profitable lines. But, like his father, he was a devout Christian and also a patriotic Englishman, and he believed that the cinema could be used as an instrument for good in the world.

The first step was the formation, in 1934, of a modest company named British National Films and by 1935 the first film, *Turn of the Tide*, was ready for release. It was a simple story describing the rivalry between two Yorkshire fishing families, with a cast that included Geraldine Fitzgerald, Wilfrid Lawson, Sam Livesey and Moore Marriott. It was a good film, but not very commercial. It not only lost money (which was unimportant) but it brought J. Arthur Rank into conflict with the distributors. Thus he learnt the first lesson of the film industry, which is that making films is one thing; getting the right distribution is another. He therefore decided that it would be necessary for him to become ultimately his own distributor and exhibitor. Thus, having committed himself to film production, he now began to commit himself to far more. His aim, already formulating in his mind, was not only to control production and distribution, but to rid Wardour Street of the stranglehold which Hollywood had upon it.

The empire which he subsequently built up was partly the result of his shrewdness, and partly of circumstance. Several of his chief rivals in the film industry died, and so did his chief adviser, C. M. Woolf, leaving J. Arthur Rank standing almost alone. The war years helped his expansion, and the tentacles of the Rank Organization began to spread into every sphere of film production.

Most remarkable of all was the fact that a man who had reached middle age without ever considering the possibility of being a film magnate should now become in his late fifties the most influential figure in the British Film Industry. He acquired control of the Gaumont-British circuit, and of the Odeon circuit; of the Denham studios, Pinewood studios, Gainsborough studios and Gaumont-British studios. These studios turned out a succession of films which always sought after quality, even if they did not achieve it. He chose Earl St. John,* a large and genial American with a shrewd knowledge of public taste, to supervise his productions. He selected John Davis, a most capable and far-seeing business executive, as his right-hand man.

He was often criticized in his life-time. It was said of him that he never really understood the entertainment world which he so largely influenced. This was probably true. But he was fully conscious of his limitations, and placed his trust in those who *did* understand it. His producers, directors, writers and actors were given a free hand; he never attempted to tell them how to do their job. Even extravagant eccentrics such as Gabriel Pascal were allowed to plan productions in their own way.

It was also said of him that he was a monopolist; that he sought to make a corner in British talent. He certainly did tend to monopolize the British film industry, especially after his major rivals, such as Alexander Korda, were dead; but he never used creative talent simply as a medium for making money. As a business man he sought to make films that were profitable, but as a man of high principle he would never make a film of which he might feel ashamed, no matter how much money it might earn for him.

It was Hollywood that held the monopoly in the years between 1920 and 1950, and it was J. Arthur Rank who was determined to make the British film industry a power in itself, respected throughout the world. In this he was successful. His biographer, Alan Wood, quotes the comment made by one of his chief rivals some years after the end of the Second World War. "Had it not been for Rank, there would be no British film industry today." It is a remarkable epitaph for a man who was born into the world to be a miller.

March 30, 1972.

John Crowe Ransom, the American poet, who died on July 3, 1974 at his home in Gambier, Ohio, at the age of 86, was also one of the most influential of modern critics; the founder, with Allen Tate and Robert Penn Warren, of "The New Criticism".

The son of a Methodist minister, he was born on April 30, 1888, in Pulaski, Tennessee. After attending Vanderbilt University in Nashville, he went to Oxford as a Rhodes scholar and read classics and mathematics at Christ Church from 1910 to 1913. In 1914 he returned to Vanderbilt, as a member of the English Faculty. There —apart from service in the First World War as a Lieutenant in the field artillery, and a year at University College, Exeter— he remained until 1937, when he became a professor of English at Kenyon College, Ohio. He was editor of *The Kenyon Review* from its inception, and was responsible for the foundation of the "Kenyon School" (of Letters, later transferred to the University of Indiana), to which many distinguished poets and critics lectured.

Ransom's reputation as a poet rests on *Chills and Fever* (1924) and *Two Gentlemen in Bonds* (1927), since his first book, *Poems About God* (1919), became unobtainable soon after its publication, and he declined to reprint any poems from it in subsequent collections. *Grace After Meat* (1924) was a selection prepared for publica-

tion in England. *Selected Poems* (1945) was also published in England, the last five poems of this volume representing the poet's slender output since 1927.

His verse ranges from the fragile evocation of *Vision by Sweetwater* to the subtle polemic of *Antique Harvesters*, yet a similar tone is common to both. It is the tone of irony. By comparing the facts of a situation with the ideal of what it might have been, Ransom was able to make a series of poetic comments which were both sharp and wise. His poems are metaphysical, precise, finely-wrought, slightly archaic in diction, tough-minded and strangely haunting. For all their use of mannered diction they are never precious or sentimental; the impression they give is of a courtly elegance which was typical of the man himself. It is the voice of a Southerner brought up in the classical tradition and clinging to the best standards of his region; Ransom was, in the most literal sense of the word, a gentleman.

He was not, however, without a sense of humour. "And now he is hungry and tired", says Ransom in *Sunset*.

". . . But he is a Southern gentleman
And will not whimper once
Though you keep him waiting forever".

In the field of criticism he became known as a "formalist", that is, a critic who devotes more attention to the form and style of a poem than to its "content". The scope of his criticism, however, was much larger than this. In *God Without Thunder* (1931), he attacked both the values of science and liberalism in religion. His ideas of science were considerably different from those of an earlier Southern poet, Edgar Allan Poe, since Ransom saw it only as a materialistic force. Art, he maintained, was a more satisfactory "alternative" since it tended to check the impulses of Rousseau's natural man.

Ransom's concept of a great critic was that he should be "ontological", concerned with the very being of a poem. Like his fellow New Critics, however, he always emphasized the value of close textual reading. Through study of the literary art, Ransom believed, the reader might come close to what he called "the world's body", which was in danger of being reduced to "types and forms" by science.

Apart from his contributions to poetry and criticism, Ransom will be remembered chiefly as one of the "Fugitives", since, in 1922, he was founder, and subsequently editor for three years, of *The Fugitive*, a journal devoted not only to the publication of original verse and to the propagation of ideas concerning Southern agrarianism, but also to the perpetuation of high literary standards. Although the magazine has long since ceased to exist, its name is as alive as ever where American literature is read and taught.

It would be tempting to say that, with Ransom's death, a valuable part of America had disappeared. But this is not so. Manners change; but the spirit lives on. What-

ever news the papers may be full of—the latest outrages, the peril of the streets— there are still Americans (and they are not few) who stand for what Ransom stood for: faith, hope and charity, no less than liberty, equality and fraternity.

Ransom was married to Robb Reavill and they had three children.

July 5, 1974.

Alan Rawsthorne, C.B.E., who died in a Cambridge hospital on July 24, 1971 at the age of 66, was a composer whose early works promised him a greater future than fashions allowed him to achieve.

The works of his early maturity, notably the Theme and Variations for two Violins and the orchestral Symphonic Studies, first heard at I.S.C.M. festivals in London and Warsaw in 1938 and 1939, announced the arrival of a composer with a distinctive style, an impressive clarity of mind and utterance, and a decisive command of all the materials necessary for his work. As fashions changed in the late 1950s, Alan Rawsthorne did not change with them; the often astringent clarity, the decisiveness and the complete intellectual control continued to display themselves in works which, because they did nothing superficially novel, won less popularity than they deserved.

Alan Rawsthorne was born in Haslingden, Lancashire, on May 2, 1905, and educated at Sandringham School, Southport. In his entry in *Who's Who* he wrote "did not begin serious study of music till the age of 20 owing to parental opposition; previously a student of dentistry and architecture". He was 21 before he entered the Royal Manchester College of Music, where he studied under Frank Merrick and the cellist Carl Fuchs. In 1930 he went abroad to study under Egon Petri. From 1932 to 1938 he was at Dartington Hall, responsible, among other things, for music in the School of Dance Mime.

Settled in London to devote himself to composition, Rawsthorne quickly made his voice heard and, after the success of his Symphonic Studies, his reputation grew rapidly. He served in the Army from 1941 to the end of the war, but continued to write works at an apparent speed which made their precision and high finish all the more surprising.

His first piano concerto was heard at a Promenade Concert in 1942; his Overture Cortèges in 1944. The Cheltenham Festival commissioned his oboe concerto of 1947 and his violin concerto of 1948. His first symphony was written for the Royal Philharmonic Society in 1950, and his second piano concerto, probably the most popular of all his works, was commissioned by the Arts Council for the Festival of Britain in 1951.

Though Rawsthorne continued to compose industriously, and never without both point and clarity of intention, the acclaim he won in the late forties and the early fifties did not endure. His second and third symphonies are no less impressive than his first; his cello concerto of 1966 and his concerto for two pianos of 1968 show perhaps less wit and ebullience than the popular second piano concerto, but they are works of complete integrity and precise intention. They were welcomed by critics rather than taken to the public's heart. In the last 10 years of his life he ranged from a setting for tenor chorus and harp of Skelton's "Lament for a Sparrow", a setting for speaker and orchestra of T. S. Eliot's* "Practical Cats", three impressive cantatas for chorus and orchestra, to the Mediaeval Diptych for baritone and orchestra, which is the most frequently heard of his later works. At the same time, he continued to write scrupulously precise, fastidiously unexaggerated chamber music.

If Alan Rawsthorne was the victim of changing fashions he was, perhaps, also the victim of his own characteristically exact sense of his own limitations. He wrote nothing that does not display a vigorous sense of purpose, a fine intellectual awareness of the means it must adopt to realize its ends, and an honesty aimed always at complete lucidity. But his music had no ambition to startle or to shock; it accepts a range of emotional expression which never attempts the grandiose, the extremely intense or the sensational.

"Composers have to take upon themselves the integrity of their own styles", he once said, apologizing immediately for a phrase which, he suspected, sounded dangerously high-flown. But he did precisely that, observing disciplines and limitations which clearly defined the integrity and value of his own works. He was created C.B.E. in 1961.

He married first in 1934 Jessie Hinchliffe, the violinist, and secondly in 1954 Isabel Lambert.

July 26, 1971.

Ernest Raymond, O.B.E., F.R.S.L., an accomplished and popular novelist, died on May 14, 1974 at the age of 85.

He was the author of the resounding best-seller *Tell England* which has been through many editions since it was first published over 50 years ago.

A fluent storyteller, Ernest Raymond found occasion in many of his novels to illustrate his social and religious convictions. These were radical and Anglo-Catholic, and he presented them, as a rule, with a dramatized earnestness which was very much in character. In the earlier ones, which have a pronounced autobiographical colouring, he drew much from his years of schoolmastering and as an Anglican chaplain in the war of 1914-18. As he developed, his scope widened and many novels were based upon various aspects of life in the London which he loved, and

upon the north-west of England which was also near to his heart. In the first part of his career he might be described as a man of sentiment, but this trait became less marked in his maturity.

Born on December 31, 1888, the son of William Bell Raymond, he was educated at Colet Court and St. Paul's School. He taught at a school in Eastbourne during 1908-11 and at a school in Bath during the following year. Then, under a strong sense of vocation, he proceeded to Chichester Theological College and took a degree preliminary to holy orders at Durham University. Ordained in 1914, he was attached to the 10th Manchester Regiment during 1915-17, and to the 9th Worcestershire Regiment 1917-1919, serving in Gallipoli, Egypt, France, Mesopotamia, Persia and Russia.

Raymond returned to England, but bruised and critical in spirit and resigned holy orders in 1923.

In the previous year he had published his first novel, *Tell England*, a story of a school and war, with an Anglo-Catholic priest for one of the leading characters. The book (later to be made into a film by Anthony Asquith*) was extremely popular and immediately established the author.

Later in the same year came *Rossenal*, a simple tale of school and schoolmastering, with a hero preparing to become a novelist; next year, *Damascus Gate;* and in the following year, *Wanderlight*, the story of a young ordinand who draws back from the Anglican priesthood.

Thereafter Raymond firmly maintained his position as a popular writer, producing a book every year. One of his most successful, *We the Accused* (1935), in which he combined a genuinely moving murder story with informed criticism of our legal system, began a series of sixteen novels which he called *A London Gallery*—each, as the name implies, dealing with some aspect of life in London. The last of the series was *The City and the Dream*, which appeared in 1958.

In all he published well over forty novels, and the success of *A Georgian Love Story* (1971) showed that he could still command a considerable public for the type of story which he wrote. Apart from two further novels he wrote some volumes of autobiography, beginning with *The Story of my Days* (1968), and three volumes of essays, of which the best, *Through Literature to Life* (1928), commanded a steady public for more than forty years.

He was made O.B.E. in 1972.

He married, first, Zoe Irene Maude, daughter of Captain Doucett, R.N.R., by whom he had a son and a daughter.

This marriage was dissolved and he married, secondly, Diana, only daughter of Professor William Thomas Young; they had one son.

May 16, 1974.

Eva, Marchioness of Reading, C.B.E., widow of the Second Marquess of Reading, Minister of State for Foreign Affairs, 1953-57, died on August 14, 1973 at the age of 78.

She was president of the British Section of the World Jewish Congress, a member of its world executive, and a devoted social worker. She was a past president of the National Council of Women.

She was born on August 6, 1895, the daughter of Alfred Mond, first Lord Melchett, and educated privately. In her reminiscences published earlier in 1973 (*For the Record*) she describes how her maternal grandmother exhorted her never to marry a Jew and never to go slumming. She did both, for she married Gerald Isaacs, son of Rufus Isaacs, first Marquess of Reading, sometime Viceroy of India and Foreign Secretary, and she gave of herself without stint in work for children's welfare.

Brought up a Christian, her growing sympathy with the Jews in Palestine culminated in her making a profession of faith as a Jewess in 1933, when the accession to power of Adolf Hitler made her feel that "the Star of David was stamped on my inner conscience". Unknown to his sister, Henry, second Lord Melchett, had taken the same decision at the same time.

She was chairman of the Sun Babies Day Nursery Home, Hoxton, 1929-39; a member of the General Nursing Council 1935-37; and during the Second World War was adviser to the Ministry of Health on child care. In 1957 she was created C.B.E. and in 1971 the Hebrew University, Jerusalem, made her an honorary Fellow.

Her husband died in 1960. They had a son, the third Marquess of Reading, and two daughters.

August 15, 1973.

Stella, Dowager Marchioness of Reading, G.B.E., founder and chairman of the Women's Royal Voluntary Service, died at her London home on May 22, 1971. She was 77.

The creation of the Women's Voluntary Service organization was the crowning achievement of Lady Reading's life. It was not only unique in conception, but eventually eclipsed in membership every other society seeking or providing opportunities for the activities of women in public life. And it owed everything to the self-sacrificing efforts and genius of its leader. Before its advent there had been many attempts on similar lines, but in most cases the interests fostered were either sectional in their appeal, violently political, or discriminatory to the point of class distinction. But the W.V.S., as it became familiarly known, suffered from none of these drawbacks. Its policy was broadly based on the promotion of the welfare of the community and the application of sympathy, kindliness, and understanding.

The W.V.S. (which became the W.R.V.S.

in 1966) was formed under the chairmanship of Lady Reading in 1938 "to encourage and coordinate the recruitment of women into the Air Raid Precautions Services", but its immediate objects were soon sublimated into the more vital activities which the outbreak of war rendered no less imperative. Thenceforward it undertook all types of work for local authorities and government departments, such as evacuation, feeding, clothing and rehousing civilians who suffered from enemy air raids. By 1942 the membership exceeded a million, and it had become a source of comfort and help in many directions.

No wonder that at the end of the war its leader and her devoted followers were asked by the Government to continue their beneficent work for a further possible two years of post-war reconstruction, and that this was followed in 1947 by an official request to keep the organization in being indefinitely. The Government provided offices and other essential facilities, and the W.V.S. acted as the distributing agent for the many gifts of food and clothing sent to British people from abroad. Their work included the care of old people and children, especially those in institutions, the general rehabilitation of families, and welfare work for British troops in all parts of the world. Perhaps the greatest attraction of the organization was that it provided an opportunity of practical service for all women.

Stella, Lady Reading, was born in Constantinople in 1894, the daughter of Charles Charnaud. As a child her health was bad, making it necessary for a great part of her education to be undertaken by private tutors. But this had its compensations, for it resulted in study of a wide range of subjects and engendered a thoughtfulness and philosophy which were afterwards reflected in all her work. In the 1914-18 war she worked in the British Red Cross Society, gaining much valuable experience.

In 1925 she went to India, where Lord Reading was Viceroy, as the woman member of the Viceroy's staff. She married Lord Reading as his second wife in 1931, and until his death in 1935 helped in all his public work. In 1932, during the worst period of post-war trade depression, Lady Reading headed the Personal Service League formed to help the victims of unemployment in distressed areas. Appointed a member of the Ullswater Royal Commission on Broadcasting in 1935, she was its only woman member, and later she became a member of the B.B.C. Advisory Council. Amid all her preoccupations she found time to serve as a Justice of the Peace.

As a member of the Overseas Settlement Board and the Imperial Relations Trust, she found an outlet for the keen interest in international and Commonwealth affairs which she shared with her husband. She travelled extensively, and just before the last war motored across the United States as Mrs. Reed, lodging in private houses where tourists were accommodated at a dollar a night, or in camps or hotels wherever she chanced to be at nightfall.

In 1938 the Home Secretary appointed her chairman of the new Women's Voluntary Services for Air Raid Precautions. Under her guidance the organization grew in numbers and influence, first as an auxiliary of civil defence, and later an army of zealous women prepared to cope with every type of war-time emergency. To bring about this result needed not only vision but organizing ability of the highest order but Lady Reading proved equal to the task. She inspired the million volunteers who had been recruited by her enthusiasm, and in spite of the fact that most of them were serving on a part-time basis, and the majority were housewives with many other responsibilities their efforts were untiring. Lady Reading spent at least a third of her time during the war in touring the country for recruits, encouraging individual workers, and trying to smooth out inevitable difficulties. In 1946 she became a Governor of the B.B.C., and its vice-chairman from 1947 to 1951. She was also vice-chairman of the Imperial Relations Trust, a member of the Central Housing Advisory Council of the Ministry of Health, the Ministry of Labour Factory and Welfare Board, the Overseas Settlement Board, and the first woman member of the National Savings Committee. She was chairman of the Advisory Council on Commonwealth Immigration from 1962 to 1965.

Even then she found time for other duties, and when, as a result of her readiness to adopt new ideas, a new company—Women's Home Industries Ltd.—was formed, she became its chairman. Launched in October 1947, the company aimed to stimulate the craftsmanship of the women of Britain in knitting, tapestry work, and needlework in their own homes to earn dollars for the country. A first-class needlewoman herself, she took an interest in every detail of the work and was seldom found in her leisure moments without knitting, embroidery or tapestry in her hands.

An enthusiastic gardener, she was often seen wearing out one of her old W.V.S. uniforms, pruning rose trees or weeding in the delightful garden of her Sussex home. Lady Reading was several times honoured for her services, being made a Dame of the British Empire in 1941, and in 1944 raised to the highest rank in the Order—Dame Grand Cross.

In 1947 Lady Reading received an honorary degree of Doctor of Literature at Reading University; she also held honorary degrees from Yale, Manitoba, and Leeds. In 1948 she received the American National Achievement Award for Women.

In 1958 she was created a life peeress, and took the title Baroness Swanborough. She was a woman of great personal charm and refinement and had the happy knack of making all with whom she came into contact feel completely at ease.

May 24, 1971.

Professor R. O. Redman, F.R.S., who died on March 6, 1975 at the age of 69, was a leading British optical astronomer who played a prominent part in the development of his subject after the Second World War.

After attending Marling School, Stroud, Roderick Oliver Redman went to St. John's College, Cambridge, where he took the Mathematical Tripos. He had a talent for music and gained the John Stewart of Rannoch Scholarship in Sacred Music in 1925. Throughout his life music gave him great pleasure, in which all his family shared.

At Cambridge he came under the influence of Professor Sir Arthur Eddington, Plumian Professor of Astronomy and Director of the Cambridge University Observatory, and decided to make astronomy his future work. After taking his Ph.D. his first appointment was to the staff of the Dominion Astrophysical Observatory at Victoria, British Columbia, where he remained until his return to Cambridge in 1931.

The Cambridge Observatory had assimilated the Solar Physics Observatory of South Kensington about 18 years previously, and Redman became its Assistant Director in succession to Dr. John A. Carroll, later Sir John Carroll. In 1935 he married Kathleen Bancroft, and they lived in a house on the observatory site. He was elected a Fellow of St. John's College in 1932.

In 1937 he again left Cambridge to become Chief Assistant at the Radcliffe Observatory in Pretoria, South Africa, under Dr. H. Knox-Shaw. Although he greatly enjoyed his nine years in South Africa, and did important work in its clear skies, the period was one of frustration for him because the 74in. telescope, which had been ordered by the Radcliffe trustees from Sir Howard Grubb Parsons and Co., could not be put into operation until after the war.

It was in South Africa that he started his researches on astronomical photometry, which he later continued at Cambridge. In 1947 he returned to Cambridge as Professor of Astrophysics. He was elected to the Royal Society in 1946. One of his first administrative actions at Cambridge was to integrate fully the Solar Physics Observatory into a new unit that was called The Cambridge Observatories.

Under his energetic direction the Cambridge Observatories rapidly recovered from the difficulties and restraints of the war years and the unit was reequipped with good modern instruments, including a 36in. telescope, a 16/24in. Schmidt camera, both by Grubb Parsons, and a large solar installation.

Observing at Cambridge was never easy, but the staff and students were inspired by Redman's enthusiasm, so that all the instruments were put to excellent use. The 36in. telescope in particular was used for the development of an important new technique that he had devised for the study of narrow wavelength bands in the spectra of stars.

While in South Africa he made an expedition to the total solar eclipse of 1940, where he obtained high dispersion chromospheric spectra that were superior to any previously obtained. The success of this expedition led Redman to head another one, equally successful, to Khartum in 1952. Although after this he did not participate in expeditions, he recognized their importance and encouraged members of his staff, and others, to make such expeditions for a variety of astronomical purposes. He served as President of the Royal Astronomical Society from 1959 to 1961.

Redman's life was exceptionally busy and he never spared himself. In the few years before retirement he devoted much of his time and energy to the planning and construction of the 150in. Anglo-Australian telescope, and the success of this instrument owes much to him. This duty involved him in frequent long visits to Australia, which were continued for some years after his retirement.

He enjoyed working with large telescopes and was delighted to have the opportunity of taking part after his retirement in the planning of the Northern Hemisphere Observatory as a consultant to the Science Research Council.

Redman had a warm and generous personality with a wry sense of humour and a complete absence of grandeur. Under his direction the Cambridge Observatories was a happy place, and all who visited the family will remember the warmth and affection there.

March 10, 1975.

Lord Reid, P.C., C.H., Q.C., a Lord of Appeal in Ordinary from 1948 until his retirement early in 1975, died at the age of 84 on March 29, 1975.

From 1962 he was the senior law lord and as such he was, as Lord Devlin observed, "the most important judge in Britain". It is probable that he did more to influence the course of the English common law then any other judge since the Second World War.

As *The Times* Legal Correspondent, Marcel Berlins, wrote on the occasion of Reid's retirement: "Lord Reid was in control in the heady decade of the sixties when traditional social and legal assumptions were coming under incessant challenge. During that period he guided the House of Lords down the middle path between the slavish acceptance of old judicial concepts and the radicalism which some critics were demanding."

Although conscious of the need to avoid substituting judicial for parliamentary law-making, he did not hesitate to call for legislative reform where he felt this was needed, nor to develop existing law to its limits without cutting across what he felt

was the job of Parliament.

Reid sat on about 600 appeals during his years as a law lord. In the majority of these he gave a full judgment, often the main judgment. He also played the dominant role during the hearing of the case itself. The influence which Reid exerted is hard to assess and certainly cannot be gauged either by inspecting the statistics or by reading his written judgments.

James Scott Cumberland Reid was born on July 30, 1890, the son of James Reid, Writer to the Signet, of Drem, East Lothian. His father, as well as being a partner in an Edinburgh legal firm, had a farm at Drem, so that Scott Reid, as he was known to his family and friends, grew up in an atmosphere conditioned by these two interests which remained his own throughout his life.

He was educated at Edinburgh Academy, the training ground of so many Scottish lawyers, which he left for Jesus College, Cambridge, where he had been elected to a scholarship in Natural Science. At Cambridge he took a first class in the Natural Science Tripos and followed this with a first class in law and the degree of LL.B.

He returned to Edinburgh to study the law of Scotland at the University of Edinburgh and qualify for the Scots Bar. At the university he was contemporary with several who were later to achieve distinction in the legal profession, chief among them being the late Lord Cooper.

In accordance with Scottish custom he spent several months in one of the leading Edinburgh legal offices, where he gained a knowledge of the practical side of the profession, learning much about the feudal law and acquiring that grasp of principle which was so marked in his subsequent career.

At the same time he joined the Speculative Society where he made friends and learned what Lord Dunedin, in recalling his own debt to the society, has called "the first elements of disputatiousness" which he was to show to such a marked degree in the House of Commons. "The Spec", as it is affectionately called by its members, has many distinguished names on its roll and it was a proud moment in Reid's life when in 1964 he presided at the dinner held to commemorate the two-hundredth anniversary of the founding of the society.

His university course had just been completed when the 1914-18 War broke out and immediately he joined the 8th Royal Scots, the Territorial unit for the area in which Drem lay. It was the practice at that time for a would-be entrant to the Faculty of Advocates to present his petition for admission a year before admission could take place, during which year he was allowed to "devil" to a practising advocate.

Reid had planned to be admitted in November 1914, and when that time came he had the distinction of being the first person to be admitted wearing uniform instead of wig and gown. As the war went on he transferred to the Machine Gun

Corps and saw service in Mesopotamia.

It was not until 1919 that he was able to begin the practice of his profession. The years of absence were a handicap to the returning lawyer. The old men who had remained at home were not, as a rule, understanding about the difficulties which faced the ex-service men and were far from sympathetic. Progress for Reid was slow for a time, even though an outstanding performance in the case of *Galloway v Earl of Minto*, the subject of which was teinds and their effect on ministers' stipends, had made a great impression in the Parliament House as showing his unusual knowledge and his skill in dealing with a most complicated matter.

In the years of comparative idleness he busied himself with legal writing, acting as one of the compilers of the *Faculty Digest*, that book so invaluable to Scottish practitioners, and publishing a book on the Agricultural Holdings (Scotland) Act of 1923. These were the early days of wireless and he amused himself by making his own receiving set and discussing with those of his brethren who were like-minded the various problems which wireless transmission involved.

But his acute legal mind and the wide knowledge of law which had been the admiration of his friends could not remain unrecognized for long. His advancement when it came was rapid, and in 1932 he was able to take silk. From a busy practice in the Parliament House he passed to the House of Commons in 1931 as Unionist member for Stirling and Falkirk Burghs, a seat which he held until 1935.

He was again returned to Parliament in 1937 as member for the Hillhead Division of Glasgow, and, as long as he remained in the House of Commons, it was as member for that division. He was Solicitor-General for Scotland from 1936 to 1941 and Lord Advocate from 1941 to 1945.

In the House of Commons he made his mark as a skilled debater and a wise administrator. In 1945 his brethren elected him Dean of Faculty of Advocates, an office which every member of the Scottish Bar regards as the summit of professional achievement for a practising advocate, depending as it does not only on skill as a pleader but on outstanding qualities of character as a man.

In 1948 he was made a Lord of Appeal in Ordinary and was given a life peerage under the title of Baron Reid, of Drem.

He will perhaps best be remembered by lawyers for his judgments in two seminal cases of the early 1960s. *Ridge v. Baldwin,* in 1963, not only had a profound effect on the law governing the individual's right to natural justice in his relationship with "authority", but also heralded a new liberal approach to the law in general on the part of the law lords.

In *Shaw v. D.P.P.* (the *Ladies' Directory* case) the House of Lords decided that the crime of conspiracy to corrupt public morals existed under English law. Lord

Reid, in what many lawyers believe was his finest hour, gave a dissenting judgment in which he argued passionately against judicial encroachment into the field of public morals and judicial lawmaking.

He was chairman of the Malayan Constitutional Commission in 1956 and 1957. As was natural, other honours fell to him. He was given the degree of LL.D. by the University of Edinburgh in June 1945; he was made an honorary Fellow of his old college, Jesus, Cambridge; and he was an honorary bencher of Gray's Inn. In 1971 Oxford made him an honorary D.C.L. He was made a Companion of Honour in 1967.

As a man he was shy and reserved and difficult to know, but his kindliness and courtesy were apparent to all, and he was held in high respect. To those who gained his friendship he was a lively and stimulating companion.

He married in 1933 Esther Mary, daughter of the late C. B. Nelson and widow of G. F. Brierley. There were no children of the marriage.

March 31, 1975.

Admiral Sir Peter Reid, G.C.B., C.V.O., Vice-Admiral of the United Kingdom from 1966 until 1973, died on September 26, 1973 at the age of 70. He was Third Sea Lord and Controller of the Navy, 1956-61.

John Peter Lorne Reid was born on January 10, 1903, the second son of Sir James Reid, the first Baronet of Ellon, who was physician to Queen Victoria at Balmoral, and of Susan, daughter of the first Baron Revelstoke. He was educated at the Royal Naval Colleges Osborne and Dartmouth.

Reid specialized in signals, taking the Jackson-Everett prize. He was fleet wireless officer in the Mediterranean during the Italo-Abyssinian war of 1935-36. In 1937 he joined the staff of the Tactical School, Portsmouth.

Early in the Second World War, in which he was twice mentioned in dispatches, Reid took part in operations off Norway and later off Oran in H.M.S. Valiant. He was still in Valiant when she passed with H.M.S. Illustrious through the Sicilian Narrows to reinforce the Mediterranean Fleet at Alexandria in the autumn of 1940; and when the ship took part in the battle of Cape Matapan.

Promoted to captain at the end of 1941, Reid flew from Alexandria to Java to be chief signals officer to Lord Wavell during the defence of the Netherlands East Indies. When the Japanese occupied the East Indies Reid escaped to Ceylon with Wavell; they were taken on board an old Singapore steamer, which broke down on the journey and had to be towed in to Colombo.

In Ceylon Reid joined the staff of Admiral of the Fleet Sir James Somerville, then Commander-in-Chief, East Indies, and served as Captain (Operations).

In 1943 he was appointed Deputy Director of the Signals Division, Admiralty, where he served until selected for work with the Pacific Fleet in 1944. In the Pacific he introduced to a British fleet for the first time the United States Navy's signalling system.

After the war Reid commanded the cruisers Dido and Cleopatra, and then engaged on special duties at the Ministry of Defence in connexion with defence research policy. He was promoted to rear-admiral in January 1951, becoming Chief of Staff to the Commander-in-Chief, Portsmouth, and Allied Commander-in-Chief Channel and North Sea the following May.

From February 1954 to August 1955 he was Flag Officer (Air) Mediterranean and Flag Officer Second-in-Command Mediterranean, working under Lord Mountbatten of Burma, also a signals specialist. He was promoted to vice-admiral in 1954.

Reid became a Lord Commissioner of the Admiralty, Third Sea Lord, and Controller of the Navy, in October 1956, retiring in 1961. He was promoted to admiral in 1958. He was Rear-Admiral of the United Kingdom and of the Admiralty from 1962 to 1966.

He was made G.C.B. in 1961 (K.C.B. 1957, C.B. 1946), and C.V.O. in 1953. He was appointed a deputy Lieutenant of East Lothian in 1962, and was Vice-Lieutenant in 1964, and 1967. He became Vice-Convenor of East Lothian County Council in 1969, and was president of the British Legion, Scotland.

Reid had a strong presence, despite his lack of height, having an obvious sincerity and a technical competence well above the average. He was quiet and kind, with a keen sense of humour, and he remained calm under every circumstance.

He married in 1933 Jean, only daughter of Sir Henry Dundas, third Baronet of Arniston, and of Beatrix, daughter of the twelfth Earl of Home; she died in 1971. They had a son and a daughter.

September 28, 1973.

Helene Reinhardt—See Thimig.

Lord Reith, K.T., G.C.V.O., G.B.E., C.B., who will long be remembered as the creator of British broadcasting, and the first Director General of the British Broadcasting Corporation, died on June 16, 1971 at the age of 81.

He was one of the outstanding personalities of his time, an engineer with a turn for business management, who, by sheer force of character and intellect, established himself as autocrat of a new realm of human expression. He was destined and well equipped to be a pioneer. He saw far and clearly—none the less because at times he focused narrowly. He had too a zest for the development of freshly dis-

covered possibilities. A keen sense of the practical told him how far he would be allowed to go; but he possessed in addition the courage to force issues and the strength frequently to secure the decisions he desired.

He made of the B.B.C. a model for many other countries, and an ideal that could be admired in others with different systems. It would almost seem as if, in spite of his energy and comparative youth, fate had regarded this great achievement as sufficient for one man. When he moved into other spheres of administration his performance, though the gifts he brought were the same, was far less conspicuous. The reason is, perhaps, that his early successes were the result of a coordination of his many qualities and that his later tasks engaged as a rule only a few of them.

His great gifts were never given the same scope again. It is true that in the difficult and invidious position of Minister of Information he succeeded in effecting valuable reforms in organization and might well, if he had remained to operate the mechanisms he devized, have done much more. At the Ministry of Transport, however, his field was restricted, while that of Works and Buildings, though it offered wider possibilities, yielded no fame. Relegated then to minor executive positions in the Admiralty and Combined Operations Headquarters, he earned the praise of his superior officers; and after the war as chairman successively of the New Towns Committee, of the Commonwealth Telecommunications Board and of the Colonial Development Corporation he made his own characteristically solid contribution to thought and practice in all these new ventures; but none of these achievements can compare with his creation of the B.B.C.

Towering well over 6ft. 6in. in height, and with strongly marked features accentuated by beetling eyebrows and a conspicuous scar, he was a formidable figure. On most occasions stern, unbending, withdrawn, he had few of the arts which charm strangers into friendship and more often than not seemed deliberately to repel by his air of self-sufficiency. Yet his quiet, deep voice belied these externals and on occasion his face would light up with a smile of great beauty and warmth. He seldom gave confidences, but when he did there was no reserve and his friends, who knew this trait, found under his stern exterior a sensitive, if proud, nature singularly attractive and worthy of their regard and loyalty. His first volume of autobiography, *Into the Wind*, published in 1949, reveals something of this dichotomy to a wider public. By then he had indeed "warmed both hands before the fire of life"; it no longer burned fiercely as in his youth and the period of his greatest achievement, but it still glowed warmly. He published a second look at his own life in *Wearing Spurs* (1966).

John Charles Walsham Reith was born at Stonehaven on July 20, 1889. He was the fifth son of the Very Rev. George

Reith, D.D., a saintly man who at the time was minister of the College Church at Glasgow and later Moderator of the United Free Church of Scotland. His earliest days were therefore spent in a deeply religious household and his character developed in conformity with it. To the end he was to remain a devotional and a pious man.

He was educated at Glasgow Academy, Gresham's School, Holt, and the Royal Technical College at Glasgow, whence after two years' study he entered upon a long apprenticeship in locomotive works in his own city. In 1913 he obtained a post in London with Messrs. S. Pearson and Sons.

Early in the war he joined the Scottish Rifles—he had had some previous military experience as a Territorial—but was shortly transferred to the Royal Engineers with the rank of lieutenant. He served in France during the winter of 1914 and was severely wounded in the following autumn. A sniper's bullet, which travelled through his face, almost ended his life. It left a conspicuous scar. At the end of 1916, unfit for further active service, he was transferred as a major to special duties. He did well and was sent on a mission to North America in charge of contracts for munitions. He liked the warmth of American friendship, the speed and directness of their working methods, and seriously considered settling there for life; but after two years there he was appointed to the Department of the Civil Engineer-in-Chief of the Admiralty. When the war ended he was put in charge of the liquidations of ordnance and engineering contracts for the Ministry of Munitions.

At the end of the war he found himself a lonely young Scot in London. He would have liked to enter politics, but he had few friends and soon found himself travelling back to Scotland to become general manager of the Coatbridge works of Messrs. Beardmore, and it was during this period that he married Miss Muriel Katherine Odhams, whose father had given his name to the well-known publishing firm. Though he was a successful engineer and got positive joy from the processes of construction he was not satisfied. "I still believe there is some great work for me to do in the world", he noted in his diary after hearing a stirring sermon.

In 1922 the newly-formed British Broadcasting Company advertised for, among other officials, a general manager. Reith answered the advertisement and received the appointment. The company was small, somewhat speculative in character, and financed by a group of electrical manufacturers. Its resources were limited and its prospects doubtful. Reith threw himself none the less wholeheartedly into his new duties, organizing, experimenting and innovating. In early 1923 progress permitted the business to move from its first home in Magnet House to Savoy Hill. By the end of the first year it had surmounted a number of initial difficulties and was growing to considerable dimensions.

As a result of the report of the Sykes Committee of 1923 its licence, originally limited to two years, was extended by two more. Reith, conscious by this time of the almost unlimited possibilities of the instrument he controlled, believed that broadcasting must eventually become a public service. Consequently he began to shape his organization with a view to such a development. In 1925 the Government appointed a committee under the chairmanship of Lord Crawford to consider the future of British broadcasting. On their invitation Reith prepared and placed before them a plan for a public broadcasting service. In doing so he deliberately jeopardized both the future of his company and his own position. He had thought deeply and seen far, for the ideas which he presented were those which were subsequently to govern British broadcasting. Some of his recommendations, such as that of Sunday observance, on which he always insisted, were calculated to provoke criticism. He was, however, concerned solely with the public welfare as he conceived it.

At this time Reith published *Broadcast over Britain*, a book which summarised his views. It was in the nature of an apologia for a monopoly; but he argued convincingly that any practical alternative presented still greater objections. Throughout he insisted—much of the success was due to it—that only the best was good enough for the new medium. Characteristically, he presented broadcasting as a means to social betterment rather than as an end in itself. While the committee were deliberating, the General Strike broke out, and the value of broadcasting as a governmental and political instrument became apparent both to Parliament and the country, but Reith stood out against those in the Government, including Sir Winston Churchill*, who wanted to commandeer the organization. On January 1, 1927, the British Broadcasting Corporation came into being with Reith, to whom its establishment and form were so largely due, as Director-General.

His aim achieved, he found himself in a new and in some ways difficult relationship both to the state and to his listeners. Within the broad limits of its Charter the B.B.C. was autonomous. For all practical purposes of administration and selection of programmes he was a dictator, though it is true that as time went on he increasingly delegated responsibility. It was for him to decide between the rival claims of culture and entertainment, and to solve, among other problems, those of controversial broadcasting, censorship of scripts and many others. He had, moreover, to establish the relationship of the new institution to its nation-wide constituency. Most difficult of all was his task to develop a system of broadcasting which should be attuned to the peculiar temperament of the British people. At Broadcasting House—the physical monument to his period of office as Director-General—he was in even a greater degree than at Savoy Hill a pioneer of what was truly a new form of statecraft, the government of a huge field of national education and diversion with the consent of the governed. His functions were in some ways comparable with those of the press; but the press is a competitive institution while he was an entrenched monopolist.

The magnitude of his achievement is not to be discounted because of the criticism which indeed he sometimes seemed to court. It is to be measured rather by the fact that he had always behind him a huge if silent reserve of national support. The vocal critics would be counted on to offset each other; but his judgment was such that he never aroused that slumbering force of British opinion which has only to stir to bring down governments and could when roused have swept him and his system away.

A man of Reith's forcefulness and even uncouthness of personality was bound to make enemies. As an administrator he was often open to criticism, for he trusted to precept and discipline rather than in more human arts of leadership. Possibly to his own sorrow, he made friends with difficulty and must often have been conscious of the loneliness of the austere. Like many formidable men he was deeply sensitive. He was, however, able to inspire affectionate respect among those of his staff who learned to understand him. Experimenting as he did— he could do no other—he made some mistakes; at times he appeared obtuse; but on the whole it is surprising how little to his discredit those who attacked him were able to disclose. He was, no doubt, ambitious; but in the outcome it was his country which gained.

In 1938, his difficulties largely overcome and his ideals established as traditions, he left the B.B.C. to become chairman of Imperial Airways. It was his second venture in developing a new application of science to human uses. Unlike the B.B.C., however, it offered scope only to some of his many powers. The outbreak of war in 1939 not only robbed him of any chance to do much, it also meant that at a time of national crisis the all-important instrument of broadcasting lacked the hand which had formed it and knew it best.

In 1940, to the general surprise, Chamberlain appointed him to the Ministry of Information. A safe seat was found at Southampton and he was returned for it unopposed. His prestige was high, and no one should have understood publicity on the home front better. He had, however, only time to achieve the internal reorganization essential in a huge and top-heavy improvisation.

Meanwhile, Chamberlain had been succeeded by Churchill and Reith was transferred to the Ministry of Transport, again deprived of the variety of stimuli he needed to achieve his best. His stay was brief, and in 1941 he moved on to the Ministry of Works and Buildings, where he was charged with the preparations for physical reconstruction after the war. He said of his task: "I have to prepare now, as it were, a physical framework within which the great postwar national policies can be fitted." During the period the centres of Coventry, Plymouth and Portsmouth were destroyed and Reith urged the local authorities to make bold and ambitious plans for their postwar rebuilding. In early February 1942, all the Town and Country planning functions formerly exercised by the Minister of Health were transferred to him, and the title of his office was changed to that of Minister of Works and Planning. Only a fortnight later, to the concern of many who regarded him as both a dynamic and stabilizing element in the Government, he ceased to be a member of it for reasons hardly adequately explained by Churchill's curt remark that he found Reith "difficult to work with".

Shortly afterwards he joined the R.N.V.R. as a lieutenant-commander, on the staff of the Rear-Admiral Coastal Services, and in 1943 was promoted Captain, R.N.V.R., and appointed Director of the Combined Operations Material Department at the Admiralty, a post he held until early in 1945. His strange relegation to these comparatively minor positions was the subject of a question in the House of Commons, but no satisfactory explanation was ever vouchsafed. That at this time he felt that his talents were buried in the ground was no secret to his friends.

While he was still, as chairman of the Commonwealth Telecommunications Board —a post he held from 1946 to 1950— bringing his mind to bear on the engineering and administrative problems of a worldwide network of communications, he was appointed chairman of the New Towns Committee. The task of the committee was not only complicated but urgent, and Reith lent his best efforts to lay down the principles on which the public corporations responsible for the creation of the new towns should work. The committee issued three reports in quick succession—the final report appearing in July 1946, nine months after the appointment of the committee.

Reith himself became chairman of the Hemel Hempstead Development Corporation in 1947 and so had the task, which until 1950 he carried out with his characteristic single-mindedness, of implementing his own principle in practice. As though to prove the point made in his remarkable letter to Churchill, that he still had energy and mind to spare, he accepted an invitation in 1948 to become chairman of the National Film Finance Corporation and held office until 1951.

The letter, itself, is worth quoting for its disconcerting candour: "Even in office I was nothing like fully stretched; and I was completely out of touch with you. You could have used me in a way and to an extent you never realized. Instead of that there has been the sterility, humiliation, and distress of all those years—'eyeless in Gaza'—without even the consolation Sam-

son had in knowing it was his own fault." This was the protest of a proud man conscious of his worth and intent only to have the opportunity to serve his fellow men to the best of his great abilities. From 1950 to 1959 he was chairman of the Colonial Development Corporation.

He later held a number of commercial directorships at different times, including those of the Phoenix Assurance Company, Tube Investments, Ltd., and the British Oxygen Company.

He was Lord Rector of Glasgow University in 1965-68. In 1967 he was appointed Lord High Commissioner to the General Assembly of the Church of Scotland. In February 1969 he was made K.T.

In establishing the Reith Lectures in 1947 the B.B.C. expressed a sentiment, warmly applauded by the great majority of listeners—in practice the great majority of the men and women of Britain—which did signal and deserved honour to the man who had cast the finely-wrought mould in which a great new medium of communication had its being and its life.

In 1967 he appeared in three memorable television programmes, discussing his life and work with Malcolm Muggeridge.

His widow survives him, with a son and a daughter, and the title passes to his son, the Hon. Christopher John Reith.

June 17, 1971.

Michael Rennie, the film actor and star of *The Third Man* television series, died on June 10, 1971 in Harrogate. He was 61.

Rennie was born in Bradford, the son of a mill owner, on August 25, 1909, and educated at the Leys School, Cambridge. He left the family business to take up acting and made his stage debut in *Pygmalion* in 1938. His first film, *Dangerous Moonlight*, came two years later and he went on to appear in well-known British pictures of the 1940s such as *Pimpernel Smith, Caesar and Cleopatra*, and two Margaret Lockwood vehicles, *I'll Be Your Sweetheart* and *The Wicked Lady*.

Soon afterwards he was put under contract by 20th Century Fox and left for Hollywood where he had a steady succession of mainly supporting parts in films like *The Robe, King of the Khyber Rifles, Désirée, Rains of Ranchipu, Island in the Sun* and *The Lost World*. He became a United States citizen in 1960.

He never reached the top rank as a film star, however, and his international fame rests mainly on the television series based on the Graham Greene—Carol Reed film, *The Third Man*. Rennie was chosen for the part of the cynical adventurer, Harry Lime, and though physically the antithesis of the original Lime, Orson Welles, his portrayal won him a large following.

June 11, 1970.

Lord Renwick, industrialist and member of the London Stock Exchange, died on October 30, 1973. He was one of the City of London's best known and most popular figures.

Robert Burnham Renwick, second baronet and first baron, was born on October 4, 1904, the son of Sir Harry Renwick, Bt., and Frederica Louisa, daughter of Robert Laing of Stirling. He was educated at Eton, where he was duly elected a member of Pop.

Stocky in build and ebullient by nature, Renwick was a natural athlete. He was joint Keeper of the Field, played for the Oppidan Wall and the Mixed Wall, and was a member of the rugger team in Eton's unbeaten year in 1923.

At Trinity College, Oxford, he played hooker for Trinity. He is remembered for a remarkable run, starting in his own half, when he scored the only, and winning, try which gave Trinity the Inter-College Cup. The exploit was the more remarkable because at the time Renwick was still convalescent from influenza and had just cured himself by a self-invented and much-admired prescription of six tumblers of vintage port a day, topped off by a whisky toddy at night.

At the end of his first year Renwick left Oxford to be near his father, who was in failing health. He entered the stockbroking firm of W. Greenwell and Co. At the age of 24 he joined the board of the County of London Electric Supply Company, where his father was chairman and managing director. Four years later he became deputy chairman. He succeeded to the chairmanship while still under 40.

Renwick became widely recognized as a skilful negotiator in other than ordinary financial and business matters. After Munich his role changed. In the summer of 1939 he was invited to join a private mission, undertaken with the full knowledge and approval of the Foreign Office, to present the British case to Field Marshal Goering.

After the declaration of war, Renwick's abilities were promptly sought by Lord Beaverbrook,* who appointed him, as a civilian within the Ministry of Aircraft Production, to take charge of the four-engine bomber programme. Renwick laid down new lines of policy which rationalized that part of the industry.

Already, however, the threat of enemy bombing had become paramount, and Renwick was appointed the chief architect of the radar chain then being built around Britain.

In wartime Whitehall, Renwick soon acquired a reputation as a large-scale administrator, and new responsibilities were placed upon him. The post of Controller of Communications at the Air Ministry and that of Controller of Communication Equipment for the Ministry of Aircraft Production had just been created. It is characteristic of Renwick's cheerful self-confidence, and of his overall grasp of the situation, that, having been offered either appointment, he accepted both because it meant that he could save time by not having to "ring up the other fellow".

Renwick was responsible for the research, development and production of radar for all Services, and for its application within the Royal Air Force. Together with Sir Robert Watson-Watt, he became identified with the success of that supreme weapon of war.

The demand for Renwick's gift of leadership was such that he was unanimously selected by all three Services to act as chairman of the newly formed Airborne Forces Committee. In 1946 he was made K.B.E. for his services.

At the end of the war Renwick returned to W. Greenwell and Co. as a joint senior partner. He soon began to diversify his interests in industry. He became a director of A.E.I.; the first chairman of British Relay Wireless; chairman of Clifton Reliance; chairman of Power Securities (Balfour Beatty); chairman of East African Power and Light; and a director of the Nigerian Electric Company.

His energies were inexhaustible. In 1948 he joined Sir Edward Spears on the Council of the Institute of Directors, when the membership was only 400. By the time he became chairman, in 1965, largely through his efforts the membership had risen to more than 42,000.

The nationalization in 1948 of the County of London Electric Supply Company brought Renwick into public life. A fervent believer in free enterprise and a determined opponent of state intervention, in 1949 he became chairman of British United Industrialists, the principal instrument for financing campaigns to fight the policies of the Labour Government.

Always close to the Conservative Party, and much sought after for counsel and assistance, Renwick was never himself active in politics. Created a peer in 1964, he preferred his personal contacts with the leaders and refrained from intervening in debates.

One of the campaigns that was closest to Renwick's heart was that of introducing competition into broadcasting and breaking the monopoly of the B.B.C. He was a notable figure in the public controversy that raged at the time, and was a founder member of the first Independent Television company to be formed. Renwick was a director of Associated Television when it was awarded a licence, and became chairman in 1961.

The wide range of his interests and the magnetism of his personality meant that he had an immense circle of friends. To more than one generation in all walks of life he was affectionately known as "Uncle Bob".

Throughout his 68 years he lived the full life. He was a born host, and always conducted even the most intricate of affairs over a luncheon table in preference to an office desk.

His hobbies were as energetically pursued as his business career. He was a lover of gardens, and a keen shot. He was also a discerning collector of ceramics, jade, silver and pictures.

Never appearing in the least rushed or harassed, he presided over his multiple affairs by telephone as much from his home as from his office. In short, throughout every hour of his waking day he enjoyed himself.

He married in 1929 Dorothy Mary, elder daughter of the late Major Harold Parkes, and they had a son and three daughters. That marriage was dissolved in 1953. He married secondly, in 1953, Joan, widow of Major J. O. Spencer, daughter of the late Sir Reginald Clarke, C.H. His heir is the Hon. Harry Andrew Renwick, who was born on October 10, 1935.

September 1, 1973.

Charles Revson, the co-founder and president of Revlon, the giant cosmetic firm, died in New York on August 24, 1975 at the age of 68. In a forty-year career begun in 1932 with the launching of a non-streak nail polish from a room on Manhattan's West Side, Revson built up a business which, by 1974, was selling 3,500 individual items in 85 countries, earning 50 million dollars net.

Charles Haskell Revson was born in Boston on October 11, 1906, the son of a cigar packer who had emigrated from Russia. Schooled in Manchester, New Hampshire, he went to New York at the age of 17 and got a job selling dresses on Seventh Avenue. His first contact with the cosmetics business was with the Elka Company, for whom he sold the nail polish which was currently on the market, a semi-transparent product in only a few basic colours.

In 1932 he left Elka after being refused the job of national distributor, and with a modest investment of 300 dollars founded Revlon with his brother Joseph and a chemist named Charles Lachman whom the brothers had met in the same year. In experiments conducted over a Bunsen burner, Lachman had produced a formula for a different kind of nail polish, non-streak, creamy and opaque. Pooling their resources the triumvirate, acknowledging Lachman by incorporating the initial "L" of his name into their own brandname, went into business in New York.

These were the depression years but Revson's selling experience stood him and his two colleagues in good stead. A man with inbuilt market antennae, he decided to concentrate his company's efforts on beauty salons, then in the hectic flush of the permanent wave boom. In 10 years he had a near monopoly of sales to America's (by then) one hundred thousand salons.

Throughout, generally recognized as the moving impulse behind Revlon's success, Revson's own personal involvement with his products drove the company on.

From the early days he often walked round with his nails daubed with polish and his hands and arms striped with different shades of lipstick. As he diversified he continued to try all his products on himself—to comply with his standards even the company's tweezers had to be fine enough to be capable of nipping the taut skin on the resistant heel of his thumb. It was this intensity of application which brought him such astonishing success in that largely women's world.

Elizabeth Arden,* it is said, used to refer to Revson as "That Man". When this came to his ears he riposted by naming a whole range of men's toiletries by the title.

His advertising campaigns, which included sponsorship of the *64,000 Dollar Question* programme, amplified the Revlon name in the public's mind. Revlon shares nearly trebled in price within three months of the launch of the programme in 1955. Thereafter cosmetics, skin care products, shampoos, hair sprays, perfumes and man's toiletries poured in seemingly unending succession from the Revlon laboratories, to take the company to the top in the beauty industry.

August 26, 1975.

Peter Revson, the 35-year old American driver who was killed racing in South Africa on March 22, 1974, was one of the most versatile and internationally successful drivers his country has produced.

Equally at home in a single-seater at Indianapolis, in a 1,000h.p. sports car in the Can-Am championship, or at the wheel of a Formula One car, he seemed to be on the brink of Grand Prix stardom as the new leader of the British-based U.O.P. Shadow team, after scoring two Grand Prix victories with a Yardley McLaren, including the John Player British Grand Prix at Silverstone, in 1973.

Throughout his career he was an immaculate driver, invariably fast but always extremely smooth, yet he was a formidable contender when the going became tough. It was only his inherent modesty which caused him to take rather longer to reach the top echelons of motor racing than his very considerable talent deserved, and his loss not only as a top driver but as one of the most friendly of people will be keenly felt within the motor racing scene.

Peter Jeffrey Revlon Revson was born in New York City on February 27, 1939, the son and nephew of cosmetics manufacturers. Educated at Hotchkiss, Connecticut, and Willeston Academy, Massachusetts, he later studied mechanical engineering at Cornell University before working as a market research analyst, trainee Wall Street stockbroker, and reading economics and philosophy at Columbia University.

He made his racing debut in February 1960 with a Morgan, while a student at University of Hawaii, and then turned to

Formula Junior racing in the United States and Canada. He went to England in March 1963, and took part in a full programme of European races with an F. J. Cooper-Ford, winning the Copenhagen G.P. He made his Formula 1 debut in Reg Parnell's Lotus-B.R.M. at the Oulton Park Gold Cup meeting in September 1963. He went into partnership in 1964 with Tim Parnell and drove a F1 Lotus 24 as an independent.

Between 1967 and 1969, Revson was active mainly in the United States and Canada in TransAm. events in Javelin and Cougar cars and in U.S.A.C. single-seater racing. In 1970 he competed in the lucrative CanAm. series in a Lola, and in 1971 he joined the McLaren team as partner to New Zealander Denny Hulme. Driving superbly, Revson won five races out of 10 (Road Atlanta, Watkins Glen, Elkhart Lake, Donnybrooke and Laguna Seca) and scored two seconds and a third to become the CanAm. champion. In the 1971 Indianapolis 500 race, Revson finished second in a McLaren-Offy.

Wishing to return to Formula 1 racing, Revson joined Yardley-McLaren for 1972, finishing third in the South African and British G.P.s and fifth in the Spanish G.P. He was well-placed in several other Formula 1 races during the rest of the season and was placed fifth in the final table. He achieved his first Grand Prix win at Silverstone in July 1973, driving a Yardley-McLaren M23. In the final standings for 1973 he was again a consistent fifth with 38 points. That autumn in a confused race he emerged the winner in the Canadian Grand Prix at Mosport, Ontario.

March 23, 1974.

Wilfred Rhodes, who had strong claims to be considered England's greatest all-round cricketer—W. G. Grace apart—died on July 8, 1973 at the age of 95.

He was the last surviving member of the team that played the Australians at Edgbaston in 1902, a side reckoned by older cricket-lovers to be England's most glorious eleven. In that game he and George Hirst, his fellow-villager, dismissed their opponents for 36, Rhodes having the amazing figures of seven for 17. Though the most matter-of-fact of mortals, his career had a touch of fantasy.

Born in 1877 at Kirkheaton, near Huddersfield, he joined Yorkshire in 1898 and played, missing only the war years, till 1930. In that time he scored just under 40,000 runs and captured 4,187 wickets. (Only three other bowlers in history have taken 3,000.) His England caps were 58, of which 41 were worn against Australia.

His first Test (which was also W.G.'s last) was in 1899 and his own last in 1926, when he returned triumphantly three months before his forty-ninth birthday. Even his astonishing figures as an all-rounder—16 doubles, 21 times 1,000 runs and 23 times 100 wickets—do not tell the whole story of his superb skills. No other cricketer has started as England's subtlest bowler, risen to be an England batsman second only to Hobbs*, and then, at the age when many cricketers retire, returned to his first love with unchallenged success.

One of Yorkshire's majestic line of slow left-hand bowlers, he followed Peate and Peel, handing on the torch to Hedley Verity. With his smooth, deceptive delivery he was destructive on bad wickets and exasperating on good ones. On his first Australian tour with Warner's 1903-04 side, he bowled unchanged throughout the second Test, taking 15 wickets for 124. (A month later he took five for 6 in helping Arnold to dismiss Victoria for 15.) In the first Test on a Sydney pitch that was as innocuous as Melbourne's was to be hostile, he bowled 40 nagging overs under a broiling sun to take five for 94, wringing from the dazzling Victor Trumper the wry supplication: "Please, Wilfred, have a bit of mercy."

Even before he rose from No. 11 to No. 2 in England's batting order he had shown his mettle: first in the legendary last-wicket stand with Hirst in "Jessop's match" at the Oval in 1902 ("fifteen runs to get and two Yorkshiremen to do it . . ."), and then in that first Sydney Test of 1903-04 when, with the scintillating R. E. Foster, he shared a last-wicket partnership of 130, still a record against Australia.

His blossoming as Hobbs's opening partner came with a tour of South Africa in 1910-11 and then, after 1911, one of his two best batting seasons, came the historic visit to Australia of 1911-12 in which he and Hobbs showed themselves the greatest opening pair of the era, laying the foundations of an even greater partnership and evolving that uncanny precision in running between the wickets which Hobbs and Sutcliffe brought to perfection. Hobbs and Rhodes were the batting stars of the series and their score of 323 in the fourth Test remained a record for 35 years. In their successes Hobbs was the more brilliant performer but Rhodes's batting was the rock on which the attack broke in vain.

After the war he went back to bowling and never since the heroic days of the turn of the century, when he had captured 725 wickets in three seasons, did he bowl so devastatingly. The old magic of length, spin and flight again took its toll and in the five summers of 1919-23 he led the English bowling averages four times. In 1926, recalled for the last Test after four had been drawn, he reached his ultimate peak. "Can you still pitch 'em there?" was the selector's query. "There or thereabouts", Rhodes replied. In the side were three players, including the captain, who had not been born when he first played for England, but the veteran's contribution was vital. In Australia's second innings he took four for 44 and England recovered the Ashes after 14 years. His comment was: "That pitch was improving. They should have put me on sooner."

For four years more, including a successful West Indies tour, he went on playing with undiminished competence. After his retirement in 1930 his remarkable eyesight gradually worsened and in his last years he was completely blind. He bore this affliction with high courage and his keenness for the game was never dimmed. At Lord's and Headingley Tests and at the Scarborough Festival he would regularly be seen, often escorted by an old warrior, Sydney Barnes*, "watching" the game by sound.

His reputation as one of the greatest of slow bowlers is secure, whether for length, spin, flight, or remorseless persistence. His was an unsleeping cricket brain, probing the batsman's weaknesses as a dentist probes a hollow tooth. Hirst and Rhodes in their heyday were names to conjure with, both for Yorkshire and England; the one genial, dashing, cavalier in spirit, the other less genial (though he mellowed pleasantly in later years), steadfast, compounded in spirit of all the Ironside virtues.

If Rhodes was a less successful coach at Harrow after his days in the first-class game were over than Hirst had been at Eton, it was because he was a perfectionist and impatient of anything less than the best. His dry humour was all his own. "The cut was never a business stroke." Or: "In Yorkshire we don't play cricket for foon." Or, confidentially revealing the secret of perfect running between the wickets, "When I'm coming, I say yes; when I'm not, I say no." Gruff or mellow, he was all of a piece, a fighting Yorkshireman, superbly gifted.

July 9, 1973.

Sir Harry Ricardo, an engineer who made notable contributions to the theory and design of the internal combustion engine, died on May 18, 1974 at the age of 89. From 1919 to 1964 he was chairman and technical director of Ricardo and Company Ltd.

Born in London on January 26, 1885, the son of the architect and artist, Halsey Ralph Ricardo, he was educated at Rugby and Trinity College, Cambridge. At Rugby he spent all his available spare time in the school workshops, where he produced a number of mechanical devices, including a coal-fired steam motor-cycle.

At Cambridge he worked under Professor Bertram Hopkinson and, while still an undergraduate, built an experimental two-stroke petrol engine—the forerunner of many others—for his own amusement. On leaving Cambridge he joined his grandfather's firm, Messrs. Rendel & Robertson (later Rendel, Palmer & Tritton), consulting engineers in Westminster, as mechanical engineer for locomotives, steam plant and oil engines. In 1916 he was appointed consulting engineer to the Mechanical Warfare Department, and in the years 1917-1919 designed and superintended the manufacture of 7,000 heavy-duty 150h.p. petrol engines for tanks.

In 1918 he became consulting engineer for aero engines to the Air Ministry. About the same time he established an organization for systematic research on internal-combustion engines and initiated in his laboratory at Shoreham a long series of investigations on the shape of the combustion chamber, the design of pistons and valves, the wear of cylinder liners and other factors affecting the performance and efficiency of petrol and oil engines. His research on sleeve-valve engines in particular was most fruitful.

He delivered the Thomas Lowe Gray lecture of the Institution of Mechanical Engineers in 1933, when he suggested the employment for ship propulsion of a multitude of light high-speed Diesel engines transmitting their power to the screws electrically, and in 1935 he was the Melchett medallist and lecturer of the Institute of Fuel.

In 1929 he became a Fellow of the Royal Society, which awarded him its Rumford Medal in 1944, and he was elected an honorary member of the American Society of Mechanical Engineers in 1942. He received the honorary degree of LL.D. from Birmingham University in 1943, when he was described as "the high priest of the internal-combustion engine", and in 1944 he became president of the Institution of Mechanical Engineers. In 1948 he became a member of the Scientific Advisory Council to the Ministry of Fuel. The Institution of Mechanical Engineers awarded him the James Watt medal in 1953 and in 1970 Sussex University made him an honorary D.Sc. His book *The High Speed Internal Combustion Engine*, first published in 1923, went into a fifth edition in 1968.

He was knighted in 1948.

He married, in 1911, Beatrice Bertha Hale, daughter of Dr. Charles Hale. There were three daughters of the marriage.

May 20, 1974.

Rudolph Richard, one of the most eminent and successful of hoteliers in modern times, died on June 12, 1973 at the Connaught Hotel, London, of which he was managing director.

Born in Switzerland in 1898, but later a British subject, of which he was immensely proud, he learnt the rudiments of his profession by practical experience in several of the leading hotels of Britain and abroad. Among the more important of these was the Carlton in London, which preserved the standards of Ritz and Escoffier, who had gone there from the Savoy when it was opened. Later, Richard moved to the much smaller Stafford Hotel in St. James's, leaving there in 1931 to go to Gibraltar to open the Rock Hotel there for the Marquess of Bute. This accomplished and the hotel established, he returned to England and was appointed in 1935, at the early age of 37, the manager of the Connaught Hotel, then in poor shape and not rated in the front rank of London hotels.

For the rest of his life of 38 years he devoted his outstanding gifts as a hotelier to the Connaught, of which he became managing director in 1943, and he raised its status and its standard to that of one of the leading hotels of quality in the world. His profound knowledge of wines and his skill in the cooking and presentation of food attracted attention, and this ability, coupled with exceptional skill as a hotelier, achieved year by year a higher reputation. Rather gentle and reserved in manner, belying his immensely energetic nature, he had an eye for detail and a passion for perfection. It can be said of him that he made the Connaught Hotel as it is now known.

It was not surprising that his professional advice was in great demand and generously given. In addition to his responsibility for the Connaught Hotel, he was a director of the Mount Nelson Hotel in Cape Town, Reid's Hotel in Madeira, Stone's Chop House in London, chairman of the Lancaster Hotel in Paris and of the Burlington Hotel in Folkestone, which was near his country house at Sandgate, where he was very fond of his garden.

In spite of these interests and responsibilities, the Connaught was the apple of his eye. He had no desire to impress by the number of establishments he ruled; his concern was only that the Connaught should be the best that could be found.

He often mentioned the thrill he received when, arriving at a London station, he said to the taxi driver, "Take me to the Connaught", and for the first time did not have to explain where it was.

June 13, 1973.

Ceri Richards, C.B.E., who died in London on November 9, 1971 at the age of 68, was one of the most gifted British artists of the past 50 years, and one of those most notable for what in French is called *un tempérament de peintre.*

Born in Dynfant, five miles west of Swansea, on June 6, 1903, Ceri Giraldus Richards was the son of a Welsh-speaking tinplate worker who had in full measure, and passed on to his son, a passion for music, poetry and the theatre.

Ceri Richards became in due time a gifted pianist and organist, and he was the prized friend of many Welsh poets: above all, of Vernon Watkins and Dylan Thomas. His inclination towards art first manifested itself in a preoccupation with engineering drawing, and on leaving school he joined a small firm of electricians in Morriston, only to find when the firm closed down that his true gifts lay rather in the direction of fine art.

From 1920-24 at Swansea School of Art, and from 1924-27 at the Royal College of Art in London, Richards proved himself a most nimble-minded student, and one outstandingly attentive to such intimations of modernity as came his way. From the writings of Apollinaire and Kandinsky, and from the example above all of Matisse and Max Ernst, he devised for himself a personal style first glimpsed in 1933, when together with Victor Pasmore, Ivon Hitchens and Rodrigo Moynihan he showed in the historic Objective Abstractionist exhibition at the Zwemmer Gallery. Between 1934 and 1939 he turned to collage-constructions which took something from Picasso, something from an art of pure form, something from continental surrealism, and something from the wild humour and uninhibited fancy of Welsh story-telling—and yet were unmistakably his own. For 20 years unsung, unbought and unrecognized, these now stand with Henry Moore's early carvings and the white reliefs of Ben Nicholson as Britain's most lasting contribution to the European art of the 1930s.

Richards's oil-paintings of this period were described by C. G. Jung*, in a letter to the artist, as "a confession of the secret of our time"; and Mondrian was among the foreign visitors to Richards's studio who came away with a heightened respect for British art. In later years there was no falling-off in the energy, the darting imagination and the disdain for routine and compromise which were the mark of Ceri Richards in every department of life.

His polymorphous activity was revealed in panorama at a retrospective exhibition at Whitechapel in 1960, and two years later he represented Great Britain at the Venice Biennale, where he was awarded the Einaudi Prize. Major commissions in recent years included an altarpiece for St. Edmund Hall, Oxford (1958), two large windows for Derby Cathedral (1964-65), and the tabernacle, reredos and stained glass windows for the Metropolitan Cathedral of Christ the King in Liverpool. One of his last professional commitments was the group of free paraphrases of Titian's "The Death of Actaeon," which he produced with characteristic generosity and profusion in the hope of saving that great canvas for the nation.

In private life, Ceri Richards was the most stimulating and vivacious of companions, ever ready to look for quality in the work of others and never content, when in his own studio, to fall back on what he had done to acclamation the season before.

He was created C.B.E. in 1960, and from 1958-65 he was a trustee of the Tate Gallery. He was married to Frances Richards, herself a gifted painter, and had two daughters.

November 11, 1971.

The Very Rev. Dr. Alan Richardson, K.B.E., Dean of York since 1964, who died suddenly, two days before the enthronement of the Archbishop of York, on February 23, 1975 at the age of 69, had been suffering from heart trouble for a number of years.

Alan Richardson was a man of remarkable vigour of mind, and of constant industry both as teacher and writer. He also had unusually wide and valuable experience. He won high academic distinction as a young man both at a modern university (Liverpool) and at Oxford.

He had four years in charge of a country parish, and then five years as study secretary of the Student Christian Movement before his appointment in 1943 to the Sixth Canonry of Durham Cathedral which he held until 1953, when he became Professor of Christian Theology in the University of Nottingham.

He was therefore particularly well acquainted with the problems and opportunities of the Church, and, as he combined very wide reading with a lively power of expression and exposition, it was natural that he became a prolific and forcible speaker and writer. His work kept him closely in touch with young minds and contemporary thought, and although he held his own opinions with tenacity and lively force, he did not form them without full awareness of other points of view.

Several of his books deserved and obtained wide circulation: they were admirably written and arranged, and as a rule commendably free from the jargon of much modern theological literature. These good qualities, and there were many others, were the more remarkable because the scope and volume of his religious writing were great.

He produced a large book on *Christian Apologetics,* another on the *Theology of the New Testament,* another on *History Sacred and Profane* (the Bampton Lectures for 1962).

Besides these, there was a host of smaller works, brief commentaries, studies of the Creeds and of the Gospel miracle stories, and expositions on biblical studies generally. He also edited a useful *Theological Word Book of the Bible.*

In all these works there was admirable and often outstandingly good material. It is, however, perhaps a fair criticism that he cast his net rather too wide and that, keen as his mind was, he could be overconfident in pressing a doubtful argument. His sympathy with the outlook of the "Biblical Theology" movement was strong; he tended to exalt "Hebraism" against "Hellenism" (not least in his Bampton Lectures), and to underrate the complex diversities of the New Testament background.

There were signs of haste in his judgment, not surprisingly, for he was a busy man who did not spare himself in answering the calls of others. But on any showing there is no question of the value and the distinction of his achievement.

In Durham, where no professorship was annexed to his canonry, he and his wife, who played an active part in the life of the city, had much to give and much to gain.

For his reading he found a good and growing university library, as well as the cathedral library, close at hand. A deep and informed concern for the Anglican Communion and for the Church in the world as a whole, was strengthened and enlarged; he was always ready to give his best mind in conference and discussion, and was much in demand both within and outside the diocese.

Richardson was invited by the University of Nottingham to become Professor and Head of the Department of Theology on the resignation of Professor John Marsh, in 1953. His influence on the department was incalculable: he increased its staff numbers, reputation and scope, the last made possible very largely by his versatility in the large and varied sphere of study loosely called theology, and by that of Dr. R. P. C. Hanson who succeeded him in the chair.

Indeed, at one time Richardson could claim that he was the only member of staff at the university who lectured on the philosophy of science; but his chief labours at this time were concerned with the Bible, a fact amply proved by his publications.

He always took a full part in the life of the university as a whole and in its administration, being opposed to any divorce between theology and life. His circle of friends among the staff was wide and varied; students and former students, not only those of his own department, made continuous demands on his time, knowing his accessibility, complete absence of pomp, and above all what sound advice he could give.

The opening of a chapel for the use of all denominations and the establishment of a whole-time Anglican chaplain in the university in 1956 could not have happened without his patient work to these ends. In all this activity he was magnificently supported by Mrs. Richardson, their home being a centre of hospitality for both university and diocese as well as for innumerable visitors from all over the world.

Vacations gave him little leisure: for example, 1960 saw him and his wife on a world tour preaching and lecturing, 1962 saw him in Africa, and 1963 both of them in Toronto for the Anglican Congress. On returning he was always ready to give students a lively and informal account of what he had discovered to be going on in the parts of the world they had been visiting. In 1966 he undertook a lecture tour of the United States.

At York his activities included endless appeals for funds to preserve the structure of the Minster, and it was for this work that he was created K.B.E. in 1973.

February 24, 1975.

T. D. Richardson, O.B.E., the foremost British authority on ice figure skating, died on January 7, 1971. He was 83.

His long life was devoted to the improvement of the art he loved, and he was one of the few skaters of his generation who thoroughly understood the complex new techniques developed since the Second World War.

Born in Yorkshire in 1887, Thomas Dow Richardson was educated at Scarborough and Lausanne, and later at Trinity Hall, Cambridge. In his own words, he was first "put on the ice during the great frost of 1891," when he was four; at the turn of the century he was taken for the first time to Grindelwald, and became an enthusiastic skater in the stiff, formal "English" style. He joined the National Skating Association in 1905, and in the same year saw an exhibition of the then new "International" style which was later adopted by skaters throughout most of the world. He was so attracted by its freedom, grace, and athleticism that he took lessons from some of its leading exponents—the Adams brothers and the Swedish master Bror Meyer—and became a gold medallist.

Between 1912 and 1914 he won several ice dancing competitions with Mildred Allingham, whom he afterwards married. After the 1914-18 War, during which he became a captain in the Army, he and Mrs. Richardson competed with success as pair skaters. Runners-up in the British championship in 1923, they were selected to skate in the 1924 Winter Olympic Games at Chamonix.

In 1930, after several years of intensive research, Richardson published his remarkable book, *Modern Figure Skating,* in which he analysed all the possible causes of skating faults, and expounded his "Theory of the Sixteen Positions". By this time he had become a judge of international championships, and his outspoken views sometimes brought him into conflict with his colleagues. His relations with the International Skating Union were not, in general, very happy, but his outstanding abilities were more readily recognized in Britain. He was for many years chairman or member of the principal N.S.A. committees, and on three occasions was responsible for major revisions of the Association's test schedules. In 1955 he was appointed O.B.E. for his services to British skating.

He contributed to *The Field, Country Life, Encyclopaedia Britannica, Skating World,* and other publications. He was winter sports correspondent of *The Times* from shortly after World War II until 1958, and from 1958 to 1960 he wrote for the *Daily Telegraph.* He was also the author of several books, among them *Champions All* (1939), in conjunction with the photographer and racing driver E. R. Hall; *Ice Skating* (1956), a splendidly-illustrated blend of history and reminiscences; and *The Art of Figure Skating* (1962).

In his younger days he was a keen oarsman; he twice rowed in the Cambridge Trial Eights, and at Henley stroked the Thames R.C. in the Grand Challenge Cup. He was a boxing blue, and enjoyed golf and curling.

"Tyke" Richardson's forthright personality made him an entertaining companion, and his circle of friends was not confined to skaters. It was he who aroused the skating ambitions of Viscount Templewood (then Sir Samuel Hoare), the former Foreign Secretary, who eventually became an N.S.A. silver medallist.

"T.D." was not an easy man to work with, and never concealed his impatience with anyone who disagreed with him. Many of the beneficial changes which he introduced in figure skating met with considerable opposition, partly because he was not always very diplomatic in dealing with official organizations. He was never deterred by controversy, however, and least of all in 1958 when, in spite of many odds, he founded the first Commonwealth Winter Games. He was a gifted man in many ways, and a towering personality in the small world of figure skating.

January 8, 1971.

Captain Eddie Rickenbacker, the American air ace during the First World War, and former president of Eastern Air Lines, died in hospital in Zurich on July 23, 1973. He was 82.

Rickenbacker shot down in all 26 German aircraft. During the Second World War he served as adviser on aviation to the Secretary of State for War.

He came from Columbus, Ohio, where he was born on October 8, 1890. From his earliest days he was familiar with the mechanism of the motor cars which were manufactured near his home. He was soon a skilful driver, daring though confident, and before long he became a familiar figure on the motor racing tracks in the country; particularly that at Indianapolis, where he won many national and international events. At Daytona Beach, Florida, he drove a car at 134 m.p.h.

When the United States entered the war he joined up as a driver and went to France in June as chauffeur to General Pershing. He was transferred at his own request to the Air Service of the American Army. He learned to fly and was given a commission in the 94th Aero Pursuit Squadron. He was a member of the first American unit to take part in action on the Western Front. This was credited with 69 enemy machines destroyed, of which Rickenbacker himself took 26. He was the first to conduct his own squadron into Coblenz when the Americans advanced to the Rhine. He retired with the rank of captain. He wrote a book on the air war called *Fighting the Flying Circus.*

After the war he was head of his own company, the Rickenbacker Motor Car Company, for a while until its dissolution,

and then joined the Cadillac company. Later he was associated with General Aviation. By the mid 1920s he was in the airline business with ideas for developing commercial flying on a strictly planned basis. In 1935 he began his career with Eastern Airlines, rising from general manager to president. The line was said never to have had a subsidy, at one time carrying mail for nothing; yet it regularly made a profit.

When the Second World War came he was called back for service. He visited various theatres of operations on special missions for the American Air Force. On one of these his aircraft came down in mid-Pacific and he and the crew took to a life raft and were in the sea for 24 days. This experience provided him with material for the book, *Seven Came Through,* published in 1943.

Rickenbacker was a much-decorated airman. He held the Congressional Medal of Honour, and also the Medal of Merit, the D.S.C. with nine oakleaves, was a member of the Legion of Honour, and held the Croix de Guerre. Numerous honorary degrees came to him from universities all over the United States.

He married, in 1922, Mrs. Adelaide F. Durant, and they had two sons.

July 24, 1973.

Sir Eric Rideal, M.B.E., F.R.S., the distinguished physical chemist, notable for his service to Britain in peace and in two world wars, and great friend and leader of his many pupils, died on September 25, 1974 at the age of 84.

Born on April 11, 1890, the son of a well-known consulting chemist, Dr. Samuel Rideal, he went to Oundle School, whence he won a scholarship to Trinity Hall, Cambridge, to which college as a Fellow he afterwards gave devoted service and which rewarded his distinction and lifelong affection with an honorary Fellowship that he greatly prized. After taking First Class Honours in Chemistry in the Natural Science Tripos, he studied next at Bonn, earning his Ph.D. in 1913.

Two years' service in the Royal Engineers in France resulted in his being invalided in 1916 to the Munitions Inventions Board, his services there being rewarded with the M.B.E. A short period of research and teaching in the United States as Visiting Professor of Physical Chemistry at the University of Illinois was followed by his appointment in 1920 to be Humphrey Owen Jones Lecturer in Physical Chemistry at Cambridge. There he rapidly built up a flourishing personal research school and 10 years later he became the first Professor of Colloidal Physics, later redesignated John Humphrey Plummer Professor of Colloid Science. In this independent position he attracted students from all over the world.

Rideal's quarter of a century of research

leadership at Cambridge was broken by his appointment in 1946 as Director of the Davy-Faraday Research Laboratory and Fullerian Professor at the Royal Institution, where he did much to instil new life into the researches in those laboratories, then languishing as a result of the war.

Perhaps he was never entirely happy there, in an organization dissimilar to the university world to which he was accustomed, operating in immediate post-war conditions which made it very difficult for him and his wife to maintain as they would both have wished the full traditions of hospitality associated with Albemarle Street. So, when he had succeeded in getting research at the Royal Institution well re-established, he was pleased in 1950 to accept the Chair of Physical Chemistry at King's College London, which he held till his retirement in 1955. Then, indefatigable in his own researches, he accepted, with great pleasure, accommodation offered to him by one of his many old pupils now holding Chairs of their own, Professor R. M. Barrer, at Imperial College, London, where he happily continued to work.

Rideal's public honours were mainly professional, in offices in which he habitually gave more than he received. He was, at various times, president of the Faraday Society, of the Society of Chemical Industry, of the Chemical Society, and of the Chemical Council. From 1953 to 1958 he was chairman of the Ministry of Supply Advisory Council on Scientific Research and Technical Development, in which task he was singularly successful in relating scientific practices to national requirements and in making personal contact with the bench workers in the Government Laboratories with which he was concerned. He received a knighthood in 1951, and in the same year the Davy Medal of the Royal Society.

Rideal's greatest strength was his power to encourage good students. Probably he was not a profound chemical scholar, but he was intensely interested in problems of mechanism, especially involving catalytic or structural surface actions. In the 1920s he was much influenced by the late Sir William Hardy's approach to biological studies and this was really the origin of his own wide researches on surface activity. He read the scientific literature extremely thoroughly, and he was always anxious to adapt new techniques to current problems. His publications, jointly with his pupils, ranged over an immense field and were of great number. As a formal teacher of undergraduates he was good only with the best, but as a special lecturer on one of his own subjects, at colloquia or student societies he was quite outstanding, bubbling with enthusiasm. His advice as an industrial consultant was widely sought and, on research matters, was good.

Astonishingly fertile in ideas, not all sound but some brilliant, Rideal needed good students to work with, and the result was then an excellent combination, for he was most stimulating to good men, though a good leader to the slightly less gifted. He was immensely interested in the professional careers of his men, many of whom owe much to him and gladly acknowledge the debt.

An illness and a major operation in 1936 left him with a physical disability which he never allowed to handicap him in his work or travels and which indeed even his closest friends were inclined to forget, such was his own mastery of himself. It was probably in the belief that his health would not stand the strain that he was not elected in 1937 to the Chair of Physical Chemistry at Cambridge—a major disappointment to him at the time, though in retrospect he probably enjoyed more the greater variety his subsequent career provided.

Rideal's major scientific contributions lie in the general field of surface chemistry, especially the study of interfaces of possible biological interest. He was, too, no mean polymer chemist in his own right; he foresaw and encouraged early the use of infrared techniques; he contributed in photochemistry and electro-chemistry, in reaction kinetics and particularly in heterogenous catalysts. Himself not a particularly gifted experimenter, the encouragement he gave to the late J. K. Roberts in his fundamental and refined work on the true conditions of clean metallic surfaces was very characteristic of his versatility of mind. He was elected a fellow of King's College London in 1953.

Rideal took his social responsibilities to his students very seriously and in this he was greatly helped, as his whole life was enriched, by his wife Peggy, an American lady of great beauty, charm and courage, whom he married in 1921 and who died in 1964. He leaves one daughter.

September 27, 1974.

Dr. E. V. Rieu, C.B.E., translator of the Penguin *Odyssey* and *Iliad*, and editor of the Penguin series of translations, died on May 11, 1972. He was 85.

For the first 25 years of his working life he was a publisher, first with the Oxford University Press, then with Methuen & Co. Ltd. At the age of almost 50 he reverted to his first interest, the Greek and Latin classics, and won a considerable reputation for his prose translations. In addition he edited from 1946 to 1963 the Penguin series of translations, a series by no means confined to the classics but including works from many European living languages. An agnostic for half his life, he became an Anglican at the age of 60, made a new translation of *The Four Gospels*, and was a member of the joint Churches' committee for the new translation of the Bible.

Emile Victor Rieu was born in London on February 10, 1887, the seventh child of Dr. C. P. H. Rieu, Keeper of Oriental M.S.S. at the British Museum and Professor of Arabic at Cambridge, a very distinguished scholar who spoke or read twenty languages. He was educated at St. Paul's School and Balliol College, Oxford, at both of which he was a Scholar. His career at Oxford did not, however, end with academic distinction of the kind confidently expected of him though he obtained a First in Honour Mods. He suffered a breakdown of health and left the university at the end of his seventh term without a degree.

In 1912 at the age of 24 he was appointed manager of the Oxford University Press in India. The Press had at that time no establishment in India, and Rieu's task was to open and organize first a head office in Bombay and then smaller branch offices in Calcutta and Madras. He was instructed to go out to Bombay by a circuitous route, more than half way round the world, in order to visit and examine an unsatisfactory representative of the Press in Shanghai. Armed with a power of attorney, young Rieu travelled by the old Trans-Siberian Railway and reached Shanghai via Berlin, Brest-Litovsk, Moscow, Harbin, and Peking in about six weeks. There he carried out the daunting duty, for a man of his age, of dismissing the representative.

In Bombay he was soon to be hampered by the outbreak of the First World War, and was himself eventually commissioned in the 105th Mahratta Light Infantry. But his military service was short and uneventful and he was soon back at work in Bombay. Attacks of malaria, however, so repeated as to have become almost chronic, undermined his health and at the end of 1919 he returned to England with his wife (Nelly Lewis, daughter of H. T. Lewis of Pembrokeshire, whom he married in 1914) and young children.

In 1923 he was appointed Educational Manager of Methuen & Co. Ltd., a post he filled with distinction for 10 years. It was for Methuen that in 1925 he edited a *Book of Latin Poetry*, intended primarily for schools.

Rieu's verses for children were collected in a volume entitled *Cuckoo Calling* in 1932, and reissued with additions in 1962 as *The Flattered Flying Fish and Other Poems*. Some of them were also included in *A Puffin Quartet of Poets* in 1958.

In 1933 he was somewhat abruptly appointed managing director of Methuen & Co. With the consequent considerable expansion of his responsibilities into fields for which he was not well equipped and which did not greatly interest him, he was not happy, and in 1936 he resigned, though he remained adviser to the company on academic books.

Adversity was to have an extraordinarily stimulating effect on Rieu. With more spare time on his hands than he had had since he came down from Oxford, he returned to his first love, the classics. For some years it had been his practice to spend evenings at home making extempore oral translations to his wife of the *Odyssey*, the *Argonautica*, Lucretius, Euripides, Aeschylus, and half a dozen dialogues of Plato (but not, oddly enough, the *Iliad*). This now led to the decision to tackle the *Odyssey* seriously and to write down the translation. The work was interrupted in 1940, when he returned to full-time work with Methuen to replace younger men who had joined the services, and by his service with the Home Guard, but he continued slowly and by the end of 1945 he had finished the *Odyssey*. He offered it to Penguin Books and Sir Allen Lane* speedily accepted it. Publication was an immediate and immense success. No other Penguin book had, up to that time, sold so many copies. In the United States it was equally successful. On the strength of this success he was invited to translate the *Iliad*, which appeared in 1950, and also to edit a long series of new translations for Penguin. He continued to edit the series for 20 years.

Rieu held strong views on the problems of translation. He always believed that foreign verse, especially long works, should be translated into contemporary English prose. The few examples of poems in foreign languages successfully translated into English poetry he looked upon as happy accidents. The translation of foreign poetry into English verse he distrusted, despite the arguments and practice of his friend Dorothy Sayers, who translated Dante into English verse. In his own translations, he was fortunate in the choice of subjects for his two best works, the *Odyssey* and the *Iliad,* these being (as was pointed out by the translator of one of the other volumes in his series, David Wright, who was responsible for *Beowulf) primary* epics, in which to a large degree the poetry is in the story. The *Aeneid* and *Paradise Lost* are examples of the other kind of epic in which the poetry lies essentially in the treatment. Rieu's prose translation of Virgil's *Pastoral Poems* was markedly less successful than his *Odyssey* and *Iliad*. His last translation was the Penguin *Argonautica* (*Voyage of Argo*).

Between 1949 and 1952, some years before he was invited to join the committee which produced the *New English Bible*, he undertook to make, single-handed, for Penguin Books, a translation of *The Four Gospels*. One of his sons, hearing of this undertaking, said: "It will be very interesting to see what father makes of the Gospels. It will be still more interesting to see what the Gospels make of father." It seemed that the Gospels made Rieu a formal member of the Church of England.

Rieu's personality was a curious mixture of the very serious and the light-hearted, even the facetious. It may have been the disappointment of his university career which made him tense and stiff through much of his business life. With his success as a translator, though it occurred so late in his life, and doubtless also with his acquisition of an assured view of life, his nature burgeoned, and colleagues who had found him intractable came to feel far stronger affection as well as admiration for him. His curious walk, a crab-like gait with the left shoulder advanced as if defensively, appeared in later years at odds with the new confidence and geniality of his manner and propensity to joke.

He took a charming simple pleasure in the public honours bestowed on him in his later years—Hon.Litt.D.(Leeds) in 1949; C.B.E. in 1953; the Presidency of the Virgil Society in 1951; a Vice-Presidency of the Royal Society of Literature in 1958; and the award of the Benson Medal (the two previous recipients of which were Dame Rebecca West and Professor J. R. R. Tolkien in 1968.

He leaves a widow, two sons and two daughters.

May 13, 1972.

Former Bishop of Ripon—See Chase.

Lord Ritchie of Dundee, Chairman of the Stock Exchange from 1959 to 1965, died on October 20, 1975 at the age of 72.

Born on September 22, 1902, the second and eldest surviving son of the Second Baron Ritchie of Dundee, John Kenneth Ritchie was educated at the Royal Naval College, Osborne, Winchester and Magdalen, Oxford. He served in the Second World War as a captain in the K.R.R.C., was Chairman of Poplar Hospital in 1948, and from 1948 to 1958 was Chairman of the Bow Group of Hospitals. He succeeded his father in 1948.

He became a senior partner of the stockbrokers, Norris Oakley Richardson & Glover, and was a director of the English Association of American Bond and Share-holders Ltd.

As the Hon. Kenneth Ritchie he was first elected to the Council of the Stock Exchange in 1947 and it was as Ken or Kenneth that he remained to his many friends in and out of the House. He soon became acquainted with the affairs of the Country Exchanges and of agents of the Stock Exchange, being appointed Chairman of the Standing Committee in 1952. In the same year he also became chairman of a special committee which reviewed the scale of commissions as well as the proportion returnable to agents. He was faced with the difficult task of picking up the threads left by the debacle of 1948, but was able to put forward a revised scheme which was to prove generally acceptable.

In 1954 he was the obvious choice to fill the vacancy caused by the resignation of one of the Deputy Chairmen. Shortly after this Ritchie became a Joint Chairman of the Quotations Committee and Vice-Chairman of the Property and Finance Committee. He served as a Deputy Chairman until Sir John Braithwaite resigned in 1959. The Chairman of the Stock Exchange is elected yearly by the Council

at their first meeting following the June elections. Ritchie was accepted with acclamation as the successor to Braithwaite and in every subsequent year his re-election was a foregone conclusion.

His predecessor had made both the Council and the members conscious of public relations. For Sir John Braithwaite this had been brought about of necessity by political criticism and widespread lack of knowledge. Ritchie found the public relations policy already in good running order and in this he was prepared to play a full part, perhaps fuller than he originally intended. He was against the cult of personality, nor did he think it was right for the Chairman of the Stock Exchange to speak for any other institution or interest than his own. But within three years he found himself publicly criticizing the Government in the name of the City. Ritchie had taken over the leadership of the Stock Exchange at a time when it had come to feel more confident and sure of its purpose than perhaps ever before. It resented unfair criticism which contributed financial scandals to the City and the Stock Exchange. The evidence of the Jenkins Committee bore this out.

Meanwhile the Stock Exchange was taking active steps to keep up with the times. Stricter rules for membership and for firms' accounts were introduced, and departmental mechanization was started, although initially on a simple scale. It was somewhat exasperating to Ritchie that a supposedly friendly government was continually ignoring the requests and advice of the Stock Exchange—even to the extent of introducing the upopular tax on short-term gains.

At this time Ritchie was heading the City committee on the new procedure for the transfer of stocks and shares. This committee's recommendations were met with the bleak reply from the authorities that the Government's parliamentary time would not be available for the introduction of the necessary legislation. It was therefore a cause of great satisfaction when in 1962-63 the Government decided to take over a private member's Stock Transfer Bill and at the same time promoted a Bill restricting invitations to depositors and, finally in 1963, after 12 years in office in each of which they had received a deputation from the Stock Exchange, halved the transfer stamp duty.

Prior to this Ritchie had found that the time was ripe for two more important matters to be considered, the closer relationship of the Stock Exchanges in Great Britain and Ireland and the rebuilding of the London Stock Exchange. A committee representing the London, the Associated and the Provincial Stock Exchanges formed under his chairmanship in 1961 was to ensure that federation became a reality.

If externally the Stock Exchange felt more sure of itself, internally it had become financially able seriously to consider the formidable task of rebuilding. A special committee under Lord Ritchie was formed

in 1962, plans were prepared, and the long duel with the authorities for planning permission commenced. The new Stock Exchange eventually appeared in 1972.

Ritchie was a keen follower of lawn tennis all his life. Unlike his brother, C. N. O. Ritchie, he was never in the top flight of players, but between the wars was prominent at tournaments all over the country. After the Second World War he became particularly interested in the administration of the game. He was the president of the Sussex Lawn Tennis Association and for many years organized and ran a popular invitation tournament at a club near his home in Rye.

He became a member of the All England Lawn Tennis Club in 1946, and was elected to the committee in 1954. In this capacity he was closely connected with the running of the club and the Wimbledon championships.

After relinquishing the chairmanship of the Stock Exchange in 1965, Lord Ritchie continued to be elected to the Council and served as deputy chairman for a further period from 1965 to 1972.

He was made a Privy Councillor in 1965.

He married Joan Beatrice, daughter of the Rev. H. C. L. Tindall, in 1945. They had no children. His brother, the Hon. Colin Neville Ower Ritchie, succeeds him.

October 21, 1975.

General Lord Robertson of Oakridge, BT., G.C.B., G.B.E., K.C.M.G., K.C.V.O., D.S.O., M.C., who died on April 29, 1974 at the age of 77, will be remembered as an administrator of the highest order.

His brilliant success in dealing with the supply problems of the 8th Army in the Desert Campaigns led to his appointment as Chief Administrative Officer to the Commander-in-Chief, Italy. After the war he dealt equally successfully with administrative problems of a different character in Germany, first as Deputy Military Governor and Military Governor and, later, as British High Commissioner. He was chairman of the British Transport Commission from 1953 till 1961.

He was a tall, slim man, fair haired, with blue eyes, and shaggy eyebrows like his father's. The memory of his father, who began as a trooper and ended as a field-marshal, was a great influence in his life; and he frequently reminded his staff of some principle which he held to be worth fighting for, because "my old father taught me that". He inherited much of his father's ability. He had a clear brain and was a great worker, and, although he was naturally reserved in manner, those who knew him well valued his friendship. He was a man of high purpose and strong resolve. He was an able public speaker and he had a special aptitude for happy cooperation with his subordinates.

Brian Hubert Robertson was born on

July 22, 1896, the eldest son of Field-Marshal Sir William Robertson, who was C.I.G.S. in the 1914-18 War. He was educated at Charterhouse and R.M.A., Woolwich, from which he was commissioned in the Royal Engineers. After acting as A.D.C. to his father and then to Sir Douglas Haig, he served as brigade major on the Western Front and in Italy, and was awarded the D.S.O. and M.C. and was three times mentioned in dispatches. He saw further active service on the North West Frontier of India in 1922 and 1923, and was again mentioned in dispatches and was given a brevet majority. He then passed through the Staff College and thus laid the basis of a successful military career. But promotion in the army was slow, and in 1933, the year in which his father died, he decided to leave the service and went to South Africa, where he became managing director of the Dunlop Rubber Company.

Six years later, on the outbreak of the Second World War, he was recalled from the Army Reserve and served in Sir Alan Cunningham's Abyssinian Campaign. In 1942 he was appointed chief administrative officer of the 8th Army with the rank of major-general, and it was in this post that he made an outstanding reputation as an organizer. After being G.O.C. Tripolitania for a time, he was appointed chief administrative officer to Field-Marshal Alexander* in Italy, and he held this post until the end of the war in Europe.

In January 1945 Robertson was about to return to Dunlop's when he was offered, and accepted, the appointment of Field-Marshal Montgomery's deputy in Germany. In this post he combined duties of purely military administration with diplomatic negotiation at the highest level. After a year he became Military Governor and Commander-in-Chief of the British Zone, and, when the Federal Government was set up in 1949, he was seconded from the Army to become the first British High Commissioner.

For four years after the war Robertson was, in effect, viceroy of a quarter of Germany responsible in great measure for getting industry on its feet again, for the restoration of the administration, for negotiations with the Russians and the Americans, and for handling the problems of the Berlin blockade and air lift. He applied himself with the utmost devotion to the task of creating order out of confusion.

By virtue of his personality and experience, he became the dominant figure in the Allied Commission, and he played a leading part in every phase of the allied occupation of Germany. The tasks which fell to him were both varied and involved, and he discharged them with consistent firmness, efficiency, integrity and calm.

In him Ernest Bevin found a faithful and reliable agent of the Foreign Office, and, although he had no final independence of decision, he was much more than a mechanical amplifier of his Government's views. It was his cool judgment and diplomacy that greatly helped the western powers through the dangerous situations created by Russian hostility to their policies. He won the friendship of the German people, and, in particular, of their trade unions, by his understanding of their problems. When he left his departure was marked by warm demonstrations of good will.

In 1950 Robertson returned to the Army for the second time on appointment as Commander-in-Chief Middle East Land Forces. He served in this post for three years in the course of which he had to deal with the beginning of Mau Mau in Kenya and with the negotiations for the return of the Suez Canal base to Egypt. On the conclusion of his tenure of command he was selected to be adjutant general to the forces but, before he could take up this appointment, Churchill* offered him the chairmanship of the British Transport Commission.

Robertson took up his new duties in September 1953, and thus became controller of one of the largest, as well as one of the most run down, industrial undertakings in the world. He started work in a period of readjustment to the Government's new policy for transport, which involved the decentralization of management and the disposal of most of the road haulage services. He was appointed for a term of five years, but his tenure was renewed in 1958; and, when the Transport Commission was broken up, he had completed eight years in this difficult assignment.

As head of the Transport Commission Robertson had to bear the massive public critcism unceasingly directed against the railways. Yet much of the criticism was unfair. He was subjected to constant political pressure from successive Ministers of Transport. If he appeared at times to have no policy, it was because the Government had no consistent plan. Robertson was at his best when the man behind him knew his own mind, as Ernest Bevin did.

His colleagues in the commission often felt that he was too much the model public servant, and that he should have resigned in protest when faced with the directives of the politicians, and he may have been too ready to obey without question when a tough line of his own might have done more for the railways. Indeed he was never allowed to run the railways like an industry.

Robertson was A.D.C. General to King George VI and later to the Queen; he was Colonel Commandant of the Royal Engineers from 1950 till 1960 and of the Royal Electrical and Mechanical Engineers from 1951 till 1961. He was created a baron in 1961.

He married in 1926 Edith Christina, daughter of J. B. Macindoe, and they had one son and two daughters. The son, Major the Hon. William Ronald Robertson, born in 1930, succeeds his father.

April 30, 1974.

Dr. Muriel Robertson, F.R.S., who died on June 14, 1973, at the age of 90, was one of a generation of pioneering British scientists who turned their talents to the scientific gold-mines of the newly opened-up territories of Africa and elsewhere.

Educated at Glasgow University, she went to Ceylon in 1905 and subsequently joined the Royal Society's Commission investigating the then recently-discovered disease of sleeping sickness in Uganda in 1911. Within a few years she had published a number of scientific papers completely elucidating (and beautifully illustrating) the development of the causative organism (*Trypanosoma*) in its transmitting insect, tsetse fly.

This work has never been superseded. She thus contributed enormously to the understanding, and hence eventual control of this disease, which had been responsible at the turn of the last century for the deaths of perhaps 200,000 Africans in Uganda alone, at no small risk to herself— for the infection was then incurable.

It is said that she rode a bicycle through the forests of Uganda, a rare if not unique feminine accomplishment at that place and time. During the First World War, Muriel Robertson did invaluable work on gangrene. Subsequently she extended her work to a variety of parasitic protozoa, mainly in the relative seclusion of Elstree. Her contributions to knowledge of the parasitic protozoa were immense, as was recognized by her election to a Fellowship of the Royal Society in 1947. She was always helpful to young scientists who sought her advice and encouragement.

Latterly Miss Robertson lived quietly in Ireland. The personal loss to those who knew her must be irreplaceable. Science is more fortunate—the fruits of her long full life remain in the literature; truly Miss Robertson will be immortalized in her works.

June 22, 1973.

James Robertson-Justice, the actor, died at his home in Stockbridge on July 2, 1975 at the age of 70.

He was a late starter in acting and did not achieve his greatest fame until he was nearly fifty, when he played the irascible surgeon Sir Lancelot in the film of *Doctor in the House.*

This led, inevitably, to his being "typed" as a peppery doctor, professor, lawyer, sailor, senior spy or whatever his height (over six foot), his age and his indispensable grizzled, once-red beard might lend themselves to. And he had the great advantage among character actors of seeming at home with literate dialogue in plot circumstances which required a touch of class and some evidence of advanced education.

This was no doubt because he himself was quite at home in such a situation. He was born in North-west Scotland in 1905, was educated at Marlborough and went on to get his Ph.D. at Bonn University.

He was often said to speak ten languages: he himself admitted to French, German, Italian, Dutch and Gaelic. At various times he taught, wrote, sold insurance and, according to his own account, steered a barge and dug sewers before he came to acting, more or less by accident. He was appearing as chairman in music-hall at the Players Theatre Club when he was noticed by the director Harry Watt and given a small role in his film *Fiddlers Three*, followed by other Ealing films including *Scott of the Antarctic* in which he played Commander Evans.

In 1951 he went to Hollywood for the first time to appear in *David and Bathsheba* and played dramatic roles in various other films such as *Land of the Pharaohs, Moby Dick* and *Orders to Kill*. But then in 1954 came *Doctor in the House* and the die was cast: almost all his subsequent roles were comic, and they tended to be very nearly identical. He repeated the *Doctor in the House* characterization in three sequels, and variations on it in dozens of other English comedies. One of the rare changes of pace was in *Mayerling*, where he played the Prince of Wales, obvious physical typecasting; another was, somewhat improbably, as a victim of Brigit Bardot's charm in Roger Vadim's *Le Repos du Guerrier*.

In private life he was an enthusiast for flying falcons and very active in wildlife conservation; stood as a Labour candidate (unsuccessful) in the 1950 election; and was Rector of Edinburgh University from 1957 to 1960 and from 1963 to 1966.

July 3, 1975.

Edward G. Robinson, one of the screen's most celebrated gangster stars, died on January 26, 1973. He was 79.

He was originally a stage actor and did not make his first film until he was 30; and it was some years after that when his brilliant portrayal of the vicious gang leader in *Little Caesar* made him a world star almost overnight. But after this late start he remained in constant demand for another 40 years and it is a measure of his quality as a screen actor that he was able to survive the typecasting which inevitably followed the success of *Little Caesar*.

As his career developed he revealed himself as a very polished comedy actor and when, later on, he took to character parts rather than leads, he often upstaged the nominal stars. Physically he was the antithesis of the conventional film star—very short in build, with an ugly crumpled face (later softened by a beard) and a rasping voice which could really grate on the nerves. He naturally exploited these attributes to the full in his early gangster roles but his professionalism and natural screen presence was able to sustain his career long after the initial fame had evaporated.

He was born in Bucharest, Romania, in December 1893; the family emigrated to the United States when he was nine. He was educated at public schools in New York and, briefly, at Columbia University, before deciding to train for the stage, when he changed his name from Emmanuel Goldenberg to Edward G. Robinson. After some years in the theatre, playing a variety of modern and classical parts, he got his first star role in a play called *The Racket* in 1927. Significantly he was cast as a gangster and it was from this time on that his film career started to develop, with one gangster part after another until *Little Caesar* in 1930 made him a star.

One of the first (and still one of the best) talking gangster pictures, *Little Caesar* tells the archetypal story of the rise and fall of the hoodlum, starting in the gutter and ending in the gutter. Robinson's dying words, as he lies riddled with bullets, have become part of cinema lore: "Mother of mercy, is this the end of Rico?"

For the same director, Mervyn LeRoy, Robinson played a ruthless newspaper editor in *Five Star Final*, and there followed a string of generally less distinguished films in the same mould. Evidence that Robinson was capable of more came in 1935 when he played two parts in John Ford's comedy, *The Whole Town's Talking:* one was the now familiar gang leader, but the other (slightly sending up his screen persona) was a timid little clerk who gets mistaken for the villain. Robinson completed his change of image, as it were, the following year when for the first time he sided with the law against Humphrey Bogart in *Bullets or Ballots*.

The 1940s were a particularly rich period, embracing the "biopic", *Dr. Ehrlich's Magic Bullet;* another biographical film in which he played Reuter (of news agency fame); and the famous Billy Wilder thriller, *Double Indemnity*. Robinson also played with great effect opposite Joan Bennett in the Fritz Lang "films noirs", *The Woman in the Window* and *Scarlet Street*. He was the war crimes commissioner tracking Orson Welles in *The Stranger,* the head of the family in Arthur Miller's *All My Sons,* and yet another memorable gang leader in John Huston's *Key Largo*.

In the fifties, after a brush with the Un-American Activities Committee about alleged communist leanings, his career had a temporary lapse and he spent some time in rather unworthy "B" pictures. After an absence of 20 years, he returned to the stage in Koestler's *Darkness At Noon,* and Paddy Chayefsky's *The Middle of the Night*.

At the end of the decade he made a triumphant return to the cinema in Henry Hathaway's *Seven Thieves,* a comedy-thriller about a robbery of the casino at Monte Carlo. In 1963 he was a diamond smuggler in the British film, *Sammy Going South,* and two years later played his last substantial role as an old poker player with too many tricks for the younger Steve

McQueen in *The Cincinnati Kid*.

Earlier in 1973 the Motion Picture Academy announced in Hollywood that it would award Robinson a special Oscar to mark his outstanding contribution to the cinema.

Robinson, who was married twice, was in private life a man of refinement and taste. He put together a magnificent collection of Impressionist paintings which fetched more than £1m. when it was sold in 1957.

January 29, 1973.

Jackie Robinson, the baseball star, who in 1947 became the first Negro to play in major American professional league games, died on October 24, 1972 at the age of 53.

Robinson made his first national debut when he played for the then Brooklyn Dodgers in 1947 and quickly became one of the game's best second basemen. Before that he was a star with the Kansas City Monarchs in the all-Negro Baseball League. Earlier, Robinson had been a star athlete at the University of California, where he excelled at football, sprinting and basketball.

When Robinson became the first Negro to play major league baseball, he opened the door for a succession of other black players from the U.S. and the Caribbean to enter the sport.

Robinson, elected to baseball's Hall of Fame in 1962, was honoured only a week before he died at a world series game for his contributions to the sport. After his retirement from baseball in 1957, following a 10-year career with Brooklyn, Robinson devoted much of his time to fighting racial prejudice.

October 25, 1972.

Sir Robert Robinson, O.M., F.R.S., one of the greatest scientists Britain has ever produced, and a Nobel Prize winner, died on February 8, 1975 at the age of 88.

Robert Robinson was born at Chesterfield, Derbyshire, in 1886, the son of W. B. Robinson, surgical dressing manufacturer of Chesterfield, one of the inventors of cotton wool; he was always proud of his father's inventiveness.

He was educated at Fulneck School and at the University of Manchester, where he studied under the late Professor W. H. Penkin, Jnr., and soon became an outstanding member of the school of research which even at that time, had a wide international reputation.

Robinson later became Perkin's close friend and they collaborated in many brilliant investigations dealing largely with the structures of natural compounds, notably the alkaloids.

His first independent appointment was

to the University of Sydney where he occupied the Chair of Organic Chemistry from 1912 to 1915. By now his quite exceptional gifts were widely recognized and in rapid succession he occupied chairs of organic chemistry in the universities of Liverpool, St. Andrews and Manchester.

After six years in Manchester, he was for a short period Professor of Organic Chemistry in University College London. From 1930 to 1955 he held (in succession to Perkin) the Waynflete Chair of Chemistry at Oxford: the university extended his tenure for four years after the normal retiring age.

Robinson's brilliance in research was maintained throughout his life and his work has illuminated many of the most important fields of organic chemistry.

Among other notable work, that dealing with the structures of the authocyanin pigments remains, even after several decades, one of the most brilliant experimental achievements of modern organic chemistry.

His deep insight into chemical problems astonished his colleagues; his synthesis of tropinone in a test-tube (1917) quickly followed Willstätter's classical synthesis involving more than 20 stages; the idea of the aromatic sextet rationalized the study of substitution in aromatic compounds. During his stay in Manchester, his happy collaboration with Professor Arthur Lapworth laid the foundation of the modern electronic theory of organic chemical reactions.

Students flocked from all over the world to work under R. R. (Robbie, as he was usually called).

Robinson received numerous honours in Britain and abroad. He was president of the Chemical Society from 1939 to 1941 and president of the British Association for the Advancement of Science in 1955. He was elected a Fellow of the Royal Society in 1920 and in 1930 was awarded its Davy Medal. In 1932 he recived one of its Royal Medals, and in 1942 he was given the Copley Medal, the highest honour the Royal Society can bestow. He served on the council of the Royal Society from 1932 to 1934 and was president from 1945 to 1950.

Further honours which gave him and his many friends and colleagues outstanding pleasure were the Paracelsus Medal of the Swiss Chemical Society in 1939, of which he was the first recipient, the Albert Gold Medal of the Royal Society of Arts in 1947, the Franklin Medal of the Franklin Institute, Philadelphia, 1947, the Nobel Prize for Chemistry in 1947 and the Priestley Medal of the American Chemical Society in 1953.

Robinson was knighted in 1939 and during the Second World War he made unique contributions to the national effort, notably concerning chemical warfare, explosives and medicinals. These further public services were recognized by his inclusion in the Order of Merit in 1949.

During 1920 and 1921 Robinson had turned his attention to industry and became Director of Research of the British Dyestuffs Corporation.

By his death the world has lost one of its preeminent leaders in classical organic chemistry and a man who, through his high intellectual qualities and genial personality, was held in affection and esteem by all with whom he came in contact.

His marriage to Miss Gertrude Maud Walsh, M.Sc., a fellow student, in 1912 marked the beginning of a long and happy collaboration in many research activities, which ended only with her death in 1954. In 1957 he married Mrs. S. Hillstrom, of New York.

February 10, 1975.

Folke Rogard, the former president of the World Chess Federation, died in Stockholm on June 11, 1973 as the result of a cerebral haemorrhage.

Born on July 6, 1899, he was in his 74th year, still practising law when his end came quite suddenly. He had a highly successful career as a lawyer but he will be remembered most of all for the immense work and skill he lavished on the task of making the Fédération Internationale des Échecs a truly representative and authoritative world body.

Though never a particularly strong chess player, his keen intellect and his intuitive knowledge of men gave him an insight into the way both strong and weak players regarded the game.

Rogard's career as a chess administrator started in Sweden, where he succeeded the celebrated Ludwig Collijn as president of the Swedish Chess Federation in 1939. *The Times* chess correspondent, Harry Golombek, meeting Rogard for the first time at the Chess Olympiad in Stockholm in 1937, was at once impressed with the remarkable character of a man who belonged to that wonderful strain of natural Swedish diplomats of which perhaps Dag Hammerskjöld* was the supreme example.

By 1947 a vice-president of F.I.D.E., he succeeded in 1949 the kindly but not particularly effective Dutchman, Dr. Rueb, in the post of president. He at once set to and busied himself with the task of first bringing such great chess-playing countries as the U.S.S.R. and West Germany into the F.I.D.E. fold, and then of asserting the authority of the parent body over all the national units that were affiliated to it.

He brought to the task an ideal temperament, consisting of an iron will-power encased in a velvet glove. Quite a good actor, he would seem to explode with rage when he thought it necessary to blast away unwarranted opposition; but underneath he remained as cool as a cucumber. He and only he was able to come between the mighty clashing opposites of the U.S.S.R. and the U.S.A., and, by observing a strict neutrality, he was able to reconcile the very different aims of East and West.

As a lawyer, the subject of the laws of chess was dear to his heart and Golombek had the privilege of working with him on the project of creating a clear codex of the rules over many years. In that formidable task he proved patient, clear-sighted and always ready to see another's point of view.

Oddly enough, for a man of his acute intelligence, he was possessed of some petty vanities that usually go with stupidity, and he was wont to wear a resplendent chain of office with almost childlike satisfaction. Warts and all, though, this was a man of whom Sweden could be justly proud and in his own way he did more for the peace of the world by smoothing over national and international differences than many a Nobel prizewinner. "We were friends for many years and I shall miss him," Golombek wrote. "The world of chess has already done so ever since his retirement from the presidency in 1970."

June 25, 1973.

General Gustavo Rojas Pinilla, the dictator who ruled Colombia from 1953 to 1957, died in Bogotá on January 17, 1975 at the age of 75.

His four dramatic years in the presidency were described by an eminent and usually mild historian as "one of the most savage, venal and altogether incompetent administrations in the history of the nation".

Before Rojas emerged on the political scene, Colombia had suffered many years of hardship. A civil war between the Conservatives and Liberals had broken out in 1948—known as *La Violencia*—and Laureano Gomez, an admirer of Hitler who was elected in 1950, had proved to be a tough authoritarian with no admiration for the niceties of democracy. In 1953 Gomez's harsh measures exasperated the country, he was deposed and Rojas was made President. He was to offer Colombia no respite.

Rojas, with his sad smile, had risen through the ranks to become Commander-in-Chief of the armed forces and Minister of Communications. Born in 1900, he attended the Military Academy of Bogotá and then went to the United States where he gained an engineering degree from Tri-State College in Indiana, supporting himself by working at night on an assembly line in a car factory.

His most melodramatic act as President, still a much discussed issue with Colombians, was to place his secret police among the crowd at a bullfight in the Bogotá bullring in February 1956. Those who did not applaud his banner were beaten or killed.

There was a law which decreed that anyone who spoke disrespectfully of Rojas could be fined or sent to prison, and newspapers were censored or forced to close. It was a classic brutal dictatorship, of which Latin America has seen many.

A constituent assembly, set up by Rojas in place of a parliament, by-passed the constitution which laid down that a president had to be elected by popular vote, and declared him president in 1954 and again in 1957. On the second occasion, there was an upsurge of feeling against his excesses and for a return to some form of democracy.

With the church, the students and the business community against him, he was forced to give up and flee to Spain. One positive result was that the Liberals and Conservatives put aside their feuding and agreed on a coalition, with the presidency passing alternately to each party. This pact lasted for 16 years.

But that was not the end of Rojas. He was allowed to return in 1958 and, although stripped of his political rights, organized a new movement called the Alianza Nacional Popular (A.N.A.P.O.) which looked for its support to the mass of the poor. He thundered against the coalition and ran, illegally, for the presidency in 1962. In the following year, he was arrested for allegedly plotting a coup d'état against the government.

A.N.A.P.O. continued to grow; it became violently anti-United States and appealed to both extreme conservatives and communists and those who felt that the two parties in the coalition had created a political oligarchy. It won a third of the votes in the 1966 election.

Aided by his daughter Maria Eugenia, Rojas stood again in 1970 and, according to the official figures, lost by a small margin to Misael Pastrana Borrero, the coalition's candidate. Rojas alleged fraud, declared himself the winner and was promptly put under house arrest. As he was too old to stand in the 1974 elections, his daughter put forward her candidature and came third, behind the Liberals and Conservatives.

January 20, 1975.

L. T. C. Rolt, the transport historian, who died on May 9, 1974 at the age of 64, won a high reputation for his books on waterways, railways, motoring and topography, and for his clutch of imaginative biographies of famous engineers, including Watt, Newcomen, Telford, Brunel and George and Robert Stephenson.

He was fortunate in his time for his excursions into industrial archaeology both coincided with and helped to create a growing public appetite for the subject.

Rolt was a popularizer in the best sense of the word and all that he wrote reflected his love of good engineering, the English language and the English countryside.

The son of Lionel Caswall Rolt, he was born in Chester on February 11, 1910, and educated at Cheltenham College. His youth and early manhood he described in a delightful volume of autobiography called *Landscape with Machines*, which was published in 1971. An early passion for things mechanical was sublimated in an engineering apprenticeship wide in scope which brought him face to face with large locomotives being built for export; milk separators for English farms; early diesel lorries; the distinguished and lamented Sentinel steam wagons and the Fowler ploughing engine.

Unless one has seen a ploughing engine at work it is hard to imagine the beauty and majesty of the thing; Rolt not only drove one but had the literary ability to describe the experience.

In the 1930s with a partner he was "involved" in selling and maintaining vintage cars and shortly before the Second World War he acquired the narrow boat *Cressy* and voyaged over much of the canal system of the Midlands. It was this experience which he described so richly in *Narrow Boat* (1944).

This was the pathfinder for the whole postwar revival of interest in canals for pleasure purposes. He joined Robert Aickman and Charles Hadfield in founding the Inland Waterways Association in 1945, and was its first secretary. He published two other classics of the waterways, *Green and Silver*, in 1949 about cruising in Ireland, and *The Inland Waterways of England* in 1950.

Already involved in the world of vintage cars, his interests now moved to narrow gauge railway restoration with the Talyllyn Railway Preservation Society. He wrote an account of the railway's reopening in *Railway Adventure* and was general manager of the line during and after its restoration. In later life his principal interests were industrial archaeology and the history of engineering—he was, for instance, the general editor of Longman's industrial archaeology series—and also the struggle for authors' public lending right.

He was vice-president of the Newcomen Society, a member of the Science Museum Advisory Council and of the York Railway Museum Committee; an honorary M.A. of Newcastle and an honorary M.Sc. of Bath.

May 11, 1974.

Jules Romains, novelist and playwright, author of the imposing *roman-fleuve, Les Hommes de bonne volonté*, and since 1947 a member of the French Academy, died on August 14, 1972 in Paris at the age of 86.

His death removes from the scene one of the three or four French authors who enjoyed wide fame in the contemporary English-speaking world. In the United States, indeed, Romains was probably the best known of all "serious" French writers, while his role as president of the French Centre of P.E.N., the international writers' organization, brought him to the notice of his professional colleagues in most parts of Europe and of the American continent. In France he was not taken quite so seriously as he thought was his due. Gide and Claudel, Giraudoux and Cocteau,* Mauriac* and Montherlant—these delighted the sophisticated more than Romains did.

Jules Romains was a pen name. His real name was Louis Farigoule. He was born on August 26, 1885. He was an Auvergnat, a native of that eastward frontier of the Massif Central, the Forez. It was in this region, round Ambert, that he set the scene for his entertaining and uninhibited essay in picaresque fiction, *Les Copains*. It was from this region that he went as a student to that goal of the brilliant provincial schoolboy, the École Normale Supérieure, the official gateway to the upper ranks of the French teaching profession. The impact of Paris on this type of young Frenchman is one of the most telling features of his long novel series *Men of Good Will*.

Like a great many young *normaliens,* Romains had no very strong vocation for teaching, although some critics may have felt that as a political preacher something of the *"oiustre"* always survived in him. After 10 years teaching philosophy in various *lycées* he became, in 1919, a full-time writer. The experience of the 1914-18 War had affected him more than the experience of the *lycées*. It shook Romains out of some at least of his more ingenuous political views; it awakened him to the importance of leadership; and it provided him with a hero in the person of Marshal Pétain. The contrast drawn between Pétain and the political soldier (probably Sarrail) in two of the volumes of *Men of Good Will* devoted to the fighting at Verdun was of no little assistance in France, and probably of even greater assistance in America, in preparing public opinion for the acceptance in 1940 of the victor of Verdun as the saviour of France.

Les Copains was published in 1914, three years after the promising but very different *Mort de quelqu'un*, a characteristically Gallic feat of subtle, if also rather tenuous, psychological drama. From these beginnings Romains as a novelist developed—how seriously it is hard to tell—the method or motive or philosophy of *unanimisme,* by which he sought to reproduce in fiction the verities of group psychology, the general collective aspect and social multiplicity of modern life. It was to further this philosophy that, with his friends Vildrac and Duhamel* he founded the group called "l'Abbaye", and published in 1908 its verse manifesto, *La Vie Unanime*.

His first notable success, however, was less ambitious than either his earlier or later literary projects. He had written two not very successful plays, *Cromedeyre-le-Vieil* (1920) and *Monsieur le Trouhadec* (1923) when, in the latter year, appeared *Knock ou le triomphe de la médicine*, a brilliant farce, deriving from a sound Molièresque tradition of doctor-baiting and adorned by a happy flow of observation of provincial types and manners. Louis Jouvet, who first produced it, kept it in his repertory all his life.

Later plays included *Le Mariage de M. le Trouhadec*, (1925); *La Scintillante*, (1925); *Jean le Maufranc*, (1926); *Demetrios*, (1926); *Le Dictateur* (1926), in a rather simplified philosophical vein; *Donogoo*, (1931), produced on the extravagantly elaborate stage of the Théâtre Pigalle; *Jean Musse* (1930) was disappointing; but his French adaptation of Stefan Zweig's German adaptation of Ben Jonson's *Volpone* was so successful in 1929 that there was talk of making an English adaptation of it—talk which happily came to nothing. His long novel, *Le Dieu des corps* (1928), translated into English under the title of *The Body's Rapture*, on the theme of love, was well received, and was followed by another novel *Quand le Navire* (1929).

It was possibly a desire to be taken seriously as a great artist that led Romains to erect the vast scaffolding of *Les Hommes de Bonne volonté*, of which the earliest volume, *Le 6 octobre*, was published in 1932. This prodigious structure, in the author's opinion, marked off his work from what might otherwise appear to be similar feats by Georges Duhamel* or Roger Martin du Gard. Romains's chronicle, planned from the start to fill 27 volumes, was to be on the lines of Romain Rolland's *Jean Christophe*, but better articulated.

In working out his plan, he exhibited conspicuous ingenuity and something more than ingenuity; there were sections that might very fairly be described as first-rate second-class work. But the political naivety which Romains revealed in the years just before and during the war of 1939-45 explains in some degree why, as a *unanimiste* totality, *Men of Good Will* fails to come off. It covers the quarter of a century from 1908 to 1933; it peoples the French scene of that period with an immense procession of characters, a few of whom have admittedly almost assumed reality for French readers and penetrated below the surface of French life; and yet it comes far short of creating the illusion of a period of contemporary history. As Romains showed in his absurd *Seven Mysteries of Europe*, he was a victim of his own creation. At his average best he recalls the more romantic parts of Balzac or Disraeli; at the worst—but perhaps it is better to leave the names unspoken.

Romains regarded himself in all good faith as a political leader. He was on terms of friendship with several French politicians during the 1930s and was used by astute Germans to throw dust in French eyes. But he was an innocent partner in the mystification.

He married a Jewish bride, Mlle. Lise Dreyfus in 1936, and after the collapse of France he went to the United States, and from there attempted to carry on the work of the French P.E.N.—to the annoyance of colleagues who thought that their organization should be less detached from the battle than that. With the American entry into the war he strongly opposed Vichy; he contributed to the organs of French resistance published in London; he published a paean of praise of the United States entitled *Salsette Discovers America;* he went to Mexico, where in 1944 he completed his *Men of Good Will* by writing volumes 26 and 27. On his return to France in 1947 he was elected to the Academy and generally reinstated in popular favour.

After the war he published several volumes of essays on various social and political subjects, including one on the atomic bomb, under the title of *Le problème no. 1*, and a series which he called *Les Cahiers des hommes de bonne volonté*, including *l'Amitié, le Crune, la Notion d'homme de bonne volonté* and *Où va le monde?* These consisted largely of comments by friends and readers of the *roman-fleuve*, under the editorship of Romain's friend, A. Cuisenier. His wife also brought out a book of extracts, called *Le Paris des hommes de bonne volonté*, with illustrations and plans. He himself made and published a selection of his poems and wrote another play, *Grace encore pour la terre!*

August 18, 1972.

Françoise Rosay, the distinguished French actress died in Paris on March 28, 1974 at the age of 82.

From childhood, and indeed from infancy, she was destined for the stage. Her father was a count and an army officer, but her mother was a successful actress who was determined that her daughter should follow in her footsteps. Françoise was born on April 19, 1891, in Paris—near the Place Pigalle. Her real name was Françoise de Nalèche, and she did not change it to Rosay until she had started her acting career. As a child she travelled widely with her mother, and was educated at a number of schools, including one in Hove, Sussex.

At the age of 16 she began to show exceptional talent as a soprano, but her mother refused to allow her to consider opera as a career. So she became Françoise Rosay, the actress, and one of her first parts was in one of Sacha Guitry's earliest plays.

She also studied acting under Paul Mounet, of the Comédie Française, and played small parts in a number of classical works.

At the age of 21 she found herself playing in the same theatre in St. Petersburg as her mother had performed in years before. On her return, she determined to turn her attention to opera, despite the opposition of her mother, and appeared in *Castor et Pollux* at the Paris Opera House.

It was at this point in her career that she met the French film director, Jacques Feyder, whom she married in 1917. This altered her whole life, and although she did not at first appear in any of his films, she did accompany him to Hollywood in 1929 when he went out there to direct Greta Garbo in the silent film, *The Kiss*. Feyder's producer, Al Lewin, offered her a part in *The Magnificent Lie*, and this led to a number of other parts in American films, including *The Trial of Mary Dugan* and *Jenny Lind*. She and her husband returned to France in 1931, and she then became one of the leading film actresses of the French cinema. She appeared under her husband's direction in *La Kermesse Héroïque*, in which she played the Burgomaster's wife; under Julien Duvivier's* direction in *Un Carnet de Bal;* and under that of Marcel Carné in *Jenny* and *Drôle de Drame*.

When war broke out, she was one of the first persons in France to be heard in propaganda broadcasts to the German people, and as a result was condemned to death by the Nazi regime and was forced to flee, first to the South of France, and finally to North Africa. When the Allies captured Tunis, she was flown to safety in England.

Her husband died in 1948, and thereafter she divided her time between the cinema and the theatre. Her English films included *Halfway House, Johnny Frenchman, Saraband for Dead Lovers*, and *Quartet*. She made several appearances on the London stage.

Although born to the theatre, Rosay's preference was for the cinema, where an error in a performance could be corrected before it was seen by the public. Acting was her *métier*; and she once concluded an article on herself with words which summed up her life's aim: "I would be a young actress, I would be a middle-aged actress, I would be an old actress, and I would die. Acting was a life's work."

From 1958 to 1967 she taught acting in Paris, while continuing her film career. In 1970 she was seen on the Paris stage in Anouilh's *Cher Antoine*.

Her final screen appearance is still to be released—a role in *The Pedestrian*, shot in 1973 in Munich by Maximilian Schell. A book of her memoirs is scheduled for publication in Paris.

March 30, 1974.

Sir Alan Rose, K.C.M.G., Q.C., M.A., LL.B., who was Chief Justice of Ceylon and later of Singapore, died on June 20, 1975 at the age of 75.

Alan Edward Percival Rose was born on October 8, 1899 and educated at Aldenham School and Trinity College, Cambridge. During the First World War he served as a Second Lieutenant in the 1st Battalion, Rifle Brigade, and was called to the Bar in 1923.

He entered the Colonial Legal Service in 1929 and became Chief Police Magistrate for Fiji in the same year. Subsequent service saw him as Crown Counsel, Northern Rhodesia, in 1931, Solicitor General in Palestine in 1936, and Puisne Judge in the same country in 1939.

He chaired the Commissions of Enquiry into the loss of s.s. Patria in 1940 and into corruption in the Customs Department in 1942.

He was subsequently a Judge of the Supreme Court of Ceylon in 1945, Legal Secretary in 1946 and 1947 and Attorney General of the Dominion of Ceylon from 1947 to 1951.

In 1951 he was selected by the Prime Minister of Ceylon as Chief Justice. This, occurring as it did after full independence, as well as after the post had been filled successively by two Ceylonese, was recognition of the value of the British connexion as well as being a tribute to the personal qualities of Rose himself.

At the end of his tenure of this appointment in 1955 he retired, but was not to remain idle. In 1956 he chaired the Commission of Enquiry into the affairs of Nairobi City Council.

Later, on the strength of his Ceylon career, he was selected as Chief Justice of Singapore in a "nightwatchman" capacity for the period of the state's evolution to complete independence.

He held this post from 1958 to 1963.

He was knighted in 1950 and made a K.C.M.G. in 1955. Sir Alan Rose was unmarried.

June 27, 1975.

Lord Rosebery, K.T., P.C., D.S.O., M.C., distinguished soldier, politician, administrator and sportsman, died on May 31, 1974 at the age of 92.

Although never deeply enmeshed in politics, Rosebery was for a time a Liberal M.P., a leader of the National Liberals, and was a member of Sir Winston Churchill's* war-time administration, first as Regional Commissioner for Scotland and then as Secretary of State. He was a shrewd owner of great estates in England and Scotland, and the knowledgeable possessor of many art treasures. He added lustre to his father's name on the turf. In his youth he had been an outstanding games player. Had circumstances permitted it, he would probably have made a remarkable military career. His was a life in some respects almost as varied as that of his famous father, and he was, in his own right, a remarkable man.

Albert Edward Harry Meyer Archibald Primrose ("names enough in all conscience", as his father remarked), sixth Earl of Rosebery, was born on January 8, 1882 at Dalmeny House, and was the elder son of the fifth Earl.

He was the heir to truly vast possessions. His parents' marriage had brought together the considerable Rosebery estates in Scotland and the wealth and properties of Baron Meyer de Rothschild, whose only daughter was perhaps the greatest heiress of her time. The family moved between Dalmeny, Mentmore, The Durdans, and 38, Berkeley Square. Later, there was the beautiful Villa Rosebery at Posilipio, which Rosebery presented to the Italian Government in 1932. None of these imposing establishments was administered with undue regard to economy, and the splendour of the Rosebery *grande tenue* was legendary and even intimidating. The Prince of Wales (later King Edward VII) was one of the new heir's godfathers.

Rosebery, both in appearance and personality, grew up almost as unlike his taut, febrile, introspective, brilliant father as could seem possible. Although he was highly intelligent, spirited, and strong-willed, it was his younger brother, Neil Primrose, who had definitely inherited the father's glamour and flair. Although Rosebery's relationship with his father was always close, that between Neil and the fifth Earl was, as Lord Birkenhead has written, more like that between brothers, and "was among the most touching in a life full of idealized love". Neil Primrose's death in action in 1917, after a brief but richly promising political career, was a blow from which the father never recovered.

After leaving Eton, Rosebery went to the Royal Military Academy and was commissioned in the Grenadier Guards. But in 1903, at his father's insistence, he very reluctantly resigned his commission to stand as Liberal candidate for Midlothian, which he represented from 1906 to 1910. Sir Henry Campbell-Bannerman, in an attempt to heal old wounds, invited him to second the Address at the opening of the new Parliament, but his father peremptorily forbade him to accept the offer. This quenched what little political aspirations he had.

He captained Surrey at cricket from 1905 to 1907, and was a more familiar figure at the Oval than Westminster. He followed his father staunchly as the fifth Earl moved with disconcerting swiftness to the right, and the critical murmurings of the Liberals of Midlothian became increasingly more evident. The compromises and artifices of politics were wholly uncongenial to such a blunt and straightforward personality, and it was with relief on both sides that in 1908 he announced his intention not to seek re-election.

On the outbreak of war in 1914 he at once rejoined the Grenadiers. He was severely wounded, mentioned in dispatches four times, and was awarded the D.S.O., the M.C., and the Legion of Honour. He rose to become Assistant Military Secretary to General Allenby. This was a most remarkable and happy relationship. Each had the reputation of being difficult to get on with. Certainly, each was outspoken, suffered fools ungladly, and possessed great common sense. They worked together so well that at times the relationship more resembled that between a commander-in-chief and his chief-of-staff.

The death of Neil Primrose and his father's severe stroke in 1918 obliged Rosebery to return home at the end of the war. He was now the actual head of the family, although it was not until May 1929 that his father's long life ended and he succeeded to the title.

Rosebery was a dutiful rather than an enthusiastic participant in party politics, and he had firmly resisted strong pressures to make him return to the Commons in the immediate post-war years. Early in the 1930s his disillusionment with Lloyd George became so complete that he joined the National Liberals, ultimately becoming the party's president. But he never took the final step into the Conservative ranks. Perhaps something of the traditional family distaste for Tories lingered on.

From 1941 until the beginning of 1945 Rosebery was Regional Commissioner for Scotland. Like his father, he had an almost passionate love of Scotland, and he worked indefatigably at his difficult task. He never courted popularity, and at times almost seemed to go out of his way in the opposite direction. But this, both with the Prime Minister and the Scottish people, did him no harm at all in the long run. In 1945 he became Secretary of State for Scotland in the brief "caretaker" government, and after its defeat he led the National Liberals in the Lords for a time. In 1947 he was created a Knight of the Order of the Thistle.

Henceforth his public interests, although varied, were uncontroversial. He was chairman of the Fine Arts Commission for Scotland and president of the Royal Scottish Corporation. He was president of Surrey Cricket Club from 1947 to 1949 and of the M.C.C. from 1953 to 1954. He was a member of the Royal Commission on Justices of the Peace and presided over the committee of inquiry set up by the Labour Government into the export and slaughter of horses. He was for many years a Justice of the Peace and Lord Lieutenant for Midlothian. In 1955 he took on the chairmanship of the Scottish Tourist Board. These constituted only a part of his many and varied public services.

It was, however, his long connexion with the British turf that will be best remembered. For close on 70 years he played an active part, first as an owner and then as a breeder, legislator and influential member of the Jockey Club. In 1932 he succeeded Lord D'Abernon as president of the newly formed Thoroughbred Breeders' Association. Meanwhile it was at his famous Mentmore stud in Buckinghamshire that he bred so many winners. He won five classic races with Blue Peter, Ocean Swell, Sandwich and Sleeping Partner, the first named being undoubtedly the best horse he ever bred. Most of his horses were trained at Newmarket by Sir Jack Jarvis*, who died in 1968. Seldom has there been a longer or more successful partnership, for it began in 1921 when his father, the fifth earl, sent 18 horses to the Park Lodge trainer.

In his youth he had been an outstanding games player. He was a beautiful cricketer, and could hit the ball with rare ferocity. He scored 52 for Eton against Harrow, and, when just 20, a memorable 197 against the M.C.C. He played for Middlesex before captaining Surrey; in 1905 he and J. N. Crawford put on 260 for the sixth wicket against Leicestershire, his contribution being 138. He played for Scotland against the Australians.

He was always a first-class shot, and indeed he excelled at every sport he took up. In later years, when president of the Heart of Midlothian Football Club, his knowledge of the game—to say nothing of the vociferous encouragements and admonitions which could make the directors' box a lively place—made him far more than a titular head.

His first marriage to Lady Dorothy, younger daughter of Lord Henry Grosvenor, which took place in 1909, was dissolved by divorce in 1919. They had a son and a daughter, of whom the daughter survives.

Rosebery's second marriage, to the Hon. Eva Isabel Marian Bruce, daughter of the second Lord Aberdare, in 1924 was supremely happy. It was by no means a union of opposites. Each had a strong will and an invigorating spirit. Each had a profound sense of public service, and Lady Rosebery's D.B.E. gave great happiness to her husband. By his second wife he had a son, Lord Primrose, who succeeds him, and a daughter who died in infancy.

Rosebery's wealth and position gave not merely the opportunity but the justification for public service. No one could have been less of a snob; he was devoid of all pomposity, and he was no respecter of persons and reputations. His often disconcertingly blunt manner sometimes gave a false impression of rudeness and insensitiveness, but this façade concealed his fundamental kindness, generosity and sympathy, particularly to young people. He was an excellent mixer in any company. He was a witty, astringent, and commonsense speaker. His father had been a superb actor and a polished orator; Rosebery was neither of these things, but in the opinion of some people, who had heard both, he was the more persuasive and certainly the less ambiguous speaker.

When in the mood he was an entrancing companion. In all weathers he was a staunch friend. If his anger could be intimidating, there was more bark than bite in it. His snort of contempt or disbelief was uniquely expressive. He read far more deeply and widely than superficial acquaintances ever dreamed. He had his blind spots about men and events, and some ineradicable prejudices. But there was no concealment, no dissimulation, no artifice, no humbug. You took him as you found him.

June 1, 1974.

Lord Rosenheim, K.B.E., F.R.S., Emeritus Professor of Medicine at University College Hospital, London, and president of the Royal College of Physicians from 1966 until March 1972, died on December 2, 1972. He was 64. From 1950 to 1971, he was Professor of Medicine at London University and Director of the Medical Unit at University College Hospital medical school.

During his presidency he played a leading part in the campaign on smoking and health. Rosenheim was created a life peer in the 1970 Birthday Honours. In December 1971 he was appointed chairman of the Medicines Commission.

Max Leonard Rosenheim was born in 1908 and educated at Shrewsbury School and St. John's College, Cambridge. At school (1922 to 1926) he was not outstanding either at games or work, but his cheerful and easy relationship with others gave an indication of that kind and friendly temperament which made him such a loved and successful leader in later life. At Cambridge he took first class honours in the natural science tripos, and went on to University College Hospital in 1929. After taking his M.B. in 1933 he held resident appointments at U.C.H. and was appointed first assistant to the Medical Unit in 1939 under Professor Sir H. Himsworth. He took his M.D. Camb. in 1938 and was elected a Fellow of the Royal College of Physicians in 1941.

Though his interests were mainly in research he was equally happy in the wards and he brought to all his work the realistic outlook of the practical clinician. His deep concern for his patients and his kind and sympathetic regard for their problems made him immensely popular and he was able to impart to his students this same quiet attitude of care and understanding. No one could better combine the scientific approach to clinical problems with the sensitivity of the practising doctor. As a teacher he was direct and undramatic but with a quick and sparkling sense of humour and an imperturbability which was most impressive. At U.C.H. his research work went steadily forward and his discovery of the use of mandelic acid (in 1930) for the treatment of kidney infections was one of major importance. This arose from his study of the value of the ketogenic diet which was then being employed for these conditions, and it was Max Rosenheim who recognized that the beneficial effects of this form of diet was due to substances from which sodium mandelate was the later outcome.

After Sir Harold Himsworth moved to become Secretary of the Medical Research Council, Max Rosenheim was appointed to the chair of medicine at U.C.H. in 1950 and he continued to hold this post until 1971. During the 1939-45 war he served in the R.A.M.C.—first as O.C. Medical Division in the Middle East, North Africa, Sicily and Italy—and later as consultant in S.E. Asia, with the rank of colonel. Here he visited Java, Sumatra and other areas which increased his love of travel and his fascination with far-off countries.

After the war he settled down again to his work at U.C.H. and became deeply concerned with the various boards of London University especially as they were related to the medical curriculum and examinations. He was an expert committeeman and his advice was widely sought. He was greatly responsible for the change from "external" to "internal" examinations and took an especial interest in the overseas colleges with which London University was in special relationship. His travels as Sims Fellow (1958), as adviser or examiner for London University, and for the British Council (of which he was chairman of the medical panel) took him to Nigeria, Ceylon, the West Indies, India and many other countries.

In 1966 he was elected P.R.C.P. and was knighted the following year. He was thus in a position to guide the college at the time of its 450th anniversary and to grasp the opportunity to expand its activities which the move from Trafalgar Square to Regent's Park in 1964 had made possible. It was then that Rosenheim's magnificent qualities of calm decision and expert judgment showed at their best. Quick to assess a situation and supremely skilful in his relationship with others he was very soon recognized as one of the ablest and most successful presidents the college had ever had. He seemed to have time to give to any member of the college who came to see him and his unruffled and confident control of college affairs was remarkable; he could deputize well which was perhaps partly the secret of how he was able to achieve so much and find such abundant energy to keep up his travels as well as his teaching and clinical research at University College Hospital.

Besides sailing and fishing "Max" was fond of music, books and especially of good conversation. He wrote clearly with a fine economy of words, and became an excellent after-dinner speaker, again with admirable brevity.

Rosenheim was a bachelor and lived at Hampstead with his Swiss mother, to whom he was devoted. In spite of the distinguished position he occupied he made little change in his mode of life; his total lack of affectation or insincerity and his modest and cheerful manner brought him countless friends; to innumerable doctors overseas and at home the name "Max" conveyed an affection and happiness which his warm and generous nature most fully deserved.

December 4, 1972.

Milton Rosmer, the actor, died on December 7, 1971 at the age of 89. During his varied career in the theatre which extended over half a century he played a remarkably wide range of parts. He had played many leading parts in works by Shaw, Ibsen and Galsworthy.

Born at Southport on November 4, 1882 and educated at Manchester Grammar School, he made his first stage appearance in the burlesque *Don Quixote* in 1899 and at the end of the following year he joined Osmond Tearle's touring company.

He was then for three years with Walter Melville and by the age of 21 he had appeared as Hamlet, Orlando and Mark Antony. He was with Sir John Martin Harvey for two seasons and during that period made his first London appearance at the Coronet Theatre, Notting Hill Gate. He toured in America in *Everyman* and many Shakespearian plays, and for four years was with Miss Horniman's company at the Gaiety Theatre, Manchester. He was director of the company on American and Canadian tours and in September 1913 he began a short spell of management, and among the plays he presented were Masefield's* *The Tragedy of Nan* and Galsworthy's *The Fugitive*.

He joined the Army in 1916 and when he resumed his stage career he played an enormous number of parts and helped the Stage Society, the Play Actors and the Fellowship of Players. He directed the Stratford-on-Avon Memorial Theatre company during the 1943 season and did some admirable work. But he declined the invitation of the Governors to continue in the following year. His decision was generally regretted, as the company had played to large audiences in wartime for 23 weeks, but Rosmer explained that owing to conditions arising largely out of the war he found it difficult to reach the high standard which the festival and his own ambition demanded.

He appeared in many films, playing Jan Ridd and Heathcliff in silent versions of *Lorna Doone* and *Wuthering Heights* and was seen in a number of television productions.

He owed much of his success to the invaluable support he received from his wife Irene Rooke, herself a player of considerable ability. She died in 1958.

December 9, 1971.

Sir David Ross, K.B.E., Vice-Chancellor of Oxford University from 1941 to 1944, and Provost of Oriel College from 1929 to 1947, died on May 5, 1971 in Oxford at the age of 94. He was chairman of the Royal Commission on the Press from 1947 to 1949; its report in 1949 led to the creation of the Press Council.

William David Ross, son of John Ross, Principal of the Maharajah College, Tranvancore, was born at Thurso in 1877. He was educated at the Royal College, Edinburgh; at Edinburgh University, where he graduated in 1895 with first class honours; and at Balliol College, Oxford, where he won the Jenkyns exhibition and first classes in classical moderations and in literae humaniores. Elected a fellow of Merton by examination in 1900, he began in that year his long association with Oriel, becoming in succession lecturer (1900-02), fellow and tutor in philosophy (1902-29), senior tutor (1924-29), and Provost (1929-47); to this office he was elected unanimously. After sitting for long periods on most of the important university boards and committees he did especially valuable work as Delegate of the Press—he was from 1941 to 1944 Vice-Chancellor.

During 1915-19 he was engaged in war work, being secretary of the N.E. Coast Armaments Committee (1915-16), serving in the Munitions Inspection Department (1916-18) and acting as a deputy assistant secretary at the Ministry of Munitions (1918-19). From 1920 onwards he served on various trade boards, on the Departmental Committee on Holidays with Pay, on an Appeal Tribunal for Conscientious Objectors (1940-41) and on the National Arbitration Tribunal (1941-52). He was chairman of the Civil Service Arbitration Tribunal (1942-52).

The distinctions he received were numerous. In 1918 he was made O.B.E. and in 1938 K.B.E. He was elected to honorary fellowships at Merton, Balliol and Oriel, and received honorary degrees from Trinity College, Dublin, and from Edinburgh, London, Manchester, Columbia, Paris and Oslo universities. In 1927 he was made a Fellow of the British Academy, and from 1936 to 1940 was its president. In 1932 he was president of the Classical Association.

As a philosopher Ross was ready and effective in debate, and his sanity and willingness to reconsider almost any problem made private discussion with him valuable. He excelled as an Aristotelian scholar. He was editor, at first jointly with Professor J. A. Smith, of the Oxford translations of Aristotle's works: he himself translated the *Metaphysics* (1908), the *Ethics* (1925) and select fragments, and revised Jowett's translation of the *Politics*. His book on Aristotle (1923) was considered by good judges to be by far the most accurate and readable survey of that philosopher's writings. His editions of the *Metaphysics* (1924), the *Physics* (1935) and the *Analytics* (1949), which included recensions of the texts, long introductions and elaborate commentaries, have established themselves as on the whole giving the best available texts and the most helpful expositions of these difficult books. Before the Second World War he also collaborated with F. H. Fobes in producing an edition, commentary and translation of Theophrastus' *Metaphysics* (1929).

He sought to work out the truth for himself, as was natural in one whose interests were primarily those of a thinker, though even here he attached importance, and possibly excessive importance, to considering what others had said. The result was the publication of *The Right and the Good* (1930) and of his Gifford Lectures, *Foundations of Ethics* (1939); the latter considers problems which the earlier book had either ignored or treated only cursorily. *The Right and the Good* was for some time the most widely read of any work on moral philosophy and occasioned much controversy, though it is less in tune with postwar philosophical interests.

In the leisure of retirement, when he had reached the age of seventy, Ross published a series of works that would have been remarkable in the whole career of another man. Besides books on *Plato's Theory of Ideas* (1951) and Kant's *Ethical Theory* (1934), he produced editions with commentaries of Aristotle's *Analytics* (1949), *Parva Naturalia* (1955) and *De Anima* (1956), and texts of his *Select Fragments* (1954), *Politics* (1957), *Topica and Elenchi* (1958), and *Rhetoric* (1959). He thus sought to provide the student with revised texts of many of Aristotle's works. He was not very interested in the history and collation of manuscripts but rather in applying his uniquely wide and long familiarity with Aristotle to the selection of what he thought the best readings, or occasionally to conjectural emendations. Many would have preferred him to have concentrated more on interpretation. But he made a large and permanent contribution to the understanding of a philosopher whose calm and dispassionate judgment resembled his own.

Ross had a modesty most unusual in a man of his attainments. He was remarkably cool and judicious in approaching practical questions. This made him so valued a member and chairman of public committees and tribunals. In earlier years he gave the impression of being unwilling to force his views on others, but this was not so striking a characteristic in later life, and though the phrase "if you can convince me" was a favourite of his, it was not easy to overcome a man formidable in argument.

His most outstanding characteristic was perhaps his astonishing capacity for work, although it was combined with a reticence about himself and his own doings which tended to conceal the extent of his activity. Even on a holiday he seldom took a complete rest. His work on Aristotle alone would have been for most men the work of a lifetime. Yet this and his other writings did not prevent him from throwing himself wholeheartedly into tutorial work, from lecturing to large audiences on a variety of subjects and from multifarious public services. Even in old age he read widely in current philosophical literature. The key to all this activity lay in several factors. He had a first rate constitution; he was a keen tennis player and golfer. He was business-like and prompt; he never wasted words and had no time for small talk. His memory was excellent. He could switch his mind from scholarship to business with astonishing ease; hence he was accessible at almost all times as Provost, undisturbed by interruptions. His temperament was equable. Above all he had an exacting conscience.

He married Miss Edith Ogden (who died in 1953) of Manchester in 1906, and they had four daughters.

May 6, 1971.

Dr. Ernst Roth, the noted music publisher, died at his home on July 17, 1971.

Roth was born in Prague on June 1, 1896. He started piano lessons at the age of five and from that time his interest in music was never interrupted. His advanced educational studies at Prague University included music, philosophy and law, and after serving in the First World War on the Eastern Front he took his doctorate in law at Prague University in March 1921. He continued his musical studies under Guido Adler at the University of Vienna and in 1922 began his long career in music publishing with the Wiener Philharmonischer Verlag.

In 1928 he joined the publishing house of Universal Edition, Vienna, and during this time came into close contact with the leading figures in European music, such as Schoenberg, Berg, Webern, Bartók and Kodály*; especially close was his friendship with Richard Strauss which lasted until the latter's death and continued thereafter towards his family. At the time of the Anschluss Roth was invited by Ralph Hawkes to join the publishing house of Boosey & Hawkes in London, and from that moment began an association that was to build the fortunes of that house.

At the time of his death he was chairman of the board of the music publishing company.

Roth dedicated throughout his life his talents, which included a prodigious memory, fluency in most of the European languages, a profound musical knowledge as well as his legal expertise, to the service of music and of composers, to so many of whom he acted as adviser and "father confessor". His work as a translator alone would have sufficed for one man's life's work, but on the practical side a further achievement was his work as architect, together with his colleagues Dr. George Straschnov and René Domanges, of the whole system of standard contracts with the European broadcasting stations, which in an ever-expanding medium enabled publishers to look after the interests of their composers.

He published several books—among them *A Tale of Three Cities* (1971) and *The Business of Music* (1969).

Finally, Roth should be remembered as the close friend and adviser of Igor Stravinsky who died in April. A touching inscription on the back of a photograph of the composer in Roth's house enjoins him to "promise not to leave until I am going away". The promise was kept.

July 21, 1971.

Sir Leslie Rowan, K.C.B., C.V.O., who died on April 29, 1972 at the age of 64, was an outstanding administrator, who after a brilliant career in the Civil Service retired early to go into industry as a director of Vickers Ltd., of which he later became chairman.

He will be remembered by all who knew him as a man with remarkable gifts of personality and leadership who brought to his work qualities of deep conviction and integrity, as well as understanding and concern for the welfare of his staff. From 1971 he was chairman of the British Council.

Thomas Leslie Rowan was born on February 22, 1908, the son of the Rev. Thomas Rowan of Dromore, co. Sligo. Perhaps the influence of heredity can be seen in some of the qualities that distinguished him most, his gift of fluent and forceful expression, the depth and firmness of his convictions, his loyalty to the institutions which he served.

His early years were spent in British India where his father was working at the time. (Perhaps this left its mark, too.) He was afterwards educated at Tonbridge and at Cambridge where he was captain of the hockey team in 1929 and 1930. He captained England in 1937, 1938, and 1947.

As a young civil servant in the Colonial Office he quickly made his mark, and was transferred to the Treasury, where he soon became Assistant Private Secretary to the Chancellor. This was a role in which he excelled and, when a few years later he became one of Churchill's* secretaries, it was not long before he took over the position of Principal Private Secretary, subsequently serving Clement Attlee* in the same position. His service with Churchill was the beginning of a close friendship which continued in later years. And it was while crossing the Atlantic with him in the Duke of York that he met the charming member of the W.R.N.S. who later became his wife.

In 1947, after six years at Number Ten, Rowan was promoted at one step to the rank of Permanent Secretary, becoming head of the newly formed Office of the Minister for Economic Affairs, Sir Stafford Cripps; and when later that year Sir Stafford became Chancellor of the Exchequer Rowan went back with him to the Treasury as a Second Secretary.

He was particularly concerned with the international work of trade and payments negotiations and European economic cooperation, which was placed under the leadership of a special section of the Treasury. In this work, too, Rowan showed outstanding ability and won the trust both of his own Minister and of other departments in Whitehall. But the demands which it made on him, coming on top of the stress of the war years, affected his health and for a time this was something of a handicap to him. He showed it very little and, when in 1949 it was decided to appoint a senior official as Economic Minister to

the Embassy in Washington, to strengthen the liaison in economic affairs between the British and United States Governments, Rowan was chosen for the post. He served there for two years with remarkable success, much helped by his wife, and they both left behind many friends.

He returned, in 1951, to the Treasury as head of the Overseas Finance Division, where he served till his retirement in 1958. These were years of constant difficulty in economic affairs, in which the balance of payments was under continuous strain, accentuated by the international disputes first over Abadan, then over Suez. In these troubles Rowan's advice was always robust and determined on the side of what he felt to be the justified defence of British interests, and this led sometimes to controversy with other departments. A subject of even more intense controversy was the plan for restoring sterling convertibility at a floating exchange rate, the so-called Robot plan, worked out by the Treasury and the Bank of England in 1952. This, as is well known, led to deep divisions of opinion not only in Whitehall but within the Treasury itself. In this and other disputes over policy Rowan never shirked difficulties and was always completely honest and courageous in stating his point of view. There were times when these qualities exercised a critical influence in leading to the right decisions.

By 1958, however, he was perhaps ready for a change and was glad to accept the offer of Lord Knollys* to join the board of Vickers as Finance Director. At Vickers his progress was steady. He became first managing director, then deputy chairman, and finally chairman. The operations of this great company must have posed problems just as obstinate and difficult as those with which he had grappled in the Treasury. But he appeared to thrive on it and his health became noticeably stronger as the years passed.

He combined with his main task many subsidiary roles. He sat on the boards of a number of companies concerned with banking and insurance, and exercised his talents for organization in the formative years of the Overseas Development Institute. He was the moving spirit in a number of clubs and dining groups. To all of these varied institutions he gave the same unstinted service. In private life he showed himself a loyal and constant friend.

He is survived by his wife, Catherine Patricia, daughter of Brigadier R. H. A. D. Love, two sons and two daughters.

May 1, 1972,

Harry Roy, one of the best-known and most popular of British band-leaders of the 1930s, died at his home in London on February 1, 1971. He was 69.

He was one of the great characters in the heyday of the dance bands, a born showman who got the very most out of any number his band played. A highly extrovert feeling characterized the band's performances; there was never a dull moment from the playing of "Bugle Call Rag"—Roy's signature tune—right up to the last number.

Harry Roy was born in North London. In their teens he and his brother Sid were strongly attracted to the music of the Dixieland band, which was causing a sensation.

They practised hard, with Harry on the soprano saxophone and Sid on the piano; four other instrumentalists were booked and Sid Roy's Lyricals were in business.

They played at Rector's Club and the Hammersmith Palais de Danse and soon built up a large following. In 1924, with Sid still in charge, but with the irrepressible Harry coming more and more to the fore as instrumentalist/performer, they opened at the Café de Paris. They were to stay there for three years, and then toured as a variety attraction in South Africa, Australia and Germany.

After the disbandment of the Lyricals Harry set up on his own account with a modest group at the Bat Club, known as the Bat Club Boys; their pianist was Ivor Moreton.

The emergence of Harry Roy as a big band leader dates from the opening of the Leicester Square Theatre, London. "Big pictures" were screened and, as an added draw, a spectacular band act was staged. Later leading his band on the clarinet, Roy played at the Café Anglais and the May Fair Hotel. He became a regular broadcaster.

In 1935 he married Elizabeth, daughter of Sir Charles Vyner Brooke*, Rajah of Sarawak. For his bride he wrote "Sarawaki", which became a hit. They had two children and were divorced in 1947. He remarried a year later.

He retired as a night-club band leader about 1963, but had recently been leading a Dixieland band in Brighton.

February 2, 1971.

Professor James Alexander Roy, teacher, biographer and Professor of English in Queen's University, Kingston, Ontario, from 1920 to 1950, died on November 26, 1973.

He was one of those innumerable adventurous Scots who gave the best part of their lives to Canada. The son of the Rev. W. F. Roy, a Presbyterian minister, he was born in Kirriemuir, Angus, in 1884. He graduated from Edinburgh University in 1906 with first-class honours, and for the next two years was a Lector in English at Giessen.

Thence he returned to Scotland to teach English language and literature at the University of St. Andrews.

The outbreak of war in August 1914 found him in Heidelberg, and in immediate

danger of arrest. By posing as a Cook's agent, he managed to attach himself to a party of Americans, secure their passports (in the days when photographs were not obligatory) and pass through the lines near Liège as an American citizen. From April 1916 to January 1919 he served as Intelligence Officer in France, for a time with the 51st Highland Division, and through the 1917 follies of attrition with the 42nd Lancashire Division. He was twice wounded and three times mentioned in dispatches.

As a junior member of the Inter-Allied Commission of Control set up in Teschen, Silesia, he took out the first trainload of Red Cross supplies to Prague, and his experiences which reflected the chaos and tragedy of Central Europe at the end of the war have been recounted vividly and sensitively in *Pole and Czech in Silesia,* published in 1921. In 1920 he accepted an appointment as assistant professor of English in Queen's University, Kingston, Ontario, where he remained until retirement in 1950, and where the bulk of his writing was accomplished.

Although his considerable creative gifts showed themselves in poetry, fiction and criticism, Roy's most important work was in biography. In 1914 he wrote his first book, a thorough-going study of *Cowper and his Poetry.* Twenty years later, *Joseph Howe,* the study of a great Nova Scotian father of Confederation, went far towards solving the riddle of Howe's enigmatic personality. On the life of his friend, *James Matthew Barrie: An Appreciation* (1937), which appeared almost at the moment of Barrie's death, he was at his best. With a Scottish background that constantly evoked memories and emotions of moors and burns and craggy hills, Roy proved himself a master in the art of blending poetry, fact and fantasy to serve his creative purposes. The elusive, nostalgic quality of his writing is especially apparent in *The Scot and Canada* and *The Heart is Highland,* both of which were published in 1947. His farewell salute to Canada on his retirement to Edinburgh took shape in the form of a history of *Kingston: The King's Town* (1952), a labour of love based on many years of research.

Roy was a Celt of incredible energy, warm, generous, often impulsive in his judgments of men and events, but a disciplined and learned romantic when he put pen to paper.

He was also a great teacher, one whose memory will be cherished by hundreds of Queen's students who loved him for his humanity, his liveliness, his freedom from all cant and pomposity, and his disarming eccentricities.

In 1951 he married Margaret Gordon Fleming, of London, whom he had known since his early days in St. Andrews. Mrs. Roy died in June.

November 29, 1973.

Rulers of Fujaira, Zanzibar, etc.—See names of those countries.

John Russell, 3rd Baron Ampthill—See **Ampthill.**

Senator Richard Brevard Russell, a commanding figure in the United States Senate for nearly 40 years, died on January 21, 1971. He was 73.

He was one of the last exemplars of the old world school of southern gentlemen. As chairman of the Senate Armed Services Committee and a close friend of President Johnson, he exerted much influence on the prosecution of the Vietnam conflict. "Hawk" he certainly was, but he came to modify his position to the extent of urging that American forces should be withdrawn at once if the South Vietnamese did not want them. He did not believe in the so-called "domino theory"; withdrawal, in his opinion, would not result in most of Asia falling to the Chinese communists. He was a member of the Warren Commission, which investigated the assassination of President Kennedy*.

Russell, the senior senator from Georgia, was at the height of his powers as a parliamentarian of exceptional skill and subtlety in leading the southern Democrats against civil rights legislation for Negro advancement. He knew the Senate rules backwards, and soon made himself the master tactician of the filibuster, for which he marshalled his forces with the precision of a field commander. He led a dozen memorable battles in the Senate before the eruption of mob violence in the city streets turned such feats of endurance into academic exercises. In 1935 he and his colleagues spent 30 days, with adjournments, in talking an anti-lynching Bill to death; and in 1960, sitting round the clock, they held the Senate floor for over five days to surpass a 45-year record for an unbroken session.

A courtly champion of the southern way of life, Russell was the antithesis of the white supremacist. He liked and admired Negroes, but like most of his generation took his stand on the "separate but equal" doctrine of civil rights. His style and wide understanding earned the respect of both Democrats and Republicans, and he was often chosen to undertake missions requiring tact and diplomacy. As chairman of the joint committee that investigated the dismissal of General Douglas MacArthur* during the Korean War, he won the esteem of the whole country for his fairness and diligence.

No doubt the poverty of Georgia caused Russell to take a jaundiced view of all foreign aid, though he was a strong supporter of his country's efforts to promote international cooperation. As leader of a senatorial group visiting war theatres, he stung British opinion in 1943 by remarking that the United States must keep a close check on the "expensive tools of war we are dealing out". Although he refuted any anti-British animus, he later voted against the post-war loan to Britain, apparently preferring to see the British Isles admitted to the American Union as four separate states.

Given his strong position in the "inner club", the White House might not have been beyond his attainments had he come from a state less compromised on the civil rights issue than Georgia. He stood against President Truman's nomination in 1948 and again ran as the South's "favourite son" at the Democratic convention of 1952, but Georgia's racial policies were more than the party could stomach.

Russell, a bachelor, was brought up with six brothers and six sisters, the family of a struggling lawyer who became chief justice of the Georgia Supreme Court. His ancestors were landowners in revolutionary times, but the destruction of his grandfather's cotton mills during the war between the States left the family impoverished.

Born in 1897, he, too, practised law after taking his degree at Georgia University only to show an early bent for politics. He was elected to the State Assembly in his early twenties, and was never to lose an election throughout his long career. The inordinate capacity for taking pains that marked his later career found him serving as Speaker of the state legislature for four years from 1927 before he became the youngest Governor ever elected in Georgia. He went to Washington as the youngest member of the Senate two years later.

January 22, 1971.

Dame Margaret Rutherford, D.B.E., (Mrs. Stringer Davis), the actress, died on May 22, 1972 aged 80, having, in the words of one of her characters in a play by Jean Anouilh, survived the birth of the airplane, the death of the corset, short hair and two world wars.

Eccentric middle-aged ladies were her speciality. That they were unconscious of their eccentricity, that they combined it with shrewdness and an air of authority, and that they liked the world and felt at home there, were among the reasons why a large public found them irresistible.

She made a late beginning and a slow one. Born at Balham on May 11, 1892, and educated at Wimbledon and Seaford, she qualified as a Licentiate of the Royal Academy of Music, but did nothing to further her wish to act professionally till, at the age of 33, she inherited a small income from an aunt. A letter of introduction from John Drinkwater then led to her joining the Old Vic Company as a student player in 1925. She actually played Juliet's mother to the nurse of Edith Evans, but at the end of the season she had to go back to teaching at Wimbledon, and two

more years passed before her engagement by Nigel Playfair as an understudy at the Lyric, Hammersmith, enabled her to start afresh.

From Hammersmith she went to Croydon, to Epsom, and to the old Oxford Playhouse, working in weekly repertory, and at Oxford she made the acquaintance of Tyrone Guthrie. Under his direction, as a member of a cast headed by Marie Tempest, Margaret Rutherford caught the eye of the critics—incidentally incurring and surviving the professional jealousy of Miss Tempest—as a village spinster in a comedy by Robert Morley. Next year she made her first two films, one of them for Carol Reed. Two parts she played in the theatre in productions by John Gielgud in 1938 and 1939, Miss Bijou Furse, the surreptitious punter in *Spring Meeting*, and Miss Prism in *The Importance of Being Earnest*, established her in comedy and farce as a star performer.

The baleful housekeeper in *Rebecca* showed an entirely different side of her, but the occasion of a triumph in her special comic line was provided by Mme. Arcati, the medium, in Noël Coward's *Blithe Spirit:* "you have taken up my pen and written it yourself", said the author. On this performance, she was also congratulated by members of Mme. Arcati's profession, because she had avoided guying it. At later stages of the war she was seen in company with Ivor Novello on a tour of France and Belgium, and in London in *Alice in Wonderland*, alternating as the White Queen with Sybil Thorndike.

After supporting Novello in his stage musical *Perchance to Dream*, she took over Lady Bracknell from Edith Evans when the Gielgud company played Wilde's farce in New York in 1947. On her return there was unqualified praise for her headmistress in a new farce, *The Happiest Days of Your Life*, and for her châtelaine in Anouilh's *Ring Round the Moon*, but in the Gielgud revival of *The Way of the World* she seemed inhibited, possibly by the heartlessness of Congreve's characterization. Nevertheless she again played the part in John Clements's revival in 1956.

Meanwhile, she had continued to make films in England, but her roles, when they were not old friends from the theatrical past like Mme. Arcati and Miss Prism, were either too short or too obviously contrived to offer scope. In 1962, however, film audiences in the United States began to take her measure on seeing her amateur detective, Miss Marple, in an adaptation of a novel by Agatha Christie, renamed *Murder She Said*, and presented by M.G.M. (She was to play Miss Marple again in at least two other "murder" films). By then she had completed a long tour of Australia in Anouilh's *Time Remembered;* had starred on Broadway in a short-lived English comedy; and at home had appeared "in the round" in a programme of distinguished one-act plays, and at the Haymarket under Gielgud's direction as Mrs. Candour in *The*

School for Scandal. In 1963 she was chosen by the Academy of Motion Picture Arts and Sciences as the best supporting actress of the year for her support of the Burtons in Anthony Asquith's* *The V.I.Ps.*

Margaret Rutherford was married in 1945 to Mr. Stringer Davis, the actor. They had met as fellow-members of the company at the Oxford Playhouse in 1930, and they often acted together in the theatre and in films after their marriage. She never turned her back on the position to which the public had elected her, that of its favourite feminine exponent of robust eccentricity, but she once said that, if she could choose her work, it would be to help people to understand the beauty of words; and her poetry recitals for the Apollo Society and in association with Malcolm Troup, the pianist, in Norway and elsewhere were important to her.

May 23, 1972.

Patrick Ryan, C.B.E., an Assistant Editor of *The Times* from 1948 to 1965 and Literary Editor until 1968, died on July 1, 1972 in hospital. He was 72.

He was an outstanding journalist, a man of great courage and wide knowledge, a lifelong student of history and of current affairs, an acute commentator, and a literary critic with wide ranging sympathies. His resources were such that he could write readily on almost anything at any time. He was helped in this by an ability to get quickly to the nub of an argument.

Alfred Patrick Ryan was born at St. Leonards on March 3, 1900, the son of Frederick Ryan, of the Eastern Telegraph Company. He was educated at Whitgift School, Croydon, and enlisted in September 1918, and was made a second lieutenant in the Royal Field Artillery. He went up to Balliol College, Oxford, in 1919. He was a Brackenbury Scholar and took a first in Modern History.

From the beginning his inclination was to be a journalist. He first joined the editorial staff of the *Manchester Guardian* in 1922 and from there went to the *Daily Telegraph*. In 1926 he married Rachel Montague, daughter of C. E. Montague, the well-known author and critic on the *Manchester Guardian*. It was a particularly happy marriage, for rarely could two people have been more in tune with each other and shared more exactly the same interests. They had one daughter.

In 1926 the newly emerging profession of promotion and publicity attracted him and he joined the secretariat of the Empire Marketing Board. In 1931 he was appointed Publicity Manager of the Gas, Light & Coke Co, and was the originator of the advertising symbol "Mr. Therm", which became nationally famous and which was discontinued only in 1964. He was a member of the General Post Office Publicity Committee.

It was still in the field of publicity that in 1936 he joined the B.B.C. as Assistant Controller, Public Relations (Sir Stephen Tallents, formerly of the Empire Marketing Board, being Controller.)

In 1939-40 he was briefly a squadron leader in the Royal Air Force Volunteer Reserve and a war correspondent. In May 1940 he returned to the B.B.C. as Controller (Home). Difficulties arose between the B.B.C. and the Government in those early days of the war, and in March 1941 Ryan was seconded to the Ministry of Information to be "Adviser to the B.B.C. on Home Affairs". His task was to put the Government's point of view to the B.B.C. on domestic matters in the same way as Mr. (later Sir Ivone) Kirkpatrick* was putting the Foreign Office's point of view to the corporation.

His position was a manifestly absurd one, in that he was a member of the corporation's staff set to advise his superiors in the corporation. Within six months, following the setting up of the Political Warfare Executive, the internal arrangements of the corporation, particularly in the Overseas Division, were reorganized; Kirkpatrick joined the corporation as Controller of the section dealing with enemy-occupied countries, and Ryan returned as Controller for the coordination of news services in English. He also became B.B.C. adviser on home policy affecting its programmes.

In effect this move meant that Ryan returned to his original journalistic career and he never left it for the rest of his life. In 1942 he was appointed Controller (News) of the B.B.C., a post he held—in 1946 there was a mere change of title to Editor (News)—until he left the corporation in October 1947.

In those five years he completely reorganized the B.B.C.'s news services. He gave the bulletins a professionalism, an authority, and an independence they had hitherto lacked. He gathered round him particularly in the later years, a staff of journalists of outstanding calibre. He gave to this team drive and judgment. In the earlier days of the war the authority of the B.B.C.'s news bulletins had largely derived from the knowledge that they were official. In Ryan's later years with the corporation, under a director-general who was himself a journalist, he gave the bulletins an authority of their own; streamlining them and tightening them but, at the same time, giving them an individuality that got away from Civil Service jargon and journalese. He was made a C.B.E. in 1946.

The task of being responsible for all the B.B.C.'s home news bulletins was an exacting one and at times an exciting one. It caused Ryan to travel to many parts of the world. From his point of view, however, it had one drawback. There was no scope in it for writing—and he was a born writer.

It was this attraction of being able to write again which led him to join *The Times* in October 1947. He had done some occasional work for the paper and particularly for *The Times Literary Supplement* before he became a member of the staff. At first he was employed as a special writer.

On July 1, 1948 he became an Assistant Editor. His course thereafter was set. His versatility has already been noted; he could turn his hand equally readily to a first or a fourth leader. He loved reporting. At the same time he specialized in a small number of subjects. One of the most notable of them was South African affairs. He visited the Union many times during his life; he knew its history in great detail and most of the contemporary political figures there. While he was implacably opposed to apartheid, the Nationalists recognized him as one of the fairest of their critics, and in the Press Commission Report published in 1964 he was singled out for qualified approval. Another of his specialities was Ireland. He paid many visits to North and South, knew everybody in both parts—politicians, scholars, clergy and genial characters of all sorts and in all professions. They trusted his judgment as much as he enjoyed their company.

Another of his special fields was English political history from 1850 to 1914. He knew his way among all the memoirs, political speeches, writings, and byways of the period. In 1956 he wrote a short book *Mutiny at the Curragh* which was a useful contribution to history (three years earlier he had published a short study of *Lord Northcliffe*). He was never happier than when delving through the mid-nineteenth century files of *The Times*, checking up this or that fact against the newest historian's "revelations", uncovering some curiosity or oddity of political history. He was also a ready speaker on these subjects, and anyone who heard him give a lecture at the National Portrait Gallery, for instance, could not help being impressed. He was a keen student of country life and sports, and had an enthusiasm for cricket. He was also a keen beagler and, until the last year or so, a tireless walker.

His third enthusiasm was for literature generally. When the post-war Books Page of *The Times* was started in 1955 he was put in charge of it. To this task also he brought judgment and knowledge. He not only knew instinctively which books were likely to be important and which were merely newsworthy, he also had a care for the books that *ought* to be written, discreetly making this or that suggestion to publishers and authors. This responsibility he continued to exercise as Literary Editor after he had ceased to be an assistant editor in 1965.

As a colleague Ryan was the easiest of men to work with. He liked to go at his own pace, would sometimes be missing for hours during the day and then be found in his office well after midnight on some weekend when he was supposed to be off. He had a ready sense of humour and was a clubable man (he belonged to the Garrick, the Beetsteak, and the United University). Wherever he was, he was eager to engage in discussion or speculation or gossip. He was not an introverted man; at the same time there can rarely have been such an outgoing man who was less of an extrovert. He was unobtrusively kind and encouraging to younger colleagues and warmed many a heart by a favourable comment on a piece of work; but he was also frank and if he thought a report or a leader inadequate said so at once.

Humbug and sloppy writing he could spot a mile off, and his zest in exposing them was only equalled by his pleasure in sharing the process of exposure with colleagues who, he flatteringly assumed, were as right-minded and knowledgeable as himself.

July 3, 1972.

Nikolai Rytjkov, the Russian actor who defected to the West in the mid-1960s, died in London on September 1, 1973 at the age of 60.

Educated at the A. Lunacharsky Academy of Dramatic Art, he was a leading actor at the Lenin-Komsomol Theatre in Moscow. At the age of 24 he was arrested during the 1938 purge because of his activities in connexion with Esperanto. He was sent to Siberia, where he was allowed to work in the theatres of Magadan and Norilsk.

He was released 18 years later on being officially declared innocent of all crime. In the years that followed he starred in the Moscow theatre, films, radio and television, acting the part of Lenin.

Rytjkov also acted in Esperanto. He presented his first important recital in the language during the World Esperanto Congress in Sophia in 1963. Two years later he accepted an invitation to a European Esperanto congress in Vienna, where he defected. He later gave recitals throughout Western Europe. In London in 1971 he performed at the Festival Hall.

In 1967 he played Lenin in a West German television film, *Civil War in Russia*. In June 1973 he played the part of Lenin in the play *Magnificence* at the Royal Court Theatre.

In recent years he was, however, best known for his recitals of Solzhenitsyn in both Esperanto and Russian. In the B.B.C. Overseas Service, where he was an announcer, actor and language supervisor in the Russian section, he regularly read excerpts from *First Circle* and *Cancer Ward*, as well as from Solzhenitsyn's Nobel Prize speech. He also broadcast some programmes in Esperanto directed at Eastern Europe.

At the time of death he was producing an Esperanto radio course.

September 5, 1973.

S

Louis Saillant, general secretary of the communist-dominated World Federation of Trade Unions from 1945 to 1969, died in Paris on October 28, 1974 at the age of 63.

He was born on November 27, 1910, in Valence, France. Shortly before the Second World War, Saillant, then an official of the Woodworkers' Union and an anticommunist, came to the notice of Leon Jouhaux, the veteran leader of the French Confédération Génerale du Travail. The ageing Jouhaux secured a place on the C.G.T. administrative committee for him. When Jouhaux and others of the older generation were in prison or otherwise inactive during the war, responsibility for leading the clandestine C.G.T. fell on a group of young men, including Saillant. While in the resistance movement, he transferred his allegiance to the communists.

An arrangement between the late Sidney Hillman, of the American Congress of Industrial Organizations and Vassili Kuznetsov, of the Soviet trade unions, made Saillant general secretary of the W.F.T.U. at its inaugural conference in Paris in September 1945. The British Trades Union Congress and some other west European trade union centres would have preferred to see Walter Schevenels, Belgian-born anticommunist general secretary of the old International Federation of Trade Unions, in the new post but they could not prevail against the powerful Americans and Russians.

When the British and others, led by Arthur Deakin, walked out of the W.F.T.U. at an executive board meeting in Paris in January 1949 because it had become a Moscow agent, Saillant remained at his post. He took his headquarters to Vienna, where the Russians were still in occupation, when the W.F.T.U. was expelled from Paris by the French Government. Later the W.F.T.U. was ordered by the Austrian Government—after the Russians had left—to leave Vienna. This time Saillant moved the headquarters behind the iron curtain—to Prague. He often made approaches to the anti-communist International Confederation of Free Trade Unions, established after the W.F.T.U. split, for a "united front"; but the suspicious "once-bitten, twice-shy" democratic trade unionists held coldly aloof. Left-wing attempts to obtain support for the W.F.T.U. overtures at the annual British Trades Union Congress were always heavily defeated.

It is believed that Saillant was never actually a member of the Communist Party but he was one of its most valuable fellow travellers in the world trade union field. It was fortuitous circumstances which brought him to a position of international reputation as a communist "front man".

He painstakingly operated Moscow policy from his lucrative post, controlling agents in all parts of the world, including Britain. His chief function seemed to be to arouse industrial strife in the western democracies and in the emerging countries of Africa and Asia, for whose workers he demanded better pay and conditions than obtained behind the iron curtain.

At the W.F.T.U. conference at Leipzig in December 1962, Saillant urged that plans should be discussed for joint action against the European Community. He was made honorary president of the W.F.T.U. in 1969 and he then became secretary of the C.G.T.

October 30, 1974.

F. E. N. St. Barbe, who died on July 2, 1975 aged 82, was the last of the founder directors of the de Havilland Aircraft Co. Ltd., from whose board he retired on March 31, 1961.

He was the youngest of the five men—of whom Sir Geoffrey de Havilland*, F. T. Hearle*, C. C. Walker* and W. E. Nixon were the others—who formed the company in 1920 and who directed its activities right through to the postwar years.

Francis St. Barbe devoted his career to selling aircraft. He conducted the sales of de Havilland products for more than a quarter of a century and established the world-wide aircraft marketing organization which now serves Hawker Siddeley Aviation. In his time he was internationally acknowledged the industry's best salesman.

Born in 1892 and educated at Felsted, he joined George Holt Thomas's firm, Aircraft Manufacturing Co. Ltd., in 1912. When "Mr. de Havilland" went to the company as chief designer in May 1914 St. Barbe was already a useful young member of the business office. When the de Havilland company was formed in 1920 he had become the obvious choice as business manager.

It was the Moth that gave St. Barbe his first chance to sell aeroplanes in numbers. He travelled extensively abroad to negotiate sales, to appoint agents and to establish after-sales service. He arranged the formation of the Australian company in 1927, the Canadian company in 1928, the Indian branch in 1929, the South African company in 1930, the New Zealand company in 1939, and the American company in 1953.

By frequent world travel he learnt his market countries well, and likewise by experience he came to eye aircraft—or their drawings—with the shrewdness of a horse dealer.

In later years, with decentralization, St. Barbe's responsibilities broadened and he devoted more time to the coordination of marketing policies of the home and overseas companies. He was a director of nearly all of these for long periods, and was deputy chairman of de Havilland Holdings Ltd., the parent company formed at the end of 1955. He served on the council and the management committee of the Society of British Aerospace Companies and as chairman of the sales and export committee for many years.

July 10, 1975.

Michel Jacques Saint-Denis, who died on July 31, 1971 at the age of 73, had exercised influence upon the British theatre ever since 1931, when a French company under his direction first visited England. Residing in London, he there was responsible for several productions and initiated two drama schools, in the years immediately preceding and following the Second World War. The value of his example and of his interest in their own work has more recently been acknowledged by some of our most enterprising producers and players. From 1961 he shared the direction of the Royal Shakespeare Company with Peter Hall and Peter Brook, and in 1966 became consultant director.

He himself was trained at the Théâtre du Vieux Colombier in Paris, whose founder, Jacques Copeau, is now regarded as having been the great pioneer of twentieth-century play-production in France—as André Barsacq has it, all contemporary French directors are Copeau's children or grandchildren. Saint-Denis was, literally, Copeau's nephew. Born at Beauvais on September 13, 1897, the son of Charles Saint-Denis and of Copeau's sister Marguerite, he joined his uncle in 1919 and worked with him for the next 10 years; as (in turn) private secretary, actor and assistant producer at the Vieux Colombier, later in the village of Pernand-Vergelesses in Burgundy, where "Les Copeaux", as the company was called by the peasants, set up a theatre-workshop on leaving Paris. Saint-Denis wrote, in collaboration with Jean Villard ("Gilles"), a couple of plays for it, and on its dissolution became the leader of a succession-group which, taking the name of La Compagnie des Quinze, reopened the Vieux Colombier with André Obey's *Noë* in 1931.

After eight plays, including four more by Obey, had been produced, a crisis arose, and Saint-Denis considered starting afresh at Beaumanoir near Aix-en-Provence. He hoped to raise the funds for this project in London, since the Quinze had been enthusiastically acclaimed by the critics and the theatrical profession of Britain on the occasions of their three visits; but it was now suggested to him by John Gielgud, Sir Bronson Albery and Tyrone Guthrie that he should make his fresh start in England, working with British actors, and found a drama school in London. Saint-Denis agreed to this. In 1935 he directed John Gielgud in *Noah* at the New Theatre, and with the assistance of George Devine and Marius Goring from the same company, he established the London Theatre Studio at Islington, which remained open until the beginning of the Second World War.

In addition to conducting this school, he

directed two plays—*The Witch of Edmonton* and, with Laurence Olivier in the chief part, *Macbeth*—at the Old Vic; and one of the plays, *The Three Sisters*, presented by John Gielgud during a season at the Queen's. Saint-Denis was allowed as much as seven weeks for his rehearsals of Chekhov and made such brilliant use of them—the production probably received higher praise for its style and team-work than anything else seen in London between the wars—that plans were laid for following it up with a series of plays to be performed under his direction by a permanent company including Peggy Ashcroft, Michael Redgrave and other members of John Gielgud's old company at the Queen's. This new venture did not thrive. The production of *The White Guard*, coming on top of the Munich Conference of September 1938, was untimely; the failure of *Twelfth Night* brought the season at the Phoenix to an abrupt end; and *The Cherry Orchard*, which went into rehearsal in 1939, was abandoned when war became imminent.

Saint-Denis was then mobilized. He served in France as a liaison officer, got out through Dunkirk with the B.E.F. and was demobilized in London in June 1940.

At the request of the B.B.C. he now organized a group for the giving of daily broadcasts to France, and on June 14, 1940 this service, *Les Français Parlent Aux Français*, was inaugurated. A few months later, on October 21, he had the experience of "directing" Sir Winston Churchill* in his first broadcast in French to France, and of sitting on the Prime Minister's knee while announcing him at the microphone. "We have made history", said Sir Winston when it was over.

Saint-Denis often broadcast under the pseudonym Jacques Duchesne in his programmes of news-commentary, and was appointed C.B.E. (Hon.), Chevalier de la Légion d'Honneur and Chevalier de l'Ordre de Léopold in recognition of his services.

In 1945 the Old Vic Theatre Centre was formed with Saint-Denis as its general director and as a director of the Old Vic School. That same year he produced the Old Vic Company headed by Laurence Olivier and Ralph Richardson in *Oedipus Rex*, and he attached such importance to this new field of activity that when the post of Administrator of the Comédie Française was offered to him, he refused it.

In 1951, however, he resigned from the Old Vic together with his two chief associates, Glen Byam Shaw and George Devine, and in 1952 Saint-Denis went back to France to take over the duties of head of the Centre Dramatique de l'Est, his intention being to train a company for the regular playing of "one-night stands" in 52 towns of the Eastern region.

This plan was carried out; a theatre was built at Strasbourg to the designs of Pierre Sonrel, who helped Saint-Denis to reconstruct the stage and auditorium of the Old Vic; but the latter was again a freelance by the end of 1957. He turned his attention

for a year to the drama in Canada, and to the theatrical sides of the Julliard School of Music and of the projected Lincoln Centre for the Performing Arts in New York. Then, in April 1959, the French Government announced his appointment as Inspecteur des Spectacles. A special responsibility for the Comédie Française was joined to this, but Saint-Denis was only twice invited to set foot in it between the date of his assuming office and January 1960, when he was the principal speaker on the contemporary theatre in Europe and America at a producers' seminar organized by the British Drama League in London.

His lectures there were followed by his first production in England for nine years, that of the Stravinsky-Cocteau* opera-oratorio *Oedipus Rex* at Sadler's Wells. He produced *The Cherry Orchard* at the Aldwych in 1965 and at the same theatre *Squire Puntila and his Servant Matti*. He was made an honorary D.Litt. of Birmingham University in 1962.

Saint-Denis was twice married.

August 2, 1971.

Louis Stephen St. Laurent, P.C., Q.C., LL.D., one of Canada's most distinguished Liberal Prime Ministers, died in Quebec City on July 25, 1973 at the age of 91.

St. Laurent looked every inch the Prime Minister with his white hair and trim white moustache, speaking with quiet authority in Parliament and with sparkling wit and vigour on the public platforms. He was capable of momentary flashes of fire and real anger, a legacy of his Irish-French ancestry. One well remembers him during the great debate on the Suez issue in late 1956 when, obviously infuriated by the Anglo-French action in Egypt, he spoke witheringly of the "supermen of Europe". Yet he remained strangely silent, almost embarrassed by the famous pipe-line furore in Parliament but a few months earlier. Indeed, at the end of the Liberal regime in the summer of 1957 after 22 years of continuous office, St. Laurent, on whom Mackenzie King himself had placed the hand of approving successorship, had no further taste for the cut and thrust of parliamentary debate.

One could not say he was, like Diefenbaker, a "House of Commons man". He had never had any real experience in the hard school of the Opposition benches. Soon after Diefenbaker took office he slipped out of Ottawa one summer evening without any fanfare and returned to his favourite Quebec City. There was only a brief note in the deserted Parliamentary Press Gallery to say that he had gone. He had retired to private life and the practice of law.

In a sense the St. Laurent regime, that had lasted from November 1948 until June 1957, was the end of an era in Canadian politics. After he had given his blessing to

Lester Pearson to carry on in his place as leader of the Liberal Party, there was much political turmoil in the country, with four general elections in eight years. It was perhaps inevitable, as Quebec began finding her own identity and the emphasis on regionalism became more pronounced.

It would not be true to say that St. Laurent did not savour political life; although he may not have liked the House of Commons very much in his latter days there, he enjoyed the atmosphere on the hustings or the role of the elder statesman at party conventions at whose feet the younger men came to sit and seek advice. He practised law almost up to the end and kept a finger very much on the pulse of the nation. It might be said of him, as Mackenzie King said of himself in 1948 almost at the end of his stewardship of the nation, "If I cease to lead the party, I shall never cease to have the party's interests near to my heart".

The son of a French-Canadian father, J. B. Moise St. Laurent, and an Irish-Canadian mother, Mary Broderick, St. Laurent once said that when he was a child he thought men spoke French and women English. He was completely bilingual. He was born at Compton, Quebec, on February 1, 1882, and, when a boy, would drive out of the town with a wagon, helping with deliveries from the family shop. He was accustomed to the easy conversation of those who visited the store and took time to chat; when he became Liberal leader and campaigned across Canada in later years, this ability to be at home with small groups, as well as large audiences, was a factor in his popularity.

At St. Charles College, Sherbrooke, and later at Laval University, Quebec City, he proved a diligent student, making friends who remained in his circle all his life. He settled down to the practice of law in his home province, where his ancestors had come from France hundreds of years before.

He became an authority on constitutional law and crossed the Atlantic on many occasions to appear before the Privy Council as the last court of appeal. He always spoke of this body with the highest esteem, but when he became Prime Minister in 1948 one of his first acts was to set in motion legislation which, when passed, made the Supreme Court of Canada the final court. St. Laurent took the position that Canada as a nation had reached the stature where she should have complete control of her own affairs.

He was not active in politics as a younger man, but he was widely known for his court work and for his participation in the activities of the Canadian Bar Association which made him honorary life president in 1949.

In 1941 Mackenzie King, then Prime Minister, sought a successor to Ernest Lapointe, his chief lieutenant in Quebec, who had died after a strenuous campaign to persuade his province of the rightness of Canadian participation in the war.

St. Laurent was surprised when the Prime Minister offered him a Cabinet appointment, but after seeking the advice of friends he accepted, being sworn Minister of Justice and Attorney General for Canada on December 10, 1941.

He entered Parliament a political unknown, a man of 59, and in the growing tension of wartime debates he proved himself an invaluable aide to Mackenzie King. In 1944, the issue of compulsory military service abroad for Canadians divided the Cabinet, and Defence Minister Ralston, who wished for conscription to fill the ranks of Canadian units overseas, resigned. Later the Government decided to recommend that a certain number of conscripts should be sent overseas and was condemned by some Quebec members of Parliament with bitter memories of conscription being enforced in their province in the 1914-18 War. St. Laurent stood by the Cabinet majority and his support was a factor in ensuring that reinforcements required were obtained without racial divisions in Canada being accentuated.

Immediately after the war, as Minister of Justice, he was confronted with the delicate problem created when a cipher clerk fled the Soviet Embassy in Ottawa with documents which revealed an espionage ring in Canada. St. Laurent set up a Royal Commission to investigate and examine witnesses who had been arrested, and this was followed by trials resulting in several convictions.

He began to be spoken of as a prospective party leader in 1946 when he was sworn of the Privy Council of the United Kingdom. In the same year he was made Secretary of State for External Affairs, an office Mackenzie King had long retained for himself.

In 1948 Mackenzie King became ill when in London for a Commonwealth Prime Ministers' meeting, and St. Laurent flew to London to take his chief's place at the Downing Street sessions. Soon after his return from London the Prime Minister resigned and St. Laurent, already chosen as Liberal party leader, was appointed to the Cabinet command on November 15, 1948.

Seven months later, after an arduous campaign in which he visited every province, St. Laurent led his party to reelection and repeated this success in 1953.

During the next four years, not years of distinction for the Liberal Party, there were growing signs of arrogance, summed up perhaps in the attitude of C. D. Howe, who said in the weeks preceding the pipeline debate of 1956, "Who's to stop us?". Earlier Howe had tried to get some legislative amendments through the Commons that would have increased the powers of his sprawling empire in the Department of Trade, but a surprisingly vigilant opposition managed to stop him in his tracks in the nick of time and the amendments had to be withdrawn. St. Laurent had pulled the rug from under the feet of his powerful Trade Minister, and in return Howe insisted on his full support for the passage of the controversial pipeline Bill in the summer of 1956. What happened in the Commons on that "Black Friday" during those stormy scenes of debate did irreparable damage to the Liberals, who had been in power for 22 continuous years, and one suspects that by the time the debate ended St. Laurent had little further taste for parliamentary life. Even so, the Liberals were confident of victory in the general election of 1957; however, they underestimated the feeling of "time for a change" in the country, a change that brought Diefenbaker to power. St. Laurent, like Howe and some other Liberal Ministers, could not really stomach the idea of being in opposition, and so in September of that year he retired as party leader.

Looking back over the first five years of his stewardship, St. Laurent could point to a number of important decisions and changes of attitude on the domestic and the international scene. They included the recommendation that a Canadian should be Governor-General; and in 1952 Massey became the first native-born Canadian to take up residence at Rideau Hall. It was under St. Laurent's regime, too, that Newfoundland entered the confederation; while on the international front Canada became an active partner in Nato. Furthermore Ottawa undertook a military responsibility under United Nations auspices in the Korean conflict, supplying an infantry brigade that was part of the Commonwealth divisions in that theatre.

He was the recipient of many honorary degrees from Canadian, American and foreign universities. In 1955 he was presented with the Freedom of the City of London.

He married in 1908 Jeanne, daughter of P. F. Renault. She died in 1966. They had five children.

July 27, 1973.

Lord Salisbury, K.G., P.C., F.R.S., who died on February 23, 1972 at the age of 78, was a patrician whose place at the centre of affairs of state came to him partly by ability and partly by right—for the old social order still had some life in it during the greater part of his career. Political acumen, which is presumably bred in the bone of a Cecil, marked his leadership of an overwhelmingly Conservative House of Lords during the Labour governments of 1945-51, and his persistent endeavours to get the composition of the chamber reformed. Independence of mind and position caused him to resign office twice.

On the first occasion, when Anthony Eden resigned from the Foreign Office over his Prime Minister's parleys with Mussolini in 1938, general opinion retrospectively applauds his reasons. The same opinion looks less kindly on the reasons for his second resignation, over colonial policy in 1957. The immediate occasion was release from detention in the Seychelles of Archbishop Makarios before, in Lord Salisbury's opinion, he had done sufficient penance for Eoka terrorism. His disagreement with the Government was soon seen to extend to attitudes towards Africa generally.

Vulnerable on account of his lineage to depiction as an archaic reactionary, he was easily neutralized as a political force when his unfashionable opinions about Rhodesia and his ill-disguised contempt for some of the more up-to-date Conservative politicians threatened to embarrass his former colleagues. Instead of ending up in the safe anchorage of elder statesmanship he became known, according to the unaccommodating convention of British political description, as an extremist.

Salisbury's charm and courtesy clothed a will of steel. He stood in awe of no man. He was certainly no "yes man" in the Churchill* Government, still less in Harold Macmillan's. He affirmed his beliefs with a patrician serenity which sometimes was mistaken for arrogance. His persistence in pursuing a point could be disconcerting, indeed exasperating, to those peers whose flow of oratory he was moved to interrupt. But there was nothing pompous about "Bobbety", as his intimates affectionately knew him. He had no need to put on airs. He was the most equable of men except when high principles were at stake. Then passion could galvanize his slight frame and lift his light voice to icy disdain. More than once he became involved in sharp conflict with political associates as well as with opponents. His attack on Iain Macleod* in March 1961 brought stinging rebukes from Lord Hailsham and Lord Chancellor Kilmuir*.

Salisbury had all the aristocrat's faith in the essential good sense of ordinary people. This explained his attitude to the Labour Government's Parliament Bill and his insistence that the electorate should be consulted on it. He was suspicious of overcleverness in politicians, though he was no mean tactician himself. His intellectual honesty and his instinct for public service were part of his Cecil heritage, deeply rooted as it is in a long religious tradition.

Robert Arthur James Gascoyne-Cecil, fifth Marquess of Salisbury, was born on August 27, 1893, eldest son of the fourth marquess. He was educated at Eton and at Christ Church, Oxford. He was gazetted in 1914 to a commission in the Grenadier Guards, saw service in France and won the Croix de Guerre before being invalided home in September 1915. In 1916 he was Personal Military Secretary to the Secretary of State for War (the Earl of Derby).

After the war he joined a City billbroking firm and it was 10 years before he took up politics. At the 1929 election he was returned as Conservative member for South Dorset and sat for that constituency until his elevation to the peerage in January 1941. Minor office came to him first in 1934. He was Parliamentary Private Secretary to Anthony Eden during Eden's tenure of the posts of Lord Privy Seal and Minister without Portfolio. When Eden succeeded Sir Samuel Hoare at the Foreign Office in October 1935, Viscount Cranborne, as he then was, went with him as Under-Secretary. The two men worked in close accord, striving untiringly for peace during the troubled period of the Abyssinian and Spanish wars.

When Eden resigned in February 1938, refusing to support any approach to Mussolini, Cranborne resigned also. He could brook no compromise with systems which he regarded as essentially evil. In a moving personal statement to the Commons he described the intention to enter into conversations with the Italians as "a surrender to blackmail". He continued throughout 1938 to urge the need for the democracies to arm themselves against the threat of the dictatorships. He was deeply disturbed by the Munich agreement and described Czechoslovakia as "a country thrown to the wolves".

After a short term as Paymaster-General he entered Churchill's Cabinet in October 1940, as Secretary of State for the Dominions, an office in which his reputation steadily grew. In January 1941 he was called to the Lords in his father's barony of Cecil of Essendon, in the County of Rutland, in order that he might answer in the Upper House for foreign affairs. In early 1942 he went to the Colonial Office and in November he was appointed Lord Privy Seal, so that he could devote himself more closely to the leadership of the Lords. His return to the Dominions Office in 1943 was widely welcomed.

The election to office of the Labour Government in 1945 opened a notable phase of his career, as Leader of the Opposition peers. In October 1947, six months after his succession to the marquessate, he raised the battle-cry against the Labour project for amending the 1911 Parliament Act as deriving from a "shabby political deal". When the new Parliament Bill came forward in January 1948, he denounced it as a "bomb in a battle of flowers" and appealed for its postponement, to facilitate inter-party talks on the possibility of reforming both the composition and powers of the House. Eventually he got his way, and it was his patient skill and diplomacy which helped to shape a rough outline of the possible composition of a reformed Chamber. But early in May the talks foundered on differences over its delaying powers.

About a month later he moved the rejection of the Bill—with a biting Cecilian contempt for the "single chamber men". The Lords rejected it in three successive sessions, and it became law without their consent in December 1949.

Meanwhile, Salisbury deployed his forces against the iron and steel nationalization measure. His tactics were good. His conviction was that the electorate should have the last word on an issue for which the

Government had only a shaky mandate. The Lords under his generalship passed an amendment to defer the operation of the Bill until after the general election. The Commons reversed the decision and the Lords carried their own insistence on it by a big majority. But, having flung down their challenge, they accepted a compromise substantially fulfilling their aim. Salisbury won a mounting weight of respect for his exercise of what someone called the flair of Herbert Morrison (later Lord Morrison of Lambeth*) "with the advantage of four centuries' start".

When the Conservatives were returned in 1951 he became Lord Privy Seal and once more Leader of the Lords. In March 1952 he was appointed Secretary of State for Commonwealth Relations, but in November he was freed from these duties to become Lord President of the Council, responsible for presenting Government policies. He carried the Sword of State at the young Queen's Coronation.

When Eden's health removed him temporarily from the Foreign Office in the summer of 1953 Salisbury became acting Foreign Secretary—and was much criticized by the Opposition for his conduct of the Government's case in the "Little Bermuda" conference.

When Eden became Prime Minister in 1955 Salisbury was confirmed in office, and supported him loyally during the Suez crisis.

Eden resigned in January 1957, and it is a good indication of Salisbury's standing in the Conservative Party at the time that it was he whom the Queen sent for in order to learn the views of the Cabinet and party concerning a successor. With Kilmuir, the Lord Chancellor, Salisbury had interviewed each member of the Cabinet singly, putting the question "Well, which is it, Wab or Hawald?" They also interviewed the Chief Whip and the chairman of the party, and the chairman of the 1922 Committee consulted them by telephone. Their soundings indicated a strong preference for Macmillan over Butler—advice which Churchill, whom the Queen also consulted, is believed to have independently duplicated.

In the new Administration Salisbury was again Lord President and Leader of the Lords. It came, therefore, as a surprise to the public when they learnt on March 29, 1957, that he had resigned from office over the release of Archbishop Makarios.

His divergences from Government policy did not stop there. When he broke his self-imposed silence at last on May 14 it was to criticize their decision to allow British ships to use the Suez Canal again on Egypt's terms.

Increasingly he strove to exert all his influence against the perilous trend, as he saw it, towards allowing Western influence to be edged out of Africa, a process which he feared that Government policies were inadequate to halt. Other aspects of their approach to African affairs carried him farther out of accord with Macmillan and his colleagues, and in March 1961 he ex-

pressed his fears partly by way of a biting attack on Iain Macleod, then Colonial Secretary. His charge was that Macleod had outwitted the European representatives at the Kenya Constitutional Conference and that he was mainly responsible for the fact that among the white settlers in Central Africa there had been created suspicion, contempt and almost hatred of the British Government. Macleod, he said, had been "too clever by half", and he woundingly suggested that the Colonial Secretary had brought the techniques of bridge, at which he was an expert, into this political sphere.

Two days later it became known that Salisbury had decided to relinquish his presidency of the Hertfordshire Constituency Conservative Association. Soon afterwards he resigned similar offices in other constituency bodies. He felt it wrong to accept office in organizations which existed to support a Government with whose policy in Africa he was in strong disagreement. In 1965 and 1966 at the Conservative Party conferences Salisbury spoke out against the use of sanctions against Rhodesia.

Salisbury had been a Knight of the Garter since 1946 and was appointed Chancellor of the Order in 1960. He was a Fellow of the Royal Society, High Steward of Hertford, Chancellor of the University of Liverpool, Chairman of the Royal Commission on Historical Monuments, and for some years a trustee of the National Gallery.

In 1915 he married Elizabeth Vere, eldest daughter of Lord Richard Cavendish. They had three sons, the second of whom died in 1934. The youngest, the Hon. Richard Hugh Vere Cecil, a sergeant pilot, was killed in a motor accident in August 1944 while on active service. The new marquess is the eldest son, Robert Edward Peter, Viscount Cranborne, who was M.P. for Bournemouth West from 1950 to 1954.

February 24, 1972.

Bishop of Salisbury—See Fison.

Former Bishop of Salisbury—See Anderson.

Ernst von Salomon, who died on August 9, 1972 at his home near Hamburg, was a German writer who, though the number of his books was comparatively small, attained international fame—or perhaps notoriety might by a better term—with three books before and after the Second World War.

He was born at Kiel on September 29, 1902; he was partly French, partly Venetian in descent, and always emphasized that, in spite of his name, he had no Jewish blood in him. This is indeed probable, as otherwise he would not have been employed, as he was, under the Nazi regime, as a cinema script-writer.

He was passionately attached to Schleswig-Holstein, and then to Prussia. He was too young to take much part in the 1914–18 War, but as a Prussian cadet he went to fight the Bolsheviks in the Baltic States in 1919. Returning to Berlin after the signature of the peace-treaty, he felt the humiliation of defeat intensely and joined one of the illegal military organizations that sprang up during the Allied occupation of Germany.

His fanaticism, his hatred of democracy, of the leaders of the Weimar Republic, found expression in the "Freikorps" in when he served while earning his living at various casual jobs. He was implicated in the murder of Walther Rathenau in 1922. Von Salomon and his comrades regarded the German-Jewish economist and politician as a symbol of the hated policy of "fulfilment" of the Allied peace conditions.

Von Salomon was sentenced to five years imprisonment, during which he discovered, and was able to practise, a considerable gift for writing. The result was two books, *Die Geächteten*, translated into English as *The Outlaws*, and *Die Stadt* (*The City*), called in the English edition *It Cannot be Stormed*. Both were autobiographical. The first revealed, with extraordinary vividness and brutal frankness, the detestation which the writer, and so many of his generation, felt for the "system", the Socialist or democratic regime in power. The second dealt especially with the exploitation of the peasants by the "system" in the cities, above all in the writer's native province. At the time of their publication, in the early nineteen-thirties, there were many readers who regarded the books as the best expression in literature of the turmoil and spirit of revolt that was to erupt soon in the National Socialist revolution.

Von Salomon was rejected for military service in 1939 and worked as a script-writer for Ufa, the German Government's chief film organization. He lived in Berlin until 1942, then moved to Munich. He was arrested by the Allied authorities in 1945 and detained for a considerable time, and subjected to an interrogation from which he emerged with nothing criminal held against him.

From this experience came his third and probably his best piece of autobiography, *Der Fragebogen*, published in 1951. In a few months it had sold some 250,000 copies, and in 1954 it was translated and published in an English version (a compressed version of the original) entitled *The Answers of Ernst von Salomon*. Its immense popularity was regarded as a disquieting sign that the spirit of aggressive German nationalism was by no means dead. However that might be, the book was a fascinating mixture of candour, humour and sarcasm, exposing the Allied occupying authorities to mockery and ridicule, and giving a brilliant description and defence of the writer's whole career. Audaciously it was suggested that some of the methods of the National Socialist Party—of which the writer claimed he was

never a member—were being followed by the victorious allies, especially the Americans. The "answers" were those which the writer gave to the 131 questions put to him during the interrogation already mentioned. It was certainly a remarkable document, of permanent value as a key to one side of the German national psychology.

In 1960 von Salomon published *Das Schicksal des A.D.*, published in English in 1961 as *The Captive; the Story of an Unknown Political Prisoner*. This purports to be the story of a man who, though strongly nationalist after the 1914-18 War, fell in love with a girl whose father was a communist. For her sake he warns the man, and is imprisoned first by the pre-Hitler government, then under the Nazis, and finally by the Americans, who accused him of assisting a concentration camp doctor to conduct medical experiments on the inmates.

August 11, 1972.

Dame Barbara Salt, D.B.E., died on December 28, 1975 at the age of 71.

When Miss Salt, as she then was, was appointed Ambassador to Israel in November 1962, she was the first woman to be appointed as a British Ambassador, but shortly after the announcement of her appointment she became ill and was unable to take it up. She was for long the most senior woman member of the Diplomatic Service. She retired in 1972.

Barbara Salt was born on September 30, 1904, the granddaughter of Sir Thomas Salt who was chairman of Lloyds Bank and one time M.P. for Stafford. She was educated at Downs School, Seaford, Sussex, and Munich and Cologne Universities.

After wartime work as Vice-Consul at Tangier, Miss Salt joined the United Nations Department of the Foreign Office in 1946 as a temporary First Secretary. She later became a permanent member of the Foreign Service (as it then was) and in 1950 was appointed First Secretary (Commercial) at Moscow; but illness made it necessary for her to return to London in the same year.

In 1951 she was appointed First Secretary at Washington and in 1955 was promoted Counsellor *sur place*. In 1957 Miss Salt was appointed Counsellor and Consul-General at Tel Aviv, where on a number of occasions she acted as Chargé d'Affaires. In 1960 Barbara Salt, on promotion to Minister, was appointed Deputy Head of the United Kingdom Disarmament delegation to the United Nations at Geneva, and transferred to New York in the following year as United Kingdom representative on the Economic and Social Council of the United Nations.

It was in October 1962, when she returned to the United Kingdom for leave and to prepare for her appointment as Ambas-

sador to Israel, that she became ill and it was this illness which led to the loss of first one leg and then the other.

Miss Salt was advanced to D.B.E. in June 1963; she had been made C.B.E. in 1959.

Although Dame Barbara's brilliant diplomatic career was interrupted by ill-health she showed great courage and her spirits remained high even when her appointment as Britain's first woman Ambassador had to be cancelled. It was characteristic of her that she called a press conference at her London home less than three months after leaving hospital and, from her wheelchair, said that she had plenty of energy to continue working and that she hoped to do so. The press reports at that time were unanimous in their praise of her courage.

Although she did not take up another overseas appointment she continued to work in the Foreign Office. She led the United Kingdom delegation at the Anglo-Israel financial negotiations of 1963-64; the United Kingdom delegation to the Anglo-Romanian negotiations in 1966; and from 1967 to 1972 was head of the S.O.E. section at the Foreign and Commonwealth Office.

She never lost touch with those in the morning of their lives, and she took a deep interest in the briefing of new entrants to the service. Those who attended her meetings are unlikely to forget the sparkle, and the deep wisdom, of her talks with them.

December 31, 1975.

Lord Salter, P.C., G.B.E., K.C.B., who died on June 27, 1975 aged 94, had been a high civil servant, both British and international, an Oxford professor, a successful author, and a Minister of the Crown. In two world wars he made an important contribution to victory through his work in connexion with the control and allocation of shipping.

James Arthur Salter—the eldest of four brothers—was born on March 15, 1881.

After an Oxford dame's school, Salter was sent to the Oxford High School for Boys. At the age of 18 he won a scholarship at Brasenose College and this opened the door to the university world within.

He read Greats, in which he won a double first, and at the end of his college career he widened his reading, sat for the Civil Service, and won a place which enabled him to choose between the Home, Indian, and Colonial services. He opted for the first of these—a decision which set the tone of an unusually active life and remained with him to the end.

From the day Salter started on his chosen career the next 60 years were divided into two periods of nearly equal length. The first consisted of the years of public employment first in the British Civil Service and then in international service mainly with the League at Geneva. The second period, in which he made a fresh start in a great variety of public activities—as professor, member of Parliament, minister, adviser to overseas governments, journalist and author—began after his resignation from the League in 1931.

Salter served his apprenticeship to the Civil Service in a small self-contained department of the Admiralty which dealt with the chartering of merchant ships—a post into which he stumbled more by accident than design. But he found it boring and seven years later was offered a transfer to a new office organized to operate Lloyd George's National Health Insurance scheme. There he found himself among a group of young officials cooperating enthusiastically in the birth of the welfare state. This experiment which included old age pensions, health insurance, unemployment insurance, trade boards, labour exchanges, and progressive taxation, brought Salter into personal contact with Lloyd George and his colleagues—in particular, with C. F. G. Masterman, the Minister in charge of the health scheme, to whom Salter was soon appointed private secretary.

This was a field of the greatest activity, where almost every action was a fresh adventure. There he made the acquaintance of the major figures in British public life. He also found an outlet for his very great gift of "contrivance"—the art of planning action to meet a special situation without breaking any crockery.

When therefore the First World War broke out (three years later) Salter was called back to the Admiralty, for his humble little backwater had suddenly assumed major importance. In 1914 Great Britain possessed by far the largest commercial fleet in the world and the only one that had any substantial surplus of tonnage that could be allotted to allies or to new or unusual tasks.

But by 1917 unrestrained submarine warfare had almost brought us to our knees. The most economical use of all the merchant ships under allied control had become the supreme need both of our war effort and of our food supply. The decision to send a great and growing American Army across the Atlantic in 1917 and 1918 gave shipping an even higher priority. The planning of the voyages of British and allied shipping was one of three ways which together defeated the German submarines in the last two years of the war. These three were the convoy of almost all allied ships at sea, the big increase of launchings from American shipyards in 1917 and 1918, and the allocation and the routing of tonnage under allied control.

Soon after Salter returned to the Admiralty he was put in charge of the financial branch of that rapidly growing transport department. He introduced a card index which grew, in the later stages of the war, into an instrument that enabled the department—which in January 1917 became the Ministry of Shipping—to keep track of the great bulk of the world's ships.

In his appointment as Director of Ship Requisitioning at the British Ministry of Shipping and Chairman of the Inter-Allied Maritime Transport Executive, Salter's role was decisive in achieving the stage of maximum collaboration in the last year of the war, and then only when the allied and associated powers were on the verge of defeat.

Salter had been so close to almost every problem of war planning that he was inevitably marked as a man who would have an important role to play in establishing the League of Nations. With the exception of a little over two years, during which he was transferred to the post of Secretary-General of the Reparation Commission, Salter spent the next 13 or 14 years as an international civil servant in the post of Director of the Economic and Financial section of the League. In that post his gifts as a "contriver" had ample scope.

The reconstruction scheme for Austria with the aid of a loan guaranteed by half a dozen of the financially stronger powers succeeded in stopping the depreciation of Austria's currency and setting it on the way to stability. The scheme became the example for Hungary and for several other countries, though without requiring the Hungarian or other budgets to be approved in detail by an expert on behalf of the Council of the League. After a dozen years of service, however, Salter realized that the League lacked the powers it needed if it was to fulfil its primary purpose. Though many extremely interesting tasks came his way—including that of organizing the first World Economic Conference in 1927—he and those who thought as he did began to feel the urge freely to speak their minds.

So in 1931 Salter resigned from the Secretariat of the League and the second half of his life began with a very full programme of many tasks in the field for public affairs. His long experience, however, in working out political institutions for different party governments was not easily set aside. Though brought up as a Gladstonian Liberal, it was 20 years before he again allied himself with any political party.

Apart from journalism and writing books he was for five of the years which preceded the Second World War chairman of the Railway and Roadway Undertakings Conference and later chairman of the National Railway Staff Tribunal.

In 1934 he was appointed to the newly created chair of Gladstone Professor of Political Theory and Institutions at Oxford. Throughout the thirties he associated himself with the growing number of those who were unwilling to accept the discipline of any political party; for example, he collaborated with the authors of *The Next Five Years* in the hope of "uncovering agreement" on a widely accepted programme of immediate action. At that time there was a tendency, though in no sense a rule, for the University franchise to return members calling themselves Independents, and in 1937 Salter was approached by representatives of all three parties in Oxford University to stand for the vacancy created when Lord Hugh Cecil resigned. The Conservatives failed to agree on their candidate and Salter was elected with an absolute majority of the votes cast. He continued to represent Oxford until the University franchise was abolished in February 1950.

In the Second World War the organization of the first war was well known; from the outset we had to meet the attack of the U-boats, a Ministry of Shipping was quickly set up, and Salter was soon back in office—but this time as a joint Parliamentary Secretary—a politician, instead of a senior executive.

As a result of the Labour Government's abolition of university representation, Salter no longer had a seat in the House after February 1950. In March 1951 he was chosen by the Ormskirk Divisional Conservative Party to contest the by-election caused by the appointment of Sir Ronald Cross* as Governor of Tasmania. He was returned to the Commons with a slightly increased Conservative majority, and he held the seat at the general election in the following October.

Churchill*, in forming his Government in 1951, appointed Salter as Minister of State for Economic Affairs. A year later he became Minister of Materials, where he carried out a difficult task in planning for the wind-up of that ministry and disposing of surplus government stocks. He resigned in September 1953, when the Government was reconstructed, and was raised to the peerage as Baron Salter of Kidlington.

Salter's rich experience was reflected in several rewarding books, *Personality in Politics* (1947) which consisted of studies of contemporary statesmen and included a penetrating study of Lloyd George; *Memoirs of a Public Servant* (1961), which was much more than a personal record; and *Slave of the Lamp* (1967). Like Keynes, Salter found that his years in the corridors of power sharpened his interest in his fellow human beings and his comments on contemporary statesmen showed the closeness with which he had watched them in action.

He married Mrs. Arthur Bullard, widow of Arthur Bullard, of Washington, D.C., in 1940. Lady Salter died in 1969. There is no heir to the title.

June 30, 1975.

John Saltmarsh, a distinguished Cambridge historian and antiquary with a particular devotion to his college of King's, died on September 25, 1974 at the age of 66.

He was the perfect answer to those who say that colleges no longer breed eccentric bachelor "characters". In appearance he was Pickwickian. He grew whiskers during the Second World War, long before they became fashionable, and later impressive long white hair. Sandals were his normal footgear, and he wore breeches he called "plus-twos" when he went on his 25-mile walks (which he took well into his sixties) out into Suffolk, or along the Norfolk coast, or wherever Oxfam prescribed. He was a fund of anecdotes, whether of folk-lore or about his innumerable relations, told with a twinkle and in a high tenor voice, *andante* with *presto* climaxes. There was a certain element of deliberate eccentricity, originally designed perhaps to amuse his nephews and nieces, for he was very fond of children and good with them.

He was born at Oakington, near Cambridge, on May 7, 1908, the son of H. A. Saltmarsh.

Going up to King's as a history scholar in 1926, he was greatly influenced by his tutor and supervisor, the economic historian Sir John Clapham. After getting a First with Distinction in both parts of the Tripos and being elected a Fellow at the age of 22 for a dissertation on the history of the college's estates, he became absorbed in the college not only as a teacher but as librarian from 1937 to 1947. His tenure was interrupted by the war, which swept him off to Bletchley, where he did confidential work for the Foreign Office with such devotion that he had to be invalided back to Cambridge.

By the time the flood of postwar pupils had subsided the psychological impetus for his projected major work on the college's muniments was long past; but he did produce in 1958 for Volume III of the *Victoria County History of Cambridgeshire* a masterly history of King's, full of original research. From then on he was engaged on a history of its great chapel, a long process because he was always thinking of new ways of deducing information. (It is hoped that this may prove publishable with expert editing of the notes he left.)

Not that his researches, specializing in the medieval and early modern periods, were by any means confined to Cambridge. His article on *Plague and Economic Decline in England in the Later Middle Ages* had the distinction of being condemned as deviationist by the Soviet Academy. G. M. Trevelyan* borrowed his lecture-notes on the sixteenth century for use, suitably acknowledged, in his *Social History of England.*

He was a stickler for accuracy, which made him not only an exemplary teacher but a superb editor. His technical proficiency was shown not only in his chosen field of manorial records, but in such things as the newly discovered manuscript of a medieval love lyric.

He wrote very well, but his *forte* was as a lecturer. His university lectures drew large audiences; but even more popular were his two-hour tours of King's Chapel, to which, frequent though they were, he always seemed to bring fresh enthusiasm. (His small illustrated book on it sold like hot cakes.) Then there was his class on medieval Cambridge, first map-work, then perambulation from this site to that in relentlessly chronological sequence; and

another in Grantchester Meadows with sixteenth century field books. He was a pioneer in the study of local history.

September 27, 1974.

Dr. L. F. Salzman, C.B.E., who died on April 4, 1971 at the age of 93, was formerly Editor of the Victoria County Histories.

Louis Francis Salzman, the son of a Brighton physician, was born on March 26, 1878 and educated at Haileybury and at Pembroke College, Cambridge, where he studied medicine. Endowed with a small private income while still quite young, he settled at Hailsham and abandoned medicine for historical research. The first evidence of his new interest was his *History of Hailsham*, published in 1901. Henceforth until an advanced age Salzman's literary output, especially in the fields of local and medieval economic history, was unceasing.

During the 1914-18 War he taught in a school. Thereafter he settled at Cambridge and did coaching and supervision for the historical tripos. In 1935 he succeeded Dr. William Page as editor of the *Victoria History of the Counties of England*, the management of which had been assumed two years before by the Institute of Historical Research of the University of London. He retained the post until his retirement in 1949.

His near contemporaries probably thanked Salzman most for his *English Industries in the Middle Ages* (1913, 2nd edtn. 1923) and *English Trade in the Middle Ages* (1931), pioneering works which must have provided many students with their first introduction to medieval economic history. Both are based on extensive searches among medieval documents, particularly the public records, and, like so much that their author published, make full and judicious use of pictures. A chapter on building in the earlier book was later expanded, out of all recognition, into *Building in England down to 1540* (1952, 2nd edtn. 1967). This deals in detail with the early organization of the building trade, the technique of construction and the materials used, and prints a substantial body of documents, including many building contracts. An outcome of this most original and scholarly composition was the Vernacular Architecture Group, of which Salzman was one of the founders.

Of less profundity were *Medieval Byways* (1913) and *More Medieval Byways* (1926). Somewhat episodic in treatment and tending to suggest that the Middle Ages were a changeless chronological entity, these books are none the less a valuable repository of curious stories, many drawn from unpublished material. The pleasures of exploring such material were ever apparent to the author, who extolled them in *Original Sources of English History* (1921), the outcome of a course of lectures to schoolboys. Salzman's other popular works comprised

Hastings (1921) in the English Towns series, *English Life in the Middle Ages* (1926), *England in Tudor Times* (1926), and *A Survey of English History* (1930); also two titles in an incomplete series of royal biographies promoted by Page—*Henry II* (1914) and *Edward I* (1968).

The *Victoria County Histories* had been running only a few years when Salzman began to contribute to the Sussex volumes. This experience helped to fit him for the general editorship of the whole series. In that capacity he brought out some 15 volumes, and made substantial contributions of his own to three of them. He took charge of the History at a time when its fortunes were very low and the University of London had but slender funds with which to maintain it. In such circumstances his performance, if below his own ambitions, was remarkable, for he managed to resume the histories of Oxfordshire and Warwickshire, to start Cambridgeshire and to drive forward with Sussex. In his time the hundredth volume was issued (1938).

The History under his editorship has sometimes been criticized for a narrowness of scope, but few of the critics can have appreciated the difficulties of maintaining so great an enterprise, partly in wartime, with very little money or staff, and some of them can have had scant understanding of the immensity of the task even in ideal conditions. His somewhat severe handling of some of his contributors was dictated by the need both to make progress with the History and to economize words.

Students of the antiquities of Sussex are deeply in his debt. He joined the Council of the Sussex Archaeological Society in 1903 and rose to be its President in 1954 and 1955. From 1909 to 1959 he edited its annual *Transactions*, 45 volumes in all, and often contributed to them. He published a history of the Society in 1946. He helped to excavate several Sussex sites— Pevensey Castle and the Saxon cemetery at Alfriston in his earlier years, and Robertsbridge Abbey in 1935. He was a foundation member of the Sussex Record Society and its Literary Director, either alone or in conjunction with a colleague, from 1905. From 1941 he was also its Secretary. He prepared the text of ten volumes for that productive body, the most notable being perhaps *The Lewes Cartulary* (1932-43). Most fittingly he was made an honorary D.Litt. of the University of Sussex in 1965.

April 6, 1971.

Air Chief Marshal Sir Arthur Sanders, G.C.B., K.B.E., who died on February 8, 1974 aged 75, was Deputy Chief of the Air Staff 1950-52, Commander-in-Chief of the Middle East Air Force 1952-53, and Commandant of the Imperial Defence College 1954-55.

Arthur Penrose Martyn Sanders was born on March 17, 1898, the son of Prebendary

H. Martyn Sanders. He went to Haileybury before entering the Royal Military College Sandhurst in 1915. He was commissioned in the Northumberland Fusiliers but after a few months was seconded to the Royal Flying Corps. He went to France with No. 5 Squadron in July 1916.

His operational flying career ended in May 1917. In a flight commanded by Captain J. C. Slessor, who later became Chief of the Air Staff, he was badly wounded in an encounter with seven or eight Halberstadts. He lost his right arm but got his aircraft back to base.

The disability limited the scope of his employment and he spent the remainder of the war on staff duties, getting a permanent commission in 1919.

In 1940 Sanders was appointed Director of the new Air Staff Directorate of Ground Defence. The plans he drew up for a new force were pushed ahead as fast as the tight reins of priorities would allow, and there was formed in February 1942 the R.A.F. Regiment.

Sanders was made C.B.E. in June 1942. He was appointed Assistant Chief of Staff (Air) to General Eisenhower* for the planning of Operation Torch, the Allied landings in North-West Africa. He went with Eisenhower, first to Gibraltar and then to Algiers, to supervise the launching of the air operations at the opening of the campaign.

He was recalled to the United Kingdom and appointed Air Officer in Charge of Administration, Bomber Command, in January 1943. He spent nearly two years in that exacting post. When peace came, he was appointed Commandant of the R.A.F. Staff College, and was made C.B. While at the college he was advanced to K.B.E. In December 1947 he was appointed A.O.C.-in-C. British Air Forces of Occupation (Germany). The inception of the Air Lift brought an additional burden. His service as A.O.A. at Bomber Command and his close liaison with the U.S.A.A.F. proved invaluable in pushing through the vigorous action required to build the air bridge from the western zones to the German capital.

Sanders returned to England to succeed Sir James Robb* as Vice-Chief of the Air Staff. He undertook an extensive examination of general air staff problems and evolved proposals for reorganization.

In March 1950 he became Deputy Chief of the Air Staff. He was able to concentrate more on the development of the international and inter-service organizations with which he had been particularly associated. He was made G.C.B. in 1955 and retired in 1956.

In spite of having one arm he was an active man. He spent his leisure in yachting and fishing.

He married in 1928 Edith Mary, daughter of Herbert Arnould Olivier, the portrait painter; they had two daughters.

February 9, 1974.

George Sanders, the suave and supercilious film actor whose distinctive gallery of cads, crooks and romantic heroes sustained a successful career of more than 30 years, was found dead in a hotel room near Barcelona on April 25, 1972. He was 65.

Among his immense output was inevitably a fair proportion of the mediocre and the bad; but given the right vehicle, the right script, and a sympathetic director, he could turn in performances of chilling brilliance. Perhaps the most memorable was his portrayal of the drama critic, Addison de Witt, opposite Bette Davis in *All About Eve*, for which he deservedly won the Oscar for Best Supporting Actor.

His voice, world-weary and lazily offensive, was like that of no other actor on the screen. He could be utterly charming but he could also extract the very last drop from an insult.

Sanders was born in St. Petersburg in Russia in 1906, the son of a rope manufacturer and his British wife. The family went to Britain during the 1917 Revolution. He was educated at Brighton College and Manchester Technical College and spent some time in the textile business and in a tobacco enterprise in South America, before deciding to make a career on the stage. He had a succession of smallish roles during the twenties and early 1930s, including Noël Coward's *Conversation Piece*, before making his film debut in *Find the Lady* in 1936. After a few more pictures in Britain he went to Hollywood and signed a long-term contract with 20th Century Fox.

For a while, however, the rival R.K.O. Company claimed him for a series based on Leslie Charteris's *The Saint*, with Sanders in the name part. During the war years he made a speciality of leering Nazis, notably in *Confessions of a Nazi Spy*, with Edward G. Robinson; Fritz Lang's *Manhunt* (based on the Geoffrey Household thriller *Rogue Male*); and Jean Renoir's *This Land is Mine*. He also appeared to considerable effect at this time in two Hitchcock pictures, *Rebecca*, playing the cousin, and *Foreign Correspondent*; and had a big success as the hero of Somerset Maugham's* *The Moon and Sixpence*.

After the war he went through a period of costume films, including two excursions into Wilde—*The Picture of Dorian Gray* and *Lady Windermere's Fan*—*Forever Amber* (playing Charles II) and De Mille's *Samson and Delilah*.

All About Eve, in 1950, stood out as a peak which he was unable to reach afterwards, and he returned to Europe two years later for *Ivanhoe* with Robert Taylor,* his first film in Britain for 13 years, and the Rossellini-Ingrid Bergman *Voyage to Italy*. Back in Hollywood, he landed the leading male part opposite Ethel Merman in one of the major musicals of 1953, *Call Me Madam*. He went on to appear in two of Fritz Lang's last American pictures, *Moonfleet* and *While the City Sleeps*, and later in the decade started his own television series, The George Sanders Mystery Theatre.

His later career was mostly in Britain or on the Continent. Among the films were *Village of the Damned* (an adaptation of John Wyndham); *The Rebel* with Tony Hancock*; and *The Cracksman* with Charlie Drake; *The Quiller Memorandum; The Best House in London;* and perhaps his last role of consequence as the drag queen in John Huston's *The Kremlin Letter*.

He published in 1960 *Memoirs of a Professional Cad*, fluent, tart, objective, highly readable and containing an excellent portrait of Rossellini at work.

Sanders was one of the directors of Cadco Developments Ltd., the Glenrothes piggery firm, which collapsed in 1964. A Board of Trade investigation, which published its findings in December 1966, sharply criticized Sanders's behaviour.

He was married several times: to Ruth Larsen, Zsa Zsa Gabor, Benita Hume, the English actress, and Magda Gabor.

April 26, 1972.

Brigadier Daniel Arthur Sandford, C.B.E., D.S.O., who played a leading role during the Second World War in Emperor Haile Selassie's return to his throne in Ethiopia, died near Addis Ababa on January 22, 1972. He was 89.

"Dan" Sandford was a legend in Ethiopia, where he lived for more than 50 years, apart from a five-year period during the Italian invasion from 1936 to 1941. When the Italian forces swept into the country he left with the Emperor, a close friend. Three years later he joined the British officers' emergency reserve. Sandford was the leader of a special mission— known as "Mission 101"—which entered Ethiopia in 1940 to help the patriots organize six months before General Orde Wingate's British army began its victorious campaign against the Italians. This culminated in the emperor's triumphal entry into Addis Ababa in May 1941. With the defeat of the Italians, Sandford became principal military and political adviser to the Emperor.

Dan Sandford, the eldest of eight children, was born at the vicarage at Landkey, North Devon, on June 18, 1882. His father, a distinguished Oxford athlete, later Canon and Archdeacon of Exeter, had been Chaplain to Archbishop Frederick Temple, then Bishop of Exeter. When the time came for Dan to go to St. Paul's School he lived at Fulham Palace with Archbishop and Mrs. Temple. He passed into Woolwich in 1900. He was commissioned into the Royal Artillery and later served in Bombay and Karachi until 1906, when he was posted to Aden. In 1907 he was posted home for a gunnery course. He returned to Aden in 1909.

In 1910 he joined the Sudan Civil Service as a contract officer and was posted to the British Legation in Addis Ababa as

Sudan Government Liaison Officer.

He rejoined the Army in 1913, served with distinction in France and was awarded the D.S.O. and bar and the French Legion of Honour. One of his brothers won a V.C. at Zeebrugge. In 1918, he married Christine, daughter of H. S. Lush; it was a most successful and happy marriage, for his wife identified herself completely with his work and interests.

In 1919 he accompanied Lord Lugard to Ethiopia to inspect the Abyssinian Corporation, and was appointed general manager, a position he held until the corporation went into liquidation in 1921. By this time he had developed a deep and abiding affection for Ethiopia and decided to make it his home. He retired from the Army in 1922 and acquired a lease of a farm at Mulu, some 30 miles to the north of Addis Ababa. Until the world slump in 1931 he combined farming with trading in coffee and hides and skins, and for two of these years practised as an advocate. In 1935 he was appointed as adviser to the newly appointed governor of Maji, a province which marches with Kenya. His instructions were to advise on the suppression of the slave trade and to assist in creating a model province. Shortly after his arrival there the Italo-Ethiopian war broke out and when he heard of the Emperor's departure from Ethiopia he made his way down to Kenya and back to England.

With the imminence of war he was selected for appointment in the Middle East Intelligence Centre and in 1939 he went to Cairo. There he laid plans for fostering patriot activity in Ethiopia. In 1940, when British Somaliland, Moyale in Kenya, and Kasala in the Sudan were in the hands of the Italians, he entered Ethiopia from the Sudan at the head of Military Mission 101. The main objects of the mission were to encourage the activities of the patriots, pin down Italian troops, and when the moment was propitious prepare for the reentry of the Emperor into Ethiopia. As soon as he reached the Ethiopian plateau he was involved in a drive being made against the patriots by Toselli with a brigade. Perhaps the military authorities in the Sudan were not over-enthusiastic about the mission, for the last message he received prior to his departure was to the effect that "We want no Lawrence nonsense".

The mission was an unqualified success and it is certain that it accelerated the reconquest of Ethiopia. For nearly a year after the reentry of the Emperor into Addis Ababa he was the Emperor's principal military and political adviser with the rank of brigadier. For his services he was created O.B.E. in 1941 and advanced to C.B.E. in 1942.

In May 1942, after the signing of the Anglo-Ethiopian Agreement, he was appointed adviser to the Ministry of the Interior, and three years later was appointed Director General in the Municipality of Addis Ababa.

In 1948 he gave up direct employment with the Ethiopian Government and devoted all his energies to the development of his farm at Mulu, which again had been leased to him, after the war had ended in Ethiopia. His wife had rejoined him in 1942 together with the two youngest children, and she gave together with a friend lessons to her children and a number of Ethiopians. So successful was this enterprise that she found it necessary to move these classes to the British Council in 1946, by which time the number of pupils under instruction had increased to more than 80. It soon became apparent that an English School was required, premises were leased, and the school was run under the direction of Sandford and his wife.

He leaves a widow, two sons, and four daughters.

January 24, 1972.

Dame of Sark—See **Hathaway.**

David Sarnoff, for many years chairman and chief executive officer of the Radio Corporation of America, and one of the pioneers in the development of radio, television and electronics in the United States, died on December 12, 1971. He was 80. He was chairman of R.C.A. until 1970 when he was made honorary chairman.

In his chosen field Sarnoff was both a visionary and a man of action. In 1916 he wrote a memorandum to his superiors in the Marconi Wireless Telegraph Company of America in which he proposed a plan for broadcasting programmes into the home by means of a "radio music box". By 1923 he was forecasting the advent of television as a parallel service to radio. In 1926 he formed the National Broadcasting Corporation, the first network established in the United States. In 1929, when the gramophone was suffering from what its supporters regarded as the competition of radio, he bought the rights to the "His Master's Voice" trademark, set up the R.C.A. Victor record company and proved that the radio and gramophone were complementary.

By 1930 he was president of the corporation which was both developing and enjoying the commercial success of these new adventures. He worked for and presided over the introduction of television into America, for which the industry awarded him the title of "Father of American Television", and much of his last years were spent in developing electronic, fully-compatible colour television. His insistence that R.C.A. should pioneer the development of colour television cost his company more than £130m. and earned him a reputation for imperiousness, but Sarnoff argued that R.C.A. was one of the few companies strong enough to be able to do it without permanent harm, and his enlightened determination began to add returns to scientific achievements.

Sarnoff's personal story was remarkable—a classic in the favoured American tradition of opportunity prepared for, seized and exploited to the limit. Taken to the United States at the age of nine, the child of penniless immigrants, he was earning money two days after landing in New York by selling newspapers in the streets. In less than 30 years he was president of one of the largest and most glamorous enterprises in America. He was extremely proud of his success, and of all the many awards he received in his life one of his favourites was the gold medal which is awarded to immigrants who have "made good".

David Sarnoff was born at Uzlian, near Minsk, in Russia, on February 27, 1891. After travelling to the United States with his mother and two younger brothers in 1900 he began helping to support his family by taking whatever casual jobs were available. In 1906 he joined the Marconi Wireless Telegraph Company as a clerk, having prepared for bigger things by investing what money he had been able to save in an experimental telegraph machine and by enrolling in evening classes both in wireless technique and in electrical engineering.

In 1912, while working at the Marconi Station on top of Wanamaker's department store in New York City, Sarnoff picked up the distress signals from the Titanic shortly after the liner had struck an iceberg on its maiden voyage. For 72 hours he stayed on duty relaying details of the tragedy and the names of survivors, while all other wireless stations on the East coast of America were silenced by presidential order to prevent interference with his work.

This dramatic demonstration of the potential of radio communications promoted the advance both of the new medium and of David Sarnoff. By 1915 he was assistant traffic manager of the Marconi Company, and it was at this time that he put forward his now famous memorandum suggesting the development of radio as a "household utility".

In 1919, when the Radio Corporation of America was formed at the request of the United States Government, Sarnoff was absorbed into it along with the Marconi Company and was appointed commercial manager. He became general manager in 1921, vice-president in the following year and president in 1930.

He at once proved his value to the company by successfully steering it through the disasters of the depression and the legal difficulties following the dissolution of the original agreements by which R.C.A. had been formed. The company emerged as an independent, self-contained organization with its headquarters in a 70-storey building in the new Rockefeller Centre and with Sarnoff firmly in control of its growing operations.

As head of this vast complex, which embraces broadcasting, radio and television manufacturing, electronics, international communications including space satellite development, and education through the

David Sarnoff Research Centre at Princeton, New Jersey, Sarnoff never hesitated to experiment nor to risk his company's resources in expensive but possibly profitless research. He was fond of visualizing the future, where he saw a world deriving immense benefits from the effective harnessing of solar energy and the farming of the sea, from the growth of automation, from the spread of instant communication throughout the world. He was a man who constantly strove to translate his visions into practice, and by his achievements added to the wealth of civilization.

He married, in 1917, Miss Lizette Hermant, of Paris, who survives him together with three sons of the marriage. His son Robert succeeded him as chief executive officer of R.C.A. in 1967.

December 14, 1971.

Eisaku Sato, who died on June 3, 1975, aged 74, was the longest serving Japanese Prime Minister in the history of parliamentary government in Japan.

Elected leader of the Liberal-Democratic Party in 1964, he presided over the most intensive era of Japan's economic growth as the able manager of the political factions that made up the party. But the later years of his rule found him wanting, in a Japan that looked for other satisfactions than those of climbing so high in the world table of gross national product.

His handling of the return of Okinawa, followed soon after by the "shock" of the announcement of Richard Nixon's impending visit to Peking, made his firm attachment to the American alliance suddenly seem to be a worthless subservience. It became essential for Japan to show its own independence in relation to China. But Sato was too much influenced by supporters of Taiwan's cause in his own party and he was slow to respond to public feeling. In July 1972 Tanaka defeated him in the contest for the party leadership and Sato's eight-year rule came to an end.

In October 1974, he was somewhat surprisingly nominated for one of the Nobel peace prizes, though it was later revealed that a campaign to win him this nomination had been assiduously pressed by a leading Japanese businessman.

The award, if questionable in the personal sense, was nevertheless welcomed by the Japanese as an acknowledgement of their own constitutional commitment to pacifism still dominant even thirty years after the war's end.

He was a leader among the youthful bureaucrats who made good in postwar politics through the vacuum caused by the Occupation purge. The old and the young had their chance, and Sato was picked out from relative obscurity in the Transport Ministry, where he had served 28 years, by the chief elder, Shigeru Yoshida*, under whose patronage his career, bar one notable

stumble, was secured.

He assumed the succession in November 1964, from another Yoshida protégé, the late Hayato Ikeda*, who retired through illness. Once in office he found himself uncomfortably hemmed in by the constitutional inhibitions on Japan's "self defence forces" which made the country totally reliant on the United States for defence, and by the need to maintain the delicate balance in the politico-business-bureaucrat oligarchy which virtually characterized Japanese government. Abroad he found the way to a smoother understanding with Peking barred by previous governments' commitments to the Nationalists on Formosa. And he was stymied by Vietnam, where he had to pick an uncomfortable way between his own inclination to give at least moral support to the Americans— soon after he assumed office American nuclear-powered submarines began calling at Japanese ports—and a dismayed public opinion which was strongly pacifist. At home he was immediately confronted with a domestic recession, and severe inflation, and, even more damagingly, by a succession of corruption scandals involving members of his party. This seemed to some to mock his slogan of marching towards the affluent society, but undeniably the Japanese continued to prosper under his stewardship.

He was criticized for more words than action, but there were some notable achievements. The decade of haggling over normalizing relations with South Korea was quickly ended during his term with a big settlement for South Korea of all occupation claims, and a resumption of serious economic relations. He also broke through hesitations, and Japan began to shoulder responsibility in fostering economic development in south-east Asia; ministerial conferences were initiated; Japan became main Asian participant in the Asian Development Bank.

Sato's most serious failing, perhaps, was his passivity towards the strengthening of democratic stability. As leader of a party that faced no serious opposition, he was neither worse nor better than his predecessors in this. But it was during Sato's time that signs emerged of frustration and disenchantment with political parties, which aroused some anxiety for the future of the system.

A personable and markedly handsome man to western eyes, Sato tried hard but failed to get the Japanese public to like him. To many Japanese his charm was suspect. In the popular view there was something "dark and shadowy" about him. This had its springs in his reputation for shrewd political dealings, in his close association with his more outspokenly right-wing brother, Nobosuke Kishi (Prime Minister 1957-61), and with his having been linked with a shipbuilding bribery scandal in 1953-54.

Sato was born in 1901 the third son (the eldest, Ichiro, became an admiral) of a solid middle-class *sake* brewer in western

Japan, whose forebears had been *samurai*. Sato acknowledged a debt to his elder brother Kishi (the names are due to both having been adopted into their wives' families) as the more brilliant, and after studying German law at Tokyo Imperial University Sato went into the Railways Ministry.

He then rose through the hierarchy steadily and, untouched by the purge, in 1947 was suddenly appointed Minister by the Allied Administration after his tough handling of a strike. However, with his brother Kishi purged, it was suddenly felt unseemly he should appear as Minister, and he became deputy instead.

There followed an offer from the interim Socialist Government to join them, but he turned it down in favour of Yoshida's Liberal Party, and entered the Cabinet as Chief Cabinet Secretary. In 1949 he was elected for the first time from his native Yamaguchi prefecture.

Sato married his cousin, a niece of Yosuke Matsuoka, who as Foreign Minister walked out of the League of Nations and signed the Axis Pact. They had two sons.

June 3, 1975.

King Faisal of Saudi Arabia, who was shot dead in his palace at Riyadh by his nephew [later executed] on March 25, 1975, was ruler of a country believed to store beneath its sands between one half and one third of all the oil reserves of the non-communist world.

His elevation to a position of global power was remarkable. Born the son of a then unknown desert shaikh, he was to become late in life a man whose squeeze on the oil supplies of great nations gave him more power and influence than that given to any Arab leader for centuries.

He was the fourth son born to Abdul Aziz Ibn Saud, the first King of Saudi Arabia, but the second of the two survived to be known to the western world. His mother, Bint al Shaikh, who died young, was one of the half dozen women who, according to Philby, left the deepest impression on Ibn Saud's affections.

Faisal was born in 1905, when his father was already established in Riyadh as ruler of Nejd. He came into prominence very early, for at the age of 14 he was sent by his father to the United Kingdom, at the head of a mission to congratulate the Allies on their victory in the 1914-18 War and to discuss problems of common interest. In 1924, when Ibn Saud wished to issue a protest against the assumption of the Caliphate by King Hussein of the Hejaz, he put Faisal's name on the protest as sole signatory. In the same year Faisal headed the main force directed by Ibn Saud against the Hejaz and in 1925 he commanded at the siege of Jeddah, and when, at the end of the year, the town surrendered to the Wahhabi forces, he became Governor of Mecca and Viceroy of the Hejaz.

In the young state of Saudi Arabia, lacking in administrative experience and testing various organs of government, Faisal was used by his father, as later by his brother, in many responsible positions, often in several at one time. Thus in 1931, while still Viceroy of the Hejaz, he was President of the Consultative Assembly and Minister of the Interior, and he was then appointed by Ibn Saud President of the Council of Deputies also. Yet in that same year he was employed on an important foreign mission visiting a number of European countries, in particular Turkey and the Soviet Union. In 1934, when the Imam of the Yemen* quarrelled with Ibn Saud, Faisal led the Saudi forces which, by advancing along the coast and capturing Hodeidah while his brother Saud's army was still entangled in the mountains, compelled the Imam to give in. In the negotiations about Palestine, in London, which were followed by the White Paper of 1939, Faisal headed the Saudi delegation.

During the war, in 1943, Faisal went to the United States—the first Saudi royalty to visit that country. In 1945 he was chairman of the Saudi delegation to San Francisco, when Saudi Arabia joined the United Nations Organization, and he was Saudi representative at the San Francisco World Security Conference: and when the conference of heads of Arab League states was held in Egypt in 1946, he represented his father there.

The last office to which Faisal was appointed by his father was that of Vice-President of the Council of Ministers, of which Saud the Crown Prince was President. When Saud came to the throne on the death of Ibn Saud in 1953 Faisal succeeded him, not only as President of the Council of Ministers but also as Crown Prince.

Early in 1958 Saudi Arabia, in spite of the huge revenue from oil, was in grave financial straits, and in March King Saud virtually handed the government of the country over to Faisal, giving him control of finance, internal and foreign affairs, and defence. In December 1960, however, the King said that he had accepted Faisal's resignation as Prime Minister and he retired into relative obscurity, but there was no sign that he resented his relegation to the background.

Less than two years later (October 1962) King Saud was obliged to recall his brother to power. Faisal became Prime Minister and Minister for Foreign Affairs. He found the finances much sounder than when he was recalled four years earlier, which suggested that the measures he had taken then had been successful. Already in August it had been announced that the budget had been balanced, and that in another two years the national debt would have been liquidated. The budget of November 1962, which also balanced, made a significant cut in the allocation to the royal family. In that same month it was announced that a programme of legal and social reform, within the framework of Islam, was to be undertaken, and in particular that slavery was to be finally abolished.

For much of 1963 King Saud was abroad, ill and under treatment. There were clear signs that his reputation was falling, and that the more progressive members of the royal family were supporting Faisal.

In March 1964 the latter, by decree of the Council of Ministers, assumed full powers, and the following November he acceded to the throne when the Council further decreed Saud's deposition. Saud appeared to accept the verdict and on January 4, 1965 formally pledged allegiance to Faisal; and although two years later he unexpectedly took up residence in Egypt and launched a series of violent attacks on his brother through Cairo Radio, he was obviously a sick man acting under the influence of President Nasser* and did little harm to Faisal's position.

Meanwhile, since 1963, Faisal's relations with Nasser had been steadily worsening. The two rulers represented the poles of the Arab World, Faisal standing for tradition and conservatism, Nasser for revolution and Socialism; but whereas Nasser cherished a burning ambition to become the acknowledged leader of a united Arab World, Faisal sought only to preserve his position and his dominions. They were in direct confrontation in the Yemen, where in 1962 a Nasser-inspired revolt had overthrown the Monarchy but had failed to overcome Royalist resistance; for Faisal was supporting the Royalists with money and arms lest a Nasserite satellite state be established on his southern frontier, whereas Nasser had felt compelled to send in Egyptian troops and aircraft to aid the revolutionaries lest their defeat should injure his prestige. A series of conferences between the rulers to end the confrontation resulted in deadlock and merely increased their enmity.

In 1966 King Faisal, during a visit to the Shah of Iran, spoke in the Iranian Parliament of the need for closer cooperation between Muslim states against "alien and atheist influences". This advocacy of Islamic solidarity was generally taken to be meant as a political counterblast to the conception of Arab unity of which Nasser was the chief protagonist; in the event, however, it merely served to demonstrate the declining influence of Islam in an increasingly secular Arab world, for after receiving lip-service from the more conservative Arab rulers, Kings Hassan of Morocco, Idris of Libya, and Hussein of Jordan, it came to nothing. King Faisal continued, however, to encourage Islamic cooperation by a series of visits to states with Islamic affiliations; and in 1969, after the fire in the El-Aqsa Mosque in Jerusalem, he was responsible for the convening of an Islamic conference in Rabat, at which Israeli responsibility for this disaster was alleged and roundly condemned.

The defeat of the Arabs by the Israelis in the "Six-Day War" of 1967 was not without its effects on Saudi Arabia, even though Saudi forces were not directly engaged. At a subsequent Arab "summit conference" at Khartum, King Faisal joined the rulers of other oil-producing states in offering substantial subsidies to the principal losers, Egypt and Jordan; and another important result was the patching-up of an agreement between him and Nasser over the Yemen, Faisal agreeing to cease subsidizing the Royalists in return for Nasser's undertaking to withdraw from the Yemen the forces now so desperately needed for the defence of the Suez Canal frontier of Egypt against Israel. On the other hand, King Faisal had no sympathy for the leftward trend, and especially for the increased influence of Soviet Russia, which the defeat had occasioned in some Arab states.

The announcement in 1968 that Great Britain, the protector of the string of Arab Sheikhdoms along the eastern frontiers of Saudi Arabia, intended to withdraw her forces from the Persian Gulf area by 1971 posed many problems for King Faisal, not least that of Iranian claims in the region. In November of that year, however, he received a state visit from the Shah of Iran, during which these questions were discussed and an agreement signed delimiting the offshore areas in the Gulf claimed by each monarch. King Faisal, nevertheless, remained suspicious of any Iranian initiative in the region; and while he at first supported a project to form a Union of Arab Emirates in the Gulf, he refused to recognize it when formed, on the grounds that one of its members, Abu Dhabi, remained in occupation of the oases of Buraimi, his father's claims to which remained outstanding. He also had trouble on his southern frontiers: despite the withdrawal of Egyptian forces from North Yemen the Republicans had triumphed over the Royalists and established the régime which he did not recognize until 1970; while South Yemen, after the withdrawal of the British from the Aden Protectorate, had fallen into the hands of a militantly left-wing régime with which Saudi forces clashed in 1969 and which King Faisal likewise refused to recognize.

Within Saudi Arabia left-wing attempts at revolt in 1969 proved abortive. On the other hand, the spread of education and wider reception of radio broadcasts, especially from Cairo, were gradually creating a demand among the rapidly growing educated class for the reform and modernization of the administration, and also for the closer involvement of the country in the Arab-Israel conflict, which was now obsessing the Arab world. These demands were opposed by the majority of the huge royal family, who constituted the largest vested interest in the country and desired only a continuance of the status quo; but the King recognized that their opposition risked setting up dangerous pressures and could endanger the family paramountcy. He therefore intensified the programmes of education and economic development, especially agricultural, which he had long since initiated; and from 1972 onwards he or his spokesmen began ever more openly to advocate the recovery of the Arab lands in Israeli occupation.

In July 1973, he for the first time referred to the possibility of a cutback in Saudi oil deliveries to the Americans if their support for Israel were not modified; and although his long friendship with the United States and collaboration with American oil companies operating in his country for the moment held up execution of this threat, a visit by the Egyptian President in August seems to have finally convinced him that the time to use the oil weapon in the interests of the Arabs as a whole was approaching. When, therefore, hostilities between Egypt, Syria, and Israel broke out in October the King first announced a 10 per cent overall reduction in Saudi oil exports and then, a few days later, a complete stoppage of these exports to the United States. The enormous oil potential of Saudi Arabia made this measure a grave menace to American industry, and King Faisal found himself for the first time in a dominant position in the Arab world. Once a ceasefire had been proclaimed, he made clear his determination that Arab claims against Israel should be satisfied; and, as befitted the Guardian of the Holy Places of Islam, he made clear to the Americans his concern that any settlement should include the return of the Old City of Jerusalem to Arab control.

Throughout 1974 and in the early months of 1975 he was in regular consultation with President Sadat and other Arab leaders who were anxious for the continuation of the King's massive backing vital for their struggle with Israel.

King Faisal's outstanding characteristics were loyalty, to his family and people; conservatism; and a realism which often bordered on cynicism. His 50 years' experience of dealing with men of all kinds and races in widely differing circumstances enabled him to sum up almost unfailingly the elements of a situation and to adopt the course of action best calculated to further his constant aims—the preservation of the realm which his father had created and of his family's interests therein. He was often criticized for excessive caution; but under his rule his once hopelessly backward country made real progress, and his subjects owe him a debt of gratitude.

In appearance he was slim and of medium height, with the thin aquiline features so often found among Arabs, but a somewhat saturnine expression, perhaps due to constant ill-health which involved him in several operations. He was deeply religious and his way of life unusually austere; unlike his father and most of his family, he lived for many years with one wife (his third). He had seven sons.

March 26, 1975.

Air Marshal Sir Robert Saundby, K.C.B., K.B.E., M.C., D.F.C., A.F.C., who died on September 25, 1971 at the age of 75, will be chiefly remembered for his long period of service at Bomber Command Headquarters during the 1939-45 war, where he served first as Senior Air Staff Officer and later as Deputy Air Officer Commanding-in-Chief under Sir Arthur Harris. He was at the High Wycombe headquarters longer than his chief, and for both of them it was their last appointment in the Service.

Perhaps no part of wartime operations aroused more controversy than strategic bombing, both during and after hostilities, and to Saundby, in the absence of his former Commander-in-Chief from the country, fell the postwar task of attempting to correct some of the misconceptions and ill-founded criticisms of what R.A.F. Bomber Command had been directed to do and the extent to which it succeeded in that task. After his retirement he devoted himself with great vigour to the furtherance of the Royal Air Forces Association.

Robert Henry Magnus Spencer Saundby was born on April 26, 1896, son of Dr. Robert Saundby, Professor of Medicine at Birmingham University for over 40 years. Leaving King Edward VI School, Birmingham, in 1913, he entered the traffic department of the London and North Western Railway as a probationer. In June 1914 he obtained a commission in the 5th Battalion, Royal Warwickshire Regiment (Territorial Force) but in January 1916 he was seconded to the Royal Flying Corps. He served with No. 24 squadron in France and was wounded in July; but he won the M.C. the following year by shooting down an airship at night near Saxmundham.

In the latter part of the war he was engaged on flying duties at the experimental station at Orfordness, and on instructor duties. In 1919 he received his permanent commission in the Royal Air Force, took a seaplane course at Lee-on-Solent, studied at the R.A.F. and Naval Cooperation School at Calshot and was awarded the A.F.C.

Wing Commander Saundby took the Imperial Defence College course in 1933 and returned to the R.A.F. Staff College afterwards as an instructor for two years. In 1937 he was appointed Deputy Director of Operations and from 1938 until the end of 1940 held successively at the Air Ministry the posts of Deputy Director and Director of Operational Requirements, and Assistant Chief of Air Staff (Operational Requirements and Tactics), being promoted to Air Vice-Marshal on taking up the latter appointment.

On retirement he quickly found an outlet for his energies in work for ex-servicemen and in promoting the regrowth of the Auxiliary and Reserve Forces. He became chairman of the council of the Royal Air Forces Association and a life vice-president, president of the metropolitan area of the British Legion, as well as taking an active part in the central and Berkshire organiza-

tions of the Territorial and Auxiliary Forces Association. In 1960 he was appointed a deputy-lieutenant for Berkshire.

He was devoted to the sport of fly-fishing and was a president of the Piscatorial Society, whose centennial publication, *The Book of the Piscatorial Society, 1836-1936,* he edited.

September 27, 1971.

Elsa Schiaparelli, the fashion designer, died on November 13, 1973. By the originality and daring of her ideas she made fashion history between the two world wars. Cecil Beaton once wrote of her: "She injected a healthy note into the thirties, inventing her own particular form of ugliness and salubriously shocking a great many people".

Hers indeed was the shot in the arm which fashion needed at that dull period, for she designed to amuse rather than to impress, to shock rather than to charm; and this, as it turned out, was the approach that the international smart set which she catered for was in the mood to adopt at that time. An intimate knowledge of American women—their whims and passion for accessories—which she had picked up and noted during a working trip to the United States after the war, was an important contributing factor in her success.

The first Paris heard of Elsa Schiaparelli was in the mid-twenties, when she began attracting attention by designing "amusing" knitwear, jumpers and cardigans decorated with the modernistic designs in vogue in decoration at that time. This she did in an hotel bedroom on the Left Bank; but by 1927 she had moved to modest quarters on the top floor of No. 4 rue de la Paix, where, encouraged by her almost immediate success with knitwear, she branched out into informal sportwear.

The handrail of the winding stairs that led up to these salons was a rope, a gimmick copied by decorators the world over. That rope, in a sense, was symbolic of the new, gay, often crazy, sometimes outrageous styles that began to flow from the rue de la Paix salons and later from the handsome John Law mansion on the Place Vendôme which she took over in 1934. It had become fashionable to be dressed by "Schiap".

Schiaparelli had a flair for fabrics and was the first dressmaker to use rough-surfaced woollens, linens, heavy crepes and "tree-bark" cloques for formal as well as for sports clothes. It was said that she always asked manufacturers to show her their throw-outs, which she often put to good account.

Her colours were rich, daring, often crude; "shocking" pink has since passed into the everyday vocabulary of colour. She made a feature of heavily encrusted, barbaric embroideries for evening, and from her many travels brought back new and exciting ideas. The most far-reaching of these was the squared shoulder line, which had been suggested, it is said, by the husky build of the ski instructors in Switzerland. The built-up shoulder line was launched in the winter of 1931-32 and remained a fashion feature for the next two decades.

Schiaparelli was the first to use the zipper fastening in dressmaking (1935) and the first to use nylon and other man-made fibres. Her buttons were always amusing, often provocative; and button and allied accessory manufacturers everywhere still owe a debt of gratitude to Schiaparelli for the new turn given to their trade by her restless inventiveness.

There was often a touch of surrealism in Schiaparelli designs. A suit decorated with bureau doors for pockets was said to have been inspired by Salvador Dali; a divan in her boutique, made in the form of a giant pair of scarlet lips, came from the same source.

Vividly aware of the present and the topical, any outstanding international event was grist to the Schiaparelli mill. Lease-lend produced the dollar sign button; cash-and-carry, giant pockets. And when on one occasion the Paris seamstresses came out on strike just before the collections, Schiaparelli, unlike the other houses, opened on time, the unfinished models held together by tacking threads and pins.

Despite the surface nonsense and the shock element inherent in every Schiaparelli collection, the models themselves were not only good but wearable; and for more than a decade it was the ambition of elegant women the world over to possess a "Schiap" dress or a "Schiap" suit. She received the 1940 Neiman-Marcus (Texas) award for distinguished service in the fields of fashion.

Elsa Schiaparelli was born in Rome. She became a French subject in 1931, partly, it was said, because of her dislike of the Fascist regime in Italy. There was never general agreement about her age, a subject on which she was herself reticent.

Before becoming a fashion designer she worked in the United States as a film script-writer and as a translator for an importing company; and she engaged in freelance writing and did some sculpture. Her marriage was dissolved. Her book, *Shocking Life*, was published in 1954.

She leaves a daughter and two grand-daughters.

November 15, 1973.

Baldur von Schirach, the former leader of the Hitler Youth, died on August 8, 1974 in a small hotel in a resort on the River Mosel. He was 67.

Narrow and fanatical though he was, his idealism appeared to have been genuine and his character exempt from the worst traits of his Nazi associates. The most reputable—as he was the youngest—of Hitler's circle, for that very reason he exercized perhaps the most dangerous moral influence of them all. Intoxicated by the personality of Hitler and by Rosenberg's racial theories, his enthusiasm was extremely infectious. He had an undoubted power of inspiring youth, and to countless thousands of German children and adolescents he became the embodiment of their ideals.

A born organizer and first-class propagandist, he reinforced his own spiritual appeal by every device known to human ingenuity and was as successful in his results as any of Hitler's lieutenants. His teaching naturally gave deep concern to the churches of Germany. He subordinated both religion and the family to an extravagant political theory, but even more serious than his heresies was the fact that young Germany was instinctively on his side, and that his impress seemed to possess a lasting quality.

Baldur von Schirach was born on May 9, 1907, the son of a German father and an American mother. His maternal great-grandfather, he claimed, was a Union officer who lost a leg in the Battle of Bull Run.

In 1924, having heard Hitler speak, he, like so many others, became immediately a passionate admirer and disciple. As soon as he could he went to Munich, threw himself heart and soul into the organization of the students there, and in virtue of his enthusiasm and ability persuaded great numbers of students not only in Munich but from many other parts of Germany to join the party.

Hitler was swift to realize his special gifts and was also flattered by his open worship. As a result, when he was barely of age, Schirach was permitted to form the Nazi *Studentenbund* and was shortly afterwards appointed to represent youth in the councils of the party. Because of these greater opportunities, he was able to add enormously to the number of his converts. Then, having largely succeeded in his original object, he turned his attention to the pupils of the secondary schools. Eventually all young people of Germany between five and 20 were placed under his leadership. An indefatigable worker, who went here, there and everywhere, he also possessed a considerable attraction for the young—he was personable, vital and eloquent—and became the idol of countless numbers of them.

The gospel which Schirach carried into the nurseries, schools and universities of Germany was primarily one of self-immolation in a blind devotion to the Führer and the party. "For life is nothing", he said, "loyalty is everything and everything is the love of Adolf Hitler; the leader of the German Youth and the German nation." In conformity with Rosenberg he taught that whereas their blood made Germans a lordly race apart and the obligation of preserving its purity lay on all, they owed in return for this privilege a complete subservience to the national idealism as dictated to them. It was, of course, a philosophy closely correlated with the military ambitions of the Nazi Party, but it exacted an allegiance more complete than any which European militarism had hitherto ventured to demand. Unfortunately its mystical quality struck deep into the German soul.

Schirach's exultation of patriotism, as defined by the Nazis, above the claims of religion and family naturally caused many heart-searchings in Germany; but he was a Pied Piper who, because his tunes were subtly flattering to adolescence, drew the young after him.

Schirach was to claim later that he became an anti-Semite after reading Henry Ford's book *The Eternal Jew*. In 1939 he was making speeches declaring that Jewry and England were "so closely linked that one could regard them as identical conceptions" and that the English were "a people of classic mediocrity" living in a "spiritual desert in which cultural life and any higher human existence were unthinkable".

In October 1939 it was announced that he, the pattern of German manhood, had been rejected for army service by a medical board. In January 1940, conscious possibly of loss of prestige, he was said to have enlisted as a volunteer. In August, however, the Führer relieved him of his position as leader of the Hitler Youth and appointed him *Reich Statthalter* and *Gauleiter* of Vienna, where he helped organize the deportation of Jews to extermination camps in the east.

Arrested by the Allies in Austria at the end of the war, Schirach professed a change of heart and at the Nuremberg trial launched into a tirade against Hitler, the man he had once considered the saviour of Germany. He would have to live with the guilt, he said, that he had educated the youth for a man "who committed murders a millionfold". Auschwitz he called "the most devilish mass murder in history".

On October 1, 1946 Schirach was sentenced to 20 years' imprisonment. The verdict read: "After the Nazi Party had come to power, Schirach, using physical violence and other methods, drove out of existence all youth groups which competed with the Hitler Youth. He established the Hitler Youth as a source of replacement for the Nazi Party formations. The Tribunal finds that Schirach, although he did not originate the policy of deporting Jews from Vienna, participated in this deportation though he knew that the best they could hope for was a miserable existence in the ghettos of the east."

He served out his term in Spandau prison in the company of Rudolf Hess and Albert Speer. Schirach later wrote his memoirs called *I Believed in Hitler* and appeared on television in Britain, repeating the denial that he made at his trial—that he did not know that the Jews who were deported from Austria, while he was *Gauleiter* of Vienna, were going to their deaths. He had read about this in foreign publications, but had dismissed it as propaganda.

He married Henriette Hoffman, the

daughter of Hitler's photographer, and had four children. In 1950, while he was in Spandau, his wife divorced him.

August 9, 1974.

Professor Daniel Schlumberger, the French archaeologist, died on October 20, 1972 at Princeton, New Jersey, where he had been doing research. He was 67. He was on leave from his duties at the University of Strasbourg, where he occupied a chair.

Born at Muhlhouse, he was educated there and also at the universities of Strasbourg and Paris. Between 1929 and 1941 he was first Assistant Inspector and then Inspector of Antiquities for the French High Commission in the Levant.

He was well known in England as one of the most distinguished of the French archaeologists working overseas during the postwar years. Equally at home in Islamic archaeology as in that of the Classical civilizations, as early as 1936-38 he had conducted excavations at the Umayyad palace of Qasr-al-Khayr-al-Gharbi in the Syrian desert. Soon after the war he completed the publication of its important frescoes.

In 1945 he went to Kabul as Director of the Délégation Archéologique Française en Afghanistan, and undertook prospection at the fabled site of Balkh, capital of the Hellenistic successors of Alexander the Great in the East. Local interest in the investigation of Islamic civilization led him next to Lashkari Bazar in Southern Afghanistan, near the confluence of the rivers Helmand and Arghandab, and the site of a palace and barracks of the Ghaznavid dynasty (11th century A.D.), where excavations revealed architectural remains, and important frescoes illustrating the Turkish guards with their gold or silver maces.

Perhaps his greatest discoveries began in 1951, when news reached him of the finding in the northern town of Pul-i Khumri (during roadwork at a place called Surkh Kotal) of discontinuous stone blocks bearing large Greek letters, but apparently text in a previously unknown language. Excavations quickly set in hand exposed a great sanctuary, sited on a spur, and reached by monumental steps ascending from the plain. The shrine emerged as a Mazdaean fire-temple, dedicated to the memory of Kanishka, legendary emperor of the Kushan dynasty ruling in much of Central Asia, who became famous in Buddhist scripture. The origin of the temple was explained by a long inscription in Greek characters found in 1957.

Professor Schlumberger always presented a figure of the greatest distinction, and either in French or in English (which as a result of wartime residence he spoke perfectly, with an attractive trace of accent) was one of the most commanding lecturers of the day, as those who heard his Albert Reckitt Archaeological Lecture at the British Academy in 1961 will recall. The occasion was enlivened by his studied use of suspense to grip the audience, and some charming touches of humour.

The ten years' campaigns of excavations at Surkh Kotal formed the subject of a series of reports in the *Journal Asiatique.*

Finally, on the eve of his retirement from the *délégation* in 1963, Daniel Schlumberger played his part in an even more capital discovery. Following up the reports of no less a personage than H.M. the King of Afghanistan, he was able to identify architectural remains at Ay Khanum, a village on the river Oxus close to the Soviet border, as those of a Hellenistic city dating back to the time of Alexander himself. This was the first such Greek city discovered in Afghanistan, and excavations have continued subsequently under the direction of his successor.

Soon afterwards, he returned to a professorship at Strasbourg University. Several years later he took over charge of the Institut Française d'Archéologie at Beirut where, in 1969, his friends were grieved to learn that he had suffered a severe stroke, as a result of which he remained disabled for many months. However, his recovery made progress, and in September 1972 at the Sixth International Congress of Iranian Art and Archaeology at Oxford, it was a delight to see him, though still somewhat frail, moving freely about the gathering, and conversing animatedly with colleagues. News of his death at Princeton just over a month later came as a bombshell. He leaves a wife and five children.

As a scholar, Schlumberger's impressive discoveries were fully matched by his scientific caution and restraint. He would never jump to conclusions, but subjected each new piece of evidence to scrupulous examination, a seeming hesitancy which was more than justified by the enhanced authority of his final results. His latest book, *L'Orient Hellénisé*, published in German (Holle Verlag, Baden-Baden) in 1969, and in French in 1970 (Éditions Albin Michel), gave a perceptive and extremely comprehensive survey of the Greek artistic heritage in the Middle East, from Syria and Lebanon to Afghanistan and India, illuminated everywhere by his unrivalled first-hand experience.

October 25, 1972.

Sir Basil Schonland, C.B.E., F.R.S., director of the Atomic Energy Research Establishment from 1958 to 1960, died on November 24, 1972 at the age of 76.

Basil Ferdinand Jamieson Schonland was born at Grahamstown in South Africa in February 1896. He was educated at St. Andrews College and later at Rhodes University College, Grahamstown, where he obtained First Class Honours in Mathematics.

In the 1914-18 war he joined the Signals Corps of the Royal Engineers and served in France between 1915 and 1918. He was wounded at Arras and twice mentioned in despatches. He was responsible for building a trench wireless set, a forerunner of the Walkie-Talkie of the 1939-45 World War. This was at a time when one of the earlier means of communication was the so-called "power buzzer" whose operation immediately brought down a shower of shells round the transmitting station. He was in charge of telephone communications on the Somme. He retired with the rank of Captain, R.E. and an O.B.E.

After the war he went to Gonville and Caius College, Cambridge, where he was a George Green Scholar and a College Exhibitioner and took the Natural Sciences Tripos in 1919. He then joined Lord Rutherford in the Cavendish Laboratory and carried out research work on the scattering and absorption of B particles from radioactive elements, obtaining his Ph.D. in 1924.

He returned to South Africa as a Lecturer and later became Professor of Physics in the University of Cape Town. He went back to Cambridge for a sabbatical year in 1929.

In 1936 he was appointed the first Director of the Bernard Price Institute of Geophysics in Witwatersrand University and carried out his well-known work on lightning which was recorded in popular form in his book *The Flight of Thunderbolts.* He was elected F.R.S. in 1938.

He joined the South African Corps of Signals as a Brigadier in 1941 and when he visited Britain in that year renewed his friendship with Sir John Cockcroft*, who at that time was Chief Superintendent of the Air Defence Research and Development Establishment and was temporarily responsible for the Army Operational Research Group located at Richmond in Surrey. Cockcroft was able to persuade Schonland to take over the post of Superintendent, and under his direction the operational research group carried out important work on the effectiveness of Anti-Aircraft Radar and measures required to improve its performance.

His interests broadened during the war and he became Scientific Adviser to General Montgomery during his command of the 21st Armoured Group. In this post Schonland's group made important contributions to the effectiveness of a number of operations. Later he became Scientific Adviser on Operational Research to General Eisenhower*. For this distinguished work he was awarded the C.B.E. in 1945.

On his return to South Africa in 1945 he was appointed Science Adviser to the Prime Minister, General Smuts, and became the first President of the South African Council for Scientific and Industrial Research. During his directorship in 1950 he was responsible for the basic planning and direction of the organization. Schonland was especially interested in the exploitation of the uranium which was found in the gold-bearing ores of the Rand and this has made a major contribution to the economy of South Africa.

In 1954 he returned to Britain as Deputy Director of the Atomic Energy Research Establishment at Harwell, and he remained at Harwell till his retirement. In 1958 he succeeded Cockcroft as Director and in 1960 became the Director of the Research Group of the A.E.A. During his period at Harwell he was responsible for a great deal of the administration. He was knighted in 1960.

Schonland was awarded the Hughes Medal of the Royal Society in 1945 for his work on atmospheric electricity and the Faraday Medal of the Institution of Electrical Engineers for his work in nuclear energy in 1962. He held a number of honorary degrees. In 1968 he published *The Atomists, 1805-1933.*

He leaves a widow, a son and two daughters.

November 25, 1972.

General Sir Geoffry Scoones, K.C.B., K.B.E., C.S.I., D.S.O., M.C., who died on September 19, 1975 at the age of 82, won fame as the Commander of the Fourth Army Corps in Burma which met and defeated the Japanese offensive against Imphal in 1944. He was High Commissioner for the United Kingdom in New Zealand from 1953 to 1957.

Scoones was one of the finest leaders produced by the Indian Army in the Second World War. He was a small man. His modesty and diffidence of manner concealed from those who did not know him well his sterling qualities of courage and determination. He inspired confidence by his calmness in action and by his good judgment, as well as by his quiet humour. In Burma he knew every unit under his command, and his Jeep, bouncing along the rough roads and tracks, with its red and white flag in front, was a familiar sight well known to his men all over the vast front which he controlled.

Geoffry Allen Percival Scoones was born at Quetta on January 25, 1893, the eldest son of Major Fitzmaurice Scoones, The Royal Fusiliers. He was educated at Wellington College and the Royal Military College Sandhurst. He was commissioned in his father's regiment in 1912, but, a year later, he transferred to the 2/8 Gurkhas, with whom he served in the First World War on the Western Front. He was awarded the D.S.O. and the M.C.

In 1938 he passed through the Imperial Defence College. His next appointment was as Deputy Director of Military Operations at Army Headquarters in India. He continued to serve in this post after the outbreak of the Second World War, and, in 1941, he was advanced to be Director of Military Operations and Intelligence. In 1942 he was given command of a division,

but, after a few months, he was appointed Commander of the 4th Corps.

When he took over his corps, it was deployed on a defensive front of some two hundred and fifty miles in Assam. Under Slim's* direction, Scoones was soon engaged in preparations for an advance to the Chindwin, but, before it could be begun, the Japanese forestalled the plan by launching an all-out offensive in an attempt to invade India. The second and heaviest phase of the Japanese attack, following their repulse in the Arakam, was directed, in March 1944, against the central sector of the front which was held by the 4th Corps. Anticipating the enemy's action, Slim and Scoones had come independently to the same conclusion that the best course would be to concentrate the corps in the Imphal plain and fight the decisive battle on ground of their own choosing. The plain was therefore put in a state of defence. This entailed a concentration of scattered administrative units, headquarters and airfields in fortified areas capable of all-round resistance and completely self-contained in ammunition and supplies. The garrisons of these fortified areas or keeps were found mainly by the administrative troops themselves, so that the fighting units and formations were left free to manoeuvre offensively.

Owing to a miscalculation of the enemy's strength, the withdrawal of the troops to their prepared positions was left a little late by Scoones, and for a time one of his three divisions, the 17th, was cut off. But, by means of counter attacks, he extricated his troops and, after a month's heavy fighting, completed his concentration in the defensive positions.

For some weeks the fate of Imphal and Kohima, the two key points on the single line of communication with India, hung in the balance. The 4th Corps was completely cut off, but the situation was saved by Scoones's skill in the direction of the fighting, by the steadfastness of the troops, and by the employment of transport aircraft to fly in reinforcements and supplies. Large numbers of aircraft were at the time engaged on carrying supplies to China by the "Hump" route, and these were immediately switched to this new role. By the beginning of April Scoones had four divisions for the all-round defence of Imphal, and under his leadership the tide was slowly turned.

There now followed three months of bitter fighting, in which the Japanese suffered terrible casualties, and, a month later, Scoones was able to pass to the offensive. At the end of May he launched attacks on his north and east fronts with two of his divisions, the 20th and 23rd. The difficulties of the operations were vastly increased by the onset of the monsoon, but the Japanese were near the end of their tether. They had lost nearly half their fighting strength. Their morale suddenly broke and their army began to disintegrate. By the third week of June the 4th Corps

had fought its way through to make contact with Stopford's 33rd Corps which had been attacking simultaneously from Kohima. The road behind was reopened and Scoones received the first overland supply convoy to reach him since the end of March.

The pursuit of the enemy was pressed with relentless vigour all through the monsoon, and Scoones's corps, on the right of the advance, was directed down the Tiddim road. At this stage of the operations it became evident that the Japanese had suffered so heavily that it would be possible to withdraw, for a much needed rest, the troops and headquarters which had been longest in action and had had the hardest time. Among these was the 4th Corps Headquarters and, at the end of July, it was returned to reserve in India.

The battle in which Scoones had played such a splendid part was the first victory over the Japanese army in the open field, and they never recovered from it. The permanent losses they had suffered were estimated at over 27,000 men. It was one of the most remarkable battles of the whole war.

Scoones was soon afterwards appointed to be Commander-in-Chief of the Central Command in India, and so was not with the 4th Corps when it was brought back to take part in the final phases of the Burma campaign. On completing his tenure of the Central Command, where he was promoted General, he was appointed Principal Staff Officer of the Defence Staff at the Commonwealth Relations Office, where he served from 1947 to 1953.

He married, in 1918, Angela, daughter of the Rev. Spencer Buller, and had one son and two daughters.

September 20, 1975.

Cyril Scott, who died on December 31, 1970 at the age of 91, was an English composer who made a greater impression in Germany and Austria than in his own country, more particularly before the first European war, though an opera of his, *The Alchemist,* was produced at Essen in 1925.

He had an individual talent which was not submerged into a colourless cosmopolitanism by his German training, and his songs and short pieces for piano won him fame at home by reason of a lyrical appeal that was fundamentally English. But he remained outside the nationalist revival and made no decisive impression with his larger works, where Continental influence and his own kind of musical thought ran counter to traditional English ways. In his early days he was a daring innovator, but in middle life he attached himself to none of the experimental schools of thought which flourished after 1918. It deserves to be remembered that in his day he was admired by Debussy; claimed as "original" by Strauss; and was admitted to be an innovator by Elgar.

He continued to compose well into his old age. After his 90th birthday in 1969 he went to the Queen Elizabeth Hall to hear Moura Lympany and the Polyphona Orchestra perform the piano concerto he wrote in 1913-14 (first performed under Sir Thomas Beecham's* baton in 1915).

He was born on September 27, 1879, at Oxton in Cheshire, the only son of Henry and Mary Scott. His father was a Greek scholar and his mother a gifted amateur musician. At an early age he showed signs of exceptional musical talent; in fact he was a prodigy, writing his first compositions at the age of seven and playing the piano remarkably well.

When 12 years old, he was sent to study piano with Uzielli at the Conservatorium in Frankfurt. He was the youngest pupil in the Conservatorium. Scott returned to England for a short period to further his English education, but then went back to Frankfurt at the age of 17 to resume his lessons and work at composition under Iwan Knorr. There he became a fellow student and friend of Percy Grainger*, Balfour Gardiner, Norman O'Neill and Roger Quilter. All who came into contact with him during his youth testified to the wonderful natural musical gifts with which he was endowed. The outpouring of finely wrought and long-drawn melodies, a flow of rhythmical and original arabesques, a sensitive feeling for beautiful and daring harmonies were his conspicuous qualities.

Scott's output during the years 1898 to 1920 was considerable. An extraordinary pianistic ability enabled him to write with the greatest ease for the piano, and his innumerable pieces, covering a great range of style and grade of difficulty, ought to have become a treasure store for teachers and pianists alike. Certainly "Water-Wagtail" and "Lotus Land" are not forgotten.

His lyrical sense of poetry, his melodic and harmonic gifts fitted him also for song writing. The public knows his "Lullaby" and "Blackbird Song", which became widely popular, but he wrote a great number of other original and beautiful songs, such as the two Chinese songs, "Waiting" and "A Picnic", and the "Villanelle", "Song of London", "Rondel of Rest", and many others.

Of Scott's chamber music works, perhaps the pianoforte quintet is the best. A string quartet was widely performed in Germany. Of his orchestral works, many written between the ages of 20 and 30 were given their first performances in Germany. He was 20 when his First Symphony was played in Darmstadt. His Second Symphony had a hearing at a Promenade concert under Sir Henry Wood; and his "Heroic Suite" was performed under Richter at Manchester. The "Princess Maleine" overture with chorus was given in Vienna. "Aubade" was performed in London, Darmstadt, Dresden and Berlin. Other works were "Two Passacaglias"; a pianoforte concerto; a setting of "La Belle Dame Sans Merci"

for baritone solo, chorus and orchestra, given at the Leeds Festival of 1934; and a "Nativity Hymn", which was selected by the Carnegie Trust for publication in 1934.

Scott was also the winner of the *Daily Telegraph* prize of £100 for a new concert overture for full orchestra which was performed by the B.B.C. orchestra at one of their London Festival concerts in May 1934. To these must be added "Mystic Ode" for chorus and orchestra, "Noel" for orchestra, and a violin concerto. Besides *The Alchemist* Scott wrote two other operas, *The Shrine* and *The Saint of the Mountain*.

That Cyril Scott failed to develop into a more mature and greater composer, and did not fulfil the high promise he displayed in early life, was due to lack of concentration and self-criticism. Many other interests were allowed to compete with his music. He very seriously took up the study of esoteric religions, theosophy, mysticism, and transcendental philosophy; and in his later years unorthodox medicine. Scott wrote some interesting books on these different subjects, among them *Music: Its Secret Influence Throughout the Ages; The Philosophy of Modernism; An Outline of Occultism; Man Is My Theme;* and on medical subjects *Doctors, Disease and Health* and *Victory over Cancer.*

As a young man he wrote some poems, which have a certain rhythmic quality. He also translated some of Stefan George's poems into English (Scott was a great friend of the poet). In 1925 he published some memoirs called *My Years of Indiscretion.* In 1969 he produced an autobiography *Bone of Contention.*

In all these sidelines there were glimpses of intuition and originality, if not always very happily expressed. But it was in music that Scott's natural gifts and inspiration lay. Had these been allowed to grow unhindered, they might have culminated in greater achievements. His larger works lacked that perfection of technique and artistic mastery which is acquired and developed only through years of assiduous and concentrated study, and often of heartbreaking effort. Nevertheless, he will be remembered as a maker of sweet music, music naturally inspired, melodious and richly coloured.

As a man and personality he endeared himself to all his friends by his charming, loyal, affectionate qualities, his ever-boyish spirit and his sense of humour.

January 1, 1971.

Elisabeth Scott, F.R.I.B.A., (Mrs. George Richards), who won the competition for designing the new Shakespeare Memorial Theatre, Stratford on Avon, in 1928, died on June 19, 1972.

In order to ensure that the new theatre to be erected on the site of the old—a very Gothic building destroyed by fire—should be worthy and adequate, the governors of

the Shakespeare Memorial Theatre had appointed an advisory council consisting of Reginald McKenna, Sir Charles Holmes, Sir James Barrie, E. Guy Dawber and H. Granville Barker, representing finance, art, literature, architecture and the drama. This council recommended that an architect should be chosen by public competition under the auspices of the Royal Institute of British Architects, who appointed as assessors E. Guy Dawber, president of the R.I.B.A., Cass Gilbert, president of the Academy of Design of the United States, and Robert Atkinson, director of education of the Architectural Association. In the second stage of the competition, Raymond Hood replaced Gilbert.

The competition was not limited to the United Kingdom but an invitation to compete was sent to the architects of Canada and the United States of America, and more than 12 months was allowed for the preparation of designs.

Originally 72 designs were submitted and six were selected for the final competition. In their report of January 1928, the assessors said that they had unanimously selected Design No. 3 as the most suitable design submitted. This was Miss Scott's. Moving the adoption of the assessors' report, A. D. Flower, chairman of the executive committee of the governors, said that a further stage had been reached in the great movement to develop the Bayreuth ideal at Stratford on Avon, and, seconding the adoption, George Bernard Shaw said that Miss Scott's plan was the only one that showed any theatre-sense.

The Shakespeare Memorial Theatre, for the construction of which Miss Scott went into partnership with Maurice Chesterton, to whom she had previously acted as assistant, was a radical building in England for its time and the brickwork has aged well. The external sculpture in cut brick was by Eric Kennington. The treatment of the site, with a landing stage, steps and terraced gardens leading up from the river, is admirable. Seen from across the Avon, with the horizontal lines of the building according with its movement and the vista closed by the spire of the parish church where Shakespeare lies buried, the effect of a celebration is irresistible.

Subsequently, Miss Scott worked on the expansion of Newnham College, Cambridge, of which the first completed portion was opened by Queen Mary in 1938. In this work she had for partners J. C. Shepherd—who had joined her and Chesterton during the progress of the Shakespeare Memorial Theatre—and John Breakwell A.R.I.B.A.

Elisabeth Whitworth Scott was born at Bournemouth in 1898. Her father Bernard Scott was a doctor, but she had architectural connexions. Her paternal grandfather, also a doctor, was brother to Sir Gilbert Scott, the great Victorian architect, and her grandmother was a sister of another notable architect, George Frederick Bodley. Sir Giles Gilbert Scott, architect of Liverpool Cathedral, was a cousin.

Educated at Redmoor School, Bournemouth, Miss Scott received her professional training at the school of the Architectural Association, taking the full five years' course and gaining her diploma in 1924. Afterwards she was assistant successively to Louis de Soissons*, at Welwyn Garden City, Oliver Hill, in London, and Maurice Chesterton—with whom she afterwards entered into partnership—in Hampstead.

June 24, 1972.

The Very Rev. R. F. V. Scott, D.D., who was for 22 years Minister of St. Columba's Church of Scotland, Pont Street, London, and Moderator of the General Assembly of the Church of Scotland, 1956-57, died in Edinburgh on March 1, 1975, aged 77.

Dr. Scott's years at St. Columba's were eventful and exacting, for he went there the year before the Second World War broke out. One night in May 1941, he saw the church destroyed by fire from incendiary bombs, and then had to wait 14 years, years burdened by money raising and negotiations for building licences, before he saw the new church completed, an imposing white building in Portland stone replacing the old brick one of 1884. That had been the first Pont Street St. Columba's, an off-shoot of the Scottish National Church, Covent Garden.

In the 14 years between the old and the new, Dr. Scott had the particularly difficult task, which he performed with zeal and good humour, not only of holding together what is inevitably a scattered congregation, but also of continuing to provide a centre for "exile" Scots.

St. Columba's is one of the largest charges in the Church of Scotland but it has come to fill a singular role in London life. First, it provides regular church life for resident Scots; then it is a port of call for travellers, not only Scots but also those from overseas whose church connexions are rooted in the work of Scottish missionaries.

It has, also, for reasons not always apparent even to its ministers, become a place where countless people, who have no Scottish link at all, but who have come adrift in the hectic life of the capital, decide to seek help.

Robert Forrester Victor Scott was born on August 11, 1897, at the manse of Logie Buchan, Aberdeenshire, and ministering came naturally to him partially, no doubt, because it was in the family. He was the son of the Rev. William Scott, and on his mother's side there was a long line of Church of Scotland ministers.

He went to Morrison's Academy, Crieff, then to the Royal High School, Edinburgh, and by the time he left there war had broken out. He served in the ranks, rising to the rank of sergeant, with the 13th Battalion, The Royal Scots, and was wounded three times.

He studied at Edinburgh University, was ordained to the parish of Strathbogie, Fife, in 1923, went to St. Andrew's Parish, Dundee in 1926 and nine years later became colleague and successor to the great John White, of The Barony, Glasgow.

It was John White who, on learning that St. Columba's needed a colleague and successor to his friend, Dr. Archibald Fleming, recommended "Robin Scott with his many great gifts".

Scott moved to London in 1938, became a chaplain to the London Scottish Regiment on the outbreak of war, but was released by the War Office in 1940 and resumed full charge of the congregation. Dr. Fleming had become ill, and died in 1941.

Dr. Scott undertook a wide variety of public work. He was chairman of the West London Committee for the Protection of Children, a member of a Home Office Committee on Prostitution and Homosexual Practices, and Presbyterian Chaplain to the Royal Hospital, Chelsea. He was the first Church of Scotland Moderator to be drawn from a ministry within the Presbytery of England.

It was always his wish, while in London, to return eventually to Scotland and take a country parish. This wish was fulfilled in 1960 when he went to Auchterhouse, near Dundee. Scott was recognized from the early years of his ministry as a preacher of great power, what is often called "a people's preacher".

In 1924 he married Phyllis Lee: they had two daughters and one son. His wife died in 1969.

March 3, 1975.

Edward Seago, R.W.S., R.B.A., died on January 19, 1974 in a London hospital. He was 63.

A fluent and prolific painter, he had a very large following spread all over the world and his exhibitions, whether they were held in London or Toronto or Johannesburg or San Francisco, were extremely successful.

Edward Seago is particularly associated with East Anglia where he was born and where he lived and it is in portraying his native countryside that his impressionistic style is perhaps seen to greatest advantage. He had a distinct gift for seizing the peculiarly brilliant quality of the light to be found in Norfolk and Suffolk and for relating it to the beaches, boats, grey-flint church towers and scattered villages of the eastern region.

He by no means confined his work to depicting East Anglia; he was a widely travelled man who during the Second World War while serving with the Royal Engineers produced some interesting work of the Allied forces in Italy, where he often went painting with Field-Marshal Lord Alexander* with whom he formed a close friendship, and who, as readers of Nigel Nicolson's biography *Alex* will remember, was a painter all his life. They had met earlier at Wilton, where Seago was in charge of a corps camouflage section. Of his time in Italy Seago wrote in *With the Allied Armies in Italy.*

The son of Francis Brian Seago, a coal merchant, Edward Brian Seago was born on March 31, 1910. In an introduction which Laurens van der Post wrote to the catalogue of Seago's 1972 London exhibition he told how Seago had little formal education and that his time at a conventional school could be measured in months rather than years. His parents, though well-to-do, discouraged his early desire to become a painter. When seven Seago was struck down by a heart complaint and lay in bed for some years, but it was in a sense a rewarding period for he painted and repainted through the windows of his room all he could see of the Norfolk scene. As his health improved he began to paint hard and to ride and hunt, spending as much of his time as possible in the open air. He had very little regular artistic training, but he was a "star" pupil of the Royal Drawing Society, winning a special prize at the age of 14, and he had some tuition in landscape painting under Bertram Priestman, R.A.

Seago's contact with the circus began early, and when he was about 18 he joined Bevin's Travelling Show, and thereafter for several years spent much of his time with circuses, touring with them throughout the greater part of the British Isles and on the Continent, sharing the ups and downs of life on the road and becoming thoroughly intimate with circus folk. The first fruits of this experience was a book, *Circus Company*, written and illustrated by himself. The introduction was by John Masefield*.

The original drawings for *Circus Company*, together with pictures of the hunting field and racecourse, formed Seago's first London exhibition at the Sporting Gallery in 1933. The exhibition was opened by Lord Harewood, and it had a great success. A year later Seago published *Sons of Sawdust*, which dealt with the fortunes and misfortunes of a small travelling circus in the West of Ireland. It was warmly praised both for its sympathetic understanding of circus life and for its evocation of landscape mood.

In 1937 Seago's association with the Poet Laureate was renewed by the reproduction of 42 of his paintings to accompany the same number of poems by Dr. Masefield in *The Country Scene*. He was a sympathetic illustrator and this gift will be remembered particularly by Norfolk people at the mention of two books on which he worked in collaboration with Lilias Rider Haggard, *I Walked by Night*, and *The Rabbitskin Cap.*

January 21, 1974.

Sir Eric Seal, K.B.E., C.B., Deputy Secretary, Ministry of Works, 1951-59, died on March 31, 1972 at the age of 73. He was Principal Private Secretary to Winston Churchill* when he was First Lord of the Admiralty and later as Prime Minister.

Born in 1898 he was trained as an engineer. Before he joined the air force he was apprenticed to an aeronautical firm and attended night classes at the (then) Northampton Polytechnic; after the war he attended a civil engineering course at the City and Guilds of London College, Finsbury.

In the First World War he served as a 2nd lieutenant in the R.F.C. and later in the R.A.F. as an Observer in France with 62 Squadron.

He originally entered the Civil Service as an assistant examiner in the Patent Office in 1921, when it was virtually impossible due to the slump to get going in engineering. He studied hard privately, mainly at economics and history, and took sixth place in the first postwar open Administrative Competition in 1925.

In 1938, on the day the Navy was mobilized for the Munich crisis, he became the Principal Private Secretary to the First Lord of the Admiralty. He served Duff Cooper for three days until he resigned, and then Lord Stanhope*.

On the day the war with Germany was declared, Winston Churchill became First Lord, and Seal was appointed his Private Secretary. He stayed with him until May 1941, and was thus by the Prime Minister's side during Dunkirk, the Battle of Britain, the night Blitz, and the great initial successes against the Italians in Africa.

When Lend-Lease became a reality, and the ports were being severely bombed, before Hitler attacked Russia, it was decided to set up a fully-equipped Admiralty Delegation in North America, and Seal was appointed by the Prime Minister Deputy Secretary of the Admiralty for North America.

After the war he became Chief of Trade and Industries in the Control Commission for Germany; Director-General of Building Materials in the Ministry of Works; Deputy P.U.S. for Germany in the Foreign Office; and finally Deputy Secretary of the Ministry of Works.

He married in 1926 Gladys, daughter of Frank Leadbitter; they had three sons.

April 3, 1972.

Mary Ethel Seaton, who was an authority on medieval literature, died on June 17, 1974.

She was the daughter of Francis Lambert Seaton, one of the last members of The Honourable the East India Company's Navy. She herself was born in Rangoon. She was educated at The Ladies College, Guernsey, and at Portsmouth High School, and in 1906 won a Goldsmith's Scholarship at Girton College. After obtaining "firsts" in three parts of the Medieval and Modern Languages Tripos in 1909 and 1910, she held the post of Lecturer in English Literature at Girton from 1911 to 1916. In 1925 she became Fellow and Tutor at St. Hugh's College, Oxford; in 1939 received the University appointment of Lecturer in English Literature; she was among the first women to examine in the Final Honour School of English, and in 1951 was made Doctor of Letters. She was awarded the Rose Mary Crayshaw Prize and was a Fellow of the Royal Society of Literature.

Mary Seaton's publications included the considerable work on the *Literary Relations of England and Scandinavia in the Seventeenth Century* (1939), *Venus and Anchises and Other Poems by Phineas Fletcher* (1926), *Sir Richard Roos, Lancastrian Poet* (1961), and a number of articles, among which *"Marlowe's Map"* and *"Comus and Shakespeare"* (*Essays and Studies by Members of the English Association, Vols. X and XXXI*), *"Marlowe's Light Reading"* in *Elizabethan and Jacobean Studies* (1959), are perhaps the best known. She contributed a number of articles to the *Review of English Studies* and to *Medium Aevum*, and had five entries in Hastings' *Encyclopaedia of Religion and Ethics*.

She was an authority on the literature of the late Middle Ages and the Renaissance, and her knowledge of some of the obscurer corners of this long period was probably unrivalled. In her retirement her interests were focused on, though by no means confined to, the fifteenth century and she occupied herself with investigating the style and canon of authors between Chaucer and Wyatt, and notably with the work of Sir Richard Roos. Though many took exception to the exposition of the ingenious anagrammatic methods used by Roos in her lengthy investigation of his work, more discerning critics responded to the admirably reconstructed picture of courtly life and literature of the fifteenth century and the excellent style of this impressive book.

Her love of literature and her scholarship and, equally, the wholesome influence of her sane and kindly personality (exercised perhaps unconsciously and certainly always unpretentiously) were a very real benefit to the English School at Oxford and to her college.

June 22, 1974.

George Seferis, the Greek poet, diplomatist and scholar, who won the Nobel Prize for Literature in 1963, died on September 20, 1971 at the age of 71. He was Greek Ambassador to Britain between 1957 and 1961, at a critical time for Anglo-Greek relations in view of the Cyprus problem.

He refused to publish poetry under military rule in Greece and lived quietly in his beautiful house in Athens. He spoke out against the régime in 1969, when he called for an early end to dictatorship before it degenerated into a tragedy: "It is this tragic ending that consciously or unconsciously torments us, as in the age-old choruses of Aeschylus". Earlier in 1971 he signed a manifesto by 130 Greek intellectuals appealing for freedom and democracy.

He was born George Seferiadis in 1900 in Smyrna, Turkey, the eldest son of a jurist who was an expert in international law but also translated ancient Greek tragedy into demotic Greek, and even had a go at Lord Byron's poetry without knowing a word of English. George went to school in Athens where the family had moved since 1914. It was then that he composed his first verse. "Seferis" was a pen-name.

As his family had strong Republican traditions, the political upheavals in Greece forced them to move in 1917, to Paris, where he studied law and literature at the university, graduating in 1924. It was then decided by the family that he should pursue a career in diplomacy and he was sent to London to brush up his English. There he composed his "Fog", the first verse to be published.

He joined the Greek diplomatic service in 1926 and by 1931 he was appointed consul in London. This period greatly influenced his evolution in poetry and led to a lifelong association and friendship with T. S. Eliot*.

When he became head of the Foreign Ministry's press department in 1938, he continued to compose and translate, this time Archibald Macleish's *Letter from America*.

One day before the German occupation of Athens in 1941 he and his wife fled with the Greek government to Cairo, then to the Greek embassy in South Africa. In 1942 he was appointed to the press department of the government-in-exile in Cairo. He returned to liberated Athens in 1944 after three and a half years of exile.

Recognition of his poetic work came in 1947 when he was awarded the Paiamas prize, named after the Greek poet laureate. But he pursued his diplomatic career which took him to Ankara, London, the Middle East, and finally to London again in 1947 as Ambassador.

It was while there that he was awarded an honorary degree in philosophy at Cambridge (1960), and the Foyle Prize (1961), the first ever given for foreign verse. In August 1961 he returned to Athens, and four years later he retired from the diplomatic service.

One year after the Nobel Prize award, he was made an honorary Doctor of Literature at Oxford in 1964 and at Princeton in 1965. In 1969 the Greek régime refused to grant him a diplomatic passport, to which he was entitled, in order to travel abroad. Later, however, he was given an exit permit and travelled to Western Europe for the last time. He is survived by his widow Maria.

September 25, 1971.

Lord Sefton, the sporting peer and former Lord Mayor of Liverpool, who died on April 13, 1972 at his home, was widely known as an administrator, owner and breeder in racing and coursing. He had been Constable of Lancaster Castle since 1942.

His extensive Lancashire estates had included the famous Aintree racecourse, over which the Grand National is run, and Altcar, home of the coursing classic, the Waterloo Cup.

Hugh William Osbert Molyneux, the seventh earl, was born in December 1898. He went to Harrow and Sandhurst, and served in the Royal Horse Guards. After a period of service as A.D.C. to the Governor-General of Canada he went to India, first as A.D.C. in Madras to the G.O.C. and then in 1926 as A.D.C. to the Viceroy. He was Lord in Waiting to King Edward VIII.

Lord Sefton was Lord Mayor of Liverpool 1944-45. He sold the Kirkby estate, which had been in his family since the Norman Conquest, to Liverpool for £375,000 in 1947. Soon afterwards, 1,000 acres of his Croxteth Park estate were acquired by Liverpool Corporation as a new park, one of the largest in Britain. The greater part of the estate was leased to him for 40 years.

Lord Sefton's famous colours—white, primrose sleeves, black cap—had a big public following, especially at Cheltenham and at Aintree, with which he had such a close family connexion. Perhaps his most popular horse was Irish Lizard, and few who were present at Cheltenham's Christmas meeting in 1954 will forget the reception given to this locally trained steeplechaser when he scored his fourteenth success in a brilliant career.

Although Lord Sefton never won a classic race, he had many triumphs with such high-class performers as Titian, Gaul, Kipling, Andros, Nassau, and St. Lucia, who was later to join his select band of brood mares. His service during the First World War with the Royal Horse Guards ensured that he always had a keen and friendly interest in National Hunt racing, and it gave him great pleasure when he won the 1942 Cheltenham Gold Cup with Medoc II. He had horses first with the late Atty Persse; then with Captain Peter Hastings-Bass, whose early death in 1964 shocked the racing community; and with "Frenchie" Nicholson, his former steeplechase jockey, at Cheltenham. All had good reason to remember his knowledge, understanding and kindness throughout those years.

He acted as a local steward at Newmarket, Liverpool, Ascot, Chester, Manchester and Newbury; and, as a member of the National Hunt Committee and the Jockey Club, sat on innumerable committees. During the last war, when racing and bloodstock interests required special attention and protection, he did invaluable work in association with the late Lord Ilchester and Lord Harewood as a Jockey Club steward,

being senior steward from 1941 to 1943.

In 1949 he sold Aintree racecourse to Topham's Ltd., and then in July 1964 the company's chairman, Mrs. Mirabel Topham, suddenly announced that the controlling interest was to be sold to Capital & Counties Property Company for development. Lord Sefton applied for an injunction restraining this action, on the grounds that a clause in the sale precluded such a transaction. Judgment was given later that year for Lord Sefton, but this was reversed on appeal to the House of Lords. Thus the future of his favourite racecourse remained unsolved at the time of his death: a sad epilogue to a life dedicated to the welfare of the British turf.

Lord Sefton married in 1941 Mrs. Josephine Armstrong Gwynne, of Virginia, U.S.A.

April 15, 1972.

Antonio Segni, President of Italy from 1962 to 1964, when he retired after suffering a cerebral stroke, died on December 1, 1972 in Rome at the age of 81.

The election of Segni to the Presidency of the Republic in May 1962 was in more than one way the culmination of his public career: he won his majority after the stiffest battle which he had ever had to fight, and emerged from it as the first official candidate of the governing Christian Democratic Party to achieve the highest place in the state. And yet apart from his undoubted claims as a man rich in ministerial experience much was heard in the aftermath of the conflict about qualities of modesty and moderation.

The varied facets of his character were in fact inclined to conceal one another rather than combining into a single impression, which made a summary judgment of his personality unusually difficult.

More than one close observer of the Italian political scene confessed to being unable to understand Antonio Segni. He was able to stimulate eulogies, and bitter ill-feeling, invoke confidence as well as resentments, and the extremes grew sharper the nearer people were to him: the wider public was inclined to accept him as a reassuringly venerable symbol. Essentially he was a man who loved office as much as he loved supervising his extensive Sardinian estates; and was as suited to his share in the inner machinations of the Christian Democratic Party as he was to the comparative serenity of lecturing in law at Rome University.

He was provincial in the sense that his native Sardinia never ceased to be one of his main concerns. He was born at Sassari on February 2, 1891, of a well established landed family of Ligurian origin, a connexion quite frequently encountered in Sardinian life. Throughout his long career he took every possible opportunity of returning to his country home at weekends,

the aircraft which took him back in itself adding to the pleasure because he loved flying after his experiences as a reconnaissance pilot in the 1914-18 War.

He took his degree in law at the age of 22 at Sassari University and went on seven years later to the chair of civil procedure in Perugia, where he taught until 1925. He later held chairs at Cagliari, Pavia, and Sassari, becoming Rector Magnificus of Sassari University in 1946, a post which he gave up seven years later when he was appointed Minister of Public Instruction. From 1954 he lectured in the faculty of law—when a member of successive Governments—at Rome.

From the beginning his political career was inseparable from his activities as a militant Roman Catholic. It was this consideration which aroused much of the opposition to his candidature for the Presidency and it must be said that he did not, when faced with a possible clash, show much inclination to give preeminence to affairs of state. He was one of the founders of the earliest Catholic Action Club in Sassari. As soon as the Popular Party— the first Roman Catholic Political group to be authorized by the Vatican—was founded he became a member. By 1923 he sat on its national council and in the following year was designated candidate for the Sassari province to the Chamber of Deputies.

This stage in his political career was cut short by the rise of Fascism and by 1942 he was among the organizers of Christian Democracy, the successor to the Popular Party, becoming its leading figure in Sardinia. As important for his future was his nomination after the clearing of Fascist nominees from various local offices to the presidency of the Sassari union of farmers. With his claims to national office based on the sure grounds of being a prominent Christian Democrat, an eminent Sardinian —the island required a representative at the centre of governmental and party affairs—and a recognized agriculturalist it was natural that his first taste of government should come soon and that the office was the under-secretaryship for agriculture in the second Bonomi Government formed in December 1944. The same month saw the law conceding regional autonomy to Sardinia, in the elaboration of which Segni had a notable hand. He was elected Deputy to the Constituent Assembly and retained his seat in the Chamber continuously until his elevation to the Presidency.

In July 1946, he was given the Ministry of Agriculture in the second de Gasperi administration, a portfolio which he was to hold in successive Governments for the next five years. His tenure of it was distinguished by the passage of the legislation for introducing agrarian reform. It is a measure with which his name is closely linked and he had always insisted that he and the Christian Democratic Pary deserved full credit for the reform in face of left-wing claims that Communist pressure forced their hand.

From July 1951 until January 1954, with the exception of one brief period, he was Minister for Public Instruction.

He formed his first Government in July 1955, after the resignation of Signor Scelba. It was a coalition in which the Christian Democrats were joined by the Liberals and the Social Democrats. With a sure political hand he kept his Government in office for 20 months, a period which, almost at its close, saw the signing of the Treaty of Rome setting up the Common Market. On the fall of his administration he returned to the chairmanship of the permanent commission of the Chamber for education. After the general election of spring 1958, he took the deputy premiership and the Ministry of Defence in the short-lived Government of Fanfani, which was a premature attempt at a centre-left coalition.

Throughout much of his career Segni was himself considered to be left of the centre line within his own party. He was later to show that fundamentally he was a conservative and this natural position was enhanced by his personal antipathy towards Fanfani—another provincial professor of uncertain temper. Segni could in fact have himself tried his hand at a centre-left administration; in March 1960 he was asked by President Gronchi to try to form such a Government. He abandoned the task, but not before his prospective allies in the smaller lay parties had acidly referred to "outside" influences from which one was allowed to suppose that the Vatican was meant. As it turned out, Fanfani's views were carried to victory at the Naples Congress of the Christian Democratic Party in early 1962, and as promptly put into governmental practice, including the historic agreement made with the Socialists which was the basis of Fanfani's next Government. Segni did nothing to oppose the move leftward of the party, and within a few months was president.

Before that development he was, however to enjoy a surprisingly diverse series of tenure of office. After Fanfani's defeat in February 1959, he formed his own second administration based on the outside support of the Liberals and the extreme right, retaining for himself the Ministry of the Interior. The full rightward looking interlude which was to colour these months only came about after Segni was succeeded by Tambroni in the summer of 1960. It was the first Government in which the Christian Democrats were supported in Parliament only by the Neo-Fascists. Segni took Foreign Affairs.

Rioting brought that Government to an end and he retained the portfolio of Foreign Affairs in the next two Governments, both of them led by Fanfani, one based on the centre formula and the other, following the Naples Congress, a true centre-left administration. It was from this post that he passed to the presidency. As Foreign Minister he was a purely orthodox supporter of Italy's place in the western alliance and in the integration of western Europe. He had no deep interest in diplomacy, but there was never doubt about the depth of his convictions on these broad lines of policy.

It was characteristic of him that in his speech accepting the 1964 Charlemagne Prize, awarded annually to politicians who have furthered the cause of European unity, he took the opportunity of emphasizing that the unity of Europe must develop within the framework of Atlantic partnership. It was not the first time that he had expressed his opposition to the Gaullist conception of a narrow Europe.

In 1921 he married Laura Carta. They had four sons.

December 2, 1972.

André de Segonzac—See Dunoyer.

Sir Nicholas Sekers, whose notable career epitomized the British textile scene, particularly in the 1950s, died on June 23, 1974 while on holiday with his wife in Yugoslavia. He was 61 years of age and had been for many years also a great patron of the arts, especially music.

Born of Hungarian parents, "Miki" Sekers progressed from school in Budapest to specialist study at the Textile Technological College at Krefeld, Germany, and at the age of 21 became director of the Adria Silk Mills in Budapest until 1937.

In that year he went to England and chose Cumberland in which to set up the weaving business that became a household word as the West Cumberland Silk Mills. At Whitehaven, where industry was depressed and Government help was available, Sekers obtained labour in part by teaching miners' daughters to weave. The business flourished, in the wholesale and retail spheres, based on Sekers's talented designs, so that in a remarkably short time he became a great name in fashion and his brocades were used widely in private homes and public buildings at home and abroad. The concern "went public" in 1955, as Sekers Fabrics Limited, and in 1963 his services for fashion were recognized by the award of an M.B.E.

In 1962 he received the Duke of Edinburgh's award for elegance in fabrics.

Already he had gathered around him at his home, Rosehill, in Whitehaven, lovers of music and other arts, and in 1959 he had set up the Rosehill Arts Trust which built an opera house in the grounds there, to the design of Oliver Messel.

Sekers had been since 1954 a trustee-founder of the Glyndebourne Arts Trust Ltd. and from 1962 vice-chairman of the London Mozart Players, as well as director of the Meadow Players, Oxford.

In 1965, the year in which he was knighted for his services to the arts, he became chairman of the newly-formed London Philharmonic Orchestra Council, with Sir Adrian Boult as president of the Orchestra, at a time when the L.P.O. was still on a free-lance basis following the financial troubles of 1957 which almost led to its disbanding.

Later he was a member of the council of the Royal Opera House, Covent Garden and the Shakespeare Theatre Trust, and he was a governor of the Yehudi Menuhin School. He also served on the Council of Industrial Design.

It was with these achievements behind him that in 1970 he underwent an operation for replacement of a heart valve, and he had retired as managing director of his company. But by early 1973 he had made a magnificent recovery and started out on a second career as a design consultant, forming M. W. Design Associates, which was retained by many British firms. In that year he produced his first collection of furnishing fabrics for the Bradford Lister group, and his new enterprise showed what could be done by original use of materials for men's clothes.

Sir Nicholas would never allow that the British textile industry was inferior to those on the Continent, and his own example showed what presentation could do, allied to superb craftsmanship and good design. He believed that we had only to lose our inhibitions and become less introvert and we could again lead the world. He produced fashions in bold and often untried colours, with specially successful ventures into printed velvets.

Sekers married in 1941 Agota Anna, daughter of Kalman Balkanyi of Budapest.

June 26, 1974.

Lord Selborne, C.H., Minister of Economic Warfare during the Second World War, died on September 3, 1971 at the age of 84. He was chairman of the House of Laity, Church Assembly, from 1955 to 1959.

As Viscount Wolmer he had a long and distinguished career in the House of Commons, though he did not attain the heights his gifts entitled him to expect. This was largely due to his steadfast hold on Tory principles at a time when the Tory party was abandoning one position after another in the hopeless effort to hold the Empire together, to keep the peace with the dictators, to support the League of Nations, and retain the domestic rate by starving the country's defences.

His great administrative capacity and his gift for lucid, conciliatory exposition gave him the opportunity to be an asset to his party, but his uncompromising principles and independence of mind often made him seem like the embodiment of an uneasy conscience in a party busy abandoning so many tenets of its former faith. It was not until after Churchill* became Prime Minister that Selborne's worth was recognized by conferment of high office. They had become close friends during the fight over the Government of India Bill, had great admiration for each other's gifts, and had much in common politically.

The Rt. Hon. Roundell Cecil Palmer, C.H., third Earl of Selborne, was born on April 15, 1887, and was educated at Winchester, and University College, Oxford. As the son of a First Lord of the Admiralty and Governor-General of South Africa, and grandson on his father's side of a Lord Chancellor, and on his mother's of a Prime Minister, he felt he must make his career in politics and plunged into the Oxford political maelstrom with zest. He was secretary of the Canning Club and founded the New Tory Club which rivalled, briefly, the Union in its ability to attract distinguished visiting speakers. Before he was 23 he went up to Lancashire to fight Newton-le-Willows in 1910. Defeated at the first attempt in that year of rumbustious campaigning and constitutional crisis, he won the seat at the second election just before the end of the year and held it for some eight years, during the last four of which he served in The Hampshire Regiment.

He resigned his commission in 1922 and meanwhile in 1918 he had won the Aldershot Division of Hampshire, a seat he held until called to the House of Lords in his father's subsidiary title, Baron Selborne, in 1941. In the few years before the outbreak of war in 1914 he had shown great energy and capacity which promised a fine career, especially after he had made his mark as Assistant Director of Trade from 1916 to 1918. He was rewarded with minor office in 1922 when he was appointed Parliamentary Secretary to the Board of Trade, a post he held until 1924.

When the Tory party was returned to power in 1924 Wolmer was appointed Assistant Postmaster-General and devoted considerable administrative talents to examining and making proposals for remedying weaknesses in the organization. This led to the setting up of the Bridgeman Committee and ultimately to important reforms. These did not go as far as he wanted and after he left office in 1929 he was able to speak with greater freedom, and published three articles in The Times and a book with the same title as Rowland Hill's pamphlet which led to the penny post, Post Office Reform: Its Importance and Practicability, in which he argued for control by a public utility corporation—an interesting anticipation by some 40 years of the present Government's policy.

As early as 1913 he had become a member of the House of Laymen of the Province of Canterbury and later on he sat in the House of Laity of the Church Assembly, latterly as chairman. He took an active part in the Church Self-Government League and published a pamphlet advocating the "Scottish Solution" for the problem of the relationship between Church and State.

In spite of his many other preoccupations, he determined to make the family estate a thoroughly up to date and efficient agricultural unit. Lying in the small hop-growing area crossing the Surrey and Hampshire border, hops had originally been the staple crop. To these were added dairy farming and sugar beet and finally fruit—originally apples grew on the dairy pasture but latterly pears and soft fruit as well. As the bushes came to maturity the sales of fruit became ever more profitable. Grading in size and colour was introduced and a gas-storage plant was installed to keep an even flow of fruit to the markets. Today Blackmoor Nurseries sells not only fruit but well nurtured trees and bushes as well, and is in the forefront among British fruit nurseries.

When war broke out in 1939, he had been chairman of the Cement Makers' Federation for some five years and so was well qualified to become Director of Cement in the Ministry of Works and Buildings.

In 1941, in order to relieve him of constituency work, he was summoned to the House of Lords as Baron Selborne and so father and son as earl and baron were members. The year 1942 saw the death of his father and of his eldest son, and his appointment as Minister of Economic Warfare. The function of the department was primarily to deny the enemy any materials that could nourish his war effort. This meant the fullest use of the regular intelligence channels of the Service departments and other government agencies.

When the war in Europe ended, Selborne resigned office on the ground that the problem of waging economic war against Japan could be more effectively handled by the United States. He was created C.H. He returned to the Cement Makers' Federation and remained chairman until 1951 when he was elected chairman of the National Provincial Bank, a post he held until 1954. He had been a director of Boots Pure Drug Co. since 1936 and resigned from the post of deputy chairman in 1963.

He married in 1910 Grace, youngest daughter of the first Viscount Ridley. There were three sons and three daughters of the marriage. The eldest son was killed while serving in the Army in 1942 and Lady Selborne died in 1959. He married in 1966 Valerie Irene de Thomka de Tomkahaza et Folkusfalva and became a widower for the second time in 1968.

The heir to the title is his grandson, Viscount Wolmer.

September 6, 1971

Gerald Seligman, founder of the International Glaciological Society, died on February 21, 1973 at the age of 86.

He was born on March 26, 1886 and was educated at Harrow and the South-Eastern Agricultural College, Wye. There he became interested in the lectures on geology and chemistry, the latter given by Sir John Russell*. From Wye he went up to Trinity Hall, Cambridge, where he took the Natural Sciences Tripos.

After a visit to North America, where he climbed his first mountains, he joined his elder brother, Richard Seligman, in a newly founded chemical engineering business. During the First World War he served at home and in East Africa and then returned to his brother's business.

At an early age he had become fascinated by mountains and by skiing, so that he spent nearly all his holidays in the Alps or Norway and became a competent ski-mountaineer. His inventive mind produced numerous new gadgets for the use of skiers. He had joined the Ski Club of Great Britain soon after its foundation, and was elected to its committee in 1921. He also took over the editorship of the club's news bulletin, *Ski Notes and Queries*, which he developed from a small leaflet to a sizable publication during the next 14 years. He became vice-president of the club in 1925 and president two years later.

In the late 1920s, Arnold Lunn, then editor of the *British Ski Year Book*, invited him to review a German work on snow and avalanches. The fascination of snow had always held him firmly, and in 1931 he resigned from business to devote full time to its study. He was then able to spend whole winters in the Alps and to devote himself to writing articles, papers and reviews on glaciological and kindred subjects. His early investigations were concerned with the nature of falling snow and the mechanics of avalanches. The results of his work were published in a series of articles over three years in the *British Ski Year Book*. Later he spent a year at the Scott Polar Research Institute in Cambridge, bringing these articles up to date in a book, *Snow Structure and Ski Fields*, published in 1936.

What came particularly to intrigue Seligman was the evolution of the snow crystal into glacier ice, and in 1936 he decided to visit the Jungfraujoch with the intention of following this transition from surface down to the bottom layers of the Aletsch Glacier. The next year he also spent some time there in company with J. D. Bernal, F. P. Bowden, M. F. Perutz, T. P. Hughes and H. Bader, the latter being at that time a member of the Swiss Snow and Avalanche Commission. In 1938 he spent the whole summer at the Jungfraujoch as leader of a research party of which Perutz was again a member; several important papers were published and some of these went much farther into glacier physics than Seligman's original theme.

Just before the first Jungfraujoch expedition, J. E. Church of the Agricultural Experiment Station, Reno, Nevada, had invited him to form a British Group within the International Commission of Snow, as it was then called. This group became the Association for the Study of Snow and Ice, and later still—through a transitional name British Glaciological Society—the

International Glaciological Society. The society, devoted to the study of snow and ice in all forms, has, since 1952, been at the Scott Polar Research Institute. It has grown into an organization with a thousand members in thirty-three countries, an international council and branches in many parts of the world.

March 10, 1973.

Jean-Marie Serreau, the stage director who played a large part in introducing dramatists like Brecht, Beckett, Genet, Ionesco and Max Frisch to postwar France, as well as being an actor himself, died in May 1973 at the age of 58.

Serreau, an architect by training, opened in May 1952 the little Paris Left Bank Théâtre de Babylone, and there in two years staged some seventeen plays which helped to launch the European *avant garde* theatre of the period after the war, notably Samuel Beckett's *Waiting for Godot.*

A decade later he went on to discover "third world" playwrights like Aime Cesaire and Kateb Yacine, and in turn took and played Brecht in black Africa with a black African cast.

Serreau was among the pioneers, too, with what has become a commonplace of contemporary theatre-going-plays seeking to make an impact on society, and not permitting pleasurable escapism for an evening.

"The theatre must have an immediate rapport with the fundamental problems of the day", Serreau once remarked.

May 24, 1973.

Doria Shafik, the suffragette whose campaigns won the vote for women in Egypt, died in September 1975, falling from her sixth floor flat in Cairo. She was 65.

Known especially as a champion of women's rights, as well as noted for her beauty, Madame Shafik fought campaigns on a number of fronts, both social and political. A doctor of philosophy from the Sorbonne, she returned to Egypt and founded the Bint El Nil (Daughters of the Nile), a movement which not only represented repressed Egyptian womanhood but was also trained in guerrilla warfare to play its part in the nationalistic movement against Britain at the time of the Suez crisis.

Bint El Nil's most spectacular gesture was the invasion in 1951 of the Egyptian parliament by 1,500 women, bringing proceedings to a standstill. Continuing demonstrations, including a week-long hunger strike by Madame Shafik and her followers, eventually resulted in the extension of the franchise to women in 1956.

Thereafter her campaigns included protest against Nasser's regime and demands for the restoration of democracy in Egypt. This brought considerable official and public odium on her and she lived in seclusion in Cairo in her latter years.

She had married, in Paris, Nour Ragai, an Egyptian lawyer, and had two daughters.

September 23, 1975.

Geoffrey Sharp, founder and editor of *The Music Review,* died in hospital on March 29, 1974. He was 59.

A student of engineering at Trinity College, Cambridge, in the early 1930s, the young Sharp's passion for music led to a friendship with the late Edward J. Dent, then Professor of Music, which developed his musical interests in the directions of opera and orchestral music.

On going down from Cambridge in 1935 Geoffrey Sharp took a postgraduate course with a prominent radio manufacturer, where he worked on problems of acoustics and amplification.

This was as near to music as Sharp's engineering skills could take him; and for him it was not near enough.

In 1937 he entered the Royal College of Music and, with the help of the printing firm of Heffers in Cambridge he decided to establish an independent journal in which he hoped to provide a medium for in-depth musicological studies and critical essays. He continued meanwhile his two years' study of music history.

At the outbreak of war the first number was in proof and appeared in February 1940. With a filled pipeline of articles from distinguished contributors to draw on, his wife miraculously kept the young publication alive. It has appeared quarterly ever since, maintaining the beauty of print and presentation that Sharp insisted on and preserving the highest standards of contributed essays. It has a worldwide sale.

From the start Sharp attracted the work of some distinguished Continental musicologists and critics.

This throws light on one endearing aspect of his character.

During the war many musicians and writers had left Germany, Austria and elsewhere to escape from Nazism. Some of the most distinguished saw in *The Music Review* an opportunity to continue their work. All, including some young unknowns, who approached the editor received help and encouragement and some outstanding reputations have been made from these beginnings.

Geoffrey Sharp's own critical writings appeared in numerous publications both in Britain and abroad. He was a past president of the Critics' Circle.

He leaves no family; tragically, his wife Mary died a few months before his own death.

April 10, 1974.

Major Alexander de Seversky—See de Seversky.

Sir Richard Sharples, K.C.M.G., O.B.E., M.C., who was Governor of Bermuda from October 1972, was shot dead with his aide-de-camp, Captain Hugh Sayers of the Welsh Guards, in the grounds of Government House, Hamilton, Bermuda, on the night of March 10, 1973. He was 56.

Though not of the first political rank—his final appointment in London was that of Minister of State at the Home Office—Sharples was an influential, well-liked and respected figure in the Conservative Party throughout his 18 years in the House of Commons. He was for a time a vice-chairman of the party, with responsibility for parliamentary candidates—an office calling for tact and good judgment, to which he was well suited.

Slight of build, of dapper appearance, courteous and considerate, he was in many respects the epitome of the "traditional" well-to-do Tory M.P., and his tragic death will be mourned by members of all parties in the House.

Sharples, an Old Etonian and Welsh Guards officer, held a number of posts under the Conservatives. He became Minister of State, Home Office, in Edward Heath's Government of June 1970, resigning in a re-shuffle in April 1972.

Born in 1916, Richard Christopher Sharples was educated at Eton and Sandhurst. He had an exceptional war record with the Welsh Guards, winning the M.C. and being mentioned in dispatches. He was awarded his M.C. for gallantry at Boulogne in 1940, and the O.B.E. in 1953. From 1951 to 1953 he had been Military Assistant to Field Marshal Lord Montgomery. He was also a holder of the Silver Star of the United States.

A farmer and an accomplished yachtsman, Sharples retired from the Army in 1953 and, after a year working in the economic section of the Conservative Research Department, he entered the Commons as M.P. for Sutton and Cheam in 1954. He was Parliamentary Private Secretary from 1955 to 1956 to Anthony Nutting, the Minister of State for Foreign Affairs, and from 1957 to 1959 to R. A. Butler, the Home Secretary. He later held office as Assistant Government Whip (1959-60); Joint Parliamentary Secretary, Ministry of Pensions and National Insurance (1961-62); and Parliamentary Secretary, Ministry of Building and Works (1962-64). When the Conservatives were in opposition he was spokesman on Home Office affairs (1964-67).

In September 1970, following riots in Northern Ireland, Sharples paid a four-day visit to the province. At one time he was tipped to become Britain's first Minister for Ulster.

He was a Liveryman of the Merchant Taylors' Comapny and a Freeman of the

City of London.

He married in 1946 Pamela, daughter of Lieutenant-Commander Keith Newall, and they had two sons and two daughters.

March 12, 1973.

Shaikh Mohammed Bin Hamed al Sharqi— See **Fujairah.**

Professor Trevor Ian Shaw, F.R.S., who died on September 26, 1972 at the age of 44, was one of the most brilliant of Britain's physiologists. He was born in York and was educated at Bootham School and at Clare College, Cambridge.

Shaw's research, carried out successively at Cambridge, Plymouth, and Queen Mary College (where he was Professor of Zoology) was outstanding both for its originality and its breadth of interest. A continuing theme of his work was the investigation of the permeability properties of living membranes, an interest which he acquired as a research student of Sir Alan Hodgkin. His early work was concerned with the investigation of the latter phenomena in such diverse objects as red blood cells and seaweed.

The full quality of his abilities as an experimental scientist was, however, most clearly revealed in his later work on the ionic basis of excitability in invertebrate nerve cells. In a series of publications, which were invariably characterized by a refreshing clarity and elegance, he successfully eludicated a number of aspects of neural function in the squid and in crustacean species. In particular, his achievement in recording impulses from squid nerve fibres, in which the contents were replaced by an artificial saline, represented a major contribution to his chosen field of study. Latterly, he developed a uniquely valuable technique, involving a laser beam, to study (as he believed) the movements of the vesicles during synaptic transmission.

Much of Shaw's most creative and interesting work was carried out during regular visits to the marine laboratory at Plymouth. In the absence of administrative duties, which were always a burden to him, he enjoyed to the full the collaboration and companionship of his research students and his Cambridge colleagues at Plymouth. His infectious enthusiasm and widely enquiring mind was an invaluable asset to the neurophysiological work of the Plymouth laboratory.

Trevor Shaw was a direct, humorous and sincere person. Almost totally lacking in worldly ambition he even had to be persuaded to accept such honours as came his way.

His loss represents a grievous blow to his many colleagues and friends.

October 4, 1972.

Rear-Admiral Robert St. Vincent Sherbrooke, V.C., C.B., D.S.O., who died on June 13, 1972 at the age of 71, won his V.C. for beating off a German naval raid on a Russian-bound British arms convoy. During the action he lost his left eye, and eventually had to retire on medical grounds at the age of 53.

Sherbrooke was serving in H.M.S. Onslow as senior officer in command of the destroyers escorting the convoy. On New Year's Eve, 1942, in semi-darkness and with visibility further reduced by snow-storms, Captain Sherbrooke led his destroyers into attack. Four times the enemy force, which included the battleship Lutzow and the heavy cruiser Admiral Hipper, tried to molest the convoy, but each time was forced to withdraw behind smoke to avoid the threat of torpedoes. These engagements lasted about two hours, but after the first 40 minutes the Onslow was hit and her captain seriously wounded in the face, losing the use of one eye. He continued to direct his ship until satisfied that the next senior officer had assumed control, and afterwards, until the convoy was out of danger, he insisted on receiving all reports of the action. No merchant ship was lost or damaged.

For his courage, fortitude and skill Sherbrooke was awarded the V.C., and the First Lord of the Admiralty, A. V. Alexander (later Lord Alexander of Hillsborough*) said of his conduct that "there was never anything finer in the annals of the Royal Navy".

Sherbrooke, the third generation of his family to serve in the Royal Navy, entered the Royal Naval College at Osborne in 1913. During the First World War he served as a midshipman in the Canada from 1917 to 1918.

During the Second World War he won the D.S.O. at the second battle of Narvik in March 1940. In 1945 he was Captain of the cruiser H.M.S. Aurora in the Mediterranean.

From 1946 to 1948 Sherbrooke was Director of Craft and Amphibious Material at the Admiralty, and from 1948 to 1950 Commodore of the R.N. barracks of the Fleet Air Arm at Lee-on-Solent. Following his promotion to rear-admiral in 1951, he was appointed Flag Officer, Germany, and Chief British Naval Representative on the Allied Control Commission. He retired in 1954 and was appointed Gentleman Usher of the Scarlet Rod in the Order of the Bath and from 1964 to 1968 was Registrar and Secretary of the Order.

In 1958 he became a deputy-lieutenant and High Sheriff for Nottinghamshire, and in 1960 he was appointed a J.P. for Nottinghamshire. He became Lord Lieutenant of Nottingham in 1968.

Sherbrooke married in 1929 Rosemary Neville, daughter of Lieutenant-Colonel P. N. Buckley, and they had two daughters.

June 15, 1972.

R. C. Sherriff, F.S.A., F.R.S.L., a volunteer soldier of the First World War who lived to be the author of the most famous play to be written about it anywhere, *Journey's End,* died on November 13, 1975 at the age of 79.

Robert Cedric Sherriff ("Bob" Sherriff) was born on June 6, 1896, at Hampton Wick, Surrey. On leaving Kingston-on-Thames Grammar School, where he was captain of rowing and cricket and edited a magazine, he became a clerk in the Sun Assurance Company in 1914. A few months later he enlisted in the 9th East Surrey Regiment. He was commissioned, served at Vimy and Loos, and was severely wounded at Ypres in 1917. Discharged with the rank of Captain, he returned to insurance work —he was now an adjustor—and to his favourite sports and hobbies.

The latter included playwriting, and soon an amateur society at Kingston-on-Thames unofficially adopted Sherriff as their resident playwright. *Journey's End*, which he worked on while recovering from a bout of scarlet fever, was based on his letters from the Front to his mother. Although no play such as this with a dug-out for setting and an all male cast had yet been seen in postwar London, it was accepted by the Stage Society and given two performances in December 1928, under the direction of James Whale, after three other directors had been offered the job and had turned it down.

Harold Monro of the Poetry Bookshop was in the audience at the first performance, on a Sunday night, and at the end of it rang up to tell his friend, Maurice Browne, who was then contemplating going into management in London, that this wonderful play by an unknown author was the very one for Browne to put on. Browne succeeded in acquiring an option on it some days later, and in January 1929 he presented it in the West End, with Colin Clive in the part of the young company commander, Stanhope, originally taken by Sir Laurence Olivier.

When it came off after 594 performances, most countries in the world possessing a theatre had heard of it and in some 20 of them it had been produced. Stresemann, the German Foreign Minister, and Einstein were among those who regarded the play as a contribution to the cause of international brotherhood and world peace, and helped to organize a gala performance of it in Berlin.

Film versions were made in English and (with Conrad Veidt as Stanhope) in German; the sale of the manuscript raised £1,500 for the League of Nations Union. The general verdict at the height of all this success might have been summarized as follows: a great play, no; a great warplay, yes; a play fulfilling what is surely a great purpose in bringing home to audiences everywhere what modern warfare really is like. And the most recent revivals of the play have all tended to confirm that *Journey's End* has, on any count, matured into a period piece of great durability.

Sherriff, in collaboration with Vernon Bartlett, turned the play into a novel, and in 1930 he allowed Maurice Browne to present an early comedy of his, *Badger's Green*. But it was still not known what his next play was to be. Was it perhaps about Captain Scott's journey to the Pole? Apparently it was not; when a senior playwright, St. John Ervine, asked Sherriff point blank what he was going to do now, he replied: "I'm going up to Oxford to read History". "And to take up rowing again", he might have added, for that is what this modest man who had just made a fortune did on arriving at New College in 1931, having read reviews of his new novel *The Fortnight in September* during the journey up.

From Oxford he moved to Hollywood, where the film scripts he worked on included those of Remarque's* *The Road Back*, Wells's *The Invisible Man* and Galsworthy's *One More River*. A play about Napoleon in exile, *St. Helena*, written by Sherriff jointly with Jeanne de Casalis*, the actress, who was then married to Colin Clive, was produced at the Old Vic in 1934. This, apart from *Journey's End*, was the one theatrical occasion on which he succeeded in using his laconic style to distinguished purpose and carried public praise from eminent persons, including Sir Winston Churchill*.

A new play by him was not again seen in London until 1948, but in the meantime he brought out four more novels, was appointed literary adviser to Alexander Korda, and was engaged during the war years on the screen plays of *Lady Hamilton* and *This Above All*. His most notable piece of work in that time was by common consent *The Dam Busters*, a war film that was not shown until 1955.

By then Sir Ralph Richardson had appeared in two new plays by him, *Home at Seven* (1950) and *The White Carnation* (1953). These were followed by the production of *The Telescope* (1957) first as a straight play, later as a musical *Johnny the Priest*, and of a play set in Roman Britain during the last days before the withdrawal of the Roman garrisons, *The Long Sunset* (1955). He also wrote for radio *Cards With Uncle Tom* (1958) and for television *The Ogburn Story* (1963) and published his autobiography *No Leading Lady* in 1968.

The sunset of men's lives, whether it comes down in earnest as in *Journey's End*, or is a false sunset, the mere threat of a disaster that is averted, as in *Home at Seven* and *A Shred of Evidence*, provided Sherriff with the theme of most of his plays. It appears in *Greengates*, too, a novel published in 1936, probably the most substantial of all his novels, being the story of what happened to an insurance clerk after his retirement from business.

As Sherriff grew older, the place in his life of cricket and rowing was taken by archaeology; he helped to excavate a Roman villa at Angmering and the fort of Procolita on Hadrian's Wall; but once he had discovered playwriting, he stayed with it. He liked best to practise it in the big study of his house at Esher, coming into and going out of the room as his characters entered or left the stage, and trying over their speeches in his own voice till he got them right. He founded a scholarship at his old college at Oxford in 1937. He was unmarried.

November 18, 1975.

Dmitri Shostakovich died in Moscow on August 9, 1975 at the age of 68.

The greatest figure in Soviet music over the last two decades, he will probably come to be seen as the last great composer to have expressed himself in the traditional musical forms: the string quartet, the concerto, and above all, the symphony. He saw himself equally as a Soviet citizen and a composer; and on those occasions when Soviet officialdom frowned on his music he searched deeply within himself to reconcile his own musical instincts with the declared requirements of the role of music in Soviet society.

Outside the Soviet Union his stature as a composer, and particularly as a symphonist, has long been unequivocally accepted, and the sympathy accorded to him in the West in his conflicts with Soviet doctrine has been strong, though he himself would scarcely have countenanced Western support against Soviet communist belief, which at a basic level he shared.

He was widely honoured: in the Soviet Union he won at least six prizes, and he was awarded a Royal Philharmonic Society gold medal (1966) and a Dublin honorary doctorate (1972).

Shostakovich was born in St. Petersburg on September 25, 1906, and showed unusual musical gifts as a boy. A pupil of Glazunov, he studied at the Conservatory in his home city from 1919 to 1925, and gained at the age of 17 the Diploma in Composition, and, two years later, an equivalent qualification in piano playing. As his success in the first International Chopin Festival in Warsaw in 1927 showed, the career of a piano virtuoso was open to him.

His First Symphony, however, completed in 1925 and first performed in Leningrad four months before his twentieth birthday, showed an individual, witty and at times freakishly humorous personality as well as a completely assured technique. Earlier works (the Symphony is his Op. 10) showed the influence of Glazunov, an individual lyrical quality and a complete mastery of his materials; but the First Symphony was a fruit of the early years of communist rule when experiment was encouraged, and showed that Shostakovich, as any lively minded young composer of the period would have done, had assimilated the influence of Stravinsky and Prokofiev (who was then in the West) as well as interested himself in the work of other Western composers; either by knowledge or by instinct, in the easily-controlled eclecticism of the work we see his colourful orchestral style reaching towards the sound-world of Gustav Mahler, and Mahlerian intensities and colourings grew more frequent in his work as he developed. His point of departure, however, was not post-war experimentalism but the fundamental discipline of traditional symphonic form handled with a gift for drama and tension.

It was natural that Shostakovich's next two symphonies, the "October" and the "May Day" (composed in 1927 and 1929), should be inspired by a communism which was beginning to turn from artistic liberalism and freedom of experiment to the doctrine which eventually solidified into "Socialist Realism", and perhaps inevitable that they should fail to achieve the stature of their predecessor.

Each has a chorale finale to a socialist text that serves as the work's culmination, or indeed its justification. They are strongly dramatic works, and foreshadow aspects of his later symphonic technique; yet the influence of progressive Western music, including the techniques associated with labels like Futurism and Expressionism, were not easily reconcilable with a manner apt to the choral texts. Both works were set aside for many years—Shostakovich is on record as calling them childish—and it was not until the 1960s that they became generally available.

In his opera based on Gogol's *The Nose*, completed in 1929, his wit and individuality took a step forward; it matched Gogol's sarcasm with equally acrid music and successfully set everyday Russian speech to taut, declamatory vocal lines. It was an immediate success, but there were official grumblings and it rapidly disappeared from the stage. It was, however, merely a stepping-stone to a second opera, *Lady Macbeth of Mtsensk*, based on a story by Leskov and hailed at its first performance in 1934 as a masterpiece. Socialist realism, however, asks a composer not for an interpretation of things as they are (a standard by which *Lady Macbeth of Mtsensk* would be an exciting but stylistically inconsistent work), but for a use of music for moral and social ends. As the excitement of its first performance abated the authorities, though not at first the professional critics, could find nothing in the work to uplift the public consciousness and openly teach the good life. After the grumblings against the "formalism" of *The Nose*—"formalism" was the communist term for a style investigating musical materials and styles for their own sakes instead of applying them to social and political ends, and therefore "decadent"—Shostakovich rehabilitated himself in official eyes by the stylistically acceptable Piano Concerto of 1933, an engaging and lively work. The second opera, however, roused not grumbling but a real storm of official protest and displeasure. The story of the faithless wife who inspired her lover to murder her husband was denounced as bourgeois, formalistic, unhealthy and stylistically unintelligible to the people. The composer defended his work with some dignity but there has never been any question of the sincerity with which he held the communist faith; the work was condemned and, for the moment, disappeared.

For some time thereafter Shostakovich was regarded by the Soviet authorities with suspicion, as a wayward but untrustworthy genius. The authorities, conscious of his earlier deviations, were ready to sense an undesirable "modernism" in anything he wrote. As the function of music is to reflect the achievements of the people in both material and moral spheres, and, by doing so, to inspire them to new achievements, any style which drew attention to itself as new, presenting an audience with difficulties in their efforts to accept it, was frowned upon. Such symptons of modernism could be found, if they were looked for, in the ballet *Bright Rivulet*, produced in Leningrad in 1935. The next year, no doubt in anticipation of criticism, he withdrew his Fourth Symphony while it was still in rehearsal. The work did not come into general circulation until the 1960s, and it then became clear that the main reason for the withdrawal of this remarkable, highly individual and passionately felt work lay in its bleak, pessimistic tone. Shostakovich followed it up with his Fifth, a much more unified work, superior in its formal control to the rambling No. 4, and more optimistic in tone. It was subtitled "A Soviet Artist's Reply to Just Criticism", and the work's strength attests to Shostakovich's own acceptance of the criticism's justice.

The success of the Fifth Symphony enabled Shostakovich to return to official favour, and in 1940 his Piano Quintet was awarded a Stalin Prize. During these years he composed much film music and incidental music for the theatre. The *Leningrad* Symphony, his Seventh, in which he discussed the experiences of an artist in a beleaguered, war-torn city, portrays an epical struggle in appropriately large-scale terms, and ultimately portrays triumph. It raised him to the rank of a war hero, not only in the Soviet Union but also in the U.S.A. and Britain where it was much performed. His Eighth was equally admired, though, like the second Piano Trio of 1944, it reflects not so much the heroism and determination of an embattled people fighting for their homeland as the artist's despair at the horror, agony, and wickedness of the conflict.

The bitter, ironic tone of the Ninth Symphony, though it may now be seen as in the established traditions of Russian humour, was severely criticized; and when the infamous Conference of Musicians met in 1948 to consider the failure of Russian composers to write the music which the people needed for inspiration and relaxation (and, incidentally, to try to turn them all into composers of popular songs), under the leadership of Andrei Alexandrovich Zhdanov, it condemned the leading Russian symphonic composers and reserved its bitterest attacks for Shostakovich. Shostakovich again defended himself with some dignity and several noticeable reservations, but again loyally toed the line. His return to grace was marked by *The Song of the Forests*, a patriotic oratorio and his first large-scale choral work, in 1948. The new condemnation did nothing to check his outpourings of music, and the decisions of the 1948 conference were disavowed after 10 years, by which time Shostakovich had written his entirely personal Tenth Symphony, one of the noblest, most spacious and most profoundly reflective of his works, and the more public Eleventh, a commemoration of the abortive 1905 revolution, an uneven work full of martial sounds and rhythms yet characteristically dark-toned and brooding in its slow music. It won him a Lenin Prize, one of many awards he received for his music (which also include World Peace Council Prize, 1954).

The 1958 reinterpretation of the composer's social duties introduced a far greater liberalism into Russian musical thinking and came to recognize Shostakovich as by far the most important Russian composer of the age. Not only were the later string quartets, the First Violin Concerto and the Twelfth Symphony accepted as much for their musical quality as for their potentially inspiring reflection of Russian life, but the forbidden Fourth Symphony was heard, recognized and published, and *Lady Macbeth of Mtsensk*, revised and rechristened *Katerina Ismailova*, was revived and judged on its own rather than on doctrinaire and irrelevant grounds. It was given at Covent Garden in 1963.

In the last years of his life, the tone of Shostakovich's music grew increasingly bleak and austere, and his idiom more concentrated. It is significant that he turned particularly to the string quartet, a favourite form of his since the war years, but one specially suited to personal and inward expression. His zigzag career as a symphonist continued to the end. His last big, public symphony was No. 12, in which the patriotic, martial tone is heard for the last time in his orchestral music. No. 13, which took a decade to be published and released to the West, is a powerful and direct series of settings of early protest poems by Yevtushenko, some of them dealing with anti-semitism. No. 14, for two voices and chamber orchestra, shows a preoccupation with death, and the tone is trenchantly ironic, even morbid. If No. 15 is superficially more extrovert, it is so only in the sharp and ironic manner of No. 9; certainly there is no hint of optimism about it, nor any suggestion that socialist realism offers the answers to the formidable problems facing man today, as individual or as social animal. It contains enigmatic quotations from earlier music (Wagner motifs, and a phrase from *William Tell* overture used in a coarse, parodistic context), and the "ticking of life's clock" in its slow movement again shows Shostakovich's preoccupation with ultimate things—a preoccupation reflected equally in his last, also fifteenth, quartet, whose elegiac tone is manifest in its form of six slow movements.

Shostakovich's profoundest thoughts are usually in his slow music; it has been said that he never composed a true symphonic allegro, and the nearest he came to doing so is, perhaps surprisingly, in his concertos for violin and cello (he composed two for each); it is characteristic that their cadenzas are strong points of emotional focus. His idiom, most obviously derived from Mahler, is none the less deeply Russian; Mussorgsky's music, with its dark and reflective tone, echoes more strongly in Shostakovich than do, for example Tchaikovsky's or Rimsky-Korsakov's. Benjamin Britten has been suggested as a late influence, notably on Symphony No. 14; certainly the two had shown much in common in the last few years. Shostakovich's symphonic technique is based on monothematic procedures of working outwards from an idea and later focusing back on to it, an approach not always reconcilable with the traditional manner of the symphonic allegro, although his debt to Beethoven (which includes the actual citation of themes, for example in the Twelfth Quartet) is strong. In all his music, thematic cross-reference, within and between movements, is notable.

Shostakovich was a courageous and articulate man. His defence against criticism of his music was always guarded, because he generally believed in the criticism's fairness; he was however prepared to condemn those who used terms like "formalism" mindlessly as critical brickbats. He spoke forcefully about modern Western music, deprecating 12-note methods in strong terms (though using aspects of them in his own late music); he was forthright, too, on the avantgarde and late Stravinsky. On non-musical matters, he was among those who lately spoke out in support of Sakharov.

It is easy to see, in Shostakovich's life and works, the history of a composer in whom important tensions were never fully resolved. But it would be facile to see them as too firmly rooted in the political ambience in which he lived; part of them doubtless lay in the restless temperament of the man himself, his searching mind, his typically Russian mixture of humour and despair, which manifested itself in the irony or the parody with which his deepest thoughts are so often overlaid. His principal legacy consists of the quartets and symphonies (15 of each), the handful of concertos, the two operas, chamber works, piano music and songs. His film music, which includes a much-praised *Hamlet* score, and his choral works (including several heroic cantatas) are less known in the West, and due account must be taken of them before a rounded picture of Shostakovich can emerge. That he is the last great symphonist, however, is beyond doubt.

He left a daughter, Galina, and a son, Maxim, an eminent conductor and pianist and a noted interpreter of his father's music.

August 11, 1975.

Amy Shuard, C.B.E., one of the leading English lyric and, later, dramatic sopranos of the postwar era, died suddenly on April 18, 1975 at the age of 50.

Following in the steps of her eminent teacher Dame Eva Turner, she was one of the very few and outstanding exponents in Britain and abroad of the roles of Turandot and Brünnhilde, for which her magnificently sustained and bright clarion tone eminently suited her. And her dramatic gifts, allied to her intense singing, were ideal for the parts of Janacek's Katya Kabanova and Jenufa, which she created in Britain.

She was born on July 19, 1924, in London and studied at the Trinity College of Music before beginning her career in South Africa. On her return in 1949, she was engaged by Sadler's Wells Opera, where she remained until she joined the Covent Garden company at the beginning of 1955. While at Rosebery Avenue, she sang most of the leading lyrical roles, breaking off in the middle for a period of beneficial study in Milan under Rosetta Pampanini. Her outstanding performances during that time were her Magda (*The Consul*), Butterfly, her fresh, ardent Tatiana in *Eugene Onegin,* still remembered with pleasure by many opera goers, and her fine Katya. But she also stepped significantly out of her *fach* to sing Eboli in the 1951 *Don Carlos.*

At Covent Garden she soon began to make her mark as a singer of international calibre, especially when in December 1958 she became the first British Turandot since Turner. It was a role she repeated with increasing authority in subsequent seasons. Then came her first Wagnerian roles, Sieglinde and Gutrune, her intense tragic Santuzza in the famous Zeffirelli *Cavalleria,* Lady Macbeth and Aïda.

In 1964 she became the first English-born singer to undertake the complete Brünnhilde at Covent Garden, and she sang the part in several further cycles of the *Ring* there in the following seasons. Strauss's *Elektra,* another performance of tragic power, followed in 1965.

Abroad, she made appearances at Vienna, Buenos Aires, San Francisco and Milan in various other roles. Her sole appearance at Bayreuth was as Kundry, another of her Covent Garden parts, in 1965.

In 1972, at a time when Italian opera houses were going through a chauvinistic period, she was poorly received at the San Carlo opera house, Naples, and left Naples without singing in two final performances of *Turandot.*

More recently at the Royal Opera House she had transferred in *Jenufa* from the title role to that of the dominating matriarch, Kostelnicka, and it was in that part

that she made her final, memorable performances at Covent Garden in May 1974. It was typical of her most un-prima-donna-like manner that she did not want audiences to know these were to be her last stage appearances.

She is survived by her husband, Dr. Peter Asher.

April 19, 1975.

Vasili Shukshin, who died suddenly in Moscow on October 2, 1974 at the age of 45, was reckoned one of the outstanding new talents of the Soviet cinema, as well as a writer of accomplishment.

He was born in Siberia in 1929, and grew up in the sort of village and peasant family he described in his second film, *Your Son and Brother.* He worked as a fitter, served in the navy, and tried his hand as a writer. Arriving in Moscow homeless, he was befriended by people of the cinema world, and entered the director's department of the Moscow Cinema Institute (V.G.I.K.) under the veteran director, Mikhail Romm. Graduating in 1961, he at first worked as an actor (appearing among other films in Sergei Gerasimov's *The Journalist*). His short stories began to appear at about the same time in *Novy Mir;* and he was soon identified with the group of writers known as the "New Slavophiles".

His chance to direct came in 1964, with *There was a Lad,* which he also scripted and which won the Golden Lion of St. Mark at the Venice Festival of Children's Films. *Your Son and Brother* followed in 1966; and in 1970 *Strange People,* taken from three of Shikshin's own stories and characterized by his ironic sense of comedy.

His last completed film, *Kalina Krafnaya* (*The Red Snowball Tree*) created a sensation when it was shown in the Soviet Union earlier in 1974. Shukshin himself played the hero, an ex-professional criminal who returns from his fifth term in a labour camp, but is murdered by his former confederates. Despite heavy cutting both by the director himself and by the censorship (allegedly some 25 minutes), the film's depiction of the effects of urban life on migrants from the country, and its satire upon officialdom, were unprecedented. It was warmly praised by official critics.

Shukshin was not permitted to realize another favourite project, *Stenka Razin;* evidently the seventeenth century peasant revolutionary was considered as politically dangerous as the fifteenth century icon painter Andrei Rublev, in Tarkovski's ill-fated film.

At the time of his death, Shukshin was working in Mosfilm Studios on an adaptation of Mikhail Sholokhov's epic *They Fought for the Motherland.*

October 4, 1974.

Vittorio de Sica—See de Sica.

Lord Sieff, president of Marks and Spencer, Ltd., since 1967, who died on February 14, 1972, was joint architect with his brother-in-law, Lord Marks of Broughton*, of the Marks and Spencer empire and thus of the retail revolution which their imaginative methods brought about.

The son of Ephraim Sieff, Israel Moses Sieff was born in Manchester on May 4, 1889, and educated at Manchester Grammar School, where he was in the same class throughout as his life-long friend, Simon Marks. On leaving school Sieff took a degree in commerce at the University of Manchester. His friendship with Simon Marks became even closer when each married the other's sister. It was Simon Marks's father, Michael Marks, whose market stall in Kirkgate, Leeds, in 1884 was the beginning of the Marks and Spencer business. Sieff joined Simon Marks in 1915 but also maintained an interest in his family textile business until 1926. In 1926, when Marks and Spencer became a public company and was entering into its formative years, Sieff joined Simon Marks on a full-time basis as vice-chairman and joint managing director. The two formed a remarkable team, with common interests both inside and outside the business. They were friends and associates for 63 years. Marks died in December 1964, and Sieff became the chairman and joint managing director.

It was a remarkable combination of two very different minds and personalities which produced the amazing success of Marks and Spencer. The immense practical genius of Lord Marks balanced the percipient, sensitive fascination with any piece of pioneering which was characteristic of Sieff. He was from the beginning deeply interested in all the social and economic implications of commerce on the scale with which he now found himself involved, and introduced many novelties in the relations of the firm with their customers, their employees, and their suppliers.

It was Sieff who went to the United States in the early 1930s and spent several weeks in the merchandise development of Sears, Roebuck and returned to see through the last stage of the Marks and Spencer revolution. "We put the technologist behind the retail counter", he remarked, "and once you start selling quality, and quality control, there is no limit".

During the 1920s, a time of great tension and stress for the British economy, Sieff, in a series of contributions in the national press and on the radio, pointed out the direction in which a permanent solution to the country's problems could be found. These views were well ahead of their time and are just as relevant today. They inspired public support for an independent, political, and economic planning research body, P.E.P. Sieff, who at his death was president, was chairman of P.E.P. from 1931 to 1939 and vice-chairman from 1939 to 1964.

As chairman during the thirties, Sieff built up P.E.P. as an effective team for research and policy-forming on an entirely non-party basis. Sieff was not among the original founders, most of whom came from pre-existing discussion groups of more limited scope. They felt increasingly frustrated during the winter of 1930-31 by their inability to deal with more than a fragment of the whole complex problem of enabling the economy and social system to revive and by their lack of resources and channels of communication.

In its earliest days P.E.P. was already well provided with supporters and contacts at a high level in many important activities, but these hardly included manufacturing industry, and from the moment of joining the young organization Sieff set himself with brilliant success to remedy this weakness, which he recognized as cardinal. His Industry Group attracted men of first-rate standing who were well aware of some of the fundamental problems and ready frankly to discuss even radical methods of solving them with economists, administrators and others holding independent positions. Under Sieff's dynamic and confident lead, impressive and well-documented reports were produced on cotton, iron and steel, coal-mining and other great industries, which were frequently acknowledged by industrial leaders to have deeply influenced their thought and action in moving towards industrial reconstruction.

Among Sieff's guiding concepts at this time was the reform of the structure of the economic system so as to make finance no longer the master but the handmaid of industry, which in turn should be guided by a dynamic and research-minded marketing organization, able to forecast reliably much longer and more economical runs of a range of merchandise scientifically designed to meet the maximum number of customer demands. Although himself a distributor he took a keen interest in every stage of the process from the raw material to the eventual consumer, and he was insistent that all must share fairly in the team effort and in its rewards. Sieff's counsel was an irresistible blend of vision and prophetic idealism with the most down-to-earth commonsense based on detailed mastery of his subject. He saw fear in all its forms as the basic obstacle to industrial advance and as the chronic disease afflicting all parties in the productive process.

The deep and lasting impression which he made in many meetings spread the influence of his ideas much more widely than many realized. This influence was furthered by the practice, which under his guidance was adopted on the basis of Zionist experience, of issuing periodic broadsheets outlining research and study group results at frequent intervals to a wide and influential band of sympathizers.

His abundant hospitality, in which he was partnered by his wife Becky, gave a special charm and friendliness to his role and the more intimately he became known the more the warmth and wisdom of his personality impressed itself. Although as the thirties advanced the shadows of the Hitlerite tragedy deepened over him he never gave up his intense interest in this work.

As young businessmen both Sieff and Simon Marks were enthusiastic disciples of Chaim Weizmann, then a lecturer in Manchester University, and they helped him largely in the Zionist work which led to the Balfour Declaration. Sieff was appointed secretary of the Zionist Commission which visited Palestine in March 1918, with a mandate to "act as an advisory body to the British authorities in all matters relating to Jews". There he came into contact with Sir Wyndham Deedes, the Political Officer concerned with the area, and formed a life-long friendship with him on the basis of their common belief in Zionism. The result was the Anglo-Israel Association. His concern with Zionist causes provided one of the mainsprings of his life, though for many years he preferred to work behind the scenes rather than through prominent office in Zionist organizations. But he later became honorary president of the British Zionist Federation. In 1970 he published his memoirs.

The tragic death of a son, Daniel, who had intended to devote himself to science, inspired Sieff and his family to create a memorial in the form of a scientific institute in Palestine at Rehovoth, and it was here that Dr. Weizmann and other Jewish scientists did much of the research work which made the agricultural and industrial development of the country possible. Sieff himself developed substantial orange groves at Tel Mond in the maritime plain. He was concerned with every aspect of its life and was constantly host to its leaders when they visited England. His other main Jewish interest was channelled through the World Jewish Congress, of whose European executive he was an active chairman, but he was also a benefactor of scholarly bodies such as the Royal Anthropological Society —of which he was a Fellow—or the Centre for the Study of Relations between the Jewish and non-Jewish worlds associated with the Parkes Library.

In his later years his fascination with pioneering was shown by his various successful activities as a farmer and horticulturist. He acquired a considerable amount of land in Berkshire, where he became a successful stockbreeder, strawberry grower, and cultivator of orchids. He would show himself more delighted at having increased the sales of strawberries by £1,000 than the sales of Marks and Spencer by £1m.

His wife, Rebecca, sister of Lord Marks, shared many of his interests, especially those centring on Israel, where she made her home in the years before her death in 1966.

February 15, 1972.

Jo Siffert, the Swiss team leader for B.R.M., who died in a motor racing accident at Brands Hatch on October 24, 1971, was at the peak of his career. After years in the shadows of Grand Prix driving, he was finding success with the British team and some thought it possible he would give them the world championship in 1972. He was one of the world's greatest sports car drivers, too, giving Porsche a string of great wins over his last three years.

He was born on July 7, 1936 in Fribourg, Switzerland, south-west of Berne, the son of a motor trader. Before taking up four-wheeled motor sport Siffert had a successful career as a motor-cycle racer. A brilliant mechanic, he rapidly mastered racing machinery and did well in the gruelling Isle of Man T.T. and many continental events. He was Swiss 350cc. champion in 1959.

He moved on to motor racing in 1960 with a Formula Junior Lotus 18, and leapt to prominence in the fiercely-fought Junior category in 1961, winning at Cesenatico, Lake Garda, the Nürburgring, Castello-Teramo, Pergusa, Cadours and Montlhéry—sharing the European F.J. championship with the South African, Tony Maggs.

Siffert moved into Formula I racing in 1962 and made his world championship debut in the Belgian Grand Prix (Lotus, 10th place). Since then he had driven a variety of Formula I cars, including Lotus-B.R.M., Brabham-B.R.M., Cooper-Maserati, Lotus-Cosworth, Ford, and March-Cosworth-Ford.

Siffert was recognized as a fast and extremely tidy Grand Prix driver. He scored his first world championship victory in the 1968 British Grand Prix at Brands Hatch, when he drove Rob Walker's new Lotus 49B and went on to score further successes in this class. He was placed ninth in the championship table of 1969.

Apart from his Formula I record, Siffert was one of the leading sports and prototype drivers of his time, his phlegmatic character being well suited to long drives at racing speeds. In 1968 and 1969 he had a string of successes in this class, including the Daytona 24 hours, the Sebring 12 hours, the Monza 1,000, and the Austrian Grand Prix 1,000 km., which he won in both years.

His sports car win in the Buenos Aires 1,000 km. in 1971, together with his Austrian F1 victory and his second place at Watkins Glen in the United States, gave him back the "fire" he had had in earlier days, and at Brands Hatch in his fatal race he started from the front of the grid and was strongly tipped to win.

October 25, 1971.

Igor Sikorsky, who died on October 26, 1972 at the age of 83, was an aeronautical pioneer in the truest sense, one who spent his own and his family's money to break into this adventure, who continued as designer and engineer until he retired when he was nearly 70, and never contrived to retain such financial control of the undertaking that bore his name as would yield him a fortune.

When he retired his position in the Sikorsky Aircraft Division of the United Aircraft Corporation was still that of engineering manager, though he had built up the original company and piloted it through days of difficulty and near-extinction. He had no hard feelings about that. On the contrary, he was grateful right through to the land that gave him his second chance when Russia was, as he thought, betrayed by the Marxists; and he got all the satisfactions he desired from realizing his dreams and bringing his ideas to completion.

Born on May 25, 1889, he was the youngest child of a professor of psychology in Kiev University and before he broke away to take up engineering he had served three years in the Naval Academy at Petrograd.

The young Sikorsky had made himself a model helicopter as a boy of 12, inspired by the tales his mother told him of Leonardo da Vinci; and his toy rose into the air. In 1908, at the age of 19, he embarked on a full-scale helicopter, and with it his first primitive scientific experiments, testing the lifting power of his rotors with weights.

Off he went to Paris to find out something about flying and, in the course of his four months' visit, bought an Anzani engine, had transmission and shaft made to his own drawings, and returned to Kiev to tackle problems which were not to be fully solved for another three decades. He built two helicopters, both with twin rotors, one above the other, arranging a system of piano wires and turnbuckles to alter the pitch of the blades; and he got the second one to rise carrying a certain amount of load but not enough to represent a man. By the spring of 1910 he was turning to fixed wing aircraft and half a dozen progressive types allowed him to teach himself to fly and to learn enough about first principles and structures to advance to the design of The Grand.

Up to that point his work had been financed by members of his family and by loans from friends. Now, early in 1912, he satisfied the chairman of the Baltic Railway Car Factory at Petrograd of the soundness of his ideas, was appointed chief designer and engineer of its new aircraft division and was given authority to go ahead with his huge aeroplane of 92ft span, using four 100 h.p. water-cooled engines. In that first essay in multi-engined aircraft, as in his first attempts at the helicopter, he learnt a lesson he never forgot.

In The Grand, he had his engines in tandem pairs with one airscrew pulling and the other pushing. That he never repeated, just as he never again sought to have two helicopter rotors turning on concentric shafts. In later big aircraft the engines were all tractors set near the loading edge of the wing. When his Ilia Mourametz came

forward in 1914, he had the satisfaction of flying it to his home town of Kiev. For a whole year, he was the only pilot in Russia capable of flying these big craft and so was test pilot as well as designer, and when the army adopted the type, he became first instructor and then technical expert attached to the squadron on active service.

As a young man of 24 his fame began to spread beyond the frontiers of his native Russia with the first successful four-engined aircraft, complete with enclosed cabin and provision for mechanics to adjust the engines in the air. In the next two years he produced improved versions of his monster which served in large numbers (75 were built) with the Russian army on bombing and reconnaissance duty so long as Russia remained in the war against the Kaiser's Germany.

It was, in its day, a fantastic piece of aeronautical development and imaginative engineering. He himself described it as "something out of Jules Verne", but his triumph ended with the revolution in the spring of 1917—a "foolish and inglorious event" as he called it—and within a year he had left Russia for ever. He was welcomed in Paris by the Allied authorities and set to work on the design of a big bomber. The armistice late in 1918 put a stop to that too, and, with a few hundred pounds, he arrived as an immigrant in New York in March 1919. Nearly ten years were to pass before he found his feet.

His persistence was as remarkable as his foresight. Those early days in New York tested it fully. His first engineering enterprise failed and he kept himself for two years by giving lectures on aviation, and teaching some of his fellow exiles mathematics and, of all things, astronomy. He infected some of these artisans and labourers with his own passion for aircraft and in 1923 formed a company of small shareholders to undertake aircraft construction. Some invested cash; some promised their labour; the company started with 1,000 dollars in cash and a huge fund of enthusiasm. Work was begun at Roosevelt Field, partly in an unheated hangar and partly in the open, with improvized tools and a good many of the materials obtained from junk yards. There was a period of financial crisis and for 20 weeks the workmen got no pay but a two-engined commercial aeroplane was built, test flown by the designer, and then set to earn its keep by means of charter flights.

This revenue and more investment funds from various New England parties who recognized the quality of the man enabled him to embark on his first amphibian. René Fouck came to him for an Atlantic craft of this kind and although Lindbergh got in first and robbed Sikorsky of a likely success, the association had proved valuable.

His next amphibian was designed with such assurance that a production line of ten was laid down. Not only were these promptly sold but orders rolled in faster than they could be met. In the end more

than 100 S.38s. were sold, a new company with five million dollars of capital was formed and Sikorsky Aircraft moved to Bridgeport, Connecticut.

That was in 1928: the following year it became a subsidiary of United Aircraft. It was set now for big business. Pan-American Airways had become a customer and Sikorsky was moving into the sphere of wind tunnels and testing tanks where Clipper ships of the air were to be conceived and brought triumphantly to the air routes of the world.

For the next ten years he was to be fully engaged in the design and construction of big flying boats for the ocean routes. This was the real fulfilment of the promise in 1913 of The Grand, that biplane of 9,000lb loaded weight and of the Ilia Mourametz which followed it.

In the S.42 class of flying-boats of a loaded weight of around 70,000lb. Sikorsky had greatly increased wing loading and brought to his aid new devices like flaps and variable-pitch propellers, and had produced a vehicle which could defy the landplane of that period because it could employ for take-off stretches of water far longer than the runways available at most airports. Its preeminence as the long-range aircraft disappeared in the war when wheeled bombers and transports and bigger airfields gave the advantage back to the landplane. The transition threw Sikorsky back to his first love, the helicopter, and the rest of his working days were given exclusively to it.

Sikorsky was proud of his achievements and yet remained a modest man. The acquisition of wealth troubled him little but twice in his life he was glad to be well enough off to pay his debts—at Petrograd to repay the loans of his friends and at Roosevelt Field to see that every one of his original supporters ultimately got back twice his investment in that struggling company.

He married Elizabeth Semion in New York in 1924 and became a naturalized citizen of the United States in 1928. They had four sons and a daughter.

October 27, 1972.

Lord Silkin, P.C., C.H., Deputy Leader of the Opposition in the House of Lords from 1955 to 1964, died on May 11, 1972. He was 82.

He had been a life-long supporter of the Labour movement, and was appointed Minister of Town and Country Planning at the end of the Second World War. He thus had an important influence on every aspect of the third Labour Government's rebuilding policy.

He was responsible for steering through Parliament the New Towns Act of 1946; the Town and Country Planning Act of 1947; and the National Parks and Access to the Countryside Act of 1949. He was the Minister in power who decided Stevenage was to be the first postwar new town.

Silkin introduced an Abortion Bill in the House of Lords in 1966 which was rewritten in committee and at the report stage. The Bill's tortuous progress indicated that the Lords had no clear idea of what it wanted to do. The debates showed, however, that there was a need for abortion reform. David Steel's Bill, introduced in the Commons, came into force in 1968.

Silkin had previously been in charge of the L.C.C.'s rehousing campaign and was closely associated with the County of London Plan. As Labour member of Parliament for Peckham for 14 years, he had a large following in south London and was well known for his wide understanding of civic affairs. A sound administrator, his shy manner and soft way of speaking concealed a capacity for an immense amount of work. As a Parliamentary reformer he made up in diligence what he lacked in brilliance. He was sworn of the Privy Council in 1945, and was raised to the peerage in 1950.

He was born on November 14, 1889, of parents who had come from one of the Baltic states. Lewis Silkin, the eldest of seven children, was educated at a junior school at Stoke Newington and the Central Foundation School, City Road, London. He won an open scholarship in mathematics to Worcester College, Oxford, but his parents were too poor to allow him to take it up. However he managed a year's study ar London University. Later he worked as a clerk in the docks, joined a solicitor who wanted a "bright boy", became his managing clerk and, after qualifying, set up in partnership with another solicitor. He later brought in one of his brothers and the firm of Lewis Silkin and Partners was founded.

In 1922 he stood for Central Wandsworth but was unsuccessful. His young, voluntary unpaid agent was Hartley Shawcross (now Lord Shawcross), who drove Silkin round on a small motor-cycle and sidecar hired for the election. Subsequently Silkin became associated with the I.L.P. and in 1925 was elected to the London County Council.

The bad conditions in the London slums had made a lasting impression on him and he soon became known as an authority on public housing and health. In 1934 he was elected chairman of the L.C.C. housing and public health committee and took on the leadership of the council's rehousing drive. In the following year a visit to study continental housing methods helped to convince him that flats—rather than individual houses, however desirable in themselves—were the only solution for the densely populated areas under his care: but at the same time he felt it important to make use of the best traditions of English domestic architecture and to preserve the separate identity of areas like the East End.

The success of the licensing scheme un-doubtedly owed much to his leadership and depended on a mass of detailed work and knowledge, ranging from rent restriction and gas charges to the schemes for building on Hackney Marshes and for mechanical car parks. While Herbert Morrison (later Lord Morrison of Lambeth*) was Minister of Transport in the second Labour Government, Lewis Silkin led the Labour Opposition in the L.C.C.; in 1935 he was appointed a member of the Central Housing Advisory Committee. The following year he was elected M.P. for Peckham.

During the war years he came to the forefront of the Parliamentary Labour Party and in 1944 he was elected a member of its executive. By this time as chairman of the L.C.C.'s town planning committee he had been closely associated with Professor Abercrombie's plan for reshaping the County of London. Envisaging the tremendous task ahead, he became more than ever conscious of the advantages of flats over houses, of the need for reducing the County of London's population, for the rational location of industry, and for positive as well as negative powers to be held by the planning authorities.

When Clement Attlee* formed his Cabinet after the general election in 1945, Silkin became Minister of Town and Country Planning. The destruction of so many built-up areas and the endorsement by the electorate of the principle of centralized planning presented him with unprecedented opportunities. The need to build temporary houses as quickly as possible, the shortage of labour and supplies and the difficulty of finding time for the legislation necessary to acquire control of land and property were, however, against him. The question was to find some way of modifying private ownership so as to make planning possible, and at the same time deal fairly with the complications of betterment and compensation.

Slkin was able to get ahead with the job of setting up the machinery of planning, and to formulate his ideas. He believed that the overall control of the building and planning should rest with the Government, but that responsibility for particular areas and much of the detailed work should devolve on the local authorities. The location of industry should follow a national plan related to transport and the sources of raw materials, housing districts should be separated as far as possible from industrial districts, and the countryside should enjoy many of the amenities of the towns, and the towns the advantage of open spaces and easy access to green belts and the country itself. He had strong objections to unsightly advertising, and believed that landscape artists should be brought in at the initial stages of all building schemes.

One of his first practical opportunities came when he introduced the New Towns Bill, which provided for the surplus population of the larger towns. Sites were chosen which were likely to attract industry, and usually with an already existing town as a nucleus. In the cases of towns like Stevenage and Hemel Hempstead he had to meet much opposition from the citizens whose lives were about to be unsettled. His answer was to explain to them personally the necessity and opportunities of the step.

In 1947 the complicated Town and Country Planning Bill proved for Silkin a great trial of Parliamentary skill. He emerged from the long debates on the floor of the House and in Committee with much credit.

In the summer of 1950 Silkin was raised to the peerage as Baron Silkin, of Dulwich.

In November 1955, he was elected deputy leader of the Labour Party in the House of Lords.

Silkin's ability found expression in several fields other than politics. He was among the best players of chess in the House of Commons in his day. He wrote a number of pamphlets and gave frequent lectures, although he had a poor speaking voice which was, however, compensated by a cheerful manner and forthright approach. He was a director of the City and Commercial Investment Trust and a governor of Alleyn's School, Dulwich.

He was three times married. His first wife, Rosa Neft, whom he married in 1915, died in 1947, leaving three sons, the eldest of whom, the Hon. Arthur Silkin, now succeeds to the peerage. The second marriage, in 1948, was to Mrs. Frieda M. Johnson, daughter of Canon Pilling, of Norwich, and widow of J. F. F. Johnson. She died in 1963 and he married, thirdly, in 1964 Marguerite Schlageter.

May 12, 1972.

Shena Lady Simon of Wythenshawe, widow of the first Lord Simon of Wythenshawe, died on July 17, 1972 in Manchester.

Shena Simon, a daughter of John Wilson Potter, married Ernest D. Simon (later Lord Simon of Wythenshawe) in 1912. Educated privately and at Newnham, she was as a young graduate, like her husband, profoundly interested in social reform: and their marriage marked the beginning of a notable partnership.

In 1921 Ernest Simon became the youngest Lord Mayor of Manchester in the history of the city, and with their intellectual gifts and remarkable good looks the Simons made a great impression as Lord Mayor and Lady Mayoress. Hospitality was a feature of their reign for they believed strongly in the value of bringing small groups together for informal discussions about matters of moment. They continued this excellent practice throughout their married life; and the small parties that they arranged at Broomcroft, their hospitable Manchester home, or in their London flat, stimulated good talk and constructive argument.

Of the several enterprises shared together, probably the one that gave them most pleasure was their munificent gifts to their beloved city—Wythenshawe Hall and its 250 acres of surrounding parkland. Well described as "an act of imaginative statesmanship", it initiated a housing programme on a grand scale. Lady Simon had a major role in the pioneer planning of Wythenshawe, being a member of the Wythenshawe committee from its inception in 1926, concluding her service on it as chairman from 1931 to 1933. A member of its council, she shared fully in Lord Simon's interest in and affection for Manchester University; and after his death in 1960 she crowned a great record of generosity by deciding to bequeath Broomcroft with its beautiful grounds to the university.

One of the happiest moments in her life was when in 1932 she was elected with acclamation chairman of the Manchester education committee. She was also in the 1930s a vigorous member of the city council's finance committee. The demand for retrenchment made it a crucial period for education, and Lady Simon's grasp of its problems, her moral courage, and her gift for marshalling statistical data made her a powerful adversary to those too ready to look to education for the imposed "cuts". She never hesitated to stand up for her convictions, however formidable the odds; and it was largely because of this quality that she, later, lost her seat as a councillor. But, coopted to the education committee, she continued to give devoted service. She was elected a Freeman of Manchester in 1964 for her services to the city and education.

Prominent in the affairs of the Workers Educational Association, she was also a member of the Spens Committee, participating in the extensive survey of secondary education that led to its constructive report. An early advocate of comprehensive schools, she published in 1948 *Three Schools or One*.

But of all her various writings the most characteristic is her scholarly *A Century of City Government*, a masterly and graphic description of local government in Manchester, 1818-1938. This she dedicated appropriately to her heroine, Beatrice Webb, describing her with pride as "a grand-niece of the first mayor of Manchester who, in partnership with her husband, laid the foundations of a science of local government".

July 18, 1972.

Michel Simon, whose face, if not the most lively, was certainly among the best-loved in the French cinema for almost half a century, died in May 30, 1975 in hospital. He was 80.

He was in fact Swiss; as Michel-François Simon he was born in Geneva on April 9, 1895. His family were poor, and as a young man he tried a variety of jobs, among them boxer, street vendor, acrobat, and photographer's assistant. Despite a face and physique that were deemed "impossible", he began to act with the Pitoëff Company in Geneva in 1918. On the strength of his performance as Shaw's *Androcles*, he became a regular member of the company and went with them to Paris.

The French at first only unwillingly accepted his unlikely appearance, strong Swiss accent, and slow diction, but his enormous comic gift could not be obscured. From Pitoëff he moved on to the Palais Royal, and then on to the Théâtre des Arts and the Mathurins.

His fame came with his work for the cinema. His first screen appearance was in Marcel L'Herbier's *Feu Mathias Pascal*, adapted from Pirandello. Three years later, in 1928, he was one of the judges, with the face of a medieval grotesque, in Carl Dreyer's *Trial of Joan of Arc*. The same year he made the first of the memorable series of films in which he was directed by Jean Renoir, *Tire au flanc*. It was followed by the Feydeau farce, *On Purge Bébé*; but the two films which revealed the full range of his means were *La Chienne* and *Boudu Sauvé des Eaux*. The roles were in sharp contrast. In *La Chienne* he was the deceived middle-aged husband. In *Boudu* he was the reprehensible *clochard* who reckons that the kindly bookseller who has saved him from drowning has thereby won him as a permanent responsibility, and thereafter uses books as spitoons and in every other way disrupts the bourgois calm of his benefactor's household. Alongside these his most notable creation remains Père Jules in Jean Vigo's *L'Atalante*, the barge's eccentric old mate whose cabin of bric-à-brac includes the pickled hands of an erstwhile friend.

Two highly successful films of the late 1930s in which he was seen were Carné's *Drôle de Drame*, with a classic cast, Françoise Rosay, Louis Jouvet, and Jean-Louis Barrault; and *Quai des Brumes*, in which the stars were Jean Gabin and Michèle Morgan.

Simon continued to work in films, albeit increasingly more intermittently, until late in life. Recent appearances had included John Frankenheimer's *The Train* and Walerian Porowczyk's *Blanche*. The extent of Simon's work, under almost every French director of note during four decades is bewildering for its variety and staggering for his ability to sustain the integrity of his playing through more then 100 roles which even included Inspector Maigret.

In private life he was gentle and modest, but with a zestful and often ribald sense of fun.

Michel's son François Simon, a notable Swiss stage director and actor who himself first appeared on screen as a child in *Sans Lendemain*, has recently been seen in Claude Goretta's *The Invitation*.

May 31, 1975.

Lord Simonds, P.C., who died on June 28, 1971 in London, became Lord Chancellor in October 1951, when the Prime Minister (then Winston Churchill*) formed his Government after the general election which had just taken place. The appointment of Simonds to the Woolsack did not follow the generally recognized course of choice. He was at the time a law lord, but he had never held one of the law officerships, and he was not an active participant in politics. Though his elevation to the chief judicial position in Britain came as a surprise to the public, the refreshing departure from conventional practice, whatever the reason, resulted in that great office being filled by a man whose high qualities well fitted him to carry out its difficult, onerous and important work.

Gavin Turnbull Simonds, the first Viscount, the son of Louis de Luze Simonds, of Audley's Wood, Basingstoke, was born on November 28, 1881; he came of a family of brewers well known in the south of England.

He was educated first at Winchester, where he was a scholar, and at New College Oxford, where he was an exhibitioner, and he took a first in Moderns in 1902 and a first in Litt. Hum. in 1904. He was elected an Honorary Fellow of New College in 1944. Always a loyal and enthusiastic Wykehamist, he had been a Fellow of Winchester College since 1933 and was Warden in 1946.

He was called to the Bar by Lincoln's Inn in 1906, and was for many years in chambers with Austen-Cartmell, afterwards the Treasury "devil". He took silk in 1924, and as a leader he was an immediate success.

In those days of Lord Greene's preeminence at the Bar, Simonds was one of his principal rivals, and when Greene was made a Lord Justice in 1935 some of his practice naturally fell to Simonds, and for ten years or so there were few heavy cases in the Chancery Courts in which he was not listed as a leader. Early in 1929 he appeared for members of the High Council in the litigation that arose out of the dispute over the leadership of the Salvation Army, then held by General Bramwell Booth. In the upshot the High Council in February 1929 elected Commissioner E. J. Higgins, Chief of Staff, to succeed him.

In 1936 Simonds appeared more prominently before the public as a Commissioner with Mr Justice (afterwards Lord) Porter and Mr (later Mr. Justice) Roland Oliver*, appointed to investigate the circumstances of the Budget leakage of that year.

For nearly twenty years Simonds, with his thorough knowledge of equity principles and practice, his fine presence, deep voice, burly figure and aggressive eyebrows, had been a dominant personality in the Chancery Division. It was no surprise when, in March 1937 he was nominated by the the Lord Chancellor to fill the vacancy on the Chancery bench created by the retirement of Mr. Justice Eve; and his learning, shrewdness, rapidity and courtesy made him as popular and successful on the Bench as he had been at the Bar. While a Judge of first instance he was appointed in July 1940, chairman of the National Arbitration Tribunal set up to establish compulsory arbitration in industrial disputes during the war. In those years, when the conditions of war deprived the courts of a great deal of their business, much of his time was occupied in that duty, and many important settlements were reached under his guidance.

When Lord Romer retired in April 1944, Simonds was named as his successor as a Lord of Appeal in Ordinary; he thus followed in the footsteps of two famous equity Lawyers, Lord Parker of Waddington and Lord Tomlin, in reaching the House of Lords without passing through the Court of Appeal. Two of his judgments in the House of Lords on the law of charities were given in cases which might justly be described as landmarks in that branch of jurisprudence: *National Anti-Vivisection Society v Commissioners of Inland Revenue* (1947), in which it was held that an anti-vivisection society was not in law a good charity, and *Gilmour v Coates* (1949), in which an Order of enclosed nuns suffered a similar fate.

Though several other better known names had been mentioned for the Lord Chancellorship, the appointment of Simonds to the post in October 1951 was received by the legal profession with great satisfaction. He was a strong and lively occupant of the Woolsack, as he also was when, as a law lord, he sometimes presided over the hearing of appeals in the House and before the Judicial Committee of the Privy Council. He kept the cases within bounds, and no time was lost, as with decisive and confident mind he pressed forward the hearings with considerable vigour. Behind his robust manner an innate kindliness was always discernible, and there never was any doubt about his judicial and administrative ability as Lord Chancellor.

If Simonds's appointment had come as a surprise, so did his resignation which occurred when the Government was reconstructed in October 1954. In a letter to the Prime Minister he wrote that "the nature of this great office, political, administrative and judicial, is a heavy burden to bear. For myself I should be glad to return to the work in which I have spent my life and there to do such service as I can". It was generally believed, at least in legal circles, that Simonds, in spite of the gracious terms in which he offered his resignation, felt, perhaps not without reason, that he had been somewhat brusquely displaced; but his forensic and judicial experience and gifts had not qualified him for conducting the business of the House, and it was no doubt with genuine relief that he resumed his role as Lord of Appeal in Ordinary. At the end of October 1954, it was announced that a viscountcy had been conferred on him, and he became

Viscount Simonds of Sparsholt, in the County of Southampton. He retired in March 1962, but continued to lend occasional assistance at judicial sessions of the House of Lords and in the Privy Council.

Simonds was a Chancery lawyer through and through, and his opinions, when they touched on questions of general concern, usually upheld a conservative view of the functions of the Law, in particular as the guardian of public morality, a view that he expressed robustly in the well-known "Ladies Directory" case (*Shaw v. Director of Public Prosecutions*).

In December 1959 the Government decided to set up a committee to consider the important question of the use of subpoenas to secure the attendance of witnesses and the production of documents before disciplinary tribunals, and in particular whether subpoenas should be issuable to secure the production before such tribunals of evidence obtained by police officers in the course of criminal investigations. The committee, which consisted of three members, Simonds being the chairman, presented their report in May 1960.

He had been made a Bencher of his Inn in 1929 and was elected Treasurer in 1951. In that year he was appointed Professor of Law, Royal Academy of Arts. In 1954 he became High Steward of Oxford University; he was also made an Hon. F.R.C.O.G. The degree of D.Litt. (Reading University) was conferred on him in 1947; of Docteur en droit (Laval University) in 1953; and of Hon. D.C.L. (Oxford University) in the following year.

He married in 1912 Mary Hope, daughter of Judge K. H. Mellor.

June 29, 1971.

Lieutenant-General Guy Granville Simonds, C.B., C.B.E., D.S.O., who died in Toronto on May 15, 1974 at the age of 71, was a distinguished soldier, who after holding a series of important commands in the Canadian army was its Chief of General Staff from 1951 to 1955.

He was born at Ixworth Abbey, Bury St. Edmunds, in April 1903, the son of Lieutenant-Golonel C. B. Simonds, R.A. In his boyhood he was taken to Canada and was educated at Ashbury College in Ottawa. Passing into the Royal Military College at Kingston, Ontario, he graduated with distinction in 1925 and was immediately given a commission in the Royal Canadian Artillery. He was sent to attend a gunnery staff course in Britain and the Staff College at Camberley. In his early thirties, when he was a captain, he was appointed an instructor in tactics at the Royal Military College.

On the outbreak of the Second World War he was posted to the headquarters staff of the 1st Canadian Infantry Division with the rank of major. In 1943, as a brigadier, he was one of a group of Cana-

dian officers sent to North Africa in the role of observers. He was then selected to command the 2nd Canadian Infantry Division. Soon afterwards, however, he was transferred to the command of the 1st Canadian Infantry Division, which had been training for the invasion of Sicily, and, as its leader in this campaign, he established his reputation as a skilful and energetic commander in action. He remained in command of it for the invasion of Italy and by his excellent work won the confidence of Field-Marshal Lord Montgomery. He was promoted lieutenant-general in January 1944, when he was recalled to Britain to assume command of the 2nd Canadian Army Corps, then training for the invasion of Normandy.

As its leader in the assault upon the beaches and subsequent battles, he set the seal upon his reputation as a first-class fighting soldier. For a period in the autumn of 1944 he was in command of the 1st Canadian Army, when General Crerar* was on sick leave. After Crerar's return Simonds resumed command of the 2nd Canadian Corps and led it in the final campaign, which led to the crossing of the Rhine and to the collapse of the resistance of the German armies.

After the cessation of hostilities, he was in command of the Canadian forces in the Netherlands and Germany. He left them in 1945 to attend the Imperial Defence College in Britain, where he was appointed an instructor in 1946.

In 1949 he returned to Canada to assume command of the National Defence College and the Canadian Army Staff College, both established at Kingston, and directed their activities until he was appointed Chief of the Army Staff in February 1951. He held this post for a little over four years and worked strenuously to bring the Canadian regular army and the territorial militia to a high pitch of efficiency; but his tenure of this important office was not uniformly happy.

The Liberal ministry then in power was intent upon paring down military expenditure to the lowest possible scale, and Simonds felt constantly frustrated by lack of the funds which he felt essential for the accomplishment of his plans. His relations with ministers became strained and as a result, although he was admitted to be Canada's most competent soldier and at the age of 52 was in the prime of his powers, his appointment was not renewed.

In 1955 he retired on pension and soon incurred the displeasure of the St. Laurent ministry by criticizing its programme of defence in public speeches and by his advocacy of military conscription.

He married in 1932 Kathleen, daughter of C. M. Taylor, of Winnipeg, by whom he had a son and a daughter. After this marriage was dissolved in 1959, he married secondly in 1960 Dorothy Flavelle Sinclair.

May 17, 1974.

The Rt. Rev. Bertram Fitzgerald Simpson, M.C., who was Bishop of Southwark from 1942 to 1958, died on July 16, 1971. He was 87.

He was one of the really great preachers of the Church of England. A strong case could be made for the claim that he was the greatest in this generation, and that upon him had fallen the mantle of Liddon. He never used a note, but just stood in the pulpit, or leaned characteristically on its edge, and the works gushed out in a torrent. Much of the secret of his success was that he always preached "as a dying man to dying men". His sermons were not leading articles or carefully polished essays on contemporary events, but fervent impassioned appeals for a verdict—for God. Like Saul and Jonathan in their deaths, he and his sermon could not be divided. The sermon was the man, and the man was the sermon. Coupled with his command of language was a remarkable lucidity of thought—the two qualities are not always found combined.

Simpson was essentially a speaker and not a writer. He published only one book, a study of the Lord's Prayer called *The Prayer of Sonship*, and that did not do him justice. He always said that he could not write his sermons; and that perhaps is why the British Broadcasting Corporation used him so seldom; he thought them out as he mowed the lawn, drove his car or dug his allotment, to which he was deeply attached.

Bertram Fitzgerald Simpson was born on September 25, 1883, the son of William and Mary Ann Simpson, and educated at University College, Durham, where he took a first-class in theology and was Hebrew and Barry scholar in addition to winning the Gabbett Prize. He took his B.D. (London) in 1906 and was ordained deacon in St. Paul's Cathedral in 1907 and priest in 1908.

Simpson was curate of St. Anne's, Soho, from 1907 to 1911, London Diocesan Home Missioner at St. Peter's, Harrow, from 1911 to 1913, and first vicar of that parish from 1913 to 1920. He was a temporary Chaplain to the Forces for the last two years of the First World War, and won the M.C. in 1918.

From 1920 to 1926 he was Rector and Rural Dean of Stepney—possibly the least happy years of his life. During that period he was offered the living at St. Mary's, Hornsey, but he decided to stay in East London. He was Boyle Lecturer in 1923, 1924 and 1925, and twice lectured on Pastoral Theology in the University of Durham.

He was also Golden Lecturer in 1925. In 1926 he was appointed vicar of St. Peter's, Cranley Gardens, where his first sermon electrified the large congregation. After he had been there for about two years the Bishop of London (Dr. Winnington-Ingram) asked him to be his Suffragan Bishop of Stepney, but he declined on the grounds that he ought not to leave St.

Peter's after so short a time. He was Chaplain to the King from 1919 to 1932, when he was consecrated Bishop of Kensington, becoming Rector of St. Botolph's, Bishopsgate, in 1935. He was translated to Southwark in 1942, where his ability, sincerity and geniality at once made their mark, and the diocese was greatly strengthened by his appointment.

In 1946 he was asked to become Bishop of Salisbury but he decided that he ought to stay in Southwark and so declined to be translated. He remained there until 1958 when he retired.

He was utterly devoted to his diocese and rarely accepted an engagement outside it.

He was not an originator of new ideas but generously encouraged the plans of his colleagues. Perhaps his chief work was the preservation of Church schools.

He had a gift (rare among Bishops) of answering letters by return and toiled at routine office work which others would have delegated. He loved his clergy and they loved him and so did their wives, whom he liked to help with the washing-up. He was not afraid to deal with miscreants but he dealt with them gently and hated doing it. Perhaps he lacked that touch of ruthlessness, and the capacity to say a few well-frozen words which are said to be essential in a leader.

At every ordination he told his new clergy to come to him if they got into any difficulties, and those in trouble rarely failed to go to him and make a clean breast of it.

He suffered terribly at times from doubts—a consequence of his keenness of intellect, straightforwardness and ability to see every point of view. He once said that though he started as a mild Anglo-Catholic he tended to become broader in his views as he grew older.

From 1958 until his death Simpson was the Preacher of Lincoln's Inn. The Inn was exceedingly fortunate to have him to conduct its services in chapel. Sunday by Sunday while the Courts were sitting, until the last fortnight of his life, he preached sermons which inspired and delighted his congregation. His sermons, carefully prepared and delivered without notes, would usually last about 20 minutes; he could describe a scene from the Old or New Testament so vividly that his congregation could believe that they as well as he had been present, and he was equally graphic when dealing with current doubts and difficulties.

Besides being a great preacher Simpson was also a kind and sympathetic pastor to his congregation sharing their joys and sorrows and visiting them in times of sickness and bereavement.

He married in 1912 Ethel Mary Penistan (who died in 1952) and they had a son and a daughter.

July 19, 1971.

The Rev. Frederick Arthur Simpson, Fellow of Trinity College, Cambridge, died on February 8, 1974.

Born on November 22, 1883, the son of the Rev. W. F. Simpson, a Cumberland rector, and of Frances Fidler, daughter of a Cumberland J.P., he came from Rossall School as an exhibitioner to The Queen's College, Oxford, where he took a first class in modern history in 1906, and became Simcox Research Student. His first book, *The Rise of Louis Napoleon*, was eagerly greeted for its acute scholarship and its brilliant style, constantly hitting the nail on the head by a neat phrase or an illuminating paradox, which was then justified by close argument. The book went into its sixth edition in 1968.

He was ordained in 1909 and from that year until 1911 was Curate of Ambleside. He was brought from his northern lair to be a Fellow of Trinity in 1911 partly at the instance of G. M. Trevelyan*, to whom his second volume was later dedicated. After three years (1915-18) as a Chaplain to the Forces, he returned to be senior dean there (1919-23), and continued to do his share of college teaching until 1937 and to lecture for the university until 1949.

His lectures always had the same two titles, "Theory of the Modern State" and "The Eastern Question in the Nineteenth Century", and were always given at the same times and in the same places; but they were continually revised and polished and were very far from being repetitious.

As a college supervisor, he could be intimidating and whimsical. His tall, sinuous body was either reclining, inert but for the smoke of a cigar curling from his mouth, or else moving restlessly round the room. Legend has it that he once in passing turned on his wireless set while a pupil was reading a dull essay; but his comments at the end, though brief, were always alarmingly pointed and relevant. His features were severe in repose, but readily broke into a quick smile.

Meanwhile his reputation as a preacher spread from the college chapel to the public schools, and for some years he readily accepted invitations, sometimes causing a sensation by arriving in his own aeroplane, piloted by a succession of distinguished R.A.F. officers. He was twice select preacher at Oxford, and three times at Cambridge. His sermon in 1913 on clerical subscription ("ambassadors in bonds") was long remembered.

Always a fastidious perfectionist, he found it harder, as time passed, to make a normal contribution to college duties; after his "last sermon" on Remembrance Day 1947 he could hardly be persuaded to preach, but when he did so it was something of an event (for example, his sermon in 1959 in Southwark Cathedral at the consecration of Mervyn Stockwood as Bishop).

His reputation rests solidly on the volume already mentioned (1909) and on its successor, *Louis Napoleon and the Recovery of France* (1923, fifth edition 1965), which carried the story from December 1848 to the peak of Napoleon III's career in 1856. Everybody hoped and expected two more volumes on the same theme, but they were disappointed. It seems certain that Simpson deliberately abandoned the task through an oversensitive reaction to one or two critical reviews which need not have shaken him so deeply.

The two volumes continue to be read, both for instruction and for sheer delight in their elegance and their eloquence. The French foreign archives were not open at that time, but full use was made of the British ones. To Simpson, the angels were on the side of national and liberal causes, but he was quick to see the growing divergence between the two. He made use of every art to please the reader, such as a catchword at the top of each page and plentiful illustrations; he succeeded without sacrificing scholarship to wit.

His *A Remembrance Day Sermon* went into its fourth editing in 1971; *Lytton Strachey on Manning* had a fourth edition in 1972 and *A Fragment of Autobiography* a second edition in the same year.

February 9, 1974.

Lieut-Gen. Yadavindra Singh—See Patila.

Robert Siodmak, the American film producer and director, died on March 10, 1973. He was 72.

Born in Memphis, Tennessee, on August 8, 1900, his German parents took him back to Berlin before he was one, and most of his early life was spent there. After completing his studies at school and university he tried his hand at various jobs before gravitating towards films, and his first work in the medium was an independently made minor classic of realistic observation, *Menschen am Sonntag*, on which a number of Germany's more notable younger talents, among them Billy Wilder, Fred Zinnemann and Eugen Schufftan, lent a hand. This film established Siodmak as a talented director, and its light and graceful realism, so far removed from the generality of German silent films (of which it was almost the last), pointed the way towards the style favoured by the new talking films. Siodmak was rapidly put under contract by the influential U.F.A. company as director.

His first work for them consisted of two films in dual language versions—a device much favoured at the time for overcoming the new language bar—the second of which, *Stürme der Leidenschaft (Tumultes)*, teamed Emil Jannings and a new French actor, Charles Boyer.

With the advent of Hitler he left Germany and settled in France. On his arrival he collaborated with another German émigré, Henry Koster, on a comedy, *Le Sexe Faible*, adapted from a successful stage play of the time, despite the fact that neither of them knew a word of French. A series of successful popular films followed, of which the most interesting were probably *Mister Flow*, a diverting pastiche of the classic Lubitsch manner, and *Pièges*, which gave Maurice Chevalier his only opportunity to play a straight role.

On the outbreak of war he left France for the United States. In the next three years he directed five pot-boilers and did some screen writing before, in 1943, he was persuaded to take on the direction of *Son of Dracula*, one of Universal's current cycle of run-of-the-mill horror films, and seizing his chance directed it for considerably more than it was worth, with a subtle use of the black and white photography to build up an eerie atmosphere of death and decay. Before the film was even completed Universal had offered him a seven-year contract, and from that time on he rapidly became one of the studio's star directors. In the same year he directed *Phantom Lady*, one of the best thrillers ever made in Hollywood, distinguished by a mastery of dramatic lighting and some characteristic studies of morbid psychology.

Phantom Lady and his five subsequent films form the core of Siodmak's work and his most strikingly individual contribution to the cinema: in all of them a subtle psychological penetration is allied with an atmosphere of quite gothic horror which puts them, in the opinion of many, head and shoulders above the rest of their genre, the psychological thriller which had its vogue in the mid-1940s. *Christmas Holiday* suffered to some extent from the casting of Deanna Durbin in a dramatic role—an experiment never repeated—but *The Suspect*, based loosely on the Crippen case, and *The Strange Affair of Uncle Harry* were both almost completely successful, with Charles Laughton* giving one of his strongest performances in the former and George Sanders by far his best screen portrayal in the latter.

In 1945 followed Siodmak's masterpiece, *The Spiral Staircase*, one of the most terrifying films ever made. Finally in 1946 the cycle was concluded with *The Dark Mirror*, with Olivia de Havilland giving a chilling performance as identical twins, one sane and one a homicidal maniac.

By this time, however, the psychological thriller was being replaced in popularity by the realistic drama made on location, and Siodmak turned his hand to this form in *The Killers*, based on a story by Hemingway, *Criss Cross*, and most successfully, *Cry of the City*, a beautifully shaped story of a policeman and a criminal from the same background and the way their paths cross and recross during 24 hours.

In 1952 he returned to Europe and made first a surprisingly successful comedy, *The Crimson Pirate*. Then after a French-made pot-boiler he went back to Germany and directed three films of considerable interest, *Die Ratten*, based on Hauptmann, *Mein Vater der Schauspieler* and *Nachte Wenn der Teufel Kam*, a powerful picture of Nazism in dissolution centred on the case of a mentally subnormal killer.

Robert Siodmak tended to be underestimated among serious film students because his best work was done in the despised genres of the psychological thriller and the horror film, but within the limits imposed by his personal tastes and inclination his mastery was complete.

March 14, 1973.

Viliam Siroky, former Prime Minister of Czechoslovakia, died on October 6, 1971 at the age of 69.

Siroky was born in Slovakia on May 31, 1902. He was of Hungarian, or Magyarised Slovak descent, and was said even in later life to speak Hungarian better than Czech or Slovak. He went to work on the railways at the age of 15, joined the Social Democratic Party, and in 1921 was a founder member of the Communist Party in Bratislava.

He served several terms of imprisonment for his political activities in the twenties and early thirties. From 1935 he was one of the secretaries of the Czechoslovak Communist Party, and when the Czechoslovak Party was dissolved in 1938 he took over the leadership of the Slovak Communist Party under the cover name of Rudolf Rehak. After the Munich Agreement he went to Paris to assist in planning underground work in Czechoslovakia, and in 1940 moved to Moscow. He returned to Slovakia in 1941, was arrested by the Gestapo, and some time later handed over to the Slovak puppet government which condemned him to death but commuted the sentence to life imprisonment. He escaped in February 1945, and at once became Deputy Prime Minister in Dr. Fierlinger's Provisional Government.

As chairman of the Slovak Communist Party from 1945 to 1954 Siroky presided over its fusion with the Czech Party. He became a member of the Presidium of the Czechoslovak Communist Party in 1945. In the state apparatus Siroky rose even higher. He succeeded Vladimir Clementis as Foreign Secretary in March 1950, a post he held until January 1953, when he became for a brief period Deputy Prime Minister. In March of that year the President of the Republic, Klement Gottwald, died and Antonin Zapotcky moved from the premiership to the presidency. Zapotcky's successor as Prime Minister was Viliam Siroky, who was to retain the premiership for more than 10 years.

A crisis within the Czechoslovak Communist Party in the years 1962-63 finally brought Siroky's political career to a close. This was a period of serious economic difficulties and it was clear that Siroky, as Prime Minister, could not entirely escape responsibility for mismanagement of the economy. Even more important was the attitude of the Slovaks to Siroky. A revived Slovak nationalism in the early sixties was a major contributory factor to the party crisis and this made Siroky particularly vulnerable. The demand for the rehabilitation of Slovaks unjustly convicted in the purges of 1952-54 naturally led to a call for Siroky's dismissal, for Siroky had played a prominent part in carrying the purges through. His animosity towards the leaders of the Slovak National Rising of 1944 helped to ensure the conviction of Husak, Novomesky and others as Slovak "bourgeois nationalists", and when a party commission reported in 1963 that these Slovaks had been unjustly sentenced, Siroky's days as Prime Minister were numbered.

In May 1963, he was the target of an audacious public attack. Miro Hysko, a former editor of *Pravda* (Bratislava), at a Congress of Slovak Journalists, denounced Siroky for his role in the purges while still Prime Minister. Antonin Novotny put the full weight of his authority as First Secretary of the Party and as President behind Siroky in an effort to stem the tide of criticism, but the pressures were too great even for him to withstand and after some months of conflict he found it prudent to sacrifice Siroky. A communique of September 22, 1963, explained Siroky's dismissal by "deficiencies in his work, insufficient application of the Party line in directing the activities of the government, some faults in his political activity in the past, and his unsatisfactory health". Little official stress at this time was put upon Siroky's record in the fifties, for it was not very different from that of President Novotny's, a fact which Novotny and his supporters were not anxious to emphasize.

Siroky was in many ways typical of the generation of communist leaders brought to the fore by the "Stalinisation" of the movement at the end of the twenties; stern, fanatical, unapproachable, a courageous and energetic organizer in the days of adversity and, as it turned out, an ineffectual administrator after the seizure of power.

October 7, 1971.

Kenneth Sisam, Secretary to the Delegates of the Clarendon Press from 1942 to 1948 and formerly Fellow of Merton College, Oxford, died on August 26, 1971. He was 83.

He was born on September 2, 1887, at Opotiki, Bay of Plenty, New Zealand, the youngest son of A. J. Sisam, who had emigrated from Warwickshire in 1863. The family name represents the pronunciation of the Northamptonshire village of Syresham. Opotiki was then a small settlement in a Maori area, and young Sisam was brought up to a life of pioneer farming. A capacity for hewing his way through obstructions to the heart of a matter—indeed a kind of relish for obstructions—

stayed with him all his days.

He was educated at Auckland Grammar School, where he found himself primarily interested in games (rugby football and cricket), but access to a copy of the *Oxford English Dictionary*, which had then advanced half way through the alphabet, produced an inclination towards historical English philology, which was further developed at Auckland University College. He was elected to a Rhodes Scholarship in 1910 and entered Merton in October. There he fell in with the Merton Professor of English Literature, A. S. Napier, with whose help he learnt, in his own words, "the rudiments of research". He became Napier's personal assistant in January 1912, and did not take schools.

Sisam acclimatized badly, and had always a difficulty in reconciling mental effort with good health. He was almost incapable of working with anything less than intense concentration, which led in 1913 to a severe illness.

He worked for a time in the Oxford Dictionary under Henry Bradley, and made contact with the Clarendon Press through the kindness of the Secretary, Charles Cannan. Research for a dissertation on Anglo-Saxon Psalters brought him the friendship of Edmund Bishop, whose *Liturgica Historica* he helped to see through the press after Bishop's death in 1917. By the autumn of 1917 he was sufficiently recovered in physical health to enter the Ministry of Food. There he became director of a major trading department (bacon) in 1919, and remained until 1923 to clear up.

In 1923 he returned to Oxford to join the publishing staff of the Clarendon Press. He became Assistant Secretary to the Delegates in 1925, and succeeded R. W. Chapman as Secretary in 1942. On Boar's Hill he became intimate with his neighbour, Robert Bridges. He was an active member of the committee of the Society for Pure English which Bridges founded, and piloted *The Testament of Beauty* through the press.

As a publisher Sisam had an unerring eye for quality, and for what was central and important in any subject. He made decisions rapidly, but by referring them to principles rather than by impulse. He had a wide and tenacious memory, and great powers of assembling and presenting complicated groups of facts, powers of which he made notable use as secretary to the Bodleian Commission in 1930. His outstanding contributions to the development of the press were in the fields of science and reference books. In the former he found no handicap in his own innocence of scientific knowledge, for he knew how to select and encourage the right advisers. In the latter he found full scope for his strong sense of form, his powers of organization, and his perseverence.

Sisam knew the limits of his energy, and had long determined to retire at his own time. Shortly before the war he found in the Isles of Scilly his ideal resting place, and

built a small and carefully planned house on a rock ledge of St. Mary's. There he and his family spent several summer holidays, and there he and his wife made their home on his retirement in 1948.

The burden of his work at the press and his exacting standards, which he applied with special austerity to his own work, had hitherto hindered him from publication, apart from a handful of learned articles, a standard edition of *Fourteenth Century Verse and Prose*, and two admirable school editions of the *Nun's Priest's Tale* and the *Clerk's Tale*. From Scilly he now added *Anglo-Saxon Genealogies* (a paper from the British Academy, of which he had been elected a Fellow in 1941), a collection of *Studies in the History of Old English Literature*, and (in collaboration with his daughter Celia) an edition of the Salisbury Psalter (Latin and Anglo-Saxon) for the Early English Text Society, which he had begun, and dropped, as long ago as 1915. He collaborated again with his daughter in the editing of *The Oxford Book of Medieval Verse* which came out in 1971. He also "dabbled in local history" in contributions to the *Scillonian,* and kept up a lively correspondence with scholars in his field.

His wife, Naomi, daughter of R. P. Gibbons, died in 1958, and he leaves a son and a daughter.

August 28, 1971.

Otto Skorzeny, the wartime S.S. Lieutenant Colonel who gained celebrity for his daring rescue from captivity of Mussolini in 1943, died on July 5, 1975 at the age of 67.

Born in 1908, Skorzeny wanted to join the Luftwaffe but was rejected because of his age. In 1940 he joined the S.S. Regiment but it was not until 1943 that he was selected to form and command a commando unit to conduct irregular warfare.

His career to that point had been undistinguished. (Indeed it was said that a comparative nonentity like him had been given the job to neuter Hitler's plans for commando formations.) But he turned his observations in the S.S. on the predictable reactions of disciplined troops to good account, in a career which gave him a reputation in Allied circles as one of the more unorthodox components of the German war machine. His physique, a height of 6ft. 6in. and a prominent scar added to this aura and earned him the nickname, "Scarface".

He studied British Commando tactics and learnt a lot from them, especially about the importance of kidnapping the enemy's senior "brains".

Not all his missions were notable but in September 1943 his dashing rescue of Mussolini from his imprisonment by the new Italian government, which was trying to negotiate an armistice with the Allies, caught the imagination of both sides in the war. With a glider-borne force of 90 men,

Skorzeny landed at the mountain top hotel where Mussolini was captive, overpowered the numerically superior garrison and spirited the Duce away to Axis territory in a light aircraft.

Later operations included sabotaging Hungarian hopes of negotiating a peace with the Russians in 1944 by kidnapping the chief negotiator, and effective confusing action (if only for the alarming rumours it spread) during the von Runstedt counter-offensive in the Ardennes.

Skorzeny was tried as a war criminal at Nuremberg but acquitted largely on the evidence of a British officer that he and his troops had done nothing that their Allied counterparts would not have attempted.

July 8, 1975.

Dean Charles Edward Smalley-Baker, who died on November 2, 1972 in his native Canada at the age of 81, will be remembered by many practising and academic lawyers in Britain as the founder of the Faculty of Law at Birmingham University.

He may be called one of the last of the Edwardians, for he was a man of impressive personality whose methods of exercising his functions were definitely paternalistic, and far from what a younger generation of university teachers—let alone students—would call democratic. Yet his wholehearted interest in the lives and careers of students and former students aroused in them an admiration for him which they always retained.

Smalley-Baker had already graduated at Acadia University, Nova Scotia, and Harvard Law School before he served in Europe from 1915 as a lieutenant with the Canadian Overseas Military Forces. For a year after hostilities ended in 1918 he directed the teaching of law at the Khaki University of Canada in London. A short law degree course at St. John's College, Oxford, which was Sir William Holdsworth's college, was followed by call to the English bar (certificate of honour) by the Inner Temple and several years' practice.

In 1924 Birmingham University decided to create a law department in the Faculty of Arts, and Smalley-Baker was appointed to the first chair of law just endowed by Sir Henry Barber. Under Grant Robertson as vice-chancellor the university obtained from the Privy Council an amendment to the statutes three years later permitting the creation of a law faculty, and so in 1928 Smalley-Baker became the first Dean of the Faculty of Law and Director of Legal Studies. The 21 years during which he held these two posts saw the development of one of the leading law faculties in the country, a special feature of which is the Holdsworth Club for both graduate and undergraduate members, whose list of annual presidents includes a glittering array of judges and jurists of international repute. Smalley-Baker must also share the credit for the fact that among the benefits the university received under the Barber Trust were a chair of jurisprudence and other bequests.

He was a member of the Lord Chancellor's Committee on Advanced Legal Studies in 1938, president of the Society of Public Teachers of Law in 1946-47, and in 1954 a president-adjoint of the Fourth International Congress of Comparative Law held in Paris. The Freedom of the City of London was conferred on him in 1956.

It was perhaps providential that, after a lengthy illness in the postwar period, Smalley-Baker received a call to return to Canada in 1949 as Dean of Osgoode Hall Law School, Ontario. He took on a new lease of life, for challenging problems in the administration of legal education faced him in Ontario. He became a Q.C. of that province and received the honorary degree of D.C.L. from his old University of Acadia. When he retired in 1958 Osgoode Hall made him Dean Emeritus and provided him with a room to work in for life.

Smalley-Baker was married in 1921 to Mary Hadland, who died in 1966.

November 18, 1972.

A. L. F. Smith, C.B.E., M.V.O., a talented educationist and Rector of Edinburgh Academy from 1931 to 1945, died on June 4, 1972 in Edinburgh, at the age of 91.

He was one of those rare people of whom, by reason of their talents, character, and friendships, it is rightly said they "could have done anything". If the record shows that he shunned success this was not because he despised ambition, or had anything but respect for those who scaled the heights, but rather because of an intense scrupulosity, in which a sense of duty played an even greater part than a natural and always evident modesty.

Arthur Lionel Forster Smith was born on August 19, 1880, the eldest of the nine children of A. L. Smith (Master of Balliol, 1916-24). He went from the Dragon School, Oxford, to Rugby, where R. H. Tawney* and William Temple were among his contemporaries, and from there to Oxford (Balliol), where he read Greats. When he got a second a popular story ran that an influential examiner said: "The fellow doesn't know his Plato", whereas Smith's papers were steeped in Plato, only he was a master of the quiet and modest and indirect, and was no more capable of writing "As Plato says . . ." than of pushing himself forward in any other way. In 1904 he took a First in History and got a fellowship at All Souls.

Lionel, as he was always called—partly in affection, partly to distinguish him from his father, "A.L."—was a remarkable natural athlete. In his first winter at Rugby he won the school skating championship; he was about 55 when he gave up squash, in which he was still unbeaten among Edinburgh Academicals. At Balliol he was in the cricket XI and the hockey team; he twice won the lawn tennis singles; and he was captain of the Boat Club, 1901-2. He played hockey for England in 1903, 1904 and 1913.

Smith was a tireless walker: doubtless it helped to avert fatigue that he had a wonderful eye for country (he never read on a train journey, however long, but looked out of the window) and a great knowledge of flowers and birds, especially birds. He and Charles Fisher, a fellow don, used to go to Italy on a walking tour every Easter vacation. They wore short black coats, dark flannel trousers and bowler hats, and carried umbrellas, and they claimed that they were thus ready for anything, from the heaviest rain to politest society.

From 1908 Smith was a fellow of Magdalen, where he was one of the tutors of the then Prince of Wales when the Prince was at Oxford just before the war. Surviving pupils recall with amusement and affection his quiet efficiency as a tutor, his extreme modesty, his dry humour, and his remarkable and sometimes slightly eccentric character. An eyewitness declares that when, after a bump supper, a bonfire was lighted on the lawn in Magdalen, "Lionel came down in pyjamas and a bowler hat, said 'I wouldn't if I were you', and thereby quelled the riot".

When war broke out Smith obtained a commission in the Hampshire Regiment, and eventually he was made a captain. He went to India with his unit, the 9th Battalion, and remained there until about the end of the war, when it was transferred to Iraq. He was seconded to the Civil Administration and became Director of Education. When the Arab Government was set up in 1921 he was made Adviser on Education and signed a fifteen-year contract, but in 1931, finding that his advice was no longer listened to and that standards he considered essential were being lowered, he resigned.

Smith would now have been warmly welcomed at Oxford, as he would have been immediately after the war, but he looked elsewhere for a post—doubtless because Oxford was associated in his mind with many friends, among them Charles Fisher, who had been killed in the war. In 1931 he was appointed Rector of Edinburgh Academy, and in the following year he married Mary Hodgkin, widow of G. L. Hodgkin. It was an open secret (not that he revealed it) that he was offered the headmastership of Eton when he had been at the Academy about a year. He refused the offer, one reason being his unwillingness to compel the Academy to find another headmaster so soon.

Smith was made Hon. LL.D. both by Edinburgh and by St. Andrews. He undertook no regular work after his retirement in 1945 except when, in answer to an appeal by Sir John Masterman, he spent a year at Worcester College, Oxford, as History Tutor.

June 5, 1972.

Cyril Smith, the noted solo pianist, who also formed a celebrated duo with his wife, Phyllis Sellick, died suddenly at his home at East Sheen, London, on August 1, 1974 aged 64.

He was born at Middlesbrough and was educated there at the High School. He went to the Royal College of Music in 1926. During his four years there he won many prizes, and in addition the *Daily Express* Piano Contest in 1928.

He made the first of many notable Prom appearances in 1929, and from then on his career blossomed sucessfully both in Britain and on the continent until interrupted by the war when, however, he was one of many artists who toured with E.N.S.A.

Meanwhile in 1941 he formed his two-piano partnership with Miss Sellick, a duo that proved highly rewarding in the concert hall and on radio and television. Several well-known British composers wrote works for them, and Vaughan Williams rearranged his piano concerto for four hands.

In 1956 he was invited to tour the Soviet Union in a party of musicians led by Sir Arthur Bliss, something of a trail blazing engagement for future cultural exchanges. Unfortunately, during the visit, Smith was struck down by a stroke which left his left hand paralysed. Undaunted, he returned to the concert platform, and much of the four-handed repertory was rearranged for three hands, a process which, as he explained less than a month before he died in a *Face the Music* appearance, was often as effective as the originals or more so.

That part of his and his wife's career continued unabated until his death and their diary was full for the coming season. He described the second career in *Duet for Three Hands,* which was published in 1958.

Smith was also a notable teacher. He had been a Professor at the R.C.M. since 1934 and adjudicated a great deal, most recently at the B.B.C. Piano Competition in 1974. As a player he judiciously balanced the needs for musicianship and virtuoso display. He was appointed O.B.E. in 1971.

August 3, 1974.

Lord Delacourt-Smith—See Delacourt-.

Eric Eph Smith, who was found dead on August 12, 1972, rode 2,313 winners during his 35 years as a flat race jockey. Among these were Aureole for the Queen in the 1954 King George VI and Queen Elizabeth States at Ascot, and Above Board for King George VI in the 1950 Cesarewitch Stakes at Newmarket. He retired at the end of 1965.

His early upbringing played an important part in his success on the turf, for his father was a renowned point-to-point rider farming at Shottesbrooke, near Maidenhead. It was there that he and his two brothers, Charles and Douglas, were born.

Thus he could ride almost before he could walk and it needed no persuasion for him to become an apprentice with Major Sneyd at Sparsholt where many famous jockeys had received their early instruction.

At the age of 15 he scored his first success on Red Queen at Windsor, beating Gordon Richards by a short head. Three years later he became first jockey to Sir Jack Jarvis*, a partnership that was to last for 15 years and provide him with two classic wins on Lord Rosebery's* Blue Peter, the best horse he ever rode. From 1949 to 1963 he was retained by H. J. Joel, among whose horses were Predominate, four times successful at Goodwood, Major Portion and Ragusa. One of his lucky races was the former Lincolnshire Handicap which he won three times on Flamenco, Phakos and Fair Judgment, all Jarvis-trained.

A fine shot, an intrepid rider both on the racecourse and in the hunting field, he had a delightful but sardonic sense of humour to suit most occasions.

An example of this was the legendary story concerning his Ascot ride on Aureole. The Queen's horse had suffered from some minor eye trouble, while Eph because of an ear affliction had for years had to wear a hearing aid. Having in the parade ring expressed his confidence in his mount, he added for the benefit of Her Majesty that they could prove to be a triumph for a blind horse ridden by a deaf jockey. Aureole threw him on the way to the post but they won the big prize by three quarters of a length. Overshadowed though he was by Douglas, he was nevertheless a great jockey and a most agreeable friend and companion who will be sadly missed.

August 14, 1972.

Frederick Smith, 2nd Earl of Birkenhead—See Birkenhead.

Leslie Fleetwood-Smith—See Fleetwood-.

Stevie (Florence Margaret) Smith, the poet, died on March 7, 1971 at the age of 68. In 1969 she was awarded the Queen's Gold Medal for Poetry.

She was one of the most original and individual artists of her time in her poems, in her novels, and in her comic drawings, which illustrated her poems. The drawings recalled Thurber and Edward Lear but one might occasionally also think a little uneasily of Blake, just as the poems were often ostensibly funny poems but at a deeper level suggested not only, like Lear's, pathos and loneliness, but a strange visionary quality. Miss Smith rejected the Christian religion, which seemed to her to hide the hook of cruelty under the bait of kindness, but she had been much affected by a Christian upbringing, and would compose, and intone, many of her poems to the tunes of popular hymns.

There could be, among some of her readers, a tendency to take her as a kind of Douanier Rousseau or Grandma Moses* of poetry. She was, in fact, though a very kindly woman, a sharp and sometimes wittily malicious observer of her fellows. Her little book of drawings *Some Are More Human than Others* (1958) is very funny but also very frightening. Her three works of fiction, *Novel on Yellow Paper* (1936), *Over the Frontier* (1938) and *The Holiday* (1950) use an informal, scatty, off-the-cuff technique, and farcical incidents, to project a vision of the world that takes full account of human wickedness, misery, and folly. Perhaps the complexity of her view of life is best expressed in the title of one of her best volumes of verse, *Not Waving But Drowning* (1957). The hero of the title poem, of whom there is an amusing drawing, seems, on a seaside holiday, to be waving cheerily to his friends on shore; actually, he is going down.

Without any sentimentality, and indeed with a rather chilling gift in her verse, prose and drawings, or blocking sentimental responses, Miss Smith was nevertheless deeply aware of the "quiet desperation" of the common human situation. She was aware, also, that misery may express itself in a gauche or inept way, and look comic to the outsider. It would be wrong, though, to exaggerate the more sombre side of her talent. Her poems owe much not only to hymns but to nursery rhymes, children's dancing and riddle games, the broadsheet ballad style. She liked the fun of writing, and had a zest in life which she often expresses directly, though often with a little turn of phrase that suggests she is aware that her enthusiasms may look absurd.

She never married and began to publish only in her middle thirties. Born in Hull, she was educated at Palmers Green High School and the North London Collegiate School for Girls. She had some Ulster Protestant ancestry and, during the Ulster troubles of 1970, wrote a letter to *The Times* expressing a sympathy with and understanding of Protestant fears by no means usual at that time. Politics did not interest her much but she was always utterly indifferent to whether a point of view was popular or not. Till 1953, she had a successful career in a publisher's office in London, looked after in Palmers Green by an elderly aunt to whom she was devoted, and who did all the housekeeping and cooking. When the aunt became bedridden, Miss Smith learned to cook and housekeep and devoted very much of her time to the old lady, whose death left her very lonely, though it left her more time for outside friends and interests.

In the 1960s, when large-scale poetry readings began to become very popular in England and elsewhere, Miss Smith found herself somewhat of a star of the circuits, even taking part in an international pop poetry festival in Brussels. She also made several very effective recordings and broadcasts of her poetry. She sang rather than spoke her poems, to what she described as "her own music, based largely on Gregorian chant and hymn tunes". The truth is that like many fine poets, including Yeats, she had an exact sense of pause and rhythm, but an imperfect sense of pitch, so that "her own music" often sounded like familiar hymns sung slightly out of tune. The timbre of her voice and the ease, gaiety and amenity of her platform manner made these readings, however, delightful occasions.

There was a touch in her platform manner of the demure little girl doing her party piece but also a touch of the comedian aware of a joke, or jokes, that the audience could not be expected to see. She was always amused by the world and by what people said to her, and her amusement, though she was the politest and kindest of women, could at times be felt as disconcerting.

She had very many devoted friends but many of them must have felt that, whereas she with her strange gifts must remain largely a mystery to them, they themselves were being observed with uncomfortable penetration. That penetration and an ever-vigilant curiosity and polite surprise about people's motives and attitudes lay behind the comic achievement of her novels, perhaps, even more than behind her poetry.

She was a public-spirited and sociable woman who sat on the Arts Council Literary panel, was an assiduous attender of P.E.N. club meetings, and could even be found occasionally sitting in one of the pubs near the B.B.C. where young poets meet to gossip and drink beer. Yet, though she put up no barriers, she was always in some sense a person apart. She was one of these "sports", these wholly individual, unconventional, and unpredictable talents which, in recent centuries, only England seems to produce.

March 9, 1971.

Sydney Goodsir Smith, the poet, who died on January 15, 1975 at the age of 59, often hailed as the most powerful after Mac-Diarmid of all the Scots-writing poets of the Scottish Renaissance movement, was actually born not in Scotland but in Wellington, New Zealand, on October 26, 1915. This experience left no discernible mark on his verse, however. Despite the further handicap of his name, Smith grew up as a poet as Scottish as they come:

Rin and rout, rin and rout,
Mahoun gars us birl about,
He skirls his pipes, he stamps his heel,
The globe spins wud in a haliket reel.

It was verses like these, from "The Deevil's Waltz", that won him his reputation. Mac-Diarmid's slogan, "Not Burns—Dunbar!" had been well-heeded. Smith's wildness and vigour frequently call Dunbar to mind, particularly the grotesque merriment of such a poem as "The Dance of the Sevin Deidly

Synnis". But he was fundamentally his own man, and modern too.

The son of Professor Sir Sydney Smith, sometime Professor of Forensic Medicine at Edinburgh University, he was educated at Edinburgh and Oxford Universities, and then followed a variety of occupations: work with the War Office, teaching English to the Polish Army in Scotland, employment with the British Council, writing art criticism for the *Scotsman*, freelance journalism, broadcasting, writing plays. Pursuit of the craft of verse was always the central concern. His first volume, *Skail Wind* (1941), gave one or two hints of the goodness to come. *The Wanderer and Other Poems* (1943) and *The Deevil's Waltz* (1946) won him the attention of Edith Sitwell.*

But it was not until *Under the Eildon Tree* (1948) that Smith revealed the full stretch of his talent. In this series of elegies the lyrical and exuberant energy which came naturally to him is put to the service of a single theme. That theme is love, the unhappy love of the poet. Personal and subjective elements are subdued to the myth of Thomas the Rhymer and his seven-year sojourn in the lands of the Queen of Elphame, and autobiographical material is also interwoven with meditations upon the fate of the great lovers of classical mythology—Orpheus and Eurydice, Dido and Aeneas. These are literate and intelligent poems, the work of a highly educated man who has chosen to express his experience of life and of books in a vernacular form which will least distort the movement of his mind as he broods upon both.

Smith's play *The Wallace* was performed at the Edinburgh Festival in 1960, with some success. Its distinguishing features were patriotism and word-intoxication. The latter quality also characterizes his one novel, *Carotid Cornucopius* (1964), an extraordinary fantasy that owes a great deal to Joyce and Rabelais, but contains passages redolent of a certain kind of Scottish literary life—the sort which revolved about Milne's Bar, a basement tavern where Smith himself was almost part of the furniture.

In his person he combined elegance and carelessness in a distinctive balance. If his clothes always looked untidy, they still looked as though they had at some point passed under the hand of the best tailor in Edinburgh. He was a witty and entertaining talker, of the sort who can always cap one story with another until well past closing time. He once listed his recreations as "drinking and blethering".

In 1946 he was the recipient of a Rockefeller Atlantic Award; in 1951 he won a Festival of Britain Scots Poetry Prize; and in 1972 the Scottish Arts Council gave him a Bursary in recognition of his services to Scots poetry. Among other honours which came his way may be mentioned an award from the magazine *Poetry Chicago* in 1956, and the Sir Thomas Urquhart Award in 1962. The last might be considered the most appropriate honour of all, since Smith had

much in common with that Scottish translator and transmogrifier of Rabelais, who is reported to have died of laughing when told of the Restoration of Charles II.

January 21, 1975.

Josef Smrkovsky, close associate of the Czechoslovak former reformist leader, Alexander Dubcek, died of cancer in Prague on January 14, 1974. He was 62.

Josef Smrkovsky spent most of his life in the resistance. During the German occupation he was a key figure in the "underground"; in 1948 he was one of the organizers of the communist *coup d'état*; in the fifties he faced disgrace and a life-sentence rather than submit to Stalinism; in 1968 he was one of those against Novotny and the hardliners; and after the Russian invasion he became one of the most popular fighters for national independence.

In 1968 the weekly *Mlady Svet* held a series of opinion polls in which its readers were asked to state which Czechoslovak politician they trusted most. One contributor answered: Dubcek, Svoboda and Smrkovsky, but I am worried in case Smrkovsky should disappear from political life". His fears were justified in the event.

Smrkovsky was born at Velenka near Cesky Brod in Central Bohemia. He started as a baker, but already at the age of 19 was holding a responsible post in the Czechoslovak Communist Youth Union and was eventually to become secretary of its Prague branch after a brief period of party schooling in Moscow. In 1937 at the age of 26 he was appointed secretary of the Regional Committee of the Party for Brno.

During the war he became leader of the Fourth (underground) Central Committee of the Party, and during the Prague rising of 1945 in the vacuum created by the non-arrival of the Soviet troops from the East and the enforced halt of the United States troops at Pilsen he was elected deputy-chairman of Czech National Council, formed of resistance groups.

Faced with a situation in which the citizens of Prague had already taken up arms against the Germans and no outside help seemed immediately available, Smrkovsky negotiated a cease-fire with the German High Command, an act which was to cost him dear in the fifties.

During the period before the *coup d'état* Smrkovsky was in charge of the redistribution of sequestered land and the Democrats found his radical methods distasteful. In March 1964, he became a member of the Praesidium of the Central Committee of the Communist Party and shortly afterwards a deputy of the National Assembly.

When February 1948 came, Smrkovsky, like the other later "reformists", Kriegl and Pavel, was an active organizer of the *coup d'état*, but in August 1951 he was arrested, subpoenaed as a witness in the Slansky trial and sentenced to life imprisonment.

Released in 1955, he was allowed to work first in forestry and then as a chairman of a collective farm. Only in 1963 did he receive full Party rehabilitation and he became first Minister and Chairman of the Central Water Conservancy Board and later Minister of Forests.

After January 1968 Smrkovsky sided with the reformists and was elected a member of the Party Praesidium in March. Shortly afterwards he was elected chairman of the National Assembly, a post of importance even under the Communist-inspired constitution and of increasing responsibility in the more democratic conditions of 1968.

Smrkovsky was a ready and popular speaker who had considerable influence on the workers. The Russians were not slow to observe this and as early as May 1968 they conveyed their disapproval of him by deliberately omitting his name from a telegram of congratulations. This was followed by other slights.

None the less in June Smrkovsky was made a member of the Political Commission of the Central Committee working on the preparation of the XIVth extraordinary congress of the Party, which was interrupted by the Soviet invasion in July.

In spite of Soviet antagonism Smrkovsky succeeded in maintaining his position on the Executive Committee of the Central Committee from November 1968 until April 1969. But when federalization was introduced the Russians refused to have him as chairman of the new Federal Assembly (the Chamber of the People). Husák obliged them in this by insisting that a Slovak nominee should be preferred. A large-scale sympathy strike threatened, but Smrkovsky damped it down by acquiescing in the appointment of Dr. Colatka. He himself had to be content with the vice-chairmanship and the chairmanship of the less important Chamber of Nationalities.

In the purge of September 28, 1969, Smrkovsky was expelled from the Central Committee of the Party and removed from the chairmanship of the Chamber of Nationalities. The following March he was expelled from the Party.

Smrkovsky was a refreshing contrast to the other Czech politicians of the Novotny era. He was courageous, blunt, honest and human. During the difficult provocative period after the Soviet invasion he tried to enjoin moderation on his followers. His qualities not only made him a fitting representative of the regime which tried to preserve "Socialism with a human face" but won for him a lasting place in the affection of the Czech and Slovak people.

On the twentieth anniversary of the Prague Rising of 1945 he was awarded the "Memorial Medal". In addition he won the Czechoslovak War Cross of 1939, the Order of the Republic (1966), the Order of the 25th February of the First Class, and the Order of Klement Gottwald.

January 16, 1974.

Group Captain Joseph Ruscombe Wadham Smyth-Pigott, C.B.E., D.S.O., who died on October 8, 1971 at the age of 81, had his roots in Brockley, Somerset, where his family had held various manors since the sixteenth century. He can truly be described as a pioneer airman, a legendary figure in his day.

In 1914, when in the R.N.A.S., he crashed at the Central Flying School, Upavon, suffering severe injuries especially to his legs.

Trenchard, then Assistant Commandant, is said to have ordered preparations for a military funeral but was outwitted by Smyth-Pigott's formidable mother. She was probably the only woman in the country who could have crushed the almost equally formidable Trenchard, and her son was accordingly conveyed—"no expense must be spared"—to Sister Agnes's Hospital in London, where he recovered.

He made his name in the Gallipoli campaign, flying with leg-irons, virtually hoisted by cranes into his cockpit, based on Imbros under Gerrard's command. He took off one night in a BE-2C, propelled by a Renault 70 h.p. engine and found his target. This was in 1915, and it was a flight of previously unheard-of dimensions; his target was the Kurelf Burggas bridge at Adrianople, a total distance there and back of 300 miles. The difficulties were appalling; the little aircraft was overloaded with petrol —he eventually landed back at his airfield with approximately one pint of fuel in the tanks; night navigation in those days was a quite new art; yet he struck the bridge with two 25lb bombs. For this he was awarded the first of his well-earned D.S.O.s.

As Air Attaché in Paris from 1925-29 he was at the hub of events and proved himself as good a diplomat as he was aviator.

Later, as a retired R.A.F. officer, he was made Chief of Staff, seconded to the Peruvian Air Force. He once had to force-land his little aeroplane on a strip 15,000ft. high on the Andes.

During the Spanish Civil War, he was invited by the Foreign Office, in company with Lt-Col. F. B. Lejeune, R.A., to act as observer of effects of bomb damage. This tiny mission based itself on Toulouse and went into Spain by invitation. The only invitations they received were from the Republicans. The reports on these invitations can be seen in the Imperial War Museum, among other places, and are of immense interest.

The difficulties under which the little mission worked might be illustrated by a plea he made: "In view of the fact that we have no typists may typed copies of this letter and of the enclosed reports and plans be forwarded to us please? They are essential for our files and future work."

Smyth-Pigott was a man of the highest integrity and intellect, but he was far too turbulent a person to conform and he suffered accordingly, being placed on the retired list long before he achieved the pinnacle deserving of his unique qualities.

The cap-badge worn today by Royal Air Force Officers represents the Albatross. The badge suitable for Smyth-Pigott's temperament could only have been one designed on the lines of a Stormy Petrel. Incidentally, it was natural that though over 50 years of age, he should fly as rear-gunner under command of sergeant-pilots in the Second World War.

He married in 1919 Lady Clare Feilding, fifth daughter of the ninth Earl of Denbigh. They had one daughter. His wife died in 1966.

October 11, 1971.

Edgar P. Snow, the American journalist widely known as an interpreter of Communist China, died on February 15, 1972 in Geneva. He was 66.

Snow's career was remarkable, not simply for being the first serious journalist to explore and describe the Chinese Communist movement at the moment when it consolidated itself under Mao Tse-tung's leadership in North West China in 1936, but in being one of the tiny handful of Westerners who established a personal and lasting contact with Mao Tse-tung himself.

Snow's character and temperament in its combination of honesty, simplicity and forthrightness must have appealed to Mao and it would not be fanciful to say that when Mao believed in the virtues of the American people, at a time when he must have despaired of the policy of their rulers, it would have been Edgar Snow who would have embodied those qualities in his imagination.

In recent years Snow's lengthy talks with Mao offered very rare direct contact with the mind of China's leader. Thus in 1965 Mao's apprehension of his own death, and of the danger that China's youth might be corrupted and the regime might be deflected from his ideals, foreshadowed the Cultural Revolution.

Snow's last journey to China was in the autumn of 1970 when he stayed for almost six months, attending the National Day Ceremony in October in the company of Mao in Peking. Snow's account of that stay has yet to be published, but an abbreviated version of his long talks with Mao in December 1970 was published in the West in 1971 and was remarkable in particular for Mao's reflection on the possibility of improved relations with the United States. Few readers of Snow's article foresaw at the time so dramatic an outcome as President Nixon's visit, though it is possible that Mao may have raised the possibility in that part of the interview which was not allowed to be published.

He was born in Kansas City, Missouri, on July 19, 1905. After attending the Kansas City Junior College he went to the University of Missouri for two years and then spent a year at Columbia. He arrived in China in 1928, a young journalist working his way round the world.

In 1936 he was smuggled through the Chinese Nationalist Army lines to Paoan headquarters of the Chinese Red Army, the first foreign journalist to make the trip. There he met Mao Tse-tung, Chou En-lai, General Chu Teh the commander of the Red Army, and other Communist leaders. In a series of long talks, Mao Tse-tung told him the story of his life, which Snow incorporated into the now famous account of his visit, *Red Star Over China,* which had a large sale.

An earlier book, *The Far Eastern Front,* which appeared in 1934, gave his first impressions of Japanese aggression, the creation of Manchukuo, and the quarrels between the Kuomintang and the Communists.

In 1938 Snow and his first wife, Nym Wales, the writer, were co-founders with a number of others, Chinese and foreign, of the Chinese Industrial Co-operatives, small mobile village industries which helped to provide employment for refugees from the Japanese advance, and to clothe and provision the Chinese armies.

After the United States entered the war he was offered a job in the American Army Air Force intelligence service, but instead, on President Roosevelt's advice, he joined the *Saturday Evening Post* (later becoming one of its assistant editors) and wrote a series of brilliant journalistic reports from India, China (behind the Japanese lines) and the Soviet Union.

In 1960 he visited China for several months as correspondent for *Look* magazine, which published a long authorized interview with Chou En-lai, the Chinese Prime Minister; Snow followed this in 1962 with a massive book *The Other Side of the River* giving an account of his trip, and, for American readers, putting the developments in China under the communists into perspective against the background of the China he had known before the war.

Earlier the Harvard Centre for Asian Studies had published his *Random Notes on Red China,* containing a large amount of new biographical material on many members of the Chinese communist government, and *Journey to the Beginning,* an account of his life and experiences as a journalist.

His marriage to Nym Wales was dissolved in 1949 and he married, secondly, Lois Wheeler. There are two children of the marriage.

February 16, 1972.

Lydia Sokolova, who died on February 5, 1974 at the age of 77, was one of the leading ballet dancers of the Diaghilev period. By her success she proved that it was possible for an English girl to be accepted as the equal of the Russians and thus helped to pave the way for the next generation which pioneered British ballet.

She was born Hilda Munnings at Wanstead, Essex, on March 4, 1896. Her pro-

fessional career began in 1911 with appearances with Mikhail Mordkin's company known (perhaps too grandly) as the Imperial Russian Ballet, and then with a small company run by Theodore Kosloff. In 1913 she became the first English dancer to be accepted into Diaghilev's Russian Ballet. Except for short breaks when she danced with Massine's company in London and made some music hall appearances, Sokolova remained with Diaghilev until the company broke up on his death in 1929.

It was not long before Fokine singled out "the English girl" for a small solo in *Daphnis and Chloë,* and when the company was depleted by wartime conditions, Sokolova soon acquired several more roles, including further parts in Fokine's ballets, notably as both Columbine and Papillon in *Carnaval,* the ballerina in *Petrushka* and the girl in *Spectre de la Rose,* which she danced with Nijinsky.

Sokolova came to be particularly associated, however, with Massine's ballets. She was in the cast of his first completed work, *Le Soleil de Nuit,* and among the roles he later created on her were Kikimora in *Contes russes,* the tarantella in *La Boutique fantasque* and the friend in *Les Matelots.* She also danced the role of the miller's wife in *The Three Cornered Hat.*

Her most challenging role was in Massine's new version of *The Rite of Spring* in 1920. She had danced in the ensemble when Nijinsky created this ballet in 1913, but Massine cast her as the chosen maiden. This part was not only arduous, but demanded an acute sense of rhythm and considerable dramatic power; it brought a great success for the young dancer.

Diaghilev's dancers were expected also to show a degree of versatility, and Sokolova's range extended from the fairy solos of *The Sleeping Princess* to the part of the hostess in Nijinska's *Les Biches,* from Nijinsky's *Faune* to Balanchine's *Le Bal.*

Sokolova was accepted entirely by the Russian members of the company as one of them, and Diaghilev personally showed special affection for her. When the company disbanded on his death in 1929, her career came almost to an end. She did, however, come out of retirement in 1935 to appear with Leon Woizikovski's company in 1935, and again in 1962 to play the role of the Marquise Silvestra in Massine's revival for the Royal Ballet of *The Good Humoured Ladies.*

Sokolova's memoirs, written with the aid of Richard Buckle, were published in 1960 under the title *Dancing for Diaghilev.* They provide the most vivid of the many accounts of what it was like to work in that great man's company and throw unexpected light on many incidents and works of the past. Also, they reveal the liveliness of humour and sharpness of character which must have been among her distinctive qualities as a dancer.

February 6, 1974.

Theodore Howard Somervell, O.B.E., died on January 23, 1975 at the age of 84. His death deprives mountaineering of a distinguished and accomplished exponent, and India of a devoted surgeon who for 22 years was head of the largest group of mission hospitals in the world at Neyyoor, in Travancore.

Born at Kendal in 1890, Somervell was a son of W. H. Somervell, J.P., head of the well-known Kendal footwear manufacturing firm. Somervell's early days on the Lake District fells inspired him with a love of mountains, and when he went from Rugby to Gonville and Caius College, Cambridge, where he took a double first class honours in the Natural Science tripos, he showed promising form on both Swiss and British mountains.

As a boy, on a family holiday, he had already shown his stamina and his passion for music by cycling repeatedly from Rye in Sussex to the Queen's Hall in London, to hear Beethoven programmes at the Promenade Concerts, each time a round distance of 130 miles. A medical student at University College Hospital he took his F.R.C.S. in 1920 and graduated M.B., B.Ch. in 1921.

General Bruce chose him to be a member of the 1922 Everest expedition and, two years later, of the 1924 attempt. It was in the 1924 expedition that Somervell earned fame for his courageous rescue of four Sherpa porters marooned on the North Col.

The anxious men had to be persuaded to cross a steep slope of snow above a great crevasse. Somervell climbed obliquely up the slope, secured on the rope by Norton and Mallory. Twenty feet from the top, the rope gave out. Somervell untied, went on unsecured, and grabbed each porter in turn, bringing him to safety.

Norton has described Somervell on this occasion: "It was a fine object lesson in mountain craft to see him, balanced and erect, crossing the ruined track without a slip or mistake. Somervell's humour, wit and uncomplaining comradeship were invaluable assets for both expeditions."

On June 2, 1924 Somervell and Norton began their assault up the Everest north face, reaching 28,000 feet: "a couple of crocks" (Somervell afterwards wrote) "slowly and breathlessly struggling up, with frequent rests and a lot of puffing, and blowing and coughing. Most of the coughing and probably most of the delay, came from me".

Half a mile from the summit Somervell's throat became intensely painful, and he was obliged to stop, leaving Norton to continue for a short distance until he too was defeated. The two had a terrible descent, with Norton half snowblind. Conditions were as good as Everest offers, "no fresh snow, no blizzards, no intense cold had driven us off the peak," (Somervell wrote)." We were just two frail mortals, and the biggest task Nature has yet set to man was too much for us".

In between the two Everest expeditions Somervell had volunteered to be a surgeon in the London Missionary Society's Neyyoor hospitals. He was appalled by the physical suffering and misery in rural India, and the claim of the villagers on his surgical skill won a whole-hearted response.

His simple, evangelical Christian faith and the utter need of India's people turned him from his contemplated career as a London consultant, and the growth of the Neyyoor Medical Mission is a monument to his leadership, in both surgery and organization. He and his colleagues dealt with 200,000 cases a year, performing more than 15,000 large and small operations.

Somervell specialized in abdominal operations and always congratulated himself that he got more work in India than he would in London. Although he was officially head of the Neyyoor hospitals, Somervell always worked in an honorary capacity.

Skilled as a musician and artist, Somervell's ability as a mountaineer lay in his immense strength (he once climbed 32 Alpine peaks in a six weeks' holiday) and poise, and he thought of mountaineering as the peerless expression of all the arts he practised. An individualist, going his own way, and quite fearless in criticism of authority and superficial prestige, he was never ungenerous in his judgments.

Reviewing his book, *After Everest*, General Bruce wrote: "It bears out all that the friends of Somervell expected from him, and his negation and complete self sacrifice during his professional work are only what you would expect of so fine a character."

Somervell retired from his medical missionary service in 1945 and was greatly in demand as a speaker to university students. He will always be remembered among the eminent Christian men who have given their best days and skill to the relief of suffering in India. He was president of the Alpine Club from 1961 to 1964.

In 1925 he married Margaret Hope Simpson, the daughter of Sir James Hope Simpson, the Liverpool banker, and they had three sons.

January 25, 1975.

T. V. Soong, brother-in-law of Chiang Kai-shek, and one of the ablest financial brains in the Chinese Nationalist government, died on April 25, 1971 in San Francisco.

Sung Tzu-wen, who adopted the style of T. V. Soong, was born in Shanghai of a wealthy Christian family in 1891. He was educated at the missionary foundation, St. John's University, and later at universities in the United States. After taking a degree in economics at Harvard he gained further experience in the banking world of New York, before returning to China after the 1914-18 war. There, his family connexions and his financial ability soon drew him into public life. His eldest sister had married Sun Yat-sen; his second sister married the banker H. H. K'ung; and his youngest sister was to marry Chiang Kai-shek.

He was first appointed to office as Minister of Finance in the government set up at Canton, where he began the task of reforming the national finances along orthodox western lines. He went to Hankow when the government moved there but when Chiang Kai-shek married his sister he threw in his lot with his brother-in-law's faction and was appointed Minister of Finance in the government formed at Nanking in 1928. His main purpose in his new post was to gain the support of banking circles in Shanghai, and it was the confidence they had in his ability rather than faith in the Kuomintang party which was to bring them over in support. For, outside the westernized fringes of China, and particularly among the warlord generals who gave their tentative support to the Kuomintang, Soong was never popular and in the party itself he built up no following.

Never happy in the chaotic conditions with which he was trying to deal, Soong resigned in 1931 but returned to public office in 1935 as chairman of the Board of the Bank of China. On the outbreak of the Japanese war he was put in charge of economic warfare and after the outbreak of the Pacific war he was sent to the United States as special envoy. While there he was appointed Minister of Foreign Affairs, a post he filled while remaining in Washington. After the war he led the Chinese delegation to the San Francisco conference, and, having added the post of Premier to that of Foreign Affairs, he also went to Moscow at the end of 1945 to negotiate the Sino-Soviet treaty. When the civil war broke out again at the end of 1946 the fissures in the Kuomintang Party began to grow and Soong, whose influence had never been strong, resigned in 1947.

Later in that year he was persuaded by Chiang Kai-shek to accept the governorship of Kwangtung province, perhaps with the intention that he should prepare the base on which the Nationalist armies might soon have to fall back. His operations in the large corporations which the Communists were later to stigmatise as "bureaucratic capitalism" had already built up for him a powerful fortune and his tenure of office in Kwangtung—as the reverses in the civil war mounted—were increasingly devoted to the same ends. In March 1949, a month before Nanking fell to the Communists, he resigned and left for Europe and later the United States.

April 27, 1971.

Air Marshal Sir Ralph Sorley, K.C.B., O.B.E., D.S.C., D.F.C., F.R.AE.S., who died on November 17, 1974 at the age of 76 was A.O.C.-in-C. Technical Training Command, R.A.F., from 1945 to 1948 and from 1948 to 1960 managing director of De Havilland Propellers, Ltd., Hatfield.

He was responsible for the original eight-gun fighter aircraft concept, and in an article in *The Times* in 1957 described its birth which occurred while he was serving in the 1930s in the Air Staff Department (Operational Requirements).

It was found that in order to build up a density of bullets which would be lethal over almost any part of an enemy aircraft the Browning guns' fire must be at their maximum; for this reason the guns must be clear of the propeller.

To sustain maximum accuracy a fighter's wings had to be built to a high degree of strength and rigidity. Sorley described in his article how he convinced Sydney Camm,* designer of the Hurricane, and Reginald Mitchell, designer of the Spitfire, of the necessity of their brainchildren having eight guns. Earlier, with his friend Major Thompson on the Shoeburyness ranges, he had the exhilarating experience of shooting to ribbons an old aircraft with eight Browning guns firing in short bursts.

Ralph Squire Sorley was born on January 9, 1898, and educated at University School, Hastings. He joined the R.N.A.S. in 1914 and won a D.S.C. in 1918 for day and night bombing attacks on the enemy ships Breslau and Goeben—which lay in the Dardanelles. He was at that time serving in the aircraft carrier Ark Royal. He became a highly experienced test pilot and later in life estimated that he had flown 170 different aircraft types. He won his D.F.C. for gallantry in Mesopotamia in 1921.

Early in the Second World War he commanded the Aircraft and Armament Experimental Establishment at Boscombe Down.

From 1941 to 1943 he was Assistant Chief of Air Staff (Technical Requirements) and from 1943 to 1945 Controller of Research and Development, Ministry of Aircraft Production.

He married in 1925 Mary Eileen Gayford, sister of Air Commodore O. R. Gayford, well-known as a long-distance flyer and planner of non-stop flights. There were two daughters of the marriage.

November 20, 1974.

Lord Soulbury, P.C., G.C.M.G., G.C.V.O., O.B.E., M.C., who died on January 30, 1971 at the age of 83, was a former Governor-General of Ceylon.

As Herwald Ramsbotham he held with distinction several ministerial posts, but it was at the old Board of Education that he found his most congenial and valuable sphere of work.

To all his tasks he brought a great capacity for hard work, a refreshing vein of common-sense and shrewd judgment. His popularity with departmental colleagues was a tribute to a genial and friendly personality. His contributions to debate were not spectacular, but they were lucid, graceful and based on careful thought and patient

SOULBURY

research. He was the best type of Parliamentarian, a devoted public servant and a man of cultivated tastes, charm and good-humour.

He was born on March 6, 1887, the son of Herwald Ramsbotham. He was educated at Uppingham and at University College, Oxford, where he obtained a First Class in Mods. and Greats. In 1911 he was called to the Bar. In the 1914-1918 War he commanded a company in the 7th Battalion of The Bedfordshire Regiment; was Staff-Captain of the 53rd Infantry Brigade, and D.A.A.G. of the Eighth Division. He was awarded the M.C., was made O.B.E. and was mentioned three times in dispatches.

He was returned Conservative member for Lancaster in 1929 and represented the same constituency until his elevation to the peerage in 1941. When the National Government was reformed after the 1931 general election he was appointed Parliamentary Secretary to the Board of Education, a position which he held until 1935.

He was Parliamentary Secretary to the Ministry of Agriculture for a year, and was then promoted to be Minister of Pensions, an office in which he assisted the Minister of Agriculture in the House of Commons. In 1939 he was appointed First Commissioner of Works, and was sworn of the Privy Council. In September of that year he achieved the distinction of sitting in the Parliamentary Press Gallery for half-an-hour—the only Minister or M.P. to be allowed to do so. The invitation to visit the Gallery was conveyed to him in Latin in a letter beginning: *Quare non venis nos videre aliquando ut ait Maia Occidentalis?* (Why don't you come up and see us some time, as Mae West would say?) Ramsbotham accepted the invitation (the object of which was to test the acoustics of the Gallery) in the same tongue. As a result of his visit he admitted he could hear nothing of the speakers on the floor of the Gallery. Hearing experiments were held in the recess, but it was not until the Commons Chamber and Press Gallery were rebuilt after the war that microphones and amplifiers were provided on an adequate scale.

Ramsbotham had often said that at no time in his public life had he been happier than during his years as Parliamentary Secretary at the Board of Education. His pleasure in returning there as President in April 1940 was widely shared. Under his leadership the education system, which had suffered such grievous fragmentation from the effects of evacuation, was restored to coherence. His determination to make the state system once more a going concern was reinforced with an equally passionate resolve to plan for the future.

In July 1941 he was appointed chairman of the Assistance Board and was raised to the peerage as Baron Soulbury, of Soulbury. In 1942 he became chairman of the Standing Joint Committees on Teachers' Salaries—the Burnham Committees—and retained the post until 1949. In November 1944 he accepted the chairmanship of the Commission on Constitutional Reform for Ceylon. It reported in October 1945 and recommended self-government for the island on the British model, as a step to full dominion status. A month later the government proposals were issued, embodying the bulk of the Commission's recommendations.

In 1948 Ceylon reached fully responsible status within the Commonwealth, when the Ceylon Independence Act came into force. It was fitting that in 1949 Soulbury should have been appointed Governor-General of Ceylon.

Soulbury arrived in Colombo in July 1949 to take up his post as Governor-General. It was typical of the man that, a month later, replying to an address by the mayor of Kandy, he made his first speech in Sinhalese, a language he had been studying since his appointment. During his term of office he suffered a tragic personal loss when his wife was killed by a bus in a London street early in 1954. His appointment ended in July of that year.

After his return to England, Soulbury made occasional interventions in Lords debates. In August 1956 he accepted the invitation of the Archbishop of Canterbury to become the chairman of the National Society. He had been president of the Classical Association in 1948, and was chairman of the board of governors of the Royal Ballet School from 1956 to 1964.

His first wife, whom he married in 1941, was Doris Violet, daughter of the late Sigmund de Stein. There were two sons and a daughter of the marriage. He married secondly in 1962 Mrs. Ursula Wakeham. She died in 1964.

February 2, 1971.

Former Bishop of Southwark—See Simpson.

Paul-Henri Spaak, the Belgian statesman, died on July 31, 1972 in Brussels at the age of 73.

Spaak, who was born in Brussels in January 1899, not only served Belgium through a long and distinguished diplomatic career but, after the Second World War, overstepped the boundaries of his small country to become one of the acknowledged statesmen of the new Europe. As the chairman of the six-nation team which achieved the drafting of the Rome Treaty in 1957 in spite of innumerable political and economic obstacles, he attained the European reputation which caused him to be widely known as "Mr. Europe".

His interest in Europe did not develop early in his career, however, although he inherited from his family a lifelong passion for politics. He was the grandson of Paul Janson, the most renowned barrister and left-wing parliamentarian nineteenth-century Belgium had known; his mother, formerly Marie Janson, was a Socialist member of the Belgian Senate. From his father Paul Spaak, a translator of Shakespeare and co-director of the Brussels Monnaie Tehatre, Spaak perhaps inherited the gift of dramatic and eloquent exposition which was to be a marked feature of his public career.

As a young man he spent two years in a German prisoner-of-war camp, but subsequently passed his Bar examinations in record time at Brussels University. His brief career as a barrister was marked by his defence of the young Italian, de Rosa, who attempted to assassinate the Italian heir apparent Prince Umberto at Brussels in 1929.

He was already acquiring a reputation as a militant Socialist orator and writer; and when in 1932 he was elected as a Socialist deputy for Brussels he continued to advocate revolutionary action until he unexpectedly attained office as Minister of Transport in the van Zeeland Government of 1935. He then swung over to the right-wing of his party. His ambition, as a good Socialist, was to transfer to the Ministry of Labour, but a few months later he was offered the Foreign Ministry, where he remained until he became Belgium's first Socialist Prime Minister in May 1938, at the age of 39.

As Foreign Minister he shared King Leopold III's belief that Belgium should return to a policy of neutrality, the more so because internal political pressure from the Flemings ruled out any possibility of allying Belgium with France, and because he believed, as he told the Chamber in February 1938, that the League of Nations was then unable to provide collective security for anyone.

On his appointment as Premier he retained the portfolio of Foreign Affairs, but resigned both offices early in 1939, and resumed the post of Foreign Minister in the Pierlot Government one day after the declaration of war between Britain and Germany on September 3. For the next few months his whole endeavour was to keep Belgium out of the war. "No country," he said in April 1940, "agrees to be a battlefield."

The German invasion of Belgium on May 10, 1940, marked the end of the attempt at neutrality. Spaak immediately invoked the help of Britain and France, and wished to continue the struggle from French soil after the May 28 capitulation of the Belgian forces. King Leopold's determination to remain in Belgium precipitated the long and bitter quarrel that subsequently divided Spaak and the King.

The fall of France and the moves of the Belgian Government to Poitiers, Bordeaux, and Vichy were a nightmare for Spaak. The decision that he and the Prime Minister should leave France for Spain was welcome action after enervating weeks of indecision, but was followed by nearly two months of restricted movement at Barcelona before they escaped to Lisbon, reaching London in October. During their years in London the exiled Ministers attempted to heal the breach between themselves and their

500

sovereign; but when they returned, to an ovation from liberated Brussels on September 8, 1944, the absent King refused to collaborate with them in any future government unless they publicly retracted their former criticisms.

In June 1945 the Socialists, like the Communists, repudiated King Leopold. At that time Spaak was himself absent in San Francisco, at the founding of the United Nations; but he soon realized that if he wished to remain in public life he had no choice but to adopt his party's line on the royal question. For the next few years he was one of the King's most dangerous opponents; indeed, he appeared to have reverted to his early militant days when, in July 1950, he led a crowd of demonstrators to the Palace of Laeken, forcing the King's abdication in favour of his son Baudouin.

But before this episode Spaak had entered the international scene. The war had convinced him of the vital necessity of a united Europe and of collective action for world peace. Already in 1944 he and Jonkheer van Kleffens, the Netherlands Foreign Minister in London, conceived the idea of Benelux, which they dreamed might be the nucleus of a larger unit. On January 10, 1946 he became first president of the United Nations General Assembly; and two years after, while both Prime Minister and Foreign Minister of Belgium, he was elected chairman of the newly-founded Organization for European Economic Cooperation. Sixteen months later, he was made president of the Consultative Assembly of the Council of Europe. By a coincidence, the Socialist Government in Belgium fell just as the first Assembly of the Council of Europe was preparing to elect its president. Hearing that Spaak was free, the delegates held up the election until he could reach Strasbourg to be given the office spontaneously and unanimously.

In 1950 he commended to the Assembly the Schuman* plan for a supranational coal-steel pool—the pilot scheme for the Common Market. In December 1951 he suddenly resigned his Strasbourg office, disappointed in the Council of Europe and dismayed also to find that in Britain the new Conservative Government was as disinclined as Labour had been to lead a new United Europe. Soon after he was given the task of presiding over the Assembly of the abortive European Political Community which failed, as did the project for the European Defence Community. Both were severe blows to Spaak's hopes.

Back in office in Belgium in 1954 as Foreign Minister, Spaak threw himself with zest into the negotiations that followed the Messina Conference, for the creation of the European Economic Community and Euratom—the European Atomic Energy Community. He drew up the Spaak report and helped draft the Rome Treaty, after months of relentless and powerful effort, during which time he amazed everyone by his persistence and resourcefulness in complex bargaining. Never losing sight of basic principles, he wheedled, bullied, and cajoled the delegates of the six countries until the Rome Treaty was at last signed in May 1957. In the same year he was awarded the Charlemagne Prize at Aachen for his work for the ideal of European unity.

In 1957 he succeeded Lord Ismay* as Secretary-General of Nato, just before the successful launching of the first Russian Sputnik forced that organization to consider the defence of the west in a new, global perspective instead of concentrating on the military situation west of the iron curtain. His views on these problems were expressed in a Penguin Special, *Why Nato?*, published in 1959. He resigned from Nato in March 1961, but subsequently had several private talks with Khrushchev on east-west affairs. After the last meeting, in Kiev during July 1963, he reported to the Nato Council his conviction that Khrushchev was permanently converted to the principle of coexistence.

He returned to serve Belgium as Foreign Minister in April 1961 and set about the difficult task of restoring good relations between his country, the United Nations, and the Government of the independent Congo. Against considerable opposition from his fellow-citizens he supported the principle of United Nations action, and did much to achieve the merging of the province of Katanga with the Congolese government.

His visit of March 1964 to the Adoula Government in Leopoldville marked a considerable improvement of relations between the two countries, but the widespread Congolese rebellions of the same year culminated in the siege of Stanleyville, where Belgian citizens were left without protection. On Spaak's orders, Belgian paratroopers relieved the town at dawn on November 24. "It was one of the most difficult decisions of my life," he later said; and one of the most popular in his own country. In February of the following year he signed a treaty with Moise Tshombe,* then Congolese Prime Minister, settling financial difficulties of some importance, which had been outstanding since 1960.

In January 1963 the sudden breakdown of the negotiations for the entry of Britain into the Common Market provoked Spaak into severe protests against the veto of General de Gaulle*. Spaak had supported British entry because he believed that "little" Europe could not achieve its true stature without Britain. Moreover he was shocked by the French president's arbitrary manner of imposing his views, fearing, with justice, that this would precipitate a severe crisis of confidence among the Six. But his faith in the Community that he had helped to create led him to take a leading part in the revival of its activities later in the same year. He also came to believe that the Common Market partners should go forward towards political union without waiting for Britain, and made proposals on these lines at a meeting of the Western European Union in September 1964. But French intransigence, culminating in the walk-out from Brussels of June 1965, distressed Spaak by plunging the Community into the long crisis of France's "empty chair", only resolved seven months later at Luxembourg, when the French agreed to return to Brussels on terms whose main practical outcome was weakening of the importance of the common market commission.

Spaak's keen concern, as a pioneer "European", with the political aspects of the European Community, demanded much of his time, as did his patient efforts to untangle relations between Belgium and the Congo. However, the Catholic-Socialist coalition government which he headed together with Théo Lefèvre, from 1961 to 1965, was severely shaken by increasingly frequent linguistic quarrels between Flemings and Walloons. A similar coalition, formed in July 1965 and led by Pierre Harmel, faced similar difficulties in its relations with Belgium's two ethnic groups.

As this issue came to dominate Belgian politics, it became increasingly distasteful to Spaak, who was reproached by his countrymen for his disregard of his country's domestic concerns in his obvious preference for international affairs. No doubt this question helped to precipitate Spaak's resignation from his Foreign Affairs Ministry in July 1966, when for the first time in his life he joined an industrial firm with world-wide connexions, as an international adviser.

He himself was not able to speak his country's second language, Flemish, and indeed found great difficulty in speaking any foreign language. He learnt English during his exile in London, and commented during that time: "I am often told that I look like Winston Churchill* and speak English like Charles Boyer, but I wish it were the other way round." In his native French, however, his mastery of language was superb. Beside his gift of eloquence, he shared Churchill's characteristics of warmth and spontaneity, his capacity for work as well as for relaxation, and enjoyment of food and drink. He made friends widely, among all circles and nationalities. He once said of himself, "I am a good European" and that is perhaps his best epitaph.

His many distinctions included membership of the Belgian Royal Academy of Languages and Literature and doctorates *honoris causa* of the University of Pennsylvania and of Columbia University. His decorations included the Civil Medal 1st Class and Grand Cross, Order of the Crown (Belgium), Cordons of the Crown of Yugoslavia, White Rose of Finland, Vasa of Sweden, Vytuatas-le-Grand of Lithuania, and St. Michael and St. George of the United Kingdom.

He had two daughters and a son by his first wife, née Marguerite Malevez, who died in August 1964. In April 1965 he married Madame Simone Dear, of Antwerp.

August 1, 1972.

General Carl ("Tooey") Spaatz, who was the Commanding General of the United States Strategic Air Forces directed against Germany in the Second World War, and who was later Chief of Staff of the United States Air Force, died on July 14, 1974. He was 83.

He was born on June 28, 1891, in Boyertown, Pennsylvania, the son of the publisher of the local newspaper. He graduated from the United States Military Academy at West Point in 1914 and served first with the infantry. In 1916 he became one of the first military aviators and was in action on the Mexican border against Pancho Villa. He served with the American Expeditionary Force in France, where he was in command of United States Army Air Corps flight training at Issoudun. When granted a fortnight's leave in 1918 he went to the front and, joining the 2nd Pursuit Group, shot down two enemy planes. For this the French awarded him the Croix de Guerre saying, "What we need is more mad majors".

Major Spaatz testified in support of General "Billy" Mitchell at the famous court martial in 1925 in which General Mitchell defended his attack on the inadequate defence strategy and the incompetence of the United States Navy and War Departments; his indignation was based largely on the United States Navy's refusal to recognize the test sinking of naval vessels by aerial bombardment which he had conducted in 1923. After the Second World War Spaatz was instrumental in the posthumous award of the Congressional Medal of Honour to General Mitchell, whose theories on the use of air power had been proved in action.

In 1929 Spaatz commanded the record 6-day endurance flight of a three-engined biplane called the "Question Mark", which involved refuelling by a hose, dropped from a plane hovering above, which was caught by the commander or one of his crew crawling out on the wings.

In the summer of 1940 Colonel Spaatz, as he then was, was sent as an official observer to England. He reported on the Battle of Britain and the success of the Royal Air Force in intercepting the Luftwaffe bombers which he considered were wrongly directing their force to the saturation bombing of England's cities. This report, and General Donovan's special report on the morale of the British, convinced President Roosevelt that Britain would survive and should be given all possible help.

In 1941 Spaatz was promoted and appointed Chief of Air Staff, United States Army Air Force Headquarters. In 1942 he was sent to England to command the United States Army Air Forces in the European Theatre, including the 8th Air Force. This was followed by command of the Northwest African Air Force in 1943 supporting the Allied operations there.

In 1944 Spaatz was given command of the U.S. Strategic Air Forces in Europe for operations against Germany—being directly responsible to the Combined Chiefs of Staff. He believed strongly in the precision bombing of the enemy's war industry and fuel supplies and was opposed to diverting his long-range bomber forces from this main task. With the development of long-range fighter support and the great raids of the week of February 20-26 (when the weather was unusually clear), Spaatz believed that his campaign, particularly against oil refineries, would achieve results which would be decisive. But the Combined Chiefs of Staff were adamant that the railway system leading to the planned invasion area be subjected to intensive bombing over a long period—and that this be done by the strategic bombing force. Finally, in September 1944, the oil refineries were made the priority target with the predicted results; as has since been confirmed by German war records and the memoirs of Albert Speer.

In 1945 General Spaatz was made Commanding General, U.S. Strategic Air Forces in the Pacific, and supervised the final stages of the strategic bombing of Japan which included the dropping of an atomic bomb on Hiroshima. It has been stated that Spaatz argued against this act and it is known that he looked back on it with great distress. He was very sensitive about the crude taking of human life.

From 1946 he commanded the U.S. Army Air Forces and in 1947, when the Air Force became separate and independent of the Army, he became the first Chief of Staff of the U.S. Air Force. He retired in 1948. He was awarded many United States and foreign decorations. He was created hon. K.B.E. in 1944 and advanced to hon. G.B.E. the following year.

July 16, 1974.

Major-General Sir Edward Spears, BT., K.B.E., M.C., who took General de Gaulle to Britain in 1940, died on January 27, 1974 aged 87.

Edward Spears, "Louis" to his intimates, was talented and versatile: soldier, politician, author and man of business. He was a dominating personality who made many friends, and a fair number of foes. He excelled in the art of conversation; relatively rare nowadays. He enjoyed taking the floor in a company of a dozen or more, and holding it against high-class competition. In his affairs he was quiet in manner but tough and tenacious, almost impossible to shift from his course even by the most persuasive objector.

The start of his rise to distinction at the age of 28 had in it an element of good fortune. His abilities did the rest. Because the lieutenant of the 11th Hussars spoke French as perfectly as he spoke English, he was in 1914 appointed liaison officer between Sir John French, the British Commander-in-Chief, and General Lanrezac, commanding the French army on his right.

For the remainder of the war he was in one liaison post after another and from 1917 head of the British Military Mission in Paris. A considerable proportion of the time was spent with the army group of General (later Marshal) Franchet d'Espérey, with whom he became very friendly and for whom he always cherished deep admiration. He afterwards recounted his experiences at Mons and during the retreat in his book *Liaison 1914*, a brilliant and valuable performance.

He ended the war with the acting rank of brigadier-general, having been wounded four times in its course. During the war or just afterwards he was awarded the M.C., was created C.B.E. and C.B., became a Commander of the French Legion of Honour, and received the Croix de Guerre with three palms.

Edward Louis Spiers—the name he bore when he entered the Army, afterwards changing the form because it had a German air—was born on August 7, 1886, the eldest son of Charles McCarthy Spiers and Marguerite Melicent Hack. He was gazetted to the 8th Hussars from the Kildare Militia and transferred to the 11th Hussars in 1910. He retired from the Army in 1920.

From 1922 to 1924 he was National Liberal M.P. for the Loughborough Division of Leicestershire. In the following year he joined the Conservative Party. In 1931 he became M.P. for Carlisle. His long connexion with that constituency ended in the landslide of 1945. He was an active member, polished and well informed as a speaker, and a stalwart in the group most strongly opposed to "appeasement" of Germany. He did good service as chairman of the Anglo-French Parliamentary Committee, devoted to the fostering of the relations between the two countries. Since he was an equally active company director, he led a full life.

In May 1940, Spears was sent to France by Winston Churchill* to act as his representative with Paul Reynaud* (in their capacities as Ministers of Defence). There, now plunged into deep sadness, now burning with anger, but working all day and a great part of the night, he witnessed the agony of France at close quarters. His final *coup* was to take General de Gaulle over to England, thus initiating the Free French movement.

De Gaulle, who would probably have been arrested had his intention been known, stood at the bottom of the steps as though saying farewell to Spears and at the last moment, with the engine going, Spears hauled him into the aircraft. It was sad that they should later have disagreed.

In July Spears became Head of the British Mission with de Gaulle. In 1941 he led a mission to Syria and Lebanon, and in February 1942 was appointed envoy extraordinary to the two new-born republics. He returned amid an international tempest in June 1945, when he was publicly accused by de Gaulle of having intrigued to force France out of the republics, and warmly defended by Churchill. Spears was convinced that the French, who had maintained forces there and were sending more, were trying to put the screw on Syria and Lebanon so as to force them to sign treaties agreeable to France.

The accusation against him was a wild one. Spears may have been hard and unfriendly to the French, possibly unreasonable, but that he intrigued against them is unbelievable. He had become deeply interested in and attracted by the Arab peoples, as was later shown by his opposition to Zionism and criticism of Israel.

Spears was promoted to K.B.E. in 1942 and received a baronetcy in 1953. He returned to his business pursuits. He was the leading figure in the foundation of the Institute of Directors, of which he became chairman, president and finally chancellor. On the death of the Earl of Athlone he became president of the United Services Corps, to which, both before and after his assumption of that office, he gave unstinted service. He was for many years chairman of Ashanti Gold Fields.

Though not a prolific writer, perhaps for want of time, Spears wrote several admirable volumes. *Liaison 1914* has been mentioned. The second, *Prelude to Victory*, though dealing with the Nivelle offensive of 1917, did not appear until 1939 and was somewhat muffled by the outbreak of another war. It is a most vivid and informative study. More exciting still are the two volumes of *Assignment to Catastrophe*, on his experiences in France in 1940. Remarkable descriptive gifts were here coupled with mordant and sombre wit.

Perhaps the truth is that Spears, whose sentiments regarding France had been all love, became when he saw her at her worst, possessed by a "love-hate complex"—and that de Gaulle sensed it long before the books appeared. There are certainly very bitter lines in both.

In 1967 he published *The Picnic Basket*, a book of recollections concerned with his childhood, his family and many aspects of war.

A year earlier appeared *Two Men Who Saved France*, a study of Pétain and de Gaulle. Speaking in November 1970, on the occasion of de Gaulle's death, he recalled Churchill's doubts in 1940 as to the stature of de Gaulle, then a little-known officer. He recalled that the aircraft carrying de Gaulle and himself had been fired on by French troops. He had only fairly recently learned from the pilot that as they crossed the Normandy coast the fuel gauge of the aircraft registered "empty". They had put down at Jersey to refuel. "It is interesting to think," said Spears, "what the course of history might have been had the plane crashed. Nobody at that time would have missed de Gaulle, or me, or the pilot."

In 1918 Spears married Mary, daughter of William Borden of Chicago. Lady Spears was a successful and a prolific writer. Their only son died. She died in 1968.

He married secondly, in 1969, Nancy,

daughter of Major-General Sir Frederick Maurice.

January 28, 1974.

Lord Spencer, a connoisseur and patron of the arts, died on June 8, 1975 at the age of 83. He was the 7th Earl.

Albert Edward John Spencer was born on May 23, 1892, the son of the Hon. C. R. Spencer, at that time M.P. for Mid-Northants, by his wife Margaret Baring, daughter of the 1st Lord Revelstoke. His father was a half-brother of John Poyntz, the 5th Earl (who died in 1910 leaving no children), and so succeeded as 6th Earl. The 6th Earl died in September 1922, when Jack Spencer, the 7th Earl, succeeded.

In several respects Jack Spencer's career departed from the family tradition. In the first place he served in the Army and not the Navy, as several of his ancestors did. He served in the First Life Guards, and was wounded in the First World War.

Secondly, although he attended the House of Lords he took no part in national politics, nor did he hold any prominent position in the Court or the Government. Thirdly, he was a Conservative (he was for many years president of the Kettering Division Conservative Association), whereas the Spencer tradition had been emphatically Whig and Liberal (his uncle was Lord President of the Council in Gladstone's administration). He, however, played a prominent part in the affairs of the County of Northampton, being the longest serving member of the County Council, where he was a member of the Planning Committee. He was also Chairman until a few years ago of the Hospital Management Committee of the Northampton General Hospital. As chairman, he took the hospital from its old role as a voluntary hospital into its new one as a constituent part of the Oxford Regional Board. Under his chairmanship the hospital was enlarged and the new outpatients' and casualty wards were built.

He was also a trustee of the Wallace Collection, and a member of the Standing Commission on Museums and Galleries, and he brought an informed taste and skill to these appointments.

The Spencers have always been connoisseurs and patrons of the arts, but none before him had an equal knowledge of the many art treasures at Althorp and was as well informed about artistic matters generally.

The great Althorp library had been sold to Mrs. Rylands by his uncle, but the pictures and art treasures remained, and Lord Spencer devoted much time to their arrangement, restoration and display. Althorp was opened to the public, who were thus able to see the splendid and unrivalled collection expertly displayed. There is no house which has so many and such fine examples of Reynolds's art. It was entirely typical of him that he chose Augustus

John[*] to paint his own portrait.

No less attention was paid to the calendaring and arrangement of the muniment room, which he allowed scholars to use. There is no such well-arranged Record Office in private hands.

Lord Spencer also lent generously to special exhibitions at the Royal Academy, the Tate Gallery and elsewhere.

He edited a Roxburgh Club publication of Garrick's letters to Lady Spencer, which was enriched by his notes, and reproductions of his portraits of Garrick and Lady Spencer.

Locally, he took a great interest in Northampton Museum, and was for many years president, and patron of "The Friends". He was mainly responsible for organizing some special exhibitions at the Art Gallery, including a loan exhibition, Paintings from Northamptonshire Houses (1938), and Country Life Pictures (1966). Mention should be made of his interest in embroidery. Finding how expensive it was to get tapestry chairs repaired, he learnt the art of petit point, and many chairs at Althorp bear witness to his skill. He was for many years Chairman of the Royal School of Needlework.

He married in 1919 Lady Cynthia Hamilton, second daughter of the third Duke of Abercorn. They had one son, Viscount Althorp, who succeeds his father, and one daughter. Lady Spencer died in 1972.

June 10, 1975.

Lieutenant-Colonel F. Spencer Chapman, author, explorer, and leader in jungle warfare, was found dead on August 8, 1971 in the grounds of Reading University, where he was Warden of Wantage Hall.

Frederick Spencer Chapman was born on May 10, 1907; both his parents dying when he was very young, he was brought up by his guardian, an elderly clergyman, and his wife in a village on the edge of the Lake District. It was due to these surroundings that Chapman acquired a love of the country and nature at an early age.

At St. John's College, Cambridge, where he took an honours degree in history and English, he spent many happy hours with the mountaineer Geoffrey Winthrop Young, and suddenly found himself in a set where talk was all of belays, pitches and cornices. Chapman became ski expert and naturalist to the British Air Route Expedition 1930-31. This was Gino Watkins's third expedition, the story of which was told by Chapman in his first book *Northern Lights*, published in 1932. In 1933 Watkins returned to Greenland with three companions of the previous year, Chapman, John Rymill and Quintin Riley, but lost his life in a kayak only 12 days after their return. Chapman's next book *Watkins' Last Expedition* (1934) describes that party's activities.

For two years he taught at Aysgarth School, Bedale. Then in 1936 he was invited by Marco Pallis to join an expedition he was planning in the Himalayas to the Kangchenjunga district of Northern Sikkim. He could not miss the chance of visiting the highest peaks in the world and so he arranged to take a term's leave. While there he was asked by the Political Officer in Sikkim, with whom he was staying, if he would be interested in taking a job in Tibet should the opportunity occur. "I felt," he said, "there was nothing I would rather do than spend the rest of my life in the practically unknown country of Tibet." He joined the British Diplomatic Mission on July 31, 1936. The mission remained in Lhasa until the end of February 1937. Chapman wrote of his impressions of the Holy City and of the journey through Tibet in *Lhasa: The Holy City*.

On the way to and from Lhasa they had spent the night at Phari, on the most bleak and windswept part of the great Tibetan plateau from which the remarkable peak of Chomolhari (24,000ft.) rises 10,000ft. sheer from the dusty plain. It is even more sacred to the Tibetans than Everest but Chapman eventually secured permission from Lhasa to climb it, and invited Charles Crawford, who was working for I.C.I. in Calcutta, to join him. With three porters Chapman and Crawford left Kalimpong for Gantok on May 7. Crawford had to leave the party and Chapman and Pasang made the attempt on the summit.

Never before had two men attempted such a climb; an error of judgment on either side would have resulted in a fall of thousands of feet. Furthermore at this height the desire to succeed is almost negligible, and it is a continual mental fight. The heading of the account in *The Times* read: "The Ascent of Chomolhari—24,000 ft. for £20;" and the leader compared "this modest ascent of two men with the yak loads of luxuries which periodically march upon Everest."

Returning to England, Chapman once again became a schoolmaster, this time as a housemaster at Gordonstoun. Early in 1940 he joined the 5th Battalion Scots Guards, which had been formed as a ski battalion.

In August 1941 Chapman was posted to Singapore, and given command of a small school of guerrilla warfare, the primary object of which was to organize and train "stay behind" parties in various parts of the Far East which the Japanese might overrun. Early in January 1942 operations began behind and among the advancing Japanese, and were to continue for three years and four months. As an example of his work, it was recorded that in one fortnight in 1942 with two companions he wrecked seven trains, cut the railway in about 60 places, including the demolition of fifteen bridges, destroyed or damaged some 40 motor vehicles, and killed or wounded some hundreds of Japanese.

One day he walked by accident into the middle of a Japanese camp and was immediately taken prisoner. He escaped into the jungle during the night, survived sickness, malaria and other fevers, and made his exit by submarine to Ceylon in April 1945, after having been officially reported as "missing, believed killed".

Promoted to lieutenant-colonel, Chapman managed to persuade the authorities that his return to Malaya was essential, and on August 26 he did his first parachute drop near Raub and joined Force 136 (the Far East code name for S.O.E.), where he remained until the Japanese surrender. For his courage and fortitude, not on one day but on many days over the years, he was awarded the D.S.O. and Bar. The full story of his incredible adventures he told in *The Jungle is Neutral*.

Demobilized in 1946, he became the first organizing secretary of the Outward Bound Trust until December 1947, when he once more became a schoolmaster at King Alfred School, Plon, Germany, where he was its first head. He married in 1946 Faith Mary Townson and had three sons.

After five years in South Africa as headmaster of St. Andrew's College, Grahamstown, he was appointed in 1962 Warden of the Pestalozzi Village Settlement, near Battle in Sussex, for displaced children, many of them Tibetans whom he understood so well. He could converse with, and was indeed a father to, them. But four years in one place was long enough for Spencer Chapman, and in 1966 he became Warden of Wantage Hall, a post he enjoyed as much as all his previous occupations, with his outstanding satisfaction from the present and optimism for the future.

In addition to his D.S.O. and bar, Chapman was awarded the Polar Medal (Arctic Clasp), 1931; the Gill Memorial Medal by the Royal Geographical Society, 1941; the Mungo Park Medal by the Royal Scottish Geographical Society, 1948; *The Sunday Times* Special Award and Gold Medal, 1949; and the Lawrence of Arabia Memorial Medal by the Royal Central Asian Society. He was a brilliant lecturer and photographer; his books speak for themselves.

Freddie was all his life an incurable optimist; he based his philosophy on a saying of Gino Watkins, who was perhaps his model hero: "There's nothing good or bad but thinking makes it so."

August 10, 1971.

John Spencer-Churchill, 10th Duke of Marlborough—See Marlborough.

Lord Spens, K.B.E., Q.C., who died on November 15, 1973 at the age of 88, had a remarkably varied career as an advocate. He was Conservative M.P. for Ashford, Kent, from 1933 to 1943; he was Chief Justice of the Federal Court of India in the last four years of British rule, and then sat in the Commons as M.P. for South Kensington from 1950 to 1959.

William Patrick Spens was the son of the late Nathaniel Spens and was born on August 9, 1885. He was educated at Rugby, where he won a scholarship. In 1904 he went up to New College, Oxford, where he took seconds in Mods. and Lit. Hum. He was called to the Bar by the Inner Temple in 1910.

In the 1914-18 war, he served in the Queen's Royal Regiment and as captain and adjutant of the 5th Battalion. From 1915 to 1918, he fought in Mesopotamia, was thrice mentioned in dispatches and was awarded the Military O.B.E. On resuming his practice at the Bar he quickly obtained a large business in the Chancery Courts, especially in company work.

He took silk in 1925, and attached himself, under the old Chancery custom to the Court of Mr. Justice (afterwards Lord) Tomlin. When the custom was abolished and the Courts were thrown open, Spens practised generally as a leader inside and outside the Chancery Division, in appeals to the House of Lords and before the Judicial Committee of the Privy Council.

He was on the executive committee of the Bar Council, and was elected a Master of the Bench of the Inner Temple in 1934. In May 1929 he unsuccessfully contested in a by-election, as a Conservative, the South-Western Division of St. Pancras. In March 1933, however, he was elected member for the Ashford Division of Kent, winning the seat by an unexpectedly large majority. A strongly built man of genial personality and a keen sense of humour, he was a popular figure in the House.

In 1942, Sir Maurice Gwyer, the first Chief Justice of the Federal Court of India, retired on attaining the age limit of 65. Spens, who was knighted, was appointed to succeed him. The selection was received with mixed feelings in India on the ground that an Indian jurist has not been chosen. But if Spens did not begin his judicial career under the best auspices, it was generally agreed when power was transferred in 1947 that his tenure had been successful. He took pains to bring the machinery of his court up to the standard of modern requirements. He visited most of the Indian High Courts, to familiarize himself with their methods and procedure with a view to bringing his own into line with them.

In 1946 he presided over a commission which reported upon the causes of the serious inter-communal Calcutta riots in August of that year.

In the 1950 general election Spens was returned for South Kensington with the largest Conservative majority vote outside Ulster. His interventions in debates were always lively and pertinent. In 1953 he was appointed to the Privilege Committee of the House.

For 12 years before going to India Spens was a member of the War Graves Commission; and he was reappointed in 1949. He had been co-opted as a member of the Bacon Marketing Board in 1935. He was a director of the Southern Railway from 1941 to 1943.

He was made O.B.E. in 1918 and made K.B.E. in 1948.

Spens married in 1913 Hilda, a daughter of Lieutenant-Colonel Wentworth Grenville Bowyer. Their younger son was killed during the Second World War in 1942. The elder son and two daughters survive. His wife died in 1962 and he married, secondly, in 1963 Kathleen Annie Fedden, daughter of Roger Dodds.

November 16, 1973.

Spiers—See Spears.

Arthur Rawdon Spinney, C.B.E., died on August 7, 1973 while on holiday in England.

For literally millions of men and women of many races the name of Spinney represented English enterprise and integrity throughout the whole of the period, and over all the terrain, of British ascendancy in the Levant. From Haifa in the north, to Baghdad in the east, Aden and Aqaba in the south and Nicosia in the west, Spinney enterprises were a visible and reassuring proof that trade not only followed, but, as often as not, preceded the flag.

This beneficial "empire" was the creation of one man. Arthur Rawdon Spinney was born in 1889, a son of the Rev. Thomas Herbert Spinney, vicar of Newborough, Staffordshire. He was educated at Burton upon Trent Grammar School. After experience in banking and business, he found himself on the outbreak of war in 1914 a young man of 25 eager to join the forces. He was five times rejected on account of deficient eyesight.

Eventually he obtained a commission in the Staffordshire Yeomanry, and fought in Allenby's victorious Levant campaign. He took part in three famous cavalry charges. After the final victory, he was sent, as a staff officer, to Beirut to organize supplies for the 4th Cavalry Division, in the course of which he established a N.A.C.B., the forerunner of N.A.A.F.I.; and it was then that his flair for "providing provisions" was first recognized.

In 1924 he founded his own business. To his care was entrusted not only the Palestine Railways department as before, but also the provisioning of the British Police in Palestine. With the run-down of British service in Palestine in the late 1920s, Spinney's business was faced with severe contraction; but in 1931 the advent of the Iraq Petroleum Company provided an opportunity for service on a national scale which probably only Spinney was capable of undertaking. The desert pipe-line, the first of its kind in the region, had to be constructed and pumping-stations erected in what was then a trackless waste, extending for some thousand kilometres. Spinney, employing specially equipped vehicles, ensured that

whatever the climatic conditions might be, and however hazardous the access, the provisions arrived exactly as scheduled. It was a great feat, and really laid the foundation of his future fortunes. He was similarly employed by the Kuwait Oil Company. Thus it came about that the chain of Spinney stores came into operation all over the Levant. In labour relations, as in much else, Spinney was a pioneer, specially as regards his profit-sharing scheme with his multi-racial staffs.

During the Second World War, Abadan, Qatar, Bahrein, other Gulf centres and Aden itself came to rely on Spinney for sustenance. He also commanded the Haifa Company of the Palestine Volunteers which he had helped to found. It was Rawdon Spinney, too, who introduced the bacon industry in Palestine and promoted it in Cyprus as well. He organized the Aqaba fisheries.

To many, undoubtedly, Spinney was a name on a door or window which indicated that on the other side of it there would be provisions of the first quality available at equitable prices. But there was far more to Rawdon Spinney than the merchant prince. He became the confidant of many men in many walks of life. Not seldom his advice was sought by those in power: had it been more consistently taken, more than one disaster might have been averted. He was uncompromisingly honest and fairminded. He was also extremely generous.

August 9, 1973.

Sir Ivan Stedeford, G.B.E., life president of Tube Investments and one of Britain's leading industrialists until his retirement in 1963, died on February 9, 1975 at the age of 78.

Ivan Arthur Rice Stedeford was born on January 28, 1897, in Exeter, the son of the Rev. Charles Stedeford, a former president of the United Methodist Church. He was educated at Shebbear College, North Devon, and King Edward VI Grammar School, Birmingham, before becoming an engineer apprentice with Wolseley Motors. During the First World War he volunteered for service in the Royal Naval Air Service and gained a commission as an observation officer.

After the demobilization he established his own automobile business in Birmingham, and in 1928 accepted an offer to become sales director of Tubes Ltd., a founder member of the T.I. Group. His progress in T.I. was rapid. In three years he became joint managing director of Tubes, Ltd., and two years later was elected to the T.I. board. He became managing director of T.I. in 1939 and five years later added the chairmanship. He held the combined posts for 19 years, during which time T.I. developed from a small group into one of the biggest companies in the United Kingdom.

Sir Ivan always carried his responsibility with a lack of fuss and drama. A tall, slim man, with a rich sense of humour and a scholarly turn of mind he possessed remarkable reserves of energy. He was an engaging conversationalist and writer and a doughty debater.

Though he always looked upon the welfare of all employees as a major charge there was no paternalism in his attitude. He expected every employee to make his or her own effort. When this was done they were given every encouragement to develop to the full extent of their ability. This encouragement took the form of many schemes sponsored by him, such as comprehensive training up to free university courses for the outstandingly talented. T.I.'s residential training centre was the first of its kind in the country. He also sponsored pensions and free life assurance for all employees at a time when such benefits were rare.

He was a governor of the B.B.C. from 1950 to 1955, having previously been a member of the Beveridge Committee on radio. He was a part-time member of the United Kingdom Atomic Energy Authority, on the executive council of the Department of Scientific and Industrial Research and a member of the board of the Commonwealth Development Finance Company. In addition, he was chairman of a committee appointed by Harold Macmillan, then Prime Minister, to report on the British Transport Commission. He was created a K.B.E. in 1954 and advanced to G.B.E. in 1961 for public service.

He leaves a widow and three daughters.

February 11, 1975.

Sir Christopher Steel, G.C.M.G., M.V.O., British Ambassador to Bonn from 1957 to 1963, died on September 17, 1973 at the age of 70 in the Princess Margaret Hospital, Swindon.

His experience of German affairs was exceptional. He first served in Berlin as second Secretary in 1936. Nine years later against a very different political background he went back to Germany as head of the political division of the Allied Control Commission for Germany (British Element), in which post he exercised a marked influence in the framing of British policy towards occupied Germany.

He became Political Adviser to the C.-in-C. in 1947 and Deputy High Commissioner in 1949. After three years, 1950-53, as Minister in Washington and four as the United Kingdom Permanent Representative on the North Atlantic Council he returned to Germany as Ambassador to the German Federal Republic. The post was never a quiet one; it was no small tribute to his ability as a diplomat and his qualities as a man that throughout the ups and downs of Anglo-German relations during his term as ambassador he never compromised his convictions or lost the respect of the Germans.

He took immense pains to persuade a hostile public opinion, a not always enthusiastic Government at home, and an initially suspicious Chancellor that good relations between the two countries was in the interest of both. He did a great deal to get Germany into Nato and it was not altogether unknown for "Der Alte", Dr. Adenauer* himself, to turn to Steel for advice first when faced with some difficulty with the High Commission.

After Macmillan's visit to Moscow, which resurrected in Adenauer's mind all the repressed fears of the perfidy of Albion, it was Steel who urged a reluctant Prime Minister to go to Bonn in the summer of 1959. The journey was successful for Adenauer willingly gave Britain a pledge of German support in her efforts to enter the European Economic Community.

Christopher Eden Steel was born on February 12, 1903, the elder son of Colonel Richard Steel, and educated at Wellington College and Hertford College, Oxford. He was a scholar of both. He entered the Diplomatic Service in 1927. For a year in the mid-1930s he was Assistant Private Secretary to the Prince of Wales, later King Edward VIII. From 1966 he was chairman of the Anglo-German Association.

He married in 1932 Catherine, elder daughter of Lieut-Gen. Sir Sidney Clive. They had two sons and one daughter.

September 18, 1973.

Marguerite Steen, the novelist and playwright, died on August 4, 1975 at the age of 81.

Marguerite Steen was a novelist of dash and bravura whose books tackled a wide range of imagination-catching subjects and ensured her a steady popular success over many years. She wrote with an exuberance of fancy and phrase that seemed to be very much in character and that she also cultivated with some deliberation.

One or two of her earliest books, though in some degree unpractised, attempted a fair correspondence with nature, but romanticism and a general taste for the opulent gained steadily on her. Hers was, in fact, a florid manner of writing, which now and then ran to garishness and in period fiction left an all too obvious impression of undiscriminating colour. Yet as a story-teller she had energy, resource and a rich and abundant invention, and, together with the technical skill on which she could in time draw with unfailing confidence, they enabled her to achieve most of what she intended.

Miss Steen came to novel writing by way of a varied early career. Educated privately, she became, in turn, a teacher in a private school during the First World War, a dancing mistress and an actress, spending three years as a member of the company with Fred Terry and Julia Neilson. What was

apparently her first novel, *Gilt Cage*, came out in 1927, and further novels appeared regularly at yearly intervals. It was with *Unicorn,* published in 1931, a brisk and lively tale about a small German principality, done in what was then a stylish fashion of historical fiction, at once dramatic and naturalistic, that she secured favourable notice. Then, in *Stallion,* published two years later, a full-blooded story of a country cottage family, she achieved a fair degree of popular success; while *Matador*, in the following year, a long, romantic novel with a Granada setting and a retired bull-fighter for central character—an exuberant but theatrical effort, marked by rather turgid philosophizing—was a still more signal success both in Britain and in the United States.

After that Miss Steen produced a novel dealing with the subject of euthanasia, *Return of a Heroine* (1936); *Family Ties* (1939), with a publisher's office for background; and *The Sun is my Undoing* (1941), a novel of prodigious size about Bristol's share in the slave trade, a vigorous but tinselly essay in romanticism, which was also notably successful both in Britain and in America.

Rose Timson appeared in 1946, an elaborate and skilfully drawn portrait of a heroine who is by no means admirable but yet retains the reader's sympathy. This was her most sound and accomplished work of fiction up to that point. She also produced a critical study, *Hugh Walpole* (1933), and a biography of Sir William Nicholson (1943).

Further books—biography and descriptive memoir as well as novels—followed in a steady stream. *Granada Window* (1949) was an exclusively novelist's outlook on the Spain of the years before the Civil War, concerned with atmosphere, people and manners rather than politics.

Further novels included *Twilight on the Floods* (1949), *The Swan* (1951), *Phoenix Rising* (1952), which completed a trilogy on the Flood family, *Anna Fitzalan* (1953), *Bulls of Parral* (1954), *The Unquiet Spirit* (1955), *The Little White King* (1956), *The Woman in the Back Seat* (1959), *The Tower* (1959) and *A Candle in the Sun* (1964).

She ventured further into biography with *A Pride of Terrys* (1962) and autobiography with two colourful volumes, *Looking Glass* (1966) and *Pier Glass* (1968).

Before the Second World War she had had two plays produced in London, *Matador* (1936) and *French for Love* (1939).

August 6, 1975.

Leonid Stein, the Soviet chess grandmaster, died suddenly of a heart attack at the age of 38 on July 4, 1973 just as he was due to set out from Moscow to take part in the European team chess finals at Bath.

Stein was born in Lvov in 1934 and soon developed into a strong chess player, winning the championship of the Ukraine in

his early twenties. His first major success was a second place in the Soviet championship in 1961 when he beat, among others, Spassky and Petrosian. His career in the Soviet championships was a distinguished one as he came first on no less than three occasions, in 1963, 1965 and 1967.

His international tournament record was also a fine one. Three times he only just failed to get to the penultimate stage of the world championship, the candidates' series. In fact, at Stockholm in 1962 and at Amsterdam in 1964 he would have qualified had it not been for the then existing rule that limited the number of Soviet participants in the candidates.

A short downward phase in his career was then followed by more major achievements; first, in the very strong Moscow international tournament of 1967 and then two more first places at Kecskemet, 1968 and at Tallinn in 1969. Then, in the Alekhine Memorial Tournament at Moscow in 1971 he came equal first with Karpov, and was first again in June 1973 in the Las Palmas international tournament. A player of great originality, he still belonged to the finest classical tradition and his premature passing represents a blow for both Soviet and world chess.

July 9, 1973.

The death of **Hugh Stenhouse,** Scottish businessman and head of Govan Shipbuilders, in a road accident in Leicestershire on November 25, 1971 tragically deprived Scotland of a man who in recent years had emerged as an outstanding public figure.

Tributes to his far-sighted and energetic leadership in both personal business activities and the economic and industrial affairs of his country have shown how great a void his loss has created both in the United Kingdom and in the countries overseas in which he had business interests.

Hugh Cowan Stenhouse was born at Kilsyth, near Glasgow, in 1915, the youngest son of Alexander Rennie Stenhouse, founder of the Stenhouse group of insurance broking and industrial companies. He was educated at Warriston preparatory school, Moffat, and at Sedbergh.

His career began in 1932 in Glasgow with the old Caledonian Insurance Company from which, thoroughly grounded in a business for which he showed a remarkable aptitude, he moved into the family insurance broking company in 1938.

A Territorial officer in 1939, Stenhouse served throughout the Second World War in the R.A.S.C. (T.A.), in which he became a lieutenant-colonel. He fought in France and at Dunkirk and later was with the Eighth Army in the North African and Italian campaigns.

After the war, he returned to the Stenhouse group and was responsible for the development of its insurance broking activities outside Scotland, in London and overseas in Australia, New Zealand, Southern Africa and, latterly, in Europe.

He became chairman of Stenhouse Holdings in 1957, at which time the company's profits stood at £35,000. By 1970 his guidance of the group's policy had raised those profits to more than £2m. and its operations had grown to embrace the industrial companies of the former John Wallace group, of which he became chairman in 1963.

Stenhouse travelled extensively in the U.K. and abroad. He believed that the principals in any undertaking should maintain as frequent personal contact with all employees as possible. It was while on one of his periodic visits to the group's hosiery factories in Leicestershire that he was killed.

In September he became chairman of Govan Shipbuilders Ltd., a company set up by him at the Government's request to examine the potential of a reorganized shipbuilding industry on the Upper Clyde and, if that was found viable, to reshape and run two or three of the four yards involved.

The critical initial negotiations with the Department of Trade and Industry, the trade unions, and especially with the Upper Clyde shop stewards, set Stenhouse a complex and delicate task in what seemed a deadlock threatening the end of one of Clydeside's major industries. Yet, by his direct, bluntly expressed logic, sincere and deep concern for the prosperity of Clydeside, and innate good humour, he gained the confidence of all parties and won universal admiration.

Hugh Stenhouse's conviction that the Clyde region held invaluable advantages as an international deep water ocean port led him to demonstrate his initiative in August 1971 by establishing and becoming chairman of the Hunterston Development Company, a project to study and possibly exploit the sea trade and industrial potential of that part of the Ayrshire coast.

Management education was another of his great interests. He established a scholarship in business administration at Strathclyde University and, through the Hugh C. Stenhouse Foundation, endowed a new campus building—to be named in memory of his father—to house the university's growing school of business and administration.

He became a member of the Court of Strathclyde University, which in 1971 conferred on him the honorary degree of Doctor of Laws. Recently Stenhouse was appointed a governor of Sedbergh School, and he was a governor of Drumley House School, Ayr.

Among his many other commitments in business was his chairmanship of the Great Northern Investment Trust. His staunch political affiliation led him to act for some years as the national treasurer of the Scottish Conservative and Unionist Party, an office he relinquished on becoming chairman of Govan Shipbuilders. Outspoken in his views on political affairs, he plainly

related them to the economic needs of Scotland and frequently described himself as "a Scottish realist".

His private interests and relaxation lay in the management of the farms he owned in Renfrewshire and Dumfriesshire, in the restoration of his home, historic Maxwelton House at Moniaive in the Borders, in occasional shooting over the Maxwelton estate, and summer spells of rest at a second home on the shores of Loch Fyne.

November 27, 1971.

Vice-Admiral Sir Gilbert O. Stephenson, K.B.E., C.B., C.M.G., who died on May 27, 1972 at the age of 94, returned to active service in the Second World War, and at the age of 62 was given charge of the special training at Tobermory for the crews of anti-submarine vessels in the use of their new and complex equipment.

Ships' companies were welded into efficient teams to locate and fight U-boats, each ship receiving individual attention from specialist officers, and by the end of the war over 1,000 had worked up at Tobermory. The success of the establishment owed much to Stephenson's unflagging energy and leadership.

He was an active worker for various societies and institutions, and in 1949 succeeded Admiral Sir Lionel Halsey as honorary Commodore of the Sea Cadet Corps.

His immense energy, high spirits and the intense enthusiasm with which he threw himself into every task he had to perform, both during his active careers in the Navy and after it, were an inspiration to all who served with or under him. He was a formidable man, something of a legend in the Royal Navy. Some idea of what he was like as a mentor can be had from reading *The Terror of Tobermory* by Richard Baker (1972).

Gilbert Owen Stephenson, born on February 13, 1878, the son of R. M. Stephenson, entered the Britannia as a naval cadet in July, 1892. As a midshipman he served in the cruisers Endymion and Forte, and from the latter was landed to take part in the punitive expedition under Rear-Admiral H. Rawson against the King of Benin, West Africa, for the massacre of a political expedition. Benin city was captured in February 1897, and Stephen was among those awarded the General Africa Medal, with Benin clasp. He became a sub-lieutenant in June 1898 and a lieutenant two years later. After serving in the Ramillies under Lord Charles Beresford in the Mediterranean he joined the Vernon in September 1901 to specialize in torpedoes.

In the First World War he was variously employed; first in the Naval Intelligence Division; then as executive officer in the battleship Canopus at the Dardanelles; and later in command of the gunboat Hussar and the mobile barrage force in the Straits of Otranto.

For two years from July 1924, he was chief of staff to Admirals Sir Sydney Fremantle and Sir Osmond Brock in the Portsmouth Command, and for the next two years he was Commodore of Portsmouth Naval Barracks. He retired on his promotion to rear-admiral in 1929, and was promoted to vice-admiral on the retired list in February 1934. From 1932 to 1935 he was general Secretary of the Navy League.

Returning to active service when the Second World War broke out in September 1939, he was commodore of convoys for a few months. In 1940 after serving afloat during the withdrawal of the Army from Dunkirk, he was appointed Commodore in Charge of the Anti-Submarine Training School at Tobermory, where he served until after the end of the war in Europe.

He married in 1903 Helen Chesney, daughter of Colonel R. F. Williamson. There were two sons and a daughter of the marriage. His wife died in 1954.

May 30, 1972.

Sir Hugh Stephenson, G.B.E., K.C.M.G., C.I.E., C.V.O., who was Ambassador to South Africa from 1963 to 1966, and to Vietnam from 1954 to 1957, died on September 23, 1972 in London. He was 65. Stephenson was Consul-General in New York from 1957 to 1960 and a deputy Under-Secretary of State at the Foreign Office from 1960 to 1963.

Hugh Southern Stephenson, whose father was a Governor of Burma, was born on November 29, 1906, and educated at Winchester and Christ Church, Oxford, where he took a first class degree in jurisprudence. He was called to the Bar by the Inner Temple.

In 1931 Hugh Stephenson entered the Indian Civil Service. He was Under-Secretary to the Government of India from 1935 to 1938 and Secretary to the Governor of the United Provinces from 1940 to 1944. He served as Collector and District Magistrate at Cawnpore until 1947 when he joined the Foreign Office.

Stephenson was in the British Middle East Office in Cairo for two years before being appointed Ambassador to Vietnam in 1954. He became the doyen of the Saigon diplomatic corps; he was there for the tumultuous period immediately after the end of the Indo-China war and the vast migration of refugees from North Vietnam.

In 1963 he succeeded Sir John Maud as Ambassador to South Africa. He was High Commissioner of Basutoland, the Bechuanaland Protectorate and Swaziland until this office was abolished in 1964. He was the first Chancellor of the new University of Basutoland, Bechuanaland and Swaziland which was opened at Roma, Basutoland, in 1964. After Rhodesia declared unilateral independence, Stephenson took part in consultations between South Africa and Britain regarding the international oil embargo.

When he retired he became Director-General of St. John Ambulance Brigade.

Stephenson's past experience in the Indian Civil Service gave him a natural sense of administration. As a diplomat he had excellent judgment of people and a calm and balanced view of political situations. He had learned from the beginning never to panic and that things were never so good or so bad as when first reported. Stephenson and his wife had a ready facility for making friends wherever they were posted. He also had a stern sense of duty in that no long hours were ever too long when duty demanded them.

He married in 1936 Patricia Elizabeth, daughter of Major-General Sir Arthur Mills, and they had three sons.

September 25, 1972.

G. B. Stern, the novelist, died on September 19, 1973 at the age of 83.

Always a fluent, animated and accomplished writer, Miss Stern in her earlier work exhibited a lively talent for the serio-comic and gave promise of commanding achievement as a novelist. To the cleverness and high spirits of novels like *Grand Chain* and *Larry Munro* she added an integrity of feminine feeling that gave depth to her comedy and seriousness and strength to her irony.

The liveliness, the ironical humour remained with her always, more particularly in the novels devoted to the fortunes of the protean and cosmopolitan Jewish Rakonitz family.

However, she did not quite live up to the promise of her work in the early 1920s. She became professionally competent and vivacious, often too studiously light and amusing.

Gladys Bertha Stern was born in London on June 17, 1890, the daughter of Albert Stern. (Though christened Bertha, she did not care for the name and adopted the name of Bronwyn.) She was educated at the Notting Hill High School, which she left at the age of 16; travelled for a time in Germany and Switzerland; had thoughts of the stage as a career, and studied for two years at what was then the Academy of Dramatic Art.

By talent and temperament, however, she was clearly a writer above everything else, and had indeed written continuously since as a small girl she had produced quantities of verse and a number of plays.

Her first novel was written while she was still only 20. But it was not until the appearance in 1916 of *Twos and Threes*, an amusing and delicately pointed piece of fiction, that she earned attention. Subsequent work confirmed her merits. The deeper and more serious note that she introduced into a seemingly innocent flow of comedy did not always carry conviction; for instance in *Children of No Man's Land* (1919), which is entertainingly set in wartime England, it has an artificial and rather forced quality.

In 1924 she published *Tents of Israel*, the first of a series of novels about the numerous branches of the fecund and idiosyncratic Rakonitz family. Energetic, shrewd, lively and varied, the style of the novel seemed to derive from the distinctive character of that prodigious cosmopolitan clan. *Tents of Israel* was followed by *A Deputy was King* (1926), *Mosaic* (1930), *Shining and Free* (1935) and *The Young Matriarch* (1942).

These Rakonitz novels were punctuated by other volumes of fiction of more than one kind, though increasingly in a light and inconsequent vein, and by several volumes of a discursive and semi-autobiographical character: *Monogram* (1936), *Another Part of the Forest* (1941); *Trumpet Voluntary* (1944); *Benefits Forgot* (1949); and *A Name to Conjure With*, which made for the most part lively reading.

There was much to be learnt in these books of Miss Stern's catholic personal tastes and enthusiasms. Hers was a wholehearted gift of enjoyment; she enjoyed travel, food, wine, music, good company, talk, Jane Austen (about whom she and Sheila Kaye-Smith wrote a book); was a lover of dogs, especially dachsunds, and cats; and in general had a frank relish for the good things of life.

She continued to write fiction until well on in life.

She married in 1919 Geoffrey Lisle Holdsworth, with whom she occasionally collaborated in authorship. She also wrote several plays.

September 20, 1973.

Sir John Stevens, K.C.M.G., D.S.O., O.B.E., who died on October 27, 1973 at the age of 59, was chairman and chief executive of Morgan Grenfell and Co., Ltd., and would have succeeded Viscount Harcourt as chairman of Morgan Grenfell Holdings Ltd. later in 1973.

Born in 1913 the son of a solicitor, he went to Winchester and was articled to a solicitors' firm, becoming a partner of the family house of Petch and Company in 1937. A very active war in Special Operations Executive in Belgium, France, the Middle East and Italy left him an hon. Colonel with an O.B.E. and D.S.O.

During the war he was parachuted into Italy as a member of S.O.E. to run the underground Piedmont Liberation Committee which he financed by means of banknotes parachuted into the area by supply drops collected by local partisans.

The Bank of England took him on in 1946 as an acting adviser and for some years he travelled extensively for the Bank, sorting out monetary postwar problems in Europe, north and south America.

In 1951 he was appointed a full adviser to the governors of the Bank. Besides his quick mind and forceful negotiating ability he had a working knowledge of French, Spanish, Russian, German, Swedish and modern Greek. He was always taking refresher courses in one or the other of these languages together with his wife.

In the 1950s Stevens became one of the most useful senior officials of the Bank. From 1954 to 1956 he was seconded to Washington to become director of European operations at the International Monetary Fund; on his return in 1956 he became an assistant to the governors of the Bank and in the following year an executive director.

In 1958 he went to Moscow to make the first official contact between the Bank of England and the Soviet State Bank and his unsuspected ability to speak Russian caused a sensation both in Moscow and in London.

In the early 1960s he was talked of as a possible future governor of the Bank of England if the government decided to nominate an official rather than a banker. Nothing came of the idea but in 1965 he was appointed Economic Minister in Washington, with the concurrent posts of Treasury Delegate and United Kingdom Executive Director of the Monetary Fund and World Bank.

These posts had been held before him by Lord Cromer who was then Governor of the Bank. On his return to London in 1968 he accepted an invitation to join Morgan Grenfell and Company.

In recent years Stevens concentrated on his work as a leading merchant banker. At work he was always intense, constructive and often original, though off duty he could be cheerful and friendly. He contributed much to the reputation of the City as a source of practical ideas and a focus of world finance. His death will leave a painful gap and he will be missed by friends in many countries.

He married in 1940 Frances Anne, daughter of C. D. Hely Hutchinson, M.C. They had one son and two daughters.

October 30, 1971.

Professor E. A. Stewardson, Emeritus Professor of Physics, Leicester University, who died on August 24, 1973, at the age of 68, was born in 1904 and educated at Hawarden County School, North Wales, and at the University of Liverpool where he graduated in 1924 with first class honours in physics and took his M.Sc. in 1925.

After two years' research at Cambridge under Sir J. J. Thomson he returned to Liverpool, first as Oliver Lodge Fellow in Physics and then as a lecturer. In 1935 he was appointed professor of physics at the National Central University, Nanking (which was moved to Chungking in 1937), and was on leave in England when the outbreak of the European war in 1939 prevented his return to China. In 1940 he was appointed head of the physics department at Leicester University College and in 1946 became the first professor of physics. He retired in 1969.

Stewardson was greatly interested in the fundamental properties of atoms and by the problems posed by astronomical observations. His research work at Cambridge with its emphasis on careful experimental techniques enabled him on arrival at Liverpool to take part in and to make contributions to the research work pioneered there by Professor Skinner on the production and the detection of soft (i.e., weakly penetrating) X-rays. This difficult area of research remained a continuing interest for the rest of his life. Although his research was frequently interrupted by events beyond his control his life-long commitment to soft X-ray spectroscopy—and his strong enthusiasm for astronomy—set the stage for a very fruitful collaboration with University College London in the late 1950s.

It had been decided as part of the United Kingdom space research programme to measure with the aid of rockets the soft X-ray radiation coming from the sun. At that time soft X-ray spectroscopy was carried out at Liverpool and at Leicester. When approached by Sir Harrie Massey, Professor Stewardson agreed to help in any way he could. In the event United Kingdom researchers were able in 1961 to obtain the first direct spectral data on the solar soft X-ray spectrum and this achievement was due in large part to the unique facilities provided by Stewardson's soft X-ray spectroscopy group at Leicester.

In 1960 as a direct result of the successful cooperation in the previous two years a group devoted to the soft X-ray side of space physics was set up at Leicester. For the next four to five years the growing Leicester group worked in close harmony with University College London. In particular the very successful solar X-ray spectro-meters flown on orbiting solar observatories D. and F. (in 1967 and 1969) and the recently acclaimed X-ray telescope array launched on the O.A.O. in 1972 were all joint proposals to N.A.S.A. with Professor Boyd and Professor Stewardson named as joint principal investigators.

In parallel with the space application of soft X-ray spectroscopy Professor Stewardson maintained a strong interest in other aspects of atomic physics. He was particularly fascinated by electron nuclear collision and supervised the building and operation of a van de Graaf accelerator—a substantial project for the relatively small physics department which existed at that time. The impetus this gave to the department to develop means of detecting charged particles, and to discriminate against unwanted effects, led to real expertise in electronic counting methods and still represents a significant area of departmental research.

Professor Stewardson married in 1937 Winefred Muriel Jones.

August 29, 1973.

Ebe Stignani, the foremost Italian mezzo of her generation, died on October 5, 1974 in Imola at the age of 70.

Born at Naples on July 10, 1904, she made her stage debut at that city's San Carlo Opera in 1925 as Amneris. At the instigation of Toscanini she joined the company of La Scala, Milan, shortly afterwards, first appearing at the theatre as Eboli in *Don Carlos* in 1926, and she quickly became established as one of that notable company's leading singers. As well as the main mezzo roles in Italian opera, she sang Wagnerian parts and that of Marina in *Boris Godunov* during her early Scala seasons.

When Victor De Sabata became the theatre's musical director, she widened her repertory still further, adding Delilah in Saint-Saëns's opera. It became her favourite role, and it was described at the time as an "unforgettable portrayal". She began to travel abroad, all over Europe and to South America. Her first Covent Garden appearance was as Amneris during the Coronation season of 1937, and she returned in the same part and as Azucena in 1939. The noted critic Dyneley Hussey described her Amneris as "one of those rare performances that provide a pattern of how a particular role should be sung".

She returned to the Royal Opera House after the war to sing Adalgisa to Callas's Norma in the now legendary performances of 1952, looking a bit like the younger singer's matronly aunt. No matter: the vocal performance was unforgettable, particularly the duets with Callas, one of which had to be repeated, a very rare occurrence at Covent Garden. Her Amneris was heard again in 1955, and her Adalgisa, once more with Callas, in 1956.

Her voice was a regal and dramatic mezzo of noble, expressive power. She was capable of considerable subtlety in her vocal if not in her histrionic performances, but she never moved with less than dignity on stage. Fortunately her complete Amneris and Adalgisa are preserved on long-playing records, although her voice is perhaps to be heard at its most opulent and beautiful on her "78" discs.

October 11, 1974.

Lady Stocks, who was made a life peer in 1966, died on July 6, 1975 at the age of 83. As Mrs. Mary Stocks she had been widely known as an economist, writer and broadcaster. But in July 1974 Baroness Stocks announced that she was leaving the Labour Party because she was unhappy about Harold Wilson's leadership and the Government's policies, including nationalization.

Mary Stocks was a woman of great courage and natural ability. She was unusually well equipped to meet the challenges presented by the changing circumstances of her life and to make the adaptations usually required of women who combine family life with professional and public work.

She had high talents of different kinds, as an exponent of ideas, a promoter of social causes, a narrator of events and a playwright. Intellectual vigour and independence of mind were her outstanding qualities.

The daughter of Dr. R. D. Brinton, she was born on July 25, 1891 and educated at St. Paul's Girls' School, London.

She took her degree at the London School of Economics, and throughout her life it was with the social aspect of economic questions that she was especially concerned. Perhaps it was also because her father had been a London doctor that she took so deep an interest in the work of the London Executive Council of the health service on which she served for years.

Before she completed her degree course she became engaged to J. L. Stocks, then a Fellow and tutor at St. John's College, Oxford. They married in 1913 and, until his death in 1937, they shared a number of social and political interests. They had two daughters and a son, and their friends have memories of the warmth of their family life.

Mary Stocks's earliest social activity was in the women's suffrage movement, where she worked in the constitutionalist camp. During the war years she lectured at the London School of Economics and at King's College for Women, her husband being on war service for most of that time.

In 1924 she and her husband left Oxford on his election to the Chair of Philosophy in Manchester University. There she found great opportunities, as a lecturer for the extramural department of the university, as a magistrate for the city and as a partner with her husband in the development of the work of the university settlement and of the Wilbraham community associations. It was for members of these associations that her plays were written and they were performed by them.

Her departure for Liverpool in 1936, when her husband was appointed Vice-Chancellor of the university, was a great loss to the social and intellectual life of Manchester, and for her it meant a new and perhaps somewhat alien role.

After her husband's sudden death she acted for a brief period as general secretary of the London Council of Social Service, and in 1939 she was appointed principal of Westfield College, London, where she stayed until her retirement in 1951.

There her wide social interests and force of character brought new ideas and new modes, not in easy conformity with tradition. The college gained a new public recognition through the fame of its principal, although within the university she was criticized for views tenaciously held and within the college for an unorthodox conception of her office.

She continued to play an active part in public life not only while principal but also after retirement. She was a member of various government committees including, in particular, the Unemployment Insurance Statutory Committee, and in this work the penetrating and analytic qualities of her mind enabled her to make a valuable contribution.

These same powers were shown in her work for the B.B.C. On the *Brains Trust,* her vigour and independence of mind and her forthright speech won her national recognition.

She also took part regularly in the B.B.C. radio programme *Any Questions.* She maintained her lively interest in the Workers' Educational Association, with which she had worked closely in Manchester, and was for several years its deputy president.

She had been much influenced by William Temple and her faith in education and social reform was coloured by his approach to these matters. But in religion and in politics, as a Christian and as a member of the Labour Party, she maintained a high degree of individuality.

In her publications she again showed her preoccupation with social and educational questions, writing with discernment and wit the histories of the Manchester University Settlement, the Workers' Educational Association and the District Nursing Service, as well as a life of her friend and fellow worker, Eleanor Rathbone.

Her services, and their scope, were recognized by the honorary degrees conferred upon her, the degree of LL.D. by the University of Manchester in 1955 and of Litt.D. by the University of Liverpool in 1956. She was also appointed a member of both the Observer and Cassel Trusts.

She will be remembered by many in a characteristic pose with chin thrust forward and eyes lit by clear and honest purpose. She was a friendly as well as an indomitable woman, forthright in manner but humane in all her intentions; and an excellent comrade and companion.

She published lives of Eleanor Rathbone and Ernest Simon of Manchester and in 1970 a volume of autobiography entitled *My Commonplace Book.* These were followed by *Still More Commonplace* (1974), and a play *Hail Nero!*

July 7, 1975.

Adrian Stokes, who died on December 15, 1972 in London, wrote primarily about art, but over a period of more than 40 years his work was increasingly concerned with the whole relationship of mental life with the physical world. It has been recognized as a deeply original achievement.

Adrian Durham Stokes was born in 1902. He remembered the surroundings of his childhood in Bayswater as discordantly ill-matched to imaginative life. From Rugby he went as a Demy to Magdalen College, Oxford, to read philosophy, politics and economics and gained a second class in 1923. During his first winter as an undergraduate he had been to Italy for the first

time and recognized an agreement of spirit and environment which he instinctively sought.

After Oxford, his father—a perceptive and eccentric stockbroker who had stood as a Liberal candidate—sent him to India. He returned by way of China and America with a sense of what is specific to the European tradition and a belief in art as the key to an order of understanding unattainable by other means, which were reflected in his first book, *The Thread of Ariadne,* in 1925.

Another of the unread juvenilia addressed perhaps, chiefly to himself, *Sunrise in the West,* focused attention on the Mediterranean, and on the medium of prose in preference to poetry. A further formative experience which it noted was the Russian ballet, and when the Diaghilev company was in difficulties, the young man offered his whole private means to maintain it.

The offer was declined and Stokes remained independent all his life, able to devote himself in seclusion to his own line of thought unconcerned with position or reward. He first settled in Venice in 1925, looking at the basic material of the Renaissance world—stone, building and carving in themselves. The richly allusive studies that made him known began with *The Quatro Cento* in 1932.

In 1934 when *The Stones of Rimini* appeared, he was back in Hampstead; in Parkhill Road the best artists in the country were his neighbours, and the gain was mutual. Stokes, who thought of himself as a writer first and last, had always painted and there is no more sensitive discussion of colour as a function of shape than *Colour and Form,* published in 1937. He spent the war years in Cornwall, occupied with market gardening and hospitality to the artists who gathered round him. With the peace he went to live in Ascona where an idyllically happy second marriage began.

During these years he produced the beautiful trilogy which combined studies of the art that meant most to him with extended autobiographical meditations—*Inside Out* (1947), *Art and Science* (1949) and *Smooth and Rough* (1951). His subject was now not art alone so much as the whole field of meaning which mental life attaches to the material world. Psychoanalysis had made him aware of the emotional background of standpoints to reality and he proceeded to examine the roots of art in the light of it. Returning to England he had to find a new publisher and an audience prepared for effort. *Michelangelo* (1955) and the essays which followed showed not only more systematic insight but wider sympathies than before. As the argument developed from book to book, illuminating the present as well as the past, and extending beyond art to life and its environment, it proved persuasive; the obscurity formerly ascribed to him seemed to lighten, perhaps because his readers were catching up.

With some 20 books behind him, Stokes felt that the masterly *Reflections on the*

Nude, published in 1967, completed his critical work, but his vitality was undiminished. The iridescent objectivity of his paintings developed an extraordinary consistency and strength; exhibitions in 1965 and 1968 made a deep impression.

More surprisingly, he began to write poetry, which he had turned away from 45 years earlier. In his last illness—still painting, with wonderful freedom, and remarking that things looked more beautiful than ever—he saw the proof of a collection of his poetry to appear in 1976. A reviewer of a selection of his writings has lately suggested, with justice, that his influence will be as positive and perhaps more benign than Ruskin's.

December 19, 1972.

Lord Stonham, P.C., O.B.E., Minister of State at the Home Office from 1967 to 1969, died on December 22, 1971 in Enfield.

Having sat in the House of Commons as a Labour member for nine years—first for Taunton and later for Shoreditch and Finsbury—he was created a life peer in 1958. When the Labour Government were returned to power in 1964 he held office as a junior Minister, later Minister, and worked ardently for the reform of a prison system which he had once described as being "a disgrace to a civilized country".

It was before he came to office that he made this criticism. At that time he was president of the Prison Reform Council and he had long felt that prison treatment was ill adapted to rehabilitation and that the after-care system for prisoners was pitifully inadequate. Holding these views it was fitting that at the Home Office he should have been given a special responsibility for prisons. He quickly saw that gross overcrowding was the first evil to be tackled.

Stonham helped contribute several penal reforms—the prison parole scheme introduced under the 1967 Criminal Justice Act had an "extraordinarily encouraging start". The first step towards prisoners joining trade unions while serving sentences was taken in 1969. New security fences were installed round prisons to prevent escapes but also secure a freer regime inside prisons. In 1967 Stonham took over the responsibility for talks about Radio Caroline and the independence movement in the Isle of Man with its government. During 1969 Stonham had special responsibilities for Northern Ireland. In the Lords, Stonham was responsible for handling important Home Office legislation, as well as Ministry of Power legislation.

Stonham—himself a former industrialist—was also deeply interested in plans to rationalize prison industries. He wished to see one industry concentrated in a single prison, the adoption of business efficiency methods, and the creation in prison workshops of a factory atmosphere so that men might take pride in useful work and be equipped to adapt themselves more easily to work in industry on leaving prison. His aim was to have the 36 industries carried on in prisons reduced to about nine. In one speech he visualized a prison with a first-class laundry being able to "take in washing over a whole region".

Victor John Collins was born on July 1, 1903, the son of Victor Collins. Educated at the Regent Street Polytechnic and London University, he entered the family business of J. Collins & Sons, in Shoreditch, at the age of 20. This is a furniture and basket making firm, and later in life Collins became the governing director. He was descended from Huguenot ancestors who had been weaving silk in Spitalfields in the seventeenth century, and his own family business dated from that period. He also had a 70-acre farm at Earl Stonham, in Suffolk, where he specialized in growing willows for his own factory. He held office as president or chairman of various trade organizations and during the Second World War he acted on behalf of the Ministry of Supply in buying and distributing willows. From 1942 to 1964 he was chairman of the National Basket and Willow Trades Advisory Committee. He was active in promoting consultation with the workers in industry and established one of the first works' councils.

Collins had joined the Labour Party in 1942 and became chairman of the British Socialist Agricultural Society. In 1945 he turned his attention to national politics and in the general election of that year he won a notable victory at Taunton, Somerset, which he captured for Labour for the first time. He lost the seat at the 1950 general election but in October, 1954, he was back again in the House of Commons as Labour member for Shoreditch and Finsbury, for which constituency he was returned at a by-election after the death of Ernest Thurtle. This was the area of London in which he had his business and with which he had been identified all his life. He retained the seat with an increased majority at the general election in the following year.

In 1958 Collins was included in the first list of life peers to be created, on the recommendation of Harold Macmillan after consultation with the Leader of the Opposition. He took the title of Baron Stonham and was a valuable recruit to the Labour benches in the House of Lords. In 1962 he became chairman of the newly formed Standing Joint Council on Inland Transport and engaged in many wordy battles with Lord Beeching about the pros and cons of closing branch lines as one means of improving the economic health of British Railways.

He took a lively interest in the welfare of young people and in 1963 he became chairman of the National Society for Mentally Handicapped Children. He was also chairman of Youth Ventures from 1959 to 1964. He had served, too, on the South-West Regional Hospital Board and as chairman of the Mental Health Committee. But prison reform was perhaps the subject about which he cared most and his appointment in 1964 to be a Parliamentary Under-Secretary and in 1967 Minister of State (until 1969) at the Home Office enabled him to work effectively for that cause.

He married, in 1929, Violet Mary Savage and they had one son.

December 23, 1971.

General Sir Montagu Stopford, G.C.B., K.B.E., D.S.O., M.C., died on March 10, 1971. He was 78.

In the Second World War he commanded a corps with outstanding success in the campaign for the reconquest of Burma, and after the war was Commander-in-Chief of the Allied Land Forces in South East Asia.

He inspired his troops by his energy and optimism and gained their loyalty and affection by his kindliness and sense of humour. He was the most delightful of companions; he had a quick wit, a gift for repartee, and a fund of good stories. His zest for life and enjoyment of everyday affairs enabled him to get pleasure and laughter out of even the dullest day's work.

Montagu George North Stopford, who was born on November 16, 1892, the eldest son of Major-General Sir Lionel Stopford, came of a family with a long tradition of naval and military service. He was educated at Wellington and Sandhurst, and was commissioned in 1911 in the Rifle Brigade. He spent the first three years of his service with the 2nd Battalion in India. In the First World War he served without a break in France and Belgium from 1914 to 1918, for the first few months with his battalion, and afterwards on the staff, as A.D.C. Staff Captain, G.S.O.3., Brigade Major, and G.S.O.2.

When the Second World War broke out he was a Chief Instructor at the Staff College, Camberley. In October 1939 he became Commander of the 17th Infantry Brigade which was to play so splendid a part in the fighting in France and Flanders in 1940. His Brigade fought a rearguard action on the River Senne near Brussels. Soon afterwards it was heavily engaged at Arras and on the Ypres-Comines Canal in the two great battles fought to cover the evacuation of the B.E.F. from Dunkirk. At Arras it narrowly escaped being cut off by the Germans who practically surrounded the town, and, with the rest of the 5th Division, by what seemed almost a miracle, it marched out by night along the only road which had not been blocked by the enemy.

He did not see active service again till he was appointed, at the end of 1943, to command the 33rd Indian Corps in Burma. When the Japanese launched their offensive in March 1944, Scoones's 4th Corps was cut off in the mountain plateau of Imphal, and settled down to a prolonged resistance, sustained by air supply. Stopford's Corps was brought into the line at Kohima. He was then given the task of holding the enemy to the north of Imphal and of driving them back from the Dimapur road in order to relieve Scoones. His corps headquarters at that time had no experience and had done little training, but the success and speed with which they overcame their teething troubles was a measure of Stopford's ability and leadership.

The battle of Kohima was a bloody one. The absence of roads, the jungle, the hills, the monsoon clouds and the pelting rain made the development of the British strength slow and difficult. There was heavy fighting in which the Japanese were held and suffered heavy casualties. Then Stopford made a series of attacks which threw them on the defensive and removed the threat to the beleaguered 4th Corps. In the final stages of the battle he launched his three divisions to relieve Imphal, and succeeded in opening the road. The Japanese resistance suddenly broke, and they fell back in full retreat, having lost 50 per cent of their attacking troops. The Imphal-Kohima battle, which had lasted four months and was one of the longest of the war, was the first considerable defeat of the Japanese by British and Indian troops, and they never recovered from it.

His Corps next took part in the pursuit of the enemy into Central Burma. This operation was made possible only by the remarkable system of air supply which had been developed at Imphal and Kohima. In spite of the appalling difficulties of the climate and the terrain, the Japanese were pressed so hard that they were given no time to rest or reform, and they were driven over the Chindwin River before they could prepare defences. After an advance of some 400 miles, the 33rd Corps reached the Irrawaddy by the middle of January.

In the battles which followed at Mandalay and Meikteila, Stopford's corps was brought from the left to the right flank of 14th Army by a remarkably clever strategic "scissors" movement which took the Japanese by surprise, and after marches through the most difficult country it seized a crossing over the Irrawaddy below Mandalay.

The fighting was severe and went on for two months, after which the enemy found themselves between two fires, and they abandoned their guns and transport and withdrew into the Shan Hills, leaving the road to Rangoon open. In the final race southward to beat the monsoon, Stopford's corps had to overcome considerable resistance in the Irrawaddy valley, and had reached Prome when the main operations came to an end.

This campaign was one of the most remarkable of the whole war and the 33rd Corps had played an outstanding part in it. It had been conducted in a theatre which had previously been held to be one of the regions of the world where powerful and highly equipped armies could not fight. The Corps had covered a distance greater than from Land's End to John o'Groats, and had had a record of unbroken success.

On Slim's* departure, Stopford was appointed to command the forces remaining in Burma, which were formed into a new 12th Army. It fell to him, as Army Commander, to complete the clearing up of the country in operations which went on for a further three months.

In January 1946 Stopford was appointed G.O.C. in C. Allied Forces in the Netherlands East Indies, where he coped successfully with the difficult military and political aftermath of the war. Six months later he succeeded General Dempsey* as Commander-in-Chief Allied Land Forces, South East Asia, a post which he held until his return to England early in 1947 to take up the appointment of G.O.C. in C. Northern Command. He was Colonel Commandant of the Rifle Brigade from 1951 to 1958.

He married in 1921 Dorothy, daughter of Lieut. Colonel Henry Foulkes Deare, 8th Hussars.

March 11, 1971.

Lesley Storm, the dramatist, died on October 19, 1975 at the age of 71. She wrote a dozen plays, of which two, *Black Chiffon* and *Roar Like a Dove* (this ran for over 1,000 performances), had protracted lives in the West End. Her special gift was for crisp and authoritative dialogue.

A clergyman's daughter—her real name was Margaret Cowie—she was born in Maud, Aberdeenshire, graduated from Aberdeen University, and married a London director, the late James Doran Clark.

One of her first pieces, a light comedy called *Tony Draws a Horse*, opened at the Criterion early in 1939 and lasted through the first months of the war. Later in the war she wrote an English book for the Johann Strauss operetta *A Night in Venice* which had a long run at the Cambridge; but *Great Day* (Playhouse, 1945), about the preparation for Mrs. Eleanor Roosevelt's* arrival in an English village, had to end prematurely when President Roosevelt died. Her major play reached the West End four years later.

Then *Black Chiffon* began a run of more than a year with Flora Robson in one of her most affecting studies: a mother so "emotionally locked" with her son that, when he is on the verge of marriage, her psychological strain forces her to shoplifting.

Though Lesley Storm did nothing to transcend *Black Chiffon*, she wrote in *Roar Like a Dove* (Phoenix, 1957) a wittily-developed comedy that lasted for well over twice as long. Described by one critic as "a kind of fertility rite", and set in a Scottish castle, it was about an American woman and her husband, a singleminded laird who does not see that, for a change, she wants to wear her tiara in London.

In spite of her professional method and varied themes, none of Lesley Storm's other plays (including *The Day's Mischief, The Long Echo* and *Time and Yellow Roses*) was comparably successful. She was co-author of the much-praised film *The Fallen Idol*. She leaves two sons and two daughters.

October 20, 1975.

Rex Stout, the creator of Nero Wolfe, the detective with a passion for collecting orchids, died on October 27, 1975 aged 88.

Rex Stout was among the most distinguished of American mystery writers, and one of the last to create a great detective in the grand manner; his obese chair-bound sleuth, Nero Wolfe, became the New Yorker's own detective, in almost as intimate a sense as Sherlock Holmes belongs to London. He was president, at various times, of the Authors' Guild, the Authors' League of America, and the Mystery Writers of America.

Rex Todhunter Stout was born in December 1886 into a large Quaker family at Noblesville, Indiana. His father, John Wallace Stout, was a teacher. The family soon moved to Topeka, Kansas, where he won prizes for spelling, and, having read extensively in his father's library, was considered something of an infant prodigy. He abandoned the University of Kansas prematurely, however, to join the United States Navy, where he eventually became Yeoman Paymaster in President Theodore Roosevelt's yacht, Mayflower. He purchased his discharge in 1908.

He then had four wandering years, which included law studies and a succession of jobs as cook, clerk, bell-hop, plumber, cigar salesman, stable hand, tourist guide and hotel manager. One day he wrote an article on palmistry, about which he knew nothing, with the aid of two political celebrities he had met on board the Mayflower, who contributed their palm-prints. He sold the article for $200 and decided to write.

He began churning out magazine fiction and articles, but was diverted by his invention of a school banking system, the Educational Thrift Service, which he sold in 400 towns. When America entered the First World War, he adapted his system to the sale of War Savings Stamps and became manager of the campaign.

In 1927, having accumulated a modest fortune, he went to Paris and began serious writing. His first novel, *How Like a God* (1929), had a good critical reception. It was a dramatic study of sex psychosis, and he followed it with three more psychological novels. Perhaps fortunately, the Wall Street crash forced him to try a more lucrative type of fiction. His first detective story, *Fer-de-Lance*, which introduced Nero Wolfe and his assistant, Archie Goodwin, appeared as a book in 1934, having already been serialized in *The Saturday Evening Post.* It was an immediate success.

Through the long series of novels and three-to-a-volume stories which followed, Wolfe's admirers became familiar with every detail of his old brownstone house on West 35th Street, with his eccentricities, his love of orchids and beer and good food, with the household routine and with Archie Goodwin's edged but affectionate style. These things mattered more than the detective problem, though the detection itself was always fair and intelligent.

The best of the Nero Wolfe books, such as *Too Many Cooks* (1938), *Some Buried Caesar* (1939) or *Plot It Yourself* (1959) (published in Britain under the title *Murder in Style*) are highly literate, soundly constructed and delightfully amusing. Rex Stout did experiment with other detectives, Tecumseh Fox in *Double for Death* (1939), which he considered, oddly, his best book; Dol Bonner in *The Hand in the Glove* (1937) (published in Britain as *Crime on Her Hands*) and the eponymous *Alphabet Hicks* (1941), but it was Nero Wolfe whom his readers loved.

Stout was a man of leftish views. During the Second World War he was heavily involved in the broadcasting of propaganda, and quarrelled with his associates because of his uncompromising demand for hard peace terms and the permanent separation of the Ruhr from Germany. Only with difficulty was he brought to admit that there might be some good Germans. After the war he gave his support to the idea of world government and to the campaign for nuclear disarmament. Wisely, however, he kept his politics and his detective stories almost entirely apart, except that a few of his later books such as *A Right to Die* (1964) and, an exceptionally good one, *The Doorbell Rang* (1965), had themes connected with current liberal preoccupations.

Unlike Nero Wolfe, he was an energetic man, but he shared Wolfe's fondness for cooking and gardening. "I love books, food, music, sleep, people who work, heated arguments, the United States of America and my wife and children", he said. "I dislike politicians, preachers, genteel persons, people who do not work or are on vacation, closed minds, movies and television, loud noises and oiliness."

He was married twice: his first marriage, in 1916, to Fay Kennedy of Topeka, Kansas, ended in divorce, and in 1932 he married Pola Hoffman of Vienna, a well-known fashion designer and interior decorator. They had two daughters.

October 29, 1975.

Christopher Strachey, Professor of Computation at Oxford University, and one of the pioneers of computing in Britain, died on May 18, 1975 aged 58.

He was the son of Oliver Strachey, a cryptographer and Lytton Strachey's brother, and his second wife, Ray Costelloe, a leading suffragist. He was educated at Gresham's School and King's College, Cambridge. Experience with a differential analyser during the war awakened his interest in mathematical machines.

In 1950, while a schoolmaster at Harrow, he suddenly appeared at the National Physical Laboratory with a draughts-playing programme for their Pilot A.C.E.: this was extraordinarily sophisticated work, particularly for an unknown amateur. His next big achievement, a simulator for the Manchester Mark 1, was far larger than any previous programme for that machine and firmly established his position in computing.

In 1951 he joined the National Research and Development Corporation where he was responsible for the overall design for the Ferranti Pegasus computer which successfully embodied his belief that ease of programming should guide the design of machines. Seconded to Toronto, he programmed most of a backwater simulation for the St. Lawrence Seaway. This was another *tour de force* and advanced the opening of the Great Lakes to shipping by many years. Later, along with one or two others, he became interested in the use of one computer for several concurrent tasks; indeed he published the earliest paper on this, though he attached little significance to the fact.

After a time as a private consultant, in 1962 he moved to Cambridge and became a Fellow of Churchill College. He took charge of the design of the high-level language C.P.L. and its compiler for the new Atlas computer. This language was never widely used, but its elegance encouraged the analysis of underlying concepts and its effects can be seen in several later languages.

After a year at the Massachusetts Institute of Technology where he influenced the development of their computing science curriculum, he moved in 1965 to Oxford to set up the Programming Research Group; he became professor there in 1971. Working on C.P.L. had made him realize the need for a coherent theory of programming language semantics, on which he had already published his initial ideas.

At Oxford he developed these into a comprehensive description technique which collaborators supported on the one hand with firm mathematical foundations, and on the other with methods for proving the correctness of implementations. He had just completed a book on this with a colleague; unfortunately he could not see its publication. Meanwhile he had continued his work on software and machine design. In 1972 the British Computer Society had made him one of its first distinguished fellows.

In research his chief talent was choosing the right notions for the right problems. He had a gift for inspiring younger colleagues and students, and endowed his group at Oxford with a distinctive sense of purpose. At Wolfson College, too, students particularly appreciated his sympathetic understanding; he enjoyed taking a vigorous part in the development of the new college.

He loved to hear and play music and also revelled in solving and constructing puzzles. Though a scientist he was a typical member of his notable family, recognizably a Strachey in feature and voice, and a master of words. He was ruthless to all forms of self-deception, but warmly tolerant, generous and irreverently witty. He would often say that his philosophy had been best summed up by Bertrand Russell* in the precept that one's life should be prompted by love and guided by intelligence.

May 23, 1975.

Professor Jaroslav Stransky, the former Czech minister, who died on August 12, 1973 in Canvey Island, was a historian and legal expert and had been a member of all the governments of Dr. Benes from 1940. He served in the government in exile in London and later after 1945 in Prague. He had been Minister of Education and Minister of Justice and was at one period deputy Prime Minister. When the Communists took over power in 1948 he fled to Britain for the second time.

His special position was underlined by his ownership of a daily and evening paper called *Lidove Noviny* (*People's News*) which was founded by his father, Dr. Adolf Stransky, who was Minister of Trade in the first Masaryk Government after liberation in 1918. Professor Stransky maintained the high standards of his journals and among their staff members and contributors were leading journalists, writers and politicians.

He broadcast during the war for the B.B.C. and his weekly talks became an event in the occupied country. They were later issued in book form. During his second exile Stransky was a regular commentator for Radio Free Europe. It is believed that his regular talks contributed greatly to the rebirth of the Czech nation experienced during the 1968 events, sometimes called the Czechoslovak spring.

August 11, 1973.

Dr. Otto Strasser, one of the early leaders of the Nazi Party, who later became Hitler's enemy, died in Munich on August 27, 1974 at the age of 76.

Born in Bavaria on September 10, 1897, Strasser, with his elder brother Gregor, fought in the First World War and then studied political economy, becoming a socialist and editing a Social Democratic newspaper. Deciding that the party was weak and rigidly dogmatic, and yielding to the influence of his brother, he joined the Nazi Party in 1925.

Soon there were, in effect, two National Socialist parties in Germany—the one led by Hitler and the other led by the Strassers. The Strassers wanted a revolutionary party, one that would fight for common cause with the trade unions and for serious social reforms and would stand firm against a dictatorship.

This struggle between the totalitarian tendencies of Hitler and the more democratic beliefs of the Strassers became violent and in 1930 Otto withdrew completely and founded his own group called the Black Front. Gregor remained with Hitler, loyal but discontented, believing that he might persuade Hitler to take a different course and hoping that he might at some time become leader of the party. As a reward for this loyalty, Hitler had him murdered in the bloodbath of June 30, 1934.

Realizing that Otto Strasser was the party's most dangerous enemy, Goering ordered that he be assassinated. Many members of the Nazi Party were at this stage disappointed, felt themselves betrayed by Hitler and were attracted to the alternatives offered by Strasser. The Gestapo reported that influential army officers, the young, and the peasants were sympathetic to Strasser; he was a serious danger threatening the system from inside.

Fleeing to Vienna and Prague, then, as war approached, to Zurich and Paris, Strasser continued his opposition to the Nazis. Founding the Free German Movement in France, he soon had to move on again, this time to Canada and the United States. His campaign, even if energetic, was largely ignored although he won some support for his views in Britain, the United States and in Germany after the war when he organized a new movement, the League for German Revival.

His muddled vision of a new Socialist Germany was not welcomed by the victorious allies, who continued to see the ghost of Nazism in Strasser's ideas, despite his vigorous fight against Hitler. His opposition to Hitler, it was thought, had been personal rather than ideological.

Deprived of his citizenship, Strasser fought through the courts to have it restored and in 1955 he returned to West Germany from Canada. In 1956 he founded another political party, the German Social Union, but his Nazi past hindered its progress. His claim of a conversion to political respectability was somewhat suspect.

August 29, 1974.

Igor Stravinsky, who died on April 6, 1971 in New York at the age of 88, was for three generations and for more than half a century the most influential and the most discussed composer of the day. His life was long; in his youth he met not only Tchaikovsky and Balakirev, but Ibsen, Monet, Petipa, Réjane, Sarah Bernhardt, Proust; he reached maturity as a composer just before Diaghilev launched his revolution in the Russian ballet, and he lived to keep pace with the most audacious musical explorers of the 1960s.

He seemed ageless in his music, because he never closed his mind to the evolution of the art, or to the creative musician's place as a reflector of current attitudes; in his younger days he led musical fashion, and in his old age he observed, translated and revealed afresh whatever he found new and exciting and fruitful in the work of composers with a quarter of his years. He was too serious ever to count as an *enfant terrible*, and too lively (too determined) of mind ever to become an old master. He became the acknowledged G.O.M. of music, but unwillingly for, as he wrote in 1960: "All my life I have thought of myself as 'the youngest one'."

Stravinsky's chief contribution to 20th century music was without doubt the new rhythmic possibilities, especially of asymmetrical pattern, that were suggested, and are still being suggested, in his ballet score *The Rite of Spring*, a work which, with *Tristan and Isolde*, (though some would say *Parsifal*), is fundamental to modern music. Language, the manner of self-expression, was an inexhaustible preoccupation for Stravinsky in music, perhaps because also in words he declared himself a "convinced etymologist", concerned with "problems of language all my life". He seems never to have been at a loss for something worth while to say—in age as in youth his intellect was as clear, as radiant and as sharp as a diamond; it was the choice between alternative methods of formulating the truth that perennially absorbed and stimulated him. When invited to contribute to an Old Testament symposial oratorio, Stravinsky typically chose *Babel*. Whatever the language, there was never any doubt about the identity of the speaker.

His linguistic inheritance and history are closely connected with the chameleonic versatility which he displayed in his music, particularly in the years between 1910 (when he left Russia) and 1952 (the beginning of his overt preoccupation with serial techniques). Stravinsky's father came of a Polish family, his mother from the Ukraine; he was brought up by a German nanny, speaking German as fluently as Russian. After leaving St. Petersburg he sided linguistically with France, and eventually became a French citizen in 1934, but in 1939 destiny took him to America, and in 1945 he adopted American nationality. His writings show an eloquence and feeling for niceties of language as remarkable in English and French as in the tongues with which he grew up, though he acknowledged Russian as his prime vehicle of thought to the end of his days, and musically, too, he never lost a trace of Russian accent; in the *Requiem Canticles* (1966) it is still strongly discernible.

Igor Stravinsky was born at Oranienbaum, near St. Petersburg, in June 1882. His father was principal bass-baritone at the St. Petersburg Opera, his mother an amateur of music, but there was no strong family heritage of musicianship. Thanks to his father's post Igor (the third of four sons) was able to attend rehearsals and performances of opera and ballet whenever he wished; in his teens he took full advantage of this. Almost as important to his development was his father's extensive library; Igor Stravinsky was an omnivorous reader all his life, and enjoyed the retentive memory of a polymath.

His father was sceptical of his son's musical gift, though Igor had, at two years old, correctly reproduced the songs of peasants in the neighbourhood. He began piano lessons at nine years, harmony and counterpoint a little later. He was already composing music when, in 1900, he stayed at the country home of his schoolfellow, Vladimir Rimsky-Korsakov, and from then onward he showed his compositions to Nicolai Rimsky-Korsakov until in 1902 he became that composer's pupil for orchestration and form.

Stravinsky was destined for a legal career and during these years read jurisprudence at St. Petersburg University, from which he graduated in 1905. But by this time music absorbed his whole interest and there was no question of another career. His father had died in 1902; Stravinsky's first catalogued work, a piano sonata (now lost) dates from 1904. He was still Rimsky-Korsakov's pupil when, in 1906, he married his first cousin, Catherine Nossenko, and began his Symphony in E flat major, a rather Wagnerian piece still occasionally performed (it was with this symphony that he made his conducting debut in Montreux, at Ansermet's* invitation, in 1914).

When Rimsky-Korsakov died in 1908 he had passed on to Stravinsky the serviceable, even virtuoso orchestral technique which can be found in two orchestral works of that year, the *Scherzo fantastique* and *Fireworks*. It was a performance of this last which aroused the interest of Sergei Diaghilev, then preparing to launch his Russian Ballet company. Diaghilev gave Stravinsky some orchestration work (for *Les Sylphides*) and then asked him to write music for Fokine's ballet *The Firebird*, since Liadov, the original choice, was working too slowly. Stravinsky, now in revolt against the methods and ideals of Rimsky, did not care for the subject, but accepted the commission.

The Firebird (1910) made his name in Paris and subsequently all over Europe; the score does show Rimsky's influence, particularly in the full orchestral version which Stravinsky later reduced, and is strongly Russian in character, though Diaghilev's company found it perplexing and unmelodious. For Stravinsky it was an artistic necessity to abandon the voluptuous style to create hard, bright colours and lines, crisp and invigorating rhythms. He and his family had now left Russia (apart from a brief visit in 1914 he did not return to his native soil until 1962) and were living in Switzerland; Stravinsky began work on a piano concerto which Diaghilev soon persuaded him to transform into *Petrushka* (1911). These two ballets and a third, *The Rite of Spring*—at its first performance in 1913 there was a riot—triumphantly proclaimed the viability of the one-act ballet as a medium of dance-drama, and not merely more or less trivial *divertissement;* as such they are of first importance in the history of ballet. But in *Petrushka*, and still more in *The Rite of Spring*, Stravinsky was increasingly preoccupied with musical structure in terms of phrases and rhythmic shapes for their own non-associative shape; significantly he took exception to the work of his choreographers in these ballets and significantly too they have been as successful in the concert hall as in the theatre.

Stravinsky's fortunes were now firmly involved with Diaghilev's enterprise; when Diaghilev had produced *The Nightingale* (1908 to 1913) Stravinsky turned his back on Russian romantic nationalism and when war broke out he was obliged to proceed without Diaghilev's support. During the war years in Switzerland he composed a succession of short works for small groups—the best known are the opera-ballet *Renard* (1917) and *The Soldier's Tale* (1918)—and these forced Stravinsky to sharpen and subtilize his invention, as well as allowing him to develop his rhythmic experiments. *The Ragtime* for 11 instruments (1918) signalled a new interest in jazz rhythms and tone-colours, and, similarly, the study for pianola (1917, subsequently orchestrated as "Madrid") inaugurated an extensive interest in the possiblities of the mechanical piano and eventually in the piano itself which the composer cultivated once more as the vehicle of his own performances.

His piano concerto was the first of these; later his second son Soulima (an old Polish family name) became an exponent of his piano music, and the majestic, very difficult concerto for two solo pianos (1935) was composed for father and son together. From the mechanical piano to the gramophone was a single, logical step. Stravinsky welcomed every opportunity to record his own performances partly to fix tempo and phrasing for the aid of other performers, partly because he abominated the "recreative" type of interpreter who labours to make another man's work his own (he compared the ideal conductor to a bell-ringer at the end of a rope).

After the armistice, in 1919, Stravinsky worked occasionally for Diaghilev, notably in *Pulcinella* (1919), in which he rearranged Pergolesi to suit his own features; *The Wedding* (1923), a tough, heavily-stylized, and earthy evocation of Russian peasant life with an orchestra consisting of four pianos; and *Apollon Musagete* (1928) which most strongly typifies the statuesque neoclassicism that was Stravinsky's chief ideal at this time. The choreography of this ballet was by George Balanchine, with whom Stravinsky was to enjoy a further, very fruitful period of collaboration in New York. In the same year Stravinsky and Diaghilev parted company after the composer had accepted a commission from a "rival", Ida Rubinstein.

The ballet in question, *The Fairy's Kiss*, took its thematic material from Tchaikovsky, and showed that Stravinsky's command of his own style was sufficiently assured to absorb features of romanticism without sounding like nineteenth century music. Traces of a Tchaikovskian texture could, however, have been remarked already in the aria "Non erubescite" from the sombre and monumental opera-oratorio *Oedipus Rex*, to a Latin text by Cocteau* (of which Diaghilev mounted a concert performance in 1927), though the predominating traits of the work derive more obviously from Bach and Handel. The grandest and most granite-like of these neo-classic works is the *Symphony of Psalms,* composed in 1930 for the jubilee of the Boston Symphony Orchestra; its noble, monolithic texture looks back to the exalted *Symphonics of Wind Instruments* (1920, in memory of Debussy), and forward to the gravely hieratical *Threni* (1958), Stravinsky's first completely serial composition—all three are strongly "Russian" in character, though the Russia of Mussorgsky rather than Rimsky-Korsakov.

Stravinsky had, indeed, re-embraced the Russian Orthodox faith in 1926, but his cast of mind and way of life had become west European and, particularly, French. His major works of the 1930s reflected the nationality which he adopted in this decade: the melodrama *Persephone*, text by Gide (1934), in which the composer took deliberate liberties with the stress of the French language, believing that words should no more limit the metre and phrasing than the musical themes should; the concerto for two pianos; and *Jeu des Cartes* (1937), another ballet for Balanchine.

In 1939 Stravinsky was offered the chair of Poetics at Harvard University. Happiness in his Paris home had been broken by the deaths of his mother, his wife, and his daughter Ludmilla, within a year. When French friends advised him to accept the chair, he left his new homeland on the eve of war. He settled in California, gave his lectures on the *Poetics of Music*, married the painter Vera de Bosset in 1940, and in 1945 became an American citizen. Stravinsky plunged enthusiastically into the musical life of America; he made an arrangement of *The Star-Spangled Banner* in 1941 (forbidden as being too peculiar), wrote a *Circus Polka* (1942) for Barnum and Bailey's elephants, a *Tango* (1941) for a "pop" music publisher, and the *Scènes de Ballet* (1944) for a Billy Rose revue. He flirted with film music, but without becoming seriously involved—the *Norwegian Moods*, the slow movement of the 1945 symphony, and the middle movement of *Ode*, all originated as film music; and he returned to American jazz in the *Ebony Concerto* (1945) for Woody Herman's Band.

He also collaborated again with Balanchine, most notably in *Orpheus* (1947) and the outstanding *Agon* (1957). And he returned to the orchestral symphony with the works in C (1940), and in three movements (1945), the latter a masterpiece of argument and invention which sums up all

Stravinsky's diverse explorations since *The Rite of Spring*. This immensely fruitful period closed in 1951 with *The Rake's Progress*, the three-act opera to an English text by W. H. Auden, in which Stravinsky adopted the techniques of Viennese classical *opera buffa*. The remarkable beauties of this "number-opera" cannot disguise the distinction between self-assertive *pastiche* and original compostion; unlike the Tchaikovsky and Pergolesi transcriptions, or the neo-Baroque *Dumbarton Oaks* (1940), which are evocatively timeless and therefore modern, this opera represented a bid to take over the assets of another century, to compose not neo-classical but actually classical music.

For 30 years Stravinsky had been acclaimed the antipode of 12-note music, the high priest of diatonicism. From 1952 onwards his works moved steadily towards the 12-note principle, at first in the *Septet* (1953) only through diatonic serial construction; later with less overt dependence upon tonality in the *Canticum Sacrum* (1955) to honour St. Mark's Cathedral in Venice, until in *Threni* (1958) he adopted the 12-note row entirely.

A halfway house was the ballet *Agon,* which begins and ends in C major but also includes strictly atonal and serial dance numbers. Stravinsky was undoubtedly attracted to serial methods by their application to his predilection for asymmetrical metres and rhythmic phraseology, but also by its non-associative "pure" significance—Webern, rather than Schoenberg, was his starting-point in this new adventure, and it is of Webern that one is reminded, both in the exiguous but oddly moving *Epitaphium* for the *Prince of Furstenberg* (1959), and in the epigrammatic concentration of the *Movements* for piano and orchestra (1959), which cultivate and harvest a broad field of textures and moods within the confines of eight minutes.

In 1962 Stravinsky celebrated his eightieth birthday by revisiting Russia and by composing three new works: a short, exquisite anthem *The Dove Descending*, to lines by T. S. Eliot*; a miniature oratorio *A Sermon, A Narrative and a Prayer*, which returned to a more direct style than that of *Movements*, and included a splendid setting of St. Stephen's last sermon; and a morality, *The Flood*, to be sung, spoken, acted, and danced on television.

He followed these with *Abraham and Isaac* in 1963, a stern rather hermetic setting of the Hebrew Bible text for baritone and orchestra; in 1964 the orchestral *Variations* in memory of Aldous Huxley*, and the tiny but marvellously concentrated *Elegy for J.F.K.* (to a *haiku* text by W. H. Auden), then in 1966 the *Requiem Canticles*, whose hieratic, deeply moving music aims to sum up the essence of all Stravinsky's religious composition.

Stravinsky's 85th birthday in 1967 was marked by world-wide celebrations. The composer had planned to take part in many of these, but age had begun to make in-

roads on his physical, if not mental, vitality, and his doctors would not let him travel.

In his late seventies Stravinsky was persuaded by his young American disciple, Robert Craft, to talk at length about his early life, his recollections of his works and his views on other music. The four conversation-books derived from these talks made stimulating reading, and provide invaluable source material for biographers and students of musical psychology alike. He regarded them as more self-revealing and faithful than the *Chronicles of My Life* (1935) written with Walter Nouvel, or the *Poetics of Music*, in which his collaborator was Roland-Manuel. The conversations revealed the broad range of his interests, and also his intolerance of many other musicians; there was an attractive streak of malice, including self-deflation, behind the eager bonhomie that his slight, bird-like figure presented. One could identify the deep mysticism of the Slav, and the debonair gaiety of the Frenchman, the affability and thirst for knowledge of the American; but these traits were personal rather than environmental, just as his music remained completely idiosyncratic, whether Grieg, Bach or Machauf or Boulez was his model. He may have hidden his face behind masks of other men, but his personality imprinted itself upon the whole face of music for over half a century, perhaps for the rest of time.

In March 1971, less than a month before he died, in a letter to *The Times*, he crossed swords with a critic on the subject of *The Firebird*. His letters are now being prepared for publication and he remarked that the one he was then writing might well be his last.

April 7, 1971.

Fred Streeter, the B.B.C. broadcaster on gardening, died on November 1, 1975 at the age of 98. A great gardener who from humble beginnings achieved distinction in the world of horticulture, he endeared himself to millions of garden lovers through his sound and television broadcasts and his writing.

It was a short broadcast talk on runner beans in the 1930s which triggered off a career that was to make him a talisman of horticultural rectitude in the average home. The talk itself attracted 200 letters and from there Streeter never looked back. Forty years as the compassionate radio sage, who, above all things, advocated kindness and consideration for plants, awaited him. His influence in disseminating a knowledge of the basics of gardening into millions of homes is incalculable.

Frederick Streeter was born the son of a shepherd at Pulborough, in Sussex, in June 1877. He attended Reigate Grammar School and was an extremely promising pupil. But at the age of 12 years he left school because he was determined to become a gardener.

In those days, the road to success as a professional gardener was long and hard. Fred Streeter started work at 3s. 6d. a week from 6 a.m. to 6 p.m. including Saturdays, at Colley Lodge, Reigate.

There followed various jobs in nurseries and private service, until in 1897 he went to work in the world-famous nursery of James Veitch & Sons at Chelsea for 12s. a week. For 14 years Fred Streeter never had a day's holiday, and except for one short visit to Paris on his employer's business had never been away from home for a holiday in his life.

There followed a period of service in Ireland at Shaffan House, in County Kildare. Back to England again, as foreman at Basing Park, then, to gain further experience, to Birtley House at Bramley, to Lavington Park, and to the girls' school at Caldecote Towers, near Watford.

In 1915 Fred Streeter joined the Royal Fusiliers, and after service was invalided out of the Army and went back to Ireland. In 1923 he was back in England as head gardener to Major Pam, at Wormley Bury. Then followed a period at Aldenham, under that great gardener Edwin Beckett, and finally to Petworth Park in 1929 as head gardener to Lord Leconfield.

During the Second World War years Fred Streeter saw, as so many other gardeners did, the glory of his garden dwindle away. A staff of 40 or more was reduced to half a dozen. Streeter became a superintendent of the Special Constabulary. Where he had grown fabulous begonias and orchids, he now produced food crops.

But in his heyday he won over 50 gold medals for superb exhibits at the Royal Horticultural Society's shows. One that will long be remembered was a large group of the original wild form of *Cyclamen persicum*, heavily scented—a plant he was able to grow outside in the woods at Petworth. The Royal Horticultural Society gave him its highest honour, the Victoria Medal of Honour, in 1945. He was made an M.B.E. in 1973.

Always ready to help every listener or reader, he coped with thousands of letters a month without a secretary—he never lost his enthusiasm for gardening, or his love of plants, even though his beloved Petworth Gardens were reduced to a shadow of their prewar magnificence.

His wife died in 1965.

November 3, 1975.

Lieutenant Colonel Arnold Nugent Strode Strode-Jackson, C.B.E., D.S.O., who died on November 13, 1972, won the 1,500 metres at the Olympic Games at Stockholm in 1912 in a time of 3min. 56.8sec., a new record time. He was up against a group of outstanding American milers, Abel Kiviat, John Paul Jones and Mel Sheppard, who had won both the 800 and 1,500 metres events at the London Olympic Games of 1908.

In his book *Olympic Cavalcade*, Lieutenant-Colonel F. A. M. Webster writes of the 1912 race: "Jackson was beaten in the race for the first bend and could find no place in the runners winding round the track, but he had the support of the Cambridge president, P. J. Baker [Mr. Philip Noel-Baker, the Labour statesman] . . . one of the most unselfish athletes who ever lived. Baker piloted Jackson yards wide of the field until 'Jackers' sprang his surprise which broke up the Americans and raced past them to victory in the new record time of 3min. 56.8sec."

Educated at Malvern and B.N.C., Oxford, he represented his college at football, hockey and rowing, while his prowess as a long-distance runner raised him to the position of President of the O.U.A.C. in 1914. He ran second for the mile in the Freshman's Sports; won the mile in the O.U.A.C.'s sports in 1912, the mile and a half at the O.U.H.C. Sports in 1913; and the mile in the inter-university sports in 1912, 1913 and 1914.

Strode-Jackson had a most distinguished career in the First World War, on the Western Front with the K.R.R.C., winning the D.S.O. with three bars and being mentioned six times in dispatches. He was thrice wounded. In 1919-20 he was a member of the British delegation to the Paris Peace Conference and was created C.B.E. for his services.

During the Second World War he was a colonel on the staff of the Governor of Kentucky and was also involved in official anti-sabotage precautions.

November 17, 1972.

Lord Stuart of Findhorn, C.H., M.V.O., M.C., Joint Chief Whip in the wartime Coalition Government from 1941 to 1945 and Secretary of State for Scotland from 1951 to 1957, died on February 20, 1971. He was 74.

He was not only one of the most popular Parliamentary figures of his generation, but one of the shrewdest. He had a great political flair which, during his many years at the Whips' Office and later as Secretary of State, he exercised with immense benefit to the House and his party. His soundness of judgment was highly prized by his Cabinet colleagues.

Before his elevation to the peerage in 1959 he had been Conservative member for Moray and Nairn for 36 years and he had unrivalled knowledge of Parliamentary affairs. He was a great success as Chief Whip, both in government and in opposition. The job was probably more congenial to him than his work at the Scottish Office. But his achievements as Secretary of State were of solid worth which his dislike of publicity led many to underestimate. Any judgment of him based on his Parliamentary performances would be wide of the mark. His gift for economy of effort was deceptive. He got a lot done without appearing to, and his most valuable contributions to the work of government seldom came to light.

His laconic, rather languid manner in the House concealed an immense capacity for hard work. He took great pains to perfect himself in a subject. Before a debate he would spend half the night in preparation; but he saw no point in burdening the House with a lot of gratuitous information. He never wasted words, in public or private. His training as a Whip had bred in him a firm conviction that a politician who talked too much was likely to get himself into trouble. He distrusted oratory and made no claim to any gift for it. It was an opposition criticism of him as a Minister that he took too little part in debate. He certainly did not believe in overdoing it. Indeed he sometimes gave the impression that he found the making of speeches a boring occupation. He once yawned in the middle of one of his own. During a stormy meeting in the country his wife passed him a note. The audience challenged him to disclose its contents. Having told them that she had written: "Try not to look so bored", he assured his audience, "But I *am* bored". Such frankness was one of his most endearing traits—and he had many.

He inherited in full measure the charm and intelligence of his Stuart ancestry—he was descended from King James V of Scotland. He was the soul of courtesy, but his hatred of humbug and claptrap could find devastating expression. With his robust attitude to life, his modesty, elegance, courage and commonsense, he brought something of a Renaissance quality to the political scene.

James Gray Stuart, third and youngest son of the 17th Earl of Moray, scion of an historic Scottish family, was born on February 9, 1897. He was sent to Eton and was intended for Cambridge but before he was due to go up the 1914-18 War broke out and he joined the Army. He was commissioned in the 3rd (Special Reserve) Battalion of the Royal Scots and by January 1915 he was at the front. Two months later he was invalided home. In 1916 he returned to France, fought on the Somme, gained the Military Cross and was promoted adjutant. After the Battle of Arras in 1917 he was awarded a Bar to the M.C. Before the end of the war he was Brigade-Major, serving with the 15th Infantry Brigade.

When peace came, Stuart read for the Scottish Bar in Edinburgh. He tried the law for nearly a year but, as he put it years later, "the law won and I retreated in disorder." In 1920 he was appointed First Equerry to Prince Albert, the future King George VI, and served him for 18 months. King George V conferred on him the M.V.O.

Stuart decided on a business career and went to the United States to learn about oil production. He spent three months in the offices of the American Petroleum Company in New York and 10 months in the Oklahoma oilfields. Home on leave in 1923, he was invited to be Conservative Candidate for Moray and Nairn. He was elected in the same year.

In 1935 he was appointed a Lord of the Treasury and Scottish Whip. Two years later he became deputy to the Conservative Chief Whip, Captain Margesson, afterwards Lord Margesson.* He was sworn of the Privy Council in 1939. When Margesson was appointed Secretary of State for War in January 1941, Stuart succeeded him as Joint Chief Whip with the late Sir Charles Edwards, Chief Whip of the Labour Party, in the wartime Coalition Government. With Edwards, and later with William Whiteley, who succeeded him in 1942, Stuart worked in easy harmony. Stuart became one of Winston Churchill's* closest and most trusted colleagues and friends. As Harold Macmillan wrote years later on Stuart's retirement: "To have been Chief Whip in a world war, and intimate adviser to the greatest of British Prime Ministers, is something to be proud of." On the formation of the "Caretaker" Government in 1945, Stuart became the sole Chief Whip. When the Conservatives went into opposition he was the party's Chief Whip until indifferent health compelled him to resign in 1948.

He had been perhaps the ideal man for the job. One of the secrets of his success was that he knew how to talk to men in language they could understand, in spite of a natural reserve. It was said of him that he had a habit of talking out of the side of his mouth and rarely finished a sentence. He had a sixth sense for detecting signs of trouble and dealt with it decisively before it could develop. Indeed he had an uncanny knack of knowing everything that was going on without appearing to make any effort to do so. But he had the poker player's art of not giving anything away. He never fussed and seldom raised his voice. As Herbert Morrison (later Lord Morrison of Lambeth*) once wrote of him, he was quiet and gentle. But he stood no nonsense from tiresome members of his party. His methods were sharp and effective. He handled his political troops like a good officer, and they responded with trust and affection.

His health improved and in 1950 he took on the duties for which the Scottish Unionist Whip had hitherto been responsible. This was useful experience for his next ministerial office as Secretary of State for Scotland, to which he was appointed when the Conservatives came back to power the next year.

Early in his term of office two additional ministers were appointed to deal with Scottish Affairs, and a Royal Commission was appointed whose recommendation that responsibility for Scottish highways and certain minor matters should be transferred to the Secretary of State were accepted by the Government. This and other measures of devolution, including the transference to his office of responsibility for the generation of electricity, had a marked effect in softening nationalist extremism.

His health continued to trouble him, and on the formation of a new Government in January 1957 he took the opportunity of resigning. Harold Macmillan described him as one of the most successful Secretaries of State for Scotland for many years —"a great achievement". In the Dissolution Honours of September 1959, he was raised to the peerage and took the style and title of Viscount Stuart of Findhorn, of Moray. His shrewd and salty interventions in debate were relished by their lordships.

Stuart published his autobiography *Within the Fringe* in 1967. He married in 1923, Lady Rachel Cavendish, fourth daughter of the ninth Duke of Devonshire.

February 22, 1971.

Sir Campbell Stuart, G.C.M.G., K.B.E., who died on September 14, 1972 at the age of 87, was a Canadian who settled in England after the First World War and touched London life at many points.

Northcliffe gave him a flying start. "Campbell is the only person I have yet found who understands the harmonising of my newspapers," he said, and appointed his young lieutenant managing director of *The Times* and Managing Editor of the *Daily Mail*. After Northcliffe's death Stuart ceased to hold a commanding position in newspapers, but he remained an active director of *The Times* until 1960. Dedicated though he was to journalism on both its managerial and editorial sides, he by no means confined himself to it. He sat on innumerable boards and threw himself into work in many fields of Commonwealth, especially Canadian, activities.

A lifelong bachelor, he enjoyed entertaining a wide circle of acquaintances, with his mother—to whom he was devoted— acting for many years as hostess. Dinner parties at his Chelsea and Brighton houses and, later, at The Grove, Highgate, brought leading figures from the journalistic, diplomatic and business world together round his table. He was no less an enthusiastic diner-out and club man. His tall, lean figure and eager, expressive face, quick to break into smiles, were familiar in Embassies and drawing-rooms in Mayfair and in Montreal, Cape Town and other centres of the old Empire. His friends and acquaintances were as many as any man of his generation. He aroused, too, hostility in those who distrusted his sometimes subtle ways of getting things done. He was, in fact, devotedly loyal to people and causes.

Even in his old age he kept up his habit—his hobby, it can be called—of entertaining at his Highgate home. Visitors would be astonished at how much he knew of what was happening behind the scenes in the City, in industry, and in the newspaper world. His information was always up-to-date. Sometimes it was even ahead of events, for no one had more sensitive antennae, and no one knew better by intuition and experience what was likely to happen. His guests always left him knowing much more than when they arrived. He would also go to endless lengths to help young people in their careers or when they were in difficulties.

Born in Montreal in 1885, he came of an old Canadian family that had migrated from the United States as Empire Loyalists. His father was a prominent lawyer and his maternal grandfather, Charles John Brydges, head of the Grand Trunk Railway. Stuart recruited an Irish-Canadian Regiment in 1915, drawn from both Protestant and Roman Catholic inhabitants of Quebec province. As a demonstration of solidarity he managed to arrange for it to march through Ireland before its officers and men went to France. This was the first of many diplomatic successes his remarkable gift of persuasion enabled him to achieve.

Sir Robert Borden, the Canadian Prime Minister, then dispatched him on a political mission to Pope Benedict XV to engage the interest of the Pontiff in recruiting in Quebec. Borden next sent him as Assistant Military Attaché in Washington, making him the first Canadian to be appointed officially to a post in the British Diplomatic Service. When Northcliffe arrived in Washington he got Stuart seconded to his mission as Military Secretary. He did well and was made a K.B.E. at 32. Returning to England in 1918, Stuart was appointed Deputy Director of Propaganda in Enemy Countries, again under Northcliffe.

There followed the most strenuous period of his career, acting as a buffer between Northcliffe and the "editorial troglodytes" of *The Times*. Working until 4 o'clock in the morning and, then, having to walk and talk business on Hampstead Heath with "The Chief", he was tested to the limit of his physical and emotional resilience. Northcliffe's decline into madness gave him some hectic moments. He was most active in the negotiations that led to the controlling interest in *The Times* going, after Northcliffe's death in 1922, to Major Astor. For many years he remained one of the most active members of the board of *The Times*.

In 1924 he was responsible for the foundation in France of the Canadian Historical Society. Characteristically he contrived to get it launched at the Palace of Versailles where, by consent of the French Government, he invited the living representatives of the English and French families which had played a leading part in Canadian history to a lunch, attended by members of the French and Canadian Governments, in the Galerie des Batailles.

The Pilgrims owed him much. He was on the committee for 40 years and resigned the chairmanship in 1958 after serving for 10 years. He was a moving spirit in the planning and erection of the Roosevelt Memorial in Grosvenor Square. Stuart performed many services for his native Dominion. He represented the Government of Canada at the Imperial Wireless Cables Conference in 1928, and in 1933 was elected chairman of the Imperial Communications Advisory Committee. He was chairman of the Beit Foundation for Scientific Research, the Wolfe Memorial Committee at Greenwich, the Quebec House Committee at Westerham and the Hudson's Bay Record Society. He was treasurer of King George's Jubilee Trust and Fields Foundation. In 1938 he received the honorary degree of Doctor of Laws of the College of William and Mary in Virginia, of which, when a colony, his ancestor, Robert Dinwiddie, had been Lieutenant Governor. In 1939 he was created a Knight Grand Cross of the Order of St. Michael and St. George.

Chairman of the Advisory Committee on the Ministry of Information in 1939, he became, on the outbreak of war, Director of Propaganda in Enemy Countries, throwing himself with typical energy into a task that called for much improvisation. He recruited at home and in France a staff that included Ray Shaw of *The Times* as his Deputy, Sir Dallas Brooks*, then a major of Royal Marines, Noël Coward and others, some of whom later rose high in the war-time services. He relinquished the post in 1940.

He wrote his biography *Opportunity Knocks Once* in 1952, and in *Secrets of Crewe House* gave the official record of enemy propaganda in the 1914-18 war.

September 15, 1972.

Kay Summersby—See Morgan.

Lady Swanborough—See Reading (Stella, Dowager Marchioness of Reading).

King Gustaf VI Adolf of Sweden, who died at Helsinborg on September 15, 1973 at the age of 90, was held in the warmest affection by his people. Their great concern for him was shown strikingly in his last days, when large numbers of well-wishers kept a vigil as he lay gravely ill in hospital, and the whole country anxiously followed reports of his progress. Although the position of the monarchy had been revised for the new constitution due to take effect in 1975, King Gustaf's place in the hearts of the Swedish public was never in doubt. Gustaf himself was expressly excluded from the new constitution's provisions.

Gustaf was 68 before he succeeded his father after 43 years as Crown Prince. The intellectual gifts of the Bernadottes, allied with a strong sense of duty and a taste for simple life, perfectly accommodated him to the development of a people's monarchy which had been less welcome to his more sternly spirited father.

He was also a good friend to Britain, making both his marriages in England, visiting London regularly, and tempering Swedish neutrality in the allied interest during the Second World War, when he was still Crown Prince.

As a scholar he achieved enough eminence as an archaeologist to justify by itself the many honorary degrees and fellowships of learned societies awarded him in many countries.

As a connoisseur of Far Eastern art he became one of the leading authorities in Europe. One of his favourite distinctions, attained in 1926, was that he was the first person to hold the famous Keishu Crown, discovered in a dig of a seventh-century grave excavated in Korea to mark his stay, and the only westerner ever to enter Peking, the "Forbidden City", by the Wu Men Gate.

He was born on November 11, 1882, the first of the Bernadotte line to trace descent from the ancient Vasa dynasty. His mother, born Princess Victoria of Baden, was the great-grand-daughter of Gustav IV, deposed in 1809.

Gustaf was educated at a state school and the universities of Oslo and Uppsala, and had a formal training in the Guards, although differing from his father in having little interest in military matters.

He became Crown Prince when his father succeeded in 1907, and during the 1914-18 War served as a staff officer. The easy days of the twenties allowed him to indulge his taste for archaeology—he sponsored and took an active part in Swedish expeditions to Greece and Cyprus—and to lead popular movements of an uncontroversial kind suitable for a future king who was to reign but not to rule.

He held office in a number of cultural organizations, some of which he initiated, and was a leader of the open-air movement. Although not a notable athlete himself, he shared the family vigour and approved the social effects of sport and country pursuits: gardening and fishing were lifelong interests. He was a mildly ascetic man who neither smoked nor drank, and was always accessible, whether to lend a hand with mounting an exhibition, or hear the views of a rank-and-file member of the athletic association with a grievance.

At the same time he followed the detail of public affairs and industrial and social change. His father in his later years became a venerable figure whose early brushes with the politicians had long been forgotten when he died at 91 in 1950. The Crown Prince's diligence and amiability had made him a highly popular figure by the time he succeeded.

It was characteristic of his sense of appropriate tradition that he should revive the medieval custom of the *Eriksgatan*, the King's progress through his provinces. It took him four years. He exercised in turn local functions from mayor or chairman of local councils to inspector of schools, inexhaustibly questioning and mixing with his temporary colleagues on their own level. He dealt with his own correspondence and became affectionately known as the king who tipped his hat.

Education is highly esteemed in Sweden, which was an important reason why the King was so admired. His intellect regularly awed certain of the Social Democratic ministers who served him over the years.

The Socialists were never able to raise seriously the question of proclaiming a republic. When the issue was once discussed, the King was reported to have said: "All forms of government have their advantages and disadvantages. But you are not likely to get one that costs less than a monarchy."

In a conversation with Bernard Berenson, the art historian, Berenson said: "I don't envy your Majesty. Kingship is a hereditary form of slavery." The King replied: "Don't say that. You have no idea how interesting this post, such as it is, can be; and how much it enables me to do about things I think are essential, right and interesting."

"This post such as it is" carried a few residual powers which are being abolished when the new Swedish constitution goes into effect on January 1, 1975: it essentially reduces the monarch to a ceremonial figurehead, although Parliament provided that the change would not have taken place during King Gustaf Adolf's lifetime.

The new constitution states that the King's formal assent is no longer required for formal government decisions. His presence would be optional at the opening of Parliament each year; and the Speaker of Parliament, and not the King would designate the man to form the Government.

The Swedish monarch would retain immunity from civil prosecution. But the reforms end the "King-in-Council" procedure in which he presides over weekly cabinet meetings. During the King's lifetime his advice and counsel were often very much sought on those occasions.

His ties with Britain began with his first marriage, in 1905 at Windsor, to Princess Margaret of Connaught, daughter of the Duke of Connaught, third son of Queen Victoria. They had five children, including Queen Ingrid of Denmark. His eldest son was killed in an air accident in 1947, and his grandson, Prince Carl Gustav, born a year earlier, now succeeds to the kingship.

Princess Margaret died in 1920, and in 1923 the Crown Prince married in London Lady Louise Mountbatten, younger daughter of the first Marquess of Milford Haven and a sister of Lord Mountbatten. She died in 1965.

The King was almost an annual visitor to Britain thereafter. He held honorary degrees of Oxford, Cambridge, Leeds and London (as well as Princeton, Harvard and Yale), and was an F.R.S. and one of three honorary F.B.A.s. He was created K.G. by the Queen during his state visit to London in 1954.

September 17, 1973.

Lord Swinton, P.C., G.B.E., C.H., M.C., the first Earl, who was a prominent figure in political life for nearly 40 years, died at his home in Masham on July 27, 1972 at the age of 88. His record of public service was outstanding.

Swinton entered the House of Commons in 1918 and within four years Bonar Law made him a member of the Cabinet, at the age of 38. Thirty years later, when he was past 70, he was serving as Secretary of State for Commonwealth Relations in Sir Winston Churchill's* last Government. In the years between he held office as President of the Board of Trade in four Governments, was Secretary of State for the Colonies, Secretary of State for Air, Minister Resident in West Africa, the first Minister of Civil Aviation, Chancellor of the Duchy of Lancaster and Minister of Materials. From 1951 to 1955 he was also Deputy Leader of the House of Lords.

In several of the offices that he held Swinton did notable work in stimulating and expanding both Commonwealth trade relations and the trade of the Colonial Empire. Within a year of swift advancement to Cabinet rank he presided over the Imperial Economic Conference of 1923—the first of its kind ever held—which brought agreement on an extension of the system of reciprocal tariff preferences.

In 1925, during his second term of office as President of the Board of Trade, Swinton turned his attention to the condition of the struggling British film industry, then fighting a losing battle against the imported products of Hollywood. Having ascertained that the Commonwealth Governments also attached great importance to the maintenance of a thriving British film industry, he introduced in 1927 the legislation which established a compulsory quota in cinemas for British films and helped the industry in other ways to get back on its feet.

But what must be regarded as Swinton's main achievement was in the office of State for Air in the critical years from 1935 to 1938. During that period, with ominous events casting their shadow before, he applied his immense enthusiasm and driving power to the expansion and reequipment of the Royal Air Force. With the growing threat from Hitler's Germany much of what Swinton accomplished in these years was veiled from public knowledge at the time. In 1935 the former Sir Philip Cunliffe-Lister became Viscount Swinton and it was as a Minister in the House of Lords that he set about his new task, at the request of Baldwin.

Starting from slender foundations, Swinton managed to bring about a threefold expansion of the R.A.F. in as many years. This involved not only a big increase in the number of squadrons—with total manpower stepped up from 29,000 to 90,000—but also the expansion of the aircraft industry, the building and equipment of "shadow" factories, the ordering of new and unproved types of aircraft direct from the drawing board because there was no

time for the testing of prototypes, and the provision of new airfields, both at home and overseas. From the first Swinton insisted that the highest standards of quality must be maintained, both in men and machines.

Robert Rhodes James, writing in *The Times* in 1967 on the centenary of Baldwin's birth, recalled that Baldwin put his full authority behind Swinton's heroic decision to order the Spitfire and Hurricane fighters straight off the drawing board.

It was Swinton, too, who brought in Sir Robert Watson-Watt, then a young scientist working with the Department of Scientific and Industrial Research, to develop the revolutionary new techniques of radar.

One other thing that Swinton did at this time was characteristic of his intuition. Churchill was still in the political wilderness, his warnings of the gathering storm all too little heeded. But Swinton thought it would be valuable to have a man of Churchill's experience and imaginative genius as a member of the Committee on Air Defence Research, set up in 1935 as a subcommittee of the Committee of Imperial Defence. Chamberlain agreed to this and Churchill accepted—although nothing was known of his association with the Government at the time. Churchill took part in the secret work of this committee for four years and contributed some stimulating ideas to the work on air defence research. This surreptitious harnessing of his services also proved of great value to Churchill.

In spite of his hard work under inhibiting conditions Swinton's position was prejudiced by the fact that he sat in the Lords and was not able to reply to critics of the pace of air rearmament face to face in the Commons. After a stormy debate in May 1938 Chamberlain decided that his Air Minister must be in the Commons and Swinton had to go.

Philip Swinton was a hard-headed Yorkshire squire—and a Wykehamist—who had been trained as a lawyer and was a very shrewd man of affairs. His appearance and manner were deceptive and the unwary were apt at first sight to regard him as something akin to the Frenchman's conventional image of a dilettante English "milord". Anybody who fell into this error was quickly disabused on closer acquaintance. He was a man of tough fibre who did not suffer fools gladly. He detested stuffiness and red tape and his vigorous personality blew strong gusts of fresh air through many Government departments and offices.

Philip Cunliffe-Lister was born on May 1, 1884, the youngest son of Lieutenant-Colonel Yarburgh G. Lloyd-Greame, of Sewerby House, Bridlington. In 1924 he and his wife assumed by Royal Warrant the name of Cunliffe-Lister under the will of Lady Cunliffe-Lister's aunt, who was a daughter of Samuel Cunliffe-Lister, first Lord Masham of Swinton, a great York-

shire captain of industry. He went to Winchester in 1897 and afterwards to University College, Oxford. In 1908 he was called to the Bar and four years later he married Mary Constance, daughter of the Rev. Ingram Boynton, rector of Barmston, Driffield. During the 1914-18 War he served with the King's Royal Rifle Corps, attained the rank of major and won the Military Cross.

Towards the end of the war Swinton was chosen by Auckland Geddes, the Minister of National Service—on whose staff he had been previously serving as a junior officer at the War Office—to be Joint Secretary to the Ministry.

After the war Swinton went into politics and in December 1918 he was elected Conservative M.P. for Hendon. He represented this constituency continuously until he received his peerage in 1935. His first Government office was as Parliamentary Secretary to the Board of Trade, in 1921, and he served there first under Sir Robert Horne and afterwards under Baldwin.

In 1922 he was appointed Secretary of the Department of Overseas Trade and accompanied Lloyd George to the ill-starred Genoa Conference, where he took part in the economic negotiations with Russia and Germany. He and Lord Kennet later led the British delegation to the subsequent conference at The Hague. After the downfall of Lloyd George's Coalition Government Swinton became President of the Board of Trade in the Conservative Government formed by Bonar Law in 1922. He retained this post under Baldwin's two succeeding Governments and again in the National Government of 1931, until he was appointed Colonial Secretary.

During his four years in office he brought in businessmen as advisers, advanced young men to posts of authority, started an immediate economic survey of the Colonies, established a system of entry to the Colonial Service by selection and required all new entrants to the Colonial Office to be prepared to serve overseas as well as at home. He also insisted that there should be more business done by direct contacts and less writing of voluminous minutes. "I ribaldly suggested", he wrote, " a motto to hang in every room: 'Bumph breeds bumph'." He gave a strong stimulus to economic development in the Colonies, and at the Ottawa Conference of 1932—at which the Colonial Empire was represented by him for the first time as a whole—tariff preferences hitherto given by some Commonwealth countries to some Colonies on a bilateral basis were replaced by preferences for Colonial products "across the board".

In the early part of the Second World War Swinton reentered Government service as chairman of what was known as the United Kingdom Commercial Corporation, the agency which was the executive arm of the Ministry of Economic Warfare in the preemptive purchasing in neutral countries if supplies and materials which were also being urgently sought after by the enemy for purposes of war production.

The doings of the U.K.C.C., which included the substantial denial of imports of wolfram and chrome to Germany from the neutrals, and the organization of non-military supplies to Russia by lorry convoys from the Persian Gulf, were in themselves an important chapter in the history of the war.

At Churchill's invitation in 1940 Swinton also became chairman of the Security Executive, which was concerned with security measures both in Britain and at many places overseas where British ships or supplies were liable to sabotage.

Then, in June 1942, he accepted Churchill's invitation to become Minister Resident in West Africa, where he remained for more than two years. With the Mediterranean closed to British shipping, and North Africa a vital theatre of war, Swinton's new post was one of high importance. His official terms of reference required him "to ensure the effective cooperation in the prosecution of the war of all Services, civil and military, throughout the British Colonies in West Africa". This was a political and administrative task after Swinton's own heart and from his base at Accra he inspired and organized the mobilization of West Africa's war effort in a way that won him high praise.

In October 1944 he was called back by Churchill from West Africa to become the first Minister of Civil Aviation. He was busily engaged in planning for the development of Britain's civil aviation after the war when the Conservatives were defeated at the general election of 1945. This gave him an interval in which to write some of his reminiscences. When Sir Winston Churchill next formed a Conservative Government in 1951 Lord Swinton was pressed into service again as Chancellor of the Duchy of Lancaster and Minister of Materials. In the following year he became Secretary of State for Commonwealth Relations. This was very much to his liking and he increased his already considerable knowledge of Commonwealth countries by further travels.

The elder of Lord Swinton's two sons, John Cunliffe-Lister, died of wounds during the fighting in North Africa. His younger son died in 1956. The family honours now pass to Lord Swinton's grandson, David Yarburgh Cunliffe-Lister, Lord Masham, who was born in 1937.

July 29, 1972.

Admiral Sir Neville Syfret, G.C.B., K.B.E., died on December 10, 1972 at the age of 83.

He had a distinguished record in the Second World War, particularly in command of forces in the Mediterranean. He fought through two important convoys to Malta and conducted other operations in which the fortress was reinforced by air-craft flown from carriers.

He also commanded the naval force which covered the first landings in Madagascar, forestalling the Japanese at this vital base in the Indian Ocean. For the last two years of war he was Vice-Chief of the Naval Staff, taking a prominent part in the direction of operations, particularly during the absence of the First Sea Lord at the various international conferences.

Edward Neville Syfret was born on June 20, 1889, the son of E. R. Syfret, of Cape Town, where he received his early education at the Diocesan College. He entered the Britannia as a naval cadet in 1904, and became a chief cadet captain. During the First World War he was gunnery officer of the cruisers Aurora, Centaur and Curacoa, all of which were for a time flagships of Admiral Sir Reginald Tyrwhitt in the Harwich Force.

In the Second World War he commanded the Rodney in the Home Fleet until November, 1939, when he became Naval Secretary to the First Lord (Winston Churchill*). Promoted to flag rank in 1940, he remained as Naval Secretary with A. V. Alexander* until June 1941, when he was given command of a cruiser squadron in the Home Fleet. In January 1942 he succeeded Vice-Admiral Sir James Somerville in command of Force H at Gibraltar, and during the next 18 months conducted a series of important operations with distinction.

He commanded the naval forces which were present at the capture of Diego Suarez, Madagascar, in the spring of 1942, and in August of that year, "for bravery and dauntless resolution in fighting an important convoy through to Malta in the face of relentless attacks by day and night from enemy submarines, aircraft and surface forces", he was promoted to K.C.B. (having been made a C.B. for a similar Malta convoy operation with a force detached from the Home Fleet in 1941).

At the landings in North Africa in November 1942, he commanded Force H in the Central Mediterranean, providing cover against interference from the Italian battle fleet.

In 1943, Syfret was promoted to vice-admiral and appointed Vice-Chief of the Naval Staff, and held this post until after the end of the war.

From 1945 to 1948, he was Commander-in-Chief of the Home Fleet, at a most difficult period of transition from war to peace routine, a large part of his force having to be immobilized for various lengths of time so that trained men might relieve others due for return from foreign service. The manner in which he maintained the morale and efficiency of his command in such circumstances was of great service to Britain.

He married in 1913 Hildegarde Warner, and had one son and one daughter.

December 11, 1972.

Joseph Szigeti, the Hungarian violinist, died on February 19, 1973 at the age of 80 at Lucerne, Switzerland.

He was for many years an important figure in European music.

He was recognized as a virtuoso who subordinated virtuosity to truthfulness of utterance and accuracy of style, a musician whose interests extended from Bach to Bartók and comprehended, among other things, music by Elgar which he transcribed for the violin. The singular purity of his tone and honesty of his style were always impressive.

As a classical player his performance of the unaccompanied violin music of Bach was justly and enthusiastically admired. He was an enthusiastic advocate of much modern music, responsible for the first performance of the violin concertos of Busoni, Casella and Hamilton Harty and included in his repertoire works by Prokofiev, Bloch, Bartók and Stravinsky.

Szigeti was born in Budapest on September 5, 1892. He was a pupil of Jenö Hubay and began his public career at the age of 13.

The Budapest High School for Music gave him an honorary degree, and as an adult his travels in Europe seemed to be interrupted only by tours of America and the Far East. There was never anything in his manner to draw attention to the brilliance of his technique; he was always a player who, by avoiding showmanship, made virtuosity seem easy, so that the brilliance was in the music, not superimposed upon it, and brilliance disappeared into the remarkable authenticity of his interpretations.

His style of playing, even in works like Stravinsky and Bartók concertos and Bartók's Rhapsodies for Violin and Orchestra, seemed always old-fashioned. His stance was rigid and his right arm kept close to his side in a way which seemed to deny his bow freedom of movement. But this undemonstrative and apparently limiting manner seemed to give power and lucidity to his playing of ferociously difficult chordal passages in unaccompanied Bach. The "white" purity of his tone was not designed simply to allure; the listener quickly discovered that its purpose was to convey the composer's thought, whatever the period or style of his music, with singular qualties of conviction, honesty and understanding.

A master of the now all-but-forgotten art of transcription, Szigeti translated music of all sorts into the language of the violin. As well as Elgar's Serenade for Strings and movements from Warlock's *Capriol* Suite and music by Rameau, Bach and Weber, obviously transcribed for no other reason than the pleasure they gave him, Szigeti translated a number of exacting explorations of piano technique into equally exacting violin studies.

February 21, 1973.

T

Wasfi Tal, Prime Minister of Jordan and the most prominent political figure of recent years in that country, was assassinated in Cairo on November 28, 1971. He was 51.

He became Prime Minister for the first time in 1962, a post he held for a year. He was Prime Minister again between 1965 and 1967 and took up the post once more in 1970.

He was noted for his tough line against the Palestinian guerrillas operating in his country. Tal was at the centre of a storm between Jordan and Egypt in 1970 when King Husain insisted on taking Tal with him on a visit to Cairo. Egypt expressed reservations and Husain cancelled the visit.

Tal was known for his toughness and was popular with the Jordanian armed forces. But he gained the enmity of the Palestinians because of his firm stand on the Arab Commando problem after he formed his last government.

Born in 1920 in Irbid he was educated at the American University of Beirut and also entered the teaching profession, but later enlisted in the British army and became liaison officer in London. From 1945 to 1948 he was employed in the Arab Office which was established in London by Musa Alami to make known the Arab case on Palestine. After the partition of Palestine he returned to Jordan and in 1951 married the daughter of Ihsan Jabri, a well-known Syrian statesman whose influence played an important part in his later career.

After serving in a number of minor administrative posts, he was in 1955 put in charge of the Jordan Government's Press Bureau, where he came out strongly in favour of Jordan joining the Baghdad Pact. Left-wing opposition to this step, fanned by President Nasser* of Egypt, brought about the fall of the Jordan Government and its replacement by one with whose views Wasfi Tal found himself in disagreement. As a result he was sent abroad as counsellor in the Jordan Embassy in Bonn, where he remained for the next two years.

In 1957, after a further change of government, he returned to Amman as Director of Ceremonies in the Palace. In 1959, after a short spell as counsellor in Tehran, he was appointed Director-General of the Hashemite broadcasting station, the official Jordan radio. In this capacity he adopted a generally pro-western and anti-Nasser attitude, which reflected his close friendship with the then Prime Minister, Hazza Majali. His anti-Nasser views commended themselves to King Husain, in whose confidence he clearly was after the Prime Minister had been assassinated; but, later, differences arose with the palace staff which resulted in his being sent abroad again, this time as ambassador to Iraq.

Early in 1962, to the general surprise, King Husain recalled him and charged him with the formation of a government which would be a complete change from its somewhat ineffective predecessor. He failed to induce any of the regular politicians to cooperate with him, so formed his Cabinet entirely of under-secretaries and other officials. He succeeded in inspiring this new team with commendable energy, especially in the domain of economic development, and during his period of office the internal state of the country showed marked improvement. He was, however, less successful in foreign affairs, where he was generally judged to lack subtlety and foresight; in particular he was responsible for King Husain's open support for the Royalist cause in the civil war in the Yemen, which by bringing him into direct opposition with President Nasser (who was supporting the Republicans) had the effect of increasing Jordan's isolation in the Arab world without any compensating gain. In 1963 criticism rose to the point where the King found it expedient to part with him.

It was, however, noticeable that his absence coincided with a deterioration in administrative activity and effectiveness, and in 1965 the King, who by that time had improved his relations with Nasser, felt able to send for Wasfi Tal again. The Cabinet which he formed was to last, with one or two reshuffles, for two years; the tempo of economic activity at once quickened, and that autumn the Prime Minister felt sufficiently confident of the future to launch the slogan of "Viability by 1970", an admittedly ambitious target, but one which would have been unthinkable a few years previously.

In November 1966 the King and his Prime Minister faced a stern test, when an Israeli "punitive expedition" destroyed a village in South Jordan for having allegedly harboured saboteurs, and the Prime Minister was somewhat unfairly blamed for the inability of the Jordan army to intercept the raiders; for the chronic dissatisfaction of the ex-Palestinians at what they regarded as the Jordan Government's "appeasement" of Israel, fomented by broadcasts from Cairo, flared up into dangerous riots in all the West Bank towns. Wasfi Tal, however, kept his head and received full backing from the King, so that the situation was gradually brought under control.

He was, above all, a man of action, expressing himself in curt phrases occasionally flavoured with sardonic wit. His rivals described him as opportunist and unreliable, and he was certainly apt to take impulsive decisions and ready to profit from any circumstance which could be turned to his advantage. But he served his King faithfully, and in doing so displayed a degree of energy and resolution which matched his master's.

November 29, 1971.

Talal ibn Abdullah—See Jordan.

Constance Talmadge, the younger of the two famous film star sisters and—as events proved—the wiser, died on November 23, 1973 in California at the age of 73.

She was wiser because, unlike Norma Talmadge, she foresaw the pitfalls when the era of talking pictures began and decided to retire. Norma, who was three years her senior, continued in talking pictures for a time, and a Hollywood legend relates that when Norma made her début in sound pictures in *New York Nights* in 1930, Constance sent her a wire which read: "Leave them while you're looking good and thank God for the trust funds Momma set up".

There were in fact three acting Talmadge sisters, the third being Natalie, but her career was not long. Their parents lived in Brooklyn, New York City, and it was here that Constance was born on April 19, 1900. She grew up and was educated in Brooklyn, and followed the path of Norma by joining the Vitagraph Company as a small part player when she was 14. Her career was given its initial impetus, as was that of so many other players of the day, by the work of D. W. Griffith, the father of the American film.

Griffith is remembered as a great star-maker, but in fact his strength lay in making brilliant and imaginative pictures which carried their leading players forward to an inevitable popularity with the rapidly increasing film public. C. A. Lejeune, writing of Griffith in 1931, noted that "he did give a shop-window display to the caprices of the young Constance Talmadge"; but the strength of the two sisters lay in the fact that they could play comedy as well as romance, and Constance was the better comedienne of the two.

Both sisters had become film stars before they left their teens, but a turning point in their careers was reached in 1919, when First National, who already had Charlie Chaplin and Mary Pickford under contract, added Norma and Constance Talmadge to their team. Constance made her initial appearance for First National in *A Temperamental Wife*. Both sisters made a large number of films for First National during the 1920s.

Nevertheless another important change occurred in their lives when, towards the end of the decade, they each transferred their allegiance to the powerful United Artists Corporation, following the lead of Joseph M. Schenck*, who had been their producer for a number of years, and who was himself a great maker of film stars. Norma had married Schenck, whom she later divorced.

Norma made several films for United Artists, but Constance retired from the screen soon after she had made *Venus* for them in 1929, with André Roanne, Jean Murat and Max Maxudian—names already long since forgotten. Her retirement was due to the advent of sound, and not to any failure to keep abreast of the times, for she had taken to playing the sophisticated "vamp" type of woman-of-the-world. The young Joan Crawford was soon to establish this kind of role as a part of the American scene.

November 27, 1973.

Dr. Igor Yegenyevich Tamm, one of the fathers of Russia's hydrogen bomb, died on April 12, 1971 at the age of 75, *Izvestia* reported.

All announced Soviet work on controlling the energy of the hydrogen bomb is based on the idea of the "pinch effect" which Tamm advanced in 1950. The idea was developed independently elsewhere as well.

In October 1958 Tamm was one of three Soviet scientists awarded the Nobel Prize in Physics. It was the first time this award was won by Soviet citizens. The prize honoured Tamm's work in helping explain the so-called Cerenkov effect in nuclear physics. This effect, which was first described by Cerenkov in 1934, is concerned with the emission of light waves by electrons moving at very high speeds and is of great importance for the study of nuclear physics.

Tamm, a professor at Moscow University, and his co-worker Frank, provided a theoretical explanation of the Cerenkov effect in 1937.

He was to become one of the best-known Soviet physicists and a member of the Academy of Sciences of the U.S.S.R.

In 1946 Tamm shared the Stalin Prize with Cerenkov and Frank for their joint work on electron radiation. He worked on the quantum theory of diffused light in solid bodies, on the photo-effect on metals, and on methods for the control of thermonuclear reactions. His technique of interpreting the interaction of elementary nuclear particles is known as the Tamm method.

Tamm was a candid and courageous scientist who spoke out about irresponsible Soviet boasting about doubtful scientific theories.

He was in effect the leader of a partly successful revolt against the dictatorial control of the Soviet Academy of Sciences in 1956; he attacked the bureaucracy which, he claimed, permeated many aspects of the academy's work.

Many of Tamm's major scientific works have been published in English or German rather than in Russian. His fame has been based on his ability to combine quantum mechanics with Einstein's relativity theory, though this theory was for many years discounted in the Soviet Union for its anti-Marxist "idealistic" nature.

Born in 1895, Tamm was able before the Bolshevik Revolution to get a first-class education at Moscow University, to which he returned as a teacher from 1924 to 1941 and again in 1954 to 1957. He became a professor in 1930 and a full member of the Academy of Sciences in 1953. He was not a member of the Communist Party.

April 14, 1971.

Alma Taylor, who died in late January 1974, was one of the best-known stars of the British silent cinema. In 1915 she headed a *Pictures and Picturegoer* poll in which Charles Chaplin, still a newcomer to films, was placed third; and nine years later she still topped a newspaper poll of favourite British stars, alongside Betty Balfour.

She was born in London on January 3, 1895 and made her first appearance in films for the pioneer British producer Cecil Hepworth in 1907. Hepworth soon teamed her with Chrissie White in a series of comedies about two tomboys, the Tilly Girls; and she quickly became and remained one of the stars of the company. Her forte was sentimental comedy, and her biggest successes were perhaps two films she made in 1916, *Annie Laurie* and *Coming Thro' the Rye,* both with Stewart Rome.

Earlier she had played in Thomas Bentley's creative film adaptation of *David Copperfield* (1913), *Oliver Twist* (1913) and *The Old Curiosity Shop* (1914). She appeared with Albert Chevalier in a film version of the favourite old moral melodrama *The Bottle* in 1915.

Hepworth was something of a technical innovator; and in 1920 Miss Taylor, aided by some ingenious double exposure photography, played a dual role in *Anna the Adventuress,* a year before Mary Pickford was to achieve the same feat in *Little Lord Fauntleroy.*

In the same year Alma appeared opposite Leslie Henson in a film version of W. A. Darlington's *Alf's Button*; and it was largely due to the huge popular success of that film that Darlington subsequently adapted his novel to the stage, in 1924.

Her career did not really outlast the silent period; although she made a couple of talking pictures, *Bachelor's Baby* (1932) and *Everybody Dance* (1936), which starred Cicely Courtneidge. In 1935 she was one of the first British film stars to act for television.

An actress of delicacy and restraint, she never used makeup on the screen. Hepworth, who directed practically all her career (and never paid her more than £60 a week) said that when she cried on the screen, her tears were invariably real.

January 28, 1974.

Elizabeth Taylor, the novelist and short story writer, died on November 19, 1975 at the age of 63.

A writer of considerable elegance, she produced 17 novels and collections of short stories.

Many of these works showed considerable perception of the foibles of middle class life of a certain kind and if the comparison, often voiced, with Jane Austen, was never a great help to an objective consideration of Mrs. Taylor, yet her writing—at its best in the short stories—puts her achievement distinctively above that of midcult success.

Elizabeth Taylor was born Elizabeth Coles, the daughter of Oliver and Elsie Coles, in 1912. She was educated at the Abbey School, Reading, and began writing, somewhat secretively, there and at home. Her apprenticeship to writing novels was to be a long one before anything saw the light of day.

She worked as a governess; married, in 1936, Mr. John William Kendall Taylor, a manufacturer of confectionery; but still continued working away at the craft of writing until in 1946 her first novel, *At Mrs. Lippincote's,* was published.

Its unassuming but subtle wit and veiled, reticent conversations were to be the hallmark of a stream of books all dealing with life as she observed it from her Penn, Buckinghamshire, home.

Palladian followed in 1947 and thereafter she produced a novel roughly every two years, including *A Wreath of Roses* (1950), her best seller though to be surpassed in quality by later books: *The Sleeping Beauty* (1953); *In a Summer Season* (1961), one of her best with its exploration of boredom and hurt lying underneath wellbred exteriors; *The Wedding Group* (1968) and *Mrs. Palfrey at the Claremont* (1972), a study of the pathos of lonely old age. The last was dramatized for television, with Celia Johnson giving a noted performance in the title role.

In the novel form this most restful of writers never perhaps gave full enough play to her undoubted perception of human character, always stronger on her astutely observed women than in creating men. Her wit and penetration were seldom in doubt but the true asperities of modern life seemed to elude her.

The short stories encouraged claims of a different kind. The short form was her metier. In it her "warm heart, sharp claws and exceptional powers of formal balance", as Angus Wilson styled them, were given their best scope. The three collections *Hester Lilly* (1954), *The Blush* (1958) and *The Devastating Boys* (1972) showed greater control as well as the ability to catch poignant flashes of human experience and still them under her microscopic eye.

These, as did many of her novels, had a considerable following in the United States—one, *The Dedicated Man,* became a television play there—and *The New Yorker,* which published over 20, played its part in fostering her transatlantic reputation.

She is survived by her husband and two children.

November 21, 1975.

Sir Geoffrey (Ingram) Taylor, O.M., F.R.S., who died on June 27, 1975 at the age of 89, was one of the most notable scientists of this century. Over a period of more than 50 years he produced a steady stream of contributions of the highest originality and importance to the mechanics of fluids and solids and to their application in meteorology, aeronautics, and many branches of engineering. He occupied a leading place in applied mathematics, in classical physics, and in engineering science, and was equally at home with the methods and attitudes of these three disciplines.

By a combination of penetrating insight, deceptively simple mathematical analysis, and correspondingly ingenious experiments, he was able to illuminate a large number of phenomena of different kinds. Many of his scientific contributions opened up whole new fields; he had the knack of being first. He was the personification of the peculiarly British tradition of applied mathematics, and carried forward the type of thought represented by Newton, Maxwell, Stokes and Rayleigh.

Profoundly original scientific thought came easily to him, and his character was entirely free from strain, artificiality or vanity.

He was born in London on March 7, 1886, to a family in which genius had already appeared. His mother Margaret was the second daughter of George Boole, one of the pioneers of mathematical logic whose third daughter Alice also had remarkable mathematical ability but no formal training. His father was an artist. At University College School Taylor had already been attracted to mathematics and science; and later at Cambridge, where he began a life-long association with Trinity College, he took first the Mathematical Tripos Part I and next the Natural Sciences Tripos Part II.

Embarking on research, he made his mark immediately by two successful pieces of work, one an experiment undertaken at J. J. Thomson's suggestion to test the new quantum theory, and the other a mathematical determination of the thickness of a shock wave. In 1910 he was elected into a Prize Fellowship at Trinity. A year later he was appointed Reader in Dynamical Meteorology at Cambridge, which was a temporary office founded to encourage the study of meteorology. Taylor's newly aroused interest in atmospheric motions was retained for many years and led to several important advances, including his pioneering work on turbulence.

In 1913 he acted as meteorologist on the ship Scotia sent to initiate an ice patrol in the North Atlantic, following the sinking of the Titanic; and in his spare time he flew kites from the mast head in order to get measurements of pressure, humidity and temperature at various heights above the sea surface, on which he based new theories about the vertical transfer of heat and water vapour by turbulent mixing of the air.

Soon after the outbreak of war in 1914 Taylor and a number of other Cambridge men joined the Royal Aircraft Factory at Farnborough to assist in experimental work in aeronautics. Characteristically adding adventure to his intellectual pursuits, Taylor decided that he should learn to fly as a part of this new work, and to parachute also, and did so. Aeronautics became another field of science in which he was to remain interested and to which he continued to make fundamental contributions.

After the war he returned to Trinity College as a lecturer in mathematics, and became a close friend of Rutherford. Rutherford gave him facilities for work in the Cavendish Laboratory, in a room alongside his own. This happy association with the Cavendish Laboratory and Taylor's appointment in 1923 to a Yarrow Research Professorship, newly-established by the Royal Society, opened up a tremendously productive phase of his research life which was to last until 1939.

In that period he made his most substantial and significant contributions to continuum mechanics, two of which stand out for comment. While at Farnborough he had been concerned with calculations of the strength of aircraft spars, and this led him later to think about the mechanism of plastic deformation of metals under load. A series of papers led him in 1934 to the idea that plastic strain of a metal crystal occurs by the sliding of one plane of atoms over another, over a finite area of the slip-plane which is bounded by an irregularity, or "dislocation", in the arrangement of the atoms. The concept of a dislocation and the related theory of strain hardening have provided the basis of much of the subsequent research in metal physics.

The other of the two major advances concerned the turbulent motion of fluids. As early as 1921 he had realized that analysis of the eddying and irregular motion of a fluid involved the statistics of continuous functions, and that the current representation of the fluid as a collection of discrete lumps was not adequate. But he was far ahead of his contemporaries, and it was not until after he had consolidated and extended his statistical description of turbulence in a series of papers published between 1935 and 1938 that the full significance of his work was appreciated. Both these major advances opened up new fields of work which were taken up by many scientists, and this was Taylor's cue to move on to other problems; he preferred always the simple mathematics and experiments that are appropriate for initial discoveries.

During the Second World War his services were much in demand by government committees, and he worked on a wide variety of defence problems, including underwater explosions and their effects on structures, dispersal of fog from aeroplane runways by lines of burners, the fragmentation of bomb casings, the ranges of large rockets, shaped charges for piercing armour plating, spherically expanding blast waves due to release of a large amount of energy (an atomic bomb), and a host of others.

In the closing phase of his scientific life, from 1945 onwards, he continued, with undiminished zest and enjoyment, to devise beautiful investigations of whatever new phenomena took his fancy. He retired from his research professorship in 1952, although the Royal Society continued to support him and there was no change whatever in his mode of life. His research in this phase followed no strategic plan, and to others he seemed sometimes to be equally interested in the trivial and the profound; but anything he touched turned to scientific gold and no longer looked trivial.

He studied the method of swimming of very small creatures such as spermatazoa, the movement of large gas bubbles through water, thin sheets of liquid in air, the hydrodynamics of paper-making machines, a novel form of cavitation bubble in viscous liquids, and many other by-ways of fluid dynamics. All these problems were relatively untouched; they could be studied by experiments performed on a small table and by mathematics covering one or two sheets of paper, and he saw that they had potentialities.

Taylor wrote over 200 scientific papers, of uniformly high quality and value, which have been collected and republished by Cambridge University Press in four large volumes.

Taylor was honoured for his work by a host of universities and learned societies in many countries. He enjoyed being fêted, with the simple pleasure of one who never took it for granted that his work deserved recognition. He was appointed O.M. in 1969.

He was passionately fond of small boats and sailing from boyhood, and sailed with his wife in their 19-ton cutter to the Shetlands, to Norway and to the Lofoten Islands. The anchor of the boat was awkwardly heavy, so Taylor designed a new one with a blade like a ploughshare which buried itself to the right depth in the seabed when dragged along; the new anchor was subsequently used by the Admiralty, in particular for holding "Mulberry" harbours in position.

Travel always appealed to him, especially if it took him to strange places unknown to tourists and "unspoiled" by material development. With his wife he explored Borneo in 1929 after attending a Pacific Science Congress.

He was a keen and perceptive botanist, and took great pleasure in the familiar plants of his well-stocked garden in Cambridge and in what he saw elsewhere in England and abroad. All these pleasures made no demands on other people, and were shared with a few only.

In 1925 he married Stephanie Ravenhill and began a happy and life-long partnership. They had no children. His wife died in 1967.

June 30, 1975.

Herbert Wilfred Taylor, M.C., the great South African batsman, who died in that country on February 7, 1973, played 42 Test matches for South Africa in an era when there were fewer opportunities at international level than nowadays.

One of the best remembered performances in cricket history was Taylor's superlative batting against S. F. Barnes* during the 1913-14 series between South Africa and England. Until the advent in recent years of R. G. Pollock and Barry Richards, Taylor was widely acknowledged as the finest batsman produced by South Africa.

Taylor, captaining South Africa for the first time, scored 508 runs in the 1913-14 series won 4-0 by England, while his colleagues floundered, Barnes, virtually unplayable on the matting wickets, missed one match but still took 49 wickets in the rubber at 10.93 each. Taylor also obtained 91 and 100 for Natal that season when the province inflicted the only defeat of their tour on the M.C.C. side. Barnes on that occasion is reputed to have declined to bowl against Taylor towards the end of the match. "Taylor, Taylor, Taylor—always Taylor", he groaned, so the story goes.

Taylor also passed 500 runs against England in the 1922-23 series which was again played on matting. He never quite reached these standards on the less predictable turf wickets outside the Union, as it then was, but even with this reservation had no rivals among his contemporaries for style and effectiveness combined.

A strictly correct technique, allied to a quick eye for length and flexible footwork, were the fundamentals Taylor possessed. He used every stroke equally well but got closer than most people to the stumps when playing on the back foot. He is generally credited with having introduced forceful back play to South African cricket, the product of early coaching at school from George Cox senior, of Sussex, who used to winter regularly on the Veldt.

Taylor made the first of his three tours to England in 1912 and also visited Australia and New Zealand. He led South Africa in 18 successive Test matches which at that time was a record sequence. In all Test matches he scored 2,936 runs, average 40.77, scoring seven hundreds, six of them in South Africa. In his first-class career he scored 13,105 runs, average 41.87, with 30 centuries.

In the First World War Taylor served 18 months in the Royal Field Artillery and later two years in the Flying Corps, winning the Military Cross.

A gentle, pleasant man, Taylor invariably made a point of encouraging young players.

February 10, 1973.

Mrs. J. W. K. Taylor—See Elizabeth Taylor.

Ellaline Terriss (Lady Hicks), widow of Sir Seymour Hicks the comedy actor, died on June 16, 1971 at the age of 100. She was an actress of great freshness and sweetness.

Daughter of William Terriss, the famous hero in Adelphi melodrama, she shared with him and with her husband the secret of perpetual youth; and she acquired consummate skill without losing a breath of nature.

One of the half-dozen or more professions which William Terriss tried before he found his proper field—the stage—was that of sheep farmer in the Falkland Isles; and it was there, in the Ship Hotel, Stanley, that his daughter Ellaline was born on April 13, 1871. Her father taught her acting; and before she was quite 17 she had been engaged by Beerbohm Tree, to pass almost immediately into the company of Charles Wyndham at the Criterion Theatre in the days of *Two Roses, David Garrick* and *Betsy*. Four years later she went to the Court Theatre to act for Arthur Chudleigh in Pinero's *The Amazons*, among other plays. A turning-point came at Christmas 1893, when she played the title part in Oscar Barrett's pantomine *Cinderella*. Her success was so great that she had to cross the Atlantic and repeat it to America. She was marked out for the lyric stage; and in 1895 she was engaged by George Edwardes for the Gaiety, where she was seen in *The Shop Girl, My Girl, The Circus Girl, A Runaway Girl*. She was a performer whose skill and accomplishment were equal to her charm. It may have been easy to caricature her famous smile; it was very hard not to fall a victim to it.

After the Gaiety days, which for her ended with *A Runaway Girl*, there was a multitude of activities in comedy, lyric drama, fairy play, and the rest, chiefly under the managements of her husband and of Charles Frohman. No Alice in Wonderland had ever come so close to the Alice of Lewis Carroll and of Tenniel.

She toured the world and played in sketches in music-halls all over Britain. And she never became stagey, never seemed to flag, and never let slip her technique. During the 1920s she was often to be seen with her husband, in Canada as well as Great Britain, in the two standing successes, *Sleeping Partners* and *The Man in Dress Clothes*, and near the end of the decade she published a modest and amusing book of reminiscences. Her husband died in 1949.

June 17, 1971.

Lionel Tertis, C.B.E., virtuoso of the viola, who died on February 22, 1975 at the age of 98, unlike most musicians whose executive art dies with them, perpetuated his greatness as a performer upon the viola by the far-reaching consequences which he wrought upon English composition and upon instrument making.

He found the viola a neglected instrument of variable dimensions played by violinists as a secondary occupation, without a repertory of its own and with its special properties unrealized. By his own study, example and experiment he extended its practicable compass, enhanced its prestige and made a distinctive contribution to the English musical renaissance.

Among his friends were Arthur Rubinstein and Pablo Casals, who was born on the same day in the same year as Tertis.

The son of the Rev. Alexander Tertis, he was born at West Hartlepool on December 29, 1876, began his musical life as a juvenile pianist at the age of six, but by the time he was 13 was playing the violin in a Hungarian band of British musicians in imaginary Hungarian uniforms at Scarborough.

He went to Trinity College in 1892 and to the Royal Academy of Music in 1895, having had six months between at the Leipzig Conservatorium. It was Sir Alexander Mackenzie who directed Tertis's attention to the viola for purposes of quartet playing. He joined Henry Wood's Queen's Hall Orchestra and played in it from 1897 to 1904, when the break came which led to the formation of the L.S.O. Tertis then decided to make solo playing his career; he gave recitals, made transcriptions of violin music for his instrument, played Mozart's Sinfonia Concertante with Wessely and so far advanced as in 1908 to play a concerto by York Bowen at a Philharmonic concert.

This and Benjamin Dale's *Romance and Finale* were the first of a whole series of large-scale works written for Tertis by McEwen, Bax, Ernest Walker, Cyril Scott, Frank Bridge, Vaughan Williams and Arthur Bliss. Tertis himself continued to make transcriptions, including Bach's Chaconne and Elgar's cello concerto. He took part in some memorable performances with the violinist Albert Sammons with whom he recorded Mozart's Sinfonia Concertante in 1933. The orchestra was the L.P.O. under Hamilton Harty.

In 1937 Tertis decided to retire from the concert platform because of fibrositis in his bow arm, and he passed on his Montagnana to his pupil Bernard Shore. In his retirement, which, however, was not destined to be permanent, he began to design a viola which accorded with his ideal of the right size for the instrument. In association with Arthur Richardson, the violin maker, of Crediton in Devon, over 60 of these instruments were made within a few years and Tertis staged his own "comeback" at Wigmore Hall on one of these. The specification he published for anyone's use in *Music and Letters* in 1947.

The Tertis model viola was followed by a newly-designed cello built to his specifications and heard by the public for the first time at a concert in the Wigmore Hall in May 1960. His life work has, however, been the complete emancipation of the viola from its very humdrum occupation to the full rank of a solo instrument in its own right. He was presented with the Gold Medal of the Royal Philharmonic Society in 1964—when he was 87. In 1950 he was made C.B.E.

He married Ada, daughter of the Rev. Hugh Gawthrop. She died in 1951 and he married secondly in 1959 Lillian Warmington, the well-known cellist.

February 25, 1975.

U Thant, Secretary-General of the United Nations from 1961 until 1971, died in New York on November 25, 1974 from cancer.

He was appointed Acting Secretary-General by the General Assembly on the recommendation of the Security Council on November 3, 1961, after the death of Dag Hammarskjöld*, to fill Hammarskjöld's unexpired term, and was again unanimously appointed by the General Assembly, on November 30, 1962, for a term of office to expire on November 3, 1966; this was extended, and then he was reappointed for another five-year term in December 1966.

U Thant was born at Pantanaw, Burma, on January 22, 1909, and was educated at the National High School in Pantanaw and at University College, Rangoon.

Prior to his diplomatic career U Thant's experience was in educational and information work. He served as senior master and then as headmaster of his old high school in Pantanaw and was a member of a number of educational committees.

U Thant was appointed Press Director of the Government of Burma in 1947, and in 1948 became Director of Broadcasting. In the following year he became Secretary to the Government of Burma in the Ministry of Education. In 1953 he became Secretary for Projects in the Office of the Prime Minister and in 1955 also became Executive Secretary of Burma's Economic and Social Board.

U Thant served on a number of occasions as adviser to Prime Ministers of Burma. He accompanied U Nu to the first and second Colombo Prime Ministers' Conferences, to the Bandung Asian-African Conference of 1955, and to the Belgrade Non-Aligned Conference in 1961.

In 1957 U Thant became Permanent Representative of Burma to the United Nations, a post which he held until his appointment as Acting Secretary-General. During that period he headed the Burmese delegation to the General Assembly and in 1959 served as a vice-president of the General Assembly's fourteenth session. In 1961 he was chairman of the United Nations Conciliation Committee for the Congo, and chairman of the committee on a United Nations Capital Development Fund.

In spite of his varied previous experience of public and international life, the task of succeeding Hammarskjöld was a formidable one. Not only was his predecessor a man of remarkable character, attainments and reputation, but the Secretary-Generalship itself had, in the last year of his stewardship, become the centre of violent controversy.

From the start, his discharge of his responsibilities was marked by diffidence, approachability, and a marked lack of dogmatism. U Thant was far more prepared to decentralize work and responsibility and to listen to advice than Hammarskjöld had been.

Hammarskjöld and U Thant had one important characteristic in common. Both had a private routine of contemplation and meditation which gave them calm and staying power. Hammarskjöld was a northern mystic and U Thant a practising Buddhist, but the effect of their religious exercises on their public performances was similar.

In taking over the Secretary-Generalship in November 1961 U Thant found no shortage of troubles and difficulties. Apart from the dispute over the Secretary-Generalship itself, the United Nations Operation in the Congo was, at that time, a source of violent controversy, and even of violent action. The September fighting in Katanga, which had culminated in the death of Hammarskjöld, had left an extremely explosive and unstable situation, which again exploded into fighting on December 5, 1961.

The year 1962 saw, in November, the dispute over the Soviet missile installations in Cuba, when the world seemed to come perilously near to a nuclear confrontation between the two super-powers. On October 24 U Thant informed the Security Council that he had appealed to President Kennedy* and Chairman Khrushchev to suspend the United States arms quarantine and the Soviet arms shipments voluntarily for two or three weeks while they negotiated a peaceful solution. He also appealed to Castro to help find a way out of the impasse by halting work on the disputed installations and made himself available to all the parties for whatever services might be useful. U Thant received conciliatory replies from Kennedy and Khrushchev and later from the authorities in Havana. While it would be difficult to say what effect these interventions had on the course of the crisis, they eventually helped Khrushchev to back away from a direct confrontation with the United States.

In December 1962 fighting flared up again in Katanga, initiated, for reasons which no logic can explain, by Tshombe's* Gendarmerie itself. This time, with a minimum of violence or loss of life the United Nations Force, with the full support of the Secretary-General, established throughout Katanga the right to complete freedom of movement which it had always, in principle, possessed, and Tshombe's secession, which had for three years made the problems of the Congo insoluble, came to an end. The United Nations Force in the Congo was finally withdrawn in June, 1964.

As the Vietnam war escalated U Thant faced a dilemma. His peace-keeping efforts could merely be "personal" ones, since neither North Vietnam nor Red China was a member of the United Nations. The image of the United Nations was "somewhat tarnished by its seeming impotence in this, the greatest crisis of present times", as U Thant once put it.

In 1968 U Thant made two personal initiatives to bring the parties involved in the Vietnam war to the conference table. He visited Britain and the Soviet Union—the co-chairmen of the Geneva conference—and spoke to North Vietnamese representatives in Paris. He still called for a halt to American bombing before any cease-fire could be negotiated. Although the Americans were sceptical about these moves, President Johnson did meet U Thant in New York before his second visit to Paris. In May talks on ending the bombing opened in Paris; and in October the N.L.F. and the South Vietnamese were admitted to the talks and Johnson halted the bombing. Yet the war which U Thant in an unguarded moment had described as "barbarous" dragged on, as did the peace talks in Paris.

In September 1965 the war between India and Pakistan confronted most of the members of the Security Council with a serious dilemma caused by conflicting alliances with both sides. In this situation the Council asked the Secretary-General to proceed urgently to the theatre of war to exert every possible effort to secure an end to the hostilities.

U Thant left New York on September 7, 1965. In Rawalpindi and New Delhi he had intensive talks with President Ayub Khan and Prime Minister Shastri* in an effort to bring about a cease-fire, and secured the assent of both in principle. He returned to New York on September 16 and although his efforts did not secure an immediate cease-fire they paved the way for the cease-fire demanded by the Security Council on September 20 and complied with by the parties on September 22, 1965. The Secretary-General then organized the observation of the cease-fire over the entire front between the armies of India and Pakistan. These arrangements functioned successfully until the agreement at Tashkent between the two Governments under the chairmanship of Kosygin allowed both armies to withdraw to the previous positions in March, 1968.

Throughout 1966 U Thant had made it clear that he did not wish to be reelected to another term of office as Secretary-General. Although his main reasons for this decision were personal, he was influenced also by certain political considerations, not least of which was the failure of his efforts to secure peace negotiations on Vietnam and the failure of the membership to agree on a sound basis for United Nations peace-keeping operations and for the financing of them. However, after intense pressure had been put on him from all sides he reversed his decision and was reelected unanimously on December 2, 1966, for another term of office ending on December 31, 1971.

From the early days of 1967 tension between Israel and her Arab neighbours, and especially between Israel and Syria, rose steadily. From January, 1967, U Thant had by various means, including appeals to the parties and efforts to secure, through the armistice machinery, discussion of at least some of the causes of tension, sought to preserve peace in the Middle East. In April the situation between Syria and Israel worsened, and the United Arab Republic was challenged by other Arab States to show some practical evidence of its proclaimed leadership of the Arab world, especially in regard to the Israeli threat to Syria. On May 18 U Thant was faced with the demand by the United Arab Republic for the immediate withdrawal of the United Nations Emergency Force (U.N.E.F.) from the armistice lines and frontier between Israel and Egypt in Gaza and Sinai, where it had maintained relative tranquillity for more than 10 years.

According to the arrangements made with Egypt in 1956 by Dag Hammarskjöld for the introduction of U.N.E.F. on to Egyptian soil and the undoubted sovereign right of Egypt to withdraw its agreement for the presence of foreign troops on Egyptian soil, U Thant had no legal grounds upon which to refuse this request, and as a purely practical matter the Egyptian Army by moving up to its own frontier, from which it had voluntarily stayed away for 10 years, on May 17 and 18, 1967, had already rendered the buffer function performed by U.N.E.F. troops, in small numbers and with no right to fire except in self-defence, completely ineffective.

U Thant's attempts to get President Nasser* to rescind the withdrawal request and to get the Government of Israel to accept U.N.E.F. on the Israel side of the line were both met with brusque and strongly worded refusals.

Not surprisingly, the decision to withdraw U.N.E.F. was violently criticized, especially in western countries, and frequently in a manner which showed that the critics had no idea either of the nature of the U.N.E.F. operation or of the basis for its presence on Egyptian soil. To find a scapegoat was most desirable for a number of governments caught in a bewildering situation, and because of his withdrawal of U.N.E.F. (which, in fact, did not leave the area until several weeks later), U Thant perfectly filled the bill.

U Thant made all possible efforts to improve the extremely dangerous situation which had arisen in the Middle East with the direct confrontation for the first time in 10 years of the Egyptian and Israeli armies. But on June 5 war broke out with the Israeli air strike against Egyptian and Jordanian airfields and the subsequent advances of the Israel army into the Sinai, up to the West Bank of the Jordan and, three days later, into Syria. Throughout this period U Thant played an essential role in the efforts to secure a cease-fire and in the arrangements, once the cease-fire was secured, to establish a proper policing of it by United Nations observers.

In November 1967 an initiative by the United Kingdom representative in the Security Council, Lord Caradon, resulted at last, to the surprise of almost everyone concerned, in a unanimous Security Council resolution on the Middle East.

It would be impossible to label or classify U Thant politically or to assign his views to any one regional affiliation or tradition. If the word "non-aligned" has any meaning left then the word could justly be applied to him. The world was his parish and his interests and sympathies were both comprehensive and tolerant. His Burmese origin gave him a particular interest in the problems of underdeveloped countries in general and of South-East Asia in particular, and he was especially concerned with such United Nations activities as the Technical Assistance Programme, the Special Fund and the Development Decade. U Thant's feelings about the East and West were not predominantly political. He summarized them once as follows: "In the West the stress is on the intellectual development of man. . . . I think the purpose of Eastern education has been to find the truth inside of us, to discover what is happening inside of us, while at the same time something external to us has been ignored, more or less. I feel that, in these tense times, what is necessary is some sort of compromise between these two concepts".

He was above all a humane man, unswayed by prejudice or vanity, and in spite of his great eminence and public success he maintained throughout his Secretary-Generalship a genuine modesty and open-mindedness which were irresistible to those he dealt with. With him it was impossible to imagine sinister or egotistical motives, and for this reason he could say and do things which would have been impossible for someone of a more complex or devious character.

U Thant was the author, before his duties as Secretary-General left him no time for writing, of several books, including *Cities and their Stories, League of Nations* (1933), *Democracy in School* (1952) and a two-volume *History of Post-War Burma* (1961).

He was married and had two children. His son was tragically killed in an accident while a student at the University of Rangoon. His married daughter lives in the United States.

November 26, 1974

Helene Thimig, widow of the Austrian theatrical director and impresario Max Reinhardt, and one of the German-speaking theatre's foremost actresses, died on November 6, 1974 in Vienna.

Born in the capital on June 5, 1889, into the celebrated theatrical family whose name she bore, Frau Thimig left Europe with her Jewish husband in 1938 when the Nazis occupied Austria and accompanied him to the United States where he died on October 10, 1943. Daughter of Hugo Thimig, leading actor and one-time director of the Vienna Burg Theatre, Frau Thimig first trod the boards in Baden in 1907. For the next two years she was apprenticed to the Meiningen Players, the company that established a tradition of naturalism which had caught the eye of Stanislavsky and led to his founding of the Moscow Arts Theatre. In 1911 she moved to Max Reinhardt's company in Berlin and when, in 1917, he took over the Deutsches Theater, which today bears his name, she followed him there.

From then on, both in Berlin and in Vienna, where Reinhardt took over the Theater an der Josefstadt in 1924, and until his expulsion by the Nazis, she appeared in a wide variety of parts, often in new plays in which she created the role for the first time. After Goethe's Stella, both in Vienna and in Berlin in 1920, the praises of the most eminent critics were showered on her. From 1920 onwards she also worked for Reinhardt at the Salzburg Festival, which he founded in that year, most memorably in the morality play of *Everyman*, the annual festival production which she was to revive and act in for many years after the Second World War.

The compass of her juvenile roles in the classics was particularly wide, from Solveig in *Peer Gynt*, Natalia in *A Month in the Country*, and Luisa in *Intrigue and Love*, in which her father Hugo played her stage father with her, to Viola in *Twelfth Night*, Cordelia in *King Lear*, Elizabeth in *Mary Stuart*, and Iphigenia in Goethe's tragedy, in which she appeared opposite the Orestes of Alexander Moissi.

Landmarks in the modern repertoire were her Dorothea Angermann in Hauptmann's drama of that name, *The Gay Countess*, Helen in von Hofmannsthal's *Der Schwierige*, and the radiant 19-year-old Inken Peters in the world première of Hauptmann's *After Sunset* in 1932, which also turned out to be Reinhardt's last German production before the Nazis seized power. Admired for her bodily grace and beauty as much as for the serene sensitivity of her talent, Frau Thimig was at all times a devoted companion, an inspiration and an aide to the man she was to marry.

In 1926 theatrical history of a sort was made at the Josefstadt when Reinhardt directed a musical farce by Nestroy that featured all four members of the Thimig family—Helene, her father Hugo, and her two brothers Hermann and Hans, respectively 18 months and 10 years her junior. This combination was to recur several times, most notably in a celebrated revival of Goldoni's *A Servant of Two Masters*, in which she glittered as Smeralda, one of several plays, *Intrigue and Love* among them, that toured the United States with "the Thimigs" in the 1927-28 season.

Among English plays in which she shone were the German premières of Galsworthy's *Loyalties*, Shaw's *The Apple Cart*, in which she played Lysistrata, and, in Vienna in 1958, Rattigan's *Separate Tables*.

During their American exile, she and Reinhardt founded a school of Film and Drama, the Max Reinhardt Workshop, in Hollywood, where she divided her time between teaching and playing in films, as the family's sole breadwinner (*The Moon is Down, Edge of Darkness, This Love of Ours*, and in 1946 Fritz Lang's *Cloak and Dagger*). On returning to Vienna after the war she acted both at her father's old Burg Theatre and, from 1954, at the Josefstadt. She became a Professor at the Vienna Music Academy and also took over the "Reinhardt Seminar", the famous theatre school in Schloss Leopoldskron that her husband had founded half a century before.

November 19, 1974.

Sir Clement Price Thomas—See Price Thomas.

Sir George Thomas, the seventh baronet, who was for a generation and more one of the strongest chess players in Britain, died on July 23, 1972 at the age of 91.

Already coming into prominence before the 1914-18 War, he did not reach his full strength until afterwards. In the earlier postwar period he shared with F. D. Yates the preeminence in British chess. Between them (except for the rare emergences of H. E. Atkins from retirement and the all too brief career in Britain of Mir Sultan Khan) they carried off most of the honours at home and did their country stout service in the international field.

Thomas won the British championship in 1923 (in which year he also won the badminton championship for the last time) and again in 1934 when, after the death of Yates, he was for a time undoubtedly the foremost player in the country. The 1934 championship at Chester was one of the strongest ever held, but Thomas won it without loss of a game. In the same year, too, he achieved perhaps his finest performance, tieing for first place in the Hastings Congress with Euwe and Flohr, ahead of Capablanca, Lilenthal, Botvinnik and others.

Thomas was almost the permanent holder of the championship of the City of London Chess Club, which he won in all 15 times, the last occasion being in 1939 shortly before the club was wound up.

Thomas was for many years captain of the English team in the international team tournaments, in which he had a splendid record. In the first contest, which was held in London, he was unbeaten and shared with the Danish player K. Norman Hansen the prize for the best individual record. He also captained England for many years in the series of international matches with Holland. Thomas continued to play in first-class chess until well on in his sixties, and continued to hold his own with the younger generation until his retirement.

The characteristic features of Thomas's style were subtlety and finesse rather than aggression. He could make combinative attacks when he wanted to, but preferred to achieve his results by more patient and less spectacular methods. He was an exceptionally good end-game player; in this branch of the game he was one of the few English players to hold his own with the continental masters.

Never a "bookish" player (except for the profound knowledge of the Ruy Lopez which years of experience had given him) Thomas preferred to go his own way. It is doubtful if he ever had a book on the opening. A habit of getting behind on his clock—though he played very well in time trouble—may partly have accounted for his singular proneness to commit elementary blunders, an idiosyncrasy which prevented his results from being even better than they were, or as good as the real excellence of his style would have justified. He was particularly good at defending himself against speculative attacks, and indeed often appeared deliberately to invite them in order to profit from the subsequent reaction.

As a sportsman "Sir Thomas", as he was almost invariably known among continental chess masters, won for himself a unique position. He represented for the foreign chess players the best traditions of British sport, and no reputation was better deserved. Quiet and unassuming in his manner, courteous and charming both in victory and defeat, Thomas was known intimately by only a few of his contemporaries. To the younger generation of English chess players he was always kind and generous, and he took a particular interest in schoolboys' chess, which he did a great deal to foster.

In the opinion of many good judges of the game Thomas was the best badminton player of his own, if not of any age. He was singles champion from 1920 to 1923, and both before and after the 1914-18 War he won the mixed and the men's doubles championship on many occasions.

Apart from his preeminence at badminton and at chess, Thomas was also a very fine lawn tennis player, and in one of the early post-1918 Wimbledons his fierce forehand driving carried him into the last eight of the singles.

July 31, 1972.

General Sir Ivor Thomas, G.C.B., K.B.E., D.S.O., M.C., who was Quarter-Master-General to the Forces from 1950 to 1952, died on August 29, 1972.

The highlight of his distinguished career in the Army was the command of the 43rd (Wessex) Division which he held for three years, the last on active service under Montgomery in the campaign in Europe. His methods both in training and in battle were sometimes described as German in their thoroughness and earned him the nickname of "Von Thoma".

He was a fine leader and he enjoyed the complete confidence of his division which he led in person in the forefront of the battlefield.

Gwilym Ivor Thomas was born on July 23, 1893, the son of John Thomas (Pencerdd Gwalia), harpist to Queen Victoria and King Edward VII. He was educated at Cheltenham College and the Royal Military Academy, Woolwich, and was commissioned in the Royal Artillery in 1912. In the 1914-18 War he served for three years on the Western Front, commanded a battery, and was twice wounded and won the M.C. and bar, and the D.S.O. His D.S.O. was awarded for an act of great gallantry and exceptional coolness.

Between the wars he passed through the Staff College, Camberley, and the Royal Naval Staff College, was adjutant of a Royal Artillery Unit of the Territorial Army, and Brigade Major, R.A., of the 1st Division. In 1938 he was posted as G.S.O. 1st Grade to the Plans Division of the Home Office where he did useful work in the organization of the Air Raids Precautions system which had to be hurriedly created as relations with Germany worsened.

A few months before war was declared Thomas was appointed Deputy Director of Recruiting and Organization at the War Office, and a year later he became Director of Organization. When he left the War Office, he commanded the artillery of a division and then of a corps before being promoted to major-general in 1942 on his appointment to command the 43rd (Wessex) Division.

Thomas commanded the 43rd Division for three years—two years of training in England and a third year of almost continuous fighting. His long tenure of this command gave him an exceptional opportunity of impressing his personality and theories of warfare upon his officers and men, and this he did with marked and incisive effect. In conformity with the doctrine established by Sir Bernard Paget*, the division was trained under conditions of austerity and hardship. Its main training area, in the enclosed country near Folkestone, by a lucky chance strikingly resembled the Normandy bocage in which the division had to fight when it landed in France in June 1944.

The division arrived in Normandy in time to take part in the operations for the capture of Caen in the holding attacks by which Montgomery pinned the bulk of the German forces on his left in order to facilitate the break-out by the Americans on his right. For the first few weeks of the campaign it was engaged in the heavy fighting on the River Orne.

The next operation undertaken by the division, as one of the divisions of 30th Corps, was the capture of Mont Pincon, a key point in the German defence system which it was necessary to occupy in order to cover the flank of the American drive on Paris and to dislodge the enemy from his new defence line on the River Vire. Here the division was faced with tough fighting in enclosed country, and the progress of the whole Corps was slow. Thomas's division acquitted itself with skill and gallantry in this action.

When the Falaise pocket had been eliminated the division accomplished a considerable feat when it raced to the Seine at Vernon, a distance of ninety miles, and within six days threw a bridge over the river for the passage of the armoured divisions which then surged forward in their spectacular dash to Brussels.

In the third week of September, the 43rd Division was engaged in the abortive attempt to relieve Urquhart's airborne forces at Arnhem. Thomas's failure here has been attributed by some critics to his cautious and methodical nature and his dislike of launching his infantry attacks without extremely thorough organization and overwhelming fire support.

Thomas's division, which still formed part of Horrocks's Corps, was engaged for some months in the winter operations in Belgium, and it played a notable part in the grim and gruelling fighting in the Reichswald in February and March, when the Allied armies were closing up to the Rhine. This bitterly contested battle, fought in appalling conditions of waterlogged and flooded ground, was perhaps one of the division's greatest triumphs.

After the war, Thomas commanded the 1st Corps District in the British Army of the Rhine until 1947, when he was appointed Administrator of the Polish Forces in Great Britain. From 1948 to 1950 he was G.O.C.-in-C. of the Anti-Aircraft Command and was then promoted General. He took up his final appointment as Quarter-Master-General to the Forces in 1950. As Quarter-Master-General it fell to him to make the arrangements for the movement and supply of troops employed in the Korean War and in the operations against the communist guerrillas in Malaya.

He was made C.B. in 1944 and was created K.B.E. in 1947, K.C.B. in 1950, and G.C.B. in 1952. He was an Officer of the Legion d'Honneur, a Knight Grand Officer of the Order of Orange Nassau, a Commander of the Order of Leopold, and had the French and Belgian Croix de Guerre. He was a Colonel Commandant of the Royal Artillery from 1947 to 1957.

He married first, in 1931, Kathleen, daughter of Alexander Heard of Coolmain Castle, County Cork, widow of Colonel Joseph Paterson, C.M.G. This marriage was dissolved in 1948, and in 1949 he married Elliott Ellen, only daughter of Major Ronald Van Kriekenbeck, Indian Army, formerly wife of Sir Archibald Forbes.

September 1, 1972.

Sir Eric Thompson, K.B.E., F.B.A., the world's leading authority on ancient Maya civilization, and one of the greatest experts of this century on American archaeology, died at Cambridge on September 9, 1975 at the age of 76.

Thompson was a man of many and diverse achievements in the field of Maya studies, but his most important contributions came in three aspects of this field: at the beginning of his career he carried out a number of important archaeological excavations at sites in the Crown Colony of British Honduras (now Belize), while throughout his life he expounded the value of ethnographic and documentary forces for illuminating the fragmentary evidence provided by archaeology; his greatest work, however, in a field in which he was for nearly half a century the pre-eminent scholar, was in forwarding the decipherment of Maya hieroglyphic writing, the most sophisticated means of recording and communication ever developed in the ancient Americas.

One of his earliest achievements was to calculate the correlation between the Maya and Christian calendars which enables events in the history of Maya civilization to be precisely placed in time; it was not the first such correlation, and was only days different from those made by Goodman and Martinez Hernandez, but its precision has resulted in its acceptance down to the present day, and it is generally known as "the Thompson Correlation".

John Eric Sidney Thompson was born on New Year's Eve, 1898, the younger son of George Thompson, F.R.C.S. He was educated at Winchester College, and dedicated one of his books to William of Wykeham; he left the school to join the Army, under age, during the First World War, and fought in France with the Coldstream Guards. His family had Argentine connexions and for some time after the war he worked as a *gaucho* on a cattle ranch in South America.

A growing interest in archaeology, and particularly in the ancient Maya, sent him to Cambridge in 1924 to study under A.C. Haddon. He was a member of what was then Fitzwilliam House, now Fitzwilliam College, which made him an Honorary Fellow in 1973.

From Cambridge he went to work for Sylvanus T. Morley on the Carnegie Institution of Washington's major project of research and restoration at the great Maya site of Chichénitzá in Mexico, having impressed Morley with his self-taught command of Maya hieroglyphics and what was then known of their meaning. For nine years, from 1926 to 1935, he was on the staff of the Field Museum of Natural History in Chicago, and in 1930 he married Florence Keens, who now survives him after forty-five years of marriage.

During his term at the Field Museum Thompson carried out most of his purely archaeological fieldwork. In 1927 he was seconded to the British Museum Expedition to British Honduras, which was excavating at the Maya site of Lubaantun under the direction of T. A. Joyce. Within weeks he first disagreed with, then disproved Joyce's major conclusions of the 1926 season; although Joyce did not accept Thompson's conclusions he was fair-minded enough to have them published, with his own comments, in the expedition's report, and Thompson retained a fierce loyalty to Joyce, and to Joyce's amateur collaborator Dr. Thomas Gann, and could be sharp with those who were younger and with hindsight thought themselves wiser than these men.

During this 1927 season Thompson discovered the important Maya site of Busilha, some 20 miles from Lubaantun, which possessed a unique Maya bridge across the Rio Moho, and also a number of stone stelae with hieroglyphic inscriptions, the dates in which formed the subject of one of his earliest papers.

In the late 1920s and early 1930s he led a number of Field Museum expeditions to excavate British Honduras, in the Cayo District and at San Jose, a modest Maya site chosen explicitly for its smallness and lack of grandeur because Thompson felt that it might reflect the nature of Maya culture more accurately than the huge sites that had claimed the most attention so far.

During the same period he spent some weeks in the Mopan Maya village of San Antonio, near Lubaantun, and from the people there, as from his workmen at San Jose, he culled information on their agricultural and religious practices and folklore, documenting the persistence of Pre-Columbian beliefs in a formally Catholic society.

Much of his subsequent work used ethnographic and documentary sources, of which he was a master, to illuminate by back-projection the fragmentary archaeological record. In this field his studies of the Maya deities, of trade and of the role of products such as cacao and tobacco in ritual as well as commerce, are exemplary.

The final season of excavations at San Jose took place in 1936 under the auspices of the Carnegie Institution of Washington, which Thompson joined in 1935 and where he remained for 23 years until his retirement in 1958. During this second phase of his career he worked increasingly on the decipherment of Maya hieroglyphs, the state of which he reported in 1950 in his monograph *Maya Hieroglyphic Writing*. This was followed in 1962 by *A Catalogue of Maya Hieroglyphs*, the essential concordance for all future investigation, and in 1972 by a commentary on the Dresden Codex, the earliest and most important of the three surviving Maya manuscripts.

During his years with the Carnegie Institution he published numerous papers on aspects of Maya Epigraphy and Ethnography, and unobtrusively ensured the publication of such important discoveries as the assemblage of early Maya polychrome vessels from Nohmul in Northern Belize.

In 1941 he was made an honorary Professor of the Museo Nacional de Mexico, and in 1953 a consultant of the Centro de Investigaciones Antropologicas Mexicanas. Both posts he held until his death.

In spite of spending his working lifetime in the United States, he remained a British citizen, and when the International Congress of Americanists was held in Cambridge in 1952 he was an obvious choice as president. When he retired to England he was swiftly elected a Fellow of the British Academy (1959), and received honorary doctorates from the Universities of Yucatan (1959) and Pennsylvania (1962).

A further honorary doctorate came from Tulane University in 1972, and in the same year the Sahagún Medal from Mexico. In 1973 the University of Cambridge made him Lit.D. *honoris causa*, the Aztec Eagle being elegantly latinized by the Public Orator as *aquila Mexica*. Finally his achievements were recognized by the bestowal of a K.B.E. earlier in 1975. In the spring Thompson had the honour of showing the Queen and the Duke of Edinburgh the great Maya sites of Uxmal and Chichénitzá during their State visit to Mexico.

His son is Professor Donald Thompson, the Peruvian archaeologist.

September 11, 1975.

Mrs. E. Roffe Thompson—See C. A. Lejeune.

Sir George Thomson, F.R.S., died in Cambridge on September 10, 1975 at the age of 83.

He was the second of his family to make a major contribution to the development of physics. His father, the great "J. J.", founded modern physics when he discovered the electron in 1897. The achievement for which "G. P." will chiefly be remembered was the demonstration that this fundamental entity, which his father had proved in the face of considerable scepticism to be a discrete particle, had after all some of the properties of a wave.

Both father and son were professors at the age of thirty, both were knighted, both were Nobel Laureates, both became Master of a Cambridge college. It is a remarkable example of inherited talent, and perhaps of the strong influence of a Cambridge environment.

George Paget Thomson was born in Cambridge on May 3, 1892. He went to the Perse School and then to Trinity College. Like many physicists of his generation he was educated in the first place as a mathematician, for he took Parts I and II of the Mathematical Tripos and obtained a first class in both; only then did he go on to study physics and to get another first class in Part II of the Natural Sciences Tripos. When he was elected a Fellow of

Corpus Christi College in 1914, only a year after taking his degree, he was appointed a college lecturer in mathematics, not physics. By temperament, however, he was always an experimenter rather than a theoretician, a man who enjoyed using his hands and making things. One of his hobbies was making beautiful and exact model boats; it illustrates not only his manual skill but also a lifelong enthusiasm for ships and sailing.

The war interrupted his academic career. He joined the Special Reserve at its outbreak and later fought in France with the 1st Battalion of the Queen's Regiment. In 1915 he transferred to the R.F.C. and he spent the rest of the war at Farnborough, as one of a team of outstanding scientists researching on aeronautical problems. He went back to Cambridge and to Corpus in 1919, but in 1922 he was appointed Professor of Natural Philosophy at Aberdeen University. Here he continued to work for a while on aerodynamics, until he became involved in the spectacular development of wave mechanics.

The suggestion that material particles might have a wave-like character, just as light waves and X-rays were known to behave in some circumstances as particles, was first made by de Broglie in 1925. Thomson decided to put it to the test of experiment, stimulated by some results published by Dymond in 1926 on the scattering of electrons by helium. In 1927 he successfully demonstrated that a beam of electrons passing through a thin metal foil was diffracted, very much like a beam of X-rays, by the regularly spaced atoms in the crystal lattice. This is one of the classic experiments of physics, and for it Thomson was awarded a Nobel Prize in 1937, together with C. Davisson who had performed a related experiment in America at much the same time.

Thomson was quick to realize the potentialities of electron diffraction as a technique for studying the structure of thin films and thin surface layers. He pursued this line at research at Aberdeen, and later at Imperial College, London, where he became Professor of Physics in 1930. After the discovery of the neutron by Chadwick in 1932, moreover, exciting possibilities began to open up in nuclear physics and Thomson became more and more interested in this field. He would confess of himself that in all research it was the possibility of practical applications that most appealed to him, and he was probably one of the first people to appreciate the practical significance of nuclear physics. Certainly he went to the Air Ministry in 1939 to point out the feasibility of the uranium bomb, and he was largely responsible for setting up the wartime atomic energy project in Britain. He was chairman of the first British Committee on Atomic Energy in 1940-41.

He was a man who tended to see political and moral issues in black and white, and having once made up his mind that

an atomic bomb was inevitable he would not have been troubled by qualms of conscience in helping to make it. It is only fair to add that the peaceful potentialities of atomic energy appealed much more to his imagination. His lively book, *The Foreseeable Future*, published in 1955, shows how exciting and encouraging he found the prospect of a world with unlimited power at its disposal. When the war was over and he was free to return to academic research (he had been engaged once more with aeronautical problems as well as with atomic energy) he started looking ahead with characteristic vision to the achievement of thermonuclear fusion as a source of useful power. He started work in his laboratory on a method of reaching the very high temperatures needed, using an apparatus which was the direct prototype of the large toroidal machines that were built at Harwell 10 years later. The project was taken over by an industrial group with the resources to develop it fruitfully, but Sir George (he was knighted in 1943) continued to take a vigorous interest in it, despite an increasing load of other responsibilities.

In 1952 he retired from his professorship, having been elected Master of Corpus in succession to Sir Will Spens. He remained a member of many government committees concerned with nuclear physics, fuel research and scientific administration, not to mention the University Grants Committee, but he found time nevertheless to play an active part in the life and administration of his college, to which he was much devoted. His influence was felt in a variety of ways, but especially perhaps by a gradual increase in the proportion of scientific Fellows. Science was always the main object for his grand, infectious enthusiasm, though the range of his interests and knowledge outside science was remarkably wide; he could talk omnisciently about anything from medieval warfare to Christian heresies. Only in aesthetic and personal matters did his scientific understanding occasionally let him down. But although he found it hard to be patient with committees which failed to behave with the reproducibility to be expected in a decent experiment, he dealt with individuals with genuine sympathy and charm. All who experienced his warm friendliness were much attached to him.

He relinquished the Mastership in 1962 but throughout a long and active retirement he continued to contribute to the intellectual life of the society. He is commemorated by the George Thomson building at Leckhampton.

He was elected F.R.S. in 1930; was president of the Institute of Physics, 1958-60; and of the British Association for the Advancement of Science in 1960.

He wrote a variety of papers in scientific journals and a number of books: *Applied Aerodynamics; The Atom; Wave Mechanics of the Free Electron; Conduction of Electricity through Gases* (with his father); *Theory and Practice of Electron Diffraction* (with W. Cochrane). His many academic honours included medals from the Franklin Institute, the Royal Society and the Institute of Electrical Engineers, an honorary Fellowship at Trinity College, Cambridge, and honorary doctorates from eight universities at home and overseas.

In 1924 he married Kathleen Buchanan, daughter of the Very Rev. Sir George Adam Smith. He and his family of two sons and two daughters suffered a great loss when she died in 1941.

September 12, 1975.

Russell Thorndike, the actor and writer, who died on November 7, 1972 at the age of 87, was the younger brother of Dame Sybil Thorndike. Of the two Russell was (in the opinion of Dame Sybil's husband, Lewis Casson*) the born actor, but he seems to have been lacking in just those qualities, imagination amd power of application, which, to quote Casson again, enabled Sybil to reach the top of the profession that she turned to on giving up professional piano playing.

Russell's first love was writing, and to this he devoted more and more time after service in the First World War had handicapped him physically for the prosecution of his stage-career.

Two and a half years younger than Sybil, Arthur Russell Thorndike was born on February 6, 1885, at Rochester, where their father had recently taken up residence as a minor canon. He was educated at St. George's School, Windsor Castle, being a chorister of the Chapel Royal.

When Sybil was advised on grounds of health temporarily to stop work as a pianist, Russell made the inspired suggestion that they both go on the stage.

In 1903 they were fellow students at Ben Greet's Academy and two years later fellow-members of his company on a North American tour. He remained in all three and a half years with the company, once giving three performances as Hamlet in three different versions of the text on the same day.

After accompanying Matheson Lang to South Africa and Asia, he was for a time reunited with Sybil, who had married Lewis Casson in 1908, in Miss Horniman's Manchester-based repertory company, and he had finished writing a novel of romantic adventure on Romney Marsh, *Dr. Syn*, when he was called up in 1914 as a trooper in the 1st Westminster Dragoons. Together with his brother Frank, who had also gone on the stage, he sailed for Egypt, leaving Sybil to throw in her lot with Lilian Baylis and Ben Greet in the former's new enterprise of presenting Shakespeare at the Old Vic.

Severely wounded at Gallipoli and invalided out of the Army with a dislocated spine, he joined Greet and his sister at the Old Vic in 1916. In the course of two wartime seasons he was the first man to play King John, Richard II and King Lear for Miss Baylis—he and Sybil as Lear's Fool did the storm scene on the first night against the background of an air raid—and he was leading man and joint-director of plays with an Old Bensonian named Charles Warburton for the 1919-20 season. Thereafter he went to the Little Theatre in John Adam Street to support the Cassons and Jose Levy in their attempt to establish an English Grand Guignol. He acted there in six consecutive programmes of plays, collaborating with Reginald Arkell in writing two of them, and making his chief success as an actor in Reginald Berkeley's *Eight O'Clock*, a drama set in the condemned cell during a prisoner's last half hour. He was released to appear as Peer Gynt in what was said to be the first fully professional production of Ibsen's play in London, at the Old Vic in 1922 under the direction of Robert Atkins.

No subsequent performance of his aroused so much interest, though he continued for nearly 40 years to work on the stage. During that time he was seen as W. G. Wills's Charles I and Tennyson's Thomas Becket, roles "created" by Henry Irving; as Hamlet at Irving's old theatre at a matinee in aid of the Sadler's Wells Fund; in many roles in Shakespeare on tour with Greet's company, and in Regent's Park with Robert Atkins; as his own *Dr. Syn*, and as a character in another play of his, in which Dame Sybil acted with him during the Second World War; and as Smee the Nonconformist pirate in 10 revivals of *Peter Pan*.

For the most part these were no doubt sound performances, but with the coming of middle age, with the establishment of the Cassons in partnership with Bronson Albery in the West End, and with the arrival of a younger generation at the Old Vic, it was as though he felt that the adventure of life in the theatre was over for him. It seemed doubtful whether his heart was in stage-work that had ceased to be pioneering.

It was, however, open to the born romancer to turn himself into a writer of romances, and the author of *The Slype* and other novels appearing in succession to *Dr. Syn*, a film version of which was made by George Arliss, did this with some success: "anything may happen; anything does happen; Mr. Thorndike's masterly plot is indescribable", wrote a reviewer in *The Times* of his *The House of Jeffreys*.

Thorndike married in 1918 Rosemary Dowson, a daughter of the well-known actress Rosina Filippi.

November 9, 1972.

Hessell Tiltman, F.R.AE.S., the aircraft designer who, with the author Nevil Shute, founded the aircraft company Airspeed Ltd., died on October 28, 1975 at the age of 84.

Alfred Hessell Tiltman graduated in engineering from London University and served his apprenticeship with the Daimler Co. in 1910-11. He was subsequently involved for three years in Canada on design work on the Quebec Bridge, and after that spent two years in structural steel design with Sir Edward Wood & Co. from 1914 to 1916 before he turned to the sphere to which he was to devote the major part of his life, aircraft design.

He joined Sir Geoffrey de Havilland's* company, Airco, in 1916 and at the end of the war was involved in testing the record breaking DH 9R. When the De Havilland Aircraft Company was formed in 1921, Tiltman was invited to join. As an assistant designer he was involved in the building and testing of a number of DH aircraft, ranging from the small DH 60 Moth to the DH 66 Hercules airliner.

Later he worked with Nevil Shute, at that time the aircraft designer N. S. Norway, on the airship R 100 which had been designed by Barnes Wallis. Shute himself had been responsible for the stressing of the airship's structure. Though airships never mounted an effective challenge to heavier-than-air craft, the R 100 still remains the most successful of the breed in marked contrast to the Government's R 101.

The shelving of further airship projects after the R 101 disaster put the future Shute and Tiltman out of work but they decided, notwithstanding the slump, to go into business as aircraft manufacturers themselves. Raising as much money as the pair could, and with an order from Sir Alan Cobham for two aeroplanes to provide joyrides for an air circus, the thereafter remarkably successful company, Airspeed, came into being, in a garage in York.

During its life it produced several basic aircraft which became R.A.F. equipment, notably the Airspeed Oxford, the standard twin engined trainer during the Second World War. Airspeed also pioneered many other now standard ideas, the retractable undercarriage, in-flight refuelling and self sealing petrol tanks. Tiltman was joint Managing Director of the company—later, when Norway left to pursue the career of Shute, sole Managing Director—and designed about 15 different types of aircraft.

A noteworthy aircraft from the latter end of his regime was the Horsa glider which was to carry troops into action on D-Day, at Arnhem and in several other theatres after the invasion. A priority project for the second front, Horsa had to be got from the drawing board into the air with considerable speed. And it was—in ten months, which, as Tiltman remarked afterwards, "was not so bad considering the drawings had to be made suitable for the furniture trade who were responsible for all production".

Tiltman himself left Airspeed shortly after that, but in 1948 co-founded Tiltman Langley Ltd., of which he was Technical Director and Chairman for six years.

November 4, 1975.

Cardinal Eugène Tisserant, who was appointed Dean of the Sacred College of Cardinals in 1951, died in February 21, 1972. He was 87.

No one could have been more Dean of the Sacred College than Eugène Tisserant, son of a veterinary of Nancy. He looked like Schoenberg's Moses and remained as French and as militarily unaccommodating as he must have been before the long years spent in Rome. He was handsome, touchy, recognized as one of the greatest living human repositories of knowledge about the Near East, and enjoyed the unusual distinction for a Curia Cardinal of having the reputation of looking after his diocese well.

There was no certainty how Tisserant would react. In this he remained the excellent Army officer which he had been in his youth. He was fond of reminiscing about his experiences as a soldier in France and the Levant. He would sometimes sit and talk philosophically and amazingly frankly about life at the court of the Popes. He served under six of them from the days as a young professor when Pius X set him teaching in Rome before Tisserant had even been ordained. He was deeply hurt and complained lengthily in private conversation when John XXIII*, in whose election he was said to have had a hand, failed to put him back at the head of the Sacred Congregation for the Oriental Churches which he had directed for years, after he had followed the custom of high-ranking Curial officials in formally placing his offices at the disposal of the new Pope.

He could at times act with imperious high temper, as when he ordered out of the Vatican at a few hours' notice the famous housekeeper of Pius XII, Sister Pasqualina, who was accustomed to allot the amount of time that even leading cardinals could spend with his Holiness. He wasted no time at all in seeing her over the threshold once Pius was dead, together with the old Pope's pet canaries.

Tisserant had no fear in speaking his mind on great subjects. He was understood to have tried to convince Pius XII against pronouncing the dogma of the Virgin's bodily assumption, the one Papal statement unquestionably having the accoutrements of infallibility since that doctrine was formulated in 1870. In 1969 he personally wrote to Cardinal Suenens in an effort to correct the Belgian prelate's view that the Sacred College should no longer have the election of Popes to themselves. But Tisserant's more general testiness tended to cause his weightier advice to be undervalued simply because he was regarded as cantankerous.

He was last prominently in the public eye when protesting against Pope Paul VI's decision to bar cardinals of over 80 years of age from the Conclave, and for having allegedly said on French television that Paul VI (about whom he could be rather impatient) would probably not survive to the age of retirement for bishops. He was a great scholar and seeker-out of precious manuscripts with which he enriched the Vatican library. He was one of the few examples of cardinals from countries other than Italy who refused to become romanized.

Born on March 24, 1884, he was ordained in August 1907. He was created cardinal in 1936 by Pius XI who was a close friend of Tisserant before his election as Pope. He was consecrated bishop 13 months later in July 1937. He held the two suburbicarian dioceses of Ostia and of Porto and Santa Rufina which, to his annoyance, became titular sees in November 1966 and were placed for administrative and pastoral purposes under the Vicariate of Rome. Tisserant liked to recall that in 1917 he was a staff officer with the Anglo-French expeditionary force in Palestine and, when the Queen visited the Pope in 1961, he took pains to point out to her that he had served in the British army. He was an academician of France.

February 22, 1972.

Professor Richard Titmuss, C.B.E., scholar, writer, teacher and adviser to the Labour Party in Britain and to many governments abroad, died on April 6, 1973 in London. He had an immense influence on social thought both in Britain and overseas. He moulded the subject of social administration into its modern form in Britain and the vast expansion in this field of study since the Second World War has been spearheaded by professors, the majority of whom have been his pupils or members of his department at the L.S.E.

Titmuss was almost unique for this age in having first entered university life as a professor. His formal education ended at the age of 15. Though five universities throughout the world awarded him degrees, all of them were honorary. He was born in 1907, the son of a Bedfordshire small farmer. For 17 years he worked in an insurance company and became a London inspector at an early age. In his spare time he wrote three books *Poverty and Population* (1938), *Our Food Problem* (1939) with a friend, F. Le Gros Clark, and *Parents Revolt* (1942) with his wife, to which Beatrice Webb contributed a foreword. Owing to poor health he was unable to join the armed forces.

The reception of his books was such that in 1942 he was invited by Keith (later Sir Keith) Hancock to join the team of historians writing the civil history of the war. It was not until 1949 that his first masterpiece, *Problems of Social Policy*, was published. More copies of it were sold than of any other volume in the series. Titmuss drew out all the moral dilemmas of planning the social services in war-time—from health services and social security services to the evacuation of children. While much of the Webb's writing had been flat and dull, Titmuss made social problems enthral-ling by writing not only from the administrator's point of view, but also with deep insight into the impact of services on families and individuals. It was this book and Keith Hancock's strong recommendation which won him his chair.

At the London School of Economics, where he became Professor of Social Administration in 1950, he rapidly attracted to him a group of young academics, who fell under his spell and influence. While his own list of publications is extremely impressive in both quality and quantity, a high proportion of the major studies of social policy undertaken by others in the fifties and sixties were conducted under his guidance, and were subjected to his criticism before publication. He was never too busy to comment on the work of others. And his help consisted not just of a hasty reading and a few general remarks, but of meticulous criticism of every line of manuscript for style and arrangement as well as content.

Titmuss did not, however, confine himself to writing and teaching. He was one of the first to appreciate the disadvantages of the plethora of specialized courses in social work and pushed for all-purpose "generic" training in this field. He thus anticipated the introduction of combined social services departments in local government on the training side by more than a decade.

He was much, if not more, concerned about the problems of the developing countries as those of Britain, Europe, and North America. Called in by the Government of Mauritius to advise on social security and health services, he soon recognized that the key problem of that country was population growth, and recommended social policies which were aimed above all else at family limitation. Though the Titmuss report—*Social Policies & Population Growth in Mauritius* (1961)—was highly controversial when presented, the main recommendations were accepted. The wide publicity given to the population problem led to action and within 10 years the birth rate in Mauritius had fallen dramatically.

It was in 1956 that Titmuss published the most significant of his shorter works—his lecture on the *Social Division of Welfare*, later republished as one of his *Essays on 'The Welfare State'* (1957). This seminal essay examined the relationship between the public social services, fringe benefits (such as sick pay and occupational pensions), and allowances in the income tax to meet social needs. He criticized the divisive character of current provisions and pleaded for an integrated social policy. In this essay are the intellectual roots of the Labour Party's plans for social security—particularly National Superannuation and the clawback of child tax allowances when family allowances were increased in 1967-68. In the Labour Party's policy planning from 1956 onwards Titmuss played a central role either by acting as adviser himself or through his closest colleagues and friends, who were constantly consulting him.

Rarely if ever did Titmuss take the initiative to seek out ministers to press his ideas upon them. It was the ministers who sought out Titmuss.

Unlike much of Titmuss's other writing, which was essentially philosophical in approach, his *Income Distribution & Social Change* (1962) is a statistical critique. It is a massive onslaught on those who had argued from such published statistics as were available that the distribution of income had become less unequal since the war. He put under a microscope the official statistics of personal incomes in the United Kingdom since 1938 and found them grossly inadequate for the use to which some had put them, and indicated the wide variety of methods by which resources could be manipulated to avoid income tax, surtax, and death duties.

Just as Titmuss spent seven years, with many interruptions, ferreting out details on tax statistics, so he spent seven years examining human blood—how it was collected for transfusion and other purposes, and how it was distributed throughout the world. His book, *The Gift Relationship* (1970), is a critique of the commercial market in human blood. Having chosen the theme, he mastered all the techniques needed to study it. The book is of immensely wide intellectual scope; it covers legal, political, and medical issues, it applies concepts from sociology, anthropology and economics, and is above all else an essay on altruism. The book became a best-seller, particularly in the United States. Within a few months, Richardson, the United States Secretary of State of Health, Education and Welfare, was privately consulting him on the problem. Within a year legislation was before Congress to regulate the private market in blood.

Throughout his life he played an active part in the detailed administration of the social services and sat on an unending chain of government committees.

He will be greatly missed by his wife, daughter, and friends throughout the world.

April 7, 1973.

When **George Todd** died in Torquay on January 17, 1974 at the age of 79, a great chapter in the history of English racing ended. In fact Todd's life was not so much a chapter but a story in itself rich with fascination. It is to be regretted that he never commissioned anyone to write his biography because surely it would have been a best-seller, a treasured volume in every racing home.

Todd was one of racing's great characters and a marvellous exponent of the art of training thoroughbreds. He adored his horses and his horses responded to his affection. He would have dearly loved to spend his last days in the surrounds of his beloved Manton, the 1,500 acre estate a couple of miles west of Marlborough which he bought in 1948 on the advice of Fred Darling. But life decreed otherwise and when ill health forced him to retire at the end of the last flat racing season he sold Manton as well.

George Edward Todd was born on December 12, 1894. Tall and erect throughout all his life, he preferred to keep his age a secret from the majority, but when he received his Derby Award at the Horserace Writers Association's annual lunch in December 1972 he had, only 24 hours earlier, celebrated his 78th birthday among some of his closest friends at a party given for him in London—with all the *joie de vivre* of a man half his age.

This was typical of Todd, whose eye for a pretty girl matched his eye for a horse and whose love of life was infectious. He was English through and through. Having been wounded in Flanders in 1915, he vowed never to leave these shores again and not once did he break that vow. His dislike of travel even stopped him going to Ireland in 1966 to see his colt Sodium win the Irish Sweeps Derby.

After the First World War Todd spent five years working for Bert Lines at Exning on the outskirts of Newmarket. He then became head lad to Tom Coulthwaite, a position that he held for two years. He once said that it was while he was working for Coulthwaite that he learnt how to keep horses sound, relaxed and happy, and the art of feeding.

In 1928 Todd decided that the moment was ripe to set up his own shop, so to speak, and he rented a small yard at Royston. But he moved soon to East Ilsley in Berkshire, where he trained for a number of years before he took his string in 1948 to Manton. It was there that his career really blossomed.

Alec Taylor and Joe Lawson had been his predecessors at Manton. They, too, were legendary characters and having made the place famous they were not easy men to follow, but Todd maintained the tradition of Manton. When Dramatic won the Lincolnshire Handicap in 1950 he landed such a gamble for his trainer that Todd was able to pay off his mortgage in one fell swoop.

Todd, bookmakers were soon to realize, was not only a shrewd judge of a horse but of the form book as well. He always fed his horses himself and perhaps this partially explains why he knew every one so intimately. His rare insight into their character was perhaps also the reason why he had such success with elder horses and especially those which others deemed unmanageable. Latterly he listed Sodium, Roan Rocket, Oncidium, Dramatic, River Chanter, Trelawny, Parthian Glance and Double Red as the best horses that he trained, but in his memory old favourites such as Caught Out, Blazing Scent, Bradfield, Square Deal, Shira and Penharbour meant every bit as much to him.

No one was more admired or respected in racing circles than George Todd, and one feels privileged to have known the Master of Manton and to have seen him at work on those hallowed gallops. He leaves a widow, Audrey, whom he married in 1931.

January 19, 1974.

Professor Samuel Tolansky, F.R.S., who died on March 4, 1973 at the age of 65, was one of the first group of scientists chosen to examine dust brought to earth by the crews of the Apollo moon missions. This articulate and energetic physicist soon became known to millions of television viewers because of his prediction that the surface of parts of the moon was covered in "marble". In fact he was describing how microscopic beads of glass could be formed by the impact of a meteorite or by volcanic activity. A shower of molten material would be ejected to produce millions of glass droplets.

Analyses at his laboratory at Royal Holloway College, London University, showed the accuracy of his predictions, and they also revealed a mineral composition that was inexplicably dissimilar from substances on earth. What Professor Tolansky brought to the lunar investigation was an extraordinary expertise in scientific instrument techniques.

He contributed a significant amount to the revolution in understanding of optical and electronic phenomena that over the past 30 years has produced many new tools of investigation for the research worker. Before enlightening the wider audience of Apollo-watchers, Samuel Tolansky had already been key man for producers in the education and documentary departments of the B.B.C. In one of his characteristically irrepressible moments, he demonstrated to a television audience a device that could make viewers smell things which were in the studio. In response to his closing remarks, hundreds telephoned to say they could smell the onions and coffee he had displayed on that particular *April 1!*

Professor Tolansky was elected a fellow of the Royal Society in 1952. He joined Royal Holloway College from Manchester University in 1947. During the Second World War he had worked on nuclear physics. He was married in 1935, and had one son and one daughter.

March 6, 1973.

Professor J. R. R. Tolkien, C.B.E., Rawlinson and Bosworth Professor of Anglo-Saxon at Oxford from 1925 to 1945, and from 1945 to 1959 Merton Professor of English Language and Literature, died at the age of 81 on September 2, 1973.

He was the author of *The Hobbit* and *The Lord of the Rings*, two much loved and immensely popular books, which sold millions of copies and have been translated into scores of languages. He was created C.B.E. in 1972.

John Ronald Reuel Tolkien was born on January 3, 1892, at Bloemfontein, South Africa, where his father died in 1896. The family returned to England, where Tolkien's early years were passed in what was then Worcestershire country, though now buried in the red brick of outer Birmingham.

He was taught by his mother, from whom he derived all his bents and early knowledge, linguistic, romantic, and naturalist. To his descent through her, from the Suffields (originally of Evesham) he used to attribute that love for the Western Marches which manifested itself alike in Mercian studies (his primary philological interest) and in the elvish or "hobbity" strain in his imagination. In those days he had an "almost idolatrous" love of trees and flowers and a hunger for Arthurian romance, classical mythology, and especially George Macdonald.

In 1903 he went with a scholarship (gained by his mother's teaching) to King Edward's School, Birmingham, of which he reported much good and little evil. His form master, George Brewerton (a "fierce teacher"), introduced him to Chaucer in the correct pronunciation and lent him an Anglo-Saxon grammar; and R. W. Reynolds introduced him to literary criticism. In 1900 he had already, with his mother and brother, been received into the Church of Rome, and on his mother's death in 1904 Fr. Francis Morgan, of the Birmingham Oratory, became his guardian. Of Fr. Morgan, Tolkien always spoke with the warmest gratitude and affection.

In 1910 he won an exhibition at Exeter College, Oxford. By the high standards of King Edward's School the award was tolerable rather than praiseworthy, and indeed Tolkien used to describe himself as "one of the idlest boys Gilson (the Headmaster) ever had". But "idleness" in his case meant private and unaided studies in Gothic, Anglo-Saxon and Welsh, and the first attempt at inventing a language—of which more hereafter.

He went into residence in 1911. Dr. Jackson was still Rector and the College had no resident classical tutor until the appointment of E. A. Barber. He came too late to be of much help and Tolkien took only a 2nd in Honour Moderations, having somewhat neglected his studies in favour of "Old Norse, festivity, and classical philology". "My love for the classics," he once said, "took ten years to recover from lectures on Cicero and Demosthenes."

It was at this period that he first came under the influence of Joseph Wright; and he was now busily engaged on the invention of the "Elvish language". This was no arbitrary gibberish but a really possible tongue with consistent roots, sound laws, and inflexions, into which he poured all his imaginative and philological powers; and strange as the exercise may seem it was undoubtedly the source of that unparalleled

richness and concreteness which later distinguished him from all other philologists. He had been inside language. He had not gone far with his invention before he discovered that every language presupposes a mythology; and at once began to fill in the mythology presupposed by Elvish.

In 1915 he took a First in English. Sisam and Craigie had been his tutors and Napier his professor. Immediately after Schools he entered the Lancashire Fusiliers. In 1916 he married Edith Bratt, whom he had known since boyhood. In 1918 he was back at Oxford, invalided out of the Army, and began to teach for the English School; E. V. Gordon was among his first pupils.

From 1920 to 1925 he worked at Leeds, first as Reader in English and later as Professor of English Language. George Gordon, E. V. Gordon and Lascelles Abercrombie were his colleagues, and some of his best work was done in building up a flourishing department of English Philology from small beginnings.

In 1925 he succeeded Craigie at Oxford as Rawlinson and Bosworth Professor of Anglo-Saxon, and in 1945 vacated that chair to become Merton Professor of English Language and Literature.

His Middle English Vocabulary had appeared in 1922. His edition of *Sir Gawain and the Green Knight* (in collaboration with E. V. Gordon) followed in 1925; *Beowulf: the Monsters and the Critics* in 1937; his Andrew Lang Lecture (on Fairy Tales) in 1939. He became an Hon.D.Litt. of University College, Dublin, and of Liège in 1954.

His most extensive researches were in the West Midland dialect from the Anglo-Saxon period to that of the *Ancrene Riwle;* in this work his most distinguished pupil was Professor d'Ardenne. He retired from the Merton professorship on reaching the age limit in 1959 and was later elected an emeritus fellow of the college.

During the years 1925-35 he was, more than any other single man, responsible for closing the old rift between "literature" and "philology" in English studies at Oxford and thus giving the existing school its characteristic temper. His unique insight at once into the language of poetry and into the poetry of language qualified him for this task.

Thus the private language and its offshoot, the private mythology, were directly connected with some of the most highly practical results he achieved, while they continued in private to burgeon into tales and poems which seldom reached print, though they might have won him fame in almost any period but the twentieth century.

The Hobbit (1937) was in origin a fragment from this cycle adapted for juvenile tastes but with one all important novelty, the Hobbits themselves. It is doubtful how far he realized that these comfort-loving, unambitious, and (in aspiration) unheroic creatures embodied what he loved best in the English character and saw most en-

dangered by the growth of "subtopia", bureaucracy, journalism, and industrialization.

They soon demanded to be united with his heroic myth on a far deeper level than *The Hobbit* had allowed, and by 1936 he was at work on his great romance *The Lord of the Rings*, published in three volumes (1954 and 1955) and often reprinted and translated. The ironic destiny which links the humble happiness of Hobbits to the decision of vast issues which they would gladly ignore, and which even makes civilization itself momentarily dependent on their latent and reluctant courage, is its central theme. It has no allegory.

These things were not devised to reflect any particular situation in the real world. It was the other way round: real events began, horribly, to conform to the pattern he had freely invented. Hence those who heard the growing work read chapter by chapter in the months that followed the fall of France found it as relevant, as stern, and as tonic, as Churchill's* promise of blood, sweat and tears. It cut right across all contemporary canons of criticism, and its success, when published, surprised and delighted the author and his friends.

Tolkien's spirited farce *Farmer Giles of Ham* (1954) was work of a wholly different type.

Only a tithe of the poems, translations, articles, lectures and notes in which his multifarious interest found expression ever reached the printer. His standard of self criticism was high and the mere suggestion of publication usually set him upon a revision, in the course of which so many new ideas occurred to him that where his friends had hoped for the final text of an old work they actually got the first draft of a new one.

He was a man of "cronies" rather than of general society and was always best after midnight (he had a Johnsonian horror of going to bed) and in some small circle of intimates where the tone was at once Bohemian, literary, and Christian (for he was profoundly religious).

He has been described as "the best and worst talker in Oxford"—worst for the rapidity and indistinctness of his speech, and best for the penetration, learning, humour and "race" of what he said. C. L. Wrenn, R. B. McCallum of Pembroke, H. V. D. Dyson of Merton, C. S. Lewis* of Magdalen, and Charles Williams were among those who most often made his audience (and interrupters) on such occasions.

September 3, 1973.

Nicholas Tomalin, who was killed in Israel on October 17, 1973, was one of the finest reporters of his generation. He was a brave, clever, witty and scrupulously honest man; these qualities, together with a wide and natural compassion, informed his writing throughout a brilliant, varied and increasingly successful career.

The word "reporter" is used with care. Although he filled many other roles in journalism—as a creative editor, as a wise and generous executive, to whom many other men owed the decisive moments in their careers, and as a perceptive and well read literary critic—it is as a reporter that he will above all be remembered.

It takes no credit away from anyone else to say that it was probably Tomalin's despatches in *The Sunday Times* which did more than any other one piece of reporting to bring home to people in Britain the dimensions of the Vietnamese tragedy. He was able to do that because he could combine the analytical powers of a first-class intellect with an unsurpassed fluency and vigour of language.

He once wrote that "a journalist's . . . required talent is the creation of interest". This was a self-set standard by which he never failed; if it is true to say that he never wrote a coarse or callous line, it is also true to say that he never wrote a dull one.

Tomalin was born in London in 1931. He was evacuated to Canada during the war, and then educated at Bryanston School and Trinity Hall, Cambridge. He was President of the Cambridge Union in 1954 and was editor of *Granta*. He first made his name in Fleet Street as a *Daily Express* gossip columnist. He edited the *Evening Standard* Londoner's Diary, and wrote *The Sunday Times's* Atticus column.

In between times he was editor of *Town Magazine* and of the news weekly *Topic*. Some people were, perhaps, surprised when the brilliantly entertaining columnist developed into the foreign correspondent and investigator. Such surprise must have been due to a confusion between seriousness and solemnity—a confusion which Tomalin never made.

In 1967 he left *The Sunday Times* and served for a time as literary editor of the *New Statesman*. As if there were any further need to demonstrate his versatility, he also worked with notable success in television. In 1969 he wrote, with his colleague Ron Hall, a biography of the yachtsman Donald Crowhurst. And shortly before he left for his last assignment in Israel, he completed a history of the National Theatre.

In the paper of Sunday, October 14, he reported, with characteristic irony, on the honour of being the first Englishman to be bombed by the new Russian Sukhoi bomber. In the incident his Israeli taxi driver suffered a broken leg. The last message Tomalin sent to London was to ask *The Sunday Times* to make arrangements for the taxi driver to be looked after and compensated for loss of work.

Nicholas Tomalin was one of the best journalists of his generation. He had a feeling for the way in which the world was changing; he responded to the changes without many illusions, but with the quick and curious eye which made his writing so vivid.

Like many good journalists he had always an element of insecurity in his response to the world; he never seemed quite sure that the world he reported was a party to which he had been invited. He wrote with the irony that insecurity gives, and was equally ironically surprised to find himself in Gray's Inn Road or observing the Zapping of Charlie Cong in Vietnam.

His friends will all be surprised that he is dead. He did not seem the sort of man to whom that would happen, not because he did not take risks, but because his vitality seemed to divorce him from the possible consequences of those risks. He is a great loss to English reporting, and nobody will cover his kind of story again the way he did.

Tomalin leaves his wife, Claire, three daughters and a son.

October 18, 1973.

Henri Tomasi, French composer and conductor, died in Avignon on January 13, 1971 in his 70th year.

Born in Marseilles, of Corsican descent, on August 17, 1901, Tomasi studied music in his home town and at the Conservatoire in Paris, where he carried off the Grand Prix de Rome at the age of 26 for his Cantata *Coriolan*. He was musical director of the French Radio between the wars and also conducted in Indo-China, before becoming musical director of the Monte Carlo Opera from 1946 to 1950. He was considered to be an exemplary interpreter of the works of Debussy, Ravel and Dukas, and reached the first rung of the ladder of international recognition—that took him to Dublin, Switzerland, and other parts of Europe—with the Concertgebouw Orchestra at the Interlaken Festival in 1946.

After 1955 he devoted himself exclusively to composition, using a lyrical mode of expression in all his writing (orchestral and otherwise) that was especially notable in a series of operas (and ballets) that deserve a greater acceptance, for their mellifluous neoclassicism, than they ever earned. His acknowledged operatic masterpiece, *Don Juan de Manara*, was written in unoccupied France but not staged until 1956 by the Bavarian State Opera in Munich. It was brilliantly revived in Mulhouse two years later. His *L'Atlantide*, based on Pierre Benoit's novel, had first been heard in Mulhouse in 1954 while his *Sampiero Corso*, inspired by recollections of Corsica, inaugurated the Bordeaux Festival of 1956 before being repeated at the Holland Festival in the same year.

Many of his operas were staged throughout France, Belgium and Germany. *Poverello*, a chamber opera about St. Francis, won him the City of Paris music prize in 1957, and he set Vercors's wartime story, *Le Silence de la Mer*, to music two years later.

The Opéra Comique put on his *Princess Pauline* in 1962. The lyrical quality of much of his writing was not without an exotic element, which clearly had its roots in Provence in particular and in the Mediterranean in general. Two of his most recent compositions were a symphony, inspired by Aimé Césaire's drama *Season in the Congo*, and a "Hymn to Vietnam", with words by Jean-Paul Sartre.

January 22, 1971.

Brigadier Sir Philip Toosey, C.B.E., D.S.O., died on December 22, 1975 at the age of 71.

Although Philip Toosey was distinguished in many other walks of life, and gave freely of his time and energy in charitable works—particularly to the Liverpool School of Tropical Medicine—it is as a leading figure in the Far Eastern Prisoners of War Federation, of which he became President on the death of General Percival*, that he will be chiefly remembered.

It was during the F.E.P.O.W.s' grim years of captivity during the last war, in which 10,000 of them died in the Japanese prison camps and on the notorious Railway of Death, that Toosey displayed those qualities of leadership which made him a most beloved and legendary figure. As Commandant of many of the prison camps, he stood up for them, often at the risk of severe physical punishment to himself. He, better than anyone, knew how to handle his own fellow prisoners, British, Dutch and Australian, and also how to handle their often very brutal Japanese jailers.

He knew that in order to have a chance of survival the military prisoners must retain their discipline, their self-respect, their morale and—above all—their sense of humour. And perhaps most important of all, he played a leading part in the very hush-hush "V. Scheme", whereby money was obtained—at the risk of the death penalty—from sources outside the prison camps to buy medicines and extra food which saved the lives of so many F.E.P.O.W.s.

After the war, when some 38,000 British ex-prisoners of war returned to Britain, Philip Toosey played a leading part in their rehabilitation and in the development of their federation into one of the finest ex-Service Associations in Britain.

But the war years had taken toll of even Toosey's fine physique and in his last years he had been living, as he himself put it, "very much on borrowed time". But he never allowed his rapidly increasing physical disabilities to deter him from his work for his hospitals and his F.E.P.O.W.s. He accepted the borrowed time with gladness and put it to the greatest advantage up to the last days of his life.

December 23, 1975.

Admiral of the Fleet Lord Tovey, of Langton Matravers, G.C.B., K.B.E., D.S.O., who died on January 12, 1971 at the age of 85, first made his name as a destroyer-captain in the 1914-18 War, gaining special promotion to the rank of commander for "the persistent and determined manner in which he attacked enemy ships" during the Battle of Jutland (1916).

In between the wars his service ashore and afloat gained him further rapid promotion, and in 1935 he achieved Flag rank.

On the outbreak of the Second World War he held the important command of the Mediterranean Fleet's destroyer flotillas under Sir Andrew Cunningham (later Lord Cunningham of Hyndhope*). In that capacity he took part in the early convoy operations to supply Malta and the Middle East forces, and contributed much to building up the great fighting reputation of the Mediterranean flotillas, which was to stand the fleet and the nation in very good stead during the successive crises of 1941-42. In July 1940 the Mediterranean commands were reorganized and Tovey took over the whole of the light forces on the station, as well as becoming second-in-command to Cunningham. He led the light forces in the action with the Italian fleet off the coast of Calabria on July 9, 1940, but in the following autumn he was recalled to Britain to take command of the Home Fleet in succession to Admiral Sir Charles Forbes.

Though the threat of invasion was by that time no longer imminent, Tovey had to face a very difficult situation. In addition to the rising onslaught by enemy submarines and aircraft on the Atlantic lifeline, made possible by the acquisition of bases in western France, powerful German surface warships several times broke out by one or other of the far northern passages to attack the lightly defended convoys.

Early in 1941 the battle cruisers Scharnhorst and Gneisenau were at large for more than two months, evaded Tovey's pursuing forces and got safely into Brest harbour. The climax came in the following May, when the newly completed battleship Bismarck and the heavy cruiser Prinz Eugen broke out by the Denmark Strait between Iceland and Greenland. Tovey, forewarned of the movement, had stationed cruisers on patrol and taken the main fleet to sea; but the first contact led to the destruction by the Bismarck of the 25-year-old battle cruiser Hood. Her loss was avenged three days later when, after a long and anxious chase, Tovey's battleships caught and sank the Bismarck, whose speed had been drastically reduced by carrier aircraft, when she had nearly reached safety.

With the German attack on Russia in June 1941 Tovey had to undertake the prolonged and hazardous operations of passing supply convoys to Murmansk and Archangel. In March 1942 he narrowly failed to catch the Bismarck's sister-ship Tirpitz when she tried to attack one such convoy.

But the conduct of the Arctic convoys and the lack of what Tovey regarded as a proper contribution by the R.A.F. to the Atlantic battle, particularly in relation to the effort put into bombing German cities, brought the C.-in-C. into conflict with both the Admiralty and the Prime Minister, Winston Churchill*. As to the former, the climax came in July 1942, when the Admiralty, anticipating attack on an Arctic convoy by greatly superior German forces based in north Norway, ordered the convoy to scatter in the Barents Sea. The result was disastrous, and Tovey, who was never a man to pull his punches or mince his words, made it plain that he regarded the Admiralty's constant interference in the conduct of his operations as the chief cause of the calamity. There is no doubt that at this time Churchill wished to have Tovey, whom he once described as "a stubborn and obstinate man", relieved from his command. At a meeting at Chequers he tried to persuade Cunningham to take over the Home Fleet; but Cunningham flatly declined to do so unless Tovey, who undoubtedly enjoyed the confidence of his whole fleet, fell sick.

In July 1943 Tovey, having served the normal 2½ years in command of the Home Fleet, was appointed Commander-in-Chief, The Nore. Preparations for the return of the Allied armies to Europe were then actively in hand, and the Nore Command played a very large part in all aspects of the greatest combined operation ever launched. Tovey, who had been promoted Admiral of the Fleet in 1943, received a special expression of the Admiralty's appreciation of the "outstanding contribution" made by his command to the success of the invasion of Normandy. He became a peer in 1946.

John Cronyn Tovey was born on March 7, 1885 the son of Lieutenant-Colonel Hamilton Tovey, R.E., and joined the training ship Britannia just before his fifteenth birthday. His first sea service was in the Majestic under Admiral Sir A. K. Wilson.

The outbreak of war found him serving as first lieutenant of the light cruiser Amphion. By sinking the German minelayer Königin Luise on August 5, 1914, she was the first British warship to be in action; but the very next day she was herself sunk by one of the mines laid by her victim. Tovey then moved to the destroyer Faulknor, still as first lieutenant; but at the beginning of 1915 he achieved the first of a long series of destroyer commands, during most of which he was attached to Admiral Sir David Beatty's Battle Cruiser Fleet. It was in the Onslow of the 13th Flotilla that at Jutland Tovey first of all "harassed the German battle fleet" and there, in spite of being severely damaged, attacked one of Admiral Hipper's battle cruisers. Forty-eight hours later the Onslow reached Aberdeen in tow of another damaged destroyer.

In 1932 he took command of the battleship Rodney in the Home Fleet. This was the period when Admiral Sir John Kelly, the C.-in-C., was pulling the Navy out of the slough of despond into which it had fallen at the time of the Invergordon mutiny, and Tovey certainly contributed greatly to Kelly's success.

Tovey married in 1916. His wife died in 1970.

January 13, 1971.

Professor Arnold Toynbee, C.H., Emeritus Professor of International History in the University of London, died on October 22, 1975 at the age of 86.

He was among the outstanding intellectual figures of our time. In his annual Surveys of International Affairs he brought the historian's impartiality and detachment to bear upon contemporary affairs, and in his study of history he used his lively knowledge of mankind to set forth his views on the recurrent rise and fall of civilization and the general directions and meaning of human events.

Arnold Joseph Toynbee was born on April 14, 1889, and was a scholar both of Winchester and of Balliol. His Oxford record included a Craven scholarship as well as a first in Mods and Greats, and after a year at the British School of Athens he became a fellow of his college. Soon after the outbreak of war in 1914 he entered government service and was a member of the Middle Eastern section of the British delegation to the Paris Peace Conference.

In 1919 Toynbee was appointed to the newly founded Koraes Professorship of Byzantine and Modern Greek Language, Literature and History at King's College, London, and two years later was given leave to travel in Greece and Asia Minor for the further study of the subjects of his chair. Before leaving England he had expressed his readiness to resign if his view of the Greco-Turkish quarrel, then moving towards its climax, embarrassed the college authorities. In *The Western Question in Greece and Turkey: A Study in the Contact of Civilizations*, published in 1922, he revealed the drift of his thought. The Turkish Empire, like its Byzantine predecessor, was founded on religion and classified its subjects according to their faith. The equilibrium thus established was disturbed by the introduction of western ideas of nationality and finally upset by the Greek occupation of Smyrna. In other writings he attacked the action of the Greek authorities, though it was not till the end of 1923 that his resignation of his chair became effective. Toynbee explained and defended his conduct in a letter to *The Times*.

In 1926 a foundation by the late Sir Daniel Stevenson opened a new and more constructive chapter in Toynbee's life. Convinced that hatreds were generated by the nationalist teaching of history, and desirous that the subject should be taught and studied "internationally and as far as possible without bias", Sir Daniel Stevenson founded a Professorship of History in the

University of London to be held in conjunction with the Directorship of Studies at Chatham House. Toynbee was appointed to the joint post and used his position to issue the annual Surveys of International Affairs which, throughout the period between the two wars, established themselves as indispensable works of reference. In the preparation of these detailed studies Toynbee was assisted throughout by Miss V. M. Boulter and as time went on he gathered round him disciples who became responsible for particular sections. Much of each survey, however, came from his own vigorous if sometimes too fluent pen.

Toynbee was not wholly uncritical in his careful exposition of international developments. Like Acton, he was above all things a moralist and when he came upon conduct which violated his ethical standards his detachment fell away from him and he became merciless in his castigation. The other duties of his chair were by no means overlooked. His *Journey to China*, published in 1931, gave his impressions of things seen on his travels to and from the Institute of Pacific Relations Conference at Kyoto; he edited the proceedings of the British Commonwealth Relations Conference at Toronto in 1933; and he delivered occasional public lectures.

In spite of all the calls thus made on his time and energy, Toynbee pushed steadily ahead with the *Study of History*. The first three volumes of this great work were published in 1934 and Oxford recognized their quality by conferring an honorary degree upon their author. The practical purpose of the study was to widen the limits of historical knowledge by a more general and comprehensive treatment of events. To this end Toynbee took as the unit of his study not particular nations but whole civilizations, of which he distinguished 21—seven of them still extant. What particularly impressed him was the rhythm manifest in human affairs, the regular recurrence of periods of growth and decay, and he found the explanation of those in profound collective experiences of an essentially moral or religious nature.

Volumes IV, V, VI, published just before the outbreak of war, extended this treatment to the later stages of civilizations. In the course of their growth civilizations almost inevitably commit the sin of *hubris,* which is expressed in nationalism, in militarism, and in the tyranny of a dominant minority. This moral breakdown brings with it its own *nemesis*. In a last desperate attempt to preserve their rule the dominant minority create a Universal State and thus obtain a brief reprieve before succumbing to the attacks of internal and external proletariats. Yet in the death-throes of a civilization human suffering is regarded by a new religious insight, the beginning of a Universal Religion which in turn engenders a new civilization.

As regards our own civilization, the western European, Toynbee was on the whole pessimistic. He felt that it had almost reached the stage at which a Universal State would be formed, and that its *nemesis* was not far off. He repudiated, however, any rigid determinism and held that western man might yet be saved if he would abandon his *hubris* and turn again to God.

The outbreak of war brought these activities to a close. The unpublished conclusion of the Study was sent for safety to the United States and Toynbee became head of the Foreign Research and Press Service —in effect a branch of the Foreign Office— set up in Oxford. In 1943, after its transfer to London, the service was renamed the Foreign Office Research Department and Toynbee continued to act as its director.

After the war he returned to Chatham House, where a grant from the Rockefeller Foundation enabled him to devote the greater part of his time to the completion of what could for once aptly be described as his *magnum opus*. The publication in 1947 of a one-volume abridgment of the first six volumes of *A Study of History* made his views known to a much wider public, especially in America, where his name became almost a household word. He spent one or two winters at the Institute of Advanced Study in Princeton, New Jersey, and in 1952 delivered the Reith Lectures, which were later published under the title *The World and the West*. Here he argued that the arrogance with which the Europeans had treated the colonial peoples of Asia and Africa was typical of the behaviour of a dominant minority towards an external proletariat. The appropriate retribution could be avoided only by a total change of attitude, a genuine humility and sense of brotherhood with all mankind.

With the appearance of the last four volumes of *A Study of History* in 1954, the religious basis of Toynbee's teachings, which had previously been latent, now became predominant. Civilizations were to be looked on as essentially occasions for sin and suffering, as stepping-stones towards ever richer and deeper religious insights, in which lay the true progress of mankind. In boldly prophetic passages of an almost visionary character, he looked forward to the day when Civilization itself would be replaced by Religion, when a synthesis of the existing historical religion would bring to earth the Kingdom of Heaven and the Communion of Saints. He completed the work by recounting, with a disarming frankness, the various experiences and influences, some of them of a mystical character, which had affected and inspired his work.

But the completed work was much less well received than its earlier volumes. It now attracted a torrent of hostile criticism from other historians and sociologists which surprised and wounded Toynbee, whose own mind was as uncritical as his temper was uncontroversial.

The religious theme was taken up again in his Gifford Lectures, published as *An Historian's Approach to Religion* (1956), in which he set forth his views on the essence of all religions. The great historical religions, Toynbee held, each contained an essential aspect of the truth, though perverted and distorted by man's *hubris*. The true nature of God was inexpressible. It could best be experienced in the extreme suffering entailed by voluntary acts of love, suffering through which the sin inherent in human existence and human action was finally purged. Thus what had begun as a scientific examination of history was finally revealed as a message of redemption through suffering and through love.

In 1955 Toynbee retired from Chatham House and his chair. His retirement was spent in almost incessant travel, lecturing and writing. His aim, as he himself characteristically put it, was to continue his education, and especially to see with his own eyes places he had known only from books and maps. An 18-month journey round the world was recorded in his second historical travel book, *East to West* (1958). The following year his *Hellenism* was published for the Home University Library, a history of Greco-Roman civilization that he had planned and begun in 1914. But he continued to be preoccupied with the elaboration and defence of *A Study of History*. He added to it a volume of maps and a final volume of "Reconsiderations" (1961), in which he tried to meet and profit from his critics. Here he showed once more the extraordinary absorptiveness and flexibility of his mind, as well as the poetical inspiration and philosophical simplicity that governed his intellectual system.

He continued to publish prolifically. His later books included *Acquaintances* (1967); *Man's Concern with Death* (1968); *Experiences* (1969); *Some Problems of Greek History* (1969); *Cities on the Move* (1970); *Constantine Porphyrogenitus and his World* (1972), a magisterial study of the tenth-century Byzantine emperor; a further illustrated abridgement of *A Study of History* (1972); and *Half the World* (ed. 1973), a cultural history of China and Japan.

The breadth of Toynbee's views and the sweeping nature of his generalizations were little compatible with the empirical and specialist character of contemporary English historical scholarship. The philosophy of history is generally looked on in Britain as an aberrant product of German romanticism. Toynbee's religious preoccupations, moreover, were out of keeping with the excessively rationalist character of our times. Yet the most severe of his critics could not deny his vast erudition, his astonishing industry and the splendours of his style, enriched as it was by all the resources of classical learning and a deep literary familiarity with the Christian scriptures.

Whatever judgment posterity may make of his views of history, it must praise him for undertaking to solve some of the most fundamental of human problems. His work will always remain a rich mine of insights and perspectives for those condemned to labour in narrower fields. In his personal life, those who knew him can testify to his extraordinary modesty and humility. The serenity of his expression and the charming kindliness of his manner spoke of one who had lived his religion as well as written about it.

In 1913 Toynbee married Rosalind, daughter of Professor Gilbert Murray, O.M., by whom he had two sons. The marriage was dissolved in 1946. He married secondly Veronica Marjorie, daughter of the Rev. Sidney Boulter, who had been for many years his assistant at Chatham House and whom he came to regard as the collaborator in his later works.

He was made a Companion of Honour in 1956 and showered with honorary degrees by universities in Britain and America.

October 23, 1975.

Sir Humphrey de Trafford—See de Trafford.

Lord Trevethin and Oaksey—See Oaksey.

Professor Lionel Trilling, University Professor Emeritus at Columbia University, died in New York on November 5, 1975 at the age of 70.

He was one of the three or four finest American literary critics of his time. His lucid and urbane prose and the liberal-conservative temper of his mind made him particularly attractive to English readers and, indeed, his earliest important books were on two English writers, E. M. Forster* and Matthew Arnold, who had done so much to shape his own attitudes. He shared with Forster a belief in the intelligent heart and with Arnold a deeply serious concern for the wider cultural context of literature. Two of his best essays were on Dickens's *Little Dorrit* and on Jane Austen's *Mansfield Park*. Like Matthew Arnold, he was an enemy of provincial self-complacency and a friend of the "free play of mind", a subject which preoccupied him with increasing urgency in the last year of his life. He sharply criticized what is called in America liberalism, and what might be called in Britain an uncritical progressivism; but always, like Arnold, from an essentially liberal point of view.

The influence of Forster can be seen in Trilling's one novel, *The Middle of the Journey*, a study of an honest man steering a lonely path between fellow-travelling and reactionary obscurantism. This novel, re-issued earlier in 1975, is perhaps too much of a tract for the times to be wholly satisfactory as a work of art, but at least one of Trilling's short stories, *Of This Time, Of That Place*, based on his long experience as a teacher of English, is a masterpiece. He was an exciting teacher, and a gifted administrator who had much to do with organizing the Kenyon School of Letters, subsequently the School of Letters at Indiana University. It is, however, as a subtle, deep and humane critic of literature and society that he will be mainly remembered.

Lionel Trilling was born in New York in 1905 of Jewish parents, and educated in public schools in that city, and took his M.A. at Columbia in 1926. From 1926 to 1932, he taught at the University of Wisconsin and at Hunter College, New York, and made his reputation as a sparkling and authoritative reviewer. In 1932, he became an instructor in English at Columbia, in 1938 he took his doctorate there, and in 1948 was made Professor of English Literature, a post he held until 1965. His wider fame began with the studies of Arnold and Forster (respectively, 1938 and 1943), and most of all with the publication of *The Liberal Imagination* in 1950. The essays in this book and in Trilling's other important collection of the 1950s, *The Opposing Self* (1955), are remarkable for the persuasiveness with which they draw the attention of a perhaps recalcitrant American reader to the importance, for very much if not all great literature, of the tragic, the ironical, and the basically unjust elements in life. Trilling was never tired of emphasizing that certain aspects of social life of which we cannot abstractly approve—frustration, division, even snobbery—though they are things which a generous democratic spirit wants to sweep away, are things also which richly nourish the creative imagination.

An apostle of maturity and of fine discrimination, Trilling could fiercely attack the crudities that can sometimes go with the progressive spirit. One of his best essays, outside the field of pure literary criticism, is an attack on the subhuman attitude to man's sexual nature which seemed to him to underlie the Kinsey reports. His attitude to literature, though scrupulously serious, was never narrowly academic, and he could bring his interest in politics, in the philosophy of Hegel, in the psychology of Freud, or (for he was always profoundly loyal to his Jewish heritage) in Rabbinical wisdom, illuminatingly to bear on the task of critical appreciation. He was a better critic of prose than verse—in his book on Arnold, for instance, the critic of literature and society gets more concentrated attention than the poet—and was, perhaps, with his almost intuitive grasp of social atmospheres, at his most brilliant as a critic of the novel.

He was George Edward Woodberry Professor of Literature at Columbia from 1964 to 1970 and George Eastman Visiting Professor at Oxford from 1964 to 1965. His later collections of essays and lectures—*Beyond Culture* (1966) and *Sincerity and Authenticity* (1972)—together with the Jefferson Lecture, *Mind in the Modern World* (1972), comprise an increasingly aggressive defence of the moral liberalism and intellectual standards which came under fierce attack in the cultural and educational crisis of the 1960s. He was profoundly shocked by the violent events of 1968 at Columbia, after which his faith in the University as a refuge of clear thinking and Jeffersonian equality was never quite the same; yet those events did nothing if not confirm his own earlier anxieties and warnings.

Starting from the belief, in *Beyond Culture*, that the characteristic element in modern literature was "the bitter line of hostility to civilization that runs through it", he examined with some depth the reviving strength of this "adversary culture", itself a phenomenon at once more literary and more deeply established than the "counter-culture" of the 1960s and traced by Trilling from Diderot's *Neveu de Rameau* to Nietzsche's *Birth of Tragedy* and Conrad's *Heart of Darkness*, the last especially a text to which he paid great attention in the last decade of his life.

Trilling believed that moral life was indeed "in process of reviving itself" and it was entirely characteristic of his approach to the Apollonian and Dionysiac antithesis of Nietzsche, the Id and Ego of Freud, that Trilling was concerned to show how twentieth-century man has deliberately misinterpreted both men, choosing to regard them as perpetrators of division between the elements of human consciousness rather than agents of reconciliation. Trilling's own scholarship was always conceived in a spirit of healing.

The teaching of literature itself came under fire after 1968, and Trilling's position became, as one reviewer noted, both lonelier and stronger. On the one hand he was fearful that literature might follow mathematics, science and philosophy into areas of specialization where the reasonably educated man might never pass; on the other he sensed both the injustice of continuing inequalities and the dangers of rounding down, rather than up, the standards of instruction. He resisted as courageously as anyone of his generation the attacks on objectivity, the cult of "authenticity" (otherwise known as doing your thing) and the widespread distrust of mind over instinct all of which have become common in the last ten years.

The conclusion of the first Thomas Jefferson Lecture in the Humanities sums up as nobly as anything can his continuing faith in the human mind as well as his unique intellectual descent from Jefferson and Arnold, Conrad and Freud. "When mind", he told his Washington audience, "far from being ornamental, part of the superstructure of society, is the very model of the nation-state, as it is now for us, any falling off in its confidence in itself must be felt as a diminution of national possibility, as a lessening of the social hope. It is out of this belief that I have ventured to urge upon you the awareness that mind at the present time draws back from its own freedom and power, from its own delight in itself. That my having done so is not a counsel of despair is assured by one characteristic of mind, its wish to be conscious of itself, with what this implies of its ability to examine a course it has taken and to correct it."

Twentieth-century scholarship does not often point the state towards self-knowledge as purposefully as this.

Lionel Trilling's personality was a modest and charming one, and on visits to England he made many friends; he spoke of London with great warmth and affection. He leaves a widow, Diana Trilling, whose reviews and critical articles breathe the same spirit as his own. He will be long regretted, by his colleagues, pupils and by the general reader, as a fine, civilizing influence.

November 10, 1975.

Harry S. Truman, who died in the United States on December 26, 1972, at the age of 88, was perhaps the most surprising President of the United States within memory.

It was not just the unexpected circumstances under which he entered the White House in 1945, nor merely his fortuitous choice as Vice-President the year before. What did take his countrymen and the world by surprise was his remarkable capacity to grow in office, and in directions that were not to be foreseen in his background and experience.

He became a President of great decisions and routine failures. In the sphere of foreign policy in an era of more rapid and bewildering change for the United States than any similar period in her history, he met the challenge. There was the end of the Second World War with the historic decision to drop the atomic bombs on Japan—whatever the rights and wrongs of this act, it was determined by Truman on at least understandable grounds and he never wavered in judgment under the impact of later controversy. There was the reversal of attitude to Russia in the light of Soviet diplomatic hostility and national aggrandizement in eastern Europe. There were military aid to Greece and Turkey, the Marshall Plan and the establishment of Nato—all marking the advance from isolationism, and for some Truman has not received his fair share of personal credit. The Point 4 programme inaugurated technical aid to underdeveloped countries. The Korean War, however unpopular it has since become in American mythology, deserves to be remembered as a prompt, courageous, and immensely significant response to communist aggression. Finally, there was one of the most difficult actions of all, the replacement of General MacArthur* and with it the assertion of civil over military authority.

It is an imposing record. Taken together these initiatives set the pattern for American foreign policy for succeeding decades—and none was as inevitable at the time as it may later have seemed. In particular, that the United States did not with the coming of peace retreat once more into her traditional isolationism owes much to Truman's readiness to face facts as he saw them, acknowledge his mistakes and change course where necessary. Not for nothing did he have on his desk a notice: "The buck stops here!"

This ability to grapple with the great issues of his time was especially striking in a man whose political experience with one of the notorious Democratic city machines, and as a respected, but certainly not outstanding, member of the Senate had hardly seemed to fit him for the task. That he was able to assume the burdens of world leadership for his country can be attributed not only to his innate toughness of mind and body, but also to a lifelong study and sense of history. But it was equally surprising that having passed the most acid of tests he, the machine politician, should fail in his control of the machine. His Administrations lacked the necessary stringent supervision and discipline in terms of both governmental efficiency and integrity. His personal honour was never in question, but there seemed to many Americans to be sufficient truth in the accusation of "the mess in Washington" for the phrase to have a damaging effect on Democratic fortunes in the 1952 election. Nor could he, a former Senator, establish a fruitful relationship with Congress.

The presidential paradox of Truman applied to his political campaigning as well. His defeat of Dewey for the presidency in 1948 was the most unforeseen electoral result this century, and remains to this day the pollster's nightmare. Yet he never established with his audiences the rapport of an Eisenhower*; he never commanded the eloquence of a Stevenson* or the magnetism of a Kennedy*. What he did possess was an enormous earthy relish for the rough and tumble of the hustings; he revelled in attack on a folksy level. That is why he can have had few superiors in the art of whistle-stop campaigning. As the pugnacious little man in battle with the giants of political and economic life, he somehow struck a chord of identification with so many of the American people. That is how he will probably be remembered—as the little man who rose to great places and did great deeds, but who yet remained an ordinary fellow with no aura of power, his fair share of faults and a few endearing idiosyncrasies.

Born on May 8, 1884, on his father's farm in Missouri, he had an ordinary state school education, the highlight of which was his acceptance, at the age of 17, by West Point, the American military academy. Because of poor eyesight, however, he was unable to take up his appointment and instead drifted into various jobs, including that of railroad timekeeper, bank clerk and newspaper mailing-room clerk.

When America entered the 1914-18 War in 1917 he volunteered for the Army, and saw service in France as an artillery captain—an experience which left him with a lasting respect for the American regular officer, reflected years later in his choice of General Marshall as his Secretary of State. On his return he went into business and started a men's clothing store in Kansas City. The venture failed and landed him in debts, which, during the next 15 years, he scrupulously paid off.

At the age of 38, out of work, and penniless, he obtained his first opening in politics through the good offices of the notorious Thomas J. Pendergast, the Democratic "boss" of Kansas City, who arranged for Truman's election as a county judge. The job itself was more administrative than legal but Truman took the opportunity of studying law at Kansas City Law School. As a judge he showed marked ability and unusual integrity, and 12 years later, in 1934, Pendergast, who had nothing in principle against honesty in others, particularly his dependants, chose him to be Democratic candidate for the Senate. Truman never forgot his debt to Pendergast—who subsequently went to prison—and in spite of the risk of being spattered with Pendergast mud, which his enemies never succeeded in doing, he always defended his old benefactor and, later in his life, travelled from Washington to his funeral. Truman's sense of personal loyalty, which was to earn him many hard political knocks as President, was a constant feature of his private and public life.

During Truman's first six years in the Senate, from 1934 to 1940, he was a reliable but obscure New Dealer. He was reelected in 1940, and soon sprang into the public eye partly as an early and outspoken critic of Nazi Germany, but principally by presiding over a special Congressional Committee to investigate waste in the national defence effort. Under his vigorous chairmanship the committee, which took his name, was credited with saving the United States more than $1,000m. Clearly this was an enviable accomplishment for any politician, and at the Democratic Presidential Convention in 1944 it soon bore fruit with Truman's nomination as vice-presidential candidate. The delegates at the Democratic Convention who, with Roosevelt's backing, chose Truman knew full well that Roosevelt was an ailing man, and they picked Truman believing that he might inherit the supreme office in the near future.

It was not really a choice so much as the reflection of the current political deadlock. The alternatives to Truman were the incumbent of the day, Henry Wallace*, whose extreme New Deal sympathies made him anathema to the South and to the conservative elements in the party, or James Francis Byrnes, whose anti-civil rights convictions, and conservative attitude made him unacceptable to the Northern wing of the party. What was needed was a man of the centre, a "border" politician uncommitted to either political extreme or geographical division. This, roughly speaking, was what Truman was—a compromise candidate—and just as its implications secured his nomination so later did they dominate his administration, both in domestic and to a lesser extent in foreign policy.

But realities of the American political deadlock which made Truman the inevitable Democratic choice looked dismayingly irrelevant when, on Roosevelt's death on April 12, 1945, the new President arrived in the White House face-to-face with the awesome challenge of international affairs. Roosevelt had made no effort to equip him for the task.

As Vice-President he had neither been informed of, nor consulted about, the intricacies and dangers of the world situation. His initiation to power politics was the fateful Potsdam Conference, which followed the allied victory in Europe. At the same time, at home, the first atomic bomb was exploded at Los Alamos, and on his return to Washington, Truman was called upon to decide whether the only two remaining bombs at that time in the possession of the United States should be dropped on Japan. He accepted the argument that to use them would save tens of thousands of allied lives, and issued the orders for the bombing of Hiroshima and Nagasaki. This was the first of the dramatic decisions the new President was called upon to take.

With the surrender of Japan the first shadows of the cold war fell across Truman's path. Such, however, was the momentum of Roosevelt's optimism about the Soviet Union that the pace of demobilization was continued as if all was well. Soon, failure to agree with Russia on a German peace treaty, Russian expansion in eastern Europe, the subversion of Czechoslovakia, the Berlin blockade, all combined to force the United States to initiate, first tentatively, but with growing boldness, the policy of containment, the first formal expression of which was the "Truman doctrine". Under this new development of United States policy, military aid was not only given to Greece and Turkey but a warning was issued to Soviet Russia that any further aggression anywhere in the world might involve war with the United States. The cold war was thereby well and truly joined.

In the same year, 1948, the Marshall Plan, for the adoption of which by Congress Truman, as President, must take the principal credit, came into operation. In the next year Truman delivered his historic inaugural address defining a programme of "peace and freedom" out of which arose the North Atlantic Treaty Organization—the first peacetime alliance ever concluded by the United States with European nations—and the "Point 4" programme for technical assistance to underdeveloped countries—another revolutionary conception.

Arising out of Nato, and the continuing Russian threat, there came the signature of the Bonn and Paris Conventions, designed to bring West German strength into the allied camp within a European Defence Community. It was under Truman's administration that E.D.C. was adopted in Washington as the kernel of American policy in Europe. Between 1945 and 1952, therefore, President Truman initiated and to a large extent implemented the great American postwar task of saving Europe, first from economic disaster and then from the threat of Russian military aggression. Faults—

some of them serious—in diplomatic timing, tactics, and judgment may mar Truman's record in Europe, but its broad achievement will surely stand the test of history.

In the Far East, however, the Truman administration was less fortunate, except in its successful negotiation of the peace settlement with Japan. All the American efforts to bring the Chinese civil war to a compromise peace ended in failure. It was in the Far East, however, that Truman was called upon to take the most urgent and spontaneous of his many historic decisions. On June 25, 1950, the North Korean army invaded South Korea. Two days later Truman committed United States forces to stop communist armed aggression—a step which was taken in conjunction with the United Nations, but which, for its effectiveness, depended on Truman's willingness to commit the might of the United States to a distant peninsula of no major strategic importance. Truman, in this action, proved himself to be the first world leader to support the principle of collective security with deeds as well as words.

The dismissal of General MacArthur from his command in the Far East in April 1951 showed the same quality of courageous decision which President Truman repeatedly exercised when dramatic, spontaneous gestures rather than a protracted exercise of political willpower could suffice, although he might well have done better to take this action earlier.

In domestic politics, Truman's freedom of action was circumscribed from the beginning. He inherited a political deadlock which, year by year during the Roosevelt era, had become more and more difficult to resolve. The national unity of war had only disguised it. It was Truman's misfortune—although in different circumstances he would never have become President—to reach the White House just when all the old tensions and frustrations were again coming to the surface. Not only was his own party bitterly divided, and the Republican Party, too long starved of responsibility, in a mood for political blood-letting, but the American economy, no less than international affairs, demanded measures which only an executive strongly entrenched in Congress could possibly carry through. Failing this, the only practicable course for Truman was compromise. As Lubell has wisely written in his celebrated study: "Compromise made Truman President and—despite the controversies he has stirred, the officials he has fired, and the terrible-tempered letters he has written—compromise has remained the unswerving objective of his presidency." This interpretation of a man so often attacked for wilful impetuousness may seem paradoxical.

The fact is, however, that compromise can, at a time when extremes are struggling for supremacy, appear to each disappointed side as inexcusable provocation. This was true as much in the foreign field, where to many Truman's policy of containment should have been replaced by liberation,

as in the domestic, where his half-hearted encouragement of free enterprise exasperated businessmen and "New Dealers" alike. Similarly, while Truman earnestly sought to win favour with the labour vote, his relations with trade union leaders were marked by an alternation of toughness and conciliation which defeated its purpose. His actions to stop or prevent strikes—two seizures of the nation's railways in 1948 and 1950 and one seizure of the steel industry in 1952, which was later ruled illegal by the Supreme Court—provoked the fierce hostility of both union leaders and owners.

Soon after he succeeded to the Presidency the Republicans, in the off-year elections of 1946, won both Houses of Congress—usually assumed to be a sure indication of the Presidential prospects two years later. With a Republican Congress, Truman's Fair Deal programme had little chance. He could, however, afford to gain popularity by advocating such radical measures as repeal of the Taft-Hartley Act, greater social security, civil rights for Negroes, etc., in the sure knowledge that the Republicans and the Southern Democrats would save him from suffering the political reprisals which would follow the enactment of such controversial Bills. He was therefore able to campaign in 1948 on a winning ticket (although at the time it only seemed "winning" to Truman himself) of a radical programme, and yet not risk, to any disastrous extent, betrayal by his own party machine or revolutionary political realignments.

His electoral victory in 1948, was, nevertheless, a personal triumph, as all the portents favoured Governor Dewey. To some considerable extent, Truman's success was due to internal Republican divisions and to Dewey's shortcomings as a popular candidate (many Republicans, in fact, abstained from voting); but even so, Truman's tempestuous and courageous campaign, his dogged refusal to accept defeat in advance, contributed vastly to the ultimate result. But having won his victory, he was able to do very little with it. The combination of Republican and Southern votes blocked his legislative efforts in his second term as surely as had the Republican majority in his first. It took all Truman's energy and bravado to prevent the New and Fair Deals from being whittled down, and indeed at times he was forced to run, politically speaking, at full speed to stay where he was—which explains the contrast between the impression of activity and the absence of legislative results.

The impact of foreign affairs also gravely added to the political deadlock. The communist victory in China gave the Republicans a major stick with which to beat the party in power and when, with the Hiss and other trials, the accusation of treason could be added to that of diplomatic blundering the stick was wielded with merciless ferocity. Truman's ingrained principle of personal loyalty made it doubly difficult for him to measure up to the challenge of subversive elements within the higher ranks of Government service, and for the same reason corruption and incompetence were afforded strange latitude. Both these Presidential shortcomings added much to the bitterness of party warfare, and introduced a new and sinister note into the built-in party deadlock. As the costs and frustrations of continued stalemate grew more burdensome, Lubell has written, "the middle ground on which Truman pitched his political tent cracked and crumbled" until, in 1952, it gave way under his party's feet.

In March 1952 Truman announced that he would not be a candidate for a third term as President, and at the party convention later in the year he lent his support to Adlai Stevenson as Democratic candidate. In the ensuing campaign he played an active part, but it is doubtful whether he greatly added to the Democratic chances of victory, limited as they already were by the Republican's choice of General Eisenhower as their candidate.

In the campaigns of 1956 and 1960 he remained an unpredictable ally of his party. His reputation for political judgment was not enhanced by supporting an unsuccessful candidate for the nomination at the Democratic Convention in each case. In 1956 he declared his backing for Governor Averell Harriman of New York too late to have any hope of swinging the majority away from Adlai Stevenson. Perhaps this action could be attributed to the former president's growing disapproval of Stevenson—an antipathy which was more clearly revealed in his book, *Mr. Citizen*, an account of his return to private life which was published in 1960 and which followed the two volumes of his autobiography published in 1955 and 1956. There can be no such easy explanation of his vain and clumsy efforts to secure the nomination for Senator Stuart Symington in 1960. This was a sad example of a politician still trying to play the kingmaker long after his influence had waned.

Nevertheless his record in office remained. During seven tumultuous years as President of the United States, he stood out as a man of integrity and simplicity in both his public and private life, endearing in his unpredictable outbursts, fearless of criticism, loyal to his friends but—and it is a large but—not always able to control the conflicting forces of contemporary American politics.

An endearing recollection of Truman comes from an English band leader who played in one of the Service bands in the Second World War and after. During a banquet held at one of the big postwar conferences Stalin asked for some Russian music to be played; this was performed apparently to his satisfaction. Whereupon Truman sat down at a piano and played pleasingly, and with something more than amateur competence, a piece by Mozart.

In 1919 he married a childhood friend, Bess Wallace. They had one daughter, Margaret, whose career as a concert singer sometimes led her father into undignified, if endearing, fracas with those who did not entirely share his high opinion of her musical attainments. She married Mr. Clifton Daniel, a New York journalist.

December 27, 1972.

Jan Tschichold, the distinguished typographer, died in Switzerland at the age of 72 in August 1974. Stanley Morison* and he were the two most influential typographers of the twentieth century—Morison as historian and purposeful adviser and director of others' skills, Tschichold above all as teacher and practitioner.

He was born in Leipzig, the son of a signwriter, and came to books and type from calligraphy which he began to teach at the precocious age of 18 and to which he gave a lifetime's study and affection.

In 1923, outraged by the low standards of jobbing typography and inspired by what he had seen at the first Bauhaus exhibition at Weimar, Tschichold launched the battle for a revolution in typographic design. It was a time of manifestos, and his, entitled *Elementare Typographie* (followed three years later by his first book, *Die neue Typographie*), was a trumpet-call for simplicity and clarity the effects of which were profound. In later years, when he had returned to a traditional style of the utmost purity, he was sometimes accused of having betrayed the revolutionary concepts of his youth; but he insisted that there was no fundamental conflict between his modernism and traditionalism, both being informed by the same sense of order and reason.

In 1926 Tschichold had accepted a teaching post at the Munich College of Printing, but with the advent of Hitler he was at once under attack for the alleged *Kulturbolschewismus* of his ideas. Like Morison 17 years before him, though in much more alarming circumstances, he was briefly imprisoned. He found refuge in Switzerland, but the country whose grateful citizen he was to become nine years later did not welcome him at first. He had to struggle hard to establish himself, though his reputation abroad was growing. A course of lectures in Denmark in 1935 was soon followed by an exhibition in London under the auspices of the firm of Lund Humphries. But his most fruitful period in England, and perhaps the summit of his work as a book designer, was to be the three years he worked for Allen Lane* at Penguin Books in the late forties. The strict typographic rules he devised and the high standards he demanded for mass-produced paperbacks may at the time have seemed dogmatic: in retrospect they are seen to have been of lasting benefit to British book production in general. For many years after his return to Switzerland at the end of 1949 the Harmondsworth aviary had a remarkable visual unity within its varied plumage.

In everything Tschichold did he aimed at expertise and excellence. Thus he was acknowledged as one of the world's most learned authorities on the history and technique of Chinese woodcut printing. His many publications in this field culminated in the book, *Chinese Colour Prints from the Ten Bamboo Studio*, 1972. He collected the works of the great writing-masters, eighteenth and nineteenth-century trade cards, and of course books. Always he classified and ordered; often he wrote, invariably in a spare and lucid style. In type design his crowning achievement was the completion in 1967 of the Sabon series, the first typeface in the history of printing (and the last?) that is indistinguishably uniform in its Linotype, Monotype and typefoundry versions.

For the past eight or 10 years Tschichold and his wife Edith, the friend of artists such as Arp* and Schwitters, lived in hospitable and active retirement in a remote mountain village in the Ticino, with Max Frisch, Alfred Andersch and Golo Mann as neighbours. Frequently they sallied forth, nowhere more often than to London.

Tschichold was an Honorary Royal Designer for Industry, a Corresponding Member of the Germany Academy of Arts, and a Gold Medallist of the American Institute of Graphic Arts. The Double Crown Club, London, made him an Honorary Member, and the City of Leipzig awarded him the Gutenberg Prize.

He leaves a widow and one son.

August 19, 1974.

President William Tubman, President of Liberia since 1944, died on July 23, 1971 in a London hospital. He was 75.

William Vacanararat Shadrach Tubman was born in November 1895 in Harper, Maryland County. Harper is in Liberia's extreme east, so the late President, though "Americo-Liberian", was not a Monrovia man. His father was a former Speaker of the House of Representatives, descended from settlers who emigrated to the then colony of Maryland in 1834 from Georgia, from which state Alexander Tubman's wife, Rebecca, was also later to go to Liberia.

Although William began life as a teacher, he came from that inner circle of Americo-Liberians who are expected to hold high office. He was called to the Bar, and began his public career as a court official. In 1923, at the age of 28, he became the youngest Liberian ever elected to the 10-man Senate. He was already popularly known as a "poor man's lawyer". In 1937 he became a judge, and in 1943 President-Elect.

It is astonishing that when he was first elected President, it was thought that he was to be a "front man" for the outgoing President Barclay, who himself constitutionally had to vacate the office. From the first Tubman made it plain that he was going to run things his own way, and since then he had stamped his personality indelibly on Liberia.

He was fortunate that his administration, much the longest in Liberia's history, coincided with the discovery of great deposits of very high-grade iron ore in Liberia, with the growth of "aid" from the richer countries to Africa, and with the development of independent Africa as an international force.

All this might explain Liberia's emergence, in spite of her small area and tiny population, as an important African country. It would not explain the President's hold over his fellow-countrymen, which was due to three things. First was his personality, combining dignity and shrewdness with warmth and humour. He made even the humblest of his people feel that this man really was his father. Second was his attitude to the "tribal" people who, until his time, were virtually excluded from any say in the Republic's government. Now, although the True Whig Party still monopolizes political power and appointments, and the indigenous peoples are not represented in proportion to their numbers in Congress, the old division between "tribal" and "county" (i.e. Americo-Liberian areas) administration has been ended, and people of tribal origin are found in very important appointments. The old antagonism between "Americo-Liberians" and "tribesmen" has almost lost its bitterness and, unless Tubman's successors revive it, it must give way to the political antipathies found in other states.

The President also shook his country free from what used to be regarded as the American economic stranglehold. This he did not by throwing the Americans out, but by encouraging other countries to come in. Today not only the Americans but the Swedes, Germans, and many other countries participate in mining, and even the former monopoly of Firestone in rubber cultivation has disappeared. Yet politically the President always kept his country on the side of the United States, and "the west". He was particularly attached to Britain, as the country which first recognized and helped Liberia, and during his state visit to London in 1962 made a great impression on all who met him.

Tubman's capacity for handling even small details of administration was astonishing. Although after he came to office Liberia's revenues had increased by over 10 times and government activity had become more complex, he was able to make even minor appointments personally, and personally to authorize even minor items of expenditure.

In 1963, because of a sharp decline in world rubber prices and the delays in the opening up of iron ore mines from which revenue was expected, Liberia ran into a budget deficit and into external payments difficulties. The International Bank and the International Monetary Fund came to the rescue, and now once again Liberia appears to be one of the few African countries to look forward to continuing rising revenues and national income. Social services are still relatively undeveloped, though there have been great advances in recent years. The test of Liberian statesmanship will be whether increasing wealth and revenues are reflected in the general standard of living.

Even when he began his third term of office in 1956 it was said that President Tubman had done far more for Liberia than any other president. At that time he was little known abroad. At his death he was an international figure, who had played an important role in Pan-African conferences, and was recognized both by Africans and by the rest of the world as one of the continent's elder statesmen.

July 24, 1971.

Andrei Tupolev, one of the Soviet Union's pioneer aircraft builders and head of a design team that produced the TU 144 supersonic airliner, died in Moscow on December 23, 1972 at the age of 84.

Tupolev watched the maiden flight of the bird-shaped TU 144, rival of the Anglo-French Concorde, soon after his eightieth birthday. The aircraft was in fact designed by his son Alexei, but Tupolev senior, as chief of the design bureau, took overall responsibility for the project. Tupolev's own major design achievements came in the years after the Second World War, when he and his team developed the TU 16 "Badger" jet-engined strategic bomber, later adapted for passenger use as the TU 104.

Until the last day of the year 1968 Andrei Nikolaevich Tupolev, although highly regarded by aeronautical specialists everywhere, was hardly known to the general public of the western world. Yet the TU 144 supersonic airliner, which brought the name of Tupolev wider recognition by making its first flight ahead of the Concorde, on December 31, 1968, was no more than the culmination of a long series of aircraft designs of remarkable variety, astonishing inventiveness and unwavering engineering competence.

In 1918 he had helped to found Moscow's Central Aerodynamical Institute and his early piston-engined aircraft built for him a reputation as a safe and competent if conventional engineer. The coming of the turbojet, however, provided him with great opportunities and did much to release his inventive genius. After he had produced the twin-engined bombers of the 1940s, the especially fruitful period of the 1950s saw Tupolev, then over 60 years of age, entering the jet era with enthusiasm. He designed and built aircraft which were capable of high performance and which had the robustness and simplicity which enabled them to work satisfactorily on the scheduled airline services.

At least 100 twin-jet TU 104 passenger machines were in regular use with Aeroflot. Other airlines also used it. In its developed form it carried 70 passengers at a speed of nearly 1,000 kilometres an hour. People in Britain showed great interest in the TU 104 when one flew to London early in 1956. A later mark, introduced by Aeroflot in 1959, accommodated 100 passengers. This aeroplane's configuration, with its unusual anhedral angle on the wings, hinted at Tupolev's individual way of thinking. It had a fairly marked sweep back and was fitted with slotted flaps.

When Tupolev's work on this and other aircraft is traced, it becomes tantalizing to find how little direct information has been issued from official Soviet sources. In fact for foreign observers Tupolev's achievements are best authenticated by the confirmed records of the Fédération Aéronautique Internationale. Thus the TU 104's speed with payload on a 2,000 kilometre closed circuit was clearly established in an F.A.I. record in 1960 at 959.94 kilometres an hour or 596.47 miles an hour. F.A.I. records are even more valuable in assessing the qualities of Tupolev's most distinctive and controversial aeroplane, the TU 114—a forerunner of the American monsters which were heralded by the Boeing 747.

At 180 metric tons the TU 114 was, in its day, the largest and heaviest commercial aircraft and also a tribute to its designer's farsightedness. Powered by four turboprops driving huge, contra-rotating airscrews, it was arranged for a standard complement of 220 passengers with a crew of from 10 to 15. Aeroflot introduced it into service in 1961. It had previously made a profound impression when exhibited at the Paris salon. Even so it is doubtful if its almost futuristic qualities would have been accepted had it not been for the groups of F.A.I. records which it set, all under the stringent conditions imposed by that body and all listed, as is the F.A.I.'s custom, under the name, not of the aircraft designer or builder, but under the name of the pilot, in this instance, Ivan Sukholmlin.

Official recognition of Tupolev's greatness came slowly at first. He held the post of Assistant Director of the Central Aerodynamical Institute from 1918 to 1935 and was appointed head of the Designing Bureau in 1922 and Chief Engineer in 1923. He was a Deputy to the Supreme Soviet and a Member of the Academy of Sciences of the U.S.S.R. He was designated Honoured Worker of Science and Technology in 1933 and received State prizes for his aeronautical work in 1943 and 1948. The Order of Lenin was conferred upon him in 1947 and again in 1949 and he won the Lenin Prize in 1957. He won a Stalin prize of 150,000 roubles and in 1959 he was given the F.A.I. Gold Medal. In 1970 he became an honorary fellow of the Royal Aeronautical Society.

Born on November 11, 1888, Tupolev was educated at the Higher Technical Institute.

December 27, 1972.

Veronica Turleigh, the actress, wife of James Laver [q.v.], died at her home on September 3, 1971 at the age of 68. She was, before her marriage, Bridget Veronica Turley.

For forty years the work of some of those producers whose names are honoured in the English theatre profited by the intelligence and cool distinction that her performances showed.

The first was her compatriot, the Irishman J. B. Fagan, who, after she left R.A.D.A., engaged her for the Oxford Playhouse, where her Deirdre of the Sorrows in Synge's play and her Hedda Gabler, not to mention her Rosaline in *Love's Labour's Lost* for the O.U.D.S. impressed undergraduate audiences in the mid-1920s.

In London she appeared for the 300 Club in D. H. Lawrence's Biblical play *David;* for Peter Godfrey at the Gate; and, with Joan Maude, Peggy Ashcroft, and the dancer Pearl Argyle, in the dramatization of *Jew Süss.*

She joined Harcourt Williams's company at the Old Vic to play Shakespeare's Hermione and Sheridan's Lady Sneerwell, and in the following year she and the young Stephen Haggard shared the honours of Gordon Daviot's *The Laughing Woman,* in which Haggard's role recalled the French artist Henri Gaudier and Miss Turleigh's Sophie Brzeska, whose name Gaudier added to his own.

Miss Turleigh was also in the dramatization of Richard Oke's *Frolic Wind;* in *The Dog Beneath the Skin,* the first joint production of W. H. Auden and Christopher Isherwood: and, as the mother of Alec Guinness's Hamlet, in Guthrie's modern-dress production in 1938.

After the Second World War Barry Jackson* invited her to join his first company at Stratford-on-Avon, where she was in two plays directed by Peter Brook; and Gielgud, setting up his classical season at the Lyric, Hammersmith, engaged her to play the Duchess of Gloucester to Scofield's Richard II.

In later years she supported John Clements and Kay Hammond in a comedy by Benn Levy, returned to the Old Vic for a revival of *The Cenci,* and was the Abbess to Sybil Thorndike's Saint in Ross Williamson's *Teresa of Avila.*

Gordon Daviot's "The Laughing—better still the Smiling—Woman" would be no bad epitaph for an actress who held her head high in the theatre.

September 8, 1971.

Sir George Turner, K.C.B., K.B.E., who died on May 10 1974 at the age of 78, was Permanent Under-Secretary of State of the War Office from 1949 to 1956, and rose to this position from the lowest grade of the civil service clerical class.

George Wilfred Turner was born on January 22, 1896, and, as he used to say,

his father, John W. Turner of Rotherham, was a turner by trade as well as in name. George Turner was educated at Rotherham Grammar School, and in 1911 joined the War Office as a boy clerk. In 1914 he qualified as a second division clerk, and spent some months in the Home Office and the Post Office before returning to the War Office after the outbreak of war. In December 1916 he joined the army, and served as a private in the Grenadier Guards. He was wounded twice in 1918 and was demobilized in February 1919.

On his return, he became a founder member and secretary of the staff side of the War Office Whitley Council, and took a leading part in obtaining staff consultation on the post-war reorganization proposals. When in 1921 he was himself promoted under their provisions to the administrative grade as an assistant principal, it was a tribute both to his own ability and to management policy. Nine years later he became private secretary to successive junior Ministers, including Duff Cooper (Viscount Norwich) when Financial Secretary of the War Office, and he was promoted to principal in 1934.

In 1936, the rearmament drive brought Vice-Admiral Sir Harold Brown into the Army Council in the new appointment of Director-General of Munitions Supply, and the experienced Turner was made his civil assistant. This assignment, which Turner regarded as a form of relegation, proved the ladder to success. In an early example of services' integration, the Admiral was soon to add the department of the M.G.O. to his own.

This was the nucleus of the future Ministry of Supply; and when it was formed in 1939, Turner accompanied the Admiral there, and rose to be principal assistant secretary in 1939, under secretary in 1941, and second secretary in 1942. He did not gain further promotion in the Ministry, but returned to the War Office in 1949 as permanent secretary, a promotion which he modestly referred to as "geographical". His tenure saw the Korean War, with its sequel of longer national service, and a new rearmament programme; and this was followed by the troubles in Egypt, Malaya, East Africa, and Cyprus. Towards the end of his service, the army in Egypt was withdrawn from the Suez Canal Zone, and the vast base installations were handed over, under arrangements in which Turner took a close interest, to the specially formed companies of the Suez Contractors.

He retired in 1956 and, perhaps because he was disappointed when the arrangements he proposed for his succession were not adopted, declined to remain in charge while alternatives were sought. A regular holiday visitor to Scilly, he then took up residence at Penzance, with the intention of devoting himself to the grocery business of his wife's family. Later, however, he accepted a number of directorships; and he was a member of the Royal Commission on the Police Force.

Turner's career was remarkable, not merely because he rose from boy clerk to permanent secretary, but because it was in no way hindered by his notable participation in staff group activities. Others who achieved the same success soon assumed the patina of the permanent secretary, but he went out of his way to emphasize the origins from which he had sprung. To the end he preserved, and used effectively, the broadest of Yorkshire accents, and, up to his retirement, continued to live in the same small house in Ealing, which served him at the beginning of his administrative career.

He was deeply conscious of the interests of the grades he had served, and of the demerits of their competitors. No greater crisis arose in his war service than when, as sentry at G.H.Q., he was faced with a requirement to present arms to the Financial Adviser, a Brigadier and member of the rival accountant grade. He was loyal to old associates, and, even when he could not help them in their careers, continued to share their social life. His version of the Three Musketeers, of widely differing fortunes, continued active much more than 20 years after.

In the Ministry of Supply Turner readily penetrated the veil of money to deal in the realities of production. He claimed to have withstood, and he certainly survived, both the aggressions and the allurements of Lord Beaverbrook* as Minister.

He was made C.B. in 1942, K.B.E. in 1944, and K.C.B. in 1947. He married in 1921 Elizabeth Chirgwin, and had one son.

May 13, 1974.

Alexander Tvardovsky, one of Russia's greatest contemporary poets and former editor of *Novy Mir,* the literary weekly, died in Moscow on December 18, 1971 at the age of 61.

Tvardovsky did his best to encourage liberal trends in the rough world of Soviet politics. As editor of *Novy Mir* (new world) he introduced Alexander Solzhenitsyn to the Soviet public, printing his work, *One Day in the Life of Ivan Denisovich,* in November 1962.

Tvardovsky's admirers considered him second only to Ilya Ehrenburg* as a literary figure. His war verses won him popular fame with the ordinary reader in his country of poetry lovers.

Alexander Trifonovich Tvardovsky, who was born in 1910, was an established and widely read Russian poet well before his appointment in 1952 for two years (and later in 1958) to the editorship of the literary monthly *Novy Mir.* His courage and skill in this job made the magazine a focal point for those who sought a new honesty in politics and literature after the years of Stalin. Official reaction to the contents of the magazine became one of the indicators of the general political climate in the U.S.S.R. But Tvardovsky will perhaps be longest remembered as the editor who, alone in the Soviet Union, published some of the work of Alexander Solzhenitsyn, the greatest Russian novelist of his generation, and in so doing saved a little of the honour of the Union of Writers of the Soviet Union, whose organ *Novy Mir* is.

Tvardovsky came from the family of a village smith in Smolensk province. His first writing was published locally and it was as a correspondent for Smolensk newspapers that he witnessed the period of collectivisation. His prose diary of a *Kolkhoz Chairman* (1932) and *Strana Muraviva* (Stalin Prize 1941) both deal with the countryside and the collective farm theme. Much of Tvardovsky's later poetry, too, is set in the countryside, and always his style is simple, lucid, sometimes enlivened with proverbs and folk sayings.

His experiences in the Finnish and Second World War deepened his writing, and in a late poem he confesses that he could never quite rid himself of guilt for having survived the war. *Vassily Tyorkin* (Stalin Prize 1946) deals with the experience of an ordinary soldier in the war, and *Cruel Memory* (1951) achieved great popularity, the latter selling several million copies in the Soviet Union. Perhaps it was a combination of his humble background, his staunch communism (he became a party member in 1940), his rugged "Soviet" personal appearance, his war experience, and his popularity beyond the circle of the Moscow intelligentsia, that led to his appointment to *Novy Mir*.

The magazine had a tradition of independence before Tvardovsky's arrival which he fully maintained. Of the many attacks on the magazine one can mention that which followed publication of Yashin's *The Vologda Wedding* in 1962 and those connected with the publication of Solzhenitsyn's writings. Although Khrushchev had authorized the publication in *Novy Mir* of *One Day in the Life of Ivan Denisovich*, the magazine was subsequently criticized for publishing it as well as two shorter stories by the same author. Solzhenitsyn's *Cancer Ward* was later set up in type for *Novy Mir* but the authorities intervened to stop publication. In 1966 Tvardovsky nevertheless managed to publish a third Solzhenitsyn short story.

His courage took the form less of defiance in open letters (although his letters were forceful) than of persistence, and quiet pressure behind the scenes. In this he resembled Ilya Ehrenburg*, the other protecting father of the new generation of Soviet writers. But the conservative tide of the past few years, which swept Solzhenitsyn out of the Writers' Union at the end of 1969, removed Tvardovsky from the editorship of *Novy Mir* early in 1970. It is some consolation that he should have lived to see the award of the Nobel prize to Solzhenitsyn.

December 20, 1971.

U

Walter Ulbricht, Chairman of the Council of State of the German Democratic Republic, and until May 1971 First Secretary of the Socialist Unity (Communist) Party, died on August 1, 1973 at the age of 80.

Ulbricht was from its birth the unquestioned dictator of the D.D.R., whose foundation he supervised immediately after the war, and which he ruled continuously from 1945. From the beginning, he was the leader of the group of German Communists (the "Ulbricht Group") which returned from Russia to Germany in the footsteps of Marshal Konev's army, and though he was not at first alone at the top of the hierarchy, he consolidated his power by securing the loyalty of his potential rivals, or else eliminating them. In the eyes of Germans in both parts of the country, he was the symbol of the separate existence of a German Communist state, and was widely regarded in Europe as the chief obstacle to a rapprochement between the two parts of Germany. But in spite of his reputation as a ruthless Stalinist, he was more pragmatic than he was commonly thought to be—though just as ruthless—and showed great skill in adapting himself and his methods to changing circumstances.

Towards the end of his reign, he presided over a coalition of different forces inside the Communist Party, which allowed scope for change inside the D.D.R. and for adjustments in its foreign policy. At the same time, the administrative machinery of the party was entirely under his control.

Walter Ulbricht was born in Leipzig on June 30, 1893, the son of a tailor. His anti-clerical parents initiated him early into Socialism. As a boy, he distributed leaflets, and, while apprenticed as a carpenter, joined the Socialist youth movement in 1906. Four years later he became a member of the Socialist-orientated Woodworkers' Union, and in 1912 entered the Socialist Party. He soon established for himself a reputation as one of the most active party functionaries in Leipzig. During the 1914-18 War, Ulbricht upheld the radical policy of Liebknecht and at the end of 1918 joined the Spartakusbund. When the Socialist revolution at the end of the war failed to fulfil these expectations, a radical group including Ulbricht founded the German Communist Party.

After a long period of training in Russia as a leading official, he returned to Germany to introduce into the party organization Stalin's "cell" system. In 1928 he was also elected to the Reichstag for South Westphalia, and obtained the key post of secretary for the district of Berlin-Brandenburg.

But Ulbricht's hour really struck with the destruction by Hitler of the Communist Party in 1933, when Thälmann, Schehr, and the greater part of the underground party leadership were sent to concentration camps.

There only remained part of the bureaucracy, and the Stalinist faction in the central committee with Wilhelm Pieck and Ulbricht at its head. They were provided with money and false papers and smuggled out of the country.

The exiles, who constituted the "Auslandskomitee" in Paris, were entirely without resources and completely dependent on Stalin. He imposed Ulbricht on them as Party Secretary—and little opposition was voiced this time. During those years Ulbricht perfected his method of eliminating potential rivals in the party hierarchy.

He was sent to Spain from 1936 to 1938 in charge of a G.P.U. detachment at the republican army headquarters, specially entrusted by Moscow with the liquidation of all party members whose loyalty was suspect, and of all social democrats, anarchists and anti-Stalinists. From 1934 onwards, Ulbricht had been in all but name the head of the German Communist Party, and the real power behind the aging and somewhat avuncular Pieck, who offered no serious obstacle to his ambitions.

Ulbricht returned to Germany in 1945, a week before the capitulation, and immediately began to establish, in the administrative no-man's-land created by the Soviet advance, the framework of a communist administration. At a time of great uncertainty, and in spite of changes of decision on the part of Stalin himself, Ulbricht picked his way with skill. He was careful at first to secure the cooperation of the "bourgeois" parties in the government, while retaining all the keys to real power in the hands of individually chosen communists. But by 1946, the political liquidation of the socialists was achieved in the Eastern Zone (though not in Berlin) through the creation of the Socialist Unity Party, the S.E.D. After this merger campaign, carried out with the help of supervision by the Soviet forces, socialists who did not conform either fled or were put away. Similarly, those communist leaders who had spent years in prisons or concentration camps were soon made aware that this was no claim to a voice in affairs. Indeed Ulbricht carried out an effective purge of the Communist Party, somewhat along the lines of Stalin's purges in the 1930s, and with the same end in view: to eliminate the old guard and ensure the creation of an élite personally dependent on himself.

In 1949, the Soviet Union established the "German Democratic Republic", in retaliation for the creation of the Federal Republic in the West. But Stalinist policy was still ambiguous, and during the next four years he showed by political and diplomatic overtures that he had not abandoned the hope of a reunified Germany, though one which would have been achieved on conditions which made it permanently dependent on the Soviet Union. In the face of such ambiguity, Ulbricht forced the pace of "Socialization" in the D.D.R.—though at the same time he was careful not to alienate the support of the peasants, which had been won by land reforms after the war. Collectivization was slower and for a time more symbolic in the D.D.R. than elsewhere; but among the industrial workers, reconstruction and socialization demanded continuing tightening of the Stakhanovite screws. It was this treatment of the industrial workers which led to the revolt of June 1953. It was the last, and only real, challenge to Ulbricht's position, although there were repeated purges thereafter.

In the D.D.R. itself, a campaign for full collectivization was launched, which reached a terrible intensity in 1960, when collectivization was carried through totally.

As the situation over Berlin deteriorated, the number of refugees increased since rumours abounded of threats to the escape route. In August daily figures exceeded 2,000. Ulbricht's demands for some action to seal the escape hatch in Berlin had hitherto been resisted by the Soviet government, but it now gave way. The Berlin Wall which was begun on August 13 was, however, even more significant than it appeared at the time. It aroused abhorrence throughout the world, but it marked the end of the most acute phase of the Berlin crisis: it meant that the economic fortunes of the D.D.R. were now to improve dramatically, and it prompted a long process of rethinking in the Federal Republic about the future relations between the two parts of the country.

But in 1963, at the Sixth Party Congress of the S.E.D., Ulbricht showed that he was prepared to experiment more radically than anyone else in Eastern Europe at the time. He took up the "Liberman theses" on the economic reform which had been published in the Soviet Union some months previously, and declared that the whole economic system of East Germany must be overhauled. Although he never envisaged the introduction of a market mechanism, even in a limited form, in the formation of prices, he showed that he was ready to restructure the whole system of planning—and that in doing so he was ready to draw upon the skills not only of economists but also of sociologists—hitherto a breed of intellectual untouchables in the D.D.R. Coupled with these economic experiments went a renewed insistence on political orthodoxy; but orthodoxy itself gradually became more flexible. Ulbricht encouraged the promotion of young men, drew on advisers from intellectual as well as political life, and began to create a new balance of forces at the highest level. In the mid-1960s he also showed a greater disposition to seek better relations with the Federal Republic, and made a number of overtures to the West German S.P.D.

Ulbricht was not prepared to stomach the developments in Czechoslovakia. In many ways the invasion of Czechoslovakia meant a crisis for Ulbricht. It shook the S.E.D. to its foundations, though very little was heard of its internal dissensions in the outside world. It wrecked his hopes of inching

more closely towards the Federal Republic to take economic advantage of the general East-West détente; and finally it induced the Soviet Union to assert far greater authority than before in the conduct of affairs in Eastern Europe.

Indeed, the Soviet government was now more inclined than it had ever been before to seek a rapprochement with the Federal Republic, and was certainly encouraged in this inclination by the knowledge that after the invasion of Czechoslovakia, no amount of West German *Ostpolitik* was likely to represent a threat to Soviet interests or the Soviet position in Eastern Europe. The Soviet (and Polish) willingness to take advantage of the new Soviet position in Eastern Europe to come to terms with the Federal Republic transformed the political position of the D.D.R. Whereas it had previously enjoyed a virtual veto over the contacts between East European countries and West Germany (particularly after Romania had opened diplomatic relations with Bonn in 1967) Ulbricht now found that he was being forced into an unwelcome policy of rapprochement by Soviet pressure.

In 1969, and into 1970, relations between the East German leaders were strained, as were relations between Ulbricht personally and the leadership in the Kremlin. In the different statements made by the East German leadership, there was evidence of dissension over the new position which had been created by the invasion of Czechoslovakia; but eventually the government of the D.D.R. was induced to participate in the rounds of talks that were being pursued simultaneously in Moscow, Warsaw, and ultimately East Germany too, with representatives of the West German government of Herr Brandt. Ulbricht's position was not made the easier by the treaties which Herr Brandt signed with Moscow and Warsaw in 1970.

He retained his sense of pragmatism throughout. In spite of a generalized view in Western Europe that no more diehard and inflexible leader could possibly be produced by the D.D.R., and that after his departure relations between the two parts of Germany were bound to improve, it was far from being automatically true. To his opponents at any moment he was invariably ruthless, but in his later years showed that he was less dogmatic than was commonly assumed.

Personally, he was cruel, unappealing and uninspiring. He seems to have enjoyed his position as a withdrawn, hard-working, efficient functionary, wielding immense power in an anonymous manner. His goatee beard and high-pitched voice inspired ridicule in East Germany; and even in personal relations, his contempt for all human considerations was evident. His withdrawn public manner was evidence of his character all through. His manner of life was generally extremely simple, even after 1960, when, upon the death of President Pieck, he achieved supreme power in name as well as in fact, and became Chairman of the

newly created Council of State, and head of the armed forces, thus combining leadership of both government and party.

His health had been bad for some years, and before the invasion of Czechoslovakia he was a regular visitor to the springs at Karlovy Vary. One of the few things that he positively enjoyed was ice-skating, and the biggest ice rink in Berlin was closed to the public from time to time so that he and his wife could go skating under the supervision of his bodyguards.

August 2, 1973.

Leon Underwood, a fiercely independent and original force in British art for over 50 years, died on October 9, 1975 at the age of 84 in the Hostel of God, Clapham, S.W. He was a sculptor, painter and printmaker whose appearance since his first exhibition at Knewstub's Chenil Gallery in 1922 often showed him to be in the forefront of developments, but whose increasingly isolated philosophy and life-long distrust of the gallery system allowed him on occasions almost to be forgotten. Sir John Rothenstein has written of him: "No artist of his generation of remotely comparable achievement has been so little honoured; indeed, so neglected."

George Claude Leon Underwood was born on Christmas Day, 1890 and won a scholarship to the Royal College of Art in 1910. Painting at Minsk in Poland in 1913-14, he was cut off by the outbreak of war and escaped round the Baltic by way of Finland and Sweden, the first of many eventful journeys to influence his career. After the war, in which he served in the R.E. Camouflage Section, he spent a year in Professor Tonks's class at the Slade before setting up what was to become a highly influential school of his own, the Brook Green School in Girdlers Road, Hammersmith, in the studio he occupied until his death. Among his first students were: Aileen Agar, Blair Hughes-Stanton and Gertrude Hermes. In the early 1920s he also taught part-time at the R.C.A. and, on his resignation, was followed to Girdlers Road by a group which included Vivian Pitchforth, Henry Moore and Raymond Coxon.

He made a seminal contribution to the development of English sculpture through his response to primitive art studied on his travels in Europe, Iceland and Central America, and later in West Africa. His activity as a carver was largely superseded in the 1940s by an astonishing sequence of metal sculptures, comparable at times to those of his exact contemporary, Zadkine*, which continued with great inventiveness and originality until his last few months, when his sight began to fail.

In earlier years his "African Madonna", a carving in lignum vitae, exhibited in 1935 at the Beaux Arts Gallery and destined for a Johannesburg school where native pupils were encouraged to develop their natural artistic talent, had been greeted as possibly a first instance of an English artist handing back to African people a little of the aesthetic principle which the Western races had received from African art.

Nearly 30 years later, an exhibition at the Kaplan Gallery, St. James's, was a reminder that he commanded a world of joyous movement and exuberant vitality. From his ideas energy flowed through the material, causing his figures to soar and spring with animation hard to parallel.

To take two examples of his work in the 1950s or early 1960s, he conceived fresh agony in themes biblical and classical—namely his "Jacob and the Angel" and his "Laocoon".

His publications include *Animalia* (verse and woodcuts), 1926; a novel, *The Siamese Cat*, 1927; *The Red Tiger*, with Phillips Russell, about a journey through Mexico, 1928; *Art for Heaven's Sake*, 1934; and three important books on West African sculpture which appeared in the late 1940s. *The Cycle of Styles in Art, Religion, Science and Technology*, a work which had occupied him for many years, remained unpublished at his death.

He married in 1917 Mary Coleman, who survives him with one son and a daughter.

October 11, 1975.

Lord Upjohn, P.C., C.B.E., a Lord of Appeal in Ordinary since 1963, died on January 27, 1971. He was 67.

Gerald Upjohn was of tall, handsome presence, gifted with a fine mind and personal charm. He was one of the best Chancery judges of our time. He was a master of the principles of equity and applied them with consummate skill and understanding. He repudiated the technical rules by which they are often overlaid. His judgments at first instance were models of their kind and were nearly always upheld in the higher courts. In the Court of Appeal and House of Lords his qualities were seen at their best. He combined in a unique degree both clarity of thought and forcefulness of expression. He carried his colleagues with him, so much so that rarely if ever was he in the minority.

He was devoted to Lincoln's Inn, of which he was Treasurer in 1965. He took the leading part in the restoration of the old gateway in Chancery Lane and in the building of the new Hale Court.

He had wide interests outside the law. He contributed much to the St. George's Hospital Medical School, of which he was chairman for 10 years. He loved to sail and to fish. He will be much missed by his colleagues.

Gerald Ritchie Upjohn was born on February 25, 1903, the youngest son of W. H. Upjohn, K.C. Educated at Eton and at Trinity College, Cambridge, he was an exhibitioner in 1924. Called to the Bar by Lincoln's Inn in 1925 (he gained a certificate of honour in the finals), he soon became a busy junior in the work of the Chancery division. The problems of equity law are many, varied and often difficult, but Upjohn took them all in his stride.

In the Second World War he joined the Welsh Guards, and from 1941 to 1943 he held the rank of captain and technical adjutant to their 2nd Armoured Battalion. In the latter year he was promoted to colonel and in 1944 to brigadier. He was appointed Chief Legal Adviser to the Allied Control Commission (Italy) in 1943, and from 1944 to 1945 was vice-president of the Allied Control Commission. He was mentioned in dispatches, was made a C.B.E. in 1945, and in 1946 an officer of the Legion of Merit.

In the latter year, after his return to practice, he was honorary treasurer to the General Council of the Bar. The same year saw his appointment as deputy chairman of the Board of Referees. In 1947 he became Attorney-General of the Duchy of Lancaster, an office of antiquity which has existed since the Duchy was united to the Crown in 1399. He was a member of the Committee on Practice and Procedure of the Supreme Court, which sat from 1947 to 1953 under the chairmanship of Lord Evershed.*

During 1947 he was made a member of the tribunal chairmen's panel under the Coal Industry (Nationalisation) Act. He carried out the work of those offices, in addition to a busy practice, till his appointment as a judge. In addition, he was a member of the tribunal, of which Mr. Justice Lynskey was chairman, set up in 1948 under the Tribunals of Inquiry (Evidence) Act 1921, to inquire into allegations of irregularities affecting certain Ministers of the Crown and other public servants. In the same year he was made a bencher of his Inn, and was elected Treasurer for the year 1965. In June 1951 the then Lord Chancellor selected him to inquire into the dispute which arose over the Gambia poultry scheme.

In November of that year he was appointed a Judge of the Chancery Division, and, as was said at the time: "The loss to the Chancery Bar of so eminent a colleague will be balanced by the gain in having on the Bench so profound a lawyer."

In 1956 he became No. 2 Judge in the Restrictive Practices Court. After a most successful term of office as a puisne judge he was made a Lord Justice of Appeal in January 1960. The appointment and promotion of judges is often affected by the chance of circumstance, and advancement may be unexpectedly delayed. So high did the reputation of Upjohn stand that, when a vacancy occurred among the Law Lords in November 1963, he was appointed to fill it, thus becoming a Lord of Appeal in Ordinary after being less than four years in the Court of Appeal.

On being granted a barony he took the title of Baron Upjohn, of Little Tey in the County of Essex. He was a prominent Freemason, and a Grand Lodge Officer.

In 1947 he married Marjorie, youngest daughter of the late Major E. M. Lucas.

January 28, 1971.

Mary Ure, who died on April 3, 1975, aged 42, on the day after her return to the London stage in *The Exorcist*, will first be remembered as the original Alison in John Osborne's *Look Back in Anger*.

This was not her best performance. But that image of the exquisite debutante slaving over an ironing board famously reflected the theatrical climate of the late 1950s, and it also does something to suggest her range.

From the time of her 1954 London debut as Amanda in Anouilh's *Time Remembered*, she was apt to figure as the beauteous victim. She radiated a type of virgin innocence that invited corruption.

Alison, Abigail Williams in *The Crucible*, Beatrice in *The Changeling*, and other parts she played at the Royal Court, amount to several variations on this pattern.

And when she joined the Stratford Memorial Theatre, it was again in roles like Desdemona and Ophelia in Peter Brook's Moscow *Hamlet*. At that time, the ultimate Ure role (although she never played it) would have been Lavinia in *Titus Andronicus*.

After her marriage to John Osborne was dissolved, she married Robert Shaw and was not seen on the London stage from 1961 until a brief return in Tennessee Williams's *Two Character Play* in 1967. In spite of her film and television work, it was an interrupted career.

Her final performance, again in a submissive and intuitive role, led up to a climax of passionate assertion frankly drawing its power from her Scottish origins. This lay well outside her past range, and it suggests that her delicate talent was developing into something altogether more robust.

She was born in Glasgow and was educated at the Mount School, York, and the Central School of Speech Training and Dramatic Art. Her first stage appearance was in *Simon and Laura* in 1954 at the Opera House, Manchester.

Her films included *Windom's Way, Sons and Lovers, The Mindbenders, Where Eagles Dare* and *Reflections of Fear*. She had also appeared on television in Britain and the United States.

Miss Ure had two sons and two daughters by Mr. Shaw.

April 4, 1975.

Nadia Ustinov—See **Nadia Benois.**

U Thant—See **Thant.**

V

Dr. Guillermo León Valencia, Conservative president of Colombia in 1962-66, died in New York on November 5, 1971 at the age of 62. From 1967 until 1971 he was Ambassador to Spain.

Valencia was elected president as head of the National Union—the Conservative-Liberal coalition—in one of the most peaceful elections the country had known for the past few decades. Under an agreement between the Liberals and the Conservatives—written into the constitution—to alternate the presidency between them, it was the turn of the Conservatives to assume this office.

Valencia was vigorously pro-American. Only later, after American intervention in the Dominican Republic, did he give way to the anti-American student rioters. Their demand that he dismiss the rector of the university (which he did) was to cost him the resignation of his own minister of foreign affairs. But in his inauguration speech he pledged full cooperation with Kennedy's* Alliance for Progress, and proclaimed Colombia "in the orbit of the United States".

His country—with its serious inflationary problems because of its reliance on the world price of coffee—was extremely dependent on American aid. In 1965, American aid bailed it out of threatening bankruptcy: however, even though the government appeared to be on the point of collapse, the five service chiefs supported it with an open declaration that the "solution for the nation's economic and political difficulties lay in democratic processes".

Valencia was born in Popayán in 1909—the son of a famous romantic poet, who ran for the presidency twice but lost each time. The son was to succeed in his second attempt. He became a journalist and entered politics in 1935 as a state assemblyman in the Cauca district. He served his country in Spain and in the United Nations. In 1957 his arrest had been ordered by the dictator Rojas Pinilla. But Valencia took refuge in the house of a friend, defied the cordon of troops with a pistol and was rescued by a Catholic bishop.

Later he became a rallying figure in a coalition of Liberals and Conservatives which overthrew Rojas Pinilla.

Valencia was married and had two sons and two daughters. His wife Susana died in 1964.

November 6, 1971.

Dickie Valentine, one of the most popular young singers of the 1950 pre-"rock" period, died in a road crash on May 6, 1971. He was 41.

His father was a lorry driver, and his first introduction to the stage was as a 14-year-old page boy at the Palace Theatre, Manchester. When his father's work took him to London, Dickie Valentine also transferred as page boy to the Palladium. He was sacked for being cheeky and moved on to the Haymarket as a call-boy, running errands for the stars. But he returned to the Palladium in the mid-1950s, topping the Palladium bill.

He was one of the first singers to break away from the usual "featured spot" with a band, to become a solo star in his own right.

He grew up professionally in the heyday of the big bands, and first achieved prominence with the Ted Heath orchestra. In fact, he came by his stage name through joining Heath on St. Valentine's Day, 1949, and lived up to it by becoming the idol of thousands of girls during the era when ballad singers of his type were known as "crooners". It was said that he never had a soprano voice, even as a child, and his romantic, deep brown tones took him to the top of the hit parade twice in 1955, with "Finger of Suspicion" and "Christmas Alphabet". There were never any muttered lyrics for Valentine; he had a big voice and made the most of it. He was one of the first British singers to challenge the top American stars at their own game, by appearing on the television shows of Ed Sullivan and Eddie Fisher.

An unfailing highlight of his act was a sequence of impersonations of famous entertainers: Al Jolson, Billy Daniels, the Ink Spots, and Johnny Ray were among his specialities. By 1957, his following was so large that he was able to book the Royal Albert Hall on a Sunday afternoon, for his annual Fan Club get-together.

With the advent of rock 'n roll he fell from favour and gracefully changed his act, becoming more of an entertainer. He returned to television in 1966 with his own programme on I.T.V.

His marriage to Elizabeth Flynn, a professional ice skater, was dissolved in 1967 after 13 years. They had two children. In 1968 Valentine married the actress Wendy Wayne.

May 7, 1971.

Eamon de Valera—See de Valera.

van—See substantive surnames.

Sir Douglas Veale, C.B.E., a senior civil servant who became an able and respected Registrar of Oxford University, died on September 27, 1973 at the age of 82.

He was born in Bristol on April 2, 1891, the third son of Edward Woodhouse Veale, solicitor, and educated at Bristol Grammar School. He gained a classical scholarship at Corpus Christi College, Oxford, in 1910 and took a first class in Classical Moderations in 1912 and a second in Greats in 1914.

As a Territorial he was called up in 1914 to serve in the 4th Battalion Gloucester Regiment. He took the Civil Service examination in August 1914, then returned to his regiment, serving in France and Belgium in 1915. Invalided home, he became captain and adjutant of his Reserve battalion until 1917, when he was released to take up a second class clerkship in the Local Government Board. In that office, later the Ministry of Health, he became private secretary to the Permanent Secretary in 1920 and then to successive Ministers of Health from 1921 to 1928.

He played a conspicuous part under Neville Chamberlain in the work which led to the passing of the important and complicated Local Government Act of 1929. In recognition of that he was made C.B.E.

Veale had proved himself a first class administrator. He was liked and respected. He would have had an outstanding Civil Service career if he had stayed on, but his thoughts were turning to public work outside the central government and in 1930 the opportunity came.

The Royal Commission on Oxford and Cambridge Universities of 1922 had recommended that the office of Registrar of Oxford University should be given extended duties and responsibilities in order to take some of the weight of business from the Vice-Chancellor, and to secure unity and continuity of administration. It was intended that the new registrar should be a trained administrator, and probably from outside the university.

The first opportunity of a new appointment in those terms came in 1930. There were other distinguished outside candidates for the post, but Veale was selected. He was released, with the blessing of the ministry, on "approved service".

From the beginning Veale showed that the office had become of cardinal importance in the university. At first there was some suspicion of this young "bureaucrat" and dons were inclined to wonder whether a new and dangerous power had been raised up. Soon they came to realize that in Veale the university had a great public servant who understood the politic limits of his influence and power.

In the shifting magistracy of the university, with a new vice-chancellor every three years and two new proctors annually, it was of the utmost value to have a permanent officer who could collate and remember the different problems with which the different boards and committees had to deal.

One of Veale's admirable qualities was his ability to find time to hear any who had to transact business, and in the press of his manifold affairs he could, with apparent ease, put his knowledge at their disposal. The difficult problem of the building of the new Bodleian was solved, the first of many elaborate projects which Veale had to assist in guiding to fruition.

In 1939 the war increased the contacts

with government, and the fact that Veale knew and understood the Civil Service was of the utmost value. When the war was over the situation became no easier, the grants were larger and the conflicting claims of departments in the university more difficult to reconcile.

By this time Veale had become the doyen of university administrators and his influence in the meetings of university heads and officers grew ever greater. He was especially concerned to improve relations between Oxford and the other universities; he worked hard to improve them and was not afraid to make himself temporarily unpopular in Oxford in that respect.

He was much concerned with the foundation of the Nuffield Institute of Medical Research, with the foundation of Nuffield College and later St. Antony's. The legal problems created by M. Besse's benefaction for St. Antony's were especially difficult.

He was also called in to help the growing universities of West Africa and the Sudan and made frequent visits to them. The development of the Radcliffe as a teaching hospital owed much to Veale's advice and brought many problems of administration. The acquisition of the Wytham estate was largely due to his enterprise. His interest in Commonwealth education was shown by the efforts he made which resulted in the foundation of Queen Elizabeth House in Oxford.

He brought to his work a splendid physical endowment. He was a walker of the old school and refreshed himself on Sundays by tramps of over 20 miles. One walk, described by him as the Shorter Bablockhithe, has been known to knock out much younger men. His holidays were given to the same spartan pursuits. He was especially fond of boating on the sea and, despising the aid of sail or engine, would row, tirelessly, happily, for hours on end.

His retirement brought no slackening of activity. He served for five years as secretary of the Oxford Preservation Trust and promoted the important report on city development by Sir William [Lord] Holford. He worked for the Marriage Guidance Council and on a committee on the rating of university premises. He was asked by the King of Jordan for help in the foundation of a university there. The South African Protectorates also asked him to help, and after several visits to Basutoland he was able by great diplomacy to secure agreement on the establishment of a university on the basis of federation of several religious colleges to provide higher education for the peoples of the protectorates.

A loyal Anglican, he was a regular communicant at his parish church and attended Sunday evening chapel at his college, Corpus. There he had his deepest loyalties and his closest friendships, and there will his loss be most deeply felt.

Veale was knighted in 1954. On his retirement he received the honorary degree of D.C.L. from the University; Corpus and St. Edmund Hall elected him to honorary fellowships.

He married in 1914 Evelyn Annie, daughter of Mr. J. A. Henderson. They had a son and two daughters.

September 29, 1973.

Marian Veitch, (Mrs. Donald Barnie), who died on July 24, 1973 at Chertsey, aged 60, was national woman officer of the General and Municipal Workers' Union from 1960 until her illness forced her early retirement at the age of 57.

She will be chiefly remembered for placing women workers on the road to equal pay, the result of a battle with eight male members of the executive of the Confederation of Shipbuilding and Engineering Unions, on which she was the only woman.

In October 1968, during protracted talks concerning the threatened strike of engineering workers, she made headline news with what was termed a "last-minute petticoat revolt", starting off a fresh crisis about the wages of 500,000 women workers. She accused her male colleagues of "selling women workers down the river", and found firm support for her action from Mrs. Barbara Castle, then Secretary of State for Employment and Productivity.

Born on July 8, 1913, Marian Veitch was the daughter of Arthur Edward and Elizabeth Veitch. She was educated at Huntsman's Gardens School, Sheffield, and Ruskin College, Oxford.

She was a member of the Food Standards Committee from 1965-68; the Confederation of Shipbuilding and Engineering Unions executive committee 1962-70; the International Metal Workers Association Women Workers' Committee 1962-70; the International Union of Food and Allied Workers Association 1964-70; and the International Federation of Industrial Organizations Women's Committee, of which she was chairman in 1969-70.

She married in 1965 Donald Barnie, lecturer at a polytechnic in Hendon.

She started her political career as a Sheffield city councillor, serving from 1945-56. Later she became a union official in Yorkshire.

Since childhood she had suffered from a serious heart condition. In 1965 she underwent an operation to replace a heart valve. With the support and care of her husband she made a spectacular recovery, and quickly returned to the battlefield for five more years of arduous work involving constant travel at home and abroad.

During her enforced retirement she began her autobiography, which must, unfortunately, remain unfinished. One title she considered using was *She's 'Ere!*, the cry she so often heard as she stepped out of her car inside factory gates, prepared, as always, for action.

July 27, 1973.

Panaghis Vergottis, the veteran London-based Greek shipowner, died in London on March 30, 1972 at the age of 83. He will be remembered in his native island of Cephalonia, to which he gave £200,000 for the establishment of a naval academy on the island. After the destructive earthquakes in the Ionian islands in 1953, he paid for rebuilding his ancestral village.

He opened his first shipping office in Cardiff in 1915 and later moved his headquarters to London, paying occasional visits to his native island where he had built a sumptuous villa. For nearly one quarter of a century however his residence was the Mayfair hotel in London. His understanding with the hotel management apparently was that the Greek flag would be displayed outside the hotel on Greek national holidays. He later moved to the Ritz.

In 1967 Vergottis made headlines throughout the world in a court case involving a colleague, Aristotle Onassis, and Maria Callas, the opera singer. He was then made to pay £38,000 in costs after unsuccessfully contesting that Madame Callas had acquired a share in one of his ships.

April 4, 1972.

V. E. Vincent, who died in hospital on June 16, 1971, was a great innovator in the construction field.

Born in 1893, one of three sons of the late Samuel H. Gluckstein (he changed his name in 1937), Vincent Esmé Vincent was educated at St. Paul's School and afterwards studied construction at the Regent Street Poly. After a period with J. Lyons & Company's building department, he volunteered in 1915 for the Royal Observer Corps, serving in the Balloons section (which he rejoined for the period of the 1939-45 war). On demobilization in 1919, he joined the building firm of Bovis Ltd.

In the early 1920s, as a result of first-hand experience of the wastefulness of the practice of placing building contracts by open tendering methods, he was instrumental in devising the Bovis system of contracting to erect buildings for an agreed fee, the prime cost of the works having been agreed previously as between the firm and the building client. The accolade of success was given to Vincent's idea when, in 1937, the firm was appointed by Marks and Spencer to execute the building work on all their branches. This arrangement still operated in 1971.

Vincent was also one of the founders of the London Builders' Conference—an organization which, while subsequently developing features which did not make it wholly acceptable to those who commission building work, played nevertheless an important role in checking the wasteful system by which 30 or more firms could be required to compete for the same contract. A much saner system exists today.

Blessed with an inventive mind, Vincent

set up within his firm the first school of building of its kind, and was the first to offer guaranteed employment to the firm's bricklayers; he invented a new method of establishing water levels below buildings and designed the Compactom wardrobe.

More importantly, he played a leading part in establishing the first Building Centre in 1932, then in New Bond Street. This he did in collaboration with a group of leading London architects and with the late Frank Yerbury, the Centre's first director, then secretary of the Architectural Association, from whose Samples Room the Centre was developed. Vincent and his brother Sidney put up the whole of the capital required by the new venture.

Vincent lost his wife Esmée some years ago. He is survived by two daughters.

June 17, 1971.

Madeleine Vionnet, the great French couturière who invented the revolutionary bias cut, died in Paris, aged 98, on March 2, 1975.

With her death France has lost a woman whose influence on the fashions of her times—the 1920s and 1930s—and indeed on the dressmaking techniques that followed, has no parallel in contemporary fashion.

The credit of freeing women from the bondage of the corset and of petticoats has often been given to Gabrielle Chanel; but it is more than likely that she was following the lead given in this direction by her contemporary, Madeleine Vionnet.

That change, reaction, liberation in modes as well as manners were in the air at that time is certain, but Madeleine Vionnet was undoubtedly the first dressmaker to appreciate and to exploit the relation between the dress and the structure of the body.

This she did by what can only be called the invention of the bias cut. With her scissors she changed fashion and dressmaking techniques, and the manner in which she manipulated fabric has never been equalled. Cecil Beaton has said of her art: "She made a Greek dress in a way the Greeks could never have imagined".

Everything that she created had to hang and cling, and she chose her materials accordingly—slippery satins, fluid velvets, heavy crepes. "You must dress a body in a fabric, not construct a dress", was her guiding rule in dressmaking.

Her first essays in bias technique are said to have been a skirt with a straight-cut back and bias-cut front, and a straight-cut dress with a bias look, finished at the neck with the bias-cut cowl drape that has ever since been connected with her name. Then came the handkerchief point inset on skirts and at necklines.

In 1926 she launched the first all-bias-cut dress, which tradition says sagged a bit at the hem. The principle of form-fit by hang was thus established as a dressmaking technique and although it was difficult to copy, the first slip-over-the-head dresses were on the market surprisingly soon.

The author of this break with past techniques was, like Chanel, a little wiry woman and, like Channel, a provincial. She came from the Jura, an origin that no doubt accounted for her small, tough physique, bright eyes set in a small brown face, her vivacity, good business sense and the firm precision of her gestures, and by no means least, her beautifully balanced intelligence.

From the age of three she lived with her father. Her mother had gone off to Paris where she founded Le Petit Casino, one of the best café-concerts of the period, at Aubervilliers, Seine. When she failed in her *prix d'excellence* at school, at the age of 11, her teacher apprenticed her to a local dressmaker where for the next five years she worked 12 hours a day.

At 16, with a solid knowledge of dressmaking in hand, she went to the house of Vincent in the Rue de la Paix. Married at 18, divorced at 19, she then went to London where she worked for five years in a tailoring establishment; and it was on her return to Paris, at the age of 24, that her career can be said to have begun.

She went to Callot, then to Madame Gerber, one of three sisters, whom she considered a better designer than her contemporary Poiret. From Madame Gerber she learnt the basic formulas that were to govern her future career as a designer and creator.

In 1907 she left Madame Gerber to go to Doucet and it was in this house that she created her first models. Finally in 1914 she opened her own house at 212 Rue de Rivoli. After the war, and backed by Bader of the Galeries Lafayette, she reopened in the vast mansion in the Avenue Montaigne which was soon to become the centre of elegance.

In the 20 years that she reigned over French couture (she closed her house in 1939), Madeleine Vionnet dressed many of the most elegant women of that period and as she put it "in dresses that went with their bodies".

March 6, 1975.

Vera Volkova, one of the leading ballet teachers of the past three decades, died on May 5, 1975.

Born at St. Petersburg in 1904, Volkova began her dance studies at the Imperial Ballet School there under Maria Romanova (the mother of Galina Ulanova) and Nicholas Legat. Later, at the private school founded in 1920 by Akim Volinsky, she studied with Agrippina Vaganova, who was then developing the theories upon which the Leningrad and Moscow schools are based today.

Volkova joined the company at the former Maryinsky (now Kirov) Theatre, where her partners included Alexander Pushkin, who later became the greatest male ballet teacher of his day. Volkova danced there until 1929 when she went with a group of colleagues to Japan and China.

She and George Goncharov left the party when it returned home; they settled in Shanghai where Goncharov founded both a company and a school in which Volkova worked. Margot Fonteyn, as a child, was one of the school's pupils, and Volkova advised her mother, at what ever cost, to take her little girl back to London to pursue her career.

Volkova herself, having married the English painter Hugh Williams, moved with him first to Hongkong, then in 1936 to London. She opened her own school in 1943 and rapidly made a high reputation. Partly that was because she introduced many of Vaganova's logical and carefully developed reforms of the old classical methods, but Volkova's success also derived from her own inspiring gifts as a teacher.

She had the ability to express herself in metaphors which immediately made the dancer visualize the kind of movement wanted. To cite only one instance, she instructed a ballerina to imagine she had tiny lungs growing on her wrists, thus evoking the gently breathing arm movements she intended. Her commands were couched in a vivid flow of language although she never lost a heavy accent.

Volkova was also for a time attached to the Sadler's Wells Ballet as an instructor, and most leading English dancers, from Fonteyn down, attended her classes. She thus played a vital part in the rise in standards that was vital to the success of the Sadler's Wells Ballet's move to Covent Garden after the war. As well as teaching, Volkova was a gifted and enthusiastic coach, especially for the great classical ballerina roles.

In 1950 she went to take charge of the ballet at La Scala, Milan, but soon afterwards moved to Copenhagen where she was given the responsible task of widening the scope of the Royal Danish Ballet to encompass the Russian classics and a range of modern works without weakening their indigenous romantic tradition. For this work she was awarded in 1956 the Order of the Dannebrog.

Copenhagen remained her home ever after, but her fame spread wide. Rudolf Nureyev was only one of many illustrious dancers or ambitious aspirants who made the journey to Denmark specially to work with her. She was also in demand throughout the world as a guest teacher.

Small, chic and elegant, assiduous in attending performances, fanatically enthusiastic about her work, but also a devoted wife, Volkova inspired great affection in her pupils and friends. In spite of a serious illness and operation, she remained active until the end.

May 6, 1975.

---

von. . . .—See substantive surnames.

Jennifer Vyvan, the English soprano, died on April 5, 1974 in London at the age of 49. She was noted particularly for her fluent singing of Purcell, Handel and Mozart, and for her very individual creations of several roles in modern British operas.

She was born at Broadstairs on March 13, 1925, and studied piano and singing at the Royal Academy of Music with Roy Henderson and Fernando Carpi. In 1951 she won first prize at the Concours International in Geneva. Her first professional stage appearance was as Jenny Diver in the English Opera Group's 1947 production of *The Beggar's Opera* in Britten's realization. That was soon followed by Nancy in Britten's *Albert Herring* and the Female Chorus in *The Rape of Lucretia* with the same company.

She came into her own as an operatic artist in 1952 with her secure, brilliant Constanze in Sadler's Wells' *The Seraglio* and sang Donna Anna for the same company that season. The following year she created the part of Penelope Rich in Britten's *Gloriana* at Covent Garden, a role she repeated with success when Sadler's Wells Opera took the work into its repertory in the late 1960s. She created three other parts in Britten's operas: the Governess in *The Turn of the Screw* at Venice (1954), Titania in *A Midsummer Night's Dream* at Aldeburgh (1960), and Mrs. Julian in *Owen Wingrave* on B.B.C. T.V. (1971) and at Covent Garden. Other parts written for her were the Countess of Serendin in Malcolm Williamson's *The Violins of St. Jacques* at Sadler's Wells in 1966, and various roles in the same composer's *Lucky Peter's Journey* at the Coliseum in 1969. At Glyndebourne she appeared as Electra in *Idomeneo* in 1953.

She sang at concerts in various European cities and in the United States, specializing in choral works such as Britten's *Spring Symphony* and *War Requiem*, in Beethoven's 9th symphony, and in the Passions of Bach. She also sang in the first performance of Bliss's *The Beatitudes* for the opening of the new Coventry Cathedral in 1962. She frequently appeared with the Handel Opera Society in stage and concert performances. She made many records, outstandingly *The Turn of the Screw* and Purcell's *The Fairy Queen* (twice).

Her singing was always marked by sure intonation, subtle phrasing and, in florid music, astonishing flexibility. In opera, she displayed her considerable dramatic gifts in vivid, sometime idiosyncratic portrayals. Sensibly, she never attempted to step outside her vocal or histrionic range and this allowed her to pursue a long career with her vocal powers largely undiminished. Her personality and generous nature will be sorely missed in British musical circles. She is survived by her husband, Lee Crown, and her son.

April 6, 1974.

W

Canon H. M. Waddams, general secretary of the Church of England Council on Foreign Relations from 1945 to 1959 and a well-known figure in the Church, died suddenly on May 13, 1972 at the age of 60.

Herbert Waddams touched the life of the Church at many points, but he will be best remembered as one of the architects of the Church of England Council on Foreign Relations. The council was founded in 1932 by the late Bishop Headlam of Gloucester and Canon J. A. Douglas. Waddams was one of a group of young men, concerned with the relations between the Church of England and foreign churches, which Douglas called his "kindergarten".

In 1946 Douglas resigned from the office of general secretary of the council and Waddams, who had been working in the religious division of the Ministry of Information, was the obvious choice as his successor. He already had a wide knowledge of the churches of Europe and under him the work of the council was not only consolidated, but widely expanded so that the initials "C.F.R." became a password to good relations in all parts of divided Christendom.

In the work of inter-church relations Waddams's primary interests were in the Church of Sweden and East Orthodox churches, on both of which he subsequently published books. But his ecumenical interest was active for good in many other parts of the Christian world. His concern for Christian unity was the result of a spiritual life which was rooted and grounded in Jesus Christ as the reconciler of men; this was a constant theme in various books published since his settlement in Canterbury in 1962. The Church of England Council on Foreign Relations has lately been contracted into a small group of experts known as the Archbishop of Canterbury's counsellors on foreign relations, and of this body H.M.W. was a valued member.

At Canterbury he entered fully into the life of the cathedral and of the city, and an echo of his past activity was that he was never happier than when groups of foreign visitors were at the cathedral. That the celebrations of the eighth centenary of the martyrdom of St. Thomas Becket in 1970 had so international a character was mainly due to him. Of late years he had made something of a name for himself as a moral thinker.

Herbert Montague Waddams was born on November 15, 1911, the son of W. H. Waddams, C.B.E., and educated at King's School, Bruton, King's College, Cambridge, and Cuddesdon College. He was ordained in 1935 and from then until 1937 he was assistant missioner at the Corpus Christi College, Cambridge, Mission. From 1937 to 1941 he was assistant priest at the Grosvenor Chapel and chaplain of Liddon House.

In 1941-42 he was priest-vicar and Sub-Dean of Chichester Cathedral, and from 1942 until the end of the Second World War he worked in the Religious Division of the Ministry of Information.

After leaving the Church of England Council on Foreign Relations in 1959 he went to Canada as rector of Manotick, Ontario.

In 1962 Waddams was appointed Canon Residentiary of Canterbury Cathedral and Examining Chaplain to the Archbishop of Canterbury. He had earlier been for some years an honorary Canon of Canterbury. He was chairman of the Hansard Society for Parliamentary Government from 1970 and a member of the Court of Essex University from 1971.

He was a prolific author. Among his publications were *The Swedish Church; Communism and the Churches; Meeting the Orthodox Churches; Life and Fire of Love; A New Introduction to Moral Theology; Companion to the Book of Common Prayer; The Church and Man's Struggle for Unity; Basic Question of Life and Death;* and *The Church in the 60s.*

He married in 1940 Margaret Mary Burgess. They had one son and one daughter.

May 15, 1972.

Professor C. H. Waddington, C.B.E., SC.D., F.R.S., the noted geneticist, died on September 26, 1975 at the age of 69.

Conrad Hal Waddington, who was born in 1905, was one of the significant figures of this century, and left his mark on more areas of current thought than is generally realised.

Waddington's massive body of writing comprises several books, contributions to critical volumes, editorship of scientific texts, and some two hundred papers and articles—academic, semi-popular and popular. It includes scientific contributions, mainly in theoretical and experimental biology, writings on the interaction between science and society and the organization of science, the relationship between art and scientific knowledge, and analyses ranging from the nature of ethics to the requirements of the human race as a whole for long-term studies on balanced ecology and planning for the future.

In many of these writings his statement of a problem or adumbration of a relationship was well ahead of his time—a bold exercise in intelligence, imagination and a grasp of the interrelationships between findings often not yet seen as significant by many of his contemporaries. These apparently diverse interests were aspects of a fascination with process rather than object, and an interest in the generation of form both in scientific and artistic terms, which provided a continuing thread throughout his life.

Joseph Needham stimulated his move to

embryology and he won the Brachet Prize for embryology in 1936. His real contribution was as a synthesizer, and, among his books, significant contributions to the development of biological thought were made in *Introduction to Modern Genetics* (1939), *Organizers and Genes* (1940) and *Principles of Embryology* (1956).

His best experimental contributions also partook of the nature of syntheses. For example, he resolved, in 1953, the problem posed by the apparently irreconcilable natures of the evolutionary process on the one hand, involving mutation and natural selection, and, on the other hand the apparently purposeful way in which development produces an organism fitted for its environment. He demonstrated that the apparent inheritance of acquired characters was in fact a very different process which contradicted neither the genetic principles of evolution nor the dynamic ones of embryology.

He was as interested in the mathematical expression of pattern formation as a resultant of biological equilibria, as in the ultrastructural features of cells as revealed by the electron microscope, and was involved in both areas.

Believing that science influences society profoundly and that an understanding of the interaction of the two is essential, he was especially active as a popularizer. His book *The Scientific Attitude* (1941) is still widely read. His practical involvements in scientific affairs include pioneering in Operational Research, the presidency of the International Union of Biological Sciences (1961-67) and the setting up and vice-presidency of the International Biological Programme (1963-66), which attempted to instigate global studies in responsible ecology. He was a founder member of the Pugwash Conference and The Club of Rome.

An interest in philosophy, which won him the Gerstenberg Prize in 1927, led him to write *Science and Ethics* (1942) and *The Ethical Animal* (1960). This interpretation of ethics as a result of a process of evolution was exciting and sympathetic to many who were not impressed by the intellectual content of formal religious morality and not converted by the abstractions of philosophy which relied more on logic than on the given facts of living organisms.

His enjoyment of poetry and painting was life-long and in *Behind Appearances* (1970) he discussed the way in which scientific knowledge and the elucidation of natural form have influenced the vision of modern art.

All his life he showed an eager interest in and a sharp appreciation of the potential impact of advances in one field upon another, and he frequently initiated organizations which brought together people of diverse interest. For example, on moving to Edinburgh in 1947 as Buchanan Professor of Animal Genetics, he built up the Institute of Animal Genetics to a large research group which has influenced biologists throughout the world; he founded an international graduate school in epigenetics arising from a research group that he formed in 1962; and established The School of the Man-made Future in 1972.

Towards a Theoretical Biology I and *II* (1968 and 1969) are the proceedings of an interdisciplinary symposium that he organized.

Waddington's last written contributions in 1973 include joint editorship of a book on insect development and an important contribution on biology in *The Twentieth Century Mind* (edited by Cox and Dyson). Over the same period he contributed to discussions on "The Nature of Mind" and gave a series of lectures on technological extrapolations, social structures and futures forecasting in Edinburgh University.

His many honours include F.R.S. (1947), C.B.E. (1958), foreign membership of the American Academy of Arts and Sciences, of the Finnish Academy, and of the New York Academy of Sciences, several honorary doctorates, and numerous visiting lectureships and fellowships.

He had one son by his first marriage in 1926 to Cecil Elizabeth Lascelles and two daughters by his second marriage in 1934 to Margaret Justin Blanco White.

September 29, 1975.

Wadiyar—See Mysore.

Major Richard Wakeford, v.c., a master of the Chancery Division of the Supreme Court since 1964, died on August 28, 1972 at the age of 51. Wakeford won his award in 1944 while serving as a captain in The Hampshire Regiment in Italy.

He was a warrior and a hero in the classic mould. He joined the Army after the outbreak of the last war immediately on leaving Westminster, where he was captain of boats and captain of shooting. He was commissioned in The Hampshire Regiment and served with them in North Africa, Italy and Greece, ultimately commanding his battalion.

The Hampshires were a name to conjure with in the Italian Campaign, and Wakeford illuminated even their reputation. He won his Victoria Cross leading his company in an advance on strongly held enemy positions near Cassino on May 13 and 14, 1944.

According to eye-witnesses his skill and courage were fantastic. At all times he led his men in the literal sense, preceding the painful advance with his orderly. Wakeford was a superb pistol shot, and used his favourite weapon, a Colt .45 automatic, with deadly effect. The withering fire of the enemy never stopped him, and with pistol and grenade he attacked every strongpoint, until at last he consolidated his depleted company at their objective.

Wakeford was wounded in the face, both arms and both legs, and by the time he reached his goal was in severe pain and weak with loss of blood. It was then he showed that he possessed not only dash and courage but the even rarer qualities of infinite endurance and patient gallantry.

He refused morphia, and took all necessary steps to defend what was an advanced and isolated position, where a counter-attack was probable, with the handful of men who were left of a company that had been only 80 strong initially. It was seven hours before stretcher bearers and other assistance arrived, and Wakeford continued his incomparable devotion to duty by finding the strength to laugh and joke with the other wounded and keep morale at a high level during that dangerous period.

After surviving a further wound, Wakeford was demobilized, and in early 1946 went up to Trinity College, Oxford, to study law. He had always wanted to be a surgeon, but one of his wounds had affected his left hand and he decided to become a solicitor.

It was typical of Wakeford that despite the fact that his wounds had caused him some disability he took up rowing again with enthusiasm. Trinity had become head of the river shortly before the war, and in the Summer VIIIs of 1946 the position was critical, in that some of the celebrated oarsmen had not returned from war service. Those who were up at that time will never forget how, as stroke, Wakeford with his usual implacable defiance fought off all challenges, and how he stroked Trinity to success for two classic seasons.

There can be no doubt that he was a man of indomitable courage; but that was only one facet of his character. While he would have been horrified at any suggestion that he was intellectual, he had a powerful mind, and an innate sensitivity, which accounted for his successful career as a solicitor and his appointment as a master in the Chancery Division of the Supreme Court.

Wakeford was painstaking, immensely shrewd, and undeviatingly just. The loss to the law is a sad one, but his loss to his friends, and to humanity in general, is tragic.

It is difficult to realize that a man whose deeds sound like a fanfare of trumpets was at heart a diffident and sensitive person; but Wakeford was just that. It would be wrong to suggest that as a young man he was frightened of nothing: he was frightened of women. He would quite simply run away if his friends brought them near.

It was a joy to his friends when the limited opportunities of seclusion offered by a ship enabled him to stand still long enough to notice the charm of Denise Corlson, and be wholly conquered by it. She became his wife and made him the happiest of men for the rest of his life.

August 30, 1972.

Professor Selman Waksman, discoverer of streptomycin, who won the Nobel Prize for medicine in 1952, died on August 16, 1973 at Hyannis, Massachusetts, aged 85.

Selman Abraham Waksman, born in the Ukraine in 1888, emigrated to the United States in 1910, and from then on, first as a student in Rutgers University and later as an experimenter and in various professional capacities there, he devoted his entire life to the study of soil microbiology. For his researches in that field he was richly rewarded when in 1942 he discovered streptomycin, an antibiotic effective against tuberculosis and other diseases resistant to penicillin. Ten years afterwards he was awarded for this discovery the Nobel Prize in Medicine.

At Rutgers he won the degrees of Bachelor of Science and Master of Science. After his graduation he attended the University of California, where he was given the degree of doctor of philosophy. Meanwhile he became an American citizen.

In 1918 he returned to Rutgers for good, starting his teaching career as a lecturer in soil microbiology and director of the university's experiment stations. His progress was rapid. In 1930 he was made a full professor and head of the department of microbiology. In this position, and as director of the Institute of Microbiology, he served until 1958, when he became Professor Emeritus.

At various times Dr. Waksman held industrial positions and served as consultant to several government, industrial and scientific organizations. He was an honorary member or fellow member of a number of scientific organizations in the United States and other countries, including the National Academy of Sciences, the American Academy of Arts and Sciences, and the International Society of Soil Science, and he was a foreign associate of the French Academy of Sciences. He was given awards and other honours by many countries and was the holder of numerous honorary degrees from American, European, and Far Eastern universities.

He wrote alone, or with others, 20 books in his field of work, including *Streptomycin, Its Nature and Application; The Soil and the Microbe;* and *My Life with Microbes.* Besides his own foundation for Microbiology, there are Waksman foundations in France, Italy, and Japan.

August 18, 1973.

Sir John Waldron, K.C.V.O., Commissioner of the Metropolitan Police from 1968 to 1972, died on August 24, 1975 at the age of 65.

Sir John's period in command of the Metropolitan Force was not an easy one. Crime was soaring, demonstrations reached a vehement climax and two policemen, whose corruption was exposed by *The Times,* were later sent to prison. Sir John's

home, like those of some other prominent people, was the target of a bomb attack.

It seemed to Sir John at the time that the values of the world he knew were being corroded. He spoke of his keenness to remove "any rotten apples from the barrel". He looked the part of Commissioner. Tall, erect, with a piercing gaze and sometimes misleadingly gruff manner, he was a person of authority and dignity. Above all, he was immensely loyal to the values he prized and to his Force.

To some, who did not appreciate that beneath the stiff exterior there was much humanity, he seemed to be old-fashioned and paternal. But it was because he believed deeply in the traditional qualities of policing that his Force was not trapped into following the example of some police forces abroad into greater confrontation with the demonstrators.

To some, the protests which reached a climax in 1968 in Grosvenor Square, and led to some of his men being injured, seemed to require a different police approach. There was a feeling that the police ought to have visors and riot shields to protect them.

Not to change took courage and faith in his men and the tradition he believed in. One day in 1968, a large part of his Force was assembled and told what the decision meant and the philosophy behind it. Later that year, helped by extra training, they faced a demonstration in Grosvenor Square, which won world wide praise for British police methods. More important, the way it was handled halted any escalation in London towards violent conflict on the scale that had occurred elsewhere, and thus to any change in the understanding between public and police.

After his retirement, when he was called in to help plan the modernization and improvement of the Miami police department, he again turned to the best of British traditions. *The Blade* reported in Toledo, Ohio: "One of Sir John's concerns is keeping qualified policemen on the beat."

In London, however, a serious shortage of men eroded the traditional ideal. Moreover, the pace of change in society, symbolized by the arrival of immigrants, meant that relations with the public demanded much more of the police.

This tended to put the police on the defensive. Sir John, loyal as ever to his men, defended them. His comments sometimes betrayed an irritation that the efforts the police were making were not appreciated. He knew that no man, particularly a policeman, is an island, yet he did not want to undermine the police duty of enforcing the law. The dilemma is still there, although experience has made policemen more aware of the complications.

Sir John, who took over as Commissioner in April 1968, after the death of Sir Joseph Simpson*, was given much to do and little time in which to do it. Even the comparative isolation of the C.I.D. was a deepseated legacy which had aroused the con-

cern of a Royal Commission as long ago as 1929.

Behind the scenes, particularly in traffic regulation, technological change was being introduced. But the traditions of the police provided them with a sense of direction, reassurance and stability. If Sir John emphasized them, they also provided a base from which change could later increase without eroding the policeman's understanding of himself and his role.

John Lovegrove Waldron was born in 1909 at Hedge End, Hampshire. He was educated at Charterhouse and Clare College, Cambridge, where he obtained an Honours Degree in history. He joined the Metropolitan Police in 1934 as one of the first graduate recruits by direct entry into the Metropolitan Police College, Hendon.

In 1943, he was seconded to the Ceylon Police to help in reorganizing the Force and acted as Deputy Inspector General (C.I.D.) from 1944 to 1947 before returning to the Metropolitan Police. In 1951, he was appointed Assistant Chief Constable of Lancashire. Three years later, he became Chief Constable of Berkshire.

It was in 1959 that he rejoined the Metropolitan Force as Assistant Commissioner in charge of traffic and transport, and four years later he transferred to the administrative and operations department, where he remained until being appointed Deputy Commissioner in 1966.

He was made a Commander of the Royal Victorian Order in 1959 and advanced to Knight Commander in 1966.

Sir John was also a governor of Sutton's Hospital in Charterhouse. He leaves a widow and two daughters.

August 25, 1975.

Former Archbishop of Wales—See Morris.

Alexander Burns Wallace, C.B.E., who died suddenly on December 14, 1974, was a plastic surgeon of international renown. This position he achieved not only because of his technical skill but also by virtue of his integrity, character and devotion to duty.

In many ways he was the supreme example of the specialist who never became lost in the technicality of his job. The patient always came first; he was never a "case", but always a human being.

Above all, he resisted any attempt to prostitute his speciality. In plastic surgery this was a particularly valuable attribute, for at one time it was threatened with domination by the more exuberant money-grabbing exponents of cosmetic surgery.

Face lifting, abolition of wrinkles, straightening of noses, unnecessary plastic operations on the breast, particularly for those to whom money was no consideration—none of these would Wallace tolerate.

Plastic surgery in his opinion was a

serious branch of surgery which should devote itself to the service of those to whom plastic surgery was of real practical and psychological assistance, whether it was the victim of burns, road or industrial accident, or congenital deformity. For these he had an infinite compassion and would labour for them morning, noon and night.

A graduate of Edinburgh University, where he qualified in 1929, he proceeded to the Fellowship of the Royal College of Surgeons of Edinburgh in 1932. Apart from a happy spell as a demonstrator in surgery in McGill University, Montreal, where he graduated M.Sc., he spent his entire professional career in Edinburgh as surgeon in charge of the plastic and jaw injuries unit at Bangour Hospital, assistant surgeon at the Royal Hospital for Sick Children, Edinburgh, and Reader in Plastic Surgery at Edinburgh University.

He also served a term as president of the British Association of Plastic Surgeons. Such was his international reputation that he was appointed general secretary of the International Society of Burn Injuries, an aspect of plastic surgery in which he had for long been a leading figure, and the University of Upsaala made him an honorary M.D. in 1970.

It was typical of his zest for life, and his refusal to give in, that when a cerebral vascular episode finally forced him to retire from other work and settle in Fife about 1970, he not only continued to run the secretariat of the International Society of Burn Injuries but also matriculated at St. Andrews University and graduated Ph.D. in 1973.

In addition, at the time of his death, he was busy on an historical project of the Edinburgh Surgical School of the nineteenth century in relation to plastic surgery.

December 18, 1974.

Wang Ming, the Chinese Communist Party's most prominent exile in Moscow, died on March 27, 1974 at the age of 69.

Wang Ming (the pseudonym of Ch'en Shao-yü) will be remembered more for his place in the Maoist record as the "third leftist deviationist" in a roll that now amounts, with Liu Shao-ch'i and Lin Piao, to 10 in all, than for the power or the offices he held in the Chinese Communist Party. As many Chinese in the twenties and thirties acquired the culture and the manner of America or other European countries in which they studied, Wang became a fluent Russian speaker, a trusted disciple of Stalin and a man steeped in the Comintern's view of the world communist movement.

As a young man Wang went to Moscow to study at the newly founded Sun Yat-sen University. In 1930 he returned at the head of the "28 Bolsheviks" who were escorted by Pavel Mif, the Comintern representative for China, with the aim of taking over the weak party and giving it a modern look.

Thus Wang's first intra-party struggle was against the then leader Li Lisan. In 1931 the new men were installed and Wang found himself—not yet out of his twenties —a member of the political bureau and secretary-general of the party.

But by then the "liberated areas" of China were gaining peasant strength and the official party leadership soon found life underground in Shanghai too hot for them. Some—such as Chou En-lai —went to Kiangsi; Wang chose to go, or possibly was summoned back, to Moscow as the Chinese party's representative on the Comintern. There he remained a distant spectator of the struggle between the communists and Chiang Kai-shek, the Long March and the establishment of a new headquarters in Yenan.

Returning to China in 1937 as spokesman of the Comintern's newly adopted united front policy, Wang soon found himself at odds with the Maoist style. He had little sympathy for peasant guerrillas and his view of the united front allowed far greater concessions to the Kuomintang than Mao Tse-tung would accept. His Soviet indoctrination and sympathies made him an obvious target of the 1942 reform campaign. "Foreign dogmatists" and those Marxists who were unable to adapt their doctrine to Chinese realities were under attack and Wang was the outstanding example.

Although he was given some minor posts, he found himself isolated. At the seventh party congress of 1945 his decline was marked by election as forty-third of 45 members of the central committee. When the new government was formed in 1949 he was given the chairmanship of minor committees and was briefly prominent in the new Sino-Soviet Friendship Association. When the cracks began to appear in that friendship in 1956, Wang sank farther yet. His election as the last of 97 candidates to the central committee was indication enough that he had no future and he made his way at the end of that year to Moscow, where he spent the rest of his life.

Nothing is known of any part he may have played in the Sino-Soviet dispute. He surfaced during the cultural revolution with an article attacking Maoism in a Canadian communist journal and some broadcasts were also attributed to him.

March 29, 1974.

Maisie Ward (Mrs. F. J. Sheed), author, publisher and speaker, died in America on January 28, 1975 at the age of 86.

Maisie Ward was best known as the biographer of G. K. Chesterton, and for her studies of Newman and the Roman Catholic revival of the late nineteenth century, which supplemented her father's important biographies of Newman and Manning.

In addition to her literary work, she was

an active partner in the publishing house of Sheed and Ward, founded by her husband, Francis J. Sheed. She was deeply interested also in the work of the Catholic Evidence Guild, speaking regularly from the guild platform in Hyde Park, assisting in the training of speakers and taking charge over a period of years of the training courses prepared for its members.

Maisie Ward was the daughter of Wilfrid Ward. She was born at Shanklin, Isle of Wight, where her grandfather, W. G. Ward, the neighbour and close friend of Tennyson had settled on his inherited property. W. G. Ward—"Ideal" Ward—was the Fellow of Balliol who played so prominent a part in the Oxford Movement, leading to the deprivation of his degree by Convocation and his expulsion from Balliol and his subsequent secession to the Roman Catholic Church.

Maisie Ward was deeply interested in her family's literary and religious traditions. One of her earliest memories was as a young girl of three or four, going for a walk with her father and Tennyson, and Tennyson saying, "Would you mind stepping back just a bit, my dear, I am going to tell your father a dirty story".

She married in 1926 Frank Sheed, the Australian lecturer and writer. They had spoken together for the Catholic Evidence Guild in Hyde Park and elsewhere. On their marriage they established the publishing house of Sheed and Ward.

Maisie Ward was herself a prolific writer, mainly on the literary and religious topics on which her family had been brought up. She wrote an attractive book on Newman, but perhaps her most considerable work was the official biography of G. K Chesterton, which appeared in 1944. She was a fervent disciple and admirer of Chesterton, adopting his views on distributism and, in defiance of her family's tradition, on the Irish question.

The book was generally hailed as a success although there were those who thought that her keenly aesthetic habits were not quite suited to do full justice to the wine, water and song side of Chesterton.

In recent years she had turned her pen to less directly apologetic topics, writing both of Robert Browning and of his son, Pen. She leaves one son, the well-known writer, and one daughter.

January 30, 1975.

Earl Warren, the former Chief Justice of the United States Supreme Court, who died on July 10, 1974 at the age of 83, presided over the Court during a particularly dramatic era.

There have been times in its history when its judgments have concentrated on interpreting the law as it stands, leaving it to Congress to make whatever changes it deemed necessary; and there have been other periods when the Court has placed the emphasis upon reinterpreting the law in the light of changing social conditions and the development of public opinion. Warren's Court followed the second course. It was liberal and activist. It kept pace with, and some would say outstripped, the movement of public opinion.

At a time of conservative political leadership in the United States, which there was for the first half of Warren's reign, the Court became the most important vehicle of social change. This applied particularly, but not solely, in the area of civil rights. Whether Warren was a great lawyer is open to question, but he must be numbered among the great Chief Justices who made their mark upon the history of the United States.

His concept of his office was not in fact surprising for a man of his background. He made his name as a politician rather than as a lawyer, and as a politician of a special kind. He was one of those whose great political gift lay in his capacity to appeal to moderate people in the opposing party. For three terms he served as Republican Governor of California at a time when there was a natural Democratic majority in the state. This was the record of a moderate conservative who could run before the wind of change. It was a gift that he developed as Chief Justice to the point where the wind may sometimes have had a bit of a job in keeping up. The vigour of his liberalism is said to have surprised President Eisenhower,* who appointed him in 1953. But it was natural that his contribution lay in sensing the kind of laws that the country needed at that time. That was bound to be controversial, but he himself always commanded an authority and respect that went to the man as well as to the office.

Warren was born in California on March 19, 1891, of Scandinavian stock, both his parents having gone to the United States as children. His father was a craftsman building railway carriages, and an active trade unionist. The family knew hard times, and young Warren had the kind of upbringing approved in American folklore, tackling a variety of casual jobs while still in high school; but later the father prospered modestly as a small property owner and was able to support his son at the University of California at Berkeley, where he studied political science before graduating in law and being admitted to the California Bar in 1914.

Warren served in the 1914-18 War, though not overseas. On demobilization he was quickly diverted from private practice into a variety of public law offices. As district attorney of his county from 1925 to 1938 he earned a reputation for severity; but it was also observed that no conviction he secured was ever reversed on appeal. During these years he became active in Republican politics, serving as chairman of the party's state committee from 1934-36 and national committeeman 1936-38.

Warren's political instincts—and talents—were, however, for moderation and compromise. When he was elected attorney general of the state of California in 1938, it was as the nominee of all three parties, Republican, Democratic and Progressive. His years as attorney general were notably efficient and free from corruption (though perhaps marred by treatment of Japanese Americans on the outbreak of war, which is now generally regarded as harsh, and which later came to trouble Warren himself), and in 1942 he was elected governor. He ran as a Republican, but he had made an impressive showing in the Democratic primary also (as Californian law permits), and in the election he carried every county. In fact it was by now clear that Warren's appeal was his own rather than that of his party. A big, burly, bluff man, his ancestry, his upbringing, his attractive wife and handsome, growing family made him the voters' delight and the despair of his opponents. He was easily reelected in 1946 as the nominee of both major parties, and elected yet again in 1950 (when the Democrats chose James Roosevelt, son of F.D.R.), to become the only man in California's history to win three terms as governor.

Inevitably he had meanwhile developed national political ambitions. As early as 1944 he had the support of the California delegation for the presidential nomination. He himself backed Governor Dewey, but he resisted Dewey's suggestion that he, Warren, should run for Vice-President. In 1948 he again lost the nomination to Dewey, but this time he agreed to take the second place and was nominated for the Vice-Presidency by acclamation. He tried yet again to win the presidential nomination in 1952.

In all these contests Warren showed that he could hold the loyalty of his delegates till a late stage in the bargaining, and that he could avoid making needless enemies; but he failed to project his local popularity to the nation at large. In 1952, particularly, many professional politicians sensed the advantages of a candidate with Warren's cross-party appeal, but a figure with more status was needed and was available. In the early months of 1956, when President Eisenhower's health made it uncertain that he could run again, opinion polls identified Warren as the only other Republican who could beat Adlai Stevenson.* But Warren then made clear his determination not to run, and the issue was of course, settled by the President's recovery.

Eisenhower had persuaded Warren, with some hesitation, to accept appointment as Chief Justice on the death of Fred J. Vinson. The court to which he came was notoriously divided. There is no direct evidence that the President deliberately chose Warren as a moderator, but that was the task which the new Chief Justice undertook; his natural inclination was perhaps reinforced by his consciousness that he lacked judicial experience. His role was quickly and strikingly symbolized. When he was appointed the court was believed to be sharply divided over *Brown v. Board of Education*, the famous case which tested the validity of segregation in public schools. In a matter of months Warren was able to write the decision, and read it as unanimous. The court's decision was remarkable not merely because it was unanimous, but for the range of non-legal evidence which the court was prepared to cite in its support. Yet the court was careful not to press integration too hard. Only after a further year did it provide instruction for lower courts.

Brown v. Board of Education was symbolic in a second and more lasting sense. Warren had been a conciliator, an administrator, a cross-party politician through conviction, not through lack of it. On the court his good sense and tact did something to make agreement easier, but in the main debate which divided his colleagues he found himself drawn more and more to one side. This was the contest between those who took a narrow view of their judicial function—those for whom Mr. Justice Frankfurter* expounded with fire and eloquence and unique learning the doctrine of his great predecessor Holmes—and those —among whom Mr. Justice Black was the leader—who saw their task in much more positive social terms, who were willing to use the court as an instrument of reform. Increasingly it became clear where the new Chief Justice's sympathies lay. He was not a lawyer of profound learning or piercing intellect. What he had was a passion for justice—indeed, in simpler terms, a passion for fair play.

This quality found scope in a time when the concern of the court shifted strikingly towards questions of human rights. Perhaps half the cases that now come before it can be brought under this head; hardly one in a hundred could have been brought under it 25 years ago. Under Chief Justice Warren the victory increasingly went to the pragmatic reforming party. For that he was not, of course, solely responsible. Other activist justices were appointed; Mr. Justice Frankfurter retired, leaving no successor of equal stature; and Frankfurter himself, like Holmes before him, had been more "liberal" in civil rights cases than in others. But when the Court makes a mark, the Chief Justice is inevitably singled out, as the John Birch Society's attempt to "Impeach Earl Warren" bears witness.

Alarm was not confined to the lunatic fringe. Lawyers of learning, conscience and sense argued that the Court was abandoning the exposition of law and was expounding rather the prejudices of its members. Even non-lawyers feared that by moving outside its proper role, the Court would endanger its prestige and so its constitutional position. To this the reformers retorted that not over-activity but over-restraint had in the past endangered the standing of the Court; and so far the facts have not justified the alarm of their critics. There can hardly be better evidence than the choice of the Chief Justice to head the inquiry into the murder of President Kennedy,* an inquiry which undoubtedly roused violent political emotions.

This was an especially difficult task. The force of public emotion and anxiety demanded a speedy verdict. Fears, some of them bizarre, needed either to be established or set at rest. But the Commission was confronted by a plethora of evidence of different kinds and varying quality. Perhaps understandably, therefore, its methods were not always so careful as they might have been. Some corners were cut. The report failed to quieten dissent, then or later. Indeed, the production of conflicting versions of the assassination became for a time one of the growth industries of the United States. Yet despite all the criticism, the Commission's judgment that Oswald was solely responsible for the deed has not been overturned. That still stands as the verdict of history.

Warren first announced his resignation in June 1968, but agreed to stay on because of President Johnson's inability to get his choice as successor, Abe Fortas, approved by Congress. Warren finally retired the following June after President Nixon had come to office, so that he had served as Chief Justice under four Presidents.

He married in 1925 Mrs. Nina Meyers, a widow, and they had three sons and three daughters.

July 11, 1974.

Sir Mortimer Warren, who was Secretary (1954-64) and Financial Secretary (1948-54) to the Church Commissioners for England, died on February 18, 1972. He was 68.

Warren was educated at Cranleigh and qualified as a chartered accountant in 1927. He joined Queen Anne's Bounty as Assistant Accountant in the same year, and in 1942 became Assistant Secretary and Finance Officer. On the amalgamation of Queen Anne's Bounty and the Ecclesiastical Commissioners in 1948 to form the Church Commissioners, he became Financial Secretary to the new body.

Tim Warren brought a professional and farseeing outlook to their financial affairs. He saw that in a world where the value of money was falling the static income of the Church would be inadequate to meet the needs of the clergy. His first opportunity to take positive action came on the extinguishment of tithe rentcharge in 1936 when Queen Anne's Bounty received £50m. of long-term government stock as compensation. On his advice and by his efforts the whole of this sum was reinvested to give increased income as well as greater security of capital.

During the war years he ran the office of Queen Anne's Bounty in London with a small staff but played his full part in the Home Guard in Orpington where he lived. After the war he was given, in conjunction with Sir James Brown, Secretary of the Ecclesiastical Commissioners, the task of preparing for the amalgamation of Queen Anne's Bounty and the Ecclesiastical Commissioners. Through their efforts this amalgamation was most efficiently and happily carried out and in 1948 Warren, as Financial Secretary, became responsible for a portfolio of fixed Stock Exchange investments of over £100m. and property of over £50m., leased almost entirely on very long leases. The situation which he had foreseen earlier had now become very much worse as a result of the war, and it was he who advised the Commissioners that they must make the revolutionary change of investing for growth, including investing in equity shares. This advice was accepted.

With strong support from Sir Malcolm Trustram Eve (now Lord Silsoe), the then First Church Estates Commissioner, Warren embarked on the huge task of converting over £150m. of fixed assets into assets yielding income which would grow sufficiently to keep abreast of inflation. On his retirement in 1964 80 per cent of the Stock Exchange portfolio was in equities and the income had been more than doubled. At the same time the Commissioners' holdings in property had been so rationalized that the income had been more than trebled.

In achieving this success Warren made many friends for the Commissioners and for himself, in both the Stock Exchange and the property worlds, all of whom will be sad at his death. His efforts earned the Commissioners a high reputation as a well-advised business-like institution who could be relied on to act in accordance with the best standards.

Warren gave the benefit of his experience and advice to a number of charitable bodies including Guy's Hospital.

After his retirement he served as chairman of Barro Equities and as a director of a number of companies, including Trustees Corporation Ltd., Great Portland Estates Ltd., and Ellis (Kensington) Ltd.

He leaves a widow and one daughter.

February 21, 1972.

Dr. Doreen Warriner, O.B.E., Emeritus Professor of Economic History at London University and an outstanding authority on the problems of underdeveloped countries, died suddenly on December 17, 1972 at Jordans, Buckinghamshire, at the age of 68.

Doreen Warriner was educated at Malvern Girls' College and St. Hugh's College, Oxford, where she obtained a first in P.P.E. and then went to London University to obtain the degree of Ph.D. in 1931. She then held a research studentship at the L.S.E. and later a research fellowship at Somerville College, Oxford.

She had by this time begun to specialize on the economic and social problems of eastern Europe, work which was to lead to the publication of her book *Economic Problems of Peasant Farming.* For this work she had to travel extensively in eastern Europe for which she received a Rockefeller Travelling Fellowship. She made many friends among economists who were working on these intractable problems and she worked closely with Professor Rudi Bicanic of Yugoslavia.

She became assistant lecturer at University College London, but in 1939 gave up academic life temporarily to work in Czechoslovakia for the British Committee for Refugees. For this work she was made O.B.E. in 1941. Her exceptional knowledge of economic conditions in eastern Europe determined her wartime career, which was spent working in the Ministry of Economic Warfare (in England and at the Middle East supply centre in Cairo) and in the political intelligence department of the Foreign Office. From 1944 to 1946 she was chief of the food supply department in the U.N.R.R.A. mission to Yugoslavia. In 1947 she became lecturer, later reader and then professor at the School of Slavonic Studies in the University of London. She had by this time become an internationally famous expert on economic problems in underdeveloped countries, especially on land reform.

She travelled indefatigably in the Middle East and South America, collecting materials for a report on land reform which was published by the United Nations. She also published many books and articles on various aspects of land reform and economic development in different parts of the world.

Her genial and very human personality, her kindly help to students of all ages and nationalities and not least her irreplaceable expertise will be sadly missed.

December 21, 1972.

Professor D. M. S. Watson, F.R.S., the distinguished zoologist and palaeontologist, died at Midhurst on July 23, 1973 at the age of 87.

David Meredith Seares Watson was the son of David Watson, a pioneer in the electrolytic refining of copper. He was born on June 18, 1886, and educated at Manchester Gammar School and Manchester University, where he was trained as a chemist and geologist. His interest in science was first aroused by visits to his father's works. Through early work in palaeobotany he became interested in palaeontology. He had, however, no formal education in zoology.

In the first war he was able to travel extensively in South Africa and Australia collecting fossil vertebrates. He would tell how he travelled in a Cape cart, from farm to farm across the Karroo with its wealth of reptilian remains. It was there that he obtained some of the material which enabled him to trace the evolution of the mammalian skeleton from that of primitive reptiles, work which led to election in 1922 to the Royal Society. When, two years later, the society invited Watson to give the Croonian lecture he chose to speak on early amphibians, on which he was a leading authority.

His connexion with University College London began in 1912. At the end of the first war, during which he served with the R.N.V.R., he returned to London to carry out research at the Natural History Museum and, at the invitation of Professor J. P. Hill, to lecture at University College. In 1921 he succeeded Hill as Jodrell Professor of Zoology and Comparative Anatomy, a post he held for 30 years until his retirement.

At University College Watson gave an annual introductory course in Zoology, lectures which were recalled many years later by those who had been privileged to attend them. Watson was a gifted lecturer. J. B. S. Haldane* regarded him as one of the two best speakers he had heard. Watson paid great attention to his research students, visiting them each working day. Shy and reserved, with no small talk, he would open out immediately a scientific subject was introduced. However, far more than science attracted his attention, for he was a man of wide learning and could discourse as readily about the design of a Chinese crossbow as the anatomy of a fossil reptile.

He took particular pleasure in his service as a Trustee of the British Museum and at University College was as much in the company of archaeologists and historians as biologists. His international reputation attracted many students to University College where he arranged for the continuation of the work on embryology which J. B. Hill had instituted, gave G. P. Wells responsibility for comparative physiology and later welcomed J. B. S. Haldane to develop his work on genetics.

When Watson was appointed to the Chair of Zoology at University College the Department was in cramped quarters; there is a story that one Sunday he and the then secretary of the college scaled the wall of neighbouring stables housing the delivery horses of a well-known store. Following this unofficial excursion the college obtained the property, and with generous support from the Rockefeller Foundation converted these to house a greatly expanded department.

During the last war when the department was evacuated to North Wales, David Watson served as secretary of the Scientific Food Policy Committee. After his retirement he retained a room at University College and with the assistance of Miss Joyce Townend, who for many years figured and prepared material with him, he continued his output of scientific research, working in some instances on material he had collected in Australia nearly fifty years earlier.

His distinctions included the Wollaston and Darwin Medals, the Gold Medal of the Linnean Society and Foreign Member-

ship of the Academy of Sciences, U.S.S.R. In 1928 he gave the Romanes Lecture.

Physically Watson was a striking figure, short and broad with a remarkable profile. He was neatfingered, skilled in the preparation of fossils and an excellent cabinet maker. He had a great interest in manual skills and he knew all the University College carpenters of his time. He could recall objects he had seen with clarity and once pointed out correctly that the other half of a certain fossil on exhibition was to be found in a museum on the opposite side of the Atlantic. In 1916 he married Katherine Parker who had been carrying out research in embryology under J. P. Hill. It gave Professor and Mrs. Watson great pleasure to see their daughters carrying on the family scientific tradition—the elder, Mrs. Mary Powell as a farmer, the younger, Dr. Janet Watson as a geologist.

July 25, 1973.

Sir Reginald Watson-Jones, F.R.C.S., who died on August 9, 1972, was a leading British specialist in orthopaedic surgery and enjoyed an international reputation as an authority in this field. He was orthopaedic surgeon to King George VI from 1946 to 1952 and to the Queen from 1952, and before being appointed director of the Orthopaedic and Accident Department of the London Hospital in 1943, he had practised with great success at Liverpool.

Reginald Watson-Jones was born in 1902, and received his medical training at Liverpool University, when he graduated B.Sc. with first-class honours (1922), M.R.C.S., L.R.C.P. (1924), and M.B., Ch.B. (1924). He greatly distinguished himself in the course of his university career, winning the Mitchell Banks Medal (1920), senior Lyon Jones scholarship and George Holt medal (1921), Robert Gee prize and George Holt fellowship in orthopaedic surgery (1926), and Robert Jones fellowship in orthopaedic surgery (1928). He obtained the degree of M.Ch.(Orth.), winning a gold medal, in 1926, and became F.R.C.S. England in 1927. After qualifying he held lectureships and demonstratorships in anatomy, physiology and physiotherapy at Liverpool, and was then resident house surgeon at the Royal National Orthopaedic Hospital and clinical assistant at the Hospital for Sick Children, Great Ormond Street.

He returned to Liverpool in 1926 to become senior surgical tutor and registrar at the Royal Infirmary, and his election to the honorary staff as orthopaedic surgeon soon followed. Success came early to Watson-Jones and his services were in great demand. His advice was sought by almost every official body concerned with accidents and the care of the disabled. At the Royal College of Surgeons he was a member of the Council and was Hunterian professor in 1945.

As well as his many notable contributions to surgical literature and the care of a host of patients in an extremely busy and active surgical life, Watson-Jones will long be remembered for three outstanding contributions to orthopaedic surgery.

The first is his textbook on *Fractures and Joint Injuries* first published in January 1940, 15 times reprinted, translated into many languages, and famous the world over.

His second great contribution was his organization of orthopaedic services in the R.A.F. during the Second World War when he held the position of Consultant in Orthopaedic Surgery to the Royal Air Force and devoted almost the whole of his time during the war to this work.

His third great achievement was the foundation of the *British Journal of Bone & Joint Surgery*, first published in the late 1940s. This venture was in partnership with the *American Journal of Bone & Joint Surgery*, a unique partnership. The American and British numbers combined are the leading source of information on orthopaedic advances in all countries of the world. Watson-Jones was the first editor.

R. W.-J. was a man of remarkable vitality and drive. He had a great gift for inspiring loyalty and affection from his disciples and junior colleagues; and the success of his work in the Royal Air Force, and of all his other surgical contributions, was due in no small measure to these personal qualities. His name will be remembered in surgical history along with two other great pioneers of orthopaedic surgery from Liverpool, Hugh Owen Thomas and Robert Jones.

He was president of the British Orthopaedic Association in 1952–53 and senior vice-president of the Royal College of Surgeons of England, 1953-54. He was knighted in 1945.

August 11, 1972.

Air Chief Commandant Dame Katherine Watson-Watt, D.B.E.—Lady Watson-Watt, wife of Sir Robert Watson-Watt, F.R.S., the inventor of radar—died on June 18, 1971 at the age of 72.

As Dame Katherine Trefusis Forbes she was the first Director of the Women's Auxiliary Air Force. She married Sir Robert Watson-Watt as his third wife in 1966.

The daughter of Edmund Forbes, A.M.I.C.E., she was born on March 21, 1899, in Chile, and had travelled through most countries in South and North America, Europe and the Middle and Far East. During the First World War, she served from 1916-18 in the Women's Volunteer Reserve.

Together with Dame Helen Gwynne-Vaughan* in 1935 Dame Katherine started Emergency Service, an officers training corps which was a forerunner to the A.T.S. She was Chief Instructor, A.T.S. in 1938, and seconded for service with the R.A.F. Companies of the A.T.S. in that year.

In 1939 Dame Katherine was appointed the first Director of the W.A.A.F., with the rank of Senior Controller, and in 1943 was promoted to the rank of Air Chief Commandant; she was created a Dame Commander (military division) of the Order of the British Empire in 1944, in which year she retired from the Service.

In 1946-48 she served with the Control Commission for Germany and was appointed Director of Welfare. In 1968 she was made an honorary LL.D. by St. Andrews University.

June 21, 1971.

Sir Robert Watson-Watt, C.B., F.R.S., who died in an Inverness hospital on December 5, 1973 at the age of 81, will be remembered above all for his pioneering work on the development of radar and associated systems immediately before and during the Second World War. So rewarding were his efforts in that sphere, which quickly flourished and provided "electronic eyes" for night fighter and bomber aircraft and Allied ships at sea, that the German High Command ultimately recognized radar as the greatest single device, even including the atomic bomb, that brought total victory to the Allies.

Although Watson-Watt became widely known as the "father of radar", a title which he believed to be justified, there was never an occasion when its origins were being discussed that he failed to give generous acknowledgement to the work of others in the field, some of which contributed to the successful emergence of radar.

He was born at Brechin, Angus, on April 13, 1892, and started his education at the town's Damacre Road Board School; it was there (Watson-Watt said years later) that "Bessie Mitchell did more than any other teacher to make me whatever I am". A local bursary won in open competition led to Brechin High School; another, this time to the University of St. Andrews, took him to University College, Dundee. He graduated with special distinction as a B.Sc. (Engineering).

With an interest in radio-telegraphy, Robert Alexander Watson-Watt—his knighthood was conferred in 1942—went to London in 1915 and joined the staff of the Meteorological Office, where he devoted some time to research directed towards the radio location of thunderstorms. This was seen as a profitable line to pursue because it might be made to give timely danger warnings to aviators.

By the end of the First World War thunderstorms were being located hundreds of miles away. But at that stage his work on thunderstorm plotting, although providing some new techniques which were to prove useful in a more advanced form of radio-location, had nothing directly to do with radar. He defined radar later as the art of detecting by means of radio echoes the presence of objects, determining their bearing and distance, recognizing their character and employing the information collected to some useful purpose. This, in general terms, was good enough; but subsequent developments quickly showed, with the coming of "secondary radar", that the definition overlooked several other important features.

In 1921 he joined the Department of Scientific and Industrial Research as superintendent of its radio research stations at Aldershot and Slough. Later he became superintendent of the radio department of the National Physical Laboratory, responsible for an increasing amount of important work for the Air Ministry, especially in connexion with radio direction-finders and radio beacons.

This led to the establishment of the ministry's research station at Bawdsey in 1936 which was to become so closely identified with the birth of radar. He remained there as superintendent for two years, when (in 1938) he became Director of Communications Development and later Scientific Adviser on Telecommunications to the Air Ministry and the Ministry of Aircraft Production. An outstanding feature of those appointments was that in all except at the Meteorological Office Watson-Watt was the first appointee.

For his "initiation of radar and his contribution to the development of radar installations" Watson-Watt received an *ex gratia* award of £50,000. It was believed to be the largest sum ever recommended by the Royal Commission on Awards to Inventors for payment to an individual. The Royal Society conferred a fellowship on him, citing Watson-Watt as "distinguished for his contribution to radio engineering, particularly in relation to aerial and marine navigation".

Many other awards were bestowed on this genial Scot during his busy lifetime, much of which was spent in Canada. He belonged to many professional institutions, wrote a number of scientific works, broadcast occasionally and lectured frequently.

He was three times married. His third wife, Air Chief Commandant Dame Katherine Trefusis Forbes, formerly Director of the W.A.A.F., died in 1971.

December 7, 1973.

Ava Lady Waverley, who died on December 22, 1974, was the widow of Sir John Anderson, later Viscount Waverley.

Only daughter of the great historian and friend of France, J. E. Courtenay Bodley, Ava (born in 1896) was brought up in a climate of rigorous intellectual discipline. The slightest grammatical error would be punished by long standings in the corner. The château at Sucy-en-Brie, near Paris, was at the turn of the century filled with the formidable frock-coated representatives of the Académie Française. The world revolved largely round the British Embassy in the Rue du Faubourg Saint Honoré. Lord Dufferin and Ava, H.M. Ambassador from 1891 to 1896 was a friend of the Bodleys, and it was after the Ambassador himself that the Bodleys' blonde daughter was quite fittingly named.

Bodley died in 1925. A few months previously his daughter had married Ralph Wigram, then a young secretary in the Paris Embassy. It was an ideal match. Sensitive, gifted, ambitious, extremely shy, Wigram, who had been drawn to social work after the War but who had nevertheless entered the Diplomatic Service in 1920, had need of a wife who would draw him out and see that his talents were recognized. But only a year or so after the marriage "Wigs" contracted polio, becoming a permanent cripple.

"Wigs" himself died in 1936 but in 1933 he had gone back to head the Central Department of the Foreign Office. In that capacity he played a major role in the high diplomacy of the early 1930s. Thanks largely to his wife, the house in Lord North Street became a centre of political activity. Sir Winston Churchill* was a frequent visitor, Lord Vansittart a presiding genius. The brilliant young couple formed a "salon" for the pro-French and anti-Nazi school of thought.

After her husband's death his widow continued the tradition. With the State visits of 1937 and 1938 she had much to do. By this time she had become a political personage in her own right. Statesmen and ambassadors constantly asked her opinion. She knew everybody. All the great houses and Embassies were open to her and even if the invitation was sometimes contrived, nobody would dream of putting her off except with a very valid excuse. Nor did they usually want to. She could be maddening, she could be catty, but she was always good value and appreciated as such. Besides, it did no harm to keep on the right side of the Cumaean Sybil in whom even Prime Ministers had been known to confide.

In 1940 she met her match. Sir John Anderson, as he then was, was one of the most powerful men in Britain. An extraordinary career in the Civil Service had been followed by the Governorship of Bengal and entry into politics. When Ava came into his life he was Home Secretary. If anything had happened to Sir Winston Churchill and to Anthony Eden, he might very well have been Prime Minister. To this pawky and rather prudish Scot Ava was a wee woman who could not be supposed to know much about politics but who could initiate him into the mysterious ways of culture and high society. He proposed and was accepted. They were married in October 1941, when he was Lord President of the Council.

An even more influential "salon" was the result. Later, when the Tory Government fell, Lord Waverley, as he then was, was made chairman of the Port of London Authority and of the Covent Garden Opera. It must be admitted that she was not herself very musical and had no great natural taste, but she had high intelligence and could therefore absorb enough of the background to converse with the cognoscenti who rubbed shoulders in her box with the socially great.

What does one chiefly remember about Ava? Beyond a little gardening and some early practice in painting she had no hobbies. She published nothing, she did not play or sing. Though charitably inclined and sincerely religious, she took no part in public life. She was no good on committees. Politics, as such, interested her very little. Why then was she so extraordinary? Why did she probably exercise more indirect influence than any woman of her generation? Partly, no doubt, because of her astonishing memory, her immense erudition, and her superb gifts as a writer of letters. But chiefly because she could detect talent—any talent. She had indeed an infallible nose for the first class and a sincere detestation of the mediocre.

She had no hesitation in showing up the pompous and the dull and in flattering the gifted. In her presence it was extremely difficult not to be indiscreet. That was why so many were frightened of her. "But don't you *want* to be Foreign Secretary?" "Why *is* it that you dislike the P.M. so?" Insidiously the voice echoes on. The charm, the spell, can never be forgotten.

December 24, 1974.

Sir David Webster, K.C.V.O., the architect-in-chief of the Royal Opera House's development since the end of the Second World War and of its present eminence, died in London on May 11, 1971 at the age of 67.

He retired in 1970 from his post as General Administrator after 25 years' tenure, but remained as adviser to the board. In February 1971 he was presented with his portrait commissioned from David Hockney by 500 musicians and staff of the Royal Opera House.

A business man by early training, he brought his own expertise, together with a trained enthusiasm for music, to the task of creating the conditions through which Covent Garden became one of the world's greatest operatic and balletic centres.

David Lumsden Webster was born in Dundee on July 3, 1903, and educated at the Holt School and Liverpool University. From 1932 to 1940 he was occupied at the Bon Marché, Liverpool, a large department store of which he eventually became general manager, and he moved, as general manager, to Lewis's (Liverpool) Ltd, for a year before he joined the Ministry of Supply, where he was concerned until 1944 with special methods of production in ordance factories.

By the outbreak of war, however, his concern for music had already begun to break into his business career, and from 1940 until 1945 he was Chairman of the Liverpool Philharmonic Society, assisting in steering the Liverpool Philharmonic Orchestra, until that time an *ad hoc* collection of players from Manchester and Liverpool, engaged to appear for the season only under a series of guest conductors, through its early years as a permanent orchestra under the conductorship of Sir (then Dr.) Malcolm Sargent*. When, in 1944, the Covent Garden Preliminary Committee was set up to plan the future of the Royal Opera House, which had been used as a dance hall during the war, Webster became its chairman, and he was appointed General Administrator of the newly formed Royal Opera Company when it was created in 1946, with Dr. Karl Rankl as its musical director. After several months of planning and auditions, the new company began operations in December 1946, with a musically respectable and visually splendid production of Purcell's *The Fairy Queen,* performed in collaboration with the Sadler's Wells Ballet, which became Covent Garden's resident ballet company.

From this point onwards, Webster's biography is the story of the Royal Opera House and its post-war achievements. The early years of the Webster-Rankl regime were not easy. Originally, the policy adopted was that of opera in English, but the supply of native singers with even minimal operatic experience was limited; foreign artists whose English fitted bizarrely into the scheme of things or broke down altogether in the course of a performance often showed up the deficiencies of the home team almost cruelly, and the period of growing pains was made more difficult by outbreaks of criticism from the press and from such combative musical personalities as Sir Thomas Beecham;* complaints, although they often had at this period a good deal of substance, had little contact with the realities of building up a company from the foundations, a policy which Webster patiently followed and from which he refused to be deflected by his opponents.

By 1950 the company was able to provide 170 performances, playing to 87 per cent of the theatre's capacity, a situation in marked contrast from the short though gorgeous international seasons which had been the custom before the war. The same year marked the return of guest conductors to the orchestra pit; Erich Kleiber provided, among other characteristically notable performances, London's first view of *Wozzeck* on the stage, and Berg's once frightening opera gradually proved to be a popular success; Clemens Krauss returned to London, and Beecham, despite his animadversions against the management, conducted a production of *Die Meistersinger* not only flighted by his light, lyrical view of Wagner but played and sung with as much finesse as could be expected in any European opera house. For the Festival of Britain Beecham returned to *The Bohemian Girl* in a new edition of his own, but Webster's comments on a revival which seemed to be so far from the policy which he had followed with such determination have not been recorded.

At the same time, under Webster's leadership, the Covent Garden company set out to make opera visually exciting. The young and brilliant Peter Brook was appointed director of productions, and what was seen on the stage was often splendid. Care for action, movement and decor, admirable in themselves, sometimes gave rise to productions based on preconceptions which worked directly against the music and which from time to time raised storms of protest which reached a resounding *fortissimo* over the eccentric sets designed by Salvador Dali for Strauss's *Salome*. Again, Webster was patiently prepared to let these excesses be cured by accumulating experience, and however loud the noises of discontent over eccentricities could be, it could not obscure the first-rate work being done in the theatre by, among others, Michael Ayrton, Oliver Messel and Leslie Hurry; like the company's other growing pains, visual excesses began to pass away. The repertory of the company continually expanded, and Bliss's *The Olympians*, in 1949, became the first English opera to have its first production in Covent Garden for over a century. In 1951 it was followed by both Britten's *Billy Budd* and Vaughan Williams's *The Pilgrim's Progress*.

The resignation of Karl Rankl at the end of the 1951 season, and four years spent without a musical director, increased both the weight on Webster's shoulders and his authority over the company. The interregnum saw the first performances of Tippett's *The Midsummer Marriage* in 1952, and of Britten's *Gloriana*, to celebrate the coronation of Queen Elizabeth II in 1953. These adventures were undertaken in spite of stringent economies in the first post-Rankl season, in which only two new productions—*Aïda* and *Turandot*—were presented. They were conducted by Sir John Barbirolli,* who was responsible for some splendid work, including a vividly lyrical *Tristan and Isolde*, in the years before the musical directorship was accepted by Rafael Kubelik in 1955. The year 1955 saw, too, the first new postwar production of Wagner's *Ring,* which was instrumental in beginning Rudolf Kempe's long association with music in London. And 1956 saw the fulfilment of one of Webster's long standing ambitions in the production of Berlioz's *The Trojans*.

By 1960 the Royal Opera House had achieved a consistently high standard and an artistic vitality sufficient to induce George Solti, for some years the operatic dictator of Frankfurt, to undertake the musical directorship and consolidate the work of 12 eventful and rewarding years. English opera remained within the repertory, with Britten's *Peter Grimes, Billy Budd* and *A Midsummer Night's Dream* as well as

Tippett's secound opera, *King Prain*. In 1964, Schoenberg's *Moses and Aaron* proved to be a great popular success. Webster's final triumph was to send his entire opera company on an immensely successful tour of Germany in 1970.

At the same time, while foreign singers were invited to play the great roles with which they were particularly associated so that English opera lovers were not deprived of the voices of the great stars familiar to them on record, the native singers of the home team found themselves well able to play such roles as Simon Boccanegra, Baron Ochs and even Wotan in productions otherwise glorified by great European stars, and, in 1963, Webster put on an entirely authentic production of Mussorgsky's *Khovantschina* without any help from abroad except that of a producer. British singers who had won their experience at Covent Garden became, for the first time, familiar and admired artists at La Scala, Bayreuth and the Vienna State Opera. This new prestige, Webster justly claimed, was the almost natural result of a policy which had set out to develop the talent and extend the range of its singers, while offering them the wildest possible experience.

Though the creation of a great opera company and the extension of its repertory were Webster's primary concern, his musical interests and authority ramified in a number of directions. From 1948 he was chairman of the Orchestral Employers' Association; he became governor and treasurer of the Royal Ballet School in 1955, governor and general administrator of the Royal Ballet Company in 1957, and in 1962 general administrator of the London Opera Centre. In all he did he allied a businessman's shrewd sense of the practical with wide musical tastes and a perfectionism more often found among artists than among those who watch over their work and interests.

The success of his work at Covent Garden, however, was largely the result of a far-sighted patience which realized that the ends he had set for himself and for the Royal Opera House were not easy of attainment and could not be quickly achieved. His loyalty to the executive musicians among his colleagues, who in the difficult years bore the brunt of criticism, ultimately strengthened his position. His public duties were carried out with a genial dignity, a skill in dealing with people in general as well as with musicians and with the old-fashioned sociability which, never reaching the familiar or the free and easy, used to be called "clubable."

David Webster was knighted in 1961. He was also an Officer of the Legion of Honour, a Commendatore al merito della Republica Italiana, and a Commander of the Order of the North Star, of Sweden, and of the Portuguese Military Order of Christ. In 1970 he was created K.C.V.O.

He was unmarried.

May 12, 1971.

Margaret Webster, the actress and stage director, who died in London on November 13, 1972 at the age of 67, had had a career in some ways more distinguished than that of any member of the four previous generations of the Webster family who had contributed to English theatrical history.

Herself an actress, she was one of the few women to have established themselves both in England and the United States as a director of plays, and the only woman in the latter country to have been conspicuously successful as a director of Shakespeare.

She was the daughter of Ben Webster ("Ben Webster the Third") and his actress wife May Whitty, who was created D.B.E. for her services to good causes during the First World War. Her father—"the handsomest actor England has sent us for years", *The Stage* called him—was acting in New York in 1905, and Margaret was born there on March 15.

She went to school in England, however, and began her career in London in 1924. She appeared with Dame Sybil Thorndikes' company on tour, understudying Dame Sybil in *Saint Joan;* with the Macdona Players; with J. B. Fagan's Oxford Players; with Ben Greet's Shakespearian company; with the company at the Old Vic led by John Gielgud in 1929; and, in her mother's daughter, she fought in the campaigns for the establishment of British Equity in the early 1930s. In the course of those years she again supported Gielgud in Ronald Mackenzie's *Musical Chairs* and in *Richard of Bordeaux*, and in 1935, while continuing to work on the London stage, she began directing plays there.

In 1937 Maurice Evans, with whom she had acted in England while both were still amateurs, sent for her to direct in New York (his first venture in actor-management) a play not seen on Broadway since 1878, *Richard II*. In the following year she directed him in what was said to be the first production of *Hamlet* in its entirety ever seen in America, and in 1939 she staged, in addition to *Henry IV (Part I)* on Broadway, condensed versions of four Shakespearian comedies in a replica of Shakespeare's Globe Theatre at the New York World's Fair. During this period in America she also at different times directed both her parents, not to mention the Lunts in *The Seagull* and Judith Anderson in *Family Portrait.*

Othello, presented under her direction in 1943 with herself playing Emilia to Paul Robeson's Moor, there set up a record in Shakespearian production of 295 performances, and her handling of *The Tempest* in 1945 caused George Jean Nathan the dramatic critic to describe her as "the best director of the plays of William Shakespeare that we have", and the one that had "given him back to the groundlings". In 1948, after the dissolution of the American Theatre Company Incorporated, which she had founded in conjunction with Eva

Le Gallienne and Cheryl Crawford, she formed a Shakespearian company of her own, touring with it 36 states of the Union and three Canadian provinces—it became known as the "bus and truck company" and its territory as "the gymnasium circuit".

Margaret Webster was the first woman to direct a production at the Metropolitan Opera House, New York. She there staged *Don Carlos* and *Aïda* early in the 1950s and later staged four other operas for the New York City Opera Company. Having returned to the English theatre, she directed Donald Wolfit* in *The Strong are Lonely,* and in the late 1950s *The Merchant of Venice* at Stratford-on-Avon and *Measure for Measure* at the Old Vic. But it is probable that her book *Shakespeare Today* gives a fairer notion of the quality of her work in the classical theatre than either of those two productions.

In 1960, thirty-six years after the Cassons* had given her her first job in the chorus of *The Trojan Women*, Margaret Webster had the pleasure of directing both Cassons in Noël Coward's *Waiting in the Wings.*

Honorary degrees were conferred on her by four American colleges, Lawrence College, Russell Sage College, Rutger's University and D.H.L. Smith College. The Women's National Press Club of America elected her one of the 10 outstanding Women of the Year for 1946.

November 14, 1972.

Professor T. B. L. Webster, Emeritus Professor of Greek and honorary Fellow of University College London, and Emeritus Professor of Classics at Stanford University, California, died in Stanford at the age of 68 on May 31, 1974.

He will be remembered as an outstanding scholar of his time—adventurous, prolific and wide ranging in his writing; as a teacher and colleague, both inspiring and inspired.

Son of Sir Thomas Lonsdale Webster, Clerk to the House of Commons, and given his names with Bertram, T.B.L. Webster was educated at Charterhouse and Christ Church, Oxford. Later he was to win the hearts of audiences at school speech days by his opening words: "It is a cardinal rule of ancient rhetoric to get your audiences on your side from the very first sentence. I won all the prizes at my school." After Oxford he studied in Germany at Leipzig, where the humane lectures of Alfred Körte, above all on Menander, to whose text and interpretation he was to make distinguished contributions, had a great effect on him. He returned to teach as a Student of Christ Church, and in 1931 at the age of 26 was appointed to the Hulme Chair of Greek in Manchester. The university and the people claimed his undying affection: articles, book notices, even leading articles in the *Manchester Guardian* flowed from his pen, the buying policy of the local galleries came under his influence, and with the help of a brilliant band of young classical scholars his teaching made a deep impact. More than 20 years after he left in 1948 to take up the Chair of Greek in University College London, good young scholars from Rochdale and Wigan still pursued him to London.

University College, his centre for 20 years of unremitting activity, knew him as scholar, teacher, dean, effective committee man; and above all as inventor and inspirer of the Institute of Classical Studies of the University of London, a focus for the dispersed colleges of a federal university and a forum for international scholarship. His activity as president of the Hellenic Society and vice-president, later president, of the Classical Association and of the Joint Association of Classical Teachers was used by him to promote collaboration at all levels of classical study. He set an admirable example by promoting inter-disciplinary seminars, most notably the London seminar on Linear B, in which Michael Ventris himself participated. Webster's own book *Mycenae to Homer* emerged from this interest in 1958.

Richness of ideas, wide reading in modern (including scientific) literature, a retentive memory, a capacity for instant articulation of an argument were among the assets he brought to classical scholarship. One could not submit to him a problem—for instance, the reconstruction of a damaged new text on a papyrus roll—without instantly receiving in return a corona of scintillating possibilities for investigation. In truth he had little time or patience for second thoughts, and balanced criticism sometimes needs slow mulling over a problem. This was the great difference between his scholarship and that of his wife Madge (A. M. Dale), whom he married in 1944. She tested every hypothesis with patient care; he would back a brilliant insight. For small objects— vases, terracottas, dramatic masks—he had a veritable passion, and books based on them, such as *Greek Theatre Production, Greek Dramatic Monuments* and (with A. D. Trendall) *Illustrations of Greek Drama*, have deeply influenced modern production techniques of Greek drama as well as the ideas of scholars.

T. B. L. Webster had a gift for friendship and a total lack of pomposity or complacency. A sixth sense enabled him to see possibilities latent in others and to bring them out by encouragement, trust and talk. The number of his pupils holding chairs and important positions is large. His own honours and distinctions were many; they included Fellowship of the Society of Antiquaries, the British Academy and eight Academies overseas; and honorary doctorates of Dublin and Manchester.

In 1967 the death of his wife, whose affection was the centre of his life in London, made him wish to leave a scene indissolubly bound up with her memory, and he accepted the post of Professor of Greek at Stanford University, where he found and

made good friends. He had for some years given up tennis and squash, which he played well; he continued to find relaxation in the quieter activities of walking and listening—perhaps after a specially frustrating committee—to Berg's violin concerto or Bartok string quartets on the gramophone.

June 6, 1974.

Harry Weetman, one of the leading English professional golfers since the war, died on July 19, 1972 in hospital. He was 51. He had not regained consciousness after being injured in a car crash on the Caterham by-pass on July 14.

In the 1950s and 1960s, when professional golf tournaments were largely a domestic affair, attended by an occasional overseas player, Weetman was one of the principal attractions. Broad of shoulder and of thigh, he hit the ball for all he was worth with a kind of sullen fury. His style was rough and he took up his stance in almost truculent fashion, flat-footed and upright. He frequently drove off line but scorned to reduce his power, and huge hands as frequently contrived a recovery that would startle his opponent. It was not surprising that he should win the match play championship twice, in 1951 and 1958, and was runner-up three times in 1956, 1959, and 1961. In one of his Ryder Cup appearances between 1951 and 1963, that of 1953 at Wentworth, he scored a resounding victory over Sam Snead, who was then at the height of his powers, after being four down with six to play.

As often happens, he combined great strength with an almost velvet touch on and around the greens and this contributed to numerous victories, principal among them being the Dunlop Masters' tournament in 1952 and 1958, the Irish Open in 1953 and the German Open in 1957. He was a delightful putter to watch. Bold and uncomplicated, he made it all look simple and even pleasant where others turn it into a torture. A certain fierceness of expression gave a general impression of violence when he was playing, but off the course he had a ready smile and a countryman's engaging humour.

He was born in Shropshire on October 25, 1920, and served as professional at Hartsbourne before moving to Selsdon Park.

July 20, 1972.

Helene Weigel, the widow of Bertolt Brecht and co-founder with him of the Berliner Ensemble, died on May 6, 1971 in East Berlin. She was 70.

Born in Vienna, she was the product of a school run on militantly suffragette lines which supplied one source of her powerful character. A great actress, she was also a

great leader and organizer whose work was sustained by a sense of collective responsibility towards her theatre company and towards society at large. Her 30-year marriage with Brecht, half of which was spent off-stage in exile, was one of the great reciprocal alliances in theatre history.

She began her stage career at the Frankfurt Neues Theater in 1919, and marriage to Brecht followed in 1928 after her appearance in his *Man is Man*. It was a major period for German acting, and Weigel and Brecht were among the constellation of talent associated with Piscator's revolutionary management at the Berlin Theater am Nollendorfplatz. From then onwards she specialized in the main Brechtian roles, Vlassova, Senora Carrar, and Mother Courage—her most legendary performance which laid the foundations of the Berliner Ensemble when it was seen at the East Berlin Deutsches Theater in 1948. It was this performance, too, which demolished British prejudice against "epic theatre" when the Ensemble visited London in 1956. The images of Weigel's silent scream over her son's corpse, and her final solitary return to the war between the shafts of her cart, are permanently imprinted on the memory of all who saw them. Brecht wrote of her, "She showed not only one art, but many arts: how, for instance, goodness and wisdom were also arts that could be learned".

She is survived by a daughter, Barbara, and a son, Stefan.

May 8, 1971.

Sir John Weir, G.C.V.O., Physician to the Queen until his retirement in 1968, died on April 17, 1971 at the age of 91. He did much to repair the breach which had for too long separated physicians practising orthodox medicine—the allopaths— from the followers of Hahnemann—the homœopaths.

He was barely 40 when the Duke of Windsor, then Prince of Wales, appointed him his physician. He promptly responded by putting the Prince on a diet which banned cigars, allowed him only four cigarettes a day, and specified two small slices of cold beef for lunch.

Weir attended Queen Mary in her last months. In addition to attending the Queen, then Princess Elizabeth, at the birth of her children, Weir attended the Duchess of Gloucester at the birth of her sons.

Weir believed in the value of exercise. He was a useful golfer, and it was on his advice that King George VI played the game more regularly.

In his biography of King George VI, Sir John Wheeler-Bennett mentions how the King became a convinced believer in homœopathy under the influence of his physician, Sir John Weir. He was one of the doctors who signed the bulletin which gave first news to the public of the King's illness in 1949, and of the cancellation of the Royal visit to Australia and New Zealand.

The birth of Prince Andrew at Buckingham Palace in 1960, when Weir was one of the doctors present, was the first birth to a reigning sovereign since 1857, when Princess Beatrice, the youngest of Queen Victoria's nine children, was born.

Weir was an excellent diagnostician and this, combined with his pleasing bedside manner, went far to explain his popularity with all sections of the community from the royal households down to his humblest hospital patients. Fame never went to his head and in spite of the inevitable popularity that accompanies any medical appointment to the reigning monarch (more so at one time perhaps than today) Weir never lost the common touch. He was inordinately proud of his royal appointment but it never went to his head. He was in the best tradition of the pawky Scot of the Harry Lauder school. Never an aggressive nationalist, he yet was proud of his origins and few things gave him more pleasure than his annual holiday at Dunbar, a habit dating from the days when this resort on the east coast of Scotland was one of the more select middle-class holiday centres for homing Scots.

One of the things that probably gave him as much if not more pleasure was the telling of stories. He was a delightful raconteur, much of his popularity in this respect being due to the accent that he never lost. Typical of his almost unlimited repertoire was a perfectly true story how, as he came away from Buckingham Palace after a consultation, Queen Mary gave him a magnificent bunch of flowers to take to the homœopathic hospital. On arrival at the hospital he had them sent up to his wards. When some time later he reached one of his wards the flowers were on display. Opposite one of the most magnificent bunches was a small six-year-old Cockney patient. As much at home with children as adults, Weir said to the young man: "Aren't these flowers lovely? Wasn't it kind of the Queen to send them to you?" With characteristic Cockney sharpness back came the reply: " 'Ow did she know I was 'ere?"

Well educated, genial and with a distinct personality, Sir John Weir gained admission to the British Medical Association and the Royal Society of Medicine while he was still physician to the Homœopathic Hospital in Great Ormond Street, Bloomsbury.

Born in October 1879, the son of John Weir, of Glasgow, he was educated at Allan Glen School and at Glasgow University, where he graduated M.B., Ch.B., and acted as House Physician and House Surgeon at the Western Infirmary. He went to London on his appointment as house physician to the Homœopathic Hospital where, in due course, he became assistant physician, physician and consulting physician. He was also honorary physician to the homœopathic hospitals in Bristol,

Birmingham, Bromley and Eastbourne, and, while still taking an active part in his profession, served as president of the British Homœopathic Society. The passing of the Faculty of Homœopathy Act through Parliament in 1947 owed much to Weir's initiative.

Acceptable in Court circles, he was Physician to the Prince of Wales from 1923 to 1936, to the Queen of Norway from 1928 to 1938, Queen Mary from 1936 until her death in 1953, the Duke and Duchess of York in 1936, and reappointed when His Royal Highness came to the throne in 1937. In 1926 he was decorated C.V.O., and was advanced to K.C.V.O. in 1932, and to G.C.V.O. in 1939. Later, in 1949, King George VI conferred on him the Royal Victorian Chain.

He wrote *Homœopathic Philosophy, its Importance in the Treatment of Chronic Disease* in 1915; *The Trend of Modern Medicine* in 1922, and contributed a paper on "Samuel Hahnemann and his Influence on Modern Thought" to the Royal Society of Medicine in 1933.

April 19, 1971.

Professor Torkel Weis-Fogh, Professor of Zoology in the University of Cambridge, died suddenly at his home on November 13, 1975 at the age of 53.

Born on March 22, 1922 in Aarhus, Denmark, the son of a banker and accountant, he was a wartime student in Copenhagen University. In 1947 he became assistant in research to the distinguished Danish physiologist August Krogh, then taking advantage of his retirement for a renewed outburst of scientific creativity; and this apprenticeship in the discipline of critical experimentation was the most formative influence in Weis-Fogh's career.

After Krogh's death in 1949, Weis-Fogh continued for four years as head of the laboratory, before taking up in turn a lectureship in the Copenhagen Institute of Neurophysiology, a Rockefeller Fellowship and the Balfour studentship in Cambridge University. In 1958 he returned to Copenhagen as Professor of Zoophysiology and head of the Zoophysiological Laboratory, where he worked and taught for eight years before being elected Professor of Zoology at Cambridge and Fellow of Christ's College in 1966.

Weis-Fogh retained his Danish citizenship and remained in close touch with the Danish academic world. He was a member of the Danish State Research Foundation and Chairman of its Natural Sciences committee, a Fellow of the Royal Danish Academy and of the Academy of Technical Sciences. He also maintained close ties with colleagues in the United States, where he was Prother lecturer in Zoology at Harvard in 1961 and was elected a Foreign Honorary member of the American Academy of Arts and Sciences in 1974.

The work of the Krogh laboratory was centred on the desert locusts, and Weis-Fogh's subsequent research can be traced back to this origin. While Krogh himself was concerned with respiration and metabolism, Weis-Fogh studied the muscles and mechanism of flight, publishing several aerodynamical papers with the engineer Martin Jensen. A discrepancy between expected and actual performance led to the discovery of a new type of elastic protein at the wingbase. And the interest in muscle led to the study of a novel contractile material in protozoa. This involved electronprobe X-ray microanalysis, a powerful technique of wide application in biology, which was being developed in Cambridge by a team brought together and inspired by Weis-Fogh.

Returning to insect flight he showed that orthodox theory failed to account for the flight of very small insects, and this led to the discovery of "the Weis-Fogh mechanism of lift generation", so named by Sir James Lighthill with whom, at the time of his death, Weis-Fogh was planning a major collaborative project in biological fluid dynamics.

In himself, Weis-Fogh combined an endearing charm, an absolute integrity and a relentless pursuit of his objectives. Never deflected by unfamiliar ground, he would only pause to master a new discipline before pushing on. Yet for all this concentration of purpose, his mind was always turning to the long term future of zoology among the biological sciences; and, no less, to the research problems of others. What his colleagues will now so sadly miss is the eager enthusiasm, the instant grasp, the surge of new ideas. They will remember him in admiration for his brilliance, in gratitude for his inspiration, and most of all in simple affection for him as a person.

He was twice married, first, in 1946, to Hanne Heckscher, who died in 1971, and secondly, in 1972, to Shirley Stevenson.

November 20, 1975.

Gerald Wellesley, 7th Duke of Wellington —See **Wellington.**

Dr. Egon Wellesz, C.B.E., who died on November 9, 1974 aged 89, was a musician and musicologist of international reputation, eminent both as a composer and as historian of music; he wrote on Byzantine music, on opera, and on the period just before and after the First World War, a period in the musical history of which he had himself played a distinguished part. He was Professor of the History of Music at Vienna University from 1929 to 1938 and a Fellow of Lincoln College, Oxford.

The last years of his life were a triumph. He went back, more and more, to his beloved Vienna, and his Ninth Symphony had its first performance there in 1972. It is fitting that his manuscripts should find their permanent home in a city which honoured him as one of the great modern masters. And his own teaching and research still went on, side by side with his composing to the end of his life.

He basked in the distinction achieved by his pupils—his disciples rather—for what it meant to them, not only for the assurance that the studies he had done so much to promote would continue after him. In his own personality, it was the singular mixture of rare intellectual quality, and extreme simplicity, that made him one of the most dearly loved figures in the Oxford of his later years.

Wellesz was born in Vienna in 1885, and grew up in a world in which the influence of the classical composers and of Schoenberg was nicely balanced. He became one of Schoenberg's first pupils (and later his biographer); and throughout his life his work showed this balance between the traditional and the modern. As time went on his scholarship was exercised on models which had hitherto been inaccessible. He was the first to interpret the neumatic notation of Byzantine music, and his work on it opened a new field; a field he found to be not so far removed from that of western music as had once been assumed to be likely, but one from which his own compositions were greatly enriched, as they were also from his studies of baroque opera.

Wellesz was richly creative after the First World War, five operas and four ballets alone belong to the period 1918-1930. The libretto of the opera *Alkestis* was written by Hugo von Hofmannsthal, a friend and neighbour.

He was always an individualist, sometimes striding out ahead of the vanguard (in pursuit of atonality, of wide melodic leaps, of chamber opera, of neo-Handelism, long before these became fashionable), sometimes pursuing a path of apparently diehard conservatism.

He wrote a body of chamber music and vocal chamber music, including a setting of Gerard Manley Hopkins's *The Leaden Echo and the Golden Echo*, written in 1944 and first performed in London in 1959, and a number of songs. Oxford bestowed on him an honorary doctorate of music in 1932, and a year later he visited London to give three lectures on opera which were seen by many as the perfect apologia for opera as an art form. These were later reprinted.

At the time of Hitler's march into Vienna he happened to be in Holland, conducting. Though a Roman Catholic, he was of partly Jewish descent. He was invited immediately to Oxford and in due course became Reader in Byzantine Music. Oxford became his home, and in the Department of Music at Oxford and the Lincoln College Common Room he found the focus of his later life, though in the years following the war he returned frequently to the Continent for learned gatherings or for private visits, and at the time of his seventieth birthday was shown special honour in Vienna as well as in America.

That occasion marked something of a turning point in his fortunes. There were still years of activity before him which from that time onwards drew wider and wider recognition, symbolized by the two volumes of papers in his honour presented to him, one on his eightieth, the other on his eighty-first birthday. But nothing gave him greater pleasure than the recognition accorded to him, by performances of his work and the commissioning of new compositions, in his native Vienna where his manuscripts will find their permanent home. And those compositions are not only scholarly. They have a deeply human and introspective quality typical of himself. It has been well said of him that his operatic creations sometimes "lifted to the height of almost religious rituals". His Seventh Symphony was composed in his eighty-second year, when he was still teaching regularly, and contributing extensively to musical scholarship.

His detailed scholarship did not in any way dim his vision of the sweep of musical history, and he edited two volumes in the *New Oxford History of Music*, the plan of which, with its recorded musical examples, appealed directly to his ideas of musical history. His compositions included six operas and a number of symphonies and string quartets—performed far more frequently abroad than in England; while his greatest work in scholarship was the editing of the *Monumenta Musicae Byzantinae*, a task in which he had various collaborators both in England and on the Continent.

He was created C.B.E. in 1957, and in the same year was awarded the Grand Silver Medal of the City of Paris. He held the Austrian Order of Merit Pro Musica, and in 1961 received the Austrian Great State Prize for work as a composer.

Though his response to a festive occasion was so eager, he was wholly unspoilt. He was indeed a man of exceptional charm, who spoke always as if he were imparting to his hearers some rich secret; his delightful habit of leaving the sentence unfinished often gave the impression that the secret was too exciting and indeed too secret ever to be disclosed. So the anecdote would end with a beaming smile, the perfect epilogue. His personal life was serene and his transparent goodness disarmed opposition. The warmth of his friendship and the generosity of his encouragement found its response in a personal discipleship and veneration on the part of those he taught. He married while still a young man Emmy Francisca Stross, who shared his interest in the visual arts, as well as in music, and published work on medieval and Persian illumination. There were two daughters of the marriage. A portrait of him painted before the First War was one of the most striking pictures in the Kokoschka exhibition in the Tate Gallery in 1963.

November 11, 1974.

Lieutenant-Colonel the Duke of Wellington, K.G., F.R.I.B.A., died on January 4, 1972 at the age of 86. He was Lord Lieutenant of Hampshire, 1949-60; of the County of London 1944-49; Governor of the Isle of Wight 1956-65; and a former Chancellor of the University of Southampton.

Gerald Wellesley, seventh Duke of Wellington, was born on August 21, 1885, the third son of the fourth Duke of Wellington. He inherited the family honours when his nephew, the sixth Duke, was killed in action in 1943 at the age of 31. After being educated at Eton in Mr. White-Thomson's house, he entered the diplomatic service in 1908 serving as Secretary at Constantinople, Rome and St. Petersburg.

After retiring from the diplomatic service in 1919 he articled himself to H. Goodhart-Rendel, P.P.R.I.B.A. In 1921 he became a F.R.I.B.A. and again afterwards set up in partnership with Trenwith Wills, F.R.I.B.A. thus becoming the first English duke to have practised as an architect and probably the first member of the peerage to have done so in a qualified professional capacity since the death of Lord Burlington. The firm specialized in alterations and decorations to existing buildings. He worked at Mount Clare, Roehampton, Hinton Ampner, Hampshire, and at Castle Hill in Devon. In 1934 Lord Gerald undertook the redecoration of the Italian Embassy in Grosvenor Square, but the domed classical church of S.S. Mary and George at Sands is probably the most frequently noticed of his buildings, for it forms a prominent and curiously Italianate feature of the landscape from the main Western Region trains passing through High Wycombe.

His taste in the arts was conservative, with a strong bias towards Regency period, and in the years before the war he formed a small but interesting collection of works of art, especially furniture and sculpture, in his Regency house at Chester Gate, Regent's Park. On the subject of the decorative arts he was unusually well informed, and it was this which doubtless led to his appointment as Surveyor of the King's Works of Art in 1936, a post which he relinquished shortly after inheriting the dukedom.

At the outbreak of the Second World War he enlisted in the Grenadier Guards and rose to the rank of (temporary) Lieutenant-Colonel. There was something especially appropriate in the unexpected inheritance by Lord Gerald Wellesley of the dukedom conferred on his distinguished ancestor, for he had always been particularly devoted to the Iron Duke's memory. In 1935 he had published *The Iconography of the First Duke of Wellington* in collaboration with John Steegman, and later on edited several works relating to the Duke, notably *The Journal of Mrs. Arbuthnot, 1820-1832* (with Francis Bamford) and *The Conversations of William Chad with the First Duke of Wellington*. He was also the author of an entertaining and unusual travel book *Desert Journey* (1939), an account of a visit to Sinai and Judea. In 1965 he edited *Wellington and His Friends,* a selection he had made from the Duke's correspondence.

It was above all with the intention of providing a memorial to his ancestor that shortly after inheriting the dukedom he formed the intention of handing over the Duke's house at Hyde Park Corner, together with its contents, to the nation as the Wellington Museum, reserving only a small part of the house for the use of himself and his heirs as long as the dukedom continued. This magnificent gesture embodied in an Act of Parliament in 1947 (which gave the house and its contents the status of a national museum administered by the Victoria and Albert Museum) met with a less generous response in certain sections of the press than it deserved. The gift included not only important militaria associated with the Iron Duke, but a group of paintings of outstanding quality (including the equestrian portrait of the Duke by Goya which was specially transferred from the collections at Stratfield Saye) and remarkable porcelain, silver and other works of art of the Napoleonic period of a type not to be found in any other public museum in Britain.

In the event, too, the duke's generous gift saved a notable London landmark, for, had it remained in private hands, there can be little doubt that "Number One, London" would never have escaped the destruction which overtook its neighbours when the traffic routes at Hyde Park Corner were reorganized in 1960-61.

The arts and literature of the eighteenth and early nineteenth century remained an abiding interest throughout his life. On inheriting Stratfield Saye, the house presented to the great Duke by the nation, he immediately set about putting the muniment room and the art collections there, which had been long neglected, in proper order. He served as a Trustee of the National Gallery from 1950 to 1957 and was for many years a member of the Committee of the National Art-Collections Fund. His expert knowledge of the arts and literature in the period he was interested in caused him to be more widely consulted by museum officials and historians than is generally realised.

In 1914 he married Miss Dorothy Violet Ashton, who later became one of the best-known English poets of her generation. By her he had one son and daughter. She died in 1956.

He is succeeded by his son the Marquess Douro, M.V.O., O.B.E., M.C.

January 5, 1972.

William Wellman, the Hollywood film director, died on December 9, 1975 at the age of 79.

He never achieved the fame or the intensity of critical attention arrived at by his close contemporaries in Hollywood, John Ford and Howard Hawks, but a glance at the immense list of distinguished films he directed makes it very difficult to understand why.

The problem, no doubt, was his great variety, which makes him difficult to place in any particular pigeonhole. His prime reputation among Hollywood producers was probably as a maker of action pictures, and in his private life he was very much a man of action, with a becoming disdain for the frills and fancies of conscious art.

He was born in Brookline, Massachusetts, in 1896, educated in Boston, and during the First World War joined the Lafayette Escadrille—whence, no doubt, the recurrent interest shown by his films in flying, most notably in the silent classic *Wings.* At this time he had vague ambitions to be an actor, but after playing one role in films, as a juvenile in Douglas Fairbanks's *The Knickerbocker Buckeroo* (1919), he decided that his real interest was in direction, and so moved to the production side of film-making. He took first a job as property man in Fox studios, soon became an assistant director, and in 1923 directed his own first film, *The Man who Won.* From then on he was continuously productive, and prolific, until 1958 when he retired after making, appropriately enough, *Lafayette Escadrille.*

Few of Wellman's silent films have been readily seeable in recent years, apart from his first great success, *Wings* (1927), famed for its spectacular air fights (enlarged on its first showings, in curious anticipation of modern showmanship techniques, to giant screen proportions) and for introducing Gary Cooper* to the screen in a small but memorable role. During this period, and subsequently, he was willing to turn his hand to anything, and gangster films, comedies, westerns, war films, message films (usually of a decidely right-wing, conservative cast) follow each other with bewildering profusion. It is possible that the films we know are not the best, but any list of films in the 1930s which includes James Cagney's definitive gangster movie *Public Enemy,* the first version of *A Star is Born,* with Janet Gaynor, the great screwball comedy *Nothing Sacred,* the Gary Cooper/Ray Milland/Robert Preston version of *Beau Geste,* and *The Light that Failed,* with one of Ronald Colman's most famous performances, can hardly be accused of mediocrity or dullness.

The 1940s started out with Wellman's most brilliant films, and one of the last of the crazy comedies, *Roxie Hart* (1942), in which Ginger Rogers as a burlesque dancer tries to make publicity out of being tried for murder. For most of the decade, though, Wellman was occupied with war films such as *The Story of G.I. Joe* and *Battleground,* and westerns like *Buffalo Bill* and *The Oxbow Incident,* the latter an unsparing study of a lynching which was for long considered Wellman's masterpiece. In the 1950s he made some of his best westerns, among them *Yellow Sky* and *Westward the Women,* and showed signs of relaxing into a new ease and mellowness of expression. *Island in the Sky,* for instance, about a group of men stranded on a mountain-top, is a large-scale film, beautifully designed and curiously contemplative. *Track of the Cat,* the most extraordinary of his later films, slowly builds up an atmosphere of brooding mystery, and contains some remarkable formal innovations in the symbolic use of sparing colour against wide snowy backgrounds. *Goodbye, My Lady,* is a wholly charming piece of rural Americana about a boy and a dog. And if *Lafayette Escadrille* seems to suffer from a general air of poverty, there is something touching about this late return to sources.

Wellman was married to the actress Dorothy Coonan, and had two children. He devoted his later years to writing his autobiography *A Short Time for Insanity.* Of a generation of giants in the American cinema, he has benefited least from revaluation at the hands of intellectual French critics and consistent, comprehensive revival of his films. But it seems likely that a revival in his reputation cannot be too long delayed.

December 11, 1975.

Sir Harold Wernher, G.C.V.O., the millionaire industrialist and friend of the Queen, and one of Britain's best-known racehorse owners, died on June 30 1973. He was 80.

Wernher, president of Electrolux and a former chairman of the Plessey electronics company, died at his home at Luton Hoo, where he often entertained the Queen and the Duke of Edinburgh.

Sir Harold, who leaves a widow, Lady Zia, and two daughters, had an art collection reputedly worth £2m. at his home. There is no heir to the baronetcy.

The Queen and Prince Philip spent wedding anniversaries at Luton Hoo. It was at Luton Hoo that Princess Alexandra met her husband, Angus Ogilvy, for the first time. Many of Europe's royalty were frequently guests.

Wernher inherited about £1,500,000 from his diamond magnate father—Sir Julius Wernher—and then built up another personal fortune in business and property. He served in the army in both world wars.

He became chairman of Electrolux, the giant electrics empire, in 1926 and president in 1963.

Wernher was also a keen pedigree cattle and sheep breeder, polo player and Master of Foxhounds.

The best horse that Wernher owned, the illustrious Brown Jack, set up a record by winning Royal Ascot's Queen Alexandra Stakes six years in succession from 1929 to 1934. Brown Jack, a great character, and his jockey partner Steve Donoghue, must have been the perfect racing combination.

Other good horses owned by Wernher were Aggressor, winner of the King George VI and Queen Elizabeth Stakes at Ascot, the Chesterfield Cup at Goodwood, and the Hardwicke Stakes; High Perch; and Harmony Hall.

Lady Zia bred the great Meld, winner of the 1,000 Guineas, Oaks and St. Leger in 1955, and Precipitation, who won the Ascot Gold Cup among many other races, and Charlottetown, winner of the 1966 Derby and Coronation Cup

In 1951 he became vice-patron of University College Hospital, and he was chairman of King Edward VII's Hospital for Officers from 1941 to 1969, when he became life vice-president.

His widow, Lady Zia Wernher, is one of Britain's greatest women racehorse owners. The elder daughter of Grand Duke Michael of Russia, and Countess Torby, she married Sir Harold Wernher in 1917. Her two daughters were contemporaries of the Queen.

July 2, 1973.

Michael West, who died on March 19, 1973 at the age of 84, was the elder statesman of the teaching of English to foreigners. He wrote over 150 books, including the pioneering New Method Course and dictionaries; and edited versions of children's books and the classics of English literature.

There can be few indeed among the countless millions of people overseas who have learnt English who have not used his books. His influence on the position of English as the international means of communication in the world today is incalculable. Many would regard him as the most significant figure in the establishing of English Language Teaching as a discipline in its own right.

Born in 1888, Michael West was educated at Marlborough and Christchurch. He went to India in 1912, and was in succession Vice-Principal of David Hare College, Principal of Dacca Training College, and Inspector of Schools in Chittagong and Calcutta. It was in the 1920s, while an inspector of schools, that he first concerned himself with the problems of schoolchildren wrestling with lessons in an unfamiliar language. In 1926 he wrote a version of *Robinson Crusoe* within a restricted vocabulary. This led him to study the whole problem of grading English for foreign students, and he left India to study the subject for a D.Phil at Oxford, and then to collaborate on the General Service List of English Words in Canada and the United States. This analysis of the English language is still the foundation for much English teaching material produced today.

For the last 20 years of his life, Michael West lived in a converted pub in Painswick. He was a familiar figure in the Cotswold area, taking his constitutional in a battered old pork-pie hat, pointing with relish

and approval to the stocks outside the church ("that's where they should put the people who throw bombs"), stopping for a chat with everyone.

He sat on committees for old people's homes, schools and various educational trusts. He gave generously from his royalties to good causes. He loved his roses. But his first interest remained his work, and he was still writing two weeks before he died. It is fitting that his last book (published after his death) should be a beautiful retelling of legends from Ireland and Scotland. The simplicity, humour, humanity and essential truth of these stories reflect the quintessence of the man who told them.

He married Joan Hardy in 1919. She died in 1961. He had three sons, Peter, Henry and Alan. Henry was killed in the Second World War.

March 24, 1973.

Archbishop of Westminster—See Cardinal John Heenan.

Sir Jack Allan Westrup, a leading figure in British academic musical life over three decades, died at Headley, Hampshire, on April 21, 1975 aged 70.

He was educated at Dulwich College and Balliol College, of which he was Nettleship Scholar from 1922 to 1925. He was still at Oxford when his name came to the notice of the musical world through his notable productions of Monteverdi operas, *Orfeo* (1925) and *L'Incoronazione di Poppea* (1927) with the Opera Club. In 1928 he returned to Dulwich College, where for six years he taught classics and played a prominent part in the school's musical life before going to *The Daily Telegraph*, where he served as music critic from 1934 to 1940; during this period he was engaged in intensive research into the life and music of Purcell, which bore fruit in his masterly study of the composer (1937).

He lectured at the Royal Academy of Music from 1938 to 1940, was editor of *Monthly Musical Record* from 1933 to 1945. A selection from his penetrating, pungent editorials and newspaper essays was reprinted in 1940 under the title *Sharps and Flats*.

Westrup entered the university world in 1941 as Lecturer in Music at King's College, Newcastle upon Tyne. Within six years he attained what he later avowed to have been his life's ambition. He left Newcastle in 1944, to become Peyton and Barber Professor of Music at Birmingham, and in 1946 was elected to the Heather Professorship at Oxford.

Although a Faculty of Music was instituted at Oxford in 1944, the Oxford Honours School was not established until 1950. The syllabus for the Preliminary and Final examinations, which included papers on general musical history, a special period

and set books in a foreign language as well as harmony and counter-point, was intended to give an education similar to that of the other arts faculties. The preparation of the Statutes for the Honours School, against some opposition, was largely inspired by Westrup.

During his professorship the Faculty's premises in Holywell doubled in size and the library became one of the finest of its kind. He was responsible for the restoration of the Holywell Music Room to its original design.

Besides the academic side of musical study, Westrup was always an ardent believer in the educational value of music making. He conducted the Oxford University Orchestra, as well as the Oxford Bach Choir and Orchestral Society, and as musical director of the University Opera Club he was responsible for a long sequence of successful productions, including such rare works as *Les Troyens* (1950), *Hans Heiling* (1955) and Scarlatti's *Mitridate Eupatore* (1962). He translated many of them himself. Westrup's devotion to the classics did not lead him to neglect modern composers: in 1951 he staged Wellesz's *Incognita*, and he directed the first English stage performance of *Oedipus Rex*.

In addition to this full life within the Faculty of Music, Westrup got through a prodigious amount of other work. He was continually asked to give lectures. A course delivered at Cape Town University appeared as the main part of *An Introduction to Musical History* (1955). In 1952 he published a skilfully revised edition of Ernest Walker's *History of Music in England*, and in 1969 a similar revision of E. H. Fellowes's *English Cathedral Music*. He collaborated with Frank Harrison in the *Collins Music Encyclopedia* (1959).

From 1958 to 1963 he was President of the Royal Musical Association, from 1964 to 1966 President of the Royal College of Organists. From 1959 he edited *Music & Letters*, and contributed to it editorials and a large number of reviews; in the same year he took over the editorship of the Master Musicians series. In 1971 he was made master of the Worshipful Company of Musicians.

He was concerned in virtually every scholarly musical enterprise in Britain, including the *New Oxford History of Music* (to which he contributed a distinguished chapter on "Mediaeval Song", and was editor of the forthcoming sixth volume), *Musica Britannica, Early English Church Music*, the Purcell Society (as chairman) and *The History of Music in Sound*. A number of important articles in the fifth edition of *Grove* and in *Die Musik in Geschichte und Gegenwart* bear his name. He contributed a continual stream of essays to symposia, journals, *Festschriften* and Congress reports. He organized, more or less single-handed, the Oxford Congress of the International Musicological Society in 1955. He was knighted in 1961.

Westrup was one of the finest musical

scholars of his day. His learning was wide as well as deep, with an especial devotion to the music of the seventeenth century; his book on Purcell, a classic of its kind, represents only one side of his knowledge. Another is found in his brilliant short study of Monteverdi, contributed to volume 3 of *The Heritage of Music*.

It is regrettable that apart from *Purcell* and his contributions to the *New Oxford History of Music* Westrup published nothing substantial that did full justice to his eminence and capacity as a scholar, and particularly that his extensive study on music and society under the Stuarts, which he regarded as his lifetime's work, remained unfinished.

In manner he tended to be dry and reserved, especially with those whom he did not know well: as a lecturer, he was polished and erudite, rather than inspiring; it was as a public speaker that his sardonic wit and his gift for quick, clear thinking were most happily employed. He was always impatient of any kind of pretension or muddled thinking. He typified the pragmatic, commonsense English approach to musical scholarship, with a firm emphasis on practical music making.

Westrup's published compositions were not numerous, mostly for voices, and in the smaller forms.

He married in 1938 Solweg Maria, younger daughter of Musikdirektor Johan Rosall, of Linköping, Sweden, by whom he had a daughter and three sons.

April 23, 1975.

Sir Charles (Reginald) Wheeler, K.B.E., chairman of the Sheerness Steel Company and chairman of Associated Electrical Industries at the time of its controversy-provoking takeover by the General Electric Company in 1967, died on November 25, 1975 at the age of 70.

Charles Wheeler was born in London on December 5, 1904 and educated at St. Paul's School. In 1922 he joined the steel company, Baldwins Ltd., moving to the sales side after two years on the shop floor. It was in this sphere that he soon found an outlet for his talents, rising swiftly to London manager. At the age of only 25 he became commercial manager of Guest Keen Baldwins Iron and Steel Company Ltd. when it was formed in 1930, and became a director of the firm in 1940.

At the outbreak of the Second World War he was sent to the Ministry of Supply on the strength of his growing reputation as one of the noted younger men in the steel industry. An Assistant Controller of Supply (Raw Materials) Iron and Steel Control in 1939, he became Deputy Controller in 1943 and finally Controller in 1945.

The war over, he returned to what was now the Guest Keen Iron and Steel Company as joint managing director, a post he

retained until 1959 when he became chairman. He was to remain chairman only one year. At that point Lord Chandos, then A.E.I.'s chairman, asked him to join the company's board. He was vice-chairman of A.E.I. from 1961 to 1962, deputy chairman in 1962 and became the group's first overall managing director in the same year. He became chairman of A.E.I. in 1964.

At the outset Wheeler's sales flair boosted the group's profits, while on the management side he always insisted that young men with the necessary ability should be appointed to managerial positions within A.E.I. But in 1967 Sir Arnold Weinstock, managing director of the General Electric Company, surprised industrial and financial circles by making a £120m bid for A.E.I. Given its blessing by the Industrial Reorganization Corporation, the bid was bitterly opposed by both Sir Charles Wheeler and his chief executive, Sir Joseph Latham, as well as arousing dislike in many other financial and industrial quarters. Wheeler, himself a member of the I.R.C., resigned from its board, stating in his letter to the Prime Minister, Harold Wilson, that I.R.C.'s endorsement of G.E.C.'s bid to acquire his company made his future membership impossible.

The resignation at that point of the I.R.C.'s managing director and deputy chairman, Ronald Grierson, though not directly connected with the takeover bid, did nothing to allay a general feeling that considerable friction had been generated, at many official levels, by the idea. Nevertheless the shareholders voted in favour of the takeover—General Electric's profit record was superior to that of A.E.I.—and the companies merged. But it was a battle which left much acrimony in its wake and though Wheeler was offered a place on the board of G.E.C. he never played a practical part in the affairs of the company. Thereafter he held a number of directorships but in 1969 turned to steel again when he co-founded the Sheerness Steel Company Ltd. For Wheeler this represented a return to the sphere in which he had first played an important role in industry, and the foundation and success of the independent company was a step dear to his heart.

Outside his work Wheeler was a keen sportsman. He was a vice-president of the British Olympic Association as well as being a participant and a supporter and patron of many sports.

A member of London Rowing Club, and of Leander, he served on many committees, on which his business experience and wide connexions were invaluable. As a member of the executive committee of the Sixth British Empire and Commonwealth Games in Cardiff in 1958, he was largely responsible for the achievement of a first class rowing course on Llyn Padarn, in Wales. But perhaps the greatest service he rendered to rowing was his regular support of British crews in international championships abroad. Whether as an international umpire, an Amateur Rowing Association dele-

gate to the Fédération Internationale des Sociétés d'Aviron, or simply as a spectator, he was a regular member of the British contingent, and always ready to help and encourage. He was also a president of the Cardiff Sea Cadet Corps and Joint Master of the Old Berkeley Beagles.

He was President of the Iron and Steel Institute in 1958, of the British Iron and Steel Federation in 1961 and of the British Electrical and Allied Manufacturers' Association in 1965. He was High Sheriff of Glamorgan in 1955. He was made a C.B.E. in 1946, K.B.E. in 1966.

He was twice married, first in 1929, to Frieda Close, who died in 1972. They had one son and two daughters. His second marriage, in 1973, was to Marcelle Ades.

He was made an Officer of the Legion of Honour in 1966 and an Honorary D.Sc. of Salford in 1967.

November 26, 1975.

Sir Charles (Thomas) Wheeler, K.C.V.O., C.B.E., P.P.R.A., who died on August 22, 1974, was widely known as the sculptor of many monumental, memorial and decorative works and as a President of the Royal Academy whose term of office (1956-66) was one of the longest in recent times. He was 82.

His architectural commissions were executed with a competency to which the skill acquired from a thorough training and an extensive professional practice both contributed. It is likely, however, that the more personal qualities of the sculptor were to some extent obscured by the work best known to the public. A possible comparison is that of the lyric poet commissioned to write narratives or epics. This is far from saying that he was unsuccessful in the sculpture carried out for Sir Herbert Baker at the Bank of England or the groups for the Jellicoe Memorial Fountain, Trafalgar Square, in collaboration with Sir Edwin Lutyens; but other works may be considered more typical of the artist's personal aspirations.

An example is the bronze statue, "Spring", exhibited in the Academy of 1930 and purchased through the Chantrey Bequest for the Tate Gallery; a gracefully mannered figure of the Botticelli type, elongated in form and lovingly finished. This more intimate impression of Wheeler is also given by the bronze angel for the Bishop Jacob memorial church at Ilford designed by Sir Herbert Baker, the bronze bust, "The Infant Christ", another Chantrey purchase for the Tate (1924), a portrait of the artist's nine-month-old son early in 1920, and the head in black marble, "Night" of 1929.

As often happens when an artist of delicate talent turns to work on a large scale, his reliefs and figures for the Bank of England (1930), his most elaborate undertaking, were inclined to over-emphasis. This applies particularly to the six buttress figures representing the "Guardians and Bearers of Wealth", which link the old building with the new. The three bronze doors below give a good idea of his lighter manner, and in the relief of the "Old Lady of Threadneedle Street" on the pediment of the central pavilion he made an individual interpretation of the symbolic "Britannia" figure, originally derived from a Roman coin. "My design", he said, "represents the new spirit of the age, the spirit of reconstruction after the war. The 'Old Lady' grasps her spear and shield and holds a model of the building that symbolizes reconstruction."

Wheeler was responsible for sculpture in other parts of the Bank building such as the figure of Ariel surmounting the Treasury dome, and the relief panel over the fireplace in the Court Room. His association with Sir Herbert Baker which began with the Angel for the church at Ilford was fruitful. For the Indian Memorial to the Missing at Neuve Chapelle he executed the two great sitting tigers and the decorative work for the pillars; for Electra House, the headquarters of Cable and Wireless, the two bronze figures of Mercury; and for Church House, Westminster, the relief of "Dedication" over the doorway to the Assembly Hall. His lively "Springbok" in gilt bronze over the corner entrance to South Africa House is familiar to all London passers-by.

The long list of his commissions also includes works at India House, Rhodes House, Oxford, The Royal Empire Society, Haileybury College Chapel, Winchester College War Memorial Cloisters, the R.A.F. Memorial, Malta, and the Merchant Navy Memorial, Tower Hill. In his non-architectural work in stone, marble and wood he practised direct carving with much regard for material texture and quality of surface.

Charles Thomas Wheeler, the son of a journalist, was born at Codsall, Staffordshire, on March 14, 1892. He elected to leave school when fifteen to study sculpture at the Wolverhampton School of Art, where he received a sound training under R. J. Emerson. Wolverhampton later accorded him the freedom of the borough. In 1912 he gained a scholarship to the Royal College of Art, where he became a pupil of Edward Lanteri and assistant to that celebrated professor in his private work. He made a posthumous portrait of Lanteri.

Wheeler exhibited at the Royal Academy from 1914, was made A.R.A. in 1934 and R.A. in 1940. He was President of the Royal Society of British Sculptors from 1944 to 1949, in the latter year receiving the Society's gold medal for services to sculpture. One of the overseas honours that came to him was the gold medal of the National Academy of Design, U.S.A., in 1963. He was a Trustee of the Tate Gallery, 1942-49 and a member of the Royal Fine Art Commission, 1946-52. In 1956 he was elected President of the Royal Academy (the first sculptor to be elected) in succession to Sir Albert Richardson*, and continued in office until 1966.

It was a period marked by the sale of the Leonardo Cartoon, the £800,000 raised to preserve the famous work for the nation in 1962 placing the Academy in a much improved position financially. It was the period also of two of the Academy's most ambitious Winter Exhibitions, those devoted to Goya and to Bonnard. He published an autobiography *High Relief* in 1968.

A mild and friendly man in personal contact, short in stature but as sturdy and athletic-looking as a sculptor might be expected to be, with clear-cut, eager features and a distinctive sweep of hair, Wheeler was a vigorous controversialist and an active propagandist for the arts in general.

Wheeler married Muriel, younger daughter of A. W. Bourne, herself a talented painter and sculptor and a regular exhibitor at the Royal Academy, and they had a son and a daughter.

August 24, 1974

General Earle Wheeler, who served as chairman of the United States Joint Chiefs of Staff during most of the Vietnam War, and held the post longer than any predecessor, died on December 18, 1975 in hospital at Frederick, Maryland. He was 67.

By the time he came to retire in 1970 Wheeler's Vietnam involvement spanned the administrations of three presidents. It was President Kennedy* who made him Army Chief of Staff, President Johnson who promoted him to chairman of the chiefs, and President Nixon who began the slow and fierce American disengagement.

So far much of the military débâcle has been attributed to the field commanders, but it is unlikely that history will be generous with General Wheeler and the staff chiefs back in Washington.

Among the many Vietnam controversies two stand out. In 1968 Wheeler was much more heavily involved than was apparent at the time in inciting General William Westmoreland to make his fateful request for over 200,000 more American troops, in addition to the half million already in Vietnam. The request convulsed President Johnson's Administration, and the American disengagement effectively began with its refusal.

Wheeler's role has since been documented as attempting to exploit the Tet offensive to gain approval for the Joint Chiefs' pet scheme for one last massive expansion of American effort to gain the elusive knockout blow. Politically it was impossible.

The other controversy was the secret bombing of Cambodia—another Joint Chiefs' longing—begun under President Nixon in 1969. When the scandal broke in 1973 Wheeler admitted that President Nixon personally ordered the massive raids against the North Vietnamese, abusing a nominally neutral country, and that records were falsified in order to keep them a total secret, even from such top officials as the Air Force Secretary. Wheeler said he could live with the deception since he was following orders.

As a soldier his claim to fame was as master of logistics and centralized planning. The phenomenal speed with which the American expeditionary force to Vietnam was built up in the 1965-66 period is tribute to the skills that could be applied when money was no object.

During his career he saw combat for only a few months in Germany in the Second World War, but he visited Vietnam many times. For the rest he excelled at staff work, although he held several important commands. Under President Kennedy he distinguished himself by being the only member of the Joint Chiefs who supported the first partial nuclear test ban agreement in 1963.

December 20, 1975.

Sir John Wheeler-Bennett, G.C.V.O., C.M.G., O.B.E., the distinguished historian and authority on international affairs, died on December 9, 1975 in a London hospital at the age of 73.

John Wheeler Wheeler-Bennett was born on October 13, 1902, a son of J. W. Wheeler-Bennett, C.B.E., a prosperous general importer, of Keston, Kent. His mother was a Canadian from Nova Scotia. He went to school at Westgate on Sea, and after that to Malvern College. His schooldays, he told his friends, were not particularly happy, in part because his health was always delicate, an impression that was reinforced in later years by the slight but noticeable nervous stammer which at times impeded his rapid and fluent conversation.

Shortly after the end of the First World War instead of entering a university he accepted the offer of a post as honorary assistant to General Sir Neil Malcolm, on whose staff he worked in the Far East and Berlin. This first awakened his interest in international affairs, and in particular in the role played by Germany in the postwar settlement of Europe, and laid the foundation of a life-long curiosity about, and knowledge of, Germany and Germans. Adequately provided with private means, curious, perceptive with a quick, darting intelligence and a romantic, slightly theatrical, sense of political life, he was intrigued, and indeed entranced, by anything that was picturesque, dramatic, out of the ordinary; this was allied, however, with an exceedingly sober and accurate sense of facts, so that, while he might tend to view a situation in terms of a political or psychological drama, he never left the solid ground of verified data, and did not exaggerate or colour the facts, even in his own imagination.

Beginning as a convinced internationalist in his youth, he worked in the publicity department of the League of Nations Union in 1923-24, and was closely associated with the work of the Royal Institute of International Affairs—indeed he was the founder and organizer of its information service in the twenties, and founder and editor of its *Bulletin of International News* until 1932. He lived in Germany a good deal in the twenties, and came to know the leading political personalities of that country better perhaps than any other Englishman. He remained all his life fascinated by Germany and the Germans: particularly by Junkers, generals, diplomats, politicians and other members of the military-political élites which flourished in Germany during the inter-war years.

His judgment of Germany always remained sharply critical: he was not deceived into accepting nationalistic German versions of the history of the twentieth century. He watched Germany, and took delight in his meetings with prominent Germans, like a specialist fascinated by particularly rich or exotic specimens of a genus which he had spent his life in studying, but towards which, with some exceptions, he preserved an attitude of absorbed and objective scientific curiosity. He spent much of his time in the twenties in breeding horses in Northern Germany (interrupted by frequent and lengthy visits to England) and acquiring an expert knowledge of international affairs, on which he was to become a leading authority.

His principal interest lay in the theory and practice of diplomacy, and in the interplay of personalities in that field. With his warm-hearted, gay, responsive nature he was ready to catch fire from anything that stirred his imagination. In the twenties and thirties his political views and interests brought him into contact with a good many of the best known members of political London society at that time, particularly with those who shared his international interests; with many of these he remained bound by devoted friendships. He held at this time no official post, but he tended to be consulted by British officials on questions concerned with Germany, since he had early acquired a reputation as an expert on Central Europe, and he was the author of a growing number of articles and books principally dealing with problems of disarmament, security, reparations and the like, most of them published by Chatham House.

He sympathized with the moderate Right in Europe; and with his tendency towards interpretation of events in terms of arresting personalities (resembling in this his friend John Buchan, to whose works—as well as those of Anthony Hope—he was greatly addicted) he developed a great admiration for Dr. Brüning*, at one time Chancellor of Germany, whom he assisted to escape from Germany after Hitler's advent to power. Indeed Brüning was the hero of the first of Wheeler-Bennett's major

works—*Hindenburg*, published in 1936, a full-scale analysis of the rise of German chauvinism between the wars. He came to alter his glowing opinion of Brüning as a result of differences during and after the Second World War. This book was followed by his masterpiece, *The Forgotten Peace*, a volume on the Peace of Brest Litovsk, based on comprehensive and imaginative research, and in particular on interviews with General Hoffman, Kühlmann, Trotsky and lesser *dramatis personae.*

The Forgotten Peace gave Wheeler-Bennett a firm reputation in academic, as well as government and journalistic circles. He was a passionate opponent of the settlement of Munich, and based his views on his expert knowledge of Germans and the German Army. The outbreak of war found him established as a lecturer on International Relations in the University of Virginia in the U.S.A.—he felt a nostalgic love for the Southern States, and found his deeply loved wife and a second home there—and his friends, Bruce Lockhart*, Lord Lothian and Sir Robert Vansittart, persuaded him to use his knowledge of Europe and America, and his very wide personal popularity in American political and journalistic circles, in the cause of Anglo-American understanding.

He was one of the triumvirate charged by the Ministry of Information with the task of overhauling the peacetime British information machinery in New York, and with A. N. Morgan and Alan Dudley he established the British Information Services in New York, an institution which played a significant part in the evolution of American opinion during the Second World War. His frequent visits to London during the war were highly valued by his friends in the Cabinet and the ministries, who looked to him as a unique source of accurate information and good judgment, based on his remarkably wide personal contacts.

In 1942 he became the representative in America of the British Political Warfare organization, and later European adviser and Assistant Director General of the Political Intelligence Department. He worked in the Political Adviser's Department in S.H.A.E.F. in the last year of the war, and was attached to the British Prosecution Team to the Nuremberg War Criminals Tribunal in 1946. He had no doubt that these trials were wholly just, and this caused a rift between him and some of his old anti-Nazi German friends. In the same year he was appointed British Editor-in-Chief of the captured archives of the German Foreign Ministry, and was retained as general adviser to the Foreign Office on publications of this type.

In the last year of the war he married Miss Ruth Risher of Charlottesville, Virginia, and they lived in the beautiful manor house of Garsington, near Oxford, which a quarter of a century before had been made famous by the literary *salon* of Lady Ottoline Morrell. After the war he became

a lecturer of New College and a Fellow of St. Antony's, and taught international relations in Oxford. His generous and genial personality made him friends in Oxford, as everywhere. In 1948 he published a book on the Munich settlement, and in 1953 *The Nemesis of Power,* a notable volume on the German Army.

In 1958 he published the official biography of King George VI, a life of Lord Waverley in 1962, and a record of the post-war period—*The Semblance of Peace* —written with Anthony Nicholls. He was made a K.C.V.O., and appointed Historical Adviser to the Royal Archives, which of all his many posts and honours probably gave him the keenest pleasure. In 1974, he was advanced to G.C.V.O. In that year he published his last book *Knaves, Fools and Heroes.*

All his life he laboured under an acute consciousness of his amateur status among professional historians, and remained modest, and indeed diffident, in the presence of experts; yet his own attainments were, judged even by the severest academic standards, as a rule higher than those of most of the specialists whom he held in such high esteem. Erudite and sagacious as he was, he looked upon the world to the end of his days with something of the freshness of an impressionable schoolboy brought up on historical romances.

What fascinated him most was the interplay of heroic or unusual personalities, the part played by audacity, by intrigue, espionage, by the sinister, the gallant, the unforeseen, the fortuitous in human affairs. He liked the pageantry of history. His vision was indeed somewhat Churchillian, but with this he remained an indefatigable, scrupulous and minute researcher, and his books, although not devoid of rhetoric and occasional purple, were based on vast and careful labours, and were free from facile generalizations.

He was happily married. He was a practising Anglican, much attached to his village church. He loved life in all its manifestations, and was a connoisseur of odd personalities and political situations.

A generous, imaginative, amusing, affectionate, warm-hearted man, full of romantic loyalties and fancies and admirations, he was much and widely loved. With his life-enhancing talk, his many acts of kindness and his enchanting personality he will be deeply missed by his many friends.

December 10, 1975.

Dr. Paul Dudley White, the Harvard heart specialist, who died on October 31, 1973 at the age of 87, was the international doyen of cardiology. For nearly half a century he was universally recognized as the outstanding clinical cardiologist of the day, and his clinic at the Massachusetts General Hospital was the Mecca of cardiologists, young and old, from all five continents.

His output and his energy were tremendous, even by United States standards. A special issue of the *American Journal of Cardiology*, the official journal of the American College of Cardiology, published in his honour in April 1965, gave a list of 710 papers he had written; and his pen had not been still since then.

His zeal as a traveller equalled that as a writer, and there can be few countries that he had not visited, to lecture, found, open or bless institutes of cardiology; or to study heart disease as it occurred in different countries. Thus, in 1946 he was chairman of the American Medical Mission to Czechoslovakia; two years later he was chairman of the American Medical Mission to Greece and Italy; while in 1952 he was a member of the Four Point Mission to Pakistan, India, Israel and Greece. He paid two visits to the U.S.S.R., a country in which, like so many of his fellow countrymen, he showed a special interest with a view to improving relationships.

Old age could not damp his ardour for novelty and travel, and in September 1971, as the guest of the Chinese Medical Association, he paid a 12-day visit to China, together with Dr. Grey Dimond, a fellow cardiologist.

The writing and travelling, however, were incidental. Above all he was a brilliant clinician, and it was his reputation as the outstanding clinical cardiologist of the day that attracted to his department in Boston post-graduates from all over the world.

Unassuming, of rather short build, he was no prima donna or orator, but he could hold an audience for an hour and more, and still have them asking for more.

Paul Dudley White was born in Roxbury, Massachusetts, on June 6, 1886, the son of a family doctor who lived even longer than his son, dying at the age of 92. The son graduated from Harvard in 1912, and, with the exception of war service and a year with a travelling fellowship at University College Hospital Medical School, London, he spent the whole of his professional career on the staff of Harvard Medical School and the Massachusetts General Hospital.

In 1916 he was in France with the British Expeditionary Force, and from 1917 to 1919 he served in France with the American Expeditionary Force, ending his war career with the American Red Cross in Greece.

Honours fell on him thick as autumn leaves in Vallambrosa from all parts of the world, including medals, government and academic, honorary university degrees and honorary membership of medical societies, such as the Royal Society of Medicine. Not least was he honoured in his own country, where he received the award of the Presidential Medal of Freedom. He was physician to President Eisenhower* and looked after the President when he had his heart attack in 1955.

Here he demonstrated his gift for public relations. His communiqués on the Presi-

dent's progress, and his interviews with the press were little masterpieces, and there can be little doubt that it was the confidence they aroused in the public that convinced the nation that, in spite of his heart attack, the President was physically fit to continue in office.

Behind this flair for public relations lay his deep interest in health education, which became one of his major concerns, particularly in his later years. He had always been a stern advocate of physical exercise. On one occasion, it is said, he walked the seven miles from the headquarters of the American Heart Association at the corner of 23rd Street and Madison Avenue to La Guardia airport.

Another episode in the same strain is the tale of the importunate reporter who asked him for an interview as he came out from an official lunch in his hotel. "Fine", Dr. White said, "just come along with me to my room". His room happened to be on the twelfth floor; and by the time the unfortunate reporter had kept pace with Dr. White up to the twelfth floor he was in no state to carry on with the interview.

One of White's many aphorisms for healthy living and long life was: "Walk more; eat less; sleep more." In his later years he modified that slightly by advocating "cycling to health". He certainly practised what he preached, and his spare, lithe figure was, literally, a walking testimony to the value of his advice, even making allowance for his longevity genes.

November 1, 1973.

Sir Edgar Whitehead, K.C.M.G., O.B.E., Prime Minister of Southern Rhodesia from 1958 to 1962, died in a nursing home in Newbury, Berkshire, on September 23, 1971 at the age of 66.

His prime ministership proved to be a transitional period between the radicalism of Garfield Todd, from whose authoritarianism and mismanagement the United Federal Party (Southern Rhodesian branch) had revolted, and the outright white suprematism of the Rhodesia Front, which subsequently led to the break with Britain. Whitehead tried to tread the middle path, fighting an African nationalism that saw itself within an ace of power as in Ghana and Kenya, on the one hand, and the white backlash of Ian Smith and Winston Field,* on the other. Intellectually brilliant, at times arrogant, tough minded and brave, he saw what was needed in a unique situation, but, like the Federal Prime Minister, Sir Roy Welensky (with whom he enjoyed more identity of political thinking than of personal rapport) he failed to achieve it.

Edgar Cuthbert Fremantle Whitehead was born on February 8, 1905, in the British Embassy in Berlin, the third son of the chancellor at the Embassy, Sir James Beethom Whitehead and Lady Marian Whitehead. Educated at Shrewsbury and

University College, Oxford, where he took a degree in history, he left England in 1928 on his doctor's advice, and entered the Southern Rhodesia service for two years. He then took up farming at Vumba, and became a leading figure in farming organizations which led him naturally into politics. He was elected for Umtali North in 1939 as a supporter of Sir Godfrey Huggins (later Lord Malvern).

He served throughout the war with the British Army and on his release as an acting Lieutenant-Colonel briefly became Rhodesian High Commissioner in London. Soon after, he re-entered Parliament, and was Minister of Finance and Posts and Telegraphs in the Huggins government from 1946 to 1953. He strained the economy, it is said, in his efforts to encourage white settlement, and he worked hard to bring about the federation of the two Rhodesias and Nyasaland, of which his chief became first federal Prime Minister.

Whitehead, however, was forced to retire temporarily from politics because of failing eyesight, but in 1957 he was fit enough to accept Sir Roy Welensky's invitation to be the Federation's minister in Washington, on attachment to the British Embassy.

He was recalled by the warring factions of the party to take over the territorial government from Garfield Todd, and, defeated in a by-election, dissolved the house and narrowly beat the right-wing Dominion party in a general election.

He set about creating a multi-racial society by appealing to moderate Africans and white liberals through the gradual removal of discriminatory legislation, which at once infuriated the hardliners, who, under Ian Smith, set about creating the Front, and the Africans who set about creating monolithic mass political parties based largely on intimidation.

The monument to Whitehead's political faith was the Sandys-Whitehead constitution of 1961, which first brought Africans into the Southern Rhodesian parliament, and remains the legal constitution, conforming to the "five principles" adumbrated later on, because it could have led to an African majority in the House by about 1976 on Whitehead's calculation—and (as he always insisted) vested sovereignty jointly in Salisbury and London, though British lawyers contended that it left Westminster legally supreme.

But both Joshua Nkomo and Sithole rejected such gradualism, and fomented a degree of disorder that forced Whitehead to bring in the Law and Order Maintenance Act (subsequently much extended) and to declare a state of emergency. This, the events in the Congo, and the determination of the British Government to end the Federation, produced the victory of Winston Field in 1961. Whitehead, who foresaw the extremism to which this victory would lead, soon abandoned his post as leader of the opposition and moved to Britain, where his opponents, no doubt relieved to be rid of his brilliant mind and fine oratory, voted him a pension.

His liberal work in developing African education and breaking down the colour bar in Salisbury and other towns (he pledged himself to end the Land Apportionment Act also) has been obliterated, but subsequent events have ensured that Edgar Whitehead will be judged indulgently by history, despite his many tactical mistakes, which arose partly from his intellectual aloofness and genuine shyness. Bad at "mixing", his charm and magnetism in small gatherings were irresistible. There never was a more informal prime minister, and even his occasional gaffes endeared him. He never married.

September 24, 1971.

Richard Whitney, formerly president of the New York Stock Exchange, who was credited with attempting to halt the Wall Street panic of 1929, but later went to prison for embezzlement, died on December 5, 1974 at the age of 86.

Educated at Groton and Harvard, he bought a seat on the New York Stock Exchange at the age of 23 and soon became principal broker for J. P. Morgan and Co. He captured the public imagination on October 24, 1929, "Black Thursday", the day when deals of 12,894,650 shares clogged the tape until just after 7 p.m. On that day Whitney, then vice-president of the New York Stock Exchange, was in charge.

At 1.30 he appeared on the floor with an order for 10,000 shares of United States Steel at 205. Since the stock was being offered at less than 200 a share, Whitney's spectacularly uneconomic bid had the almost instantaneous effect of convincing jittery brokers and investors that the bankers had confidence in the market. Next day there were headlines, "Richard Whitney halts stock panic".

He was elected president of the Stock Exchange in 1930 and so remained until 1935. However, all the while his personal financial affairs were getting into a disastrous state. In April 1938 he pleaded guilty to two indictments for grand larceny and was sentenced to from five to 10 years' imprisonment on each count.

It was found that over a period of six years Whitney had unlawfully used securities belonging to customers of his firm Richard Whitney and Co, but without the knowledge of his partners. The firm went bankrupt.

In his endeavours to keep the firm from failing Whitney borrowed $1m. from his brother, a partner in J. P. Morgan and Co., and large amounts from friends, but concealed from them the true position of his affairs. He was paroled after a little over three years.

December 7, 1974.

Hazel Hotchkiss Wightman, the "first lady of American tennis," and the donor of the Wightman Cup in 1923, died on December 5, 1974 in Boston, Massachusetts. She was 87.

Mrs. Wightman won 48 United States national tennis titles, the first in 1909 and her last in 1954, retiring from veterans' competitions at the age of 78. The Wightman Cup is awarded to the winner of women's team tennis competition between the United States and Britain, and Mrs. Wightman was playing and non-playing captain of the American team on a number of occasions.

Speaking of her playing days, she said in 1973 at the celebration of the fiftieth anniversary of Wightman Cup competition: "I have always been small . . . but I was fast and I had courage. Tennis needs courage." She and Helen Wills were never beaten in doubles and they won the Wimbledon and United States doubles in 1924. They won the United States doubles again in 1928.

Mrs. Wightman began playing tennis at the age of 16. "About the only sport a girl could play was tennis," she said, noting the difficulty women had in being accepted as athletes at the turn of the century. Tennis also had its worries. As a teenager, she would get up at dawn to play because the courts were reserved for men after 8 a.m.

In 1934 Mrs. Wightman published *Better Tennis*. It was described by *The Times* critic as "very good reading . . . once one has recovered from the shock of seeing a book about tennis written by a woman".

In it, Mrs. Wightman made it clear that at no time had she lived for the game, but had played it because she liked it, and that she had never let it interfere with a normal life.

But, while disclaiming the game as the chief interest in her life, she held it to be not only a stimulating pastime but also a builder of character and health and "a channel of intensified life". During her career, Mrs. Wightman kept closely in touch with the game all over the world and met everyone with any claim to fame.

She and her husband, George, had five children, 13 grandchildren and nine great-grandchildren.

December 7, 1974.

Thornton Wilder, the American novelist and playwright, died in New Haven, Connecticut, on December 7, 1975 at the age of 78.

A writer who continued to the end to ply his craft, he would have been accepted for many years as the most outstanding of contemporary American men-of-letters had prizes and popularity been taken into account. But for several reasons the critics have looked at him askance, and for every serious paragraph on him there must have been a hundred articles and books on Hemingway* and Faulkner.* It is an, as yet, unresolved question which was right:

the instinctive judgment of the reading public, or the informed opinion of the critics.

Thornton Niven Wilder was born in 1897 at Maddison, Wisconsin, the son of the editor and publisher of a newspaper. His parents were Protestants and deeply religious. He was educated partly in Hongkong, where his father was American Consul-General for a time, and in California. He attended Oberlin College, transferring in 1917 to Yale. He returned to Yale in 1919 after serving for a year with the Coast Artillery, the only force that would accept him because of his poor eyesight. He took his B.A. in 1920.

Wilder taught French in high school for a time and studied at Princeton for his M.A., which he took in 1926, but he quickly determined to make writing his profession. After 1928 he devoted his life to his writing, except for a period of part-time teaching in the University of Chicago from 1930 to 1936. He built a house for his mother close to the Yale campus after his first success in 1928, and continued to make his home there for the rest of his life. His sister, Isabel Wilder, herself a distinguished novelist, largely looked after his affairs.

Wilder published his first work of fiction, *The Cabala*, in 1926. The three stories which make up the work are interesting and well written but failed to attract much notice. In 1927, however, he published *The Bridge of San Luis Rey*, a novel which had as great a success in England as in the United States, where it was awarded a Pulitzer Prize, the first of Wilder's many prizes. The story is set in eighteenth-century Peru and is a skilful interlocking account of the lives of the five characters who are crossing the bridge at the moment of its collapse. It is so artfully constructed and un-American in tone that it was sometimes mistaken by the unwary for a translation from some Spanish original.

The Bridge of San Luis Rey was very much at variance with the spirit and style of the naturalistic American novel of the day and hostility to Wilder broke out on the publication in 1930 of his next novel *The Woman of Andros*, which is taken from Terence's *Andria*. Wilder's methods and manner were violently attacked and his religion was described by his most outspoken critic as being "Anglo-Catholicism, that last refuge of the American snob"—a fair example of the level of the criticism.

Wilder once declared that the "novel is preeminently the vehicle of the unique occasion, the theatre of the generalized one;" an observation that hardly fits most novels and plays but that certainly enlightens Wilder's own practice. He had published six one-act plays, *The Long Christmas Dinner and Other Plays,* in 1931, but his first theatrical success came in 1938 with *Our Town;* and a resounding success it was, winning another Pulitzer Prize. The play has hardly any plot, being concerned with the ordinary happenings of life in a village in New Hampshire, seen out of chronological order across many years, but these incidents are handled with deep feeling and arranged with all the skill needed "to find a value above all price for the smallest events in our daily life," as Wilder himself put it.

He was not as successful at first with his next play, *The Merchant of Yonkers*, produced in 1938, but when it was later modified and produced in 1954 under the title of *The Matchmaker*, it went much better—and better still in its musical adaptation, *Hello, Dolly* (1963).

Wilder's greatest theatrical success—and a third Pulitzer—came in 1942 with *The Skin of Our Teeth*. The chronicle of the Antrobus family surviving all the great cataclysms of history, in spite of the odds against them, was especially appropriate to the circumstances of wartime. The play was as ingenious in construction as it was simple in effect—a sophisticated morality. The London production was made even more of an occasion by the brilliant performance of Vivien Leigh* as Mrs. Antrobus (Eve). Wilder's triumph was only spoilt by an acrimonious dispute whether his borrowings from James Joyce's *Finnegan's Wake* constituted plagiarism or not.

Wilder had published another novel, *Heaven's My Destination*, in 1935. The hero is an American salesman seen as Don Quixote; like his great original, he maintains his integrity through goodness of heart and simplicity of mind. A further novel, *The Ides of March*, a study of dictatorship in the guise of Julius Caesar, appeared in 1948. And in 1967, he published *The Eighth Day*, a novel with which he won the National Book Award for fiction, in spite of the competition of his much belauded and publicized juniors. His last novel, *Theophilus North* (1974), was more autobiographical than its predecessors, and in places heavy, but essentially a sunny book, recounting the progress of a young man through life.

Wilder was awarded the first National Medal for Literature in 1965, which proved conclusively his standing in the public's regard—a standing that will now depend on a long overdue objective review of his achievements.

He remained unmarried.

December 9, 1975.

Sir Arthur Willert, K.B.E., who died on March 11, 1973 at the age of 90, had a long career of public service which began on *The Times*, continued in the Foreign Office, and ended in the Ministry of Information.

His dispatches to the paper from Washington immediately before and during the First World War are recognized as having made a valuable contribution to Anglo-American understanding, a cause which he had much at heart during the whole of his life. He was seconded from *The Times* to serve on Lord Northcliffe's War Mission in the U.S.A. in the year 1917; and after peace was signed was invited by the Foreign Office to be the first head of its newly created News Department. He relinquished that post in 1935; and after a few years of independent writing, lecturing and travel he joined the Ministry of Information during the Second World War and became Head of its Southern England Branch with headquarters at Reading. He was the author of four short books on foreign policy.

Arthur Willert was born on May 19, 1882, and was educated at Eton and Balliol. He began his journalistic career under good auspices. The prompting of Sir Harold Hartley and his father's friendship with Arthur Walter took him to Printing House Square at the age of 24, and he was soon sent to serve under two masters of their craft, Lavino and Saunders, Correspondents of *The Times* respectively in Paris and Berlin. Thence he was called back to work directly under the Foreign Editor, Sir Valentine Chirol. Chirol completed his journalistic education and then sent him to Washington as assistant to R. P. Porter, who was expected to retire shortly. He was recalled for another brief spell in the London Office in 1909; and in the next year, on the retirement of Porter, he was given, at the early age of 28, the post of Washington Correspondent of *The Times*. He soon made his mark there, and the post became more and more important year by year owing to the growing American influence in international affairs. Willert's messages attracted increasing attention both in London and Washington. By 1914 his position was firmly established not only as an exponent of American political thinking but also—even more important in President Wilson's day—as an intelligent interpreter to the Americans of the British view.

After the First World War had begun, a British official who was serving in the United States at the same time recorded that Willert's universal popularity and many friendships in governmental, Congressional, and private circles attuned his senses to the variable breezes of public opinion, and that his contacts and information were of great value to the British official machine. In this context Willert himself often insisted how much he owed to Lady (then Mrs.) Willert, who made many friends in circles other than those whom he would normally meet in the course of his professional duties. One of his own chief contacts was the future President, Franklin Roosevelt, then Assistant-Secretary of the Navy, and he was in almost daily touch with the British Ambassador, Sir Cecil Spring-Rice.

Spring-Rice performed excellent work in settling the difficult questions of contraband that vexed Anglo-American relations as soon as war began, but failing health and impatience with the detached and cautious approach to war of the United States rendered him irascible in the last years of his life (he died at his post); and Willert occasionally was able to soothe ruffled feelings on either side. This happened also when Lord Northcliffe was sent to Washington at the head of a British War Mission. Spring-Rice was perhaps naturally upset that a special envoy should be thought necessary, and refused to send a representative of the Embassy to greet him on arrival, at which Northcliffe did not conceal his annoyance. That the two men soon worked well together was largely due to the mediation of Willert, in whom both placed absolute confidence. Northcliffe in fact chose Willert to be the secretary to his mission, which involved handing over his journalistic work to a deputy. Willert at the same time became Washington representative of the British Ministry of Information. For his services during this period he was made a K.B.E.

When the war was over he served for a short time under Wickham Steed in Paris during the peace negotiations. When Steed became Editor of *The Times* on the resignation of Geoffrey Dawson, Willert was an obvious candidate for the post of Foreign Editor vacated by Steed. He did not get the appointment. Willert resigned from *The Times* and accepted the Foreign Office's invitation to become Head of its News Department.

There Willert's ability to get on with persons of the most varied temperaments—as had already been known by his close cooperation with both Northcliffe and Geoffrey Dawson—served him well, and journalists of every shade of opinion came to like and trust one who was so well versed in the work of a newspaper. He combined the art of telling as much as he properly could with never giving away what for the time had to remain secret; and he always knew when it was possible to impart secret information in confidence. Willert attended the Naval Conference in Washington (1921-22), the London Economic Conference (1924), the Disarmament Conference at Geneva, and most of the meetings of the League of Nations there. He was given the rank of temporary Counsellor in the Foreign Office.

He resigned this post in 1935 to the general regret of members of the press, who gave him a parting gift of a silver rosebowl. Then for four years Willert travelled, lectured and wrote books, notably *The Frontiers of England*, and *The Road to safety*.

When the Second World War broke out Willert went into harness again, serving in the Ministry of Information from 1940 till 1945—at first as one of the liaison officers between the Head Office in London and the 12 Regional Offices, and then as Head of the Information Office for all Southern England, with headquarters at Reading.

Lady Willert, who was the daughter of Sir Walter Simpson, Bt., of Balabraes, Scotland, died in 1955. Their son survives.

March 13, 1973.

Prince William—See Gloucester.

Sir (Arthur) Leonard Williams—See Sir Len Williams.

Dr. Harley Williams, O.B.E., M.D., author and until shortly before his death Director-General of the Chest and Heart Association, died on April 12, 1974.

John Hargreaves Harley Williams was born at Birkenhead and attended school there. He began the medical course at Edinburgh University when he was still under 17 years of age and graduated M.B., Ch.B. in 1923. At the university he found the main interests of his life and a lasting love of Edinburgh. He was at once attracted to the work in the dispensary which Dr. Robert Philip had founded for the detection and care of tuberculous patients, and 56 years later when Williams retired from the Chest and Heart Association he was awarded its Sir Robert Philip medal. At the university he was editor of the student magazine and was an attractive pianist of classical music. In debate he made a spirited attack with a quick, provocative wit.

After graduation Williams worked in Stornoway, Isle of Lewis. He found there tuberculosis in an acute form and he wrote his first novel, *Northern Lights and Western Stars*, which has an evocative account of scenery and life in the Outer Hebrides. During a lifetime of writing three more novels followed and six volumes of biographies of over forty men and women, medical and political.

Harley Williams's great interest in the psychological aspects of organic disease was shown in *A Doctor Looks at Miracles*, his M.D. thesis was published as *A Century of Public Health in Britain*, and his last book, published in 1973, was *A Requiem for a Great Killer*—a history of tuberculosis.

In 1927 Harley Williams joined the National Association for the Prevention of Tuberculosis and as travelling lecturer throughout Great Britain he was probably the first doctor engaged whole-time in health education.

In 1939 he became Secretary-General of the National Association and Director-General when it was renamed the Chest and Heart Association in 1958. Williams fully used his talents to improve the detection of tuberculosis (by encouraging miniature X-rays), the treatment and after-care of patients and the training of doctors, nurses and social workers for this purpose. He spoke and wrote copiously, edited periodicals, arranged conferences at home and abroad, and organized visits between Britain and other countries, for the sharing of experience. He lectured in North America and India.

When modern drug treatment reduced the importance of tuberculosis in Britain, Williams gave more attention to the disease in many countries of the Commonwealth and to other chest diseases and heart disease.

He succeeded as a health educationist by his lively imagination and personality. He was a barrister of the Middle Temple, where he lived, and was married to Elizabeth Mackay Pascoe.

April 15, 1974.

Sir Len Williams, G.C.M.G., the man whose organizing ability helped the Labour Party to election victories in 1964 and 1966, died on December 27, 1972. He was 68.

Since 1968 Sir Leonard had been Governor-General of Mauritius. His big, slightly stooping figure, and decisive manner fitted into the pomp and circumstance of that office as readily as into the political battles to which his early life had attuned him. But he will be remembered mainly for his work at the Labour Party headquarters at Transport House as national agent and then, from 1962 to 1968, as general secretary.

He was a natural choice for the general secretaryship at the time of his appointment, not only because of his own personality, but because he had shouldered many of the responsibilities of the office during the illness of his predecessor, Morgan Phillips.* Moreover, he was not a man who was feared as a possible political rival.

He regarded his job as organization and devoted himself to it with a fierce determination. Inefficiency or laziness provoked him to outbursts of impatience which became something of a byword at Transport House.

However, he was liked and respected by almost everyone there, because of his open and direct character, qualities not always to be found in top men in the political world.

He did not seek to interfere in policy-making, but neither would he brook interference by others in his running of the party machine. Nor would he easily accept that the decisions of the party conference should be ignored by the Parliamentary leadership, even when they were the Government of the country. His appointment to Mauritius, not long before he would have reached retiring age, was followed by a struggle for the succession which eventually went to Harry Nicholas, in preference to Anthony Greenwood, by 14 votes to 12 on the national executive committee.

Arthur Leonard Williams was born at Birkenhead on January 22, 1904, and started work at the age of 14 as a junior railway porter in the Merseyside town. He joined the National Union of Railwaymen and at an unusually early age was made a branch official. He showed such promise that his union sponsored him, at 17, as a student at the old London Labour College, where he stayed for two years. He returned to work on the railway and joined the Independent Labour Party. When the I.L.P. decided to break with the Labour Party, he refused to be separated from the main stream of the working class movement.

In his early twenties he was appointed a full-time tutor-organizer by the National Council of Labour Colleges. For 12 years he conducted adult classes on Merseyside, in North Lancashire and in South Wales.

He was twice a Parliamentary Labour candidate—at Southport in 1929 and Winchester in 1935.

In 1936 he was appointed secretary of the Leeds Labour Party and took over the editorship of the *Leeds Weekly Citizen*, one of the oldest and most efficiently managed Labour papers. Six years later he was made Yorkshire Regional organizer and was credited with much of his party's success in the northern counties in the 1945 general election.

In 1946 he was transferred to the party's Transport House headquarters as Assistant National Agent and became the National Agent in 1951, a post he held until 1962.

He leaves a widow.

December 28, 1972.

Sir Thomas Parry-Williams—See Parry-.

Vera Williams—See Volkova.

Roger Williamson, the Leicester racing driver, who was killed in the Dutch Grand Prix on July 27, 1973 at the age of 25, was one of Britain's most promising young racing drivers. A distinguished career in grand prix racing had been predicted for him.

After some outstanding performances at the wheel of a Ford Anglia in saloon car racing, Williamson was taken under the wing of another Leicester motor racing enthusiast, Tom Wheatcroft, who during the past three years did much to further Williamson's progress in motor racing.

After moving into single-seater racing, Williamson became a formula three champion in 1970 at a time when competition in that class was at its height. He graduated into formula two, winning his first major victory at Monza in late June 1973.

In July the March-Ford which he was driving at Silverstone for his formula one debut was one of eight cars badly damaged in the multi-car accident at the beginning of the British Grand Prix. It was the replacement of that car that he was driving at Zandvoort. He lost control of it when lying in thirteenth place.

Williamson's talent as a racing driver had been widely acclaimed for several years. It is doubly sad that he should have met his death when seemingly on the threshold of a grand prix career.

July 28, 1973.

Sir Henry Willink, BT., P.C., M.C., Q.C., Master of Magdalene College, Cambridge, from 1948 until 1966; Vice-Chancellor of Cambridge University from 1953 to 1955; and a former Minister of Health, died on January 1, 1973 in Cambridge.

He was a man of exceptional gifts, and in his time played many parts. After a distinguished record of service in the First World War, he became a successful barrister, taking silk in 1935. Abandoning his legal practice soon after the outbreak of the Second World War, he entered Parliament and became Minister of Health. At the age of 53 he entered upon a third career, forsaking politics to become Master of Magdalene College, Cambridge, where perhaps his happiest days were passed. He found time for many interests outside the college and university, though in no sense neglecting these, and was in constant demand as chairman of Royal Commissions and other important committees.

Henry Urmston Willink was the son of William Edward Willink, F.R.I.B.A., of Diggle Bank, Liverpool, joint architect of the Cunard Building. Born on March 7, 1894, he was educated at Eton, where he was a King's Scholar, and later won the Newcastle Scholarship and also an entrance scholarship to Trinity College, Cambridge. His university career was cut short by the war of 1914, in which he distinguished himself in the R.F.A. (T.F.), reaching the rank of captain and acting major, and obtaining an M.C., the French Croix de Guerre, and mention in dispatches. He took his degree in 1919.

He was called to the Bar by the Inner Temple in 1920. His rise was rapid and by the time he took silk he was doing a large business in commercial and the best type of common law litigation. He was a standing counsel to the Board of Trade.

In June 1940 he was returned as Conservative and National Government member for North Croydon. Three months after becoming M.P. Willink made his entry into official life as a Commissioner for the London Region. This post he held until October 1943 and in the following month was appointed Minister of Health, and was sworn a member of the Privy Council.

One of his chief tasks in his new office was to implement the decision which the Government had taken in accepting the principle of a national health service. In February 1944 a White Paper was published setting out in detail the Government's proposals.

Willink was also active in preparing housing plans for peace, but Aneurin Bevan and other Labour members were critical. Willink's public statement that he hoped "to improve on Beveridge" did not help. Between the B.M.A. on the one hand, and Bevan and his friends on the other, the Minister's life was far from being a bed of roses, particularly when Nazi flying bombs and rockets increased the housing shortage.

When the Coalition broke up, Willink, in the short-lived "Caretaker" Government, retained the post of Minister of Health. Though the Government was routed at the General Election in the summer of 1945, Willink just managed to hold his seat.

In Opposition Willink was not happy. He was not a born political fighter, for one of his qualities, that of being able to see the other man's point of view, was a political weakness. But his personality and sincerity won him a host of friends, not confined to his own party.

In May 1947 he was appointed to the Mastership of Magdalene College, Cambridge, in succession to A. B. Ramsay. He quickly proved himself to be an admirable Master of Magdalene and was perhaps happier in this post than in any other of his career; he was outstanding as a host to visitors at the lodge and at the high table and to his undergraduates, in whom he took a great personal interest. It gave him great satisfaction also in the final years of his mastership—extended, to his great pleasure, by the invitation of the Fellows beyond the normal term—to preside over the college appeal, the success of which was largely achieved by the personal approach which he himself made to a very large number of Magdalene men. He had always a most jealous care to preserve all that was good against reforms which he felt too drastic. He was not opposed to change, but like a true Conservative needed to be convinced that the change really was for the better.

But his interests were not entirely confined to the college or to the university. On his appointment to Magdalene he became also vice-chairman of the Central Board of Finance of the Church of England and Chancellor of the dioceses of Norwich and of St. Edmundsbury and Ipswich, and in 1955 the Archbishop of Canterbury made him Dean of the Court of Arches, Master of the Court of Faculties and Vicar-General and Official Principal of the Province of Canterbury: he held many other offices in both Sees.

During his mastership of Magdalene he was made chairman of a Royal Commission on Betting, Lotteries and Gaming, which reported in 1951, recommending wide changes in the law, the most controversial being the reintroduction of cash betting shops. No action was taken for many years, in spite of the chairman's protest in a letter to *The Times* in 1955, but R. A. Butler four years later embodied most of the recommendations in a comprehensive Bill and subsequently much-criticized Act. He presided over a steering committee to study the formation of a College of General Practitioners, which reported in 1952, and was chairman of a committee on medical manpower which reported in 1957, but the report, which recommended a reduction in the annual supply of qualified doctors, came in for considerable criticism in later years.

The committee's calculations were shortly shown to have been fallacious. Their implementation by the Government of the day led to a reduction of places in medical schools which had a considerable bearing on the discontents of general practitioners within the Health Service in the immediate years following. The policy was reversed within five years.

In 1957 Willink examined the position of the minorities in Nigeria, and he subsequently became chairman of the Royal Commission on the Police. The commission's report, though cautious, led to substantial pay increases for the police and laid the groundwork for successive Home Secretaries, enabling them to break up the Victorian pattern into which police organization had ossified.

He married in 1923 Cynthia, daughter of H. Morley Fletcher, M.D., F.R.C.P., and had two sons and two daughters. His wife died in 1959. He married secondly in 1964 Mrs. Doris Preston. He is succeeded in the baronetcy, which he accepted in 1957, by his eldest son, Charles William Willink.

January 2, 1973.

Edmund Wilson, the American literary and cultural critic and commentator, died on June 12, 1972. He was 77.

Edmund Wilson was perhaps—as Sherman Paul's study of him in the year of his seventieth birthday emphasized—the pre-eminent American man of letters of his time. He was writer, critic, social analyst and representative intellectual; and though in various of these roles he was excelled by others—by his friend Scott Fitzgerald as novelist, for instance, though Wilson's *I Thought of Daisy* (1929) is an important and too-little-read book—he lived the literary life with a range and fullness achieved by no other American writer. His task, as he saw it, was to use his own life and literary imagination as a way of both responding to and criticizing the enormous and complicated history and development of his American society. As a writer of fiction he was important; as a literary critic, he was greatly influential.

His *Axel's Castle* (1931) was a classic introduction to the French symbolists and to an aesthetic of enormous importance in modern literature and art. But, as other critical studies like *The Triple Thinkers* (1938) and *The Wound and the Bow* (1941) make clear, he considered criticism as a humanistic and a social activity. And though he recognized that the paradox of the writer was the paradox of an obligation to art as well as to society, he himself persisted in pursuing a ceaseless dialogue with the world and his times. Literature, he said, is "a history of man's ideas and imaginings in the setting of the conditions which have shaped them". Much of his own writing took the form of reports en route—essays and memoirs, journalism and chronicle. But the route was a large one, and led him through many of the crucial experiences of his own culture and of

Western culture generally.

Born in Red Bank, New Jersey, on May 8, 1895, the son of Edmund Wilson and Helen Mather Kimball, he came from an American patrician background, many of whose manners he always continued to share. In *A Prelude,* the first of a projected five or six-volume version of his journals, he describes both his involvement in and his reaction against this background. At Princeton he knew Fitzgerald and John Peale Bishop, he became immersed in the developing intellectual *ferment* of his time, and his literary ambitions grew.

Immediately afterwards he became a reporter on the New York *Evening Sun.* On American entry into the war he served with the United States Army in the United States, England, and France. Returning to journalism, he was briefly managing editor of *Vanity Fair:* but, except for his associate editorship of the *New Republic* during 1926-31, where his articles attracted notice in left-wing circles, he did not tie himself down to a regular journalistic post.

In 1922 came his first volume. *The Undertaker's Garland,* with John Peale Bishop. Plays, fiction and verse followed; then *Axel's Castle,* his first critical work; then *The American Jitters,* a panorama of the economic situation in slump-time America, and the first of a series of chronicles recording the age.

More travel-sketches, criticism and plays were followed in 1940 by *To the Finland Station,* a study in the writing and acting of history, tracing the evolving pattern of the Socialist conception of history through the individual careers of those who tried to make revolutionary history by writing it. Wilson's half-sceptical involvement with socialism and historical hope informs *Europe Without Baedeker,* attacked in Britain on appearance in 1947 for its anti-British bias, but better seen as an unresolved attempt to postulate an egalitarian yet civilized future for the world. More chronicles —*Classics and Commercials* (1950), *The Shores of Light* (1952) and *The Bit Between My Teeth* (1965)—followed; and in other books Wilson looked at the American Civil War, the Dead Sea Scrolls, the American Indian, and Canada. He travelled widely, acquired new languages, and—often for the *New Yorker*—produced situation reports which his learning, curiosity and historical sense, often illuminated by a radical and at times even cranky independence, made into much more than occasional pieces. This persistently open curiosity meant that much of his work is not precisely resolved or complete (though that does not apply to his literary criticism); but the fruitful engagement with history was always his end in view, and is his final achievement.

Latterly his early books were reissued and he embarked on a biography by journal, starting with *A Prelude.* He was four times married; first in 1923 to Mary Blair, by whom he had a daughter; second in 1930 to Margaret Canby; third to Mary McCarthy, by whom he had a son; fourth to Elena Thornton, by whom he had a daughter.

June 13, 1972.

Sir Horace Wilson, G.C.B., G.C.M.G., C.B.E., who was Neville Chamberlain's chief confidant during the appeasement period leading to Munich, died on May 19, 1972. He was 89.

From 1939 to 1942 he was Permanent Secretary of the Treasury and official Head of the Civil Service.

Wilson possessed to a preeminent degree the gifts appropriate to a higher civil servant: clarity and rapidity of thought, impartiality, mediating skill, and (most useful to his harassed chiefs) the ability to summarize complicated matters faithfully and succinctly. These gifts were recognized and increasingly drawn on by three successive Prime Ministers, MacDonald, Baldwin and Chamberlain; until, freed from departmental duties and established in an office in 10, Downing Street, Wilson achieved a position of general influence unique in his profession.

In the personal diplomacy of appeasement he was Chamberlain's *fidus Achates* and one of the principal actors in the drama of Munich. He was eclipsed in the general ruin that overtook the reputations of the men who were implicated in that mistaken policy; and his long retirement was more truly a retirement than that achieved by most elderly and distinguished public servants.

Herbert von Dirksen, who was the German ambassador in London from May 1938, recorded his opinion that Chamberlain, "aware of the ingrained power of passive resistance of the Foreign Office officials to a line of foreign policy with which they were not in sympathy . . . relied in his foreign political plans on Sir Horace Wilson, 'Secretary of State in the Reich Chancellery'". Any suggestion the last phrase may carry that Wilson had the makings of a Quisling can be instantly dismissed. The point of Dirksen's remark is that the presence of Wilson at Chamberlain's elbow suited the book of the Nazi leaders; and the reason for this was not merely that he was good at seeing the German point of view.

So close was the rapport between Chamberlain's mind and Wilson's that the Prime Minister automatically turned to him as an agent for his diplomacy; while various Nazi emissaries believed that through their conversations with Wilson they were becoming privy to the workings of Chamberlain's mind. The two men shared the same attitude to war, the same belief in the efficacy of concessions, and the same credulity concerning Hitler's promises. Wilson can no more be made a scapegoat for the policies which followed from these promises than he can be exculpated by invoking the doctrine of ministerial responsibility. He made a fundamental misassessment of issues about which his official advice was sought, and the consequences of this misassessment were deplorable. Failure in such a matter and at such a time necessarily overshadows the long and distinguished service he rendered in other directions.

Horace John Wilson was the son of the late Henry Wilson, a furniture dealer, of Bournemouth, and was born on August 23, 1882. He was educated at Kurnella School, Bournemouth, and at the London School of Economics. He entered the Civil Service in 1900, in the old Second Division. His outstanding ability had impressed his many chiefs, notably Lloyd George when at the Board of Trade, and in 1915 he was made secretary to the Committee on Production and the Special Arbitration Tribunal at the Ministry of Munitions. At the end of the war in 1918 he was appointed an assistant secretary at the lately constituted Ministry of Labour. With Sir D. J. Shackleton he was associated in the Conciliation Department of the ministry. In 1921 he was made its Permanent Secretary.

He proved himself singularly successful in the settlement of labour disputes, and others often got the credit for what was really Wilson's doing, and his skilful intervention in the great cotton crisis of 1929 earned him the gratitude of the whole country. One of the great assets that Wilson brought to methods of conciliation was his absolute impartiality, and his good faith was never in doubt either by employers or employed. He had known every important trade union official and employers' organization long before there was a Ministry of Labour at all, so when it came to a crisis he was able to sum up accurately the elements with which he had to deal.

In 1930 the Prime Minister, Ramsay MacDonald, with a view to more active cooperation by the Government in developing and reorganizing industry both for production and marketing, appointed Wilson to the new post of Chief Industrial Adviser to the Government. His reorganization of the cotton industry in 1935 may in this connexion be regarded as his outstanding success.

In July 1932 the Chief Industrial Adviser (who was already chairman of the Imperial Economic Committee) accompanied the British delegation to the Imperial Economic Conference at Ottawa. There, his intimate knowledge of trade and industry and his vision into the heart of any question under discussion impressed all observers. He virtually took over the spade-work of the delegation, and at the time, it was said, was chiefly responsible for the agreement. On his return he was created a G.C.M.G.

In 1935 Wilson was seconded by the Prime Minister, Stanley Baldwin, for the new and somewhat anomalous post described as "for service with the Prime Minister", which appointment was to bring him three years later upon the stage of world politics; and when Chamberlain succeeded as Prime Minister in 1937, Wilson's services were retained in the same capacity. He and the new Prime Minister were old friends and their characters and tastes were similar and their minds moved in unison. Wilson's position, as may be supposed, was not viewed with complete approval by the departments, least of all by the Foreign Office, where feelings were not assuaged by the removal of the Permanent Under-Secretary, Sir Robert Vansittart, to the sinecure post of Chief Diplomatic Adviser to the Government towards the end of 1937. Foreign Office officials often had reason to resent Wilson's direct interference with their work.

The first notification the public had of Wilson's intimate association with foreign policy was when Chamberlain set off for Berchtesgaden on September 15, 1938, taking Wilson with him. It was Chamberlain's first journey by aeroplane and Wilson's first diplomatic mission, and their enterprise has been likened (by Sir Harold Nicolson*) to "the bright faithfulness of two curates entering a pub for the first time". Wilson accompanied the Prime Minister on his two other visits to Hitler later in the month. He also made one of his own, to Berlin on September 26.

This solo flight occurred soon after Hitler's Godesberg ultimatum to the Czechs had smashed Chamberlain's fair hopes of his previous meeting with the Führer. Hitler was due to deliver one of his apocalyptic harangues in the Sportspalast on the evening of the 26th, and Wilson was dispatched to confront him before he launched forth. He took a letter from Chamberlain, in which it was proposed that there should be direct negotiations between Germany and Czechoslovakia about the cession of territories in the Sudetenland, and that the British Government should be represented if both parties so desired. Wilson caught the Führer in a bad mood, impatient and irascible, and it was not until the next day that he had an opportunity to deliver the second leg of his message, which was that "if, in pursuit of her treaty obligations, France became actively engaged in hostilities against Germany, the United Kingdom would feel obliged to support her". Wilson was ranted at and hectored for transmitting this evanescent display of determination on the part of the British Government, and he seems to have supported the ordeal with his customary imperturbability.

Munich was a disillusionment neither for Chamberlain nor for Wilson, and the latter's continuing explorations of the possibility of a settlement with Germany came to the surface again in July 1939. Herr Wohlthat, who held subordinate economic responsibilities in the German Government, was over in London for a whaling conference. He was invited to see Wilson, who presented him with a memorandum setting out heads of agreement which might be reached between the two countries. The paper, which Wohlthat thought had the

approval of the Prime Minister, included proposals for a joint declaration to abstain from aggression, for limitation of armaments, and for economic cooperation. Wilson's visitor gained the impression that the British Government were looking out for some way in which they could disembarrass themselves of their commitments to Poland; and Wilson "said on parting that he saw the possibility of a common foreign trade policy for the two greatest European states". Wohlthat, who was beginning to feel out of his depth as the recipient of these important confidences, asked for instructions as to what reply he should return. None has been found.

Ribbentrop frowned on the conversations (Wohlthat being Goering's man); and indeed, although the overtures are indicative of the sort of hopes Wilson was still capable of entertaining, and although they were interpreted in Berlin as further evidence of British compliance, they were of small intrinsic importance since German policy was by then already set on another course.

Meanwhile early in 1939 Wilson had been promoted Permanent Secretary of the Treasury and Head of the Civil Service in succession to Sir Warren Fisher. It was a position he was clearly destined to achieve, and one to which his talents and experience well suited him. Had it not been for the unhappy excursus into diplomacy which he undertook at Chamberlain's insistence, this final promotion would have rounded off a blameless and orthodox career.

He was made G.C.B. in 1937. He was an Hon. LL.D. of Aberdeen and Liverpool. He married in 1908 Emily, daughter of the late John Sheather of Beckley. They had one son and two daughters.

May 26, 1972.

Walter Winchell, the American journalist and broadcaster, who died on February 20, 1972 at the age of 74, was for many years one of the best known of all the columnists writing for the newspapers of the United States.

"Other columnists may print it—I make it public", said Winchell, who was a pioneer of modern gossip-writing. His self-description, typical of his brash, egotistical manner, was remarkably accurate.

Millions read "On Broadway", his daily column that appeared locally in the *New York Daily Mirror* and was syndicated nationally; and more millions listened to his weekly radio broadcasts that he addressed to "Mr. and Mrs. America—and all the ships at sea."

"W.W.," as he often styled himself, or "Mrs. Winchell's little boy, Walter," purveyed a mixture of intimate news about personalities, mostly in show business and politics; "inside" items about business and finance; bits and pieces about the underworld; denunciations of Italian and German

fascism; diatribes against communism; puffs for people, stocks and events that pleased him—and a large smattering of innuendos.

He was born the son of a second-generation Jewish immigrant in a poor district of New York on April 7, 1897, and left school at the age of 14 to become a music hall song-and-dance man. He saw service in the United States Navy in the First World War. After the war, back in vaudeville, he began to put up a typewritten gossip sheet called "Newsense" on the rehearsal board of the troupe he worked with.

Then he began to submit show business gossip to *Billboard* and later to *Vaudeville News,* for which weekly he went to work as a reporter-cum-advertising salesman. The *New York Evening Graphic* hired Winchell as dramatic critic in 1924 and five years later the Hearst organization, realizing his potential as a columnist, engaged him. He served them for more than 30 years until the death of the *New York Daily Mirror.* He moved to another Hearst New York newspaper, the *Journal American,* and then to a combination of this newspaper with two others, the *Herald Tribune* and the *World Telegraph.*

February 22, 1972.

Professor Edgar Wind, Professor Emeritus of the History of Art in the University of Oxford and Honorary Fellow of Trinity College, Oxford, died on September 12, 1971. He was 71.

Edgar Wind was born in Berlin in 1900, and educated in the Universities of Berlin, Freiburg and Hamburg; in 1922 he took his doctorate in the history of art; he was also, however, a philosopher by vocation; his teaching career, and his publications, reflect this dual interest.

After having taught philosophy at the University of North Carolina (1925-27), he went back to Hamburg as a Privatdozent at the university, and became a research assistant at the Warburg Institute in 1928. The institute at that time gathered round the Faustian figure of Aby Warburg such outstanding scholars as Saxl and Panofsky.

When it was transferred to London in 1933 Wind became its deputy director and a joint editor of *A Bibliography on the Survival of the Classics;* at the same time he was honorary lecturer in philosophy at University College (1939-42).

The next 13 years he spent again in America as Professor of Art in the University of Chicago, then as Professor of Philosophy and of Art at Smith College. During that period he was visiting scholar of the American Academy in Rome, and he lectured extensively in the United States. His talent for lecturing was unsurpassed for ease and brilliance, erudition and wit. These qualities dazzled his Oxford audiences when he was invited to give the Chichele lectures in 1954; when the chair of the History of Art was founded in 1955 in the University of Oxford he became its first incumbent, and a Fellow of Trinity.

A powerful personality, with a belligerent temper disguised under a suave manner, he soon inflamed controversy; but even his critics agreed on his rare gifts. A bewitching conversationalist, he also knew how to stimulate interest in his newly imported discipline. His lectures on Michelangelo, Raphael, Leonardo, eighteenth century English painting, and modern art exerted a truly magnificent attraction; they drew extraordinary numbers; but he also conducted seminars on aesthetic and iconographic problems for the happy few; and he applied his formidable learning to solving the most recondite problems in his favourite field, the Rinascimenta; he explored enigmatic aspects of Venetian humanism (*The Feast of the Gods*, 1948); and his *Pagan Mysteries in the Renaissance* (1958) combined once more, with supreme skill, the approach of the philosopher and that of the iconographer. The aesthetician revealed again his full brilliance in the Reith lectures which Wind delivered in 1960, and which were published under the title *Art and Anarchy*.

He married in 1942 Margaret Kellner.

September 18, 1971.

Wolfgang Windgassen, the German tenor and producer, died in Stuttgart at the age of 60, on September 8, 1974.

He was born at Annemasse, Switzerland, in June 1914 of German parents; his father was Fritz Windgassen, leading tenor of the Stuttgart Opera from 1923 to 1944 and his mother was the soprano Vally von der Osten, sister of Eva von der Osten the first Octavian in *Der Rosenkavalier*. Windgassen heard his first opera when nine years of age, d'Albert's *Tiefland*, in which both his parents sang leading roles, and he decided to become a singer. He studied in Stuttgart with Maria Ranzow and Alfons Fischer and made his debut in 1941 at Pforzheim as Alvaro in *La Forza del Destino*.

After the end of the Second World War he was engaged by the Stuttgart Opera where he sang regularly from 1945 to 1972, appearing first in the Italian repertory and in such roles as Tamino, Hoffmann and Florestan. In 1949 he began to study the Wagnerian repertory with his father and in 1950 sang his first Siegmund. In the same year he appeared in a Wagner concert in Munich conducted by Hans Knappertsbusch* who suggested to Wieland Wagner* that he engage him for Parsifal at the first postwar Bayreuth Festival. Windgassen accordingly made his Bayreuth debut in the summer of 1951 and sang there regularly until 1970 as Parsifal, Siegmund, Siegfried, Lohengrin, Tannhäuser, Walther, Erik, Loge and Tristan.

He quickly established himself as the leading *Heldentenor* in postwar opera and appeared regularly at Covent Garden in the Wagnerian repertory between 1955 and 1966 and at the Royal Festival Hall with the Stuttgart Opera in 1955 and at the Edinburgh Festival in 1958. He made his United States debut at the Metropolitan Opera, New York, in 1957 and sang regularly at the Vienna State Opera, La Scala, Milan, and other leading European houses. His repertory also included Adolar in *Euryanthe*, Rienzi the emperor in *Die Frau ohne Schatten* and *Otello*.

In 1970 he began to produce opera and from 1972 until his death was opera director at Stuttgart. Windgassen's voice was light by prewar *Heldentenor* standards but he knew how to conserve it and sang with great feeling and musicality. Few Tristans or Siegfrieds have been able to impart such beauty to the lyrical portions of their music.

September 10, 1974.

The recent history of British Monarchy presents no figure of stranger or more contrasted interest than that of the **Duke of Windsor,** who died at his home in Paris on May 28, 1972—the only British Sovereign who, of his own will, resigned the Crown.

In early manhood he possessed—he held it all his life to a considerable degree—a magnetic quality which made him one of the most popular characters in the world. In his ways and tastes he was of his age, charming to those who met him, and impatient of all except the minimum of ceremonial. He was, too, a remarkable speaker and had many of a leader's gifts. In the years after the 1914-18 War he seemed the embodiment of a new era in which youth had come into its own. He became the hope of an Empire which, knowing him, was proud to possess him, and the envy of foreign peoples. When, as King Edward VIII, he succeeded to the Throne, his popularity had scarcely diminished, and his subjects throughout the Empire felt assured of a reign which would be both "happy and glorious". That it was not, and that there was much unhappiness and little surviving glory, is, sadly indeed, a matter of history. But the manner of his going should not be allowed to eclipse the preceding years of strenuous service to the Commonwealth and its peoples.

His father's views on discipline allowed the young Prince but little freedom; and the Navy, with its strict code and proud tradition, reinforced an upbringing of stern imperatives. He was contented in it, worked hard, and although in some ways curiously immature, he was popular and well reported on. Then he was taken away and sent to Oxford. In his dismay at this course, which was by no means to his liking, and in his introduction there for the first time to a relaxed and tolerant society, may be traced the beginning of an impatience with older heads and with their counsels of prudence. Oxford brought out no latent aptitude for study in the Prince, and before war came in 1914 it had already been decided that he should go down and take a commission in the Grenadier Guards.

In France and Flanders he proved that he possessed courage in a high degree. So much so that his constant and often successful efforts to reach the front line were an embarrassment to his commanding officers. There he found, not for the last time, how irksome could be the restrictions imposed on him by his station in life. After the war came the triumphal series of Dominion tours and visits abroad, which, though raising him to a pinnacle of popularity, placed a heavy strain on his physically nervous constitution.

By the time of his accession he had become very much a man of his age. He was impatient of tradition for its own sake, he had developed a social conscience about urban squalor and the armies of unemployed, he was an ally of change. He had no taste for the solid domesticity and stately rhythm of his father's way of life, preferring a less predictable programme and more stimulating company. His private life and his public routine had grown apart. These characteristics, applauded as modern in a Prince of Wales, were, in a profoundly conservative society, less readily accepted in a King. But Edward VIII was not a man to play a role in a way that was consistently false to his character. He had ideas about modernizing the monarchy, of adapting the tone of its constitutional functions to the changing conditions of society. He thought to dispense with some of the ceremonial, and if this was found impossible he suffered it with a not very good grace. He entered upon drastic economies in the royal estates, which hurt the feelings and the prospects of many faithful retainers. In his impatience of some of the business of state his former courtesy was known to desert him. These rather precipitous changes might have been tolerated and later approved, given time. But before the first painful impression had faded his modernity in the matter of marriage and divorce had brought his reign to an end.

He was no doubt right in thinking that the movement of opinion was in the direction of his own views about the remarriage of divorced persons. But he failed altogether to distinguish between what people will approve of in themselves and among their acquaintances and what they will approve of in their Sovereign. Nor did he appear to understand the full consequences in this respect of his being the head of the Church of England. During the years after the 1914-18 War he had been greatly attracted by a succession of women, none of whom was free to marry him; finally, when he was 40, he fell deeply in love with a married woman who already had two husbands living. He was brought to see, though it seems to have been anything but clear to him at first, that he could not marry Mrs. Simpson as King without precipitating a grave constitutional convulsion. So he took what he insisted in his last broadcast was necessarily his decision and his alone: for the sake of his love, he who had been born with the ability to sustain it at its highest, renounced the greatest of all crowns.

Thereafter his life presented in its public aspect the appearance of tragedy. The exception taken to his marriage, having lost him his Throne, continued so as to perpetuate his exile and, except for his term as Governor of the Bahamas, to deny him office in the service of the Commonwealth. The judgment that he brought these consequences on himself does not diminish the tragic contrast between the adulation in which he was once held and the long functionless years that followed. He bore with dignity and without bitterness the equivocal status of a royal duke with no public role to fill, and found in his fateful marriage much to compensate him for the sense of loss.

The Duke of Windsor was born Prince Edward of York at White Lodge, Richmond Park, on Saturday, June 23, 1894. Never before in the history of these islands had the reigning Sovereign seen three male descendants in the direct line of inheritance; and, during the remainder of her life, a deep affection united the aged Queen Victoria and the Boy Prince. Three days after his birth she drove from Windsor to see him. On July 16 he was christened by the Archbishop of Canterbury (Dr. Benson) by the family names of Edward Albert Christian, to which were added those of the four patron saints of the British Isles, George Andrew Patrick David. Officially he used to sign himself "Edward P.", but to his family and close friends he was and remained David.

The chief landmarks of his early years were the departure of his parents on their world tour of 1901, when he and their other children were constantly with King Edward and Queen Alexandra; the death and funeral of Queen Victoria, and the Accession and Coronation of King Edward VII. Apart from his share in these public events, he lived the quiet, active, happy life of an ordinary English boy. He romped and played rounders with King Edward VII, who loved and understood him thoroughly, practised cricket with boys from Eton, and football with others from the Sandringham estate. He did his lessons with Mme. Bricka, his mother's former governess, and with H. P. Hansell, the Ludgrove and Rossall master, who was his tutor from 1902 until he went to the 1914-18 War.

Hansell, whose opinion it was that the Prince would have been better off at a boarding school, did what he could to reproduce the conditions of a school in the regimen of private tuition. He was, on the evidence of his pupil's recollection, a conscientious but uninspiring teacher. The task of grounding the Prince in the doctrines of the Church of England was entrusted to Canon J. N. Dalton (the father of Hugh Dalton*), who some 30 years

earlier had been selected by Queen Victoria to be tutor to his new pupil's father. The canon had only qualified success, though he did arouse in the Prince a certain dread of the society of Church dignitaries which was to accompany him throughout life.

He learnt to talk French and German, to recite long lists of poems, and he studied dancing, singing, and voice production. He worked too at his lathe at Sandringham and learnt the elements of seamanship in a model brig on Virginia Water. The more formal part of the curriculum was geared to the entrance examination at the Royal Naval College; and when his mathematics looked like letting him down they were brought on by special coaching. He was in some trepidation lest he fail the examination, for he stood at that time in considerable awe of his father, whose stern admonitions and insistence on punctilio and punctuality made, naturally enough, a deep impression on him.

In 1907, just before his thirteenth birthday, he went to Osborne, to live the life of the ordinary cadet. In 1909 he passed on to Dartmouth. He worked hard and happily in the engineering shops; was whip to the beagles; had measles; and did his fair share of punishment drills. In 1910, while he was still there, King Edward VII died and he became Duke of Cornwall. On his sixteenth birthday he was created Prince of Wales. The next day he was confirmed by the Archbishop of Canterbury (Dr. Davidson). In March 1911 he left the College. On June 10 he was invested with the Garter and in July went to Caernarvon for his investiture, the first of 19 English Princes of Wales who was invested in the Principality. The ceremony in the castle was picturesque and splendid. As its Constable Lloyd George received him, and, thanks to his coaching, the Prince was able to introduce a phrase or two of Welsh into his speech. He was afterwards to use them with telling effect upon Welsh audiences.

In October, 1912, he went up to Magdalen College, Oxford, accompanied by his valet, H. P. Hansell, and an equerry, Major the Hon. William Cadogan, to live (so far as this retinue allowed) the normal life of an undergraduate. During his vacations he paid two visits to Germany and one to Scandinavia, when he gave early expression in his diary to his impatience with ceremonial: "What rot and a waste of time, money, and energy all these state visits are! ! This is my only remark on all this unreal show and ceremony! ! "

At Oxford he played football with the Magdalen second XI, joined the University O.T.C., ran with the beagles, began to hunt, saw through Sir Herbert Warren, the head of his college, and read with Sir William Anson and other hand-picked tutors. No particular love of scholarship was kindled in him, and it was decided that he should leave at the end of the academic year in 1914 and go for a period of soldiering.

When war came he was gazetted to the Grenadier Guards, but Lord Kitchener, to

the Prince's deep distress, would not allow him to proceed to France. Seeking an interview with Lord Kitchener, he asked what it would matter if he were killed since he had four brothers. Kitchener replied that the line of battle was not then stabilized and he could not take the risk of his being captured. A little later, however, he had his way and in November he was posted to the staff of G.H.Q. in France. He was next assigned to H.Q. Guards Division, where he contrived to spend much of his time in or near the front and was occasionally under fire. He was not, however, allowed to return to regimental duties. After a visit to the Mediterranean theatre and Egypt he was appointed to H.Q. 14 Corps, and in 1917 moved with the corps headquarters to Italy, to shore up the defences after Caporetto, and there made the acquaintance of the King of Italy. Throughout his service he was only too ready to endanger his life and he had the satisfaction of one narrow escape.

Less than a year after the Armistice he sailed for Canada in H.M.S. Renown. He went with a war reputation which made him the comrade of every veteran. He had in addition "the smile that conquered Canada", the appeal of his boyishness, and his own way of identifying himself with the peoples among whom he moved. His personal dignity when he asserted it required no accessories, his memory for faces was exceptional, and he could talk well. Moreover, his voice, memory and resourcefulness as a public speaker, together with his command of French, gave him an immense additional advantage. Lloyd George did not exaggerate his qualities in calling him "our greatest Ambassador".

On August 12, 1919, he struck at St. John's, Newfoundland, the key-note of his tour. After the official reception the inhabitants, many of whom had served in the war, surged round him, an enthusiastic escort. They enjoyed themselves immensely. So did he. It was the same all over Canada and in Washington and New York as well. Right across the continent to Victoria and back again there was never a moment's slackening of the delirium of welcome. It was such that the newspaper correspondents were suspected of exaggerating it. To do so would have been well-nigh impossible. Before long he was saying that he was just a Canadian, and later he bought a ranch to prove it.

In Quebec he was a French Canadian, talking the language of the people. In the Eastern Provinces he became an Easterner; in the Western, a Westerner; to the farmers, a farmer; to all a sportsman and to the ex-Service men everywhere one of themselves. Above all, he never patronized. The task was heavy, but he made it seem easy by the pleasure which he so plainly took in it.

In March 1920 the Renown sailed with him again, by Barbados, the Mexican coast to San Diego and the Panama Canal, to Honolulu across the Line (he was ducked by Father Neptune) to Fiji and at last to

Auckland, which was sighted on the morning of April 24. His tour of both the North and South Islands of New Zealand was triumphal. In Australia, too, he came, and smiled, and conquered. He sailed away on August 19; but Australia had laid a spell on him: never to be effaced.

He went home victorious but, it was felt, in need of rest. The claims upon him and his own active disposition would not, however, permit it. Public speeches, appeals for ex-Service men, printers' orphans, the Boy Scouts, and many other objects followed each other rapidly. The conferring of honorary degrees by Oxford and Cambridge, and of a Fellowship of the Royal College of Surgeons, created important occasions. It was only indeed in the late summer of 1921 that he took a holiday, and then he used it chiefly to prepare for the arduous undertaking of his Indian tour.

Since the days of the Indian Mutiny disloyalty to the Crown had never been so widespread as in 1921, and to pit the personality of the Prince against the influence of the extremist agitators was a grave and anxious experiment. It was chiefly his individual charm and his real sympathy with his father's Indian subjects which carried it through. On October 26 he sailed again in the Renown from Portsmouth. After a long exhaustive and exhausting journey he returned in July.

Shortly afterwards he was elected Captain of the Royal and Ancient Golf Club at St. Andrews and was invested as Senior Grand Warden of the United Grand Lodge of Ancient Free and Accepted Masons of England.

In March 1925 he sailed in the Repulse to Africa. It was a time of acute political division in South Africa; but, thanks to a loyal unanimity of welcome given by the respective leaders of the parties, General Hertzog and General Smuts, and to his own unfailing tact, the harmony of his tour was undisturbed by racial or party feeling. He travelled all through the Union area and on to Southern and Northern Rhodesia.

He was away for seven months and on reaching England received magnificent ovations both at Portsmouth and in London. Perhaps, however, the governing feeling of the public was that he needed the rest he had so richly earned. In the winter of 1925-26 he hunted, for the second time broke a collarbone, and rode in one or two regimental point-to-points. He took much delight in the hunting field and in the company it provided, at Melton Mowbray in particular. His frequent falls, however, attracted the solicitous notice of the King, who requested him, and of the Prime Minister (Ramsay MacDonald), who appealed to him, to give up the sport. During the next four or five years the Prince's life was one of a perpetual round of visits to every part of Great Britain varied by occasional trips to France and Spain and rather longer stays in Africa and Canada. By 1930 he must have set foot in more British towns than even the hardiest of commercial

travellers and delivered a greater number of speeches than any politician in the same length of time. Their range was as wide and varied as his travels.

In the autumn of 1928 he went to East Africa with the Duke of Gloucester. While there he learnt of his father's illness and sped home from Dar es Salaam in what was then the undreamed-of time of 10 days. During King George V's convalescence, which entailed extra work for him, he sold his stud of hunters, gave up point-to-point racing, and instead took to flying. Later he purchased a light Moth aeroplane of his own, the precursor of others. Thus he saved the time he always grudged.

The serious illness of King George V marked a change in the Prince's life. Before 1928 he was acquiring experience of the Empire and the outer world; after it he took an increasing interest in national affairs, particularly in trade and unemployment. In 1931 he undertook the most important of all his later visits abroad. Accompanied by Prince George (afterwards Duke of Kent) he went to open the British Exhibition at Buenos Aires. The Princes also travelled through Peru, Bolivia, Chile, and Brazil, spending their time almost exclusively with South Americans.

When in 1931 the economic crisis raised unemployment to an appalling level, the Prince felt that the efforts made by the State, the municipalities, and industry were not enough. He thought that through his experience of the British Legion, Toc H, the National Council of Social Service, and the Boy Scouts organization, which he had always been eager to assist, he had detected a remedy in voluntary service. At a meeting at the Albert Hall he said there was no central machinery which could provide a substitute for the good neighbour. He did not rest content with speech making. In April 1932 he began a series of visits to unemployment clubs all over the country. In the year of his accession some 200,000 unemployed men and women were associated in occupational clubs as a result of the campaign he started. Yet he was often uncomfortably conscious of the contrast between the eminence of his position and the political importance it forced upon him.

The formal splendour of great houses never appealed to him. His favourite residence was Fort Belvedere, a country house near Virginia Water which his father assigned to him in 1930 with the words, "What could you possibly want that old place for? Those damn weekends, I suppose." In the Fort, as he called it, he enjoyed as nowhere else the pleasures of privacy and possession. There indeed he spent much more time with his own small circle than was generally known, and latterly slept only now and then in London. Consequently, although he performed his public duties, he withdrew increasingly from London social life. This, and his preference for company which could not be admitted to his father's Court—a matter of general comment in London society—caused

anxiety to the advisers of the Crown and, not least, to King George V himself.

He had, of course, his various hobbies, into which he threw himself with tremendous though sometimes transitory enthusiasm—music, hunting, flying, golf, angling and gardening. He also began to take a keen interest in pictures, became at his own request a Trustee of the National Gallery, and although his knowledge was not deep, he was a first-class guide to the royal collection.

In 1930 the Prince's friendship with Mr. and Mrs. Simpson began. Mrs. Simpson was born on June 19, 1896, the only child of Teakle Walter Warfield, whose family had long settled in Maryland. Her mother was a Virginian. In 1915 she married Lieutenant Spencer, of the American Navy, but she divorced him in 1927, and in 1928 married in London Ernest Simpson, a member of a shipping firm, who had served in the Coldstream Guards during the 1914-18 War. The Simpsons became known in some Anglo-American circles, and the Prince, who first met her casually at a party, became attracted by her amusing talk and gifts as a hostess. He began to entertain her and her husband frequently at Fort Belvedere. In 1934 she and her aunt, Mrs. Merriman, were among his guests when he cruised in his chartered yacht Rosaura along the Riviera. In February 1935 Mrs. Simpson, with other guests of his, was with him at the winter sports at Kitzbühel.

About this time he took enthusiastically to gardening at Fort Belvedere, and Mrs. Simpson helped him. By 1934 he was deeply in love with her. In 1914 Queen Alexandra had done her best to engage him to a charming and suitable princess. He refused even to consider it and told his grandmother that he would in no circumstances marry any woman unless he loved her. The sincerity of his devotion to Mrs. Simpson is beyond doubt. There is authority for believing that as early as 1935 he did not discount the possibility of renouncing his right to the Throne in order that he might marry Mrs. Simpson, but he had not spoken to the King before the latter's illness and death removed the opportunity.

On January 20, 1936, the life of King George V closed in peace and the Prince of Wales ascended the Throne as King Edward VIII. The next day he flew to London in his Dragon aeroplane for his Accession Council. To it he pledged himself to follow in his father's footsteps; to the Empire he broadcast: "I am better known to most of you as the Prince of Wales—as a man who, during the war and since, has had the opportunity of getting to know the people of nearly every country in the world under all conditions and circumstances. And, although I speak to you as the King, I am still the same man who has had that experience and whose constant effort it will be to continue to promote the well-being of his fellow men."

He had, he protested many years later, no intention of upsetting the proud traditions of the Court. "All that I ever had in mind was to throw open the windows a little and to let into the venerable institution some of the fresh air that I had become accustomed to breathe as Prince of Wales." However that may be, he managed to create a draught that chilled the warmth of his own reception. For instance, the 20 "privileged bodies" to whom custom accords the right of presenting singly their loyal addresses to a new Sovereign he decided to receive *en bloc*—"a most unfortunate decision" as one of the disappointed parties said. In matters of ceremony and official business he was apt to question things which had long been immune from question. He shocked his advisers by asking if it was necessary to preface his Speech from the Throne at the opening of Parliament with a declaration maintaining the Protestant succession. It was necessary.

Then in March he abolished the royal stud at Sandringham, which had been formed in 1877; an act which caused circles enjoying much influence to fear for the soundness of the King's judgment in matters of moment. He also set in train measures of economy in the royal estates which caused hard feelings among his father's old retainers. These innovations, which showed that he intended to be King after his own fashion, occasioned apprehension in those connected with the Court who believed his predecessors' methods to be right if not immutable.

On July 16, when he was returning to Buckingham Palace, after presenting colours to battalions of the Guards, a man threw a loaded revolver into the roadway on Constitution Hill. It fell between the King and the following troops. He saw what happened, reined his horse, and after a surprised look in the direction from which the missile came, calmly proceeded to the centre gateway of the Palace and took the salute as had been arranged. The assailant was afterwards convicted at the Central Criminal Court of wilfully producing a pistol near the person of the King with the intention of alarming His Majesty. The judge who tried him was satisfied that there was no intention of harming the King, and sentenced him to 12 months' imprisonment with hard labour.

In July he unveiled the Canadian National Memorial at Vimy Ridge. He had intended to spend August at Cannes, but cancelled his arrangements as he did not wish to add to the responsibilities of the French authorities, already much increased by the civil war in Spain. Instead he chartered Lady Yule's yacht Nahlin, and left in early August for a cruise along the Dalmation coast. He travelled incognito as Duke of Lancaster, though a Cabinet Minister was in attendance for part of the time. Some friends accompanied him; among them was Mrs. Simpson, whose society he had courted no less assiduously since his accession. He visited the Prince Regent of Yugoslavia and the King of the Hellenes, and went to Istanbul, where he established

friendly relations with Mustapha Kemal. In September he returned overland, visiting President Miklas and Chancellor von Schuschnigg on his way.

Scarcely was he home before he had a house party at Balmoral for Mrs. Simpson, and asked some prominent guests to it. The Duke and Duchess of York, and the Duke and Duchess* of Kent, and other members of the Royal Family also either visited or stayed at the Castle. If it were intended for the social advantage of Mrs. Simpson it was scarcely a success. Leaving Scotland, Mrs. Simpson went to stay at Felixstowe and was therefore able to enter her action for divorce at the Assizes at Ipswich. Mr. Simpson did not appear or contest the case and, after what is known as hotel evidence had been tendered, a decree *nisi* was granted on October 27.

In November King Edward VIII opened Parliament, and after a visit to the Home Fleet at Portland made a tour of the distressed areas in South Wales, showing deep sympathy with the personal histories he learnt from talks with unemployed men on the dole. The emotion aroused prompted him to declare that "something will be done", which led to a comparison by certain newspapers of the King's personal concern with the supposed apathy of his Government.

For months American papers of a sensational kind had been enlarging on the King's friendship with Mrs. Simpson with preposterous exaggeration and frequently sheer invention, and in November 1936 had announced his forthcoming marriage. The most responsible American and Canadian journals began at the same time to publish statements which betrayed anxiety and bewilderment at the extraordinary campaign of publicity. Though enough of the facts were well known in every newspaper office in Britain, no public reference to it appeared in any reputable journal there until December 2. On the previous day the Bishop of Bradford (Dr. Blunt), speaking at his diocesan conference on the Coronation Service, commended the King "to God's grace, which he will so abundantly need, as we all need it, if he is to do his duty faithfully. We hope he is aware of his need. Some of us wish that he gave more positive signs of his awareness". The press, realizing that the American campaign of publicity had gone beyond that side of the King's life which might be regarded as private, broke, first in the North and then in London, its self-imposed ordinance of restraint. The Bishop said he was surprised at this.

Meanwhile by October 18 the Prime Minister (Stanley Baldwin) had become sufficiently perturbed to ask for an urgent audience of the King. It was principally the knowledge of the impending Simpson divorce case that caused the Prime Minister to break the studied inactivity with which he had been watching the approaching crisis. The audience took place at Fort Belvedere on the following Tuesday. Baldwin expressed his fears, explaining the peril

he saw to the integrity of the British Monarchy. His immediate object was to see if Mrs. Simpson could be persuaded to withdraw her divorce petition. In this he received no encouragement from the King. On November 16 the King sent for Baldwin again and, having been told that the marriage was not one that would receive the approbation of the country, he declared that he intended to marry Mrs. Simpson as soon as she was free and that if the Government opposed the marriage he was "prepared to go". Baldwin answered, "Sir, that is most grievous news, and it is impossible for me to make any comment on it today". On November 25 there was a further audience at which the King mooted the possibility of a morganatic marriage. Baldwin said that his first reaction was that Parliament would not pass such a Bill, but at the King's request he agreed to consult the Cabinet and the Prime Ministers of the Dominions. At their next meeting on December 2 Baldwin assured the King that such a proposal was impracticable. The issue was therefore narrowed to one fateful choice. In all the conversations the King had repeated that if he went he would go with dignity and with as little disturbance of his Ministers and his people as possible.

In the course of the memorable speech in the House of Commons in which, after the King's final decision had been disclosed, Baldwin gave an account of the preceding events, he asserted that there had been no kind of conflict. The King's action had been dictated by a determination to avoid the gossip and rumours which would be dangerous not only at home but throughout the Empire to the moral force of the Crown. His own efforts had been directed in trying to help the King to make the choice which he had not made, and they failed. But Baldwin felt that he had left nothing undone which he could have done to move the King from his decision. He added that on December 9 the Cabinet had pleaded for reconsideration and had been told that the King was unable to alter his mind. The Bill of Abdication was passed on December 11 and at 1.52 p.m. on that day the Royal Assent was given; the reign of King Edward VIII ended and that of King George VI began.

The same evening "His Royal Highness Prince Edward" broadcast to the Empire from Windsor Castle. "You all know," he said, "the reasons which have impelled me to renounce the throne. . . . But you must believe me when I tell you that I have found it impossible to carry the heavy burden of responsibility and to discharge my duties as King as I would wish to do without the help and support of the woman I love. And I want you to know that the decision I have made has been mine and mine alone. This was a thing I had to judge, entirely for myself; the other person concerned has tried up to the last to persuade me to take a different course." There had never, he went on to say, been any constitutional difference between Ministers and himself or between himself and Parliament. "Bred in the constitutional traditions by my father, I should never have allowed any such issue to arise." In conclusion he added: "I now quit altogether public affairs, and I lay down my burden. It may be some time before I return to my native land. But I shall always follow the fortunes of the British race and Empire with profound interest, and if at any time in the future I can be found of service to his Majesty in a private station I shall not fail."

In his own account of the Abdication drama, published some 15 years afterwards in his memoirs, the Duke of Windsor did not disguise his feeling of resentment against Baldwin, whose part in the fateful proceedings he understood as that of a deep and relentless politician bent upon creating an alignment of forces—the Established Church, the Conservative Party organization, *The Times*, and the Opposition leaders included—sufficiently powerful to force the King's hand. The impression does not do justice to Baldwin, but it is easy to understand how it arose. As the strain of the crisis increased, so did the King's isolation. At the climax he retired to Fort Belvedere—for the wholly creditable reason that he did not want to excite popular demonstrations by his appearance in London—and was there besieged by reporters and photographers. He chose, or was able, to consult chiefly those who wished him to keep both his intended marriage and his Throne; and he had, early in the proceedings, withdrawn his confidence in matters relating to his marriage, from his Private Secretary, Lord Hardinge of Penshurst. In these circumstances it was easy for him to imagine a vast and only partly discernible conspiracy working against him.

At a late stage, urged by some of his unofficial advisers and detecting signs of a popular movement in his favour, he entertained the idea of challenging his Ministers and appealing direct to his subjects. On reflection he put the project firmly aside in the belief that it would do irreparable damage to the institution of the monarchy. He believed, however, after the storm, as he had believed before it, that with a better disposed set of ministerial advisers it should have been possible for him both to have continued his reign with the full confidence of his peoples and to have taken Mrs. Simpson for his wife.

The first act of the new King was to declare his brother Duke of Windsor. No minor title was added. Subsequently, since it had lapsed, he restored to the Duke the membership of all his orders of Knighthood and his ranks in the Royal Navy, Army, and Royal Air Force. By letters patent of May 1937, the King declared that his brother should be entitled to hold and enjoy for himself alone the title of Royal Highness, but that neither his wife nor descendants should possess it. It was a limitation that the Duke of Windsor deeply resented. Arms were recorded for the Duke. They

were those he bore as King differenced by a label of three points charged with the Imperial Crown proper. All the Duke's official income had ceased; but no application was made to the Parliament for a grant since it was understood that adequate income would be provided for him by the other members of the Royal Family in concert. King George VI purchased outright the Sandringham and Balmoral estates which the Duke had inherited from his father.

On the early morning of December 12, having driven there through the night, the Duke of Windsor left Portsmouth in the destroyer Fury. He went to Baron Eugene de Rothschild's residence at Enzesfeld, near Vienna. His sister (the Princess Royal*), the Earl of Harewood, and the Duke of Kent visited him there. In May 1937 Mrs. Simpson's decree was made absolute, and in June, as Mrs. Wallis Warfield, the Duke married her according to French law at the Château de Candé, near Tours, the home of their friends, Mr. and Mrs. Charles Bedaux. No member of the Royal Family was present. There was a subsequent marriage service of the Church of England conducted by an incumbent from the diocese of Durham, who had volunteered without ecclesiastical permission or sanction to celebrate it. The honeymoon was spent in Carinthia.

The first three years after their marriage were spent in restless movement between hotels and hired houses in Paris, Versailles, and the Côte d'Azur. The Duke had no wish to become an expatriate; he missed moreover the ordered life of public service. In 1938 he sounded the Prime Minister (Neville Chamberlain), who happened to be in Paris, about the possibility of his return to England now that his brother was firmly established on the Throne. Chamberlain was non-committal but said he would explore the ground. The matter disappeared in the no-man's-land between Downing Street and Buckingham Palace and the Duke heard no more about it.

The war, however, and its opportunities for service seemed to offer the chance the Duke awaited. In September he was summoned to England, being given to understand that he would be offered a choice of employment with the Military Mission at French G.H.Q. or as Commissioner for Wales in the civil defence organization. He leant towards the latter which contained the prospect of becoming established once again in his own country. He found, however, that that way was not open, and he accordingly went again to France with the rank of major-general. The role of a former monarch in a subordinate military post was not an easy one either for the Duke or for his fellow-soldiers.

When France was overrun the Duke and Duchess made their way, with some difficulty, to Spain. There he received a message that Sir Winston Churchill* wanted him to return to England by way of Portugal. Much as this coincided with his own wishes,

he insisted upon two conditions; that he should be given notice of the kind of job the Government had in mind for him, and that the Duchess should be accorded equality with the wives of the other royal dukes. The refusal of the Court to receive her when they were in England the year before had wounded him. The attitude was the cause of continuing estrangement between the Duke and other members of his family, and the continuing obstacle to his permanent return to England. Although his pride was touched, England's "darkest hour" was an unfortunate moment at which to make an issue of this matter. His conditions remained unsatisfied, and he was offered instead the post of Governor of the Bahamas, which he immediately accepted.

While the Duke of Windsor was in Lisbon with his future still unsettled, the German Minister there got wind of the argument with Churchill and duly reported it to Ribbentrop. The latter wired to the German Embassy in Madrid that the Duke should be lured back to Spain, told that Germany wanted peace with England and that only the Churchill clique stood in the way, and further that Germany "would be prepared to accommodate any desire expressed by the Duke, especially with a view to the assumption of the English throne by the Duke and Duchess". There followed various farcical and half-hearted attempts by German agents to delay the Duke's departure for the Bahamas. This curious story was told in the official publication in 1957 of an instalment of *Documents on German Foreign Policy*. The British Government prefaced the volume with a note saying that the Duke of Windsor "never wavered in his loyalty to the British cause or in his determination to take up his official post as Governor of the Bahamas". That the Germans thought they could tamper with his loyalty is of value only as evidence of the grotesque unreality of German foreign intelligence of the period.

In mid-August 1940 the Duke and Duchess arrived at Nassau. His four and a half years there were the most satisfying period he was granted after his abdication. The sphere of action was, it is true, narrow but it was not without its importance and its problems. The Bahamas were in the process of transformation into a major military base, and the Governor was also able to give a new impetus to the islands' commercial and industrial enterprise, as well as organize their war effort. His energy, habit of command, and long training for public service were given something to work on, and his life was once again afforded a round of ordered duties. From the point of view of colonial administration too the term was a success. Towards its close the Duke began to chafe at his isolation from the main theatres of the war, and when no prospect of a new appointment nearer to his wishes was held out to him, he resigned.

After the war the Duke and Duchess returned to Paris. In October 1945 he made a short visit to England to see Queen Mary and the King, his first since the early days of the war. Fairly frequent though always short visits followed over the succeeding years. He attended the funeral of King George VI and that of Queen Mary. He did not attend the Coronation of Queen Elizabeth, having stated that it would not be in accordance with constitutional usage for the sovereign or former sovereign of a state to attend.

In 1964 the Duke underwent an operation in Texas for an aneurysm of the abdominal aorta and in the following year several operations were performed in London on his left eye. He was visited in hospital by the Queen, the Princess Royal and other members of the Royal Family. In May Jack Le Vien's film *A King's Story*, made with the Duke's cooperation, was shown in London. The Duke saw it in Paris at a private showing to some 300 of his friends. In the summer of 1967 both the Duke and the Duchess attended at the invitation of the Queen the unveiling of a plaque to Queen Mary at Marlborough House. This was the first time the Duchess had attended an official public ceremony with members of the Royal Family.

May 29, 1972.

Godfrey Winn, well-known as a writer and broadcaster since the 1930s, collapsed and died on his private tennis court on June 19, 1971. He was 62.

He was the professional writer par excellence, prodigiously hard-working, commercially successful, a household name to millions. Columnists, popular oracles, crusading journalists came and went but Godfrey Winn was perennial. He had been meeting people of every class and in every income bracket for something like 40 years writing about them in a snug, readable way that looked artless but was in fact achieved by taking great pains. He had also two natural gifts which were of incalculable value to him, a remarkable memory, and a sympathy with the human condition which was entirely unfeigned.

He survived prosperous and intact to the last; in spring 1971 it was estimated that he had in all five contracts going, and two books on the go; one a third volume of autobiography and another a work on the Royal Family to be published to coincide with the silver wedding anniversary of the Queen. In addition he was a regular broadcaster on radio and on television.

Uninhibited sympathy (which some people called sentimentality) combined with a steely journalistic professionalism, were the qualities which characterized Godfrey Winn. At least, they constituted his public character. He was among the most highly-paid journalists of his day because he was one of the most reliable. His articles always arrived on the editors' desk at the right time, the right length and striking the

right note. He was among the most popular journalists of his day, particularly with women, because he wrote what they wanted to read; he put their feelings into words.

He was genuinely interested in people and their troubles, genuinely moved by suffering, by bereavement, by loneliness, genuinely anxious to help, as some of the men who served with him in the Navy during the war could testify. It was the blend of this ostentatiously common touch with such obviously enjoyed success which irritated his critics.

There was no astringency in his work and not much intellectual subtlety, but it was always unashamedly on the side of decency and kindness. If warm-hearted popular journalism has a legitimate and comforting social role, it was one which Godfrey Winn played sincerely and to perfection.

He was born Godfrey Herbert Winn, on October 15, 1908, the son of Ernest Winn and his wife Joan. All his life he was entirely devoted to his mother. He was a brother of Lord Justice Winn and was educated at St. Christophers, Eastbourne, and King Edward's, Birmingham. His father failed financially when he was young and he suffered years of partial social eclipse during which he decided that bankruptcy should never happen to him. When he was 13 and the youngest competitor, he won the South of England Junior Lawn Tennis championship at Eastbourne, a success which was to give him satisfaction all his life. Later he became a boy actor and appeared in John Galsworthy's *Old English*, in *St. Joan* and Noel Coward's *The Marquise*.

By now he had got a footing in the theatrical world, making friends rapidly, among them Sir Edward Marsh and Somerset Maugham.* At 20 he had a first novel, *Dreams Fade*, published. To Maugham, whom he coached at tennis, he reckoned that he owed his ability to report accurately and there are some highly pertinent recollections of the famous novelist in *The Infirm Glory*, Winn's first volume of autobiography.

In 1936 he was approached by Hugh Cudlipp, then features editor of the *Daily Mirror*, to write a column each day on whatever subject took his fancy. The outcome was the extraordinarily successful "Personality Parade" which brought him, literally, fame and fortune. "I hadn't believed Cudlipp", he said later, "when he said he would make me a star. I was going to play in tennis championships and Hugh, in his turn, couldn't believe that." In 1938 he moved to the *Sunday Express*, with whom he stayed until 1942.

In the Second World War he was the first British correspondent to visit the Maginot line and later wrote about many of the human aspects of war. In 1942 he joined the Royal Navy as an ordinary seaman and saw service on the hazardous Russian convoys including the disastrous P.Q. 17.

He eventually wrote several books based on his war-time experiences and two volumes of autobiography, *The Infirm Glory* (1967) and *The Positive Hour* which appeared in November 1970. Both were entertaining, but perplexing and revealing more of himself. He was unmarried.

June 21, 1971.

Sir Rodger Winn, P.C., C.B., O.B.E., a Lord Justice of Appeal from 1965 to 1971, died on June 4, 1972. He was 68. From 1964 to 1971 Winn was chairman of the Permanent Security Commission. Winn had a distinguished career in Naval Intelligence during the Second World War; he was in charge of the U-boat tracking room in the Admiralty.

He was born on December 22, 1903, the son of Ernest Winn and a brother of Godfrey Winn [q.v.], and as a boy set his heart on joining the navy. Before going to Dartmouth he was stricken with poliomyelitis which left him severely handicapped with his body bent and the use of his legs impaired. With indomitable courage and perseverance he taught himself to walk and he became able to play a full part in life.

He proved himself to be a brilliant student and won scholarships which enabled him to pay his way. He went to Oundle and afterwards to Trinity College, Cambridge where he took three first classes in classics one, in law two and in the LL.B. He went to Yale as Davison Scholar in 1925 and to Harvard as Choate Fellow in 1927.

Returning to England he was called to the Bar by the Inner Temple in 1928. He was in distinguished chambers, those of Sir Patrick Hastings, Fearnley-Whittingstall and Lord Shawcross.

He had an outstanding war-time career in the Admiralty Citadel between the years 1941 and 1945. His work there brought him the unusual distinction for an R.N.V.R. officer of four stripes and a C.B., O.B.E. and the U.S. Legion of Merit. His skill and authority became legendary.

In the casual way that some of the best intelligence men were recruited into Whitehall, Winn offered himself for the interrogation of prisoners of war. By a mysterious bureaucratic process he was allotted to the submarine tracking room, which had been started under Paymaster Commander Thring in 1938. Thring was one of the few survivors of the famous Room 40 which in the First World War had applied the study of decoded German signals to the destruction of U-boats and the diversion of convoys. Thanks to the training and advice of Thring—who had some notable encounters with First Lord Winston Churchill* over claims of U-boats sunk—Winn had by 1941 become so adept at the work that he was chosen by the Director of Naval Intelligence, with the approval of the Director of Anti-Submarine Warfare, to succed Thring when his health made retirement necessary. For a civilian to take on such responsibility, even under supervision by R.N. officers in the Operational Intelligence Centre, was a notable innovation which proved entirely successful.

Using information from a multiplicity of sources, which varied in volume and accuracy at different times, the tracking room staff under Winn were able to compile the biography of virtually every U-boat that went to sea. This required the most painstaking fitting together of fragments, in which Winn's legal training was invaluable. Still more it meant the exercise of judgment when it came to routeing important convoys away from known or suspected concentrations of U-boats. In the final stage every decision had to be made by Winn and his colleagues in the Trade Division, and there were errors as well as successes. It is nonetheless true that, until sufficient escort destroyers and aircraft were available in 1943 to capture the initiative from Doenitz's wolf packs, the main obstacle to German success in the Battle of the Atlantic was the work of the section known as "8(s)".

The technique of estimating the course and position of U-boats was at first regarded by regular naval officers as sheer guesswork, but in time not only Winn, but also his young assistants, came to be trusted completely. Their advice was always offered and treated as the advice of "the Room". More than once forecasts and diagnoses of U-boat strategy offered by this section affected Admiralty decisions over a wide field. For example it discouraged in the months leading up to the invasion of Normandy in 1944 too easy optimism about the inability of the Germans to recapture the initiative in the U-boat war.

Winn was a hard taskmaster, who drove his colleagues mercilessly. Their admiration and devotion was none the less for that, and they realized more than once during four years of war—notably in 1942—that the man was being driven to the limits of his strength by continuous work: 14 hours a day of controversial and deeply disturbing decisions about the destination and fate of precious men, equipment and supplies. He was almost persuaded in late 1942 by his doctor to resign. Fortunately he refused, knowing, without any immodesty, that his departure at that stage in the U-boat war would have been a national disaster.

After the war he returned to practice at the Bar and soon established himself as a leading junior. He had an exceptionally quick and clear mind. He could always see the real point in a case and would contemplate upon it and discard the others. He was forceful in argument yet brief. His qualities were so well recognized that he was appointed counsel to the G.P.O. and afterwards in 1954 attained the coveted position of "Treasury devil" (i.e. Junior Counsel to the Treasury).

Here he proved a strong and wise adviser of the Government departments. He would

not allow them to take a bad point nor would he countenance any inefficiency. After being Treasury devil for five years he was, according to custom, appointed a judge of the Queen's Bench Division.

Here his strength of character showed itself. He was a first-rate judge in criminal cases and a sound judge of fact and of law in the civil causes. In 1961 after a 40-day hearing he declared that J. T. Byrne was general secretary of the Electrical Trades Union; and that the election of F. Haxell as general secretary, in 1959, was void.

He did so well that in 1965 he was appointed to be a Lord Justice of Appeal. Here he was able fully to show his worth. He mastered every detail of the cases. He brought to bear his knowledge of the law. He was forceful in discussion and trenchant in expression. He contributed much to the correct decision of every case. He was naturally enough always called in to sit on Admiralty cases.

In addition to his work on the bench he was chairman of the Security Commission. This is a commission which investigates leaks and defects in the security of the country. Here his knowledge of intelligence enabled him to handle the secrets of the services, and to recommend improvements which have been of lasting benefit. He served on law reform committees and in particular he rendered valuable service in regard to the reform of personal injury litigation.

Apart from all these activities he took a great interest in St. Thomas's Hospital of which he was a governor and chairman of the medical school. Often after a hard day in court he would go to a meeting at the hospital which would last two or three hours. His advice was sought on the building contracts, on the finances and indeed on much of the business of the hospital, and never in vain. He did much to keep them on the right lines to their gratitude and appreciation. His record is a record of courage and skill which triumphed over physical disability. In all his career he was supported by his wife Joyce, whom he married in 1930, to whom he was devoted, and who was his mainstay in all he did. She and one daughter survive him.

June 5, 1972.

Tom Wisdom, one of Britain's best-known racing and rally drivers in the later 30s and 40s, died on November 12, 1972 in a Birmingham nursing home. He was 65.

Motoring editor of the *Daily Herald, Sporting Life* and *The Sunday People* for more than 30 years, he was a founder member and past chairman of the Guild of Motoring Writers.

Wisdom was a familiar sight at Brooklands, driving Rileys and the Leyland Thomas Straight 8. He competed 12 times in the Le Mans 24-hour race, failing to

finish only once, when his Bristol caught fire at 140 m.p.h. He also took part in 25 Monte Carlo rallies—the last in 1969, when he was in the highest placed British car—and won the Grand Touring Class three times in the nine Mille Miglia Alpine Trials in which he raced.

Wisdom was an R.A.F. Wing Commander during the Second World War. He was always impeccably dressed, carrying his personal trade mark of a Homburg hat, monocle, and a constant cigarette. In 1949, he was in a team which broke the world speed records on the Bonneville Salt Flats.

His wife "Bill", who died earlier in the year, competed with him in many events, as well as racing at Brooklands; and his daughter Anne drove with Pat Moss when they were the world's top ladies' rally driving team.

November 13, 1972.

Elizabeth Wiskemann, writer on modern and contemporary history, was found dead at her home in London on July 5, 1971.

When she received an honorary degree from Oxford University she was described as a "Cassandra who had lived to record the war she had foretold" and as "a historian who had obtained international recognition".

Elizabeth Wiskemann was an anti-Nazi from the earliest days. She saw the dangers that were not so apparent to others in more responsible posts—from Arnold Toynbee to Neville Chamberlain. She formed part of a devoted group of anti-Nazis in Berlin that centred round Norman Ebbutt* —Darsie Gillie and Ernest Rowe-Dutton among them.

She wrote for Chatham House the first scholarly account of the Sudeten crisis—a rush job which she carried off with flying colours. During the war she did intelligence work in Berne and made many useful contacts with people in occupied territories, particularly in Czechoslovakia. Her heart was with the Czechoslovaks and she had many friends among them. The brutal Russian aggression in 1968 came as a great shock to her.

Elizabeth Wiskemann, the daughter of Hugo Wiskemann and Myra Burton, was educated at Notting Hill High School, London, and Newnham College, Cambridge, where she took a first class degree in history.

Her career as a travelling scholar-journalist started in 1930 when she was not awarded a Ph.D. degree. She then decided to make a break with Cambridge and go to Berlin. As she later wrote: "If I had remained an academic specializing in the nineteenth century I suppose my life would have been considerably duller than it became."

During the next nine years Miss Wiskemann spent long periods on the Continent trying to "get inside" the countries she visited. In the intervals she taught history.

In Germany Miss Wiskemann witnessed the rise of Nazism in the early thirties; from the start she sensed the full significance of it, and stated her views in print. She heard Goebbels speak in 1931, and toured Berlin during the "nightmare" of the election of March 1933, the first after Hitler took over. In July 1936 she was expelled from Germany after the Gestapo had arrested her in Berlin.

Her first book, *Czechs and Germans*, appeared in 1938—it was the result of a study of the Czech-German question which the Royal Institute of International Affairs had asked her to undertake. In 1937 she had plunged "with hurricanes blowing up" into "the uncharted seas" of the dispute. The book appeared just in time for Runciman to take it off to Prague.

During the Second World War Miss Wiskemann was assistant Press Attaché at the British Legation in Berne. She spent her time collecting political intelligence from Hitler's Europe and transmitting it to London. Her book *The Rome-Berlin Axis*, published in 1949, was written "while the feeling of Nazi Germany was still with me and that of Fascist Italy was so near".

After the Second World War Miss Wiskemann became Rome correspondent of *The Economist* for a year, but gave this up to write her book on Italy (1948). She contributed to many journals, among them the *New Statesman, The Times Literary Supplement* and *The Listener*, as well as to daily newspapers.

Her books included *Undeclared War* (1939), *Germany's Eastern Neighbours* (1956), *Europe of the Dictators* (1966) and *The Europe I Saw* (1968).

From 1958 to 1961 she was Montague Burton Professor of International Relations at Edinburgh University, and from 1961 to 1964 Tutor in Modern European History at the University of Sussex. In 1965 she received an honorary D.Litt. from Oxford University.

July 6, 1971.

Professor Rudolf Wittkower, the art historian, died in America on October 11, 1971 at the age of 70.

His death deprives art history of a great scholar and a great teacher. It was Wittkower's achievement to have brought the history of architecture, which had lagged behind other branches of art-history, into line with the sister-discipline by applying to it the scientific approach and sensitive analysis which had long been in use by historians of painting. In addition to developing method he also "discovered" new territories, and was the first writer systematically to chart the field of Baroque architecture.

Wittkower was born in Berlin in 1901 and was trained at the universities of Berlin and Munich. From 1923 to 1932 he worked at the Hertziana Library in Rome,

first as assistant and later as research fellow, and it was in these years that he laid the foundation of his vast knowledge of Roman art of the Renaissance and Baroque periods.

In 1932 he was appointed lecturer in art-history at the University of Cologne, but with the accession of Hitler to power in the following year he immediately decided to leave Germany for England, partly, no doubt, because he could claim British nationality as his father had been born in England. After a very difficult initial period he was appointed by Fritz Saxl to a post on the staff of the Warburg Institute, which had recently moved to England from Hamburg.

For the next 20 years the Warburg was the centre of his life, and he played a great part in establishing its position in Britain and developing it as part of London University, in which it was incorporated in 1944. His efforts to obtain work which would have enabled him to take part in the war effort were unsuccessful, and he continued to work for the Institute and was one of its most active supporters during the years when it was evacuated from London to Denham. With Saxl and Frances Yates he bore the main weight of running the *Journal of the Warburg Institute,* which had been founded in 1937, and played an active part in the community at Denham which became a refuge for art historians during the war years. At the same time he gave generous support to the Courtauld Institute—reduced to a skeletal staff and for part of the war evacuated to Guildford —by teaching the few remaining students. His support was continued after the war, and until his departure to America in 1956 generations of Courtauld students benefited from his teaching.

In 1949 he was appointed Durning–Lawrence Professor at University College London. Here his main duty was to teach art history to the students of the Slade School and with the encouragement of Sir William Coldstream, the director, he rapidly showed that he possessed the rare talent of expounding art-history in a way that appealed to practising artists, stimulated their imaginations and helped them in their own creative work. It is not too much to say that his achievement at the Slade was in great part responsible for the establishment of art-history as part of the normal curriculum in an art school.

In 1956 he was offered a chair at Columbia University and moved to New York, though he went to Europe for several months every year and kept a flat in London. As chairman of the department of art-history he rapidly built up a great school at Columbia, and many of the best American historians of the younger generation were his pupils. In 1969, on retiring from Columbia, he was appointed Kress Professor at the National Gallery, Washington, and during the academic year 1970-71 he was Slade Professor at Cambridge, where he lectured on the art of sculpture, thus

taking up again a theme which had fascinated him since his early studies of Bernini.

His published works cover a wide field. At the Hertziana he collaborated with E. Steinmann in his great Michelangelo bibliography. In 1931 he published a complete catalogue of the drawings of Bernini, in which Heinrich Brauer collaborated but in a minor way. The book is much more than a catalogue, since it is packed with information based on Wittkower's researches in Roman archives.

His studies of Bernini were later incorporated in a monograph published in 1955 by the Phaidon Press. In 1952 appeared his catalogue of the Carracci drawings at Windsor, a model of precise scholarship and wise attribution. During the years just after the war he collaborated with Saxl in *British Art and the Mediterranean*, one of the first attempts to see the art of Britain in a European perspective.

More revolutionary was his *Architectural Principles in the Age of Humanism* in which, by a close study of texts as well as buildings, he was able to define the ideas and ideals which architects of the Renaissance consciously set before themselves, as opposed to those which a modern student might read into their works. At his death he left unfinished several works, including a monograph on Lord Burlington and a work on English architectural treatises.

He will be remembered by his many friends as essentially a huge man—huge in size, huge in energy and huge in kindliness.

He leaves a widow—who had collaborated with him in *Born under Saturn*, a study in the psychology of artists—and one son.

October 19, 1971.

Sir Pelham Wodehouse (P. G. Wodehouse), who died on February 14, 1975 in a Long Island hospital at the age of 93, was a comic genius recognized in his lifetime as a classic and an old master of farce. His span as an author was as long as the biblical span of man. His first fans were schoolboys at the turn of the century; seventy years later he had them in the whole English-speaking world and beyond— he was translated into many languages, including Chinese and Japanese. He was that rare literary phenomenon, a best-seller who became a cult among highbrows.

Popularity did not inflate him any more than the burst of hostility provoked by his wartime broadcasts from Berlin upset his balance. He remained always a modest, retiring man, avoiding the limelight, absorbed in the technicalities of his craft and happy in his circle of friends, to whom he was affectionately known as "Plum".

To the surprise of some and to the pleasure of many he was created K.B.E. in the New Year Honours, six weeks before he died.

Pelham Grenville Wodehouse was born

on October 15, 1881, at Guildford, the third son of Henry Ernest Wodehouse, C.M.G., a judge in Hongkong. The family had its roots in Norfolk and had sent many members to Parliament. While his parents were in the Far East, Wodehouse stayed with aunts, several of whom were married to country clergymen. He spent part of his youth in Shropshire, a county he was to people with some of his happiest characters and in which he sited Blandings Castle.

He went to school at Dulwich College, doing well as a classical scholar and playing in the first football and cricket teams. He remained loyal to Dulwich throughout his life. A career as a banker in the East was planned for him. But he soon discovered (as did his employers at the Hongkong and Shanghai Bank) that he was not cut out for a career in commerce. He left the bank to earn his living as a journalist and story-writer. For some years he wrote the "By The Way" column in a London evening paper, the *Globe*, and he contributed a series of school stories, *The Gold Bat, The White Feather* and others, to the *Captain*, a magazine for boys that was popular in the early years of this century. By 1910, still largely unknown to grown-ups, he had won an enthusiastic following of schoolboys. His stories, coming out in monthly parts, were more realistic and true to public school life than most of their predecessors. He created in them two outstanding characters, one of whom was to keep in the foreground of his later popularity. Mike, the brilliant cricketer and solid citizen, was a pin-up for the average schoolboy, and a perfect foil to his friend, Psmith. It was with Psmith that Wodehouse tried his first experiment in fooling with English prose, an art that he subsequently carried to such dizzy heights.

Going to New York before the first war, he quickly made it his second home and found there a market for other than school stories. At the same time he began his connexion with the stage which was to make him part author and writer of lyrics of 18 musical comedies, including *Kissing Time, The Golden Moth* and *The Cabaret Girl*. His recognition as a new star in the small constellation of really funny writers—those who can provoke spontaneous laughter in a reader as opposed to a smile—began before the first war was over and spread like wild fire in the twenties. This was his great creative period which saw the births of Jeeves and Bertie Wooster. The books poured out and so did praise of them. The Earl of Emsworth, the Drones Club, and other names and places in the canon became household words. *Punch* said that to criticize their author was like taking a spade to a soufflé. V.I.P.s were known to carry the latest Wodehouse to bed with them on day of publication. Among the admirers of this quickly maturing vintage comic were Asquith, Gilbert Murray, Kipling, Wells and Montague James. Belloc called him the best living writer of English.

Correspondents, learned and facetious, argued in the columns of *The Times* about the evidence for and against Bertie having a receding chin. Wodehouse joined in with the official statement that the chin is "undoubtedly opisthognathous". The Public Orator at Oxford asked, when the Vice-Chancellor was admitting Wodehouse to a D.Litt., "*Petroniumne dicam an Terentium nostrum?*" Such of Bertie Wooster's old school chums as remembered their Latin might have told the Public Orator that Wodehouse was much funnier than Petronius and Terence put together. But the Public Orator deserved praise for the ingenuity with which he worked Bertie and Jeeves, Mulliner and Lord Emsworth, Psmith, the Hon. Augustus Fink-Nottle, and the Empress of Blandings into Latin verse. Thus Wodehouse was given the accolade of the Establishment in 1939. There had been nothing like it since the crazes for the *Diary of a Nobody* and the Sherlock Holmes stories.

Captured by the Germans at Le Touquet in 1940, Wodehouse was sent to an internment camp in upper Silesia. As he turned 60 he was released, but not allowed to leave Germany, and in Berlin he was approached by the representative of an American broadcasting company who persuaded him to talk over the air to the United States. The broadcasts were attacked with savagery and Duff Cooper, then Minister of Information, ordered the B.B.C., against the wishes of its chairman, to allow William Connor,* "Cassandra" of the *Daily Mirror*, to broadcast a vulgar blackguarding onslaught on Wodehouse. This was in its turn attacked by correspondents in *The Times*, angrily protesting against the hounding down of a man, without regard to what he had actually said. The words were indeed free from suspicion of favouring the Nazis. But anyone less naive than Wodehouse would have kept his mouth shut.

He made his own confession in 1953 in *Performing Flea*, a self-portrait in letters to his old school friend, W. Townend. "Of course I ought to have had the sense to see that it was a loony thing to do to use the German radio for even the most harmless stuff, but I didn't. I suppose prison life saps the intellect." He claimed without resentment that he had been falsely accused of having accepted favours from the enemy and denied having spoken over the air against his own country, expressed unpatriotic sentiments or been indifferent to the outcome of the war.

As a result of this sorry business Wodehouse could only have returned to England after the war at the risk of being the centre of a major row, involving a demand for his trial for treason. So he went from Paris to New York and, taking American citizenship in 1955, never came back. He would have liked to do so; but feelers put out on his behalf showed that the risk of trouble was too great and he remained in exile until he was too old to revisit his old haunts.

Exile was far from leading to sterility.

Through the fifties and sixties Jeeves staged a come-back and there was a steady flow of books that pleased his old admirers and won him others in a new generation. The remarkable thing about the work of his old age was that it stayed true to the formula of earlier days without seeming to date. His mind as an artist had been set in his teens and, superb and accomplished craftsman though he was, he remained a teenager even in his eighties—and a late Victorian one at that. Boat Race night of Mafeking year may be said to be roughly the point at which he came to a standstill. Yet, paradoxically, he never took on a period flavour. His "eggs", "old beans" and "crumpets" lived in a timeless fairy land in which it was irrelevant whether transport was by Hansom cab or jet aircraft. Theirs was a permissive society, only cramped in style by Aunt Agatha and that super-aunt, Jeeves; as with Saki, the memory of the aunts of his youth remained green with Wodehouse. The boundaries of this unfading, escapist fairyland were never crossed by serious sex or crime. Its inhabitants never grew up. A member of the Drones Club once lamented that he was "twenty-bally-six and no getting away from it". But that was an exaggeration. Like their creator, Bertie and his buddies were Peter Pans. They stayed adolescents.

Wodehouse knew what he was doing. He was a professional to the tips of his fingers. "I believe", he declared, "there are two ways of writing novels. One is mine, making the thing a sort of musical comedy without music and ignoring real life altogether; the other is going right deep down into life and not caring a damn. The ones that fail are the ones where the writer loses his nerve and says: 'My God! I can't write this, I must tone it down'."

He classed all his characters as if they were living salaried actors, being convinced that this was the right way of casting a novel. "The one thing actors—important actors I mean", he wrote, "won't stand is being brought in to play a scene which is of no value to them in order that they may feed some less important character, and I believe this isn't vanity but is based on an instinctive knowledge of stage craft. They kick because they know the balance isn't right."

This discipline, which kept him consistently within chosen limits, is reflected in his hundred books and came through in the successful television versions of them. It guided, too, his excursions into drama and films. He collaborated with Ian Hay in farce writing in the thirties and gave British films *Summer Lightning* in which Ralph Lynn appeared. He told something of himself in *Bring on the Girls* with Guy Bolton (1954) and his autobiographical *Over Seventy* (1957). He continued to write until the last.

There was nothing of the literary man about Wodehouse. He might have been a retired master from Wrykyn, the public school of some of his best early stories.

Dressed in blue blazer and grey flannel trousers, figure kept trim by golf, swimming and leading the simple life, he made no attempt to shine in any company.

Wodehouse married in 1914 Ethel, widow of Leonard Rowley, of Dee Bank, Cheshire, whose daughter Leonora he adopted. She married Peter Cazalet, the racehorse trainer, and died in 1944. There were no children of the Wodehouse marriage.

February 17, 1975.

Leon Woizikovski, who died on February 23, 1975 in Poland, aged 78, was a leading member of Diaghilev's Russian Ballet for the greater part of its history and, in the opinion of many, was probably the finest character dancer of his generation.

Born in Poland, Leon Woizikovski studied dancing in Warsaw where he made his debut at the Grand Theatre. There he was seen by Serge Diaghilev who, recognizing an exceptional talent, invited the young dancer in 1915 to join his company. It was not long before Woizikovski was dancing solo roles. He showed a special affinity for the new style of choreography being developed at that time by Leonide Massine.

Among the new works in which he appeared were *The Good Humoured Ladies,* where his vivid gift for expressive dancing revealed itself as Niccolo the waiter; *La Boutique Fantasque,* in which he was the original Tarantella dancer and later appeared in the choreographer's own part of the Cancan dancer; and *The Three Cornered Hat,* in which he created the grotesque role of the Corregidor besides understudying, and later replacing, Massine as the Miller.

In Diaghilev's celebrated production of *The Sleeping Princess,* Woizikovski had a great success as the leading Ivan in the interpolated Russian dance. After the disruption of the company, caused by the financial failure of this production, he appeared in 1922 with Massine in some hastily concocted programmes at Covent Garden and was engaged as leading dancer for one of Charles Cochran's revues, *Phi-Phi,* at the London Pavilion.

The following year saw him back with Diaghilev in time to dance a leading role in Nijinski's creation of *Les Noces.* This was followed, among many other specially created parts, by the Spanish sailor in Massine's *Les Matelots,* the title part in *Barabau* and the Shepherd in *The Gods Go A-Begging,* the two last being by Balanchine.

Some of Woizikovski's most noted roles, however, were those he inherited from other dancers, including the leading Polovtsian warrior in *Prince Igor* and the title part in *Petrushka.*

After Diaghilev's death in 1929 and the disbanding of the company, Woizikovski danced with Anna Pavlova until her death in 1931. He also made several guest appearances in 1930 and 1931 with the newly formed Ballet Rambert, for which he mounted Fokine's *Carnaval* and Nijinski's *L'Après-midi d'un Faune,* and himself danced as Harlequin, Bluebird, and in a specially created role in *Waterloo and Crimea.*

Joining Colonel de Basil's Ballets Russes de Monte Carlo, he created other notable roles including the Tatterdemalian in *La Concurrence,* the Conductor of the Dance in *Cotillon,* an athlete in *Jeux d'enfants* and Fate in *Les Présages.*

During 1935 and 1936 he directed his own company which toured Europe. Subsequently he returned to his native land, accepting the post of ballet master and principal teacher at Warsaw. After the war he also mounted works from time to time for various companies including London's Festival Ballet, a curiously revised *Petrushka* and a splendid *Scheherazade.* Latterly he had directed a large ballet school in Cologne.

Short, dark and stocky, Woizikovski had a pale complexion and features that would scarcely have attracted attention off stage. When dancing, however, he was possessed of a remarkable vitality, ease, poise and sense of timing. The suppleness and rhythm of his performances were as much admired as were his vigour, precision and virility.

March 8, 1975.

Arthur Wood, wicket-keeper and humourist, died at the age of 74, on April 3, 1975.

He was born in August 1898 and played for Eccleshill (Bradford League) as a batsman at the age of 13. Later he joined the Bradford club and, developing his gifts with the gloves, he got into the Yorkshire first eleven on the retirement of Arthur Dolphin at the end of 1926.

From then he held this exacting post till the 1939 season and returned for a few matches in 1946 to help in the reorganization of the county side. *Wisden* that year called him "the happiest of cricketers". His gay, effervescent humour carried him along throughout his playing career and indeed his drollery on the field was so infectious that batsmen were known to have returned to the pavilion wryly lamenting that they had not been caught or stumped but *laughed out* by Wood.

There was, however, little levity in his vigilance and no flaw in his technical ability, for he gave Yorkshire splendid service behind the stumps and over one period in the 1930s he appeared in 222 consecutive county games, a Yorkshire record broken only by Binks in the years 1955 to 1962.

His England caps were four—one against Australia in 1938 and three against the West Indies in 1939. As a batsman he appeared lighthearted, but possessed a repertory of handsome strokes and was adept at forcing the pace when the game demanded it. Between 1927 and the outbreak of the Second World War he scored over 8,000 runs for Yorkshire. His best season was 1935, when he made 1,249 runs, including a hard-hit 123 not out against Worcestershire.

Stories of his fun are numberless. The most famous concerns the historic Oval Test of 1938 when Sir Leonard Hutton scored 364. When Wood went to the wicket the total was 770 for six. With a series of dashing hits he swiftly scored 53 and then, attempting another big hit, was caught and bowled. Rushing to the pavilion, he flung down his bat in mock despair. "Just like me", he exclaimed, "I *would* lose my head in a crisis!"

April 4, 1975.

Oliver Woods, M.C., Chief Assistant to the Editor-in-Chief of Times Newspapers Limited from 1967 to 1970, died on December 13, 1972 aged 61.

In nearly a quarter of a century of service in Printing House Square he filled many roles, all of them with distinction. But it is no disparagement to the value of what he did in other posts to say that his 13 years in charge of Colonial affairs for *The Times,* from 1948-1961, were the most important. His sympathy for underdeveloped countries, his shrewd appraisal of men of all races and his ability to get on friendly terms with them, and his calm unemotional judgment of political situations wherever they arose led him to become at one time probably the most knowledgeable man about the Colonial "empire".

His judgment was as sound about the governors as about the government. He travelled regularly in Africa, in the Caribbean, and elsewhere. His writings in *The Times* provided a wealth of information and wisdom. He was consulted by ministers in Whitehall and in territories overseas. At the same time, as he showed in his years of service both before and after this spell, he was an all-round journalist.

Oliver Frederick John Bradley Woods was born in London on November 21, 1911. His father, the late Maurice Woods, was the son of the Rev. H. G. Woods, President of Trinity College, Oxford, and later Master of the Temple. His mother had been Viola Taylor, a grand-daughter of Sir Henry Taylor, the poet and the author of *The Statesman.* After Maurice Woods's death she married J. L. Garvin, the Editor of *The Observer.* Oliver Woods therefore came from a learned and literary background and was brought up in a home in which great affairs and great writings were common talk.

He went to New College, Oxford, from Marlborough College. He was not enough of a scholar to gain more than seconds in Honour Mods. and in Litt. Hum. From the beginning he was keen to get the full savour out of life as a whole. It seemed natural that he should become a journalist. He joined *The Times* in 1934.

Sent for a period as assistant to the Munich correspondent, he returned to Printing House Square where he undertook various editorial duties, including subediting and work in the Letters to the Editor department.

To many who knew Oliver Woods it seemed strange that so sensitive and peaceful a man should have been such a fine soldier. He became interested in military theory while quite young, and some years before 1939 he obtained a commission in the 23rd (London) Armoured Car Company (Sharpshooters). When the Second World War broke out he was already trained in the handling of mechanized units and threw himself with passionate eagerness into active service.

He fought in the Western Desert, in Sicily, in Italy, and in north-west Europe. He was a brave man; over and over again he had the narrowest escapes. He gained the Military Cross in 1943 and was later mentioned in dispatches. In the ensuing years of peace military men remained among his closest friends. When he was most fully immersed in the work of Colonial Correspondent he could still always find time—and indeed was eager to do so—to write about military tactics or the latest reorganization of the armed forces.

As independence removed the colonial status from different countries one by one, Woods's responsibilities in the field inevitably diminished. For five years from 1956-61 he joined the role of Colonial Editor with that of Assistant Foreign Editor. In 1961 he was switched to the home side of *The Times* and became Assistant Editor (Home). In 1965 he was appointed Deputy Managing Editor of *The Times* and when the merger with *The Sunday Times* took place in 1967 he became Chief Assistant to C. D. Hamilton, the Editor-in-Chief of Times Newspapers Limited, a post of varied responsibilities covering both newspapers.

Until his 45th year Oliver Woods was a bachelor. The constant travel his work entailed and the social demands made upon him when he was in London left him no time to look after himself. It was, therefore, a great pleasure to his friends and relief to their anxieties when in 1956 he married Joan Waters, the widow of the former Managing Director of the *News Chronicle*. She was the daughter of Nancy Price* the actress, the great granddaughter of Jenny Lind, and the niece of Cyril Maude. She herself had, before her first marriage, been well known on the stage as Joan Maude. With common interests, an already acquired knowledge of newspaper life and personalities, and great social charm, Joan Woods was the ideal partner for this

serious and sociably-inclined journalist. She devoted herself to Oliver Woods's welfare and interests. The inner serenity of his later years was her reward.

December 14, 1972.

Admiral Sir Wilfrid Woods, G.B.E., K.C.B., D.S.O., who died on January 1, 1975 at the age of 68, was Commander-in-Chief, Home Fleet, and Nato C.-in-C., Eastern Atlantic Area, 1960-62, and from 1963 to 1965 Commander-in-Chief, Portsmouth and Allied C.-in-C. Channel. In his retirement after 1965 he was a Deputy Lieutenant for Hampshire and for four years chairman of the R.N.L.I.

His chairmanship of the R.N.L.I. from 1968 to 1972 was highly successful. When he took office there was a deficit of about £400,000, which he wiped out during his term. It was also while he was chairman that the boat building programme was greatly expanded.

Wilfrid Woods was born at Southsea, Hampshire, on February 19, 1906, the son of the late Sir Wilfrid Woods, K.C.M.G., K.B.E., a distinguished colonial civil servant. He was educated at Seabrooke Lodge, Hythe, Kent, and at the Royal Naval Colleges, Osborne and Dartmouth, being commissioned as a sub-lieutenant in 1926.

He specialized in submarines in 1927, and obtained his first command in the submarine Seahorse as a lieutenant in 1935. He was promoted to lieutenant-commander in H.M.S. Nelson the following year, and remained in that ship until he attended R.N. Staff College early in 1939.

At the outbreak of the Second World War, he was serving on the staff of the Sixth Submarine Flotilla in home waters, but went to the Mediterranean in 1940 in command of the submarine Triumph. For his services in that submarine he was awarded the D.S.O. and bar, and also the Order of the White Eagle of Yugoslavia. He was promoted to commander in 1941.

He next served as Staff Officer (Operations) on the staff of the Commander-in-Chief, Mediterranean, before assuming command of the old battleship Centurion for her passage from the Mediterranean to the United Kingdom, and her preparations for the Normandy landings. He took the Centurion to Normandy for the landings, and scuttled her there according to plan, as part of Mulberry Harbour.

He was appointed captain of H.M.S. Forth and of the 3rd Submarine Flotilla in 1945, and Chief Staff Officer to the Flag Officer Submarines in 1947. He was next appointed to the Admiralty as Director of Torpedo, Anti-Submarine and Mine Warfare, and thence to the Imperial Defence College in 1951.

He commanded the aircraft carrier Indomitable in 1952, and 18 months later was appointed as Chief of Staff to the Commander-in-Chief, Mediterranean, in the rank

of commodore. He was promoted to rear-admiral in 1955.

From December 1955 to November 1957, he served as Flag Officer Submarines and on promotion to vice-admiral in 1958 was appointed to the Nato post of Deputy Supreme Allied Commander, Atlantic.

In July 1960, he was appointed in the rank of admiral to the posts of Commander-in-Chief, Home Fleet, and Nato Commander-in-Chief, Eastern Atlantic Area, and in May 1962, was appointed First and Principal Naval A.D.C. to the Queen. He was awarded the C.B. in 1957, and was made a K.C.B. in 1960.

January 3, 1975.

Sir (Ernest) Llewellyn Woodward—See Sir Llewellyn Woodward.

Professor Joan Woodward, head of the Industrial Sociology Unit at the Imperial College of Science and Technology, died on May 18, 1971 at the age of 54.

She had an outstanding academic career, which began with first class honours in P.P.E. at Oxford in 1936, followed by an M.A. in Medieval Philosophy from Durham in 1938, and the Diploma in Social and Public Administration from Oxford in 1939. The war temporarily interrupted her academic career, but typically she made an outstanding and unusual contribution to the war effort. For seven years she was a manager, ending the war as Senior Labour Manager of the Royal Ordnance Factory at Bridgwater. During this period she gained practical insights into industrial problems which illuminated and became one of the distinguishing features of her subsequent work in the field of industrial sociology.

After a brief period as a civil servant she returned to academic life, first at the University of Liverpool, then at the South East Essex Technical College and at the Department of Social and Administrative Studies at Oxford. In 1962 she was appointed Senior Lecturer in Industrial Sociology in the Department of Mechanical Engineering at Imperial College and in 1969 the title of professor was conferred upon her; she was only the second woman to become a professor at Imperial College. She also became head of the newly formed Industrial Sociology Unit at the college.

Her early publications such as *The Dockworker* (1954) and *The Saleswoman* (1960) were important contributions to industrial sociology. But the publication of *Industrial Organization: Theory and Practice* was a landmark in the development of organization theory. It inspired a whole new body of interest in this important area among sociologists both in Britain and abroad. It also immediately made a practical appeal to managers.

She attracted a group of research workers

to the Industrial Sociology Unit, and inspired work which has already gained an international reputation. The first fruits of the Unit's research are to be seen in *Industrial Organization: Behaviour and Control* which Professor Woodward edited in 1970.

During her time at Imperial College she developed a unique teaching programme which introduced post-graduate students in science and technology to industrial sociology, and undergraduates to the social and economic environment in which their work is carried out.

Her modest manner, her emphasis upon practical common sense combined with her keen analytical mind made her much in demand as a consultant to industry and as an adviser to bodies like the G.P.O. and the former Department of Employment and Productivity. She also made a considerable contribution, both through research and as an adviser, to the training of nurses and to the administration of hospitals.

She was a member of a number of government committees including two sub-committees of the Social Science Research Council, the Mallabar Committee on Government Industrial Establishments, and from 1968 to 1970 was a part-time member of the National Board for Prices and Incomes.

All these activities she sustained despite the increasing burden of ill-health.

She is survived by Leslie Thompson Blakeman, whom she married in 1951.

May 19, 1971.

Sir Llewellyn Woodward, the distinguished historian, died on March 11, 1971 at the age of 80.

Ernest Llewellyn Woodward was born at Ealing on May 14, 1890, the only son of G. E. Woodward, C.B.E., a civil servant in the Admiralty. This naval background in the era of imperialism later informed one of the historian's best works, *Great Britain and the German Navy.*

Woodward's happy childhood, suburban and evangelical, is described in his attractive autobiography, *Short Journey.* The slight, nervous boy was classically drilled at the old Merchant Taylors' School and took to books in the Hampstead Public Library. A scholarship to Corpus Christi College, Oxford, led on to a second class in Greats, a first in modern History and a senior scholarship to St. John's College.

During the First World War Woodward became something of a horseman. He served as a junior officer in Flanders and later on the staff at Salonika. In 1918 illness brought him back to write a Foreign Office handbook, for the peace conference, on the Congress of Berlin. After a brief interlude as an Eton master, Woodward emerged as an Oxford don at Keble College and in 1919 gained a distinction which he specially valued. This was a fellowship of All Souls'

where he remained until the next World War, while also becoming a lecturer at New College.

Woodward had mainly turned to modern history. In the decade up to 1938 he published three volumes of telling essays on European history in the nineteenth century, his important study of Anglo-German naval rivalry and a standard work on *The Age of Reform 1815-1870,* in the Oxford History of England. This massive volume confirmed that Woodward's range extended beyond politics, and it won deserved success.

The Second World War redirected Woodward to the Foreign Office where, had he been so minded, he might perhaps have succeeded Sir Stephen Gaselee as Librarian. Woodward was, however, to make an outstanding contribution to the annals of British diplomacy as the founding editor, for a decade after 1944, of the great series of *Documents on British Foreign Policy 1919-1939.* Also in 1944, he was appointed Professor of International Relations at Oxford where, three years later, he became the first holder of a new chair of Modern History. Woodward's interest in expanding modern studies had further taken him to Nuffield College, and his successive professorships made him a fellow first of Balliol, then, most congenially, of Worcester.

He thus established something of a record by having had a working association with eight Oxford colleges. He was later elected to honorary fellowships at Worcester and Corpus, and at All Souls to a distinguished fellowship, an honour rather rarely accorded to academics.

In 1951 Woodward exchanged his chair at Oxford for a research-professorship, held for a decade, at the Institute for Advanced Study at Princeton.

Woodward in his seventies produced a revised edition of *The Age of Reform* and a large history of *Great Britain and the War, 1914-1918.* Here, if the treatment may sometimes seem a little dated, it is notable as one of the last substantial estimates of that war from a participant. Already, however, Woodward had written his magisterial *British Foreign Policy in the Second World War,* based upon extensive research in governmental archives. The publication of a condensed version was followed in 1970 by the first of the full five volumes.

March 13, 1971.

Sir William Worsley, BT., died on December 4, 1973 at the age of 83. By his death the county of Yorkshire and the North of England in a wider sense has lost an outstanding personality. He was the father of the Duchess of Kent.

William Arthington Worsley was born on April 5, 1890, the elder son of Sir William Henry Arthington Worsley, third

baronet, and was educated at Eton and New College, Oxford. He was commissioned into the Green Howards in 1912. During the 1914–18 War he was seriously wounded in the retreat from Mons and taken prisoner. He retained his commission for a few years after the end of hostilities, retiring in 1922.

For many years he was a county councillor and alderman of the North Riding, a magistrate, a member and chairman of Malton Rural Council, and a deputy lieutenant. At the outbreak of war in 1939 he rejoined The Green Howards, with which he served for two years.

In all other respects, too, William Worsley was the cultivated country gentleman. He was deeply interested in agriculture, and a keen supporter of good husbandry, particularly of sound forestry. His estate was in many ways a model of good management.

But it is perhaps as a cricketer that he will always be thought of. At Hovingham he had one of the finest private cricket grounds in the country, and he was still playing at an age when most people think they are much too old for the game.

A hard-hitting batsman who had played for Eton, he captained the Yorkshire team in 1928-29. In 45 innings with his side, he scored 733, an average of 16.28. He was president of M.C.C. in 1961-62.

From 1951 to 1965 he was Lord Lieutenant of the North Riding.

He was devoted to the collection of fine art which he inherited at Hovingham, and gradually cleaned, restored and catalogued the paintings and sculpture. The collection, which was formed by the first baronet to furnish the new hall which he himself had designed (it includes a fine riding school), is an exceptionally well preserved example of the connoisseurship of that age, and includes the work of many Italian, French and Flemish masters. The famous statue of Samson slaying the Philistines by Giovanni da Bologna was acquired by the Victoria and Albert Museum during Sir William's lifetime; but some part of the proceeds was devoted to the purchase of other works of art, including two panels by Boucher.

Sir William's main enthusiasm was directed to the early English watercolour drawings in the collection, to which he made substantial additions, including several examples of Francis Towne, an artist for whom he had a particular liking.

Hovingham Hall is also associated with what was perhaps the first of the country house music festivals. The Hovingham Festival, originally instituted at the end of the nineteenth century by a local clergyman who was a friend of Joachim (who used to play at Hovingham), lapsed at the beginning of the First World War but was revived under Sir William's patronage in 1951.

He married in 1924 Joyce Morgan, daughter of Sir John Brunner, Bt. They had three sons and a daughter. The eldest,

Mr. Marcus Worsley, who succeeds his father, is Conservative M.P. for Chelsea.

December 6, 1973.

W. T. Wren, a former chairman of Allied Ironfounders, died in a London hospital on May 24, 1971. He was 69.

He had a considerable influence on British housing during the post-war shortage —especially in the establishment of higher standards of fittings and equipment—and was also one of the leaders of a campaign for the improvement and conversion of existing house property with the aid of Government grants to the owners, and for higher standards of comfort in small and agricultural housing.

Walter Thomas Wren started his business life at the age of 14 as an office boy at Chubb & Sons in St. James's Street. He subsequently joined the original Aga Company, and made such a success of introducing this hitherto unknown concept in heating and cooking to the British and Commonwealth markets that he became its managing director. On its amalgamation into Allied Ironfounders, he joined the board.

After a distinguished wartime career in the Foreign Service, he returned to a Britain much of whose housing had been destroyed by bombing, and where effectively no building had taken place for six years. A number of official reports laid down the housing standards that would be required in the future, including the Egerton Report on standards of housing, but neither their provisions nor the means of attaining them seemed to be widely understood by local authorities.

Ideas on communication and publicity were still restricted, but Wren commissioned an exhibition train which would carry the necessary information direct to the major urban centres throughout the country. It included an air-conditioned cinema for the showing of instructional films.

This was typical of a number of campaigns which had a wide influence on official thinking. In order to urge local authorities to make greater use of their powers to give improvement grants for the conversion of old property, and to expose some shortcomings in the existing grant system, Wren bought four old working class houses and, in what became known as "the Stockton test", converted them under controlled conditions to modern standards, keeping exact records of the costs involved. The Housing Act of 1954, in which the grants were modified, was to a large extent a result of the Stockton test— the brainchild of a man who wanted every resident in old houses to have hot water "on tap".

He retired from Allied Ironfounders in 1957, and never returned to full-time business, although he remained an active figure

in housing and planning circles. A born communicator, he was also able to devote more time to broadcasting and to the writing not only of books but also of film scripts and plays.

May 27, 1971.

Lieutenant-Colonel Harold Wyllie, O.B.E., who died in London on December 22, 1973 at the age of 93, was a man of unusual talent and experience.

He was most widely known for his work as a marine painter in oils and watercolours and as an engraver and sculptor. Much of his talent with a brush and engraving tool and his love of the sea were inherited from his father, W. L. Wyllie, R.A., who stimulated his talent and guided him in his early work.

Indeed, it was to avoid having to compete directly with his father which led Harold Wyllie to select one specific field as a painter, that of chronicling the activities of the men of the Royal Navy, and their ships, in all the ages of sail.

This specialization led to extensive research and ultimately to a degree of expertise in this subject that put him among the greatest authorities in the world on the manning, manoeuvring and naval architecture of Britain's wooden walls.

Examples of his work in this category among many others will be found as basreliefs and murals in R.N. buildings at Chatham, Portsmouth and Devonport. At another level his profound knowledge of ships and their rigging led to his being the member of the Victory Committee who had direct responsibility for the rebuilding and re-rigging in the mid-1920s of Nelson's flagship and to his building a model of Victory under full sail, which was commissioned by Lord Mountbatten and is now in the Victory Museum. Later he had executive responsibility for the start which was made on the restoration of the Implacable and the Foudroyant.

Harold Wyllie saw active service in the Boer War and in the 1914-18 War, and commanded the Implacable, then H.M.S. Implacable, as a training establishment during the Second World War.

At the start of his war service in South Africa he was commissioned in 1900 at the age of 20 in the Royal West Kent Regiment and served later with The Buffs. In 1914 he was one of the first men to volunteer for the R.F.C. and to fly in action. He commanded squadrons both in France and in the defence of England, one of them being the first night fighter squadron assigned to attack intruding Zeppelins.

December 24, 1973.

John Wyndham, 1st Baron Egremont—See Egremont.

Harry Vincent Yorke—See Green.

Gladys Young, O.B.E., one of the first generation of radio and television actresses, died on August 18, 1975.

She had been an actress in the "live" theatre, on sound radio and in television, but she will be remembered principally for her pioneering work in the second of these. During the first 20 years in the history of radio drama she, by her own excellence as a broadcaster, did much to arouse interest in it among the public and to reveal its possibilities to the theatrical profession generally.

Gladys Young, the daughter of a ship owner, William Michael Young, and the sister of Miss E. H. Young, the novelist, was born at Newcastle upon Tyne, but went to school in the South, to Sutton High School, where she joined an amateur dramatic society and so came to know Mabel Constanduros. As a pupil at R.A.D.A. she won the Silver and the Gold Medals, and shortly before the outbreak of the First World War she joined Vedrenne and Eadie's company at the old Royalty Theatre in Soho. In one of the plays there she understudied Gladys Cooper and Lynn Fontanne, but she left in 1916 in order to do war-work and did not return to the stage after the war, since she had meanwhile married Algernon West, the actor, and wished to devote herself to bringing up her son.

In 1926 she broadcast for the B.B.C. in *Milestones*, and in the same year was suggested by her old friend, Mabel Constanduros, for a part in a play that the latter had written specially for radio. She was soon being used not only by the drama department but in Children's Hour and in readings from books. When the B.B.C. Repertory Company was formed at the beginning of the Second World War for the purpose of ensuring the continuance of a drama service, she was engaged for it.

Other broadcasters did particular things as well as or better than she, but it seemed to the public, listening to her four, five or even six times a week in very varied programmes over the next 10 years, that the standard, a high one, in this new form of acting was set, rather than by anyone else, by Gladys Young. She became almost a national figure with the introduction in 1943 of Saturday Night Theatre, her performances on the air in popular plays like *The Silver Cord* and *The First Mrs. Fraser* having every bit as much authority as those originally given on the stage by Lilian Braithwaite and Marie Tempest in the same parts. Thanks, it was said, to the elastic wavelength of her voice, Gladys Young could bring characters to life for a "blind" audience, as stars of the "live" theatre similarly placed, with only the microphone to help them, often failed to do.

In 1951, soon after she resigned from the B.B.C. Repertory Company and resumed freelancing, she was appointed O.B.E., and she was on three occasions nominated for the National Radio Award as the year's best actress. She appeared only once in her career in a film; but on television, a medium in which her experience dated from the first dramatic production in Britain by the Baird Office, a few important parts such as the ex-headmistress in Pamela Hansford Johnson's *Corinth House* came her way, and she made a brief return to the stage in 1954, touring in a play directed by her son, Richard West.

August 20, 1975.

Whitney Young, executive director of the National Urban League, New York, since 1961, and a moderate civil rights leader, died in Lagos on March 11, 1971 at the age of 49. Young transformed the Urban League from an old-fashioned welfare agency into the most concrete effective civil rights organization in America.

Whitney Young's argument against segregated housing was that segregation always leads towards Negroes getting the worst— the worst houses, schools, streets, police, meat in the shops, rubbish disposal.

Whitney Young visited Negro troops in Vietnam in the sixties. With Martin Luther King* and Roy Wilkins, he had direct access to President Johnson. In order not to lose the support of the masses he joined the Meredith March.

The National Urban League, as a voluntary community service agency of civic, professional, business, labour and religious leaders is dedicated to the removal of "all forms of segregation and discrimination based on race or colour".

When Young took over the Urban League, it was a drowsy and very nearly bankrupt agency, with a reputation as little more than an employment agency for the Negro middle class. Young increased its staff from 34 to 200, set up new local Leagues, and prodded the organization into more work in the black slums.

Young, the son of a headmaster, was educated at the Massachusetts Institute of Technology and the University of Minnesota. He also studied at Harvard. He began working for the Urban Leagues in 1947.

In 1968 Young endorsed the black power philosophy instead of integration as the way ahead for Negroes in America. He announced this change of tactics at the closing session of the annual meeting of the Congress for Racial Equality. In 1970 he commended President Nixon for his "real concern" over pleas for more Government action in providing housing, education and jobs for blacks and other minorities.

Young was awarded the Medal of Free-dom by President Johnson in 1969 and several times went on television in 1967 to try to calm black rioters rampaging through a number of American cities.

March 12, 1971.

Prince George of Yugoslavia died in Belgrade on October 17, 1972 at the age of 85.

He was born in 1887 in Tsetinje, the capital of his maternal grandfather, Prince Nicholas of Montenegro. When his mother, Princess Zorka, died, his father, the exiled Karageorgevich pretender to the throne of Serbia, moved to Geneva, and George was later sent to school in Russia. In 1903, his father's accession as King Peter I took him to Serbia, as heir apparent, being the elder son.

He was given a commission in the Army; threw himself with zeal into his military duties and acquired popularity in army circles, especially among those officers of markedly anti-Austrian outlook. The eccentricity of his private character, however, had long given rise to grave anxiety on the part of those who knew him intimately. He had a passionate temper and did not lightly brook any crossing of his will. In 1909 his father took action and the Prince renounced his rights of succession to the Serbian throne.

He served with courage in the Balkan war of 1912 and in the early part of the First World War was twice wounded; on the second occasion he was hit by a bullet while leading a battalion of infantry in a charge. But the ensuing years were clouded because of his unpredictable behaviour and he was put under the supervision of a doctor.

In 1934 his brother the King was assassinated at Marseilles.

The Germans freed Prince George in 1941 and allowed him to live in Belgrade where he remained after the liberation and the Communist take-over. As a royal victim of the monarchy, he was left undisturbed, and even granted a retired army officer's pension. The Prince, who seemed to have mellowed with age, was to be seen in the streets, the trams and the shops. A tall, gaunt figure, he was a familiar sight to the inhabitants of Belgrade who had come to recognize him, and show respect for this still eccentric, but now dignified, old gentleman.

In 1968, Prince George published his memoirs (*George Karageorgevich, The Truth About My Life*). The book is an interesting and candid clinical document about a sad life.

Until latterly Prince George was a regular customer at the Hunters' Café near the British Embassy in Belgrade; dressed in old clothes and a Basque beret, he would sit for hours, drinking brandy and Turkish coffee, chatting with friends.

October 19, 1972.

Z

The Ruler of Zanzibar, Shaikh Abeid Amani Karume, who was both chairman of the Zanzibar Revolutionary Council and First Vice-President of Tanzania, was assassinated on April 7, 1972. He was 67.

Karume began his working life as a boat-boy on the Zanzibar waterfront, after something like 18 months of primary school education. He left school at 15, and for 18 years travelled the world as a sailor on cargo boats. He at one time belonged to the British seamen's union.

Karume returned to Zanzibar in 1938 and worked with a syndicate running a shore launch service. In 1954 he became a town councillor, and went into Zanzibari politics. He became president of the African Association, which merged with the Shirazi Association. The union, later the Afro-Shirazi Party, represented Zanzibaris supposedly of Persian descent and those of mainland descent against the Arab élite under the Sultans. Karume's family had gone to Zanzibar from the mainland.

Karume, as president of the Afro-Shirazi Party, had varying electoral successes. He gained power in 1964 when a violent African revolution a month after the island's independence overthrew the Sultan's government, and killed or drove out thousands of Arabs.

Karume became president and he and his colleagues turned to communist powers, particularly East Germany and China, for help, while western states appeared sympathetic to the deposed Sultan, who went into exile in Britain.

After three months Karume negotiated an Act of Union between Zanzibar and the mainland, then Tanganyika. In the new Tanzania, Karume became First Vice-President of the United Republic, but almost no progress was made on the intended integration. Karume retained nearly absolute powers in Zanzibar which he kept isolated from the mainland, and from the rest of the world.

Karume was regarded inside and outside Zanzibar as a tyrant. Though he was a powerful public speaker in Swahili, he felt keenly his lack of formal education. He had also a deep sense of bitterness about the discrimination that Europeans and Arabs had traditionally shown against Africans in Zanzibar. Karume tried to force the pace of social change, including symbolic and actual demands for inter-racial marriages.

He acted harshly against those who remained of the mercantile class after the revolution. Though he tried to introduce social measures, such as cheap housing, to benefit the mass of Zanzibari people, he was unable to coordinate planning. Zanzibar, with large revenues from spices, had frequent shortages of essential foods. He had strong ideas about eventual benefit that the single-party rule of the Revolutionary Council could bring to the islanders, but he had not the skill and restraint to put ideas into practice.

April 10, 1972.

Paul van Zeeland, a former Prime Minister of Belgium, who died on September 22, 1973 at the age of 79, was an economist and financier of exceptional gifts who won an international reputation during the 1930s as the Keynes of his country.

The devastations of the 1914-18 War, followed by a decade of uncertain recovery and social unrest, left Belgium particularly unfitted to face the fresh economic disasters which befell her during the years of the Great Depression. Van Zeeland, in 1935 vice-governor of the Belgian National Bank, was called in by King Leopold III to lead an all-party government facing national bankruptcy. His swift and brilliant action —which included devaluation of the Belgian franc but fidelity to the gold standard —led to the restoration of Belgian solvency in little over a year; it was accompanied by a thorough reform of the country's finances and its banking and credit structure, on lines which Belgium has never since abandoned.

Paul van Zeeland was born at Soignies on November 11, 1893, and won the Croix de Guerre on the battlefield in 1914. He studied law, economics and political science at Louvain University; after obtaining his LL.D., he continued his studies at Princeton University, New Jersey, where he took an M.A. degree in economics before returning to teach at Louvain. He remained closely connected with the university throughout his long life.

In April 1937, Belgians demonstrated their gratitude to their prime minister by giving him a resounding victory in a Brussels election over Léon Degrelle, despite the latter's meteoric rise to fame as leader of the extreme right-wing Rexist movement. Yet in October of the same year he was compelled to resign because of a scandal in the National Bank—to the particular regret of King Leopold who had formed, and retained, a high regard for his minister's talents.

It was during van Zeeland's second ministry (1936-37), with the young Paul-Henri Spaak as his Foreign Minister, that Germany occupied the Rhineland. Van Zeeland, in close agreement with King Leopold, announced that his country would meet the challenge of German troops at her frontiers by adopting a policy of military independence. Later this developed into a policy of open neutrality and included the abrogation of the 1920 Franco-Belgian military agreement—partly at the insistence of anti-French elements in the Belgian parliament.

Van Zeeland was not in office when Nazi troops overran Belgium in May 1940; but later he crossed the Pyrenees and arrived in London in August 1940. During the war he lived mainly in America, returning to Belgium at the end of 1944 at the head of a commission for repatriation.

In 1946 van Zeeland was elected Senator, and in 1949 he became a coopted member of the Belgian Senate. He was appointed Minister of State in 1948. In 1949 he joined the Eyskens Christian-Social/Liberal coalition as Foreign Minister, and retained this portfolio in successive coalition governments until 1954. During 1950, the last months of King Leopold's exile, van Zeeland argued and laboured in support of the King's return and became very popular with the Leopoldist royalists. However, when Leopold returned in July of that year van Zeeland was playing a leading role in the formation of the European Payments Union, and was thus absent from the cabinet meeting during which King Leopold agreed to abdicate—a decision which van Zeeland bitterly deplored.

During these years as Foreign Minister van Zeeland shared in the negotiations for the launching of Robert Schuman's* European Coal and Steel Community (the pilot scheme for the Common Market venture of 1958).

He was also associated closely with the abortive attempts to create a European Defence Community, with the setting up of the Council of Europe in Strasbourg, as well as playing a leading role in the formation of the Organisation for European Economic Cooperation (O.E.E.C.).

Throughout his life he was devoted to the idea of a united Europe, in partnership with the United States; even when he had withdrawn from public office he still continued to work towards this long-term goal, notably by his activities as one of the founder members of the Atlantic Institute set up in 1957.

September 24, 1973.

Marshal Georgi Zhukov, who prepared and carried out the final Soviet offensive against the German armies on the Eastern front and later commanded the Russian armies of occupation in Germany, died on June 18, 1974 at the age of 77.

Zhukov was perhaps the most brilliant of the Soviet soldiers who fought in the Second World War. Although, like Rokossovsky*, he was not an outstanding veteran of the Russian Civil War, his victories over the Germans at Moscow, on the Don, in the Ukraine, and finally in Berlin have guaranteed him a significant place in military history.

A great popular hero, he bulked too large on the political scene to suit either Stalin's autocracy or Khrushchev's brand of personal rule. At the end of the war Stalin moved him into a comparatively minor post and in 1957 in highly dramatic circumstances Khrushchev removed him from the party praesidium and the Ministry of Defence. He was accused of resisting party control of the armed forces, of "adventurism" in foreign affairs, promoting the cult of his own personality, and was even blamed for the unpreparedness of the Soviet forces when the Nazis invaded in 1941.

It was not until May 1965, on the occasion of a large military parade to mark the twentieth anniversary of the end of the Second World War, that he again made a public appearance, standing with other leading commanders and being greeted with a special burst of applause.

Georgi Konstantinovitch Zhukov was born in 1896 in the village of Strelkova, near the spot where Kutozov defeated Napoleon. Of peasant stock, his early education was neglected and at the age of 11 he was apprenticed to a furrier in Moscow. During the 1914-18 War he served with the 10th Novgorod Dragoons as an n.c.o. and was twice awarded the Russian George Cross for gallantry and daring. He was an ardent supporter of the October Revolution, and in the newly formed Red Army he was elected to his regimental council and became the chairman of his squadron committee.

In 1919 he joined the Communist Party. During the civil war, as a young cavalryman, he took part in the defence of Tsaritsyn, under Voroshilov,* where he was wounded. When internal peace was at last restored to Russia, he continued to serve in the Red Army, rising to command a cavalry corps. Between the wars he commanded the Stalin Cossack Corps and for his work in the field of military training he was decorated with the Order of Lenin. In 1939 he saw fighting at Khalingol, Mongolia, against the Japanese Sixth Army, and his abilities as a general on this occasion won him the title of "Hero of the Soviet Union".

In February 1941 Stalin appointed Zhukov Chief of the General Staff, in which post he was responsible for working out the Soviet defence plan in the spring of 1941, completed in outline by May; in this post Zhukov began his wartime service when Germany invaded the Soviet Union; he was dispatched almost at once to assist with the defence of the Ukrainian frontiers, and when in August Shaposhnikov was installed once more as Chief of the General Staff, Zhukov was assigned to command of the Reserve Front, the main covering force for Moscow. On September 12 he was flown to Leningrad to organize the last-ditch defence of the city against Army Group North, and he was recalled from Leningrad on October 8 to take command of the Western Front when Army Group Centre broke through the centre and drove for Moscow.

In this post he was responsible for the defence of the capital, before which Army Group Centre was finally halted. Having taken part in planning the Soviet counterblow, Zhukov commanded the Western Front armies until February 1, 1942, when he was appointed "Commander of the

Western Axis" to supervise the encirclement and destruction of Army Group Centre. This, however, was not accomplished and Zhukov remained in command at the centre before Moscow throughout the summer of 1942. The crisis developed not at the centre but in the south-west, and in the autumn of 1942 Zhukov was dispatched to Stalingrad as "Stavka (G.H.Q.) representative" to supervise the defence of the city and to take part in planning and supervising the counter-offensive where he coordinated the operations of the South-western and Don Fronts (while Vasilevski of the General Staff controlled the Stalingrad Front proper).

In January 1943 he was appointed a Marshal of the Soviet Union and once again in the spring and summer of 1943 acted as planner and "Stavka co-ordinator" of the giant battles at Kursk in 1943. Zhukov was also Stalin's "deputy", a post later formalized as First Deputy or Deputy Supreme Commander. During the third winter campaign, 1943-44, Zhukov planned and coordinated the operations of the 1st and 2nd Ukrainian Fronts, but when General Vatutin was killed by anti-Soviet guerrillas in February 1944 Zhukov assumed personal command of the 1st Ukrainian

Front, which, in spite of considerable successes, failed to accomplish the total inner and outer encirclement of the German forces in the south-west.

Zhukov was also at this time associated with the planning of the major offensive operations in Belorussia, Operation Bagration, in which Zhukov and Vasilevski again collaborated in planning and co-ordination. Zhukov assumed responsibility for the 1st and 2nd Belorussian Fronts, which expelled German forces from Soviet territory, and which reached into Poland.

After the planning conference on operations in Germany (October 1944) Stalin appointed his "First Deputy" Zhukov on November 16 to command the 1st Belorussian Front, to which Stalin assigned the task of taking Berlin.

On January 26, 1945, Zhukov presented his plans for the offensive, while a certain delay was imposed by clearing the Soviet flanks, principally in Pomerania. At the end of March, after the conclusion of the first stage of operations in Germany, the General Staff worked out the final version of the Berlin attack plans; on April 16, Zhukov's 1st Belorussian and Konev's 1st Ukrainian Fronts began their offensive on the Oder and Neisse respectively, Zhukov being held

up for three days by the remaining German defences.

With Konev moving on Berlin from the south-east, Zhukov's troops struck from the east and north-east, and the final battle for Berlin began on April 25, the encirclement of Berlin having been completed on April 21-22. On May 2 the Berlin garrison under General Weidling capitulated to Zhukov, whose troops had stormed the Reichstag and raised the Soviet flag over it. Soon afterwards he was appointed C.-in-C. of the Soviet occupation forces in Germany; he also became a member of Allied Control Commission.

In *The Memoirs of Marshal Zhukov*, which he published in 1971, he recounts how Stalin became hesitant, fearful and near despair when the German invasion became a certainty, and how the Russians grew suspicious, after the fall of Nazi Germany, that the western allies were plotting against them. He also graphically described his early life in poverty when his family had to live for a while in a shed, and his father, a cobbler, had to journey to Moscow in search of work.

June 20, 1974.

OBITUARIES OF THE SIXTIES

Many obituaries reprinted in this volume contain references in the text to persons who died in the 1960s. Those whose names are shown in this volume with an asterisk * were the subject of biographies in the previous volume, *Obituaries from The Times 1961-1970*, which is available from Newspaper Archive Developments Limited.

Below appear the names concerned, in each case with the year of death, and the page in the 1961-70 volume of this work in which their obituaries begin:-

GUIDE TO SUBJECTS OF THE OBITUARIES, 1971-1975

The following guide to the fields of activity of the persons whose obituaries have been reprinted in this volume lists some names under more than one heading – e.g., a head of state who was a soldier:–

INDEX OF OBITUARIES AND TRIBUTES 1971—1975

EXPLANATION OF INDEX

This index has been compiled from the last edition of *The Times* each day, for the years 1971 to 1975. It contains references to all obituaries —including the 'after rules' the short death notices at the foot of the Obituary Section of the paper— and tributes, published during the period.

Where a name is printed in black type, it signifies that the full text of the Obituary is reprinted in the main section of this book, which is arranged in alphabetical order.

In each entry the first numeral(s) indicate the day of the month, the second the page, and the letter the column: for reference purposes the columns of each page are supposed to be lettered from left to right—a, b,c,d,e,f,g,h. The final numerals appearing in parenthesis indicate the year. Thus July 15, 9c (72) denotes the issue of July 15, Page 9, column 3, of the year 1972.

The first date after each name refers to the date the obituary appeared in *The Times*, and each subsequent date refers to a tribute; the only exception being where the letter (t) appears, thus indicating that there was no obituary and that all references are to tributes.

Andrews, Prof. P. W. S.—Mar. 8, 14f (71); 20, 14h (71)

Andrews, Wilfrid—Feb. 20, 16f (75)

Andric, Ivo—Mar. 14, 16g (75)

Androulidakes, George—July 20, 14g (74)

Androvskaya, Olga—Apr. 8, 16g (75)

Angeli, **Pier**—Sept. 13, 16g (71)

Angrolillo, Renato—Aug. 18, 14h (73)

Angus, James G.—Dec. 5, 18f (72)

Anneon, Nikolas of—Oct. 19, 19h (72)

Annesley, Hilda—Sept. 27, 14g (72)

Anns, Bryan H.—July 10, 17f (75); 24, 16h (75)

Anokhin, Prof. Peter—Mar. 9, 16h (74)

Anson, Peter F.—July 19, 14g (75)

Anson, Sir Wilfred—Feb. 27, 20h (74); Mar. 6, 14h (74); 14, 18h (74)

Antoniutti, Card. Ildebranda—Aug. 15, 14h (74)

Antrim, Lady—Apr. 24, 18h (74)

Anwyl-Davis, Dr. Thomas—(t.), Nov. 2, 17h (71)

Appleby, Lt.-Col. Charles B.—Mar. 7, 16h (75); 10, 14g (75)

Appleby, William—Oct. 31, 20h (73)

Arab, Maroun—May 4, 18g (72)

Araoz, Card. Arturo T.—June 18, 20g (75)

Aras, Dr. Terfik Rustu—Jan. 7, 14h (72)

Arbenz, Col. Jacobo—Jan. 29, 17h (71)

Arbuthnot, Lady Elizabeth—June 13, 16h (72)

Archer, David A.—Oct. 21, 19h (71)

Archibald, Lord—Mar. 4, 16g (75)

Arcis, Evelyn d'—(t.), Sept. 24, 15h (74)

Arden, Lt.-Col. Eric C.—Aug. 31, 14h (73)

Arendt, Dr. Hannah—Dec. 6, 14h (75); 12, 18g (75)

Argenti, Philip—Apr. 16, 14h (74)

Argyll, Duke of—Apr. 9, 14f (73); 18, 21g (73)

Arie, Lt.-Col. Tuira—Nov. 7, 17g (72)

Arieli, Celia—Oct. 19, 16h (71)

Aris, Dr. Peter—May 18, 21h (72)

Arisfeld, Boris—Dec. 8, 16h (73)

Aristov, Averky—July 12, 18g (73)

Arkle, Harry—(t.), Mar. 20, 16h (73)

Arkwright, Maj.-Gen. Robert H. B.—Nov. 15, 14g (71); 18, 17f (71)

Arkwright, Robert O.—Sept. 29, 14h (73)

Arlen, Stephen—Jan. 20, 16g (72); 25, 16h (72)

Armand, Louis—Aug. 31, 12f (71); Sept. 3, 14g (71)

Armfield, Lillian—Aug. 28, 14g (71)

Armfield, Maxwell—Jan. 25, 16g (72); Feb. 2, 16f (72)

Armgard, Princess—Apr. 29, 18h (71)

Armitage, Gen. Sir Clement—Dec. 17, 17g (73); 24, 12g (73)

Armitage, William—Mar. 3, 14g (72)

Armstrong, Lord—July 11, 16g (72)

Armstrong, Arthur Henry—Jan. 13, 14h (72)

Armstrong, Hamilton F.—May 4, 20g (73)

Armstrong, John—May 23, 21h (73)

Armstrong, Louis—July 7, 16g (71)

Armstrong, Martin—Feb. 27, 20g (74)

Armstrong, Robert—Apr. 23, 8h (73)

Arndt, Dr. Adolf—Feb. 15, 17g (74)

Arndt, Dr. Klaus-Dieter—Feb. 2, 14h (74)

Arnold, Cecily—Oct. 22, 16g (74)

Arnold, Sir William—July 23, 14h (73); Aug. 1, 14h (73)

Arnott, Maj.-Gen Stanley—Oct. 28, 16h (72)

Aroch, Arie—Oct. 17, 18h (74)

Aron, Robert—Apr. 21, 16g (75)

Arnbay Castro, Cardinal—Mar. 9, 20h (73)

Arndt, Adolf—Feb. 15, 17g (74)

Arthur, Sir Raynor—Dec. 5, 21g (73)

Artsimovich, Prof. Lev. A.—Mar. 3, 16h (73); 8, 18f (73)

Aruttunyan, Dr. A. A.—Apr. 8, 16h (71)

Ascroft, Lady Eve—Dec. 7, 18g (74)

Asgeirsson, Asgeir—Sept. 18, 15h (72)

Ash, Frankie—May 3, 21h (73)

Ashbridge, Sir Noel—June 6, 17g (75)

Ashby, Miss Mabel K.—(t.), Oct. 31, 17g (75)

Ashby, Prof. W. Ross—Nov. 25, 16h (72)

Ashcombe, Lady (Jean)—(t.), Mar. 22, 20h (72)

Ashford, Daisy—Jan. 17, 12g (72)

Ashkanasy, Maurice—Apr. 8, 16h (71)

Ashmore, Vice-Adm. L. H.—Jan. 12, 14h (74); 24, 16h (74)

Ashrafi, Mukhtar—Dec. 18, 14f (75)

Ashtan, Lt.-Col. John L.—Nov. 15, 14h (75)

Ashworth, Mrs. Elizabeth J.—June 27, 18h (72)

Ashworth, Sir John—Sept. 27, 14h (75); 30, 14g (75); Oct. 1, 16g (75)

Askew, R. Kirk—(t.), Apr. 11, 22h (74)

Askew, Ray P.—(t.), Apr. 10, 18g (75)

Askey, May—Apr. 16, 14h (74)

Askochensky, Alexander—Mar. 8, 18h (73)

Askwith, Arthur V.—Apr. 28, 16g (71)

Asparoukohov, Georgi—July 6, 14h (71)

Aspinal, Prof. Arthur—May 6, 16g (72)

Assunto, Frank—Feb. 27, 20h (74)

Astor of Hever, Lord—July 20, 14e (71); 21, 14g (71); 22, 16g (71); 30, 17h (71); 27 15h (71)

Asturias, Miguel A.—June 11, 16h (74)

Athenagoras, Patriarch—July 8, 16g (72)

Atkins, Robert—Feb. 11, 16f (72); 17, 18h (72)

Atkinson, Lady Elsie—June 19, 16g (75)

Atkinson, Lt.-Col. Philip York—Apr. 13, 21h (72)

Atlas, Charles—Dec. 27, 5h (72)

Attenborough, Frederick L.—Mar. 23, 20g (73); 28, 21h (73)

Auckland, Lady Evelyn—Nov. 26, 19h (71)

Auden, W. H.—Oct. 1, 19f (73)

Audley, Lady—Oct. 26, 23g (73)

Auerbach, Dr. Erna—June 27, 14h (75)

Austin, Clive G.—Dec. 17, 17g (74)

Austin, Gene—Jan. 26, 16f (72)

Austin, Prof. George W.—Mar. 12, 18g (75)

Austin, Herschel L.—Apr. 11, 22h (74)

Austin, Robert S.—Sept. 21, 18g (73); 27, 22g (73); 29, 14g (73)

Austin, Prof. Roland—Oct. 11, 16g (74); 18, 19h (74)

Avebury, Lord—June 23, 19g (71)

Avery, Dr. Harold—Feb. 16, 16g (72); 18, 14h (72)

Avgheris, Adm. Spyridon—Jan. 8, 16g (72)

Awdry, Mrs. Evelyn D. A.—Oct. 20, 16g (71)

Axon, James—Apr. 17, 18h (73)

Aykroyd, Col. H. H.—Jan. 8, 14h (74)

Aylen, Rt. Rev. Charles A. W.—Aug. 16, 12g (72)

Ayre, Lady—Jan. 15, 14h (73)

Ayre, Leslie—Aug. 1, 16h (74)

Ayre, Sir Wilfrid—Aug. 13, 13h (71)

Ayrton, Michael—Nov. 19, 18f (75); 22, 14h (75); 25, 17h (75)

Ayub Khan, F.-M. Mohammad Ayub—Apr. 22, 16g (74)

Azcaratey y Florez, Don Pablo de—Dec. 16, 17g (71)

B

Babock Gove, Dr. Philip—Nov. 20, 19g (72)

Babin, Dr. Victor—Mar. 4, 14g (72); 10, 16g (72); 22, 18g (72)

Babington, Sir Anthony B.—Apr. 13, 21g (72)

Bacci, Cardinal Antonio—Jan. 21, 16g (71)

Bach, Dr. Francis—Nov. 21, 18g (75)

Bach, Dr. Stefan J.—Mar. 28, 21g (73)

Bachelet, Gen. Alberto—Mar. 14, 18h (74)

Bachmann, Ingeborg—Oct. 19, 20g (73)

Bach-Zelewsky, Erich van—Mar. 21, 16h (72)

Bacilek, Karol—Mar. 27, 18h (74)

Backer, George—(t.), May 18, 16g (74)

Bacon, Stuart L.—Aug. 13, 12h (73); 17, 16g (73)

Baddeley, John H.—Oct. 24, 19h (72)

Badenoch, Sir Cameron—Aug. 16, 16h (73)

Badenoch, Lady Jess—Sept. 30, 16h (72)

Bader, Thelma—Jan. 25, 12h (71); 30, 14g (71)

Badham, Rev. Leslie S. R.—July 5, 14g (75)

Badillo, Pablo Vargas—Sept. 6, 16h (71)

Baerlein, E. M.—June 5, 12g (71)

Bagdasarian, Russ—Jan. 18, 14g (72)

Bagnall-Wild, Brig. Ralph E.—Mar. 17, 14f (75)

Bailey, Lady Janet—Jan. 4, 14g (73)

Bailey, Lady Margaret—July 6, 14h (71)

Bailey, Lady Phyllis—Apr. 10, 14h (71)

Bailey, Air Comm. George Cyril—June 2, 16h (72)

Bailey, Gerald—(t.), May 18, 21h (72)

Bailey, James A. N.—Feb. 3, 16h (72)

Bailey, John—Apr. 12, 14h (75)

Bailey, John—(t.), Nov. 30, 19f (72)

Bailey, Sir Kenneth—May 5, 14g (72); 19, 18h (72)

Bailey, Col. S. W.—(t.), July 9, 17g (74)

Baillie, Lady Maud—Apr. 1, 14h (75)

Baillie, Lady Olive—(t.), Sept. 12, 20g (74)

Baillie, Brig. Allister C.—June 15, 17h (71)

Baillieu, Lord—Apr. 21, 14g (73)

Baily, Robert E. H.—Sept. 24, 16h (73)

Bain, Dr. William A.—Aug. 25, 14g (71); 27, 14h (71)

Baines, Rt. Rev. Henry W.—Dec. 2, 18h (72); 5, 18f (72); 15, 16h (72)

Baines, Jocelyn—(t.), Dec. 15, 16g (72)

Baird, Teddy—(t.), Mar. 27, 20g (75); Apr. 2, 16h (75)

Baissac, Maj. Claude de—Jan. 7, 14g (75)

Baker, Lady Doris—Dec. 22, 15g (72)

Baker, Beatrice M.—Oct. 17, 23h (73)

Baker, Dr. Doris M.—Oct. 1, 19g (71)

Baker, Rev. Dr. Eric—Sept. 24, 16f (73)

Baker, J. N. L.—Dec. 18, 14h (73)

Baker, John—Nov. 29, 14g (71)

Baker, Josephine—Apr. 14, 14g (75)

Bakladjis, Emmanouel—Dec. 2, 18f (71)

Bakstansky, Lavy—(t.), Feb. 3, 14 (71)

Balachova, Tania—Aug. 7, 14h (73)

Balchen, Bernt—Oct. 20, 18h (73)

Baldick, Dr. Robert—Apr. 25, 14g (72)

Brasch, Charles—(t.), May 24, 20h (73)

Brasher, William K.—May 27, 16g (72)

Brass, Lady—July 18, 15h (72)

Brasseur, Pierre—Aug. 16, 12g (72)

Brauer, Mat—Feb. 3, 16g (73)

Braun, Otto—Aug. 17, 14h (74)

Braun, Baron Otto von—Aug. 31, 14f (72)

Braunthal, Julius—(t.), May 1, 16g (72)

Brazier, Fred—Apr. 5, 14g (75)

Brean, Herbert J.—May 11, 22g (73)

Brebner, Lady Margaret—Dec. 27, 10g (74)

Brebner, John—Feb. 20, 16g (74)

Breene, Very Rev. Richard—Feb. 8, 18h (74)

Breffort, Alexandre—Feb. 26, 16g (71)

Bremner, Brig. Richard M.—Dec. 28, 10h (73)

Brennan, Charles J.—May 10, 18g (72)

Brennan, Walter—Sept. 23, 14g (74)

Brenner, Otto—Apr. 17, 16g (72)

Brent, Evelyn—June 9, 16g (75)

Bret, Paul-Louis—Nov. 23, 21g (72)

Bretcher, Dr. Egon—Apr. 17, 18h (73)

Brett, Louis J.—Aug. 14 17f (75)

Brett, Prof. Peter—(t.), May 13, 16g (75)

Bretton Frank—Aug. 25, 14h (71)

Brewis, Rev. John S.—Mar. 3, 14f (72)

Brewster, Dr. George—July 3, 18h (73)

Breyfogle, Robert J.—Sept. 4, 14h (72)

Brezanoczy, Dr. Pal—Feb. 14, 14h (72)

Brian, Havergal—Nov. 29 18g (72)

Brickell, Harry T.—Apr. 16, 18h (71)

Bridge, Ann: see O'Malley, Lady

Bridge, George W.—Mar. 24, 16h (71); Apr. 16, 18h (71)

Bridge, Kathleen E.—Feb. 9, 16h (73)

Bridge, Adm. Sir Robin—Feb. 23, 14h (71)

Bridgeford, Lt.-Gen. Sir William—Sept. 24, 14h (71)

Bridgeman, Geoffrey J. O.—Oct. 17, 18g (74)

Bridgeman, Col. Henry G. O.—May 20, 16f (72)

Bridges, Daisy C.—Dec. 2, 18h (72)

Bridges, Victor—Dec. 1, 18f (72)

Bridges, Yscult—(t.), Aug. 5, 14h (71)

Bridgewater, Leslie—Mar. 21, 18h (75)

Brierley, Lady Zoe—Sept. 12, 17h (75)

Brigard, Dr. Camilo de—Jan. 19, 16h (72)

Briggs, Albert—(t.), June 4, 17h (71)

Briggs, D. H. C.—Oct. 1, 16h (74)

Briggs, W. Gerald—(t.), Jan. 13, 16g (75)

Brigstocke, Geoffrey—(t.), Mar. 7, 18g (74)

Brigstocke, Rev. George E.—Oct. 26, 14h (71)

Brigstocke, Reginald—Dec. 17, 16g (71)

Brill, Joseph E.—May 23, 16h (75)

Brinitzer, Dr. Carl—Oct. 29, 19f (74)

Brink, Lt.-Gen. George—May 1, 14h (71)

Brinkmann, Rolf D.—May 7, 18f (75)

Brinson, Derek—(t.), Jan. 6, 14h (75)

Brinton, Jasper Yeates—Aug. 15, 16g (73)

Briscoe, Grace Lady—Oct. 5, 21h (73)

Brise, Tony—Dec. 1, 14g (75)

Brittain, Lady—Sept. 26, 18g (73)

Brittain, Sir Harry—July 10, 1e 20h (74)

Brittan, Cliff—Dec. 3, 18h (75)

Britten, Lt.-Col. F. C. R.—Apr. 15, 16h (72)

Britton, Lionel—Jan. 19, 14h (71)

Broad, Prof. Charles W.—Mar. 15, 14h (71)

Broad, H. S.—(t.), Aug. 5, 14h (75); 15, 14g (75)

Broadbent, Prof. T. A. A.—Jan. 31, 16g (73)

Broadbridge, Lord—Nov. 22, 18g (72)

Broadwood, Capt. Evelyn—June 26, 18g (75)

Brocket, Lady Angela—Aug. 25, 8h (75)

Brocklebank, Lady Lucy—Nov. 13, 16h (75)

Brocklebank, Sir John—Sept. 17, 17g (74)

Brocklehurst, Lady Gladys—Feb. 12, 14g (72)

Brocklehurst, Mark D.—(t.), Sept. 14, 19g (72)

Brocklehurst, Sir Philip—Jan. 30, 18g (75)

Brodie, Sir Benjamin—Aug. 6, 14h (71); 10, 14h (71)

Brodrick, Rev. James P.—Aug. 28, 14h (73)

Brogan, Sir Denis—Jan. 7, 12g (74)

Bromet, William G. H.—Jan. 4, 12f (71)

Brommage, Joseph Charles—Feb. 16, 16h (72)

"Bronco Billy": see Anderson, Gilbert

Bronfman, Samuel—July 13, 14h (71)

Bronk, Dr. Detlev W.—Nov. 19, 18h (75)

Bronowski, Dr. Jacob—(t.), Sept. 11, 17h (74)

Brook, Clive—Nov. 19, 17g (74)

Brook, Rev. Victor J. K.—July 3, 18g (74)

Brooke, Sylvia Lady—Nov. 13, 14g (71)

Brookeborough, Lord—Aug. 20, 15e (73)

Brookes, Dame Mabel—May 2, 17g (75)

Brookes, Roy—(t.), Sept. 2, 16f (72)

Brooks, Cicely—Feb. 14, 18g (75)

Brooks, Herbert W.—Nov. 26, 18g (74)

Brooks, Neil—Aug. 21, 14h (75)

Brooks, Phillips—Jan. 14, 16g (75)

Brooks, Roy—Sept. 1, 14h (71)

Broughshane, Lady Constance—July 23, 15g (71)

Brown, Lady—Apr. 30, 16f (73)

Brown, Lady—Sept. 16, 16h (75)

Brown, Lady Jane—Mar. 26, 18h (75)

Brown, Lady Joanna—May 13, 19h (71)

Brown, Alan Grahame—Jan. 6, 12h (72)

Brown, Brig. Alan W.—Sept. 3, 14g (71)

Brown, Charles Gordon—Feb. 10, 16f (72)

Brown, Dr. Felix—June 17, 16g (72); 20, 16h (72)

Brown, Harold J.—Dec. 29, 10g (75)

Brown, Hugh B.—Dec. 8, 14h (75)

Brown, Ivor—Apr. 23, 18g (74)

Brown Jackie—Mar. 16, 17h (71)

Brown, Jacques—Apr. 4, 18h (75)

Brown, Joe E.—July 7, 14h (73)

Brown, Johnny M.—Nov. 16, 16h (74)

Brown, Sir Lindor—Feb. 23, 14f (71)

Brown, Maurice J. E.—Sept. 30, 14g (75)

Brown, Pamela—Sept. 20, 14g (75); 23, 17g (75); 27, 14g (75)

Brown, Robert—Jan. 6, 12g (72)

Brown, Prof. Robert J.—Sept. 5, 14g (72)

Brown, Robert V.—(t.), Apr. 27, 18g (72); June 2, 16h (72)

Brown, Robson C.—Dec. 17, 16g (71)

Brown, Robley—(t.), Jan. 20, 16g (73)

Brown, Sandy—(t.), Mar. 22, 16g (75); 25, 19g (75)

Brown, Spencer—Jan. 19, 16g (73)

Brown, Wilfred—Mar. 9, 16h (71); 11, 18g (71)

Brown, Prof. William—Jan. 25, 14g (75)

Brown, Sir William R.—Feb. 27, 16h (75)

Browne, Cardinal Michael—Apr. 1, 18g (71)

Browning, Prof. Andrew—May 11, 18g (72)

Brownjohn, Gen. Sir Nevil—Apr. 23, 8h (73); 27, 21g (73); May 2, 20g (73)

Bruce, Charles—Dec. 21, 14h (71)

Bruce, Sir Hervey—June 22, 14h (71)

Bruce, Maj.-Gen. J. G.—Feb. 2, 16f (72)

Bruce, Sir John—Dec. 31, 12f (75)

Bruce, Capt. John B.—Aug. 5, 14g (71)

Bruce, Robert E. S.—Mar. 24, 16g (71)

Bruen, Jimmy—(t.), May 5, 14h (72)

Brundage, Avery—May 10, 16f (75)

Brundage, Mrs. Avery—July 8, 16h (71)

Brundrett, Sir Frederick—Aug. 6, 14g (74); 8, 16h (74); 12, 14h (74)

Bruner, Dr. Herbert—Aug. 7, 16h (74)

Brunot, Andre—Aug. 8, 16g (73)

Brunt, Lady Claudia—Feb. 23, 14h (72)

Bruntisfield, Lady Dorothy—July 3, 17g (75)

Bryan, Rev. Frank—(t.), May 9, 16g (72)

Buasir, Saleh M.—Feb. 27, 16h (73)

Bubanj, Col.-Gen. Viktor—Oct. 16, 14h (72)

Buccleuch, Duke of—Oct. 5, 21f (73); 18, 20h (73)

Buchanan, Lady—Sept. 5, 21h (73)

Buchanan, Maj.-Gen. Alan G. B.—Feb. 27, 14g (71)

Buck, Dr. John L.—Sept. 30, 14h (75)

Buck, Pearl S.—Mar. 7, 18f (73)

Buck, Tim—Mar. 16, 18h (73)

Buckland, Lady Gwladys—Oct. 1, 19f (71)

Buckley, Bill—Apr. 21, 14h (73)

Buckley, Henry—Nov. 11, 18g (72); 15, 19h (72)

Buckley, Maj-Gen. John—(t.), Oct. 28, 16g (72)

Buckley, Prof. John—Apr. 18, 16g (72)

Buckmaster, Lord Owen—Nov. 26, 18g (74)

Budberg, Lady Marie—Nov. 2, 14g (74)

Budden, Geoffrey—Mar. 16, 17g (71)

Budenny, Marshal S. M.—Oct. 29, 17f (73)

Budenz, Louis—Apr. 29, 16h (72)

Budgen Frank—(t.), Apr. 29, 18f (71)

Buist, "Gladdie"—July 4, 19g (72)

Bulganin, Nikolai—Feb. 26, 17g (75)

Bulgaranov, Boyan—Dec. 30, 16h (72)

Bullard, Lady—Jan. 2, 12f (73)

Buller, Amy—(t.), Mar. 18, 14h (74)

Buller, Annie G.—Jan. 23, 16h (73)

Bullock, Lady Barbara—Dec. 20, 14h (74)

Bullock, Sir Christopher L.—May 19, 18g (72); 20, 16f (72)

Bullock-Marsham, Brig. Francis W.—Dec. 23, 12g (71)

Bulman, Prof. Oliver—Feb. 20, 16g (74)

Bum, Dr. John L.—Jan. 3, 14g (74)

Bunche, Dr. Ralph—Dec. 10, 16f (74)

Bundy, May S.—Oct. 8, 16g (75)

Bunker, Alfred S.—May 7, 16h (74)

Bunker, Dr. H. J.—(t.), Aug. 15, 14g (75)

Burchnall, Prof. Joseph L.—May 2, 17g (75); 8, 16g (75)

Burckhardt, Dr. Carl—Mar. 5, 16f (74)

Burgess, Clarkson L.—July 18 14h (75)

Burgess, Geoffrey—May 22, 16g (72)

Burke, Lady—Mar. 4, 17h (71)

Burke, Denis E.—(t.), Aug. 3, 14h (71)

Burke, Don—Jan. 20, 11h (73)

Burke, Mick—Sept. 30, 14g (75)

Burke, Roger—Dec. 23, 12h (74)

Burke-Gaffney, Dr. H.—Feb. 6, 16h (73)

Burkitt, Miles C.—Aug. 24, 13h (71); 26, 12g (71); 16, 18h (71)

Burleigh, T. H.—Sept. 15, 17g (71)

Burling, Group Capt.—(t.), Dec. 13, 20g (74)

Burman, William F.—Oct. 25, 18g (74)

Burmeister, Vladimir—Mar. 8, 14f (71)

Burnell, Cmdr. John B.—Apr. 10, 14h (71)

Burnett, Al—Apr. 21, 14g (73)

Burnett, Col. Geoffrey A.—Nov. 6, 14g (72)

Burnett, Col. Robert R.—Nov. 6, 17g (75)

Burnett, Whit—May 7, 18h (73)

Burnley, Fred—July 10, 17g (75)

Burns, Emile—Feb. 9, 14h (72)

Burns, Henry S.—Oct. 29, 16f (71)

Burns, Jack—Mar. 15, 18h (74)

Burns, John—Nov. 28, 16g (72)

Burns, Robert—July 16, 14h (71)

Burnside, Thomas Allan—Jan. 17, 12h (72)

Burrell, John P.—Oct. 4, 16f (72)

Burrough, Lady—Sept. 6, 17h (72)

Burrows, Lady Eleanor—Feb. 18, 16g (75)

Burrows, Sir Frederick—Apr. 24, 14f (73)

Burrows, Larry—Feb. 12, 14g (71)

Burt, Lady—Sept. 17, 17h (74)

Burt, Sir Cyril—Oct. 12, 15e (71); 15, 16h (71); 16, 14g (71)

Burton, Lady Doris—Nov. 20, 21h (73)

Burton, Beatrice B. E.—Feb. 24, 16h (75)

Burton, David C. F.—Oct. 1, 19h (71)

Burton, Sir Geoffrey Pownall—Apr. 11, 16g (72)

Burton, Maj. Henry M.—(t.), July 1, 16h (72)

Burton, John—Oct. 24, 21g (73)

Burton, Mary—Mar. 27, 20g (75)

Burton, Richard—Feb. 2, 14h (74)

Bush, Cmdr. Athelstan P.—Sept. 21, 16g (72)

Bush, Maj. Christopher—Sept. 27, 22h (73)

Bush, Dr. Vannevar—July 1, 16g (74)

Bushell, W. F.—Nov. 22, 19h (74)

Bushnell, George H.—Aug. 13, 12h (73)

Bustard, Col. F.—Jan. 23, 16g (74)

Butchart, Lt.-Col. Henry J.—Aug. 31, 12h (71); Sept. 14, 15g (71)

Butcher, Rt. Rev. Reginald A. C. —Nov. 24, 19h (75)

Butler, Lady Helen—Jan. 15, 16g (72)

Butler, Charles H. A.—Mar. 23, 14h (74)

Butler, Ewan—Oct. 5, 16h (74)

Butler, Grace—Apr. 10, 14h (71)

Butler, Harold E.—May 16, 21g (73)

Butler, Herbert W.—Nov. 19, 16g (71)

Butler, Hugh M.—Apr. 26, 16g (72)

Butler, Prof. Sir James—Mar. 3, 16g (75); 13, 18h (75); 24, 16g (75)

Butler, Sir Nevile—Nov. 13, 18g (73)

Butler, Olive—(t.), Oct. 21, 19f (71)

Butler, Maj. Robert A. P.—Aug. 23, 16h (7)

Butler, William Boynton—Mar. 28, 17h (72)

Butterfield, Frederick V.—Mar. 11, 14f (74)

Butterworth, W. Walton—Apr. 2, 16h (75); 4, 18g (75)

Buxton, Richard G.—Jan. 1, 16g (73)

Buzzard, Rear Adm. Sir Anthony —Mar. 11, 14g (72)

Buzzati, Dino—Jan. 29, 14g (72)

Byas, Don—Aug. 31, 14g (72)

Byington, Spring—Sept. 9, 16f (71)

Byl, Maj. P. V. G. van der—Jan. 23, 19h (75)

Byrne, Dr. Alfred—July 16, 14g (71)

Byrne, Cecily—July 4, 16g (75)

Byrne, Mgr. Canon John H.— Nov. 28, 16g (72)

Byrnes, James Francis—Apr. 10, 15e (72)

Bywaters, Maj. John—(t.), Apr. 18, 12g (73)

C

Cabon, Marcel—Feb. 5, 16h (72)

Cabot, Bruce—May 5, 14g (72)

Cabral, Amilcar—Jan. 22, 16h (73)

Cabrolier, Dr. Henri—Nov. 19, 16g (71)

Caceres, Ernie—Jan. 13, 12h (71)

Cade, Sir Stanford—Sept. 21, 18f (73)

Cadorna, Gen. Raffaile—Dec. 22, 12h (73)

Caetano, Donna Maria T.—Jan. 16, 14h (71)

Caffrey, Jefferson—Apr. 16, 14h (71)

Cain, Maj. Robert—May 4, 14h (74)

Caine, Lady Doris—Dec. 13, 21g (73)

Cakobau, Ratu Sir Edward—July 2, 16g (73); 11, 18h (73)

Calamai, Capt. Pietro—Apr. 12, 18h (72)

Caldecott, Lady Evelyn—May 14, 18g (74)

Calder, J. W.—May 30, 16g (75)

Caldwell, Prof. John—Aug. 30, 16h (74)

Callan, B. J. T.—Sept. 22, 17g (72)

Callaway, A. V.-M. William B.— Aug. 31, 14g (74)

Callejon, Eduardo Propper y—(t.), Jan. 29, 14f (72)

Calley, Joan M.—May 9, 18f (73)

Callori, Cardinal Federico—Aug. 11, 12g (71)

Calpin, G. H.—July 22, 16h (74)

Cals, Joseph Maria—Jan. 1, 18f (72)

Calvert, John C.—May 4, 14g (74)

Calwell, Arthur—July 10, 16g (73)

Cameron, Lady Jane—Jan. 29, 14g (74)

Cameron, Basil—June 28, 14g (75)

Cameron, Ald. Sir Cornelius— May 10, 16f (75)

Cameron, Douglas—(t.), Aug. 29, 16h (74)

Cameron, Maj.-Gen. Roderic D.— May 3, 16g (75)

Cameron-Ramsay-Fairfat, Maj. Sir Brian F.—Jan. 24, 16h (74)

Cameron-Webb, Brig. John H.— Sept. 12, 17h (75)

Campbell, Lady Janet—June 13, 18h (75)

Campbell, Alfred E.—Mar. 6, 18h (73)

Campbell, Prof. Alistair—Feb. 11, 16g (74)

Campbell, Prof. Archibald D.— Jan. 13, 16g (75)

Campbell, C. Douglas—May 31, 14h (75)

Campbell, Prof. Charles—Mar. 19, 16g (74); 20, 18h (74)

Campbell, Colin—Nov. 22, 14g (71)

Campbell, Edmund G.—Nov. 27, 16g (72)

Campbell, Elidor—July 8, 16g (75)

Campbell, Ewen—Nov. 17, 18h (75)

Campbell, Brig. H.—(t.), Apr. 19, 17h (72)

Campbell, Capt. Ian—Dec. 22, 13g (71)

Campbell, Isobel—(t.), Jan. 9, 12g (71)

Campbell, John M.—July 6, 14h (74)

Campbell, Dr. Maurice—Aug. 9, 14g (73)

Campbell, Rt. Rev. Montgomery —(t.), Jan. 2, 14g (71)

Campbell, Richard M.—Nov. 19, 17h (74); Dec. 4, 18g (74)

Campbell, Dr. Sidney—June 6, 18g (74); 8, 14h (74)

Campbell, Lt-Col. Sir Walter— May 24, 20g (73)

Campbell, Wilson W.—Jan. 15, 17g (75); 16, 21h (75)

Campigli, Massimo—June 4, 17f (75)

Campling, Rev. Canon William C. —Feb. 26, 14h (73)

Camps, Prof. Francis E.—July 10, 16g (72); 14, 18g (72)

Cane, H. P.—May 28, 10h (73)

Cang, Joel—Nov. 29, 20h (74)

Cannon, James P.—Aug. 30, 16g (74)

Canny, Lady (Mary)—Nov. 25, 16g (72)

Cantlie, Sir Neil—May 20, 16h (75)

Canty, Joe—Mar. 9, 16g (71)

Cao Hoai Sang—Apr. 26, 15h (71)

Capener, Norman—Apr. 2, 16g (75); 5, 14g (75)

Capon, Prof. Norman—Jan. 10, 16g (75)

Carandini, Count Nicolo—Mar. 21, 16g (72); 22, 18h (72); 27, 14g (72)

Carden, Winifred Lady—(t.), Jan. 17, 14h (74)

Cardew, A. Evelyn—May 18, 21h (72)

Cardew, Dr. Bruce—(t.), June 23, 19h (71)

Cardona, Dr. Jose M.: see Miro Cardona, Dr. Jose

Cardus, Sir Neville—Mar. 1, 14f (75); 7, 16g (75)

Carey, Lady Elizabeth—Apr. 17, 16g (72)

Carey, Maj.-Gen. De Vic—Oct. 4, 16h (72)

Carey, Dr. Fraser—(t.), Nov. 30, 19g (72)

Carleton, John D.—Nov. 7, 18g (74); 13, 18g (74)

Carlisle, Lt.-Col. Denton—Mar. 14, 16h (72)

Carlson, Bo—(t.), May 17, 14g (75)

Carmichael, Dr. James—Mar. 25, 18f (72)

Carnegy, Lieut.-Col. U. E.—Feb. 5, 14h (73)

Carneiro, Levi—Sept. 7, 12h (71)

Carnell, Edward John—Mar. 25, 18h (72)

Carney, Harry—Oct. 11, 16h (74)

Caroe, Frederik T. K.—(t.), Jan. 5, 14h (71)

Carpenter, Edward H. O.—Jan. 16, 14g (74)

Carpenter, Sir Eric—Aug. 6, 14g (73)

Carpenter, Peter—Mar. 31, 16h (71)

Carpentier, Georges—Oct. 29, 16g (75)

Carpmael, Kenneth S.—Nov. 28, 19g (75)

Carr, Lady—Feb. 9, 16h (73)

Carr, Ralph Edward—Jan. 13, 14g (72)

Carr, Air Marshal Sir Roderick— Dec. 18, 14g (71)

Carr, Rupert E.—May 17, 22h (74)

Carrero Blanco, Adm. Luis—Dec. 21, 17 (73)

Carrington, Lady—Jan. 19, 16h (73)

Carrington, Mabel Ruby: see Peeler, Mrs. Ruby

Carrington, Most Rev. Philip— Oct. 7, 14g (75)

Carrington, Richard—Sept. 28, 14f (71)

Carrington, Dr. Roger C.—July 13, 14h (71)

Carrington, Sir William—May 13, 16h (75); 15, 20h (75)

Carroll, Sir John—May 4, 14g (74); 9, 22h (74); June 7, 21h (74)

Carroll, Leo G.—Oct. 19, 19h (72)

Carruthers, James N.—(t.), Mar. 24, 14h (73)

Carse, H. P.—(t.), May 28, 10h (73)

Carson, Anthony—May 18, 22f (73)

Carter, Dr. C. W.—(t.), May 18, 16g (74); 21, 18g (74)

Carter, Hodding—Apr. 6, 15h (72)

Carter, John—Mar. 19, 19f (75)

Carter, Jonas Harry—Oct. 10, 21h (73)

Carter, Julius—Jan. 22, 16f (71)

Carter, Robert E.—Oct. 24, 20g (74)

Carter, Walter—Feb. 13, 16g (75)

Carthy, Dr. John D.—Mar. 14, 16g (72)

Cartier, Raymond—Feb. 11, 14h (75)

Cartmel, Lt.-Col. A E—June 10, 16h (74)

Carton, Jane—Jan. 4, 14h (71)

Carton, Pauline—June 19, 18g (74)

Carty, Francis—Apr. 10, 15g (72)

Carver, David—May 11, 16g (74); 16, 21h (74)

Casadesus, Robert—Sept. 20, 17h (72)

Casals, Pablo—Oct. 23, 18g (73)

Casaus, Gregorio Modrego—Jan. 18, 14g (72)

Caseley, J. R.—Feb. 12, 14g (72)

Cash, Alan J.—Feb. 22, 16h (74)

Cashman, Rt. Rev. David—Mar. 15, 14f (71)

Cashmore, Francis M.—July 23, 15f (71)

Cashmore, Herbert M.—June 20, 19g (72)

Caslon, Vice-Adm. C.—Feb. 13, 18g (73)

Cassels, Sir James Dale—Feb. 8, 14g (72); 14, 14g (72)

Cassidy, A. V.-M. John R.—Dec. 10, 16h (74)

Castagneto, Sig. Renzo—Feb. 19, 16h (71)

Castellani, Prof. Marchese Sir Aldo—Oct. 5, 16f (71)

Castle, Prof. Edgar B.—Sept. 11, 18g (73); 19, 21f (73)

Castro, Dr. Augusto de—July 26, 14h (74)

Castro, Jose M. F. de—July 4, 18h (74)

Catchpool, Jack—Mar. 16, 17f (71)

Cater, Percy—(t.), Feb. 18, 16h (71); 19, 16g (71)

Catling, Lady—Jan. 29, 14g (74)

Cator, Geoffrey—Apr. 23, 8h (73)

Cavan, Romilly—(t.), Aug. 13, 14h (75)

Cavendish, Richard E. O.—Aug. 22, 14h (72); Sept. 2, 16f (72)

Cawadias, Dr. Alexander—Nov. 23, 17g (71)

Cawthorne, Lady Lilian—Apr. 19, 16g (75)

Cayley, Elizabeth Lady—Jan. 22, 16g (74)

Cazalet, Peter—May 30, 20f (73)

Ceausescu, Andruta—Apr. 18, 16h (72)

Cederstrom, Baroness Hermione—Jan. 18, 14g (72)

Celsing, Prof. Peter—Mar. 23, 14g (74)

Ceran-Maillard, Roger—May 16, 21h (74)

Cerf, Bennett—Aug. 30, 8h (71)

Cerny, Joseph—Jan. 5, 14g (71)

Cerutty, Percy—Aug. 15, 14h (75)

Cervi, Sig. Gino—Jan. 4, 14g (74)

Cevert, Francois—Oct. 8, 19h (73)

Chabou, Col. Abdelkader—Apr. 8, 16g (71)

Chacko, Mangalam E.—Mar. 14, 18h (73)

Chadwick, Sir James—July 25, 20g (74)

Chadwick, Nora K.—Apr. 26, 16h (72)

Chagrin, Francis—Nov. 11, 18g (72); 13, 16g (72)

Chakrabongse, Princess Chula—Dec. 2, 18g (71)

Chaliha, Bimala P.—Feb. 27, 14g (71)

Chalkley, Lady—Feb. 5, 16g (71)

Chalmers, Canon R.—Feb. 8, 18g (74)

Chalmers, Rear-Adm. William S.—June 15, 17h (71)

Chaloner, Lenore—Dec. 7, 18g (74)

Chamberlain, Brenda—July 31, 12h (71)

Chamberlain, Rt. Rev. Frank N.—July 23, 16h (75)

Chamberlain, Samuel—Jan. 21, 16f (75)

Chamberlayne, Edith A.—Apr. 30, 16f (73)

Chambers, Philip Cecil—Mar. 24, 16g (72)

Chambure, Count Gerard de—July 6, 14h (71)

Chamier, Air-Comm. Sir John—May 4, 14h (74)

Champion, Frederick H.—Jan. 9, 17g (75)

Chancellor, Francis B.—Oct. 12, 18f (72)

Chandos, Lord—Jan. 22, 14f (72); 27, 18g (72)

Chanel, Gabrielle—Jan. 12, 14f (71)

Chaney Jnr., Lon—July 14, 1f (73); 14, 14h (73)

Chang Chien—Mar. 29, 20h (74)

Chang Hsi-Jo—Jul. 30, 14h (73)

Chang Kuo-Hua—Feb. 29, 16g (72)

Chang Li-Sheng—Apr. 21, 16h (71)

Chang Shih-chao—July 3, 18h (73)

Chaplin, Dowager Lady Gwladys—Oct. 20, 16h (71)

Chaplin, Sir George—Apr. 28, 14h (75)

Chaplin, Mary—(t.), June 7, 21g (74)

Chapman, Helen Lady—July 17, 14h (72)

Chapman, Charles H.—July 18, 14g (72)

Chapman, Guy—July 1, 16f (72)

Chapman, A. V.-M. Hubert Huntlea—Apr. 11, 16g (72)

Chapman, James—Nov. 24, 16h (71)

Chapman, Raynor D.—Feb. 28, 18g (73)

Chappell, Lady Eileen—Mar. 25, 18g (72)

Chapple, Dr. Peter A. C.—(t.), Dec. 2, 14g (75)

Charbonneau, Pierre—Oct. 6, 14h (75)

Charie, Lt.-Col. Pierre—Mar. 16, 18h (73)

Charlemont, Lord—Nov. 20, 14h (71)

Charles, Dr. Enid—Apr. 3, 8e (72)

Charles, Ezzard—May 29, 16f (75)

Charles, Maj. Ivor—Aug. 24, 12h (74)

Charles, Sir John—Apr. 8, 16g (71); 21, 16g (71)

Charles, Sir Noel—Sept. 12, 17g (75); 22, 14g (75)

Charlesworth, Prof. John Kaye—Jan. 31, 14g (72)

Charlet, Armand—(t.), Dec. 5, 16g (75)

Charlton, Andrew—Dec. 15, 13g (75)

Charnley, Leonard—Aug. 15, 16h (73)

Charon, Jacques—Oct. 16, 16g (75)

Charriere, Henri—July 31, 14g (73)

Charrington, Jack—(t.), Apr. 4, 22h (74)

Chase, Rt. Rev. George A.—Dec. 1, 17g (71); 4, 14h (71)

Chatterton, Ernest—Jan. 26, 14h (71)

Chatterton, Vivienne—Jan. 10, 16h (74)

Chaudbury, Abdul H.—Mar. 20, 14f (71)

Chaundler, Christine—Dec. 22, 15g (72)

Chave, Alf—Aug. 16, 12g (71)

Checchi, Andrea—Apr. 1, 17g (74)

Chehab, Gen. Fuad—Apr. 26, 18h (73)

Chen Pheng-Jen—Apr. 15, 16g (72)

Chen Po-Chun—Feb. 12, 16h (74)

Chen Yi, Marshal—Jan. 12, 12f (72); 15, 16h (72)

Chen Yuan—July 1, 19h (71)

Chenebenoit, Andre—Feb. 26, 14g (74)

Chenevix-Trench, Christopher J.—July 20, 14f (71); 21, 14g (71)

Chenevix-Trench, Brig. Ralph—May 7, 16g (74)

Cheng Wei-san—Aug. 5, 14h (75)

Chesham, Marian Lady—Sept. 8, 14g (73)

Cheshire, Dame Mary—Apr. 4, 14h (72)

Chesselet, Dr. Robert—Nov. 3, 18f (72)

Chesser, Dr. Eustace—Dec. 6, 18h (73)

Chester, Alfred I.—Aug. 3, 14h (71)

Chesterton, A. K.—Aug. 17, 16h (73)

Chetham-Strode, Warren—Apr. 27, 16h (74)

Chetwood, Denis—(t.), Jan. 31, 16h (73)

Chevalier, Maurice—Jan. 3, 12f (72)

Chevins, Hugh—Aug. 12, 14g (75)

Cheylesmore, Lord—May 7, 16g (74)

Cheylesmore, Lady Pearl—May 18, 16h (74)

Chiang Kai-shek, Gen.—Apr. 7, 16f (75)

Chiarini, Luigi—Nov. 15, 14h (75)

Chichester, Lt.-Col. Arthur—Mar. 10, 16h (72)

Chichester, Sir Francis—Sept. 8, 18h (72)

Chick, Sir Louis—(t.), May 11, 18h (72)

Chiesman, Sir Walter—Aug. 15, 16h (73)

Child, Lady (Barbara)—Dec. 31, 10h (71)

Child, Sir John—May 28, 18g (71)

Child, Rev. Robert L.—Jan. 4, 12g (71)

Childers, Erskine—Nov. 18, 16g (74)

Childs, Dr. E. C.—May 26, 16g (73)

Chinn, Wilfred H.—(t.), Jan. 14, 16h (71)

Chipembere, Henry B. M.—Oct. 8, 14g (75)

Chisholm, Ven Alexander—Dec. 27, 10h (75)

Chisholm, Dr. Brock—Feb. 5, 16g (71)

Chisholm, Most Rev. John W.—May 29, 16g (75)

Chisholm, Ronal G.—July 12, 16h (72)

Chitepo, Herbert—Mar. 19, 19h (75)

Chitham, Sir Charles—Sept. 27, 16g (72)

Chitty, Ethel Lady—Jan. 4, 14h (71)

Chitty, Rev. Derwen—(t.), Mar. 2, 16f (71)

Chivers, Stephen O.—Aug. 23, 14g (75)

Choi Doo-Sun—Sept. 12, 20g (74)

Cholerton, A. T.—(t.), Mar. 21, 17f (73); 26, 14h (73)

Chotiner, Murray—Jan. 31, 18h (74)

Chowdhury, Fozlul Q.—July 25, 18g (73)

Chowdhury, Zaher Ahmed—July 2, 16f (74)

Chrimes, Sir Bertram—Dec. 22, 15h (72)

Chrissoveloni, Nicholas—Oct. 19, 19h (72)

Christ, George—May 25, 21h (72); 27, 16h (72)

Christiains, Louis—Feb. 6, 19f (75)

Christian, Harry—Sept. 27, 16g (74)

Christie, Sir Harold—Sept. 27, 22h (73)

Christie, Group Capt. Malcolm G.—Nov. 17, 19h (71); 24, 16g (71)

Christison, Lady Betty—Mar. 27, 18h (74)

Christopher, John—Feb. 3, 14g (71)

Chunhawan, Marshal P.—Jan. 27, 16h (73)

Church, Eric E. R.—(t.), Jun. 29, 18f (72)

Church, Esme—June 1, 16f (72); 6, 16h (72); 6, 16h (72); 10, 14h (72)

Church, Richard—Mar. 6, 17f (72); 9, 16g (72); 11, 14g (72); 17, 16h (72)

Churcher, Harry—June 28, 16h (72)

Churchill, Lord—Dec. 24, 12g (73)

Churchill, Arnold R.—(t.), May 5, 16g (75)

Churchill, Capt. Peter—May 2, 16g (72)

Chye, Dato Aw Cheng—Aug. 25, 14g (71)

Cicognani, Card. Amleto—Dec. 18, 16g (73)

Citrine, Lady Doris—July 17, 16g (73)

Clair-Erskine, J. A. W.—(t.), Jan. 12, 14h (74)

Clancarty, Lord—Sept. 18, 16g (75)

Clancarty, Lord Richard—Jun. 8, 14h (71)

Clapp, Verner—(t.), July 4, 19h (72)

Clapperton, G. D.—Oct. 21, 19h (71); 23, 14g (71)

Clare, Brother—Jan. 20, 16g (71)

Clark, Douglas—Feb. 26, 14h (73)

Clark, Frank—Apr. 3, 16g (71)

Clark, Geoffrey de N.—(t.), Jan. 19, 16h (72)

Cooper, Merian—(t.), Apr. 23, 8h (73)

Coopland, Prof. George W.—Apr. 3, 16g (75); 8, 16h (75)

Coote, Lady Alice—Aug. 14, 17h (75)

Cope, Sir Mordaunt—Nov. 9, 21h (72)

Cope, Sir Vincent Zachery—Dec. 31, 14g (74)

Copeland, George—June 24, 16g (71)

Copeman, William O.—Nov. 1, 21g (73)

Copland, Sir Douglas—Sept. 28, 14f (71)

Copnall, Bainbridge—Oct. 19, 20g (73)

Coppel, Alec—Jan. 25, 16g (72)

Coppen, Hazel—Apr. 14, 14g (75)

Coppock, Lady Ursula—Sept. 8, 17h (71)

Coppock, Sir Richard—Feb. 5, 16g (71); 13, 12h (71)

Coppola, Piero—Mar. 19, 22h (71)

Copson, William H.—Sept. 15, 17g (71)

Corbett, Jane—(t.), Jan. 25, 18g (73)

Cord, Errett L.—Jan. 4, 14h (74)

Cordier, Dr. Andrew—Jul. 14, 14g (75)

Corkran, Lady Winifred—Jan. 31, 14g (72)

Cormack, Prof. J. M. R.—June 12, 20g (75)

Cornell, Katharine—June 11, 16e (74)

Cornwallis, Lady—Apr. 5, 21h (73)

Cornwallis, Capt. O. W.—Feb. 5, 14g (74)

Cornwallis-West, Georgette—Nov. 22, 18g (72)

Correll, Charles J.—Sept. 28, 18h (72)

Corrigan, Fr. Terence—May 12, 16g (75)

Corsini, Donna Lucrizia—(t.), Sept. 7, 12f (71)

Cortinez, Adolfo R.—Dec. 5, 21h (73)

Cory, Ven Alexander—Apr. 17, 18h (73)

Cost, March—Feb. 10, 18h (73)

Costello, Sir Leonard—Dec. 5, 18f (72)

Costes, Dieudonne—May 19, 16h (73); 21, 16h (73)

Costin, Maj.-Gen. Eric B.—Feb. 25, 16g (71)

Cotes, Harold—Jan. 23, 16h (74)

Cottom, Dr. Dennis G.—(t.), Aug. 23, 12h (71)

Cotton, Rene—July 29, 20f (71)

Cottrell, Leonard—Oct. 9, 20h (74)

Coudenhove-Kalergi, Countess Lilly—Apr. 10, 18g (75)

Coudenhove-Kalergi, Count—July 29, 16h (72); Aug. 7, 16h (72)

Coulon, Johnny—Oct. 31, 20g (73)

Coulon, Roger—Jan. 23, 14h (71)

Coulson, Prof. Charles A.—Jan. 8, 14f (74); 11, 16g (74); 17, 14g (74)

Coulson, Dr. Michael—(t.), Oct. 27, 14g (75)

Coultas, William W.—Nov. 16, 23f (73)

Coulthard, Prof. Gabriel R.—Aug. 31, 14g (74)

Courage, Nina E.—May 7, 18g (73)

Court, Prof. W. H. B.—Oct. 6, 16g (71)

Courtauld, Lady—Jan. 4, 14h (73)

Courtney, Lady Constance—Aug. 9, 18g (74)

Courtney, Dame Kathleen—Dec. 10, 16g (74); 19, 16g (74)

Courtown, Cicely Lady—Feb. 8, 19h (73)

Courtown, Lord—July 24, 16h (75)

Coutanche, Lady Ruth—Aug. 9, 14h (73)

Coutanche, Lord—Dec. 19, 16f (73)

Coutinho, Gen. Vicente De P. D. —May 27, 8h (74)

Covell, Sir Gordon—Oct. 7, 14g (75)

Cowan, Clyde L.—May 27, 8h (74)

Cowan, Jerome—Jan. 27, 18h (72)

Coward, Arthur—May 20, 17h (71); June 12, 18h (74)

Coward, Sir Noel—Mar. 27, 18f (73); 29, 18h (73); Apr. 4, 20h (73); 5, 21h (73)

Cowell, Maj.-Gen. Sir Ernest—Feb. 27, 14g (71)

Cowell, Prof. Stuart J.—Aug. 3, 14g (71)

Cowley, Lord—Dec. 15, 13h (75); 24, 12h (75)

Cox, Lady Mary—Dec. 28, 10g (73); Jan. 2, 14h (74)

Cox, Anthony B.—Mar. 11, 18f (71)

Cox, Freddie—Aug. 8, 16g (73)

Cox, H. H.—(t.), July 9, 17g (74)

Cox, Harry—May 8, 14g (71)

Cox, Sir Herbert—Sept. 24, 16h (73)

Cox, Wally—Feb. 16, 21g (73)

Cozens-Hardy, Lady—June 21, 14h (75); Sept. 13, 14g (75)

Crabbe, Lady—July 28, 18h (72)

Crabbe, Sir Cecil—Dec. 22, 13f (71); 31, 10g (71)

Cracroft-Amcotts, Lieut.-Col. Sir Weston—Sept. 24, 14g (75)

Craddock, George—May 1, 18h (74)

Craddock, Maj. Guy H.—May 3, 16g (75)

Craddock, Col. Sir Walter—Dec. 28, 14h (72); Jan. 8, 14h (73)

Craig, Sir Arthur—May 8, 14g (72)

Craig, Irene—Mar. 22, 18f (74)

Craig, Patrick W. D.—Aug. 22, 14h (72)

Craig, Prof. W. S. M.—June 24, 16g (75)

Craigavon, Lord—May 20, 16h (74)

Crane, Howard H.—Jan. 11, 14g (71)

Cranko, John—June 27, 21 (73)

Craske, Rt. Rev. Frederick W. T. —Mar. 11, 18f (71)

Craske, Rt. Rev. Tom—(t.), Apr. 1, 18h (71)

Craster, Sir John—Dec. 13, 16g (75)

Craven, Countess Mary of—Sept. 18, 18g (74)

Crawford, Lady (Margaret)—May 18, 22h (73)

Crawford and Balcarres, Lord David of—Dec. 16, 14g (75); 24, 12f (75); 29, 10g (75)

Crawshay, Maj. Owen T. R. —Mar. 8, 16g (72)

Craxton, Harold—Mar. 31, 16h (71); Apr. 6, 18f (71)

Creamer, Muriel—Mar. 24, 16h (72)

Crean, Robert—May 9, 22g (74)

Creasey, John—June 11, 16g (73)

Creasy, Adm. of the Fleet Sir George E.—Nov. 2, 18f (72); 9, 21f (72)

Creasy, Lady Monica—Nov. 10, 14h (75)

Cree, Donald—Sept. 28, 18h (72)

Creedy, Sir Herbert—Apr. 5, 21g (73)

Cremin, Eric—Jan. 9, 17f (74)

Cressall, Nellie—Nov. 8, 23g (73)

Creswell, Sir Archibald—Apr. 13, 14g (74)

Cresswell, Rev. Cyril L.—Mar. 27, 18h (74)

Cresswell, Warneford—Oct. 22, 17h (73)

Cretney, Sir Godfrey—May 19, 19g (73)

Crew, Prof. F. A. E.—May 30, 20f (73)

Crewdson, Col. William D.—Feb. 21, 14g (72)

Crews, L. G.—Sept. 30, 14g (75)

Crick, Rt. Rev. Douglas H.—Aug. 8, 16h (73); 16, 16g (73)

Cripps, William P.—Dec. 23, 13g (72)

Crisp, Donald—May 28, 16g (74)

Critchley, Alexander—Sept. 7, 14h (74)

Crocker, Lady Hilda—May 14, 18g (71)

Crocker, Sir William—Oct. 1, 19h (73)

Crofton, Lord—June 18, 16f (74)

Crofton, Brig. R.—Aug. 1, 17h (72)

Crofts, Prof. John E. V.—May 17, 16h (72)

Crombie, George E.—Dec. 22, 15g (72)

Crombie, Rear-Adm. John H. F.— Sept. 1, 14g (72)

Crompton, James—Dec. 8, 14h (75)

Cronin, Harley—May 16, 21f (73)

Crooks, Richard—Oct. 2, 17h (72)

Crooks, Richard M.—Feb. 9, 16h (73)

Crookshank, Arthur P. U.—Dec. 1, 17h (71)

Crookshank, Dr. Henry—Aug. 12, 14h (72)

Crosbie, Cmdr. George—Feb. 9, 14f (72)

Crosland, Brig. Harold Powell— July 11, 18h (73)

Cross, Lady Louise—June 27, 14h (75)

Cross, Claude B.—Oct. 19, 14h (74)

Cross, Douglas—Jan. 14, 16g (75)

Cross, George—(t.), Nov. 30, 19g (72)

Cross, Rev. Leslie B.—Apr. 15, 8h (74); 19, 18f (74)

Crossley, Sir Julian—Jan. 27, 14f (71); 30, 14g (71)

Crossman, Richard H. S.—Apr. 6,

16f (74); 15, 8h (74); 17, 16h (74)

Crosthwaite, Sir B. M.—Jan. 19, 14g (74)

Crowe, T. A.—May 4, 14g (74)

Crowell, Air Comm. P. L.—Oct. 9, 14g (71)

Crowley, Dave—Dec. 13, 20g (74)

Crowther, Lord Geoffrey—Feb. 7, 14f (72); 10, 16h (72); 12, 14h (72)

Crowther, Capt. Denys—May 29, 16h (74)

Crowther, Harold—Oct. 25, 14g (75)

Crowther, Maj.-Gen. William A.— Oct. 8, 16h (75)

Crowther, Capt. William R. D.— May 25, 14h (74)

Crozier, Lt.-Col. Norman L.— Apr. 6, 15g (72)

Cruikshank, Prof. Robert—Aug. 19, 14g (74); 21, 14h (74); 23, 15f (74)

Csaky, Joseph—May 5, 18f (71)

Csanadi, Dr. Gyorgy—May 4, 14h (71)

Csatorday, Dr. Karoly—July 28, 18h (72)

Cuddon, George U.—Aug. 3, 16g (72)

Cullen, J. Brian—(t.), Aug. 19, 14h (72)

Culley, Group Capt. S. D.—June 18, 20g (75); 20, 20h (75)

Culshaw, Rev. Wesley—(t.), Apr. 5, 14h (75)

Cumber, William—Feb. 26, 14g (74)

Cuming, Lady Beryl—Aug. 7, 14h (75)

Cumings, Prof. John N.—(t.), Aug. 26, 8h (74)

Cumming, Brig. Arthur E.—Apr. 14, 16g (71)

Cumming, Stephen—(t.), Jan. 19, 14f (74)

Cummins, William Ashley—Mar. 16, 19g (72)

Cummins, Phyllis D.—(t.), May 15, 18g (73)

Cundall, Charles—Nov. 6, 14g (71); 11, 18g (71)

Cundall, Howard G.—June 17, 14g (74)

Cunliffe, Jack—Feb. 13, 18h (73)

Cunningham, Rt. Rev. James— July 12, 20h (74)

Cunnington, Phillis—(t.), Nov. 4, 16h (74)

Curran, Charles—Sept. 18, 15g (72); 21, 16g (72)

Cursley, Norman—May 4, 18g (72)

Curteis, Capt. Sir Gerald—Feb. 25, 17g (72)

Curthoys, Roy L.—Sept. 28, 14h (71)

Curtin, Elsie—June 27, 14h (75)

Curtis, Frederick F. C.—June 19, 16g (75)

Curtis, Sir George—Jan. 18, 14h (72)

Curtis, Dame Myra—June 29, 17f (71)

Curtis, A. V.-M. Walter J. B.— Nov. 14, 21h (73)

Curtis-Bennett, Lady Lilian—Feb. 14, 14g (72)

Dering, Sir Rupert—Mar. 20, 17h (75)

de Rothschild, Mrs. Lionel—(t.), Jan. 2, 14h (75)

Derry, Dr. D. C. L.—(t.), July 24, 16h (75); 28, 14h (75)

Derujinsky, Gleb M.—Mar. 17, 14g (75)

Desai, C. C.—Sept. 23, 16h (72)

Desai, Visant—Dec. 24, 12h (75)

De Salis, Capt. Rudolph H. F.—June 6, 16h (72)

de Seversky, Major Alexander—Aug. 27, 12g (74)

Desbrow, Laurence W.—(t.), Nov. 30, 20h (73)

de Selincourt, Prof. Oliver—(t.), Aug. 22, 16g (74); 26, 8h (74)

des Forges, Sir Charles Lee—Sept. 16, 14h (72)

De Sica, Vittorio,—Nov. 14, 19b (74)

Desjardins, Claude—Dec. 10, 19f (75)

de Smith, Prof. S. A.—Feb. 14, 24g (74); 20, 16g (74)

Desmond, Astra—Aug. 17, 16g (73)

Desnoyer, Francois—July 22, 14h (72)

Desta, Prince Alexander—Nov. 30, 16g (74)

des Voeux, Lady Jean—May 22, 22h (74)

de Trafford, Sir Humphrey Oct. 8, 19f (71)

Deval, Jacques—Dec. 21, 14f (72)

de Valera, Eamon—Aug. 30, 14d (75)

Devas, Godfrey C.—July 30, 17h (71)

Devay, Jean-Francois—July 27, 15g (71)

Devenport, Lord—Mar. 31, 16h (73)

Deverell, Lady Hild—June 13, 18g (75)

Deverson, Harry—Sept. 21, 16g (72)

de Visscher, Prof. C.—Jan. 5, 14h (73)

Devlin, Mrs. Margaret: see Ashford, Daisy

Devon, William Allan—Apr. 15, 16h (72)

Dewar, Rear Adm. Alan R.—Nov. 7, 17g (72)

de Wet, Hugh O.—Nov. 27, 16g (75)

Dewey, Cyril M.—Sept. 18, 21h (73)

Dewey, Thomas E.—Mar. 17, 18f (71)

De Wilde, Brandon—July 11, 16h (72)

De Wolfe, Billy—Mar. 7, 18h (74)

d'Eyncourt, Sir Gervais T.—Nov. 26, 19h (71)

Dhammasiddhi, Madugalle Sri S. S.—Jan. 9, 14g (73)

Dhannivat, Prince—(t.), Sept. 16, 16h (74); 20, 18h (74)

Dhar, Durga Prasad—June 13, 18g (75)

Diakite, Capt. Yoro—Aug. 16, 16h (73)

Diamond, Bobby—Oct. 31, 17g (72)

Diamond, Howard—Aug. 26, 14h (72)

Dible, Prof. James H.—July 3, 14h (71)

Dible, William C.—Mar. 10, 16h (71)

Dick, Jack R.—Jan. 9, 17f (74); 16, 14h (74)

Dick, Prof. Marcus—(t.), May 3, 14h (71); 6, 18g (71); 7, 18g (71)

Dickens, Lady Ena—Jan. 20, 16g (71)

Dickens, Air-Comm. T. C.—Jan. 17, 12h (72)

Dickson, Alex—Oct. 17, 14g (75)

Diepen, Frederick J. L.—July 9, 17h (74)

Dies, Martin—Nov. 16, 21h (72)

Dieterle, William—Dec. 20, 14g (72)

Dietze, Prof. Constantin von—Mar. 22, 20f (73)

Diggle, Rev. Reginald F.—Jan. 27, 12g (75)

Dijk, Fr. Stephen van—Mar. 23, 19h (71)

Dillon, Josephine—Nov. 13, 14g (71)

Dineley, Mark—(t.), Oct. 14, 17g (75)

Dinwiddie, Dr. Melville—June 17, 16g (75)

Diomede, Miguel—Oct. 17, 18h (74)

Diringer, Dr. David—Feb. 19, 17g (75)

Disney, Roy—Dec. 22, 13h (71)

Diu, Sayed Buth—Sept. 27, 14g (75)

Dixon, Maj.-Gen. B. E. C.—Oct. 10, 21h (73)

Dixon, John Reginald—Mar. 6, 17h (72); 13, 14h (72)

Dixon, Sir Owen—July 10, 16g (72); 13, 18h (72)

Doak, Sir James—July 10, 17h (75)

Dobell, Lady Elizabeth—Mar. 22, 18h (72)

Dobie, Margaret—Apr. 13, 12h (71)

Dobie, Marryat R.—(t.), Nov. 2, 19f (73)

Dobree, Prof. Bonamy—Sept. 4, 16g (74); 6, 16h (74); 7, 14h (74)

Dodd, Prof. Arthur H.—May 21, 17g (75)

Dodd, Dr. Charles—Sept. 24, 16f (73); 26, 18g (73); 28, 20f (73)

Dodd, Charles E. S.—Sept. 3, 14g (74)

Dodd, Claire—Nov. 26, 17g (73)

Dodd, Sir John—Sept. 6, 18h (73)

Dodd, Thomas—May 25, 14f (71)

Dodds, Lady Etelka—Dec. 23, 12g (74)

Dodds, Sir Charles—Dec. 18, 16g (73); 28, 10h (73)

Dodds, Sir James—Aug. 14, 14f (72)

Dodds, Madeline H.—(t.), June 28, 16h (72)

Dodge, Dr. Bayard—July 18, 14g (72)

Dolansky, Dr. Jaromir—July 18, 18g (73)

Dollfuss, Alwine—Mar. 7, 18h (73)

Dolphin, Albert E.—Sept. 2, 16h (72)

Dolphin, John R. V.—May 4, 20h (73)

Domville, Adm. Sir Barry—Aug. 16, 12f (71)

Don, Lt.-Col. John A.—Dec. 1, 17g (71)

Donahue, Sam—(t.), Apr. 27, 16g (74)

Donald, William C.—Apr. 29, 18h (74)

Donaldson, Malcolm—Mar. 19, 16g (73); 22, 20g (73)

Donegall, Lord—May 26, 8g (75)

Donlevy, Brian—Apr. 7, 16h (72)

Donn-Byrne, St. John—(t.), Nov. 24, 16h (73)

Donnelly, Desmond—Apr. 5, 18g (74); 13, 14g (74)

Donohue, Mark—Aug. 21, 14g (75)

Dietze, Prof. Constantin von—Mar. 22, 20f (73)

Donovan, Lord—Dec. 13, 14g (71); 24, 12h (71)

Donovan, John—Nov. 16, 17h (71)

Doonan, George—Apr. 21, 14g (73)

Doran, Group Capt. K. C.—Mar. 9, 16g (74)

Doren, Mark van—Dec. 13, 17h (72)

Dorey, Dr. S. F.—Sept. 1, 14h (72)

Dorgeles, Roland—Mar. 20, 16h (73)

Dorham, Kenny—Dec. 8, 21f (72)

Dori, Lt.-Gen. Yaakov—Jan. 30, 16h (73)

Dormer, Lord—Sept. 1, 12h (75)

Dorrell, Geoffrey—Dec. 6, 18g (73)

Dorrell, Lt.-Col. Thomas—Jan. 9, 12h (71)

Dostalova, Leopolda—June 19, 14g (72)

Dott, Prof. Norman—Dec. 12, 19g (73)

Doubleday, Sir Leslie—Feb. 11, 14g (75)

Doughty, Charles—July 12, 18g (73)

Douglas, Lady Vera—Apr. 13, 14g (74)

Douglas, Archibald Roderick Sholto—Jan. 7, 14g (72)

Douglas, Capt. Cosmo A. O.—Mar. 4, 16h (71)

Douglas, Frank—(t.), Nov. 10, 17h (71)

Douglas, Very Rev. G. J. C.—Jan. 9, 14h (73)

Douglas, Maj.-Gen. John P.—Sept. 9, 14h (75)

Douglas, Lewis—Mar. 9, 16g (74)

Douglas, Stanley—Dec. 31, 10g (71)

Douglas Pennant, Winifred—Dec. 12, 19g (72)

Douglas-Scott, Col. Montagu—Jan. 28, 14h (71)

Douglas-Whyte, F.—May 29, 14g (73)

Douglass, Kingman—Oct. 12, 15h (71)

D'Ouince, Rev. Rene—Jan. 16, 14h (74)

Douthwaite, Dr. Arthur H.—Sept. 26, 16g (74)

Dovas, Gen. Constantine—July 25, 18h (73)

Dove-Edwin, George F.—(t.), Jan. 2, 14h (74)

Dovey, Ray—Jan. 7, 14h (75)

Dowding, Lady—Jan. 30, 16h (73)

Downing, Prof. Richard—Nov. 25, 17h (75); 29, 16h (75)

Downing, Sam—Feb. 22, 16h (74)

Dowty, Sir George—Dec. 9, 19g (75)

Doxiadis, Prof. Constantinos—July 1, 16g (75); 2, 18g (75)

Dozza, Giuseppe—Dec. 30, 10h (74)

Drage, Lady—Feb. 3, 14h (71)

Drain, Job H. C.—July 31, 16g (75)

Drake, Donald H. C.—Aug. 14, 14g (74)

Dreaper, Thomas W.—Apr. 30, 20g (75)

Dress, Michael—(t.), Apr. 21, 16h (75)

Drew, Lt.-Col. George—Jan. 5, 14g (73)

Drewe, Basil—June 12, 18g (74)

Drewe, Sir Cedric—Jan. 22, 16f (71); 30, 14g (71)

Drewery, Alfred—Mar. 17, 14h (75)

Drewett, Preb. Alfred J.—Jan. 23, 16h (73)

Dreyfuss, Henry—Oct. 9, 14h (72)

Driver, Sir Godfrey—Apr. 24, 18g (75); 30, 20h (75)

Driver, Gordon—June 21, 16h (72)

Driver, Harry—Nov. 27, (73)

Driver, Peter—(t.), Nov. 19, 16g (71)

Driz, Oosei—Feb. 19, 16h (71)

Drouillet, Rene—Sept. 26, 16h (74)

Drower, Lady Ethel Stefane—Jan. 31, 14h (72)

Drucquer, Sir Leonard—Apr. 1, 14h (75)

Druitt, Sir Harvey—Feb. 7, 18g (73); 9, 16g (73)

Drummond-Jackson, Stanley L.—Dec. 10, 19f (75)

Drury, Lady Daphne—Jan. 31, 16h (73)

Drury, George—June 22, 21h (72)

Drury, Henry—Oct. 9, 14g (71)

Dryden, Bruce—Mar. 6, 18h (73)

D'Silva, Prof. John L.—Aug. 23, 16h (73); 29, 16g (73)

Dubas, Marie—Feb. 25, 17g (72)

Duchesne, Brig. C. C.—May 24, 20g (73)

Duckwitz, Georg—Feb. 17, 16g (73); 24, 14h (73)

Duckworth, F. V.—May 27, 8h (74)

Duckworth-King, Sir John—May 17, 16g (72)

Duclos, Jacques—Apr. 28, 14g (75)

Duclos, Pierre—Nov. 28, 22h (73)

du Cros, Sir Philip—Oct. 15, 14g (75)

Duddington, Natalie—June 24, 16h (72)

Dudley, Sir Alan—Sept. 14, 15g (71); 16, 18f (71); 28, 14h (71)

Dudley, Prof. Donald R.—(t.), Sept. 7, 16g (72)

Dudly, Lord Ferdinando—Apr. 21, 16g (72)

Duel, Pete—Jan. 1, 18h (72)

Duff, Maj.-Gen. Alan C.—Nov. 6, 22h (73)

Duff, Sir Patrick—Dec. 20, 14h (72); 22, 15h (72)

Duffield, Alec C.—Jan. 20, 16g (73)

Dufhues, Sir Joseph H.—Mar. 27, 14h (71)

Duggan, Mary—Mar. 14, 18g (73)

Duggan, Maurice—(t.), Jan. 13, 16g (75)

Duke, Leonard—Dec. 23, 12h (71)

Dulay, Arthur—June 22, 14f (71)

Dumaine, Alexandre—Apr. 24, 18h (74)

Dumbrille, Douglas—Apr. 15, 8h (74)

Dun, Rt. Rev. Angus—Aug. 14, 14h (71)

Dunbar, Maj.-Gen. C. I. H.—May 19, 19h (71)

Duncan, Sir James—Oct. 2, 17h (74)

Duncan, Sir Val—Dec. 20, 14g (75); 30, 10g (75)

Dundas, Sir Ambrose—May 3, 21h (73)

Dundonald, Countess Aphra of—Jan. 19, 16g (72)

Dunhill, Alfred—July 9, 14g (71)

Dunlop, Dr. Annie I.—Apr. 11, 18h (73)

Dunlop, Isobel—May 14, 18g (75)

Dunlop, Sir John—Apr. 29, 18g (74); May 1, 18h (74)

Dunlop, R. O.—May 19, 16g (73)

Dunn, Michael—Aug. 31, 14h (73)

Dunne, James—Feb. 24, 18f (72)

Dunne, Prof. James H.—June 13, 20h (74)

Dunning, John A.—June 29, 17g (71); July 6, 14h (71)

Dunning, Dr. John R.—Aug. 29, 14g (75)

Dunning, Prof. T. P.—(t.), May 8, 18h (73)

Dunoyer, de Segonzac, André,—Sept. 18, 18g (74)

Dupre, Desmond—(t.), Aug. 23, 15f (74)

Dupre, Marcel—June 1, 12h (71); 4, 17g (71)

Dupree, Sir Vernon—Sept. 6, 16h (71)

Durand, Brig. Sir Alan—Feb. 19, 16h (71)

Durfee, Minta—Sept. 17, 18g (75)

Durham, Yancey—Aug. 31, 14h (73)

Durieux, Frau Tilla—Feb. 25, 16f (71)

Durnford-Slater, Brig. John—(t.), Feb. 9, 14g (72)

Durr, Clifford—May 17, 14g (75)

Durrant-Wright, Geoffrey—(t.), Feb. 24, 18g (72)

Dusen, Dr. Henry P. van—Feb. 15, 16g (75)

Dutra, Marshal Enrico G.—June 12, 18h (74)

Dutrey, Marius—(t.), Nov. 13, 16g (75)

Dutt, Palme—Dec. 21, 12g (74)

Dutton, Maj. Eric A. T.—Nov. 29, 20f (73)

Dutton, Pamela—Dec. 10, 16f (71)

Duvalier, Dr. Francois—Apr. 23, 18f (71)

Duveen, Sir Geoffrey—Nov. 17, 18h (75)

Dvornik, Rev. Prof. Francis—(t.), Nov. 15, 14h (75)

Dwyer, Allan—Feb. 14, 18h (75)

Dye, Arthur G.—Dec. 28, 8f (71)

Dyer, Sir Leonard—June 12, 20g (75)

Dyke, Lady Zoe Hart—Feb. 14, 18h (75); 24, 16g (75)

Dyke, Dr. Sidney C.—Mar. 7, 16g (75)

Dykman, Henry J.—Apr. 26, 16g (72)

Dyment, Clifford—June 8, 14f (71)

Dyrenforth, James—(t.), Jan. 11, 16g (74)

Dysart, Lady—June 5, 16g (75)

Dyson, Lady Mildred—Jan. 31, 16h (75)

Dyson, Henry V. D.—June 11, 17f (75); 24, 16h (75)

Dyson, Maureen—Sept. 3, 14h (74)

E

Eades, Sir Thomas—June 22, 14f (71)

Earle, Lady Gladys—May 3, 21h (73)

Easby, Thomas L.—May 25, 14f (71)

Easmon, Dr. McCormack C. F.—May 9, 16g (72)

Eassie, Maj.-Gen. William J. F.—May 16, 21h (74)

Eastman, Brig. Henry C. W.—Sept. 24, 14g (75)

Easton, John Murray—Aug. 23, 14g (75)

Eccles, Lady Madeleine—Apr. 8, 16g (75)

Eccles, Guy—(t.), July 7, 16h (71)

Eccles, Col. John G.—Jan. 2, 14g (75)

Eckman, Maurice I.—(t.), Nov. 14, 19f (74)

Eddis, Sir Basil—Nov. 9, 17g (71)

Eddy, John P.—July 15, 14g (75); 25, 14h (75)

Ede, Prof. Allan J.—Oct. 14, 17g (75)

Edelman, Maurice—Dec. 15, 13g (75)

Eden, Guy—June 14, 14g (71)

Eden, William A.—(t.), Apr. 17, 18h (75)

Edgar, Frederick P.—Apr. 22, 16h (72)

Edgcumbe, John A. P.—Oct. 31, 19h (74)

Edge, Ada Lady—Mar. 17, 16g (73)

Edinger, Jacques—May 29, 14g (73)

Edmenson, Lady Doris—Oct. 8, 16g (75)

Edmondson, Robert—July 24, 18h (74)

Edmunds, Col. John F.—July 12, 18h (73)

Edwards, Lady Kathleen—Dec. 10, 19g (75)

Edwards, A. Trystan—Jan. 31, 16g (73); Feb. 3, 16g (73); 14, 17g (73)

Edwards, Dean—(t.), Feb. 22, 19h (73)

Edwards, George P.—Aug. 4, 14h (75); 6, 14g (75)

Edwards, Lt.-Col. Harold W.—May 16, 21f (73)

Edwards, Group Capt. Hugh R. A.—Dec. 23, 12g (73)

Edwards, Very Rev. Irven D.—Feb. 15, 20g (73)

Edwards, Rev. Maldwyn L.—Oct. 17, 18g (74)

Edwards, Canon R. A.—Sept. 24, 16h (73)

Edwards, Lt.-Col. Walter M.—Jan. 23, 14h (71)

Egbert, Prof. D. D.—Jan. 8, 14g (73)

Egerton, Vice-Adm. Henry J.—Apr. 18, 16g (72)

Eggers, Dr. Reinhold—(t.), Nov. 16, 16g (74)

Eggert, Prof. John—Oct. 6, 14g (73)

Eglington, Charles—June 30, 16h (71)

Egremont, Lord—June 7, 18f (72); 9, 16h (72); 19, 14g (72)

Egtvedt, Claire L.—Oct. 22, 19g (75)

Ehrenberg, Prof. W.—Dec. 2, 14g (75)

Eid, Guy—Mar. 6, 18f (73); 9, 20g (73)

Einstein, Dr. Hans A.—July 28, 14g (73)

Einzig, Dr. Paul—May 9, 18f (73)

Eisemann, Henrick—(t.), Dec. 12, 19h (72)

Eisenberg, Maurice—Dec. 20, 14g (72)

Eisendrath, Rabbi Maurice—Nov. 12, 21h (73)

Eisenhower, Edgar—July 14, 14g (71)

Eissfeldt, Dr. Otton—(t.), May 7, 18h (73)

Eklund, Ernst—Aug. 12, 14g (71)

el-Aref, Aref—Aug. 1, 14g (73)

Eleanor, Sister—(t.), Feb. 1, 19g (73)

Elgood, Walter S.—Dec. 18, 14g (75)

Elifas, Chief Filemon—Aug. 18, 12f (75)

Elkington, A. E. H.—(t.), Oct. 16, 16h (74)

Ellender, Allen—July 29, 16h (72)

Ellerman, Sir John—July. 18, 18g (73); 20, 18h (73); 21, 14h (73)

Ellicott, Langford P.—Aug. 22, 14g (72)

Ellington, Duke—May 25, 14g (74)

Elliot, Lady—Mar. 4, 17g (71)

Elliot, Lt.-Col. Henry Hawes—Mar. 8, 16g (72)

Elliot, Sir William—June 28, 14f

Elliot, Hugh—Oct. 31, 19h (74) (71); 30, 16h (71); July 1, 19h (71); 9, 14h (71)

Elliot-Smith, Arthur—Aug. 8, 14h (72)

Elliott, Cass—July 31, 18g (74)

Elliott, Sir Claude—Nov. 24, 16g (73); Dec. 10, 19h (73)

Elliott, John M.—Jan. 6, 12g (72)

Elliott, Vice-Adm. Sir Maurice—Mar. 28, 17g (72)

Ellis, Charles H.—July 16, 17g (75); 21, 12g (75)

Ellis-Rees, Sir Hugh—July 20, 14g (74); 26, 17h (74)

Elmhirst, Leonard K.—Apr. 18, 16f (74); 23, 18h (74)

Elphinstone, Lord—Nov. 19, 18f (75); Dec. 3, 18g (75)

Elphinstone, Rev. Andrew—(t.), Mar. 31, 8h (75)

Elphinstone, Sir Howard—May 21, 17h (75)

Elphinstone-Dalrymple, Lady—May 4, 20g (73)

El-Saadaweyah, Awad Mustapha—(t.), Mar. 6, 18g (73)

Elston, Roy—(t.), Oct. 7, 16h (71)

Elton, Lord—Apr. 19, 20g (73)

Elton, Sir Arthur—Jan. 2, 12h (73); 5, 14g (73); 6, 18h (73); 8, 14h (73)

Elvin, Lady—June 18, 16g (74)

Elwes, Dominic—(t.), Sept. 13, 14g (75)

Elwes, Gloria E.—Oct. 11, 16h (71)

Elwes, Simon—Aug. 9, 14g (75)

Elwin, Bill—Dec. 20, 14h (75)

Elwin, Malcolm—Oct. 29, 17f (73)

Ely, Gen. Paul—Jan. 23, 19f (75)

Emberton, Sybil C.—Oct. 21, 14h (74)

Embleton, Philip—May 23, 18h (74); 24, 16h (74)

Emery, Douglas—Dec. 3, 16g (74)

Emery, Walter—June 26, 20f (74); July 1, 16g (74)

Emery, Prof. Walter B.—Mar. 13, 14f (71); 20, 14h (71); 29, 14h (71)

Emmanuel, Philip—(t.), Jan. 2, 14g (75)

Emmett, E. V. H.—(t.), June 14, 14h (71)

Emsden, Lt.-Col. Leslie G.—Aug. 20, 14g (74)

Enfield, Sir Ralph—Feb. 19, 14g (73)

Engelhard, Charles—Mar. 3, 14g (71)

Engelmann, Franklin—Mar. 3, 14g (72)

English, John—Sept. 1, 14h (73)

English, Prof. Joseph S.—Nov. 22, 14h (71)

Enthoven, H. J.—(t.), July 5, 14g (75)

Entwistle, Betty—Aug. 7, 14g (75)

Entwistle, Sir Cyril—July 10, 20h (74)

Erdtman, Prof. Gunnar—Mar. 6, 18f (73)

Erhard, Luise—July 15, 14g (75)

Eriksen, Erik—Oct. 9, 14g (72)

Erith, Raymond C.—Dec. 3, 17h (73); 5, 20h (73); 11, 18g (73)

Errington, Lady Marjorie—Dec. 1, 18h (73)

Erskine, Lady (Ruby)—Jan. 25, 18g (74)

Erskine, Capt. Francis W.—Sept. 22, 17g (72)

Erskine, G. B.—May 24, 20g (73)

Erskine, Keith—Apr. 24, 18g (74)

Erskine Crum, Lt.-Gen. V. F.—Mar. 19, 22f (71); 23, 19f (71); 25, 18f (71); 29, 14h (71)

Ervine, St. John—Jan. 25, 12g (71); Feb. 1, 12g (71)

Escande, Maurice—Feb. 12, 14h (73)

Escombe, Capt. William M. L.—Nov. 28, 22h (73)

Escriva, Mgr. Josemaria—June 28, 14g (75)

Espil, Felipe A.—Jan. 25, 16g (72)

'Espinasse, Prof. Paul G.—May 13, 16g (75)

Espley, Arthur J.—July 27, 15g (71)

Essely, Col. Cyril—Sept. 14, 16h (74)

Essex, Tony—May 17, 14g (75)

Esterel, Jacques—Apr. 15, 8h (74)

Estridge, Delme G.—(t.), Sept. 16, 18h (71)

Etchegoyen, Martin—May 23, 18g (74)

Etchells, Frederick—Aug. 18, 14g (73)

Etches, Matilda—(t.), Apr. 26, 20h (74)

Ethiopia, former Emperor Haile Selassie of—Aug. 28, 1g (75)

Ettinghausen, Dr. Maurice L.—Nov. 20, 19f (74)

Eugster, Prof. J.—Feb. 18, 16g (74)

Eustace, Edward A. R.—Sept. 11, 14h (72)

Evans, Dr. Alice—Sept. 9, 14h (75)

Evans, Rev. Arthur N.—May 26, 8h (75)

Evans, Air Chief Marshal Sir Donald—Apr. 11, 16g (75)

Evans, Donald—Apr. 14, 14g (75)

Evans, Eve V.—Aug. 16, 12h (71)

Evans, Dr. Frankis—Aug. 29, 16g (74)

Evans, Dr. Herbert M.—Mar. 9, 16g (71)

Evans, Father Illtud—Aug. 2, 17h (72)

Evans, Maj. James J. P.—Feb. 7, 17h (74)

Evans, Dr. Jenkin A.—Jan. 10, 16h (75)

Evans, John F.—(t.), Oct. 19, 19f (72)

Evans, Sir John H.—May 31, 18h (73)

Evans, Merlyn—Nov. 3, 16f (73)

Evans, Thomas S.—Oct. 21, 14g (75)

Evans, Prof. Trefor E.—Apr. 19, 18f (74)

Evans, Walter—Apr. 12, 14g (75)

Evans, Warwick—Mar. 11, 14h (74)

Evans-Bevan, Sir David—Sept. 12, 16h (73)

Evans-Lombe, Vice-Adm. Sir Edward M.—May 15, 21h (74)

Evans-Pritchard, Sir Edward—Sept. 14, 18f (73); 18, 21g (73)

Everard, Penelope B.—Sept. 2, 14h (75)

Evert, Anghelos—Jan. 1, 12h (71)

Evill, Sir Douglas—Mar. 24, 16g (71)

Ewan, Robert W.—(t.), Mar. 23, 20g (73)

Ewing, Dr. A. C.—May 16, 21h (73)

Ewing, James—Mar. 25, 19g (75)

Exham, Maj.-Gen. K. G.—Mar. 6, 14h (74); 9, 16h (74)

Exeter, Dowager Lady—Oct. 30, 19h (73)

F

Fadden, Sir Arthur—Apr. 23, 8f (73)

Fagan, Mary (Mrs. V. E.)—see Gray

Fairbairn, William A.—Dec. 20, 14h (72)

Fairbrother, Nan—Nov. 25, 18g (71); Dec. 6, 17g (71); 11, 14h (71)

Fairchild, Sherman M.—Mar. 30, 16h (71)

Fairclough, Alan—Jan. 2, 14g (74)

Fairfat-Jones, James—(t.), Apr. 9, 14h (73)

Fairfat-Lucy, Sir Brian—(t.), Feb. 5, 14h (74)

Fairhaven, Lord—Apr. 9, 14h (73); 28, 16h (73)

Fairley, Prof. G. Hamilton—Oct. 24, 18g (75); 25, 14g (75); 31, 17g (75)

Fairweather, Lady Patricia—Aug. 31, 14h (73)

Fairweather, Ian—May 23, 18h (74)

Faisal, King: see Saudi Arabia

Falck, Giovanni—Jan. 8, 16g (72)

Falconer, Alun—Sept. 29, 14g (73)

Falk, Oswald T.—Nov. 20, 18g (72); 22, 18h (72)

Fallers, Prof. Lloyd A.—July 8, 16g (74)

Fallons, Jack—Jan. 22, 16h (74)

Falls, Capt. Cyril—Apr. 24, 14f (71)

Fanner, John L.—Dec. 23, 10g (75)

Farber, Dr. Sidney—(t.), Apr. 13, 18g (73)

Farey-Jones, Frederick—Feb. 20, 16g (74)

Farkas, Karl—May 20, 17g (71)

Farley-Jones, F. W.—(t.), Mar. 1, 16h (74)

Farmer, Norman W.—Dec. 23, 12g (71)

Farr, Thomas H.—May 24, 14h (71)

Farrar, John C.—Nov. 8, 18g (74)

Farrell, M. J.—Oct. 30, 16g (75)

Farrington, Prof. B.—(t.), Nov. 21, 16f (74)

Farsio, Gen. Ziaoddin—May 5, 18g (71)

Fassi, Muhammad Allal al—May 15, 21f (74)

Faulder, Emily—Jan. 4, 14h (75)

Faulkner, Harry—Jan. 13, 12h (71)

Faulkner, James A.—Feb. 13, 17f (74)

Fawcett, Eric—(t.), Jan. 10, 14h (72)

Fay, Gen. Pierre—Feb. 2, 12g (71)

Fayer, Yuri—Aug. 5, 14g (71)

Fayle, Brig. Lindley R. E.—Feb. 5, 16h (72)

Fealy, John—May 20, 16g (74)

Fearon, George—Dec. 11, 17h (72)

Featherstonehaugh, Lt.-Col. A. J. S.—Dec. 4, 17g (72)

Fechner, Max—Sept. 15, 14g (73)

Fedden, Sir Roy—Nov. 22, 18h (73); 26, 17h (73)

Fegan, Ethel S.—Aug. 19, 14g (75)

Feiling, Dr. Anthony—May 23, 16g (75); June 9, 16g (75)

Felkin, Group Capt. D. S.—Jan. 27, 16h (73)

Fellowes, Sir Edward—Jan. 2, 14h (71)

Fellows, Ernest—Apr. 3, 16h (71)

Felsenstein, Dr. Walter—Oct. 9, 16h (75); 10, 17f (75)

Feltin, Card. Maurice—Oct. 1, 16g (75)

Felton, Felix—Oct. 26, 18g (72); 28, 16h (72); Nov. 10, 18g (72)

Feltrenelli, Giangiacomo—Mar. 18, 14g (72)

Fenby, Charles—Apr. 8, 16g (74)

Fenn, Prof. H. R. B.—Jan. 14, 14h (74)

Fenton, Billy—Apr. 17, 18h (73)

Fenwick, Kathleen—Oct. 16, 18h (73)

Feola, Vicente Italo—Nov. 15, 14h (75)

Ferens, Henry C.—June 6, 17g (75)

Ferguson, Maj. Sir John—May 28, 14h (75)

Ferguson, Lt.-Col. William H.—Aug. 9, 16h (72)

Fergusson, Lady—Sept. 15, 17g (71)

Fergusson, Sir Ewen—Nov. 7, 18g (74)

Fergusson, Sir James—Oct. 27, 16h (73)

Fernandel—Mar. 2, 16f (71)

Ferrar, Lt.-Col. Michael L.—Mar. 2, 16g (71)

Ferraris, Ines Maria—Dec. 16, 17h (71)

Ferraro, Prof. V. C. A.—Jan. 15, 16g (74)

Ferreira de Castro, Hose Maria—July 4, 18h (74)

Ferretto, Cardinal—Mar. 19, 16h (73)

Ferrier, Arthur—(t.), May 31, 18g (73)

Fesenkov, Prof. Vasilii G.—Mar. 17, 16g (72)

Feyer, Dr. Dorothy—(t.), Mar. 20, 18h (74)

Ffrench Blake, Lt.-Col. Arthur O. B.—Oct. 30, 19h (73)

Fidler, Ald. M.—Jan. 11, 16g (74)

Field, Arnold—Sept. 13, 18h (73)

Field, Betty—Sept. 17, 19h (73)

Field, Sir Ernest—Aug. 20, 14g (74)

Field, Olive—(t.), July 6, 18h (73)

Fielden, Lady Reva—Oct. 12, 15g (71)

Fielden, Arthur N.—Apr. 4, 18g (75)

Fielden, Lt.-Col. Edward A.—Sept. 8, 18g (72)

Fielden, Lionel—June 4, 16g (74); 10, 16h (74)

Fielden, Thomas P.—Sept. 17, 17h (74)

Fields, Dorothy—Mar. 30, 16g (74)

Fifoot, Cecil—Feb. 7, 16g (75); Mar. 27, 20g (75)

Figgures, Lady Aline—Feb. 18, 16g (75)

Fildes, Sir Paul—Feb. 6, 14f (71)

Finberg, Prof. Herbert P. R.—Nov. 5, 16g (74); 11, 17g (74)

Findlay, Brig. Patrick H. L.—Aug. 22, 16h (73)

Findlay, Sidney A.—June 15, 17g (71)

Finer, Sir Morris—Dec. 16, 15f

(74); 20, 14h (74); 27, 10h (74)

Fini, Telesforo—Jan. 18, 14g (72)

Finnemore, Sir Donald—May 11, 16g (74); 14, 18g (74); 21, 18h (74)

Finney, John E.—Nov. 22, 18h (72)

Firebrace, Sir Aylmer—June 12, 15h (72)

Firth, Lady—Sept. 12, 16h (73)

Firth, Capt. Charles L.—July 13, 14h (71)

Fischer, Bram—May 9, 18f (75); 13, 16g (75)

Fischer, Ernst—Aug. 3, 18h (72)

Fischtrum, Harvey: see Zemach, Harve

Fish, Sir Wilfred—July 22, 16h (74)

Fish Armstrong, Hamilton—Apr. 25, 18f (73); 28, 16g (73)

Fisher of Lambeth, Lord—Sept. 16, 14c (72); 22, 17g (72); 26, 14h (72)

Fisher, Lady Geraldine—Jan. 6, 15h (71)

Fisher, Brig. Arthur F.—Sept. 9, 16h (72)

Fisher, Lt.-Col. Sir Bertie—Aug. 3, 18g (72)

Fisher, Dorothea W.—Oct. 4, 18h (74)

Fisher, Cmdr. John P.—Dec. 18, 17g (74)

Fisher, Norman—Feb. 3, 16f (72)

Fisher, Patrick—May 17, 14g (75)

Fisher, Sir Woolf—Jan. 21, 16h (75)

Fishlock-Lomax, Norman—Mar. 26, 16h (71)

Fisk, Dorothy—Nov. 17, 18h (72)

Fiske, Lord—Jan. 14, 16g (75); 16, 21g (75)

Fison, Rt. Rev. Joseph E.—July 3, 16h (72); 13, 18h (72)

Fison, Robert—Aug. 7, 14g (72)

Fitzalan-Howard, Magdalen—Nov. 28, 18g (74)

Fitzgerald, Mrs. Barbara—Aug. 25, 14g (73)

Fitzmaurice, Lady Nancy—Feb. 3, 14h (75)

Fitzwilliam, Lady Olive—Dec. 29, 10g (75)

Flach, Karl-Hermann—Aug. 27, 8g (73)

Flaiano, Ernie—Nov. 22, 18g (72)

Flanders, Allan—Oct. 2, 18g (73)

Flanders, Michael—Apr. 16, 18f (75); 18, 16g (75)

Flannelly, Most Rev. J. F.—May 29, 14g (73)

Fleck, Peter H.—Oct. 15, 14g (75)

Fleetwood-May, Cecil—(t.), Oct. 15, 16h (71)

Fleetwood-Smith, Leslie—Mar. 17, 18g (71)

Fleischer, Max—Sept. 13, 14g (72)

Fleischer, Nat—June 27, 18h (72)

Fleisser, Marieluise—Feb. 7, 17h (74)

Fleming, H. M.—Nov. 28, 16g (72)

Fleming, Lionel—Mar. 5, 16g (74)

Fleming, Col. Peter—Aug. 20, 14g (71)

Fleming, Maj. Philip—Oct. 14, 18h (71)

Flemming, Brig. Gordon—Oct. 3, 18g (74)

G

Godfrey, Adm. John H.—Aug. 31, 12f (71); Sept. 3, 14h (71); 7, 12h (71)

Godfree, Leslie—(t.), Nov. 24, 16g (71)

Godfrey, Sir William M.—Nov. 27, 16h (71)

Goetze, Prof. Albrecht E. R.—Aug. 19, 12h (71)

Goff, Tom R. C.—(t.), Mar. 18, 16g (75); 22, 16h (75)

Golby, Colin—(t.), Oct. 23, 14h (74)

Goldschmidt-Rothschild, Lady Marie-Anne de—Dec. 13, 21g (73)

Goldie, Robert George—Mar. 8, 14f (71)

Goldsmith, Maj. John Gilbert—Jan. 4, 12h (72)

Goldsmith, Dr. William Noel—Apr. 9, 16g (75)

Goldston, Eli—(t.), Feb. 7, 17g (74)

Goldwyn, Samuel—Feb. 1, 20f (74)

Gollancz, Lady—Apr. 30, 16g (73); May 5, 14g (73)

Golovanov, Alexander—Oct. 2, 17g (75)

Gombell, Minna—Apr. 17, 18h (73)

Gomez, Thomas—June 21, 14h (71)

Gonard, Samuel—May 6, 16g (75)

Gonsalves, Paul—May 18, 16g (74)

Goodale, Lady Gwendolen—June 24, 16h (72)

Goodbody, Buzz—Apr. 15, 16g (75)

Goodfellow, Basil—(t.), Oct. 21, 16g (72)

Goodman, B. M.—(t.), July 25, 18g (73)

Goodman, Paul—Aug. 5, 14g (72); 8, 14h (72)

Goodrich, Dame Matilda—Aug. 15, 12g (72)

Goodsall, Robert H.—Nov. 19, 18f (75)

Goodson, Arthur—Mar. 20, 17h (75)

Gorbach, Dr. Alfons—Aug. 1, 17f (72)

Gorbatov, Gen. Alexander—Dec. 13, 21f (73)

Gordon, Lady Aileene—Nov. 26, 17g (73)

Gordon, Sir Archibald—Nov. 29, 20g (74); Dec. 5, 20h (74)

Gordon, Colin—Oct. 11, 18g (72)

Gordon, Sir Eyre—Aug. 3, 18h (72)

Gordon, Sir Garnet H.—Aug. 18, 12h (75); 27, 12g (75)

Gordon, John—Dec. 11, 18g (74)

Gordon, Richard M.—May 27, 8h (74)

Gordon-Dean, Air Comm. Horace—Apr. 11, 16g (72)

Gore, Phillip—June 20, 20h (75)

Gorham, Maurice—Aug. 19, 14g (75)

Gorin, Daniel—Apr. 26, 16f (72)

Gornall, Col. James M.—Oct. 6, 14g (73)

Gorst, Elliot M.—Nov. 29, 20h (73)

Gort, Lord—May 24, 14g (75)

Gort, Lady Bessy—Apr. 17, 16g (72)

Goschen, Maj.-Gen. Arthur A.—July 5, 14h (75)

Gosling, Maj. Cecil H.—May 21, 18g (74)

Gostling, Col. Bertrand W. W.—Aug. 17, 12f (71)

Gotfurt, Frederick—Feb. 24, 14h (73)

Gott, John—Sept. 4, 14h (72)

Gottlieb, Adolph—Mar. 6, 14g (74)

Gotts, John B.—July 24, 14g (71)

Gough, Prof. Michael—(t.), Nov. 7, 21g (73)

Goulandris, George P.—Oct. 19, 14h (74)

Gould, Lady—Aug. 21, 14h (73)

Gould, Sir Robert—Nov. 12, 16f (71)

Gouriet, Geoffrey—(t.), May 25, 20f (73)

Gourlay, Col. Clifford W.—July 23, 16h (75)

Gower, Lady Enid Leveson—Aug. 12, 14h (75)

Gower, Janet L.—May 9, 22h (74)

Grable, Betty—July 4, 18h (73)

Grace, John—Dec. 12, 19h (72)

Grace, Capt. Norman V.—Feb. 21, 16h (75)

Graf, Herbert, Apr. 9, 14h (73)

Graff, George—Jan. 27, 16h (73)

Graham, Lord Malise—Dec. 2, 16g (74)

Graham, Clive—Aug. 21, 14g (74)

Graham, Maj.-Gen. Douglas A. H.—Sept. 30, 17g (71); Oct. 6, 16h (71)

Graham, G. Michael—Jan. 11, 14h (72)

Graham, Dr. George—Nov. 15, 14g (71)

Graham, Sir George—Jan. 18, 16h (74)

Graham, John—Aug. 9, 18g (74)

Graham, Michael—Jan. 14, 14g (72)

Graham, Stephen—Mar. 20, 17g (75)

Graham, Col. William J.—May 20, 17h (71)

Graham-Jones, Aileen—(t.), Nov. 12, 17h (74)

Granard, Countess Beatrice of—Feb. 4, 14h (72)

Grand, Maj.-Gen. Laurence D.—Nov. 25, 17h (75); 28, 19h (75)

Grandjany, Marcel—Feb. 27, 16h (75)

Grange, Claude—Sept. 24, 14g (71)

Grange-Bennett, Rev. Canon Ronald du Pre—June 15, 21g (72)

Gransden, Sir Robert—Apr. 13, 21g (72)

Grant, Lord—Nov. 21, 17g (72)

Grant, Lady Margaret—Apr. 10, 14g (71)

Grant, C. R. A.—(t.), Jan. 31, 14g (72)

Grant, Col. James W.—Nov. 28, 16g (72)

Grant, John L.—Feb. 26, 17h (75)

Grant, Leonard Bishopp—Mar. 6, 14g (74)

Grant, Peter F.—Feb. 5, 14g (74); 8, 18g (74); 12, 16h (74)

Grant, William T.—Aug. 8, 14h (72)

Granville, Richard St. L.—Aug. 18, 12h (72)

Grasett, Lt.-Gen. Sir Edward—Dec. 6, 17g (71)

Gratiaeu, E. F. N.—(t.), Feb. 27, 16g (73); Mar. 2, 16h (73)

Grattan-Doyle, Lady—Mar. 17, 16g (72)

Graves, Charles—Feb. 22, 12f (71)

Graves, Diana—(t.), Feb. 6, 19h (75)

Graves, Sir Hubert—Apr. 6, 15f (72); 12, 18h (72)

Gray, Allan—Sept. 15, 14g (73)

Gray, Anthony—Apr. 29, 16g (72)

Gray, Charles D. S.—June 18, 16g (74)

Gray, Prof. Hamilton R.—May 13, 16h (72)

Gray, Harold—Dec. 29, 12h (72)

Gray, Sir James—Dec. 16, 14g (75); 24, 12g (75)

Grazebrook, Owen F.—Apr. 2, 16h (74)

Greece, Princess Aspasia of—Aug. 9, 16h (72); 14, 14g (72)

Green, Abel—May 12, 14g (73)

Green, Dr. Arnold T.—July 20, 14h (74)

Green, Charles—Oct. 10, 17f (72)

Green, Charles—Sept. 28, 16h (74)

Green, Eric—(t.), Dec. 29, 12h (72)

Green, F. L.—Jan. 17, 16h (75)

Green, Henry—Dec. 15, 14g (75); 24, 12g (74)

Green, Lawrence—(t.), June 9, 16g (72)

Green, Leslie—July 3, 18h (73)

Green, Brig. M.—(t.), Dec. 31, 10f (71)

Green, Martyn—Feb. 11, 14g (75)

Green, Neal—Sept. 23, 14g (74)

Green, Prof. R. B.—(t.), May 5, 14h (73)

Green, Roland—Dec. 21, 14f (72)

Green, Brig. Valentine C.—Nov. 6, 14g (72)

Greenberg, Dr. Len—Nov. 11, 15h (75)

Greenberg, Dr. Martin—(t.), Jan. 29, 14g (72)

Greenidge, Charles—(t.), May 17, 16h (72)

Greenlaw, Rev. Karl S. G.—Feb. 1, 16h (75)

Greenleaves, Herbert L.—Sept. 6, 14h (75)

Greenshields, Lt.-Col. David J.—Mar. 9, 20g (73)

Greenway, Lord—Sept. 16, 16g (75)

Greenwood, John E.—July 25, 14g (75)

Greenwood, Walter—Sept. 16, 16g (74)

Greer, Lady Marguerite—Aug. 26, 12h (71)

Greer, Rt. Rev. William D. L.—Nov. 1, 16f (72)

Gregg, Col. W. T. H.—June 11, 17h (75)

Gregory, Lady Dorothy—June 3, 16g (72)

Gregory, Lady Florence—Nov. 24, 19h (75)

Gregory, Sir David—(t.), Mar. 26, 18f (75)

Gregory, J. M.—Aug. 8, 16g (73)

Gregory, R. J.—Oct. 16, 18g (73)

Gregory, Sir Theodore—Jan. 19, 14h (71); Feb. 3, 14g (71)

Gregory, Theophilus S.—Aug. 18, 12h (75)

Gregson, John—Jan. 10, 16g (75)

Gregson, Lady Violet—Sept. 28, 16h (74)

Greig, Lady Phyllis—Mar. 9, 16g (72)

Greig, Charles—July 28, 18g (72)

Greig, William—Dec. 27, 10g (75)

Grenfell, Hilda—June 12, 15f (72)

Gresley, Sir Nigel—Jan. 16, 14h (74)

Gresson, Lady—Feb. 27, 14f (71)

Gresson, Sir Kenneth—Oct. 8, 18g (74)

Greswell, William T.—Feb. 15, 14h (71)

Grettan, Stanley—June 19, 16g (75)

Grew, Mary—Mar. 22, 14g (71)

Grey, Mary—Oct. 12, 14h (74)

Griebling, Otto—Apr. 21, 16h (72)

Grierson, Edward—(t.), June 5, 16g (75); 10, 18g (75)

Grierson, Francis D.—Sept. 27, 16h (72)

Grierson, Henry—(t.), Feb. 3, 16h (72)

Grierson, John—Feb. 21, 14f (72); 28, 14f (72); Mar. 4, 14g (72)

Griffies, Ethel—Sept. 16, 16g (75)

Griffin, Maj.-Gen. John A. A.—Mar. 28, 17g (72)

Griffith, Cyril C.—Aug. 1, 17h (72)

Griffith, Eric—(t.), Oct. 15, 18h (74)

Griffith, Prof. John S.—Apr. 27, 18g (72)

Griffith, Robert E.—Nov. 27, 16g (75)

Griffiths, Alex—Apr. 3, 16h (75)

Griffiths, James—Aug. 8, 14e (75); 12, 14g (75)

Griffiths, Jane—June 20, 20h (75)

Griffiths, Dr. Ruth—(t.), Dec. 24, 12h (73)

Griffiths, William—Apr. 16, 16f (73)

Griff-Smith, Rev. Canon Thomas—Oct. 23, 14g (71)

Grime, Alan—July 30, 16h (74)

Grimes, William Henry—Jan. 17, 12g (72)

Grimsditch, Herbert B.—Oct. 13, 17f (71)

Grimswade, Harold J.—Nov. 2, 19e (73)

Grinnell-Milne, Duncan—(t.), Dec. 13, 21f (73)

Gripper, Canon Francis H.—(t.), Dec. 4, 18g (73)

Grisconi, Frances—Mar. 31, 16h (75)

Grisewood, Freddie—Nov. 16, 21f (72); 20, 18g (72); 22, 18h (72)

Grivas, Gen. George—Jan. 29, 14f (74)

Grofe, Ferde—Apr. 5, 14f (72)

Gromaire, Marcel—Apr. 13, 12g (71); 15, 18g (71)

Groom, Prof. Bernard—(t.), Apr. 11, 16h (75)

Groom, Donald—Aug. 21, 12g (72)

Kennedy, Dr. Douglas P.—Dec. 13, 17h (72)

Kennedy, Duncan—(t.), July 17, 18g (74)

Kennedy, Frank Robert—Jan. 7, 14h (71)

Kennedy, Dr. Peter—(t.), Feb. 8, 14g (75)

Kennedy, Col. Sydney—(t.), Jan. 23, 19f (75)

Kenner, Prof. James—July 4, 18h (74)

Kenny, Sean—June 12, 18 (73)

Kent, Lady Margaret—June 13, 20h (74)

Kent, Lt.-Col. Anthony E.—(t.), Apr. 12, 18g (72)

Kent, L. E.—Feb. 8, 14h (72)

Kent, Rockwell—Mar. 15, 14f (71)

Kenward, Lady Ruth—Dec. 16, 15f (74)

Keogh, Malcolm—Apr. 21, 16g (71)

Keppel-Palmer, Col. C. M.—Nov. 8, 23h (73)

Kerby, Capt. Henry B.—Jan. 5, 14f (71); 8, 12h (71)

Kerensky, Olga—Oct. 3, 16h (75) (75)

Keres, Paul—June 6, 17g (75)

Kermode, A. V. M. Alfred C.—Feb. 26, 14g (73); Mar. 1, 18h (73)

Kernan, Thomas—(t.), May 19, 14g (75)

Kernick, Jack—Mar. 26, 16h (74)

Kerr, Lady—Sept. 12, 20h (74)

Kerr, Mrs. Anne—July 30, 14g (73); Aug. 4, 14h (73)

Kerr, Bertie—Nov. 29, 20g (73)

Kerr, Sir Hamilton—Dec. 28, 12g (74); Jan. 4, 14h (75); 6, 14g (75)

Kerr, Sir Reginald—Nov. 7, 18g (74)

Kerr, Col. William H.—Feb. 25, 16h (71)

Kerr-Muir, R. J.—Feb. 16, 18g (74)

Kerrigan, Berrard W.—Mar. 20, 17g (75)

Kerrigan, Daniel P.—Nov. 3, 17f (71); 6, 14g (71)

Kerrison, Roger F.—Nov. 13, 16h (72)

Kershaw, Capt. Cecil A.—(t.), Nov. 4, 16g (72)

Kerslake, Reginald—(t.), Mar. 20, 17g (75)

Kertesz, Istvan—Apr. 18, 21g (73)

Kewley, Brig. Edward Rigby—Mar. 8, 16g (72)

Keyes, Dowager Lady Eva—Aug. 31, 14h (73)

Keynes, Lady Margaret—Dec. 31, 14h (74)

Keyworth, Prof. William G.—Aug. 27, 12g (75)

Khadouri, Sasson—May 25, 14h (71)

Khalipor, Col.-Gen. Ivan—Aug. 4, 14h (75)

Khan, Field Marshal Ayub: see Ayub Khan

Khan, Ustad Allauddin—(t.), Sept. 14, 19h (72)

Khetagurov, Gen. Georgi—Sept. 8, 14h (75)

Khrushchev, Nikita—Sept. 13, 7a (71)

Khudadad Khan—Mar. 10, 16h (71)

Khvostov, Prof. Vladimir—Mar. 11, 14h (72)

Kiamarsangpei, Gen.—July 10, 20g (74)

Kidd, Dr. Franklin—May 10, 24h (74)

Kidd, Frederic W.—July 8, 16g (71)

Killby, Leonard G.—Aug. 14, 17f (75)

Killick, Brig. Sir Alexander—Feb. 6, 19f (75)

Killick, John—Sept. 16, 18e (71)

Kilmarnock, Lord—Mar. 16, 18h (75)

Kimball, Maj. Lawrence—Jan, 18g (72)

Kindinger, Gerd—Feb. 21, 14h (72)

King, Sir Alexander—Feb. 16, 21g (73)

King, Archdale—(t.), July 13, 18h (72)

King, Cyril—June 27, 18f (72)

King, Adm. Edward L. S.—May 10, 14g (71)

King, Geoffrey—(t.), Apr. 3, 8h (72)

King, Gordon R.—Apr. 12, 8h (71)

King, Capt. Herbert R.—June 12, 16h (71)

King, Hetty—Sept. 29, 16h (72)

King, William C. H.—May 14, 14h (73)

King-Hall, Magdalen—Mar. 3, 14g (71)

King-King, Capt. Eustace—Jan. 10, 16g (75)

Kingdon, Dr. Frank—(t.), Mar. 8, 16h (72)

Kingsmill, Lt.-Col. William H.—July 5, 12h (71)

Kingston-McCloughry, A. V. M. Edgar J.—Nov. 14, 16f (72); 16, 21g (72)

Kinmant, Col. George M.—Dec. 13, 21f (73)

Kinnaird, Lord—July 11, 16g (72); 14, 18h (72)

Kinnell, Rev. Gordon—Nov. 22, 14g (71)

Kintore, Countess of—Sept. 25, 18h (74)

Kintore, Helena Lady—Dec. 16, 17h (71)

Kippax, A. F.—Sept. 6, 17h (72)

Kirby, Allan Price—May 7, 18h (73)

Kiril, Patriarch—Mar. 8, 14g (71)

Kirk, Lady Mary—July 10, 20g (74)

Kirk, Adam K.—Mar. 13, 18h (75); Apr. 15, 16h (75)

Kirk, Geoffrey W.—July 31, 16h (75)

Kirk, Norman—Sept. 2, 14g (74); 3, 14g (74); 5, 16g (74)

Kirkpatrick, Rev. Canon Herbert F.—July 24, 14h (71)

Kisch, Lady—Apr. 27, 18h (71)

Kisfaludi-Strobl, Zsigmond—Aug. 16, 14f (75)

Kitson, Col. Geoffrey H.—Nov. 9, 18h (74)

Kitson Clark, Dr. G. S. R.—Dec. 11, 16g (75)

Kittermaster, Ronald—Mar. 16, 19g (72)

Klausner, Mrs. Margot—Nov. 27, 16g (75)

Klein, John W.—Sept. 6, 18h (73)

Klein, Louis—Aug. 2, 14h (75)

Klein, Dr. Viola—Oct. 18, 20h (73)

Kleinwort, Lady Davina—Mar. 8, 18h (73)

Klemperer, Otto—July 9, 193 (73)

Kletzki, Paul—Mar. 7, 18f (73); 17, 16h (73)

Knatchbull-Hugessen, Sir Hughe—Mar. 23, 19f (71); 31, 16f (71); Apr. 12, 8g (71)

Knight, Jasper—Jan. 28, 16f (72)

Knott, Lt.-Gen. Sir Harold—Aug. 30, 16g (74)

Knowland, William—Feb. 25, 14g (74)

Knowles, Prof. David—Nov. 26, 18g (74); Dec. 6, 18g (74)

Knowles, Sir Francis—July 18, 20g (74)

Knowles, Joshua K.—July 11, 18f (74)

Knox, Lady Dorothy—Mar. 28, 18h (74)

Knox, Edmund V.—Jan. 4, 12f (71)

Knox, Gen. Sir Harry—June 11, 16f (71)

Knox, Teddy—Dec. 4, 18h (74)

Knox-Johnston, Anthony—(t.), Jan. 11, 18g (73)

Knox-Shaw, Thomas—Aug. 2, 17g (72)

Koch, Mrs. Bodil—Jan. 8, 16h (72)

Koch, Helmut—Jan. 31, 16h (75)

Koch, Dr. Ludwig—May 7, 16g (74)

K'O-Chen, Dr. Chu—Feb. 15, 17f (74)

Kochetov, Vsevolod—Nov. 7, 21g (73)

Kohlmeyer, Werner—Mar. 29, 20h (74)

Koita, Youssouf—Oct. 6, 16h (71)

Kokkas, Panos—June 28, 20g (74)

Kollis, Costas—Apr. 15, 16g (75)

Kolnai, Aurel—Jul. 7, 14h (73)

Komarovski, Gen. Alexander—Nov. 24, 16g (74)

Kominek, Card. Boleslaw—Mar. 16, 16h (74)

Komissarov, Alexander—Aug. 9, 14g (75)

Komocsin, Zoltan—May 30, 18h (74)

Konenkov, Sergei—Oct. 13, 17f (71)

Konev, Marshal of the Soviet Union Ivan—May 22, 18f (73)

Korayim, Mohamed—May 29, 10h (72)

Kormendi, Ferenc—July 22, 14h (72)

Korneichuk, Alexander—May 17, 16h (72)

Korner, Prof. Asher—(t.), Sept. 28, 14f (71)

Kossamak, Sisowath—Apr. 28, 14g (75)

Kozintsev, Grigon—May 14, 14g (73); 19, 16h (73)

Kozub, Ernst—Jan. 5, 12h (72)

Krainer, Josef—(t.), Dec. 2, 18e (71)

Kratochvil, Dr. Bohnslav—Sept. 2, 16h (72)

Krichefski, Wilfred—(t.), Dec. 20, 14g (74)

Kripalani, Mrs. Sucheta—Dec. 3, 16g (74)

Krips, Jose—Oct. 14, 16h (74)

Krishnamachari, T. T.—Mar. 9, 16g (74); 18, 14h (74)

Krishna Menon, Vengalil Krishnan—Oct. 7, 14g (74); 12, 14h (74); 14, 16h (74); 18, 19h (74); 23, 14h (74)

Kriza, John—Aug. 22, 12h (75)

Krock, Arthur—Apr. 15, 8g (74)

Kroyer-Kielberg, Lady Margaret—May 17, 16g (72)

Kruger, Otto—Sept. 9, 14h (74)

Krummacher, Rt. Rev. Friedrich W.—June 22, 10h (74); 27, 20g (74)

Krupa, Gene—Oct. 19, 20g (73)

Krylov, Marshal Nikolai—Feb. 11, 16g (72)

Kschessinska, Mathilda—Dec. 9, 16f (71); 15, 17h (71)

Kuen, Herr Felix—Jan. 25, 18h (74)

Kuentscher, Prof. Gehard—Dec. 20, 14g (72)

Kuhnle-Woods, Walter—(t.), Nov. 7, 21h (73)

Kuiper, Dr. Gerald—Jan. 11, 16g (74)

Kukiel, Lt.-Gen. Marian—Aug. 25, 14h (73)

Kulesov, Nikolai V.—May 27, 14g (75)

Kuper, Charles—(t.), Aug. 14, 17h (75)

Kurella, Alfred—June 16, 16h (75)

Kurtz, Harold—Dec. 23, 12h (72); 30, 16f (72); Jan. 1, 16g (73); 2, 12g (73)

Kurz, Prof. Otto—Sept. 8, 14f (75)

Kuts, Vladimir—Aug. 18, 12f (75)

Kuusinen, Hertta—Mar. 22, 18h (74)

Kuyck, Hugo van—Oct. 10, 17g (75)

Kuznetsov, Vice-Adm. Nikolai—Dec. 9, 14h (74)

Kwan, Sir Cho-Yio—Dec. 8, 17h (71)

Kydd, Ronald R.—Oct. 12, 18g (72)

Kyes, Roger—Feb. 15, 14h (71)

Kyrillos VI, Pope—Mar. 10, 16h (71)

Kyrou, Kyros—Apr. 10, 20h (74)

L

La Bedoyere, Count Michael de—July 16, 14h (73)

Laborde, Gerard—(t.), Feb. 13, 16h (74)

Labric, Pierre—May 19, 18g (72)

Labroca, Mario—July 3, 18h (73)

Lacassagne, Prof. Antoine—Dec. 17, 16h (71); 18, 14h (71)

Lacasse, Joseph—Oct. 31, 17g (75)

Lack, Dr. David Lamber—Mar. 13, 16f (73)

Lacore, Mme Suzanne—Nov. 17, 18h (75)

Ladborough, Dr. Richard W.—May 3, 18g (72)

L'Estrange, Comdre. H. O.—Dec. 6, 19h (72)

Letchworth, Thomas E.–Feb. 6, 16 (73)

Letham, James—Jan. 19, 16h (72)

Lethbridge, Dorothy M. B.—Apr. 21, 14g (73)

Lethbridge, Thomas C.—Oct 2, 14g (71); 6, 16g (71)

Letourneur, Alfred—Jan. 8, 17g (75)

Levant, Oscar—Aug. 16, 12h (72)

Levén and Melville, Dowager Countess Rosamund of—Apr. 13, 14h (74)

Levene, Philip—Apr. 8, 21g (73)

Lever, Elizabeth R.—Apr. 20, 19h (72)

Lever, Prof. J. W.—Nov. 20, 19g (75)

Lever, Sir Tresham—May 2, 17g (75)

Leverhulme, Lady Margaret—Aug. 23, 16h (73)

Leveson-Gower, Miss Janet—(t.), May 13, 18h (74)

Levi, Dr. Carlo—Jan. 7, 14g (75)

Levin, Rabbi—Nov. 19, 16h (71)

Levin, Dr. Daniel—Jan. 21, 16h (71)

Levy, Benn W.—Dec. 8, 16g (73); 15, 14g (73)

Levy, Prof. Hyman—Feb. 28, 16f (75); Mar. 1, 14f (75)

Levy, Leonard—Jan. 26, 14f (71)

Lewin, Rabbi Itzhak Meir—Aug. 9, 12h (71); 16, 12h (71)

Lewis, Sir Aubrey—Jan. 22, 14g (75)

Lewis, Frank R.—Dec. 6, 19h (72)

Lewis, J. Haydon—Sept. 18, 14g (71)

Lewis, Hilda—Feb. 6, 16h (74)

Lewis, Joe E.—June 7, 16f (71)

Lewis, Michael—Mar. 15, 16h (75)

Lewis, Prof. Morris M.—Oct. 4, 14h (71)

Lewis, Neville—June 28, 16g (72)

Lewis, Brig. R. M. H.—Oct. 20, 21h (72)

Lewis, Ted—Aug. 26, 12g (71)

Lewisohn, William—July 15, 14h (74)

Lewthwaite, Dr. Raymond—Mar. 22, 18g (72); 24, 16g (72)

Ley, Frank—Jan. 28, 16g (72)

Lichine, David—July 21, 14g (72)

Lichtheim, George—Apr. 24, 14f (73); 26, 18g (73)

Liddell, Mrs. Calypso—Oct. 29, 19f (74)

Lidderdale, Alan W.—(t.), Feb. 26, 16g (71)

Liénart, Cardinal Achille—Feb. 16, 21g (73)

Lier, Bertus Van—(t.), Feb. 29, 16h (72)

Liesching, Lady—Feb. 13, 17f (74)

Liesching, Sir Percivale—Nov. 6, 22h (73); 8, 23g (73)

Lieven, Albert—Dec. 23, 12f (71)

Li Fu-Chun—Jan. 16, 21g (75)

Lightfoot, Lionel—(t.), Aug. 7, 14g (72)

Lilley, Frank—Aug. 24, 13g (71)

Lilley, Joseph J.—Jan. 4, 12f (71)

Limón, Jose—Dec. 5, 18g (72)

Lin Piao—July 29, 16g (72)

Linaker, William H.—July 9, 16g (75)

Lincoln, G. Gould—Dec. 4, 18 (74)

Lincoln, Brig-Gen. George A.—May 27, 14g (75)

Lindbergh, Col. Charles—Aug. 28, 15e (74); 30, 16h (74)

Lindblom, Prof. Johannes—Oct. 24, 20g (74)

Linder, Leslie—Apr. 11, 18g (73)

Lindgren, Lord—Sept. 10, 14g (71)

Lindgren, Ernest—July 24, 16h (73)

Lindley, William N.—Sept. 19, 21h (73)

Lindrum, Horace—June 22, 10h

Lindsay, Dr. Eric M.—July 30, 16g (74)

Lindsay, Kevin—Apr. 30, 20h (75)

Lindsay, Nancy—Jan. 4, 14g (73)

Lindsay, Sir William—Oct. 22, 19g (75)

Lindsay-Carnegie, M.P. G. M.—Jan. 3, 14h (74)

Lindsay-Rea, Robert—Apr. 30, 16f (71)

Lindsell, Herbert G.—May 16, 21h (73)

Lindsell, Sir Wilfred—May 3, 21g (73)

Lindstrom, Erik—Oct. 10, 18h (74)

Linehan, Prof. Patrick A.—Mar. 8, 18f (73)

Lines, Walter—Nov. 24, 17g (72)

Linfield, Sir Arthur—Apr. 19, 18f (74)

Link, Prosper—Aug. 8, 14h (72)

Linklater, Eric—Nov. 8, 18g (74); 13, 18g (74)

Linnett, Prof. John W.—Nov. 10, 14f (75); 13, 16g (75)

Linton, Sir Andrew—Jan. 13, 12h (71)

Linton, Prof. David L.—Apr. 14, 16h (71); 26, 15g (71)

Linzell, Dr. James L.—Dec. 31, 12f (71)

Lipchitz, Jacques—May 29, 14g (73)

Lippmann, Walter—Dec. 16, 15f (74)

Liro, Dr. Hermenegildo A.—May 19, 18g (72)

Lisiewicz, Mrs. Theodozya—May 14, 18h (75)

List, Field-Marshal Wilhelm—Aug. 18, 14e (71)

Lister, Arthur—Apr. 9, 16h (75); 17, 18g (75)

Lister, Lt-Col. Frederick H.—Nov. 11, 18h (71)

Lister-Kaye, Lady Jean—Sept. 26, 19g (75)

Liston, Sonny—Jan. 7, 14f (71)

Li Szu-Kuang—May 5, 18h (71)

Li Te-Ch'uan, Mrs.—Apr. 29, 16f (72)

Lithgow, Lady Gwendolyn—Sept. 19, 16g (75)

Little, Adm. Sir Charles—June 22, 23h (73)

Little, Dr. Clarence C.—Dec. 24, 12h (71)

Little, Tom—Feb. 28, 16f (75)

Littlefair, Ald. Joseph—Oct. 8, 18h (74)

Littler, Prince—Sept. 14, 18f (73)

Litvak, Anatole—Dec. 17, 17f (74)

Liu Shao-Chi—Nov. 4, 16g (74)

Liu Shou-Kwan—Oct. 9, 16g (75)

Livanov, Boris N.—Sept. 25, 14g (72)

Livingston, William B.—May 25, 21h (72)

Llewellyn, Redvers—May 29, 16f (75)

Lloyd, Lady—Dec. 11, 17h (72)

Lloyd, Guy V.—Aug. 14, 17g (75)

Lloyd, Harold—Mar. 10, 16f (71); 16, 17h (71)

Lloyd, James—Mar. 12, 16h (74)

Lloyd, A. V. M. Kennedy B.—Aug. 9, 14h (73)

Lloyd, L. J.—June 9, 16h (75)

Lloyd, Lt-Col. Roderick Croil—Feb. 17, 18h (72)

Lloyd, Dr. William E.—May 30, 16g (75)

Lloyd, Woodrow—Apr. 10, 15h (72)

Lloyd, Wynne H.—May 28, 10g (73)

Lloyd-Baker, Olive K. L.—June 5, 16h (75); 11, 17f (75)

Lloyd George, Frances Lady—Dec. 7, 21f (72)

Lloyd-Williams, Dr. Katharine—Jan. 13, 16g (73)

Lloyd-Williams, Trefor—Apr. 21, 16h (72)

Loch, Brig. D. G.—(t.), Jan. 17, 16g (75)

Loch, Col. John C.—June 7, 21g (74)

Lockhart, Dr. Laurence—(t.), May 9, 18h (75)

Lockspeiser, Edward—Feb. 6, 16f (73)

Lockton, Johnny H.—July 4, 19h (72); 7, 14h (72)

Lockwood, James H.—Nov. 30, 19f (72)

Lockwood, Cmdr. Rev. Oliver John Frank—Aug. 8, 14h (72)

Locmaria, Marquis du Parc—Mar. 28, 21h (73)

Loeb, Harold A.—Jan. 29, 14h (74)

Loeb, Milton B.—Feb. 9, 14h (72)

Loeb, Otto—Aug. 8, 16h (74)

Loeb, Dr. Robert F.—Oct. 27, 16h (73); 31, 20g (73)

Lofthouse, Dr. C. T.—(t.), Mar. 8, 18g (74); 13, 18h (74)

Lohr, Miss Marie—Jan. 24, 16f (75)

Lojendio, Juan Pablo de—Dec. 15, 14h (73)

Lomax, Maj.-Gen. Cyril E. N.—Sept. 1, 14g (73)

Lombardo, Carmen—Apr. 19, 14g (71)

Lomenie, Emmanuel B. de—Feb. 12, 16h (74)

Londos, Jim—Aug. 23, 14g (75)

Londoun-Shand, Col. Eric—(t.), Aug. 24, 14h (72)

Long, Sir Bertram—May 13, 16g (75)

Longdon-Davies, John—Dec 6, 17h (71)

Longhurst, Stanley Charles—Jan. 25, 16g (72)

Longland, Austin C.—July 5, 18g (72); 12, 16g (72)

Longley, Lady—Jan. 18, 14g (71)

Longman, Mark—Sept. 7, 16g (72)

Longman, Robert—(t,), June 28, 14g (71)

Longmore, Brig. John A.—Aug. 21, 14h (73)

Longmuir, Very Rev. James B.—Oct. 24, 21f (73)

Longstreth-Thompson, Francis—Mar. 21, 17f (73); Apr. 16, 16g (73)

Lonsdale, Dame Kathleen—Apr. 2, 18d (71)

Loomis, Alfred L.—Aug. 13, 14h (75)

Lopez, Eugenio—July 17, 16g (75)

Lopez, Vincent—Sept. 22, 14h (75)

Lopukhov, Fyodor—Feb. 8, 19f (73)

Lord, Sir Frank—May 2, 20h (74)

Lord, Commissioner Herbert—Apr. 15, 18g (71)

Lord, John H.—Oct. 29, 17h (73)

Lorenz, Max—Jan. 13, 16h (75)

Lorenzo, Ange—Apr. 26, 15g (71)

Losch, Tilly—Dec. 27, 10g (75)

Loughrey, Miss H. M.—Dec. 18, 14h (75)

Love, Herbert Gordon—Aug. 30, 8g (71)

Love, Robert J. M.—Oct. 4, 18h (74)

Lovell, Prof. Reginald—Mar. 13, 14h (72)

Lovely, Percy—Jan. 25, 14h (75)

Loveridge, Arthur J.—Aug. 14, 17f (75)

Lovet-Lorski, Boris—Mar. 6, 18h (73)

Low, Lady—Jan 16, 14g (73)

Low, David M.—June 26, 14f (72)

Low, Sir Francis—Sept. 20, 17f (72); 28, 18g (72)

Lowe, Edmund—Apr. 23, 18g (71)

Lowe, Sir Francis Gordon—May 19, 18g (72)

Lowe, Lt-Col. William H.—May 4, 16f (71)

Lowenfeld, Frances G.—Feb. 3, 16h (73)

Lowndes, Noble F.—May 10, 18g (72)

Lowndes, Norman—(t.), Nov. 29, 20g (74)

Lowry-Corry, Sir Henry—Jan. 3, 14h (74)

Lowson, Sir Denys—Sept. 11, 16g (75); 18, 16g (75)

Lowther, Lady Dorothy—Oct. 9, 16h (75)

Loyd, Gen. Sir Henry—Nov. 12 21f (73); 15, 21g (73)

Loyd, Vivian Graham—Mar. 30, 18g (72)

Lozier, Marguerite—Oct. 11, 16f (71)

Lu Han—May 20, 16g (74)

Lubarda, Petar—Feb. 14, 24h (74)

Lubke, Heinrich—Apr. 7, 16 (72)

Lucan, Dowager Countess Violet of—Feb. 4, 14h (72)

Lucas, Lady Thelma—Jan. 30, 16g (74)

Lucas, Bernard G.—(t.), Dec. 10, 16g (74)

Lucas, Claude A.—June 4, 16g (74)

Lucas, Prof. Wilfrid J.—May 11, 12g (73); 11, 22g (73)

Luce, Adm. Sir David—Jan. 7, 14h (71); 9, 12h (71)

Luce, Canon Harry K.—Nov. 28, 16g (72)

Petushkov, Vladimir—Apr. 29, 18g (74)

Pham Dang Lam—June 6, 17h (75)

Phelps, Edwin—Mar. 16, 16h (74)

Phelps, Harry T.—Dec. 19, 16f (73)

Phelps, Tom J.—Aug. 28, 14h (71)

Philips, Lady Dorcas—Aug. 24, 12h (74)

Phillimore, Sir Henry J.—June 5, 19g (74); 10, 16h (74)

Phillimore, Miles—Sept. 20, 17h (72)

Phillips, Lady Gertrude—Dec. 29, 10h (75)

Phillips, Prof. A. W. H.—Mar. 6, 16g (75)

Phillips, Cabell—Dec. 1, 14h (75)

Phillips, Sir Charles—Aug. 14, 14g (74)

Phillips, Maj.-Gen. Sir Edward— May 18, 22h (73)

Phillips, Peter J.—Sept. 27, 14h (75)

Phillips, Sid—May 26, 16h (73)

Phillips, Wendell—Dec. 6, 14g (75)

Phipps, Maj.-Gen. Herbert C.— Nov. 10, 14f (75)

Phipson, Col. E. S.—May 29, 14h (73)

Picasso, Pablo—Apr. 9, 14e (73)

Pickford, Lady Lillian—Dec. 24, 12h (75)

Pickles, Sir John—Nov. 7, 17h (72)

Pickthorn, Sir Kenneth—Nov. 13, 16g (75)

Pidgeon, Very Rev. George C.— June 17, 17h (71); 18, 18h (71)

Pierre-Bloch, Jean—Aug. 10, 14g (73)

Piggott, Capt. George B.—Apr. 21, 16g (72)

Pigott, Lady Christabel—May 1, 18g (74)

Pike, Most Rev. Robert B.—Dec. 29, 12h (73)

Pilditch, Sir Denys—Sept. 6, 14g (75)

Pilkington, Geoffrey L.—Jan. 10, 14g (72)

Pilkington, Miss Margaret—Aug. 7, 16h (74); 10, 14g (74)

Pilkington, Canon Ronald J.—Jan. 28, 17g (75)

Pilkington Jackson, Mr. D. d'O.— —Sept. 27, 22g (73)

Pincus, Louis A.—July 26, 18h (73)

Pinder, Brig. Harold—Dec. 23, 12f (74)

Pinheiro, Israel—July 10, 16h (73)

Pinna, Mgr. Giovanni M.—June 24, 16h (71)

Pintacuda, Carlo—Mar. 9, 16g (71)

Pinto, Edward—(t.), May 11, 18h (72); 20, 16g (72)

Pinto, Mrs. Eva—Mar. 14, 16g (72); 20, 16g (72)

Pinto Basta, Dr. A.—Aug. 29, 12f (72)

Piovene, Count Guido—Nov. 14, 19f (74)

Pipon, Sir James—Jan. 16, 14h (71)

Pirandello, Fausto—Dec. 2, 14g (75)

Pirandello, Stefano—Feb. 10, 16g (72)

Pirelli, Alberto—Oct. 21, 19f (71)

Pirolley, Mgr. Emile—July 6, 14h (71)

Piron, Gen. J.—(t.), Sept. 6, 16h (74)

Pitcairn, Lieut-Col. John F. A.— July 27, 15g (71)

Pitcairn, Rev. Theodore—Dec. 21, 17f (73)

Pitman, Capt. Charles R. S.—Sept. 22, 14h (75)

Pitt, Col. Robert—Apr. 16, 14g (74)

Pitz, Wilhelm—Nov. 23, 18g (73)

Pixton, C. H.—Feb. 9, 14f (72)

Plamenatz, Prof John—Feb. 27, 16f (75); Mar. 24, 16h (75)

Plastov, Arkadi—May 17, 16g (72)

Platnauer, Maurice—Dec. 23, 12f (74)

Platt, James W.—Dec. 20, 14h (72)

Platt, Gen. Sir William—Sept. 29, 14f (75)

Playfair, Maj.-Gen. Ian S. O.— Mar. 25, 18h (72)

Playfair, Sir Patrick H. L.—Nov. 26, 18g (74)

Plesch, Arped—Dec. 19, 16g (74)

Pletkus, Mgr. Juozas—Oct. 1, 16g (75)

Plomer, Brig. Geoffrey—Aug. 7, 14h (75)

Plomer, William—Sept. 22, 16g (73); 28, 20f (73); Oct. 8, 19h (73)

Plume, Alan—Feb. 22, 16h (74)

Plummer, Lady—June 14, 18g (72); 15, 21h (72); 16, 18h (72)

Plunket, Lord Patrick—May 29, 16h (75); June 7, 14g (75)

Pochin, Victor Robert—Sept. 6, 17g (72); 9, 16h (72)

Poe, Col. John P.—May 30, 18h (74)

Poelchau, Dr. Harold—May 4, 18h (72)

Pol, Herman Van de—Mar. 31, 16f (71)

Poliakov, Nikolai—Sept. 26, 16g (74)

Pollitt, Charles—(t.), Oct. 14, 17g (75)

Pollock, Sir Ronald—Mar. 11, 14h (74)

Pommier, Jean—Feb. 21, 16h (73)

Pompidou, Pres. Georges—Apr. 3, 1a (74); 8, 16g (74)

Pontoppidan, Clara—Jan. 25, 14h (75)

Pook, Brian—Nov. 5, 17h (71)

Pool, Phoebe—(t.), Dec. 28, 8g (71)

Poole, Lt.-Col. Gilbert S.—Jan. 14, 14g (72)

Pope-Hennessy, James—Jan. 26, 16g (74)

Popenchenko, Valery—Feb. 22, 14h (75)

Popovic, Milentije—May 12, 16h (71)

Porcella, Prof. Amadore—Jan. 4, 12g (72)

Portal of Hungerford, Lord—Apr. 24, 14f (71); 30, 16g (71); May 7, 18g (71); 8, 14g (71)

Portarlington, Countess Winna-freda of—Apr. 19, 16h (75)

Porteous, Douglas A.—Dec. 12, 16h (74)

Porter, Air Vice-Marshal Cedric E. V.—Apr. 19, 16h (75)

Porter, Sir George—Feb. 13, 16h (74)

Porter, Harold E. L.—(t.), July 12, 18g (73)

Porter, Col. James H.—Mar. 23, 20g (73)

Porter, Nicholas H. A.—Aug. 14, 14h (73)

Porter, Mrs. Rose—Oct. 10, 17h (75)

Porter, William D.—Aug. 2, 14h (75)

Portman, Lady Sybil—July 9, 16g (75)

Portman, Davina—(t.), Nov. 10, 17g (71)

Portman, Genevere—Mar. 20, 16f (73)

Portway, Col. Cedric—Feb. 28, 18g (73)

Post, Majorie M.—Sept. 17, 19h (73)

Postgate, Mrs. Daisy—Apr. 22, 18g (71); 30, 16h (71)

Postgate, Raymond—Mar. 30, 26f (71)

Pott, Mrs.—Dec. 12, 16g (74)

Potter, Lady—Feb. 5, 14h (73)

Potter, Prof. David—Feb. 26, 16g (71)

Potter, Gillie—Mar. 5, 16g (75)

Poulet, Gaston—Apr. 29, 18g (74)

Poulett, Lord—Mar. 2, 16h (73)

Pound, Mrs. Dorothy—Dec. 11, 18g (73); 13, 21h (73)

Pound, Ezra—Nov. 2, 18f (72)

Powell, Adam Clayton—Apr. 6, 15f (72)

Powell, Alan R.—Oct. 14, 17g (75)

Powell, Frank J.—Nov. 2, 17h (71)

Powell, Ioan L.—Apr. 2, 16g (75)

Powell, Rear-Adm. James—Sept. 9, 16h (71)

Powell, Lawrence—(t.), July 18, 18h (73)

Powell, Dr. Lawrence F.—July 18, 14g (75)

Powell, Lewis—(t.), Sept. 8, 18g (72)

Powell, Michael C. L.—July 27, 15g (71); 30, 17h (71); 31, 12h (71)

Powell, Prof. Thomas G. E.—July 10, 17g (75); 15, 14g (75); 17, 16g (75)

Power, Miss Beryl—(t.), Nov. 15, 21g (74)

Power, Lt-Col. Gervase B.—Sept. 30, 17h (74)

Powerscourt, Lord—Apr. 5, 21g (73)

Powis, Lord—Jan. 17, 14g (74)

Powl, Robert G.—(t.), Oct. 26, 18g (72)

Prats, Gen. Carlos—Oct. 1, 16h (74)

Pratt, Sir Bernard—Dec. 15, 13h (75)

Pratt, Rear-Adm. Charles B.— Aug. 16g (73)

Pratt, Miss Claire A.—(t.), June 20, 20h (75)

Pratt, John L.—Dec. 23, 10g (75)

Pratt, Sydney E.—May 22, 18h (73)

Prawdin, Michael—(t.), Jan. 11, 14h (71)

Preetorius, Emil—Feb. 3, 16g (73)

Prefontaine, Steve—(t.), May 31, 14g (75)

Preiswerk, William—(t.), July 3, 18h : 74)

Prendergast, Lady—Aug. 3, 18h (72)

Preobrazenskiy, Rear-Adm. Valery —Nov. 1, 14h (75)

Prescott, Mrs. Hilda—May 6, 16h (72); 16, 18g (72)

Prescott, Robin—(t.), May 28, 14g (75)

Preston, Lady—Dec. 16, 17h (71)

Preston, Prof. G. D.—June 29, 18h (72); July 13, 18g (72)

Preston, Kerrison—Jan. 18, 16h (74)

Preston, Adm. Sir Lionel G.— Sept. 25, 14h (71)

Preston, W. Cmdre Raphael C.— Nov. 13, 16h (72)

Prestwich, Irene—(t.), Aug. 21, 14h (74)

Pretty, Air Marshal Sir Walter— Jan. 23, 19h (75); Feb. 5, 17h (75)

Prevett, Cmdr. Harry—Mar. 3, 14g (72)

Prevost, Alain—Dec. 21, 14h (71)

Price, Dennis—Oct. 8, 19g (73)

Price, Rt. Rev. Dudley W.—Jan. 4, 12f (71)

Price, M. Philips—Sept. 25, 18h (73)

Price, Col. Rees Thomas—Mar. 15, 18h (74)

Price, Thomas E.—Aug. 11, 12g (71)

Price, Tom—Feb. 2, 16g (73)

Price, William R.—Aug. 1, 17h (75)

Price Thomas, Sir Clement—Mar. 20, 16f (73)

Prichard, Ian—Aug. 3, 18h (72)

Prichard, Sir John—Apr. 15, 18h (71)

Prichard, Sir Norman—Apr. 13, 21g (72)

Prickard, Thomas F. V.—July 9, 16g (73)

Prickelt, Rear-Adm. Cecil B. —Oct. 11, 18g (72)

Pridham, Sir Francis—Jan. 29, 19h (75)

Priestley, Sir Raymond E.—June 27, 20g (74)

Priestman, Lady Marie—Aug. 5, 14g (71)

Prince, John—Aug. 13, 14g (74)

Prince-White, Frederick G.—July 19, 14h (75)

Pringle, Lady Laura—Jan. 18, 14g (72)

Pringle, Don—Oct. 14, 17h (75)

Prins, George—(t.), Apr. 13, 18h (73)

Prior, Sir Geoffrey—Oct. 14, 18h (72); 19, 19f (72)

Pritchett, Lady—June 5, 12h (71)

Prititski, Sergei—June 15, 17f (71)

Pritt, Denis N.—May 24, 18g (72); 27, 16h (72); 31, 17h (72); June 3, 16h (72)

Probert, Arthur—Feb. 15, 16h (75)

Prochazka, Jan—Feb. 23, 14f (71)

Procter, Dod—Aug. 3, 18h (72)

Reid, Col. Andrew McK—Feb. 19, 14h (73); 22, 19h (73)

Reid, Sir Douglas—Sept. 1, 14g (71)

Reid, Sir Edward—Feb. 25, 17f (72); Mar. 23, 19g (72)

Reid, Harold A.—Oct. 31, 19h (74)

Reid, Adm. Sir Peter—Sept 28, 20f (73); Oct. 25, 23g (73)

Reid, Robert—(t.), May 31, 18h (74)

Reinhard, Prof. Max—(t.), Sept. 5, 16g (74)

Reith, Lord—June 17, 17e (71); 19, 12g (71); 23, 19g (71)

Relton, Dr. Maurice—Dec. 2, 18g (71)

Renault, Lucien—Mar. 28, 21g (73)

Rendulic, Lt.-Gen. Lothar—Jan. 23, 14h (71)

Rennie, James—Nov. 29, 20g (73); Dec. 1, 18h (73)

Rennie, Michael—June 11, 16h (71)

Renny, Brig. George D.—Feb. 25, 16h (71)

Renton, Edward—Apr. 18, 16g (75)

Renton, Maj.-Gen. James M.L.—Jan. 14, 14g (72); 21, 14g (72)

Renwick, Lord—Sept. 1, 14g (73); 4, 17f (73)

Renwick, Sir Eustace—Nov. 6, 22h (73)

Repond, Dr. Andre—Mar. 17, 16h (73)

Reuter, Hanna—June 19, 18h (74)

Revell-Smith, Eleana—May 18, 22h (73)

Revers, Gen. Georges—Apr. 4, 22h (74)

Revson, Charles—Aug. 26, 12g (75)

Revson, Peter—Mar. 23, 14g (74)

Rew, Charles H.—(t.), Oct. 16, 14h (72)

Rey, Roberto—June 1, 16h (72)

Reynardson, Lt.-Col. H. Birch—(t.), Feb. 17, 18g (72)

Reynolds, Col. Lewis—July 9, 17h (74)

Reynolds, Paul K. Baillie—Aug. 25, 14g (73)

Rezola, Jose—Dec. 29, 10h (71)

Rhoden, Harry G.—Apr. 24, 14h (72)

Rhodes, Geoffrey—June 24, 12g (74)

Rhodes, Sir Godfrey—Feb. 22, 12h (71)

Rhodes, Wilfred—July 9, 16h (73)

Rhys-Roberts, Thomas E. R.—June 10, 18g (75)

Ribiero, Col. Helder—Nov. 13, 18g (73)

Ricardo, Lady Beatrice—Sept. 6, 14h (75)

Ricardo, Sir Harry—May 20, 16g (74); 22, 22g (74)

Rice, Prof. David Talbot—Mar. 15, 16g (72); 17, 16g (72); 20, 14h (72)

Rice-Oxley, Dr. Douglas G.—July 3, 16g (72)

Rich, Cecil—May 8, 16h (75)

Richard, Rudolph—June 13, 18h (73)

Richards, Ceri—Nov. 11, 18g (71); 17, 19h (71)

Richards, Prof. Melville—(t.), Nov. 17, 16g (73)

Richards, Morley—(t.), Jan. 22, 16g (74)

Richardson, Dr. Alan—Feb. 24, 16g (75); Mar. 7, 16g (75)

Richardson, Arnold—July 3, 18g (73)

Richardson, Blair—Mar. 8, 14g (71)

Richardson, Charles A.—Jan. 1, 16g (73)

Richardson, Henry G.—(t.), Sept. 10, 16g (74)

Richardson, Justin—(t.), Sept. 5, 16h (75)

Richardson, Kenneth—Aug. 15, 14h (74)

Richardson, Linetta de C.—June 7, 14g (75)

Richardson, Thomas D.—Jan. 8, 12g (71)

Richardson, Sir William W.—Nov. 17, 16h (73)

Richey, Dr. Margaret—Nov. 21, 16f (74)

Richman, Harry—Nov. 6, 14g (72)

Richmond and Gordon, Hilda Duchess of—Dec. 30, 12h (71); Jan. 8, 16g (72)

Richter, Dr. Gisela—Dec. 28, 14f (72)

Ricken-Backer, Capt. Eddie—July 24, 16g (73)

Riddell, Prof. Athol G.—May 23, 18g (74)

Riddell-Webster, Gen. Sir Thomas—May 28, 16h (74)

Rideal, Sir Eric—Sept. 27, 16f (74)

Ridehalgh, Arthur—Sept. 9, 16h (71)

Ridgeway, Charles C.—(t.), Sept. 12, 16h (73)

Ridrueoj, Dianisio—July 1, 16h (75)

Rieder, Mrs. Gertrude E.—Apr. 1, 17h (74)

Rienits, Rex—May 6, 18h (71)

Rieu, Lady Eileen—June 8, 14h (71)

Rieu, Dr. Emile V.—May 13, 16f (72)

Rigal, Georges—Mar. 27, 18h (74)

Rigby, Arthur—Apr. 27, 18h (71)

Rihtniemi, Juha—Jan. 14, 16g (71)

Riisager, Knudage—Jan. 9, 17g (75)

Ryneveld, Gen. Sir Pierre van—Dec. 4, 17h (72)

Rinaldi, Luigi—May 22, 16h (72)

Ringham, Reginald—Dec. 29, 12h (73)

Riordan, William—Jan. 16, 14h (73)

Riseborough, Harry T.—Aug. 22, 12h (75)

Ritchie, Lady Florina—Dec. 1, 14g (75)

Ritchie of Dundee, Lord—Oct. 21, 14g (75); 31, 17g (75)

Ritchie Kilner, Maj. E. E.—Sept. 26, 18h (73)

Rito, Ted Fio—July 26, 14h (71)

Ritter, Tex—Jan. 4, 14h (74)

Rittner, Thomas H.—Mar. 13, 18h (75)

Rivera, Card. Jose G. y—May 30, 14g (72)

Rivelt-Carnac, Sir Henry—Jan. 1, 16g (73)

Rivett-Carnac, Lt-Col. John C. T.—Aug. 2, 14h (75)

Rizo-Rangabe, H. E. Alexander—(t.), Feb. 10, 16h (72)

Road, Sir Alfred—Feb. 17, 18h (72)

Rob, John V.—Mar. 12, 18h (71)

Robbins, Francis W.—Dec. 2, 18g (72)

Robbins, Sidney—(t.), Aug. 7, 12g (71)

Roberson, R. S.—Jan. 25, 16g (72)

Roberts, Lady—May 3, 14f (71)

Roberts, Alf—Sept. 24, 14h (71)

Roberts, Bruce—(t.), July 31, 18g (74)

Roberts, Charles W.—Apr. 12, 14h (75)

Roberts, Rev. Dr. Colin—Dec. 12, 18g (75)

Roberts, Ald. Edwin—Apr. 5, 21g (73)

Roberts, Sir Howard—May 8, 16g (75)

Roberts, Sir James D.—July 12, 18h (73); 17, 16h (73)

Roberts, John P.—Mar. 28, 21h (73)

Roberts, Sir Norman S.—Nov. 4, 16h (72)

Roberts, Paddy—Sept. 6, 14g (75)

Roberts, Paul—Aug. 16, 18h (74)

Roberts, Raymond—(t.), Aug. 15, 16h (74)

Roberts, Robert David V.—May 11, 12h (73); 11, 22h (73)

Roberts, Teddy—Mar. 4, 14g (72)

Roberts, Sir William—June 18, 18g (71)

Robertshaw, Vice-Adm. Sir Ballin J.—July 16, 14g (71); 21, 14h (71)

Robertson of Oakridge, Lord—(t.), May 1, 18g (74); 7, 16h (74)

Robertson, Lady May—July 12, 20h (74)

Robertson, Algar R. W.—June 9, 16g (75)

Robertson, Bruce—Mar. 25, 18f (72)

Robertson, Dr. Edward G.—Dec. 29, 10g (75)

Robertson, Prof. Jean—(t.), Nov. 21, 16h (74)

Robertson, John F.—Sept. 28, 18h (72)

Robertson, Dr. Muriel—(t.), July 18, 18g (73)

Robertson, Vernon A. M.—Feb. 13, 12g (71)

Robertson-Justice, James—July 3, 17g (75); 10, 17g (75)

Robiette, Dr. A. G.—(t.), Dec. 20, 14g (74)

Robins, Lady Mary—Dec. 18, 17g (74)

Robinson, Lady—July 11, 18h (73)

Robinson, Lady Charlotte—June 18, 20h (75)

Robinson, A. Esmond—(t.), Dec. 5, 16g (75)

Robinson, Prof. Abraham—May 6, 16g (74); 9, 22g (74)

Robinson, Comm. David Samuel—Jan. 5, 12g (72)

Robinson, Edward G.—Jan. 29, 14g (73)

Robinson, Eric—July 25, 20g (74)

Robinson, Sir Frederick—Mar. 25, 19h (75)

Robinson, Rev. Godfrey C.—June 21, 14h (71)

Robinson, Jackie—Oct. 25, 21g (72)

Robinson, Air Comm. John A.—Sept. 9, 14h (75)

Robinson, Sir Leslie—Apr. 26, 20h (74); 29, 18h (74); May 2, 20h (74)

Robinson, Prof. P. L.—(t.), Mar. 15, 18h (73)

Robinson, R. H. O. B.—Feb. 7, 18g (73)

Robinson, Sir Robert—Feb. 10, 14g (75); 21, 16g (75)

Robinson, Col. Victor O.—Oct. 31, 17g (72)

Robinson, W. Kay—(t.), Oct. 22, 14h (71)

Robo, Rev. Etienne—(t.), July 7, 14g (72)

Robson, Prof. William—Jan. 25, 14g (75)

Rockefeller, Martha B.—Jan. 27, 14g (71)

Rockefeller, Winthrop—Feb. 23, 19e (73)

Rocyn-Jones, Arthur—Feb. 14, 14h (72); 18, 14h (72)

Rodney, Lord—Dec. 21, 17e (73)

Rodrigo, Sir Philip—July 9, 16h (75)

Rodriguez, Pedro—July 12, 14h (71)

Rodwell, Air Cmdre, Robert J.—Jan. 4, 14h (71)

Roe, Dr. Edna—(t.), Aug. 4, 12f (71)

Roe, Raymond—June 20, 20f (74)

Roenue, Torben—Oct. 20, 18h (73)

Rogard, Folke—(t.), June 25, 14h (73)

Roger, Lady Helen—Apr. 8, 16g (75)

Rogers, Charlie—July 27, 15g(71)

Rogers, His Hon. Graham—Apr. 18, 21g (73)

Rogers, John—(t.), Aug. 22, 12f (75)

Rojas Pinilla, Gen.—Jan. 20, 15g (75)

Rolin, Dr. Henri—Apr. 21, 14g (73); 28, 16h (73)

Rollason, Prof. Ernest C.—May 8, 14g (72)

Rolleston, Susan—Aug. 22, 14g (72)

Rolleston, Col. William—July 30, 16h (74)

Rolt, L. T. C.—May 11, 16g (74); 14, 18h (74)

Rolz Bennett, José—Dec. 21, 14g (72)

Rom, Luis Alvarez—Jan. 20, 16g (72)

Romains, Jules—Aug. 18, 12g (72)

Romanis, W. H. C.—Jan. 28, 16h (72)

Romanoff, Michael—Sept. 3, 14g (71)

Romer, Dr. Alfred S.—Nov. 8, 23g (73); 22, 18h (73)

Romero, Adelino—July 15, 14h (74)

Romm, Mikhail Ilyich—Nov. 3, 17f (71)

Romney, Lord—Sept. 8, 14f (75)

Rooney, John J.—Oct. 31, 17h (75)

Sofer, Cyril—(t.), Mar. 22, 18h (74)

Soglo, Mrs. Paule J.—Nov. 17, 16g (73)

Sokolova, Lydia—Feb. 6, 16g (74)

Soloman, Charles J.—May 3, 16h (75)

Solovyov, Rear-Adm. Nikolai V.—Sept. 9, 14h (75)

Somervell, Lady Dorothy—June 8, 18g (72)

Somervell, Theordore H.—Jan. 25, 14g (75)

Sommer, Francois—Jan. 10, 16g (73)

Sonov, Mikhael—Jan. 5, 14h (74)

Soong, T. V.—Apr. 27, 18g (71)

Sorensen, Lord—Oct. 11, 16f (71); 15, 16g (71)

Soriano, Gonzalo—May 17, 16g (72)

Sorley, Sir Ralph—Nov. 20, 19f (74)

Sorrell, Alan—Dec. 31, 14h (74)

Sotomayor, Alberto U.—Apr. 14, 14h (75)

Soucek, Prof. Josef B.—Sept. 15, 14h (72)

Soulbury, Lord—Feb. 2, 16g (71); 4, 16g (71)

Souter, Lady—Feb. 3, 14g (71)

Southan, Miss Joyce—(t.), Apr. 28, 16h (71)

Southborough, Dorothy Lady—Aug. 5, 14g (72)

Southby, Lady Phyllis—Apr. 29, 18h (74)

Southgate, Dr. B. A.—Oct. 6, 14g (75)

Southwell, Miss Lorna V.—(t.), Feb. 17, 18g (72)

Sowerby, Lt.-Col. Michael—Mar. 19, 16h (74)

Soysa, Rt. Rev. Charles H. W. de —May 7, 18f (74)

Spaak, Charles—Mar. 6, 16g (75)

Spaak, Paul-Henri—Aug. 1, 17f (72); 8, 14h (72)

Spaatz, Gen. Carl—(t.), July 18, 20g (74); 20, 14g (74)

Spackman, A. V-M. Charles B. S. —Dec. 15, 17h (71)

Spafford, Brig. Percy L.—June 20, 16g (72)

Spalla, Erminio—Aug. 17, 12f (71)

Spanier, Eric—(t.), Mar. 14, 18g (73)

Sparham, Rev. Louis C.—(t.), Jan. 23, 14h (71)

Sparke, Michael E. B.—Apr. 25, 20h (73)

Sparshott, Donald—(t.), Apr. 10, 18h (75)

Spater, Ernest G.—(t.), Aug. 1, 17g (75)

Spaven, John R.—Aug. 31, 12h (71)

Spears, Lady Nancy—May 20, 16g (75)

Spears, Sir Edward—Jan. 28, 14f (74); 31, 18g (74); Feb. 8, 18h (74)

Specter, Edward—Mar. 15, 18h (74)

Speed, Sir Eric—June 30, 16g (71); July 9, 14g (71)

Spekke, Dr. Arnolds—July 31, 14h (72)

Spencer, Lady—Dec. 6, 19f (72); Jan. 31, 16g (73)

Spencer, Lord Albert—June 12, 20g (75)

Spencer, Lt.-Col. A. V.—Jan. 8, 14h (73)

Spencer, Brig. Francis Elmhirst—Mar. 8, 16g (72)

Spencer, George—Aug. 11, 12h (71)

Spencer, George H.—Mar. 15, 18h (74)

Spencer-Chapman, Lt.-Col. Frederick S.—Aug. 10, 14g (71)

Spender-Clay, Mrs. Pauline—May 6, 16h (72); June 20, 16h (72)

Spens, Lord—Nov. 16, 23g (73)

Spens, Lady Dorothy—Jan. 2, 14h (74)

Spewack, Samuel—Oct. 16, 14g (71)

Spicer, Capt. Frank—Oct. 9, 22h (73)

Spinks, Lady Marguerite—Apr. 25, 14g (75)

Spinney, Arthur R.—Aug. 9, 14g (73)

Spofforth, Brig. Percy L.—June 17, 16h (72)

Sprague, Capt. William N.—Mar. 28, 21f (74)

Spreckley, Capt. Herbert M.—Jan. 31, 18g (74)

Sprigge, Miss Elizabeth—Dec. 11, 18g (74)

Sprott, Prof. Walter J. H.—Sept. 6, 16h (71); 9, 16f (71); 11, 14g (71); 13, 16h (71); 14, 15g (71)

Sproul, Dr. Robert G.—Sept. 13, 14h (75)

Sprules, Miss Dorothy W.—Sept. 12, 14h (72)

Spurgeon, Miss Freda—Oct. 22, 14f (71)

Spurrier, John M.—Jan. 2, 14h (74)

Squance, Col. Thomas C.—Sept. 19, 16h (75)

Squires, Charles—(t.), May 23, 18g (74)

Stacey, Sir Ernest—May 18, 22h (73)

Stacey, Prof. R. S.—Feb. 16, 18g (74); 21, 16g (74)

Stagg, J. M.—June 25, 16g (75)

Stainless, Stephen—Jan. 14, 16g (71)

Stallard, Col. C. F.—June 14, 14g (71)

Stallard, Henry B.—(t.), Nov. 2, 19f (73); 9, 23g (73)

Stallard, Hyla B.—Oct. 25, 23g (73)

Stamer, Lady Mary—June 13, 20h (74)

Stamp, Lady Mildred—May 14, 18g (71)

Stamp, A. Reginald—Nov. 9, 18h (74)

Stampe, Lady Agatha—June 27, 14h (75)

Stancu, Zaharia—Dec. 7, 18h (74); Jan. 2, 14g (75)

Stanford, Lt.-Col. John K.—Sept. 28, 14g (71); Oct. 26, 14g (71)

Stanham Truscott, Sir Eric H.—May 19, 16h (73)

Stanley, Rev. Howard—Oct. 24, 18g (75)

Stanley, Rev. Victor—(t.), Oct. 15, 18g (74)

Stanley, Prof. Wendell M.—June 16, 16h (71)

Stanley-Wrench, Margaret—Jan. 15, 16h (74)

Stansfield, Capt. John—July 12, 14g (75)

Stanton, Lt.-Col. John P.—Aug. 27, 12h (74)

Stapledon, Sir Robert—Sept. 2, 14h (75)

Stapleton, Cyril—Feb. 26, 14g (74)

Starey, Capt. Stephen H.—June 13, 16h (72)

Stark, Adm. Harold—Aug. 22, 14g (72)

Starkey, Lt.-Col. Lewis S.—Sept. 9, 14h (75)

Starkey, Maj. Morey J. P.—Dec. 31, 14g (74)

Statham, Dr. Heathcote—Oct. 31, 20g (73)

Staub, Roger—July 2, 16h (74)

Stchoukine, Ivan—Oct. 9, 16g (75)

Steavenson, Dr. W. H.—Sept. 25, 16g (73)

Stebbins, Henry E.—Apr. 3, 16g (73)

Steckel, Sir Leonard—Feb. 12, 14g (71)

Stedeford, Sir Ivan—Feb. 11, 14g (75)

Stedman, Dr. Edgar—May 26, 8h (75)

Steeds, William—(t.), May 10, 24h (74)

Steel, Dr. Anthony—Oct. 6, 14g (73); 11, 21g (73)

Steel, Sir Christopher—Sept. 18, 21g (73); 21, 18f (73)

Steel, Dr. Frederick—(t.), Apr. 9, 16f (74)

Steele, Lady Joan—Nov. 22, 18h (72)

Steele, Air Marshal Sir Charles—Feb. 17, 16h (73)

Steele, Gen. Sir James—July 26, 14g (75); 31, 16h (75); Aug. 4, 14g (75); 12, 14g (75)

Steen, Marguerite—Aug. 6, 14g (75)

Stehelin, Dr. John—Apr. 28, 16h (73)

Stehman, Jacques—May 29, 16f (75)

Steichen, Edward—Mar. 27, 18f (73)

Stein, Leonard—Apr. 25, 20f (73)

Stein, Leonid—July 7, 14g (73); 9, 16f (73)

Steinberg, Dr. Aaron—(t.), Aug. 20, 14g (75)

Steiner, Max—Dec. 30, 12g (71)

Steiner, Otto—(t.), Feb. 29, 16g (72)

Stengel, Charles D.—Oct. 1, 16g (75)

Stenhouse, Lt.-Col. Edward E.—July 17, 14h (71)

Stenhouse, Hugh C.—Nov. 27, 16g (71)

Stenton, Lady Doris—Dec. 30, 12h (71); Jan. 4, 12h (72)

Stephens, Esca—Oct. 30, 16h (75)

Stephenson, Lady Daphne—Dec. 24, 12h (71); 31, 10h (71)

Stephenson, Rev. Canon Colin—Aug. 17, 16h (73); 25, 14g (73)

Stephenson, Sir Gilbert—May 30, 14g (72); June 3, 16h (72)

Stephenson, Sir Hugh—Sept. 25, 14g (72); 27, 16h (72)

Stephenson, T. H.—Aug. 25, 14g (73)

Stephenson, Thomas—Mar. 15, 18h (74)

Stephenson, William H.—June 6, 18g (73)

Sterling, Brig. Walter A.—Dec. 21, 14h (72)

Stern, Lady Helen—Nov. 16, 16h (74)

Stern, Lady Sybil—July 18, 15h (72)

Stern, Alan H.—Dec. 18, 17h (74)

Stern, Gladys B.—Sept. 20, 20h (73)

Stevens, Arthur H.—(t.), Jan. 23, 16h (74)

Stevens, Sir Bertram—Mar. 26, 14g (73)

Stevens, George—Mar. 11, 18g (75)

Stevens, George C.—Aug. 2, 14h (75)

Stevens, Sir John—Oct. 30, 19g (73); Nov. 2, 19h (73); 9, 23g (73)

Stevens, William C.—Jan. 3, 14h (74)

Stevenson, Dorothy E.—Jan. 5, 12h (74)

Stevenson, Ellen B.—July 31, 14g (72)

Stevenson, Maj. Sir Hubert C.—June 14, 14h (71)

Stevenson, J. A. R.—Apr. 17, 16h (74)

Stevenson, Dr. Suzanne S.—Apr. 3, 16g (73)

Steward, Maj.-Gen. Reginald H. R.—Dec. 8, 14h (75)

Stewardson, Prof. E. A.—Aug. 29, 16g (73)

Stewart, Lady MacTaggart—Feb. 28, 16h (75)

Stewart, Dr. Alexander B.—Nov. 22, 19h (74)

Stewart, Andrew—Aug. 25, 14h (72); Sept. 2, 16h (72)

Stewart, Dr. Clara—Feb. 9, 16g (73)

Stewart, Dr. Donald—Nov. 3, 18g (72)

Stewart, Maj.-Gen. Herbert W. V. —Jan. 31, 16h (75)

Stewart, Maj.-Gen. Keith—Nov. 14, 16h (72)

Stewart, Sir Kenneth—May 22, 16h (72); 27, 16g (72)

Stewart, Maj.-Gen. Robert Neil—June 22, 21h (72)

Stewart, William—Feb. 27, 16f (75)

Stewart-Clark, Sir Stewart—Dec. 3, 16f (71)

Stewart-Roberts, Walter—Mar. 7, 16h (75)

Stewart-Stevens, Maj. Greville—June 15, 21f (72)

Stewartson, Prof. E. A.—(t.), Sept. 11, 18g (73)

Stickney, Mrs. Jean Noble—Jan. 22, 14h (72)

Stignani, Ebe—Oct. 11, 16f (74)

Still, Dr. Robert—(t.), Jan. 21, 16h (71)

Stirling, Carl L.—July 17, 16g (73)

Stirling, Sir James—Feb. 7, 17g (74); 12, 16g (74); 15, 17f (74)

Stirling, Sir John—Mar. 24, 16g (75)

Stirling, Mrs. Margaret—Aug. 14, 14h (73)

Stirling, Raymond S.—Nov. 5, 16h (74)

Stirling, Gen. Sir William—Aug. 30, 14g (73)

Stirling Boyd, T.—Jan. 5, 14g (73)

Stocks, Lady Mary—July 7, 14g (75); 15, 14g (75)

Stocks, Charles—Feb. 22, 14g (75)

Stocks, Mrs. Cheridah A. de B.— May 7, 18h (71)

Stockwell, Thomas H.—May 14, 14g (73)

Stoddart, Alexander F. R.—Nov. 8, 23g (73)

Stode-Jackson, Col. A. N. S.—(t.), Nov. 28, 16h (72)

Stoica, Chiva—Feb. 19, 17g (75)

Stokes, Lady Alice—Jan. 10, 16g (75)

Stokes, Adrian—Dec. 19, 18f (72)

Stolz, Robert—June 28, 14g (75); July 2, 18g (75)

Stone, Lt.-Gen. Robert G. W. H.— July 5, 16g (74)

Stonehewer-Bird, Lady Franceska —July 16, 17h (75)

Stonham, Lord—Dec. 23, 12e (71); 24, 12g (71); Jan. 17, 12h (72); 18, 14h (72)

Stopford, Miss Eveleen E.—Oct. 1, 19f (71)

Stopford, Mrs. Kathleen—(t.), July 17, 16g (73)

Stopford, Gen. Sir Montague— Mar. 11, 16f (71)

Storch, Anton—Nov. 29, 16h (75)

Storey, Capt. Alan T. T.—Dec. 30, 10g (75)

Storey, Leslie H.—Dec. 12, 16g (74)

Storey, Percy—Oct. 7, 14h (75)

Storm, Miss Lesley—Oct. 20, 14g (75)

Stossel, Ludwig—Feb. 6, 16g (73)

Stout, Rex—Oct. 29, 16g (75)

Stovin-Bradford, Capt. F.—Oct. 8, 18h (74)

Stracey, Sir Michael G. M.—Oct. 16, 14h (71)

Strachey, Alix—(t.), May 7, 18h (73)

Strachey, Prof. Christopher—May 23, 16g (75); 26, 8h (75)

Strachie, Lord—May 19, 16g (73)

Stranders, Michael O'C.—Feb. 21, 16h (73); Mar. 27, 18f (73)

Strang, Lady Elsie—Sept. 25, 18h (74)

Strange, Lady—Oct. 21, 14h (75)

Strangman, Sir Thomas—Oct. 12, 15h (71)

Stransky, Prof. Jaroslav—Aug. 14, 14h (73)

Strasser, Dr. Otto—Aug. 29, 16g (74)

Strath, Sir William—May 10, 16f (75)

Strathcarron, Lady Diana—May 2, 20g (73)

Strathmore, Lord Timothy—Sept. 14, 19g (72)

Stratton, David G.—May 25, 21g (72)

Strauss, Rear-Adm. L.—Jan. 23, 16g (74)

Strauss, Robert—Feb. 24, 16h (75)

Stravinsky, Igor—Apr. 7, 16f (71)

Street, A. F.—June 27, 20g (74)

Street, Peter—(t.), July 14, 14h (73)

Streeter, Fred—Nov. 3, 14g (75)

Strickland-Constable, Sir Henry— Apr. 1, 14g (75)

Strode-Jackson, Col. Arnold N.— Nov. 17, 18g (72)

Strong, Dr. Donald E.—Sept. 28, 20h (73); Oct. 3, 17g (73)

Strutt, Vice-Adm. Arthur C.—Feb. 12, 14h (73)

Strutt, Geoffrey St. John—Oct. 25, 15g (71)

Strutt, Mrs. Irene—(t.), May 2, 20g (74)

Struye, M. Paul—Feb. 18, 16h (74)

Stuart of Findhorn, Lord—Feb. 22, 12f (71)

Stuart, Sir Campbell—Sept. 15, 14f (72)

Stuart, Hilda V.—Mar. 19, 19h (75)

Stuart Snr, Robert D.—Jan. 8, 17h (75)

Stuart-Clark, Arthur Campbell— May 14, 14g (73); 23, 21g (73)

Stubbs, W. E.—(t.), Sept. 15, 14h (73)

Studd, Lady Alexandra—Nov. 30, 16h (74)

Studd, Lady Kathleen—Dec. 29, 10h (75)

Studd, Sir Eric—June 13, 18g (75)

Studdert, Ven. Augustine John de Clare—Mar. 22, 18g (72)

Studdy, Sir Henry—Nov. 11, 15h (75)

Studholme, Lady Alice—Jan. 8, 14h (74)

Stutchfield, R. E.—(t.), Apr. 10, 18g (75)

Suarez-Dominguez   Lt.-Col. Manuel—Aug. 17, 12f (71)

Suburov, Maj.-Gen. Alexander— Apr. 19, 18f (74)

Suddaby, Rowland—Nov. 13, 16g (72); 17, 18h (72)

Sugden, Group Capt. Ronald S.— Apr. 2, 18h (71)

Suginome, Harusada—(t.), Apr. 20, 19h (72)

Sukhoi, Pavel—Sept. 18, 16g (75)

Sullivan, Mrs. Doris—May 16, 18h (72)

Sullivan, Ed.—Oct. 15, 18h (74)

Sullivan, Joe—Oct. 15, 16g (71)

Sullivan, Sir William—June 23, 19g (71); 28, 14f (71)

Sumantri, Dr. Iwa K. K.—Nov. 30, 15g (71)

Sumiya, Morio—Sept. 12, 17g (75)

Summerhayes, Victor S.—Jan. 7, 14g (75)

Summers, Lady Margaret—Mar. 12, 18h (75)

Summers, Sir Geoffrey—Jan. 18, 14h (72); 26, 16h (72)

Sumner, John R. H.—May 14, 18g (71)

Sumner, Dr. William L.—(t.), Aug. 24, 14g (73)

Sun Fo, Dr.—Sept. 17, 19f (73)

Sung Tzu-wen: see Soong, T. V.

Susann, Jacqueline—Sept. 23, 14g (74)

Suschitzky, Dr. Joseph—Dec. 19, 16g (75)

Susini, Pierre—Oct. 21, 16g (72)

Suslov, Mrs. Elizaveta—Sept. 16, 14h (72)

Sutch, H. A.—(t.), Feb. 16, 18h (74)

Sutch, Ven. Ronald H.—Feb. 27, 16g (75)

Sutch, Dr. William B.—Oct. 2, 17h (75); 11, 14g (75)

Sutcliffe, Jean—(t.), Feb. 24, 14g (73)

Sutcliffe, John E.—July 8, 16g (75)

Sutherland, David M.—Sept. 22, 16g (73); Oct. 2, 18h (73)

Sutherland, Miss Mary E.—Oct. 23, 14h (72); 26, 18h (72)

Sutton, Charles E.—Jan. 27, 14h (71)

Sutton, Claude—July 14, 18g (72)

Sutton, Ernest P. F.—Aug. 14, 14f (72)

Svedberg, Prof. Theodor—Feb. 27, 14f (71)

Swabey, Christopher—Apr. 13, 21g (72)

Swaelens, Donald—Apr. 29, 18h (75)

Swan, Albert W.—Aug. 14, 17g (75)

Swan, Sir Kenneth—Oct. 15, 19g (73); 20, 18h (73)

Swann, Lady Dorothy—May 1, 14h (71)

Swanson, John L.—Feb. 16, 18h (74)

Swarowsky, Hans—Sept. 13, 14h (75)

Swart, Antoinette—(t.), Aug. 16, 18h (74)

Swartz, Tom—Sept. 20, 14h (75)

Sweden, King Gustaf VI Adolf of —Sept. 17, 19f (73)

Sweden, Princess Sibylla of—Nov. 29, 18g (72)

Swim, Dudley—Feb. 2, 16g (72)

Swinarski, Konrad—Aug. 22, 12h (75); 26, 12g (75)

Swinburne, Lady Millicent—Nov. 9, 17h (71)

Swinburne, Col. Hugh L.—Nov. 26, 17h (73)

Swindell, Rev. Frank G.—Dec. 24, 12h (75)

Swindlehurst, Joseph E.—Dec. 28, 14h (72)

Swiney, Lady—Mar. 29, 14h (75)

Swinton, Lord—July 29, 16e (72); Aug. 2, 17g (72)

Swinton, Countess Mary of—Oct. 1, 16h (74); 22, 16h (74)

Swinton, Brig. Alan H. C.—Apr. 24, 14g (72)

Swire, Col. Roger—Nov. 22, 19h (74)

Swynnerton, Maj.-Gen. Charles R. A.—Mar. 6, 18f (73)

Sydney, Granvile—Feb. 16, 18g (74)

Sye, Tan Lark—Sept. 20, 17g (72)

Syfret, Adm. Sir Neville—Dec. 11, 17g (72)

Sykes, Lady Evelyn—Jan. 2, 14h (74)

Sykes, Lt.-Col. Peter T. W.—Nov. 22, 14g (75); Dec. 3, 18h (75)

Sykes-Wright, Col. Cecil E.—(t.), Sept. 13, 14g (75)

Symon, Sir Alexander—July 19, 17g (74)

Symon, Harold—Nov. 16, 17h (71)

Symonds, Lt.-Col. Ralph F.—(t.), Sept. 2, 14g (71)

Symonds-Tayler, Sir Richard—Feb. 20, 14h (71)

Symons, Prof. Hubert W.—Feb. 26, 14g (73)

Szamuely, Dr. Tibor—Dec. 11, 17g (72); 12, 19g (72)

Szepan, Fritz—Dec. 17, 17g (74)

Szigeti, Joseph—Feb, 21, 16f (73); 22, 19h (73)

Szu-cheng, Liang—Jan. 14, 14g (72)

T

Tabenkin, Yitzhak—July 7, 16g (71)

Tabori, Dr. Paul—Nov. 12, 17g (74)

Taek, Chong Jun—Jan. 13, 16g (73)

Tahir, Kemal—Apr. 26, 18h (73)

Taih Khiet, Ven. Thich—Feb. 27, 16h (73)

Tailby, T.—June 2, 14g (71)

Tailyour, Lady Priscilla—**June 14,** 14h (71)

Taimur, Sayid Said bin: see Muscat and Oman, Sultan of

Tait, Sir John—Aug. 10, 14h (72)

Takriti, Air Marshal Hardan— Mar. 31, 16h (71)

Tal, Wasfi—Nov. 29, 14g (71)

Talantov, Boris—May 13, 19g (71)

Talbot, Lady Helene—May 30, 16h (75)

Talbot, Bridget E.—Dec. 3, 16g (71)

Talbot de Malahide, Lord—Apr. 16, 16f (73); May 15, 18h (73)

Talmadge, Constance—Nov. 27, 21h (73)

Tamiroff, Akim—Sept. 20, 17g (72)

Tamm, Dr. Igor Y.—Apr. 14, 16g (71); May 4, 16h (71)

Tanaka, Kotaro—Mar. 2, 16h (74)

Tankerville, Lord—Dec. 3, 16h (71)

Tann, Bert—July 8, 16h (72)

Tanner, Herbert G.—Mar. 27, 18h (74)

Tanzi, Madrandele—Feb. 13, 16h (74)

Taqa, Shazel—Oct. 21, 14h (74)

Tarasconi, Antonio M. L. di S.— Aug. 26, 12h (71)

Tarasov, Alexander M.—July 10, 17h (75)

Tarasova, Alla—Apr. 6, 23g (73)

Tarjan, George—(t.), Jan. 5, 12h (74)

Tarn, Adam—July 23, 16h (75)

Tarrant, Prof. Dorothy—Sept. 7, 18g (73); 10, 14h (73)

Tarrant, John—Jan. 24, 16h (75)

Tasker, Lady Jessie—Sept. 7, 14h (74)

Tatarashvili, Shota M.—Aug. 21, 14h (75)

Tatham, Allen R.—Nov. 24, 19h (75)